# TENNESSEANS IN THE WAR OF 1812

Byron Sistler & Samuel Sistler

*Tennesseans in the War of 1812*

Copyright © 1992
Byron and Samuel Sistler

Originally published by:
Byron Sistler & Associates, Inc.
Nashville, Tennessee
1992

Reprinted
Janaway Publishing, Inc.
2007

Janaway Publishing, Inc.
2412 Nicklaus Dr.
Santa Maria, California 93455
(805) 925-1038
www.janawaygenealogy.com

ISBN 10:  1-59641-087-6
ISBN 13:  978-1-59641-087-9

*Made in the United States of America*

# INTRODUCTION

This book is an attempt to list all persons who served in Tennessee units during the War of 1812. Information contained herein was taken from so-called "Service Records" which consist of a typewritten card file which is available on microfilm at the Tennessee State Library and Archives in Nashville. The card file, in turn, was produced from photostats of the original muster rolls.

The exact source of this card file is shrouded in mystery. Kendall Cram, former head of the Library section of the TSLA, thinks the copies of the muster rolls were obtained by the then State Librarian, John Trotwood Moore, during the 1920s, and that before his death in 1929, he supervised preparation of the card file. As such there could be some variation in these records from the "Service Records" available at the National Archives in Washington. It is clear, however, that the source of the records in each case were the muster rolls.

Since there was more than one muster roll for each unit during the course of the war, there are numerous duplications of names on the cards. In transcribing this data we attempted to eliminate any complete duplications, but where there was any doubt as to whether we were dealing with a single individual or several individuals with the same name, we left the second or third entry in.

Almost all the information we felt was pertinent was copied from the microfilm. This includes name, rank, regimental commander and company commander, branch of service and, where shown, place of residence of the soldier. Unfortunately very few of the records indicated place of residence, but if one refers to the "Officers" section of the book, the county of residence of the unit (usually company or battery) may be given. A very useful tool in determining place of residence is the book *Record of Commissions of Officers in the Tennessee Militia 1796-1815*, by Mrs. John Trotwood Moore (Baltimore, 1977). The county where the officer was living when commissioned is shown in this indexed volume.

In addition to the data indicated above, we also included other information of interest, such as date wounded or died--if while in service--whether deserted or absent without leave, or if discharged for inability to serve.

It should be emphasized that not all Tennesseans who served in the War of 1812 are included in this work; members of the Regular Army, Navy and Marines are not here, and possibly some who enlisted in the Volunteer U. S. Army specifically for this war are absent. Where a Tennessee militia unit was called into Federal service, as in the case of the 24th Infantry and 39th Infantry, it appears they have been listed on this set of service records.

Almost all the men named herein, where involved in actual campaigning, served in the Creek War of 1813-14 (a sub-conflict of the War of 1812) or in the New Orleans campaign which culminated in the victory of the Americans at Chalmette in January 1815. Ironically, most deaths of Tennesseans were the result of an apparent epidemic of some unknown malady after the war was over, in the late winter and spring of 1815. History books do not seem to mention this epidemic but a perusal of the service records clearly reveals its existence.

Genealogists are sometimes confused about where persons lived who were in units designated as "West Tennessee." At the time of this war what we consider West Tennessee still belonged to the Indians, and what we call Middle Tennessee was then West Tennessee. Thus a Bedford County regiment, for example, would be "West Tennessee Infantry."

The Sistlers
Nashville, TN
January, 1992

## GLOSSARY OF ABBREVIATIONS

| | | | |
|---|---|---|---|
| Adjt | Adjutant | Fgmstr | Foragemaster |
| ADC | Aide de Camp | Gen | General |
| Artif | Artificer | Inf | Infantry |
| Arty | Artillery | KIA | Killed in Action |
| AWOL | Absent without Leave | Lt | Lieutenant |
| Blksmth | Blacksmith | 1 Lt | First Lieutenant |
| Bn | Battalion | 2 Lt | Second Lieutenant |
| Brig | Brigadier or Brigade | 3 Lt | Third Lieutenant |
| Capt | Captain | Lt Col | Lieutenant Colonel |
| Cav | Cavalry | Maj | Major |
| Chap | Chaplain | Mil | Militia |
| Co | Company | Mtd | Mounted |
| Col | Colonel | Mus | Musician |
| Comm | Commissary | Pvt | Private |
| Cor | Cornet | QM | Quartermaster |
| Cpl | Corporal | Regt | Regiment |
| d | Died | Sdlr | Saddler |
| Det | Detachment | Sqdn | Squadron |
| Dmr | Drummer | Svce | Service |
| Drm Maj | Drum Major | Tptr | Trumpeter |
| Ens | Ensign | Wgnr | Wagoner |
| Far | Farrier | Wgnmstr | Wagonmaster |

## Officers, War of 1812

ABBOTS, David, 2 Maj, Col Jas Raulston, W TN Mil Inf, Res omitted

ABELS, John, Ens, Col Thomas Williamson & Capt Robert Steel, Vol Mtd Gunmen, Res omitted; Div of Maj Gen A Jackson

ADAMS, David, Ens, Col Edwin E Booth & Capt John McKamey, E TN Mil, Res Greene Co

ADAMS, John A, 1 Lt, Col Philip Pipkin & Capt Peter Searcy, Mil Inf, Res Hickman Co

ADAMS, Wm, 2 Lt, Col R H Dyer & Capt Cuthbert Hudson, Branch Srvce omitted, Res omitted

ADKINS, Drury, Capt, Col R C Napier, 1st Regt W TN Mil Inf, Res Dickson Co

AIKMEN, William E, Ens, Col John K Wynne & Capt James Cole, Inf, Res omitted

AKIN, Harrison, 3 Lt, Col James Raulston & Capt Charles Wade, Inf, Res Wilson Co; d 2-18-1815

ALCORN, John, 1 Lt Col, Col John Coffee, TN Vol Cav & Mtd Riflemen, Res omitted

ALCORN, John, Col, Field & Staff Officer, Cav, Nashville

ALEXANDER, Adam C, 1 Lt & 2 Master, Col Thos McCrory, 2nd Regt TN Mil, Res omitted

ALEXANDER, Alexander B, 3 Lt, Col Alexander Loury, Capt John Looney, 2nd Regt W TN Mil, Res omitted

ALEXANDER, Benj, 1 Lt, Col Stephens Copeland & Capt G W Stell, Mil Inf, Res omitted

ALEXANDER, Cyrus, Ens, Col N T Perkins, Capt Jas McMahan, Mtd Gunmen, Res omitted

ALEXANDER, Richard, Lt, Col William Hall, 1st Regt TN Vol Inf QM Corp, Res omitted

ALEXANDER, Silas, Ens, Col William Metcalf & Capt John Hill & Capt John Cunningham, Mil Inf, Res omitted; promoted 3 Lt

ALEXANDER, William I, Capt, Col William Hall, 1st Regt TN Vol Mil, Nashville

ALEXANDER, William L, Capt, Col William Hall, Vol Inf, Res omitted

ALEXANDER, William L, Maj, Col Edward Bradley, 1st Regt TN Vol Inf, Res omitted

ALEXANDER, William, Capt, Col William Hall, Vol Inf, Res omitted

ALEXANDER, William, Capt, Col William Johnson, 30th Regt TN Drafted Mil, Rhea Co

ALEXANDER, William, Capt, Col William Johnson, Det E TN Drafted Mil, Res omitted

ALFORD, Wm, 2 Lt, Col Newton Cannon & Capt Ota Cantrell, W TN Mtd Inf, Res omitted

ALLCOM, John, 1 Lt Col, Col John Coffee, TN Vol Cav, Res omitted

ALLEN, Abraham, Capt, Brig Gen Thos Johnson, Mil Inf, Res omitted

ALLEN, Abraham, Capt, Col R C Napier, 1st TN Regt Mil Inf, Montgomery Co

ALLEN, Bethel, Capt, Col Robert Dyer, Vol Mtd Gunmen, Res omitted

ALLEN, Bethel, Capt, Col Robert H Dyer, 1st Regt TN V Cav Mtd Gunmen, Smith Co

ALLEN, Chas, Capt, Col Thos McCrory & Capt Wm Dooly, Res omitted

ALLEN, Isaac, 2 Maj, Col Sam'l Bunch, E TN Mil, Res omitted

ALLEN, Isaac, 2 Maj, Col Wm Lillard, E TN Vol Mil, Res omitted

ALLEN, James, Capt, Col Samuel Bunch, E TN Mil, Knoxville?

ALLEN, James, Capt, Commander omitted, Branch Srvce omitted, Res omitted

ALLEN, Jas, Capt, Col Ewen Allison, E TN Mil, Res omitted

ALLEN, Jno, Ens, Col T McCrory & Capt Isaac Patton, Inf, Res omitted

ALLEN, Robert, Capt, Col N Cannon & Capt James Walton, Mtd Riflemen, Res omitted; promoted to Lt Col

ALLEN, Robert, Capt, Col Newton Cannon, Mtd Riflemen, Smith Co

ALLEN, Sam, Lt, Gen Andrew Jackson, Pack Horse Guards, Res omitted

ALLEN, Samuel A, Capt, Col William Y Higgins, Mtd Gunmen, Madison Co

ALLEN, Samuel, Capt, Co Pack Horse Guards, W TN Mil, Madison Co

ALLEN, Valentine, 1 Lt, Col William Metcalf & Capt Andrew Patterson, Mil Inf, Res omitted

ALLEN, Wm, 2 Lt, Commander omitted, Branch Srvce omitted, Res omitted; in hospital sick

ALLEN, Wm, 2 Lt, Gen Andrew Jackson & Capt Joel Parrish, Arty, Res omitted

ALLEY, Levin, Ens, Capt Jno Miller, Spies, Res omitted

ALLISON, Ewen, Col, Commander omitted, E TN Mil, Res omitted

ALLISON, Ewen, Col, Field & Staff Officers, E TN Mil, Res omitted

ANDERSON, James, Capt, Maj James P H Porter, E TN Mil Cav, Res omitted

ANDERSON, James, Capt, Maj James Porter, Cav Sqdn of E TN Mil, Res omitted

ANDERSON, John H, 2 Lt, Col Thomas Benton, Capt George Gibbs, Vol Inf, Res omitted

ANDERSON, John H, Capt, Col William Pillow, 2nd TN Vol Inf, White Co

ANDERSON, John H, Capt, Col William Pillow, Vol Inf, Res omitted

ANDERSON, John, Lt Col, Brig Gen Nathaniel Taylor, Col William Johnson, 3rd Regt E TN Drafted Mil; d 10-27-1814

ANDERSON, Joseph M, Judge Advocate, Brig Gen Geo Doherty, E TN Mil, Res omitted

ANDERSON, Lewis, Chap, Col Samuel Bayless, 4th Regt E TN Mil, Res omitted

ANDERSON, Tafley, Lt, Col T. McCrory, Capt Jas. Shannon, Mil Inf; sick absent

ANDERSON, Thomas, Ens, Col William Johnson, Capt Elihu Milikin, 3rd Reg TN Mil

ANTHONY, Joseph, Asst Adjt Gen, Maj Gen Andrew Jackson, Div of TN Mil

ANTHONY, William, 1 Lt, Col James Raulston, Capt Mathew Neal, Inf

ARGENBRIGHT, Geo, Capt, Col Wm Lillard, E TN Vol Riflemen, Res omitted

- 1 -

## Officers, War of 1812

ARGENBRIGHT, George, Capt, Col William Lillard, E TN Mil, Rogersville

ARMS, Edward, Ens, Col Samuel Bunch & Capt Francis Berry, E TN Mil, Res omitted

ARMSTRONG, David, 1 Lt, Col Newton Cannon & Capt John Hanley, Mtd Riflemen

ARMSTRONG, Jas L, Surgeon, Brig Gen John Coffee, Vol Mtd Gunmen, Res omitted

ARMSTRONG, Jas L, Surgeon, Col John Alcorn, TN Vol Cav, Res omitted

ARMSTRONG, Jas L, Surgeon, Col John Coffee, TN Vol Cav Nat'l Riflemen, Res omitted

ARMSTRONG, Jas L, Surgeon, Col John Coffee, TN Vol Cav, Res omitted

ARMSTRONG, Jno M, Ens, no other information

ARMSTRONG, Jno, Ens, no other information

ARMSTRONG, Robert, 2 Lt, Maj Gen Andrew Jackson & Capt David S Deadrick, Arty, Res omitted

ARMSTRONG, William, Adjt & 1 Lt, Col Edward E Booth, E TN Mil, Res omitted

ARMSTRONG, Wm, Ens, Col Wm Sitton & Capt Wm Metcalf, Mil Inf, Res omitted

ARRASMITH, Thos, 2 Lt, Col Wm Metcalf & Capt Barbee Collins, Mil Inf, Res omitted

ASHMORE, Samuel, Capt, Col R C Napier, 1st TN Regt Inf, Maury Co

ASHMORE, Samuel, Capt, Col R C Napier, Mil Inf, Res omitted

ASHWORTH, Jasper, Lt, Maj James Porter, Sqdn of E TN Cav, Res omitted

ASKEW, Josiah, Capt, Col John Coffee, 26th Regt TN Mil, Res omitted

ASKEW, Josiah, Capt, Commander omitted, Inf, Res omitted

ATCHESON, Peter, Ens, Col William Hall & Capt John Moore, Vol Inf, Res omitted

ATCHISON, Adam, 2 Lt, Col Edward Bradley & Capt John Moore, Vol Inf, Res omitted

AUSTIN, Benj, Ens, Col Samuel Bunch & Capt Solomon Dobkins, E TN Mil, Res omitted

AVERY, Wm, Ens, Col Jas Raulston & Capt Chas Wade, Inf, Res omitted

AWALT, John, Lt, Col S Copeland & Capt John Holshouser, Inf, Res omitted

BACON, Allen I, Capt, Col John Brown, E TN Mil Inf, Res omitted

BACON, Allen J, Capt, Col John Brown, Branch Svce omitted, Res omitted

BACON, Joseph B, Capt, Col Samuel Bayless, E TN Drafted Mil, Washington Co

BAIRD, John, 2 Lt, Col Newton Cannon & Capt Isaac Williams, Mtd Riflemen, Res omitted

BAIRD, John, 2 Lt, Col R H Dyer & Maj Wm Russell & Capt Isaac Williams, Separate Bn of TN Vol Mtd Gunmen, Res omitted

BAKER, Andrew, Ens, Col R C Napier & Capt John Chism, Mil Inf, Res omitted

BAKER, Israil, Lt, Col R C Napier & Capt Thomas Preston, Mil Inf, Res omitted

BAKER, William, 1 Lt, Capt Edwin S Mmoore, Mtd Riflemen, Res omitted

BAKER, William, 1 Lt, Col William Lillard & Capt William Hamilton, E TN Vol Inf, Res omitted

BALCH, Elijah, Ens, Col Wm Lillard & Capt Jacob Dyke, Vol Inf, Res omitted

BANDY, Jamison, 1 Lt, Regt Commander omitted, Capt George Smith, Spies

BANDY, Jamison, 2 Lt, Col Thomas Williamson, Capt Robert Moore, Vol Mtd Gunmen

BANDY, Jamison, 2 Lt, Maj Gen John Cocke, Co Commander omitted, T V M Gunmen

BARKLEY, Robert, Ens, Col Edward Bradley, Capt Brice Martin, Vol Inf, promoted from Sgt

BARKSDALE, John, Lt & Adjt, Col John K Wynn, no Co Commander, 1 Regt TN Mil

BARNES, George, Capt, Col John Cocke, Capt self; Inf

BARNES, George, Capt, Col John Cocke, TN Mil Inf, Res Omitted

BARNES, Turner, 3 Lt, Col James Raulston & Capt Henry Hamilton, Inf, Res omitted

BARNETT, John, 1 Lt, Regt Commander omitted, Capt Nathan Peoples, Branch Srvce omitted, Res omitted

BARNETT, Jos H, 3 Lt, Col Wm Metcalf & Capt Alexander Hill & Capt John Cunningham, Mil Inf; promoted to 2 Lt

BARNHART, John, Capt, Col William Metcalf, W TN Mil Inf, Res Omitted

BARRETT, Isaac, Lt, Capt Nathan Davis, W TN Mil Inf, Bedford Co

BARRON, Amon, Capt, Col S Bunch & Capt George McPherson, E TN Mil, Res omitted; resigned 4-4-1814

BARRON, Amos, Capt, Col Samuel Bunch, E TN Mil, Res Omitted

BARRY, James, Surgeon, Maj William Woodfolk, Separate Bn of W TN Mil, Res omitted

BARTHOLOMEN, Guin, Lt, Col William Lillard & Capt John Neatherton, E TN Vol Inf, Res omitted

BARTLETT, John L, Cor (3 Lt), Col Thomas Williamson & Capt Beverly Williams, Vol Mtd Gunmen, Res omitted

BARTLETT, John L, Cor (3 Lt), Maj Gen John Cocke, TN Vol Mtd Gunmen, Res omitted

BARTON, Eli, Ens, Capt Jas Williams, Mil Cav, Res omitted

BARTON, Eli, Ens, Col Samuel Bunch & Capt Joseph Duncan, E TN Drafted Mil, Res omitted

BARTON, Eli, Ens, Col Samuel Bunch & Capt Moses, E TN Mil, Res omitted

BARTON, Hugh, Capt, Col Jno Brown, E TN Mil Inf, Res omitted

BARTON, Hugh, Capt, Col John Brown, Branch Svce omitted, Res Omitted

BARTON, Samuel, 1 Lt, Col Newton Cannon & Capt John Harpole, Mtd Gunmen, Res omitted; killed at Talledgeda 11-9-1813

BARTON, Wm S, 2 Maj, Col Stephen Copeland, 3rd Regt TN Mil, Res omitted

BASKERVILLE, John, 3 Lt & Adjt, Col Robt H Dyer, Regt TN Vol Mtd Gunmen, Res omitted; promoted to Maj

BASKERVILLE, John, Capt, Col John Alcorn, Vol Cav, Sumner Co
BASKERVILLE, John, Lt & Adjt, Brig Gen John Coffee, TN Vol Mtd Gunmen, Res omitted
BASS, Ezekial, Capt, Maj William Woodfolk, Mil Inf Separate Bn, Wilson Co
BASSETT, Spencer, Ens, Col Samuel Bunch & Capt Jas Cumming, E TN Vol Mtd Inf, Res omitted
BATES, Wm, Ens, Maj John Chiles & Capt Jas Cummings, E TN Vol Mtd Inf, Res omitted
BAUTON, Jobbtt?, 1 Lt, Col N Cannon & Capt Ota Cantrell, W TN Mtd Inf, Res omitted; promoted to Capt
BAXTER, James, Inspector Gen, Maj Gen William Carroll, TN Mil, Res omitted
BAXTER, James, Lt Adjt, Col John Alcorn, TN Vol Cav, Res omitted
BAXTER, James, Lt Adjt, Col John Coffee, TN Vol Cav & Mtd Riflemen, Res omitted
BAYLES, Samuel, Lt, Col William Lillard & Capt Jacob Hartsell, E TN Inf, Res omitted
BAYLESS, John, Capt, Col Samuel Wear & Capt John Bayless, Mtd Inf, Res omitted
BAYLESS, John, Capt, Col Samuel Wear, E TN Mil Mtd Inf, Res omitted
BAYLESS, Samuel, Col, Commander omitted, 4th Regt E TN Mil, Res omitted
BAYLESS, Samuel, Col, Field & Staff Officers, Res omitted; Div of Maj Gen Wm Carro 2
BAYLESS, William, 3 Lt, Col Samuel Bayless & Capt Joseph Hale, E TN Mil, Res omitted; promoted to 2 Lt
BAYLESS, William, Adjt, Col Samuel Bayless, 4th Regt E TN Mil, Res omitted; 1st Lt in the line
BEAN, Jesse, 1 Lt, Gen John Coffee, Commander of Spies, Res omitted
BEAN, Jesse, 1 Lt, Gen John Coffee, TN Vol Mtd Gunmen Spies, Nashville
BEAN, Jesse, Lt, Capt Wm Mitchell, Spies, Res omitted
BEAN, Russell, 1 Lt, Col Wm Lillard & Capt Wm McLin, E TN Inf, Res omitted; detached to the armory
BEATTY, John, Ens, Col Stephens & Capt William Evans, Mil Inf, Res omitted
BEEN, Leroy, 2 Lt, Maj William Russell & Capt John Cowan, Vol Mtd Riflemen, Res omitted; resigned 1-12-1815
BELL, James C, 1 Lt, Col Ewen Allison & Capt Jacob Hoyal, E TN Mil, Res omitted
BELL, John, 1 Lt, Maj Gen Andrew Jackson & Capt William Rupee, Mtd Spies, Res omitted; wounded 4-22-1814
BENGE, William, 2 Lt, Cor, Col J Coffee, Capt Alexander, Cav; promoted from Cornet to 2 Lt
BENNET, Noah, 3 Lt, Col Philip Pipkin, Capt Ebenezer Kirkpatrick, Mil Inf
BENNETT, James, Capt, Col Robert Steele, 4th Regt TN Mil Inf, Jackson Co
BENNETT, James, Capt, Col Robert Steele, Capt self, Mil Inf
BENSON, Early, Capt, Col R C Napier, 1st Regt W TN Mil Inf, Nashville
BENSON, Mathias, 1 Lt, Col Edwin Booth, Capt Alexander Biggs, Inf
BENSON, Richard, Capt, Col A Cheatham, Capt self, Mil Inf
BENSON, Richard, Capt, Col Archar Cheatham, 2nd Regt Mil Inf, Robertson Co
BENTON, Thomas H, Col, 2 Regt TN Vol Inf
BENTON, Thomas H, Col, Field & Staff Officers, 2nd Regt TN Vol Inf, Nashville
BERDIT, Jills, Capt, Maj Gen John Cocke, other commanders omitted, T Vol Mtd Gunmen
BERDIT, William, 1 Lt, Maj Gen John Cocke, Co commander omitted, T Vol Mtd Gunmen
BERRY, Francis, Capt, Col Samuel Bunch, Capt self, E TN Mil
BERRY, Francis, Capt, Col Samuel Bunch, E TN Mil Inf, Knoxville
BERRY, James, 1 Lt, Col N Cannon, Capt Brice Martin, Mtd Gunmen; promoted from 2 Lt
BERRY, James, 1 Lt, Commanders omitted, Mtd Riflemen; killed in battle 3-27-1814
BERRY, James, 3 Lt, Col John Cocke, Capt George Barnes, Inf
BERRY, James, Lt, Col R H Dyer, Det Mtd Riflemen Vol Cav, Williamson Co
BETHERAL, Lewis, 2 Adjt, Col John Brown, E TN Vol Mtd Gunmen, Res omitted
BEVERLEY, William, Capt, Maj Gen John Cocke, TN Vol Mtd Gunmen
BEWLEYS, Jacob M, 3 Lt, Col William Johnson, Capt Christopher Cook; 3 Regt E TN Mil; promoted from Cpl
BIBLE, John, 3 Lt, Col Samuel Bayless, Capt Branch Jones, E TN Drafted Mil
BIDWILL, Charles, 2 Lt, Col William Metcalf, Capt Obidiah Waller, Mil Inf
BIGGS, Alexander, Capt, Col Edwin Booth, Inf
BIGGS, Alexander, Capt, Col Edwin E Booth, 5th Regt TN Drafted Mil, Knoxville
BILER, John, Capt, Col S Copeland, 3rd Regt Militia Inf, Bedford Co
BILES, John, Capt, Col S Copeland, Inf
BINGHAM, William, Ens, Col N Cannon, Capt Williams, Mtd Riflemen; absent sick
BIRD (BAIRD), Robert, 3 Lt, Col R H Dyer, Maj William Russell, Capt Beverly Williams, TN Vol Mtd Gunmen
BIRD, Thomas, Cor, Col Thomas Williamson, Capt John Crane, Capt James Cook, Vol Mtd Gunmen
BIRD, William C, 1 Lt, Col Thomas Benton, Capt William Moore, Vol Inf
BIRD, William, Ens, Col James Raulston, Capt Matthew Neal, Inf; promoted from Pvt
BIRDWELL, Hugh, Capt, Col A Cheatham, Inf
BIRDWELL, Hugh, Capt, Col Archer Cheatham, 2nd Regt Tn Mil Inf, Davidson Co
BLACK, George V, 1 Lt, Col William Johnson, Capt David McKamy, E TN Draft Mil
BLACK, George, 2 Lt, Col Edward Bradley, Capt William Lauderdale, Vol Inf
BLACK, George, Ens, Col William Hall, Capt William

Alexander, Vol Inf
BLACK, James A, Capt, Col James Raulston, 3rd Regt TN Mil Inf, Res omitted
BLACK, James A, Capt, Col James Raulston, Inf
BLACK, Joseph, 3 Lt, Maj John Childs, Capt Charles Conway, E Tn Mtd Gunmen; Regt Co--13-Anderson
BLACKMAN, Launer (Learner), Chap, Maj Gen Andrew Jackson, Det TN Vol, Res omitted
BLACKMAN, Learner, Chap, Brig Gen Andrew Jackson, Det TN Vol, Res omitted
BLACKWELL, Jas, 3 Lt, Col Jno Brown & Capt Jas Preston, E TN Mil Inf, Res omitted
BLAIR, Samuel, 1 Lt, Col Edwin E Booth, Drafted Mil, Res omitted
BLAIR, Solomon, 3 Lt, Col Newton Cannon & Capt James Walton, Mtd Riflemen, Res omitted; sick absent
BLAIR, William A, 1 Lt, Maj William Woodfolk & Capt Abner Pearce, Inf, Res omitted
BLAKEMORE, James, Capt, Col Philip Pipkin, 1st Regt W TN Mil, Res omitted
BLAKEMORE, Jas, Capt, Col Philip Pipkin, Mil Inf, Res omitted
BLAKEMORE, Jno D, 3 Lt, Col Alexander Loury & Capt Geo Sarver, Inf, Res omitted
BLANTON, James P, Ens, Capt S Bunch & Capt Francis Register, E TN Mil, Res omitted
BLANTON, Jas D, Ens, Capt S Bunch & Capt Francis Register, E TN Mil, Res omitted
BLEDSOE, Abraham, Capt, Col William Hall, 1st Regt TN Vol, Res omitted
BLEDSOE, Abraham, Capt, Col Wm Hall, Vol Inf, Res omitted
BLEDSOE, Abram, Capt, Col Edward Bradley, 1st Regt TN Vol Inf Riflemen, Sumner Co
BLEDSOE, Henry, 1 Lt & QM, Col Edward Bradley, 1 Regt TN Vol Inf, Res omitted
BLOUNT, Richard, Adjt, Commander omitted, Mil Inf, Res omitted
BOATRIGHT, William, 1 Lt, Col Samuel Bayless & Capt Jonathan Waddell, E TN Mil, Res omitted
BOAZ, Thos, 1 Lt, Col William Y Higgins & Capt William Doake, Mtd Riflemen, Res omitted
BOND, Nicholas, Cpt, Col John Brown & Capt John Childs, E TN Vol Mtd Gunmen, Res omitted
BONE, Henry P, Ens, Col S Copeland, Capt Moses Thompson, Inf, Res omitted
BOOTH, Edwin E, Col, Commander omitted, E TN Mil, Res omitted
BOOTH, Edwin E, Col, Field & Staff Officers, 5th 2 Regt TN Mil, Knox Co
BOTTS, Seth, 2 Lt, Col William Lillard, Capt William Hamilton, E TN Vol Inf, Res omitted
BOWDERY, Samuel, 2 Lt, Col Ewen Allison & Capt William King, Drafted Mil, Res omitted
BOWEN, Wm, Ens, Col N Cannon & Capt Ota Cantrell, W TN Mtd Inf, Res omitted
BOWMAN, Samuel, Capt, Col Samuel Wear, E TN Mil Mtd Inf, Res omitted
BOWMAN, Samuel, Capt, Col Samuel Wear, Mtd Inf, Res omitted
BOWMAN, William, 2 Lt, Capt John Alcorn, Capt William Locke, Cav, Res omitted
BOWMAN, William, Cor (3 Lt), Col John Coffee, Capt Blackman Coleman, Cav, Res omitted
BOYAKIN, Willie, Ens, Col Robert Steele & Capt Robert Campbell, W TN Mil Inf, Res omitted
BOYD, Henry, Ens, Col Ewen Allison & Capt Adam Winsell, E TN Drafted Mil, Res omitted; on furlough
BOYD, James, 1 Lt, Col Philip Pipkin, Capt Ebenezer Kirkpatrick, Mil Inf
BOYD, James, 3 Lt, Col Edwin Booth, Capt John Lewis, E TN Inf, Res omitted
BOYD, James, Ens, Col Edwin Booth, Capt Alexander Biggs, Inf, Res omitted
BOYD, Richard, 2 Maj, Col Newton Cannon, Tn Vol Mtd Riflemen
BOYD, Richard, Capt, Col John Coffee & John Alcorn, Mtd Gunmen, Nashville
BOYD, Richard, Capt, Col John Coffee, Capt Daniel Ross, Mtd Gunmen; promoted to 2 Maj, Col N Cannon Regt
BOYD, Richard, Maj, Col Newton, Field Staff
BOYLES, John, 1 Lt, Maj Gen A Jackson, Capt John Craine, Mtd Gunmen
BRADEN, James, Ens, Regt Commander omitted, Capt Robert Evans, Mtd Spies; raised from Sgt
BRADEN, Robert, Capt, Col John K Wynne, Mil Inf 1st Regt W TN, Robertson Co
BRADEN, Robert, Ens, Col Newton Cannon, Capt John Harpole, Mtd Gunmen; promoted to 2 Lt
BRADFORD, Daniel M, 1 Lt, Col William Carroll, Capt Lewis Dillahunty, Vol Inf
BRADFORD, Daniel M, Capt, Col Wm Metcalf, TN Mil Inf, Res omitted
BRADFORD, Davis, Ens, Col N Cannon, Capt James Walton, Mtd Riflemen
BRADFORD, Larkin, 1 Lt, Regt Commander omitted, Capt George Smith, Spies; K at Battle of Talledge
BRADIN, Robert, Capt, Col John K Wynne, Inf
BRADLEY, Edward, Col, Commander omitted, 1st Regt TN Vol Inf, Res omitted
BRADLEY, Edward, Col, Field & Staff Officers, 1st Regt Vol Inf, Res omitted
BRADLEY, Edward, Lt Col, Col Wm Hall, Inf, Res omitted
BRADLEY, Hugh, Cor (3 Lt), Col J Alcorn, Capt Thomas Bradley, Branch Srvce omitted, Res omitted
BRADLEY, Hugh, Cor (3 Lt), Col John Coffee, Capt Thomas Bradley, Branch Srvce omitted, Res omitted
BRADLEY, Isaac, Ens, Col Stephen Copeland, Capt William Hodges, Inf, Res omitted
BRADLEY, Jas, 1 Lt, Col Bradley, Capt Martin, Vol Inf, Res omitted
BRADLEY, Jas, 1 Lt, Col Wm Hall, Capt Brice Martin, Vol Inf, Res omitted
BRADLEY, Thomas, Capt, Col J Alcorn, Cav, Res omitted
BRADLEY, Thomas, Capt, Col John Alcorn, Vol Cav,

Res omitted

BRADLEY, Thomas, Capt, Col John Coffee, Cav Vol, Res omitted

BRADLEY, Wm, Maj, Col Wm Lillard, E TN Vol Mil, Res omitted

BRADLY, Wm, 2 Maj, Col John Brown, E TN Mtd Gunmen Vol, Res omitted

BRADSHAW, Christopher, Lt, Col William Lillard, Capt Robert McCalpin, E TN Inf, Res omitted

BRANCH, Robt, 1 Lt, Col Thomas Benton, Capt Henry Douglas, Vol Inf, Res omitted

BRANDON, George, Capt, Col N Cannon, Mtd Riflemen, Res omitted

BRANDON, George, Capt, Col Newton Cannon, Capt George Brandon, Mtd Riflemen, Res omitted; sick absent

BRANNER, Michael, Lt, Col William Lillard, Capt John Ruper, E TN Vol Inf, Res omitted

BRANSTETTER, Daniel, 2 Lt, Col Ewin Allison, Capt Joseph Everett, E TN Mil, Res omitted

BRATTON, Joshua, 2 Lt, Col William Higgins, Capt Adam Dale, Mtd Gunmen, Res omitted

BRAY, Solomon, Capt, Col Ewen Allison, Capt William King, Drafted Mil; left at Ft Williams 4-28-1814 in service

BREARDEN, Andrew, 2 Lt, Col Jno Brown, Capt Lunsford Oliver, E TN Mil, Res omitted

BREDEN, Andrew, Capt, Col Samuel Bunch, E TN Mil, Res omitted

BREDEN, Robert, Capt, Col John K Wynne, Mil Inf 1st Regt W TN, Nashville?

BREEDLOVE, Chas, 3 Lt, Col Wm Johnson, Capt Henry Hunter, E TN Mil, Res omitted

BREVARD, Cyrus W, 1 Lt, Col Thomas Williamson, Capt Anthony Metcalf, Vol Mtd Gunmen, Res omitted

BREVARD, Cyrus, Lt, Maj Gen John Cocke, TN Vol Mtd Gunmen, Res omitted

BRIDGEWATER, Richard, 1 Lt, Col Robert Steele, Capt Robert Campbell, W TN Mil Inf, Res omitted

BRIGGS, Rich'd, 3 Lt, Maj Gen A Jackson, Col Thomas Williamson, Capt Robert Steele, Vol Mtd Gunmen, Res omitted

BRIGHAM, James H, Capt, Lt Col Jno Edmonson, Cav, Res omitted

BRIGMORE, Thomas, 1 Lt, Col John Brown, Capt Allen I Bacon, E TN Mil Inf, Res omitted

BRITTON, Joseph, 2 Lt, Col Samuel Bayless, Capt Allen Bacon, E TN Mil, Res omitted

BROCK, John, Capt, Col Samuel Bayless, E TN Drafted Mil, Tazewell TN

BROOKS, Henry, Surgeon, Col S Copeland, 3rd Regt Mil Inf, Res omitted; on furlough 4-18-1814

BROOKS, Sam'l I, 1 Lt, Brig Gen John Coffee, TN Vol Mtd Gunmen, Res omitted

BROOKS, Sam'l T, 1 Lt, Col N T Perkins, Capt James McMahan, Mtd Gunmen, Res omitted

BROOKS, Wm, 2 Lt, Maj John Childs, Capt Jas Cummings, E TN Vol Mtd Inf, Res omitted

BROWN, Allen, Adjt, Col Samuel Bunch, Capt Alexander Smith, E TN Mil, Res omitted

BROWN, Dudley, Ens, Col N T Perkins, Capt John B, Vol Mtd Inf

BROWN, George, 1 Lt, Col William Metcalf, Capt Thomas Marks, Mil Inf

BROWN, John, Col, E Tn Vol Mtd Gunmen

BROWN, John, Col, Field & Staff Officers, E TN Vol Mtd Gunmen, Kingston TN

BROWN, Jos, Cor (3 Lt), Brig Gen John Coffee, TN Mtd Gunmen, Res omitted

BROWN, Joseph, Cor (3 Lt), Col R H Dyer, Capt James McMahan, TN Mtd Vol Gunmen, Res omitted

BROWN, Thomas, Surgeon, Col Samuel Bunch, Maj Alexaner Smith, E TN Mil, Res omitted; furloughed at Ft Strother

BROWN, Washington, Ens, Maj Wm Woodfolk, Capt McCully, Inf, Res omitted

BROWNING, James, Ens, Col R C Napier, Capt James McMurry, Mil Inf, Res omitted; on furlough

BROWNLOW, Joseph, 3 Lt, Col Samuel Bayless, Capt James Landen, E TN Mil, Res omitted; resigned 12-27-1814

BRUNSON, Robert, Cor (3 Lt), Lt Col John Edmonson, Cav, Res omitted

BRYAN, Henry H, Lt Col, Commander omitted, Mil Inf, Res omitted

BRYAN, Morgan, 1 Lt, Col Robert Steele, Capt James Randals, Inf, Res omitted

BRYANT, Henry H, Lt Col, Det Mil Inf 6th Brig, Res omitted

BRYERS, James, 1 Lt & B? Inspector, Gen Andrew Jackson, Brig Gen Isaac Roberts, W TN Mil, Res omitted

BUCHANAN, David, Capt, Col Samuel Bunch, Capt Edward Buchanan, E TN Drafted Mil, Res omitted

BUCHANAN, Edward, Capt, Col Samuel Bunch, E TN Drafted Mil, Res omitted

BUCK, Ephraim, 1 Lt, Col Ewen Allison, Capt Adam Winsell, E TN Drafted Mil, Res omitted

BUCKNER, John, Cor (3 Lt), Col William Higgins, Capt Stephen Griffith, Mtd Riflemen, Res omitted

BUFORD, Thos, 2 Lt, Col Philip Pipkin, Capt David Smith, Mil Inf, Res omitted

BUNCH, Samuel, Capt, Col Jno Williams, Mtd Vol, Res omitted

BUNCH, Samuel, Capt, Col John Williams, E Tn Mtd Vol, Res omitted

BUNCH, Samuel, Col, Commander omitted, E TN Mil, Res omitted

BUNCH, Samuel, Col, Field & Staff Officers, E TN Mil, Res omitted

BURCH (BUNCH), John, 2 Lt, Col Alexander Loury, Col Leroy Hammonds, Capt Araheal Rains, Inf, res omitted; sick absent

BURD, Thos, Cor (3 Lt), Maj Gen John Cocke, TN Vol Mtd Gunmen, Res omitted

BURDEN, Eli, 2 Lt, Col Edward Braley, Capt John Kennedy, Riflemen, Res omitted

BURDETT, Giles, Capt, Col Thomas Williamson, 2nd Regt Vol Mtd Gunmen, Nashville

BURDETT, Wm, 1 Lt, Col Thomas Williamson, Capt Giles Burdett, Vol Mtd Gunmen, Res omitted

## Officers, War of 1812

BURDON, Hawkins, 2 Lt, Col John Brown, Capt Jesse G Reany, Mtd Gunmen, Res omitted

BURGESS, Richard, 2 Lt, Lt Col L Hammonds, Lt Col A Loury, Capt Thomas Delaney, Inf, Res omitted

BURGIS, William, 1 Lt, Col Samuel Bayless, Capt James Landen, E TN Mil, Res omitted

BURNETT, Zachriah, Lt, Col Samuel Bunch, Capt John McNare, E TN Mil, Res omitted; resigned 1-18-1814

BURNS, John, 3 Lt, Maj William Woodfolk, Capt John Sutton, Inf, Res omitted

BURTON, John H, 2 Maj, Col John Cocke, 2nd Regt W TN Mil Inf, Res omitted

BUTLER, Baily, Capt, Col John K Wynne, Mil Inf 1st TN Regt, Jackson Co

BUTLER, Edmond, Ens, Col John K Wynne, Capt Butler, Inf, Res omitted

BUTLER, Isaac, 1 Lt, Col N T Perkins, Capt Mathew Patterson, Mtd Vol, Res omitted

BUTLER, Price, Lt, Col John K Wynne, Capt Butler, Inf, Res omitted; sick present

BUTLER, Wm, Surgeon, Commander omitted, 2nd Regt TN Vol Inf, Res omitted

BYLER, John, Ens, Col N Cannon, Capt John B Demsey, Mtd Gunmen, Res omitted

BYRAM, Ebenezer, 1 Lt, Capt J Prewitt, Mtd Vol, Res omitted

BYRD, Richard, 1 Lt, Col John Alcorn, Capt Winton, Mtd Riflemen, Res omitted

BYRN, John W, Capt, Col Jno Coffee, Cav, Res omitted

BYRN, John W, Capt, Col John Alcorn, Cav, Res omitted; sick

BYRN, John W, Capt, Col John Alcorn, Mtd Mil Vol Cav, Sumner Co

BYRNE, John W, Capt, Col John Coffee, Cav, Res omitted

CALLOWAY, Joseph, Capt, Col Samuel Wear, E TN Mtd Inf, Res omitted

CAMPBELL, Robert, Capt, Col Robert Steele, 4th Regt Mil Inf, Columbia Maury Co

CANNON, Newton, Capt, Col Newton Cannon, TN Regt Mtd Gunmen, Res illegible

CANNON, Newton, Col, Commander omitted, Regt TN Mtd Riflemen Vol, Williamson Co

CANNON, Robert, Capt, Col Thomas Benton, Inf, Res omitted

CANTRELL, Ota, Capt, Col N Cannon, Mtd Gunmen, Rutherford Co

CAPERTON, George, Capt, Col Thomas Benton, 2nd Regt TN Mil Inf, Res omitted

CAPERTON, George, Capt, Col William Pillow, 2nd Regt TN Vol Inf, Winchester

CARROLL, William, Capt, Col William Hall, TN Vol Inf 1st Regt, Res omitted

CARROLL, William, Inspector Gen, Div of Maj Gen Andrew Jackson, TN Mil, Nashville

CARROLL, William, Maj Gen, Commander omitted, TN Mil, Res omitted

CARSON, Robert, Capt, Col Archer Cheatham, Mil Inf, Rutherford Co

CARUTHERS, Samuel M, Capt, Col John Cocke, Mil Inf, Nashville? TN

CARUTHERS, William, Capt, Col John K Wynne, Mil Inf, Bedford Co

CATLETT, John, 1 Lt, Col Samuel Bunch & Capt Isaac Williams, E TN Drafted Mil, Kingston

CHAPMAN, George G, Capt, Col A Cheatham, TN Mil 2nd Regt, Robertson Co

CHEATHAM, Archer, Col, Field & Staff Officers, 2nd Regt TN Mil, Fayetteville

CHEATHAM, Archer, Lt Col, Commander omitted, Mtd Inf of the 6th Brig Mil, Res omitted

CHEATHAM, John B, Capt, Col William Y Higgins, Mtd Riflemen, Robertson Co

CHILDS, John, Maj, Field & Staff Officer, Bn E Tn Mtd Vol, Knox Co; Brigade--Brig Gen John Coffee

CHILES, John, Capt, Col John Brown, Mtd Inf, Res omitted

CHILES, John, Capt, Col Samuel Weer?, Vol Mil Inf, Res omitted

CHISM, John, Capt, Col R C Napier, 1st Regt W Tn Mil Inf, Maury Co

CHISM, William, Capt, Maj William Russell, TN Vol Mtd Gunmen, Warren Co

CHITWOOD, John, Capt, Col Robert Steele, Mil Inf, Fayetteville

CHRISTIAN, William, Capt, Col John Brown, Branch Svce omitted, Res omitted

CHURCHMAN, James, Capt, Col Samuel Bayless, E TN Drafted Mil, Res omitted

COCKBURN, George, Ens, Col William Metcalf, Capt Bird L Hurt, Mil Inf

COCKE, Benjamin, Lt & QM, Col John Cocke, no Co Commander, 2 Regt W TN Mil Inf

COCKE, James W, 3 Lt, Maj William Woodfolk, Capt Abner Pearce, Inf

COCKE, John, Maj Gen, E TN Vol Mil

COCKE, John, Maj Gen, Field & Staff Officers, E TN Mil, Res omitted

COCKE, John, Maj, Col John Williams, Branch omitted

COCKE, John, Maj, Col John Williams, E TN Vol, Res omitted

COCKE, William E, 1 Lt, Cool Samuel Bunch, Capt Thomas Mann, E TN Vol Mtd Inf

COFFEE, John, Brig Gen, Staff Officer, TN Vol Mtd Gunmen, Nashville

COFFEE, John, Brig Gen, TN Mtd Mil; also TN Vol Cav & TN Vol Mtd Gunmen

COFFEE, John, Col, Field & Staff Officers, TN Vol Cav, Res omitted

COFFEE, John, Col, TN Vol Cav & Mtd Riflemen

COLBERT, William, 1 Lt, Col Samuel Bunch, Capt Joseph Duncan, E TN Mil; joined Capt Allen's Co

COLBERT, William, 1 Lt, Regt Commander omitted, Capt Joseph William, Mil Cav

COLE, James, Capt, Col John K Wynne, Mil Inf 1st Regt TN, White Co

COLE, James, Capt, Col John Wynne, Inf, Res omitted

COLE, Jesse, Capt, Col Samuel Wear, Vol Inf, Res omitted

COLEMAN, Blackman, Capt, Col John Coffee, Cav, Res omitted

COLEMAN, William, 3 Lt, Maj Wm Woodfolk, Capt

## Officers, War of 1812

Ezekial Ross, Capt McCulley, Inf, Res omitted; d 12-29-1814

COLLIN, John, 2 Lt, Col Ewen Allison, Capt Henry McCray, E TN Mil, Res omitted; transferred to Capt Register Co

COLLINS, Barba, Ens, Col Thos H Benton, Capt Geo Caperton, Vol Inf, Res omitted

COLLINS, Barba, Ens, Col William Pillow, Capt Geo Caperton, Inf, Res omitted

COLLINS, Barbee, Capt, Col William Metcalf, Mil Inf W TN, Res omitted

COLLINS, Barbee, Capt, Col Wm Metcalf, Mil Inf, Res omitted

COLLINS, Barbee, Ens, Col Thos H Benton, Inf, Res omitted

COLLINS, William C, 2 Lt, Col James Raulston, Capt James Black, Inf, Res omitted

COLLINS, William, Lt, Col Robert Steele, Capt John Chitwood, Mil Inf, Res omitted

COLLOM, John, 1 Lt, Col Samuel Bunch, Capt Francis Register, E TN Mil, Res omitted

COMPTON, John, 2 Lt, Col Jas Raulston, Capt Chas Wade, Inf, Res omitted

CONDON, Wm, 3 Lt, Col Wm Lillard, Capt Wm Hamilton, E TN Drafted Mil; elected 10-12-1813

CONN, Jophus H, 2 Maj, Col Jno K Wynn, Regt TN Mil, Res omitted

CONRAD, William, 1 Lt & Assistant B QM, Maj Gen Andrew Jackson, Brig Gen Thomas Johnson, W TN Mil, Res omitted

CONWAY, Charles, Capt, Commander omitted, E TN Mtd Inf Vol, Knoxville; Bn of Maj John Childs

CONWAY, Charles, Capt, Maj John Childs, E TN Mtd Gunmen, Regimental Co 40 Knox

COOK, Christopher, 2 Lt, Col William Johnson, E TN Mil, Res omitted; promoted to Capt

COOK, Christopher, 3 Lt, Col William Johnson, Capt Joseph Kirk, Mil, Res omitted

COOK, James, Capt, Col Thomas Williamson, 2nd Regt TN Vol Mtd Gunmen, Robertson Co

COOK, James, Capt, Col Thomas Williamson, Capt John Crane, Vol Mtd Gunmen; replaced John Crane (d 1-23-1815)

COOK, Joseph, 1 Lt, Maj Gen John Cocke, TN Vol Mtd Gunmen, Res omitted

COOKS, Christopher, Capt, Col William Johnsonn, 3rd Regt E TN Mil, Knoxville

COOKSEY, Jessee, Ens, Col William Hall, Capt James Hamilton, Vol Inf, Res omitted

COOKSEY, John T, 1 Lt, Col Phillip Pipkin, Capt Geo Mebane, Mil Inf, Res omitted

COOKSIE, Jesse, Lt, Lt Col H Dryan, Inf, Res omitted

COONS, Jas, 1 Lt, Col S Bunch, Capt Geo Gregory, E TN Drafted Mil, Res omitted

COOPER, John, 3 Lt, Col Jas Raulston, Capt Jas A Black, Inf, Res omitted

COOPER, Mathew D, 1 Lt, Col Wm Pillow, Capt C E McEwen, Vol Inf, Res omitted

COOPER, Robert, 1 Maj, Lt Col A Cheatham, Mtd Inf, Res omitted

COOPER, Robert, Maj, Commander omitted, Mtd Riflemen, Res omitted

COOPER, Robert, Maj, Commander omitted, Mtd riflemen 26th Regt TN Mil, Res omitted

COOPER, Stephen, 2 Lt, Maj William Russell, Capt George Mitchie, Vol Mtd Gunmen, Res omitted

COOTHE, Daniel, 3 Lt, Maj William Russell, Capt John Cown, Vol Mtd Gunmen, Res omitted

COPELAND, Stephen, Col, Commander omitted, 3rd Regt TN Mil, Res omitted

COPELAND, Stephen, Col, Field & Staff Officers, 3rd Regt TN Mil, Fayetteville

COPELAND, Zacheus, Capt, Col Wm Lillard, Capt Wm Copeland, E TN Vol Inf, Res omitted

CORBET, Jas, 2 Lt, Col S Bayless, Capt Jas Churchman, E TN Mil, Res omitted

COTTON, Noah, 2 Lt, Col John Coffee, Capt John W Byrns, Cav

COTTON, Noah, 2 Lt, Col William Alcorn, Capt John W Byrns, Cav

COULTER, Alex, Ens, Col John Brown, Capt James Standifer, E TN Vol Mtd Mil

COULTER, Alexander, B Q M, Brig Gen Thomas Coulter, E TN Draft Mil; resigned 12-18-1814

COULTER, Thomas, Brig Gen, Div of Maj Gen William Carroll, Div of TN Drafted Mil, Knoxville

COWAN, Andrew, Adjt Gen, Maj Gen John Cocke, E TN Vol Mil

COWAN, Andrew, Capt, Brig Gen James White, Mtd Spies, Res omitted

COWAN, Andrew, Lt, Col John Brown, Capt John Trimble, E TN Mtd Gunmen

COWAN, David, 3 Lt, Maj William Woodfolk, Capt Abner Pearce, Inf; promoted from Cpl

COWAN, James, Capt, Commander omitted, Mtd Inf, Res omitted; guarded Franklin Co under Wm Blount

COWAN, James, Capt, Regt Commander omitted, Mtd Inf

COWAN, John, Capt, Maj William Russell, 1st TN Vol Mtd Gunmen, Fayetteville Lincoln Co

COWAN, John, Capt, Maj William Russell, Vol Mtd Gunmen

COWAN, Mathew, Capt, Col James Raulston, 3rd Regt TN Mil, Res omitted

COWAN, Mathew, Capt, Col James Raulston, Inf

COWAN, Samuel, Capt, Bn of Maj James P H Porter, E TN Cav Vol, Res omitted

COWAN, Samuel, Capt, Maj James Porter, Cav

COZBY, Jas, Adjt, Col Samuel Bunch, E TN Mil, Res omitted

CRABB, Thos, 2 Lt, Col John Alcorn, Capt John J Winston, Mtd Riflemen, Res omitted; resigned 12-8-1813

CRAFTON, John B, Ens, Col John Cocke, Capt James Gault, Inf, Res omitted; promoted to 3 Lt

CRAGS, John, Ens, Col Alexander Loury, Lt Col Leroy Hammonds, Capt Thomas Delaney, Inf

CRAIG, Alexander, Lt, Col A Cheatham, Capt William Creel, Inf, Res omitted

CRAIG, James, Capt, Col A Loury, 2nd Regt W TN Mil Inf, Humphreys Co

CRAIG, James, Capt, Col Leroy Hammonds, 2nd Regt W

TN Mil, Res omitted
CRAIG, James, Capt, Commander omitted, Mil Inf, Res omitted
CRAIG, James, Capt, Commander omitted, Mtd inf, Res omitted
CRAIG, Jas, Capt, Lt Col Leroy Hammonds, Inf, Reynoldsburg?
CRANE, John, Capt, Brig Gen Thomas Johnson, 6th Brig TN Mil Mtd Inf, Res omitted
CRANE, John, Capt, Col Thomas Williamson, 2nd Regt TN Vol Mtd Gunmen, Fayetteville
CRANE, John, Capt, Col Thomas Williamson, Capt James Cook, Vol Mtd Gunmen, Res omitted
CRANE, John, Capt, Col Wm Y Higgins, Mtd Gunmen, Springfield
CRANE, John, Capt, Commander omitted, Mtd Inf, Res omitted
CRANE, John, Capt, no other information
CRANE, Newell, Ens, Col S Copeland, Capt John Biles, Inf, Res omitted
CRAWFORD, John, Adjt, Col Samuel Bunch, E TN Mil, Res omitted
CRAWFORD, John, Capt, Brig Gen Thomas Washington, 9th Brig Mtd Inf, Res omitted
CRAWFORD, John, Capt, no other information
CRAWFORD, Samuel, 2 Lt - Capt, Col Robert Dyer, Capt James McMahon, 1st TN Mtd Vol Gunmen, Res omitted; promoted to Capt
CRAWFORD, Samuel, 2 Lt, Brig Gen John Coffee, TN Vol Mtd Gunmen, Res omitted
CRAWFORD, Samuel, Capt, Col Robert H Dyer, Mtd Gunmen TN Vol Cav, Res omitted
CRAWFORD, Samuel, Ens, Col Samuel Bunch, Capt N Gibbs, E TN Mil, Res omitted
CREEL, William, Capt, Col Archer Cheatham, Mil Inf, Res omitted
CREEL, Wm, Capt, Col A Cheatham, Inf, Res omitted
CRIDDLE, Ed, Lt, Brig Gen Thomas Washington, Branch Srvce omitted, Res omitted
CRIM, John, Ens, Capt William J Smith, Vol Inf, Res omitted
CRIM, John, Ens, Col Thomas Benton, Capt William Smith, Vol Inf, Res omitted
CRIM, John, Ens, Col William Pillow, Capt William J Smith, Vol Inf, Res omitted; deserted 12-6-1813
CROSS, James, 2 Lt, Col Edwin E Booth, Capt John Porter, Drafted Mil, Res omitted
CROSWELL, Nelson, Lt, Col John Cocke, Capt James Gray, Inf, Res omitted
CRUNK, Richard, Capt, Col John Cocke, Inf
CRUNK, Richard, Capt, Col John Cocke, Mil Inf, Nashville
CRUNK, Richard, Ens, Lt Col A Cheatham, Co Commander omitted, Mtd Inf
CUMMING, James, Capt, Bn of Maj John Childs, E TN Mil Vol Mtd Gunmen, Rogersville (Hawkins Co)
CUMMING, James, Capt, Col Samuel Bunch, E TN Vol Mtd Inf, Hawkins Co
CUMMING, James, Capt, Col Samuel Bunch, Mtd Inf, E TN Mil, Rogersville (Hawkins Co)
CUMMING, James, Capt, Maj John Chiles, E TN Vol Mtd Inf, Hawkins Co
CUMMINS, Uriah, 1 Lt, Col John Alcorn, Capt Wm Locke, Cav, Res omitted
CUMMINS, Urich, 2nd Lt, Col John Coffee, Capt Blackman Coleman, Cav, Res omitted
CUNNINGHAM, Alexander, Ens, Col John Wynne, Capt Wm McCall, Inf, Res omitted
CUNNINGHAM, David, Lt, Col S Bunch, Capt William Jobe, E TN Vol Mtd Inf, Res omitted
CUNNINGHAM, John, 1 Lt, Col Wm Metcalf, Capt Hill, Mil Inf, Res omitted; promoted to Capt
CUNNINGHAM, John, Capt, Col William Metcalf, 1st Regt TN Militia, Nashville
CUNNINGHAM, John, Lt, Col John Wynne, Capt James Cole, Inf, Res omitted
CUNNINGHAM, Robert, 3 Lt, Col Wm Metcalf, Capt Wm Sitton, Mil Inf, Res omitted
CURRBY, Isaac, 1 Lt, Col Wm Metcalf, Capt William Mullen, Mil Inf, Res omitted
CURRIN, Jonathan, 2 Lt, Capt David Mason, Cav, Res omitted
CURTIS, Joshua, 1 Lt, Col A Cheatham, Inf, Res omitted
DABZELL, David, 3 Lt, Col Edwin Booth, Capt Samuel Thompson, E TN Mil, Res omitted
DALE, Adam, Capt, Col Wm Higgins, Mtd Gunmen, Res omitted
DALF, Adam, Capt, Col William Y Higgins, Mtd Gunmen, Carthage Smith Co
DALTON, John, Capt, Col John Cocke, Mil Inf, Nashville
DANIEL, Sale O, 2 Lt, Brig Gen John Coffee, Co Commander omitted, TN Vol Mtd Gunmen, Res omitted
DAVIDSON, William, Ens, Col John Brown, Capt Lunsford Oliver, E TN Mil, Res omitted
DAVIS, James, 1 Lt & Paymaster, Commander omitted, 2nd Regt TN Vol Inf, Res omitted
DAVIS, Moses, Capt, Col Samuel Bunch, Drafted Inf E TN Mil, Res omitted
DAVIS, Nathan, Capt, Commander omitted, Inf, Res omitted; promoted from 1 Lt
DAVIS, Nathan, Capt, Div of Maj Gen Andrew Jackson, Vol Mil Inf, Fayetteville
DAVIS, Thomas, Lt Col, Col Samuel Bunch, E TN Mtd Vol Inf, Res omitted
DAWBINS, John, 1 Lt, Maj Gen John Cocke, Co Commander omitted, TN Vol Mtd Gunmen
DAWSON, John, Capt, Col S Copeland, 3rd Regt Military Inf, Fayetteville
DAWSON, John, Capt, Col S Copeland, Inf
DEADERICK, D H, Capt, Gen Andrew Jackson, Arty
DEADERICK, David S, 1 Lt, Maj Gen Andrew Jackson, Capt William Carroll, Vol Inf
DEADERICK, David S, Capt, Div of Maj Gen Andrew Jackson, Arty, Nashville
DEAN, I, 2 Lt, Col John Coffee, Capt Charles Kavanaugh, Cav
DEENS, Jeremiah, 2 Lt, Col John Coffee, Capt Charles Kavanaugh, Cav
DEENS, Jeremiah, 2 Lt, Regt Commander omitted, Capt Archibald McKenney, Cav; resigned 12-10-1813
DEERY, Daniel, Cor, Regt Commander omitted, Capt

## Officers, War of 1812

Archibald McKinney, Cav; quit the service
DEERY, Jeremiah, 2 Lt, Regt Commander omitted, Capt A McKenney, Cav; Resigned 12-10-1813
DEGRAFFENREED, Metcalf, 2 Lt, Col Thomas Benton, Capt James McEwen, Vol Inf
DELANEY, Thomas, Capt, Col Alexander Loury, W TN Mil, Res omitted
DELANY, Thos, Capt, Lt Col A Hammonds, Capt A Loury, Inf, Res omitted
DELL, John, 2 Lt, Col Thomas Benton, Capt Benj Reynolds, Vol Inf, Res omitted
DEMENT, Cador, 3 Lt, Col John Cocke, Capt James Gault, Inf, Res omitted
DEMSEY, John B, Capt, Col N Cannon, Mtd Riflemen, Shelbyville Bedford Co
DENTON, Joel, 2 Lt, Col John Williams, Capt William Walker, Vol, Res omitted
DERMOND (DEDMOND), Thomas D, 2 Lt, Col William Johnson, Capt David McKamy, E TN Drafted Mil, Res omitted
DERRET, John G, 2 Lt, Col Edwin Booth, Capt Richard Marshall, Drafted Mil, Res omitted
DERRICK, William E, Lt, Col Samuel Bunch, Capt David Vance, E TN Mtd Inf, Res omitted
DEVER, Alexander, 2 Lt, Col Edwin Booth, Capt Vernon, E TN Mil, Res omitted
DEW, Robert, 3 Lt, Col William Johnston, Capt James Tunnell, E TN Mil, Res omitted
DEWETT, Richard B, Lt, Col S Bunch, Capt Henry Stephens, E TN Inf, Res omitted
DICKASON, John H, 1 Lt, Col Edward Bradley, Capt Wm Lauderdale, Vol Inf, Res omitted
DICKERSON, John H, 2 Lt, Col William Hall, Capt Wm L Alexander, Vol Inf, Res omitted
DICKERSON, John H?, Lt, Col Wm Hall, Capt Wm L Alexander, Vol Inf, Res omitted
DICKINSON, Jacob, 1 Lt & Paymaster, Col Robert Steele, 4th Regt TN Mil, Res omitted
DICKSON, Ephraim D, Capt, Brig Gen John Coffee, TN Vol Mtd Gunmen, Res omitted
DICKSON, Ephraim D, Capt, Col R H Dyer, 1st TN Mtd Vol Gunmen, Res omitted
DICKSON, Ephraim D, Capt, Col Robert H Dyer, Vol Mtd Gunmen 1st Regt, Nashville
DICKSON, Ezekiel, Cor, Col Newton Cannon, Capt Thomas Yardley, Mtd Riflemen, Res omitted
DICKSON, John B, 2 Lt, Col Robert H Dyer, Capt Dickson, TN Mtd Vol Gunmen, Res omitted
DILL, John, 2 Lt, Col Wm Pillow, Capt Renshaw, Inf, Res omitted
DILLAHUNT, Lewis, Lt, Col Thomas Benton, Capt Thomas Williamson, Vol Inf, Res omitted
DILLAHUNTY, Lewis, 1 Lt, Capt Thos Williamson, Det TN Vol Inf; transferred to Col Cheatham's Regt of Mil & appointed Adjt
DILLAHUNTY, Lewis, 1 Maj, Col Wm Metcalf, Co Commander omitted, 1st Regt W TN Mil Inf, Res omitted
DILLAHUNTY, Lewis, 2 Lt, Col Thomas Benton, Capt Thomas Williamson, Vol Inf, Res omitted
DILLAHUNTY, Lewis, 2 Lt, Col Wm Pillow, Capt Thos Williamson, Vol Inf, Res omitted
DILLAHUNTY, Lewis, Capt, Maj Gen Wm Carroll, Vol Inf, Res omitted; promoted to Maj & transferred to 1st Regt TN Mil
DILLEHUNTY, Lewis, 2nd Lt & Adjt, Col Wm Pillow, 2nd Regt TN Vol Inf, Res omitted
DILLIHUNTY, Lewis, 1 Lt & Adjt, Col A Cheatham, 2nd Regt TN, Res omitted
DOAK, John, 1 Lt, Col Thomas Benton, Capt Isaiah Renshaw, Vol Inf, Res omitted
DOAK, John, 1 Lt, Col Wm Pillow, Capt Isaiah Renshaw, Inf, Res omitted
DOAK, John, Capt, Col N T Perkins, 1st Regt W TN Mil Mtd Riflemen, Fayetteville
DOAK, John, Capt, Col N T Perkins, Capt John Doak, Mtd Riflemen Vol, Res omitted
DOAK, John, Capt, Col Thomas Williamson, 2nd Regt Vol Mtd Gunmen, Fayetteville
DOAK, Robert, Capt, Col Samuel Wear, Capt Robert Doak, E TN Vol Inf, Res omitted
DOAK, Samuel, Lt & Adjt, Gen John Coffee, TN Vol Mtd Inf, Res omitted
DOAKE, John, Lt Col, Col Nicholas Perkins, 1st Regt TN Mtd Vol, Res omitted
DOAKE, William, Capt, Col William Y Higgins, Mtd Riflemen, Fayetteville
DOAKE, William, Capt, Col Wm Higgins, Capt Wm Doake, Mtd Riflemen, Res omitted
DOBBINS, Carson, Lt, Col R S Napier, Capt James McMurry, Mil Inf, Res omitted
DOBBINS, John, Capt, Col Thomas Williamson, 2nd Regt Vol Mtd Gunmen, Nashville
DOBBINS, John, Capt, Col Thomas Williamson, Capt John Dobbins & Capt James Cook, Vol Mtd Gunmen
DOBBINS, Solomon, Capt, Col S Bunch, Capt S Dobbins, E TN Mil, Res omitted
DOBKINS, Solomon, Capt, Col Samuel Bunch, Mil E TN, Washington TN
DODSON, Joshua, Ens, Col Thomas Benton, Capt Wm Moore, Vol Inf, Res omitted
DOHERTY, George, Brig Gen, Field & Staff Officers, E TN Mil, Jefferson Co
DOHERTY, George, Brig Gen, no other information
DOHERTY, Robert, Ens, Col Thomas H Benton, Capt Benjamin Hewett, Vol Inf
DOHERTY, William, 2 Lt, Col Thomas Williamson, Vol Mtd Gunmen
DOKE, John, Capt, Maj Gen John Cocke, TN Vol Mtd Gunmen
DONALDSON, John, Lt, no other information
DONCARLOS, Robert C, Adjt, no commanding officer named, E TN Vol Mil Inf
DONELSON, Alex, Lt & Aide de Camp, Brig Gen John Coffee, TN Mtd Mil; killed in battle 1-22-1814
DONELSON, Alex, Lt & Paymaster, Col John Coffee, no Co Commander, TN Vol Cav & Mtd Riflemen
DOOLEY, Thomas, 2 Lt, Col John Alcorn, Capt Thomas Bradley, Vol Cav; promoted to 1 Lt
DOOLEY, William, Capt, Col Thos McCrory, 2nd Regt Mil Inf, Columbia Maury Co

## Officers, War of 1812

DOOLY, William, Capt, Col T McCrory, Inf

DORAN, Alexander, 2 Lt, Col Samuel Wear, Capt Jesse Cole, Vol Inf

DORAN, Robert L, 1 Lt, Col Samuel Wear, Capt Jesse Col, Vol Inf

DORRIS, Joseph, Chap, Brig Gen I Roberts, W TN Mil; in Gen Andrew Jackson's Division

DORRIS, Joseph, Chap, Brig Gen John Coffee, TN Mtd Mil; transferred from Gen Roberts' Brig

DORRISS, Joseph, Ens, Col A Cheatham, Capt George G Chapman, Inf

DORSEY, John S, Lt QM, Brig Gen John Coffee, TN Vol Mtd Gunmen

DOUGLAS, James, Lt, Lt Col Ed Edmondson, Cav, Res omitted

DOUGLASS, Alfred A, 1 Lt, Col John Coffee, Capt John W Byrns, Cav, Res omitted

DOUGLASS, Harry L, Capt & Aid Camp, Brig Gen Wm Hall, Vol Inf, Res omitted

DOUGLASS, Harry L, Capt, Col Ed Bradley, Vol Inf, Res omitted

DOUGLASS, Harry L, Capt, Col Edward Bradley, Vol Inf 1st Regt, Lebanon Wilson Co

DOUGLASS, Harry L, Capt, Col William Hall, Inf 1st Regt TN Vols, Res omitted

DOUGLASS, Henry L, Capt, Col Thomas Benton, Vol Inf, Res omitted

DOUGLASS, William, Capt, Col S Copeland, 3rd Regt Mil Inf, Warren Co

DRAKE, John, 2 Lt, Col Leroy Hammonds, Capt J N Williamson, 2nd Regt TN, Res omitted

DRAKE, John, 2 Lt, Col Leroy Hammonds, Capt Joseph Williamson, Inf, Res omitted

DRAKE, John, Lt, Col A Loury, Capt Jos Williamson, Mil Inf, Res omitted

DRENMEN, James, 2 Lt, Col Thomas Benton, Capt Henry L Douglass, Vol Inf, Res omitted

DREWRY, John, 3 Lt, Col Philip Pipkin, Capt Wm McKay, Mil Inf, Res omitted

DRUMMONS, James, 2 Lt, Col Edward Bradley, Capt Harry Douglass, Vol Inf, Res omitted

DRUMOND, James, 2 Lt, Col Thomas Benton, Capt Henry Douglass, Vol Inf, Res omitted

DUDNEY, Abraham, Capt, Commander omitted, 3rd Regt Mil Inf, Fayetteville

DUGGER, John, Ens, Col Ewen Allison, Capt Adam Winsell, E TN Drafted Mil, Res omitted; elected from Pvt

DUNAWAY, Sam'l, 2 Lt, Col John Cocke, Capt James Gault, Inf, Res omitted

DUNCAN, John, 1 Lt, Col John Cocke, Capt Richard Crunk, Inf, Res omitted

DUNCAN, Joseph, Capt, Capt Joseph Williams, Mil Cav, Res omitted

DUNCAN, Joseph, Capt, Col Samuel Bunch, E TN Drafted Mil, Res omitted

DUNCAN, Joseph, Capt, Col Samuel Bunch, E TN Mil, Res omitted

DUNN, John C, 1 Lt & Adjt, Col Thomas McCrory, 2nd Regt TN Mil, Res omitted; resigned 11-12-1813

DUNN, John C, Lt, Col S Copeland, Capt John Biles, Inf,
Res omitted; promoted to Adjt in the 3rd Regt

DUNNAWAY, Patrick, 1 Lt, Col S Bayless, Capt John Brock, E TN Mil, Res omitted

DYER, John, Ens, Col William Johnson, Capt Joseph Scott, E TN Drafted Mil, Res omitted; promoted from Sgt

DYER, R H, Col, no other information

DYER, Robert H, 1 Lt Col, Col John Alcorn, TN Vol Cav, Res omitted

DYER, Robert H, 2 Lt Col, Col John Coffee, TN Vol Cav, Res omitted

DYER, Robert H, Col, Div of Maj Gen Andrew Jackson/Brigade of Brig Gen John Coffee, 1st Regt TN V Cav, Res omitted

DYER, Robert H, Col, Maj Gen Andrew Jackson, TN Mtd Gunmen Vol, Res omitted; in Gen Coffee's Brig

DYER, Robert, Col, Brig Gen John Coffee, TN Vol Mtd Gunmen, Res omitted

DYER, William, Lt & Adjt, Col Robert H Dyer, TN Vol Mtd Gunmen, Res omitted

DYER, Wine H, Lt Adjt, Brig Gen John Coffee, TN Vol Mtd Gunmen, Res omitted

DYKE, Jacob, Capt, Col William Lillard, Vol Mil Inf, Res omitted

DYKE, Jacob, Capt, Col Wm Lillard, Mil Inf Vol, Res omitted

EAGEN, William, 2 Lt, Maj Gen Jackson, Capt J Kirkpatrick, Mtd Gunmen, Res omitted; killed 1-22-1814

EARHART, Rodney, 2 Lt, Col Philip Pipkin, Capt George Mebane, Mil Inf, Res omitted

EATON, James, 3 Lt, Col Samuel Bayless, Capt Solomon Hendrich, E TN Mil; promoted 2 Lt

EATON, William B, 1 Lt, Regt Commander omitted, Capt David Mason, Cav

ECHOLS, John jr, 3 Lt, Col Leroy Hammonds, Col Alexander Loury, Capt Thomas Wells, Inf

EDGE, Henry, Ens, Col Philip Pipkin, Capt David Smith, Mil Inf, Res omitted

EDMONDSON, Andrew I?, Ens, Col Thomas Benton, Capt Thomas Williamson, Vol Inf, Res omitted

EDMONDSON, Andrew J, Ens, Col William Pillow, Capt Thomas Williamson, Vol Inf, Res omitted

EDMONDSON, John, Lt Col, Mil Cav 6th Brig, Res omitted

EDMONDSON, Robert, Lt, Lt Col John Edmondson, Co Commander omitted, Cav, Res omitted

EDMONSON, John, Lt Col, Commander omitted, Cav, Res omitted; against Creek Indians

EDMONSTON, Robert, 2 Lt, Capt Davis Smith, Cav Vol, Res omitted; promoted from Cor

EDMONSTON, Robert, Capt, Brig Gen John Coffee, Col R H Dyer, TN Vol Mtd Gunmen, Res omitted

EDMONSTON, Robert, Capt, Col Robert H Dyer, TN Vol Cav Mtd Gunmen, Fayetteville

EDMONSTON, T I, 3 Lt, Brig Gen John Coffee, TN Vol Gunmen, Res omitted

EDMONSTON, Wm, Lt, Brig Gen John Coffee, TN Vol Mtd Gunmen, Res omitted

EDWARDS, William, Capt, Col Newton Cannon, Mtd Rifleman, Res illegible

EDWARDS, William, Capt, Col Newton Cannon, Regt Command, Res omitted

EGNEW, George M, 1 Lt, Col Thomas McCrory, Capt William Dooley, Inf, Res omitted

ELDREDGE, Thomas, Capt, Col Wm Higgins, Mtd Gunmen, Res omitted

ELDRIDGE, Benj, 1 Lt, Col John Brown, Capt Allen Bacon, E TN Mil Inf, Res omitted

ELGIN, Robert, Corn, Brig Gen John Coffee, TN Mtd Gunmen, Res omitted

ELIOT, George, 1 Lt Col, Gen John Coffee, TN Vol Mtd Gunmen, Res omitted

ELLIOT, Benj, Capt, Lt Col A Cheatham, Inf 6th Brig, Res omitted

ELLIOT, George, Capt, Col George Eliot, Capt N T Perkins, Mtd Riflemen, Res omitted

ELLIOTT, George, Capt, Col Nicholas T Perkins, 1st Regt W TN Mtd Mil Vol, Gallatin Sumner Co

ELLIOTT, George, Lt Col, Brig Gen John Coffee, TN Mtd Gunmen, Res omitted

ELLIOTT, Isaac, 2 Lt, Brig Gen John Cocke, Col Thomas H Williamson, Co Commander omitted, Vol Mtd Gunmen

ELLIOTT, Isaac, Lt, Col Newton Cannon, Capt Wm Edwards, Regt Command, Res omitted

ELLIS, Francis S, Capt, Col John Cocke, TN Mil 2nd Regt, Nashville

ELLIS, Francis, Capt, Lt Col Richard Napier, Inf, Res omitted

ELLIS, Francis, Capt, Maj Gen Carroll, Inf, Res omitted

ELLIS, James, Brig Maj, Brig Gen George White, E TN Mil, Res omitted; discharged at Knoxville by general's orders

ELLIS, Samuel, Ens, Col John Winn, Capt Wm McCall, Inf, Res omitted

ELMORE, Henry, Ens, Col Alexander Loury, Capt Gabriel Martin, Inf, Res omitted

EMERSON, James H, 2 Lt, Col Metcalf, Capt Hurt, Mil Inf, Res omitted

EMERSON, John, Ens, Col Burton, Capt Reynolds, Vol Inf, Res omitted

ENGLISH, James, 1 Lt, Col S Bunch, Capt John English, E TN Drafted Mil, Res omitted; furloughed for bad health

ENGLISH, James, Ens, Col Higgins, Capt Allen, Mtd Gunmen, Res omitted

ENGLISH, John, Capt, Col S Bunch, E TN Drafted Mil, Res omitted

ENGLISH, John, Capt, Col Samuel Bunch, E TN Drafted Mil, Res omitted

ENGLISH, Thomas, 2 Lt, Col S Bunch, Capt John English, E TN Drafted Mil, Res Rhea? County

ENGLISH, Thos, 1 Lt, Col Metcalf, Capt Hurt, Mil Inf, Res omitted

ERWIN, Thomas, Ens, Col Thomas Benton, Capt Isaiah Renshaw, Vol Inf, Res omitted

ESCUM, James W, 2 Lt, Brig Gen John Coffee, TN Mtd Gunmen, Res omitted

ESPERY, William, Ens, Col John Cocke, Capt Bird Nance, Inf, Res omitted

ESTES, Robert, 1 Lt Brig Inspector, Brig Gen T Johnson, Maj Gen Andrew Jackson, W TN Mil, Res omitted

ESTES, Robert, Adjt, Brig Gen Johnson, Vol, Res omitted

EVANS, Henry, Ens, Capt Francis Register, E TN Mil, Res omitted

EVANS, Henry, Ens, Col Samuel Bunch, E TN Mil, Res omitted; also under Capt F Register

EVANS, John, 2 Lt, Brig Gen John Coffee, TN Vol Mtd Gunmen, Res omitted

EVANS, John, 2 Lt, Col Robert Dyer, Capt Robert Evans, Vol Mtd Gunmen, Res omitted

EVANS, John, Ens, Col William Hall, Capt John Kennedy, Vol Inf, Res omitted

EVANS, Robert, 1 Lt, Col John Coffee, Capt Daniel Ross, Mtd Gunmen, Res omitted; promoted Capt of Co of Spies

EVANS, Robert, Capt, Brig Gen John Coffee, Col Robert Dyer, Capt Robert Evans, TN Mtd Vol Gunmen, Res omitted

EVANS, Robert, Capt, Col Robert H Dyer, Mtd Gunmen 1st TN Vol Cav, Williamson Co

EVANS, Robert, Capt, Commander omitted, Co of Spies Mtd Vol Gunmen, Davidson Co

EVANS, Robert, Capt, Commander omitted, Spies Gunmen, Res omitted

EVANS, William, Capt, Col S Copeland, Mil Inf, Res omitted

EVANS, William, Capt, Col Stephen Copeland, 3rd Regt Mil Inf, Overton Co

EVERETT, Joseph, Capt, Col Ewen Allison, E TN Mil, Res omitted

EVERETT, Joseph, Capt, Cox Ewen Allison, E TN Mil, Knoxville

EVIN, Wallen, Lt, Col Wm Johnson, Capt Benj Powell, E TN Mil, Res omitted; resigned 1-3-1815

EWEN, Ephraim, Ens, Col Thomas McCrory, Capt Wm Dooley, Inf, Res omitted

EWENS, Joseph, Ens, Col Samuel Bunch & Col Samuel Wear, Capt Wm Mitchell, E TN Mtd Inf; in place of Andrew Stephenson

EXUM, James W, 2 Lt, Col Robert Dyer, Capt Thomas Jones, Mtd Vol Gunmen, Res omitted; promoted to Adjt of Regt

EXUM, James W?, 1 Lt, Col John Coffee, Capt James Terrell, Vol Cav, Res omitted

FAIRLER, Jesse, 1 Lt, Col Williamson, Capt Hutchings, Vol Mtd Gunmen, Res omitted; d 4-22-1815

FARLEY, Jesse, 1 Lt, Maj Gen John Cocke, TN Vol Mtd Gunmen, Res omitted

FARMER, Nathan, Capt, Col R H Dyer, TN Vol Cav Mtd Rifleman, Res omitted

FARMER, Nathan, Capt, Commander omitted, Mtd Riflemen, Res omitted

FARNSWORTH, David, 1 Lt, Col S Bayless, Capt Joseph Hale, E TN Mil, Res omitted; promoted from 2 Lt

FARRER, Nathaniel, Ens, Col Leroy Hammonds, Capt James Tubb, Inf, Res omitted

FARRIS, James, Regt Chap, Col Phillip Pipkin, Capt Wm Pegram, W TN Mil Det of Capt David Smith, Res omitted

FEARN, Thomas, Surgeon, Col Wm Pillow, 2nd Regt TN Vol Inf, Res omitted

## Officers, War of 1812

FENFLY, Wm, Lt, Col Wm Lillard, Capt George Argenbright, E TN Vol Riflemen, Res omitted

FENTRESS, James, Ens, Col James Raulston, Capt Elijah Haynie, Inf, Res omitted

FERGUSON, James C, Ens, Col John K Winn, Capt Holleman, Inf, Res omitted

FERREL, E, Lt & Adjt, Gen John Coffee's Brig, TN Vol Mtd Inf, Res omitted

FERRELL, James, Capt, Col Alcorn, no other information

FERRELL, Larkin, Capt, Commander omitted, 7th Brig Inf, Res omitted

FERRILL, Larkin, Capt, Commander omitted, Mtd Inf 7th Brig W TN Mtd Inf, Williamsburg Jackson co

FINCH, Edward, Ens, Col S Copeland, Capt Richard Sharp, Mil Inf, Res omitted

FINE, Jonathan, B Maj, Brig Gen Thomas Coulter, E TN Drafted Mil, Res omitted

FINE, Lidgard, Lt, Col Wm Lillard, Capt J Lillard, E TN Inf Vol, Res omitted

FITE, Joseph, 1 Lt, Col William Higgins, Capt Adam Dale, Mtd Gunmen, Res omitted

FLENNEKEN, James W, 2 Lt, Maj Childs, Capt Tipton, E TN Vol Mtd Inf, Knox 10th; promoted from Pvt

FORD, Moses, Capt, Lt Col Henry Bryan, Inf, Res omitted

FORD, Wm, Lt, Lt Col Henry Bryan, Mil Inf, Res omitted

FORE, G P, Surgeon, Brig Gen John Coffee, TN Vol Mtd Gunmen, Res omitted

FORE, Gree P, Surgeon, Col Robert H Dyer, TN Vol Mtd Gunmen, Res omitted; transferred to Gen'l Staff

FORE, Green P, Surgeon, Col N Cannon, Vol Mtd Gunmen, Res omitted

FORE, Grun P, Surgeon, Col N T Perkins, TN Mtd Vol, Res omitted

FORE, Wrigh P, Surgeon, Col Robert H Dyer, no other information

FORGASON, James C, Ens, Col Robert Steele, Capt Samuel Maxwell, Mil Inf, Res omitted

FOSTER, George, Chap, Col Wm Metcalf, 1st Regt W TN Mil Inf, Res omitted

FRANCIS, Miller, 2 Lt, Col John Brown, Co Commander omitted, Regt E TN Mil Inf, Res omitted

FRANKLIN, Isaac, 2 Lt, Col Newton Cannon, Capt Wm Edwards, Regt Command, Res omitted

FRAZIER, John, Lt, Col Cheatham, Capt Birdwell, Inf, Res omitted

FRISTOC, Richard, Lt, Col Samuel Wear, Capt Daniel Price, E TN Vol Inf, Res omitted

FRISTOE, Richard, 1 Lt, Maj John Chiles, Capt Daniel Price, E TN Vol Mtd Inf, Res omitted

FRISTOE, Thomas, Ens, Maj John Childs, Capt Daniel Price, E TN Vol Mtd Inf, Res omitted

FROST, Joseph, Surgeon, Maj Wm Russell, Separate Bn of TN Vol Mtd Gunmen, Res omitted

FRYE, John, Ens, Col Wm Johnson, Capt James Tunnell, E TN Mil, Res omitted

FUGIT (FUGATT), Evan, 2 Lt, Col Wm Johnson, Capt Joseph Scott, E TN Drafted Mil, Res omitted

GAMBLE, James H, 1 Lt, Col Benton, Capt Hewett, Vol Inf, Res omitted

GAMBLE, John H, Judge Advocate, Maj Gen John Cocke, E TN Mil Inf, Res omitted

GAMBLE, Wm, Ens, Col Cheatham, Capt Benson, Inf, Res omitted

GANAWAY, Walker, 1 Lt, Col Alcorn, Capt McKern, Cav, Res omitted

GANNAWAY, Walker, 1 Lt, Col J Coffee, Capt McKenn, Cav, Res omitted

GANT, Edward, Hospital Surgeon, Brig Gen George Doherty, E TN Mil, Res omitted

GARDINER, Peter, Ens, Col Bayless, Capt Bacon, E TN Mil, Res omitted

GARDNER, James, 2 Lt, Col Samuel Wear, Capt James Gillespie, E TN Vol Inf, Res omitted

GARNER, John, Ens, Col A Cheatham, Mtd Inf 6th Brig, Res omitted

GARNER, John, Ens, Lt Col John Edmonson, Cav, Res omitted

GAULT, Edward, Surgeon, Col Sam'l Bunch, Co Commander omitted, E TN Mil, Res omitted

GAULT, James, Capt, Col John Cocke, Mil Inf 2nd Regt, Nashville

GAUNT, Edward, Surgeon, Col Ewin Allison, Co Commander omitted, E TN Mil, Res omitted; appointed Hospital Surgeon

GEE, Edmond W, 1 Lt, Col Hammond, Capt Craig, 2nd Regt W TN Mil, Res omitted

GEORGE, Solomon, 2 Lt, Col Dyer, Maj Russell, Capt Russell, Vol Mtd Gunmen

GEORGE, Solomon, Capt, Col Copeland, Inf

GEORGE, Solomon, Capt, Col S Copeland, 3rd Regt Mil Inf, Winchester Franklin Co

GHOLSON, John, 2 Lt, Maj Thomas Williamson, Co Commander omitted

GIBB, George W, Capt & ADC, Brig Gen Bird Smith, no Co Commander; no service performed

GIBB, George W, Capt, Col Thomas Benton, Vol Inf

GIBBONS, Samuel G, 2 Lt, Col James Raulston, Maj Gen William Carroll, Capt Edward Robinson, Inf

GIBBS, George W, 1 Lt & ADC, Brig Gen Bird Smith, W TN Mil Inf; in Maj Gen William Carroll Division

GIBBS, George W, Capt, Col Thomas Benton, Vol Inf

GIBBS, George W, Capt, Col Thomas H Benton, 2nd Regt TN Mil Inf, Nashville

GIBBS, N, Capt, Capt, Col S Bunch, E TN Mil; killed in action 3-27-1814

GIBBS, Nicholas, 2 Lt, Col Samuel Wear, Capt John Bayless, Mtd Inf

GIBSON, David, Ens, Col Ewen Allison, Capt Jacob Hoyal, E TN Mil; trans. from Capt McPherson

GIBSON, J. H., Lt Col, Col R H Dyer, Branch omitted

GIBSON, John H, 1 Maj, Col John Alcorn, TN Vol Cav

GIBSON, John H, 2 Lt Col, Brig Gen John Coffee, TN Vol Mtd Gunmen

GIBSON, John H, 2 Lt, Col R H Dyer, Co Commander omitted, Regt TN Vol Mtd Gunmen

GIBSON, John H, 2 Maj, Col John Coffee, TN Vol Cav & Mtd Riflemen

GIBSON, John H, Lt Col, Col R H Dyer, Branch omitted

GIBSON, John H., 2 Maj, Col John Coffee, TN Vol Cav

GIBSON, John W, Lt Col, Lt Col E? H Dyer, Regt of TN Vol Mtd Gunmen

GIBSON, Sam G, 3 Lt, Maj Gen Carroll, Col Raulston,

## Officers, War of 1812

Capt Robinson, Inf
GIBSON, Samuel D, 3 Lt, Maj Gen Carroll, Col Raulston, Capt Robinson, Inf
GIBSON, Spencer E, Hospital Surgeon, Brig Gen N Taylor
GIBSON, Thomas, Ens, Col S Bunch, Capt George McPherson, E TN Mil, Res omitted
GIDDENS, James, Capt, Col A Cheatham, Mil Inf, Res omitted
GIDDINS, James, Capt, Col Cheatham, Inf, Res omitted
GILBERT, Jesse, Ens, Capt Gray, Inf, Res omitted
GILBERT, Jesse, Ens, Col Philip Pipkin, Capt Peter Searcy, Mil Inf, Res omitted
GILIENWATER, William, Capt, Col William Lillard, E TN Mil Inf, Hawkins Co
GILLELAND, James, Ens, Col Thomas Benton, Capt Jas McFerrin, Vol Inf, Res omitted
GILLELAND, James, Ens, Col Wm Pillow, Capt James McFerrin, Inf, Res omitted
GILLENWATER, Wm T, Lt, Col Wm Lillard, Capt Wm Gillenwater, E TN Vol Inf, Res omitted
GILLENWATER, Wm, Capt, Col Wm Lillard, E TN Vol Mil Inf, Res omitted
GILLESPIE, James, Capt, Col Samuel Wear, E TN Vol Inf, Res omitted
GILLESPIE, James, Capt, Col Samuel Wear, E TN Vol Mil Inf, Kingston
GILLESPIE, John, Cor, Maj James Porter, Capt Sam Cowan, Cav, Res omitted
GILLILAND, Wm, 1 Lt, Col Samuel Bayless, Capt Joseph Bacon, E TN Mil, Res omitted
GIVENS, James, Chap, Brig Gen John Coffee, TN Vol Mtd Gunmen, Res omitted
GLASS, Alexander, Lt, Brig Gen John Coffee, TN Vol Mtd Gunmen, Res omitted
GLASS, Alexander, Lt, Col Robert Dyer, Capt Jas McMahon, TN Mtd Vol Gunmen, Res omitted; promoted from 3 Lt to 1 Lt
GLASS, Robert, Cor, Brig Gen John Coffee, TN Vol Mtd Gunmen, Res omitted
GOLD, David, 2 Maj, Lt Col John Edmonson, no other information
GOODALL, John, Cor, Maj Gen John Cocke, TN Vol Mtd Gunmen, Res omitted
GOODALL, John, Ens, Col Williamson, Capt Metcalf, Vol Mtd Gunmen, Res omitted
GOODIN, Lawson, 3 Lt, Col Bayless, Capt Waddle, E TN Mil, Res omitted
GOODMAN, Behajah, 2 Lt, Capt Archibald McKenney, Cav, Res omitted
GOODMAN, Benj, 2 Lt, Capt Archibald McKenney, Cav, Res omitted
GOODSON, Jos, Capt, Col Bayless, E TN Mil, Res omitted
GOODSON, Joseph, Capt, Col Samuel Bayless, E TN Drafted Mil, Knoxville
GORDON, John, Capt, Commander omitted, Mtd Spies, Res omitted
GORDON, John, Capt, Div of Maj Gen Andrew Jackson, Mtd Spies, Hickman Co
GORDON, John, Ens, Capt Nathan Farmer, Mtd Riflemen, Res omitted
GORDON, Thomas K, Capt, Col Thomas McCrory, 2nd Regt TN Mil Inf, Giles Co
GORDON, Thos K, Capt, Col T McCrory, Inf, Res omitted
GORDON, Wm, Ens, Col R C Napier, Capt Andrew McCarty, Mil Inf, Res omitted
GORE, Henry, 2 Lt, Maj Gen Wm Carroll, Capt James Raulston, Capt Wiley Huddleston, Inf, Res omitted
GORELY, Robert, Ens, Col S Bayless, Capt James Churchman, E TN Mil, Res omitted
GOULD, David, Lt, Col N T Perkins, Capt George Marr, Mtd Vol, Res omitted
GRAHAM, Joseph, 1 Lt, Col Ewen Allison, Capt Thos Wilson, E TN Draft Mil
GRANT, Zachariah, 1 Lt, Brig Gen Thos Johnson, Capt Allen, Branch Srvce omitted, Res omitted
GRANT, Zachariah, 2 Lt, Col John Cocke, Capt John Weakley, Inf, Res omitted
GRASON, Benjamin, 2 Lt, Col Wm Johnson, Capt James Stuart, E TN Drafted Mil, Res omitted
GRAVES, Henry, 1 Lt, Col Samuel Wear, Capt Samuel Bayless, Mtd Inf, Res omitted
GRAY, James, Capt, Col Cocke, Inf, Res omitted
GRAY, James, Capt, Col John Cocke, Mil Inf, 2nd Regt, Nashville?
GRAY, James, Capt, Col John Coffee, Branch Srvce omitted, Res omitted
GRAY, James, Ens, Col Winn, Capt Spinks, Inf, Res omitted
GRAY, Robert, 3 Lt, Col Johnson, Capt Lawson, E TN Drafted Mil, Res omitted
GRAY, Thomas, Capt, Col John Coffee, Branch Srvce omitted, Res omitted
GRAY, Thomas, Capt, Col Napier, Capt Gray, Mil Inf, Res omitted
GRAY, Thomas, Capt, Col R C Napier, 1st Regt Mil Inf, Dover Stewart Co
GRAY, Thomas, Capt, Commander omitted, Inf, Res omitted
GRAY, Thomas, Ens, Maj Cooper, 26th TN Regt Mtd Riflemen, Res omitted
GRAY, William S, 2 Lt, Col Benton, Capt Caperton, Inf, Res omitted
GRAY, William S, 2 Lt, Col Pillow, Capt Caperton, Inf, Res omitted
GRAYSON, Benjamin, Lt, Col Wm Johnson, Capt Stewart, 3rd Regt E TN Mil, Res omitted
GRAYSON, Peter, Adjt Gen, Maj Gen Wm Carroll, TN Mil, Res omitted
GREEG, Abraham, Ens, Col William Lillard & Lt Col William Snodgrass, 2nd Regt Vol Inf, Res omitted
GREEN, James Y, 1 Lt QM, Maj Gen Andrew Jackson, Col T McCrory, 2nd Regt TN Mil, Res omitted
GREEN, John, 2 Lt, Col John Williams, Capt Sam Bunch, Mtd Vol, Res omitted
GREEN, Lewis, 1 Lt, Col Thomas Williamson, Capt Robert Moore, Vol Mtd Gunmen, Res omitted
GREEN, Lewis, 1 Lt, Maj Gen John Cocke, E TN Vol Mtd Gunmen, Res omitted

- 13

## Officers, War of 1812

GREEN, Lewis, Ens, Capt George Smith, Spies, Res omitted

GREENFIELD, Samuel, Lt, Capt David Smith, Cav, Res omitted

GREENFIELD, William, Lt, Col John Coffee, Capt Smith, Vol Cav, Res omitted

GREER, Andrew, Lt, Col Thos Benton, Capt Isaiah Renshaw, Vol Inf, Res omitted

GREER, Andrew, Lt, Col Thos Benton, Capt James Renshaw, Vol Inf, Res omitted

GREER, James, Lt? & Forage Master, Maj Wm Russell, TN Vol Mtd Gunmen, Res omitted

GREGG, Abraham, Ens, Col Wm Lillard, Capt Benj H King, E TN Vol Inf, Res omitted

GREGG, Abraham, Ens, Lt Col Wm Snodgrass, Det of Inf of 2nd Regt E TN Mil Vol, Res omitted

GREGORY, Edmund D, Lt & QM, Col John K Wynne, 1st Regt TN Mil, Res omitted

GREGORY, George, Capt, Col S Bunch, E TN Drafted Mil, Res omitted

GREGORY, George, Capt, Col Samuel Bunch, E TN Drafted Mil, Knoxville

GRIFFIN, Jones, Capt, Col S Bunch, E TN Drafted Mil, Res omitted

GRIFFIN, Jones, Capt, Col Samuel Bunch, E TN Mil, Res omitted

GRIFFITH, Stephen, Capt, Col Higgins, Capt Griffith, Mtd Riflemen, Res omitted

GRIFFITH, Stephen, Capt, Col William Higgins, Mtd Riflemen, Madison Co MS

GRIFFY, William, Ens, Capt Gray, Inf, Res omitted

GRIMES, Charles, 1 Lt, Col Copeland, Capt Douglass, Inf, Res omitted

GUEST, Joshua, 2 Lt, Capt Robert Evans, Spies, Res omitted; promoted from Pvt

GUINN, William, Cor, Col John Coffee, Capt John Baskerville, Branch Srvce & Res omitted

GUNNER, Elisha, Ens, Col R C Napier, Capt Drury Adkins, Mil Inf, Res omitted

GUNNER, Elisha, Ens, Col Stephen Copeland, Capt Wm Evans, Mil Inf, Res omitted

GUNTER, Sterling, Lt, Col John Cocke, Capt John Dalton, Inf, Res omitted

GWIN, John, Cor, Brig Gen John Cocke, TN Vol Mtd Gunmen, Res omitted

GWINN, John, Cor, Col T Williamson, Capt Thos Scurry, Vol Mtd Gunmen, Res omitted

GWINN, William, Cor, Col John Alcorn, Capt John Baskerville, Vol Inf, Res omitted

HABBERT, James, 1 Lt, Maj Wm Russell, Capt Wm Chism, Vol Mtd Gunmen, Res omitted

HACKWORTH, John, 2 Lt, Col Samuel Wear, Capt John Childs, E TN Vol Inf, Res omitted

HAGGARD, James, Capt, Col Robert R? Dyer, Mtd Gunmen, Stewart Co

HAGGARD, James, Capt, Commander omitted, Mtd Gunmen, Res omitted

HAIL, John, 2 Lt, Col Edwin Booth, Capt John Slatton, E TN Mil, Res omitted; d 2-6-1815?

HAILE, George, Lt, Col R H Dyer, Capt Thos White, Vol Mtd Gunmen, Res omitted

HAILEY, Elijah, 1 Lt, Col John Cocke, Capt Nance, Inf, Res omitted; in place of Thos Ross (dismissed)

HALE, George, Cor, Col N T Perkins, Capt Philip Pipkin, Mtd Riflemen, Res omitted

HALE, John, Cor, Capt Wm Peacock, Cav, Res omitted

HALE, Joseph, Capt, Col Samuel Bayless, Capt Jos Hale, E TN Mil, Res omitted

HALE, Joseph, Capt, Col Samuel Bayless, E TN Mil Inf, Res omitted

HALE, Leroy, Lt, Col Samuel Bunch, Capt George McPherson, E TN Mil, Res omitted

HALEY, Elijah, Lt, Col Thos McCrory, Capt John Reynolds, Mil Inf, Res omitted

HALEY, Lysaniouz, 3 Lt, Capt J Williams, Cav, Res omitted

HALL, Garret, 1 Lt, Col John Brown, Capt Wm White, E TN Vol Mtd Inf, Res omitted

HALL, James, Cor, Col John Alcorn, Capt Robert Jetton, Vol Cav, Res omitted

HALL, James, Cor, Col John Coffee, Capt Robert Jetton, Cav, Res omitted

HALL, Philip, Ens, Capt Jas Gray, Inf, Res omitted

HALL, William, Brig Gen, Commander omitted, Vol Inf, Res omitted

HALL, William, Brig Gen, Staff Officers, Vol Inf, Res omitted; Div of Maj Gen Andrew Jackson

HALL, William, Col, Commander omitted, 1st Regt TN Vol Inf, Res omitted

HALL, William, Col, Field & Staff Officers, 1st Rgt TN Vol, Res omitted; Div of Maj Gen Andrew Jackson

HALLADAY, David, 3 Lt, Col Jas Raulston, Capt John Cowan, Inf, Res omitted

HALLOWAY, William, Ens, Col John K Wynne, Capt Bayless Prince, Inf, Res omitted

HAMBLENTON, James, Capt, Col William Hall, TN Vol 1st Regt Inf, Nashville

HAMBLETON, James, Capt, Col Edward Bradley, Vol Inf, Res omitted

HAMBLETON, James, Capt, Col William Y Higgins, Mtd Gunmen, Madison Co MS

HAMBLETON, James, Capt, Col Wm Hall, Vol Inf, Res omitted

HAMBLETON, James, Capt, Col Wm Y Higgins, Mtd Gunmen, Res omitted

HAMBLETON, Peter, Ens, Col Sam Wear, Capt Jos Calloway, Mtd Inf, Res omitted

HAMILTON, Alex, 2 Lt, Col Wm Lillard, Capt Thos Sharpe, Inf 2nd Regt, Res omitted; discharged - unfit for duty

HAMILTON, Henry, Capt, Col James Raulston, 3rd Regt TN Mil Inf, Res omitted

HAMILTON, Henry, Capt, Col Jas Raulston, Inf, Res omitted; also served under Maj Gen Carroll

HAMILTON, Isaiah, Capt, Capt Ephram Dickson, Branch Service & Res omitted

HAMILTON, Isaiah, Capt, Col Robert Jarman, 6th Brig TN Mil Mtd Inf, Res omitted

HAMILTON, James, Capt, Col Edward Bradley, Vol Inf, Res omitted

HAMILTON, John T, Ens, Col N T Perkins, Capt Mathew

## Officers, War of 1812

Johnson, Mil Inf, Res omitted
HAMILTON, William, Capt, Col William Lillard, E TN Vol Mil Inf, Knoxville?
HAMMEL, Robert, Lt, Col Edwin Booth, Capt S Thompson, Mil, Res omitted
HAMMONDS, Leroy, Lt Col, Field & Staff Officers Regt of Col Loury, 2nd Regt W TN Mil, Res omitted
HAMMONS, Leroy, Lt Col, Col A Loury, 2nd Regt W TN Mil, Res omitted
HAMPTON, John, Capt, Col Ewen Allison, Capt Hampton, Mil, Res omitted
HAMPTON, John, Capt, Col Ewen Allison, Mil, Washington
HANBY, John, Capt, Col Newton Cannon, Capt John Hanley, Mtd Riflemen, Res omitted
HANBY, John, Capt, Col Newton Cannon, Mtd Riflemen W TN, Res omitted
HANCOCK, William, Ens, Col Ewen Allison & Capt Thomas Wilson, E TN Mil, Res omitted
HANCOCK, William, Ens, Col Ewen Allison, Capt Thos Wilson, E TN Drafted Mil, Res omitted
HANEY, Thos B, 1 Lt, Col Wm Hall, Capt Henry M Newlin, Inf, Res omitted
HANIS, Joel D, Cor, Col John Alcorn, Capt Alexander McKeen, Cav, Res omitted
HANNAH, John, 3 Lt, Col Wm Metcalf, Capt Wm Mullin, Mil Inf, Res omitted
HARDAMAN, Thomas J, 1 Lt, Col Robert Dyer, Capt Glen Owen, TN Vol Mtd Gunmen, Res omitted
HARDEMAN, Bailey, 1 Lt, Col N Cannon, Capt Cantrell, W TN Mtd Inf, Res omitted; promoted from Pvt
HARDEMAN, Peter, 1 Lt, Maj Gen Carroll, Capt Ellis, Inf, Res omitted
HARDEN, William, Cor, no other information
HARGRAVES, Shelton, 1 Lt, Lt Col L Hammonds, Capt Jos Williamson, Inf, Res omitted
HARGROVE, Stephen, Ens, Col Philip Pipkin, Capt E Kirkpatrick, Mil Inf, Res omitted
HARGROVES, Shelton, Lt, Col A Loury, Capt Jos Williamson, W TN Mil Inf, Res omitted
HARKINS, Joseph, 1 Lt, Col Philip Pipkin, Capt John Robertson, Mil Inf, Res omitted
HARMON, Peter, 1 Lt, Col Wm Lillard, Capt Maloney, E TN Vol Inf, Res omitted
HARNEY, Robert, 1 Lt, Gen A Jackson, Capt David Deaderick, Arty, Res omitted
HARPOLE, John, Capt, Col N Cannon, Mtd Gunmen, Res omitted
HARPOLE, John, Capt, Col Newton Cannon, Mtd Gunmen, Wilson Co
HARRINGTON, Whitmill, 2 Lt, Maj Gen A Jackson, Capt John Crane, Mtd Gunmen
HARRIS, Arthur, Capt; no other information
HARRIS, James W, Asst Topograph Eng, Maj Gen Wm Carroll, no Co Commander, TN Mil; appt Top Engr
HARRIS, James, 2 Lt, Regt Commander Omitted, Capt Jas Williams, Mil Cav; resigned
HARRIS, James, Cor, Col John Coffee, Capt Michael Molton, Cav
HARRIS, Joel D, Cor, Col John Coffee, Capt Alexander McKeen, Cav; promoted to Cor from Sgt
HARRIS, John, Lt, Col S Bunch, Lt John Harris, E TN Mil
HARRIS, Mark W?, 2 Lt, Col Newton Cannon, Capt Francis Jones, Mtd Riflemen
HARRIS, Mathew H, 1 Lt, Col Wm Hall, Capt John Moore, Vol Inf
HARRIS, Mathew H, 2 Lt, Col Edward Bradley, Capt John Moore, Vol Inf
HARRIS, Thomas, 2 Lt, Col N T Perkins, Capt Nathan Johnson, Mil Inf, Res omitted
HARRIS, William, 1 Maj, Col Samuel Wear, E TN Vol Mil Inf, Res omitted
HARRISON, Benjamin, Surgeon, Col John Brown, E TN Vol, Res omitted
HARRISON, Charles, 2 Lt, Col S Bunch, Capt Francis Berry, E TN Mil, Res omitted; promoted from Pvt
HARRISON, Charles, 2 Lt, Col Samuel Bunch, Capt John Houk, E TN Mil, Res omitted; joined from Capt Berry's Co
HARRISON, James, 1 Lt, Col Edward Bradley, Capt John Kennedy, Riflemen, Res omitted
HARRISON, James, 2 Lt, Col Wm Hall, Capt John Kennedy, Vol Inf, Res omitted
HART, Robert W, Adjt, Col R C Napier, 1st Regt W T Mil, Res omitted; appointed Adjt in place of John L McRae
HART, Robert W, Asst Adj Gen, Brig Gen Nathaniel Taylor, On Command In W TN, Res omitted
HARTGROVES, John, Ens, Col John Coffee, Capt Daniel Ross, Mtd Gunmen, Res omitted
HARTSELL, Isaac, Lt, Col Wm Lillard, Capt Jacob Hartsell, E TN Vol Inf, Res omitted
HARTSELL, Jacob, Capt, Col William Lillard, Mil Inf Vol, Jonesborough
HARTSFIELD, William, 1 Lt, Col Thos Williamson, Capt Beverly Williams, Vol Mtd Gunmen, Res omitted
HARTSFIELD, William, 1 Lt, Maj Gen John Cocke, Co Commander omitted, TN Vol Mtd Gunmen, Res omitted
HARVEY, Allen, 1 Lt & QM, Col Jas Raulston, W TN Mil Inf, Res omitted
HASKELL, Joshua, Fgmstr, Col John Coffee, no Co Commander, TN Vol Cav & Mtd Riflemen
HASKELL, Joshua, Lt & Asst Fgmstr, Brig Gen John Coffee, TN Mtd Mil
HATSEL, Jacob, Capt, Col Wm Lillard, E TN Vol Inf
HAWS, William M, Lt, Col John Wynne, Capt Jas Jolleman, Inf
HAYES, Stokley D, Lt & B Inspector, Brig Gen John Coffee, no Co Commander, TN Vol Mtd Gunmen
HAYNES, Thomas B (Haynie), Capt, Col Edward Bradley, Vol Inf, Res omitted
HAYNIE, Elijah, Capt, Col James Raulston, 3rd Regt Mil Inf, Nashville
HAYNIE, Elijah, Capt, Col Jas Raulston, Inf
HAYNIE, Thomas B, 1 Lt, Col Edw Bradley, Vol Inf
HAYNIE, Thomas B, 1 Lt, Col Wm Hall, Capt Henry M Newlin, Inf
HAYS, Hugh, Cor, Col Thos Williamson, Capt Ricahrd Tate, Vol Mtd Gunmen; wounded 12-25-1814
HAYS, Hugh, Cor, Maj Gen John Cocke, Co Commander

omitted, TN Vol Mtd Gunmen
HAYS, Joseph, 1 Lt, Col S Bunch, Capt F Register, E TN Mil
HAYS, Robert, 1 Lt & Sub Inspt, Maj Gen A Jackson, detachment TN Vol
HAYS, Robert, Asst Inspector Genl, Maj Genl Andrew Jackson, Div of TN Mil
HAYS, Robert, Asst Inspector Genl, Maj Genl Wm Carroll, TN Mil; cashiered
HAYS, Stokely D, 1 Lt & Paymaster, Col John Coffee, no Co Commander, TN Vol Cav
HAYS, Stokely D, QM Gen, Maj Gen A Jackson, Div of TN Mil
HAYTOR, James, Ens, Col S Bunch, Capt John English, E TN Draft Mil
HEDDLESTON, Isiah D, 2 Lt, Col Thomas Williamson, Capt James Cook, Vol Mtd Gunmen; promoted from 3 Lt in place of A Clark
HEDDLESTON?, Josiah, 3 Lt, Maj Gen John Cocke, TN Vol Mtd Gunmen, Res omitted
HEMBREE, Joel, 1 Lt, Col Edwin E Booth, Capt John McKamey, E TN Mil, Res omitted
HENDERSON, James, 1 Lt Brig QM, Brig Gen Andrew Jackson, Det of TN Vol, Res omitted
HENDERSON, William, Capt, Brigade of Brig Gen Nathan Taylor, E TN Spies, Res omitted
HENDERSON, William, Capt, Commander omitted, Spies, Res omitted
HENDERSON, William, Ens, Col Samuel Bunch, Capt Geo Gregory, E TN Drafted Mil, Res omitted
HENDRICKS, Solomon, Capt, Col Samuel Bayless, E TN Mil, Knoxville?
HENDRIX, Solomon, Capt, Col S Bayless, E TN Mil, Res omitted
HENRY, James, 2 Lt, Maj John Childs, Capt James Cummings, E TN Vol Mtd Inf, Res omitted
HERD, James, Ens, Col Samuel Bunch, Capt Thomas Menn, E TN Vol Mtd Inf, Res omitted
HESS, William, Principle Forage Master, Maj Gen Andrew Jackson, TN Mil, Res omitted
HEWETT, Benjamin, Capt, Col Thomas H Benton, 2nd Regt TN Vol Inf, Nashville
HEWETT, Benjamin, Capt, Col Thos Benton, Capt Giles Burdett, Vol Mtd Gunmen, Res omitted
HICKS, John C, Lt & Adjt, Col Philip Pipkin, 1st Regt TN Mil, Res omitted
HICKS, Stephen T, Lt & QM, Maj William Russell, Separate Bn of TN Vol Mtd Gunmen, Res omitted
HIGGINS, William Y, Col, Field & Staff Officers Div of Maj Gen Andrew Jackson, 2nd Regt Mtd TN Vol, Madison Co
HIGGINS, William, Col, no other information
HILL, Alexander, 2 Maj, Col William Metcalf, 1st W TN Mil Inf, Res omitted; promoted to 2 Maj
HILL, Alexander, Capt, Col William Metcalf, Mil Inf, Res omitted; promoted to 2 Maj
HILL, Allen, 1 Lt, Lt Col Alexander Loury & Lt Col Leroy Hammonds, Capt Thomas Wells, Inf, Res omitted
HILL, James, 1 Lt, Col Thomas Williamson, Capt James Pace, Lt Neely, Vol Mtd Gunmen; promoted from 2 Lt

HILL, James, 2 Lt, Maj Gen John Cocke, TN Vol Mtd Gunmen, Res omitted
HILL, Joab, Lt Col, Col Samuel Bayless, 4 Regt E TN Mil
HILL, John, 2 Lt, Maj Gen John Cocke, Co Commander omitted, TN Vol Mtd Gunmen
HILL, John, 3 Lt, Col Thomas Williamson, Capt Richard Tate, Vol Mtd Gunmen
HILL, John, 3 Lt, Col William Lillard, Capt Thomas Sharpe, 2 Regt E TN Inf
HILL, John, Capt, Col Wm Y Higgins, Mtd Gunmen, Wilson Co
HILL, John, Capt, Maj Gen Andrew Jackson, Capt Joseph Kirkpatrick, Mtd Gunmen; killed 1-22-1814
HILL, John, Ens, Col S Copeland, Capt William Douglass, Inf
HILL, Samuel, 2 Lt, Col James Raulston, Capt James A Black, Inf
HILL, Thomas L, Ens, Maj William Woodfolk, Capt Ezekiel Ross & Capt McCulley, Inf; apptd 2 Lt
HOBBS, Collin, Ens, Col A Cheatham, Capt Wm Creel, Inf, Res omitted
HODGE, Robert, Capt, Lt Col L Hammond, Col Alex Loury, Capt Thos Wells, Inf, Res omitted; promoted from Pvt
HODGE, Samuel, Chap, Col Jas Raulston, W TN Mil Inf, Res omitted
HODGES, Fleman, Capt, Maj William Russell, Vol Mtd Gunmen, Murfreesboro
HODGES, Flemming (Fleman), Capt, Maj Wm Russell, Vol Mtd Gunmen, Res omitted
HODGES, William, Capt, Col S Copeland, Inf, Res omitted
HODGES, William, Capt, Col Stephen Copeland, 3rd Regt Mil Inf, Res omitted
HOGAN, David, 2 Maj, Col Archer Cheatham, Regt of TN, Res omitted
HOGAN, David, 2 Maj, Lt Col Richard Napier, Inf, Res omitted
HOGAN, David, Capt, Col N Cannon, Mtd Gunmen, Res omitted; promoted to Maj in A Cheatham's Regt
HOGAN, Isaac, 2 Lt, Capt Jas Terrill, Cav, Res omitted
HOGAN, Johiah, 2 Lt, Capt Jas Terrill, Cav, Res omitted
HOGG, Samuel, Hospital Surgeon, Maj Gen Andrew Jackson, TN Mil, Res omitted
HOGG, Samuel, Hospital Surgeon, Maj Gen William Carroll, TN Mil, Res omitted
HOGG, Samuel, Surgeon, Col W Hall, Inf, Res omitted
HOLLEMAN, James, Capt, Col John K Wynne, Mil Inf, 1st TN Regt, Res omitted
HOLLEMAN, James, Capt, Col John Wynne, Capt James Holleman, Inf, Res omitted
HOLLOWAY, Elliott, 2 Lt, Col Sam Bunch, Capt Edward Buchanan, E TN Mil, Res omitted
HOLMES, I L, Lt, Col Sam Copeland, Capt Richard Sharp, Mil Inf, Res omitted
HOLSHOUSER, John, Capt, Col S Copeland, 3rd Regt Mil Inf, Res omitted
HOLSHOUSER, John, Capt, Col S Copeland, Inf, Res omitted
HOLT, Michael, Ens, Lt I Barrett, Capt Nathan Davis, W TN Bn Inf, Res omitted

## Officers, War of 1812

HOMES, J L, 1 Lt & QM, Col S Copeland, 3rd Regt TN Mil, Res omitted

HOOPER, Absolom, 1 Lt, Col John Coffee, Capt Frederick Stump, Cav, Res omitted

HOOPER, Nimrod, 2 Lt, Commander omitted, Vol Mtd Gunmen, Res omitted

HOPE, James, 2 Lt, Col John Brown, Capt William White, E TN Vol Mtd Inf, Res omitted

HOPSON, George, Surgeon, Brig Gen Thomas Johnson, no other information

HOPSON, James, Ens, Col Samuel Bayless, Capt Jonathan Waddell, W TN Mil, Res omitted

HORD, Thomas, Ens, Col Thomas McCrory, Capt Abel Willis, Mil Inf, Res omitted; promoted from Sgt

HORDEMAN, Thomas I, 1 Lt, Brig Gen John Coffee, TN Vol Mtd Gunmen, Res omitted

HORN, Thomas, 1 Lt, Col Philip Pipkin, Capt John Strother, Mil, Res omitted

HORSLER, Adam, Ens, Col John Brown, Capt James McKemey, E TN Mtd Gunmen, Res omitted

HOUK, John, Capt, Col Samuel Bunch, Capt John Houk, E TN Mil, Res omitted

HOUK, John, Capt, Col Samuel Bunch, E TN Mil, Knox Co

HOUSTON, John P, Brig Maj, Brig Gen Jas White, no other information

HOWEL, John, Capt, Col S Bunch, Lt Jno Harris, E TN Mil, Res omitted

HOWELL, John, Capt, Col Samuel Bunch, E TN Mil, Knoxville

HOYAL, Jacob, Capt, Col Ewen Allison, Capt Jacob Hoyal, E TN Mil, Res omitted

HOYAL, Jacob, Capt, Col Ewen Allison, E TN Mil, Res omitted

HUBBARD, G K, 3 Lt, Maj Gen John Cocke, Co Commander omitted, TN Vol Mtd Gunmen, Res omitted

HUBBARD, Green K, 3 Lt, Col William _____, Capt James Pace, Vol Mtd Gunmen, Res omitted

HUBBARD, Vincent, Cor, Col Thomas Williamson, Capt James Pace & Capt Neely, Vol Mtd Gunmen, Res omitted

HUBBARD, Vincent, Cor, Maj Gen John Cocke, TN Vol Mtd Gunmen, Res omitted

HUBBART, Benjamin, 1 Lt, Col S Wear, Capt Simeon Perry, E TN Mtd Inf, Res omitted

HUDDLESTON, John, Ens, Col Alexander Loury, Capt John Looney, Inf, Res omitted

HUDDLESTON, John, Col John Cocke, Capt Richard Crunk, Inf, Res omitted

HUDDLESTON, Wiley R, Capt, Maj Gen Carroll, Capt Jas Raulston, Inf, Res omitted

HUDDLESTON, Wiley, Capt, Col James Raulston, 3rd Reg TN Mil Inf, Res omitted

HUDNALL, William W, Cor, Col John Alcorn, Capt Fredrick Stump, Cav, Res omitted

HUDSON, Andrew G, 2 Lt, Col Wm Metcalf, Capt John Barnhat, Mil Inf, Res omitted

HUDSON, Cuthbert, 1 Lt, Col Newton Cannon, Capt David Hogan, Mtd Gunmen, Res omitted

HUDSON, Cuthbert, Capt, Brig Gen John Coffee, TN Vol Mtd Gunmen, Res omitted

HUDSON, Cuthbert, Capt, Col R H Dyer, Mtd Gunmen Vol, Lincoln Co

HUDSON, Cuthbert, Capt, Col Robert Dyer, Vol Mtd Gunmen, Res omitted

HUDSON, Edward G, Ens, Col John Cocke, Capt Joseph Price, Inf, Res omitted

HUFFMASTER, Joseph, 1 Lt, Col S Bunch, Capt Jones Griffin, E TN Drafted Mil, Res omitted

HUMPHREY, David, Lt & Adjt, Col Wm Hall, 1st Regt TN Vol Inf, Res omitted

HUMPHREYS, David, Lt & Brig Maj, Brig Gen Wm Hall, Vol Inf, Res omitted

HUMPHREYS, Lesly, 3 Lt, Col W Johnson, Capt A Lawson, E TN Drafted Mil, Res omitted; replaced by Robert Gray

HUNT, David, 1 Lt, Col N Cannon, Capt F Jones, Mtd Riflemen, Res omitted

HUNT, James, 2 Maj, Col Robert Steele, 4th Regt TN Mil, Res omitted

HUNTER, Henry, Capt, Col William Johnston, 3rd Regt E TN Mil, Knoxville

HUNTER, Henry, Capt, Col Wm Johnston, Capt Henry Hunter, E TN Mil, Res omitted

HUNTER, Joseph, Ens, Col William Johnson & Capt Christopher Cooks, 3rd Regt E TN Mil, Knoxville

HUNTER, Joseph, Ens, Col Wm Johnson, Capt Christopher Cook, 3rd Regt E TN Mil; transferred to Capt Henry Hunter's Co

HUNTER, Joseph, Ens, Col Wm Johnson, Capt Henry Hunter, E TN Mil, Res omitted; transferred from Capt Kirk's Co

HUNTER, Joseph, Ens, Col Wm Johnson, Capt Joseph Kirk, Mil, Res omitted

HUNTER, Joseph, Ens, Col Wm Lillard, Capt Wm Hamilton, E TN Inf Vol, Res omitted

HUNTER, Sherod, 2 Lt, Col Thos Benton, Capt Wm Moore, Vol Inf, Res omitted

HUNTER, Sherod, 2 Lt, Col W Pillow, Capt Wm Moore, Inf, Res omitted

HURT, Bird L, Capt, Col William Metcalf, W TN Mil Inf, Res omitted

HURT, Bird L, Capt, Col Wm Metcalf, Mil Inf, Res omitted

HUSTON, William, Capt, Col Samuel Bunch, E TN Mil Mtd Inf, Knoxville

HUTCHERSON, John T, Ens, Col John Cocke, Capt John Weakley, Inf, Res omitted

HUTCHINGS, John, Asst Dept QM Gen, Maj Gen Andrew Jackson, TN Mil, Res omitted

HUTCHINGS, John, Capt, Col Thomas Williamson, 2nd Regt TN Vol Mtd Gunmen, Shelbyville TN

HUTCHINS, John, Capt Maj Gen John Cocke, TN Vol Mtd Gunmen, Res omitted

HUTCHINS, John, Capt, Maj Gen John Cocke, TN Vol Mtd Gunmen, Res omitted

HUTCHINS, John, Deputy QM Gen, Maj Gen Andrew Jackson, Branch Srvce omitted, Res omitted

HUTCHINSON, John T, Ens, Col John Cocke, Capt John Weakley, Inf, Res omitted

HUTCHINSON, John, Capt, Col Williamson, Vol Mtd

## Officers, War of 1812

Gunmen, Res omitted

HUTCHINSON, John, Ens, Lt Col Henry Bryan, Inf, Res omitted

HYNES, Andrew, 1 Lt & Aid, Maj Gen A Jackson, Det TN Vol, Res omitted

HYNES, Andrew, Capt & Aid-de-camp, Maj Gen Wm Carroll, TN Mil, Res omitted

HYNES, Benjamin, 1 Lt, Col W Y Higgins, Capt J Hambleton, Mtd Gunmen, Res omitted

HYNES, Bryant, 2 Lt, Col W Y Higgins, Capt Thos Eldridge, Mtd Gunmen, Res omitted

IDLETT, Thomas, Ens, Col Wm Metcalf, Capt Jas Jackson, Inf, Res omitted

IGOW, James, 3 Lt, Col Edwin Booth, Capt Vernon, E TN Mil, Res omitted; returned home because of sickness

INGRAM, Samuel, 2 Lt, Col Newton Cannon, Capt John Demsey, Mtd Gunmen, Res omitted

INMAN, John, Capt, Col Samuel Bunch, TN Mtd Vol, Jefferson Co

INMAN, Joseph, 2 Maj, Col Alex Loury, Capt Lt L Hammonds, 2nd Regt W TN Mil, Res omitted

INMAN, Joseph, 2 Sgt & 1 Maj, Lt Col Hammonds, 2nd Regt TN Mil, Res omitted

INMON, Benjamin, Ens, Col William Lillard, Capt Thos McChristian, E TN Vol Inf, Res omitted

IRVINE, David, 1 Maj, Col R C Napier, 1 Regt W TN Mil

ISBELL, Templel?, 2 Lt, Col Samuel Bunch, Capt Jones Griffin, E TN Draft Mil

JACKSON, Andrew, Maj Gen, Div of TN Mil

JACKSON, Andrew, Maj Gen, TN Vol, Davidson Co

JACKSON, Isham, 1 Lt, Col James Raulston, Capt Charles Wade, Inf, Res omitted

JACKSON, John, Capt, Col William Metcalf, Mil Inf W TN, Bedford Co

JACKSON, John, Capt, Maj Gen Wm Carroll, Col Wm Metcalf, Capt J Jackson, Mil Inf, Res omitted

JACOBS, Solomon D, Judge Advocate 2nd Lt In Line, Maj Gen John Cocke, E TN Mil Inf, Res omitted

JACOBS, Solomon D, Lt, Col Samuel Wear, Capt R Morgan, E TN Vol Inf, Res omitted

JAMISON, Samuel, Ens, Col Sam Bayless, Capt Joseph Hale, E TN Mil, Res omitted; promoted from the ranks

JARMAN, Robert, Lt Col, Col John Cocke, 2nd Regt W TN Mil Inf, Res omitted

JARMON, Robert, Col, Brigade of Gen Thomas Johnson, 6th Brig TN Mil Mtd Inf, Res omitted

JARMON, Robert, Col, Gen Thos Johnson, 6th Brig TN Mil Mtd Inf, Res omitted

JENERSON, Samuel, 2 Lt, Col Ewen Allison, Capt Thomas Wilson, E TN Drafted Mil, Res omitted

JENKINS, John G, Ens, Maj William Woodfolk, Capt John Sutton, Inf, Res omitted; promoted from Pvt

JENKINS, Walter, Lt, Regt Commander omitted, Capt Nathan Farmer, Mtd Riflemen, Res omitted

JENNINGS, James, 1 Lt, Col Samuel Bayless, Capt Branch Jones, E TN Drafted Mil, Res omitted

JERNIGAN, David, Ens, Col John Wynn, Capt Robert Breden, Inf, Res omitted; promoted from Pvt

JERRELL, Berja?, Lt, Capt Jos Williams, Mil Cav, Res omitted; promoted from Cpl

JESTER, Isaac, Cor?, Col John Brown, Capt Charles Lewin, E TN Mtd Inf, Res omitted

JESTIN, Jonathan, Ens, Col S Bayless, Capt John Brock, E TN Mil, Res omitted

JETTON, Robert, Capt, Col John Alcorn, Capt Robert Jetton, Vol Cav, Res omitted

JETTON, Robert, Capt, Col John Alcorn, Vol Cav, Rutherford Co

JETTON, Robert, Capt, Col John Coffee, Capt Robert Jetton, Cav, Res omitted

JETTON, Robert, Capt, Col John Coffee, Cav Vol, Murfreesboro Rutherford Co

JIMARSON, Samuel, 2 Lt, Col Samuel Bunch, Capt Francis Register, E TN Mil; transferred

JOBE, Samuel, 1 Lt, Col Phillip Pipkin, Capt William Pipkin, Mil Inf, Res omitted

JOBE, William, Capt, Col S Bunch, Capt William Jobe, E TN Vol Mtd Inf, Res omitted

JOBE, William, Capt, Col Samuel Bunch, Regt E TN Mil, Res omitted

JOHNSON, Burrell, Ens, Regt Commander omitted, Capt Sam Allen, Pack Horse Guards

JOHNSON, Cave, 1 Lt, Brig Gen Thos Johnson, Co Coimmander omitted, W TN Mil

JOHNSON, Charles, 2 Lt, Col Wm Metcalf, Capt Wm Mullin, Mil Inf

JOHNSON, Charles, Capt, Col A Cheatham, Mil Inf 2nd Regt, Res omitted

JOHNSON, James J, Ens, Col Jno Williams, Capt David Vance, W TN Vol

JOHNSON, John, 2 Lt, Col Sam Bunch, Capt Jonas Griffin, E TN Draft Mil; joined Capt Everett Co

JOHNSON, John, 2 Lt, Col Samuel Bunch, Capt Joseph Duncan, E TN Drafted Mil

JOHNSON, Joseph, Lt, Col William Lillard, Capt Jacheus? Copeland, E TN Vol Inf

JOHNSON, Mathew, Capt, Col N T Perkins, Mil Inf

JOHNSON, Richard, Ens, Col Edward Bradley, Capt Abraham Bledsoe, Riflemen; promoted to adjt 1 Regt

JOHNSON, Richard, Ens, Col William Hall, Capt Abraham Bledsoe, Vol Inf

JOHNSON, Robert G, 1 Lt, Regt Commander omitted, Capt David Smith, Cav

JOHNSON, Robert, Lt, Col R C Napier, Capt Andrew McCarty, Mil Inf

JOHNSON, Thomas, Brig Gen, Div of Maj Gen Andrew Jackson, W TN Mil, Res omitted

JOHNSON, William, Col, Brig Gen N Taylor, Drafted Mil (3rd Regt E TN Mil?), Res omitted

JOHNSON, William, Col, Field & Staff Officers, 3rd Regt E TN Mil, Knoxville

JOHNSTON, Charles, 2 Lt, Col Wm Metcalf, Capt William Mullen, Mil Inf, Res omitted

JOHNSTON, Mathew, Capt, Col Nicholas T Perkins, 1st Regt Vol Mil Mtd Inf, Franklin TN Williamson Co

JOHNSTON, Richard, Ens, Col Edward Bradley, Capt Abraham Bledsoe, Riflemen; promoted to Adjt in Col Bradley's 1st Regt

## Officers, War of 1812

JOHNSTON, Richard, Ens, Col William Hall, Capt Abraham Bledsoe, Vol Inf, Res omitted
JOHNSTON, Thomas, Brig Gen, Staff Officers, W TN Mil, Res omitted
JONES, Andrew, Ens, Col Sam Wear, Capt Rufus Morgan, E TN Vol Inf, Res omitted
JONES, Branch, Capt, Col Sam Bayless, E TN Mil Inf, Res omitted
JONES, Branch, Capt, Col Samuel Bayless, E TN Mil Drafted, Knoxville?
JONES, Francis, Capt, Col N Cannon, Capt B Jones, Mtd Riflemen, Res omitted
JONES, Francis, Capt, Col Newton Cannon, Mtd Riflemen, Franklin Co Winchester
JONES, George B, 2 Lt, Col S Bayless, Capt J Brock, E TN Mil, Res omitted
JONES, Isaiah, Lt, Col S Bunch, Capt Dobkins, E TN Mil Drafted, Res omitted
JONES, Jesse, 3 Lt, Col Wm Metcalf, Capt O Waller, Mil Inf, Res omitted
JONES, Richard, Lt, Col Edwin Booth, Capt SAmuel Thompson, Mil
JONES, Robert, Lt, Regt Commander omitted, Capt Abner Pearce, Inf
JONES, Thomas, Capt, Brig Gen John Coffee, TN Vol Mtd Gunmen
JONES, Thomas, Capt, Col Robert Dyer, Mtd Vol Gunmen
JONES, Thomas, Capt, Col Robert H Dyer, Mtd Gunmen 1st Regt TN Vol, Lincoln Co (Nashville?)
JONES, Thornton, 2 Lt, Col John Cocke, Capt Richard Crunk, Inf
JONES, Zachariah, Ens, Col James Raulston, Capt Daniel Newman, Inf, Res omitted
JORNAGAN, Spencer, Secretary to General, Maj Gen John Cocke, E TN Vol Mil; Capt of the Maury Co Vol
JORROD (JARRAD), William, 2 Lt, Col Phillip Pipkin, Capt Ebenezer Kirkpatrick, Mil Inf, Res omitted
JUSTICE, Julius, Ens, Regt Commander omitted, Capt John Crane, Mtd Inf, Res omitted
JUSTICE, Moses, 2 Lt, Col Wm Metcalf, Capt John Cunningham & Capt Alexander Hill, Mil Inf; promoted to 1 Lt
KAVANAUGH, Charles, 2 Maj, Brig Gen John Coffee, TN Vol Gunmen, Res omitted
KAVANAUGH, Charles, 2nd Maj, Col Robt H Dyer, no other information
KAVANAUGH, Charles, Capt, Capt Arch McKinney, Cav, Res omitted; promoted to Maj
KAVANAUGH, Charles, Capt, Col John Coffee, Capt C Kavanaugh, Cav, Res omitted
KAVANAUGH, Charles, Capt, Col John Coffee, Cav, Nashville?
KAVANAUGH, Charles, Capt, Col Robert Dyer, Cav TN Vol, Williamson Co
KAVANAUGH, Charles, Maj, Col Robert Dyer, TN Vol Mtd Gunmen, Res omitted
KAVANAUGH, James, 1 Lt, Brig Gen Coffee, TN Vol Mtd Gunmen, Res omitted
KAVANAUGH, Lee, 1 Lt, Capt Arch McKinney, Cav, Res omitted
KELLY, Nathan, 3 Lt, Col Wm Johnson, Capt James Stewart, E TN Drafted Mil, Res omitted
KELLY, Nathaniel, Lt, Col Wm Johnson, Capt James Stewart, 3rd Regt E TN Mil, Res omitted
KELLY, William, 3 Lt, Col John Brown, Capt Wm D Nelson, E TN Vol Mil, Res omitted
KENDELL, John, 2 Lt, Col Samuel Bunch, Capt F Register, E TN Mil, Res omitted
KENDRE, Peter, Capt, Maj Cooper, 26th Regt TN Mtd Riflemen, Res omitted
KENNEDY, Avender, Cor, Capt Arch McKenney, Cav, Res omitted; promoted from Pvt
KENNEDY, John, Capt, Col Edward Bradley, 1st Regt TN Vol Riflemen, Res omitted
KENNEDY, John, Capt, Col Edward Bradley, Riflemen, Res omitted
KENNEDY, John, Capt, Col William Hall, 1st Regt TN Vol Inf, Res omitted
KENNEDY, John, Capt, Col William Hall, Vol Inf, Res omitted
KENNIS, Jacob, 1 Lt, Col S Bunch, Capt J Griffin, E TN Drafted Mil, Res omitted; resigned 4-6-1814
KERKINDALL, James, 3 Lt, Col A Loury, Capt L Hammonds & Capt Arahel Rains, Inf, Res omitted; deserted 10-3-1814
KERLEY, William, Lt, Col Thos McCrory, Capt Thos Gordon, Inf, Res omitted; promoted from Sgt
KERR, Hugh, Capt, Commander omitted Div of Gen Andrew Jackson, Mtd Rangers, Res omitted
KERR, Hugh, Capt, Maj Gen A Jackson, Mtd Rangers, Res omitted
KERR, William, Ens, Capt I Williams, E TN Mil, Res omitted
KERR, William, Ens, Col S Bunch, Capt I Williams, E TN Mil, Res omitted
KERR, William, Ens, Col S Bunch, Capt Jno Houk, E TN Mil; joined from Capt Williams' Co, discharged for inability
KERR, Wilson, 1 Lt, Col J Alcorn, Capt R Jetton, Vol Inf, Res omitted; d 12-24-1813
KERR, Wilson, 1 Lt, Col Jno Coffee, Capt R Jetton, Cav, Res omitted
KEYES, George, Capt, Col William Lillard, Capt George Keys, E TN Inf, Res omitted
KEYES, George, Capt, Col William Lillard, Vol Inf Mil, Res omitted
KILGORE, James, 3 Lt, Col S Bayless, Capt Thomas Gordon, E TN Mil, Res omitted
KILLEREASE, John, 1 Lt, Gen A Jackson, Capt Nathan Davis, Inf, Res omitted
KILPATRICK, Ebenezer, Capt, Col Philip Pipkin, 1st Regt TN Mil Inf, Fayetteville
KINCAID, James, Capt, Col A Lowry, Capt Jas Kincaid, Inf, Res omitted
KINCAID, James, Capt, Col Alexander Loury, 2nd Regt TN Mil Inf, Res omitted
KINDRED, Edmond, 2 Lt, Col John Brown, Capt Wm D Neilson, E TN Vol Mil, Res omitted
KING, Benjamin H, Capt, Col Wm Lillard, Capt Benj H King, E TN Vol Inf, Res omitted

## Officers, War of 1812

KING, Benjamin H, Capt, Col Wm Lillard, E TN Vol Inf, Res omitted

KING, Henry, 2 Lt, Capt Jas Haggard, Mtd Gunmen, Res omitted

KING, James, Aid De Campe, Brig Gen Jas White, no other information

KING, James, Surgeon, Col Jno Williams, Vol, Res omitted

KING, Jonathan, Ens, Col L Hammonds, Capt James Craig, 2nd Regt W TN Mil, Res omitted; left sick & never returned

KING, William, 1 Lt, Col R C Napier, Capt Thomas Gray, Mil Inf, Res omitted

KING, William, Capt, Col Ewen Allison, Capt Wm King, Drafted Mil, Res omitted

KING, William, Capt, Col Ewen Allison, Drafted Mil, Res omitted

KIRK, Joseph, Capt, Col William Johnson, 3rd Regt E TN Mil, Knoxville

KIRK, Joseph, Capt, Col Wm Johnson, Capt James Cook, E TN Mil, Res omitted

KIRKPATRICK, Charles, 2 Lt, Col Samuel Bunch, Capt Andrew Breden, E TN Mil, Res omitted; transferred to Capt Bacon's Co

KIRKPATRICK, James, 1 Lt, Col Jno Brown, Capt H Barton, E TN Mil Inf, Res omitted

KIRKPATRICK, Joseph, 1 Lt, Maj Gen A Jackson, Capt Joseph Kirkpatrick, Mtd Gunmen, Res omitted; promoted from 1 Lt

KIRKPATRICK, Joseph, Capt, Col Wm Y Higgins, Branch Srvce omitted, Wilson Co

KIRKPATRICK, Martin, Ens, Col Samuel Wear, Capt John Bayless, Mtd Inf, Res omitted

KNIGHT, Josiah, 2 Lt, Col Nichols T Perkins, Capt Mathew Johnston, Mil Inf

KRISEL (KRISSELL), Andrew, 2 Lt, Col Alexander Loury, Capt Gabriel Martin, Inf

LADEN, James, Capt, Col Samuel Bayless, E TN Mil; cashiered

LAMB, Isaac, Ens, Col T McCrory, Capt T K Gordon, Inf, Res omitted

LAMB, John, 1 Lt, Col Samuel Wear, Capt John Doak, E TN Vol Inf, Res omitted

LAMBERT, Aaron, 1 Lt, Col Samuel Bunch, Capt Joseph Duncan, E TN Drafted Mil, Res omitted

LANDEN, James, Capt, Col Samuel Bayless, E TN Drafted Mil, Knoxville

LANE, Garret, Capt, Commander omitted, Mtd Riflemen Pack Horse Guards, Hickman Co

LANE, Garrett, Capt, Commander omitted, Mtd Riflemen, Res omitted

LATURE, Christopher, 2 Lt, Col S Bayless, Capt Solomon Hendricks, E TN Mil, Res omitted

LATURE, Samuel, 3 Lt, Col S Bayless, Capt Joseph Hale, E TN Mil, Res omitted

LAUDERDALE, James, 1 Lt Col, Brig Gen John Coffee, TN Vol Mtd Gunmen, Res omitted

LAUDERDALE, James, 1 Maj, Col John Coffee, TN Vol Cav, Res omitted

LAUDERDALE, James, 2 Lt Col, Col John Alcorn, Co Commander omitted, TN Vol Cav, Res omitted; wounded at Talledega

LAUDERDALE, James, Lt & Lt Col, Col Robert H Dyer, TN Vol Mtd Gunmen; killed in battle 12-23-1814

LAUDERDALE, Jonah, 1 Lt, Col John Coffee, Capt John Baskerville, Cav, Res omitted

LAUDERDALE, Josiah, 1 Lt, Col John Alcorn, Capt John Baskerville, Vol Inf, Res omitted

LAUDERDALE, Samuel D, Lt Col, Col Edward Bradley, 1st Regt TN Vol Inf, Res omitted

LAUDERDALE, Samuel D, Maj, Col Wm Hall, 1st Regt TN Vol, Res omitted

LAUDERDALE, William, 1 Lt & Paymaster, Col Wm Hall, 1st TN Regt Vol, Res omitted

LAUDERDALE, William, 1 Lt, Col William Hall, Capt William Alexander, Vol Inf, Res omitted

LAUDERDALE, William, Capt & Paymaster, Col Edward Bradley, 1st Regt TN Vol Inf, Res omitted

LAUDERDALE, William, Capt, Col Edward Bradley, 1st Regt Vol Inf, Gallatin

LAUDERDALE, William, Capt, Col Edward Bradley, Vol Inf, Res omitted

LAWERY, A, Col, Commander omitted, 2nd Regt W TN Mil, Res omitted; resigned 11-20-1814

LAWRENCE, Jesse, 1 Lt, Col Thomas Williamson, Capt Doak & Capt John Dobbins, Vol Mtd Gunmen

LAWRENCE, William P, Surgeon, Col Jas Raulston, no Co Commander, W TN Mil

LAWSON, Andrew, Capt, Col William Johnson, 3rd Regt E TN Mil Drafted, Knoxville

LAWSON, Andrew, Capt, Col Wm Johnson, E TN Draft Mil

LAWSON, Eppy, 2 Lt, Col A Cheatham, Capt Richard Benson, Inf; died 4-21-1814

LEATH, Willie, 3 Lt, Col Samuel Bunch, Capt Andrew Breden, E TN Mil, Res omitted

LEE, James, Ens, Col S Bunch, Capt Jones Griffin, E TN Drafted Mil, Res omitted; furloughed for inability

LEFTWICH, John, Adjt, Col John Brown, Capt Jesse C. Reany, Mtd Gunmen; also 3 Lt

LEFTWICH, John, Ens, Regt Commander omitted, Capt Wm D Neilson, E TN Vol Mil

LEMB, Adam, 1 Lt, Col Jno Brown, Capt W Christian, E TN Vol Inf, Res omitted

LENIER, Buchanan, 2 Lt, Col John Alcorn, Capt Frederick Stump, Cav

LENIER, Buchanan, 2 Lt, Col John Coffee, Capt Fred Stump, Cav, Res omitted

LEWEN, Charles, Ens, Col Samuel Bunch, Capt Henry Stephens, E TN Mtd Inf, Res omitted

LEWIN, Charles, Capt, Col John Brown, 2nd Regt TN Vol Mtd Gunmen, Kingston

LEWIN, Charles, Chap, Col John Brown, E TN Mtd Inf, Res omitted

LEWIS, Christian, 3 Lt, Col Wm Lillard, Capt George Argenbright, E TN Vol Riflemen, Res omitted

LEWIS, Elijah, 2 Lt, Col James Raulston, Capt Daniel Newman, Inf, Res omitted

LEWIS, Grein, Ens, Capt George Smith, Spies, Res omitted

LEWIS, John, Capt, Col Edwin Booth, E TN Drafted Mil, Res omitted

LEWIS, John, Capt, Col Edwin E Booth, 5th Regt TN Mil Inf, Knoxville
LEWIS, John, Ens, Col Samuel Wear, Capt John Chiles, E TN Vol Inf, Res omitted
LEWIS, Thomas W, 1 Lt, Col John Cocke, Capt James Gray, Inf, Res omitted
LEWIS, Tipton, 1 Lt, Maj Wm Russell, Capt Geo Mitchie, Vol Mtd Gunmen; promoted to Adjt of Maj Russell's Bn
LEWIS, Tipton, Lt & Adjt, Maj Wm Russell, Separate Bn of TN Vol Mtd Gunmen, Res omitted
LEWIS, Washington, Lt, Gen A Jackson, Capt Hugh Kerr, Mtd Rangers, Res omitted; promoted from Sgt
LEWTON (LUTEN), Henry, 1 Lt, Col John Cocke, Capt Samuel M Caruthers, Inf, Res omitted
LILLARD, James, Capt, Col William Lillard, Vol Mil, Newport
LILLARD, James, Capt, Col Wm Lillard, Capt Jas Lillard, E TN Inf Vol, Res omitted
LILLARD, John, Ens, Col Samuel Bayless, Capt B Jones, E TN Drafted Mil, Res omitted
LILLARD, William, Col, Commander omitted, Vol E TN Mil, Res omitted
LILLARD, William, Col, Field & Staff Officers, 1st Div E TN Mil & 2nd Regt Vol Inf, Res omitted
LINN, Joseph, 1 Lt, Capt Garrett Lane, Mtd Riflemen, Res omitted
LISBY, Moses, Ens, Col Samuel Wear, Capt Daniel Price, E TN Vol Inf, Res omitted
LITTER, J W, 1 Lt, Gen Andrew Jackson, Capt D Deaderick, Arty, Res omitted; appointed Adjt Gen
LOCKE, William, 1 Lt, Col John Coffee, Capt Blackman Coleman, Cav, Res omitted
LOCKE, William, Capt, Col John Alcorn, Cav, Res omitted
LOCKE, William, Capt, Col John Alcorn, Cav, Rutherford Co
LONG, Benjamin, Cor, Brig Gen John Coffee, TN Vol Mtd Gunmen, Res omitted
LONG, Benjamin, Cor, Capt Ephraim Dickson, no other information
LONG, Isaac, Ens, Col Wm Lillard, Capt George Argenbright, E TN Vol Riflemen, Res omitted
LONG, James, Lt, Regt Commander omitted, Capt Robt Evans, Mtd Gunmen, Res omitted
LONG, John B, 1 Lt, Col Thos H Benton, Capt George Gibbs, Vol Inf, Res omitted
LONGACRE, Richard, 2 Lt, Col Wm Johnson, Capt Elihu Milliken, 3rd Regt E TN Mil, Res omitted
LONY, Benjamin, Cor, Col Robt H Dyer, Capt Ephraim D Dickson, TN Mtd Vol Gunmen, Res omitted
LOONEY, John, 2 Lt, Col N T Perkins, Capt J Doak, Vol Mtd Riflemen, Res omitted
LOONEY, John, Capt, Col Alex Loury, Capt John Looney, 2nd Regt of W TN Mil, Res omitted
LORANCE, Jesse, Cor, Maj Gen John Cocke, TN Vol Mtd Gunmen, Res omitted
LOUGHMILLER, Frederick, 2 Lt, Col Wm Lillard, Capt Geo Argenbright, E TN Vol Riflemen, Res omitted
LOUGHMILLER, James (Jonas), Capt, Col Ewen Allison, Mil, Res omitted
LOUGHMILLER, Jonas, Capt, Col Ewen Allison, E TN Mil, Res omitted
LOURY, Alexander, Col, Field & Staff Officers, 2nd Regt W TN Mil, Fayetteville
LOVE, Robert, 1 Lt, Col S Bunch, Capt Daniel Yarnell, E TN Mil, Res omitted
LOVELL, Daniel, Ens, Col John Cocke, Capt George Barnes, Inf, Res omitted
LOWDESS, Jacob, 1 Lt, Col Samuel Bayless, Capt Joseph Hale, E TN Mil, Res omitted; resigned 11-29-1814
LOWERY, Alexander, Col, Commander omitted, 2nd Regt W TN Mil, Res omitted; resigned 11-2-1814
LUALLEN, Charles, 3 Lt, Col Edwin Booth, Capt Richard Marshall, Drafted Mil, Res omitted
LUCAS, George A, 1 Lt, Col Edward Bradley, Capt John Wallace, Inf, Res omitted
LUCAS, John, 1 Lt, Col Samuel Bunch, Capt James Cummings, E TN Vol Mtd Gunmen, Res omitted
LUCAS, P W, 3 Lt, Brig Gen John Cocke, TN Vol Mtd Gunmen, Res omitted
LUCAS, Peter W, 3 Lt, Col Thomas Williamson, Capt Thomas Scurry, Vol Mtd Gunmen, Res omitted
LUCAS, William, Ens, Col Newton Cannon, Capt David Hogan, Mtd Gunmen, Res omitted
LUNA, James, Ens, Col John K Wynn, Capt John Porter, Inf, Res omitted
LUNDAY, Richard, Ens, Maj Wm Woodfolk, Capt Abner Pearce, Inf, Res omitted; resigned 10-3-1814
LUNG, Isaac, Lt, Col J K Winn, Capt Wm McCall, Inf, Res omitted
LUSK, Andrew M, Topograph Ens, Maj Gen Wm Carroll, TN Mil, Res omitted; resigned 1-10-1815
LYNES, James, 2 Maj, Lt Col Henry Bryan, Inf, Res omitted
LYNN, John, Ens, Col Thos McCrory, Capt Thos Gordon, Inf, Res omitted; elected from Pvt
LYON, Will, 2 Lt, Col Wm Hall, Capt Henry M Newlin, Inf, Res omitted
LYON, William, 2 Lt, Col Edward Bradley, Capt Thos B Haynie, Vol Inf; promoted to 1 Lt
LYONS, Williams, 2 Lt, Col Wm Hall, Capt Henry M Newlin, Inf, Res omitted
MACADOO, John, 2 Lt, Co Wm Johnson, Capt James Tunnell, E TN Mil, Res omitted; promoted to 1 Lt
MACKAY, William, Capt, Col Philip Pipkin, 1st Regt TN Mil Inf, Res omitted
MACKAY, William, Capt, Col Philip Pipkin, Capt Wm Mackay, Mil Inf, Res omitted
MACKEY, William, Ens, Col Wm Lillard, Capt George Keyes, E TN Inf, Res omitted
MADDING, Absalom, Cor, Regt Commander omitted, Capt Jno Williams, Mil Cav; promoted to 2nd then 1st Lt
MAHAN, Archer, 3 Lt, Col Edwin Booth, Capt Porter, Drafted Mil, Res omitted
MAHAN, James W, Capt, Brig Gen John Coffee, TN Vol Mtd Gunmen, Res omitted
MAHAN, S D W, 3 Lt, Brig Gen John Coffee, TN Vol Mtd Gunmen, Res omitted

MAJORS, Absalem, 3 Lt, Col Edwin Booth, Capt George Winton, E TN Mil, Res omitted; resigned 12-28-1814
MALCOM, Alexander, Ens, Col Samuel Wear, Capt John Stephens, E TN Vol Inf, Res omitted
MALLERY, Benjamin, 3 Lt, Col John Cocke, Capt John Weakley, Inf, Res omitted
MALLOCK, Charles, 1 Lt, Col Wm Hall, Capt John Kennedy, Vol Inf, Res omitted
MALONE, Michael, Ens, Col Wm Johnston, Capt Joseph Scott, E TN Drafted Mil, Res omitted
MALONE, William, Ens, Col Wm Johnson, Capt Andrew Lawson, E TN Mil, Res omitted
MALONEY, Robert, Capt, Col William Lillard, Vol Mil Inf., Greeneville
MALONEY, Robert, Capt, Col Wm Lillard, E TN Vol Inf, Res omitted
MANEY (MURRAY), Blank, 2 Lt, Lt Col L Hammond, Capt James Tubb, Inf, Res omitted
MANEY, Bland, Lt, Col Leroy Hammonds, Capt Jas Tubb, Inf, Res omitted
MANLEY, James, 2 Lt, Col Phillip Pipkin, Capt John Strother, Mil, Res omitted
MANN, Thomas, Capt, Col S Bunch, E TN Mtd Vol Inf, Res omitted
MANTON, Charles, Judge Advocate, Maj Sam W Carroll, TN Mil, Res omitted
MAPLES, Wilson (William), Capt, Col Edwin E. Booth, Capt John Porter, E TN Drafted Mil, Knoxville
MAPLES, Wilson, Capt, Col E E Booth, Drafted Mil, Res omitted; resigned 12-23-1814
MARKHAM, Jasper, Ens, Col James Raulston, Capt Mathew Neal, Inf, Res omitted; d 2-2-1815
MARKS, Thomas, Capt, Col William Metcalf, 1st Regt W TN Mil Inf, Res omitted
MARKS, Thomas, Capt, Col Wm Metcalf, Capt Thomas Marks, Mil Inf, Res omitted
MARLIN, William, Capt, Col Newton Cannon, Mtd Riflemen, Res omitted
MARR, George W L, Capt, Col N T Perkins, 1st Reg Mil Mtd Vol, Montgomery Co
MARR, George W L, Capt, Col N T Perkins, Mtd Vol; wounded at Enuckfan 1-22-1814
MARR, William M, 1 Lt, Col N T Perkins, Capt Quarles, Vol Mtd Riflemen
MARSHALL, Hardy, Ens, Col Samuel Bunch, Capt Andrew Breden, E TN Mil
MARSHALL, Richard, Capt, Col Edwin Booth, Drafted Mil
MARSHALL, Richard, Capt, Col Edwin E Booth, TN Drafted Mil, Washington
MARTAIN, William, 1 Maj, Col A Cheatham, TN Mil
MARTIN, Brice, Capt, Col Edward Bradley, 1st Reg Vol Inf, Smith Co
MARTIN, Brice, Capt, Col William Hall, 1st Reg TN Vol Inf, Res omitted
MARTIN, Brice, Capt, Col Wm Hall, Vol Inf
MARTIN, Bruce, Capt, Col Edward Bradley, Vol Inf
MARTIN, G W, ADC, Brig Gen John Coffee, TN Vol Mtd Gunmen
MARTIN, G W, Lt & Paymaster, Col Thomas Williamson, Res omitted
MARTIN, G W, Lt & Paymaster, Col Thomas Williamson, no other information
MARTIN, Gabrial, Capt, Lt Col Archer Cheatham, 6 Brig Inf
MARTIN, Gabriel, Capt, Col A Loury, Inf
MARTIN, Gabriel, Capt, Col Alexander Loury, W TN Mil Inf, Madison Co?
MARTIN, George W, Lt & ADC, Brig Gen Jno Coffee, TN Vol Mtd Gunmen
MARTIN, George W, Lt & Paymaster, Gen John Coffee, Tn Vol Mtd Gunmen
MARTIN, George, 2 Lt, Col James Raulston, Capt Henry Hamilton, Inf; also served under Gen Wm Carroll
MARTIN, George, Ens, Col Philip Pipkin, Capt Wm Mackay, Mil Inf
MARTIN, Hugh, Capt, Col William Lillard, Vol Mil, Knoxville
MARTIN, Hugh, Capt, Col Wm Lillard, Capt Hugh Martin, E TN Vol Inf
MARTIN, James G, 1 Lt, Col Philip Pipkin, 1st Regt TN Mil, Res omitted
MARTIN, John D, 2 Lt, Col Thomas H Williamson, Capt Wm Martin, Vol Mtd Gunmen, Res omitted
MARTIN, John L, 2 Lt, Col R H Dyer, Capt Bethel Allen, Vol Mtd Gunmen, Res omitted; mustered sick & never joined
MARTIN, John, 2 Maj, Col Edwin E Booth, E TN Mil, Res omitted
MARTIN, John, 3 Lt, Col James Raulston, Capt Mathew Neal, Inf, Res omitted
MARTIN, Patrick, Lt & Adjt, Col John Coffee, TN Vol Mtd Gunmen, Res omitted; d 3-30-1815
MARTIN, Samuel, 1 Lt, Maj Gen John Cocke, TN Vol Mtd Gunmen, Res omitted
MARTIN, William, Capt, Col N Cannon, Mtd Gunmen, Res omitted; promoted from 1 Lt
MARTIN, William, Capt, Col Thomas Williamson, 2nd Reg TN Vol Mtd Gunmen, Williamson Co
MARTIN, William, Capt, Col Thos Williamson, Vol Mtd Gunmen, Res omitted
MARTIN, William, Capt, Maj Gen John Cocke, TN Vol Mtd Gunmen, Res omitted
MARTIN, William, Ens, Col Edwin E Booth, Capt John Slatton, E TN Mil, Res omitted
MARTIN, William, Lt Col, Col Wm Pillow, TN Vol Inf, Res omitted; promoted from Maj
MARTIN, William, Maj, Commander omitted, TN Vol Inf, Res omitted
MASON, David, Capt, Commander omitted, Cav, Res omitted
MASON, David, Capt, Commander omitted, Mil Cav, Res omitted
MASON, Isaac, Ens, Col Thomas Benton, Capt N Cannon, Inf, Res omitted
MASON, Isaac, Ens, Col William Pillow, Capt Mason, Vol Inf, Res omitted
MASON, James, 1 Lt, Col Thomas Benton, Capt N Cannon, Inf, Res omitted
MASON, Joseph, 1 Lt, Col William Pillow, Capt Mason, Vol Inf, Res omitted

MASON, Joseph, Lt, Col William Pillow, Capt Mason, Vol Inf, Williamson Co
MASON, Robert, 2 Lt, Col John Coffee, Capt Molton, Cav, Res omitted
MASSINGALE, Robert, 1 Maj, Col Samuel Bunch, E TN Mil, Res omitted
MATHEWS, Abner, 1 Lt, Col R C Napier, Capt Samuel Ashmore, Mil Inf, Res omitted
MATHEWS, Sampson, 1 Lt, Col A Cheatham, Capt George Chapman, Inf, Res omitted
MATLOCK, Charles, 1 Lt, Col Wm Hall, Capt John Kennedy, Vol Inf, Res omitted
MATLOCK, David, Ens, Col Edward Bradley, Capt John Kennedy, Riflemen, Res omitted
MAURIAN, Charles, Aide De Camp, Brig Gen Bird Smith, Capt William Carroll, TN Mil, Res omitted
MAURY, Thomas T, 1 Lt, Col Thomas Benton, Capt James McEwen, Vol Inf, Res omitted
MAURY, Thomas T, 2 Maj, Col Nicholas T Perkins, TN Vol, Res omitted
MAURY, Thomas, 1 Maj, Col N Cannon, Vol Mtd Riflemen, Res omitted
MAXEY, Bennett, Ens, Col R T Perkins, Capt Patterson, Vol Mtd Gunmen, Res omitted
MAXWELL, Daniel, Ens, Col Wm Metcalf, Capt Patterson, Mil Inf, Res omitted; promoted from Sgt
MAXWELL, Samuel, Capt, Col Robert Steele, Capt Samuel Maxwell, Mil Inf, Res omitted
MAXWELL, Samuel, Capt, Col Robert Steele, Mil Inf, Jackson Co
MAXWELL, Thomas, Lt, Col Samuel Wear, Capt James Tedford, E TN Vol Inf, Res omitted
MAY, Charles P, 2 Lt, Col T McCrory, Capt William Dooley, Inf, Res omitted
MAY, John, 2 Lt, Brig Gen John Coffee, Co Commander omitted, TN Vol Mtd Gunmen, Res omitted
MAY, John, 2 Lt, Col R H Dyer, Capt Joseph Williams, Vol Mtd Gunmen, Res omitted
MAYS, William, 2 Maj, Col Samuel Bayless, 4th Regt E TN Mil, Res omitted
MCALEB, John, 3 Lt, Col John Brown, Capt John Childs, E TN Vol Mtd Gunmen, Res omitted
MCBRIDE, Samuel, 2 Lt, Col A Loury, Capt John Looney, 2nd Regt W TN Mil, Res omitted
MCBRIDE, William, 1 Maj, Col Edwin E Booth, E TN Mil, Res omitted
MCCALL, William, Capt, Col John K Wynn, Inf, Res omitted
MCCALL, William, Capt, Col John K Wynne, 1st Regt Mil Inf, Sumner Co
MCCALPIN, Robert, Capt, Col William Lillard, E TN Vol Mil Inf, Res omitted
MCCALPIN, Robert, Capt, Col Wm Lillard, E TN Inf, Res omitted
MCCAMPBELL, James, Capt & Brig Inspector, Brig Gen Bird Smith, W TN Mil Commanded by Maj Gen Wm Carroll, Res omitted
MCCAMPBELL, William A, Lt, Maj P H Porter, Capt James Anderson, Cav, Res omitted
MCCANN, Michael, 1 Lt, Maj Jno Chiles, Capt James Cumming, E TN Vol Mtd Inf, Res omitted

MCCARTNEY, James, Ens, Col Samuel Wear, Capt James Tedford, E TN Vol Inf, Res omitted
MCCARTY, Andrew, Capt, Col R C Napier, 1st Regt TN Mil Inf, Maury Co
MCCARTY, Andrew, Capt, Col R C Napier, Capt Andrew McCarty, Mil Inf, Res omitted
MCCAULEY (MANLEY), James, 2 Lt, Col Phillip Pipkin, Capt John Strother, Mil, Res omitted
MCCHRISTIAN, Thomas, Capt, Col Wm Lillard, E TN Vol Inf, Res omitted
MCCLANAHAN, Alexander, 3 Lt, Col Samuel Bayless, Capt James Churchman, E TN Mil, Res omitted
MCCLURE, John, Chap, Col John Cocke, no Co Commander, 2 Regt W TN Mil Inf
MCCONNELL, James, Ens, Col Samuel Bunch, Capt Jno McNare, E TN Mil
MCCONNELL, Moses, 1 Lt, Col Thomas Benton, Capt James McFerrin, Vol Inf
MCCONNELL, Moses, 1 Lt, Col Wm Pilloe, Capt James McFerrin
MCCORKLE, Joel, 1 Lt, Col Samuel Bunch, Capt Edward Buchanan, E TN Mil Draft
MCCORMACH, Absolom, 1 Lt, Col R C Napier, Capt Early Benson, Mil Inf
MCCOY, Henry, Adjt, Maj Thos Williamson, Branch Srvce & Res omitted
MCCRACKEN, Hugh, Sgt Maj Brig QM, Brig Gen Geo Doherty, E TN Mil, Res omitted
MCCRAY, Elisha, 1 Lt, Col Ewen Allison, Capt John Hampton, Mil, Res omitted; promoted to Ens
MCCRAY, Henry, Capt, Col Ewen Allison, Capt Henry McCray, E TN Mil, Res omitted
MCCRAY, Thomas, Ens, Col Ewen Allison, Capt Henry McCray, E TN Mil, Res omitted; promoted to Sgt
MCCRORY, Thomas, Col, Commander omitted, TN Mil, Res omitted
MCCRORY, Thomas, Col, Field & Staff Officers Div of Maj Gen Andrew Jackson, 2nd Regt TN Mil, Williamson Co
MCCULLEY, William, Capt, Bn of Maj William Woodfolk, Branch Srvce omitted, Res omitted
MCCULLOCK, Alexander, Lt & Aide De Camp, Brig Gen John Coffee, TN Mtd Mil, Res omitted; in place of Alex Donelson
MCCULLOCK, James, Lt, Capt Nathan Farmer, Mtd Riflemen, Res omitted; promoted to 1 Lt
MCCULLY, William, 1 Lt, Maj Wm Woodfolk, Capt Ross, Inf
MCCUTCHEN, William, Ens, Col Wm Metcalf, Capt Wm Mullin, Mil Inf
MCCUTCHER, Robert, 3 Lt, Col Robert Dyer, Capt Geo Edmonston, TN Mtd Vol Gunmen
MCCUTCHIN, William, Ens, Col Wm Metcalf, Capt Wm Mullen, Mil Inf
MCDANIEL, Moses, Cor, Maj Wm Russell, Capt Wm Chism, Vol Mtd Gunmen, Res omitted
MCDOWELL, Benjamin, 3 Lt, Col Wm Metcalf, Capt Wm Sitton, Mil Inf, Res omitted
MCELDER, Thomas, 1 Lt, Maj John Childs, Capt Reuben Tipton, E TN Vol Mtd Inf, Res omitted
MCELDRY, Thomas, 1 Lt, Col John Brown, Capt John

## Officers, War of 1812

Childs, E TN Mtd Gunmen, Res omitted
MCEWEN, C D, Ens, Col T H Benton, Capt Jas McEwen, Vol Inf, Res omitted
MCEWEN, C E, Capt, Col William Pillow, 2nd Regt TN Vol Inf, Williamson Co
MCEWEN, C E, Capt, Col Wm Pillow, Vol Inf, Res omitted
MCEWEN, Christopher, Ens, Col T H Benton, Capt Jas McEwen, Vol Inf, Res omitted
MCEWEN, James, Capt, Col T H Benton, Vol Inf, Res omitted
MCEWEN, James, Capt, Col Thomas H Benton, 2nd Regt TN Vol Mil, Res omitted
MCEWEN, James, Maj, Col Wm Pillow, 2nd Regt TN Vol Inf, Res omitted; promoted from a Capt
MCEWEN, Robt H, 3 Lt, Col John Brown, Capt Wm White, E TN Vol Mtd Inf, Res omitted; appointed Regt QM
MCEXUM, James, 1 Lt, Capt Jas Terrill, Cav, Res omitted
MCFALL, Samuel P, 2 Lt, Col Jno Cocke, Capt S M Caruthers, Inf, Res omitted
MCFARLAND, William, Ens, Col Wm Lillard, Capt Zacheus Copeland, E TN Vol Inf, Res omitted
MCFERRAN, Thomas, 3 Lt, Col Leroy Hammond, Capt James Tubb, Inf, Res omitted
MCFERRIN, Benton L, 2 Lt, Col Wm Pillow, Capt James McFerrin, Inf, Res omitted
MCFERRIN, Burton L, 2 Lt, Col Thomas H Benton, Capt James McFerrin, Vol Inf, Res omitted
MCFERRIN, James, Capt, Col Thomas H Benton, 2nd Regt TN Vol Inf, Res omitted
MCFERRIN, James, Capt, Col William Pillow, 2nd Regt TN Vol Inf, Rutherford Co
MCFERRIN, James, Capt, Col Wm Pillow, Capt James McFerrin, Inf, Res omitted
MCGEE, James C, 2 Maj, Brig Gen Nathaniel Taylor, 3rd Regt E TN Drafted Mil; resigned 2-7-1815
MCGEE, Samuel, Lt & Forage Master, Maj Wm Russell, Separate Bn E TN Mtd Gunmen, Res omitted; resigned 1-14-1815
MCKAMEY, James, Capt, Col John Brown, E TN Mtd Gunmen, Res omitted
MCKAMEY, John, Capt, Col Edwin Booth, E TN Mil, Res omitted
MCKAMEY, John, Capt, Col Edwin E Booth, E TN Drafted Mil, Washington; Division of Maj Gen Wm Carroll
MCKAMY, David, 2 Lt, Col Samuel Wear, Capt James Tedford, E TN Vol Inf, Res omitted
MCKAMY, David, Capt, Col William Johnson, 3rd Regt E TN Mil, Res omitted
MCKAMY, David, Capt, Col Wm Johnson, Capt David McKamey, E TN Drafted Mil, Res omitted
MCKAMY, James, Capt, Col John Brown, E TN Vol Mtd Gunmen, Kingston; Gen George Doherty's Brigade
MCKEAN, Alexander, Capt, Col Jno Coffee, Capt Alexander McKeen, Cav, Res omitted
MCKEE, Robert, 2 Lt, Col Wm Johnson, Capt Andy Lawson, E TN Drafted Mil, Res omitted
MCKEEN, Alexander, Capt, Col John Acorn, Cav, Rutherford Co; Div of Maj Gen Andrew Jackson
MCKEEN, Alexander, Capt, Col John Alcorn, Capt Alexander McKeen, Cav, Res omitted
MCKEEN, Alexander, Capt, Col John Coffee, Cav W TN Vol, Rutherford Co
MCKENNEY, Archibald, Capt, Col Robert H Dyer, Cav TN Vol, Williamson Co
MCKENNY, Archibald M, Capt, Commander omitted, Cav, Res omitted; promoted from 1 Lt
MCKINNEY, Archibald, Pvt, no other information
MCKNIGHT, David, Lt & Adjt, Col John Cocke, no Co Commander, 2 Regt W TN Mtd Inf
MCKNIGHT, Samuel B, Capt, Col Thomas McCrory, 2nd Regt TN Mil Inf, Maury Co
MCKNIGHT, Samuel B, Capt, Col Thos McCrory, Mil Inf
MCLIN, William, Capt, Col William Lillard, E TN Mil Vol Inf, Res omitted
MCMAHAN, Abraham, Ens, Col S Copeland, Capt J Holshouser, Inf
MCMAHAN, James, Capt, Col N T Perkins, 1st Regt Vol Mil Mtd Gunmen, Maury Co
MCMAHAN, James, Capt, Col N T Perkins, Mtd Gunmen
MCMAHAN, James, Capt, Col R H Dyer, TN Mtd Vol Gunmen; died of wounds, battle of 12-6-1814
MCMAHAN, Richard, Cor, Regt Commander omitted, Capt Jas Terrill, Cav
MCMAHON, James, Capt, Col Robert H Dyer & Capt Samuel Crawford, TN Vol Cav Mtd Gunmen, Nashville
MCMAHON, Samuel D, Sgt--3 Lt, Col Robert H Dyer, Capt Jas McMahon, Tn Vol Mtd Gunmen; elected to 3 Lt
MCMEKIN, Elisha, 1 Lt, Col Alexander Loury, Capt John Looney, W Tn Mil
MCMILLIN, Thomas, Ens, Col Wm Johnson, Capt Christopher Cook, E TN Mil
MCMURRY, James, Capt, Col R C Napier, 1st Regt TN Mil Inf, Res omitted
MCMURRY, James, Capt, Col R C Napier, Capt Jas McMurray, Mil Inf, Res omitted
MCNAIR, John, Capt, Col Samuel Bunch, E TN Mil, Res omitted
MCNARE, John, Capt, Col S Bunch, E TN Mil, Res omitted
MCNIGHT, William, Ens, Col Thomas McCrory, Capt James Shannon, Mil Inf, Res omitted
MCNUTTE, Joseph, Ens, Col T McCrory, Capt Samuel McKnight, Inf, Res omitted
MCPHERSON, George, Capt, Col Samuel Bunch, E TN Mil, Res omitted; Sub Capt to Amos Parsons
MCPHERSON, George, Lt, Col Samuel Bunch, Capt Geo McPherson, E TN Mil, Res omitted; elected from Pvt
MCPHERSON, John, 1 Lt, Col Wm Lillard, Capt Thomas Sharpe, 2nd Regt Inf, Res omitted
MCPHETERS, James, 2 Lt, Col Wm Lillard, Capt Thomas Sharpe, 2nd Regt Inf, Res omitted; elected from Ens
MCRAE, John L, 1 Lt & Adjt, Col R C Napier, 1st Regt W TN Mil, Res omitted
MCRAEE, John L, Lt & Paymaster, Col R C Napier, 1st

## Officers, War of 1812

Regt W TN Mil, Res omitted
MCRUNOLD, Joseph H, 2 Lt, Col Newton Cannon, Capt Andrew Patterson, Mtd Riflemen, Res omitted
MCVAY, Thomas, 1 Lt, Col Wm Johnston, Cap Joseph Kirk, E TN Mil, Res omitted
MCVEY, Thomas, Lt, Col Wm Johnson, Capt Christopher Cook, E TN Mil, Res omitted; d 12-31-1814
MEBANE, George, Capt, Col Philip Pipkin, 1st Reg Mil Inf, Fayetteville
MEBANE, George, Capt, Col Philip Pipkin, Mil Inf, Res omitted
MECUTCHEON, Robert, 3 Lt, Brig Gen John Coffee, TN Vol Mil Gunmen, Res omitted
MELTON, Elijah, 3 Lt, Col William Metcalf, Capt Thomas Marks, Mil Inf, Res omitted; d 2-27-1815
MENESS, Benjamin, 2 Maj, Lt Col Arch Cheatham, 6th Brig Inf, Res omitted
MENIFEE, Willis, 1 Lt, Col Philip Pipkin, Capt David Smith, Mil Inf, Res omitted
MEREDITH, Richard, 1 Lt, Capt John Williams, Vol, Res omitted
MEREDITH, Richard, 1 Lt, Col Jno Williams, Capt William Walker, E TN Mtd Vol, Res omitted
MEREDITH, Richard, Deputy QM Gen - 1st Lt in Line, Maj Gen John Chiles, E TN Mil Inf, Res omitted
MEREDITH, Richard, Deputy QM Gen, Brig Gen Geo Doherty, E TN Mil, Res omitted; continued under Gen Cocke
MEREDITH, Samuel, 1 Lt & Paymaster, Col R C Napier, 1st Regt W TN Mil, Res omitted; resigned 3-19-1814
MEREDITH, Samuel, Adjt, Col Newton Cannon, TN Vol Mtd Riflemen, Res omitted
MEREDITH, Samuel, Lt & Brig Inspector, Brig Gen John Coffee, TN Mtd Mil, Res omitted; appointed in place of Basil Shaw
MERIDETH, Samuel, 1 Lt & Adjt, Col N T Perkins, 1st Regt TN Mtd Vol, Res omitted
MERIDITH, Richard, 1st Lt, Col Samuel Wear, Capt John Chiles, E TN Vol Mil, Res omitted
METCALF, A H, Capt, Maj Gen John Cocke, TN Vol Mtd Gunmen, Res omitted
METCALF, Anthony M., Capt, Col Thomas Williamson, 2nd Reg TN Vol Mtd Gunmen, Carthage (Smith Co)
METCALF, Anthony, Capt, Col Thomas McCrory, 2nd Reg TN Mil, Smith Co
METCALF, Anthony, Capt, Col Thomas McCrory, Capt William Metcalf, Mil Inf, Res omitted
METCALF, William, Col, Commander omitted, 1st Regt W TN Mil Inf, Res omitted
METCALF, William, Col, Field & Staff 1st Reg W TN Mil Inf, Nashville
MICHIE, George, Capt, Col Thomas Williamson, Capt Geo Michie, TN Vol Mtd Gunmen, Res omitted
MICHIE, George, Capt, Maj William Russell, Capt Geo Mitchie, Vol Mtd Gunmen, Res omitted
MILES, Bird A, 2 Lt, Lt James Berry, Mtd Riflemen, Res omitted; promoted from Sgt
MILES, Charles, 1 Lt, Capt Jas Haggard, Mtd Gunmen, Res omitted

MILES, Richard, Cor, Maj Gen Jackson, Capt John Crane, Mtd Gunmen, Res omitted; payroll says Ens instead of Cor
MILIKEN, Elisha, Capt, Col William Johnson, Capt Elihu Milliken, E TN Mil, Res omitted
MILLER, Isael, Ens, Brig Gen Thos Johnson, Capt Robert Carson, Inf, Res omitted
MILLER, John, Capt, Col R H Dyer, unit omitted, Overton Co
MILLER, John, Capt, Regt Commander omitted, Capt John Miller, Spies, Res omitted
MILLER, Peter, 1 Lt, Col William Johnson, Capt Andrew Lawson, E TN Drafted Mil, Res omitted
MILLER, Samuel, Lt, Capt John Miller, Spies, Res omitted
MILLICAN, Hugh, 1 Lt, Col S Bunch, Capt Andrew Breden, E TN Mil, Res omitted
MILLIKEN, Alexander, 1 Lt, Col William Johnson, Capt Joseph Scott, E TN Drafted Mil, Res omitted
MILLIKEN, Elihu, Capt, Col William Johnson, 3rd Reg E TN Mil, Res omitted
MILLS, Johns, 2 Lt, Col William Higgins, Capt William Doak, Mtd Riflemen, Res omitted
MITCHEL, George, 2 Lt, Col N T Perkins, Capt Quarles, Vol Mtd Inf, Res omitted
MITCHELL, Arthur, Lt, Col S Copeland, Capt David Williams, Mil Inf, Res omitted
MITCHELL, David, 2 Lt, Col P Pipkin, Capt Jno Robertson, Mil Inf, Res omitted
MITCHELL, Granberry, 3 Lt, Col Wm Lillard, Capt Thos Sharpe, 2nd Regt E TN Inf, Res omitted; promoted from Sgt
MITCHELL, James C, 1 Maj, Col Wm Johnson, 3rd Regt E TN Mil, Res omitted
MITCHELL, Marcus, 2 Lt, Maj Wm Woodfolk, Capt John Sutton & Capt A Dudney, Inf, Res omitted; promoted to 1 Lt
MITCHELL, William, 1 Maj, Gen John Coffee's Brig, TN Vol Mtd Gunmen
MITCHELL, William, Capt, Col Robert H. Dyer, Spies-- TN Vol Cav, Res Ru____(Rutherford?)
MITCHELL, William, Capt, Col Samuel Bunch, Col Samuel Wear, E TN Mtd Inf
MITCHELL, William, Capt, Regt Commander omitted, Spies
MITCHIE, George, Capt, Maj William Russell, TN Vol Mtd Gunmen, Wilson Co
MOLTON, Michael, 1 Maj, Brig Gen John Coffee, TN Vol Mtd Gunmen
MOLTON, Michael, 1 Maj, Col Robert Dyer, Field & Staff Officers, W Tn Mil
MOLTON, Michael, Capt, Col John Coffee, Cav
MOLTON, Michael, Capt, Col John Coffee, Cav, Res omitted
MOLTON, Michael, Capt, Col Robert H. Dyer, Vol Cav, Dixon Co, promoted to 1st Maj
MONTGOMERY, James, 2 Lt, Col N T Perkins, Capt James McMahan, Mtd Gunmen
MONTGOMERY, Samuel, Ens, Col Samuel Wear, Capt James Gillespie, E TN Vol Inf
MONTGOMERY, William, 2 Maj, Col R C Napier, 1 Regt

W TN Mil
MOORE, Achalas, Lt, Col Robert Steele, Capt Samuel Maxwell, Mil Inf
MOORE, Aldred, Surgeon, Col John Brown, no Co Commander, E TN Vol Mtd Gunmen
MOORE, Bennett W, 3 Lt, Col Wm Metcalf, Capt Andrew Patterson, Mil Inf
MOORE, Cleon, 3 Lt, Col Samuel Bunch, Capt James Cummings, E Tn Vol Mtd Gunmen
MOORE, David A, Cor, Brig Gen John Coffee, Co Commander omitted, TN Vol Mtd Gunmen
MOORE, David A, Cor, Col R H Dyer, Capt Glen Owen, 1 Tn Vol Mtd Gunmen
MOORE, Edwin S (G?), Capt, Col Robert H. Dyer, TN Vol Cav Mtd Riflemen, Nashville
MOORE, Edwin S, Capt, Regt Commander omitted, Mtd Riflemen
MOORE, George, Cor, Col Thomas H Williamson, Capt John Doak & Capt John Dobbins, Vol Mtd Gunmen; died 1-25-1815
MOORE, Henry, 2 Lt, Col William Pillow, Capt William Moore, Inf
MOORE, Hugh A, 2 Lt, Col John Brown, Capt Wm White, Regt E Tn Mil Inf
MOORE, Isaac, Ens, Col Thomas H Benton, Capt Harry L Douglas, Vol Inf
MOORE, Issac, Ens, Col Edward Bradley, Capt Harry L Douglas, Vol Inf
MOORE, James, 1 Lt, Col John Cocke, Capt Daniel Price, Inf, Res omitted
MOORE, James, Ens, Capt Craig, Inf, Res omitted
MOORE, James, Ens, Col A Cheatham, Capt Wm Smith, Inf, Res omitted
MOORE, John, Capt, Col Edward Bradley, 1st Reg TN Vol Inf, Res omitted
MOORE, John, Capt, Col Edward Bradley, Capt John Moore, Vol Inf, Res omitted
MOORE, John, Capt, Col William Hall, 1st Reg TN Vol, Fayetteville
MOORE, John, Capt, Col William Hall, Capt John Moore, Vol Inf, Res omitted
MOORE, Robert, 1 Lt, Col John Alcorn, Capt Thomas Bradley, Vol Cav, Res omitted; killed in battle 11-9-1813
MOORE, Robert, 1 Lt, Col John Coffee, Capt Thomas Bradley, Vol Cav, Res omitted
MOORE, Robert, Capt, Col Thomas Williamson, 2nd Reg TN Vol Mtd Gunmen, Nashville
MOORE, Robert, Capt, Col Thos Williamson, Capt Robt Moore, Vol Mtd Gunmen, Res omitted
MOORE, Robert, Capt, Maj Gen John Cocke, TN Vol Mtd Gunmen, Res omitted
MOORE, Robert, Cor, Maj Gen John Cocke, TN Vol Mtd Gunmen, Res omitted
MOORE, Samuel, 2 Lt, Capt George Smith, Spies, Res omitted
MOORE, Travis, Lt, Capt James Gray, Inf, Res omitted
MOORE, Warren, Capt, Col Thomas H Benton, Capt William Moore, Vol Inf, Res omitted
MOORE, William, Capt, Col Thomas H Benton, Capt Wm Moore, Vol Inf, Res omitted

MOORE, William, Capt, Col Thomas H. Benton, 2nd Reg TN Vol Mil, Res omitted
MOORE, William, Capt, Col William Pillow, 2nd Reg TN Vol Inf, Fayetteville
MOORE, William, Capt, Col Wm Pillow, Inf, Res omitted
MOORE, William, Cor, Brig Gen John Coffee, TN Vol Mtd Gunmen, Res omitted
MOORE, William, Lt, Lt Col Richard Napier, Inf, Res omitted
MORELY, Thomas, Cor, Lt Col Jno Edmonson, Cav, Res omitted
MORGAN, Daniel, 1 Lt, Col R H Dyer, Capt James Wyatt, Vol Mtd Gunmen, Res omitted
MORGAN, Rufus, Capt, Col Samuel Wear, E TN Vol Mil Inf, Res omitted
MORRIS, John, Ens, Col Philip Pipkin, Capt Robertson, Mil Inf, Res omitted; resigned 8-10-1814
MORRIS, Morris, Cor, Capt David Smith, Cav Vol, Res omitted; promoted from Cpl
MORRIS, William H, Cor, Col Robert Dyer, Capt Bethel Allen, Vol Mtd Gunmen, Res omitted; promoted to 2 Lt
MORRISS, William, Pvt, 3 Lt, Col Philip Pipkin, Capt Henry M Newlin, Mil Inf, Res omitted
MORTON, Quin, Brig Chaplain, Brig Gen Thos Coulter, E TN Drafted Mil, Res omitted
MOSELY, Thomas, Cor, Lt Col Jno Edmonson, Cav, Res omitted
MOSES, Davis, Capt, Col Samuel Bunch, E TN Drafted Inf, Res omitted
MOTLOW, Michael, Capt, Capt Jos Williams, Mil Cav, Res omitted; promoted to 1 Maj
MOYER, Henry, Lt, Col Samuel Bayless, Capt Branch Jones, E TN Drafted Mil, Res omitted
MUHLIN (MCLINER), Wm A, 1 Lt, Col Jas Raulston, Capt James A Black, Inf, Res omitted
MULLEN, William, Capt, Col William Metcalf, W TN Mil Inf, Res omitted
MULLIN, Swift, 1 Lt & Adjt, Col Wm Metcalf, 1st Regt W TN Mil Inf, Res omitted
MULLIN, William, Capt, Col Wm Metcalf, Mil Inf, Res omitted
MUNIPOWER, Benjamin, Ens, Col Samuel Bayless, Capt S Hendricks, E TN Mil; promoted 3 Lt; died 2-11-1815
MUNIPOWER, Benjamin, Ens, Col Wm Lillard, Capt Thos Sharpe, 2 Regt E Tn Inf
MURDOCK, James G, 1 Lt, Col Wm Pillow, Lt Jno Anderson, Vol Inf
MURDOCK, James G, Ens, Col T H Benton, Capt G W Gibbs, Vol Inf
MURDOCK, James G, Ens-2 Lt, Maj William Carroll, Capt L Dillahunty, Vol Inf; also under Capt D Bradford
MURPHY, Joseph, Chap, Lt Col L Hammonds, no Co Commander, 2 Regt W TN Mil; also under Col Alexander Lowry
MURRAY (MAURY), Thomas, 1 Maj, Col Newton Cannon, TN Vol Mtd Riflemen
MURRAY, George, Ens, Col Wm Johnson, Capt James Stewart, 3 Regt E TN Mil

## Officers, War of 1812

MURRY, James, Ens, Col James Raulston, Capt Henry West, Inf

MYLES, Byrd A, 2 Lt--1 Sgt, Regt Commander omitted, Lt James Berry, Mtd Riflemen

MYNATT, William C, ADC, Maj Gen John Cocke, E TN Vol

MYNATT, William, ADC, Maj Gen John Cocke, E TN Vol Mil

NAIL, John L, 1 Lt, Brig Gen John Coffee, TN Mtd Gunmen, Res omitted

NAIL, Joseph, 2 Lt, Col Jno Brown, Capt Jas Standifer, E TN Vol Mil, Res omitted

NAIL, Matthew, 1 Lt, Col John Brown, Capt Jas Standifer, E TN Vol Mil, Res omitted

NAIL, Samuel, Ens, Col Wm Metcalf, Capt Walker, Mil Inf, Res omitted

NANCE, Bird, Capt, Col John Cocke, 2nd Reg Tn Mil, Nashville

NANCE, Bird, Capt, Col John Cocke, Inf, Res omitted

NAPIER, E W, Surgeon, Col R C Napier, W TN Mil, Res omitted

NAPIER, R C, Col, Commander omitted, W TN Mil, Res omitted

NAPIER, Richard C, Lt Col, Commander omitted, 6th Brig Inf, Res omitted

NAPIER, Richard C., Col, Field & Staff 1st Reg W Tn Mil, Dickson Co

NASH, Francis C, Capt, Col Edward Bradley, Capt Travis Nash, Vol Inf, Res omitted

NASH, Travis C, Capt, Col Wm Hall, Inf, Res omitted

NASH, Travis C., Capt, Col Edward Bradley, 1st Reg TN Vol Inf, Rutherford Co

NASH, Travis C., Capt, Col W Hall, 1st Reg TN Vol Rifle Inf, Res omitted

NEAL, Mathew, 2 Lt, Col N T Perkins, Capt Geo Eliot, Mil Inf, Res omitted

NEAL, Matthew, Capt, Col James Raulston, 3rd Reg W TN Mil, Res omitted

NEALE, Mathew, Capt, Col Jas Raulston, Inf, Res omitted

NEALY, James, Capt, Col Thos Williamson, Capt James Pace, Vol Mtd Gunmen; promoted from 1 Lt

NEATHERTON, John, Capt, Col William Lillard, Vol Mil Inf, Newport?

NEATHERTON, John, Capt, Col Wm Lillard, E TN Vol Inf, Res omitted

NEBLETT, Benjamin, 1 Lt, Col R C Napier, Capt Edward Neblett, Mil Inf, Res omitted

NEBLETT, Edward, Capt, Col R C Napier, 1st Reg TN Mil Inf, Montgomery Co

NEBLETT, Edward, Capt, Col R C Napier, Mil Inf, Res omitted

NEELLY, Charles, 1 Lt, Col N T Perkins, Capt Marr, Mtd Vol, Res omitted

NEELY, James, 1 Lt, Maj Gen John Cocke, TN Mtd Gunmen, Res omitted

NEELY, James, Capt, Col Thomas Williamson, 2nd Reg TN Vol Mtd Gunmen, Rutherford Co

NEIL, James C, Capt, Maj William Woodfolk, 1st Bn 3rd Reg TN Mil Inf, Fayetteville

NEIL, James C, Capt, Maj William Woodfolk, Inf, Res omitted

NEILL, John L, Lt, Col R H Dyer, Capt Ephraim Dickson, TN Vol Mtd Gunmen, Res omitted

NEILSON, William D, Capt, Col John Brown, E TN Vol Mil, Res omitted

NEITF?, Solomon, 2 Lt, Col Samuel Bayless, Capt James Landen, E TN Mil, Res omitted

NELSON, David, Surgeon, Col Samuel Bayless, 4th Regt E TN Mil, Res omitted

NELSON, John, Ens, Col Wm Lillard, Capt Wm Lillard, E TN Vol Inf, Res omitted

NESBITT, Thomas, 3 Lt, Col L Hammond, Capt James Craig, 2nd Regt W TN Mil, Res omitted

NEVILL, John, 1 Maj, Lt Col Jno Edmonson, Cav, Res omitted

NEWLAN, Henry M, Capt, Col Wm Hall, Capt Henry M Newland, Inf, Res omitted

NEWLIN, Henry M, Capt, Col Edward Bradley, 1st Reg TN Vol Inf, Res omitted

NEWLIN, Henry M, Capt, Col Edward Bradley, Capt Thos B Haynes, Vol Inf, Res omitted

NEWLIN, Henry M, Capt, Col Philip Pipkin, 1st Reg TN Mil Inf, Res omitted

NEWLIN, Henry M., Capt, Col William Hall, 1st Reg Inf, Res omitted

NEWMAN, Daniel, Capt, Col James Raulston, 3rd Reg W TN Mil Inf, Res omitted

NEWMAN, John, Ens, Col Edwin Booth, Capt Richard Marshall, Drafted Mil, Res omitted

NEWTON, Robert, 3 Lt, Maj Woodfolk, Inf, Res omitted

NICHOLS, Solomon, Ens, Col William Metcalf, Capt B Collins, Mil Inf, Res omitted

NOLAN, Thomas, Adjt, Col Wm Lillard, E TN Vol Mil, Res omitted

NORMAN, Ezekial, 3 Lt, Col Philip Pipkin, Capt David Smith, Mil, Res omitted; d 9-24-1814

NORMAN, John, 1 Lt, Col S Copeland, Capt Solomon George, Inf, Res omitted

NORMAN, Thomas, Lt, Col Robert Steele, Capt James Shenault, Branch Srvce omitted

NORWOOD, Henry, Cor, Maj William Russell, Col Robert Dyer, Capt William Russell, Vol Mtd Gunmen

NORWOOD, Samuel, 1 Lt, Col Thomas Benton, Capt Geo Caperton, Vol Inf

NORWOOD, Samuel, 1 Lt, Col William Pillow, Capt Geo Caperton, Inf

NOURSE, Lawson, Regt Surgeon, Col Phillip Pipkin 1 Regt TN Mil

NOWELL, Moses, 2 Lt, Maj Gen Andrew Jackson, Capt Carroll, Vol Inf

NURSE, Lawson, Surgeon, Lt Col Hammonds, W TN Mil

OBAN, Daniel, Capt, Col John Coffee, Lt Col William Phillips, 36th Reg TN Mil Inf, Hickman Co

OBAN, David, Capt, Gen Thos Johnston's Brig, 36 Regt Inf

ODENEAL, Tate, 2 Lt, Col John Coffee, Capt John W Byrns, Cav

ODENEAL, Tate, 2 Lt, Regt Commander omitted, Capt David Smith, Cav Vol; promoted from Sgt

ODGEN, John, Ens, Col Ewen Allison, Capt James Allen, E Tn Mil

- 27

ODLE, Bartlert H, 2 Lt, Col Samuel Bayless, Capt John Brock, E TN Mil
OLIVER, Lunsford, Capt, Col John Brown, E Tn Mil
OLIVER, Lunsford, Capt, Col John Brown, E Tn Mil; Res omitted
ORTON, Richard, 1 Lt & QM, Col N T Perkins, 1 Regt TN Mtd Vol
OSBORN, Thomas, Ens, Lt Col Leroy Hammonds, Capt Joseph Williamson, Inf
OSBORNE, Alfred, 3 Lt, Regt Commander omitted, Capt David Deadrick, Arty
OSBURN, John, Lt, Col John Winn, Capt William Willson, Inf
OSBURN, Thomas, Ens, Col Alexander Loury, Capt J Williamson, W TN Mil
OUTLAW, Alexander, ADC, Maj Gen J Cocke, E TN Vol Mil
OVERALL, Abraham, 2 Maj, Col Wm Higgins, TN Mtd Vol
OVERTON, John W, 1 Lt, Col N Cannon, Capt Jas Walton, Mtd Riflemen
OWEN, Glen, Capt, Col R H Dyer, TN Vol Mtd Gunmen
OWEN, Glen, Capt, Col Robert H. Dyer, 1st Reg TMV Gunmen, Williamson Co
OWEN, William, 1 Surgeon Mate, Maj Wm Woodfolk, Separate Bn W TN Mil; promoted to Asst Hospital Surgeon
OWEN, William, 3 Lt, Lt Col L Hammond, Capt A Loury & Capt Thos Delaney, Inf
OWENS, Michael, Lt, Col Wm Lillard, Capt George Keyes, E TN Inf
OWENS, Moses, Ens, Col James Raulston, Capt James A Black, Inf
OWENS, Samuel, Surgeon, Col Wm Metcalf, 1 Regt W TN Mil Inf; died 1-4-1815
PACE, James, 1 Lt, Col Newton Cannon, Capt Thos Yardley, Mtd Riflemen
PACE, James, Capt, Col Thomas Williamson, 2nd Reg TN Vol Mtd Gunmen, Rutherford Co
PACE, James, Capt, Col Thos Williamson, Vol Mtd Gunmen; killed in battle 12-23-1814
PACE, James, Capt, Maj Gen John Cocke, TN Vol Mtd Gunmen
PAGE, Lewis, Ens, Col Wm Y Higgins, Capt Thos Eldridge, Mtd Gunmen
PARISS, Joel, 1 Lt, Col Jas Raulston, Capt Wiley Huddleston, Gen Carroll, Inf
PARKER, David, 1 Lt, Maj William Russell, Capt Fleman Hodges, Vol Mtd Gunmen
PARKER, Robert, Ens, Col S Copeland, Capt David Williams, Mil Inf
PARRISH, Joel, Capt & Brig Inspector, Gen John Coffee, no Co Commander, TN Vol Mtd Gunmen
PARRISH, Joel, Capt, Gen Andrew Jackson, Art, Res omitted
PARROT, Benjamin, Lt, Col Stephen Cole, Capt Wm Evans, Mil Inf
PARROT, John, Ens, Col Wm Lillard, Capt John Roper, E TN Vol Inf
PATE, Kinchen, 2 Lt, Lt Col L Hammonds, Col Alexander Loury, Capt Thos Wells, Inf

PATTERSON, Andrew, Capt, Col A Metcalf, Mil Inf
PATTERSON, Andrew, Capt, Col Newton Cannon, Mtd Riflemen
PATTERSON, Andrew, Capt, Col Newton Cannon, Mtd Riflemen, Bedford Co.
PATTERSON, Andrew, Capt, Col William Metcalf, 1st Reg W TN Mil Inf, Res omitted
PATTERSON, James, Lt, Regt Commander omitted, Capt Jno Gordon, Mtd Spies
PATTERSON, Mathew, Capt, Col N T Perkins, 1st Reg TN Mil Mtd Vol, Nashville
PATTERSON, Mathew, Capt, Col N T Perkins, Mtd Vol
PATTON, Isaac, Capt, Col T McCrory, Inf
PATTON, Isaac, Capt, Col Thomas McCrory, 2nd Reg TN Mil Inf, Williamson Co
PATTON, Thomas C, 1 Lt, Col Ewen Allison, Capt T McCrory, E Tn Mil
PAXTON, James, 2 Lt, Col Wm Metcalf, Capt Thomas Marks, Mil Inf
PAYNE, Charles, Ens, Col S Bunch, Capt S Roberson, E TN Drafted Mil
PAYNE, Charles, Ens, Regt Commander omitted, Capt Samuel Richardson, E TN Drafted Mil
PAYNE, Ephraim, ADC, Brig Gen Thos Johnson, Branch omitted
PAYNE, Greenwood, 1 Lt, Col Wm Metcalf, Capt John Barnhardt, Branch omitted
PAYNE, Mathew, 2 Lt, Col Wm Y Higgins, Capt James Hambleton, Mtd Gunmen
PAYNE, Simpson, 2 Lt, Col Wm Hall, Capt John Moore, Vol Inf
PEACOCK, William, Capt, Col Jno Edmondson, Branch omitted; det protecting Western Frontier
PEACOCK, William, Capt, Col John Edmonson, Detach Mil Cav 6th Brig, Res omitted
PEARCE, Abner, Capt Maj Wm Woodfolk, 1 Bn Inf 3 Regt
PEARCE, Abner, Capt, Col John Coffee, Inf, Res omitted
PEARGOLL, Benjamin, Lt, Regt Commander omitted, Capt Jos Williams, Cav Mil
PEARSOLL, Benjamin, Cor, Capt Jos Williams, Mil Cav; promoted to 2 Lt
PECK, Moses L, 1 Lt, Col Wm Johnson, Capt Elihu Milliken, 3rd Regt QM E TN Mil, Res omitted
PECK, Nicholas S, Lt, Col Wm Lillard, Capt Thomas McChristian, E TN Vol Inf, Res omitted
PEEBLES, Nathan, Capt, Col Robert Johnson, Inf, Res omitted
PEGRAM, William, Ens, Col Philip Pipkin, Capt William Smythe, 1st Reg W TN Mil, Res omitted
PEGRAM, William, Ens, Col Philip Pipkin, Det of Capt David Smythe Co W TN Mil, Res omitted
PENNY, James, Capt, Col Samuel Bunch, E TN Mil Mtd Inf, Res omitted
PENNY, James, Capt, Col Samuel Bunch, E TN Mtd Inf, Res omitted
PEOPLES, Nathan, Capt, Col Robert Jarmon, Mil Inf, Res omitted
PERKINS, Nicholas T, Col, 1st Reg W TN Mtd Vol, Franklin (Williamson Co)
PERKINS, Nicholas T, Col, Commander omitted, 1st

## Officers, War of 1812

Regt W TN Mtd Vol, Res omitted

PERKINS, William O, 1 Lt, Col N T Perkins, Capt Mathew Johnson, Mil Inf, Res omitted

PERREN, John, 2 Lt, Maj John Childs, Capt Daniel Price, E TN Vol Mtd Inf, Res omitted

PERREN, John, Lt, Col Samuel Wear, Capt Jos Calloway, Mtd Inf, Res omitted

PERRIN, William, Ens, Lt Jno Harris, Capt Samuel Bunch, E TN Mil, Res omitted

PERRY, Alexander, Lt QM, Col Wm Metcalf, W TN Mil Inf, Res omitted; resigned 1-10-1815

PERRY, Ramson, 3 Lt, Maj John Childs, Capt Jas Cunningham, E TN Vol Mtd Inf, Res omitted

PERRY, Simeon, Capt, Col S Wear, E TN Vol Mtd Inf, Res omitted

PERRY, Simeon, Capt, Col Samuel Wear, E TN Vol Mil Mtd Inf, Sevierville

PERRY, Simeon, Lt, Col Brig? Nathan Taylor, Capt Wm Henderson, Spies, Res omitted

PETERS, John, Lt, Gen Jackson, Capt Hugh Kerr, Mtd Rangers, Res omitted; resigned 12-10-1813

PHILLIPE, William, 2 Lt, Col Jas Raulston, Capt Elijah Haynie, Inf, Res omitted

PHILLIPS, William, 1 Maj, Col Nicholas Perkins, 1st Regt TN Mtd Vol, Res omitted

PHILLIPS, William, 2 Maj, Gen John Coffee, TN Vol Mtd Gunmen, Res omitted

PHILLIPS, William, Lt Col, Commander omitted, Inf, Res omitted

PHILLIPS, William, Lt Col, Gen Thomas Johnson, 6th Brig Mil Mtd Inf, Res omitted

PICKEL, George, 3 Lt, Col Wm Johnson, Capt James Rogers, E TN Drafted Mil, Res omitted

PILLOW, Abner, 1 Lt & Aid, Brig Gen Roberts, W TN Mil, Res omitted; in Gen A Jackson's Div

PILLOW, William, Col, Field & Staff Officers, 2nd Reg TN Vol Inf, Nashville?

PILLOW, William, Lt Col, Commander omitted, 2nd Regt TN Vol Inf, Res omitted

PIPKIN, Philip, Capt, Col N T Perkins, 1st Reg TN Mil Mtd Riflemen, Res omitted

PIPKIN, Philip, Capt, Col N T Perkins, Capt P Pipkin, Mtd Riflemen, Res omitted

PIPKIN, Philip, Col, Commander omitted, 1st Regt TN Mil, Res omitted

PIPKIN, Philip, Col, Field & Staff, 1st Reg TN Mil, Fayetteville

PIPKIN, Stewart, Cor, Brig Gen John Coffee, TN Vol Mtd Gunmen, Res omitted

PIPKIN, Stuard, Cor, Col R H Dyer, Capt C Hudson, Vol Mtd Gunmen, Res omitted

PIPKINS, Thomas B, 1 Lt, Col Jno Coffee, Capt Dan'l Ross, Mtd Gunmen, Res omitted; promoted from 2 Lt

PITT, William, Cor, Col N Cannon, Capt William Edwards, Command, Res omitted; deserted

PITTS, Burwell, Lt, Col William Higgins, Capt A Cheatham, Mtd Riflemen, Res omitted

POLK, Andrew, Lt, Lt Col Phillips, Inf, Res omitted

POLK, William, 2 Lt, Col Thomas H Benton, Capt Robert Cannon, Inf, Res omitted

POLK, William, 2 Lt, Col Wm Pillow, Capt Joseph Mason, Vol Inf, Res omitted

PORTER, James P H, 2 Maj, Commander omitted, Cav, Res omitted

PORTER, James P H, Maj, Field & Staff Officers, E TN Mil Cav, Res omitted

PORTER, John, Capt, Col Edwin E Booth, Capt Wilson Maples, E TN Drafted Mil, Res omitted

PORTER, John, Capt, Col John K Winn, Inf, Res omitted

PORTER, John, Capt, Col John K Wynne, 1st TN Reg Mil Inf, Lincoln Co

PORTER, John, Capt, Maj Gen James Cook, Col Edwin Booth, Drafted Mil, Res omitted

PORTER, Joseph, 1 Lt, Col John K Winn, Capt John Porter, Inf, Res omitted; wounded at Talledega 11-9-1813

PORTER, Thomas, Capt, Col Thomas Williamson, 2nd Reg TN Vol Mtd Gunmen, Res omitted

PORTER, Thomas, Capt, Col Thos Williamson, Capt John Porter, Vol Mtd Gunmen, Res omitted

PORTER, Thomas, Capt, Maj Gen John Cocke, TN Vol Mtd Gunmen, Res omitted

PORTER, William B, 3 Lt, Col John Cocke, Capt Richard Crunk, Inf, Res omitted

PORTER, William, Ens, Capt John Porter, Drafted Mil, Res omitted

POSTON, Richard, Ens, Lt Col Henry Bryan, Inf, Res omitted

POTTER, Archibald, Deputy QM Gen, Maj Gen A Jackson, Div of TN Mil, Res omitted; resigned 2-25-1814

POTTER, Wilson, 1 Lt, Col S Bayless, Capt Solomon Hendrix, E TN Mil, Res omitted

POTTS, Thomas, Ens, Col Wm Hall, Capt Travis C Nash, Inf, Res omitted; promoted to 1 Lt

POWELL, Benjamin, Capt, Col William Johnson, 3rd Reg E Tn Mil, Res omitted

POWELL, Mathew, 2 Lt, Col John Cocke, Capt James Gray, Inf, Res omitted

POWELL, S? Benjamin, Capt, Col Wm Johnston, E TN Mil, Res omitted

POWERS, Lewis, 1 Maj, Col Jno Cocke, 2nd Regt W TN Mil Inf, Res omitted

POWERS, Nathaniel, 1 Maj, Col Wm Higgins, 2nd Regt TN Mtd Vol, Res omitted

PRESTON, James, Capt, Col Jno Brown, E TN Mil Inf, Res omitted

PRESTON, Thomas, Capt, Col R C Napier, 1st Reg TN Mil Inf, Sumner Co

PRESTON, Thomas, Capt, Col R C Napier, Mil Inf, Res omitted

PREWETT, Jacob, Capt, Commander omitted, Pack Horse Guard--Mtd Vol, Huntsville

PREWITT, Jacob, Capt, Gen A Jackson, Mtd Vol, Res omitted

PRICE, Daniel, Capt, Col S Wear, E TN Vol Inf, Res omitted

PRICE, Daniel, Capt, Col Samuel Wear, E TN Mil Mtd Inf, Knoxville

PRICE, Daniel, Capt, Gen John Coffee, Maj John Childs, E TN Vol Mtd Gunmen, Knoxville?

PRICE, Daniel, Capt, Maj John Childs, E TN Mtd Inf Vol, Res omitted
PRICE, Joseph, Capt, Col John Cocke, 2nd Reg Mil Inf, Nashville
PRICE, Joseph, Capt, Col John Cocke, Inf, Res omitted
PRICE, William J, Lt, Col John Wynn, Capt Jas Cole, Inf, Res omitted; promoted from Ens
PRICE, William, 1 Lt, Col Jas Raulston, Capt Henry West, Inf, Res omitted
PRIESTLY, William, 2 Lt, Maj Wm Carroll, Capt Lewis Dillahunty, Vol Inf; also under Capt Bradford, promoted to 1 Lt
PRINCE, Bayless E, Capt, Col John K. Wynne, 1st Reg Vol Mil Inf, Montgomery Co
PRINCE, Bayless E, Capt, Col John Wyne, Vol Inf, Res omitted
PRINCE, Bayless E, Lt & Adjt, Col John Cocke, 2nd Regt W TN Mtd Inf, Res omitted; resigned 3-2-1815
PRIOR, Joseph, Ens, Col Wm Lillard, Capt Hugh Martin, E TN Vol Inf, Res omitted
PROVINE, Alexander, Capt, Col S Copeland, Mil Inf, Res omitted
PROVINE, Alexander, Capt, Col S Copeland, Mil Inf, Wilson Co
PRUIT, Moses H, 2 Lt, Col Wm Metcalf, Mil Inf, Res omitted
PUCKET, Robert, 1 Lt, Col James Raulston, Capt Daniel Newman, Inf, Res omitted
PUGH, Daniel, Ens, Col Edwin Booth, Capt John Sharpe, E TN Mil, Res omitted
PULLIAM, William P, 1 Lt, Col William Metcalf, Capt William Sitton, Mil Inf, Res omitted
PUNSHARD, William, Surgeon, Col William Higgins, TN Mtd Vol, Res omitted
PURRIS, William, Surgeon, Col Samuel Wear, E TN Mil Inf, Res omitted
PURSLEY, Jarnes, Cor, Maj John Porter, Capt Jas Anderson, Cav, Res omitted
PURSLEY, Robert, 3 Lt, Maj Gen John Cocke, TN Vol Mtd Gunmen, Res omitted
PURSLEY, Robert, Lt, Col Thomas Williamson, Capt Wm Metcalf, Vol Mtd Gunmen, Res omitted
QUARLES, John B, Capt, Col N T Perkins, 1st Reg TN Mil Mtd Inf, Wilson Co
QUARLES, John B, Capt, Col N T Perkins, Vol Mtd Inf, Res omitted; killed 1-24-1814 at Enotechopca
QUILLIN, Will, Ens, Col John Cocke, Capt John Dalton, Inf, Res omitted
RAGLAND, John D, 2 Lt, Col N Cannon, Capt Jas Walton, Mtd Riflemen
RAGLAND, John, 2 Lt, Regt Commander omitted, Capt Jno Walton, Branch omitted
RAGSDALE, Edward, 1 Lt, Col John Coffee, Capt Charles Kavanaugh, Cav
RAGSDALE, John, Cor, Col John Coffee, Capt Charles Kavanaugh, Cav
RAINS, Arahel, Capt, Col Alexander Loury, 2nd Reg W TN Mil Inf, Res omitted
RAINS, Asahel, Capt, Col A Loury, Lt Col L Hammons, Inf
RALSTON, Alexander, 2 Maj, Col Philip Pipkin, 1 Regt TN Mil
RANDALS, James, Capt, Col Robert Steele, 4th Reg TN Mil Inf, White Co
RANDALS, James, Capt, Col Robert Steele, Inf
RANKIN, Anthony, Ens, Col Ewen Allison, Capt Jacob Hoyal, E Tn Mil
RANKIN, David, 1 Lt, Col Samuel Bunch, Capt Francis Berry, E TN Mil; killed 3-27-1814
RATHER, John T, Lt, Gen A Jackson, Capt Hugh Kerr, Mtd Rangers
RATTAN (ROTTON), Richard W, Lt & QM, Col Alexander Lourey, no Co Commander, 2 Regt W TN Mil
RATTON (ROTTON), Richard M, Capt, Col Robert Steele, 4th Reg TN Mil Inf, White Co
RATTON, Richard W, Capt, Col Robert Steele, Mil Inf
RAULSTON, James, Col, Field & Staff Officers, 3rd Reg TN Mil Inf, Res omitted
RAWLINGS, Asahel, ADC, Brig Gen Thos Coulter, E TN Draft Mil
RAWLSTON, James, Col, W Tn Mil Inf
RAY, John, Lt, Col Jno Cocke, Capt Geo Barnes, Inf
READ, James, Capt, Gen A Jackson, Inf
READ, James, Capt, Gen Andrew Jackson, Inf, Res omitted
READ, John H, Lt, Col Jno Coffee, Capt Alexander McKeen, Cav
READ, John, 1 Lt & ADC, Maj Gen Andrew Jackson, Div of TN Mil
READ, Leon, Cor, no other information
READ, Robert, 3 Lt, Col R H Dyer, Capt Bethel Allen, Vol Mtd Gunmen; promoted to 2 Lt
READ, Sion S, Cor, Col John Alcorn, Capt Wm Locke, Cav; promoted from Sgt
REAMY, Jesse G, Capt, Col John Brown, Capt James Standifee, Branch Srvce omitted, Res omitted
REANY (RAINEY), Jesse G, Capt, Col John Brown, Capt James Standifer, E TN Vol Mtd Gunmen, Res omitted
RECTOR, Richard, 3 Lt, Col Edwin Booth, Capt John McKamey, E TN Mil, Res omitted
REDFENNEN, Isaac, Ens, Col A Cheatham, Capt Gabriel Martin, Mtd Inf, Res omitted
REDMON, William, 3 Lt, Col James Raulston, Capt Elijah Haynie, Inf, Res omitted
REECE, George, Capt, no other information
REED, George, Capt, Lt Col Phillips, Inf, Res omitted
REED, Robert, 3 Lt, Brig Gen John Coffee, TN Vol Mtd Gunmen, Res omitted
REED, Thomas, Lt, Col S Bunch, Capt S Robertson, E TN Drafted Mil, Res omitted
REEVES, Samuel, Ens, Col Sam'l Bayless, Capt Jas Lauden, E TN Mil, Res omitted
REGISTER, Francis, Capt, Col S Bunch, Capt Francis Register, E TN Mil, Res omitted
REGISTER, Francis, Capt, Col Samuel Bunch, E TN Mil, Res omitted
REGNA, Henry, 1 Lt, Maj John Childs, Capt Chas Conway, E TN Mtd Gunmen, Knox County
REID, Andrew, Ens, Brig Gen Thos Washington, Capt Jno Crawford, Mtd Inf, Res omitted
RENSHAW, Isaiah, Capt, Col Thomas H Benton, 2nd Reg

## Officers, War of 1812

Tn Vol Inf, Res omitted

RENSHAW, Isaiah, Capt, Col Thos Benton, Capt Benj Renshaw, Vol Inf, Res omitted

RENSHAW, Isaiah, Capt, Col William Pillow, 2nd Reg Tn Vol Inf, Rutherford Co

RENSHAW, Isiah, Capt, Col Wm Pillow, Inf, Res omitted

REUBEN, George, Lt, Col Samuel Bunch, Capt N Gibbs, E TN Mil, Res omitted; took command on death of Capt Gibbs

REYNOLDS, Benjamin, Capt, Col Thos Benton, Vol Inf, Res omitted

REYNOLDS, Benjamin, Capt, Gen Isaac B Roberts, 5th Brig Mtd Rangers, Res omitted

REYNOLDS, Benjamin, Capt, Gen Isaac B Roberts, Col Benjamin Reynolds, Mtd Rangers, Res omitted

REYNOLDS, Benjamin, Col, Col Thomas H Benton, Mtd Rangers, Res omitted

REYNOLDS, Benjamin, Col, Gen Isaac B Roberts, Mtd Rangers, Res omitted

REYNOLDS, John, 1 Lt, Col Samuel Bunch, Capt Jesse Williams, Mtd Vol, Res omitted

REYNOLDS, John, 2 Maj, Col Samuel Wear, E TN Vol Mil Inf, Res omitted

REYNOLDS, John, Capt, Col T McCrory, Mil Inf, Res omitted

REYNOLDS, John, Capt, Col Thomas McCrory, 2nd Reg TN Mil Inf, Murfreesboro

REYNOLDS, Reuben, 1 Lt, Col John Cocke, Capt James Gault, Inf, Res omitted

RHEA, George, 3 Lt, Col Samuel Bayless, Capt Joseph Rich, E TN Inf, Res omitted; promoted from Ens

RHEA, Robert, 1 Maj, Col Ewen Allison, E TN Draft Mil; mustered at Knoxville

RHEA, Robert, Maj, Col Ewen Allison, Mil, Res omitted

RICE, David, 2 Lt, Col William Lillard, Capt Robert Maloney, E TN Mil Vol Inf, Res omitted

RICE, Elijah, Ens, Col Jno Coffee, Capt Henry Byron, Cav, Res omitted

RICE, John, 1 Lt, Col Jno Brown, E TN Mil Inf, Res omitted

RICE, John, Adjt, Brig Gen Nathaniel Taylor, 3rd Regt E TN Drafted Mil, Res omitted; resigned 10-5-1814

RICE, Laban, 2 Lt, Maj William Russell, Capt William Chism, Vol Mtd Gunmen, Res omitted

RICH, Joseph, Capt, Col S Bayless, E TN Inf, Res omitted

RICH, Joseph, Capt, Col Samuel Bayless, E TN Drafted Mil, Res omitted

RICHARDSON, Mason, Cor, Brig Gen John Coffee, TN Vol Mtd Gunmen, Res omitted

RICHARDSON, Mason, Cor, Col R H Dyer, Capt Robt Evans, Vol Mtd Gunmen, Res omitted

RICHARDSON, Samuel, Capt, Commander omitted, E TN Drafted Mil, Res omitted

RICHERSON, Samuel, Capt, Col Samuel Bunch, E TN Drafted Mil, Res omitted

RICHMAN, Alexander P, Ens, Col S Copeland, Capt G W Stell, Mil Inf, Res omitted

RIDLEY, Henry, Ens, Regt Commander omitted, Capt Joel Parrish, Branch omitted

RIDLEY, Vincent, 1 Lt, Col T McCrory, Capt S McKnight, Inf; died 12-11-1813

RIGGLE, Jacob, 2 Lt, Col E Booth, Capt Geo Winton, E Tn Mil

RIGNEY, Henry, Ens, Col Jno Brown, Capt Jno Childs, E Tn Vol Mtd Gunmen

ROADMAN, William C, 1 Maj, Col Samuel Bayless, 4 Regt E Tn Mil

ROANE, James, 3 Lt, Col Thomas Williamson, Capt Beverly Williams, Vol Mtd Gunmen

ROARK, Amos, 2 Lt, Col Thomas Williamson, Capt A Metcalf, Vol Mtd Gunmen

ROARK, Amos, Lt, Maj Gen John Cocke, Co Commander omitted, Tn Vol Gunmen

ROBERTS, Elijah, 1 Lt BQM, Brig Gen Isaac Roberts, W Tn Mil

ROBERTS, Isaac B, Brig Gen, Gen Andrew Jackson, Brig W TN Mil, Res omitted

ROBERTS, Isaac, B Gen, W Tn Mil; consigned in Gen Andrew Jackson Div

ROBERTS, Philip, Ens, Col John Brown, Capt Wm White, E Tn Mll Inf

ROBERTSON, David, Ens, Col Samuel Bunch, Capt David Vance, E Tn Mtd Inf

ROBERTSON, Hughes, 2 Lt, Gen Andrew Jackson, Capt Wm Russell, Mtd Spies; arm broken, left unfi

ROBERTSON, John, 3 Lt, Col Phillip Pipkin, Capt John Robertson, Mil Inf

ROBERTSON, John, Capt, Col Philip Pipkin, 1st Reg Tn Mil Inf, Res omitted

ROBERTSON, John, Capt, Col Philip Pipkin, Mil Inf; died 11-9-1814

ROBERTSON, Sterling, Asst QM Gen, Maj Gen Wm Carroll, TN Mil, Res omitted

ROBINSON, Edward, Capt, Col James Raulston, 3rd Reg Mil Inf, Res omitted

ROBINSON, Edward, Capt, Maj Gen Carroll, Col James Raulston, Inf, Res omitted

ROBINSON, Nathaniel, 2 Lt, Col Edwin Booth, Capt John Sharp, E TN Mil, Res omitted

RODGERS, John, 2 Lt, Col John Brown, Capt Chas Lewin, E TN Mtd Inf, Res omitted; promoted from Cpl

RODGERS, Micajah, Ens, Col Jarmon, Capt Hamilton, Inf, Res omitted

RODGERS, Reuben, Ens, Col Ewen Allison, Capt John Hampton, Mil, Res omitted; promoted from Sgt

RODGERS, Samuel, Cor, Maj Wm Russell, Capt Isaac Williams, Separate Bn of TN Vol Mtd Gunmen; also under Col R H Dyer

RODGERS, William, Chap, Maj Gen John Cocke, E TN Mil Inf, Res omitted

RODGERS, William, Ens, Col Edwin Booth, Capt John Lewis, E TN Mil, Res omitted

ROGERS, David, 2 Maj, Col Samuel Bunch, E TN Mil, Res omitted

ROGERS, James R, Capt, Col Wm Johnson, E TN Mil, Res omitted

ROGERS, James R., Capt, Col William Johnston, 3rd Reg E TN Mil, Res omitted

ROGERS, William, Chap, Brig Gen Geo Doherty, E TN Mil, Res omitted; also under Maj Gen John Cocke

RONE, James, 3 Lt, Maj Gen John Cocke, TN Vol Mtd

Gunmen, Res omitted
ROOK, Aaron, 1 Lt, Col Samuel Bayless, Capt Joseph Rich, E TN Inf, Res omitted
ROPER, John, Capt, Col William Lillard, E TN Vol Mil Inf, Res omitted
ROPER, John, Capt, Col Wm Lillard, E TN Vol Inf, Res omitted
ROSE, Neal B, Lt & Brig QM, Brig Gen John Coffee, TN Vol Mtd Gunmen
ROSS (BASS), Ezekial, Capt, Maj William Woodfolk, Mil Inf Sep Bn, Wilson Co
ROSS, Daniel, Capt, Col John Alcorn & John Coffee, Mtd Gunmen, Davidson Co
ROSS, Daniel, Capt, Col John Coffee, Capt Ezekial Ross, Mtd Gunmen, Res omitted; promoted from Pvt
ROSS, Ezekial, 1 Lt, Col A Loury, Capt Geo Sarver, Inf, Res omitted
ROSS, Ezekiel, Capt, Maj Wm Woodfolk, Inf, Res omitted
ROSS, Jesse S, 1 Lt, Brig Gen John Coffee, TN Vol Mtd Gunmen, Res omitted
ROSS, Jesse S, 1 Lt, Col R H Dyer, Vol Mtd Gunmen, Res omitted
ROSS, Nathan, Lt, Maj Robert Cooper, Mtd Riflemen, Res omitted
ROSS, Samuel, Ens, Lt Col Wm Phillips, no other information
ROSS, Thomas, 1 Lt, Col John Cocke, Capt Bird Nance, Inf, Res omitted
ROSS, William, Ens, Col Samuel Bunch, Capt James Penny, E TN Mtd Inf, Res omitted
ROTTAN, R W, Lt & QM, Lt Col Leroy Hammond, 2nd Regt W TN Mil, Res omitted
ROWARK, Rubin, Ens, Col S Copeland, Capt Allen Wilkinson, Mil Inf, Res omitted
ROWEN, John, Lt, Col A Cheatham, Mtd Inf, Res omitted
ROYSTON, John, 2 Lt, Col John Allison, Capt Adam Winsell, Mil, Res omitted; changed to Wgnr
RUCKER, William R, Hospital Surgeon's Mate, Maj Gen Wm Carroll, TN Mil, Res omitted; appointed Regt Surgeon
RUCKER, William R, Surgeon, Col Wm Metcalf, TN Mil Inf, Res omitted
RUFF, John, 3 Lt, Col Wm Metcalf, Capt Thomas Marks, Mil Inf, Res omitted
RUSHING, Elijah, Capt, Col John Coffee?, unit omitted, Res omitted
RUSHING, Elijah, Capt, no Regt Commander, Det of Inf
RUSSELL, Alexander, Ens, Col Wm Lillard, Capt Robt Maloney, E TN Vol Inf, Res omitted
RUSSELL, John, Brig Maj, Brig Gen Nathan Taylor, no other information
RUSSELL, Nathaniel, Ens, Col John Wynne, Capt Geo Carothers, W TN Mil Inf, Res omitted
RUSSELL, William, Capt, Col Robert Dyer, Maj William Russell, TN Vol Mtd Gunmen, Franklin Co
RUSSELL, William, Capt, Commander omitted Bn of Maj William Russell, TN Vol Mtd Gunmen, Murfreesboro
RUSSELL, William, Capt, Commander omitted Div of Maj Gen Andrew Jackson, Mtd Spies, Res omitted
RUSSELL, William, Capt, Gen Andrew Jackson, Mtd Spies, Res omitted
RUSSELL, William, Ens, Capt Wm Mitchell, Spies, Res omitted
RUSSELL, William, Maj, Commander omitted, TN Vol Mtd Gunmen, Res omitted
RUSSELL, William, Maj, Field & Staff Officers Col Dyer, TN Vol Mtd Gunmen, Murfreesboro
RUSSWORM, John S, 2 Lt, Col N Cannon, Capt Martin, Mtd Gunmen, Res omitted; promoted from Ens
RUTH, Daniel, Lt, Col Robert Steele, Capt Jas Bennett, Mil Inf, Res omitted
SAILING, Peter, 2 Lt, Maj Gen Wm Carroll, Col Wm Metcalf, Capt John Jackson, Inf, Res omitted
SANDERDALL, William, 1 Lt, Col Wm Hall, Capt Wm Alexander, Vol Inf, Res omitted
SANDERS, Nathaniel, Surgeon, Col John K Wynne, 1st Regt TN Mil, Res omitted
SANDERSON, Edward, 1 Lt, Col P Pipkin, Capt Jas Blakemore, Mil Inf, Res omitted
SANDFORD, Robert, 2 Lt, Col A Cheatham, Capt Wm Smith, Inf, Res omitted; promoted from Ens
SARVER, George, Capt, Col Alex Loury, Inf, Res omitted
SARVER, George, Capt, Col Alexander Loury, 2nd Regt Mil Inf, Res omitted
SAUNDERS, Benjamin L, Ens, Col John Alcorn, Capt John Winston, Mtd Riflemen, Res omitted
SAWYER, James, Maj, Col A Cheatham, Capt Ben Elliott, Mtd Inf, Res omitted
SCAMP, Thomas, 1 Lt, Col N T Perkins, Capt Geo Eliot, Mil Inf, Res omitted
SCOBY, James, 1 Lt, Col Thos Williamson, Capt Thos Scurry, Vol Mtd Gunmen, Res omitted
SCOBY, Joseph, Cor, Col Jno Coffee, Capt John Byrn, Branch Srvce omitted, Res omitted
SCOBY, Joseph, Cor, Col John Alcorn, Capt John W Burn, Cav, Res omitted
SCOTT, Hercules, 2 Lt, Col Jno Brown, Capt Wm Christian, E TN Mil Inf, Res omitted; promoted from Pvt
SCOTT, James, Ens, Col N T Cannon, Capt Martin, Mtd Gunmen, Res omitted; promoted from a Sgt
SCOTT, John, 1 Lt, Col John Coffee, 36th TN Mil, Hickman?
SCOTT, John, Ens, Maj Jno Childs, Capt Chas Conway, E TN Mtd Gunmen, Res omitted
SCOTT, John, Lt, Regt Commander omitted, Lt Jno Scott, Detachment of Inf, Res omitted
SCOTT, Joseph, Capt, Col Wm Johnson, E TN Drafted Mil, Res omitted
SCOTT, Joseph, Capt/Chap, Col William Johnson, 3rd Regt E TN Mil, Res omitted
SCOTT, Joseph, Chap, Col Wm Johnson, 3rd Regt E TN Mil, Res omitted
SCOTT, Nehemiah, 1 Lt, Col Robt Dyer, Capt I Williams, Vol Mtd Gunmen, Res omitted
SCOTT, Neth, 1 Lt, Brig Gen John Coffee, TN Vol Mtd Gunmen, Res omitted
SCOTT, Williams, Lt, Col Jno Brown, Capt Jas McKamy, E TN Mtd Gunmen, Res omitted
SCRUGGS, Thofalus, Ens, Col Leroy Hammond, Col A

## Officers, War of 1812

Loury, Capt Thomas Wells, Inf
SCURRY, Thomas, Capt, Col Thomas Williamson, 2nd Regt TN Vol Mtd Gunmen, Nashville
SCURRY, Thomas, Capt, Col Thos Williamson, Vol Mtd Gunmen
SEAGRAVES, William, Capt, Lt Col Henry Bryan, Maj Robt Searcy, Mil Inf
SEARCA, Reuben, Ens, Col James Raulston, Capt Henry Hambleton, Inf; apptd from Sgt
SEARCY, James, Ens, Col Edward Bradley, Capt John Moore, Vol Inf
SEARCY, Peter, Capt, Col Philip Pipkin, 1st Regt TN Mil Inf, Fayetteville
SEARCY, Robert, 1 Lt & ADC, Maj Gen Andrew Jackson, Div of TN Mil
SEARCY, Robert, 1 Maj, Lt Col Henry Bryan, Mil Inf
SEBASTON, Issac, 1 Lt, Col A Loury, Lt Col Leroy Hammons, Capt Thomas Delaney, Inf
SELLS, William, Lt, Regt Commander omitted, Capt Gray, Inf
SEVEIR, Archibald, Ens, Col T McCrory, Capt Abel Willis, Mil Inf
SEVIER, Charles, Maj, no other information
SHANNON, James, Capt, Col Thomas McCrory, 2nd Regt Mil Inf, Williamson Co
SHANNON, James, Capt, Col Thos McCrory, Capt Jas Shannon, Mil Inf
SHARP, John, Capt, Col Edwin Booth, E TN Mil
SHARP, John, Capt, Col Edwin Booth, E TN Mil Drafted, Knox Co
SHARP, M D L F, Surgeon Mate, Col Edward Bradley, 1 Regt TN Vol Inf; later apptd Surgeon
SHARP, Richard, Capt, Col S Copeland, 3rd Regt Mil Inf, Res omitted
SHARP, Richard, Capt, Col S Copeland, Mtd Inf
SHARP, Thomas, Capt, Col William Lillard, E TN Mil Inf, Res omitted
SHARPE, Joseph, Ens, Col Samuel Wear, Capt John Doak, E TN Vol Inf
SHARPE, Thomas, Capt, Col Wm Lillard, 2 Regt Inf
SHAW, Basil, 1 Lt & 1 Adj, Col John Coffee, Tn Vol Cav
SHAW, Basil, Lt & Brig Insp, Brig Gen John Coffee, TN Mtd Mil
SHAW, Bazil, Asst Adj Gen, Maj Gen Wm Carroll, TN Mil
SHEFFIELD, Arthur, 1 Lt, Col Newton Cannon, Capt Andrew Patterson, Mtd Riflemen
SHELBY, John D, Surgeon, Col Edward Bradley, 1 Regt E TN Vol Inf; apptd Hospital Surgeon
SHELBY, John, Hospital Surgeon, Maj Gen Andrew Jackson, Div of TN Mil
SHELTON, Chrispan, Ens, Col Sam'l Bayless, Capt Jos Rich, E TN Inf, Res omitted; promoted from Sgt
SHELTON, George, Ens, Maj Gen Wm Carroll, Capt F Elliss, Inf, Res omitted; d 2-25-1815
SHELTON, Jonathan, 3 Lt, Col Jno Cocke, Capt Saml Caruthers, Inf, Res omitted
SHELTON, William, Adjt, Col Nicholas T Perkins, 1st Regt TN Mtd Vol, Res omitted
SHENAULT, James, Capt, Col Robert Steele, 4th Regt TN Mil Inf, Bedford Co

SHIELDS, Robert, Ens, Col S Bunch, Capt Jno Houk, E TN Mil, Res omitted; joined from? Capt Williams Co
SHIELDS, Robert, Ens, Col S Bunch, Capt S Richerson, E TN Mil, Res omitted
SHIELDS, William, Adjt, Col Ewin Allison, E TN Mil, Res omitted
SHINAULT, James, Capt, Col Robert Steele, Mil Inf, Res omitted
SHINAULT, Walter, Lt, Col John Wynne, Capt Jas Carothers, W TN Inf, Res omitted
SHIPLEY, Ben, Ens, Gen Andrew Jackson, Capt Nathan Davis, Inf, Res omitted; killed at Tehoopa 3-27-1814
SHOCKLY, Thomas H, Ens, Maj Wm Woodfolk, Capt James C Neil, Inf, Res omitted
SHORT, Caleb, 2 Lt, Col James Raulston, Capt Henry West, Mil Inf, Res omitted; d 3-7-1815
SHOULTS, Martin, 3 Lt, Col Edwin Booth, Capt Geo Winton, E TN Mil; promoted from Ens
SHROPSHIRE, David, Ens, Lt Col Napier, Inf, Res omitted
SHUFFIELD, Ephraim, Ens, Col N T Cannon, Capt M Patterson, Mtd Riflemen, Res omitted
SHUMATE, William, 1 Lt, Col Thomas H Williamson, Capt Richard Tate, Vol Mtd Gunmen, Res omitted
SHUMATE, William, 1 Lt, Maj Gen John Cocke, TN Vol Gunmen, Res omitted
SHUMMELL, Joseph, Lt, Col A Loury, Inf, Res omitted
SIMMONS, James, Ens, Col E Bradley, Capt Thos Haynes, Vol Inf; promoted to 2 Lt
SIMMONS, James, Ens, Col Wm Hall, Capt Henry Newlin, Inf, Res omitted
SIMPSON, John W, 1 Maj, Col Wm Metcalf, Mil Inf, Res omitted; promoted to Lt Col
SIMPSON, Thomas, Ens, Col Philip Pipkin, Capt John Strother, Mil, Res omitted
SIMS, Newton, Capt, Maj Robt Searcy, Inf, Res omitted
SISKE, James, Ens, Col S Copeland, Capt Solomon George, Inf, Res omitted
SITLER, James, Adjt Gen, Maj Gen A Jackson, Div of TN Mil, Res omitted
SITTLER, James W, Ens, Maj Gen A Jackson, Capt Wm Carroll, Vol Inf, Res omitted
SITTON, William, Capt, Col William Metcalf, W TN Mil Inf, Nashville
SITTON, William, Capt, Col Wm Metcalf, Mil Inf, Res omitted
SLATTON, John, Capt, Col Edwin Booth, Capt John Slatton, E TN Mil, Res omitted
SLATTON, John, Capt, Col Edwin E Booth, E TN Drafted Mil, Knox Co?
SLAUGHTER, Reuben, Cor, Col Thos Williamson, Capt Robt Moore, Vol Mtd Gunmen, Res omitted
SLAUGHTER, Reuben, Cor, Maj Gen John Cocke, TN Vol Mtd Gunmen, Res omitted
SMART, Phillip, 2 Lt, Maj Wm Woodfolk, Capt Ross & Capt McCully, Inf, Res omitted; promoted to 1 Lt
SMART, William C, 1 Maj, Col Alexander Loury, W TN Mil; under Lt Col Leroy Hammond; Field/Staff Officer

## Officers, War of 1812

SMILEY, Thomas, 2 Lt, Maj Russell, Capt Mathew Cowan, Vol Mtd Gunmen
SMITH, Abe, 1 Maj, Brig Gen George Doherty, E TN Mil; continued on Maj Gen John Cocke's Roll
SMITH, Alexander, 1 Maj, Col Samuel Bunch, Regt E TN Mil
SMITH, Alexander, Insp Gen, Maj Gen John Cocke, E TN Vol Mil
SMITH, Amos, 1 Lt, Col A Loury, Col Leroy Hammonds, Capt Arahel Raines, Inf; deserted
SMITH, Bird, Brig Gen, Div of Maj Gen William Carroll, 2nd Brig W TN Mil Inf, Camp Hynes?
SMITH, Bird, Brig Gen, Maj Gen Wm Carroll, 2 Brig Tn Mil; died 2-19-1815
SMITH, David, Capt, Col John Coffee, Cav Vol
SMITH, David, Capt, Col Robert Dyer, TN Vol Cav, Nashville?
SMITH, Edward, 3 Lt, Brig Gen John Coffee, Co Commander omitted, TN Vol Mtd Gunmen
SMITH, Edward, 3 Lt, Col R H Dyer, Capt Cuthbert Hudson, Vol Mtd Gunmen; died 2-23-1815
SMITH, Elijah, 1 Lt, Maj Gen Wm Carroll, Col Wm Metcalf, Capt John Jackson, Inf, Res omitted
SMITH, G W, Lt & Adjt, Brig Gen John Coffee, TN Vol Mtd Gunmen, Res omitted
SMITH, George, 2 Lt Col, Brig Gen John Coffee, TN Mtd Vol Gunmen, Res omitted
SMITH, George, 2 Lt, Col John Coffee, Capt Jas Terrell, Vol Cav, Res omitted
SMITH, George, Capt, Col Robert H Dyer, TN Vol Cav Spies, Sunmen Co
SMITH, George, Capt, Commander omitted, Spies, Res omitted
SMITH, Gray, Lt, Col Thos Benton, Capt Smith, Vol Inf, Res omitted
SMITH, Guy, 2 Lt, Col Thos Benton, Capt Smith, Vol Inf, Res omitted
SMITH, Jasper, 1 Maj, Col Philip Pipkin, 1st Regt TN Mil, Res omitted
SMITH, John M, 2 Lt, Col John Williams, Capt David G Vance, E TN Mtd Vol, Res omitted; killed in action 2-10-1813
SMITH, John, Adjt, Col Newton Cannon, TN Vol Mtd Riflemen, Res omitted
SMITH, John, Lt & Adjt, Col Robt H Dyer, no other information
SMITH, John, Lt & Adjt, Gen John Coffee, Brig TN Vol Mtd Inf, Res omitted
SMITH, Joseph, 2 Maj, Maj Wm Woodfolk, Separate Bn of W TN Mil, Res omitted
SMITH, Meriwether, 1 Maj, Brig Gen Nathaniel Taylor, Col Wm Johnson, Drafted Mil, Res omitted; resigned 10-12-1814
SMITH, Nathan, 1 Lt, Col Wm Higgins, Capt Stephen Griffith, Mtd Riflemen, Res omitted
SMITH, Patrick, 2 Lt, Col Samuel Wear, Capt John Doak, E TN Vol Inf, Res omitted
SMITH, Sam, 2 Lt, Gen Jno Coffee, Mtd Spies, Res omitted
SMITH, Samuel, 2 Lt, Lt Jesse Bean, Mtd Spies, Res omitted
SMITH, Samuel, Lt & Aide de Camp, Maj Gen Wm Carroll, Brig Gen Bird Smith, 2nd Brig TN Mil, Res omitted
SMITH, Thomas, 2 Lt, Col Wm Metcalf, Capt B Collins, Mil Inf, Res omitted
SMITH, William J, Capt, Col Thomas H Benton, 2nd Regt TN Vol Mil, Res omitted
SMITH, William J, Capt, Col William Pillow, 2nd Regt TN Vol Inf, Res omitted
SMITH, William J, Capt, Col Wm Pillow, Capt Wm Smith, Vol Inf, Res omitted
SMITH, William, 2 Lt, Maj Gen A Jackson, Col Thos Williamson, Capt Robt Steele, Vol Mtd Gunmen, Res omitted
SMITH, William, Aid De QM Gen?, Brig Gen Geo Doherty, E TN Mil, Res omitted
SMITH, William, Capt, Col A Cheatham, Inf, Res omitted
SMITH, William, Capt, Col A Cheatham, Mil Inf 2nd Regt, Rutherford Co
SMITH, William, Capt, Col Thos Benton, Capt Wm Smith, Vol Inf, Res omitted
SMITH, William, Lt, Col Sam'l Bayless, Capt Jas Goodson, E TN Mil, Res omitted
SMITH, William, QM Gen, Maj Gen Wm Carroll, TN Mil, Res omitted
SMITH, _____, Lt & ADC, Brig Gen Bird Smith
SMYTHE, David, Capt, Col Philip Pipkin, 1st Regt Mil Inf, Warren Co
SMYTHE, David, Capt, Col Philip Pipkin, Capt Smyth, Mil Inf, Res omitted
SNODDEY, James, 2 Lt, Col Saml Bayless, Capt Jos Goodson, E TN Mil
SNODGRASS, William, Lt Col, Col Wm Lilllard, E TN Vol Mil Cherokee Indians, Res omitted
SNODGRASS, William, Lt Col, commanding Cherokee Indians at Ft Armstrong
SONAS, Jacob, 2 Lt, Col Edwin Booth, Capt John Lewis, E TN Inf, Res omitted
SOUTHERLAND, George, QM 1 Lt, Col Edwin Booth, E TN Mil, Res omitted
SPEAR, Isaac, Surgeon, Col Samuel Bunch, Regt E TN Mil, Res omitted
SPEARMAN, Samuel, Lt, Col John Wynne, Capt Robt Bradin, Inf, Res omitted
SPINKS, John, Capt, Col John K Wynne, 1st Regt Mil Inf, Wilson Co
SPINKS, John, Capt, Col John Wynne, Inf, Res omitted
SPOER (SPOOR), Cornelius F, Adjt, Col Saml Wear, E TN Mil Inf Vol, Res omitted
SPOOR, Cornelius F, Brig Gen ADC, Brig Gen Geo Doherty, E TN Mil
SPOOR, Cornelius F, Judge Advocate, Brig Gen N Taylor
SPRATT, John, 2 Lt, Brig Gen John Coffee, Co Commander omitted, TN Vol Mtd Gunmen
SPRATT, John, 2 Lt, Col R H Dyer, Capt Glen Owen, TN Vol Mtd Gunmen
SPRATT, John, Ens, Col A Cheatham, Capt Jones Giddens, Mil Inf
SPRING, John, 1 Lt, Col Wm Johnson, Capt James Tunnell, E TN Mil
SPURLOCK, Josiah, Ens, Col James Raulston, Capt

Edward Robinson, Inf
STALLCUP, James, 2 Lt, Col Jas Raulston, Capt Mathew Neal, Inf
STANDERFORD, Luke, Ens, Col Jno Brown, Capt Wm Christian, E Tn Mil Inf
STANDIFER, James jr, 1 Lt, Col John Brown, Capt Jesse G Reany, Mtd Gunmen
STANDIFER, James, Capt, Col John Brown, E TN Vol Mtd Mil; promoted to Lt Col
STANFORD, Thomas, 1 Lt, Col T McCrory, Capt Thos R Gordon; deserted & cashiered
STARKS, James, 2 Lt, Col A Cheatham, Capt Geo C Chapman, Inf
STARMEN, George, Ens, Col Wm Lillard, Capt Jacob Hartsell, E TN Vol Inf
STARROTT, Joseph, 2 Lt, Maj Wm Woodfolk, Capt James Neil, Inf
STEAD, Abner, Paymaster, Col Wm Higgins, TN Mtd Vol
STEEL, James R, Ens, Col Wm Metcalf, Capt Thos Marks, Mil Inf; died 2-2-1815
STEEL, John, 1 Lt, Gen Jackson, Capt J Reed, Inf
STEELE, Robert, Capt, Col Thomas Williamson, 2nd Regt Vol Mtd Gunmen, Res omitted
STEELE, Robert, Capt, Col Thos Williamson, Maj Gen A Jackson, Vol Mtd Gunmen
STEELE, Robert, Col, 4 Regt TN Mil
STEELE, Robert, Col, Field & Staff Officers, 4th Regt TN Mil, Fayetteville
STELL, G W, Capt, Col S Copeland, Mil Inf
STELL, G W, Capt, Col Stephen Copeland, 3rd Regt Mil Inf, Wilson Co
STEPHENS, Gilbert, 2 Lt, Col Philip Pipkin, Capt Peter Searcy, Mil Inf, Res omitted
STEPHENS, Henry, Capt, Col Samuel Bunch, Capt Henry Stephens, E TN Mtd Inf, Res omitted
STEPHENS, Henry, Capt, Col Samuel Bunch, E TN Mil Mtd Inf, Res omitted
STEPHENS, Henry, Lt, Maj Jas Porter, Capt Samuel Cowan, Cav, Res omitted
STEPHENS, John, Capt, Bn of Maj John Childs Brig of Brig Gen John Coffee, Mtd Inf, Res omitted
STEPHENS, John, Capt, Col Samuel Wear, Capt John Stephens, E TN Vol Inf, Res omitted
STEPHENS, John, Capt, Col Samuel Wear, E TN Mil Inf, Knoxville
STEPHENS, John, Ens, Col Samuel Bunch, Capt Isaac Williams, Mtd Vol, Res omitted
STEPHENSON, Andrew, Lt, Col Samuel Wear & Col Samuel Bunch, Capt Wm Mitchell, E TN Mtd Inf; deserted
STEWART, James, Capt, Col William Johnson, 3rd Regt E TN Mil, Res omitted
STEWART, James, Capt, Col Wm Johnson, 3rd Regt E TN Mil, Res omitted
STEWART, William, Lt, Col T McCrory, Capt Isaac Patton, Inf, Res omitted
STOKES, Henry, Lt, Gen A Jackson, Capt Hugh Kerr, Mtd Rangers, Res omitted; resigned 12-27-1813
STOLTZ, Henry, Lt, Col A Cheatham, Capt Richd Benson, Inf, Res omitted

STONE, Drury, Ens, Col E Bradley, Capt Wm Lauderdale, Vol Inf, Res omitted
STONE, John, Cor, Col Jno Alcorn, Capt Wm Locke, Cav; d 11-6-1813
STONE, Thomas G, Cor, Col Thos Williams, Capt Giles Burdett, Branch Srvce omitted, Res omitted
STONE, Thomas, Cor, Maj Gen John Cocke, TN Vol Mtd Gunmen, Res omitted
STONE, William B, 2 Lt, Col Thomas H Williamson, Capt Burdett, Vol Mtd Gunmen, Res omitted
STONE, William, 2 Lt, Maj Gen John Cocke, TN Vol Mtd Gunmen, Res omitted
STONE, William, Ens, Col John Brown, Capt Reamy, Mtd Gunmen; promoted from Sgt
STORY, Samuel, 1 Lt, Col R C Napier, Capt Drury Adkins, Mil Inf, Res omitted
STOVER, John, 2 Lt, Col Samuel Bayless, Capt Joseph Rich, E TN Inf, Res omitted
STRAIN, Robert, Ens, Col Wm Lillard, Capt Wm McLin, E TN Inf, Res omitted
STROTHER, John, Capt, Col Philip Pipkin, 1st Regt Mil Inf, Fayetteville
STROTHER, John, Capt, Col Philip Pipkin, Mil, Res omitted
STUART, David, 1 Lt, Maj Wm Woodfolk, Capt A Turner, Inf, Res omitted
STUART, James, Capt, Col Wm Johnson, Drafted E TN Mil, Res omitted
STUART, John, 1 Lt, Col John Brown, Capt Charles Lewin, E TN Mtd Inf, Res omitted
STUMP, Frederick, Capt, Col John Alcorn, Cav W TN Vol, Davidson Co
STUMP, Frederick, Capt, Col John Alcorn, Cav, Res omitted
STUMP, Frederick, Capt, Col John Coffee, Capt Frederick Stump, Cav, Res omitted
STUMP, Frederick, Capt, Col John Coffee, Vol Cav, Nashville
STUMP, John, Lt Col, Maj Gen Andrew Jackson, Capt John Craine, Mtd Gunmen, Res omitted
SUGGS, Herbert, 1 Lt, Maj William Woodfolk, Capt Mathew Neal, Inf, Res omitted
SUMMERS, Isaac, Ens, Col John Wynne, Capt Wm Wilson, Inf, Res omitted
SUTOR, William, Lt, Regt Commander omitted, Capt Jas Craig, Inf
SUTTIN, James, Lt, Regt Commander omitted, Capt L Ferrell, Inf
SUTTON, John, 1 Lt, Maj Wm Woodfolk, Capt Dudney, Inf; promoted to Capt
SUTTON, John, Capt, 3rd Regt Mil Inf, Res omitted; Bn of Maj William Woodfolk
SWAN, John, 1 Lt, Col Edwin Booth, Capt John Lewis, E TN Mil
SWANSON, Richard, 3 Lt, Col Philip Pipkin, Capt Geo Mebane, Mil Inf
SWIFT, Thomas, 3 Lt, Maj Gen Carroll, Capt Elliott, Inf
TAIT, James, Capt, Col S Copeland, 3rd Regt Mil Inf, Warren Co
TAIT, James, Capt, Col S Copeland, Inf
TAPPER, John, 3 Lt, Maj Wm Russell, Capt Wm Chism,

Vol Mtd Gunmen

TATE, Richard, Capt, Col Thomas Williamson, 2nd Regt TN Vol Mtd Gunmen, Davidson Co

TATE, Richard, Capt, Col Thomas Williamson, Vol Mtd Gunmen, Res omitted

TATE, Richard, Capt, Maj Gen John Cocke, TN Vol Mtd Gunmen, Res omitted

TATE, Z, Capt, Brig Gen John Coffee, TN Vol Mtd Gunmen, Res omitted

TATOM, Bernard, Ens, Gen Jackson, Capt Hugh Kerr, Mtd Rangers, Res omitted; promoted from Sgt

TAYLOR, Eli, 2 Lt, Col Thos Williamson, Capt Jno Doak & Capt Jno Dobbins, Vol Mtd Gunmen; promoted from Sgt

TAYLOR, Gilbert, Surgeon, Col Thos McCrory, 3rd(2nd?) Regt TN Mil, Res omitted

TAYLOR, James, 1 Lt, Regt Commander omitted, Capt James Cowan, Inf

TAYLOR, Joel, 3 Lt, Col Robt Dyer, Capt Robt Evans, Vol Mtd Gunmen, Res omitted

TAYLOR, John, Ens, Col R C Napier, Capt Early Benson, Mil Inf, Res omitted; elected from 1 Sgt

TAYLOR, Nathan, Brig Gen, no other information

TAYLOR, Nathaniel, Brig Gen, General & Staff of Brig of Inf, Inf, Res omitted

TAYLOR, Samuel, 1 Lt & 2 Adjt, Col John Coffee, TN Vol Cav, Res omitted

TAYLOR, Samuel, 1 Lt, Col Edwin Booth, Capt Richard Marshall, Drafted Mil, Res omitted

TAYLOR, Samuel, 1 Maj, Col Jno K Wynn, 1st Regt TN Mil, Res omitted

TEARNE, Thomas, Hospital Surgeon, Maj Gen Andrew Jackson, Div of TN Mil, Res omitted

TEAS, William, Capt, Col Robert Jarmon, 6th Brig TN Mil Mtd Inf, Res omitted

TEAS, William, Capt, Commander omitted, Mtd Inf, Res omitted

TEDFORD, James, Capt, Col Samuel Wear, E TN Vol Inf, Res omitted

TEDFORD, James, Capt, Col Samuel Wear, E TN Vol Mil, Kingston TN

TEDFORD, James, Ens, Col Wm Johnson, Capt David McKamy, E TN Drafted Mil, Res omitted

TEMPLETON, John, 3 Lt, Maj Wm Woodfolk, Capt James C Neil, Inf, Res omitted

TERRELL, E, 2 Maj, Col R H Dyer, no other information; resigned 3-22-1814

TERRELL, James, Capt, Col John Coffee, Vol Cav, Res omitted

TERRELL, James, Capt, Col Robert H Dyer, Cav Vol, Davidson Co

TERRILL, James, Capt & 1 Adjt, Col R H Dyer, no other information

TERRILL, James, Capt, Col John Coffee, Cav, Nashville?

THOMAS, Isaac, 2 Lt, Col Wm Pillow, Capt John H Anderson, Vol Inf, Res omitted; resigned 12-4-1813

THOMAS, Isaac, Ens & Adjt, Col Wm Pillow, 2nd Regt TN Vol Inf, Res omitted

THOMAS, John, Ens, Regt Commander omitted, Capt Geo Smith, Spies; promoted from Pvt

THOMAS, Tristrim B, 2 Lt, Col L Hammond, Capt James Craig, 2nd Regt W TN Mil, Res omitted

THOMPSON, Allen, 2 Lt, Col N T Perkins, Capt Mathew Patterson, Mtd Vol, Res omitted

THOMPSON, James, 2 Lt, Col Ewin Allison, Capt Jacob Hoyal, E TN Mil, Res omitted

THOMPSON, James, 2 Lt, Col S Bunch, Capt George McPherson, E TN Mil, Res omitted

THOMPSON, James, 2 Lt, Col Thomas H Benton, Capt Isiah Renshaw, Vol Inf, Res omitted

THOMPSON, Moses, Capt, Col S Copeland, 3rd Regt Mil Inf, Wilson Co

THOMPSON, Moses, Capt, Col S Copeland, Inf, Res omitted

THOMPSON, Samuel, Capt, Col Edwin Booth, TN Mil, Res omitted

THOMPSON, Samuel, Capt, Col Edwin E Booth, E TN Drafted Mil, Knoxville; Div of Maj Gen Wm Carroll

THOMPSON, William, 1 Lt, Col Wm Johnson, Capt James Stewart, Drafted E TN Mil, Res omitted

THOMPSON, William, Lt, Col Wm Johnson, Capt James Stewart, 3rd Regt E TN Mil, Res omitted

THRESHOUN, Henry, Ens, Maj Wm Russell, Capt John Trimble, Vol Mtd Gunmen

TILLETT, James, 1 Lt, Col S Bunch, Capt Geo Gregory, E Tn Drafted Mll

TILLETT, James, 2 Lt, Col S Bunch, Capt Jno English, E Tn Drafted Mil

TINDALL, Samuel, Lt, Col S Wear, Capt Saml Bowman, Mtd Inf

TIPTON, Jacob, Ens, Maj Jno Childs, Capt R Tipton, E TN Vol Mtd Inf; Regt from Blount Co

TIPTON, Reuben, 3 Lt, Col Saml Wear, Capt Jos Calloway, Mtd Inf

TIPTON, Reuben, Capt, Bn of Maj John Childs Brig of Brig Gen John Coffee, E TN Vol Gunmen, Knoxville

TIPTON, Reuben, Capt, Maj Jno Childs, Capt R Tipton, E TN Vol Mtd Inf; Regt from Knox Co

TITTLE, James, Ens, Col A Loury, Lt Col L Hammons, Capt A Rains, Inf

TODD, William, 1 Lt, Col Alex Loury, Capt Jas Kincaid, Inf

TOLE, George W, Ens, Col Wm Lillard, Capt Robt McCalpin, E TN Inf

TOWNSEND, William, 3 Lt, Col R H Dyer, Maj Wm Russell, Capt Wm Russell, Vol Mtd Gunmen

TRAMELL, David, Ens, Col Edwin Booth, Capt Saml Thompson, Mil

TRAP, John, 1 Lt, Col Thos Benton, Capt Wm J Smith, Vol Inf

TRAPP, John, 1 Lt, Col Wm Pillow, Capt Wm J Smith, Vol Inf

TREADWELL, Daniel C, Cor, Col R H Dyer, Capt Thos Jones, Vol Mtd Gunmen

TRICE, James, 1 Lt, Col John K Wynne, CApt Bayless Prince, Inf

TRIMBLE, John, Capt, Col John Brown, E TN Mtd Gunmen

TRIMBLE, John, Capt, Col John Brown, E TN Vol Gun-

## Officers, War of 1812

men, Res omitted
TRIMBLE, John, Capt, Maj William Russell, TN Vol Mtd Gunmen, Res omitted
TRIMBLE, John, Capt, Maj Wm Russell, Vol Mtd Gunmen
TRISTOE, Richard, 1 Lt, Gen Coffee, Maj John Childs, Capt Daniel Price, Vol Mtd Gunmen, Res omitted
TRISTOE, Thomas, Ens, Gen Coffee, Maj John Childs, Capt Daniel Price, Vol Mtd Gunmen, Res omitted
TROUSDALE, William, Cor, Col N Cannon, Capt William Edwards, Command, Res omitted
TRUPP, John, 1 Lt, Col Thos Benton, Capt Geo Smith, Vol Inf, Res omitted
TUBB, James, Capt, Col Alexander Loury, W Tn Mil Inf, Carthage?
TUBB, James, Capt, Lt Col Leroy Hammonds, Capt Geo Tubb, Inf, Res omitted
TUNNELL, James, Capt, Col William Johnson, 3rd Regt E TN Mil, Res omitted
TUNNELL, James, Capt, Col Wm Johnson, E TN Mil, Res omitted
TUNNELL, Robert, 2 Lt, Col John Brown, Capt John Childs, E TN Vol Mtd Inf, Res omitted
TUNNELL, William, Lt Col, Col Edwin E Booth, E TN Mil, Res omitted
TUPPER, John, 3 Lt, Maj Wm Russell, Capt Wm Chism, Vol Mtd Riflemen, Res omitted
TURNER, Anthony S, 1 Maj, Gen Andrew Jackson, Col Thomas McCrory, Field & Staff Officers, 2nd Regt TN Mil
TURNER, James, Capt, Bn of Maj William Woodfolk, Mil Inf, Monroe Overton Co
TURNER, James, Capt, Maj Wm Woodfolk, Inf, Res omitted
TURNEY, George, 1 Lt, Maj Gen Wm Carroll, Col Jas Raulston, Capt E Robinson, Inf, Res omitted
TURNEY, George, Ens, Col Wm Higgins, Capt A Dale, Mtd Gunmen, Res omitted
TUTEN, John, 1 Lt, Col Jno Brown, Capt Wm D Neilson, E TN Vol Mil, Res omitted
TUTON, John, 1 Lt, Col Wm Johnson, Capt Jas Rogers, E TN Drafted Mil, Res omitted
TYRE, Richmond C, 2 Lt, Col Alex Loury, Capt Geo Sarver, Inf, Res omitted
TYRELL, James, Capt & Adjt, Col Jno Alcorn, TN Vol Cav, Res omitted
TYRELL, James, Capt & Adjt, Col Jno Coffee, TN Vol Cav & Mtd Riflemen, Res omitted
UNDERWOOD, James, Capt, Col John Brown & Capt James Standifer, E TN Vol Mil, Res omitted
UNDERWOOD, James, Capt, Col John Brown, Capt James Standifer, E TN Vol Mil, Res omitted
UNDERWOOD, John, Capt, Col John Brown, E TN Vol Mtd Mil, Res omitted
UPTON, William, 1 Lt, Maj John Childs, Capt Jas Cummings, E TN Mtd Inf
UPTON, William, 2 Lt, Col Saml Wear, Capt John Stephens, E TN Vol Inf
USSERY, Richard, Lt, Regt Commander omitted, Capt Jas Gray, Inf
USSERY, Richard, Lt, Regt Commander omitted, Capt Josiah Askew, Inf
VANALT, William H, Cor, Brig Gen John Coffee, Co Commander omitted, E TN Vol Mtd Gunmen
VANCE, David G, Capt, Col John Williams, E TN Mtd Vol
VANCE, David G, Capt, Col John Williams, E Tn Mtd Vol, Res omitted
VANCE, David G, Capt, Col Saml Bunch, E TN Mtd Inf
VANCE, David G, Capt, Col Samuel Bunch, E TN Mtd Inf, Knoxville
VANDERPOOL, Vincent, 2 Lt, Col Wm Johnson, Capt Henry Hunter, E TN Mil, Res omitted
VANDYKE, Thomas J, Surgeon, Col Wm Johnson, 3rd Regt E TN Drafted Mil, Res omitted; d 12-27-1814
VANDYKE, Thomas, Surgeon, Col Wm Lillard, E TN Vol Mil, Res omitted
VANHOOK, Aaron, 3 Lt, Brig Gen John Coffee, TN Vol Mtd Gunmen, Res omitted
VANHOOK, Aaron, 3 Lt, Col R H Dyer, Capt Joseph Williams, Vol Mtd Gunmen, Res omitted
VARAIL, John, Ens, Col S Wear, Capt Mitchell & Capt S Bunch, E TN Mtd Inf, Res omitted
VARNALL, William, Cor, Col Robert Dyer, Capt Thomas Williams, Vol Mtd Gunmen, Res omitted
VAUGHN, Archibald, Ens, Col Wm Johnson, Capt Jas Rogers, E TN Drafted Mil, Res omitted
VERNON, Miles, Capt, Col Edwin Booth, E TN Mil
VERNON, Miles, Capt, Col Edwin E Booth, E TN Mil, Res omitted
VINYARD, John, 1 Lt, Regt Commander omitted, Capt Saml Richardson, E TN Draft Mil
WADDELL, Johnathan, Capt, Col Samuel Bayless, E TN Mil Drafted, Washington Co
WADDLE, Elias, 2 Lt, Col Ewen Allison, Capt Jonas Loughmiller, Mil, Res omitted; killed in battle 3-27-1814
WADDLE, Jonathan, Capt, Col Samuel Bayless, E TN Mil, Res omitted
WADE, Austin M, 2 Lt, Col Philip Pipkin, Capt Wm Mackay, Mil Inf, Res omitted
WADE, Charles, Capt, Col James Raulston, 3rd Regt TN Mil Inf, Res omitted
WADE, Charles, Capt, Col Jas Raulston, Inf, Res omitted
WAGGONER, Jacob, 1 Lt, Maj Gen A Jackson, Col Thos Williamson, Capt Robt Steele, Vol Mtd Gunmen
WAGGONER, Solomon, 1 Lt, Maj Wm Russell, Capt John Cowan, Vol Mtd Gunmen, Res omitted
WAIR, George F, 1 Lt & 2 Maj, Col Archer Cheatham, 2nd Regt of TN, Res omitted
WALKER, Andrew, 3 Lt, Col A Loury, Capt Gabriel Martin, Inf, Res omitted
WALKER, E R, Cor, Maj Gen John Cocke, TN Vol Mtd Gunmen, Res omitted
WALKER, Elias R, Cor, Col T Williamson, Capt Thos Porter, Vol Mtd Gunmen, Res omitted
WALKER, John A, 1 Lt, Brig Gen John Coffee, TN Vol Mtd Gunmen, Res omitted
WALKER, John A, 1 Lt, Col R H Dyer, Capt Thos Jones, Mtd Vol Gunmen, Res omitted
WALKER, Meredith, Capt, Lt Col A Cheatham, Capt

Meredith Walker, Mtd Inf, Res omitted
WALKER, Robert, Capt, Lt Col Wm Phillips, Inf, Res omitted
WALKER, Robert, Lt, Capt Gray, Inf, Res omitted
WALKER, William, Capt, Col John Williams, E TN Mtd Vol, Res omitted
WALKER, William, Capt, Col John Williams, Mtd Vol, Res omitted
WALLACE, John, Capt, Col Edward Bradley, 1st Regt Vol Inf, Sumner Co
WALLACE, John, Capt, Col Edward Bradley, Vol Inf, Res omitted
WALLACE, John, Capt, Col William Hall, Inf 1st Regt TN Vol, Res omitted
WALLACE, John, Capt, Col Wm Hall, Branch Srvce omitted, Res omitted
WALLACE, William, Ens, Col Wm Pillow, Capt C E McEwen, Vol Inf, Res omitted; promoted from a Pvt
WALLER, Obadiah, Capt, Col Wm Metcalf, Capt Obidiah Waller, Mil Inf, Res omitted
WALLER, Obidiah, Capt, Col William Metcalf, 1st Regt W TN Mil Inf, Res omitted
WALTON, James, Capt, Col N Cannon, Mtd Riflemen, Smith Co
WALTON, James, Capt, Col Newt Cannon, Mtd Riflemen, Res omitted; promoted from 1 Lt
WALTON, Josiah, 1 Lt, Col John Alcorn, Capt John Byrn, Cav, Res omitted
WALTON, Meredith, Capt, Lt Col Jno Edmonson, Cav, Res omitted
WARD, Anthony, 1 Lt, Col S Copeland, Capt John Dawson, Inf, Res omitted
WARD, Burwell, Ens, Col John Cocke, Capt Sam Caruthers, Inf, Res omitted
WARD, Dickin, 3 Lt, Col Philip Pipkin, Capt Jas Blakemore, Mil Inf, Res omitted
WARD, John, Ens, Col Saml Bunch, Capt Wm Jobe, E TN Vol Mtd Inf, Res omitted
WARMICK, John P, Ens, Col E Booth, Capt Geo Winton, E TN Mil, Res omitted; promoted from the ranks
WARTERS, John, Lt, Col A Cheatham, Capt Charles Johnson, Inf, Res omitted
WASSUM, Jonathan, 3 Lt, Col Wm Johnson, Capt Joseph Scott, E TN Drafted Mil, Res omitted
WATKINS, Charles, 1 Maj, Col Jas Raulston, W TN Mil Inf, Res omitted
WATKINS, Henry, 1 Lt, Col A Cheatham, Capt Wm Smith, Inf, Res omitted
WATKINS, Isaac, 1 Lt, Col R T Perkins, Capt Phillip Pipkin, Mtd Riflemen, Res omitted
WEAKLEY, John, 1 Lt, Col Wm Hall, Capt Jas Hambleton, Vol Inf
WEAKLEY, John, Capt, Col John Cocke, Capt John Weakley, Inf
WEAKLEY, John, Capt, Col John Cocke, Mil Inf, Nashville
WEAKLEY, John, Capt, Lt Col Henry Bryan, Co Commander omitted, Inf
WEAKLEY, John, Lt, Col Edward Bradley, Capt Jas Hambleton, Vol Inf

WEAKLEY, Robert, Capt, Lt Col Henry Bryan, Inf
WEAR, John, 1 Lt, Col Saml Bunch, Capt Jno Hawk, E Tn MII; joined from Capt Davis Co
WEAR, Samuel jr, Ens, Col Saml Wear, Capt Simeon Perry, E TN Vol Mtd Inf
WEAR, Samuel, Col, E TN Vol Mil Inf
WEAR, Samuel, Col, Field & Staff Officers, E TN Mil, Res omitted
WEATHEREAD, Francis, 1 Lt, Col Edward Bradley, Capt Abraham Bledsoe, Riflemen, Res omitted
WEAVER, Abraham, Ens, Maj Wm Woodfolk, Capt James Turner, Inf, Res omitted
WEAVER, Benjamin, Lt, Col Robert Steele, Capt Richard M Ratton, Mil Inf, Res omitted
WEAVER, Jesse, 2 Lt, Col Jno Coffee, Capt John Baskerville, Cav, Res omitted
WEAVER, Jesse, 2 Lt, Col John Alcorn, Capt John Baskerville, Vol Inf, Res omitted
WEBB, Martin, 3 Lt, Maj Wm Woodfolk, Capt A Pearce, Inf, Res omitted; d 2-15-1815
WEBB, Ross, 3 Lt, Maj Gen Jno Cocke, TN Vol Mtd Gunmen, Res omitted
WEBSTER, Peter, Ens, Col Thos McCrory, Capt A Metcalf, Mil Inf, Res omitted
WEEKS, Solomon, Ens, Col P Pipkin, Capt Jas Blakemore, Mil Inf, Res omitted; AWOL
WELLS, Thomas, Capt, Col Alexander Loury, 2nd Regt Mil Inf, Fayetteville
WELLS, Thomas, Capt, Lt Col L Hammond, Col A Loury, Inf, Res omitted
WEST, George, 1 Lt QM, Col Wm Pillow, Vol Inf, Res omitted
WEST, George, Adjt, Lt Col Jno Edmonson, Cav, Res omitted
WEST, Henry, Capt, Col James Raulston, 3rd Regt TN Mil Inf, Res omitted
WEST, Henry, Capt, Col Jas Raulston, Inf, Res omitted
WEST, John B, Ens, Col John Brown, Capt Allen I Bacon, E TN Mil Inf, Res omitted; promoted from 2 Sgt
WETHERALL, James, Lt, Col S Copeland, Capt Jas Tait, Inf, Res omitted
WETHEREL, Francis M, 1 Lt, Col Wm Hall, Capt Geo Bledsoe, Vol Inf, Res omitted
WHITE, Frederick, Lt, Col Wm Lillard, Capt Jacob Dyke, TN Vol Inf, Res omitted
WHITE, James, Brig Gen, Field & Staff Officers, Spies E TN Mil, Res omitted
WHITE, James, Brig Gen, no other information
WHITE, John, 3 Lt, Col John Brown, Capt Wm White, E TN Mil Inf, Res omitted; transferred from Capt Underwood's Co
WHITE, Richard, Lt, Col S Bunch, Capt Geo McPherson, E TN Mil, Res omitted
WHITE, Thomas, Capt, Brig Gen John Coffee, TN Vol Mtd Gunmen, Res omitted
WHITE, Thomas, Capt, Col R H Dyer, Capt Thos White, Vol Mtd Gunmen, Res omitted
WHITE, Thomas, Capt, Col R H Dyer, TN Vol Cav Mtd Gunmen, Davidson Co
WHITE, Thomas, Lt, Col Jno Alcorn, Capt F Stump, Cav, Res omitted

## Officers, War of 1812

WHITE, Thomas, Lt, Col Wm Lillard, Capt Benj King, E TN Vol Inf, Res omitted

WHITE, William, Capt, Col Jno Brown, Capt Wm White, E TN Mtd Inf Vol, Res omitted

WHITE, William, Capt, Col Jno Brown, E TN Mil Inf, Res omitted

WHITE, William, Judge Advocate, Maj Gen Andrew Jackson, Div of TN Mil, Res omitted

WHITENBARGER, Mathew, 3 Lt, Col Edwin Booth, Capt Geo Biggs, Inf, Res omitted

WHITESIDE, Abraham, 3 Lt, Col Wm Metcalf, Capt Bird Hurt, Mil Inf, Res omitted

WIATT, Edwin, Surgeon, Col Edwin E Booth, E TN Mil, Res omitted

WILBORN (WILBURN), Robert, 1 Lt, Lt Col L Hammond, Capt James Tubb, Inf, Res omitted

WILBOURN, William, Cor, Col R H Dyer, Capt James Wyatt, Vol Mtd Gunmen, Res omitted

WILEY, John, 1 Lt, Col John Brown, Capt Wm White, E TN Mil Inf, Res omitted

WILKERSON, Hinchen T, Surgeon, Col John Cocke, 3rd Regt W TN Mil, Res omitted

WILKES, Benjamin, Ens, Capt Edwin S Moore, Mtd Riflemen, Res omitted

WILKINSON, Allen, Capt, Col S Copeland, 3rd Regt Mil Inf, Smith Co

WILKINSON, Allen, Capt, Col S Copeland, Mil Inf, Res omitted

WILKINSON, Thomas, 2 Lt, Lt Col Hammons, Capt Joseph Williams, Inf, Res omitted

WILKINSON, Thomas, 3 Lt, Col A Loury, Capt Jos Williams, W TN Mil Inf, Res omitted

WILLIAMS, Beverly, 2 Lt, Col Newton Cannon, Capt John Harpole, Mtd Gunmen, Res omitted; promoted to 1 Lt

WILLIAMS, Beverly, Capt, Col Thomas Williamson, 2nd Regt TN Vol Mtd Gunmen, Wilson Co

WILLIAMS, Coleman, 1 Lt, Maj Gen A Jackson, Capt Jos Kirkpatrick, Mtd Gunmen, Res omitted; promoted from Ens

WILLIAMS, David, Capt, Col S Copeland, 3rd Regt Military Inf, Monroe Overton Co

WILLIAMS, David, Capt, Col S Copeland, Mil Inf, Res omitted

WILLIAMS, Eli, Lt, Col Saml Bunch, Capt Moses, E TN Mil Drafted; transferred to Capt Hanks Co

WILLIAMS, Garland, Lt, Lt Col Archer Cheatham, 6th Brig Mtd Inf, Res omitted

WILLIAMS, George, 2 Lt, Capt Edwin S Moore, Mtd Riflemen, Res omitted

WILLIAMS, Isaac, Capt, Col Newton Cannon, Capt Isaac Williams, Mtd Riflemen, Res omitted; wounded 11-9-1813 at Taledega

WILLIAMS, Isaac, Capt, Col Newton Cannon, Mtd Riflemen, Bedford Co

WILLIAMS, Isaac, Capt, Col Robert Dyer, Vol Mtd Gunmen, Shelbyville Bedford Co; Bn of Maj William Russell

WILLIAMS, Isaac, Capt, Col S Bunch, E TN Mil, Res omitted

WILLIAMS, Isaac, Capt, Col Samuel Bunch, E TN Drafted Mil, Res omitted

WILLIAMS, James H, Ens, Col Philip Pipkin, Capt Henry M Newlin, Mil Inf, Res omitted

WILLIAMS, James, Ens, Capt Jas Haggard, Mtd Gunmen, Res omitted

WILLIAMS, John S, Ens, Maj Gen Carroll, Capt Huddleston & Capt Raulston, Inf, Res omitted; promoted to 2 Lt

WILLIAMS, John, Col, Commander omitted, E TN Vol, Res omitted

WILLIAMS, Joseph, 1 Lt, Capt Jas Williams, Mil Cav, Res omitted; promoted to Capt

WILLIAMS, Joseph, 1 Lt, Col John Coffee, Capt Michael Molton, Cav, Res omitted

WILLIAMS, Joseph, Capt, Brig Gen John Coffee, TN Vol Mtd Gunmen, Res omitted

WILLIAMS, Joseph, Capt, Col R H Dyer, Mtd Gunmen Vol, Dixon Co

WILLIAMS, Joseph, Capt, Col Thos Dyer, Vol Mtd Gunmen, Res omitted

WILLIAMS, Joseph, Lt, Capt Elijah Rushing, Det of Inf, Res omitted

WILLIAMS, Matthew, 2 Lt, Col William Johnson, Capt Rogers, E TN Drafted Mil, Res omitted; resigned 10-22-1814

WILLIAMS, Nathaniel, 1 Lt, Maj Wm Russell, Capt Isaac Williams, Separate Bn of TN Vol Mtd Gunmen, Res omitted

WILLIAMS, Nathaniel, Lt, Col Newton Cannon, Capt Isaac Williams, Mtd Riflemen, Res omitted

WILLIAMS, Thomas L, Judge Advocate, Maj Gen Jno Cocke, E TN Mil Inf, Res omitted

WILLIAMS, William, 2 Lt, Col Wm Higgins, Capt S Griffith, Mtd Riflemen, Res omitted

WILLIAMSON, James N, Lt, Col Thos Benton, Capt Thos Williamson, Vol Inf, Res omitted

WILLIAMSON, Joseph A, Capt, Col A Loury, W TN Mil Inf, Res omitted

WILLIAMSON, Joseph N, 1 Lt, Col Thos Benton, Capt J N Williamson, Vol Inf, Res omitted

WILLIAMSON, Joseph N, 1 Lt, Col Thos Benton, Capt Thos Williamson, Vol Inf, Res omitted

WILLIAMSON, Joseph N, Capt, Col Alexander Loury, 2nd Regt TN Mil Inf, Nashville

WILLIAMSON, Joseph, 1 Lt, Col Wm Pillow, Capt Thos Williamson, Vol Inf, Res omitted

WILLIAMSON, Joseph, Capt, Col Leroy Hammond, Capt J N Williamson, 2nd Regt Inf, Res omitted

WILLIAMSON, Joseph, Capt, Col Leroy Hammond, Capt Thos Williamson, Inf, Res omitted

WILLIAMSON, Thomas, Capt, Col Thomas H Benton, 2nd Regt TN Vol Mil Inf, Res omitted

WILLIAMSON, Thomas, Capt, Col Thos Benton, Capt Thos Williamson, Vol Inf, Res omitted

WILLIAMSON, Thomas, Capt, Col William Pillow, 2nd Regt Vol Inf, Davidson Co

WILLIAMSON, Thomas, Capt, Col Wm Pillow, Capt Jos Williamson, Vol Inf, Res omitted

WILLIAMSON, Thomas, Col, Brig Gen Jno Coffee, E TN Vol Mtd Gunmen, Res omitted

WILLIAMSON, Thomas, Col, Brigade of Brig Gen John

Coffee Div of Maj Gen Andrew Jackson, W Tn Vol Mtd Gunmen, Res omitted

WILLIAMSON, Thomas, Maj, Field & Staff Officers Col R H Dyer, Bn of Mtd Gunmen & Cav, Davidson Co

WILLIAMSON, Thomas, Maj, no other information

WILLIS, Abel, Capt, Col T McCrory, Mil Inf, Res omitted

WILLIS, Abel, Capt, Col Thomas McCrory, 2nd Regt Mil Inf, Monroe Overton Co

WILLIS, Benjamin, 1 Lt & Pay Master, Col R C Napier, 1st Regt W TN Mil, Res omitted; resigned 2-9-1814

WILLIS, Nimrod, 2 Lt, Col Wm Lillard, Capt Wm McLin, E TN Inf, Res omitted

WILLIS, Plummer, 1 Lt & Brig Maj, Brig Gen Thomas Johnson, no other information

WILLIS, Plummer, Aide de Camp, Brig Gen Thomas Johnson, no other information

WILLSON, William, Capt, Col John K Wynne, Inf, Res omitted

WILSON, James M, Ens, Col John Cocke, Capt James Gault, Inf, Res omitted; promoted from Pvt

WILSON, Jason H, Lt & Adjt, Maj Wm Woodfolk, Separate Bn of W TN Mil, Res omitted; resigned 12-20-1814

WILSON, John, 1 Lt, Col Williamson, Capt Porter, Vol Mtd Gunmen, Res omitted

WILSON, John, 1 Lt, Maj Gen John Cocke, TN Vol Mtd Gunmen, Res omitted

WILSON, John, 1 Lt, Maj Wm Russell, Capt John Trimble, Vol Mtd Gunmen, Res omitted

WILSON, John, 2 Lt, Maj Wm Woodfolk, Capt Jas Turner, Inf, Res omitted

WILSON, John, Ens, Col John Brown, Capt Geo Trimble, E TN Mtd Gunmen, Res omitted

WILSON, Samuel, 1 Lt, Col John Walker, Capt David Vance, Mtd Mil, Res omitted

WILSON, Samuel, 1 Lt, Col John Williams, Capt David G Vance, E TN Mtd Vol, Res omitted

WILSON, Thomas, 2 Lt, Col Wm Higgins, Capt Samuel Allen, Mtd Gunmen, Res omitted

WILSON, Thomas, Capt, Col Ewen Allison, E TN Drafted Mil, Res omitted

WILSON, Thomas, Capt, Col Ewen Allison, E TN Mil, Greenville

WILSON, William, 2 Lt, Col John Wynne, Capt John Porter, Inf, Res omitted

WILSON, William, Capt, Col John K Wynne, Mil Inf, Res omitted

WINGFIELD, Foster, 3 Lt, Col Wm Johnson, Capt Benj Powell, E TN Mil, Res omitted

WINHAM (WINCHUM), Robert, Ens, Col Wm Hall, Capt John Wallace, Inf, Res omitted

WINN, Thomas P, Brig QM, Brig Gen N Taylor, no other information

WINNE, William W, Surgeon, Col Philip Pipkin, 1st Regt TN Mil, Res omitted; d 11-9-1814 at Ft Jackson

WINSELL, Adam, Capt, Col Ewen Allison, E TN Drafted Mil, Res omitted

WINSELL, Adam, Capt, Col Ewin Allison, E TN Drafted Mil, Res omitted

WINSTON, Anthony, Lt, Gen Jackson, Capt Kerr, Mtd Rangers, Res omitted; resigned 12-14-1813

WINSTON, John I, Capt, Col John Alcorn, Capt George Winston, Mtd Riflemen, Res omitted

WINSTON, John J, Capt, Col John Alcorn, Mtd Riflemen TN Vol, Res omitted

WINTON, George, Capt, Col Edwin Booth, E TN Mil, Res omitted

WINTON, George, Capt, Col Edwin E Booth, E TN Drafted Mil, Res omitted; Div of Maj Gen William Carroll

WIRICK, Fredrick, 1 Lt, Col Wm Johnson, Capt Henry Hunter, E TN Mil, Res omitted

WISDOM, William, 2 Lt, Col Philip Pipkin, Capt Henry Newlin, Mil Inf, Res omitted

WISNER, Henry, 3 Lt, Col Philip Pipkin, Capt Peter Searcy, Mil Inf, Res omitted; d 11-27-1814 at Ft Pearce

WISNER, Joseph, Ens, Col A Cheatham, Capt Chas Johnson, Inf, Res omitted

WITTEN, James, Lt, Col Edwin Booth, Capt Vernon, E TN Mil, Res omitted

WOLF, William, 2 Lt, Col John Cocke, Capt John Dalton, Inf, Res omitted

WOOD, William, 2 Maj, Col Wm Metcalf, W TN Mil Inf, Res omitted; resigned 1-11-1815

WOODFOLK, Austin, Lt & QM, Maj Wm Woodfolk, Separate Bn W TN Mil Inf, Res omitted

WOODFOLK, William, 1 Maj, Commander omitted, Separate Bn W TN Mil, Res omitted

WOODFOLK, William, Maj, Field & Staff Officers Col John K Wynne, Separate Bn of W TN Mil, Res omitted

WOODLEY, John, 3 Lt, Maj Gen John Cocke, TN Vol Mtd Gunmen, Res omitted

WOODROUGH, William B, Ens, Col Wm Y Higgins, Capt Dake, Mtd Riflemen, Res omitted

WOODS, Joseph B, Ens, Col S Bunch, Capt John English, E TN Draft Mil; trans from Capt Jos Duncan's Co

WOODS, Joshua, 3 Lt, Col Wm Metcalf, Capt Barbee Collins, E TN Vol Riflemen

WOODS, Peter, 2 Lt, Regt Commander omitted, Capt Jas Cowan, Branch omitted

WOODWARD, William, 1 Lt, Col Edwin Booth, Capt Geo Winton, E TN Mil

WOODWARD, William, Lt, Col Wm Johnson, Capt Wm Alexander, Det of E TN Draft Mil

WOODY, John, 3 Lt, Col Thos Williamson, Capt John Doak & Capt John Dobbins, Vol Mtd Gunmen

WOSLEY, Nathan, Capt, Col Edward Bradley, Capt Harry Douglas, Vol Inf

WRIGHT, Bird, Capt Brig QM, Brig Gen Bird Smith, W TN Mil Inf

WRIGHT, Henry, Cor, Col John Coffee, Capt Terrell, Vol Cav

WRIGHT, Nelson S, 2 Lt, Maj John Childs, Capt John Stephens, E TN Vol Mtd Inf

WYATT, James, Capt, Col R H Dyer, Vol Mtd Gunmen

WYATT, James, Capt, Col Robert H Dyer, Vol Mtd Gunmen, Fayetteville

WYATT, Thomas, Adjt, Col Wm Y Higgins, 2 Regt TN

Mtd Vol
WYNN, James T, 1 Lt & Adjt, Lt Col L Hammond, 2 Regt W TN Mil; Field & Staff Officer
WYNN, John K, Col, 1 Regt TN Mil
WYNNE, James T, Lt & Adjt, Col Alexander Loury, Lt Col L Hammond, 2 Regt W TN Mil
WYNNE, John K, Col, Field & Staff Officers, W TN Mil 1st TN Regt, Wilson Co
YANDALL, John, Ens, Col R C Napier, Capt Jas McMurray, Mil Inf; cashiered 3-14-1814
YARDLEY, Thomas, Capt, Col Newton Cannon, Mtd Riflemen, Res omitted
YARDLEY, Thomas, Capt, Col Newton Cannon, Mtd Riflemen, Rutherford Co
YARNELL, Daniel, Capt, Col Samuel Bunch, E TN Mil, Res omitted
YARNELL, Daniel, Capt, Col Samuel Bunch, E TN Mil, Rhea Co
YOE, Perigrim G, Ens, Maj John Childs, Capt Cunningham, E TN Vol Mtd Inf, Res omitted
YOUNG, William B, 1 Lt, Col John Cocke, Capt John Weakley, Inf, Res omitted
YOURE, Joseph, 2 Lt, Col N Cannon, Capt Geo Brandon, Mtd Riflemen, Res omitted
YOUREE, William, 2 Lt, Col Jno Alcorn, Capt Robt Jetton, Vol Cav, Res omitted
YOUREE, William, 2 Lt, Col John Coffee, Capt Robt Jetton, Cav, Res omitted

## Enlisted Men, War of 1812

----, Albert, Waiter, Col James Raulston, Co Commander omitted, W TN Mil Inf; black man no last name

AARON, Alexander, 1st Cpl, Col Wm Pillow, Capt Wm Moore, Inf

AARON, Jacob, Pvt, Maj Gen A Jackson, Capt Wm Carroll, Vol Inf

AARON, John, Pvt, Col John Cocke, Capt Thos Gray, Inf

AARON, Thomas, Pvt, Col Philip Pipkin, Capt Wm Mackay, Mil Inf

ABANATHA, Laban, Pvt, Col Jno Coffee, Capt Fredrick Stump, Cav

ABANATHY, Robert, Pvt, Col A Loury & Lt Col L Hammons, Capt Thos Delaney, Inf

ABAR, John, Pvt, Col Philip Pipkin, Capt Henry M Newlin, Mtd Vol

ABBOT, David, Pvt, Commanders omitted, Branch Svce omitted

ABBOT, Jonathan, Pvt, Col Samuel Bunch, Capt Geo McPherson, E TN Mil

ABBOT, William, Pvt, Col William Metcalf, Capt Barbee Collins, Mil Inf

ABBOTT, David, Pvt, Regt Commander omitted, Capt Wm Mitchell, Spies

ABBOTT, Geo, Pvt, Col Thos Williamson, Capt Thomas Scurry, Vol Mtd Gunmen

ABBOTT, Jas, Pvt, Col Edward Bradley, Capt John Moore, Vol Inf; deserted 11-12-1813

ABBOTT, John, Pvt, Col Philip Pipkin, Capt Henry M Newlin, Mil Inf

ABBOTT, Lewis, Pvt, Col John K Wynne, Capt Wm Caruthers, W TN Mil

ABBOTT, Samuel, Pvt, Col Samuel Bunch, Capt Jno Houk, E TN Mil; d 4-27-1814

ABEL, Michael, Pvt, Col Wm Johnson, Capt Jas R Rogers, E TN Drafted Mil

ABELS, John, Cpl, Col S Copeland, Capt John Houshouser, Inf

ABERNATHA, Robert, Pvt, Col William Metcalf, Capt Thomas Marks, Mil Inf

ABERNATHY, Allen, Pvt, Gen Andrew Jackson, Capt Nathan Davis, Inf

ABERNATHY, Chas, Sgt, Gen Andrew Jackson, Capt Nathan Davis, Inf

ABERNATHY, David, Pvt, Col William Y Higgins, Capt Thomas Eldridge, Mtd Gunmen

ABERNATHY, Jno, Pvt, Gen Andrew Jackson, Capt Nathan Davis, Inf

ABERNATHY, Littleton, Pvt, Col Thomas McCrory, Capt Samuel B McKnight, Inf

ABLE, Anthony, Pvt, Col William Hall, Capt John Wallace, Inf

ABLE, Charles, Pvt, Col A Cheatham, Capt George Chapman, Inf

ABLE, Philip, Pvt, Col Edwin Booth, Capt John Lewis, E TN Inf

ABLE, Philip, Pvt, Col Samuel Wear, Capt James Gillespie, E TN Vol Inf

ABLES, William, Pvt, Col Stephen Copeland, Capt William Evans, Mil Inf

ABNER, John, Blksmth, Col R H Dyer, Capt Cuthbert Hudson, Vol Mtd Gunmen; d 2-23-1815

ABNEY, Elias, Pvt, Col R C Napier, Capt Drury Adkins, Mil Inf

ABNEY, Isaac, Pvt, Col A Cheatham, Capt James Giddens, Inf

ABNEY, Joshua, Pvt, Col Leroy Hammonds & Col Alexander Loury, Capt Thomas Wells, Inf

ABNEY, William, Pvt, Col A Cheatham, Capt William Creel, Inf

ACARD, John, Pvt, Col John Williams, Capt David Vance, Mtd Mil

ACARD, Joseph, Pvt, Col John Brown, Capt Allen I Bacon, E Tn Mil Inf

ACHLAND, Samuel, Pvt, Col Samuel Wear, Capt John Stephens, E TN Vol Inf

ACHLEY, Isaac, 3 Cpl, Col William Johnson, Capt Andrew Lawson, E Tn Drafted Mil

ACHLEY, Jesse, Pvt, Col William Johnson, Capt Andrew Lawson, E TN Mil

ACHLEY, Joshua, Cpl, Col William Johnson, Capt Andrew Lawson, E TN Drafted Mil

ACHOR, James, Pvt, Maj Gen Andrew Jackson, Capt John Craine, Mtd Gunmen

ACKER, Joseph, Pvt, Col R H Dyer, Capt Beverly Williams, 1st Regt TN Vol Mtd Gunmen

ACKERSON, Henry, Pvt, Col Philip Pipkin, Capt James Blakemore, Mil Inf; Des 1-13-1815

ACKLAND, Alexander S, 2nd Mate, Col John K Wynne, Co Commander omitted, 1st Regt TN Mil

ACORD, Jonos, Pvt, Gen Andrew Jackson, Capt David S Deaderick, Arty

ACRIDGE, John, Pvt, Col William Metcalf, Capt Bird L Hurt, Mil Inf

ACRIDGE, John, Pvt, Col William Metcalf, Capt Thomas Marks, Mil Inf; Died 2-9-1815

ACTON, James, Pvt, Col Samuel Bayless, Capt Joseph B Bacon, E TN Mil

ACUFF, Carter, Pvt, Col R C Napier, Capt Drury Adkins, Mil Inf

ACUFF, Carter, Pvt, Col William Johnson, Capt Benjamin Powell, E TN Mil

ACUFF, Carter, Pvt, Col William Lillard, Capt Wm Gillenwater, E TN Vol Inf

ACUFF, Chas, Pvt, Col R C Napier, Capt Drury Adkins, Mil Inf

ACUFF, Hamilton, Pvt, Col R C Napier, Capt Drury Adkins, Mil Inf

ACUFF, Isaac, Pvt, Brig Gen Isaac B Roberts, Capt Benj Reynolds, Mtd Rangers

ACUFF, Isaac, Pvt, Commanders & Branch Srvce omitted

ACUFF, Isaac, Sgt, Col Thomas McCrory, Capt William Dooley, Inf

ACUFF, Spencer, Pvt, Col William Lillard, Capt William Gillenwater, E TN Vol Inf

ACUFF, William, Cpl, Col William Johnson, Capt Benjamin Powelll, E TN Mil

ACUFF, William, Pvt, Col William Johnson, Capt Benjamin Powell, E TN Mil

ADAIR, Alexander, Pvt, Col Samuel Wear, Capt John Bayless, Mtd Inf

ADAIR, Jacob, Pvt, Col Jno Brown, Capt Wm D Neilson, Regt E TN Vol Mil

ADAIR, James, Pvt, Col Wm Lillard, Capt Wm McLinn, E Tn Inf
ADAIR, Jas, Pvt, Brig Gen Jas White, Regt Commander & Branch Srvce omitted; appointed spy
ADAIR, Jas, Pvt, Col Alexander Loury, Capt John Looney, 2nd Regt W TN Mil
ADAIR, John, Pvt, Col Robert H Dyer, Capt Jas McMahan, TN Mtd Gunmen
ADAM, Eli, Cpl, Col Newton Cannon, Capt William Edwards, Regular Command
ADAM, Henry, Pvt, Col Robert H Dyer, Capt Bethel Allen, Vol Mtd Gunmen
ADAMS, Aaron L, Pvt, Col Edward Bradley, Capt Brice Martin, Vol Inf
ADAMS, Aaron L, Pvt, Col Wm Hall, Capt Brice Martin, Vol Inf
ADAMS, Abraham, Pvt, Lt Col Archer Cheatham, Co Commander omitted, 6th Brig Mtd Inf
ADAMS, Abraham, Pvt, Maj Wm Russell, Capt Geo Mitchie, Vol Mtd Gunmen
ADAMS, Abraham, Sgt, Col Thomas Williamson, Capt John Crane & Capt Jas Cook, Vol Mtd Gunmen
ADAMS, Amos, Pvt, Col John Coffee, Capt Jas Terrell, Vol Cav; out of the State
ADAMS, Bailey, Pvt, Col Thomas Williamson, Capt Richard Tate, Vol Mtd Gunmen
ADAMS, Buckner, Cpl, Col John Cocke, Capt George Barnes, Inf
ADAMS, Dan'l, Pvt, Col Samuel Wear & Col Bunch, Capt William Mitchell, E TN Mtd Inf
ADAMS, David, Pvt, Col Ewin Allison, Capt Joseph Everett, E TN Mil; Transferred to Capt Jones Griffin
ADAMS, David, Pvt, Col S Bunch, Capt Jones Griffin, E TN Drafted Mil
ADAMS, David, Pvt, Col Thomas Williamson, Capt John Crane & Capt Jas Cook, Vol Mtd Gunmen
ADAMS, Edwin, Pvt, Col Alexander Loury, Capt Gabriel Martin, Inf
ADAMS, Enos, Pvt, Col S Copeland, Capt Moses Thompson, Inf
ADAMS, Geo, Pvt, Col A Cheatham, Capt William Creel, Inf
ADAMS, Hardin S, Pvt, Col Robert H Dyer, Capt Ephraim G Dickson, TN Mtd Vol Gunmen
ADAMS, Howell, 2 Lt, Col N Cannon, Capt David Hogan, Mtd Gunmen; Died 1-1814
ADAMS, Isaac, Pvt, Maj William Russell, Capt Fleman Hodges, Vol Mtd Gunmen
ADAMS, Isaac, Sgt, Col Samuel Bunch, Capt Joseph Duncan
ADAMS, James, Pvt, Lt Col Archer Cheatham, Co Commander omitted, 6th Brig Mtd Inf
ADAMS, James, Pvt, Regt & Co Commanders omitted, Branch Srvce omitted
ADAMS, Jas, Pvt, Col Edward Bradley, Capt John Moore, Vol Inf; Des 11-19-1813
ADAMS, Jas, Pvt, Col Edwin Booth, Capt Samuel Thompson, Mil
ADAMS, Jas, Pvt, Regt Commander omitted, Capt Jas Haggard, Mtd Gunmen
ADAMS, Jno, Pvt, Regt Commander omitted, Capt David Mason, Cav
ADAMS, John, Cpl, Lt Col Richard Napier, Co Commander omitted, Inf
ADAMS, John, Pvt, Brig Gen Roberts, Capt Benjamin Reynolds, W TN Brig Mtd Rangers
ADAMS, John, Pvt, Col Edward Bradley, Capt Brice Martin, Vol Inf
ADAMS, John, Pvt, Col Ewen Allison, Capt James Allen, E TN Mil
ADAMS, John, Pvt, Col John Alcorn, Capt William Locke, Cav
ADAMS, John, Pvt, Col N T Perkins, Capt John B Quarles, Vol Mtd Inf
ADAMS, John, Pvt, Col R H Dyer, Capt Beverly Williams, Vol Mtd Gunmen
ADAMS, John, Pvt, Col S Bunch, Capt John Houk, E TN Mil; Trans to Capt Duncan's Co
ADAMS, John, Pvt, Col Samuel Bunch, Capt Joseph Duncan, E TN Drafted Mil; Joined from Capt Allen's Co
ADAMS, John, Pvt, Col Thomas McCrory, Capt William Dooley, Inf
ADAMS, John, Pvt, Col Thomas Williamson, Capt John Crane & Capt Jas Cook, Vol Mtd Gunmen
ADAMS, John, Pvt, Col William Hall, Capt Brice Martin, Vol Inf
ADAMS, John, Pvt, Col Wm Lillard, Capt Robert Maloney, E TN Vol Inf
ADAMS, John, Pvt, Maj William Russell, Capt George Michie, Vol Mtd Gunmen
ADAMS, John, Pvt, Regt & Co Commanders omitted, Branch Srvce omitted
ADAMS, Joseph, Pvt, Col Alexander Loury, Capt James Kincaid, Inf
ADAMS, Joshua, Pvt, Col Robert H Dyer & Maj William Russell, Capt William Russell, Vol Mtd Gunmen
ADAMS, Joshua, Pvt, Col William Y Higgins, Capt William Doake, Mtd Riflemen
ADAMS, Laban, Cpl, Col John Brown, Capt William White, E TN Mil Inf
ADAMS, Martin, Cpl, Col Robert H Dyer, Capt Ephriam D Dickson, 14th Mtd Vol Gunmen
ADAMS, Peter, Pvt, Col Stephen Copeland, Capt James Tait, Inf; d 3-19-1814
ADAMS, Reeves, Pvt, Lt Col John Edmondson, Co Commander omitted, Cav
ADAMS, Robert I, Pvt, Col John Coffee, Capt James Terrill, Vol Cav; out of state
ADAMS, Robert J, Pvt, Col R H Dyer, Capt Thomas Jones, Vol Mtd Gunmen
ADAMS, Robert J, Pvt, Regt Commander omitted, Capt Archibald McKenney, Cav
ADAMS, Robert L, Pvt, Regt Commander omitted, Capt Archibald McKenney, Cav
ADAMS, Robert S, Pvt, Col John Coffee, Capt James Terrill, Vol Cav; out of state
ADAMS, Simon, Ffr, Col S Bunch, Capt Isaac Williams, E TN Mil
ADAMS, Simon, Pvt, Col S Bunch, Capt John English, E TN Drafted Mil

## Enlisted Men, War of 1812

ADAMS, Thomas, Pvt, Col John Brown, Capt William White, E TN Mil Inf
ADAMS, Thomas, Pvt, Col N Cannon, Capt David Hogan, Mt Gunmen
ADAMS, Thomas, Pvt, Col S Bunch, Capt Joseph Duncan, E TN Drafted Mil
ADAMS, Thomas, Sgt, Col R H Dyer, Capt Cuthbert Hudson, Vol Mtd Gunmen
ADAMS, Toliver, Pvt, Col S Copeland, Capt Richard Sharpe, Mil Inf
ADAMS, Toliver, Pvt, Maj William Russell, Capt John Cowan, Vol Mtd Gunmen
ADAMS, Will, Pvt, Lt Col Richard Napier, Co Commander omitted, Branch Srvce omitted
ADAMS, William, 3 Cpl, Col John Cocke, Capt George Barnes, Inf
ADAMS, William, Cpl, Col R H Dyer, Capt James McMahon, 1st TN Vol Gunmen
ADAMS, William, Pvt, Col John Coffee, Capt David Smith, Vol Cav
ADAMS, William, Pvt, Col S Copeland, Capt Richard Sharpe, Mil Inf
ADAMS, William, Pvt, Col Thomas McCrory, Capt Thomas K Gordon, Inf
ADAMS, Willie, Pvt, Maj Wm Russell, Capt John Trimble, Vol Mtd Gunmen
ADAMS, Wm G, Pvt, Col Newton Cannon, Capt Andrew Patterson, Mtd Riflemen
ADAMS, Wm, Pvt, Col N Cannon, Capt David Hogan, Mtd Gunmen
ADAMS, Wm, Pvt, Col R H Dyer, Capt William Russell & Maj Wm. Russell, Vol Mtd Gunmen
ADAMS, Wm, Pvt, Maj William Russell, Capt John Cowan, Vol Mtd Gunmen
ADAMS, Wm, Sgt, Capt James Cowan, Mtd Inf
ADAMSON, David, Pvt, Maj John Childs, Capt Daniel Price, E TN Vol Mtd Inf
ADAMSON, Jos, Pvt, Col Samuel Wear, Capt Joseph Calloway, Mtd Inf
ADCOCK, Ariel, Pvt, Col Jno Brown, Capt Lunsford Oliver, E TN Mil
ADCOCK, Barney, Pvt, Col Edward Bradley, Capt Travis Nas, Vol Inf
ADCOCK, David, Pvt, Col S Copeland, Capt Jas Tait, Inf
ADCOCK, Henderson, Pvt, Col Edward Bradley, Capt Travis Nash, Vol Inf
ADCOCK, Jas, Pvt, Col Edwin Booth, Capt Richard Marshall, Drafted Mil
ADCOCK, John, Pvt, Dol Ewen Allison, Capt Jonas Loughmiller, Mil
ADCOCK, Jos, Pvt, Col William Lillard, Capt William Gillenwater, E TN Vol Inf
ADCOCK, Mark, Pvt, Col John Cocke, Capt George Barnes, Inf
ADCOCK, Tyree, Pvt, Col Wm Johnson, Capt Jas Tunnell, E TN Mil
ADCOCK, Wm, Pvt, Brig Gen Thomas Johnston, Capt Robert Carson, Inf
ADCOCK, Wm, Pvt, Col T McCrory, Capt Jno Reynolds, Mil Inf
ADDAIR, Jas, Pvt, Col Samuel Bunch, Capt Andrew Breden, E TN Mil
ADDINGTON, Vardy, Pvt, Lt Col Leroy Hammons, Capt Thomas Delaney, Inf
ADEAR, John, Pvt, Maj William Woodfolk, Capt Abner Pearce, Inf
ADELYOTTE, Arthur, Cpl, Regt Commander omitted, Capt David Mason, Cav
ADINS, Anderson, Pvt, Col William Johnson, Capt Henry Hunter, E TN Mil
ADKERSON, Absolem, Pvt, Col Edwin E Booth, Capt John McKamey, E TN Mil
ADKERSON, David, Pvt, Col Edwin E Booth, Capt John McKamey, E TN Mil
ADKERSON, Jas, Pvt, Col Wm Johnston, Capt Jas R Rogers, E TN Drafted Mil
ADKERSON, Walker, Pvt, Col Wm Johnson, Capt Jas R Rogers, E TN Drafted Mil
ADKINS, Andrew, Pvt, Col Samuel Bayless, Capt James Landen, E TN Mil
ADKINS, David, Pvt, Col Thomas Williamson, Capt Richard Tate, Vol Mtd Gunmen; d 1-17-1815
ADKINS, Elijah, Mus, Col Edwin Booth, Capt Richard Marshall, Drafted Mil
ADKINS, Ephraim, Pvt, Col Alexander Loury, Capt James Kincaid, Inf
ADKINS, Gabriel, Pvt, Col Edwin Booth, Capt __ Vernon, E TN Mil
ADKINS, Jackson, Pvt, Col John Cocke, Capt John Weakley, Inf
ADKINS, Jacob, Pvt, Col Edwin Booth, Capt Vernon, E TN Mil
ADKINS, Jacob, Pvt, Col Wm Johnson, Capt Jas Tunnell, E TN Militia
ADKINS, Jas, Pvt, Regt Commander omitted, Capt Geo Smith, Spies
ADKINS, Joseph, Pvt, Col John Coffee, Capt Blackman Coleman, Inf
ADKINS, Levi, Cpl, Col Edwin Booth, Capt Richard Marshall, Drafted Mil
ADKINS, Owen, Pvt, Col William Hall, Capt John Kennedy, Vol Inf
ADKINS, Read, Sgt, Col William Y Higgins, Capt Samuel A Allen, Mtd Gunmen
ADKINS, Sherod, Pvt, Col S Bunch, Capt John English, E TN Drafted Mil
ADKINS, Thomas, Pvt, Col John Coffee, Capt Blackman Coleman, Cav
ADKINS, William, Pvt, Col William Johnson, Capt Elihu Millikin, 3rd Regt E TN Mil
ADKINS, Zedekiah, Sgt, Regt Commander omitted, Capt James Gray, Inf
ADKINSON, Arthur, Pvt, Col Newton Cannon, Capt Andrew Patterson, Mtd Riflemen
ADKINSON, Ephraim, Pvt, Col William Lillard, Capt William Gillenwater, E TN Vol Inf
ADKINSON, Jordan, Pvt, Col James Raulston, Capt Henry Hamilton, Inf
ADKINSON, Joseph, Pvt, Col Ewen Allison, Capt Jonas Loughmiller, Mil
ADKINSON, William, Pvt, Col S Copeland, Capt G W STell, Mil Inf

## Enlisted Men, War of 1812

ADWELL, John, Pvt, Col Wm Lillard, Capt Hugh Martin, E TN Vol Inf

ADYELETTE, Arthur, Cpl, Commanders omitted, Branch Srvce omitted

AEBURTHROTT, Jno, Pvt, Regt Commander omitted, Capt Jas Haggard, Mtd Gunmen

AERAS, Uriah R, Pvt, Col Thos Williamson, Capt Robert Moore, Vol Mtd Gunmen

AFFIL, Jesse, Pvt, Col Wm Lillard, Capt Benj King, E TN Vol Inf

AGE, Moses, Pvt, Col Philip Pipkin, Capt John Strother, Mil; deserted 9-20-1814 & 12-21-1814

AGEE, Ambrose, Cpl, Col Jno Brown, Capt Wm Christian, E TN Mil Inf

AGEE, Edmund, Pvt, Col Samuel Wear, Capt Robert Doak, E TN Vol Inf

AGEE, Jas, Pvt, Col R C Napier, Capt Ed Neblett, Mil Inf

AGEE, Jas, Pvt, Col Samuel Wear, Capt Robert Doak, E TN Vol Inf

AIKEN, Benj, Pvt, Col S Bunch, Capt John Williams, Mtd Vol

AIKEN, John, Sgt, Col S Bunch, Capt Jos Duncan, E TN Drafted Mil

AIKEN, Saml, Pvt, Regt Commander omitted, Capt Wm Henderson, Spies

AIKINS, William, Pvt, Col Robert Steele, Capt Robert Campbell, Mil Inf

AINSWORTH, Josiah, Pvt, Col John Cocke, Capt John Weakley, Inf

AKARD, John, Pvt, Col Edwin Booth, Capt John Slatton, E TN Mil

AKENS, Samuel, Pvt, Col Samuel Wear & Col Samuel Bunch, Capt William Mitchell, E TN Mtd Inf

AKER?, Jos, Pvt, Col N Cannon, Capt Beverly Williams, Mtd Riflemen

AKERD, Adam, Pvt, Col Ewen Allison, Capt William King, Drafted Mil

AKIN, Abraham, Pvt, Maj Gen Andrew Jackson, Capt Ebenezer Kirkpatrick, Mtd Gunmen

AKIN, John, Pvt, Col Thomas Williamson, Capt John Doak & Capt John Dobbins, Vol Mtd Gunmen

AKINS, George, Pvt, Col William Metcalf, Capt Alexander Hill & Capt John Cunningham, Mil Inf

AKINS, Jesse, Pvt, Col Edwin Booth, Co Commander omitted, Drafted Mil

AKINS, John, Pvt, Col Thomas McCrory, Capt Samuel McKnight, Inf

AKINS, Joseph, Pvt, Commanders omitted, Brnch Srvce omitted

AKINS, Thomas, Pvt, Col William Higgins, Capt Samuel Allen, Mtd Gunmen

AKINS, William, Pvt, Col Thomas Williamson, Capt Richard Tate, Vol Mtd Gunmen

AKUFF, Jesse B, Pvt, Col William Lillard, Capt Thomas Sharpe, 2nd Regt Inf

ALBERSON, Solomon, Dmr, Col William Metcalf, Capt John Cunningham & Capt Alexander Hill, Mil Inf; promoted to Drm Maj

ALBERTSON, William, 4 Sgt, Col William Hall, Capt John Moore, Branch Srvce omitted

ALBION, John, Pvt, Col N Cannon, Capt Martin (Marlin?), Mtd Gunmen

ALBRIGHT, Lewis, Pvt, Col Philip Pipkin, Capt James Blakemore, Mil Inf

ALBUTT, James, Pvt, Col William Hall, Capt John Moore, Vol Inf

ALDEN, Barnabas, Pvt, Col Samuel Wear, Capt Robert Doak, E TN Vol Inf

ALDENS, Thomas, Waiter, Maj William Russell, Capt William Chism, Branch Srvce omitted

ALDERSON, Curtis, Pvt, Regt Commander omitted, Capt Thomas Gray, Inf

ALDERSON, John D, Pvt, Col Robert Steele, Capt Robert Campbell, Mil Inf

ALDERSON, John, Pvt, Col S Copeland, Capt Moses Thompson, Inf

ALDRIDGE, Enoch, Pvt, Col S Bunch, Capt Daniel Yarnell, E TN Mil

ALDRIDGE, Enoche, Pvt, Col S Bunch, Capt Daniel Yarnell, E TN Mil

ALDRIDGE, James, Sgt, Col William Johnson, Capt James Stewart, 3rd Regt E TN Mil

ALDRIDGE, John, Pvt, Brig Gen Thomas Johnson, Capt Robert Carson, Inf

ALDRIDGE, John, Pvt, Col Edward Bradley, Capt Travis Nash, Vol Inf

ALDRIDGE, John, Pvt, Col William Hall, Capt Travis Nash, Inf

ALDRIDGE, Nathaniel, Pvt, Col John Cocke, Capt James Gault, Inf

ALEXANDER, Aaron, Cpl, Col Thomas Benton, Capt William Moore, Vol Inf

ALEXANDER, Aaron, Pvt, Col Robert H Dyer, Capt Wyatt, Vol Mtd Gunmen

ALEXANDER, Adam, Pvt, Col Thos McCrory, Capt William Dooley, Inf

ALEXANDER, Alec P, Pvt, Regt Commander omitted, Capt David Smith, Cav

ALEXANDER, Alexander B, Pvt, Col Thos McCrory, Capt Samuel B ____, Inf

ALEXANDER, Alexander P, Pvt, Regt Commander omitted, Capt David Smith, Cav Vol

ALEXANDER, Andrew M, Pvt, Col Thomas Williamson, Capt Robert Moore, Vol Mtd Gunmen

ALEXANDER, Andrew, Pvt, Gen Jno Coffee, Co Commander omitted, Mtd Spies; d 12-23-1814

ALEXANDER, Aquilla, 2 Cpl, Lt Col Leroy Hammonds, Capt Jas Tubb, Inf

ALEXANDER, Dan'l, Pvt, Maj William Woodfolk, Capt Ezekial Ross & Capt ____ McCulley, Inf

ALEXANDER, David, Pvt, Col Samuel Wear, Capt John Chiles, E TN Inf

ALEXANDER, Delaney U, 1 Sgt, Col Samuel Bunch, Capt ____ Moses, E TN Drafted Inf

ALEXANDER, Edwin, Cpl, Col John Alcorn, Capt John Baskerville, Vol Inf

ALEXANDER, Ezekiel, Pvt, Col Jas Raulston, Capt Jas A Black, Inf

ALEXANDER, Horatio G, 4 Cpl, Col Jas Raulston, Capt Jas A Black, Inf

ALEXANDER, James, Pvt, Col S Copeland, Capt Allen Wilkinson, Mil Inf

## Enlisted Men, War of 1812

ALEXANDER, James, Pvt, Lt Col Archer Cheatham, Capt Gabriel Martin, 6th Brig Mtd Inf

ALEXANDER, Jas W, 1 Sgt, Col Edward Bradley, Capt Abraham Bledsoe, Riflemen

ALEXANDER, Jas W, Pvt, Col William Hall, Capt Abraham Bledsoe, Vol Inf

ALEXANDER, Jas W, Pvt, Col Wm Hall, Capt Abraham Bledsoe, Vol Inf

ALEXANDER, Jas, Cpl, Col Edward Bradley, Capt Travis Nash, Vol Inf

ALEXANDER, Far, Col Newton Cannon, Capt Andrew Patterson, Mtd Riflemen

ALEXANDER, Jas, Ffr, Col William Hall, Co Commander omitted, Vol Inf

ALEXANDER, Jas, Pvt, Col Alexander Loury, Capt John Looney, 2 Regt W TN Mil

ALEXANDER, Jas, Pvt, Col N Cannon, Capt John B Dempsey, Mtd Gunmen

ALEXANDER, Jas, Pvt, Col Wm Johnson, Capt Jas Tunnell, E TN Mil

ALEXANDER, Jas, Sgt Maj, Col Philip Pipkin, Co Commander omitted, 1st Regt TN Mil

ALEXANDER, Jas, Sgt, Col Philip Pipkin, Capt Ebenezer Kirkpatrick, Mil Inf

ALEXANDER, John W, Pvt, Col N Cannon, Capt Ota Cantrell, W TN Mtd Inf

ALEXANDER, John, Pvt, Col Ewin Allison, Capt Henry McCray, E TN Mil

ALEXANDER, John, Pvt, Col Wm Johnson, Capt Jas Tunnell, E TN Mil

ALEXANDER, Jos, Pvt, Col Alexander Loury, Capt James Kincaid, Inf

ALEXANDER, Joseph, Pvt, Capt Nathan Dane, Lt Isaac Barrett, Inf

ALEXANDER, Joseph, Pvt, Gen Andrew Jackson, Capt Nathan Davis, Branch Srvce omitted

ALEXANDER, Josiah, 2 Cpl, Col Philip Pipkin, Capt Henry M Newlin, Mil Inf

ALEXANDER, Josiah, Pvt, Gen Andrew Jackson, Capt Nathan Davis, Inf

ALEXANDER, Lawson, Pvt, Col Jno Brown, Capt Allen I Bacon, E TN Mil Inf

ALEXANDER, Milton K, Sgt, Col R H Dyer, Capt James Wyatt, Vol Mtd Gunmen

ALEXANDER, Moses, Pvt, Col John K Wynne, Capt Wm Carruthers, Branch Srvce omitted; deserted 11-19-1813

ALEXANDER, Moses, Pvt, Col N Cannon, Capt Jas Walton, Mtd Riflemen

ALEXANDER, Moses, Pvt, Lt Col Leroy Hammons, Capt Thomas Delaney, Inf

ALEXANDER, Nathaniel, 4 Cpl, Col William Hall, Capt Henry M Newlin, Inf

ALEXANDER, Nathaniel, Sgt, Col Edward Bradley, Capt Elijah Haynie, Vol Inf

ALEXANDER, Peter, Pvt, Maj Gen Andrew Jackson, Capt William Carroll, Vol Inf

ALEXANDER, Richard, Pvt, Col William Hall, Capt Brice Martin, Vol Inf

ALEXANDER, Samuel, Pvt, Col John K Wynne, Capt James Cole, Inf

ALEXANDER, Silas, Pvt, Col Thomas McCrory, Capt William Dooley, Inf

ALEXANDER, Squire, Pvt, Brig Gen Thomas Johnson, Capt Robert Carson, Inf

ALEXANDER, Stephen, Sgt, Col Ewen Allison, Capt Jacob Hoyal, E TN Mil

ALEXANDER, Thomas H, Pvt, Col James Raulston, Capt James Black, Inf

ALEXANDER, Thomas, Cpl, Col Edward Bradley, Capt Travis Nash, Vol Inf

ALEXANDER, Thomas, Pvt, Col William Hall, Capt Travis C Nash, Inf

ALEXANDER, William, Pvt, Capt Nathan Davis, Lt Isaac Barrett, Inf

ALEXANDER, William, Pvt, Col John Brown, Capt Childs, E TN Vol Mtd Gunmen

ALEXANDER, William, Pvt, Regt Commander omitted, Capt Archibald McKenney, Cav

ALEXANDER, Zebulon, Pvt, Col Philip Pipkin, Capt John Robertson, Mil Inf

ALEXIS, Alexander, Dmr, Col James Raulston, Capt James Black, Inf

ALFIN, John, Pvt, Col Philip Pipkin, Capt John Strother, Mil Inf; deserted 9-20-1814 returned & left 12-21-1814

ALFORD, Burtus, Pvt, Col A Cheatham, Capt Charles Johnson, Inf

ALFORD, David, Pvt, Maj William Russell, Capt Felman Hodges, Vol Mtd Gunmen

ALFORD, John, Pvt, Col Thomas Benton, Capt William J Smith, Vol Inf

ALFORD, John, Pvt, Col Thomas Benton, Capt William Smith, Inf

ALFORD, John, Sgt, Col Beverly Williams, Capt Richard Tate, Vol Mtd Gunmen

ALFORD, Lee, Pvt, Col Newton Cannon, Capt Ota Cantrell, W TN Mtd Inf

ALFORD, Nelson, Pvt, Brig Gen Thos Washington, Capt Jno Crawford, Branch Srvce omitted

ALFORD, Nelson, Pvt, Col Thomas Benton, Capt Thos Williamson, Vol Inf

ALFORD, Nelson, Pvt, Maj William Carroll, Capt Lewis Dillahunty & Capt Daniel M Bradford, Vol Inf

ALFORD, Wm, Sgt, Col Samuel Wear & Col Samuel Bunch, Capt William Mitchell, E TN Mtd Inf

ALFRED, John, Pvt, Col Wm Pillow, Capt Thos Williamson, Vol Inf

ALFRED, Nelson, Pvt, Col N T Perkins, Capt Philip Pipkin, Mtd Riflemen

ALFRED, Nelson, Pvt, Col Thos H Benton, Capt Thos Williamson, Vol Inf

ALFRED, Washington, Pvt, Col Robert Steele, Capt John Chitwood, Mil Inf

ALIVER, Shadrick, Pvt, Col William Hall, Capt John Wallace, Inf

ALLBRIGHT, Adam, Pvt, Col Jno Brown, Capt Hugh Barton, E TN Mil Inf

ALLDRIDGE, Hiram, Pvt, Maj John Childs, Capt Chas Conway, E TN Mtd Gunmen; Regt County Knox

ALLDRIDGE, John, Pvt, Col Jno Brown, Capt Hugh Barton, Regt E TN Mil Inf

ALLEN, Abraham, 1 Cpl, Col William Lillard, Co Commander omitted, E TN Vol Inf
ALLEN, Abraham, Pvt, Commanders omitted, Branch Srvce omitted
ALLEN, Abraham, Pvt, Lt Col Henry Bryan, Co Commander omitted, Inf
ALLEN, Archibald P, Pvt, Col James Raulston, Capt Charles Wade, Inf
ALLEN, Benjamin, Pvt, Col William Metcalf, Capt Bird Hurt, Mil Inf
ALLEN, Bethel, Pvt, Col N Cannon, Capt James Walton, Mtd Riflemen
ALLEN, Charles, Pvt, Col William Metcalf, Capt Bird Hurt, Mil Inf
ALLEN, Charles, Sgt, Col Thomas Benton, Capt Benjamin Reynolds, Vol Inf
ALLEN, Daniel, Mus, Col Nicholas Perkins, Capt George Eliot, Mil Inf
ALLEN, David, Pvt, Col S Copeland, Capt Richard Sharp, Mil Inf
ALLEN, David, Pvt, Col William Metcalf, Capt John Barnhart, Mil Inf
ALLEN, David, Sgt, Col John Winn, Capt William McCall, Inf
ALLEN, Eli, Pvt, Col John Coffee, Capt James Terrell, Vol Cav; out of state
ALLEN, Felix, Pvt, Maj Gen Carroll, Capt Francis Ellis, Inf
ALLEN, Gabriel, Pvt, Col Philip Pipkin, Capt John Strother, Mil; deserted 9-20-1814 returned 10-11-1814
ALLEN, Gabriell, Pvt, Col William Woodfolk, Capt Abner Pearce, Inf; promoted to Sgt
ALLEN, Geo A, Sgt, Col N Cannon, Capt ____ Martin, Mtd Gunmen
ALLEN, Geo, Pvt, Maj William Woodfolk, Capt Ezekial Rose & Capt ____ McCulley, Inf
ALLEN, Geo, Sgt, Col Samuel Bayless, Capt Branch Jones, E TN Mil
ALLEN, Hyram M, Pvt, Col T McCrory, Capt Abel Willis, Mil Inf
ALLEN, Isaac, Pvt, Col Jas Rawlston, Capt Mathew Cowan, Inf
ALLEN, Isaac, Pvt, Col Jno Brown, Capt Wm D Neilson, Regt of E TN Vol Mil; d 12-24-1814
ALLEN, Jacob, Pvt, Col Robert H Dyer, Capt Joseph Williams, Vol Mtd Gunmen
ALLEN, Jacob, Pvt, Col S Copeland, Capt Moses Thompson, Inf
ALLEN, James, Pvt, Brig Gen Roberts, Capt Benj Reynolds, Branch Srvce omitted
ALLEN, James, Pvt, Col Jno Brown, Capt Allen I Bacon, E TN Mil Inf
ALLEN, James, Pvt, Col John Brown, Capt William White, Regt E TN Mil Inf; discharged on account of inability
ALLEN, James, Pvt, Commanders omitted, Branch Srvce omitted
ALLEN, Jas, 1 Lt, Col Thos Benton, Capt Benjamin Reynolds, Vol Inf
ALLEN, Jas, Pvt, Col Edwin E Booth, Capt John McKamey, E TN Mil
ALLEN, Jas, Pvt, Col Jas Raulston, Capt Chas Wade, Inf; d 1-6-1815
ALLEN, Jas, Pvt, Col S Bunch, Capt James Griffin, E TN Drafted Mil; deserted 3-4-1814
ALLEN, Jas, Pvt, Col Samuel Wear, Capt Rufus Morgan, E TN Vol Inf
ALLEN, Jas, Pvt, Col Thomas McCrory, Capt William Dooley, Inf
ALLEN, Jno, 1 Lt, Gen Andrew Jackson, Capt Joel Parrish, Arty
ALLEN, Jno, 2 Lt, Gen Andrew Jackson, Capt Deaderick
ALLEN, Jno, Pvt, Regt Commander omitted, Capt Edwin S Moore, Mtd Riflemen
ALLEN, Job, Pvt, Col Samuel Wear, Capt Jas Tedford
ALLEN, John, 2 Lt, Gen Andrew Jackson, Capt Deadrick, Branch Srvce omitted
ALLEN, John, Cpl, Col Edwin Booth, Capt John McKamey, E TN Mil
ALLEN, John, Pvt, Col John Brown, Capt Jesse G Reany, Mtd Gunmen
ALLEN, John, Pvt, Col John Raulston, Capt Charles Wade, Inf; d 3-14-1815
ALLEN, John, Pvt, Col S Copeland, Capt Moses Thompson, Inf
ALLEN, John, Pvt, Col William Metcalf, Capt William Mullen, Mil Inf
ALLEN, John, Pvt, Col Wm Metcalf, Capt William Mullen, Mil Inf
ALLEN, John, Pvt, Maj Gen A Jackson, Capt Carroll, Vol Inf
ALLEN, John, Pvt, Maj Gen Andrew Jackson, Capt William Carroll, Vol Inf
ALLEN, John, Pvt, Maj William Russell, Capt John Cowan, Vol Mtd Gunmen
ALLEN, John, Pvt, Regt Commander omitted, Lt John Scott, Det of Inf
ALLEN, Joseph, Pvt, Col R C Napier, Capt Thomas Gray, Mil Inf
ALLEN, Joseph, Pvt, Col Thomas Williamson, Capt Richard Tate, Vol Mtd Gunmen
ALLEN, Joseph, Pvt, Col William Hall, Capt Travis Nash, Inf
ALLEN, Joshua, Pvt, Col James Raulston, Capt Daniel Newman, Inf
ALLEN, Levi, Pvt, Col Edward Bradley, Capt John Wallace, Vol Inf
ALLEN, Levi, Pvt, Col James Raulston, Capt Daniel Newman, Inf
ALLEN, Levi, Pvt, Col William Hall, Capt John Wallace, Inf
ALLEN, Lewis, Cpl, Col T McCroy, Capt Isaac Patton, Inf
ALLEN, Lewis, Pvt, Gen Andrew Jackson, Capt David Deaderick, Arty
ALLEN, Mark, Pvt, Col Ewin Allison, Capt Joseph Everett, E TN Mil; deserted 3-4-1814
ALLEN, Mark, Pvt, Col S Bunch, Capt Jones Griffin, E TN Drafted Mil; furloughed 6-1-1815 on account of inability
ALLEN, Matthew H, Pvt, Col James Raulston, Capt Henry Hamilton, Inf

## Enlisted Men, War of 1812

ALLEN, Moses, Pvt, Col William Hall, Capt Henry Newlin, Inf

ALLEN, Nathaniel H, 3 Sgt, Col N T Perkins, Capt George Marr, Mtd Vol

ALLEN, Neuben, Pvt, Col S Bayless, Capt Joseph Hale, E TN Mil

ALLEN, Ralph, Pvt, Col A Cheatham, Co Commander omitted, Inf

ALLEN, Ralph, Pvt, Col Ewin Allison, Capt Thomas McCrory, E TN Mil

ALLEN, Ralph, Pvt, Col S Bunch, Capt F Register, E TN Mil

ALLEN, Ralph, Pvt, Col S Bunch, Capt Francis Register, E TN Mil

ALLEN, Reuben B, Pvt, Col William Johnson, Capt Joseph Scott, E TN Drafted Mil

ALLEN, Richard, Pvt, Maj Gen Carroll & Col William Metcalf, Capt John Jackson, Inf

ALLEN, Robert, Pvt, Col Thomas Williamson, Capt Anthony Metcalf, Vol Mtd Gunmen

ALLEN, Robert, Pvt, Col Thomas Williamson, Capt Richard Tate, Vol Mtd Gunmen

ALLEN, Sampson, Pvt, Col William Higgins, Capt Adam Dale, Mtd Gunmen; wounded 1-22-1814 & absent

ALLEN, Samuel H, Sgt, Col Jas Raulston, Capt Elijah Haynie, Inf

ALLEN, Samuel, Capt, Gen Andrew Jackson, Co Commander omitted, Pack Horse Guards

ALLEN, Samuel, Pvt, Col Edwin Booth, Capt Richard Marshall, Drafted Mil

ALLEN, Samuel, Pvt, Col Ewin Allison, Capt Joseph Everett, E TN Mil

ALLEN, Samuel, Pvt, Col N T Perkins, Capt John Quarles, Vol Mtd Inf

ALLEN, Samuel, Pvt, Col S Bunch, Capt Jones Griffin, E TN Drafted Mil; left sick at Ft Strother 7-13-1814

ALLEN, Starling, Pvt, Col John Cocke, Capt Joseph Price, Inf; d 2-11-1815

ALLEN, Stephen, Pvt, Col Thos Benton, Capt George W Gibbs, Vol Inf

ALLEN, Stephen, Pvt, Col Thos H Benton, Capt George W Gibbs, Inf Vol

ALLEN, Stephen, Pvt, Col Wm Pillow, Capt John H Anderson, Vol Inf

ALLEN, Sutton F, 2 Mate, Col Philip Pipkin, Co Commander omitted, 1st Regt TN Mil; sick absent at Fort Strother

ALLEN, Sutton F, Surg Mate, Col Wm Pillow, Co Commander omitted, 2nd Regt TN Vol Inf

ALLEN, Terrel, Pvt, Col Philip Pipkin, Capt Jas Blakemore, Mil Inf

ALLEN, Thos, Pvt, Col R C Napier, Capt John Chism, Mil Inf

ALLEN, Valentine, Pvt, Col John K Wynne, Capt Wm Carothers, W TN Inf

ALLEN, William, 2 Cpl, Gen Andrew Jackson, Capt David S Deadrick, Arty?

ALLEN, William, Pvt, Col Alexander Loury, Capt James Kincaid, Inf; sick at Fayetteville 9-25-1814

ALLEN, William, Pvt, Col Thos McCrory, Capt Isaac Patton, Inf

ALLEN, William, Pvt, Col Thos McCrory, Capt Jno Reynolds, Mil Inf

ALLEN, William, Pvt, Maj Robert Cooper, Co Commander omitted, Mtd Riflemen

ALLEN, Wm jr, Pvt, Maj William Woodfolk, Capt Abner Pearce, Inf

ALLEN, Wm sr, Pvt, Maj Wm Woodfolk, Capt Abner Pearce, Inf

ALLEN, Wm, 2 Sgt, Col Edward Bradley, Capt Abraham Bledsoe, Riflemen; wounded at Talledega & furloughed 11-9-1813

ALLEN, Wm, 3 Cpl, Col Jas Raulston, Capt Chas Wade, Inf; promoted to 2 Sgt

ALLEN, Wm, Pvt, Col Ewen Allison, Capt William King, Drafted Mil

ALLEN, Wm, Pvt, Col Philip Pipkin, Capt Jas Blakemore, Mil Inf; deserted 9-20-1814

ALLEN, Wm, Pvt, Col R H Dyer, Capt Beverly Williams, Vol Mtd Gunmen

ALLEN, Wm, Pvt, Col Samuel Wear, Capt Rufus Morgan, E TN Vol Inf

ALLEN, Wm, Pvt, Col Thos Benton, Capt Benj Reynolds, Vol Inf

ALLEN, Wm, Pvt, Col Wm Hall, Capt Abraham Bledsoe, Vol Inf

ALLEN, Wm, Pvt, Col Wm Hall, Capt Abraham Bledsoe, Vol Inf; promoted

ALLEN, Wm, Pvt, Col Wm Metcalf, Capt William Mullin, Mil Inf

ALLEN, Wm, Pvt, Maj Gen A Jackson, Capt William Carroll, Vol Inf; missing

ALLEN, Wm, Pvt, Maj John Chiles, Capt Jas Cummings, E TN Vol Inf

ALLEN, Wm, Sgt, Brig Gen Roberts, Capt Benj Reynolds, Mtd Rangers

ALLEN, Wm, Sgt, Col Wm Y Higgins, Capt William Doake, Mtd Riflemen

ALLEN, Wm, Sgt, Commanders omitted, Branch Srvce omitted

ALLEN, Zachariah, Pvt, Col Wm Metcalf, Capt Bird L Hurt, Mil Inf

ALLEWAY, Archilans, Sgt, Col Thos Williamson, Capt Anthony M Metcalf, Vol Mtd Gunmen

ALLEY, Henry, Pvt, Col S Bunch, Capt George Gregory, E TN Drafted Mil

ALLEY, Hoebert, Pvt, Col A Cheatham, Capt Richard Benson, Inf; sick absent

ALLEY, Nicholas, 4 Cpl, Col Wm Metcalf, Capt Alexander Hill & Capt John Cunningham, Mil Inf

ALLEY, Nicholas, Pvt, Col S Copeland, Capt Jas Tait, Inf

ALLEY, Wm, Pvt, Col Jas Raulston, Capt Matthew Neal, Inf

ALLIMONEY, John, Pvt, Col Ewen Allison, Capt William King, Drafted Mil

ALLING, John, Pvt, Col Newton Cannon, Capt Thos Williamson, Mtd Riflemen

ALLISON, David, Pvt, Col Wm Lillard, Capt Robert Maloney, E TN Vol Inf

ALLISON, Ewen, Pvt, Col Samuel Bunch, Capt James Penny, E TN Mtd Inf

## Enlisted Men, War of 1812

ALLISON, Holbert, Pvt, Col Wm Metcalf, Capt Thomas Marks, Mil Inf

ALLISON, Jas, Pvt, Maj Gen Carroll & Col Jas Raulston, Capt Edward Robinson, Inf

ALLISON, Jesse, Pvt, Col Wm Johnson, Capt Benj Powell, E TN Mil

ALLISON, John, Pvt, Col Edwin Allison, Capt McCrory, E TN Mil

ALLISON, Thos, Ffr, Col Leroy Hammond, Capt Jas Tubb, Inf

ALLISON, Vernon, Pvt, Capt James Gray, Inf

ALLMAN, Geo, Pvt, Col R H Dyer, Capt Bethel Allen, Mtd Gunmen

ALLMAN, Jacob, Pvt, Col R H Dyer, Capt Bethel Allen, Vol Mtd Gunmen

ALLMAN, Jeremiah, Pvt, Col William Hall, Capt John Kennedy, Vol Inf

ALLON, Benj, Pvt, Col Alex Lowry & Leroy Hammonds, Capt Arahel Rains, Inf

ALLOWAY, Archelus, Sgt, Col Thos McCrory, Capt Anthony Metcalf, Inf

ALLOWAY, Archiball, Pvt, Col Thos McCrory, Capt Anthony Metcalf, Mil Inf; promoted to Sgt

ALLRED, John, Pvt, Col Robt Steele, Capt John Chitwood, Mil Inf

ALLRED, Reuben, Pvt, Col Alex Loury, Capt James Kincaid, Inf; sick at Fayetteville 9-25-1814

ALLRED, Wm, Pvt, Col John K Wynne, Capt Wm Carruthers, W TN Inf

ALLSTON, James, Pvt, Col Lt Wm Phillips, Co Commander omitted, Inf

ALLSUP, David, Pvt, Regt Commander omitted, Capt Josiah Askew, Inf

ALLSUP, Harry, Pvt, Col Samuel Bunch, Capt Thos Mann, E Tn Vol Mil Inf

ALLSUP, John, Pvt, Capt Josiah Askew, Inf

ALLSUP, Samuel, Pvt, Col R C Napier, Capt Thos Gray, Mil Inf

ALMAN, Jacob, Pvt, Col N Cannon, Capt Jas Walton, Mtd Riflemen

ALMOND, Jermiah, Pvt, Col William Hall, Capt John Kennedy, Vol Inf

ALMOND, Thos, Pvt, Col John Cock, Capt James Gray, Inf

ALREAD, Samuel, Pvt, Col Alex Loury, Capt John Kincaid, Inf; sick at Fayetteville 9-25-1814

ALRID, Samuel, Pvt, Brig Gen Thos Johnson, Capt Robt Carson, Branch Srvce omitted

ALSIP, David, Pvt, Col Leroy Hammonds, Capt Jas Craig, Inf; d 2-17-1815

ALSOP, Asaph, Pvt, Maj William Woodfolk, Capt Zekial Ross & Capt McCalley, Branch Srvce omitted

ALSOP, David, Pvt, Col Leroy Hammonds, Capt Jas Craig, 2nd Regt W TN Mil, d 2-15-1815

ALSOP, John, Pvt, Col Philip Pipkin, Capt Peter Searcy, Mil Inf; deserted 9-20-1814 & 12-21-1814

ALSOP, Thos, Pvt, Col Robert Steele, Capt Thomas Williamson, Vol Mtd Gunmen

ALSTADT, Nichols, Pvt, Col John Brown, Capt John Chiles, E TN Vol Mtd Gunmen; d 3-2-1814 at Ft Williams

ALSTON, Jno W, Pvt, Col No? Williams, Capt Wm Walker, Vol

ALSUP, Drury, Pvt, Col Thos McCrory, Capt Thos K Gordon, Inf

ALSUP, John, Cpl, Col S Copeland, Capt Moses Thompson, Inf

ALSUP, William, Pvt, Regt Commander omitted, Capt Askew, Inf

ALT, Jacob, Pvt, Gen Andrew Jackson, Capt Nathan Davis, Inf

ALTHERSON, John, Pvt, Maj William Russell, Capt John Cowan, Vol Mtd Riflemen

ALTON, Jas, Pvt, Col S Bunch, Capt Jones Griffin, E TN Drafted Mil

ALTON, Wm, Pvt, Col S Bunch, Capt Jones Grffin, E TN Drafted Mil

ALTUM, James, Pvt, Col Philip Pipkin, Capt James Blakemore, Mil Inf

ALTUM, Robert, Pvt, Col William Johnson, Capt Benjamin Powell, E TN Mil; sick at Ft Jackson 11-11-1814 left 5-3-1815

ALTUM, Robert, Pvt, Col William Pillow, Capt John Anderson, Vol Inf

ALTUM, Spencer, Pvt, Col S Bunch, Capt Andrew Breden, E TN Mil

ALVATT, George, Pvt, Lt Col Leroy Hammons, Capt Thomas Delaney, Inf

ALVICE, Shadrick, Pvt, Col Thomas Williamson, Capt Thomas Scurry, Mtd Gunmen

ALVIS, Abraham, Pvt, Col Thomas McCrory, Capt Anthony Metcalf, Inf

ALVIS, Abraham, Pvt, Col Thomas Williamson, Capt Anthony Metcalf, Vol Mtd Gunmen

ALVIS, Ashley, 4 Cpl, Col Edward Bradley, Capt Brice Martin, Vol Inf

ALVIS, Ashley, Pvt, Col William Hall, Capt Brice Martin, Vol Inf

ALVIS, Ashley, Sgt, Col Thomas Williamson, Capt Anthony Metcalf, Vol Mtd Gunmen

ALVIS, David, Pvt, Col John Brown, Capt William White, E TN Vol Mtd Inf

ALVIS, Moses, Pvt, Col John Robertson, Capt Philip Pipkin, Mil Inf

ALVIS, Shadrick, Pvt, Col John Alcorn, Capt John Byrn, Cav

ALVISON, John, Pvt, Col Samuel Bayless, Capt John Brock, E TN Mil

ALY, King, Pvt, Col S Bunch, Capt George Gregory, E TN Drafted Mil

AMBRESTER, Mickael (Michael?), Pvt, Col S Bunch, Capt Isaac Williams, E TN Mil

AMBROUSE, John, Private Servant, Maj William Russell, Co Commander omitted, TN Vol Mtd Gunmen; servant to Lt Lewis

AMES, Hardin, Pvt, Col Thomas Williamson, Capt Beverly Williams; sick absent

AMES, Willis, Pvt, Col S Bunch, Capt Jones Griffin, Branch Srvce omitted

AMINETTE, Israel, Pvt, Col Edwin Booth, Capt John Porter, Drafted Mil

AMMON, William B, Cpl, Col John Alcorn, Capt Freder-

## Enlisted Men, War of 1812

ick Stump, Cav
AMMONS, Henry, Pvt, Col Thomas Williamson, Capt Thomas Proter?, Vol Mtd Gunmen
AMMONS, Thomas, Pvt, Regt Commander omitted, Capt Garrett Lane, Mtd Riflemen
AMONDS, William B, Pvt, Regt Commander omitted, Capt John Gordon, Mtd Spies Co
AMONTH, Reuben, Sgt, Col Philip Pipkin, Capt David Smith, Mil Inf; d 9-24-1814
AMY, Willie, Pvt, Col S Bunch, Capt S Boerson, E TN Drafted Mil; discharged for inability
AMY, Willie, Pvt, Regt Commander omitted, Capt Samuel Richardson, E TN Drafted Mil; discharged for inability
ANALT, Jacob, Pvt, Col Thomas Benton, Capt William Moore, Vol Inf
ANALT, John, Pvt, Col Thomas Benton, Capt William Moore, Vol Inf
ANDERS, David, Pvt, Col Thomas McCrory, Capt Samuel McKnight, Inf
ANDERS, Henry, Pvt, Col N Cannon, Capt Gabriel Martin, Mtd Gunmen
ANDERS, James, Pvt, Col N Cannon, Capt Gabriel Martin, Mtd Gunmen
ANDERS, John, Pvt, Col Robert Steele, Capt John Chitwood, Mil Inf
ANDERS, William, Pvt, Col N Cannon, Capt Gabriel Martin, Mtd Gunmen
ANDERSON, Abraham, Pvt, Col John Cocke, Capt James Gault, Inf; d 3-10-1815
ANDERSON, Alexander O, Pvt, Col S Bunch, Capt Henry Stephens, E TN Mtd Inf
ANDERSON, Andrew, Pvt, Col Ewen Allison, Capt William King, Drafted Mil
ANDERSON, Andrew, Pvt, Col S Bunch, Capt John English, E TN Drafted Mil
ANDERSON, Andrew, Pvt, Col S Bunch, Capt Moses, E TN Drafted Inf
ANDERSON, Barney, Pvt, Col Thomas McCrory, Capt Isaac Patton, Mil Inf
ANDERSON, Benjamin, Pvt, Col William Johnson, Capt David McKamey; sick absent
ANDERSON, Burrel, Col John Winn, Capt James Holleman, Inf
ANDERSON, Charles, Col William Johnson, Capt Benjamin Powell, E TN Mil
ANDERSON, Daniel, Pvt, Commanders omitted, Branch Srvce omitted
ANDERSON, Daniel, Pvt, Lt Col Archer Cheatham, Co Commander omitted, Mtd Inf
ANDERSON, David F, Pvt, Col John Winn, Capt William Wilson, Branch Srvce omitted
ANDERSON, David O, Pvt, Commanders omitted, Branch Srvce omitted
ANDERSON, David P, Pvt, Col T McCrory, Capt James Shannon, Mil Inf
ANDERSON, David, Pvt, Col S Bunch, Capt William Houston, E TN Vol Mtd Inf
ANDERSON, David, Pvt, Col William Lillard, Capt William Hamilton, E TN Vol Inf
ANDERSON, David, Pvt, Lt Col John Edmondson, Co Commander omitted, Cav
ANDERSON, David, Pvt, Maj Gen Andrew Jackson, Capt William Russell, Mtd Spies
ANDERSON, Elkaner, Pvt, Maj Gen William Carroll, Capt Francis Ellis, Inf
ANDERSON, George H, Pvt, Col William Johnson, Capt James Rogers, E TN Drafted Mil
ANDERSON, George, Pvt, Col James Raulston, Capt Elijah Haynie, Inf
ANDERSON, George, Pvt, Col William Metcalf, Capt John Barnhart, Mil Inf
ANDERSON, Isaac, Pvt, Capt Nathan Davis, Lt Isaac Barrett, Inf
ANDERSON, Isaac, Pvt, Col S Bunch, Co Commander Omitted, E TN Drafted Mil
ANDERSON, Isaac, Pvt, Lt Col Leroy Hammons & Col Alexander Lowry, Capt Thomas Wells, Inf; sick Ft Montgomery 12-16-1814
ANDERSON, James, Pvt, Col John Brown, Capt Jesse Reany, Mtd Gunmen
ANDERSON, James, Pvt, Col John Brown, Capt John Childs, E TN Vol Mtd Gunmen
ANDERSON, James, Pvt, Col N T Perkins, Capt Mathew Patterson, Mtd Vol
ANDERSON, James, Pvt, Col S Bunch, Capt Edward Buchanan, E TN Draft Mil
ANDERSON, James, Pvt, Col S Bunch, Capt Francis Berry, E TN Mil
ANDERSON, James, Pvt, Col S Copeland, Capt John Holshouser, Inf
ANDERSON, James, Pvt, Col Samuel Bayless, Capt Jones, E TN Drafted Mil
ANDERSON, James, Pvt, Col Samuel Wear, Capt Simeon Perry, E TN Vol Mtd Inf
ANDERSON, James, Pvt, Col William Johnson, Capt James Rogers, E TN Drafted Mil
ANDERSON, James, Pvt, Col William Johnson, Capt James Stewart, 3rd Regt E TN Mil
ANDERSON, James, Pvt, Col William Johnson, Capt James Stewart, E TN Drafted Mil
ANDERSON, James, Pvt, Col William Metcalf, Capt John Cunningham & Capt Alexander Hill, Mil Inf
ANDERSON, Jesse, Pvt, Col William Johnson, Capt James Stewart, 3rd Regt E TN Mil
ANDERSON, Jesse, Pvt, Col William Johnson, Capt James Stewart, E TN Drafted Mil
ANDERSON, John G, Drm, Col Philip Pipkin, Capt Henry Newlin, Mil Inf
ANDERSON, John J, Sgt, Maj William Woodfolk, Capt Abner Pearce, Inf
ANDERSON, John, 2 Sgt, Col Thomas Benton, Capt George Gibbs, Vol Inf
ANDERSON, John, Cpl, Maj William Woodfolk, Capt John Sutton & Capt Abraham Dudney, Inf; promoted to Sgt
ANDERSON, John, Pvt, Col A Loury, Capt Joseph Williamson, W TN Mil
ANDERSON, John, Pvt, Col John Brown, Capt John Childs, E TN Vol Mtd Gunmen
ANDERSON, John, Pvt, Col John Coffee, Capt Charles Kavanaugh, Cav; absent without leave

## Enlisted Men, War of 1812

ANDERSON, John, Pvt, Col L Hammonds, Capt Joseph Williamson, 2nd Regt Inf

ANDERSON, John, Pvt, Col Philip Pipkin, Capt George Mebane, Mil Inf; deserted 12-24-1814

ANDERSON, John, Pvt, Col R C Napier, Capt Thomas Gray, Mil Inf

ANDERSON, John, Pvt, Col Robert Steele, Capt Samuel Maxwell, Mil Inf

ANDERSON, John, Pvt, Col Thomas Williamson, Capt Anthony Metcalf, Vol Mtd Gunmen

ANDERSON, John, Pvt, Col William Johnson, Capt Andrew Lawson, E TN Drafted Mil

ANDERSON, John, Pvt, Lt Col Lery Hammons, Capt Joseph Williamson, Inf; left sick at Ft Montgomery

ANDERSON, John, Pvt, Maj Gen Andrew Jackson, Capt William Carroll, Vol Inf

ANDERSON, John, Pvt, Maj Gen Carroll, Capt Francis Ellis, Inf

ANDERSON, John, Pvt, Regt Commander omitted, Capt Thomas Gray, Inf

ANDERSON, Jonathan, Pvt, Col Edwin Booth, Capt John Lewis, E TN Mil

ANDERSON, Jonathan, Sgt, Col Thomas Williamson, Capt John Doak & Capt John Dobbins, Vol Mtd Gunmen

ANDERSON, Jordan, Pvt, Col Philip Pipkin, Capt Peter Searcy, Mil Inf

ANDERSON, Jorden, Pvt, Col Wm Metcalf, Capt Barbee Collins, Mil Inf

ANDERSON, Jos, Pvt, Col Samuel Bunch, Capt Isaac Williams, E TN Mil

ANDERSON, Joseph, Pvt, Col Edwin Booth, Capt Alexander Biggs, Inf

ANDERSON, Joseph, Pvt, Col S Bunch, Capt Isaac Williams, E TN Mil

ANDERSON, Joshua, Pvt, Col Philip Pipkin, Capt Geo Mebane, Mil Inf; deserted for Ft Jackson 9-20-1814

ANDERSON, Jubilee, Pvt, Col Jas Rawlston, Capt Mathew Cowan, Inf

ANDERSON, Levi, Pvt, Col Leroy Hammonds, Capt Jas Craig, 2nd Regt W TN Mil

ANDERSON, Levi, Pvt, Col Leroy Hammonds, Capt Jas Craig, Inf

ANDERSON, Maber, Cpl, Col James Raulston, Capt Mathew Neal, Inf; promoted to Sgt

ANDERSON, Mathew, Pvt, Maj Gen A Jackson & Col Thomas Williamson, Capt Robert Steele, Vol Mtd Gunmen

ANDERSON, Michael, Pvt, Col Samuel Bunch, Capt Dan'l Yarnell, E TN Mil

ANDERSON, Michael, Pvt, Col Samuel Bunch, Capt Joseph Duncan, E TN Drafted Mil

ANDERSON, Michael, Pvt, Col Wm Johnson, Capt Jas R Rogers, E TN Drafted Mil

ANDERSON, Pleasant, Pvt, Col Edward Bradley, Capt John Wallace, Vol Inf

ANDERSON, Pleasant, Pvt, Col Philip Pipkin, Capt Henry M Newlin, Mil Inf

ANDERSON, Pleasant, Pvt, Col Philip Pipkin, Capt Henry M Newlin, Mil Inf; substitute for Wm Abbott

ANDERSON, Pleasant, Pvt, Col Wm Hall, Capt John Wallace, Inf

ANDERSON, Presley, Pvt, Col Wm Pillow, Capt Geo Caperton, Inf

ANDERSON, Robt, Pvt, Col N T Perkins, Capt Mathew Patterson, Mtd Vol

ANDERSON, Robt, Pvt, Col Thomas Williamson, Capt Thomas Scurry, Vol Mtd Gunmen

ANDERSON, Robt, Pvt, Maj Gen Carroll, Col William Metcalf, Capt John Jackson, Inf

ANDERSON, Russell, Pvt, Col Wm. Johnson, Capt Jas. Stewart, E TN Draft Mil

ANDERSON, Samuel R., Pvt, Col Newton Cannon, Capt John Harpole, Mtd Gunmen

ANDERSON, Samuel, Pvt Col Edwin Booth, Capt Richard Marshall, Drafted Mil

ANDERSON, Samuel, Pvt, Col Samuel Wear, Capt John Chiles, E TN Vol Inf

ANDERSON, Samuel, Pvt, Col Wm. Hall, Capt Abraham Bledsoe, Vol Inf

ANDERSON, Samuel, Pvt, Maj Gen A. Jackson, Capt William Carroll, Vol Inf; on furlough or AWOL

ANDERSON, Samuel, Pvt, Maj William Russell, Capt John Cowan, Vol Mtd Gunmen

ANDERSON, Solomon, Pvt, Col John Coffee, Capt John W. Byrns, Cav

ANDERSON, Thomas, Pvt, Col John Brown, Capt James Preston, E TN Mil Inf

ANDERSON, Thomas, Pvt, Col Leroy Hammons, Capt Thomas Delaney, Inf

ANDERSON, Thomas, Pvt, Maj Gen A. Jackson, Gen William Carroll, Capt John Jackson, Inf

ANDERSON, Vincent, Sgt, Col William Lillard, Capt Robert Maloney, E TN Vol Inf

ANDERSON, Washington, Pvt, Col William Johnson, Capt James R. Rogers, E TN Draft Mil

ANDERSON, William E., Pvt, Maj James Porter, Cav, Sqdn of E TN Mil

ANDERSON, William P., Pvt, Maj William Woodfolk, Capt Abner Pearce, Inf

ANDERSON, William, Cpl, Col T. McCrory, Capt A. Metcalf, Mil Inf

ANDERSON, William, Pvt, Col John Alcorn, Capt Fredrick Stump, Cav

ANDERSON, William, Pvt, Col John Brown, Capt John Childs, E TN Vol Mtd Gunmen

ANDERSON, William, Pvt, Col John Coffee, Capt Fredrick Stump, Cav

ANDERSON, William, Pvt, Col Newton Cannon, Capt Thomas Yardley, Mtd Riflemen

ANDERSON, William, Pvt, Col Robert Steele, Capt James Randals, Inf; AWOL

ANDERSON, William, Pvt, Col S. Bunch, Capt S. Roberson, E TN Draft Mil

ANDERSON, William, Pvt, Col Thomas Williamson, Capt Robert Moore, Vol Mtd Gunmen

ANDERSON, William, Pvt, Col William Pillow, Capt John H Anderson, Vol Inf; Substitute for William Burden

ANDERSON, William, Pvt, Col omitted, Capt Samuel Richardson, E TN Draft Mil
ANDERSON, William, Pvt, Maj James Porter, Cav Sqdn E TN Mil
ANDERSON, William, Sgt Major, Col omitted, Capt James Anderson, Cav
ANDES, Adam, Cpl, Col Wm Lillard, Capt Jacob Hartsell, E TN Vol Inf
ANDES, Solomon, Pvt, Col Samuel Wear, Capt Simson Perry, E TN Vol Inf
ANDREW, David, Pvt, Col R. C. Napier, Capt Thomas Gray, Mil Inf; sick absent
ANDREW, David, Pvt, Col Thomas Benton, Capt Isaiah Renshaw, Vol Inf
ANDREW, James, Pvt, Col T. McCrory, Capt James Shannon, Mil Inf
ANDREW, Phillips, Pvt, Col S. Bunch, Capt John English, E Tn Draft Mil; left sick at Camp Ross
ANDREW, Robert, Pvt, Maj John Childs, Capt Daniel Price, E TN Vol Mtd Inf
ANDREWS, Adam, Pvt, Col R. C. Napier, Capt Samuel Ashmore, Mil Inf
ANDREWS, Anderson, Sgt, Maj Robert Cooper, Capt omitted, 26th TN Reg Mtd Riflemen
ANDREWS, Charles L., Sgt, Col William Lillard, Capt William Gillenwater, E TN Vol Inf
ANDREWS, Charles A., Pvt, Maj Gen A. Jackson, Capt William Carroll, Vol Inf
ANDREWS, David, Pvt, Col N. Cannon, Capt George Brandon, Mtd Riflemen
ANDREWS, David, Pvt, Col Thomas Benton, Capt Isaiah Renshaw, Vol Inf
ANDREWS, David, Pvt, Col Wm Pillow, Capt Isaiah Renshaw, Inf
ANDREWS, David, Pvt, Col omitted, Capt Thomas Gray, Inf
ANDREWS, Drewsey, Pvt, Col Philip Pipkin, Capt James Blakemore, Mil Inf; AWOL
ANDREWS, Drury, Pvt, Col John Coffee, Capt Charles Kavanaugh, Cav
ANDREWS, Drury, Pvt, Col T. McCrory, Capt A. Metcalf, Mil Inf
ANDREWS, Ephraim, Pvt, Col John Coffee, Capt Charles Kavanaugh, Cav; AWOL
ANDREWS, George, Pvt, Col John Coffee, Capt Charles Kavanaugh, Cav; AWOL
ANDREWS, Henry, 4 Sgt, Col Thomas Benton, Capt Robert Cannon, Inf
ANDREWS, Henry, Cornet, Col Thomas Williamson, Maj Gen John Cocke, Capt William Martin, Vol Mtd Gunmen
ANDREWS, Henry, Pvt, Col Thomas Williamson, Capt William Martin, Vol Mtd Gunmen
ANDREWS, James, Cpl, Maj William Woodfolk, Capt James C. Neil, Inf
ANDREWS, James, Pvt, Col N. T. Perkins, Capt John Quarles, Vol Mtd Inf; killed 1-24-1814 at Enotechopea
ANDREWS, James, Pvt, Col Philip Pipkin, Capt George Mebane, Mil Inf; deserted
ANDREWS, James, Pvt, Col omitted, Capt James Gray, Inf
ANDREWS, James, Pvt, Col omitted, Lt James Berry, Mtd Riflemen
ANDREWS, James, Pvt, Maj William Woodfolk, Capt James C. Neil, Inf
ANDREWS, John, Pvt, Col T. McCrory, Capt Isaac Patton, Mil Inf
ANDREWS, John, Pvt, Col omitted, Capt Nathan Farmer, Mtd Riflemen
ANDREWS, John, Pvt, no other information
ANDREWS, John, Trumpet, Col omitted, Capt Nathan Farmer, Mtd Riflemen
ANDREWS, Lazarus, Pvt, Lt Col Leroy Hammonds, Col Alexander Loury, Capt Thomas Wells, Inf
ANDREWS, Samuel, 3 Cpl, Col A. Cheatham, Capt James Giddins, Inf
ANDREWS, William G., 4 Cpl, Col John Cocke, Capt John Dalton, Inf
ANDREWS, William, Sgt, Col A. Cheatham, Capt Charles Johnson, Inf
ANDREWS, William, Sgt, Col Thomas Williamson, Capt William Martin, Vol Mtd Gunmen
ANDREWS, _____, Pvt, Col T. McCrory, Capt A. Metcalf, Mil Inf
ANGLIN, Aaron, Pvt, Col Thomas Benton, Capt Henry Douglass, Vol Inf
ANGLIN, Samuel, Pvt, Col R. C. Napier, Capt John Chism, Mil Inf
ANGLIN, William, Pvt, Col Thomas Benton, Capt Henry Douglass, Vol Inf
ANGLING, Drury, Pvt, Col John Cocke, Capt James Gray, Inf; sick absent
ANLEY, Frederick, Pvt, Col Samuel Bayless, Capt Jones (Branch Capt), E TN Draft Mil
ANNIS, James, Pvt, Col John Williams, Capt David Vance, Mtd Mil
ANNYS, Isaac, Pvt, Col Edwin Booth, Capt John Slatton, E TN Mil
ANTHONY, Hiram, Pvt, Col William Metcalf, Capt Bird Hurt, Mil Inf
ANTHONY, Lewis C., Pvt, Col John Coffee, Capt Blackman Coleman, Cav
ANTHONY, Milton, Pvt, Col omitted, Capt Nathan Farmer, Mtd Riflemen
ANTHONY, William B., Pvt, Col Thomas Williamson, Capt William Moore, Vol Mtd Gunmen, killed in battle 12-3-1814
ANTHONY, William B., Pvt, Col omitted, Capt George Smith, Spies
ANTHONY, William, Pvt, Col Nicholas Perkins, Capt George Eliot, Mil Inf
ANTHONY, Zeph. H. B., Pvt, Col A. Cheatham, Capt William Smith, Inf
ANTRY, William, Pvt, Col omitted, Capt Garrett Lane, Mtd Riflemen
APERSON, Isaac, Pvt, Col Ewen Allison, Capt Jacob Hoyal, E TN Mil
APPLEGATE, Nathan, Pvt, Col John Brown, Capt John Trimble, E TN Mtd Gunmen
APPLETON, James, Pvt, Maj Gen Carroll, Capt Francis Ellis, Inf

## Enlisted Men, War of 1812

APPLETON, John, Pvt, Col A Cheatham, Capt Geo G Chapman, Inf

ARANT, Wm, Pvt, Col Wm Metcalf, Capt William Mullin, Mil Inf

ARBAUGH, Jacob, Sgt, Maj Wm Russell, Capt Fleman Hodges, Vol Mtd Gunmen

ARCH, Geo, Pvt, Col Philip Pipkin, Capt Henry M Newlin, Mil Inf

ARCHER, Geo, Pvt, Col Philip Pipkin, Capt Henry M Newlin, Mil Inf; furlowed on the line of march 6-30-1814

ARCHER, Hezekiah, Pvt, Col Wm Pillow, Capt John H Anderson, Vol Inf

ARCHER, Joe, Pvt, Lt Col Jno Edmonson, Capt McCray, Cav

ARCHER, Jos, Pvt, Col Ewin Allison, Capt Henry McCray, E TN Mil; discharged by a surgeon 1-14-1814

ARCHER, Joseph, Pvt, no other information

ARCHER, Thomas, Pvt, Col Leroy Hammonds, Capt Jas Craig, 2 Regt W TN Mil; d 3-12-1815

ARCHER, Thos, Pvt, Lt Col Leroy Hammond, Capt James Craig, Inf; d 3-12-1814

ARCHEY, Elisha, Pvt, Maj Gen A Jackson, Capt Hugh Kerr, Mtd Rangers

AREHEART, Abraham, Artif, Col A Cheatham, Capt Geo G Chapman, Inf

ARMER, Davis W, Pvt, Col Alexander Loury, Capt John Looney, 2 Regt W TN Mil

ARMER, Robert, Pvt, Col Alexander Loury, Capt John Looney, 2 Regt W TN Mil

ARMES, Moses, Pvt, Col S Copeland, Capt William Douglas, Inf

ARMFIELD, Isaac, Sgt, Col Jas Raulston, Capt Henry Hamilton, Inf; also served under Maj Gen Carroll

ARMITAGE, John, Cpl, Col Wm Lillard, Capt Robert Maloney, E TN Vol Inf

ARMONT, Robert, Sgt, Regt Commander omitted, Capt Elijah Rushing, Det of Inf

ARMOR, Joseph D, Pvt, Gen Andrew Jackson, Capt Nathan Davis, Inf

ARMOUR, Robert, Sgt, Regt Commander omitted, Capt Thos Gray, Inf

ARMOUR, Wm, Cpl, Regt Commander omitted, Capt Elijah Rushing, Det of Inf

ARMS, Archibold, Pvt, Maj Gen Wm Carroll & Col Jas Raulston, Capt Wiley Huddleston, Inf

ARMS, Moses, Pvt, Col Wm Metcalf, Capt Alexander Hill & Capt John Cunningham, Mil Inf

ARMSFIELD, Jacob, Pvt, Col John Cocke, Capt Joseph Price, Inf; d 1-6-1813

ARMSTRONG, Aaron, Pvt, Col Samuel Bunch, Capt Jno McNair, E TN Mil

ARMSTRONG, Abram, Pvt, Col Thos McCrory, Capt Samuel McKnight, Inf

ARMSTRONG, Andrew, Pvt, Col William Johnson, Capt Christopher Cook, E TN Mil

ARMSTRONG, Andrew, Pvt, Col William Johnson, Capt Joseph Kirk, Mil; substitute for Jac Atlinger

ARMSTRONG, Andrew, Pvt, Col Wm Lillard, Capt Robert McCalpin, Inf

ARMSTRONG, Arthur G, 1 Sgt, Col Wm Lillard, Capt George Argenbright, E TN Vol Riflemen; appointed Issuing Comm

ARMSTRONG, Arthur G, Regt(?) Comm, Col Wm Lillard, Co Commander omitted; E TN Vol Mil

ARMSTRONG, Barefoot D, Pvt, Col Samuel Bayless, Capt Joseph Rich, E Tn Inf

ARMSTRONG, Benjamin, Pvt, Col Samuel Bayless, Capt Jas Churchman, E TN Mil

ARMSTRONG, Daniel, Pvt, Col Edward Booth, Capt Winton, E TN Mil; transferred to Capt Jos Rich Co

ARMSTRONG, Daniel, Pvt, Col Samuel Bayless, Capt Joseph Rich, E TN Inf; joined from Capt Winton's Co

ARMSTRONG, Daniel, Pvt, Col Samuel Wear & Col Samuel Bunch, Capt Wm Mitchell, E TN Mtd Inf

ARMSTRONG, Drury, Pvt, Col John Cocke, Capt John Dalton, Inf

ARMSTRONG, Eliisha, Pvt, Col William Johnson, Capt Christopher Cook, E TN Mil

ARMSTRONG, Elisha, Pvt, Col Wm Johnston, Capt Joseph Kirk, Mil; substitute for Peter Wilson

ARMSTRONG, Ephraim, Pvt, Col John K Wynne, Capt John Spinks, Inf

ARMSTRONG, Ezekiel, Pvt, Col Alex Loury, Capt James Kincaid, Inf

ARMSTRONG, Geo, Pvt, Col William Hall, Capt John Kennedy, Vol Inf; removed out of the county

ARMSTRONG, Hugh C, 4 Sgt, Col Edward Bradley, Capt John Kennedy, Riflemen; furlough to wait on the sick

ARMSTRONG, Hugh P, Cpl, Col Edward Bradley, Capt John Kennedy, Riflemen; furlough sick

ARMSTRONG, James, Pvt, no other information

ARMSTRONG, Jas S, Pvt, Col Thos McCrory, Capt Jno Reynolds, Mil Inf

ARMSTRONG, Jas, Pvt, Col John Cocke, Capt Geo Barnes, Inf

ARMSTRONG, Jas, Pvt, Col S Bunch, Capt Geo Gregory, E TN Drafted Mil; discharged 2-4-1814

ARMSTRONG, Jas, Pvt, Col William Hall, Capt John Kennedy, Vol Inf

ARMSTRONG, Jas, Pvt, Regt Commander omitted, Capt Archibald McKinney, Cav

ARMSTRONG, Jesse, Pvt, Col Thos Benton, Capt Wm Smith, Vol Inf

ARMSTRONG, Jno, 4 Sgt, Gen Andrew Jackson, Capt Jeol Parrish, Arty

ARMSTRONG, Jno, Pvt, Col Wm Hall, Capt Newton, Inf; discharged under age & objected to by father

ARMSTRONG, Jno, Pvt, Regt Commander omitted, Capt Archibald McKinney, Cav

ARMSTRONG, John, 4 Sgt, Commanders & Branch Srvce omitted; in hospital sick

ARMSTRONG, John, Cpl, Col Thos McCrory, Capt Abel Willis, Mil Inf

ARMSTRONG, John, Pvt, Col John Cocke, Capt John Dalton, Inf

ARMSTRONG, John, Pvt, Col N Cannon, Capt John B Demsey, Mtd Gunmen

ARMSTRONG, John, Pvt, Col R C Napier, Capt Thos

## Enlisted Men, War of 1812

Preston, Mil Inf; transferred to Arty Co
ARMSTRONG, John, Pvt, Col Robert H Dyer, Capt McMahon, 1st TN Mtd Gunmen
ARMSTRONG, John, Pvt, Col Thos McCrory, Capt Wm Dooley, Inf
ARMSTRONG, John, Pvt, Col Thos Williamson, Capt Giles Burdett, Vol Mtd Gunmen; dismissed from service 11-20-1814
ARMSTRONG, John, Pvt, Maj Wm Russell, Capt John Cowan, Vol Mtd Gunmen
ARMSTRONG, Jos, Pvt, Col Thos McCrory, Capt Samuel McKnight, Inf
ARMSTRONG, Nathaniel, Pvt, Col John Cocke, Capt John Dalton, Inf
ARMSTRONG, Rial (Royal), Pvt, Col Jas Raulston, Capt Daniel Newman, Inf
ARMSTRONG, Robt, Sgt, Maj Gen Andrew Jackson, Capt William Carroll, Vol Inf
ARMSTRONG, Samuel, Pvt, Col Wm Lillard, Capt Robert McCalpin, E TN Vol Inf
ARMSTRONG, Wm, Pvt, Col Alex Loury, Capt Gabriel Martin, Inf
ARMSTRONG, Wm, Pvt, Col Jas Raulston, Capt Elijah Haynie, Inf; discharged on account of age 11-28-1814
ARMSTRONG, Wm, Pvt, Col Jno Williams, Capt Wm Walker, Mtd Vol
ARMSTRONG, Wm, Pvt, Col No? Williams, Capt Sam Bunch, Mtd Vol
ARNET, Jas, Pvt, Col John Cocke, Capt James Gault, Inf
ARNET, Jas, Pvt, Col William Metcalf, Capt Andrew Patterson, Mil Inf
ARNET, Samuel, Pvt, Brig Gen Thomas, Capt Robert Carson, Inf
ARNET, William, Pvt, Col S Copeland, Capt Allen Wilkinson, Mil Inf; sick absent
ARNETT, Andrew, Pvt, Col Edward Bradley, Capt John Kennedy, Riflemen
ARNETT, Jas, Sgt, Maj William Woodfolk, Capt Abraham Dudney, Inf
ARNETT, Peter, Pvt, Regt Commander omitted, Capt Jno Miller, Spies
ARNETT, William, Sgt, Maj Wm Woodfolk, Capt Abraham Dudney & Capt John Sutton, Branch Srvce omitted
ARNETT, Wm, 2 Sgt, Maj Wm Woodfolk, Co Comm omitted, Separate Bn of W TN Mil; promoted to jr Master Sgt
ARNETTE, Peter, Pvt, Regt Commander omitted, Capt Jno Miller, Spies
ARNINGTON, Thomas, Pvt, Col Samuel Bunch, Capt Francis Bunch, E TN Mil; joined from Capt McCrea's Co
ARNINGTON, Thos, Pvt, Col Samuel Bayless, Capt Solomon Hendrix, E TN Mil
ARNINGTON, Thos, Pvt, Col Samuel Bunch, Capt Francis Register, E TN Mil
ARNOLD, Alexander, Pvt, Col Samuel Bayless, Capt Solomon Hendricks, E TN Mil
ARNOLD, Andrew, Pvt, Col Samuel Wear, Capt Jesse Cole, Vol Inf

ARNOLD, Benj, Pvt, Col Alexander Loury, Capt John Looney, 2 Regt W TN Mil
ARNOLD, Butler, Pvt, Col Thomas Williamson, Capt Beverly Williams, Vol Mtd Gunmen; sick absent
ARNOLD, David T, Pvt, Col T McCrory, Capt William Cooley, Inf
ARNOLD, David, Pvt, Col Thos Benton, Capt Benjamin Reynolds, Vol Inf; refused to march
ARNOLD, Elisha, Pvt, Col Philip Pipkin, Capt John Strother, Mil; deserted 9-20-1814
ARNOLD, Elisha, Pvt, Maj Gen Carroll, Capt Francis Ellis, Inf
ARNOLD, Ephraim, Pvt, Col John Coffee, Capt Michael Molton, Cav
ARNOLD, Ephraim, Pvt, Regt Commander omitted, Capt Jos Williams, Mil Cav
ARNOLD, Ezekiel, Pvt, Col John Cocke, Capt James Gault, Inf
ARNOLD, Francis, Pvt, Col Alexander Loury & Lt Col Leroy, Capt Thomas Wells, Inf; sick
ARNOLD, Henry, Pvt, Maj William Woodfolk, Capt McCalley, Inf
ARNOLD, Hezekiah, Pvt, Col R M Dyer, Capt Robert Evans, V Mtd Gunmen
ARNOLD, Israel, Pvt, Regt Commander omitted, Capt Jos Williams, Mil Cav; discharged
ARNOLD, Israll (Ezra), Pvt, Col R H Dyer, Capt Joseph Williams, Vol Mtd Gunmen; left sick at Nachey
ARNOLD, Jarrett, Pvt, Col Samuel Wear, Capt Jesse Cole, Vol Inf
ARNOLD, Jas L, Pvt, Col Philip Pipkin, Capt Ebenezer Kirkpatrick, Mil Inf; deserted 9-20-1814
ARNOLD, Jas, Pvt, Col John Coffee, Capt Michael Molton, Cav
ARNOLD, Jas, Pvt, Col Wm Johnston, Capt Jas R Rogers, E TN Drafted Mil
ARNOLD, Jas, Pvt, Col Wm Metcalf, Capt William Sitton, Mil Inf
ARNOLD, John, Blksmth, Col John Alcorn, Capt William Locke, Cav
ARNOLD, John, Pvt, Col R H Dyer, Capt Joseph Williams, V Mtd Gunmen; killed in action 12-23-1814
ARNOLD, John, Pvt, Col William Johnson, Capt Joseph Scott, E TN Drafted Mil; deserted 10-29-1814
ARNOLD, John, Pvt, Col William Lillard, Capt George Keys, E TN Inf
ARNOLD, Lindsay, Pvt, Col Robert Steele, Capt Jas Randals, Inf; on furlough
ARNOLD, Little B, Pvt, Col Edwin E Booth, Capt John Slatton, E TN Mil
ARNOLD, Michael, Cpl, Col John Brown, Capt Jas McKamy, E TN Mtd Gunmen; an artificer
ARNOLD, Richard, Pvt, Col Samuel Wear, Capt Jesse Cole, Vol Inf
ARNOLD, Stephen, Pvt, Col Samuel Bunch, Capt Jas Cumming, E Tn Vol Mtd Gunmen
ARNOLD, Thos, Pvt, Col John Coffee, Capt Michael Molton, Cav
ARRANTS, Richard, Pvt, Col William Johnson, Capt Joseph Scott, E TN Drafted Mil

ARRINGTON, Demsey, Pvt, Col John Cocke, Capt John Dalton, Inf
ARRINGTON, Drury, Pvt, Col John Cock, Capt John Dalton, Inf
ARRINGTON, John, Pvt, Col Wm Lillard, Capt Wm McLin, E TN Inf
ARRINGTON, Richard S, Pvt, Col N Cannon, Capt John B Dempsey, Mtd Gunmen
ARRINGTON, Stephen, Pvt, Col R C Napier, Capt Early Benson, Mil Inf; sick present
ARRINGTON, Thomas, Pvt, Col Wm Lillard, Capt Wm McLin, E TN Inf
ARRINGTON, Thos, Pvt, Col Ewin Allison, Capt Henry McCray, E TN Mil; substitute for Jas Arrington
ARRINGTON, Whitemel, Pvt, Col Thomas Benton, Capt Henry L Douglass, Vol Inf; sick absent before marching orders
ARRINGTON, Wm, Pvt, Col R C Napier, Capt Early Benson, Mil Inf
ARRNAT, Wm, Pvt, Col Wm Metcalf, Capt William Mullen, Mil Inf
ASHFORD, John, Pvt, Col S Copeland, Capt Moses Thompson, Inf
ASHFORD, Moses, Pvt, Col Leroy Hammonds, Capt James Tubb, Inf; left sick at Camp Mandarville near Mobile
ASHFORD, Muchael, Pvt, Col John Winn, Capt John Spinks, Inf
ASHINS, James, Pvt, Lt Col Leroy Hammonds, Capt Joseph Williamson, Inf; left sick at Ft Pierce
ASHLEY, Edward, Pvt, Col Alexander Loury, Capt James Kincaid, Inf; sick absent at Ft Montgomery
ASHLEY, Edward, Pvt, Col William Lillard, Capt William Hamilton, E TN Vol Inf
ASHLEY, James, Pvt, Maj William Russell, Capt Isaac Williams, 1 Regt Separate Bn of TN Mtd Gunmen
ASHLEY, Joseph, Ffr, Col William Johnson, Capt James Rogers, E TN Drafted Mil
ASHLEY, Thomas, Pvt, Col Philip Pipkin, Capt George Mebane, Mil Inf; deserted from Ft Jackson 9-20-1814
ASHLEY, William, Pvt, Col Edwin Booth, Capt John McKamey, E TN Mil
ASHLEY, William, Pvt, Col John Williams, Capt Samuel Bunch, Branch Srvce omitted
ASHLEY, William, Pvt, Col Samuel Bayless, Capt Joseph Bacon, E TN Mil
ASHLOCK, Benjamin, Pvt, Col John Alcorn, Capt John Baskerville, Vol Inf
ASHLOCK, Benjamin, Pvt, Col John Coffee, Capt John Baskerville, Cav
ASHLOCK, Obidiah, Sgt, Col John Brown, Capt Oliver Lunsford, E TN Mil
ASHLOCK, Philip, Pvt, Col Thomas Williamson, Capt Thomas Surry, Vol Mtd Gunmen
ASHLOCK, William, Pvt, Maj Gen Carroll & Col James Raulston, Capt Wiley Huddleston, Inf
ASHLOCKE, Philip, Pvt, Col John Coffee, Capt John Baskerville, Cav
ASHMORE, David, Pvt, Col Samuel Bayless, Capt James Churchman, E TN Mil
ASHMORE, David, Pvt, Col William Lillard, Capt John Ruper, E TN Vol Inf
ASHMORE, James, Pvt, Col N T Perkins, Capt John Quarles, Vol Mtd Inf
ASHMORE, James, Pvt, Col S Bunch, Capt George Gregory, E TN Drafted Mil
ASHMORE, James, Pvt, Col Samuel Bunch, Capt John English, E TN Mil
ASHMORE, James, Sgt, Col Samuel Bayless, Capt Joseph Goodson, E TN Mil
ASHWORTH, Austin, Mus, Col Samuel Wear, Capt John Chiles, E TN Vol Inf
ASHWORTH, Jasper, Cpl, Col John Brown, Capt John Childs, E TN Mtd Gunmen
ASHWORTH, John C, Pvt, Maj James Porter, Co Commander omitted, Sqdn of E TN Mil Cav
ASHWORTH, John, Pvt, Col John Brown, Capt John Childs, E TN Vol Mtd Gunmen
ASHWORTH, Thomas, Pvt, Col John Brown, Capt John Childs, E TN Vol Mtd Gunmen
ASKEL, Champ, Pvt, Col T McCrory, Capt James Shannon, Mil Inf; sick absent
ASKEW, Allen, Pvt, Col William Hall, Capt John Wallace, Inf
ASKEW, Benjamin, Pvt, Col James Raulston, Capt Charles Wade, Inf
ASKEW, Elisha, Pvt, Capt Josiah Askew, Inf
ASKEW, Isaac, Pvt, Col Edward Bradley, Capt John Wallace, Vol Inf
ASKEW, Isaac, Pvt, Col William Hall, Capt John Wallace, Inf
ASKEW, James, Pvt, Col James Raulston, Capt Henry Hamilton, Inf; also served under Maj Gen Carroll
ASKEW, John C, Pvt, Col A Cheatham, Capt Charles Johnson, Inf; discharged for inability to do duty
ASKEW, Josiah, Pvt, Regt Commander omitted, Capt James Gray, Inf
ASKEW, Samuel, Pvt, Col John Cocke, Capt John Dalton, Inf
ASKINS, James, Pvt, Col A Loury, Capt J Williamson, W TN Mil
ASKINS, James, Pvt, Col L Hammonds, Capt J Williamson, 2 Regt Inf
ASKINS, James, Pvt, Col N Cannon, Capt Ota Cantrell, W TN Mtd Inf
ASKINS, Joseph, Pvt, Col Edwin Booth, Capt John Slatton, E TN Mil
ASLINGER, Gasper, Cpl, Col Samuel Bayless, Capt Jones (Branch), E TN Mil
ASPLEY, William, Pvt, Col William Hall, Capt William Alexander, Vol Inf
ASTEAN, Samuel, Ffr, Col Thomas Benton, Capt Robert Cannon, Inf
ASTEN, James, Pvt, Col N T Perkins, Capt John Doak, Vol Mtd Gunmen
ASTEN, James, Pvt, Col William Metcalf, Capt Obidish Waller, Mil Inf
ASTER, Benjamin, Pvt, Regt Commander omitted, Capt George Smith, Spies
ATCHBY, Thomas, Pvt, Col Samuel Wear, Capt Simeon Perry, E TN Vol Mtd Inf

## Enlisted Men, War of 1812

ATCHESON, Nathan, Pvt, Col William Hall, Capt John Moore, Vol Inf
ATCHISON, Adam, Sgt, Col William Hall, Capt John More, Vol Inf
ATCHISON, Henry, Pvt, no other information
ATCHISON, Mathew, Cpl, Col Edward Bradley, Capt John Moore, Vol Inf; on furlough
ATCHISON, William, Pvt, Col William Hall, Capt John Moore, Vol Inf
ATCHISON, Willis, Pvt, Col Edward Bradley, Capt John Moore, Vol Inf; on furlough
ATCHLEY, Abraham, Pvt, Col William Johnson, Capt Andrew Lawson, E TN Drafted Mil
ATCHLEY, Benjamin, Cpl, Col Edwin Booth, Capt John Porter, Drafted Mil
ATCHLEY, Jos, Pvt, Col S Bunch, Capt Isaac Williams, E TN Mil
ATCHLY, Benjamin, Pvt, Col William Johnson, Capt Elihu Milliken, 3rd Regt E TN Mil; transferred from Capt Churchman
ATCHLY, Jos, Pvt, Col Wm Johnson, Capt Elihu Millikin, 3rd Regt E Tn Mil
ATHA, Benj L, Pvt, Col Thomas Williamson, Capt James Pace & Lt Nealy, Vol Mtd Gunmen
ATHEY, Abraham, Pvt, Col Jno Brown, Capt Jas Preston, E TN Mil Inf
ATHEY, Edgmore, Pvt, Col Jno Brown, Capt Jas Preston, E TN Mil Inf
ATHINSON, Thomas, Pvt, Gen Andrew Jackson, Capt Nathan Davis, Inf
ATIN, Sam'l S, Pvt, Regt Commander omitted, Capt Archibald McKenney, Cav
ATKERSON, Adam, Pvt, Col Wm Hall, Capt John Moore, Branch Srvce omitted
ATKERSON, Jas, Pvt, Col Wm Johnson, Capt Jas A Rogers, Branch Srvce omitted
ATKINS, David, Pvt, Col William Hall, Capt Henry M Newland, Inf
ATKINS, Jackson, Pvt, Col John Cocke, Capt John Weakley, Inf
ATKINS, James, Pvt, Gen Andrew Jackson, Capt Joel Parrish, Arty
ATKINS, James, Pvt, Lt Col Archer Cheatham, Co Commander omitted, 6th Brig Mtd Inf; sick
ATKINS, Jas T, Pvt, Maj Gen A Jackson, Capt William Carroll, Vol Inf
ATKINS, John, Pvt, Col William Hall, Capt Henry M Newland, Inf; not found
ATKINS, Jos, Pvt, Col John Alcorn, Capt William Locke, Cav
ATKINSON, David, Pvt, Col Jno Brown, Capt Wm D Neilson, Regt E TN Vol Mil
ATKINSON, Jesse, Pvt, Col N T Perkins, Capt Jas McMahan, Mil Inf
ATKINSON, John, Pvt, Col N T Perkins, Capt Jas McMahan, Mtd Gunmen
ATKINSON, Jordan, Pvt, Col Wm Pillow, Capt C E McEwen, Vol Inf
ATKINSON, Leroy, Pvt, Col Samuel Bunch, Capt Thomas Mann, E TN Vol Mtd Inf
ATKINSON, Welton M, 2 Sgt, Col Samuel Bunch, Capt Thomas Mann, E TN Vol Mtd Gunmen
ATLEY, Nimrod, Pvt, Col William Johnson, Capt Joseph Scott, E TN Drafted Mil; sick absent
ATLEY (UTLEY), Seth, Pvt, Regt Commander omitted, Capt James Gray, Inf
ATWOOD, Wm, Pvt, Col John K Wynne, Capt Jas Cole, Inf; deserted 11-18-1813
ATWOOD, Wm, Pvt, Col Robert H Dyer, Capt James Wyatt, V Mtd Gunmen; dismissed 9-28-1814
AUGAN, John, Pvt, Col William Higgins, Capt James Hambleton, Mtd Gunmen
AULT, John, Pvt, Col S Bunch, Capt Jno McNare, E TN Mil
AUSBURN, Jas, Pvt, Col Thomas McCrory, Capt Thomas K Gordon, Inf
AUSTIN, David, Pvt, Maj Gen Andrew Jackson, Capt Wm Russell, Mtd Spies
AUSTIN, David, Pvt, Regt Commander omitted, Capt James Cowan, Mtd Inf
AUSTIN, David, Pvt, no other information
AUSTIN, Jas, Pvt, Col Samuel Wear, Capt Jesse Cole, Vol Inf; d 1-19-1814
AUSTIN, John, Pvt, Col John Cocke, Capt John Dalton, Inf
AUSTIN, John, Pvt, Col N T Perkins, Capt John Doak, Vol Mtd Gunmen
AUSTIN, John, Pvt, Col Samuel Bunch, Capt William Houston, E TN Vol Mtd Inf; d 1-5-1814
AUSTIN, John, Pvt, Maj John Chiles, Capt Chas Conway, E TN Mtd Gunmen; Regt County Bledsoe
AUSTIN, John, Rank omitted, Col John Cocke, Capt Bird Nance, Inf
AUSTIN, Jos, Pvt, Col Samuel Bayless, Capt Jas Churchman, E TN Mil
AUSTIN, Jos, Pvt, Col Wm Lillard, Capt Zacheus Copeland, E TN Vol Inf
AUSTIN, Levi, Cpl, Col Thos Williamson, Capt Wm Metcalf, Vol Mtd Gunmen
AUSTIN, Pleasant, Pvt, Col T McCrory, Capt Abel Willis, Mil Inf
AUSTIN, Samuel S, Pvt, Col Nicholas Perkins, Capt John Doak, Vol Mtd Gunmen
AUSTIN, Thos, Pvt, Col Samuel Bayless, Capt Solomon Hendricks, E TN Mil; d 12-1-1814
AUSTIN, Will, Pvt, Col Joseph Hale, Capt Wm Hamilton, Vol Inf
AUSTIN, Wm, Cpl, Col Robert H Dyer, Capt Cuthbert Hudson, Vol Mtd Gunmen
AUSTIN, Wm, Pvt, Col John K Wynne, Capt Wm Carothers, W TN Inf
AUSTIN, Wm, Pvt, Col Thos Bradley, Capt James Hambleton, Vol Inf
AUSTIN, Wm, Pvt, Maj Gen A Jackson, Capt Wm Russell, Mtd Spies
AVANS, Amos, Pvt, Col John Coffee, Capt Jas Terrill, Vol Cav; out of state
AVENSHINE, John, Pvt & Dmr, Col Wm Metcalf, Capt Alexander Hill & Capt John Cunningham, Mil Inf
AVENT, Harris, Pvt, Col Philip Pipkin, Capt Jas Blakemore, Mil Inf; d 9-12-1814
AVENT, Herbert, Pvt, Col Jno Coffee, Capt Byrn, Cav

AVENT, John, Pvt, Col Wm Hall, Capt John Wallace, Inf
AVERETT, Thos, Pvt, Col Edwin Booth, Capt Samuel Thompson, Mil
AVERETT, Washington, Pvt, Col Wm Hall, Capt Wm Alexander, Vol Inf
AVERITE, John, Pvt, Col Alexander Loury, Capt John Looney, 2 Regt W TN Mil; sick absent
AVERY, Allen, Pvt, Col Jas Raulston, Capt Chas Wade, Inf
AVERY, Wm, Pvt, Col Thos Benton, Capt Henry L Douglas, Vol Inf
AVERY, Wm, Pvt, Lt Col Rich Napie, no other information
AVORITE, Larkin, 3 Cpl, Col R C Napier, Capt Early Benson, Mil Inf
AWALT, Michael, Pvt, Col R H Dyer & Maj Wm Russell, Capt Wm Russell, Vol Mtd Gunmen
AYDELOTTE, Arthur, 1 Cpl, Col Thos Benton, Capt Robert Cannon, Inf
AYDETOTE, Arthur, Pvt, Col Alexander Loury, Capt John Looney, 2 Regt W TN Mil; d 3-18-1815
AYERS, Arthur, Pvt, Maj Gen Wm Carroll & Col Wm Metcalf, Capt John Jackson, Inf
AYERS, Daniel, Pvt, Maj Woodfolk, Capt McCulley, Inf
AYERS, Jos, Pvt, Col Wm Metcalf, Capt Barbee Collins, Mil Inf
AYERS, Marshall, Pvt, Col Jno Williams, Capt Wm Walker, Vol
AYNESWORTH, Isaac, Pvt, Col John Cocke, Capt John Weakley, Branch Srvce omitted
AYRES, Henry, Pvt, Maj Gen A Jackson, Capt John Craine, Mtd Gunmen
AYRES, Jas, 3 Sgt, Col R C Napier, Capt John Chism, Mil Inf
AYRES, Jesse, Pvt, Maj John Childs, Capt Chas Conway, E TN Mtd Gunmen; Regt County Knox
AYRES, John, Pvt, Col Wm Lillard, Capt Thos McChristian, E TN Vol Inf
AYRES, Jos, Pvt, Col Alexander Loury, Capt John Looney, 2 Regt W TN Mil
AYRES, William, Pvt, Col S Copeland, Capt Richard Sharp, Mil Inf
AYRS, Ezakiel, Pvt, Col Wm Metcalf, Capt Barbee Collins, Mil Inf
AYRS, Jos, Pvt, Col Wm Metcalf, Capt Barbee Collins, Mil Inf
BABB, David, Pvt, Col S Bunch, Capt F Register, E TN Mil
BABB, David, Pvt, Col William Lillard, Capt Jacob Dyke, Vol Inf; deserted
BABB, Err, Pvt, Col Samuel Bayless, Capt Solomon Hendricks, E TN Mil
BABB, Hiram, Pvt, Col Samuel Bayless, Capt Solomon Hendricks, E TN Mil
BABB, Isaac, Pvt, Col S Bunch, Capt F Register, E TN Mil
BABB, Israel, Pvt, Regt Commander omitted, Capt I Prewitt, Pack Horse Guards
BACHELOR, John, Tptr, Col Jno Coffee, Capt John Baskerville, Cav
BACHELOR, John, Tptr, Col John Alcorn, Capt John Baskerville, Vol Inf; on furlough since 10-17-1813
BACON, Aaron, Pvt, Col Ewin Allison, Capt Joseph Everett, E TN Mil; transferred to Capt McPherson
BACON, Aaron, Pvt, Col S Bunch, Capt Geo McPherson, E TN Mil; joined from Capt Everett's Co
BACON, Allen S, Pvt, Col John Williams, Capt Wm Walker, Mtd Vol
BACON, Chas, Pvt, Col Ewen Allison, Capt Jacob Hoyal, E TN Mil; transferred from Capt McPherson's Co
BACON, Chas, Pvt, Col S Bunch, Capt Geo McPherson, E TN Mil
BACON, Edmond, Pvt, Col S Bunch, Capt Jones Griffin, E TN Drafted Mil; furloughed from Ft Williams for inability
BACON, Edmund, Pvt, Col Ewin Allison, Capt Joseph Everett, E TN Mil
BACON, Jas, Cpl, Col Samuel Bayless, Capt Joseph B Bacon, E TN Mil
BACON, Jeremiah, Pvt, Col Ewin Allison, Capt Jacob Hoyal, E TN Mil
BACON, Jeremiah, Pvt, Col S Bunch, Capt Geo McPherson, E TN Mil
BACON, Jesse, Pvt, Col Ewen Allison, Capt Jacob Hoyal, E TN Mil
BACON, Jesse, Pvt, Col S Bunch, Capt Geo McPherson, E TN Mil
BACON, Jos B, Pvt, Col S Bayless, Capt Joseph B Bacon, E TN Mil
BACON, Thos, Pvt, Col S Bayless, Capt Joseph B Bacon, E TN Mil
BAGBY, Nathaniel, Pvt, Col John Coffee, Capt Charles Kavanaugh, Cav; absent without leave
BAGGETT, Silas, Pvt, Col S Copeland, Capt John Holshouser, Inf
BAGGETT, Silas, Pvt, Col Thomas Benton, Capt William J Smith, Vol Inf
BAGGETT, Silas, Pvt, Regt Commander omitted, Capt William J Smith, Vol Inf
BAGGETT (BAGGATE), Allen, Pvt, Maj William Woodfolk, Capt Abner Pearce, Inf
BAILES, Josiah, Pvt, Col Leroy Hammonds, Capt James Tubb, Inf
BAILES, Thomas D, Pvt, Col William Lillard, Capt Jacob Hartwell, E TN Vol Inf
BAILEY, Benjamin 4 Sgt, Col William Higgins, Capt Samuel Allen, Mtd Gunmen
BAILEY, Chandler, Pvt, Col James Raulston, Capt Charles Wade, Inf
BAILEY, Charles, Pvt, Gen Andrew Jackson, Capt H Kerr, Mtd Rangers
BAILEY, David, Pvt, Maj William Russell, Capt Felman Hodges, Vol Mtd Gunmen
BAILEY, Dempsey, Pvt, no other information
BAILEY, Duncan, Pvt, Col William Hall, Capt James Hambleton, Vol Inf
BAILEY, Duncan, Pvt, Lt Col H Bryan, no other information
BAILEY, Elias, Cpl, Maj Gen Andrew Jackson, Co Commander omitted, Mtd Spies
BAILEY, Geo, Pvt, Col William Hall, Capt Henry M Newland, Inf

## Enlisted Men, War of 1812

BAILEY, George, Pvt, Col Edward Bradley, Capt Elijah Haynie, Vol Inf
BAILEY, Henry, Pvt, Col Robert Steele, Capt Jas Shenault, Mil Inf; on furlough
BAILEY, Henry, Pvt, Col S Copeland, Capt David Williams, Inf; sick absent
BAILEY, Henry, Pvt, Regt Commander omitted, Capt David Williams, Branch Srvce omitted
BAILEY, Isaac, Cpl, Col William Johnson, Capt James Rogers, E TN Drafted Mil
BAILEY, Jeremiah, Cpl, Col James Raulston, Capt Henry Hamilton, Inf
BAILEY, John, Pvt, Col Ewin Allison, Capt Henry McCray, E TN Mil
BAILEY, John, Pvt, Col John Cocke, Capt John Weakley, Inf
BAILEY, John, Pvt, Col S Bunch, Capt F Register, E TN Mil
BAILEY, John, Pvt, Col Samuel Bayless, Capt James Landen, E TN Mil
BAILEY, Merdith, Pvt, Col R C Napier, Capt Jas McMurray, Mil Inf
BAILEY, Montgomery, Pvt, Col Wm Metcalf, Capt William Mullen, Mil Inf
BAILEY, Moses, Pvt, Maj Wm Woodfolk, Capt Ezekial Ross, Inf
BAILEY, Robt, Pvt, Col Samuel Bayless, Capt James Landern, E TN Mil
BAILEY, Samuel, 4 Sgt, Capt George Argenbright, E TN Vol Riflemen
BAILEY, Samuel, Pvt, Col Samuel Wear, Capt Jesse Cole, Vol Inf
BAILEY, Sib, Pvt, Col Edwin Booth, Capt Richard Marshall, Drafted Mil
BAILEY, Sterling, Pvt, Col John Coffee, Capt Jas Terrell, Vol Cav
BAILEY, Thos L, Pvt, Maj John Chiles, Capt Jas Cummings, E TN Vol Mtd Inf
BAILEY, Thos, Pvt, Col Philip Pipkin, Capt John Strother, Mil; substitute for Jacob Bailey
BAILEY, William, Pvt, Col Ewen Allison, Capt Jacob Hoyal, E TN Mil
BAILEY, Wm, Pvt, Col Thos McCrory, Capt Anthony Metcalf, Mil Inf
BAILEY, Wm, Regt Commander omitted, Capt Jacob Hoyal, Branch Srvce omitted
BAILY, Absolom, Pvt, Col John Wynne, Capt John Porter, Inf
BAILY, Jacob, Pvt, Col Philip Pipkin, Capt David Smyth & Ens Wm Pegram, W TN Mil; replaced by Thos Baily
BAILY, Jas, Sgt, Col Wm Johnson, Capt Elihu Milliken, 3rd Regt E TN Mil
BAILY, John, Pvt, Col John Coffee, Capt Blackman Coleman, Cav
BAILY, John, Pvt, Col Samuel Bayless, Capt Joseph Hale, E TN Mil
BAILY, Jos, Pvt, Col John Cocke, Capt George Barnes, Inf
BAILY, Michael, Cpl, Col Thos McCrory, Capt Anthony Metcalf, Mil Inf

BAILY, Sterling A, Sgt, Col Robert H Dyer, Capt Thomas Jones, Vol Mtd Gunmen
BAILY, Thos, Pvt, Col Robert Steele, Capt Jas Randals, Inf
BAILY, Thos, Pvt, Col S Copeland, Capt John Biles, Inf
BAILY, William, Pvt, Col Wm Lillard, Capt George Argenbright, E TN Vol Riflemen
BAILY, Wm, Pvt, Col T McCrory, Capt A Metcalf, Branch Srvce omitted
BAILY, Wm, Pvt, Col Wm Johnson, Capt Elihu Millikin, 3rd Regt E TN Mil
BAINS, Samuel, 1 Sgt, Col Edward Bradley, Capt Brice Martin, Vol Inf
BAION, Chas, Pvt, Col S Bunch, Capt Geo McPherson, E TN Mil
BAIR, Geo, Pvt, Col Wm Lillard, Capt Hugh Martin, E TN Vol Inf
BAIRD, Henry, Pvt, Col Wm Hall, Capt James Hamilton, Vol Inf
BAIRD, Henry, Sgt, Lt Col H Bryan, no other information
BAIRD, Josiah, Pvt, Col Jas Raulston, Capt Edward Robinson, Inf
BAIRD, Robt, Pvt, Col Alex Loury & Lt Col Hammonds, Capt Thos Delaney, Inf
BAIRD, Wm, Pvt, Col Thos Benton, Capt Geo Caperton, Vol Inf
BAIRDING, William, Pvt, Col Alex Loury, Capt Gabriel Martin, Inf
BAIRNES (BAINES), Samuel, 1 Sgt, Col Wm Hall, Capt Brice Martin, Vol Inf
BAITES, Wm, Pvt, Maj Wm Woodfolk, Capt Abner Pearce, Vol Inf
BAITES (BAILES), Caleb, Sgt, Col S Bayless, Capt John Brock, E TN Mil
BAITY, Davis, 4 Cpl, Col John K Wynne, Capt Bayless E Prince, Inf
BAITY, Jos, Sgt, Col Thos McCrory, Capt Jno Reynolds, Mil Inf
BAKE (BECK), Wm, Pvt, Col William Johnson, Capt Joseph Scott, E TN Drafted Mil
BAKELY, Wm, Pvt, Col A Cheatham, Capt Richard Benson, Inf
BAKER, Abraham, Pvt, Col John K Wynne, Capt Wm Carruthers, W TN Inf; deserted 10-25-1813
BAKER, Abraham, Pvt, Col Thomas Benton, Capt Isaiah Renshaw, Vol Inf
BAKER, Abraham, Pvt, Col Wm Pillow, Capt Isaiah Renshaw, Inf
BAKER, Abraham, Pvt, Col Wm Pillow, Capt Isaiah Renshaw, Vol Inf
BAKER, Abraham, Pvt, Maj William Woodfolk, Capt Jas Turner, Inf; reduced from fifer
BAKER, Ambrose, Pvt, Col Philip Pipkin, Capt Peter Searcy, Mil Inf; sick absent
BAKER, Ambrose, Pvt, Col Philip Pipkin, Capt William Mackay, Mil Inf
BAKER, Ambrose, Pvt, Col Philip Pipkin, Capt William Mackay, Mil Inf; left sick at Fayetteville 6-26-1814
BAKER, Anderson, Pvt, Col William Johnston, Capt Henry Hunter, E TN Mil; substituted Hawkins

## Enlisted Men, War of 1812

Bowman (not found)

BAKER, Benj, Pvt, Col Alexander Loury, Capt James Kincaid, Inf

BAKER, Chas, Cpl, Col John Coffee, Capt Michael Molton, Cav

BAKER, Chas, Pvt, Col Wm Johnson, Capt Jas Stewart, E TN Drafted Mil

BAKER, Chas, Sgt, Col R H Dyer, Capt Joseph Williams, Vol Mtd Gunmen

BAKER, Chas, Sgt, Regt Commander omitted, Capt Jas Williams, Mil Cav

BAKER, Christopher, Pvt, Col Samuel Bunch, Capt Andrew Breden, E TN Mil

BAKER, David, Pvt, Col Samuel Bayless, Capt Jas Churchman, E TN Drafted Mil

BAKER, Edmund, Pvt, Col A Cheatham, Capt William Creel, Inf

BAKER, Elias, Pvt, Col Alexander Loury, Capt James Kincaid, Inf; d 1-13-1815?

BAKER, Elias, Sgt, Col Wm Johnson, Capt Jas Tunnell, E TN Mil

BAKER, Elijah, Pvt, Col Samuel Bunch, Capt Francis Berry, E TN Mil

BAKER, Gabriel, Pvt, Maj William Woodfolk, Capt Abraham Dudney & Capt John Sutton, Inf

BAKER, Geo, Cpl, Col William Johnson, Capt Benjamin Powell, Branch Srvce omitted

BAKER, Geo, Pvt, Col S Bunch, Capt Geo Gregory, E TN Drafted Mil

BAKER, Geo, Pvt, Col William Johnson, Capt Benjamin Powell, E TN Mil

BAKER, Isaac, Cpl, Col Jno Brown, Capt Jas Preston, E TN Mil Inf

BAKER, Isaiah, Pvt, Col William Metcalf, Capt Bird L Hurt, Mil Inf

BAKER, Jacob, Cpl, Col Robert H Dyer, Capt Bethel Allen, Vol Mtd Gunmen; left sick 4-2-1815

BAKER, Jacob, Pvt, Col Samuel Bayless, Capt Joseph Rich, E TN Inf

BAKER, Jacob, Pvt, Col Wm Lillard, Capt Thomas Sharpe, 2nd Regt Inf

BAKER, Jas D, Pvt, Col Thomas Williamson, Capt Thomas Scurry, Vol Mtd Gunmen

BAKER, Jas, Pvt, Col John Cocke, Capt James Gault, Inf

BAKER, Jas, Pvt, Col William Johnson, Capt Elihu Milliken, 3rd Regt E TN Mil

BAKER, Jas, Pvt, Maj Gen Wm Carroll & Col William Metcalf, Capt John Jackson, Inf

BAKER, Jas, Pvt, Maj Gen Wm Carroll, Capt Francis Ellis, Inf

BAKER, Jeremiah, Pvt, Col Newton Cannon, Capt Isaac Williams, Mtd Riflemen

BAKER, Joel, Pvt, Col William Johnson, Capt Henry Hunter, E TN Mil; left sick near Portock Springs 10-2-1814

BAKER, John jr, Pvt, Col John Coffee, Capt David Smith, Vol Cav

BAKER, John, Far, Regt Commander omitted, Capt Joseph Williams, Mil Cav; discharged

BAKER, John, Pvt, Col Alexander Loury & Lt Col Leroy Hammonds, Capt Thomas Wells, Inf

BAKER, John, Pvt, Col Robert Steele, Capt Richard Ratton, Mil Inf; on furlough sick since 4-25-1814

BAKER, John, Pvt, Col S Bunch, Capt George Gregory, E TN Drafted Mil

BAKER, John, Pvt, Col Samuel Bayless, Capt Solomon Hendricks, E TN Mil

BAKER, John, Pvt, Lt Col Henry Bryan, no other information

BAKER, John, Pvt, Lt Col R Napier, no other information

BAKER, John, Pvt, Maj John Childs, Capt Reuben Tipton, E TN Vol Mtd Inf; Regt County Jefferson

BAKER, John, Sgt Mate, Col Edward Bradley, Co Commander omitted, 1st Regt TN Vol Inf

BAKER, Joseph N, Pvt, Col William Johnson, Capt James Stuart, E TN Drafted Mil

BAKER, Joshua, Pvt, Col Thomas Williamson, Capt Robert Steele, Vol Mtd Gunmen

BAKER, Josiah, Pvt, Col N Cannon, Capt Francis Jones, Mtd Riflemen

BAKER, Major, Pvt, no other information

BAKER, Martin, Pvt, Col Thomas Williamson, Capt Robert Moore, Vol Mtd Gunmen; sick absent since 3-1815

BAKER, Nathan, Pvt, Maj William Russell, Capt Fleman Hodges, Vol Mtd Gunmen; substitute for Richard Priest

BAKER, Nicholas, Cpl, Col R H Dyer, Capt Cuthbert Hudson, Vol Mtd Gunmen

BAKER, Nicholas, Pvt, Col John Coffee, Capt Michael Molton, Cav; sick absent

BAKER, Nicholas, Pvt, Col R H Dyer, Capt Cuthbert Hudson, Vol Mtd Gunmen; reduced from Cpl

BAKER, Nicholas, Pvt, Regt Commander omitted, Capt David Smith, Cav Vol; discharged his horse killed 11-3-1813

BAKER, Peter, Pvt, Col Ewen Allison, Capt Thomas Wilson, E TN Drafted Mil

BAKER, Richard, Pvt, Col William Johnson, Capt Andrew Lawson, E TN Drafted Mil; never appeared

BAKER, Robert, Cpl, Maj William Woodfolk, Capt Ezekial Ross & Capt McCulley, Inf

BAKER, Robert, Pvt, Col R C Napier, Capt Edward Neblett, Mil Inf

BAKER, Samuel, Pvt, Col John Brown, Capt Charles Lewis, E TN Mtd Inf Vol

BAKER, Samuel, Pvt, Col John Winn, Capt Bailey Butler, Inf; deserted 11-9-1813

BAKER, Samuel, Pvt, Col Robert Dyer, Capt Bethel Allen, Vol Mtd Gunmen

BAKER, Samuel, Pvt, Maj William Woodfolk, Capt John Sutton & Capt Abraham Dudney, Inf

BAKER, Simon, Pvt, Col L Hammond, Capt J Williamso, 2nd Regt Inf

BAKER, Solomon, Pvt, Col Thomas Benton, Capt George Gibbs, Vol Inf

BAKER, Solomon, Pvt, Col William Pillow, Capt John Anderson, Vol Inf

BAKER, Thomas W, Pvt, Col Samuel Wear, Capt Joseph Calloway, Mtd Inf

BAKER, Thomas, Pvt, Col John Brown, Capt Charles Lewis, E TN Vol Mtd Inf

## Enlisted Men, War of 1812

BAKER, William, Pvt, Col John Alcorn, Capt William Locke, Cav

BAKER, William, Pvt, Col John Brown, Capt John Childs, E TN Mtd Gunmen Vol

BAKER, William, Pvt, Col Robert Dyer, Capt Robert Edmonston, 1 TN Vol Mtd Gunmen; d 1-21-1815

BAKER, William, Pvt, Col S Bunch, Capt George Gregory, E TN Drafted Mil

BAKER, William, Pvt, Col T McCrory, Capt John Reynolds, Mil Inf

BAKER, William, Pvt, Col Thomas Williamson, Capt Giles Burdett, Vol Mtd Gunmen

BAKER, William, Pvt, Col Thomas Williamson, Capt James Pace & Lt Nealy, Vol Mtd Gunmen; dismissed on muster date

BAKER, William, Pvt, Col William Johnson, Capt Benjamin Powells; sick absent

BAKER, William, Pvt, Lt Col John Edmonson, Co Commander omitted, Cav

BAKER, William, Pvt, Maj John Childs, Capt Reuben Tipton, E TN Vol Mtd Gunmen; Regt County Knox

BAKER, William, Pvt, Maj William Russell, Capt Fleman Hodges, Vol Mtd Gunmen; substitute for James Myers

BAKER, William, Pvt, Regt Commander omitted, Capt Thomas Gray, Inf

BALANCE, Abraham, Pvt, Col Robt M Dyer, Capt Robt Evans, Vol Mtd Gunmen

BALCH, John B, Pvt, Col John K Wynne, Capt Wm Carruthers, W TN Inf

BALCH, John, Pvt, Col Alex Loury & Lt Col Leroy Hammonds, Capt Thos Delaney, Inf

BALCH, John, Pvt, Col Wm Lillard, Capt Jacob Dyke, Vol Inf

BALCH, Jos, Pvt, Col John K Wynne, Capt John Proter, Inf

BALCH, Philonius B, Pvt, Col Thos Benton, Capt Benj Hewett, Vol Inf; refused to march

BALDON, Aaron, Pvt, Col R H Dyer, Capt Cuthbert Hudson, Vol Mtd Gunmen

BALDRIDGE, Andrew, Sgt, Col Thos Benton, Capt Thos Williamson, Vol Inf

BALIEW, Jonathan, Pvt, Col Robert Steele, Capt Jas Shenault, Mil Inf

BALLARD, Jas, Pvt, Col Thos McCrory Capt Anthony Metcalf, Mil Inf; not being fit for duty

BALLARD, Jesse, Pvt, Col Thos Williamson, Capt James Pace & Lt James Neely, Vol Mtd Gunmen; d 2-5-1815

BALLARD, John, Pvt, Col Jas Raulston, Capt Edward Robinson, Inf

BALLARD, John, Pvt, Col Philip Pipkin, Capt David Smith, Inf; deserted 9-20-1814

BALLARD, Jos, Pvt, Col Newton Cannon, Capt Francis Jones, Mtd Riflemen

BALLARD, Micajah, Pvt, Col Edwin Booth, Capt Samuel Thompson, Inf

BALLARD, Richard, Pvt, Col Samuel Bayless, Capt Joseph Rich, E TN Mil Inf

BALLENGER, Henry, Pvt, Col Wm Lillard, Capt Thos McChristian, E TN Vol Inf

BALLENGER, Jas, Pvt, Col Edward Booth, Capt Samuel Thompson, Mil

BALLENGER, Jas, Pvt, Col Wm Johnston, Capt Henry Hunter, E TN Mil

BALLENGER, Jos, Pvt, Col Edward Booth, Capt Samuel Thompson, Mil

BALLEW, Isaac, Pvt, Col John Cocke, Capt James Gray, Inf; d 1-8-1815

BALLEW, John, Pvt, Regt Commander omitted, Capt N Davis, Inf

BALLINGER, Henry, Pvt, Col Wm Johnson, Capt Elihu Millikin, 3rd Regt E TN Mil

BALLINGER, Jacob, Pvt, Col William Johnston, Capt Henry Hunter, E TN Mil; left sick at Camp Ross 10-16-1814

BALLINGER, Jas, Pvt, Col William Johnston, Capt Henry Hunter, E TN Mil; left sick at Ft Claiborn 11-20-1814

BALLION, Wm, Pvt, Lt Col Jno Edmonson, Co Commander omitted, Cav

BALLSON, Joshua, Pvt, Col Wm Y Higgins, Capt Samuel A Allen, Mtd Gunmen

BALUE, Jos, Sgt, Col Pillow, Capt Isaiah Renshaw, Inf

BANDY, Briant, Pvt, Col Ewen Allison, Capt Jas Allen, E TN Mil

BANDY, Elihu, Pvt, Col S Copeland, Capt David Williams, Mil Inf

BANDY, Eperson, Pvt, Regt Commander omitted, Capt George Smith, Spies

BANDY, Eperson, Sgt, Col Thomas Williamson, Capt Robert Moore, Vol Mtd Gunmen

BANDY, Jamison, Pvt, Col Philip Pipkin, Capt Peter Searcy, Mil Inf

BANDY, Perrin, Cpl, Col Thomas Williamson, Capt Robert Moore, Vol Mtd Gunmen

BANDY, Richard, Sgt, Regt Commander omitted, Capt George Smith, Spies

BANDY, Robert, Pvt, Col Ewen Allison, Capt James Allen, E TN Mil

BANDY, Robert, Pvt, Col James Raulston, Capt Elijah Haynie, Inf

BANDY, Robert, Pvt, Col Joseph Duncan, Capt Joseph Duncan(?), E TN Drafted Mil

BANDY, Solomon, Pvt, Col Nicholas Perkins, Capt George Eliot, Mil Inf

BANGER, Henry, Far, Col Newton Cannon, Capt George Brandon, Mtd Riflemen

BANGER, Joseph, Ffr, Col Thomas Benton, Capt Renshaw, Vol Inf; Discharged

BANGERS, Enijah, Pvt, Maj John Chiles, Capt Charles Conway, E TN Mtd Gunmen

BANKHEAD, James, Pvt, Col John Alcorn, Capt Alexander McKeen, Cav

BANKHEAD, John, Cor, Col N Cannon, Capt George Brandon, Mtd Riflemen

BANKHEAD, Robert, 1 Lt, Col N Cannon, Capt George Brandon, Mtd Riflemen

BANTON, Joel H (Joab), Pvt, Col John Coffee, Capt Blackman Coleman, Cav

BARBA (BARBOUR), Major, Pvt, Col William Hall,

- 61

Capt John Moore, Vol Inf
BARBER, J John, Pvt, Maj Gen William Carroll, Capt Francis Ellis, Inf
BARBER, James, Pvt, Lt Col Leroy Hammons, Capt Thomas Delaney, Inf
BARBER, John, Pvt, Lt Col John Edmonson, Co Commander omitted, Cav
BARBER, John, Pvt, Regt Commander omitted, Capt G Martin, Mtd Inf 6 Brig
BARBER, Thadins W, Sgt, Col John Coffee, Capt John Baskerville, Cav
BARBER, William, Sgt, Col John K Wynne, Capt William Carruthers, W TN Inf; deserted, brought back, reduced to Pvt
BARBER, William, Sgt, Col Leroy Hammonds, Capt James Craig, 2 Regt W TN Mil
BARBOUR, T W, Master Swords, Col R H Dyer, Co Commander omitted, branch svce omitted
BARBOUR, Thaddeus, Master Swords, no other information
BARBOUR, Thadens W, Sgt, Col John Alcorn, Capt John Baskerville, Vol Inf
BARBOUR (BARBER), Lawson, 4 Sgt, Col Nicholas T. Perkins, Capt George Eliot, Mil Inf
BARBY, James, Pvt, Lt Col Leroy Hammons, Lt Col Alexander Loury, Capt Thomas Delaney, Inf
BARE, John, Pvt, Col William Lillard, Capt Thomas McChristian, E TN Vol Inf
BAREFIELD, Frederick, Pvt, Col John Cocke, Capt Joseph Price, Inf
BAREFIELD, James, Pvt, Col William Hall, Capt Travis Nash, Inf
BAREFIELD, James, Pvt, Maj Gen William Carroll, Capt Francis Ellis, Inf
BAREFOOT, Jonathan, Pvt, Col John Cocke, Capt John Dalton, Inf; died 12-10-1814
BAREN, Greenberry, Pvt, Col Ewen Allison, Capt Jacob Hoyal, E TN Mil
BARFIELD, James, Pvt, Col John Alcorn, Capt Alexander McKeen, Cav
BARFIELD, Lewis, Pvt, no other information
BARGE, Frederick, Pvt, Col William Lillard, Capt George Keyes, E TN Inf
BARGER, Daniel D, Pvt, Col L Hammond, Capt J Williamson, 2 Regt Inf
BARGER, Henry, Pvt, Col William Lillard, Capt William McLin, E TN Inf
BARGER, John, Pvt, Col John Brown, Capt John Chiles, E TN Vol Mtd Inf; left sick in Madison Co
BARGER, John, Pvt, Col S Barry, Capt Jones Griffin, E TN Draft Mil
BARGO, Isaac, Pvt, Col Samuel Bunch, Capt James Cummings, E TN Vol Mtd Inf
BARGO, Jacob, Pvt, Col Samuel Bunch, Capt James Cummings, E TN Vol Mtd Inf
BARGO, Jacob, Pvt, Maj John Childs, Capt James Cummings, E TN Vol Mtd Inf; died Ft Deposit 12-10-1814
BARHAM, William, Pvt, Maj Gen Andrew Jackson, Capt J Parrish, Arty
BARHEE, Major, Pvt, Lt Col H Dryan, no other information
BARKER, Daniel, Pvt, Col Thomas Benton, Capt George Caperton, Vol Inf
BARKER, David, Pvt, Col Thomas Benton, Capt George Caperton, Vol Inf
BARKER, Isaac N, Pvt, Col John K. Wynne, Capt William McCall, Inf
BARKER, John, Pvt, Lt Col H Bryan, no other information
BARKER, Joshua, Pvt, Col James Raulston, Capt Henry Hamilton, Inf; also served under Gen Carroll
BARKER, Lemon, Pvt, Lt Col Hammons, Capt Thomas Williamson, Inf; left sick at Ft Pierce
BARKER, William, Pvt, Col Stephen Copeland, Capt Wilkinson, Mil Inf
BARKER, Younger, Pvt, Regt Commander omitted, Capt James Haggard, Mtd Gunmen
BARKER, Zachariah, Pvt, Col John Cocke, Capt Joseph Price, Inf
BARKLEY, James, Pvt, Col Philip Pipkin, Capt George Mebane, Mil Inf
BARKLEY, James, Pvt, Col Thomas Benton, Capt Isiah Renshaw, Vol Inf
BARKLEY, James, Pvt, Col William Pillow, Capt Isiah Renshaw; waggoner
BARKLEY, Robert, 3 Sgt, Col William Hall, Capt Brice Martin, Vol Inf
BARKMAN, Henry, Pvt, Col S Copeland, Capt John Dawson, Inf
BARKS, Henderson, Pvt, Col James Raulston, Capt Mathew Cowan, Inf
BARKS, Sutton, Pvt, Col James Raulston, Capt Mathew Cowan, Inf
BARKS, Sutton, Pvt, Col Robert Stelle, Capt Richard Ratton, Mil Inf
BARKSDALE, John, Pvt, Col N Cannon, Capt John Harpole, Mtd Gunmen; to Col Wynn Regt & promoted
BARKSDALE, Randolph, Col John Alcorn, Capt William Locke, Cav
BARKSDALE, Randolph, Pvt, Col Thomas Williamson, Capt John Hutchings, Vol Mtd Gunmen
BARKSDALE, William, 3 Sgt, Col John Coffee, Capt Blackman Coleman, Cav
BARKSDALE, William, Pvt, Col Thomas Williamson, Capt Richard Tate, Vol Mtd Gunmen
BARNARD, Barkett, Pvt, Maj William Woodfolk, Capt Abraham Dudney, Inf
BARNARD, James T, Pvt, Col Thomas Williamson, Capt Thomas Scurry, Vol Mtd Gunmen
BARNARD, James, Pvt, Col William Hall, Capt John Moore, Vol Inf
BARNARD, Moses, Pvt, Col Philip Pipkin, Capt William Mackay, Mil Inf
BARNARD, Thomas, Pvt, Col Philip Pipkin, Capt William Mackay, Mil Inf
BARNARD, William, Pvt, Col William Hall, Capt John Moore, Vol Inf
BARNES, Abraham, Cpl, Col S Bunch, Capt George Gregory, E TN Draft Mil
BARNES, Abraham, Ffr, Col Samuel Bayless, Capt James

## Enlisted Men, War of 1812

BARNES, Abraham, Pvt, Col William Lillard, Capt John Roper, E TN Vol Inf
BARNES, Alexander S, Pvt, Col William Metcalf, Capt Bird Hurt, Mil Inf
BARNES, Ansylum, Sgt, Col A Cheatham, Capt Charles Johnson, Inf
BARNES, Benjamin, Pvt, Col Philip Pipkin, Capt William Mackay, Mil Inf
BARNES, Benjamin, Pvt, Col William Metcalf, Capt William Mullin, Mil Inf
BARNES, Collum, Sgt, Col Thomas Williamson, Capt Thomas Scurry, Vol Mtd Gunmen
BARNES, Daniel T, Pvt, Col Thomas Williamson, Capt James Pace, Lt James Nealy, Vol Mtd Gunmen; died 10-10-1815
BARNES, Daniel, Pvt, Col Newton Cannon, Capt Thomas Yarkley, Mtd Riflemen
BARNES, Daniel, Pvt, Col Thomas McCrory, Capt James Shannon, branch svce omitted
BARNES, Dempsey, Pvt, Col N T Perkins, Capt Philip Pipkin, Mtd Riflemen
BARNES, Dempsey, Pvt, Col Thomas Benton, Capt Thomas Williamson, Vol Inf
BARNES, Dempsey, Pvt, Col William Pillow, Capt Thomas Williamson, Vol Inf; deserted
BARNES, James, Cpl, Col Samuel Bunch, Capt Frances Register, E TN Mil; transferred from McPherson's Co
BARNES, James, Cpl, Col Samuel Bunch, Capt George McPherson, E TN Mil
BARNES, James, Pvt, Maj William Woodfolk, Capt Abraham Dudney, Inf
BARNES, Jesse, Pvt, Col William Pillow, Capt Thomas Williamson, Vol Inf
BARNES, Joel, Pvt, Col N T Perkins, Capt Philip Pipkin, Mtd Riflemen
BARNES, John, Pvt, Col John Brock, Capt Samuel Bayless, E TN Mil
BARNES, John, Pvt, Col Robert Dyer, Capt Ephraim Dickson, 1st TN Mtd Vol Gunmen
BARNES, John, Pvt, Regt Commander omitted, Capt Josiah Askew, Inf
BARNES, John, Sgt, Col William Johnson, Capt Joseph Scott, E TN Drafted Mil; sick absent
BARNES, Jordon, Pvt, Col Thomas Benton, Capt Thomas Williamson, Vol Inf
BARNES, Joshua, 3 Sgt, Maj Gen Jackson, Capt Joseph Kirkpatrick, Mtd Gunmen
BARNES, Joshua, Pvt, Col Thomas Williamson, Capt Richard Tate, Vol Mtd Gunmen
BARNES, Moses, Pvt, Col Samuel Bayless, Capt James Churchman, E TN Mil
BARNES, Moses, Pvt, Col Samuel Bunch, Capt John Houk, E TN Mil
BARNES, Traylous, Sgt, Col Samuel Bayless, Capt James Churchman, E TN Mil
BARNES, Turner, 2 Cpl, Col William Hall, Capt John Wallace, Inf
BARNES, Turner, 3 Cpl, Col Edward Bradley, Capt John Wallace, Vol Inf

BARNES, Wm, Pvt, Col John K Wynne, Capt Bayless E Prince, Inf; deserted 12-12-1813
BARNES, ____, Cpl, Col S Bunch, Capt F Register, E TN Mil
BARNET, Elijah, Pvt, Col Thomas Benton, Capt William Smith, Vol Inf
BARNET, James, Pvt, Col Philip Pipkin, Capt David smith, Inf
BARNET, John, Pvt, Col Samuel Bunch, Capt William Houston, E TN Mil; deserted 10-19-1813
BARNET, Lewis, Pvt, Col Wm Lillard, Capt Wm Hamilton, E TN Vol Inf; never came out camp
BARNET, Moses, Pvt, Col J Alcorn, Capt Thos Bradley, Vol Cav
BARNETT, Abraham, Pvt, Maj John Childs, Capt John Stephens, E TN Vol Mtd Inf
BARNETT, Elijah, Pvt, Regt Commander omitted, Capt Wm J Smith, Vol Inf
BARNETT, Jacob, Pvt, Col Edwin Booth, Capt Samuel Thompson, Mil
BARNETT, James, Pvt, no other information
BARNETT, Jas H, Pvt, Col Wm Lillard, Capt George Keys, E TN Inf
BARNETT, Jas P, Pvt, Col Thos Williamson, Capt Wm Martin, Vol Mtd Gunmen
BARNETT, Jas, Pvt, Col William Johnson, Capt Christopher Cook, E TN Mil
BARNETT, Thomas, Pvt, Col S Bunch, Capt Jno Houk, E TN Mil
BARNETT, Thos, Pvt, Col Samuel Wear, Capt John Stephens, E TN Vol Inf
BARNETT, Thos, Pvt, no other information
BARNHAM, Talbot, Pvt, Col John Brown, Capt Allen Bacon, E TN Mil Inf
BARNHAM, Wm N, Pvt, Col A Cheatham & Maj A Jackson, Capt Wm Creel, Inf; transferred to artillery
BARNHART, Adam, Pvt, Col Wm Metcalf, Capt John Barnhart, Mil Inf
BARNHART, Andrew, Pvt, Col Wm Metcalf, Capt John Barnhart, Mil Inf
BARNHART, Andrew, Pvt, Maj A Jackson & Col A Cheatham, Capt Wm Creel, Inf
BARNHART, Conrad, Pvt, Col S Bunch, Capt Geo McPherson, E TN Mil
BARNHART, John, Capt, Col Wm Metcalf, Capt John Barnhart, Mil Inf
BARNHART, ____, Pvt, Col S Bunch, Capt F Register, E TN Mil
BARNHART, ____rod, Pvt, Col Samuel Bunch, Capt Francis Register, E TN Mil
BARNS, Chas, Pvt, Col R C Napier, Capt Early Benson, Mil Inf
BARNS, Henry, Pvt, Col Jno Coffee, Capt John W Byrns, Cav
BARNS, Henry, Tptr, Col Wm Alcorn, Capt John W Byrne, Cav; killed at battle of Talledega 11-9-1813
BARNS, Hugh, Pvt, Col Wm Metcalf, Capt John Cunningham & Capt Alexander Hill, Mil Inf
BARNS, John, Pvt, Col William Lillard, Capt Benjamin H

- 63

## Enlisted Men, War of 1812

Kings, E TN Vol Inf
BARNS, John, Pvt, Regt Commander omitted, Capt Ephraim Dickson, Branch Srvce omitted
BARNS, John, Sgt, Col William Johnson, Capt Joseph Scott, E TN Drafted Mil
BARNS, Moses, Pvt, Col S Bunch, Capt Geo Gregory, E TN Drafted Mil
BARNS, Moses, Pvt, Col S Bunch, Capt Geo Gregory, E TN Drafted Mil; substituted for Abraham Barnes
BARNWELL, Robt, Pvt, Col S Bunch, Capt Jno English, E TN Mil Drafted
BARNWELL, Robt, Pvt, Col S Bunch, Capt Solomon Dobkins, E TN Drafted Mil
BARNWELL, William, Pvt, Col Samuel Bayless, Capt John Brock, E TN Mil; furloughed 1-31-1815 on account of inability
BARR, Eli, Pvt, Col Nicholas Perkins, Capt George Eliot, Mil Inf
BARR, Hezekiah, Pvt, Col Alexander Loury, Capt Geo Sarver, Inf
BARR, Hugh, Pvt, Col R C Napier, Capt Jas McMurry, Mil Inf
BARR, Hugh, Pvt, Col Thomas H Benton, Capt Jas McEwen, Vol Inf
BARR, Hugh, Pvt, Maj A Jackson & Col A Cheatham, Capt William Creel, Inf
BARR, Hugh, Sgt, Gen Thos Washingotn, Capt Jno Crawford, Mtd Inf
BARR, Jno D, Pvt, Regt Commander omitted, Capt David Smith, Cav Vol
BARR, John W, Pvt, Col Jas Raulston, Capt Henry West, Inf
BARR, John, Sgt, Col Alexander Loury, Capt Geo Sarver, Inf
BARR, Peter, Pvt, Col S Bunch, Capt Jas Cummings, E TN Vol Mtd Inf
BARR, Silas, Pvt, Col A Cheatham, Capt George Chapman, Inf
BARR, Thomas, Sgt, Col James Raulston, Capt Mathew Neal, Inf
BARRETT, George, Sgt, Col Alexander Loury, Capt George Sarver, Inf
BARRETT, Henry, Pvt, Col Thomas Benton, Capt William Moore, Vol Inf
BARRETT, James, Pvt, Col Philip Pipkin, Capt David Smith, Inf
BARRETT, John, Pvt, Maj William Russell, Capt John Cowan, Vol Mtd Gunmen
BARRETT, Joseph, Sgt, Col Thomas Williamson, Capt John Moore, Vol Mtd Gunmen
BARRETT, Samuel S, Cpl, Col Philip Pipkin, Capt David Smith, Inf; deserted 9-20-1814
BARRETT, Samuel S, Cpl, Col S Copeland, Capt Richard Sharp, Mil Inf
BARRETT, Samuel S, Pvt, Col Philip Pipkin, Capt William Pegram, W TN Mil Det of Capt David Smyth Co; deserted 9-20-1814
BARRETT, Samuel, Pvt, Col John Cocke, Capt Joseph Price, Inf; d 3-20-1815
BARRETT, William, Pvt, Col John Wynne, Capt Bayless Prince, Inf

BARRETT, William, Pvt, Col S Copeland, Capt Alexander Provine, Mil Inf; sick absent 3-10-1814
BARRIER, Charles, Pvt, Col Alexander Loury & Lt Col Leroy Hammonds, Capt Thomas Delaney, Inf
BARRINGER, Daniel, Pvt, Col S Bunch, Capt George Gregory, E TN Drafted Mil
BARRON, Edmund, Pvt, Col Edward Bradley, Capt John Wallace, Vol Inf
BARRON, Thomas, Pvt, Col William Lillard, Capt Jacob Hartsell, E TN Vol Inf
BARROW, William, Pvt, Col Thomas Williamson, Capt John Doak, Vol Mtd Gunmen
BARROW, William, Pvt, Regt Commander omitted, Capt N Davis, Inf
BARROWS, Edmond, Pvt, Col William Hall, Capt John Wallace, Inf
BARRY, James T, 3 Cpl, Col John Coffee, Capt James Terrill, Vol Cav
BARTEN, Robert, Pvt, Brig Gen Thomas Johnson, Capt Robert Carson, Inf
BARTHELL, Thomas, Pvt, Lt Col John Edmonson, Co Commander omitted, Cav
BARTLET, Elisha, Pvt, Col James Raulston, Capt Daniel Newman, Inf; d 2-11-1815
BARTLET, Isaac, Pvt, Col James Raulston, Capt Charles Wade, Inf
BARTLET, John, Pvt, Col S Bunch, Capt Solomon Dobkins, E TN Mil
BARTLETT, Benjamin, Pvt, Col R C Napier, Capt Drury Adkins, Mil Inf
BARTLETT, Jesse, Pvt, Col John Williams, Capt William Walker, Mtd Vol
BARTLETT, John L, Pvt, Col John Bradley, Capt Thomas Alcorn, Vol Cav
BARTLETT, John, Pvt, Col John Coffee, Capt Thomas Bradley, Vol Cav
BARTLETT, Joshua, Pvt, Col John Wynn, Capt James Holleman, Inf
BARTLEY, John, Pvt, Col S Bunch, Capt James Penny, E TN Mtd Inf
BARTLEY, Walker, Pvt Tptr, Maj John Chiles, Capt Daniel Price, Mil Inf
BARTLEY, William, Pvt, Col William Metcalf, Capt Barbee Collins, Mil Inf
BARTON, David, Pvt, Cool Edwin Booth, Capt Thomas Bradley, Vol Cav
BARTON, Elijah, Pvt, Col Samuel Bunch, Capt John English, E TN Drafted Mil
BARTON, Gabriel, 3 Sgt, Col Jas Raulston, Capt Chas Wade, Inf
BARTON, Isaac, Pvt, Col Samuel Bayless, Capt Joseph Rich, E TN Inf
BARTON, James, Pvt, Col Samuel Bunch, Capt Joseph Duncan, E TN Drafted Mil
BARTON, Jno, Pvt, Col S Bunch, Capt Jno Hauk, E TN Mil
BARTON, Jno, Pvt, Col Samuel Bunch, Capt Geo Gregory, E TN State Mil
BARTON, Jno, Pvt, Regt Commander omitted, Capt Jas Haggard, Mtd Gunmen
BARTON, John H, Pvt, Regt Commander omitted, Capt

*Enlisted Men, War of 1812*

Isaih Hamilton, Branch Srvce omitted
BARTON, John, Pvt, Col R C Napier, Capt Drury Adkins, Mil Inf
BARTON, John, Pvt, Col Samuel Bayless, Capt Jas Churchman, E TN Mil
BARTON, John, Pvt, Col Samuel Bunch, Capt Francis Berry, E TN Mil
BARTON, John, Pvt, Col Wm Johnson, Capt Elihu Millikin, 3rd Regt E TN Mil
BARTON, John, Pvt, Col Wm Lillard, Capt Thos McChristian, E TN Vol Inf
BARTON, John, Sgt, Col Samuel Bayless, Capt Joseph Goodson, E TN Mil; d 2-15-1815
BARTON, Joseph, Pvt, Col J Alcorn, Capt Thos Bradley, Vol Cav
BARTON, Joseph, Pvt, Col John Coffee, Capt Thos Bradley, Vol Cav
BARTON, Lemuel, Pvt, Lt Col H Bryan, no other information
BARTON, Robt, Pvt, Regt Commander omitted, Capt Jas Haggan, Mtd Gunmen
BARTON, Smith H, Pvt, Col Phillip Pipkin, Capt John Strother, Mil Inf
BARTON, Stephen, Pvt, Col J Allcorn, Capt Thomas Bradley, Vol Cav
BARTON, Stephen, Pvt, Col John Coffee, Capt Thomas Bradley, Vol Cav
BARTON, Stephen, Sgt Maj, Maj Wm Woodfolk, Co Commander omitted, Separate Bn W TN Mil
BARTON, Thos, Pvt, Col John K Wynne, Capt Bayless E Prince, Inf
BARTON, Thos, Pvt, Col R C Napier, Capt Early Benson, Mil Inf
BARTON, William, Pvt, Col Francis Ellis, Capt Maj Gen Carroll, Inf; d 2-13-1815
BARTON, William, Pvt, Col J Allcorn, Capt Thos Bradley, Vol Cav
BARTON, Wm, Pvt, Col Newton Cannon, Capt John Handly, Mtd Riflemen
BARTON, Wm, Pvt, Col Thos Williamson, Capt Robt Steele, Vol Mtd Gunmen
BARTON, Wm, Pvt, Lt Col John Edmonson, Co Commander omitted, Cav
BASE, Geo, Pvt, Col Edwin Booth, Capt John Slatton, E TN Mil
BASETER, Aaron, Pvt, Col John Bayless, Capt Francis Jones, E TN Drafted Mil
BASHAM, Drury, Pvt, Col N T Perkins, Capt John Doak, Vol Mtd Inf
BASHAM, Minyard, Pvt, Col John K Wynne, Capt John Porter, Inf; sick, present since discharged
BASHAM, Richard, Cpl, Col Thos Williamson, Capt John Doak & Capt John Dobbins, Vol Mtd Gunmen
BASHEARS, John, Pvt, Col Zacheus Copeland, Capt Fait, Inf
BASHEARS, Wm, Pvt, Col Zacheus Copeland, Capt Fait, Inf
BASKELL, Samuel, Pvt, Col Wm Hall, Capt Henry M Newlin, Vol Inf
BASKERVILLE, John, Capt, Col Jno Coffee, Capt Jno Baskerville, Cav

BASKERVILLE, John, Capt, Col John Alcorn, Capt Jno Baskerville, Vol Inf
BASKERVILLE, Samuel, Pvt, Col Philip Pipkin, Capt David Smith, Mil Inf
BASKERVILLE, Wm B, Pvt, Col Philip Pipkin, Capt David Smith, W TN Mil
BASKERVILLE, Wm H, Pvt, Col N T Perkins, Capt Matthew Patterson, Mtd Vol
BASKERVILLE, Wm H, Pvt, Col Philip Pipkin, Capt David Smith, Inf
BASKETT, Mathias, Pvt, Col William Johnson, Capt Christopher Cook, E TN Mil
BASKINS, Moses, Cpl, Col John Brown, Capt William White, Regt E TN Mil Inf
BASKINS, Moses, Pvt, Col Wm Hall, Capt Martin, Vol Inf; deserted
BASKINS, Robert, Cpl, Col A Cheatham, Capt Wm Smith, Inf
BASKINS, Wm, 3 Sgt, Col Jas Raulston, Capt Jas A Black, Inf
BASS, Cader, Pvt, Col Thos Williamson, Capt Robert Moore, Vol Mtd Gunmen
BASS, Charles, 6 Cpl, Col John Cocke, Capt James Gray, Inf
BASS, Dread, Cpl, Col S Copeland, Capt Moses Thompson, Inf
BASS, Elijah, Pvt, Col John K Wynne, Capt John Spinks, Inf
BASS, Elijah, Pvt, Col N T Perkins, Capt John Doak, Vol Mtd Gunmen
BASS, Hudson, Pvt, Lt Col H Boyan, no other information
BASS, Jesse, Pvt, Col John Coffee, Capt Michael Molton, Cav
BASS, John, Cpl, Maj Gen Wm Carroll, Capt Dan'l M Bradford & Capt Lewis Dillahunty, Vol Inf
BASS, John, Pvt, Col Stephen Copeland, Capt G W Stell, Mil Inf
BASS, John, Sgt, Col Thos Williamson, Capt John Doak & Capt John Dobbins, Vol Mtd Gunmen
BASS, Lyon, Pvt, Col Thos Williamson, Capt Robert Moore, Vol Mtd Gunmen
BASS, Orrion, Pvt, Maj Gen A Jackson, Capt Joseph Kirkpatrick, Mtd Gunmen; sick absent
BASSELL, Miles, Pvt, Col Wm Pillow, Capt Thos Williamson, Vol Inf
BASTES (BASTIC), John, Pvt, Col Samuel Wear, Capt James Gillespie, E TN Vol Inf
BATEMAN, Arail?, Pvt, Col S Copeland, Capt Alexander Provine, Mil Inf; sick absent 4-1-1814
BATEMAN, Asahel (Isail), Pvt, Col Jas Raulston, Capt Charles Wade, Inf
BATEMAN, Bemiah, Pvt, Commanders & Branch Srvce omitted; deserted 1-22-1813
BATEMAN, Benniah, Sgt, Col Robert Dyer, Capt Robert Evans, Vol Mtd Gunmen
BATEMAN, Enoch, Pvt, no other information
BATEMAN, Hoseah, Pvt, Col Robert M Dyer, Capt Robert Evans, Vol Mtd Gunmen
BATEMAN, Simon, Pvt, Commanders omitted, David Mason Cav
BATEMAN, Spencer, Pvt, Commanders & Branch Srvce

- 65

## Enlisted Men, War of 1812

omitted; sick--sent home
BATES, Benj, Pvt, Col Stephen Copeland, Capt William Hodges, Inf; sick absent
BATES, Drury, Pvt, Col J Alcorn, Capt Thomas Bradley, Vol Cav
BATES, Hampton, Pvt, Col Samuel Bunch, Capt Francis Berry, E TN Mil
BATES, James, Pvt, Col J Alcorn, Capt Thomas Bradley, Branch Srvce omitted
BATES, James, Pvt, Col John Coffee, Capt Thomas Bradley, Vol Cav
BATES, Jas, Pvt, Col John K Wynne, Capt Wm Carruthers, W TN Inf; sick absent
BATES, Jas, Pvt, Col Philip Pipkin, Capt John Robertson, Mil Inf
BATES, John B, Pvt, Col Philip Pipkin, Capt John Robertson, Mil Inf; left sick at Ft Jackson 11-19-1814
BATES, Jos, Pvt, Col Edward Bradley, Capt John Kennedy, Riflemen; absent without leave 12-12-1813
BATES, Jos, Pvt, Col William Hall, Capt John Kennedy, Vol Inf
BATES, Robt, Pvt, Col Alexander Loury & Lt Col Leroy Hammonds, Capt Thomas Wells, Inf
BATES, Royal R, Pvt, Col Jno Brown, Capt Wm D Neilson, E TN Vol Mil
BATES, Royal, Sgt, Col Edwin E Booth, Capt John McKamey, E TN Mil
BATES, Umphrey, Pvt, Col Jno Coffee, Capt John Baskerville, Cav
BATES, William, Pvt, Maj William Woodfolk, Capt Abner Pearce, Inf
BATES, Wm, Pvt, Col Philip Pipkin, Capt John Robertson, Mil Inf; left sick at Ft Strother 10-25-1814
BATES, Wm, Sgt, Col S Wear, Capt John Stephens, E TN Vol Inf
BATEY, David, Pvt, Col John Cocke, Capt John Weakley, Inf
BATEY, Robt, Pvt, Col John Alcorn, Capt John J Winston, Mtd Riflemen
BATEY, Robt, Pvt, Maj John Childs, Capt John Stephens, E TN Vol Mtd Inf
BATH, Thos, Pvt, Col Smith, Co Commander omitted, Inf
BATSON, Richard, Pvt, Regt Commander omitted, Capt Jos Williams, Mil Cav; discharged
BATTE, Benj D, Pvt, Col Thomas H Benton, Capt George W Gibbs, Vol Inf
BATTLE, Benj, Pvt, Col Thomas Benton, Capt Isaiah Renshaw, Vol Inf
BATTLE, Benjamin, Pvt, Col John Coffee, Capt Jas Terrill, Vol Cav; delinquent
BATTLE, Oren D, Pvt, Col John Coffee, Capt David Smith, Vol Cav; sick & absent
BATTRUP, Wm, Pvt, Col William Johnson, Capt Henry Hunter, E TN Mil
BATTS, Benj D, Pvt, Col Thomas Benton, Capt George W Gibbs, Vol Inf
BATTS, Jeremiah, Pvt, Col A Cheatham, Capt Richard Benson, Branch Srvce omitted
BATTS, Jno, 3 Sgt, Regt Commander omitted, Capt Joel Parrish, Arty
BATTS, John, Pvt, Maj Gen A Jackson & Col A Cheatham, Capt William Creel, Inf; transferred to Arty
BATTS, John, Pvt, Maj Gen A Jackson, Capt William Carroll, Vol Inf
BATTS, Jonathan, Pvt, Col Philip Pipkin, Capt John Strother, Mil; deserted 9-20-1814
BATY, James, Pvt, Col J Alcorn, Capt Thomas Bradley, Vol Cav
BATY, Sam'l, Pvt, Col Edwin E Booth, Capt Alexander Biggs, Inf
BATY, Wm, Pvt, Col N T Perkins, Capt John Quarles, Vol Mtd Inf
BAUCHMAN, John, Pvt, Maj Gen Wm Carroll, Capt Daniel M Bradford & Capt Dillahunty, Vol Inf
BAUGH, Jeremiah, Pvt, Col Philip Pipkin, Capt Henry Newlin, Mil Inf
BAUGHMAN, Christopher, Pvt, Col Thomas Benton, Capt George Gibb, Vol Inf
BAUGUS, Filus L, Pvt, Col John Brown, Capt John Lewis, E TN Vol Mtd Inf
BAULCH, John, Pvt, Col Ewen Allison, Capt Jacob Hoyal, E TN Mil; deserted 1-18-1814
BAULDWIN, Moses, Sdlr, Col N T Perkins, Capt Mathew Patterson, Mtd Vol
BAUSWELL, Walter, Cpl, Col John Cocke, Capt James Gray, Inf
BAW, Bartholomew, Pvt, Col Thomas McCrory, Capt Isaac Patton, Mil Inf
BAWDRY, Benj, 1 Cpl, Col William Lillard, Capt George Keyes, E TN Inf
BAWMAN, William, Pvt, Col William Johnson, Capt Andrew Lawson, E TN Drafted Mil
BAWSER, George, Pvt, Col William Lillard, Capt William McLin, E TN Inf
BAXTER, Alexander, Pvt, Col William Higgins, Capt Stephen Griffith, Mtd Riflemen
BAXTER, James, Pvt, Col William Metcalf, Capt William Mullin, Mil Inf
BAXTER, James, Pvt, Lt Col H Bryan
BAXTER, Jesse, Pvt, Col William Hall, Capt John Kennedy, Vol Inf
BAXTER, John, Pvt, Col Samuel Bunch, Capt David Vance, E TN Mtd Inf
BAXTER, Levi, Pvt, Col Samuel Bayless, Capt Joseph Hale, E TN Mil
BAXTER, Samuel, Pvt, Col Thomas Williamson, Capt James Pack & Lt James Nealy, Vol Mtd Gunmen
BAXTER, Stephen, Pvt, Col Samuel Bunch, Capt James Cummings, E TN Vol Mtd Inf
BAXTER, William, Pvt, Col Samuel Wear, Capt Robert Doak, E TN Vol Inf
BAY, Thomas, 1 Cpl, Maj Gen Andrew Jackson, Capt Joseph Kirkpatrick, Mtd Gunmen
BAYAR, Welcome, Pvt, Maj William Russell, Capt John Trimble, Vol Mtd Gunmen
BAYLES, William, Pvt, Col Samuel Bunch, Capt David Vance, E TN Mtd Inf
BAYLESS, Daniel, Pvt, Col Ewen Allison, Capt John Hampton, Mil

## Enlisted Men, War of 1812

BAYLESS, Daniel, Pvt, Col Ewin Allison, Capt Henry McCray, E TN Mil

BAYLESS, George L, Pvt, Col Philip Pipkin, Capt Henry Newlin, Mil Inf; promoted to 3 Cpl

BAYLESS, George, Pvt, Col Samuel Bayless, Capt John Waddle, E TN Mil

BAYLESS, George, Pvt, Col William Lillard, Capt Jacob Hartsell, E TN Vol Inf

BAYLESS, Harold, Pvt, Col John Brown, Capt Allen I Bacon, E TN Mil Inf

BAYLESS, Hezekiah, Pvt, Col Samuel Bayless, Capt Jonathan Waddle, E TN Mil; promoted QM Sgt

BAYLESS, Hezekiah, Pvt, Col Samuel Bunch, Capt David Vance, E TN Mtd Inf

BAYLESS, Hezekiah, Pvt, Maj William Russell, Capt William Chism, Vol Mtd Gunmen

BAYLESS, Hezekiah, Sgt, Col Samuel Bayless, Co Commander omitted, 4th Regt E TN Mil QM Corps

BAYLESS, John, Pvt, Maj John Childs, Capt Charles Conway, E TN Mtd Gunmen; Regt County Knox

BAYLESS, John, Sgt, Brig Gen Johnson, Capt Bethel Allen, Mil Inf

BAYLESS, Reese, Pvt, Col John Williams, Capt Samuel Bunch, Mtd Vol

BAYLESS, Reuben L, Pvt, Col Samuel Bunch, Capt David Vance, E TN Mtd Inf

BAYLESS, Thomas, Pvt, Maj William Russell, Capt Isaac Williams, Separate Bn TN Vol Mtd Gunmen

BAYLESS, William, Pvt, Col John Williams, Capt Samuel Bunch, Mtd Vol

BAYLESS, William, Pvt, Lt Col John Edmonson, Co Commander omitted, Cav

BAYLEY, Jas, Pvt, Col S Bunch, Capt N Gibbs, E TN Drafted Mil; discharged by Doctor King 1-17-1814

BAYLEY, Samuel, Pvt, Col Thos Williamson, Capt Robert Moore, Vol Mtd Gunmen

BAYLEY, Wm, Pvt, Col Robert H Dyer, Capt Joseph Williams, Vol Mtd Gunmen; d 1-3-1815

BAYLISS, Joel, Pvt, Lt Col John Edmonson, Co Commander omitted, Cav

BAYS, Williams A, Pvt, Gen Andrew Jackson, Capt William Rupee, Mtd Spies

BAYSE, James T, 3 Cpl, Col John Coffee, Capt James Terrell, Vol Cav

BEACHBOARD, William, Pvt, Col William Lillard, Capt George Keys, E TN Inf

BEADFORD, Joseph, Pvt, Col Robert Dyer, Capt Bethel Allen, Vol Mtd Gunmen

BEADLE, Philip, Pvt, Col Samuel Wear, Capt Daniel Price, E TN Vol Inf

BEADLES, Thomas, Pvt, Col James Raulston, Capt James Black, Inf

BEADLES, William, Pvt, Col James Raulston, Capt James Black, Inf

BEADY, Edmund, Pvt, Col John Brown, Capt James Standifer, E TN Vol Mtd Mil

BEAGLEY, Ephraim, Pvt, Col John Coffee, Capt Charles Kavanaugh, Cav

BEAIRD, William, Pvt, Col Thomas Benton, Capt George Caperton, Inf

BEAL, George, Pvt, Col Edwin Booth, Capt John Slatton, E TN Mil

BEAL, Thomas, Pvt, Col William Metcalf, Capt Thomas Marks, Mil Inf

BEALAND, Edward W, 4 Cpl, Col Alexander Loury, Capt John Looney, 2 Regt W TN Mil; d 3-17-1815

BEALE, Thomas, Pvt, Col William Hall, Capt Henry Newlin, Inf

BEALER, Peter, Pvt, Col William Johnson, Capt Henry Hunter, E TN Mil; d 11-20-1814

BEALER, William, Pvt, Col William Johnson, Capt Christopher Cook, E TN Mil

BEALER, William, Pvt, Col William Johnson, Capt Joseph Kirk, Mil

BEAMER, William, Pvt, Col John Brown, Capt Charles Lewis, E TN Vol Mtd Inf

BEAMSTETTER, Fred, Pvt, Col Samuel Bayless, Capt James Landen, E TN Mil

BEAN, Baxter, Pvt, Col Jno Williams, Capt Samuel Bunch, Mtd Vol

BEAN, Charles, Artif, Div of Maj Gen John Cocke, Master Artificer Aron Yarnell, E TN Mil

BEAN, Charles, Pvt, Col Wm Lillard, Capt Wm McLin, E TN Inf; appointed Armorer

BEAN, Chas, Pvt, Col Ewen Allison, Capt Henry McCray, E TN Mil

BEAN, Isaac, Cpl, Col Samuel Bayless, Capt Jonathan Waddell, E TN Mil

BEAN, Isaac, Pvt, Col Ewen Allison, Capt Henry McCray, E TN Mil

BEAN, Isaac, Pvt, Col Ewen Allison, Capt John Hampton, Mil

BEAN, Isaac, Pvt, Col S Bunch, Capt F Register, E TN Mil

BEAN, Jas C, Pvt, Col Jno Coffee, Capt Alexander McKeen, Cav; absent

BEAN, Jesse, Pvt, Col S Wear, Capt James Gillespie, E TN Vol Inf; appointed QM

BEAN, Jesse, Pvt, Col Thomas Williamson, Capt James Pace & Lt Nealy, Vol Mtd Gunmen; promoted to Lt of Spies

BEAN, Jesse, QM, Col Sam'l Wear, Co Commander omitted, E TN Vol Mil Inf

BEAN, Joab, Pvt, Col Jno Coffee, Capt McKean, Cav; absent

BEAN, Joel, Pvt, Col R H Dyer & Maj Wm Russell, Capt William Russell, Vol Mtd Gunmen

BEAN, Joel, Pvt, Col Thos Benton, Capt Geo Caperton, Vol Inf; substitute for Isaac Estus

BEAN, Joel, Pvt, Gen John Coffee, no other information

BEAN, Joel, Pvt, Regt Commander omitted, Capt Wm Mitchell, Spies

BEAN, Mark, Pvt, Col Samuel Bunch, Capt David G Vance, E TN Mtd Inf; AWOL

BEAN, Mordica, Pvt, Col Edwi E Booth, Capt John Slatton, E TN Mil

BEAN, Pleasant H, Pvt, Col Wm Pillow, Capt Geo Caperton, Inf

BEAN, Robert, Pvt, Col Samuel Bayless, Capt Joseph Rich, E TN Inf

BEAN, Russell Jno, Pvt, Col Wm Lillard, Capt Wm

- 67

## Enlisted Men, War of 1812

McLin, E TN Inf
BEAN, Russell, Pvt, Col Thos Benton, Capt Geo Caperton, Vol Inf
BEAN, Russell, Pvt, Gen John Coffee, no other information
BEAN, William, Pvt, Col Edwin Booth, Capt Samuel Thompson, Mil
BEANAD, Jno, Pvt, Maj William Woodfolk, Capt Abner Pearce, Inf; substitute for Richard Beacon
BEANE, Chas, Artif, Maj Gen John Cock, Co Commander omitted, E TN Mil
BEARD, Alexander, Pvt, Col William Y Higgins, Capt Thomas Eldridge, Mtd Gunmen
BEARD, David, Pvt, Col Wm Hall, Capt John Wallace, Inf
BEARD, Davis, Pvt, Col Edward Bradley, Capt John Wallace, Vol Inf; wounded on furlough 11-28-1813
BEARD, Elike, Pvt, Col Samuel Bayless, Capt Jas Churchman, E TN Mil
BEARD, Francis, 3 Cpl, Col Thos McCrory, Capt Thos K Gordon, Inf
BEARD, Geo W, Pvt, Col a Lowry, Capt J N Williamson, W TN Mil
BEARD, Geo W, Pvt, Lt Col Hammons, Capt Jos N Williamson, Inf
BEARD, Geo W, Pvt, Lt Col Leroy Hammons, Capt J N Williamson, W TN Mil
BEARD, Hiram, Pvt, Col Stephen Copeland, Capt G W Stell, Mil Inf
BEARD, Jas C, Pvt, Col John Coffee, Capt Alexander McKenn, Cav
BEARD, Jeremiah, Pvt, Brig Gen Johnson, Capt Abraham Allen, Mil Inf
BEARD, John C, Pvt, Col Samuel Bayless, Capt Jas Churchman, E TN Mil
BEARD, John, 2 Cpl, Col William Hall, Capt Henry Newland, Inf
BEARD, John, Cpl, Col Edward Bradley, Capt Thomas B Haynie, Vol Inf
BEARD, John, Pvt, Col John Brown, Capt Jesse G Reany, Mtd Gunmen
BEARD, John, Pvt, Col Thomas Williamson, Capt Thomas Scurry, Vol Mtd Gunmen
BEARD, Martin, 2 Sgt, Col N T Perkins, Capt Geo W Marr, Mtd Vol
BEARD, Martin, Pvt, Col William Hall, Capt Henry M Newland, Inf
BEARD, Nathan, 4 Cpl, Col R C Napier, Capt John Chism, Mil Inf
BEARD, Robt, Pvt, Col John Alcorn, Capt Alexander McKeen, Cav
BEARD, Samuel, Pvt, Col Edward Bradley, Capt Abraham Bledsoe, Riflemen; deserted 11-27-1813
BEARD, Samuel, Pvt, Col Edward Bradley, Capt John Wallace, Vol Inf
BEARD, Samuel, Pvt, Col Thos Williamson, Capt Thomas Scurry, Vol Mtd Gunmen
BEARD, Samuel, Pvt, Col Wm hall, Capt John Wallace, Inf
BEARD, Thos C, 4 Sgt, Col Edward Bradley, Capt John Wallace, Vol Inf
BEARD, Thos C, 4 Sgt, Col Wm Hall, Capt John Wallace, Inf
BEARD, Thos, Pvt, Col William Higgins, Capt Thomas Eldridge, Mtd Gunmen
BEARD, William, Pvt, Col Thomas Benton, Capt Isaiah Renshaw, Vol Inf
BEARD, Wm, Pvt, Col James Raulston, Capt Mathew Neal, Inf
BEARD, Wm, Pvt, Col Thomas Benton, Capt Geo Caperton, Vol Inf
BEARD, Wm, Pvt, Col Wm Hall, Capt Abraham Bledsoe, Vol Inf
BEARD, Wm, Pvt, Col Wm Pillow, Capt Geo Caperton, Inf
BEARD, Wm, Pvt, Maj John Childs, Capt Daniel Price, E TN Mtd Inf
BEARDEN, John, Pvt, Col Edward Bradley, Capt Abram Bledsoe, Vol Inf
BEARDEN, John, Pvt, Col Wm Hall, Capt Abraham Bledsoe, Vol Inf
BEARKLY, Isaac, Pvt, Col Phillip Pipkin, Capt Wm Mackey, Mil Inf
BEARMAN, Wm, Pvt, Col Wm Johnson, Capt Jas R Rogers, E TN Drafted Mil
BEARRY, Gilbert, Pvt, Col R Jarmon, Co Commander omitted, Inf
BEARSON, Jacob, Pvt, Gen Andrew Jackson, Capt H Kerr, Mtd Rangers
BEARSON, Jonathan, Pvt, Gen Andrew Jackson, Capt H Kerr, Mtd Rangers
BEASLEY, Archibald, Pvt, Col John Coffee, Capt Charles Kavanaugh, Cav
BEASLEY, Benjamin, Pvt, Regt Commander omitted, Capt Wm Tear, 6th Brigade
BEASLEY, Ephraim, Pvt, Col John Coffee, Capt Charles Kavanaugh, Cav
BEASLEY, Johnson, Pvt, Col Jas Raulston, Capt Elijah Haynie, Inf
BEASLEY, Jos, Pvt, Col John Cocke, Capt Bird Nance, Branch Srvce omitted
BEASLEY, Major A, Pvt, Col Thos Williamson, Capt Anthony Metcalf, Vol Mtd Gunmen
BEASOM, John, Cpl, Col Wm Higgins, Capt Stephen Griffith, Mtd Riflemen; killed 1-22-1814
BEASON, Jacob, Pvt, Col John K Winn, Capt William McCall, Inf
BEASON, Richard, Pvt, Maj William Woodfolk, Capt Jas Turner, Inf
BEATON, John, Pvt, no other information
BEATS, Russell, Pvt, Col Samuel Wear, Capt John Stephens, E TN Vol Inf
BEATTY, David, 3 Cpl, Col Cock, Capt Weakly, Inf
BEATTY, David, Pvt, Col Stephens Copeland, Capt William Evans, Mil Inf
BEATTY, John jr, Pvt, Col Stephen Copeland, Capt William Evans, Mil Inf; sick at Ft Strothers about 3-27-1814
BEATY, Arthur, Pvt, Col Alexander Loury, Capt John Looney, 2 Regt W TN Mil; sick absent
BEATY, David, Pvt, Col Ewen Allison, Capt Jonas Loughmiller, Branch Srvce omitted

## Enlisted Men, War of 1812

BEATY, Eliazer, Pvt, Brig Gen Johnson, Capt Carson, Inf

BEATY, John, Pvt, Col Thomas McCrory, Capt Samuel McKnight, Inf

BEATY, John, Sgt, Col Samuel Wear, Capt John Stephens, E TN Vol Inf

BEATY, Jos, Pvt, Col John Cocke, Capt George Barnes, Inf

BEATY, Robt, Pvt, Col Samuel Wear, Capt John Stephens, E TN Vol Inf

BEATY, Watson, Pvt, Col Ewen Allison, Capt Jonas Loughmiller, Mil

BEATY, Wm jr, Pvt, Col Edward Bradley, Capt John Kennedy, Riflemen; AWOL 12-12-1813

BEAVER, Edmund, Pvt, Col John K Wynne, Capt Rober? Brader, Inf

BEAVER, James, Pvt, Regt Commander omitted, Capt John Gordon, Mtd Spies

BEAVER, Jas, Pvt, Col Edward Bradley, Capt William Lauderdale, Vol Inf

BEAVER, Jas, Pvt, Col Philip Pipkin, Capt Jas Blakemore, Mil Inf; sick at Ft Strother 11-1-1814

BEAVER, Laurence, Pvt, Col Edward Bradley, Capt William Lauderdale, Vol Inf

BEAVER, Laurence, Pvt, Col Philip Pipkin, Capt Jas Blakemore, Mil Inf

BEAVER, Laurence, Pvt, Col Wm Hall, Capt William L Alexander, Vol Inf

BEAVERS, Abraham, Far, Col Thomas Williamson, Capt Wm Martin, Vol Mtd Gunmen

BEAVERS, Abraham, Pvt, Col Robert Steele, Capt Robert Campbell, Mil Inf; on furlough

BEAVERS, Jas, Pvt, Col Thomas Benton, Capt Thomas Williamson, Vol Inf

BEAVERS, Jas, Pvt, Col Thomas H Benton, Capt Benj Hewett, Vol Inf; refused to march

BEAVERS, Jas, Pvt, Col Thomas Williamson, Capt Hugh Martin, Vol Mtd Gunmen; d 2-8-1815

BEAVERS, Jas, Pvt, Col William Pillow, Capt Thomas Williamson, Vol Inf; transferred to Capt Gordon's Spies

BEAVERS, Jesse, Pvt, Col John K Wynne, Capt Robert Brader, Inf

BECK, Wm, Pvt, Col S Bunch, Capt Jno Houk, E TN Mil

BECK, Wm, Pvt, Col Samuel Bunch, Capt Francis Berry, E TN Mil

BECKELHIMER, John D, Pvt, Col Robert Steele, Capt John Chitwood, Mil Inf

BECKETT, Chas, Pvt, Col Thomas Williamson, Capt John Doak & Capt John Dobbins, Vol Mtd Gunmen; subst for Jos McCracken

BECKNEL, Lindsay, Pvt, Col Ewen Allison, Capt Thomas Wilson, E TN Drafted Mil

BECKNEL, Sam'l, Pvt, Col Ewen Allisoon, Capt Thomas Wilson, E TN Drafted Mil; appointed QM Sgt

BEDEN, Briant, Pvt, Col S Bunch, Capt Solomon Dobkins, E TN Mil; furloughed on account of inability

BEDFORD, Benjamin, Pvt, Maj Gen Carroll, Capt Francis Ellis, Inf

BEDFORD, Clement R, Pvt, Col Thomas Williamson, Capt James Pace, Vol Mtd Gunmen

BEDFORD, Robt, 4 Cpl, Col John Coffee, Capt Blackman Coleman, Cav

BEDFORD, Stephen, Tptr, Col John Alcorn, Capt Alexander McKeen, Cav; d 10-15-1813

BEELAR, James, 3 Cpl, Maj John Chiles, Capt James Cummings, E TN Vol Mtd Inf; sick at Ft Deposit, deserted

BEELER, Abraham, Cpl, Col Samuel Bunch, Lt John Harris, E TN Mil

BEELER, Benjamin, Pvt, Col Ewen Allison, Capt William King, Drafted Mil; left with the sick at Ft Williams

BEELER, Daniel, Pvt, Col Samuel Bayless, Capt John Brock, E TN Mil

BEELER, George, Pvt, Col Samuel Bayless, Capt John Brock, E TN Mil

BEELER, Joseph, Pvt, Col Ewen Allison, Capt William King, Drafted Mil; left sick at Ft Williams & returned

BEEN, Charles, Pvt, Col Samuel Bunch, Capt Francis Register, E TN Mil

BEEN, Edmond, Pvt, Col John Brown, Capt James Preston, E TN Mil Inf; promoted to Cpl

BEEN, Jonathan, Pvt, Maj William Woodfolk, Capt Ezekial Ross & Capt McCulley, Inf

BEEN, Russel, Pvt, Col William Johnson, Capt Andrew Lawson, E TN Mil Drafted; substitute for Cotten Cullin

BEEN, Russell, Pvt, Col Thomas Benton, Capt George Caperton, Inf; substitute for C Lee

BEEN, William, Pvt, Col Samuel Bunch, Lt John Harris, E TN Mil

BEETS, John, Pvt, Col Samuel Bunch, Capt Andrew Bacon, E TN Mil

BEIRD, John, Pvt, Col Ewen Allison, Capt Jonas Loughmiller, Mil; deserted 3-5-1814

BELAMY, Jesse, Pvt, Col L Hammond, Capt J Williamson, 2 Regt Inf

BELATE, Geo, Pvt, Col Philip Pipkin, Capt Jas Blakemore, Mil Inf; replaced by Whitwell Hill

BELCHER, James, Cpl, Col S Bunch, Capt John English, E TN Drafted Mil; joined from Capt Gregory's Co

BELCHER, James, Cpl, Col Samuel Bunch, Capt Solomon Dobkins, E TN Drafted Mil; transferred to Capt English Co

BELCHER, John, Pvt, Col A Cheatham, Capt James Giddens, Inf

BELEN, Joseph, Pvt, Col Thomas Benton, Capt James McFerrin, Vol Inf; transferred to Capt Renshaw's Co

BELEN, William H, 3 Sgt, Col Thomas Benton, Capt Robert Cannon, Inf

BELL, Alfred, Pvt, Col John Alcorn, Capt John W Byrn, Cav; sick absent

BELL, Archibald, Pvt, Col Samuel Wear, Capt John Bayless, Mtd Inf

BELL, Brooksey, Pvt, Col William Lillard, Capt William McLin, E TN Inf

BELL, Buchannon, Pvt, Col Thomas Williamson, Capt Thomas Scurry, Vol Mtd Gunmen

BELL, Daniel, Pvt, Col William Metcalf, Capt John Barnhart, Mil Inf; d 1-2-1815

BELL, David, Pvt, Col William Pillow, Capt Thomas Williamson, Vol Inf; sick absent continued service
BELL, David, Pvt, Regt Commander omitted, Capt Thomas Williamson, Det TN Vol Inf
BELL, Edward, Pvt, Col William Higgins, Capt Thomas Eldridge, Mtd Gunmen
BELL, Garrett, Pvt, Regt Commander omitted, Capt James Gray, Inf
BELL, Henry, Pvt, Col Samuel Bayless, Capt James Churchman, E TN Mil
BELL, Isaac H, Pvt, Col Newton Cannon, Capt John Dempsey, Mtd Gunmen; transferred from Capt Carothers
BELL, James I, Pvt, Lt Col John Edmonson, Co Commander omitted, Cav
BELL, James L, Pvt, Col John Coffee, Capt Michael Molton, Cav
BELL, James, Pvt, Col Newton Cannon, Capt John Harpole, Mtd Gunmen
BELL, James, Pvt, Col Samuel Wear, Capt Rufus Morgan, E TN Vol Inf
BELL, James, Pvt, Lt Col John Edmonson, Co Commander omitted, Cav
BELL, James, Pvt, Maj William Russell, Capt Felman Hodges, Vol Mtd Gunmen
BELL, Jared, Pvt?, Col R C Napier, Capt Thomas Gray, Mil Inf
BELL, Jesse, 5 Cpl, Col John Cocke, Capt Richard Crunk, Inf
BELL, Jesse, Pvt, Col A Cheatham, Capt Richard Benson, Inf
BELL, Joel, Pvt, Col John Wynne, Capt John Porter, Inf
BELL, John B, Pvt, Col Samuel Bayless, Capt Jonathan Waddell, E TN Mil
BELL, John jr, Pvt, Maj William Russell, Capt John Cowan, Vol Mtd Riflemen
BELL, John jr, Pvt, Regt Commander omitted, Capt Jas Cowan, Branch Srvce omitted; on furlough 3-20-1814
BELL, John sr, Pvt, Maj William Russell, Capt John Cowan, Vol Mtd Riflemen
BELL, John, Cpl, Col A Cheatham, Capt Richard Benson, Inf
BELL, John, Pvt, Col John Alcorn, Capt John Byrn, Cav
BELL, John, Pvt, Col John Cocke, Capt Richard Crunk, Inf
BELL, John, Pvt, Col Robert Steele, Capt John Chitwood, Mil Inf
BELL, John, Pvt, Col Thomas Williamson, Capt Richard Tate, Vol Mtd Gunmen
BELL, John, Pvt, Col William Metcalf, Capt John Cunningham & Capt Alexander Hill, Mil Inf
BELL, John, Pvt, Col William Metcalf, Capt William Mullin, Mil Inf
BELL, John, Pvt, Regt Commander omitted, Capt James Cowan, Mtd Inf
BELL, John, Pvt, Regt Commander omitted, Capt William Rupee, Gen Jackson's Mtd Spies
BELL, John, Pvt, no other information
BELL, Jos E, Pvt, Col William Johnson, Capt Andrew Lawson, E TN Drafted Mil; furloughed sick at Knoxville 9-27-1814
BELL, Jos H, Pvt, Col Samuel Bayless, Capt Joseph E Bacon, E TN Mil
BELL, Jos, Pvt, Col William Johnson, Capt Andrew Lawson, E TN Drafted Mil; substitute for Jas Bishop
BELL, Nathaniel, Pvt, Col Thomas Benton, Capt Thomas Williamson, Vol Inf; missing
BELL, Nathaniel, Pvt, Col William Pillow, Capt Thomas Williamson, Vol Inf; continued in service
BELL, Nathaniel, Pvt, Regt Commander omitted, Capt Thos Williamson, Det TN Vol Inf
BELL, Philip, Pvt, Col S Bunch, Capt Jno McNare, E TN Mil; d 3-19-1814
BELL, Robt, Pvt, Col Robert Steele, Capt John Chitwood, Mil Inf
BELL, Sam'l, Pvt, Col Ewen Allison, Capt John Hampton, Mil; deserted 3-4-1814
BELL, Sam'l, Pvt, Col N Cannon, Capt John B Dempsey, Mtd Gunmen
BELL, Sam'l, Pvt, Col Thomas Benton, Capt Thomas Williamson, Vol Inf
BELL, Sam'l, Pvt, Col Thomas Williamson, Capt Giles Burdett, Vol Mtd Gunmen
BELL, Sam'l, Pvt, Col Thomas Williamson, Capt Wm Martin, Vol Mtd Gunmen
BELL, Sam'l, Pvt, Col William Pillow, Capt Thomas Williamson, Vol Inf
BELL, Sam'l, Pvt, Col William Y Higgins, Capt John B Cheatham, Mtd Riflemen
BELL, Sam'l, Pvt, Col Wm Johnson, Capt Jas Stewart, E TN Drafted Mil
BELL, Sam'l, Pvt, Col Wm Johnson, Capt Jas Stewart, E TN Mil
BELL, Samuel, Pvt, Lt Col Jas Edmonson, Co Commander omitted, Cav
BELL, Samuel, Pvt, Regt Commander omitted, Capt G Martin, Mtd Inf 6th Brig
BELL, Thos, Pvt, Col Alexander Loury, Capt Gabriel Martin, Inf; left sick at Mount by order of Col Loury
BELL, Wm, Pvt, Col William Johnston, Capt Henry Hunter, E TN Mil; substitute for Jas Brown
BELL, Wm, Pvt, Regt Commander omitted, Capt Jas Haggard, Spies
BELL, Zedcock, Pvt, Brig Gen Thomas Johnson, Capt Robert Carson, Inf
BELLAMY, Jesse, Pvt, Col A Loury, Capt J Williamson, W TN Mil
BELLAMY, Jesse, Pvt, Col Jno Coffee, Capt Fredrick Stump, Cav
BELLAMY, Jesse, Pvt, Col John Alcorn, Capt Fredrick Stump, Cav
BELLEMY, Jesse, Pvt, Col Leroy Hammonds, Capt Joseph N Williamson, Inf; left sick at Ft Pierce
BELLER, Peter, Pvt, Maj Wm Russell, Capt Geo Mitchie, Vol Mtd Gunmen
BELLEW, Bryant, Pvt, Col Thomas Benton, Capt Isaiah Renshaw, Vol Inf
BELLOW, Jas, Pvt, Col Jas Raulston, Capt Edward Robin-

son, Inf; detached to work with principal artificer
BELLOW, Peter, Pvt, Col Thomas Williamson, Capt Geo Mitchie, 2 Regt TN Vol Mtd Gunmen
BELLOW (BELLOM), Moses, Pvt, Col Jas Raulston, Capt Edward Robinson, Inf
BELOATT, Smith C, Sdlr, Col Robert H Dyer, Capt Bethel Allen, Vol Mtd Gunmen
BELT, Middleton, Pvt, Col Jas Raulston, Capt Jas A Black, Inf; d 2-4-1815
BELT, Thos, Pvt, Col Jas Raulston, Capt Jas A Black, Inf
BELYAE, John, Pvt, Col Edward Bradley, Capt John Kennedy, Riflemen; furlough
BELYEW, Isaac, Pvt, Col John Cocke, Capt James Gray, Inf; d 1-8-1815
BEMAN, Martin, Pvt, Col S Copeland, Capt Allen Wilkinson, Mil Inf
BENAN, William, Pvt, Lt I Barrett, Capt Nathan Davis, Inf
BENBY, William, Pvt, Regt Commander omitted, Capt Thomas Gray, Inf
BENCE, Peter, Pvt, Col Samuel Wear, Capt John Stephens, E TN Vol Inf
BENCH, Peter, Pvt, Col William Johnson, Capt David McKamy, E TN Draft Mil; sick absent
BENGE, Richard, Pvt, Col R H Dyer, Maj William Russell, Capt William Russell, Vol Mtd Gunmen
BENGE, Richard, Pvt, Col Thomas Benton, Capt George Caperton, Vol Inf
BENHAM, John, Pvt, Col Philip Pipkin, Capt John Strother, Mil; deserted
BENHAM, William, Pvt, Col Ewen Allison, Capt William King, Drafted Mil; deserted
BENJAMIN, Henry, Pvt, Maj William Russell, Capt Isaac Williams, Separate Bn V M Gunmen
BENJAMIN, Thomas, Pvt, Col Leroy Hammonds, Capt James Craig, Inf
BENNEFIELD, James H, Pvt, Col T McCrory, Capt James Shannon, Mil Inf
BENNEFIELD, Ranson, Pvt, Col Stephen Copeland, Capt William Evans, Mil Inf
BENNEFIELD, Robert, Cpl, Col Stephen Copeland, Capt William Evans, Mil Inf
BENNET, Aaron, Pvt, Lt Col Leroy Hammonds, Capt Joseph N Williamson, Inf
BENNET, Jacob, Pvt, Col Philip Pipkin, Capt George Mebane, Mil Inf; deserted from Ft Jackson
BENNET, James, Pvt, Col William Lillard, Capt Jacob Dyke, Vol Inf; deserted
BENNET, Pvt, Col James Raulston, Capt Henry West, Inf
BENNET, William, Pvt, Col William Alcorn, Capt John W Byrne, Cav
BENNETT, Aaron, Pvt, Col L Hammond, Capt J N Williamson, 2nd Regt Inf
BENNETT, Benjamin, Pvt, Col Edwin Booth, Capt John Sharp, E TN Mil
BENNETT, Cooper M, Pvt, Col Thomas Benton, Capt Robert Cannon, Inf
BENNETT, Cornelius, Pvt, Col Thomas Benton, Capt George Caperton, Inf
BENNETT, Daniel, Pvt, Col Thomas Benton, Capt George Caperton, Inf

BENNETT, George, Pvt, no other information
BENNETT, Green, Pvt, Col Thomas Benton, Capt George Caperton, Inf
BENNETT, Hardy, Sgt, Col N T Perkins, Capt John Doak, Mtd Vol Riflemen; wounded 1-22-1814?
BENNETT, Haywood, Pvt, Col Edwin Booth, Capt John Lewis, E Tn Mil; promoted to asst wgnmstr
BENNETT, James D, Forage Master, Maj Gen John Cocke, Co Commander omitted, E TN Vol Mil
BENNETT, James, Pvt, Col John Brown, Capt Jesse Reany, Mtd Gunmen
BENNETT, James, Pvt, Col Samuel Bayless, Capt John Brock, E TN Mil
BENNETT, James, Pvt, Col William Johnson, Capt Joseph Kirk, Mil
BENNETT, John, Pvt, Col John Brown, Capt William Christian, E TN Mil Inf
BENNETT, John, Pvt, Col William Metcalf, Capt John Barnhart, Mil Inf
BENNETT, Solomon, 3 Sgt, Col N T Perkins, Capt John Doak, Mtd Vol Riflemen
BENNETT, Thomas, Pvt, Col James Raulston, Capt Charles Wade, Inf
BENNETT, Walker, Mus, Col Thomas Benton, Capt George Gibbs, Vol Inf
BENNETT, Walter, Mus-Dmr, Col Thomas Benton, Capt George Gibbs, Vol Inf
BENNETT, Walter, Pvt, Col William Pillow, Capt John Anderson, Vol Inf; deserted
BENNETT, William E, Pvt, Col Newton Cannon, Capt John Harpole, Mtd Gunmen
BENNETT, William, Pvt, Col William Hall, Capt John Wallace, Inf
BENNETT, William, Pvt, no other information
BENNINGFIELD, Robert, Pvt, Col R H Dyer, Capt Thomas White, Vol Mtd Gunmen; absent sick
BENSOLL, James, Pvt, Maj William Russell, Capt William Russell, Vol Mtd Gunmen
BENSON, Charles, Pvt, Col William Lillard, Capt Jacob Dyke, Vol Inf
BENSON, Daniel, Pvt, Col William Lillard, Capt Jacob Dyke, Vol Inf; deserted
BENSON, David, Pvt, Col Samuel Bayless, Capt Joseph Rich, E TN Inf
BENSON, Early, Capt, Col R C Napier, Capt self, Mil Inf
BENSON, James, Pvt, Col John Cocke, Capt James Gault, Inf
BENSON, James, Pvt, Col Robert Dyer, Maj William Russell, Capt William Russell, Vol Mtd Gunmen
BENSON, James, Pvt, Col S Copeland, Capt Richard Sharp, Mil Inf; absent sick
BENSON, James, Sgt, Col Edwin Booth, Capt James Porter, Drafted Mil
BENSON, John, Pvt, Col John Coffee, Capt Charles Kavanaugh, Cav
BENSON, John, Pvt, Col Thomas Williamson, Capt John Crane, Capt James Cook Vol Mtd Gunmen
BENSON, John, Pvt, Regt Commander omitted, Capt Archibald McKenney, Cav
BENSON, Labin, Pvt, Col John Coffee, Capt Charles Kavanaugh, Cav; AWOL

## Enlisted Men, War of 1812

BENSON, Labin, Sgt, Regt Commander omitted, Capt Archibald McKenney, Cav

BENSON, Philip, Cpl, Regt Commander omitted, Capt N David, Inf

BENSON, Richard, Pvt, Col S Copeland, Capt David Williams, Inf

BENSON, William, Pvt, Col Thomas Williamson, Capt John Crane, Capt James Cook, Vol Mtd Gunmen

BENSON, William, Pvt, Col William Higgins, Capt John Cheatham, Mtd Riflemen

BENSOW, Benjamin, Pvt, Col Edwin Booth, Capt James Porter, Drafted Mil

BENTAL, Enos, Cpl, Col Thomas Williamson, Capt Thomas Scurry, Vol Mtd Gunmen

BENTON, David, Pvt, Col S Copeland, Capt James Tait, Inf

BENTON, James, Pvt, Col John Cocke, Capt Richard Crunk, Inf

BENTON, James, Pvt, Col John Wynne, Capt Robert Breden, Inf

BENTON, James, Pvt, Regt Commander omitted, Capt David Smith, Cav Vol

BENTON, John, Cpl, Col Samuel Bunch, Capt John Houk, E TN Mil; from Berry's Co to Houk & promoted

BENTON, John, Pvt, Col John Alcorn, Capt Thomas Bradley, Vol Cav

BENTON, John, Pvt, Col Samuel Bunch, Capt Francis Berry, E Tn Mil

BENTON, John, Pvt, Col Samuel Wear, Capt Samuel Bowman, Mtd Inf

BENTON, John, Pvt, Col William Higgins, Capt John Cheatham, Mtd Riflemen

BENTON, John, Pvt, Lt Col John Edmonson, Co Commander omitted, Cav

BENTON, Samuel, Pvt, Col Thomas Benton, CaptJames McEwen, Vol Inf; promoted to 1 Sgt

BENTON, William, Pvt, Col Edwin Booth, Capt John Sharp, E TN Mil

BENTON, Willie, Pvt, Col Newton Cannon, Capt Ota Cantrell, W TN Mtd Inf

BENTY, Jacob, Cpl, Col William Johnson, Capt Joseph Kirk, Mil

BENZEY, Benjamin, Pvt, Col Robert Dyer, Capt Joseph Williams, 1st Regt Tn Vol Mtd Gunmen

BERAS, James, Pvt, no other information

BERCEAN, John, Pvt, Col Thomas Benton, Capt George Caperton, Inf

BERGER, Michael, Pvt, Col William Lillard, Capt James Lillard, E TN Vol Inf

BERK (BURK?), John, Pvt, Col James Raulston, Capt Henry West, Inf

BERKEEN, Lemuel, Pvt, Col N Cannon, Capt Ota Cantrell, W Tn Mtd Inf

BERKET, Mathias, Pvt, Col William Johnson, Capt Joseph Kirk, Mil

BERKLEY, Archibold C, Cpl, Col Thomas Benton, Capt Isaiah Renshaw, Vol Inf

BERKLEY, Benjamin E, Pvt, Col John K. Winn, Capt Robert Brader, Inf

BERLEY, Dillard, Pvt, Col S Copeland, Capt Alexander Provine, Mil Inf

BERNARD, George, Pvt, Col Robert H Dyer, Capt Thomas Jones, V M Gunmen

BERNARD, James, Pvt, Col Edward Bradley, Capt John Moore, Vol Inf; deserted

BERNARD, Valentine, Pvt, Col S Copeland, Capt G W Stell, Mil Inf

BERNARD, William L, Pvt, Col John Alcorn, Capt Fredrick Stump, Cav; transferred to Capt Gordon's Spies

BERNARD, William, Pvt, Col Edward Bradley, Capt John Moore, Vol Inf; deserted

BERNARD, William, Pvt; transferred to Capt White's Co; no other information

BERRY, Adam H, Pvt, Col Thomas H Benton, Capt James McEwen, Vol Inf

BERRY, Adam, Pvt, Col Robert H Dyer, Capt Robert Edmonson, 1 TN M V Gunmen

BERRY, Adam, Pvt, Col Thomas H Benton, Capt James McEwen, Vol Inf

BERRY, Adam, Pvt, Gen Thomas Washington, Capt John Crawford, Mtd Inf

BERRY, Adam, Pvt; no other information

BERRY, Barrel, Pvt, Col William Pillow, Capt C E McEwen, Vol Inf

BERRY, Bazel, Pvt, Col Thomas H Benton, Capt James McEwen, Vol Inf

BERRY, Enoch, Pvt, Col Thomas Williamson, Capt Giles Burdett, Mtd Vol Gunmen

BERRY, Francis, Pvt, Col Samuel Bunch, E TN Vol Mtd Inf

BERRY, George, Pvt, Col A Cheatham, Capt Richard Benson, Inf

BERRY, George, Pvt, Commanders omitted, Det of Inf of 26 Regt

BERRY, George, Pvt, Regt Commander omitted, Capt James Gray, Inf

BERRY, George, Sdlr, Regt Commander omitted, Capt James Haggard, Mtd Gunmen

BERRY, Gilbert, Pvt, Col John Coffee, Capt Michael Molton, Cav, absent sick

BERRY, Hugh, Pvt, Col John Brown, Capt James Preston, Regt E TN Mil Inf

BERRY, Jacob, Pvt, Col John Coffee, Capt Michael Molton

BERRY, James, Pvt, Col Edwin Booth, Capt Winton, E TN Mil

BERRY, James, Pvt, Col Samuel Wear, Col Samuel Bunch, Capt William Mitchell, E TN Mtd Inf

BERRY, John M C, Pvt, Col John Cocke, Capt John Weakley, Inf

BERRY, Lewis, Pvt, Lt Col R Napier, Co Commander & Branch omitted

BERRY, Lewis, Pvt, Regt Commander omitted, Capt James Williams, Mil Cav

BERRY, Richard, 4 Sgt, Col L Hammond, Capt J N Williamson, 2 Regt Inf

BERRY, Richard, Sgt, Col A Loury, Capt J Williamson, W TN Mil

BERRY, Robert, Pvt, Col William Higgins, Capt James Hambleton, Mtd Gunmen

## Enlisted Men, War of 1812

BERRY, Samuel, 2 Sgt, Col Thomas Benton, Capt George Caperton, Vol Inf

BERRY, Samuel, 2 Sgt, Col William Pillow, Capt George Caperton, Inf

BERRY, Samuel, Pvt, Regt Commander omitted, Capt John Goodson

BERRY, Thomas, Cpl, Col Edwin Booth, Capt John Slatton, E TN Mil

BERRY, William, Pvt, Col William Metcalf, Capt William Sitton, Mil Inf

BERRYHILL, William, Pvt, Col Newton Cannon, Capt Francis Jones, Mtd Riflemen

BERRYMAN, John, Pvt, Col Philip Pipkin, Capt Peter Searcy, Mil Inf; left sick at Ft Jackson

BERT, Jeremiah, Pvt, Col John Brown, Capt Allen I Bacon, E TN Mil Inf

BERTON, John, Cpl, Col R H Dyer, Capt James Wyatt, Vol Mtd Gunmen

BESON, Alfred, Pvt, Col Robert Dyer, Capt James McMahon, 1 TN Mtd Vol Gunmen

BEST, John, Pvt, Col James Raulston, Capt Henry Hamilton, Inf; also served under Gen Carroll

BETHA, Phillip, Pvt, Lt Col Leroy Hammonds, Capt Thomas Wells, Inf

BETHEL, Larkin, Pvt, Col S Copeland, Capt Richard Sharp, Mtd Inf; deserted

BETHEL, Larkin, Pvt, Maj William Russell, Capt John Cowan, Vol Mtd Riflemen

BETHELL, Sampson, 2 Sgt, Lt Col Leroy Hammonds, Capt James Tubb, Inf

BETHELL, Samuel, Pvt, Col Robert Dyer, Capt Bethel Allen, Vol Mtd Gunmen

BETHEY, Rederick, Pvt, Lt Col Leroy Hammonds, Capt James Craig, Inf

BETTERELL, Richard, Pvt, Lt Col John Edmonson, Co Commander omitted, Cav

BETTESS, James, Pvt, Col John Cocke, Capt Bird Nance, Inf

BETTEY, Drewry, Pvt, Col John Coffee, Capt Thomas Bradley, Vol Cav

BETTEY, Wyatt, Pvt, Col John Coffee, Capt Thomas Bradley, Vol Cav

BETTINGTON, Permical, Pvt, Col John Wynne, Capt William Carruthers, W TN Inf

BETTIS, Bradley, Pvt, Col Samuel Bayless, Capt James Churchman, E TN Mil

BETTIS, David, Pvt, Col William Lillard, Capt Thomas McChristian, E TN Vol Inf

BETTIS, John, Pvt, Col John Alcorn, Capt John Byrn, Cav

BETTIS, John, Pvt, Col Newton Cannon, Capt John Harpole, Mtd Gunmen

BETTIS, William, Pvt, Col William Lillard, Capt Thomas McChristian, E Tn Vol Inf

BETTS, John, Pvt, Regt Commander omitted, Capt Edwin S Moore, Mtd Riflemen

BETTY, John, Pvt, Col James Raulston, Maj Gen William Carroll, Capt Edward Robinson, Inf

BEVERS, Spencer, Pvt, Regt Commander omitted, Capt William Henderson, Spies

BEVILL, Edward, 5th Sgt, Lt Col Leroy Hammonds, Col Alexander Loury, Capt Thomas Wells, Inf

BEWLEY, Jacob M, Cpl, Col William Johnson, Capt Christopher Cook, E TN Mil

BEZZEL, Isaac, Pvt, Col John Coffee, Capt Charles Kavanaugh, Cav

BEZZEL, William, Pvt, Col John Coffee, Capt Charles Kavanaugh, Cav

BIARD?, William, Pvt, Maj John Childs, Capt Daniel Price, Vol Mtd Gunmen

BIBB, David, Pvt, Col Edward Bradley, Capt Abraham Bledsoe, Riflemen

BIBB, David, Pvt, Col William Hall, Capt Abraham Bledsoe, Branch omitted

BIBB, Henry, Pvt, Col William Pillow, Capt Thomas Williamson, Vol Inf

BIBB, Prior, Pvt, Col S Copeland, Capt Solomon George, Inf

BIBB, Thomas, Pvt, Col Thomas Benton, Capt Thomas Williamson, Vol Inf

BIBLE, Lewis, Dmr, Col Samuel Bayless, Capt Joseph Hale, E TN Mil

BIBLE, Philip, Pvt, Col Ewen Allison, Capt Jacob Hoyal, E TN Mil

BIBLE, Philip, Pvt, Col Samuel Bunch, Capt Francis Register, E TN Mil

BIBLE, Phillip, Pvt, Col Samuel Bayless, Capt Joseph Hale, E TN Mil, died 2-11-1815

BIBY, Caswell, Pvt, Maj William Russell, Capt John Cowan, Vol Mtd Riflemen

BIBY, Price, Pvt, Col Samuel Bayless, Capt Joseph Goodson, E TN Mil

BICKENSTAFF, Henry, Pvt, Regt Commander omitted, Cpl Elisha Green, Mtd Spies

BICKERSTAFF, John, Sgt, Col Robert Perkins, Capt James McMahon, Mtd Gunmen

BICKLHIMER, John, Pvt, Col Philip Pipkin, Capt Henry Newlin, Mil Inf; deserted

BIDDIX, Robert, Pvt, Col Robert Dyer, Capt Ribert? Evans, Vol Mtd Gunmen

BIDDLE, John, Pvt, Gen Andrew Jackson, Capt D Deaderick, Arty

BIDWELL, Reuben, Pvt, Col John Wynne, Capt William Carothers, W TN Inf

BIERD, John C, Pvt, Col William Johnson, Capt Elihu Millikin, 3 Regt E TN Mil

BIERDEN, John, Pvt, Col Samuel Wear, Capt Rufus Morgan, E TN Vol Inf

BIERNET, Charles, Pvt, (Col) William McPherson, no other information

BIFFLE, John, Pvt, Col Thomas McCrory, Capt Samuel McKnight, Inf

BIFFLE, Valentine, Pvt, Col Samuel Bayless, Capt James Landen, E TN Mil

BIGBIE, Archibald, Sgt, Col Alexnader Loury, Capt Gabriel Martin

BIGERSTAFF, Wallace, Sgt, Col Robert Steele, Capt James Bennett, Mil Inf

BIGGS, Ara, Sgt, Maj Robert Cooper, Co Commander omitted, Mtd Riflemen

BIGGS, Dennis, Cpl, Maj William Russell, Capt William Chism, Vol Mtd Gunmen

BIGGS, Elias, Pvt, Maj William Russell, Capt William

- 73

Chism, Vol Mtd Gunmen
BIGGS, John, Pvt, Lt Col Leroy Hammonds, Capt James Craig, Inf
BIGGS, Reulin P C, Pvt, Col John Coffee, Capt James Terrill, Vol Cav
BIGHAM, William, Pvt, Maj William Russell, Capt John Cowan, V M Riflemen
BIGHAM, William, Pvt, Regt Commander omitted, Capt James Cowan, Mtd Inf
BIGLEY, Patrick, Pvt, Col William Metcalf, Capt William Muller, Mil Inf
BILBERRY, Benton, Pvt, Col S Copeland, Capt David Williams, Mil Inf
BILBERY, James, Pvt, Maj Woodfolk, Capt Turner, Inf
BILBO, William, Pvt, Capt Thomas Eldridge, Col William Y Higgins, Mtd Gunmen
BILDERBACK, Thomas, Pvt, Col William Hall, Capt John Moore, Vol Inf
BILL, Boy, waiter to Capt Owen, Col Robert H Dyer, Capt Glen Owen, 1 TN Vol Mtd Gunmen
BILLINGTON, Elias, Pvt, no other information
BILLINGTON, James, Pvt, Maj William Woodfolk, Capt James C Neil, Inf
BILLINGTON, John, Pvt, Col Thomas Williamson, Capt John Hutchings, Vol Mtd Gunmen
BILLINGTON, Pennual, Pvt, Col Winn, Capt Williams, Inf; transferred to Capt Carrothers
BILYAE, William, Pvt, Col Edward Bradley, Capt John Kennedy, Riflemen; sick on furlough
BILYON, Isaac, Pvt, Col Edward Bradley, Capt John Kennedy, Riflemen
BINCKNEY, Jacob, Pvt, Col William Johnson, Capt Andrew Lawson, E TN Draft Mil; never appeared
BINGE (BENGE), William B, 2 Lt, Col John Alcorn, Capt Alexander McKeen, Cav
BINKLEY, David, Pvt, Col John Cocke, Capt John Weakley, Inf
BINKLEY, Frederick, Pvt, Col John Alcorn, Capt Fredrick Stump, Cav; absent sick
BINKLEY, Frederick, Pvt, Col John Coffee, Capt Fredrick Stump, Cav; absent
BINKLEY, Henry, Pvt, Col William Metcalf, Capt John Barnhart, Mil Inf
BINKLEY, John, Pvt, Lt Col Archer Cheatham, Co Commander omitted, 6 Brig Mtd Inf
BINKLEY, Peter, Pvt, Col John Alcorn, Capt Fredrick Stump, Cav
BINNAM (BENEHAM), James, Pvt, Col Alexander Loury, Lt Col Leroy Hammonds, Capt Delany, Inf
BINUM, Turner, Pvt, Col William Metcalf, Capt Bird L Hurt, Mil Inf
BIRD, Alexander, Pvt, Col S Copeland, Capt John Holshouser, Inf
BIRD, Ary, Pvt, Regt Commander omitted, Capt Lane Garrett, Mtd Riflemen
BIRD, Bartley, Pvt, Col Thomas Benton, Capt William Moore, Vol Inf
BIRD, Howell L, Pvt, Col William Metcalf, Capt William Muller, Mil Inf
BIRD, James, Pvt, Col R C Napier, Capt Thomas Gray, Mil Inf
BIRD, John, Pvt, Col Edward E Booth, Capt John Porter, Drafted Mil
BIRD, John, Pvt, Col John Cocke, Capt John Weakley, Inf
BIRD, John, Pvt, Col John K Wynne, Capt Bayless Prince, Inf
BIRD, John, Pvt, Col R C Napier, Capt Thomas Gray, Mil Inf
BIRD, John, Pvt, Col Thomas McCrory, Capt Isaac Patton, Inf
BIRD, John, Pvt, Col Thomas Williamson, Capt Thomas Porter, Vol Mtd Gunmen
BIRD, John, Sgt, Col Robert Steele, Capt James Shenault, Mil Inf
BIRD, Joseph, Pvt, Col John Cocke, Capt Richard Crunk, Inf
BIRD, Joseph, Pvt, Maj John Chiles, Capt Charles Conway, E TN Mtd Gunmen; Regt Co--14-Roane
BIRD, Levi, Pvt, Col William Johnson, Capt Benjamin Powell, E TN Mil
BIRD, Levy, Pvt, Col S Bunch, Capt Jones Griffin, E TN Draft Mil; deserted
BIRD, Nathan, Pvt, Col John Cocke, Capt Sam M Carothers, Inf
BIRD, Richard, Pvt, Maj William Woodfolk, Capt Abner Pearce, Inf; transferred from Capt Dudney
BIRD, Richard, Pvt, Regt Commander omitted, Capt Gerome Smith, Spies; deserted
BIRD, Robert, Pvt, Lt Col Leroy Hammonds, Col Alexander Loury, Capt Delany, Inf
BIRD, Thomas, Pvt, Col John Cocke, Capt Richard Crunk, Inf
BIRD, William C, 1 Sgt, Col William Fillow, Capt William Moore, Inf
BIRD, William C, Sgt, Col Thomas Benton, Capt William Moore, Vol Inf
BIRD, William, Cpl, Col A Cheatham, Capt George G Chapman, Inf
BIRDSONG, William, Pvt, Col John Brown, Capt James Preston, Regt E TN Mil Inf
BIRDWELL, Armstead, Pvt, Col Ewin Allison, Capt Joseph Everett, E TN Mil
BIRDWELL, Benjamin, Pvt, Col Samuel Bunch, Capt David G Vance, E TN Mtd Inf
BIRDWELL, George, Cpl, Col Samuel Wear, Capt John Chiles, E TN Vol Inf
BIRDWELL, George, Pvt, Gen Andrew Jackson, Capt H Kerr, Mtd Rangers
BIRDWELL, James, Pvt, Col William Lillard, Capt Hugh Martin, E TN Vol Inf
BIRDWELL, Morris, Pvt, Gen Andrew Jackson, Capt H Kerr, Mtd Rangers
BIRDWELL, Moses, Pvt, Maj William Russell, Capt William Chism, V M Gunmen
BIRDWELL, Moses, Pvt, Regt Commander omitted, Capt I Prewitt, Branch omitted; Pack Horse
BIRDWELL, Robert, Cpl, Col Robert Steele, Capt Samuel Maxwell, Mil Inf
BIRK, Arnold, Pvt, Col John K Wynn, Capt William McCall, Inf
BIRKLOE, Isaac, Pvt, Col N Cannon, Capt Brice Martin,

## Enlisted Men, War of 1812

Mtd Gunmen; deserted & returned to duty

BIRNET, Daniel, Pvt, Col William Pillow, Capt George Caperton, Inf

BIRRIS, Martin, Ffr Maj, Col Philip Pipkin, Co Commander omitted, 1 Regt Tn Mil

BIRTHRIGHT, Williamson, Pvt, Maj William Carroll, Capt Lewis Dillahunty, Capt Daniel M Bradford, Vol Inf

BIRTLY, William, Pvt, Col William Metcalf, Capt Barbee Collins, Mil Inf

BISHOP, Abner, Pvt, Maj William Russell, Capt Fleman Hodges, V Mtd Gunmen

BISHOP, Charles, Pvt, Maj John Childs, Capt James Cummings, E TN Vol Mtd Inf

BISHOP, Collin, Pvt, Gen A Jackson, Capt D Deaderick, Arty

BISHOP, Eli, Pvt, Col William Johnson, Capt Andrew Lawson, Drafted E TN Mil

BISHOP, Elijah, 3 Sgt, Col William Bunch, Capt Moses, E TN Draft Inf

BISHOP, Elijah, Pvt, Col William Lillard, Capt William Hamilton, E TN Vol Inf

BISHOP, Empson, Pvt, Col R H Dyer, Capt Cuthbert Hudson, V M Gunmen

BISHOP, Isaac, 1 Cpl, Col Samuel Bunch, Capt James Cummings, E TN Vol Mtd Gunmen

BISHOP, Jacob, Pvt, Col Edwin Booth, Capt John Lewis, E TN Mil

BISHOP, James (Hawkins R Co), Pvt, Col William Johnson, Capt Benjamin Powell, E TN Mil

BISHOP, John, 1 Sgt, Maj John Childs, Capt James Cummings, E TN Vol Mtd Inf

BISHOP, John, __, Col John Williams, Capt David Vance, Mtd Vol

BISHOP, John, Pvt, Col N Cannon, Capt James Walton, Mtd Riflemen

BISHOP, John, Pvt, Col S Copeland, Capt Allen Wilkinson, Mil Inf

BISHOP, John, Pvt, no other information except--I Berry's Roll

BISHOP, Jonathan, Pvt, Col William Lillard, Capt William Hamilton, E TN Vol Inf

BISHOP, Joseph, no other information

BISHOP, Mason, Pvt, Col John Williams, Capt David Vance, Mtd Vol

BISHOP, Mason, Pvt, Maj John Childs, Capt James Cummings, E TN Vol Mtd Inf

BISHOP, Nathan, Pvt, Col James Raulston, Maj Gen William Carroll, Capt Edward Robinson, Inf

BISHOP, Nathan, Pvt, Col N Cannon, Capt James Walton, Mtd Riflemen

BISHOP, Samuel, Pvt, Col William Johnson, Capt Joseph Scott, E TN Draft Mil; deceased 3-3-1815

BISHOP, Samuel, Pvt, Col William Lillard, Capt John Neatherton, E TN Vol Inf

BISHOP, Samuel, Pvt, Col William Lillard, Capt William Gillenwater, E TN Vol Inf

BISHOP, Stephen, Pvt, Col John K Wynne, Capt James Holleman, Inf; deserted

BISHOP, Stephen, Pvt, Col S Bunch, Capt S Robinson, E TN Draft Mil

BISHOP, Stephen, Pvt, Maj William Russell, Capt William Chism, V Mtd Gunmen

BISHOP, Stephen, Pvt, Regt Commander omitted, Capt Sam Richardson, E TN Draft Mil

BISHOP, William, Pvt, Col Samuel Bayless, Capt Joseph B Bacon, E TN Mil

BISHOP, Willie, Pvt, Col T McCrory, Capt John Reynolds, Mil Inf

BITNER, Samuel, Pvt, Col William Johnson, Capt Andrew Lawson, E TN Draft Mil; died 11-19-1814

BITNER, William, Pvt, Col Samuel Bayless, Capt Joseph Hale, E TN Mil

BITTICK, John R, Pvt, no other information

BIVEN, Stephen, Pvt, Col N T Perkins, Capt George W L Marr, Vol Mtd Gunmen

BIVINS, John, Pvt, Col William Metcalf, Capt Barbee Collins, Mil Inf

BIZOLE, William, Pvt, Col R H Dyer, Capt Glen Owen, T V Mtd Gunmen

BIZZELL (BIZZLE), Isaac, Sgt, Regt Commander omitted, Capt Archibald McKinney, Cav

BIZZELL (BIZZLE), William, Tptr, Regt Commander omitted, Capt Archibald McKinney, Cav

BIZZLE, William, Pvt, Maj William Russell, Capt Isaac Williams, V Mtd Gunmen

BLACK, Alarameer C, Pvt, Col William Johnson, Capt David McKamey, E TN Draft Mil

BLACK, Alexander, Dmr, Maj William Woodfolk, Capt Abner Pearce, Inf

BLACK, Alexander, Pvt, Col William Johnson, Capt David McKamy, E TN Draft Mil

BLACK, Amon William D, Pvt, Maj William Russell, Capt John Cowan, Vol Mtd Riflemen

BLACK, Charles, Pvt, Col William Lillard, Capt John Neatherton, E TN Vol Inf

BLACK, David, Pvt, Col Ewen Allison, Capt Jacob Hoyal, E TN Mil

BLACK, David, Pvt, Col Samuel Bayless, Capt Joseph Hale, E TN Mil

BLACK, David, Pvt, Col Samuel Bunch, Capt James Penny, E TN Mtd Inf

BLACK, David, Sgt, Col T McCrory, Capt Isaac Patton, Inf

BLACK, Edmond, Pvt, Col Philip Pipkin, Capt John Strother, Mil Inf

BLACK, Edmund, Cpl, Col R H Dyer, Maj William Russell, Capt William Russell, V Mtd Gunmen; died 11-20-1814

BLACK, George, Pvt, Col Philip Pipkin, Capt James Blakemore, Vol Inf; AWOL

BLACK, George, Pvt, Col Samuel Bayless, Capt Branch Jones, E TN Draft Mil

BLACK, George, Pvt, Maj William Woodfolk, Capt Abraham Dudney, Capt John Sutton, Inf; deserted

BLACK, George, Pvt, Regt Commander omitted, Capt Joel Parrish, Arty; also served under Jackson

BLACK, Jacob, Pvt, Col Edward Bradley, Capt William Lauderdale, Vol Inf

BLACK, Jacob, Pvt, Col William Hall, Capt William L. Alexander, Vol Inf

BLACK, Jacob, Pvt, Regt Commander omitted, Capt

-75

*Enlisted Men, War of 1812*

William Henderson, Spies
BLACK, James H, Cpl, Col R H Dyer, Capt Glen Owen, T V Mtd Gunmen
BLACK, James, Pvt, Col John Coffee, Capt Michael Molton, Cav
BLACK, James, Pvt, Col John K Wynne, Capt John Spinks, Inf
BLACK, James, Pvt, Col Robert Jarmon, Capt I Hamilton, Branch omitted
BLACK, James, Pvt, Col William Metcalf, Capt John Cunningham, Capt Alexander Hill, Mil Inf; elected to Cpl
BLACK, John, Cpl, Col Samuel Bunch, Capt Edward Buchanan, E TN Draft Mil
BLACK, John, Pvt, Col Edwin Booth, Capt Richard Marshall, Drafted Mil
BLACK, John, Pvt, Col N T Perkins, Capt John Quarles, Vol Mtd Inf
BLACK, John, Pvt, Col Thomas Benton, Capt C E McEwen, Vol Inf; missing
BLACK, John, Pvt, Maj Gen Andrew Jackson, Col Thomas Williamson, Capt Robert Steele, Vol Mtd Gunmen
BLACK, John, Pvt, Maj John Childs, Capt James Cummings, E TN Vol Mtd Inf
BLACK, Joseph, Cpl, Col William Johnson, Capt Christopher Cook, E TN Mil
BLACK, Joseph, Cpl, Col William Johnson, Capt Joseph Kirk, Mil
BLACK, Joseph, Pvt, Col John Brown, Capt Charles Lewin, E TN Vol Mtd Inf
BLACK, Joseph, Pvt, Col Samuel Bunch, Capt James Penny, E TN Mtd Inf
BLACK, Josiah B, Pvt, Maj William Russell, Capt John Dyer, Capt William Russell, Vol Mtd Gunmen
BLACK, Lemuel, Pvt, Col John Dyer, Maj William Russell, Capt William Russell, Vol Mtd Gunmen
BLACK, Lewis, Pvt, Maj John Chiles, Capt John Stephens, E TN Vol Mtd Inf
BLACK, Mark, Pvt, Col Thomas McCrory, Capt James Shannon, Mil Inf; sick absent
BLACK, Peter, Pvt, Col Newton Cannon, Capt James Walton, Mtd Riflemen
BLACK, Peter, Pvt, Col R Jarmon, Capt Isiah Hamilton, Inf
BLACK, Robert, Pvt, Col Samuel Bayless, Capt Josiah Hale, E TN Mil
BLACK, Samuel N, Pvt, Col Newton Cannon, Capt Brice Martin, Mtd Gunmen; transferred to Capt Evan's Spies Co
BLACK, Samuel, Pvt, Maj Gen Andrew Jackson, Col Thomas Williamson, Capt Robert Steele, Vol Mtd Gunmen
BLACK, Samuel, Pvt, no other information
BLACK, Uriah, Pvt, Col Samuel Bunch, Capt Edward Buchanan, E TN Drafted Mil
BLACK, William, Cpl, Col Samuel Wear, Capt James Tedford, E TN Vol Inf
BLACK, William, Pvt, Col Samuel Bunch, Capt Isaac William, E TN Mil
BLACKAMORE, Edward, Pvt, Col Thomas Williamson, Capt Thomas Scurry, Vol Mtd Gunmen; dismissed from service 3-1-1815
BLACKAMORE, Fielding, Pvt, Col Thomas Williamson, Capt Thomas Scurry, Vol Mtd Gunmen; dismissed from service 1-1815
BLACKAMORE, George D, Pvt, Col Thomas Williamson, Capt Thomas Scurry, Vol Mtd Gunmen
BLACKAMORE, Thomas T, Pvt, Col John Coffee, Capt John Baskerville, Cava
BLACKARD, Blanch H, Pvt, Col A Cheatham, Capt James Giddins, Inf
BLACKARD, Branch, Pvt, Regt Commander omitted, Capt Archibald McKenney, Cav
BLACKARD, Levi H, Pvt, Col William Metcalf, Capt Bird Hurt, Mil Inf
BLACKBLEY, Thos, Pvt, Col John Williams, Capt Samuel Bunch, Mtd Vol
BLACKBURN, James, Pvt, Col William Johnson, Capt James Tunnell, E TN Mil; substitute for Geo Smith
BLACKBURN, Joel, Pvt, Col John Brown, Capt Hugh Barton, E TN Mil Inf
BLACKBURN, John A, Pvt, Col John Brown, Capt John Trimble, E TN Mtd Gunmen
BLACKBURN, John W, Pvt, Maj William Russell, Capt Fleman Hodges, Vol Mtd Gunmen
BLACKBURN, John, Pvt, Col John K Wynne, Capt John Spinks, Inf; deserted 11-23-1813
BLACKBURN, Lemuel, 5 Sgt, Lt Col Leroy Hammond, Capt Thomas Wells, Inf
BLACKBURN, Matthew H, Pvt, Maj Jas Porter, Capt John Cowan, E TN Inf
BLACKBURN, Thomas, Cpl, Col Wm Lillard, Capt Wm McLin, E TN Inf
BLACKEMORE, Chas N, 1 Sgt, Col Philip Pipkin, Capt Jas Blakemore, Mil Inf; sick at Ft Jackson 11-11-1814
BLACKLEY, Chas, Pvt, Col Samuel Wear, Capt Joseph Calloway, Mtd Inf
BLACKLEY, Chas, Pvt, Maj John Childs, Capt Daniel Price, E TN Vol Mil Inf
BLACKLEY, John, Pvt, Col John K Wynne, Capt Bayless E Price, Inf; deserted 12-12-1813
BLACKLEY, John, Pvt, Col Wm Johnson, Capt Jas Stewart, E TN Drafted Mil
BLACKLEY, John, Pvt, Maj John Chiles, Capt Daniel Price, E TN Vol Mil Inf
BLACKLEY, Thos, Pvt, Col Samuel Bunch, Capt David G Vance, E TN Mtd Inf
BLACKLY, Jos, Pvt, Col Samuel Wear, Capt Joseph Calloway, Mtd Inf
BLACKMAN, John, Pvt, Col N T Perkins, Capt Phillip Pipkin, Mtd Riflemen
BLACKMAN, Moses, Pvt, Col William Johnson, Capt Benjamin Powells, Branch Srvce omitted; deserted
BLACKMAN, Moses, Pvt, no other information
BLACKMAN, Olby, Pvt, Col John Coffee, Capt Byrne, Cav
BLACKMAN, Oley, Cpl, Col John Alcorn, Capt Henry Bryan, Cav

BLACKMAN, Reubin, Sgt, Col John Alcorn, Capt John Baskerville, Vol Inf
BLACKMORE, Reubin, Sgt, Col John Coffee, Capt John Baskerville, Cav
BLACKMORE, Thos T, Pvt, Col John Alcorn, Capt John Baskerville, Vol Inf
BLACKSHARE, Luke, Pvt, Col Wm Y Higgins, Capt Adam Dale, Mtd Gunmen
BLACKSHIER, Ezekiel, Pvt, Col McCrory, Capt Isaac Patton, Mil Inf; transferred to Capt Shannon Co, absent
BLACKSHIRE, Elisha, Pvt, Commanders & Branch Srvce omitted; deserted 1-22-1813
BLACKSTON, Arggle, Pvt, Col Wm Johnson, Capt Joseph Scott, E TN Drafted Mil
BLACKSTON, Pleasant, Pvt, Maj John Chiles, Capt Daniel Price, E TN Mtd Inf
BLACKWELL, Henry, Pvt, Col Robt H Dyer, Capt Thomas Jones, Vol Mtd Gunmen
BLACKWELL, James, Pvt, Lt Col Jno Edmonson, Co Commander omitted, Cav
BLACKWELL, Jas, Pvt, Col Edwin Booth, Capt George Wintons, E TN Mil; transferred to Capt John Sutton's Co
BLACKWELL, Jas, Pvt, Maj Wm Woodfolk & Capt John Sutton, Capt Dudney, Inf; substitute for John Carte
BLACKWELL, John, Pvt, Maj Wm Russell, Capt John Trimble, Vol Mtd Gunmen
BLACKWELL, Noel (Noevell), Pvt, Col John Cocke, Capt Bird Nance, Inf; cleared by Court Martial 11-17-1814
BLACKWELL, Robt, Pvt, Brig Gen Johnson, Capt Carson, Inf
BLACKWELL, Strodder, Pvt, Col Edwin Booth, Capt John Lewis, E TN Mil
BLACKWELL, W Geo, Pvt, Col Edwin Booth, Capt John Lewis, E TN Mil
BLACKWELL, William, Sgt, Col Thomas Williamson, Capt Jas Cook, Capt John Crane, Vol Mtd Gunmen
BLACKWELL, Wm, Sgt, Lt Col Cheatham, Co Commander omitted, 6th Brig Mtd Inf
BLAGG, Isaac, Pvt, Col Wm Hall, Capt John Moore, Vol Inf
BLAGG, Kelton H, Pvt, Col Wm Hall, Capt John Moore, Vol Inf
BLAGG, Kelton, Pvt, Col James Raulston, Capt Mathew Neal, Inf; d 2-6-1815
BLAGRAVE, Jas, Pvt, Col Alexander Loury, Capt John Looney, 2 Sgt W TN Mil
BLAIN, John, Pvt, Col N T Perkins, Capt Mathew Johnson, Mil Inf
BLAIR, Alexander, Pvt, Maj William Woodfolk, Capt Abraham Dudney, Capt John Sutton, Inf
BLAIR, Alford, Pvt, Col Thomas Williamson, Capt Giles Burdett, Vol Mtd Gunmen
BLAIR, Andrew, Pvt, no other information
BLAIR, George, Pvt, Col James Raulston, Capt Henry Hamilton, Inf; also served under Maj Gen William Carroll
BLAIR, Hayes, Pvt, Maj William Russell, Capt Thomas Williamson, Separate Bn TN Vol Mtd Gunmen
BLAIR, John, Pvt, Col John Coffee, Capt Frederick Stump, Cav
BLAIR, John, Pvt, Col S Bunch, Capt George McPherson, E TN Mil
BLAIR, John, Pvt, Col Samuel Bunch, Capt Francis Register, E TN Mil
BLAIR, John, Pvt, Col Samuel Bunch, Capt Thomas Mann, E TN Vol Mtd Inf
BLAIR, Jonathan, Pvt, Col William Higgins, Capt James Hambleton, Mtd Gunmen
BLAIR, Joseph, Cpl, Maj William Carroll, Capt Daniel Bradford, Capt Lewis Dillahunty, Vol Inf; d 1-13-1815
BLAIR, Joseph, Pvt, Col Ewin Allison, Capt Henry McCray, E TN Mil; deserted 3-4-1814
BLAIR, Joseph, Pvt, Col John Brown, Capt Charles Lewin, E TN Mtd Inf
BLAIR, Joseph, Pvt, Col John Wynne, Capt William McCall, Inf
BLAIR, Joseph, Pvt, Col Thomas Williamson, Capt William Martin, Vol Mtd Gunmen; killed in battle 1-8-1814
BLAIR, Joseph, Pvt, Col William Metcalf, Capt Thomas Marks, Mil Inf
BLAIR, Ralph, Cpl, Col Thomas Williamson, Capt William Martin, Vol Mtd Gunmen
BLAIR, Richard, Pvt, Col William Lillard, Capt George Keys, E TN Inf
BLAIR, Robert B, Pvt, Col Thomas Williamson, Capt Robert Moore, Vol Mtd Gunmen
BLAIR, Samuel, Pvt, Col N T Perkins, Capt Mathew Patterson, Mtd Vol
BLAIR, Taylor H, 3 Cpl, Col Philip Pipkin, Capt William Mackay, Mil Inf
BLAIR, Thos, Pvt, Col Robt Stelle, Capt Jas Shenault, Mil Inf; on furlough
BLAIR, Thos, Pvt, Maj Wm Russell, Capt John Trimble, Vol Mtd Gunmen
BLAIR, William, Pvt, Col Thomas Benton, Capt Isaiah Renshaw, Vol Inf
BLAIR, Wm, Pvt, Col Edward Bradley, Capt Travis Nash, Vol Inf
BLAIR, Wm, Pvt, Col Samuel Bunch, Capt Thomas Mann, E TN Vol Mtd Inf
BLAIR, Wm, Pvt, Col Wm Hall, Capt John Kennedy, Vol Inf
BLAIR, ___, Pvt, no other information
BLAKE, Wm, Pvt, Col Thomas Benton, Capt Geo Caperton, Inf
BLAKE, Wm, Pvt, Col Wm Pillow, Capt Geo Caperton, Inf
BLAKELEY, Jesse, Pvt, Col John Brown, Capt John Chiles, E TN Mtd Gunmen
BLAKELEY, Jno, Pvt, Col Samuel Bunch, Capt John McNair, Inf; attached to Capt Duncan's Co
BLAKELEY, John, Pvt, Maj John Chiles, Capt Daniel Price, Vol Mtd Gunmen
BLAKELEY, Wm, Pvt, Col Samuel Bayless, Capt Jonathan Waddell, E TN Mil

## Enlisted Men, War of 1812

BLAKELY, Chas, Pvt, Col John Brown, Capt John Chiles, E TN Vol Mtd Gunmen
BLAKELY, Chas, Pvt, Col John Childs, Capt Daniel Price, Vol Mtd Gunmen
BLAKELY, Daniel, Pvt, no other information
BLAKELY, James, Pvt, Gen Andrew Jackson, Capt N Davis, Inf
BLAKELY, Jas, Cpl, Col Ewen Allison, Capt Jonas Loughmiller, Mil
BLAKELY, John, Cpl, Col S Bunch, Capt Geo McPherson, E TN Mil; joined from Capt Griffin Co
BLAKELY, Samuel, Pvt, Col N T Perkins, Capt Mathew Johnston, Mil Inf
BLAKEMAN, Moses, Pvt, Col William Johnson, Capt Benjamin Powell, E TN Mil; sick absent at Ft Strother
BLAKEMAN, Moses, Pvt, Regt Commander omitted, Capt Samuel Richardson, E TN Drafted Mil
BLAKLEY, John, Pvt, Col Wm Johnson, Capt Jas Stewart, E TN Mil
BLANCHARD, Peter, Pvt, Col S Bunch, Capt S Roberson, E TN Drafted Mil
BLANCHARD, Peter, Pvt, Regt Commander omitted, Capt Sam'l Richardson, E TN Drafted Mil
BLANCHET, Archibald, Pvt, Col Alexander Loury & Lt Col Leroy Hammonds, Capt Arahel Rains, Inf; deserted 11-8-1814
BLANETT, Jas, Pvt, Col Wm Metcalf, Capt John Cunningham, Capt Alexander Hill, Mil Inf
BLANKENSHIP, Roland, Tptr, Col John Brown, Capt John Childs, E TN Vol Mtd Gunmen
BLANKENSHIP, William, Pvt, Col William Higgins, Capt Stephen Griffith, Mtd Riflemen
BLANKINSHIP, Gad, Pvt, Maj William Carroll, Capt Lewis Dillahunty, Capt Daniel Bradford, Vol Inf
BLANKS, Jas, Sgt, Regt Commander omitted, Capt Jas Haggard, Mtd Gunmen
BLANNET, John, Pvt, Col Wm Metcalf, Capt John Cunningham, Capt Alexander Hill, Mil Inf
BLANTON, Alexander, Pvt, Maj Gen Wm Carroll, Col William Metcalf, Capt John Jackson, Inf; d 3-5-1815
BLANTON, Isaac, Pvt, Col Samuel Bayless, Capt John Brock, E TN Mil
BLARE (BLAIR), Sam'l, Pvt, Col Edwin E Booth, Capt Alexander Biggs, Inf
BLASANGAME, Wm, Pvt, Col Wm Hall, Capt Abraham Bledsoe, Vol Inf
BLASENGAME, John, Pvt, Col James Raulston, Capt Henry Hamilton, Inf; also served under Maj Gen Wm Carroll
BLASSENGAME, Wm, Pvt, Col Wm Metcalf, Capt Thomas Marks, Mil Inf
BLASSENGER, Wm, Pvt, Col Wm Hall, Capt Abraham Bledsoe, Vol Inf
BLASSINGAME, Wm, Pvt, Col William Metcalf, Capt Bird L Hurt, Mil Inf
BLASSINGHAM, Wade, Pvt, Col Thomas McCrory, Capt Thomas K Gordon, Inf
BLATON, John, Pvt, Lt Col H Bryan, no other information
BLAXTON, Henry, Pvt, Col Samuel Bayless, Capt Jas Churchman, E TN Mil
BLAYLOCK, Henry, Pvt, Maj Gen Wm Carroll, Capt Francis Ellis, Inf
BLAZER, Dan'l, Pvt, Col S Bunch, Capt Jno English, E TN Mil Drafted
BLAZIER, Dan'l, Pvt, Col Ewen Allison, Capt Jas Allen, E TN Mil
BLEAK, Adam, Pvt, Col Jno Brown, Capt Lunsford Oliver, E TN Mil
BLEDSAW, Lewis, Pvt, Col Wm Pillow, Capt Geo Caperton, Inf
BLEDSO, Cheakam, Pvt, Col Thomas Benton, Capt Geo Caperton, Inf
BLEDSO, Lewis, Pvt, Col Thomas Benton, Capt Geo Caperton, Inf
BLEDSOE, Abraham, Pvt, Col Thomas Benton, Capt Geo Caperton, Vol Inf; substituted by Stephen Hall
BLEDSOE, Abram, Capt, Col Edward Bradley, Capt Abraham Bledsoe, Riflemen
BLEDSOE, David, Pvt, Col Jno Brown, Capt Hugh Barton, Regt E TN Mil Inf
BLEDSOE, Henry, Pvt, Col Jno Coffee, Capt John Baskerville, Cav
BLEDSOE, Henry, Pvt, Col William Hall, Capt Abraham Bledsoe, Vol Inf
BLEDSOE, Isaac, Pvt, Col Jno Coffee, Capt John Baskerville, Cav
BLEDSOE, John, Dmr, Col Jno Brown, Capt Hugh Barton, E TN Mil Inf
BLEDSOE, Lewis, Pvt, Regt Commander omitted, Capt Jas Cowan, Mtd Inf
BLEDSOE, Wm, Pvt, Col Wm Pillow, Capt C E McEwen, Vol Inf
BLEVENS, Rich'd, Pvt, Col Wm Johnston, Capt Jas Tunnell, E TN Mil; substitute for Jesse Patton
BLEVENS, Robt, Pvt, Col Ewen Allison, Capt William King, Drafted; left at Ft Strother 5-2-1814 in service
BLEVENS, Robt, Pvt, Col S Bunch, Capt Geo McPherson, E TN Mil; joined from Capt King's Co
BLEVENS, Russell, Pvt, Col Ewen Allison, Capt William King, Drafted Mil
BLEVIN, Abraham, Pvt, Col William Johnston, Capt Benjamin Powell, E TN Mil; substitute for Beiler Washington
BLEVINS, Armstead, Pvt, Regt Commander omitted, Capt Wm Mitchell, Spies; discharged
BLEVINS, Geo, Ens, Col Samuel Bayless, Capt Joseph Goodson, E TN Mil; d 2-15-1815
BLEVINS, Hugh, 3 Sgt, Col Wm Metcalf, Capt John Cunningham, Capt Alexander Hill, Mil Inf
BLEVINS, John, Pvt, Regt Commander omitted, Capt Wm Mitchell, Spies; discharged
BLEVINS, Preston, Pvt, Col William Lillard, Capt Benjamin H Kings, E TN Vol Inf
BLEVINS, Richard, Pvt, Col Jno Brown, Capt Hugh Barton, E TN Mil Inf
BLEVINS, Robert, Pvt, Col William Johnson, Capt Joseph Scott, E TN Drafted Mil; substitute for Jos Neulin

## Enlisted Men, War of 1812

BLEVINS, Robt, Pvt, Col William Lillard, Capt Benjamin Kings, E TN Vol Inf

BLEVINS, Walter, Pvt, Col William Lillard, Capt Benjamin Kings, E TN Vol Inf

BLEVINS, Wm, Pvt, Regt Commander omitted, Capt Wm Mitchell, Spies; discharged

BLITHE, Benj, Pvt, Regt Commander omitted, Capt Archibald McKenney, Cav

BLITHE, Champion, Pvt, Gen A Jackson, Capt Wm Rupee, Spies

BLITHE, John, Pvt, Col Nicholas T Perkins, Capt Mathew Johnson, Mil Inf

BLITHE, Joseph, Pvt, Col R H Dyer, Capt Glen Owen, TN Vol Mtd Gunmen

BLITHE, Wm, Pvt, Col Nicholas T Perkins, Capt Mathew Johnson, Mil Inf

BLITHE, Wm, Pvt, Col Wm Johnson, Capt David McKamy, E TN Drafted Mil; sick absent

BLIZZARD, Thos, Pvt, Col Wm Metcalf, Capt Barbee Collins, Mil Inf

BLOCK, Josiah, Pvt, Col Robert Steele, Capt Jas Bennett, Mil Inf

BLOMFIELD, Elijah, Pvt, Lt Col Leroy Hammonds, Col Alexander Loury, Capt Thomas Wells, Inf

BLOODSWORTH, Isaiah, Pvt, Col Robert Steele, Capt Samuel Maxwell, Mil Inf

BLOODWORTH, Edward, Pvt, Col R C Napier, Capt Thomas Preston, Mil Inf; on furlough 3-4-1814

BLOODWORTH, Henry, Pvt, Maj Gen Carroll, Col James Raulston, Capt Henry Hamilton, Inf

BLOODWORTH, Jesse, Pvt, Maj Gen A Jackson, Capt Joseph Kirkpatrick, Mtd Gunmen; wounded on furloe 1-27-1814

BLOODWORTH, John, Pvt, Maj Gen Carroll, Capt Henry Hamilton, Inf

BLOODWORTH, John, Pvt, Maj Gen Carroll, Col James Raulston, Capt Henry Hamilton, Inf

BLOODWORTH, Samuel, Pvt, Maj Gen Carroll, Col James Raulston, Capt Henry Hamilton, Inf

BLOODWORTH, William, Pvt, Maj Gen Carroll, Capt Henry Hamilton, Inf

BLOODWORTH, Wm, Sgt, Col Newton Cannon, Capt John Harpole, Mtd Gunmen

BLOOMER, John, Pvt, Maj John Chiles, Capt Jas Cummings, E TN Vol Mtd Inf

BLOUNT, Benjamin, Pvt, Col Alexander Loury, Lt Col Leroy Hammonds, Capt Thomas Wells, Inf

BLOUNT, Isaac, Pvt, Lt Col Leroy Hammonds, Col Alexander Loury, Capt Thomas Wells, Inf; left sick at Ft Cont. 12-1814

BLOUNT, Rich B, Pvt, Capt D Deadrick, Capt Wade, Branch Srvce omitted

BLOUNT, Wilson, 2 Cpl, Maj Gen Carroll, Capt Francis Ellis, Inf

BLOYD, Tubby, Pvt, Col S Copeland, Capt John Sharp, Mil Inf

BLUE, Abraham, Pvt, Regt Commander omitted, Capt Jas Terrill, Cav; not mustered, present

BLUE, David, Pvt, Maj Gen Carroll, Col Jas Raulston, Capt Edward Robinson, Inf

BLUE, Neill, Pvt, Brig Gen Thos Johnson, Capt Abraham Allen, Mil Inf

BLUFORD, Jas, Pvt, Col Robert Steele, Capt Jas Randals, Inf

BLUNT (BLOUNT), Reading, Pvt, Col Philip Pipkin, Capt William Mackay, Mil Inf

BLURTON, Bryant, Pvt, Maj Gen A Jackson, Capt Joseph Kirkpatrick, Mtd Gunmen; sick absent

BLURTON, Henry, Pvt, Col William Pillow, Capt Thos Williamson, Vol Inf

BLURTON, Hinton, Pvt, Col Thos Williamson, Capt Robert Moore, Vol Mtd Gunmen

BLURTON, John, Pvt, Col Thos Williamson, Capt Richard Tate, Vol Mtd Gunmen; sick absent since 4-10-1815

BLYTHE, Benjamin, Pvt, Regt Commander omitted, Capt Archibald McKinney, Cav

BLYTHE, Hugh, Pvt, Col S Copeland, Capt John Holshouser, Inf

BLYTHE, John, Tptr, Col William Y Higgins, Capt James Hambleton, Mtd Gunmen

BLYTHE, Jos, Pvt, Col Philip Pipkin, Capt Geo Mebane, Mil Inf; deserted

BLYTHE, Wm, Pvt, Col Wm Metcalf, Capt Thomas Marks, Mil Inf

BLYTHE (BLYE), Hugh, Pvt, Col Alexander Loury, Lt Col Leroy Hammonds, Capt Delany, Inf

BOAK (BOKE), William, Pvt, Col Alexander Loury, Capt James Kincaid, Inf

BOALTON, Josiah, Pvt, Col John K Wynne, Capt Wm Carrothers, W TN Inf

BOAN, John, Pvt, Col Alexander Loury, Capt James Kincaid, Inf

BOAN (BOWEN), Allen, Pvt, Col R H Dyer, Capt Cuthbert Hudson, Vol Mtd Gunmen

BOAN (BOWEN), Eldridge, Pvt, Col R H Dyer, Capt Cuthbert Hudson, Vol Mtd Gunmen

BOANENER, Edward, Pvt, Maj John Childs, Capt C Conway, Mtd Gunmen; Regt Co 10th Knox

BOATMAN, Ezekirl, Pvt, Col Samuel Bayless, Capt John Reynolds, E TN Inf

BOATRIGHT, Lewis, Pvt, Col Alexander Loury, Capt James Kincaid, Inf

BOATRIGHT, Thos, 4 Cpl, Col Thomas Benton, Capt Robert Cannon, Inf

BOATRIGHT, Thos, Cpl, Col Wm Pillow, Capt Joseph Mason, Vol Inf; sick absent

BOATRIGHT, Thos, Pvt, Col A Cheatham, Capt Charles Johnson, Inf

BOATRIGHT, Thos, Pvt, Col Alexander Loury, Capt James Kincaid, Inf; sick at Fayetteville 9-25-1814

BOATRIGHT, Thos, Pvt, Col Thomas Benton, Capt Robert Cannon, Inf

BOATWRIGHT, Thos, Pvt, Col R H Dyer, Capt Joseph Williams, Vol Mtd Gunmen

BOATWRIGHT, Tinney, Pvt, Col John Cocke, Capt James Gray, Inf

BOAZ, Elipaz, Pvt, Col William Y Higgins, Capt William Doake, Mtd Riflemen

BOAZ, Jas, Pvt, Col Samuel Bunch, Capt Edward Buchanan, E TN Drafted Mil; d 5-17-1814

BOAZ, Migdom, Pvt, Col Edwin E Booth, Capt _____

## Enlisted Men, War of 1812

Porter, Drafted Mil
BOAZE, Bennett, Pvt, Col Philip Pipkin, Capt John Rovertson, Mil Inf
BOBBETT, Jubal, Pvt, Col S Copeland, Capt John Dawson, Inf; deserted 2-12-1814
BOBBIT, Jubal, Pvt, Maj William Woodfolk, Capt Ezekiel Ross, Inf
BOBBITT, Wm A, Pvt, Maj Gen Wm Carroll, Col Wm Metcalf, Capt John Jackson, Inf
BOBO, Wm, 3 Sgt, Col Wm Metcalf, Capt Obidiah Waller, Mil Inf
BOCKER, Younger, Pvt, Col John Cocke, Capt Joseph Price, Inf
BOCKMAN, Christopher, Pvt, Col Wm Pillow, Capt John H Anderson, Vol Inf; on furlough
BODDY, Elijah, Pvt, Col James Raulston, Capt Henry Hamilton, Inf; also served under Maj Gen Wm Carroll
BODEN, Jacob, Pvt, Col John Cocke, Capt James Gray, Inf; d 2-14-1815
BODINE, Thos, Pvt, Col S Copeland, Capt Alexander Provine, Mil Inf
BODWELL (BIDWELL), Archibald, Pvt, Col John K Wynne, Capt William Wilson, Inf; transferred to Capt Caruthers Co
BOGAR, E Elijah, Pvt, Maj John Childs, Capt Reuben Tipton, E TN Vol Mtd Inf; transferred from Capt Connaway's Co
BOGAR, Giles S, Pvt, Maj John Childs, Capt Reuben Tipton, E TN Vol Mtd Inf
BOGARD, Benj, Pvt, Col R C Napier, Capt Early Benson, Mil Inf
BOGARD, Jas, Pvt, Maj Gen A Jackson, Col Thomas Williamson, Capt Robert Steele, Vol Mtd Gunmen
BOGARD, Wm, Pvt, no other information
BOGART, Alexander, Pvt, Col Samuel Bayless, Capt Solomon Hendricks, E TN Mil
BOGEL, Andrew, Sgt, Col Samuel Wear, Capt John Stephens, E TN Vol Inf
BOGGESS, Giles L, Pvt, Col S Wear, Capt Simeon Perry, E TN Vol Mtd Inf
BOGGOTS (BAGGET), Henry, Pvt, Col John Cocke, Capt Joseph Price, Inf
BOGGS, Geo C, Pvt, Col Thomas Williamson, Capt Richard Tate, Vol Mtd Gunmen
BOGGS, John O, Pvt, Col William Higgins, Capt Stephen Griffith, Mtd Riflemen
BOGGS, Sam'l, Pvt, Col William Higgins, Capt Stephen, Griffith, Mtd Riflemen
BOGLE, Jos L, Pvt, Col Edwin Booth, Capt Samuel Thompson, Mil
BOGLE, Sam, Pvt, Maj Porter, Capt John Cowan, Cav
BOGLE, Thos, Pvt, Col Jas Raulston, Capt Jas A Black, Inf
BOGOL, John, Pvt, Col R C Napier, Capt Jas McMurry, Mil Inf
BOHANAN, Davis, Pvt, Col James Raulston, Capt Mathew Neal, Inf
BOHANNON, John, Ens, Regt Commander omitted, Capt Nathan Peoples, Branch Srvce omitted
BOHANNON, Peter, Pvt, Col Leroy Hammond, Capt Jas Craig, Inf
BOILS, John R, Pvt, Col S Copeland, Capt John Holshouser, Inf
BOIN, Henry, Pvt, Col Wm Johnson, Capt David McKamy, E TN Drafted Mil
BOINAN, Jas, Pvt, Col Edwin Booth, Capt John McKamey, Inf
BOIT, Jas, Cpl, Regt Commander omitted, Capt Archibald McKinney, Cav
BOLAND, Jas, Pvt, Col Thomas Williamson, Capt John Doak, Vol Mtd Gunmen
BOLAND, John A, Pvt, Col Wm Metcalf, Capt John Cunningham, Capt Hill, Mil Inf
BOLEN, Davis, Pvt, Col Samuel Bunch, Capt Thomas Mann, E TN Vol Mtd Inf
BOLES, David, Pvt, Col Wm Lillard, Capt Thomas Sharpe, 2nd Regt Inf
BOLES, John, Pvt, Col John Alcorn, Capt William Locke, Cav; transferred to Capt Mitchel's Co
BOLES, Thos, Pvt, Col William Lillard, Capt Geo Keyes, E TN Inf
BOLIN, Larkin, Pvt, Col S Booth, Capt John Porter, Drafted Mil
BOLIN, Solomon R, Pvt, Col N T Perkins, Capt Jas McMahan, Mtd Gunmen
BOLIN, Wm, Pvt, Col S Bunch, Capt Jas Harris, E TN Mil; sick at Ft Strother
BOLING, John A, Pvt, Col S Bunch, Capt F Register, E TN Mil; joined from Capt McPherson's Co
BOLING, Phillip, Pvt, Col Samuel Bayless, Capt Jonathan Waddell, E TN Mil; promoted to Artif
BOLING, Stephen, Pvt, Col Wm Johnson, Capt David McKamy, E TN Drafted Mil
BOLINGER, Frederick, Artif, Div of Maj Gen John Cocke, Co Commander omitted, E TN Mil
BOLINGER, Frederick, Artif, Maj Gen John Cocke, Master Artif Aron Yarnell, E TN Mil
BOLTON, Evan, Cpl, Col Phillip Pipkin, Capt David Smith, Inf
BOLTON, Josiah, Pvt, Maj Gen Carroll, Col Wm Metcalf, Capt John Jackson, Inf
BOLTON, Wm, Pvt, Regt Commander omitted, Capt David Smith, Cav Vol
BOMAN, Samuel, Pvt, Col Phillip Pipkin, Capt Ebenezer Kirkpatrick, Mil Inf; deserted
BONAS, Zachariah, Pvt, Col John K Winn, Capt William McCall, Inf
BOND, Banister, Pvt, Col William Y Higgins, Capt James Hambleton, Mtd Gunmen
BOND, Benj, Pvt, Edwin E Booth, Capt Alex Bigg, Inf
BOND, Geo, Pvt, Col Edward Bradley, Capt Thomas M Haynie, Vol Inf
BOND, Geo, Pvt, Col Wm Hall, Capt Henry M Newland, Vol Inf
BOND, John, Pvt, Col Edwin E Booth, Capt Alex Biggs, Inf
BOND, Joshua, Pvt, Col Edward Bradley, Capt Thomas Haynie, Vol Inf
BOND, Joshua, Pvt, Col Wm Hall, Capt Henry M Newland, Inf
BOND, Maurice, Sgt, no other information

## Enlisted Men, War of 1812

BOND, Nelson, Pvt, Maj William Russell, Capt Isaac Williams, Mtd Gunmen

BOND, Robt, Pvt, Col Philip Pipkin, Capt John Robertson, Mil Inf

BOND, Thos, Pvt, Col Jas Raulston, Capt Jas A Black, Inf; d 2-9-1815

BOND, William, Pvt, Col Alex Loury, Capt Arahel Rains, Inf

BONDS, Allen, Pvt, Col Thomas Williamson, Capt Anthony M Metcalf, Vol Mtd Gunmen

BONDS, Drury, Pvt, Col R C Napier, Capt Edward Neblett, Mil Inf

BONDS, Larry, Pvt, Col Alexander Loury, Capt Geo Sarver, Inf

BONDS, Lewis, Pvt, Maj William Woodfolk, Capt Ezekial Ross, Inf

BONDS, Lewis, Sgt, Maj William Woodfolk, Capt McCulley, Inf

BONDS, Nelson, Pvt, Col Newton Cannon, Capt Isaac Williams, Mtd Riflemen

BONDS, Wright, 1 Sgt, Col N T Perkins, Capt Geo W L Marr, Mtd Vol

BONE, Elisher, Sgt, Col S Copeland, Capt Moses Thompson, Inf

BONE, Jas, Pvt, Col John K Wynne, Capt John Spinks, Inf; sick absent

BONE, Jas, Pvt, Col Newton Cannon, Capt John Harpole, Mtd Gunmen

BONE, Jas, Sgt, Col S Copeland, Capt Moses Thompson, Inf

BONE (BANE), Levy, Pvt, Col Philip Pipkin, Capt John Strother, Mil; attached to Capt D Smith

BONER, Henry, Pvt, Col R H Dyer, Capt Thos White, Vol Mtd Gunmen

BONFIELD, John, Pvt, Col Philip Pipkin, Capt Geo Mebane, Mil Inf; deserted

BONLEY, Philip, Pvt, Col John Brown, Capt William White, E TN Mil Inf

BONNER, Geo, Pvt, Col Ewen Allison, Capt Jonas Loughmiller, Mil; transferred from Capt Griffin's Co

BONNER, Geo, Pvt, Col S Bunch, Capt Jones Griffin, E TN Drafted Mil; on command to E TN to be discharged

BONNER, Jas, Pvt, Col Wm Metcalf, Capt Barbee Collins, Mil Inf

BONNER, Williamson, Pvt, Col Jas Raulston, Capt Chas Wade, Inf

BOOKER, Adam, Pvt, Col William Johnson, Capt Joseph Scott, E TN Drafted Mil

BOOKER, Isaac, Pvt, Col Samuel Bayless, Capt James Landen, E TN Mil

BOOKER, John, Pvt, Col Samuel Bayless, Capt James Landen, E TN Mil

BOOKER, Martin, Pvt, Col Ewen Allison, Capt William King, Drafted Mil

BOOKER, Peter, Pvt, Col William Lillard, Capt Benjamin H King, E TN Vol Inf

BOOKER (BROOKER), Pink D, Pvt, Lt Col Leroy Hammonds, Capt Jas Tubb, Inf; furloughed on march to muster out of service

BOOKOUT, Jos, Pvt, Col Samuel Bunch, Capt Andrew Breden, E TN Mil

BOOKY, Dan'l, Blksmth, Col Thomas Williamson, Capt John Crane, Capt Jas Cook, Vol Mtd Gunmen

BOOLE, Jas, 1 Cpl, Maj John Childs, Capt John Stephens, E TN Vol Mtd Inf

BOON, Jas, Pvt, Col Wm Hall, Capt John Wallace, Inf

BOON, Phillip, Pvt, Col Alexander Loury, Capt Geo Sarver, Inf

BOON, Wm, Pvt, Col Wm Hall, Capt John Wallace, Inf; on furlough

BOON (BOOM), Briant, Pvt, Col Robert M Dyer, Capt Robert Evans, Vol Mtd Gunmen

BOONE, Byrd, Pvt, Regt Commander omitted, Capt Jas Gray, Inf

BOONE, Jas, Pvt, Col James Raulston, Capt Henry Hamilton, Inf; also served Maj Gen Wm Carroll

BOONE, Nathan, Pvt, Regt Commander omitted, Capt James Gray, Inf

BOONE, Thos, Pvt, Col Thomas Williamson, Capt Robert Moore, Vol Mtd Gunmen

BOONETT, Chas, Pvt, Col Ewen Allison, Capt William King, Drafted Mil

BOOSMAN, Caleb, Pvt, Col James Raulston, Capt Henry Hamilton, Inf; also served under Maj Gen Wm Carroll

BOOTH, Benj, Cpl, Col Thomas Williamson, Capt John Hutchins, Vol Mtd Gunmen

BOOTH, Benj, Pvt, Col N Cannon, Capt John B Dempsey, Mtd Gunmen

BOOTH, David, Pvt, Col Philip Pipkin, Capt Peter Searcy, Mil Inf

BOOTH, Geo C, Pvt, Col Robert Steele, Capt Robert Campbell, Mil Inf

BOOTH, Henry, Pvt, Col John K Winn, Capt William McCall, Inf

BOOTH, Jas, Dmr, Col Phillip Pipkin, Capt William Mackay, Mil Inf; one roll gives Fifer? as rank

BOOTH, John, Cpl, Col John Coffee, Capt Michael Molton, Cav

BOOTH, Jos, Cpl, Col Ewen Allison, Capt John Hampton, Mil

BOOTH, Samuel, Pvt, Col John Cocke, Capt Samuel M Carrothers, Inf; killed 1-1-1815

BOOTH, Zachariah, Pvt, Col Samuel Wear, Capt Rufus Morgan, E TN Vol Inf

BORDAN, Adam, Cpl, Maj Wm Woodfolk, Capt Abraham Dudney, Inf

BORDEN, Adam, Pvt, Maj Wm Woodfolk, Capt Abraham Dudney, Capt John Sutton, Inf; reduced from Cpl

BORDEN, Augustus, Pvt, Col William Johnson, Capt Andrew Lawson, E TN Drafted Mil

BORDEN, John, Pvt, Col John Brown, Capt Jesse G Reaney, Mtd Gunmen

BORDEN, William, Pvt, Col John Brown, Capt Jesse G Reaney, Mtd Gunmen

BORDON, Jacob, Pvt, Col Samuel Bunch, Capt Edward Buchanan, E TN Drafted Mil

BORDON, John, Pvt, Col John Brown, Capt Charles Lewin, E TN Mtd Inf

## Enlisted Men, War of 1812

BORDSON, John, Pvt, Col Samuel Bayless, Capt Joseph B Bacon, E TN Mil

BOREN, Amon, Pvt, Col S Bunch, Capt Geo McPherson, E TN Mil

BOREN, Aron, Pvt, Col Samuel Wear, Capt Jesse Cole, Vol Inf; transferred to Capt McLin

BOREN, Dossa, Sgt, Col Samuel Bayless, Capt Joseph B Bacon, E TN Mil

BOREN, Greenberry, Pvt, Col S Bunch, Capt Geo McPherson, E TN Mil

BOREN, Jacob, Pvt, Col Philip Pipkin, Capt Geo Mebane, Mil Inf

BOREN, Jas F, Cpl, Col A Cheatham, Capt Geo G Chapman, Inf

BOREN, Jeremiah, Pvt, Col Alexander Loury, Capt Gabriel Martin, Inf; left sick by order of Col Loury at Montgomery

BOREN, John, Pvt, Col A Cheatham, Capt Geo G Chapman, Inf

BOREN, Thos, Pvt, Lt Col Jno Edmonson, Co Commander omitted, Cav

BOREN, ___ B, Cpl, Col S Bunch, Capt F Register, E TN Mil; joined from Capt McPherson's Co

BORING, Amon, Pvt, Col Wm Lillard, Capt Wm McLin, E TN Inf

BORING, Dorsey, Pvt, Col Wm Lillard, Capt Wm McLin, E TN Inf

BORING, Greenbury, Pvt, Col William Johnson, Capt Andrew Lawson, E TN Drafted Mil; substitute for Henry Bowens

BORING, Jacob, Sgt, Gen A Jackson, Capt Hugh Kerr, Mtd Rangers

BORING, Nicholas, Pvt, Col Wm Johnson, Capt David McKamy, E TN Drafted Mil; sick absent

BORING, Wm, Pvt, Col Samuel Bayless, Capt Jonathan Waddle, E TN Mil

BORUM, Edward, Pvt, Maj Gen Andrew Jackson, Capt Joseph Kirkpatrick, Mtd Gunmen; wounded on furlough 1-27-1814

BORWELL, Andrew, Pvt, Col A Cheatham, Capt Wm Smith, Inf

BOSELE, Jas, Pvt, Regt Commander omitted, Capt Archibold McKemaey, Cav

BOSS, Kinchen T, Pvt, Col Alexander Loury, Capt John Looney, W TN Inf

BOSSELL (BOSWITH), Miles, Pvt, Col Thos H Benton, Capt Thos Williamson, Vol Inf

BOSTIC, John, Cpl, Col S Bunch, Capt Geo McPherson, E TN Mil; joined from Capt Everett's Co

BOSTICK, Don F, 1st Mate, Col John K Wynne, Co Commander omitted, 1st Regt TN Mil

BOSTICK, Don Ferdinand, Hospital Surg Mate, Maj Gen A Jackson, Co Commander ommitted, Div of TN Mil

BOSTICK, Jno, Pvt, Regt Commander omitted, Capt Edwin S Moore, Mtd Riflemen

BOSTICK, John, Cpl, Col Ewen Allison, Capt Joseph Everett, E TN Mil; transferred to Capt McPherson's Co

BOSTON, Geo, Pvt, Col Philip Pipkin, Capt Jas Blackmore, Mil Inf

BOSWELL, Jas, Pvt, Col Alex Loury, Capt James Kincaid, Inf

BOSWELL, Jas, Pvt, Regt Commander omitted, Capt Jno Miller, Spies

BOSWELL, John, Pvt, Col Wm Hall, Capt John Kennedy, Vol Inf

BOSWELL, Samuel, Pvt, Regt Commander omitted, Capt Jno Miller, Spies

BOSWELL, Walter, Cpl, Col John Cocke, Capt James Gray, Inf

BOSWELL, Wm, Pvt, Regt Commander omitted, Capt John Miller, Spies

BOTHOON, Kenith, Pvt, Col T McCrory, Capt John Reynolds, Mil Inf; on furlough

BOTHWELL, Davis, Pvt, Col Robert Steele, Capt John Chitwood, Mil Inf

BOTTELES, Wm, Pvt, Col Wm Lillard, Capt Jacob Hartsell, E TN Vol Inf

BOTTOM, Claibon, Pvt, Col Robert Steele, Capt Jas Shenault, Mil Inf

BOTTOM, Jos L, Pvt, Maj William Russell, Capt William Chism, Vol Mtd Gunmen

BOTTOMS, Wm, Pvt, Col Wm Hall, Capt Henry M Newland, Inf

BOTTS, Thos, Cpl, Col William Lillard, Capt William Hamilton, E TN Vol Inf

BOUGH, Bartholeum, Pvt, Col T McCrory, Capt Jno Shannon, Mil Inf; transferred from Capt Patton's Co

BOUGHER, Jacob, Ffr, Col Thomas Benton, Capt Isaiah Renshaw, Vol Inf

BOUGHMAN, John, Pvt, Col Edward Booth, Capt Porter, Drafted Mil

BOULTON, John, Cpl, Col Samuel Bayless, Capt Joseph Rich, E TN Mil

BOULTON, John, Pvt, Col N T Perkins, Capt Philip Pipkin, Mtd Riflemen

BOUNDS, James, Ffr, Col Jno Brown, Capt Lunsford Oliver, E TN Mil

BOUNDS, Jesse, Pvt, Col Jno Brown, Capt Lunsford Oliver, E TN Mil

BOVLEN, James, Pvt, Col A Cheatham, Capt Wm Smith, Inf; discharged for want of arms

BOWDRY, Benj, Pvt, Col Samuel Bayless, Capt James Landen, E TN Mil

BOWEN, Allen, Cpl, Col R H Dyer, Capt Cuthbert Hudson, Vol Mtd Gunmen

BOWEN, Benj, Pvt, Maj Gen Andrew Jackson, Capt Ebenezer Kirkpatrick, Mtd Gunmen; on furlough

BOWEN, Chas, Pvt, Col Samuel Wear, Capt Rufus Morgan, E TN Vol Inf

BOWEN, Jas, Pvt, Col John K Wynne, Capt John Spinks, Inf; sick absent since 1-1-1814

BOWEN, Robert G, Pvt, Regt commander omitted, Sgt John Patton, Inf

BOWEN, William, Pvt, Col John Cocke, Capt Bird Nance, Inf

BOWER, Jas, Pvt, Col Jno Brown, Capt Jas Standifer, Branch Srvce omitted

BOWERMAN, David, Cpl, Col S Bunch, Capt Daniel Yarnell, E TN Mil

## Enlisted Men, War of 1812

BOWERMAN, John, Pvt, Col Samuel Wear, Capt John Chiles, E TN Vol Inf

BOWERMAN, Peter, Pvt, Col Ewin Allison, Capt Joseph Everett, E TN Mil; deserted 3-4-1814

BOWERS, John, Drm Maj, Col Phillip Pipkin, Co Commander omitted, 1st Regt TN Mil

BOWERS, John, Pvt, Col Ewen Allison, Capt Adam Winsell, E TN Drafted Mil

BOWERS, John, Pvt, Col Phillip Pipkin, Capt William Mackay, Mil Inf; promoted to Drm Maj

BOWERS, John, Sgt, Maj William Woodfolk, Capt Abner Pearce, Inf; promoted to Ens

BOWERS, Jos, Sgt, Col John Cocke, Capt Joseph Price, Inf

BOWERS, Valentine, Pvt, Col Ewen Allison, Capt Adam Winsell, E TN Drafted Mil

BOWERS, Wm, Pvt, Col Wm Johnston, Capt Jas R Rogers, E TN Drafted Mil

BOWERS, Wm, Sgt, Col Ewen Allison, Capt Adam Winsell, E TN Drafted Mil

BOWGARD, Wm, Pvt, Col Wm Metcalf, Capt Obidiah Waller, Mil Inf

BOWLEN, Enoch, Pvt, Col Wm Johnston, Capt Jas R Rogers, E TN Drafted Mil; substitute

BOWLEN, John A, Pvt, Col Ewen Allison, Capt William King, Drafted Mil; left at Ft Williams 4-28-1814 in service

BOWLEN, Lewis, Pvt, Brig Gen Thomas Johnston, Capt Robert Carson, Inf

BOWLENGER, Frederick, Dmr, Col William Lillard, Capt William Hamilton, E TN Vol Inf; Armorer

BOWLES, Chas L, Pvt, Col Philip Pipkin, Capt John Robertson, Mil Inf; deserted from Ft Jackson 9-20-1814

BOWLES, Robt, Pvt, Lt Col R Napier, no other information

BOWLES, Sampson, Pvt, Lt Col R Napier, no other information

BOWMAN, Ezekiel, Pvt, Maj Gen Wm Carroll, Col Jas Raulston, Capt Edward Robinson, Inf

BOWMAN, Geo, Pvt, Maj John Childs, Capt Reuben Tipton, E TN Vol Mtd Inf; Regt Co Jefferson

BOWMAN, Hawkins, Pvt, Col Samuel Wear, Capt Jesse Cole, Vol Inf

BOWMAN, Henry, Pvt, Col Samuel Bunch, Capt James Penny, E TN Mtd Inf

BOWMAN, Jas, Pvt, Col Edwin E Booth, Capt John Slatton, E TN Mil

BOWMAN, Jeremiah, Pvt, Col William Johnston, Capt Henry Hunter, E TN Mil; left sick at Ft Jackson

BOWMAN, John, Pvt, Col John Brown, Capt William White, E TN Vol Mtd Inf

BOWMAN, Levi, Pvt, Col Robert Steele, Capt Jas Randals, Inf; d 4-15-1814

BOWMAN, Peter, Pvt, Col John Brown, Capt Hugh Barton, E TN Mil Inf

BOWMAN, Samuel, Pvt, Col Samuel Bunch, Capt James Penny, E TN Mtd Inf

BOWMAN, Samuel, Pvt, Col William Johnson, Capt David McKamy, E TN Drafted Mil; substitute for John Boman

BOWMAN, William, Pvt, Col William Johnson, Capt Benjamin Powell, E TN Mil

BOWMAN, William, Pvt, Col William Johnson, Capt David McKamey, E TN Drafted Mil

BOWRY, John, Pvt, Col Samuel Bayless, Capt James Landen, E TN Mil

BOWS, Hardy, Pvt, Col Thomas Williamson, Capt Anthony Metcalf, Vol Mtd Gunmen

BOX, John, 2 Sgt, Col William Metcalf, Capt Barbee Collins, Mil Inf

BOX, Robert, Sgt, Col Stephen C Copeland, Capt George, Inf

BOY, Andrew, Pvt, Col Samuel Bayless, Capt James Landen, E TN Mil

BOY, Champion, Pvt, Maj William Russell, Capt John Cowan, Vol Mtd Gunmen

BOYAKEN, Joel, Pvt, Col James Raulston, Capt Mathew Neal, Inf; d 3-25-1815

BOYAKEN, Lemuel, Pvt, Col James Raulston, Capt Mathew Neal, Inf; d 1-7-1815

BOYCE, Macklin, Pvt, Col S Copeland, Capt Richard Sharp, Mil Inf

BOYCE, Nicholas, Pvt, Col John Coffee, Capt John Byrn, Cav

BOYCE, Richard, Pvt, Col John Alcorn, Capt John Byrn, Cav

BOYCE, Richard, Pvt, Col John Coffee, Capt John Byrn, Cav

BOYD, Andrew, Rank omitted, Col William Metcalf, Capt William Mullin, Mil Inf

BOYD, Aron, Pvt, Col William Metcalf, Capt Obidiah Waller, Mil Inf

BOYD, Barkley, Pvt, Col Ewen Allison, Capt Adam Winsell, E TN Drafted Mil; deserted 3-4-1814, enlisted w/US 39th Inf

BOYD, David, Pvt, Col Ewen Allison, Capt John Hampton, Mil

BOYD, Elijah, Pvt & Wgnr, Col R C Napier, Capt Samuel Ashmore, Mil Inf

BOYD, George, Pvt, Col R C Napier, Capt Thomas Gray, Mil Inf

BOYD, George, Pvt, Commanders omitted, Det Inf 26th Regt TN

BOYD, James, Cpl, Col William Higgins, Capt John Cheatham, Mtd Riflemen

BOYD, James, Pvt, Col A Loury, Capt Joseph Williamson, W TN Mil

BOYD, James, Pvt, Col Ewen Allison, Capt Joseph Everett, E TN Mil

BOYD, James, Pvt, Col L Hammond, Capt Joseph Williamson, 2nd Regt Inf

BOYD, James, Pvt, Col Thomas McCrory, Capt William Dooly, Inf

BOYD, James, Pvt, Lt Col John Edmonson, Co Commander omitted, Cav

BOYD, James, Pvt, Lt Col Leroy Hammonds, Capt Thomas Williamson, Inf; sick

BOYD, James, Pvt, Maj William Russell, Capt John Tremble, Vol Mtd Gunmen

BOYD, Jeremiah, Cpl, Col S Bunch, E TN Drafted Mil; furloughed from Ft Williams to care for a sick

## Enlisted Men, War of 1812

man

BOYD, Jno R, Cpl, Col T McCrory, Capt Jas Shannon, Mil Inf

BOYD, Joel, Pvt, Col Philip Pipkin, Capt Geo Mebane, Mil Inf; deserted from Ft Jackson 9-20-1814

BOYD, John, Cpl, Col William Pillow, Capt E C McEwen, Vol Inf

BOYD, John, Cpl, Maj William Woodfolk, Capt Abraham Dudney, Inf; also under Capt John Sutton

BOYD, John, Pv, Lt Col John Edmonson, Co Commander omitted, Cav

BOYD, John, Pvt, Col John Brown, Capt William White, E TN Vol Mtd Inf; promoted to Sgt Maj

BOYD, John, Pvt, Col Philip Pipkin, Capt George Mebane, Mil Inf

BOYD, John, Pvt, Col R C Napier, Capt Samuel Ashmore, Mil Inf

BOYD, John, Pvt, Col Samuel Bunch, Capt Thomas Mann, E TN Vol Mtd Inf; made Wgnmstr

BOYD, John, Pvt, Col Thos Benton, Capt Benjamin Reynolds, Vol Inf

BOYD, John, Pvt, Col Thos Benton, Capt Benjamin Reynolds, Vol Inf; joined Capt McEwen's Co

BOYD, John, Pvt, Col Thos H Benton, Capt Jas McEwen, Vol Inf

BOYD, John, Pvt, Gen A Jackson, Capt N Davis, Inf

BOYD, John, Pvt, Maj William Russell, Capt John Trimble, V Mtd Gunmen

BOYD, John, Pvt, Maj William Woodfolk, Capt Abraham Dudney, Inf

BOYD, John, Sgt Maj, Col John Brown, Co Commander omitted, E TN Vol Mtd Gunmen

BOYD, John, wgnmstr, Maj Gen John Cocke, Co Commander omitted, TN Vol Mil

BOYD, Joseph, Pvt, Col A Cheatham, Capt Charles Johnson, Inf

BOYD, Joseph, Pvt, Col S Bunch, Capt Daniel Yarnell, E TN Mil

BOYD, Joseph, Pvt, Maj Gen Carroll, Capt Francis Ellis, Inf

BOYD, Michael, Pvt, Col Williams, Capt David Vance, Mtd Vol

BOYD, Robert, 3 Lt, Col Samuel Wear, Capt James Gillespie, E TN Vol Inf

BOYD, Robert, Pvt, Col Thomas Williamson, Capt Robert Moore, Vol Mtd Gunmen

BOYD, Spencer, Pvt, Col John Cocke, Capt Richard Crunk, Inf

BOYD, Thomas, Pvt, Capt James Haggard, Mtd Gunmen

BOYD, Thomas, Pvt, Col R C Napier, Capt Early Benson, Mil Inf, died 4-17-1814

BOYD, Thomas, Pvt, Regt Commander omitted, Capt James Haggard, Spies

BOYD, William, 1 Cpl, Gen John Coffee, Co Commander omitted, Branch omitted

BOYD, William, Pvt, Col John Alcorn, Capt John Baskerville, Vol Inf

BOYD, William, Pvt, Col Thomas Benton, Capt Henry L. Douglass, Vol Inf

BOYD, William, Pvt, Col Thomas Williamson, Capt Beverly Williams, Vol Mtd Gunmen; transferred to Benas spies

BOYD, William, Pvt, Col William Johnson, Capt Benjamin Powell, E TN Mil

BOYD, William, Sgt, Col Edward Bradley, Capt Harry L Douglass, Vol Inf

BOYD (BOYTE), Thomas, Pvt, Col R H Dyer, Capt James Wyatt, Vol Mtd Gunmen

BOYE, Abednego, Pvt, Col Edwin Booth, Capt Alexander Biggs, Inf

BOYED, Jeremiah, Pvt, Col Edwin Allison, Capt Henry McCray, E TN Mil; transferred to Capt F Register

BOYER, John K, Pvt, Col Philip Allison, Capt James Allen, E TN Mil

BOYER, John, Pvt, Col Thomas Williamson, Capt Anthony M Metcalf, Vol Mtd Gunmen

BOYETT (BOYT), Lemuel, Sgt, Maj William Woodfolk, Capt Abner Pearce, Inf

BOYKIN, Williamson, Pvt, Col Philip Pipkin, Capt William Mackay, Mil Inf

BOYLE, Joseph, Pvt, Maj William Woodfolk, Capt Ezekial Ross, Capt McCulley, Inf; died 12-31-1814

BOYLER, Abram, Pvt, Col N T Perkins, Capt John B Quarles, Vol Mtd Inf

BOYLES, James, Pvt, Col Thomas Benton, Capt Isaiah Renshaw, Vol Inf; absent

BOYLES, James, Pvt, Col Thomas Williamson, Capt William Moore, Vol Mtd Gunmen

BOYLES, James, Sgt, Col Thomas H Benton, Capt William Moore, Vol Inf

BOYLES, John R, Pvt, Col Robert Steele, Capt Robert Campbell, Mil Inf

BOYLES (BOYLS), John, Pvt, Col John Coffee, Capt Blackman Coleman, Cav

BOYLSTON, Nathaniel, Pvt, Col Samuel Bayless, Capt Branch Jones, E TN Draft Mil

BOYRS, Rice, Pvt, Lt Col Richard Napier, no other information

BOYS, William, Pvt, Maj William Russell, Capt John Cowan, Vol Mtd Riflemen

BOYS (BAYS), John A, Pvt, Col Edwin Booth, Capt Samuel Thompason, Mil

BOYT, Benjamin, Sgt, Regt Commander omitted, Capt Thomas Gray, Inf

BOYT, James, Pvt, Col John Coffee, Capt Charles Kavanaugh, Cav; AWOL

BOYT, Jesse, Pvt, Regt Commander omitted, Capt Archibold McKemay, Cav

BRABSON, Ephriam, Pvt, Col John Williams, Capt David Vance, Mtd Vol

BRABSON, William B, Cpl, Col Samuel Bayless, Capt Joseph Rich, E TN Inf

BRACEDAYWAY, Drura, Pvt, Col S Bunch, Capt Isaac Williams, E TN Mil

BRACHENORR, Benjamin, Pvt, Col William Johnson, Capt Benjamin Powell, E TN Mil

BRACHINS, William, Pvt, Col William Johnson, Capt Henry Hunter, E TN Mil

BRACK, Durham, Pvt, Col Edward Bradley, Capt Abraham Bledsoe, Riflemen

BRACK, Durham, Pvt, Col William Hall, Capt Abraham

## Enlisted Men, War of 1812

Bledsoe, Vol Inf
BRACKAS, Thomas, Pvt, Col William Johnson, Capt James Stewart, E TN Draft Mil
BRACKBELL, Peter, 3 Sgt, Col William Johnson, Capt David McKamy, E tn Draft Mil
BRACKENRIDGE, Richard, Pvt, Col Thomas Williamson, Capt John Doak & Capt John Dobbins, Vol Mtd Gunmen
BRACKOW, Levi, Pvt, Col Samuel Bayless, Capt James Landen, E TN Mil
BRADBERRY, Elijah, Pvt, Maj William Woodfolk, Capt Ezekial Ross & Capt McCulley, Inf
BRADEN, Alex, Pvt, no other information
BRADEN, James sr, Pvt, Col William Johnson, Capt James Stewart, E Tn Mil
BRADEN, James, Pvt, Col Edwin E. Booth, Capt Richard Marshall, Drafted Mil
BRADEN, James, Pvt, Col John Coffee, Capt James Terrill, Vol Cav
BRADEN, James, Pvt, Col Samuel Wear, Capt John Bayless, Mtd Inf
BRADEN, James, Pvt, Col William Johnson, Capt James Stewart, E TN Draft Mil
BRADEN, Joseph jr, Pvt, Col William Johnson, Capt James Stewart, E TN Draft Mil
BRADEN, Robert, 1 Cpl, Col John Coffee, Capt James Terrill, Vol Cav
BRADEN, Sand, Pvt, Regt Commander omitted, Capt Joseph Williams, Mil Cav
BRADEN, Thomas, Pvt, Col Samuel Wear, Capt John Bayless, Mtd Inf
BRADEN, Thomas, Pvt, Col William Johnson, Capt James Stewart, E TN Drafted Mil
BRADEN, William, Pvt, Col Thomas Williamson, Capt John Crane & Capt Cook, Vol Mtd Gunmen
BRADEN, William, Pvt, Regt Commander omitted, Capt James Haggard, Mtd Gunmen
BRADFORD, David, Pvt, Col Thomas McCrory, Capt John Reynolds, Mil Inf
BRADFORD, Hugh, Pvt, Col R C Napier, Capt Andrew McCarty, Mil Inf
BRADFORD, Hyram, Pvt, Gen Andrew Jackson, Capt D Deadrick, Arty
BRADFORD, Ira, Wgnmstr, Maj Gen William Carroll, Co Commander omitted, TN Mil
BRADFORD, Priestly, Pvt, Col N T Perkins, Capt George Eliot, Mil Inf
BRADFORD, Robert, Sdlr, Col Thomas Williamson, Capt James Neeley & Capt James Pace, Vol Mtd Gunmen
BRADFORD, Samuel, Pvt, Col James Raulston, Capt Elijah Haynie, Inf
BRADFORD, Thomas, Pvt, Col S Copeland, Capt Allen Wilkerson, Mil Inf
BRADFORD, William, Principle Eng, Maj Gen Andrew Jackson, no Co Commander, Div of TN Mil
BRADLEY, Aaron, Pvt, Col William Metcalf, Capt William Sitton, Mil Inf
BRADLEY, Abraham, Pvt, Col Thomas Williamson, Capt Thomas Scurry, Vol Mtd Gunmen
BRADLEY, Caldwell, Pvt, Col William Johnson, Capt Benjamin Powell, E TN Mil
BRADLEY, David, Pvt, Maj Gen A Jackson, Capt Ebenezer Kirkpatrick, Mtd Gunmen
BRADLEY, Emond, Pvt, Col Wm Johnson, Capt John Rogers, E TN Drafted Mil; substitute
BRADLEY, Geo, Pvt, Col Jas Raulston, Capt Elijah Haynie, Inf
BRADLEY, Geo, Pvt, Col R C Napier, Capt Early Benson, Mil Inf
BRADLEY, James, Pvt, Col J Alcorn, Capt Thomas Bradley, Vol Cav
BRADLEY, Jas A, Pvt, Col A Lowry, Capt J N Williamson, W TN Mil
BRADLEY, Jas A, Pvt, Col L Hammond, Capt J N Williamson, 2nd Regt Inf
BRADLEY, Jas, Pvt, Col Thomas Williamson, Capt Thomas Scurry, Vol Mtd Gunmen
BRADLEY, Jesse, Pvt, Col Thomas Williamson, Capt Thomas Scurry, Vol Mtd Gunmen
BRADLEY, John, Asst to Master, Brig Gen John Coffee, Co Commander omitted, E TN Mtd Gunmen
BRADLEY, John, Pvt, Col J Alcorn, Capt Thomas Bradley, Vol Cav
BRADLEY, John, Pvt, Col James Raulston, Capt Elijah Haynie, Inf
BRADLEY, John, Pvt, Col Jas Raulston, Capt Chas Wade, Inf
BRADLEY, John, Pvt, Col John Coffee, Capt Thomas Bradley, Vol Cav
BRADLEY, John, Pvt, Col R C Napier, Capt Drury Adkins, Mil Inf
BRADLEY, John, Pvt, Col Wm Hall, Capt Brice Martin, Vol Inf
BRADLEY, Joseph, Pvt, Col William Metcalf, Capt Thomas Marks, Mil Inf
BRADLEY, Joseph, Pvt, Col William Metcalf, Capt William Mullin, Mil Inf
BRADLEY, Joshua, Pvt, Maj Gen Wm Carroll, Col Jas Raulston, Col Jas Hamilton, Inf
BRADLEY, Luke, Pvt, Col Wm Higgins, Capt Bethel Allen, Mtd Gunmen
BRADLEY, Nathaniel, Pvt, Col A Cheatham, Capt Richard Benson, Inf
BRADLEY, Richard, Pvt, Gen Coffee, no other information
BRADLEY, Robt, Cpl, Col Joseph Hale, Capt Gabriel Martin, Branch Srvce omitted
BRADLEY, Robt, Sgt, Col Wm Pillow, Co Commander omitted, 2nd Regt TN Vol Inf QM Corps
BRADLEY, Samuel, 4 Sgt, Maj Gen Wm Carroll, Col Jas Raulston, Inf
BRADLEY, Thomas, Pvt, Col Edward Bradley, Capt Brice Martin, Vol Inf
BRADLEY, Thomas, Pvt, Col John Coffee, Co Commander omitted, Vol Cav
BRADLEY, Thomas, Pvt, Col R C Napier, Capt Thos Preston, Mil Inf
BRADLEY, Thos, Pvt, Col Thos Williamson, Capt Anthony Metcalf, Vol Mtd Gunmen
BRADLEY, Wiley, Pvt, Col John Brown, Capt John Chiles, E TN Vol Mtd Gunmen

- 85

## Enlisted Men, War of 1812

BRADLEY, Wm R, Pvt, Col N T Perkins, Capt James McMahan, Mtd Gunmen

BRADLY, Evan B, Pvt, Col Alexander Loury, Lt Col Leroy Hammonds, Capt Arahel Rains, Inf

BRADLY, Isaac, Pvt, Col Samuel Wear, Capt Joseph Calloway, Mtd Inf

BRADLY, Jas A, Pvt, Lt Col Leroy Hammonds, Capt Joseph N Williamson, Inf

BRADLY, John, Pvt, Col Thomas Williamson, Capt James Pace, Lt Nealy, Vol Mtd Gunmen; promoted to assist forage master

BRADLY, John, Pvt, Maj William Woodfolk, Col Ezekial Ross, Inf; appointed Hospital Stewart

BRADLY, Pleasant, Pvt, Maj William Woodfolk, Capt Ezekial Ross, Capt McCulley, Inf

BRADSHAW, David, Pvt, Col James Raulston, Capt Mathew Neal, Inf

BRADSHAW, Eli G, Pvt, Col Thomas McCrory, Capt William Dooley, Inf

BRADSHAW, Geo, Pvt, Col William Metcalf, Capt Barbee Collins, Mil Inf; d 2-10-1815

BRADSHAW, Henry, Pvt, Col John K Wynne, Capt John Spinks, Inf; deserted 11-16-1813

BRADSHAW, Ishmael, Pvt, Col Edward Bradley, Capt Harry L Douglass, Vol Inf

BRADSHAW, Ishmael, Pvt, Col Thomas Benton, Capt Henry L Douglass, Vol Inf

BRADSHAW, Jas, Pvt, Col William Lillard, Capt George Keys, E TN Inf

BRADSHAW, John, Pvt, Col R C Napier, Capt James McMurry, Military Inf

BRADSHAW, John, Pvt, Col Robert Steele, Capt Richard M Ratton, Mil Inf; sick absent

BRADSHAW, John, Pvt, Col Thomas Benton, Capt Isaiah Renshaw, Vol Inf

BRADSHAW, John, Pvt, Col Thomas H Benton, Capt Benjamin Hewett, Vol Inf

BRADSHAW, John, Pvt, Col William Metcalf, Capt Barbee Collins, Mil Inf; d 3-6-1815

BRADSHAW, Jos, Pvt, Col John Cocke, Capt John Weakley, Inf

BRADSHAW, Jos, Pvt, Maj John Childs, Capt James Cummings, E TN Vol Mtd Inf

BRADSHAW, Rich'd, Pvt, Brig Gen Thomas Johnston, Capt Abraham Allen, Mil Inf; sick absent

BRADSHAW, Rich'd, Pvt, Col John Cocke, Capt John Weakley, Inf

BRADSHAW, Rich'd, Pvt, Col William Lillard, Capt Thomas McChristian, E TN Vol Inf

BRADSHAW, Sam'l, Pvt, Col Thomas Benton, Capt Isaiah Renshaw, Vol Inf

BRADSHAW, Solomon, Pvt, Col R C Napier, Capt Camuel? Ashomore?, Mil Inf

BRADSHAW, Wm, Pvt, Col Samuel Wear, Capt William Carothers, W TN Inf; sick absent

BRADSHAW, Wm, Pvt, Col William Metcalf, Capt Barbee Collins, Mil Inf

BRADY, Alexander, Pvt, Gen A Jackson, Capt N Davis, Inf

BRADY, Frederick, Pvt, Maj William Woodfolk, Capt James C Neil, Inf; substitute for Jas Morrow

BRADY, Geo, Pvt, Col John Cocke, Capt Joseph Price, Inf

BRADY, Jas, Pvt, Col Robert M Dyer, Capt Robert Evans, Vol Mtd Gunmen; substitute

BRADY, Tolliver, Pvt, Regt Commander omitted, Capt Archibald McKenney, Cav

BRADY, William, Pvt, Col John Alcorn, Capt Alexander McKeen, Cav

BRADY, Wm, Pvt, Col A Cheatham, Capt William Smith, Inf

BRADY (BRADA), John, Pvt, Col John Cocke, Capt Samuel Carrothers, Inf; died 12-7-1814

BRAG, John, Pvt, Col Samuel Bayless, Capt James Churchman, E TN Mil

BRAGG, Ben, Cpl, Col William Higgins, Capt Stephen Griffith, Mtd Riflemen

BRAGG, John, 3 Cpl, Col John Brown, Capt Charles Lewin, E TN Mtd Inf

BRAGG, John, Pvt, Col Thomas McCrory, Capt Isaac Patton, Mil Inf

BRAGG, Jos, Pvt, Col William Johnson, Capt Joseph Scott, E TN Drafted Mil

BRAGG, Thos, Sgt, Col William Higgins, Capt Stephen Griffith, Branch Srvce omitted

BRAGG, Wm, Pvt, Regt Commander omitted, Capt Wm Mitchell, Spies

BRAKE, Levi, Pvt, Col Hammond, Capt Tubb, Inf

BRAKEBELL, John, Pvt, Col Wm Johnson, Capt David McKamay, E TN Drafted Mil; sick absent substitute for Henry Breakbell

BRAKEFIELD, Abraham, Pvt, Col Bayless, Capt Jones, E TN Drafted Mil

BRALEY, John, Pvt, Col S Copeland, Capt Alexander Provine, Mil Inf

BRALEY, John, Pvt, Col Thomas Benton, Capt Isaiah Renshaw, Vol Inf

BRALEY, Levi, Pvt, Col Wm Pillow, Capt Isaiah Renshaw, Inf; sick on furlough

BRAMBLETT, Sanford, Pvt, Col John Cocke, Capt James Gray, Inf

BRAMBY, John, Pvt, Col Wear, Capt Simeon Perry, E TN Mtd Inf

BRAMEN, Farmer, Pvt, Col Booth, Capt Porter, Drafted Mil

BRANCH, Henry, Pvt, Col Robert H Dyer, Capt Jas McMahon, 1st TN Mtd Vol Gunmen

BRANCH, John, Pvt, Col T McCrory, Capt A Metcalf, Mil Inf

BRANCH, John, Pvt, Col Thomas Williamson, Capt Robert Steele, Vol Mtd Gunmen

BRANCH, Nicholas, Pvt, Gen Andrew Jackson, Col Thos Williamson, Capt Robert Steele, Vol Mtd Gunmen

BRANCH, Nicholas, Pvt, Maj Russell, Capt Williams, TN Vol Mtd Gunmen

BRANCH, Valentine, Pvt, Col S Bunch, Capt Jno Harris, E TN Mil

BRANCH, _____, Servant, Col Pipkin, Co Commander omitted, 1st Regt TN Mil; servant to Regt Master Elisha B Clark

BRANDON, Chas, Pvt, Col John Cocke, Capt James Gray, Inf

## Enlisted Men, War of 1812

BRANDON, Cornelius, Pvt, Col N Cannon, Capt Geo Brandon, Mtd Riflemen; wounded Dec 1813 and furloughed

BRANDON, George, Pvt, Col William Pillow, Capt Isiah Renshaw, Inf; substitute for Thos Cameron

BRANDON, George, Pvt, Lt Col William Philips, Co Commander omitted, Inf

BRANDON, George, Pvt, Maj John Coffee, Co Commander omitted, Mtd Riflemen

BRANDON, Iareo, Pvt, Regt Commander omitted, Capt Joseph Williams, Mil Cav

BRANDON, Jared, Pvt, Regt Commander omitted, Capt Michael Mullin, Branch Srvce omitted

BRANDON, John D, Pvt, Col John Wynne, Capt William Carothers, W TN Inf; sick absent

BRANDON, John, Pvt, Col William Johnson, Capt Joseph Scott, 3rd Regt Mil; left sick at Ft Jackson 11-18-1814

BRANDON, John, Pvt, Col William Johnson, Capt Joseph Scott, E TN Drafted Mil; d Nov 1814

BRANDON, Joseph, Pvt, Col William Metcalf, Capt Barbee Collins, Mil Inf

BRANDON, Laris, Pvt, Regt Commander omitted, Capt Joseph Williams, Mil Cav

BRANDON, Thomas, Pvt, Col Philip Pipkin, Capt George Mebane, Mil Inf; deserted

BRANDON, William, Pvt, Col Edward Bradley, Capt William Lauderdale, Vol Inf

BRANDON, William, Pvt, Col William Hall, Capt William Alexander, Vol Inf

BRANEN, Edward, Pvt, Maj John Chiles, Capt Charles Conway, E TN Mtd Gunmen

BRANHAM, Beverage, Pvt, Col William Johnson, Capt Henry Hunter, E TN Mil; attached to Corp of Armors

BRANHARR, Turner, Pvt, Col Samuel Wear, Capt Rufus Morgan, E TN Vol Inf

BRANNER, Casper, 1 Cpl, Col William Lillard, Capt John Ruper, E TN Vol Inf

BRANNING, Christopher, Pvt, Regt Commander omitted, Capt James Gray, Inf

BRANNON, George, Sgt, Col John Cocke, Capt George Barnes, Inf

BRANNON, James, Cpl, Col A Cheatham, Co Commander omitted, Inf

BRANNON, James, Cpl, Col Robert Dyer, Capt Robert Evans, Vol Mtd Gunmen

BRANNON, James, Pvt, Lt Col Leroy Hammonds, Capt James Tubb, Inf; furloughed on march to muster out of service

BRANNON, John, Pvt, Lt Col Hammonds, Col James Tubb, Inf; furloughed on march to mustering out of service

BRANNON, Thomas, Pvt, Col Ewen Allison, Capt Henry McCray, E TN Mil

BRANNON, William, Pvt, Col S Copeland, Capt Solomon George, Inf

BRANSFORD, Arthur, Pvt, Col R C Napier, Capt James McMurry, Mil Inf

BRANSFORD, John, Pvt, Col Edward Bradley, Capt Brice Martin, Vol Inf

BRANSFORD, John, Pvt, Col William Hall, Capt Brice Martin, Vol Inf

BRANSON, Richard, Pvt, Maj William Woodfolk, Capt Abner Pearce, Inf

BRANSTADER, Frederick, Pvt, Col William Lillard, Capt Hugh Martin, E TN Vol Inf

BRANSTATER, John, Pvt, Col Ewen Allison, Capt Adam Winsell, E TN Drafted Mil; furloughed till better health 3-10-1814

BRANTLETT, Sandford, Pvt, Regt Commander omitted, Capt James Gray, Inf

BRANTLEY, Hugh, Pvt, Col William Hall, Capt James Hambleton, Vol Inf

BRANTLEY, James, Pvt, Col Philip Pipkin, James Blakemore, Mil Inf; substitute for Hudson Howell deserted 9-20-1814

BRANTLEY, Thomas, Pvt, Col William Hall, Capt James Hambleton, Vol Inf; absent by consent

BRANTON, Thomas Pvt, Maj Gen William Carroll, Col William Metcalf, Capt John Jackson, Inf; d 3-5-1815

BRANUM, Thomas, Pvt, Col Samuel Bunch, Capt John English, E TN Drafted Mil

BRASEL, Green, Pvt, Col James Raulston, Capt Henry West, Inf

BRASHEAR, Jene, Pvt, Col Thomas Benton, Capt Isiah Renshaw, Vol Inf; out of state

BRASHEAR, Lemuel, Pvt, Col James Raulston, Capt Henry Hamilton, Inf

BRASHEAR, Samuel, Pvt, Col Thomas Benton, Capt Isiah Renshaw, Vol Inf; joined from Capt Huett's Co

BRASHEAR, Zays, Pvt, Col John Brown, Capt William White, E TN Vol Mtd Inf

BRASHEARS, Walter, Pvt, Col John Brown, Capt William Neilson, E TN Vol Mil

BRASHIRES, John, Pvt, Col Robert Dyer, Maj William Russell, Capt William Russell, Vol Mtd Gunmen

BRASNER, Michael, Pvt, Col John Williams, Capt Samuel Bunch, Mtd Vol

BRASSELL, Elias, Pvt, Maj William Russell, Capt William Chism, Vol Mtd Gunmen

BRASSFIELD, Dennis, Pvt, Col Samuel Bayless, Capt John Brock, E TN Mil

BRASSFIELD, James (Joseph), Pvt, Col Samuel Bunch, Co Commander omitted, E TN Drafted Inf

BRATTON, Daniel, Pvt, Lt Col Leroy Hammonds, Capt James Tubb, Inf

BRATTON, David, Pvt, Col Edward Bradley, Capt Brice Martin, Vol Inf

BRATTON, David, Pvt, Col William Hall, Capt Brice Martin, Vol Inf

BRATTON, David, Pvt, Lt Col Leroy Hammonds, Capt James Tubb, Inf; left sick at Ft Jackson

BRATTON, James, Pvt, Col Leroy Hammonds, Capt James Tubb, Inf; furloughed on march to mustering out of service

BRATTON, John, Cpl, Maj Gen William Carroll, Col William Metcalf, Capt John Jackson, Inf; d 3-11-1815

BRATTON, Joseph, Pvt, Col John Coffee, Capt John

Baskerville, Cav
BRATTON, Robert, Pvt, Col Thomas Williamson, Capt Anthony Metcalf, Vol Mtd Gunmen
BRATTON, Thomas, Pvt, Col Philip Pipkin, Capt James Blakemore, Mil Inf
BRAWLEY, John, Pvt, Col Thomas Benton, Capt Isiah Renshaw, Vol Inf
BRAWLEY, Thomas, Pvt, Col N T Perkins, Capt John Quarles, Vol Mtd Inf
BRAWLEY, William, Pvt, Maj Gen Andrew Jackson, Capt James Reed, Inf
BRAWNER, Joel, Pvt, Col William Hall, Capt Travis Nash, Vol Inf
BRAWNER, Wm, Pvt, Col Samuel Wear, Capt John Chiles, E TN Vol Inf
BRAXTON, Mitchell, Pvt, Col William Johnson, Capt Elihu Mitchell, 3rd Regt E TN Mil; transferred to Capt Churchman's Co
BRAY, Solomon, Pvt, Col S Bunch, Capt F Register, E TN Mil
BRAY, Solomon, Sgt, Col Samuel Bunch, Capt F Register, E TN Mil; joined from Capt King's Co
BRAY, Stogner, Pvt, Col Wm Johnson, Capt Christopher Cook, E TN Mil
BRAY, Stogner, Pvt, Col Wm Johnson, Capt Joseph Kirk, Mil
BRAY, Thomas, Pvt, Col Wm Lillard, Capt Geo Argenbright, E TN Vol Riflemen
BRAYDEN, Jas jr, Pvt, Col Wm Johnson, Capt Jas Stewart, E TN Mil
BRAYDEN, Jas sr, Pvt, Col Wm Johnson, Capt Jas Stewart, E TN Mil
BRAYDEN, Jesse, Pvt, Col Wm Johnson, Capt Jas Stewart, E TN Mil
BRAYDEN, Thos, Pvt, Col Wm Johnson, Capt Jas Stewart, E TN Mil
BRAZEALE, John, Sgt, Col John Brown, Capt Allen I Bacon, E TN Mil Inf
BRAZEL, David, Pvt, Col John Brown, Capt Wm White, E TN Vol Mtd Inf
BRAZELL, Archibald W, Pvt, Col John Cocke, Capt George Barnes, Inf
BRAZELL, Geo, Pvt, Col John Cocke, Capt George Barnes, Inf
BRAZELLE, John, Pvt, Col Wm Johnson, Capt Elihu Millikin, 3rd Regt E TN Mil; d 12-20-1814
BRAZELTON, Solomon, Pvt, Col Jno Brown, Capt Allen I Bacon, E TN Inf
BREADEN, William, Rank omitted, Col Jno Brown, Capt Lunsford Oliver, E TN Mil
BREADON, Richard, Pvt, Col S Bunch, Capt George Gregory, E TN Drafted Mil
BREANT, Littleberry, Pvt, Col Jno Brown, Capt William White, E TN Mil Inf
BRECHER, Jas, Pvt, Col Phillip Pipkin, Capt Ebenezer Kirkpatrick, Mil Inf; furloughed 10-7-1814
BRECKEN, John, Pvt, Col Wm Pillow, Capt Geo Caperton, Inf
BRECKENRIDGE, Richard, Pvt, Col N T Perkins, Capt John Doak, Vol Mtd Gunmen
BRECKINRIDGE, John, Pvt, Col Wm Metcalf, Capt Obidiah Waller, Mil Inf
BREDEN, Andrew, Capt, Col S Bunch, Capt Breden, E TN Mil
BREDEN, Jos, Pvt, Col S Bayless, Capt Joseph Goodson, E TN Mil; discharged for inability
BREDEN, Mark, Pvt, Col S Bunch, Capt Geo Gregory, E TN Drafted Mil
BREDEN, Richard, Pvt, Col S Bunch, Capt Geo Gregory, E TN Drafted Mil
BREEDEN, Wm, Pvt, Col William Lillard, Capt R H Dyer, Vol Inf
BREEDING, Mason, Pvt, Regt Commander omitted, Capt N Davis, Inf
BREEDLOVE, Chas, Pvt, Col Samuel Wear, Capt John Bayless, Mtd Inf
BREEDLOVE, David W, Pvt, Col Newton Cannon, Capt John Harpole, Mtd Gunmen
BREEDLOVE, Thos, Pvt, Maj Gen Andrew Jackson, Capt Jos Kirkpatrick, Mtd Gunmen
BREEDLOVE, William, Pvt, Col John Brown, Capt John Chiles, E TN Vol Mtd Gunmen
BREEDON, Elijah, Cpl, Col Allison, Capt Allen, E TN Mil
BREMER, John, Pvt, Col Ewen Allison, Capt Jacob Hoyal, E TN Mil
BRENCEFIELD, Jas, Pvt, Col Wm Johnson, Capt Jas Tunnell, E TN Mil; substitute for Willie Warrick
BRENER, Geo, Mtd Ranger, Brig Gen Roberts, Capt Benj Reynolds, Branch Srvce omitted
BRENSEN, Jas, Pvt, Col A Cheatham, Capt William Creel, Inf
BRESSIE, Murrell, Sgt, Col Thomas Williamson, Capt Wm Martin, Vol Mtd Gunmen
BRETE, Prichet, Pvt, Col Samuel Bayless, Capt James Landen, E TN Mil
BRETON, Robt, Pvt, Col Ewen Allison, Capt Jonas Loughmiller, Mil; transferred to Capt Griffin's Co
BREVARD, Cyrus W, Pvt, Col Edward Bradley, Capt Brice Martin, Vol Inf
BREVARD, Hugh, 4 Sgt, Col Wm Hall, Capt Brice Martin, Vol Inf
BREVARD, Hugh, Lt Master Sgt, Col Edward Bradley, Co Commander omitted, Vol TN Inf
BREVARD, Lewis W, Pvt, Col Wm Hall, Capt Brice Martin, Vol Inf
BREVARD, Wm F, Pvt, Col Wm Hall, Capt Brice Martin, Vol Inf
BREVARD, Wm T, Pvt, Col Edward Bradley, Capt Brice Martin, Vol Inf
BREVARD, Wm, Pvt, Col Wm Hall, Capt Brice Martin, Vol Inf
BREWER, Cayce, Pvt, Col Edwin Booth, Capt John Sharp, E TN Mil
BREWER, Cornelius, Pvt, Col Thos Benton, Capt Benj Reynolds, Vol Inf
BREWER, Elias, Pvt, Col Jas Raulston, Capt Mathew Cowan, Inf
BREWER, Erasmus, Pvt, Col Leroy Hammond, Capt Jas Craig, 2 Regt W TN Mil
BREWER, Geo, Pvt, Col Wm Metcalf, Capt Andrew

## Enlisted Men, War of 1812

Patterson, Mil Inf
BREWER, James, Pvt, Col Thomas McCrory, Capt Isaac Patton, Inf; sick absent
BREWER, Jas, Ffr, Col Wm Metcalf, Capt William Mullen, Mil Inf
BREWER, Jas, Pvt, Col Samuel Wear, Capt Joseph Calloway, Mtd Inf
BREWER, Jno, Pvt, Lt Col John Edmonson, Co Commander omitted, Cav
BREWER, John, Pvt, Col Edwin E Booth, Capt John Slatton, E TN Mil
BREWER, Lewis, Pvt, Regt Commander omitted, Capt Askew, Inf
BREWER, Lion, Pvt, Col S Bunch, Capt Jno Harris, E TN Mil
BREWER, Meridith, Pvt, Col Edward Bradley, Capt John Kennedy, Riflemen; furloughed to wait on the sick
BREWER, Russell, Cpl, Col S Copeland, Capt William Douglass, Inf
BREWER, Thos, Pvt, Col Samuel Wear, Capt Joseph Calloway, Branch Srvce omitted
BREWER, Thos, Pvt, Regt Commander omitted, Capt Josiah Askew, Inf
BREWER, Wm, Pvt, Col Philip Pipkin, Capt William Mackay, Mil Inf
BREWER, Wm, Pvt, Col Samuel Wear, Capt Joseph Calloway, Mtd Inf
BRIAN, Abijah, Pvt, Col J Alcorn, Capt Thos Bradley, Vol Cav
BRIAN, John, Pvt (Private Waiter), Col William Johnson, Capt Benjamin Powell, E TN Mil; private waiter to Capt Powell
BRIANT, David O, Cpl, Col A Cheatham, Capt Charels Johnson, Inf
BRIANT, John, Pvt, Col S Copeland, Capt William Douglass, Inf
BRIANT, John, Pvt, Col Samuel Bayless, Capt Jas Churchamn, E TN Mil
BRIANT, John, Pvt, Col Thos Benton, Capt Henry L Douglass, Vol Inf; in Capt Bradley's troop
BRIANT, Joshua, Pvt, Col John Cocke, Capt Samuel M Caruthers, Inf
BRIANT, Lewis, Pvt, Col Samuel Bayless, Capt Jas Churchman, E TN Mil
BRIANT, Nathan, Pvt, Maj William Russell, Capt John Cowan, Vol Mtd Riflemen
BRIANT, Philip, Pvt, Col Philip Pipkin, Capt David Smith, Inf
BRIANT, Sterling, Pvt, Col Alexander Loury, Capt Geo Sarver, Inf
BRIANT, Tarlton, Pvt, Col S Bunch, Capt Jno English, E TN Drafted Mil; joined from Capt Allen's Co
BRIANT, Thos, Pvt, Col William Y Higgins, Capt William Doake, Mtd Riflemen
BRIANT, William, Pvt, Col L Hammonds, Capt Jno Williamson, 2nd Regt Inf
BRICE, Castleton, Pvt, Col S Bunch, Capt Jones Griffin, E TN Drafted Mil
BRICE, Robert, Pvt, Col William Lillard, Capt William Gillenwater, E TN Vol Inf

BRICE, William, Pvt, Col Robert Steele, Capt James Shenault, Mil Inf
BRICKER, Wm, Pvt, Col Samuel Bayless, Capt Jonathan Waddle, E TN Mil
BRICKEY, Jeremiah, Pvt, Col William Lillard, Capt James Lillard, E TN Vol Inf
BRICKEY, Peter, Pvt, Col William Lillard, Capt James Lillard, E TN Vol Inf
BRICKEY, William, Pvt, Col Edwin E Booth, Capt Alexander Biggs, Inf
BRICKEY, Wm, Pvt, Col S Bunch, Capt Jno Houk, E TN Mil; sick in the hospital at Ft Strothers
BRICKY, Wm, Pvt, Col Ewen Allison, Capt Jas Allen, E TN Mil
BRIDE, Jas M, 2 Sgt, Col N Cannon, Capt John B Demsey, Mtd Gunmen; reduced to the ranks
BRIDGEMAN, Jno, Sgt, Col S Bunch, Capt Jno English, E TN Drafted Mil; discharged by Gen orders
BRIDGES, Benjamin, Pvt, Col John Cocke, Capt Joseph Price, Inf
BRIDGES, Benjamin, Pvt, Regt Commander omitted, Capt Archibald McKinney, Cav
BRIDGES, Brickel (Brickley), Pvt, Col Jas Raulston, Capt Chas Wade, Inf
BRIDGES, Britain, Pvt, Col John Coffee, Capt David Smith, Vol Cav
BRIDGES, Ephram, Pvt, Col Edwin E Booth, Capt John McKamey, E TN Inf
BRIDGES, James, Pvt, Gen Andrew Jackson, Capt Nathan Davis, Branch Srvce omitted
BRIDGES, Jas, Pvt, Col S Bunch, Capt N Gibbs, E TN Drafted Mil; left sick at Camp Ross 3-6-1814
BRIDGES, Jas, Pvt, Col Wm Johnson, Capt Henry Hunter, E TN Mil; d 1-20-1815
BRIDGES, John, Pvt, Col A Cheatham, Capt James Giddens, Inf
BRIDGES, John, Pvt, Col N T Perkins, Capt Philip Pipkin, Mtd Riflemen
BRIDGES, Jos, 2 Cpl, Col William Lillard, Capt John Neatherton, E TN Vol Inf
BRIDGES, Jos, Pvt, Col William Johnson, Capt Jos Scott, 3rd Regt Mil; left sick a few miles below Knoxville
BRIDGES, Robert, Pvt, Col John Cocke, Capt James Gray, Inf
BRIDGES, Sampson, Cpl, Col Thos Williamson, Capt Robert Moore, Vol Mtd Gunmen
BRIDGES, Terry, Pvt, Col Alexander Loury, Capt John Looney, 2nd Regt W TN Mil
BRIDGES, Thos, Pvt, Lt Col Leroy Hammonds, Capt James Tubb, Inf
BRIDGES, Wm, Pvt, Col N Cannon, Capt Brice Martin, Mtd Gunmen
BRIDGES, Wm, Pvt, Col Philip Pipkin, Capt John Robertson, Mil Inf; left sick at Ft Jackson 11-11-1814
BRIDGEWATER, Alexander, Pvt, Col A Loury, Capt J N Williamson, W TN Mil
BRIDGEWATER, Elias, Pvt, Col John Alcorn, Capt Fredrick Stump, Cav
BRIDGEWATER, Elias, Pvt, Col L Hammonds, Capt J N

## Enlisted Men, War of 1812

Williamson, 2nd Regt Inf
BRIDGEWATER, Isaac, 4 Cpl, Col Thomas McCrory, Capt Gordon, Inf
BRIDGEWATER, Wm, Pvt, Col Edin E Booth, Capt Richard Marshall, Drafted Mil
BRIDGMAN, Jos, Pvt, Col Jas Raulston, Capt Matthew Cowan, Inf
BRIENT, William, Pvt, Col Alexander Loury, Capt J N Williamson, W TN Mil
BRIGANCE, Chas N, Pvt, Col John Alcorn, Capt John Byrn, Cav
BRIGANCE, Chas, Pvt, Col Jno Coffee, Capt John Byrn, Cav
BRIGANCE, Chas, Pvt, Col John Alcorn, Capt John W Byrn, Cav
BRIGANCE, David, Far, Col Newton Cannon, Capt William Edwards, Regt Commander
BRIGANCE, Geo S, Far, Col John Alcorn, Capt John W Byrn, Cav; on furlough
BRIGANCE, Jas, Pvt, Col John Alcorn, Capt John W Byrn, Cav
BRIGANCE, John, Pvt, Col Jno Coffee, Capt John W Byrn, Cav
BRIGANCE, Nicholas, Pvt, Col Jno Coffee, Capt John Byrn, Cav
BRIGANCE, Stewart, Far, Col Jno Coffee, Capt John W Byrn, Cav
BRIGES, John, Sgt, Col John Coffee, Capt Charles Kavanaugh, Cav
BRIGES, Jos, Pvt, Col William Johnson, Capt Joseph Scott, E TN Drafted Mil; substitute for Spencer Torbin
BRIGES, Wm, Pvt, Col Thomas Benton, Capt Robert Cannon, Inf
BRIGGINS, Chas M, Pvt, Col Thomas Williamson, Capt Thomas Scurry, Vol Mtd Gunmen
BRIGGS, Ephriam, Pvt, no other information
BRIGGS, Jno, Pvt, Regt Commander omitted, Capt Jno Miller, Spies
BRIGGS, Merrill, Pvt, Maj William Russell, Capt John Cowan, Vol Mtd Gunmen
BRIGGS, R P C, Blksmth, Col John Coffee, Capt James Terrill, Vol Cav
BRIGGS, Sam'l, Pvt, Col Thomas Williamson, Capt John Doak, Capt John Dobbins, Vol Mtd Gunmen
BRIGHAM, David, Pvt, Regt Commander omitted, Capt Gray, Inf
BRIGHAM, William, 5 Cpl, Col John Cocke, Capt James Gray, Inf
BRIGHAM, William, Pvt, Regt Commander omitted, Capt Gray, Inf
BRIGHT, Cabit, Pvt, Col R C Napier, Capt Durry Adkins, Mil Inf
BRIGHT, Elijah, Pvt, Col Philip Pipkin, Capt Henry M Newlin, Mil Inf; left sick at Ft Williams 11-4-1814
BRIGHT, Jas, Pvt, Col James Raulston, Capt Edward Robinson, Inf
BRIGHT, Jasper, Pvt, Col Samuel Wear, Capt James Gillespie, E TN Vol Inf
BRIGHT, John, Pvt, Maj Gen Wm Carroll, Col James Raulston, Capt Edward Robinson, Inf
BRIGHT, Michael, Cpl, Col William Johnson, Capt Christopher Cooks, E TN Mil
BRIGHT, Michael, Cpl, Col William Johnson, Capt Joseph Kirk, Mil
BRIGHT, Wm, 2 Cpl, Col Nicholas T Perkins, Capt Mathew Johnston, Mil Inf
BRIGHTWELL, Reynolds, Pvt, Col Robert Steele, Capt Richard M Ratton, Mil Inf
BRILES, Dempsey, Pvt, Col John Cocke, Capt Joseph Price, Inf
BRILES, Jas, Pvt, Col James Raulston, Capt Henry Hamilton, Inf; also served under Maj Gen Wm Carroll
BRILES, Thomas, Pvt, Col John Brown, Capt Jesse G Reany, Mtd Gunmen
BRILEY, Joshua, Pvt, no other information
BRIMER, Vinyard, Pvt, Col Samuel Bayless, no other information
BRINEFIELD, Robt, Pvt, Col Edward Bradley, Capt John Kennedy, Riflemen
BRINKLEY, Peter, Pvt, Col Jno Coffee, Capt Frederick Stump, Cav
BRINKLEY, Samuel, Pvt, Col James Raulston, Capt Henry Hamilton, Inf; d 3-8-1815 also served under Maj Gen Wm Carroll
BRINKLEY, Stephen, Pvt, Col William Hall, Capt John Wallace, Inf
BRINKLEY, Thos, Pvt, Col William Hall, Capt John Wallace, Inf; absent suspended
BRINSON, Drury, Pvt, Regt Commander omitted, Capt Gray, Inf
BRINSON, Josiah, Cpl, Col A Cheatham, Capt Hugh Birdwell, Inf
BRIRE, Dan'l, Blksmth, Col Thomas Williamson, Capt James Cook, Capt John Crane, Vol Mtd Gunmen
BRIRON, John, Pvt, Col James Raulston, Capt James A Black, Inf
BRISBY, David, Pvt, Col John Cocke, Capt John Dalton, Inf
BRISBY, John, Pvt, Col John Cocke, Capt John Dalton, Inf
BRISBY, John, Pvt, Regt Commander omitted, Capt Gray, Inf
BRISCO, John, 1 Sgt, Col Thomas Benton, Capt George Caperton, Branch Srvce omitted
BRISCO, John, 1 Sgt, Col William Pillow, Capt Geo Caperton, Inf
BRISCOE, John, Pvt, Regt Commander omitted, Capt Jas Cowan, Mtd Inf; d 2-10-1814
BRISCOE, Thos, Pvt, no other information
BRISEN (BRYSEN), Sam'l, Pvt, Col Samuel Bunch, Capt David G Vance, E TN Mtd Inf
BRISKEY, Wm, Pvt, Col Samuel Bunch, Capt Joseph Duncan, E TN Drafted Mil; joined from Capt Allen's Co
BRISKINS, John, Pvt, Col Thomas Benton, Capt George Caperton, Vol Inf
BRISON, Andrew, Pvt, Col William Y Higgins, Capt Thomas Eldridge, Mtd Gunmen
BRISON, Dan'l, Pvt, Maj William Woodfolk, Capt Ezekial Ross, Capt McCulley, Inf; d 12-1-1814

## Enlisted Men, War of 1812

BRISTOE, Eliza, Pvt, Col William Hall, Capt John Kennedy, Vol Inf

BRISTON, Elijah, Pvt, Col Edward Bradley, Capt John Kennedy, Riflemen; AWOL

BRISTOR, William, Pvt, Col William Lillard, Capt Thomas Sharpe, 2nd Regt Inf

BRIT, Benj, Pvt, Col Ewen Allison, Capt Joseph Everett, E TN Mil

BRIT, Robt, Pvt, Col John K Wynne, Capt James Cole, Inf

BRIT, Wm, Pvt, Col Ewen Allison, Capt Joseph Everett, E TN Mil; deserted 3-4-1814

BRITCHER, Jas, Pvt, Col William Johnson, Capt Christopher Cook, E TN Mil

BRITER (BRILES), Wm, Pvt, Col Samuel Bayless, Capt Joseph Hale, E TN Mil

BRITEY, John, Pvt, Col William Pillow, Capt Thomas Williamson, Vol Inf

BRITON, John, Pvt, Col R C Napier, Capt Early Benson, Mil Inf

BRITON, Jos, Pvt, Lt Col Wm Snodgrass, Ens Abraham Gregg, 2nd Regt E TN Mil Vol Det of Inf

BRITT, Anderson S, Pvt, Col Philip Pipkin, Capt John Strother, Mil; deserted

BRITT, Benj, Pvt, Col S Bunch, Capt Jones Griffin, E TN Drafted Mil; joined from Capt Everett's Co

BRITT, Jas, Pvt, Lt Col Hammond, Capt Thomas Delaney, Inf; also served Col Alexander Loury

BRITT, Wm, Pvt, Col S Bunch, Capt Jones Griffin, E TN Drafted Mil; joined fromm Capt Everett's Co

BRITTAIN, Andrew, Pvt, Maj John Childs, Capt James Cummings, E TN Vol Mtd Inf

BRITTAIN, John, Pvt, Maj John Childs, Capt James Cummings, E TN Vol Mtd Inf; substitute for Joab Moore

BRITTEN, John, Pvt, Col Ewen Allison, Capt Joseph Everett, E TN Mil

BRITTIS, Michael, Pvt, Col Samuel Bayless, Capt Jonathan Waddell, E TN Mil

BRITTIS, William, Pvt, Col Samuel Bayless, Capt Jonathan Waddle, E TN Mil

BRITTON, Abraham, Pvt, Col Ewen Allison, Capt Henry McCray, E TN Mil; deserted

BRITTON, Abraham, Pvt, Col William Hall, Capt Brice Martin, Vol Inf; sick absent

BRITTON, Alsolom, Pvt, Col Samuel Bunch, Capt Francis Register, E TN Mil; joined from Capt McCrea's Co

BRITTON, Cornelius, Pvt, Col William Johnson, Capt Joseph Scott, E TN Drafted Mil; substitute for John Shipley

BRITTON, Harvey, Pvt, Col Thomas Williamson, Capt Anthony Metcalf, Vol Mtd Gunmen

BRITTON, Hugh, Pvt, Col John Brown, Capt Hugh Barton, E TN Mil Inf

BRITTON, Jackett, Pvt, Maj William Carroll, Capt Lewis Dillahunty, Vol Inf; d 2-11-1815, Also served Capt Danl Bradford

BRITTON, James H, Pvt, Col Thomas Williamson, Capt Anthony Metcalf, Vol Mtd Gunmen

BRITTON, James, Pvt, Col Samuel Bayless, Capt Joseph Goodson, E TN Mil

BRITTON, Joseph, Pvt, Col Samuel Bunch, Capt Francis Berry, E TN Mil

BRITTON, Joseph, Pvt, Col William Lillard, Capt Jacob Hartsell, E TN Vol Inf

BRITTON, Robert, Pvt, Col Samuel Bunch, Capt Francis Berry, E TN Mil; transferred to Capt Griffin's Co

BRITTON, Robert, Pvt, Col Samuel Bunch, Capt Jones Griffin, E TN Drafted Mil

BRITTON, Samuel, Pvt, Col S Copeland, Capt Allen Wilkinson, Mil Inf

BRITTON, William, Pvt, Col Samuel Bayless, Capt Allen Bacon, E TN Mil

BRIXLER, Joseph, Pvt, Col Ewen Allison, Capt Samuel Allen, E TN Mil

BRIZENDINE, Thomas, Pvt, Col Samuel Bayless, Capt Branch Jones, E TN Drafted Mil

BROADAWAY, John, Pvt, Maj William Russell, Capt Felman Hodges, Vol Mtd Gunmen

BROADHURST, John, Pvt, Col William Lillard, Capt Robert McCalpin, E TN Vol Inf

BROADWAY, Drury, Pvt, Col Samuel Bunch, Capt John English, E TN State Mil Drafted; joined from Capt William's Co

BROADWAY, Jesse, Pvt, Gen Andrew Jackson, Capt N Davis, Inf

BROCK, Allen, Pvt, Col William Hall, Capt John Kennedy, Vol Inf

BROCK, Barnes, Pvt, Col Samuel Bayless, Capt John Brock, E TN Mil

BROCK, Basset, Pvt, Col James Raulston, Capt James Black, Inf

BROCK, David, Pvt, Col John Cocke, Capt James Gray, Inf

BROCK, David, Pvt, Regt Commander omitted, Capt James Gray, Inf

BROCK, George A, Pvt, Regt Commander omitted, Capt N Davis, Inf

BROCK, George, Pvt, Col Samuel Bayless, Capt Jonathan Waddle, E TN Mil

BROCK, George, Pvt, Col William Johnson, Capt Henry Hunter, E TN Mil; never appeared

BROCK, James, Pvt, Col John Dyer, Maj William Russell, Capt William Russell, Vol Mtd Gunmen

BROCK, James, Pvt, Col Samuel Wear, Capt Rufus Morgan, E TN Vol Inf

BROCK, James, Pvt, Maj Gen William Carroll, Col James Raulston, Capt Wiley Huddleston, Inf

BROCK, Joel, 2 Sgt, Maj Gen William Carroll, Col James Raulston, Capt Wiley Huddleston, Branch Srvce omitted

BROCK, John, Capt, Col Samuel Bayless, Capt John Brock, E TN Mil

BROCK, John, Pvt, Col Alexander Loury, Lt Col Leroy Hammonds, Capt Thomas Delaney, Inf

BROCK, John, Pvt, Maj William Woodfolk, Capt Abner Pearce, Inf

BROCK, John, Pvt, Regt Commander omitted, Capt James Haggard, Mtd Gunmen; on furlough

BROCK, Leonard, Pvt, Col Samuel Wear, Capt Daniel Price, E TN Vol Inf

BROCK, Russell, Pvt, Col R H Dyer, Capt Cuthbert

## Enlisted Men, War of 1812

Hudson, Vol Mtd Gunmen; reduced from Sdlr
BROCK, Thos, Pvt, Col S Bunch, Capt Dan'l Yarnell, E TN Mil; deserted
BROCKAS, Thos, Pvt, Col William Johnson, Capt James Stewart, E TN Mil
BROCKETT, Thos, Pvt, Col Thomas Williamson, Capt Anthony M Metcalf, Vol Mtd Gunmen
BROCKS, Wm, Pvt, Col William Johnston, Capt Henry Hunter, E TN Mil; left sick at Ft Strothers
BRODSHAM, William, Pvt, Col Samuel Bayless, Capt James Landen, E TN Mil
BROGAN, Runalds, Pvt, Col William Johnston, Capt Henry Hunter, E TN Mil; deserted 10-27-1814 & reported
BROOCKS, Thos, Pvt, Col William Johnson, Capt James Stewart, E TN Drafted Mil; substitute
BROOK, Isaac, Pvt, Col William Johnson, Capt David McKamy, E TN Drafted Mil; deserted notified but never appeared
BROOK, Samuel, Pvt, Col N Cannon, Capt Martin, Mtd Gunmen; wounded 11-3-1813 at Tallashatchez
BROOK, Thomas, Pvt, Col Samuel Bunch, Capt Joseph Duncan, E TN Mil Drafted; joined from Capt Gibbs Co
BROOKS, Archibald, Pvt, Col William Pillow, Capt George Caperton, Inf
BROOKS, Chas, Pvt, Regt Commander omitted, Capt Sam'l Richardson, E TN Drafted Mil
BROOKS, Geo, Pvt, Col William Lillard, Capt William Hamilton, E TN Vol Inf; left at the lookout as guard
BROOKS, Henry, Pvt, Col Robert H Dyer, Capt James McMahon, TN Vol Mtd Gunmen
BROOKS, Isaac, Pvt, Col N T Perkins, Capt James McMahan, Mtd Gunmen
BROOKS, James, Pvt, Commanders omitted, Ferrell Inf
BROOKS, James, Pvt, Gen Thos Washington, Capt Jno Crawford, Mtd Inf
BROOKS, Jas, Pvt, Col N T Perkins, Capt James McMahan, Mil Inf
BROOKS, Jas, Pvt, Col S Copeland, Capt William Douglass, Inf
BROOKS, Jas, Pvt, Col William Pillow, Capt C E McEwen, Vol Inf
BROOKS, John, 5 Sgt, Col Philip Pipkin, Capt Henry M Newlin, Mil Inf; substituted Geo Brooks
BROOKS, John, Pvt, Col S Bunch, Capt Jno McNeil, E TN Mil
BROOKS, Philip, Sgt, Col S Bunch, Capt Jno English, E TN Drafted Mil
BROOKS, Price W, Cpl, Col William Pillow, Capt C E McEwen, Vol Inf
BROOKS, Price W, Pvt, Col Thomas H Benton, Capt James McEwen, Vol Inf
BROOKS, Robert, Pvt, Maj William Russell, Capt John Cowan, Vol Mtd Gunmen
BROOKS, Robt, Pvt, Col Edwin Booth, Capt John Sharp, E TN Mil; d 2-7-1815
BROOKS, Robt, Pvt, no other information; on furlough 3-20-1814
BROOKS, Sam'l, Pvt, Col Thomas Benton, Capt Robert Cannon, Inf
BROOKS, Sam'l, Pvt, Col Thomas McCrory, Capt William Dooley, Inf
BROOKS, Samuel T, 1 Lt, Col Robert H Dyer, Capt James McMahon, TN Vol Mtd Gunmen, Res omitted; KIA 12-23-1814
BROOKS, Stephen, Pvt, Col William Lillard, Capt Jacob Dyke, Vol Inf
BROOKS, Thomas, Pvt, Col Robt H Dyer, Capt Robert Edmonston, TN Vol Mtd Gunmen
BROOKS, Thomas, Pvt, Col Samuel Bayless, Capt Joseph Rich, E TN Inf; transferred from Capt Churchman
BROOKS, Wm, 4 Sgt, Col S Bunch, Capt Jas Cummings, E TN Vol Mtd Gunmen
BROOKS, Wm, 4 Sgt, Col William Metcalf, Capt William Mullin, Mil Inf
BROOKS, Wm, Sgt, Col R H Dyer, Maj William Russell, Capt William Russell, Vol Mtd Gunmen; d 12-14-1814
BROOKS, Wm, Sgt, Col S Bunch, Capt Jones Griffin, E TN Drafted Mil; promoted from Cpl
BROOKSHARE, Thos, Pvt, Col Nicholas Perkins, Capt Geo Eliot, Mil Inf
BROOKSHARES, Manning, Pvt, Col Robert Steele, Capt John Chitwood, Mil Inf
BROOKSHEAR, Minering, 2 Cpl, Col Higgins, Capt Dake, Mtd Riflemen
BROOKSHER, Nathan, Pvt, Col Wm Metcalf, Capt Barbee Collins, Mil Inf
BROOKSHERE, E Wm, Pvt, Maj Gen Andrew Jackson, Capt William Carroll, Vol Inf
BROOKSHIRE, Thos, 3 Cpl, Col John Coffee, Capt John Baskerville, Cav
BROOM, Brittain, 3 Sgt, Col John Cocke, Capt Joseph Price, Inf; d 3-8-1815
BROOM, Jonathan, Pvt, Col Robert Steele, Capt Robert Campbell, Mil Inf; sick on furlough
BROOM, Miles, Pvt, Col Jas Raulston, Capt Elijah Haynie, Inf
BROOM, Wm, Pvt, Regt Commander omitted, Capt Davis Smith, Cav Vol
BROTH, Davis, Pvt, Lt John Steele, Det of Inf
BROTHERS, Phillip, Pvt, Col Wm Hall, Capt William Alexander, Vol Inf
BROTHERS, Sampson, Pvt, Col Samuel Bayless, Capt James Landen, E TN Mil
BROTHERTON, John T, Cpl, Col William Johnson, Capt Christopher Cook, E TN Mil
BROTHERTON, John, Cpl, Col William Johnson, Capt Joseph Kirk, Mil
BROTHERTON, John, Pvt, Col Samuel Bayless, Capt Solomon Hendrix, E TN Mil
BROTHERTON, Robert, Pvt, Col Samuel Bayless, Capt Solomon Hendrix, E TN Mil
BROUGHTON, Thos, Sgt, Col Thos McCrory, Capt John Reynolds, Mil Inf
BROW, Robert, Pvt, Col James Raulston, Capt Mathew Neal, Inf
BROW, Robert, Pvt, Col Samuel Wear, Capt Robert Doak, E TN Vol Inf
BROWDER, Williams, Pvt, Col Jno Brown, Capt Allen I

## Enlisted Men, War of 1812

Bacon, E TN Mil Inf
BROWDER, Wm, Pvt, Commanders & Branch Srvce omitted; ill health
BROWN, Abraham, Pvt, Col Alex Loury, Capt John Looney, 2nd Regt W TN Mil
BROWN, Absolom, Pvt, Col S Copeland, Capt Jas Tait, Inf
BROWN, Adam, 4 Cpl, Col R C Napier, Capt Edward Noblett, Mil Inf
BROWN, Alex, Pvt, Col Samuel Wear, Capt Joseph Callaway, Mtd Inf
BROWN, Alexander, Pvt, Col Wm Lillard, Capt Robert Maloney, E TN Vol Inf
BROWN, Alexander, Sgt, Col Robert M Dyer, Capt Robert Evans, Vol Mtd Gunmen
BROWN, Allen, Adjt, Col Ewin Allison, E TN Mil, Res omitted; transferred to Col Bunch Regt
BROWN, Allen, Adjt, Col Samuel Bunch, E TN Mil, Res omitted
BROWN, Allen, Pvt, Col Ewen Allison, Capt Thomas Wilson, E TN Drafted Mil; appointed Adjt
BROWN, Armistead, Pvt, Col J Alcorn, Capt Thomas Bradley, Vol Cav
BROWN, Armistead, Pvt, Col John Coffee, Capt Jas Terrell, Vol Cav; attached himself to Capt Bradley
BROWN, Armistead, Pvt, Col John Coffee, Capt Thomas Bradley, Vol Cav
BROWN, Azekiah, Pvt, Col John Coffee, Capt Byrns, Cav
BROWN, Benj H, Pvt, Col John Coffee, Capt John Baskerville, Cav
BROWN, Benj, Pvt, Col Samuel Bunch, Capt David G Vance, E TN Mtd Inf
BROWN, Benj, Pvt, Col Wm Metcalf, Capt Hill, Capt John Cunningham, Mil Inf
BROWN, Bernard, Pvt, Col John K Wynne, Capt John Spinks, Inf
BROWN, Berry H, Pvt, Col John Coffee, Capt J Baskerville, Cav
BROWN, Chas, Pvt, Col Thos Williamson, Capt Richard Tate, Vol Mtd Gunmen
BROWN, Chas, Pvt, Maj Gen Wm Carroll, Capt Francis Ellis, Inf; d 2-9-1815
BROWN, Clairborne, Pvt, Col John Brown, Capt Lunsford Oliver, E TN Mil
BROWN, Dan'l, Pvt, Col Wm Metcalf, Capt Bird L Hurt, Mil Inf
BROWN, Daniel, Pvt, Col Newton Cannon, Capt Harpole, Mtd unmen
BROWN, Daniel, Pvt, Col Thos Williamson, Capt John Williams, Vol Mtd Gunmen
BROWN, David (Daniel), Pvt, Col Zacheus Copeland, Capt William Douglass, Inf
BROWN, David G, Pvt, Col Samuel Bayless, Capt Joseph Goodson, E TN Mil
BROWN, David W, Pvt, Col William Johnson, Capt James Tunnell, E TN Mil
BROWN, David, Pvt, Col John K. Wynne, Capt James Cole, Inf
BROWN, David, Pvt, Col Philip Pipkin, Capt William Mackay, Mil Inf; deserted
BROWN, David, Pvt, Col Philip Pipkin, Ens Wm Pegram,
Capt David Smith Co of E TN
BROWN, David, Pvt, Col R C Napier, Capt Early Benson, Mil Inf
BROWN, David, Pvt, Col Samuel Bayless, Capt Jonathan Waddell, E TN Mil
BROWN, David, Pvt, Col William Johnson, Capt Andrew Lawson, E TN Draft Mil
BROWN, David, Sgt, Col Samuel Bayless, Capt Joseph Hale, E TN Mil
BROWN, Ebbenezer, Pvt, Col William Y Higgins, Capt William Doake, Mtd Riflemen
BROWN, Edward, Far, Col Thomas Williamson, Capt Robert Moore, Vol Mtd Gunmen
BROWN, Edward, Pvt, Col Samuel Bayless, Capt Joseph B Bacon, E TN Mil
BROWN, Eli, Pvt, Col Edwin Booth, Capt Richard Marshall, Drafted Mil
BROWN, Ezekiel, Pvt, Col James Raulston, Capt Daniel Newman, Inf; deceased 2-21-1815
BROWN, Felix, Pvt, Col Samuel Wear, Capt Joseph Calloway, Mtd Inf
BROWN, Francis, Pvt, Col R H Dyer, Capt Cuthbert Hudson, Vol Mtd Gunmen
BROWN, Francis, Pvt, Col S Bunch, Capt John McNare, E TN Mil
BROWN, Francis, Pvt, Col Samuel Bunch, Capt James Duncan, E TN Drafted Mil; from Capt McNares Co
BROWN, Francis, Pvt, Col Samuel Wear, Capt Joseph Calloway, Mtd Inf
BROWN, Francis, Pvt, Col William Lillard, Capt Thomas Sharpe, 2 Regt Inf; transferred to Calloway's Co
BROWN, Francis, Pvt, Col William Metcalf, Capt Alexander Hill & Capt John Cnningham, Mil Inf
BROWN, Francis, Pvt, Maj John Chiles, Capt Daniel Price, E TN Vol Mtd Inf
BROWN, Francis, Pvt, Maj John Chiles, Capt Daniel Price, Vol Mtd Gunmen; in Coffee's Brig
BROWN, Gabriel, Pvt, Col Ewen Allison, Capt James Allen, E TN Mil
BROWN, George, Pvt, Col Edwin Booth, Capt John Slatton, E TN Mil
BROWN, George, Pvt, Col Ewen Allison, Capt Jonas Loughmiller, Mil; transferred to Capt Griffin
BROWN, George, Pvt, Col S Bunch, Capt John Griffin, E TN Draft Mil; joined from Capt Loughmiller Co
BROWN, George, Pvt, Col Samuel Wear, Capt Jesse Cole, Vol Inf
BROWN, George, Pvt, Col Samuel Wear, Capt Rufus Morgan, E TN Vol Inf
BROWN, George, Pvt, Col William Lillard, Capt Robert Maloney, E TN Vol Inf
BROWN, George, Sgt, Maj William Woodfolk, Capt Ezekial Ross & Capt McCulley, Inf; elected 3 Lt
BROWN, Hardy, Pvt, Col John Alcorn, Capt John W Byrn, Cav
BROWN, Henry, Pvt, Col S Bunch, Capt Jones Griffin, E TN Drafted Inf; deserted 3-4-1814
BROWN, Henry, Sgt, Col Edward Bradley, Capt Harry L Douglass, Vol Inf
BROWN, Hezekiah, Pvt, Col James Raulston, Capt Daniel

## Enlisted Men, War of 1812

Newman, Inf
BROWN, Hugh, Pvt, Col William Metcalf, Capt Alexander Hill, Mil Inf
BROWN, Isaac N, Sgt, Col Ewen Allison, Capt Allen, E TN Mil
BROWN, Isaac W, Pvt, Col Ewen Allison, Capt John Hampton, Mil
BROWN, Isaac, Pvt, Col H C Napier, Capt Drury Adkins, Mil Inf
BROWN, Isaac, Pvt, Col R H Dyer, Capt Beverly Williams, Vol Mtd Gunmen
BROWN, Isaac, Pvt, Col R H Dyer, Capt Cuthbert Hudson, Vol Mtd Gunmen; transferred from Joseph Williams Co
BROWN, Jacob, Col S Bunch, Capt David G Vance, E TN Mtd Inf
BROWN, Jacob, Pvt, Col William Johnson, Capt Andrew Lawson, E TN Mil Draft
BROWN, James, 3 Cpl, Col Newton Cannon, Capt John Demsey, Mtd Gunmen
BROWN, James, Ffr, Col Alexander Loury, Lt Col Leroy Hammonds, Capt Thomas Delaney, Inf
BROWN, James, Pvt, Col James Raulston, Capt Daniel Newman, Inf
BROWN, James, Pvt, Col John Brown, Capt Jesse G Reany, Mtd Gunmen
BROWN, James, Pvt, Col John Coffee, Capt James Terrell, Vol Cav; not fit for service
BROWN, James, Pvt, Col John Dyer, Capt Joseph Williams, Vol Mtd Gunmen
BROWN, James, Pvt, Col Samuel Bayless, Capt Solomon Hendricks, E TN Mil
BROWN, James, Pvt, Col Thomas Williamson, Capt John Dobbins & Capt John Doak, Vol Mtd Gunmen; died 2-2-1813 (SB 1815?
BROWN, James, Pvt, Col William Higgins, Capt William Doake, Mtd Riflemen; killed 1-22-1814 at Emuckfaw
BROWN, James, Pvt, Col William Johnson, Capt David McKamy, E TN Draft Mil
BROWN, James, Pvt, Gen Andrew Jackson, Capt James Reed
BROWN, James, Pvt, Lt Col Leroy Hammonds, Capt Thomas Delaney, Inf; also served under Col Loury
BROWN, James, QM Sgt, Col William Higgins, no Co Commander, 2 Regt Mtd Vol
BROWN, Jeremiah, Pvt, Col Newton Cannon, Capt John Harpole, Mtd Gunmen
BROWN, Jesse, Cpl, Maj Gen Andrew Jackson, Col Thomas Williamson, Capt Robert Steele, Vol Mtd Gunman
BROWN, Jesse, Pvt, Col Ewin Allison, Capt Jonas Loughmiller, Mil
BROWN, Jesse, Pvt, Col John Wynne, Capt John Spinks, Inf; deserted
BROWN, Jesse, Pvt, Col N T Perkins, Capt John Quarles, Vol Mtd Inf
BROWN, Joel, Pvt, Col Thomas Williamson, Capt Robert Moore, Vol Mtd Gunmen, died 2-4-1815
BROWN, Joel, Pvt, Regt Commander omitted, Capt George Smith, Spies
BROWN, John B, 1 Sgt, Maj Gen William Carroll, Capt Francis Ellis, Inf
BROWN, John G, Pvt, Maj William Woodfolk, Capt Abraham Dudney & Capt John Sutton, Inf, deserted
BROWN, John L, Sgt, Col William Hall, Capt John Kennedy, Vol Inf
BROWN, John M, Pvt, Col William Johnson, Capt Henry Hunter, E TN Mil; attached to Wgnr Corp, replaced Benjamin Gentry
BROWN, John S, Pvt, Col Edward Bradley, Capt John Kennedy, Riflemen
BROWN, John S, Pvt, Col William Hall, Capt John Kennedy, Vol Inf
BROWN, John, Pvt, Col A Cheatham, Capt James Giddins, Inf
BROWN, John, Pvt, Col A Cheatham, Capt William Creel, Inf; promoted to Surgeon
BROWN, John, Pvt, Col Edward Bradley, Capt Elijah Haynie, Vol Inf
BROWN, John, Pvt, Col Edwin Booth, Capt George Winton, E TN Mil
BROWN, John, Pvt, Col James Raulston, Capt Mathew Cowan, Branch omitted
BROWN, John, Pvt, Col John Childs, Capt Daniel Price, E TN Vol Mtd Inf
BROWN, John, Pvt, Col John Coffee, Capt James Terrell, Vol Cav
BROWN, John, Pvt, Col John Wynne, Capt James Cole, Inf
BROWN, John, Pvt, Col Leroy Hammonds, Capt Arahel Rains, Inf
BROWN, John, Pvt, Col R C Napier, Capt Early Henson, Mil Inf
BROWN, John, Pvt, Col S Copeland, Capt James Tait, Inf
BROWN, John, Pvt, Col S Copeland, Capt Moses Thompson, Inf
BROWN, John, Pvt, Col S Copeland, Capt Solomon George, Inf
BROWN, John, Pvt, Col Samuel Bayless, Capt Jonathan Waddell, E TN Mil
BROWN, John, Pvt, Col Samuel Bunch, Capt John McNare, E TN Mil
BROWN, John, Pvt, Col Samuel Bunch, Capt Joseph Duncan, E TN Drafted Mil; joined from Capt McNare's Co
BROWN, John, Pvt, Col Samuel Bunch, Capt Thomas Mann, E TN Vol Mtd Inf
BROWN, John, Pvt, Col Samuel Wear, Capt John Childs, E TN Vol Inf
BROWN, John, Pvt, Col Thomas Williamson, Capt Robert Steele, Vol Mtd Gunmen
BROWN, John, Pvt, Col William Hall, Capt Abraham Bledsoe, Vol Inf
BROWN, John, Pvt, Col William Lillard, Capt George Keyes, E TN Inf
BROWN, John, Pvt, Col William Lillard, Capt Jacob Hartsell, E TN Vol Inf
BROWN, John, Pvt, Col William Lillard, Capt Robert McCulpin, E TN Vol Inf; deserted

## Enlisted Men, War of 1812

BROWN, John, Pvt, Col William Lillard, Capt William McLin, E TN Inf
BROWN, John, Pvt, Col William Metcalf, Capt Thomas Marks, Mil Inf
BROWN, John, Pvt, Col William Metcalf, Capt William Mullin, Mil Inf
BROWN, John, Pvt, Maj William Woodfolk, Capt Abner Pearce, Inf
BROWN, John, Pvt, Maj William Woodfolk, Capt Abraham Dudney, Inf
BROWN, John, Pvt, Regt Commander omitted, Capt Lane Garrett, Mtd Riflemen
BROWN, Jonathan, Pvt, Regt Commander omitted, Capt Jas Haggard, Mtd Gunmen
BROWN, Jos, Pvt, Col Ewen Allison, Capt Jonas Loughmiller, Mil; transferred to Capt McPherson's Co
BROWN, Jos, Pvt, Col Thos McCrory, Capt William Dooley, Inf; promoted to Wgnmstr
BROWN, Jos, Pvt, Col William Johnson, Capt David McKam, E TN Drafted Mil; sick absent
BROWN, Jos, Pvt, Regt Commander omitted, Capt Geo Smith, Spies
BROWN, Jos, Sgt, Col S Bunch, Capt Francis Register, E TN Mil
BROWN, Jos, Sgt, Col S Bunch, Capt James Penny, E TN Mtd Inf
BROWN, Joseph, Pvt, Col Samuel Bunch, Capt Isaac Williams, Mtd Vol
BROWN, Joshua, 5 Sgt, Maj John Childs, Capt Chas Conway, E TN Mtd Gunmen
BROWN, Joshua, Cpl, Commanders omitted, E TN Mil Inf
BROWN, Joshua, Pvt, Col S Bunch, Capt N Gibbs, E TN Drafted Mil; left sick at Camp Ross 3-6-1814
BROWN, Joshua, Pvt, Col Samuel Bayless, Capt Jonathan Waddell, E TN Mil
BROWN, Joshua, Sgt, Col S Bunch, Capt Breden, E TN Mil
BROWN, Josiah, Cpl, Col Samuel Bunch, Capt Joseph Duncan, E TN Drafted Mil
BROWN, Jothan, Pvt, Col Wm Lillard, Capt Robert Malone, E TN Vol Inf
BROWN, Leonard, Pvt, Col Alex Loury, Capt John Looney, 2nd Reg W TN Mil
BROWN, Leonard, Pvt, Col Wm Y Higgins, Capt Samuel Allen, Mtd Gunmen
BROWN, Lindsey, Pvt, Col William Woodfolk, Capt Abner Pearce, Inf
BROWN, Lindsey, Pvt, Maj William Woodfolk, Capt James C Neil, Inf
BROWN, Mackey, Pvt, Col William Metcalf, Capt Andrew Patterson, Mil Inf
BROWN, Michael T, Pvt, Col S Bunch, Capt Houston, E TN Vol Mtd Inf
BROWN, Nathaniel, Pvt, Col Alex Loury, Capt Leroy Hammonds, Capt Thos Delaney, Inf
BROWN, Nathaniel, Pvt, Col Wm Hall, Capt Henry Newlin, Inf; substituted Jos Johns
BROWN, Nathaniel, Pvt, Gen Thos Washington, Capt Jno Crawford, Mtd Inf

BROWN, Richard, Pvt, Col Alex Loury, Capt Carver, Inf; furloughed by the surgeon to Deposit
BROWN, Richard, Pvt, Col Edwin Booth, Capt John Slatton, E TN Mil
BROWN, Richard, Pvt, Col John Alcorn, Capt John Baskerville, Vol Inf; on furlough wounded 11-9-1815
BROWN, Richard, Pvt, Col John Cocke, Capt Samuel Caruthers, Inf
BROWN, Richard, Pvt, Col Philip Pipkin, Capt Peter Searcy, Mil Inf; left sick at Ft Jackson
BROWN, Richard, Pvt, Col Wm Hall, Capt John Kennedy, Vol Inf
BROWN, Richard, Sgt, Col Edward Bradley, Capt John Kennedy, Riflemen
BROWN, Robert, Pvt, Col William Woodfolk, Capt James C Neil, Inf
BROWN, Samuel, Pvt, Col Edward Bradley, Capt Abraham Bledsoe, Riflemen; wounded and furloughed
BROWN, Samuel, Pvt, Col Ewen Allison, Capt Jonas Loughmiller, Mil
BROWN, Samuel, Pvt, Col James Raulston, Capt Mathew Neal, Inf
BROWN, Samuel, Pvt, Col Leroy Hammonds, Capt Thomas Delaney, Inf
BROWN, Samuel, Pvt, Col Thomas Williamson, Capt John Hutchings, Vol Mtd Gunmen
BROWN, Samuel, Pvt, Col William Johnson, Capt Benj Powell, E TN Mil
BROWN, Samuel, Pvt, Col Wm Benton, Capt Thomas Williamson, Vol Inf
BROWN, Samuel, Pvt, Col Wm Hall, Capt Abraham Bledsoe, Vol Inf
BROWN, Samuel, Pvt, Col Wm Pillow, Capt Thomas Williamson, Vol Inf
BROWN, Sanders, Pvt, Col Jas Raulston, Capt Elijah Haynie, Inf
BROWN, Seaton, Pvt, Col Wm Lillard, Capt George Argenbright, E TN Vol Riflemen
BROWN, Solomon, Pvt, Col William Johnson, Co Commander omitted, E TN Drafted Mil
BROWN, Solomon, Pvt, Maj William Russell, Capt Isaac Williams, Vol Mtd Gunmen; Col Dyer 1st Regt TN Vol Mtd Gunmen
BROWN, Spicer, Pvt, Col R C Napier, Capt Drury Adkins, Mil Inf
BROWN, Spicer, Pvt, Maj Wm Woodfolk, Capt A Turner, Inf
BROWN, Stanley, Pvt, Col Edwin Booth, Capt John Sharpe, E TN Mil
BROWN, Step, Pvt, Col Thomas Williamson, Capt Robert Moore, Vol Mtd Gunmen
BROWN, Stephen, Pvt, Col Ewin Allison, Capt Henry McCrory, E TN Mil; discharged having furnished substitute
BROWN, Stephen, Pvt, Col Wm Hall, Capt Brice Martin, Vol Inf
BROWN, Tarlton, Pvt, Col John Coffee, Capt John Baskerville, Cav
BROWN, Thomas B, Pvt, Maj Woodfolk, Capt Neil, Inf

BROWN, Thomas L, Pvt, Col Alcorn, Capt Edward Bradley, Vol Cav
BROWN, Thomas, Pvt, Regt Commander omitted, Capt John Roper, E TN Vol Inf
BROWN, Thos S, Pvt, Col Robert H Dyer, Co Commander omitted, Vol Mtd Gunmen; KIA 12-23-1814
BROWN, Thos, Hospital Surgical Mate, Maj Gen Andrew Jackson, Div of TN Mil Expedition against Creek Indians
BROWN, Thos, Pvt, Col Anthony Metcalf, Co Commander omitted, Mil Inf
BROWN, Thos, Pvt, Col Jas Raulston, Capt Mathew Cowan, Inf
BROWN, Thos, Pvt, Col Robert H Dyer, Capt Cuthbert Hudson, Vol Mtd Gunmen
BROWN, Thos, Pvt, Col Samuel Bayless, Capt Jas Churchman, E TN Mil
BROWN, Thos, Pvt, Col Thos H Benton, Capt George Caperton, Vol Inf
BROWN, Thos, Pvt, Col Wm Lillard, Capt Hugh Martin, E TN Vol Inf
BROWN, Thos, Pvt, Col Wm Pillow, Capt Geo Caperton, Inf
BROWN, Thos, Pvt, Maj William Woodfolk, Capt Jas Turner, Inf
BROWN, Thos, Sgt, Col Samuel Bayless, Capt Johnathan Waddell, E TN Mil
BROWN, Tod, Pvt, Regt Commander omitted, Capt George Smith, Spies
BROWN, Wadkins, Pvt, Col Robert H Dyer, Capt Thomas H Jones, Vol Mtd Gunmen
BROWN, Walter, Pvt, Regt Commander omitted, Capt Elijah Rushing, Det of Inf
BROWN, Walter, Sgt, Col R C Napier, Capt James Gray, Mil Inf
BROWN, Washington, Pvt, Maj Wm Woodfolk, Capt Ezekial Ross, Inf
BROWN, Washington, Sgt, Col Zacheus Copeland, Capt Moses Thompson, Inf
BROWN, Watkins, Pvt, Col Thomas Benton, Capt Thomas Williamson, Vol Inf; missing
BROWN, William, Pvt, Col Edwin Booth, Capt Porter, Drafted Mil
BROWN, William, Pvt, Col John Brown, Capt Jesse G Reany, Mtd Gunmen
BROWN, William, Pvt, Col Samuel Bayless, Capt Jonathan Waddell, E TN Mil
BROWN, William, Pvt, Col Thomas Benton, Capt Thomas Williamson, Vol Inf
BROWN, William, Pvt, Col Thomas Benton, Capt William Moore, Vol Inf
BROWN, William, Pvt, Col William Lillard, Capt Robert Maloney, E TN Vol Inf
BROWN, William, Pvt, Col William Lillard, Capt William McLin, E TN Inf
BROWN, Wm L, Pvt, Regt Commander omitted, Capt David Smith, Cav
BROWN, Wm M, Pvt, Col Robert H Dyer, Capt Robert Edmonston, TN Vol Mtd Gunmen
BROWN, Wm jr, Pvt, Col Edward Bradley, Capt Abraham Bledsoe, Riflemen
BROWN, Wm jr, Pvt, Col William Hall, Capt Abraham Bledsoe, Vol Inf
BROWN, Wm sr, Pvt, Col Edward Bradley, Capt Abraham Bledsoe, Riflemen
BROWN, Wm sr, Pvt, Col William Hall, Capt Abraham Bledsoe, Vol Inf
BROWN, Wm, Pvt, Col Ewen Allison, Capt James Allen, E TN Mil
BROWN, Wm, Pvt, Col James Raulston, Capt Mathew Cowan, Inf; d 1-24-1815
BROWN, Wm, Pvt, Col Jno Brown, Capt Wm Christian, E TN Mil Inf
BROWN, Wm, Pvt, Col John Brown, Capt William White, E TN Vol Mtd Inf
BROWN, Wm, Pvt, Col John K Wynne, Capt James Cole, Inf
BROWN, Wm, Pvt, Col John K Wynne, Capt John Spinks, Inf
BROWN, Wm, Pvt, Col S Bunch, Capt David G Vance, E TN Mtd Inf
BROWN, Wm, Pvt, Col S Bunch, Capt F Register, E TN Mil; joined from Capt McCrea's Co
BROWN, Wm, Pvt, Col Samuel Bayless, Capt Joseph Hale, T TN Mil
BROWN, Wm, Pvt, Col Samuel Brown, Capt David G Vance, E TN Mtd Inf
BROWN, Wm, Pvt, Col Samuel Wear, Capt Joseph Calloway, Mtd Inf
BROWN, Wm, Pvt, Col Thomas Williamson, Capt Thomas Scurry, Vol Mtd Gunmen
BROWN, Wm, Pvt, Col William Hall, Capt Abraham Bledsoe, Vol Inf
BROWN, Wm, Pvt, Col William Pillow, Capt Thomas Williamson, Vol Inf
BROWN, Wm, Pvt, Maj John Childs, Capt Daniel Price, Mil Inf
BROWN, Wm, Pvt, Regt Commander omitted, Capt Archibald McKinney, Cav
BROWN, Wm, Pvt, Regt Commander omitted, Capt David Smith, Cav
BROWN (BOREN), Jos, Pvt, Maj Gen Wm Carroll, Capt Francis Ellis, Inf; d 3-1-1815
BROWNE, Wm, Pvt, Col Ewen Allison, Capt Thomas Wilson, E TN Drafted Mil
BROWNEN, John, Pvt, Col Edwin Booth, Capt John Sharp, E TN Mil
BROWNING, Caleb, Pvt, Col A Cheatham, Capt George C Chapman, Inf
BROWNING, Edmond, Pvt, Col Thomas Williamson, Capt James Cook, Capt John Crane, Vol Mtd Gunmen
BROWNING, Edw, Pvt, Lt Col A Cheatham, Co Commander omitted, 6th Brig Mtd Inf
BROWNING, James, 1 Sgt, Col R C Napier, Capt James McMurry, Mil Inf; promoted to Ens
BROWNING, James, Pvt, Col Newton Cannon, Capt John Harpole, Mtd Gunmen
BROWNING, John, Pvt, Col R C Napier, Capt Early Benson, Mil Inf
BROWNING, Joshua, 1 Sgt, Col William Metcalf, Capt

Barbee Collins, Mil Inf

BROWNING, Joshua, Pvt, Col Thomas Williamson, Capt Giles Burdett, Vol Mtd Gunmen

BROWNING, Richard, Pvt, Col John K Wynne, Capt William McCall, Inf; deserted 11-17-1813

BROWNING, Robert, Pvt, Col Thomas Williamson, Capt John Crane, Capt James Cook, Vol Mtd Gunmen

BROWNING, Thomas, Pvt, Col R C Napier, Capt Early Benson, Mil Inf

BROWNING, William, Pvt, Col A Cheatham, Capt Richard Benson, Mil Inf

BROWNLOW, Samuel, Pvt, Col Ewen Allison, Capt William King, Drafted Mil; promoted to Wgnmstr

BROWNLOW, Samuel, Wgnmster, Brig Gen George Doherty, E TN Mil; discharged at Camp Ross by Gen order

BROWNLOW, William, Cpl, Col Edward Bradley, Capt Elijah Haynie, Vol Inf

BROWNLOW, William, Pvt, Col William Hall, Capt Henry Newlin, Inf

BROWNSON, Asahel, 2 Sgt Mate, Col John Cocke, 2nd Regt W TN Mil Inf; d 2-15-1815

BROYLE, Cornelius S, Pvt, Col William Lillard, Capt William McLin, E TN Inf

BROYLES, Jacob, Pvt, Col Samuel Bunch, Capt George McPherson, E TN Mil; joined from Capt Everett's Co

BROYLES, James, Pvt, Col Thomas McCrory, Capt Thomas Gordon, Inf

BROYLES, ___, Pvt, Col Samuel Bunch, Capt Francis Register, E TN Mil; transferred to Capt McPherson's Co

BRUCE, James, Pvt, Col Alexander Loury, Capt George Sarver, Inf; substituted by Thomas Kirkman

BRUCE, James, Pvt, Col N T Perkins, Capt John Doak, Vol Mtd Gunmen

BRUCE, Jesse, Pvt, Col Leroy Hammonds, Capt James Tubb, Inf

BRUCE, John, Pvt, Col John K Wynne, Capt James Walton, Mtd Riflemen

BRUCE, John, Pvt, Col R H Dyer, Capt Bethel Allen, Vol Mtd Gunmen

BRUCE, John, Pvt, Col Robert Steele, Capt James Shenault, Mil Inf

BRUCE, Robert, 3 Cpl, Col R C Napier, Capt James McMurry, Mil Inf

BRUCE, Robert, Pvt, Col Philip Pipkin, Capt James Blakemore, Mil Inf

BRUCE, Seaburn, Pvt, Col Thomas Williamson, Capt John Doak, Vol Mtd Gunmen

BRUCE, Uriah (Ezariah), Pvt, Col James Raulston, Capt Charles Wade, Inf

BRUFF, Samuel, Asst Topograph Engineer, Brig Gen N Taylor, Branch Srvce omitted

BRUFF, Samuel, Sgt, Maj William Woodfolk, Co Commander omitted, Separated Bn of W TN Mil QM Corps; reduced to ranks

BRUFFS, Sam, Pvt, Regt Commander omitted, Capt Larkin, Branch Srvce omitted

BRUMER, Jacob, Pvt, Col Ewen Allison, Capt Jacob Hoyal, E TN Mil; discharged on account of inability

BRUMETTE, John, Pvt, Col Leroy Hammonds, Capt Thomas Delaney, Inf; also served Col Alexander Loury

BRUMLEY, John, Pvt, Col R C Napier, Capt Early Benson, Mil Inf; sick absent

BRUMLEY, John, Pvt, Col Thomas Williamson, Capt John Doak, Capt John Dobbins, Vol Mtd Gunmen; substitute for M Harbor

BRUMLEY, Samuel, Pvt, Col Thomas Williamson, Capt John Doak, Capt John Dobbins, Vol Mtd Gunmen

BRUMLEY, William, Pvt, Col Samuel Bunch, Capt John English, E TN Drafted Mil; furnished a substitute 5-31-1814

BRUMLEY, William, Pvt, Maj William Russell, Capt John Cowan, Vol Mtd Gunmen

BRUMMET, Owen, Pvt, Col Samuel Bunch, Capt John Hauk, E TN Mil; deserted 3-4-1814

BRUMMETT, John, Pvt, Col Edwin Booth, Capt George Winton, E TN Mil; transferred to Capt James Turner's Co

BRUMMETT, John, Pvt, Col Samuel Bunch, Capt George McPherson, E TN Mil

BRUNER, John, Pvt, Col William Lillard, Capt John Roper, E TN Vol Inf

BRUNNET, George, Pvt, Col Edwin Booth, Capt Richard Marshall, Drafted Mil

BRUNSON, Joab, Pvt, Col William Lillard, Capt William Hamilton, E TN Vol Inf

BRUSHEARS, John, Pvt, Col Edwin Booth, Capt John Slatton, E TN Mil; appointed QM Sgt

BRYAN, Allen 1 Cpl, Col Samuel Wear, Capt Simeon Perry, E TN Vol Mtd Inf; reduced from Sgt

BRYAN, Elijah, Pvt, Col Stephen Copeland, Capt G W Stell, Mil Inf

BRYAN, Hardy, Pvt, Col Alexander Loury, Capt Gabriel Martin, Inf

BRYAN, Harriett, Sgt, Col William Pillow, Capt Thomas Williamson, Vol Inf

BRYAN, Henry M, 4 Sgt, Col Thomas Benton, Capt Thomas Williamson, Vol Inf

BRYAN, Henry M, Sgt, Col Thomas Benton, Capt Thomas Williamson, Vol Inf

BRYAN, Jas, Drm Maj, Col Samuel Bunch, Maj Alexander Smith, E TN Mil

BRYAN, John, Pvt, Col William Johnson, Capt Andrew Lawson, E TN Mil Drafted

BRYAN, Lewis C, Pvt, Col A Cheatham, Capt Richard Benson, Inf; transferred to Arty

BRYAN, Wm Bethel, Pvt, Regt Commander omitted, Capt I Previtt, Pack Horse Guards

BRYAN, Wm, Pvt, Col N T Perkins, Capt Philip Pipkin, Mtd Riflemen

BRYAN, Wm, Pvt, Col Samuel Bayless, Capt Branch Jones, E TN Drafted Mil

BRYANS, William J, Pvt, Col R H Dyer, Capt Ephraim D Dickson, TN Vol Mtd Gunmen; transferred to Capt Isaac Williams Co

BRYANT, Burwell, Pvt, Maj William Woodfolk, Capt James Turner, Inf

BRYANT, Cornelius, Pvt, Col Robert Steele, Capt Ri-

cahrd M Ratton, Mil Inf
BRYANT, Greg, Pvt, Col Edward Bradley, Capt John Wallace, Vol Inf
BRYANT, James, Pvt, Gen A Jackson, Capt N Davis, Gen Jackson's Inf
BRYANT, Jas, Drm Maj, Col Sam'l Bunch, Co Commander omitted, E TN Mil
BRYANT, Jas, Pvt, Col Robert Steel, Capt Richard M Ratton, Mil Inf
BRYANT, Jas, Pvt, Col S Bunch, Lt Col Jno Harris, E TN Mil
BRYANT, Jas, Pvt, Col William Lillard, Capt Zacheus Copeland, E TN Vol Inf
BRYANT, John, Pvt, Col John Alcorn, Capt William Locke, Cav
BRYANT, John, Pvt, Col John Coffee, Capt Thomas Bradley, Vol Cav
BRYANT, John, Pvt, Gen A Jackson, Capt Hugh Kerr, Mtd Rangers
BRYANT, Joseph, Pvt, Col Jno Brown, Capt Wm D Neilson, Regt E TN Vol Mil
BRYANT, Joshua, Pvt, Col John Cocke, Capt Samuel M Caruthers, Inf
BRYANT, Josiah, Pvt, Col Robert Steele, Capt Richard M Ratton, Mil Inf
BRYANT, Lewis C, Pvt, Gen A Jackson, Capt J Parrish, Arty
BRYANT, Phil, Pvt, no other information
BRYANT, Philip, Pvt, Col John K Wynne, Capt James Holleman, Inf
BRYANT, Philip, Pvt, Col Philip Pipkin, Capt David Smythe, W TN Mil; attached to Capt John Srother's Co 7-27-1814
BRYANT, Robt, Pvt, Col John Coffee, Capt David Smith, Vol Cav
BRYANT, Sterling, Pvt, Col Edward Bradley, Capt Abraham Bledsoe, Riflemen
BRYANT, Tarlton, Pvt, Col Ewen Allison, Capt James Allen, E TN Mil
BRYANT, William, Sdlr, Col John Coffee, Capt David Smith, Vol Cav
BRYANT, Willis, Pvt, Col John Coffee, Capt Thomas Bradley, Vol Cav
BRYANT, Willis, Pvt, Col S Copeland, Capt G W Stell, Mil Inf; sick absent since 3-19-1814
BRYANT, Willis, Pvt, Col Thomas Williamson, Capt Beverly Williams, Vol Mtd Gunmen
BRYANT, Wm I, Pvt, Maj William Russell, Capt Isaac Williams, Separate Bn TN Vol Mtd Gunmen; joined from Capt Dickson
BRYANT, Wm, Pvt, Col James Raulston, Capt Henry Hamilton, Inf; also served Maj Gen Wm Carroll
BRYANT, Wm, Pvt, Col John K Wynne, Capt John Porter, Inf
BRYANT, Wm, Pvt, Col Philip Pipkin, Capt Peter Searcy, Mil Inf; deserted from Ft Jackson
BRYANT, Wm, Pvt, Col Samuel Bunch, Capt Isaac Williams, E TN Mil
BRYANT, Wm, Pvt, Col Thomas Williamson, Capt Beverly Williams, Vol Mtd Gunmen; transferred to Lt Bean's Spies

BRYEANS, Wm S, Pvt, Regt Commander omitted, Capt Ephraim Dickson, Branch Srvce omitted
BRYSON, Peter, Blksmth, Col John Alcorn, Capt John Baskerville, Vol Cav
BRYSON, Peter, Blksmth, Col John Coffee, Capt John Baskerville, Cav
BRYSON, William, Pvt, Col William Metcalf, Capt William Mullin, Mil Inf
BUCHANAN, Alexander, Pvt, Col Newton Cannon, Capt Brice Martin, Mtd Gunmen
BUCHANAN, Alexander, Pvt, Col William Metcalf, Capt Obidiah Waller, Mil Inf
BUCHANAN, Andrew, Pvt, Regt Commander omitted, Capt Archibald McKenney, Cav
BUCHANAN, David, Pvt, Col Philip Pipkin, Capt James Blakemore, Mil Inf; deserted
BUCHANAN, Hugh, Pvt, Lt Col A Cheatham, Capt G Martin, Mtd Inf -- 6th Brig
BUCHANAN, Hugh, Pvt, Lt Col John Emonson, Co Commander omitted, Cav
BUCHANAN, John B, Pvt, Capt Archibald McKenney, Co Commander omitted, Cav; AWOL 12-14-1813
BUCHANAN, John B, Pvt, Regt Commander omitted, Capt Archibald McKinney, Cav; AWOL
BUCHANAN, John, Pvt, Col James Raulston, Capt Daniel Newman, Inf
BUCHANAN, John, Pvt, Col John Dyer, Capt Ephraim D Dickson, TN Vol Mtd Gunmen; no service performed
BUCHANAN, John, Pvt, Col Newton Cannon, Capt Andrew Patterson, Mtd Riflemen
BUCHANAN, John, Pvt, Regt Commander omitted, Capt James Gray, Inf
BUCHANAN, Robert jr, Pvt, Regt Commander omitted, Capt Archibald McKenney, Cav
BUCHANAN, Robert, Cpl, Col Thomas Williamson, Capt John Doak, Capt John Dobbins, Vol Mtd Gunmen
BUCHANAN, Robert, Pvt, Regt Commander omitted, Capt Archibald McKenney, Cav
BUCHANAN, Samuel, Pvt, Col John Dyer, Capt Thomas Jones, Vol Mtd Gunmen
BUCHANAN, William, Pvt, Col James Raulston, Capt Daniel Newman, Inf; substituted in room of David Comins
BUCHANNON, Hugh, Pvt, Col Alexander Loury, Capt Gabriel Martin, Inf; left sick at Montgomery by order of Col A Loury
BUCHANNON, John B, Pvt, Commanders & Branch Srvce omitted; transferred to Capt McKinney's Co
BUCHANNON, John, 3 Sgt, Col William Metcalf, Capt Andrew Patterson, Mil Inf
BUCHANNON, John, Pvt, Col Robert Dyer, Capt Thomas Jones, Vol Mtd Gunmen
BUCHANNON, John, Pvt, Col William Johnson, Capt William Alexander, Det of E TN Drafted Mil
BUCHANNON, John, Pvt, Regt Commander omitted, Capt Ephraim Dickson, Branch Srvce omitted
BUCHANNON, Samuel, Pvt, Col Robert Dyer, Capt

## Enlisted Men, War of 1812

Thomas Jones, Vol Mtd Gunmen
BUCHANON, John, Pvt, Col John Cocke, Capt James Gray, Inf
BUCHANON, John, Pvt, Col S Copeland, Capt Allen Wilkinson, Mil Inf
BUCHANON, John, Pvt, Col S Copeland, Capt John Biles, Inf
BUCK, Bethel, Pvt, Col Ewen Allison, Capt Adam Winsell, E TN Drafted Mil
BUCK, Bethiel, Pvt, Col Samuel Bunch, Capt George McPherson, E TN Mil; joined from Capt Winsell's Co
BUCK, Cornelius, Pvt, Col S Copeland, Capt Alexander Provine, Mil Inf
BUCK, Daniel, Pvt, Col William Higgins, Capt William Doake, Mtd Riflemen
BUCKALEW, Moses, Pvt, Col Newton Cannon, Capt Thomas Yardley, Mtd Riflemen; transferred to Capt Smith's Spies Co
BUCKALOE, Jonathan, Pvt, Col William Lillard, Capt Hugh Martin, E TN Vol Inf
BUCKALOO, William, Pvt, Col Samuel Bunch, Capt N Gibbs, E TN Drafted Mil
BUCKEART, Peter, Pvt, Col Ewen Allison, Capt William King, Drafted Mil
BUCKHANNON, James, Pvt, Col Philip Pipkin, Capt George Mebane, Mil Inf; deserted from Ft Jackson 9-20-1814
BUCKHANNON, James, Sgt, Col John Brown, Capt William Nielson, E TN Vol Mil
BUCKHANNON, John, Pvt, Col William Metcalf, Capt Andrew Patterson, Mil Inf
BUCKHANNON, John, Sgt, Col William Metcalf, Capt Andrew Patterson, Mil Inf
BUCKHANNON, Samuel S, Pvt, Col Thomas Williamson, Capt John Dobbins, Capt John Doak, Vol Mtd Gunmen
BUCKHANNON, Samuel, Pvt, Col Newton Cannon, Capt Francis Jones, Mtd Riflemen
BUCKHANNON, William, Pvt, Col Newton Cannon, Capt Francis Jones, Mtd Riflemen
BUCKHANNON, William, Pvt, Col William Johnson, Capt William Alexander, Det of E TN Drafted Mil
BUCKHANNON, James, Pvt, Gen John Coffee, no other information
BUCKHANON, John, Pvt, Col N T Perkins, Capt Mathew Johnson, Mil Inf
BUCKHANON, William G, Pvt, Col Robert Steele, Capt John Chitwood, Mil Inf
BUCKHART, John, Pvt, Col William Lillard, Capt Benjamin King, E TN Vol Inf
BUCKHOLDER, John, Pvt, Col Samuel Wear, Col Samuel Bunch, Capt William Mitchell, Inf
BUCKINHAM, Thomas C, 4 Sgt, Col William Johnson, Capt Andrew Lawson, E TN Drafted Mil
BUCKLEY, Garland, Pvt, Col Wm Benton, Capt Jas McEwen, Vol Inf
BUCKLEY, Jas R, Pvt, Col Wm Benton, Capt Jas McEwen, Vol Inf
BUCKLEY, Payton, Pvt, Col Cocke, Capt Wesley, Inf
BUCKLEY, Samuel R, Pvt, Col Thomas H Benton, Capt Jas McEwen, Vol Inf
BUCKLEY, Tapley, Pvt, Col Bradley, Capt Hambelton, Vol Inf
BUCKLEY, Taply, Pvt, Col Wm Hall, Capt James Hambleton, Vol Inf
BUCKLEY, Tatein, Pvt, Col John Cocke, Capt John Weakley
BUCKNAL, Daniel, Pvt, Col Samuel Bayless, Capt Joseph Hale, E TN Mil
BUCKNAL, Nelson, Pvt, Col Samuel Bayless, Capt Joseph Hale, E TN Mil
BUCKNEL, Samuel, Lt M? Sgt, Col Ewin Allison, Co Commander omitted, E TN Mil
BUCKNER, Ezra, Pvt, Col S Bunch, Capt N Gibbs, E TN Drafted Mil; transferred to Capt Duncan
BUCKNER, Ezra, Pvt, Col Samuel Bunch, Capt Joseph Duncan, E TN Drafted Mil; joined from Capt Gibb Co
BUCKNER, John, Pvt, Col Samuel Wear, Capt Daniel Price, E TN Inf
BUCKNER, Presley, Pvt, Regt Commander omitted, Capt Samuel Richardson, E TN Drafted Mil
BUCKNER, Thos, Pvt, Col William Johnson, Capt Andrew Lawson, E TN Drafted Mil
BUCKNER, William, Pvt, Col Samuel Wear, Capt Jesse Cole, Vol Inf
BUFORD, Bird jr, Pvt, Col John Coffee, Capt Jas Terrell, Vol Inf
BUFORD, Bird, Pvt, Col John Coffee, Capt Jas Terrell, Vol Inf
BUFORD, John, Pvt, Col Wm Hall, Capt Brice Martin, Vol Inf
BUG, Willis, Pvt, Col R C Napier, Capt Thomas Gray, Mil Inf; sick absent 5-6-1814
BUGG, Ephraim M, Sgt Maj, Col Newton Cannon, Co Commander omitted, TN Vol Mtd Gunmen
BUGG, Ephraim, Sgt, Col N Cannon, Capt Martin, Mtd Gunmen
BUGG, Samuel, Pvt, Maj Gen Carroll, Capt Ellis, Inf
BUGG, Styles, Pvt, Col A C Napier, Capt Drury Adkins, Mil Inf
BUGG, Willis, Ffr, Maj Gen Carroll, Capt Ellis, Inf
BULL, Balam, Pvt, Col R C Napier, Capt Edward Neblett, Mil Inf
BULL, Elisha, Pvt, Col Samuel Bunch, Capt David Vance, E TN Mtd Inf
BULL, Jesse, Pvt, Col Brown, Capt Vance, E TN Mtd Inf
BULL, Jos, Pvt, Col William Johnson, Capt Benj Powell, E TN Mil; deserted 10-27-1814, substitute for Needham Lee
BULLARD, Asia L, Pvt, Col William Woodfolk, Capt Abner Pearce, Inf
BULLARD, Benj, Pvt, Col Thomas Williamson, Capt James Pace, Lt Neely, Vol Mtd Gunmen
BULLARD, Jesse, Pvt, Col T McCrory, Capt John Reynolds, Mil Inf
BULLARD, Jesse, Pvt, Col Thomas Williamson, Capt Richard Tate, Vol Mtd Gunmen; transferred to Capt Pace Co
BULLARD, Jno, Pvt, Col T McCrory, Capt Jno Reynolds, Mil Inf

## Enlisted Men, War of 1812

BULLARD, John, Pvt, Col John Cocke, Capt George Barnes, Inf

BULLARD, John, Pvt, Col Phillip Pipkin, Capt John Robertson, Mil Inf

BULLARD, Jos, Pvt, Col Dyer, Capt Russell, Vol Mtd Gunmen

BULLARD, Joseph, Pvt, Regt Commander omitted, Capt Wm Rupee, Mtd Spies

BULLARD, Josiah, Pvt, Col John Cocke, Capt James Gault, Inf

BULLARD, Reubin N, Pvt, Col Phillip Pipkin, Capt John Storther, Mil; attached for Wgnr

BULLARD, Ruben, Pvt, Regt Commander omitted, Capt Jas Hagan, Mtd Gunmen

BULLARD, Rubin, Pvt, Regt Commander omitted, Capt Jas Haggard, Spies

BULLARD, Wm G, Pvt, Col William Woodfolk, Capt Abner Pearce, Inf

BULLENER, Jacob, Pvt, Col Ewen Allison, Capt Adam Windell, E TN Drafted Mil; deserted 1-9-1814

BULLENER, Peter, Pvt, Col Ewen Allison, Capt Adam Windell, E TN Drafted Mil

BULLICK, Chas, Pvt, Maj Gen Andrew Jackson, Capt William Carroll, Vol Inf

BULLIN, Jas, Pvt, Col S Bunch, Capt S Robinson, E TN Drafted Mil

BULLING, Thos, Pvt, Col Philip Pipkin, Capt Henry Nowlin, Mil Inf

BULLION, Jas, Pvt, Regt Commander omitted, Capt Samuel Richardson, E TN Drafted Mil

BULLMAN, Thos, Pvt, Col R C Napier, Capt Richard Benson, Mil Inf

BULLOCK, Elyjah, Pvt, Col Bayless, Capt Bacon, E TN Mil

BULLOCK, Jos, Pvt, Col Edwin Booth, Capt John McKamy, E TN Mil

BULLOCK, Nathaniel, Pvt, Col John Cocke, Capt John Dalton, Inf

BULLOCK, William, Pvt, Col William Johnson, Capt Joseph Scott, E TN Drafted Mil

BUMBELOE, Lewis, Pvt, Col John K Winn, Capt Robert Bradin, Inf

BUMBELOW, Jesse, Pvt, Col Alexander Loury, Capt James Kincaid, Inf; prisoner at Ft Rogers 3-1-1815

BUMBLETON, John, Pvt, Col A Cheatham, Capt Wm Smith, Inf; discharged for want of arms

BUMBLETON, Jos, Pvt, Col A Cheatham, Capt Wm Smith, Inf; discharged for want of arms

BUMPAS, Robert, Pvt, Col Philip Pipkin, Capt John Strothers, Mil; promoted to Cpl

BUMPASS, Hartwell, Pvt, Col Thos Williamson, Capt John Doak, Capt John Dobbins, Vol Mtd Gunmen; substitute for L Bruce

BUMPASS, John, 2 Cpl, Col R C Napier, Capt Edward Neblett, Mil Inf

BUMPASS, Tompkins, Pvt, Col R C Napier, Capt Edward Noblett, Mil Inf

BUNCH, Anderson, Pvt, Col William Johnson, Capt Henry Hunter, E TN Mil; never appeared

BUNCH, David, Pvt, Col R C Dyer, Capt Cuthbert Hudson, Vol Mtd Gunmen; transferred from Capt Jos Williams Co

BUNCH, David, Pvt, Col R H Dyer, Capt Beverly Williams, Vol Mtd Gunmen; transferred to Capt Hudson's Co

BUNCH, David, Pvt, Col Wm Lillard, Capt Thomas Sharpe, 2nd Regt Inf

BUNCH, David, Sgt, Col Wm Lillard, Capt William Hamilton, E TN Vol Inf

BUNCH, Elijah, Pvt, Col Samuel Bunch, Capt Jones Griffin, E TN Drafted Mil; deserted 3-4-1814

BUNCH, Harry, Pvt, Col John Cocke, Capt John Weakley, Inf

BUNCH, Henry, Pvt, Col John Cocke, Capt John Weakley, Inf

BUNCH, Henry, Pvt, Lt Col H Bryan, no other information

BUNCH, Jas, Pvt, Col Thos McCrory, Capt Gordon, Inf

BUNCH, John, Pvt, Col Wm Lillard, Capt William Hamilton, E TN Vol Inf

BUNCH, Joshua C, Pvt, Col Wm Johnson, Capt Henry Hunter, E TN Mil; never appeared

BUNCH, Nathaniel, Pvt, Col Thos McCrory, Capt Abel Willis, Mil Inf

BUNCH, Roderick, Pvt, Col John Cocke, Capt John Weakely, Inf

BUNCH, William, Pvt, Col John Brown, Capt Jesse G Reany, Mtd Gunmen

BUNCH, William, Pvt, Col Samuel Bayless, Capt Joseph Rich, E TN Inf

BUNCH, William, Pvt, Col Wm Lillard, Capt Wm Hamilton, E TN Vol Inf

BUNCH, Wm, Pvt, Col Thomas H Benton, Capt Geo Caperton, Inf; substitute

BUNCH, Wm, Pvt, Col Wm Johnson, Capt Henry Hunter

BUNCHAN, Eli, Pvt, no other information

BUNDAY, Henry, Sgt, Col Ed Bradley, Capt Wm Lauderdale, Vol Inf

BUNDY, Henry, 3 Cpl, Col Wm Hall, Capt Wm L Alexaner, Vol Inf

BUNDY, Henry, Cpl, Col Wm Hall, Capt Wm L Alexander, Vol Inf

BUNDY, Henry, Pvt, Col Thos Williamson, Capt Thomas Scurry, Vol Mtd Gunmen; dismissed from service 1-1-1815

BUNDY, John, Pvt, Col Samuel War, Capt James Gillespie, E TN Vol Inf; unable to perform duty

BUNDY, Nathan, Pvt, Col Edward Bradley, Capt Wm Lauderdale, Vol Inf

BUNDY, Nathan, Pvt, Col Philip Pipkin, Capt Jas Blakemore, Mil Inf

BUNDY, Thos, Pvt, Col Edward Bradley, Capt Wm Lauderdale, Vol Inf

BUNDY, Thos, Pvt, Col R C Napier, Capt Jas McMurray, Mil Inf

BUNDY, Thos, Pvt, Col Wm Hall, Capt Wm L Alexander, Vol Inf

BUNDY, William, Pvt, Col Alexander Loury, Capt George Sarver, Inf

BUNTON (BUNTER), William, Pvt, Col John Cocke, Capt James Gray, Inf; sick absent 3-14-1815

BURBEY, Robert, Pvt, Col Alexander Loury, Capt John Looney, 2nd Regt W TN Mil
BURCH, Geo, Pvt, Col W Johnson, Capt Elihu Milliken, 3rd Regt E TN Mil
BURCH, Henry, Pvt, no other information
BURCH, John, Pvt, Col Wm Johnson, Capt Elihu Milliken, 3rd Regt E TN Mil
BURCHAM, Eli, Pvt, Lt Col H Bryan, no other information
BURCHEN, Isaiah, Pvt, Col S Copeland, Capt John Holshouser, Inf
BURCHETT, Doglas, Pvt, Col S Copeland, Capt Allen Wilkinson, Mil Inf
BURCHETT, Edward, Pvt, Col Philip Pipkin, Capt Jas Blakemore, Mil Inf; deserted
BURCHFIELD, Elijah, Cpl, Regt Commander omitted, Capt Wm Henderson, Spies
BURCHFIELD, Thos, Tptr, Col William Higgins, Capt Stephen Griffith, Mtd Riflemen
BURD, Isaac, Pvt, Lt Col Leroy Hammonds, Lt Col Alexander Loury, Capt Thomas Delaney, Inf
BURD (BEARD), Alexander, Pvt, Col Alexander Loury, Capt George Sarver, Inf
BURD (BEARD), Thos, Pvt, Col Alexander Loury, Capt George Sarver, Inf
BURDEN, Eli, Pvt, Col William Hall, Capt John Kennedy, Vol Inf; a substitute for Jas Armstrong
BURDEN, Hawkins, Pvt, Col Jno Brown, Capt Jas Standifer, Regt E TN Vol Mtd Mil
BURDEN, Jas (Thos?), Pvt, Col John Cocke, Capt Samuel M Caruthers, Inf; discharged by loss of eye
BURDEN, Wm, Pvt, Col Thomas H Benton, Capt George W Gibbs, Vol Inf
BURDETT, Giles, Capt, Col Thomas Williamson, Capt Giles Burdett, Vol Mtd Gunmen
BURDINO (BODINE), Thos, Pvt, Col James Raulston, Capt Charles Wade, Inf
BURDON, Wm, Pvt, Col Thomas H Benton, Capt George W Gibbs, Vol Inf
BURDY, Nathan, Pvt, Col Edward Bradley, Capt William Lauderdale, Vol Inf
BUREHAM, Isaiah (Isaac), Pvt, Lt Col Leroy Hammonds, Lt Col Alexander Loury, Capt Thomas Delaney, Inf
BURFORD, John M, Pvt, Col R C Napier, Capt John Chism, Vol Mtd Gunmen
BURFORD, John, Pvt, Col Edward Bradley, Capt William Martin, Vol Inf
BURFORD, John, Pvt, Col Newton Cannon, Capton James Walton, Mtd Gunmen
BURFORD, John, Pvt, Col William Hall, Capt Brice Martin, Vol Inf
BURFORD, John, Pvt, Col William Johnson, Capt Elihu Milliken, 3rd Regt E TN Mil
BURGAN (BURGEN), John, Pvt, Col John Cocke, Capt Joseph Price, Inf; d 1-3-1815
BURGASS (BURGESS), John, Pvt, Col John Cocke, Capt James Gray, Inf; d 1-22-1815
BURGE, Drury, Pvt, Col Robert Steele, Capt Samuel Maxwell, Mil Inf
BURGER, John, Pvt, Col Samuel Wear, Capt John Stephens, E TN Vol Inf
BURGERS, William, Pvt, Lt Col Leroy Hammonds, Capt Thomas Delaney, Inf; also under Col A Loury
BURGES, Drury, Pvt, Col William Metcalf, Capt William Sitton, Mil Inf
BURGES, Warren, Pvt, Lt Col Leroy Hammonds, Col Alexander Loury, Capt Arahel Rains, Inf; d 2-17-1815
BURGESS, Geo, Pvt, Col William Metcalf, Capt John Cunningham, Capt Alexander Hill, Mil Inf
BURGESS, Harrison, Pvt, Col Thomas Williamson, Capt John Doak, Capt John Dobbins, Vol Mtd Gunmen
BURGESS, Jacob, Pvt, Col William Metcalf, Capt Alexander Hill, Mil Inf
BURGESS, John, Pvt, Regt Commander omitted, Capt Gray, Inf
BURGESS, Nathaniel, Pvt, Col R H Dyer, Capt James McMahan, TN Mtd Vol Gunmen
BURGESS, Nathl G, Pvt, Col R H Dyer, Capt James McMahan, TN Mtd Vol Gunmen
BURGESS, Richard, Sgt, Regt Commander omitted, Capt N Davis, Inf
BURGETT, Henry, Pvt, Lt Col Leroy Hammonds, Col Alexander Loury, Capt Thomas Delaney, Inf
BURGIS, Wm, Pvt, Col S Bunch, Capt Moses, E TN Drafted Mil
BURK, David H, Sgt Maj, Col Wm Johnson, Co Commander omitted, 3rd Regt E TN Mil
BURK, David, Pvt, Col William Johnston, Capt James Tunnell, E TN Mil; appointed Sgt
BURK, Isaac, Pvt, Col S Bunch, Capt N Gibbs, E TN Drafted Mil; left sick at Camp Ross 3-6-1814
BURK, Isaac, Pvt, Col Samuel Wear, Capt Daniel Price, E TN Vol Inf
BURK, John, Pvt, Col Edwin Booth, Capt Vernon, E TN Mil; deserted 3-15-1815
BURK, John, Pvt, Col Jno Brown, Capt Wm D Neilson, Regt E TN Vol Mil
BURK, Martin, Pvt, Col John Brown, Capt William White, E TN Vol Mtd Inf
BURK, Robt, Pvt, Col Samuel Bunch, Capt David Vance, E TN Mil Inf
BURK, Robt, Pvt, Col William Johnson, Capt Elihu Milliken, 3rd Regt E TN Mil
BURK, Rubin, Pvt, Col William Johnson, Capt Joseph Scott, E TN Drafted Mil; substitute for Henry Ketren
BURKE, Isaac, Pvt, Maj John Childs, Capt Daniel Price, E TN Mil Inf
BURKE, Isaac, Pvt, Maj John Childs, Capt Daniel Price, Vol Mtd Gunmen; in Gen John Coffee's Brig
BURKE, John B, Pvt, Col Thomas Williamson, Capt Richard Tate, Vol Mtd Gunmen
BURKE, John R, Sgt, Col Thomas Williamson, Capt Robert Steele, Vol Mtd Gunmen
BURKE, John, Pvt, Col Philip Pipkin, Capt Henry M Newlin, Mil Inf; left sick at Ft Montgomery by order of Col Pipkin
BURKE, Wm, Pvt, Col Robert Steele, Capt James Bennett, Mil Inf
BURKES, Jas, Pvt, Maj William Russell, Capt Isaac Wil-

liams, Separate Bn Vol Mtd Gunmen; also under Col R H Dyer
BURKES, John R, Pvt, Col Thomas McCrory, Capt James Shannon, Mil Inf; sick absent
BURKET, Mathias, Pvt, Col Samuel Bunch, Lt John Harris, E TN Mil; deserted 3-24-1814
BURKET, Thomas, Pvt, Col John Coffee, Capt Thomas Bradley, Vol Cav
BURKETT, George, Pvt, Col Edwin Booth, Capt John Slatton, E TN Mil
BURKILL, Ephraim, Pvt, Maj Gen William Carroll, Capt Francis Ellis, Inf
BURKLOE, Isaac, Pvt, Col Philip Pipkin, Capt William Mackay, Mil Inf
BURKS, James L, Sgt, Col S Copeland, Capt Moses Thompson, Mil
BURKS, James, Pvt, Brig Gen Thomas Johnson, Capt Robert Carson, Inf; discharged for want of arms
BURKS, Leaory, Pvt, Col Thomas McCrory, Capt John Reynolds, Mil Inf
BURKS, Leroy, Pvt, Maj William Russell, Capt Isaac Williams, 1st Regt TN Vol Mtd Gunmen Separate Bn; also under Dyer
BURLESON, Hill R, Pvt, Col Newton Cannon, Capt Ota Cantrell, W TN Mtd Inf
BURLESON, Isaac, Pvt, Col Robert Dyer, Capt Thomas Jones, Vol Mtd Gunmen
BURLESON, James, Pvt, Maj William Russell, Capt Fleman Hodges, Vol Mtd Gunmen; substitute for Henry Stiles'
BURLEY, Michael, Pvt, Col Samuel Bayless, Capt Allen Bacon, E TN Mil
BURLISON, James jr, Pvt, Col William Metcalf, Capt William Mullin, Mil Inf
BURLISON, William, Pvt, Col William Metcalf, Capt William Mullin, Mil Inf
BURLISTON, David, Pvt, Col John Cocke, Capt Bird Nance, Inf
BURMINGHAM, James, Pvt, Col N T Perkins, Capt John Doak, Vol Mtd Gunmen
BURN, Charles, Pvt, Col John Wynne, Capt James Holleman, Inf; on furlough
BURNARD, Reuben, Pvt, Col Ewin Allison, Capt Jonas Loughmiller, Mil
BURNES, Abery, Pvt, Maj William Woodfolk, Capt Abner Pearce, Inf
BURNES, Asbury, Pvt, Maj William Woodfolk, Capt Abner Peace, Inf
BURNES, Elijah I, Cpl, Maj William Woodfolk, Capt Abner Pearce, Inf
BURNES, James, 2 Cpl, Regt Commander omitted, Capt James Haggard, Mtd Gunmen
BURNES, James, Pvt, Col William Hall, Capt John Wallace, Inf
BURNES, James, Pvt, Col William Pillow, Capt John Anderson, Vol Inf; sick absent
BURNES, Joseph, Pvt, Col Thomas Benton, Capt Thomas Williamson, Vol Inf; transferred from Hewett's Co
BURNES, Joseph, Pvt, Col William Pillow, Capt Thomas Williamson, Vol Inf

BURNET, Cornelius, Pvt, Col Thomas Benton, Capt George Caperton, Vol Inf
BURNET, Daniel, Pvt, Col Thomas Benton, Capt George Caperton, Vol Inf
BURNET, Green, Pvt, Col Thomas Benton, Capt George Caperton, Vol Inf
BURNET, Joseph, Tptr, Col N T Perkins, Capt Philip Pipkin, Mtd Riflemen; on furlough
BURNET, Swepston, Pvt, Col William Metcalf, Capt William Mullin, Mil Inf
BURNET, William, Pvt, Col Philip Pipkin, Capt William Mackay, Mil Inf; transferred to Capt Searcy
BURNETE, John S, Pvt, Col Samuel Wear, Capt James Gillespie, E TN Vol Inf; reduced from Cpl
BURNETT, Berry, Pvt, Col Edwin Booth, Capt Samuel Thompson, Mil
BURNETT, Isham, Pvt, Col William Metcalf, Capt William Sitton, Mil Inf
BURNETT, James D, Pvt, Regt Commander omitted, Capt William Walker, Mtd Vol
BURNETT, James, 4 Cpl, Col John Brown, Capt William White, E TN Vol Mtd Inf
BURNETT, Joseph, Pvt, Col Robt Dyer, Capt Thomas Jones, Vol Mtd Gunmen
BURNETT, Pumphrey, Pvt, Maj William Russell, Col Robert Dyer, Capt William Russell, Vol Mtd Gunmen
BURNETT, Sweepston J, Pvt, Col William Metcalf, Capt Alexander Hill, Capt John Cunningham, Mil Inf
BURNETT, Thomas, Pvt, Col Thomas Williamson, Capt Anthony Metcalf, Vol Mtd Gunmen
BURNETT, Vincent, Pvt, Col Samuel Wear, Capt Simeon Perry, E TN Vol Mtd Inf
BURNETT, Zachariah M B, Pvt, Col Edwin Booth, Capt John Porter, Drafted Mil
BURNHAM, Joseph, Pvt, Col Alexander Loury, Lt Col Leroy Hammonds, Capt Thomas Wells, Inf
BURNHAM, William, Pvt, Regt Commander omitted, Capt N Davis, Inf
BURNIM, Hickerson, Cpl, Col Thomas Williamson, Capt John Hutchings, Vol Mtd Gunmen
BURNIM, Jesse, Pvt, Col Thomas Williamson, Capt John Hutchings, Vol Mtd Gunmen
BURNINE, Moses, Pvt, Col William Johnson, Capt Joseph Scott, E TN Drafted Mil; sick absent
BURNS, Absalom, Pvt, Col Alexandery Loury, Capt James Kincaid, Inf
BURNS, Charles, Pvt, Lt Col R T Napier, no other information
BURNS, Edward, Pvt, Col Alexander Loury, Capt James Kincaid, Inf
BURNS, Elijah J, Pvt, Maj William Woodfolk, Capt Abner Pearce, Inf; reduced from Cpl
BURNS, Frederick A, Pvt, Col Philip Pipkin, Capt Henry M Newlin, Mil Inf
BURNS, James, Pvt, Col John Cocke, Capt Joseph Price, Inf
BURNS, Jas, 3 Cpl, Col John Cocke, Capt John Weakley, Inf
BURNS, Jas, Pvt, Col James Raulston, Capt Henry West, Inf

## Enlisted Men, War of 1812

BURNS, Jas, Pvt, Col John Cocke, Capt James Gault, Inf; substitute for John Griggs

BURNS, Jas, Pvt, Col Philip Pipkin, Capt David Smythe, Inf; d 11-6-1814

BURNS, Jas, Pvt, Col R C Napier, Capt Samuel Ashmore, Mil Inf; sick absent

BURNS, Jas, Pvt, Col Thomas Williamson, Capt Richard Tate, Vol Mtd Gunmen

BURNS, John, Pvt, Col John Cocke, Capt James Gray, Inf

BURNS, John, Pvt, Col Newton Cannon, Capt John B Demsey, Mtd Gunmen

BURNS, John, Sgt, Col R C Napier, Capt Andrew McCarty, Mil Inf

BURNS, Jonathan, Pvt, Col Samuel Wear, Capt Jesse Cole, Vol Inf

BURNS, Jonathan, Pvt, Col William Johnston, Capt James Tunnell, 3rd Regt E TN Mil; sick absent

BURNS, Jonathan, Pvt, Col William Johnston, Capt James Tunnell, E TN Mil; left sick at Ft Strother 10-31-1814

BURNS, Jos, Pvt, Col Thomas Benton, Capt Thomas Williamson, Vol Inf; transferred from Hewett's Co

BURNS, Josiah, Pvt Col Newton Cannon, Capt Andrew Patterson, Mtd Riflemen

BURNS, Robt, Pvt, Col Robert H Dyer, Capt Ephraim D Dickson, TN Mtd Vol Gunmen

BURNS, Sam'l, Pvt, Col Samuel Wear, Capt Jesse Cole, Vol Inf

BURNS, Stephens, Pvt, Col Alexander Loury, Capt James Kincaid, Inf

BURNS, Wm, Pvt, Col James Raulston, Capt Mathew Cowan, Inf

BURNS, Wm, Pvt, Col William Hall, Capt Henry M Newland, Inf

BURNS, Wm, Sgt, Col Samuel Wear, Capt Jesse Cole, Vol Inf

BURNS (BARNS), John, Pvt, Col N T Perkins, Capt Mathew Johnston, Mil Inf; sick on furlough

BURNSIDE, Andrew, Pvt, Col John Wynn, Capt James Cole, Inf

BURREP, Jacob, Pvt, Col T McCrory, Capt Abel Willis, Mil Inf; on detachment

BURRES, Swanny, Pvt, Col T McCrory, Capt Abel Willis, Mil Inf

BURRESS, Chas, Pvt, Maj William Woodfolk, Capt James Turner, Inf

BURRIS, Elijah, Pvt, Col Robert Steele, Capt James Bennett, Mil Inf

BURRIS, John, Pvt, Col Philip Pipkin, Capt David Smythe, Inf; deserted 9-23-1814

BURRIS, Martin, Pvt, Col William Johnson, Capt Elihu Milliken, 3rd Regt E TN Mil

BURRIS, Wm, Pvt, Col R C Napier, Capt Andrew McCarty, Mil Inf

BURRIS, Wm, Pvt, Col Samuel Bunch, Capt Andrew Breden, E TN Mil

BURRIS (BURNS), Hawkey, Pvt, Col S Copeland, Capt David Williams, Inf; sick absent

BURRIS (BURNS), Wm, Pvt, Col S Copeland, Capt David Williams, Inf

BURRISS, Thos, Cpl, Col Philip Pipkin, Capt David Smythe, Inf

BURROW, Green, Pvt, Col Robert H Dyer, Capt Bethel Allen, Vol Mtd Gunmen

BURROW, James, Pvt, Gen A Jackson, Capt N Davis, Inf

BURROW, Jas, Drm Maj, Col Wm Lillard, Co Commander omitted, E TN Vol Mil

BURROW, Jas, Drm, Col William Lillard, Capt George Keys, E TN Inf

BURROW, John, Cpl, Col Philip Pipkin, Capt Henry M Newlin, Mil Inf

BURROW, John, Pvt, Col John Alcorn, Capt John R Winston, Mtd Riflemen

BURROW, John, Pvt, Col Philip Pipkin, Capt Henry M Newlin, Mil Inf; left sick at Ft Montgomery 11-27-1814

BURROW, John, Pvt, Col William Lillard, Capt Hugh Martin, E TN Vol Inf

BURROW, Robt, Ffr Maj, Col Wm Lillard, Co Commander omitted, E TN Vol Mil

BURROW, Robt, Ffr, Col William Lillard, Capt George Keys, E TN Inf

BURROW, Sandy, Pvt, Col R H Dyer, Capt James McMahan, TN Vol Gunmen; d 2-16-1815

BURROWS, Hutson, Pvt, Col William Metcalf, Capt Barbee Collins, Mil Inf

BURRUS, John, Pvt, Maj William Woodfolk, Capt Abraham Dudney, Inf

BURTISON, Wm, Pvt, Col William Metcalf, Capt John Hill, Capt John Cunningham, Mil Inf

BURTON, Benj, Pvt, Col Robert H Dyer, Capt Bethel Allen, Vol Mtd Gunmen

BURTON, Edward D, Pvt, Col Alexander Loury, Capt James Kincaid, Inf

BURTON, Henry, Pvt, Col Robert Steele, Capt James Randals, Inf

BURTON, Jas, Pvt, Col Edwin E Booth, Capt John Slatton, E TN Mil

BURTON, John K, Cpl, Col Philip Pipkin, Capt William _____, Branch Srvce omitted

BURTON, John, Cpl, Col Robert Steele, Capt John Chitwood, Mil Inf

BURTON, John, Pvt, Col A Lowry, Capt Jas Kincaid, Inf

BURTON, John, Pvt, Col John Cocke, Co Commander omitted, Inf

BURTON, Jonathan, Pvt, Col Newton Cannon, Capt James Walton, Mtd Riflemen

BURTON, Martin H (Wm H), Sgt, Col R H Dyer, Co Commander omitted, Vol Mtd Gunmen

BURTON, Maurice G (Morris), Pvt, Col Cocke, Col Bird Nance, Co Commander omitted, Inf; substitute for Robert Goodman

BURTON, Robert, Pvt, Regt Commander omitted, Capt Jas Cowan, Mtd Inf

BURTON, Samuel H, Pvt, Col Philip Pipkin, Capt John Strother, Mil; deserted 9-20-1814

BURTON, Theodrick, Pvt, Col Newton Cannon, Capt Jas Walton, Mtd Riflemen

BURTON, Wiley, 3 Sgt, Col Philip Pipkin, Capt Geo Mebane, Mil Inf

BURTON, Willie, Pvt, Col A Cheatham, Capt Wm J

Smith, Inf

BURTON (BARTON), Chas A H, Pvt, Col John Cocke, Capt Joseph Price, Inf; d 3-6-1815

BURTON (BLURTON), John, Pvt, Col Copeland, Co Commander omitted, Mil Inf; sick absent since 3-10-1814

BUSBY, Elijah, Pvt, Col John Wynne, Capt William Wilson, Inf

BUSBY, Elisha, Pvt, Col John K Wynne, Capt William McCall, Inf

BUSBY, Elisha, Pvt, Col Thomas Williamson, Capt Thomas Scurry, Vol Mtd Gunmen; dismissed from service 3-1-1815

BUSBY, James, Pvt, Col Thomas Benton, Capt Robert Cannon, Inf

BUSBY, James, Pvt, Col Thomas Williamson, Capt William Martin, Vol Mtd Gunmen

BUSBY, Reeves, Pvt, Col William Higgins, Capt Samuel Allen, Mtd Gunmen

BUSBY, Robert, Pvt, Col Alexander Loury, Capt John Looney, W TN Inf

BUSBY, Robert, Pvt, Col Robert Dyer, Capt Isaac Williams, Vol Mtd Gunmen

BUSBY, William, Pvt, Col Samuel Bunch, Capt Francis Berry, E TN Mil; attached to Capt Houk Co

BUSBY, William, Pvt, Col Samuel Bunch, Capt John Hauk, E TN Mil; joined from Capt Berry Co, discharged for inability

BUSH, Andrew, Pvt, Maj James Porter, Capt Sam Cowan, Cav

BUSH, Benjamin, Pvt, Col Philip Pipkin, Capt Peter Searcy, Mil Inf; deserted

BUSH, George, Waiter to Col Tunnell, Col Edwin Booth, Capt John Lewis, E TN Mil

BUSH, John, Pvt, Col Samuel Wear, Col Samuel Bunch, Capt William Mitchell, E TN Mtd Inf

BUSH, Oliver, Pvt, Col William Hall, Capt John Wallace, Inf; deserted

BUSH, Oliver, Pvt, Col William Hall, Capt John Wallace, Inf; substitute for James Philips

BUSH, Thomas, Pvt, Col John K Wynne, Capt James Holleman, Inf

BUSHON, George, Pvt, Col Ewen Allison, Capt William King, Drafted Mil

BUSLER, Henry, Pvt, Col Ewen Allison, Capt Thomas Wilson, E TN Drafted Mil; discharged for inability

BUSSELL, Benjamin L, Pvt, Maj John Childs, Capt James Cummings, E TN Vol Mtd Inf; appointed pack horse carrier

BUSSEY, Daniel, Pvt, Col Robert Dyer, Capt Ephraim Dickson, TN Vol Mtd Gunmen

BUSSY, George, Pvt, Col Newton Cannon, Capt Andrew Patterson, Mtd Riflemen

BUSTARD, Michael W, Sgt, Col Ewen Allison, Capt Thomas Wilson, E TN Drafted Mil

BUTCHER, Daniel, Pvt, Col John Brown, Capt Hugh Barton, E TN Mil Inf

BUTCHER, James, Pvt, Col William Johnson, Capt Henry Hunter, E TN Mil; transferred to Capt Kirk's Co

BUTHIN, Daniel, Pvt, Col William Lillard, Capt Robert Maloney, E TN Vol Inf

BUTHIN, John, Pvt, Col William Lillard, Capt Robert Maloney, E TN Vol Inf

BUTLAR, Elias, Pvt, Maj John Childs, Capt Charles Conway, E TN Mtd Gunmen; Regt Co 14 Roan

BUTLER, Abraham, Pvt, Col William Hall, Capt Brice Martin, Vol Inf

BUTLER, Bailey, Capt, Col John K Wynne, Capt Butler, Inf

BUTLER, Benjamin, Pvt, Col Robert Steele, Capt John Chitwood, Mil Inf

BUTLER, Benjamin, Pvt, Col William Higgins, Capt William Doake, Mtd Riflemen

BUTLER, Edmond, Pvt, Col John Brown, Capt James Standifer, E TN Vol Mtd Mil

BUTLER, Edward, Pvt, Col William Hall, Capt John Moore, Vol Inf; missing before 12-10-1812

BUTLER, George T, Pvt, Maj William Woodfolk, Capt John Sutton, Capt Abraham Dudney, Inf

BUTLER, Henry, Pvt, Col John Brown, Capt Lunsford Oliver, E TN Mil

BUTLER, Henry, Pvt, Col Philip Pipkin, Capt George Mebane, Mil Inf

BUTLER, Henry, Pvt, Col William Hall, Capt Abraham Bledsoe, Vol Inf

BUTLER, James, Pvt, Col Robert Steele, Capt James Bennett, Mil Inf

BUTLER, James, Pvt, Col Thomas Williamson, Capt James Pace, Lt Nealy, Vol Mtd Gunmen

BUTLER, James, Pvt, Col William Hall, Capt Travis Nash, Inf

BUTLER, John, Pvt, Col Thomas Williamson, Capt Giles Burdett, Vol Mtd Gunmen

BUTLER, John, Pvt, no other information

BUTLER, Joshua, Pvt, Col R C Napier, Capt Drury Adkins, Mil Inf

BUTLER, Moses, Pvt, Col Edwin Booth, Capt John Sharp, E TN Mil; d 12-26-1814

BUTLER, Pleasant H, Pvt, Col Edwin Booth, Capt Richard Marshall, Drafted Mil; appointed QM Sgt

BUTLER, Pleasant H, Sgt, Col Edwin Booth, E TN Mil QM Corps

BUTLER, Richard, Pvt, Col Alexander Loury, Capt John Looney, 2nd Regt W TN Mil; d 2-7-1815

BUTLER, Samuel, Pvt, Col John Cocke, Capt George Barnes, Inf

BUTLER, Samuel, Pvt, Col Thomas Benton, Capt Henry Douglass, Vol Inf; AWOL before 12-10-1812

BUTLER, Thomas, Pvt, Col John Brown, Capt Wm White, Regt E TN Mil Inf

BUTLER, Wm, Pvt, Col John K Winn, Capt Bailey Butler, Inf; on furlough, wounded 11-9-1814

BUTLER, Wm, Pvt, Col William Hall, Capt Travis C Nash, Inf

BUTLER, Wm, Pvt, Maj Gen A Jackson, Col Thos Williamson, Capt Robert Steele, Vol Mtd Gunmen

BUTRAGE, Henry, Pvt, Maj John Childs, Capt R Tipton, E TN Mtd Inf; Regt Co 6th Jefferson

BUTRIDGE, Henry, Pvt, Col Wm Lillard, Capt John Roper, E TN Vol Inf

BUTRON, Seth, Sgt, Col Newton Cannon, Capt Jas Wal-

## Enlisted Men, War of 1812

BUTT, Hasdell, Pvt, Col William Hall, Capt Abraham Bledsoe, Branch Srvce omitted
BUTT, Hazel (Hasdell), Pvt, Col Edward Bradley, Capt Abraham Bledsoe, Riflemen
BUTTER, Alexander, Pvt, Col Thomas Benton, Capt Thomas Williamson, Vol Inf; deserted
BUTTER, William jr, Pvt, Col Edwin Booth, Capt Richard Marshall, Drafted Mil
BUTTER, William, Cpl, Col Edwin Booth, Capt Richard Marshall, Drafted Mil; discharged 1-6-1815 for inability
BUTTRACE, Henry, Pvt, Maj John Childs, Capt R Tipton, E TN Vol Mtd Inf
BUTTS, Hazel, Pvt, Col Wm Hall, Capt Abraham Bledsoe, Col Inf
BUTTS, Willie, Pvt, Maj Gen Wm Carroll, Col Jas Raulston, Capt Edward Robinson, Inf
BYERS, Andrew, Pvt, Regt Commander omitted, Capt Nathan Davis, Inf
BYERS, James, Pvt, Lt Col Jno Edmondson, Co Commander omitted, Cav
BYERS, Nathan, Pvt, Col John K Wynne, Capt Jas Cole, Inf; deserted
BYERS, Wm, Pvt, Brig Gen Thos Johnson, Capt Robert Carson, Inf
BYERS (BYNES), David, Pvt, Lt Col Leroy Hammonds, Capt Thomas Wells, Inf; left sick at Fayetteville 9-25-1814
BYET, Wm, Pvt, Col John K Winn, Capt Robert Bradin, Inf
BYFORD, Wm, Pvt, Brig Gen Thos Johnson, Capt Robert Carson, Inf
BYNUM, Pumphrey, Cpl, Maj Gen Wm Carroll, Col Wm Metcalf, Capt John Jackson, Inf; no service performed
BYNUM, Wm, Pvt, Col John K Winn, Capt Wm Carruthers, W TN Inf; sick absent
BYRD, Bryan, Pvt, Regt Commander omitted, Capt Thos Gray, Inf
BYRD, Henry, Pvt, Lt Col H Bryan, no other information
BYRD, Howell L, Pvt, Col Wm Metcalf, Capt William Sitton, Mil Inf
BYRD, Joseph, Cpl, Col John Brown, Capt Wm D Neilson, Regt E TN Vol Mil
BYRD, Richard, Pvt, Col John Alcorn, Capt Winton, Mtd Riflemen; promoted to 1 Lt
BYRD, Wm, Pvt, Regt Commander omitted, Capt Jno Crane, Mtd Inf
BYRES, Moses, Pvt, Col Robert Steele, Capt Samuel Maxwell, Mil Inf
BYRN, Jas, Pvt, Col Jno Coffee, Capt John W Byrn, Cav
BYRN, John, Pvt, Col Jno Coffee, Capt John Baskerville, Cav
BYRN, Wm P, Pvt, Col Wm Alcorn, Capt John W Byrn, Cav
BYRNE, Isaac, Pvt, Maj Gen Wm Carroll, Col Wm Metcalf, Capt John Jackson, Inf
BYRNE, Jas, Pvt, Col Jas Raulston, Capt Henry Hamilton, Inf; d 2-14-1815, also served Maj Gen Carroll

BYRNE, John, Pvt, Col Edward Bradley, Capt Abraham Bledsoe, Riflemen
BYRNE, John, Pvt, Col John Alcorn, Capt John Baskerville, Vol Inf
BYRNES, Daniel, Pvt, Maj Gen A Jackson, Capt Wm Carroll, Vol Inf; replaced C S Hobbs
BYRNS, Stephen, Cpl, Col Wm Woodfolk, Capt Ezekial Ross, Inf
BYRNS, Stephen, Pvt, Maj William Woodfolk, Capt McCulley, Inf
BYRNS, Thos, 1 Sgt, Col Jas Raulston, Capt Jas A Black, Inf
BYRON, Alden, Pvt, Gen A Jackson, Capt H Kerr, Mtd Rangers
BYRT, Henry, Pvt, no other information
CABBAGE, John, Pvt, Col Wm Johnson, Capt Henry Hunter, E TN Mil
CABES, Thos, Pvt, no other information
CABLE, Conrad, Pvt, Col Ewen Allison, Capt Winsell, E TN Drafted Mil
CABLE, Jacob, Sgt, Col Samuel Bayless, Capt Solomon Hendricks, E TN Mil
CABLE, John, Pvt, Col Samuel Wear, Capt Jesse Cole, Vol Inf
CABLE, Peter, Pvt, Col Samuel Wear, Capt Jesse Cole, Vol Inf
CABLER, Jno, Pvt, Gen Andrew Jackson, Capt Joel Parrish, Arty
CABLER, John, Pvt, no other information
CADE, Hughes, Dmr, Col Wm Lillard, Capt Hugh Martin, E TN Vol Inf
CADE, Samuel, Pvt, Col Wm Lillard, Capt Hugh Martin, E TN Vol Inf
CADE, Samuel, Pvt, Maj John Childs, Capt Chas Conway, E TN Mtd Gunmen; Regt Co 40 Knox
CADLE, Benjamin, Pvt, Col Thos Benton, Capt Henry L Douglass, Vol Inf; missing
CAFFA, John, Pvt, Maj William Russell, Capt John Cowan, Vol Mtd Gunmen; sick absent
CAFFEE, Jno, Sgt, Regt Commander omitted, Capt Samuel Richardson, E TN Drafted Mil
CAFFEE, John, Pvt, Col A Cheatham, Capt Charles Johnson, Inf
CAFFEY, Meaford, Tptr, Col N Cannon, Capt Thos Bradley, Mtd Riflemen
CAFFS, Jeremiah, Pvt, Col Jno Coffee, Capt Chas Kavanaugh, Cav
CAGA, Dan'l, Pvt, Col Thomas Benton, Capt William Moore, Vol Inf
CAGE, Albert, 2 Cpl, Col Nicholas F? Perkins, Capt George Eliot, Mil Inf
CAGE, Allen, Sgt, Maj Wm Carroll, Capt Daniel M Bradford, Capt Lewis Dillahunty, Vol Inf
CAGE, Harry, Ens, Col N T Perkins, Capt Geo Eliot, Mil Inf, Res omitted
CAGE, Harry, Pvt, Col Jno Coffee, Capt John W Byn, Cav
CAGE, Henry, Pvt, Col Thos Williamson, Capt Thos Scurry, Vol Mtd Gunmen; appointed Asst Depy Sgt Master General
CAGE, Henry, Sgt Maj, Col Wm Hall, 1st Regt TN Vol Inf

## Enlisted Men, War of 1812

CAGE, Jesse, 1 Lt & Pay Master, Col N T Perkins, 1st Regt TN Mtd Vol, Res omitted

CAGE, Jesse, Pvt, Col N T Perkins, Capt Geo Eliot, Mil Inf

CAGE, John, Pvt, Col N T Perkins, Capt John B Quarles, Vol Mtd Inf

CAGE, John, Pvt, Col Thos Benton, Capt Henry L Douglass, Vol Inf; promoted to QM Sgt

CAGE, John, Sgt, Col Wm Hall, Co Commander omitted, 1st Regt TN Vol QM Corps

CAGLE, Chas, Pvt, Col Jno Coffee, Capt Fredrick Stump, Cav

CAGLE, Nathan, Pvt, Col John K Cocke, Capt Carruthers, Inf; died ___

CAHELL, Jonathan, Cpl, Col R C Napier, Capt Samuel Ashmore, Mil Inf

CAHFFIN, Edward H, Pvt, Col Thomas Williamson, Capt James Pace, Capt James Nealy, Vol Mtd Gunmen

CAHOON, Andrew, Pvt, Col Philip Pipkin, Capt Henry M Newlin, Mil Inf; left sick at Ft Williams 11-4-1814

CAHOON, Samuel, Sgt, Col S Copeland, Capt Alexander Provine, Mil Inf; sick absent since 3-15-1814

CAHORN, Alexander, Pvt, Col Samuel Wear, Capt Jas Tedford, E TN Vol Inf

CAILBREATH?, John, Pvt, Col Wm Hall, Capt Brice Martin, Vol Inf

CAILES, Jacob, Pvt, Col Samuel Wear, Capt Jas Tedford, E TN Vol Inf

CAIN, David, Pvt, Col Wm Hall, Capt Wm L Alexander, Vol Inf; AWOL

CAIN, Geo, Pvt, Regt Commander omitted, Capt Jno Miller, Spies

CAIN, Hardy, Pvt, Col John Williams, Capt David Vance, Mtd Mil

CAIN, Jas, Pvt, Regt Commander omitted, Capt James Gray, Inf

CAIN, Jas, Pvt, Regt Commander omitted, Capt Jas Haggard, Mt Gunmen; d 2-24-1814

CAIN, Jesse, Pvt, Col William Hall, Capt William L Alexander, Vol Inf; substitute for David Cain

CAIN, Jesse, Pvt, Col Wm Lillard, Capt Wm Hamilton, E TN Vol Inf

CAIN, Jesse, Pvt, Commanders omitted, Det of Inf of 26th TN Regt

CAIN, Jesse, Pvt, Regt Commander omitted, Capt Jas Haggard, Mtd Gunmen; d 5-7-1814

CAIN, Lemuel, Pvt, Maj John Childs, Capt Charles Conway, E TN Mtd Gunmen; discharged for inability, Regt Co 40 Knox

CAIN, Peter, Pvt, Col William Johnson, Capt Andrew Lawson, E TN Drafted Mil

CAIN, Walter, 4 Sgt, Maj John Childs, Capt James Cummings, E TN Vol Mtd Inf

CAIN, Wm, Pvt, Maj John Childs, Capt Charles Conway, E TN Mtd Gunmen; discharged for inability, Regt Co 40 Knox

CAIREY, Benj, Pvt, Col S Bunch, Capt F Register, E TN Mil; joined from Capt McPherson's Co

CAISSERSON, Daniel, Pvt, no other information

CALAHAN, Asa, Pvt, Col Philip Pipkin, Capt William Mackay, Mil Inf

CALAHAN, Joshua, Sgt, Col William Higgins, Capt Adam Dale, Mtd Gunmen

CALBOUGH, Jacob, Pvt, Col Samuel Bunch, Capt George McPherson, E TN Mil; joined from Capt Winsell's Co

CALBREATH, John, 1 Sgt, Col Leroy Hammonds, Capt James Tubb, Inf

CALBREATH, John, Pvt, Col William Hall, Capt Brice Martin, Vol Inf

CALDHOUN, James, Pvt, Col John Coffee, Capt Thomas Bradley, Vol Cav

CALDWELL, Alexander, Cpl, Maj John Childs, Capt Charles Conway, E TN Mtd Gunmen; Regt Co 10 Knox

CALDWELL, Alexander, Pvt, Maj John Childs, Capt Charles Conway, E TN Mtd Gunmen; reduced from Cpl

CALDWELL, Amos, Pvt, Col R H Dyer, Capt James McMahan, TN Vol Mtd Gunmen

CALDWELL, Benj, Pvt, Maj John Childs, Capt Charles Conway, E TN Mtd Gunmen; Regt Co 10 Knox

CALDWELL, Beuoni, 2 Lt, Col Samuel Bunch, Capt James Cummings, E TN Vol Mtd Inf, Res omitted

CALDWELL, David, 2 Sgt, Regt Commander omitted, Capt Jos Williams, Mil Cav

CALDWELL, David, Pvt, Col Robert H Dyer, Capt James Wyatt, Vol Mtd Gunmen

CALDWELL, David, Pvt, Col William Johnston, Capt Henry Hunter, E TN Mil

CALDWELL, David, Pvt, Maj William Russell, Capt John Trimble, Vol Mtd Gunmen

CALDWELL, David, Sgt, Regt Commander omitted, Capt Jos Williams, Mil Cav

CALDWELL, Davidson, Pvt, Col S Copeland, Capt William Douglass, Inf

CALDWELL, Hardy, Pvt, Col Robert Steele, Capt Robert Campbell, Mil Inf

CALDWELL, Hugh, Pvt, Col John Brown, Capt John Childs, E TN Vol Mtd Inf

CALDWELL, James, Pvt, Col Jno Brown, Capt Hugh Barton, E TN Mil Inf

CALDWELL, Jas, Ens, Col R C Napier, Capt Edward Neblett, Mil Inf, Res omitted

CALDWELL, Jas, Pvt, Col John Alcorn, Capt Frederick Stump, Cav

CALDWELL, Jas, Pvt, Maj John Childs, Capt John Stephens, E TN Vol Mtd Inf; transferred to Capt Trimble's Co

CALDWELL, John C, 2 Sgt, Maj Gen Wm Carroll, Col William Metcalf, Capt John Jackson, Inf; appointed Sgt Maj

CALDWELL, John C, Sgt Maj, Col Wm Metcalf, Co Commander omitted, 1st Regt W TN Mil Inf

CALDWELL, John C, Sgt, Col Robert Steele, Capt James Shenault, Mil Inf

CALDWELL, John, Ffr Maj, Col John Cocke, Co Commander omitted, 2nd Regt W TN Mil Inf

CALDWELL, John, Pvt, Maj Jas Proter, Co Commander omitted, Cav

CALDWELL, Jos, Pvt, Col John Cocke, Capt John Weakley, Inf

## Enlisted Men, War of 1812

CALDWELL, Joseph, Col John Coffee, Capt David Smith, Vol Cav
CALDWELL, Robt, Pvt, Col Philip Pipkin, Capt George Mebane, Mil Inf
CALDWELL, Robt, Pvt, Maj John Childs, Capt Charles Conway, E TN Mil Gunmen; Regt Co 10 Knox
CALDWELL, Sam'l, Pvt, Col N T Perkins, Capt John Doak, Vol Mtd Gunmen
CALDWELL, Sam'l, Pvt, Regt Commander omitted, Capt Jas Haggard, Mtd Gunmen
CALDWELL, Sam'l, Sgt, Col Samuel Wear, Capt James Tedford, E TN Vol Inf
CALDWELL, Silas M, Pvt, Col Samuel Wear, Capt James Gillespie, E TN Vol Inf
CALDWELL, Silas, Surgeon's Mate, Col Sam'l Bunch, Co Commander omitted, E TN Mil
CALDWELL, Thos, Cpl, Maj Gen Wm Carroll, Col Wm Metcalf, Capt John Jackson, Inf
CALDWELL, Thos, Pvt, Col Samuel Wear, Capt John Stephens, E TN Vol Inf
CALDWELL, Wallis, Pvt Col Thomas Williamson, Capt Beverly Williams, Vol Mtd Gunmen
CALDWELL, William, 1 Lt, Col William Hall, Capt Travis Nash, Vol Inf
CALDWELL, William, Pvt, Col John Cocke, Capt George Barnes, Inf
CALDWELL, William, Pvt, Col Thomas Williamson, Capt Anthony Metcalf, Vol Mtd Gunmen; d 3-9-1815
CALDWELL, Wm, Pvt, Col John Alcorn, Capt Frederick Slump, Cav
CALDWELL, Wm, Pvt, Maj John Childs, Capt John Stephens, E TN Vol Mtd Inf; discharged for inability
CALFFE, Henry, Pvt, Col John Brown, Capt Charles Lewin, E TN Vol Mtd Inf
CALHOON, Charles, Pvt, Col R H Dyer, Capt Ephraim Dickson, TN Mtd Vol Gunmen
CALHOUN, John, Pvt, Maj Gen William Carroll, Capt John Jackson, Inf
CALHOUN, Wilson, Pvt, Col John Cocke, Capt James Gault, Inf
CALL, Richard K, 2 Lt, Col John K Wynne, Capt Prince Bayless, Inf, Res omitted
CALL, Richard, Pvt, Lt Col John Edmonson, Co Commander omitted, Cav
CALLAHAN, Andrew M, Pvt, Col N T Perkins, Capt John Quarles, Vol Mtd Inf
CALLAHAN, William, Pvt, Col N T Perkins, Capt John Quarles, Vol Mtd Riflemen
CALLANGHAN, James, Pvt, Col Samuel Bayless, Capt Branch Jones, E TN Drafted Mil
CALLAWAY, John E, Tptr, Col R H Dyer, Capt Bethel Allen, Vol Mtd Gunmen; d 1-21-1815 from his wound
CALLEHAN, Thomas, Cpl, Maj William Russell, Capt John Cowan, Vol Mtd Gunmen
CALLEN, Achibald, Pvt, Maj John Childs, Capt Daniel Price, Vol Mtd Gunmen
CALLEN, Archibald, Pvt, Maj John Childs, Capt Daniel Price, E TN Vol Mtd Inf
CALLEN, Henry, 1 Sgt, Maj John Childs, Capt Daniel Price, Vol Mtd Gunmen
CALLEY, Peleg, Pvt, Col Newton Cannon, Capt George Brandon, Mtd Riflemen; sick absent
CALLICUT, James, Pvt, Col Edwin Booth, Capt John Slatton, E TN Mil; d 12-17-1814
CALLIHAN, William, Pvt, Maj Gen Andrew Jackson, Col Thomas Williamson, Capt Robert Steele, Vol Mtd Gunmen
CALLISON, Robert, Pvt, Col Edwin Booth, Capt George Winton, E TN Mil
CALLOWAY, Richard, Pvt, Maj William Russell, Capt John Coan, Vol Mtd Gunmen
CALLOWAY, Richard, Pvt, Regt Commander omitted, Capt William Mitchell, Spies
CALLOWAY, Thomas, Pvt, Maj Gen William Carroll, Col James Raulston, Capt Edward Robinson, Inf
CALTEN, Archibald, Pvt, Col Samuel Wear, Capt Samuel Bowman, Mtd Inf
CALTEN, Charles, Pvt, Col Samuel Wear, Capt Samuel Bowman, Mtd Inf
CALVERD, John D, Pvt, Col Alexander Loury, Capt John Looney, 2nd Regt W TN Mil
CALVERT, Samuel, Pvt, Col Philip Pipkin, Capt Henry Newlin, Mil Inf; substituted James Cochran
CALVERT, Samuel, Pvt, Col R C Napier, Capt John Chism, Mil Inf; substituted Jourdon Dodson
CALVERT, William, 1 Lt, Col Ewen Allison, Capt Samuel Allen, E TN Mil, Res omitted
CALVERT, William, Pvt, Maj William Russell, Capt Isaac Williams, Separate Bn of TN Vol Mtd Gunmen
CALVERY, Edward, Pvt, Col Samuel Wear, Capt Simeon Perry, E TN Vol Mtd Inf
CALVERY, Leonard, Pvt, Col William Lillard, Capt Jacob Hartsell, E TN Vol Inf
CALVIL, Young, Pvt, Col Samuel Wear, Capt Simeon Perry, E TN Vol Mtd Inf
CALVIN, Ananias, Pvt, Col William Lillard, Capt George Argenbright, E TN Vol Riflemen
CALVIN, John, Pvt, Col William Lillard, Capt Geore Argenbright, E TN Vol Riflemen
CALVIN, John, Pvt, Col William Lillard, Capt Thomas Sharp, 2nd Regt Inf; deserted 11-1-1813
CAMBEL, John, Pvt, Brig Gen T Johnston, Capt Robert Carson, Inf; deserted 3-4-1814
CAMBELL, Zeno, Pvt, Col Philip Pipkin, Capt Ebenezer Kirkpatrick, Mil Inf; substitute for Samuel D McNealy
CAMBLE, S William, Pvt, Col Edwin Booth, Capt John Lewis, E TN Mil
CAMERON, Daniel, Pvt, Col William Hall, Capt John Kennedy, Vol Inf
CAMERON, Elisha, Pvt, Col Samuel Bunch, Capt William Houston, E TN Vol Mtd Inf
CAMERON, George, Cpl, Col Ewen Allison, Capt Samuel Allen, E TN Mil
CAMERON, George, Pvt, Col Samuel Bunch, Capt John English, E TN Drafted Mil; furloughed from Ft Strother for bad health
CAMERON, William, Pvt, Col Samuel Bayless, Capt

## Enlisted Men, War of 1812

Branch Jones, E TN Drafted Mil; d 2-1-1815
CAMMEL, Hamilton C, Pvt, Col N T Perkins, Capt John Quarles, Vol Mtd Inf
CAMP, Bird, Pvt, Col Edwin Booth, Capt John McKamey, Inf
CAMP, Byrd, Pvt, Col John Brown, Capt James McKamy, E TN Mtd Gunmen
CAMP, Thomas, Div Quarter Master Gen, Maj Gen Andrew Jackson, Div of TN Mil, Res omitted
CAMP, Thomas, Pvt, Gen Andrew Jackson, Capt William Carroll, Vol Inf
CAMP, Thomas, Pvt, Regt Commander omitted, Capt David Deaderick, Arty; made Adj
CAMP, Thomas, Pvt, no other information
CAMPBELL, Alexander, Pvt, Col David Williams, Co Commander omitted, Vol
CAMPBELL, Alexander, Pvt, Col Thomas Williamson, Capt Anthony Metcalf, Vol Mtd Gunmen
CAMPBELL, Alexander, Pvt, Col William Hall, Co Commander omitted, Vol Inf; substitute
CAMPBELL, Alexander, Pvt, Col William Lillard, Co Commander omitted, E TN Drafted Mil
CAMPBELL, Alexander, Pvt, Regt Commander omitted, Capt William McLin, E TN Inf
CAMPBELL, Andrew, Pvt, Col John K Wynne, Capt William Caruthers, W TN Inf
CAMPBELL, Archibald, Pvt, Col William Lillard, Capt Brice Martin, E TN Vol Inf
CAMPBELL, Argile, Pvt, Col Nicholas Perkins, Capt John Doak, Vol Mtd Gunmen
CAMPBELL, Arter, Pvt, Col John K Wynne, Capt William Caruthers, W TN Inf
CAMPBELL, Arter, Pvt, Col John K Wynne, Capt William Wilson, Inf; transferred to Capt Caruthers Co
CAMPBELL, Arthur, 2 Lt, Col Samuel Bunch, Capt Edward Buchanan, E TN Drafted, Res omitted
CAMPBELL, Artur L, Pvt, Col Samuel ____, Capt William Houston, E TN Mtd Inf
CAMPBELL, Benjamin, Pvt, Col Thomas McCrory, Capt Abel Willis, Mil Inf
CAMPBELL, Chas, Ffr, Col McCrory, Capt Samuel McKnight, Inf
CAMPBELL, Colin, Pvt, Col Thomas Bradley, Co Commander omitted, Vol Inf
CAMPBELL, Colin, Pvt, Col W Hall, Capt John Wallace, Inf
CAMPBELL, Daniel, Pvt, Col Samuel Bayless, Capt John Brock, E TN Mil
CAMPBELL, Daniel, Pvt, Col Wm Johnson, Capt Samuel Allen, Mil Inf
CAMPBELL, Daniel, Pvt, Maj John Childs, Capt Chas Conway, E TN Gunmen
CAMPBELL, Daniel, Pvt, Maj Wm Woodfolk, Capt Abner Pearce, Inf
CAMPBELL, Daniel, Sgt, Commander omitted, Inf
CAMPBELL, Daniel, Sgt, no other information
CAMPBELL, David, Pvt, Col Samuel Bunch, Capt John Dobbins, E TN Drafted Mil
CAMPBELL, Duncan, Pvt, Col T McCrory, Capt Isaac Patton, Mil Inf
CAMPBELL, Edward, Pvt, Col R C Napier, Capt Drury Adkins, Mil Inf
CAMPBELL, Ezekiel, Pvt, Col S Bunch, Capt G Gregory, E TN Drafted Mil
CAMPBELL, Ezekiel, Pvt, Col S Bunch, Capt Jno Houk, E TN Mil; discharged for inability
CAMPBELL, Ezekiel, Pvt, Col Samuel Bunch, Capt John Inman, E TN Mtd Inf
CAMPBELL, Eziekiel, Pvt, Col Samuel Bunch, Capt Francis Berry, E TN Mtd Inf
CAMPBELL, Forance, Pvt, Col William Johnston, Capt James Stewart, E TN Drafted Mil
CAMPBELL, Francis, Pvt, Col N T Perkins, Capt Philip Pipkins, Mtd Riflemen
CAMPBELL, Geo A, Pvt, Col Jas Raulston, Capt Jas A Black, Inf
CAMPBELL, Geo, Pvt, Col Samuel Wear, Capt Simeon Perry, E TN Mtd Inf
CAMPBELL, Hiram, Pvt, Col Jno Brown, Capt Hugh Barton, E TN Mil Inf
CAMPBELL, Isaac, 1 Sgt, Col Samuel Wear, Capt Daniel Price, Branch Srvce omitted
CAMPBELL, Isaac, Pvt, Col R C Napier, Capt Wm Russell, Vol Mtd Gunmen
CAMPBELL, Isaac, Pvt, Regt Commander omitted, Capt Jas Cole, Vol Inf
CAMPBELL, James B, Pvt, Col John Coffee, Capt David Smith, Vol Cav
CAMPBELL, James, Cpl, Regt Commander omitted, Capt J Anderson, Branch Srvce omitted
CAMPBELL, James, Pvt, Col Jno Brown, Capt Jas Preston, E TN Mil Inf
CAMPBELL, James, Pvt, Col Robert H Dyer, Capt Jas McMahon, TN Mtd Vol Gunmen
CAMPBELL, James, Pvt, Col Samuel Bunch, Capt Joseph Duncan, E TN Drafted Mil; joined from Capt Allen's Co
CAMPBELL, James, Pvt, Gen Jackson, Capt N Davis, Inf
CAMPBELL, Jas A, Pvt, Col Ewen Allison, Capt Robert Allen, E TN Mil
CAMPBELL, Jas B, Tptr, Regt Commander omitted, Capt Davis Smith, Cav Vol
CAMPBELL, Jas M, Adjt, no other information; promoted from Pvt
CAMPBELL, Jas M, Capt & Brig Ins, Brig Gen Bird Smith, Maj Gen Wm Carroll, 2nd Brig TN Mil, Res omitted
CAMPBELL, Jas, Pvt, Col Ewen Allison, Capt Robert Allen, E TN Mil
CAMPBELL, Jas, Pvt, Col John Brown, Capt John Childs, E TN Vol Mtd Gunmen
CAMPBELL, Jas, Pvt, Col N T Perkins, Capt Philip Pipkin, Mtd Riflemen
CAMPBELL, Jas, Pvt, Col S Bunch, Capt Geo Gregory, E TN Drafted Mil; furloughed 1-28-1814 not returned
CAMPBELL, Jas, Pvt, Col Samuel Bayless, Capt Solomon Hendricks, E TN Mil
CAMPBELL, Jas, Pvt, Col Samuel Wear, Capt John Childs, E TN Vol Inf
CAMPBELL, Jas, Pvt, Col Samuel Wear, Capt Robert Doak, E TN Vol Inf

## Enlisted Men, War of 1812

CAMPBELL, Jas, Pvt, Col Thomas McCrory, Capt Samuel McKnight, Inf
CAMPBELL, Jas, Pvt, Col William Johnson, Capt Andrew Lawson, E TN Drafted Mil
CAMPBELL, Jas, Pvt, Col William Lillard, Capt James Lillard, E TN Vol Inf
CAMPBELL, Jas, Pvt, Col Wm Lillard, Capt Hugh Martin, E TN Vol Inf
CAMPBELL, Jas, Pvt, Col Wm Lillard, Capt Robert Maloney, E TN Vol Inf
CAMPBELL, Jas, Pvt, Maj John Childs, Capt Chas Conway, E TN Mtd Gunmen
CAMPBELL, Jas, Pvt, no other information
CAMPBELL, Jesse, Pvt, Col Edward Booth, Capt Porter, Drafted Mil
CAMPBELL, Jno B, Pvt, Col S Copeland, Capt James Tait, Inf
CAMPBELL, Jno S, Pvt, Col A Loury, Capt J Williamson, W TN Mil
CAMPBELL, Jno, Pvt, Col S Bunch, Capt Jones Griffith, E TN Drafted Mil; furloughed at Ft Williams for inability
CAMPBELL, Jno, Pvt, Col Thomas Benton, Capt Henry Douglas, Vol Inf
CAMPBELL, Jno, Pvt, Gen Thos Washington, Co Commander omitted, Mtd Inf
CAMPBELL, Jno, Pvt, Regt Commander omitted, Capt Jas Terrell, Cav; promoted to Sgt in Col McCrory's Regt
CAMPBELL, Jno, Sgt, no other information
CAMPBELL, Joal, Pvt, no other information
CAMPBELL, Joel, Pvt, Col John Coffee, Capt David Smith, Vol Cav
CAMPBELL, Joel, Pvt, Col John K Wynne, Capt John Spinks, Inf
CAMPBELL, Joel, Pvt, Regt Commander omitted, Capt David Smith, Cav; deserted 9-30-1813
CAMPBELL, Joel, Pvt, no other information
CAMPBELL, John S, Pvt, Col Nicholas T Perkins, Capt Mathew Johnston, Mil Inf
CAMPBELL, John W, Pvt, Col William Lillard, Capt Thomas Sharpe, 2nd Regt Inf
CAMPBELL, John, 1 Lt & Adjt, Col Thos McCrory, 3rd Regt TN Mil, Res omitted
CAMPBELL, John, 1 Lt, Col Stephen Copeland, Capt William Hodges, Inf, Res omitted
CAMPBELL, John, Ens, Col William Johnson, Capt Benjamin Powell, E TN Mil, Res omitted
CAMPBELL, John, Pvt, Col A Cheatham, Capt William Smith, Inf; transferred to Capt Carson's Co
CAMPBELL, John, Pvt, Col Edward Bradley, Capt Martin, Vol Inf
CAMPBELL, John, Pvt, Col Edwin Booth, Capt Porter, Drafted Mil
CAMPBELL, John, Pvt, Col Edwin Booth, Capt Richard Marshall, Drafted Mil
CAMPBELL, John, Pvt, Col Ewen Allison, Capt Joseph Everett, E TN Mil; transferred to Capt Griffin Co
CAMPBELL, John, Pvt, Col Ewen Allison, Capt Thomas Wilson, E TN Mil Drafted
CAMPBELL, John, Pvt, Col James Raulston, Capt Mathew Cowan, Inf
CAMPBELL, John, Pvt, Col John Brown, Capt Jas Preston, E TN Mil Inf
CAMPBELL, John, Pvt, Col Leroy Hammonds, Capt Joseph N Williamson, Inf
CAMPBELL, John, Pvt, Col S Bunch, Capt F Register, E TN Inf; joined from Capt Winsel's Co
CAMPBELL, John, Pvt, Col S Bunch, Capt F Register, E TN Mil; joined from Capt Winsel's Co
CAMPBELL, John, Pvt, Col Samuel Wear, Capt Joseph Galloway, Mtd Inf
CAMPBELL, John, Pvt, Col Thomas Williamson, Capt Anthony M Metcalf, Vol Mtd Gunmen
CAMPBELL, John, Pvt, Col Thomas Williamson, Capt Giles Burdett, Vol Mtd Gunmen; d 1-23-1815
CAMPBELL, John, Pvt, Col William Hall, Capt Brice Martin, Vol Inf
CAMPBELL, John, Pvt, Col William Hall, Capt James Hambleton, Vol Inf; dead
CAMPBELL, John, Pvt, Col William Johnson, Capt Andrew Lawson, E TN Drafted Mil; substitute for John Keynester
CAMPBELL, John, Pvt, Col William Pillow, Capt Thomas Williamson, Vol Inf
CAMPBELL, John, Pvt, Maj William Russell, Capt John Cowan, Vol Mtd Riflemen
CAMPBELL, John, Sgt, Col John Cocke, Capt James Gault, Inf
CAMPBELL, John, Sgt, Lt Col H Bryan, Co Commander omitted, Inf
CAMPBELL, Jonathan A, Pvt, Col Robert H Dyer, Capt Bethel Allen, Vol Mtd Gunmen; d 1-15-1815
CAMPBELL, Jonathan A, Pvt, Col T McCrory, Capt A Metcalf, Mil Inf
CAMPBELL, Jos, Pvt, Col Ewen Allison, Capt Adam Winsell, E TN Drafted Mil
CAMPBELL, Jos, Pvt, Col Samuel Bayless, Capt Branch Jones, E TN Drafted Mil
CAMPBELL, Jos, Pvt, Col William Lillard, Capt James Lillard, E TN Inf Vol
CAMPBELL, Jos, Pvt, Col William Lillard, Capt John Neatherton, E TN Vol Inf
CAMPBELL, Jos, Pvt, Maj Gen Wm Carroll, Capt Henry Hamilton, Inf
CAMPBELL, Michael, Pvt, Col R H Dyer, Capt James McMahan, TN Vol Mtd Gunmen
CAMPBELL, Parker, Pvt, Col R H Dyer, Capt James Wyatt, Vol Mtd Gunmen
CAMPBELL, Robert, Pvt, Col William Lillard, Capt William Gillenwater, E TN Inf
CAMPBELL, Robt E, Pvt, Col James Raulston, Capt Henry Hamilton, Inf
CAMPBELL, Robt, Pvt, Col N T Perkins, Capt James McMahan, Mtd Gunmen
CAMPBELL, Russell, Sgt, Col William Lillard, Capt James Lillard, E TN Inf Vol
CAMPBELL, S William, Pvt, Col Edwin Booth, Capt John Lewis, E TN Mil
CAMPBELL, Sam'l, Pvt, Col John Alcorn, Capt Frederick Stump, Cav
CAMPBELL, Sam'l, Pvt, Col R H Dyer, Capt Joseph

*Enlisted Men, War of 1812*

Williams, Vol Mtd Gunmen
CAMPBELL, Sanders, Pvt, Col Samuel Bunch, Capt William Jobe, E TN Vol Mtd Inf
CAMPBELL, Shadrack, Pvt, Col S Bunch, Capt Geo Gregory, E TN Drafted Mil
CAMPBELL, Shadrack, Pvt, Col S Bunch, Capt Jno Hoak, E TN Mil; joined from Capt Williams Co
CAMPBELL, Shadrack, Sgt, Col Samuel Bunch, Capt John Inman, E TN Vol Mtd Inf
CAMPBELL, Silas, Pvt, Col John Cocke, Capt John Weakley, Inf; substituted Jas Burns
CAMPBELL, Thadrick, Pvt, no other information
CAMPBELL, Thomas, Pvt, no other information
CAMPBELL, Thos J, Asst Insp Gen, Maj Gen John Cocke, E TN Vol Mil, Res omitted
CAMPBELL, Thos J, Dept Ins Gen, Brig Gen Geo Doherty, E TN Mil, Res omitted; discharged at Washington by Gen order
CAMPBELL, Thos, Cpl, Col Alexander Loury, Col Leroy Hammonds, Capt Arahel Rains, Inf; sick present
CAMPBELL, Thos, Pvt, Col Alexander Loury, Capt Gabriel Martin, Inf
CAMPBELL, Thos, Pvt, Regt Commander omitted, Capt Jas Craig, Inf
CAMPBELL, William, 3 Cpl, Gen Andrew Jackson, Capt John Crane, Mtd Gunmen
CAMPBELL, William, Pvt, Col Alexander Loury, Capt John Looney, 2nd Regt W TN Mil
CAMPBELL, William, Pvt, Col Edward Bradley, Capt Harry L Douglass, Vol Inf
CAMPBELL, William, Pvt, Col John Alcorn, Capt Thomas Bradley, Vol Cav
CAMPBELL, William, Pvt, Col Philip Pipkin, Capt George Malone, Mil Inf; deserted from Ft Jackson 9-20-1814
CAMPBELL, William, Pvt, Col S Copeland, Capt Moses Thompson, Inf
CAMPBELL, William, Pvt, Col William Hall, Capt James Hambleton, Vol Inf
CAMPBELL, William, Pvt, Col William Johnson, Capt Andrew Lawson, E TN Drafted Mil
CAMPBELL, William, Sgt, Lt Col H Bryan, Co Commander omitted, Inf
CAMPBELL, _____, Pvt, Col Samuel Bayless, Capt Colomon Hendricks, E TN Mil
CAMPE, John, Cpl, Col Newton Cannon, Capt Isaac Williams, Mtd Riflemen
CAMRON, Daniel, Pvt, Col Edward Bradley, Capt John Kennedy, Riflemen
CAMRON, John, Cpl, Maj William Woodfolk, Capt James Turner, Inf
CAMRON, John, Pvt, Maj William Woodfolk, Capt James Neil, Inf
CAMRON, Thomas, Pvt, Maj William Woodfolk, Capt James Turner, Inf
CAMRON, William, 5 Sgt, Col James Raulston, Capt Mathew Cowan, Inf
CAMRON, William, Pvt, Col James Raulston, Capt Daniel Newman, Inf
CANADA, Milbery, Pvt, Col N T Perkins, Capt Mathew Patterson, Mtd Vol

CANADA, Robert, Pvt, Maj Gen Andrew Jackson, Col A Cheatham, Capt William Creel, Inf
CANADAY, John, Pvt, Col William Metcalf, Capt Thomas Marks, Mil Inf
CANADY, Elijah, Pvt, Col Edwin Booth, Capt John McKamey, E TN Mil
CANADY, Evander, Pvt, Col William Hall, Capt Henry Newlin, Inf
CANADY, James, Pvt, Col Samuel Bunch, Capt Francis Berry, E TN Mil
CANADY, John, Pvt, Col Robert Steele, Capt Samuel Maxwell, Mil Inf; transferred
CANADY, John, Pvt, Col William Hall, Capt Henry Newlin, Inf
CANADY, John, Pvt, Col William Johnson, Capt James Rogers, E TN Drafted Mil; substitute
CANAGES, John, Pvt, Col William Johnson, Capt Henry Hunter, E TN Mil; sick absent
CANARD, Philip, Pvt, Col Robert Steele, Capt James Shenault, Mil Inf; on furlough
CANBIER, Thomas, Pvt, Col R H Dyer, Capt James McMahon, 1st TN Mtd Vol Gunmen
CANE, George, Pvt, Col James Raulston, Capt Henry West, Inf
CANE, Hardy, Pvt, Col Alexander Loury, Capt Gabriel Martin, Inf
CANE, John P, Pvt, Col Thomas McCrory, Capt Abel Willis, Mil Inf
CANNADY, George, Pvt, Col Edwin Booth, Capt John Lewis, E TN Mil
CANNADY, James, Pvt, Col William Johnson, Capt Elihu Milliken, E TN Mil
CANNADY, Samuel, Col William Metcalf, Maj William Carroll, Capt Jackson, Inf
CANNADY, William, Pvt, Regt Commander omitted, Capt James Haggard, Mtd Gunmen
CANNOLE, William, Ens, Col Ewen Allison, Capt William King, Drafted Mil, Res omitted
CANNON, Andrew, Pvt, Col Thomas Williamson, Capt John Hutchings, Vol Mtd Gunmen
CANNON, Clement, Pvt, Col Newton Cannon, Capt John Demsey, Mtd Gunmen
CANNON, Elisher, Pvt, Col William Johnson, Capt Andrew Lawson, E TN Drafted Mil
CANNON, George, Pvt, Col Edwin Booth, Capt Alexander Biggs, Inf
CANNON, James, Pvt, Col Samuel Bayless, Capt James Landen, E TN Mil
CANNON, John, Pvt, Capt S Roberson, Capt Samuel Bunch, E TN Drafted Mil
CANNON, John, Pvt, Col Samuel Bunch, Capt George McPherson, E TN Mil; joined from Capt Hoyal's Co
CANNON, John, Pvt, Col Samuel Bunch, Capt John Harris, E TN Mil; waited on sick at Highwassee
CANNON, John, Pvt, Col William Johnson, Capt David McKamy, E TN Drafted Mil
CANNON, John, Pvt, Regt Commander omitted, Capt Samuel Richardson, E TN Drafted Mil
CANNON, Lewis, Pvt, Col Samuel Bunch, Capt George McPherson, E TN Mil; transferred to Capt Regis-

## Enlisted Men, War of 1812

ter's Co
CANNON, Robert, Pvt, Col Newton Cannon, Capt Martin, Mtd Gunmen; AWOL
CANNON, Steven, Pvt, Regt Commander omitted, Capt Sam Allen, Pack horse guard
CANON, John, Pvt, Col William Johnson, Capt David McKamy, E TN Draft Mil
CANOWAY, Benjamin, Pvt, Col John Cocke, Capt Richard Crunk, Inf; died 2-20-1815
CANTERBERRY, Andrew, Pvt, Col William Higgins, Capt Thomas Eldridge, Mtd Gunmen
CANTRARELS, William, Pvt, Col Newton Cannon, Capt William Edwards, Regt Command; transferred to Burn's Co
CANTREL, Elijah, Pvt, Col John Cocke, Capt Samuel Caruthers, Inf
CANTRELL, Alfred, Adjt, Col William Higgins, 2nd Regt TN Mtd Vol
CANTRELL, Alfred, Sgt Maj, Col Newton Cannon, no Co Commander, Vol Mtd Riflemen
CANTRELL, Alfred, Sgt, Col Newton Cannon, Capt Ota Cantrell, W TN Mtd Inf; promoted to Sgt Maj
CANTRELL, Prior, Pvt, Col Alexander Loury & Col Leroy Hammonds, Capt Arahel Rains, Inf
CANTRELL, Samuel, Pvt, Regt Commander omitted, Capt James Haggard, Mtd Gunmen
CANTRELL, William, Cpl, Col John Coffee, Capt John Byrn, Cav
CANTRELL, William, Pvt, Gen John Coffee, Co Commander omitted, Mtd Spies
CANTRELL, William, Pvt, Regt Commaner omitted, Capt James Haggard, Mtd Gunmen
CANTRELL, William, Sgt, Col John Alcorn, Capt John Byrn, Cav
CAPEHORN, Thomas, Pvt, Col R H Dyer, Capt Robert Edmondston, 1 TN Vol Mtd Gunmen
CAPERTON, Arch, Pvt, Col R H Dyer, Maj William Russell, Capt William Russell, Vol Mtd Gunmen
CAPERTON, Archibald, pvt, Regt Commander omitted, Capt James Cowan, Inf
CAPERTON, Archible, Pvt, Col Thomas Benton, Capt George Caperton, Inf
CAPERTON, Archibold, Pvt, Col Thomas H. Benton, Capt George Caperton, Vol Inf
CAPERTON, George, Capt, Col William Pillow, Inf
CAPERTON, Hugh, Pvt, Regt Commander omitted, Capt James Cowan, Inf
CAPERTON, John, Pvt, Col John Cocke, Capt John Dalton, Inf
CAPERTON, Samuel, Pvt, Col John Cocke, Capt John Dalton, Inf
CAPERTON, Thomas, Pvt, Maj William Rssell, Capt John Cowan, Vol Mtd Gunmen
CAPERTON, Thomas, Pvt, Regt Commander omitted, Capt James Cowan, Branch omitted
CAPERTON, William jr, Pvt, Regt Commander omitted, Capt James Cowan, Inf
CAPERTON, William, Pvt, Maj William Russell, Capt John Cowan, Vol Mtd Gunmen
CAPLINGER, George, Pvt, Lt Col L Hammonds, Capt James Tubb, Inf
CAPLINGER, Samuel, Lt, Col S Copeland, Capt Moses Thompson, Inf
CAPLINGTER, Leonard, Pvt, Col James Raulston, Capt James A Black, Inf
CAPP, John, Pvt, Col S Bayless, Capt Jonathan Waddle
CAPP, John, Pvt, Col Samuel Bunch, Capt F Register, E TN Mil
CAPP, John, Pvt, Col William Johnson, Capt Andrew Lawson, E TN Draft Mil
CAPP, John, Pvt, Col William Johnston, Capt Joseph Kirk, Mil Inf
CAPPS, Benjamin, Pvt, Col John Coffee, Capt James Terrill, Vol Cav
CAPPS, John, Pvt, Col S Bunch, Capt S Robertson, E TN Draft Mil; deserted
CAPPS, John, Pvt, Regt Commander omitted, Capt Samuel Richardson, E TN Draft Mil
CAPPS, Josiah, Pvt, Col S Bunch, Capt S Robinson, E TN Draft Mil
CAPPS, Willis, Pvt, Col Samuel Bunch, Capt S Robertson, E TN Draft Mil
CAPPS, Willis, Pvt, Regt Commander omitted, Capt Samuel Richardson, E TN Draft Mil
CAPS, Benjamin, Pvt, Col Robert Steele, Capt John Chitwood, Mil Inf
CAPS, Richard, Pvt, Col William Johnson, Capt Benjamin Powell, Branch omitted
CAR, David, Sgt, Col William Johnson, Capt Joseph Kirk, Mil
CARALEY, John, Pvt, Regt Commander omitted, Capt James Craig, Inf
CARARAHAN, Thomas, Pvt, Col Thomas Benton, Capt Isaiah Renshaw, Vol Inf
CARATHERS, John, Pvt, Col N T Perkins, Capt John Doak, Vol Mtd Gunmen
CARBACK, Elisha, Pvt, Col S Bunch, Capt S Robertson, E TN Draft Mil
CARBERRY, John, Pvt, Col S Bunch, Capt F Register, E TN Mil; joined from Capt McPherson Co
CARBETT, Allen, Pvt, Col A Cheatham, Capt William Johnson, Inf
CARBOUGH, Daniel, Pvt, Col Samuel Bayless, Capt Joseph Hale, E TN Mil
CARBY, John, Pvt, Col John Coffee, Capt John Byrn, Cav
CARDEN, James, Pvt, Col William Johnson, Capt James Tunnell, E TN Mil
CARDER, Benjamin, Pvt, Col Edward Bradley, Cap Harry L Douglass, Vol Inf
CARDIN, Joseph W, Pvt, Col Edwin Booth, Capt John Slatton, E TN Mil; appt Surgeon Mate
CARDWELL, Caleb, Pvt, Col James Ralston, Maj Gen William Carroll, Capt Edward Robinson, Inf
CARDWELL, James, Pvt, Col James Raulston, Maj Gen William Carroll, Capt Edward Robinson, Inf
CARDWELL, James, Pvt, Col R C Napier, Capt James McMurray, Mil Inf
CARDWELL, John, Pvt, Col John Bayless, Capt John Brock, E TN Mil
CARDWELL, Nelson, Pvt, Col R C Napier, Capt James McMurray, Mil Inf
CARDWELL, Nelson, Pvt, Col William Pipkin, Capt

## Enlisted Men, War of 1812

Blakemore, Mil Inf
CARDWELL, Richard, Sgt, Col Samuel Wear, Capt Rufus Morgan, E TN Vol Inf
CARE, John, 2 Lt, Col William Hall, Capt Gabriel Martin, Vol Inf
CARE, Walter, 2 Lt, Maj Gen John Cocke, Co Commander omitted, TN Vol Mtd Gunmen
CARE (CARR), Andrew, Pvt, Col A Loury, Capt George Sarver, Inf
CARETHERS, Robert, Ens, Col R C Napier, Capt Ashburn, Mil Inf
CARETHERS, William, 1 Maj, Col Robert Steele, 4 Regt TN Mil
CARETHERS, William, Ens, Col Robert Steele, Capt James Chenault, Mil Inf
CAREY, Benjamin, Pvt, Col Samuel Bunch, Capt George McPherson, E TN Mil; transferred to Capt Register's Co
CAREY, Jesse, Pvt, Col Johnson, Capt Joseph Scott, E TN Draft Mil
CAREY, John, Cpl, Col Charles Johnson, Capt Benjamin Powell, E TN Mil
CAREY, Miles, Pvt, Col John Cocke, Capt Barnes, Inf
CARGALL, John H, Pvt, Col Zacheus Copeland, Capt John Biles, Inf
CARGILL, James, Pvt, Maj William Russell, Capt William Chism, Vol Mtd Gunmen
CARIGAN, Arthur W, Cpl, Col John K Wynn, Capt James Cole, Inf
CARIMON, Jacob, Pvt, Regt Commander omitted, Capt Nathan Farmer, Mtd Riflemen
CARLES, Robert, Pvt, Col Samuel Wear, Capt Joseph Calloway, Mtd Inf
CARLEY, William, Pvt, Col R C Napier, Capt James McMurry, Mil Inf
CARLILES, William, Pvt, Col Thomas Williamson, Co Commander omitted, Vol Mtd Gunmen
CARLIN, Hugh, Pvt, Col Philip Pipkin, Capt Mebane, Mil Inf
CARLIN, John, Pvt, Col S Copeland, Capt Provine, Mil Inf
CARLISH, James, Sgt, Maj Woodfolk, Capt Abraham Dudney, Inf
CARLISLE, William, Pvt, Col John K Wynne, Capt Baily Butler, Inf
CARLISLE, William, Pvt, Col Philip Pipkin, Capt David Smythe, Inf
CARLISLE, William, Pvt, Col Philip Pipkin, Capt William Mackey, Mil Inf
CARLISLE, William, Pvt, Col Robert Steele, Capt James Shenault, Inf
CARLOCK, Abraham, Pvt, Col James Raulston, Maj Gen William Carroll, Capt Wiley Huddleston, Inf
CARLOCK, Isaac, Pvt, Col Edward Bradley, Capt John Kennedy, Riflemen
CARLOCK, Joseph, Pvt, Col Thomas McCrory, Capt William Dooley, Inf
CARLOCK, Reuben, Pvt, Col Edward Bradley, Capt John Kennedy, Riflemen
CARLTON, Thomas, Pvt, Col Philip Pipkin, Capt William Mackey, Mil Inf
CARLTON, Thomas, Pvt, Col Thomas Benon, Capt Robert Cannon, Inf
CARLTON, Thomas, Pvt, Col William Pillow, Capt David Mason, Vol Inf
CARMAC, Cornelius, Cpl, Col Alexander Loury, Capt Gabriel Martin, Inf
CARMAC, John, Pvt, Col William Y Higgins, Capt John B Cheatham, Mtd Riflemen
CARMAC, John, Pvt, Regt Commander omitted, Capt Elijah Rushing, Det of Inf
CARMAC, Neil, Pvt, Regt Commander omitted, Capt Jno Miller, Spies
CARMACK, Jesse, Pvt, Regt Commander omitted, Capt Gray, Inf
CARMACK, Jno, Pvt, Lt Col A Cheatham, Co Commander omitted, Mtd Inf
CARMACK, Jno, Pvt, no other information
CARMACK, Wm, Ens, Col William Lillard, Capt William Gillenwater, E TN Vol Inf, Res omitted
CARMAN, John, Sgt, Col S Copeland, Capt Allen Wilkinson, Mil Inf
CARMAN, William, Ffr Maj, Lt Col L Hammonds, Co Commander omitted, 2nd Regt W TN Inf; promoted from Pvt in Capt Tubb's
CARMAN, William, Pvt, Col Leroy Hammonds, Capt James Tubb, Inf; promoted to Ffr Maj
CARMICALE, William, Pvt, Lt Col A Loury, Lt Col L Hammonds, Capt Thomas Delaney, Inf; substitute for Jesse Parker
CARMICEL, Arch'd Pvt, Maj William Woodfolk, Capt James C Neil, Inf
CARMICHAEL, Dan'l, Pvt, Col William Y Higgins, Capt James Hambleton, Mtd Gunmen
CARMICHAEL, Hugh, Pvt, Col S Bunch, Capt N Gibbs, E TN Drafted Mil
CARMICHAEL, Jno, Pvt, Col S Bunch, Capt N Gibbs, E TN Drafted Mil
CARMICHAEL, William, Pvt, Col William Lillard, Capt William McLin, E TN Inf
CARMOLE, Wm, Ens, Col Ewen Allison, Capt William King, Drafted Mil, Res omitted
CARMON, Stephen, Pvt, Col John Alcorn, Capt John Winston, Mtd Riflemen
CARMUT, Jas, Pvt, Col Edwin Booth, Capt Richard Mashall, Drafted Mil
CARN, Sam'l 3 Cpl, Col Thomas Benton, Capt George Caperton, Vol Inf
CARNAHAM, Jas, Pvt, Col R C Napier, Co Commander omitted, Mil Inf; on furlough
CARNAHAN, John, Pvt, Col John Alcorn, Capt John Winston, Mtd Riflemen
CARNAHAN, Thos, Pvt, Col Jno Coffee, Capt Robert Jetton, Cav
CARNES, Jas, Pvt, Col R H Dyer, Capt Joseph Williams, 1st Regt TN Vol Mtd Gunmen
CARNES, Levi, Pvt, Col William Lillard, Capt William Hamilton, E TN Vol Inf
CARNES, Michael, Pvt, Col S Bunch, Capt Dan'l Yarnell, E TN Mil; substitute
CARNEW, Thos, Pvt, Lt Col J Edmonson, Co Commander omitted, Cav

## Enlisted Men, War of 1812

CARNEW, Thos, Pvt, no other information
CARNEY, Jas W, 2 Lt, Col Philip Pipkin, Capt John Strother, Mil, Res omitted
CARNON, Howard, Cpl, Col R C Napier, Capt Samuel Ashmore, Mil Inf; sick absent
CARNS, Thos, Pvt, Maj William Russell, Capt John Trimble, Vol Mtd Gunmen
CARODINE, Andrew, Sgt, Col William Metcalf, Capt Bird L Hurt, Mil Inf
CAROTHERS, Geo, Pvt, no other information
CAROTHERS, Jno, Pvt, no other information
CAROTHERS, John, 2 Lt, Col Thomas Williamson, Capt John Doak, Capt John Dobbins, Vol Mtd Gunmen, Res omitted; d 2-8-1815
CAROTHERS, Wm, Capt, Col John K Wynne, Capt William Carruthers, W TN Inf, Res omitted
CAROTHERS, Wm, Pvt, Col Jno Coffee, Capt John Baskerville, Cav
CARPENTER, Asa, Pvt, Col Alexander Loury, Capt James Kincaid, Inf
CARPENTER, Austin, Pvt, Col Edward Bradley, Capt Thomas B Haynes, Vol Inf
CARPENTER, Austin, Pvt, Col Robert Steele, Capt James Randals, Inf
CARPENTER, Fielding, Pvt, Col S Bunch, Capt Jones Griffin, E TN Drafted Mil; deserted 3-4-1814
CARPENTER, Frederick, Pvt, Col John Cocke, Capt John Weakley, Inf
CARPENTER, Frederick, Pvt, Col William Metcalf, Capt John Barnhart, Mil Inf
CARPENTER, Jacob, Pvt, Maj James Porter, Co Commander omitted, Cav
CARPENTER, James, Pvt, Col Edward Bradley, Capt John Kennedy, Riflemen; AWOL 12-12-1813
CARPENTER, James, Pvt, Col Samuel Bunch, Capt William Houston, E TN Vol Mtd Inf
CARPENTER, John, Cpl, Col Robert Steele, Capt Ricahrd Ratton, Mil Inf
CARPENTER, John, Pvt, Col Leroy Hammonds, Capt James Tubb, Inf
CARPENTER, John, Pvt, Col Newton Cannon, Capt John Hanley, Mtd Riflemen
CARPENTER, John, Pvt, Col R H Dyer, Capt James Wyatt, Vol Mtd Gunmen
CARPENTER, John, Pvt, Col William Metcalf, Capt William Sitton, Mil Inf
CARPENTER, Lewis, Pvt, Col Edward Bradley, Capt John Kennedy, Riflemen; furloughed to wait on the sick
CARPENTER, Owen, Pvt, Col John Wynne, Capt John Porter, Inf
CARPENTER, Robert, Pvt, Col Philip Pipkin, Capt David Smith, Mil Inf
CARPENTER, Robt, Pvt, Col Philip Pipkin, Capt William Mackay, Mil Inf; left sick at Ft Jackson 11-11-1814
CARPENTER, Solomon, Pvt, Col James Raulston, Capt Daniel Newman, Inf
CARPENTER, Solomon, Pvt, Col Robert Steele, Capt Richard Ratton, Mil Inf
CARPENTER, William, Pvt, Col William Metcalf, Capt William Mullin, Mil Inf
CARPENTER, William, Pvt, Regt Commander omitted, Capt James Cowan, Inf
CARPENTER, William, Pvt, no other information
CARPENTER, Willis, Pvt, Col William Lillard, Capt Thomas Sharpe, 2nd Regt Inf
CARPENTER, Yelenton, Pvt, Col Samuel Bunch, Capt Jones Griffin, E TN Drafted Mil
CARPMEN, Jacob, Pvt, Col John Cocke, Capt James Gault, Inf
CARR, Andrew, Pvt, Commanders omitted, Inf; on command at Ft Montgomery by order of Col Hammonds
CARR, Benjamin, Pvt, Maj John Childs, Capt Reuben Tipton, E TN Vol Mtd Inf; Regimental Co 40th Knox
CARR, James, Ffr, Col James Raulston, Capt John Cowan, Inf
CARR, James, Pvt, Col Edward Bradley, Capt Martin, Vol Inf
CARR, James, Pvt, Col James Raulston, Capt Mathew Neal, Inf
CARR, James, Pvt, Col Newton Cannon, Capt Ota Cantrell, W TN Mtd Inf
CARR, James, Pvt, Col William Hall, Capt Brice Martin, Vol Inf; substituted for King Carr
CARR, James, Sgt, Col Thomas Williamson, Capt Anthony Metcalf, Vol Mtd Gunmen
CARR, John, 2 Lt, Col Edward Bradley, Capt Martin, Vol Inf, Res omitted
CARR, Joseph, Pvt, Col Samuel Bayless, Capt Joseph Goodson, E TN Mil
CARR, King, Pvt, Col William Hall, Capt Brice Martin, Vol Inf
CARR, Richardson, Sgt, Maj William Woodfolk, Capt Ezekiel Ross, Capt McCulley, Inf
CARR, Samuel, Pvt, Col Alexander Loury, Col Leroy Hammonds, Capt Arahel Rains, Inf
CARR, Samuel, Pvt, Col Samuel Wear, Col Samuel Bunch, Capt William Mitchell, E TN Mtd Inf
CARR, Thomas, 3 Cpl, Gen Andrew Jackson, Capt Ebenezer Kirkpatrick, Mtd Gunmen
CARR, Walter, 2 Lt, Col Thomas Williamson, Capt Beverly Williams, Vol Mtd Gunmen
CARR, Walter, Cpl, Maj William Woodfolk, Capt James Turner, Inf
CARR, Walter, Pvt, Col John K Wynne, Capt James Cole, Inf
CARR, Walter, Pvt, Maj William Woodfolk, Capt McCulley, Inf
CARR, William, 2 Cpl, Col William Hall, Capt Brice Martin, Vol Inf
CARR, William, 2 Sgt, Col Edward Bradley, Capt Martin, Vol Inf
CARR, William, Pvt, Col James Raulston, Capt Mathew Neal, Inf
CARR, William, Pvt, Col Thomas Williamson, Capt Anthony Metcalf, Vol Mtd Gunmen
CARR, William, Pvt, Commanders omitted, Branch Srvce omitted; discharged 4-4-1814 from Capt Gordan's Co

## Enlisted Men, War of 1812

CARR, William, Pvt, Commanders omitted, Mtd Spies; from Capt Gordon 4-4-1814

CARR, William, Pvt, Regt Commander omitted, Capt James Anderson, Branch Srvce omitted

CARRAHAN, Thomas, Pvt, Col Thomas Benton, Capt Isiah Renshaw, Vol Inf

CARRAHAN, William P, Pvt, Col Philip Pipkin, Capt David Smith, Mil Inf

CARRAWAY, Jas, Pvt, Col Phillip Pipkin, Capt John Strother, Mil; deserted 9-20-1814

CARRICK, Addison B, Asst Dept QM Gen, John Cocke, E TN Mil Vol

CARRICK, Addison, 2 Lt, Col Samuel Bunch, Capt Thomas Mann, E TN Vol Mtd Inf

CARRICK, Addison, A D Q M Gen'l, Brig Gen Geo Dorherty, E TN Mil; continued service for Maj Gen Cocke Roll

CARRIGAN, Leonard, Pvt, Col John K Wynne, Co Commander omitted, Inf

CARROLL, Geo, Pvt, Regt Commander omitted, Capt N Davis Butt, Branch Srvce omitted

CARROLL, Geo, Pvt, no other information

CARROLL, Henry, Dmr, Col Samuel Bayless, Capt Jonathan Waddell, E TN Mil; promoted to Drm Maj

CARROLL, Henry, Drm Maj, Col Samuel Bayless, Co Commander omitted, 4th Regt E TN Mil

CARROLL, James, Pvt, no other information

CARROLL, Jas, Pvt, Col Wm Pillow, Capt C E McEwen, Vol Inf

CARROLL, Jas, Pvt, Regt Commander omitted, Capt Geo Smith, Spies

CARROLL, John, Pvt, Col Phillip Pipkin, Capt Peter Searcy, Mil Inf

CARROLL, John, Pvt, Col Samuel Bunch, Capt James Cummings, E TN Vol Mtd Inf

CARROLL, Joseph A, Pvt, Maj William Woodfolk, Capt James Turner, Inf

CARROLL, Joseph, Pvt, Col Thomas Williamson, Capt John Dobbins, Capt John Doak, Vol Mtd Gunmen

CARROLL, Joseph, Pvt, Col William Hall, Capt James Hambleton, Vol Inf

CARROLL, Luke, 1 Lt, Col Ewen Allison, Capt John Hampton, Mil, Res omitted; resigned his command 2-28-1814

CARROLL, Samuel, Pvt, Col William Metcalf, Capt William Mullin, Mil Inf

CARROLL, Stephen, Pvt, Col John Cocke, Capt George Barnes, Inf; cleared by Court Martial 11-18-1814

CARROLL, Thomas, Pvt, Col John Brown, Capt Hugh Barton, E TN Mil Inf

CARROLL, William, Capt & Brig Inspector, Brig Gen Andrew Jackson, Det TN Vol, Res omitted

CARROLL, William, Capt, Maj Gen Andrew Jackson, Capt William Carroll, Vol Inf, Res omitted

CARROLL, William, Pvt, Col Ewen Allison, Capt John Hampton, Mil

CARROT, Jesse, Pvt, Col John Coffee, Capt Charles Kavanaugh, Cav; sick at home

CARROTHERS, James, Sgt, no other information

CARROTHERS, John, Pvt, Brig Gen Isaac Roberts, Capt Benjamin Reynolds, Branch Srvce omitted

CARROTHERS, Robert, Pvt, no other information

CARROTHERS, William, Sgt, Maj Gen William Carroll, Col William Metcalf, Capt John Jackson, Mil Inf

CARRUTH, Walter, Pvt, Col Samuel Wear, Capt James Gillespie, E TN Vol Inf

CARRUTHERS, Ezekial, Pvt, Col James Raulston, Capt Mathew Neal, Inf

CARRUTHERS, James, Pvt, Gen Thomas Washington, Co Commander omitted, Mtd Inf

CARRUTHERS, James, Sgt, Regt Commander omitted, Capt Archibald McKinney, Cav

CARRUTHERS, John, Sgt, no other information

CARSON, Alexander, Pvt, Col Samuel Bunch, Capt Francis Berry, E TN Mil; attached to Capt Houk's Co

CARSON, Alexander, Pvt, Col Samuel Bunch, Capt John Houk, E TN Mil; joined from Capt Berry's Co

CARSON, David, Pvt, Maj William Woodfolk, Capt James Neil, Inf

CARSON, Hugh, Pvt, Col William Hall, Capt William Alexander, Vol Inf

CARSON, James, Pvt, Col Edward Bradley, Capt William Lauderdale, Vol Inf

CARSON, John L, Pvt, Col Samuel Bunch, Capt Francis Berry, E TN Mil

CARSON, John, Pvt, Col Edwin Booth, Capt James Porter, Drafted Mil

CARSON, Lamuel, Pvt, Regt Commander omitted, Capt Joseph Williams, Mil Cav

CARSON, Levi jr, Pvt, Col William Metcalf, Capt Andrew Patterson, Mil Inf

CARSON, Levi sr, Pvt, Col William Metcalf, Capt Andrew Patterson, Mil Inf

CARSON, Major, Pvt, Gen Andrew Jackson, Capt William Russell, Mtd Spies

CARSON, Moses, Pvt, Col Samuel Bayless, Capt Jonathan Waddell, E TN Mil

CARSON, Robert, Capt, Brig Gen Thomas Johnson, Inf, Res omitted

CARSON, Robert, Pvt, Col John Cocke, Capt Samuel Caruthers, Inf; left at Clarksville 11-1814

CARSON, Robert, Pvt, Col Samuel Bayless, Capt Joseph Goodson, E TN Mil; sick at Mobile 3-29-1815

CARSON, Samuel, Pvt, Col John Cocke, Capt James Gault, Inf; d 3-16-1815

CARSON, Samuel, Pvt, Regt Commander omitted, Capt Joseph Williams, Mil Cav; discharged

CARSON, Thomas, Pvt, Col William Lillard, Capt Benjamin King, E TN Vol Inf; substitute

CARSON, Thomas, Rank omitted, Gen Andrew Jackson, Capt William Russell, Mtd Spies

CARSON, William, 1 Sgt, Col William Lillard, Capt Zacheus Copeland, E TN Vol Inf; discharged on account of inability

CARSON, William, Pvt, Col Edwin Booth, Capt Alexander Biggs, Inf

CARSON, William, Pvt, Col Ewen Allison, Capt Henry McCray, E TN Mil; transferred to Capt Register's Co

CARSON, William, Pvt, Col Samuel Bunch, Capt Francis Berry, E TN Mil; attached to Capt Houk's Co

## Enlisted Men, War of 1812

CARSON, William, Pvt, Col Samuel Bunch, Capt Francis Register, E TN Mil; joined from Capt McCrea's Co

CARSON, William, Pvt, Col Samuel Bunch, Capt John Houks, E TN Mil; joined from Capt Berry's Co

CARSON, William, Pvt, Col William Lillard, Capt Benjamin King, E TN Vol Inf

CARSON, Willis, Cpl, Col Thomas Williamson, Capt William Martin, Vol Mtd Gunmen; d 2-23-1815

CARSONBURY, Paul, Pvt, Col John Cocke, Capt Richard Crunk, Inf; d 4-24-1814

CARSONBURY, Solomon, Pvt, Col John Cocke, Capt James Gray, Branch Srvce omitted; substituted b Jesse Weston

CARSWELL, Eli, Pvt, Col S Copeland, Capt Robert Steele, Mil Inf

CARTAIN, Joseph, Pvt, Col Ewen Allison, Capt Henry McCray, E TN Mil; discharged by surgeon

CARTELOW, James, Pvt, Col Leroy Hammonds, Capt Joseph Williamson, Inf; left sick at Ft Strother

CARTER, Adams, Pvt, Maj John Childs, Capt Reuben Tipton, E TN Vol Mtd Inf; Regimental Co 6th Jefferson

CARTER, Alexander, Pvt, Col Alexander Loury, Capt George Sarver, Inf

CARTER, Benjamin, Pvt, Col A Cheatham, Capt James Giddins, Inf

CARTER, Benjamin, Pvt, Col John Brown, Capt Allen Bacon, E TN Mil Inf

CARTER, Benjamin, Pvt, Col William Johnson, Capt Christopher Cook, 3rd Regt E TN Mil; deserted

CARTER, Benjamine, Pvt, Col William Johnson, Capt Joseph Kirk, Mil

CARTER, Bernard, Cpl, Maj William Woodfolk, Capt Ezekial Ross, Capt McCulley, Inf

CARTER, Bradley, Pvt, Maj William Woodfolk, Capt Abner Pearce, Inf

CARTER, Chas, Pvt, Capt James Raulston, Capt Henry Hamilton, Inf; also served Maj Gen Wm Carroll

CARTER, Dan'l, Pvt, Col Nicholas T Perkins, Capt Mathew Johnston, Mil Inf

CARTER, David B, Ens, Col Robert Steele, Capt James Randals, Inf, Res omitted

CARTER, David, Dmr, Lt Col L Hammonds, Capt James Tubb, Inf; furloughed on march to place of mustering out of service

CARTER, Elijah, Pvt, Col Ewen Allison, Capt Jacob Hoyal, E TN Mil; furloughed on account of inability

CARTER, Elijah, Pvt, Col William Lillard, Capt Robert Maloney, E TN Vol Inf; deserted 10-29-1813

CARTER, Ellis, Pvt, Col William Lillard, Capt Robert Maloney, E TN Vol Inf

CARTER, Geo, Pvt, Col William Hall, Capt Brice Martin, Vol Inf

CARTER, George, Pvt, Col Jno Brown, Capt Allen I Bacon, E TN Mil Inf

CARTER, Gideon, Pvt, Col William Hall, Capt William L Alexander, Vol Inf

CARTER, Giles, Pvt, Lt Col L Hammonds, Capt James Tubb, Inf; furloughed on march to muster out of service

CARTER, Harris, Pvt, Col Leroy Hammonds, Capt George Sarver, Inf

CARTER, Jas, Cpl, Col Robert H Dyer, Capt Thomas Jones, Vol Mtd Gunmen; furnished substitute Moses Matlock

CARTER, Jas, Pvt, Col Philip Pipkin, Capt David Smythe, Inf

CARTER, Jas, Pvt, Col Philip Pipkin, Capt David Smythe, W TN Mil, attached to Capt John Strother's Co

CARTER, Jas, Pvt, Col Philip Pipkin, Capt Henr M Newlin, Mil Inf; sick at Ft Williams 11-4-1814

CARTER, Jas, Pvt, Col Philip Pipkin, Capt James Blakemore, Mil Inf; transferred from Capt H Newlin Co

CARTER, Jesse, Pvt, Col Philip Pipkin, Capt Ebenezer Kirkpatrick, Mil Inf

CARTER, Jno, Pvt, Col S Bunch, Capt Dan'l Yarnell, E TN Mil; furnished as substitute

CARTER, Jno, Pvt, Regt Commander omitted, Capt Wm Teas, Inf

CARTER, Jno, Sgt, Regt Commander omitted, Capt Edwin S Moore, Mtd Riflemen

CARTER, Joel W I, Pvt, Lt Col L Hammonds, Capt James Tubb, Inf

CARTER, Joel, 1 Cpl, Maj John Childs, Capt Charles Conway, E TN Mtd Gunmen

CARTER, Joel, Pvt, Col John Coffee, Capt James Terrill, Vol Cav; delinquent

CARTER, Joel, Pvt, Maj John Childs, Capt Charles Conway, E TN Mtd Gunmen; Regimental Co 40-Knox

CARTER, John C, Pvt, Col N T Perkins, Capt Mathew Johnston, Mil Inf

CARTER, John N, Sgt, Regt Commander omitted, Capt Jno Gordon, Mtd Spies

CARTER, John W, Pvt, Col John K Wynne, Capt John Spinks, Inf

CARTER, John, 3 Lt, Col Jno Brown, Capt Allen I Bacon, E TN Mil Inf, Res omitted

CARTER, John, Pvt, Col Ewen Allison, Capt Jacob Hoyal, E TN Mil; joined from Capt McPherson's Co

CARTER, John, Pvt, Col John Alcorn, Capt William Locke, Cav

CARTER, John, Pvt, Col Nicholas T Perkins, Capt Mathew Johnston, Mil Inf

CARTER, John, Pvt, Col Robert H Dyer, Capt Ephraim D Dickson, TN Mtd Vol Gunmen; no service performed

CARTER, John, Pvt, Col Robert H Dyer, Capt James Wyatt, Vol Mtd Gunmen

CARTER, John, Pvt, Col Robert Steele, Capt John Chitwood, Mil Inf

CARTER, John, Pvt, Col S Bunch, Capt Geo McPherson, E TN Mil; joined from Capt Hoyle Co

CARTER, John, Pvt, Col William Johnson, Capt Christopher Cooks, E TN Mil

CARTER, John, Pvt, Col William Johnson, Capt Joseph Kirk, Mil

CARTER, John, Pvt, Maj Gen Wm Carroll, Col James Raulston, Capt Edward Robinson, Inf

CARTER, John, Pvt, Regt Commander omitted, Capt

## Enlisted Men, War of 1812

Ephraim Dickson, Branch Srvce omitted
CARTER, Johnson, Pvt, Col William Metcalf, Capt Alexander Hill, Mil Inf
CARTER, Jos, Pvt, Col William Hall, Capt William L Alexander, Vol Inf
CARTER, Jos, Pvt, Col William Hall, Capt Wm L Alexander, Vol Inf
CARTER, Jos, Pvt, Maj William Woodfolk, Capt Abraham Dudney, Inf
CARTER, Jos, Pvt, Maj William Woodfolk, Capt James Turner, Inf; in place of Eli Hubbard transferred to Capt McCulley
CARTER, Josiah R, Pvt, Col Stephen Copeland, Capt William Evans, Mil Inf
CARTER, Leaven, Pvt, Col James Raulston, Capt James A Black, Inf
CARTER, Levin, Pvt, Col Robert Steele, Capt James Bennett, Mil Inf
CARTER, Levy, Pvt, Col Samuel Bayless, Capt Joseph Goodson, E TN Mil
CARTER, Lewis, Pvt, Col James Raulston, Capt James A Black, Inf
CARTER, Martin, 5 Cpl, Col John Cocke, Capt John Weakley, Inf
CARTER, Nelson, Cor (3 Lt), Maj William Russell, Capt John Cowan, Vol Mtd Gunmen, Res omitted; promoted from Sgt
CARTER, Randolph, Pvt, Col Alexander Loury, Capt Gabriel Martin, Inf; left sick at Mount? by order of Col Loury
CARTER, Reuben, Cpl, Col Thomas McCror, Capt William Dooley, Inf
CARTER, Richard, Pvt, Col Jno Brown, Capt Allen I Bacon, Regt E TN Mil Inf
CARTER, Robt M, Pvt, Maj Gen Wm Carroll, Capt Daniel M Bradfod, Capt Lewis Dillahunty, Vol Inf
CARTER, Sam'l L, Pvt, Regt Commander omitted, Capt Archibald McKinney, Cav
CARTER, Sam'l L, Pvt, Regt Commander omitted, Lt Jas Berry, Mtd Riflemen; joined from L Hogan Co
CARTER, Thos, Pvt, Col William Johnson, Capt James Stewart, E TN Drafted Mil
CARTER, William, Pvt, Col Edward Bradley, Capt Brice Martin, Vol Inf
CARTER, William, Pvt, Col John Cocke, Capt Joseph Price, Inf
CARTER, Wm B, Pvt Forage Master, Brig Gen M Taylor, Branch Srvce omitted; resigned 10-17-1814
CARTER, Wm D, Pvt, Lt Col L Hammonds, Capt Jas Craig, Inf
CARTER, Wm L, 3 Lt, Col Wm Metcalf, Capt Muttin, Mil Inf, Res omitted
CARTER, Wm L, 3 Sgt, Col Wm Metcalf, Capt Wm Mullin, Mil
CARTER, Wm, Pvt, Col S Copeland, Capt Fait, Inf
CARTER, Wm, Pvt, Col Wm Hall, Capt Brice Martin, Vol Inf
CARTER, Wm, Pvt, Maj Gen Wm Carroll, Col James Raulston, Capt Wiley Huddleston, Inf
CARTER, Wm, Pvt, Sgt John Patton, Det of Inf
CARTETT, Benjamin, Pvt, Regt Commander omitted, Capt William Henderson, Spies
CARTEZ, Benj, Pvt, Maj John Childs, Capt John Stephens, E TN Vol Mtd Inf
CARTRIGHT, Daniel, Pvt, Col John Cocke, Capt John Dalton, Inf
CARTRIGHT, Enoch, Pvt, Col John Cocke, Capt John Dalton, Inf
CARTRIGHT, Jordan, Pvt, Col Thos Benton, Capt Thos Williamson, Vol Inf; missing
CARTRIGHT, Lemuel, Pvt, Col Wm Lillard, Capt Benj H King, E TN Vol Inf
CARTRIGHT, Robert, Pvt, Col Edward Bradley, Capt Henry L Douglass, Vol Inf
CARTRIGHT, Robert, Pvt, Col Thos Benton, Capt Henry L Douglass, Vol Inf; deserted
CARTRIGHT, Robt, Pvt, Col Jno Coffee, Capt Jas Terrell, Vol Cav
CARTRIGHT, Thos, Pvt, Col Samuel Wear, Capt Jas Tedford, E TN Vol Inf
CARTWRIGHT, Robt, 2 Cpl, Regt Commander omitted, Capt Jas Terrell, Cav; Old Volunteer discharged
CARTWRIGHT, Thos, Pvt, Col Jas Raulston, Capt Chas Wade, Inf
CARTWRIGHT, Vinson, Pvt, Col R H Dyer, Capt Robert Evans, Vol Mtd Gunmen; d 1-1-1815
CARUTH, Jas, Pvt, Maj Wm Russell, Capt John Trimble, Vol Mtd Gunmen
CARUTH, Thos, Pvt, Col Wm Hall, Capt Brice Martin, Vol Inf
CARUTHERS, Andrew, Pvt, Col Edwin Booth, Capt John Sharp, E TN Mil
CARUTHERS, David S, Pvt, Col Philip Pipkin, Capt Jas Blakemore, Mil Inf; sick at Ft Strother 11-1-1814
CARUTHERS, Ezekiel, Pvt, Col Wm Hall, Capt John Wallace, Inf
CARUTHERS, James, Pvt, no other information
CARUTHERS, Jas, Pvt, Col Jno Coffee, Capt Chas Kavanaugh, Cav
CARUTHERS, Jas, Pvt, Col N T Perkins, Capt Matthew Johnston, Mil Inf
CARUTHERS, Jas, Sgt, Regt Commander omitted, Capt Archibold McKinney, Cav
CARUTHERS, John, 2 Lt, Maj Gen John Cocke, TN Vol Mtd Gunmen, Res omitted
CARUTHERS, John, Pvt, Col N T Perkins, Capt Matthew Johnston, Mil Inf
CARUTHERS, John, Pvt, Col Wm Lillard, Capt Hugh Martin, E TN Vol Inf
CARUTHERS, John, Sgt, Brig Gen Thos Washington, Co Commander omitted, Inf
CARUTHERS, Robt, Pvt, Regt Commander omitted, Capt Archibold McKinney, Cav
CARUTHERS, Samuel M, Capt, Col John Cocke, Capt S M Caruthers, Inf, Res omitted
CARUTHERS, Samuel, Pvt, Maj Wm Russell, Capt John Trimble, Vol Mtd Gunmen
CARUTHERS, Thos, Pvt, Col Jas Raulston, Capt Matthew Neal, Inf
CARUTHERS, William, Pvt, Col John Alcorn, Capt John Baskerville, Vol Inf
CARUTHERS, William, Pvt, Col S Copeland, Capt Thos

Williamson, Mil Inf; on furlough 5-6-1814
CARVER, Cornelius, Pvt, Col Jas Raulston, Capt Mathew Cowan, Inf
CARVER, Edward, Pvt, Maj Wm Woodfolk, Capt Abraham Dudney, Inf
CARVER, Isaac, Pvt, Col Jas Raulston, Capt Chas Wade, Inf
CARVER, Michael, Pvt, Col Ewen Allison, Capt Henry McCray, E TN Mil; deserted
CARVER, Michael, Pvt, Col S Bunch, Capt F Register, E TN Mil; joined from Capt Winsel's Co
CARVER, Wm, Pvt, Col Ewen Allison, Capt Henry McCray, E TN Mil; transferred to Capt Register's Co
CARY, Francis, Pvt, Maj Gen Wm Carroll, Capt Francis Ellis, Inf
CARY, John, Pvt, Col Wm Johnson, Capt Jas Stewart, E TN Drafted Mil
CARY, Thos, Pvt, Col S Bunch, Capt Wm Houston, E TN Vol Mtd Inf; substitute for Nathaniel McNabb
CARY, Wm, Pvt, Col Wm Johnson, Capt Christopher Cook, E TN Mil; d 11-8-1814
CARY, Wm, Pvt, Col Wm Johnston, Capt Joseph Kirk, Mil Inf
CASBELL, Jas, Pvt, no other information
CASBY, Garland, Pvt, Col Wm Pillow, Capt C E McEwen, Vol Inf
CASCA, Wm, Pvt, Col Wm Johnston, Capt Joseph Kirk, Mil
CASELMAN, Abraham, Sgt Maj, Col Philip Pipkin, Co Commander omitted, 1st Regt TN Mil; d at Ft Strother 9-23-1814
CASELMAN, Jacob, Pvt, Col Thos Williamson, Capt Beverly Williams, Vol Mtd Gunmen
CASEY, Ambelar (Ambler), Pvt, Col Wm Johnson, Capt Jas R Rogers, E TN Drafted Mil; left at home sick in Sept
CASEY, Geo, Pvt, Maj John Chiles, Capt Chas Conway, E TN Mtd Gunmen; Regimental Co-Bledsoe
CASEY, Hughes, Pvt, Regt Commander omitted, Capt James Anderson, Branch Srvce omitted
CASEY, John, Pvt, Col Jno Coffee, Capt Robert Jetton, Cav
CASEY, Nathaniel, Pvt, Maj Wm Carroll, Capt Lewis Dillahunty, Vol Inf
CASH, D John, Pvt, Col Edwin Booth, Capt John Lewis, E TN Mil
CASH, Jas, Pvt, Col Edwin Booth, Capt John Lewis, E TN Mil
CASH, John D, Pvt, Col Samuel Wear, Capt Robert Doak, E TN Vol Inf
CASKIN, Martin, 2 Sgt, Regt Commander omitted, Capt Jas Haggard, Mtd Gunmen
CASKIN, Martin, Sgt, Regt Commander omitted, Capt Jas Haggard, Mtd Gunmen
CASKY, John, Pvt, Col Jas Raulston, Capt Chas Wade, Inf
CASLEMAN, Abram, Sgt, Col Thomas Benton, Capt Joseph Williamson, Vol Inf
CASON, Isaac N, Pvt, Col Wm Lillard, Capt Wm McLin, E TN Inf
CASON, Jas, Pvt, Col Edward Bradley, Capt William Lauderdale, Vol Inf
CASON, Jas, Pvt, Col Wm Hall, Capt William L Alexander, Vol Inf
CASON, Jas, Pvt, Col Wm Hall, Capt Wm Alexander, Vol Inf
CASON, Seth, Pvt, Col Robert Steele, Capt John Chitwood, Mil Inf
CASON, Thos, Pvt, Lt Col Leroy Hammonds, Capt Thomas Wells, Inf; sick at Ft Montgomery 12-16-1814
CASSADY, Jas, Sgt, Col Wm Lillard, Capt Jacob Hartsell, E TN Vol Inf
CASSAN, David, Pvt, Col A Cheatham, Capt Charles Johnson, Inf
CASSAN, Levi, Pvt, Col A Cheatham, Capt Charles Johnson, Inf
CASSELMAN, Sylvenas, Cpl, Col N T Perkins, Capt Phillip Pipkins, Mtd Riflemen; AWOL
CASTEAL, Barney, Pvt, Col Samuel Wear, Capt James Gillespie, E TN Vol Inf
CASTEAT, Caleb, Pvt, Col Samuel Wear, Capt James Gillespie, E TN Vol Inf
CASTEEL, Abednigo, Pvt, Col John Brown, Capt John Chiles, E TN Vol Mtd Inf
CASTEEL, Caleb, Pvt, Col Samuel Bunch, Capt Joseph Duncan, E TN Drafted Mil; transferred to Capt Buchanan's Co
CASTEEL, Daniel, 3 Cpl, Col Wm Lillard, Capt Hugh Martin, E TN Vol Inf
CASTEEL, Daniel, Cpl, Col William Johnston, Capt Joseph Scott, E TN Drafted Mil
CASTEEL, Henry, Pvt, Col Edwin Booth, Capt Alexander Biggs, Inf
CASTEEL, Isaac, Pvt, Col Phillip Pipkin, Capt William Mackay, Mil Inf
CASTEEL, Jacob, Pvt, Col Edwin Booth, Capt Alexander Biggs, Inf
CASTEEL, Jas, Pvt, Col S Bunch, Capt Jones Griffin, E TN Drafted Mil; deserted 3-4-1814
CASTEEL, John, Pvt, Col Samuel Bunch, Capt Edward Buchanan, E TN Drafted Mil
CASTEEL, John, Pvt, Col Samuel Bunch, Capt Joseph Duncan, E TN Drafted Mil
CASTEEL, Jos, Pvt, Col Samuel Bunch, Capt Edward Buchanan, E TN Drafted Mil
CASTEEL, Jos, Pvt, Col Samuel Bunch, Capt Joseph Duncan, E TN Drafted Inf; transferred to Capt Buchanan Co
CASTEEL, Meshac, Pvt, Col Samuel Bunch, Capt Joseph Duncan, E TN Drafted Mil; transferred to Capt Buchanan Co
CASTEEL, Zachariah, Pvt, Col Ewen Allison, Capt Jacob Hayal, E TN Mil
CASTEEL, Zachariah, Pvt, Col William Johnson, Capt Joseph Kirk, Mil
CASTEEL, _____, Pvt, Col Wm Johnson, Capt John Scott, E TN Drafted Mil; substitute for David Odele
CASTELL, James, Pvt, Regt Commander omitted, Capt N Davis Butts, Branch Srvce omitted
CASTELL, Zachariah, Pvt, Col William Johnson, Capt

## Enlisted Men, War of 1812

Christopher Cook, E TN Mil
CASTELOW, Jas, Pvt, Col Jno Coffee, Capt Fredrick Stump, Cav; absent
CASTILL, Isaac, Pvt, Col William Pillow, Capt Thomas Williamson, Vol Inf
CASTLE, Geo, Pvt, Col Samuel Bunch, Capt Geo Gregory, E TN Drafted Mil; substitute Shadrack Campbell
CASTLEMAN, A, Sgt, Col Wm Pillow, Capt Thos Williamson, Vol Inf
CASTLEMAN, Abraham (Adam), 1 Sgt, Col Thomas Benton, Capt Thomas Williamson, Vol Inf
CASTLEMAN, Jacob, Pvt, Col N Cannon, Capt Martin, Mtd Gunmen
CASTLEMAN, Jas, Pvt, Col Williamson, Capt Dake, Vol Mtd Gunmen
CASTLEMAN, John, Pvt, Col Thomas Williamson, Capt James Neeley, Capt James Pace, Vol Mtd Gunmen; transferred to Capt Comp
CASTLEMAN, John, Pvt, Col Williamson, Capt Dake, Vol Mtd Gunmen; joined by transfer for Capt Pace
CASTLEMAN, Joseph, Pvt, Col Alcorn, Co Commander omitted, Vol Cav
CASTLEMAN, Sylvanius, Pvt, Gen Thos Washington, Co Commander omitted, Mil Inf
CASTLES, Sylvanius, Pvt, no other information
CATCHERS, Saymore, Lt, Col Wm Johnson, Capt Elihu Millikin, 3rd Regt E TN Mil, Res omitted
CATE, Aaron, Pvt, Col S Bunch, Capt Geo Gregory, E TN Drafted Mil
CATE, Aaron, Pvt, Col Samuel Bunch, Capt Francis Berry, E TN Mil
CATE, Elisha, Pvt, Col Samuel Bunch, Capt Francis Berry, E TN Mil
CATE, Ephraim, Pvt, Col N T Perkins, Capt George Eliot, Mil Inf
CATE, Jas, Pvt, Col N T Perkins, Capt George Eliot, Mil Inf
CATE, John, Pvt, Col Samuel Bunch, Capt Francis Berry, E TN Mil
CATE, Robt, Cpl, Col Samuel Bayless, Capt Jas Churchman, E TN Mil
CATES, Jos, Pvt, Col Thomas Williamson, Capt Thomas Scurry, Vol Mtd Gunmen
CATES, Thos, Pvt, no other information
CATES, Wm, Pvt, Col Robt Steele, Capt Jas Shenault, Mil Inf; furloughed since 4-2-1814
CATHEY, Alexander, Pvt, Col John Coffee, Capt Blackman Coleman, Cav
CATHEY, James, Pvt, Regt Commander omitted, Capt Kavanah, Branch Srvce omitted
CATHEY, Jas, Pvt, Col John Cocke, Capt George Barnes, Inf
CATHEY, Jas, Pvt, Regt Commander omitted, Capt Archibald McKinney, Cav
CATHEY, John, Pvt, Col William Metcalf, Capt Andrew Patteson, Mil Inf
CATHEY, John, Pvt, Regt Commander omitted, Capt Elijah Rushing, Det of Inf
CATHEY, Mathew B, Pvt, Col Robert Dyer, Capt James McMahon, 1st TN Mtd Vol Gunmen
CATHEY, _____, Pvt, no other information
CATHY, Alexander, Pvt, Col N Cannon, Capt Geo Brandon, Mtd Riflemen
CATHY, Andrew, Pvt, Col John Cocke, Capt James Gray, Inf; d 2-13-1815, substitute for Jas Taylor
CATHYE, Jas, Pvt, Regt Commander omitted, Capt Archibald McKinney, Cav
CATLETE, Benjamin, Pvt, Col Samuel Bunch, Capt Isaac Williams, E TN Mil
CATLETE, Richard, Pvt, Col Samuel Bunch, Capt Joseph Williams, E TN Mil
CATLETT, John, 1 Lt, Capt Isaac Williams, E TN Mil, Res omitted
CATLETT, Richard, Pvt, Col Samuel Wear, Capt Simeon Perry, E TN Vol Mtd Inf
CATO, Henry, Pvt, Regt Commander omitted, Capt James Gray, Inf
CATO, Nehemiah, Pvt, Regt Commander omitted, Capt James Gray, Inf
CATO, Robert, Pvt, Col N T Perkins, Capt George Eliot, Mil Inf
CATOE, Rouland, Pvt, Col John Coffee, Capt James Terrill, Vol Inf
CATRON, Jacob, Pvt, Col William Pillow, Capt John Anderson, Vol Inf
CATRON, John, Pvt, Col William Pillow, Capt John Anderson, Vol Inf; promoted to Sgt Maj, resigned 11-23-1813
CATRQN, John, Sgt Maj, Col William Pillow, Co Commander omitted, 2nd Regt TN Vol Inf; resigned 11-20-1813
CATTETT, Richard, Pvt, Regt Commander omitted, Capt William Henderson, Mtd Spies
CATTREN, Daniel, Pvt, Col Ewen Allison, Capt Joseph Everett, E TN Mil; transferred to Capt McPherson's Co
CAUBLE, Peter, Pvt, Col Robert Steele, Capt Richard Ratton, Mil Inf
CAUCE, James M, Pvt, Col John Williams, Capt David Vance, Mtd Mil
CAUGH, Martin, Pvt, Col Thomas Benton, Capt Henry Douglass, Vol Inf
CAUGHN, Samuel, Pvt, Col William Lillard, Capt James Lillard, E TN Mil Inf Vol
CAUGHRAN, Aun D, Pvt, Col Newton Cannon, Capt Isaac Williams, Mtd Riflemen; transferred
CAULTHRAP, James, Pvt, Col Edwin Booth, Capt John Slatton, E TN Mil; d 2-27-1815
CAULY, Robert, Pvt, Col William Higgins, Capt Adam Dale, Mtd Gunmen
CAUSBY, James, Pvt, Col William Metcalf, Capt Andrew Patterson, Mil Inf; d 3-26-1815
CAVEATH, Simpson, Pvt, Maj John Childs, Capt Charles Conway, E TN Mtd Gunmen
CAVEN, John, Pvt, Col Philip Pipkin, Capt David Smith, Inf
CAVENDER, Edward, Pvt, Col John Cocke, Capt Samuel Caruthers, Inf
CAVENDER, Henry, Pvt, Col Samuel Bunch, Capt S Roberson, E TN Drafted Mil

## Enlisted Men, War of 1812

CAVENDER, Henry, Pvt, Regt Commander omitted, Capt Samuel Richardson, E TN Drafted Mil

CAVENDER, Jarrett, Pvt, Col John Cocke, Capt Samuel Caruthers, Inf

CAVENDER, Jarrett, Pvt, Col William Metcalf, Capt Thomas Marks, Mil Inf

CAVENDER, Stephen, Pvt, Col John Coffee, Capt Frederick Stump, Cav

CAVENDER, Stephen, Pvt, Col Robert Dyer, Capt White, Vol Mtd Gunmen

CAVENDER, William, Pvt, Col Robert Dyer, Capt James Wyatt, Vol Mtd Gunmen

CAVENOR, John, Cpl, Col Ewen Allison, Capt Jacob Hoyal, E TN Mil

CAVERN, John, Pvt, Col Philip Pipkin, Capt David Smith, W TN Mil; attached to Capt John Strother's Co

CAVET, Andrew, Pvt, Col John Cocke, Capt John Weakley, Inf

CAVETT, John, Pvt, Col John Coffee, Capt Thomas Bradley, Vol Cav

CAVETT, Joseph, Pvt, Col Philip Pipkin, Capt John Strother, Mil; substitute for John Smith, attached to Capt Smith Co

CAVETT, Joseph, Pvt, Col Philip Pipkin, Capt Peter Searcy, Mil Inf

CAVINDER, Stephen, Pvt, Col John Alcorn, Capt Frederick Stump, Cav

CAVINOR, William W, Pvt, Maj William Russell, Capt John Cowan, Vol Mtd Gunmen; d 12-19-1814

CAVIT, George, Pvt, Col Robert Steele, Capt Robert Campbell, Mil Inf

CAVITT, Andrew, Pvt, Col John Cocke, Capt John Weakley, Inf

CAVITT, Moses, Pvt, Col William Higgins, Capt Stephen Griffith, Mtd Riflemen

CAVITT, Thomas, Pvt, Col William Higgins, Capt Stephen Griffith, Mtd Riflemen

CAWHORN, Alexander, Pvt, Maj John Childs, Capt John Stephens, E TN Vol Mtd Inf

CAWHORN, John, Pvt, Col John Cocke, Capt John Dalton, Inf

CAWHORN, William, Drm Maj, Lt Col Leroy Hammonds, Co Commander omitted, 2nd Regt W TN Mil; also served Col Alex Loury

CAWLEY, Charles, Pvt, Col Newton Cannon, Capt John Hanley, Mtd Riflemen; wounded at Battle of Talledaga 1-1813

CAWOOD, Thomas, Pvt, Col Ewen Allison, Capt Joseph Everett, E TN Mil; transferred to Capt McPherson Co

CAWOOD, Thomas, Sgt, Col William Lillard, Capt George Keys, E TN Inf

CAYCE, Thomas, 4 Sgt, Col N T Perkins, Capt Mathew Patterson, Mtd Vol

CAYGLE, Abraham, Pvt, Col John Cocke, Capt Samuel Caruthers, Inf

CAYGLE, Adam, Pvt, Col John Cocke, Capt Samuel Caruthers, Inf

CAYGLE, Charles, Pvt, Col John Cocke, Capt Samuel Caruthers, Inf

CAYGLE, Henry, Pvt, Col John Cocke, Capt Samuel Caruthers, Inf

CAYWOOD, Edward, Pvt, Col John Brown, Capt John Trimble, E TN Mtd Gunmen

CAYWOOD, Jeremiah, Pvt, Col Samuel Bayless, Capt James Landen, E TN Mil

CAZA, Ala, Pvt, Col Thomas Benton, Capt William Moore, Vol Inf

CAZA, Ala, Pvt, Col William Pillow, Capt William Moore, Inf

CAZA, Daniel, Pvt, Col Thomas Benton, Capt William Moore, Vol Inf

CA_____, John, Pvt, Regt Commander omitted, Capt James Gray, Inf

CEAL, Isam, Pvt, Col Robert Steele, Capt James Shenault, Mil Inf; on furlough

CEASA (CASCA), Wm, Pvt, Col William Johnson, Capt Christopher Cook, E TN Mil

CEDERS, Solomon J, Pvt, Col James Raulston, Capt Henry West, Inf

CENTER, John, Pvt, Col Leroy Hammonds, Capt George Sarver, Inf

CENTER, Martin, Pvt, Col Edwin E Booth, Capt John McKamey, Inf

CENTRE, John, Pvt, Col John Brown, Capt John Trimble, E TN Mtd Gunmen

CERBY (CIRBEY), Jonathan, Pvt, Maj William Woodfolk, Capt Abner Pearce, Inf

CERTAIN, Jno, Pvt, Col S Bunch, Capt Geo Gregory, E TN Drafted Mil; discharged for inability

CETCHEN, Jacob, Pvt, Col Edwin Booth, Capt Vernon, E TN Mil

CEWEN, Hugh, Pvt, Col John Brown, Capt Charles Lewin, E TN Vol Mtd Inf

CGA, Daniel, Pvt, Col William Pillow, Capt William Moore, Inf; sick absent

CHADWELL, Valentine, Pvt, Col Robert Steele, Capt Samuel Maxwell, Mil Inf

CHAFFEN, Abner, Cpl, Maj William Woodfolk, Capt Abraham Dudney, Inf; substitute for Robt Thompson

CHAFFEN, Wm, Pvt, Col T McCrory, Capt A Metcalf, Mil Inf

CHAFFIN, Edward H, 2 Sgt, Regt Commander omitted, Capt Wm Mitchell, Spies

CHAFFIN, Edward H, Pvt, Col Jno Coffee, Capt A McKeen, Cav

CHAFFIN, Edward H, Pvt, Col John Alcorn, Capt Alexander McKeen, Cav; transferred to Mitchell's Spies

CHAFFIN, Edwin H, Sgt, Regt Commander omitted, CApt Wm Mitchell, Spies

CHAFFIN, Moses, Pvt, Col R C Napier, Capt Samuel Ashmore, Mil Inf

CHAFFIN, William, Pvt, Col T McCrory, Capt A Metcalf, Inf

CHAFFIN, William, Pvt, Maj William Woodfolk, Capt Abraham Dudney, Capt John Sutton, Inf

CHAFFIN, Wm, Pvt, Col T McCrory, Capt A Metcalf, Mil Inf

CHAKE, Anderson, Sgt, Col William Johnson, Capt

## Enlisted Men, War of 1812

Benjamin Powell, E TN Mil; discharged for inability
CHAMBERLAIN, Dan'l, Pvt, Col S Bunch, Capt Thomas Mann, E TN Vol Mtd Inf
CHAMBERS, Alexander, Sgt, Col S Copeland, Capt A Provine, Mil Inf; sick absent 3-20-1814
CHAMBERS, Dan'l, Pvt, Col R C Dyer, Maj William Russell, Capt William Russell, Vol Mtd Gunmen
CHAMBERS, Elias, Pvt, Col Robert H Dyer, Capt Robert Edmonston, TN Vol Gunmen
CHAMBERS, Green, Pvt, Col John Cocke, Capt James Gray, Inf
CHAMBERS, Hardy, Pvt, Lt Col L Hammonds, Capt James Craig, Inf
CHAMBERS, Hardy, Pvt, no other information
CHAMBERS, Henry, Pvt, Col John Cocke, Capt James Gray, Inf
CHAMBERS, Henry, Pvt, Col Robert Steele, Capt Robert Campbell, Mil Inf
CHAMBERS, Henry, Pvt, Regt Commander omitted, Capt Josiah Askew, Inf
CHAMBERS, Jas, Sgt, Regt Commander omitted, Capt Gray, Inf
CHAMBERS, Jas, Sgt, Regt Commander omitted, Capt Josiah Askew, Inf
CHAMBERS, John, Pvt, Regt Commander omitted, Capt Gray, Inf
CHAMBERS, John, Pvt, Regt Commander omitted, Capt Josiah Askew, Inf
CHAMBERS, Mark, Pvt, Brig Gen T Williamson, Capt Allen, Mil Inf; sick absent
CHAMBERS, Reuben, Pvt, Col John Cocke, Capt Joseph Price, Inf
CHAMBERS, William, Pvt, Col Philip Pipkin, Capt Peter Searcy, Mil Inf; left sick at Ft Pearce 11-1814
CHAMBERS, Wm, Pvt, Col Newton Cannon, Capt David Hogan, Mtd Gunmen
CHAMBERS, Wm, Pvt, Col R H Dyer, Capt Cuthbert Hudson, Vol Mtd Gunmen
CHAMLESS, Drury, Pvt, Col Alexander Loury, Capt James Kincaid, Inf
CHAMNESS, William, Pvt, Col William Johnston, Capt James R Rogers, E TN Drafted Mil
CHAMP, Asel, Pvt, Col T McCrory, Capt Isaac Patton, Mil Inf; transferred to Capt Shannon's Co
CHAMP, Golesberry, Pvt, Col N T Perkins, Capt Philip Pipkin, Mtd Riflemen
CHAMP, Robt, Pvt, Col T McCrory, Capt William Dooley, Inf
CHAMP, Wm, Pvt, Col N T Perkins, Capt Philip Pipkin, Mtd Riflemen
CHAMPLAIN, Benj H, Cpl, Col William Lillard, Capt Robert McCalpin, E TN Inf
CHAMPLIN, Benj H, Pvt, Col Samuel Bayless, Capt Joseph Hale, E TN Mil
CHANCE, Robt, Pvt, Maj Gen Wm Carroll, Capt Francis Ellis, Inf
CHANDLER, Andrew, Pvt, Col Thomas Williamson, Capt Beverly Williams, Vol Mtd Gunmen
CHANDLER, Benj, Pvt, Col Samuel Wear, Col Samuel Bunch, Capt William Mitchell, E TN Mtd Inf
CHANDLER, Edins, Pvt, Maj Wm Woodfolk, Capt McCulley, Inf
CHANDLER, Henry, Pvt, Col Edward Bradley, Capt Harry I Douglass, Vol Inf; on furlough
CHANDLER, Isaac, Pvt, Col S Bunch, Col Jno McNare, E TN Mil; attached to Capt Berry's Co
CHANDLER, James, Pvt, Lt Col A Cheatham, Capt Gabriel Martin, Mtd Inf
CHANDLER, James, Pvt, no other information
CHANDLER, Jas, Pvt, Col A Cheatham, Capt Richard Benson, Inf
CHANDLER, Jas, Pvt, Col John Cocke, Capt Samuel M Caruthers, Inf; d 3-13-1815
CHANDLER, John, Pvt, Col Newton Cannon, Capt James Walton, Mtd Riflemen
CHANDLER, John, Pvt, Col Thomas Williamson, Capt John Crane, Capt James Cook, Vol Mtd Gunmen
CHANDLER, Parks, Pvt, Col Thomas Williamson, Capt Beverly Williams, Vol Mtd Gunmen
CHANDLER, Pitts, Pvt, Col Thomas Williamson, Capt Beverly Williams, Vol Mtd Gunmen
CHANDLER, Robt, 1 Cpl, Col Samuel Wear, Capt Daniel Price, E TN Vol Inf
CHANDLER, Robt, 4 Sgt, Maj John Childs, Capt Daniel Price, E TN Vol Mtd Inf; promoted from Pvt
CHANDLER, Robt, Pvt, Col Edward Bradley, Capt Harry L Douglass, Vol Inf
CHANDLER, Robt, Pvt, Maj John Childs, Capt Daniel Price, E TN Vol Mtd Inf
CHANDLER, Thos, Pvt, Col Philip Pipkin, Capt David Smythe, Mil Inf
CHANDLER, Thos, Pvt, Col S Copeland, Capt John Dawson, Inf; d 4-16-1814
CHANDLER, William, Pvt, Col Alexander Loury, Capt Gabriel Martin, Inf
CHANDLER, William, Pvt, Col Edward Bradley, Capt Harry Douglass, Vol Inf
CHANDLER, William, Pvt, Col William Metcalf, Capt William Mullin, Mil Inf
CHANDLER, William, Pvt, Maj William Woodfolk, Capt Ezekial Ross, Capt McCulley, Inf
CHANDLER, William, Sgt, Lt Col A Cheatham, Co Commander omitted, Mtd Inf
CHANEY, Joseph, Pvt, Col S Copeland, Capt William Hodges, Inf; sick absent
CHANLY, John, Pvt, Regt Commander omitted, Capt J Prewitt, Mtd Vols & Pack Horse Guards
CHANY, Robert, Pvt, Col William Johnson, Capt Henry Hunter, E TN Mil
CHAPEL, Trom, Pvt, Maj William Woodfolk, Capt Ezekial Ross, Inf
CHAPLINGER, George, Pvt, Col John Alcorn, Capt John Baskerville, Vol Inf
CHAPMAN, Benjamin, Pvt, Col Philip Pipkin, Capt James Blakemore, Mil Inf
CHAPMAN, Daniel, Pvt, Col Newton Cannon, Capt James Walton, Mtd Riflemen; wounded at Talledega
CHAPMAN, Daniel, Pvt, Col Robert H. Dyer, Capt Bethel Allen, Vol Mtd Gunmen; died 2-15-1815
CHAPMAN, Daniel, Pvt, Col Samuel Bayless, Capt Jon-

## Enlisted Men, War of 1812

athan Waddle, TN Mil
CHAPMAN, George G, Capt, Col Cheatham, Inf
CHAPMAN, George, Lt, Regt Commander omitted, Capt Meredith Walker, Lt Cheatham, Mtd Inf
CHAPMAN, Isaac, Pvt, Col S Copeland, Capt John Dawson, Inf
CHAPMAN, John A, 1 Lt & Adjt, Col Robert Steele, no Co Commander, 4 Regt TN Mil
CHAPMAN, John A, 1 Lt, Col Pillow, Capt Moore, Inf; apptd Adjt of 4 Reg TN Mil
CHAPMAN, John A, Lt, Col Thomas Benton, Capt John Moore, Vol Inf
CHAPMAN, John D, Pvt, Col Philip Pipkin, Capt William Mackay, Mil Inf
CHAPMAN, John, Pvt, Col Charles Johnsonn, Capt Kirk, Mil
CHAPMAN, John, Pvt, Col Philip Pipkin, Capt Seracy, Mil Inf
CHAPMAN, John, Pvt, Col Thomas Williamson, Capt John Crane, Vol Mtd Gunmen
CHAPMAN, John, Pvt, Col William Johnson, Capt James Cook, E TN Mil
CHAPMAN, John, Pvt, Col William Metcalf, Co Commander omitted, Mil Inf; promoted to Cpl
CHAPMAN, John, Sgt, Col Alexander Loury, Capt George Sarver, Inf
CHAPMAN, Joseph, Cpl, Col R H Dyer, Capt Bethel Allen, Vol Mtd Gunmen
CHAPMAN, Joseph, Pvt, Col Ewen Allison, Capt Jonas Loughmiller, Mil; transferred from Capt Griffin Co
CHAPMAN, Joseph, Pvt, Col S Copeland, Capt John Dawson, Inf
CHAPMAN, Joseph, Pvt, Col Samuel Bunch, Capt George McPherson, E TN Mil
CHAPMAN, Joseph, Pvt, Col Samuel Bunch, Capt Jones Griffin, E TN Draft Mil
CHAPMAN, Robert, Pvt, Col N T Perkins, Capt John Doak, Vol Mtd Riflemen
CHAPMAN, Robert, Pvt, Col Samuel Bayless, Capt Jonathan Waddle, E TN Mil
CHAPMAN, Thomas, Pvt, Maj William Woodfolk, Capt James Zeil, Inf
CHAPMAN, William, Pvt, Col Thomas Williamson, Capt Thomas Scurry, Vol Mtd Gunmen; appt asst depy QM Gen
CHAPMAN, William, Pvt, Col William Johnson, Capt Benjamin Powell, E TN Mil
CHAPPEL, Hiram, Pvt, Maj William Woodfolk, Capt Abraham Dudney & Capt John Sutton, Inf
CHAPPELL, James, Pvt, Col William Metcalf, Maj Gen William Carroll, Capt John Jackson, Inf
CHAPPELL, Miles, Pvt, Maj Gen William Carroll, Col William Metcalf, Capt John Jackson, Inf
CHARFER, John N, Pvt, no other information; promoted to Sgt
CHARLES, Anderson, Pvt, Col William Johnson, Capt Benjamin Powell, E TN Mil
CHARLES, John, Pvt, Col William Metcalf, Capt Alexander Hill & Capt John Cunningham, Mil Inf
CHARLES, Oliver, Pvt, Maj William Russell, Capt John Cowan, Vol Mtd Gunmen
CHARLES, Solomon I, Pvt, Maj William Woodfolk, Capt Abner Pearce, Inf
CHARLES, Stephen, Pvt, Maj William Russell, Capt John Cowan, Vol Mtd Gunmen
CHARLES, William B, Pvt, Col William Metcalf, Capt Barbee Collins, Mil Inf
CHARLES, William, Pvt, Col John Brown, Capt John Childs, E TN Vol Mtd Inf
CHARLES, William, Pvt, Col Robert Dyer, Capt Robert Evans, Vol Mtd Gunmen
CHARLETON, Thomas, Pvt, Col William Lillard, Capt Jacob Hartsell, E TN Vol Inf
CHARLOCK, Isaac, Pvt, Maj William Woodfolk, Capt Abner Pearce, Inf
CHARLOCK, Reuben, Pvt, Maj William Woodfolk, Capt Abner Pearce, Inf
CHARLTON, James D, Pvt, Col Alexander Loury, Lt Col Leroy Hammonds, Capt Thomas Wells, Inf; enl US svce
CHARLTON, John K M, Pvt, Col John Williams, Capt David Vance, Mtd Mil
CHARMING, Richard, Pvt, Col S Copeland, Capt G W Stell, Mil Inf
CHARY, John, Pvt, Col Thomas Williamson, Capt James Pace & Capt James Neely, Vol Mtd Gunmen
CHASTEN, Elisha, Pvt, Col John Wynne, Capt John Spinks, Inf
CHASURE, Thornton, Pvt, Col Samuel Bayless, Capt Allen Bacon, TN Mil
CHATMAN, Erasmus, Pvt, Col Robert Steele, Capt John Chitwood, Mil Inf
CHEAK, Elijah, Pvt, Col Edward Bradley, Capt John Moore, Vol Inf
CHEATHAM, Anderson, Sgt Maj, Brig Gen Thomas Robinson, no Co Commander
CHEATHAM, Archer, Col, 2 Regt TN Mil
CHEATHAM, Archer, Lt Col, Mtd Inf of 6 Brig
CHEATHAM, Edmund, Pvt, Col Thomas McCrory, Capt Samuel McKnight, Inf
CHEATHAM, Edward, Pvt, Col Thomas McCrory, Capt Anthony Metcalf, Mil Inf
CHEATHAM, John A, Pvt, Regt Commander omitted, Capt David Smith, Cav Vol
CHEATHAM, John B, Capt, Lt Col John Edmonson, Cav
CHEATHAM, John B, Pvt, Col Newton Cannon, Capt Andrew Patterson, Mtd Riflemen; promoted to Capt in Higgins Regt
CHEATHAM, L P, Paymaster, Col Archer Cheatham, 2 Regt of TN
CHEATHAM, Leonard, Capt, Col J W Edmonson, Cav
CHEATHAM, Richard, Lt Col, no other information
CHEATHAM, Thomas, Lt, Regt Commander omitted, Capt John Crane, Mtd Inf
CHEATHAM, Thomas, Pvt, Col Newton Cannon, Capt Andrew Patterson, Mtd Riflemen
CHEATHAM, Thomas, Pvt, Regt Commander omitted, Capt Archibald McKenney, Cav
CHEATHAM, Thomas, Pvt, no other information
CHEATHAM, ____, Pvt, Regt Commander omitted, Capt Archibald McKenney, Cav

CHEEK, Andrew, Sgt, Col William Johnson, Capt Benjamin Powell, E TN Mil
CHEEK, Chason, Pvt, Col William Lillard, Capt Zacheus Copeland, E TN Vol Inf
CHEEK, Edmund, Cpl, Maj William Woodfolk, Capt James C Weil, Inf
CHEEK, Elijah, 2 Sgt, Col Philip Pipkin, Capt John Strother, Mil Inf
CHEEK, Randolph, Pvt, Col A Loury, Capt J N Williamson, E TN Mil
CHEEK, Randolph, Pvt, Col L Hammonds, Capt Joseph N Williamson, Inf
CHEEK, Robert, Pvt, Col James Raulston, Capt Elijah Haynie, Inf; died 2-20-1815
CHEEK, William H, 2 Lt, Col Philip Pipkin, Capt James Blakemore, Mil Inf
CHEEK, William, 1 Lt, Col T McCrory, Capt A Metcalf, Inf
CHEEK, William, Pvt, Maj Gen Andrew Jackson, Capt John Gordon, Inf
CHEEK, Willis, Pvt, Col William Lillard, Capt Thomas Sharpe, 2 Regt Inf
CHEEKE, Randolph, Pvt, Col I Hammond, Capt J N Williamson, 2 Regt Inf
CHEETWOOD, John, Capt, Col Robert Steele, Mil Inf
CHELTON, James, Pvt, Col Samuel Bunch, Capt Francis Barry, E TN Mil
CHENEY, William, Pvt, Lt Col William Phillips, Co Commander omitted, Inf
CHENNY, John, Cpl, Col James Raulston, Capt Mathew Neal, Inf; promoted to Sgt
CHERRY, Benjamin, 3 Lt, Col William Johnston, Capt James Tunnell, E TN Mil; promoted to 2 Lt
CHERRY, Benjamin, Pvt, Col Edward Bradley, Capt John Kennedy, Riflemen; AWOL
CHERRY, Benjamin, Pvt, Col John Brown, Capt William Christian, E TN Mil Inf
CHERRY, Benjamin, Pvt, Col William Hall, Capt John Kennedy, Vol Inf
CHERRY, Caleb, Pvt, Col Robert Dyer, Capt Robert Evans, Vol Mtd Gunmen
CHERRY, Cary, Pvt, Col Jas Raulston, Capt Henry West, Inf
CHERRY, Elijah, Brig Chap, Brig Gen N Taylor, no other information
CHERRY, Elijah, Chap, Brig Gen N Taylor, no other information
CHERRY, Elijah, Pvt, Col Wm Johnston, Capt Jas Tunnell, E TN Mil; substituted for John Burk, appointed Brig Chap
CHERRY, Ezekiel, 2 Lt, Col Wm Hall, Capt John Wallace, Inf, Res omitted
CHERRY, Harvey, Pvt, Commanders omitted, Mil Inf
CHERRY, Jerred, Pvt, Col Philip Pipkin, Capt Jas Blakemore, Mil Inf
CHERRY, John, Pvt, Col Stephen Copeland, Capt William Evans, Mil Inf
CHERRY, Sam, Pvt, Col John Coffee, Capt Jas Terrell, Vol Cav; out of state
CHERRY, William, Pvt, Col John K Wynne, Capt James Holleman, Inf

CHERRY, William, Pvt, Col Stephen Copeland, Capt William Evans, Mil Inf; sick absent 3-27-1814 at Ft Strother
CHERRY, William, Pvt, Col William Pillow, Capt Thomas Williamson, Vol Inf
CHERRY, Wilson, Pvt, Col Jas Raulston, Capt Henry West, Inf
CHERRY (CHARRY), John, Pvt, Col Thomas Williamson, Capt Pace, Capt Jas Neel, Vol Mtd Gunmen
CHERUM, Guilletone, Pvt, Col Thomas H Benton, Capt George Gibbs, Vol Inf
CHESER, John, Pvt, Col Samuel Wear, Capt Joseph Calloway, Mtd Inf
CHESHER, Baptist, Pvt, Col Wm Lillard, Capt Thomas Sharpe, 2nd Regt Inf
CHESNEY, John, Pvt, Col Samuel Wear, Capt John Bayless, Mtd Inf
CHESNUT, Anderson (Andrew), Pvt, Col William Johnson, Capt Benj Powell, E TN Mil
CHESSER, William, Pvt, Col Wm Metcalf, Capt Hill, Capt John Cunningham, Mil Inf
CHESTER, John, Lt, Col William Lillard, Capt Hugh Martin, E TN Vol Inf, Res omitted
CHESTER, John, Pvt, Col John Cocke, Capt James Gray, Inf; d 1-22-1815
CHESTER, Mark, Pvt, Col William Johnson, Capt Joseph Scott, E TN Drafted Mil
CHESTER, Robert, QM - 1 Lt, Col Samuel Bayless, 4th Regt E TN Mil, Res omitted
CHESTER, Robt, Cpl, Col Samuel Bayless, Capt James Landen, Branch Srvce omitted
CHETHAM, John, Asst Topograph, Maj Gen A Jackson, Co Commander omitted, Div of TN Mil
CHEVERS, Jordon, Pvt, Col Alexander Loury, Capt James Kincaid, Inf
CHICOAH, Thomas, Pvt, no other information
CHIHOLM, Alexander, 3 Cpl, Col John Coffee, Capt Alexander McKeen
CHILCOAT, Jas, Pvt, Col William Pillow, Capt Geo Caperton, Inf
CHILCOAT, Thomas, Pvt, Regt Commander omitted, Capt James Cowan, Inf
CHILCOUT, Jas, Pvt, Col Thomas Benton, Capt Geo Caperton, Vol Inf
CHILCUTT, Peter, Sgt, Maj Wm Woodfolk, Capt James G Neil, Inf
CHILDERS, David, Pvt, Col Wm Lillard, Capt Hugh Martin, E TN Vol Inf; hired a substitute
CHILDERS, Henry, Pvt, Col Samuel Wear, Capt Jesse Cole, Col Inf
CHILDERS, Lindsey, Cpl, Col Edwin Booth, Capt John Lewis, E TN Mil
CHILDERS, Wm, Pvt, Col Wm Pillow, Capt Jas McFerrin, Inf; deserted 11-19-1813
CHILDRESS, Benj, Pvt, Col S Copeland, Capt John Dawson, Inf; sick absent
CHILDRESS, David, Pvt, Regt Commander omitted, Capt Jas Craig, Inf
CHILDRESS, David, Pvt, no other information
CHILDRESS, Edwin H, Pvt, Maj Gen A Jackson, Capt Wm Carroll, Vol Inf

## Enlisted Men, War of 1812

CHILDRESS, Elisha, Pvt, no other information
CHILDRESS, Elishes, Pvt, Regt Commander omitted, Capt David S Deadrick, Arty
CHILDRESS, George, Pvt, Col Samuel Bayless, Capt James Landen, E TN Mil
CHILDRESS, George, Pvt, Col W Metcalf, Capt Barbee Collins, Mil Inf; d 3-24-1815
CHILDRESS, Henry, Pvt, Col Jno Coffee, Capt Chas Kavanaugh, Cav
CHILDRESS, Henry, Pvt, Regt Commander omitted, Capt David Mason, Cav
CHILDRESS, Henry, Pvt, no other information
CHILDRESS, Jas, Pvt, Col S Bunch, Capt Dan'l Yarnell, E TN Mil
CHILDRESS, Jas, Pvt, Maj John Chiles, Capt Chas Conway, E TN Mtd Gunmen; d 3-12-1815, Regimental Co 40-Knox
CHILDRESS, Joel, 5 Cpl, Col John Cocke, Capt Joseph Price, Inf
CHILDRESS, Joel, Pvt, Lt Col Leroy Hammonds, Capt James Craig, Inf
CHILDRESS, John, Pvt, Maj John Childs, Capt Charles Conway, E TN Mtd Gunmen; discharged for inability, Regt Co 4-Knox
CHILDRESS, John, Sgt, Col Ewen Allison, Capt Allen, E TN Mil
CHILDRESS, John, Sgt, Col Samuel Bunch, Capt John English, E TN Drafted Mil; joined from Capt Allen's Co
CHILDRESS, Joseph, Pvt, Col John Cock, Capt John Weakley, Inf
CHILDRESS, Lemuel, Div QM General, Maj Gen Andrew Jackson, Div of TN Mil, Res omitted; resigned 1-31-1814
CHILDRESS, Lemuel, Pvt, Commanders omitted, Branch Srvce omitted; appointed QM
CHILDRESS, Lemuel, Pvt, Regt Commander omitted, Capt D Deaderick, Arty; appointed QM
CHILDRESS, Mitchell, Pvt, Col Robert Dyer, Capt Isaac Williams, Vol Mtd Gunmen
CHILDRESS, Mitchell, Pvt, Col Samuel Wear, Capt John Childs, E TN Vol Inf
CHILDRESS, Nathaniel G, Ens, Col A Cheatham, Capt Birdwell, Inf, Res omitted
CHILDRESS, Nathaniel G, Tptr, Col Robert Dyer, Capt Thomas Jones, Vol Mtd Gunmen; transferred to Capt Donelson's Co
CHILDRESS, Robert, Pvt, Maj John Childs, Capt Reuben Tipton, E TN Vol Mtd Inf; Regimental Co 12th Blount
CHILDRESS, Stephen, Pvt, Col John Brown, Capt John Childs, E TN Vol Mtd Gunmen
CHILDRESS, Thomas C, Pvt, Col John Brown, Capt James Standifer, E TN Vol Mtd Mil
CHILDRESS, Walter, Pvt, Maj John Childs, Capt Reuben Tipton, E TN Vol Mtd Inf; Regimental Co 40th Knox
CHILDRESS, William G, Pvt, Col William Pillow, Capt C H McEwen, Vol Inf; sick absent
CHILDRESS, William, 2 Sgt, Col S Copeland, Capt John Dawson, Inf; sick absent
CHILDRESS, William, Pvt, Col N T Perkins, Capt Mathew Johnson, Mil Inf
CHILDRESS, William, Pvt, Maj John Childs, Capt Reuben Tipton, E TN Vol Mtd Inf; Regimental Co 40th Knox
CHILDRY, Joseph, Pvt, Col John Cocke, Capt Weakley, Inf
CHILES, Edmond, Pvt, Col Edward Bradley, Capt Travis Nash, Vol Inf
CHILES, Edward, Pvt, Col William Hall, Capt Travis Nash, Inf
CHILES, James, Pvt, Col Edwin Booth, Capt John Slatton, E TN Mil
CHILES, John, Capt, Col John Brown, Capt John Childs, E TN Vol Mtd Gunmen, Res omitted
CHILES, John, Capt, Col Samuel Wear, Capt John Chiles, E TN Vol Mtd Inf, Res omitted
CHILES, John, Ens, Col John Williams, Capt William Walker, Vol, Res omitted
CHILES, John, Maj, Commander omitted, E TN Vol Mtd Inf, Res omitted
CHILES, Millington, Pvt, Col William Pillow, Capt Thomas Williamson, Vol Inf
CHILES, Paul, 2 Lt, Maj John Chiles, Capt Charles Conway, E TN Mtd Gunmen, Regimental Co 40 Knox
CHILES, Thomas, Cpl, Col John Brown, Capt John Childs, E TN Vol Mtd Gunmen
CHILTY, Benjamin, Pvt, Maj William Woodfolk, Capt James Turner, Inf
CHISM, Jas, Pvt, Col T McCrory, Capt Abel Willis, Mil Inf; transfer to Capt Russell Spies
CHISM, John, Pvt, Col John Alcorn, Capt John J Winston, Mtd Riflemen
CHISM, John, Pvt, Col N T Perkins, Capt Geo Marr, Mtd Vol
CHISM, John, Pvt, Col T McCrory, Capt Abel Willis, Mil Inf; transfer to Capt Russell Spies
CHISM, Taylor, Pvt, Col John Cocke, Capt John Weakley, Inf
CHISM, Wm, Pvt, Col Philip Pipkin, Capt Ebenezer Kirkpatrick, Mil Inf; deserted
CHISTEN, Mark, Cpl, Col Wm Johnson, Capt Joseph Scott, E TN Drafted Mil
CHISTUM, Jno, Pvt, no other information
CHISUM, Dempsey, Pvt, Col Robert Jarmon, Capt Nathan Peoples, Inf
CHISUM, Guillentine, Pvt, Col Thos H Benton, Capt George W Gibbs, Vol Inf
CHISUM, James, Pvt, Maj Gen A Jackson, Capt Wm Russell, Mtd Spies
CHISUM, James, Pvt, no other information
CHISUM, Jno jr, Pvt, Maj Gen A Jackson, Capt Wm Russell, Mtd Spies
CHISUM, Jno, Pvt, Maj Gen A Jackson, Capt Wm Russell, Mtd Spies
CHISUM, Richard P, Pvt, Col A Loury, Capt Gabriel Martin, Inf
CHISUM, Taylor, Pvt, Col John K Wynne, Capt Bayless E Prince, Inf
CHISUM, Wm, 1 Cpl, Commanders & Branch Srvce omitted; wounded 1-22-1814

- 123

## Enlisted Men, War of 1812

CHISUM, Wm, 1 Cpl, Maj Gen A Jackson, Capt Wm Russell, Mtd Spies; wounded 1-22-1813

CHITWOOD, Mathew, Pvt, Col Thos Williamson, Capt John Doak, Capt John Boddins, Vol Mtd Gunmen; replaced Morgan Clayton

CHITWOOD, Richard, Pvt, Lt Col L Hammonds, Capt Jas Tubb, Inf; furloughed on march to muster out of service

CHOAT, Gidean, Pvt, Col Thomas Williamson, Capt John Crane, Capt James Cook, Vol Mtd Gunmen

CHOAT, Sibert, Pvt, Col Thomas Williamson, Capt John Crane, Capt James Cook, Vol Mtd Gunmen

CHOAT, Valentine, Ffr, Col John Cocke, Capt Richard Crunk, Inf

CHOAT (SHOAT), Austin, Pvt, Col John Cocke, Capt Richard Crunk, Inf

CHOAT (SHOAT), Edward, Pvt, Col John Cocke, Capt Richard Crunk, Inf; d 1-14-1814

CHOAT (SHOAT), Gabriel, Pvt, Col John Cocke, Capt Richard Crunk, Inf; left sick 11-19-1814 & never joined the army

CHOATE, Nicholas, Pvt, Regt Commander omitted, Capt Archibald McKinney, Cav

CHOATE, Silas, Pvt, Col John K Wynne, Capt James Cole, Inf

CHOATE, Thomas, Cor (3 Lt), Lt Col John Edmonson, Cav, Res omitted

CHOLANS, Jonathan, Pvt, Col William Lillard, Capt Jacob Hartsell, E TN Vol Inf

CHOLANS, Joshua, Pvt, Col William Lillard, Capt Jacob Hartsell, E TN Vol Inf

CHORMLEY, John, Pvt, Col Wm Johnson, Capt David McKamy, E TN Drafted Mil; discharged

CHOTE, Nicholas, Pvt, Regt Commander omitted, Capt Archibald, McKenney, Cav

CHOWING, Robt, Pvt, Col Archer Cheatham, Co Commander omitted, Inf

CHOWNING, John, Pvt, Lt Col John Edmonson, Co Commander omitted, Cav

CHOWNING, John, Pvt, no other information

CHRISM, Alex, Cpl, Col John Alcorn, Capt Alexander McKeen, Cav

CHRISMAN, Aaron, Pvt, Col T McCrory, Capt Jas Shannon, Mil Inf

CHRISTIAN, Benjamin, Pvt, Col Booth, Capt Vernon, E TN Mil

CHRISTIAN, Benjamin, Pvt, Regt Commander omitted, Capt Jesse Reany, Mtd Gunmen

CHRISTIAN, James, Pvt, Col Booth, Capt Slatton, E TN Mil

CHRISTIAN, Jas, Cpl, Col R H Dyer, Capt Culbort Hudson, Vol Mtd Gunmen; appointed Cpl from Pvt

CHRISTIAN, John, Pvt, Col William Metcalf, Capt Cunningham, Capt Alexander Hill, Mil Inf

CHRISTIAN, Nathaniel, Pvt, Col Thomas H Benton, Capt Benjamin Reynolds, Vol Inf; refused to march

CHRISTIAN, Nathaniel, Pvt, Col Thomas McCrory, Capt Wm Dooley, Inf

CHRISTIAN, Robt, Pvt, Col Samuel Bunch, Co Commander omitted, E TN Vol Mtd

CHRISTIAN, Thos M, 1 Lt, Col Newton Cannon, Capt John B Dempsey, Mtd Gunmen

CHRISTIAN, Thos, 2 Cpl, Col Wm Lillard, Capt Argenbright, E TN Vol Riflemen

CHRISTIAN, Thos, Pvt, Col Edward Booth, Co Commander omitted, E TN Mil

CHRISTIAN, William, Capt, Col Jno Brown, E TN Mil Inf, Res omitted

CHRISTIAN, Wm, Pvt, Col Ed W Booth, Capt Vernon, E TN Mil

CHRISTOPHER, John, Pvt, Col John Williams, Capt David Vance, Mtd Mil

CHRISTOPHER, John, Pvt, Col Robert Steele, Capt Samuel Maxwell, Mil Inf

CHRISTOPHER, Mathias, Pvt, Commanders & Branch Srvce omitted; enlisted in 3rd Regt US Infantry

CHRISTOPHER, Mathias, Pvt, Gen Andrew Jackson, Capt Nathan Davis, Inf

CHRISTY, Wm, Pvt, Col A Cheatham, Capt Richard Benson, Inf

CHUM, Wm, Pvt, Col Edward Bradley, Capt Thos B Hanie, Vol Inf

CHUMBLEY, Jos, Far, Col Jno Coffee, Capt Fredrick Stump, Cav

CHUN, Wm, Pvt, Col Wm Hall, Capt Henry M Newlin, Inf

CHUNING, Jesse, Sgt, Col S Bunch, Lt Jno Harris, E TN Mil; sick absent on command Ft Williams

CHURCH, Abram, Pvt, Col Wm Hall, Capt Henry M Newlin, Inf; refused to appear

CHURCH, Asa, Tptr, Col N Cannon, Capt Williams, Mtd Riflemen

CHURCH, George, Pvt, Col Ewen Allison, Capt Jonas Loughmiller, Mil; furloughed to drive his own wagon

CHURCH, George, Pvt, Col Samuel Bunch, Capt Jas Cummings, E TN Vol Mtd Inf

CHURCHILL, John, Pvt, Maj Gen Wm Carroll, Col Wm Metcalf, Capt John Jackson, Inf; d 2-4-1815

CHURCHMAN, Edward, Pvt, Col Samuel Wear, Capt Joseph Calloway, Mtd Inf

CHURCHMAN, Jas, Capt, Col S Bayless, Capt Jas Churchman, E TN Mil, Res omitted

CHURCHMAN, John, Pvt, Col Wm Lillard, Capt Thos McChristian, E TN Vol Inf

CHURCHMAN, Jos, Pvt, Col Samuel Bayless, Capt Jas Churchman, E TN Mil

CHURCHMAN, Stephen, Pvt, Col Samuel Bayless, Capt Jas Churchman, E TN Mil; transferred from Capt Milliken's Co

CHURCHMAN, Stephen, Pvt, Col Wm Johnson, Capt Elihu Milliken, 3rd Regt E TN Mil; transferred to Capt Churchman's Co

CHURCHMAN, Stephen, Sgt, Col Wm Johnson, Capt Jas Milliken, 3rd Regt E TN Mil

CHURCHWELL, John, Pvt, Col John Cocke, Capt James Gault, Inf

CHURCHWELL, John, Pvt, Col R C Napier, Capt John Chism, Mil Inf; on furlough

CHURCHWELL, John, Pvt, Col Wm Hall, Capt Henry M Newlin, Inf; deserted from camp

CHURCHWELL, John, Pvt, Maj Wm Woodfolk, Capt

## Enlisted Men, War of 1812

James C Neil, Inf
CHURCHWELL, William, Pvt, Col Robert H Dyer, Capt Jas McMahan, 1st TN Mtd Vol Gunmen
CHURCHWELL, Wm, Pvt, Col N T Perkins, Capt Jas McMahan, Mtd Gunmen
CIMBROUGH, Elisha, Pvt, Col Wm Johnson, Capt Henry Hunter, E TN Mil; transferred from Capt Millikan's Co
CIMBROUGH, M D, Pvt, Col Edward Bradley, Capt Wm Lauderdale, Vol Inf
CINKS, Jesse, Pvt, Col John Cocke, Capt Joseph Price, Inf
CIRUS, Burnett, Pvt, Regt Commander omitted, Capt Jas Terrill, Cav
CLABAUGH, John, Pvt, Col Wm Lillard, Capt John Roper, E TN Vol Inf
CLABES, William, Sgt, no other information
CLABS, Wm, Pvt, Col Wm Metcalf, Capt Alexander Hill, Capt John Cunningham, Mil Inf
CLACK, John jr, Pvt, Regt Commander omitted, Capt Wm Henderson, Spies
CLACK, John, Pvt, Regt Commander omitted, Capt Jas Anderson, Branch Srvce omitted
CLACKSON, John, 3 Cpl, Brig Gen Thos Johnson, Capt Robert Carson, Inf
CLACKSON, Raleigh, Pvt, Regt Commander omitted, Capt Jas Anderson, Branch Srvce omitted
CLACKSTON, Jonathan, 3 Sgt, Col N Cannon, Capt John B Demsey, Mtd Gunmen
CLAIBORN, Thos, 1 Lt & De Camp, Brig Gen Thos Johnson, W TN Mil, Res omitted; on furlough
CLAIMAN, Geo, Pvt, Col Wm Lillard, Capt Hugh Martin, E TN Vol Inf
CLAIMAN, John, Pvt, Col Wm Lillard, Capt Hugh Martin, E TN Vol Inf
CLAIR (ST CLAIR), Wm, Pvt, Col William Hall, Capt John Kennedy, Vol Inf
CLANA, Robert Y, Pvt, Col Samuel Wear, Capt John Childs, E TN Vol Inf
CLANAHAN, Jos, Pvt, Col Samuel Bunch, Capt Samuel Richardson, E TN Drafted Mil; discharged 5-18-1814
CLANCEY, Cornelious, Pvt, Col Robert Steele, Capt Jas Bennete, Mil Inf
CLANHAN, Matthew, Lt, Capt Robert Evans, Mtd Spies, Res omitted
CLANSEN (CLOSSIN), Josiah, Cpl, Col William Lillard, Capt Robert McCalpin, E TN Mil Inf
CLARDY, Abraham, Pvt, Maj William Russell, Capt Isaac Williams, TN Mtd Gunmen
CLARDY, Jas, Pvt, Maj William Russell, Capt Isaac Williams, TN Vol Mtd Gunmen
CLARDY, Richard, Pvt, Maj William Russell, Capt Isaac Williams, Vol Mtd Gunmen
CLARK, Absolom, Ens, Col R C Napier, Capt Jas Gray, Mil Inf, Res omitted; sick absent 5-6-1814
CLARK, Alijah, Pvt, Regt Commander omitted, Capt Edward Neblett, Mil Inf; on furlouh 4-28-1814 & absent
CLARK, Amos, Pvt, Col Samuel Booth, Capt Porter, Drafted Mil
CLARK, Andrew, Pvt, Col N Cannon, Capt Jas Walton, Mtd Riflemen
CLARK, Andrew, Pvt, Maj Gen Jackson, Col Williamson, Capt Robert Steele, Vol Mtd Gunmen
CLARK, Archibald, 1 Lt, Col Thomas Williamson, Capt Crane, Capt Christopher Cook, Vol Mtd Gunmen, Res omitted
CLARK, Archibald, 2 Lt, Maj Gen John Cocke, TN Vol Mtd Gunmen, Res omitted
CLARK, Archibald, Pvt, Col A Cheatham, Capt Geo G Chapman, Inf
CLARK, Archibald, Pvt, Col John Coffee, Capt David Smith, Vol Cav
CLARK, Archibald, Pvt, Lt Col A Cheatham, Co Commander omitted, Mtd Inf
CLARK, Archibald, Pvt, no other information
CLARK, Barnes (Barnhill), Blksmth, Col Jon Coffee, Capt Robert Jetton, Cav
CLARK, Benj, 3 Sgt, Col John Cocke, Capt John Weakley, Inf
CLARK, Benj, Pvt, Col A Cehatham, Capt Geo G Chapman, Inf
CLARK, Benj, Pvt, Col John K Wynne, Capt Bayless E Prince, Inf
CLARK, Benj, Pvt, Col Thomas Williamson, Capt Thomas Scurry, Vol Mtd Gunmen
CLARK, Benj, Pvt, Lt Col Richardson Napier, Co Commander omitted, Inf
CLARK, Benj, Pvt, no other information
CLARK, Bolin, Pvt, Col A Cheatham, Capt James Giddens, Inf
CLARK, Chas, Pvt, Col Thomas Benton, Capt Isaiah Renshaw, Vol Inf
CLARK, Daniel, Pvt, Regt Commander omitted, Capt David Smith, Vol Cav
CLARK, Daniel, Sgt, Col Thomas Williamson, Capt Jas Cook, Capt Crane, Vol Mtd Gunmen
CLARK, David, Lt, Col S Copeland, Capt Alexander Provine, Mil Inf, Res omitted
CLARK, David, Pvt, Regt Commander omitted, Capt David Smith, Cav
CLARK, Davis, Pvt, Col S Copeland, Capt John Holshouser, Inf
CLARK, Edward, Pvt, Maj William Woodfolk, Capt James C Neil, Inf
CLARK, Elijah, Pvt, Col John Cocke, Capt Joseph Price, Inf
CLARK, Elisha B, 1st Mate, Col Philip Pipkin, Co Commander omitted, 1st Regt TN Mil; resigned 10-13-1814
CLARK, Geo, Pvt, Col William Johnston, Capt Henry Hunter, E TN Mil
CLARK, Gettin, Pvt, Regt Commander omitted, Capt J Prewitt, Mtd Vol
CLARK, Henry, Pvt, Col John Cocke, Capt Samuel Caruthers, Inf
CLARK, Isaac, Cpl, Col Samuel Bayless, Capt Joseph Bacon, E TN Mil
CLARK, Isaac, Pvt, Col Samuel Bunch, Capt Geo Gregory, E TN Drafted Mil
CLARK, Isaac, Pvt, Col Samuel Bunch, Capt John Inman, E TN Mtd Inf

CLARK, Isaac, Pvt, Regt Commander omitted, Capt Geo Smith, Spies
CLARK, James, Pvt, Col Samuel Bunch, Capt Priter, Drafted Mil
CLARK, James, Pvt, Lt Col A Cheatham, Co Commander omitted, Mtd Inf
CLARK, James, Pvt, Regt Commander omitted, Capt Lane Garrett, Mtd Riflemen
CLARK, Jas, Cpl, Col John K Wynne, Capt William Wilson, Inf
CLARK, Jas, Pvt, Col John K Wynne, Capt John Porter, Inf
CLARK, Jas, Pvt, Col Philip Pipkin, Capt Blakemore, Mil Inf
CLARK, Jas, Pvt, Col Samuel Bunch, Capt Andrew Breden, E TN Mil
CLARK, Jas, Pvt, Col William Johnson, Capt Benj Powell, Branch Srvce omitted; d 11-13-1814
CLARK, Jas, Pvt, Col William Johnson, Capt Benj Powell, E TN Mil; sick absent
CLARK, Jas, Pvt, no other information
CLARK, Jno, Pvt, Col John Brown, Capt Wm Christian, E TN Mil Inf
CLARK, Jno, Pvt, Lt Col A Cheatham, Co Commander omitted, Mtd Inf
CLARK, John G, Pvt, Col Philip Pipkin, Capt John Strother, Inf; appointed Cpl
CLARK, John T, Pvt, Col Wm Johnson, Capt Andrew Lawson, E TN Drafted Mil
CLARK, John W, Sgt, Col Thomas Williamson, Capt Thomas Scurry, Vol Mtd Gunmen
CLARK, John, 1 Lt, Brig Gen Thos Johnson, Capt Robert Carson, Inf, Res omitted
CLARK, John, 1 Sgt, Col N T Perkins, Capt John Doak, Mtd Vol Riflemen
CLARK, John, Pvt, Col John K Wynne, Capt Bayless Prince, Vol Inf
CLARK, John, Pvt, Col Samuel Bayless, Capt Joseph Rich, E TN Inf
CLARK, John, Pvt, Col Samuel Wear, Capt Jesse Cole, Vol Inf
CLARK, John, Pvt, Col Samuel Wear, Capt John Chiles, E TN Vol Inf
CLARK, John, Pvt, Col William Higgins, Capt Stephen Griffith, Mtd Riflemen; sick, AWOL
CLARK, John, Pvt, Col William Johnson, Capt Andrew Lawson, E TN Drafted Mil
CLARK, John, Pvt, Maj John Childs, Capt Jas Cunningham, E TN Mtd Inf
CLARK, Jonn E, Pvt, Col N T Perkins, Capt Mathew Patterson, Mtd Vol
CLARK, Josiah (Joshua), Pvt, Col John Cock, Capt Gray, Inf
CLARK, Mark, Pvt, Col N T Perkins, Co Commander omitted, Mil Inf
CLARK, Nathan, Pvt, Regt Commander omitted, Capt David Smith, Cav Vol
CLARK, Reuben, Pvt, Col John Cocke, Co Commander omitted, Inf
CLARK, Richard, Pvt, Col John Cocke, Capt Wm Caruthers, Inf; d 2-14-1815
CLARK, Robt, Pvt, Maj Gen Andrew Jackson, Col Thomas Williamson, Capt Robt Steele, Branch Srvce omitted
CLARK, Robt, Sgt, Col Newton Cannon, Capt Thomas Yardley, Mtd Riflemen
CLARK, Silas, Pvt, Col James Raulston, Capt Henry West, Inf
CLARK, Thomas C, 2 Maj, Commander omitted, E TN Vol, Res omitted
CLARK, Thos C, 1 Maj, Col Sam'l Bunch, E TN Mil, Res omitted
CLARK, Thos C, Lt Col, Col Wm Johnson, E TN Mil 3rd Regt; replaced Lt Col John Anderson
CLARK, Thos, Pvt, Col Edwin Booth, Capt Vernon, E TN Mil
CLARK, Thos, Pvt, Col Robert Steele, Capt James Randals, Inf
CLARK, Thos, Pvt, Col William Higgins, Capt Stephen Griffith, Mtd Riflemen; sick AWOL
CLARK, Walter, Lt, Col S Bunch, Capt James Penny, E TN Mtd Inf, Res omitted
CLARK, Walter, Pvt, Col S Bunch, Capt F Register, E TN Mil; appointed Sgt Maj
CLARK, Walter, Sgt Maj, Col Ewin Allison, Co Commander omitted, E TN Mil
CLARK, Watson, Pvt, Col T McCrory, Capt Thomas K Gordon, Inf
CLARK, William, Cpl, Col William Johnson, Capt James Stewart, E TN Mil Drafted
CLARK, William, Pvt, Col S Bayless, Capt Joseph B Bacon, E TN Mil
CLARK, Willis C, Pvt, Col John Coffee, Capt James Terrill, Vol Cav; d 1-31-1813
CLARK, Wm C, Pvt, Col Jno Coffee, Capt Frederick Stump, Cav
CLARK, Wm, 3 Sgt, Col William Hall, Capt Travis C Nash, Inf
CLARK, Wm, Pvt, Col W Metcalf, Capt Alexander Hill, Mil Inf
CLARKE, Andrew, Pvt, Col James Raulston, Capt Mathew Neal, Inf; d 3-15-1815
CLARKE, Eli, Pvt, Col William Lillard, Capt Thomas Sharpe, 2nd Regt E TN Inf; hired a substitute Thos Stafford
CLARKE, Getlin, Pvt, no other information
CLARKE, Isaac, Pvt, Col S Bunch, Capt Geo Gregory, E TN Drafted Mil; discharged for inability
CLARKE, Levi, Pvt, Col William Lillard, Capt Thomas Sharpe, 2nd Regt Inf; discharged by order of Col Lillard
CLARKE, Richard, Pvt, Col S Copeland, Capt Wilkinson, Mil Inf
CLARKE, Wm, Pvt, Col N T Perkins, Capt Mathew Johnston, Mil Inf
CLARKE, Wm, Pvt, Col William Lillard, Capt Thomas Sharpe, 2nd Regt Inf
CLARKSON, Aquilla, Pvt, Col Jno Brown, Capt Hugh Barton, Regt E TN Mil Inf
CLARKSTON, Jas, Pvt, Col S Bunch, Capt Francis Berry, E TN Mil; AWOL 2-1-1814
CLARY, Elisha, Pvt, Col James Raulston, Capt Daniel

## Enlisted Men, War of 1812

Newman, Inf
CLARY, John, Cpl, Col S Copeland, Capt David Williams, Mil Inf
CLARY, John, Pvt, Col William Johnson, Capt Elihu Milliken, 3rd Regt E TN Mil; transferred to Capt Churchman Co
CLARY, Spencer, Pvt, Col Thomas Benton, Capt William J Smith, Vol Inf
CLARY, Spencer, Pvt, Col Thomas Williamson, Capt Thomas Scurry, Vol Mtd Gunmen
CLARY, Spencer, Pvt, Col William Pillow, Capt William J Smith, Inf
CLARY, Thos M, Pvt, Col Jno Williams, Capt David Vance, Mtd Mil
CLARY, Wm, Pvt, Col Thomas Williamson, Capt Robert Moore, Vol Mtd Gunmen; d 2-24-1815
CLARY, Zachariah, Cpl or Pvt, Col S Bunch, Capt Geo Gregory, E TN Drafted Mil; discharged for inability
CLASS, Solomon, Pvt, Col Samuel Wear, Capt Daniel Price, E TN Vol Inf
CLATON, Frederick, Pvt, Col Jno Coffee, Capt Frederick Stump, Cav
CLATON, Henry, Pvt, Col L Hammonds, Capt J N Williamson, Inf; sick
CLAXTON, Jas, Pvt, Col S Bayless, Capt John Brock, E TN Mil; d 2-11-1815
CLAXTON, John, Pvt, Col John Brown, Capt Jesse G Reany, Mtd Gunmen
CLAY, John, Pvt, Maj Gen Wm Carroll, Col T Metcalf, Capt John Jackson, Inf
CLAY, Jonathan, Pvt, Col Wm Metcalf, Capt John Barnhart, Mil Inf
CLAY, Mark, Pvt, Col William Pillow, Capt Thomas Williamson, Vol Inf
CLAY, Woody, Pvt, Col William Pillow, Capt Thomas Williamson, Vol Inf
CLAYBORN, Ephraim, Pvt, Col Edwin Booth, Capt John Lewis, E TN Mil
CLAYBROOK, Levi, Pvt, Col Philip Pipkin, Ens Wm Pegram, W TN Mil; detachment of Capt David Smyth Co
CLAYBROOKS, Levi, Pvt, Col Philip Pipkin, Capt William Mackay, Mil Inf
CLAYMORE, Phillip, Pvt, Col Samuel Bayless, Capt Joseph Rick, E TN Inf; transferred to Capt Churchman's Co
CLAYTON, Baze, Pvt, Col Alexander Loury, Capt John Looney, W TN Inf
CLAYTON, Bazye, Pvt, Col R C Napier, Capt John Chism, Mil Inf
CLAYTON, Dan'l, Pvt, Col Samuel Bayless, Capt Jonathan Waddell, E TN Mil
CLAYTON, Elijah, Pvt, Col William Johnson, Capt Benjamin Powell, E TN Mil
CLAYTON, Henry, Pvt, Col A Loury, Capt J N Williamson, W TN Mil
CLAYTON, Henry, Pvt, Col L Hammond, Capt J N Williamson, 2nd Regt Inf
CLAYTON, John, Pvt, Col Alexander Loury, Capt John Looney, 2nd Regt W TN Mil

CLAYTON, Morgan, Pvt, Col Thos Williamson, Capt John Doak, Vol Mtd Inf
CLAYTON, Osten, Cpl, Col Samuel Bayless, Capt Joseph B Bacon, E TN Mil
CLAYTON, Richard, Pvt, Col Jas Raulston, Capt Mathew Neal, Inf
CLAYTON, Robert, Pvt, Regt Commander omitted, Capt Archibold McKinney, Cav
CLAYTON, Stephen, Pvt, Col Thos Williamson, Capt John Doak, Vol Mtd Gunmen
CLAYTON, Wm, Pvt, Col Jno Coffee, Capt Alexander McKeen, Cav
CLAYTON, Wm, Pvt, Col Philip Pipkin, Capt Peter Searcy, Mil Inf; Edward Pickett substitute deserted
CLEAK, Jacob, Pvt, Col Ewen Allison, Capt Jonas Loughmiller, Mil
CLEAR, Henry, Pvt, Maj John Childs, Capt Daniel Price, E TN Mtd Inf Vol
CLEAR, Henry, Pvt, Maj John Childs, Capt Daniel Price, Vol Mtd Gunmen
CLEAVELAND, Milton, Pvt, Col Philip Pipkin, Capt Jas Blakemore, Vol Inf
CLEAVELAND, Oliver, Pvt, Regt Commander omitted, Capt Nathan Farmer, Mtd Riflemen
CLEAVES, Wm, Col Jno Coffee, Capt Fredrick Stump, Cav
CLEAVLAND, Carter H, Pvt, Regt Commander omitted, Capt Nathan Farmer, Mtd Riflemen
CLEEK, Adam, Pvt, Col S Bunch, Capt Geo Gregory, E TN Drafted Mil; substitute for Peter Cleek
CLEEK, Adam, Pvt, Col S Bunch, Capt Jno English, E TN Drafted Mil; from Capt Gregory Co, furloughed for bad health
CLEEK, John, Pvt, Col Samuel Wear, Col S Bunch, Capt Wm Mitchell, E TN Mtd Inf
CLEEK, Peter, Pvt, Col S Bunch, Capt Geo Gregory, E TN Drafted Mil; furnished a substitute, Adam Cleek
CLEMENS, Christopher, Ens, Col Robert Steele, Capt Jas Bennett, Mil Inf, Res omitted; on furlough
CLEMENTS, C, Pvt, Col Wm Pillow, Capt Thos Williamson, Vol Inf
CLEMENTS, Curtis, Pvt, Col Thos Benton, Capt Thos Williamson, Vol Inf
CLEMENTS, Edward, 1 Lt, Col Wm Y Higgins, Capt Thos Eldridge, Mtd Gunmen, Res omitted
CLEMMONS, Curtis, Pvt, Col Wm Metcalf, Capt Wm Mullins, Mil Inf
CLEMMONS, Isaac, Pvt, Regt Commander omitted, Capt David S Deadrick, Arty
CLEMMONS, Jas, Pvt, Col Jno Coffee, Capt Blackman Coleman, Cav
CLEMONS, Arthur, Pvt, Maj Wm Woodfolk, Capt Ezekial Ross, Inf
CLEMONS, Curtis, Pvt, Col Wm Metcalf, Capt Wm Mullins, Mil Inf
CLEMONS, John, Pvt, Col John Alcorn, Capt Alexander McKeen, Cav
CLENDENEN, John, Ens, Col S Bunch, Capt John Inman, E TN Vol Mtd Inf, Res omitted
CLENDENEN, William, Pvt, Col William Lillard, Capt

- 127

## Enlisted Men, War of 1812

James Lillard, E TN Inf Vol

CLENDENING, Anthony, 2 Lt, Col Wm Hall, Capt Abraham Bledsoe, Vol Inf, Res omitted

CLENDENING, Thos, Pvt, Col Thos Williamson, Capt Thos Scurry, Vol Mtd Gunmen; d 1-31-1815

CLENTON, Henry, Cpl, Col Alexander Loury, Capt James Kincaid, Inf; transferred to Artif returned to ranks as Pvt

CLENTON, Isaac, Pvt, Col Alexander Loury, Capt James Kincaid, Inf

CLEPPER, David, Pvt, Col William Lillard, Capt William Gillenwater, E TN Inf

CLERK, Benjamin, Pvt, Maj Gen William Carroll, Col James Raulston, Capt Edward Robinson, Inf

CLEVELAND, John, Pvt, Col William Metcalf, Capt John Barnhart, Mil Inf; deserted 11-19-1814

CLEVELAND, William, Ens, Col William Hall, Capt Brice Martin, Vol Inf, Res omitted

CLEVENGER, Elias, Pvt, Col Samuel Bunch, Capt John English, E TN Drafted Mil; furloughed from Ft Strother for inability

CLEVENGER, Samuel, Pvt, Col Samuel Bunch, Capt William Jobe, E TN Vol Mtd Inf

CLEVENGER, Zacharia, Pvt, Col William Lillard, Capt James Lillard, E TN Mil Inf Vol

CLEVINGER, Elias, Pvt, Col Ewen Allison, Capt Allen, E TN Mil; discharged at Ft Strother

CLEVINGER, Jesse, Pvt, Col Samuel Bayless, Capt Branch Jones, E TN Drafted Mil

CLEVINGER, Richard, Pvt, Col Ewen Allison, Capt Allen, E TN Mil; discharged

CLICK, George, Pvt, Col Samuel Bunch, Capt Francis Register, E TN Mil; deserted 3-4-1814

CLICK, Henry, Pvt, Col William Lillard, Capt Jacob Hartsell, E TN Vol Inf

CLICK, Henry, Pvt, Regt Commander omitted, Capt Sam Bunch, Branch Srvce omitted

CLICK, Lewis, Tptr, Maj William Russell, Capt John Cowan, Vol Mtd Riflemen

CLICK, Mathias, 3 Cpl, Col Samuel Bunch, Capt James Cummings, E TN Vol Mtd Gunmen

CLICK, Mathias, Pvt, Col Edwin Booth, Capt John Slatton, E TN Mil

CLICK, Michael, Pvt, Col William Metcalf, Capt Andrew Patterson, Mil Inf

CLIFT, Bejamin D, Drm Maj, Col Samuel Bunch, Co Commander omitted, E TN Mil; deserted 3-4-1814

CLIFT, Benj D, Pvt, Col S Bunch, Capt Dan'l Yarnell, E TN Mil; deserted

CLIFT, Benj D, Pvt, Col Samuel Bunch, Capt Joseph Duncan, E TN Drafted Mil; joined from Capt Yarnell's Co

CLIFT, Benjamin B, Pvt, Regt Commander omitted, Capt Yarnell, Branch Srvce omitted

CLIFT, Jas, Pvt, Col Edwin Booth, Capt John Sharp, E TN Mil

CLIFT, Jesse, Pvt, Col T McCrory, Capt Jno Reynolds, Mil Inf

CLIFT, John, Pvt, Maj William Woodfolk, Capt James C Neil, Inf

CLIFTEN, Alexander, Sgt, Col A Cheatham, Capt William Creel, Inf; transferred to Arty

CLIFTEN, Jesse, Pvt, Col William Johnson, Capt Elihu Milliken, 3rd Regt E TN Mil

CLIFTON, Alex H, Pvt, Gen Andrew Jackson, Capt Joel Parrish, Branch Srvce omitted

CLIFTON, Ezekiel T, Sgt, Maj William Carroll, Capt Lewis Dillahunty, Capt Daniel M Bradford, Vol Inf; reduced to ranks

CLIFTON, Harry C, Pvt, Col Thomas Williamson, Capt George Mitchie, 2nd Regt TN Vol Mtd Gunmen

CLIFTON, Harry, 3 Sgt, Maj William Russell, Capt George Mitchie, Vol Mtd Gunmen

CLIFTON, Henry, Pvt, Col S Copeland, Capt Moses Thompson, Inf; on furlough since 3-4-1814

CLIFTON, Jesse, Pvt Col S Bunch, Capt Jno Houk, E TN Mil

CLIFTON, Sam'l, Pvt, Col S Bunch, Capt S Roberson, E TN Drafted Mil

CLIFTON, Sam'l, Pvt, Regt Commander omitted, Capt Sam'l Richardson, E TN Drafted Mil; deserted 4-11-1814

CLIFTON, Thos, Pvt, Col Thomas Williamson, Capt Beverly Williams, Vol Mtd Gunmen

CLIFTON, Turner, Pvt, Col S Copeland, Capt Moses Thompson, Inf; on furlough since 3-4-1814

CLIFTON, Turner, Pvt, Maj William Russell, Capt George Mitchie, Vol Mtd Gunmen

CLIFTON, William, Pvt, Col John Alcorn, Capt Thomas Bradley, Vol Cav

CLIFTON, Wm, Pvt, Col Thomas Williamson, Capt Beverly Williams, Vol Mtd Gunmen

CLIMER, Aaron, Pvt, Col John Wynne, Capt John Spinks, Inf

CLIMER, Thos, Pvt, Regt Commander omitted, Capt Jas Craig, Inf

CLIMORE, Eleam, Pvt, Col Samuel Bayless, Capt James Churchman, E TN Mil

CLIMORE, Elkany, Pvt, Col S Bunch, Capt Francis Berry, E TN Mil

CLIMORE, Jas, Pvt, Col S Bunch, Capt Geo Gregory, E TN State Mil; transferred to Capt Francis Berry Co

CLIMORE, Jos, Pvt, Col Samuel Bunch, Capt Francis Berry, E TN Mil

CLIMORE, Phillip, Pvt, Col S Bunch, Capt Francis Berry, E TN Mil

CLIMORE, Phillip, Pvt, Col Samuel Bayless, Capt James Churchman, E TN Mil; d 4-22-1815

CLINARD, Henry, Pvt, Maj Gen A Jackson, Col A Cheatham, Capt William Creel, Inf

CLINARD, Lawrence, Cpl, Regt Commander omitted, Capt Jno Crane, Mtd Inf

CLINARD, Lawrence, Pvt, Lt Col A Cheatham, Co Commander omitted, Mtd Inf

CLINDINING, Anthony, 2 Lt, Col Edward Bradley, Capt Abraham Bledsoe, Riflemen, Res omitted

CLINDINING, Anthony, 2 Sgt, Col Edward Bradley, Capt Abraham Bledsoe, Riflemen, Res omitted

CLINE, John, Pvt, Col Samuel Wear, Capt Daniel Price, E TN Vol Inf

## Enlisted Men, War of 1812

CLINE, John, Pvt, Col William Johnston, Capt James Tunnell, E TN Mil; and never returned

CLINE, John, Pvt, Lt Col L Hammonds, Capt Arahel Rains, Inf; joined by transfer from Capt Wells Co

CLINE, John, Pvt, Lt Col Leroy Hammonds, Capt Thomas Wells, Inf; transferred to W Winston Rains

CLINE, Sam'l, Pvt, Col William Lillard, Capt Thomas McChristian, E TN Vol Inf

CLINE, Wm, Pvt, Col S Bunch, Capt Francis Berry, E TN Mil

CLINGAN, Geo W, Tptr, Regt Commander omitted, Capt David Smith, Cav

CLINGAN, John P, Pvt, Col William Lillard, Capt Jacob Hartsell, E TN Vol Inf; a wagoner for US Service

CLINGAN, Wm, Pvt, Col William Johnson, Capt Henry Hunter, E TN Mil; d 11-30-1814, substituted Thos Gill

CLINGAN, Wm, Pvt, Col William Lillard, Capt Thomas Sharpe, 2nd Regt Inf

CLINGHAM, Geo, Pvt, Col Samuel Bayless, Capt Jonathan Waddell, E TN Mil

CLINGINBEARD, Robt, Pvt, Col S Wear, Col S Bunch, Capt William Mitchell, E TN Mtd Inf

CLINGING, Thos, Pvt, Col S Bayless, Capt John Brock, E TN Mil; substituted John Harris 11-13-1814

CLINNARD, Lawrence, Pvt, no other information

CLINTON, Jas, Pvt, Col William Pillow, Capt Thomas Williamson, Vol Inf

CLINTON, John, Pvt, Col Newton Cannon, Capt Andrew Patterson, Mtd Riflemen

CLIPPER, Frederick, Pvt, Regt Commander omitted, Capt David Smith, Cav Vol

CLOEN, Wm, Pvt, Col James Raulston, Capt Mathew Neal, Inf

CLOUD, Jacob, Pvt, Col Wm Lillard, Capt Wm Hamilton, E TN Vol Inf; substitute for Jas House

CLOUSE, Aaron, Pvt, Col Ewin Allison, Capt Henry McCray, E TN Mil; transferred from Capt Hampton's Co

CLOUSE, Christian, Pvt, Col Wm Johnson, Capt Christopher Cook, E TN Mil

CLOUSE, Christian, Pvt, Col Wm Johnston, Capt Joseph Kirk, Mil Inf

CLOWERS, Daniel, Cpl, Col Wm Lillard, Capt Thos Sharpe, 2nd Regt Inf

CLOWERS, James, Pvt, Col Wm Lillard, Capt Thos Sharpe, 2nd Regt Inf

CLOWN, Wm, Pvt, Col Ewen Allison, Capt John Hampton, Mil

CLOWS, Aaron, Pvt, Col Ewen Allison, Capt Hampton, Mil Inf; transferred to Capt McCrea's Co

CLOYD, Jas B, Pvt, Col Ewen Allison, Capt Henry McCray, E TN Mil

CLOYD, John, Pvt, Col Wm Lillard, Capt Jacob Hartsell, E TN Vol Inf

CLOYD, Philip, Pvt, Col Thos McCrory, Capt Isaac Patton, Mil Inf; sick absent

CLOYD, Samuel, Pvt, Col Ewen Allison, Capt Henry McCray, E TN Mil

CLOYD, Stephen, Pvt, Col Philip Pipkin, Capt John Robertson, Mil Inf

CLUMER, Thos, Pvt, no other information

CLUTS, Andrew, Pvt, Col John Brown, Capt John Childs, E TN Vol Mtd Inf

CLYATT, Samuel, Pvt, Regt Commander omitted, Capt Sam Bunch, Branch Srvce omitted

CLYNARD, John, Pvt, Col Thos Williamson, Capt John Crane, Capt Jas Cook, Vol Mtd Gunmen

CLYNE, Adam, Pvt, Col Wm Hall, Capt Wm L Alexander, Vol Inf

CLYNES, Jacob D, Pvt, Col John Coffee, Capt David Smith, Vol Cav; dead

COAGIL, Martin, Pvt, Col Thomas Benton, Capt Henry Douglass, Vol Inf

COAL, Abraham, Pvt, Col Thomas McCrory, Capt Thomas Gordon, Inf; deserted 11-18-1813

COAL, John, Pvt, Col Thomas McCrory, Capt Thomas Gordon, Inf; deserted 11-18-1813

COAL, Joshua, Pvt, Col Samuel Bunch, Capt John English, E TN Drafted Mil; joined from Capt Gibbs Co

COAL, Joshua, Pvt, Col Samuel Bunch, Capt N Gibbs, E TN Drafted Mil; transferred to Capt English Co

COALE, James (Joseph), Pvt, Col Thomas Williamson, Capt John Crane, Capt James Cook, Vol Mtd Gunmen

COALE, Stephen, Pvt, Col Thomas Williamson, Capt John Crane, Capt James Cook, Vol Mtd Gunmen; dismissed from service

COALE, Temple, Pvt, Col Thomas Williamson, Capt John Crane, Capt James Cook, Vol Mtd Gunmen; d 2-22-1815

COALSON, William, Pvt, Col John Cocke, Capt James Gray, Inf

COAR, Jonathan, Pvt, Col John Coffee, Capt Charles Kavanauh, Cav; AWOL

COATES, Barton, Pvt, Col A Cheatham, Capt Richard Benson, Inf

COATES, James, Cpl, Col Thomas Benton, Capt William Moore, Vol Inf

COATES, Lesly, Pvt, Col John Williams, Capt David Vance, Mtd Mil

COATES, William, Sgt, Regt Commander omitted, Capt Nathan Davis, Branch Srvce omitted

COATS, Benjamin, Pvt, Col Samuel Bayless, Capt Joseph Rich, E TN Inf

COATS, Christopher, Pvt, Col Ewen Allison, Capt Jonas Loughmiller, Mil

COATS, David, Pvt, Col John Brown, Capt John Childs, E TN Vol Mtd Gunmen

COATS, Henry (Kinsey), Pvt, Col Samuel Wear, Capt Joseph Calloway, Mtd Inf

COATS, James, 2 Cpl, Col Thomas Benton, Capt William Moore, Vol Inf

COATS, James, 3 Cpl, Maj Gen William Carroll, Col James Raulston, Capt Edward Robinson, Inf

COATS, James, Cpl, Col Thomas Benton, Capt William Moore, Vol Inf

COATS, James, Pvt, Col John Brown, Capt John Childs, E TN Vol Mtd Gunmen

COBB, Howel, Pvt, Col William Johnson, Capt Elihu Milliken, 3rd Regt E TN Mil

## Enlisted Men, War of 1812

COBB, Jesse, Ens, Col John Brown, Capt William White, E TN Vol Mtd Inf, Res omitted

COBB, Jesse, Pvt, Col Samuel Bayless, Capt Branch Jones, E TN Drafted Mil

COBB, Jesse, Pvt, Maj John Childs, Capt James Cummings, E TN Vol Mtd Inf; Regimental Co Hawkins

COBB, John, Pvt, Col S Copeland, Capt John Holshouser, Inf

COBB, Joseph, Pvt, Col Samuel Bunch, Capt Thomas Mann, E TN Vol Mtd Inf

COBB, Lewis, W, Pvt, Col John Coffee, Capt Robert Jetton, Cav

COBB, Rice, Pvt, Col Phillip Pipkin, Capt Peter Searcy, Mil Inf; ____ Herald substitute

COBB, William, Pvt, Col John Brown, Capt William White, E TN Vol Mtd Inf

COBBLE, Daniel, Pvt, Regt Commander omitted, Capt Archibald McKenney, Cav

COBBLE, George, Pvt, Regt Commander omitted, Capt Archibald McKenney, Cav

COBBS, B L, Surgeon, Col Archer Cheatham, 2nd Regt of TN, Res omitted

COBBS, David, Pvt, Col William Metcalf, Capt William Sitton, Mil Inf

COBLE, Daniel, Pvt, Regt Commander omitted, Capt Archibald McKenney, Cav

COBLER, Chris, Cpl, Col Thomas Benton, Capt Thomas Williamson, Vol Inf

COBLER, Christopher, 4 Cpl, Col Thomas H Benton, Capt Thomas Williamson, Vol Inf

COBLER, Christopher, Cpl, Col William Pillow, Capt Thomas Williamson, Vol Inf

COBLER, Christopher, Pvt, Col A Loury, Capt J Williamson, W TN Mil

COBLER, Christopher, Pvt, Col L Hammond, Capt J N Williams, 2nd Regt Inf

COBLER, Christopher, Pvt, Col N T Perkins, Capt Philip Pipkin, Mtd Riflemen

COBLER, Christopher, Pvt, Lt Col Hammons, Co Commander omitted, Pvt

COBLER, Francis, Pvt, Col A Loury, Co Commander omitted, W TN Mil

COBLER, Francis, Pvt, Col L Hammond, Capt J N Williamson, 2nd Regt Inf

COBLER, Francis, Pvt, Lt Col Hammonds, Capt Joseph Williamson, Inf

COBLER, Hansley, Pvt, Col T McCrory, Capt Isaac Patton, Mil Inf

COBLER, Jno, Pvt, Col John Coffee, Capt McKeene, Cav

COBLER, John, 2 Lt, Col Thomas Williamson, Co Commander omitted, Vol Mtd Gunmen

COBLER, John, 3 Lt, Maj Gen J Cocke, Co Commander omitted, TN Vol Mtd Gunmen

COBLER, John, Pvt, Col A Cheatham, Capt Charles Johnson, Inf; transferred to Arty

COBLER, John, Pvt, Col Jno Coffee, Co Commander omitted, Cav; substitute for Zebulon Jetton

COBLER, John, Pvt, Col John Alcorn, Co Commander omitted, Cav

COBY, French, Pvt, Regt Commander omitted, Capt David Smith, Cav Vol

COCHRAN, Alexander, Pvt, Col S Bunch, Capt Geo McPherson, E TN Mil; transferred from Capt Register Co

COCHRAN, Edward, Pvt, Col A Loury, Capt John Looney, E TN Mil

COCHRAN, Jacob, Pvt, Col Philip Pipkin, Capt Henry M Newlin, Mil Inf

COCHRAN, Jas L, Pvt, Col Philip Pipkin, Capt Henry M Newlin, Mil Inf; replaced by Sam'l Calvert

COCHRAN, Jas, Pvt, Col Philip Pipkin, Capt John Robertson, Mil Inf; left sick at Ft Pearce 11-26-1814

COCHRAN, Jas, Sgt, Col T McCrory, Capt Jno Reynolds, Mil Inf

COCK, Jaster, Pvt, Maj William Woodfolk, Capt James C Neil, Inf; substituted John Givens

COCK, Jesse W, Pvt, Col Robert Steele, Capt John Chitwood, Mil Inf

COCK, William, Pvt, Regt Commander omitted, Capt R Evans, Mtd Spies

COCK (FACK), John, Pvt, Col John Coffee, Capt Thomas Bradley, Vol Cav

COCKBURN, George, Pvt, Col T McCrory, Capts William Dooley, Inf

COCKBURN, Henry, Pvt, Col Robert Steele, Capt Robert Campbell, Mil Inf

COCKBURN, John, Pvt, Col Ewen Allison, Capt Thomas Wilson, E TN Draft Mil; deserted

COCKBURN, Patrick, Pvt, Col Ewen Allison, Capt Thomas Wilson, E TN Draft Mil; deserted

COCKE, Benjamin, Pvt, Regt Commander omitted, Capt David Smith, Cav Vol

COCKE, James W, Pvt, Col N T Perkins, Capt George Marr, Mtd Vol; residence Montgomery Co, wounded at Emuckfaw

COCKE, John I, Pvt, Col John Coffee, Capt James Terrell, Vol Cav; missing

COCKE, John, Col, 2 Regt W TN Mil Inf

COCKE, John, Pvt, Col John Alcorn, Capt Thomas Bradley, Vol Cav

COCKE, John, Pvt, Col William Johnson, Capt Christopher Cook, E TN Mil

COCKE, Stephen, Pvt, Col Samuel Bunch, Capt James Cummings, E TN Vol Mtd Gunmen

COCKE, Stephen, Pvt, Col Samuel Bunch, Capt Thomas Mann, E TN Vol Mtd Inf; transferred to Capt Cummings Co

COCKE, Sterling, Pvt, Col John Williams, Capt D Vance, Mtd Mil

COCKE, Thomas J, Pvt, Col John Coffee, Capt James Terrell, Vol Cav; missing

COCKE, Thomas, 5 Sgt, Col Samuel Bunch, Capt James Cummings, E TNl Vol Mtd Gunmen

COCKE, William, Pvt, Col John Williams, Capt David Vance, Mtd Mil

COCKE (COX), William, Pvt, Col William Johnson, Capt Christopher Cook, E TN Mil

COCKLE, Joseph M, Pvt, Col John Williams, Capt David Vance, Mtd Mil

COCKRAL, William, Pvt, Col T Benton, Capt Benjamin

## Enlisted Men, War of 1812

Reynolds, Vol Inf; refused to march
COCKRAN, Aaron D, Pvt, Regt Commander omitted, Capt Archibald McKenney, Cav
COCKRAN, Abner, Rank omitted, Col John Brown, Capt Lunsford Oliver, Regt E TN Mil
COCKRAN, Alexander?, Pvt, Col Samuel Bunch, Capt F Register, E TN Mil; joined from Capt McPherson's Co
COCKRAN, James, Pvt, Col Philip Pipkin, Capt Henry M Newlin, Mil Inf
COCKRAN, James, Pvt, Col S Bayless, Capt Joseph B Bacon, E TN Mil
COCKRAN, _____, Pvt, Col S Bunch, Capt F Register, E TN Mil; joined from Capt McPherson's Co
COCKRON, John, Pvt, Col Philip Pipkin, Capt Ebenezer Kirkpatrick, Mil Inf
COE, Isaiah, 5 Sgt, Col James Raulston, Capt James A Black, Inf
COE, Joseph, Sgt, Col T McCrory, Capt William Dooly, Inf
COE, William H, Pvt, Maj Gen A Jackson, Capt William Carroll, Vol Inf
COFFEE, Bennett, Pvt, Col Ewen Allison, Capt Jonas Loughmiller, Mil; joined from Capt Griffin's Co
COFFEE, Bennett, Pvt, Col S Bunch, Capt Jones Griffin, E TN Draft Mil
COFFEE, Charles, Pvt, Col William Lillard, Capt John Neatheron, E TN Vol Inf
COFFEE, George, Pvt, Col Samuel Bayless, Capt Joseph Rich, E TN Inf
COFFEE, Jesse, 3 Sgt, Col William Hll, Capt John Kennedy, Vol Inf
COFFEE, Jesse, Sgt, Col William Hall, Capt John Kennedy, Vol Inf
COFFEE, Joel, Pvt, Col Ewen Allison, Capt Jonas Loughmiller, Mil; joined from Capt Griffin Co
COFFEE, Joel, Pvt, Col S Bunch, Capt George McPherson, E TN Mil; joined from Capt Griffin Co
COFFEE, Joel, Pvt, Col S Bunch, Capt Jones Griffin, E TN Mil
COFFEE, John, Pvt, Col R C Napier, Capt Andrew McCarty, Mil Inf
COFFEE, Reuben, Pvt, Col Ewen Allison, Capt Adam Winsell, E TN Draft Mil; disch for inability
COFFEE, _____, Pvt, Col S Bunch, Capt Geo McPherson, E TN Mil; joined from Capt Griffin's Co
COFFER, Elijah, Pvt, Col William Pillow, Capt George Caperton, Inf
COFFEY, Pleasant, Pvt, Col Edward Bradley, Capt John Kennedy, Riflemen
COFFMAN, Harmon, Pvt, Col Ewen Allison, Capt Jacob Hoyal, E TN Mil
COFFMAN, Isaac, Pvt, Maj Gen Andrew Jackson, Capt John Crane, Mtd Gunmen
COFFMAN, Jacob, Pvt, Col Samuel Bunch, Capt Jones Griffin, E TN Draft Mil
COFFMAN, Joseph, Pvt, Col Samuel Bunch, Capt George Gregory, E TN Draft Mil
COFFMAN, Pvt, Regt Commander omitted, Capt Samuel Richardson, E TN Draft Mil; deserted
COFFMAN, Rhinehart, Pvt, Regt Commander omitted,

Capt Samuel Richardson, E TN Draft Mil; deserted
COFFMAN, Robert, Pvt, Col Samuel Bunch, Capt Jones Griffin, E TN Draft Mil
COFFMON, Samuel, Pvt, Col William Lillard, Capt Copeland, E TN Vol Inf
COFFORD, John, Pvt, Col Ewen Allison, Capt William King, Draft Mil
COFMAN, Andrew, Pvt, Col William Lillard, Capt Zacheus Copeland, Branch omitted; appt 3 Sgt
COFMAN, Courad, Pvt, Col Samuel Bayless, Capt Jonathan Waddle, E TN Mil
COFMAN, Daniel, Cpl, Col Samuel Bayless, Capt Joseph Hale, E TN Mil
COFMAN, David, Pvt, Col William Lillard, Capt Thomas McChristian, E TN Vol Inf
COFMAN, Isaiah, Pvt, Col Samuel Bayless, Capt Joseph Hale, E TN Mil
COFMAN, Jacob, Pvt, Col Ewen Allison, Capt Jonas Loughmiller, Mil
COFMAN, Jacob, Pvt, Col Samuel Bayless, Capt Jonathan Waddle, E TN Mil
COFMAN, Robert, Pvt, Col Ewen Allison, Capt Jonas Loughmiller, Mil
COFMAN, William, Pvt, Col William Lillard, Capt George Argenbright, E TN Vol Riflemen
COFT, Dan B, Pvt, Col J Alcorn, Capt Thomas Bradley, Vol Cav
COFY, Josh?, Pvt, Col William Lillard, Capt Thomas Sharpe, 2 Regt Inf
COGBELL, Charles C, Pvt, Col James Raulston, Capt Mathew Neal, Inf
COGGHILL, Samallowood, Pvt, Col John Coffee, Capt James Terrill, Vol Cav
COGHAN, Jordan, Pvt, Col Philip Pipkin, Capt James Blakemore, Vol Inf
COGHILL, Smallwood, Pvt, Col John Coffee, Capt James Terrill, Vol Cav
COGIN, Rich'd, Pvt, Col A Loury, Capt Gabriel Martin, Inf
COHEN, George, 4 Cpl, Col Philip Pipkin, Capt John Strother, Mil
COHOON, Samuel, 5 Cpl, Col James Raulston, Capt Charles Wade, Inf
COHORN, William, Dmr, Col Alexander Loury, Capt George Sarver, Inf
COHORN, William, Pvt, Col R C Napier, Capt Thomas Preston, Mil Inf
COHOUN, Andrew, Pvt, Col Philip Pipkin, Capt Henry Newlin, Mil Inf
COHRAN, John, 5 Sgt, Col John Cocke, Capt John Dalton, Inf
COIL, Michael, Pvt, Maj William Russell, Co Commander omitted, Vol Mtd Gunmen
COILL, Michiel, Pvt, Col John Alcorn, Capt John Winston, Mtd Riflemen
COKER, Austin, Pvt, Col Philip Pipkin, Capt Ebenezer Kirkpatrick, Mil Inf
COKER, George, Pvt, Col Edward Bradley, Capt John Kennedy, Riflemen
COKER, James, Pvt, Col Samuel Wear, Capt Joseph Cal-

loway, Mtd Inf
COKER, Jesse, Pvt, Col Alexander Loury, Capt George Sarver, Inf
COKER, Joel, Pvt, Col Samuel Wear, Capt Joseph Caloway, Mtd Inf
COLANS, David, Pvt, Col Wiliam Johnson, Capt James Stewart, E TN Mil
COLBAUGH, Jacob, Pvt, Col Ewen Allison, Capt Adam Winsell, E TN Draft Mil
COLBAUGH, John, Pvt, Col Ewen Allison, Capt William King, Drafted Mil
COLDWELL, James, Pvt, Maj William Russell, Capt John Trimble, Vol Mtd Gunmen; transferred from Capt Stephen's Co
COLDWELL, John, Pvt, Col Samuel Wear, Capt James Tedford, E TN Vol Inf
COLDWELL, Nathaniel, Sgt, Col John Wynne, Capt William Carothers, W TN Inf
COLDWELL, Silas M, Surgeon Mate, Col Ewen Allison, no Co Commander, E TN Mil; attached to Col Bunch Regt
COLDWELL, William, Pvt, Col Samuel Wear, Capt James Tedford, E TN Vol Inf
COLE, Abram, Pvt, Col William Higgins, Capt William Doake, Mtd Riflemen
COLE, Andrew, Pvt, Col A Cheatham, Capt Charles Johnson, Inf
COLE, Caleb, Pvt, Col Samuel Wear, Capt John Bayless, Mtd Inf
COLE, David, Cpl, Col Thomas Williamson, Capt Beverly Williams, Vol Mtd Gunmen
COLE, David, Pvt, Col John Alcorn, Capt Thomas Bradley, Vol Cav
COLE, David, Pvt, Col John Coffee, Capt Thomas Bradley, Vol Cav
COLE, Elisha, Pvt, Col John Coffee, Capt Thomas Bradley, Vol Cav
COLE, Elisha, Pvt, Col Thomas Williamson, Capt Beverly Williams, Vol Mtd Gunmen
COLE, Ezekiel, Pvt, Col John Brown, Capt John Childs, E TN Vol Mtd Gunmen
COLE, George, Pvt, Col Ewen Allison, Capt John Hampton, Mil
COLE, Hyram, Pvt, Col Thomas Williamson, Capt William Martin, Vol Mtd Gunmen
COLE, Isaiah, Pvt, Maj William Woodfolk, Capt Abraham Dudney, Inf
COLE, Jacob, Pvt, Col John Wynne, Capt James Cole, Inf
COLE, James, Pvt, Col Alexander Loury, Capt George Sarver, Inf; discharged by surgeon 9-24-1814
COLE, Jeremiah, Pvt, Col Samuel Bayless, Capt Joseph Rich, E TN Inf
COLE, John, 3 St, Col Philip Pipkin, Capt John Strother, Mil
COLE, John, Pvt, Brig Gen William Johnson, Capt Robert Carson, Inf; discharged for want of arms
COLE, John, Pvt, Col William Higgins, Capt William Doake, Mtd Riflemen
COLE, Jos, Pvt, Col Ewen Allison, Capt John Hampton, Mil; deserted
COLE, Mark, Pvt, Col R H Dyer, Capt Bethel Allen, Vol Mtd Gunmen
COLE, Mark, Pvt, Col Stephen Copeland, Capt William Hodges, Inf
COLE, Rosco, Pvt, Col R H Dyer, Capt Thomas Gunmen, Vol Mtd Gunmen
COLE, Sam'l, Pvt, Col A Cheatham, Capt Charles Johnson, Inf
COLE, Wm, Pvt, Regt Commander omitted, Capt A Metcalf, Mil Inf
COLEMAN, Benj, Pvt, Col William Lillard, Capt James Lillard, E TN Vol Inf
COLEMAN, Blackman, Capt, Col John Coffee, Capt Blackman Coleman, Cav
COLEMAN, Chas, Pvt, Col Samuel Bayless, Capt Solomon Hendrix, E TN Mil; deserted 12-24-1814
COLEMAN, David, Pvt, Gen Thomas Johnson, Capt Daniel Oban, 36 Inf
COLEMAN, Hardy, Pvt, Col A Loury, Capt John Looney, 2nd Regt W TN Mil
COLEMAN, Henry, Pvt, Col A Loury, Lt Col L Hammonds, Capt Thomas Wells, Inf; d 11-7-1814 by an accident
COLEMAN, Henry, Pvt, Col Robert Steele, Capt James Bennett, Mil Inf
COLEMAN, Jesse, Pvt, Col Samuel Bayless, Capt Branch Jones, E TN Drafted Mil
COLEMAN, John, Pvt, Col Philip Pipkin, Capt Peter Searcy, Mil Inf
COLEMAN, Thos B, Sgt, Col R H Dyer, Capt James McMahan, TN Mtd Vol Gunmen; promoted from Pvt
COLEMAN, Thos, 2 Sgt, Col R C Napier, Capt John Chism, Mil Inf; acted as Hospital Steward
COLEMAN, W Wm, Pvt, Maj Gen Wm Carroll, Capt Francis Ellis, Inf
COLEMAN, Wm B, Pvt, Col Thomas Williamson, Capt Richard Tate, Vol Mtd Gunmen; d 3-9-1813
COLEMAN, Wm, Pvt, Col Samuel Bayless, Capt Branch Jones, E TN Drafted Mil
COLES, Burwell, Pvt, Regt Commander omitted, Capt Abner Pearce, Inf
COLES, John, 6 Cpl, Col James Raulston, Capt Daniel Newman, Inf
COLEY, French, Pvt, Regt Commander omitted, Capt David Smith, Cav
COLINS, Erastus, 1 Sgt, Regt Commander omitted, Lt Jas Berry, Mtd Riflemen
COLINS, John, Pvt, Lt Col L Hammonds, Capt Arahel Rains, Inf
COLINS, Solomon, Pvt, Col Ewen Allison, Capt Jonas Loughmiller, Mil
COLISON, Jos, Pvt, Col John Cocke, Capt Joseph Price, Inf
COLLANS, David, Pvt, Col William Johnson, Capt Henry Hunter, E TN Mil; transferred from Capt Stewart's Co
COLLEN, David, Pvt, Col William Lillard, Capt William Hamilton, E TN Vol Inf
COLLENS, Elijah, Pvt, Col William Lillard, Capt William Hamilton, E TN Vol Inf
COLLET, Andrew, Pvt, Col William Johnson, Capt Jo-

## Enlisted Men, War of 1812

seph Kirk, Mil
COLLET, Andrew, Pvt, Col William Lillard, Capt Jacob Dyke, Vol Inf
COLLET, Isaac, Pvt, Col William Johnston, Capt Joseph Kirk, Mil; on furlough
COLLET, John, Pvt, Col William Johnston, Capt Joseph Kirk, Mil
COLLETT, Isaac, Pvt, Col William Johnson, Capt Christopher Cook, E TN Mil
COLLETT, Jacob, Pvt, Col S Bunch, Capt F Register, E TN Mil; furnished Jno Jones as substitute
COLLETT, Jacob, Pvt, Regt Commander omitted, Capt F Register, E TN Mil; furnished John A Jones as substitute
COLLETT, John, Pvt, Col William Johnson, Capt Christopher Cook, E TN Mil
COLLIER, Barnett, Pvt, Maj William Russell, Capt John Cowan, Vol Mtd Gunmen
COLLIER, Chas B, Pvt, Col John Cocke, Capt George Barnes, Inf
COLLIER, Dan'l, Pvt, Col John Cocke, Capt John Weakley, Inf
COLLIER, Daniel, Pvt, Lt Col H Bryans, Co Commander omitted, Inf
COLLIER, Daniel, Pvt, no other information
COLLIER, David, Pvt, Col William Hall, Capt John Kennedy, Vol Inf
COLLIER, Ingram B, Sgt, Col A Loury, Capt James Kincaid, Inf; reduced to ranks, transferred to Artif
COLLIER, John, Pvt, Col R C Napier, Capt Thomas Gray, Mil Inf
COLLIER, Jonathan, Pvt, Col William Lillard, Capt Robert McCalpin, E TN Vol Inf
COLLIER, Lee, Pvt, Col Philip Pipkin, Capt James Blakemore, Mil Inf; AWOL 1-13-1815
COLLIER, Lewis, Pvt, Regt Commander omitted, Capt William Henderson, Spies
COLLIER, Randall, Cpl, Col S Wear, Capt Robert Doak, E TN Vol Inf
COLLIER, Randel, Pvt, Col Thomas Benton, Capt Geo W Gibbs, Vol Inf
COLLIER, Thos, Pvt, Col John Cocke, Capt Joseph Price, Inf
COLLIER (COLLINS), Jas, Pvt, Col Samuel Bayless, Capt Branch Jones, E TN Drafted Mil
COLLIHAN, Jas, Pvt, Col William Lillard, Capt Robert Maloney, E TN Inf Vol
COLLIN, Jas L, Dmr, Col William Metcalf, Capt William Mullin, Mil Inf
COLLIN, Sampson, 2 Cpl, Col John Cocke, Capt John Weakley, Inf
COLLINGSWORTH, Coventon, Ffr, Col William Lillard, Capt William Hamilton, E TN Vol Inf
COLLINS, Abner, Sgt, Col Robert Steele, Capt John Chitwood, Mil Inf
COLLINS, Absolom, Pvt, Col Thomas Williamson, Capt John Dobbins, Capt John Doak, Vol Mtd Gunmen
COLLINS, Barba, Pvt, Col John Cocke, Capt John Weakley, Inf
COLLINS, Barlow, Pvt, Capt John Cocke, Capt Weakley, Inf

COLLINS, Bartlett, Pvt, Col Robt Steele, Co Commander omitted, Mil Inf
COLLINS, Chas, Pvt, Col R H Dyer, Co Commander omitted, Vol Mtd Gunmen
COLLINS, Chas, Pvt, Maj Woodfolk, Capt James Turner, Inf
COLLINS, David, Pvt, Col Chas Johnson, Capt Jas Stuart, E TN Drafted Mil; transferred to Capt Hunter Co
COLLINS, Deram, Sgt, Col N Cannon, Co Commander omitted, Mtd Riflemen
COLLINS, E T, Paymaster, Lt Col L Hammons, Co Commander omitted, 2nd Regt W TN Mil; also served Col Alexander Loury
COLLINS, Edmond, Pvt, Col James Raulston, Capt James Hamilton, Inf; also served Maj Gen Carroll
COLLINS, Erastus, 1 Sgt, Lt Col L Hammond, Capt Wells, Inf
COLLINS, Erastus, Sgt, Regt Commander omitted, Lt Jas Berry, Mtd Riflemen
COLLINS, Frances, Pvt, Maj John Childs, Capt Tipton, E TN Vol Mtd Gunmen; Regimental Co 6th Jefferson
COLLINS, Francis, Pvt, Col John Williams, Capt William Walker, Vol
COLLINS, Griffith, Pvt, Col S Bunch, Capt S Robinson, E TN Drafted Mil; discharged for inability
COLLINS, Griffith, Pvt, Regt Commander omitted, Capt Samuel Richardson, E TN Drafted Mil
COLLINS, Henry, 1 Sgt, Maj John Childs, Co Commander omitted, E TN Vol Mil
COLLINS, Henry, Pvt, Col Edwin Booth, Capt Winton, E TN Mil
COLLINS, Henry, Sgt, Col Charles Johnson, Capt William Alexander, Det of E TN Drafted Mil
COLLINS, Isaac, Pvt, Col R H Dyer, Co Commander omitted, Mtd Gunmen; transferred to Capt Bean's Co
COLLINS, Isaac, Pvt, Gen Jno Coffee, Co Commander omitted, Mtd Spies
COLLINS, Isaac, Pvt, no other information
COLLINS, Jas S, Dmr, Col William Metcalf, Capt Mullins, Mil Inf
COLLINS, Jas, Pvt, Col Newton Cannon, Capt Ota Cantrell, W TN Mtd Inf
COLLINS, Jesse, Pvt, Col Samuel Bunch, Capt Francis Register, E TN Mil; deserted 3-4-1814
COLLINS, John, Pvt, Col James Raulston, Capt James Black, Inf
COLLINS, John, Pvt, Col Wm Metcalf, Co Commander omitted, Mil Inf; d 2-11-1815
COLLINS, John, Pvt, Commanders omitted, E TN Mil
COLLINS, John, Pvt, Lt Col Hammond, Capt Arahel Raines, Inf
COLLINS, John, Pvt, Maj Gen Andrew Jackson, Col A Cheatham, Capt Creel, Inf; transferred to Arty
COLLINS, John, Pvt, Maj Woodfolk, Capt Turner, Inf
COLLINS, John, Pvt, Regt Commander omitted, Capt Joel Parrish, Arty; also served Gen Andrew Jackson
COLLINS, John, Sgt, Col Samuel Bayless, Capt James Churchman, E TN Mil; deserted 12-30-1814

- 133

## Enlisted Men, War of 1812

COLLINS, Jonathan, Pvt, Col W Snodgrass, Ens Gregg, Det of Inf of E TN Vol Mil
COLLINS, Jonathan, Pvt, Col Wm Johnson, Capt Andrew Lawson, E TN Drafted Mil
COLLINS, Jos, Pvt, Col Thomas Williamson, Capt Thomas Scurry, Vol Mtd Inf
COLLINS, Joseph, Pvt, Col Edward Badley, Capt Abraham Bledsoe, Riflemen
COLLINS, Joseph, Pvt, Col Samuel Bunch, Capt S Roberson, E TN Drafted Mil; discharged for inability
COLLINS, Joseph, Pvt, Col William Hall, Capt Abraham Bledsoe, Vol Inf
COLLINS, Joseph, Pvt, Regt Commander omitted, Capt Samuel Richardson, E TN Drafted Mil; discharged for inability
COLLINS, Joseph, Sgt, Col Robert Dyer, Capt Bethel Allen, Vol Mtd Gunmen
COLLINS, Lewis, Pvt, Col Robert Dyer, Capt Joseph Williams, Vol Mtd Gunmen
COLLINS, Luns, Pvt, Col R C Napier, Capt Drury Adkins, Mil Inf
COLLINS, Meredith, Pvt, Col Thomas Williamson, Capt Richard Tate, Vol Mtd Gunmen
COLLINS, Meredith, Pvt, no other information
COLLINS, Nathan, Pvt, Col Robert Steele, Capt John Chitwood, Mil Inf
COLLINS, Nathaniel, Pvt, Col Robert Dyer, Capt James McMahon, 1st TN Mtd Vol Gunmen
COLLINS, Samuel, Pvt, Col William Johnson, Capt Joseph Kirk, Mil; discharged
COLLINS, Samuel, Pvt, Col William Lillard, Capt William Hamilton, E TN Vol Inf; never came into camps
COLLINS, Solomon, Pvt, Col Samuel Bunch, Capt John Houk, E TN Mil
COLLINS, Thomas, Pvt, Col Thomas Williamson, Capt Richard Tate, Vol Mtd Gunmen
COLLINS, Thomas, Pvt, Regt Commander omitted, Capt James Cowan, Inf
COLLINS, Uriah, Pvt, Col William Johnson, Capt Christopher Cook, E TN Mil
COLLINS, Uriah, Pvt, Col William Johnson, Capt Joseph Kirk, Mil
COLLINS, William, Cpl, Col Samuel Wear, Col Samuel Bunch, Capt William Mitchell, E TN Mtd Inf
COLLINS, William, Pvt, Col Alexander Loury, Lt Col Leroy Hammonds, Capt Arahel Rains, Inf
COLLINS, William, Pvt, Col N T Perkins, Capt John Quarles, Vol Mtd Inf
COLLINS, William, Pvt, Col Newton Cannon, Capt John Demsey, Mtd Gunmen
COLLINS, William, Pvt, Col William Higgins, Capt William Doak, Mtd Riflemen
COLLINS, William, Sgt, Col Edwin Booth, Capt George Winton, E TN Mil
COLLINSWORTH, Edmond, Pvt, Col Robert Dyer, Capt Thomas Jones, Vol Mtd Gunmen
COLLINSWORTH, Edwin, Pvt, Col N T Perkins, Capt Mathew Patterson, Mtd Vol; wounded in battle
COLLINSWORTH, John, Pvt, Col William Lillard, Capt William Hamilton, E TN Vol Inf

COLLISON, Samuel, Pvt, Col Samuel Bunch, Lt John Harris, E TN Mil
COLLOM, Charles, 6 Cpl, Col James Raulston, Capt Mathew Cowan, Inf
COLLOM, William, Pvt, Col Ewen Allison, Capt Henry McCray, E TN Mil; transferred to Capt Register's Co
COLLOMS, Bartlett, Pvt, Col James Raulston, Capt Charles Wade, Inf
COLLUM, Charles, 6 Cpl, Col James Raulston, Capt Mathew Cowan, Inf
COLLUM, William, Pvt, Col James Raulston, Capt Mathew Cowan, Inf
COLLUM, William, Pvt, Col Samuel Bunch, Capt Francis Register, E TN Mil; joined from Capt McCray's Co
COLSON (COLSEN), Wm, Pvt, Col Robert Steele, Capt Jas Randals, Inf
COLT (GOLT?), Joshua, Pvt, Col Bunch, Capt Vance, E TN Mtd Inf
COLTHARP, Strange, Pvt, Col Wm Lillard, Capt Zacheus Copeland, E TN Vol Inf
COLTHARP, William, Pvt, Col John Alcorn, Capt Fredrick Stump, Cav
COLTHORP, Wm, Pvt, Col R H Dyer, Capt Thos White, Vol Mtd Gunmen
COLTON, Chas, Sgt, Gen Thos Washington, Co Commander omitted, Mtd Inf
COLWELL, James, Pvt, Col Alexander Loury, Capt George Sarve, Inf; d 3-8-1815
COLWELL, Jos, Pvt, Col John Cocke, Capt John Weakley, Inf
COLWELL, Jos, Pvt, Regt Commander omitted, Capt David Smith, Cav
COLWELL, Jose, Pvt, Regt Commander omitted, Capt David Smith, Cav Vol
COLWELL, Nathaniel, 5 Cpl, Col Philip Pipkin, Capt Henry M Newlin, Mil Inf; promoted to 1 Sgt
COLYER, Charles, Pvt, Col Newton Cannon, Capt Hamby, Mtd Riflemen
COMAN, Archibald, Pvt, Col Thomas Williamson, Capt Robert Moore, Vol Mtd Gunmen
COMBS, Geo M, Pvt, Col S Bunch, Capt Thos Mann, E TN Vol Mtd Inf; promoted to Regt QM
COMBS, Geo M, QM, Col Samuel Bunch, Co Commander omitted, E TN Mil; absent on command
COMBS, John, Pvt, Col John K Winn, Capt Bailey Butler, Inf; deserted 11-19-1813
COMBS, Jos, Pvt, Col S Bunch, Capt Jno English, E TN Drafted Mil
COMBS, Jos, Pvt, Col Samuel Bunch, Capt Geo Gregory, E TN Drafted Mil
COMBS, Laburn, Pvt, Commander omitted, Mtd Inf
COMER, Allen, Pvt, Lt Col L Hammonds, Capt Jas Craig, Inf
COMER, Martin, Pvt, Brig Gen Thos Johnson, Capt Robert Carson, Inf
COMER (CROMER), Adam, Pvt, Col Philip Pipkin, Capt Geo Mebane, Mil Inf
COMICAEL, Lemuel, Pvt, Col Samuel Bayless, Capt Jas Churchman, E TN Mil

## Enlisted Men, War of 1812

COMINS (CUMMINS), Geo, Pvt, Maj Wm Woodfolk, Capt Ezekiah Ross, Capt McCulley, Inf

COMMIN, John, Cpl, Col A Cheatham, Capt Wm Smith, Inf

COMMINS, Jas, Pvt, Lt Col L Hammonds, Col Alexander Loury, Capt Thos Delany, Inf

COMPERRY, Francis, Pvt, Col Philip Pipkin, Capt John Strother, Mil; deserted

COMPTON, John, Pvt, Col Edward E Booth, Capt John Proter, Drafted Mil

COMPTON, John, Pvt, Col S Copeland, Capt Alexander Provine, Mil Inf

COMPTON, John, Pvt, Col Samuel Wear, Capt Simeon Perry, E TN Mtd Inf Vol

COMPTON, Jos, Pvt, Col S Bunch, Capt Jno Houk, E TN Mil; transferred to Capt English Co

COMPTON, Wm, Pvt, Col Jas Raulston, Capt Chas Wade, Inf

COMPTON, Wm, Pvt, Col Samuel Wear, Capt John Stephens, E TN Vol Inf

COMPTON, Zachariah, Pvt, Col Edward E Booth, Capt John Porter, Drafted Mil

COMPTON, Zachariah, Pvt, Col S Bunch, Capt Jno Houk, E TN Mil; transferred to Capt English Co

CON, Josiah, Sgt, Col Robert Steele, Capt Jas Randals, Inf; on furlough

CONATSER, Andrew, Pvt, Col Wm Johnson, Capt Andrew Lawson, E TN Drafted Mil

CONDON, Jas, Pvt, Maj Gen A Jackson, Capt Wm Carroll, Vol Inf

CONDRA, James, Pvt, Col N Cannon, Capt John Hanley, Mtd Riflemen

CONDRA, Jas, Pvt, Col William Pillow, Capt William Moore, Inf; transferred to Capt Hamby's Co

CONDRAY, Bird, Pvt, Col R H Dyer, Maj Wm Russell, Capt Wm Russell, Vol Mtd Gunmen

CONDRAY (CONARD), Geo, Pvt, Col Robert Dyer, Maj Wm Russell, Capt Wm Russell, Vol Mtd Gunmen

CONDRAY (CONDRY), Martin, Pvt, Maj John Childs, Capt James Cummings, E TN Vol Mtd Inf

CONDRIN, John, Pvt, Col Wm Lillard, Capt John Roper, E TN Vol Inf

CONDRY, Bird, Pvt, no other information

CONDUIT, Willis, Pvt, Col William Johnson, Capt Joseph Kirk, Mil; substitute for Dan'l Byran

CONDUIT, Wm, Pvt, Col William Johnson, Capt Christopher Cook, E TN Mil

CONELEY, John L, Pvt, Col Samuel Bayless, Capt Joseph Rich, E TN Inf; d 1-23-1815

CONGER, Adam, Blcksmith, Col John Alcorn, Capt John W Byrn, Cav

CONGER, Eli, Pvt, Col R H Dyer, Capt Bethel Allen, Vol Mtd Gunmen

CONGO, Eli, Pvt, Col William Higgins, Capt Adam Dale, Mtd Gunmen

CONKIN, John, Cpl, Col Samuel Bayless, Capt Jonathan Waddell, E TN Mil

CONKLING, Moses, Pvt, Col Wm Lillard, Capt Jacob Hartsell, E TN Vol Inf

CONLER, Enoch, Pvt, Col Jno Brown, Capt Allen I Bacon, E TN Mil Inf

CONLEY, Wm, Pvt, Col N T Perkins, Capt Philip Pipkin, Mtd Riflemen

CONLEY (COWLEY), Chas, Pvt, Col Wm Higgins, Capt Wm Doak, Mtd Riflemen

CONLSON, Isaac, Pvt, Col Robert Steele, Capt Richard M Ratton, Mil Inf

CONLY, John, Sgt, Col S Copeland, Capt Wm Douglass, Inf

CONNARD, Burket, Pvt, Maj Wm Woodfolk, Capt Abraham Dudney, Capt John Sutton, Inf; deserted 9-29-1814

CONNELL, Enoch, Pvt, Lt Col A Cheatham, Co Commander omitted, Mtd Inf

CONNELL, Giles, Pvt, Brig Gen T Johnson, Capt Abraham Allen, Mil Inf

CONNELL, Giles, Pvt, Lt Col A Cheatham, Co Commander omitted, Mtd Inf

CONNELL, Jno, Pvt, Lt Col A Cheatham, Co Commander omitted, Mtd Inf

CONNELL, John, Pvt, Col A Loury, Capt Gabriel Martin, Inf

CONNELL, Sampson, 2 Cpl, Col John Cocke, Capt John Weakley, Inf

CONNELL, Sampson, Pvt, Regt Commander omitted, Capt Jas Haggard, Mtd Gunmen

CONNELL, Sampson, Sgt, Lt Col A Cheatham, Co Commander omitted, Mtd Inf

CONNELL, William, Pvt, Col John Cocke, Capt John Weakley, Inf

CONNELL, Wm, Pvt, Col John Cocke, Capt John Weakley, Inf; d 1-25-1815

CONNELL, Wm, Pvt, Col Wm Metcalf, Capt John Barnhart, Mil Inf

CONNELLY, Jas B, Pvt, Maj Gen Jackson, Capt Wm Carroll, Vol Inf

CONNELLY, John, Pvt, Col John Cocke, Capt Joseph Price, Inf

CONNELY, Peter, Pvt, Col R C Napier, Capt Drury Adkins, Mil Inf

CONNER, Arthur, Pvt, Col Wm Metcalf, Capt Wm Mullen, Mil Inf; d 4-23-1815

CONNER, Edward, Pvt, Col James Raulston, Capt Daniel Newman, Inf

CONNER, Jacob, Pvt, Col Thomas Benton, Capt George W Gibbs, Vol Inf

CONNER, James, Pvt, Maj John Childs, Capt John Stephens, E TN Vol Mtd Inf

CONNER, John, Pvt, Col Ewen Allison, Capt Jacob Hoyal, E TN Mil; transferred to Capt McPherson's Co

CONNER, John, Pvt, Col S Copeland, Capt G W Stell, Mil Inf

CONNER, John, Pvt, Col William Metcalf, Capt William Sitton, Mil Inf

CONNER, Julias, Pvt, Col Samuel Bunch, Capt James Cummings, E TN Vol Mtd Inf

CONNER, Lewis, Sgt, Col Samuel Bunch, Capt Daniel Yarnell, E TN Mil

CONNER, Samuel, Pvt, Col S Copeland, Capt G W Stell, Mil Inf

CONNER, Thomas, Cpl, Col Edwin Booth, Capt John

Lewis, E TN Mil
CONNER, Thomas, Pvt, Col Edwin Booth, Capt John Lewis, E TN Mil; promoted to Cpl
CONNER, Thomas, Pvt, Col Edwin Booth, Capt Moses Thompson, Mil
CONNER, William S, Pvt, Col Philip Pipkin, Capt Ebenezer Kirkpatrick, Mil Inf; substitute Samuel DeLooch who left sick
CONNER, William, Sgt, Col Samuel Bunch, Capt Daniel Archibald, E TN Mil
CONNOR, Edward, Pvt, Col John Williams, Capt David Vance, Mtd Mil
CONOWAY, Wm, Pvt, Col Wm Metcalf, Capt Obidiah Waller, Mil Inf
CONRAD, William C, Pvt, Regt Commander omitted, Capt David Smith, Cav
CONRAD, William C, Pvt, Regt Commander omitted, Capt David Smith, Cav Vol
CONSTABETE, Joseph, Pvt, Col William Johnson, Capt Henry Hunter, E TN Mil
CONSTABLE, Jacob, Pvt, Col Ewen Allison, Capt John Hampton, Mil; furloughed & did not return
CONSTABLE, Jacob, Pvt, Col William Johnson, Capt Henry Hunter, E TN Mil; d 11-31-1814
CONWAY, Benjamin, Pvt, Col John Cocke, Capt Richard Crunk, Inf
CONWAY, Charles, Pvt, Col Philip Pipkin, Capt Ebenezer Kirkpatrick, Mil Inf
CONWAY, Christopher, Pvt, Col Philip Pipkin, Capt Ebenezer Kirkpatrick, Mil Inf; substituted for John Ellis
CONWAY, John, Pvt, Col William Johnson, Capt James Stewart, E TN Drafted Mil
CONWAY, John, Pvt, Col William Johnson, Capt James Stewart, E TN Mil
CONWAY, Richard, Pvt, no other information
CONWAY, William, Pvt, Regt Commander omitted, Capt Sam Bunch, Branch Srvce omitted
CONWELL, Thomas, Pvt, Col Thomas Williamson, Capt Giles Burdett, Vol Mtd Gunmen
CONYERS, John, Pvt, Col Newton Cannon, Capt John Harpole, Mtd Gunmen
CONYERS, John, Pvt, Col Thomas Williamson, Capt Beverly Williams, Vol Mtd Gunmen
CONYERS, Samuel, Pvt, Col Thomas Williamson, Capt Beverly Williams, Vol Mtd Gunmen
CON____, Stephen, Pvt, Col Thomas McCrory, Capt Thomas Gordon, Inf; sick on furlough
COOK, Adam, Dmr, Col A Cheatham, Capt George Chapman, Inf
COOK, Adam, Pvt, Col Samuel Bayless, Capt James Landen, E TN Mil
COOK, Alexander, Pvt, Col Samuel Wear, Capt James Tedford, E TN Vol Inf
COOK, Augustine, Pvt, Col Thomas Williamson, Capt John Crane, Capt James Cook, Vol Mtd Riflemen
COOK, Augustus, Pvt, Col William Higgins, Capt John Cheatham, Mtd Riflemen; on furlough 1-5-1814
COOK, Christian, Pvt, no other information
COOK, Christopher, Pvt, Regt Commander omitted, Capt Nathan Davis, Branch Srvce omitted
COOK, Daniel, Pvt, Col Alexander Loury, Capt Gabriel Martin, Inf
COOK, Green, Pvt, Col John Coffee, Capt Thomas Bradley, Vol Cav
COOK, Henry, 2 Sgt, Col William Johnson, Capt Andrew Lawson, E TN Drafted Mil
COOK, Henry, Pvt, Col Samuel Bunch, Capt William Houston, E TN Vol Mtd Inf; transferred to Capt Hamilton Co
COOK, Henry, Pvt, Col William Pillow, Capt John Anderson, Vol Inf; deserted 11-18-1813
COOK, Isaac, Pvt, Col Samuel Bunch, Capt Francis Register, E TN Mil; joined from Capt McPherson's Co
COOK, Jacob C, Pvt, Col John Coffee, Capt John Baskerville, Cav
COOK, James, Ffr, Col Samuel Bayless, Capt John Brock, E TN Mil; d 1-25-1815
COOK, James, Pvt, Col Samuel Bayless, Capt Joseph Rich, E TN Inf
COOK, James, Pvt, Lt Col A Cheatham, Co Commander omitted, Mtd Inf
COOK, James, Pvt, Regt Commander omitted, Capt Elijah Rushing, Det of Inf
COOK, James, Pvt, no other information
COOK, Jesse, Pvt, Col John Alcorn, Capt Thomas Bradley, Vol Cav
COOK, Jesse, Pvt, Col John Coffee, Capt Thomas Bradley, Vol Cav
COOK, Joel, Pvt, Col Ewen Allison, Capt Adam Winsell, E TN Mil
COOK, John, Pvt, Col John Brock, Capt Samuel Bayless, E TN Mil
COOK, Joseph, Pvt, Col Samuel Bunch, Capt Francis Register, E TN Mil; transferred to Capt McPherson Co
COOK, Joseph, Pvt, Col Samuel Bunch, Capt Francis Register, E TN Mil; transferred to Capt McPherson's Co
COOK, Joseph, Pvt, Col Samuel Bunch, Capt George McPherson, E TN Mil; joined from Capt Register's Co
COOK, Joseph, Pvt, Maj William Russell, Capt John Trimble, Vol Mtd Gunmen
COOK, Oston, Pvt, Col S Copeland, Capt Solomon George, Inf
COOK, Peter, Pvt, Col Edwin Booth, Capt John Lewis, E TN Mil
COOK, Richard, 4 Sgt, Col Robert Steele, Co Commander omitted, W TN Mil Inf; sick on furlough
COOK, Simeon, Pvt, Col Edwin E Booth, Co Commander omitted, E TN Mil
COOK, Theophilus, Pvt, Col Thos Williamson, Capt Robert Moore, Vol Mtd Gunmen
COOK, Theophilus, Pvt, Regt Commander omitted, Capt Geo Smith, Spies
COOK, Thomas B, Pvt, Maj Woodfolk, Capt Mathew Neal, Inf
COOK, Thomas, Pvt, Col John Alcorn, Capt Edward Bradley, Vol Cav
COOK, Thomas, Pvt, Col R H Dyer, Capt McMahon, TN

## Enlisted Men, War of 1812

Vol Mtd Gunmen
COOK, Thos, Pvt, Regt Commander omitted, Capt Jos Williams, Mil Cav
COOK, William, Pvt, Col Edwin Booth, Capt Samuel Thompson, Mil
COOK, William, Pvt, Col Edwin E Booth, Co Commander omitted, Inf
COOK, William, Pvt, Col N Cannon, Capt Jas Walton, Mtd Riflemen
COOK, William, Pvt, Col Samuel Bunch, Capt F Register, E TN Mil
COOK, William, Pvt, Col Samuel Bunch, Capt Francis Register, E TN Mil
COOK, William, Pvt, Col Samuel Wear, Capt Stephens, E TN Vol Inf
COOK, William, Pvt, Maj Wm Russell, Capt John Trimble, Vol Mtd Gunmen
COOK, William, Sgt, Col John Cocke, Capt Bird Nance, Inf
COOK, Willie, Pvt, Col John K Winn, Capt William McCall, Inf
COOK, Wm P, Pvt, Col William Metcalf, Capt Andrew Patterson, Mil Inf
COOK, Wm, Pvt, Col A Cheatham, Capt Wm A Smith, Inf
COOK, Wm, Pvt, Col Jas Raulston, Capt Haynie, Inf
COOK, Wm, Pvt, Regt Commander omitted, Capt Larkin Ferrell, Inf
COOKE, Greene, Pvt, Col J Alcorn, Capt Thomas Bradley, Vol Cav
COOKE, Hezekiah G, 2 Lt, Col Alexander Loury, Capt James Kincaid, Inf; left sick at Ft Montgomery 3-20-1815?
COOKE, James, Pvt, Col John Coffee, Capt David Smith, Vol Cav
COOKE, Jas, 2 Sgt, Regt Commander omitted, Capt David Smith, Vol Cav
COOKE, Reuben, Dmr, Col James Raulston, Capt Henry Hamilton, Inf; also served Gen Carroll
COOKE, Richard, Sgt, Maj William Woodfolk, Capt Abraham Dudney, Capt Sutton, Inf
COOKE, Thomas, Pvt, Col John Coffee, Capt David Smith, Vol Cav
COOKE, Thos B, Cpl, Maj William Woodfolk, Capt James K Neil, Inf
COOKE, Thos, Pvt, Col Thomas Williamson, Capt John Doak, Vol Mtd Gunmen
COOKE, Thos, Pvt, Regt Commander omitted, Capt Jno Crane, Mtd Inf
COOKSEY, Andrew, Pvt, Maj William Carroll, Capt Ellis, Inf
COOKSEY, Jesse, Cpl, Col Robert H Dyer, Capt Robert Edmonston, TN Mtd Vol Gunmen
COOKSEY, Nat, Pvt, Col Edward Bradley, Capt James Hamilton, Vol Inf; sick absent
COOKSEY, Nat, Pvt, Col William Hall, Capt James Hamilton, Vol Inf
COOKSEY, Vincent, Pvt, Col Jas Raulston, Capt Elijah Haynie, Inf
COOKSEY, Vincent, Pvt, Col Thomas Benton, Capt William Smith, Vol Inf
COOKSEY, Vincent, Pvt, Regt Commander omitted,

Capt Smith, Vol Inf
COOLEY, Cornelius, Pvt, Col John Cocke, Capt James Gray, Inf
COOLEY, Cornelius, Pvt, Regt Commander omitted, Capt Thos Gray, Inf
COOLEY, Joel, Pvt, Regt Commander omitted, Capt Thos Gray, Inf
COOLEY, William, Pvt, Col Alexander Loury, Capt Geo Sarver, Inf
COOLEY, Wood, Pvt, Brig Gen Johnston, Capt Allen, Mil Inf
COOLY, Johnathan, Tptr, Regt Commander omitted, Capt Jas Haggan, Mtd Gunmen; on furlough 4-6-1814 & absent
COON, Jas, Pvt, Col John Alcorn, Capt Frederick Stump, Cav
COON (KUHN), Peter, Pvt, Col Wm Lillard, Capt Wm McLin, E TN Inf
COONCE, Henry, Pvt, Col S Copeland, Capt George, Inf
COONCE, Martin, Pvt, Col Robert Steele, Capt Jas Bennett, Mil Inf
COONCE, Nathaniel, Pvt, Col Robert Steele, Capt Jas Bennett, Mil Inf
COONTS, Jacob, Pvt, Col Wm Johnson, Capt Jas Stewart, E TN Mil
COOP, Richard, Pvt, Col Robert Steele, Capt Jas Shenault, Mil Inf
COOPER, Abraham, Pvt, Col Robert H Dyer, Capt James Wyatt, Vol Mtd Gunmen
COOPER, Abraham, Pvt, Maj Wm Russell, Capt Geo Mitchi?, Vol Mtd Gunmen
COOPER, Archibald, Pvt, Col Samuel Bayless, Capt John Brock, E TN Mil
COOPER, Benj, Pvt, Col Edwin Booth, Capt Porter, Drafted Mil
COOPER, Carmady, Pvt, Col James Raulston, Capt Wiley Huddleston, Capt Gen'l Carroll, Inf
COOPER, David, Pvt, Col Loury, Capt Gabriel Martin, Inf
COOPER, David, Pvt, Col S Bunch, Capt Jones Griffin, E TN Drafted Mil; deserted 3-4-1814
COOPER, Edmund, Pvt, Col Thomas McCrory, Capt William Dooley, Inf
COOPER, Elijah, Pvt, Regt Commander omitted, Capt N Davis, Branch Srvce omitted
COOPER, Geo, Pvt, Col John Coffee, Capt John Baskerville, Cav
COOPER, Geo, Pvt, Col S Copeland, Capt Jas Tait, Inf
COOPER, Geo, Pvt, Col Thomas Benton, Capt William Moore, Vol Inf
COOPER, Geo, Pvt, Col Wm Pillow, Capt William Moore, Inf
COOPER, Geo, Pvt, Gen Andrew Jackson, Capt Hugh Kerr, Mtd Rangers
COOPER, Henry, Pvt, Regt Commander omitted, Capt David Deadrick, Arty
COOPER, Jacob, Pvt, Col Edward Bradley, Capt John Kennedy, Riflemen
COOPER, Jno, Pvt, Col S Bunch, Capt Jno Houk, E TN Mil; joined from Capt Berry's Co
COOPER, Jno, Pvt, Regt Commander omitted, Capt Geo Smith, Spies

- 137

## Enlisted Men, War of 1812

COOPER, Jno, Pvt, Regt Commander omitted, Capt Jos Williams, Mil Cav
COOPER, John, Pvt, Col Edward Bradley, Capt John Kennedy, Riflemen
COOPER, John, Pvt, Col Jno Coffee, Capt Michael Molton, Cav
COOPER, John, Pvt, Col John K Wynne, Capt John Porter, Inf
COOPER, John, Pvt, Col Newton Cannon, Capt Francis Jones, Mtd Riflemen
COOPER, John, Pvt, Col R C Napier, Capt Drury Adkins, Mil Inf
COOPER, John, Pvt, Col R H Dyer, Capt Beverly Williams, Vol Mtd Gunmen
COOPER, John, Pvt, Col S Bunch, Capt Francis Berry, E TN Mil; attached to Capt Hauk's Co
COOPER, John, Pvt, Col Samuel Bayless, Capt Branch Jones, E TN Drafted Mil
COOPER, John, Pvt, Col Stephen Copeland, Capt Fait, Inf
COOPER, John, Pvt, Col Thos Bradley, Capt Brice Martin, Vol Inf
COOPER, John, Pvt, Col Wm Hall, Capt Brice Martin, E TN Drafted Mil
COOPER, John, Pvt, Maj John Childs, Capt John Stephens, E TN Vol Mtd Inf
COOPER, John, Pvt, Regt Commander omitted, Capt Thos Gray, Inf
COOPER, John, Sgt, Col Jno Brown, Capt Lunsford Oliver, E TN Mil
COOPER, Jonathan, Pvt, Col Wm Lillard, Capt Hugh Martin, E TN Vol Inf
COOPER, Jos, 4 Cpl, Col Wm Metcalf, Capt Wm Mullen, Mil Inf
COOPER, Jos, Pvt, Col Samuel Wear, Capt Jesse Cole, Vol Inf
COOPER, Joshua F (Joseph), Pvt, Col John Cocke, Capt John Dalton, Inf
COOPER, Len, Pvt, Regt Commander omitted, Capt Nathan Davis, Branch Srvce omitted
COOPER, Leon, Pvt, no other information
COOPER, Matthew D, Pvt, Col Thos Benton, Capt Jas McEwen, Vol Inf
COOPER, Meridith, Pvt, Col T McCrory, Capt A Metcalf, Mil Inf; wounded at battle of Talledege 11-9-1813
COOPER, Peter, Pvt, Col S Bunch, Capt Andrew Breden, E TN Mil
COOPER, Richard, Pvt, Col Samuel Wear, Capt John Doak, E TN Vol Inf
COOPER, Richard, Pvt, Lt Col A Cheatham, Co Commander omitted, Mtd Inf
COOPER, Robert M, Pvt, Col William Metcalf, Capt Bird Hurt, Mil Inf
COOPER, Robert, Cpl, Col Edwin Booth, Capt Samuel Thompson, Mil
COOPER, Robert, Pvt, Col Edwin Booth, Capt John Sharp, E TN Mil
COOPER, Samuel, Pvt, Col Newton Cannon, Capt Francis Jones, Mtd Riflemen
COOPER, Stephen, Pvt, Col Edward Bradley, Capt Martin, Vol Inf
COOPER, Stephen, Pvt, Col S Copeland, Capt Moses Thompson, Inf
COOPER, Stephen, Pvt, Col Thomas Williamson, Capt George Mitchie, 2nd Regt TN Vol Mtd Gunmen
COOPER, Stephen, Pvt, Col William Hall, Capt Brice Martin, Vol Inf
COOPER, Thomas, Pvt, Col Samuel Wear, Capt James Tedford, E TN Vol Inf
COOPER, Wells, Pvt, Col Edward Bradley, Capt Travis Nash, Vol Inf
COOPER, Wells, Pvt, Col William Hall, Capt Travis Nash, Inf
COOPER, William, 2 Cpl, Col N T Perkins, Capt Philip Pipkin, Mtd Riflemen
COOPER, William, Pvt, Col John Brown, Capt William White, E TN Vol Mtd Inf
COOPER, William, Pvt, Col Robert Dyer, Capt Glen Owen, 1st TN Vol Mtd Gunmen
COOPER, William, Pvt, Col Robert Dyer, Capt Robert Edmonston, 1st TN Vol Mtd Gunmen; d 1-5-1815
COOPER, William, Pvt, Col Robert Steele, Capt James Shenault, Mil Inf; on furlough
COOPER, William, Pvt, Col Samuel Wear, Capt James Tedford, E TN Vol Inf
COOPER, William, Pvt, Maj William Woodfolk, Capt James Neil, Inf
COOPER, ___, Pvt, Col William Johnson, Capt Joseph Scott, E TN Drafted Mil; substitute for John Gamble
COOPWOOD, Thomas, Pvt, Col William Higgins, Capt Adam Dale, Mtd Gunmen
COOPWOOD, William, Pvt, Col William Higgins, Capt Adam Dale, Mtd Gunmen
COOPWOOD, Woodson, Pvt, Col William Higgins, Capt Adam Dale, Mtd Gunmen
COOS, Adam, Rank omitted, Col Samuel Bunch, Lt John Harris, E TN Mil
COOS, William, Pvt, Col Samuel Bunch, Lt John Harris, E TN Mil
COOSE, Barachias, Pvt, Col Samuel Bunch, Capt Joseph Duncan, E TN Drafted Mil
COOSE, William, Pvt, Col Samuel Bayless, Capt Joseph Rich, E TN Inf
COOSE, William, Pvt, Col Samuel Bunch, Capt Joseph Duncan, E TN Drafted Mil; joined from Capt Howel's Co
COOTHE, John, Sgt, Maj William Russell, Capt John Cowan, Vol Mtd Gunmen
COOTY, Daniel, Pvt, Col Samuel Bunch, Capt Solomon Dobkins, E TN Mil Drafted; furloughed for inability
COPEL, James, Pvt, Col John Brown, Capt William Neilson, E TN Vol Mil
COPELAN, Hugh, Dmr, Col Edwin Booth, Capt John Sharp, E TN Mil
COPELAND, Anthony, Pvt, Col Thomas McCrory, Capt Samuel McKnight, Inf
COPELAND, Jas, Pvt, Col Edwin Booth, Capt Vernon, E TN Mil
COPELAND, Jas, Pvt, Col Thomas McCrory, Capt William Dooley, Inf; sick absent

## Enlisted Men, War of 1812

COPELAND, Jno, Pvt, Col S Bunch, Capt Geo Gregory, E TN Drafted Mil; substitute James Haskins until better health

COPELAND, Jno, Pvt, Col S Bunch, Capt Geo Gregory, E TN Mil

COPELAND, Jno, Pvt, Regt Commande omitted, Capt Jno Miller, Spies

COPELAND, John, 2 Cpl, Col William Lillard, Capt Zacheus Copeland, E TN Vol Inf; exchanged places with James Haskins

COPELAND, John, Pvt, Col Abraham Allison, Capt Allen, E TN Mil

COPELAND, John, Pvt, Col Edward Bradley, Capt John Kennedy, Riflemen; sick on furlough

COPELAND, John, Pvt, Col John Cocke, Capt John Weakley, Inf

COPELAND, John, Pvt, Col John K Wynne, Capt William Wilson, Inf

COPELAND, John, Pvt, Col William Hall, Capt John Kennedy, Vol Inf; absent

COPELAND, Jos jr, Pvt, Col Wm Lillard, Capt Zacheus Copeland, E TN Vol Inf; exchanged places with Joseph McChristian

COPELAND, Jos, Pvt, Col S Bunch, Capt Geo Gregory, E TN Drafted Mil; sub for Jos McQuister furloughed till better health

COPELAND, Jos, Pvt, Col William Johnston, Capt Elihu Milliken, 3rd Regt E TN Mil

COPELAND, Jos, Sgt, Col William Johnston, Capt Elihu Milliken, 3rd Regt E TN Mil

COPELAND, Joseph sr, 3 Cpl, Col William Lillard, Capt Zacheus Copeland, E TN Vol Inf

COPELAND, Richard, Pvt, Col T McCrory, Capt Abel Willis, Mil Inf; sick absent

COPELAND, Stephen jr, Pvt, Col S Copeland, Capt David Williams, Inf

COPELAND, Stephen jr, Pvt, Col S Copeland, Co Commander illegible, 3rd Regt E TN Mil

COPELAND, Westley, Pvt, Col S Copeland, Capt John Biles, Inf

COPELAND, William, Pvt, Col Ewen Allison, Capt Allen, E TN Mil

COPELAND, William, Pvt, Col Wm Johnston, Capt Elihu Milliken, 3rd Regt E TN Mil

COPELAND, Willis, Pvt, Col Wm Metcalf, Capt Andrew Patterson, Mil Inf

COPELAND, _____, Pvt, Maj William Woodfolk, Capt James C Neil, Inf; substitute for Thos Bell

COPELIN, David, Pvt, Col Samuel Bayless, Capt Solomon Hendricks, E TN Mil

COPELIN, John, Pvt, Col John Cocke, Capt John Weakley, Inf

COPLE, Sam'l, Pvt, Col Wm Higgins, Capt Sam'l Allen, Mtd TN Gunmen

COPP, John, Pvt, Col Ewen Allison, Capt Henry McCray, E TN Mil; transferred to Capt Register

CORALEY, John, Pvt, no other information

CORAM, Robt, Pvt, Col Wm Hall, Capt B Martin, Vol Inf

CORAM (CORUM), Henry, Pvt, Col Wm Hall, Capt Brice Martin, Vol Inf

CORBAN, Isaac, Pvt, Col S Bunch, Capt Dan Yarnell, E TN Mil

CORBAN, Isaac, Pvt, Col S Bunch, Capt Jos Duncan, E TN Drafted Mil; joined from Capt Yarnell Co

CORBELL, Thos, Pvt, Col John Cocke, Capt G Barnes, Inf; d 1-9-1815

CORBET, John, Pvt, Col N T Perkins, Capt Philip Pipkin, Mtd Riflemen

CORBETT, Allen, Pvt, Col John Alcorn, Capt Alex McKeen, Cav

CORBETT, Allen, Pvt, Col Thomas Williamson, Capt Richard Tate, Vol Mtd Gunmen; on furlough since 11-23-1814 sick

CORBETT, Benj, Pvt, Col C? Bayless, Capt Branch Jones, E TN Drafted Mil

CORBETT, Jesse, Pvt, Col N Cannon, Capt J B Demsey, Mtd Gunmen

CORBIN, Isaac, Pvt, Col Johnson, Capt Jas Terrell, E TN Mil

CORBITT, Allen, Pvt, Col John Coffee, Capt Alex McKeen, Cav

CORBY, Hamer, Pvt, Regt Commander omitted, Capt Arch McKenney, Cav

CORBY, William, Pvt, Regt Commander omitted, Capt Arch McKenney, Cav

CORDAN (CORDE), Ezeriah, Pvt, Col John Cocke, Capt Bird Nance, Inf

CORDELL, Isom, Pvt, Maj Wm Russell, Capt John Trimble, Vol Mtd Gunmen

CORDELL, John, Pvt, Col Alex Loury, Capt Gabriel Martin, Inf

CORDELL, Thos, Pvt, Col R C Napier, Capt Jas McMurray, Mil Inf

CORDER, Elijah, Pvt, Col Wm Johnson, Capt Christopher Cook, E TN Mil

CORDER, Elijah, Pvt, Col Wm Johnson, Capt Joe Kirk, Mil

CORDER, Jas, Pvt, Col Philip Pipkin, Capt Geo Mebane, Mil Inf

CORDER, William, Pvt, Col John Alcorn, Capt John Baskerville, Vol Inf

CORDER, William, Pvt, Col John Coffee, Capt John Baskerville, Cav

CORE, Geo, Pvt, Col Alexander Loury, Lt Col Simmons, Capt Thos Delaney, Inf

CORE, Jonathan, Pvt, Regt Commander omitted, Capt Arch McKinney, Cav

CORGAN, Patrick, Pvt, Col John Cocke, Capt John Dalton, Inf; appointed hospital Stewart

CORLEE, Calvin, Pvt, Col Thomas Benton, Capt Jas McFerrin, Vol Inf; absent

CORLEE, Cullen, Pvt, Col Thomas Benton, Capt Jas McFerrin, Vol Inf

CORLEY, Geo, Ens, Col S Copeland, Capt John Dawson, Inf

CORLEY, Harm, Pvt, Regt Commander omitted, Capt Archibald McKinney, Cav

CORLEY, Mathew, Pvt, Col S Copeland, Capt John Dawson, Inf

CORLEY, Wm, Pvt, Regt Commander omitted, Capt Archibald McKinney, Cav

CORLOCK, Reuben, Pvt, Col Edward Bradley, Capt John

Kennedy, Riflemen
CORMS, John, Pvt, Col Samuel Bayless, Capt Jas Churchman, E TN Mil
CORN, Samuel, 2 Cpl, Col Wm Pillow, Capt Geo Caperton, Inf
CORN, Samuel, 4 Cpl, Col Thomas Benton, Capt Geo Caperton, Inf
CORNELIUS, Edmond, Pvt, Col John Coffee, Capt L Ferrill, Vol Cav
CORNELIUS, Edmond, Pvt, Maj William Russell, Capt Fleman Hodges, Vol Mtd Gunmen; substitute for Lewis Broadaway
CORNELIUS, Edmond, Pvt, Regt Commander omitted, Capt Jas Terrell, Cav; old Vol discharged
CORNELL, Sampson, Pvt, Regt Commander omitted, Capt Jas Haggard, Mtd Gunmen
CORNETT, Davis, Pvt, Col Samuel Bunch, Capt Robert Breden, E TN Mil; transferred to Capt Bacon Co
CORNETT, John, Pvt, Col Samuel Bunch, Capt Andrew Breden, E TN Mil
CORPOCK, Geo, Pvt, Col Samuel Bunch, Capt Daniel Yarnell, E TN Mil
CORPOCK, Jacob, Sgt, Col Samuel Bunch, Capt Geo Gregory, E TN Drafted Mil; appointed for Private
CORPS, George, Pvt, Maj William Russell, Capt Fleman Hodges, Vol Mtd Gunmen
CORRETHERS, Jas, Pvt, Col Alexander Loury, Lt Col Leroy Hammonds, Capt Thomas Delaney, Inf
CORRY, Jas, Pvt, Col Samuel Wear, Capt James Gillespie, E TN Vol Inf
CORT (KORTY), John, Sgt, Col William Lillard, Capt Wm McLin, E TN Inf
CORTENY, John, Pvt, Col Wm Johnson, Capt Jas Stewart, E TN Mil Drafted; substitute
CORTNEY, Wm, Pvt, Col Samuel Bayless, Capt Jonathan Waddell, E TN Mil
CORUM, Henry, Pvt, Col Wm Hall, Capt Brice Martin, Vol Inf
CORUM, Robert, Pvt, Col Edward Bradley, Capt Brice Martin, Vol Inf
CORUM, Robert, Pvt, Col Wm Hall, Capt Brice Martin, Vol Inf
CORY, Wm, Pvt, Col William Johnson, Capt Elihu Millikin, 3rd Regt E TN Mil
COSBY, Garland, Pvt, Col Thomas Benton, Capt Jas McEwen, Vol Inf
COSBY, George, Pvt, Col John Brown, Capt William White, E TN Mil Inf
COSBY, Jas, Surgeon Mate, Col John Brown, Co Commander omitted, E TN Mtd Gunmen
COSBY, John, Pvt, Col John Brown, Capt Jesse G Reany, Mtd Gunmen
COSBY, Wm, Pvt, Col Wm Metcalf, Capt William Mullin, Mil Inf
COSLEY, George, Pvt, Col John Brown, Capt Jesse G Reany, Mtd Gunmen
COSSEY, Chas, Pvt, Col Thomas Williamson, Capt Richard Tate, Vol Mtd Gunmen
COSTEELE, Jeremiah, Pvt, Col Wm Lillard, Capt Robert Maloney, E TN Vol Inf
COSTILLO, Jas, Pvt, Col A Loury, Capt J N Williamson, W TN Mil
COSTILOW, James, Pvt, Col S Hammonds, Capt J N Williamson, 2nd Regt Inf; unable to perform duty left sick at Ft Strother
COTHAM, Elijah, Pvt, Col Thomas Williamson, Capt John Dobbins, Capt Robert Doak, Vol Mtd Gunmen
COTHRAN, Hutson, Pvt, Col Thomas Scurry, Capt Thomas Williamson, Vol Mtd Gunmen; no service performed
COTHRAN, Jeremiah, Pvt, Col A Cheatham, Capt Thomas Benson, Inf
COTHRONS (COTRON), Adam, Pvt, Col Wm Lillard, Capt Robert McCalpin, E TN Inf
COTLER, Wm, Pvt, Col John Cocke, Capt George Barnes, Inf; cleared by Court Martial 11-18-1814
COTLETT, Benj, Pvt, Col S Bunch, Capt Jno Houch, E TN Mil; joined for Capt Williams Co, discharged for inability
COTLETT, John, Pvt, Col William Johnson, Capt Jas Cook, E TN Mil
COTNER, John, Pvt, Col Wm Lillard, Capt Thomas Sharpe, 2nd Regt Inf
COTNER, Marlin, Pvt, Col Samuel Bayless, Capt Joseph Rich, E TN Inf
COTRELL, Pryer, Pvt, Col Robert Steele, Capt Samuel Maxwell, Mil Inf
COTTEN, Alexander, Cpl, Col Alcorn, Capt Byrn, Cav
COTTEN, Caleb, Pvt, Col N Cannon, Capt Ota Cantrell, W TN Mtd Inf; deserted 10-14-1813
COTTEN, Jas W, Pvt, Col Samuel Bunch, Capt Thomas Mann, E TN Vol Mtd Inf
COTTEN, John, Pvt, Col Robert Dyer, Capt Isaac Williams, Vol Mtd Gunmen
COTTENGIN, William, Pvt, Regt Commander omitted, Capt Archibald McKinney, Cav
COTTENHAM, John, Pvt, Col John Cocke, Capt James Gray, Inf; discharged by court martial
COTTENHAM, William, Pvt, Col Robert Dyer, Capt Isaac Williams, Vol Mtd Gunmen
COTTER, John, Pvt, Col S Booth, Capt Archibald McKinney, E TN Mil
COTTER, John, Pvt, Col Samuel Bayless, Capt Joseph Hale, E TN Mil
COTTER, William, Pvt, Col Samuel Bunch, Capt Francis Register, E TN Mil; deserted
COTTERILL, Allen, Pvt, Col S Copeland, Capt John Dawson, Inf
COTTERILL, Martin, Pvt, Col S Copeland, Capt John Dawson, Inf
COTTESREN, Daniel, Pvt, Col S Bunch, Capt George McPherson, E TN Mil
COTTINGER, Jonathan, Pvt, Gen Anddrew Jackson, Capt Hugh Kerr, Mtd Rangers
COTTINGHAM, William, Pvt, Regt Commander omitted, Capt Gray, Inf
COTTINS, Owen, Pvt, Col Samuel Bayless, Capt John Brock, E TN Mil
COTTON, Alexander, Cpl, Col John Coffee, Capt John W Byrns, Cav
COTTON, Allen, Pvt, Gen Thomas Washington, Co

## Enlisted Men, War of 1812

COTTON, Allen, Tptr, Col John Coffee, Capt John W Byrn, Cav
Commander omitted, Mtd Inf
COTTON, Alton, Pvt, Col William Metcalf, Capt William Sitton, Mil Inf
COTTON, Caleb, Pvt, Col William Metcalf, Capt Thomas Marks, Mil Inf
COTTON, Caleb, Pvt, Col William Metcalf, Capt William Mullen, Mil Inf
COTTON, Charles, Sgt, no other information
COTTON, James, Sgt, Col William Y Higgins, Capt Thomas Eldridge, Mtd Gunmen
COTTON, John, 3 Sgt, Col William Metcalf, Capt William Sitton, Mil Inf
COTTON, John, 4 Sgt, Col John Coffee, Capt John W Byrns, Cav
COTTON, John, Pvt, Col John Wynne, Capt John Porter, Inf
COTTON, John, Pvt, Col R H Dyer, Capt Ephraim D Dickson, TN Mtd Vol Gunmen; no service performed
COTTON, John, Pvt, Col S Copeland, Capt John Holshouser, Inf
COTTON, John, Pvt, Col Thomas Williamson, Capt Richard Tate, Vol Mtd Gunmen
COTTON, John, Pvt, Col William Lillard, Capt William Hamilton, E TN Vol Inf
COTTON, John, Pvt, Regt Commander omitted, Capt Ephraim Dickson, Branch omitted
COTTON, John, Sgt, Col William Alcorn, Capt John W Byrne, Cav
COTTON, Nathaniel, Waiter to Maj Powers, Col John Cocke, 2 Regt W TN Mil Inf
COTTON, Peter, Pvt, Col William Lillard, Capt William Hamilton, E TN Vol Inf
COTTON, Peter, Pvt, Regt Commander omitted, Capt J Previtt, Mtd Vol
COTTON, Shadrack, Pvt, Col S Bunch, Capt John English, E TN Draft Mil
COTTON, Shadrick, Pvt, Col S Bunch, Capt Solomon Dobkins, E TN Draft Mil
COTTON, Thomas, Pvt, Col A Cheatham, Capt William Smith, Inf
COTTON, William, Pvt, Col John K Wynne, Capt James Holleman, Inf
COTTON, William, Pvt, Lt Col L Hammonds, Capt James Craig, Inf
COTTON, William, Pvt, Regt Commander omitted, Capt John Craig, Inf
COTTRELL, John, Pvt, Maj John Childs, Capt Charles Conway, E TN Mtd Gunmen
COTTRELL, William, Pvt, Col Newton Cannon, Capt James Walton, Mtd Riflemen; killed 11-2-1813 at Tellesche
COUCH, David, Pvt, Col Samuel Wear, Capt John Childs, E TN Vol Inf
COUCH, Jacob, Pvt, Col William Johnson, Capt Christopher Cooks, E TN Mil
COUCH, James, Pvt, Col Philip Pipkin, Capt David Smythe, Inf
COUCH, John, Pvt, Col Ewen Allison, Capt Jacob Hoyal, E TN Mil; transferred to Capt Register's Co
COUCH, John, Pvt, Col S Bunch, Capt F Register, E TN Inf; joined from Capt Hughes' Co
COUCH, John, Pvt, Col Samuel Bayless, Capt Branch Jones, E TN Draft Mil; transferred to Capt Goodson's Co
COUCH, John, Pvt, Col Samuel Bayless, Capt Goodson, E TN Mil; joined from Capt Jones' Co
COUCH, John, Pvt, Col Samuel Bunch, Capt F Register, E TN Mil; joined from Capt Hoyles' Co
COUCH, John, Pvt, Col William Johnson, Capt James Cook, E TN Mil
COUCH, John, Pvt, Gen Thomas Johnston, Capt Daniel Oban, 36 Inf
COUCH, Jonathan, Pvt, Col Samuel Wear, Capt John Childs, E TN Vol Inf
COUCH, Joseph, Pvt, no other information; died 3-12-1814
COUCH, Thomas, Pvt, Regt Commander omitted, Capt Nathan Davis Batton, Branch omitted
COULBOURN, Richard, Pvt, Col Samuel Bayless, Capt Joseph Hale, Branch omitted; died 3-8-1815
COULTER, Abraham S, Pvt, Maj John Childs, Capt John Stephens, E TN Vol Mtd Inf
COULTER, Eli, Pvt, Col William Lillard, Capt Thomas Sharpe, 2 Regt Inf
COULTER, James, Asst Wgnmstr, Brig Gen George Doherty, no Co, E TN Mil
COULTER, James, Pvt, Col Thomas Williamson, Capt John Crane & Capt James Cook, Vol Mtd Gunmen
COULTER, Jesse, Pvt, Col William Hall, Capt John Moore, Vol Inf
COULTER, John, Pvt, Col Edwin Booth, Capt John Slatton, E TN Mil
COULTER, Thomas, 2 Lt, Col John Brown, Capt Allen I Bacon, E TN Inf Mil; promoted from 2 to 3 Lt
COULTER, Thomas, Brig Gen, E TN Draft Mil; cashiered 3-31-1815
COULTER, Thomas, Sgt, Col Samuel Bayless, Capt Joseph Rich, E TN Inf
COUNCE, Isaac, Pvt, Col Thomas Benton, Capt George W Gibbs, Vol Inf; AWOL
COUNCEL, Dudley, Pvt, Col A Lour, Capt Gabriel Martin, Inf
COUNCELL, Jesse, 6 Cpl, Col Philip Pipkin, Capt William Mackay, Mil Inf
COUNCIL, Jesse, Col Philip Pipkin, Capt William Mackay, Mil Inf
COUNCIL, William, Pvt, Col John Alcorn, Capt John Baskerville, Vol Inf
COUNCIL, William, Pvt, Gen John Coffee, no Co Commander, Mtd Spies
COUNCILL, William, Pvt, Col Thomas Williamson, Capt Richard Tate, Vol Mtd Gunmen; transferred to Lt Bean's Spies
COUNSET, Will, Pvt, Col John Coffee, Capt John Baskerville, Cav
COUNT, Adam, Pvt, Maj William Woodfolk, Capt Abner Pearce, Inf
COUNT, Henry, Pvt, Col S Bunch, Lt John Harris, E TN

- 141

## Enlisted Men, War of 1812

Mil
COUNTS, Adam, Cpl, Maj William Woodfolk, Capt Abner Pearce, Inf; promoted from Pvt to Cpl
COUNTS, George, no other information
COUNTS, Henry, Pvt, Col William Metcalf, Capt William Sitton, Mil Inf
COUNTS, Jacob, Pvt, Col William Johnson, Capt James Stewart, E TN Draft Mil
COUNTS, John, Pvt, Regt Commander missing, Capt George McPherson, Branch omitted
COUNTS, John, Sgt, Col Ewen Allison, Capt Jonas Loughmiller, transferred to Capt McPherson's Co
COUNTS, John, Sgt, Col S Bunch, Capt George McPherson, E TN Mil; joined from Capt Everett's Co
COUNTS, Peter, Pvt, Col William Metcalf, Capt William Sitton, Mil Inf
COURRY, Lewis, Pvt, Col Thomas Benton, Capt George Caperton, Vol Inf
COUTCH, Jacob, Pvt, Col William Johnson, Capt Joseph Kirk, Mil
COUTCH, John, Pvt, Col William Johnson, Capt Joseph Kirk, Mil
COUTS, William, Sgt, Col Thomas Williamson, Capt John Crane & Capt James Cook, Vol Mtd Gunmen
COVENDER, Edward, Pvt, Col John Cocke, Capt Samuel M Caruthers, Inf
COVEY, Russell R, 1 Cpl, Col William Metcalf, Capt Bird L Hurt, Mil Inf
COVINGTON, Henry, Pvt, Col John Cocke, Capt Richard Crunk, Inf; died 3-11-1815
COVINGTON, Jesse, Pvt, Col T McCrory, Capt John Reynolds, Mil Inf
COVINGTON, John, Pvt, Col Edwin Booth, Capt John Lewis, E TN Mil
COVINGTON, Larkin (Larkington), Pvt, Col Alexander Loury, Capt James Kincaid, Inf
COVINGTON, Lewis, Pvt, Col Ewen Allison, Capt James Allen, E TN Mil
COVINGTON, Lewis, Pvt, Col S Bunch, Capt John English, E TN Draft Mil
COVINGTON, Richard, Pvt, Col S Bunch, Capt Daniel Yarnell, E TN Mil; deserted
COVINGTON, Richard, Pvt, Col William Johnson, Capt Stuart, E TN Draft Mil
COVINGTON, William, Pvt, Col John Coffee, Capt John Byrn, Cav
COWADIC, William, Sgt, Col William Johnston, Capt Christopher Cook, E TN Mil
COWAN, Andrew, Pvt, Brig Gen James White, no other information; app spy
COWAN, Andrew, Pvt, Col John Williams, Capt William Walker, Vol
COWAN, Andrew, Pvt, Col Thomas Benton, Capt George W Gibbs, Vol Inf
COWAN, Andrew, Pvt, Col William Lillard, Capt Benjamin H Kings, E TN Vol Inf
COWAN, Andrew, Sgt, Col Robert Steele, Capt James Randals, Inf; AWOL
COWAN, Andrew, Sgt, Col William Pillow, Capt John H Anderson, Vol Inf

COWAN, David, Pvt, Col Thomas H Benton, Capt George W Gibbs, Vol Inf
COWAN, James P, Pvt, Col Thomas H Benton, Capt George Caperton, Inf
COWAN, James, Pvt, Col Alexander Loury, Lt Col Leroy Hammonds, Inf
COWAN, James, Pvt, Col John Alcorn, Capt Wm Locke, Cav
COWAN, James, Pvt, Maj William Russell, Capt John Cowan, Vol Mtd Gunmen
COWAN, Joel W, Pvt, Col Samuel Bayless, Capt James Churchman, E TN Mil; transferred from Capt Jones Co
COWAN, John, Pvt, Col N T Perkins, Capt John Quarles, Vol Mtd Inf
COWAN, John, Pvt, Col William Lillard, Capt William McLin, E TN Inf
COWAN, John, Pvt, Regt Commander omitted, Capt James Cowan, Inf
COWAN, Joseph, Cpl, Col John Coffee, Capt Charles Kavanaugh, Cav
COWAN, Robert, Pvt, Capt James Cowan, Mtd Inf
COWAN, Samuel, Pvt, Col John Brown, Capt James Standifer, E TN Vol Mtd Mil
COWAN, Samuel, Pvt, Col John Brown, Capt Jesse G Reany, Mtd Gunmen
COWAN, Thompson, Pvt, Col William Lillard, Capt Zacheus Copeland, E TN Vol Inf
COWAN, Wesley, Pvt, Col Philip Pipkin, Capt Ebenezer Kirkpatrick, Mil Inf
COWAN, William, 2 Cpl, Col John Cocke, Capt John Dalton, Inf
COWAN, William, Pvt, Col John Coffee, Capt Chas Kavanaugh, Cav
COWAN, William, Pvt, Col William Lillard, Capt Benjamin H Kings, E TN Vol Inf
COWARD, Elisha, Pvt, Col William Lillard, Capt William Gillenwater, E TN Inf
COWARD, Isaac, Pvt, Col Samuel Bunch, Capt Bacon, E TN Mil
COWARD, James, Pvt, Col Allison, Capt Joseph Everett, E TN Mil; transferred to Capt McPherson's Co
COWARD, John, Pvt, Col John Cocke, Capt James Gault, Inf
COWARD, John, Pvt, Col William Johnson, Capt James Tunnell, E TN Mil
COWARD, John, Pvt, Col William Lillard, Capt William Gillenwater, E Tn Inf
COWARD, Lewis, Pvt, Maj John Childs, Capt Cummings, E Tn Vol Mtd Inf
COWARD, Thomas, Pvt, Col William Johnson, Capt James Stewart, E TN Draft Mil
COWARD, William, Pvt, Col John Cocke, Capt James Gault, Inf
COWDEN, Elisha, Pvt, Col William Metcalf, Capt Andrew Patterson, Mil Inf
COWDEN, Henry, Pvt, Col R H Dyer, Capt Evans, Vol Mtd Gunmen; deserted
COWDEN, Josiah, Pvt, Regt Commander omitted, Capt Nathan Davis Batt, Branch omitted
COWDEN, William, Pvt, Regt Commander omitted, Capt

James Cowan, Inf
COWELL, Colby, Pvt, Col S Bunch, Capt Daniel Yarnell, E TN Mil
COWELL, James B, Pvt, Col John Cocke, Capt Gray, Inf
COWELL, James B, Pvt, Col John Cocke, Co Commander omitted, Inf; died 2-14-1815
COWEN, Davice, Cpl, Maj William Woodfolk, Capt Pearce, Inf
COWEN, Isaac, Pvt, Col James Raulston, Capt Charles Wade, Inf
COWEN, James B, Pvt, Col Thomas H Benton, Capt Caperton, Vol Inf
COWEN, James, Pvt, Col William Metcalf, Capt Waller, Mil Inf
COWEN, Joseph, Pvt, Col A Cheatham, Capt James Giddens, Inf
COWEN, Joseph, Pvt, Col William Pillow, Capt John H Anderson, Vol Inf
COWEN, W Wallis, Pvt, Col Johnson, Capt Elihu Millikin, 3 Regt E TN Mil
COWEN, West, Pvt, Col Philip Pipkin, Capt Ebenezer Kirkpatrick, Mil Inf
COWEN, William, Pvt, Col Samuel Wear, Col Samuel Bunch, Capt William Mitchell, E TN Mtd Inf
COWERY, William Pvt, Lt Col Richard Napier, Co Commander omitted, Inf
COWGER, Adam, Blksmth, Col John Coffee, Capt J W Byrn, Cav
COWGER, John, Cpl, Col Thomas Williamson, Capt Beverly Williams, Vol Mtd Gunmen
COWGILL, Henry, Pvt, Col William Metcalf, Capt William Mullen, Mil Inf
COWGILL, Martin, Pvt, Col Edward Bradley, Capt Harry Douglass, Vol Inf
COWSAER, Andrew, Far, Regt Commander omitted, Capt Arch McKinney, Cav
COWSER, John F, Pvt, Col John Coffee, Capt Blackman Coleman, Cav
COWSERT, Andrew, Far, no other information
COWSERT, Andrew, Pvt, Col John Coffee, Capt Charles Kavanaugh, Cav, AWOL
COX, Abraham, Pvt, Col Ewen Allison, Capt Allison, E TN Mil
COX, Adam, Pvt, Col John Coffee, Capt B Coleman, Cav
COX, Amon, Pvt, Col Thomas Benton, Capt George Caperton, Vol Inf; refused to march
COX, Archillar, Pvt, Col Thomas Benton, Capt Thomas Williamson, Vol Inf
COX, Archillar, Pvt, Col William Pillow, Capt Thomas Williamson, Vol Inf
COX, Archillus, Pvt, Col Thomas Benton, Capt Thomas Williamson, Vol Inf
COX, Bartlett, Pvt, Col Sam Bayless, Capt Joseph Bacon, E TN Mil
COX, Bartley, Pvt, Col William Lillard, Capt Roper, E TN Mil Inf
COX, Benjamin, Pvt, Col William Lillard, Capt Thomas Sharpe, 2 Inf
COX, Benjamin, Pvt, Maj Woodfok, Capt Ezekial Ross, Inf; enlisted in Regular Svce
COX, Bowsley, Pvt, Col Ewen Allison, Capt William King, Draft Mil
COX, Caleb, Pvt, Col S Copeland, Capt John Biles, Inf
COX, Coleman, Pvt, Col John Williams, Capt William Walker, Vol
COX, Edmund, Pvt, Col S Bunch, Capt T Roberson, E TN Draft Mil
COX, Edmund, Pvt, Regt Commander omitted, Capt Samuel Richardson, E TN Draft Mil
COX, Elisha jr, Pvt, Col Thomas Williamson, Capt John Hutchings, Vol Mtd Gunmen
COX, Elisha, Pvt, Col Thomas Benton, Capt George Gibbs, Vol Inf; AWOL
COX, Elisha, Pvt, Col Thomas Williamson, Capt Richard Tate, Vol Mtd Gunmen
COX, Francis B, Pvt, Col John Alcorn, Capt Wm Locke, Cav
COX, Francis B, Pvt, Col John Coffee, Capt B Coleman, Cav
COX, Francis B, Pvt, Col Thos Williamson, Capt Richard Tate, Vol Mtd Gunmen
COX, Francis B, Sgt, Col Thos Williamson, Capt John Hutchings, Vol Mtd Gunmen
COX, Gails, Pvt, Col Ewen Allison, Capt Wm King, Drafted Mil; promoted to QM
COX, Gate, Regt QM, Col Ewen Allison, Co Commander illegible, E TN Mil; left sick at Ft Williams 3-18-1814
COX, George, Pvt, Col Leroy Hammonds, Capt Jas Tubb, Inf
COX, Godfrey, Pvt, Col Saml Bayless, Capt Jas Landen, E TN Mil
COX, Henry, Sgt, Col Thos Williamson, Capt Richard Tate, Vol Mtd Gunmen
COX, Hopkin, Pvt, Col Sam'l Bunch, Capt Francis Berry, E TN Mil
COX, Isaac, Pvt, Col S Bunch, Capt F Register, E TN Mil; joined Capt McPherson Co
COX, Isaac, Pvt, Col S Bunch, Capt Francis Berry, E TN Mil, transferred to Capt Richardson Co
COX, Isaac, Pvt, Col S Bunch, Capt Geo McPherson, E TN Mil
COX, Isaac, Pvt, Regt Commander omitted, Capt Sam Richardson, E TN Mil
COX, Isham, Pvt, Col John Brown, Capt Wm White, E TN Mil Inf
COX, Isham, Sgt, Col John Brown, Capt Jas McKamey, E TN Mtd Gunmen
COX, Jacob, Pvt, Col John Williams, Capt Wm Walker, Vol
COX, Jacob, Pvt, Col Sam Wear, Capt John Bayless, Mtd Inf
COX, James, Pvt, Regt Commander omitted, Capt James Cowan, Inf
COX, Jas (Col), Waiter, Col Wm Metcalf, Co Commander omitted, 1st Regt W TN Inf; waiter to Daniel Owens, Surgeon
COX, Jas, Pvt, Col Edwin Booth, Capt John Lewis, E TN Mil
COX, Jas, Pvt, Col John Cocke, Capt John Dalton, Inf
COX, Jas, Pvt, Col Wm Russell, Capt John Cowan, Vol Mtd Gunmen

COX, Jas, Pvt, Maj Wm Russell, Capt I Williams, Separate Bn Col Dyer - 1st Regt Vol Mtd Gunmen
COX, Jeremiah, Pvt, Col Wm Lillard, Capt Thos Sharpe, 2nd Regt Inf
COX, Jess, Pvt, Col S Bunch, Capt S Roberson, E TN Drafted Mil
COX, Jesse, 3 Sgt, Col N T Perkins, Capt Phillip Pipkin, Mtd Riflemen
COX, Jesse, Cpl, Brig Gen Thomas Washington, no other information
COX, Jesse, Pvt, Col Wm Metcalf, Capt Mullen, Mil Inf
COX, John, Cpl, Regt Commander omitted, Capt David Mason, Cav; promoted to Sgt
COX, John, Pvt, Col Philip Pipkin, Capt Ebenezer Kirkpatrick, Mil Inf
COX, John, Pvt, Col Robert Steele, Capt James Shenault, Mil Inf
COX, John, Pvt, Col S Bunch, Capt S Roberson, E TN Drafted Mil
COX, John, Pvt, Col S Copeland, Capt David Williams, Inf
COX, John, Pvt, Col Samuel Bunch, Capt James Cumming, E TN Vol Mtd Inf
COX, John, Pvt, Col Samuel Wear, Capt Robert Doak, E TN Vol Inf
COX, John, Pvt, Col Thomas Williamson, Capt Giles Burdett, Vol Mtd Gunmen; d 2-1-1815
COX, John, Pvt, Col Thomas Williamson, Capt John Doak, Capt John Dobbins, Vol Mtd Gunmen
COX, John, Pvt, Col William Johnson, Capt Henry Hunter, E TN Mil; left sick at Ft Strother 10-30-1814
COX, John, Pvt, Col Wm Lillard, Capt G Argenbright, Vol Riflemen E TN
COX, John, Pvt, Maj Gen A Jackson, Col A Cheatham, Capt William Creel, Inf
COX, John, Pvt, Regt Commander omitted, Capt Sam'l Richardson, E TN Drafted Mil
COX, Jonathan, Pvt, Col John Brown, Capt John Childs, E TN Mtd Gunmen
COX, Jonathan, Pvt, Col Samuel Wear, Capt John Childs, E TN Vol Inf
COX, Jos, Pvt, Col Wm Pillow, Capt Isaiah Renshaw, Inf
COX, Joshua, Pvt, Col John Brown, Capt William White, E TN Vol Mtd Inf; appointed Sgt Maj
COX, Joshua, Sgt Maj, Col John Brown, Co Commander omitted, E TN Vol Mtd Gunmen; resigned 3-11-1814
COX, Larkin, Pvt, Maj Gen Wm Carroll, Col James Raulston, Capt Wiley Huddleston, Inf
COX, Lewis, Pvt, Col Wm Metcalf, Capt Obidiah Waller, Mil Inf; d 3-21-1815
COX, Linanlar (Lincalow), Pvt, Col William Johnson, Capt James R Rogers, E TN Drafted Mil
COX, Philip, Pvt, Col Samuel Bayless, Capt Joseph Goodson, E TN Mil
COX, R Crelis, Pvt, Col A Cheatham, Capt William Creel, Inf
COX, Reed, Pvt, Col Samuel Bunch, Capt Thomas Mann, E TN Vol Mtd Inf
COX, Richardson, Pvt, Col S Bunch, Capt Dan'l Yarnell, E TN Mil
COX, Robt, Pvt, Col R C Napier, Capt Early Benson, Mil Inf; sick absent
COX, Robt, Pvt, Col Thomas Williamson, Capt John Coak, Vol Mtd Gunmen
COX, Sam'l, Pvt, Col S Copeland, Capt John Holshouser, Inf
COX, Sam'l, Surgeon Mate, Col Samuel Bayless, Co Commander omitted, 4th Regt E TN Mil; resigned 1-28-1815
COX, Samuel, Pvt, Regt Commander omitted, Capt Jno Crane, Mtd Inf
COX, Thos, Pvt, Col S Copeland, Capt Moses Thompson, Inf
COX, Thos, Pvt, Regt Commander omitted, Capt Gray, Inf
COX, William, Pvt, Col Samuel Bayless, Capt James Landen, E TN Mil
COX, Willison (William), Pvt, Col Thomas Benton, Capt James McFerrin, Vol Inf
COX, Willison, Pvt, Col Wm Pillow, Capt James McFerrin, Inf; furloughed by the doctor 11-30-1813
COX, Wm, Pvt, Col S Bunch, Capt Geo McPherson, E TN Mil
COX, Wm, Pvt, Col William Johnson, Capt Joseph Kirk, Mil Inf
COX, Wm, Pvt, Lt Col R Napier, Co Commander omitted, Inf
COY, Jacob M, Pvt, Col Jno Williams, Capt D Vance, Mtd Mil
COZBY, David, Pvt, Col Samuel Bunch, Capt Moses, E TN Mil Drafted
COZINE, Shelby, 1 Cpl, Col N T Perkins, Capt Mathew Johnston, Mil Inf; wounded 1-24-1814 & returned home
CRAB, Jos, Pvt, Col Edwin Booth, Capt John Sharp, E TN Mil
CRABTREE, Hyram, Pvt, Col Edwin Booth, Capt Vernon, E TN Mil
CRABTREE, Jno P, Cpl, Commanders & Branch Srvce omitted; promoted from Pvt
CRABTREE, Jno P, Pvt, Lt Col J N Edmonson, Co Commander omitted, Cav
CRABTREE, Jno P, Pvt, Regt Commander omitted, Capt Jno Crane, Mtd Inf
CRABTREE, John, 3 Cpl, Col James Raulston, Capt Henry West, Inf
CRABTREE, John, Pvt, Regt Commander omitted, Capt Larkin Ferrell, Inf
CRABTREE, Ransom, Pvt, Col Wm Metcalf, Capt Barbee Collins, Mil Inf
CRABTREE, Westley, Pvt, Regt Commander omitted, Capt Jno Crane, Mtd Inf
CRABTREE, Wm, 5 Sgt, Col James Raulston, Capt Henry West, Inf; promoted from Pvt
CRABTREE, Wm, Pvt, Col James Raulston, Capt Henry Hamilton, Inf
CRABTREE, Wm, Pvt, Col James Raulston, Capt Henry West, Inf
CRACE, John, Pvt, Col Edwin Booth, Capt Richard Marshall, Drafted Mil; discharged for inability

## Enlisted Men, War of 1812

CRADDOCK, Martin, Pvt, Lt Col Jno Edmonson, Co Commander omitted, Cav
CRADDOCK, Martin, QM Sgt, Col Wm Metcalf, 1st Regt W TN Mil Inf; dismissed 11-26-1814
CRADIC, Wm, Pvt, Col William Johnson, Capt Joseph Kirk, Mil
CRADIC, Wm, Sgt, Col William Johnson, Capt Joseph Kirk, Mil
CRAFFORD, Craig, Pvt, Regt Commander omitted, Capt Ephraim Dickson, Branch Srvce omitted
CRAFFORD, Moses, 5 Cpl, Lt Col L Hammonds, Lt Col A Loury, Capt Thomas Delaney, Inf
CRAFFORD, Smith, Pvt, Col Robert Steele, Capt James Shenault, Mil Inf
CRAFFORD, William, Pvt, Brig Gen Isaac Roberts, Capt Benjamin Reynolds, Branch Srvce omitted
CRAFT, Archalaus, Pvt, Maj William Russell, Capt Fleman Hodges, Vol Mtd Gunmen
CRAFT, Archelus, Sgt, Gen Andrew Jackson, Capt Kerr, Mtd Rangers; promoted from Pvt
CRAFT, Jesse, Pvt, Maj William Russell, Capt Fleman Hodges, Vol Mtd Gunmen
CRAFT (CROFT), Elias, Pvt, Col Edwin E Booth, Capt Alexander Biggs, Inf
CRAFTON, Fountain, Pvt, Commanders & Branch Srvce omitted; died
CRAFTON, Fountain, Pvt, Regt Commander omitted, Capt David Mason, Cav; d 6-19-1812?
CRAFTON, John B, Pvt, Col Newton Cannon, Capt Brice Martin, Mtd Gunmen
CRAFTON, Robert C, Pvt, Col Alexander Loury, Capt J N Williamson, W TN Mil
CRAFTON, Robert W, Pvt, Col Leroy Hammonds, Capt J N Williamson, 2nd Regt Inf
CRAFTON, Robert W, Pvt, Lt Col Leroy Hammonds, Capt J N Williamson, Inf; transferred to Capt Wells Co
CRAFTON, Robert, Pvt, Lt Col Leroy Hammonds, Capt Thomas Wells, Inf; substitute for Jos Lamb
CRAG, Thomas, Pvt, Col William Y Higgins, Capt Samuel A Allen, Mtd Gunmen
CRAGE, Jno, Pvt, no other information
CRAGE, John, Pvt, Regt Commander omitted, Capt Jason Craig, Inf
CRAGE, Robert, Pvt, no other information
CRAGE (CRAGG), John, Pvt, Col Edwin E Booth, Capt John Porter, Drafted Mil
CRAGE (CRAIG), John, Pvt, Col R H Dyer, Capt Beverly Williams, Vol Mtd Gunmen
CRAGG, Hugh, Cpl, Col William Johnson, Capt Elihu Milliken, 3rd Regt E TN Mil
CRAGG, Hugh, Cpl, Col Wm Johnson, Capt Henry Hunter, E TN Mil; transferred to Capt Milliken Co
CRAGG, Wm, Pvt, Gen Andrew Jackson, Capt High Kerr, Mtd Rangers
CRAIG, Adam, Pvt, Col John Brown, Capt Lunsford Oliver, E TN Mil
CRAIG, Alexander, Pvt, Col R H Dyer, Capt Robert Evans, Vol Mtd Gunmen
CRAIG, Andrew, Pvt, Col Edwin E Booth, Capt John Lewis, E TN Mil

CRAIG, Andrew, Pvt, Col John Brown, Capt Hugh Barton, E TN Mil Inf
CRAIG, Andrew, Pvt, Col Newton Cannon, Capt Brice Martin, Mtd Gunmen; absent from 12-8-1813
CRAIG, David, Pvt, Col John Brown, Capt William White, E TN Vol Mtd Inf
CRAIG, David, Pvt, Col Thomas McCrory, Capt Samuel B McKnight, Inf
CRAIG, David, Pvt, Commanders & Branch Srvce omitted; discharged
CRAIG, David, Pvt, Commanders & Branch Srvce omitted; pay stopped for absence
CRAIG, David, Pvt, Regt Commander omitted, Capt David Mason, Cav
CRAIG, David, Pvt, Regt Commander omitted, Capt R Evans, Mtd Spies
CRAIG, Hiram, Pvt, Col Jas Raulston, Capt Elijah Haynie, Inf; d 2-9-1815
CRAIG, James, Pvt, Col Thomas McCrory, Capt William Dooley, Inf
CRAIG, James, Pvt, Gen Andrew Jackson, no other information
CRAIG, John B, Cpl, Col Wm Metcalf, Capt Barbee Collins, Mil Inf
CRAIG, John B, Pvt, Regt Commander omitted, Capt Robert Evans, Mtd Spies
CRAIG, John, Pvt, Col John Brown, Capt William White, E TN Vol Mtd Inf
CRAIG, John, Pvt, Col N T Perkins, Capt John Doak, Vol Mtd Gunmen
CRAIG, John, Pvt, Col R H Dyer, Capt Beverly Williams, Vol Mtd Gunmen
CRAIG, John, Pvt, Col Thomas McCrory, Capt Thomas K Gordon, Inf
CRAIG, John, Pvt, Col Wm Johnson, Capt Jas Tunnell, 3rd Regt E TN Mil
CRAIG, John, Pvt, Col Wm Johnson, Capt Jas Tunnell, E TN Mil; sick absent
CRAIG, Leonard, Pvt, Col Edwin E Booth, Capt Vernon, E TN Mil
CRAIG, Leonard, Pvt, Col S Copeland, Capt Fait, Inf
CRAIG, Moses, Pvt, Regt Commander omitted, Capt Thomas Gray, Inf
CRAIG, Reuben, Pvt, Col Samuel Wear, Capt Robert Doak, E TN Vol Inf
CRAIG, Samuel, Pvt, Col Edwin E Booth, Capt John Sharp, E TN Mil
CRAIG, Thomas, Pvt, Col Edwin Booth, Capt Richard Marshall, Drafted Mil
CRAIG, Thomas, Pvt, Col N T Perkins, Capt Philip Pipkin, Mtd Riflemen; transferred from Capt Daniel Ross' Co
CRAIG, William W, Sgt, Regt Commander omitted, Capt Archibald McKinney, Cav; promoted from Sgt to Maj
CRAIG, William, Pvt, Col John Brown, Capt William White, E TN Mil Inf
CRAIG, William, Sdlr, Col Robert H Dyer, Capt James Wyatt, Vol Mtd Gunmen
CRAIG, William, Sgt, no other information
CRAIG, Wm, Pvt, Brig Gen Roberts, Capt Benjamin

Reynolds, Mtd Rangers
CRAIG, Wm, Pvt, Col Edwin Booth, Capt Vernon, E TN Mil
CRAIG, Wm, Pvt, Col John Cocke, Capt Joseph Price, Inf; d 1-16-1815
CRAIG, Wm, Pvt, Col John Coffee, Capt Charles Kavanaugh, Cav; transferred for the Inf
CRAIG, Wm, Pvt, Col Robert H Dyer, Capt Jas McMahon, TN Mtd Vol Gunmen; transferred to Capt Wyatt Co
CRAIG, Wm, Pvt, Col Wm Hall, Capt Henry Newlin, Inf
CRAIG, Wm, Sgt, Gen Andrew Jackson, Capt N Davis, Inf
CRAIG, Wm, Sgt, Maj William Russell, Capt Fleman Hodges, Vol Mtd Gunmen
CRAIG (CRAGE), Eli, Pvt, Col R H Dyer, Capt Beverly Williams, Vol Mtd Gunmen
CRANCH, Wm, Pvt, Col Samuel Wear, Capt Simeon Perry, E TN Vol Mtd Inf; deserted from Camp Coosa 11-4-1813
CRANE, Charles, Cpl, Col William Johnson, Capt Henry Hunter, E TN Mil
CRANE, Isaac, Pvt, Col Thomas Williamson, Capt John Crane, Capt Cook, Vol Mtd Gunmen; dismissed from service
CRANE, Isaac, Pvt, Lt Col John Edmondson, Co Commander omitted, Cav
CRANE, Isaac, Pvt, Regt Commander omitted, Capt John Crane, Inf
CRANE, Jason, Pvt, Col Robert Steele, Capt Jas Randals, Inf; on furlough
CRANE, Joel, Pvt, Col Edwin Booth, Capt John Sharpe, E TN Mil; private waiter to Dr E Wyatt
CRANE, John, Pvt, Lt Col Jno Edmondson, Co Commander omitted, Cav
CRANE, John, Pvt, no other information
CRANE, John, Sgt, Maj Woodfolk, Capt Ross, Capt McNully, Inf
CRANE, Lemel, Pvt, Regt Commander omitted, Capt Jno Crane, Mtd Inf
CRANE, Lemuel, Pvt, Lt Col A Cheatham, Co Commander omitted, Mtd Inf
CRANE, Newell W, Pvt, Col Wynne, Capt Bailey Butler, Inf
CRANE, Newton, Pvt, no other information
CRANGHRON, John, Pvt, Col R C Napier, Capt John Chism, Mil Inf
CRANK, Ira, Pvt, Regt Commander omitted, Capt George Smith, Spies
CRANTFORD, Hardy, Pvt, Col R C Napier, Capt John Chism, Mil Inf
CRASSRO, Thomas, Pvt, Col S Copeland, Capt Solomon George, Inf
CRATCH, Everitte, Pvt, Col Philip Pipkin, Capt George Mebane, Mil Inf
CRATCH, George, Pvt, Col Philip Pipkin, Capt George Mebane, Mtd Inf
CRATON, McNeal, Pvt, Col Dyer, Capt Russell, Maj Russell, Vol Mtd Gunmen
CRATON, Thomas, Pvt, Col Robert Dyer, Capt James Wyatt, Vol Mtd Gunmen

CRATON (CREATON), McNeal, Pvt, Col S Copeland, Co Commander omitted, Inf
CRATSINGER, Jacob, Pvt, Col William Lillard, Capt George Keys, E TN Inf; deserted Camp Williams 10-6-1813
CRAVAN, Wm P, Pvt, Col Thomas Williamson, Capt Anthony Metcalf, Vol Mtd Gunmen; dismissed 3-8-1815
CRAVENS, James, Pvt, Col Thomas Williamson, Capt Richard Tate, Vol Mtd Gunmen
CRAVENS, John, Pvt, Col L Hammonds, Capt J N Williamson, 2nd Regt Inf
CRAVENS, John, Pvt, Col Leroy Hammonds, Capt Joseph Williamson, Inf
CRAVENS, John, Pvt, Col Loury, Capt J N Williamson, W TN Mil
CRAVIN, Elijah, Pvt, Col John Cocke, Capt Richard Crunk, Inf
CRAWELY, Gabriel, Pvt, Maj John Childs, Capt Henry Stephens, E TN Mtd Vol Inf
CRAWELY, Samuel, Pvt, Col William Johnson, Capt Benjamin Powell, E TN Mil
CRAWFORD, Alex C, Pvt, Col Robert H Dyer, Capt Jas McMahon, TN Vol Gunmen
CRAWFORD, Arthur H, Pvt, Col Loury, Capt Looney, 2nd Regt W TN Mil
CRAWFORD, David, Cpl, Col John Wynne, Capt Wm Caruthers, W TN Inf; promoted from Pvt
CRAWFORD, David, Pvt, Col A Metcalf, Capt William Metcalf, Mil Inf
CRAWFORD, David, Pvt, Maj Gen Andrew Jackson, Capt Joseph Kirkpatrick, Mtd Gunmen
CRAWFORD, David, Sgt, Col S Copeland, Capt Richard Sharpe, Mil Inf; sick absent
CRAWFORD, Edmond, Pvt, Col James Raulston, Capt Charles Wade, Inf
CRAWFORD, Elias, Pvt, Col Thomas Benton, Capt Henry Douglass, Inf
CRAWFORD, English, Pvt, Capt William Walker, Col John Williams, Vol
CRAWFORD, Guzuway, Pvt, Col John Brown, Capt William Christian, E TN Mil
CRAWFORD, Hardin W, Pvt, Col Robert Dyer, Capt James McMahon, 1st TN Mtd Vol Gunmen
CRAWFORD, Jackson, Pvt, Col James Raulston, Capt Charles Wade, Inf
CRAWFORD, James, 2 Sgt, Col James Raulston, Capt Charles Wade, Inf; reduced to the ranks
CRAWFORD, James, 4 Sgt, Col Philip Pipkin, Capt John Strother, Mil
CRAWFORD, James, Cpl, Col William Hall, Capt John Kennedy, Vol Inf
CRAWFORD, James, Pvt, Col Edward Bradley, Capt John Kennedy, Riflemen; AWOL 12-12-1813
CRAWFORD, James, Pvt, Col John Wynne, Capt Robert Breden, Inf
CRAWFORD, James, Pvt, Col Samuel Wear, Capt Robert Doak, E TN Vol Inf
CRAWFORD, James, Sgt, Col John Wynne, Capt John Spinks, Inf; sick absent since 11-11-1813
CRAWFORD, Jessee, Pvt, Col John Alcorn, Capt Jetton,

## Enlisted Men, War of 1812

CRAWFORD, Jessee, Pvt, Col John Coffee, Capt Jetton, Vol Cav
CRAWFORD, John, 2 Cpl, Col Wm Metcalf, Capt Andrew Patterson, Mil Inf
CRAWFORD, John, Capt, Brig Gen Thomas Washington, Co Commander omitted, Inf
CRAWFORD, John, Pvt, Col Edwin Booth, Capt Ricahrd Marshall, Drafted Mil
CRAWFORD, John, Pvt, Col Philip Pipkin, Capt Peter Searcy, Mil Inf
CRAWFORD, John, Pvt, Col Wm Lillard, Capt Hugh Martin, E TN Vol Inf; deserted 11-8-1813
CRAWFORD, John, Pvt, Regt Commander omitted, Capt John Miller, Spies; transferred to Capt Russell's Spies
CRAWFORD, John, Pvt, Regt Commander omitted, Capt William Mitchell, Spies
CRAWFORD, John, QM, Col Ewen Allison, Co Commander omitted, E TN Mil
CRAWFORD, John, Rank omitted, Maj Gen John Cocke, Co Commander omitted, E TN Vol Mil
CRAWFORD, Jonathan, Ffr, Col William Johnson, Capt James Tunnell, E TN Mil
CRAWFORD, Jonathan, Pvt, Col Edwin Booth, Capt Richard Marshall, Drafted Mil
CRAWFORD, Joseph, Pvt, Col John Brown, Capt John Childs, E TN Vol Mtd Inf
CRAWFORD, Robert, Pvt, Col John Wynne, Capt Butler, Inf
CRAWFORD, Samuel, Pvt, Col S Copeland, Capt James Tait, Inf
CRAWFORD, Samuel, Pvt, Lt Col Wm Phillips, Co Commander omitted, Inf
CRAWFORD, Samuel, Pvt, Regt Commander omitted, Capt David Mason, Cav
CRAWFORD, Samuel, Pvt, no other information
CRAWFORD, Smith, Pvt, Cpl, Maj Gen William Carroll, Col Wm Metcalf, Capt John Jackson, Inf
CRAWFORD, Thomas, Pvt, Col Samuel Wear, Capt John Bayless, Mtd Inf
CRAWFORD, Thomas, Pvt, no other information
CRAWFORD, Vincent, Far, Col John Coffee, Capt Robert Jetton?, Cav
CRAWFORD, Vinyard, Far, Col John Coffee, Capt Robert Jetton, Cav
CRAWFORD, Vynard, Far, Col John Alcorn, Capt Robert Jetton, Vol Cav
CRAWFORD, William, Pvt, Col John Coffee, Capt Thomas Bradley, Vol Cav
CRAWFORD, William, Pvt, Col Thomas Benton, Capt Henry Douglass, Vol Inf; in Capt Bradley's Troop Cav
CRAWFORD, William, Pvt, Col Wm Johnson, Capt Joseph Scott, E TN Drafted Mil
CRAWLEY, Isam, Pvt, Col Edwin Booth, Capt Samuel Thompson, Mil
CRAWLEY, John, Pvt, Col John Cocke, Capt Daniel Price, Inf; substitute for John Hunter & d 12-2-1814
CRAWLEY, Kemp, Pvt, Col John Cocke, Capt Daniel Price, Inf
CRAWLEY, Samuel, Pvt, Col Samuel Bunch, Capt Moses, E TN Drafted Inf
CRAWLEY, Samuel, Pvt, Col Thomas Benton, Capt George Gibbs, Inf
CRAWLEY, Samuel, Pvt, Col Thomas Benton, Capt George Gibbs, Vol Inf
CRAWMER, James, Pvt, Col Wm Johnson, Capt Wm Alexander, Det of E TN Drafted Mil
CRAWSON, John, Pvt, Col Samuel Bunch, Capt Daniel Yarnell, E TN Mil
CRAWSON, John, Pvt, Col Samuel Bunch, Capt Joseph Duncan, E TN Drafted Mil; joined from Capt Yarnell's Co
CRAYTON, John, Cpl, Col William Lillard, Capt Thomas Sharpe, Branch Srvce omitted
CREASY, Archibald, Pvt, Regt Commander omitted, Capt Larkin Ferrell, Inf
CREASY, Joe, Pvt, Col James Raulston, Co Commander omitted, Inf; d 2-26-1815
CREECH, Jessee, Pvt, Col Edwin E Booth, Co Commander omitted, E TN Mil
CREECH, Zacock, Cpl, Col S Copeland, Co Commander omitted, Inf
CREED, John, Pvt, Col Wm Metcalf, Capt John Sutton, Mil Inf
CREED, Wilson, Pvt, Maj John Childs, Capt James Cummings, Branch Srvce omitted; appointed Master Sgt by Maj Chiles
CREED, Wilson, QM Sgt, Commanders omitted, E TN Vol Mtd Inf
CREEK, George, Pvt, Col Thomas Benton, Capt Newton Cannon, Inf
CREEL, Thos W, Pvt, Col A Cheatham, Capt Creel, Inf
CREEVES, John, Pvt, Col William Higgins, Co Commander omitted, Mtd Gunmen
CRENSHAW, Cornelius, Pvt, Col S Copeland, Capt Moses Thompson, Inf
CRENSHAW, Corter C, Pvt, Col Wm Hall, Capt Wm Alexander, Vol Inf
CRENSHAW, Freeman, Pvt, Maj Gen Andrew Jackson, Col A Cheatham, Capt Wm Creel, Inf
CRENSHAW, Garland, Pvt, Col Wm Hall, Capt Wm L Alexander, Vol Inf
CRENSHAW, Henry?, Pvt, Col John Coffee, Capt Alexander McKeen, Cav
CRENSHAW, Jack, Pvt, Col Wm Hall, Capt William L Alexander, Vol Inf
CRENSHAW, Jack, Pvt, Col Wm Hall, Capt Wm L Alexander, Vol Inf; AWOL, waiter to Col Cradley
CRENSHAW, Nathaniel, Pvt, Col S Bunch, Capt John English, E TN Drafted Mil; left sick at Camp Ross 3-1814
CRES, John, Pvt, Maj Gen William Carroll, Capt Francis Ellis, Inf; substitute for Benj Crews
CRESILES, Philip, Pvt, Col William Lillard, Capt John Hartsell, E TN Vol Inf
CREW, Jas, Pvt, Col Edwin Booth, Capt John Slatton, E TN Mil
CREW, William jr, Pvt, Col Edwin E Booth, Capt John Slatton, E TN Mil

## Enlisted Men, War of 1812

CREW, Wm sr, Pvt, Col Edwin E Booth, Capt John Slatton, E TN Mil
CREWS, Benjamin, 5 Cpl, Maj Gen Wm Carroll, Capt Francis Ellis, Inf
CREWS, Gilleon, Pvt, Maj John Childs, Capt Reuben Tipton, E TN Vol Mtd Inf; Regimental Co Knox 10
CREWS, Jas, Pvt, Col Samuel Wear, Capt Joseph Calloway, Mtd Inf
CREWS, John, Pvt, Maj John Childs, Capt Reuben Tipton, E TN Vol Mtd Inf; Regimental Co Knox 10
CREWS, Pleasant, Cpl, Col R H Dyer, Capt Cuthbert Hudson, Vol Mtd Gunmen
CREWS, Pleasant, Pvt, Col R H Dyer, Capt Cuthbert Hudson, Vol Mtd Gunmen
CREWS, Pleasant, Pvt, Maj Gen Wm Carroll, Col Wm Metcalf, Capt John Jackson, Inf
CREWS, Pleasant, Pvt, Regt Commander omitted, Capt James Haggard, Mtd Gunmen
CREWS, Sam'l, Pvt, Col John Cocke, Co Commander omitted, Inf; substituted for Andrew Robertson
CREWS, William, Pvt, Col William Johnson, Capt Joseph Scott, E TN Drafted Mil; sick absent
CREWS, Wm, Pvt, Col Wm Hall, Capt Wm L Alexander, Vol Inf
CRIBS, Jonathan (Johnson), Pvt, Lt Col A Loury, Lt Col L Hammonds, Capt Thomas Delaney, Inf
CRICK, John, Pvt, Col Wm Metcalf, Capt Wm Mullin, Mil Inf
CRIDDLE, Ed, Pvt, Col Newton Cannon, no other information
CRIDDLE, Edward, Pvt, Col N Cannon, Capt Martin, Mtd Gunmen; promoted to Regt QM
CRIDDLE, Edward, QM, Col Newton Cannon, Co Commander omitted, TN Vol Mtd Riflemen
CRIDER, George, Pvt, Col Wm Johnson, Capt David McKamy, E TN Drafted Mil
CRINSHAW, Cornelius, Pvt, Col Robert H Dyer, Capt Robert Evans, Vol Mtd Gunmen
CRIPPEN, George, Pvt, Brig Gen I B Roberts, Capt Benj Reynolds, Mtd Rangers
CRIPPEN, George, Pvt, Col Thomas Benton, Capt Benj Reynolds, Vol Inf
CRISCO (CRISCOE), Jas, Pvt, Col John Brown, Capt William White, E TN Vol Mtd Inf
CRISNOW (CROSNOW), Jacob, Pvt, Regt Commander omitted, Capt Thomas Gray, Branch Srvce omitted
CRISP, Prescott, Pvt, Regt Commander omitted, Capt Abner Pearce, Inf
CRISP, Wm M, Pvt, Col S Copeland, Capt John Biles?, Inf
CRISWELL, Andrew, Pvt, Col R C Napier, Capt Edward Neblett, Mil Inf
CRISWELL, Saml, Pvt, Maj Jas Porter, Co Commander omitted, Cav
CRITCHES, John, Pvt, Col R C Napiet, Capt S Ashmore, Mil Inf
CRITCHFIELD, Lemuel, Pvt, Col John Williams, Capt David Vance, Mtd Mil
CROACKETT, John, Pvt, no other information
CROCKEL, William, Pvt, Regt Commander omitted, Capt Sam Bunch, Brnch Srvce omitted
CROCKER, Chas, Pvt, Col Edward Bradley, Capt John Kennedy, Riflemen
CROCKER, Eli, Pvt, Col Thomas Benton, Capt Henry Douglass, Vol Inf; d before 12-10-1814
CROCKER, Stephen, Pvt, Col James Raulston, Capt Henry West, Inf
CROCKETT, Aaron, Pvt, Col Wm Lillard, Capt Gabriel Martin, E TN Vol Inf
CROCKETT, David, Pvt, Col Newton Cannon, Capt Francis Jones, Mtd Riflemen
CROCKETT, David, Pvt, Col Thomas Benton, Capt James McFerrin, Vol Inf
CROCKETT, David, Pvt, Col Wm Pillow, Capt James McFerrin, Inf; deserted 11-19-1813
CROCKETT, David, Sgt, Maj Wm Russell, Capt John Cowan, Vol Mtd Gunmen
CROCKETT, James, Pvt, Col Stephen Copeland, Capt Wm Evans, Mil Inf
CROCKETT, James, Pvt, Maj Gen Jackson, Capt John Crane, Mtd Gunmen
CROCKETT, James, Pvt, no other information
CROCKETT, John, Pvt, Col Samuel Bayless, Capt James Churchman, E TN Mil
CROCKETT, John, Pvt, Maj Gen Jackson, Capt John Crane, Mtd Gunmen
CROCKETT, John, Pvt, Regt Commander omitted, Capt John Crane, Mtd Inf
CROCKETT, John, Pvt, Regt Commander omitted, Capt William Teas, Inf
CROCKETT, Joseph, Pvt, Regt Commander omitted, Capt D Mason, Cav
CROCKETT, Nathan, Pvt, Col S Bunch, Capt S Roberson, E TN Drafted Mil
CROCKETT, Nathan, Pvt, Regt Commander omitted, Capt Sam Richardson, E TN Drafted Mil
CROCKETT, Nathaniel, Pvt, Col Thomas Williamson, Capt John Crane, Vol Inf
CROCKETT, William, Blksmth, Maj Gen Jackson, Capt John Crane, Mtd Gunmen
CROCKETT, William, Pvt, Col Edward Bradley, Capt John Kennedy, Riflemen
CROCKETT, William, Pvt, Col Stephen Copeland, Capt William Evans, Mil Inf
CROCKETT, William, Sgt, Col Newt Cannon, Capt William Edwards, Regimental Command
CROFF, Jacob, Pvt, Maj Woodfolk, Capt James Neil, Inf; d 1-21-1815
CROFF, William, Pvt, Col Robert Steele, Capt Jas Randals, Inf; on furlough
CROFFORD, Anthony, Pvt, Col Wm Russell, Capt John Cowan, Vol Mtd Gunmen
CROFFORD, Craig, Pvt, Col R H Dyer, Capt E C Dickson, TN Mtd Gunmen
CROFFORD, Jas, 1 Sgt, Col Alexander Loury, Capt John Looney, 2nd Regt W TN Mil
CROFFORD, Jesse, Pvt, Maj Wm Russell, Capt John Cowan, Vol Mtd Gunmen
CROFFORD, Sabert S, Pvt, Col Sam Bayless, Capt Joseph Hale, E TN Mil
CROFFORD, Saml, Pvt, Col Samuel Bayless, Capt Joseph

## Enlisted Men, War of 1812

Hale, E TN Mil
CROFFORD, Thomas, Pvt, Maj Wm Russell, Capt John Cowan, Vol Mtd Gunmen
CROFT, Sam'l, Pvt, Col S Bunch, Capt J Griffin, E TN Drafted Mil; furloughed for inability
CROFT, Saml, Pvt, Col Ewen Allison, Capt Jos Everett, E TN Mil; transferred to Capt Griffin
CROGSIL, David, Pvt, Col Ewen Allison, Capt William King, Mil Drafted
CROMLEY, Sam'l, Pvt, Col S Bunch, Capt F Register, E TN Mil; discharged for inability
CRONESTER, Mathias, Pvt, Col Robert Coffee, Capt Robert Jetton, Cav
CRONESTER, Philip, Pvt, Col John Cocke, Capt George Barnes, Inf
CRONK, Jacob, Pvt, Col Thomas Benton, Capt Wm Smith, Vol Inf
CRONSON, John, Pvt, Col Edwin Booth, Capt John Slatton, E TN Mil
CROOK, James, 3 Cpl, Col Wm Metcalf, Capt Wm Mullen, Mil Inf
CROOK, James, Cpl, Col Wm Metcalf, Capt Wm Mullen, Mil Inf
CROOKS, Robert, Pvt, Maj Woodfolk, Capt McCulley, Inf
CROSBY, James, Pvt, Col Richard Tate, Capt Stephen Copeland, Inf
CROSBY, Saml, Pvt, Col Wm Hall, Capt Henry Newland, Inf; deserted from camp
CROSBY, Thomas, Pvt, Col Wm Lillard, Capt Z Copeland, E TN Vol Inf
CROSBY, William, Pvt, Col Richard Tate, Capt Stephen Copeland, Inf
CROSBY, William, Pvt, Col Wm Johnson, Capt Joseph Kirk, Mil
CROSBY, William, Pvt, Col Wm Johnston, Capt Christopher Cook, E TN Mil
CROSMORE, Jacob, Pvt, Col John Cocke, Capt James Gray, Inf; sick absent 3-18-1815
CROSNOE, George, Pvt, Col Thomas Benton, Capt Henry L Douglas, Vol Inf
CROSON, John, Pvt, Col William Lillard, Capt William Gillenwater, E TN Inf
CROSS, Abraham, Pvt, Col Samuel Bayless, Capt James Landen, E TN Mil
CROSS, Arthur, Pvt, Col Edward Bradley, Capt William Lauderdale, Vol Inf
CROSS, Arthur, Pvt, Col Wm Hall, Capt William L Alexander, Vol Inf
CROSS, Ashee, Pvt, Col Robert Steele, Capt James Bennett, Mil Inf
CROSS, Elijah, 2 Cpl, Maj Thomas Benton, Capt Henry L Douglass, Vol Inf
CROSS, Elijah, 2 Sgt, Col Ewen Allison, Capt William King, Drafted Mil
CROSS, Elijah, Cpl, Col Edward Bradley, Capt Harry L Douglass, Vol Inf
CROSS, Elijah, Cpl, Col Thomas Benton, Capt Harry L Douglass, Vol Inf
CROSS, Elisha, Pvt, Col Wm Johnson, Capt Joe Scott, E TN Drafted Mil; sick absent
CROSS, John B, 1 Maj, Col S Copeland, Co Commander omitted, 3rd Regt TN Mil
CROSS, John, Pvt, Col Philip Pipkin, Capt George Mebane, Mil Inf
CROSS, John, Pvt, Col R C Napier, Co Commander omitted, Mil Inf
CROSS, John, Pvt, Col S Bayless, Capt John Brock, E TN Mil
CROSS, John, Pvt, Col Wm Johnson, Capt Joe Scott, E TN Mil
CROSS, John, Pvt, Col Wm Lillard, Capt Martin, E TN Vol Inf
CROSS, Jos, Pvt, Col Ewin Allison, Co Commander omitted, Drafted Mil
CROSS, Macklen, Pvt, Col R H Dyer, Maj Wm Russell, Capt Wm Russell, Vol Mtd Gunmen
CROSS, Macklen, Pvt, no other information
CROSS, Marlin (Maclin), Pvt, Maj John Chiles, Co Commander omitted, E TN Mtd Gunmen; transferred to Maj Russell Bn
CROSS, Samuel, Pvt, Col James Raulston, Co Commander omitted, Inf
CROSS, William, Pvt, Col William Lillard, Capt Hugh Martin, E TN Vol Inf
CROSS, Wm, Pvt, Col Edward Bradley, Capt Harry Douglass, Vol Inf
CROSS, Wm, Pvt, Col Wm Johnson, Capt David McKamy, E TN Drafted Mil
CROSSLEN, John, Pvt, Col Wm Metcalf, no other information
CROSSNER, Henry, Pvt, Col Wm Hall, Capt Henry Newlin, Inf
CROSSNO, Thos, Far, Col R H Dyer, Capt Cuthbert Hudson, Vol Mtd Gunmen
CROSWELL, Elisha, Pvt, Col John Cocke, Capt James Gray, Inf
CROUCH, Hardin, Pvt, no other information
CROUCH, Harelin, Pvt, Lt Col H Bryan, Co Commander omitted, Inf
CROUCH, Jacob, 4 Cpl, Col Wm Pillow, Capt Wm Smith, Vol Inf
CROUCH, Thomas, Pvt, Col Philip Pipkin, Capt David Smythe, Inf
CROUSE, Wm, Pvt, Col William Lillard, Capt Thomas Sharpe, 2nd Regt Inf
CROW, George, Pvt, Col John Brown, Capt William White, Regt E TN Mil Inf
CROW, Isaac, Sgt, Col John Coffee, Capt Charles Kavanaugh, Cav
CROW, James, Pvt, Col Jno Brown, Capt Wm D Neilson, Regt E TN Vol Mil
CROW, Jas, Pvt, Col John Coffee, Capt Charles Kavanaugh, Cav
CROW, John, Pvt, Col Wm Johnson, Capt Joseph Scott, E TN Drafted Mil
CROW, Levi, Pvt, Regt Commander omitted, Capt N David, Branch Srvce omitted
CROW, Mansfield W, Cpl, Col Newton Cannon, Capt Isaac Williams, Mtd Riflemen
CROW, Mansfield W, Pvt, Col John Coffee, Capt Robert Jetton, Cav

- 149

## Enlisted Men, War of 1812

CROW, Mansfield W, Pvt, Col S Copeland, Capt Moses Thompson, Inf
CROW, Robert, Pvt, Col John Brown, Capt William White, E TN Vol Mtd Inf
CROW, Thomas, Pvt, Col Ewen Allison, Capt Adam Winsell, E TN Drafted Mil
CROW, William, Pvt, Col Edwin E Booth, Capt John McKamey, Inf
CROW, William, Pvt, Col John Brown, Capt Wm D Neilson, E TN Vol Mil
CROW, Willis, Pvt, Col John Brown, Capt William D Neilson, E TN Vol Mil
CROWDER, Green, Pvt, Col R H Dyer, Capt Bethel Allen, Vol Mtd Gunmen
CROWDER, Greenham, Pvt, Col Samuel Wear, Capt Rufus Morgan, E TN Vol Inf
CROWDER, James A, Pvt, Col Samuel Wear, Capt Rufus Morgan, E TN Vol Inf
CROWDER, Nelson, Pvt, Col S Bunch, Capt John English, E TN Drafted Mil; substitute for James J Vaughn
CROWDER, Nelson, Pvt, Col Samuel Wear, Capt James Gillespie, E TN Vol Inf; deserted 11-13-1813
CROWDER, Thos, Pvt, Col William Hall, Capt John Wallace, Inf; on furlough & sick
CROWDER, William, Pvt, Col Philip Pipkin, Capt James Blakemore, Mil Inf
CROWDER (CROWDON), Philip, Pvt, Col John Cocke, Capt George Barnes, Inf
CROWLEY, Sam'l, Pvt, Col Thos H Benton, Capt George W Gibbs, Vol Inf
CROWLEY, Sam'l, Pvt, Col William Johnson, Capt Benjamin Powell, E TN Mil
CROWNOVER, Dan'l, Pvt, Col John K Wynne, Capt James Cole, Inf; absent
CROWNOVER, Dan'l, Pvt, Col Thomas Benton, Capt Isaiah Renshaw, Vol Inf; absent
CROWNOVER, James, Cpl, Col Robert Steele, Capt Richard M Ratton, Mil Inf
CROWNOVER, Theodorus, Pvt, Col John K Wynne, Capt James Cole, Inf
CRROAK, Jacob, Pvt, Regt Commander omitted, Capt Smith, Vol Inf
CRUCH, Elisha, Pvt, Col T McCrory, Capt A Metcalf, Mil Inf
CRUCHFIELD, Sam B, Pvt, Col Newton Cannon, Capt James Walton, Mtd Riflemen
CRUDRUNE, Bennett, Pvt, Col Phillip Pipkin, Capt William McKay, Mil Inf
CRUISE, Ellison, Pvt, Col John Brown, Capt John Childs, E TN Vol Mtd Gunmen
CRUISE, James, Pvt, Col John Brown, Capt John Chiles, E TN Vol Mtd Inf
CRUISE, Sam'l, Pvt, Col John Brown, Capt William McCall, Inf
CRUISE (CREWS), James, Pvt, Col William Johnson, Capt James Tunnell, E TN Mil
CRUISE (CREWS), Walter, Pvt, Col William Johnson, Capt James Tunnell, E TN Mil
CRUIZ, Hardeman, Pvt, Col S Bunch, Capt John McNare, E TN Mil

CRUIZE, John, Pvt, Col William Johnson, Capt David McKamy, E TN Drafted Mil; substitute for Andrew Rogers (deserted)
CRUMLESS, James, Cpl, Col William Johnson, Capt Jas R Rogers, E TN Drafted Mil
CRUMLEY, Aaron, Pvt, Col Ewen Allison, Capt Jacob Hoyal, E TN Mil; discharged for inability
CRUMLEY, Jacob jr, Pvt, Col Ewen Allison, Capt William King, Drafted Mil
CRUMLEY, Jacob sr, Pvt, Col Ewen Allison, Capt William King, Drafted Mil; deserted 4-28-1814
CRUMLEY, John, Pvt, Col Samuel Bayless, Capt Branch Jones, E TN Drafted Mil
CRUMLEY, Samuel, Pvt, Col Ewen Allison, Capt Jacob Hoyal, E TN Mil; transferred from Capt Hampton Co
CRUMLEY, Samuel, Pvt, Col Ewen Allison, Capt John Hampton, Mil; transferred to Capt Hail Co
CRUMLEY, William, Pvt, Col Ewen Allison, Capt Jacob Hoyal, E TN Mil; discharged for inability
CRUMP, Adam, Sdlr, Col N T Perkins, Capt George Eliot, Mil Inf
CRUMP, George, Pvt, Col Thomas Williamson, Capt Giles Burdette, Vol Mtd Gunmen
CRUMPLER, Edward, Pvt, Col R C Napier, Capt Drury Adkins, Mil Inf
CRUMPLER, Matthews, Pvt, Lt Col Richard Napier, Co Commander omitted, Inf
CRUNK, George, Pvt, Col Thomas Williamson, Capt Robert Moore, Vol Mtd Gunmen
CRUNK, Ira, 3 Cpl, Col N T Perkins, Capt George Eliot, Mil Inf
CRUNK, Ira, Pvt, Col R H Dyer, Capt Ephraim E Dickson, 1 TN Mtd Vol Gunmen; no service performed
CRUNK, Ira, Pvt, Regt Commander omitted, Capt Geore Smith, Spies
CRUNK, Ira, Tptr, Col Thomas Williamson, Capt Robert Moore, Vol Mtd Gunmen
CRUNK, James, Pvt, Col Alexander Loury, Capt Gabriel Martin, Inf
CRUNK, John, Pvt, Col Thomas Williamson, Capt Robert Moore, Vol Mtd Gunmen
CRUNK, William, Pvt, Col John Cocke, Capt Richard Crunk, Inf
CRUNK, William, Pvt, Col William Y Higgins, Capt A Cheatham, Mtd Riflemen
CRUSE, Edward, Pvt, Col Edwin E Booth, Capt John Lewis, E TN Mil; died 12-22-1814
CRUSE, James, Pvt, Maj William Russell, Capt John Cowan, Vol Mtd Gunmen
CRUSE, William, Pvt, Col William Lillard, Capt Thomas Sharpe, 2 Regt Inf
CRUTCHER, Carter, Pvt, Col John Coffee, Capt Thomas Bradley, Vol Cav
CRUTCHER, Carter, QM Sgt, Col John Coffee, no Co Commander, TN Vol Cav
CRUTCHER, George, Pvt, Col John K Wynne, Capt Bayless E Prince, Inf; transferred to Capt Marr's Co
CRUTCHER, George, Pvt, Col N T Perkins, Capt W L George Marr, Mtd Vol; transferred from Capt

## Enlisted Men, War of 1812

Prince's Co
CRUTCHER, John, Cpl, Col N Cannon, Capt Ota Cantrell, W TN Mtd Inf
CRUTCHER, Thomas B, 2 Sgt, Col John K Wynne, Capt Bayless E Prince, Inf; died 1-2-1814
CRUTCHER, Thomas B, Pvt, Col William Hall, Capt James Hambleton, Vol Inf; joined Clarksville
CRUTCHER, Thomas B, Pvt, Lt Col H Bryan, Co Commander omitted, Inf
CRUTCHFIELD, John, Pvt, Col A Cheatham, Capt William Smith, Inf
CRUTCHFIELD, Parmer, Pvt, Col Samuel Bayless, Capt John Brock, E TN Mil
CRUTCHFIELD, William, Pvt, Regt Commander omitted, Capt Sam Bunch, Branch omitted
CRUTHER, William, 3 Sgt, Col A Cheatham, Capt James Giddens, Inf
CRUZE, William, Cpl, Col Edward Bradley, Capt William Lauderdale, Vol Inf
CRY, John, Pvt, Col John K Winn, Capt James Holleman, Inf
CRY, John, Pvt, Col John K Winn, Capt Samuel M Carothers, W TN Inf transferred to Capt Hollom's Co
CUDD, Jarrett, Pvt, Col Alexander Loury, Capt James Kincaid, Inf
CUDE, John, Pvt, Col John Cocke, Capt Samuel Carothers, Inf
CUFF, Cates, Pvt, Lt Col Richard Napier, Co Commander omitted, Inf
CUFF, David, Pvt, Col N T Perkins, Capt Philip Pipkin, Mtd Riflemen
CUFF, David, Pvt, Col Thomas Williamson, Capt John Doak & Capt John Dobbins, Vol Mtd Gunmen
CUFF, Robert, Pvt, Col Thomas Williamson, Capt John Doak & Capt John Dobbins, Vol Mtd Gunmen
CUFFMAN, Thomas, Pvt, Col John Coffee, Capt John Byrn, Cav
CULBERSON, John, Pvt, Col Edward Bradley, Capt John Moore, Vol Inf
CULBERSON, Joseph, Pvt, Col William Hall, Capt John Moore, Vol Inf
CULBERTSON, Benjamin, Pvt, Col Thomas H Benton, Capt Newton Cannon, Inf
CULBERTSON, James B, Pvt, Col John K Winn, Capt Robert Braden, Inf
CULBERTSON, Jesse, Pvt, Col Edward Bradley, Capt John Moore, Vol Inf
CULBERTSON, Jesse, Pvt, Col William Hall, Capt John Moore, Vol Inf
CULBURTH, Daniel, Pvt, Col Thomas McCrory, Capt William Dooley, Inf
CULIFER, Isaac, Pvt, Col Edward Bradley, Capt William Lauderdale, Vol Inf
CULLA, James M, Pvt, Maj James Porter, Co Commander omitted, Cav
CULLEN, Edward, Pvt, Col Alexander Loury, Capt George Sarver, Inf
CULLEN, Jesse, Pvt, Col L Hammonds, Capt J N Williamson, 2nd Regt Inf
CULLER, Sam M, Pvt, Maj James Porter, Co Commander omitted, Cav

CULLOM, Jesse, Pvt, Col Alexander Loury, Capt _ N Williamson, W TN Mil
CULLOM, Jesse, Pvt, Lt Col L Hammonds, Capt Thomas Williamson, Inf
CULPH, John, Pvt, Col Samuel Wear, Capt James Gillespie, E TN Vol Inf
CULTS, William, Pvt, Col Ewen Allison, Capt Joseph Everett, E TN Mil; deserted 3-4-1814
CUMMING, John, Pvt, Col Samuel Bunch, Capt James Cumming, E TN Vol Mtd Gunmen
CUMMING, Thomas, Pvt, Maj John Childs, Capt James Cumming, E TN Vol Mtd Inf; Regimental Co Blount
CUMMINGS, George, Cpl, Col John Cocke, Capt Bird Nance, Inf; promoted from Pvt
CUMMINGS, George, Pvt, Col John Cocke, Capt Bird Nance, Inf
CUMMINGS, Malakiah, Pvt, Regt Commander omitted, Capt Larkin Ferrels, Inf
CUMMINGS, Moses, Pvt, Regt Commander omitted, Capt Larkin Ferrels, Inf
CUMMINGS, Richard, Pvt, Col Newt Cannon, Capt Thos Yardley?, Mtd Riflemen; transferred to Capt Smith Spies
CUMMINGS, Seth, Pvt, Col John Cocke, Capt Bird Nance, Inf
CUMMINGS, William, Pvt, Regt Commander omitted, Capt Larkin Ferrels, Inf
CUMMINS, George, Pvt, Maj Wm Woodfolk, Capt Ezekial Ross, Inf
CUMMINS, John, Pvt, Col S Bunch, Capt George McPherson, E TN Mil
CUMMINS, Richard, Pvt, Regt Commander omitted, Capt George Smith, Spies
CUMMINS, Thomas, Pvt, Col Robert Dyer, Capt James Wyatt, Vol Mtd Gunmen
CUMMINS, Thomas, Pvt, Col Samuel Wear, Capt James Tedford, E TN Vol Inf
CUMMINS, William, Pvt, Col James Raulston, Capt James Black, Inf
CUMPTON, Jos, Pvt, Col S Bunch, Capt John English, E TN Drafted Mil
CUMPTON, Richard, Pvt, Col John Cocke, Capt Sam Caruthers, Inf
CUMPTON, Thomas, Pvt, Col Thos Williamson, Capt Beverly Williams, Vol Mtd Gunmen; d 4-10-1815
CUMPTON, Zachariah, Pvt, Col S Bunch, Capt John English, E TN Drafted Mil; joined from Capt Howel's Co
CUNG, David, Pvt, Col R C Napier, Capt Drury Adkins, Mil Inf
CUNNINGHAM, Aaron, Pvt, Col John Wynne, Capt James Porter, Inf
CUNNINGHAM, Aaron, Pvt, Col John Wynne, Capt Wm Wilson, Inf; transferred to Capt Porter's Co
CUNNINGHAM, Andrew, Pvt, Col Wm Johnson, Capt James Stewart, E TN Drafted Mil
CUNNINGHAM, Benjamin, Pvt, Col Edwin Booth, Capt Alex Biggs, Inf
CUNNINGHAM, Elijah, Pvt, Col Thos McCrory, Capt

## Enlisted Men, War of 1812

Thos Gordon, Inf
CUNNINGHAM, George, Pvt, Col Maj Wm Russell, Capt Isaac Williams, Separate Bn of TN Vol Mtd Gunmen
CUNNINGHAM, George, Pvt, Col Wm Lillard, Capt Robert Maloney, E TN Vol Inf
CUNNINGHAM, George, Secretary, Maj Gen Andrew Jackson, Co Commander omitted, Div TN Mil; sick absent
CUNNINGHAM, Hance M, Pvt, Col Thomas Williamson, Capt Giles Burdett, Vol Mtd Gunmen
CUNNINGHAM, Hance, Pvt, Col Thomas Benton, Capt Benj Hewett, Vol Inf; refused to march
CUNNINGHAM, Hugh, Pvt, Maj James Porter, Co Commander omitted, Cav
CUNNINGHAM, Isaac, Pvt, Col James Raulston, Capt James M Neal, Inf; d 1-31-1815
CUNNINGHAM, Isaac, Pvt, Maj Wm Woodfolk, Capt Abner Pearce, Inf
CUNNINGHAM, James, Pvt, Capt Sam Bunch, no other information
CUNNINGHAM, James, Pvt, Regt Commander omitted, Capt Sam Bunch, Branch Srvce omitted
CUNNINGHAM, James, Sgt, Col John Brown, Capt John Trimble, E TN Mtd Gunmen
CUNNINGHAM, Jas, 2 Lt, Maj Wm Russell, Capt John Trimble, Vol Mtd Gunmen
CUNNINGHAM, Jas, Pvt, Col A Cheatham, Capt Wm Smith, Inf
CUNNINGHAM, John B, Pvt, Gen Thos Washington, Co Commander omitted, Mtd Inf
CUNNINGHAM, John, Cpl, Col S Bunch, Capt Solomon Dobkins, E TN Drafted Mil; discharged for inability
CUNNINGHAM, John, Pvt, Col Edwin Booth, Capt John Porter, Drafted Mil
CUNNINGHAM, John, Pvt, Col Stephen Copeland, Capt G W Stell, Mil Inf
CUNNINGHAM, John, Pvt, Col Wm Metcalf, Capt Hill & Capt John Cunningham, Mil Inf
CUNNINGHAM, Jonathan, Pvt, Col John Brown, Capt Charles Lewin, Mil
CUNNINGHAM, Jos, Pvt, Col John Brown, Capt Charles Lewin, E TN Vol Mtd Inf
CUNNINGHAM, Jos, Pvt, Col Philip Pipkin, Capt John Robertson, Mil Inf; left sick at Ft Pierce 11-2-1814
CUNNINGHAM, Jos, Pvt, Col Sam Bunch, Capt Wm Jobe, E TN Vol Mtd Inf
CUNNINGHAM, Mordica, Pvt, Col Sam Bunch, Capt Wm Houston, E TN Vol Mtd Mil
CUNNINGHAM, Moses, Pvt, Col Philip Pipkin, Capt John Robertson, Mil Inf; left sick at Ft Pierce 11-26-1814
CUNNINGHAM, Moses, Pvt, Maj Wm Russell, Capt John Trimble, Vol Mtd Gunmen
CUNNINGHAM, Robert, Pvt, Col Wm Higgins, Capt Wm Doak, Branch Srvce omitted
CUNNINGHAM, Thomas, Pvt, Regt Commander omitted, Capt James Craig, Branch Srvce omitted
CUNNINGHAM, William, Pvt, Col Ed Bradley, Capt Thos Haynie, Vol Inf
CUNNINGHAM, William, Pvt, Col Ewen Allison, Capt Sam Allen, E TN Mil
CUNNINGHAM, William, Pvt, Col Sam'l Bunch, Capt Joseph Duncan, E TN Drafted Mil
CUNNINGHAM, William, Pvt, Col Wm Hall, Capt Henry Newland, Inf
CUP, Davis, Pvt, Col Wm Johnson, Capt Jas McKamey, E TN Drafted Mil; sick absent
CURD, Chas, Pvt, Col S Bunch, Capt ? Gibbs, E TN Drafted Mil
CURE, Jarrett, Pvt, Col Thomas Williamson, Capt Thomas Porter, Vol Mtd Gunmen
CURENTON, Richard, Pvt, Col Ewen Allison, Capt Haynie, E TN Mil
CURINGTON, James, Pvt, Col Wm Collins, Capt Barbee Metcalf, Mtd Inf; d 3-24-1814
CURL, Wm, Pvt, Lt Col Phillips, Co Commander omitted, Inf
CURLEE, Cullin, Tptr, Col N Cannon, Capt George Brandon, Mtd Riflemen
CURLEN, Calvin, 4 Sgt, Regt Commander omitted, Capt George Brandon, Mtd Riflemen
CURLEY, John, Pvt, Col John Coffee, Capt John Byrn, Cav
CURRELL, George, Pvt, Col S Bayless, Capt James Churchman, E TN Mil
CURRIER, William, Pvt, Col Edwin Booth, Capt John Lewis, E TN Mil
CURRIN, Thomas, Pvt, Col Samuel Bayless, Capt John Brock, E TN Mil
CURRY, Alexander, Pvt, Col Wm Johnson, Capt William Alexander, Det of E TN Drafted Mil
CURRY, David, Pvt, Lt Col John Edmondson, Co Commander omitted, Cav
CURRY, Edward, Pvt, Maj Wm Woodfolk, Capt Abner Pearce, Inf; transferred from Capt Searcy Co
CURRY, Elijah, 2 Cpl, Col Thomas Benton, Capt Henry Douglass, Vol Inf
CURRY, Elijah, Cpl, Col Edward Bradley, Capt Henry Douglass, Vol Inf
CURRY, George, Pvt, Col S Copeland, Capt John Holshouser, Inf
CURRY, Isaiah, 1 Lt, Col Wm Metcalf, Capt Wm Mullen, Mil Inf
CURRY, James, Pvt, Brig Gen Johnson, Capt Robert Carson, Inf
CURRY, James, Pvt, Col William Hall, Capt Travis C Nash, Inf
CURRY, John L, Pvt, Col John Brown, Capt John Trimble, E TN Mtd Gunmen
CURRY, John, Col John K Winn, Capt William McCall, Inf
CURRY, John, Pvt, Col James Raulston, Capt Henry Hamilton, Inf; also served Gen Wm Carroll
CURRY, John, Pvt, Col Philip Pipkin, Capt Henry M Newlin, Mil Inf
CURRY, John, Pvt, Col Thomas Benton, Capt William Moore, Vol Inf
CURRY, Jos, Pvt, Col R C Napier, Capt Andrew McCarty, Mil Inf

## Enlisted Men, War of 1812

CURRY, Riley, Pvt, Brig Gen Thos Johnson, Capt Robert Carson, Inf
CURRY, Sam'l, Pvt, Col Samuel Bunch, Capt James Cummings, E TN Vol Mtd Gunmen
CURRY, William, Pvt, Col William Johnson, Capt James Stewart, E TN Drafted Mil
CURRY, Wm, Pvt, Col William Hall, Capt Travis C Nash, Inf
CURSWELL, Samuel, Pvt, Col Carroll, Capt Dillahanty, Capt Bradford, Vol Inf
CURTIS, Arthur, Pvt, Col Philip Pipkin, Capt James Blakemore, Mil Inf; deserted 9-20-1814
CURTIS, Dan'l, Cpl, Col R C Napier, Capt Thomas Gray, Mil Inf
CURTIS, Elijah, Pvt, Col Samuel Wear, Capt Robert Doak, E TN Vol Inf
CURTIS, George Washing, Pvt, Col A Cheatham, Capt Charles Johnson, Inf; sick absent
CURTIS, James, Pvt, Col William Metcalf, Capt William Sitton, Mil Inf
CURTIS, Joce, Pvt, Maj William Woodfolk, Capt Abraham Dudney, Inf
CURTIS, Joel, Pvt, Col John Cocke, Capt Joe Price, Inf
CURTIS, John B, Pvt, Maj Woodfolk, Capt Dudley, Inf
CURTIS, John D, Pvt, Col Edwin E Booth, Co Commander omitted, E TN Mil; joined Capt Sutton's Co
CURTIS, John, Pvt, Col R H Dyer, Capt Williams, Vol Mtd Gunmen
CURTIS, John, Pvt, Col Samuel Bayless, Co Commander omitted, E TN Mil
CURTIS, John, Pvt, Col T McCrory, Capt Isaac Patton, Mil Inf; sick absent
CURTIS, Joseph, Pvt, Regt Commander omitted, Capt Larkin Ferrell, Inf
CURTIS, Noah, Pvt, Col Wm Metcalf, Capt Cunningham, Mil Inf; d 12-30-1814
CURTIS, Solomon, Pvt, Col Philip Pipkin, Co Commander omitted, Mil Inf
CURTIS, Thomas, Cpl, Col R C Napier, Co Commander omitted, Mil Inf
CURTIS, Thomas, Pvt, Col Cocke, Capt Price, Inf
CURTIS, Thos, Pvt, Col Samuel Wear, Capt Calloway, Mtd Gunmen
CURTIS, William D, Pvt, Col Leroy Hammond, Capt James Craig, Inf
CURTIS, William, Pvt, Col John Alcorn, Capt Alexander McKeen, Cav
CURTIS, Wm, Pvt, Regt Commander omitted, Capt James Williams, Mil Cav
CURTNER, Jacob, Pvt, Col Ewen Allison, Capt Adam Winsell, E TN Drafted Mil
CURTON, Robert, Pvt, Col Samuel Bayless, Capt Branch Jones, E TN Drafted Mil; discharged by general 12-7-1814
CUSICK, David, Pvt, Col Samuel Wear, Capt John Stephens, E TN Vol Inf
CUTCHIN, Joshua, Pvt, Col James Cocke, Capt James Gault, Inf
CUTTER, Jesse, Pvt, Col Thomas Benton, Capt Thomas Williamson, Vol Inf

CUTTER, John, Pvt, Regt Commander omitted, Capt Wm Camp, Vol Inf
CYPERT, Lawrence, Pvt, Col John Alcorn, Capt Thomas Bradley, Vol Cav
CYPRET, William, Pvt, Col Thomas Williamson, Capt Beverly Williams, Vol Mtd Gunmen
CYPRETT, Lawrence, Pvt, Regt Commander omitted, Capt A McKinney, Cav
CYPRETT, Stephen, Pvt, Col Newton Cannon, Capt John Harpole, Mtd Gunmen
CYPRETT, William, Pvt, Col Newton Cannon, Capt John Harpole, Mtd Gunmen
CYRUS, Burnett, Pvt, Regt Commander omitted, Capt James Terrill, Cav
DABBS, Richard, Pvt, Col A Cheatham, Capt Charles Johnson, Inf
DABNEY, England, Pvt, Col John Brown, Capt William Neilson, E TN Vol Mil
DABZELL, William, Sgt, Col Edwin Booth, Capt Samuel Thompson, Mil
DAGGAD, Chatten, Pvt, Regt Commander omitted, Capt Garrett Lane, Mtd Riflemen
DAGLEY, Benjamin, Pvt, Col Edwin Booth, Capt John Lewis, E TN Mil
DAGLEY, John, Pvt, Col Alexander Loury, Capt John Looney, 2nd Regt W TN Mil
DAIL, Mathew, Pvt, Col S Copeland, Capt William Evans, Mil Inf; on furlough sick 4-21-1814
DAILEY, George, Pvt, Col S Copeland, Capt Solomon George, Inf
DAILEY, James, Cpl, Col Samuel Bayless, Capt Hale, E TN Mil; reduced to the ranks
DAILEY, John, Pvt, Col Ewen Allison, Capt Jacob Hoyal, E TN Mil
DAILY, James, Pvt, Col Alexander Provine, Co Commander omitted, Mil Inf
DAILY, William, Cpl, Col S Copeland, Capt David Williams, Inf
DAIMWOOD, Henry, Pvt, Col John Cocke, Capt Richard Crunk, Inf
DALE, Abner, Pvt, Col William Lillard, Capt Thomas Sharpe, 2nd Regt Inf
DALE, Dan'l, Pvt, Col Richard Steele, Capt Richard M Ratton, Mil Inf
DALE, George, Pvt, Col William Y Higgins, Capt James Hambleton, Mtd Gunmen
DALE, Isaac A, Pvt, Col William Higgins, Capt Adam Dale, Mtd Gunmen
DALE, James, Pvt, Maj Gen Wm Carroll, Col James Raulston, Capt Wiley Huddleston, Inf
DALE, John, Pvt, Col T McCrory, Capt Abel Willis, Mil Inf
DALE, John, Pvt, Maj Gen William Carroll, Col James Raulston, Capt Edward Robinson, Inf
DALE, Jonathan, Pvt, Col S Bunch, Capt S Richardson, E TN State Mil
DALE, Jonathan, Pvt, Col S Bunch, Capt S Robertson, E TN Drafted Mil
DALE, Sam'l, Pvt, Col S Copeland, Capt James Taite, Inf
DALE, Squire, Cpl, Col S Copeland, Capt David Williams, Inf

## Enlisted Men, War of 1812

DALE, Thomas A, Sgt, Col Thomas McCrory, Capt Abel Willis, Mil Inf; reduced from Capt, sick absent
DALE, Thomas, Pvt, Col William Higgins, Capt Adam Dale, Mtd Gunmen
DALE, William, Pvt, Col Wm Higgins, Capt James Hambleton, Mtd Gunmen
DALLIS, Evans, Pvt, Col John Cocke, Capt Joe Rich, E TN Inf
DALLIS, John, Capt, Col John Cocke, Capt John Dalton, Inf
DALLIS, John, Pvt, Col Philip Pipkin, Capt Wm Smith, Vol Mil; transferred from Capt John Strothers
DALLIS, Tolbert, Pvt, Col Philip Pipkin, Capt John Robertson, Mil Inf; left sick at Ft Jackson 11-11-1814
DALLIS, William, Pvt, Col Ewen Allison, Capt J Laughmiller, Mil
DALY (DAILY), John, Pvt, Col Alexander Loury, Capt James Kincaid, Inf
DAM, Henry, Pvt, Lt Col Archer Cheatham, Co Commander omitted, Mil Inf (with 6th Brig)
DAME, John, Pvt, Col Wm Johnson, Capt James Tunnell, E TN Mil; reduced from Sgt
DAMEWOOD, Nathaniel, Pvt, Col Wm Johnson, Capt James Stewart, E TN Drafted Mil
DAMEWOOD, Watson, Pvt, Col Wm Johnson, Capt James Stewart, E TN Drafted Mil
DAMOON (DAMOTE), Henry, Pvt, Col John Cocke, Capt Richard Crunk, Inf
DAMWOOD, Nath, Pvt, Col Wm Johnson, Capt James Stewart, E TN Mil
DANAWAY, William, Pvt, Col Philip Pipkin, Capt Eb Kirkpatrick, Mil Inf; deserted 9-24-1814
DANBY, Hezekiah, Pvt, Col Ewen Allison, Capt Henry McCray, E TN Mil
DANCER, Henry, Pvt, Col Wm Hall, Capt William Alexander, Vol Inf
DANEL, Nicholas, Pvt, Regt Commander omitted, Capt David Smith, Cav
DANIEL, Anderson, Pvt, Col Wm Higgins, Capt Sam Allen, Mtd Gunmen
DANIEL, Andrew (Anderson), Pvt, Lt Col L Hammons, Capt Arahel Raines, Inf
DANIEL, Barton, Pvt, Col Alex Loury, Capt James Kincaid, Inf; d 12-18-1814
DANIEL, Barton, Pvt, Col John Cocke, Capt John Weakly, Inf
DANIEL, Dandy, Pvt, Maj William Russell, Capt John Cowan, Vol Mtd Gunmen
DANIEL, Daniel, Pvt, Lt Col L Hammons, Capt Arahel Raines, Inf
DANIEL, David, Pvt, Lt Col Archer Cheatham, Co Commander omitted, Mtd Inf 6th Brig
DANIEL, Edward, Pvt, Col S Bunch, Capt John Harris, E TN Mil
DANIEL, Henry B W, Pvt, Lt Col Hammons, Capt James Tubb, Inf
DANIEL, Isaac, Pvt, Maj Gen Jackson, Col Thos Williamson, Capt Robt Steele, Vol Mtd Gunmen
DANIEL, James, Pvt, Col James Raulston, Capt Daniel Newman, Inf; d 12-22-1814

DANIEL, James, Pvt, Regt Commander omitted, Capt James Williams, Mil Cav
DANIEL, Jas, Pvt, Col R H Dyer, Capt Jos Williams, Vol Mtd Gunmen
DANIEL, Jeremiah, Pvt, Col Thomas Williamson, Capt James Cook, Capt John Crane, Cav
DANIEL, Jesse, Pvt, Col Newton Cannon, Capt John Hanly, Mtd Riflemen
DANIEL, Jesse, Pvt, Col Wm Alcorn, Capt John Byrn, Cav; sick absent
DANIEL, Joe, Pvt, Col S Bunch, Lt John Harris, E TN Mil
DANIEL, John, Pvt, Col Wm Pillow, Capt John Anderson, Vol Inf
DANIEL, Martin, Pvt, Col John Cocke, Capt John Weakley, Inf
DANIEL, Nathaniel, Pvt, Col S Copeland, Capt John Holshouser, Inf
DANIEL, Paul, Pvt, Col Edward Bradley, Capt John Kennedy, Riflemen
DANIEL, Paul, Pvt, Col Wm Hall, Capt John Kennedy, Vol Inf
DANIEL, Peter, Pvt, Col S Copeland, Capt David Williams, Mil Inf; d 4-2-1814
DANIEL, Robert, Pvt, Col Ewen Allison, Capt Jacob Hoyal, E TN Mil
DANIEL, Robert, Pvt, Col John Cocke, Capt John Weakley, Inf
DANIEL, Robert, Pvt, Col S Copeland, Capt Wm Douglass, Inf
DANIEL, Samuel, Pvt, no other information
DANIEL, Stephen, 3 Sgt, Col Wm Lillard, Capt John Roper, E TN Vol Inf
DANIEL, Thomas, Pvt, Col Alex Loury, Capt George Sarver, Inf
DANIEL, Thos, Pvt, Col John Alcorn, Capt John Byrns, Cav
DANIEL, Thos, Pvt, Col Wm Hall, Capt John Kennedy, Vol Inf
DANIEL, Thos, Pvt, Col Wm Hall, Capt John Wallace, Inf
DANIEL, Thos, Pvt, Lt Col Henry Byrn, Co Commander omitted, Inf
DANIEL, William, Pvt, Col Alcorn, Capt Bryan, Cav
DANIEL, William, Pvt, Col John Coffee, Capt Henry Bryan, Cav
DANIEL, William, Pvt, Col R C Napier, Capt Thomas Gray, Inf
DANIEL, William, Pvt, Col Robert Dyer, Capt James Wyatt, Vol Mtd Gunmen
DANIEL, William, Pvt, Col Robert Steele, Capt Richard Ratton, Mil Inf
DANIEL, William, Pvt, Col Wm Lillard, Capt John Roper, E TN Vol Inf
DANIEL, William, Pvt, Regt Commander omitted, Capt Jas Gray, Inf
DANIEL, Wm R, Pvt, Col John Brown, Capt William White, E TN Inf
DANIEL, Wm, 5 Sgt, Col Alexander Loury, Capt Thomas Delaney, Inf; transferred to the Horse Camp by order of Gen Taylor
DANIEL, Wm, Pvt, Col Thomas McCrory, Capt Wm Dooley, Inf

## Enlisted Men, War of 1812

DANIEL, Wm, Pvt, Col Wm Hall, Capt John Wallace, Inf
DANIEL, Zachariah, Pvt, Col Samuel Bayless, Capt Jonathan Waddell, E TN Mil
DANIELS, Marmeduke, Pvt, Col S Bunch, Capt G McPherson, E TN Mil
DANIL, Thos, Pvt, Col John Coffee, Capt Henry Byrn, Cav
DANIL, William, Pvt, Col Alex Loury, Lt Col Hammond, Capt Thos Delaney, Inf
DANLEY, Andrew, Pvt, Col John Cocke, Capt John Dalton, Inf
DANSLEY, Daniel, Pvt, Col Robert Dyer, Capt Robert Evans, Vol Mtd Gunmen
DARBY, Ebenezer, Pvt, Col Thomas Benton, Capt James McEwen, Vol Inf
DARBY, George, Pvt, Regt Commander omitted, Capt James Williams, Mil Cav
DARBY, Izor, Pvt, Col Wm Y Higgins, Capt A Cheatham, Mtd Riflemen
DARBY, John, Pvt, Col Thomas Williamson, Capt John Doak & Capt Dobbins, Vol Mtd Gunmen
DARBY, Phillip, Pvt, Col R C Napier, Capt Thos Benton, Mil Inf
DARDEN, Charnell, Pvt, Col Thos Williamson, Capt Giles Burdett, Vol Mtd Gunmen; d 2-15-1815
DARDIN, Carnal, Pvt, Col Robert H Dyer, Capt Joseph Williams, TN Vol Mtd Gunmen
DARE, Hubbard, Pvt, Col Thomas Williamson, Capt Anthony Metcalf, Vol Mtd Gunmen
DARE, John, Pvt, Col Wm Lillard, Capt Thos McChristian, Vol Inf
DARIN, Mann, Pvt, Col N T Perkins, Capt Philip Pipkin, Mtd Riflemen
DARIS, Stuten, Pvt, Regt Commander omitted, Capt Edwin S Moore, Mtd Riflemen
DARK, James, Pvt, Col Thomas Williamson, Capt Beverly Williams, Vol Mtd Gunmen
DARK, Josiah, Pvt, Col S Copeland, Capt John Holshouser, Inf
DARK, Josiah, Pvt, Col Wm Metcalf, Capt William Sitton, Mil Inf
DARNAL, Thomas, Far, Regt Commander omitted, Capt David Smith, Cav Vol
DARNALD, Aaron, Pvt, Col William Johnson, Capt Joseph Scott, E TN Drafted Mil
DARNALD, Henry, Ffr, Col William Johnson, Capt Joseph Scott, E TN Drafted Mil
DARNALD, Henry, Pvt, Col William Johnson, Capt Joseph Scott, E TN Drafted Mil; promoted to Ffr Maj
DARNALD, John B, Pvt, Maj Gen Carroll, Col William Metcalf, Capt Andrew Jackson, Inf
DARNALL, Nicholas, Pvt, Col John Coffee, Capt David Smith, Vol Cav
DARNELL, Benjamin, Cpl, Lt Col A Cheatham, Co Commander omitted, Inf
DARNELL, Benjamin, Tptr, Col John Coffee, Capt David Smith, Vol Cav
DARNELL, Henry, Ffr Maj, Col Wm Johnson, Co Commander omitted, E TN Mil
DARNELL, Thos, 2 Cpl, Col John Coffee, Capt Alexander McKeem, Cav
DARNELL, William, Pvt, Regt Commander omitted, Capt Wm Mitchell, Spies
DARNING, John, Pvt, Col Thomas Williamson, Capt John Cook & Capt John Dobbins, Vol Mtd Gunmen
DARNING, William, Pvt, Col Thomas Williamson, Capt John Doak, Vol Mtd Gunmen
DARNOLD, John, Pvt, Col Edward Bradley, Capt Travis Nash, Vol Inf
DARNOLD, John, Pvt, Col William Hall, Capt Travis Nash, Inf
DARR, John, Pvt, Col John Chiles, Capt Reuben Tipton, E TN Vol Mtd Inf; Regimental Co 6th Jefferson
DARROW, John B, Pvt, Lt Col Archer Cheatham, Co Commander omitted, Mtd Inf
DARTER, Michael, Pvt, Col William Lillard, Capt George Argenbright, E TN Vol Riflemen
DASONLY, Wm, Pvt, Regt Commander omitted, Capt James Cowan, Mtd Inf
DAUGHERTY, John, Pvt, Col William Metcalf, Capt Hill & Capt John Cunningham, Mil Inf
DAUGHERTY, Joseph, Rank omitted, Regt Commander omitted, Capt Larkin Ferrell, Inf
DAUSET, Philip, Pvt, Col Samuel Wear, Capt Robert Doak, E TN Vol Inf
DAUSET, Robert, Pvt, Col Samuel Wear, Capt Robert Doak, E TN Vol Inf
DAUSON, Ezekiel, Pvt, Col Thomas McCrory, Capt James Shannon, Mil Inf
DAUSON, William, Pvt, Col John Coffee, Capt Daniel Ross, Mtd Gunmen
DAVALT, Samuel, Pvt, Col William Lillard, Capt Benj King, E TN Vol Inf
DAVENPORT, Absalom, Pvt, Col James Raulston, Capt James A Black, Inf
DAVENPORT, Charles, Pvt, Col James Raulston, Capt John Cowan, Inf
DAVENPORT, Francis, Pvt, Col James Raulston, Capt Charles Wade, Inf
DAVENPORT, Henry, Pvt, Maj William Woodfolk, Capt John Sutton, Capt Dudney, Inf
DAVENPORT, Joseph, Pvt, Col James Raulston, Capt Elijah Haynie, Inf
DAVENPORT, Thomas, Pvt, Col James Raulston, Capt Charles Wade, Inf
DAVENPORT, William, 1 Cpl, Col Edwin Booth, Capt John Sharpe, E TN Mil
DAVEY, Ashburn, Pvt, Col R H Dyer, Capt Joseph Williams, Vol Mtd Gunmen
DAVID, David, Pvt, Col John Brown, Capt James Preston, E TN Mil Inf
DAVID, Henry, Pvt, Col Edwin Booth, Capt John McKamey, Inf; deserted 12-8-1814
DAVID, Isiah, Pvt, Col James Raulston, Capt James Black, Inf
DAVID, John, Pvt, Regt Commander omitted, Capt James Craig, Inf
DAVIDSON, Abner, Pvt, Maj William Woodfolk, Capt Abner Pearce, Inf; joined from Capt Neil's Co
DAVIDSON, Abner, Pvt, Maj William Woodfolk, Capt

## Enlisted Men, War of 1812

James Neil, Inf

DAVIDSON, Abraham, Pvt, Col William Hall, Capt James Hambleton, Vol Inf

DAVIDSON, Alin, Pvt, Col William Johnson, Capt James Stewart, E TN Mil; transferred

DAVIDSON, Allen, Pvt, Col Alexander Loury & Col Leroy Hammonds, Capt Arahel Rains, Inf; attached to Gen Taylor's Guard

DAVIDSON, Asa, Cpl, Col Samuel Bunch, Capt Daniel Yarnell, E TN Mil

DAVIDSON, Benjamin, Pvt, Col James Raulston, Capt James Black, Inf

DAVIDSON, Benjamin, Pvt, Col William Hall, Capt John Moore, Vol Inf; on furlough

DAVIDSON, Benjamin, Pvt, Col William Johnson, Capt Elihu Millikin, E TN Mil

DAVIDSON, Brasket, Pvt, Col Robert Dyer, Capt James McMahon, 1st TN Mtd Vol Gunmen

DAVIDSON, Bryan, Pvt, Col Edwin Booth, Capt Porter, Drafted Mil

DAVIDSON, Charleton, Sgt, Lt Col Archer Cheatam, Co Commander omitted, Mtd Spies

DAVIDSON, Charlton, 2 Sgt, Col John Coffee, Capt James Terrell, Vol Cav

DAVIDSON, Edward, Pvt, Col S Bunch, Capt S Roberson, E TN Drafted Mil; deserted 4-12-1814

DAVIDSON, Edward, Pvt, Regt Commander omitted, Capt Samuel Richardson, E TN Drafted Mil; deserted 4-12-1814

DAVIDSON, Ephraim E, Sgt Maj, Col Thomas McCrory, Co Commander omitted, 2nd Regt TN Mil; resigned

DAVIDSON, Ephraim, Cpl, Brig Gen Isaac Roberts, Capt Benjamin Reynolds, Mtd Rangers

DAVIDSON, Ephraim, Pvt, Col Thomas McCrory, Capt William Dooley, Inf

DAVIDSON, George, Cpl, Regt Commander omitted, Capt Robert Evans, Mtd Spies

DAVIDSON, George, Pvt, Col Newt Cannon, Capt Martin, Mtd Gunmen; transferred to Capt Evan's Spies Co

DAVIDSON, George, Pvt, Regt Commander omitted, Capt James Cowan, Mtd Inf

DAVIDSON, Gilbert, Pvt, Brig Gen Isaac Roberts, Capt Benjamin Reynolds, Mtd Rangers

DAVIDSON, Green, Pvt, Lt Col Henry Bryan, Co Commander omitted, Inf

DAVIDSON, Jacob, Pvt, Col S Wear, Capt Joseph Calloway, Mtd Inf

DAVIDSON, James L, Pvt, Col Alexander Loury, Capt John Loone, W TN Inf; d 4-15-1815?

DAVIDSON, James, Pvt, Col John Brown, Capt Lunsford Oliver, E TN Mil

DAVIDSON, James, Pvt, Col Philip Pipkin, Capt David Smith, Inf

DAVIDSON, James, Pvt, Col Robert Dyer, Capt Williams, Vol Mtd Gunmen; d 11-14-1814

DAVIDSON, John E, Pvt, Brig Gen Isaac Roberts, Capt Benjamin Reynolds, Mtd Rangers

DAVIDSON, John O, Pvt, Col Robert Dyer, Capt Ephraim Dickson, 1st TN Mtd Vol Gunmen

DAVIDSON, John O, Pvt, Gen Andrew Jackson, Capt Nathan Davis, Inf

DAVIDSON, John O?, Pvt, Regt Commander omitted, Capt David Mason, Cav; promoted to Cpl

DAVIDSON, John jr, Pvt, Col John Brown, Capt Lunsford Oliver, E TN Mil

DAVIDSON, John, Pvt, Col John Cocke, Capt John Weakley, Inf

DAVIDSON, John, Pvt, Col N T Perkins, Capt John Doak, Vol Mtd Gunmen; sick on furlough 2-7-1814

DAVIDSON, John, Pvt, Col N T Perkins, Capt Marr, Mtd Vol

DAVIDSON, John, Pvt, Col Robert Dyer, Capt Cuthbert Hudson, Vol Mtd Gunmen

DAVIDSON, John, Pvt, Col Robert Dyer, Capt Williams, Vol Mtd Gunmen

DAVIDSON, Joseph, Pvt, Col S Copeland, Capt William Evans, Mil Inf; sick absent 3-27-1814 at Ft Strother

DAVIDSON, Joseph, Sgt, Lt Col John Edmondson, Co Commander omitted, Cav

DAVIDSON, Joshua, Pvt, Col N T Perkins, Capt James McMahon, Mtd Gunmen

DAVIDSON, Joshua, Pvt, Col Robert Dyer, Capt James McMahon, 1 TN Mtd Vol Gunmen

DAVIDSON, Joshua, Pvt, Col William Lillard, Capt William Hamilton, E TN Vol Inf; substitute for Martin Miller

DAVIDSON, Richard, Pvt, Col James Raulston, Capt Mathew Cowan, Inf

DAVIDSON, Robert, Pvt, Col Edwin Booth, Capt John Sharp, E TN Mil

DAVIDSON, Robert, Pvt, Col Samuel Bunch, Capt S Robertson, E TN Drafted Mil

DAVIDSON, Robert, Pvt, Regt Commander omitted, Capt Samuel Richardson, E TN Drafted Mil

DAVIDSON, Samuel C, Pvt, Maj John Childs, Capt John Stephens, E TN Mtd Vol Mil

DAVIDSON, Samuel I, 1 Lt, Col John Brown, Capt Lunsford Oliver, E TN Mil

DAVIDSON, Thomas, Pvt, Col William Johnson, Capt Elihu Milliken, 3rd Regt E TN Mil; substitute for Buck Sutton

DAVIDSON, Thomas, Pvt, Maj Gen William Carroll, Co Commander omitted, Inf; promoted to Cpl, d 1-30-1815

DAVIDSON, Thomas, Pvt, Maj William Woodfolk, Capt John Sutton, Capt Abraham Dudney, Inf

DAVIDSON, William jr, Pvt, Col John Brown, Capt Lunsford Oliver, E TN Mil

DAVIDSON, William, Pvt, Col Leroy Hammonds, Capt James Craig, Inf

DAVIDSON, William, Pvt, Col Samuel Bayless, Capt Allen Bacon, E TN Mil

DAVIDSON, William, Pvt, Col William Metcalf, Capt William Sitton, Mil Inf; d 3-20-1815

DAVIDSON, William, Pvt, Lt Col A Cheatham, Co Commander omitted, Inf

DAVIDSON, William, Pvt, Lt Col Henry Bryan, Co Commander omitted, Inf

DAVIDSON, William, Pvt, Maj John Childs, Capt John

## Enlisted Men, War of 1812

Stephens, E TN Vol Mtd Inf
DAVIS, Absolom, Pvt, Maj Gen Andrew Jackson, Col A Cheatham, Capt William Creel, Inf
DAVIS, Alexaner, Pvt, Col Metcalf, Co Commander omitted, Mil Inf
DAVIS, Alford, Pvt, Lt Col Hammond, Co Commander omitted, Inf
DAVIS, Amos, Cpl, Col Robert Steele, Co Commander omitted, Mil Inf
DAVIS, Amos, Pvt, Col Thomas Williamson, Capt John Doak & Capt John Dobbins, Vol Mtd Gunmen
DAVIS, Amy R, Pvt, Col Thomas H Benton, Capt Benjamin Reynolds, Vol Inf
DAVIS, Andrew, Pvt, Col R C Napier, Co Commander omitted, Mil Inf
DAVIS, Andrew, Pvt, Col R H Dyer, Capt Edmondson, TN Vol Mtd Gunmen
DAVIS, Andrew, Pvt, Col Samuel Wear, Capt Tedford, E TN Vol Inf
DAVIS, Archibald, Pvt, Col Nicholas Perkins, Capt John Doak, Vol Mtd Gunmen
DAVIS, Archibald, Pvt, Col Samuel Bunch, Capt Edward Buchanan, E TN Drafted Mil
DAVIS, Archibald, Pvt, Col Samuel Bunch, Capt Joseph Duncan, E TN Drafted Mil
DAVIS, Archibald, Pvt, Col Wm Johnson, Capt Benjamin Powell, E TN Mil
DAVIS, Arthur N, Cpl, Regt Commander omitted, Capt Archibald, Cav
DAVIS, Baker, Pvt, Col William Lillard, Capt Zacheus Copeland, E TN Vol Inf
DAVIS, Barton, Pvt, Col Alexander Loury, Capt James Kincaid, Inf
DAVIS, Barton, Pvt, Col Alexander Loury, Capt John Looney, W TN Inf; joined from Capt Craig Co
DAVIS, Barton, Pvt, Col Leroy Hammonds, Capt James Craig, Inf
DAVIS, Basdal, Pvt, Col Newton Cannon, Capt James Walton, Mtd Riflemen, Drafted
DAVIS, Benj A, Pvt, Col John Cocke, Capt John Dalton, Inf
DAVIS, Benj A, Pvt, Maj Wm Carroll, Capt Daniel M Bradford & Capt Lewis Dillahunty, Vol Inf
DAVIS, Benj, Pvt, Col S Bunch, Capt James Cummings, E TN Vol Mtd Gunmen
DAVIS, Benj, Pvt, Regt Commander omitted, Capt Thomas Gray, Inf
DAVIS, Benjamin, Pvt, Col Edwin Booth, Capt Richard Marshall, Drafted Mil
DAVIS, Benjamin, Pvt, Col Samuel Bayless, Capt James Churchman, E TN Mil
DAVIS, Benjamin, Pvt, Col Wm Metcalf, Capt Thomas Marks, Mil Inf
DAVIS, Benjamin, Pvt, Regt Commander omitted, Capt Archibald McKinney, Cav
DAVIS, Cadwell, Cpl, Col Robert Steele, Capt Samuel Maxwell, Mil Inf
DAVIS, Charles, Ffr, Col Edwin Booth, Capt John Sharp, E TN Mil
DAVIS, Charles, Pvt, Col John Brown, Capt Hugh Barton, E TN Mil Inf

DAVIS, Chisley, Pvt, Col Edwin Booth, Capt John Sharp, E TN Mil
DAVIS, Coleman, Pvt, Col R H Dyer, Capt Bethel Allen, Vol Mtd Gunmen
DAVIS, Dan'l, Pvt, Col Thomas Benton, Capt William J Smith, Vol Inf; absent?
DAVIS, Dan'l, Pvt, Maj John Childs, Capt Daniel Prcie, E TN Vol Mtd Inf
DAVIS, Elijah, Pvt, Col S Copeland, Capt David Williams, Inf; sick absent
DAVIS, Elisha, Pvt, Col Wm Pillow, Capt C E McEwen, Vol Inf; on furlough
DAVIS, Enoch, Pvt, Col Thomas McCrory, Capt John Gordon, Inf
DAVIS, Enoch, Pvt, Maj William Woodfolk, Capt Dan Ross, Inf
DAVIS, Ephraim, Pvt, Col Edwin Booth, Capt John Slatton, E TN Mil
DAVIS, Ephraim, Pvt, Col Ewen Allison, Capt ? Laughmiller, Mil; transferred to Capt Register Co
DAVIS, Ephraim, Pvt, Col S Bunch, Capt F Register, E TN Mil; joined from Capt Laughmiller Co
DAVIS, Furfulow, Pvt, Col Edwin Booth, Capt John Slatton, E TN Mil
DAVIS, Hardy, Pvt, Col Alex Loury, Capt James Kincaid, Inf; d 12-18-1814
DAVIS, Henry A, Pvt, Col Thomas Benton, Capt John Reynolds, Vol Inf
DAVIS, Henry R, Pvt, Col Wm Pillow, Capt C E McEwen, Vol Inf
DAVIS, Henry, 3 Sgt, Lt Col Hammonds, Capt James Tubb, Inf; absent sick at Ft Montgomery
DAVIS, Henry, Pvt - Cpl, Col John Brown, Capt Allen Bacon, E TN Inf Mil
DAVIS, Henry, Pvt, Col Edward Bradley, Capt John Kennedy, Riflemen
DAVIS, Henry, Pvt, Col Thomas Benton, Capt Isaiah Renshaw, Vol Inf
DAVIS, Hezekiah, Pvt, Col S Copeland, Capt Alex Provine, Mil Inf
DAVIS, Hugh, Pvt, Col Sam Wear, Capt John Bayless, Mtd Inf
DAVIS, Isaac, Pvt, Col Ewen Allison, Capt Jacob Hoyal, E TN Mil
DAVIS, Isaac, Pvt, Maj William Woodfolk, Capt James Neil, Inf
DAVIS, Isaac, Pvt, Maj Wm Woodfolk, Capt James Turner, Inf; in place of Wilson Petty (transferred to Capt Neil)
DAVIS, Isaih, Pvt, Col Robert Dyer, Capt Ephraim Dickson, TN Mtd Gunmen
DAVIS, Jaba, Pvt, Col R C Napier, Capt John Chism, Mil Inf
DAVIS, Jacob, Pvt, Brig Gen Johnson, Capt Robert Carson, Inf
DAVIS, Jacob, Pvt, Col Edward Bradley, Capt John Kennedy, Riflemen
DAVIS, Jacob, Pvt, Col Edwin Booth, Capt Porter, Drafted Mil
DAVIS, James, 2 Cpl, Col Samuel Bunch, Capt James Cummings, E TN Vol Mtd Gunmen

- 157

## Enlisted Men, War of 1812

DAVIS, James, Pvt, Col A Cheatham, Capt James Giddins, Inf

DAVIS, James, Pvt, Col Alexander Loury, Capt John Looney, 2nd Regt W TN Mil

DAVIS, James, Pvt, Col Edwin Booth, Capt Richard Marshall, Drafted Mil; deserted 1-5-1815

DAVIS, James, Pvt, Col N T Perkins, Capt John Doak, Vol Mtd Gunmen

DAVIS, James, Pvt, Col Robert Dyer, Capt Bethel Allen, Vol Mtd Gunmen

DAVIS, James, Pvt, Col Thomas Benton, Capt George Caperton, Vol Inf; promoted to paymaster

DAVIS, James, Pvt, Col William Johnson, Capt Elihu Milliken, 3rd Regt E TN Mil

DAVIS, James, Pvt, Col William Johnson, Capt James Tunnell, E TN Mil; notified & never appeared

DAVIS, James, Pvt, Maj John Childs, Capt John Stephens, E TN Vol Mtd Inf

DAVIS, James, Pvt, Regt Commander omitted, Capt David Mason, Cav

DAVIS, James, Pvt, Regt Commander omitted, Sgt Wyatt Fussel, Det of Inf

DAVIS, Jesse, Pvt, Regt Commander omitted, Capt John Miller, Spies

DAVIS, John B, Pvt, Col John Cocke, Capt George Barnes, Inf

DAVIS, John H, Far, Col Robert Dyer, Capt Robert Evans, Vol Mtd Gunmen

DAVIS, John H, Pvt, Col S Copeland, Capt William Hodges, Inf; sick absent

DAVIS, John P, Pvt, Col Thomas Benton, Capt Isaiah Renshaw, Vol Inf

DAVIS, John P, Pvt, Col Wm Pillow, Capt Isaiah Renshaw, Inf

DAVIS, John jr, Pvt (Blksmth), Col Thomas Williamson, Capt John Doak, Capt John Dobbins, Vol Mtd Gunmen; substitute

DAVIS, John jr, Pvt, Col S Bunch, Capt F Register, E TN Mil; joined from Capt Noyles Co

DAVIS, John jr, Pvt, Col T McCrory, Capt A Metcalf, Mil Inf

DAVIS, John sr, Pvt, Col S Bunch, Capt F Register, E TN Mil

DAVIS, John sr, Pvt, Col T McCrory, Capt A Metcalf, Mil Inf

DAVIS, John, 1 Cpl, Col N T Perkins, Capt John Doak, Vol Mtd Riflemen

DAVIS, John, 4 Sgt, Col R C Napier, Capt Early Benson, Mil Inf

DAVIS, John, Blksmth, Col N T Perkins, Capt Philip Pipkin, Mtd Riflemen

DAVIS, John, Cpl, Col Ewen Allison, Capt Jacob Hoyal, E TN Mil; transferred to Capt Register Co

DAVIS, John, Cpl, Col William Metcalf, Capt John Barnhart, Mil Inf

DAVIS, John, Pvt, Col A Cheatham, Capt Richard Benson & Capt Charles Johnson & Capt James Giddins, Inf

DAVIS, John, Pvt, Col Alexander Loury, Capt Arahel Rains, Capt Leroy Hammonds, Inf

DAVIS, John, Pvt, Col John Brown, Capt James Standifer, E TN Vol Mtd Mil

DAVIS, John, Pvt, Col John Coffee, Capt Daniel Ross, Mtd Gunmen

DAVIS, John, Pvt, Col John Wynne, Capt John Porter, Inf

DAVIS, John, Pvt, Col Philip Pipkin, Capt James Blakemore, Mil Inf

DAVIS, John, Pvt, Col R C Napier, Capt John Chism, Mil Inf; on furlough

DAVIS, John, Pvt, Col Robert Steele, Capt James Randals, Inf; substitute for G Fitzgerald

DAVIS, John, Pvt, Col S Copeland, Capt William Hodges, Inf; sick absent

DAVIS, John, Pvt, Col Samuel Bayless, Capt Solomon Hendrix, E TN Mil

DAVIS, John, Pvt, Col Samuel Bunch, Capt Daniel Yarnell, E TN Mil

DAVIS, John, Pvt, Col Thomas Williamson, Capt John Hutchings, Vol Mtd Gunmen

DAVIS, John, Pvt, Col William Johnson, Capt Joseph Scott, E TN Drafted Mil; deserted

DAVIS, John, Pvt, Col Wm Metcalf, Capt Andrew Patterson, Mil Inf

DAVIS, John, Sgt Maj, Col John Brown, Co Commander omitted, E TN Vol Mtd Gunmen

DAVIS, Jonathan, Pvt, Col William Lillard, Capt Robert McCalpin, E TN Inf

DAVIS, Jos, Pvt, Col John Cocke, Capt James Gault, E TN Mil Inf

DAVIS, Jos, Pvt, Col T McCrory, Capt William Dooley, Inf

DAVIS, Jos, Pvt, Col Thomas Williamson, Capt John Dobbins, Capt John Doak, Vol Mtd Gunmen; substituted Will Hawkins

DAVIS, Jos, Pvt, Maj William Woodfolk, Capt James C Neil, Inf

DAVIS, Joshua, Pvt, Col John Brown, Capt Hugh Barton, E TN Mil Inf

DAVIS, Joshua, Pvt, Col Robert H Dyer, Capt Robert Evans, Vol Mtd Gunmen

DAVIS, Josiah, Pvt, Col Thomas Benton, Capt Newton Cannon, Inf

DAVIS, Josiah, Pvt, Col Wm Pillow, Capt David Mason, Vol Inf; sick absent since 10-29-1813

DAVIS, Julian, Pvt, Col Newton Cannon, Capt David Hogan, Mtd Gunmen

DAVIS, Lelbourn, Pvt, Col Wm Lillard, Capt George Argenbright, E TN Vol Riflemen

DAVIS, Lemuel, Pvt, Col T McCrory, Capt Abel Willis, Mil Inf; sick absent

DAVIS, Levi, Pvt, Col William Johnson, Capt Henry Hunter, E TN Mil; left sick at Ft Jackson, substituted Elias Davis

DAVIS, Lewis, Pvt, Col Edwin Booth, Capt John Slatton, E TN Mil

DAVIS, Lewis, Pvt, Maj John Childs, Capt James Cummings, E TN Vol Mtd Inf

DAVIS, Major, Pvt, Col Wm A Metcalf, Capt Bird L Hurt, Mil Inf

DAVIS, Mathew, Pvt, Col S Copeland, Capt Allen Wilkinson, Mil Inf

DAVIS, Mathew, Pvt, Col T McCrory, Capt Abel Willis,

## Enlisted Men, War of 1812

DAVIS, Miles, Pvt, Col Ewen Allison, Capt Wm King, Mil Inf Drafted Mil
DAVIS, Moses, Pvt, Col N T Perkins, Capt Mathew Johnson, Mil Inf
DAVIS, Moses, Pvt, Col R H Dyer, Capt Cuthbert Hudson, Vol Mtd Gunmen
DAVIS, Nathaniel, Pvt, Col S Bunch, Capt F Register, E TN Inf
DAVIS, Newell H, 3 Cpl, Col S Bunch, Capt Thomas Mann, E TN Vol Mtd Inf
DAVIS, Peter, Pvt, Col William Johnson, Capt David McKamy, E TN Drafted Mil
DAVIS, Phillip E, 3 Cpl, Col William Pillow, Capt George Caperton, Inf
DAVIS, Phillip E, 4 Cpl, Col Thomas Benton, Capt George Caperton, Inf
DAVIS, Phillip E, Pvt, Col Thomas Benton, Capt George Caperton, Inf
DAVIS, Phillip, Pvt, Col T McCrory, Capt John Reynolds, Mil Inf
DAVIS, Price, Pvt, Col William Hall, Capt John Kennedy, Vol Inf
DAVIS, Richard, Pvt, Col Wm Metcalf, Capt Barbee Collins, Mil Inf
DAVIS, Richmond, Pvt, Col William Johnson, Capt David McKamy, E TN Drafted Mil
DAVIS, Robert C, Pvt, Maj Gen Andrew Jackson, Capt Joseph Kirkpatrick, Mtd Gunmen; wounded on furlough 1-27-1814
DAVIS, Robert, Pvt, Col Samuel Wear, Capt Rufus Morgan, E TN Vol Inf
DAVIS, Robert, Pvt, Regt Commander omitted, Capt James Haggard, Mtd Gunmen
DAVIS, S Henry, Pvt, Col Edwin Booth, Capt Alex Biggs, Inf
DAVIS, Samuel, Pvt, Col Newton Cannon, Capt James Walton, Mtd Riflemen
DAVIS, Samuel, Pvt, Col R C Napier, Co Commander omitted, Mil Inf; on furlough
DAVIS, Samuel, Pvt, Col Samuel Bayless, Capt Solomon Hendrickx, E TN Mil
DAVIS, Sterling, Pvt, Col Thomas H Benton, Co Commander omitted, Vol Inf
DAVIS, Sterling, Pvt, Col Wm Pillow, Capt Thomas Williamson, Vol Inf
DAVIS, Sterling, Pvt, Regt Commander omitted, Capt Edwin S Moore, Mtd Riflemen
DAVIS, Thomas C, Pvt, Col Thomas Williamson, Capt Robert Moore, Vol Mtd Gunmen
DAVIS, Thomas, Pvt, Col Edwin E Booth, Capt Bigg & Capt Moore, Inf
DAVIS, Thomas, Pvt, Col John Brown, Capt Charles Lewin, E TN Mtd Vol Gunmen
DAVIS, Thomas, Pvt, Col John Williams, Capt William Walker, Vol
DAVIS, Thomas, Pvt, Col Philip Pipkin, Co Commander omitted, Mil Inf
DAVIS, Thomas, Pvt, Col Robert Steele, Capt Richard M Ratton, Mil Inf
DAVIS, Thomas, Pvt, Col Samuel Bunch, Capt Edward Buchanan, E TN Drafted Mil
DAVIS, Thomas, Pvt, Regt Commander omitted, Capt George Smith, Spies
DAVIS, Thomas, Pvt, Regt Commander omitted, Capt Joseph Duncan, E TN Drafted Mil; transferred to Capt Buchanan Co
DAVIS, Thos, Pvt, Col Samuel Bunch, Capt Moses, E TN Mil Drafted; discharged by Gen George Doughtery
DAVIS, Thos, Pvt, Col Samuel Bunch, Capt Penny, E TN Mtd Inf
DAVIS, Thos, Pvt, Col Wm Lillard, Co Commander omitted, E TN Vol Inf
DAVIS, Weekli, Pvt, Col Philip Pipkin, Capt Blakemore, Mil Inf; substituted William Allen
DAVIS, William H, Pvt, Col Ewen Allison, Capt Robert Moore, Vol Mtd Gunmen
DAVIS, William H, Pvt, Col S Bunch, E TN Mil; joined Capt Laughmiller
DAVIS, William, Pvt, Col Edwin Booth, Capt Porter, Drafted Mil
DAVIS, William, Pvt, Col John K Wynne, Capt John Spinks, Inf; sick absent 1-1-1813
DAVIS, William, Pvt, Col John Wynne, Capt James Cole, Inf
DAVIS, William, Pvt, Col S Bunch, Capt James Cummings, E TN Vol Mtd Gunmen
DAVIS, William, Pvt, Col Sam Wear, Capt Daniel Price, E TN Vol Inf
DAVIS, William, Pvt, Col Sam Wear, Capt Joseph Callaway, Mtd Inf
DAVIS, William, Pvt, Col Samuel Bunch, Co Commander omitted, E TN Drafted Mil
DAVIS, William, Pvt, Col Thomas Williamson, Capt Robert Moore, Vol Mtd Gunmen
DAVIS, William, Pvt, Regt Commander omitted, Capt William Russell, Mtd Spies
DAVIS, Willie, Pvt, Col Newton Cannon, Capt David Hogan, Mtd Gunmen
DAVIS, Willie, Pvt, Col R H Dyer, Capt Cuthbert Hudson, Vol Mtd Gunmen
DAVIS, Wilson, Pvt, Col Philip Pipkin, Capt E Kirkpatrick, Mil Inf
DAVIS, Wilson, Pvt, Col Robert Steele, Capt R M Patton, Mil Inf
DAVIS, Zachariah, Pvt, Col James Raulston, Capt Charles Wade, Inf
DAVISON, Hudson, Pvt, Lt Col John Edmondson, Capt William Peacock, Cav
DAVISON, James L, Pvt, Col Thomas McCrory, Capt William Dooley, Inf
DAVISON, James, Pvt, Col S Copeland, Capt Richard Sharpe, Mil Inf
DAVISON, Joshua, Pvt, Col Samuel Bunch, Capt William Houston, E TN Vol Mtd Inf
DAVISON, Josiah, Pvt, Regt Commander omitted, Capt William Peacock, Cav
DAVISON, Thomas, Pvt, Col Samuel Bayless, Capt Jonathan Waddle, E TN Mil; Artif & Actic
DAVITT, Robert, Pvt, Col John Cocke, Capt John Weakley, Inf

DAW, Henry, Pvt, Maj Gen Andrew Jackson, Capt John Crane; killed 1-22-1814
DAWDY, Allison, Pvt, Col Philip Pipkin, Capt Ebenezer Kirkpatrick, Mil Inf; deserted
DAWSON, Abraham, Pvt, Col Samuel Bayless, Capt Joseph Hale, E TN Mil
DAWSON, Jesse, Pvt, Regt Commander omitted, Capt John Miller, Spies
DAWSON, John, Pvt, Col Philip Pipkin, Capt Henry Newlin, Mil Inf; died 10-10-1814
DAWSON, John, Pvt, Col William Metcalf, Capt William Mullin, Mil Inf
DAWSON, Willis L., 3 Cpl, Maj Gen William Carroll, Capt Francis Ellis, Inf
DAY, David, Pvt, Col Edwin Booth, Capt George Winton, E TN Mil; transferred to Capt Milliken's Co
DAY, David, Pvt, Col William Johnson, Capt Elihu Milliken, 3 Regt E TN Mil; joined from Capt Winton's Co
DAY, Edward, Pvt, Col William Lillard, Capt Maloney, E TN Vol Inf; unable to perform duty
DAY, Francis, Pvt, Col William Hall, Capt Abraham Bledsoe, Vol Inf
DAY, John, Cpl, Col Samuel Bunch, Capt Francis Berry, E TN Mil
DAY, John, Mus, Col Samuel Bunch, Capt Solomon Dobkins, E TN Mil; deserted
DAY, Joseph, Cpl, Col William Johnson, Capt Elihu Milliken, 3 Regt E TN Mil
DAY, Joseph, Sgt, Col Samuel Bunch, Capt Andrew Breden, E TN Mil
DAY, Samuel, 5 Sgt, Col Alexander Loury, Capt John Looney, 2 Regt W TN Mil; promoted to QM
DAY, Samuel, QM, Lt Col Leroy Hammonds, Col Alexander Loury, 2 Regt W TN Mil
DAY, Thomas, Pvt, Col Thomas Williamson, Capt Anthony Metcalf, Vol Mtd Gunmen
DAYLY, James, Pvt, Col Samuel Bayless, Capt Joseph Hale, E TN Mil; reduced from Cpl
DEAN, Benjamin, Pvt, Col John Williams, Capt William Walker, Vol
DEAN, Benjamin, Sgt, Col Samuel Wear, Capt Rufus Morgan, E TN Vol Inf; appointed QM
DEAN, Benjamin, asst Fgmstr Sgt, Maj Gen John Cocke, no Co Commander, E TN Vol Mil
DEAN, Daniel, Cpl, Col John Coffee, Capt Charles Kavanaugh, Cav
DEAN, Francis M, Pvt, Col Thomas H Benton, Capt James McEwen, Vol Inf
DEAN, Jacob, Pvt, Lt Col L Hammons, Capt James Craig, Inf
DEAN, Jacob, Pvt, Regt Commander omitted, Capt Garrett Lane, Mtd Riflemen
DEAN, Joab, Pvt, Col Thomas Williamson, Capt James Pace, Lt Nealy, Vol Mtd Gunmen
DEAN, Job, Pvt, Maj William Woodfolk, Capt Ezekiel Ross & Capt McCulley, Inf
DEAN, Luke H, 3 Cpl, Col John Coffee, Capt Robert Jetton, Cav
DEAN, Luke H, Cpl, Col John Alcorn, Capt Robert Jetton, Vol Cav; died 10-24-1815
DEAN, Luke, Pvt, Col John Coffee, Capt Robert Jetton, Cav
DEAN, Robert L, Far, Col John Coffee, Capt Charles Cavanaugh, Cav
DEAN, Robert L, Far, Regt Commander omitted, Capt Archibald McKinney, Cav, transferred to Evans Co of Spies
DEAN, Robert L, Far, Regt Commander omitted, Capt Archibald McKinney, Cav, transferred to Evary Co
DEAN, Robert, Far, no Regt Commander, Carp Robert Evans, Mtd Spies
DEAN, Thomas, Cpl, Col A Loury, Capt Gabriel Martin, Inf
DEAN, Thomas, Pvt, Col John Cocke, Capt Samuel W Caruthers, Inf
DEAN, William, Pvt, Col Edward Bradley, Capt John Moore, Vol Inf
DEAN, William, Pvt, Col William Hall, Capt John Moore, Vol Inf
DEAN, Willis, Pvt, Col James Raulston, Capt Elijah Haynie, Inf
DEANE, William, Pvt, Maj William Russell, Capt Isaac Williams, Tn Vol Mtd Gunmen; Sep Bn
DEARING, Alfred, Ffr, Maj William Woodfolk, Capt Abner Pearce, Inf
DEARMAN, David, Pvt, Col Samuel Wear, Capt John Stphens, E TN Vol Inf
DEARMAN, George, Pvt, Col William Lillard, Capt Benjamin H King, E TN Vol Inf
DEARMAN, John, Pvt, Col William Johnson, Capt James Stewart, E TN Draft Mil
DEARMAN, John, Pvt, no Regt Commander, Capt William Henderson, Spies
DEARMAN, Thomas G, Pvt, Col Samuel Wear, Capt John Stephens, E TN Vol Inf
DEARMAND, James, 3 Sgt, Col John Brown, Capt James Standifer, Regt E TN Vol Mtd Inf
DEARMOND, James, Pvt, Col Thomas Benton, Capt Benjamin Reynolds, Vol Inf
DEARMOND, Richard, Pvt, Col Samuel Wear, Capt Joseph Calloway, Mtd Inf
DEARMOND, William, Pvt, Maj John Childs, Capt Reuben Tipton, E TN Vol Mtd Inf; Knox County
DEARMONS, William, Pvt, Col Samuel Wear, Capt Joseph Calloway, Mtd Inf
DEASON, Absolom, Pvt, Col Philip Pipkin, Capt John Robertson, Mil Inf
DEASON, John, Pvt, Col Newton Cannon, Capt John B Dempsey, Mtd Gunmen
DEAVULT, William, Pvt, Col Thomas Benton, Capt Henry L Douglas, Vol Inf
DEBENPORT, Absolem, Pvt, Col William Johnson, Capt Henry Hunter, E TN Mil
DEBERRY, Benjamin, Pvt, Col R H Dyer, Capt James McMahon, TN Vol Mtd Gunmen
DEBOW, Solomon, Pvt, Col Edward Bradley, Capt Brice Martin, Vol Inf
DEBRELL, Charles, Pvt, Col Samuel Bunch, Capt Gibbs, Vol Inf
DEBRILL, Charles, Pvt, Col William Pillow, Capt John H

## Enlisted Men, War of 1812

Anderson, Vol Inf
DECK, Daniel, Pvt, Col Samuel Bunch, Capt James Cummings, E TN Vol Mtd Gunmen
DECKARD, Benjamin, Pvt, Col Thomas Benton, Capt George Caperton, Inf
DECKARD, George, Pvt, Maj William Woodfolk, Capt James C Neil, Inf
DECKHART, John, Pvt, Col Ewen Allison, Capt Jonas Laughmiller, Mil
DECOLP, John H, Dmr, Col Philip Pipkin, Capt Peter Searcy, Mil Inf
DEEDS, Michael, Pvt, Col Ewen Allison, Capt John Hampton, Mil
DEEK (DICK), Frederick, Pvt, Col James Raulston, Maj Gen William Carroll, Capt Wiley Huddleston, Inf
DEEN, Charles, Sgt, Col Newton Cannon, Capt Isaac Williams, Mtd Riflemen
DEEN, Jeremiah, Pvt, no other information
DEEVAL, Alexander, Pvt, Col Thomas Williamson, Capt Thomas Scurry, Vol Mtd Gunmen; no service performed
DEFEW, James, Pvt, Col Ewen Allison, Capt Jacob Hoyal; transferred from McPherson
DEFRIES, Hiram A, Pvt, Maj John Childs, Capt John Stephens, E TN Vol Mtd Inf
DEGRAFFENRED, M T, Pvt, Col William Pillow, Capt James McEwen, Vol Inf
DEGRAFFENREED, M F, Pvt, Col Thomas Benton, Capt James McEwen, Vol Inf
DEGRAFFENREED, Mathew F, Pvt, Col Thomas Benton, Capt James McEwen, Vol Inf
DEGRAFFENRIED, Metcalf, 2 Lt, Col Thomas Benton, Capt James McEwen, Vol Inf
DEGRAFFINRIED, A M, Pvt, Regt Commander omitted, Capt David Mason, Cav
DEGRIFFENRIED, F D, QM Sgt, Col Nicholas T Perkins, Co Commander omitted, 1st Regt TN Mtd Vol
DEILL?, David, Pvt, Regt Commander omitted, Capt Larkin Ferrell, Inf
DELANY, John, Pvt, Col Thos Williamson, Capt Giles Burdett, Vol Mtd Gunmen; d 2-15-1815
DELANY, John, Pvt, Lt Isaac Barrett, Capt Nathan Davis, Inf; d 3-14-1814
DELANY, John, Sgt, Col S Copeland, Capt John Holhouser, Inf
DELANY, William, Pvt, Col Thomas Benton, Capt George Caperton, Inf
DELARNEE, Jess, Pvt, Col Edwin Booth, Capt John McKamey, E TN Mil
DELES, Demois, 3 Cpl, Col Ler Hammonds, Capt Joseph Williamson, Inf; sick
DELF, Phillip, Pvt, Col Johnston, Capt Allen, Mil Inf
DELL, Frederick, Pvt, Col Thomas Benton, Capt Thomas Williamson, Vol Inf
DELL, Frederick, Pvt, Col Wm Pillow, Capt Thomas Williamson, Vol Inf
DELL, James, Pvt, Col John Walker, Capt John Williams, Vol
DELL, Maxey, Pvt, Col John Williams, Capt William Walker, Vol
DELLAHUN, William, Pvt, Col N T Perkins, Capt Philip Pipkin, Mtd Riflemen
DELLIS, Dennie, Pvt, Col Wm Pillow, Capt George Caperton, Inf
DELLIS, Dennis, Pvt, Col L Hammonds, Capt John Williams, 2nd Regt Inf; promoted to Cpl
DELLIS, John, Pvt, Col Philip Pipkin, Capt David Smith, Mil Inf
DELLIS, John, Pvt, Col S Copeland, Capt S George, Inf
DELOACH, Boiken, Pvt, Col Thomas Benton, Capt George Caperton, Vol Inf
DELOACH, Elias F, Cpl, Col John Coffee, Capt David Smith, Vol Cav
DELOACH, Sam'l, Pvt, Col Newton Cannon, Capt George Brandon, Mtd Riflemen; deserted 10-5-1813
DELOACH, Sam'l, Pvt, Col Philip Pipkin, Capt E Kirkpatrick, Mil Inf
DELOACH, Sam'l, Pvt, Maj Gen Woodfolk, Capt McCully, Inf
DELOACH, Samuel, Pvt, Col Philip Pipkin, Capt E Kirkpatrick, Mil Inf
DELOACH, Simon, Pvt, Lt Col R Napier, Co Commander omitted
DELOACH, Simon, Pvt, Maj Gen Carroll, Capt Ellis, Inf
DELOACH, Solomon, Pvt, Maj Gen Woodfolk, Capt Daniel Ross & Capt McCully, Inf
DELOACH, Solomon, Pvt, Maj William Woodfolk, Capt Abner Pearce, Inf
DELOACH, William, Pvt, Col Newt Cannon, Capt George Brandon, Mtd Riflemen
DELORIER, Asa, Pvt, Maj John Childs, Capt Reuben Tipton, Vol Mtd Inf; Regimental Co Blount
DELPH, Michael, Pvt, Col John Cocke, Capt John Weakley, Inf
DELPH, Michael, Pvt, Col John Cocke, Capt John Weakley, Inf; d 2-16-1815
DELPH, Michael, Pvt, Lt Col Henry Bryan, Co Commander omitted, Inf
DEMAHOO, John, Pvt, Col John Alcorn, Capt John Winston, Branch Srvce omitted
DEMASCUS, Solomon, Pvt, Col Edwin Booth, Capt Richard Marshall, Drafted Mil; discharged for inability
DEMASTERS, Jess, Sgt, Col Allison, Capt Allison, E TN Mil
DEMASTERS, John, 1 Cpl, Col John Brown, Capt Charles Lewin, E TN Mtd Inf
DEMENT, James, Pvt, Col Philip Pipkin, Capt James Blakemore, Mil Inf
DEMERY (DEMRA), Allen, Pvt, Col James Raulston, Capt James Black, Inf
DEMONBREUM, Timothy, Pvt, Regt Commander omitted, Capt John Gordon, Mtd Spies
DEMONBRY, Timothy, Pvt, Col T McCrory, Capt Isaac Patton, Mil Inf; transferred to Gordon's Spies
DEMOSS, Ike, Pvt, Regt Commander omitted, Capt William Russell, Mtd Spies; transferred to Maj Williamson's Bn
DEMOSS, James, Pvt, Col John Cocke, Capt Dan'l Ross, Mtd Gunmen
DEMOSS, John, 2 Lt, Col N T Perkins, Capt Philip Pipkin,

- 161

## Enlisted Men, War of 1812

Mtd Gunmen; wounded--returned home 1-27-1814
DEMOSS, Thomas, 5 Cpl, Col John Cocke, Capt John Dalton, Inf
DEMOSS, William, 5 Cpl, Col Robert Dyer, Capt Robert Evans, Vol Mtd Gunmen
DEMOSS, William, Pvt, Col R H Dyer, Capt Robert Evans, Vol Mtd Gunmen
DEMPSEY, John, Pvt, Col R C Napier, Capt Thomas Prescom, Mil Inf; on furlough 3-4-1814
DEMUMBREUM, Felix, Pvt Col John Coffee, Capt Fred Stump, Cav; absent
DENAHM, Philip, Pvt, Col William Johnson, Capt Elihu Milliken, 4th Regt E TN Mil; transferred to Capt Hunter's Co
DENARY, James, Pvt, Col Robert Dyer, Capt Glen Owen, TN Vol Mtd Gunmen
DENHAM, Franklin, Pvt, Col Ewen Allison, Capt J Laughmiller, Mil
DENHAM, John S, Pvt, Col Sam Bunch, Capt James Cummings, E TN Vol Mtd Inf
DENHAM, John, Pvt, Col William Johnston, Capt Henry Hunter, E TN Mil
DENHAM, Phillip, Pvt, Col William Johnson, Capt Henry Hunter, E TN Mil; transferred to Capt William Co
DENHAM, Thomas, Pvt, Col Samuel Bunch, Capt George McPherson, E TN Mil
DENHAM, William, Pvt, Col William Lillard, Capt Hugh Martin, E TN Vol Inf; substitute for David Childress
DENING, William, Pvt, Col Philip Pipkin, Capt James Blakemore, Mil Inf
DENNINGTON, Elijah, Pvt, Col Samuel Bayless, Capt Joseph Goodson, E TN Mil
DENNINGTON, Reubin, Pvt, Col William Johnson, Capt James Tunnell, E TN Mil
DENNIS, Beverly, Pvt, Col James Raulston, Capt Henry Hamilton, Inf; also served Maj Gen Carroll
DENNIS, Edward, Pvt, Col William Johnson, Capt Christopher Cook, E TN Mil; joined from Capt Hunter Co
DENNIS, George, Pvt, Lt Col Hammond, Capt A Loury & Capt Thos Delaney, Inf
DENNIS, James, Pvt, Col S Copeland, Capt Wm Evans, Mil Inf
DENNIS, Jeremiah, Pvt, Col Philip Pipkin, Capt George Mebane, Mil Inf
DENNIS, Joseph, Pvt, Col S Bayless, Capt Branch Jones, E TN Mil; discharged for inability
DENNIS, Levi, Pvt, Col S Bunch, Capt S Roberson, E TN Drafted Mil
DENNIS, Levi, Pvt, Regt Commander omitted, Capt Samuel Richardson, E TN Drafted Mil
DENNIS, Thomas, Pvt, Col John Cocke, Capt James Gray, Inf; sick absent 3-18-1815
DENNIS, Thomas, Pvt, Col John Coffee, Capt Dan'l Ross, Mtd Gunmen; promoted to 2 Lt
DENNIS, Thomas, Pvt, Regt Commander omitted, Capt Thomas Gray, Inf
DENNIS, Thos, 4 Sgt, Col Wm Metcalf, Capt John Hill & Capt John Cunningham, Mil Inf; sick

DENNY, Edward, Pvt, Col William Johnson, Capt Henry Hunter, E TN Mil; transferred to Capt Kirk's Camp
DENNY, James, Pvt, Col S Bayless, Capt Branch Jones, E TN Drafted Mil
DENNY, James, Pvt, Col William Lillard, Capt James Lillard, E TN Mil Inf
DENNY, Johnathan, Pvt, Col S Copeland, Capt William Hodges, Inf
DENNY, Jonathan, Pvt, Lt Col Hammond, Capt James Tubb, Inf
DENNY, William, Cpl, Col S Copeland, Capt Wm Hodges, Inf
DENNY, William, Pvt, Col Edwin Booth, Capt Porter, Drafted Mil
DENNY, William, Pvt, Col Newton Cannon, Capt James Walton, Mtd Riflemen
DENNY, William, Pvt, Col Robert Dyer, Capt Bethel Allen, Vol Gunmen
DENSON, Christopher, Pvt, Col Robert Dyer, Capt White, Vol Mtd Gunmen
DENSON, George, Pvt, Col Robert Jarmon, Capt Nathan Peoples, Inf
DENSON, I, Pvt, Col Wm Russell, Co Commander omitted, Spies; transferred to Maj Williamson Bn
DENSON, James, Pvt, Col Philip Pipkin, Capt Peter Searcy, Mil Inf
DENSON, Jesse, Pay Master, Col John K Wynne, Co Commander omitted, 1st Regt TN Mil
DENSON, Jesse, Pvt, Col John Brown, Capt William White, E TN Vol Mil Inf; transferred to Capt Mullen
DENSON, Jesse, Pvt, Col John Wynne, Capt Robert Breden, Inf
DENSON, Jesse, QM Sgt, Maj Thomas Williamson, Co Commander & Branch Srvce omitted
DENSON, Jessee, Pvt, Col John Miller, Co Commander omitted, Spies; transferred to Capt White
DENSON, Robert, Pvt, Col Thomas Williamson, Capt John Hutchings, Vol Mtd Gunmen
DENSON, Tearl, Pvt, Regt Commander omitted, Capt Nathan Peoples, Inf
DENTON, B G, Pvt, Col S Bunch, Capt John Houk, E TN Mil; joined from Capt Gregory Co
DENTON, Benj, Pvt, Col Edwin Booth, Capt Vernon, E TN Mil
DENTON, Cornelius, Pvt, Regt Commander omitted, Capt William Henderson, Spies
DENTON, Edwin, Pvt, Col Robert Steele, Capt James Randalls, Inf; on furlough
DENTON, Isaac, Pvt, Col William Johnson, Capt Elihu Milliken, 3rd Regt E TN Mil
DENTON, Jacob G, Pvt, Col S Bayless, Capt James Churchman, E TN Mil
DENTON, Jacob, Pvt, Col S Bunch, Capt George Gregory, E TN Drafted Mil
DENTON, James, Pvt, Regt Commander omitted, Capt John Miller, Spies
DENTON, John G, Pvt, Col S Bayless, Capt James Churchman, E TN Mil
DENTON, John G, Pvt, Col S Bunch, Capt John Houk, E

## Enlisted Men, War of 1812

TN Mil; joined from Capt Gregory Co
DENTON, John S, Pvt, Col Robert Dyer, Capt Bethel Allen, Vol Mtd Gunmen
DENTON, John, Pvt, Col S Bayless, Capt James Churchman, E TN Mil; transferred to Capt Milliken Co
DENTON, John, Pvt, Col S Bayless, Capt James Landen, E TN Mil
DENTON, John, Pvt, Col S Bunch, Capt George Gregory, E TN Drafted Mil
DENTON, John, Pvt, Col Wm Johnson, Capt Elihu Milliken, 3rd Regt E TN Mil; transferred to Capt Churchman's Co
DENTON, Jonathan, Sgt, Col Edwin Booth, Capt Vernon, Branch Srvce omitted
DENTON, Joshua, Pvt, Maj Wm Woodfolk, Capt Sutton, Capt Abraham Dudney, Inf
DENTON, Josiah, Pvt, Regt Commander omitted, Capt Wm Johnson, Spies
DENTON, Solomon G, Pvt, Col S Bayless, Capt Joseph Goodson, E TN Mil; substituted for John Clay
DENTON, Solomon, Pvt, Col S Bunch, Capt George Gregory, E TN Drafted Mil
DENTON, Solomon, Pvt, Col S Bunch, Capt John Houk, E TN Mil; joined from Capt Gregory Co
DENTON, Thos, Pvt, Col Edwin Booth, Capt Sam Thompson, Mil
DENTON, William, Pvt, Regt Commander omitted, Capt Wm Henderson, Spies
DENTON (DENTONG), Solomon, Pvt, Col Wm Johnson, Capt Elihu Milliken, 3rd Regt E TN Mil; transferred to Capt Churchman's Co
DENVER, William, Pvt, Col William Johnson, Capt David McKamy, E TN Drafted Mil
DENWOODY, John, Pvt, Col S Bayless, Capt S Hendris?, E TN Mil
DEPREST, George C, Pvt, Col N Cannon, Capt Martin, Mtd Gunmen
DEPREST, George C, Pvt, Col Thomas Benton, Capt Benj Hewett, Vol Inf
DEPREST, Randolph, Pvt, Col John Cocke, Capt Sam Caruthers, Inf
DEPRIEST, George, Pvt, Col Thos Benton, Capt Isaiah Renshaw, Vol Inf
DEPRIEST, John C, Pvt, Col Thomas Benton, Capt I Renshaw, Vol Inf
DEPRIEST, Moses, Pvt, Maj John Chiles, Capt Charles Conway, E TN Gunmen; Regimental Co Roan
DEPRIEST, Will, Pvt, Col Thomas Benton, Capt Isaiah Renshaw, Vol Inf
DEPRIEST, William, 1 Sgt, Col Thomas Benton, Capt Benj Hewitt, Vol Inf
DEPRIEST, ____, Pvt, Col Thomas Benton, Capt Isaiah Renshaw, Vol Inf; joined from Capt Hewett's Co
DEPRIEST, ____, Pvt, Col William Pillow, Capt Isaiah Renshaw, Inf
DERHAM, Henry, Pvt, Col R C Napier, Capt James McMurry, Mil Inf
DERHAM, Samuel, Pvt, Col R C Napier, Capt James McMurry, Mil Inf
DERHAM (DURAM), Leroy, Pvt, Col N Cannon, Capt James Walton, Mtd Riflemen; deserted 10-15-

1813
DERICK, Jacob, Pvt, Col William Johnson, Capt Andrew Lawson, E TN Drafted Mil
DERICK, John, Pvt, Col William Y Higgins, Capt James Hambleton, Mtd Gunmen
DERICKSON, Jos, Cpl, Col Thomas McCrory, Capt Isaac Patton, Inf
DERICKSON, Jos, Ffr, Col A Loury, Capt J N Williamson, W TN Mil
DERMAND, Richard, Pvt, Col John Williams, Capt William Walker, Vol
DEROSIT, Elijah, Pvt, Col Phillip Pipkin, Capt John Robertson, Mil Inf
DERRICK, Jacob, Pvt, Col William Lillard, Capt George Argenbright, E TN Mil Vol Riflemen
DERRICK, James (Jonez), Pvt, Col John Brown, Capt Charles Lewin, E TN Vol Mtd Inf
DERRICK, Michael, Pvt, Col John Williams, Capt Samuel Bunch, Mtd Vol
DERRICK, William E, Pvt, Col John Williams, Capt David Vance, Mtd Vol
DERRICKSON, Jos, Dmr, Col Leroy Hammonds, Capt Joseph Williamson, Inf
DERRICKSON, Joseph, Dmr, Col L Hammonds, Capt J N Williamson, 5th Regt Inf
DERRON, Christopher, Pvt, Col Cheatham, Capt Birdwell, Inf
DERRUM, John, Pvt, Col William Y Higgins, Capt James Hamberton, Mtd Gunmen; transferred to Capt Eldridge Co
DERWIM, James, Pvt, Col James Raulston, Capt Mathew Cowan, Inf
DESHANE, Aaron, Sgt, Regt Commander omitted, Capt Samuel Richardson, E TN Drafted Mil
DESKINS, Smith, Sgt, Col William Y Higgins, Capt Stephen Griffith, Mtd Riflemen; sick absent
DEVALT, Michael, Pvt, Col William Lillard, Capt Benj King, Enlisted in service of U S
DEVAS, Alexander, Pvt, Col John Brown, Capt William Christian, E TN Mil Inf
DEVASEUR, William, Pvt, Col Alexander Loury, Capt Peter Looney, W TN Mil
DEVAULT, Adam, Pvt, Col William Lillard, Capt Benj King, E TN Vol Inf
DEVAULT, Daniel, Pvt, Col Edward Bradley, Capt Henry L Douglass, Vol Inf
DEVAULT, Daniel, Pvt, Col Thomas Benton, Capt Henry Douglas, Vol Inf
DEVAULT, David, Pvt, Col Thomas Benton, Capt Henry Douglas, Vol Inf
DEVAULT, Jacob, Sgt, Col S Bayless, Capt Joseph Macon, E TN Mil
DEVAULT, John, Pvt, Regt Commander omitted, Capt Samuel Richardson, E TN Drafted Mil
DEVAULT, Samuel, Pvt, Col Wm Snodgrass, Ens Gregg, E TN Vol Mil 2nd Regt
DEVAULT, William, Pvt, Col Edward Bradley, Capt Harry L Douglass, Vol Inf
DEVER, Jesse, Pvt, Col William Lillard, Capt William Hamilton, E TN Vol Inf
DEVER, Mathew, Pvt, Col William Y Higgins, Capt

James Hambleton, Mtd Gunmen
DEVERIX, W C, Pvt, Regt Commander omitted, Capt David Mason, Cav
DEVERS, James, Pvt, Col Alexander Loury, Capt James Kincaid, Inf
DEVINEY, Charles, Pvt, Regt Commander omitted, Capt John Gordon, Mtd Spies
DEVINPORT, Francis, Pvt, Col James Raulston, Capt Charles Wade, Inf
DEVORIX, William C, Pvt, Col Newt Cannon, Capt Gabriel Martin, Mtd Gunmen
DEW, Archibald, Pvt, Col Edward Bradley, Capt Harry Douglas, Vol Inf
DEW, Robert, Sgt, Col Wm Johnson, Capt James Tunnell, E TN Mil
DEW, William C, 1 Cpl, Gen A Jackson, Capt Joel Parrish, Arty
DEWEL, Archibal, 2 Cpl, Col A Loury, Capt J N Williamson, W TN Mil
DEWEL, Archibald, 2 Cpl, Col L Hammond, Capt J N Williamson, Inf
DEWELL, Archibald, Cpl, Col A Cheatham, Capt William Creel, Inf; sick absent
DEWELL, Archibald, Cpl, Col John Coffee, Capt Daniel Ross, Mtd Gunmen
DEWETT, Wm, Pvt, Col S Bunch, Capt Henry Stephens, E TN Mtd Inf
DEWHITT, Samuel, Cpl, Col S Copeland, Capt Allen Wilkerson, Mil Inf; sick absent since 3-4-1814
DEWISE, James, Pvt, Col Robert Steele, Capt Richard Ratton, Mil Inf
DEWISE, Morgan, Ens, Col Robert Steele, Capt Richard Ratton, Mil Inf
DEWLY, John, Cpl, Col A Cheatham, Capt William Creel, Inf; promoted
DEWLY, John, Pvt, Col A Cheatham, Capt William Creel & Capt Jackson, Inf
DEWS, Nathaniel, 5 Cpl, Col James Raulston, Capt James A Black, Inf
DEXON, Tilma T, Pvt, Col Newton Cannon, Capt James Walton, Mtd Riflemen
DEZELL, James, Pvt, Maj John Childs, Capt John Stephens, E TN Mtd Inf
DEZELL, Robert, Pvt, Col Samuel Wear, Capt John Stephens, E TN Mtd Inf
DEZERNE, Hezekiah, Pvt, Col Wm Johnson, Capt Benj Powell, Branch Srvce omitted; d 6-3-1815
DIAL, Henry, Pvt, Col Robert Steele, Capt James Shenault, Mil Inf
DIAL, James, 6 Cpl, Maj John Childs, Capt Charles Conway, E TN Mtd Gunmen
DIAL, James, Cpl, Maj Gen Andrew Jackson, Capt Jos Kirkpatrick, Mtd Gunmen; wounded on furlough 1-1814
DIAL, James, Pvt, Maj John Childs, Capt Charles Conway, E TN Mtd Gunmen; Regt Co Knox
DIAL, Jeremiah, Pvt, Col Robert Steele, Capt James Shenault, Mil Inf
DIAL, Jos, Pvt, Col Thos Williamson, Capt Richard Tate, Vol Mtd Gunmen
DIAL, Reuben, Pvt, Col James Raulston, Capt Charles Wade, Inf
DIAL, Wm, Pvt, Col Samuel Wear, Capt Rufus Morgan, E TN Vol Inf
DIALL, Isaac, Pvt, Maj Wm Russell, Capt John Trimble, Vol Mtd Gunmen
DIAMOND, I I, Dmr, Col Thomas Benton, Capt Isiah Renshaw, Vol Inf; joined from Capt Hewett's Co
DIAMOND, Robert, Pvt, Col John K Wynne, Capt Robert Breden, Inf
DIAMOND, Sam'l T, Dmr, Col Thomas Benton, Capt Benj Hewett, Vol Inf
DIAS, Thos, Pvt, Col Newton Cannon, Capt James Walton, Mtd Riflemen
DICAS, Jas, Pvt, Col William Hall, Capt James Hambleton, Vol Inf; not well
DICER, Edward, Pvt, Lt Col Henry Bryan, Co Commander omitted, Inf
DICKASON, Benj, Pvt, Col William Hall, Capt Abraham Bledsoe, Vol Inf
DICKEN, Absolem, Pvt, Col T McCrory, Capt A Metcalf, Inf
DICKENS, Jesse, Pvt, Col S Copeland, Capt Allen Wilkinson, Mil Inf
DICKENS, Reuben, Pvt, Col Edward Bradley, Capt Harry Douglass, Vol Inf; sick absent
DICKERSON, Benj, Pvt, Col William Hall, Capt Abraham Bledsoe, Vol Inf
DICKERSON, John, Pvt, Col Wm Metcalf, Capt Christopher Cook, E TN Mil
DICKERSON, John, Pvt, Maj Wm Russell, Capt Isaac Williams, Separate Bn of TN Vol Mtd Gunmen; joined from Capt Dickson Co
DICKERSON, Olive, Pvt, Col Edward Bradley, Capt William Lauderdale, Vol Inf
DICKERSON, Oliver, Pvt, Col Edward Bradley, Capt William L Alexander, Vol Inf; AWOL, substitute for Philip Brothers
DICKERSON, Ralph, Pvt, Col John Coffee, Capt John Baskerville, Cav
DICKERSON?, John, Pvt, Col John Coffee, Capt McKeen, Cav
DICKEY, Ephraim, Pvt, Col Wm Y Higgins, Capt Thos Eldridge, Mtd Gunmen
DICKIE, Mathew, Pvt, Col John Coffee, Capt Blackman Coleman, Cav
DICKINS, James, Pvt, Col Thomas Benton, Capt Henry Douglass, Vol Inf
DICKINS, Jos, Pvt, Maj Wm Woodfolk, Capt James C Neil, Inf
DICKINS, Sam'l, Pvt, Col Thomas Williamson, Capt Beverly Williams, Vol Mtd Gunmen
DICKINS (DICKING), Jesse, Pvt, Col Thomas Benton, Capt Henry L Douglass, Vol Inf; deserted
DICKINSON, Griffin, Pvt, Col Robert H Dyer, Capt Thomas Jones, Vol Mtd Gunmen
DICKINSON, Hugh, Pvt, Col John Coffee, Capt Michale Molton, Cav
DICKINSON, Oliver, Pvt, Col James Raulston, Capt Mathew Neal, Inf
DICKINSON, Sam, Pvt, no other information
DICKISON, Lewis, Pvt, Col Thomas Williamson, Capt

## Enlisted Men, War of 1812

Thomas Crane & Capt James Cook, Vol Mtd Gunmen
DICKMAN, Wm, Pvt, Col Samuel Bunch, Capt Isaac Williams, E TN Mil
DICKS, James B, Pvt, Col Thomas Benton, Capt George Caperton, Vol Inf
DICKSON, Abner, Pvt, Regt Commander omitted, Capt Joseph Williams, Vol Mtd Gunmen
DICKSON, Alexander, Pvt, Col John Coffee, Capt Michale Molton, Cav
DICKSON, Alexander, Pvt, Col Robert Steele, Capt James Bennett, Mil Inf; on furlough
DICKSON, Alexander, Pvt, Col S Bunch, Capt John Houk, E TN Mil; joined from Capt Williams Co
DICKSON, Alexander, Pvt, Maj Wm Russell, Capt John Cowan, Vol Mtd Gunmen
DICKSON, Ezekiel, 3 Cpl, Col John Coffee, Capt Robert Jetton, Cav
DICKSON, James, Pvt, Col Samuel Wear, Capt James Tedford, E TN Vol Inf
DICKSON, John, Pvt, Col R H Dyer, Co Commander omitted, TN Vol Mtd Gunmen
DICKSON, John, Pvt, Col Steele, Capt James Bennett, Mil Inf; on furlough
DICKSON, John, Pvt, Maj Wm Russell, Capt John Cowan, Vol Mtd Gunmen
DICKSON, John, Pvt, Regt Commander omitted, Capt Ephraim Dickson, Branch Srvce omitted
DICKSON, Joseph, Pvt, Regt Commander omitted, Capt Joseph Williams, Mil Cav
DICKSON, Levin, Cpl, Col R C Napier, Capt Drury Adkins, Mil Inf
DICKSON, Mathew, 1st Surgeon Mate, Col Edwin E Booth, Co Commander omitted, E TN Mil
DICKSON, Molton, Pvt, Col R H Dyer, Capt Beverly Williams, Vol Mtd Gunmen
DICKSON, Robert, Pvt, Col A Loury, Co Commander omitted, Inf
DICKSON, Robert, Pvt, Col Robert H Dyer, Capt Williams, Vol Mtd Gunmen
DICKSON, Samuel, Pvt, Col Philip Pipkin, Capt Searcy, Mil Inf; substituted for Wm McCord
DICKSON, Samuel, Sgt, Col Philip Pipkin, Co Commander omitted, Mil Inf
DICKSON, Wm, Cpl, Col Ewen Allison, Capt Joseph Everett, E TN Mil; furnished a substitute (Henry Myers)
DICKSON (DIXON), Thomas, Pvt, Col Samuel Bunch, Capt Penny, E TN Mtd Inf
DICKY, Beonionio, Pvt, Regt Commander omitted, Capt Robert Evans, Mtd Spies
DICKY, Mathew, Pvt, Col John Alcorn, Capt Wm Locke, Cav
DICK___?, James, Pvt, Col Thomas Benton, Capt George Caperton, Inf; substitute for Aldham
DICUS, Edward, Pvt, Col L Hammond, Capt J N Williamson, 2nd Regt Inf; appointed Artif
DICUS, Edward, Pvt, Col Wm Hall, Capt Hambleton, Vol Inf
DICUS, John, Pvt, Col John K Winn, Capt James Holleman, Inf

DIDKIN, Absolom, Pvt, Col T McCrory, Capt A Metcalf, Mil Inf
DIEU, William C, Sgt, Col A Cheatham, Capt Creel, Inf; transferred to Arty
DILDINE, Hezekiah, Pvt, Col Robert Steele, Capt James Randals, Branch Srvce omitted
DILDINE, James, Pvt, Col Robert Steele, Capt Randals, Inf
DILE (DILL), Arthur, Pvt, Maj Woodfolk, Capt John Sutton & Capt Abraham Dudney, Inf
DILL, Frederick, Pvt, Col R H Dyer, Capt Evans, Vol Mtd Gunmen
DILL, Frederick, Pvt, Col Thomas H Benton, Capt Williams, Vol Inf
DILL, Joel, Pvt, Col James Raulston, Capt Charlie Wade, Inf
DILL, John, Pvt, Brig Gen Roberts, Capt Benjamin Reynolds, Mtd Rangers
DILL, John, Pvt, Maj Gen Wm Carroll, Capt James Raulston & Capt Robinson, Inf; deserted 11-1814
DILL, Stephen, Cpl, Maj Woodfolk, Capt Dudney & Capt Sutton, Inf
DILL, Thomas, Pvt, Maj Gen Jackson, Capt Joseph Kirkpatrick, Mtd Gunmen
DILL, William, Pvt, Col A Lowry, Co Commander omitted, 2nd Regt W TN
DILL, Wm, Pvt, Maj Gen Carroll, Col James Raulston, Capt John Robinson, Inf
DILLARD, Austin (Osten), Pvt, Col James Raulston, Capt Mathew Cowan, Inf
DILLARD, Dan'l, Pvt, Col Stephen Copeland, Capt William Hodges, Inf
DILLARD, Edward, Pvt, Maj William Woodfolk, Capt Ezekiel Ross, Capt McCulley, Inf
DILLARD, Elijah, Pvt, Col S Copeland, Capt G W Stell, Mil Inf
DILLARD, Elijah, Pvt, Col Thomas Williamson, Capt Robert Moore, Vol Mtd Gunmen
DILLARD, Joel, Pvt, Maj Gen Wm Carroll, Col James Raulston, Capt Edward Robinson, Inf
DILLARD, John B, Pvt, Col John Alcorn, Capt Frederick Stump, Cav
DILLARD, Lewis H, Pvt, Maj Gen A Jackson, Col Thomas Williamson, Capt Robert Steele, Vol Mtd Gunmen
DILLARD, Lewis H, Sgt, Maj Gen Jackson, Col Thomas Williamson, Capt Robert Steele, Vol Mtd Gunmen; promoted from Pvt
DILLARD, Nicholas, Pvt, Col John Coffee, Capt Charles Kavanaugh, Cav; AWOL
DILLARD, Nicholas, Pvt, Maj Gen A Jackson, Col Thos Williamson, Capt Robert Steele, Vol Mtd Gunmen; promoted to Sgt Maj
DILLARD, Nicholas, Pvt, Regt Commander omitted, Capt Archibald McKinney, Cav; promoted to Sgt
DILLARD, Nicholas, Sgt Maj, Maj Wm Russell, Co Commander omitted, Separate Bn of TN Vol Mtd Gunmen
DILLARD, Wm, Pvt, Col S Copeland, Capt G W Stell, Mil Inf; sick absent
DILLARD, Wm, Pvt, Col Thomas Williamson, Capt

- 165

## Enlisted Men, War of 1812

Robert Moore, Vol Mtd Gunmen

DILLEN, James, Pvt, Col Wm Lillard, Capt James Lillard, E TN Vol Inf

DILLENDER, Joseph, Pvt, Lt James Berry, Co Commander omitted, Mtd Riflemen; transferred from Capt Cannon's Cav Co

DILLION, Henry, Pvt, Maj Gen Wm Carroll, Col James Raulston, Capt Wiley Huddleston, Inf

DILLION, John, Pvt, Col Ewen Allison, Capt James Allen, E TN Mil

DILLIS, Dennis, Pvt, Col A Loury, Capt J N Williamson, E TN Mil

DILLON, Charles R, Pvt, Maj Gen Andrew Jackson, Capt Wm Carroll, Vol Inf

DILLON, Daniel, Pvt, Col S Copeland, Capt Allen Wilkinson, Mil Inf

DILLON, Jas, Pvt, Col John Cocke, Capt John Dalton, Inf

DILLON, Jesse, Pvt, Col Copeland, Capt Allen Wilkinson, Mil Inf

DILWORTH, Thomas, Pvt, Maj Wm Carroll, Capt Lewis Dillahunty, Capt Daniel M Bradford, Vol Inf

DIMARY, Stephen, Pvt, Col S Copeland, Capt Moses Thompson, Inf

DIMERY, John, Pvt, Col John K Wynne, Capt James Cole, Inf

DIMOND, John, Pvt, Col John Cocke, Capt Richard Crunk, Inf

DIMOND, Samuel F, Tptr, Col Newton Cannon, Capt John B Demsey, Mtd Gunmen

DIMOND, Samuel T, Pvt, Col R H Dyer, Capt Ephraim Dickson, TN Mtd Vol Gunmen

DINES, Wm, Pvt, Col S Bunch, Capt John English, E TN Drafted Mil

DINNEL, Thomas, Pvt, Col S Bunch, Capt George Gregory, E TN Drafted Mil

DINNELLS, Thos, Pvt, Col S Bunch, Capt John Houk, E TN Mil; joined from Capt Gregory's Co

DINON (DIXON), Robert, Pvt, Col Samuel Wear, Capt Rufus Morgan, E TN Mil Inf

DINSMORE, Adam, Pvt, Col Samuel Bunch, Capt Joseph Duncan, E TN Drafted Mil; left sick at Ft Strother 3-21-1814

DINWIDDLE, James, Pvt, Regt Commander omitted, Capt James Cowan, Mtd Inf

DINWIDDLE, William, Pvt, Col William Johnson, Capt Christopher Cook, E TN Mil

DIRE, Isaac, Pvt, Col William Lillard, Capt Thomas Sharpe, 2nd Regt Inf; sick 10-30-1813 went home

DIRHAM (DURHAM), William, Pvt, Col S Copeland, Capt Alexander Provine, Mil Inf

DISCON, Sam'l, Tptr, Regt Commander omitted, Capt John Miller, Spies

DISCUS, Edward, Pvt, Col Loury, Capt Joseph N Williamson, W TN Mil

DISENTON, Joseph, Cpl, Col Thomas McCrory, Capt Isaac Patton, 2nd Regt TN Mil

DISERN, Francis, Pvt, Col S Bunch, Capt James Cumming, E TN Vol Mtd Gunmen; deserted from Camp Williams 10-22-1813

DISERT, William, Pvt, Maj Wm Woodfolk, Capt James C Neil, Inf; waggoner

DISMUKES, George R, Sgt, Regt Commander omitted, Capt George Smith, Spies

DISON, Wm, Pvt, Col Newton Cannon, Capt Isaac Williams, Mtd Riflemen; sick absent

DITTEMORE, Michael, Pvt, Col Ewen Allison, Capt Thomas Wilson, E TN Drafted Mil; discharged for inability

DITTER, Elijah, Pvt, Col Robert H Dyer, Capt Bethel Allen, Vol Mtd Gunmen

DITTON, Shadrack, Pvt, Col A Loury, Capt J N Williamson, W TN Mil

DITTON, Shadrack, Pvt, Col Archer Cheatham, Capt Hugh Birdwell, Inf

DITTON, Shadruth, Pvt, Lt Col L Hammonds, Capt J N Williamson, Inf; left scik at Ft Montgomery

DIXON, Alexander, Pvt, Col S Bunch, Capt John English, E TN Drafted Mil; joined from Capt Houk's Co

DIXON, Amos, Pvt, Col James Raulston, Capt Henry West, Inf

DIXON, Amos, Pvt, Col John K Wynne, Capt Butler, Inf

DIXON, David, Pvt, Regt Commander omitted, Capt Larkin Ferrell, Inf

DIXON, George W, Sgt, Col Robert Steele, Capt James Bennett, Mil Inf

DIXON, Hugh, Pvt, Col S Bunch, Capt Andrew Breden, E? TN Mil

DIXON, Jeremiah, Pvt, Col S Bunch, Lt John Harris, E TN Mil

DIXON, John D, Pvt, Col N T Perkins, Capt Mathew Johnson, Mil Inf

DIXON, John, Pvt, Col John Alcorn, Capt Alexander McKean, Cav

DIXON, John, Pvt, Col Thomas Williamson, Capt James Pace, Lt Neely, Vol Mtd Gunmen; appointed QM in Col Dyer's Regt

DIXON, John, QM, Brig Gen John Coffee, Co Commander omitted, TN Vol Mtd Gunmen

DIXON, John, QM, Col Robert Dyer, Co Commander omitted, Regt of TN Vol Mtd Gunmen

DIXON, Joseph, Pvt, Regt Commander omitted, Capt George Smith, Spies

DIXON, Joseph, Pvt, Regt Commander omitted, Capt Joseph Williams, Mil Cav

DIXON, Michael, Pvt, Regt Commander omitted, Capt Isaiah Hamilton, Inf

DIXON, Reuben, Pvt, Col John Wynne, Capt John Porter, Inf

DIXON, Robert, Pvt, Col James Raulston, Capt Henry West, Inf; d 2-9-1813

DIXON, Samuel, Cpl, Brig Gen Thomas Johnson, Capt Abraham Allen, Inf

DIXON, Samuel, Tptr, Regt Commander omitted, Capt John Miller, Spies

DIXON, Thomas, Ens, Col John Brown, Capt Hugh Barton, E TN Mil Inf

DIXON, William, Ffr, Col Samuel Bayless, Capt Joseph Goodson, E TN Mil

DIXON, Wm, Pvt, Col John Brown, Capt William D Neilson, E TN Vol Mil

DIXON, Wm, Pvt, Col N T Perkins, Capt John Quarles, Vol Mtd Inf; sick absent

## Enlisted Men, War of 1812

DIXON (DICKSON), Edmund, Pvt, Col William Metcalf, Capt Barbee Collins, Mil Inf; d 1-31-1815

DIZERN, Francis, Pvt, Col Edwin Booth, Capt Richard Marshall, Drafted Mil

DIZINEY, William, Pvt, Col Edwin Booth, Capt Richard Marshall, Drafted Mil

DLINGER?, David, Pvt, Col Ewen Allison, Capt Allen, E TN Mil

DOAK, John, Capt, Col Thomas Williamson, Capt John Doak & Capt John Dobbins, Vol Mtd Gunmen; d 20-16-1815

DOAK, Joseph, Pvt, Col Thomas Benton, Capt Isaiah Renshaw, Vol Inf

DOAK, Samuel S, Pvt, Col Thomas Williamson, Capt John Dobbins, Vol Mtd Gunmen; promoted to Sgt Maj

DOAK, Wm, Cpl, Col Newt Cannon, Capt John Harpole, Mtd Gunmen

DOAKE, Jonathan, Pvt, Col Newton Cannon, Capt John Harpole, Mtd Gunmen; on furlough wounded 11-9-1813 at Talledga

DOAKS, Joseph, Pvt, Col Wm Pillow, Capt Isaiah Renshaw, Inf

DOBBINS, Alexander, Pvt, Col Edward Bradley, Capt John Wallace, Vol Inf

DOBBINS, Alexander, Pvt, Col Thomas Williamson, Capt John Dobbins & Capt John Doak, Vol Mtd Gunmen

DOBBINS, Alexander, Pvt, Col Thomas Williamson, Capt Thomas Scurry, Vol Mtd Gunmen

DOBBINS, Alexander, Pvt, Col William Hall, Capt John Wallace, Inf

DOBBINS, Andrew, Pvt, Col Wm Lillard, Capt Jacob Dyke, Vol Inf

DOBBINS, Wm, Pvt, Col Perkins, Capt Johnson, Mil Inf

DOBBS, Caleb, Cpl, Col S Bunch, Capt Dobbins, E TN Drafted Mil; discharged for inability

DOBBS, David (Dan'l), Pvt, Col S Copeland, Capt Wm Hodges, Inf

DOBBS, David, Pvt, Col Philip Pipkin, Capt James Blakemore, Mil Inf

DOBBS, George, Pvt, Col Philip Pipkin, Capt James Blakemore, Mil Inf; d 9-13-1814

DOBBS, George, Pvt, Col S Copeland, Capt Wm Hodges, Inf

DOBBS, Henry, Pvt, Col Robert Dyer, Capt E Dickson, TN Mtd Gunmen

DOBBS, Henry, Pvt, Col S Bayless, Capt John Brock, E TN Mil

DOBBS, Henry, Pvt, Regt Commander omitted, Capt E Dickson, Branch Srvce omitted

DOBBS, James, Cpl, Col L Hammond, Capt James Tuhbb, Inf

DOBBS, Joel, Pvt, Col S Bunch, Capt Wm Houston, E TN Vol Mtd Service

DOBBS, John, Pvt, Col Wm Johnson, Capt Joe Kirk, Mil

DOBBS, John, Pvt, Col Wm Johnston, Capt Christopher Cook, E TN Mil; promoted to Sgt

DOBBS, Thomas, Pvt, Col Wm Lillard, Capt Wm Hamilton, E TN Vol Inf

DOCKREY, Able, Pvt, Col Philip Pipkin, Capt Henry Newlin, Mil Inf; left sick at Ft Williams 11-4-1814

DODD, Daniel, Pvt, Lt Col Hammond, Capt James Craig, Inf

DODD, James, Pvt, Lt Col Wm Phillips, Co Commander omitted, Inf

DODD, John, Cpl, Col Wm Metcalf, Capt John Barnhart, Mil Inf

DODD, John, Pvt, Col S Bunch, Capt F Register, E TN Mil

DODD, Richard, Pvt, Maj John Childs, Capt Reuben Tipton, E TN Vol Mtd Inf; Regimental Co Knox

DODD, Robert, Pvt, Col N T Perkins, Capt Mathew Patterson, Mtd Vol

DODD, Samuel, Pvt, Col Robert Dyer, Capt Glen Owen, TN Vol Mtd Gunmen

DODD, Samuel, Pvt, Col Thomas Benton, Capt Henry Douglas, Vol Inf

DODD, Samuel, Pvt, Regt Commander omitted, Capt David Mason, Cav

DODD, William, Pvt, Col Sam Wear, Capt Joe Calloway, Mtd Inf

DODDY (DOWDY), Alanson, Pvt, Col Philip Pipkin, Capt E Kirkpatrick, Mil Inf; deserted 9-20-1814

DODS (DADS), Joe, Pvt, Col Wm Higgins, Capt Wm Doak, Mtd Riflemen; wounded 1814 at Emuckafan

DODSON, Bird, Pvt, Col John Cocke, Capt John Dalton, Inf

DODSON, Elisha, Pvt, Col Philip Pipkin, Capt Henry Newlin, Mil Inf

DODSON, John, Pvt, Col S Bayless, Capt Joe Rich, E TN Inf

DODSON, John, Pvt, Lt Col Hammond, Capt James Tubb, Inf

DODSON, Joshua, Pvt, Col Wm Pillow, Capt Wm Moore, Inf

DODSON, Jourdon, Pvt, Col R C Napier, Capt John Chism, Mil Inf; substituted for Sam'l Calvert

DODSON, Sam'l, Pvt, Col S Bayless, Capt Joe Bacon, E TN Mil

DODSON, Thomas, Pvt, Col Philip Pipkin, Capt Henry M Newlin, Mil Inf

DODSON, Wm, 2 Cpl, Col N T Perkins, Co Commander omitted, Mtd Gunmen

DOGGETT, Jesse, Pvt, Col S Bunch, Capt Francis Berry, E TN Mil; transferred to Capt Richardson's Co

DOGGETT, Jesse, Pvt, Regt Commander omitted, Capt Samuel Richardson, E TN Drafted Mil

DOGGETT, Thomas, Pvt, Col S Roberson, Capt S Bunch, E TN Drafted Mil; substitute for Jessee Doggett

DOGGETT, Thomas, Pvt, Regt Commander omitted, Capt Samuel Richardson, E TN Drafted Mil; substitute for Jesse Doggett

DOHERTY, Cornelius, Pvt, Col Edward Bradley, Capt John Kennedy, Riflemen; sick on furlough

DOHERTY, Cornelius, Pvt, Maj Woodfolk, Capt Pearce, Inf; transferred for Capt Nail's Co

DOHERTY, Dennis, Pvt, Lt Col Mite Archer, Co Commander omitted, Mtd Inf 6th Brig

DOHERTY, Innis, Pvt, no other information

DOHERTY, Isaac, Pvt, Col Samuel Bayless, Co Com-

- 167

## Enlisted Men, War of 1812

mander omitted, E TN Mil

DOHERTY, James, Pvt, Col Samuel Bunch, Capt Francis Berry, E TN Mil; transferred to Capt Hank Co

DOHERTY, James, Pvt, Col Samuel Bunch, Capt John Houk, E TN Mil; joined for Capt Berry's Co

DOHERTY, John, Pvt, Col William Y Higgins, Capt S Allen, Mtd Gunmen

DOHERTY, John, Pvt, Col Wm Johnson, Capt Powell, E TN Mil; sick absent, substitute for Elisha Butcher

DOHERTY, John, Pvt, Col Wm Lillard, Capt Wm Hamilton, E TN Vol Mil

DOHERTY, Josiah, Pvt, Col Samuel Bayless, Capt James Churchman, E TN Mil

DOHERTY, Robert, Pvt, Col John L Coffee, Capt Blackman Coleman, Cav; substitute for Lewis C Anthony

DOKE, Robert, Pvt, Col John Williams, Capt Sam Bunch, Mtd Vol

DOLE, Shadrick M, Pvt, Col R C Napier, Capt Early Benson, Mil Inf

DOLEY, Thomas, Pvt, Lt Col Leroy Hammonds & Lt Col Alexander Loury, Capt Thomas Delaney, Inf

DOLINGS, David, Pvt, Col Edwin Booth, Capt John Slatton, E TN Mil

DOLLINS, John, Pvt, Col S Copeland, Capt John Holshouser, Inf

DOLLOHIDE, Asa, Pvt, Col Philip Pipkin, Capt David Smith, Inf

DOLTON, Bradley, Pvt, Col John Brown, Capt Lunsford Oliver, E TN Mil

DOLTON, Thomas, Pvt, Col Ewen Allison, Capt Jones Loughmiller, Mil

DONAHO, Anthony, Pvt, Col James Raulston, Capt Henry Hamilton, Inf; also served under Gen Wm Carroll

DONAHO, Thomas, Pvt, Col Edward Bradle, Capt William Lauderdale, Vol Inf

DONAHOO, James, Pvt, Col R C Napier, Capt Thomas Preston, Mil Inf

DONAHOO, Patrick, Pvt, Col Robert Steele, Capt James Randels, Inf

DONAHOO, Walter, Pvt, Col R C Napier, Capt Thomas Preston, Mil Inf

DONALD, Jesse, Pvt, Regt Commander omitted, Capt Edwin S Moore, Mtd Riflemen

DONALD, Samuel, Pvt, Col William Metcalf, Capt Thomas Marks, Mil Inf

DONALDSON, Francis, Pvt, Regt Commander omitted, Capt George Smith, Spies

DONALDSON, Thomas, Pvt, Maj William Russell, Capt Fleman Hodges, Vol Mtd Gunmen; deserted

DONALDSON, William, Pvt, Col William Johnson, Capt David McKamy, E TN Draft Mil

DONATHAN, James, Cpl, Maj William Russell, Col Robert Dyer, Capt William Russell, Vol Mtd Gunmen

DONATHAN, Stephen, Pvt, Col S Copeland, Capt Solomon George, Inf

DONAVIN, Andrew, Sgt, Col John Brown, Capt John Childs, E TN Vol Mtd Gunmen; promoted from Cpl

DONCARLOS, Robert, Pvt, Col John Brown, Capt John Childs, E TN Vol Mtd Gunmen

DONE, John, Pvt, Col Edwin Booth, Capt Samuel Thompson, Mil

DONEHOS, Joseph, Pvt, Col William Higgins, Capt Stephen Griffith, Mtd Riflemen

DONEHOS, Walter, Pvt, Col John Alcorn, Capt John Byrn, Cav

DONELL, James, Pvt, Col Thomas Benton, Capt William Smith, Vol Inf

DONELSON, Birkley, Pvt, Col A Cheatham, Capt James Giddins, Inf

DONELSON, Francis, Pvt, Col W T Perkins, Capt Marr, Mtd Vol

DONELSON, John, Pvt, Col Thomas Williamson, Capt Robert Moore, Vol Mtd Gunmen

DONELSON, Lemuel, Pvt, Col Thomas Williamson, Capt John Hutchings, Vol Mtd Gunmen

DONELSON, Samuel, Pvt, Regt Commander omitted, Capt Edwin S Moore, Mtd Riflemen

DONELSON, William, Pvt, Col Thomas Williamson, Capt Robert Moore, Vol Mtd Gunmen

DONELSON, Willis, Pvt, Col Edward Bradley, Capt John Moore, Vol Inf; deserted

DONNALD, Eli, Pvt, Col Newton Cannon, Capt John Harpole, Mtd Gunmen

DONNEL, John, Pvt, Col Robert Dyer, Capt Wyatt, Vol Mtd Gunmen

DONNEL, Robert, Pvt, Col Thomas Williamson, Capt Beverly Williams, Vol Mtd Gunmen

DONNELL, James, Pvt, Col Thomas Benton, Capt William Smith, Vol Inf

DONNELL, Lul, Pvt, Col N T Perkins, Capt John Quarles, Vol Mtd Inf

DONNELL, Thomas, Pvt, Col John Wynne, Capt John Spinks, Inf

DONNELSON, Barnet, Pvt, Col John Cocke, Capt John Dalton, Inf

DONNELSON, Thomas, Pvt, Col Samuel Wear, Capt Jesse Cole, Vol Inf

DONOHO, Archibald, Pvt, Col Edward Bradley, Capt Abraham Bledsoe, Riflemen

DONOHO, Benjamin, Pvt, Col William Hall, Capt John Moore, Vol Inf; missing

DONOHO, Coleman, Pvt, Col Thomas Williamson, Capt Anthony Metcalf, Vol Mtd Gunmen

DONOHO, Coleman, Sgt Maj, Col Edward Bradley, no Co Commander, TN Vol Inf Regt

DONOHO, Coleman, Sgt, Col William Hall, Capt William Alexander, Vol Inf

DONOHO, Goldman, 1 Sgt, Col William Hall, Capt William Alexander, Vol Inf

DONOHO, Isaac, Pvt, Col Alexander Loury, Capt George Sarver, Inf

DONOHO, Isaac, Pvt, Col William Hall, Capt John Moore, Vol Inf

DONOHO, James, Pvt, Col Edward Bradley, Capt Abraham Bledsoe, Riflemen

DONOHO, James, Pvt, Col Newton Cannon, Capt William Edwards, Regt Command

DONOHO, James, Pvt, Col Philip Pipkin, Capt John

## Enlisted Men, War of 1812

Robertson, Inf
DONOHO, John, Pvt, Col Alexander Loury, Capt George Sarver, Inf
DONOHO, Joshua, Pvt, Col William Metcalf, Capt Bird Jurt, Mil Inf; died 12-16-1814
DONOHO, Walter, Pvt, Col Alexander Loury, Capt George Sarver, Inf
DONOHO, William, 2 Cpl, Col William Hall, Capt Abraham Bledsoe, Vol Inf
DONOHO, William, Pvt, Col Edward Bradley, Capt Abraham Bledsoe, Riflemen
DONOHOO, Benjamin, Pvt, Col Edward Bradley, Capt John Moore, Vol Inf; deserted
DONOHOO, Isaac, Pvt, Col Edward Bradley, Capt John Moore, Vol Inf; deserted
DONWORTH, Thomas, Pvt, Col Samuel Bayless, Capt Jonathan Waddell, E TN Mil
DOOLEY, Esom B, Pvt, Col T McCrory, Capt William Dooley, Inf
DOOLEY, Esom, Pvt, Col Thomas Benton, Capt Henry L Douglass, Vol Inf
DOOLEY, Jacob, Pvt, Col Robert H Dyer, Capt Glen Owen, TN Vol Mtd Gunmen
DOOLEY, James, Pvt, Col John Alcorn, Capt James Bradley, Vol Cav
DOOLEY, James, Pvt, Col John Coffee, Capt Thomas Bradley, Vol Cav
DOOLIN, Amos, Pvt, Col William Johnson, Capt James Stewart, E TN Draft Mil
DOOLIN, John, Pvt, Col Samuel Bayless, Capt John Brock, E TN Mil
DOOLLEY (DOWLIN), Thomas, Pvt, Col Robert H Dyer, Capt White, Vol Mtd Gunmen
DOOLY, Jacob, Pvt, Col A Cheatham, Capt Charles Johnson, Inf
DORCH, David, Pvt, Col Thomas Williamson, Capt Beverly Williams, Vol Mtd Gunmen
DORCH, David, Sgt, Col Thomas Williamson, Capt Beverly Williams, Vol Mtd Gunmen
DORHAM (DURHAM), Bedford, Pvt, Maj William Woodfolk, Capt James C Neil, Inf
DORHERTY, Cornelius, 5 Cpl, Maj Gen William Carroll, Col James Raulston, Capt Wiley Huddleston, Inf
DORIS, James, Pvt, Col John Cocke, Capt George Barnes, Inf
DORKINS, Allen, Pvt, Col Edward Bradley, Capt Harry L Douglass, Vol Inf
DOROUGH, Henry, Pvt, Col William Hill, Capt William L Alexander, Vol Inf
DORRETY-DAUGHERTY, Cornelius, Pvt, Maj William Woodfolk, Capt James C Neil, Inf
DORRIS, Elijah, Pvt, Col James Raulston, Capt Henry Hamilton, Inf; also served under Gen Wm Carroll
DORRIS, Isaac, Pvt, Col Alexander Loury, Capt Gabriel Martin, Inf
DORRIS, Nathaniel, Pvt, Col Thomas Williamson, Capt James Cook & Capt John Crane, Vol Mtd Inf
DORRIS, Robert, Pvt, Col Alexander Loury, Capt George Sarver, Inf
DORSAN, David, Pvt, Col William Johnson, Capt Henry Hunter, E TN Mil; deceased 10-29-1814

DORSAN, Edmond H, Pvt, Col William Johnston, Capt Henry Hunter, E TN Mil; died 11-1-1814
DORTON, Andrew, Pvt, Col Thomas Benton, Capt James McEwen, Vol Inf
DORY, John, Pvt, Col Newton Cannon, Capt Thomas Bradley, Mtd Riflemen
DOSER, William, Pvt, Col Samuel Bayless, Capt Johnathan Waddell, E TN Mil
DOSET, Emonds, Pvt, Col William Johnson, Capt David McKamy, E TN Drafted Mil
DOSIER, Peter, Pvt, Col Robert H Dyer, Capt White, Vol Mtd Gunmen; sick absent since 12-1-1814
DOSIT, Edmond, Pvt, Col S Bunch, Capt John Houk, E TN Mil; joined from Capt English Co
DOSS, Azeriah, Pvt, Col John Wynne, Capt Robert Braden, Inf
DOSS, Exeriah, 5 Cpl, Col John Crocke, Capt Richard Crunk, Inf
DOSS, James, Pvt, Col A Cheatham, Capt George Chapman, Inf
DOSS, John, Pvt, Col Edwin Booth, Capt John McKamey, E TN Mil
DOSS, John, Pvt, Col John Brown, Capt William Christian, E TN Mil Inf
DOSS, William, Pvt, Regt Commander omitted, Capt James Cowan, Mtd Inf
DOSSET, Edmond, Pvt, Col William Johnson, Capt Benjamin Powell, E TN Mil
DOSSETT, John, Pvt, Col John Coffee, Capt John Byrn, Cav; killed at Telledga 11-3-1813
DOSSETT, William, Pvt, Col John Coffee, Capt John Byrn, Cav
DOSSEY, John, Pvt, Col R C Napier, Capt John Chism, Mil Inf
DOSSIT, Edmond, Pvt, Col Samuel Bunch, Capt John English, E TN Drafted Mil
DOSSITT, Moses, Pvt, Col Samuel Bunch, Capt John English, E TN Drafted Mil
DOTSON, Charles, Pvt, Col S Copeland, Capt Richard Sharp, Mil Inf
DOTSON, Daniel, Pvt, Col Samuel Bunch, Capt F Register, E TN Mil
DOTSON, Green, Pvt, Maj Gen Andrew Jackson, Capt James Reed, Inf
DOTSON, Hightower, Pvt, Col Robert Dyer, Capt James McMahon, 1st TN Mtd Vol Gunmen
DOTSON, Jordon, Pvt, Gen Andrew Jackson, Capt James Reed, Inf
DOTSON, Nimrod, Pvt, Maj William Russell, Capt William Chism, Vol Mtd Gunmen
DOTSON, Reuben, Pvt, Regt Commander omitted, Capt David Mason, Cav; AWOL from 6-22-1812
DOTSON, Thomas, Pvt, Col A Cheatham, Capt James Giddins, Inf; sick absent
DOTTY, Thomas, Pvt, Lt Col Leroy Hammond, Capt James Craig, Inf; d 1-25-1815 at Camp Manderville
DOTY, Reuben, Pvt, Col William Johnson, Capt Christopher Cook, E TN Mil
DOTY, Robert, Pvt, Maj Gen William Carroll, Capt Francis Ellis, Inf

DOTY, Thomas, Pvt, Col Wm Johnson, Capt James Tunnell, E TN Mil
DOUBTY, Reuben, Pvt, Col William Johnson, Capt Joseph Kirk, Mil Inf
DOUBY, Reubein, Pvt, Col S Bayless, Capt James Churchman, E TN Mil; transferred to Capt Jones Co
DOUGAN, John, Pvt, Col Thomas Benton, Capt George Caperton, Vol Inf
DOUGAN, John, Pvt, Col William Pillow, Capt George Caperton, Vol Inf
DOUGAN, Robert, Pvt, Col Thomas Benton, Capt Goerge Caperton, Vol Inf
DOUGAN, Robert, Pvt, Col Wm Pillow, Capt George Caperton, Inf
DOUGAN, Sharp, Pvt, Col Wm Pillow, Capt George Caperton, Inf
DOUGAN, Thomas, Pvt, Col Thomas Benton, Capt George Caperton, Vol Inf
DOUGAN, Thomas, Pvt, Col William Pillow, Capt George Caperton, Inf
DOUGHERTY, Charles, Pvt, Col S Copeland, Capt Wm Douglass, Inf
DOUGHERTY, Cornelius, Pvt, Capt John Kennedy, Vol Inf; 2nd KY Vol
DOUGHERTY, Dennis, Pvt, Col S Copeland, Capt Wm Douglass, Inf
DOUGHERTY, James, Pvt, Col S Copeland, Capt Wm Douglass, Inf
DOUGHERTY, James, Pvt, Col Wm Johnson, Capt Elihu Milliken, 3rd Regt E TN Mil
DOUGHERTY, John, Pvt, Col S Copeland, Capt Wm Douglass, Inf
DOUGHERTY, Jos, Pvt, Col Wm Johnson, Capt Elihu Milliken, 3rd Regt E TN Mil
DOUGHERTY, Moses, Pvt, Col William Johnson, Capt David McKamey, E TN Drafted Mil
DOUGHERTY, William, Pvt, Col S Bunch, Capt Jones Griffith, E TN Drafted Mil
DOUGHTY, Reuben, Pvt, Col S Bayless, Capt Branch Jones, E TN Mil; joined from Capt Churchman's Co
DOUGLAS, Alexander, Pvt, Col A Loury, Capt Joseph Williamson, E TN Mil
DOUGLAS, Alexander, Pvt, Col John Coffee, Capt Fred Stump, Cav
DOUGLAS, Alexander, Pvt, Col L Hammond, Capt J Williamson, 2nd Regt Inf
DOUGLAS, Charles, Pvt, Capt Wm Walker, Capt John Williams, Vol
DOUGLAS, Elmore, 2 Sgt, no other information
DOUGLAS, John, Pvt, Col Wm Metcalf, Capt Bird Hut, Mil Inf
DOUGLAS, John, Pvt, Maj John Childs, Capt John Stephens, E TN Vol Mtd Inf
DOUGLAS, Jos, Pvt, Col John Childs, Capt John Stephens, E TN Mtd Inf
DOUGLAS, Thomas, Pvt, Col Wm Johnson, Capt Andrew Lawson, E TN Drafted Mil; furloughed sick
DOUGLAS, Thomas, Pvt, Col Wm Walker, Capt John Williams, Vol

DOUGLASS, Edward, Pvt, Col L Hammond, Capt J N Williamson, 2nd Regt Inf; appointed Artif
DOUGLASS, Edward, Pvt, Col Newt Cannon, Capt William Edwards, Regt Command
DOUGLASS, Edward, Pvt, Col Newton Cannon, Capt John Harpole, Mtd Gunmen
DOUGLASS, Edward, Sgt, Col Williamson, Capt Sourry, Vol Mtd Gunmen
DOUGLASS, Elmore, Pvt, Col John Alcorn, Capt Thomas Bradley, Vol Cav
DOUGLASS, Elmore, Pvt, Col Thomas Williamson, Capt Thomas Scurry, Vol Mtd Gunmen; transferred to Spies
DOUGLASS, Ezekiel, Pvt, Col James Raulston, Capt Henry Hamilton, Inf
DOUGLASS, George, Cpl, Col John Coffee, Capt Robert Jetton, Cav
DOUGLASS, George, Sdlr, Col John Alcorn, Capt Robert Jetton, Vol Cav; sick, wounded at Talladega
DOUGLASS, George, Sdlr, Col John Coffee, Capt Robert Jetton, Cav
DOUGLASS, James, Pvt, Col Robert Dyer, Capt Jos Williams, Vol Mtd Gunmen
DOUGLASS, Jessee, 2 Cpl, Col R C Napier, Capt Jas McMurry, Mil Inf
DOUGLASS, John D, Cpl, Col R C Napier, Capt James McMurry, Mil Inf
DOUGLASS, John L, Pvt, Col Edward Bradley, Capt Brice Martin, Vol Inf
DOUGLASS, John jr, Pvt, Maj John Childs, Capt John Stephens, E TN Vol Mtd Inf; d 12-17-1814
DOUGLASS, John, Cpl, Col Ewen Allison, Capt Jacob Hoyal, E TN Mil; joined from Capt McPherson Co
DOUGLASS, John, Cpl, Col S Bunch, Capt George McPherson, E TN Mil; transferred to Capt Register Co
DOUGLASS, John, Pvt, Col Robert Steele, Capt Richard Ratton, Mil Inf; transferred to Capt Creel
DOUGLASS, John, Pvt, Col Sam Wear, Capt John Stephens, E TN Vol Inf
DOUGLASS, John, Pvt, Maj Gen Jackson, Col Cheatham, Capt Wm Creel, Branch Srvce omitted
DOUGLASS, Jonathan, Pvt, Col Sam Wear, Capt John Childs, E TN Vol Inf
DOUGLASS, Mathew, Cpl, Col Edwin Booth, Capt John Sharp, E TN Mil
DOUGLASS, Nathaniel, Pvt, Col Nick Perkins, Capt Mathew Johnson, Mil Inf
DOUGLASS, Sam'l, Sgt, Col Sam Bayless, Capt Joseph Bacon, E TN Mil
DOUGLASS, Saml, Pvt, Col S Bunch, Capt Francis Berry, Mil
DOUGLASS, William, Pvt, Col S Copeland, Capt Wm Douglass, Inf
DOUNALD, Jesse, Pvt, Col Newt Cannon, Capt John Harpole, Mtd Gunmen
DOUTHAT, James, Pvt, Col Wm Johnston, Capt James Tunnell, E TN Mil; promoted to Cpl
DOVE, Thos, Pvt, Maj John Childs, Capt Charles Conway, E TN Mtd Gunmen

DOVER, Joshua, Pvt, Col Wm Johnson, Capt Jas R Rogers, E TN Drafted Mil
DOWELL, Benj, Far, Col John Coffee, Capt John Baskerville, Cav
DOWELL, Colby, Pvt, Col S Bunch, Capt Daniel Yarnell, E TN Mil
DOWELL, John, Pvt, Col Edward Bradley, Capt Abraham Bledsoe, Riflemen
DOWELL, John, Pvt, Col James Raulston, Capt Mathew Neal, Inf
DOWELL, John, Pvt, Col Wm Hall, Capt Abraham Bledsoe, Vol Inf
DOWLAND, Timothy, Pvt, Col S Bayless, Capt James Landen, E TN Mil
DOWLEN, John, Pvt, Brig Gen Thomas Johnson, Capt Robert Carson, Inf; deserted 3-4-1814
DOWNIE, John, Pvt, Col James Raulston, Capt Elijah Haynie, Inf; d 3-28-1815
DOWNING, James, Pvt, Col John K Wynne, Capt John Porter, Inf
DOWNING, James, Pvt, Col Leroy Hammonds, Capt Arahel Rains, Inf
DOWNING, James, Sgt, Col John K Wynne, Capt William Wilson, Inf
DOWNING, John, Pvt, Col N T Perkins, Capt John Doak, Vol Mtd Gunmen
DOWNING, William, Pvt, Col John K Wynne, Capt John Porter, Inf
DOWNING, William, Pvt, Col John K Wynne, Capt William Wilson, Inf; attached to Capt Porter's Co
DOXEY, I S, QM Sgt, Col R H Dyer, no other information
DOXEY, John S, QM, Gen John Coffee, TN Vol Mtd Inf
DOXEY, S S, 2 Sgt, Col Robert Dyer, no other information
DOYAL, Kinchere, Pvt, Col Robert Dyer, Capt John Edmondson, TN Vol Mtd Gunmen; d 2-23-1815
DOYEL, Kenchen, Pvt, Col Thomas Pillow, Capt James McEwen, Vol Inf
DOYL, Zachariah, 3 Cpl, Regt Commander omitted, Capt David Smith, Cav Vol
DOYLE, James A, Pvt, Col S Bunch, Capt Joseph Duncan, E TN Drafted Mil
DOYLE, James A, Sgt, Col S Bunch, Capt John English, E TN Drafted; joined from Capt Duncan's Co
DOYLE, John L, 1 Sgt, Col John Cocke, Capt Richard Crunk, Inf
DOYLE, John, Pvt, Col S Wear, Capt S Bayless, Mtd Inf
DOYLE, William, Pvt, Col John Brown, Capt John Childs, E TN Vol Mtd Gunmen
DOYLE, Zachariah, Sdlr, Col Thomas Williamson, Capt John Crane, Vol Mtd Gunmen; left sick at Natchez
DOYLE, Zacharick, 4 Cpl, Regt Commander omitted, Capt Davis Smith, Cav
DRAKE, Edward, Pvt, Col John Loury, Capt John Looney, W TN Mil
DRAKE, Ephraim, QM Sgt, Col N T Perkins, TN Mtd Vol
DRAKE, Isaac, Pvt, Col Wm Metcalf, Capt John Barnhart, Mil Inf
DRAKE, James B, Pvt, Regt Commander omitted, Capt William Mitchell, Spies
DRAKE, Jesse, Pvt, Col N T Perkins, Capt Mathew Patterson, Mtd Vol
DRAKE, Timothy, Pvt, Col William Hall, Capt James Hambleton, Vol Inf
DRAKE, William I, Pvt, Col N T Perkins, Capt John Doak, Vol Mtd Gunmen
DRAKE, William, Pvt, Col Thomas Benton, Capt Thomas Williamson, Vol Inf; deserted
DRAKE, William, Pvt, Col William Pillow, Capt Wm Moore, Inf; sick absent
DRAPER, Benj, Pvt, Col John Brown, Capt William White, E TN Vol Mtd Inf
DRAPER, John, Pvt, Col Leroy Hammonds, Capt James Tubbs, Inf; left sick at Camp Manderville near Mobile
DRAPER, John, Pvt, Col Wm Johnson, Capt James R Rogers, E TN Drafted Mil
DRAPER, Joshua, Pvt, Col Wm Hall, Capt William Alexander, Vol Inf
DRAPER, William, Pvt, Col John Brown, Capt Allen I Bacon, E TN Mil Inf
DRAUGHN, Miles, Pvt, Col A Cheatham, Capt Richard Benson, Inf
DRAUGHN, Wm, Pvt, Col William Hall, Capt Wm Alexander, Vol Inf
DRAUGHTON, John, Pvt, Col John Cocke, Capt Richard Church, Branch Srvce omitted
DRENAN, William, Pvt, Col John Cocke, Capt Bird Nance, Inf; d 1-8-1815 at the hospital New Orleans
DRENNING, Robert, 1 Sgt, Col John Neatherton, Capt William Lillard, E TN Vol Inf
DRENNON, David, Pvt, Col Thomas Benton, Capt Henry Douglass, Vol Inf
DRENNON, John, Pvt, Col Stephen Copeland, Capt G W Stell, Mil Inf
DRENNON (DREMMON), Robert, Pvt, Col William Johnston, Capt James R Rogers, E TN Drafted Mil
DRESBLE, James, Pvt, Col William Lillard, Capt John Neatherton, E TN Vol Inf
DRESIEL, Elijah, Pvt, Col Philip Pipkin, Capt John Strother, Mil Inf; substitute for John McElbanny
DRESKEL, Thomas, Pvt, Col William Lillard, Capt John Neatherton, E TN Vol Inf
DREW, James, Pvt, Col Robert Dyer, Capt Thomas Jones, Vol Mtd Gunmen
DRIGGORS, Absolom, Tptr, Col Thomas Williamson, Capt John Hutchings, Vol Mtd Gunmen
DRINKARD, William, Pvt, Col Wm Pillow, Capt Joseph Mason, Mtd Inf
DRINKWATER, William, Pvt, Col Samuel Bunch, Capt John Inman, E TN Vol Mtd Inf
DRISKEL, Jessee, Pvt, Col John Cocke, Capt Richard Crunk, Inf
DRISKILL, John, Pvt, Col Samuel Bayless, Capt Branch Jones, E TN Drafted Mil
DRISKILL, Obidiah, Pvt, Col Robert Steele, Capt John Chitwood, Mil Inf
DRISKWATER, Robert, Pvt, Col Samuel Bayless, Capt Branch Jones, E TN Drafted Mil; reduced from Cpl
DRIVER, Bennett, Pvt, Col Wm Metcalf, Capt Alexander

Hill, Capt John Cunningham, Mil Inf
DRIVER, Daniel, Pvt, Maj Gen Wm Carroll, Col James Raulston, Capt Edward Robinson, Inf
DRIVER, Laban, Pvt, Maj Gen Wm Carroll, Col James Raulston, Capt Edward Robinson, Branch Srvce omitted
DRIVER, Wm, Pvt, Brig Gen Thomas Johnson, Capt Robert Carson, Inf
DRUMMONS, Milton, Pvt, Col William Lillard, Capt George Keys, E TN Inf
DRURY, George, Pvt, Col Edward Bradley, Capt Brice Martin, Vol Inf
DRURY, George, Pvt, Col William Hall, Capt Brice Martin, Vol Inf
DRURY, John, Pvt, Col Thomas McCrory, Capt Anthony Metcalf, Inf
DRYDEN, Joel, Sgt, Col Samuel Bayless, Capt Solomon Hendrix, E TN Mil
DRYDEN, Thomas, Pvt, Col John Wynne, Capt John Porter, Inf
DRYDEN, Thomas, Pvt, Col Robert Dyer, Capt Ephraim Dickson, 1st TN Mtd Vol Gunmen
DRYDEN, Thomas, Pvt, Col William Lillard, Capt Benj King, E TN Vol Inf
DRYDEN, William, 2 Sgt, Col S Copeland, Capt John Biles, Inf
DRYDESS, John, Pvt, Col John Wynne, Capt John Porter, Inf
DUAN, Samuel, 2 Lt, Col John Brown, Capt Hugh Barton, E TN Mil Inf
DUBERRY, William, Pvt, Col Alexander Loury, Capt John Looney, Regt W TN Mil
DUCK, John, Pvt, Col William Johnson, Capt James Stewart, E TN Drafted Mil
DUCKWORTH, Abel, Pvt, Col Thomas Williamson, Capt John Doak & Capt John Dobbins, Vol Mtd Gunmen
DUCKWORTH, John, Pvt, Col Wm Hall, Capt Henry Newlin, Inf
DUCKWORTH, William, Pvt, Col Thomas Williamson, Capt John Doak & Capt John Dobbins, Vol Mtd Gunmen
DUDLEY, Thomas E, Pvt, Regt Commander omitted, Capt David Mason, Cav
DUDLEY, William, Pvt, Col Philip Pipkin, Capt John Robertson, Mil Inf; left sick at Ft Pierce 11-26-1814
DUDLEY, William, Pvt, Maj John Childs, Capt Charles Conway, E TN Mtd Gunmen; Regimental Co Roan
DUDLY, William, Pvt, Col John Brown, Capt James McKamy, E TN Mtd Gunmen
DUDLY, William, Pvt, Col John Wynne, Capt Bayless Prince, Inf
DUDNEY, Abraham, Cpl, Maj Wm Woodfolk, Capt Abraham Dudney, Inf; d 11-29-1814
DUE, Joseph, Pvt, Col John Wynne, Capt John Spinks, Inf
DUFF, Dennis, Pvt, Col James Raulston, Capt Daniel Newman, Inf
DUFF, Harvard, Pvt, Col William Pillow, Capt William Smith, Vol Inf
DUFF, Hiram, Pvt, Col John Alcorn, Capt John Byrn, Cav
DUFF, Hiram, Pvt, Col John Wynne, Capt William McCall, Inf
DUFF, Hyram, Pvt, Col John Coffee, Capt John Byrn, Branch Srvce omitted
DUFF, John, Pvt, Brig Gen Thomas Johnson, Capt Abraham Allen, Mil Inf
DUFF, Josiah, Pvt, Col William Johnson, Capt James Tunnell, E TN Mil
DUFF, Thomas, Pvt, Col Thomas Benton, Capt William Smith, Vol Inf
DUFF, Thomas, Pvt, Col William Pillow, Capt William Smith, Vol Inf
DUFF, Thomas, Pvt, Regt Commander omitted, Capt William Smith, Vol Inf
DUFF, William, Pvt, Col Thomas Williamson, Capt Anthony Metcalf, Vol Mtd Gunmen
DUFFEE, Samuel, Pvt, Regt Commander omitted, Capt Joseph Williams, Mil Cav
DUFFELL, Samuel, Pvt, Col William Hall, Capt John Moore, Vol Inf
DUFFELL, William, Pvt, Col Robert Steele, Capt Samuel Maxwell, Mil Inf
DUFFELLS, William K, Pvt, Col Thomas Benton, Capt James McEwen, Vol Inf
DUFFIE, William K, Pvt, Col William Pillow, Capt C E McEwen, Vol Inf; sick absent
DUFFIE, William R, Pvt, Col Thomas Benton, Capt James McEwen, Vol Inf
DUFFIELD, George, A D Camp, Brig Gen Nathan Taylor, no other information
DUFFIELD, James, Pvt, Col Samuel Bunch, Capt N Gibbs, E TN Drafted Mil
DUFFIELD, James, Pvt, Col Samuel Wear, Capt John Bayless, Mtd Inf
DUFFIELD, James, Pvt, Maj John Childs, Capt Charles Conway, E TN Mtd Gunmen; substitute for Joseph Long
DUFFIELD, Samuel, Pvt, Regt Commander omitted, Capt Joseph Williams, Mil Cav
DUFFIELD, William, Pvt, Maj John Childs, Capt Charles Conway, E TN Mtd Gunmen; Regt Co Knox
DUGGAN, Daniel, Pvt, Col William Johnson, Capt Andrew Lawson, E TN Drafted Mil
DUGGAN, Hugh, Pvt, Col Edwin Booth, Capt Alexander Biggs, Inf
DUGGAN, William, 3 Sgt, Col Wm Johnson, Capt Andrew Lawson, E TN Drafted Mil; substitute for John Benson
DUGGAR, Abel, Rank omitted, Col Samuel Bunch, Capt George McPherson, E TN Mil; joined from Capt Winsell's Co
DUGGER, Abel, Pvt, Col Edwin Allison, Capt Adam Winsell, E TN Drafted Mil
DUGGER, Drea, Pvt, Col John Coffee, Capt Bym, Cav
DUGGER, Jarrett, Pvt, Col John Coffee, Capt Bym, Cav
DUGGER, John C, Pvt, Capt Lewis Dillahunty, Capt Daniel Bradford, Vol Inf
DUGGER, Julius A, Pvt, Col Samuel Wear, Capt Jesse Cole, Vol Inf
DUGGER, Julius A, Pvt, Col Wm Johnson, Capt Henry

## Enlisted Men, War of 1812

Hunter, E TN Mil; d 11-10-1814
DUGGER, Julius, Pvt, Col Ewen Allison, Capt Winsell, E TN Drafted Mil
DUGGER, Julius, Pvt, Col Samuel Bunch, Capt George McPherson, E TN Mil; joined from Capt Winsell's Co
DUGGER, Thomas, Pvt, Col John Alcorn, Capt John W Byrn, Cav
DUGGER, Thomas, Pvt, Col John Coffee, Capt Byrn, Cav
DUGGER, Wesley, Pvt, Col John W Byrn, Capt John W Byrn, Cav
DUGGER, Westley, Pvt, Col John Coffee, Capt John W Byrn, Cav
DUGIN, Sharp, Pvt, Maj Wm Russell, Capt John Cowan, Vol Mtd Gunmen
DUGLAS, Alexander, Pvt, Lt Col Hammons, Capt Thomas Williamson, Inf
DUGLES, Samuel, Pvt, Col Wm Lillard, Capt Jacob Hartsell, E TN Vol Inf; transferred to W TN Troop
DUKAID, Benj, Pvt, Col Thomas H Benton, Capt Caperton, Vol Inf; Joel Bean substitute
DUKE, Abraham, Pvt, Col Thomas H Benton, Capt Bushard, Vol Inf
DUKE, Joel, 2 Cpl, Col James Raulston, Capt Daniel Newman, Inf
DUKE, John, Pvt, Col Thomas Williamson, Co Commander omitted, TN Mtd Gunmen
DUKE, John, Sgt, Col Robert H Dyer, Capt Robert Edmondson, TN Vol Mtd Gunmen
DUKE, Pleasant, Pvt, Col Newton Cannon, Capt Hanby, Mtd Riflemen; sick absent
DUKE, Pleasant, Pvt, Regt Commander omitted, Capt James Haggard, Mtd Gunmen
DUKE, Robert, Pvt, Col N T Perkins, Co Commander omitted, Mtd Riflemen
DUKE, Samuel, Pvt, Regt Commander omitted, Capt David Smith, Cav Vol
DUKE, Washington, Pvt, Col John Cocke, Capt George Barnes, Inf
DUKE, William, Pvt, Col S Copeland, Capt Robert Steele, Mil Inf
DUKES, Stephen, Pvt, Col Robert Steele, Capt James Randalls, Inf
DULANEY, Isaac, Pvt, Col S Bunch, Capt F Register, E TN Mil; French Haggard substitute
DULANEY, Lewis B, Pvt, Col S Bunch, Capt F Register, E TN Mil
DULANEY, William, Pvt, Col Thomas Benton, Capt George Caperton, Vol Inf
DULING, Daniel, Pvt, Col Edwin Booth, Capt Richard Marshall, Drafted Mil
DUMWOOD, Henry, Pvt, Col S Bunch, Capt S Robersn, E TN Drafted Mil
DUMWOOD, Henry, Pvt, Regt Commander omitted, Capt Daniel Richardson, E TN Drafted Mil
DUMWOODY, William, Pvt, Col William Johnson, Capt Joseph Kirk, Mil Inf
DUN, Hugh T, Cpl, Col John Wynne, Capt Willson, Inf
DUNAGAN, Hiram, Pvt, Col Robert Dyer, Capt Cuthbert Hudson, Vol Mtd Gunmen
DUNAGAN, Thomas, Pvt, Maj Gen Carroll, Capt Ellis, Inf
DUNAWAY, Daniel, Pvt, Col James Raulston, Capt Charles Wade, Inf
DUNCAN, Abner, Pvt, Col S Bayless, Capt Sol Hendrix, E TN Mil
DUNCAN, Allen, Pvt, Col Edwin Booth, Capt Richard Marshal, Drafted Mil; left Mobile sick
DUNCAN, Allen, Sgt, Col S Bunch, Lt Col Harris, E TN Mil; d 2-14-1814
DUNCAN, David, Pvt, Col John Cocke, Capt Sam Caruthers, Inf
DUNCAN, Elijah, Pvt, Col James Raulston, Capt Edward Roberson, Inf
DUNCAN, Elijah, Pvt, Col Wm Higgins, Capt Adam Adale, Mtd Gunmen
DUNCAN, Evans, Pvt, Col Edwin Booth, Capt John McKamey, Inf
DUNCAN, Frances, Pvt, Col Ewen Allison, Capt Henry McCray, E TN Mil
DUNCAN, George, Pvt, Col Edward Bradley, Capt Brice Martin, Vol Inf
DUNCAN, James L, Pvt, Col Wm Metcalf, Capt Bird Hurt, Mil Inf
DUNCAN, James, Pvt, Col Wm Metcalf, Capt Bird Hurt, Mil Inf
DUNCAN, James, Pvt, Maj Jackson, Col A Cheatham, Capt William Creel, Inf
DUNCAN, Jephthale, Cpl, Col John Brown, Capt Wm Neilson, E TN Vol Mil
DUNCAN, Jesse, Cpl, Col Thomas Benton, Capt Wm Moore, Vol Inf
DUNCAN, Jessee, 4 Cpl, Col Thos Benton, Capt Wm Moore, Vol Inf
DUNCAN, Jessee, 4 Cpl, Col Wm Pillow, Capt Wm Moore, Inf
DUNCAN, John, Cpl, Col John Brown, Capt Lunsford Oliver, E TN Mil
DUNCAN, John, Pvt, Col Edwin Booth, Capt John McKamey, E TN Inf
DUNCAN, John, Pvt, Col Robert Steele, Capt James Shenault, Mil Inf
DUNCAN, John, Pvt, Col Wm Lillard, Capt John Roper, E TN Vol Inf
DUNCAN, John, Pvt, Col Wm Lillard, Capt Wm McLin, E TN Inf
DUNCAN, Jos, Pvt, Col Nicholas Perkins, Capt Mathew Johnson, Mil Inf
DUNCAN, Joseph, Pvt, Col Thomas Benton, Capt James McFerrin, Vol Inf; substituted by E McGonigal
DUNCAN, Joseph, Pvt, Maj Wm Woodfolk, Capt Abner Pearce, Inf
DUNCAN, Joseph, Sgt, Maj Wm Woodfolk, Capt Abner Pearce, Inf; promoted from Pvt to Cpl to Sgt
DUNCAN, Josiah, Pvt, Col John Wynne, Capt Wm Caruthers, W TN Inf
DUNCAN, Josiah, Pvt, Col John Wynne, Capt Wm Wilson, Inf
DUNCAN, Lemuel H, Pvt, Col Robert Dyer, Capt Glen Allen, Vol Mtd Gunmen
DUNCAN, Martin A, Pvt, Col John Cocke, Capt Richard Crunk, Inf

DUNCAN, Marvel, Sgt, Col Sam Bunch, Capt Joe Duncan; promoted from Cpl
DUNCAN, Moses, Pvt, Col Wm Johnson, Capt James Tunnell, E TN Mil
DUNCAN, Peter, Pvt, Col Philip Pipkin, Capt John Strother, Mil
DUNCAN, Reece, Pvt, Col S Bunch, Capt George McPherson, E TN Mil
DUNCAN, Rice, Pvt, Col S Bunch, Capt F Register, E TN Mil; joined from Capt McPherson's Co
DUNCAN, Robert, Pvt, Col John Brown, Capt John Childs, E TN Vol Mtd Gunmen
DUNCAN, Sam'l, Pvt, Col Wm Higgins, Capt John Cheatham, Mtd Riflemen
DUNCAN, Thomas, Pvt, Col Ewen Allison, Capt Jacob Hoyal, E TN Mil; joined from Capt McPherson Co
DUNCAN, Thomas, Pvt, Maj Russell, Capt John Cowan, Vol Mtd Gunmen
DUNCAN, William, Pvt, Col John Wynne, Capt Robert Breeden, Inf
DUNCAN, William, Pvt, Col N T Perkins, Capt James McMahan, Mtd Gunmen
DUNCAN, Zachariah, Pvt, Col Alex Loury, Capt Martin, Inf; left sick at Ft Calyborne by order of Col Hart
DUNCAN, Zachariah, Pvt, Lt Col A Cheatham, Co Commander omitted, Mtd Inf 6th Brig
DUNCAN, Zachariah, Pvt, Maj Gen Jackson, Capt John Crane, Mtd Gunmen
DUNCHIN, Joe, Pvt, Maj Wm Woodfolk, Capt Abner Pearce, Inf
DUNGAN, Thomas, Pvt, Col Newton Cannon, Capt John Demsey, Mtd Gunmen
DUNGE, John, Pvt, Col Thomas Williamson, Capt Richard Tate, Vol Mtd Gunmen; d 2-15-1815
DUNGY, Joseph, Pvt, Col N T Perkins, Capt Mathew Patterson, Mtd Vol
DUNHAM, Daniel, Pvt, Col William Johnson, Capt James Tunnell, E TN Mil; notified & never appeared
DUNHAM, Franklin, Pvt, Col Samuel Bunch, Capt Jones Griffin, E TN Drafted Mil; joined from Capt Loughmiller Co
DUNHAM, Franklin, Pvt, Maj John Childs, Capt James Cummings, E TN Vol Mtd Inf
DUNHAM, Henry, Pvt, Col Wm Metcalf, Capt James Cummings, E TN Vol Mtd Inf
DUNHAM, Henry, Pvt, Col Wm Metcalf, Capt John Cunningham & Capt Alexander Hill, Mil Inf
DUNHAM, John B, Pvt, Maj John Chiles, Capt James Cummings, E TN Vol Mtd Inf
DUNHAM, John S, Pvt, Maj John Chiles, Capt James Cummings, Mil Inf
DUNHAM, Lewis, Pvt, Col Wm Johnson, Capt James Tunnell, E TN Mil; notified & never appeared
DUNHAM, Phillip, Pvt, Col Wm Lillard, Capt Wm Gillenwater, E TN Inf
DUNHAM, Washington, Pvt, Col Wm Lillard, Capt William Gillenwater, E TN Inf
DUNIM, William, Pvt, Col John Brown, Capt Charles Lewin, E TN Vol Mtd Inf
DUNIVAN, John, Pvt, Col John Brown, Capt James McKamy, E TN Mtd Gunmen
DUNKEN, Anderson, Pvt, Col Philip Pipkin, Capt George Mebane, Mil Inf
DUNKIN, Anderson, Pvt, Col Philip Pipkin, Capt George Mebane, Mil Inf
DUNKIN, Andrew, Pvt, Col Samuel Bayless, Capt Jonathan Waddle, E TN Mil
DUNKIN, Charles, Pvt, Col Wm Metcalf, Capt Wm Sitton, Mil Inf; d 2-22-1815
DUNKIN, David, Pvt, Col Wm Johnson, Capt Elihu Milliken, 3rd Regt E TN Mil
DUNKIN, James H, Pvt, Col John Cocke, Capt Joseph Price, Inf
DUNKIN, James, Pvt, Col Samuel Bayless, Capt Jonathan Waddle, E TN Mil
DUNKIN, Wm, Pvt, Col Samuel Bayless, Capt Allen Bacon, E TN Mil
DUNLAP, Adam, Pvt, Brig Gen Thomas Johnson, Capt Robert Carson, Inf; discharged for want of arms
DUNLAP, Andrew, Pvt, Col John Wynne, Capt James Cole, Inf
DUNLAP, James (Joseph), Pvt, Col Wm Johnson, Capt David McKamy, E TN Drafted Mil, sick absent
DUNLAP, John, Cpl, Col Wm Lillard, Capt Robert McCalpin, E TN Inf
DUNLAP, Richard, Pvt, Col Samuel Wear, Capt Jesse Cole, Vol Inf
DUNLAP, William, Pvt, Col S Copeland, Capt G W Stell, Mil Inf; sick absent since 4-10-1814
DUNLAP, William, Pvt, Col William Johnson, Capt David McKamy, E TN Drafted Mil; sick absent
DUNLAP, Wm, Pvt, Lt Col Henry Bryan, Co Commander omitted, Inf
DUNN, Bartholomew, Pvt, Col Wm Hall, Capt Travis Nash, Inf
DUNN, Benj, Pvt, Col Wm Metcalf, Capt Wm Mullin, Mil Inf; discharged for disability
DUNN, Benjamin, Pvt, Col John Cocke, Capt James Gray, Inf
DUNN, Benjamin, Pvt, Col Wm Metcalf, Capt Wm Mullin, Mil Inf
DUNN, Daniel, Pvt, Col Samuel Bayless, Capt Solomon Hendrichs, E TN Mil
DUNN, Daniel, Pvt, Col William Johnson, Capt Elihu Milliken, 3rd Regt E TN Mil
DUNN, David, Pvt, Col Wm Johnson, Capt Elihu Milliken, 3rd Regt E TN Mil
DUNN, Francis, Cpl, Col William Lillard, Capt James Hambleton, E TN Vol Inf
DUNN, Hugh T, Pvt, Col John Wynne, Capt John Porter, Inf
DUNN, John, Pvt, Col Philip Pipkin, Capt Ebenezer Kirkpatrick, Mil Inf; deserted 9-20-1814
DUNN, John, Pvt, Col S Copeland, Capt Richard Sharp, Mil Inf; deserted 2-18-1814
DUNN, John, Pvt, Col Thomas Benton, Capt Henry Douglass, Vol Inf; d 3-8-1813
DUNN, Joseph, Pvt, Col Philip Pipkin, Capt Ebenezer Kirkpatrick, Mil Inf; deserted 9-20-1814
DUNN, Levi, Sgt, Col John Wynne, Capt Robert Breden, Inf

## Enlisted Men, War of 1812

DUNN, Michael, Pvt, Col Philip Pipkin, Capt David Smith, Inf; deserted 9-21-1814

DUNN, Thomas, Pvt, Col Philip Pipkin, Capt Peter Searcy, Mil Inf

DUNN, Thomas, Pvt, Col Wm Metcalf, Capt Wm Mullin, Mil Inf; deserted 3-20-1815

DUNN, William, Pvt, Col Thomas Benton, Capt Henry Douglass, Vol Inf; deserted

DUNN, William, Pvt, Col Thomas McCrory, Capt William Dooley, Inf

DUNN, William, Pvt, Col Thomas Williamson, Capt Richard Tate, Vol Mtd Gunmen

DUNN, William, Pvt, Col Wm Hall, Capt Travis Nash, Inf

DUNNAVENT, Leonard, 1 Sgt, Col John Cocke, Capt John Dalton, Inf

DUNNAWAY (DUMERY), Stephen, Rank omitted, Col S Copeland, Capt Moses Thompson, Inf

DUNNEGAN, John, Blksmth, Col John Coffee, Capt Daniel Ross, Mtd Gunmen

DUNNEGAN, Nicholas, Pvt, Col Wm Lillard, Capt Robert Maloney, E TN Vol Inf

DUNNEGAN, William, Pvt, Col Thomas McCrory, Capt Isaac Patton, Mil Inf

DUNSMORE, James, Pvt, Col Samuel Bunch, Capt James Penny, E TN Mtd Inf

DUNWOODY, John, Pvt, Col William Lillard, Capt Robert McCalpin, E TN Inf

DUNWOODY, William, Pvt, Col Wm Lillard, Capt Robert McCalpin, E TN Inf; unable to perform duty

DUPESS, William, Pvt, Regt Commander omitted, Capt Samuel Richardson, E TN Drafted Mil

DUPRE, James, Pvt, Col John Coffee, Capt Daniel Ross, Mtd Gunmen; sick absent since 10-16-1813

DUPRE, William, 1 Cpl, Col Wm Higgins, Capt Samuel Allen, Mtd Gunmen

DURALL (DUVALL), Alexander, Pvt, Col Wm Y Higgins, Capt Robert Doak, Mtd Riflemen; wounded 7-22-1814

DURAN, John, Pvt, Maj John Childs, Capt Charles Conway, E TN Mtd Gunmen; Regimental County - Knox

DURAS, Sam'l, Pvt, Col Wm Johnson, Capt James Stewart, E TN Drafted Mil

DURDEN, Jesse, Pvt, Maj Gen Andrew Jackson, Capt John Crane, Mtd Gunmen

DURGAN, John, Asst Forage Master, Brig Gen Nathaniel Taylor, Co Commander omitted

DURGEN (DERGEN), John, Pvt, Col Wm Johnson, Capt Elihu Milliken, 3rd Regt E TN Mil

DURHAM, Benj, Pvt, Col Samuel Bunch, Capt Joseph Duncan, E TN Mil Drafted; left sick at Ft Strother 3-21-1814

DURHAM, Eliab, Pvt, Maj Gen Carroll, Col James Raulston, Capt Edward Robinson, Inf

DURHAM, James, Pvt, Col A Loury & Hammond, Capt Arahel Raines, Inf

DURHAM, John, Pvt, Regt Commander omitted, Capt Larkin Ferrell, Inf

DURHAM, Nepha, Pvt, Maj Gen Wm Carroll, Col James Raulston, Capt Edward Robinson, Inf

DURING, Berry, Pvt, Gen Andrew Jackson, Capt Nathan Davis, Inf

DURLEY, John, Sdlr, Col Thomas Williamson, Co Commander omitted, Vol Mtd Gunmen

DURRAN, John, Pvt, Col Wm Y Higgins, Capt Thomas Eldridge, Mtd Gunmen

DURRAN, Wm, Pvt, Col John Coffee, Capt Ross, Mtd Gunmen

DURRATT, John B, Pvt, Regt Commander omitted, Capt John Crane, Mtd Gunmen

DURREN, John, Pvt, Col Samuel Wear, Capt John Chiles, E TN Vol Inf

DURRETT, John, Pvt, Col John Brown, Capt James Standifer, E TN Vol Mtd Mil

DURRETT, Martin, Sgt, Col Edwin E Booth, Co Commander omitted, E TN Mil

DURRIN (DERWIN), Wm, Pvt, Col Newton Cannon, Capt Francis Jones, Mtd Riflemen

DURRON (DURROW), John B, Col John Alcorn, Capt Frederick Stump, Cav

DURROW, Christopher, Pvt, Col R H Dyer, Capt Thomas White, Vol Mtd Gunmen

DUSHANE, Aaron, Pvt, Col S Bunch, Capt S Robertson, E TN Drafted Mil

DUTTON, Alexander, Pvt, Maj Gen Andrew Jackson, Capt Hugh Kerr, Mtd Rangers

DUTY, Benj, Pvt, Col John Coffee, Capt Baskerville, Cav

DUTY, George, Pvt, Col John Alcorn, Capt John Baskerville, Mil Inf

DUTY, George, Pvt, Col John Coffee, Capt John Baskerville, Cav

DUTY, John, Pvt, Col Philip Pipkin, Capt Blakemore, Mil Inf

DUTY, Mathew, Pvt, Col John Alcorn, Capt John Baskerville, Vol Inf

DUTY, Mathew, Pvt, Col John Coffee, Capt Baskerville, Cav

DUTY, Solomon, Pvt, Col John Coffee, Co Commander omitted, Cav

DUTY, Thomas, Pvt, Maj William Carroll, Capt Lewis Dillahunty, Capt Daniel Bradford, Vol Inf; transferred to Arty

DUVALL, Daniel, Pvt, Col John Coffee, Capt David Smith, Vol Cav

DUVALT, John, Pvt, Col Thomas Williamson, Capt Thomas Pace, Lt James Neely, Vol Mtd Gunmen

DUVALT (DUVAULT), David, Cpl, Col Thomas Williamson, Capt James Pace, Lt James Neely, Vol Mtd Gunmen

DUVAUL (DUVALLO), Alexander, Pvt, Col Wm Metcalf, Capt John Sutton, Mil Inf

DUVAULT (DEVAULT), Daniel, Pvt, Col Edward Bradley, Capt Henry Douglass, Vol Inf

DUVAULT (DEVAULT), David, Pvt, Col Edward Bradley, Capt Harry Douglass, Vol Inf

DUVAULT (DEVAULT), Wm, Pvt, Col Edward Bradley, Capt Henry Douglas, Vol Inf

DUZERN, Hezekiel, Pvt, Col Wm Johnson, Capt Powell, E TN Mil; sick at Ft Claybourne 11-20-1814

DYCUS, Daniel, Pvt, Col Thomas Benton, Capt Benj Reynolds, Vol Inf

## Enlisted Men, War of 1812

DYCUS, Edward, Pvt, Col Robert Steele, Capt Samuel Maxwell, Mil Inf

DYCUS, Hugh, Cpl, Col Brig Gen Johnson, Capt Allen, Mil Inf

DYCUS, James, Pvt, Maj Gen Carroll, Co Commander omitted, Inf; substitute for John Miller

DYCUS, Joshua, 1 Cpl, Col Wm Metcalf, Capt Wm Mullen, Mil Inf

DYCUS, Joshua, Cpl, Col Wm Metcalf, Capt Wm Mullen, Mil Inf

DYCUS, Osey (Osa), Pvt, Col Philip Pipkin, Capt Peter Searcy, Mil Inf

DYCUS, Reubin, Pvt, Col Thomas Benton, Capt Benj Reynolds, Vol Inf

DYE, Stephen, Pvt, Col N Cannon, Capt Gabriel Martin, Mtd Gunmen

DYE, Stephen, Pvt, Col Wm Hall, Capt James Hambleton, Vol Inf; deserted

DYER, Alexander, Pvt, Col S Bayless, Capt James Landen, E TN Mil

DYER, Clement, Pvt, Col N Cannon, Capt James Walton, Mtd Riflemen; deserted 10-15-1813

DYER, Clement, Pvt, Regt Commander omitted, Capt George Smith, Spies

DYER, Eli, Pvt, Regt Commander omitted, Capt George Smith, Spies; deserted 10-9-1813

DYER, Enoch, Pvt, Col Wm Johnson, Capt James Tunnell, E TN Mil; notified & never appeared for transfer

DYER, Isaac, Pvt, Col S Bunch, Capt John Harris, E TN Mil

DYER, James, Pvt, Col Thomas Benton, Capt Benj Reynolds, Vol Inf

DYER, James, Pvt, Col Thomas McCrory, Capt Wm Dooly, Inf

DYER, James, Pvt, Col Wm Lillard, Capt Zacheus Copeland, E TN Vol Inf

DYER, James, Pvt, Regt Commander omitted, Capt Larken Ferrell, Inf

DYER, Joel, Pvt, Col Thomas Benton, Capt William Moore, Vol Inf

DYER, John, Pvt, Col Ewen Allison, Capt Wm King, Drafted Mil

DYER, John, Pvt, Col S Bunch, Capt F Register, E TN Mil

DYER, John, Pvt, Col Wm Johnson, Capt Joseph Scott, Branch Srvce omitted; promoted to Sgt & Ens

DYER, John, Pvt, Col Wm Lillard, Capt Benj King, E TN Vol Inf

DYER, Joseph, Pvt, Col Philip Pipkin, Capt William MacKay, Mil Inf

DYER, Mazier, Pvt, Col N Cannon, Capt William Edwards, Regt Command; no pay & deserted

DYER, Micajah, Ffr, Col Alexander Loury, Capt George Sarver, Inf

DYER, Robert, Pvt, Col John Alcorn, Capt William Locke, Cav

DYER, Robert, Pvt, Col John Coffee, Capt Blackman Coleman, Cav

DYER, Robert, Pvt, Col Philip Pipkin, Capt Wm Mackey, Mil Inf

DYER, Robert, Pvt, Col Philip Pipkin, Ens Wm Pegram, W TN Mil

DYER, Thomas, Pvt, Col S Bunch, Capt Samuel Richardson, E TN Drafted Mil

DYER, William H, 1st Sgt Maj, Col R H Dyer, no other information

DYER, William H, Pvt, Col John Alcorn, Capt Wm Locke, Cav; transferred to Capt Mitchell's Co

DYER, William H, Pvt, Col John Coffee, Capt Blackman Coleman, Cav

DYER, William H, Pvt, Regt Commander omitted, Capt Wm Mitchell, Spies; promoted to Maj

DYER, William, Pvt, Col S Bunch, Lt John Harris, E TN Mil

DYKE, Christian, Sgt, Col Wm Lillard, Capt Jacob Dyke, Vol Inf

DYKE, Emanuel, Pvt, Col Wm Lillard, Capt Robert Maloney, E TN Vol Inf

DYKE, Henry, Cpl, Col Wm Lillard, Capt Jacob Dyke, Vol Inf

DYKE, Henry, Pvt, Col Wm Lillard, Capt Jacob Dyke, Vol Inf

DYKE, Michael, Pvt, Col Wm Lillard, Capt Jacob Dyke, Vol Inf

DYKES, William, Pvt, Col Sam Bayless, Capt Joseph Hale, E TN Mil

DYMAN, James, Pvt, Col Sam'l Bunch, Capt Francis Berry, E TN Mil

DYNEN, Quintian, Pvt, Col Sam Bunch, Capt Joseph Duncan, E TN Drafted Mil

DYNES, William, Pvt, Col S Bunch, Capt Joseph Duncan, E TN Drafted Mil; transferred to Capt English Co

DYRE, Jacob, Pvt, Col Sam Bunch, Capt Joseph Duncan, E TN Drafted Mil

DYRE, James, Sgt Maj, Col James Raulston, Co Commander omitted, Vol TN Mil Inf

DYRE, John, Pvt, Lt Col Snodgrass, Ens Gregg, 2nd Regt E TN Mil Det of Inf

DYSART, Francis, Pvt, Col Robert Dyer, Capt E Dickson, E TN Vol Mtd Gunmen

DYSART, Francis, Pvt, Regt Commander omitted, Capt Ephraim Dickson, Branch Srvce omitted

DYSART, Wm, Pvt, Maj Wm Woodfolk, Capt James Neil, Inf

EACARD, Jones, Pvt, Col N T Perkins, Capt Mathew Patterson, Mtd Vol

EADES, George, Pvt, Col Sam Bunch, Capt Moses, E TN Drafted Mil

EADES, Jesse, Pvt, Col Robert Bunch, Capt John English, E TN Drafted Mil; joined from Capt Davis Co

EADES, Jesse, Pvt, Col S Bunch, Capt Moses, E TN Mil Drafted; transferred to Capt John English Co

EADES, William, Cpl, Col A Loury, Capt J Williamson, W TN Mil

EAGEN, Jesse, Pvt, Maj Gen Jackson, Capt Joe Kirkpatrick, Mtd Gunmen

EAGERS (AGERS), George, Pvt, Col S Copeland, Capt Robert Steele, Mil Inf; sick absent since 5-6-1814

EAGLETON, Alexander, Pvt, Col Sam Wear, Capt James Tedford, E TN Vol Inf

EAGLETON, James, Pvt, Maj Childs, Capt John Stephens, E TN Vol Mtd Inf

## Enlisted Men, War of 1812

EAKIN, David, Pvt, Col N T Perkins, Capt Philip Pipkin, Mtd Riflemen; killed 1-24-1814
EAKIN, George, Pvt, Col Wm Metcalf, Capt Wm Mullin, Mil Inf
EAKIN, William, Pvt, Col S Bunch, Capt Ed Buchanan, E TN Drafted Mil; transferred from Capt Duncan's Co
EAKIN, Wm, Pvt, Col S Bunch, Capt Joe Duncan, E TN Drafted Mil; left sick at Ft Deprst 3-12-1814
EAKINS, David, Pvt, Col Thomas Williamson, Capt Richard Tate, Vol Mtd Gunmen
EAKINS, Jonathan, Pvt, Col S Bunch, Capt Joe Duncan, E TN Drafted Mil
EAKINS, Solomon, Pvt, Col Sam Bunch, Capt Joe Duncan, E TN Drafted Mil
EAKINS, William (2), Pvt, Col S Bunch, Capt Joe Duncan, E TN Drafted Mil; transferred to Capt Buchanan Co
EAKINS, William, Pvt, Col Thomas Williamson, Capt Richard Tate, Vol Mtd Gunmen
EARHART, Elijah, Pvt, Col John Coffee, Capt James Terrell, Cav; out of state
EARLEY, Andrew, 2 Sgt, Col Edwin Booth, Capt Alex Biggs, Inf
EARLEY, Daniel, 3 Sgt, Col Wm Lillard, Capt Hugh Martin, E TN Vol Inf
EARLEY, Daniel, Pvt, Lt Col Wm Phillips, Gen A Jackson, Inf
EARLEY, David, Pvt, Regt Commander omitted, Capt Garrett Lane, Mtd Riflemen
EARLEY, Joh, Pvt, Regt & Co Commanders omitted, Cpl Elisha Green, Mtd Spies
EARLEY, John, Pvt, Col John Cocke, Capt Richard Crunk, Inf
EARLEY, Millington, Pvt, Lt Col Wm Phillips, Co of Gen Andrew Jackson, Inf
EARLEY, Millington, Sgt, Regt Commander omitted, Capt Garrett Lane, Mtd Riflemen
EARLEY, Thomas, Pvt, Col Wm Johnson, Capt Andrew Lawson, E TN Drafted Mil
EARLEY, Vincent, Pvt, Col Wm Lillard, Capt Hugh Martin, E TN Vol Inf
EARLEY (EASLEY), Charles, Col Thomas Williamson, Capt John Doak & Capt John Dobbins, Vol Mtd Gunmen; d 2-7-1815
EARLY, Samuel, Pvt, Col William Johnson, Capt Al Lawson, E TN Draft Mil
EARLY, Thomas, Cpl, Col William Lillard, Capt Jacob Hartsell, E TN Vol Inf
EARLY, Thomas, Pvt, Col William Lillard, Capt Hugh Martin, E TN Vol Inf
EARNEST, Peter, Pvt, Col John Coffee, Capt Thomas Bradley, Vol Cav
EARP, Collin, Pvt, Col John Alcorn, Capt Thomas Bradley, Vol Cav
EASBY, Robert, Pvt, Col John Cocke, Capt Sam Caruthers, Inf; AWOL
EASLEY, Allen, Pvt, Col. John Cocke, Capt Sam Caruthers, Inf
EASLEY, Allen, Pvt, Regt Commander omitted, Capt Garrett Lane, Mtd Riflemen

EASLEY, Drury, Pvt, Regt Commander omitted, Capt Garrett Lane, Mtd Riflemen
EASLEY, John, Pvt, Col A Loury, Capt George Sarver, Inf
EASLEY, John, Pvt, Col James Raulston, Capt Mathew Neal, Inf
EASLEY, Joseph, Pvt, Col Alex Loury, Capt George Sarver, Inf
EASLEY, Samuel, Pvt, Col John Coffee, Capt David Smith, Vol Cav
EASLEY, Stephen, Pvt, Sgt John Patton (only commander shown); Detachment Inf
EASLEY, William, Pvt, Col William Williamson, Capt Thomas Porter, Vol Mtd Gunmen; died 4-1-1815
EASON, Carter T(D?), Sgt, Col Robert Dyer, Capt Cuthbert Hudson, TN Mtd Gunmen
EASON, Ira, Pvt, Maj William Woodfolk, Capt Ezekial Ross & Capt McCully, Inf
EASON, James, Pvt, Col John Alcorn, Capt Thomas Bradley, Vol Cav
EASON, James, Pvt, Col John Coffee, Capt Thomas Bradley, Vol Cav
EASON, James, Pvt, Lt Col Richard Napier, Co Commander omitted, Inf
EASON, John E(S?), 2 Cpl, Col James Raulston, Capt Charles Wade, Inf
EASON, Joseph, Col Robert Dyer, Capt Cuthbert Hudson, Vol Mtd Gunmen
EASON, Joseph, Pvt, Col Newt Cannon, Capt James Walton, Mtd Riflemen
EASON, Mills, Sgt, Col Robert Dyer, Capt Cuthbert Hudson, Vol Mtd Gunmen; died 11-23-1814
EAST, Addison, Pvt, Maj Gen Jackson, Capt William Carroll, Vol Inf
EAST, Henry, Pvt, Col A Cheatham, Capt George Chapman, Inf
EAST, John, 2 Sgt, Col N T Perkins, Capt John Doak, Mtd Vol Gunmen
EAST, John, Pvt, Col Philip Pipkin, Capt Peter Searcy, Mil Inf
EAST, John, Pvt, Col Philip Pipkin, Capt William Mackay, Mil Inf
EAST, John, Pvt, Maj William Woodfolk, Capt McCulley, Inf; died 1-19-1815
EAST, Joseph, Pvt, Col Thomas McCrory, Capt Anthony Metcalf, Mil Inf
EAST, Mathew, Pvt, Col John Wynne, Capt James Holleman, Inf; deserted
EAST, Mathew, Pvt, Col Robert Dyer, Capt Thomas Jones, Vol Mtd Gunmen
EAST, Robert, Pvt, Col John Cocke, Capt Richard Crunk, Inf
EAST, Tarlton, Pvt, Col Thomas McCrory, Capt Isaac Patton, Mil Inf
EASTEN, Carter T, Pvt, Lt Col John Edmondson, Co Commander omitted, Cav
EASTEN, Thomas, Cpl, Maj Gen Andrew Jackson, Capt William Carroll, Vol Inf
EASTERLY, Moses, Sgt, Col Samuel Bayless, Capt Branch Jones, E TN Mil Drafted
EASTES, Bethlem, Pvt, Col Philip Pipkin, Capt George

-177

## Enlisted Men, War of 1812

Mebane, Mil Inf
EASTES, Edward, Pvt, Col Philip Pipkin, Capt George Mebane, Mil Inf
EASTES, John H, Pvt, Col Thomas McCrory, Capt William Dooley, Inf
EASTES, John, Pvt, Col N T Perkins, Capt Mathew Johnson, Mil Inf
EASTHAM, William, Pvt, Col Thomas McCrory, Capt William McKnight, Inf
EASTIN, Thomas, Cpl, Regt Commander omitted, Capt William Carroll, Vol Inf; 2 Regt Inf
EASTIS, Andrew, Pvt, Col William Pillow, Capt George Caperton, Inf
EASTWOOD, Daniel, Pvt, Col John Alcorn, Capt Robert Jetton, Vol Cav
EASTWOOD, Daniel, Pvt, Col John Coffee, Capt Robert Jetton, Cav
EASTY, Robin, Sgt, Col William Lillard, Capt Thomas Sharpe, 2 Regt Inf
EATHARADGE, Jonathan, Pvt, Col Robert Dyer, Capt Glen Owen, 1 TN Vol Mtd Gunmen
EATHERIDGE, John, Pvt, Col Philip Pipkin, Capt James Blakemore, Mil Inf
EATON, Camel, Pvt, Col Weaver, Capt Joseph Calloway, Mtd Inf
EATON, Element?, Pvt, Maj John Childs, Capt James Cummings, E TN Vol Mtd Inf
EATON, John, Pvt, Col S Copeland, Capt John Holshouser, Inf
EATON, Jonathan, Pvt, Col S Copeland, Capt John Holshouser, Inf
EATON, Joseph, Pvt, Col Edwin Booth, Capt John Slatton, E TN Mil
EAVERY, William, Pvt, Col John Alcorn, Capt Thomas Bradley, Vol Cav
EAVES, David, Pvt, Col Philip Pipkin, Capt David Smith, Inf; died 10-6-1814
EBBEN, E, Pvt, Regt Commander omitted, Capt Gray, Inf
EBBS, John, Pvt, Col Samuel Bayless, Capt Branch Jones, E TN Draft Mil
EBLIN, Edward, Pvt, Col R C Napier, Capt Thomas Gray, Mil Inf
EBLIN, Samuel, Pvt, Maj John Childs, Capt Charles Conway, E TN Mtd Gunmen; Regt Co Roane
EBLIN, William, Sgt, Col Edwin Booth, Capt John McKamey, E TN Mil
ECHOLS, Moses, Pvt, Col N T Perkins, Capt James McMahon, Mtd Inf
ECKOLSL, John, Pvt, Col Philip Pipkin, Capt James Blakemore, Mil Inf
ECLES, Moses, Pvt, Col Philip Pipkin, Capt Henry Newlin, Mil Inf
EDDING, John, Pvt, Col Newton Cannon, Capt John Harpole, Mtd Gunmen
EDDING, Joseph, Sgt, Col Thomas Williamson, Capt Beverly Williams, Vol Mtd Gunmen
EDDINGTON, James, Sgt, Col Edwin Booth, Capt Samuel Thompson, Mil
EDDINGTON, John, Pvt, Col William Lillard, Capt William Hamilton, E TN Vol Inf
EDDINGTON, Phillip, Pvt, Col John Williams, Capt William Walker, Vol
EDDINS, John, Sgt, Col Thomas Williamson, Capt Beverly Williams, Vol Mtd Gunmen
EDDINS, Joseph, Pvt, Col Newton Cannon, Capt John Harpole, Mtd Gunmen
EDDLEMAN, Aren, Pvt, Col William Lillard, Capt Robert McCalpin, E TN Inf
EDDLEMAN, David, Pvt, Col William Metcalf, Capt Bird Hurt, Mil INf
EDDLEMAN, John, Pvt, Col William Johnson, Capt Joseph Kirk, Mil
EDDLEMON, Aaron, Pvt, Col Samuel Bunch, Capt F Register, E TN Mil
EDDLEMON, John, Pvt, Col William Johnson, Capt Christopher Cook, E TN Mil
EDDS, William P, 4 Cpl, Col Leroy Hammonds, Capt J N Williamson, 2 Regt Inf; promoted Regt QM
EDDS, William P, QM, Lt Col Leroy Hammonds, no Co Commander, 2 Regt W TN Mil
EDDS, William, Pvt, Col N T Perkins, Capt Mathew Patterson, Mtd Vol
EDDY, John, Pvt, Col S Copeland, Capt James Taft, Inf
EDEN, John, Pvt, Col Edwin Booth, Capt Samuel Thompson, Mil
EDENS, Archibald, Pvt, Maj Wm Russell, Capt John Cowan, Vol Mtd Gunmen
EDENS, Austin, Pvt, Col Samuel Bayless, Capt Solomon Hendrichs, E TN Mil
EDENS, James, Pvt, Col William Johnson, Capt James Tunnell, E TN Mil
EDENS, Jonathan, Pvt, Maj Wm Russell, Capt John Cowan, Vol Mtd Gunmen
EDENS, Samuel, Pvt, Maj William Russell, Capt John Cowan, Vol Mtd Gunmen
EDGAR, James, 2 Cpl, Col N T Perkins, Capt Mathew Patterson, Mtd Vol
EDGAR, James, Pvt, Gen Thomas Johnson, Capt Daniel Oben, 36th Inf
EDGAR, John H, Sgt, Col Samuel Bayless, Capt James Churchman, E TN Mil
EDGIN, John, Pvt, Col S Copeland, Capt Solomon George, Inf
EDGIN, William, Pvt, Col S Copeland, Capt Solomon George, Inf; d 4-6-1814
EDGING, Andrew, Pvt, Col Wm Johnson, Capt James Tunnell, E TN Mil
EDGING, John, Pvt, Maj Wm Woodfolk, Capt Abner Pearce, Inf; deserted 10-6-1814
EDGING, John, Pvt, Maj Wm Woodfolk, Capt Abraham Dudney, Inf; deserted 9-28-1814, also served Capt John Sutton
EDINGTON, David, Pvt, Col Samuel Wear, Capt Rufus Morgan, E TN Vol Inf
EDINGTON, James, Pvt, Col Samuel Wear, Capt John Stephens, E TN Vol Inf
EDINGTON, Jesse, Pvt, Col Samuel Wear, Capt Rufus Morgan, E TN Vol Inf
EDINGTON, Jos, Cpl, Col William Johnson, Capt Wm Alexander, E TN Drafted Mil
EDINGTON, Joseph, Pvt, Col Wm Johnson, Capt Elihu Millikin, E TN Mil

## Enlisted Men, War of 1812

EDINGTON, Luke T, Sgt, Col R H Dyer, Capt Bethel Allen, Vol Mtd Gunmen

EDINGTON, Luke, Sgt, Col Stephen Copeland, Capt Wm Hodges, Inf

EDINGTON, Philip, Pvt, Col Samuel Wear, Capt Joseph Calloway, Mtd Inf

EDINGTON, Samuel F, Pvt, Col Robert H Dyer, Capt Bethel Allen, Vol Mtd Gunmen

EDINGTON, Samuel, Pvt, Col Samuel Wear, Capt Joseph Calloway, Mtd Inf

EDLIN, Oswald, Pvt, Col Robert H Dyer, Capt Robert Edmondson, TN Vol Mtd Gunmen

EDMINSON, Robert, Pvt, Regt Commander omitted, Capt John Gordon, Mtd Spies; transferred to Capt Williamson Co

EDMINSON, Wm, Pvt, Col Phillip Pipkin, Capt William Mackay, Mil Inf

EDMINSON, Wm, Tptr, Regt Commander omitted, Capt Robert Evans, Mtd Spies

EDMINSON, Zubelon, Sgt, Col Wm Pillow, Capt Joseph Pillow, Vol Inf

EDMISTON, Andrew, Pvt, no other information

EDMISTON, Benj, Pvt, Regt Commander omitted, Capt David Mason, Cav

EDMISTON, Fredrick, Pvt, Col Edwin Booth, Capt Samuel Thompson, Mil

EDMISTON, James, Pvt, Col Edward Bradley, Capt Abraham Bledsoe, Riflemen

EDMISTON, John, Pvt, Col Edwin Booth, Capt Samuel Thompson, Mil

EDMISTON, John, Pvt, Regt Commander omitted, Capt David Mason, Cav

EDMISTON, Robert, Pvt, Regt Commander omitted, Capt David Mason, Cav

EDMOND, Allen, Pvt, Col William Johnson, Capt Joseph Kirk, Mil; never appeared

EDMOND, James, Pvt, Col William Lillard, Capt Benj King, E TN Vol Inf

EDMOND, Jennings, Pvt, Regt Commander omitted, Capt George Smith, Spies

EDMONDS, Allen T, Pvt, Col Robert H Dyer, Capt Thomas Jones, Vol Mtd Gunmen

EDMONDS, Daniel, Pvt, Col R C Napier, Capt James McMurry, Mil Inf; on furlough

EDMONDS, David W, Pvt, Col N T Perkins, Capt Phillip Pipkins, Mtd Riflemen

EDMONDS, David W, Pvt, Col Wm Metcalf, Capt Thomas Marks, Mil Inf

EDMONDS, Solomon, Pvt, Col Wm Lillard, Capt Jacob Dyke, Vol Inf

EDMONDS, Wm, Pvt, Col John Alcorn, Capt John J Winston, Mtd Riflemen

EDMONDSON, Andrew J, Sgt, Col Robert H Dyer, Capt Thomas Jones, Vol Mtd Gunmen; promoted to 3 Lt

EDMONDSON, Benjamin, Pvt, Col Newt Cannon, Capt Isaac Williams, Mtd Riflemen

EDMONDSON, David H, Pvt, Col Newton Cannon, Capt Francis Jones, Mtd Riflemen

EDMONDSON, James E, Pvt, Col Thomas Benton, Capt David Smith, Vol Cav

EDMONDSON, James, Pvt, Col Thomas Williamson, Capt Wm Martin, Vol Mtd Gunmen; transferred to Lt Bean's Spies

EDMONDSON, James, Pvt, Gen John Coffee, Co Commander omitted, Mtd Spies; d 1-26-1815

EDMONDSON, Richard, Pvt, Maj James Porter, Capt Sam Cowan, Cav

EDMONDSON, Robert, Pvt, Col Robert H Dyer, Capt James Wyatt, Vol Mtd Gunmen

EDMONDSON, Robert, Pvt, Col Thomas Benton, Capt Thomas Williamson, Vol Inf

EDMONDSON, Robert, Pvt, Col Thomas Benton, Capt Thomas Williamson, Vol Inf; transferred to Gordon's Spies

EDMONDSON, Robert, Pvt, Col William Russell, Capt Isaac Williams, TN Vol Mtd Gunmen

EDMONDSON, Thomas, Pvt, Col Wm Johnson, Capt James Stewart, E TN Drafted Mil

EDMONDSON, William, Pvt, Col Thomas Williamson, Capt Doak & Capt John Dobbins, Vol Mtd Gunmen

EDMONDSON, Wm, Tptr, Regt Commander omitted, Capt Archibald, Cav; transferred to Col Evans Spies

EDMONDSON, Zeb, Pvt, Gen John Coffee, Co Commander omitted, Mtd Spies

EDMONDSON, Zebulon, Pvt, Lt James Berry, Co Commander omitted, Mtd Riflemen; transferred from Capt Cannon's Co of Cav

EDMONS, Leanard, Pvt, Col James Raulston, Capt Henry Hamilton, Inf; also served Maj Gen Carroll

EDMONSON, Robert, Sgt, Col Robert Dyer, Capt Thomas Jones, Vol Mtd Gunmen

EDMONSON, Samuel, Pvt, Col John Brown, Capt Hugh Barton, E TN Mil Inf

EDMONSON, William, Pvt, Col John Coffee, Capt Charles Kavanaugh, Cav

EDMONSON, Wm, 2 Cpl, Col Philip Pipkin, Capt Wm Pegram, W TN Mil

EDMONSON, Wm, Pvt, Regt Commander omitted, Capt John Crawford, Mtd Inf

EDMONSON, Wm, Tptr, Regt Commander omitted, Capt Archibald McKinney, Cav; transferred to Evans Co of Spies

EDMONSON, Zebulon, Pvt, Lt James Berry, Co Commander omitted, Mtd Riflemen

EDMONSTON, Robert, 1 Lt, Capt David Smith, Cav Vol

EDMONSTON, Will, Tptr, Col John Coffee, Capt Charles Kavanaugh, Branch Srvce omitted

EDMONSTON, Zebulon, Pvt, Col Thomas Benton, Capt Newt Cannon, Inf

EDMONSTON, Zebulon, Pvt, Col Thomas Williamson, Capt Wm Martin, Vol Mtd Gunmen; transferred to Lt Bean's Spies

EDMUNSTON, James, Pvt, Col Edward Bradley, Capt Abraham Bledsoe, Riflemen

EDMUNSTON, Willie, Pvt, Col Sam Wear, Capt James Gillespie, E TN Vol Inf

EDNEY, Edmond, Pvt, Col Robert Dyer, Capt Robert Evans, Vol Mtd Gunmen

EDNEY, John, Cpl, Col Thomas McCrory, Capt Isaac

Patton, Inf
EDSON (EADSON), James, Pvt, Col John Coffee, Capt John Baskerville, Cav
EDSON (EIDSON), Samuel, Pvt, Col John Coffee, Capt John W Byrns, Cav
EDWARD, Harry, Blksmth, Col Robert Dyer, Capt Glen Owen, TN Vol Mtd Gunmen
EDWARD, Isaac, Pvt, Col John Coffee, Capt B Coleman, Cav
EDWARD, John, Pvt, Col S Copeland, Capt James Tait, Inf; on command as Wgnr
EDWARD, John, Pvt, Col S Copeland, Capt Moses Thompson, Inf
EDWARD, John, Pvt, Col Thomas McCrory, Capt Wm Dooley, Inf
EDWARD, Peter, Pvt, Col John Coffee, Capt Charles Kavanaugh, Cav
EDWARD, Walker, Pvt, Col Wm Johnson, Capt David McKamey, E TN Drafted Mil
EDWARDS, Andrew, Pvt, Lt I Barrett, Capt William Davis, Inf; d 3-2-1814
EDWARDS, Archibald, 5 Cpl, Col Wm Metcalf, Capt John Cunningham, Mil Inf
EDWARDS, Archibald, Pvt, Brig Gen Johnson, Capt Robert Carson, Inf
EDWARDS, Aron, Pvt, Col John Coffee, Capt James Terrell, Vol Cav
EDWARDS, Berry (Benj), Pvt, Col John Coffee, Capt John Byrns, Cav
EDWARDS, Berry, Sgt, Col John Alcorn, Capt John Byrn, Cav
EDWARDS, Bradford, Pvt, Col James Raulston, Capt James Black, Inf
EDWARDS, Charles, Pvt, Col John Cocke, Capt John Weakley, Inf
EDWARDS, Charles, Pvt, Col Thomas McCrory, Capt Wm Dooley, Inf
EDWARDS, Cullen (Colen), Pvt, Col Alex Loury, Capt George Sarver, Inf
EDWARDS, Cullen, Sgt, Col Newt Cannon, Capt Wm Edwards, Regt Command
EDWARDS, David, Pvt, Col Thomas McCrory, Capt Wm Dooley, Inf
EDWARDS, Edward, Pvt, Col Robert Evans, Capt Robert Dyer, Vol Mtd Gunmen
EDWARDS, Edward, Pvt, Col Sam Copeland, Capt Moses Thompson, Inf
EDWARDS, Eli, Pvt, Col John Coffee, Capt James Terrell, Vol Cav
EDWARDS, Enoch, Pvt, Col Alex Loury, Capt Gabriel Martin, Inf
EDWARDS, Enoch, Pvt, Col R C Napier, Capt Drury Adkins, Mil Inf
EDWARDS, Enoch, Pvt, Col Robert Dyer, Capt I Williams, Vol Mtd Gunmen
EDWARDS, Enoch, Pvt, Col William Hall, Capt John Moore, Vol Inf
EDWARDS, Franklin, Pvt, Col Wm Lillard, Capt Zacheus Copeland, E TN Vol Inf
EDWARDS, Greenberry, Pvt, Maj John Childs, Capt Charles Conway, E TN Mtd Gunmen; Regt County Knox
EDWARDS, Isaac, Pvt, Col John Alcorn, Capt Wm Locke, Cav; promoted to QM Dept
EDWARDS, James B, Cpl, Col Alex Loury, Capt George Sarver, Inf
EDWARDS, James, Cpl, Col James Raulston, Capt Henry Hamilton, Inf; also served under Maj Gen Carroll
EDWARDS, Jesse, Pvt, Col Sam Copeland, Capt Wm Douglas, Inf
EDWARDS, John M, Pvt, Col Alex Loury, Capt Gabriel Martin, Inf
EDWARDS, John, Cpl, Col Thomas Williamson, Capt Thomas Scurry, Vol Mtd Gunmen
EDWARDS, John, Pvt, Brig Gen Johnson, Capt Allen, Mil Inf
EDWARDS, John, Pvt, Col Ewen Allison, Capt John Hampton, Mil
EDWARDS, John, Pvt, Col John Brown, Capt John Trimble, E TN Vol Mtd Gunmen
EDWARDS, John, Pvt, Col John Cocke, Capt James Gray, Inf
EDWARDS, John, Pvt, Col Robert Dyer, Capt Robert Evans, Vol Gunmen
EDWARDS, John, Pvt, Col Wm Russell, Capt Fleman Hodges, Vol Mtd Gunmen
EDWARDS, Jonas, Pvt, Col James Raulston, Capt Daniel Newman, Inf; d 3-14-1815
EDWARDS, Jos, Cpl, Col Robert Dyer, Capt Jos Williams, Vol Mtd Gunmen; promoted from Pvt
EDWARDS, Joshua, Pvt, Col Philip Pipkin, Capt John Strother, Mil; attached to Capt Davis Smith
EDWARDS, Kenning, Pvt, Regt Commander omitted, Capt Thomas Gray, Inf
EDWARDS, Labern, Pvt, Col A Cheatham, Capt George Chapman, Inf
EDWARDS, Morgan, Pvt, Col William Johnson, Capt David McKamy, E TN Drafted Mil
EDWARDS, Morgan, Pvt, Col Wm Johnson, Capt Andrew Lawson, E TN Drafted Mil; substitute for John King
EDWARDS, Nicholas, 1st Sgt Mate (Surgeon), Col Wm Metcalf, Co Commander omitted, 1st Regt W TN Mil
EDWARDS, Peter, Pvt, Regt Commander omitted, Capt Archibald McKinney, Cav; promoted to Cpl
EDWARDS, Right, Pvt, Col S Bunch, Capt Joe Duncan, E TN Drafted Mil; joined from Capt Yarnell's Co
EDWARDS, Sanford, Pvt, Col R C Napier, Capt Drury Adkins, Mil Inf
EDWARDS, Simon, Pvt, Col Newton Cannon, Capt Wm Edwards, Regt Command
EDWARDS, Spencer, Pvt, Col Philip Pipkin, Capt George Mebane, Mil Inf
EDWARDS, Spencer, Pvt, Col Sam Bayless, Capt Jos Bacon, E TN Mil
EDWARDS, Thomas, Pvt, Col Nicholas Perkins, Capt George Eliott, Mil Inf
EDWARDS, Thomas, Pvt, Col Wm Hall, Capt John Wallace, Inf
EDWARDS, William, Pvt, Col James Raulston, Capt James Black, Inf

*Enlisted Men, War of 1812*

EDWARDS, William, Pvt, Col N T Perkins, Capt James McMahan, Mtd Gunmen
EDWARDS, William, Pvt, Col Philip Pipkin, Capt Peter Searcy, Mil Inf
EDWARDS, William, Pvt, Maj Gen Andrew Jackson, Capt John Craine, Mtd Gunmen
EDWARDS, William, Pvt, Regt Commander omitted, Capt John Gordon, Mtd Spies
EDWARDS, Winn, Pvt, Col Philip Pipkin, Capt Ebenezer Kirkpatrick, Mil Inf; deserted 9-20-1814
EELY, Nicholas, Pvt, Col Ewen Allison, Capt Thomas Wilson, E TN Drafted Mil
EENDALL, Epaphroditus T, Sgt, Col John Wynne, Capt Butler, Inf
EFFLER, Lawrence, Pvt, Col Samuel Wear, Capt James Cole, Vol Inf
EGNEW, James, 3 Sgt, Col R C Napier, Capt Early Benson, Mil Inf
EGNEW, Jesse G, Pvt, Regt Commander omitted, Capt John Gordon, Mtd Spies
EGNEW, Jesse, Pvt, Brig Gen Isaac Roberts, Capt Benj Reynolds, Mtd Rangers
EIDSON, James, Pvt, Col John Alcorn, Capt John Baskerville, Vol Inf
EIDSON, Samuel, Pvt, Col John Alcorn, Capt John W Byrns, Cav
ELAM, Edmond, Pvt, Col Thomas Williamson, Capt Richard Tate, Vol Mtd Gunmen
ELAM, Mathew, Pvt, Col Newt Cannon, Capt Martin, Mtd Gunmen
ELAM, Mathew, Pvt, Col P Pipkin, Capt Wm Mackay, Mil Inf
ELAM, Mathew, Pvt, Col Thomas Benton, Capt Newt Cannon, Inf
ELAM, Mathew, Pvt, Lt James Berry, Co Commander omitted, Mtd Riflemen; transferred from Carmon's Co
ELAM, Robert, Pvt, Col Thomas Benton, Capt Newt Cannon, Inf
ELAM, William I, Pvt, Col N Cannon, Capt Martin, Mtd Gunmen; transferred to the Arty
ELAM, William, Pvt, Gen Andrew Jackson, Capt Joel Parrish, Arty
ELBS, John, Pvt, Col Wm Johnson, Capt Christopher Cook, E TN Mil
ELDER, Adam Pvt, Col Samuel Wear, Capt Daniel Price, E TN Vol Inf
ELDER, James, 1 Cpl, Col Thomas Benton, Capt James McFerrin, Vol Inf
ELDER, James, Cpl, Col Thomas Benton, Capt James McFerrin, Vol Inf
ELDER, James, Pvt, Col Sam Wear, Capt Dan Price, E TN Vol Inf
ELDER, James, Sgt, Col Wm Pillow, Capt James McFerrin, Inf; deserted 11-9-1813
ELDER, Wm, Pvt, Col Sam Copeland, Capt David Williams, Inf
ELDERS, Elias, Pvt, Col Wm Pillow, Capt James McFerrin, Inf; deserted 11-9-1813
ELDING, Francis, Cpl, Col Robert Dyer, Maj Wm Russell, Capt Wm Russell, Vol Mtd Gunmen

ELDREDGE, Thomas, Pvt, Col S Copeland, Capt David Williams, Inf
ELDRIDGE, Moses, Pvt, Col John Brown, Capt Jess G Rainey, Mtd Gunmen
ELETT, James, Pvt, Col John Cocke, Capt Sam Caruthers, Inf
ELGIN, Robert I, Sgt, Col Robert Dyer, Capt Bethel Allen, Vol Mtd Gunmen; promoted to Cor
ELIAS, Edward, Pvt, Maj Woodfolk, Capt Abner Pearce, Inf; transferred from Capt Dudney Co
ELIM, Robert, Pvt, Maj Wm Woodfolk, Capt Abraham Dudney, Inf
ELINGTON, Stephen, Pvt, Regt Commander omitted, Capt George Smith, Spies
ELIOTT, Thomas, Pvt, Maj Childs, Capt Charles Conway, E TN Mtd Gunmen; Regt County Knox
ELISON, James, Pvt, Col Wm Johnson, Capt James Stewart, E TN Mil
ELKIN, George, Pvt, Col Ewen Allison, Capt Jonas Laughmiller, Mil; joined by transfer from Capt Griffith's Co
ELKINS, George, Sgt, Col S Bunch, Capt Jones Griffin, E TN Drafted Mil
ELKINS, John, Pvt, Col Edwin Booth, Capt John Slatton, E TN Mil
ELKINS, Larkin, Pvt, Col William Johnson, Capt Joseph Scott, E TN Mil Drafted; absent
ELKINS, Ralph, Pvt, Maj John Childs, Capt James Cummings, E TN Vol Mtd Inf
ELKINS, Robert, Pvt, Col S Bunch, Capt James Cummings, E TN Mtd Gunmen
ELKINS, William, Pvt, Col William Lillard, Capt John Neatherton, E TN Vol Inf
ELLEDGE, John, Pvt, Col Alex Loury, Lt Col Hammond, Capt Arahel Rains, Inf
ELLEDGE, Morgan, Pvt, Lt Col Hammons, Capt Arahel Rains, Inf
ELLERSON, Hugh, Pvt, Col S Bunch, Capt G McPherson, E TN Mil
ELLERSON, John, Pvt, Col Wm Johnson, Capt Joe Scott, E TN Drafted Mil
ELLERSON, Peter, Pvt, Col Wm Johnson, Capt Joe Scott, E TN Drafted Mil
ELLIF, James, Pvt, Col John Coffee, Capt John Byrns, Cav
ELLIFF, Everett (Everlan), Pvt, Col John Coffee, Capt John Byrns, Cav
ELLINGTON, Stephen, Pvt, Regt Commander omitted, Capt George Smith, Spies
ELLIOT, Andrew, 3 Cpl, Col A Loury, Co Commander omitted, 2nd Regt W TN Mil
ELLIOT, George, Pvt, Col Thomas Williamson, Capt Thomas Scurry, Vol Mtd Gunmen
ELLIOT, George, Pvt, Col Wm Hall, Capt John Wallace, Inf
ELLIOT, James (Jonas), Pvt, Col James Raulston, Capt Dan Newman, Inf
ELLIOT, James, Pvt, Col John Cocke, Capt Bird Nance, Inf
ELLIOTT, George S, Pvt, Col P Pipkin, Capt Peter Searcy, Mil Inf

## Enlisted Men, War of 1812

ELLIOTT, George, Pvt, Col Edward Bradley, Capt John Wallace, Vol Inf
ELLIOTT, Hyram E, Pvt, Col Wm Metcalf, Co Commander omitted, Mil Inf
ELLIOTT, Hyram, Pvt, Col Wm Metcalf, Capt Wm Mullins, Mil Inf
ELLIOTT, Ira, Pvt, Regt Commander omitted, Capt James Gray, Inf
ELLIOTT, Isaac, Cpl, Col John Coffee, Capt John W Byrn, Cav
ELLIOTT, James, Pvt, Col Thomas H Benton, Co Commander omitted, Inf
ELLIOTT, James, Pvt, Col Thomas McCrory, Capt Dooly, Inf; deserted 10-22-1813
ELLIOTT, James, Pvt, Col Wm Metcalf, Capt Alexander Hill & Capt John Cunningham, Mil Inf
ELLIOTT, James, Pvt, Col Wm Metcalf, Capt Mullins, Mil Inf
ELLIOTT, James, Pvt, Lt Col Henry Bryan, Co Commander omitted, Inf
ELLIOTT, John, 1 Cpl, Col Wm Metcalf, Capt Thomas Marks, Mil Inf
ELLIOTT, John, Pvt, Col Wm Pillow, Lt Joseph Mason, Vol Inf
ELLIOTT, Moses, Pvt, Col P Pipkin, Capt E Kirkpatrick, Mil Inf
ELLIOTT, Reuben, Pvt, Regt Commander omitted, Capt Josiah Askew, Inf
ELLIOTT, Robert, Pvt, Col Wm Pillow, Lt Joseph Mason, Vol Inf
ELLIOTT, Samuel, Pvt, Lt Col John Edmondson, Co Commander omitted, Cav
ELLIOTT, Samuel, Pvt, Maj John Childs, Capt Charles Conway, E TN Mtd Gunmen; Regt County Knox
ELLIOTT, Samuel, Pvt, Regt Commander omitted, Capt John Crane, Mtd Inf
ELLIOTT, Stephen, Pvt, Col Wm Metcalf, Capt Alexander Hill & Capt John Cunningham, Mil Inf
ELLIOTT, Thomas, Sgt, Col Wm Y Higgins, Capt Stephen Griffith, Mtd Riflemen
ELLIOTT, Walter T, Pvt, Col Thomas H Benton, Capt Newton Cannon, Inf
ELLIOTT, Walter T, Pvt, Col Wm Pillow, Lt Joseph Mason, Vol Inf
ELLIOTT, William, Pvt, Col Thomas McCrory, Capt Thomas Gordon, Inf
ELLIOTT, Wm, Pvt, Col Wm Metcalf, Capt Andrew Patterson, Mil Inf; d 1-22-1815
ELLIOTTE, Robert, Dmr, Col Thomas H Benton, Capt Robert Cannon, Inf
ELLIS, Benjamin, Cpl, Col S Copeland, Capt Richard Sharp, Mil Inf; reduced to Pvt
ELLIS, Edward S, Pvt, Col A Cheatham, Co Commander omitted, Inf
ELLIS, Edward T, Pvt, Col Hammond, Capt James Tubb, Inf
ELLIS, Ellison, Pvt, Col R H Dyer, Maj Russell, Capt Wm Russell, Mtd Gunmen
ELLIS, Ezekiel, Pvt, Col Samuel Wear, Capt J Cole, Vol Inf
ELLIS, Ezekiel, Pvt, Col Wm Johnson, Capt Andrew Lawson, E TN Drafted Mil; transferred from Capt Scott's Co
ELLIS, Ezekiel, Pvt, Col Wm Johnson, Capt Joseph Scott, E TN Drafted Mil; transferred to Capt Lawson
ELLIS, George, Pvt, Col Wm Johnson, Capt Andrew Lawson, E TN Drafted Mil; never appeared
ELLIS, Hardy, Pvt, Col R H Dyer, Capt Edmondson, TN Vol Mtd Gunmen
ELLIS, Hardy, Pvt, Regt Commander omitted, Capt James Haggard, Mtd Gunmen
ELLIS, James, Pvt, Col John K Wynne, Capt Porter, Inf
ELLIS, James, Pvt, Col Philip Pipkin, Co Commander omitted, Mil Inf; substitute for Wm Pittman
ELLIS, James, Pvt, Col R C Napier, Capt Thomas Preston, Mil Inf
ELLIS, Jesse, Pvt, Col S Bunch, Capt George McPherson, E TN Mil
ELLIS, Jesse, Rank omitted, Col Ewen Allison, Capt Jacob Hoyal, E TN Mil; transferred to Capt McPherson's Co
ELLIS, John, Pvt, Col James Raulston, Capt Henry Hamilton, Inf
ELLIS, John, Pvt, Col Philip Pipkin, Capt Eb Kirkpatrick, Mil Inf; deserted 9-20-1814
ELLIS, John, Pvt, Col Wm Hall, Capt Brice Martin, Vol Inf; deserted
ELLIS, John, Pvt, Col Wm Johnson, Capt Jos Kirk, Mil
ELLIS, Joseph, Pvt, Col Wm Lillard, Capt S Copeland, E TN Vol Inf
ELLIS, Laban, Pvt, Maj Woodfolk, Capt Abraham Dudney & Capt John Sutton, Inf
ELLIS, Luelling, Cpl, Col John Winn, Capt Wm McCall, Inf
ELLIS, Moses, Pvt, Col Wm Lillard, Capt James Lillard, E TN Vol Inf
ELLIS, William, Pvt, Col A Loury, Lt Col Hammonds, Capt Arahel Rains, Inf
ELLIS, William, Pvt, Col S Bunch, Capt David Vance, E TN Mtd Inf
ELLIS, William, Pvt, Col S Bunch, Capt John Hauk, E TN Mil; joined from Capt Berry's Co
ELLIS, Williams, Pvt, Col Wm Johnson, Capt Henry Hunter, E TN Mil; substitute for Finnas McField
ELLIS, Wm, Cpl, Col Robert Dyer, Capt Wm Evans, Vol Mtd Gunmen
ELLIS, Wm, Pvt, Col S Bunch, Capt Francis Berry, E TN Mil; attached to Capt Houk's Co
ELLIS (ELLISON), Ezekiel, Pvt, Col Philip Pipkin, Capt James Blakemore, Mil Inf
ELLISON, Henry, Pvt, Col John K Winn, Capt William McCall, Inf
ELLISON, Isaah, Pvt, Col John K Winn, Capt John Spinks, Inf
ELLISON, James, Pvt, Col Robert Dyer, Capt Eph Dickson, Branch Srvce omitted
ELLISON, James, Pvt, Col Wm Johnson, Capt James Stewart, E TN Drafted Mil
ELLISON, James, Sgt, Col John Alcorn, Capt John Winston, Mtd Riflemen
ELLISON, John, Pvt, Col S Bayless, Capt Branch Jones, E TN Drafted Mil

## Enlisted Men, War of 1812

ELLISON, John, Pvt, Col Thomas McCrory, Capt Thomas Gordon, Inf
ELLISON, Jos, Pvt, Col John Alcorn, Capt John Winston, Mtd Riflemen
ELLISON, Robert, Sgt, Col John Brown, Capt John Childs, E TN Vol Mtd Gunmen
ELLISON, Thomas, Pvt, Col John Wynne, Capt John Porter, Inf
ELLISON, Thomas, Pvt, Col Robert Dyer, Capt E Dickson, TN Mtd Gunmen
ELLISON, Thomas, Pvt, Regt Commander omitted, Capt Ephraim Dickson, Branch Srvce omitted
ELLISTON, Jonathan, Pvt, Col John Cocke, Capt Joseph Price, Inf
ELLISTON, Thomas, Pvt, Col John Cocke, Capt Joseph Price, Inf
ELLISTON, William, Pvt, Col John Cocke, Capt Bird Nance, Inf
ELLITT, Thomas W, Pvt, Col Wm Johnson, Capt Andrew Lawson, E TN Drafted Mil; discharged by the doctor
ELLITT, William, Pvt, Col S Bunch, Capt Dan Yarnell, E TN Mil; transferred from Capt McNave's Co
ELLITT, William, Pvt, Col S Bunch, Capt Dan Yarnell, Regt Service
ELLOTT, Thomas, Pvt, Col Sam Wear, Capt Jess Cole, Vol Inf
ELMORE, David, Pvt, Col S Bunch, Capt George Gregory, E TN Drafted Mil; discharged for inability
ELMORE, George, Pvt, Col Philip Pipkin, Capt William Mackay, Mil Inf
ELMORE, George, Pvt, Col Thomas Benton, Capt Thomas Williamson, Vol Inf
ELMORE, George, Pvt, Col William Pillow, Capt Thomas Williamson, Vol Inf; AWOL
ELMORE, Julius, Pvt, Col Thomas Benton, Capt Thomas Williamson, Vol Inf
ELMORE, Julius, Sgt, Regt Commander omitted, Capt Meridith Walker, Mtd Inf
ELMORE, Julius, Tptr, Col Thomas Williamson, Capt James Cook, Capt Crane, Vol Mtd Gunmen
ELROD, James, Pvt, Col Robert Steele, Capt William Smith, Vol Inf
ELROD, Jiles, Pvt, Col Thomas Benton, Capt William Smith, Vol Inf
ELSAY, John, Pvt, Col Ewen Allison, Capt John Hampton, Mil
ELSHI, John, Pvt, Col William Lillard, Capt Jacob Dyke, Vol Inf
ELSONBACK, James, Cpl, Col S Bunch, Capt John Houk, E TN Mil
ELSTON, Jonathan, Pvt, Col William Y Higgins, Capt Adams Dale, Mtd Gunmen
ELSTON, William, Pvt, Col Leroy Hammonds, Capt James Tubb, Inf
ELSWICK, Jonathan, Pvt, Col Wm Johnson, Capt James Tunnell, E TN Mil
ELSY, John, Pvt, Col Wm Hall, Capt John Hall, Vol Inf
ELY, Adam, Pvt, Col Ewen Allison, Capt Thomas Wilson, E TN Drafted Mil
ELY, Mills, Pvt, Col Wm Y Higgins, Capt A Cheatham, Mtd Gunmen
ELY, William, 1 Lt, Col S Bunch, Capt John Houk, E TN Mil
EMBERSON, James, Pvt, Col Thomas Benton, Capt George Caperton, Inf; out of state
EMBERSON, James, Pvt, Maj Wm Russell, Capt John Cowan, Vol Mtd Gunmen
EMBERSON, Maury, Pvt, Col Thomas Benton, Capt George Caperton, Inf
EMBERTON, Walter, Pvt, Maj Wm Woodfolk, Capt James Turner, Inf
EMBRA, James, Pvt, Col S Copeland, Capt Richard Sharpe, Mil Inf
EMBREY, Thomas, Pvt, Col Wm Metcalf, Capt William Mullen, Mil Inf
EMBRY, James, Pvt, Col Johnson, Capt Stewart, E TN Drafted Mil
EMBRY, Joel, Pvt, Col Cannon, Capt Jones, Mtd Riflemen
EMBRY, Jos, Pvt, Col Cannon, Capt Jones, Mtd Riflemen
EMBRY, Jos, Pvt, Col Higgins, Capt Eldridge, Mtd Gunmen
EMBRY, Thomas, Pvt, Col Wm Metcalf, Capt Thomas Marks, Mil Inf
EMBY, James, Pvt, Col Wm Johnson, Capt James Stewart, E TN Mil
EMERSON, Harry, Sgt, Col Burton, Capt Reynolds, Vol Inf
EMERSON, John, Pvt, Col Allison, Capt Loughmiller, Mil; transferred to Capt Trippen's Co
EMERY, Bald, Pvt, Col Winn, Capt Carothers, W TN Inf; transferred to Capt Hollan's Co
EMERY, Jos, Pvt, Col Brown, Capt White, E TN Vol Mtd Inf
EMET, Andrew, Pvt, Col Johnson, Capt Hunter, E TN Mil
EMET, Jacob, Pvt, Col Johnson, Capt Hunter, E TN Mil
EMMERETE, John, Pvt, Col Wear, Capt Cole, Vol Inf
EMMERETTE, Andrew, Pvt, Col Wear, Capt Cole, Vol Inf
EMMERSON, John, Pvt, Col S Bunch, Capt James Griffin, E TN Drafted Mil; joined from Capt Loughmiller's Co
EMMERT, Andrew, Pvt, Col Wear, Capt Cole, Vol Inf
EMMERT, John, Pvt, Col Bayless, Capt Hendrix, E TN Mil
EMMERT, Philip, Pvt, Col Bayless, Capt Hendrix, E TN Mil
EMMERY, Boley, Pvt, Col Winn, Capt Holleman, Inf
EMMET, Daniel, Pvt, Col S Bunch, Capt Isaac Williams, E TN Mil
EMMETT, Frederick, Pvt, Col S Bunch, Capt John Houk, E TN Mil; discharged for inability
EMMIT, Frederick, Pvt, Col S Bunch, Capt Isaac Williams, E TN Mil
EMMITT, Daniel, Pvt, Col S Bunch, Capt Isaac Williams, E TN Mil
EMORY, Murry, Pvt, Col Benton, Capt Caperton, Vol Inf
EMPISON, Gregory, Pvt, Col Winn, Capt Bradin, Inf
EMPSON, Caleb, Pvt, Col Cheatham, Capt Chapman, Inf
EMPTON, Caleb, Pvt, Col Raulston, Capt Hamilton, Inf; also served under Maj Gen Carroll

*Enlisted Men, War of 1812*

EMRY, John, Pvt, Col Hammons, Capt Rains, Inf
EMSON, William, Pvt, Regt Commander omitted, Capt Meredith Walker, Mtd Inf
ENGLAND, Anderson, Pvt, Maj Gen Carroll, Capt Ellis, Inf
ENGLAND, Benj, Pvt, Col Lowry, Capt Martin, Inf
ENGLAND, Enos, Pvt, Maj Childs, Capt Conway, E TN Mtd Gunmen
ENGLAND, Isaac, Ffr, Col Booth, Capt McKamey, E TN Mil
ENGLAND, Jos, Pvt, Maj Gen Carroll, Col Raulston, Capt Huddleston, Inf
ENGLAND, Joseph, Cpl, Col John Brown, Capt Lunsford Oliver, E TN Mil
ENGLAND, Joseph, Pvt, Maj Childs, Capt Conway, E TN Mtd Gunmen; Regt County Anderson
ENGLAND, Joseph, Pvt, Regt Commander omitted, Capt John Crane, Mtd Inf
ENGLAND, Thomas, Pvt, Col Brown, Capt White, E TN Vol Mtd Inf
ENGLAND, Titus, Pvt, Col John Brown, Capt Lunsford Oliver, E TN Mil
ENGLAND, Wm, Pvt, Col Cocke, Capt Caruthers, Inf
ENGLE, William, Pvt, Col Allison, Capt King, Drafted Mil
ENGLISH, Abraham, Pvt, Col Copeland, Capt Douglass, Inf
ENGLISH, Alexander, Pvt, Col S Bunch, Capt McPherson, E TN Mil
ENGLISH, James, Pvt, Col Wynne, Capt Cole, Inf
ENGLISH, John, Pvt, Col Dyer, Capt Allen, Vol Mtd Gunmen
ENGLISH, John, Pvt, Col Lillard, Capt Dyke, Vol Inf
ENGLISH, John, Pvt, Col Lillard, Capt Hartsell, E TN Vol Inf; discharged--unfit for duty
ENGLISH, John, Pvt, Col Wynne, Capt Cole, Inf
ENGLISH, John, Sgt, Col Allison, Capt Hoyal, E TN Mil; transferred to Capt McPherson
ENGLISH, John, Sgt, Col S Bunch, Capt George McPherson, E TN Mil; transferred to Capt Hoyle's Co
ENGLISH, Matthew, Cpl, Col John Brown, Capt William D Neilson, E TN Vol Mil; promoted from Pvt
ENGLISH, Stephen, Sgt, Col Booth, Capt Winton, E TN Mil
ENGLISH, Stephens, Pvt, Col Lillard, Capt Hamilton, E TN Mil Inf Vol
ENGLISH, Titus, Pvt, Col Bunch, Capt Breden, E TN Mil; transferred to Capt Bacon's Co
ENGLISH, Wm, Pvt, Col Johnson, Capt Scott, E TN Drafted Mil
ENGLISH, Wm, Pvt, Col Napier, Capt Chism, Mil Inf
ENNIS, Vincent, Pvt, Brig Gen Johnson, Capt Allen, Mil Inf
ENOCH, Andrew, Pvt, Col Johnson, Capt Hunter, E TN Mil
ENOCH, Isaac, Pvt, Col Loury, Lt Col Hammond, Capt Delaney, Branch Srvce omitted
ENOCHS, John, Pvt, Col Alcorn, Capt Locke, Cav
ENOCHS, Thompson, Pvt, Col Alcorn, Capt Locke, Cav
ENOCHS, Thompson, Pvt, Col Coffee, Capt Coleman, Cav

ENOCKS, John R, Pvt, Col Coffee, Capt Coleman, Cav
ENOCKS, Thompson, Pvt, no other information
ENOX, Sam'l, Pvt, Col Winn, Capt Holleman, Inf
ENSON, Thomas, Pvt, Col Allison, Capt Hampton, Mil
ENSUMING, Sam'l, Pvt, Col Higgins, Capt Eldridge, Mtd Gunmen
EOCHORT, Elijah, Pvt, Col Coffee, Capt Terrell, Vol Inf; out of state
EPERY, John, Pvt, Col Brown, Capt White, E TN Vol Mtd Inf
EPISON, James, Pvt, Col Lillard, Capt Hartsell, E TN Vol Inf
EPPERSON, Anthony, Pvt, Col S Bunch, Capt George McPherson, E TN Mil
EPPERSON, Benjamin, Pvt, Col Lillard, Capt McLin, E TN Inf; in lieu of Ransom Matlock
EPPERSON, Berry, Pvt, Col Cannon, Capt Patterson, Mtd Riflemen
EPPERSON, Joel, Pvt, Col John Brown, Capt Hugh Barton, Branch Srvce omitted
EPPERSON, John, Pvt, Col R H Dyer, Capt Joseph Williams, Vol Mtd Gunmen
EPPERSON, Jos, Pvt, Col James Raulston, Capt Mathew Neal, Inf
EPPERSON, Mark, Pvt, Regt Commander omitted, Capt Jos Williams, Mil Cav
EPPERSON, Thomas, Pvt, Col Wm Lillard, Capt Wm McLin, E TN Inf
EPPS, Daniel, Pvt, Brig Gen Thos Johnson, Capt Robert Carson, Inf
EPPS, John, Pvt, Col John Coffee, Capt Charles Kavanaugh, Cav
EPPS, Laurence, Cpl, Col Robert H Dyer, Capt James Wyatt, Vol Mtd Gunmen
EPSION, Benj, Pvt, Col Wm Lillard, Capt Jacob Hartsell, E TN Vol Inf
ERBY, Harrison, Pvt, Maj Wm Woodfolk, Capt Ross & Capt McCally, Inf
ERBY, Pleasant, Pvt, Col R H Dyer, Capt Cuthbert Hudson, Vol Mtd Gunmen
ERNAL, Henry, Pvt, Maj William Woodfolk, Capt Ross & Capt McCally, Inf
ERNST, Peter, Tptr, Col Thos Williamson, Capt Thos Scurry, Vol Mtd Gunmen
ERRINGTON, James, Pvt, Col Ewen Allison, Capt Henry McCrory, E TN Mil; furnishing a substitute
ERVIN, Alexander, Pvt, Brig Gen Roberts, Capt Benj Reynolds, Branch Srvce omitted
ERVIN, Alexander, Pvt, Col Ewen Allison, Capt Jacob Hoyal, E TN Mil
ERVIN, David, Pvt, Col Wm Johnson, Capt Jos Scott, E TN Drafted Mil
ERVIN, Emos, Cpl, Col John K Wynne, Capt Robert Breden, Inf
ERVIN, John, Sgt, Col John Brown, Capt William White, E TN Mil Regt
ERVIN, Patrick, Pvt, Col Ewen Allison, Capt McCrory, Inf
ERVIN, William L, Pvt, Col Edward Bradley, Capt Wm Lauderdale, Vol Inf
ERVIN, William, Pvt, Col Thomas Benton, Capt Newton

## Enlisted Men, War of 1812

Cannon, Inf
ERVINE, Daniel, Pvt, Col Wm Johnson, Capt Elihu Milliken, E TN Mil
ERVINE, James, Pvt, Col Samuel Bunch, Capt Joseph Duncan, E TN Drafted Mil
ERVING, Wm, Pvt, Col John Coffee, Capt Michael Molton, Cav
ERWEN, Richard, Pvt, Col James Raulston, Capt Mathew Neal, Inf; d 1-27-1815
ERWIN, Alfred, Pvt, Col James Raulston, Capt Mathew Neale, Inf
ERWIN, David, Pvt, Col Robert Steele, Capt James Randals, Inf
ERWIN, David, Pvt, Col Thomas Benton, Capt N Cannon, Inf
ERWIN, Edward, Cpl, Col Wm Lillard, Capt George Argenbright, E TN Vol Riflemen; appointed 1st Sgt
ERWIN, Elam, Pvt, Col James Raulston, Capt Mathew Neale, Inf
ERWIN, Emos, Pvt, Col John Cocke, Capt Bird Nance, Inf
ERWIN, Francis, Pvt, Col John Brown, Capt William White, E TN Vol Mtd Inf
ERWIN, Francis, Pvt, Col Wm Lillard, Capt George Argenbright, E TN Vol Riflemen
ERWIN, George, Pvt, Col John Cocke, Capt John Dalton, Inf
ERWIN, George, Pvt, Col S Bunch, Capt Edward Buchanan, E TN Drafted Mil
ERWIN, James, Pvt, Col Alexander Loury, Capt Peter Looney, W TN Mil
ERWIN, James, Pvt, Col Edward Bradley, Capt Wm Lauderdale, Vol Inf
ERWIN, James, Pvt, Col Samuel Bunch, Capt Edward Buchanan, E TN Drafted Mil
ERWIN, James, Pvt, Col Wm Johnson, Capt Powell, E TN Mil
ERWIN, James, Pvt, Col Wm Lillard, Capt George Argenbright, Vol Riflemen
ERWIN, John jr, 4 Cpl, Regt Commander omitted, Capt David Dedrick, Arty
ERWIN, John, Pvt, Col John Cocke, Capt John Dalton, Inf
ERWIN, John, Pvt, Col John Coffee, Capt Alexander McKeen, Cav
ERWIN, John, Pvt, Col Wm Johnson, Capt Millikin, 3rd Regt E TN Mil
ERWIN, John, Pvt, Col Wm Lillard, Capt Hugh Martin, E TN Vol Inf
ERWIN, Joseph, 1 Sgt, Col Wm Pillow, Capt Renshaw, Inf
ERWIN, Joseph, Drm Maj, Col Ewen Allison, Co Commander omitted, E TN Mil
ERWIN, Joseph, Sgt, Col Thomas H Benton, Capt Isaac Renshaw, Vol Inf
ERWIN, Richard, Pvt, Col Edward Bradley, Capt William Lauderdale, Vol Inf
ERWIN, Sam'l, Pvt, Col John Cocke, Capt John Dalton, Inf
ERWIN, Samuel, Pvt, Brig Gen Thomas Johnson, Capt Robert Carson, Inf
ERWIN, Samuel, Pvt, Col John Cocke, Capt John Dalton, Inf

ERWIN, William, Pvt, Col James Raulston, Capt Mathew Neal, Inf
ERWIN, William, Pvt, Col Wm Metcalf, Capt Andrew Patterson, Mil Inf
ERWOOD, William, Pvt, Col Thomas Williamson, Capt James Cook & Capt John Dobbins, Vol Mtd Gunmen
ESBY, John, Pvt, Col John Brown, Capt Wm White, E TN Vol Mtd Gunmen; reduced to ranks from Cpl
ESDALE, David, Pvt, Maj Gen Jackson, Capt Wm Carroll, Vol Inf
ESKRIDGE, Samuel, Pvt, Col Wm Metcalf, Capt John Cunningham, Mil Inf
ESKRIDGE, Samuel, Pvt, Col Wm Metcalf, Capt Wm Mullen, Mil Inf
ESLINGER, Andrew, Pvt, Col Wm Lillard, Capt Robert McCalpin, E TN Inf
ESRY, William, Pvt, Col S Copeland, Capt Wm Douglass, Inf
ESSARY, William, Cpl, Col A Loury, Capt Arahel Rains, Inf
ESSMAN, John, Pvt, Col Ewen Allison, Capt Jonas Loughmiller, Mil; joined from Capt Griffin Co
ESSMAN, John, Pvt, Col S Bunch, Capt John Griffin, E TN Drafted Mil
ESTEEL, Isaac, Pvt, Col Thomas Benton, Capt George Caperton, Vol Inf; Joel Bean substitute
ESTEIN, Buker (Burk), Pvt, Maj Russell, Capt John Cowan, Vol Mtd Gunmen
ESTEN, James W, Pvt, Maj Russell, Capt John Cowan, Vol Mtd Gunmen
ESTEP, James, Pvt, Col R C Napier, Capt Ed Neblett, Mil Inf
ESTER, John, Pvt, Col Alex Loury, Capt John Looney, 2nd Regt W TN Mil
ESTES, Andrew, Pvt, Regt Commander omitted, Capt James Cowan, Mtd Inf; substitute for Isaac Burke
ESTES, Benj, Pvt, Col S Copeland, Capt Robert Steele, Mil Inf
ESTES, Canady, Pvt, Maj Wm Woodfolk, Co Commander omitted, Inf; transferred from Capt Nail's Co
ESTES, Canna, Pvt, Maj Woodfolk, Capt Dudney & Capt Sutton, Inf; deserted 9-28-1814
ESTES, Edward, Pvt, Col William Higgins, Capt Adam Dale, Mtd Gunmen
ESTES, Gallant, Pvt, Col Wm Higgins, Capt Adam Dale, Mtd Gunmen
ESTES, George W, Pvt, Col Wm Lillard, Capt Adam Dale, Mtd Gunmen
ESTES, James, Pvt, Col Wm Higgins, Capt Adam Dale, Mtd Gunmen
ESTES, John H, Pvt, Brig Gen Roberts, Capt Benj Reynolds, Mtd Rangers
ESTES, John H, Pvt, Col Thomas Benton, Capt Robert Reynolds, Vol Inf
ESTES, John, Pvt, Col Wm Higgins, Capt Adam Dale, Mtd Gunmen; wounded & absent
ESTES, John, Rank omitted, Regt Commander omitted, Capt James Cowan, Mtd Inf
ESTES, Robert, Pvt, Col Wm Metcalf, Capt Bird Hurt, Mil

- 185

## Enlisted Men, War of 1812

ESTES, Willis, Pvt, Col Sam Bayless, Capt Joe Goodson, E TN Mil — Inf

ESTESS, Elijah, Pvt, Col Robert Dyer, Capt Joe Williams, Vol Mtd Gunmen

ESTESS, John, Dmr, Col C Bayless, Capt Sol Hendrix, E TN Mil

ESTHERLY, Conrad, Pvt, Col Ewen Allison, Co Commander omitted, E TN Drafted Mil; furnished John Jenoe as substitute

ESTHERLY, Philip, Pvt, Col Ewen Allison, Capt Wm Wilson, E TN Drafted Mil; furnished Francis Jone as Sub

ESTHIL, James, Pvt, Regt Commander omitted, Capt Archibald McKenney, Cav

ESTHILL, Isaac, Pvt, Regt Commander omitted, Capt James Cowan, Mtd Inf

ESTIS, Andrew, Pvt, Maj Russell, Capt Cowan, Vol Mtd Gunmen

ESTIS, Ansen L, Pvt, Col Bunch, Capt Mann, E TN Vol Mtd Inf

ESTIS, Floyd, Cpl, Col S Bunch, Capt Jones Griffin, Branch Srvce omitted

ESTIS, William P, Pvt, Col Raulston, Capt Wort, Inf

ESTUS, Isaac, Pvt, Col Benton, Capt Caperton, Inf

ESVIN, Joe, Dmr, Col Allison, Capt Everett, E TN Mil; promoted to Drm Maj

ETHERAGE, Mathew, Pvt, Col Raulston, Capt Neale, Inf

ETHEREDGE, John, Pvt, Col Napier, Capt McMurray, Mil Inf

ETHERIDGE, Aaron, Pvt, Regt Commander omitted, Capt Larkin Ferrell, Inf

ETHERIDGE, Acries, Pvt, Col Dyer, Capt Williams, Vol Mtd Gunmen

ETHERIDGE, David T, Pvt, Col Dyer, Capt White, Vol Mtd Gunmen

ETHERIDGE, David, Sgt, Col Dyer, Capt White, Vol Mtd Gunmen

ETHERIDGE, George, Pvt, Col Hall, Capt Bledsoe, Vol Inf

ETHERIDGE, Jared, Pvt, Col Bradley, Capt Bledsoe, Riflemen

ETHERIDGE, Jerard, Pvt, Col Hall, Capt Bledsoe, Vol Inf

ETHERIDGE, Jeremiah, Pvt, Col Dyer, Capt Williams, Vol Mtd Gunmen

ETHERIDGE, John, Pvt, Col Copeland, Capt Tait, Inf

ETHERIDGE, Peter, Pvt, Col Copeland, Capt Tait, Inf

ETHERTON, Micajah, Pvt, Col Bayless, Capt Jones, E TN Drafted Mil

ETHRIDGE, John, Pvt, no other information

ETTER, John, Pvt, Col Wm Lillard, Capt Robert McCalpin, E TN Inf

ETTER, Samuel, Pvt, Col Wm Johnson, Capt Tunnell, E TN Mil

EUBANKS, John, Pvt, Col John K Winn, Capt Wm McCall, Inf

EUBANKS, Moten (Mote), Pvt, Col Alexander Loury, Capt George Sarver, Inf

EUDALEY, Isaac, Pvt, Col A Cheatham, Capt William Smith, Inf; discharged for want of arms

EUDALY, James, Pvt, Col A Cheatham, Capt Wm Smith, Inf; discharged for want of arms

EVANS, Allen, Pvt, Col Thomas Williamson, Capt John Hutchinson, Vol Mtd Gunmen

EVANS, Andrew, Pvt, Col Robert Steele, Capt James Randals, Inf

EVANS, Andrew, Pvt, Col S Bunch, Capt John English, E TN Drafted Mil; deserted 3-4-1814

EVANS, Andrew, Pvt, Col Thomas H Benton, Capt George Gibbs, Vol Inf

EVANS, Andrew, Pvt, Col Wm Pillow, Capt John H Anderson, Vol Inf

EVANS, Andrew, Pvt, Regt Commander omitted, Capt Thos Sharpe, 2nd Regt Inf; also under Capt Wm Lillard

EVANS, Archibald, Pvt, Col S Bunch, Capt John Houk, E TN Mil; discharged for inability

EVANS, Archibald, Pvt, Col Samuel Bunch, Capt Solomon Dobkin, E TN Drafted Mil; deserted 4-1814

EVANS, Bird, 1 Cpl, Gen Andrew Jackson, Capt David Dedrick, Arty; killed at Battle of Entilope 6-24-1814

EVANS, Cornelius, Pvt, Col James Raulston, Capt Wm Hamilton, Inf; also served under Maj Gen William Carroll

EVANS, Cornelius, Pvt, Col Wm Lillard, Capt Wm Hamilton, E TN Vol Inf

EVANS, Daniel, Pvt, Col Samuel Bayless, Capt James Churchman, E TN Mil; d 3-28-1815

EVANS, Daniel, Pvt, Col Wm Johnson, Capt Elihu Millikin, 3rd Regt E TN Mil; transferred to Capt Churchman Co

EVANS, David, Cpl, Col Philip Pipkin, Capt John Robertson, Mil Inf

EVANS, David, Pvt, Col R C Napier, Co Commander omitted, Mil Inf

EVANS, David, Pvt, Col Samuel Bayless, Co Commander omitted, E TN Mil

EVANS, Dennis, Pvt, Col Wm Lillard, Capt William Hamilton, E TN Vol Inf

EVANS, Elias, Pvt, Col Samuel Bunch, Capt John English, E TN Drafted Mil; deserted 3-4-1814

EVANS, Ephram, Pvt, Lt Col Hammond, Capt James Tubb, Inf

EVANS, Evan, Pvt, Col John K Winn, Capt James Holleman, Inf

EVANS, Henry, Pvt, Col Samuel Bayless, Co Commander omitted, E TN Mil

EVANS, Henry, Pvt, Col Wm Lillard, Capt Thos Sharpe, 2nd Regt Inf

EVANS, Isham, Pvt, Col A Cheatham, Capt Wm Johnson, Inf; d 4-5-1814

EVANS, James C, Pvt, Col S Bayless, Capt Joseph Hale, E TN Mil

EVANS, James, Cpl, Col Edwin E Booth, Capt Slatton, E TN Mil

EVANS, James, Cpl, Col Robert Dyer, Capt Bethel Allen, Vol Mtd Gunmen

EVANS, James, Pvt, Col Wm Lillard, Capt Wm Gillenwater, E TN Drafted Mil

EVANS, James, Pvt, Col Wm Y Higgins, Capt Adam Dale, Mtd Gunmen

EVANS, James, Pvt, Gen Andrew Jackson, Capt Nathan Davis, Inf
EVANS, John jr, Pvt, Col S Bunch, Capt John English, E TN Drafted Mil
EVANS, John, Pvt, Col Cheatham, Maj Jackson, Capt Creel, Inf
EVANS, John, Pvt, Col Edward Bradley, Capt John Kennedy, Riflemen
EVANS, John, Pvt, Col Perkins, Capt Quarrells, Mtd Inf
EVANS, John, Pvt, Col Philip Pipkin, Capt David Smith, Inf
EVANS, John, Pvt, Col Robert Dyer, Capt Bethel Allen, Vol Mtd Gunmen
EVANS, John, Pvt, Col Robert Dyer, Capt Thomas Jones, Vol Mtd Gunmen; d 2-15-1815
EVANS, John, Pvt, Col S Bunch, Capt George McPherson, E TN Mil
EVANS, John, Pvt, Col S Bunch, Capt John English, E TN Drafted Mil
EVANS, John, Pvt, Col S Bunch, Capt Moses, E TN Drafted Mil; transferred to Capt John English
EVANS, John, Pvt, Regt Commander omitted, Lt James Berry, Mtd Riflemen
EVANS, Jonathan, Pvt, Col Allison, Capt Allen, E TN Mil
EVANS, Joseph, Pvt, Col Thomas Benton, Capt James McFerrin, Vol Inf; transferred to Renshaw's Co
EVANS, Joshua, Pvt, Col William Hall, Capt John Kennedy, Vol Inf
EVANS, Lewis, Pvt, Maj Gen Carroll, Capt Ellis, Inf; promoted to Cpl
EVANS, Louren, Pvt, Col A Cheatham, Capt Charles Johnson, Inf
EVANS, Nathan, Cpl, Col William Hall, Capt John Kennedy, Vol Inf
EVANS, Nathan, Pvt, Col Edward Bradley, Capt John Kennedy, Riflemen
EVANS, Patrick, Pvt, Col Edward Bradley, Capt John Kennedy, Riflemen
EVANS, Patrick, Pvt, Col Wm Hall, Capt John Kennedy, Vol Inf
EVANS, Patrick, Sgt, Col Stephen Copeland, Capt William Evans, Mil Inf
EVANS, Reuben, Pvt, Col James Raulston, Capt Carroll, Capt Daniel Newman, Inf
EVANS, Reuben, Pvt, Col Thomas McCrory, Capt Anthony Metcalf, Mil Inf
EVANS, Richard, Pvt, Gen Andrew Jackson, Capt Nathan Davis, Inf
EVANS, Robert, 3 Sgt, Col Samuel Wear, Capt Joseph Calloway, Mtd Inf
EVANS, Robert, Pvt, Col Alexander Loury, Capt Leroy Hammonds, Capt Thomas Delaney, Inf
EVANS, Robert, Pvt, Col Ewen Allison, Capt Adam Winsell, E TN Drafted Mil; transferred to Capt Howell's Co
EVANS, Robert, Pvt, Col Leroy Hammonds, Capt Jas Tubbs, Inf
EVANS, Robert, Pvt, Col Leroy Hammonds, Capt Thomas Delaney, Inf
EVANS, Robert, Pvt, Col Samuel Bunch, Capt Joseph Duncan, E TN Drafted Mil; transferred from Capt Howell's Co
EVANS, Robert, Pvt, Col Samuel Bunch, Lt John Harris, E TN Mil
EVANS, Samuel, Cpl, Col S Copeland, Capt Wm Evans, Mil Inf
EVANS, Samuel, Pvt, Col Samuel Wear, Capt Joseph Calloway, Mtd Inf
EVANS, Thomas, Pvt, Col John Wynne, Capt John Porter, Inf
EVANS, Thomas, Pvt, Col S Copeland, Capt Solomon George, Inf
EVANS, Thomas, Pvt, Col Samuel Bunch, Capt John Houk, E TN Mil; joined from Capt Dobkins Co
EVANS, Thomas, Pvt, Col Samuel Bunch, Capt Solomon Dobkins, E TN Drafted Mil; deserted 3-4-1814
EVANS, Thomas, Pvt, Col William Pillow, Capt George Caperton, Inf
EVANS, William (Will), Cpl, Col Thomas Benton, Capt James McEwen, Vol Inf
EVANS, William D, Cpl, Col Wm Pillow, Capt John Anderson, Vol Inf
EVANS, William R, Pvt, Col John Brown, Capt Wm White, E TN Mil Inf
EVANS, William, Pvt, Col John Coffee, Capt Michael Molton, Cav
EVANS, William, Pvt, Col Newton Cannon, Capt Ota Cantrell, W TN Mtd Inf
EVANS, William, Pvt, Col R H Dyer, Capt Bethel Allen, Vol Mtd Gunmen
EVANS, William, Pvt, Col Samuel Bunch, Capt John Houk, E TN Mil; joined from Capt Dobkins Co
EVANS, William, Pvt, Col Samuel Bunch, Capt Solomon Dobkins, E TN Mil Drafted; deserted 3-4-1814
EVANS, William, Pvt, Col Samuel Wear, Capt John Stephens, E TN Vol Inf
EVANS, William, Pvt, Col Samuel Wear, Capt Joseph Calloway, Mtd Inf
EVANS, William, Pvt, Regt Commander omitted, Capt George Smith, Spies
EVANS, Wm, Pvt, Col James Raulston, Capt Henry Hamilton, Inf; also under Maj Gen Wm Carroll
EVANS, Wm, Pvt, Col John Coffee, Capt Frederick Stump, Cav
EVANS (EVENS), George, Pvt, Col Robert Dyer, Capt Williams, Vol Mtd Gunmen
EVENS, John, Pvt, Col William Metcalf, Capt Thomas Marks, Mil Inf
EVENS, William, Pvt, Col William Metcalf, Capt Thomas Marks, Mil Inf
EVERET, Laurence, Pvt, Col A Cheatham, Capt George Chapman, Inf
EVERETT, Coleman, Pvt, Maj John Childs, Capt James Cummings, E TN Vol Mtd Inf
EVERETT, Isaac, Pvt, Col Ewen Allison, Capt Jonas Loughmiller, Mil
EVERETT, Parker, Pvt, Col John Brown, Capt James McKamey, E TN Mtd Gunmen
EVERETT, Sylvaners (Sylvanus), Pvt, Col John Brown, Capt James McKamy, E TN Mtd Gunmen
EVERETT, Thomas, Pvt, Maj John Childs, Capt Charles Conway, E TN Mtd Gunmen; Regt Co Anderson

## Enlisted Men, War of 1812

EVERETT, Wm, Pvt, Col Samuel Bunch, Capt Francis Berry, E TN Mil; transferred to Capt Berry's Co, appointed Sgt

EVERETT, Wm, Pvt, Col Samuel Wear, Capt John Stephens, E TN Vol Inf

EVERETT, Wm, Pvt, Maj John Childs, Capt Charles Conway, E TN Mtd Gunmen; Regimental Co - Anderson

EVERHART, Chrisley, Pvt, Col Samuel Bunch, Capt Jones Griffin, E TN Drafted Mil

EVERHART, Jacob, Pvt, Col Wm Lillard, Capt George Argenbright, E TN Vol Riflemen

EVERHEART, Christopher, Pvt, Col Ewen Allison, Capt Jonas Loughmiller, Mil; joined by transfer from Capt Griffin's Co

EVERITE, John, Pvt, Col A Cheatham, Capt Charles Johnson, Inf

EVERLY, George, Dmr, Lt Col Leroy Hammonds & Lt Col A Loury, Capt Thomas Wells, Inf

EVERS, James, Pvt, Regt Commander omitted, Capt William Henderson, Spies

EVES, Jonathan, Pvt, Col S Copeland, Capt James Tait, Inf

EVES, Mark, Pvt, Col William Johnson, Capt James Stewart, E TN Mil

EVETS, James, Pvt, Col James Raulston, Capt Elijah Haynie, Inf

EVETS, Joseph G, Pvt, Col John Alcorn, Capt John Byrn, Cav; transferred to Capt Evan's Co of Spies

EVETTS, George, Cpl, Col James Raulston, Capt Elijah Haynie, Inf

EVETTS, Moses, 2 Cpl, Col Thomas McCrory, Capt Thomas Gordon, Inf

EVILLS, Joseph G, Sgt, Regt Commander omitted, Capt Robert Evans, Mtd Co of Spies

EVINS, Andrew, Pvt, Col Wm Johnson, Capt Benj Powell, E TN Mil; d 3-1-1815

EVINS, Bird, Pvt, Maj Gen Andrew Jackson, Capt William Carroll, Vol Inf

EVINS, Charles, Pvt, Col Samuel Bayless, Capt Solomon Hendricks, E TN Mil

EVINS, George, Pvt, Lt Col Richard Napier, Co Commander omitted, Inf

EVINS, Harris, Pvt, Col John Brown, Capt John Childs, E TN Vol Mtd Inf

EVINS, James, Pvt, Col John Brown, Capt John Childs, E TN Vol Mtd Gunmen

EVINS, John, Pvt, Col Samuel Bunch, Capt Isaac Williams, E TN Mil

EVINS, Joseph, Pvt, Regt Commander omitted, Capt Larkin Ferrell, Inf

EVINS, Mark, Pvt, Col William Johnson, Capt James Stewart, E TN Drafted Mil

EVINS, Richard, Pvt, Capt Isaac Williams, Col Samuel Bunch, E TN Mil

EVINS, Richard, Pvt, Col Samuel Bunch, Capt Isaac Williams, E TN Mil

EWELL, William, Pvt, Col Thomas Williamson, Capt Robert Moore, Branch Srvce omitted; d 1-15-1815

EWEN, William, Pvt, Col Wm Pillow, Capt Joseph Mason, Vol Inf

EWIN, Alexander, Cpl, Col Samuel Wear, Capt James Tedford, E TN Vol Inf

EWIN, Alexander, Pvt, Col Newton Cannon, Capt Andrew Patteson, Mtd Riflemen

EWIN, David, Pvt, Col Wm Pillow, Capt Joseph Mason, Vol Inf

EWIN, Joseph, Pvt, Col Samuel Bunch, Capt Wm Jobe, E TN Vol Mtd Inf

EWIN, Mathew, Pvt, Col Edward Bradley, Capt Wm Lauderdale, Vol Inf

EWIN, Robert, 6 Cpl, Col John Cocke, Capt John Dalton, Inf

EWIN, Samuel, Pvt, Col S Copeland, Capt John Biles, Inf

EWING, Andrew, Pvt, no other information

EWING, Edley, Pvt, Col N T Perkins, Capt Philip Pipkin, Mtd Riflemen; AWOL

EWING, Henry, Pvt, Maj John Childs, Capt John Stephens, E TN Vol Mtd Inf

EWING, James, Pvt, Col John Alcorn, Capt Thomas Bradley, Vol Cav

EWING, James, Pvt, Col N T Perkins, Capt Mathew Patterson, Mtd Vol

EWING, Lee, Pvt, Regt Commander omitted, Capt David Smith, Cav Vol

EXUM, Lewis, Pvt, Col William Hall, Capt John Moore, Vol Inf

EZALL, Hensel, Pvt, Col John Cocke, Capt John Dalton, Inf; d 1-21-1815

EZALL, Belum, Pvt, Col John Cocke, Capt John Dalton, Inf

EZELL, Byham (Berum), 3 Sgt, Col Phillip Pipkin, Capt Peter Searcy, Mil Inf

EZELL, Harrison, Pvt, Col Wm Hall, Capt John Moore, Vol Inf

EZELL, Hasel, Pvt, Col Wm Hall, Capt John Moore, Vol Inf

EZELL, Parham, 3 Sgt, Col Philip Pipkin, Capt Peter Searcy, 1st Regt TN Mil

EZELL, Parham, Pvt, Regt Commander omitted, Capt Gray, Inf

EZELL, Thomas, Pvt, Regt Commander omitted, Maj Robert Cooper, Mtd Riflemen

EZELL, William, Pvt, Col William Metcalf, Capt William Mullin, Mil Inf

EZELL, Wm, Pvt, Regt Commander omitted, Capt Elijah Rushing, Det of Inf

EZRA, James, 3 Sgt, Col Wm Metcalf, Capt John Cunningham, Mil Inf; promoted from Pvt

EZZEL, Timothy, Pvt, Col Wm Metcalf, Capt Obadiah Walker, Mil Inf

FABUSH, John, Pvt, Regt Commander omitted, Capt Wyatt Fussel, Det of Inf

FAGAN, Robert, Cpl, Col Williamson, Capt Pace, Lt Nealy, Vol Mtd Gunmen

FAILIN (FELING), Evans, Pvt, Col Johnson, Capt Millikin, 3rd Regt E TN Mil

FAIN, Nicholas M, Pvt, Col Perkins, Capt Patterson, Mtd Vol

FAIN, Nicholas, Pvt, Regt Commander omitted, Capt James Terrill, Cav

## Enlisted Men, War of 1812

FAIN, Samuel, Pvt, Col Allison, Capt McCray, E TN Mil
FAIN, Thomas, Pvt, Col Allison, Capt Hampton, Mil
FAINE, Moore, Pvt, Regt Commander omitted, Capt James Terrill, Cav
FAIR, Wm, Pvt, Maj Gen Carroll, Col Raulston, Capt Robinson, Inf
FAIR (FAIN), Sam'l, 4 Cpl, Col Metcalf, Capt Marks, Mil Inf
FAIR (FAIRE), George, Pvt, Col Cannon, Capt Williams, Mtd Riflemen
FAIR (FARR), Sam'l, Pvt, Col Booth, Capt Thompson, Mil; d 3-3-1815
FAIRLESS, Robert, Sgt, Lt Col A Cheatham, Capt Meredith Walker, Inf
FAITH, John T?, Pvt, Lt Col Hammonds & Lowry, Capt Wells, Inf
FAKAWAY (FUQUAY), Nathaniel, Pvt, Col Hall, Capt Newton, Inf
FAKEWAY (FUQUAY), Thomas, Pvt, Col Hall, Capt Nowlin, Inf
FANCHER, Job, Pvt, Col Pipkin, Capt Smith, Mil Inf
FANN, Elijah, Pvt, Col Cannon, Capt Brandon, Mtd Riflemen; furloughed 11-1813 since dead
FANN, Solomon, Pvt, Col Bayless, Capt Hale, E TN Mil
FANNING, George, Pvt, Maj Gen Jackson, Capt Williamson? Steele, Vol Mtd Gunmen
FANNING, Jehu, Pvt, Col Benton, Capt Caperton, Inf
FANNING, Jesse, Pvt, Col Benton, Capt Caperton, Vol Inf
FANNING, Robert, Pvt, Col Loury, Capt Looney, 2nd Regt W TN Mil; sick absent, d 4-10-1815
FANSHAW, John, Pvt, Col S Bunch, Capt John Houk, E TN Mil
FANSHEAR, Richard, Pvt, Col Lillard, Capt Lillard, E TN Vol Inf
FANSHER, Benj, Pvt, Col S Bunch, Capt John Houk, E TN Mil
FANSHER, David, Pvt, Col Bradley, Capt Kennedy, Riflemen; d 12-24-1813
FANSHER, John, Pvt, Col S Bunch, Capt John Houk, E TN Mil; discharged for inability
FANSHER, James, Pvt, Col S Bunch, Capt John Houk, E TN Mil
FANSHER, John, Pvt, Col Brown, Capt Lewin, E TN Vol Mtd Inf
FANSHER, John, Pvt, Col S Bunch, Capt John Houk, E TN Mil
FANSHER, Richard, Pvt, Col Bunch, Capt Jobe, E TN Vol Mtd Inf
FANSHER, Westly, Pvt, Col Bradley, Capt Kennedy, Riflemen
FANSHIER, Alexander, Pvt, Regt Commander omitted, Capt John Miller, Spies
FANSHIER, James, Pvt, Regt Commander omitted, Capt John Miller, Spies
FANSHIERS, Alexander, Pvt, Regt Commander omitted, Capt John Miller, Spies
FAR, James, Pvt, Col Winn, Capt McCall, Inf
FARER, Clement, Pvt, Col T McCrory, Capt Isaac Patton, Mil Inf
FARES, George, Pvt, Col Cannon, Capt Jones, Mtd Riflemen

FARES, John, Pvt, Col Cannon, Capt Jones, Mtd Riflemen
FARGUSON, Elias, Cpl, Col John Brown, Capt James Preston, Branch Srvce omitted; reduced to ranks
FARGUSON, Thomas, Ffr, Col Loury, Lt Col Hammond, Capt Wells, Inf
FARGUSSON, Joel, Pvt, Col Branch, Capt Duncan, E TN Drafted Mil; joined from Capt Yarnell's Co
FARGUSSON, Robert, Pvt, Col Bunch, Capt Duncan, E TN Drafted Mil; joined from Capt Yarnell's Co
FARIS, James, Pvt, Col Dyer, Col Russell, Capt Russell, Vol Mtd Gunmen
FARIS, John, Pvt, Col Dyer, Maj Russell, Capt Russell, Vol Mtd Gunmen
FARIS, Major, Sgt, Col Loury & Hammonds, Capt Rains, Inf
FARLEY, John, Pvt, Col Benton, Capt Renshaw, Vol Inf; deserter
FARMER, Abraham, Pvt, Col Allison, Capt Wilson, E TN Drafted Mil
FARMER, Benj, Pvt, Col Steele, Capt Campbell, Mil Inf
FARMER, Conrad, Pvt, Lt Col Hammond, Capt Craig, Inf
FARMER, David, Pvt, Col Wear, Capt Chiles, E TN Vol Inf
FARMER, Enos, Pvt, Lt Col Hammond, Capt Craig, Inf
FARMER, Frederick, Cpl, Col Brown, Capt White, E TN Vol Inf Mtd; promoted from Pvt
FARMER, George, Pvt, Maj Woodfolk, Capt Turner, Inf
FARMER, George, Pvt, Regt Commander omitted, Capt Gray, Inf
FARMER, James A, Sgt, Col Steele, Capt Campbell, W TN Mil Inf
FARMER, James, Pvt, Col Johnson, Capt Powell, E TN Mil; d 2-21-1815
FARMER, John, Cpl, Col Booth, Capt Thompson, Mil
FARMER, John, Pvt, Col Higgins, Capt Dale, Mtd Gunmen
FARMER, John, Pvt, Col William Johnson, Capt Christopher Cook, E TN Mil
FARMER, Josiah, Pvt, Col Alexander Loury, Capt Gabriel Martin, Inf
FARMER, Lemuel, Pvt, Col John K Wynne, Capt John Spinks, Inf
FARMER, Leonard, Pvt, Col Philip Pipkin, Capt John Strother, Mil
FARMER, Luke, Pvt, Col S Bunch, Capt Andrew Breden, E TN Mil
FARMER, Nathan, Capt, Regt Commander omitted, Capt Nathan Farmer, Mtd Riflemen
FARMER, Nathan, Pvt, Maj Wm Woodfolk, Capt John Sutton & Capt Dudney, Inf
FARMER, Samuel, Pvt, Col J Alcorn, Capt Thomas Bradley, Vol Cav
FARMER, Samuel, Pvt, Col James Raulston, Capt Charles Wade, Inf
FARMER, Samuel, Pvt, Col Robert Steele, Capt Robert Campbell, Mil Inf
FARMER, Samuel, Pvt, Col Thomas Williamson, Capt Cook & Capt John Crane, Vol Mtd Gunmen
FARMER, Samuel, Pvt, Lt Col A Cheatham, Capt Meredith Walker, Inf
FARMER, Samuel, Pvt, Regt Commander omitted, Capt

## Enlisted Men, War of 1812

Nathan (Jonathan?) Farmer, Mtd Riflemen

FARMER, Stephen, Sgt, Lt Col John Edmonson, Co Commander omitted, Inf

FARMER, Thomas, 1 Cpl, Regt Commander omitted, Capt Nathan Farmer, Mtd Riflemen

FARMER, Thomas, Cpl, Col Edwin Booth, Capt Samuel Thompson, Mil

FARMER, Thomas, Pvt, Col Samuel Bunch, Capt Joseph Duncan, E TN Drafted Mil

FARMER, Thomas, Pvt, Maj John Childs, Capt Charles Conway, E TN Vol Mtd Inf

FARMER, Thomas, Rank omitted, Maj John Childs, Capt Charles Conway, E TN Mtd Gunmen; Regimental Co Anderson

FARMER, Thos, Cpl, Regt Commander omitted, Capt Nathan Farmer, Mtd Riflemen

FARMER, William, Pvt, Col Robert Steele, Capt Samuel Maxwell, Mil Inf

FARMER, William, Pvt, Col Samuel Bunch, Capt Joseph Duncan, E TN Drafted Mil

FARMER, William, Pvt, Maj John Childs, Capt John Stephens, E TN Vol Mtd Inf

FARMERS, Elijah, Pvt, Col Wm Ramsey, Capt David McKamy, E TN Drafted Mil

FARMWALT, Jacob W, Cpl, Col Edwin Booth, Capt Lewis, E TN Mil

FARNES, Jacob, Pvt, Col Wm Lillard, Capt Robert McCalpin, E TN Mil Inf

FARNEY, John, Sgt, Col Thomas McCrory, Capt William Dooley, Inf

FARNSBOROUGH, Robert, Pvt, Col John Cocke, Capt Bird Nance, Inf

FARNSWORTH, David, Pvt, Col Samuel Bayless, Capt Joseph Hale, E TN Mil

FARR, David D, Pvt, Col Robert H Dyer, Capt Glen Owen, TN Vol Mtd Gunmen

FARR, James, Sgt, Col Wm Pillow, Capt James McFerrin, Inf

FARR, John, 4 Sgt, Col Thomas Benton, Capt James McFerrin, Vol Inf

FARR, John, Sgt, Col Thomas Benton, Capt James McFerrin, Vol Inf

FARR, Samuel, Pvt, Col John Alcorn, Capt Baskerville, Vol Inf

FARR, Samuel, Pvt, Lt Col Leroy Hammonds, Capt Joseph Duncan, E TN Drafted Mil

FARR, Samuel, Pvt, Regt Commander omitted, Capt Archibald McKinney, Cav

FARR, Walter, Cpl, Col James Raulston, Capt Mathew Neal, Inf

FARRAR, Absolum, Pvt, Col Thomas Benton, Capt James McEwen, Vol Inf

FARRAR, John, Pvt, Col Wm Johnson, Capt Andrew Lawson, E TN Drafted Mil; never appeared

FARRAS, Wm, Pvt, Col A Loury, Capt James Kincaid, Inf

FARRATT, Abraham, Pvt, Col Wm Pillow, Capt C E McEwen, Vol Inf

FARRER, Abraham, Pvt, Col Thomas Benton, Capt Jas McEwen, Vol Inf

FARRER, William, Pvt, Col Thomas Williamson, Capt John Dobbins & Capt John Doak, Vol Mtd Gunmen

FARRES, John, Pvt, Maj Gen Carroll, Capt Ellis, Inf

FARRES, Robert, Pvt, Maj Gen Carroll, Capt Ellis, Inf

FARRIER, Needham, Pvt, Col Philip Pipkin, Capt John Strother, Mil

FARRIS, Davison, Pvt, Col S Copeland, Capt James Tait, Inf

FARRIS, Edward, Pvt, Col William Hall, Capt John Kennedy, Vol Inf

FARRIS, Edward, Pvt, Regt Commander omitted, Capt James Haggard, Mtd Gunmen

FARRIS, George, Pvt, Col A Loury & Col Leroy Hammonds, Capt Arahel Rains, Inf

FARRIS, James, Pvt, Col John Brown, Capt James Preston, E TN Mil Inf

FARRIS, John, Pvt, Col Phillip Pipkin, Capt Henry Newlin, Mil Inf

FARRIS, John, Pvt, Col William Hall, Capt John Kennedy, Vol Inf

FARRIS, John, Pvt, Col William Johnson, Capt Joseph Kirk, Mil

FARRIS, John, Pvt, Col Wm Hall, Capt John Kennedy, Vol Inf

FARRIS, Nathan, Pvt, Col S Copeland, Capt James Tait, Inf

FARRIS, Samuel B, Pvt, Col Alexander Loury, Capt John Looney, W TN Mil

FARRIS, Samuel, Pvt, Col Leroy Hammonds, Col Alexander Loury, Capt Thomas Delaney, Inf; d 12-6-1814

FARRIS, Thomas, Pvt, Maj Wm Russell, Capt William Chism, Vol Mtd Gunmen

FARRIS, Wm, Pvt, Col S Copeland, Capt George, Inf

FARRISTER, George, Pvt, Col T McCrory, Capt A Metcalf, Mil Inf

FARRNWALT, Jacob W, Cpl, Col Samuel Wear, Capt Rufus Morgan, E TN Vol Inf; promoted from Pvt

FARROM (FARRER), William, Pvt, Col T Williamson, Capt John Doak & Capt John Dobbins, Vol Mtd Gunmen

FARTHING, Abner, Pvt, Col John Cocke, Capt John Weakley, Inf

FARTHING, Solomon, Pvt, Col John Cocke, Capt George Barnes, Inf

FAUBUSH, Andrew, Pvt, Col Samuel Bayless, Capt Jonathan Waddell, E TN Mil

FAUCETT, Richard, Pvt, Col Philip Pipkin, Capt Peter Searcy, Mil Inf

FAUGHT, Isham, Pvt, Gen Thomas Johnson, Capt Daniel Oban, 36 Inf

FAUGHT, John, Pvt, Gen Thomas Johnson, Capt Daniel Oban, 36th Inf

FAUGHT, Moses, Pvt, Gen Thomas Johnson, Capt Daniel Oban, 36th Inf

FAUGHT, William, Pvt, Gen Thomas Johnson, Capt Daniel Oban, 36th Inf

FAULKENBERRY, David, Pvt, Col Thomas Benton, Capt Isaiah Renshaw, Vol Inf

FAUX, Levi, 2 Sgt, Col Thomas Benton, Capt Harry L Douglass, Vol Inf

FAWBASH, John, Drm Maj, Col Wm Johnson, Co Com-

## Enlisted Men, War of 1812

mander omitted, 3rd Regt E TN Mil

FAWBASH, Wm, Pvt, Col Wm Johnson, Capt Joseph Hunter, E TN Mil; substitute for John Fletcher

FEARIS, Nimrod, Pvt, Maj Gen Andrew Jackson, Capt James Reid, Inf

FEARLESS, James, Pvt, Col James Raulston, Capt Henry Hamilton, Inf; also served Maj Gen Wm Carroll, d 12-25-1814

FEARN, Robert, Pvt, Col John Alcorn, Capt John J Winston, Mtd Riflemen

FEARN, Thomas, Sgt, Col Wm Higgins, Co Commander omitted, 2nd Regt TN Mtd Vol

FEARRIS, Levi, Sgt, Col S Copeland, Capt James Tait, Inf

FEARS, Edward, Pvt, Col John K Wynne, Capt John Porter, Inf

FEARS, Edward, Pvt, Lt Col Hammonds, Capt Thomas Delaney, Inf; also under Col A Loury

FEARS, Jacob, Pvt, Col Wm Lillard, Capt Thomas Sharpe, 2nd Regt Inf

FEARS, James, Pvt, Col Wm Lillard, Capt Thomas Sharpe, 2nd Regt Inf

FEARS, Saward, Pvt, Col Robert Steele, Capt James Bennett, Mil Inf

FEATHERSTON, Burwell, Pvt, Col John Coffee, Capt A McKeen, Cav

FEATHERSTON, Dan'l, Pvt, Col James Raulston, Capt Elijah Haynie, Inf; d 2-2-1815

FEATHERSTONE, Edward, 3 Sgt, Col Wm Hall, Capt W L Alexander, Vol Inf

FEATHERSTONE, Edward, Pvt, Col T Williamson, Capt Anthony N Metcalf, Vol Mtd Gunmen

FEATHERSTONE, Edward, Sgt, Col Edward Bradley, Capt Wm Lauderdale, Vol Inf

FEILDING, Jesse, Pvt, Col Samuel Bayless, Capt Branch Jones, E TN Drafted Mil; transferred to Capt Millikin's Co

FEILDS, Bennett, Pvt, Maj Gen Jackson, Capt Metcalf, Capt Jackson, Inf

FEKES, Elisha, Pvt, Col Alexander Loury, Capt Gabriel Martin, Inf; substitute for Lewis Fekes

FEKES, Simon, Pvt, Col Alexander Loury, Capt Gabriel Martin, Inf

FELBY, Wm, Pvt, Col John Williams, Capt Sam Bunch, Mtd Vol

FELING, Jesse, Pvt, Col Wm Johnson, Capt Elihu Milliken, 3rd Regt E TN Mil; transferred from Capt Churchman Co

FELING (FAILIN?), Evans, Pvt, Col Wm Johnson, Capt Elihu Milliken, 3rd Regt E TN Mil

FELKER, Wm, Pvt, Col Wm Johnston, Capt James R Rogers, E TN Drafted Mil

FELLER, Jacob, Pvt, Col Ewen Allison, Capt Thomas Wilson, E TN Drafted Mil

FELLER (FELLOWS?), Jacob G, Cpl, Col Samuel Bunch, Capt F Register, E TN Mil

FELPS, Elisha, Pvt, Col Philip Pipkin, Co Commander omitted, Mil

FELPS, Elisha, Pvt, Col Wm Metcalf, Capt Wm Mullins, Mil Inf

FELPS, Henry, Pvt, Col John Alcorn, Capt Bradley, Vol Cav

FELPS, Jacob, Pvt, Col A Cheatham, Capt Wm Smith, Inf

FELPS (FILPS), Michael, Pvt, Col Stephen Copeland, Capt James Tait, Inf

FELTNER, Jacob, Pvt, Lt Col John Edmondson, Co Commander omitted, Inf

FELTNER, William, Pvt, Col Ewen Allison, no other information

FELTS, Cader, Pvt, Col Thomas H Benton, Capt Wm Smith, Vol Inf

FELTS, Drury, Pvt, Col A Loury, Capt G Martin, Inf

FELTS, James, Cpl, Col John K Wynne, Capt Robert Braden, Inf

FELTS, Joseph, Pvt, Col John K Winn, Capt Robert Bradin, Inf

FELTS, William, Pvt, Col A Cheatham, Capt A Birdwell, Inf

FELTZ, Elisha, Pvt, Maj Gen A Jackson, Capt Wm Cree, Inf

FENCELET?, Frederick, Pvt, Col S Bunch, Capt George McPherson, E TN Mil; joined from Capt McCrory's Co

FENN, Abednigo, Pvt, Col James Raulston, Capt Mathew Neale, Inf

FENRELLER, Frederick, Pvt, Col Ewen Allison, Capt Thomas McCrory, E TN Mil; transferred to Capt McPherson's Co

FENSHER, John, Pvt, Col Wm Lillard, Capt Maloney, E TN Vol Inf

FENTRESS, Davis, Sgt, Col R C Napier, Co Commander omitted, Mil Inf

FENTRESS, Wm, 1 Cpl, Col John K Wynne, Capt Bayless Prince, Inf

FERAN, Wyly, Pvt, Col Samuel Bunch, Capt John Inman, Branch Srvce omitted

FERGASON, James, 3 Sgt, Col Wm Pillow, Capt Wm Moore, Inf

FERGERSON, Nelson, Pvt, Lt Col Hammond, Col Loury, Capt Delaney, Inf

FERGERSON, Thomas, Pvt, Col John Coffee, Co Commander omitted, Cav

FERGUSON, Alexander, Pay Master, Brig Gen Nathaniel Taylor, Col Wm Johnson, 3rd Regt E TN Mil

FERGUSON, Alexander, Pvt, Col Thomas Williamson, Capt Wm Metcalf, Vol Mtd Gunmen

FERGUSON, Alexander, Pvt, Col Wm Metcalf, Capt John Sutton, Mil Inf

FERGUSON, James C, Pvt, Col Wm Hall, Capt Brice Martin, Vol Inf

FERGUSON, James M, Pvt, Maj Gen Wm Carroll, Capt Lewis Dillahunty & Capt Daniel Bradford, Vol Inf

FERGUSON, James, 3 Sgt, Col Thomas H Benton, Capt Wm Moore, Vol Inf

FERGUSON, James, Pvt, Col Thomas H Benton, Capt Wm Moore, Vol Inf

FERGUSON, James, Sgt, Col Thomas H Benton, Capt Wm Moore, Branch Srvce omitted

FERGUSON, Joel, Pvt, Col S Bunch, Capt Dan'l Youree, E TN Mil; substitute for James Haskins

FERGUSON, John, Pvt, Lt Col A Cheatham, Co Commander omitted, 6th Brig of Mtd Inf

## Enlisted Men, War of 1812

FERGUSON, Larkin, Pvt, Col Lillard, Capt Hamilton, E TN Vol Inf
FERGUSON, Oley, Pvt, Col John Coffee, Capt Stump, Cav
FERGUSON, Robert, Cpl, Maj Gen Carroll, Col Metcalf, Capt Jackson, Inf
FERGUSON, Robert, Pvt, Capt Nathan Davis, Lt I Barrett, Inf
FERGUSON, William D, Pvt, Col Metcalf, Capt Sitton, Mil Inf
FERGUSON, Wm, Pvt, Col Raulston, Capt Haynie, Inf
FERLONG, Martin, Pvt, Col Hall, Capt Martin, Vol Inf
FERMIN, John, Pvt, Col Bunch, Capt Inman, E TN Vol Mtd Inf
FERN, David, Pvt, Col John Williams, Capt Sam Bunch, Mtd Vol
FERRELL, Benj, Pvt, Col Williamson, Capt Moore, Vol Mtd Gunmen
FERRELL, Clement, Pvt, Col Raulston, Capt Hamilton, Inf; also under Maj Gen Carroll
FERRELL, Leonard, Pvt, Col Bradley, Capt Moore, Vol Inf
FERRELL, Levi, Pvt, Col Burton, Capt Reynolds, Vol Inf; refused to march
FERRELL, Levi, Pvt, Col McCrory, Capt McKnight, Inf
FERRELL, Thomas, Cpl, Col Hall, Capt Moore, Vol Inf
FERRELL, Thomas, Sgt, Col Bradley, Capt Moore, Vol Inf
FERRELL, Wm, Pvt, Col McCrory, Capt Gordon, Inf
FERRELL, Wm, Pvt, Col Raulston, Capt Hamilton, Inf; also under Maj Gen Carroll
FERRELL, Wm, Pvt, Col Winn, Capt Carothers, W TN Inf
FERRELL, Wm, Pvt, Col Wynne, Capt Prince, Inf
FERRETT, Thomas, Pvt, Col Cocke, Capt Gray, Inf
FERRIER, George, Pvt, Col Dyer, Capt Ephraim Dickson, TN Vol Mtd Gunmen
FERRIL, David, Pvt, Col Wynne, Capt Porter, Inf
FERRIL, Larkin, Pvt, Col Raulston, Capt Cowan, Inf
FERRILL, Thomas, Pvt, Col Cocke, Capt Gray, Inf
FERRINGTON, John, Pvt, Col Pillow, Capt Williamson, Vol Inf; transferred
FERRIS, James, Pvt, Col Philip Pipkin, Capt Smith, Inf
FERRIS, William, Pvt, Col Lillard, Capt King, E TN Vol Inf
FERRIS (FARRIS), Wm, Pvt, Col Metcalf, Capt Collins, Mil Inf
FESTLER, Charles G, Pvt, Maj Gen Jackson, Capt Craine, Mtd Gunmen; wounded 1-22-1814
FETHERSTON, Henry, 1 Sgt, Col Metcalf, Capt Waller, Mil Inf; wounded 1-1 & d 1-9-1815
FETHERSTONE, Edward, Pvt, Col Winn, Capt McCall, Inf
FETNES, James, Pvt, Col Allison, Capt Loughmiller, Mil
FEW, John, Pvt, Maj Woodfolk, Capt Neale, Inf
FIELAND, Thomas W, Pvt, Col Coffee, Capt Ross, Mtd Gunmen
FIELD, John, Pvt, Col Metcalf, Capt Patterson, Mil Inf
FIELDER, John L, Pvt, Col N Cannon, Capt Martin, Mtd Gunmen; transferred to Capt Gordon's Spies
FIELDING, Wm, Pvt, Col Dyer, Capt White, Vol Mtd Gunmen; d 2-9-1815

FIELDS, David, Pvt, Col Allison, Capt Everett, E TN Mil; killed in battle at Topopece? 3-27-1814
FIELDS, David, Pvt, Col Bunch, Capt Houston, E TN Vol Mtd Inf; substitute for Ritchee Hutson
FIELDS, George D, Pvt, Col Winn, Capt Carothers, W TN Inf
FIELDS, George, Pvt, Lt Col Hammonds & Lowry, Capt Delaney, Inf
FIELDS, Henry, 4 Cpl, Col Perkins, Capt McMahon, Mtd Gunmen
FIELDS, Isaac, Waiter, Col Bayless, Capt Goodson, E TN Mil
FIELDS, James, Pvt, Col Booth, Capt Lewis, E TN Mil
FIELDS, James, Pvt, Maj Russell, Capt Hodges, Vol Mtd Gunmen
FIELDS, John L, Pvt, Col Coffee, Capt Sault, Inf
FIELDS, John, Cpl, Maj Gen Carroll, Col Metcalf, Capt Jackson, Inf
FIELDS, Moses, Pvt, Col Higgins, Capt Eldridge, Mtd Gunmen
FIELDS, Nathaniel, Pvt, Col N Cannon, Capt Martin, Mtd Gunmen
FIELDS, Nathaniel, Pvt, Col Napper, Capt McMurray, Mil Inf
FIELDS, Nathaniel, Pvt, Lt Col Hammond & Lowry, Capt Wells, Inf
FIELDS, Richard, Pvt, Col Pipkin, Capt Mebane, Mil Inf
FIELDS, Thomas, Pvt, Col Brown, Capt White, E TN Vol Mtd Inf
FIELDS, William, Pvt, Col Brown, Capt McKenny, E TN Mtd Gunmen
FIELDS, William, Pvt, Col Williamson, Capt Martin, Vol Mtd Gunmen
FIELDS, William, Pvt, Regt Commander omitted, Capt John Gordon, Mtd Spies; wounded at Battle of Thopea, d 4-20-1814
FIFE, William, Pvt, Col Lillard, Capt McChristian, E TN Vol Inf
FIFERSE, Wm, Pvt, Maj Gen A Jackson, Capt John Crane, Mtd Gunmen
FIKE, Josiah, Cpl, Col John Brown, Capt William D Neilson, E TN Vol Mil; promoted from Pvt
FIKE, Josiah, Pvt, Col Williamson, Capt Cook & Crane, Vol Mtd Gunmen
FIKES, Elijah, Pvt, Lt Col A Cheatham, Co Commander omitted, 6th Brig of Mtd Inf
FIKES, Elkin, Pvt, Lt Col A Cheatham, Capt Meredith Walker, Inf
FIKES, John, Pvt, Col Philip Pipkin, Capt John Strother, Mil; attached to Capt Smith, deserted 9-20-1814
FILES, James, Pvt, no other information
FILES, John, Pvt, Col Robert H Dyer, Capt James McMahon, TN Vol Mtd Gunmen
FILLINGGIN, Jonathan, Pvt, Col Wm Hall, Capt John Wallace, Inf
FILLINGGIN, Sam'l, Pvt, Col Wm Hall, Capt John Wallace, Inf
FILLINGIM, Sam'l, Pvt, Col N T Perkins, Capt George W Marr, Mtd Vol
FILLINGIN, Jonathan, Pvt, Col N T Perkins, Capt George W L Marr, Mtd Riflemen Vol

## Enlisted Men, War of 1812

FILLIPS, James, Pvt, Col Thomas Williamson, Capt John Doak & Capt John Dobbins, Vol Mtd Gunmen; transferred from Marlin

FILLIPS (FLIPPO), John C, Pvt, Col Wm Metcalf, Capt Barbee Collins, Mil Inf

FIN, Greenbury, Pvt, Col T McCrory, Capt Isaac Patton, Mil Inf

FIN, John, 4 Sgt, Col James Raulston, Capt Mathew Cowan, Inf

FINCH, Aaron, Pvt, Col Wm Lillard, Capt Robert McCalpin, E TN Inf

FINCH, Edmond, Pvt, Maj Gen Wm Carroll, Col Wm Metcalf, Capt John Jackson, Inf

FINCH, Edward, Pvt, Col Newton Cannon, Capt Isaac Williams, Mtd Riflemen

FINCH, Edward, Pvt, Col Robert Steele, Capt James Shenault, Mil Inf

FINCH, Jarratt, Pvt, Col John Cocke, Capt Bird Nance, Inf

FINCH, John, Pvt, Maj Wm Russell, Capt William Russell, Vol Mtd Gunmen

FINCH, Michael, Pvt, Col Samuel Bayless, Capt James Landen, E TN Mil

FINCH, Thomas, Pvt, Col Samuel Bayless, Capt Jonathan Waddell, E TN Mil

FINCH, Wm, Cpl, Col Robert Steele, Capt James Shenault, Mil Inf

FIND, Abraham, Pvt, Col Samuel Wear & Col Samuel Bunch, Capt William Mitchell, E TN Mtd Inf; transferred to W Jobe

FINDLEY, James, Pvt, Col Edwin Booth, Capt Alexander Biggs, Inf

FINDLEY, James, Pvt, Col John Williams, Capt Sam Bunch, Mtd Vol

FINDLEY, Sam'l, Pvt, Col Philip Pipkin, Capt Wm Mackay, Mil Inf

FINDLEY, Sam'l, Pvt, Col Wm Metcalf, Capt Bird Hurt, Mil Inf; d 1-27-1815

FINDLEY, Thomas, Pvt, Col Wm Metcalf, Capt Thomas Marks, Mil Inf

FINDLEY, Travis, Pvt, Col Edwin Booth, Capt Samuel Thompson, Mil Inf

FINDLY, John, Pvt, Col Edwin Booth, Capt Samuel Thompson, Mil; detailed as Principle Artif to repair wagons

FINDLY, Thomas Pvt, Col A Cheatham, Capt George G Chapman, Inf

FINDLY, William, Pvt, Col A Cheatham, Capt George G Chapman, Inf

FINE, Abraham jr, Pvt, Col Wm Lillard, Capt James Lillard, E TN Vol Inf

FINE, Abraham sr, Pvt, Col William Lillard, Capt James Lillard, E TN Inf Vol

FINE, Abraham, Pvt, Col Lillard, Capt Jacob Hartsell, E TN Vol Inf

FINE, Abraham, Pvt, Col Samuel Bunch, Capt William Jobe, E TN Vol Mtd Inf

FINE, Isaac, Pvt, Col William Lillard, Capt James Lillard, E TN Inf Vol

FINE, John, 4 Sgt, Col John Brown, Capt Charles Lewin, E TN Mtd Inf

FINE, Levi, Pvt, Col William Lillard, Capt James Lillard, E TN Inf Vol

FINE, Peter jr, 1 Sgt, Col Samuel Bunch, Capt Henry Stephens, E TN Mtd Inf

FINES, Abraham, 1 Sgt, Col John Brown, Capt Charles Lewin, E TN Mtd Inf

FINLEY, Alexander, Pvt, Col R C Napier, Capt James McMurry, Mil Inf; deserted 2-9-1814

FINLEY, Benj, Cpl, Col Samuel Bayless, Capt John Brock, E TN Mil; promoted

FINLEY, James, Cpl, Col Samuel Bayless, Capt James Churchman, E TN Mil

FINLEY, James, Pvt, Col Wm Lillard, Capt Thomas McChristian, E TN Vol Inf

FINLEY, John, Pvt, Col Samuel Bunch, Capt Edward Buchanan, E TN Drafted Mil

FINLEY, John, Pvt, Col Samuel Bunch, Capt Joseph Duncan, E TN Drafted Mil

FINLEY, Martin, Pvt, Col Thomas Williamson, Capt Wm Martin, Vol Mtd Gunmen

FINLEY, Obadiah G, Pvt, Col N T Perkins, Capt John B Quarles, Vol Mtd Inf

FINLEY, Reuben, Sgt, Col Edwin Booth, Capt John Slatton, E TN Mil

FINLEY, Robert, Pvt, Col Thomas Williamson, Capt Wm Martin, Vol Mtd Gunmen

FINLEY, Sam'l, Pvt, Col Samuel Bayless, Capt James Churchman, E TN Mil

FINLEY, Thomas, Pvt, Col R C Napier, Capt Andrew McCarty, Mil Inf

FINLEY, William, Pvt, Col John Brown, Capt John Trimble, E TN Mtd Gunmen

FINLEY, Wm, Pvt, Col N T Perkins, Capt John Doak, Vol Mtd Gunmen

FINLEY, Wm, Pvt, Col Wm Metcalf, Capt Bird L Hurt, Mil Inf

FINLY, Thomas, Pvt, Col John Coffee, Capt John W Byrn, Cav

FINN, Edward W, Pvt, Col James Raulston, Capt James A Black, Inf

FINN, Greenberry, Pvt, Col Wm Metcalf, Capt Wm Mullin, Mil Inf

FINN, Sharick, Pvt, Regt Commander omitted, Capt Joseph Williams, Mil Cav

FINNA, Pleasant, Pvt, Col S Copeland, Capt Solomon George, Inf

FINNEY, Andrew, Cpl, Col Newton Cannon, Capt Ota Cantrell, W TN Mtd Inf; deserted 10-10-1813

FINNEY, Andrew, Pvt, Col A Cheatham, Capt Wm Smith, Inf

FINNEY, Griffin, Pvt, Col Wm Higgins, Capt Adam Dale, Mtd Gunmen

FINNEY, Joshua, Pvt, Col Samuel Bunch, Capt F Register, E TN Mil; deserted 3-4-1814

FINNING, Joshua, Sgt, Maj Wm Russell, Capt John Cowan, Vol Mtd Riflemen

FINNY, Alexander, 1 Sgt, Col Thomas Williamson, Capt Giles Burdett, Vol Mtd Gunmen

FISH, John, Pvt, Col Ewen Allison, Capt Jonas Loughmiller, Mil

FISHBARK, William, Pvt, Col Wm Hall, Capt Brice Martin, Vol Inf; deserted

FISHER, Anderson, Pvt, Col Edward Bradley, Capt Henry Douglass, Vol Inf
FISHER, Anderson, Pvt, Col Thomas Benton, Capt Henry Douglass, Vol Inf
FISHER, Benj, Pvt, Col Edward Bradley, Capt Harry Douglass, Vol Inf
FISHER, Benj, Pvt, Col Thomas Benton, Capt Henry Douglass, Vol Inf
FISHER, Benjamin, Pvt, Col Thomas Williamson, Capt Richard Tate, Vol Mtd Gunmen
FISHER, Daniel, Pvt, Col Samuel Wear, Capt Samuel Bowman, Mtd Inf
FISHER, George, Cpl, Maj William Russell, Capt Isaac Williams, Sep Bn Vol Mtd Gunmen
FISHER, George, Pvt, Col Robert Dyer, Capt Joseph Williams, 1st Regt TN Vol Mtd Gunmen
FISHER, Jacob, Pvt, Col William Johnson, Capt Christopher Cook, E TN Mil
FISHER, Jacob, Pvt, Col William Johnson, Capt Joseph Kirk, Mil
FISHER, James, Pvt, Lt Col Leroy Hammonds & Lt Col Alexander Loury, Capt Thomas Wells, Inf
FISHER, John, Pvt, Col A Cheatham, Capt Charles Johnson, Inf
FISHER, John, Pvt, Col Robert Dyer, Capt James McMahon, 1st TN Mtd Vol Gunmen
FISHER, Michael, Pvt, Col Robert Dyer, Capt Joseph Williams, 1st Regt TN Vol Mtd Gunmen
FISHER, Michael, Sgt, Maj Wm Russell, Capt Isaac Williams, Sep Bn Vol Mtd Gunmen
FISHER, Sherod, Pvt, Col Newton Cannon, Capt Andrew Patterson, Mtd Riflemen
FISHER, Thomas, Pvt, Col Philip Pipkin, Capt Ebenezer Kirkpatrick, Mil Inf
FISHER, William, Cpl, Col Robert Dyer, Capt Ephraim Dickson, 1st TN Mtd Vol Gunmen; d 3-5-1815
FISHER, William, Cpl, Regt Commander omitted, Capt Ephraim Dickson, Branch Srvce omitted
FISHER, William, Pvt, Col A Cheatham, Capt Charles Johnson, Inf
FISHER, Wm, Pvt, Col John Wynne, Capt John Spinks, Inf
FISHER, Wm, Pvt, Col Philip Pipkin, Capt Ebenezer Kirkpatrick, Mil Inf
FISK, John, Pvt, Col John Cocke, Capt James Gault, Inf
FISK, Madison, Pvt, Col Philip Pipkin, Capt David Smith, Inf
FISK, Madison, Pvt, Col Philip Pipkin, Capt William Mackay, Mil Inf
FISK, Madison, Pvt, Col Thomas McCrory, Capt Abel Willis, Mil Inf
FITCHE, John, Pvt, Maj William Russell, Capt Isaac Williams, Sep Bn Vol Mtd Gunmen; served Col Robert Dyer 1st Regt
FITE, Jacob, Cpl, Col William Johnson, Capt James Stewart, 3rd Regt E TN Drafted Mil
FITSRIGHT, Earl, Pvt, Col Thomas Benton, Capt Thomas Williamson, Vol Inf
FITSRIGHT, John, Pvt, Col Thomas Benton, Capt Williamson, Vol Inf
FITSWALD, Langford, Pvt, Col William Hall, Capt Henry Newlin, Inf
FITTS, Ambrose, Pvt, Col Alexander Loury, Capt John Looney, W TN Inf
FITTS, Reuben, Pvt, Lt Col A Cheatham, Co Commander omitted, 6th Brig Mtd Inf
FITXHUGH, Ariel, Pvt, Col Philip Pipkin, Capt William Mackay, Mil Inf
FITZGERALD, Anderson, Pvt, Col John Wynne, Capt James Hollman, Inf
FITZGERALD, Andrew, Pvt, Col John Wynne, Capt William Caruthers, W TN Inf; transferred to Capt Hollan's Camp
FITZGERALD, George, Pvt, Maj Gen Wm Carroll, Col Wm Metcalf, Capt John Jackson, Inf
FITZGERALD, Jackson, Pvt, Regt Commander omitted, Lt James Berry, Mtd Riflemen; transferred from Lt Hogan Co
FITZGERALD, Jacob, Pvt, Gen Andrew Jackson, Capt William Russell, Mtd Spies
FITZGERALD, John, Pvt, Col Wm Metcalf, Capt Andrew Patterson, Mil Inf
FITZGERALD, Langford, Pvt, Col Edward Bradley, Capt Elijah Haynie, Vol Inf
FITZGERALD, Martin, Pvt, Regt Commander omitted, Lt James Berry, Mtd Riflemen; transferred from Lt Hogan's
FITZGERALD, Nathaniel, Pvt, Col Alexander Loury, Capt John Looney, 2nd Regt W TN Mil; d 4-10-1815
FITZGERALD, Pleasant, Pvt, Col Robert Dyer, Capt James McMahon, 1st TN Mtd Vol Gunmen
FITZGERALD, Pleasant, Pvt, Regt Commander omitted, Lt James Berry, Mtd Riflemen; transferred from Lt Hogan's Co
FITZGERALD, Thomas, Pvt, Col Wm Metcalf, Capt Andrew Patterson, Mil Inf
FITZGERALD, William, Pvt, Col John Coffee, Capt Charles Kavanaugh, Cav
FITZGERALD, William, Sgt, Regt Commander omitted, Capt Archibald McKenney, Cav; promoted from Pvt
FITZHUGH, Earl, Pvt, Col Thomas Benton, Capt Thomas Williamson, Vol Inf
FITZHUGH, John, Pvt, Col Robert Dyer, Capt Thomas Jones, Vol Mtd Gunmen
FITZHUGH, John, Pvt, Col Thomas Benton, Capt Thomas Williamson, Vol Inf
FITZPATRICK, Joseph, Pvt, Col S Copeland, Capt Alexander Provine, Mil Inf
FITZUGH, Earl, Pvt, Col Wm Pillow, Capt Thomas Williamson, Vol Inf
FITZUGH, James, Pvt, Col William Pillow, Capt Thomas Williamson, Vol Inf
FITZUGH, John, Pvt, Col Wm Pillow, Capt Thomas Williamson, Vol Inf
FITZUGH, Richard, Pvt, Col Wm Pillow, Capt Thomas Williamson, Vol Inf
FLANAGAN, Thomas, Pvt, Col L Hammond, Capt J N Williamson, 2nd Regt Inf
FLANAGEN, John, Pvt, Col Cheatham, Capt Smith, Inf
FLANAGEN, John, Pvt, Col L Hammond, Capt J N Wil-

## Enlisted Men, War of 1812

liamson, 2nd Regt Inf
FLANAGEN, John, Pvt, Lt Col Hammond, Capt Williamson, Inf
FLANAGIN, John, Pvt, Col A Loury, Capt J N Williamson, W TN Mil
FLANAGIN, Thomas, Pvt, Col A Lowry, Capt J N Williamson, W TN Mil
FLANAGIN, Thomas, Pvt, Col Perkins, Capt Pipkin, Mtd Riflemen
FLANIKEN, James W, Sgt, Col Brown, Capt Childs, E TN Vol Mtd Gunmen
FLANNAKIN, John, Pvt, Col Brown, Capt Chiles, E TN Vol Mtd Inf
FLANNAKIN, Sam'l, Sgt Maj, Commanders omitted, E TN Vol Mtd Inf
FLAT, James, Pvt, Col John Brown, Capt Allen I Bacon, E TN Mil Inf
FLATT, John, Pvt, Maj Gen Carroll, Capt Raulston, Capt Huddleston, Inf
FLEMING, Beverly, Cpl, Col Hall, Capt Bledsoe, Vol Inf
FLEMING, Bird, Pvt, Col Pipkin, Capt Mackay, Mil Inf
FLEMING, Bird, Pvt, Col Pipkin, Capt Smith, Inf
FLEMING, John D, Pvt, Col Perkins, Capt Johnson, Mil Inf
FLEMING, John W, Pvt, Col Bayless, Capt Hendrix, E TN Mil
FLEMING, John, Pvt, Col Hall, Capt Kennedy, Vol Inf; disabled
FLEMING, Michel, Pvt, Col Bunch, Capt Jobe, E TN Vol Mtd Inf
FLEMING, Wm, Pvt, Col Copeland, Capt Williams, Inf
FLEMMING, Beverly, 3 Cpl, Col Hall, Capt Bledsoe, Vol Inf
FLEMMING, John, Pvt, Regt Commander omitted, Capt Robert Evans, Mtd Spies
FLEMMING, Thomas, Pvt, Gen Andrew Jackson, Capt Nathan Davis, Inf
FLEMMING, Wm, 3 Sgt, Col Napier, Capt McMurry, Mil Inf
FLEMMING, Wm, Pvt, Gen A Jackson, Capt Wm Ruppell, Mtd Spies
FLEMMING, Wm, Pvt, Regt Commander omitted, Capt Wyatt Fusul, Det of Inf
FLENNEKENS, Sam'l, Pvt, Maj Chiles, Capt Tipton, E TN Vol Mtd Inf; appointed Sgt Maj, Regt Co Knox
FLENTY, Wm, Pvt, no other information
FLEPPO, Garret, Pvt, Col Lowry, Capt Martin, Inf
FLETCHER, Henry, Cpl, no other information
FLETCHER, James, Pvt, Col Perkins, Capt Marr, Mtd Riflemen Co
FLETCHER, John, Pvt, Col Booth, Capt Vernon, E TN Mil
FLETCHER, John, Pvt, Col Cocke, Capt Crunk, Inf
FLETCHER, John, Pvt, Col Pipkin, Capt Strothers, Mil; deserted 9-20-1814
FLETCHER, John, Pvt, Lt Col Hammond, Capt Tubb, Inf; d 1-1-1815
FLETCHER, John, Pvt, Regt Commander omitted, Capt Gray, Inf
FLETCHER, John, Pvt, Regt Commander omitted, Capt James Haggard, Mtd Gunmen
FLETCHER, Lewis, Pvt, Col Pipkin, Capt Strothers, Mil
FLETCHER, Lewis, Pvt, Lt Col A Cheatham, Co Commander omitted, 6th Brig Mtd Inf
FLETCHER, Thomas, 3 Cpl, Gen Andrew Jackson, Capt David Deaderick, Arty
FLETCHER, William, Pvt, Col Alcorn, Capt Winston, Mtd Riflemen; killed 11-9-1813
FLIN, Barney H, 2 Sgt, Col Pipkin, Capt Searcy, Mil Inf
FLIN, George W, Pvt, Col Burton, Capt Moore, Vol Inf
FLIN, George, Pvt, Col Burton, Capt Moore, Vol Inf
FLINARD, Lawrence, Pvt, Regt Commander omitted, Capt John Crane, Mtd Inf
FLINN, George W, Pvt, Col Higgins, Capt Doak, Mtd Riflemen
FLINN, George, Pvt, Regt Commander omitted, Capt James Terrill, Cav; old Vol discharged
FLINT, Abajah, Pvt, Gen Andrew Jackson, Capt Nathan Davis, Inf
FLINT, Martin, Pvt, Gen Andrew Jackson, Capt Nathan Davis, Inf
FLINT, Richard, Pvt, Gen Andrew Jackson, Capt Nathan Davis, Inf
FLIPPIN, William, Pvt, Col McCrory, Capt Gordon, Inf
FLIPPO, William, Pvt, Col Higgins, Capt Eldridge, Mtd Gunmen
FLITCHEE, John, Pvt, Col Dyer, Capt Jones, Vol Mtd Gunmen
FLOID, Isaac, Pvt, Col Bayless, Capt Waddle, E TN Mil
FLOID, Richard, Pvt, Brig Gen Johnson, Capt Carson, Inf
FLORA, John, Pvt, Col Booth, Capt Slatton, E TN Mil
FLOWERS, Benj, Pvt, Col Cocke, Capt Nance, Branch Srvce omitted
FLOWERS, James, Pvt, Maj Woodfolk, Capt Pearce, Inf; transferred to Capt Turner's Co
FLOWERS, John W, Pvt, Maj Chiles, Capt Cummings, E TN Vol Mtd Inf
FLOWERS, John, Sgt, Col John Williams, Capt Sam Bunch, Mtd Vol
FLOWERS, Larry, Pvt, Col Cheatham, Capt Smith, Inf; discharged for inability to do duty
FLOWERS, William F, Sgt, Col Raulston, Capt Haynie, Inf
FLOWERS, Wm, Pvt, Col Bunch, Capt Vance, E TN Mtd Inf
FLOWERS, Wm, Pvt, Col Johnson, Capt Lawson, E TN Drafted Mil
FLOYD, David, Pvt, Col T Williamson, Capt Giles Murdett, Vol Mtd Gunmen
FLOYD, Eaders, Pvt, Col Ewen Allison, Capt Jonas Loughmiller, Mil; joined from Capt Griffin's Co
FLOYD, Enoch, Pvt, Col T Williamson, Capt Giles Burdett, Vol Mtd Gunmen
FLOYD, George, Pvt, Col T Williamson, Capt Giles Burdett, Vol Mtd Gunmen
FLOYD, Isaac, Pvt, Col Samuel Wear, Capt Jesse Cole, Vol Inf
FLOYD, Joel, Pvt, Col R H Dyer, Maj Wm Russell, Capt Wm Russell, Vol Mtd Gunmen
FLOYD, Jonathan, Pvt, Col T Williamson, Capt Giles Burdett, Vol Mtd Gunmen

## Enlisted Men, War of 1812

FLOYD, Samuel, Pvt, Col Wm Lillard, Capt Thomas Sharpe, 2nd Regt Inf
FLOYD, Wm, Pvt, Col T McCrory, Capt James Shannon, Mil Inf
FLOYED, William, Sgt, Col Robert M Dyer, Capt Robert Evans, Vol Mtd Gunmen
FLUD, Alexander, Pvt, Regt Commander omitted, Capt James Craig, Mil Inf
FLUKE, Wm, Pvt, Col S Copeland, Capt John Biles, Inf
FLUMON, John, Pvt, Col S Copeland, Capt John Biles, Inf
FLUTY, Ransom, Pvt, Col James Raulston, Capt Daniel Newman, Inf; promoted to Cpl
FLY, Elisha, 3 Sgt, Col Philip Pipkin, Capt Wm Mackay, Mil Inf
FLY, Elisha, Pvt, Col A Cheatham, Capt William Creel, Inf; transferred to Capt Johnston
FLY, Elisha, Pvt, Col Robert Steele, Capt Robert Campbell, Mil Inf
FLY, Jesse, Pvt, Col T Williamson, Capt Richard Tate, Vol Mtd Gunmen
FLY, Jesse, Sdlr, Col T Williamson, Capt Richard Tate, Vol Mtd Gunmen
FLY, John, Pvt, Col Robert Steele, Capt Robert Campbell, Mil Inf; appointed Hospital Stewart
FLY, Lawrence, Pvt, Col T McCrory, Capt Jos Shannon, Mil Inf
FLY, Micajah, Pvt, Col Wm Metcalf, Capt William Millin, Mil Inf
FOLAND, Jacob, Pvt, Regt Commander omitted, Capt James Craig, Inf
FOLKS, Edward, Pvt, Col Edward Bradley, Capt James Jamilton, Vol Inf
FOLKS, Edwin, Pvt, Col Wm Hall, Capt James Hambleton, Vol Inf
FOLKS, Ethelred, Pvt, Col R C Napier, Capt Thomas Gray, Mil Inf; transferred to Arty
FOLLIS, E, Pvt, Gen Andrew Jackson, Capt Joel Parrish, Arty
FOLLIS, Wm, Pvt, Gen Andrew Jackson, Capt Nathan David, Inf
FOLWELL, Elisha, Pvt, Col Wm Metcalf, Capt Andrew Patterson, Mil Inf
FONDERIN, Jesse, Pvt, Regt Commander omitted, Maj Wm Russell, Vol Mtd Gunmen
FONDRELL, Jesse, Pvt, Col John K Wynne, Capt Wm Caruthers, W TN Inf
FONDREN, Jesse, 4 Cpl, Col Philip Pipkin, Capt Ebenezer Kirkpatrick, Mil Inf; substituted John McDowel
FONDRIN, Jesse, Pvt, Col S Copeland, Capt Solomon George, Inf
FONDRIN, Richard, Pvt, Col S Copeland, Capt Solomon George, Inf
FONVIEL, Lewis, Pvt, Col James Raulston, Capt Mathew Neale, Inf
FOOK, Thomas, Pvt, Regt Commander omitted, Capt John Crane, Mtd Inf
FOOLKER, Isom, Pvt, Col S Copeland, Capt Moses Thompson, Inf
FOOT, Berryman H, Pvt, Regt Commander omitted, Lt James Berry, Mtd Riflemen

FOOT, Berryman, Pvt, Col N Cannon, Capt Martin, Mtd Gunmen
FOOT, Richard, Pvt, Col A Cheatham, Capt George G Chapman, Inf
FORBES, Alexander, QM Sgt, Col Samuel Bunch, E TN Mil
FORBES, John, Ffr, Lt Col L Hammonds, Capt James Craig, Inf
FORBES, John, Pvt, Col John Cocke, Capt Samuel N Caruthers, Inf
FORBES, John, Sgt, Maj Wm Woodfolk, Capt James C Neil, Inf
FORBESS, William, Pvt, Maj Wm Woodfolk, Capt James Turner, Inf
FORBIAN, John, Pvt, Col Samuel Bayless, Capt Branch Jones, E TN Mil
FORBIS, Alexander, Sgt, Col John Brown, Capt James Preston, Regt E TN Mil Inf
FORBUSH, James, Pvt, Regt Commander omitted, Capt John Miller, Spies
FORBUSH, John, Pvt, Col William Johnson, Capt Joseph Scott, E TN Drafted Mil; promoted to Drm Maj
FORBUSH, John, Pvt, Lt Col L Hammonds, Capt James Craig, Inf; d 2-22-1815 at Ft Montgomery
FORBUSH, Thomas, Pvt, Col Wm Lillard, Capt Wm McLin, E TN Inf
FORBUSH, William, Pvt, Col Wm Lillard, Capt Wm McLin, E TN Inf
FORD, Alexander, Pvt, Col James Raulston, Capt Mathew Neal, Inf
FORD, Alexander, Pvt, Col S Bunch, Capt George McPherson, E TN Mil
FORD, Andrew G, Pvt, Col Wm Hall, Capt Brice Martin, Vol Inf
FORD, Benj, Pvt, Col Samuel Bunch, Capt David Vance, E TN Mtd Inf
FORD, Benjamin, Pvt, Col Samuel Bayless, Capt James Landen, E TN Mil
FORD, Charles, Pvt, Col T Benton, Capt George Caperton, Inf
FORD, Charles, Pvt, Col Thomas Benton, Capt George Caperton, Vol Inf
FORD, Charles, Pvt, Col Wm Pillow, Capt George Caperton, Inf
FORD, Daniel, Pvt, Regt Commander omitted, Capt Gray, Inf
FORD, Ezekiel, Pvt, Col Samuel Bayless, Capt Jonathan Waddell, E TN Mil
FORD, Garrett, Sgt, Maj Wm Woodfolk, Capt Abraham Dudney, Inf; also under Capt Sutton
FORD, Grant, Pvt, Col S Bunch, Capt George McPherson, E TN Mil
FORD, Horatio, Pvt, Col William Johnson, Capt Andrew Lawson, E TN Drafted Mil
FORD, Isaac, Pvt, Col Wm Metcalf, Capt Thomas Marks, Mil Inf
FORD, James, Pvt, Col James Raulston, Capt Mathew Cowan, Inf
FORD, James, Pvt, Col S Bayless, Capt James Landen, E TN Mil
FORD, James, Pvt, Regt Commander omitted, Capt Gray,

## Enlisted Men, War of 1812

FORD, John L, Pvt, Col Robert Dyer, Capt Bethel Allen, Vol Mtd Gunmen, Inf
FORD, John, Pvt, Col James Raulston, Capt Mathew Cowan, Inf
FORD, John, Pvt, Col John Brown, Capt John Childs, E TN Vol Mtd Gunmen
FORD, John, Pvt, Col Robert Steele, Capt James Bennette, Mil Inf
FORD, John, Pvt, Col S Bayless, Capt I Bacon, E TN Mil
FORD, John, Pvt, Col S Bunch, Capt George McPherson, E TN Mil
FORD, Jos, Pvt, Col Robert Steele, Capt Samuel Maxwell, Mil Inf
FORD, Joseph, Pvt, Col Edwin Booth, Capt Adam Winsell, E TN Drafted Mil
FORD, Joseph, Pvt, Col Edwin Booth, Capt Richard Marshall, Drafted Mil; discharged for inability
FORD, Joshua, Pvt, Brig Gen Thomas Johnston, Capt Robert Carson, Inf
FORD, Lloyd, Pvt, Col Robert Steele, Capt Samuel Maxwell, Mil Inf
FORD, Lloyd, Pvt, Col S Bunch, Capt George McPherson, E TN Mil
FORD, Loide, Pvt, Col Edwin Booth, Capt Alexander Biggs, Inf
FORD, Loyd, Pvt, Col Ewin Allison, Capt Joseph Everett, E TN Mil; transferred to Capt McPherson
FORD, Micajah, Sgt, Col Edwin Booth, Capt John Slatton, E TN Mil
FORD, Micajah, Sgt, Col William Lillard, Capt Wm Hamilton, E TN Inf
FORD, Milton, Cpl, Col Robert Dyer, Capt Bethel Allen, Vol Mtd Gunmen
FORD, Mordecai, Pvt, Col Wm Johnson, Capt Andrew Lawson, E TN Drafted Mil; never appeared
FORD, Nathan, Pvt, Col Robert Steele, Capt Robert Steele, Mil Inf
FORD, Ninrod, Pvt, Col Ewen Allison, Capt John Hampton, Mil
FORD, Peter, Pvt, Col John Williams, Capt David Vance, Mtd Mil
FORD, Ralph, Pvt, Col S Bunch, Capt Penney, E TN Mtd Inf
FORD, Robert, Pvt, Col Wm Lillard, Capt Thomas McChristian, E TN Vol Inf
FORD, Thomas, Cpl, Col S Bayless, Capt Jonathan Waddle, E TN Mil
FORD, Thomas, Pvt, Col Edward Bradley, Capt James Hambleton, Vol Inf
FORD, Thomas, Pvt, Col Ewen Allison, Capt John Hampton, Mil; d 2-14-1814
FORD, Thomas, Pvt, Col Wm Hall, Capt Hamilton, Vol Inf
FORD, Waller, Pvt, Col N Cannon, Capt James Walton, Mtd Riflemen
FORD, William, Pvt, Col S Bunch, Capt Penney, E TN Mtd Inf
FORDE, Isaac, Pvt, Col Wm Metcalf, Capt William Mullen, Mil Inf
FORE, Green P, Surgeon Mate, Col John Coffee, TN Vol Cav Mtd Riflemen
FORE, Wright, Pvt, Regt Commander omitted, Capt David Smith, Cav Vol; wounded 11-1813
FOREHAM, Henry, Pvt, Col Philip Pipkin, Capt Robertson, Mil Inf; deserted 11-9-1814
FOREHAN, John, Pvt, Col Wm Metcalf, Capt Wm Mullin, Mil Inf
FOREHAN, Lambert, Pvt, Col A Cheatham, Capt James Giddens, Inf
FOREHAND, Allen, 3 Cpl, Col L Hammonds & Col Alexander Loury, Capt Thomas Wells, Inf
FOREHAND, Henry, Pvt, Col Thomas Williamson, Capt Richard Tate, Vol Mtd Gunmen
FOREHAND, Thomas, Pvt, Col Leroy Hammonds & Col Alexander Loury, Capt Thomas Wells, Inf
FOREMAN, Elijah, Pvt, Col S Copeland, Capt Allen Wilkinson, Mil Inf
FORGASON, John, Pvt, Col S Bayless, Capt John Brock, E TN Mil
FORGASON, Joseph, Pvt, Col Wm Y Higgins, Capt Wm Doak, Mtd Riflemen
FORGERSON, Wm, Pvt, Col S Bayless, Capt Solomon Hendrix, E TN Mil
FORGEY, Andrew, Pvt, Col S Bunch, Capt James Cummings, E TN Vol Mtd Inf
FORGURSON, Henry, Pvt, Col John Cocke, Capt Richard Crunk, Inf
FORGUSON, John, Pvt, Col Samuel Wear, Capt Simon Petty, E TN Vol Mtd Inf
FORGUSON, Robert, Cpl, Col Wm Johnson, Capt James Stewart, E TN Drafted Mil
FORKNEY, Lewis, Pvt, Col Alexander Loury, Capt Peter Looney, W TN Mil; d 3-18-1815
FORMWALT, Jacob, Pvt, Col John Williams, Capt Wm Walker, Vol
FORMWALT, John jr, Pvt, Col Wm Johnson, Capt James Stewart, E TN Mil
FORMWALT, John sr, Pvt, Col Wm Johnson, Capt James Stewart, E TN Drafted Mil
FORREST, James, 6 Sgt, Col John Cocke, Co Commander omitted, Inf
FORREST, John, Pvt, Col John Cocke, Capt Joseph Price, Inf
FORRESTER, Absolom, Pvt, Lt Col Hammond, Capt James Tubb, Inf
FORRESTER, Alexander, Pvt, Col Wm Alcorn, Capt Byrns, Cav
FORRESTER, Benj, Pvt, Col Wm Johnson, Capt Joseph Hunter, E TN Mil; transferred to Capt Kirk's Co
FORRESTER, Benj, Pvt, Col Wm Johnson, Capt Joseph Kirk, Mil Inf
FORRESTER, Charles, Pvt, Col Thomas H Williamson, Capt Isaac Williams, Vol Mtd Gunmen; killed in battle 12-23-1814
FORRESTER, George, Pvt, Col Thomas McCrory, Capt Wm Metcalf, Mil Inf
FORRESTER, Isaac, Pvt, Col James Raulston, Capt James C Neale, Inf; d 2-7-1815
FORRESTER, Isaac, Pvt, Col S Copeland, Capt John Holshouser, Inf; 2 Isaac Forresters
FORRESTER, Isaac, Pvt, Maj Gen Andrew Jackson, Col

Thos H Williamson, Vol Mtd Gunmen
FORRESTER, James, Pvt, Col John Brown, Capt Wm D Neilson, E TN Vol Mil
FORRESTER, James, Pvt, Col John Cocke, Capt Samuel Caruthers, Inf; d 3-16-1815
FORRESTER, James, Rank omitted, Maj Gen Andrew Jackson, Col Thos H Williamson, Vol Mtd Gunmen
FORRESTER, Joel, Pvt, Col John Cocke, Capt Sam Caruthers, Inf; d 3-20-1815
FORRESTER, Jonathan, Ffr, Col John Cocke, Capt Samuel Caruthers, Inf; d 2-22-1815
FORRESTER, Mark, Pvt, Col John K Wynne, Co Commander omitted, Inf
FORRESTER, Reuben, Pvt, Col James Raulston, Capt James Neale, Inf
FORRESTER, Robert, Pvt, Col Thomas H Williamson, Capt Beverly Williams, Vol Mtd Gunmen
FORRESTER, Robert, Sgt, Col Thos H Williamson, Capt Beverly Williams, Vol Mtd Gunmen
FORRISTER, Benj, Pvt, Col Samuel Bunch, Capt John English, E TN Drafted Mil
FORRISTER, Jacob, Pvt, Maj Wm Carroll, Capt Dillahunty & Capt Bradford, Vol Inf
FORRISTER, James, Pvt, Col S Copeland, Capt John Holshouser, Inf
FORRISTER, Stephen, Pvt, Col Thomas H Williamson, Capt Thomas Scurry, Vol Mtd Gunmen
FORRISTER, William, Pvt, Col Samuel Wear, Capt James Gillespie, E TN Vol Inf
FORSYTHE, Jeremiah, Pvt, Col R C Napier, Capt Thomas Gray, Mil Inf
FORSYTHE, John, Pvt, Col R C Napier, Capt Drury Adkins, Mil Inf
FORSYTHE, John, Pvt, Maj Gen Carroll, Capt Francis Ellis, Inf
FORT, Elias, Pvt, Lt Archer Cheatham, Co Commander omitted, 6th Brig of Mtd Inf
FORT, Henry, 1 Sgt, Capt David Smith, Co Commander omitted, Cav
FORT, Henry, 1 Sgt, Regt Commander omitted, Capt David Smith, Cav Vol
FORT, Henry, Pvt, Col John Coffee, Co Commander omitted, Vol Cav
FORT, Jacob, Pvt, Lt Col John Edmondson, Co Commander omitted, Cav
FORT, James, Pvt, Col John Coffee & Col Smith, Vol Cav
FORT, James, Pvt, Lt Col A Cheatham, Capt G Martin, Inf
FORT, Josiah, Pvt, Col John Coffee, Capt David Smith, Vol Cav
FORT, Robert, Pvt, Col A Cheatham, Capt Richard Benson, Inf
FORT, William, Pvt, Col John Coffee, Capt David Smith, Vol Cav
FORT, William, Pvt, Regt Commander omitted, Capt David Smith, Cav Vol
FORT, Wm, Pvt, Regt Commander omitted, Capt David Smith, Cav
FORTENBERRY, David, Pvt, Col Newton Cannon, Capt George Brandon, Mtd Riflemen
FORTENBERRY, David, Sgt, Maj Wm Russell, Capt John Cowan, Vol Mtd Riflemen; promoted from Cpl
FORTNER, Conrad, Pvt, Lt Col L Hammonds, Capt James Craig, Inf
FORTNER, John, Pvt, Col Wm Johnson, Capt David McKamy, E TN Drafted Mil
FORTNER, Nathan, Far, Lt Col L Hammonds, Capt James Craig, Inf
FORTUNBERRY, John, Cpl, Maj Wm Russell, Capt John Cowan, Vol Mtd Gunmen
FOSCUE, Benj, Pvt, Col Thomas Williamson, Capt Anthony Metcalf, Vol Mtd Gunmen
FOSCUE, Lewis, Pvt, Col Thomas Williamson, Capt Anthony Metcalf, Vol Mtd Gunmen
FOSESTER, Wm, Pvt, Maj Wm Russell, Capt William Chism, Vol Mtd Inf
FOSET, Richard, Pvt, Regt Commander omitted, Capt Abner Pearce, Inf
FOSHEA, Jesse, Pvt, Col Wm Lillard, Capt Robert Maloney, E TN Vol Inf
FOSHEA, Richard, Pvt, Col Wm Lillard, Capt Robert Maloney, E TN Vol Inf
FOSSETT, Alexander, Pvt, Col Robert Dyer, Capt James McMahon, 1st TN Mtd Vol Gunmen
FOSSETT, William, Pvt, Col A Cheatham, Capt Richard Benson, Inf
FOSTER, Abner, Pvt, Lt Col Hammonds, Capt James Tubb, Inf
FOSTER, Alexander, Pvt, Col Newton Cannon, Capt John Harpole, Mtd Gunmen
FOSTER, Ambrous, Pvt, Col Thomas Williamson, Capt Giles Burdett, Vol Mtd Gunmen
FOSTER, Benj, Mus, Col Thomas Williamson, Capt Giles Burdett, Vol Mtd Gunmen
FOSTER, Benj, Pvt, Col Thomas Williamson, Capt Giles Burdett, Vol Mtd Gunmen
FOSTER, Daniel, Pvt, Col Samuel Bunch, Capt Wm Houston, E TN Vol Mtd Inf
FOSTER, Edward, Principle Musician, Brig Gen Bird Smith, Maj Gen Wm Carroll, 2nd Brig TN Mil
FOSTER, Ephraim, Pvt, Gen Andrew Jackson, Capt David Deaderick, Arty; appointed Sec to Gen Jackson
FOSTER, Ephraim, Secretary, Maj Gen Andrew Jackson, Div of TN Mil; resigned 1-31-1814
FOSTER, Frederick, Pvt, Col William Pillow, Capt William Moore, Inf
FOSTER, George W, 3 Cpl, Col Wm Metcalf, Capt Bird Hurt, Mil Inf
FOSTER, George, 4 Cpl, Lt Col Leroy Hammonds, Capt Thomas Delaney, Inf; transferred to Horse Co, also under Col Loury
FOSTER, George, Pvt, Col S Copeland, Capt Richard Sharpe, Mil Inf
FOSTER, George, Pvt, Col Thomas Williamson, Capt William Martin, Vol Mtd Gunmen; joined by transfer fro Capt Tubb's Co
FOSTER, Isaiah (Josiah), Pvt, Maj Wm Woodfolk, Capt James Neil, Inf; substitute for Henry Wise
FOSTER, John jr, Pvt, Maj Wm Russell, Capt William Chism, Vol Mtd Gunmen

## Enlisted Men, War of 1812

FOSTER, John sr, Pvt, Col William Metcalf, Capt Alexander Hill & Capt John Cunningham, Mil Inf

FOSTER, John, 7 Cpl, Col John Cocke, Capt Bird Nance, Inf; promoted from Pvt

FOSTER, John, Pvt, Col Edward Bradley, Capt John Wallace, Vol Inf

FOSTER, John, Pvt, Col William Hall, Capt John Wallace, Inf

FOSTER, John, Pvt, Maj Wm Woodfolk, Capt James Neil, Inf; Reduced from 5 Sgt to ranks

FOSTER, John, Sgt, Maj Wm Woodfolk, Capt James Neil, Inf

FOSTER, Mark, Pvt, Col Samuel Bunch, Capt William Houston, E TN Vol Mtd Inf; transferred to Capt Hamilton's Co

FOSTER, Mark, Pvt, Col Wm Lillard, Capt Wm Hamilton, E TN Vol Inf

FOSTER, Martin, Pvt, Col Samuel Bunch, Capt Joseph Duncan, E TN Drafted Mil

FOSTER, Michael, Pvt, Col Philip Pipkin, Capt David Smith, Inf; d 10-10-1814

FOSTER, Richard, Pvt, Col John Wynne, Capt John Porter, Inf

FOSTER, Robert, Pvt, Col Wm Lillard, Capt Robert Maloney, E TN Vol Inf

FOSTER, Samuel, Pvt, Col John Wynne, Capt James Cole, Inf

FOSTER, Thomas, Pvt, Col Newton Cannon, Capt John Demsey, Mtd Gunmen

FOSTER, Thomas, Pvt, Col Thomas Williamson, Capt Beverly Williams, Vol Mtd Gunmen; d 2-7-1815

FOSTER, Thomas, Pvt, Maj Wm Russell, Capt Wm Chism, Vol Mtd Gunmen

FOSTER, William, Pvt, Col Newton Cannon, Capt John Harpole, Mtd Gunmen

FOSTER, William, Pvt, Col Samuel Bunch, Capt Isaac Williams, E TN Mil

FOSTER, Wm, Pvt, Col Samuel Bunch, Capt Isaac Williams, E TN Mil

FOSTER (FORESTER), James sr, Cpl, Maj William Woodfolk, Capt James Neil, Inf

FOUGHT, Isham, Pvt, Col John Cocke, Capt Samuel Caruthers, Inf

FOULKS, Herod, Pvt, Gen Andrew Jackson, Capt Nathan Davis, Inf

FOUNTAIN, Edward, Pvt, no other information

FOURBUSH, Thomas, Pvt, Col William Johnson, Capt Andrew Lawson, E TN Drafted Mil; substitute for Henry Malrackin

FOUST, George, Pvt, Col Samuel Wear, Capt Daniel Price, E TN Vol Inf

FOUST, George, Pvt, Col Wm Lillard, Capt George Keyes, E TN Inf

FOUST, John, Pvt, Col Robert Dyer, Capt Bethel Allen, Vol Mtd Gunmen

FOUST, Lewis, Pvt, Col William Johnson, Capt Joseph Scott, E TN Drafted Mil; substitute for Joseph Clark

FOUST, Philip, Pvt, Col Robert Dyer, Capt Bethel Allen, Vol Mtd Gunmen

FOWLER, Daniel, Pvt, Col James Raulston, Capt Henry Hamilton, Inf; also under Maj Gen Wm Carroll

FOWLER, Daniel, Pvt, Col Wm Hall, Capt James Hamilton, Vol Inf

FOWLER, Edward, Pvt, Regt Commander omitted, Capt James Haggard, Mtd Gunmen

FOWLER, Elijah, Pvt, Regt Commander omitted, Capt Samuel Allen, Pack Horse Guards

FOWLER, Elisha, Pvt, Col Wm Y Higgins, Capt John Doak, Mtd Riflemen

FOWLER, Enoch, Pvt, Maj Gen A Jackson, Capt John Crane, Mtd Gunmen

FOWLER, Enoch, Pvt, Regt Commander omitted, Capt John Crane, Mtd Inf

FOWLER, James, Pvt, Maj Wm Woodfolk, Capt Abner Pearce, Inf; transferred from Capt Neil's Co

FOWLER, James, Pvt, Maj Wm Woodfolk, Capt James C Neil, Inf; substitute for James Ewin

FOWLER, Jeremiah, Pvt, Col Wm Johnson, Capt Jas Tunnell, E TN Mil

FOWLER, Jos, Pvt, Col N Cannon, Capt George Brandon, Mtd Riflemen

FOWLER, Moses, Pvt, Col R H Dyer, Capt Thomas White, Vol Mtd Gunmen

FOWLER, Moses, Pvt, Maj Gen A Jackson, Capt John Crane, Mtd Gunmen

FOWLER, Nehemiah, Pvt, Maj Gen A Jackson, Capt John Crane, Mtd Gunmen

FOWLER, Robert, Cpl, Col Wm Hall, Co Commander omitted, Vol Inf; also under Capt James Hambleton

FOWLER, Robert, Pvt, Col William Hall, Capt James Hambleton, Vol Inf

FOWLER, Robert, Pvt, Lt Col Henry Bryan, Co Commander omitted, Inf

FOWLER, Sam'l, Pvt, Col N Cannon, Capt John B Dewey, Mtd Gunmen

FOWLER, Simon, Pvt, Col Samuel Wear, Capt John Chiles, E TN Vol Inf

FOWLER, Thomas, Pvt, Col Thos Williamson, Capt Wm Martin, Vol Mtd Gunmen

FOWLER, Thos, Pvt, Col Thomas Benton, Capt James McEwen, Vol Inf

FOWLER, Thos, Pvt, Col Wm Pillow, Capt C E McEwen, Vol Inf

FOWLER, Wilie, Pvt, Col R H Dyer, Capt Robert Evans, Vol Mtd Gunmen

FOWLER, William, Pvt, 4 Cpl, Col Wm Hall, Capt James Hambleton, Vol Inf

FOWLER, William, Pvt, Brig Gen T Johnson, Capt Abraham Allen, Mil Inf

FOWLER, William, Pvt, Regt Commander omitted, Capt Wm Crane, Mtd Inf

FOWLER, William, Sgt, Maj Gen Wm Carroll, Capt Wm Metcalf, Capt John Jackson, Inf

FOWLER, Wm, 1 Cpl, Col Edward Bradley, Capt James Hamilton, Vol Inf

FOWLER, Wm, Pvt, Col Ewen Allison, Capt Joseph Everett, E TN Mil; discharged - unable to perform duty

FOWLER, Wm, Pvt, Col John K Wynne, Capt Bayless E Prince, Inf

- 199

## Enlisted Men, War of 1812

FOWLKER, Nehemiah, Pvt, Regt Commander omitted, Capt John Crane, Mtd Inf
FOX, Adam, Pvt, Col Samuel Wear, Capt Simeon Perry, E TN Vol Mtd Inf
FOX, Charles, Pvt, Col R H Dyer, Capt Bethel Allen, Vol Mtd Gunmen
FOX, Enoch, Pvt, Col William Johnson, Capt Joseph Scott, E TN Drafted Mil
FOX, Enoch, Pvt, Maj Gen Wm Carroll, Col James Raulston, Capt Wiley Huddleston, Inf
FOX, George, Pvt, Col John K Wynne, Capt Jas Cole, Inf
FOX, Henry, Pvt, Col John Cocke, Capt Richard Crunk, Inf
FOX, Jacob, Pvt, Col R H Dyer, Capt Abraham Allen, Vol Mtd Gunmen
FOX, James, Pvt, Col Philip Pipkin, Capt Henry Newlin, Mil Inf
FOX, Job, Pvt, Col Samuel Bayless, Capt Branch Jones, E TN Drafted Mil
FOX, Jos, Pvt, Col R C Napier, Capt John Chism, Mil Inf
FOX, Lewis, Pvt, Col Samuel Bayless, Capt Branch Jones, E TN Drafted Mil
FOX, Mathew, Sgt, Col William Lillard, Capt James Lillard, E TN Inf Vol
FRACK, Henry, Pvt, Col Robert Steele, Capt Robert Campbell, Mil Inf
FRAGG, James, Pvt, Col Stephen Copeland, Capt Wm Hodges, Inf
FRAIZER, James, Pvt, Col Napier, Capt Patterson, Mtd Vol
FRAKER, Frederick, Pvt, Col S Bunch, Capt Gibbs, E TN Drafted Mil
FRALEY, Caleb, Pvt, Col N T Perkins, Capt George W Marr, Mtd Vol
FRALEY, Hyram, Pvt, Col N T Perkins, Capt George W Marr, Mtd Vol
FRAME, Jas, Pvt, Col R H Dyer, Maj Wm Russell, Capt Wm Russell, Vol Mtd Gunmen
FRANCE, Gideon, Pvt, Maj Gen Wm Carroll, Capt Francis Ellis, Inf
FRANCE, John, Pvt, Col Ewen Allison, Capt Jacob Royal, E TN Mil
FRANCE, John, Pvt, Col S Bunch, Capt George McPherson, E TN Mil
FRANCIS, Frizzle, Pvt, Regt Commander omitted, Capt James Haggard, Mtd Gunmen
FRANCISCO, James, Pvt, Col Wm Lillard, Capt George Argenbright, E TN Vol Riflemen
FRANK, Sam'l B, Pvt, Col Perkins, Capt McMahon, Mtd Gunmen
FRANK, Sam'l B, Pvt, Col Wm Metcalf, Capt Andrew Patterson, Mil Inf
FRANKLIN, Elijah, Pvt, Col Wm Higgins, Capt Stephen Griffith, Mtd Riflemen
FRANKLIN, Ephraim, Pvt, Col Wm Johnson, Capt James Stewart, E TN Drafted Mil
FRANKLIN, Esom, Pvt, Col Wm Hall, Capt John Kennedy, Vol Inf
FRANKLIN, George, Pvt, Col Thomas Williamson, Capt Beverly Williams, Vol Mtd Gunmen
FRANKLIN, Henry, Pvt, Col Samuel Bayless, Capt James Churchman, E TN Mil
FRANKLIN, Isaac, Pvt, no other information
FRANKLIN, John A, Pvt, Col John K Wynne, Capt James Cole, Inf
FRANKLIN, John, Cpl, Maj John Childs, Capt Reuben Tipton, E TN Vol Mtd Inf; Regt Co Jefferson
FRANKLIN, John, Pvt, Col S Bunch, Capt George Gregory, E TN Drafted Mil
FRANKLIN, John, Pvt, Col Wm Lillard, Capt John Roper, E TN Vol Inf
FRANKLIN, Lewis, Pvt, Col James Raulston, Capt Mathew Cowan, Inf
FRANKLIN, Sam'l, Pvt, Col Bayless, Capt Churchman, E TN Mil
FRANKLIN, Wesley, Pvt, Maj Russell, Capt Russell, Vol Mtd Gunmen
FRANKLIN, Wm, Cpl, Col Cannon, Capt Edwards, Regt Command
FRANKLING, Lewis, Pvt, Col Lillard, Capt Neatherton, E TN Vol Inf
FRANKS, Edmond, 4 Sgt, Col Metcalf, Capt Marks, Mil Inf; d 3-10-1815
FRANKS, Elijah, Cpl, Col Raulston, Capt Newman, Branch Srvce omitted
FRANKS, Jacob, 3 Sgt, Col Raulston, Capt Newman, Inf
FRANKS, Lemuel, Pvt, Col Steele, Capt Randals, Inf
FRANKS, Martin, Pvt, Maj Gen Jackson, Col Williamson, Capt Steele, Vol Mtd Gunmen
FRANKS, Mathew, Pvt, Maj Russell, Capt Cowan, Vol Mtd Gunmen
FRANKS, Sam'l (Lemuel), 4 Sgt, Col Raulston, Capt Newman, Inf
FRASER, Sam'l, Pvt, Col Copeland, Capt Thompson, Inf
FRASER, Thomas, Pvt, Col Steele, Capt Ralton, Mil Inf
FRASEUR, John H, Pvt, Col Lowry, Capt Looney, 2nd Regt W TN Mil; d 3-19-1815
FRASIER, John, Pvt, Col S Bunch, Capt Isaac Williams, E TN Mil
FRASIER, Wm, Pvt, Col Johnson, Capt Lawson, E TN Drafted Mil
FRASURE, John, Pvt, Col Napier, Capt Benson, Mil Inf
FRAYZER, James, Pvt, Col Allison, Capt Everett, E TN Mil; deserted 3-4-1814
FRAZER, Dan'l, Pvt, Col Williamson, Capt Moore, Vol Mtd Gunmen; d 2-7-1815
FRAZER, Ebenezer, Pvt, Regt Commander omitted, Capt Edwin S Moore, Mtd Riflemen
FRAZER, Harmon, Sgt, Col Pipkin, Capt Searcy, Mil Inf
FRAZER, James, Pvt, Col Coffee, Capt Terrill, Vol Cav
FRAZER, James, Pvt, Regt Commander omitted, Capt Nathan Farmer, Mtd Riflemen
FRAZER, James, Pvt, Regt Commander omitted, Capt Robert Evans, Mtd Spies
FRAZER, Moses, Pvt, Regt Commandre omitted, Capt Robert Evans, Mtd Spies
FRAZER, Wm, Pvt, Regt Commander omitted, Capt Nathan Farmer, Mtd Riflemen
FRAZIER, Ebenezer, Cpl, Col Dyer, Capt Jones, Vol Mtd Gunmen
FRAZIER, James, 2nd Surgeon Mate, Col R H Dyer, Co Commander omitted, Regt of Mtd Gunmen

## Enlisted Men, War of 1812

FRAZIER, Julian, Acting QM Sgt, Col Weaver, Capt Calloway, E TN Mil
FRAZIER, Julian, Pvt, Col Weaver, Capt Calloway, Mtd Inf
FRAZIER (FRAZURE), Jas, Pvt, Col Johnson, Capt Scott, E TN Drafted Mil
FRAZIEUR, James, Surgeon Mate, Brig Gen John Coffee, Co Commander omitted, TN Vol Mtd Gunmen
FRAZOR, Moses, Pvt, Col Coffee, Capt Terrill, Vol Cav
FREE, Mathew, Pvt, Col Cocke, Capt Gray, Inf; d 2-23-1815
FREE, Mathew, Pvt, Regt Commander omitted, Capt Gray, Inf
FREEMAN, Alexander, Pvt, Col John Coffee, Capt Jetton, Cav
FREEMAN, Alexander, Pvt, Col Pipkin, Capt Mebane, Mil Inf
FREEMAN, Carter, Pvt, Maj Woodfolk, Capt Ross & Capt McCully, Inf
FREEMAN, Edward, Pvt, Col Pipkin, Capt Mebane, Mil Inf
FREEMAN, Elisha, 3 Sgt, Col Cocke, Capt Crunk, Inf
FREEMAN, Elisha, Pvt, Col Cheatham, Capt Chapman, Inf
FREEMAN, Foster, Pvt, Col Brown, Capt Chiles, E TN Vol Mtd Inf
FREEMAN, Greene, Pvt, Col Winn, Capt Spinks, Inf
FREEMAN, Isum, Pvt, Col Williamson, Capt Williams, Vol Mtd Gunmen
FREEMAN, James, Pvt, Col Lillard, Capt Gillenwater, E TN Inf; deserted at Kingston 10-29-1813
FREEMAN, John P, Pvt, Col Hall, Capt Wallace, Inf
FREEMAN, John P, Pvt, Maj Carroll, Capt Dilliahunty & Capt Bradford, Vol Inf
FREEMAN, John, Pvt, Col Lillard, Capt Gillenwater, E TN Inf; deserted at Kingston 10-29-1814
FREEMAN, Joshua, Pvt, Col Wear, Capt Calloway, Mtd Inf
FREEMAN, Kenchen, Pvt, Col John Coffee, Capt Jetton, Cav
FREEMAN, Kinchen, Pvt, Col Alcorn, Capt Jetton, Vol Cav
FREEMAN, Miles, Pvt, Col Cocke, Capt Nance, Inf; d 2-5-1815
FREEMAN, Moses, Pvt, Col Lillard, Capt Dyke, Vol Inf; d 1-10-1814
FREEMAN, Obediah, Pvt, Col Pipkin, Capt Searcy, Mil Inf
FREEMAN, Parker, Pvt, Col Alcorn, Capt Byrns, Cav
FREEMAN, Reuben, Cpl, Col Raulston, Capt Newman, Inf; d 3-14-1815
FREEMAN, Reuben, Pvt, Col Bunch, Capt Vance, E TN Mtd Inf
FREEMAN, Silas, Pvt, Col Pipkin, Capt Searcy, Mil Inf
FREEMAN, William, Pvt, Col Cocke, Capt Crunk, Inf
FREEMAN, Wm, 4 Sgt, Maj Gen Carroll, Capt Ellis, Inf
FREEMAN, Zachariah, Pvt, Col Ewen Allison, Capt Jonas Loughmiller, Mil
FREEMAN, Zachariah, Pvt, Col Wm Lillard, Capt Wm Gillenwater, E TN Inf; deserted at Kingston 10-29-1813

FREG, Peter, Pvt, Lt Col A Cheatham, Co Commander omitted, 6th Brig Mtd Inf
FREMAN, Richard, Pvt, Col John Cocke, Capt Richard Crunk; substituted for John Dymont
FREMAN, Richard, Pvt, Lt Col L Hammonds & Lt Col A Loury, Capt Thomas Wells, Inf; d 1-26-1815
FREMAN, Wm, Pvt, Col Samuel Bayless, Capt John Brock, E TN Mil
FRENCH, Amos, Pvt, Maj Gen Andrew Jackson, Capt Hugh Kerr, Mtd Vol
FRENCH, Edward, Pvt, Maj Gen Wm Carroll, Capt Wm Metcalf, Capt John Jackson, Inf
FRENCH, Gideon, Pvt, Col John Cocke, Capt James Gray, Inf
FRENCH, James, Pvt, Col John Coffee, Capt David Smith, Vol Cav
FRENCH, Jeremiah, Pvt, Col Robert Dyer, Capt Bethel Allen, Vol Mtd Gunmen
FRENCH, Jeremiah, Pvt, Col S Copeland, Capt Wm Hodges, Inf
FRENCH, Jeremiah, Pvt, Col Thomas McCrory, Capt Anthony Metcalf, Mil Inf
FRENCH, Jeremiah, Sgt, Col Robert Dyer, Capt Bethel Allen, Vol Mtd Gunmen
FRENCH, Jesse, Pvt, Col Wm Higgins, Capt Samuel Allen, Mtd Gunmen
FRENCH, John P, Pvt, Col Samuel Bayless, Capt Solomon Hendrix, E TN Mil
FRENCH, John, Pvt, Col Philip Pipkin, Capt Henry Newlin, Mil Inf
FRENCH, Joshua, Pvt, Col Samuel Bayless, Capt Solomon Hendrix, E TN Mil
FRENCH, Joshua, Pvt, Col Thomas McCrory, Capt Thomas Gordon, Inf
FRENCH, Marshall, Pvt, Regt Commander omitted, Capt Josiah Askew, Inf
FRENCH, Martial, Pvt, Col John Cocke, Capt James Gray, Inf
FRENCH, Matal, Pvt, Regt Commander omitted, Capt Gray, Inf
FRENCH, Samuel C, Pvt, Col John Cocke, Capt James Gray, Inf
FRENCH, Samuel C, Pvt, Regt Commander omitted, Capt Josiah Askew, Inf
FRENCH, Samuel, Cpl, Col John Cocke, Capt James Gray, Inf
FRENCH, Samuel, Pvt, Regt Commander omitted, Capt Gray, Inf
FRENCH, Thomas, Pvt, Col Samuel Wear, Capt Rufus Morgan, E TN Vol Inf
FRENCH, Thomas, Sgt, Col John Cocke, Capt James Gray, Inf; d coming up in the steam boat 3-20-1815
FRENCH, Thomas, Sgt, Regt Commander omitted, Capt Josiah Askew, Inf
FRENCH, William, Pvt, Maj Gen Andrew Jackson, Capt Ebenezer Kirkpatrick, Mtd Gunmen
FRENCH, William, Pvt, Maj John Chiles, Capt Charles Conway, E TN Mtd Gunmen; Regimental Co Knox
FRESHOM, John, Cpl, Col Samuel Bunch, Capt James

- 201

## Enlisted Men, War of 1812

Penny, E TN Mtd Inf
FRESHOUR, George, Pvt, Col John Williams, Capt Samuel Bunch, Mtd Vol
FRESHOUR, Henry, Pvt, Col John Williams, Capt Samuel Bunch, Mtd Vol
FREZE, Jacob, Ffr, Col Samuel Bayless, Capt Solomon Hendrix, E TN Mil
FRIDAY, George, Cpl, Maj Wm Woodfolk, Capt Abner Pearce, Inf
FRIDAY, George, Pvt, Regt Commander omitted, Capt Elijah Rushing, Det of Inf
FRIEAL, Morris, Pvt, Col Thomas Benton, Capt Robert Cannon, Inf; d 2-7-1813
FRIELDS, Isaac, Cpl, Col Samuel Bunch, Capt Andrew Breden, E TN Mil
FRIELDS, John, Pvt, Col Samuel Bunch, Capt Andrew Breden, E TN Mil
FRIERSON, Elijah, Pvt, Gen Andrew Jackson, Capt Nathan Davis, Inf
FRIERSON, Thomas, Pvt, Regt Commander omitted, Capt Robert Evans, Mtd Spies
FRISTOE, Robert L, Sgt, Col John Brown, Capt John Childs, E TN Vol Mtd Gunmen
FRIZZELL, Francis, Pvt, Regt Commander, Capt Gray, Inf
FRIZZELL, Isaac, Cpl, Maj Gen Wm Carroll, Col Wm Metcalf, Capt John Jackson, Mil Inf
FROST, Alexander, Pvt, Col William Johnson, Capt James Tunnell, 3rd Regt E TN Mil; d at Ft Jackson 11-21-1814
FROST, Edward, Pvt, Maj Gen Andrew Jackson, Capt Hugh Kerr, Mtd Rangers
FROST, James, Pvt, Col S Copeland, Capt John Holshouser, Inf
FROST, John, Pvt, Col Newton Cannon, Capt William Martin (Marlin), Mtd Gunmen
FROST, John, Pvt, Col Samuel Bunch, Capt S Roberson, E TN Drafted Mil
FROST, Russell, Pvt, Col John Barton, Capt Hugh Barton, E TN Mil Inf
FROST, Stephen, Pvt, Col Samuel Bayless, Capt Allen Bacon, E TN Mil
FROST, Thomas, Pvt, Col John Brown, Capt John Childs, E TN Vol Mtd Inf
FRULL, Wm, Pvt, Col S Bunch, Capt Isaac Williams, E TN Mil; substitute for George Reed, transferred to Capt Hawk's Co
FRUSHOUR, Henry, Pvt, Col Samuel Wear, Capt James Tedford, E TN Vol Inf
FRY, Freeman, Pvt, Col John Alcorn, Capt Frederick Stump, Cav
FRY, Gabriel, Pvt, Col Edwin Booth, Capt Richard Marshall, Drafted Mil
FRY, John, Pvt, Col A Cheatham, Capt Richard Benson, Inf
FRY, John, Sgt, Col John Brown, Capt Hugh Barton, E TN Mil Inf
FRY, Peter, Pvt, Col A Cheatham, Capt Richard Benson, Inf
FRY, Peter, Pvt, Col Cheatham, Capt Richard Benson, Inf
FRY, Peter, Pvt, Col John Cocke, Capt Richard Crunk, Inf
FRY, Phillip, Pvt, Col S Bunch, Capt N Gibbs, E TN Mil
FRY, Robert, Cpl, Col Wm Johnson, Capt Joseph Hunter, E TN Mil
FRY, Robert, Cpl, Col Wm Johnson, Co Commander omitted, E TN Mil
FRY, Robert, Pvt, Col Wm Lillard, Capt Thomas Sharpe, 2nd Regt Inf
FRY, Samuel, Pvt, Maj Woodfolk, Capt James Neal, Inf
FRY, Solomon, Pvt, Col Wm Y Higgins, Capt Jas Hambleton, Mtd Gunmen
FRYAR, James, Pvt, Col Edwin E Booth, Capt John Lewis, E TN Mil
FRYAR, Jeremiah, Pvt, Col John Brown, Capt Wm Christian, E TN Mil Inf
FRYAR, Wm, Pvt, Col Edwin E Booth, Co Commander omitted, Drafted Mil
FRYAR (FRYER), Wm, Pvt, Maj John Childs, Capt Charles Conway, E TN Mtd Gunmen
FRYE, Sam'l, Pvt, Col Wm Johnson, Capt James Tunnell, E TN Mil
FRYER, James, Pvt, Col Edwin E Booth, Co Commander omitted, E TN Mil
FRYER, John H, Pvt, Maj John Childs, Capt Charles Conway, E TN Mtd Gunmen; Regimental Co Knox
FUBRELL, Dan'l L, 2 Sgt, Col John Cocke, Capt James Gray, Inf
FUGATE, Andrew, Pvt, Col R C Napier, Capt Early Benson, Mil Inf
FUGATE, John, Pvt, Col Edward Bradley, Capt Elijah Haynie, Vol Inf; deserted 11-27-1813
FUGATE, Moses, Pvt, Col Thomas H Williamson, Capt Bardette, Vol Mtd Gunmen
FUGET, John, Pvt, Col Wm Johnson, Capt Joseph Scott, E TN Drafted Mil; d 11-22-1814
FUGET, Levy, Pvt, Col Samuel Bayless, Capt John Brock, E TN Mil
FUGIT, Martin, Pvt, Col Wm Johnson, Capt James Cook, Mil
FULKS, Abel, Pvt, Col R C Napier, Capt Early Benson, Mil Inf; attached to Arty
FULKS, Abel, Pvt, Genl A Jackson, Capt Joel Parrish, Arty
FULKS, Burwell, Pvt, Col Thomas Williamson, Capt Robert Moore, Vol Mtd Gunmen; reduced from Sgt
FULKS, Elijah, Pvt, Col James Raulston & Col Carroll, Capt Edward Robinson, Inf
FULLAR, Darling, Pvt, Col John K Wynne, Capt Wm Carothers, W TN Inf; deserted 10-18-1813
FULLER, Allen, Pvt, Col Edward Bradley, Capt Harry L Douglas, Vol Inf
FULLER, Allen, Pvt, Maj Wm Woodfolk, Capt Ross & Capt McCaully, Inf
FULLER, Arthur, Pvt, Col John Cocke, Capt Bird Nance, Inf
FULLER, Benj, Cpl, Col Alexander Loury, Capt James Kincaid, Inf
FULLER, Benj, Pvt, Lt I Barrett, Capt Nathan Davis, Inf
FULLER, Benj, Pvt, Maj Wm Russell, Capt Isaac Williams, TN Vol Mtd Gunmen

FULLER, Clayton, Rank omitted, Col James Raulston, Capt Henry West, Inf
FULLER, Ezekiel, 3 Sgt, Col John Cocke, Capt Bird Nance, Inf
FULLER, Ezekiel, Pvt, Col T McCrory, Capt John Reynolds, Mil Inf
FULLER, Henry, Ffr, Col Philip Pipkin, Capt James Blackmore, Mil Inf
FULLER, Henry, Pvt, Col A Cheatham, Capt Wm Smith, Inf; d 4-11-1814
FULLER, John, Pvt, Col John Alcorn, Capt John Baskerville, Vol Inf
FULLER, John, Pvt, Col John Coffee, Capt John Baskerville, Cav
FULLER, John, Pvt, Col R C Napier, Capt Jas McMurry, Mil Inf
FULLER, Stephen, Artif, Col S Copeland, Capt Richard Sharpe, Mil Inf
FULLER, Wm, Pvt, Col A Loury, Capt Gabriel Martin, Inf
FULLER, Wm, Pvt, Col John Alcorn, Capt Robert Jetton, Vol Cav; wounded 11-3-1813, discharged 12-10-1813
FULLER, Wm, Pvt, Col Philip Pipkin, Capt Henry Newlin, Mil Inf
FULLERTON, James, Pvt, Col Wm Hall, Capt Travis Nash, Inf
FULLERTON, Robert, Pvt, Col John K Wynne, Capt John Spinks, Inf
FULLINGTON, Wm, Pvt, Col Wm Johnson, Capt Joseph Kirk, Mil; deserted from his place 9-20-1814
FULLINGTON, Wm, Pvt, Regt Commander omitted, Capt Gray, Inf
FULLMORE, George, Pvt, Col John K Wynne, Capt Wm Carothers, W TN Inf
FULMER, John, Pvt, Col Wm Lillard, Capt Jacob Hartsell, E TN Vol Inf
FULTON, James, Pvt, Col N Cannon, Capt Wm Martin, Mtd Gunmen
FULTON, John S, Sgt, Col Wm Johnson, Capt Benj Powell, E TN Mil; appointed Asst Forage Master
FULTON, John, Asst Forage Master, Brig Gen N Taylor, no other information
FULTON, Samuel, Blksmth, Col N Cannon, Capt Andrew Patterson, Mtd Riflemen
FULTON, Wm, Pvt, Col Samuel Wear, Capt Joseph Calloway, Mtd Inf
FUNK, Henry, Pvt, Brig Gen Johnson, Capt Allen, Mil Inf
FUNK, John, Pvt, Col Wm Rogers, Capt James R Rogers, E TN Drafted Mil
FUQUA, Benj, Pvt, Col James Raulston, Capt Mathew Cowan, Inf
FUQUA, Benj, Pvt, Col Robert Steele, Capt Samuel Maxwell, Mil Inf; deserted 4-29-1814
FUQUA, John, Pvt, Col James Raulston, Capt James Black, Inf
FUQUA, John, Pvt, Col T McCrory, Capt Neal Patton, Mil
FUQUA, Nathan, Pvt, Col Edward Bradley, Capt Thomas Haynie, Vol Inf
FUQUA, Thomas, Pvt, Col Edward Bradley, Capt Thomas Haynie, Vol Inf
FURGUASON, Joel, Pvt, Col S Bunch, Capt Daniel Yarnell, E TN Mil
FURGUASON, Robert, Pvt, Regt Commander omitted, Capt Daniel Yarnell, Branch Srvce omitted
FURGUSON, Andrew, Pvt, Col Edwin Booth, Capt Samuel Thompson, Mil
FURGUSON, Douglas, Pvt, Col John Alcorn, Capt Robert Jetton, Vol Cav
FURGUSON, James E, Pvt, Col Wm Hall, Capt Martin, Vol Inf
FURGUSON, John M, Pvt, Col Wm Y Higgins, Capt A Cheatham, Mtd Riflemen
FURGUSON, Joshua, Pvt, Col Wm Hall, Capt Martin, Vol Inf
FURGUSON, Samuel, Pvt, Col James Raulston, Capt Charles Wade, Inf; d 1-28-1815
FURGUSSON, Andrew, Pvt, Col Samuel Bunch, Capt Joseph Duncan, E TN Drafted Mil
FURLONG, Martin, Pvt, Col Edward Bradley, Capt Brice Martin, Vol Inf
FURLONG, Martin, Pvt, Col Wm Hall, Capt Martin, Vol Inf
FURLONG, Robert, Pvt, Col A Cheatham, Capt Birdwell, Inf
FURLORY, Hutson, Pvt, Col S Copeland, Capt Allen Wilkerson, Mil Inf
FURLORY, James, Pvt, Col S Copeland, Capt Allen Wilkerson, Mil Inf
FURRY, Daniel, Pvt, Col S Bunch, Capt Moses, E TN Drafted Mil
FUSSELL, Wyatt, Sgt, Col John Coffee, Lt Col William Phillips, 36th Regt TN Mil Inf
FUSSELL, Wyatt, Sgt, Commanders omitted, Inf
FUSTON, John, Cpl, Col Wm Y Higgins, Capt Adam Dale, Mtd Gunmen
FUTRELL, Daniel, Pvt, Col A Cheatham, Capt Wm Smith, Inf; transferred to Capt Parrish's Co
FUTRELL, Daniel, Rank omitted, Gen Andrew Jackson, Capt Joel Parrish, Arty
FUTTILL, Daniel, Pvt, Col T McCrory, Capt John Reynolds, Mil Inf
FUZZELL, Harrison, Pvt, Col Robert Dyer, Capt Thomas Jones, Vol Mtd Gunmen
FUZZLE, Wayotte, Pvt, Maj Gen Carroll, Capt Ellis, Inf
FYKES, Elisha, Pvt, Maj Gen Jackson, Capt Crane, Mtd Gunmen
FYKES, Josiah, Pvt, Maj Gen Jackson, Capt Crane, Branch Srvce omitted
GABLE, Barnabas, Pvt, Col John Coffee, Capt Daniel Ross, Mtd Gunmen
GABLE, Wm, Tptr, Col John Alcorn, Capt Robert Jetton, Vol Cav
GABLE, Wm, Tptr, Col John Coffee, Capt Robert Jetton, Cav
GABRIEL, Israel, Sgt, Col John Coffee, Capt Daniel Ross, Mtd Gunmen
GADBERRY, John, Pvt, Col John Cocke, Capt George Barnes, Inf
GAGE, Aaron, Pvt, Maj Wm Russell, Capt John Cowan, Vol Mtd Gunmen
GAGE, John, Pvt, Lt Col L Hammond, Col A Loury, Capt Thomas Delaney, Inf

## Enlisted Men, War of 1812

GAGE, John, Pvt, Maj Wm Russell, Capt Fleman Hodges, Vol Mtd Gunmen; deserted 12-23-1814
GAGE, Mathew, Pvt, Maj Wm Russell, Capt John Cowan, Vol Mtd Gunmen
GAGE, Moses, Pvt, Maj Wm Woodfolk, Capt James C Neil, Inf
GAGE, Wm, Pvt, Maj Wm Russell, Capt John Cowan, Vol Mtd Gunmen
GAIEN, John, Pvt, Col Robert Steele, Capt Samuel Maxwell, Mil Inf
GAILE, John, Pvt, Col T Williamson, Capt Anthony M Metcalf, Vol Mtd Gunmen
GAILEY, Moses, Pvt, Col John Brown, Capt John Childs, E TN Vol Mtd Inf
GAIN, Thomas, Pvt, Col Ewen Allison, Capt John Hampton, Mil
GAINER, Abner, Pvt, Col Edwin Booth, Capt Samuel Thompson, Mil
GAINER, Sam'l, Pvt, Col Samuel Wear, Capt Rufus Morgan, E TN Vol Inf
GAINER, Sam'l, Sgt, Col S Bunch, Capt Dan'l Yarnell, E TN Mil; joined Capt Parrish Co of Arty
GAINES, Dan'l, Pvt, Col Wm Hall, Capt Wm L Alexander, Vol Inf
GAINES, Francis, Pvt, Col Robert Steele, Capt Samuel Maxwell, Mil Inf
GAINES, James T, Pvt, Col Edwin Booth, Capt John Slatton, E TN Mil; appointed Asst QM
GAINES, John J, Pvt, Col John Williams, Capt David Vance, Mtd Mil
GAINES, John, Pvt, Col Wm Johnson, Capt Andrew Lawson, E TN Drafted Mil
GAINES, Joshua, Cpl, Col Wm Lillard, Capt Jacob Hartsell, E TN Vol Inf
GAINES, Joshua, Pvt, Col Wm Johnson, Capt Andrew Lawson, E TN Drafted Mil; substitute for Ephraim Drake
GAINES, Robert, Pvt, Col Samuel Wear, Capt James Gillespie, E TN Vol Inf; unable to perform duty
GAINES, Thomas, Pvt, Col Samuel Bayless, Capt Joseph D Bacon, E TN Mil
GAINES, Thomas, Pvt, Col Thomas Williamson, Capt Beverly Williams, Vol Mtd Gunmen
GAINEY, Mathew, Pvt, Col Philip Pipkin, Capt Henry M Newlin, Mil Inf; deserted from Ft Williams 9-20-1814
GAINS, Dan'l, Pvt, Col Wm Hall, Capt Wm L Alexander, Vol Inf
GAINS, Fountain III, 2 Sgt, Col N T Perkins, Capt George Eliot, Mil Inf
GAINS, James, Sgt, Col A Cheatham, Capt George C Chapman, Inf
GAINS, Moses, Pvt, Col Wm Hall, Capt Wm L Alexander, Vol Inf
GAINS, Thomas, 3 Cpl, Col James Raulston, Capt Mathew Cowan, Inf
GAINS, Thomas, Pvt, Col Wm Lillard, Capt Wm McLin, E TN Inf; joined from Capt Cole's Co
GAINS, Wm, Pvt, Col Wm Johnson, Capt Henry Hunter, E TN Mil
GAITHER, Thomas, Pvt, Regt Commander omitted, Capt I Prewitt, Mtd Vol Pack Horse Guards
GALADA, George, Pvt, Col James Raulston, Capt James A Black, Inf
GALAGLAY, George, Pvt, Col John Coffee, Capt James Terrill, Vol Cav
GALBREATH, Aneas, Pvt, Col John Williams, Capt Sam Bunch, Mtd Vol
GALBREATH, David, Pvt, Col John Brown, Capt James Standifer, E TN Vol Mtd Mil
GALBREATH, Thos, Pvt, Col John Brown, Capt James Standifer, E TN Vol Mtd Mil; transferred to Capt White
GALBREATH, Thos, Pvt, Col Samuel Wear, Capt Rufus Morgan, E TN Vol Inf
GALE, John, Pvt, Col S Copeland, Capt Wm Hodges, Inf
GALE, Thomas, Surgeon Mate, Lt Col Hammonds, 2nd Regt W TN Mil; appointed Surgeon
GALE, Thos, 1 Surgeon Mate, Col R C Napier, 1st Regt W TN Mil
GALE, Thos, 2 Surgeon Mate, Col A Loury, Lt Col L Hammonds, 2nd Regt W TN Mil; appointed surgeon
GALE, Thos, Surgeon Mate, Col Samuel Bunch, E TN Mil; attached to Regt
GALESPIE, James, 2nd Master, Lt John Edmondson, no other information
GALIGLE, Ephraim, Pvt, Maj Gen Wm Carroll, Col Wm Metcalf, Capt John Jackson, Inf
GALION, Amos, Pvt, Col Edwin Booth, Capt Porter, Drafted Mil
GALION, John, Pvt, Col Ewen Allison, Capt Jonas Loughmiller, Mil
GALION, Wm, Pvt, Col James Raulston, Capt Henry West, Inf
GALLAHER, James, Pvt, Maj James Porter, Capt James Anderson, Cav
GALLAHER, Thomas C, Pvt, Maj James Porter, Capt James Anderson, Cav
GALLAHER, Wm, Pvt, Col John Brown, Capt Wm Christian, E TN Mil Inf; not able to do duty
GALLAWAY, Charles, Pvt, Col Samuel Wear, Capt John Bayless, Mtd Inf
GALLAWAY, James, Pvt, Col Wm Lillard, Capt George Keys, E TN Inf
GALLAWAY, James, Pvt, Lt Col L Hammond, Col A Loury, Capt Thomas Wells, Inf
GALLAWAY, Jesse, Sgt, Col Samuel Wear, Capt John Bayless, Mtd Inf; promoted from Cpl
GALLAWAY, John, Pvt, Col Ewen Allison, Capt Jacob Hoyal, E TN Mil
GALLAWAY, John, Pvt, Col John Cocke, Capt Joseph Price, Inf
GALLAWAY, John, Pvt, Col Wm Lillard, Capt George Keys, E TN Inf
GALLAWAY, Wiles (Willie), Pvt, Col T Williamson, Capt James Cook & Capt John Crane, Vol Mtd Gunmen
GALLEWAY, Jesse, 2 Cpl, Maj Childs, Capt Conway, E TN Mtd Gunmen; Regimental Co Knox
GALLEY, Thos, Pvt, Col John K Wynne, Capt Robert Brader, Inf

## Enlisted Men, War of 1812

GALLIAN, Thos, Pvt, Col S Copeland, Capt Williams Evans, Mil Inf
GALLIGBY, George, Pvt, Regt Commander omitted, Capt James Terrill, Cav; old Vol discharged
GALLIGLA, Wm, Pvt, Maj Woodfolk, Capt Neil, Inf
GALLIHER, Wiatt, Pvt, Col Bayless, Capt Churchman, E TN Mil
GALLIMORE, David, Pvt, Col Brown, Capt White, E TN Vol Mtd Inf
GALLION, Jacob, Pvt, Col Steele, Capt Cheetwood, Mil Inf
GALLISPIE, Thomas, Pvt, Col Weaver, Capt Morgan, E TN Vol Mil
GALLISPIE, Wm, Pvt, Col Wear, Capt Morgan, Branch Srvce omitted
GALLOWAY, Enoch, Pvt, Col A Loury, Lt Col L Hammond, Capt Thomas Wells, Inf
GALLOWAY, John, Pvt, Col S Bunch, Capt George McPherson, E TN Mil
GALLOWAY, Wm, Pvt, Col Dyer, Capt Evans, Vol Mtd Gunmen
GALYON, Jacob, Pvt, Col S Bunch, Capt John English, E TN Drafted Mil; deserted 3-4-1814
GAMBEL, James, Pvt, Maj Woodfolk, Capt Pearce, Inf; joined by transfer from Capt Turner's Co
GAMBELL, John, Cpl, Maj Russell, Capt Hodges, Vol Mtd Gunmen; substitute for E Burleson
GAMBELL, Sam'l, Pvt, Col Williamson, Capt Tate, Vol Mtd Gunmen
GAMBIL, Martin, Pvt, Col Benton, Capt Smith, Vol Inf
GAMBILL, James, 5 Cpl, Col Pipkin, Capt Strother, Mil
GAMBLE, Francis, Pvt, Col Lillard, Capt Keyes, E TN Inf
GAMBLE, James, Pvt, Col Coffee, Capt Coleman, Cav; substitute for Benj Ward
GAMBLE, James, Pvt, Col Wear, Capt Gillespie, E TN Vol Inf
GAMBLE, James, Sgt, Maj Russell, Capt Trimble, Vol Mtd Gunmen
GAMBLE, Joe, Tptr, Col Cannon, Capt Patterson, Mtd Riflemen
GAMBLE, John, 3 Sgt, Col Raulston, Capt Cowan, Inf
GAMBLE, Kinchen G, Pvt, Col Napier, Capt McCarty, Mil Inf
GAMBLE, Moses, Pvt, Maj Childs, Capt Stephens, E TN Vol Inf
GAMBLER, James, Cpl, Col Napier, Capt Preston, Mil Inf
GAMBREL, Martin, 1 Cpl, Col Pillow, Capt Smith, Vol Inf
GAMBRELL, Milton, Cpl, Col N Cannon, Capt Martin, Mtd Gunmen
GAMMEL, Andrew, 2 Cpl, Col Metcalf, Capt Hurt, Mil Inf
GAMMON, Dozier, Pvt, Col Wear, Capt Bayless, Mtd Inf
GAMMON, Harris, Pvt, Col Wear, Capt Bayless, Mtd Inf
GAMMON, Jeremiah, Pvt, Col Bradley, Capt Martin, Vol Inf
GAMMON, Jeremiah, Pvt, Col Hall, Capt Martin, Vol Inf
GAMMON, John, Pvt, Col S Bunch, Capt N Gibbs, E TN Drafted Mil
GAMMON, Levi, Pvt, Col Williamson, Capt Metcalf, Vol Mtd Gunmen
GAMMON, Lewis, Pvt, Maj Childs, Capt Conway, E TN Mtd Gunmen; Regimental Co Knox
GAMMON, Thomas, Pvt, Col Hammond, Capt Tubb, Inf
GAMMON, Wm, Pvt, Col Steele, Capt Ratton, Mil Inf
GANES, Brandis, Pvt, Col Winn, Capt Holleman, Inf; deserted 11-19-1813
GANMISON, Hugh B, Pvt, Col Thomas Williamson, Capt Anthony Metcalf, Vol Mtd Gunmen
GANN, George, Pvt, Col Allison, Capt McCray, E TN Mil; transferred to Capt Register's Co
GANN, George, Pvt, Col S Bunch, Capt F Register, E TN Mil
GANN, Isaac, Pvt, Col John Williams, Capt Samuel Bunch, Mtd Vol
GANN, Joshua, Pvt, Col Johnson, Capt Lawson, E TN Drafted Mil; substitute for Wm Patton
GANN, Reuben, Pvt, Col John Williams, Capt Sam Bunch, Mtd Vol
GANN, Thomas, Pvt, Col Wear, Capt Bowman, Mtd Inf
GANNAWAY, Burrell, Pvt, Col Cannon, Capt Yardley, Mtd Riflemen
GANNAWAY, James, Pvt, Col McCrory, Capt Dooley, Inf
GANNELS, Joseph, Pvt, Col Hammond, Capt Rains, Inf; transferred to Capt Wells
GANT, James, Pvt, Col McCrory, Capt McKnight, Inf
GANT, James, Pvt, Col Napier, Capt Ashmore, Mil Inf
GANT, Mathew, Pvt, Col Lillard, Capt Roper, E TN Vol Inf
GANTER, George, Pvt, Col Perkins, Capt Johnston, Mil Inf
GANTER (GUNTER), Joshua, Pvt, Col Pillow, Capt McEwen, Vol Inf
GARAWAY, John, Pvt, Maj Woodfolk, Capt Turner, Inf
GARBROUGH, Ambrose, Pvt, Col McCrory, Capt Gordon, Inf
GARDENHIRE, George, Pvt, Maj Childs, Capt Conway, E TN Mtd Gunmen; Regimental Co - Roan
GARDENHIRE, Thomas, Pvt, Col Copeland, Capt Williams, Inf
GARDNER, Cullen, QM Sgt, Gen John Coffee, TN Vol Mtd Inf
GARDNER, Dan'l, Pvt, Col Copeland, Capt George, Inf
GARDNER, Dempsey, Pvt, Lt Col John Edmonson, Co Commander omitted, Cav
GARDNER, George, Pvt, Col A Loury, Capt Gabriel Martin, Inf
GARDNER, Jacob, Pvt, Col Edwin Booth, Capt Samuel Thompson, Mil; d 3-3-1815
GARDNER, James, Pvt, Regt Commander omitted, Capt Gray, Inf
GARDNER, Jesse, Pvt, Lt Col A Cheatham, Co Commander omitted, 6th Brig Mtd Inf
GARDNER, John, Pvt, Col John K Wynne, Capt John Porter, Inf
GARDNER, John, Pvt, Maj Wm Carroll, Capt Dan'l Bradford & Capt Lewis Dillahunty, Vol Inf
GARDNER, John, Sgt, Col John Wynne, Capt Wm Wilson, Inf
GARDNER, Joshua, Pvt, Lt Col John Edmonson, Co Commander omitted, Cav

- 205

*Enlisted Men, War of 1812*

GARDNER, Nathan, Pvt, Col T Williamson, Capt Beverly Williams, Vol Mtd Gunmen
GARDNER, Robert, Pvt, Col James Raulston, Capt Mathew Neal, Inf; d 1-5-1815
GARDNER, Robert, Pvt, Col R C Napier, Capt James McMurry, Mil Inf
GARDNER, Sam'l G, Pvt, Maj Wm Carroll, Capt Daniel Bradford & Capt Lewis Dillahunty, Vol Inf; promoted to Cpl
GARDNER, Thomas, 1 Cpl, Col John Brown, Capt Wm White, E TN Vol Inf
GARDNER, Wm, Pvt, Lt James Berry, Co Commander omitted, Mtd Riflemen
GARDNER (GAINER), Sam'l, 4 Cpl, Col A Cheatham, Capt James Giddins, Inf
GARIM, John, Pvt, Col John Coffee, Capt David Smith, Vol Cav
GARING (GORING), Reuben, Pvt, Col R C Napier, Capt Thomas Preston, Mil Inf
GARLAND, Jesse, Cpl, Col R H Dyer, Capt Robert Evans, Vol Mtd Gunmen
GARLAND, Jesse, Pvt, Col John Coffee, Capt Daniel Ross, Mtd Gunmen
GARLAND, Jos, Pvt, Col Samuel Bayless, Capt Jonathan Wadell, E TN Mil
GARLAND, Joshua, Pvt, Col Samuel Bayless, Capt Jonathan Waddell, E TN Mil
GARLAND, Sam'l, Sgt, Maj Gen A Jackson, Col Thomas Williamson, Capt Robert Steele, Vol Mtd Gunmen
GARLAND, Solomon, Pvt, Maj Gen A Jackson, Col Thomas Williamson, Capt Robert Steele, Vol Mtd Gunmen
GARLAND, Wm, Pvt, Col Samuel Bayless, Capt Solomon Hendricks, E TN Mil
GARLAND (GARLON), Jesse, Pvt, Col Wm Lillard, Capt Jacob Hartsell, E TN Vol Inf
GARLAND (GARLON), John, Pvt, Col Wm Lillard, Capt Jacob Hartsell, E TN Vol Inf
GARLEY, Davis, Sgt, no other information
GARMON, Jacob, Pvt, Col Wm Metcalf, Capt Andrew Patterson, Mil Inf; d 2-24-1815
GARNELL, James, Pvt, Maj Wm Woodfolk, Capt James C Neil, Inf
GARNER, Abner, Col Samuel Wear, Capt John Stephens, E TN Vol Inf
GARNER, Benj, Pvt, Col Wm Y Higgins, Capt Adam Dale, Mtd Gunmen
GARNER, Fushee, Pvt, Col Wm Pillow, Capt Wm J Smith, Vol Inf; deserted 11-16-1813
GARNER, Fushel, Pvt, Col Thomas Benton, Capt Wm J Smith, Vol Inf
GARNER, George, Pvt, Col Wm Johnson, Capt James Tunnell, E TN Mil; substitute for John Farmer
GARNER, Haislip, Pvt, Col R H Dyer, Maj Wm Russell, Capt Wm Russell, Vol Mtd Gunmen
GARNER, James, Pvt, Lt Col A Cheatham, Co Commander omitted, 6th Brig Mtd Inf
GARNER, Jeremiah, Pvt, Col John Williams, Capt David Vance, Mtd Mil
GARNER, John, Pvt, Col Thomas Benton, Capt Wm J Smith, Vol Inf
GARNER, John, Pvt, Col Wm Pillow, Capt Wm J Smith, Vol Inf
GARNER, John, Pvt, Regt Commander omitted, Capt Smith, Vol Inf
GARNER, John, Tptr, Lt Col A Cheatham, no other information
GARNER, Johns, Pvt, Lt Col L Hammond, Capt James Craig, Inf
GARNER, Jos, Cpl, Col N T Perkins, Capt John Doak, Mtd Vol Gunmen
GARNER, Richard, Pvt, Col Thomas Benton, Capt Robert Cannon, Inf
GARNER, Robert, Pvt, Maj Wm Russell, Capt John Cowan, Vol Mtd Gunmen
GARNER, Robert, Pvt, Regt Commander omitted, Capt David Smith, Cav Vol; deserted 10-19-1813
GARNER, Robert, Pvt, Regt Commander omitted, Capt Samuel Allen, Pack Horse Guards
GARNER, Sam'l, Pvt, Col Wm Y Higgins, Capt Samuel A Allen, Mtd Gunmen
GARNER, Thomas H, Pvt, Col R H Dyer, Maj Wm Russell, Capt Wm Russell, Vol Mtd Gunmen
GARNER, Wm, 4 Cpl, Maj John Childs, Capt John Stephens, E TN Vol Mtd Inf
GARNER, Wm, Pvt, Col S Bunch, Capt Jones Griffin, E TN Drafted Mil
GARNER, Wm, Pvt, Col Wm Y Higgins, Capt Samuel A Allen, Mtd Gunmen
GARNER, Wm, Pvt, Maj Wm Russell, Capt John Cowan, Vol Mtd Gunmen
GARNER, Wm, Pvt, Regt Commander omitted, Capt Samuel Allen, Pack Horse Guards
GARRAN, Peter, Pvt, Col Robert Steele, Capt James Shenault, Mil Inf
GARRET, George W, Pvt, Col John Cocke, Capt John Dalton, Inf
GARRETT, Caleb, Pvt, Maj Wm Carroll, Capt Daniel M Bradford & Capt Lewis Dillahunty, Vol Inf
GARRETT, Catlett, Pvt, Col Wm Johnson, Capt Jas R Rogers, E TN Drafted Mil; d 11-21-1814
GARRETT, Francis, Pvt, Maj Wm Carroll, Capt Daniel M Bradford & Capt Lewis Dillahunty, Vol Inf
GARRETT, George W, Pvt, Maj Wm Carroll, Capt Daniel M Bradford & Capt Lewis Dillahunty, Vol Inf
GARRETT, Jacob, Pvt, Col S Bunch, Capt John Houk, E TN Mil
GARRETT, Jacob, Pvt, Col S Bunch, Co Commander omitted, E TN Drafted Mil
GARRETT, Jacob, Pvt, Col Samuel Bayless, Capt Joseph Hale, E TN Mil
GARRETT, James, Pvt, Col N T Perkins, Capt John Doak, Vol Mtd Gunmen
GARRETT, James, Pvt, Col Thomas Williamson, Capt James Cook & Capt John Dobbins, Vol Mtd Gunmen
GARRETT, John, Pvt, Col John Alcorn, Capt Wm Locke, Cav
GARRETT, John, Pvt, Col Robert Steele, Capt John Cheetwood, Mil Inf; transferred to Arty
GARRETT, John, Pvt, Col S Copeland, Capt Wm Evans,

## Enlisted Men, War of 1812

GARRETT, John, Pvt, Col Thomas H Benton, Capt Wm Moore, Vol Inf

GARRETT, John, Pvt, Col Thomas Williamson, Capt James Cook & Capt John Dobbins, Vol Mtd Gunmen; substituted Wm Barron

GARRETT, John, Pvt, Regt Commander omitted, Capt Joel Parrish, Arty

GARRETT, Larkin, Pvt, Col S Copeland, Capt Wm Hodges, Inf

GARRETT, Lewis, Pvt, Col Thomas H Williamson, Capt James Cook & Capt John Dobbins, Vol Mtd Gunmen

GARRETT, Malicah, Pvt, Col R H Dyer, Capt Beverly Williams, Vol Mtd Gunmen; d 1-20-1815

GARRETT, Martin, Pvt, Col John Coffee, Capt Frederick Stump, Cav

GARRETT, Pleasant, Pvt, Col S Bunch, Capt George Gregory, E TN Drafted Mil

GARRETT, Pleasant, Pvt, Col S Bunch, Capt John English, E TN Drafted Mil

GARRETT, Richard, Pvt, Maj Gen A Jackson, Capt Wm Carroll, Vol Inf

GARRETT, Thomas, 4 Cpl, Maj Gen Wm Carroll, Capt Wiley Huddleston, Col Raulston, Inf; d 1-5-1815

GARRETT, Wm, Pvt, Col G W Steele, Capt John Chitwood, Mil Inf

GARRIGAS, John, Pvt, Col Wm Metcalf, Co Commander omitted, Mil Inf

GARRIGAS, Wm, Pvt, Col Wm Metcalf, Capt Bird L Hurt, Mil Inf

GARRISON, Bailey, Pvt, Col James Raulston, Co Commander omitted, Inf; d 2-27-1815

GARRISON, Benjamin, Pvt, Col James Raulston, Capt James Black, Inf

GARRISON, Elijah, Pvt, Col John Coffee, Capt Frederick Stump, Branch Srvce omitted

GARRISON, Ezekiel, Rank omitted, Col A Loury, Co Commander omitted, Inf

GARRISON, Mason, Pvt, Col James Raulston, Capt Henry Hamilton, Inf; also served Maj Gen Carroll

GARRISON, Moses, Pvt, Col Copeland, Capt Hodge, Inf

GARRISON, Moses, Sgt, Col R H Dyer, Co Commander omitted, Vol Mtd Gunmen

GARRISON, Obadiah, Pvt, Col Wm Higgins, Capt Adam Dale, Mtd Gunmen

GARTNER, Conrad, Ffr, Col S Bayless, Capt Joseph Hale, E TN Mil

GARTNER, James, Pvt, Col Samuel Bayless, Capt Joseph Hale, E TN Mil

GARY, Archibald, Pvt, Col John Coffee, Capt Daniel Ross, Mtd Gunmen

GASAWAY, John, Pt, Col Philip Pipkin, Capt George Mebane, Mil Inf; deserted from Ft Jackson 9-20-1814

GASAWAY, John, Pvt, Col John Coffee, Capt Blackman Coleman, Cav

GASKILL, Robert, Pvt, Col Wm Hall, Capt Henry Newlin, Inf

GASS, Andrew, 4 Sgt, Maj John Childs, Capt Reuben Tipton, E TN Vol Mtd Inf; Regimental Co - Jefferson

GASS, Andrew, Pvt, Maj John Childs, Capt Reuben Tipton, E TN Vol Mtd Inf; Regimental Co - Jefferson

GASS, James, Sgt, Col Bunch, Capt Penney, E TN Mtd Inf

GASS, John, Cpl, Col Lillard, Capt Maloney, E TN Vol Inf

GASS, John, Pvt, Col Lillard, Capt McCalpin, E TN Mil Inf

GASS, John, Pvt, Col S Bunch, Capt George Gregory, E TN Drafted Mil

GASS, Sam'l, Pvt, Col Bayless, Capt Hendrix, E TN Mil

GASSAWAY, Nicholas, Pvt, Col Pipkin, Capt Mebane, Mil Inf

GASTEN (GHASTON), Thomas, Pvt, Col Booth, Capt Briggs, Inf

GASTON, John, Pvt, Col Cocke, Capt Gray, Inf

GASTON, Thomas, Pvt, Col Bunch, Capt Duncan, E TN Drafted Mil; joined from Capt Buchanan's Co

GASTON, Thos, Pvt, Col Bunch, Capt Buchanan, E TN Drafted Mil

GATES, Bartholomew, Pvt, Col Lowry, Lt Col Hammons, Capt Rains, Inf

GATES, James, Pvt, Col Williamson, Capt Martin, Vol Mtd Gunmen

GATES, John, Pvt, Col Dyer, Capt Edmonson, TN Vol Mtd Gunmen; transferred to Capt Hudson

GATES, John, Pvt, Col Dyer, Capt Hudson, Vol Mtd Gunmen

GATES, John, Pvt, Lt Col Hammons, Capt Rains, Inf

GATES, Thomas, Pvt, Maj Woodfolk, Capt Neil, Inf

GATES, Valentine, Pvt, Col Copeland, Capt George, Inf

GATES (GAITS), Wm, Pvt, Maj Gen Carroll, Col Raulston, Capt Robinson, Inf

GATHIS, Sam'l, Pvt, Brig Gen Johnston, Capt Allen, Mil Inf

GATLAND, Dempsey, Pvt, Col Williamson, Capt Doak & Dobbins, Vol Mtd Gunmen

GATLAND, James, Pvt, Col Williamson, Capt Cook & Dobbins, Vol Mtd Gunmen; substitute for Isaac Gatland

GATLAND (GANTLET), John H, Pvt, Col Metcalf, Capt Jackson, Inf

GATLEN, Ephraim, Sgt, Regt Commander omitted, Capt Gray, Inf

GATLIN, Aron P, Pvt, Col Pipkin, Capt Newlin, Mil Inf

GATLIN, Edmond, Pvt, Col A Loury, Capt J N Williamson, W TN Mil

GATLIN, Edmond, Pvt, Col L Hammond, Capt J N Williamson, 2nd Regt Inf

GATLIN, Emund, Pvt, Lt Col L Hammond, Capt Williamson, Inf

GATLIN, Ephraim, Pvt, Lt Col Wm Phillips, Co Commander omitted, Inf

GATLIN, Isaac, Pvt, Col Williamson, Capt Cook & Dobbins, Vol Mtd Gunmen

GATLIN, Jethro P, Pvt, Col Coffee, Capt Coleman, Cav

GATLIN, Jethro T, Pvt, Col Cocke, Capt Barnes, Inf; d 2-14-1815

GATLIN, John, 3 Sgt, Col Napier, Capt Chism, Mtd Inf

GATLIN, John, Pvt, Col Cocke, Capt Barnes, Inf

GATLIN, Richard, Pvt, Regt Commander omitted, Capt Abner Pearce, Inf

GATTIS, Isaac, Pvt, Col Metcalf, Capt Sutton, Mil Inf
GAUF (GAUGH), Ambrose, Pvt, Col Brown, Capt White, E TN Vol Mtd Inf
GAULT, Hugh C, Ffr, Col Metcalf, Capt Waller, Mil Inf
GAULT, James, Capt, Col Cocke, Capt Jas Gault, Inf
GAUN (GANN), Wm, Pvt, Col Johnson, Capt Lawson, E TN Drafted Mil
GAUREY, John, Pvt, Col Bradley, Capt Kennedy, Riflemen
GAY, Alexander, Pvt, Col Wear, Capt Stephens, E TN Vol Inf
GAY, Mills, Pvt, Col Steele, Capt Cheetwood, Mil Inf
GAY, Richard, Pvt, Col Wear, Capt Stephens, E TN Vol Inf
GAY, Simon, Pvt, Col Perkins, Capt Eliot, Mil Inf
GAYNE, Jeremiah, Pvt, Lt Col John Edmonson, Co Commander omitted, Inf
GAYNES, Wm, Pvt, no other information
GAZAWAY (GASAWAY), Wm, Pvt, Col Pipkin, Capt Mebane, Mil Inf
GA___ (GARRET), George W, Pvt, Col John Cocke, Capt John Dalton, Inf
GEAINER, Samuel, Pvt, Maj Gen Andrew Jackson, Capt Joel Parrish, Arty
GEAR (GREER), Andrew, Pvt, Col Lowry, Capt Kincaid, Inf; deserted 9-22-1814
GEAREN, Isaac, Pvt, Maj Childs, Capt Conway, E TN Mtd Gunmen
GEAREN, Samuel, Pvt, Col Brown, Capt Reany, Mtd Gunmen
GEASON, Simeon, 1 Cpl, Col John Brown, Capt Standifer, E TN Vol Mtd Mil
GEE, David, Pvt, no other information
GEE, Henry, Pvt, Col Perkins, Co Commander omitted, Mil Inf
GEE, Henry, Pvt, Regt Commander omitted, Capt Joseph Williams, Mil Cav
GEE, James N, Pvt, Col Pipkin, Capt Searcy, Mil Inf
GEE, John S, Cpl, Col Pipkin, Capt Newlin, Mil Inf; substitute for Josiah Alexander
GEE, John S, Pvt, Col Cannon, Capt Hunby, Mtd Riflemen
GEE, John S, Pvt, Col Copeland, Capt Holshouser, Inf
GEE, John, Tptr, Col Perkins, Capt Johnson, Mil Inf
GEE, Thomas, Sgt, Col Hammond, Capt Craig, 2nd Regt W TN Mil
GEE, Wm, Pvt, Col T McCrory, Capt Isaac Patton, Mil Inf
GEE (JEE), James H, Ffr, Maj Gen Carroll, Capt Bradford & Dillahunty, Vol Inf
GEER, Frederick, Pvt, Maj Woodfolk, Capt Pearce, Inf
GEFFREY, Thos, Pvt, Col Lillard, Capt Neatherton, E TN Vol Inf
GENEA, John, Pvt, Col Wear & Col Bunch, Capt Mitchell, E TN Mtd Inf
GENNINGS, John, Pvt, Maj Woodfolk, Capt Turner, Inf
GENNINGS, Sinclair, Pvt, Col Allison, Capt Everett, E TN Mil; furnished substitute
GENNINGS, Wm, Pvt, Col Allison, Capt Everett, E TN Mil; reduced from Cpl
GENO, Francis, Pvt, Col S Bunch, Capt Jones Griffin, E TN Drafted Mil; joined from Capt Wilson's Co
GENOE, John, Sgt, Col Booth, Capt Winton, E TN Mil
GENS, John, Pvt, Col John Brown, Capt James Preston, Regt E TN Mil Inf
GENT, Josiah, Pvt, Col Steele, Capt Ratton, Mil Inf
GENTRY, Allen, Pvt, Col John Brown, Capt James Preston, Regt E TN Mil Inf
GENTRY, Charles, Pvt, Col Lillard, Capt McChiristian, E TN Vol Inf
GENTRY, Elijah, Pvt, Col Cannon, Capt Yardley, Mtd Riflemen
GENTRY, Elijah, Pvt, Col Williamson, Capt Pace, Lt Neely, Vol Mtd Gunmen; dismissed day mustered in
GENTRY, George, Pvt, Regt Commander omitted, Capt David Mason, Cav
GENTRY, James, Pvt, Col N Cannon, Capt Martin, Mtd Gunmen
GENTRY, John, Pvt, Col Metcalf, Capt Collins, Mil Inf
GENTRY, John, Pvt, Col Napier, Capt Ashmore, Mil Inf
GENTRY, John, Pvt, Col Steele, Capt Maxwell, Mil Inf
GENTRY, Martin, Ffr, Col S Bunch, Capt N Gibbs, E TN Draft Mil
GENTRY, Nicholas, Pvt, Regt Commander omitted, Capt David Mason, Cav
GENTRY, Reynolds, Pvt, Col Wear, Capt Gillespie, E TN Vol Inf
GENTRY, Samuel, Pvt, Regt Commander omitted, Capt David Mason, Cav
GENTRY, Silas, Pvt, Col Bunch, Capt Stephens, E TN Mtd Inf
GENTRY, Thomas G, Sgt, Col Cocke, Capt Dalton, Inf
GENTRY, Thomas, 1 Cpl, Col Cannon, Capt Hogan, Mtd Gunmen
GENTRY, William, Pvt, Col Cocke, Capt Gray, Inf
GENTRY, William, Pvt, Col Steele, Capt Campbell, Mil Inf
GENTRY, William, Pvt, Regt Commander omitted, Capt Abner Pearce, Inf
GENTRY, William, Sgt, Col Johnson, Capt Stuart, E TN Draft Mil
GENTRY, William, Sgt, Col S Bunch, Capt N Gibbs, E TN Draft Mil
GENTRY, William, Sgt, Col William Johnson, Capt Stewart, 3 Regt E TN Mil
GEORGE, Carroll, Pvt, Col Lillard, Capt Neatherton, E TN Vol Inf
GEORGE, Charles N, Pvt, Col S Bunch, Capt George McPherson, E TN Mil
GEORGE, Elias, Pvt, Col Copeland, Capt Tait, Inf
GEORGE, Elias, Pvt, Maj Russell, Capt Chism, Vol Mtd Gunmen
GEORGE, James, Pvt, Col Copeland, Capt Douglass, Inf
GEORGE, John, Pvt, Col Allison, Capt Wilson, E TN Draft Mil
GEORGE, John, Pvt, Col Brown, Capt Lewen, E TN Vol Mtd Inf
GEORGE, John, Pvt, Col Hall, Capt Moore, Vol Inf
GEORGE, John, Sgt, Col Bradley, Capt Moore, Vol Inf
GEORGE, Michael, Pvt, Col Allison, Capt Wilson, E TN Draft Mil
GEORGE, Reubin, Pvt, Col Wear, Capt Bayless, Mtd Inf

## Enlisted Men, War of 1812

GEORGE, Thomas, Pvt, Col Bayless, Capt Jones, E TN Draft Mil
GEORGE, Thomas, Pvt, Col Wear, Capt Stephens, E TN Vol Inf
GEORGE, William, Cpl, Col Wynne, Capt Porter, Inf; wounded at Talledega
GEREN, Panell, Sgt, Regt Commander omitted, Capt I Prewitt, Pack Horse Guards
GEREN, Silas, Cpl, Col Booth, Capt McKenny, E TN Mil; promoted from ranks
GEREN, Solomon, Pvt, no Regt Commander, Capt I Prewitt, Pack Horse Guards
GERMAN, Daniel, Pvt, no other information
GERON, Hiram, Pvt, Col Wear, Capt Bayless, Mtd Inf
GERON, Samuel, Pvt, Col John Brown, Capt James Standifer, E TN Vol Mtd Mil
GERON (GIRON), Thomas, Pvt, Col Wear, Capt Bayless, Mtd Inf
GERRET (GARRET), John, Pvt, Lt Col Hammond, Capt Craig, Inf
GERRING, Joseph, Pvt, Col John Williams, Capt William Walker, Vol
GESS, Charles, Pvt, Col Bayless, Capt Hale, E TN Mil
GESS, Christopher, Pvt, Col Raulston, Capt Haynie, Inf
GESS, James, Pvt, Maj Chiles, Capt Tipton, E TN Vol Mtd Inf; Regt Co Jefferson
GESS, John, Pvt, Col Samuel Bayless, Capt Joseph Hale, E TN Mil
GESS, John, Pvt, Col Wynne, Capt Cole, Inf
GESS, Joseph, Pvt, Col John K Wynne, Capt James Cole, Inf
GEST (GIST), Neal, Pvt, Col William Johnson, Capg James Tunnell, E TN Mil
GEST (GUEST), James, Pvt, Col William Metcalf, Maj Gen William Carroll, Capt A Jackson, Inf
GEST (GUEST), Joshua, Pvt, Col William Metcalf, Maj Gen William Carroll, Capt A Jackson, Inf
GETINGS, Asahel, Pvt, Col James Raulston, Capt Henry West, Inf
GHOLSON, Benjamin, Pvt, Col A Loury, Capt John Looney, W TN Inf
GHOLSON, Benjamin, Pvt, Col Thomas Benton, Capt Benjamin Reynolds, Vol Inf
GHOLSON, John, Pvt, Brig Gen Roberts, Capt Benjamin Reynolds, Mtd Rangers
GHOLSON, John, Pvt, Col Thomas Benton, Capt Benjamin Reynolds, Vol Inf
GHOLSON, John, Pvt, Regt Commander omitted, Capt John Gordon, Mtd Spies
GHOLSON, John, QM, Maj Thomas Williamson, no Co Commander
GHOLSON, William, 2 Sgt, Col Thomas Benton, Capt Benjamin Reynolds, Vol Inf
GHOLSON, William, SGt, Col Thomas Benton, Capt Benjamin Reynolds, Vol Inf
GHOLSTON, Reuben, Pvt, Col Samuel Bunch, Capt Andrew Breden, E TN Mil
GHOMLEY, Michael, Pvt, Col John Brown, Capt Jesse Reany, Mtd Gunmen
GIBBINS (GIBSON), Charles, Pvt, Col Ewen Allison, Capt Jonas Loughmiller, 1 Mil

GIBBON, William, Pvt, no other information
GIBBONS, Edward, Pvt, Col Copeland, Capt David Williams, Inf
GIBBONS, Epps, Pvt, Col William Lillard, Capt William Gillenwater, E TN Inf
GIBBONS, William, Pvt, Col John Alcorn, Capt William Locke, Cav
GIBBONS, William, Pvt, Col John Coffee, Capt Blackman Coleman, Cav
GIBBONS, William, Pvt, Maj John Childs, Capt James Cummings, E TN Vol Mtd Inf
GIBBS, Austin, Pvt, Col A Loury, Capt Gabriel Martin, Inf
GIBBS, Austin, Pvt, Col William Hall, Capt James Hambleton, Vol Inf
GIBBS, George, Pvt, Col William Johnson, Capt Andrew Lawson, E TN Draft Mil
GIBBS, Jacob, Pvt, Col Samuel Wear, Capt John Bayless, Mtd Inf
GIBBS, James, Pvt, Col S Bayless, Co Commander omitted, E TN Mil
GIBBS, James, Pvt, Col William Johnson, Capt James R Rogers, E TN Draft Mil
GIBBS, James, Pvt, Maj William Russell, Capt William Chism, Vol Mtd Gunmen
GIBBS, Mathew, Pvt, Col William Metcalf, Capt John Cunningham & Capt Alexander Hill, Mil Inf
GIBBS, Miles N, Pvt, Col William Metcalf, Capt William Mullen, Mil Inf
GIBBS, Miles W, Pvt, Col Al Cheatham, Maj Gen A Jackson, Capt William Creel, Inf
GIBBS, Samuel R, Pvt, Col William Johnson, Capt David McKamy, E TN B? Mil; AWOL
GIBBS, Samuel, Pvt, Col Philip Pipkin, Capt David Smythe, W TN Mil
GIBBS, Stafford, Pvt, Col Samuel Wear, Capt James Tedford, E TN Vol Inf
GIBBS, Thomas, Pvt, Regt Commander omitted, Capt Elijah Rushing, Detachment of Inf
GIBBS, Thomas, Sgt, Col R C Napier, Capt Thomas Gray, Mil Inf
GIBBS, William, Pvt, Maj William Russell, Capt William Chism, Vol Mtd Gunmen
GIBBS, William, Pvt, Regt Commander omitted, Capt Larkin Ferrell, Inf
GIBEONS, David, Pvt, Maj William Woodfolk, Capt Abner Pearce, Inf; trans. from Neil
GIBLEY, Osteen, Pvt, Lt Col Henry Bryan, Co Commander omitted, Mil Inf
GIBS, James, Pvt, Col Samuel Bayless, Capt John Brock, E TN Mil
GIBSON, Amos, Pvt, Col Samuel Wear, Capt Jesse Cole, Vol Inf
GIBSON, Byram, Pvt, Col Samuel Bayless, Capt Joseph B. Bacon, E TN Mil
GIBSON, Garrett, Pvt, Col William Lillard, Capt Thomas Sharpe, 2 Regt Inf
GIBSON, George M, Pvt, Col Thomas Williamson, Capt John Doak & Capt John Dobbins, Vol Mtd Gunmen
GIBSON, George, Pvt, Lt Col John Edmonson, Co Com-

## Enlisted Men, War of 1812

mander omitted, Cav
GIBSON, Henry, Pvt, Lt Col John Edmonson, Co Commander omitted, Cav
GIBSON, Hezekiah, Pvt, Col A Cheatham, Capt Charles Johnson, Inf
GIBSON, Hugh, Pvt, no other information
GIBSON, Isaac B, Pvt, Col Thomas Williamson, Capt Thomas Scurry, Vol Mtd Gunmen
GIBSON, Jacob, Cpl, Col John Brown, Capt William Christian, E TN Mil Inf
GIBSON, James, Pvt, Col Cannon, Capt Yardley, Mtd Riflemen
GIBSON, James, Pvt, Col E? McCrory, Capt John Reynolds, Mil Inf
GIBSON, James, Pvt, Col Hall, Capt Martin, Vol Inf
GIBSON, James, Pvt, Col William Lillard, Capt Jacob Dyke, Vol Inf
GIBSON, James, Pvt, Col Williamson, Capt Pace, Lt Neely, Vol Mtd Gunmen; dismissed day mustered in
GIBSON, James, Pvt, Col Williamson, Capt Scurry, Mtd Vol Gunmen
GIBSON, James, Pvt, Maj Woodfolk, Capt Pearce, Inf
GIBSON, James, Pvt, Regt Commander omitted, Capt Edwin S Moore, Mtd Riflemen
GIBSON, Jeremiah, Pvt, Col Raulston, Capt Black, Inf
GIBSON, Jesse, Pvt, Col Williamson, Capt Tate, Vol Mtd Gunmen
GIBSON, Jesse, Pvt, Regt Commander omitted, Capt Edwin S Moore, Mtd Riflemen
GIBSON, John S, Pvt, Col Pillow, Capt Williamson, Vol Inf; trans to Gordon's Spies
GIBSON, John, Pvt, Col Dyer, Capt Edmonston, 1 TN Vol Mtd Gunmen
GIBSON, John, Pvt, Col Metcalf, Capt Patterson, Mil Inf; died 1-25-1815
GIBSON, John, Pvt, Maj Woodfolk, Capt Neil, Inf
GIBSON, John, Pvt, Regt Commander omitted, Capt Edwin S Moore, Mtd Riflemen
GIBSON, John, Pvt, Regt Commander omitted, Capt John Gordon, Mtd Spies
GIBSON, Joseph, Pvt, Col Cocke, Capt Barnes, Inf; died 12-30-1814
GIBSON, Levi, Pvt, Col John Brown, Capt William White, E TN Mil Inf; discharged for inability
GIBSON, Levi, Pvt, Col Johnson, Capt Rogers, E TN Mil
GIBSON, Rark, Cpl, Col Williamson, Capt Cook & Dobbins, Vol Mtd Gunmen
GIBSON, Samuel, Pvt, Maj Woodfolk, Capt Ross, Capt McCulley, Inf
GIBSON, Thomas N, Pvt, Col Steele, Capt Shenault, Mil Inf
GIBSON, Thomas N, Pvt, Maj Gen Carroll, Col Metcalf, Capt Jackson, Inf
GIBSON, Thomas, Pvt, Col Williamson, Capt Tate, Vol Mtd Gunmen
GIBSON, Thomas, Pvt, Regt Commander omitted, Capt Edwin S Moore, Mtd Riflemen
GIBSON, Thos, Pvt, Col T McCrory, Capt John Reynolds, Mil Inf; d 12-15-1813
GIBSON, William, Pvt, Col Cocke, Capt Price, Inf

GIBSON, Willis, Pvt, Col Napier, Capt Preston, Mil Inf
GIBSON, Wm, Pvt, Col Bayless, Capt Churchman, E TN Mil
GIBSON, Wm, Pvt, Col Dyer, Capt Williams, Vol Mtd Gunmen
GIDDONS (GIDDINS), Edward, Pvt, Col Lilard, Capt Hamilton, E TN Vol Inf
GIDDONS (GIDDINS), Wm, Pvt, Col Lillard, Capt Hamilton, E TN Vol Inf
GIDEON, Aaron, Sgt, Col Wm Johnson, Capt Stewart, 3rd Regt E TN Mil
GIDEON, James, Pvt, Col Benton, Capt Hewitt, Vol Inf
GIDEON, James, Pvt, Col Benton, Capt Renshaw, Vol Inf
GIDEON, James, Pvt, Col John Brown, Capt Allen I Bacon, E TN Mil Inf
GIDEON, Jas, Pvt, Col Johnson, Capt Powell, E TN Mil
GIDEON, John, Pvt, Col Wynne, Capt Carothers, W TN Inf
GIDEON, John, Pvt, Col Wynne, Capt Wilson, Inf; transferred to Capt Carother's Co
GIDEON, Randolph, Pvt, Col Wear, Capt Bayless, Mtd Inf
GIDEON, Thomas, Pvt, Col Steele, Capt Bennett, Mil Inf
GIDEONS, Edwards, Pvt, Col John Williams, Capt Sam Bunch, Mtd Vol
GIDEONS, Zachariah, Pvt, Col Johnson, Capt McKarny, E TN Drafted Mil; substitute for Wm Boman
GIDIANS (GIDDEON), Aron, Sgt, Col Johnson, Capt Stuart, E TN Drafted Mil
GIFFORD, Gideon, Pvt, Col Williamson, Capt Metcalf, Vol Mtd Gunmen
GIFFORD, Ibez, Pvt, Lt Col Hammond, Capt Williamson, Inf
GIFFORD, Jabez, Pvt, Col Edward Bradley, Capt Brice Martin, Vol Inf
GIFFORD, Jabez, Pvt, Col L Hammond, Capt J N Williamson, 2nd Regt Inf
GIFFORD, Jabez, Pvt, Col Wm Hall, Capt Brice Martin, Vol Inf
GIFFORD, Tabes (Tabas), Pvt, Col R C Napier, Co Commander omitted, Mil Inf
GIFFORD, Wm, Pvt, Col Thos McCrory, Capt Samuel McKnight, Inf
GIGER, Jacob, Pvt, Col Lillard, Capt John Roper, E TN Vol Inf
GILASPY, John, Ffr, Col John Cocke, Capt George Barnes, Inf; d 2-4-1815
GILBERT, Arouthon, Pvt, Col Newton Cannon, Capt Thos Yardley, Mtd Riflemen
GILBERT, Benjamin, Pvt, Col R C Dyer, Capt Cuthbert Hudson, Vol Mtd Riflemen
GILBERT, David, Pvt, Col A Loury, Capt Gabriel Martin, Inf; enlisted to service of the United States
GILBERT, Ebenezer, Pvt, Col John K Wynne, Capt John Spinks, Inf
GILBERT, James, Pvt, Col Newton Cannon, Capt Isaac Williams, Mtd Riflemen
GILBERT, James, Pvt, Col S Copeland, Capt John Biles, Inf
GILBERT, James, Pvt, Col Thomas H Benton, Capt John Reynolds, Vol Inf

## Enlisted Men, War of 1812

GILBERT, John, Pvt, Col A Loury, Co Commander omitted, 2nd Regt W TN Mil

GILBERT, John, Pvt, Col R H Dyer, Maj Wm Russell, Capt Beverly Williams, Separate Bn of TN Vol Mtd Gunmen

GILBERT, Moulton, Pvt, Col Newton Cannon, Capt Thomas Yardley, Mtd Riflemen

GILBERT, Peter, Pvt, Col R C Napier, Co Commander omitted, Mil Inf

GILBERT, Robert, Pvt, Col Newton Cannon, Capt Thomas Yardley, Mtd Riflemen

GILBERT, Wm, Pvt, Col Robert Steele, Capt James Shenault, Mil Inf

GILBERT, Wm, Pvt, Maj Russell, Capt Williams, Separate Bn of TN Vol Mtd Gunmen

GILBREATH, Alex, Pvt, Gen Andrew Jackson, Capt D Deaderick, Branch Srvce omitted; appointed Artif

GILBREATH, Alexander, Sgt, Col John Brown, Capt Lunsford Oliver, E TN Mil

GILBREATH, Andrew, Pvt, Col Samuel Bunch, Capt James Cummings, E TN Vol Mtd Inf

GILBREATH, Robert, Pvt, Col Wm Johnson, Co Commander omitted, E TN Drafted Mil

GILBREATH, Samuel, Pvt, Col Edwin E Booth, Co Commander omitted, Mil Inf

GILBREATH, Thos, Pvt, Col Edwin E Booth, Co Commander omitted, E TN Mil

GILBREATH, Thos, Pvt, Col John Brown, Capt Wm White, E TN Mil Inf; transferred from Capt Underwood

GILBREATH, Wm, Pvt, Col Wm Lillard, Capt Thos McChristian, E TN Vol Inf

GILES, Harvey, Pvt, Lt Col Hammond, Capt Jas _____, Inf

GILES, James, Pvt, Col Thos McCrory, Capt Dooly, Inf

GILES, Jesse, Pvt, Col Wm Johnson, Capt James Rogers, E TN Drafted Mil; substitute

GILES, Joriah E, Pvt, Col John K Wynne, Co Commander omitted, Inf

GILES, Milton, Pvt, Col Thomas Williamson, Capt Thos Scurry, Vol Inf

GILFORD, Jabez, Pvt, Col A Loury, Capt J N Williamson, W TN Mil

GILL, George, Pvt, Col Wm Metcalf, Capt Andrew Patterson, Mil Inf; d 4-3-1815

GILL, Henry, Pvt, Col John Cocke, Capt Bird Nance, Inf

GILL, James, Pvt, Col Edwin E Booth, Capt John Lewis, E TN Mil

GILL, Jesse, Pvt, Col R H Dyer, Capt Bethel Allen, Vol Mtd Gunmen

GILL, Presley, Pvt, Col Philip Pipkin, Capt John Robertson, Mil Inf

GILL, Robert, Pvt, Maj Wm Woodfolk, Capt James Neil, Inf; substitute for Thomas Ellerton

GILL, Thomas, Pvt, Brig Gen Isaac Roberts, Capt Benj Reynolds, Mtd Rangers

GILL, Thomas, Pvt, Col Philip Pipkin, Capt James Blakemore, Mil Inf

GILL, Wm, Pvt, Col Robert Steele, Capt James Shenault, Mil Inf

GILL, Wm, Pvt, Col Thos McCrory, Capt Wm Dooly, Inf

GILLAM, Ezekiel, Pvt, Col Robert Dyer, Capt James Wyatt, Vol Mtd Gunmen

GILLAM, John, Pvt, Regt Commander omitted, Capt Edwin S Moore, Mtd Riflemen

GILLAM, Lemuel P, Cpl, Col Wm Pillow, Capt John Anderson, Vol Inf

GILLAM, Nathaniel, Pvt, Col John Coffee, Capt Daniel Ross, Mtd Gunmen

GILLAM, Richard, Pvt, Col Wm Johnson, Capt James Tunnell, E TN Mil; substitute for Wm Henson

GILLAM, Wm, Pvt, Col John Alcorn, Capt Frederick Stump, Cav; deserted 10-7-1813

GILLASPIE, Jacob, Pvt, Col John Alcorn, Capt John Baskerville, Vol Inf

GILLASPIE, James, Pvt, Col Edward Bradley, Capt Abraham Bledsoe, Riflemen

GILLASPIE, Jeremiah, Pvt, Col Thomas Williamson, Capt John Dobkins, Vol Mtd Gunmen?; d 3-7-1815

GILLASPIE, John, Pvt, Col Robert Dyer, Capt James McMahon, 1st TN Vol Mtd Gunmen

GILLASPIE, Thomas T, Cpl, Col Robert Dyer, Capt Ephraim Dickson, 1st TN Vol Mtd Gunmen

GILLASPIE, Thomas, Pvt, Col S Bunch, Capt Dan'l Yarnell, E TN Mil

GILLELAND, Abel, Pvt, Col Samuel Bunch, Capt Henry Stephens, E TN Mtd Inf; deserted 10-24-1813

GILLELAND, James, Pvt, Col Thomas Williamson, Capt James Pace, Lt Neely, Vol Mtd Gunmen; dismissed day of mustering in

GILLELAND, James, Pvt, Regt Commander omitted, Capt John Miller, Spies

GILLELAND, Joel, 6 Cpl, Col John Cocke, Capt Bird Nance, Inf

GILLELAND, John B, Pvt, Col Thomas Benton, Capt James McFerrin, Vol Inf

GILLELAND, John, 4 Cpl, Col Thos Benton, Capt James McFerrin, Vol Inf

GILLELAND, John, Pvt, Col Wm Pillow, Capt James McFerrin, Inf; deserted 10-16-1813

GILLELAND, Robert L, Pvt, Col John Brown, Capt Wm D Neilson, E TN Vol Mil

GILLEM, John, Pvt, Col Newton Cannon, Capt John Hanley, Mtd Riflemen

GILLENWATER, Elijah C, 1 Sgt, Col Wm Lillard, Capt Wm Gillenwater, E TN Vol Inf

GILLENWATER, Wm T, Pvt, Col John Williams, Capt David Vance, Mtd Mil

GILLES, George, Pvt, Col Wm Lillard, Capt Wm McLin, E TN Inf

GILLESPIE, Isaac, Pvt, Col Samuel Wear, Capt John Childs, E TN Vol Inf

GILLESPIE, J A, Sgt, Col Newton Cannon, Capt Wm Edwards, Regt Command

GILLESPIE, Jacob, Pvt, Col John Coffee, Capt John Baskerville, Cav

GILLESPIE, James, Pvt, Col Edward Bradley, Capt Abraham Bledsoe, Riflemen

GILLESPIE, James, Pvt, Maj James Porter, Capt Sam Cowan, Cav

## Enlisted Men, War of 1812

GILLESPIE, James, Pvt, Regt Commander omitted, Capt Wm Mitchell, Spies

GILLESPIE, John, Pvt, Col John Wynne, Capt James Holleman, Inf

GILLESPIE, John, Pvt, Col Thomas McCrory, Capt Isaac Patton, Mil Inf

GILLESPIE, Samuel V, Pvt, Col Wm Higgins, Capt Wm Doake, Mtd Riflemen

GILLESPIE, Thomas, Cpl, Col Samuel Bunch, Capt Daniel Yarnell, E TN Mil

GILLESPIE, Wm, Pvt, Col John Wynne, Capt John Spinks, Inf

GILLESPIE, Wm, Pvt, Col Wm Johnson, Capt Joseph Kirk, Mil

GILLET, John, Cpl, Col Wm Johnson, Capt Joseph Scott, E TN Drafted Mil

GILLEY, Edward, Pvt, Col S Copeland, Capt Wm Douglass, Inf

GILLEY, Jesse, Pvt, Col John Cocke, Capt George Barnes, Inf

GILLIAM, Jariet, Pvt, Col Wm Hall, Capt Brice Martin, Vol Inf

GILLIAM, John, Pvt, Col John Wynne, Capt James Holleman, Inf

GILLIAM, William, Pvt, Col John Brown, Capt Allen Bacon, E TN Mil Inf

GILLIHAM, Major, Pvt, Col John Brown, Capt James Preston, E TN Mil Inf

GILLILAND, David, Pvt, Col Thomas Benton, Capt James McFerrin, Vol Inf

GILLILAND, Elijah, Pvt, Maj Wm Russell, Capt John Cowan, Vol Mtd Gunmen

GILLILAND, Henry, Pvt, Col John Brown, Capt Charles Lewin, E TN Vol Mtd Inf

GILLILAND, Isaac H, Pvt, Col Ewen Allison, Capt Allen, E TN Mil

GILLILAND, James, Pvt, Col Ewen Allison, Capt Adam Winsell, E TN Drafted Mil; furloughed & not returned

GILLILAND, James, Pvt, Col John Brown, Capt Charles Lewin, E TN Vol Mtd Inf

GILLILAND, James, Pvt, Col Wm Johnson, Capt Henry Hunter, E TN Mil

GILLILAND, James, Pvt, Regt Commander omitted, Capt John Miller, Spies

GILLILAND, John B, 2 Sgt, Col Thomas Benton, Capt James McFerrin, Vol Inf

GILLILAND, John B, Sgt, Col Thomas Benton, Capt James McFerrin, Vol Inf

GILLILAND, John, Cpl, Col Thomas Benton, Capt James McFerrin, Vol Inf

GILLILAND, Thomas, Pvt, Col Robert Dyer, Capt James McMahon, 1st TN Vol Mtd Gunmen

GILLILAND, Thos, Pvt, Col R H Dyer, Capt Jas McMahan, TN Vol Mtd Gunmen

GILLIM, Rich, Pvt, Col John Brown, Capt Wm Christian, E TN Mil Inf

GILLION, Moses, Pvt, Col Wm Johnson, Capt Wm Alexander, Det of E TN Drafted Mil

GILLSIM, George, Pvt, Col Wm Johnson, Capt Andrew Lawson, E TN Drafted Mil

GILLSTROP, Jesse, Pvt, Col Robert Steele, Capt Jas Bennet, Mil Inf; deserted

GILLUM, Jarrot, Pvt, Col Hall, Capt Brice Martin, Vol Inf

GILLUM, John, Pvt, Col John K Wynne, Capt Wm Caruthers, W TN Inf; transferred to Capt Hollin's Co

GILMAN, David, 4 Sgt, Regt Commander omitted, Capt Jas Haggard, Mtd Gunmen

GILMAN, David, Sgt, Regt Commander omitted, Capt Jas Haggard, Mtd Gunmen

GILMORE, Elijah, Pvt, Col Wm Metcalf, Capt John Cunningham, Mil Inf

GILMORE, Hugh, Pvt, Col Samuel Bayless, Co Commander omitted, E TN Inf

GILMORE, James, Pvt, Col Wm Booth, Capt Thompson, Mil

GILMORE, John, Pvt, Col Edwin Booth, Capt Vernon, E TN Mil

GILMORE, Peter, Pvt, Col S Bayless, Capt Rich, E TN Inf

GILMORE, Robert, Pvt, Lt J Barrett, Capt Nathan Davis, Inf

GILMORE, Thomas, Pvt, Col Edwin Booth, Capt Vernon, E TN Mil

GILMORE, Thomas, Pvt, Col Wm Lillard, Capt Thomas Sharpe, Inf

GILMORE, Willie, Pvt, Col Wm Metcalf, Capt Hill & Capt John Cunningham, Mil Inf

GILMORE, Wm, Pvt, Col Edwin Booth, Capt Vernon, E TN Mil; d 2-11-1815 in service

GILPATRICK, George, Pvt, Col S Copeland, Capt David Williams, Inf

GILPIN (GRIFFIN), John, Pvt, Maj Gen Carroll, Capt Ellis, Inf

GILSON, Jarvis, Pvt, Col T McCrory, Capt John Reynolds, Mil Inf

GIN, H Therwood, Pvt, Lt Col Leroy Hammonds, Col A Loury, Capt Thomas Wells, Inf; enlisted in regular service

GINGER, John, Pvt, Col James Raulston, Capt James Haynie, Inf

GINNINGS, John, Pvt, Col Wm Metcalf, Capt Bird L Hurt, Mil Inf; d 1-31-1815

GIPSON, James P, Pvt, Col Edwin Booth, Capt Samuel Thompson, Mil

GIPSON, Jos, Pvt, Col Leroy Hammonds, Capt James Craig, Inf

GIPSON, Joseph, Pvt, Regt Commander omitted, Capt James Craig, Inf

GIRLEY, Benj, Pvt, Col John Coffee, Capt Charles Kavanaugh, Cav

GIRLEY, John, Pvt, Col N T Perkins, Capt George Marr, Mtd Gunmen Vol

GIRMAN, Zacheus, Pvt, Col Wm Pillow, Capt C E McEwen, Vol Inf

GIVANS, David, Pvt, Maj Wm Woodfolk, Capt James Neil, Inf; substitute for John E Long

GIVEN, Wm, Cpl, Col Wm Higgins, Capt Stephen Griffith, Mtd Riflemen

GIVENS, Edward, Pvt, Col Wm Johnson, Capt Wm Alexander, E TN Drafted Mil

GIVENS, Jacob, Pvt, Col S Bayless, Capt I Bacon, E TN

## Enlisted Men, War of 1812

Mil; d 2-24-1815

GIVENS, James, Pvt, Col Wm Lillard, Capt Wm McChristian, E TN Vol Inf

GIVENS, James, Pvt, Regt Commander omitted, Capt James Cowan, Mtd Inf

GIVENS, John A, Cpl, Col John Coffee, Capt Thomas Bradley, Vol Cav

GIVENS, John A, Sgt, Col John Alcorn, Capt Thomas Bradley, Vol Cav

GIVENS, Robert, Pvt, Col Edwin Booth, Capt George Winton, E TN Mil

GIVENS, Samuel, Pvt, Col Edwin Booth, Capt George Winton, E TN Mil

GIVENS, Samuel, Pvt, Col Wm Johnson, Capt David McKamy, E TN Drafted Mil

GIVENS, Thos, Pvt, Col Wm Lillard, Capt Thomas McChristian, E TN Vol Inf

GIVENS, Thos, Sgt, Col Samuel Bayless, Capt John Brock, E TN Mil

GIVENS, Wm, Pvt, Col John Cocke, Capt Barnes, Inf

GLADDEN, John, Pvt, Col John Brown, Capt Charles Lewin, E TN Vol Mtd Inf

GLADDEN, Jos, Pvt, Col Wm Lillard, Capt Robert Maloney, E TN Vol Inf

GLADDIN, James, Pvt, Col Wm Lillard, Capt Robert Maloney, E TN Vol Inf

GLADDIN, Jos, Pvt, Col Wm Lillard, Capt Robert Maloney, E TN Vol Inf

GLADLEGLY, George, Pvt, Regt Commander omitted, Capt James Terrill, Cav

GLANTON, James, Pvt, Col Thomas Williamson, Capt Beverly Williams, Vol Mtd Gunmen; d 11-16-1814

GLASBY, Robert, Pvt, Col Wm Y Higgins, Capt Thomas Etheridge, Mtd Gunmen

GLASCO, Robert, Pvt, Col Philip Pipkin, Capt Henry Newlin, Mil Inf

GLASCOCK, George, Pvt, Col John Coffee, Capt Charles Kavanaugh, Cav

GLASCOCK, Gregory, Pvt, Col Wm Johnson, Capt Joseph Kirk, Mil

GLASGOW, Thomas, Pvt, Col S Bayless, Capt Joseph Rich, E TN Inf

GLASS, David, Pvt, Col N T Perkins, Capt George Marr, Mtd Riflemen Vol

GLASS, Finden, Pvt, Col S Bunch, Capt F Register, E TN Mil

GLASS, James, Pvt, Col Wm Johnson, Capt David McKamy, E TN Drafted Mil

GLASS, James, Pvt, Maj Wm Woodfolk, Capt James Neil, Inf

GLASS, Jesse, Pvt, Col Ewin Allison, Capt Henry McCrory, E TN Mil; transferred to Capt Register Co

GLASS, Jesse, Pvt, Col S Bunch, Capt F Register, E TN Mil

GLASS, Robert, Sgt - Cor, Col Robert Dyer, Capt Jas McMahon, TN Mtd Vol Gunmen; promoted from Sgt to Cor

GLASS, Samuel, Pvt, Col S Wear, Capt John Stephens, E TN Vol Inf

GLASS, Thos, Sgt, Col Thomas McCrory, Capt Samuel McKnight, Inf

GLASS, Wm, 5th Regt?, Maj John Childs, Capt John Stephens, E TN Vol Mtd Inf

GLASS, Wm, Pvt, Col N T Perkins, Capt George Marr, Mtd Riflemen Vol

GLASS, Wm, Pvt, Col S Wear, Capt John Stephens, E TN Vol Inf

GLASS, Wm, Pvt, Col Wm Lillard, Capt Wm McLin, E TN Inf

GLASSCOCK, John, Pvt, Col Wm Johnson, Capt Jas Cook, E TN Mil

GLASSCOCK, Moses H, Pvt, Col Thomas Benton, Capt James McFerrin, Vol Inf

GLASSCOCK, Moses H, Pvt, Col Wm Pillow, Capt Jas McFerrin, Inf

GLASSCOCK, Spencer, Pvt, Col Thomas Benton, Capt James McFerrin, Vol Inf

GLASSCOCK, Spencer, Pvt, Col Wm Pillow, Capt Jas McFerrin, Inf

GLATON, Augustus, Cpl, Col John Wynne, Capt Robert Breden, Branch Srvce omitted; promoted from Pvt

GLAZE, John, Pvt, Col Alexander Loury, Capt James Kincaid, Inf

GLEDEWELL, Mark, Pvt, Lt Col Leroy Hammonds & Lt Col A Loury, Capt Thomas Wells, Inf

GLEESON, James, Pvt, Col Thomas Benton, Capt Wm Smith, Vol Inf

GLEESON, James, Pvt, Col Wm Pillow, Capt Wm Smith, Vol Inf

GLEESON, James, Pvt, Regt Commander omitted, Capt Wm Smith, Vol Inf

GLEN, Alexander, Pvt, Col Wm Johnson, Capt James Tunnell, E TN Mil

GLEN, Jonathan, Pvt, Col Thomas Benton, Capt George Caperton, Vol Inf

GLEN, William, Pvt, Lt Col Leroy Hammonds & Lt Col A Loury, Capt Thomas Wells, Branch Srvce omitted

GLENN, Daniel, Pvt, Col Philip Pipkin, Capt George Mebane, Mil Inf; appointed 5th Sgt

GLENN, James (Joseph), Sgt, Col Samuel Wear, Capt Robert Doak, E TN Vol Inf

GLENN, John P, Pvt, Col John Wynne, Capt Butler, Inf

GLENN, Jonathan, Pvt, Col Wm Pillow, Capt George Caperton, Inf

GLENN, Jonathan, Sgt, Col S Copeland, Capt Solomon George, Inf

GLENN, Robert B, Pvt, Col Thomas Benton, Capt George Gibbs, Vol Inf; AWOL

GLIDEWELL, Robert, Pvt, Maj John Childs, Capt Charles Conway, E TN Mtd Gunmen; Regt County Knox

GLISON, Henry, Pvt, Col N T Perkins, Capt George Eliot, Mil Inf

GLOVER, Charles, Pvt, Col S Copeland, Capt Wm Hodges, Inf

GLOVER, Daniel, Pvt, Col S Copeland, Capt Wm Hodges, Inf

GLOVER, David, Pvt, Col S Copeland, Capt William Hodges, Inf

*Enlisted Men, War of 1812*

GLOVER, John, Pvt, Col Wm Lillard, Capt John Neatherton, E TN Vol Inf

GLOVER, Jonathan, Pvt, Col Wm Higgins, Capt Adam Dale, Mtd Gunmen

GLOVER, Jonathan, Pvt, Maj Gen Wm Carroll, Col James Raulston, Capt Edward Robinson, Inf

GLOVER, Joshua, Pvt, Col Robert Steele, Capt Robert Campbell, Mil Inf

GLOVER, Nathaniel, 1 Sgt, Col James Raulston, Capt Mathew Cowan, Inf

GLOVER, Richard, Pvt, Col Wm Higgins, Capt Adam Dale, Mtd Gunmen; wounded 1-22-1814 & absent

GLOVER, Samuel C, Pvt, Col Thomas Benton, Capt George Caperton, Vol Inf

GLOVER, Thomas, Pvt, Col Ewen Allison, Capt Wm King, Drafted Mil

GLOVER, Wm, Pvt, Col S Copeland, Capt Allen Wilkinson, Mil Inf

GLUSSEP, Wm, Cpl, Col Wm Lillard, Capt Thomas Sharpe, 2nd Regt E TN Inf

GOAD, Marlin, Ffr, Col S Copeland, Capt John Dawson, Inf

GOAD, Reuben, Pvt, Col Robert Steele, Capt Robert Campbell, Mil Inf

GOAD, Ruelin, Pvt, Col Wm Hall, Capt Henry Newlin, Inf

GOAN, Agnes, Pvt, Col S Bunch, Capt George Gregory, E TN Drafted Mil

GOAN, James, Pvt, Col S Bunch, Capt George Gregory, E TN Drafted Mil

GOCHER, Thomas, Pvt, Col Wm Metcalf, Capt Barbee Collins, Mil Inf

GODARD, David, Pvt, Col S Bayless, Capt Joseph Goodson, E TN Mil

GODARD, Jesse, Pvt, Col Wm Lillard, Capt George Keys, E TN Inf

GODARD, Solomon, Pvt, Maj John Childs, Capt James Cummings, E TN Vol Mtd Inf

GODARD, Thornton, Pvt, Col S Bunch, Capt John McNare, E TN Mil; attached to Capt Berry's Co

GODART, John, Cpl, Col Samuel Wear, Capt Samuel Bowman, Mtd Inf

GODART, Wm, Ens, Col Samuel Wear, Capt Samuel Bowman, Mtd Inf

GODDARD, John, Pvt, Col Thomas Benton, Capt Charles Lewin, E TN Vol Mtd Inf

GODOK?, James, Pvt, Col Wm Johnson, Capt Elihu Millikin, 3rd Regt E TN Mil; never appeared

GODSEY, Benj, Pvt, Col Wm Lillard, Capt George Keys, E TN Inf

GODSEY, Solomon, Pvt, Col Samuel Bunch, Capt Andrew Breden, E TN Mil

GODSON, Benj, Pvt, Col Thomas Williamson, Capt Anthony Metcalf, Vol Mtd Gunmen

GOFF, Ambrose, Pvt, Col Edwin Booth, Capt John McKamy, E TN Inf

GOFF, John, Pvt, Regt Commander omitted, Capt Reynolds, Vol Inf

GOFF, Thomas, Pvt, Regt Commander omitted, Capt David Mason, Cav

GOFF, Wm, Pvt, Col Edwin Booth, Capt John McKamey, Inf

GOFF, Wm, Pvt, Col Thomas Benton, Capt Benj Hewett, Vol Inf

GOFF, Wm, Pvt, Regt Commander omitted, Capt David Mason, Cav

GOFORTH, Andrew (Alexander), Pvt, Col Philip Pipkin, Capt David Smith, Inf

GOFORTH, Andrew, Pvt, Col Philip Pipkin, Capt Wm Mackay, Mil Inf

GOFORTH, Hiram, 1 Sgt, Col R C Napier, Capt John Chism, Mil Inf

GOFORTH, John, Pvt, Lt Col L Hammonds & Lt Col A Loury, Capt James Tubb, Inf

GOFORTH, Wm, Cpl, Gen Andrew Jackson, Capt Nathan Davis, Inf

GOFORTH, Zachariah, Pvt, Col John Williams, Capt David Vance, Mtd Mil

GOHEEN, James, Pvt, Col Wm Hall, Capt Abraham Bledsoe, Riflemen; deserted 11-27-1813

GOHEEN, James, Pvt, Col Wm Hall, Capt Abraham Bledsoe, Vol Inf

GOHLSON, Nathaniel, Pvt, Brig Gen Isaac Roberts, Capt Benj Reynolds, Inf

GOIN, Caleb, Pvt, Col Wm Lillard, Capt Zacheus Copeland, E TN Vol Inf

GOIN, Isaac, Pvt, Col Samuel Bayless, Capt John Brock, E TN Mil

GOIN, Isom, Pvt, Col Wm Johnson, Capt Benj Powell, E TN Mil

GOIN, Wm, Pvt, Col Samuel Bayless, Capt John Brock, E TN Mil

GOINER, John, Pvt, Col Wm Lillard, Capt Hugh Martin, E TN Vol Inf

GOINER, Wm, Pvt, Col Wm Lillard, Capt Hugh Martin, E TN Vol Inf; deserted 11-20-1813

GOINS (GORMS), Nathan, Pvt, Col Samuel Bayless, Capt Joseph Goodson, E TN Mil

GOLD, David, Pvt, Col John K Wynne, Co Commander omitted, Inf; killed in battle at Talledega 11-9-1813

GOLD, John, 3 Sgt, Col Samuel Wear, Capt Joseph Calloway, Mtd Inf

GOLD, John, Pvt, Col John Brown, Capt Lewis, E TN Vol Mtd Inf

GOLD, Jonathan, Pvt, Col Robert Steele, Capt John Chitwood, Mil Inf

GOLD (GOULD), Thomas, 6 Cpl, Lt Col Hammond & Loury, Capt Thos Delaney, Inf

GOLDBERRY, James, Pvt, Col A Loury, Capt Williamson, W TN Mil

GOLDEN, Enoch, Pvt, Col James Ralston, Capt Daniel Newman, Inf

GOLDEN, Sam'l, Pvt, Regt Commander omitted, Capt Josiah Askew, Inf

GOLDEN, Thos, Pvt, Col A Loury, Co Commander omitted, E TN Mil

GOLDEN, Thos, Pvt, Maj Gen Andrew Jackson, Col Archer Cheatham, Capt Wm Creel, Inf

GOLDESBERG, James, Pvt, Lt Col Hammond, Capt Thomas Williamson, Inf

GOLDSBERRY, James B, Pvt, Col Thos McCrory, Capt

## Enlisted Men, War of 1812

Jas Shannon, Mil Inf; transferred from Capt Patton's Co

GOLDSBERRY, John E, Pvt, Col John K Wynne, Capt Wm Wilson, Inf; transferred to Capt Shannon's Co

GOLDSBY, Charles, Pvt, Col Samuel Wear, Capt James Gillespie, E TN Vol Inf

GOLDSON, Harrod L, Pvt, Col N T Perkins, Capt George Eliot, Mil Inf

GOLDSTON, Eli, Pvt, Col S Copeland, Capt Alexander Provine, Mil Inf

GOLEMAN (GOLDMAN), John, Pvt, Col A Loury, Capt George Sarver, Inf

GOLESBERRY, James, Pvt, Col L Hammond, Capt J N Williamson, 2nd Regt TN Inf

GOLIHER, Weit, Pvt, Col Wm Lillard, Capt Zacheus Copeland, E TN Vol Inf

GOLIHER, Wm, Pvt, Col Wm Lillard, Capt Z Copeland, E TN Vol Inf

GOLLAHER, John, Pvt, Col Samuel Bunch, Capt Francis Berry, E TN Mil; deserted 3-4-1814

GOLLAHER, Wm, Pvt, Col Edwin E Booth, Co Commander omitted, E TN Mil

GOLLAHER, Wm, Pvt, Col Samuel Bunch, Capt Francis Berry, E TN Mil; attached to Capt English's Co

GOLLIHORN, John, Pvt, Col Samuel Bunch, Capt Jones Griffin, E TN Drafted Mil; deserted 4-24-1814

GOLLIHORN, Wm, Pvt, Col Samuel Bunch, Capt Jones Griffin, E TN Drafted Mil

GOLLINS, ____, Pvt, Col Wm Y Higgins, Capt Stephen Griffith, Mtd Riflemen; AWOL

GOLLOW, Hugh, Pvt, Col Wm Hall, Capt John Wallace, Inf

GOLSBERRY, John B, Pvt, Col T McCrory, Capt Isaac Patton, Mil Inf; transferred to Capt Shannon's Co

GOLSON, John, Pvt, Col Thomas McCrory, Capt Dooly, Inf; transferred to Capt Gordon's Co of Spies

GOLSON, Thos, Mtd Gunmen, Col John Brown, Capt Jesse Reamy, Mtd Gunmen

GOLSTON, Benj, Cpl, Col T McCrory, Capt Wm Dooly, Inf

GOLSTON, Eli, Pvt, Col Thos Williamson, Capt Isaac Williams, Vol Mtd Gunmen

GOLSTON, Nathaniel, Sgt, Col T McCrory, Capt Wm Dooly, Inf

GOOCH, Davis, Pvt, Col N Cannon, Capt Martin, Mtd Gunmen

GOOCH, James, Cpl, Col Loury, Capt Martin, Inf

GOOCH, James, Pvt, Brig Gen Johnson, Capt Allen, Mil Inf

GOOD, David, Pvt, Col Bayless, Capt Waddle, E TN Mil

GOOD, Edward, Pvt, Col John Brown, Capt Allen I Bacon, E TN Mil Inf

GOOD, Edward, Pvt, Col John Brown, Capt James Preston, E TN Mil Inf

GOOD, Henry, Pvt, Col Cannon, Capt Brandon, Mtd Riflemen

GOOD, Hugh, 1 Cpl, Col Cannon, Capt Brandon, Mtd Riflemen

GOOD, Hugh, Pvt, Col Benton, Capt McFerrin, Vol Inf

GOOD, Isham, Pvt, Col Raulston, Capt Newman, Inf; d 1-14-1815

GOOD, John, Pvt, Col Johnson, Capt Cook, E TN Mil

GOOD, Joshua, Pvt, Col Johnson, Capt Kirk, Mil

GOOD, Peter, Pvt, Col Dyer, Capt McMahon, 1st TN Vol Mtd Gunmen

GOOD, Sam'l, 3 Sgt, Col Burton, Capt Williamson, Vol Inf

GOOD, Sam'l, Sgt, Col Benton, Capt Williamson, Vol Inf

GOOD, Samuel, Pvt, Col S Bunch, Capt F Register, E TN Mil

GOOD, William, Pvt, Col John Brown, Capt James Preston, E TN Mil Inf

GOOD, Wm, 3 Sgt, Col Napier, Capt Neblett, Mil Inf

GOOD (GOAD), Joshua, Pvt, Col Booth, Capt Marshall, Drafted Mil

GOODALL, John F, Pvt, Col Alcorn, Capt Bradley, Vol Cav

GOODALL, John T, Pvt, Col Williamson, Capt Williams, Vol Mtd Gunmen

GOODALL, Park, Pvt, Col Copeland, Capt Thompson, Inf

GOODALL, Zachariah, Pvt, Col Bradley, Capt Martin, Vol Inf

GOODE, John, Pvt, Col Copeland, Capt Evans, Mil Inf

GOODE, John, Pvt, Col Hall, Capt Kennedy, Vol Inf

GOODIN, James, Pvt, Col Lillard, Capt Maloney, E TN Vol Inf

GOODING, James, Pvt, Col Loury, Capt Kincaid, Inf

GOODMAN, Andrew, Pvt, Col Bayless, Capt Landen, E TN Mil

GOODMAN, Archibald, Pvt, Col Coffee, Capt Kavanaugh, Cav

GOODMAN, Benejah (Benjamin), Pvt, Col Coffee, Capt Kavanaugh, Cav

GOODMAN, Benj, Pvt, Col Coffee, Capt Kavanaugh, Cav

GOODMAN, George, Pvt, Col Cocke, Capt Barnes, Inf; d 2-5-1815

GOODMAN, Jesse, Pvt, Lt Col Hammond & Lowry, Capt Wells, Inf; enlisted in regular army

GOODMAN, John, Pvt, Col Cocke, Capt Nance, Inf

GOODMAN, Robert, Pvt, Col Cocke, Capt Nance, Inf

GOODNER, Henry, Pvt, Col Loury, Capt Kincaid, Inf

GOODNER, Henry, Pvt, Maj Woodfolk, Capt Neil, Inf

GOODNER, James, Cpl, Col T McCrory, Capt A Metcalf, Mil Inf

GOODNER, John, 1 Cpl, Col Benton, Capt Hewitt, Vol Inf

GOODNER, John, Pvt, Maj Gen A Jackson, Capt Hugh Kerr, Mtd Rangers

GOODNIGHT, Henry, Pvt, Regt Commander omitted, Capt James Terrill, Cav

GOODON, Frederick, Cpl, Col Williamson, Capt Porter, Vol Mtd Gunmen; d 1-25-1815

GOODRUM, John, Pvt, Col Raulston, Capt Neale, Inf

GOODSEY, Benton, Pvt, Col Bayless, Capt Jones, E TN Drafted Mil

GOODSIN, Lewis, Pvt, Regt Commander omitted, Capt Larkin Ferrell, Inf

GOODSON, Benj, Pvt, Col Bradley, Capt Martin, Vol Inf

GOODSON, Benj, Pvt, Col Hall, Capt Martin, Vol Inf

GOODSON, Benj, Sgt, Col Copeland, Capt Wilkinson, Mil Inf; promoted from Pvt
GOODSON, John A, Pvt, Col Benton, Capt Caperton, Vol Inf; joined from Capt Hewitt's Co
GOODSON (GOODDON), Jos, Pvt, Col Lillard, Capt McChristian, E TN Vol Inf
GOODWIN, Alexander, Pvt, Maj Gen Jackson, Col Williamson, Capt Steele, Vol Mtd Gunmen
GOODWIN, James, Pvt, Col John Brown, Capt Allen I Bacon, E TN Mil Inf
GOODWIN, John, Pvt, Maj Gen Jackson, Col Cheatham, Capt Creel, Inf
GOODWIN, Robert H, Dmr, Col Booth, Capt Lewis, Branch Srvce omitted
GOODWIN, Robert, Pvt, Col Bunch, Capt Buchanan, E TN Drafted Mil
GOOLSBY, Charles, Pvt, Col Booth, Capt Biggs, Inf
GORDIN, Jas, Pvt, Col Dyer, Maj Russell, Capt Russell, Vol Mtd Gunmen
GORDIN, Thomas, Pvt, Col Perkins, Capt Pipkin, Mtd Riflemen
GORDON, Arch W, Pvt, Col John Williams, Capt Wm Walker, Vol
GORDON, Chas, Ens, Col S Bunch, Capt George Gregory, E TN Drafted Mil; taken as deserter from regular service
GORDON, David, Pvt, Col R H Dyer, Capt Glen Owen, TN Vol Mtd Gunmen
GORDON, David, Pvt, Maj Gen Wm Carroll, Col Wm Metcalf, Capt John Jackson, Inf
GORDON, Francis, Pvt, Regt Commander omitted, Capt Archibald McKenney, Cav
GORDON, Francis, Sgt, Col R H Dyer, Capt Glen Owen, TN Vol Mtd Gunmen
GORDON, James, Cpl, Col R H Dyer, Maj Wm Russell, Capt Wm Russell, Vol Mtd Gunmen
GORDON, James, Pvt, Col R C Napier, Capt Thomas Preston, Mil Inf
GORDON, James, Pvt, Maj Wm Russell, Capt Wm Chism, Vol Mtd Gunmen
GORDON, Jas, Sgt, Col Thomas McCrory, Capt Samuel B McKnight, Inf
GORDON, John, Pvt, Col A Loury, Lt Col L Hammonds, Capt Arahel Rains, Inf
GORDON, John, Pvt, Col Thomas Williamson, Capt Richard Tate, Vol Mtd Gunmen
GORDON, John, Pvt, Regt Commander omitted, Capt Nathan Farmer, Mtd Riflemen
GORDON, John, Sgt, Regt Commander omitted, Capt Larkin Ferrell, Inf
GORDON, Jos, Pvt, Lt Col L Hammonds, Capt Arahel Rains, Inf
GORDON, Richard, Pvt, Col Robert Steele, Capt James Bennett, Mil Inf
GORDON, Sam'l, Pvt, Regt Commander omitted, Capt Archibald McKenney, Cav
GORDON, Samuel sr, Pvt, Col R H Dyer, Capt Glen Owen, TN Vol Mtd Gunmen
GORDON, Samuel, Sgt, Col R H Dyer, Capt Glen Owen, TN Vol Mtd Gunmen
GORDON, Wm, Pvt, Col Ewen Allison, Capt James Allen, E TN Mil
GORDON, Wm, Pvt, Col John Cocke, Capt John Weakley, Inf
GORDONS, John jr, Pvt, Gen A Jackson, Capt D Deaderick, Arty
GORE, Edward, Pvt, Col Wm Metcalf, Capt Wm Sitton, Mil Inf
GORELEY, Edward, Pvt, Col Edwin Booth, Capt Samuel Thompson, Mil
GORLY (GERLY), Hugh, Pvt, Col John K Wynne, Capt Wm McCall, Inf
GORMAN, John, Pvt, Col S Bunch, Capt Wm Jobe, E TN Vol Mtd Inf
GORMLEY, Hugh, Pvt, Maj Wm Russell, Capt John Trimble, Vol Mtd Gunmen
GORMLEY, Michael, Cpl, Maj Wm Russell, Capt John Trimble, Vol Mtd Gunmen
GORMLEY, Michael, Pvt, no other information
GORNER, John, Pvt, Col John Brown, Capt John Childs, E TN Vol Mtd Inf
GORY, Henry, Pvt, Regt Commander omitted, Capt Nathan Farmer, Mtd Riflemen
GOSETT, John, Pvt, Col Wm Higgins, Capt Adam Dale, Mtd Gunmen
GOSHAM, Jacob, Sgt, Col S Bayless, Capt James Landen, E TN Mil
GOSHEEN, James, Pvt, Col Edward Bradley, Capt Abraham Bledsoe, Riflemen; deserted 11-27-1813
GOSS, James, Pvt, Col Wm Lillard, Capt John Roper, E TN Vol Inf
GOSS, John, Pvt, Col Thos Benton, Capt Benj Reynolds, Vol Inf
GOSSAGE, Jeremiah, Pvt, Col N T Perkins, Capt Mathew Johnston, Mil Inf
GOSSAGE, Jeremiah, Pvt, Col Philip Pipkin, Capt Wm Mackay, Mil Inf
GOSSAGE, John, Pvt, Col Wm Johnston, Capt James R Rogers, E TN Drafted Mil
GOSSETT, Isaac, Pvt, Maj Wm Woodfolk, Capt John Sutton & Capt Abraham Dudney, Inf
GOSSETT, Isaac, Pvt, Regt Commander omitted, Capt Gray, Inf
GOSSETT, Isaac, Pvt, Regt Commander omitted, Capt Larkin Ferrell, Inf
GOSSETT, John, Pvt, Col John Cocke, Capt John Weakley, Inf
GOSSETT, John, Pvt, Maj Wm Woodfolk, Capt Ezekial Ross, Capt McCulley, Inf
GOSSETT, Mun, Pvt, Col Wm Johnston, Capt Jas Tunnell, E TN Mil; notified & never appeared, transferred?
GOSSETT, Wm, Pvt, Col John Alcorn, Capt Alexander McKeen, Cav
GOSSIT, John, Pvt, Col Phillip Pipkin, Capt Henry M Newlin, Mil Inf; replaced by Jas Stephens
GOTCHER, Davidson A, Pvt, Regt Commander omitted, Capt George Smith, Spies
GOTCHER, Henry A, Pvt, Regt Commander omitted, Capt George Smith, Spies
GOTCHER, Henry, Pvt, Col A Loury, Lt Col L Hammonds, Capt Thos Delaney, Inf

## Enlisted Men, War of 1812

GOTCHER, Jesse, 4 Sgt, Col A Loury, Lt Col L Hammond, Capt Thomas Delaney, Inf
GOTCHER, John, Pvt, Col A Loury, Lt Col L Hammonds, Capt Thos Delaney, Inf
GOTHER, Henry, Pvt, Maj Wm Russell, Capt John Cowan, Vol Mtd Gunmen
GOTHER, Sam'l, Pvt, Maj Wm Russell, Capt John Cowan, Vol Mtd Gunmen
GOTT, Samuel H, Sgt, Col John Brown, Capt Jesse C Reany, Mtd Gunmen
GOUGE, Martin, Pvt, Col S Bunch, Capt John English, E TN Drafted Mil
GOUGH, Asa, Pvt, Regt Commander, Capt Thos Gray, Inf
GOUGH, Wm, Cpl, Col A Loury, Capt George Sarver, Inf
GOULD, John, Pvt, Maj Wm Russell, Capt John Trimble, Vol Mtd Gunmen
GOUND, John, Pvt, Maj John Childs, Capt Chas Conway, E TN Mtd Gunmen; Regt County Knox
GOURLY, Hugh, Pvt, Col Edward Bradley, Capt John Wallace, Vol Inf
GOURLY, Hugh, Pvt, Col Thos Williamson, Capt Thos Scurry, Vol Mtd Gunmen
GOUTON, George, Pvt, Col L Hammonds, Capt Thos Wells, Inf
GOUTRE, Davis, Pvt, Col Wm Hall, Capt John Wallace, Inf
GOUZE, James, Pvt, Col William Hall, Capt James Hambleton, Vol Inf; joined at Clarksville
GOWAN, John, Pvt, Col S Bunch, Capt Dan'l Yarnell, E TN Mild; discharged for inability
GOWAN, Wm, Pvt, Col John Brown, Capt John Childs, E TN Vol Mtd Inf
GOWEN, Alexander R, Sgt, Col Wm Metcalf, Capt John Barnhart, Mil Inf; d 3-25-1815
GOWEN, Andrew, Pvt, Col Wm Metcalf, Capt Andrew Patterson, Mil Inf; d 1-30-1815
GOWEN, James, Pvt, Col Wm Johnson, Capt Elihu Millikin, E TN Mil
GOWEN, John M, Pvt, Col Thomas Benton, Capt George Caperton, Vol Inf
GOWEN, Menoah, Cpl, Col Wm Metcalf, Capt Andrew Patterson, Mil Inf; d 4-22-1815
GOWEN, Wm D, Pvt, Col Robert Dyer, Capt Bethel Allen, Vol Mtd Gunmen
GOWER, James, Pvt, Col N Cannon, Capt George Brandon, Mtd Riflemen
GOWER, Robert, Pvt, Col R H Dyer, Capt Thomas White, Vol Mtd Gunmen
GOWER, Samuel, Pvt, Col R H Dyer, Capt Thos White, Vol Mtd Gunmen
GOWER, Samuel, Pvt, Col T McCrory, Capt Isaac Patton, Mil Inf
GOWER, Wilson L, Pvt, Col R H Dyer, Capt Thos White, Vol Mtd Gunmen
GOWER, Wm E, Pvt, Col R H Dyer, Capt Thos White, Vol Mtd Gunmen; d 1-16-1815
GOWER, Wm, Pvt, Col S Bunch, Capt Dan'l Yarnell, E TN Mil
GOWER, Wm, Pvt, Regt Commander omitted, Capt Dan'l Yarnell, E TN Mil
GOWIN, Jas, Pvt, Regt Commander omitted, Capt Gregory, Branch Srvce omitted
GOWINS, Drewey, Pvt, Col S Bayless, Capt Jas Churchman, E TN Mil
GOWINS, Wishok, Pvt, Col S Bayless, Capt Jas Churchman, E TN Mil
GOYNE, Amos, Sgt, Col James Raulston, Capt Mathew Neal, Inf
GRACE, James, Dmr, Col James Raulston, Capt Mathew Cowan, Inf; promoted to Drm Maj
GRACE, James, Drm Maj, Col Jas Raulston, Co Commander omitted, W TN Mil Inf
GRACE, Levin, 6 Cpl, Maj Gen Carroll, Col James Raulston, Capt Huddleston, Inf
GRACE, Solomon, Pvt, Col Wm Johnson, Capt Allen, Mil Inf
GRACE, Thos, Pvt, Col Cocke, Capt Weakley, Inf
GRACE, Wm, Cpl, Col Cocke, Capt Weakley, Inf
GRACEY, John, Pvt, Col T McCrory, Capt Isaac Patton, Mil Inf
GRACEY, Jos, Pvt, Col Edwin Booth, Capt Thompson, Mil
GRACEY, Jos, Pvt, Col Robert Steele, Capt Chitwood, Mil Inf
GRACEY, Wm, Pvt, Col Edwin Booth, Capt Thompson, Mil
GRACY, John, Pvt, Col Robert Dyer, Capt Evans, Vol Mtd Gunmen
GRADY, Berrill, Pvt, Col John Williamson, Capt Wm Walker, Vol
GRADY, James M, Pvt, Col Wm Hall, Capt Wallace, Inf
GRADY, John, Pvt, Col S Bunch, Capt John English, E TN Drafted Mil
GRADY, Wm, Pvt, Col A Loury, Capt George Sarver, Inf
GRADY, Wm, Pvt, Col Ewen Allison, Capt Jonas Loughmiller, Mil
GRAGG, Benj, Pvt, Col S Bunch, Capt Wm Jobe, E TN Vol Mtd Inf
GRAGG, Elijah, Pvt, Col Wm Lillard, Capt Jacob Dyke, Vol Inf
GRAGG, Henry, Pvt, Gen A Jackson, Capt Hugh Kerr, Mtd Rangers
GRAGG, Henry, Pvt, Maj Wm Russell, Capt Fleman Hodges, Vol Mtd Gunmen
GRAGG, John, Pvt, Col Wm Johnson, Capt Christopher Cook, E TN Mil
GRAGG, John, Pvt, Col Wm Johnson, Capt John Scott, E TN Drafted Mil; transferred to Capt Rich
GRAGG, John, Pvt, Col Wm Johnson, Capt Joshua Kirk, Mil; substitute for Meryman
GRAGG, Thos, Sgt, Col Wm Johnson, Capt Jas Rogers, E TN Drafted Mil; substitute
GRAGG (GRAFF), Thos, 4 Cpl, Col Phillip Pipkin, Capt Wm Mackay, Mil Inf
GRAHAM, Alexander, Pvt, Col T McCrory, Capt Samuel McKnight, Inf
GRAHAM, Alexander, Pvt, Maj Wm Woodfolk, Capt Abner Pearce, Inf; trans for Capt Nail's Camp
GRAHAM, Alexander, Pvt, Maj Wm Woodfolk, Capt James Neil, Inf
GRAHAM, Charles, Pvt, Col John Williams, Capt Sam Bunch, Mtd Vol

*Enlisted Men, War of 1812*

GRAHAM, Charles, Pvt, Col S Bayless, Capt Jonathan Waddle, E TN Mil
GRAHAM, Francis, Pvt, Regt Commander omitted, Capt George Smith, Spies
GRAHAM, George, Pvt, Regt Commander omitted, Capt Gray, Inf
GRAHAM, George, Sgt, Col S Bunch, Capt Danl Yarnell, E TN Mil
GRAHAM, James, Pvt, Col Edward Bradley, Capt Wm Lauderdale, Vol Inf
GRAHAM, James, Pvt, Col S Copeland, Capt John Biles, Inf
GRAHAM, James, Pvt, Lt Col Leroy Hammonds, Capt Thomas Wells, Inf
GRAHAM, Jesse, Pvt, Col Alexander Loury, Capt George Sarver, Inf
GRAHAM, Jesse, Pvt, Col Wm Hall, Capt Wm Alexander, Vol Inf
GRAHAM, Joel, Pvt, Col S Copeland, Capt Wm Douglass, Inf
GRAHAM, John P, Cpl, Col Thos Williamson, Capt Thos Scurry, Vol Mtd Gunmen
GRAHAM, John, Pvt, Col Newton Cannon, Capt George Brandon, Mtd Riflemen
GRAHAM, John, Pvt, Col R C Napier, Capt Early Benson, Mil Inf
GRAHAM, John, Pvt, Maj Wm Woodfolk, Capt Abner Pearce, Inf; Reduced to ranks from Sgt
GRAHAM, Lewis, Pvt, Col Edward Bradley, Capt Wm Lauderdale, Vol Inf; waggoner detached
GRAHAM, Lewis, Pvt, Col Wm Hall, Capt Wm Alexander, Vol Inf
GRAHAM, Loyd, Pvt, Col Thos McCrory, Capt McKnight, Inf
GRAHAM, Nathaniel, Pvt, Col Edwin Booth, Capt John Sharp, E TN Mil
GRAHAM, Richard, Pvt, Col Newton Cannon, Capt John Demsey, Mtd Gunmen
GRAHAM, Richard, Pvt, Col Robert Dyer, Capt Ephraim Dickson, 1 TN Mtd Vol Gunmen
GRAHAM, Richard, Pvt, Regt Commander omitted, Capt Ephraim Dickson, Branch omitted
GRAHAM, Samuel, Pvt, Col Newton Cannon, Capt John Demsey, Mtd Gunmen
GRAHAM, Samuel, Pvt, Col Robert Dyer, Capt John Dickson, 1 TN Vol Mtd Gunmen
GRAHAM, Samuel, Pvt, Regt Commander omitted, Capt Ephraim Dickson, Branch omitted
GRAHAM, Solomon, Pvt, Lt Col Richard Napier, Co Commander omitted, Inf
GRAHAM, Thomas, Pvt, Col Samuel Wear, Capt John Bayless, Mtd Inf
GRAHAM, Thomas, Pvt, Col William Lillard, Capt Jacob Hartsell, E TN Vol Inf
GRAHAM, William, Pvt, Col S Bunch, Capt George McPherson, E TN Mil; joined from Capt Register
GRAINGER, James, Cpl, Col Edward Bradley, Capt John Moore, Vol Inf
GRAINGER, James, Pvt, Col Thomas Williamson, Capt Robert Moore, Vol Mtd Gunmen
GRAMMEL, Samuel, Pvt, Col Thos McCrory, Capt Isaac Patton, Mil Inf
GRAMMER, Joseph, Pvt, Col S Copeland, Capt David Williams, Inf
GRAMMER, Joseph, Pvt, Col Wm Metcalf, Capt John Cunningham & Capt Alexander Hill, Mil Inf
GRANAD, William, Pvt, Col Thos Williamson, Capt Anthony Metcalf, Vol Mtd Gunmen
GRANBY, Richard, Pvt, Col John Brown, Capt James Preston, E TN Mil Inf
GRANGER, James, Pvt, Col Wm Hall, Capt John Moore, Vol Inf
GRANGER, Noah, Pvt, Col James Raulston, Capt Mathew Neal, Inf
GRANGER, Noah, Pvt, Col John Wynne, Capt Wm McCall, Inf
GRANT, Armistead, 3 Cpl, Regt Commander omitted, Capt David Smith, Cav
GRANT, James, 3 Sgt, Regt Commander omitted, Capt David Smith, Cav
GRANT, James, Pvt, Col Wm Johnson, Capt Elihu Milliken, 3 Regt E TN Mil
GRANT, John, Col Samuel Bunch, Capt Francis Berry, E TN Mil
GRANT, John, Pvt, Col John Cocke, Capt Richard Crunk, Inf
GRANT, John, Pvt, Col John Coffee, Capt David Smith, Vol Cav
GRANT, John, Pvt, Col Samuel Wear, Capt Robert Doak, E TN Vol Inf
GRANT, John, Pvt, Lt Col John Edmonson, Co Commander omitted, Branch Col?
GRANT, John, Pvt, Regt Commander omitted, Capt David Smith, Cav Vol
GRANT, Joshua, Pvt, Col Edwin Booth, Capt John Lewis, E TN Mil
GRANT, Joshua, QM Sgt, Col Edwin E Booth, E TN Mil
GRANT, Moses, Pvt, Col John Coffee, Capt David Smith, Col? Cav
GRANT, Richard, Pvt, Col Wm Metcalf, Capt Thos Marks, Mil Inf
GRANT, Samuel, Pvt, Col Philip Pipkin, Capt John Strother, Mil
GRANT, Samuel, Pvt, Col Samuel Bunch, Capt Thos Mann, E TN Vol Mtd Inf
GRANT, Spencer, Pvt, Col A Cheatham, Capt George Chapman, Inf
GRANT, Spencer, Pvt, Col Thos Williamson, Capt James Cook & Capt John Crane, Vol Mtd Gunmen
GRANT, William, Pvt, Col Samuel Bunch, Capt Wm Jobe, E TN Vol Mtd Inf
GRANT, Wm, Pvt, Col Wm Johnson, Capt Joseph Scott, E TN Mil; substitute for Wm Kelly
GRANTURN, Annis, Pvt, Col John Williams, Capt John Vance, Mtd Mil
GRASON, Walter (A friendly Crick), Pvt, Brig Gen James White, Co Commander omitted, Spy
GRASON, Wren, Pvt, Col Wm Johnson, Capt James Tunnell, E TN Mil
GRASS, Solomon, Pvt, Regt Commander omitted, Capt James Gray, Inf
GRASTY, Israel, Pvt, Col Wm Lilard, Capt Thos Sharpe,

## Enlisted Men, War of 1812

GRATNER, Henry, Pvt, Col Samuel Bayless, Capt Joseph Bacon, E TN Mil, 2nd Regt Inf
GRATNER, John, Pvt, Col Samuel Bunch, Capt Solomon Dobkins, E TN Mil
GRAVE, George, Dmr, Col Samuel Bunch, Capt James Williams, E TN Mil
GRAVES, Adam, Pvt, Col Samuel Wear, Capt Jas Gillespie, E TN Vol Inf
GRAVES, Buman (Beeman), Pvt, Maj Woodfolk, Capt Dudney & Capt John Sutton, Inf
GRAVES, Daniel, Pvt, Col John Williams, Capt Wm Walker, Vol
GRAVES, David, Cpl, Col S Bunch, Capt N Gibbs, E TN Drafted Mil
GRAVES, George, Dmr, Col S Bunch, Capt John Houk, E TN Mil; joined from Capt William's Co, discharged for inability
GRAVES, Jacob, Pvt, Col James Raulston, Capt Mathew Neal, Inf
GRAVES, Jacob, Pvt, Col John K Wynne, Capt James Holleman, Inf
GRAVES, John R, Pvt, Col S Copeland, Capt George, Inf
GRAVES, John, Pvt, Col Philip Pipkin, Capt Jas Blakemore, Mil Inf
GRAVES, Joseph D, Pvt, Col John Coffee, Capt Alexander McKeen, Cav
GRAVES, Peter, Pvt, Col Edwin E Booth, Capt John Sharpe, Branch Srvce omitted
GRAVES, Rice, Pvt, Col Robert Steele, Capt Samuel Maxwell, Mil Inf
GRAVES, Stephen, Drm Maj, Col Samuel Wear, Co Commander omitted, E TN Vol Inf
GRAVES, Thomas, Pvt, Col Philip Pipkin, Capt John Strother, Mil
GRAVES, Thomas, Pvt, Col Raulston, Capt Jas Cowan, Inf; d 2-8-1815
GRAVES, William, Pvt, Col James Raulston, Co Commander omitted, Inf
GRAVES, William, Pvt, Col S Copeland, Capt George, Inf; d 3-27-1814
GRAVES, William, Pvt, Maj John Childs, Capt John Stephens, E TN Mtd Inf
GRAVES, Willie C, Pvt, Col Wm Hall, Capt Jas Hambleton, Vol Inf
GRAY, Abner, Pvt, Col Wm Lillard, Capt Robert McCalpin, E TN Inf
GRAY, Alex M, Pvt, Regt Commander omitted, Capt James Cowan, Mtd Inf
GRAY, Alexander M, Pvt, Commanders & Branch Srvce omitted; see original card Re: Act of Congress
GRAY, Alexander N, Pvt, Col R H Dyer, Maj Russell, Capt Wm Russell, Vol Mtd Gunmen; transferred to Capt Bean's Co
GRAY, Alexander, Pvt, Col John Coffee, Co Commander omitted, Mtd Spies
GRAY, Alexander, Pvt, Col Thos Williamson, Capt Wm Metcalf, Vol Mtd Gunmen
GRAY, Archibald, Pvt, Col Philip Pipkin, Capt Mackay, Mil Inf
GRAY, Briant, Sgt, Col A Loury, Capt George Sarver, Inf
GRAY, Daniel, Pvt, Col Philip Pipkin, Capt Mackay, Mil Inf
GRAY, David, Pvt, Regt Commander omitted, Capt Jas Haggard, Mtd Gunmen
GRAY, Deliverance, Pvt, Col R H Dyer, Capt Robert Evans, Vol Mtd Gunmen
GRAY, Frederick, Pvt, Col Philip Pipkin, Capt Blakemore, Mil Inf
GRAY, Frederick, Pvt, Col T McCrory, Capt A Metcalf, Mil Inf
GRAY, George S, 4 Sgt, Col N T Perkins, Capt Marr, Mtd Gunmen
GRAY, George, Pvt, Lt Col John Edmonson, Co Commander omitted, Cav
GRAY, Harmon, Pvt, Col Allison, Capt Loughmiller, Mil; deserted and transferred to Capt Powell Co
GRAY, Harmon, Pvt, Col Johnson, Capt Powell, Branch Srvce omitted; d 11-15-1814, joined from Capt Loughmiller's Co
GRAY, Henry T, Pvt, Col Pillow, Capt McEwen, Vol Inf
GRAY, Isaac R, Pvt, Col John Coffee, Capt Stump, Cav
GRAY, Isaac, Pvt, Col A Loury, Capt J N Williamson, W TN Mil
GRAY, Isaac, Pvt, Col John Coffee, Capt Baskerville, Cav
GRAY, Isaac, Pvt, Col L Hammond, Capt J N Williamson, 2nd Regt Inf
GRAY, Isaac, Pvt, Lt Col Hammond, Capt Williamson, Inf
GRAY, Jacob, Pvt, Col Cocke, Capt Dalton, Inf
GRAY, James, 3 Sgt, Col Raulston, Capt West, Inf
GRAY, James, Cpl, Col Johnson, Capt Scott, E TN Drafted Mil
GRAY, James, Pvt, Col Allison, Capt Allen, E TN Mil
GRAY, James, Pvt, Col Lillard, Capt King, E TN Vol Inf
GRAY, James, Pvt, Col Pipkin, Capt Newlin, Mil Inf; replaced by Wm Pew
GRAY, James, Pvt, Commanders omitted, Det of Inf of 26th Regt TN
GRAY, James, Pvt, Lt Col Hammond & Lowry, Capt Wells, Inf
GRAY, Jeremiah, Pvt, Lt Col Richard Napier, Co Commander omitted, Inf
GRAY, John H, Pvt, Col Pillow, Capt Renshaw, Inf
GRAY, John V, Pvt, Col Cheatham, Capt Johnson, Inf
GRAY, John W, Pvt, Col Pipkin, Capt Searcy, Mil Inf
GRAY, John, Cpl, Col Bayless, Capt Bacon, E TN Mil
GRAY, John, Pvt, Col Alcorn, Capt Bradley, Vol Cav
GRAY, John, Pvt, Col Allison, Capt McCray, E TN Mil
GRAY, John, Pvt, Col Bradley, Capt Martin, Vol Inf
GRAY, John, Pvt, Col Cocke, Capt Caruthers, Inf
GRAY, John, Pvt, Col Hall, Capt Martin, Vol Inf
GRAY, John, Pvt, Col Johnson, Capt Scott, E TN Drafted Mil
GRAY, John, Pvt, Col Lillard, Capt McLin, E TN Inf
GRAY, John, Pvt, Col Pillow, Capt McEwen, Vol Inf
GRAY, John, Pvt, Col Williamson, Capt Moore, Vol Mtd Gunmen
GRAY, John, Pvt, Col Wynne, Capt McCall, Inf
GRAY, Joseph, 2 Sgt, Col John Coffee, Capt Stump, Cav
GRAY, Joseph, Pvt, Col Allison, Capt Allen, E TN Mil
GRAY, Joseph, Pvt, Col Allison, Capt King, Drafted Mil

## Enlisted Men, War of 1812

GRAY, Joseph, Pvt, Col Metcalf, Capt Sitton, Mil Inf
GRAY, Joseph, Pvt, Col S Bunch, Capt George McPherson, E TN Mil; joined from Capt King's Co
GRAY, Joseph, Pvt, Col S Bunch, Capt John English, E TN Drafted Mil; joined from Capt Allen's Co
GRAY, Malcolm, Pvt, Col S Bunch, Capt Penny, E TN Mtd Inf
GRAY, Nathan, Pvt, Col Bunch, Capt Vance, E TN Mtd Inf
GRAY, Robert, Pvt, Col Bayless, Capt Jones, E TN Mil
GRAY, Sampson, Pvt, Col Perkins, Capt Johnson, Mil Inf
GRAY, Thomas, Cpl, Col Wear, Capt Stephens, E TN Vol Inf
GRAY, Thomas, Pvt, Col Brown, Capt Lewin, E TN Vol Inf
GRAY, Thomas, Pvt, Maj Childs, Capt Stephens, E TN Vol Mtd Inf
GRAY, William jr, Pvt, Col Bayless, Capt Rich, E TN Inf
GRAY, William sr, Pvt, Col Bayless, Capt Rich, E TN Inf
GRAY, Wm, Pvt, Col Pillow, Capt McFerrin, Inf
GRAYBILL, Jacob, Pvt, Col Brown, Capt Childs, E TN Vol Mtd Inf
GRAYHAN, John, Pvt, Col McCrory, Capt Gordon, Inf
GRAYSON, Benjamin, Sgt, Col Wear, Capt Childs, E TN Vol Inf
GREATHOUSE, John, Pvt, Col Pillow, Capt Caperton, Inf
GREE (GILL, GILE), William B, Pvt, Col Houston, Capt Balck?, Inf
GREEGSBY, James, Pvt, Col Samuel Wear, Capt James Gillespie, E TN Vol Inf
GREEN, Abraham, Pvt, Col Wm Lillard, Capt James Lillard, E TN Inf Vol
GREEN, Arnold, Pvt, Col John Williams, Capt Sam Bunch, Mtd Vol
GREEN, Asa, Pvt, Col A Cheatham, Capt W Smith, Inf; discharged for want of arms
GREEN, Asab, Pvt, Col A Cheatham, Capt Wm Creel, Inf
GREEN, Benjamin, Pvt, Col Edwin E Booth, Capt John Slatton, E TN Mil
GREEN, Bethel, Pvt, Col Robert Steele, Capt James Shenault, Mil Inf
GREEN, David, 2 Cpl, Col Philip Pipkin, Capt Henry M Newlin, Mil Inf; d 9-21-1814 at Ft Williams
GREEN, David, Sgt, Col Thomas Williamson, Capt Robert Moore, Vol Mtd Gunmen
GREEN, Elisha, Cpl, Commanders omitted, Mtd Spies
GREEN, Elisha, Cpl, Commanders omitted, Spies
GREEN, Elithom, Pvt, Col John K Wynne, Capt Wm Caruthers, W TN Inf; discharged for inability
GREEN, Evan, Pvt, Col Thos Williamson, Capt John Crane & Capt John Cook, Vol Mtd Gunmen; d 2-23-1815
GREEN, Ewdard, Pvt, Col R C Napier, Capt Thos Preston, Mil Inf
GREEN, Francis, Pvt, Col S Bayless, Capt Branch Jones, E TN Drafted Mil; reduced from Cpl
GREEN, George, Pvt, Brig Gen I B Roberts, Capt Benj Reynolds, Inf
GREEN, George, Pvt, Col Wm Metcalf, Capt Bird L Hurt, Mil Inf

GREEN, George, Pvt, Maj Wm Woodfolk, Capt Ezekial Ross, Capt McCulley, Inf
GREEN, Henry, Pvt, Col John Cocke, Capt George Barnes, Inf
GREEN, Isaac, Pvt, Col Ewen Allison, Capt A Allen, E TN Mil
GREEN, Isaac, Pvt, Col John Coffee, Capt Daniel Ross, Mtd Gunmen
GREEN, Isaac, Pvt, Col S Bunch, Capt John English, E TN Drafted Mil
GREEN, Isaac, Sgt, Col Wm Lillard, Capt James Lillard, E TN Inf Vol
GREEN, James Y, Pvt, Regt Commander omitted, Capt John Miller, Spies
GREEN, James, Pvt, Col A Cheatham, Capt Richard Benson, Inf
GREEN, James, Pvt, Col Edward Bradley, Capt John Kennedy, Riflemen; AWOL 12-1-1813
GREEN, James, Pvt, Col Philip Pipkin, Capt John Strother, Mil
GREEN, James, Pvt, Col S Wear, Capt Jesse Cole, Vol Inf
GREEN, James, Pvt, Col Wm Bradley, Capt Wm Martin, Vol Inf
GREEN, James, Pvt, Col Wm Hall, Capt Brice Martin, Vol Inf
GREEN, James, Pvt, Col Wm Johnson, Capt Elihu Milliken, 2nd Regt E TN Mil
GREEN, James, Pvt, Col Wm Lillard, Capt Jacob Dyke, Vol Inf
GREEN, James, Pvt, Maj Wm Russell, Capt John Cowan, Vol Mtd Gunmen; promoted to Forage Master
GREEN, Jeremiah W, Pvt, Lt Col L Hammonds, Capt James Tubb, Inf
GREEN, Jesse, Pvt, Col Edwin Booth, Capt John Sharpe, E TN Mil
GREEN, Jesse, Pvt, Col Jiggins?, Capt Allen, Mtd Gunmen
GREEN, Jesse, Pvt, Col Thos Williamson, Capt James Cook, Vol Mtd Gunmen
GREEN, Joel, Pvt, Col Thomas Williamson, Capt James Cook, E TN Mil
GREEN, Joel, Pvt, Col Wm Johnson, Capt Joseph Kirk, Mil
GREEN, John, Pvt, Col John Cocke, Capt Joseph Price, Inf
GREEN, John, Pvt, Col Philip Pipkin, Capt John Strother, Mil
GREEN, John, Pvt, Col S Bunch, Capt Jones Griffin, E TN Drafted Mil; deserted 3-4-1814
GREEN, John, Pvt, Col Thos Benton, Capt H L Douglass, Vol Inf
GREEN, John, Pvt, Col Wm Johnson, Capt Benj Powell, Branch Srvce omitted
GREEN, John, Pvt, Col Wm Lillard, Capt Robert McCalpin, E TN Mtd Inf
GREEN, John, Pvt, Maj Gen A Jackson, Capt Joseph Kirkpatrick, Mtd Gunmen
GREEN, Jonathan, Pvt, Col William Johnson, Capt Christopher Cook, E TN Mil
GREEN, Jonathan, Pvt, Col Wm Johnson, Capt Jos Kirk, Mil

GREEN, Jos, Pvt, Col Samuel Bunch, Capt John Williams, Mtd Vol
GREEN, Jos, Pvt, Col Wm Johnson, Capt Henry Hunter, E TN Mil; d 3-30-1815
GREEN, Lewis, Pvt, Col John Alcorn, Capt Frederick Stump, Cav
GREEN, Lewis, Pvt, Col John Brown, Capt Hugh Barton, E TN Mil Inf
GREEN, Lewis, Pvt, Col John Coffee, Capt Frederick Stump, Cav
GREEN, Lewis, Pvt, Col S Bunch, Capt Jones Griffin, E TN Drafted Mil
GREEN, Lewis, Pvt, Col Wm Johnson, Capt Benj Powell, E TN Mil
GREEN, Lewis, Pvt, Lt Col John Edmonson, Co Commander omitted, Cav
GREEN, Nedam, Pvt, Col Wm Hall, Capt John Wallace, Inf
GREEN, Perry, Pvt, Col John Cocke, Capt George Barnes, Inf
GREEN, Reuben, Pvt, Col Philip Pipkin, Capt Ebenezer Kirkpatrick, Mil Inf; deserted 9-20-1814
GREEN, Richard G, Pvt, Col Wm Johnson, Capt Benj Powell, E TN Mil
GREEN, Richard G, Pvt, Col Wm Johnson, Capt David McKamy, E TN Drafted Mil
GREEN, Richard, Pvt, Col S Bunch, Capt John English, E TN Drafted Mil
GREEN, Richard, Pvt, Maj Wm Russell, Col R H Dyer, Capt Wm Russell, Vol Mtd Gunmen
GREEN, Robert, Pvt, Col John Cocke, Capt Bird Nance, Inf
GREEN, Robert, Rank omitted, Regt Commander omitted, Capt Garrett Lane, Mtd Riflemen
GREEN, Ruben, Pvt, Col Philip Pipkin, Capt Fitzpatrick, Mil Inf
GREEN, Samuel, Pvt, Col S Wear, Capt Bowman, Mtd Inf
GREEN, Stephen, Pvt, Col Philip Pipkin, Capt Mebane, Mil Inf
GREEN, Stephen, Pvt, Col Wm Lillard, Capt Thos Sharpe, Inf
GREEN, Thomas, Pvt, Regt Commander omitted, Capt Elisha Green, Mtd Spies
GREEN, Thomas, Sgt, Col Edwin Booth, Capt John McKamy, E TN Mil
GREEN, Thomas, Sgt, Regt Commander omitted, Capt Garrett Lane, Mtd Riflemen
GREEN, Thos P, Sgt, Regt Commander omitted, Capt John Miller, Spies
GREEN, Wesley, Cpl, Maj Wm Woodfolk, Capt Dudney & Capt Sutton, Inf; promoted from Pvt
GREEN, Wesley, Pvt, Maj Wm Woodfolk, Capt Abraham Dudney, Inf
GREEN, Westly, Pvt, Col Wm Pillow, Capt Wm Smith, Vol Inf
GREEN, William, Cpl, Col N Cannon, Capt John Dempsey, Mtd Gunmen; promoted to 2 Lt
GREEN, William, Pvt, Col John Brown, Capt Hugh Barton, E TN Mil Inf
GREEN, William, Pvt, Col John Brown, Capt James Preston, E TN Mil Inf
GREEN, William, Pvt, Col John Cocke, Capt John Weakley, Inf; substitute for Daniel Binkley
GREEN, William, Pvt, Col S Wear, Capt James G Gillespie, E TN Vol Inf
GREEN, William, Pvt, Col Thomas Benton, Capt Joseph Smith, Vol Inf
GREEN, William, Pvt, Col Thomas Benton, Capt William Smith, Vol Inf
GREEN, William, Pvt, Col Thos Williamson, Capt Thomas Porter, Vol Mtd Gunmen; d 1-25-1815
GREEN, William, Pvt, Col William Johnson, Capt Andrew Lawson, E TN Drafted Mil
GREEN, William, Pvt, Col Wm Johnson, Capt Benjamin Powell, E TN Mil
GREEN, William, Pvt, Col Wm Johnson, Capt James Rogers, E TN Drafted Mil
GREEN, William, Pvt, Lt Col Wm Phillips, Co Commander omitted, Inf
GREEN, William, Pvt, Maj Gen Andrew Jackson, Capt Joseph Kirkpatrick, Mtd Gunmen
GREEN, William, Pvt, Maj Gen Carroll, Col Raulston, Capt Robinson, Inf
GREEN, William, Pvt, Maj Wm Woodfolk, Capt Dudney & Capt Sutton, Inf
GREEN, William, Pvt, Regt Commander omitted, Capt Gray, Inf
GREEN, William, Pvt, Regt Commander omitted, Capt Smith, Vol Inf
GREENE, David, Pvt, Col Thomas Williamson, Capt Robert Moore, Vol Mtd Gunmen; reduced from Sgt
GREENE, James, Pvt, Col Edwin Booth, Capt Winton, E TN Mil
GREENE, John, Pvt, Col Ewen Allison, Capt Jacob Hoyal, E TN Mil; deserted 1-18-1814
GREENELL, John, Pvt, Col S Bunch, Capt Lt? John Harris, E TN Mil
GREENFIELD, Peter, Pvt, Col Wm Johnson, Capt David McKamy, E TN Drafted Mil; transferred to Capt Stewart
GREENFIELD, Peter, Pvt, Col Wm Johnson, Capt James Stewart, E TN Drafted Mil
GREENFIELD, Peter, Pvt, Col Wm Lillard, Capt Wm McLin, E TN Inf
GREENFIELD, Samuel, Cpl, Col John Coffee, Capt Smith, Vol Cav
GREENFIELD, William, Pvt, Col Edwin Booth, Capt Lewin, Branch Srvce omitted
GREENFIELD, ___, Pvt, Col Wm Johnson, Capt James Stewart, E TN Mil
GREENHAM, Cloudsberry, Pvt, Gen A Jackson, Capt Hugh Kerr, Mtd Rangers
GREENHAM, Gabriel, Pvt, Regt Commander omitted, Capt Hugh Kerr, Mtd Rangers
GREENHAN, Jonathan, Pvt, Col Maj Gen Jackson, Capt Hugh Kerr, Mtd Rangers
GREENWAY, David, Pvt, Col John Brown, Capt John Trimble, E TN Vol Mtd Inf
GREENWAY, William H, Sgt, Col John Williams, Capt Wm Walker, Vol
GREENWAY, William, Pvt, Col Samuel Bayless, Capt I

## Enlisted Men, War of 1812

Bacon, E TN Mil
GREENWAY, William, QM, Capt Sam Cowan (QM), Branch Srvce omitted; loaned as a Sgt in Capt Sam Cowan's Co
GREENWOOD, George, Pvt, Col Wm Y Higgins, Capt James Hambleton, Mtd Gunmen
GREENWOOD, John, Pvt, Col N Cannon, Capt N Jones, Mtd Riflemen
GREENWOOD, Yancey, Pvt, Col T McCrory, Capt Abel Willis, Mil Inf
GREER, Alexander, Pvt, Regt Commander omitted, Capt Edwin S Moore, Mtd Riflemen
GREER, Andrew, Pvt, Col Thos Benton, Capt Benj Hewett, Vol Inf
GREER, Aquilla Jim, Pvt, Col James Raulston, Capt Chas Wade, Inf
GREER, David, Pvt, Col Thomas Williamson, Capt Giles Burnette, Vol Mtd Gunmen
GREER, James B, Pvt, Col Thos Benton, Capt Benj Hewett, Vol Inf
GREER, James, Sgt, Col John Cocke, Capt James Gray, Inf
GREER, John, Pvt, Col John Cocke, Capt James Gray, Inf
GREER, John, Pvt, Col Raulston, Capt Black, Inf
GREER, Joshua, Pvt, Col John Cocke, Capt John Dalton, Inf
GREER, Nathan, Pvt, Brig Gen T Johnson, Capt Robert Carson, Inf
GREER, Robert S, Pvt, Maj Gen Wm Carroll, Capt Daniel M Bradford & Capt Lewis Dillahunty, Vol Inf
GREER, Vincent, Pvt, Col John Cocke, Capt John Dalton, Inf
GREER, William, Pvt, Col Edward Bradley, Capt John Kennedy, Riflemen; AWOL 12-12-1815
GREER, William, Pvt, Gen T Johnson, Capt Daniel Oban, 36 Inf
GREET (GREEL), Jacob, Pvt, Col Wm Johnson, Capt Jos Scott, E TN Drafted Mil; discharged for inability
GREGORY, Boswell (Bozel), Pvt, Col Edward Bradley, Capt Abraham Bledsoe, Riflemen
GREGORY, George, Pvt, Col James Raulston, Capt Elijah Haynie, Inf; d 1-9-1815
GREGORY, Henry, Pvt, Col William Johnson, Capt Joseph Scott, E TN Drafted Mil
GREGORY, Jacob, Pvt, Col Robert Steele, Capt Robert Campbell, Mil Inf
GREGORY, John W, Pvt, Col Robert Steele, Capt James Randals, Inf
GREGORY, John, Pvt, Col T Williamson, Capt Thomas Scurry, Vol Mtd Gunmen
GREGORY, Joseph, Pvt, Col John Cocke, Capt James Gault, Inf; substitute for Green Seat
GREGORY, Maliki, Pvt, Col N T Perkins, Capt Mathew Patterson, Mtd Vol
GREGORY, Tafley, Pvt, Col S Copeland, Capt Allen Wilkinson, Mil Inf
GREGORY, Tapley, Pvt, Col James Raulston, Capt Elijah Haynie, Inf
GREGORY, Thomas, Pvt, Col John Cocke, Capt James Gault, Inf
GREGORY, Thomas, Pvt, Col T Williamson, Capt Thomas Scurry, Vol Mtd Gunmen
GREGORY, Turnstile, Pvt, Col Wm Y Higgins, Capt Wm Doake, Mtd Riflemen
GREGORY, William, Pvt, Col Alexander Loury, Capt George Sarver, Inf
GREIR, Louis, Pvt, Regt Commander omitted, Capt John Crane, Mtd Inf
GREMMETT, William, Pvt, Col R H Dyer, Capt Cuthbert Hudson, Vol Mtd Gunmen
GRENWAY, George, Pvt, Col Ewen Allison, Capt Wm King, E TN Vol Inf
GRESHAM, Austin, Pvt, Maj Gen Wm Carroll, Capt Francis Ellis, Inf
GRESHAM, Moses, Cpl, Gen Andrew Jackson, Capt Nathan Davis, Inf
GREST (GRIST), Robert, Pvt, Col Ewen Allison, Capt Henry McCray, E TN Mil
GREY, Robert, Pvt, Col Wm Metcalf, Capt Thos Marks, Mil Inf
GREZELL, Daniel, Pvt, Col S Copeland, Capt Wm Douglass, Inf
GRICE, Solomon, Pvt, Col John Cocke, Capt James Gray, Inf
GRIER, William, Sgt, Col Wm Johnson, Capt Henry Hunter, E TN Mil
GRIFFEE, John P, Pvt, Col John Coffee, Capt Frederick Stump, Cav
GRIFFEE, Richard, Pvt, Col Wm Johnson, Capt James Tunnell, E TN Mil; legally notified & never appeared
GRIFFEY, William, Pvt, Col Wm Hall, Capt John Kennedy, Vol Inf
GRIFFIN, Andrew, Pvt, Lt Col Richard Napier, Co Commander omitted, Inf
GRIFFIN, Andrew, Pvt, Regt Commander omitted, Capt James Haggard, Mtd Gunmen
GRIFFIN, Berry G, Pvt, Col Wm Hall, Capt Henry M Newlin
GRIFFIN, George, Pvt, Col Wm Metcalf, Capt Wm Mullin, Mil Inf
GRIFFIN, George, Pvt, Col Wm Pillow, Capt Thos Williamson, Vol Inf
GRIFFIN, Gilbert, Pvt, Lt Col L Hammonds, Capt James Craig, Inf
GRIFFIN, H, Pvt, Col T McCrory, Capt Wm Dooley, Inf
GRIFFIN, Ira, Sgt, Col Newton, Capt Ota Cantrell, W TN Mtd Inf
GRIFFIN, James, Pvt, Col Wm Metcalf, Capt Wm Mullin, Mil Inf
GRIFFIN, John H, Pvt, Col Philip Pipkin, Capt George Mebane, Mil Inf
GRIFFIN, John, Pvt, Col John Alcorn, Capt John Byrne, Cav; wounded 11-9-1813 at Talledega
GRIFFIN, John, Pvt, Col Thos Williamson, Capt Thos Scurry, Vol Mtd Gunmen
GRIFFIN, John, Pvt, Col Wm Hall, Capt Brice Martin, Vol Inf
GRIFFIN, John, Pvt, Col Wm Pillow, Capt George Caperton, Inf; transferred to Capt Russell's Co
GRIFFIN, John, Pvt, Gen A Jackson, Capt Wm Ruppell, Mtd Spies; joined from Capt Caperton's Co

## Enlisted Men, War of 1812

GRIFFIN, John, Pvt, Gen John Coffee, Co Commander omitted, Mtd Spies
GRIFFIN, John, Pvt, Regt Commander omitted, Capt James Haggard, Mtd Gunmen
GRIFFIN, Martin, Pvt, Col Wm Lillard, Capt George Argenbright, E TN Vol Riflemen
GRIFFIN, N Nathaniel, Pvt, Col S Bunch, Capt Henry Stephens, E TN Vol Mtd Inf
GRIFFIN, Nathan W, Pvt, Col J Brown, Capt Charles Lewin, Mtd Vol Inf
GRIFFIN, Oswell (Oswald), Pvt, Col John Cocke, Capt Samuel M Caruthers, Inf
GRIFFIN, Owen, Pvt, Col A Loury, Capt John Looney, 2nd Regt W TN Mil
GRIFFIN, Thomas, Cpl, Col S Copeland, Capt Alexander Provine, Mil Inf; promoted from Pvt
GRIFFIN, Thomas, Pvt, Col S Bunch, Capt George Gregory, E TN Drafted Mil
GRIFFIN, Thomas, Pvt, Col S Wear, Capt Joseph Calloway, Mtd Inf
GRIFFIN, Wilie, Cpl, Col R H Dyer, Capt James McMahan, TN Vol Mtd Gunmen
GRIFFIN, Wilie, Pvt, Regt Commander omitted, Capt Jas Terrill, Cav
GRIFFIN, William, Pvt, Col Bradley, Capt Douglass, Vol Inf
GRIFFIN, William, Pvt, Lt Col Richard Napier, Co Commander omitted, Inf
GRIFFIN, William, Pvt, Regt Commander omitted, Capt Jas Terrill, Cav
GRIFFIS, Anderson, 3 Cpl, Col Pipkin, Capt Kirkpatrick, Mil Inf
GRIFFIS, John, 2 Sgt, Col Cannon, Capt Hogan, Mtd Gunmen
GRIFFITH, Jacob, Pvt, Col John Brown, Capt Wm White, E TN Mil Inf
GRIFFITH, James, Pvt, Col Johnston, Capt Kirk, Mil
GRIFFITH, John, Pvt, Maj Woodfolk, Capt Dudney & Sutton, Inf
GRIFFITH, Jonathan, Pvt, Col Cocke, Capt Barnes, Inf
GRIFFITH, Thomas, Pvt, Col John Brown, Capt Wm Christian, E TN Mil Inf
GRIFFITH, William, Cpl, Regt Commander omitted, Capt Sam'l Richardson, E TN Drafted Mil
GRIFFITH, William, Pvt, Col Bayless, Capt Brock, E TN Mil
GRIFFITH, William, Pvt, Col Pipkin, Capt Mebane, Mil Inf
GRIFFITH, William, Pvt, Col S Bunch, Capt S Robinson, E TN Drafted Mil
GRIFFITS, James, Cpl, Col Johnson, Capt Hunter, E TN Mil
GRIFFON, John, Pvt, Col Edward Bradley, Capt Brice Martin, Vol Inf
GRIFFON, John, Pvt, Col Wear, Capt Stephens, E TN Vol Inf
GRIFFORD, Jabus, Pvt, Col Hall, Capt Martin, Vol Inf
GRIFFY, William, Pvt, Col Booth, Capt Marshall, Drafted Mil
GRIGG, Henry, Pvt, Maj Woodfolk, Capt Neil, Inf
GRIGGS, Berry, Pvt, Col Williamson, Capt Martin, Vol Mtd Gunmen
GRIGGS, George, Pvt, Col Copeland, Capt Tait, Inf
GRIGGS, John, Cpl, Col Steele, Capt Randall, Inf
GRIGGS, John, Pvt, Col Cocke, Capt Cocke, Inf
GRIGGS, John, Pvt, Col Napier, Capt Adkins, Mil Inf
GRIGGS, John, Pvt, Regt Commander omitted, Capt Drury Adkinson, Branch Srvce omitted
GRIGGSBY, Amos, Pvt, Col Napier, Capt Benson, Mil Inf
GRIGGSBY, John, Pvt, Col Johnson, Capt Milliken, 3rd Regt E TN Mil
GRIGGSBY, Samuel, Pvt, Col Coffee, Capt Terrill, Vol Cav; delinquent
GRIGGSBY, Samuel, Sgt, Col John Brown, Capt Wm Neilson, Regt E TN Vol Mil
GRIGGSBY, William, Pvt, Col McCrory, Capt Gordon, Inf; deserted 11-18-1813
GRIGSBY, William, Pvt, Col Metcalf, Capt Marks, Mil Inf
GRIGSBY, William, Pvt, Maj Gen Jackson, Col Williamson, Capt Steele, Vol Mtd Gunmen
GRILLET, George, Pvt, Col Pipkin, Capt David Smith, Ens Wm Pegram, Det of Ens Pegram of W TN Mil
GRIMES, Abel, Pvt, Col Hall, Capt Newlin, Inf; not found
GRIMES, David, Pvt, Col Hall, Capt Wallace, Inf
GRIMES, Jacob, Pvt, Lt Col A Cheatham, Co Commander omitted, Mtd Inf
GRIMES, James, Pvt, Col Benton, Capt Reynolds, Vol Inf
GRIMES, James, Pvt, Col Pillow, Capt McEwen, Vol Inf
GRIMES, James, Pvt, Lt Col Hammonds & Loury, Capt Wells, Inf; deserted 10-7-1814 from Deposit
GRIMES, James, Pvt, Regt Commander omitted, Capt Benj Reynolds, Mtd Rangers
GRIMES, James, Sgt, Col Dyer, Capt McMahon, TN Vol Mtd Gunmen
GRIMES, Jesse, Pvt, Col Loury, Capt Looney, W TN Inf
GRIMES, Neal, Pvt, Maj Gen Andrew Jackson, Capt Joel Parrish, Arty
GRIMES, Philip, Pvt, Col A Loury, Capt J N Williamson, W TN Mil
GRIMES, Philip, Pvt, Col L Hammond, Capt J N Williamson, 2nd Regt Inf
GRIMES, William H, Sgt, Maj James Porter, Capt Sam Cowan, Cav
GRIMES, William, Pvt, Col Dyer, Capt McMahon, 1st TN Mtd Vol Gunmen
GRIMES, William, Pvt, Col Lowry, Capt Looney, W TN Inf
GRIMES, William, Pvt, Col Pipkin, Capt Strother, Mil
GRIMES, William, Pvt, Maj Woodfolk, Capt Pearce, Inf
GRIMES, William, Pvt, Regt Commander omitted, Capt David Mason, Cav
GRIMLEY, John, Pvt, Maj Woodfolk, Capt Turner, Inf
GRIMM, Bartlett, Cpl, Col Samuel Bunch, Capt Joseph Duncan, E TN Drafted Mil
GRIMMER, Henry, Pvt, Col T McCrory, Capt James Shannon, Mil Inf
GRIMMET, Jacob, Pvt, Col Johnson, Capt Lawson, E TN Drafted Mil
GRIMMETT, Abraham, Rank omitted, Col John Brown, Capt James Preston, E TN Mil

## Enlisted Men, War of 1812

GRIMMETT, Benjamin, Cpl, Col Hammond, Capt Craig, 2nd Regt W TN Mil
GRIMMETT, William, Sgt, Col Booth, Capt Winton, E TN Mil
GRIMMIT, John, 4 Cpl, Col S Bunch, Capt F Register, E TN Mil
GRIMSLEY, John, Pvt, Col S Bunch, Capt F Register, E TN Mil
GRINDER, John, Pvt, Lt John Harris, Co Commander omitted, Det Inf
GRINDSTAFF, Nicholas, Pvt, Col S Bayless, Capt S Hendrix, E TN Mil
GRISARD, Henry, Pvt, Col Wm Hall, Capt J Hambleton, Vol Inf
GRISHAM, Charles, Pvt, Col Copeland, Capt Tait, Inf
GRISHAM, David, Pvt, Lt Col Hammond, Capt Jas Tubb, Inf
GRISHAM, Elijah, Pvt, Col Wm Lillard, Capt McChristian, E TN Vol Inf
GRISHAM, George, Pvt, Col Samuel Bunch, Capt David Vance, E TN Mtd Inf
GRISHAM, John, 2 Sgt, Col S Bunch, Capt David Vance, E TN Mtd Inf
GRISHAM, John, Pvt, Col Wm Lillard, Capt Thos McChristian, E TN Vol Inf
GRISHAM, John, Pvt, Col Wm Metcalf, Capt Thos Marks, Mil Inf
GRISHAM, Joseph, Pvt, Col Samuel Bunch, Capt George Gregory, E TN Drafted Mil
GRISHAM, Lambuth D, Pvt, Col Thos Williamson, Capt Anthony Metcalf, Vol Mtd Gunmen
GRISHAM, Michael, Pvt, Col Samuel Bunch, Capt George Gregory, E TN Drafted Mil
GRISHAM, Robert, Pvt, Col Samuel Bunch, Capt Wm Houston, E TN Vol Mtd Inf
GRISHAM, Thomas, Pvt, Col Ewen Allison, Capt John Hampton, Mil
GRISHAM, Thomas, Pvt, Col Samuel Bunch, Capt Wm Houston, E TN Vol Mtd Inf
GRISHAM, Thomas, Sgt, Col Samuel Bayless, Capt Jonathan Waddle, E TN Mil
GRISHAM, William, Pvt, Col Thos McCrory, Capt Anthony Metcalf, Mil Inf
GRISHAM (GRESHAM), George, Pvt, Brig Gen T Johnson, Capt Carson, Inf
GRISOM, Thomas, Pvt, Col Wm Metcalf, Capt John Barnhart, Mil Inf
GRISSAM, Thomas, Pvt, Col John Coffee, Capt Thomas Bradley, Vol Cav
GRISSLY, Samuel, Pvt, Col John Coffee, Capt James Terrill, Vol Cav; delinquent
GRISSOM, Benjamin, Pvt, Maj Wm Woodfolk, Capt Ezekiel Ross & Capt McCulley, Inf
GRISSOM, James, Pvt, Col Philip Pipkin, Capt George Mebane, Mil Inf
GRISSOM, James, Pvt, Col Thomas Williamson, Capt James Pace, Lt Nealy, Vol Mtd Gunmen; dismissed day of mustering in
GRISSOM, John, Cpl, Maj Wm Woodfolk, Capt Abner Pearce, Inf
GRISSOM, John, Pvt, Col Thos Williamson, Capt James Pace, Lt Nealy, Vol Mtd Gunmen
GRISSOM, Thomas, Pvt, Col S Copeland, Capt Moses Thompson, Inf
GRISSOM, William, Pvt, Col Robert Dyer, Capt Bethel Allen, Vol Mtd Gunmen
GRISSOM, William, Pvt, Col Robert Dyer, Capt Robert Edmonson, 1st TN Vol Mtd Gunmen
GRISSUM, Prior, Pvt, Col Samuel Bayless, Capt Jonathan Waddle, E TN Mil
GRISSUM, Thomas, Pvt, Col John Alcorn, Capt Thomas Bradley, Vol Cav
GRIST, Robert, Pvt, Col Samuel Bunch, Capt Francis Register, E TN Mil; joined Capt McCrea's Co
GRISUM, Richard, Pvt, Col Samuel Bayless, Capt James Churchman, E TN Mil
GRISWOULD, Carter, Pvt, Col Wm Hall, Capt Brice Martin, Vol Inf
GRIZARD, Carter, Pvt, Col John Cocke, Capt Richard Crunk, Inf
GRIZARD, Hardy, Pvt, Col John Cocke, Capt Richard Crunk, Inf
GRIZZARD, Carter, Pvt, Col Wm Hall, Capt Martin, Vol Inf
GROOMS, Bright, Pvt, Regt Commander omitted, Capt David Mason, Cav
GROOMS, Richard, Pvt, Col Nicholas Perkins, Capt George Eliot, Mil Inf
GROPE, Jonathan, Cpl, Col Samuel Bayless, Capt James Landen, E TN Mil
GROS, Henry, Cpl, Brig Gen Andrew Jackson, Capt Wm Carroll, Vol Inf
GROSS, Frederick, Pvt, Regt Commander omitted, Capt Josiah Askew, Inf
GROSS, George, Pvt, Col Ewen Allison, Capt Wm King, Drafted Mil; d 3-20-1814
GROSS, James, Pvt, Col Wm Lillard, Capt Wm Gillenwater, E TN Inf
GROSS, John, Pvt, Maj John Childs, Capt Jas Cummings, E TN Vol Mtd Inf
GROSS, William, Pvt, Maj John Childs, Capt James Cummings, E TN Vol Mtd Inf
GROSS (GROCE), Jacob, Pvt, Maj Gen Wm Carroll, Col Wm Metcalf, Capt John Jackson, Inf
GROSS (GROCHE), Jonathan, Pvt, Lt Col Hammond, Col Alexander Loury, Capt Thos Delaney, Inf
GROSSET, John, Pvt, Col John Cocke, Capt John Weakley, Inf
GROVE, George, Dmr, Col Sam Bunch, Capt Isaac Williams, E TN Mil
GROVES, Abraham, Pvt, Col Wm Pillow, Capt George Caperton, Inf; wounded 11-9-1813 at Talledega
GROVES, Isaac, 3 Sgt, Col Bradley, Capt Moore, Vol Inf
GROVES, Isaac, Pvt, Col Wm Hall, Capt Moore, Vol Inf
GROVES, Jacob, 4 Sgt, Col Wm Lillard, Capt Wm Gillenwater, E TN Vol Inf
GROVES, John, Pvt, Col Wm Lillard, Capt Wm Gillenwater, E TN Inf
GROVES, Reuben, Pvt, Col Sam Bunch, Capt David Mason, E TN Vol Mtd Inf
GRUBB, Abraham, Pvt, Col Ewen Allison, Capt Wm King, Drafted Mil

## Enlisted Men, War of 1812

GRUBB, Wesley, 3 Sgt, Col Wm Lillard, Capt Wm King, E TN Vol Inf

GRUBB, Wesley, 3 Sgt, Lt Col Wm Snodgrass, Co Commander omitted, Det of Inf of 2nd Regt of E TN Vol

GUESS, Elijah, Pvt, Col Thos H Benton, Capt Wm Moore, Vol Inf

GUESS, Ferrell, Pvt, Col Philip Pipkin, Capt Searcy, Mil Inf

GUESS, John, Pvt, Maj Wm Russell, Capt Chism, Vol Mtd Gunmen

GUESS, Morgan, Pvt, Regt Commander omitted, Sgt Wyatt Fussell, Det of Inf

GUESS, Samuel, Pvt, Maj Gen A Jackson, Col Thos Williamson, Capt Steele, Vol Mtd Gunmen

GUESS, William, Pvt, Col Thos H Benton, Capt Moore, Vol Inf; dead?

GUEST, Joshua, Cpl, Col Thos H Benton, Capt Benj Reynolds, Vol Inf

GUEST, Joshua, Pvt, Col Newton Cannon, Capt Wm Martin, Mtd Gunmen; transferred for Capt Evan's Spy Co

GUFFEE, Ephrainus, Pvt, Col Jas Raulston, Capt Mathew Cowan, Inf

GUFFEE, William, Pvt, Col Wm Hall, Capt John Kennedy, Vol Inf; substitute

GUFFREY, Henry, Sgt, Col S Copeland, Capt Evans, Mil Inf

GUICE, Solomon, Pvt, Col John Cocke, Capt Jas Gray, Inf

GUIN, Ezekiel, Pvt, Gen John Coffee, Co Commander omitted, Mtd Spies

GUIN, James, Pvt, Col John Williams, Capt David Vance, Mtd Mil

GUIN, John, Pvt, Col Wm Lillard, Capt Robert Maloney, E TN Vol Inf

GUIN, Stephen O, Pvt, Col John Cocke, Capt James Gray, Inf

GUIN, William, Cpl, Col Wm Lillard, Capt Robert Maloney, E TN Vol Inf

GUIN, William, Pvt, Col Wm Lillard, Capt Wm McLin, E TN Inf

GUINN, Barlette, Pvt, Col S Bayless, Capt Branch Jones, E TN Drafted Mil

GUINN, Christopher, Pvt, Col Alexander Loury, Capt Gabriel Martin, Inf

GUINN, Daniel, Pvt, Col Philip Pipkin, Capt John Strother, Mil; attached to Capt Peter Searcy

GUINN, Elijah, Pvt, Col Wm Lillard, Capt John Neatherton, E TN Vol Inf

GUINN, Isaac, Pvt, Col S Bayless, Co Commander omitted, E TN Mil

GUINN, John, Pvt, Col Hugh Bradley, Capt Harry L Douglass, Vol Inf

GUINN, John, Pvt, Col John Coffee, Capt John Baskerville, Cav

GUINN, Levy, Cpl, Col Bayless, Capt Solomon Hendrix, E TN Mil; d 2-23-1815

GUINN, Valentine, Pvt, Col Philip Pipkin, Capt Henry M Newlin, W TN Mil

GUINN, William, Pvt, Col Robert Steele, Capt Samuel Maxwell, Mil Inf

GUINNE, Ezekiel, Cpl, Col Thomas Williamson, Capt Robert Moore, Vol Mtd Gunmen; transferred to Lt Bosis Spies

GULLAGE, Thomas, Pvt, Col John Cocke, Capt Samuel Caruthers, Inf

GULLET, George, Pvt, Col Philip Pipkin, Capt David Smith, Inf

GULLET, John, Pvt, Col Johnson, Capt Scott, E TN Drafted Mil; substitute for Joel Mason

GULLET, Reece, Pvt, Col L Hammonds, Capt A Loury & Capt Thos Delaney, Inf

GULLET, Waitman, Pvt, Col Ewen Allison, Capt Adam Winsell, E TN Drafted Mil

GULLETT, John, Pvt, Col Wm Lillard, Capt James Lillard, E TN Inf Vol

GULLEY, Lazarus, Pvt, Col Wm Lillard, Capt George Argenbright, E TN Vol Riflemen

GULLIDGE, William, Pvt, Col A Loury, Capt Gabriel Martin, Inf

GULLIE (GULLUCK), Richard, Pvt, Lt Col L Hammond, Col A Loury, Capt Thomas Delaney, Inf

GULLIFORD, James, Pvt, Regt Commander omitted, Capt Edwin S Moore, Mtd Riflemen

GULLIHORN, James, Pvt, Col Wm Johnson, Capt Joseph Scott, E TN Drafted Mil

GULLY, Jesse, Pvt, Col Archibald McKenney, Co Commander omitted, Cav

GULLY, Jesse, Pvt, Col John Coffee, Capt Kavanaugh, Cav

GULLY, Jesse, Pvt, Regt Commander omitted, Capt Archibald McKenney, Cav

GULLY, William, Pvt, Col Philip Pipkin, Capt Ebenezer Kirkpatrick, Mil Inf

GUMBRELL, John, Pvt, Col Thomas McCrory, Capt Thomas Gordon, Inf; deserted 11-18-1813

GUN, Charles, Pvt, Maj Gen Wm Carroll, Capt Francis Ellis, Inf

GUNDLE, Geny, Pvt, Lt Isaac Barrett, Co Commander omitted, Inf; also under Col A Jackson

GUNN, Alex, Pvt, Lt Col Archer Cheatham, Co Commander omitted, Mtd Inf 6th Brig

GUNN, Alexander, Pvt, Col John Cocke, Capt Richard Crunk, Inf

GUNN, Elisha, Pvt, Lt Col Richard Napier, Co Commander omitted, Inf

GUNN, George, Pvt, Lt Col A Cheatham, Capt Meredith Walker, Inf

GUNN, Griffin, Pvt, Col John Cocke, Capt Crunk, Inf

GUNN, John, Pvt, Col John Cocke, Capt Crunk, Inf

GUNN, Lawson, Pvt, Lt Col Richard Napier, Co Commander omitted, Inf

GUNN, Richard, Sgt, Col John Coffee, Capt Ross, Mtd Gunmen; promoted to Commander of Pack Horse Co

GUNN, Richard, Sgt, Regt Commander omitted, Capt Richard Boyd, Branch Srvce omitted

GUNN, Samuel, 1 Sgt, Regt Commander omitted, Capt Isaac Prewitt, Mtd Vol; Pack Horse Guards

GUNN, William, Pvt, Lt Col Richard Napier, Co Commander omitted, Inf

GUNNALS, James, Pvt, Maj Gen Wm Carroll, Col James

## Enlisted Men, War of 1812

Raulston, Capt Wiley Huddleston, Inf; promoted to 4 Cpl
GUNNALS, William, 3 Cpl, Maj Gen Wm Carroll, Col James Raulston, Capt Wiley Huddleston, Inf
GUNNELS, James, Pvt, Col S Copeland, Capt Wm Evans, Mil Inf
GUNNELS, Nicholas, Pvt, Col Stephen Copeland, Capt Wm Evans, Mil Inf
GUNNER, Alisha, Pvt, Col R C Napier, Capt Drury Adkins, Mil Inf
GUNNER, Lauson, Pvt, Col R C Napier, Capt Drury Adkins, Mil Inf
GUNTER, Francis, Pvt, Col R H Dyer, Capt Robert Edmonson, TN Vol Mtd Gunmen
GUNTER, Hawkins, 1 Cpl, Col R C Napier, Capt Early Benson, Mil Inf
GUNTER, James, Pvt, Col T Williamson, Capt John Doak & Capt John Dobbins, Vol Mtd Gunmen
GUNTER, Joel, Pvt, Col Wm Metcalf, Capt Alexander Hill & Capt John Cunningham, Mil Inf
GURLEY, David, Pvt, Regt Commander omitted, Capt A McKinney, Cav
GURLEY, George, Pvt, Col S Copeland, Capt Wm Hodges, Inf
GURLEY, George, Pvt, Maj Gen Wm Carroll, Col James Raulston, Capt Edward Robinson, Inf
GURLEY, Jeremiah, Sgt, Regt Commander omitted, Capt A McKenney, Cav; d 1-11-1814 at Battle of Talledega
GURLEY, Martin, Pvt, Regt Commander omitted, Capt A McKenney, Cav
GURLEY, William, Pvt, Regt Commander omitted, Capt A McKenney, Cav; promoted to Sdlr
GURLEY, William, Sdlr, Col John Coffee, Capt Charles Kavanaugh, Cav
GURLY, Davis, Pvt, Regt Commander omitted, Capt Archibald McKinney, Cav
GUSSET, John, Pvt, Maj Gen Carroll, Col James Raulston, Capt Edward Robinson, Inf
GUST, John, Pvt, Regt Commander omitted, Capt Larkin Ferrell, Inf
GUTHERY, Robert, Pvt, Col John K Wynne, Capt Wm McCall, Inf
GUTHREE, Robert, Pvt, Col N T Perkins, Capt Mathew Johnston, Mil Inf
GUTHREY, John, Pvt, Col John Coffee, Co Commander omitted, Vol Cav; also under Capt Thos Bradley
GUTHREY, William, Pvt, Col Samuel Bayless, Capt Joseph E Bacon, E TN Mil
GUTHRIE, Anslem, Pvt, Col Edward Bradley, Capt John Kennedy, Riflemen
GUTHRIE, John, Pvt, Maj Gen A Jackson, Capt James Reed, Inf
GUTRY, Henry, Pvt, Col S Bunch, Capt John Houk, E TN Mil; joined from Capt Davis's Co
GUTRY, William, Pvt, Col S Bunch, Capt John Houk, E TN Mil; joined from Capt Davis's Co
GUTTERY, Anslam, Pvt, Col James Raulston, Capt Wiley Huddleston, Inf
GUTTERY, Henry, Dmr, Col S Bunch, Capt Moses, E TN Mil; transferred to Capt John Houk Co
GUTTERY, William, 2 Cpl, Col S Bunch, Capt Moses, E TN Mil Drafted; transferred to Capt John Houk
GUUY?, Thomas, Pvt, Col Philip Pipkin, Capt Ebenezer Kirkpatrick, Mil Inf; deserted 9-20-1814
GUY, Joseph, Pvt, Col William Metcalf, Capt Barbee Collins, Mil Inf
GUY, William H, Pvt, Lt Col Hammond, Capt James Tubb, Inf
GWIN, Ezekiel, Pvt, Col John Alcorn, Capt John Baskerville, Vol Inf
GWIN, James, Pvt, Col John Alcorn, Capt John Baskerville, Vol Inf
GWIN, James, Pvt, Col William Alcorn, Capt John W Byrne, Cav; killed 11-9-1813 at Talledega
GWIN, John, Pvt, Col John Alcorn, Capt John Baskerville, Vol Inf
GWIN, John, Pvt, Col Thomas Benton, Capt Henry L Douglass, Vol Inf
GWIN, Joseph, Pvt, Regt Commander omitted, Capt George Smith, Spies
GWIN, Lane, Pvt, Col Samuel Wear, Capt Jesse Cole, Vol Inf
GWIN, Samuel, 1 Cpl, Col N T Perkins, Capt George Eliot, Mil Inf
GWIN, Thomas, Pvt, Col Samuel Wear, Capt Jesse Cole, Vol Inf; transferred to Capt McLin
GWIN, Isaac, Pvt, Col Samuel Wear, Capt Jesse Cole, Vol Inf
GWINN, Samuel, Pvt, Col T Williamson, Capt Thos Scurry, Vol Mtd Gunmen
GWYN, John, 4 Cpl, Col Thos Benton, Capt H L Douglass, Vol Inf
GYLLESPIE, James, Pvt, Regt Commander omitted, Capt John Gordon, Mtd Spies; missing, supposed to be killed
GYPERT, Stephen, Pvt, no other information
HACKELL, John, Pvt, Regt Commander omitted, Capt Wm Henderson, Spies
HACKER, John, Cpl, Col John Brown, Capt Allen I Bacon, E TN Mil Inf
HACKINGS, John P, Pvt, Col John Alcorn, Capt Winston, Mtd Riflemen
HACKNEY, William, Pvt, Regt Commander omitted, Capt Edwin S Moore, Mtd Riflemen
HACKWORTH, John, Pvt, Regt Commander omitted, Capt Wm Henderson, Spies
HADDEN, Hugh, Pvt, Col T McCrory, Capt Isaac Patton, Mil Inf
HADDEN, Robert S, Pvt, Col Thos Benton, Capt George Caperton, Vol Inf
HADDEN, Robert, Pvt, Col J Raulston, Capt Neale, Inf; promoted to Cpl
HADDEN, William, Pvt, Col R H Dyer, Capt Beverly Williams, Vol Mtd Gunmen
HADDOCK, David, Pvt, Col Wm Johnson, Capt Benj Powell, E TN Mil; never appeared
HADDON, Beren, Pvt, Maj John Childs, Capt R Tipton, E TN Vol Mtd Inf; Regimental Count Blount
HADDON, Hugh, Pvt, Col Wm Metcalf, Capt John Barnhart, Mil Inf; d 3-28-1815
HAGEPETH, John, Pvt, Col J K Wynne, Capt Wm

## Enlisted Men, War of 1812

Caruthers, W TN Inf; transferred to Capt Hollan's Co

HAGEPETH, William, Pvt, Col J K Wynne, Capt Wm Caruthers, W TN Inf; transferred to Capt Hollan's Co

HAGER, Abner, Pvt, Col N Cannon, Capt John Hanley, Mtd Riflemen

HAGER, Jonathan, Pvt, Col L Hammond, Capt J N Williamson, W TN Mil

HAGEWOOD, Benjamin, Pvt, Col John Brown, Capt Allen I Bacon, E TN Mil

HAGGAN, William, Pvt, Col John Alcorn, Capt Wm Locke, Cav

HAGGARD, Alfred, Pvt, Maj John Chiles, Capt Charles Conway, E TN Mtd Gunmen; Regimental Co - Roan

HAGGARD, French, Pvt, Col John Brown, Capt Wm D Neilson, E TN Vol Mil

HAGGARD, Gray, 1 Sgt, Col John Brown, Capt Wm White, E TN Vol Mtd Inf

HAGGARD, James, Cpl, Col Sam'l Bayless, Capt Jas Churchman, E TN Mil

HAGGARD, James, Pvt, Col Copeland, Capt John Dawson, Inf

HAGGARD, James, Pvt, Col N Cannon, Capt David Hogan, Mtd Gunmen

HAGGARD, James, Pvt, Col Samuel Wear, Capt John Childs, E TN Vol Inf

HAGGARD, James, Pvt, Col Wm Metcalf, Capt A Patterson, Mil Inf; d 4-15-1815

HAGGARD, Jesse, Pvt, Col Edwin E Booth, Capt John Slatton, E TN Mil; d 12-13-1814

HAGGARD, John L, Pvt, Col John Brown, Capt Wm D Neilson, Regt E TN Vol Mil

HAGGARD, Jonathan, Pvt, Col John Brown, Capt Wm D Neilson, Regt E TN Mil

HAGGARD, Martin, Pvt, Regt Commander omitted, Capt Wm Henderson, Spies

HAGGARD, Nowel, Pvt, Col N Cannon, Capt David Hogan, Mtd Gunmen; d 12-9-1813

HAGGARD, Richard, Pvt, Col Edwin E Booth, Capt John Porter, Drafted Mil

HAGGARD, Samuel, Pvt, Maj Childs, Capt Charles Conway, E TN Mtd Gunmen; Regimental Co - Roan

HAGGARD, William jr, Pvt, Lt Col John Edmonson, Co Commander omitted, Cav

HAGGARD, William, 2 Cpl, Col N Cannon, Capt David Hogan, Mtd Gunmen

HAGGARD, William, Pvt, Col Copeland, Capt John Dawson, Inf

HAGGARD, William, Pvt, Lt Col John Edmonson, Co Commander omitted, Cav

HAGGARD, _____, Pvt, Col S Bunch, Capt F Register, E TN Mil; substitute for Isaac Dulaney

HAGLER, Benjamin J, Mus, Col John Cocke, Capt Jas Gray, Inf

HAGLER, Benjamin, Pvt, Regt Commander omitted, Capt Thos Gray, Inf

HAGLER, Garland, Pvt, Col Copeland, Capt Sol George, Inf

HAGLER, Jacob, Pvt, Col John Cocke, Capt Jas Gray, Inf

HAGLER, John, Pvt, Col John Brown, Capt Wm White, E TN Mil Inf

HAGLER, Thomas, Pvt, Col John Brown, Capt Wm White, E TN Mtd Mil Inf

HAGLER, William H, Sgt, Col John Cocke, Capt Jas Gray, Inf

HAGLER, William, Sgt, Regt Commander omitted, Capt Jas Gray, Inf

HAGOOD, Buckner, Pvt, Regt Commander omitted, Capt Davis Smith, Cav Vol

HAGOOD, John, Pvt, Col Wynne, Capt E B Prince, Inf

HAGOOD, Robert, Pvt, Col John Coffee, Capt David Smith, Vol Cav

HAGOOD, Tapley, Pvt, Regt Commander omitted, Capt Hugh Kerr, Mtd Rangers

HAHOON, Samuel, Pvt, Col Jas Raulston, Capt Charles Wade, Inf

HAIBY, David W, Asst Wagon Master, Brig Gen N Taylor, Branch Srvce omitted; stationed at Ft Taylor

HAIL, Alexander, Pvt, Col Williamson, Capt John Hutchings, Vol Mtd Gunmen

HAIL, Christopher, Pvt, Col Wm Johnson, Capt Joseph Kirk, Mil

HAIL, Ezekiel, Pvt, Maj Gen Carroll, Col Raulston, Capt Edward Robinson, Inf

HAIL, George, Cpl, Col Williamson, Capt Thos Porter, Vol Mtd Gunmen

HAIL, Gilliard, Pvt, Col John Coffee, Capt Thos Bradley, Vol Mtd Gunmen; d 1-20-1815

HAIL, Jesse, Pvt, Col Ewen Allison, Capt Henry McCray, E TN Mil

HAIL, John A, Pvt, Col N Cannon, Capt Ewdards, Regt Command

HAIL, John B, Pvt, Col S Wear, Capt Jas Gillespie, E TN Vol Inf

HAIL, Leroy, Pvt, Col Ewen Allison, Capt John Hampton, Mil; transferred to Capt Barron's Co

HAIL, Marshack, Pvt, Gen John Coffee, Co Commander omitted, Mtd Spies

HAIL, Micaja, Pvt, Col John K Wynne, Capt James Holleman, Inf

HAIL, Nicholas, 4 Cpl, Col Wm Hall, Capt Wm Alexander, Vol Inf

HAIL, Nicholas, Cpl, Col Edward Bradley, Capt Wm Lauderdale, Vol Inf

HAIL, Nicholas, Cpl, Col Wm Hall, Capt Wm Alexander, Vol Inf

HAIL, Richard, Pvt, Col William Lillard, Capt Jacob Hartsell, E TN Vol Inf

HAIL, Richard, Pvt, Col Williamson, Capt Hutchings, Vol Mtd Gunmen

HAIL, Sherwood, Pvt, Col Thomas Benton, Capt Thos Williamson, Vol Inf

HAIL, Thomas, Pvt, Col John Alcorn, Capt Fredrick Stump, Cav; d 12-1-1813

HAIL, William, Pvt, Col Thos Williamson, Capt Giles Burdette, Vol Mtd Gunmen

HAIL (HALE), Jeremiah, Pvt, Col Thomas Williamson, Capt Anthony Metcalf, Vol Mtd Gunmen; d 1-20-1815

HAILAND, Boman, Pvt, Col John Cocke, Capt Samuel

- 227

## Enlisted Men, War of 1812

Caruthers, Inf

HAILE, Chase, Pvt, Col Samuel Bunch, Capt Vance, E TN Mtd Inf

HAILE, Hezekiah, Pvt, Col S Bunch, Capt Vance, E TN Mtd Inf

HAILE, Jesse, Pvt, Col S Bunch, Capt Vance, E TN Mtd Inf

HAILE, Leroy, Pvt, Col S Bunch, Capt Vance, E TN Mtd Inf

HAILE, Nicholas, Cpl, Col R H Dyer, Capt Thos White, Vol Mtd Gunmen

HAILE, Nicholas, Pvt, Col R H Dyer, Capt Thos White, Vol Mtd Gunmen

HAILE, Richard, Pvt, Col S Bunch, Capt Vance, E TN Mtd Inf

HAILE, Samuel, Pvt, Col Thos Benton, Capt N Cannon, Inf

HAILE, Walter, Pvt, Col S Bunch, Capt Vance, E TN Mtd Inf

HAILES, Barneby, Pvt, Col Wm Metcalf, Capt Andrew Patterson, Mil Inf

HAILES, Daniel, Pvt, Col S Wear, Capt Jas Tedford, E TN Vol Inf

HAILEY, Edward, Pvt, Col A Lowry, Capt Williamson, W TN Mil

HAILEY, Edward, Pvt, Col L Hammonds, Capt J N Williamson, Inf

HAILEY, Jesse, Cpl, Maj Wm Woodfolk, Capt Abner Pearce, Inf; promoted from Pvt

HAILEY, Richard, Pvt, Col Wm Metcalf, Capt Thos Marks, Mil Inf

HAILEY, Spencer, 4 Sgt, Col John Cocke, Capt Nance, Inf

HAILEY, William B, Pvt, Col Wm Y Higgins, Capt Thos Eldridge, Mtd Gunmen

HAILEY, William, Pvt, Col Thos Williamson, Capt Wm Martin, Vol Mtd Gunmen

HAILY, David, Pvt, Regt Commander omitted, Capt Williamson, Spies

HAINE, Ephraim, Pvt, Col John Cocke, Capt Nance, Inf; substitute for Wm Marshall

HAINE, _____, Cpl, Col Thos Williamson, Capt Anthony Metcalf, Vol Mtd Gunmen

HAINES, Abraham, Pvt, Col S Bayless, Capt Solomon Hendrix, E TN Mil

HAINES, Drewry, Pvt, Col Wm Lillard, Capt Wm Lillard, E TN Inf

HAINES, Joe, Pvt, Col I Barrett, Capt Nathan Davis, Inf

HAINES, Moody P, Pvt, Col Edward Bradley, Capt Lauderdale, Vol Inf

HAINES, Moody P, Pvt, Regt Commander omitted, Capt John Gordon, Mtd Spies

HAINEY, George M, Sgt, Col S Bayless, Capt Solomon Hendrix, E TN Mil

HAINEY, Jas, Pvt, Col Jas Raulston, Capt Mathew Neal, Inf

HAIR, Archibald, Pvt, Col Philip Pipkin, Capt Smith, Inf

HAIR, Isaac, Cpl, Col S Bayless, Capt Jonathan Waddell, E TN Mil

HAIR, Joseph, Pvt, Col Wm Lillard, Capt Jacob Hartsell, E TN Vol Inf

HAIRS, Daniel, Pvt, Col Wm Lillard, Capt Wm Hamilton, E TN Vol Inf

HAIRS, John, Pvt, Col Wm Lillard, Capt Wm Hamilton, E TN Vol Inf

HAISLETT, William, Pvt, Maj Wm Russell, Capt John Cowan, Vol Mtd Gunmen

HALBERCE, Joel, Pvt, Col Leroy Hammonds & Col A Loury, Capt Thos Delaney, Inf

HALBERT, William, Pvt, Col Thos Williamson, Capt Doak & Capt John Dobbins, Vol Mtd Gunmen

HALBROOK, Ezekiel, Far, Col Thos Williamson, Capt Giles Burdette, Vol Mtd Gunmen

HALBROOK, George, Far, Regt Commander omitted, Capt Ephraim Dickson, Branch Srvce omitted

HALBROOK, George, Pvt, Col N Cannon, Co Commander omitted, Mtd Gunmen

HALCOMB, Hiram, Pvt, Regt Commander omitted, Capt John Crane, Inf

HALCOMB, James, Sgt, Col John Coffee, Capt Chas Kavanaugh, Cav

HALCOMB, John, Pvt, Col J Alcorn, Capt Thos Bradley, Vol Cav

HALCORN, Meredith, Pvt, Col Jas Craig, Co Commander omitted, Inf

HALE, Alexander, Pvt, Col John K Wynne, Capt Wm Caruthers, W TN Inf

HALE, Alexander, Pvt, Col John K Wynne, Capt Wm Wilson, Inf; transferred to Capt Caruther's Co

HALE, Bird, Pvt, Col Wm Johnson, Capt Andrew Lawson, E TN Drafted Mil

HALE, Dickerson, Pvt, Col A Cheatham, Capt Meredith Walker, Brig Mtd Inf

HALE, Ezekiel, Pvt, Col S Copeland, Capt Wm Hodges, Inf

HALE, Hugh, Pvt, Col John Williams, Capt Sam Bunch, Branch Srvce omitted

HALE, James, Pvt, Col William Johnson, Capt Andrew Lawson, E TN Drafted Mil

HALE, James, Pvt, Col Wm Johnson, Capt Elihu Milliken, 3rd E TN Mil; d 11-9-1814

HALE, Jesse, 3 Sgt, Maj Gen Wm Carroll, Col Wm Metcalf, Capt John Jackson, Mil Inf

HALE, Jesse, Sgt, Col S Bunch, Capt George McPherson, E TN Mil

HALE, John, 1 Sgt, Col S Copeland, Capt John Dawson, Inf

HALE, Joseph, Pvt, Col Ewen Allison, Capt Thos Wilson, Branch Srvce omitted

HALE, Joseph, Pvt, Regt Commander omitted, Capt Samuel Bunch, Mtd Vol; alos under Col John Williams

HALE, Lemon, Pvt, Col Jas Raulston, Capt Elijah Haynie, Inf

HALE, Masacah, Pvt, Col John Coffee, Capt Daniel Ross, Mtd Gunmen

HALE, Meshich, Pvt, Col Thos H Williamson, Capt Wm Martin, Vol Mtd Gunmen; transferred to Lt Bean's Spies

HALE, Micajah, Pvt, Col Robert Steele, Capt Samuel Maxwell, Mil Inf

HALE, Nathan G, Pvt, Col Coffee, Capt Stump, Cav

## Enlisted Men, War of 1812

HALE, Nathan O, Pvt, Col John Alcorn, Co Commander omitted, Cav
HALE, Nicholas, Pvt, Col John Coffee, Capt Daniel Ross, Mtd Gunmen
HALE, Richard, 4 Cpl, Col Philip Pipkin, Capt Jas Blakemore, Mil Inf
HALE, Samuel, Pvt, Col Newton Cannon, Capt Wm Martin, Mtd Gunmen
HALE, Sherwood, Pvt, Col Thos Benton, Capt Thos Williamson, Vol Inf
HALE, Talbot, Pvt, Maj Wm Woodfolk, Capt Abraham Dudney, Inf; also under Capt Sutton
HALE, Thomas, Pvt, Col Thomas H Benton, Capt Thos Williamson, Vol Inf
HALE, Walter, Pvt, Col John Williams, Capt David Vance, Mtd Mil
HALE, William, Pvt, Col John Brown, Capt Jas Preston, E TN Mil Inf
HALE, William, Pvt, Col John K Wynne, Capt William Caruthers, W TN Inf
HALE (HALL), James, Pvt, Col Wm Hall, Capt Henry M Newlin, Inf
HALE (HALL), William, Pvt, Col Jas Raulston, Capt Mathew Neale, Inf; d 2-5-1815
HALE (HALL), Wilson, Pvt, Col A Loury, Capt George Sarver, Inf
HALEY, David F, Pvt, Col Samuel Wear, Capt Rufus Morgan, E TN Vol Inf
HALEY, Frederick, Pvt, Col John Cocke, Co Commander omitted, Inf
HALEY, Limons, 4 Sgt, Col John Coffee, Co Commander omitted, Cav
HALEY, Lylanious, Sgt, Regt Commander omitted, Capt Jos Williams, Mil Cav
HALEY, Overton, Pvt, Col R H Dyer, Co Commander omitted, TN Vol Mtd Gunmen
HALEY, Robert K, Pvt, Col John Brown, Capt Wm D Neilson, E TN Vol Mil
HALEY, Thomas, Pvt, Col John Coffee, Capt Frederick Stump, Cav
HALEY, Thomas, Pvt, Regt Commander omitted, Capt James Haggard, Mtd Gunmen
HALEY, Thomas, Pvt, Regt Commander omitted, Lt John Scott, Det of Inf
HALEY, William B, Pvt, Col John Brown, Capt Wm D Neilson, E TN Vol Mil
HALEY, William, Pvt, Col John Steele, Capt Richard Ratton, Mil Inf
HALEY, Woodson, Pvt, Col Robert Steele, Capt John Chitwood, Mil Inf
HALEY (HOLLY), William, Pvt, Maj Gen Andrew Jackson, Col Thos Williamson, Capt Robert Steele, Branch Srvce omitted
HALFACRE, Isaac, Pvt, Col Edwin Booth, Capt John Sharp, E TN Mil
HALFACRE, Jesse, 2 Cpl, Col Edwin Booth, Capt John Sharp, E TN Mil
HALFACRE, John, Pvt, Col John Cocke, Capt James Gault, Inf; d 3-5-1815
HALIN, Charles, Pvt, Col Wm Metcalf, Capt Barbee Collins, Mil Inf

HALKIN, Grant, Pvt, Maj Gen Wm Carroll, Col Wm Metcalf, Capt John Jackson, Inf
HALL, Adam, Pvt, Col S Copeland, Capt John Holshouser, Inf
HALL, Alexander, Pvt, Col Edwin Booth, Capt Vernon, E TN Mil
HALL, Archibald, Pvt, Col R H Dyer, Capt Thos Jones, Vol Mtd Gunmen
HALL, Asa, Pvt, Col S Copeland, Capt John Holshouser, Inf
HALL, Benjamin, Pvt, Col Edwin Booth, Capt Richard Sharp, E TN Mil
HALL, Benjamin, Pvt, Regt Commander omitted, Capt John Miller, Spies
HALL, Christian, Pvt, Col Wm Johnson, Capt Christopher Cook, E TN Mil
HALL, David, 2 Sgt, Col John Coffee, Capt Robert Jetton, Cav
HALL, David, Pvt, Col A Loury, Capt Jas Kincaid, Inf
HALL, David, Pvt, Col Samuel Wear, Capt John Childs, E TN Vol Inf
HALL, Dickerson, Pvt, Col John Cocke, Capt Richard Crunk, Inf; d 2-1-1815
HALL, Drury, Pvt, Col Philip Pipkin, Capt George Mebane, Mil Inf
HALL, Edmond, Pvt, Col Samuel Bunch, Capt N Gibbs, E TN Drafted Mil; transferred to Capt Duncan's Co
HALL, Edward, Pvt, Col Samuel Bunch, Capt Joseph Duncan, E TN Drafted Mil; joined from Capt Gibb's Co
HALL, Elijah, Pvt, Col Samuel Bayless, Capt Joseph Rich, E TN Inf
HALL, Elisha, Pvt, Maj Wm Carroll, Capt Lewis Dillahunty & Capt Daniel M Bradford, Vol Inf
HALL, Frederick, Pvt, Col Ewen Allison, Capt Joseph Everett, E TN Mil; discharged - unfit for duty
HALL, Garland, Pvt, Col Wm Metcalf, Capt Barbee Collins, Mil Inf; d 3-13-1815?
HALL, Garrett, Pvt, Col John Brown, Capt Wm White, E TN Mtd Mil Inf
HALL, George, Pvt, Col John Alcorn, Capt John W Byrn, Cav
HALL, Hardin P, Sgt, Col John Coffee, Capt Charles Kavanaugh, Cav
HALL, Hardin, Pvt, Maj Gen Wm Carroll, Col Wm Metcalf, Capt John Jackson, Inf
HALL, Harvey, Pvt, Col Wm Lillard, Capt Wm Gillenwater, E TN Inf
HALL, Henry, Pvt, Col R H Dyer, Capt Bethel Allen, Vol Mtd Gunmen
HALL, Henry, Pvt, Col William Johnson, Capt Christopher Cook, E TN Mil
HALL, Henry, Pvt, Col Wm Johnson, Capt Joseph Kirk, Mil
HALL, Henry, Pvt, Col Wm Metcalf, Capt Bird L Hurt, Mil Inf
HALL, Henry, Pvt, Maj Gen Wm Carroll, Capt Francis Ellis, Inf
HALL, Isaac, Pvt, Col Robert Steele, Capt Robert Campbell, Mil Inf
HALL, James, Pvt, Col Edward Bradley, Capt Thos B

- 229

## Enlisted Men, War of 1812

Haynes, Vol Inf
HALL, James, Pvt, Col John K Wynne, Capt William Caruthers, W TN Inf; promoted to Cpl
HALL, James, Pvt, Col Loury, Lt Col L Hammonds, Capt Arahel Rains, Inf; transferred to Capt Russell
HALL, James, Pvt, Maj Wm Russell, Capt John Cowan, Vol Mtd Gunmen
HALL, Jesse, Pvt, Maj Wm Woodfolk, Capt Jas Turner, Inf; in place of James Gray, transferred to Capt McCulley
HALL, Joel, Pvt, Lt I Barrett, Capt Nathan Davis, W TN Bn Inf
HALL, John C, Pvt, Col Philip Pipkin, Capt David Smith, Inf; d 11-?-1814
HALL, John M, Pvt, Col T Williamson, Capt James Pace, Lt Nealy, Vol Mtd Gunmen
HALL, John, Pvt, Col John Alcorn, Capt Wm Locke, Cav
HALL, John, Pvt, Col John Brown, Capt William White, E TN Mtd Mil Inf
HALL, John, Pvt, Col John Coffee, Capt Blackman Coleman, Cav
HALL, John, Pvt, Col R H Dyer, Capt Cuthbert Hudson, Vol Mtd Gunmen
HALL, John, Pvt, Col Samuel Bunch, Capt Andrew Breden, E TN Mil
HALL, John, Pvt, Col Wm Lillard, Capt Wm Gillenwater, E TN Inf
HALL, John, Pvt, Lt Col Henry Bryan, Co Commander omitted, Inf
HALL, John, Pvt, Regt Commander omitted, Capt Edwin S Moore, Mtd Riflemen
HALL, John, Sgt, Col R H Dyer, Capt Cuthbert Hudson, Vol Mtd Gunmen; promoted from Pvt
HALL, Jonathan, Pvt, Col Thos Benton, Capt Isaiah Renshaw, Vol Inf
HALL, Joseph, Pvt, Col John Cocke, Capt Jas Gault, Inf; substitute for Joshua Cutchen, d 2-1-1815
HALL, Joseph, Pvt, Col S Bunch, Capt George McPherson, E TN Mil; joined from Capt Millikin's Co
HALL, Joseph, Pvt, Col Samuel Bayless, Capt James Landen, E TN Mil
HALL, Joseph, Pvt, Col Wm Metcalf, Capt Bird L Hurt, Mil Inf
HALL, Joseph, Pvt, Maj Gen Wm Carroll, Col Wm Metcalf, Capt John Jackson, Inf
HALL, Joseph, Pvt, Maj Woodfolk, Capt Jas C Neil, Inf
HALL, Joseph, Sgt, Col Wm Lillard, Capt Robert Maloney, E TN Vol Inf
HALL, Joshua, Pvt, Maj Wm Woodfolk, Capt Abraham Dudney, Inf & Sutton?
HALL, Lemuel, Cpl, Col John Alcorn, Capt Robert Jetton, Vol Cav
HALL, Lemuel, Pvt, Col John Coffee, Capt Robert Jetton, Cav
HALL, Luke, Pvt, Col John Brown, Capt Wm White, E TN Mtd Mil Inf
HALL, Moses, Pvt, Col John Coffee, Capt John W Byrn, Cav
HALL, Nathan, Pvt, Col N Cannon, Capt Jas Walton, Mtd Riflemen
HALL, Obadiah, Cpl, Col S Bunch, Capt N Gibbs, E TN Drafted Mil; promoted from Pvt
HALL, Pharaoh, Pvt, Col N Cannon, Capt Ota Cantrell, W TN Mtd Gunmen
HALL, Pharaoh, Pvt, Col Thos Williamson, Capt James Pace, Lt Nealy, Vol Mtd Gunmen
HALL, Philip S, Pvt, Col Samuel Bayless, Capt James Landen, E TN Mil; promoted to Sgt Maj
HALL, Philip S, Sgt Maj, Col Samuel Bayless, Co Commander omitted, 4th Regt E TN Mil
HALL, Randolph B, Pvt, Regt Commander omitted, Capt John Cocke & Capt George Barnes, Inf
HALL, Richard, Pvt, Col S Bunch, Capt Andrew Breden, E TN Mil
HALL, Richard, Pvt, Col Samuel Bayless, Capt Jas Landen, E TN Mil
HALL, Samuel P, Pvt, Col Edwin E Booth, Capt Vernon, E TN Mil
HALL, Samuel, Pvt, Col E Allison, Capt Allen, E TN Mil
HALL, Squire, Pvt, Col Samuel Wear, Capt John Childs, E TN Vol Inf
HALL, Stephen, Pvt, Col Thos H Benton, Capt George Caperton, Vol Inf; substitute for C Bledsoe
HALL, Stephen, Pvt, Col Wm Pillow, Capt George Caperton, Inf
HALL, Stephen, Pvt, Maj Wm Russell, Capt George Caperton, Vol Mtd Gunmen
HALL, Swan, Pvt, Col Wm Lillard, Capt Wm Gillenwater, E TN Inf
HALL, Thomas, Pvt, Col Philip Pipkin, Capt George Mebane, Mil Inf
HALL, Thomas, Pvt, Regt Commander omitted, Capt Garrett Lane, Mtd Riflemen
HALL, William, Pvt, Col John Brown, Capt J G Reany, Mtd Gunmen
HALL, William, Pvt, Col N Cannon, Capt John Harpole, Mtd Gunmen; furloughed, wounded at Talledega 11-3-1813
HALL, William, Pvt, Col N Perkins, Capt George Eliot, Mil Inf
HALL, William, Pvt, Col Thos Williamson, Capt Giles Burdett, Vol Mtd Gunmen
HALL, William, Pvt, Col William Pillow, Capt Isaiah Renshaw, Inf
HALL, William, Pvt, Regt Commander omitted, Capt Larkin Ferrell, Inf
HALL, William, Sgt, Capt Nathan Davis, Lt I Barrett, W TN Bn Inf
HALL, Willis, Pvt, Col Edwin E Booth, Capt Vernon, E TN Mil
HALL, Willis, Pvt, Col R H Dyer, Capt Robert Evans, Vol Mtd Gunmen?
HALL, Zachariah, Pvt, Col S Bunch, Capt George McPherson, E TN Mil; deserted 3-7-1814
HALL, Zachary, Pvt, Col S Bunch, Capt N Gibbs, E TN Drafted Mil; transferred to Capt Duncan's Co
HALL (HAIL), Benjamin, Pvt, Col R H Dyer, Capt Bethel Allen, Vol Gunmen
HALL (HALE), Guy, Pvt, Col Ewen Allison, Capt Jonas Loughmiller, Mil
HALL (HALE), Nathaniel, Pvt, Col Ewen Allison, Capt Loughmiller, Mil

## Enlisted Men, War of 1812

HALLAND, John, Pvt, Lt Col Hammond, Capt Jas Craig, Inf
HALLAND, William, Pvt, Lt Col John Edmonson, Co Commander omitted, Cav
HALLOWAY, Edward, Pvt, Col R Dyer, Capt Jas McMahon, TN Vol Mtd Gunmen
HALLOWAY, Joseph, Pvt, Maj John Childs, Capt Chas Conway, E TN Mtd Gunmen
HALLOWAY, Nathaniel, Cpl, Col Wm Hall, Capt Abraham Bledsoe, Vol Inf
HALLOWELL, William L, Pvt, Maj Gen Andrew Jackson, Capt Wm Carroll, Vol Inf
HALLUM, John, Sgt, Col John Coffee, Capt Thos Bradley, Vol Cav
HALLUM, William, Pvt, Col John Coffee, Capt Thomas Bradley, Vol Cav
HALLY (HOLLY), Benjamin, Pvt, Col Thos Benton, Capt George Caperton, Vol Inf
HALLYWAY, John B, Pvt, Maj Gen Andrew Jackson, Capt A Cheatham, Capt Creel, Inf
HALM, Frederick, Pvt, Maj William Woodfolk, Capt James C Neil, Inf
HALMON, Benjamin, Pvt, Lt Col John Edmonson, Co Commander omitted, Cav
HALSEL, Vardiman, Cpl, Regt Commander omitted, Capt Edwin S Moore, Mtd Riflemen
HAM, Abraham, Pvt, Col Ewen Allison, Capt Adam Winsell, E TN Drafted Mil
HAM, Abraham, Pvt, Col S Bayless, Capt Solomon Hendrix, E TN Mil
HAM, Bassengame, Pvt, Col Wm Hall, Capt Henry Newlin, Inf
HAM, Jacob, Pvt, Col Wm Hall, Capt Henry Newlin, Inf
HAM, James, Pvt, Col Wm Hall, Capt Henry Newlin, Inf
HAM, John, Pvt, Col Ewen Allison, Capt Adam Winsell, E TN Drafted Mil
HAM, Naney B, Pvt, Col T McCrory, Capt Isaac Patton, Mil Inf
HAM, Orang, Pvt, Col A Cheatham, Capt J Giddens, Inf
HAM, Orange, Pvt, Col R H Dyer, Capt Glen Owen, 1st TN Vol Mtd Gunmen
HAM, Samuel, Pvt, Col Robert Steele, Capt Samuel Maxwell, Mil Inf
HAMANTREE, James, Pvt, Col S Bunch, Capt Jos Duncan, E TN Drafted Mil; transferred to Capt Berry
HAMANTREE, William, Pvt, Col S Bunch, Capt Jos Duncan, E TN Drafted Mil; transferred to Capt Berry's Co
HAMBER, Benjamin, Pvt, Col John Brown, Capt Allen I Bacon, E TN Mil Inf
HAMBERT, Henry, Pvt, Col S Bunch, Capt George McPherson, E TN Mil; joined from Capt Register's Co
HAMBERT, Isaac, Pvt, Col S Bunch, Capt George McPherson, E TN Mil; joined from Capt Register's Co
HAMBLE, Robert, 3 Sgt, Col Anthony Metcalf, Capt Andrew Patterson, Mil Inf
HAMBLEN, Thomas, 2 Sgt, Col Wm Lillard, Co Commander omitted, E TN Vol Inf
HAMBLEN, Thomas, Pvt, Col Ewen Allison, Capt Joseph Everett, E TN Mil
HAMBLEN, William H, Sgt, Col A Cheatham, Capt Birdwell, Inf
HAMBLET, William, Pvt, Col John K Wynne, Capt McCall, Inf
HAMBLETON, Andrew, 3 Sgt, Maj Gen Wm Carroll, Capt Francis Ellis, Inf; promoted to Ward Master
HAMBLETON, Andrew, Sgt, Col John Coffee, Capt Molton, Cav
HAMBLETON, Benjamin, Pvt, Col Robert Steele, Capt Rotton, Mil Inf
HAMBLETON, David L, Pvt, Col S Copeland, Co Commander omitted, Inf
HAMBLETON, David, Pvt, Col S Copeland, Capt John Holshouser, Inf
HAMBLETON, Francis, Pvt, Col Ewen Allison, Capt Joseph Everett, E TN Mil; transferred to Capt McPherson's Co
HAMBLETON, Francis, Pvt, Regt Commander omitted, Capt David Smith, Cav
HAMBLETON, Hance, Pvt, Col R C Napier, Capt Wm Chism, Mil Inf
HAMBLETON, James, Pvt, Lt Col Hammond, Capt Jas Craig, Inf
HAMBLETON, John, Pvt, Col Ewen Allison, Capt Joseph Everett, E TN Mil; transferred to Capt McPherson
HAMBLETON, John, Pvt, Col John Cocke, Capt Crunk, Inf
HAMBLETON, John, Pvt, Col Thomas H Benton, Capt George Caperton, Vol Inf
HAMBLETON, Mathew, Pvt, Col Samuel Bunch, Capt Moses, E TN Mil Drafted; promoted to Cpl
HAMBLETON, Moses, Pvt, Col John Alcorn, Capt Winston, Mtd Riflemen
HAMBLETON, Robert, Pvt, Lt Col Hammond, Capt Jas Craig, Inf
HAMBLETON, Thomas, Pvt, Col John Alcorn, Capt Winston, Mtd Riflemen
HAMBLETON, William T, Pvt, Col Bradford, Capt Jas Hambleton, Vol Inf
HAMBLETON, William, Pvt, Col Wm Metcalf, Capt O Waller, Mil Inf
HAMBLETT, John, Pvt, Maj Wm Russell, Capt Beverly Williams, Separate Bn TN Vol Mtd Gunmen; Regimental Co - Hawkins
HAMBLIN, John, 4 Cpl, Maj John Childs, Capt Jas Cummings, E TN Vol Mtd Inf
HAMBRECK, Jerry, Pvt, Maj Wm Woodfolk, Capt Abner Pearce, Inf
HAMBRER, Benjamin, Pvt, Col Samuel Wear, Capt John Bayless, Mtd Inf
HAMBREY, William, Pvt, Maj Wm Russell, Capt John Trimble, Vol Mtd Gunmen
HAMBRICK, John, Pvt, Col Philip Pipkin, Capt Eb Kirkpatrick, Mil Inf; deserted 9-20-1814
HAMBRICK, Joseph, Pvt, Col William Higgins, Capt Jas Hambleton, Mtd Gunmen
HAMBRICK, Thomas, Pvt, Col Philip Pipkin, Capt Eb Kirkpatrick, Mil Inf; deserted 9-20-1814
HAMBRIGHT, Benjamin, Pvt, Maj John Childs, Capt Chas Conway, E TN Mtd Gunmen; Regimental

## Enlisted Men, War of 1812

HAMBY, Isaac, Cpl, Col Wm Johnson, Capt A Lawson, E TN Mil
HAMBY, Isaac, Pvt, Col Samuel Wear, Capt John Stephens, E TN Vol Inf; unable to perform duty & discharged
HAMELLE, Hugh, Pvt, Col Sam Wear, Capt Jas Tedford, E TN Vol Inf
HAMELTON, Barton, Pvt, Col Wm Y Higgins, Capt Jas Hambleton, Mtd Gunmen; wounded 1-22-1814
HAMELTON, William, Pvt, Col Wm Johnson, Capt David McKamey, E TN Drafted Mil
HAMER, Daniel, Pvt, Col N Cannon, Capt Wm Martin, Mtd Gunmen
HAMILTON, Adam C, Pvt, Col James Raulston, Capt Henry West, Inf
HAMILTON, Alexander G, Pvt, Col Wm Metcalf, Capt Bird L Hurt, Mil Inf
HAMILTON, Andrew, Sgt, Lt Col Richard Napier, Co Commander omitted, Inf
HAMILTON, Asa, Pvt, Maj Wm Russell, Capt John Cowan, Vol Mtd Gunmen
HAMILTON, Benjamin, Pvt, Col S Bunch, Capt Jno Houk, E TN Mil; transferred from Capt English to here then to Capt Rotton
HAMILTON, David F, Pvt, Col Robert Dyer, Capt Robert Evans, Vol Mtd Gunmen
HAMILTON, Eleazer, Pvt, Col N T Perkins, Capt Philip Pipkin, Mtd Riflemen
HAMILTON, Francis, Pvt, Col John Coffee, Capt David Smith, Vol Cav
HAMILTON, Francis, Pvt, Col S Bunch, Capt George McPherson, E TN Mil
HAMILTON, George, Pvt, Col Jas Raulston, Capt Henry West, Inf
HAMILTON, George, Pvt, Col John Wynne, Capt John Spinks, Inf
HAMILTON, George, Pvt, Col Wm Metcalf, Capt Bird Hurt, Mil Inf
HAMILTON, George, Pvt, Col Wm Metcalf, Capt Wm Sitton, Mil Inf
HAMILTON, Jack, Pvt, Col John K Wynne, Capt John Spinks, Inf
HAMILTON, Jacob, Pvt, Col Robert Dyer, Capt Ephraim Dickson, TN Vol Mtd Gunmen; d 2-6-1815
HAMILTON, Jacob, Pvt, Maj Wm Russell, Capt John Cowan, Vol Mtd Gunmen
HAMILTON, James E, Pvt, Col Jas Raulston, Capt Elijah Haynie, Inf
HAMILTON, James, 2 Sgt, Col John Coffee, Capt Bryan, Cav
HAMILTON, James, 3 Cpl, Col Wm Hall, Capt James Hambleton, Vol Inf
HAMILTON, James, Capt, Col Henry Bryan, Co Commander omitted, Inf
HAMILTON, James, Pvt, Col N Cannon, Capt Brandon, Mtd Riflemen
HAMILTON, James, Pvt, Col Philip Pipkin, Capt Henry Newlin, Mil Inf; d 9-21-1814
HAMILTON, James, Pvt, Lt Col John Edmonson, Co Commander omitted, Cav
HAMILTON, James, Pvt, Maj Childs, Capt Price, Vol Mtd Gunmen
HAMILTON, James, Pvt, Regt Commander omitted, Capt Wm Henderson, Spies
HAMILTON, James, Sgt, Col Alcorn, Capt Bryan, Cav
HAMILTON, James, Sgt, Col S Bunch, Lt John Harris, Branch Srvce omitted
HAMILTON, Joel, Capt, Col S Bayless, Capt Brock, E TN Mil
HAMILTON, John T, Pvt, Col Thos Benton, Capt Jas McEwen, Vol Inf
HAMILTON, John, Pvt, Col Alexander Loury, Capt Gabriel Martin, Inf
HAMILTON, John, Pvt, Col Robert Dyer, Capt Ephraim Dickson, TN Vol Mtd Gunmen; d 2-13-1815
HAMILTON, John, Pvt, Col Robert Steele, Capt Bennett, Mil Inf
HAMILTON, John, Pvt, Col S Bunch, Capt George McPherson, E TN Mil
HAMILTON, John, Pvt, Col Wm Pillow, Capt George Caperton, Inf; d 11-3-1813
HAMILTON, John, Pvt, Regt Commander omitted, Capt Ephraim Dickson, Branch Srvce omitted
HAMILTON, Joseph, Ffr, Col Wm Hall, Capt Jas Hamilton, Vol Inf
HAMILTON, Joseph, Pvt, Col Edward Bradley, Capt Jas Hambleton, Vol Inf
HAMILTON, Joseph, Pvt, Col John Cocke, Capt Joseph Price, Inf
HAMILTON, Joseph, Pvt, Col S Bunch, Capt John Harris, E TN Mil
HAMILTON, Joseph, Pvt, Col S Bunch, Capt Jos Duncan, E TN Drafted Mil; joined from Capt Howell's Co
HAMILTON, Joseph, Pvt, Maj Childs, Capt Price, E TN Vol Mil Inf
HAMILTON, Joseph, Pvt, Maj Childs, Capt Price, Mtd Gunmen
HAMILTON, Nace, Pvt, Col Edward Bradley, Capt Travis Nash, Inf; not legally enrolled or notified
HAMILTON, Nance, Pvt, Col Robert Jarman, Capt Nathan Peoples, Inf
HAMILTON, Thomas, 2 Lt, Col Wm Hall, Capt Travis Nash, Inf; transferred to Cav after resigning
HAMILTON, Thomas, Cpl, Col Thos Williamson, Capt Robert Moore, Vol Mtd Gunmen
HAMILTON, Thomas, Pvt, Col John Cocke, Capt Joseph Price, Inf
HAMILTON, Thomas, Pvt, Col John Coffee, Capt McKean, Cav
HAMILTON, Thomas, Pvt, Col John Wynne, Capt John Porter, Inf; deserted 10-5-1813
HAMILTON, Thomas, Pvt, Col Philip Pipkin, Capt Henry Newlin, Mil Inf; replaced by Samuel Harper
HAMILTON, Thomas, Pvt, Col Robert Jarman, Capt Nathan Peoples, Inf
HAMILTON, Thomas, Pvt, Col Thomas Williamson, Capt Robert Moore, Vol Mtd Gunmen
HAMILTON, Timothy, Pvt, Col Ewen Allison, Capt Joseph Everett, E TN Mil; reduced from Cpl
HAMILTON, William S, Pvt, Col N T Perkins, Capt Mathew Johnston, Mil Inf

## Enlisted Men, War of 1812

HAMILTON, William, Cpl, Col S Wear, Capt S Bayless, Mtd Inf

HAMILTON, William, Pvt, Col S Wear, Capt John Stephen, E TN Vol Inf; unable to perform duty & discharged

HAMILTON, William, Pvt, Col William Lillard, Capt William Hamilton, E TN Vol Inf

HAMILTON, William, Pvt, Col Wm Hall, Capt John Wallace, Inf

HAMILTON, William, Pvt, Maj Gen Jackson, Col A Cheatham, Inf

HAMILTON, William, Pvt, Regt Commander omitted, Capt David Vance, Mtd Mil

HAMLET, James G, Pvt, Col Wm Hall, Capt H M Newlin, Inf

HAMLET, James, Dmr, Col Wm Hall, Capt Newlin, Inf

HAMLET, James, Pvt, Col A Cheatham, Capt Richard Benson, Inf

HAMLET, Joshua, Pvt, Regt Commander omitted, Capt Thos Gray, Inf

HAMLET, Robert, Pvt, Col Philip Pipkin, Capt Peter Searcy, Mil Inf; d at Ft Deposit 7-14-1814

HAMLETT, John, Pvt, Col R C Napier, Capt Thos Preston, Mil Inf

HAMLETT, John, Pvt, Col S Bayless, Capt Joseph Hale, E TN Mil

HAMLETT, William, Pvt, Col R C Napier, Capt Thos Preston, Mil Inf

HAMLIN, Eliakin, Pvt, Col John K Wynne, Capt Jas Holleman, Inf

HAMMAC, John, Pvt, Col Edwin E Booth, Capt Vernon, E TN Mil

HAMMACK, Brice, Pvt, Col Thos Williamson, Capt A M Metcalf, Vol Mtd Gunmen

HAMMACK, Martin, Pvt, Col Thos Williamson, Capt A M Metcalf, Vol Mtd Gunmen

HAMMEL, Abraham, Pvt, Col Ewen Allison, Capt Jos Everett, E TN Mil; transferred to Capt McPherson's Co

HAMMEL, Peter, Pvt, Col Ewen Allison, Capt John Hampton, Mil

HAMMER, Jonathan, Pvt, Col Ewen Allison, Capt John Hampton, Mil; transferred to Capt McCrea 5-5-1814

HAMMILTON, James, Pvt, Maj John Childs, Capt Dan Price, E TN Vol Mtd Inf

HAMMILTON, Middleton, Pvt, Col John K Wynne, Capt Wm Caruthers, W TN Inf

HAMMOCK, John, Dmr, Col Jas Raulston, Capt E Haynie, Inf; d 2-8-1815

HAMMOCK, John, Pvt, Col S Bunch, Capt S Roberson, E TN Drafted Mil; deserted 4-12-1814

HAMMOCK, John, Pvt, Col Wm Johnston, Capt Henry Hunter, E TN Mil

HAMMOCK, John, Pvt, Regt Commander omitted, Capt Samuel Richardson, E TN Drafted Mil

HAMMOCK, Lewis, Pvt, Col S Copeland, Capt Wm Douglas, Inf

HAMMOCK, Martin, Pvt, Col Wm Hall, Capt Brice Martin, Vol Inf

HAMMOCK, William, 1 Cpl, Col Wm Metcalf, Capt Wm Sitton, Mil Inf; promoted to 5 Sgt

HAMMOND, Mickly, Pvt, Col Ewen Allison, Capt Wm King, Drafted Mil

HAMMONDS, William, Pvt, Col Ed Bradley, Capt John Moore, Vol Inf

HAMMONS, Benjamin, Pvt, Col Sam'l Bayless, Capt James Landen, E TN Mil

HAMMONS, Ezekiel, Pvt, Col Wm Metcalf, Capt Alex Hill & Capt John Cunningham, Mil Inf

HAMMONS, Hiram, Cpl, Col John Alcorn, Capt Alex McKeen, Cav; transferred to Mitchell's

HAMMONS, Hiram, Pvt, Gen John Coffee, Co Commander omitted, Mtd Spies

HAMMONS, Hiram, Pvt, Regt Commander omitted, Capt Wm Mitchell, Spies

HAMMONS, Isham, Pvt, Col A Metcalf, Capt Marks, Mil Inf

HAMMONS, James, Pvt, Col A Loury, Capt J N Williamson, W TN Mil

HAMMONS, James, Pvt, Col L Hammond, Capt J N Williamson, 2nd Regt Inf

HAMMONS, John, Pvt, Col R H Dyer, Capt Cuthbert Hudson, Vol Mtd Gunmen

HAMMONS, John, Pvt, Col Wm Metcalf, Capt Alex Hill, Mil Inf

HAMMONS, Jonathan, Pvt, Col Ewen Allison, Capt Henry McCray, E TN Mil; joined by transfer from Capt Hampton's Co

HAMMONS, Larkin, Pvt, Col Wm Metcalf, Capt Wm Sitton, Mil Inf

HAMMONS, Micajah, Pvt, Col S Bunch, Capt Jones Griffin; deserted 3-4-1814

HAMMONS, Michael, Pvt, Col Edwin Booth, Capt John Lewis, E TN Mil

HAMMONS, William, Pvt, Col Wm Hall, Capt John Moore, Vol Inf

HAMMONTREE, Jacob, Pvt, Col Sam'l Wear, Capt Jas Gillespie, E TN Vol Inf

HAMON, George, Pvt, Col Edw Bradley, Capt John Kennedy, Riflemen

HAMONDS, Hyram, 4 Cpl, Col John Coffee, Capt Alexander McKeen, Cav

HAMPTON, Hardy, Pvt, Col Edw Booth, Capt John Lewis, E TN Mil

HAMPTON, James, Dmr, Col Philip Pipkin, Capt George Mebane, Mil Inf

HAMPTON, James, Dmr, Col Thomas Benton, Capt Henry L Douglass, Vol Inf

HAMPTON, Jene, Pvt, Col Sam'l Bayless, Capt Waddle, E TN Mil

HAMPTON, Jesse, Pvt, Col Wm Lillard, Capt Jacob Hartsell, E TN Vol Inf

HAMPTON, John, Pvt, Col Edw Bradley, Capt H L Douglass, Vol Inf

HAMPTON, John, Pvt, Col Philip Pipkin, Capt George Mebane, Mil Inf; replaced by John Griffin

HAMPTON, Richard, Pvt, Col Thos Benton, Capt Henry L Douglass, Vol Inf

HAMPTON, Robert, Pvt, Col Samuel Bayless, Capt Jonathan Waddell, E TN Mil

HAMPTON, Smith, Pvt, Col Philip Pipkin, Capt John

Strother, Mil
HAMPTON, Tollison, Pvt, Col Samuel Wear, Capt Rufus Morgan, E TN Vol Inf; unable to perform duty
HAMPTON, Wade, Pvt, Col John Williams, Capt Wm Walker, Vol
HAMPTON, William, Pvt, Col Philip Pipkin, Capt David Smith, Inf; d 9-18-1814
HANAH, James, Pvt, Col Wm Johnson, Capt David McKamy, E TN Drafted Mil
HANAH, Joshua, Pvt, Col Wm Johnson, Capt Elihu Milliken, 3rd Regt E TN Mil
HANBY, John, Pvt, Col Samuel Wear, Capt Jas Gillespie, E TN Vol Inf
HANCHER, Joe, Pvt, Col Philip Pipkin, Capt David Smith, Inf; d 9-3-1814
HANCOCK, Aaron, Pvt, Lt Col Richard Napier, Co Commander omitted, Inf
HANCOCK, Benjamin, Pvt, Col Wm Johnson, Capt Christopher Cook, E TN Mil
HANCOCK, Benjamin, Pvt, Col Wm Johnson, Capt Joseph Kirk, Mil; substitute for David Nutting
HANCOCK, Benjamin, Sgt, Col A Cheatham, Capt Wm Smith, Inf
HANCOCK, Clement, Sgt, Col Jas Raulston, Capt Henry West, Inf; killed 1-8-1815
HANCOCK, Dawson, Pvt, Col Newton Cannon, Capt John Harpole, Mtd Gunmen
HANCOCK, Elijah, Pvt, Col John K Wynne, Capt Bayless E Prince, Inf
HANCOCK, James, Pvt, Maj Gen A Jackson, Capt Hugh Kerr, Mtd Rangers
HANCOCK, John, Cpl, Col James K Wynne, Capt Jas Holleman, Inf
HANCOCK, Joslma?, Pvt, Maj Gen A Jackson, Capt Hugh Kerr, Mtd Rangers
HANCOCK, William, Pvt, Col Wm Johnston, Capt Jas Tunnell, E TN Mil
HANDCOCK, Robert, Pvt, Col John Williams, Capt Wm Walker, Vol
HANDLER, John, Pvt, Col Robert Dyer, Capt Isaac Williams, Vol Mtd Gunmen
HANDLIN, William, Pvt, Col Newton Cannon, Capt David Hogan, Mtd Gunmen
HANDLY, Jordan Y, Pvt, Col John Cocke, Capt Jos Price, Inf; appointed Surgeon's Mate
HANDLY, Robert, Pvt, Maj Wm Russell, Capt John Cowan, Vol Mtd Gunmen
HANDON, James, Pvt, Col A Loury, Capt Geo Sarver, Inf
HANDY, John, Pvt, Col Wm Johnson, Capt Elihu Milliken, 3rd Regt E TN Mil
HANE, Samuel, Pvt, Col N T Perkins, Capt George Eliot, Mil Inf
HANES, Azariah, Pvt, Col S Bayless, Capt Jos Goodson, E TN Mil
HANES, John, Pvt, Col T McCrory, Capt Isaac Patton, Mil Inf
HANES, Joseph, Pvt, Col Wm Metcalf, Capt Thos Marks, Mil Inf
HANEY, Elijah, Sgt, Col Newton Cannon, Capt Wm Edwards, Regt Command
HANEY, Emanuel, Pvt, Col Newton Cannon, Capt George Brandon, Mtd Riflemen
HANEY, Francis, Pvt, Col John Brown, Capt J G Reany, Mtd Gunmen
HANEY, George, Pvt, Col Philip Pipkin, Capt John Strother, Mil
HANEY, James, Pvt, Col Thos Benton, Capt Jas McFerrin, Vol Inf; deserted 12-25-1813
HANEY, Martain, Pvt, Col Philip Pipkin, Capt E Kirkpatrick, Mil Inf; deserted 9-20-1814
HANEY, Mott, Pvt, Col Philip Pipkin, Capt Peter Searcy, Mil Inf
HANEY, Samuel, Pvt, Col Samuel Wear, Capt Joseph Calloway, Mtd Inf
HANEY, Stephen, Pvt, Col Samuel Wear, Capt Joseph Calloway, Mtd Inf
HANEY, Tallern, Pvt, Regt Commander omitted, Capt Wm Henderson, Spies
HANEY, Uriah, Pvt, Col Samuel Wear, Capt Samuel Bunch, Capt Wm Mitchell, E TN Mtd Inf
HANEY, William, 2 Sgt, Col James Raulston, Capt Henry West, Inf
HANEY, William, Sgt, Col T McCrory, Capt A Metcalf, Mil Inf
HANIS, William G, Pvt, Col Newton Cannon, Capt Thos Yardley, Mtd Riflemen
HANISON, Charles, Pvt, Col S Bunch, Capt Henry Stephens, E TN Mtd Inf; transferred from Capt Zachariah Copeland's Co
HANISON, Thomas, Pvt, Col John Cocke, Capt S M Caruthers, Inf
HANK, William, Pvt, Col Leroy Hammonds, Capt Jas Craig, Inf
HANKINGS, Absalam, Sgt, Col John Williams, Capt Sam Bunch, Mtd Vol
HANKINGS, Benjamin, Pvt, Lt Col Wm Phillips, Co Commander omitted, Inf
HANKINGS, Robert, Pvt, Col Ewen Allison, Capt Wm King, Drafted Mil
HANKINS, David, Pvt, Maj John Childs, Capt Charles Conway, E TN Mtd Gunmen; Regimental Co - Knox
HANKINS, Eli, Pvt, Regt Commander omitted, Capt Samuel Richardson, E TN Drafted Mil; discharged for inability
HANKINS, Gilbert, Pvt, Col Robert Jarmon, Capt Nathan Peoples, Inf
HANKINS, James, Pvt, Col John Brown, Capt Wm White, E TN Vol Mtd Inf
HANKINS, James, Pvt, Col S Bunch, Capt N Gibbs, E TN Drafted Mil
HANKINS, James, Pvt, Col Samuel Wear, Capt Joseph Calloway, Mtd Inf
HANKINS, John E, Pvt, Col Wm Lillard, Capt Maloney, E TN Vol Inf
HANKINS, John, Pvt, Col John Brown, Capt Wm White, E TN Mtd Mil Inf
HANKINS, John, Pvt, Col Wm Johnston, Capt Jas R Rogers, E TN Drafted Mil; Wgnr
HANKINS, John, Pvt, Maj John Childs, Capt Chas Conway, E TN Mtd Gunmen; Regimental Co - Knox
HANKINS, Joseph, Pvt, Col John Brown, Capt Allen I

## Enlisted Men, War of 1812

Bacon, E TN Mil Inf; AWOL
HANKINS, Joseph, Pvt, Col Wm Johnson, Capt Jas R Rogers, E TN Drafted Mil
HANKINS, Nimrod, Pvt, Col Wm Johnson, Capt Henry Hunter, E TN Mil; transferred from Capt Stewart's Co
HANKINS, Nimrod, Pvt, Col Wm Johnson, Capt Jas Stewart, E TN Drafted Mil; transferred to Capt Rick Co
HANKINS, Nimrod, Pvt, Col Wm Johnson, Capt Jas Stewart, E TN Mil; transferred to Capt Kirk Co
HANKINS, Richard, Pvt, Col Edwin Booth, Capt Vernon, E TN Mil; d 2-25-1815 in service
HANKINS, Richard, Pvt, Col S Bunch, Capt N Gibbs, E TN Drafted Mil; enlisted in service of U S
HANKINS, Richard, Pvt, Col Samuel Wear, Capt John Bayless, Mtd Inf
HANKINS, Right, Pvt, Col Wm Johnson, Capt James R Rogers, E TN Drafted Mil
HANKINS, Thomas, Pvt, Col John Brown, Capt Wm White, E TN Mtd Mil Inf
HANKINS, William, Pvt, Col Samuel Bunch, Capt Francis Berry, E TN Mil
HANKINS, William, Pvt, Col Samuel Wear, Capt Joseph Calloway, Mtd Inf
HANKINS, William, Pvt, Col Wm Johnson, Capt Jas R Rogers, E TN Drafted Mil
HANKINS, Wright, Pvt, Col John Brown, Capt Allen I Bacon, E TN Mil Inf
HANKINS (HARKINS), Daniel, Pvt, Col Philip Pipkin, Capt H M Newlin, Mil Inf
HANKLEWOOD, Henry, Sgt, Col Ewen Allison, Capt Wm King, Drafted Mil
HANKS, Dan'l, Pvt, Col Edward Bradley, Capt Harry L Douglass, Vol Inf
HANKS, Zachariah, Pvt, Col Jas K Wynne, Capt Jas Cole, Inf
HANLEY, John, Cpl, Regt Commander omitted, Capt Jas Cowan, Mtd Inf
HANLEY, Robert, Pvt, Regt Commander omitted, Capt Jas Cowan, Mtd Inf
HANN, John, Pvt, Col Wm Lillard, Capt Robert McCalpin, E TN Inf; deserted 11-9-1813
HANNA, John, Pvt, Col Samuel Wear, Capt Jos Calloway, Mtd Inf
HANNA, Josiah, Cpl, Lt Col Wm Phillip, Co Commander omitted, Inf
HANNA, Samuel, Pvt, Col T McCrory, Capt Samuel B McKnight, Inf
HANNAH, Alexander, Sgt, Maj Wm Russell, Capt John Trimble, Vol Mtd Gunmen
HANNAH, Avery, Cpl, Col John Brown, Capt Lunsford Oliver, E TN Mil
HANNAH, Carolinas, Pvt, Maj Wm Russell, Capt John Trimble, Vol Mtd Gunmen
HANNAH, George H, Pvt, Col Philip Pipkin, Capt John Robertson, Mil Inf
HANNAH, James jr, Pvt, Col Charles Brown, Capt Chas Lewin, E TN Vol Mtd Inf
HANNAH, James sr, Pvt, Col John Brown, Capt Charles Lewin, E TN Vol Mtd Inf

HANNAH, James, Pvt, Col Edwin Booth, Capt Samuel Thompson, Mil
HANNAH, James, Pvt, Col Samuel Wear, Capt Joseph Calloway, Mtd Inf
HANNAH, James, Pvt, Col Thos Williamson, Capt John Doak & Capt John Dobbins, Vol Mtd Gunmen
HANNAH, James, Pvt, Col Wm Lillard, Capt Benj H King, E TN Vol Inf
HANNAH, John, Pvt, Col N T Perkins, Capt Mathew Patterson, Mtd Vol
HANNAH, John, Pvt, Lt Col R C Napier, Co Commander omitted, Inf
HANNAH, John, Pvt, Maj Wm Russell, Capt John Trimble, Vol Mtd Gunmen
HANNAH, John, Sgt, Col Wm Johnson, Capt Am Alexander, Det of E TN Mil
HANNAH, Joshua, Pvt, Col John Brown, Capt Chas Lewin, E TN Vol Mtd Inf
HANNAH, Joshua, Pvt, Col Samuel Wear, Capt Jos Calloway, Mtd Inf
HANNAH, Mathew, Pvt, Maj Wm Russell, Capt John Trimble, Vol Mtd Gunmen
HANNAH, Moses, Pvt, Maj Wm Russell, Capt John Trimble, Vol Mtd Gunmen
HANNAH, Robert, Pvt, Col John Brown, Capt Charles Lewin, E TN Vol Mtd Inf
HANNAH, Robert, Pvt, Col Wm Lillard, Capt George Keys, E TN Inf
HANNAM, Mifthlin?, Pvt, Col John Cocke, Capt John Weakley, Inf
HANNAN, William, Pvt, Maj Wm Russell, Capt Jas Cowan, Vol Mtd Gunmen
HANNAS, David P, Pvt, Col Newton Cannon, Capt Thos Yardley, Mtd Riflemen
HANNEGAN, James, Sgt, Maj Wm Woodfolk, Capt Jas C Neil, Inf
HANNER, Avery, Pvt, Col Wm Johnston, Capt Jas Tunnell, E TN Mil; substitute for Reuben Williams
HANNES, David P, Asst Forage Master, Brig Gen John Coffee, E TN Vol Mtd Gunmen
HANNES, David P, Pvt, Col N T Perkins, Capt Mathew Patterson, Mtd Vol
HANNES, Enock, Pvt, Col N T Perkins, Capt Mathew Patterson, Mtd Vol
HANNEY, David P, Pvt, Col Thos Williamson, Capt Jas Pace, Lt Nealy, Vol Mtd Gunmen; appointed Asst Forage Master
HANNIS, Enoch, Pvt, Col John Coffee, Capt Robert Jetton, Cav
HANNOCK, John, Pvt, Col Wm Johnson, Capt Henry Hunter, E TN Mil
HANNUM, Miflin, Pvt, Col John Cocke, Capt John Weakley, Inf
HANRICK, Yelvanton, Pvt, Col R C Napier, Capt Edward Neblett, Mil Inf
HANS, John, Pvt, Col Wm Metcalf, Capt John Barnhart, Mil Inf; transferred to Capt Mullins Co
HANSARD, John, Pvt, Maj John Childs, Capt Chas Conway, E TN Mtd Gunmen
HANSE, Washington, Pvt, Col Edwin Booth, Capt Vernon, E TN Mil

- 235

## Enlisted Men, War of 1812

HANSLEY, George W, Pvt, Col S Bunch, Capt Andrew Breden, E TN Mil; discharged at Ft Williams for inability

HANSLEY, Ochabod, 3 Sgt, Maj John Childs, Capt Reuben Tipton, E TN Vol Mtd Inf

HANSON, George, Pvt, Maj John Childs, Capt Reuben Tipton, E TN Vol Mtd Inf; Regimental Co - Knox

HANSON, Solomon, Pvt, Col John Brown, Capt Jas Preston, E TN Mil Inf

HANSON, Thomas, Pvt, Col Newton Cannon, Capt Thos Yardley, Mtd Riflemen

HANSON (HANSARD), John, Pvt, Maj John Childs, Capt Reuben Tipton, E TN Vol Mtd Inf; Regimental Co - Knox

HANY, James, Pvt, Col Thos Benton, Capt Jas McFerrin, Vol Inf; deserted 12-23-1812, camp near Nashville

HAPPER, Thomas, Pvt, Col Samuel Bayless, Capt Jos B Bacon, E TN Mil

HARBEN, Jesse, Pvt, Maj Gen A Jackson, Capt John Crane, Mtd Gunmen

HARBEN, Masse, Pvt, Col Samuel Bayless, Capt Jas Landen, E TN Mil

HARBER, Joe, Pvt, Lt Col A Cheatham, Capt Gabriel Martin, 6th Brig Mtd Inf

HARBIN, Jarriet, Sgt, Col Wm Johnson, Capt Jas Tunnell, E TN Mil

HARBIN, Jarrot, Pvt, Col Wm Johnson, Capt Jas Tunnell, E TN Mil; substitute for Thomas Manifee

HARBIN, Jesse, Pvt, Col T Williamson, Capt Jas Cook & Capt John Crane, Vol Mtd Gunmen

HARBIN, John, Pvt, Col Edwin Booth, Capt Richard Marshall, Drafted Mil

HARBIN, Micajah, Pvt, Col Thos Williamson, Capt John Doak & Capt John Dobbins, Vol Mtd Gunmen

HARBIN, Nathaniel, Pvt, Col T Williamson, Capt John Doak, Vol Mtd Gunmen

HARBISON, James, Pvt, Regt Commander omitted, Capt Sam Bunch, Mtd Vol

HARBOUR, Adam, Pvt, Col Robert Dyer, Capt Ephraim Dickson, TN Mtd Vol

HARBOUR, Christian, Pvt, Col Robert Dyer, Capt Dickson, TN Vol Mtd Gunmen

HARDAWAY, Ed, Pvt, Lt Col Hughes, Capt Meredith Walker, Brig Mtd Inf

HARDAWAY, Edward D, Pvt, Col Wm Y Higgins, Capt John Cheatham, Mtd Riflemen

HARDBARGER, Daniel, Pvt, Col Wm Lillard, Capt George Keys, E TN Inf

HARDCASTLE, Baenet, Pvt, Col Jas Raulston, Capt John Cowan, Inf

HARDCASTLE, Ezekiel, Pvt, Col Jas Raulston, Capt John Cowan, Inf

HARDCASTLE, Hezekiah, Pvt, Col Robert Steele, Capt Samuel Maxwell, Mil Inf

HARDCASTLE, James, Pvt, Col James Raulston, Capt Newman, Inf; d 2-22-1815

HARDCASTLE, James, Pvt, Col John K Wynne, Capt Wm Caruthers, W TN Inf; deserted 11-19-1813

HARDCASTLE, William, Pvt, Col James Raulston, Capt Newman, Inf

HARDEN, Alexander, Pvt, Col Wm Metcalf, Capt Andrew Patterson, Mil Inf

HARDEN, Asa, Pvt, Col John Coffee, Capt John Baskerville, Cav

HARDEN, Henry, Pvt, Col N Cannon, Capt Alexander Patton, Mtd Riflemen

HARDEN, Jonathan, Pvt, Col John Cocke, Capt Richard Crunk, Inf

HARDEN, Jonathan, Pvt, Col Thos Williamson, Capt Cook & Capt John Crane, Vol Mtd Gunmen

HARDEN, William, Pvt, Col Cheatham, Capt Chas Johnson, Inf

HARDEN, William, Pvt, Col S Bunch, Capt Perry, E TN Mil

HARDESTER, Samuel, Pvt, Col Jas Raulston, Capt Daniel Newman, Inf

HARDIN, Asa, Pvt, Col John Alcorn, Capt John Baskerville, Vol Inf; killed 11-9-1813

HARDIN, Calloway, Sgt, Col N T Perkins, Capt Jas McMahan, Mtd Gunmen

HARDIN, David M, Sgt, Col John Coffee, Capt Daniel Ross, Mtd Gunmen

HARDIN, Francis, Pvt, Col S Copeland, Capt John Biles, Inf

HARDIN, Henry, Pvt, no other information

HARDIN, John, Pvt, Col John Wynne, Capt John Porter, Inf

HARDIN, John, Pvt, Col Wm Higgins, Capt Hamberton, Mtd Gunmen

HARDIN, John, Pvt, Col Wm Lillard, Capt Robert Maloney, E TN Vol Inf

HARDIN, John, Pvt, Regt Commander omitted, Capt David Mason, Cav

HARDIN, Mark, Pvt, Col Newton Cannon, Capt Andrew Patterson, Mtd Riflemen

HARDIN, Obadiah, Pvt, Col Thos Williamson, Capt Beverly Williams, Vol Mtd Gunmen

HARDIN, William, 2 Sgt, Regt Commander omitted, Capt Jas Terrill, Cav

HARDIN, William, 2 Sgt, Regt Commander omitted, Capt Jas Terrill, Cav; transferred to Capt McMahan

HARDIN, William, Cpl, Col Robert Steele, Capt Richard Ratton, Mil Inf

HARDIN, William, Pvt, Col N T Perkins, Capt Jas McMahan, Mtd Gunmen

HARDIN, William, Pvt, Col Samuel Wear, Capt Samuel Bowman, Mtd Inf

HARDING, Horace, 4 Cpl, Maj Gen A Jackson, Capt Joel Parrish, Arty

HARDING, Horace, Pvt, Maj Gen A Jackson, Col A Cheatham, Capt Wm Creel, Inf; transferred to Arty

HARDING, Jeremiah jr, Pvt, Col N Cannon, Capt Martin, Mtd Gunmen

HARDING, Jeremiah sr, Pvt, Col N Cannon, Capt Martin, Mtd Gunmen

HARDING, John, Cpl, Col John K Wynne, Capt William Wilson, Inf

HARDING, John, Pvt, Col John Coffee, Capt Daniel Ross, Mtd Gunmen

HARDISON, Charles, Pvt, Col Robert Dyer, Capt James

McMahan, TN Vol Mtd Gunmen
HARDISON, Joshua, Pvt, Col N T Perkins, Capt Jas McMahan, Mtd Gunmen
HARDON, William P, Pvt, Col John K Wynne, Capt Jas Cole, Inf
HARDRIDGE, William, Pvt, Col John K Wynne, Capt Jas Cook, Inf
HARDY, Asa, Pvt, Col John Coffee, Capt John Baskerville, Cav
HARDY, Coalman, Pvt, Col A Loury, Capt John Looney, W TN Inf
HARDY, James, Pvt, Col Wm Pillow, Capt Isaiah Renshaw, Inf
HARDY, Thomas, Pvt, Col N T Perkins, Capt Mathew Patterson, Mtd Vol
HARE, Archibald, Pvt, Col Philip Pipkin, Capt David Smythe, Ens Wm Pegram, W TN Mil
HARE, Joseph, 3 Lt, Col Samuel Bayless, Capt Jos B Bacon, E TN Mil
HAREN, Joseph, Pvt, Col Samuel Bunch, Capt N Gibbs, E TN Drafted Mil; transferred to Capt Duncan's Co
HARGAS, Fredrick, Pvt, Col Wm Johnson, Capt David McKamy, E TN Drafted Mil
HARGES, Nathan, Pvt, Col Wm Johnson, Capt David McKamy, E TN Drafted Mil
HARGES, William A, Pvt, Col David Pipkin, Capt David Smythe, Inf; deserted 9-20-1814
HARGES, William W, Pvt, Maj Wm Russell, Capt John Trimble, Vol Mtd Gunmen
HARGES, William, Pvt, Lt Col L Hammons, Capt Thos Delaney, Inf; also under Col A Loury
HARGESS, Abraham, Pvt, Lt Col L Hammonds, Capt Thos Delaney, Inf; also under Col A Loury
HARGIS, Solomon, Pvt, Col Samuel Wear, Capt John Childs, E TN Vol Inf
HARGROVE, Thomas, Pvt, Col Wm Lillard, Capt John Neatherton, E TN Vol Inf
HARGROVES, Ethelridge, Pvt, Col John Cocke, Capt John Weakley, Inf
HARGUS, Abram, Pvt, Col John K Wynne, Capt Wm McCall, Inf
HARGUS, Lin W W, Pvt, no other information
HARGUS, William, Pvt, Col Philip Pipkin, Capt Wm Pegram, Det of Pegram Co of W TN Mil
HARLAND, John, Pvt, Col S Bunch, Capt Henry Stephen, W TN Mtd Inf
HARLEN, Bonham, Pvt, Col John Cocke, Capt S M Caruthers, Inf
HARLER (HARLIN), Harlin, Pvt, Col Philip Pipkin, Capt E Kirkpatrick, Mil Inf; enlisted in regular army
HARLEY, David, Pvt, Col Roc? Steele, Capt Robert Campbell, Mil Inf
HARLEY, Tilman, Pvt, Col Wm Johnson, Capt Chris Cooks, E TN Mil
HARLIN, Harmen, Pvt, Col J K Wynne, Capt John Porter, Inf
HARLIN, Harmen, Pvt, Col S Copeland, Capt John Holshouser, Inf
HARLIN, Moses, Pvt, Col N Cannon, Capt John Hanley, Mtd Riflemen
HARLIP, James, Pvt, no other information

HARLOW (HARLAN), Overton, Pvt, Col Edward Bradley, Capt H L Douglass, Vol Inf
HARLTON, John, Sgt, Col Samuel Wear, Capt John Chiles, E TN Vol Inf
HARMAN, David, Pvt, Col Wm Lillard, Capt George Argenbright, E TN Vol Riflemen
HARMAN, Jacob, Pvt, Col Edwin Booth, Capt Richard Marshall, Drafted Mil; d 12-12-1814
HARMAN, Jacob, Pvt, Col S Bunch, Capt John English, E TN Drafted Mil
HARMAN, James, Pvt, Col S Bunch, Capt F Register, E TN Mil
HARMAN, John, Pvt, Col Samuel Wear, Capt Robert Doak, E TN Vol Inf
HARMAN, Richard O, Pvt, Col John Coffee, Capt Jas Terrell, Vol Cav
HARMON, Adam, Pvt, Lt Col John Edmonson, Co Commander omitted, Cav
HARMON, Conrad, Pvt, Col Ewen Allison, Capt W King, Drafted Mil
HARMON, Conrad, Pvt, Col S Bunch, Capt F Register, E TN Mil; joined from Capt King's Co
HARMON, Conrad, Pvt, Col Sam'l Bayless, Capt Jos Goodson, E TN Mil
HARMON, Daniel, Pvt, Col Ewen Allison, Capt Winsell, E TN Drafted Mil; enlisted in U S Inf
HARMON, Edward, Pvt, Col John Alcorn, Capt Wm Locke, Inf
HARMON, Gideon, Pvt, Col N Cannon, Capt John B Dempsey, Mtd Gunmen
HARMON, Jacob, Pvt, Col S Bunch, Capt John Houk, E TN Mil; joined from Capt English Co
HARMON, James, Pvt, Col Ewen Allison, Capt Wm King, Drafted Mil
HARMON, James, Pvt, Col Wm Lillard, Capt George Keys, E TN Inf
HARMON, John T, Pvt, Col N Cannon, Capt John B Dempsey, Mtd Gunmen
HARMON, John, Cpl, Col S Bunch, Capt Andrew Breden, E TN Mil
HARMON, John, Pvt, Col R C Napier, Capt Edward Neblett, Mil Inf
HARMON, Lewis, Pvt, Col Philip Pipkin, Capt Henry M Newlin, Mil Inf
HARMON, Richard D, Pvt, Col John Coffee, Capt Jas Terrell, Vol Cav
HARMON, William, 5 Sgt, Col Wm Metcalf, Capt A Patterson, Mil Inf
HARMON, William, Pvt - Sgt, Col Wm Metcalf, Capt A Patterson, Mil Inf; promoted to Sgt
HARMON, William, Pvt, Col Philip Pipkin, Capt H M Newlin, Mil Inf
HARMON, William, Pvt, Col Wm Johnson, Capt Jos Scott, E TN Drafted Mil; deserted 10-2-1814
HARMSON, Thomas, Pvt, Maj Gen A Jackson, Col T Williamson, Capt Robert Steele, Vol Mtd Gunmen
HARNETT, Daniel, Pvt, Col Samuel Bayless, Capt Branch Jones, E TN Mil
HARNEY, James, Pvt, Col Ewen Allison, Capt Henry McCray, E TN Mil; transferred to Capt McPher-

son Co
HARNEY, Robert, Pvt, Maj Gen A Jackson, Capt Wm Carroll, Vol Inf
HARNEY, Zachariah, Pvt, Col R H Dyer, Capt Robert Edmonson, 1 TN Vol Mtd Gunmen; d 12-9-1814
HARNEY (HARVEY), Jesse, Pvt, Lt Col L Hammond, Capt Jas Tubb, Inf
HARNEY (HARVEY), Thomas, Pvt, Col John Coffee, Capt Jas Terrell, Vol Cav; over age and no horse
HARO, William, Pvt, Maj Wm Woodfolk, Capt Abner Pearce, Inf
HAROLD, William, Pvt, Col S Bunch, Capt S Dobkins, E TN Drafted Mil
HARP, Elijah, Sgt, Col S Bayless, Capt John Brock, E TN Mil
HARP, Solomon, Pvt, Col Jas Raulston, Capt Dan Newman, Inf
HARP, Trya, Pvt, Col S Copeland, Capt David Williams, Inf
HARP, William, Pvt, Col Wm Johnson, Capt Jos Kirk, Mil; never appeared
HARPER, Asa, Pvt, Lt Col Hammond & A Loury, Capt Thos Wells, Inf
HARPER, Benjamin, Pvt, Col S Copeland, Capt Wm Douglass, Inf
HARPER, Britton, Pvt, Col T McCrory, Capt Isaac Patton, Mil Inf; deserted 10-19-1813
HARPER, Edward, Pvt, Col Wm Hall, Capt A Bledsoe, Vol Inf
HARPER, Enos, Pvt, Col R C Napier, Capt Jas McMurry, Mil Inf
HARPER, George, Pvt, Col Wm Metcalf, Capt Obidiah Walker, Mil Inf
HARPER, Henry, Pvt, Col Samuel Bayless, Capt Allen Bacon, E TN Mil
HARPER, Henry, Pvt, Col Wm Metcalf, Capt Wm Sitton, Mil Inf
HARPER, James, Pvt, Col Alexander Loury, Capt George Sarver, Inf
HARPER, Jesse, Pvt, Col Samuel Bayless, Capt John Brock, E TN Mil
HARPER, Joel, Pvt, Col Samuel Bayless, Capt John Brock, E TN Mil
HARPER, John, Pvt, Col John Wynne, Capt William Wilson, Inf; transferred to Capt Caruther's Co
HARPER, John, Pvt, Col John Wynne, Capt Wm Caruthers, W TN Inf
HARPER, John, Pvt, Col Philip Pipkin, Capt John Robertson, Mil Inf
HARPER, John, Pvt, Col S Copeland, Capt Allen Wilkinson, Mil Inf
HARPER, John, Pvt, Col Samuel Bayless, Capt Allen Bacon, E TN Mil
HARPER, Joseph, Pvt, Col Newton Cannon, Capt Wm Edwards, Regt Command
HARPER, Joseph, Pvt, Col Philip Pipkin, Capt George Mebane, Mil Inf; transferred to Capt McCary's Co
HARPER, Joseph, Pvt, Col Philip Pipkin, Capt Wm Mackay, Mil Inf
HARPER, Joseph, Pvt, Col Robert Steele, Capt Robert Campbell, Mil Inf
HARPER, Joseph, Pvt, Col Samuel Bayless, Capt Jas Churchman, E TN Mil; deserted 12-30-1814
HARPER, Joseph, Pvt, Col Thos Williamson, Capt Robert Moore, Vol Mtd Gunmen
HARPER, Joseph, Pvt, Lt Col Leroy Hammonds, Capt Jas Tubb, Inf
HARPER, Mark, Pvt, Col Wm Johnson, Capt Jas Rogers, E TN Drafted Mil
HARPER, Mitchell, Pvt, Col Edwin Booth, Capt John Sharpe, E TN Mil
HARPER, Moses D, Pvt, Brig Gen Roberts, Capt Benj Reynolds, Mtd Rangers
HARPER, Moses D, Pvt, Col Thomas Benton, Capt Benj Reynolds, Vol Inf
HARPER, Robert, Pvt, Col Jas Raulston, Capt Elijah Haynie, Inf
HARPER, Samuel, Pvt, Col Philip Pipkin, Capt Henry Newlin, Mil Inf
HARPER, Samuel, Pvt, Col Robert Steele, Capt John Chitwood, Mil Inf
HARPER, Samuel, Pvt, Col Thomas Williamson, Capt Giles Burdett, Vol Mtd Gunmen
HARPER, Thomas, Pvt, Col Samuel Bunch, Capt Joseph Duncan, E TN Drafted Mil; joined from Capt Howel's Co
HARPER, Thomas, Pvt, Col Samuel Bunch, Lt John Harris, E TN Mil
HARPER, Whitmore, Pvt, Brig Gen Thos Johnson, Capt Allen, Mil Inf
HARPER, William, Pvt, Col James Raulston, Capt Daniel Newman, Inf
HARPER, William, Pvt, Col Jas Raulston, Capt Mathew Neal, Inf; killed 1-8-1815
HARPER, William, Pvt, Col Samuel Bayless, Capt James Churchman, E TN Mil; joined from Capt Milliken's Co
HARPER, William, Pvt, Col Samuel Bunch, Capt S Roberson, E TN Drafted Mil
HARPER, William, Pvt, Col William Johnson, Capt Elihu Milliken, 3rd Regt E TN Mil; transferred to Capt Churchman Co
HARPER, William, Pvt, Col Wm Johnson, Capt Elihu Milliken, 3rd Regt E TN Mil
HARPER, William, Pvt, Regt Commander omitted, Capt Samuel Richardson, E TN Drafted Mil
HARPOLE, Adam, Cpl, Col Newton Cannon, Capt John Harpole, Mtd Gunmen
HARPOLE, George, Pvt, Col A Cheatham, Capt George Chapman, Inf
HARPOLE, George, Pvt, Col John Alcorn, Capt Thos Bradley, Vol Cav
HARPOLE, George, Pvt, Col John Coffee, Capt Thos Bradley, Vol Cav
HARPOLE, John, Tptr, Maj Gen Andrew Jackson, Capt E Kirkpatrick, Mtd Gunmen
HARPOLE, Martin, Pvt, Col Robert Dyer, Capt Jas Wyatt, Vol Mtd Gunmen; substitute for John Buchanan
HARRASON, Aaron, Pvt, Col Edwin Booth, Capt John Sharpe, E TN Mil
HARREFORD, Paul, Pvt, Col William Metcalf, Capt

## Enlisted Men, War of 1812

Barbee Collins, Mil Inf
HARREL, Baldwin, Pvt, Col Samuel Bunch, Capt Wm Jobe, E TN Vol Mtd Inf
HARREL, Frederick, QM Sgt, Col Philip Pipkin, 1st Regt TN Mil
HARRELL, Asa, Pvt, Col Thos McCrory, Capt Anthony Metcalf, Mil Inf
HARRELL, Eli, Sgt, Col N T Perkins, Capt John Quarles, Vol Mtd Inf
HARRELL, Isham, Pvt, Col Philip _____, Capt David Smith, Mil Inf; deserted 12-30-1814
HARRELL, John, Pvt, Col A Loury, Capt Gabriel Martin, Inf
HARRELL, Mitchell, Pvt, Col Wm Lillard, Capt George Argenbright, E TN Vol Riflemen
HARRELL, William, Pvt, Col Samuel Bayless, Capt Jos Rich, E TN Inf
HARRELL, William, Pvt, Col Wm Lillard, Capt Wm Gillenwater, E TN Inf
HARRELSON, William, 3 Lt, Col Edwin Booth, Capt John Sharp, E TN Mil
HARRELSON, William, Pvt, Col Samuel Wear, Capt Rufus Morgan, E TN Vol Inf
HARRESTON, John, Pvt, Col William Johnson, Capt Jas Stewart, E TN Drafted Mil
HARRETT, John, Pvt, Col A Loury, Capt Gabriel Martin, Inf
HARRINGTON, Charles, Pvt, Col Thos Williamson, Capt Beverly Williams, Vol Mtd Gunmen
HARRINGTON, Drury, Pvt, Col John Cocke, Capt John Dalton, Inf
HARRINGTON, Dumphrey, Pvt, Col John Cocke, Capt John Dalton, Inf
HARRINGTON, John, Pvt, Maj Gen A Jackson, Capt John Crane, Mtd Gunmen
HARRINGTON, Whitmill, Pvt, Col Thos Williamson, Capt Jas Cook & Capt John Crane, Vol Mtd Gunmen
HARRINGTON, Whitmill, Pvt, Lt Col John Demonson, Cav
HARRINGTON, Whitmill, Pvt, Regt Commander omitted, Capt John Craig, Inf
HARRIS, Adly, Cpl, Col Edwin Booth, Capt Alexander Biggs, Inf
HARRIS, Albury, Pvt, Maj Wm Woodfolk, Capt Abner Pearce, Inf
HARRIS, Alexander, Pvt, Col Jas Raulston, Capt Daniel Newman, Inf
HARRIS, Andrew, Pvt, Col Edward Bradley, Capt John Kennedy, Riflemen
HARRIS, Andrew, Pvt, Maj Gen Wm Carroll, Col Jas Raulston, Capt Wiley Huddleston, Inf
HARRIS, Archibald, Pvt, Brig Gen T Johnson, Capt Robert Carson, Inf
HARRIS, Archibald, Pvt, Col S Copeland, Capt John Biles, Inf; trans to Carson's Co
HARRIS, Archibald, Pvt, Col Wm Metcalf, Capt Thos Marks, Mil Inf
HARRIS, Archibald, Pvt, Col Wm Metcalf, Capt Wm Mullen, Mil Inf
HARRIS, Asia, Pvt, Col Philip Pipkin, Capt John Strother,

Mil; deserted
HARRIS, Bartlet, Pvt, Lt Col L Hammonds, Capt Thos Wells, Inf
HARRIS, Benjamin C, Pvt, Col Samuel Bunch, Capt David G Vance, E TN Mtd Inf
HARRIS, Benjamin F, 2 Sgt Mate, Col Wm Metcalf, 1 Regt W TN Mil Inf; died 1-6-1815
HARRIS, Benjamin, Pvt, Col John Wynne, Capt John Spinks, Inf; trans to Harpole Co
HARRIS, Benjamin, Pvt, Col Newton Cannon, Capt David Hogan, Mtd Gunmen
HARRIS, Benjamin, Pvt, Col Newton Cannon, Capt John Hanley, Mtd Riflemen
HARRIS, Benjamin, Pvt, Col Newton Cannon, Capt John Harpole, Mtd Gunmen; joined by trans from Spinks
HARRIS, Benjamin, Pvt, Col Thos Benton, Capt Benj Hewett, Vol Inf; AWOL
HARRIS, Benoni, Pvt, Col Wm Lillard, Capt George Argenbright, E TN Vol Riflemen
HARRIS, Beverly, Maj Wm Woodfolk, Capt Jas C Neil, Inf
HARRIS, Beverly, Pvt, Col A Loury, Capt Jas Kincaid, Inf
HARRIS, Chedle, Pvt, Col A Loury, Capt Gabriel Martin, Inf
HARRIS, Clabourn, Pvt, Maj Wm Russell, Col R H Dyer, Capt Wm Russell, Vol Mtd Gunmen
HARRIS, Claiborne, Pvt, Regt Commander omitted, Capt Jos Williams, Mil Cav
HARRIS, Daniel, Pvt, Regt Commander omitted, Capt Jas Cowan, Mtd Inf
HARRIS, David, Pvt, Col Wm Hall, Capt John Kennedy, Vol Inf
HARRIS, David, Pvt, Regt Commander omitted, Capt Jas Craig, Inf
HARRIS, Dorrel, Pvt, Col R H Dyer, Capt Isaac Williams, Vol Mtd Gunmen
HARRIS, Edward, Blksmth, Col John Alcorn, Capt Thos Bradley, Vol Cav
HARRIS, Edward, Pcr, Col R H Dyer, Capt Glen Owen, TN Vol Mtd Gunmen
HARRIS, Edward, Pvt, Col Thos Benton, Capt Wm J Smith, Vol Inf
HARRIS, Edwin, Pvt, Maj John Childs, Capt John Stephens, E TN Vol Mtd Inf
HARRIS, Eli, Pvt, Col John Coffee, Capt Thos Bradley, Vol Cav
HARRIS, Eli, Sgt, Col John Alcorn, Capt Thos Bradley, Vol Cav
HARRIS, Elijah, Pvt, Maj John Childs, Capt Reuben Tipton, E TN Vol Mtd Inf; Regt Knox Co
HARRIS, George C, Sgt, Col Ewin Allison, Capt Henry McCray, E TN Mil
HARRIS, George, Cpl, Col S Bunch, Capt N? Gibbs, E TN Draft Mil; appt from pvt
HARRIS, George, Pvt, Col Wm Metcalf, Capt Barbee Collins, Mil Inf; died 4-17-1815
HARRIS, George, Sgt, Col A Loury, Capt Jas Kincaid, Inf
HARRIS, Gideon, Col Philip Pipkin, Capt John Strother, Mil
HARRIS, Gideon, Pvt, Col Jas Raulston, Capt Chas Wade,

## Enlisted Men, War of 1812

HARRIS, Howel, Pvt, Col John Cocke, Capt John Weakley, Inf

HARRIS, Hugh, Pvt, Col John Cocke, Capt Joseph Price, Inf

HARRIS, Hugh, QM Sgt, Col Wm Metcalf, no Co Commander, 1 Regt W TN Mil Inf

HARRIS, Isaac, Pvt, Maj Gen Wm Carroll, Col Jas Raulston, Capt Wiley Huddleston, Inf; promoted to 3 Sgt

HARRIS, Israel, Pvt, Col Samuel Wear, Capt Daniel Price, E TN Vol Inf

HARRIS, James J, Pvt, Col Philip Pipkin, Capt E Kirkpatrick, Mil Inf

HARRIS, James, 2 Cpl, Col N T Perkins, Capt Mathew Patterson, Mtd Vol

HARRIS, James, Pvt, Col S Copeland, Capt John Biles, Inf

HARRIS, James, Pvt, Lt Col John Edmonson, Co Commander omitted, Cav

HARRIS, James, Pvt, Maj John Childs, Capt Reuben Tipton, E TN Vol Mtd Inf

HARRIS, James, Pvt, Maj Wm Woodfolk, Capt Jas C Neil, Inf

HARRIS, Jeremiah, Pvt, Col Edward Bradley, Capt John Kennedy, Riflemen

HARRIS, Jeremiah, Pvt, Col Jas Raulston, Capt Wiley Huddleston, Inf

HARRIS, Jesse, Col John Alcorn, Capt Alexander McKeen, Cav

HARRIS, Jesse, Pvt, Col John Coffee, Capt Alexander McKeen, Cav

HARRIS, Jesse, Pvt, Maj John Childs, Capt John Stephens, E TN Vol Mtd Inf; trans to Capt Trimble

HARRIS, Jesse, Pvt, Maj Wm Russell, Capt John Trimble, Vol Mtd Gunmen; trans from Capt Stephens

HARRIS, Jesse, Pvt, Maj Wm Russell, Capt Wm Chism, Vol Mtd Gunmen

HARRIS, Jesse, Pvt, Regt Commander omitted, Capt Wm Mitchell, Spies

HARRIS, John jr, Pvt, Maj John Childs, Capt John Stephens, E TN Vol Mtd Inf

HARRIS, John sr, Pvt, Maj John Childs, Capt John Stephens, E TN Vol Mtd Inf

HARRIS, John, 1 Sgt, Col Jas Raulston, Capt Chas Wade, Inf; died 3-17-1815

HARRIS, John, Cpl, Col Thos Williamson, Capt Thos Porter, Vol Mtd Gunmen, died 2-12-1815

HARRIS, John, Pvt, Col Ewen Allison, Capt Thos Wilson, E TN Draft Mil

HARRIS, John, Pvt, Col Philip Pipkin, Capt E Kirkpatrick, Mil Inf; deserted

HARRIS, John, Pvt, Col S Copeland, Capt David Williams, Inf

HARRIS, John, Pvt, Col Samuel Bunch, Capt Wm Houston, E TN Vol Mtd Inf

HARRIS, John, Pvt, Col Samuel Wear, Capt John Stephens, E TN Vol Inf

HARRIS, John, Pvt, Col Thos McCrory, Capt Abel Willis, Mil Inf

HARRIS, John, Pvt, Col William Johnson, Capt Henry Hunter, TN Mil; trans from Capt Rulton's Co

HARRIS, John, Pvt, Regt Commander omitted, Capt Jas Terrill, Cav

HARRIS, Mathew, Pvt, Col John Wynne, Capt Robert Breden, Inf

HARRIS, Mathew, Sgt, Col N T Perkins, Capt Mathew Patterson, Mtd Vol

HARRIS, Moody P, Pvt, Col Jas Raulston, Capt Chas Wade, Inf

HARRIS, Nathan, Pvt, Col Newton Cannon, Capt John Harpole, Mtd Gunmen; killed 11-9-1813 at Battle of Talledega

HARRIS, Nehemiah, Pvt, Col Thos Benton, Capt George Capreton, Vol Inf

HARRIS, Newsom, Pvt, Col Philip Pipkin, Capt Wm Mackay, Mil Inf

HARRIS, Nicholas, Pvt, Lt I Barrett, Capt Nathan Davis, Inf; Next TN Bn

HARRIS, Olin B, Sgt, Col Newton Cannon, Capt Thos Yardley, Mtd Riflemen

HARRIS, Oliver B, 1 Sgt, Col John Coffee, Capt Robert Jetton, Cav

HARRIS, Oliver, Pvt, Col John Coffee, Capt Robert Jetton, Cav

HARRIS, Peter, Pvt, Col Philip Pipkin, Capt Wm Mackey, Mil Inf

HARRIS, Peter, Pvt, Maj Wm Russell, Capt John Cowan, Vol Mtd Gunmen

HARRIS, Randolph, Pvt, Col John Coffee, Capt Michale Molton, Cav

HARRIS, Reuben, Pvt, Col T McCrory, Capt Samuel McKnight, Inf

HARRIS, Reuben, Pvt, Maj John Childs, Capt Daniel Price, E TN Vol Mtd Inf

HARRIS, Robert, Pvt, Col S Roberson, Col Samuel Bunch, E TN Drafted Mil; furnished Walter McJones as a substitute

HARRIS, Robert, Pvt, Col Thos Benton, Capt Wm Smith, Vol Inf

HARRIS, Robert, Pvt, Maj Wm Russell, Capt John Trimble, Vol Mtd Gunmen

HARRIS, Robert, Pvt, Regt Commander omitted, Capt Samuel Richardson, E TN Drafted Mil

HARRIS, Robert, Sgt, Col A Loury, Capt Jas Kincaid, Inf

HARRIS, Robert, Sgt, Regt Commander omitted, Capt Samuel Richardson, E TN Drafted Mil

HARRIS, Samuel, Pvt, Col John Cocke, Capt George Barnes, Inf

HARRIS, Samuel, Pvt, Maj Wm Russell, Capt John Cowan, Vol Mtd Gunmen

HARRIS, Samuel, Pvt, Maj Wm Russell, Capt Wm Russell, Vol Mtd Gunmen

HARRIS, Samuel, Pvt, Regt Commander omitted, Capt Jas Cowan, Mil Inf; substitute for Abram Vinyard

HARRIS, Shadrick, Pvt, Maj Wm Woodfolk, Capt Abner Pearce, Inf

HARRIS, Shadrock, Pvt, Col A Cheatham, Capt Chas Johnson, Inf

HARRIS, Simeon, Pvt, Col Edwin Booth, Capt John Sharpe, E TN Mil

HARRIS, Simpson, Forage Master, Brig Gen John Coffee,

## Enlisted Men, War of 1812

6th TN Vol Mtd Gunmen
HARRIS, Stephen, 4 Sgt, Regt Commander omitted, Capt Jos Williams, Mil Cav
HARRIS, Stephen, Pvt, Col John Coffee, Capt Michale Molton, Cav
HARRIS, Stephen, Pvt, Col Robert Dyer, Capt Jos Williams, Vol Mtd Gunmen
HARRIS, Stephen, Pvt, Regt Commander omitted, Capt Jos Williams, Mil Cav; promoted to Sgt
HARRIS, Stephen, Sgt, Regt Commander omitted, Capt Jos Williams, Mil Cav
HARRIS, Thomas A, Pvt, Col Philip Pipkin, Capt Henry Newlin, Mil Inf
HARRIS, Thomas R(K?), Pvt, Col John Coffee, Capt Jas Terrill, Vol Cav
HARRIS, Thomas S, 4 Cpl, Brig Gen Thos Johnston, Capt Robert Carson, Inf
HARRIS, Thomas, Pvt, Col Robert Moore, Co Commander omitted, Vol Mtd Gunmen
HARRIS, Thomas, Pvt, Col S Bunch, Capt Thos Mann, E TN Mtd Inf
HARRIS, Thomas, Pvt, Regt Commander omitted, Capt James Terrill, Vol Cav
HARRIS, Thomas, Sgt, Col S Bunch, Capt John Harris, E TN Mil
HARRIS, Thomas, Sgt, Col S Bunch, Capt John Houk, E TN Mil; attached from Capt Howel's Co
HARRIS, Toliver, Pvt, Col S Wear, Capt John Stephens, E TN Vol Inf
HARRIS, Toliver, Pvt, Maj John Childs, Capt John Stephens, E TN Vol Mtd Inf
HARRIS, William, 1 Sgt, Col John Coffee, Capt Alex McKeen, Cav
HARRIS, William, 1 Sgt, Regt Commander omitted, Capt Wm Mitchell, Spies
HARRIS, William, Cpl, Maj Gen A Jackson, Capt Hugh Kerr, Mtd Rangers
HARRIS, William, Pvt, Col Edwin Booth, Capt Samuel Thompson, Mil
HARRIS, William, Pvt, Col Jas Raulston, Capt Chas Wade, Inf
HARRIS, William, Pvt, Col R H Dyer, Capt Thos Jones, Vol Mtd Gunmen
HARRIS, William, Pvt, Col S Copeland, Capt Richard Sharpe, Mil Inf
HARRIS, William, Pvt, Col Wm Johnson, Capt Jas Tunnell, E TN Mil
HARRIS, William, Pvt, Col Wm Metcalf, Capt Barbee Collins, Mil Inf
HARRIS, William, Pvt, Col Wm Metcalf, Capt Wm Mullen, Mil
HARRIS, William, Pvt, Col Wm Metcalf, Capt Wm Mullen, Mil Inf
HARRIS, William, Pvt, Maj John Chiles, Capt Stephens, E TN Vol Mtd Inf; transferred to Capt Chism's Co
HARRIS, William, Pvt, Maj Wm Russell, Capt Wm Chism, Vol Mtd Riflemen
HARRIS, William, Sgt, Col John Alcorn, Capt Alex McKeen, Cav; transferred to Mitchell's Spies
HARRIS, William, Sgt, Regt Commander omitted, Capt Wm Mitchell, Spies

HARRIS, Zachariah, Pvt, Lt John Scott, Co Commander omitted, Det of Inf
HARRIS (HARRISON), William, Pvt, Col Wm Hall, Capt Wm L Alexander, Vol Inf
HARRISON, Abner, Sgt, Col Samuel Wear, Capt R Morgan, E TN Vol Inf; promoted from Cpl
HARRISON, Andrew, Pvt, Col John Cocke, Capt Richard Crunk, Inf
HARRISON, Benjamin, Ffr Maj, Col Samuel Wear, Co Commander omitted, E TN Vol Mil Inf
HARRISON, Benjamin, Pvt, Col Samuel Bayless, Capt Branch Jones, E TN Drafted Mil
HARRISON, Benjamin, Pvt, Col Samuel Wear, Capt Jas Tedford, E TN Vol Inf; appointed Sgt Maj
HARRISON, Benjamin, Pvt, Maj Gen Carroll, Col Jas Raulston, Capt Wiley Huddleston, Inf; promoted to Ens
HARRISON, Benjamin, Sgt, Col Wm Higgins, Capt Stephen Griffith, Mtd Riflemen
HARRISON, Charles, 3 Sgt, Col William Lillard, Capt Z Copeland, E TN Vol Inf; exchanged w/Jeremiah Shully-Capt Stephens
HARRISON, Charles, Pvt, Col S Bunch, Capt Francis Berry, E TN Mil; promoted to 2 Lt
HARRISON, Charles, Sgt, Col S Bayless, Capt Jas Churchman, E TN Mil
HARRISON, Cuddith, Pvt, Col John Alcorn, Capt Fred Stump, Cav
HARRISON, Cuddy, 1 Sgt, Maj Gen A Jackson, Capt John Crane, Mtd Gunmen
HARRISON, Cuddy, Pvt, Col John Coffee, Capt Fred Stump, Cav
HARRISON, Cuddy, Pvt, Col R H Dyer, Capt Thos White, Vol Mtd Gunmen
HARRISON, Cuddy, Sgt, Col R H Dyer, Capt Thos White, Vol Mtd Gunmen
HARRISON, Daniel, Pvt, Col S Bunch, Capt Solomon Dobkins, E TN Drafted Mil; transferred to Capt Houk Co
HARRISON, Daniel, Pvt, Col Samuel Bunch, Capt John Houk, E TN Mil; transferred from Capt Dobkin's Co
HARRISON, Daniel, Pvt, Col T McCrory, Capt Thos Gordon, Inf; deserted 11-9-1813
HARRISON, Daniel, Sgt, Col R H Dyer, Capt Wm Russell, Vol Mtd Gunmen
HARRISON, Daniel, Sgt, Col Wm Lillard, Capt Wm Hamilton, E TN Vol Inf
HARRISON, Edmond, Pvt, Regt Commander omitted, Capt Arch McKinney, Cav
HARRISON, Edmund, Pvt, Col Thos Benton, Capt Wm J Benton, Vol Inf
HARRISON, Edmunth, Pvt, Regt Commander omitted, Capt Arch McKinney, Cav
HARRISON, Fledge, Pvt, Col Wm Johnson, Capt Jas Stewart, E TN Drafted Mil
HARRISON, Gidian, Pvt, Maj Gen A Jackson, Capt Hugh Kerr, Mtd Rangers
HARRISON, Henry, Pvt, Maj Gen A Jackson, Capt Jas Reid, Inf
HARRISON, Hugh, Sgt, Col Wm Metcalf, Co Com-

mander omitted, 1st Regt TN Mil Inf
HARRISON, James, Cpl, Maj Wm Russell, Capt Fleman Hodges, Vol Mtd Gunmen; substitute for Jas Bailey
HARRISON, James, Pvt, Col S Bunch, Capt F Berry, E TN Mil; attached to Capt English's Co
HARRISON, James, Pvt, Col S Bunch, Capt Geo Gregory, E TN Drafted Mil; transferred from Capt Berry's Co
HARRISON, James, Pvt, Col S Bunch, Capt John English, E TN Drafted Mil; joined from Capt Berry's Co
HARRISON, Jeremiah, Pvt, Col Wm Lillard, Capt Jacob Dyke, Vol Inf; deserted
HARRISON, Jeremiah, Pvt, Col Wm Lillard, Capt Jas Lillard, E TN Vol Inf
HARRISON, Joel, Pvt, Maj Gen A Jackson, Capt Hugh Kerr, Mtd Rangers
HARRISON, John, Cpl, Maj Wm Russell, Capt Fleman Hodges, Vol Mtd Gunmen; substitute for Samuel McKinney
HARRISON, John, Pvt, Col John Brown, Capt Allen I Bacon, E TN Mil Inf
HARRISON, John, Pvt, Col R H Dyer, Maj Wm Russell, Capt Wm Russell, Vol Mtd Gunmen
HARRISON, John, Pvt, Col Wm Metcalf, Capt John Barnhart, Mil Inf
HARRISON, John, Pvt, Maj Gen A Jackson, Capt Hugh Kerr, Mtd Rangers
HARRISON, Joseph, Pvt, Col Wm Metcalf, Capt Add Patterson, Mil Inf; d 2-22-1815
HARRISON, Jurneer?, Sgt, Col S Bunch, Capt Jos Duncan, E TN Drafted Mil; joined from Capt Houk's Co
HARRISON, Nathaniel, Pvt, Col R H Dyer, Capt Glen Owen, TN Vol Mtd Gunmen
HARRISON, Nathaniel, Pvt, Col Thos H Benton, Capt Jas McEwen, Vol Inf
HARRISON, Reuben, Pvt, Col A Cheatham, Capt Richard Benson, Inf
HARRISON, Richard, Pvt, Col T Williamson, Capt George Mitchie, 2nd Regt TN Vol Mtd Gunmen
HARRISON, Richard, Pvt, Col Wm Hall, Capt Travis C Nash, Inf
HARRISON, Richard, Pvt, Maj Wm Russell, Capt George Mitchie, Vol Mtd Gunmen
HARRISON, Samuel, Pvt, Brig Gen I B Roberts, Capt Wm Teas, 6th Brig Mtd Inf
HARRISON, William, Cpl, Col Samuel Wear, Capt Jos Calloway, Mtd Inf
HARRISON, William, Pvt, Col Ewen Allison, Capt Thos Wilson, E TN Drafted Mil
HARRISON, William, Pvt, Col John Cocke, Capt Bird Nance, Inf
HARRISON, William, Pvt, Col S Copeland, Capt Wm Evans, Mil Inf
HARRISON, William, Pvt, Gen Andrew Jackson, Capt Nathan Davis, Inf
HARRISON (HARRIS), William, Pvt, Col Wm Hall, Capt Wm L Alexander, Vol Inf
HARRISS, John B, Pvt, Col Samuel Wear, Capt Jas Tedford, E TN Vol Inf
HARRISS, John, Pvt, Col Samuel Wear, Capt John Stephens, E TN Vol Inf
HARRISS, Willey, Pvt, Maj Gen A Jackson, Capt John Crane, Mtd Gunmen
HARROLD, Elisha, Pvt, Col Wm Lillard, Capt Hugh Martin, E TN Vol Inf
HARROLD, Mitchell, Pvt, Col Wm Lillard, Capt George Argenbright, E TN Vol Riflemen
HARSHAW, John, Pvt, Col John Cocke, Capt John Dalton, Inf
HARSMAN, George, 2 Sgt, Col Wm Lillard, Capt Hugh Martin, E TN Vol Inf
HART, Alex, Tptr, Maj Jas Porter, Capt Sam Cowan, Cav
HART, Eli, Pvt, Col John Brown, Capt Wm D Neilson, Regt E TN Vol Mil
HART, Hartwell, Pvt, Col John Brown, Capt Wm D Neilson, Regt E TN Vol Mil
HART, Henry, 3 Sgt, Col Robert Steele, Capt Robert Campbell, W TN Mil Inf
HART, Henry, Pvt, Col Thos Williamson, Capt Thos Scurry, Vol Mtd Gunmen
HART, Henry, Sgt, Col John Coffee, Capt David Smith, Vol Cav
HART, Isaac, Pvt, Col Samuel Bayless, Capt Solomon Hendricks, E TN Mil
HART, John, Pvt, Col Philip Pipkin, Capt Wm Mackay, Mil Inf; deserted 9-20-1814
HART, John, Pvt, Col Samuel Bayless, Capt Jas Landen, E TN Mil
HART, John, Pvt, Col Thos Williamson, Capt Thos Scurry, Vol Mtd Gunmen; no service rendered
HART, John, Pvt, Col Wm Metcalf, Capt Bird L Hurt, Mil Inf
HART, John, Pvt, Col Wm Metcalf, Capt Wm Mullin, Mil Inf
HART, John, Pvt, Maj Wm Carroll, Capt Lewis Dillahunty & Capt Daniel M Bradford, Vol Inf
HART, John, Sgt, Col John Williams, Capt Wm Walker, Vol
HART, John, Sgt, Col N T Perkins, Capt George Eliot, Mil Inf
HART, Mark, Pvt, Col John Cocke, Capt Jos Price, Inf
HART, Mark, Pvt, Col John K Wynne, Capt Bayless, Prince, Vol Inf
HART, Robert S, Pvt, Col Edward Bradley, Capt Wm Lauderdale, Vol Inf
HART, Robert W, Sgt, Col N T Perkins, Co Commander omitted, 1st Regt TN Mtd Vol
HART, Samuel, Pvt, Col Edward Bradley, Capt Wm Lauderdale, Vol Inf
HART, Samuel, Pvt, Regt Commander omitted, Capt N Davis, Inf; also under Gen Andrew Jackson
HART, Silas, Cpl, Col Samuel Bunch, Capt Edward Buchanan, E TN Drafted Mil
HART (HEART), Samuel, Pvt, Col Wm Hall, Capt Wm L Alexander, Vol Inf
HARTEN, James, Pvt, Col Jas Raulston, Capt Henry Hamilton, Inf; also served under Maj Gen Wm Carroll
HARTGRAVES, S Kelton, 1 Lt, Col Leroy Hammond, Capt J N Williamson, 2nd Regt Inf

## Enlisted Men, War of 1812

HARTGRAVES, William, Pvt, Col Wm Y Higgins, Capt Wm Doak, Mtd Riflemen
HARTGROVE, Hezekal (Isihial), Pvt, Col John Coffee, Capt Alexander McKeen, Cav
HARTGROVE, Hezekial, Pvt, Col John Alcorn, Capt Alexander McKeen, Cav
HARTGROVE, John, Pvt, Col Samuel Bunch, Capt Francis Berry, E TN Mil; AWOL 1-27-1814
HARTGROVES, Hugh, Pvt, Col Robert Steele, Capt John Chitwood, Mil Inf
HARTKROAD?, Henry, Pvt, Col Wm Johnson, Capt Jos Scott, E TN Drafted Mil
HARTLEY, Charles, Pvt, Maj Gen A Jackson, Capt Wm Carroll, Vol Inf
HARTLEY, Daniel, Pvt, Col Wm Lillard, Capt Robert Maloney, E TN Vol Inf
HARTLEY, David, Pvt, Regt Commander omitted, Capt Smith, Inf Vol
HARTLY, John, Pvt, Col Wm Lillard, Capt Wm Gillenwater, E TN Inf
HARTMAN, Marshall, Pvt, Col Wm Lillard, Capt Wm McLin, E TN Inf
HARTON, John, Pvt, Col Edward Bradley, Capt John Moore, Vol Inf
HARTSFIELD, William, Cpl, Col Newton Cannon, Capt John Harpole, Mtd Gunmen
HARTY, Daniel, Pvt, Col Wm Lillard, Capt Robert Maloney, E TN Vol Inf
HARTY, Daniel, Pvt, Col Wm Pillow, Capt Wm J Smith, Vol Inf
HARTY, David (Daniel), Pvt, Col Thos H Benton, Capt Wm J Smith, Vol Inf
HARTY, Jacob, Pvt, Col Robert Steele, Capt Richard Ratton, Mil Inf
HARTY, James, Pvt, Col Samuel Bayless, Capt Churchman, E TN Mil
HARULSON, James, Pvt, Col Robert H Dyer, Capt McMahon, TN Vol Mtd Gunmen
HARVELL, Buckner jr, QM, Col Robert Steele, 4th Regt TN Mil
HARVELL, Buckner, QM, no other information
HARVELL, James, Pvt, Col John K Wynne, Capt Jas Holleman, Inf; discharged day to enlistment
HARVESTER, Pledge, Pvt, Col Wm H Johnson, Capt Jas Stewart, E TN Mil
HARVESTON, John, Pvt, Col Wm Johnson, Capt Jas Stewart, E TN Mil
HARVEY, Charles, Pvt, Col John K Wynne, Capt Jas Holleman, Inf
HARVEY, James, Pvt, Col S Bunch, Capt George McPherson, E TN Mil
HARVEY, James, Pvt, Col Wm Hall, Capt Newlin, Inf
HARVEY, Jesse, Pvt, Col John Cocke, Capt Joseph Price, Inf
HARVEY, John, Ffr, Maj Gen William Carroll, Col Jas Raulston, Capt Edward Robinson, Inf
HARVEY, John, Pvt, Regt Commander omitted, Capt Elisha Green, Mtd Spies
HARVEY, Johnathan, Pvt, Col Wm Johnson, Capt Jas R Rogers, E TN Drafted Mil
HARVEY, Robert, Pvt, Col Wm Johnson, Capt Jas Rogers, E TN Drafted Mil
HARVEY, Thomas, Pvt, Col Wm Johnson, Capt Elihu Milliken, 3rd E TN Mil
HARVEY, Thomas, Sgt, Col Edwin E Booth, Capt McKamey, E TN Mil; transferred to Capt Milliken's Co
HARVEY (HARNEY), Thomas, Pvt, Col John Coffee, Capt Jas Terrell, Vol Cav; over age & no horse
HARWELL, Samuel, Pvt, Col Wm Metcalf, Capt Thos Marks, Mil Inf
HARWELL, Sterling, Pvt, Maj Gen A Jackson, Capt Wm Carroll, Vol Inf
HARWELL, William, Pvt, Lt Col Hammond, Capt Jas Tubb, Inf; enlisted in Regular Service
HARWOOD, Benjamin, Pvt, Col John Brown, Capt James Preston, E TN Mil Inf; discharged for inability
HARWOOD, Nathan, Pvt, Col John Brown, Capt Jas Preston, E TN Mil Inf
HARWOOD, Randolph D, Pvt, Col Wm Johnson, Capt Elihu Milliken, 3rd Regt E TN Mil; transferred to Capt Winton's Co
HARWOOD, Randolph, Pvt, Col Edwin Booth, Capt Winton, E TN Mil
HARWOOD, Randolph, Pvt, Col Wm Johnson, Capt Elihu Milliken, 3rd Regt E TN Mil
HARWOOD, Randolph, Pvt, Col Wm Johnson, Capt Mulligan, 3rd Regt E TN Mil
HARWOOD, Thomas, 1 Sgt, Regt Commander omitted, Capt Jas Terrill, Det from Ft Strother Cav
HARWOOD, Thomas, Sgt, Regt Commander omitted, Capt Jas Terrill, Cav
HASELET, Archibald D, Pvt, Col Philip Pipkin, Capt Henry M Newlin, Mil Inf
HASELIP, Wallin, Pvt, Col Thomas H Benton, Capt Caperton, Inf
HASELWOOD, Blaney, Pvt, Col Samuel Bunch, Capt George Gregory, E TN Drafted Mil; discharged for inability
HASEY (HOSEY?), James, Pvt, Col S Copeland, Capt George, Inf
HASH, Daniel, Pvt, Maj John Childs, Capt Daniel Price, E TN Mtd Inf
HASH, John, Pvt, Col Wm Lillard, Capt Zacheus Copeland, E TN Vol Inf
HASH, John, Pvt, Maj John Childs, Co Commander omitted, Vol Mtd Gunmen
HASKEN, William, Pvt, Col S Wear, Capt S Bayless, Vol Mtd Inf
HASKINS, Aaron, Pvt, Lt Col Henry Bryan, Co Commander omitted, Inf
HASKINS, James, Pvt, Col S Bunch, Capt George Gregory, E TN Drafted Mil
HASKINS, James, Pvt, Col S Bunch, Capt John Houk, E TN Mil; joined Capt Davis' Co.
HASKINS, John, Pvt, Col S Bunch, Capt Daniel Yarnell, E TN Mil
HASKINS, John, Pvt, Col Wm Johnson, Capt Jas Stewart, E TN Drafted Mil; trans to Capt Scott Co
HASKINS, Joseph, Pvt, Col N Cannon, Capt John Hanley, Mtd Riflemen
HASKINS, Thomas, Pvt, Col S Bunch, Capt Moses, E TN

## Enlisted Men, War of 1812

HASKINS, William, Ffr, Col Wm Brown, Capt Hugh Barton, E TN Mil Inf
HASLEP, David D, Pvt, Col Wm Russell, Col Maj Wm Russell, Vol Gunmen
HASLEP, James, Pvt, Col T McCrory, Capt Isaac Patton, Mil Inf
HASLEP, Wallie, Pvt, Col Thos Benton, Capt George Caperton, Vol Inf
HASLEP, William N, Pvt, Col S Loury, Capt Leroy Hammonds? & Capt Arahel Raines, Inf; deserted
HASLIP, Jeremiah, Pvt, Col Wm Williamson, Capt Doak & Capt John Dobbins, Vol Mtd Gunmen
HASLIP, John, Pvt, Col Williamson, Capt Cook & Capt Dobbins, Vol Mtd Gunmen
HASLIP, Thomas, Pvt, no other information
HASNER, Jacob, Pvt, Col Thomas Benton, Capt Geo Gibbs, Vol Inf
HASS, Albert, Sgt, Col Wm Metcalf, Capt John Cunningham & Capt Hill, Mil Inf; died 2-6-1815
HASS, Philip, Pvt, Col Philip Pipkin, Capt Jas Blakemore, Mil Inf
HASSEL, Zackews, Pvt, Col John Cocke, Capt Samuel Caruthers, Inf
HASSELL, John, Pvt, Gen Johnston, Capt Danl Oban?, E TN Inf
HASSELL, William I, Pvt, Col John Cocke, Capt Samuel Caruthers, Inf
HASSER, John, Pvt, Col Wm Hall, Capt Henry Newlin, Inf
HASSIL, Elijah M, Pvt, Col Leroy Hammonds, Capt Thos Wells, Inf; died 1-31-1815
HASTING, Henry, Pvt, Col Wm Pillow, Capt Joseph Mason, Vol Inf
HASTINGS, Henry, 1 Cpl, Col Philip Pipkin, Capt Henry Newlin, Mil Inf
HASTINGS, Henry, Pvt, Col Thos Benton, Capt N Cannon, Inf; trans for Capt Hewett's Co
HASTINGS, Henry, Pvt, Col Thos Benton, Capt Benj Hewett, Vol Inf
HASTINGS, Henry, Sgt, Regt Commander omitted, Lt I Barrett, Inf
HASTINGS, Isaac, Pvt, Col Jas Raulston, Capt Daniel Newman, Inf
HASTINGS, Richard, Pvt, Col Philip Pipkin, Capt Henry Newlin, Mil Inf
HASTINGS, Richard, Pvt, Lt (Col?) I Barrett, Capt Nathan Davis, W TN Inf
HASTON, Overton, Pvt, Col Thos Benton, Capt Thos Benton, Vol Inf
HATCHER, James, Pvt, Col S Bayless, Capt Jos Goodson, E TN Mil
HATCHER, James, Pvt, Col S Wear, Capt Perry, E TN Vol Mtd Inf
HATCHER, Thomas, Pvt, Col Wm Lillard, Capt Benj King, E TN Vol Inf
HATCHETT, John, Sgt, Col Wm Metcalf, Capt Bird Hurt, Mil Inf
HATCHETT, Thomas, Pvt, Col T McCrory, Capt John Reynolds, Mil Inf
HATFIELD, James, Pvt, Col S Wear, Capt Doak, E TN Vol Inf
HATFIELD, John, Pvt, no other information
HATFIELD, Jonathan, Pvt, Col Edwin Booth, Capt Richard Marshall, Drafted Mil
HATFIELD, Joseph, Pvt, Col S Bunch, Capt John English, E TN Drafted Mil
HATFIELD, Moses, Pvt, Col S Bayless, E TN Mil
HATFIELD, Reuben, Cpl, Col Wm Johnson, Capt Benj Powell, E TN Mil
HATFIELD, Stanley, Pvt, Col S Wear, Capt Doak, E TN Vol Inf
HATHAWAY, Abraham, Pvt, Col Wm Johnson, Capt Jos Scott, E TN Drafted Mil
HATHAWAY, Leonard, Blksmth, Col Robert Dyer, Capt Bethel Allen, Vol Mtd Gunmen
HATHAWAY, Samuel, Pvt, Col Edwin Booth, Capt Alexander Biggs, Inf
HATHCOCK, Thomas, Pvt, Col Wm Lillard, Capt Wm Lillard, E TN Inf Vol
HATLEN, Joseph, Pvt, Col R C Napier, Capt Thos Preston, Mil Inf; trans to Arty
HATTOCKS, Beveu, Pvt, Col S Bunch, Capt Edward Buchanan, E TN Mil
HATTON, Francis, Pvt, Lt Col John Edmonson, Co Commander omitted, Cav
HATTON, Joseph, Pvt, Maj Wm Russell, Capt Wm Chism, Vol Mtd Riflemen
HATTON, Peter, Pvt, Col Thos Benton, Capt Jas Renshaw, Vol Inf; deserted
HAUKE, Jacob, Pvt, Col Ewin Allison, Capt Jacob Hoyal, E TN Mil
HAUSE, William, Pvt, Col S Bayless, Capt Jos Hale, E TN Mil
HAUSSEE, Smith, Pvt, Col Thos Benton, Capt Jas McFerrin, Inf
HAVENS, Joseph, Pvt, Col Samuel Bunch, Capt Jos Duncan, E TN Drafted Mil; joined from Capt Gibb's Co
HAVINS, Howard, Pvt, Col Samuel Wear, Capt Rufus Morgan, E TN Vol Inf
HAW, John, Pvt, Col WM Metcalf, Capt Wm Mullin, Mil Inf
HAW, Samuel, Cpl, Col Thos Williamson, Capt Robert Moore, Vol Mtd Gunmen
HAWK, Abraham, Pvt, Col Samuel Bunch, Capt Jas Cunningham, E TN Vol Mtd Inf
HAWK, Benjamin, Pvt, Col Edwin Booth, Capt Porter, Drafted Mil
HAWK, John, Pvt, Col Edwin Booth, Capt Porter, Draft Mil
HAWK, Matthias, 4 Cpl, Col Jas Raulston, Capt Chas Wade, Inf
HAWK, Michael, Pvt, Col Samuel Wear, Capt Simeon Perry, E TN Vol Mtd Inf
HAWKE, Henry, Dmr, Col Wm Johnson, Capt Andrew Lawson, E TN Mil
HAWKES, Stephen, pvt, no other information except-- appt spy by Brig Gen Jas Roberts
HAWKINS, Aaron, Pvt, Col Samuel Bunch, Capt Andrew Breden, E TN Mil; trans to Capt J Berry's Co
HAWKINS, Benjamin, Pvt, Gen Thos Johnson, Capt

## Enlisted Men, War of 1812

Daniel Oban, 36th Inf

HAWKINS, Eli, Pvt, Col Samuel Bunch, Capt S Roberson, E TN Draft Mil; disch for inability

HAWKINS, Eli, Pvt, Regt Commander omitted, Capt Samuel Richardson; E TN Draft Mil; disch for inability

HAWKINS, Grant, Pvt, Maj Gen Wm Carroll, Col Wm Metcalf, Capt John Jackson, Inf

HAWKINS, James, Pvt, Col Edwin Booth, Capt Richard Marshall, Drafted Mil

HAWKINS, Jesse, Pvt, Col John Brown, Capt Lunsford Oliver, E TN Mil

HAWKINS, Joel, Pvt, Col John Brown, Capt John Childs, E TN Vol Mtd Inf

HAWKINS, John, Pvt, Col Philip Pipkin, Capt Jas Blakemore, Mil Inf

HAWKINS, Joseph, Pvt, Col Edward Bradley, Capt Wm Lauderdale, Vol Inf

HAWKINS, Joseph, Pvt, Maj Wm Woodfolk, Capt Abraham Dudney & Capt John Sutton, Inf

HAWKINS, Pleasant, Pvt, Col John Wynne, Capt Jas Cole, Inf

HAWKINS, Robert, Pvt, Gen Thos Johnson, Capt Daniel Oban, 36th Inf

HAWKINS, Stephen, Pvt, Brig Gen Jas White, no Co Commander; appt spy

HAWKINS, William A, Sgt, Col Wm Lillard, Capt Robert Maloney, E TN Vol Inf

HAWKINS, William, Pvt, Col Thos Williamson, Capt John Crane & Capt Jas Cook, Vol Mtd Gunmen

HAWKINS, William, Pvt, Col Thos Williamson, Capt John Dobbins & Capt John Doak, Vol Mtd Inf

HAWLEY, Benjamin, Pvt, Maj Wm Russell, Col Robert Dyer, Capt Wm Russell, Vol Mtd Gunmen

HAWS, John, Pvt, Col Wm Metcalf, Capt John Barnhart, Mil Inf

HAWS, John, Pvt, Col Wm Metcalf, Capt Wm Mullin, Mil Inf

HAWS, Thomas, Pvt, Col Samuel Bunch, Capt David Vance, E TN Mtd Inf

HAWTHORN, John, Pvt, Col Wm Johnson, Capt Jas Stewart, E TN Draft Mil

HAY, George, Pvt, Col Robert Dyer, Capt Nathan Farmer, Mtd Riflemen

HAY, Jeremiah, Sgt, Col Robert Dyer, Capt Ephraim Dickson, 1 TN Vol Mtd Gunmen

HAY, John, Pvt, Col N T Perkins, Capt Mathew Johnson, Mil Inf

HAYES, Andrew, Pvt, no other information

HAYES, Campbell, Pvt, Col Thos McCrory, Capt Isaac Patton, Mil Inf

HAYES, John, Sgt, Regt Commander omitted, Capt Joseph Williams, Mil Cav

HAYES, Joseph, Pvt, Col John Wynne, Capt Jas Cole, Inf

HAYES, Martin, Pvt, Col John Wynne, Capt Jas Cole, Inf; deserted

HAYGOOD, Will, Far, Col John Coffee, Capt David Smith, Vol Cav

HAYLES, Thomas, Pvt, Col Thos Williamson, Capt Thos Scurry, Vol Mtd Gunmen

HAYLEY, James, Pvt, Col Robert Dyer, Capt Jos Williams, Vol Mtd Gunmen

HAYNES, Andrew, Pvt, Col John Cocke, Capt George Barnes, Inf

HAYNES, Andrew, Pvt, Col Wm Hall, Capt Henry Newlin, Inf; deserted

HAYNES, Ephraim, Pvt, Col John Cocke, Capt George Barnes, Inf

HAYNES, George, Pvt, Col Philip Pipkin, Capt Peter Searcy, Mil Inf

HAYNES, James, Pvt, Col Wm Metcalf, Capt John Barnhart, Mil Inf

HAYNES, James, Pvt, Regt Commander omitted, Capt Abner Pearce, Inf

HAYNES, John B, Pvt, Col John Alcorn, Capt Thomas Bradley, Vol Cav

HAYNES, John, Pvt, Col John Cocke, Capt James Gault, Inf; died 1-31-1815

HAYNES, John, Pvt, Gen Andrew Jackson, Capt Nathan Davis, Inf

HAYNES, John, Pvt, Lt Col Leroy Hammonds, Capt James Craig, Inf

HAYNES, Lewis, Pvt, Col John Cocke, Capt James Gault, Inf

HAYNES, Moody P, Pvt, Col William Hall, Capt William Alexander, Vol Inf

HAYNES, Peter, 1 Sgt, Col William Hall, Capt Abraham Bledsoe, Vol Inf

HAYNES, Richard, Pvt, Col Samuel Wear, Capt Rufus Morgan, E TN Vol Inf

HAYNES, Robert, Pvt, Capt Nathan Davis, Lt I Barrett, W TN Bn Inf; deserted

HAYNES, Robert, Pvt, Col William Hall, Capt William Alexander, Vol Inf

HAYNES, Stephen, Cpl, Col Thomas McCrory, Capt James Shannon, Mil Inf

HAYNES, Sterling, Pvt, Col Samuel Bunch, Capt S Roberson, E TN Draft Mil; deserted

HAYNES, Sterling, Pvt, Regt Commander omitted, Capt Samuel Richardson, E TN Draft Mil; deserted

HAYNES, Thomas, Pvt, Col S Bunch, Capt Francis Berry, E TN Mil; AWOL

HAYNES, Thomas, Pvt, Col S Bunch, Capt S Roberson, E TN Draft Mil

HAYNES, Thomas, Pvt, Regt Commander omitted, Capt S Richardson, E TN Draft Mil

HAYNES, William, Pvt, Col S Bunch, Capt Joseph Rich, E TN Inf

HAYS, Arthur, Pvt, Col Wm Hall, Capt Jas Raulston, Vol Inf

HAYS, Blackman, Pvt, Col Wm Pillow, Capt Jas McEwen, Vol Inf

HAYS, Charles, Pvt, Col S Bunch, Capt John Inman, E Tn Vol Mtd Inf

HAYS, David, 6 Cpl, Col John Cocke, Capt John Weakley, Inf

HAYS, Elexander, Pvt, Col Wm Lillard, Capt Thos McChristian, E TN Vol Inf

HAYS, Emmon, Pvt, Col Philip Pipkin, Capt Jas Blakemore, Mil Inf

HAYS, Ezra, Pvt, Col Thos H Benton, Capt Geo W Gibbs, Vol Inf

HAYS, George, Pvt, Regt Commander omitted, Capt James Craig, Inf
HAYS, George, Pvt, Regt Commander omitted, Capt Nathan Farmer, Mtd Riflemen
HAYS, Henry, Cpl, Col Thos Williamson, Capt Richard Tate, Vol Mtd Gunmen
HAYS, Hugh, Sgt, Col A Cheatham, Capt Wm Creel, Inf; apptd from pvt
HAYS, Jacob, Pvt, Lt Col L Hammond, Capt Jas Tubb, Inf
HAYS, James, Pvt, Col A Lowry, Lt Col L Hammond, Capt Arahel Rains, Inf
HAYS, James, Pvt, Col Wm Johnson, Capt E Milliken, 3 Regt E TN Mil
HAYS, James, Pvt, Col Wm Lillard, Capt Thos McChristian, E TN Vol Inf
HAYS, John, 1 Sgt, Regt Commander omitted, Capt John Williams, Mil Cav
HAYS, John, Pvt, Col John Coffee, Capt Michael Melton, Cav
HAYS, John, Pvt, Col S Bunch, Capt Jno English, E TN Draft Mil
HAYS, John, Pvt, Maj John Chiles, Capt R Tipton, E TN Vol Mtd Inf; Regt from Jefferson Co
HAYS, Jonathan, Pvt, Col N T Perkins, Capt John Doak, Vol Mtd Gunmen
HAYS, Jonathan, Pvt, Regt Commander omitted, Capt Jas Haggard, Mtd Gunmen
HAYS, Martin, Pvt, Col A Lowry, Lt Col L Hammond, Capt Arahel Rains, Inf; trans to Capt Russell's Co
HAYS, Richard, Pvt, Col Philip Pipkin, Capt Wm Mackey, Mil Inf
HAYS, Robert, Pvt, Col S Wear, Capt Robert Doak, E TN Vol Inf
HAYS, Samuel, Pvt, Col John Cocke, Capt Bird Nance, Inf; died 2-18-1815
HAYS, Samuel, Pvt, Col Robt Steele, Capt Jas Bennett, Mil Inf
HAYS, Stephen, Pvt, Lt Col L Hammons, Capt Arahel Rains, Inf; trans to Capt Chisholm
HAYS, Thomas, Sgt, Col Robert Steele, Capt Cheekwood, Mil Inf
HAYS, Thompson, Pvt, Col John Coffee, Capt Thos Bradley, Vol Cav
HAYS, William, Pvt, Col Edward E Booth, Capt John Slatton, E TN Mil
HAYS, William, Pvt, Col Philip Pipkin, Capt Henry M Newlin, Mil Inf
HAYS, William, Pvt, Col Robert Steele, Capt R M Renton?, Mil Inf; deserted
HAYS, William, Pvt, Col S Bayless, Capt Joseph Hale, E TN Mil
HAYS, William, Pvt, Col S Copeland, Capt Wm Evans, Mil Inf
HAYS, William, Pvt, Col Thos Williamson, Capt John Coak & Capt Sol Dobkins, Vol Mtd Gunmen
HAYS, Zachariah, Pvt, Col Thos Williamson, Capt Richard Tate, Vol Mtd Gunmen; trans to Capt Burdette's Co
HAYZLETT, John, Pvt, Col H Hall, Capt John Moore, Vol Inf
HAZE, James, Pvt, Col S Bayless, Capt Jas Churchman, E TN Mil; joined from Capt Milliken's Co
HAZE, James, Pvt, Col Wm Johnson, Capt E Milliken, 3 Regt E TN Mil
HAZLEWOOD, John, Pvt, Col Jas Raulston, Capt Jas A Black, Inf
HAZLEWOOD, John, Pvt, Col John K Wynne, Capt John Spinks, Inf
HAZLIP, Henry, Pvt, Col Robert Steele, Capt Cheekwood, Mil Inf
HAZLIP, John, Pvt, Col Robert Steele, Capt Cheekwood, Mil Inf
HEAD, George, Pvt, Col Samuel Wear, Capt John Chiles, E TN Inf
HEAD, George, Pvt, Maj Gen A Jackson, Capt James Reed, Inf
HEAD, George, Pvt, Maj John Chiles, Capt Chas Conway, E TN Mtd Gunmen; Regt from Knox Co
HEADRICK, Joseph, Pvt, Col William Johnson, Capt Joseph Scott, E TN Draft Mil
HEADSPETH, George, Pvt, Col Robert H Dyer, Capt Wm Russell, Maj Wm Russell, Vol Mtd Gunmen
HEADSPETH, George, Pvt, no Regt Commander, Capt Wm Mitchell, Spies
HEADSPETH, James, Pvt, Col William Hall, Capt Henry W Newland, Inf; deserted
HEADSPETH, Major, Pvt, Col Philip Pipkin, Capt George Mebane, Inf
HEADSPETH, Seaton, Pvt, Col Robert Dyer, Maj Wm Russell, Capt Wm Russell, Vol Mtd Gunmen
HEAFLEY, Cornelius, Pvt, Maj John Childs, Capt John Stephens, E TN Vol Mtd Inf
HEARD, Jeff, Pvt, Col Edwin Booth, Capt Vernon, E TN Mil
HEARD, Jesse, Pvt, Maj William Russell, Capt John Trimble, Vol Mtd Gunmen; transferred from Capt Stephens Co
HEARD, John, Pvt, Col Edwin Booth, Capt Vernon, E TN Mil
HEARN, Ebenezer, Pvt, Col Edward Bradley, Capt Harry L Douglass, Vol Inf
HEARN, Jacob, Pvt, Col Edward Bradley, Capt Harry L Douglass, Vol Inf
HEARN, Jacob, Pvt, Col Thos Benton, Capt Henry L Douglass, Vol Inf
HEARN, John, Pvt, Col Edward Bradley, Capt Harry L Douglass, Vol Inf
HEARN, Parnell, Pvt, Col Edward Bradley, Capt Harry L Douglass, Vol Inf
HEARN, William, Sgt, Col Edward Bradley, Capt H L Douglass, Vol Inf
HEARNDON, William, Pvt, Regt Commander omitted, Lt Jas Berry, Mtd Riflemen
HEART, Edward, Pvt, Col Samuel Wear, Capt John Stephens, E TN Vol Inf
HEART, John, Pvt, Regt Commander omitted, Capt Wyatt Fussell, Det of Inf
HEART, Joseph, Pvt, Col Samuel Wear, Capt John Stephens, E TN Vol Inf
HEART, Sam, Pvt, Col William Hall, Capt William L Alexander, Vol Inf
HEART, Thomas, Pvt, Col Samuel Wear, Capt James

## Enlisted Men, War of 1812

Gillespie, E TN Vol Inf

HEART (HART), Pleasant, Cpl, Col Wm Metcalf, Capt Drury Adkins, Mil Inf

HEARTLY, Daniel, Pvt, Col Thomas Benton, Capt Wm J Smith, Vol Inf

HEASLET, George W, Pvt, Col Samuel Wear, Capt John Chiles, E TN Vol Inf

HEATH, Able, Pvt, Col R C Napier, Capt Edward Neblett, Mil Inf

HEATH, John, Pvt, Col Wm Lillard, Capt John Neatherton, E TN Vol Inf

HEATH, Philip C, Cpl, Col Samuel Wear, Capt John Bayless, Mtd Inf

HEATH, Ryland, Pvt, Col Newton Cannon, Capt Thomas Yardley, Mtd Riflemen; AWOL 10-5-1813

HEATH, William, Pvt, Col Samuel Wear, Capt John Bayless, Mtd Inf

HEATHCOAT, John, Pvt, Col Samuel Bunch, Capt John Dobbins, E TN Drafted Mil; furloughed for inability

HEATON, Amos, 3 Sgt, Maj Andrew Jackson, Capt John Crane, Mtd Gunmen; killed 1-22-1814

HECKLAN, Jonathan, Pvt, Col Samuel Wear, Capt James Gillespie, E TN Vol Inf

HECKLAN (HICKLON), James, Pvt, Col Samuel Wear, Capt James Gillespie, E TN Vol Inf

HEDDLESTON, William, Pvt, Col Thomas Williamson, Capt James Cook & Capt John Crane, Vol Mtd Gunmen; joined Capt Crucks Co

HEDGCOCK, John, Pvt, Col Thomas Benton, Capt William Moore, Vol Inf

HEDGCOCK, Thomas, Pvt, Col William Pillow, Capt William Moore, Inf; d 12-14?-1815

HEDGDON, Thomas, Pvt, Col John Cocke, Capt Samuel M Caruthers, Inf

HEDGECOCK, Thomas, Pvt, Col Thomas Benton, Capt William Moore, Vol Inf

HEDGEPETH, Council, Pvt, Maj Gen Wm Carroll, Capt John Jackson, Inf

HEDGEPETH, Hutson, Pvt, Col Robert Dyer, Maj Wm Russell, Capt Wm Russell, Vol Mtd Gunmen

HEDGEPETH, Thomas, Pvt, Col Robert Dyer, Maj Wm Russell, Capt Wm Russell, Vol Mtd Gunmen

HEDRICK, Abraham, Pvt, Col Samuel Bayless, Capt James Landen, E TN Mil

HEDRICK, Jeremiah, Pvt, Col Wm Lillard, Capt Geo Argenbright, E TN Vol Riflemen

HEDRICK, William, Pvt, Col Jno Brown, Capt Wm D Neilson, E TN Vol Mil

HEDRICK, William, Pvt, Col Samuel Bayless, Capt Solomon Hendricks, E TN Mil

HEDSPITH, John, Pvt, Col John K Wynne, Capt James Holleman, Inf

HEDSPITH, William, Pvt, Col John K Wynne, Capt James Holleman, Inf

HEFFINGTON, Henry, Pvt, Col Wm Hall, Capt John Moore, Vol Inf

HEFFLIN, Simon, Pvt, Col John K Wynne, Capt Bayless E Prince, Inf

HEFLEY, John, Pvt, Col Edwin Boothe, Capt Vernon, E TN Mil; d 3-25-1815

HEFLIN, James, Pvt, Col Philip Pipkin, Capt George Mebane, Mil Inf

HEFLIN, James, Pvt, Col Robert Dyer, Capt Robert Evans, Vol Mtd Gunmen

HEFLIN, James, Pvt, Col William Hall, Capt Travis C Nash, Inf; deserted while on furlough

HEFLIN (HUFLIN), Fielder, Pvt, Col Philip Pipkin, Capt John Strother, Mil

HEGDON (HIGDON), Gabriel, Pvt, Col S Copeland, Capt Alexander Province, Mil Inf

HEGGS, William, Pvt, Regt Commander omitted, Capt Archibald McKinney, Cav

HEGH, James, Pvt, Col John Coffee, Capt Blackman Coleman, Cav

HEGLER, Abraham, Pvt, Col John Brown, Capt Lunsford Oliver, E TN Mil

HEGLER, Benjamin S, Dmr, Col John Cocke, Capt James Gray, Inf

HEITHER, Thomas, Pvt, Col William Johnson, Capt Benjamin Powell, Branch Srvce omitted

HELBURN, Samuel, Pvt, Col S Bunch, Capt Jno Hawk, E TN Mil

HELDREATH, Lewis, Pvt, Col John Cocke, Capt Joseph Price, Inf

HELLUM, George, Pvt, Col John Brown, Capt John Chiles, E TN Vol Mtd Inf

HELLY, S, Pvt, Lt Col Richard Napier, Co Commander omitted, Inf

HELM, Hiram, Pvt, no other information

HELM, Stephen, Pvt, Col Wm Johnson, Capt Henry Hunter, E TN Mil

HELMS, Frederick, Pvt, Maj Wm Woodfolk, Capt Abner Pearce, Branch Srvce omitted; joined from Capt Neil's

HELMS, Henry, Hospital Stewart, Col Samuel Bayless, 4th Regt E TN Mil

HELMS, Henry, Pvt, Col Samuel Bayless, Capt Waddle, E TN Mil; appointed Hospital Stewart

HELMS, Hiram, Pvt, Col Robert Steele, Co Commander omitted, Inf

HELMS, Joseph, Pvt, Col T McCrory, Capt A Metcalf, Mil Inf

HELMS, Lever (Lener), Pvt, Col T McCrory, Capt Samuel McKnight, Inf

HELMS, Malachi, Pvt, Col T McCrory, Co Commander omitted, Inf

HELMS (HOLMES), William, Pvt, Col Wm Metcalf, Capt Bird L Hurt, Mil Inf

HELTON, Arnold, Pvt, Col Wm Lillard, Capt Wm Gillenwater, E TN Inf

HELTON, Henry, Cpl, Col Edwin E Booth, Capt John Lewis, E TN Mil

HELTON, Henry, Pvt, Col John Brown, Capt John Chiles, E TN Vol Inf

HELTON, James, Dmr, Col Jas Raulston, Capt Daniel Newman, Inf; d 1-13-1815

HELTON, John, Pvt, Col Wm Lillard, Capt Gillenwater, E TN Inf

HELTON, Samuel, Cpl, Col John Cowan, Capt Thos Yardley, Mtd Riflemen

HELTON, Silas, Pvt, Col Samuel Bayless, Capt Hendrix,

## Enlisted Men, War of 1812

HELTON, Stephen, Pvt, Col Wm Johnson, Capt Henry Hunter, E TN Mil

HELTON, Vaskell, Pvt, Col Johnson, Capt Benjamin Powell, E TN Mil

HELTON, Vaskell, Pvt, Col Wm Lillard, Capt Gillenwater, E TN Inf

HEMBER, Joel, Pvt, Col Jno Brown, Capt Allen I Bacon, E TN Mil Inf

HEMBRE, John, Pvt, Col Thos H Benton, Capt George W Gibbs, Vol Inf

HEMBREE, Isaac, Pvt, Col Edwin E Booth, Capt John McKamey, E TN Mil

HEMBREE, John, Pvt, Col Thos H Benton, Capt George W Gibbs, Vol Inf

HEMBREE, John, Pvt, Col Thos H Benton, Co Commander omitted, Vol Inf

HEMBY, Robert, Pvt, no other information

HEMMELLY, Temple, Sgt, Col S Bunch, Capt Jones Griffin, E TN Mil Drafted

HEMP, Jacob, Pvt, Col John Williams, Capt Sam Bunch, Mtd Vol

HEMPHILL, Robert, Cpl, Regt Commander omitted, Capt David Mason, Cav

HEMPHILL, Samuel, Pvt, Col Thos H Benton, Capt Jas McEwin, Vol Inf

HEMPHILL, Samuel, Pvt, Col Wm Johnson, Capt James Stewart, E TN Mil

HENARD, James, Pvt, Col Wm Lillard, Capt George Keys, E TN Inf

HENBY (HENLY), Joseph, Pvt, Col John Cocke, Capt John Price, Inf; d 3-13-1815

HENDERSON, Aaron, Pvt, Col Thomas McCrory, Capt Abel Wills, Mil Inf

HENDERSON, Allen, Pvt, Col S Bunch, Capt Buchanan, Mtd Inf

HENDERSON, Allen, Pvt, Col S Bunch, Capt Joseph Duncan, E TN Drafted; transferred to Capt Buchanan's Co

HENDERSON, Benjamin, Sgt, Brig Gen Thos Washington, Capt John Crawford, Mtd Inf

HENDERSON, Charles, Pvt, Col N T Perkins, Co Commander omitted, Mil Inf

HENDERSON, Daniel, Pvt, Col Wm Hall, Capt Abraham Bledsoe, Vol Inf

HENDERSON, David, Pvt, Col S Bunch, Lt J N Harris, E TN Mil

HENDERSON, David, Pvt, Col Wm Y Higgins, Capt Wm Doak, Mtd Riflemen

HENDERSON, Edward, Pvt, Col Wm Johnson, Capt Tunnell, W TN Mil

HENDERSON, Edward, Pvt, Col Wm Metcalf, Capt Alexander Hill & Capt John Cunningham, Mil Inf

HENDERSON, Eli, Cpl, Col S Bunch, Capt George Gregory, E TN Drafted Mil

HENDERSON, James W, Sgt, Col John Cocke, Capt Caruthers, Inf

HENDERSON, James, Pvt, Col Newton Cannon, Co Commander omitted, Mtd Riflemen

HENDERSON, James, Pvt, Col R Steele, Co Commander omitted, Mil Inf

HENDERSON, James, Pvt, Col S Bunch, Capt George Gregory, E TN Mil

HENDERSON, James, Pvt, Col Thos McCrory, Capt Dooly, Inf

HENDERSON, James, Pvt, Col Thos McCrory, Capt Samuel McEnigh?, Inf

HENDERSON, James, Pvt, Col Wm Hall, Capt Travis Nash, Inf; promoted to QM

HENDERSON, James, Pvt, Col Wm Metcalf, Co Commander omitted, 1st Regt W TN Mil Inf; killed in action 12-28-1814

HENDERSON, James, Sgt, Regt Commander omitted, Capt Robert Evans, Mtd Spies; deserted 11-24-1813

HENDERSON, Jeremiah, Pvt, Col S Bunch, Capt Daniel Yarnell, E TN Mil

HENDERSON, Jesse, Pvt, Col S Bunch, Capt Duncan, E TN Drafted Mil; joined from Capt Yarnell's Co

HENDERSON, Jesse, Pvt, Col Samuel Bunch, Capt Daniel Yarnell, E TN Mil

HENDERSON, Jesse, Pvt, Regt Commander omitted, Capt Daniel Yarnell, E TN Mil; transferred from Capt Gibbs Co

HENDERSON, Jesse, Sgt, Col Edwin E Booth, Co Commander omitted, E TN Mil

HENDERSON, John, 1 Sgt, Brig Gen Thos Johnson, Capt Robert Carson, Inf

HENDERSON, John, Pvt, Col John Brown, Capt Wm Christian, E TN Mil Inf

HENDERSON, John, Pvt, Col Philip Pipkin, Capt Scurry, Mil Inf

HENDERSON, John, Pvt, Col S Bunch, Co Commander omitted, E TN Mil

HENDERSON, John, Pvt, Maj Wm Russell, Capt Fleman Hodges, Vol Mtd Gunmen

HENDERSON, John, Sgt, Col Wm Johnson, Capt Christopher Cook, E TN Mil

HENDERSON, John, Sgt, Col Wm Johnson, Capt Kirk, Mil

HENDERSON, Joseph, Pvt, Regt Commander omitted, Capt Arch McKinney, Cav

HENDERSON, Lewis, Pvt, Col A Lowry, Lt Col L Hammond, Capt Thos Delaney, Inf

HENDERSON, Michael, Pvt, Maj John Chiles, Capt Chas Conway, E TN Mtd Gunmen; Regimental County Knox

HENDERSON, Nathan, Pvt, Col Wm Metcalf, Capt Thos Marks, Mil Inf; d 2-4-1814

HENDERSON, Nathaniel, Pvt, Col A Lowry, Capt John Looney, W TN Inf; promoted to Sgt

HENDERSON, Nathaniel, Pvt, Col John Alcorn, Capt Alex McKeen, Cav

HENDERSON, Nathaniel, Pvt, Col John Coffee, Capt Alex McKeen, Cav

HENDERSON, Nathaniel, Pvt, Regt Commander omitted, Capt Arch McKenney, Cav; transferred to Russell's Spy Camp

HENDERSON, Nathaniel, Pvt, Regt Commander omitted, Capt Wm Mitchell, Spies

HENDERSON, Preston, Cpl, Col Thomas Williamson, Capt Beverly Williams, Vol Mtd Gunmen

## Enlisted Men, War of 1812

HENDERSON, Preston, Pvt, Col N Cannon, Capt John Harpole, Mtd Gunmen

HENDERSON, Robert, 2 Sgt, Regt Commander omitted, Capt Nathan Farmer, Branch Srvce omitted

HENDERSON, Robert, 2 Sgt, Regt Commander omitted, Capt Nathan Farmer, Mtd Riflemen

HENDERSON, Robert, Pvt, Col Alex Loury, Capt James Kincaid, Inf; transferred to Capt Henderson

HENDERSON, Robert, Pvt, Col John Brown, Capt Wm Christian, E TN Mil, Inf

HENDERSON, Robert, Pvt, Col Thomas Benton, Capt Isaiah Renshaw, Vol Inf

HENDERSON, Robert, Sgt, Regt Commander omitted, Capt Nathan Farmer, Mtd Riflemen

HENDERSON, Sherwood, Pvt, Col Wm Metcalf, Capt John Cunningham, Mil Inf

HENDERSON, Thomas, 2 Cpl, Col Wm Lillard, Capt John Raper, E TN Vol Inf

HENDERSON, Thomas, Pvt, Col Alex Loury, Capt Geo Sarver, Inf

HENDERSON, Thomas, Pvt, Col James Raulston, Capt Mathew Cowan, Inf

HENDERSON, Thomas, Pvt, Col Sam Wear, Capt John Stephens, E TN Vol Inf

HENDERSON, Thomas, Pvt, Col William Hall, Capt Abraham Bledsoe, Vol Inf

HENDERSON, Thomas, Pvt, Col Wm Johnson, Capt David McKemey, E TN Mil

HENDERSON, Tobias, Cpl, Col Thos Williamson, Capt Beverly Williams, Vol Mtd Gunmen

HENDERSON, Tobias, Pvt, Col Newton Cannon, Capt John Harpole, Mtd Gunmen

HENDERSON, Will T, 2 Sgt's Mate, Col John Coffee, TN Vol Cav

HENDERSON, William, Pvt, Col A Loury, Capt John Looney, W TN Inf

HENDERSON, William, Pvt, Col Robert Steele, Capt James Bennett, Mil Inf

HENDERSON, William, Pvt, Col Samuel Bayless, Capt Jas Churchman, E TN Mil

HENDERSON, William, Pvt, Col Samuel Wear, Capt Wm Mitchell, E TN Mtd Inf

HENDERSON, William, Pvt, Col Thos McCrory, Capt Sam McKnight, Inf

HENDERSON, William, Pvt, Col Wm Johnson, Capt Jas Tunnell, E TN Mil; d 10-13-1814

HENDERSON, William, Pvt, Col Wm Lillard, Capt Wm Hamilton, E TN Vol Inf

HENDERSON, William, Pvt, Col Wm Russell, Capt Geo Mitchie, Vol Mtd Gunmen

HENDERSON, _____, Pvt, Col Newton Cannon, Capt Cantrell, W TN Mtd Inf; transferred to Capt Evans Co

HENDMAN, James, 1 Sgt, Maj Gen A Jackson, Capt Joel Parrish, Branch Srvce omitted

HENDON, Aaron, Pvt, Gen A Jackson, Capt Wm Carroll, Vol Inf

HENDON, Berry, Pvt, Col John Barton, Capt Hugh Barton, E TN Mil Inf

HENDON, Berry, Pvt, Col Samuel Bunch, Capt A Breden, E TN Mil; transferred to Capt Bacon's Co

HENDON, James, Pvt, Col L Hammonds, Capt James Craig, Inf

HENDON, Plijah?, Pvt, Col John Brown, Capt Lunsford Oliver, E TN Mil

HENDON, William, Pvt, no other information

HENDRICK, Campion, Pvt, Col John Alcorn, Capt Wm Locke, Cav

HENDRICK, Thomas, Pvt, Lt Col Richard Napier, Co Commander omitted, Inf

HENDRICK, Tobias, Pvt, Col Wm Johnson, Capt Joseph Scott, E TN Drafted Mil; substitute for Ben Kelley

HENDRICKSON, Jonathan, Cpl, Col Wm Higgins, Capt Adam Dale, Mtd Gunmen

HENDRIX, Abner, Pvt, Col R C Napier, Capt Andrew McCarty, Mil Inf

HENDRIX, Andrew, Pvt, Regt Commander omitted, Capt Gray, Inf

HENDRIX, Isaac, Pvt, Col Wm Metcalf, Capt Wm Sitton, Mil Inf

HENDRIX, James L, Pvt, Col T McCrory, Capt Thomas Gordon, Inf

HENDRIX, Jeremiah, Pvt, Col Newt Cannon, Capt Geo Brandon, Mtd Riflemen

HENDRIX, Jesse, Pvt, Col Gen Thos Johnston, Capt Dan Oban, 36th Inf

HENDRIX, John, Pvt, Col R C Napier, Capt Andrew McCarty, Mil Inf; service as Gun Smith

HENDRIX, John, Pvt, Col Wm Metcalf, Capt Bird Hurt, Mil Inf

HENDRIX, Tarlton, Pvt, Maj John Childs, Capt Chas Conway, E TN Mtd Gunmen; Regimental Co - Knox

HENDRIX, Thomas, Pvt, Col William Johnson, Capt Joseph Hunter, E TN Mil; substitute for Benjamin C Kelly

HENDRIX, Tobias, Pvt, Col William Johnston, Capt Henry Hunter, E TN Mil

HENERY (HENRY), John, Pvt, Col Jno Brown, Capt Jas Preston, E TN Mil Inf

HENLEY, Robert, Pvt, Col A Cheatham, Capt William Smith, Inf

HENLEY, Williams, Pvt, Col Robert Dyer, Capt Jas McMahon, TN Vol Mtd Gunmen

HENLY, Isaac, 2 Cpl, Maj Gen Andrew Jackson, Capt John Crane, Mtd Gunmen

HENLY, William, Pvt, Col Alexander Loury, Capt Gabriel Martin, Inf

HENLY (HANLY), Thomas, Pvt, Col William Johnson, Capt Andrew Lawson, E TN Drafted Mil

HENRY, Alexander, Pvt, Col Wm Metcalf, Capt William Mullen, Mil Inf

HENRY, Benjamin, 3 Cpl, Col Wm Lillard, Capt John Roper, E TN Vol Inf

HENRY, David, Pvt, Col S Bayless, Capt Jas Churchman, E TN Mil

HENRY, Eli, Pvt, Col William Johnson, Capt Andrew Lawson, E TN Drafted Mil

HENRY, Hugh, 3 Sgt, Maj John Childs, Capt John Stephens, E TN Vol Mtd Inf

HENRY, Hugh, Pvt, Col Robert Dyer, Capt Allen, Vol Mtd Gunmen

## Enlisted Men, War of 1812

HENRY, Hugh, Pvt, Col S Bunch, Capt Jno Houk, E TN Mil
HENRY, Hugh, Pvt, Col Wm Lillard, Capt John Roper, E TN Vol Inf
HENRY, Isaac, Pvt, Col A Cheatham, Capt James Gidden, Inf; transferred to the Arty
HENRY, Isaac, Pvt, Maj Gen Andrew Jackson, Capt Joel Parrish, Arty
HENRY, James L, 3 Sgt, Col William Metcalf, Capt Thomas Marks, Mil Inf
HENRY, James, Pvt, Col Samuel Wear, Capt James Gillespie, E TN Vol Inf
HENRY, John E, Pvt, Col James Raulston, Capt James Black, Inf; d 12-28-1814, a substitute for Benjamin Davidson
HENRY, John, 3 Cpl, Maj John Childs, Capt John Stephens, E TN Vol Mtd Inf
HENRY, John, Ffr, Col Ewen Allison, Capt Allen, E TN Mil
HENRY, John, Pvt, Col Edwin Booth, Capt Samuel Thompson, Mil
HENRY, John, Pvt, Col John Brown, Capt John Trimble, E TN Mtd Gunmen
HENRY, John, Pvt, Maj William Russell, Capt Fleman Hodges, Vol Mtd Gunmen
HENRY, Moess, Sgt, Col John Alcorn, Capt John Baskerville, Vol Inf; promoted to QM Sgt in Col Alcorn's Co
HENRY, Moses, Sgt, Col John Coffee, Capt John Baskerville, Cav
HENRY, Peter, Pvt, Col William Lillard, Capt William Gillenwater, E TN Inf
HENRY, Reuben, Pvt, Col Ewen Allison, Capt Allen, E TN Mil
HENRY, Robert, Pvt, Col Edwin Booth, Capt John Porter, Drafted Mil
HENRY, Samuel, Pvt, Col John E Wynne, Capt John Spinks, Inf
HENRY, Samuel, Pvt, Col Wm Metcalf, Capt Barbee Collins, Mil Inf
HENRY, Samuel, Pvt, Maj John Childs, Capt John Stephens, E TN Vol Mtd Inf
HENRY, Samuel, Sgt, Col Samuel Wear, Capt James Gillespie, E TN Vol Inf
HENRY, Spencer, Cpl, Col Ewen Allison, Capt Henry McCray, E TN Mil; transferred to Capt Register Co
HENRY, Spencer, Cpl, Col Samuel Bunch, Capt Francis Register, E TN Mil; joined from Capt McCrea's Co
HENRY, Spencer, Pvt, Col Jno Williams, Capt Sam Bunch, Mtd Vol
HENRY, Thomas, Pvt, Col Samuel Bunch, Capt Branch Jones, E TN Drafted Mil
HENRY, Thomas, Pvt, Regt Commander omitted, Capt David Smith, Cav Vol
HENRY, Vincent (Vinet), Pvt, Col James Raulston, Capt Daniel Newman, Inf
HENRY, William H, Pvt, Maj Wm Carroll, Capt Lewis Dillahunty & Capt Daniel M Bradford, Vol Inf
HENRY, William S, Pvt, Col R H Dyer, Capt Ephraim D Dickson, TN Mtd Vol Gunmen
HENSLEY, Temple, 4 Sgt, Col Ewen Allison, Capt Joseph Everett, E TN Mil; transferred to Capt Griffin at Ft Williams
HENSON, Edward, Pvt, Col Wm Johnson, Capt James Tunnell, 3rd Regt E TN Mil
HENSON, Jesse, Pvt, Col William Pillow, Capt James McFerrin, Inf
HENSON, John, Cpl, Maj Wm Woodfolk, Capt Abraham Dudney, Inf; promoted from Pvt
HENSON, John, Pvt, Col John K Wynne, Capt James Holleman, Inf; deserted 11-10-1813
HENSON, John, Pvt, Maj Wm Woodfolk, Capt Abraham Dudney, Inf
HENSON, Josiah, Pvt, Col Edward Bradley, Capt Abraham Bledsoe, Riflemen
HENSON, Josiah, Pvt, Col Wm Hall, Capt Abraham Bledsoe, Vol Inf
HENSON, Phillip, Pvt, Col William Metcalf, Capt William Mullin, Mil Inf
HENSON, Solomon, Pvt, Col Alexander Loury, Capt George Sarver, Inf
HENSON, Solomon, Pvt, Maj John Childs, Capt John Stephens, E TN Vol Mtd Inf
HENSON, Thomas, Pvt, no other information
HERALD, John, Pvt, Col William Lillard, Capt George Argenbright, E TN Vol Riflemen
HERALD, Raby, 3 Cpl, Col Edward Bradley, Capt John Wallace, Vol Inf
HERALD, Willis, Pvt, Col William Lillard, Capt George Argenbright, E TN Vol Riflemen
HERD, Charles, Pvt, Col A Cheatham, Capt William Smith, Inf
HERD, John, 3 Cpl, Col John Brown, Capt Jesse Reany, Mtd Gunmen
HERD, John, Cpl, Col John Brown, Capt William Christian, E TN Mil Inf
HERD, Reuben, Pvt, Regt Commander omitted, Capt Samuel Allen, Pack Horse Guards
HERD, Thomas, Pvt, Col Robert Steele, Capt Robert Campbell, Mil Inf
HERD, Thomas, Sgt, Col William Johnson, Capt Joseph Scott, E TN Mil; d 10-24-1814
HERICHARD, S, Drm Maj, Col Wm Hall, Co Commander omitted, Inf
HERIDON, William, Pvt, Col Edward Bradley, Capt William Lauderdale, Vol Inf
HERL, Tatlton?, Pvt, Col Samuel Bunch, Capt Joseph Duncan, E TN Drafted Mil
HERLEY, James, Sgt, Col Thomas McCrory, Capt Anthony Metcalf, Inf; promoted to QM Sgt
HERN, George, Pvt, Col Edward Bradley, Capt John Kennedy, Riflemen; AWOL 12-12-1813
HERN, George, Pvt, Regt Commander omitted, Capt Ephraim Dickson, Branch Srvce omitted
HERN, Henry, Pvt, Col John Brown, Capt John Childs, E TN Vol Mtd Inf
HERNDON, William, Pvt, Lt James Berry, Co Commander omitted, Mtd Riflemen
HERNES, James, Pvt, Maj William Russell, Capt Isaac Williams, Sep Bn of TN Vol Mtd Gunmen

## Enlisted Men, War of 1812

HEROD, Alexander, Cpl, Col John Coffee, Capt Daniel Ross, Mtd Gunmen; promoted from Pvt

HEROD, James, Pvt, Lt Col Leroy Hammonds, Capt James Tubb, Inf

HEROD, John, Pvt, no other information

HEROD, Josiah, Pvt, Maj William Russell, Capt Fleman Hodges, Vol Mtd Gunmen; substitute for Solomon Malone

HEROD, Peter, Pvt, Col Thomas Williamson, Capt Anthony Metcalf, Vol Mtd Gunmen

HEROD, Peter, Sgt, Col Newton Cannon, Capt James Walton, Mtd Riflemen

HEROD, Peter, Tptr, Col Thomas Williamson, Capt Anthony Metcalf, Vol Mtd Gunmen; promoted from a Pvt

HERRALD, Cader, Pvt, Maj Robert Cooper, Co Commander omitted, Mtd Riflemen 26th TN Regt

HERRALD, Raby, 3 Cpl, Col William Hall, Capt John Wallace, Inf

HERRALDSON, Vincent, Pvt, Col Newton Cannon, Capt George Bradon, Mtd Riflemen

HERRALL, James J, Pvt, Col S Copeland, Capt Richard Sharp, Mil Inf

HERREL, Eli, Sgt, Maj William Woodfolk, Capt Ezekial Ross, Inf

HERRELL, Asa, Pvt, Col Thomas McCrory, Capt Anthony Metcalf, Mil Inf

HERREN, John, Pvt, Col Samuel Wear, Capt John Childs, E TN Vol Inf

HERREN, Lemuel, Pvt, Col Robert Dyer, Maj Wm Russell, Capt William Russell, Vol Mtd Gunmen

HERRFORD, Paul, 5 Sgt, Col William Metcalf, Capt Barbee Collins, Mil Inf

HERRIFORD, John, Pvt, Col William Metcalf, Capt Barbee Collins, Mil Inf

HERRIN, Andrew, Pvt, no other information

HERRIN, Andrew, Sgt, Regt Commander omitted, Capt Archibald McKenney, Cav

HERRIN, David, Cpl, Col John Cocke, Capt Samuel Caruthers, Inf

HERRIN, James, Pvt, Col Thomas McCrory, Co Commander omitted, Mil Inf; transferred to Capt Shannon's Co

HERRING, Alexander, Pvt, Col William Hall, Co Commander omitted, Vol Inf

HERRING, Bright, Pvt, Col Philip Pipkin, Capt John Strother, Mil; deserted 9-20-1814

HERRING, Henry, Pvt, Col A Cheatham, Capt George Chapman, Inf

HERRING, Henry, Pvt, Col William Hall, Capt John Moore, Vol Inf

HERRING, John, Pvt, Col Philip Pipkin, Capt Peter Searcy, Mil Inf

HERRING, Solomon, Cpl, Col Robert Dyer, Capt James McMahon, 1st TN Mtd Vol Gunmen; appointed Sgt

HERRING, Stephen, Pvt, Col John K Wynn, Capt James Holleman, Inf

HERRING, William P(S?), Sgt, Col Alexander Loury, Capt Gabriel Martin, Inf; appointed in place of Chas H Pickering

HERRINGSDON, John L, Pvt, Col Phillip Pipkin, Capt Geo Mebane, Branch Srvce omitted

HERRINGTON, Charles, Pvt, Col John K Wynn, Capt Wm Carruthers, W TN Inf; transferred to Wgnr

HERRINGTON, William, Pvt, Col Wm Pillow, Capt Joseph Mason, Vol Inf

HERROD, Thomas, Pvt, Col John Cocke, Capt Nance, Inf

HERRON, Abemelic, Pvt, Col Wm Metcalf, Capt John Barnhart, Mil Inf

HERRON, Abner, Pvt, Col S Copeland, Capt John Anderson, Vol Inf

HERRON, James, Pvt, Col T McCrory, Capt Jas Shannon, Mil Inf

HERRON, Peyton, Pvt, Col T McCrory, Capt Jas Shannon, Mil Inf

HERRON, William, Pvt, Col S Copeland, Capt Richard Sharp, Mil Inf

HERTON, Joe, Pvt, Maj Gen Andrew Jackson, Capt Joel Parrish, Arty

HESHION, John, Pvt, Col Thomas Williamson, Capt Anthony Metcalf, Mtd Vol Gunmen

HESLEP, David D, Pvt, Col R H Dyer, Maj William Russell, Capt William Russell, Vol Mtd Gunmen

HESLEP, William, Pvt, Col R H Dyer, Maj Wm Russell, Vol Mtd Gunmen

HESLIP, Thomas, Pvt, Col John Alcorn, Capt John Winston, Mtd Riflemen

HESNER, Jacob, Pvt, Col Thos Benton, Capt Geo Gibbs, Vol Inf

HESSON, Andrew, Pvt, Col Jas Raulston, Capt Elijah Haynie, Inf

HESSON, Andrew, Pvt, Col William Hall, Capt Henry Newlin, Inf

HESTER, Abraham, Pvt, Col R Napier, Capt Samuel Ashmore, Mil Inf

HESTER, James, Pvt, Maj Wm Woodfolk, Capt Dudney & Capt John Sutton, Inf; deserted

HESTER, Jesse, Pvt, Col William Johnson, Capt William Alexander, E TN Drafted Mil

HESTER, Samuel, Pvt, Col William Metcalf, Capt Andrew Patterson, Mil Inf

HESTER, William, Pvt, Col Ewin Allison, Capt Joseph Everett, E TN Mil

HETHER, Thomas, Pvt, Col William Johnson, Capt Benj Powell, E TN Mil

HEWELL, William, Pvt, Brig Gen William Johnson, Capt Allen, Mil Inf

HEWETT, Benjamin, Pvt, Regt Commander omitted, Capt Wm Mitchell, Spies

HEWETT, George, Pvt, Col R H Dyer, Capt James Wyatt, Vol Mtd Gunmen

HEWETT, Hayal, Sgt, Col N T Perkins, Capt Phillip Pipkin, Mtd Gunmen

HEWITT, Benjamin, Pvt, Col N Cannon, Capt John Demsey, Mtd Gunmen

HEWS, Daniel, Pvt, Col Phillip Pipkin, Capt Henry Newlin, Mil Inf

HEWS, Ennis, Pvt, Col S Copeland, Capt Tait, Inf

HEWSTON, James, Pvt, Maj Gen Andrew Jackson, Capt Hugh Kerr, Mtd Rangers

HEY, Jeremiah, Sgt, Regt Commander omitted, Capt

-251

## Enlisted Men, War of 1812

Ephraim Dickson, Branch Srvce omitted
HIBBET, David C, Pvt, Col William Hall, Capt Brice Martin, Vol Inf
HIBBIT, David C, Pvt, Col Edward Bradley, Capt Brice Martin, Vol Inf
HIBBS, Jeremiah, Pvt, Col John Brown, Capt Allen Bacon, E TN Mil Inf
HIBBS, John, Cpl, Col John Brown, Capt Hugh Barton, E TN Mil Inf
HIBBS, John, Pvt, Col Alexander Loury, Capt John Looney, W TN Inf
HIBBS, William, Pvt, Col John Brown, Capt Hugh Barton, E TN Mil Inf
HICH, Henry, Pvt, Regt Commander omitted, Capt Sam Cowan, Cav; also served under Maj James Porter
HICKERSON, Charles, Pvt, Maj Gen Andrew Jackson, Capt William Carroll, Vol Inf
HICKERSON, David, Pvt, Col John Coffee, Capt John Baskerville, Cav
HICKERSON, Isaac, Cpl, Regt Commander omitted, Capt Robert Evans, Mtd Spies
HICKERSON, Isaac, Pvt, Col John Alcorn, Capt John Byrn, Cav; transferred to Capt Evan's Co of Spies
HICKERSON, John, Cpl, Regt Commander omitted, Capt Robert Evans, Mtd Spies
HICKERSON, John, Pvt, Col John Alcorn, Capt John Byrn, Cav; transferred to Capt Evan's Co of Spies
HICKERSON, Samuel D, Pvt, Col William Hall, Capt William Alexander, Vol Inf
HICKERSON, Samuel, Pvt, Col Edward Bradley, Capt William Lauderdale, Vol Inf
HICKERSON, William L, Pvt, Col John Alcorn, Capt John Byras, Cav; transferred to Capt Evan's Co of Spies
HICKERSON, William, 3 Cpl, Col William Higgins, Capt Samuel Allen, Vol Mtd Gunmen
HICKERSON, William, Pvt, Col James Raulston, Capt Mathew Neal, Inf
HICKERSON, William, Sgt, Regt Commander omitted, Capt Robert Evans, Mtd Spies; transferred to the 60 Day Men
HICKEY, James, Pvt, Col Samuel Bunch, Capt Andrew Breden, E TN Mil; transferred to Capt J Berry's Co
HICKEY, John, Pvt, Col John Brown, Capt William White, E TN Mil Inf
HICKEY, John, Pvt, Col S Bunch, Capt A Breden, E TN Mil; transferred to Capt J Berry's Co
HICKEY, Joseph, Pvt, Col Wm Johnson, Capt Jas Stewart, E TN Mil
HICKEY, Michael, Pvt, Col T McCrory, Capt Abel Willis, Mil Inf
HICKMAN, Caleb, Pvt, Col Samuel Wear, Capt Saml Bowman, Mtd Inf
HICKMAN, Edward, Pvt, Gen A Jackson, Capt D Deaderick, Arty
HICKMAN, Edwin, Pvt, Regt Commander omitted, Capt David Mason, Cav; appointed to Navy
HICKMAN, Elias, Pvt, Maj John Childs, Capt Daniel Price, Vol Mtd Gunmen
HICKMAN, Frederick, Pvt, Col Samuel Wear, Capt Samuel Bowman, Mtd Inf
HICKMAN, George, Pvt, Col S Bunch, Capt F Register, E TN Mil
HICKMAN, George, Pvt, Col S Bunch, Capt Geo McPherson, E TN Mil
HICKMAN, Isaac, Pvt, no other information
HICKMAN, John, Pvt, Col John Brown, Capt Jas Standifer, E TN Vol Mtd Mil
HICKMAN, John, Pvt, Col Philip Pipkin, Capt Geo Mebane, Mil Inf
HICKMAN, John, Pvt, Col S Copeland, Capt Alex Provine, Mil Inf
HICKMAN, Lemuel, Pvt, Col John K Wynne, Capt John Spinks, Inf
HICKMAN, Nathaniel, Pvt, Col A Cheatham, Capt Chas Johnson, Inf
HICKMAN, Olias, Pvt, Maj John Childs, Capt Daniel Price, E TN Vol Mtd Inf
HICKMAN, Pleasant, Pvt, Col John Cocke, Capt S M Caruthers, Inf
HICKMAN, Thomas, Pvt, Col Samuel Wear, Capt Samuel Bowman, Mtd Inf
HICKMAN, Thomas, Pvt, Col William Johnson, Capt Jas Stewart, E TN Mil; substitute
HICKMAN, William, Pvt, Col Edwin Booth, Capt John Sharp, E TN Mil
HICKMAN, William, Pvt, Col John Coffee, Capt Chas Kavanaugh, Cav
HICKMAN, William, Pvt, Col S Bunch, Capt Isaac Williams, E TN Mil
HICKMAN, William, Pvt, Col Wm Johnson, Capt David McKamy, E TN Drafted Mil; substitute for John Brandon
HICKMAN, William, Pvt, Regt Commander omitted, Capt David Mason, Cav
HICKMAN, Windson, Pvt, Col Samuel Wear, Capt Rufus Morgan, E TN Vol Inf
HICKS, Benjamin, Pvt, Col Robert Steele, Capt Sam Maxwell, Mil Inf
HICKS, James, Pvt, Col Samuel Bunch, Capt Andrew Breden, E TN Mil
HICKS, James, Pvt, Col Wm Lillard, Capt Geo Argenbright, E TN Vol Riflemen
HICKS, James, Pvt, Regt Commander omitted, Capt Jas Craig, Inf
HICKS, John C, Pvt, Maj Gen Jackson, Capt Wm Carroll, Vol Inf
HICKS, John C, Pvt, Maj William Russell, Capt Isaac Williams, Separate Bn of TN Vol Mtd Gunmen
HICKS, John, Pvt, Col Edwin E Booth, Capt Alex Biggs, Inf
HICKS, John, Pvt, Col Wm Metcalf, Capt Bird L Hurt, Mil Inf
HICKS, John, Pvt, Maj Gen Carroll, Capt Francis Ellis, Inf
HICKS, Joseph D, Pvt, Col Ewin Allison, Capt Joseph Everett, E TN Mil
HICKS, Joseph, Pvt, Col Samuel Bayless, Capt Joe Hale, E TN Mil; d 2-21-1815 in service
HICKS, Martin, Pvt, Col Edwin Booth, Capt Saml Thompson, Mil
HICKS, Martin, Pvt, Col S Bunch, Capt Jno Houk, E TN

252 -

## Enlisted Men, War of 1812

Mil; joined from Capt Duncan's Co

HICKS, Martin, Pvt, Col S Bunch, Capt Jos Duncan, E TN Drafted Mil; transferred to Capt Houk's Co

HICKS, Martin, Pvt, Col Samuel Bayless, Capt James Landen, E TN Mil; d 2-18-1815

HICKS, Moses, Pvt, Col Samuel Bayless, Capt Francis John, E TN Mil Drafted

HICKS, Richard B, Pvt, Col R C Napier, Capt Thomas Gray, Mil Inf

HICKS, Seet, Pvt, Col John K Wynne, Capt Robert Breder, Inf

HICKS, Stephen, Pvt, Col John Brown, Capt Jesse G Reany, Mtd Gunmen

HICKS, Stephen, Pvt, Col Wm Johnson, Capt Joseph Scott, E TN Mil Drafted; substitute for Alexander Smith

HICKS, Stephen, Pvt, Col Wm Lillard, Capt Hugh Martin, E TN Vol Inf

HICKS, Thomas, Pvt, Col Wm Johnson, Capt Jas Tunnell, 3rd Regt E TN Mil

HICKS, Vines, Pvt, Col Wm Johnston, Capt Jas Tunnell, E TN Mil

HICKS, William, Pvt, Col Edwin Booth, Capt John Slatton, E TN Mil

HICKS, William, Pvt, Col William Lillard, Capt Benjamin King, E TN Vol Inf

HICKS, William, Pvt, Col Wm Hall, Capt John Kennedy, Vol Inf

HICKS, William, Pvt, Col Wm Lillard, Capt Hugh Martin, E TN Vol Inf

HICKS, William, Pvt, Col-Maj Woodfolk, Capt Jas Neil, Inf

HICKS, William, Pvt, Maj Woodfolk, Capt James Turner, Inf

HICKS, William, Sgt, Col John Bunch, Capt John Trimble, E TN Mtd Gunmen

HICKY, Isaac, Pvt, Col Wm Phillips, Capt Wm J Smith, Vol Inf; substitute for Thos Taylor

HICKY, John, Pvt, Col Sam Wear, Capt John Stephens, E TN Vol Inf

HIDE, Henry, Pvt, Col Sam Bunch, Capt Joe Duncan, E TN Drafted Mil; joined from Capt Yarnell's Co

HIDE, Hiram, Pvt, Col Edwin Booth, Capt John McKamey, E TN Mil

HIDEN, David, Pvt, Col Wm Lillard, Capt Hugh Martin, E TN Vol Inf

HIGDEN, Charles, Pvt, Col Edwin Booth, Capt Vernon, E TN Mil

HIGGANBOTHAM, Alex, Pvt, Col N T Perkins, Capt Mathew Patterson, Mtd Vol

HIGGANBOTHAM, Alex, Pvt, Lt Col Wm Phillips, Co Commander omitted, Inf

HIGGANBOTHAM, Caleb, Pvt, Col R H Dyer, Capt C Hudson, Vol Mtd Gunmen

HIGGANBOTHAM, Caleb, Sgt, Col R H Dyer, Capt Cuth Hudson, Mtd Gunmen

HIGGERSON, Samuel, Pvt, Col Wm Hall, Capt Wm Alexander, Branch Srvce omitted

HIGGINBOTHAM, Alex, Rank omitted, Regt Commander omitted, Capt Robt Evans, Spies; transferred to Capt Patterson Co

HIGGINBOTHAM, Alexander R, Pvt, Col John Cocke, Capt Sam Caruthers, Inf

HIGGINBOTHAM, Caleb, Pvt, Lt Col Wm Phillips, Co Commander omitted, Inf

HIGGINBOTHAM, Joseph, Pvt, Lt I Barrett, Capt Nathan Davis, Inf W TN Bn

HIGGINBOTHAM, Middleton, Pvt, Col R H Dyer, Capt Cuthbert Hudson, Vol Mtd Gunmen

HIGGINS, James, Pvt, Col - Gen Thomas Johnson, Capt Robert Carson, Inf

HIGGINS, John, Pvt, Col S Bunch, Capt Jones Griffin, E TN Drafted Mil

HIGGINS, Silas, Pvt, Col John Cocke, Capt James Gault, Inf

HIGGINS, Wesley, Cpl, Col Sam Copeland, Capt Moses Thompson, Inf

HIGGINS, William B, QM, Col Wm Higgins, 2nd Regt TN Mtd Vol

HIGGINS, William Y, Col, Commander omitted, 2nd Regt TN Vol Mtd Gunmen

HIGGINS, William, Pvt, Col Thos Williamson, Capt Geo Mitchie, 2nd Regt TN Vol Mtd Gunmen

HIGGINS, William, Pvt, Maj Wm Russell, Capt Geo Mitchie, Vol Mtd Gunmen

HIGGS, Isaac, Pvt, Col Edwin Booth, Capt John Sletton, E TN Mil

HIGGS, James, Sgt, Col N T Perkins, Capt Jas McMahon, Mtd Gunmen

HIGGS, William, Pvt, Regt Commander omitted, Capt Arch McKenney, Cav

HIGH, James M, Pvt, Regt Commander omitted, Lt John Scott, Det Inf

HIGH, John, Pvt, Col William Lillard, Capt Robert Maloney, E TN Inf Vol; unable to perform duty

HIGH, Richard, Pvt, Col Leroy Hammonds, Capt James Craig, Inf

HIGH, Robert, Pvt, Col Newt Cannon, Capt Jas Walton, Mtd Riflemen

HIGHSAN, Andrew, Pvt, Gen Carroll, Capt James Raulston & Capt Wiley Huddleston, Inf

HIGHSMITH, Daniel, Pvt, Lt Col Arch Cheathain, Capt Gabriel Manbin, Mtd Inf 6th Brig

HIGHSMITH, Elias, Pvt, Col Edward Bradley, Capt Abraham Bledsoe, Riflemen

HIGHT, John, Pvt, Col Williamson, Capt Hill, Lt Neely, Vol Mtd Gunmen

HIGHT, Robert, Pvt, Col Thomas Johnson, Capt Robert Carson, Inf

HIGHT, Robert, Pvt, Col Thos Williamson, Capt Jas Pace, Lt Neely, Vol Mtd Gunmen

HIGHT, Robert, Pvt, Regt Commander omitted, Capt Jas Terrell, Cav

HIGHT, Robert, Tptr, Col John Coffee, Capt James Terell, Vol Cav

HIGHTON, Richard, Pvt, Col Ewen Allison, Capt Robert Allen, E TN Mil

HIGHTOWER, Abijah, Pvt, Col John Coffee, Capt David Smith, Vol Cav

HIGHTOWER, Epaphroditus, Pvt, Col S Bunch, Capt Thos Mann, E TN Vol Mtd Gunmen

HIGHTOWER, James, Pvt, Col R C Napier, Capt Edward

## Enlisted Men, War of 1812

Neblett, Mil Inf
HIGHTOWER, John, Pvt, Col Newt Cannon, Capt Martin, Mtd Gunmen; wounded 11-3-1813
HIGHTOWER, Stith, Pvt, Col Thos Williamson, Capt Robt Moore, Vol Mtd Gunmen
HIGHTOWER, William, Pvt, Col R C Napier, Capt Edward Neblett, Mil Inf
HIGLER, Isaac, Pvt, Col L Hammonds, Capt Jas Craig, Inf; d 2-7-1815 at Camp Maderville
HIGNIGHT, John, 4 Cpl, Col Edward Bradley, Capt Jas Hambleton, Vol Inf
HIGNIGHT, John, Pvt, Col Robert H Dyer, Capt Robert Edmondson, TN Vol Mtd Gunmen
HIGNIGHT, John, Pvt, Col Wm Hall, Capt Jas Hambleton, Vol Inf
HIGNIGHT, Joseph, Pvt, Lt Col Henry Bryan, Co Commander omitted, Inf
HIGNIGHT, Joseph, Pvt, Maj Gen Jackson, Capt Craine, Branch Srvce omitted
HIGNIGHT, Joseph, Pvt, Regt Commander omitted, Capt John Craig, Inf
HILBERTSON, Solomon, Pvt, Col Wm Metcalf, Capt Hill & Capt John Cunningham, Mil Inf
HILBURN, Levi, Pvt, Col Sam Bayless, Capt Branch Jones, E TN Drafted Mil
HILEMAN, Henry, Pvt, Col Newt Cannon, Capt James Walton, Mtd Riflemen; deserted 10-11-1813
HILL, Abel, Pvt, Col Sam Bayless, Capt Joe B Bacon, E TN Mil
HILL, Abraham, Pvt, Col Robert Dyer, Capt Ephraim Dickson, 1st TN Mtd Vol Gunmen; transferred to Capt Williams Co
HILL, Abraham, Pvt, Maj William Russell, Capt Isaac Williams, Sep Bn of TN Vol Mtd Gunmen; joined from Capt Dickson
HILL, Abraham, Pvt, Regt Commande
HILL, Abram, Pvt, Col William Higgins, Capt William Doake, Mtd Riflemen
HILL, Alexander, Pvt, Col Thomas McCrory, Capt William Dooley, Branch Srvce omitted
HILL, Alfred, Pvt, Col Thomas McCrory, Capt Abel Willis, Mil Inf
HILL, Anderson, Cpl, Col Samuel Wear, Capt John Childs, E TN Vol Inf
HILL, Asaph, Pvt, Col John Wynne, Capt James Holleman, Inf; deserted 11-13-1813
HILL, Benjamin, Cpl, Col Samuel Bunch, Capt Jones Griffin, E TN Drafted Mil
HILL, Benjamin, Pvt, Col Samuel Bunch, Capt James Cummings, E TN Vol Mtd Inf
HILL, Benjamin, Pvt, Maj John Childs, Capt James Cummings, E TN Vol Mtd Inf
HILL, Bowman, Cpl, Col Edwin Booth, Capt John Lewis, E TN Mil
HILL, Branham, Pvt, Maj John Childs, Capt James Cummings, E TN Vol Mtd Inf
HILL, Cage, Pvt, Col Thomas Williamson, Capt Thomas Scurry, Vol Mtd Gunmen
HILL, Daniel H, Pvt, Col Thomas Benton, Capt Robert Moore, Vol Inf
HILL, Edward, Pvt, Col Thomas Metcalf, Capt William Mullin, Mil Inf
HILL, Edward, Pvt, Col William Metcalf, Capt Thomas Marks, Mil Inf
HILL, George, Pvt, Col John Brown, Capt Allen Bacon, E TN Mil Inf; deserted 10-16-1813
HILL, George, Pvt, Col John Cocke, Capt Richard Crunk, Inf
HILL, George, Pvt, Col Samuel Wear, Capt Simeon Perry, E TN Vol Mtd Inf
HILL, Gurham, Pvt, Col Philip Pipkin, Capt William Mackay, Mil Inf
HILL, Henry, Pvt, Col Edwin Booth, Capt John Sharpe, TN Mil
HILL, Isaac, 2 Sgt, Col William Metcalf, Capt Alexander Hill & Capt John Cunningham, Mil Inf; promoted to Ens
HILL, Isaac, Cpl, Regt Commander omitted, Capt James Cowan, Mtd Inf
HILL, Isaac, Pvt, Col John Coffee, Capt Michael Molton, Cav
HILL, Jacob, 4 Sgt, Lt Col Leroy Hammonds & Lt Col Alexander Loury, Capt Thomas Wells, Inf
HILL, James sr, Pvt, Maj William Russell, Capt William Chism, Vol Mtd Gunmen; died 1-12-1815
HILL, James, Pvt, Col John Alcorn, Capt Alexander McEwen, Cav
HILL, James, Pvt, Col John Coffee, Capt Alexander McKean, Cav
HILL, James, Pvt, Col Robert Dyer, Capt Thomas Jones, Vol Mtd Gunmen
HILL, James, Pvt, Col Samuel Bayless, Capt Allen Bacon, E TN Mil
HILL, James, Pvt, Col Thomas Williamson, Capt Giles Burdett, Vol Mtd Gunmen
HILL, James, Pvt, Col Thomas Williamson, Capt James Pace, Lt Neely, Vol Mtd Gunmen
HILL, James, Pvt, Col William Johnson, Capt Andrew Lawson, E TN Drafted Mil
HILL, James, Pvt, Maj William Russell, Capt William Chism, Vol Mtd Riflemen
HILL, James, Pvt, Regt Commander omitted, Capt Nathan Farmer, Mtd Riflemen
HILL, Jesse, Pvt, Col William Lillard, Capt John Neatherton, E TN Vol Inf
HILL, John H, 5 Cpl, Col John Cocke, Capt Bird Nance, Inf; died 1-14-1815
HILL, John P, Pvt, Col John Cocke, Capt John Dalton, Inf
HILL, John P, Pvt, Col Robert Steele, Capt James Shenault, Mil Inf
HILL, John, Cpl, Col A Cheatham, Capt George Chapman, Inf
HILL, John, Cpl, Col Thomas Williams, Capt Richard Tate, Vol Mtd Gunmen
HILL, John, Pvt, Col Jno Coffee, Capt A McKeen, Cav
HILL, John, Pvt, Col John Alcorn, Capt Robert Jetton, Vol Cav
HILL, John, Pvt, Col John Coffee, Capt Robert Jetton, Cav
HILL, John, Pvt, Col Philip Pipkin, Capt William Mackey, Mil Inf
HILL, John, Pvt, Col S Copeland, Capt David Williams, Mil Inf

## Enlisted Men, War of 1812

HILL, John, Pvt, Col Samuel Bayless, Capt Allen Bacon, E TN Mil

HILL, John, Pvt, Col Thomas McCrory, Capt John Reynolds, Mil Inf

HILL, John, Pvt, Col Thomas Williamson, Capt William Martin, Vol Mtd Gunmen

HILL, John, Pvt, Col WIlliam Johnson, Capt Christopher Cook, E TN Mil

HILL, John, Pvt, Col William Johnson, Capt James Rogers, E TN Draft Mil

HILL, John, Pvt, Col William Johnson, Capt Joseph Kirk, Mil Inf

HILL, John, Pvt, Col Wm Metcalf, Capt John Jackson, Maj Gen Wm Carroll, Inf

HILL, John, Pvt, Maj John Childs, Capt Reuben Tipton, E TN Vol Mtd Inf; Regt from Jefferson Co

HILL, John, Pvt, Maj William Russell, Capt Isaac Williams, Separate Bn TN Vol Mtd Gunmen; joined by trans fr Dickson

HILL, John, Pvt, Regt Commander omitted, Capt Edwin S Moore, Mtd Riflemen

HILL, John, Sgt Maj, Maj Thomas Williamson, no Co Commander; branch omitted

HILL, John, Tptr, Col Thomas Williamson, Capt James Pace, Vol Mtd Gunmen

HILL, Johnson, Pvt, Col R H Dyer, Maj Wm Russell, Capt Wm Russell, Vol Mtd Gunmen

HILL, Jonathan, Cpl, Col Samuel Bunch, Capt Isaac Williams, E TN Mil

HILL, Joseph, 6 Cpl, Col William Metcalf, Capt Andrew Patterson, Mil Inf

HILL, Joseph, Pvt, Col Philip Pipkin, Capt William Mackey, Mil Inf

HILL, Joseph, Pvt, Col Thomas Williamson, Capt James Pace, Lt Neely, Vol Mtd Gunmen

HILL, Josiah, Cpl, Col Thomas McCrary, Capt Abel Williams, Mil Inf

HILL, Luke, Pvt, Col A Cheatham, Maj Gen A Jackson, Capt William Creel, Inf

HILL, Mark, Pvt, Col John Cocke, Capt James Gault, Inf

HILL, Marvel, Pvt, Col Thomas Benton, Capt William Moore, Vol Inf

HILL, Reuben, Pvt, Col T Williamson, Capt John Hill, Lt Neely, Vol Mtd Gunmen; dismissed day mustered

HILL, Richard, Pvt, Col Philip Pipkin, Capt Henry M Newlin, Mil Inf

HILL, Richard, Pvt, Col T Williamson, Capt John Doak & Capt John Dobbins, Vol Mtd Gunmen

HILL, Robert, Pvt, Col William Johnson, Capt David McKamy, E TN Mil

HILL, Robert, Pvt, Col William Lillard, Capt William McLin, E TN Inf

HILL, Robert, Pvt, Regt Commander omitted, Capt Wm Henderson, Spies

HILL, Samuel, Pvt, Col Edwin Booth, Capt Samuel Thompson, Mil

HILL, Spencer, Pvt, Col Samuel Bunch, Capt S Roberson, E TN Draft Mil; died 2-20-1814

HILL, Spencer, Pvt, Regt Commander omitted, Capt Saml Richardson, E TN Draft Mil; died 9-24-1814

HILL, Spencer, Pvt, Regt commander omitted, Capt Saml Richardson, E TN Draft Mil; died 2-24-1814

HILL, Thomas, Pvt, Col John Alcorn, Capt Thomas Bradley, Vol Cav

HILL, Thomas, Pvt, Col William Johnson, Capt Christopher Cook, 3 Reg E TN Mil; trans to Capt Henry Hunter Co

HILL, Thomas, Pvt, Col William Johnson, Capt Henry Hunter, E TN Mil; trans from Capt Kirk's Co

HILL, Thomas, Pvt, Col William Johnson, Capt Joseph Kirk, Mil

HILL, Thomas, Pvt, Col Wm Metcalf, Capt Andrew Patterson, Mil Inf

HILL, Whitmel, Pvt, Col Philip Pipkin, Capt James Blakemore, Vol Inf; trans from Capt H M Newlin

HILL, William K, Pvt, Col Alexander Loury, Capt John Looney, W TN Inf

HILL, William, 4 Cpl, Col Jno Coffee, Capt Robert Jetton, Cav

HILL, William, Cpl, Col A Cheatham, Capt George G Chapman, Inf

HILL, William, Cpl, Col John Alcorn, Capt Robert Jetton, Vol Cav

HILL, William, Maj Wm Woodfolk, Capt James C Neil, Inf

HILL, William, Pvt, Brig Gen T Johnson, Capt Robert Carson, Inf

HILL, William, Pvt, Brig Gen Thos Washington, Capt Jno Crawford, Mtd Inf

HILL, William, Pvt, Col Edwin Booth, Capt Richard Marshall, Drafted Mil

HILL, William, Pvt, Col John Brown, Capt Charles Lewin, E TN Mtd Inf

HILL, William, Pvt, Col T Williamson, Capt James Pace, Lt Neely, Vol Mtd Gunmen; died 2-1-1815

HILL, William, Pvt, Col Wm Johnson, Capt James R Rogers, E TN Draft Mil

HILL, William, Pvt, Col Wm Lillard, Capt Wm Gillenwater, E TN Inf

HILL, William, Sgt, Col Wm Johnson, Capt Henry Hunter, E TN Mil

HILLARD, John, Pvt, Col Philip Pipkin, Capt John Robertson, Mil Inf

HILLARD, Micajah, Pvt, Col Robert Steele, Capt James Shenault, Mil Inf

HILLEMS, Thomas, Pvt, Col T McCrory, Capt Thomas K Gordon, Inf; deserted

HILLEN, James, Pvt, Col R H Dyer, Capt Glen Owen, TN Vol Mtd Gunmen

HILLIS, John, Pvt, Col A Loury, Capt John Looney, W TN Inf

HILLIS, Samuel, Pvt, Col A Loury, Capt John Looney, W TN Inf

HILLIS, Samuel, Pvt, Col N T Perkins, Capt John Doak, Vol Mtd Gunmen

HILLIS, Samuel, Pvt, Col Samuel Bayless, Capt James Churchman, E TN Mil; trans to McKamey

HILLIS (HILTS), David, Pvt, Col Wm Johnson, Capt Christopher Cook, E TN Mil

HILTON, John, Pvt, no Regt Commander, Capt Geo Smith, Spies

HILTON, Marvel, Pvt, Col Samuel Bunch, Capt Jones

## Enlisted Men, War of 1812

Griffin, E TN Draft Mil
HILTON, William, Pvt, Col R H Dyer, Capt Bethel Allen, Vol Mtd Gunmen
HILTON, William, Pvt, Col S Copeland, Capt Richard Sharp, Mil Inf
HILTON, William, Pvt, Maj Wm Woodfolk, Capt John Sutten & Capt Abraham Dudney, Inf; det as waggoner
HINDON, Elijah, Pvt, Col Edwin Booth, Capt Richard Marshall, Drafted Mil
HINDS, Asa, Pvt, Col Samuel Wear, Capt John Bayless, Mtd Inf
HINES, Isaac, Cpl, Col Maj John Childs, Capt Chas Conway, E TN Mtd Gunmen; trans to Capt Tipton
HINES, Isaac, Pvt, Col Sam Wear, Capt Sam Bowman, Mtd Inf
HINES, James, Pvt, Col Maj John Childs, Capt Reuben Tipton, E TN Vol Mtd Inf; Regt from Knox Co
HINES, John, Pvt, Col Lt L Hammonds, Capt James Tubb, Inf
HINES, Peter, Pvt, Col Sam Copeland, Capt Allen Wilkinson, Mil Inf
HINES, Richard, Pvt, Col Sam Wear, Capt Joe Calloway, Mtd Inf
HINES, Robert, Pvt, Col Edward Bradley, Capt Wm Lauderdale, Vol Inf
HINES, Robert, Pvt, Col Sam Wear, Capt Sam Bowman, Mtd Inf
HINES, Robert, Pvt, Regt Commander omitted, Capt James Cowan, Mtd Inf
HINES, William B, Sgt, Col Sam Bayless, Capt Joe Rich, E TN Inf
HINESLEY, Michael, Pvt, Col Robt Steele, Capt Jas Randals, Inf
HINKLE, Anthony, Pvt, Col Sam Bayless, Capt Joe Hale, E TN Mil
HINKLE, George, Pvt, Col Ewen Allison, Capt William King, Drafted Mil
HINKLE, Peter, Pvt, Col John Cocke, Capt John Weakley, Inf
HINSHAW, George, Pvt, Col Sam Copeland, Capt David Williams, Inf
HINSHAW, William, Pvt, Col A Loury, Capt A Rains, Inf
HINSLEY, Michael, Pvt, Col Thos Benton, Capt Geo Caperton, Inf; refused to march
HINSON, Merritt, Ffr, Col Wm Metcalf, Capt A Patterson, Mil Inf
HINSON, William, Pvt, Col Cheatham, Capt Birdwell, Inf
HIPS, Jacob, Pvt, Col Wm Lillard, Capt Robt McAlpin, E TN Inf; unable to perform duty
HIR, William, Pvt, Col William Hall, Capt Travis Nash, Inf; unfit for service before first two months
HITCH, Elvin, Pvt, Col Samuel Wear, Capt John Stephens, E TN Vol Inf
HITCHCOCK, Elijah, Pvt, Col Thos Benton, Capt Wm J Smith, Vol Inf
HITCHCOCK, Elijah, Pvt, Col Wm Pillow, Capt Wm J Smith, Vol Inf
HITCHCOCK, Elijah, Pvt, Regt Commander omitted, Capt Wm J Smith, Vol Inf
HITCHCOCK, Ezakeil, Pvt, Col Wm Pillow, Capt Wm J Smith, Vol Inf
HITCHCOCK, Ezekiel, Pvt, Col Thos Benton, Capt Wm J Smith, Vol Inf
HITE, Jacob, Pvt, Col Sam Bayless, Capt Jonathan Waddell, E TN Mil
HITE, John, Pvt, Col N T Perkins, Capt John Quarles, Mtd Inf
HITE, Richard, Pvt, Col Thos McCrory, Capt Jno Reynolds, Mil Inf
HITE, Robert, Pvt, Col John Coffee, Capt Jas Terrell, Vol Cav
HITE, Samuel, Pvt, Col R C Napier, Capt Thos Preston, Mil Inf
HITE, Spencer, Pvt, Col Wm Lillard, Capt Thos Sharpe, 2nd Regt Inf; deserted 10-27-1813
HITER, Milton O, Sgt, Maj Wm Carroll, Capt Dan Bradford & Capt L Dillahunty, Vol Inf
HITTON, John, Pvt, Regt Commander omitted, Capt Geo Smith, Spies
HITTS, Richard, Pvt, Col Sam Bunch, Capt Jas Cummings, E TN Vol Mtd Inf
HIX, Isaac, Pvt, Col Wm Johnson, Capt Joe Scott, E TN Drafted Mil
HIX, Jacob, Pvt, Col Wm Johnson, Capt Joseph Scott, E TN Drafted Mil
HIX, John, Pvt, Regt Commander omitted, Capt Larkin Ferrell, Inf
HIX, Stephen, Pvt, Col Wm Johnson, Capt Joseph Scott, E TN Drafted Mil; transferred to Capt Anderson's Spy Camp
HIX, Stephen, Pvt, Regt Commander omitted, Capt Wm Henderson, Spies
HIXON, Ephraim, Pvt, Col Edwin Booth, Capt Vernon, E TN Mil
HOARD, Abraham, Pvt, Maj Wm Woodfolk, Co Commander omitted, Inf; substitute for John Murry (deserted 9-30-1814)
HOARD, William, Pvt, Col William Hall, Capt Jno Kennedy, Vol Inf
HOBBS, Brice, Pvt, Col Edwin Booth, Capt John Lewis, E TN Mil
HOBBS, Colin S, Pvt, Maj Gen Jackson, Capt Carroll, Vol Inf
HOBBS, Enos, Pvt, Col Sam Bunch, Capt Wm Houston, E TN Vol Mtd Inf
HOBBS, Ezakiel, Pvt, Col Philip Pipkin, Co Commander omitted, Mil Inf; deserted from Camp Tatum 6-25-1814
HOBBS, Frederick, Pvt, Col Wm Metcalf, Capt Wm Mullin, Mil Inf
HOBBS, Isaac, Pvt, Col Wm Johnson, Capt Christopher Cook, E TN Mil
HOBBS, Isaac, Pvt, Col Wm Johnson, Capt Joe Kirk, Mil
HOBBS, James, Pvt, Col N T Perkins, Capt John Doak, Vol Mtd Gunmen
HOBBS, John, Pvt, Col R H Dyer, Capt Glen Owen, TN Vol Mtd Gunmen
HOBBS, John, Pvt, Regt Commander omitted, Capt David Mason, Cav
HOBBS, Joseph, Pvt, Col Philip Pipkin, Capt Eb Kirkpatrick, Mil Inf; d 9-25-1814

HOBBS, Solomon, Pvt, Col Alex Loury, Capt Thos Wells, Inf
HOBBS, Solomon, Pvt, Regt Commander omitted, Capt David Mason, Cav
HOBBS, Thomas jr, Pvt, Col John Coffee, Capt Daniel Ross, Mtd Gunmen
HOBBS, Thos S, Pvt, Col John Coffee, Capt Daniel Ross, Mtd Gunmen
HOBDY (HOBBS), Burwell, Pvt, Col Philip Pipkin, Capt Peter Searcy, Branch Srvce omitted
HOBSON, Benjamin, Pvt, Col Thos Williamson, Capt Robert Moore, Vol Mtd Gunmen
HOBSON, Benjamin, Pvt, Maj Gen Jackson, Capt Eb Kirkpatrick, Mtd Gunmen; wounded 1-22-1814
HOBSON, Henry, Pvt, Col Thomas Williamson, Capt Robert Moore, Vol Mtd Gunmen
HOBSON, Henry, Pvt, Col Thos Benton, Capt Benj Reynolds, Vol Inf
HOBSON, Isaac, Pvt, Gen Andrew Jackson, Capt Nathan Dove, Inf
HOBSON, John M, Pvt, Col Thomas McCrory, Capt Thos K Gordon, Inf
HOBSON, Joseph, Pvt, Col Newton Cannon, Capt John Harpole, Mtd Gunmen
HODGE, Charles C, Pvt, Col Jno Williams, Capt Wm Walker, Vol
HODGE, Charles, Pvt, Maj John Childs, Capt Reuben Tipton, E TN Vol Mtd Inf; Regimental County Jefferson
HODGE, Edmond, Pvt, Col Allison, Capt Hoyal?, E TN Mil; joined by transfer from Capt McPherson's Co
HODGE, Edmond, Pvt, Col S Bunch, Capt Geo McPherson, E TN Mil
HODGE, Edmond, Pvt, Col Thos Benton, Capt Geo Caperton, Vol Inf
HODGE, Edward, Cpl, Col Samuel Wear, Capt Jos Calloway, Mtd Inf
HODGE, Gideon, Pvt, Col Wm Metcalf, Capt Wm Mullins, Mil Inf
HODGE, Howel, Pvt, Col E Allison, Capt Jacob Hoyal, E TN Mil; joined by transfer from Capt McPherson's Co
HODGE, Howel, Pvt, Col Saml Bayless, Capt James Landen, E TN Mil
HODGE, Howell, Pvt, Col Sam Bunch, Capt Geo McPherson, Inf; furnished a substitute in Capt Griffin's Co
HODGE, Isaac, Pvt, Col John Cocke, Capt S M Caruthers, Inf
HODGE, James, Pvt, Col Wm Johnson, Capt Jas Tunnell, E TN Mil; appointed Sgt Maj
HODGE, John, Far, Col N Cannon, Capt Martin, Mtd Gunmen; wounded 11-12-1813
HODGE, John, Pvt, Col Ewen Allison, Capt Wm King, Drafted Mil
HODGE, John, Pvt, Col R M Dyer, Capt Robert Evans, Vol Mtd Gunmen
HODGE, John, Pvt, Col Samuel Bunch, Capt D G Vance, E TN Mtd Inf
HODGE, John, Pvt, Col Thos Benton, Capt Robert Cannon, Inf
HODGE, Micajah, Pvt, Col S Bayless, Capt James Landen, E TN Mil
HODGE, Robert, Pvt, Col Alex Loury, Lt Col Hammond, Capt Thos Wells, Inf
HODGE, Robert, Pvt, Lt Col L Hammond, Capt Thos Wells, Inf
HODGE, Robert, Sgt, Col Jno Coffee, Capt J Baskerville, Cav
HODGE, William, Pvt, Col Wm Metcalf, Capt B L Hurt, Mil Inf; d 4-15-1815
HODGES, Charles, 1 Lt, Col Samuel Wear, Capt Jos Calloway, Mtd Inf
HODGES, Charles, Pvt, Maj Wm Russell, Capt F Hodges, Vol Mtd Gunmen
HODGES, Drury, Pvt, Col Wm Johnston, Capt Wm Alexander, Det of E TN Drafted Mil
HODGES, Edmund, Pvt, Col Thos Benton, Capt Geo Caperton, Inf
HODGES, Edmund, Pvt, Col Wm Pillow, Capt Geo Caperton, Inf
HODGES, Elisha, Pvt, Col S Copeland, Capt Moses Thompson, Inf
HODGES, Henry, Rank omitted, Col John Cocke, Capt John Dalton, Inf
HODGES, James, Pvt, Col N Cannon, Capt Jas Walton, Mtd Riflemen
HODGES, James, Pvt, Col S Copeland, Capt Wm Hodges, Inf
HODGES, Jesse, Pvt, Maj Wm Russell, Capt F Hodges, Vol Mtd Gunmen; d 2-23-1815
HODGES, Jesse, Pvt, Maj Wm Woodfolk, Capt E Ross & Capt McCulley, Inf
HODGES, John, Pvt, Col R C Napier, Capt Drury Adkins, Mil Inf
HODGES, John, Pvt, Col Wm Johnson, Capt Elihu Milliken, 3rd Regt E TN Mil
HODGES, John, Pvt, Maj Robert Cooper, Co Commander omitted, Mtd Riflemen
HODGES, John, Sgt, Col John Cocke, Capt Jas Gray, Inf
HODGES, John, Sgt, Col Saml Bayless, Capt Jas Churchman, E TN Mil
HODGES, Josiah, Pvt, Maj Wm Woodfolk, Capt E Ross & Capt McCulley, Inf
HODGES, Miles, Pvt, Col Wm Johnson, Capt Jos Kirk, Mil; never appeared
HODGES, Robert, Cpl, Col S Copeland, Capt Wm Hodges, Inf
HODGES, Robert, Pvt, Col R H Dyer, Capt Bethel Allen, Vol Mtd Gunmen
HODGES, Robert, Pvt, Col R M Dyer, Capt Robert Evans, Vol Mtd Gunmen
HODGES, Robert, Pvt, Col Saml Wear, Capt J Calloway, Mtd Inf
HODGES, Samuel, Pvt, Col Alex Loury, Lt Col Hammond, Capt Thomas Delaney, Inf; d 1-22-1815
HODGES, Seth, Sgt, Col S Copeland, Capt J Holshouser, Inf
HODGES, Silas, Pvt, Col Samuel Bayless, Capt Jos Goodson, E TN Mil
HODGES, Stephen, Pvt, Lt Col Hammonds, Col S Loury,

## Enlisted Men, War of 1812

HODGES, William, Pvt, Col N Cannon, Capt John Hanley, Mtd Riflemen
HODGES, William, Pvt, Col R H Dyer, Capt Bether Allen, Vol Mtd Gunmen
HODGES, William, Pvt, Col S Copeland, Capt J Holshouser, Inf
HODGES, William, Pvt, Col Wm Hall, Capt John Moore, Vol Inf
HOFFER, James, Pvt, Col N T Perkins, Capt Philip Pipkin, Mtd Riflemen
HOFFER, Thomas, Pvt, Col William Johnston, Capt Joseph Kirk, Mil; substitute for Zachariah Kinneman reenlisted
HOFFIN, Edward H, Pvt, Col Jno Coffee, Capt Alex McKeen, Cav
HOFFMAN (HUFFMAN), John, Pvt, Col Wm Metcalf, Maj Gen Carroll, Capt John Jackson, Inf
HOFLA (HOLFIN), Jesse, Pvt, Col Alex Loury, Capt James Kincaid, Inf
HOFLIN, Jesse, Pvt, Col Wm Hall, Capt T C Nash, Inf; under 18 not notified
HOGAN, Adly, Sgt, Col A Cheatham, Capt William Creel, Inf; promoted from Pvt
HOGAN, Alexander, Pvt, Col S Copeland, Capt Wm Evans, Mil Inf
HOGAN, Anderson, Pvt, Col Robert Steele, Capt Robt Campbell, Mil Inf
HOGAN, David, Pvt, Regt Commander omitted, Capt Gray, Inf
HOGAN, Ewin, Cpl, Col Robert Dyer, Capt William Russell, Vol Mtd Gunmen
HOGAN, Ewin, Pvt, Maj Wm Woodfolk, Capt Anthony Turner, Inf
HOGAN, Isaac, Pvt, Col William Hall, Capt Henry Newlin, Inf; transferred to the Cav
HOGAN, Isaah, Pvt, Col John Coffee, Capt Jas Terrill, Vol Cav
HOGAN, James, Pvt, Col R C Napier, Capt Thomas Gray, Mil Inf
HOGAN, Job, Pvt, Regt Commander omitted, Capt Elijah Rushing, Inf
HOGAN, John H, 2 Cpl, Col Phillip Pipkin, Capt Peter Searcy, Mil Inf
HOGAN, John, Pvt, Col N T Perkins, Capt Jas McMahon, Mtd Gunmen
HOGAN, John, Pvt, Col Philip Pipkin, Capt David Smith, Mil Inf
HOGAN, John, Pvt, Col Philip Pipkin, Capt Mackey, Mil Inf
HOGAN, John, Pvt, Regt Commander omitted, Capt Jas Gray, Inf
HOGAN, Josiah, Pvt, Col John Coffee, Capt Jas Terrill, Vol Cav
HOGAN, Richard, Pvt, Col John Brown, Capt Jas Standifer, E TN Vol Mtd Mil
HOGAN, Robert, Pvt, Col John Wynn, Capt Robert Brader, Inf
HOGAN, Squire E, Sgt, Col John Wynn, Capt Jas Cole, Inf
HOGAN, William, Pvt, Col A Cheatham, Capt James Giddens, Inf
HOGAN, William, Pvt, Col Wm Hall, Capt Jas Hambleton, Vol Inf
HOGAN, William, Pvt, Lt Col Henry Bryan, Co Commander omitted, Inf
HOGAN, William, Pvt, Maj Wm Woodfolk, Capt Jas Turner, Inf
HOGAN, Yewing, Pvt, Col William Hall, Capt John Kennedy, Vol Inf
HOGAS, Silas, Pvt, Col S Bunch, Capt Francis Register, E TN Mil
HOGE, Edward, Pvt, Maj William Russell, Capt Fleman Hodges, Vol Mtd Gunmen
HOGE, James, Pvt, Col Wm Metcalf, Capt Barbee Collins, Mil Inf
HOGEN, Robert, Pvt, Col Thomas Williamson, Capt John Crane, Vol Mtd Gunmen
HOGES, Jesse, Sgt, Col John Brown, Capt Jas Preston, E TN Mil Inf
HOGES, John, Pvt, Col Wm Johnson, Capt Elihu Milliken, 3rd Regt E TN
HOGES, Miles, Pvt, Col John Wynn, Capt Wm Carothers, W TN Inf
HOGG, Gidenn, Pvt, Col Robt Dyer, Capt James Wyatt, Vol Mtd Gunmen
HOGG, Gipson, Pvt, Col Phillip Pipkin, Capt Henry Newlin, Mil Inf
HOGIN, Ewin, Pvt, Col Edward Bradley, Capt John Kennedy, Riflemen
HOGINS, John, Pvt, Col Ewin Allison, Capt Joseph Everett, E TN Mil
HOGLAND, James, Pvt, Maj Wm Woodfolk, Capt Abraham Dudney, Inf
HOGUE, Andrew, Sgt, Col Jas Raulston, Capt Mathew Neal, Inf; d 1-27-1815
HOGUE, Gideon, Pvt, Col Wm Metcalf, Capt Thomas Marks, Mil Inf
HOGYE, John, Cpl, Col John Brown, Capt Jesse Reamy, Mtd Gunmen
HOILE, Peter, Pvt, Col Edwin Booth, Capt Samuel Thompson, Mil
HOLAWAY, John, Pvt, Col Wm Johnson, Capt David McKamy, E TN Mil
HOLAWAY, William, Pvt, Col Wm Johnson, Capt Elihu Millikin, E TN Mil; transferred for Capt Churchman Co
HOLBERTON, Solomon, Drm Maj, Col Wm Metcalf, Co Commander omitted, W TN Mil Inf
HOLBROOK, George, Far, Col Robert Dyer, Capt Ephraim Dickson, TN Vol Gunmen
HOLCOM, Daniel, Pvt, Col Alexander Loury, Capt John Looney, W TN Mil
HOLCOM, Daniel, Pvt, Col S Bayless, Capt Solomon Hendrix, E TN Mil
HOLDAWAY, Henry, Pvt, Col S Bunch, Capt Francis Berry, E TN Mil; attached to Capt English
HOLDAWAY, William, Pvt, Col S Bayless, Capt Jas Churchman, E TN Mil; transferred to Capt Millikin
HOLDEN, Bledso, Pvt, Col Thos Benton, Capt Geo Caperton, Vol Inf
HOLDEN, George, Pvt, Col Edward Bradley, Capt Travis

## Enlisted Men, War of 1812

Nash, Vol Inf
HOLDEN, George, Pvt, Col William Hall, Capt Travis Nash, Inf
HOLDEN, Joseph, Pvt, Col Edward Bradley, Capt Travis Nash, Vol Inf
HOLDEN, Joseph, Pvt, Col Wm Hall, Capt Travis Nash, Inf
HOLDEN, Spencer, Pvt, Col Wm Hall, Capt Travis Nash, Inf
HOLDER, Bradley, Pvt, Col Jno Coffee, Capt Fredrick Stump, Cav
HOLDER, Jas, Dmr, Col William Metcalf, Capt Andrew Patterson, Mil Inf
HOLDER, John, Pvt, Col Russell, Capt Wm Russell, Vol Mtd Gunmen
HOLDER, John, Pvt, Col T McCrory, Capt Thomas Gordon, Inf; d 11-21-1813
HOLDER, Joseph, Pvt, Col Wm Metcalf, Capt John Jackson, Inf
HOLDER, Martin, Pvt, Col Wm Pillow, Capt Caperton, Inf
HOLDER, Solomon, Pvt, Col A Cheatham, Capt Creed, Inf
HOLDER, Solomon, Pvt, Col A Loury, Capt J N Williamson, W TN Mil
HOLDER, Solomon, Pvt, Col L Hammonds, Capt J N Williamson, 2nd Regt Inf
HOLDER, Thomas, Pvt, Col A Loury, Capt J N Williamson, W TN Mil
HOLE, Jonathan, Pvt, Col Allison, Capt Hoyal, E TN Mil Inf
HOLEBROOK, William, Far, Maj Gen Andrew Jackson, Capt Joseph Kirkpatrick, Mtd Gunmen
HOLEMAN, John, Pvt, Col A Cheatham, Capt Wm Johnson, Inf
HOLEMAN, William, Pvt, Col Edwin Booth, Capt Vernon, E TN Mil
HOLEMAN, Yancey, Pvt, Col Robert Dyer, Capt Glen Owen, TN Vol Mtd Gunmen
HOLEWAY, John, Pvt, Col Wm Lillard, Capt Zacheus Copeland, E TN Mil Vol Inf
HOLIDA, Stephen, Pvt, Col Hammond, Capt James Tubb, Inf
HOLKUM, Hiram, Pvt, Regt Commander omitted, Capt Gabriel Martin, Brig Mtd Inf
HOLLADAY, Allen, Sgt, Col Robert Steele, Co Commander omitted, Mil Inf
HOLLADAY, David, Sgt, Col John K Winn, Capt James Holeman, Inf
HOLLADAY, Thomas, Pvt, Col R H Dyer, Capt Robert Evans, Vol Mtd Gunmen
HOLLAN, James, Pvt, no other information
HOLLAND, Anthony, Cpl, Col Wm Lillard, Co Commander omitted, E TN Vol Inf; also under Col Jacob Hartsell
HOLLAND, Asa, Pvt, Col Thos Williamson, Capt John Doak, Capt John Dobbins, Vol Mtd Gunmen
HOLLAND, Asa, Sgt, Col Robert Steele, Capt John Chitwood, Mil Inf
HOLLAND, Charles, Pvt, Col Samuel Bunch, Co Commander omitted, E TN Vol Mtd Inf

HOLLAND, Frederick, 3 Sgt, Col N T Perkins, Capt Johnson, Mil Inf
HOLLAND, Green, Pvt, Col R H Dyer, Co Commander omitted, Vol Mtd Gunmen
HOLLAND, Harphrey, Pvt, Col S Copeland, Capt John Dawson, Inf
HOLLAND, Jacob, Cpl, Col S Bunch, Capt John Houk, E TN Mil; discharged for inability
HOLLAND, James, 3 Sgt, Col Samuel Bunch, Capt Wm Jobe, E TN Vol Mtd Inf
HOLLAND, James, Pvt, Col Thos Williamson, Capt John Doak & Capt John Dobbins, Vol Mtd Gunmen
HOLLAND, John, Pvt, Col A Loury, Capt Brice Martin, Inf
HOLLAND, John, Pvt, Col John K Winn, Capt John Porter, Inf
HOLLAND, John, Pvt, Col Thos Williamson, Capt Giles Burdette, Vol Mtd Gunmen
HOLLAND, John, Pvt, Col Thos Williamson, Capt John Doak & Capt John Dobbins, Vol Mtd Gunmen
HOLLAND, Leven, Pvt, Col John Brown, Capt Jas White, E TN Mtd Inf
HOLLAND, Mark, Pvt, Col R C Napier, Capt Drury Adkins, Mil Inf
HOLLAND, Mark, Pvt, Lt Col Richard Napier, Co Commander omitted, Inf
HOLLAND, Martin, 2 Cpl, Col Philip Pipkin, Capt Jas Blakemore, Mil Inf
HOLLAND, Peter, Sgt, Col Robert Steele, Capt John Chitwood, Mil Inf
HOLLAND, Philip, Pvt, Col Philip Pipkin, Capt Peter Searcy, Mil Inf
HOLLAND, Thomas, Pvt, Col Robert Steele, Capt John Chitwood, Mil Inf
HOLLAND, Thomas, Pvt, Col Samuel Bayless, Capt Francis Jones, E TN Drafted Mil
HOLLAND, Thomas, Pvt, Col Stephen C Copeland, Co Commander omitted, Mil Inf
HOLLAND, Thomas, Pvt, Col Thos Williamson, Capt John Crane & Capt Jas Cook, Vol Mtd Gunmen
HOLLAND, Thomas, Pvt, Col Wm Y Higgins, Capt Archie Cheatham, Mtd Riflemen
HOLLAND, Wiley, Pvt, Lt Col Arch Cheatham, Capt Gabriel Martin, 6th Brig Mtd Inf
HOLLAND, William, Pvt, Col John Cocke, Capt Crunk, Inf
HOLLAND, William, Pvt, Maj John Childs, Capt Chas Conway, E TN Mtd Gunmen; Regimental County - Roan
HOLLAND, Willie, Pvt, Col Thos Williamson, Capt Wm Metcalf, Vol Mtd Gunmen
HOLLAND, Willis, Cpl, Col A Cheatham, Capt Richard Benson, Inf
HOLLANDSWORTH, James, Pvt, Col Sam Copeland, Capt Moses Thompson, Inf
HOLLANDSWORTH, William, Pvt, Col John Wynne, Capt John Spinks, Inf
HOLLEMAN, Thomas, Sgt, Col John Wynne, Capt James Holleman, Inf
HOLLEMAN, William, Pvt, Col S Copeland, Capt Alex Provine, Mil Inf

- 259

## Enlisted Men, War of 1812

HOLLER, Christopher, Pvt, Col John Brown, Capt Wm White, E TN Vol Mtd Inf
HOLLEY, William, Pvt, Col Wm Johnson, Capt Henry Hunter, E TN Mil
HOLLIDAY, Benjamin, Pvt, Col James Raulston, Capt Elijah Haynie, Inf; killed 12-2-1814
HOLLIDAY, Joel, Cpl, Maj Wm Woodfolk, Capt Abraham Dudney, Inf; promoted to Sgt
HOLLIDAY, Robert, Pvt, Regt Commander omitted, Capt David Mason, Cav
HOLLINGSWORTH, Ezakiel, Pvt, Col Sam Wear, Capt Robert Doak, E TN Vol Inf
HOLLINGSWORTH, Jacob, Pvt, Col Thos Williamson, Capt George Mitchie, 2nd Regt TN Vol Mtd Gunmen
HOLLINGSWORTH, Jacob, Pvt, Maj Russell, Capt George Mitchie, Vol Mtd Gunmen
HOLLINGSWORTH, John, Pvt, Col James Raulston, Capt James Black, Inf
HOLLINGSWORTH, Jonah, Pvt, Col William Lillard, Capt Thomas Sharpe, 2nd Inf
HOLLIS, Isaac, Pvt, Col Edward Bradley, Capt Jas Hamilton, Vol Inf
HOLLIS, Silas, Pvt, Col R C Napier, Capt Andrew McCarty, Mil Inf
HOLLIS, Stephen, Pvt, Maj Wm Woodfolk, Capt Abner Pearce, Inf
HOLLOMON, Malachi, Pvt, Col Edward Bradley, Capt Abraham Bledsoe, Riflemen
HOLLOWAY, Edmond, Pvt, Col Edward Bradley, Capt Abraham Bledsoe, Riflemen
HOLLOWAY, Edmond, Pvt, Col Sam Bunch, Capt Edward Buchanan, E TN Drafted Mil; discharged for inability
HOLLOWAY, Edmond, Pvt, Col Wm Hall, Capt Abraham Bledsoe, Vol Inf
HOLLOWAY, Emanuel, Pvt, Col Sam Bunch, Capt Edward Buchanan, E TN Drafted Mil
HOLLOWAY, Jesse, Pvt, Brig Gen Johnson, Capt Robert Carson, Inf
HOLLOWAY, Nathan (Anthony), 1 Cpl, Col Edward Bradley, Capt Abraham Bledsoe, Riflemen
HOLLOWAY, Nathan, 1 Cpl, Col William Hall, Capt Abraham Bledsoe, Vol Inf
HOLLOWAY, Stephen, Pvt, Maj John Childs, Capt Daniel Price, Vol Mtd Gunmen
HOLLOWAY, Thomas, Pvt, Maj Gen Jackson, Capt John Crane, Mtd Gunmen
HOLLOWAY, Whitfield, Pvt, Col Alex Loury, Capt George Sarver, Branch Srvce omitted
HOLLOWAY, William, Pvt, Col Robert Dyer, Capt Robert Edmondson, TN Vol Mtd Gunmen
HOLLY, Benjamin, Pvt, Col Thomas Benton, Capt George Caperton, Inf
HOLLY, David, Pvt, Col John Brown, Capt Wm Neilson, E TN Vol Mil
HOLLY, Frazier, Pvt, Col Jno Williams, Capt David Vance, Mtd Mil
HOLLY, Sion, Pvt, Col Wm Metcalf, Capt Wm Sitton, Mil Inf
HOLMAN, Daniel, Sgt, Col John Brown, Capt Wm Christian, E TN Mil Inf
HOLMES, Alijah, Pvt, Col John Alcorn, Capt Fred Stump, Cav; d 10-20-1813
HOLMES, James, Pvt, Col Robert Steele, Capt Robert Campbell, Mil Inf
HOLMES, James, Pvt, Col Wm Higgins, Capt Stephen Griffith, Mtd Riflemen
HOLMES, Jesse, Pvt, Regt Commander omitted, Capt J Prewitt, Mtd Vol Pack Horse Guards
HOLMES, John, 6 Sgt, Col Alex Loury, Capt Thos Wells, Inf
HOLMES, John, Pvt, Col Wm Higgins, Capt Stephen Griffith, Mtd Riflemen
HOLMES, Thomas, Pvt, Col John Alcorn, Capt Fred Stump, Cav
HOLMES, William, 4 Cpl, Col John Cocke, Capt James Gault, Inf
HOLMES, William, Pvt, Col James Raulston, Capt Elijah Haynie, Inf
HOLSHOUSER, John, Pvt, Col John Wynne, Capt Thos Porter, Inf
HOLSON, Henry, Pvt, Col Thomas Benton, Capt Benjamin Reynolds, Vol Inf
HOLT, David, Pvt, Col Wm Lillard, Capt Thomas Sharpe, 2nd Regt Inf
HOLT, Edward, Pvt, Col Wm Lillard, Capt Thomas Sharpe, 2nd Regt Inf
HOLT, Garland, Pvt, Col Wm Metcalf, Capt Barbee Collins, Mil Inf; d 3-13-1815
HOLT, Garland, Sgt, Regt Commander omitted, Capt Archibald McKenney, Cav
HOLT, H Perkins, Pvt, Col A Loury, Capt Thomas Wells, Inf
HOLT, Hardin P, Sgt, Regt Commander omitted, Capt Archibald McKenney, Cav
HOLT, Harding P, Pvt, Col N T Perkins, Capt Mathew Johnson, Mil Inf
HOLT, Henry, Pvt, Col James Raulston, Capt Henry Hamilton, Inf
HOLT, Henry, Pvt, Maj Wm Russell, Capt Isaac Williams, Separate Bn TN Vol Mtd Gunmen; also under Col R H Dyer
HOLT, Jacob, Ffr Maj, Col Ewin Allison, Co Commander omitted, E TN Mil
HOLT, Jacob, Ffr, Col Ewen Allison, Capt Joseph Everett, E TN Mil; promoted to Ffr Maj
HOLT, James, Cpl, Col Wm Johnson, Capt Elihu Milliken, 3rd Regt E TN Mil
HOLT, James, Pvt, Col R C Napier, Capt James McMurry, Mil Inf
HOLT, James, Pvt, Col Wm Johnson, Capt Henry Hunter, E TN Mil; transferred to Capt Milliken's Co
HOLT, Jesse, Pvt, Lt Col L Hammond, Capt James Tubb, Inf
HOLT, Jesse, Pvt, Maj Wm Woodfolk, Capt Ezekiel Ross & Capt McCully, Inf
HOLT, John, Pvt, Brig Gen T Johnson, Capt Robert Carson, Inf
HOLT, John, Pvt, Col R H Dyer, Capt Cuthbert Hudson, Vol Mtd Gunmen
HOLT, Joseph, Pvt, Col Wm Metcalf, Capt John Jackson,

HOLT, Laban, Pvt, Col R C Napier, Capt Edward Neblett, Mil Inf
HOLT, Michael, Pvt, Col Samuel Bunch, Capt Andrew Breden, E TN Mil
HOLT, Perkins, Pvt, Brig Gen T Washington, Capt Jno Crawford, Mtd Inf
HOLT, Perkins, Pvt, Regt Commander omitted, Capt David Mason, Cav
HOLT, Robert, 3 Sgt, Col Jno Coffee, Capt Frederick Stump, Cav; reduced to Pvt
HOLT, Robert, Pvt, Col John Alcorn, Capt Frederick Stump, Cav
HOLT, Rubin, Pvt, Brig Gen T Johnson, Capt Allen, Mil Inf
HOLT, Thornberry, Pvt, Brig Gen T Johnson, Capt Robert Carson, Inf
HOLT, Thornberry, Pvt, Col Alexander Loury, Capt James Kincaid, Inf
HOLT, Wm N, Pvt, Regt Commander omitted, Capt David Mason, Cav
HOLT, Wm jr, Pvt, Col James Raulston, Capt Elijah Haynie, Inf
HOLT, Wm sr, Pvt, Col James Raulston, Capt Elijah Haynie, Inf
HOLTON, Michael, Pvt, Regt Commander omitted, Capt Wm Peacock, Cav
HOLTSINGER, John, Pvt, Col Wm Johnson, Capt Andrew Lawson, E TN Drafted Mil
HOLTZINGER, John, 6 Cpl, Col Wm Johnson, Capt Andrew Lawson, E TN Drafted Mil
HOMER, David, Pvt, Col Samuel Bunch, Capt Francis Berry, E TN Mil
HOMERLY, Joseph, Pvt, Col Wm Johnson, Capt James Tunnell, E TN Mil
HOMES, Alijah, Pvt, Col Jno Coffee, Capt Frederick Stump, Cav
HOMES, David, Pvt, Col S Copeland, Capt David Williams, Inf
HOMES, James, Sgt, Col William Y Higgins, Capt James Hambleton, Mtd Gunmen
HOMES, John, Cpl, Col Wm Y Higgins, Capt James Hambleton, Mtd Gunmen
HOMES, Joseph, Pvt, Col Ewen Allison, Capt Jonas Loughmiller, Mil
HONEY, James T, Pvt, Col Wm Johnson, Capt James R Rogers, E TN Drafted Mil
HONEYCUTT, Ady, Pvt, Col Thomas Williamson, Capt Robert Moore, Vol Mtd Gunmen
HONEYCUTT, Bartlet, Pvt, Col Thomas Williamson, Capt Robert Moore, Vol Mtd Gunmen
HONEYCUTT, Brasey (Brady), Pvt, Col Thos Williamson, Capt Robert Moore, Vol Mtd Gunmen
HONEYCUTT, John, Pvt, Col Jno Brown, Capt Hugh Barton, E TN Mil
HONNELL, Robert, Pvt, Col R C Napier, Capt Drury Adkins, Mil Inf
HOOD, Aaron, Pvt, Col Edwin Booth, Capt John Lewis, E TN Mil
HOOD, Clas, Sgt, Col Thos Benton, Capt George Caperton, Vol Inf

HOOD, Delanson W, Pvt, Col Wm Metcalf, Capt Bird L Hunt, Mil Inf
HOOD, Elijah, Pvt, Col A Loury, Capt Thomas Wells, Inf
HOOD, Elijah, Pvt, Col John K Wynne, Capt James Cole, Inf
HOOD, Ellison, Pvt, Col Philip Pipkin, Capt Peter Searcy, Mil Inf; deserted from Ft Jackson 9-20-1814
HOOD, Frederick, Cor, Maj William Russell, Capt Fleman Hodges, Vol Mtd Gunmen
HOOD, John, 1 Cpl, Maj John Childs, Capt Reuben Tipton, E TN Vol Mtd Inf; Regimental County - Knox
HOOD, John, Pvt, Col A Loury, Capt John Looney, 2nd Regt W TN Mil; d 3-12-1815
HOOD, John, Pvt, Col Ewen Allison, Capt Jacob Hoyal, E TN Mil; deserted 3-4-1814
HOOD, John, Pvt, Col John Brown, Capt John Childs, E TN Vol Mtd Inf
HOOD, John, Pvt, Col John Cocke, Capt James Gray, Inf; d 3-20-1815
HOOD, John, Pvt, Col R C Napier, Capt Thomas Gray, Mil Inf
HOOD, John, Pvt, Col Samuel Bayless, Capt Branch Jones, E TN Drafted Mil
HOOD, John, Pvt, Col Samuel Wear, Capt Joseph Calloway, Mtd Inf
HOOD, John, Pvt, Regt Commander omitted, Capt Abner Pearce, Inf
HOOD, Robert, Pvt, Col S Copeland, Capt William Douglass, Inf
HOOD, Robert, Pvt, Col Samuel Wear, Capt James Gillespie, E TN Vol Inf; unable to perform duty
HOOD, Thomas, Pvt, Col Edwin Booth, Capt Alexander Biggs, Inf
HOODENPILE, Peter, Pvt, Maj John Childs, Capt Chas Conway, E TN Mtd Gunmen; Regimental County - White
HOOKE, Thomas, Pvt, Col Thos Williamson, Capt John Doak & Capt John Dobbins, Vol Mtd Gunmen
HOOKER, Jabez, Pvt, Col Jas Raulston, Capt Chas Wade, Inf
HOOKER, Joshua, Pvt, Col Jas Raulston, Capt Chas Wade, Inf
HOOKER, Namon, Pvt, Col Wm Metcalf, Co Commander omitted, Mil Inf; d 4-15-1815
HOOKER, Richard, Pvt, Col John K Winn, Capt Wm Caruthers, W TN Inf; deserted 11-19-1813
HOOKER, Richard, Pvt, Col John K Winn, Capt Wm Wilson, Inf
HOOKER, Thomas, Pvt, Col Philip Pipkin, Capt David Smith, Inf; deserted 9-20-1814
HOOKER, Thomas, Pvt, Col Philip Pipkin, Capt Kirkpatrick, Mil Inf
HOOKER, Thomas, Pvt, Col Robert H Dyer, Capt Bethel Allen, Vol Mtd Gunmen
HOOKER, William, Pvt, Col Thos Benton, Capt Henry L Douglas, Branch Srvce omitted
HOOKER, Willie, Pvt, Col Jas Raulston, Capt Elijah Haynie, Inf
HOOKER, Willie, Pvt, Col Stephen Copeland, Capt John Dawson, Inf

## Enlisted Men, War of 1812

HOOKS, Charles, Pvt, Col R C Napier, Capt Thos Gray, Mil Inf
HOOKS, Charles, Pvt, Regt Commander omitted, Capt Abner Pearce, Inf
HOOKS, James, Sgt, Gen Andrew Jackson, Capt Nathan Davis, Inf
HOONENPILE, Philip, Pvt, Col Wm Johnson, Capt Tinnell, E TN Mil
HOONENPILE, Philip, Pvt, Maj John Chiles, Capt Chas Conway, E TN Mtd Gunmen; Regimental County - White
HOOPER, Churchill, Pvt, Col John Coffee, Capt Daniel Ross, Mtd Gunmen
HOOPER, Jeptha, Pvt, Col John Coffee, Capt Daniel Ross, Mtd Gunmen
HOOPER, John, Pvt, Regt Commander omitted, Capt Jos Williams, Mil Cav
HOOPER, Joseph, Pvt, Maj Gen Andrew Jackson, Capt John Craine, Mtd Gunmen
HOOPER, Nathaniel, Pvt, Col Thos H Benton, Co Commander omitted, Vol Inf
HOOPER, Seamore, Pvt, Col Samuel Bayless, Capt Joseph Rich, E TN Inf
HOOPER, Will, Pvt, Col John Coffee, Capt Jas Terrell, Vol Cav
HOOPER, Wilson, 2 Sgt, Col Wm Hall, Capt Jas Hambleton, Vol Inf
HOOSER, Isaac, Dmr, Col William Hall, Capt John Kennedy, Vol Inf
HOOSER, V Wm, Pvt, Col Sam Bunch, Capt Francis Berry, E TN Mil; deserted 3-4-1814
HOOTEN, Britton, Pvt, Col Wm Metcalf, Capt Barbee Collins, Mil Inf
HOOTEN, James, Pvt, Col Wm Metcalf, Capt Barbee Collins, Mil Inf; d 4-10-1815
HOOVER, Isaac V, Pvt, Col Alex Loury, Capt Arahel Rains, Inf
HOOVER, Isaac, Sgt, Col Sam Bunch, Capt Jno English, E TN Drafted Mil
HOOVER, Jacob, Pvt, Col Wm Russell, Capt Isaac Williams, Sep Bn of TN Mtd Gunmen
HOOVER, John, Pvt, Col Newton Cannon, Capt Thos Yardley, Mtd Riflemen; transferred to Smith's Spies
HOOVER, John, Pvt, Regt Commander omitted, Capt Gen Smith, Spies
HOOVER, Martin, Pvt, Maj Gen Carroll, Col Wm Metcalf, Inf
HOOVER, Valentine, Pvt, Col Thos Benton, Capt George Gibbs, Vol Inf
HOOVER, Valentine, Pvt, Col Wm Pillow, Capt John Anderson, Vol Inf
HOPE, Adam, Cpl, Col John Alcorn, Capt John Winston, Mtd Riflemen
HOPE, Adam, Sgt, Maj William Russell, Capt Fleman Hodges, Vol Mtd Gunmen
HOPE, Eli, Tptr, Col Robert Dyer, Capt James McMahon, 1st TN Mtd Vol Gunmen
HOPE, John, 1 Cpl, Col Thomas Benton, Capt Thomas Williamson, Vol Inf
HOPE, John, Cpl, Col Thomas Benton, Capt Thomas Williamson, Vol Inf
HOPE, John, Pvt, Brig Gen Thomas Washington, Capt John Crawford, Mtd Inf
HOPE, John, Pvt, Col Robert Dyer, Capt Thomas Jones, Vol Mtd Gunmen
HOPE, John, Sgt, Col William Pillow, Capt Thomas Williamson, Vol Inf
HOPE, Samuel H, Pvt, Col Thomas Benton, Capt Thomas Williamson, Vol Inf
HOPE, Samuel W, Pvt, Col Thomas Benton, Capt Thomas Williamson, Vol Inf
HOPE, Samuel W, Pvt, Col William Metcalf, Capt John Barnhart, Mil Inf; promoted to Cpl
HOPE, Samuel W, Pvt, Col William Pillow, Capt Thomas Williamson, Vol Inf
HOPE, Thomas, Pvt, Col A Cheatham, Capt William Creel, Inf
HOPE, Thomas, Pvt, Col John Brown, Capt Hugh Barton, E TN Mil Inf
HOPE, William, Pvt, Col A Cheatham, Capt Birdwell, Inf
HOPE, William, Pvt, Col Sam Wear, Capt John Childs, E TN Vol Inf
HOPEL, Samuel, Pvt, Col Newton Cannon, Capt William Edwards, Regt Command
HOPKINS, David, Dmr, Col S Copeland, Capt John Dawson, Inf
HOPKINS, Dennis, Pvt, Maj William Russell, Capt Isaac Williams, Sep Bn of TN Vol Mtd Gunmen
HOPKINS, Derry, Pvt, Col Robert Dyer, Capt Joseph Williams, 1st Regt TN Vol Mtd Gunmen
HOPKINS, George, Pvt, Col William Lillard, Capt William Hamilton, E TN Vol Inf
HOPKINS, Helms, Pvt, Col Robert Dyer, Capt James Wyatt, Vol Mtd Gunmen
HOPKINS, Holmes, Pvt, no other information
HOPKINS, Jason, Pvt, Regt Commander omitted, Capt John Gordon, Spies; transferred to Capt Lauderdale's Co
HOPKINS, Jesse, Pvt, Col Samuel Bayless, Capt John Brock, E TN Mil
HOPKINS, John, Pvt, Col Newton Cannon, Capt Isaac Williams, Mtd Riflemen; d 12-22-1813 of wounds at Battle of Talledega
HOPKINS, John, Pvt, Col Thomas Benton, Capt William Smith, Vol Inf
HOPKINS, John, Pvt, Regt Commander omitted, Capt William Smith, Vol Inf; deserted 1-7-1813
HOPKINS, Neel, Cpl, Col John Coffee, Capt Daniel Ross, Mtd Gunmen; transferred to Capt Gordon's Co
HOPKINS, Nehemiah, Pvt, Col Samuel Bayless, Capt John Brock, E TN Mil; furloughed for inability
HOPKINS, Neil, Pvt, no other information
HOPKINS, Samuel, Sgt, Col William Johnson, Capt Joseph Scott, E TN Drafted Mil
HOPKINS, Thomas, Pvt, Col James Raulston, Capt Mathew Neal, Inf
HOPKINS, William, Pvt, Col Robert Dyer, Capt Joseph Williams, 1st Regt TN Vol Mtd Gunmen
HOPKINS, William, Pvt, Col S Copeland, Capt Moses Thompson, Inf
HOPKINS, William, Sdlr, Maj William Russell, Capt

## Enlisted Men, War of 1812

Isaac Williams, Sep Bn of TN Vol Mtd Gunmen
HOPPER, Charles, Pvt, Regt Commander omitted, Capt Samuel Richardson, E TN Drafted Mil; deserted 4-12-1814
HOPPER, James, Cpl, Col William Lillard, Capt Thomas Sharpe, 2nd Regt Inf
HOPPER, John, Pvt, Col John Coffee, Capt Alexander McKeen, Cav
HOPPER, John, Pvt, Col William Metcalf, Capt Obidiah Waller, Mil Inf; d 2-20-1815?
HOPPER, Robert, Pvt, Col James Raulston, Capt Henry West, Inf
HOPPER, Zachariah, Pvt, Col Robert Dyer, Capt Joseph Williams, Vol Mtd Gunmen; d 11-16-1814
HOPPER (HOOPER), John, Pvt, Col John Coffee, Capt Michael Molton, Cav
HOPSON, Henry, Pvt, Col Robert Dyer, Capt James McMahon, 1st TN Vol Mtd Gunmen
HOPSON, Isaac H, Pvt, Col Alexander Loury, Capt John Looney, 2nd Regt W TN Mil
HOPSON, James, Pvt, Col William Lillard, Capt William Hamilton, E TN Vol Inf; substitute for William Stallions
HOPSON, John, Pvt, Col Alexander Loury, Capt John Looney, 2nd Regt W TN Mil
HOPSON, John, Pvt, Col William Lillard, Capt William Hamilton, E TN Vol Inf
HOPSON, Joshua, Surgeons Mate, Commander omitted, 2nd Regt TN Vol Inf
HORD, John, Pvt, Col William Lillard, Capt George Argenbright, E TN Vol Riflemen
HORD, Richard, Pvt, Col Edwin Booth, Capt John Slatton, E TN Inf
HORD, William, Pvt, Col Edward Bradley, Capt John Kennedy, Riflemen
HORD, William, Pvt, Col William Hall, Capt John Kennedy, Vol Inf; not fit for ____
HORH?, Henry, Sgt, Lt Col John Edmonson, Co Commander omitted, Cav
HORIS, Abner, Pvt, Maj William Woodfolk, Capt Ezekiel Ross & Capt McCulley, Inf
HORKINS, William, Pvt, Col William Higgins, Capt Thoms Eldridge, Mtd Gunmen
HORN, Adam, Pvt, Col Samuel Bunch, Capt John Houk, E TN Mil
HORN, Frederick, Pvt, Col John Cocke, Capt John Dalton, Inf
HORN, George, Cpl, Regt Commander omitted, Capt Ephraim Dickson, Branch Srvce omitted
HORN, George, Pvt, Col James Raulston, Capt Daniel Newman, Inf
HORN, George, Pvt, Col Robert Dyer, Capt E Dickson, TN Mtd Vol Gunmen
HORN, Henry, Pvt, Col Edward Bradley, Capt John Moore, Vol Inf
HORN, Henry, Pvt, Col Wm Hall, Capt John Moore, Vol Inf
HORN, Jacob, Sgt, Maj Gen Jackson, Capt Carroll, Vol Inf
HORN, James, 1 Sgt, Col William Hall, Capt John Moore, Vol Inf
HORN, James, Cpl, Col John Brown, Capt Allen Bacon, E TN Mil; promoted from Pvt
HORN, James, Pvt, Col Edward Bradley, Capt John Moore, Vol Inf
HORN, Jeremiah, 4 Cpl, Col N T Perkins, Capt John Quarles, Vol Mtd Inf
HORN, John, Sgt, Col N T Perkins, Capt John Quarles, Vol Mtd Inf
HORN, Peter, Pvt, Col Wm Metcalf, Capt Wm Mullin, Mil Inf
HORN, Richard, Pvt, Col John Alcorn, Capt Thos Bradley, Vol Cav
HORN, Samuel, Pvt, Col Ewen Allison, Capt John Allen, E TN Mil
HORN, Theophilus, Pvt, Col Sam Copeland, Capt John Dawson, Inf; d 4-20-1814
HORN, William, Pvt, Col Wm Lillard, Capt James Lillard, E TN Vol Inf
HORN, Zachariah, Pvt, Regt Commander omitted, Capt John Mullin, Spies
HORN, Zachel, Pvt, Regt Commander omitted, Capt William Mitchell, Spies
HORNBACK, Elijah, Pvt, Col John Brown, Capt Wm Christian, E TN Inf
HORNBORGER, William, Pvt, Col R C Napier, Capt Thos Gray, Mil Inf
HORNE, Henry, Pvt, Col John Coffee, Capt Alex McKeen, Cav
HORNE, James, Pvt, Col William Hall, Capt John Moore, Vol Inf
HORNE, Peter, Pvt, Col Wm Metcalf, Capt Wm Mullin, Mil Inf
HORNE, Zachariah, Pvt, Regt Commander omitted, Capt John Russell, Spies
HORNER, Cavilleer, Pvt, Col Wm Lillard, Capt S Copeland, E TN Vol Inf
HORNER, Isaac, Pvt, Col Wm Lillard, Capt S Copeland, E TN Vol Inf
HORNER, John, Pvt, Lt Col Wm Phillips, Co Commander omitted, Inf
HORNER, John, Pvt, Regt Commander omitted, Cpl E Green, Mtd Spies
HORNER, Phillip, Pvt, Col Wm Johnson, Capt Jas Rogers, E TN Drafted Mil
HORNER, Robert, Pvt, Maj Gen Carroll, Capt Ellis, Inf
HORNSDY, Solomon, Pvt, Col John Wynne, Capt Wm Caruthers, W TN Inf
HORSEY, Smith H, Pvt, Col Philip Pipkin, Capt Eb Kirkpatrick, Mil Inf
HORSKINS, James, Pvt, Col Sam Bunch, Capt Moses, E TN Mil Drafted; transferred to Capt Hauk's Co
HORSONG, William, Pvt, Col Edwin Booth, Capt Alex Biggs, Inf
HORTEN, Francis M, 2 Cpl, Col Newton Cannon, Capt John Demsey, Mtd Gunmen
HORTLE (HORTHER), Adam, Pvt, Col Sam Wear, Capt John Childs, E TN Vol Inf
HORTON, Archibald, Pvt, Col Sam Copeland, Capt Solomon George, Inf
HORTON, Isaac, Pvt, Col Ewen Allison, Capt Jacob Hoyal, E TN Mil; joined by transfer from Capt McPherson Co

## Enlisted Men, War of 1812

HORTON, Isaac, Pvt, Col Sam Bunch, Capt George McPherson, E TN Mil

HORTON, James, Pvt, Col Wm Johnson, Capt Jas Rogers, E TN Drafted Mil

HORTON, Jesse, Pvt, Regt Commander omitted, Capt Wm Mitchell, Spies

HORTON, Joseph, Pvt, Regt Commander omitted, Capt D Deaderick, Arty; under Gen A Jackson

HORTON, Joshua, Pvt, Col Pipkin, Capt Henry Newlin, Mil Inf; substitute for Caleb Horton

HORTON, William W, Pvt, Col R H Dyer, Capt James Wyatt, Vol Mtd Gunmen

HORTON, William, Pvt, Col Ewen Allison, Capt Jacob Hoyal, E TN Mil; joined by transfer from Capt McPherson Camp

HOSKINS, John, Pvt, Col John Brown, Capt Hugh Barton, E TN Mil Inf

HOSKINS, John, Pvt, Col Wm Johnson, Capt Joseph Scott, E TN Drafted Mil

HOSKINS, Samuel, Pvt, Col William Johnson, Capt Joseph Scott, E TN Drafted Mil

HOSKINS, William N, 1 Sgt, Col Wm Lillard, Capt John Roper, E TN Vol Inf

HOSSEY, James, 6 Cpl, Col Alex Loury, Capt John Looney, 2nd Regt W TN Mil

HOSTLER, Daniel, Pvt, Col John Brown, Capt William White, E TN Mil Inf

HOTCHKISS, Hezakiah, 3 Sgt, Col John Brown, Capt William White, E TN Vol Mtd Inf

HOTH, Joseph, Pvt, Lt I Berrett, Capt Nathan Davis, W TN Bn Inf

HOU, Stephen, Pvt, Regt Commander omitted, Capt Jas Williams, Mil Cav

HOUK, John, Sgt Maj, Col Sam Wear, Co Commander omitted, E TN Vol Mil Inf

HOUK, John, Sgt, Col Sam Wear, Capt Wm Mitchell, E TN Mtd Inf; appointed Sgt Maj

HOUK, Michael, Dmr, Col Edwin Booth, Capt Porter, Drafted Mil

HOUKE, Mathias, Pvt, Col Thos Williamson, Capt John Hutchings, Vol Mtd Gunmen

HOUN, George, Cpl, Col R H Dyer, Capt Ephraim Dickson, TN Mtd Vol Gunmen; d 3-26-1815

HOUNNELL, Daniel, Pvt, Col John Brown, Capt John Childs, E TN Vol Mtd Inf

HOUSE, David, Pvt, Col Philip Pipkin, Capt Wm Mackay, Mil Inf

HOUSE, Green, Pvt, Col John Coffee, Capt Chas Kavanaugh, Cav; d 1-13-1813

HOUSE, Henry, Pvt, Col James Raulston, Capt Henry Hamilton, Inf; also served under Maj Gen Carroll

HOUSE, Jacob, Pvt, Col A Cheatham, Capt Wm Creel, Inf

HOUSE, Jacob, Pvt, Col R H Dyer, Capt Jas Wyatt, Vol Mtd Gunmen

HOUSE, James, Pvt, Col Alex Loury, Capt Geo Sarver, Inf

HOUSE, James, Pvt, Regt Commander omitted, Capt David Mason, Cav

HOUSE, John, 2 Cpl, Col Wm Hall, Capt John Moore, Vol Inf

HOUSE, John, Pvt, Col R H Dyer, Capt Jas Wyatt, Vol Mtd Gunmen

HOUSE, John, Pvt, Col Wm Hall, Capt John Moore, Vol Inf; substituted for Thos M Smith

HOUSE, John, Pvt, Regt Commander omitted, Capt David Mason, Cav; promoted to Cpl, Sgt, then to Ens

HOUSE, Mansfield, Pvt, Col John Coffee, Capt Chas Kavanaugh, Cav

HOUSE, Mansfield, Pvt, Regt Commander omitted, Capt David Mason, Cav

HOUSE, Mathew, Dmr, Col Wm Metcalf, Capt O Waller, Mil Inf

HOUSE, Samuel, Pvt, Col John Alcorn, Capt John Winston, Mtd Riflemen

HOUSE, Samuel, Pvt, Col Saml Wear, Capt Jesse Cole, Vol Inf

HOUSE, Thomas, Pvt, Col Alex Loury, Capt Geo Sarver, Inf

HOUSE, Thomas, Pvt, Col N T Perkins, Capt Geo Eliot, Mtd Inf

HOUSE, Thomas, Pvt, Col Thomas Williamson, Capt Robert Moore, Vol Mtd Gunmen

HOUSE, William, Pvt, Col Robert Steele, Capt R Campbell, Mil Inf

HOUSE, William, Pvt, Col Wm Hall, Capt John Wallace, Inf

HOUSEBY, Isaac, Pvt, Col Wm Johnson, Capt Henry Hunter, E TN Mil

HOUSING, Benjamine, Pvt, Col Robert Dyer, Capt Robert Edmondson, TN Vol Mtd Gunmen

HOUSTON, James, Cpl, Maj James Porter, Capt Sam Cowan, Cav

HOUSTON, James, Pvt, Col T H Benton, Capt Benj Hewett, Vol Inf

HOUSTON, James, Pvt, Col T Williamson, Capt Robert Steele, Vol Mtd Gunmen

HOUSTON, Joe P, Pvt, Col Jno Williams, Capt Wm Walker, Vol

HOUSTON, John, Pvt, Col N Cannon, Capt John B Dempsey, Mtd Gunmen

HOUSTON, John, Pvt, Col Thos Benton, Capt Isaiah Renshaw, Vol Inf; joined from Capt Hewett's Co

HOUSTON, John, Pvt, Maj J Childes, Capt John Stephens, E TN Vol Mtd Inf

HOUSTON, John, Sgt, Col T H Benton, Capt Benj Hewett, Vol Inf

HOUSTON, Mathew, Pvt, Maj John Childs, Capt R Tipton, E TN Vol Mtd Inf; Regimental County Knox

HOUSTON, Matthew, Pvt, Maj James Porter, Capt Sam Cowan, Cav

HOUSTON, Paxon, Sgt, Maj James Porter, Capt Sam Cowan, Cav

HOUSTON, Peter, Pvt, Col J Alcorn, Capt Thos Bradley, Vol Cav

HOUSTON, Robert, Sgt, Maj Jas Porter, Capt Sam Cowan, Cav

HOUSTON, Samuel, Pvt, Col S Bunch, Capt E Buchanan, E TN Drafted Mil; appointed Wagon Master

HOUSTON, Samuel, Pvt, Col Sam'l Wear, Capt Jas Gillespie, E TN Vol Inf

HOUSTON, William, Pvt, Col Jno Brown, Capt Wm

## Enlisted Men, War of 1812

Christian, E TN Mil Inf
HOUSTON, William, Pvt, Regt Commander omitted, Capt Larkin Ferrell, Inf
HOW, John, Pvt, Col Wm Lillard, Capt W Gillenwater, E TN Inf
HOW, Joseph, Pvt, Gen T Johnston, Capt Daniel Oban, 36 Inf
HOW, Joseph, Sgt, Col T Williamson, Capt T Porter, Vol Mtd Gunmen
HOWARD, Alexander, Pvt, Col W Johnston, Capt J H Rogers, E TN Drafted Mil
HOWARD, Allen, Mus, Col R C Napier, Capt D Adkins, Mil Inf
HOWARD, Allen, Pvt, Col Ed Bradley, Capt A Bledsoe, Riflemen
HOWARD, Allen, Pvt, Col Jas Raulston, Capt M Neal, Inf; d 1-25-1815
HOWARD, Allen, Pvt, Col Robert Steele, Capt R Campbell, Mil Inf
HOWARD, Allen, Pvt, Lt Col R Napier, Co Commander omitted, Inf
HOWARD, Allen, Pvt, Regt Commander omitted, Capt Jos Williams, Mil Cav
HOWARD, Charles, Pvt, Col Robert Dyer, Capt I Williams, Mtd Gunmen
HOWARD, Edmond, Pvt, Col Robert Dyer, Capt I Williams, Vol Mtd Gunmen
HOWARD, Edward, Pvt, Col T Williamson, Capt Jas Cook & Capt John Crane, Vol Mtd Gunmen
HOWARD, Elisha, Pvt, Col Robt Steele, Capt R M Ratton, Mil Inf
HOWARD, Ezekiel, Pvt, Col Wm Lillard, Capt R Maloney, E TN Vol Inf
HOWARD, Green B (Greenberry), Pvt, Col Wm Hall, Capt A Bledsoe, Vol Inf
HOWARD, Green B, Pvt, Col Ed Bradley, Capt A Bledsoe, Riflemen
HOWARD, Isaac, Pvt, Col Robert Steele, Capt R M Ratton, Mil Inf
HOWARD, Isaiah, Pvt, Col Robert Dyer, Capt I Williams, Vol Mtd Gunmen
HOWARD, James, 1 Sgt, Col Philip Pipkin, Capt George Mebane, Mil Inf
HOWARD, James, Pvt, Col Robert Steele, Capt Richard M Ratton, Mil Inf
HOWARD, James, Pvt, Col Samuel Bunch, Capt Francis Berry, E TN Mil; deserted 3-4-1814
HOWARD, James, Pvt, Col Samuel Bunch, Capt Geo McPherson, E TN Mil; joined from Capt Griffin's Co
HOWARD, James, Pvt, Regt Commander omitted, Capt Gray, Inf
HOWARD, James, Sgt, Col John K Wynne, Capt John Spinks, Inf
HOWARD, John, Pvt, Col Edwin Booth, Capt Vernon, E TN Mil; d 3-15-1815
HOWARD, John, Pvt, Col Ewen Allison, Capt John Hampton, Mil
HOWARD, John, Pvt, Col Robert Steele, Capt Richard M Ratton, Mil Inf
HOWARD, John, Pvt, Col Thomas Benton, Capt Isaiah Renshaw, Vol Inf
HOWARD, John, Pvt, Col Wm Metcalf, Capt Alexander Hill, Mil Inf
HOWARD, Joshua, Pvt, Col A Cheatham, Capt George G Chapman, Inf
HOWARD, Mathew, Pvt, Col Wm Metcalf, Capt Barbee Collins, Mil Inf
HOWARD, Nathan, Pvt, Lt Col A Cheatham, Capt Meredith Walker, 6th Brig Mtd Inf
HOWARD, Promineous, Pvt, Col R C Napier, Capt Samuel Ashmore, Mil Inf
HOWARD, Richard, Pvt, Col R H Dyer, Capt Joseph Williams, Vol Mtd Gunmen; died of wounds received in action 1-2-1815
HOWARD, Robert, Pvt, Col R H Dyer, Capt J Williams, Vol Mtd Gunmen
HOWARD, Robert, Pvt, Col Samuel Bayless, Capt Jas Churchman, E TN Mil
HOWARD, Samuel, Ffr, Col Edwin Booth, Capt John Lewis, E TN Mil
HOWARD, Samuel, Pvt, Col Samuel Bayless, Capt James Landen, E TN Mil
HOWARD, Samuel, Pvt, Col Wm Lillard, Capt Zacheus Copeland, E TN Vol Inf
HOWARD, Stephen, Pvt, Regt Commander omitted, Capt Jas Williams, Mil Cav
HOWARD, William, 1 Cpl, Col Alexander Loury, Capt John Looney, 2nd Regt W TN Mil
HOWARD, William, Pvt, Col John Wynne, Capt John Spinks, Inf
HOWARD, William, Pvt, Col Samuel Bayless, Capt James Churchman, E TN Mil; transferred to Capt Millikin's Co
HOWARD, William, Pvt, Col Wm Johnson, Capt Elihu Milliken, 3rd Regt E TN Mil; transferred from Capt Churchman's Co
HOWARD, William, Pvt, Col Wm Metcalf, Capt John Cunningham, Mil Inf
HOWARD, William, Sgt Maj, Col Wm Johnson, Co Commander omitted, 3rd Regt E TN Mil
HOWE, Joseph, Pvt, Col William Johnson, Capt Joseph Kirk, Mil
HOWE, William, Pvt, Col S Bunch, Capt Jones Griffin, E TN Drafted Mil
HOWEL, Anderson, Pvt, Regt Commander omitted, Capt Dan'l Yarnell, E TN Mil; joined Capt Parrish's Co of Arty
HOWEL, Henry H, Pvt, Maj Gen A Jackson, Capt Joseph Kirkpatrick, Mtd Gunmen
HOWEL, John, Pvt, Col Jno Williams, Capt David Vande, Mtd Mil
HOWEL, John, Pvt, Col Samuel Bunch, Capt John Dobbins, E TN Drafted Mil; furloughed for inability
HOWEL, William, Pvt, Col William Johnson, Capt Elihu Milliken, 3rd Regt E TN Mil
HOWELL, Abner, Pvt, Col R H Dyer, Capt Joseph Williams, 1st Regt TN Vol Mtd Gunmen
HOWELL, Abner, Sgt, Maj Wm Russell, Capt Isaac Williams, Separate Bn of Vol Mtd Gunmen
HOWELL, Absolem, Pvt, Col Samuel Bunch, Capt Geo McPherson, E TN Mil; joined from Capt Everett's

## Enlisted Men, War of 1812

HOWELL, Anderson, Pvt, Col Samuel Wear, Capt Jesse Cole, Vol Inf; transferred to Capt Morgan
HOWELL, Anderson, Pvt, Col Samuel Wear, Capt Rufus Morgan, E TN Vol Inf
HOWELL, Anderson, Pvt, Maj Gen A Jackson, Capt Joel Parrish, Arty
HOWELL, Charles, Pvt, Regt Commander omitted, Capt Gray, Inf
HOWELL, Colep, Pvt, Col A Loury, Capt John Looney, W TN Inf
HOWELL, John, Cpl, Col R C Napier, Capt Andrew McCarty, Mil Inf
HOWELL, John, Pvt, Col A Cheatham, Capt William Smith, Inf
HOWELL, John, Pvt, Col John Cocke, Capt Richard Crunk, Inf; promoted to Deputy QM
HOWELL, John, Pvt, Col Samuel Bayless, Capt Joseph Rich, E TN Inf
HOWELL, John, Pvt, Maj William Woodfolk, Capt Abner Pearce, Inf
HOWELL, John, QM, Brig Gen Thos Johnson, Branch Srvce omitted
HOWELL, Joseph B, Blksmth, Maj Wm Russell, Capt Isaac Williams, 1st Regt TN Vol Mtd Gunmen; also under Col R H Dyer
HOWELL, Laben, Pvt, Maj John Childs, Capt James Cummings, E TN Vol Mtd Inf
HOWELL, Levi, Pvt, Col Newton Cannon, Capt John Harpole, Mtd Gunmen
HOWELL, Levi, Sgt, Col Thos Williamson, Capt Beverly Williams, Vol Mtd Gunmen
HOWELL, Malachi, Pvt, Col Newton Cannon, Capt John Harpole, Mtd Gunmen
HOWELL, Malachi, Tptr, Col Thos Williamson, Capt Beverly Williams, Vol Mtd Gunmen
HOWELL, Marshall S, Pvt, Col Samuel Wear, Capt Rufus Morgan, E TN Vol Inf
HOWELL, Paul, Pvt, Col James Raulston, Capt Mathew Cowan, Inf
HOWELL, William S, Lt, Col Samuel Wear, Capt Rufus Morgan, E TN Vol Inf
HOWELL, William, Cpl, Maj Wm Woodfolk, Capt Abner Pearce, Inf
HOWELL, William, Pvt, Col John K Wynne, Capt James Cole, Inf
HOWELL, William, Pvt, Col S Copeland, Capt William Douglass, Inf
HOWSER, Henry, Pvt, Col Wm Lillard, Capt Geo Keys, E TN Inf
HOWSON, Andrew, Pvt, Col John Cocke, Capt Richard Crunk, Inf
HOYLE, Daniel, Pvt, Maj Wm Russell, Capt John Trimble, Vol Mtd Gunmen
HOYSE, John, Pvt, Regt Commander omitted, Capt Jas Haggard, Mtd Gunmen
HOZE, Cas, Sgt Maj, Col Wm Johnson, Co Commander omitted, 3rd Regt E TN Draft Mil; discharged for inability of body
HUBARD, David, Sgt, Col Thomas Williamson, Capt Pate & Capt James Neely, Vol Mtd Gunmen
HUBARD, James, Pvt, Col S Wear, Capt John Stephens, E TN Vol Inf
HUBARD, John, QM Sgt, Col S Copeland, Co Commander omitted, Mil
HUBART, Fredrick, Pvt, Col Wm Johnson, Capt David McKamey, E TN Mil
HUBB, Richard, Pvt, Col John K Wynn, Capt Bailey Butler, Inf; deserted 11-19-1813
HUBBARD, Benjamin, Pvt, Col Ewen Allison, Capt Jonas Loughmiller, Mil
HUBBARD, David, Sgt, Col Thomas Williamson, Capt James Pace, Vol Mtd Gunmen
HUBBARD, Davis, Pvt, Col Williamson, Capt Thomas Searcy, Vol Mtd Gunmen
HUBBARD, Eli, Pvt, Maj Wm Woodfolk, Capt Abner Pearce, Inf
HUBBARD, Green H, Sgt, Col John Alcorn, Capt Locke, Cav
HUBBARD, Green K, 2 Cpl, Col John Coffee, Capt Blackman Coleman, Cav
HUBBARD, Jesse, Pvt, Col Edwin Booth, Capt John Slatton, E TN Mil
HUBBARD, John, Sgt, Col S Copeland, Capt Allen Wilkinson, Mil Inf; promoted to QM Gen
HUBBARD, Joseph, Pvt, Col Robert H Dyer, Co Commander omitted, TN Vol Mtd Gunmen
HUBBARD, Thomas, Pvt, Col John Alcorn, Capt William Locke, Cav
HUBBARD, Thomas, Pvt, Col John Coffee, Capt Blackman Coleman, Cav
HUBBARD, Vincent, Pvt, Col John Alcorn, Capt Blackman Locke, Cav
HUBBARD, Vincent, Tptr, Col John Coffee, Capt Blackman Coleman, Inf
HUBBART, Mathew, Pvt, Col S Wear, Capt Simeon Perry, E TN Vol Mtd Inf
HUBBART, William, Pvt, Col S Wear, Capt Jesse Cole, Vol Inf
HUBBS, Bane, Pvt, Maj Gen Carroll, Capt Ellis, Inf
HUBBS, John, 1 Cpl, Col Philip Pipkin, Capt Peter ____, Mil Inf
HUBBS, Thomas, Pvt, Col Elish Green, Co Commander omitted, Mtd Spies
HUBBS, William, Pvt, Col S Wear, Capt Daniel Price, E TN Vol Inf
HUBBS, William, Pvt, Maj Gen Carroll, Capt Ellis, Inf
HUBEY, John, Pvt, Gen Andrew Jackson, Capt Nathan Davis, Inf
HUCHERSON, John, Pvt, Col John K Butler, Capt Bailey Butler, Inf; deserted 11-19-1813
HUCKABEL, William, Pvt, Col Edwin Booth, Capt John Porter, Drafted Mil
HUCKABY, John, Pvt, Col S Bunch, Capt Jno English, E TN Drafted Mil
HUCKABY, Nathaniel, Pvt, Col S Bunch, Capt Jno ____, E TN Drafted Mil
HUDDESDON, John, Pvt, Regt Commander omitted, Capt Jno Gordon, Branch Srvce omitted
HUDDLESON, Daniel, Pvt Col Alexander Loury, Capt John Looney, Inf
HUDDLESTON, Charles, Pvt, Col Leroy Hammonds,

## Enlisted Men, War of 1812

Capt Jas Tubbs, Inf
HUDDLESTON, Doodson, Pvt, Regt Commander omitted, Capt Jno Craig, Inf
HUDDLESTON, Fielding, Pvt, Col A Cheatham, Capt Richard Benson, Inf
HUDDLESTON, Fielding, Pvt, Lt Col Jno Edmonson, Co Commander omitted, Cav
HUDDLESTON, James, Pvt, Col A Cheatham, Capt Geo Chapman, Inf
HUDDLESTON, James, Pvt, Col John Winn, Capt James Holleman, Inf
HUDDLESTON, John, 1 Sgt, Maj Gen Carroll, Capt Huddleston & Capt Jas Raulston, Inf
HUDDLESTON, Jonah, Sgt, Col A Cheatham, Capt Geo Chapman, Inf
HUDDLESTON, Jonathan, Pvt, Col A Cheatham, Capt Merith Walker, Mtd Inf
HUDDLESTON, Jonathan, Pvt, Col Thos Dyer, Capt Cuthbert Hudson, Vol Mtd Gunmen
HUDDLESTON, Richard, Pvt, Col John Cocke, Capt John Weakley, Branch Srvce omitted
HUDDLESTON, Thomas, Cpl, Col S Bunch, Lt Jno Harris, E TN Mil
HUDDLESTON, Woodson, Pvt, Col John Cocke, Capt Samuel Caruthers, Inf
HUDDLESTON, Woodson, Pvt, Regt Commander omitted, Capt Jno Crane, Mtd Inf
HUDGEONS, Wilson, Pvt, Col S Wear, Capt James Gillespie, Inf E TN Vol; deserted 11-12-1813
HUDGING, Plaro, Pvt, Col Phillip Pipkin, Capt David Smith, W TN Mil; attached to Capt John Strother Camp
HUDGINS, Holloway, Pvt, Col John Cocke, Capt Nance, Inf
HUDGINS, Parrow, Pvt, Col Phillip Pipkin, Capt Geo Smith, Inf
HUDGINS, William, Pvt, Col Thos Dyer, Capt Thos White, Vol Mtd Gunmen
HUDGONS, William, Pvt, Col John Alcorn, Capt Fredrick Stump, Cav; wounded 11-9-1813
HUDIBURG, Lewis, Pvt, Maj James Porter, Capt James Anderson, Cav
HUDNAL, William W, Cpl, Col Jno Coffee, Capt Fredrick Stump, Cav
HUDNELL, W W, Pvt, Col John Coffee, Capt Jas Terrell, Vol Cav
HUDNELL (HUDNUL), William, Pvt, Col Robert Dyer, Capt Sam White, Vol Mtd Gunmen
HUDROY, Armstead, Pvt, Col John Childs, Capt Chas Conway, E TN Mtd Gunmen
HUDSON, Andrew G, Pvt, Regt Commander omitted, Capt Jas Terrell, Cav
HUDSON, Cuthbert, Pvt, Lt Col John Edmondson, no other information
HUDSON, Elijah, 4 Cpl, Col John Brown, Capt Jesse Reany, Mtd Gunmen
HUDSON, Elijah, Sgt, Col Wm Russell, Capt Wm Chism, Vol Mtd Gunmen
HUDSON, George, Pvt, Col John Cocke, Capt Bird Nance, Inf
HUDSON, George, Rank omitted, Col John Wynne, Capt James Cole, Inf
HUDSON, Howell, Pvt, Col Wm Russell, Capt Fleman Hodges, Vol Mtd Gunmen
HUDSON, Irby, Pvt, Col John Wynne, Capt Robert Brader, Inf
HUDSON, James, Pvt, Col James Raulston, Capt Dan Newman, Inf
HUDSON, John B, Pvt, Regt Commander omitted, Capt Jas Terrell, Cav
HUDSON, John, Pvt, Col Edwin Booth, Capt Porter, Drafted Mil
HUDSON, Noah, Pvt, Col Edward Bradley, Capt Harry Douglass, Vol Inf
HUDSON, Noah, Pvt, Col Sam Copeland, Capt Moses Thompson, Inf
HUDSON, Obadiah, Pvt, Col Edwin Booth, Capt Porter, Drafted Mil
HUDSON, Richard, Pvt, Col James Raulston, Capt James Black, Inf
HUDSON, Richard, Pvt, Col Robert Steele, Capt Richard Ratton, Mil Inf; killed 3-30-1814
HUDSON, Thomas B, Pvt, Col John Coffee, Capt James Terrell, Vol Cav
HUDSON, Thomas B, Pvt, Regt Commander omitted, Capt Jas Terrell, Cav; killed at battle of Tallehatcher 11-3-1813
HUDSON, Thomas, Cpl, Col Robert Dyer, Capt Cuthbert Hudson, Vol Mtd Gunmen; promoted from Pvt
HUDSON, Thomas, Pvt, Col A Cheatham, Capt James Giddens, Inf
HUDSON, Thomas, Pvt, Col Edwin Booth, Capt Richard Marshall, Drafted Mil; discharged for inability
HUDSON, Thomas, Pvt, Col Philip Pipkin, Capt Wm Mackay, Mil Inf
HUDSON, Thomas, Pvt, Col Robert Dyer, Capt C Hudson, Vol Mtd Gunmen
HUDSON, Thomas, Pvt, Regt Commander omitted, Lt Richard Napier, Inf
HUDSON, Wesley, Pvt, Col John Coffee, Capt George Barnes, Inf
HUDSON, William, 1 Sgt, Col Newt Cannon, Capt David Hogen, Mtd Gunmen; d 12-1-1813
HUDSON, William, Pvt, Col Robert Steele, Capt Richard Ratton, Mil Inf; deserted 4-29-1814
HUDSON (HUTSON), John, Pvt, Col J Raulston, Capt E Robinson, Inf
HUDSPETH, George, Pvt, Regt Commander omitted, Capt Wm Mitchell, Spies
HUDSPETH, William, Pvt, Col Ewen Allison, Capt Joe Everett, E TN Mil; deserted 3-4-1814
HUES, Reuben, Pvt, Col William Hall, Capt John Moore, Vol Inf
HUES (HUGES), Ezekiel, Pvt, Col Wm Johnson, Capt Elihu Milliken, 3rd Regt E TN Mil
HUETT, Robert, Sgt, Col John Brown, Capt Wm White, E TN Mil Inf
HUEY, Enoch, Pvt, Col Alex Loury, Capt Martin, Inf
HUEY, John, Far, Col Robert Dyer, Capt James McMahon, TN Mtd Vol Gunmen
HUEY, John, Pvt, Col N T Perkins, Capt John Doak, Vol Mtd Gunmen

## Enlisted Men, War of 1812

HUEY, John, Pvt, Col Wm Higgins, Capt John Cheatham, Mtd Riflemen
HUEY (HUGHY), John, Pvt, Col John Cocke, Capt Richard Crunk, Inf; d 3-17-1814
HUFF, George, Pvt, Col John Brown, Capt Chas Lewin, E TN Mtd Inf Vol
HUFF, John, 3 Sgt, Col Wm Lillard, Capt John Neatherton, E TN Vol Inf
HUFF, Joseph, Pvt, Col Wm Johnson, Capt Christopher Cook, E TN Mil
HUFF, Joseph, Pvt, Col Wm Lillard, Capt James Lillard, E TN Vol Mil Inf
HUFF, Leonard, Cpl, Col John Wynne, Capt Jas Holleman, Inf
HUFF, Richard, Pvt, Col Robert Steele, Capt James Bennett, Mil Inf
HUFF, Richard, Pvt, Maj Wm Woodfolk, Capt Abraham Dudney, Inf
HUFF, William, Pvt, Col Wm Lillard, Capt James Lillard, E TN Vol Inf
HUFFACK (HOFFAND), John, Pvt, Col Sam Wear, Capt Brownman, Mtd Inf
HUFFLIN (HEFLIN), Abelem, Pvt, Col Philip Pipkin, Capt John Strother, Mil; substituted for Solomon Odel
HUFFMAN, Adam, Pvt, Col Ewen Allison, Capt John Hampton, Mil
HUFFMAN, Jacob, Pvt, Col Wm Johnson, Capt Alex Loury, E TN Drafted Mil
HUFFMAN, Jacob, Pvt, Col Wm Johnson, Capt Andrew Lawson, E TN Drafted Mil
HUFFMAN, Jesse, Pvt, Col Saml Bunch, Capt Jos Duncan, E TN Mil; furnished a substitute
HUFFMAN, John, Pvt, Col Sam Bunch, Capt Jones Griffin, E TN Drafted Mil
HUFFMAN, William, Pvt, Col John Wynne, Capt Bayless Prince, Inf
HUFFMASTER, Daniel, Pvt, Col S Bunch, Capt Jones Griffin, E TN Drafted Mil; joined from Capt Loughmiller Co
HUFFMASTER, John, Pvt, Col Sam Bunch, Capt Jones Griffin, E TN Drafted Mil; joined from Capt Loughmiller Co
HUFFSTATLAR, Jacob, Pvt, Col Wm Johnson, Capt Jas Rogers, E TN Drafted Mil
HUFMAN, Benjamin, 2 Sgt, Col Edward Bradley, Capt John Wallace, Vol Inf
HUFMAN, William, 1 Cpl, Col Wm Hall, Capt John Wallace, Vol Inf
HUFMASTER, Daniel, Pvt, Col Ewen Allison, Capt J Laughmiller, Mil; transferred to Capt McPherson Co
HUFMASTER, John, Pvt, Col Ewen Allison, Capt Laughmiller, Mil; transferred to Capt Griffin's Co
HUFMASTER, Joseph, Pvt, Col Ewin Allison, Capt John Loughmiller, Mil
HUFSTATLER, Solomon, Pvt, Col R H Dyer, Capt Jas McMahon, TN Vol Mtd Gunmen
HUGGINS, Jonathan, Pvt, Maj Carroll, Capt Lewis Dillahunty & Capt Daniel Bradford, Vol Inf
HUGGINS, Phillip, Pvt, Maj Wm Woodfolk, Capt Abner Pearce, Inf
HUGGINS, Reuben, Pvt, Col R H Dyer, Capt Robert Evans, Vol Mtd Gunmen
HUGGINS, Reuben, Pvt, Col Robert Steele, Capt John Chitwood, Mil Inf
HUGGINS, William, Pvt, Col John Coffee, Capt Blackman Coleman, Cav
HUGGINS (HIGGINS), John, Pvt, Col Thos McCrory, Capt Thos K Gordon, Inf
HUGGINS (HIGGINS), Luke, Pvt, Col Wm Metcalf, Capt Thos Marks, Mil Inf
HUGHBANKS, John, Pvt, Col Stephen Copeland, Capt Douglas, Inf
HUGHBANKS, Morton, Pvt, Col A Loury, Capt Sarver, Inf
HUGHES, Aaron, Pvt, Col S Bunch, Capt Jones Griffin, E TN Drafted Mil
HUGHES, Aaron, Pvt, Col Wm Metcalf, Capt Alexander Hill & Capt John Cunningham, Mil Inf; d 1-30-1815
HUGHES, Cornelius, Pvt, Col Wm Johnson, Capt Benjamin Powell, E TN Mil
HUGHES, David, Cpl, Col Wm Johnson, Capt Joseph Scott, E TN Drafted Mil
HUGHES, David, Pvt, Col R C Napier, Co Commander omitted, Mil Inf
HUGHES, David, Pvt, Col William Johnson, Capt Joseph Scott, E TN Drafted Mil; substitute for Larman Arrauts
HUGHES, David, Pvt, Col Wm Lillard, Capt Benjamin King, E TN Vol Inf
HUGHES, David, Pvt, Gen Andrew Jackson, Capt D Deadrick, Arty
HUGHES, David, Pvt, Regt Commander omitted, Capt D S Deadrick, Arty
HUGHES, Francis, Pvt, Col Samuel Bunch, Capt James Penny, E TN Mtd Inf
HUGHES, George, Cpl, Col Samuel Bayless, Capt James Landen, E TN Mil
HUGHES, George, Pvt, Col John Brown, Capt Charles Lewin, E TN Vol Mtd Inf
HUGHES, George, Pvt, Col Wm Johnson, Capt Joseph Scott, E TN Drafted Mil; substitute for Ebenezer Shields
HUGHES, James A, Pvt, Col Stephen Copeland, Capt John Dawson, Inf
HUGHES, James A, Pvt, Regt Commander omitted, Capt Joe Dawson, Branch Srvce omitted
HUGHES, James, 1 Cpl, Col Wm Lillard, Capt Benjamin King, E TN Vol Mil
HUGHES, James, Pvt, Col Ewin Allison, Capt William King, Drafted Mil
HUGHES, James, Pvt, Col John K Wynn, Capt Jas Cole, Inf; deserted 10-30-1813
HUGHES, James, Pvt, Col John Williams, Capt Wm Walker, Vol
HUGHES, James, Pvt, Col William Y Higgins, Capt Thomas Eldridge, Mtd Gunmen
HUGHES, James, Pvt, Col Wm Lillard, Capt George Keyes, E TN Inf
HUGHES, James, Pvt, Col Wm Pillow, Capt McEwin, Vol

## Enlisted Men, War of 1812

HUGHES, James, Pvt, Maj Wm Russell, Capt Wm Hodges, Vol Mtd Gunmen
HUGHES, John, Pvt, Col Thos H Benton, Capt Thos M Williamson, Vol Inf
HUGHES, John, Pvt, Col Wm Lillard, Capt Thos Sharpe, 2nd Regt Inf
HUGHES, John, Pvt, Col Wm Pillow, Capt Thos Williamson, Vol Inf
HUGHES, Kibble T, Pvt, Col R H Dyer, Capt Jas McMahon, TN Vol Mtd Gunmen
HUGHES, Lewis, Pvt, Col Thos H Williamson, Capt John Doak & Capt John Dobbins, Vol Mtd Gunmen
HUGHES, Owen, Pvt, Col Thos H Benton, Capt McEwin, Vol Inf
HUGHES, Owen, Pvt, Col Wm Pillow, Capt C H McEwin, Vol Inf
HUGHES, Reuben, Pvt, Col Wm Hall, Capt William Alexander, Vol Inf
HUGHES, Reubin, Pvt, Col Thos Bradley, Capt Wm Lauderdale, Vol Inf; d 12-10-1813
HUGHES, Robert, Pvt, Col Ewin Allison, Capt Wm King, Drafted Mil
HUGHES, Robert, Pvt, Col Thomas Williamson, Capt John Doak & Capt John Dobbins, Vol Mtd Gunmen
HUGHES, Robert, Pvt, Regt Commander omitted, Capt Andrew Patterson, Branch Srvce omitted
HUGHES, Sterling, Pvt, Col Ewin Allison, Capt Wm King, Drafted Mil
HUGHES, Thomas, Pvt, Col John K Wynne, Capt John Porter, Inf
HUGHES, Thomas, Pvt, Col Thos H Williamson, Capt Robert Steele, Vol Mtd Gunmen
HUGHES, William, Pvt, Gen Thos Washington, Capt John Crawford, Mtd Inf
HUGHES, Zachariah, QM Sgt, Col John Brown, E TN Mtd Gunmen
HUGHEY, Ezekiel, Pvt, Col Thos H Williamson, Capt John Doak & Capt John Dobbins, Vol Mtd Gunmen
HUGHEY, Richard, Pvt, Col Thos H Williamson, Capt Thomas Porter, Vol Mtd Gunmen
HUGHLETT, Thomas, Pvt, Col Philip Pipkin, Capt John Strother, Mil; attached to Wgnr, substitute John Humphrey
HUGHLETT, William H, Sgt, Col Edward Bradley, Capt John Kennedy, Riflemen; AWOL 12-12-1813
HUGHS, Aaron, Ffr, Col Edwin E Booth, Capt Vernon, Branch Srvce omitted
HUGHS, Robert, Pvt, Col Newton Cannon, Capt Andrew Patteson, Mtd Riflemen; promoted to Sgt
HUGHS, William, 2 Sgt, Col N T Perkins, Capt Philip Pipkin, Mtd Riflemen; wounded
HUGHS, William, Pvt, Col John Cocke, Capt James Gault, Inf
HUGHS, William, Pvt, Col Samuel Bunch, Capt George McPherson, E TN Mil
HUGHS, Zachariah, Pvt, Col John Brown, Capt John Trimble, E TN Mtd Gunmen
HUGHSON, James, 3 Cpl, Col James Raulston, Capt Newman, Inf; promoted to Sgt
HUGHSON, James, Pvt, Col Robert Steele, Capt Rotton, Mil Inf
HUGHY (HEUY), Robert, Sgt, Col John Cocke, Capt S M Caruthers, Inf
HULCEY, John, Pvt, Regt Commander omitted, Capt N Davis, Mil Inf
HULING, David, Dmr, Col Jno Brown, Capt L Oliver, E TN Mil
HULING, Frederick, Pvt, Lt Col A Cheatham, Capt G Marbey, 6th Brig Mtd Inf
HULING, Frederick, Pvt, Lt Col J Edmonson, Co Commander omitted, Cav
HULING, Frederick, Pvt, Regt Commander omitted, Capt David Smith, Cav Vol
HULING, Jonathan, Pvt, Col Edwin Booth, Capt Richard Marshall, Drafted Mil
HULL, Alfred M, Pvt, Col Wm Lillard, Capt T McChristian, E TN Vol Inf
HULL, Daniel, Pvt, Col Saml Bayless, Capt Jos Hale, E TN Mil; d 12-15-1814
HULL, Jesse, Pvt, Maj Wm Woodfolk, Capt E Ross & Capt McCulley, Inf
HULL, John, Cpl, Col Wm Lillard, Capt Jacob Dyke, Vol Inf
HULL, John, Pvt, Col T McCrory, Capt Jos Shannon, Mil Inf
HULL, Richard, Pvt, Maj Wm Russell, Capt Wm Chism, Vol Mtd Gunmen
HULL, Zachariah, Pvt, Col Saml Bunch, Capt Jos Duncan, E TN Drafted Mil; joined from Capt Gibbs Co
HULME, John C, Pvt, Col T H Benton, Capt Jas McEwen, Vol Inf
HULME, John C, Pvt, Regt Commander omitted, Capt David Mason, Cav
HULME, John, Pvt, Col John Cocke, Capt J Dalton, Inf
HULRY, Frederick W, Pvt, Lt Col A Cheatham, Capt G Martin, Mtd Inf
HULSE, Abraham, Pvt, Col Wm Lillard, Capt Hugh Martin, E TN Vol Inf
HULVEY, Conrad, Pvt, Col Wm Lillard, Capt J Dyke, Vol Inf
HUMBART, William jr, Pvt, Col Saml Bayless, Capt Jos Rich, E TN Inf
HUMBERT, Amos, Sgt, Col S Bayless, Capt Jos Rich, E TN Inf
HUMBERT, Isaac, Pvt, Col S Bunch, Capt F Register, E TN Mil; transferred to Capt McPherson's Co
HUMBERT, Reason, Pvt, Col Wm Lillard, Capt T Sharpe, 2nd Regt Inf
HUMBERT, _____, Pvt, Col S Bunch, Capt F Register, E TN Mil
HUMBLE, George, Pvt, Col R H Dyer, Capt Jos Williams, Vol Mtd Gunmen
HUMBLE, George, Pvt, Lt Col R Napier, Co Commander omitted, Inf
HUMBLE, Jacob, Pvt, Col E E Booth, Capt John Slatton, E TN Mil
HUMES, Charles, Pvt, Col S Bayless, Capt J Rich, E TN Inf
HUMMEL, John, Pvt, Col S Bayless, Capt J Rich, E TN Inf

## Enlisted Men, War of 1812

HUMMIN, Thomas, Pvt, Col S Bayless, Capt J Waddell, E TN Mil

HUMPHREY, Daniel, Pvt, Col N Cannon, Capt Martin, Mtd Gunmen

HUMPHREY, David, Pvt, Col R C Napier, Capt Ashmore, Mil Inf

HUMPHREY, James, Pvt, Col Wm Lillard, Capt Wm McLin, E TN Inf

HUMPHREY, John, Pvt, Col P Pipkin, Capt John Strother, Mil; substitute for Thomas Hughlett

HUMPHREY, John, Pvt, Col W Johnston, Capt H Hunter, E TN Mil

HUMPHREY, Uriah, Pvt, Col T McCrory, Capt Jas Shannon, Mil Inf

HUMPHREYS, Dudleys, Pvt, Col S Bunch, Lt Jno Harris, E TN Mil

HUMPHREYS, James, Pvt, Maj Gen Jackson, Col A Cheatham, Capt Wm Creel, Inf

HUMPHREYS, John, Pvt, Col E Bradley, Capt John Moore, Vol Inf; deserted 11-24-1813

HUMPHREYS, John, Pvt, Col S Wear, Capt J Cole, Vol Inf

HUMPHREYS, Moses, Pvt, Col S Wear, Capt J Cole, Vol Inf

HUMPHREYS, Solomon, Pvt, Col S Bunch, Capt J Duncan, E TN Drafted Mil; joined from Capt Howel's Co

HUMPHRIES, Jacob, 5 Sgt, Col W Metcalf, Capt Odidiah Walker, Mil Inf

HUMPHRIES, Jacob, Pvt, Col W Metcalf, Capt T Marks, Mil Inf

HUMPHRIES, John, Pvt, Col R Dyer, Capt I Williams, Vol Mtd Gunmen

HUMPHRIES, John, Pvt, Col Wm Johnston, Capt H Hunter, E TN Mil

HUMPSTEAD, Edward, Pvt, Col Sam'l Bunch, Capt Henry Stephens, E TN Mtd Inf

HUNDLEY, Robert, Pvt, Col John Cocke, Capt Bird Nance, Inf; d 3-7-1815

HUNDLEY, Willis, Pvt, Col Wm Hall, Capt A Bledsoe, Vol Inf

HUNDLY, John S, Cpl, Col E Allison, Capt H McCray, E TN Mil

HUNGERFORD, William, Cpl, Col N T Perkins, Capt M Johnston, Mil Inf

HUNGERFORD, William, Pvt, Maj Wm Carroll, Capt D M Bradford & Capt L Dillahunty, Vol Inf

HUNLEY, John, Pvt, Col Wm Hall, Capt A Bledsoe, Vol Inf

HUNLEY, Jordan, Sgt Mate, Col John Cocke, Co Commander omitted, 2nd Regt E TN Mil Inf

HUNLEY, Lankston, Pvt, Col S Bayless, Capt J Waddle, E TN Mil

HUNNEL, Robert, Pvt, Col R H Dyer, Capt C Hudson, Vol Mtd Gunmen

HUNT, Abraham, Pvt, Col J Brown, Capt Wm D Neilson, E TN Vol Mil

HUNT, Abram, Pvt, Maj J Childs, Capt C Conway, E TN Mtd Gunmen; Regimental County - Knox

HUNT, David, Pvt, Col J Alcorn, Capt A McKenn, Cav

HUNT, David, Pvt, Col P Pipkin, Capt Geo Mebane, Mil Inf

HUNT, Ephraim, Pvt, Col Wm Hall, Capt John Wallace, Inf

HUNT, Ephraim, Sdlr, Col John Coffee, Capt John Baskerville, Cav

HUNT, George, Pvt, no other information

HUNT, Henry W, Pvt, Col R H Dyer, Capt Thomas Jones, Vol Mtd Gunmen

HUNT, James, Pvt, Col John Cocke, Capt Bird Nance, Inf

HUNT, James, Sgt, Col A Cheatham, Capt William Smith, Inf; discharged for want of arms

HUNT, John, Pvt, Col Edward Bradley, Capt Abraham Bledsoe, Riflemen

HUNT, John, Pvt, Col Samuel Bayless, Capt James Landen, E TN Mil

HUNT, John, Pvt, Col Wm Hall, Capt Abraham Bledsoe, Vol Inf

HUNT, Jonathan, Pvt, Regt Commander omitted, Capt Samuel Allen, Pack Horse Guards

HUNT, Lewis, Cpl, Col Wm Metcalf, Capt Barbee Collins, Mil Inf

HUNT, Peter, Pvt, Col Samuel Bayless, Capt James Landen, E TN Mil

HUNT, Samuel, 2 Sgt, Col John Cocke, Capt Bird Nance, Inf

HUNT, Silas, Pvt, Lt Col L Hammonds, Capt Thomas Wells, Inf; deserted 10-7-1814 from Ft Deposit

HUNT, Smith, Sgt, Col Samuel Bayless, Capt Jonathan Waddell, E TN Mil

HUNT, Theoderick, Pvt, Col N T Perkins, Capt Mathew Patterson, Mtd Vol

HUNT, Thomas, 2 Cpl, Col Edward Bradley, Capt Abraham Bledsoe, Riflemen

HUNT, Thomas, 4 Cpl, Col William Hall, Capt Abraham Bledsoe, Vol Cav

HUNT, Thomas, Cpl, Col Wm Lillard, Capt Jacob Dyke, Vol Inf

HUNT, Thomas, Pvt, Col Samuel Bunch, Capt David G Vance, E TN Mtd Inf

HUNT, William, Pvt, Col Edward Bradley, Capt John Kennedy, Riflemen

HUNT, William, Pvt, Col James Raulston, Capt James A Black, Inf

HUNTER, Aaron, Lt, Col Wm Metcalf, Capt John Jackson, Inf; d 2-20-1815

HUNTER, Abraham, Pvt, Col Wm Johnston, Capt Henry Hunter, E TN Mil

HUNTER, Alexander, Pvt, Col R C Napier, Capt Drury Adkins, Mil Inf

HUNTER, Alfred, Cpl, Col Wm Lillard, Capt Robert Maloney, E TN Vol Inf

HUNTER, Andrew, Pvt, Col L Hammond, Capt James Craig, Inf

HUNTER, Burwell, Pvt, Col Philip Pipkin, Capt James Blakemore, Mil Inf

HUNTER, Daniel, Pvt, Col Jno Brown, Capt Wm White, Regt E TN Mil Inf Mtd

HUNTER, David, Pvt, Col Samuel Bunch, Capt David G Vance, E TN Mtd Inf

HUNTER, Dempsey, Cpl, Lt Col Henry Bryan, Co Commander omitted, Inf

## Enlisted Men, War of 1812

HUNTER, Dempsey, Pvt, Col Wm Hall, Capt James Hambleton, Vol Inf
HUNTER, Demsey, Pvt, Col Edward Bradley, Capt James Hambleton, Vol Inf
HUNTER, Dickerson, Pvt, Lt Col L Hammonds, Capt Thomas Delaney, Inf; also under Col A Loury
HUNTER, Elija, 4 Sgt, Col A Cheatham, Capt James Giddins, Inf
HUNTER, Elisha, Pvt, Col John Cocke, Capt John Dalton, Inf
HUNTER, Emanuel, Pvt, Brig Gen Thos Johnston, Capt Abraham Allen, Mil Inf
HUNTER, Henry jr, Pvt, Col Wm Lillard, Capt Wm Hamilton, E TN Vol Inf; Wgnr
HUNTER, Henry sr, Pvt, Col Wm Lillard, Capt Wm Hamilton, E TN Mil Vol
HUNTER, Henry, Pvt, Col James Raulston, Capt Daniel Newman, Inf
HUNTER, Henry, Pvt, Col John Cocke, Capt Bird Nance, Inf
HUNTER, Henry, Pvt, Col R H Dyer, Capt Cuthbert Hudson, Vol Mtd Gunmen
HUNTER, Hugh, Pvt, Regt Commander omitted, Capt James Craig, Inf
HUNTER, Isaac, Pvt, Col Jno Brown, Capt Jas Preston, E TN Mil Inf
HUNTER, Isaac, Pvt, Col Jno Coffee, Capt Thomas Bradley, Vol Cav
HUNTER, John, Pvt, Brig Gen T Johnson, Capt Abraham Allen, Mil Inf
HUNTER, John, Pvt, Col A Loury, Capt Arahel Rains, Inf; transferred to Capt Russell's Co
HUNTER, John, Pvt, Col James Raulston, Capt Elijah Haynie, Inf; d 1-18-1815
HUNTER, John, Pvt, Col Jno Coffee, Capt Jno W Byrn, Cav
HUNTER, John, Pvt, Col Jno Williams, Capt David Vance, Mtd Mil
HUNTER, John, Pvt, Col John Alcorn, Capt John W Byrne, Cav
HUNTER, John, Pvt, Col John Cocke, Capt Joseph Price, Inf
HUNTER, John, Pvt, Col N T Perkins, Capt Geo W Marr, Vol Mtd
HUNTER, John, Pvt, Col Wm Johnson, Capt Christopher Cook, E TN Mil
HUNTER, John, Pvt, Col Wm Johnson, Capt Joseph Kirk, Mil; substitute for Thomas Hunter
HUNTER, John, Pvt, Maj William Woodfolk, Capt Abraham Dudney & Capt John Sutton, Inf; substitute for Patrick McBride
HUNTER, John, Pvt, Regt Commander omitted, Capt Jas Craig, Mil Inf
HUNTER, John, Sgt, Col R H Dyer, Capt James McMahan, TN Vol Mtd Gunmen
HUNTER, Joseph, Pvt, Col Philip Pipkin, Capt John Strother, Mil
HUNTER, Nicholas, Pvt, Col Newt Cannon, Capt John Harpole, Mtd Gunmen; transferred to Capt Gordon's Co
HUNTER, Nicholas, Pvt, Regt Commander omitted, Capt John Gordon, Spies
HUNTER, Sam, Pvt, Col Robert Dyer, Capt Isaac Williams, Vol Mtd Gunmen
HUNTER, Samuel, Pvt, Col Ewen Allison, Capt Jacob Hoyal, E TN Mil
HUNTER, Samuel, Pvt, Col John Alcorn, Capt Thos Bradley, Vol Cav
HUNTER, Samuel, Pvt, Col John Coffee, Capt Thos Bradley, Vol Cav
HUNTER, Samuel, Pvt, Col Samuel Copeland, Capt Wm Douglass, Inf
HUNTER, Thomas, Pvt, Brig Gen Johnson, Capt Allen, Mil Inf
HUNTER, Thomas, Pvt, Col Robert Dyer, Capt Isaac Williams, Vol Mtd Gunmen
HUNTER, Thomas, Pvt, Col Wm Johnson, Capt Joe Kirk, Mil; never appeared
HUNTER, Thomas, Pvt, Lt Col R Napier, Co Commander omitted, Inf
HUNTER, Washington, Pvt, Maj Gen Carroll, Capt Francis Ellis, Inf
HUNTER, William, Pvt, Col Edwin Booth, Capt Vernon, E TN Inf
HUNTER, William, Pvt, Col N T Perkins, Capt G W Marr, Mtd Vol
HUNTER, William, Pvt, Col Wm Lillard, Capt G Argenbright, E TN Vol Riflemen
HUNTER, William, Pvt, Regt Commander omitted, Capt James Craig, Inf
HUNTER (HUNT), Lewis, 4 Sgt, Col Wm Hall, Capt A Bledsoe, Vol Inf
HUNTER (HUNT), Lewis, Pvt, Col Wm Hall, Capt Abraham Bledsoe, Vol Inf
HUNTER (HUNT), Lewis, Sgt, Col Wm Hall, Capt Abraham Bledsoe, Vol Inf
HUNTSMAN, Lemuel, Pvt, Col Sam Wear, Capt Brownman, Mtd Inf
HUNTSMAN, Lemul, Sgt, Col Wm Johnson, Capt Elihu Milliken, 3rd Regt E TN Mil
HUPPT, Joseph, Pvt, Col Wm Johnston, Capt Joe Kirk, Mil Inf
HUPTUTLER, George, Pvt, Col Edwin Booth, Capt James McKamey, E TN Mil
HURD, Benjamin, Pvt, Col Newt Cannon, Capt Ota Cantrell, W TN Mtd Inf
HURD, Charles, Pvt, Col Newt Cannon, Capt Ota Cantrell, W TN Mtd Inf
HURD, Jesse, Pvt, Maj Wm Russell, Capt Wm Chism, Vol Mtd Gunmen
HURD, Jessee, Pvt, Maj John Childs, Capt John Stephens, E TN Vol Mtd Inf; transferred to Capt Trimble's Co
HURE, William, Pvt, Col A Loury, Capt J Williamson, W TN Mil
HURLEY, Elwin, Pvt, Col Sam Bayless, Capt Joseph Hale, E TN Mil
HURLEY, Moses, Pvt, Col Sam Bunch, Capt Jones Griffin, E TN Drafted Mil
HURLEY, Moses, Pvt, Col Wm Johnson, Capt Ben Powell, E TN Mil
HURLEY, Nehemiah, Pvt, Col S Bunch, Capt Jonas Grif-

## Enlisted Men, War of 1812

fin, E TN Drafted Mil; deserted 3-4-1814
HURLEY, Nehemiah, Pvt, Col Wm Johnson, Capt Ben Powell, E TN Mil
HURLEY, Robinson, Pvt, Col S Bunch, Capt Jonas Griffin, E TN Drafted Mil; deserted 3-4-1814
HURLEY, Tilmon, Pvt, Col Wm Johnson, Capt Joe Kirk, Mil
HURST, Bird, Pvt, Regt Commander omitted, Capt Robert Evans, Mtd Spies
HURST, Daniel, Pvt, Col Wm Lillard, Capt James Hamilton, E TN Vol Inf
HURST, George jr, Pvt, Col Sam Bunch, Capt Jno Houk, E TN Mil
HURST, George sr, Pvt, Col Samuel Bunch, Capt John Houk, E TN Mil
HURST, Hiram, Sgt, Col Sam Bayless, Capt John Brock, E TN Mil
HURST, James, Pvt, Col Sam Bunch, Capt Henry Stephens, E TN Mtd Inf; d 12-29-1813
HURST, Jeremiah, Cpl, Col Ewen Allison, Capt Henry McCray, E TN Mil; transferred to Capt Parrish Co Arty
HURST, Jesse, Pvt, Col S Bunch, Capt Jno Hauk, E TN Mil
HURST, Jesse, Pvt, Col Sam Bunch, Capt Jno English, E TN Drafted Mil; joined from Capt Dobbins Co
HURST, John, Pvt, Col Maj Wm Russell, Capt Isaac Williams, Bn of TN Mtd Gunmen
HURST, John, Pvt, Col Thos Williamson, Capt Giles Burdette, Vol Mtd Gunmen
HURST, John, Pvt, Col Wm Johnson, Capt Henry Hunter, E TN Mil; transferred from Capt Kirk's Co
HURST, Joseph, Pvt, Col Wm Johnson, Capt Christopher Cook, 3rd Regt E TN Mil; transferred to Capt Henry Hunter Co
HURST, Joseph, Pvt, Col Wm Johnson, Capt Henry Hunter, E TN Mil; transferred from Capt Kirk's Camp for Jno Childress
HURST, Thompson, Dmr, Col Wm Lillard, Capt J Hamilton, E TN Vol Inf
HURST, Uriah, Pvt, Col Sam Bunch, Capt Henry Stephens, E TN Mtd Inf
HURST, William, Pvt, Col Sam Bunch, Capt Jno English, E TN Mil Drafted; joined from Capt Dobkins Co
HURST, William, Pvt, Maj Wm Russell, Capt John Cowan, Vol Mtd Gunmen
HURT, Bird I?, Pvt, Col N Cannon, Capt Martin, Mtd Gunmen; transferred to Capt Evan's Co
HURT, Bird L, Pvt, Regt Commander omitted, Capt Robert Evans, Spies
HURT, James, Cpl, Col Wm Johnson, Capt E Milliken, 3rd Regt E TN Mil
HURT, James, Sgt, Col Wm Johnson, Capt E Milliken, 3rd Regt E TN Mil
HURT, John, Pvt, Col Philip Pipkin, Co Commander omitted, Mil
HURT, Joshua, Pvt, Col Wm Metcalf, Capt William Sitton, Mil Inf
HURT, Samuel, Pvt, Regt Commander omitted, Capt N Davis, Mil Inf
HURT, Tarlton, Pvt, Col Edwin Booth, Capt John McK-amy, E TN Mil
HURT, Thomas, Cpl, Col William Hall, Capt Abraham Bledsoe, Vol Inf
HUSBAND, John, Pvt, Col Phillip Pipkin, Capt Kirkpatrick, Mil Inf
HUSE, Aaron, Pvt, Col Ewen Allison, Capt Thomas Wilson, E TN Drafted Mil
HUSE, Jesse, Pvt, Col S Bayless, Capt James Landon, E TN Mil
HUSE, John, Pvt, Col S Bayless, Capt James Landen, E TN Mil
HUSE, William, Pvt, Col S Bunch, Capt Edward Buchanan, E TN Drafted Mil
HUSK, Joseph, Pvt, Col William Johnson, Capt Joseph Kirk, Mil
HUST, James, Sgt, Col Wm Johnson, Capt Elihu Milliken, 3rd Regt E TN Mil
HUST, William, Blksmth, Regt Commander omitted, Capt Jas Haggard, Mtd Gunmen
HUSTANDER, Jacob, Pvt, Col Jno Brown, Capt Lunsford Oliver, Mil
HUSTON, James, Pvt, Col Thomas Benton, Capt N Cannon, Inf; transferred for Hewett's Co
HUSTON, Pleasant, Pvt, Maj Gen Jackson, Capt Crane, Mtd Gunmen
HUSTON, William, Cpl, Col S Bunch, Capt William Houston, E TN Vol Mtd Inf
HUTCHENS, Aaron, Pvt, Col Alexander Loury, Capt Arahel Raines, Inf
HUTCHENS, Ezekiel, Pvt, Regt Commander omitted, Capt William Smith, Vol Inf
HUTCHENS, Jesse, Pvt, Regt Commander omitted, Capt Josiah Askew, Inf
HUTCHENS, John, 3 Cpl, Col Thomas Williamson, Capt Giles Burdett, Vol Mtd Gunmen
HUTCHENS, John, Rank omitted, Col Thomas Benton, Capt William Smith, Vol Inf
HUTCHENS, Joseph, Pvt, Col Thos Benton, Capt William Smith, Vol Inf
HUTCHENS, Stokely, Pvt, Col John Coffee, Capt Edward Bradley, Branch Srvce omitted
HUTCHENSON, Ambros, Pvt, Col Lt A Cheatham, Capt Benj Elliott, Mtd Inf
HUTCHENSON, Ambrose, Pvt, Col Alexander Loury, Capt Gabriel Martin, Inf
HUTCHERSON, George, Cpl, Col Thos Dyer, Capt William Russell, Vol Mtd Gunmen
HUTCHERSON, George, Pvt, Col Edwin Booth, Capt Richard Marshall, Drafted Mil
HUTCHERSON, James, Pvt, Col John K Wynn, Capt Robert Breden, Inf
HUTCHERSON, John (Jesse), 1 Sgt, Col William Hall, Capt James Hambleton, Vol Inf
HUTCHERSON, John, 1 Sgt, Col Edward Bradley, Capt Hamberlton, Vol Inf
HUTCHERSON, Thomas, Pvt, Col John Cocke, Capt John Dalton, Inf
HUTCHERSON, Will E, Blksmth, Col John Coffee, Capt David Smith, Vol Inf
HUTCHERSON, William E, Blksmth, Regt Commander omitted, Capt David Smith, Cav Vol

## Enlisted Men, War of 1812

HUTCHERSON, William, Pvt, Col John K Wynn, Capt Bailey Butler, Inf
HUTCHERSON, William, Pvt, Col William Hall, Capt James Hambleton, Vol Inf
HUTCHINGS, Stokely D, QM Sgt, Col John Coffee, TN Vol Cav
HUTCHINGSON, James, Pvt, Regt Commander omitted, Capt Daniel Yarnell, E TN Mil; discharged, furnished a substitute
HUTCHINS, John, Pvt, Col Wm Pillow, Capt William Smith, Vol Inf
HUTCHINS, Joseph, Pvt, Col William Pillow, Capt William Smith, Vol Inf
HUTCHINS, Joseph, Pvt, Regt Commander omitted, Capt William Smith, Branch Srvce omitted; deserted 12-15-1813
HUTCHINS, Zachariah, Pvt, Col Thomas Williamson, Capt Beverly Williamson, Vol Mtd Gunmen
HUTCHINSON, Ambrose, Pvt, Lt Col A Cheatham, Co Commander omitted, Brig Mtd Inf
HUTCHINSON, Bailey, Pvt, Col S Bunch, Capt Jones Griffin, E TN Drafted Mil; furnished A Posey as a substitute
HUTCHINSON, George, Pvt, Maj Russell, Capt John Trimble, Vol Mtd Gunmen
HUTCHINSON, Isaiah, Pvt, Col John Cocke, Capt Samuel Caruthers, Inf
HUTCHINSON, James, Pvt, Col S Bunch, Capt Daniel Yarnell, E TN Mil; furnished a substitute
HUTCHINSON, James, Pvt, Col Wm Pillow, Capt John Neatherton, E TN Vol Inf
HUTCHINSON, John, Pvt, Col S Wear, Capt S Bayless, Mtd Inf
HUTCHINSON, Luke, Pvt, Col S Wear, Capt S Bayless, Mtd Inf
HUTCHINSON, Reuben, Pvt, Col S Bunch, Capt Andrew Breden, E TN Mil; d 4-17-1814
HUTCHINSON, William, Pvt, Col John Cocke, Capt John Dalton, Inf
HUTER, Thomas, Pvt, Col S Bayless, Capt Solomon Hendrix, E TN Mil
HUTON, James, Pvt, Col Thomas Williamson, Capt Geo Mitchie, TN Vol Mtd Gunmen
HUTSON, Armistead, Pvt, Maj John Childs, Capt Jas Cummings, E TN Mtd Gunmen; Regimental County Knox
HUTSON, Cathbert B, Pvt, Col A Cheatham, Capt Wm Creel, Inf
HUTSON, Cuthbert, Pvt, Col R H Dyer, Capt R Edmonston, TN Vol Mtd Gunmen
HUTSON, Henry, Pvt, Col J Cocke, Capt R Crunk, Inf
HUTSON, Isaiah, Pvt, Col R Steele, Capt J Randals, Inf
HUTSON, Jesse, Pvt, Col R C Napier, Capt Thos Gray, Mil Inf
HUTSON, Jesse, Pvt, Regt Commander omitted, Capt Thos Gray, Inf
HUTSON, John, Sgt, Col J Raulston, Capt D Newman, Inf; d 2-7-1815
HUTSON, Mathias, 5 Cpl, Col J Raulston, Capt D Newman, Inf; d 1-15-1815
HUTSON, Noah, Pvt, Col T Benton, Capt H Douglas, Vol Inf
HUTSON, Wesley, Cpl, Col J Alcorn, Capt F Stump, Cav
HUTSON, Westley, Cpl, Col Jno Coffee, Capt F Stump, Cav
HUTSON, William, Pvt, Col R H Dyer, Maj W Russell, Capt W Russell, Vol Mtd Inf
HUTSON, William, Pvt, Lt Col Jno Edmonson, Co Commander omitted, Cav
HUTSON (HUDSON), John, Pvt, Maj Gen Carroll, Col J Raulston, Capt E Robinson, Inf
HUTTON, Charles, Pvt, Col R M? Dyer, Capt R Evans, Vol Mtd Gunmen
HUTTON, Francis, Pvt, Col R H Dyer, Capt C Hudson, Vol Mtd Gunmen; transferred to Capt J William's Co
HUTTON, Francis, Pvt, Col R H Dyer, Capt J Williams, Vol Mtd Gunmen
HUTTON, Henry, Pvt, Col A Cheatham, Capt Wm Smith, Inf
HUTTON, James, Pvt, Col J Cocke, Capt B Nance; substitute for Jas Elliott
HUTTON, John, Pvt, Regt Commander omitted, Capt Jas Cowan, Mtd Inf
HUTTON, John, Sgt, Col T McCrory, Capt A Willis, Mil Inf; killed 11-9-1813 at Talledega
HUTTON, Joseph, Pvt, Col J K Wynne, Capt J Cole, Inf; transferred to Capt Russell's Co
HUTTON, Joseph, Pvt, Gen A Jackson, Capt Wm Russell, Mtd Spies; joined from Capt Willis's Co
HUTTON, Josiah, Pvt, Col John Brown, Capt Chas Lewin, E TN Vol Mtd Inf
HUTTON, Patrick, Pvt, Col R C Napier, Capt A McCarty, Mil Inf
HUTTON, Samuel, Pvt, Col Jno Coffee, Capt Daniel Ross, Mtd Gunmen
HUTTON, William, Pvt, Col T Williamson, Capt William Doak & Capt Wm Dobbins, Vol Mtd Gunmen
HUTTON, William, Pvt, Col Wm Metcalf, Capt Wm Mullin, Mil Inf
HUZES (HUES), Ezekiel, Pvt, Col Wm Johnson, Capt E Milliken, 3rd Regt E TN Mil
HYBARGER, John, Pvt, Col Wm Lillard, Capt R Maloney, E TN Vol Inf
HYDE, Henry, Pvt, Col S Bunch, Capt Daniel Narnell?, E TN Mil
HYDE, Taswell, Pvt, Col Wm Metcalf, Capt J Barnhart, Mil Inf
HYER, John, Cpl, Col R C Napier, Capt T Gray, Mil Inf
HYLES, Peter, Pvt, Col Wm Metcalf, Capt B Collins, Mil Inf; d 1-1-1815
HYNES, Anthony, Pvt, Col Metcalf, Capt Johnson, Inf
HYNES, Benjamin, 5 Cpl, Maj John Childs, Capt Jas Cummings, E TN Vol Mtd Inf
HYNES, David, Pvt, Col R Steele, Capt R Campbell, Branch Srvce omitted
HYNES, Gabriel, Pvt, Col J Raulston, Capt E Robinson, Inf
HYNESLY, Michael, Pvt, Col T McCrory, Capt T K Gordon, Inf
HYTE, Robert, Pvt, Col J Coffee, Capt Jas Terrill, Vol Cav
H\_\_\_, David W, Asst W Master, Brig Gen N Taylor, no

-273

## Enlisted Men, War of 1812

other information

IMPSON, Alford, Pvt, Col Robert Steele, Capt Robert Campbell, Mil

IMPSON, Isaac, Pvt, Col Thos Williamson, Capt Beverly Williams, Vol Mtd Gunmen

IMPSON, Isaiah, Pvt, Col Thos Williamson, Capt Beverly Williams, Vol Mtd Gunmen

IMPSON, Josiah, Pvt, Col Thos Williamson, Capt B Williams, Vol Mtd Gunmen; deserted 12-24-1814

ING, Alford, Sgt, Col Alex Loury, Capt Geo Sarver, Inf; appointed 1 Sgt in place of Beverly Young

ING, Mathew, Pvt, Col R C Napier, Capt Thos Preston, Mil

INGE, Vincent, Pvt, Col James Raulston, Capt Edward Robinson, Inf; d 12-18-1814

INGLE, George, Pvt, Maj Wm Woodfolk, Capt Jas Turner, Inf

INGLE, John, Pvt, Col Wm Lillard, Capt Jacob Hartsell, E TN Vol Inf

INGLE, William, Pvt, Col Wm Lillard, Capt Jacob Hartsell, E TN Vol Inf

INGLEBARGER, William, Pvt, Col Wm Johnson, Capt Henry Hunter, E TN Mil; substituted James Carnet

INGLISH, James, Pvt, Col Sam Wear, Capt Robert Doak, E TN Vol Inf

INGLISH, John, Pvt, Col Jno Williams, Capt Sam Bunch, Mtd Vol

INGLISH, Joshua, Pvt, Col Jno Williams, Capt Sam Bunch, Mtd Vol

INGRAHAM, Aaron, Pvt, Col Major Jas Porter, Capt Jas Anderson, Cav

INGRAHAM, Samuel, Pvt, Col Major Jas Porter, Capt Jas Anderson, Cav

INGRAM, John, Pvt, Col Wm Johnson, Capt Jas McKamey, E TN Drafted Mil

INGRAM, John, Pvt, Col Wm Lillard, Capt Jacob Hartsell, E TN Vol Inf

INGRAM, Shadrick, Pvt, Col John Wynne, Capt John Spinks, Inf

INGRAM, Sterling, Pvt, Col John Cocke, Capt John Weakley, Inf

INGRAM, Thomas, Pvt, Col John Cocke, Capt Samuel Caruthers, Inf; d 10-12-1815

INGRAM, Willard, Pvt, Col Arch Cheatham, Capt Nathan Peoples, Mtd Inf

INGRAM, William, 3 Cpl, Col Thos Benton, Capt James McFerrin, Vol Inf

INGRAM, William, Cpl, Col Thos Benton, Capt Jas McFerrin, Vol Inf

INLOW, Benjamin, Pvt, Col Alex Loury, Capt Gabriel Martin, Inf

INLOW, John, Pvt, Col Alex Loury, Capt Gabriel Martin, Inf

INMAN, Ezekiel, Pvt, Col John Cocke, Capt John Dalton, Inf

INMAN, Ezekiel, Pvt, Gen Thos Johnson, Capt Daniel Oban, 36 Inf

INMAN, Isaac, Pvt, Col Thos Williamson, Capt Thos Porter, Vol Mtd Gunmen

INMAN, Isaac, Pvt, Gen Thos Johnson, Capt Danl Oban, 36 Inf

INMAN, Jeremiah, Pvt, Col Sam Bunch, Capt John Inman, E TN Vol Mtd Inf

INMAN, John, Cpl, Col Sam Bunch, Capt John Inman, E TN Vol Mtd Inf

INMAN, John, Pvt, Col John Cocke, Capt John Dalton, Inf

INMAN, John, Pvt, Col R C Napier, Capt Drury Adkins, Mil Inf

INMAN, John, Pvt, Col Sam Bunch, Capt John Inman, E TN Vol Mtd Inf

INMAN, John, Pvt, Col Thos Williamson, Capt Thos Porter, Vol Mtd Gunmen

INMAN, Michael, Pvt, Col Thos McCrory, Capt John Gordon, Inf; deserted 11-18-1814

INMAN, Samuel, Pvt, Gen Wm Johnson, Capt Daniel Oban, 36th Inf

INMAN, Shadrick, 2 Sgt, Col Wm Lillard, Capt Thos McChristian, E TN Vol Inf

INMAN, William, Cpl, Regt Commander omitted, Capt Wm Henderson, Spies

INSTOT, William, Pvt, Regt Commander omitted, Lt John Harris, Det of Inf

INTUS, John, Pvt, Col Wm Johnson, Capt Andrew Lawson, E TN Drafted Mil

IRBY, Henderson, Pvt, Col John Allcorn, Capt Thos Bradley, Vol Cav

IRBY, Henderson, Pvt, Col Thos Williamson, Capt Wm Williams, Vol Mtd Gunmen

IRBY, John, Pvt, Col John Allcorn, Capt Thos Bradley, Vol Cav

IRBY, John, Pvt, Col John Cocke, Capt Thos Bradley, Vol Cav

IRBY, John, Pvt, Col Philip Pipkin, Capt George Mebane, Mil Inf

IRBY, Joseph, Pvt, Col John Allcorn, Capt Thos Bradley, Vol Cav

IRBY, Joseph, Pvt, Col John Coffee, Capt Thos Bradley, Vol Cav

IRBY, Pleasant, Pvt, Col John Coffee, Capt Thos Bradley, Vol Cav

IRBY, Pleasant, Pvt, Col Robert Dyer, Capt Cuthbert Hudson, Vol Mtd Gunmen

IREDALE, John, Pvt, Gen Andrew Jackson, Capt David Deadrick, Arty

IRELAND, Daniel, Pvt, Col John Cocke, Capt Jas Gault, Inf

IRELAND, William, Pvt, Col John Brown, Capt John Childs, E TN Vol Mtd Inf

IRELAND, William, Pvt, Col Sam Bayless, Capt Joseph Bacon, E TN Mil

IRIONS, James H, Pvt, Col Wm Higgins, Capt Stephens Griffith, Mtd Riflemen

IRONS, Peter, Pvt, Col John Brown, Capt Chas Lewin, E TN Mtd Vol Inf

IRONS, Walker, Pvt, Col Wm Metcalf, Capt Bird Hurt, Mil Inf; died 3-22-1815

IRVIN, David C, Cpl, Col Jno Coffee, Capt Frederick Stump, Cav

IRVIN, Robert, Pvt, Col John Cocke, Capt James Gault, Inf

IRVINE, Andrew, Pvt, Col R C Napier, Capt Thomas

## Enlisted Men, War of 1812

Gray, Mil Inf

IRVINE, James, Pvt, Col Thos Williamson, Capt James Cook & Capt John Crane, Vol Mtd Gunmen

IRVINE, Patrick, Pvt, Col Samuel Bunch, Capt F Register, E TN Mil; joined from Capt McCree's Co

IRVINE, Patrick, Pvt, Col Samuel Bunch, Capt Geo McPherson, E TN Mil; trans to Capt Register's Co

IRWIN, Andrew, Pvt, Col Wm Johnson, Capt Ben Powell, E TN Mil

IRWIN, Benjamin, Pvt, Col Samuel Wear, Capt James Gillespie, E TN Vol Inf

IRWIN, Daniel, Pvt, Col James Raulston, Capt Wiley Huddleston, Inf

IRWIN, David, Pvt, Col Thos Williamson, Capt William Martin, Vol Mtd Gunmen

IRWIN, James, Pvt, Col William Johnson, Capt Benjamin Powell, E TN Mil

IRWIN, Robert jr, Pvt, Col John Spinks, Capt John Spinks, Inf

IRWIN, Robert sr, Pvt, Col John K Wynne, Capt John Spinks, Inf; deserted

IRWIN, Robert, Pvt, Maj James Porter, Capt Sam Cowan, Cav

IRWIN, William, Pvt, Maj Gen A Jackson, Capt Hugh Kerr, Mtd Rangers

ISABEL, Thomas, Pvt, Col A Cheatham, Capt George G Chapman, Inf

ISAM, James, Pvt, Maj John Childs, Capt Daniel Price, E TN Vol Mtd Inf

ISBEL, Abraham, Pvt, Col Alexander Loury, Capt J N Williamson, W TN Mil

ISBEL, Abraham, Pvt, Col Alexander Loury, Capt Thomas Wells, Inf;

ISBELL, Daniel, Pvt, Regt Commander omitted, Capt Jas Haggard, Mtd Gunmen

ISBELL, Jabas, Pvt, Regt Commander omitted, Capt Archibald McKinney, Cav

ISBELL, Jeptha V, Pvt, Regt Commander omitted, Capt Archibald McKinney, Cav

ISBELL, Jeptha, Pvt, Regt Commander omitted, Capt Archibald McKinney, Cav

ISBELL, John S, Pvt, Col L Hammond, Capt J N Williamson, 2 Regt Inf; apptd Artif

ISBELL, Miller, Pvt, Col William Johnson, Capt Andrew Lawson, E TN Draft Mil

ISBELL, Thomas, Cpl, Col Edwin Booth, Capt John Slatton, E TN Mil

ISBELL, Thomas, Cpl, Col Samuel Bunch, Capt Jones Griffin, E TN Draft Mil

ISBELL, Thomas, Pvt, Col Samuel Bunch, Capt James Cumming, E TN Vol Mtd Inf

ISER, Darby, Pvt, Col Archer Cheatham, Capt Nathan Peoples, Mtd Inf

ISH, Alexander, Pvt, Col Samuel Wear, Capt James Gillespie, E TN Vol Inf

ISH, Jacob, Sgt, Col John K Wynne, Capt James Cole, Inf

ISH, John, Pvt, Col William Pillow, Capt John H Anderson, Vol Inf

ISH, John, Sgt, Col Thomas Benton, Capt George W Gibbs, Vol Inf

ISHAM, Arthur, Pvt, no Regt Commander, Capt Jno Gordon, Mtd Spies

ISHAM, Charles, Pvt, Col Robert Steele, Capt James Rendals, Inf; AWOL

ISHAM, George, Pvt, Col William Johnson, Capt Henry Hunter, E TN Mil

ISHAM, George, Pvt, no Regt Commander, Capt Jno Gordon, Mtd Spies

ISHAM, Richard, Pvt, Col Alexander Loury, Capt James Kincaid, Inf

ISHAM, Richard, Pvt, Col Newton Cannon, Capt James Walton, Mtd Riflemen

ISOM, Arthur S, Pvt, Col Robert H Dyer, Capt James McMahan, TN Vol Mtd Gunmen

ISOM, Edmund, Pvt, Col Philip Pipkin, Capt James Blakemore, Mil Inf

ISOM, James, Cpl, Col Samuel Wear, Capt John Bayless, Mtd Inf

ISTIS, William, Pvt, Col Samuel Bayless, Capt Waddell, E TN Mil

IVENS, Archibald, Pvt, Col Samuel Bunch, Capt Jones Griffin, Branch omitted; trans to Capt Dobbins Co

IVES, John, Pvt, Col L Hammond, Capt J N Williamson, 2 Regt Inf

IVES, John, Pvt, Col Newton Cannon, Capt James Walton, Mtd Riflemen

IVEY, Henry, Cpl, Col Thomas Benton, Capt Iaiah Renshaw, Vol Inf; joined from Capt Hewett's

IVY, Absolom, Pvt, Col Philip Pipkin, Capt Henry M Newlin, Mil Inf; deserted

IVY, Elisha, Pvt, Col William Metcalf, Capt Andrew Patterson, Mil Inf; died 12-6-1814

IVY, Frederick, 2 Cpl, Col A Cheatham, Capt James Giddins, Inf

IVY, Henry, Cpl, Col William Pillow, Capt Isaiah Renshaw, Inf

IVY, James, Pvt, Col William Johnson, Capt Joseph Scott, E TN Draft Mil

IVY, Joseph, Pvt, Col Philip Pipkin, Capt Peter Searcy, Mil Inf; deserted

IVY, Joseph, Pvt, Maj William Woodfolk, Capt James C Neil, Inf

IVY, Phillips, Sgt, Col Samuel Bunch, Lt Jno Harris, E TN Mil

JACK, James, Cpl, Col Samuel Wear, Capt Bowman, Mtd Inf

JACK, Jeremiah, Pvt, Col Samuel Bayless, Capt Joseph Hale, E TN Mil

JACK, Jeremiah, Pvt, Col Samuel Wear, Capt Bowman, Mtd Inf; unfit for duty

JACK, John, Pvt, Col Ewin Allison, Capt Wilson, E TN Draft Mil

JACK, John, Pvt, Col Samuel Bunch, Capt John Houk, E TN Mil; joined for Capt Gregory

JACK, John, Pvt, Col Wm Lillard, Capt Jacob Dyke, Vol Inf; deserted

JACK, Melton, Pvt, Maj John Chiles, Capt John Stephens, E TN Vol Mtd Gunmen

JACK, Robert, Pvt, Maj John Chiles, Capt Reuben Tipton, E TN Vol Mtd Inf

JACK, Thomas, Pvt, Col Samuel Wear, Capt Jas Tedford, E TN Vol Inf

- 275

## Enlisted Men, War of 1812

JACK, Thomas, Pvt, Maj John Chiles, Capt John Stephens, E TN Vol Mtd Inf

JACK, William, 1 Lt, Col Samuel H Wear, Capt John Stephens, E TN Vol Inf

JACK, William, Pvt, Col Wm Lillard, Capt Thos Sharpe, 2 Regt Inf

JACKMAN, Adam, Pvt, Col R H Dyer, Capt Robert Edmondson, TN Vol Mtd Gunmen

JACKSON, Bergason, Ens, Regt Commander omitted, Co Commander omitted, E TN Mil Inf

JACKSON, Branch, Pvt, Col Wm Metcalf, Capt Andrew Patterson, Mil Inf

JACKSON, Branch, Pvt, Lt Col John Edmondson, Co Commander omitted, Cav

JACKSON, Bruce, Pvt, Col John Edmondson, Co Commander omitted, Cav

JACKSON, Burrell, Pvt, Col John K Wynn, Capt Jas Cole, Inf

JACKSON, Churchwell, Pvt, Col Edwin E Booth, Capt Marshall, Drafted Mil

JACKSON, Cravin, Pvt, Regt Commander omitted, Capt Isaac Crane, Arty

JACKSON, Daniel, Pvt, Gen Andrew Jackson, Capt Nathan Davis, Inf

JACKSON, Daniel, Pvt, Gen R H Dyer, Capt Jas McMahan, TN Vol Gunmen

JACKSON, Daniel, Pvt, Regt Commander omitted, Capt Gray, Inf

JACKSON, David, Pvt, Lt Col Hammond, Capt Craig, Inf

JACKSON, David, Pvt, Regt Commander omitted, Capt Askew, Inf

JACKSON, David, Pvt, Regt Commander omitted, Capt Edwin S Moore, Mtd Riflemen

JACKSON, Deaken, Pvt, Col Wm Johnson, Capt Jas Tunnell, TN Mil; d 11-1814, substitute for Daniel Quallen

JACKSON, Eli, Pvt, Col R C Napier, Capt Thomas Gray, Mil Inf

JACKSON, Eli, Pvt, Regt Commander omitted, Capt Elijah Rushing, Det of Inf

JACKSON, Elisha, Pvt, Col R C Napier, Capt Thomas Gray, Mil Inf

JACKSON, Epps, Pvt, Col John Cocke, Capt Joseph Price, Inf

JACKSON, Epps, Pvt, Col R C Napier, Capt Edward Neblett, Mil Inf

JACKSON, George, Pvt, Col Wm Lillard, Capt Jacob Hartsell, E TN Vol Inf

JACKSON, Graham, Pvt, Maj Gen Andrew Jackson, Capt Joseph Kirkpatrick, Mtd Gunmen

JACKSON, Henry B, Pvt, Col John Coffee, Capt Charles Kavanaugh, Cav

JACKSON, Henry B, Pvt, Regt Commander omitted, Capt Archibald McKenney, Cav

JACKSON, Henry, Pvt, Col Jas Raulston, Capt Daniel Newman, Inf; substituted in room of Elisha Stewart

JACKSON, Henry, Pvt, Regt Commander omitted, Capt Abner Pearce, Inf

JACKSON, Hezekiah, Pvt, Col John Williams, Capt Wm Walker, Vol

JACKSON, Hugh, Pvt, Lt Col Hammond, Capt Jas Craig, Inf

JACKSON, Hugh, Pvt, Regt Commander omitted, Capt Jas Gray, Inf

JACKSON, Isaac, Pvt, Col Wm Johnson, Capt Andrew Lawson, E TN Drafted Mil; substitute for Benjamin Jackson

JACKSON, Jacob, Pvt, Col Samuel Wear, Capt Rufus Morgan, E TN Vol Inf

JACKSON, Jacob, Pvt, Col Wm Lillard, Capt Jacob Hartsell, E TN Vol Inf

JACKSON, James, Cpl, Col Leroy Hammond, Capt James Craig, 2nd Regt W TN Mil; d 11-16-1814

JACKSON, James, Pvt, Col Ed Bradley, Capt J Wallace, Vol Inf

JACKSON, James, Pvt, Col Ewin Allison, Capt Jacob Hoyal, E TN Mil; transferred to Capt Register 4-27-1814

JACKSON, James, Pvt, Col J Cocke, Capt J Dalton, Inf

JACKSON, James, Pvt, Col Wm Hall, Capt J Wallace, Inf

JACKSON, James, Pvt, Maj Gen Andrew Jackson, Capt Joseph Kirkpatrick, Mtd Gunmen

JACKSON, John, Pvt, Col Edwin Booth, Capt Geo Winton, E TN Mil

JACKSON, John, Pvt, Col Ewin Allison, Capt Joseph Everett, E TN Mil

JACKSON, John, Pvt, Col P Pipkin, Capt Wm Mackay, Mil Inf

JACKSON, John, Pvt, Col S Copeland, Capt Wm Douglass, Inf

JACKSON, John, Pvt, Col Samuel Wear, Capt Jas Gillespie, E TN Vol Inf

JACKSON, John, Pvt, Col W Johnson, Capt J Scott, E TN Drafted Mil

JACKSON, John, Pvt, Lt Col L Hammond, Capt Jas Craig, Inf

JACKSON, John, Pvt, Regt Commander omitted, Capt Archibald McKinney, Cav

JACKSON, John, Sgt, Col John Brown, Capt Jas Preston, E TN Mil Inf

JACKSON, Jonathan, Pvt, Col P Pipkin, Capt E Kirkpatrick, Mil Inf; deserted 9-20-1814

JACKSON, Jordon, Pvt, Col J Raulston, Capt H Hamilton, Inf; also under Maj Gen Carroll

JACKSON, Joseph, Pvt, Col Wm Metcalf, Capt Bird L Hurt, Mil Inf

JACKSON, Joshua L, 2 Sgt, Maj J Childs, Capt D Price, E TN Mtd Riflemen Vol

JACKSON, Joshua S, Cpl, Col John Brown, Capt John Childs, E TN Vol Mtd Gunmen; promoted from Pvt

JACKSON, Josiah, Pvt, Col J Raulston, Capt Chas Wade, Inf

JACKSON, Larkin, Pvt, Col R Steele, Capt J Shenault, Mil Inf

JACKSON, Leroy, Pvt, Col P Pipkin, Capt D Smith, Inf; deserted 9-20-1814

JACKSON, Levi, Pvt, Col J K Wynne, Capt Jas Holleman, Inf

JACKSON, Lewis, Pvt, Regt Commander omitted, Capt J Askew, Inf

## Enlisted Men, War of 1812

JACKSON, Lewis, Pvt, Regt Commander omitted, Capt Jas Gray, Inf
JACKSON, Martin, Pvt, Col Wm Metcalf, Capt B Collins, Mil Inf
JACKSON, Nicholas, Pvt, Col N Cannon, Capt J Harpole, Mtd Gunmen
JACKSON, Reuben, Sdlr, Col N Cannon, Capt J Harpole, Mtd Gunmen
JACKSON, Richard, Pvt, Col A Cheatham, Capt Chas Johnson, Inf
JACKSON, Richard, Pvt, Col J Cocke, Capt J Price, Inf
JACKSON, Richard, Pvt, Lt Col L Hammonds, Col A Loury, Capt T Wells, Inf
JACKSON, Robert, Pvt, Col N Cannon, Capt J Harpole, Mtd Gunmen
JACKSON, Robert, Pvt, Col P Pipkin, Capt W Mackay, Mil Inf
JACKSON, Robert, Pvt, Col T McCrory, Capt J Shannon, Mil Inf; transferred from Capt Randol's Co
JACKSON, Roby?, Sdlr, Col Williamson, Capt Williams, Vol Mtd Gunmen
JACKSON, Samuel, Pvt, Col S Bayless, Capt J B Bacon, E TN Mil
JACKSON, Samuel, Pvt, Maj Wm Russell, Capt J Cowan, Vol Mtd Gunmen
JACKSON, Stephen, Pvt, Col P Pipkin, Capt J Blakemore, Mil Inf; substituted for Terrell Allen
JACKSON, Thomas, 2 Sgt, Col Wm Metcalf, Capt Wm Mullins, Mil Inf; d 4-25-1815
JACKSON, Thomas, Pvt, Col S Wear, Capt Robt Doak, E TN Vol Inf
JACKSON, Thomas, Pvt, Col Wm Lillard, Capt Geo Keys, E TN Inf
JACKSON, Thomas, Pvt, Lt Col L Hammonds, Col A Loury, Capt T Wells, Inf
JACKSON, Unit, Pvt, Col S Bayless, Capt J Hale, Inf
JACKSON, Uriah, Pvt, Col T McCrory, Capt A Metcalf, Mil Inf
JACKSON, Uzeriah, Pvt, Col T McCrory, Capt A Metcalf, Mil Inf
JACKSON, William, 4 Cpl, Col J Cocke, Capt J Gray, Inf
JACKSON, William, Pvt, Col J Cocke, Capt J Gault, Inf; d 3-3-1815
JACKSON, William, Pvt, Col Jas Raulston, Capt H Hamilton, Inf; also under Maj Gen Carroll
JACKSON, William, Pvt, Col S Bayless, Capt J Waddell, E TN Mil
JACKSON, William, Pvt, Col S Copeland, Capt G W Stell, Mil Inf
JACKSON, _____, Pvt, Col Samuel Bunch, Capt Francis Register, E TN Mil; joined for Capt Hoyle's Co
JACOB, Joseph, Pvt, Capt David Vance, Capt Jno Williams, Vol
JACOB, William, Pvt, Col Wm Metcalf, Capt O Waller, Mil Inf; transferred to Capt Jackson's Co in place of Rich Usrey
JACOBS, Basil, Pvt, Col J K Wynne, Capt John Spinks, Inf
JACOBS, Jeremiah, Pvt, Maj Gen Wm Carroll, Col Wm Metcalf, Capt John Jackson, Inf
JACOBS, Nathaniel, Pvt, Col Alex Loury, Capt J Looney, W TN Inf

JACOBS, Samuel, Cpl, Col John Cocke, Capt Geo Barnes, Inf
JACOBS, Samuel, Pvt, Col Wm Lillard, Capt T McChristian, E TN Vol Inf
JACOBS, Thomas, Pvt, Col W Lillard, Capt T McChristian, E TN Vol Inf
JACOBS, William, Pvt, Maj Gen Wm Carroll, Capt J Jackson, Inf
JAGGERS, John, Pvt, Col Wm Metcalf, Capt B L Hurt, Mil Inf
JAGGERS, Simon, Pvt, Col Wm Metcalf, Capt B L Hurt, Mil Inf
JAMERSON, Robert, Pvt, Col R H Dyer, Capt J Williams, Vol Mtd Gunmen
JAMERSON, Robert, Pvt, Col Robt Dyer, Capt Wm Williams, Vol Mtd Gunmen
JAMES, Alexander, Pvt, Maj Gen Carroll, Col James Raulston, Capt Edward Robinson, Inf
JAMES, Amos, Pvt, Col R C Napier, Capt Drury Adkins, Mil Inf
JAMES, Andrew, Pvt, Col Sam Wear, Capt James Gillespie, E TN Vol Inf
JAMES, Benjamin, Pvt, Col Philip Pipkin, Capt Jno Strother, Mil
JAMES, Benjamin, Pvt, Col Sam Bunch, Capt Edward Buchanan, E TN Drafted Mil; transferred to Capt Duncan Co
JAMES, Benjamin, Pvt, Col Sam Bunch, Capt Joseph Duncan, E TN Drafted Mil; transferred to Capt Buchanan Co
JAMES, Carey, Pvt, Regt Commander omitted, Capt Griffin, Branch Srvce omitted
JAMES, Elijah, Pvt, Col Robt Dyer, Capt Cuthbert Hudson, Vol Mtd Gunmen; d 2-4-1815
JAMES, Elijah, Pvt, Col Wm Lillard, Capt Thos Sharp, 2nd Regt Inf
JAMES, Elisha, Pvt, Col Sam Bunch, Capt Edw Buchanan, E TN Drafted Mil; transferred from Capt Duncan's Co
JAMES, Elisha, Pvt, Col Sam Bunch, Capt Joseph Duncan, E TN Drafted Mil; transferred to Capt Buchanan Co
JAMES, Enos, Pvt, Col R C Napier, Capt Drury Adkins, Mil Inf
JAMES, Frederick, Pvt, Col Sam Copeland, Capt Wm Douglass, Inf
JAMES, Hardy, Pvt, Col Thos Benton, Capt Isaiah Renshaw, Vol Inf; joined from Capt Hewitt's Co
JAMES, Henry, Pvt, Col John Cocke, Capt John Weakley, Inf
JAMES, Jesse, Pvt, Col Sam Wear, Capt James Gillespie, E TN Vol Inf
JAMES, John, Pvt, Col John Brown, Capt John Childs, E TN Vol Mtd Inf
JAMES, John, Pvt, Col Thos Benton, Capt Wm Smith, Vol Inf
JAMES, John, Pvt, Col Wm Pillow, Capt George Caperton, Inf
JAMES, Keerg, Pvt, Col Sam Bunch, Capt Jones Griffin, E TN Drafted Mil; deserted 3-4-1814
JAMES, Mathew, Pvt, Col Archer Cheatham, Capt

## Enlisted Men, War of 1812

Meredith Walker, Inf
JAMES, Mathew, Pvt, Regt Commander omitted, Capt David Smith, Cav
JAMES, Missey, Pvt, Col Thos McCrory, Capt A Metcalf, Mil Inf
JAMES, Nicholas, Pvt, Col Wm Lillard, Capt Thos Sharp, E TN Inf 2nd Regt
JAMES, Robert D, Pvt, Col Thos Williamson, Capt Jame Pace, Vol Mtd Gunmen
JAMES, Robert, Pvt, Col Thos Williamson, Capt John Hutchings, Vol Mtd Gunmen
JAMES, Thomas, Pvt, Col Alex Loury, Capt Martin, Inf
JAMES, Thomas, Pvt, Col Barbee Collins, Capt Wm Metcalf, Mil Inf
JAMES, Thomas, Pvt, Col Sam Bunch, Capt S Robinson, E TN Drafted Mil
JAMES, Thomas, Pvt, Col Sam Bunch, Capt Sam Richardson, E TN Drafted Mil
JAMES, Thomas, Pvt, Col Wm Pillow, Capt George Caperton, Inf
JAMES, William, Pvt, Col Ewen Allison, Capt Adam Winsell, E TN Drafted
JAMES, William, Pvt, Col James Raulston, Capt Daniel Newman, Inf
JAMES, William, Pvt, Col Sam Bunch, Capt Andrew Breeden, E TN Mil; transferred to Capt Bacon's Co
JAMES, William, Pvt, Col Sam Bunch, Capt George McPherson, E TN Mil; joined from Capt Winsell's Co
JAMES, William, Pvt, Col Wm Johnson, Capt Henry Hunter, E TN Mil; never appeared
JAMES, William, Pvt, Col Wm Johnson, Capt Jas Tunnell, E TN Mil; AWOL
JAMES, William, Pvt, Col Wm Metcalf, Capt Barbee Collins, Mil Inf
JAMES, William, Pvt, Maj Gen Jackson, Capt Eb Kirkpatrick, Mtd Gunmen
JAMES, Williams, Pvt, Col John Brown, Capt John Trimble, E TN Mtd Gunmen
JAMES, Willie, Pvt, Col Wm Metcalf, Capt John Cunningham & Capt Alex Hill, Mil Inf
JAMESON, John, Pvt, Col Sam Wear, Capt Geo Gillespie, E TN Vol Inf
JAMESON, Robert, Pvt, Lt Richard Napier, Co Commander omitted, Inf
JAMESON, Thomas, Pvt, Col Wm Hall, Capt Brice Martin, Vol Inf
JAMESS, William, Pvt, Col John Wynne, Capt James Cole, Inf; deserted 11-18-1813
JAMISON, Abraham, Pvt, Col Thos Benton, Capt I Renshaw, Vol Inf
JAMISON, D William, Cpl, Col Philip Pipkin, Capt Peter Searcy, Mil Inf
JAMISON, John R, Cpl, Col Sam Bayless, Capt Joseph Hale, E TN Mil
JAMISON, John, Pvt, Col Sam Bunch, Capt Joseph Duncan, E TN Drafted Mil
JAMISON, Samuel, Pvt, Col Thos Benton, Capt Benj Reynolds, Vol Inf; joined with KY-Vol
JAMISON, Thomas, Pvt, Col Brice Martin, Capt Wm Hall, Vol Inf
JAMISON, Thomas, Pvt, Col Joseph Hale, Capt Brice Martin, Vol Inf
JAMISON, William D, Pvt, Col John Wynn, Capt Bayless Prince, Inf; transferred
JAMISON, William, Pvt, Col John Coffee, Capt David Smith, Vol Cav
JAMMISON, Henry, Pvt, Col L Hammonds & Col Alex Loury, Capt Thomas Delaney, Inf; d 2-1814?
JANNINGS, John, Pvt, Col Wm Johnson, Capt Jas Stewart, E TN Mil
JARAGAN, Cornwell, Pvt, Col Sam Bunch, Capt Mann, E TN Vol Mil
JARMIN, John, Pvt, Col John Coffee, Capt David Smith, Vol Cav
JARMON, Daniel, Pvt, Regt Commander omitted, Capt David Smith, Cav
JARMON, Robert, Pvt, Col Robt Jarmon, Capt Isaiah Hamilton, Inf
JARMON, Stephen, Pvt, Regt Commander omitted, Capt Isaiah Hamilton, Inf
JARNAGAN, Spencer, Pvt, Col Samuel Bunch, Capt Thomas Mann, E TN Vol Mtd Inf; taken as secretary to the Maj Gen
JARNAGIN, Spencer, Pvt, Col Samuel Bunch, Capt Thomas Mann, E TN Vol Mtd Inf; taken as secretary to the Maj Gen
JARRELL, John B, Pvt, Maj Gen Wm Carroll, Col Wm Metcalf, Capt John Jackson, Inf
JARRET, John, Pvt, Lt Col L Hammonds, Capt James Craig, Inf
JARVICE, Richard, Pvt, Col Edward Bradley, Capt John Wallace, Vol Inf
JARVIS, Bennet, Pvt, Col James Raulston, Capt Henry West, Inf; d 3-20-1815
JARVIS, Elephalet, Pvt, Col Robert Steele, Capt Richard M Ratton, Mil Inf
JARVIS, William, Pvt, Col Robert Steele, Capt Richard M Ratton, Mil Inf
JEAN, Robert, Pvt, Col Jno Brown, Capt William White, E TN Vol Mtd Inf
JEFFERS, James, Pvt, Col Edwin Booth, Capt Richard Marshall, Drafted Mil
JEFFERY, Heremiah?, Pvt, Col John Brown, Capt Jesse G Reany, Mtd Gunmen
JEFFERY, William, Pvt, Maj Wm Woodfolk, Capt Abner Pearce, Inf
JEFFIS, William, Pvt, Col Samuel Bunch, Capt Jones Griffin, E TN Drafted Mil; joined from Capt Everett Co
JEFFRES, Nathaniel, Pvt, Maj John Childs, Capt John Stephens, E TN Vol Mtd Inf
JEFFRES, Samuel, Pvt, Col Edwin Booth, Capt Samuel Thompson, Mil
JEFFRES, William, Pvt, Col Samuel Bunch, Capt William Jobe, E TN Vol Mtd Inf
JEFFREY, James, Pvt, Maj William Russell, Capt John Cowan, Vol Mtd Gunmen
JEFFREY, Jeremiah, Pvt, Maj Wm Russell, Capt John Cowan, Vol Mtd Gunmen
JEFFREY, John, Pvt, Maj Wm Russell, Capt Wm Russell,

## Enlisted Men, War of 1812

Vol Mtd Gunmen
JEFFREY, Joseph, Pvt, Col Newton Cannon, Capt Francis Jones, Mtd Riflemen
JEFFREYS, James, Pvt, Regt Commander omitted, Capt James Cowan, Mtd Inf
JEMERSON, Robert, Pvt, Col R H Dyer, Capt Joseph Williams, Vol Mtd Gunmen
JENINGS, Edmund, Pvt, Regt Commander omitted, Capt Geo Smith, Spies; d 4-20-1814
JENKENS, Hiram, Pvt, Col Newton Cannon, Capt Ota Cantrell, W TN Mtd Inf; transferred to Capt Evans Co
JENKENS, Thomas, Pvt, Col William Metcalf, Capt Andrew Patterson, Mil Inf
JENKINS, Alexander, Pvt, Col Ewen Allison, Capt James Allen, E TN Mil
JENKINS, Alexander, Pvt, Col Samuel Bunch, Capt Joseph Duncan, E TN Drafted Mil; joined from Capt Allen Co, d 5-9-1814
JENKINS, Archibald, Pvt, Col Samuel Bayless, Capt Joseph Hale, E TN Mil
JENKINS, Bradly, Pvt, Col Samuel Wear, Capt Daniel Price, E TN Vol Inf
JENKINS, Emanuel, Pvt, Col Samuel Wear, Capt Jesse Cole, Vol Inf
JENKINS, Hiram, Pvt, Regt Commander omitted, Capt Wm Mitchell, Spies
JENKINS, James, Pvt, Col Robert Steele, Capt James Shenault, Mil Inf
JENKINS, James, Pvt, Col William Johnson, Capt Joseph Kirk, Mil; never appeared
JENKINS, Jesse, Pvt, Maj William Woodfolk, Capt Abraham Dudney & Capt John Sutton, Inf
JENKINS, John, Pvt, Regt Commander omitted, Capt Wm Henderson, Spies
JENKINS, Jonas, Pvt, Col Ewen Allison, Capt Abraham Allen, E TN Mil
JENKINS, Joseph, Sgt, Col R H Dyer, Capt Bethel Allen, Vol Mtd Gunmen; d 2-20-1815
JENKINS, Mathew, Cpl, Col Samuel Bunch, Capt Francis Berry, E TN Mil; promoted from Pvt
JENKINS, Nathan, Pvt, Col John K Wynne, Capt John Spinks, Inf
JENKINS, Phillip, Pvt, Col William Johnson, Capt James R Rogers, E TN Drafted Mil
JENKINS, Robert, Pvt, Col William Johnson, Capt Benjamin Powell, E TN Mil
JENKINS, Solomon, Pvt, Col Wm Metcalf, Capt Andrew Patterson, Mil Inf; enlisted in the U S Service
JENKINS, Thomas, Pvt, Col Samuel Bunch, Capt Moses, E TN Mil Drafted
JENKINS, Thomas, Pvt, Col Thos Williamson, Capt Anthony M Metcalf, Vol Mtd Gunmen
JENKINS, Walter S, 2 Lt, Regt Commander omitted, Capt Nathan Farmer, Mtd Riflemen
JENKINS, Walter, Pvt, Col Wm Metcalf, Capt Alexander Hill & Capt John Cunningham, Mil Inf
JENKINS, Walter, Pvt, Col Wm Metcalf, Capt William Mullen, Mil Inf
JENNESON, Henry, Pvt, Brig Gen T Johnson, Capt Abraham Allen, Mil Inf

JENNINGS, Martin, Pvt, Col Thomas Benton, Capt George Caperton, Vol Inf
JENNINGS, Thomas, Cpl, Col Samuel Bayless, Capt Branch Jones, E TN Drafted Mil
JENNINGS (JENNET), John, Pvt, Col Wm Johnson, Capt James Stewart, E TN Drafted Mil
JENNINS, John, Pvt, Col Samuel Bunch, Capt John Dobbins, E TN Drafted Mil; deserted 3-4-1814
JENNINS, Royal, Pvt, Col Samuel Bunch, Capt John Dobbins, E TN Drafted Mil; deserted 3-6-1814
JENOE, Francis, Pvt, Col Ewen Allison, Capt Thomas Wilson, E TN Drafted Mil
JENOE, John, Pvt, Col Ewen Allison, Capt Thomas Wilson, E TN Drafted Mil; deserted
JERNAGIN, Felix, Pvt, Col Thomas Williamson, Capt Giles Burdett, Vol Mtd Gunmen; dismissed the day mustered into service
JERNIGAN, Asa, Pvt, Col Samuel Bunch, Capt Thomas Mann, E TN Vol Mtd Inf; deserted 10-20-1813 from Camp Williams
JERNIGIN, Conwell, Pvt, Col Samuel Bunch, Capt Thomas Mann, E TN Vol Mtd Inf
JESSE, John, Pvt, Regt Commander omitted, Capt James Haggard, Mtd Gunmen
JESTER, Ar., Pvt, Maj Wm Woodfolk, Capt James Neil, Inf
JETT, Ferdanan, Pvt, Col Thos Dyer, Maj William Russell, Capt William Russell, Vol Mtd Gunmen
JETT, Humphrey, Ens, Col T McCrory, Capt Jas Reynolds, Inf
JETTON, Isaac, Pvt, Col N Cannon, Capt Jas Yardley, Mtd Riflemen
JETTON, Zebulon, Pvt, Col John Coffee, Capt Alexander McKeen, Cav; substituted by John Cobler
JEWELL, Absoleum, Sgt, Col S Copeland, Capt George, Inf
JIMISON, William, Pvt, Regt Commander omitted, Capt Davis Smith, Cav Vol
JIMKINS, John, Pvt, Col Robert Steele, Capt Jas Shenault, Mil Inf
JIMMERSON, William D, Pvt, Col N T Perkins, Capt Geo Marr, Mtd Vol; transferred fro Capt Primce? Co
JIMMING, James, Pvt, Col S Bunch, Capt William Jobe, E TN Vol Mtd Inf
JIMMING, William, Pvt, Col S Bunch, Capt William Jobe, E TN Vol Mtd Inf
JINKINS, Mathew, Pvt, Col S Bunch, Capt Francis Berry, E TN Mil
JOAB, Jermiah, Pvt, Col William Metcalf, Capt Andrew Patterson, Mil Inf
JOAS (JOSY), Allen, Pvt, Col William Hall, Capt John Wallace, Inf
JOB, Aaron, Cpl, Regt Commander omitted, Capt Archibald, McKenney, Cav
JOB, Abraham, Pvt, Col John Winn, Capt Jas Cole, Inf; deserted 10-26-1813
JOB, Abraham, Pvt, Col Robert Dyer, Capt Jas McMahon, TN Vol Mtd Gunmen
JOB, Abraham, Pvt, Gen Andrew Jackson, Capt Nathan Davis, Inf
JOB, Abraham, Pvt, Maj Wm Russell, Capt William

## Enlisted Men, War of 1812

Chism, Vol Mtd Gunmen
JOB, Enoch, Sgt, Col S Bayless, Capt Johnathan Waddell, E TN Mil
JOB, Jeremiah, Pvt, Gen Andrew Jackson, Capt Nathan Davis, Inf
JOB, John, Pvt, Col N T Perkins, Capt Mathew Patterson, Mtd Vol Mil?
JOB, Joshua, Pvt, Col Ewen Allison, Capt Adam Winsell, E TN Drafted Mil; discharged for inability
JOB, Robt, Pvt, Col N T Perkins, Capt Mathew Patterson, Mtd Vol
JOB, Samuel, Pvt, Col Ewin Allison, Capt Joseph Everett, E TN Mil
JOB, Samuel, Pvt, Gen Andrew Jackson, Capt Nathan Davis, Inf
JOB, William, Pvt, Col John K Wynn, Capt John Porter, Inf
JOB, Zacherich, Pvt, Col Ewin Allison, Capt Joseph Everett, E TN Mil
JOBE, John, Pvt, Col Wm Metcalf, Capt William Mullens, Mil Inf
JOBE, Moses, Pvt, Col Wm Lillard, Capt Jacob Hartsell, E TN Vol Inf
JOBE, Samuel, Pvt, Regt Commander omitted, Capt David Mason, Cav; promoted to Cpl
JOEL, Cobb, Pvt, Col Edwin Booth, Capt John Slatton, E TN Mil
JOH, Andrew, Pvt, Col John Brown, Capt John Childs, E TN Mtd Inf Vol
JOHN, Elias, Pvt, Col Thomas Williamson, Capt Anthony Metcalf, Vol Mtd Gunmen
JOHNES, Isaac, Pvt, Col Robert Dyer, Capt Robert Evans, Vol Mtd Gunmen
JOHNES, John, Pvt, Col Thomas Williamson, Capt Robert Moore, Vol Mtd Gunmen
JOHNS, Harvey, Pvt, Col Leroy Hammonds, Capt Jas Craig, Inf
JOHNS, Jacob, Pvt, Col John Coffee, Capt Blackman Coleman, Cav
JOHNS, Jacob, Sdlr, Col John Coffee, Capt John Coleman, Inf
JOHNS, Jesse, Pvt, Col Abner Pearce, Capt Wm Woodfolk, Inf
JOHNS, Jesse, Pvt, Col N Cannon, Capt Jas Walton, Mtd Riflemen
JOHNS, Jesse, Pvt, Col N Cannon, Capt Martin, Mtd Gunmen
JOHNS, Jesse, Pvt, Col Phillip Pipkin, Capt Geo Mebane, Mil Inf
JOHNS, Joel, Pvt, Col Robert Dyer, Capt Robert Evans, Mtd Gunmen
JOHNS, Joseph, Pvt, Col Wm Hall, Capt Henry Newlin, Inf; substitute for Nathaniel Brown
JOHNS, Joseph, Pvt, Gen Andrew Jackson, Capt Nathan Davis, Inf
JOHNS, Samuel, Pvt, Col S Bunch, Capt Jno McNair, E TN Mil
JOHNS, Stephen, Pvt, Col Robert Dyer, Capt Robert Evans, Vol Mtd Gunmen; killed in action 12-23-1814
JOHNSON, Aaron, Pvt, Col Edwin Booth, Capt Vernon, E TN Mil
JOHNSON, Abner, Pvt, Brig Gen Roberts, Capt Benj Reynolds, Mtd Rangers
JOHNSON, Absolem, Pvt, Col Edwin Booth, Capt Richard Marshall, Drafted Mil
JOHNSON, Albert S, Pvt, Maj Gen Andrew Jackson, Capt William Carroll, Vol Inf
JOHNSON, Alexander, Pvt, Col Jas Raulston, Capt Jas Black, Inf
JOHNSON, Alexander, Pvt, Col S Copeland, Capt William Douglas, Inf
JOHNSON, Alexander, Pvt, Col Thos McCrory, Capt Sam McKnight, Inf
JOHNSON, Allen, Brig QM, Brig Gen N Taylor, Branch Srvce omitted; resigned - then appointed private secretary
JOHNSON, Allen, Pvt, Col Wm Johnson, Capt Henry Hunter, E TN Mil; appointed Secretary by the Gen
JOHNSON, Andrew M, Pvt, Col Thos Williamson, Capt Wm Martin, Vol Mtd Gunmen; promoted to Cpl
JOHNSON, Andrew, Rank omitted, Col John Alcorn, Capt Robert Jetton, Vol Cav
JOHNSON, Anguish, Sgt, Col Wm Higgins, Capt Wm Doak, Mtd Riflemen
JOHNSON, Archibold, Pvt, Col John Coffee, Capt John Baskerville, Cav
JOHNSON, Arthur, Pvt, Brig Gen Thos Washington, Capt Jno Crawford, Mtd Inf
JOHNSON, Arthur, Pvt, Col John Coffee, Capt John Baskervills, Cav
JOHNSON, Ben, Pvt, Col Sam Wear, Capt Jos Calloway, Mtd Inf
JOHNSON, Benjamin, 2 Cpl, Maj John Childs, Capt Reuben Tipton, E TN Vol Inf
JOHNSON, Charles, Col A Cheatham, Capt Chas Johnson, Inf
JOHNSON, Charles, Col N T Perkins, Capt Philip Pipkin, Mtd Riflemen
JOHNSON, Charles, Pvt, Col P Pipkin, Capt Wm Mackey, Mil Inf
JOHNSON, Chatman, Pvt, Col Robert Dyer, Capt Robt Evans, Vol Mtd Gunmen
JOHNSON, Daniel, Pvt, Col John Wynne, Capt Robt Brader, Inf
JOHNSON, Daniel, Pvt, Col Robt Steele, Capt Jas Bennett, Mil Inf
JOHNSON, Daniel, Pvt, Col Sam Copeland, Capt Moses Thompson, Inf
JOHNSON, Daniel, Pvt, Col Sam Copeland, Capt Richard Sharp, Mil Inf
JOHNSON, David, Cpl, Col Thos Williamson, Capt John Crane, Vol Mtd Gunmen
JOHNSON, Edward, Pvt, Col Philip Pipkin, Capt David Smith, Inf
JOHNSON, Edward, Pvt, Col Philip Pipkin, Capt John Strother, Mil
JOHNSON, Elisha, Pvt, Col Thos McCrory, Capt J Shannon, Mil Inf
JOHNSON, Elliot, Pvt, Col SAm Wear, Capt John Childs, E TN Vol Inf
JOHNSON, Elliott, Pvt, Col John Childs, Capt Chas Con-

way, E TN Mtd Gunmen
JOHNSON, Francis, Pvt, Col John Coffee, Capt J Baskerville, Cav
JOHNSON, George, Cpl, Col Robert Dyer, Capt Wm Russell, Vol Gunmen
JOHNSON, Hardy, Pvt, Col Williamson, Maj Gen Jackson, Capt Robt Steele, Vol Gunmen
JOHNSON, Henry, 3 Sgt, Regt Commander omitted, Capt David Smith, Cav Vol
JOHNSON, Henry, Pvt, Col John Cocke, Capt Geo Barnes, Inf
JOHNSON, Henry, Pvt, Col Robt Steele, Capt Jas Randals, Inf
JOHNSON, Howell, Cpl, Col Wm Metcalf, Capt Jason Barnhart, Mil Inf; reduced to the ranks
JOHNSON, Howell, Pvt, Col P Pipkin, Capt Jas Newlin, Mil; deserted
JOHNSON, Isaac, Pvt, Col Newton Cannon, Capt David Hogan, Mtd Gunmen
JOHNSON, Isaac, Pvt, Col Thos Benton, Capt Wm Moore, Vol Inf
JOHNSON, Isaac, Pvt, Col Wm Pillow, Capt Wm Moore, Inf
JOHNSON, Jacob, Cpl, Col Sam Bunch, Capt John Houk, E TN Mil
JOHNSON, Jacob, Pvt, Col John Cocke, Capt James Gray, Inf
JOHNSON, James B, Pvt, Col Robt Steele, Capt Jas Shenault, Mil Inf
JOHNSON, James M, Pvt, Col Alex Loury, Capt Gabriel Martin, Inf; died 3-6-1815
JOHNSON, James, Cpl, Col John Coffee, Capt Jno Baskerville, Cav
JOHNSON, James, Cpl, Col Sam Bunch, Capt Jas Baskerville, Vol Inf
JOHNSON, James, Pvt, Brig Gen T Washington, Capt John Crawford, Mtd Inf
JOHNSON, James, Pvt, Col John Cocke, Capt George Barnes, Inf; died 1-27-1815
JOHNSON, James, Pvt, Col John Wynne, Capt James Cole, Inf
JOHNSON, James, Pvt, Col Robt Steel, Capt James Randals, Inf
JOHNSON, James, Pvt, Col Sam Bunch, Capt Jas Cummings, E TN Vol Mtd Inf
JOHNSON, James, Pvt, Col Williamson, Capt Peter Searcy, Vol Mtd Gunmen
JOHNSON, James, Pvt, Col Wm Johnson, Capt Jas Stewart, E TN Drafted Mil; trans to Capt Rich Co
JOHNSON, James, Pvt, Col Wm Metcalf, Co Commander omitted, Mil Inf; died 2-2-1815
JOHNSON, James, Pvt, Maj Gen Jackson, Capt John Crane, Mtd Gunmen
JOHNSON, James, Pvt, Maj John Childs, Capt Dan Price, E TN Vol Mtd Inf
JOHNSON, James, Pvt, Maj Wm Russell, Capt I Williams, Bn W TN Mtd Gunmen; also under Col Dyer 1 Regt TN Gunmen
JOHNSON, Jesse, 1 Cpl, Col Edw Bradley, Capt Brice Martin, Vol Inf
JOHNSON, Jesse, Pvt, Col Wm Hall, Capt Brice Martin, Vol Inf
JOHNSON, Jesse, Pvt, Col Wm Williamson, Maj Gen Jackson, Capt Robt Steele, Vol Mtd Gunmen
JOHNSON, John A, Pvt, Col James Raulston, Capt ELijah Haynie, Inf
JOHNSON, John W, Pvt, Col Thomas Williamson, Capt Robert Moore, Vol Mtd Gunmen
JOHNSON, John jr, Pvt, Col Samuel Bayless, Capt James Landen, E TN Mil
JOHNSON, John sr, Pvt, Col Samuel Bayless, Capt James Landon, E TN Mil
JOHNSON, John, Cpl, Col John K Wynne, Capt John Porter, Inf
JOHNSON, John, Pfr, Col William Lillard, Capt Hugh Martin, E TN Vol Inf
JOHNSON, John, Pvt, Col John Alcorn, Capt William Locke, Cav
JOHNSON, John, Pvt, Col John Cocke, Capt Joseph Price, Inf
JOHNSON, John, Pvt, Col John K Wynne, Capt William McCall, Inf
JOHNSON, John, Pvt, Col Newton Cannon, Capt Francis Jones, Mtd Riflemen
JOHNSON, John, Pvt, Col Philip Pipkin, Capt William Mackay, Mil Inf
JOHNSON, John, Pvt, Col R C Napier, Capt Andrew McCarty, Mil Inf
JOHNSON, John, Pvt, Col Thomas McCrory, Capt William Dooly, Inf
JOHNSON, John, Pvt, Col William Lillard, Capt Robert Jaloney, E TN Vol Inf; unable to perform duty
JOHNSON, John, Pvt, Col William Metcalf, Capt Alexander Hill & Capt John Cunningham, Mil Inf
JOHNSON, John, Pvt, Col William Metcalf, Capt Bird Hurt, Mil Inf
JOHNSON, John, Pvt, Maj William Woodfolk, Capt James Turner, Inf
JOHNSON, Jonathan, Pvt, Col John Cocke, Capt Samuel Caruthers, Inf
JOHNSON, Joseph, Pvt, Col William Lillard, Capt Robert Maloney, E TN Vol Inf
JOHNSON, Josiah, Pvt, Col William Johnson, Capt Andrew Lawson, E TN Draft Mil
JOHNSON, Lemuel, Pvt, Col Robert Dyer, Capt Joseph Williams, 1 Regt TN Vol Mtd Gunmen
JOHNSON, Lemuel, Pvt, Col William Johnson, Capt Andrew Lawson, E TN Draft Mil
JOHNSON, Levi, Pvt, Col Ewen Allison, Capt Jonas Loughmiller, Mil; deserted
JOHNSON, Levi, Pvt, Col Philip Pipkin, Capt David Smith, Inf
JOHNSON, Levy, Pvt, Col John Cocke, Capt James Gray, Inf
JOHNSON, Lewis, Pvt, Col James Raulston, Capt Henry West, Inf
JOHNSON, Louis, Pvt, Col Philip Pipkin, Capt Ebenezer Kirkpatrick, Mil Inf; deserted
JOHNSON, Martin, Sgt, Col S Copeland, Capt James Tait, Inf
JOHNSON, Mathew, Pvt, Col John Alcorn, Capt John Baskerville, Inf

## Enlisted Men, War of 1812

JOHNSON, Mathew, Pvt, Col John Coffee, Capt Alexander McKeen, Cav
JOHNSON, Mathew, QM Sgt, Col Robert H Dyer, no Co Commander, Regt of TN Vol Mtd Gunmen
JOHNSON, Meredith, Pvt, Col John Cocke, Capt Joseph Price, Inf
JOHNSON, Moses, Pvt, Col Ewen Allison, Capt Jonas Loughmiller, Mil
JOHNSON, Moses, Pvt, Col Samuel Wear, Capt Simeon Perry, E TN Vol Mtd Inf
JOHNSON, Nathan, Mus-Dmr, Col Philip Pipkin, Capt Henry Newlin, Mil Inf
JOHNSON, Nathaniel, Pvt, Col Philip Pipkin, Capt Henry Newlin, Mil Inf
JOHNSON, Needham, Pvt, Col John Cocke, Capt George Barnes, Inf
JOHNSON, Oliver C, Pvt, Maj Gen Andrew Jackson, Capt William Carroll, Inf
JOHNSON, Peter, Cpl, no Regt Commander, Capt George Smith, Spies
JOHNSON, Peter, Pvt, Col Thomas Benton, Capt Thomas Williamson, Inf
JOHNSON, Pleasant M, Pvt, Maj John Childs, Capt Charles Conway, E TN Mtd Gunmen
JOHNSON, Reuben, Pvt, Col Robert Dyer, Capt Joseph Williams, Vol Mtd Gunmen
JOHNSON, Richard C, Pvt, Col John Alcorn, Capt John Baskerville, Vol Inf
JOHNSON, Richard C, Pvt, Col John Coffee, Capt John Baskerville, Cav
JOHNSON, Robert, Pvt, Col James Raulston, Capt James Black, Inf
JOHNSON, Robert, Pvt, Lt Col Leroy Hammonds, Capt Arahal Rains, Inf
JOHNSON, Robert, QM Sgt, Lt Col Alexander Loury, Lt Col Leroy Hammonds, 2 Regt W TN Mil
JOHNSON, Samuel, M, Pvt, Col Alexander Loury, Capt John Looney, W TN Inf
JOHNSON, Samuel, Pvt, Col Edward Bradley, Capt William Lauderdale, Vol Inf
JOHNSON, Samuel, Pvt, Col Edwin Booth, Capt John Lewis, E TN Mil
JOHNSON, Samuel, Pvt, Col R C Napier, Capt Samuel Ashmore, Mil Inf
JOHNSON, Samuel, Pvt, Maj Gen Andrew Jackson, Col A Cheatham, Capt William Creel, Inf
JOHNSON, Samuel, Pvt, Maj John Childs, Capt John Stephens, E TN Vol Mtd Inf
JOHNSON, Samuel, Pvt, Maj William Russell, Capt Isaac Williams, Separate Bn TN Vol Mtd Gunmen
JOHNSON, Samuel, Sgt, Maj William Russell, Capt Fleman Hodges, Vol Mtd Gunmen
JOHNSON, Sanford, Pvt, Col William Lillard, Capt Thomas Sharpe, 2nd Regt Inf
JOHNSON, Seth, Pvt, Col Edwin Booth, Capt John Sharp, E TN Mil
JOHNSON, Simon, Pvt, Col William Hall, Capt Abraham Bledsoe, Vol Inf
JOHNSON, Solomon, Pvt, Col Samuel Bunch, Capt Andrew Breden, E TN Mil; transferred to Capt Bacon Co
JOHNSON, Solomon, Pvt, Col Wm Y Higgins, Capt Samuel A Allen, Mtd Gunmen
JOHNSON, Solomon, Pvt, Maj Gen Andrew Jackson, Capt Joseph Kirkpatrick, Mtd Gunmen
JOHNSON, Stephen W, Pvt, Col Philip Pipkin, Capt John Strother, Mil
JOHNSON, Theophilas, Dmr, Col Edwin Booth, Capt George Winton, E TN Mil
JOHNSON, Thomas J, 1 Lt, Col Philip Pipkin, Capt Henry M Newlin, Mil Inf; d 11-6-1814 at Ft Williams
JOHNSON, Thomas, Pvt, Col A Cheatham, Capt George G Chapman, Inf
JOHNSON, Thomas, Pvt, Col John Cocke, Capt Richard Crunk, Inf
JOHNSON, Thomas, Pvt, Col Samuel Bunch, Capt Jones Griffin, E TN Drafted Mil
JOHNSON, Thomas, Pvt, Col William Johnson, Capt James Tunnell, 3rd Regt E TN Mil; d 11-19-1814
JOHNSON, Thomas, Pvt, Col William Johnson, Capt Joseph Kirk, Mil
JOHNSON, Thomas, Pvt, Col William Lillard, Capt John Roper, E TN Vol Inf
JOHNSON, Thomas, Pvt, Col Wm Johnson, Capt Benjamin Powell, E TN Mil
JOHNSON, Thomas, Pvt, Col Wm Metcalf, Capt Wm Mullin, Mil Inf
JOHNSON, Thomas, Pvt, Regt Commander omitted, Capt Archibald McKinney, Cav
JOHNSON, Thomas, Sgt, Col Thos Williamson, Capt James Cook & Capt John Crane, Vol Mtd Gunmen
JOHNSON, Wiatt. P, Ffr, Col Philip Pipkin, Capt John Strother, Mil
JOHNSON, William, 3 Cpl, Col R C Napier, Capt Edward Neblett, Mil Inf
JOHNSON, William, Pvt, Col A Cheatham, Capt Charles Johnson, Inf
JOHNSON, William, Pvt, Col A Cheatham, Capt George G Chapman, Inf
JOHNSON, William, Pvt, Col Edwin Booth, Capt Samuel Thompson, Mil
JOHNSON, William, Pvt, Col James Raulston, Capt Daniel Newman, Inf; d 1-15-1815
JOHNSON, William, Pvt, Col Jno Coffee, Capt Alexander McKeen, Cav; substituted by Thos Rhodes
JOHNSON, William, Pvt, Col Jno Coffee, Capt Robert Jetton, Cav
JOHNSON, William, Pvt, Col John Alcorn, Capt Robert Jetton, Vol Cav
JOHNSON, William, Pvt, Col Philip Pipkin, Capt William Mackay, Mil Inf
JOHNSON, William, Pvt, Col Phillip Pipkin, Capt Henry M Newlin, Mil Inf; substituted by Peter Johnson
JOHNSON, William, Pvt, Col R C Napier, Capt James McMurry, Mil Inf
JOHNSON, William, Pvt, Col S Bunch, Capt Jno Houk, E TN Mil
JOHNSON, William, Pvt, Col S Bunch, Capt Jones Griffin, E TN Drafted Mil
JOHNSON, William, Pvt, Col Samuel Bayless, Capt Joseph Hale, E TN Mil

## Enlisted Men, War of 1812

JOHNSON, William, Pvt, Col Samuel Wear, Capt Joseph Calloway, Mtd Inf
JOHNSON, William, Pvt, Col Thomas Benton, Capt Benjamin Reynolds, Vol Inf
JOHNSON, William, Pvt, Col William Johnson, Capt Elihu Milliken, 3rd Regt E TN Mil; transferred to Capt Hunter's Co
JOHNSON, William, Pvt, Col William Johnson, Capt Henry Hunter, E TN Mil; transferred from Capt Milliken's Co
JOHNSON, William, Pvt, Col William Johnson, Capt James Stewart, E TN Drafted Mil; substitute
JOHNSON, William, Pvt, Col William Johnson, Capt James Stewart, E TN Mil; transferred
JOHNSON, William, Pvt, Col William Lillard, Capt William McLin, E TN Inf
JOHNSON, William, Pvt, Col Wm Hall, Capt John Moore, Vol Inf
JOHNSON, William, Pvt, Lt Col L Hammonds, Capt Arahel Rains, Inf; d 2-1-1815
JOHNSON, William, Pvt, Maj Gen Wm Carroll, Capt Henry Hamilton, Inf
JOHNSON, William, Pvt, Maj John Childs, Capt Daniel Price, E TN Vol Mtd Inf
JOHNSON, William, Pvt, Maj John Childs, Capt Daniel Price, Vol Mtd Gunmen
JOHNSON, William, Pvt, Maj Wm Woodfolk, Capt James C Neil, Inf
JOHNSON, William, Pvt, Regt Commander omitted, Capt Edwin S Moore, Mtd Riflemen
JOHNSON, William, Pvt, Regt Commander omitted, Capt Nathan Farmer, Mtd Riflemen
JOHNSON, Willis, Pvt, Maj Gen Wm Carroll, Col James Raulston, Capt Edward Robinson, Inf
JOHNSON, Winston, Pvt, Col Jno Coffee, Capt John W Byrns, Cav
JOHNSON, Wm A, Pvt, Col Thomas Benton, Capt Benjamin Reynolds, Vol Inf
JOHNSON, Zephemiah, Pvt, Col N T Perkins, Capt Mathew Johnson, Mil Inf
JOHNSON, _____, Pvt, Col S Bunch, Capt Francis Register, E TN Mil
JOHNSTON, Abner H, 2 Sgt, Col R C Napier, Capt Samuel Ashmore, Mil Inf
JOHNSTON, Alexander, Pvt, Col John Brown, Capt Jesse G Reany, Mtd Gunmen
JOHNSTON, Andrew M, Pvt, Col Newton Cannon, Capt Martin, Mtd Gunmen
JOHNSTON, Arthur, Sgt, Col Arch Cheatham, Capt Meredith Walker, 6th Brig Mtd Inf
JOHNSTON, Charles, Pvt, Col Newton Cannon, Capt Martin, Mtd Gunmen
JOHNSTON, Cornelius, Pvt, Col Philip Pipkin, Capt William MacKay, Mil Inf
JOHNSTON, Daeney?, Pvt, Col Samuel Bayless, Capt John Brook, E TN Mil
JOHNSTON, Daniel, Pvt, Col Edwin Booth, Capt Vernon, E TN Mil; returned home on account of sickness
JOHNSTON, Daniel, Pvt, Col S Copeland, Capt Alexander Provine, Mil Inf
JOHNSTON, David, Pvt, Col Samuel Bunch, Capt Geo McPherson, E TN Mil
JOHNSTON, David, Pvt, Col William Pillow, Capt George Caperton, Inf
JOHNSTON, Eli, Pvt, Col Edwin E Booth, Capt Porter, Drafted Mil
JOHNSTON, Elijah, Pvt, Col N Perkins, Capt Jas McMahon, Mtd Gunmen
JOHNSTON, Frederick, Pvt, Col Samuel Bayless, Capt Joseph Rich, E TN Inf
JOHNSTON, Garrett, Pvt, Col Robert Steele, Capt Robt Campbell, Mil Inf
JOHNSTON, George, Pvt, Col Robt H Dyer, Maj Wm Russell, Capt Wm Russell, Vol Mtd Gunmen
JOHNSTON, George, Pvt, Col Samuel Bunch, Capt N Gibbs, E TN Drafted Mil
JOHNSTON, Henry, Pvt, Col John Coffee, Capt David Smith, Vol Cav
JOHNSTON, Henry, Pvt, Lt Col A Cheatham, Co Commander omitted, Brig Mtd Inf
JOHNSTON, Henry, QM, Brig Gen Thos Johnston, Branch Srvce omitted
JOHNSTON, Hezekiah, Pvt, Regt Commander omitted, Capt Isaiah Hamilton, Inf
JOHNSTON, Isaac, Pvt, Col Thos Benton, Capt Wm Moore, Vol Inf
JOHNSTON, Isaac, Pvt, Maj Gen A Jackson, Capt Hugh Kerr, Mtd Rangers
JOHNSTON, Isom, Pvt, Col R H Dyer, Capt McMahan, TN Vol Mtd Gunmen
JOHNSTON, James B, Pvt, Col Philip Pipkin, Capt John Robertson, Mil Inf
JOHNSTON, James, Pvt, Capt Nathan Davis, Lt I Barrett, Inf
JOHNSTON, James, Pvt, Col John Brown, Capt Hugh Barton, E TN Mil Inf
JOHNSTON, James, Pvt, Col John Brown, Capt William White, Regt E TN Mtd Mil Inf
JOHNSTON, James, Pvt, Col Samuel Bunch, Capt John English, E TN Mil; joined from Capt David Co
JOHNSTON, James, Pvt, Col Samuel Bunch, Capt Moses, E TN Drafted Mil
JOHNSTON, James, Pvt, Col Wm Lillard, Capt Thos Sharpe, Branch Srvce omitted
JOHNSTON, James, Pvt, Col Wm Pillow, Capt Isaiah Renshaw, Inf
JOHNSTON, James, Pvt, Lt Col A Cheatham, Capt Meredith Walker, 6th Brig Mtd Inf
JOHNSTON, James, Sgt, Col Thos Benton, Capt Isaiah Renshaw, Vol Inf
JOHNSTON, Jesse, 1 Cpl, Col Wm Hall, Capt Brice Hall, Vol Inf; promoted in place of Robt Bradley
JOHNSTON, Jesse, 5 Cpl, Col Philip Pipkin, Capt James Blakemore, Mil Inf
JOHNSTON, Jesse, Pvt, Col Robert H Dyer, Maj Wm Russell, Capt Wm Russell, Vol Mtd Gunmen
JOHNSTON, Joel, Pvt, Col A Loury, Lt Col L Hammond, Capt Thos Wells, Inf
JOHNSTON, John W, 3 Cpl, Col N T Perkins, Capt Mathew Patterson, Mtd Vol
JOHNSTON, John W, Pvt, Col N T Perkins, Capt Jas McMahon, Mtd Gunmen

- 283

## Enlisted Men, War of 1812

JOHNSTON, John, 1 Sgt, Col N T Perkins, Capt Mathew Johnston, Mil Inf
JOHNSTON, John, Pvt, Col R C Napier, Capt Samuel Ashmore, Mil Inf
JOHNSTON, John, Pvt, Col R C Napier, Capt Thos Preston, Mil Inf
JOHNSTON, John, Pvt, Col Thos H Benton, Capt Isaiah Renshaw, Vol Inf
JOHNSTON, John, Pvt, Col Wm Pillow, Capt Isaiah Renshaw, Vol Inf
JOHNSTON, John, Pvt, Lt Col A Cheatham, Capt G Martin, 6 Brig Mtd Inf
JOHNSTON, John, Pvt, Lt Col L Hammond, Capt James Tubb, Inf
JOHNSTON, John, Pvt, Maj William Russell, Capt William Russell, Vol Mtd Gunmen
JOHNSTON, John, Sgt, Col John Brown, Capt Jas Preston, E TN Mil Inf
JOHNSTON, Jonathan, Pvt, Col A Cheatham, Capt Meredith Walker, Inf
JOHNSTON, Jonathan, Pvt, Col Edward Bradley, Capt John Kennedy, Riflemen; AWOL 12-12-1813
JOHNSTON, Joseph, Pvt, Col Samuel Wear, Capt James Tedford, E TN Vol Inf
JOHNSTON, Joshua, Pvt, Lt Col L Hammond, Col Alexander Loury, Capt Thos Delaney, Inf
JOHNSTON, Josiah, Pvt, Col John Brown, Capt John Childs, E TN Vol Mtd Inf
JOHNSTON, Lemuel, Pvt, Col Wm Metcalf, Capt Barbee Collins, Mil Inf
JOHNSTON, Lewis, Pvt, Col Samuel Bayless, Capt Joseph Rich, E TN Inf
JOHNSTON, Lewis, Pvt, Col Thos Williamson, Capt Beverly Williams, Vol Mtd Gunmen; deserted 12-24-1814
JOHNSTON, Mathew, Pvt, Col R H Dyer, Capt Thomas Jones, Vol Mtd Gunmen; promoted to QM Sgt
JOHNSTON, Peter, Pvt, Col Thos Benton, Capt Thos Williamson, Vol Inf
JOHNSTON, Robb, Pvt, Lt Col Richard Napier, Co Commander omitted, Inf
JOHNSTON, Robert G, 1 Sgt, Col John Coffee, Capt David Smith, Vol Cav
JOHNSTON, Robert, Pvt, Col Robert H Dyer, Capt James McMahon, TN Vol Mtd Gunmen; d 12-27-1814 of wounds in battle
JOHNSTON, Robert, QM Sgt, Lt Col L Hammond, Co Commander omitted, 2nd Regt W TN Mil
JOHNSTON, Samual, Pvt, Col William Hall, Capt Wm Alexander, Vol Inf
JOHNSTON, Samuel, Pvt, Col Thos Williamson, Capt Thos Scurry, Vol Mtd Gunmen
JOHNSTON, Simon, Pvt, Col William Hall, Capt Abraham Bledsoe, Vol Inf
JOHNSTON, Solomon, Pvt, Col William Pillow, Capt General Caperton, Inf
JOHNSTON, Swan, Pvt, Col N T Perkins, Capt Mathew Johnston, Mil Inf
JOHNSTON, Thomas J, Pvt, Col N T Perkins, Capt Jas McMahan, Mtd Gunmen
JOHNSTON, Thomas, Pvt, Col N T Perkins, Capt John Quarles, Vol Mtd Inf
JOHNSTON, Thomas, Pvt, Col William Metcalf, Capt William Mullin, Mil Inf
JOHNSTON, Thomas, Pvt, Col Wm Johnston, Capt James Tunnell, E TN Mil
JOHNSTON, Thomas, Pvt, Col Wm Lillard, Capt Wm Gillenwater, E TN Inf
JOHNSTON, Thomas, Pvt, Gen Andrew Jackson, Capt Deaderick, Arty
JOHNSTON, Thomas, Pvt, Maj Gen William Carroll, Capt Francis Ellis, Inf
JOHNSTON, Thomas, Pvt, Regt Commander omitted, Capt Arch McKinney, Cav
JOHNSTON, William, Cpl, Col Thomas Benton, Capt Jas Renshaw, Vol Inf
JOHNSTON, William, Cpl, Col Thos Benton, Capt I Renshaw, Vol Inf
JOHNSTON, William, Pvt, Col Edw Bradley, Capt John Moore, Vol Inf
JOHNSTON, William, Pvt, Col James Raulston, Capt Mathew Neal, Inf
JOHNSTON, William, Pvt, Col John Brown, Capt Jas Preston, E TN Mil Inf
JOHNSTON, William, Pvt, Col N T Perkins, Capt James McMahan, Mtd Gunmen
JOHNSTON, William, Pvt, Col Philip Pipkin, Capt John Strother, Mil
JOHNSTON, William, Pvt, Gen Andrew Jackson, Capt D Deadrick, Arty
JOHNSTON, William, Pvt, Lt Col Jno Edmondson, Co Commander omitted, Cav
JOHNSTON, William, Pvt, Maj Wm Woodfolk, Capt Mathew Neal, Inf
JOHNSTON, William, Pvt, Regt Commander omitted, Capt Jas Haggard, Mtd Gunmen
JOHNSTON, William, Pvt, Regt Commander omitted, Capt Nathan Farmer, Mtd Riflemen
JOHNSTON, Winsds? P, Pvt, Maj Gen Jackson, Capt Wm Carroll, Vol Inf
JOHNSTON, Zepaniah, Pvt, Regt Commander omitted, Capt David Smith, Cav Vol
JOICE, Bins, Pvt, Col Alex Loury, Capt James Kincaid, Inf
JOICE, Thomas, Pvt, Col N T Perkins, Capt P Pipkin, Mtd Riflemen
JOINER, Cullen (Colen), Pvt, Col Alex Loury, Capt George Sarver, Inf
JOINER, Jeptha, Pvt, Col John Cocke, Capt James Gray, Inf; died while on the boat
JOINER, John, Pvt, Col John Alcorn, Capt John Byrns, Cav
JOINER, Joshua, Pvt, Col Philip Pipkin, Capt George Mebane, Mil Inf
JOINER, Lyttleton, Pvt, Col James Raulston, Capt John Hamilton, Inf; also served under Maj Gen Carroll
JOINER, Micajah, Pvt, Col Sam Copeland, Capt Robt Steele, Mil Inf
JOINER, Thomas, Dmr, Col Thomas Benton, Capt Wm Moore, Vol Inf
JOINER, Turner, Pvt, Col Thos Williamson, Capt Robt Moore, Vol Mtd Gunmen; d 2-6-1815

## Enlisted Men, War of 1812

JOLIN (JOSLIN), Daniel, Pvt, Col Philip Pipkin, Capt Wm Mackay, Mil Inf; transferred to Capt Searcy

JOLLEY, Thomas, Pvt, Col Wm Hall, Capt John Hambleton, Vol Inf; joined at Clarksville

JOLLEY, William, Pvt, Col Wm Metcalf, Capt John Barnhart, Mil Inf; d 2-8-1815

JOLLY, Jesse, Cpl, Col Arch Cheatham, Capt Hugh Virdwell, Inf

JONAKIN?, Allen, Pvt, Col John Cocke, Capt Bird Nance, Inf

JONATHAM, Joseph, Pvt, Col Wm Lillard, Capt G Argenbright, E TN Vol Riflemen

JONES, A, Pvt, Col Sam Bunch, Capt F Register, E TN Mil; substituted for Jacob Collets

JONES, Abner, Pvt, Col R C Napier, Capt A McCarty, Mil Inf

JONES, Abner, Pvt, Col Robert Dyer, Capt George Mebane, TN Mtd Gunmen

JONES, Abner, Pvt, Maj John Childs, Capt Chas Conway, E TN Mtd Gunmen; d 12-3-1814

JONES, Abraham, Pvt, Maj Wm Woodfolk, Capt James Turner, Inf

JONES, Abram, Pvt, Col Edwin Booth, Capt Vernon, E TN Mil

JONES, Andrew, Dmr, Col Sam Bunch, Capt Jones Griffin, E TN Drafted Mil; furloughed for inability

JONES, Andrew, Sgt, Col John Brown, Capt Wm Neilson, E TN Vol Mil

JONES, Anthony, Pvt, Col John Cocke, Capt Richard Crunk, Inf

JONES, Anthony, Sgt, Col A Cheatham, Capt George Chapman, Inf

JONES, Asariah, Pvt, Col Archer Cheatham, Capt Meredith Walker, Inf

JONES, Asariah, Pvt, Regt Commander omitted, Capt David Smith, Cav

JONES, Azariah, Sgt, Regt Commander omitted, Capt Jno Crane, Mtd Inf

JONES, Benjamin, Pvt, Col John Coffee, Capt Chas Kavanaugh, Cav

JONES, Benjamin, Pvt, Col R C Napier, Capt Sam Ashmore, Mil

JONES, Benjamin, Pvt, Col Thos McCrory, Capt Sam McKnight, Inf

JONES, Benjamin, Pvt, Col Wm Hall, Capt Henry Newlin, Inf

JONES, Britton, Cpl, Col Wm Metcalf, Capt Barbee Collins, Mil Inf

JONES, Caleb, Pvt, Col Wm Lillard, Capt Robt Maloney, E TN Vol Inf

JONES, Car__, Pvt, Col Sam Bayless, Capt James Landen, E TN Mil

JONES, Charles M, Cpl, Col John Cocke, Capt John Dalton, Inf; appointed Cpl in place of Henry Whitehead

JONES, Charles M, Pvt, Col John Cocke, Capt John Dalton, Inf

JONES, Charles, Pvt, Col Newton Cannon, Capt James Walton, Mtd Riflemen

JONES, Clinton, Pvt, Col James Raulston, Capt Mathew Cowan, Inf

JONES, Clinton, Pvt, Col Robt Steele, Capt Sam Maxwell, Mil Inf

JONES, Crawford, Pvt, Col Sam Wear, Capt John Childs, E TN Vol Inf

JONES, Daniel, Pvt, Regt Commander omitted, Capt George Smith, Spies

JONES, David, Cpl, Lt Col Henry Bryan, Co Commander omitted, Inf

JONES, David, Cpl, Regt Commander omitted, Capt Jas Cowan, Mtd Inf

JONES, David, Pvt, Col S Bunch, Capt W Jobe, E TN Vol Mtd Inf

JONES, David, Pvt, Col Wm Johnson, Capt E Milliken, 3rd Regt E TN Mil

JONES, David, Pvt, Col Wm Lillard, Capt J Roper, E TN Vol Inf

JONES, David, Pvt, Maj Gen Wm Carroll, Col Wm Metcalf, Capt J Jackson, Inf; d 1-9-1815

JONES, David, Sgt, Col W Y Higgins, Capt J Hambleton, Mtd Gunmen

JONES, Edward, Pvt, Maj Gen Wm Carroll, Capt J Jackson, Inf

JONES, Edwin, Pvt, Col Alex Loury, Capt Geo Sarver, Inf

JONES, Elias (Elixes), Pvt, Col J Cocke, Capt J Gault, Inf

JONES, Elijah, Pvt, Maj Wm Woodfolk, Capt E Ross, Inf

JONES, Elijah, Sgt, Col Wm Lillard, Capt Wm Hamilton, E TN Vol Inf

JONES, Elisha, Pvt, Col N Cannon, Capt Wm Edwards, Regt Command

JONES, Enoch F(H), Pvt, Col T Williamson, Capt R Tate, Vol Mtd Gunmen

JONES, Ezekiah M, Pvt, Col J Cocke, Capt J Weakley, Inf

JONES, Ezekiel, Pvt, Col Edwin Allison, Capt J Everett, E TN Mil

JONES, Ezekiel, Pvt, Col Wm Lillard, Capt Geo Keys, E TN Inf

JONES, Foster, Cpl, Col S Bayless, Capt J Brock, E TN Mil

JONES, Francis, Pvt, Col T Benton, Capt Geo Caperton, Inf; promoted to Sgt Maj

JONES, Francis, Pvt, Col T Benton, Capt Geo Caperton, Vol Inf; reduced from Sgt Maj of 2nd Regt

JONES, Francis, Sgt Maj, Commanders omitted, 2nd Regt TN Vol Inf; resigned 3-10-1813

JONES, Freborn G, Pvt, Col Robert Steel, Capt Jas Shenault, Mil Inf

JONES, Frederick, Pvt, Col J Brown, Capt J Childs, E TN Vol Mtd Inf

JONES, George, Pvt, Col Edwin Allison, Capt J Everett, E TN Mil; deserted 1-27-1814

JONES, George, Pvt, Col Wm Johnson, Capt C Cook, E TN Mil

JONES, George, Pvt, Col Wm Johnson, Capt J Kirk, Mil

JONES, Hamlet (Hambleton), Pvt, Col J Cocke, Capt J Gault, Inf

JONES, Henry, Pvt, Col J Raulston, Capt Mathew Cowan, Inf

JONES, Hugh, Pvt, Col Wm Metcalf, Capt B Collins, Mil Inf

JONES, Isaac, Pvt, Col T Williamson, Capt Robt Moore, Vol Mtd Gunmen; d 1-13-1815

- 285

## Enlisted Men, War of 1812

JONES, Isaac, Pvt, Col Wm Lillard, Capt Hugh Martin, E TN Vol Inf
JONES, Isham, Cpl, Col R C Napier, Capt T Gray, Mil Inf
JONES, Isham, Cpl, Regt Commander omitted, Capt E Rushing, Det of Inf
JONES, Jacoriah, Pvt, Regt Commander omitted, Capt David Smith, Cav Vol
JONES, James W, Cpl, Col Wm Hall, Capt J Moore, Vol Inf
JONES, James W, Pvt, Col Wm Hall, Capt R Braden, Inf
JONES, James jr, Pvt, Col J K Wynne, Capt R Braden, Inf
JONES, James sr, Pvt, Col J K Wynne, Capt R Braden, Inf
JONES, James, Pvt, Brig Gen T Johnston, Capt R Carson, Inf
JONES, James, Pvt, Col E Allison, Capt J Hampton, Mil; transferred to Capt Mcrea's
JONES, James, Pvt, Col E Booth, Capt Geo Winton, E TN Mil
JONES, James, Pvt, Col J Coffee, Capt T Bradley, Vol Cav
JONES, James, Pvt, Col J Rawlston, Capt M Cowan, Inf
JONES, James, Pvt, Col Jno Brown, Capt Wm Christian, E TN Mil Inf
JONES, James, Pvt, Col Jno Brown, Capt Wm White, E TN Mtd Mil Inf
JONES, James, Pvt, Col S Bayless, Capt J Brock, E TN Mil; d 5-5-1815 in service
JONES, James, Pvt, Col Samuel Bunch, Capt Jas Cumming, E TN Vol Mtd Inf
JONES, James, Pvt, Col Wm Hall, Capt B Martin, Vol Inf
JONES, James, Pvt, Col Wm Lillard, Capt Wm McLin, E TN Inf
JONES, James, Sgt, Col J D Wynne, Capt R Breden, Inf
JONES, Jeremiah, Pvt, Col E Booth, Capt Geo Winton, E TN Mil
JONES, Jeremiah, Pvt, Col Jno Brown, Capt Jas Preston, E TN Mil Inf
JONES, Jeremiah, Pvt, Col Wm Lillard, Capt J Roper, E TN Vol Inf
JONES, Jesse W, Cpl, Col N Cannon, Capt I Williams, Mtd Riflemen; deserted 10-10-1813
JONES, Jesse, Pvt, Col J Alcorn, Capt G Winton, Mtd Riflemen
JONES, Jesse, Pvt, Maj Gen W Carroll, Col J Raulston, Capt W Huddleston, Inf
JONES, John A, Pvt, Col Samuel Bayless, Capt Joseph Goodson, E TN Mil
JONES, John A, Pvt, Col William Lillard, Capt Robert Maloney, E TN Vol Inf
JONES, John jr, Pvt, Col William Higgins, Capt Stephen Griffith, Mtd Riflemen; wounded 1-28-1814
JONES, John jr, Pvt, Regt Commander omitted, Capt William Henderson, Spies
JONES, John, Cpl, Col William Higgins, Capt Stephen Griffith, Mtd Gunmen
JONES, John, Master of Sword, Col John Coffee, Co Commander omitted, TN Vol Cav
JONES, John, Pvt, Brig Gen Isaac Roberts, Capt Benjamin Reynolds, Mtd Rangers
JONES, John, Pvt, Col Ewen Allison, Capt Jonas Loughmiller, Mil
JONES, John, Pvt, Col John Brown, Capt Lunsford Oliver, E TN Mil; d 12-4-1813
JONES, John, Pvt, Col John Cocke, Capt John Dalton, Inf; substitute for __ Cowan
JONES, John, Pvt, Col John Cocke, Capt Samuel Caruthers, Inf
JONES, John, Pvt, Col John Coffee, Capt John Bryn, Cav
JONES, John, Pvt, Col N Cannon, Capt Geo Brandon, Mtd Riflemen
JONES, John, Pvt, Col Philip Pipkin, Capt David Smith, Mil Inf
JONES, John, Pvt, Col Philip Pipkin, Capt George Mebane, Mil Inf
JONES, John, Pvt, Col Robert Dyer, Capt Cuthbert Hudson, Vol Mtd Gunmen
JONES, John, Pvt, Col Robert Steele, Capt James Randals, Inf
JONES, John, Pvt, Col S Bunch, Capt John Houk, E TN Mil; transferred to Capt English Co
JONES, John, Pvt, Col S Copeland, Capt M Thompson, Inf
JONES, John, Pvt, Col S Wear, Capt J Tedford, E TN Vol Inf
JONES, John, Pvt, Col S Wear, Capt S Perry, E TN Vol Mtd Inf
JONES, John, Pvt, Col Samuel Bunch, Capt John English, E TN Drafted Mil
JONES, John, Pvt, Col William Hall, Capt Henry Newlin, Inf
JONES, John, Pvt, Col William Johnson, Capt Joseph Scott, E TN Drafted Mil; deserted 10-4-1814
JONES, John, Pvt, Col William Lillard, Capt William Hamilton, E TN Vol Inf
JONES, John, Pvt, Col Wm Metcalf, Capt A Patterson, Mil Inf
JONES, John, Pvt, Col Wm Metcalf, Capt Wm Mullin, Mil Inf; discharged for inability
JONES, John, Pvt, Lt Col Henry Bryan, Co Commander omitted, Inf
JONES, John, Pvt, Lt Col John Edmonson, Co Commander omitted, Cav
JONES, John, Pvt, Maj J Childs, Capt C Conway, E TN Mtd Gunmen
JONES, John, Pvt, Maj William Russell, Capt John Cowan, Vol Mtd Gunmen
JONES, John, Pvt, Regt Commander omitted, Capt Archibald McKenney, Cav
JONES, John, Pvt, Regt Commander omitted, Capt James Haggard, Mtd Gunmen
JONES, John, Pvt, Regt Commander omitted, Capt John Crane, Mtd Inf
JONES, John, Pvt, Regt Commander omitted, Capt Joseph Williams, Mil Cav
JONES, John, Pvt, Regt Commander omitted, Sgt Wyatt Fussell, Det of Inf
JONES, Joseph, Pvt, Col John Brown, Capt William White, E TN Mil
JONES, Joseph, Pvt, Col Samuel Bunch, Capt Andrew Breden, E TN Mil
JONES, Joshua D, Pvt, Col John Alcorn, Capt William Locke, Cav
JONES, Joshua D, Pvt, Col John Coffee, Capt Blackman

## Enlisted Men, War of 1812

Coleman, Cav
JONES, Joshua T, Pvt, Col William Metcalf, Capt John Cunningham & Capt Alexander Hill, Mil Inf
JONES, Joshua, Pvt, Col Newton Cannon, Capt James Walton, Mtd Riflemen
JONES, Josiah M, Pvt, Col John Cocke, Capt John Weakley, Inf; died 2-8-1815
JONES, Josiah, Pvt, Col Robert Dyer, Capt Cuthbert Hudson, Vol Mtd Gunmen; died 2-25-1815
JONES, Judson, Pvt, Col Newton Cannon, Capt William Marlin, Mtd Gunmen
JONES, Judson, Pvt, Col William Pillow, Capt Thomas Williamson, Vol Inf
JONES, Jules, Pvt, Col Thomas Benton, Capt James McFerrin, Vol Inf
JONES, Julius, Pvt, Col Thomas Benton, Capt Isiah Renshaw, Vol Inf
JONES, Julius, Pvt, Col Thomas Benton, Capt James McFerrin, Vol Inf
JONES, Julius, Pvt, Col William Pillow, Capt James McFerrin, Inf; deserted
JONES, Kenchen, Pvt, Col Alexander Loury, Capt Gabriel Martin, Inf
JONES, Kenenen, Pvt, Col A Cheatham, Capt Meredith Walker, Inf
JONES, Lemuel, Pvt, Col Robert Dyer, Capt Robert Evans, Vol Mtd Gunmen
JONES, Lemuel, Pvt, Col Robert Steele, Capt James Shenault, Mil Inf
JONES, Leonard, Pvt, Col Edward Bradley, Capt Abraham Bledsoe, Riflemen
JONES, Leonard, Pvt, Col William Hall, Capt Abraham Bledsoe, Vol Inf
JONES, Leroy, Pvt, Col Thomas Williamson, Capt Thomas Porter, Vol Mtd Gunmen
JONES, Lewis, 2 Cpl, Lt Col Leroy Hammonds, Lt Col Alexander Loury, Capt Thomas Delany, Inf
JONES, Lewis, Pvt, Col Edwin Booth, Capt Samuel Thompson, Mil
JONES, Loten, Pvt, Col Thomas Benton, Capt Isiah Renshaw, trans to McFerrin
JONES, Mallin, Pvt, Col Ewen Allison, Capt Joseph Everett, E TN Mil
JONES, Malon, Pvt, Col S Bunch, Capt George McPherson, E TN Mil
JONES, Mark, Pvt, Col William Hillard, Capt James Hamilton, E TN Vol Inf
JONES, Martin, Pvt, Col John Alcorn, Capt William Locke, Cav
JONES, Martin, Pvt, Col Robert Dyer, Capt James Wyatt, Vol Mtd Gunmen
JONES, Marvel, Pvt, Col William Hall, Capt John Kennedy, Vol Inf
JONES, Mathew, Pvt, Col Robert Steele, Capt James Shenault, Mil Inf
JONES, Morgan, Pvt, Col Phillip Pipkin, Capt Ebenezer Kirkpatrick, Mil Inf
JONES, Moses, Pvt, Col A Cheatham, Maj Gen Jackson, Capt Creel, Inf
JONES, Moses, Pvt, Col S Copeland, Capt Stell, Mil Inf
JONES, Moses, Pvt, Col William Lillard, Capt George

Argenbright, E TN Vol Riflemen
JONES, Peter, Pvt, Col John Cocke, Capt Price, Inf; deserted
JONES, Prateman, Pvt, Col Jas Raulston, Capt Mathew Cowan, Inf
JONES, Reddins, Pvt, Col Ewin Allison, Capt Joseph Everett, E TN Mil
JONES, Reddon, Pvt, Col S Bunch, Capt Jones Griffin, joined for Capt Everett Co
JONES, Redin, Pvt, Col S Bayless, Capt James Landen, E TN Mil
JONES, Redrick, Pvt, Col A Cheatham, Capt Geo Chapman, Inf
JONES, Reuben, Pvt, Col William Pillow, Capt William Williamson, Vol Inf
JONES, Reuben, Pvt, Lt Col A Cheatham, Capt Meredith Walker, Mtd Mil
JONES, Reubeun, Pvt, Col Robert Dyer, Capt Cuther Hudson, Vol Mtd Gunmen; died 4-15-1815
JONES, Rheuben, Pvt, Col John Brown, Capt William White, E TN Vol Mtd Inf
JONES, Richard, Pvt, Col Phillip Pipkin, Capt Henry Newlin, Mil Inf
JONES, Richard, Pvt, Col William Higgins, Capt Stephen Griffith, Mtd Riflemen
JONES, Richard, Pvt, Lt Col Henry Byran, Co Commander omitted, Inf
JONES, Richard, Pvt, Regt Commander omitted, Capt James Cowan, Mtd Inf
JONES, Robert, Pvt, Col Robert Steele, Capt Jas Shenault, Mil Inf
JONES, Robert, Pvt, Regt Commander omitted, Capt Jas Haggard, Mtd Gunmen
JONES, Ruelin, Pvt, Col Thos Benton, Capt Thomas Williamson, Vol Inf
JONES, Samuel, Pvt, Col Ewin Allison, Capt Joseph Everett, E TN Mil
JONES, Samuel, Pvt, Col John K Wynn, Capt Jas Cole, Inf
JONES, Samuel, Pvt, Col Phillip Pipkin, Capt Ebenezer Kirkpatrick, Mil Inf
JONES, Spicer, Pvt, Col Thomas Williamson, Capt Thomas Porter, Vol Mtd Gunmen; died 2-10-1815
JONES, Stephen, Pvt, Col Robert Dyer, Capt Jas McMahan, TN Vol Mtd Gunmen
JONES, Stephens, Pvt, Col William Johnson, Capt Joseph Scott, E TN Drafted Mil
JONES, Theophielus, Pvt, Lt Col Jno Edmonson, Co Commander omitted, Cav
JONES, Thomas, Cpl, Col S Bunch, Capt Geo Gregory, E TN Drafted Mil
JONES, Thomas, Dmr, Col Thos Benton, Capt Geo Moore, Vol Inf
JONES, Thomas, Dmr, Col Thos Benton, Capt William Moore, Inf
JONES, Thomas, Pvt, Col A Cheatham, Capt Geo Chapman, Inf
JONES, Thomas, Pvt, Col J Alcorn, Capt Thomas Bradley, Vol Inf Cav
JONES, Thomas, Pvt, Col Jas Raulston, Capt Jas Cowan, Inf
JONES, Thomas, Pvt, Col John Cocke, Capt Geo Barnes,

## Enlisted Men, War of 1812

JONES, Thomas, Pvt, Col S Bayless, Capt William Hale, E TN Mil
JONES, Thomas, Pvt, Col S Wear, Capt Jesse Wear, Vol Inf
JONES, Thomas, Pvt, Col Thos Benton, Capt Geo Caperton, Vol Inf
JONES, Thomas, Pvt, Col Wm Metcalf, Capt Barbee, Mil Inf
JONES, Thomas, Pvt, Col Wm Pillow, Capt William Moore, Inf
JONES, Thomas, Pvt, Maj Gen Carroll, Capt Francis Ellis, Inf
JONES, Thomas, Pvt, Maj John Childs, Capt Chas Conway, E TN Mtd Gunmen
JONES, Thomas, Sgt, Col Samuel Bunch, Capt John Dobbins, E TN Drafted Mil, discharge for inability
JONES, Timothy, Pvt, Regt Commander omitted, Capt David Mason, Cav
JONES, Waddin, Pvt, Col Alexander Lowry, Capt Gabriel Martin, Inf
JONES, Waddy, Cpl, Col Alexander Loury, Capt Gabriel Martin, Inf
JONES, Wiley (Willie), Pvt, Col John Coffee, Capt Geo Coleman, Cav
JONES, William, Pvt, Brig Gen T Johnson, Capt Allen, Mil Inf
JONES, William, Pvt, Col A Cheatham, Capt Hugh Birdwell, Inf
JONES, William, Pvt, Col Edwin Booth, Capt Richard Marshall, Drafted Mil
JONES, William, Pvt, Col Ewen Allison, Capt Joseph Everett, E TN Mil
JONES, William, Pvt, Col James Raulston, Capt Daniel Newman, Inf
JONES, William, Pvt, Col John Coffee, Capt Blackman Coleman, Cav
JONES, William, Pvt, Col N T Perkins, Capt James McMahan, Mtd Gunmen
JONES, William, Pvt, Col Philip Pipkin, Capt George Mebane, Mil Inf
JONES, William, Pvt, Col S Wear, Capt Simeon Perry, E TN Vol Mtd Inf
JONES, William, Pvt, Col Wm Lillard, Capt Thomas Sharpe, 2 Regt Inf; deserted
JONES, William, Pvt, Gen A Jackson, Capt Nathan Davis, Inf
JONES, William, Pvt, Lt Col Leroy Hammonds, Capt Jas Craig, Inf; died 3-17-1815
JONES, William, Pvt, Maj Gen Wm Carroll, Capt Hamilton, Inf
JONES, William, Pvt, Maj John Childs, Capt Charles Conway, E TN Vol Mtd Inf
JONES, William, Pvt, Maj John Childs, Capt Chas Conaway, E TN Mtd Gunmen
JONES, William, Pvt, Regt Commander omitted, Capt Archibald MacKinney, Cav; trans to Capt McMannuis Co
JONES, William, Pvt, Regt Commander omitted, Capt Archibald McKinney, Cav; trans to Capt McMurry
JONES, Williams, Pvt, Col Wm Lillard, Capt Wm McLin, E TN Mil
JONES, Willie, Far, Col John Alcorn, Capt William Locke, Cav; wounded 11-9-1813
JONES, Willie, Pvt, Col Jas Raulston, Capt Elijah Haynie, Inf
JONES, Willie, Pvt, Col John Cocke, Capt Bird Nance, Inf
JONES, Willie, Pvt, Col Philip Pipkin, Capt Geo Mebane, Mil Inf; deserted 9-20-1814
JONES, Willie, Pvt, Col Robert Dyer, Capt James Wyatt, Vol Mtd Gunmen
JONES, Willie, Sgt, Brig Gen Thos Washington, Capt Jno Crawford, Mtd Inf
JONES, Wood, Pvt, Lt Col Henry Bryan, Co Commander omitted, Inf
JONES, Wyly, Pvt, Col William Johnson, Capt Joseph Scott, E TN Drafted Mil
JONES, _____, Pvt, Col Sam Bunch, Capt F Register, E TN Mil
JONICAN, Williams, Pvt, Col John Cocke, Capt Joe Price, Inf
JONY, John, Pvt, Regt Commander omitted, Capt Jos Williams, Mil Cav
JORDAN, Benjamin, Pvt, Col Jno Coffee, Capt Frederick Stump, Cav
JORDAN, Ezekiel, Pvt, Col John Cocke, Capt Joseph Price, Inf
JORDAN, George, Pvt, Col Newton Cannon, Capt William Marlin, Mtd Gunmen
JORDAN, George, Pvt, Col William Metcalf, Capt William Mullin, Mil Inf
JORDAN, George, Pvt, Col Wm Metcalf, Capt William Sitton, Mil Inf
JORDAN, James, Pvt, Col N T Perkins, Capt Mathew Johnson, Mil Inf
JORDAN, James, Pvt, Col Newton Cannon, Capt Isaac Williams, Mtd Riflemen
JORDAN, Jesse, Pvt, Col Wm T Higgins, Capt Samuel A Allen, Mtd Gunmen
JORDAN, John, Pvt, Col A Loury, Lt Col L Hammonds, Capt Arahel Rains, Inf
JORDAN, Jonas, Pvt, Col N T Perkins, Capt James McMahan, Mtd Gunmen
JORDAN, Lewis, Pvt, Col William Lillard, Capt William McLin, E TN Inf; detached as Wgnr
JORDAN, Uriah, Pvt, Maj William Russell, Capt Fleman Hodges, Vol Mtd Gunmen
JORDAN, William, Pvt, Col John Cocke, Capt John Weakley, Inf
JORDAN, William, Pvt, Col Robert H Dyer, Capt James McMahan, TN Vol Mtd Gunmen
JORDAN, Zachariah, Pvt, Col William Johnson, Capt Christopher Cook, E TN Mil
JORDON, John, Pvt, Col Philip Pipkin, Capt Peter Searcy, Mil Inf
JORDON, John, Pvt, Col Wm Y Higgins, Capt Thos Eldridge, Mtd Gunmen
JORDON, Stephen, Pvt, Col William Higgins, Capt Stephen Griffith, Mtd Riflemen
JORDON, William, Pvt, Brig Gen T Johnson, Capt Allen,

## Enlisted Men, War of 1812

JORDON, Wriah, Pvt, Maj Gen A Jackson, Capt Hugh Kerr, Mtd Rangers [Mil Inf above]

JOSA, Allen, Pvt, Col Edward Bradley, Capt John Wallace, Vol Inf

JOSA, John, Pvt, Col Edward Bradley, Capt John Wallace, Vol Inf

JOSLIN, Bird L, Pvt, Col N T Perkins, Capt Mathew Patterson, Mtd Vol

JOSLIN, Daniel, Pvt, Col Philip Pipkin, Capt William MacKay, Mil Inf

JOURDAN, John, Pvt, Col John Cocke, Capt Bird Nance, Inf; discharged by court martial 11-16-1814

JOURDAN, Jonas, Pvt, Col William Metcalf, Capt Bird L Hurt, Mil Inf

JOURDAN, Lee, Pvt, Col Archer Cheatham, Capt Meredith Walker, Inf

JOURDAN, Robert, Pvt, Col Thomas Williamson, Capt Giles Burdett, Vol Mtd Gunmen

JOURDAN, William, Pvt, Col John Cocke, Capt John Weakley, Inf

JOURDON, Benjamin, Pvt, Col Wm Metcalf, Capt Bird L Hurt, Mil Inf

JOURDON, Robert, Pvt, Col Thomas Williamson, Capt Robert Steele, Vol Mtd Gunmen

JOURDON, Thomas, Pvt, Regt Commander omitted, Capt Wm Henderson, Spies

JOY, Daniel, Pvt, Col Samuel Bunch, Capt Jno English, E TN Drafted Mil; deserted 3-4-1814

JOY, George, Pvt, Col John Alcorn, Capt Robt Jetton, Vol Cav

JOY, George, Pvt, Col Philip Pipkin, Capt David Smith, Ens Wm Pegram, Det of W TN Mil

JOY, George, Pvt, Col Philip Pipkin, Capt David Smythe, Inf

JOY, George, Pvt, Col Thomas Benton, Capt Isaiah Renshaw, Vol Inf

JOY, Henry, Pvt, Col Thomas Benton, Capt Benj Hewett, Vol Inf

JOY, Jesse, Pvt, Col Thomas Benton, Capt Isaiah Renshaw, Vol Inf

JOY, John, Pvt, Col A Lowry, Capt Williamson, W TN Mil

JOY, John, Pvt, Col Thomas Benton, Capt Isaiah Renshaw, Vol Inf

JOYCE, Bean, Pvt, Maj William Woodfolk, Capt James C Neil, Inf

JOYCE, James, Pvt, Col R H Dyer, Capt Ephraim D Dickson, TN Vol Mtd Gunmen; no service performed

JOYCE, James, Pvt, Regt Commander omitted, Capt Ephraim Dickson, Branch Srvce omitted

JOYNER, John, Sgt, Col R C Napier, Capt Thomas Preston, Mil Inf

JUDGE, James, Pvt, Maj Wm Carroll, Capt Lewis Dillahunty & Capt Daniel Bradford, Vol Inf

JULIAN, Renny, Pvt, Col Samuel Bunch, Capt Daniel Yarnell, E TN Mil

JUMAN, John, Pvt, Col N T Perkins, Capt Philip Pipkin, Mtd Riflemen

JUMP, Samuel, Pvt, Col R C Napier, Capt Thomas Gray, Mil Inf

JUMP, Samuel, Pvt, Regt Commander omitted, Capt James Gray, Inf

JUNALL, Robert, Pvt, Maj John Childs, Capt Charles Conway, E TN Mtd Gunmen; Regimental Co - Halefax VA

JURDAN, James, Pvt, Col John K Wynn, Capt James Cole, Inf

JURDON, Zachariah, Pvt, Col Wm Johnston, Capt Joseph Kirk, Mil

JUSTICE, Alfred, Pvt, Lt Col Archer Cheatham, Co Commander omitted, 6th Brig Mtd Inf

JUSTICE, Alfred, Pvt, Regt Commander omitted, Capt John Crane, Mtd Inf

JUSTICE, Buckner, Pvt, Col Thos H Williamson, Capt James Cook & Capt John Crane, Vol Mtd Gunmen

JUSTICE, James, Pvt, Col John K Wynn, Capt Jas Cole, Inf

JUSTICE, James, Pvt, Col S Bunch, Capt John English, E TN Drafted Mil; furloughed for inability

JUSTICE, John, Pvt, Col Archer Cheatham, Capt Richard Benson, Inf

JUSTICE, John, Pvt, Col Wm Johnson, Capt Christopher Cook, E TN Mil

JUSTICE, John, Pvt, Col Wm Johnson, Capt Joseph Kirk, Mil

JUSTICE, John, Pvt, Col Wm Metcalf, Capt Marks, Pvt

JUSTICE, Richard, Pvt, Col John Coffee, Capt Michael Molton, Branch Srvce omitted

JUSTICE, Samuel, Pvt, Col Robert Steele, Capt Jas Randals, Inf; enlisted in the Regular Service

JUSTICE, Thomas, Cpl, Col Samuel Bunch, Capt Jas Benny, E TN Mtd Inf

JUSTICE, Thomas, Sgt, Col John K Wyne, Capt Bailey Butler, Inf

J_____, William, Pvt, Maj Wm Woodfolk, Capt Ezekiel Ross, Inf

KAIGLER, David, 3 Cpl, Col Thomas Benton, Capt Robt Cannon, Inf

KAIN, Edward, Pvt, Col John Brown, Capt John Childs, E TN Vol Mtd Inf

KAIN, Elijah, Pvt, Col Sam Bayless, Capt James Landen, E TN Mil

KAIN, George, Pvt, Col Sam Bayless, Capt James Landen, E TN Mil

KAIN, William, Pvt, Col John Brown, Capt John Childs, E TN Vol Mtd, Inf

KAMP, Talimachus, Pvt, Col Wm Pillow, Capt George Caperton, Inf

KARMON, Thomas, Pvt, Col Wm Metcalf, Co Commander omitted, Mil Inf

KARN, Yancy B, Pvt, Maj Andrew Jackson, Col Thos McCrory, 2nd Regt TN Mil; d 1-10-1814 (against the Creek Indians)

KARR, David, Sgt, Col Wm Johnston, Capt Christopher Cook, E TN Mil

KARR, William, Pvt, Col Edwin Booth, Capt John Lewis, E TN Mil

KARRY, Thomas, Pvt, Col John Brown, Capt John Lewis, E TN Vol Mtd Inf

KARSEY (KASEY), David, Pvt, Col Thos Williamson,

## Enlisted Men, War of 1812

Capt James Cook, Vol Mtd Gunmen
KARY, Francis, Pvt, Col R C Napier, Capt Drury Adkins, Mil Inf
KASEY (KERSEY), David, Pvt, Col Thos Williamson, Capt James Cook & Capt John Dobbins, Vol Mtd Gunmen
KATHCAR, Joseph, Pvt, Col Sam Bunch, Capt Jno McNare, E TN Mil; d 4-3-1814
KAVANAUGH, Charles, Pvt, Col Philip Pipkin, Capt Jas Blakmore, Mil Inf; AWOL, promoted to 2 Maj
KAVANAUGH, James P, 1 Lt, Col Robert Dyer, Capt Bethal Allen, Vol Mtd Gunmen; d 4-5-1815
KAVANAUGH, John, Cpl, Col Robert Dyer, Capt Bethel Allen, Vol Mtd Gunmen
KAVANAUGH, John, Pvt, Col Robert Dyer, Capt Bethel Allen, TN Vol Mtd Gunmen
KAVANAUGH, Lee, Pvt, Col John Coffee, Capt Chas Kavanaugh, Cav
KAVANAUGH, Lee, Sgt, Col John Coffee, Capt Chas Kavanaugh, Cav
KAVANAUGH, William W, Pvt, Regt Commander omitted, Capt Wm Mitchell, Spies
KAVANAUGH, William, Pvt, Regt Commander omitted, Capt Arch McKinney, Cav; promoted to Cpl
KEAIS, Thomas, Pvt, Maj Wm Russell, Capt John Cowan, Vol Mtd Gunmen
KEAL, Jacob, Pvt, Col John Cocke, Capt George Barnes, Inf
KEAL?, Richard, Pvt, Col John Cocke, Capt George Barnes, Inf
KEAN, Edmond, Pvt, Col John Alcorn, Capt John Baskerville, Vol Inf
KEAN, Enoch, Pvt, Col Jno Williams, Capt David Vance, Mtd Mil
KEANE, Mathias, Pvt, Maj Wm Woodfolk, Capt James Turner, Inf
KEANEY, Michael, Pvt, Col Sam Wear, Capt Robert Doak, E TN Vol Inf
KEANEY, William, Pvt, Col Sam Wear, Capt Robert Doak, E TN Vol Inf
KEARBY, Daniel, Pvt, Col Wm Johnson, Capt James Tunnell, E TN Mil
KEARBY, William, Cpl, Col John Winn, Capt James Holleman, Inf
KEARLY (KEARBY), Daniel, Pvt, Col Wm Johnston, Capt James Tunnell, Branch Srvce omitted
KEAS, Henry, Pvt, Col Wm Williamson, Capt Anthony Metcalf, Vol Mtd Gunmen
KEATON, James, Pvt, Col Robert Steel, Capt James Randals, Inf
KEATON, Reacon, Pvt, Col Newton Cannon, Capt Francis Jones, Mtd Riflemen; substituted for James Woods
KEAVIR (KIVAR), Jonathan, Pvt, Col Wm Johnson, Capt James Stewart, E TN Drafted Mil
KEDWELL, Levy, Rank omitted, Col Philip Pipkin, Capt Peter Searcy, Mil Inf; Alexander Cotton substituted
KEE, Benjamin, Pvt, Col Sam Copeland, Capt David Williams, Mil Inf
KEE, David, Pvt, Col Sam Wear, Capt Geo Gillespie, E TN Vol Inf
KEE (KEAS), Elijah, Pvt, Col Thos Williamson, Capt Giles Burdette, Vol Mtd Gunmen
KEE (KEAS), John, Pvt, Col John Brown, Capt Lunsford Oliver, E TN Mil
KEEDY, Lewis, Pvt, Col John Brown, Capt Wm Christian, E TN Mil
KEEDY, Lewis, Pvt, Col Sam Bunch, Capt G Gregory, E TN Drafted Mil
KEEDY, William, Pvt, Col John Brown, Capt Wm Christian, E TN Mil
KEEHUM, Jacob, Pvt, Maj John Childs, Capt James Cowan, TN Mtd Gunmen; Regimental Co - Knox
KEEL, Richard, Pvt, Col Thos McCrory, Capt Jno Reynolds, Mil Inf
KEEL (KEAL), Richard, Pvt, Col John Cocke, Capt George Barnes, Inf
KEELER, Joseph, Pvt, Col Edwin Booth, Capt Thos Porter, Drafted Mil
KEELY, John S, Pvt, Col Thos Benton, Capt James McEwen, Vol Inf
KEEN, Edmond, Pvt, Col John Coffee, Capt John Baskerville, Cav
KEEN, Jacob, Pvt, Col John Allcorn, Capt John Hampton, Mil; transferred to Capt McCrea's Co
KEEN, John, Pvt, Col James Raulston, Capt Mathew Neal, Inf
KEEN, John, Pvt, Col N T Perkins, Capt George Eliott, Mil Inf
KEEN, Samuel, Pvt, Col Wm Hall, Capt Abraham Bledsoe, Vol Inf
KEENER, Howsen, Pvt, Col Robt H Dyer, Capt Thomas Jones, Vol Mtd Gunmen
KEENEY, Michael, Pvt, Col William Lillard, Capt James Lillard, E TN Vol Inf
KEENY, Jacob, Sgt, Col Samuel Bunch, Capt James Allen, E TN Drafted Mil
KEENY, John, Pvt, Col Edwin Booth, Capt Richard Marshall, Drafted Mil
KEENY, Joseph, 1 Cpl, Col Edwin Booth, Capt Richard Marshall, Drafted Mil
KEES (KEAIS), Elijah, Pvt, Col Thos Williamson, Capt Giles Burdett, Vol Mtd Gunmen
KEESEE, George, Pvt, Col Thos Williamson, Capt Thos Scurry, Vol Mtd Gunmen
KEETH, Eli, Pvt, Col John Brown, Capt Jesse G Reany, Mtd Gunmen
KEETH, James, Pvt, Col John Brown, Capt Jesse G Reany, Mtd Gunmen
KEETH, John B, Pvt, Col John Brown, Capt Jesse G Reany, Mtd Gunmen
KEETH, John, Pvt, Maj Wm Russell, Capt Samuel Cowan, Vol Mtd Gunmen
KEETH, William, Pvt, Col N T Perkins, Capt George Eliot, Mil Inf
KEETHLEY, Jesse, Pvt, Col Robert Steele, Capt James Randals, Inf
KEETHLEY, Joseph, Cpl, Col Robert Steele, Capt Jas Randals, Inf
KEETON, James, Pvt, Maj Wm Russell, Capt Geo Mitchie, Vol Mtd Gunmen

290 -

## Enlisted Men, War of 1812

KEEWOOD, Berry, Pvt, Col Ewen Allison, Capt William King, Drafted Mil

KEEWOOD, Joshua, Pvt, Col Ewen Allison, Capt William King, Drafted Mil

KEHIL, Thomas, Pvt, Col John Brown, Capt John Childs, E TN Vol Mtd Inf

KEITH, George, Pvt, Col Thos Benton, Capt Geo Caperton, Inf

KEITH, George, Sgt, Regt Commander omitted, Capt James Cowan, Mtd Inf

KEITH, John, Pvt, Col Wm Pillow, Capt Geo Caperton, Inf

KEITH, Spencer, Pvt, Col John Brown, Capt Lunsford Oliver, E TN Mil

KEITH (KYTHE), William, Pvt, Col A Loury, Capt George Sarver, Inf

KELLAM, Henry, Pvt, Col Thos Benton, Capt Benj Reynolds, Vol Inf

KELLAM, John, Pvt, Col Thos Benton, Capt Benj Reynolds, Vol Inf

KELLAN, Henry, Pvt, Brig Gen Roberts, Capt Benj Reynolds, Mtd Rangers

KELLAN, James, Pvt, Col John K Wynne, Capt Robt Breden, Inf

KELLEE, Andrew, Pvt, Maj John Childs, Capt Daniel Price, Vol Mtd Gunmen

KELLER, Austin Y, Pvt, Col William Hall, Capt Jas Hambleton, Vol Inf

KELLER, Benjamin, Pvt, Col Samuel Bayless, Capt Solomon Hendrix, E TN Mil

KELLER, Charles, Pvt, Col Robert Steele, Capt Jas Shenault, Mil Inf

KELLER, David, Pvt, Col Samuel Bayless, Capt Solomon Hendrix, E TN Mil

KELLER, Francis, Pvt, Col Robert Steele, Capt Jas Shenault, Mil Inf

KELLER, Lemuel, Pvt, Col Robert Steele, Capt Jas Shenault, Mil Inf

KELLER, Leonard, Pvt, Col Samuel Bayless, Capt Joseph Hale, E TN Mil

KELLER, Peter, Pvt, Col Samuel Bunch, Capt Andrew Breden, E TN Mil

KELLER, Samuel, Pvt, Col Wm Lillard, Capt Robt Maloney, E TN Vol Inf

KELLEY, Austin Y, Pvt, Col A Loury, Capt Martin, Inf

KELLEY, Barnabas, Pvt, Col William Lillard, Capt Wm Gillenwater, E TN Inf

KELLEY, Caperton, 4 Cpl, Gen A Jackson, Capt Wm Rupell, Mtd Spies

KELLEY, Caperton, Pvt, Maj Wm Russell, Capt Wm Russell, Vol Mtd Gunmen

KELLEY, Catruk, Pvt, Regt Commander omitted, Capt Jas Williams, Mil Cav

KELLEY, Charles U, Pvt, Col William Hall, Capt Jas Hambleton, Vol Inf

KELLEY, Charles, Pvt, Col Robt M Dyer, Capt Robt Evans, Vol Mtd Gunmen

KELLEY, Daniel, Ens, Col Philip Pipkin, Capt George Mebane, Mil Inf

KELLEY, Durham, Pvt, Maj William Russell, Capt William Russell, Vol Mtd Gunmen

KELLEY, Edward, Pvt, Col Robert Steele, Capt Robert Campbell, Mil Inf

KELLEY, James S, Sgt, Col Thos Benton, Capt Jas McEwen, Vol Inf

KELLEY, James, Pvt, Col Ewen Allison, Capt Wilson, E TN Drafted Mil; discharged for inability

KELLEY, John S, Pvt, Col Thos Benton, Capt Jas McEwen, Vol Inf

KELLEY, John, Pvt, Col John Brown, Capt Allen I Bacon, E TN Mil Inf

KELLEY, Nathan, Pvt, Col S Copeland, Capt Wm Douglass, Inf

KELLEY, Richard, Pvt, Col A Loury, Capt Barnes, Inf

KELLEY, Taylor, Pvt, Col James Raulston, Capt James A Black, Inf; substitute for Isaiah Davis

KELLEY, Thomas, Pvt, Col Samuel Bunch, Capt Andrew Breden, E TN Mil; discharged for inability

KELLEY, Thomas, Pvt, Col Thomas Williamson, Capt John Doak & Capt John Dobbins, Vol Mtd Gunmen

KELLEY, William, Pvt, Brig Gen Thos Washington, Capt John Crawford, Mtd Inf

KELLEY, William, Pvt, Col Jas Raulston, Capt Jas A Black, Inf

KELLISON, Robert R, Pvt, Col William Lillard, Capt Jas Lillard, E TN Vol Inf

KELLOUGH, Edward, Pvt, Col Wm Metcalf, Capt John Barnhart, Mil Inf

KELLOUGH, John, Pvt, Col John Coffee, Capt Robert Jetton, Cav

KELLY, Alexander, Pvt, Col William Hall, Capt Henry M Newlin, Inf

KELLY, Alfred, Pvt, Col R H Dyer, Capt Ephraim D Dickson, TN Mtd Vol Gunmen

KELLY, Allen, Pvt, Col R H Dyer, Capt Ephraim Dickson, TN Vol Mtd Gunmen

KELLY, Benjamin, Pvt, Brig Gen Thos Johnston, Capt Allen, Mil Inf

KELLY, Carey T, Pvt, Col John Coffee, Capt James Terrell, Vol Cav

KELLY, David, Sgt, Col Samuel Bayless, Capt Joseph Hale, E TN Mil

KELLY, Elijah, Pvt, Col Wm Lillard, Capt Wm McLin, E TN Inf

KELLY, Green B, Pvt, Col John Cocke, Capt Punks, Inf

KELLY, Henry, Pvt, Regt Commander omitted, Capt Archibald McKenney, Cav

KELLY, Isaac, Pvt, Col John Coffee, Capt Thomas Bradley, Vol Cav

KELLY, James S, 3 Sgt, Col Thomas H Benton, Capt C E McEwin, Vol Inf

KELLY, James, Pvt, Col Wm Lillard, Capt Dyke, Vol Inf

KELLY, James, Sgt, Col Wm Johnson, Capt Benjamin Powell, E TN Mil; promoted from Pvt

KELLY, James, Sgt, Col Wm Pillow, Capt C E McEwen, Vol Inf

KELLY, John sr, Pvt, Regt Commander omitted, Capt Archibald McKenney, Cav

KELLY, John, 3 Sgt, Col Thomas H Benton, Capt George Caperton, Inf

KELLY, John, 3 Sgt, Col Thomas H Benton, Capt George

-291

## Enlisted Men, War of 1812

Caperton, Vol Inf
KELLY, John, Ens, Col Samuel Wear, Capt Jesse Cole, Vol Inf
KELLY, John, Pvt, Col Ewin Allison, Capt John Hampton, Mil; transferred to Capt McCrea's Co
KELLY, John, Pvt, Col Ewin Allison, Capt McCray, E TN Mil; transferred from Capt Hampton's Co
KELLY, John, Pvt, Col Philip Pipkin, Capt George Mebane, Mil Inf
KELLY, John, Pvt, Col Wm Booth, Capt John Porter, Drafted Mil
KELLY, Joseph, Pvt, Col Thos Bradley, Capt Lauderdale, Vol Inf
KELLY, Joshua, Pvt, Col Samuel Bunch, Capt George McPherson, E TN Mil
KELLY, Joshua, Pvt, Col Wm Lillard, Capt James Lillard, E TN Inf Vol
KELLY, Julian, Pvt, Lt Col Hammond, Capt Arahel Raines, Inf
KELLY, Lewis, Pvt, Col John K Wynn, Capt John Spinks, Inf
KELLY, Mordicae, Far, Col Thomas H Williamson, Capt Richard Tate, Vol Mtd Gunmen
KELLY, Nimrod O, Pvt, Col Wm Johnson, Capt Elihu Milligan, 3rd Regt E TN Mil
KELLY, Patrick, Pvt, Col John Coffee, Capt Michael Molton, Cav
KELLY, Patrick, Pvt, Regt Commander omitted, Capt Beverly Williams, Mil Cav
KELLY, Robert, Pvt, Col Wm Lillard, Capt John Roper, E TN Vol Inf
KELLY, Samuel, Cpl, Col Ewin Allison, Capt Thomas Nelson, E TN Drafted Mil
KELLY, Sims, Pvt, Col R H Dyer, Maj Wm Russell, Capt Wm Russell, Vol Mtd Gunmen
KELLY, Thomas, Pvt, Col Ewin Allison, Capt Jacob Hoyal, E TN Mil
KELLY, Thomas, Pvt, Col Samuel Wear, Capt John Bayless, Mtd Inf
KELLY, William, Pvt, Col Ewin Allison, Capt McCray, E TN Mil; transferred to Capt Hampton's Co
KELLY, William, Pvt, Col John Cocke, Capt John Dalton, Inf
KELLY, William, Pvt, Col John Coffee, Capt Daniel Ross, Mtd Gunmen
KELLY, William, Pvt, Col R H Dyer, Capt McMahon, TN Vol Mtd Gunmen; killed in battle 12-23-1814
KELLY, William, Pvt, Col R H Dyer, Maj Wm Russell, Capt Wm Russell, Vol Mtd Gunmen; substitute for Nathan Kemp
KELLY, William, Pvt, Col Wm Johnson, Capt Benj Powell, E TN Mil
KELLY, William, Pvt, Col Wm Lillard, Capt James Lillard, E TN Vol Inf
KELLY, William, Pvt, Lt I Barrett, Capt Nathan Davis, Inf
KELLY, William, Sgt & Cpl, Col Ewin Allison, Capt Winsell, E TN Drafted Mil
KELLY (KEELY), John S, Pvt, Col Thomas H Benton, Capt James McEwen, Vol Inf
KELSO, Charles B, Pvt, Col S Bunch, Capt Daniel Norvell, E TN Mil
KELSO, E, Pvt, Col S Bunch, Capt John Houk, E TN Mil
KELSO, Eliphalette, Pvt, Col Samuel Bunch, Capt John Houk, E TN Mil
KELSO, Eliphalot, Pvt, Col S Bunch, Capt Geo Gregory, E TN Drafted Mil
KELSO, James E, Pvt, Maj James Porter, Capt James Anderson, Cav
KELSO, James, Pvt, Maj Wm Russell, Capt John Trimble, Vol Mtd Gunmen
KELTON, James, Pvt, Col Thomas H Williamson, Capt James Cook & Capt John Crane, Vol Mtd Gunmen
KELTON, Robert, Pvt, Col John Coffee, Capt Robt Jetton, Cav
KELTON, Thomas, Cpl, Col Thomas H Williamson, Capt John Crane & Capt James Cook, Vol Mtd Gunmen
KELTON, Thomas, Pvt, Col John K Winn, Capt Robert Braden, Inf
KELTON, Thomas, Pvt, Col Thomas H Williamson, Capt James Cook & Capt John Crane, Vol Mtd Gunmen; promoted to Cpl
KELTON, William, Pvt, Col Newton Cannon, Capt Thomas Yardly, Mtd Riflemen
KEMP, James, Pvt, Maj John Childs, Capt Reuben Tipton, E TN Vol Mtd Inf
KEMP, Telemachus, Pvt, Col Thomas Benton, Capt Geo Caperton, Vol Inf
KENADY, John, Pvt, Col Samuel Wear, Capt John Bayless, Mtd Inf
KENDRICK, Austin, Pvt, Col Philip Pipkin, Capt Peter Searcy, Mil Inf; enlisted in the 3rd Rifle Regt
KENDRICK, Chamery?, Pvt, Col Philip Pipkin, Capt Wm MacKay, Branch Srvce omitted
KENDRICK, Henry, Cpl, Col Edwin E Booth, Capt John McKamey, E TN Mil; promoted from the ranks
KENDRICK, James, Pvt, Col Samuel Wear, Capt James Gillespie, E TN Vol Mil
KENDRICK, Jones, Sgt, Brig Gen T Johnson, Capt Allen, Mil Inf
KENDRICK, Joseph, Pvt, Col Jno Coffee, Capt Blackman Coleman, Cav
KENDRICK, Thomas, Pvt, Col Philip Pipkin, Capt Peter Searcy, Mil Inf
KENDRICK, William, Pvt, Col Philip Pipkin, Capt Peter Searcy, Mil Inf; enlisted in the 3rd Rifle Regt
KENEDY, Abraham, Pvt, Col Edwin E Booth, Capt Porter, drafted Mil
KENEDY, Isaac, Pvt, Col William Lillard, Capt William McLin, E TN Inf
KENEDY, James, Pvt, Col N T Perkins, Capt John Doak, Vol Mtd Gunmen
KENEDY, James, Pvt, Col S Copeland, Capt James Tait, Inf
KENEDY, Joseph, Pvt, Col S Copeland, Capt Allen Wilkinson, Mil Inf
KENEDY, Robert S, Pvt, Col Wm Lillard, Capt William McLin, E TN Mil
KENER, Johnston, Pvt, Col William Johnson, Capt James Stewart, E TN Mil
KENES, Gilbert, Pvt, Col Samuel Bunch, Capt Andrew

## Enlisted Men, War of 1812

Breden, E TN Mil
KENESDAY (KINEDY), Jacob, Pvt, Col James Raulston, Maj Gen Wm Carroll, Capt Elijah Haynie, Inf
KENESDAY (KINEDY), Lekes, Pvt, Col James Raulston, Maj Gen Wm Carroll, Capt Elijah Haynie, Inf
KENESDAY (KINEDY), Robert, Pvt, Maj Gen Wm Carroll, Col James Raulston, Capt Elijah Haynie, Inf
KENETZER, Henry, Pvt, Col Edwin Booth, Capt Porter, Drafted Mil
KENNADY, John, Pvt, Col Samuel Bayless, Capt Joseph Hale, E TN Mil; substitute for John Tadlock
KENNALLY, James, Pvt, Maj William Russell, Capt Wm Russell, Vol Mtd Gunmen
KENNALLY, John P, Pvt, Maj Wm Russell, Capt Wm Russell, Vol Mtd Gunmen
KENNEBREW, William, Pvt, Col William Hall, Capt Jas Hambleton, Vol Inf
KENNEDA, Absolem, Pvt, Col S Copeland, Capt Moses Thompson, Inf
KENNEDAY, Eli M O, Pvt, Col Thomas Benton, Capt Benj Reynolds, Vol Inf
KENNEDAY, James, Pvt, Col Robt Steele, Capt Robt Campbell, Mil Inf
KENNEDY, Armstrong, Pvt, no other information
KENNEDY, Edward (Edmond), Pvt, Col John Cocke, Capt Geo Barnes, Inf
KENNEDY, Ei M C, Pvt, Col Thomas Benton, Capt Benj Reynolds, Vol Inf
KENNEDY, Eli Mc, Pvt, Col T McCrory, Capt William Dooley, Inf
KENNEDY, Eli, Pvt, Brig Gen Isaac B Robert, Capt Benj Reynolds, Mtd Rangers
KENNEDY, Evander, Pvt, Col R H Dyer, Capt Glen Owen, TN Vol Mtd Gunmen; transferred to Capt McMahan
KENNEDY, Evander, Pvt, Col Wm Hall, Capt Henry M Newland, Inf
KENNEDY, Evander, Sdlr, Col R H Dyer, Capt James McMahon, TN Mtd Vol Gunmen
KENNEDY, Hugh, Pvt, Maj James Porter, Capt James Anderson, Cav
KENNEDY, Isaac, Pvt, Col William Johnson, Capt Andrew Lawson, E TN Drafted Mil
KENNEDY, James, Pvt, Col Wm Metcalf, Capt Wm Mullin, Mil Inf
KENNEDY, John M, Pvt, Col R H Dyer, Capt James McMahan, TN Vol Mtd Gunmen
KENNEDY, John, Pvt, Maj Gen A Jackson, Col A Cheatham, Capt William Creel, Inf
KENNEDY, Robert, Pvt, Col S Copeland, Capt Richard Sharp, Mil Inf; deserted 3-7-1814
KENNEDY, Samuel, Pvt, Col R M Dyer, Capt R Evans, Vol Mtd Gunmen; d 2-3-1815
KENNEDY, Samuel, Pvt, Maj Gen Wm Carroll, Capt John Jackson, Inf
KENNEDY, William B, Sgt, Col Newton Cannon, Capt John Harpole, Mtd Gunmen
KENNEDY, William, Pvt, Gen Andrew Jackson, Capt Nathan Davis, Inf

KENNEDY (CANADY), John, Pvt, Col Wm Hall, Capt Henry M Newland, Inf
KENNON, James, Pvt, Col Wm Lillard, Capt T McChristian, E TN Vol Inf
KENNY, Daniel, Pvt, Col N Cannon, Capt Jas Walton, Mtd Riflemen
KENNY, Daniel, Pvt, Col T Williamson, Capt G Burdett, Vol Mtd Gunmen
KENNY, John, Pvt, Col Wm Johnson, Capt D McKany, E TN Drafted Mil; transferred
KENNY, John, Pvt, Col Wm Johnson, Capt J Kirk, Mil
KENNY, William, Pvt, Col N Cannon, Capt J Walton, Mtd Riflemen
KENNY, William, Pvt, Col Thos Williamson, Capt G Burdett, Vol Mtd Gunmen
KENNYMOON (KMORE), Philip, Pvt, Col S Bayless, Capt S Hendricks, E TN Mil
KENOR, Jacob, Rank omitted, Lt I Barrett, Capt Nathan Davis, Inf
KENOR, William, Lt I Barrett, Capt Nathan Davis, Inf
KENSALL (KINDALL), Benjamin, H Sgt, Col P Pipkin, Capt P Searcy, Mil Inf
KENSEL, Benjamin, Pvt, Col Jno Coffee, Capt J W Byrn, Cav
KENT, Henry, Pvt, Col J Raulston, Capt D Newman, Inf
KENT, Luke, Sdlr, Col J Coffee, Capt T Bradley, Vol Cav
KENT, Peter, Pvt, Lt Col L Hammons, Col A Loury, Capt T Delaney, Inf
KENT, William, Pvt, Col W Higgins, Capt S Griffith, Mtd Riflemen
KENYON, Joseph, Pvt, Col S Bunch, Capt H Stephens, E TN Mtd Inf
KEPPER, Joseph, Pvt, Regt Commander omitted, Capt Sam Bunch, Mtd Vol
KEPSINGER, William, Pvt, Col T McCrory, Capt Jas Reynolds, Mil Inf
KERBY, Clinton, Pvt, Col S Wear, Capt J Stephens, E TN Vol Inf
KERBY, Francis, Pvt, Col P Pipkin, Capt J Blakemore, Mil Inf
KERBY, Henry, Cpl, Col T Williamson, Capt A M Metcalf, Vol Mtd Gunmen
KERBY, Robert, Pvt, Maj Wm Russell, Capt Wm Chism, Branch Srvce omitted
KERBY, William, Pvt, Col R Steele, Capt J Chitwood, Mil Inf
KERHN (KERLAM), Joseph, Pvt, Col S Bayless, Capt J Waddell, E TN Mil
KERIAH, Samuel, Sgt, Col Adam Dale, Capt W Y Higgins, Mtd Gunmen
KERKINDALL, Peter, Pvt, Col Robt Steele, Capt Jas Bennett, Mil Inf
KERLEY, Daniel, Pvt, Col Wm Johnston, Capt Jas Tunnell, 3rd Regt E TN Mil
KERLEY, Henry, Pvt, Col Wm Metcalf, Capt J Cunningham & Capt A Hill, Mil Inf
KERLEY, James, QM Sgt, Col Thos McCrory, 2nd Regt TN Mil
KERLEY, James, Sgt, Col T McCrory, Capt A Metcalf, Mil Inf; promoted to QM Sgt
KERNS, William B, Sgt, Col S Wear, Capt J Bayless, Mtd

- 293

## Enlisted Men, War of 1812

KERR, Alexander, Pvt, Maj Gen Wm Carroll, Capt W Huddleston, Inf; d 1-5-1815

KERR, Daniel, Sgt, Col S Bunch, Capt I Williams, E TN Mil

KERR, Jesse, Pvt, Maj J Childs, Capt J Stephens, E TN Vol Mtd Inf

KERR, John, Pvt, Maj Gen Wm Carroll, Capt W Huddleston, Inf

KERR, Robert, Pvt, Col S Bunch, Capt I Williams, E TN Mil

KERR, Robert, Pvt, Col S Bunch, Capt Jno Houk, E TN Mil; joined from Capt Williams' Co, discharged for inability

KERR, Samuel, Pvt, Col E Bradley, Capt A Bledsoe, Riflemen

KERR, Samuel, Pvt, Col S Wear, Capt S Bowman, Mtd Inf

KERR, Samuel, Pvt, Col Wm Hall, Capt A Bledsoe, Vol Inf

KERR, William, Pvt, Col Wm Johnston, Capt Wm Alexander, Det of E TN Drafted Mil

KERR, William, Pvt, Maj W Woodfolk, Capt J Sutton & Capt A Dudney, Inf

KERR, William, Pvt, Regt Commander omitted, Capt J McMahon, TN Vol Mtd Gunmen; d 1-20-1815 (wounds caught in battle)

KERR, William, Sgt, Col E Allison, Capt J Hoyal, E TN Mil

KERR, William, Sgt, Col S Bunch, Capt I Williams, E TN Mil

KERR, _____, Pvt, Col S Bunch, Capt J Houk, E TN Mil; joined from Capt William's Co

KERR (CARR), John, Pvt, Col P Pipkin, Capt J Blakemore, Mil Inf; d 9-8-1814

KERR (KARR), Henry, Pvt, Col Wm Johnson, Capt H Hunter, E TN Mil

KERRELL, William, Pvt, Col S Wear, Capt J Cole, Vol Inf

KERSELL, John, Pvt, Col S Bayless, Capt Jas Landen, E TN Mil; d 2-15-1815

KERSEY, William, Pvt, Col Wm Hall, Capt Brice Martin, Vol Inf

KERTNA, Jacob, Pvt, Col Wm Johnston, Capt Henry Hunter, E TN Mil

KESTERSON, John, Pvt, Col Samuel Bunch, Capt John Dobbins, E TN Drafted Mil; deserted 4-6-1814

KESTERSON, Meredith, Pvt, Col Samuel Bunch, Capt John Dobbins, E TN Drafted Mil; deserted 4-6-1814

KESTERSON, Thomas, Dmr, Col Samuel Bunch, Capt Francis Register, E TN Mil

KESTERSON, Thomas, Pvt, Col Samuel Bayless, Capt Joseph Hale, E TN Mil

KESTERSON, William, Pvt, Col Samuel Bunch, Capt John Dobbins, E TN Drafted Mil; deserted 4-6-1814

KETON, Zachariah, Pvt, Maj Wm Woodfolk, Capt Ezekial Ross & Capt McCulley, Inf

KETTNER, Solomon, Pvt, Col R C Napier, Capt Early Benson, Mil Inf

KEY, James, Pvt, Maj Wm Woodfolk, Capt Abner Pearce, Inf

KEY, Job, Pvt, Maj Gen A Jackson, Capt Hugh Kerr, Mtd Rangers

KEY, John, Pvt, Col Edwin Booth, Capt Vernon, E TN Mil; d 1-29-1815

KEY, John, Pvt, Col S Wear, Capt Daniel Price, E TN Vol Inf

KEY, Macklin, Pvt, Col Jno Coffee, Capt John Baskerville, Cav

KEY, Macklin, Pvt, Col John Alcorn, Capt John Baskerville, Vol Inf

KEY, Peter, Pvt, Col S Wear, Capt Geo Gillespie, E TN Vol Inf

KEY, Ruffin, Pvt, Col Edward Bradley, Capt William Lauderdale, Vol Inf

KEY, Ruffin, Pvt, Col William Hall, Capt William Alexander, Vol Inf

KEY, Strother, Pvt, Col Thomas Williamson, Capt Thomas Scurry, Vol Mtd Gunmen

KEYS, Isaac, Pvt, Col William Lillard, Capt Wm McLin, E TN Inf

KEYS, Jerimah, Pvt, Col William Lillard, Capt Wm McLin, E TN Inf

KEYTH, William, Pvt, Col Alexander Loury, Capt Geo Sarver, Inf

KEYTON, Cornelious, Pvt, Col N T Perkins, Capt Quarles, Vol Mtd Inf

KEYWOOD, Thomas, Pvt, Col S Bunch, Capt Geo McPherson, E TN Mil

KIBBLE, John, Pvt, Col S Bunch, Capt Edward Buchanan, E TN Drafted Mil

KIBBLE, Robert, Pvt, Col R T Perkins, Capt Phillip Pipkin, Mtd Riflemen

KIBLER, John, Pvt, Col Bunch, Capt David Vance, E TN Mtd Inf

KIDD, James, Pvt, Col John K Wynne, Capt John Porter, Inf

KIDD, James, Pvt, Col Thomas Williamson, Capt Hugh Martin, Vol Mtd Gunmen

KIDDY, Henry, Pvt, Capt Nathan Davis, Lt I Barrett, Inf

KIDDY, Jacob, Pvt, Capt Nathan Davis, Lt I Barrett, Inf

KIDNER, Junior, Pvt, Col S Bunch, Capt Geo Gregory, E TN Drafted Mil

KIDWELL, James, Pvt, Col William Hall, Capt Geo Newlin, Inf; deserted

KIDWELL, Josiah, Pvt, Col S Bayless, Capt Joseph Rich, E TN Inf; d 1-10-1815

KIDWELL, Levi, Pvt, Col Jas Raulston, Capt Chas Wade, Inf

KIEGHLER, David, Pvt, Col N Cannon, Capt Martin, Mtd Gunmen

KIETH, George, Pvt, Col Thos Benton, Capt Geo Caperton, Vol Inf

KIFER, Jacob, Pvt, Col Ewen Allison, Capt Thomas Wilson, E TN Drafted Mil

KIFFER, John, Pvt, Col S Bayless, Capt Hale, E TN Mil

KILBOURN, Benjamin, Dmr, Col S Booth, Capt Samuel Thompson, Mil

KILBOURNE, William, Pvt, Col Edwin Booth, Capt Samuel Thompson, Mil

KILBREATH, John, Pvt, Col Edward Bradley, Capt Abraham Bledsoe, Riflemen

## Enlisted Men, War of 1812

KILBREATH, Thomas, Pvt, Maj Gen Carroll, Capt Jas Raulston, Inf

KILBREW, Thomas, 2 Sgt, Col R T Napier, Capt Thos Benton, Mil Inf

KILBRIETH, John, Pvt, Col Edward Bradley, Capt Abraham Bledsoe, Riflemen

KILBUCK, Robert, Pvt, Col Edward Bradley, Capt James Hambleton, Vol Inf

KILBURN, Amos, Pvt, Col T McCrory, Capt Thomas Gordon, Inf

KILBURN, William, Pvt, Maj James Porter, Capt Sam Cowan, Cav

KILCADE, David, Pvt, Gen Andrew Jackson, Capt Nathan Davis, Inf

KILE, Hyrun, Pvt, Col Thomas Williamson, Capt Doak & Capt John Dobbins, Vol Mtd Gunmen

KILE, James, Pvt, Col T McCrory, Capt Samuel McKnight, Inf

KILE, Prior, Pvt, Col William Metcalf, Capt Hill & Capt Cunningham, Mil Inf

KILE, Robert, Pvt, Col Ewen Allison, Capt Jonas Loughmiller, Mil; transferred to Capt Griffin's Co

KILE, Thomas, Pvt, Col S Copeland, Capt William Douglass, Inf

KILGORE, William, Pvt, Col S Bayless, Capt Hale, E TN Mil

KILGORE, William, Pvt, Col S Bunch, Capt James Penny, E TN Mil

KILHAM, John, Pvt, Col Jno Coffee, Capt Henry Bryan, Cav

KILLBREW, William, Sgt, Lt Col Henry Bryan, Co Commander omitted, Inf

KILLBUCK, Robert, 6 Cpl, Col Phillip Pipkin, Capt John Strother, Mil

KILLEBREW, Thomas, Cpl, Col N Cannon, Capt Jas Walton, Mtd Riflemen

KILLEBREW, Whitefield, Pvt, Regt Commander omitted, Capt David Smith, Cav

KILLEBREW, Whitfield, Cpl, Col Wm Hall, Capt James Hambleton, Vol Inf

KILLEN, Thomas, Pvt, Col Philip Pipkin, Capt Geo Mebane, Mil Inf; substituted by Nicholas Gazaway, deserted 9-20-1814

KILLENSWORTH, Thomas, Pvt, Col Samuel Wear, Capt John Chiles, E TN Vol Inf

KILLGORE, Robert, Pvt, Col Phillip Pipkin, Capt John Strother, Mil

KILLINGSWORTH, John, Pvt, Col John K Wynne, Capt Jas Holleman, Inf

KILLINGSWORTH, John, Pvt, Col Robert Dyer, Capt Bethel Allen, Vol Mtd Gunmen; rendered no service

KILLINSWORTH, Nathaniel, Pvt, Col Samuel Wear, Capt John Chiles, E TN Vol Inf

KILLION, Michael, Pvt, Col Wm Johnson, Capt Jas Tunnell, Mtd Riflemen?; substitute for Samuel Lard

KILLOUGH, John, 3 Lt, Col A Lowry, Capt Jas Kincaid, Inf

KILLOUGH, John, Pvt, Maj Wm Carroll, Capt L Dillahunty & Capt Daniel M Bradford, Vol Inf

KILLUM, Carter, Pvt, Col Thos McCrory, Capt Thos Gordon, Inf

KILNSWORTH, John, Pvt, Col Wm Y Higgins, Capt Adam Dale, Mtd Gunmen

KILOUGH, John, Pvt, Col John Alcorn, Capt Robt Jetton, Vol Cav

KILOUGH, Thomas, Pvt, Col John Alcorn, Capt Robt Jetton, Vol Cav

KILPATRICK, Felix, Pvt, Col Thos H Benton, Capt Benj Reynolds, Vol Inf

KIMBREL, Peterson, Pvt, Col Wm Johnson, Capt Jas R Rogers, E TN Drafted Mil

KIMBRO, Benney, Pvt, Col Jas Churchman, Co Commander omitted, E TN Mil

KIMBRO, Isaac, Cpl, Col Samuel Bayless, Capt Jas Churchman, E TN Mil

KIMBRO, John, Cpl, Col Samuel Bayless, Capt Jas Churchman, E TN Mil

KIMBRO, Lishua, Pvt, Col Wm Johnson, Capt Elihu Milliken, 3rd Regt E TN Mil; transferred to Capt Hunter

KIMBRO, Solomon, Pvt, Col William Hall, Capt Newlin, Inf

KIMBROUGH, Elisha L, Pvt, Col A Lowry, Capt J N Williamson, W TN Mil

KIMBROUGH, Elisha L, Pvt, Col L Hammond, Capt J N Williamson, 2nd Regt Inf

KIMBROUGH, John M, Pvt, Col A Lowry, Capt J N Williamson, W TN Mil

KIMBROUGH, John W, Pvt, Col L Hammond, Capt J N Williamson, 2nd Regt Inf

KIMBROUGH, M D, Pvt, Col William Hall, Capt Wm Alexander, Vol Inf

KIMBROUGH, Marmarduke, Pvt, Col A Lowry, Capt George Sarver, Inf

KIMBROUGH, Robert, Pvt, Gen Andrew Jackson, Capt Nathan Davis, Inf

KIMBROW, John, Pvt, Col S Copeland, Capt Solomon George, Inf

KIMBROW, John, Pvt, Col William Lillard, Capt Thos McChristian, E TN Vol Inf

KIMBROW, Joseph, Sgt, Col A Cheatham, Capt Wm Smith, Inf

KINAMORE, William, Pvt, Col Thos Benton, Capt Benj Reynolds, Vol Inf; refused to march

KINAR (KEANIR), Jonathan (Johnson), Pvt, Col William Johnson, Capt Jas Stewart, E TN Drafted Mil

KINARD, William, Pvt, Col Samuel Bunch, Capt Edward Buchanan, E TN Drafted Mil

KINATCHR, Andrew, Pvt, Col Wm Johnson, Capt Andrew Lawson, E TN Drafted Mil

KINCADE, Burris, Pvt, Col Samuel Bunch, Capt Jas Cummings, E TN Vol Mtd Inf

KINCADE, Joseph, Pvt, Col S Copeland, Capt Solomon George, Inf

KINCADE, Samuel, 6 Sgt, Col Samuel Bunch, Capt Jas Cummings, E TN Vol Mtd Gunmen

KINCADE, Samuel, Pvt, Col S Copeland, Capt Solomon George, Inf

KINCADE, Samuel, Pvt, Col Samuel Bunch, Capt Jas Cummings, E TN Vol Mtd Inf

- 295

## Enlisted Men, War of 1812

KINCADE, William, Pvt, Regt Commander omitted, Capt James Cowan, Mtd Inf
KINCAID, John, Pvt, Col Edwin Booth, Capt George Winton, E TN Mil
KINCANNON, Andrew, Sgt, Col Samuel Bunch, Capt John Houk, E TN Mil; discharged for inability
KINCANNON, James, Pvt, Col Samuel Bunch, Capt John Houk, E TN Mil; joined to Capt Rotton's Co
KINCHELOR, James, Pvt, Col Samuel Bunch, Capt Geo McPherson, E TN Mil
KINCHELOR, William, Pvt, Col Samuel Bunch, Capt Geo McPherson, E TN Mil
KINCHELUS, Enoch, Pvt, Col Samuel Bunch, Capt David G Vance, E TN Mtd Inf
KINCHLOE, Enoch, Pvt, Col John Williams, Capt David Vance, Mtd Mil
KINDEL, Ephroditus, Pvt, Col Robert Steele, Capt James Bennett, Mil Inf
KINDLE, Ephroditus, Pvt, Col R C Napier, Capt Samuel Ashmore, Mil Inf
KINDLE, William, Pvt, Col Robert Steele, Capt Jas Bennett, Mil Inf
KINDRED, Sherenton, Pvt, Col Wm Johnson, Capt Jas R Rogers, E TN Drafted Mil
KINDRED, Thomas, Pvt, Col Edwin E Booth, Capt John McKamey, E TN Mil
KINDRED, Thomas, Pvt, Col Ewen Allison, Capt William King, Drafted Mil
KINDRED, Thornton, Pvt, Col Wm Johnston, Capt Jas R Rogers, E TN Drafted Mil
KINDRED, _____, Pvt, Col Samuel Bunch, Capt F Register, E TN Mil; joined from King's Co, transferred to Bacon's Co
KINDRICK, Absolom, Pvt, Col John Brown, Capt Wm White, E TN Vol Mtd Inf
KING, Abner, Pvt, Col R H Dyer, Capt Jas McMahon, TN Vol Mtd Gunmen; killed in battle on the night 12-23-1814
KING, Abraham, Pvt, Col William Hall, Capt Abraham Bledsoe, Vol Inf; absent from the state
KING, Adam, Pvt, Col William Lillard, Capt Geo Argenbright, E TN Vol Riflemen
KING, Amos, Pvt, Col Samuel Bayless, Capt James Landen, E TN Mil
KING, Avery, Cpl, Col Thos McCrory, Capt Samuel B McKnight, Inf
KING, Backster, Pvt, Col Wm Metcalf, Capt Wm Sitton, Mil Inf
KING, Benjamin, Pvt, Regt Commander omitted, Capt David Smith, Cav
KING, Bery, Pvt, Regt Commander omitted, Capt David Smith, Cav Vol
KING, Billy F, Pvt, Col Samuel Bayless, Capt Jonathan Waddell, E TN Mil; d 4-25-1815 in service
KING, Charles, Cpl, Brig Gen Thos Johnson, Capt Allen, Mil Inf
KING, Charles, Pvt, Col Edward Bradley, Capt Jas Hambleton, Vol Inf
KING, Charles, Pvt, Col John Cocke, Capt John Weakley, Inf
KING, Charles, Pvt, Col S Copeland, Capt Solomon George, Inf
KING, Charles, Pvt, Col William Hall, Capt Jas Hambleton, Vol Inf
KING, Charles, Pvt, Lt Col Henry Bryan, Co Commander omitted, Inf
KING, Charles, Pvt, Maj John Chiles, Capt Jas Cummings, E TN Mil Inf; appointed Pack Horse Carrier, Regt Co Hawkins
KING, Charles, Pvt, Regt Commander omitted, Capt James Cowan, Mtd Inf
KING, Charles, Pvt, Regt Commander omitted, Capt Jas Haggard, Mtd Gunmen
KING, David, Pvt, Col Thomas Benton, Capt Henry L Douglass, Vol Inf
KING, David, Pvt, Col Wm Lillard, Capt Benj H King, E TN Vol Inf; detached as Wgnr
KING, Edward, 1 Lt, Col Ewen Allison, Capt Wm King, Drafted Mil
KING, Elijah, Pvt, Col Newton Cannon, Capt Martin, Mtd Gunmen; transferred to Capt Evans Co of Spies
KING, Eliza, Pvt, Regt Commander omitted, Capt Robt Evans, Mtd Spies
KING, George, Cpl, Col Edwin E Booth, Capt John Slatton, E TN Mil
KING, George, Pvt, Col Ewen Allison, Capt Jacob Hoyal, E TN Mil
KING, Harmon, Pvt, Col Wm Higgins, Capt Stephen Griffith, Mtd Riflemen
KING, Harry, Pvt, Col T Johnson, Capt Jos Scott, 3rd Regt E TN Drafted Mil
KING, Harvey, Pvt, Col T Johnson, Capt Jos Scott, E TN Drafted Mil; reduced from Cpl
KING, Henry, Cpl, Regt Commander omitted, Capt Gray, Inf
KING, Henry, Pvt, Col R H Dyer, Capt Thomas Jones, Vol Mtd Gunmen
KING, Henry, Sgt, Col Wm Phillips, Co Commander omitted, Inf
KING, Isaiah, Pvt, Col Wm Pillow, Capt Isaiah Renshaw, Inf
KING, James M, Cpl, Col R H Dyer, Capt Thomas Jones, Vol Mtd Gunmen
KING, James, Hospital Surgeon, Maj Gen John Cocke, E TN Vol Mil
KING, John A, Pvt, Col Wm Metcalf, Capt Thomas Marks, Mil Inf
KING, John T, Sgt, Col Samuel Bayless, Capt James Landen, E TN Mil
KING, John, Pvt, Col John Brown, Capt John Childs, E TN Vol Mtd Inf
KING, John, Pvt, Col John Coffee, Capt A McKeen, Cav
KING, John, Pvt, Col John K Wynne, Capt Bayless E Prince, Inf
KING, John, Pvt, Col Philip Pipkin, Capt John Strother, Mil; promoted to Cpl
KING, John, Pvt, Col R C Napier, Capt Drury Adkins, Mil Inf
KING, John, Pvt, Col Samuel Bayless, Capt James Landen, E TN Mil
KING, John, Pvt, Col Samuel Wear, Capt John Bayless, Mtd Inf

## Enlisted Men, War of 1812

KING, John, Pvt, Col Thomas Benton, Capt Geo Caperton, Inf

KING, John, Pvt, Col Thomas Benton, Capt Geo Caperton, Vol Inf

KING, John, Pvt, Col Thomas Benton, Capt Isaiah Renshaw, Vol Inf

KING, John, Pvt, Col Thomas Benton, Capt James McFerrin, Vol Inf; transferred to Capt Renshaw

KING, John, Pvt, Maj John Childs, Capt James Cummings, E TN Vol Mtd Inf

KING, John, Pvt, Regt Commander omitted, Capt Geo Caperton, 2nd Regt Vol Inf

KING, John, Sgt, Col Wm Lillard, Capt John Roper, E TN Inf

KING, Johnson, Pvt, Col John K Wynne, Capt James Holleman, Inf; deserted 11-19-1813

KING, Johnson, Pvt, Col John K Wynne, Capt Wm Carruthers, W TN Inf; transferred to Capt Hollon's Co

KING, Johnson, Pvt, Col Philip Pipkin, Capt John Roberton, Mil Inf

KING, Jonathan, Pvt, Regt Commander omitted, Capt Jos Williams, Mil Cav; deserted

KING, Jonathan, Sgt, Col Wm Lillard, Capt Benj H King, E TN Vol Inf

KING, Joseph, Pvt, Col James Raulston, Capt James A Black, Inf

KING, Joseph, Pvt, Col John Coffee, Capt Thomas Bradley, Vol Cav

KING, Mirady, Pvt, Col John K Wynne, Capt William Carruthers, W TN Inf; transferred to Capt Hollon's Co

KING, Moses, Pvt, Col Edward Bradley, Capt Abraham Bledsoe, Riflemen; wounded at Talledega, since died

KING, Moses, Pvt, Col William Hall, Capt Abraham Bledsoe, Vol Inf

KING, Nathaniel, Ffr, Col Thomas Benton, Capt Isaiah Renshaw, Vol Inf; joined from Hewett's Co

KING, Nathaniel, Ffr, Col Thomas H Benton, Capt Benj Hewett, Vol Inf

KING, Nathaniel, Ffr, Col William Pillow, Capt Isaiah Renshaw, Inf

KING, Nathaniel, Pvt, Col John Cocke, Capt John Weakley, Inf

KING, Richard P, Pvt, Regt Commander omitted, Capt David Smith, Cav Vol

KING, Robert, Pvt, Brig Gen Jas White, Co Commander omitted, Spy

KING, Robert, Pvt, Brig Gen Jas White, no other information

KING, Robert, Pvt, Col S Bunch, Capt S Richardson, E TN Drafted Mil

KING, Robert, Pvt, Col S Copeland, Capt Moses Thompson, Inf

KING, Robert, Pvt, Col Samuel Wear, Capt Joseph Calloway, Mtd Inf

KING, Robert, Pvt, Regt Commander omitted, Capt Samuel Richardson, E TN Drafted Mil

KING, Rufus, Pvt, Col Jno Brown, Capt Wm D Neilson, E TN Vol Mil

KING, Samuel, Pvt, Col James Raulston, Capt Henry Hamilton, Inf; also under Maj Gen Wm Carroll

KING, Samuel, Pvt, Col Samuel Bayless, Capt James Churchman, E TN Mil; transferred from Capt Milliken's, d 2-16-1815

KING, Sanford H, Pvt, Col John Cocke, Capt Richard Crunk, Inf

KING, Thomas, Pvt, Col John Cocke, Capt Joseph Price, Inf; substitute for James Yarborough

KING, Thomas, Pvt, Col Samuel Bayless, Capt James Landen, E TN Mil

KING, William D, Pvt, Col John Alcorn, Capt John Winston, Mtd Riflemen

KING, William S, Pvt, Col Wm Lillard, Capt Robert McCalpin, E TN Inf

KING, William, Cpl, Col John Cocke, Capt Joseph Price, Inf; joined at Clarksville

KING, William, Col Ewen Allison, Capt Henry McCray, E TN Mil; transferred to Capt Hampton's Co

KING, William, Pvt, Col Ewen Allison, Capt John Hampton, Mil; transferred from Capt McCrea's Co

KING, William, Pvt, Col John K Wynne, Capt James Holleman, Branch Srvce omitted; deserted 11-19-1813

KING, William, Pvt, Col John Wynne, Capt John Porter, Inf; deserted 11-18-1813

KING, William, Pvt, Col John Wynne, Capt William Carruthers, W TN Inf; transferred to Capt Hollon's Co

KING, William, Pvt, Col Newton Cannon, Capt Isaac Williams, Mtd Riflemen

KING, William, Pvt, Col Newton Cannon, Capt Ota Cantrell, W TN Mtd Inf

KING, William, Pvt, Col Philip Pipkin, Capt John Robertson, Mil Inf

KING, William, Pvt, Col T Williamson, Capt Anthony M Metcalf, Vol Mtd Gunmen

KING, William, Pvt, Col William Lillard, Capt Wm Gillenwater, E TN Inf

KING, William, Pvt, Col Wm Lillard, Capt Geo Argenbright, E TN Vol Riflemen

KING, William, Pvt, Col Wm Metcalf, Capt William Sitton, Mil Inf; d 3-20-1815

KING, William, Pvt, Col Wm Y Higgins, Capt Thomas Eldridge, Mtd Gunmen

KING, William, Pvt, Lt Col L Hammond, Capt Thomas Wells, Inf

KING, William, Pvt, Lt Col L Hammond, Capt Thomas Wells, Inf; Col A Loury

KING, William, Pvt, Lt Col Wm Phillips, Co Commander omitted, Inf

KING, William, Pvt, Maj Gen Robt Cooper, Co Commander omitted, Mtd Riflemen

KING, William, Pvt, Maj John Childs, Capt James Cummings, E TN Vol Mtd Inf; Regimental Co - Hawkins

KING, William, Pvt, Regt Commander omitted, Capt Sam Bunch, Mtd Vol

KINGSTON, William C, Pvt, Col Jno Brown, Capt William White, Regt E TN Mil Inf

KINNARD, Alexander, Pvt, Col Jno Brown, Capt John Trimble, E TN Mtd Gunmen
KINNARD, George, Pvt, Col Samuel Wear, Capt John Stephens, E TN Vol Inf
KINNARD, George, Pvt, Maj John Childs, Capt John Stephens, E TN Vol Mtd Inf
KINNARD, John, 4 Sgt, Col Samuel Bunch, Capt David G Vance, E TN Mtd Inf
KINNEY, John, Pvt, Col William Johnson, Capt Christopher Cook, E TN Mil
KINNEY, William, Tptr, Col Thos Williamson, Capt Giles Burdett, Vol Mtd Gunmen
KINNIGA, Miller, Pvt, Col Thos Williamson, Capt Anthony M Metcalf, Vol Mtd Gunmen
KINNY, Daniel, Pvt, Col Wm Lillard, Capt Wm McLin, E TN Inf
KINNY, John, Pvt, Col Wm Lillard, Capt Wm McLin, E TN Inf
KINOR, John, Pvt, Lt I Barrett, Capt Nathan Davis, Inf
KINRALL (KINDALL), Benjamin, Sgt, Col Philip Pipkin, Capt Peter Search, Mil Inf
KINSAL, Benjamin, Pvt, Col John Alcorn, Capt John W Byrn, Cav
KINSAL, John, Pvt, Col John Alcorn, Capt John W Byrn, Cav
KINSALL, John, Pvt, Col Thomas Williamson, Capt Robert Moore, Vol Mtd Gunmen
KINSAY, Thomas, Pvt, Col S Copeland, Capt William Douglass, Inf
KINSEY, Thomas, Pvt, Col Thomas Williamson, Capt Benjamin Powell, E TN Mil
KINSTON, John, Pvt, Col Samuel Bunch, Capt McKamey, E TN Mil
KINSTROE, Henry, Pvt, Col R C Napier, Capt Drury Adkins, Mil Inf
KIOUS, Henry, Pvt, Col S Copeland, Capt Alexander Provine, Mil Inf
KIRBY, John, Pvt, Col John Alcorn, Capt John W Byrne, Cav
KIRBY, Lewis, Pvt, Col Samuel Wear, Capt John Stephens, E TN Vol Inf
KIRBY, Richard, Pvt, Col John Brown, Capt John Childs, E TN Vol Mtd Inf
KIRK, Ezekiel, Pvt, Col William Lillard, Capt Thomas Sharpe, 2nd Regt Inf
KIRK, George, Pvt, Col John Cocke, Capt John Weakley, Inf
KIRK, George, Pvt, Col William Johnson, Capt Andrew Lawson, E TN Drafted Mil; substitute for Asa Eppison
KIRK, George, Pvt, Lt Col Henry Bryan, Co Commander omitted, Inf
KIRK, George, Pvt, Regt Commander omitted, Capt James Cowan, Inf
KIRK, Hugh, Pvt, Col Jno Coffee, Capt Robert Jetton, Cav
KIRK, Hugh, Pvt, Col Newton Cannon, Capt Thomas Yardley, Mtd Riflemen
KIRK, James, Pvt, Col Robert H Dyer, Capt Thomas Jones, Vol Mtd Gunmen
KIRK, Jesse L, Pvt, Col A Cheatham, Capt James Giddens, Inf
KIRK, John, Pvt, Col John Brown, Capt Hugh Barton, E TN Mil Inf
KIRK, John, Pvt, Col Samuel Bunch, Capt Andrew Breden, E TN Mil; transferred to Capt Bacon's Co
KIRK, John, Pvt, Col Thomas Williamson, Capt James Pace, Lt Nealy, Vol Mtd Gunmen
KIRK, Joseph, Cpl, Col Wm Johnson, Co Commander omitted, E TN Mil
KIRK, Lewis, Sgt, Regt Commander omitted, Capt Nathan Farmer, Mtd Riflemen
KIRK, Nates, Pvt, Regt Commander omitted, Capt Benjamin Reynolds, Mtd Rangers
KIRK, Thomas, Cpl, Col T McCrory, Capt John Reynolds, Mil Inf
KIRK, Thomas, Pvt, Col Thomas H Benton, Capt Isaac Renshaw, Vol Inf
KIRK, Thomas, Pvt, Col Wm Lillard, Capt Wm Hamilton, E TN Vol Inf
KIRK, William, Sgt, Regt Commander omitted, Capt John Gordon, Mtd Spies
KIRKHAM, William, Pvt, Regt Commander omitted, Capt David Vance, Mtd Mil
KIRKLAN, Jacob, Pvt, Col John K Wynn, Capt Wm Caruthers, W TN Inf; deserted 10-20-1813
KIRKLAND, Joab W, Pvt, Col Robert Steele, Capt James Shenault, Mil Inf
KIRKLAND, Zekeriah, Pvt, Col Robert Steele, Capt Samuel Maxwell, Mil Inf
KIRKMAN, Thomas, Pvt, Col A Loury, Capt George Sarver, Inf; substitute for James Bruce
KIRKPATRICK, Alex, Sgt, Col John Brown, Capt Hugh Barton, E TN Mil Inf
KIRKPATRICK, Alexander, Pvt, Col Samuel Wear, Capt Rufus Morgan, E TN Vol Inf
KIRKPATRICK, Amos, 1 Sgt, Col James Raulston, Capt Henry West, Mil Inf
KIRKPATRICK, Arthur, Pvt, Col Samuel Bunch, Capt Andrew Breden, E TN Mil; transferred to Capt Bacon's Co
KIRKPATRICK, Charles, 1 Sgt, Col John Brown, Capt James Standifer, E TN Vol Mtd Mil
KIRKPATRICK, Daniel, Pvt, Col John Brown, Capt James Standifer, E TN Vol Mtd Inf
KIRKPATRICK, Edward, Pvt, Col R C Napier, Capt Samuel Ashmore, Mil Inf
KIRKPATRICK, Eleazer, 4 Sgt, Col R C Napier, Capt Samuel Ashmore, Mil Inf
KIRKPATRICK, Henry, Pvt, Col Wm Pillow, Capt Thomas Williamson, Vol Inf
KIRKPATRICK, Henry, Pvt, Regt Commander omitted, Capt Thomas Williamson, Det of TN Vol Inf
KIRKPATRICK, James, 1 Sgt, Col John Cocke, Capt Joseph Price, Inf; d 1-28-1813
KIRKPATRICK, James, 3 Cpl, Col Wm Lillard, Capt Geo Argenbright, E TN Vol Riflemen
KIRKPATRICK, James, Cpl, Col John Wynne, Capt Butler, Inf; promoted from Pvt
KIRKPATRICK, James, Pvt, Col Edwin E Booth, Capt John McKamey, Inf
KIRKPATRICK, James, Pvt, Maj Wm Carroll, Capt Lewis Dillahunty, Capt Daniel M Bradford, Vol

## Enlisted Men, War of 1812

KIRKPATRICK, Joel, Pvt, Col Samuel Wear, Capt John Bayless, Mtd Inf; killed 1-8-1815

KIRKPATRICK, John H, Pvt, Col Edward Bradley, Capt Harry L Douglass, Vol Inf

KIRKPATRICK, John H?, Pvt, Col Thomas Benton, Capt Henry L Douglass, Vol Inf

KIRKPATRICK, John, Pvt, Col R C Napier, Capt Samuel Ashmore, Mil Inf

KIRKPATRICK, John, Pvt, Col William Johnson, Capt James Stewart, E TN Drafted Mil

KIRKPATRICK, John, Pvt, Col Wm Johnson, Capt Jas Stewart, E TN Mil

KIRKPATRICK, John, Pvt, Col Wm Lillard, Capt Zacheus Copeland, E TN Vol Inf

KIRKPATRICK, John, Pvt, Regt Commander omitted, Capt Samuel Bunch, Mtd Vol

KIRKPATRICK, Joseph, 3 Cpl, Col Philip Pipkin, Capt Peter Searcy, Mil Inf

KIRKPATRICK, Joseph, Pvt, Col William Alcorn, Capt John W Byrne, Cav

KIRKPATRICK, Martin, Pvt, Maj John Childs, Capt Charles Conway, E TN Mtd Gunmen; Regimental Co - Knox

KIRKPATRICK, Robert, Pvt, Col Jno Brown, Capt Hugh Barton, E TN Mil Inf

KIRKPATRICK, Robert, Pvt, Col Samuel Wear, Capt John Bayless, Mtd Inf

KIRKPATRICK, Samuel, Pvt, Col Wm Pillow, Capt Thos Williamson, Vol Inf

KIRKPATRICK, Samuel, Pvt, Regt Commander omitted, Capt David Mason, Cav

KIRKPATRICK, Samuel, Pvt, Regt Commander omitted, Capt Thos Williamson, Det of TN Vol Inf

KIRKPATRICK, Thomas, Pvt, Col Edward Bradley, Capt Harry L Douglass, Vol Inf

KIRKPATRICK, William, Pvt, Col William Johnson, Capt Christopher Cook, E TN Mil

KIRKPATRICK, William, Pvt, Col William Johnson, Capt Joseph Kirk, Mil; substitute for Zachariah Lurton

KIRNSEY (KINSEY), Benjamin, Pvt, Maj William Russell, Capt Isaac Williams, Sep Bn TN Vol Mtd Gunmen

KISSINGER, Jacob, Pvt, Col Thos Williamson, Capt James Pace, Lt Nealey, Vol Mtd Gunmen

KISSINGER, Solomon, Pvt, Col Thos Williamson, Capt James Pace, Lt Nealey, Vol Mtd Gunmen

KITCHELL, Iradel, Pvt, Col John K Wynne, Capt Bayless E Prince, Inf

KITCHEN, John H, Pvt, Col William Johnson, Capt Henry Hunter, E TN Mil; trans to Capt Kirk's Co

KITCHEN, John, Pvt, Maj Wm Russell, Capt John Trimble, Vol Mtd Gunmen

KITCHENS, James, Pvt, Col S Copeland, Capt Richard Sharp, Mil Inf; deserted

KITCHENS, John H, Pvt, Col William Johnson, Capt Christopher Cook, E Tn Mil

KITE, Hugh, Pvt, Col Phillip Pipkin, Capt Ebenezer Kirkpatrick, Mil Inf

KITE, Jesse, Pvt, Col William Johnson, Capt Joseph Scott, 3 Regt Mil

KITE (KYTE), Jesse, Pvt, Col William Johnson, Capt Joseph Scott, E TN Draft Mil; died 11-1-1814

KITRELL, George, Pvt, Col A Loury, Capt John Looney, W TN Inf

KITTLE, John, Pvt, Col Philip Pipkin, Capt James Blakemore, Mil Inf; deserted

KITTS, John, Pvt, Col H C Napier, Capt Thomas Gray, Mil Inf

KITTS, John, Pvt, Col Wm Johnson, Capt Christopher Cook, 3 Regt E TN Mil; trans from Capt Henry Hunter Co

KITTS, Peter, Pvt, Col Samuel Bayless, Capt Joseph B? Bacon, E TN Mil

KIVER, Jonathan, Pvt, Col William Johnson, Capt James Stewsart, E TN Draft Mil

KIZER, Benjamin, Pvt, Col R C Napier, Capt Edward Neblett, Mil Inf

KIZER, Francis, Pvt, Col John K Wynne, Capt James Cole, Inf; deserted

KIZER, John, Pvt, Col R C Napier, Capt Thomas Preston, Mil Inf

KIZON, Benjamin, Pvt, Regt Commander omitted, Capt Gray, Inf

KLEPPER, Peter, Pvt, Col Wm Lillard, Capt Geo Argenbright, E TN Vol Riflemen

KLIGAM, Thomas H, Pvt, Col Wm Johnson, Capt Henry Hunter, E TN Mil; trans to Kirk's Co

KNAVE, John, Pvt, Col Samuel Wear, Capt James Gillespie, E TN Vol Inf

KNAVE, Samuel, Pvt, Col Samuel Bunch, Capt Edward Buchanan, E TN Mil; trans from Capt Duncan's Co

KNICELY, John, Pvt, Col Ewen Allison, Capt William King, Draft Mil

KNIGHT, Absalom, Pvt, Col Wm Higgins, Capt Adam Dele, Mtd Gunmen

KNIGHT, Allen, Pvt, Col William Metcalf, Capt John Barnhart, Mil Inf

KNIGHT, Aquilla, Pvt, Col Philip Pipkin, Capt Geo Mebane, Mil Inf

KNIGHT, Henry F, Pvt, Col Philip Pipkin, Capt Peter Searcy, Mil Inf

KNIGHT, James, Pvt, Col Thomas Benton, Capt Benj Reynolds, Vol Inf

KNIGHT, James, Pvt, Col Wm Higgins, Capt Adam Dale, Mtd Gunmen; wounded 1-28-1814

KNIGHT, James, Rank omitted, Brig Gen I B Roberts, Capt Benj Reynolds, Mtd Ranger

KNIGHT, John, Cpl, Col John Coffee, Capt Blackman Coleman, Cav; promoted to QM Sgt

KNIGHT, John, Pvt, Col Edwin Booth, Capt George Winton, E TN Mil

KNIGHT, John, Pvt, Maj John Childs, Capt John Stephens, E TN Vol Mtd Inf

KNIGHT, Jonathan, Pvt, Col Edward Bradley, Capt Abraham Bledsoe, Riflemen

KNIGHT, Jonathan, Pvt, Col Wm Hall, Capt Abraham Bledsoe, Vol Inf

KNIGHT, Joseph, Pvt, Col Philip Pipkin, CApt James Blakemore, Mil Inf

## Enlisted Men, War of 1812

KNIGHT, Robert, Pvt, Col Wm Y Higgins, Capt Adam Dele, Mtd Gunmen; killed in Emuckfaw Battle 1-22-1814

KNIGHT, Stephen, Pvt, Col Edwin Booth, Capt Thomas Porter, Draft Mil

KNIGHT, Thomas, Cpl, Col John Alcorn, Capt John Baskerville, Vol Inf

KNIGHT, Thomas, Cpl, Col John Coffee, Capt John Baskerville, Cav

KNIGHT, Thomas, Pvt, Col John K Winn, Capt John Spinks, Inf

KNIGHT, Thomas, Pvt, Maj John Chiles, Capt John Stephens, E TN Vol Mtd Inf

KNIGHT, Wade H, Pvt, Col Philip Pipkin, Capt Peter Searcy, Mil Inf

KNOW, William, Pvt, Col Samuel Wear, Capt Rufus Morgan, E TN Vol Inf

KNOX, Benjamin W, Sgt, Col S Copeland, Capt Moses Thompson, Inf

KNOX, Benjamin, Pvt, Col N Cannon, Capt Geo Brandon, Mtd Riflemen

KNOX, David, Pvt, Col William Johnson, Capt Elihu Milliken, 3 Regt E TN Mil

KNOX, James, Pvt, Col Edward E Booth, Capt George Winton, E TN Mil

KNOX, John, Pvt, Col Jas Raulston, Capt Jas A Black, Inf

KNOX, Joseph, Pvt, Col N Cannon, Capt Geo Brandon, Mtd Riflemen

KNOX, Squire, Pvt, Col John Cocke, Capt George Barnes, Inf; joined at Clarksville

KNOX, Walker, Pvt, no other information

KNOX, William, Pvt, Col Edwin Booth, Capt George Winton, E TN Mil; trans to Capt Millican's Co

KNOX, William, Pvt, Col Jas Brown, Capt Jas Preston, Regt E TN Mil Inf

KNOX, William, Pvt, Col N Cannon, Capt George Brandon, Mtd Riflemen; died about 10-24-1813

KNOX, William, Pvt, Col William Johnson, Capt Elihu Milliken, 3 Regt E TN Mil

KOFFMAN, John, Col Samuel Bayless, Capt Branch Jones, E TN Draft Mil

KOKER, Jonathan, Pvt, Col Edwin Booth, Capt John Lewis, E TN Mil

KOON, John, Pvt, Col Ewen Allison, Capt Adam Winsell, E TN Mil

KOON, William, Pvt, Brig Gen Thos Johnson, Capt Abraham Allen, Mil Inf

KOONCE, George, Pvt, Col A Cheatham, Maj Gen A Jackson, Capt William Creel, Inf

KOONCE, Tobias, Pvt, Col John Cocke, Capt George Barnes, Inf

KOONS, Philip, Pvt, Col Robert H Dyer, Capt James Wyatt, Vol Mtd Gunmen

KOONSE, Christopher, Pvt, Col S Copeland, Capt G W Stell, Mil Inf

KORGOR, Josiah, Pvt, Capt Nathan Davis, Lt I Barrett, Inf

KOYLE, Robert, Pvt, Col S Bunch, Capt Jones Griffin, E TN Draft Mil; joined from Capt Longmiller's Co

KRESKY (KREECY), William, Pvt, Col Wm Metcalf, Capt Thos Marks, Mil Inf

KUK (KULL?), William, Pvt, Capt Josiah Askew, Inf

KURK, George, Pvt, Col John Cocke, Capt John Weakley, Inf

KURKENDOLL, James, Pvt, Col Wm Metcalf, Capt Barbee Collins, Mil Inf

KUTCH, Daniel, Pvt, Col Robert Steele, Capt Robert Campbell, Mil Inf

KUTON, Zachariah, Pvt, Col S Copeland, Capt Moses Thompson, Inf

KYLE, JOHN, Pvt, Col S Bunch, Capt James Penny, E TN Mtd Inf

KYLE, James, Pvt, Col Robert H Dyer, Capt Jas McMahon, 1 TN Vol Mtd Gunmen

KYLE, John, Pvt, Maj John Chiles, Capt Jas Cummings, E TN Vol Mtd Inf; Regt from Hawkins Co

KYLE, John? M?, Pvt, Col William Lillard, Capt Malone, E TN Vol Inf

KYLE, Joseph, Pvt, Col Philip Pipkin, Capt David Smith, W TN Mil; deserted

KYLE, Joseph, Pvt, Col Philip Pipkin, Capt John Strother, Mil

KYSER, Michael, Pvt, Col James Raulston, Capt Daniel Newman, Inf

KYSER, Peter, Pvt, Col Jas Raulston, Capt Daniel Newman, Inf

LA REW, George, Pvt, Col S Bunch, Capt Daniel Narnell, E TN Mil

LAATS?, James, Pvt, Maj Gen Wm Carroll, Col Wm Metcalf, Capt John Johnson, Branch omitted

LACETER, Jonathan, Pvt, Col Samuel Bunch, Capt Joseph Duncan, E TN Drafted Mil; trans to Capt Buchanan's Co

LACEY, Alexander, Blksmth, Col John Alcorn, Capt Alexander McKeen, Cav

LACEY, Andrew, Pvt, Col John Alcorn, Capt John J Winston, Mtd Riflemen

LACEY, John, Pvt, Regt Commander omitted, Capt Samuel Richardson, E TN Draft Mil; disch for inability

LACEY, Reuben, Pvt, Col Ewen Allison, Capt Adam Winsell, E Tn Draft Mil

LACEY, Thomas, Pvt, Col Ewen Allison, Capt Henry McCray, E TN Mil; trans to Capt Register's Co

LACEY, _____, Pvt, Col S Bunch, Capt F Register, E TN Mil; joined from Capt Winsell's Co

LACKARD, Charles, Pvt, Col Samuel Wear, Capt John Stephens, E TN Vol Inf

LACKEY, Alexander, Pvt, Col Jno Coffee, Capt Alexander McKeen, Cav

LACKEY, George, Pvt, Col William Johnson, Capt Christopher Cook, E TN Mil; died 11-9-1814

LACKEY, George, Pvt, Col Wm Y Higgins, Capt Wm Doake, Mtd Riflemen

LACKEY, James, Pvt, Col John Brown, Capt Allen I Bacon, E Tn Mil Inf; promoted to QM

LACKEY, Joseph, Pvt, Col S Bunch, Capt David G Vance, E TN Mtd Inf

LACKLAND, Joseph, Pvt, Col William Lillard, Capt Jacob Dyke, Vol Inf

LACKLEY, George, Pvt, Col Wm Johnston, Capt Joseph Kirk, Mil

LACKS, Abraham, Pvt, Col Wm Pillow, Capt Wm Moore,

## Enlisted Men, War of 1812

LACKY, James, Pvt, Col Thos Williamson, Capt Thos Scurry, Vol Mtd Gunmen
LACKY, Thomas, Pvt, Col J Williams, Capt David Vance, Mtd Mil
LACKY, William, Pvt, Col Thos Williamson, Maj Gen Jackson, Capt Robert Steele, Vol Mtd Gunmen
LACY, Abraham, Pvt, Col Wm Johnston, Capt Jas Rogers, E TN Draft Mil
LACY, Amos H, Pvt, Lt Col L Hammonds, Col A Lowry, Capt Thos Delaney, Inf
LACY, Claibourn, Pvt, Col Thos McCrory, Capt S B McKnight, Inf
LACY, Isaac, Pvt, Col Wm Johnson, Capt Henry Hunter, E TN Mil
LACY, James, Pvt, Col E Allison, Capt A Winsell, E TN Draft Mil
LACY, John, Pvt, Col S Bunch, Capt S Richardson, E TN Drafted Mil; deserted
LACY, John, Pvt, Col Samuel Bayless, Capt Solomon Hendricks, E Tn Mil
LACY, John, Pvt, Col Wm Johnson, Capt Jas Stewart, E TN Draft Mil
LACY, Jordon, Pvt, Col P Pipkin, Capt H M Newlin, Mil Inf
LACY, Mark, Pvt, Col Wm Lillard, Capt Thos Sharpe, 2 Regt Inf
LACY, Nehemiah, Pvt, Col S Bunch, Capt E Buchanan, E TN Draft Mil
LACY, Philemon, Pvt, Col E Allison, Capt Adam Winsell, E TN Draft Mil
LACY, Valentine, Pvt, Col Wm Johnson, Capt Jas Scott, E TN Draft Mil
LADD, Constantine, Pvt, Col N T Perkins, Capt McMahan, Mtd Gunmen
LADD, Thomas, Pvt, Col R C Napier, Capt J Chism, Mil Inf
LADD, Thomas, Pvt, Col R H Dyer, Capt Jas McMahan, TN Vol Mtd Gunmen; died 1-24-1815?
LADEN, George, Pvt, Col Thos Benton, Capt I Renshaw, Vol Inf; trans from Capt Hewett's Co
LADEN, George, Pvt, Col Thos H Benton, Capt Benj Hewett, Vol Inf
LADS, Hillery, Pvt, Gen Andrew Jackson, Capt Nathan Davis, Inf
LADY, Barker, Pvt, Col Samuel Bayless, Capt Jas Landen, E TN Mil
LADY, William, Pvt, Col Samuel Bayless, Capt Jas Landen, E TN Mil
LAFEW, Elisha, Pvt, Col S Bunch, Capt Samuel Richardson, E Tn Draft Mil; discharged for inability
LAFOLLETT, George, Pvt, Col S Bayless, Capt J Waddell, E TN Mil
LAFOLLETT, Jeremiah, Pvt, Col S Bayless, Capt J Waddell, E TN Mil
LAIN, James, Pvt, Col P Pipkin, Capt David Smith, Inf
LAIN, James, Pvt, Col Wm Pillow, Capt Jas McFerrin, Inf
LAIN, John, Pvt, Col J Brown, Capt Allen I Bacon, E TN Mil Inf
LAIN, John, Pvt, Col Wm Johnson, Capt B Powell, E TN Mil
LAIN, John, Pvt, Col Wm Johnson, Capt Jas Stewart, E TN Mil
LAIN, John, Pvt, Col Wm Johnson, Capt Jos Kirk, Mil Inf
LAIN, Jordon, Pvt, Col Wm Johnson, Capt Jas Stewart, E TN Drafted Mil
LAIN, Joseph, Pvt, Col Wm Lillard, Capt J Hartsell, E TN Vol Inf
LAIN, Middleton, Cpl, Col Jno Brown, Capt A I Bacon, E TN Mil Regt
LAIN, Richard, Pvt, Col Wm Johnson, Capt B Powell, E TN Mil
LAIN, William, Pvt, Col J Cocke, Capt S M Caruthers, Inf
LAIN, Woodson, Pvt, Col Wm Johnson, Capt Jas Stewart, E TN Mil
LAIRD, Alex, 3 Cpl, Maj Gen A Jackson, Capt Joel Parrish, Arty
LAIRD, John, Pvt, Col R C Napier, Capt J Chism, Mil Inf
LAKE, Allen D, Pvt, Lt Col L Hammond, Capt Jas Tubb, Inf
LAKE, Daniel, Pvt, Col Edward Bradley, Capt Brice Martin, Vol Inf
LAKE, George, Pvt, Col N T Perkins, Capt Mathew Johnston, Mil Inf
LAKY, Henry, Pvt, Col S Bunch, Capt Geo McPherson, E TN Mil
LAMASTER, James, Pvt, Col John Cocke, Capt John Weakley, Inf
LAMB, Archibald, Pvt, Col S Wear, Capt Wm Doake, E TN Vol Inf
LAMB, Claiburn, Pvt, Col Ewin Allison, Capt Jos Everett, E TN Mil; deserted 1-25-1812
LAMB, David, Pvt, Col Wm Hall, Capt T C Nash, Inf; transferred
LAMB, Gross, Pvt, Col S Bunch, Capt Jno English, E TN Drafted Mil
LAMB, Jacob, Pvt, Col Wm Metcalf, Capt O Waller, Mil Inf
LAMB, James, Pvt, Brig Gen Johnson, Capt Allen, Mil Inf
LAMB, James, Pvt, Col Wm Johnson, Capt Jos Scott, E TN Drafted Mil
LAMB, Jessie, Pvt, Col Alex Loury, Capt John Looney, W TN Inf
LAMB, Joseph, Pvt, Lt Col L Hammond, Col Alex Loury, Capt Thos Wells, Inf; substituted by Robt Crafton
LAMB, Longsheare, Pvt, Col Wm Hall, Capt John Kennedy, Vol Inf
LAMB, Quiller, Pvt, Col Wm Hall, Capt John Kennedy, Vol Inf
LAMB, William, Pvt, Col E Bradley, Capt A Bledsoe, Riflemen; wounded and furloughed
LAMBE, Longshore, Pvt, Col Wm Hall, Capt J Kennedy, Vol Inf
LAMBERSON, Conrad (Koonrod), Pvt, Col R H Dyer, Capt Bethel Allen, Vol Mtd Gunmen
LAMBERSON, Leonard, Sgt Maj, Lt Col Hammons, Co Commander omitted, 2nd Regt W TN Mil
LAMBERT, Aaron, Sgt, Col S Copeland, Capt Alexander Provine, Mil Inf
LAMBERT, Charles, Pvt, Col Thomas H Williamson, Co Commander omitted, Vol Mtd Gunmen

- 301

## Enlisted Men, War of 1812

LAMBERT, Daniel, Pvt, Col Samuel Bunch, Capt Joseph Duncan, E TN Drafted Mil; transferred to Capt English's Co

LAMBERT, John, Cpl, Col Samuel Wear, Capt James Gillespie, E TN Vol Inf

LAMBERT, John, Cpl, Maj W Woodfolk, Capt Ezekial Ross, Capt McCully, Inf; principle Blksmth at Ft Ross

LAMBERT, Thomas, Pvt, Col S Copeland, Capt David Williams, Inf

LAMBERT, Thomas, Pvt, Maj Gen Wm Carroll, Capt Wiley Huddleston, Inf

LAMBERTON, Leonard, Sgt Maj, Col A Loury, Lt Col Leroy Hammond, 2nd Regt W TN Mil

LAMBETH, Demsey, Pvt, Col Wm Metcalf, Capt Marks, Mil Inf

LAMBURT, Daniel, Pvt, Col Samuel Bunch, Capt John English, E TN Drafted Mil; joined Capt Duncan's Co

LAMESTER, Samuel, Pvt, Col John Cocke, Capt J Weakly, Inf

LAMKIN, William, Pvt, Col Wm Y Higgins, Capt James Hambleton, Mtd Gunmen

LAMPKIN, Elias, Pvt, Col R H Dyer, Capt Robert Edmondson, TN Vol Mtd Gunmen

LAMPKINS, Robert, Pvt, Regt Commander omitted, Capt Daniel Yarnell, E TN Mil

LANCASTER, Aaron, Pvt, Col John Cocke, Capt Samuel Caruthers, Inf

LANCASTER, Aaron, Pvt, Col R H Dyer, Capt McMahon, TN Vol Mtd Gunmen

LANCASTER, Davis, Pvt, Col Thomas Williamson, Capt Wm Martin, Vol Mtd Gunmen

LANCASTER, James, Pvt, Col John Cocke, Capt John Weakley, Inf

LANCASTER, John, Blksmth, Col Newt Cannon, Capt James Walton, Mtd Riflemen

LANCASTER, John, Pvt, Col R C Napier, Capt Andrew McCarty, Mil Inf

LANCASTER, Joseph, Pvt, Col R C Napier, Co Commander omitted, Mil Inf

LANCASTER, Michael, Pvt, Commanders omitted, Inf

LANCASTER, Richard, Pvt, Col John Cocke, Capt Samuel Caruthers, Inf

LANCASTER, Robert A, Cpl, Col Newton Cannon, Capt James Walton, Mtd Riflemen

LANCASTER, Robert, Pvt, Col Newton Cannon, Capt James Walton, Mtd Riflemen

LANCASTER, Samuel, Pvt, Col John Cocke, Capt James Gray, Inf

LANCASTER, Samuel, Pvt, Regt Commander omitted, Capt James Haggard, Mtd Gunmen

LANCASTER, Thomas A, Pvt, Col Newton Cannon, Capt James Walton, Mtd Riflemen

LANCASTER, William, Pvt, Col John Cocke, Capt Samuel Caruthers, Inf

LANCEFORD, Prior, Pvt, Col A Cheatham, Capt Chapman, Inf

LAND, Aaron, Pvt, Col Edward Bradley, Capt John Moore, Vol Inf; deserted 11-24-1813

LAND, Aaron, Pvt, Col Wm Hall, Capt John Moore, Vol Inf

LAND, James, Pvt, Col S Copeland, Capt Allen Wilkinson, Mil Inf

LANDERS, Isaac, Pvt, Col Newton Cannon, Capt Beverly Williams, Mtd Riflemen

LANDFORD, George, Pvt, Col Wm Hall, Capt John Moore, Vol Inf

LANDFORD, George, Sgt, Col A Loury, Capt Jas Kincaid, Inf

LANDIS, Levi, Pvt, Col Wm Metcalf, Capt Wm Sitton, Mil Inf; promoted from Pvt to 6 Cpl

LANDLING, William, Pvt, Col Wm Metcalf, Capt Barbee Collins, Mil Inf

LANDRITH, Thomas, Pvt, Col Wm Y Higgins, Capt Stephen Griffith, Mtd Riflemen

LANDROM, William, Pvt, Col T McCrory, Capt John Shannon, Mil Inf

LANDRUM, David, Pvt, Col Wm Johnson, Capt James Tunnell, E TN Mil; substitute for Isaac Horton

LANDRUM, Thomas, Pvt, Col John Brown, Co Commander omitted, E TN Vol Mtd Mil

LANDRUN, Thomas, Pvt, Col Wm Johnson, Capt James Stewart, E TN Drafted Mil; substitute

LANDSON, Thomas D, 4 Sgt, Col James Raulston, Capt James K Black, Inf

LANE, Abraham, Sgt, Col Thomas H Williamson, Capt Thomas Porter, Vol Mtd Gunmen

LANE, Absolom, Sgt, Col Wm Lillard, Capt John Roper, E TN Inf; transferred to Capt Berry's

LANE, Aquilla, Pvt, Col Samuel Bunch, Capt James Griffin, E TN Drafted Mil

LANE, Armstead, Pvt, Col S Copeland, Capt G W Stell, Mil Inf

LANE, Benjamin, Pvt, Col Wm Lillard, Capt Thomas Sharpe, 2nd Regt Inf; deserted 10-26-1813

LANE, Bennett, Pvt, Col James Raulston, Capt Henry West, Inf

LANE, Daniel, M, Pvt, Col Thomas H Williamson, Capt Wm Metcalf, Vol Mtd Gunmen

LANE, David, Pvt, Col R H Dyer, Capt Bethel Allen, Vol Mtd Gunmen

LANE, Dedmon, Pvt, Col Wm Johnson, Capt Elihu Milliken, 3 Regt E TN Mil; substitute for Peter King

LANE, Equilla, Pvt, Col Samuel Bunch, Capt Francis Berry, E TN Mil; attached to Capt Houk Co

LANE, George, Pvt, Col Samuel Bunch, Capt Wm Houston, E TN Vol Mtd Inf

LANE, Hardy, 3 Cpl, Col Thomas H Benton, Capt Benj Hewitt, Vol Inf

LANE, James, Pvt, Col Phillip Pipkin, Capt Mackey, Mil Inf

LANE, James, Pvt, Regt Commander omitted, Capt Samuel Richardson, E TN Drafted Mil

LANE, John, 2 Sgt, Col William Hall, Capt John Wallace, Inf

LANE, John, Cpl, Col Ewen Allison, Capt Jacob Hoyal, E TN Mil; deserted 5-4-1814

LANE, John, Pvt, Col Robt Jarmon, Capt Nathan Peoples, Inf

LANE, John, Pvt, Col Samuel Bayless, Capt Branch Jones, E TN Drafted Mil

## Enlisted Men, War of 1812

LANE, John, Pvt, Col Samuel Bayless, Capt Jas Churchman, E TN Mil
LANE, John, Pvt, Col Samuel Bunch, Capt S Richardson, E TN Drafted Mil
LANE, John, Pvt, Col Wm Johnson, Capt Christopher Cook, E TN Mil
LANE, Lewis, 3 Sgt, Col Edward Bradley, Capt John Wallace, Vol Inf
LANE, Lewis, 3 Sgt, Col William Hall, Capt John Wallace, Inf
LANE, Lewis, Pvt, Col John K Wynne, Capt John Wallace, Inf
LANE, Marlin, Pvt, Regt Commander omitted, Capt Nathan Forrest, Mtd Riflemen
LANE, Martin, Pvt, Regt Commander omitted, Capt Nathan Forrest, Mtd Riflemen
LANE, Middleton, Pvt, Col Wm Johnson, Capt Jas R Rogers, E TN Drafted Mil; substitute
LANE, Newel, Pvt, Col Philip Pipkin, Capt Ebenezer Kirkpatrick, Mil Inf
LANE, Quiller, Pvt, Col Samuel Bunch, Capt John English, E TN Drafted Mil; joined from Capt Duncan's Co
LANE, Ransom, Pvt, Col Alex Hill, Capt John Cunningham & Capt Alex Hill, Mil Inf
LANE, Robert, Pvt, Col John K Wynne, Capt John Spinks, Inf
LANE, Samuel, Pvt, Col Edwin E Booth, Capt Porter, Drafted Mil
LANE, Samuel, Pvt, Col Samuel Bayless, Capt Jos B Bacon, E TN Mil
LANE, Samuel, Sgt, Col Wm Lillard, Capt Wm McLin, E TN Inf
LANE, Tedince, Pvt, Col Wm Metcalf, Capt Alex Hill & Capt John Cunningham, Mil Inf; promoted to QM
LANE, Thomas, Pvt, Col John Cocke, Capt Geo Barnes, Inf
LANE, Thomas, Pvt, Col John Cocke, Capt James Gault, Inf
LANE, Thomas, Pvt, Col John K Wynne, Capt John Spinks, Inf
LANE, Thomas, Pvt, Col R C Napier, Capt Thos Gray, Mil Inf
LANE, Thomas, Pvt, Col Samuel Bunch, Capt F Register, E TN Mil
LANE, Thomas, Pvt, Col Wm Lillard, Capt Jacob Dyke, Vol Inf; deserted
LANE, Thomas, Pvt, Regt Commander omitted, Capt Nathan Farmer, Mtd Riflemen
LANE, Tidance, Pvt, Col Wm Lillard, Capt Zach Copeland, E TN Vol Inf
LANE, Tidence, Pvt, Col Samuel Bayless, Capt Jas Churchman, E TN Mil
LANE, Tidence, QM, Col Wm Metcalf, 1st Regt W TN Mil Inf
LANE, William H, Pvt, Col A Lowry, Capt Geo Sarver, Inf
LANE, William, Pvt, Col Edward Bradley, Capt Abraham Bledsoe, Riflemen; wounded & furloughed
LANE, William, Pvt, Col John Cocke, Capt James Gault, Inf
LANE, William, Pvt, Col S Copeland, Capt G W Stell, Mil Inf
LANE, William, Pvt, Col William Hall, Capt Abraham Bledsoe, Vol Inf
LANE, William, Pvt, Col Wm Lillard, Capt John Neatherton, E TN Vol Inf
LANE, Williston, Pvt, Col Wm Y Higgins, Capt Wm Doake, Mtd Riflemen
LANE, Wyatt, Pvt, Col Wm Y Higgins, Capt Thos Eldridge, Mtd Gunmen
LANEY, William, Cpl, Maj Wm Russell, Capt John Trimble, Vol Mtd Gunmen
LANGDON, Jonathan, Pvt, Maj John Childs, Capt Daniel Price, E TN Vol Mtd Inf
LANGFORD, Arthur, Pvt, Col Thos Williamson, Capt Anthony Metcalf, Vol Mtd Gunmen
LANGFORD, Henry, Pvt, Col Thos Benton, Capt Isaac Renshaw, Vol Inf
LANGFORD, Henry, Pvt, Col Wm Metcalf, Capt John Barnhart, Mil Inf
LANGFORD, James, Pvt, Regt Commander omitted, Capt John Gordon, Mtd Spies
LANGFORD, Jesse, Pvt, Col Phillip Pipkin, Capt Jas Blakemroe, Mil Inf
LANGFORD, John, Pvt, Col Wm Metcalf, Capt Bird L Hurt, Mil Inf
LANGFORD, Thomas, Pvt, Col Wm Lillard, Capt Geo Argenbright, E TN Vol Riflemen
LANGFORD, William, Pvt, Col Edward Bradley, Capt Brice Martin, Vol Inf
LANGFORD, William, Pvt, Col William Hall, Capt Brice Martin, Vol Inf
LANGLEY, Jonathan, Ffr, Col Wm Johnson, Capt Andrew Lawson, E TN Drafted Mil
LANGLEY, William, Pvt, Regt Commander omitted, Capt Jas Haggard, Mtd Gunmen
LANGSTON, John, Pvt, Col Wm Johnson, Capt Elihu Milliken, 3rd Regt E TN Mil
LANGSTON, Mathew, Pvt, Col Thos Williamson, Capt John Hutchings, Vol Mtd Gunmen
LANGSTON, Obidiah, Pvt, Col Thomas Williamson, Capt John Doak & Capt John Dibbins, Vol Mtd Gunmen; d 12-1-1814
LANGSTON, Zarwbobals, Pvt, Col William Johnson, Capt Elihu Milliken, 3rd Regt E TN Mil
LANING, Isaac, Pvt, Col Edwin Booth, Capt Porter, Drafted Mil
LANKFORD, Benjamin, Pvt, Col John Brown, Capt William White, E TN Vol Mtd Inf
LANKFORD, Berry, Pvt, Col Thos Benton, Capt Wm J Smith, Vol Inf
LANKFORD, James, Pvt, Lt Col L Hammonds, Capt James Craig, Inf
LANKFORD, Jesse, Pvt, Col John Cocke, Capt John Dalton, Inf
LANKFORD, John M, Pvt, Col R C Napier, Capt Andrew McCarty, Mil Inf
LANKFORD, Joseph, Pvt, Col S Copeland, Capt John Dawson, Inf
LANKFORD, William, Pvt, Col S Copeland, Capt A Provine, Mil Inf

## Enlisted Men, War of 1812

LANKSON, John, Pvt, Col N Cannon, Capt Yardley, Mtd Riflemen

LANNUM, Pleasant, Pvt, Col Wm Metcalf, Capt J Cunningham & Capt A Hill, Mil Inf

LANNUM, Tillman, Pvt, Col A Loury, Capt Jas Kincaid, Inf

LANSDEL, Abner, Pvt, Col N T Perkins, Capt J B Quarles, Vol Mtd Inf

LANSDON, Eli M, Cpl, Col N T Perkins, Capt J B Quarles, Vol Mtd Inf

LANSFORD, Samuel, Pvt, Col Thos Williamson, Capt John Crane & Capt Jas Cook, Vol Mtd Gunmen

LANSON, Thomas D, 4 Sgt, Col James Raulston, Capt James A Black, Inf

LANTSFORD, Berry, Pvt, Col Thos Benton, Capt Wm Smith, Vol Inf

LANTSFORD, Eton, Pvt, Col Thos Benton, Capt Wm Smith, Vol Inf

LANUM, Pleasant, Pvt, Col Wm Metcalf, Capt Wm Mullin, Mil Inf; never served

LARAINE, George, Pvt, Regt Commander omitted, Capt Wm Henderson, Spies

LARD, Alexander, Cpl, Col A Cheatham, Capt Wm Creel, Inf; transferred to the Arty

LARD, Samuel, Pvt, Col Alex Loury & Col Leroy Hammonds, Capt Arahel Rains, Inf

LARE, Jacob, Pvt, Col John Wynne, Capt John Porter, Inf

LAREN, Francis, 4 Cpl, Col Edwin Booth, Capt John Sharp, E TN Mil

LAREW, Benjamin, Pvt, Maj Jas Porter, Capt Jas Anderson, Branch Srvce omitted

LAREW, William Cpl, Col Wm Johnston, Capt Jas Tunnell, E TN Mil

LAREW, William, Pvt, Col Jno Brown, Capt Hugh Barton, E TN Mil Inf

LARGE, John, Pvt, Col Samuel Bayless, Capt Jos D Bacon, E TN Mil

LARGE, John, Pvt, Col Samuel Bunch, Capt Francis Berry, E TN Mil

LARGE, Thomas, Pvt, Col Samuel Bunch, Capt Francis Berry, E Tn Mil

LARGE, William, Pvt, Col Samuel Bayless, Capt Jas Churchman, E TN Mil

LARGENT, William, Pvt, Regt Commander omitted, Capt Gray, Inf

LARKEN, Robert, Pvt, Lt Col Richard Napier, Lt Col Richard Napier, Co Commander omitted, Inf

LARKIN, David, Pvt, Regt Commander omitted, Capt Jas Cowan, Mtd Inf

LARKIN, Henry S, Pvt, Col Wm Lillard, Capt Geo Argenbright, E TN Vol Riflemen

LARKIN, John, Pvt, Maj John Childs, Capt Jas Cummings, E Tn Vol Mtd Inf; Regt from Hawkins Co

LARKIN, Joseph, Pvt, Col A Cheatam, Capt Geo G Chapman, Inf

LARKIN, Joseph, Pvt, Col John Coffee, Capt M Molton, Cav

LARKIN, William, 3 Sgt, Col Wm Pillow, Capt Geo Caperton, Inf

LARKIN, William, Pvt, Col Samuel Bunch, Capt Jas Cummings, E TN Vol Mtd Inf

LARKIN, William, Pvt, Col Samuel Bunch, Capt M. Molton, Cav

LARKINS, William, 1 Cpl, Col Thos Benton, Capt Geo Caperton, Inf

LARKINS, William, 4 Sgt & Cpl, Col Thos Benton, Capt Geo Caperton, Vol Inf; in lieu of Chas Woods

LARLEY, Henry, Pvt, Regt Commander omitted, Capt Jos Williams, Mil Cav

LARNE, John, Pvt, Col Wm Lillard, Capt Hugh Martin, E TN Vol Inf

LARREMERE, John, Pvt, Col Wm Johnston, Capt Henry Hunter, E TN Mil

LARRIMORE, James, Pvt, Lt I Barrett, Capt Nathan Davis, Inf

LARRIMORE, John, Pvt, Lt I Barrett, Capt Nathan Davis, Inf

LARUE, George, Pvt, Col Samuel Bunch, Capt Joseph Duncan, E TN Drafted Mil; joined from Capt Yarnell's Co

LARUE, Isaac, Pvt, Col Thos Williamson, Capt John Doak & Capt John Dobbins, Vol Mtd Gunmen

LARUE, John, Pvt, Col Thos Williamson, Capt John Doak & Capt John Dobbins, Vol Mtd Gunmen

LASATER, Cannon, Pvt, Col S Copeland, Capt Moses Thompson, Inf

LASATER, Jacob, Pvt, Col S Copeland, Capt M Thompson, Inf

LASATER, James, Pvt, Col John Coffee, Capt Jas Terrill, Vol Cav

LASETER, James, Pvt, Col Jno Coffee, Capt Jas Terrill, Vol Cav

LASETER, John, Pvt, Regt Commander omitted, Capt Smith, Vol Inf

LASHLEY, Hugh, Pvt, Lt Col Leroy Hammond, Capt Jas Craig, Inf

LASIETER, Fred K, Pvt, Col Wm Hall, Capt Brice Martin, Vol Inf

LASITER, Abner, Pvt, Col Wm Pillow, Capt Geo Caperton, Inf

LASITER, Atener, Pvt, Col Thos Benton, Capt Geo Caperton, Inf

LASITER, Frederick, Pvt, Col Wm Hall, Capt Brice Martin, Vol Inf; refused to march

LASLEY, Jesse, Pvt, Col Samuel Bunch, Capt D G Vance, E TN Mtd Inf

LASSITER, Abner, Pvt, Col Thos Benton, Capt Geo Caperton, Vol Inf

LASSITER, Frederick, Pvt, Col Edward Bradley, Capt Brice Martin, Vol Inf

LASSITER, Johnny (John), Pvt, Col Edwin Booth, Capt Vernon, E TN Mil; deserted 12-25-1814

LASSLEY, Archibald, Pvt, Col R C Napier, Capt Thos Preston, Mil Inf

LATEM, William, Pvt, Capt Nathan Davis, Lt I Barrett, Inf

LATEN, Michael, Pvt, Regt Commander omitted, Capt Archibald McKenney, Cav

LATHAM, Charles, Pvt, Col Wm Johnson, Capt E Milliken, 3rd Regt E TN Mil

LATHAM, George, Pvt, Col Wm Johnston, Capt Jas Tunnell, E TN Mil

## Enlisted Men, War of 1812

LATHAM, Joseph, Pvt, Col N T Perkins, Capt M Johnson, Mil Inf
LATHAM, William, Pvt, Col John Cocke, Capt John Dalton, Inf
LATHAM, William, Pvt, Col N T Perkins, Capt M Johnson, Mil Inf
LATIMER, Edmond, Pvt, Col Robt Moore, Capt Thomas Williamson, Vol Mtd Gunmen
LATIMER, Nathaniel, Pvt, Col A Cheatham, Capt Chapman, Inf
LATIMORE, Hugh, Pvt, Col John Coffee, Capt John Baskerville, Cav
LATIMORE, Jonathan C (John), Pvt, Col Jno Coffee, Capt Henry Bryan, Cav
LATIMORE, Jonathan C, Pvt, Col John Alcorn, Capt Geo Bryan, Cav
LATIMORE, Nicholas, Pvt, Col Jno Coffee, Capt Geo Bryan, Cav
LATIMORE, Nicholas, Pvt, Col John Alcorn, Capt Geo Bryan, Cav
LATTA, John, Pvt, no other information
LATTA, Thomas, Pvt, Col Thomas Williamson, Capt Robt Moore, Inf
LATTEN, James, Pvt, Maj Gen Carroll, Capt Jackson, Capt A Metcalf, Inf
LATTEN, Thomas, Pvt, Maj Gen Carroll, Capt Jackson, Capt A Metcalf, Inf
LATTER, John, Pvt, Col Robert Steele, Capt Jas Raulston, Inf
LATTURE, Christopher, Pvt, Col William Lillard, Capt George Keys, E TN Inf
LAUDERDALE, D, Far, Col N T Perkins, Capt Geo Elliott, Mil Inf
LAUDERDALE, George, Rank omitted, Col S Wear, Capt S Bowman, Mtd Inf
LAUDERDALE, John, Pvt, Col Wm Lillard, Capt Robert McCalpin, E TN Inf
LAUDERDALE, William, Pvt, Col Robert Dyer, Capt Thomas Jones, Vol Mtd Gunmen; promoted to Sgt Maj
LAUDERDALE, William, Sgt Maj, Col Robt H Dyer, TN Vol Mtd Gunmen; transferred to QM the day of mustering into service
LAUDERMILK, John, Pvt, Col S Bayless, Capt Joseph Goodson, E TN Mil
LAUDERMILK, Solomon, Pvt, Col S Wear, Capt S Bowman, Mtd Inf
LAUGHLEN, Steth H, Pvt, Col William Lillard, Capt Jacob Hartsell, E TN Vol Inf; transferred to W TN
LAUGHLIN, Christopher, Pvt, Col Ewen Allison, Capt Jacob Hayal, E TN Mil
LAUGHNER, John, Pvt, Col Ewen Allison, Capt Jacob Hoyal, E TN Mil; transferred to Capt Register
LAUGHORN, Henry, Pvt, Maj Gen Carroll, Capt Hamilton, Inf
LAUGHRIDGE, Abraham, Pvt, Col William Hall, Capt John Moore, Vol Inf; substitute for Maj Barbee
LAULLETER, John, Pvt, Col S Bunch, Capt Jno English, E TN Drafted Mil
LAUN, Isaac, Pvt, Col N T Perkins, Capt Quarles, Vol Mtd Inf
LAUN, Joseph, Pvt, Col N T Perkins, Capt Quarles, Vol Mtd Inf
LAUNDERS, Thomas, Sgt, no other information
LAURANCE, Alexander, Inf, Col William Pillow, Capt Isaiah Renshaw, Branch Srvce omitted
LAURENCE, Alexander, Pvt, Regt Commander omitted, Capt Isaiah Renshaw, Vol Inf
LAURENCE, Jeremiah, Pvt, Col S Bunch, Capt Jas Berry, E TN Mil; attached to Capt English Co
LAVENDER, Nicholas, Pvt, Lt Col Alexander Loury, Capt Thomas Wells, Inf
LAVENDER, William A, Pvt, Col John Cocke, Capt John Dalton, Inf; d 12-15-1814
LAVENDER, William, Pvt, Col Phillip Pipkin, Capt William MacKay, Mil Inf
LAW, Henry, Pvt, Col Jas Raulston, Capt Mathew Neal, Inf
LAW, James, Pvt, Col Wm Johnston, Capt Joseph Kirk, Mil
LAW, Jesse, Pvt, Col S Copeland, Capt Allen Wilkinson, Mil Inf; wounded at battle of Tehopea 3-27-1814
LAW, John, Pvt, Col Samuel Bunch, Capt Joseph Duncan, E TN Drafted Mil; joined from Capt Buckhanon's Co
LAW, John, Pvt, Col Wm Lillard, Capt Benjamin H King, E TN Vol Inf
LAW, John, Pvt, Col Wm Lillard, Capt Thomas Sharpe, 2nd Regt Inf
LAW, Joshua, Pvt, Col William Johnson, Capt Christopher Cooks, E TN Mil; d 11-1-1814
LAWDER (LOWDER), Lewis, Pvt, Col John Cocke, Capt Richard Crunk, Inf
LAWDERMILK, Solomon, Pvt, Col S Bunch, Capt Joseph Duncan, E TN Drafted Mil; joined from Capt McNare's Co
LAWERY, James S, Mus, Col Thos H Benton, Capt George Gibbs, Vol Inf
LAWHORN, John, Pvt, Col John K Wynn, Capt William McCall, Inf
LAWRENCE, Beverage, Pvt, Col S Bunch, Capt Joseph Duncan, E TN Drafted Mil
LAWRENCE, Charles, Pvt, Col Lowry, Capt Geo Sarver, Inf; d 2-20-1815
LAWRENCE, George, Pvt, Col John Brown, Capt William White, E TN Mil Inf
LAWRENCE, John, 1 Cpl, Col Jno Coffee, Capt Robert Jetton, Cav
LAWRENCE, John, Pvt, Col Ewen Alcorn, Capt Henry Bryan, Cav
LAWRENCE, John, Pvt, Col Jno Coffee, Capt Henry Bryan, Cav
LAWRENCE, John, Pvt, Col Phillip Pipkin, Capt Peter Searcy, Mil Inf
LAWRENCE, John, Pvt, Col Robt H Dyer, Capt James McMahon, 1 TN Vol Mtd Gunmen
LAWRENCE, John, Pvt, Col S Bunch, Capt Jno English, Branch omitted; joined for Capt Berry's Co
LAWRENCE, John, Pvt, Maj Wm Woodfolk, Capt Ross & Capt McCully, Inf
LAWRENCE, John, Sgt, Col S Bunch, Capt Francis Berry, E TN Mil; attached to Capt English Co

## Enlisted Men, War of 1812

LAWRENCE, Joseph B, 3 Cpl, Col Phillip Pipkin, Capt Gen Mebane, Mil Inf

LAWRENCE, Lemmel, Pvt, Col Phillip Pipkin, Capt Peter Searcy, Mil Inf

LAWRENCE, Lemuel, Pvt, Col Philip Pipkin, Capt William Mackay, Mil Inf

LAWRENCE, Levi, Pvt, Maj Gen Carroll, Col James Raulston, Capt Elijah Haynie, Inf; died 1-6-1815

LAWRENCE, Pharis, Pvt, Col James Raulston, Capt Robertson & Capt Carroll, Inf

LAWRENCE, Robert, Pvt, Col Thomas Williamson, Capt Thomas Scurry, Vol Mtd Gunmen

LAWRENCE, Samuel, Pvt, Col John Alcorn, Capt John W Byrns, Cav

LAWRENCE, Samuel, Pvt, Col John Coffee, Co Commander omitted, Cav

LAWRENCE, Samuel, Pvt, Col Robert H Dyer, Capt William McMahon, 1 TN Vol Mtd Gunmen

LAWRENCE, William, Cpl, Regt Commander omitted, Capt Larkin Ferrell, Inf

LAWRENCE, William, Pvt, Col John K Wynn, Capt John Spinks, Inf

LAWRENCE, William, Pvt, Col S Bunch, Capt Francis Berry, E TN Mil; attached to Capt English Co later

LAWS, Aaron, Pvt, Col Newton Cannon, Capt David Hogan, Mtd Gunmen

LAWS, Aaron, Sgt, Col Thos H Dyer, Capt Cuthbert Hudson, Vol Mtd Gunmen; died 2-2-1815

LAWSON, Andrew Z, Pvt, Col Thos Williamson, Capt John Doak & Capt John Dobbins, Vol Mtd Gunmen

LAWSON, Clement, Pvt, Col S Bunch, Capt Jones Griffin, E TN Draft Mil; deserted

LAWSON, David, Pvt, Col Edwin Booth, Capt Richard Marshall, Draft Mil

LAWSON, Elisha, Pvt, Col Edwin Booth, Capt John Sharpe, E TN Mil

LAWSON, Elisha, Pvt, Col Wm Lillard, Capt Wm Gillenwater, E TN Inf

LAWSON, Jacob, Pvt, Col Wm Lillard, Capt Wm GIllenwater, E TN Inf

LAWSON, James, Pvt, Col Newton Cannon, Capt John Henley, Mtd Riflemen

LAWSON, John, Cpl, Col John K Wynn, Capt James Cole, Inf; wounded 11-12-1813

LAWSON, John, Pvt, Col S Bunch, Capt Jones Griffin, E TN Draft Mil

LAWSON, Joshua, Pvt, Col Edwin Booth, Capt John McKeme, E TN Mil

LAWSON, Lemuel, Pvt, Col Wm Johnson, Capt Benjamin Powell, E TN Mil

LAWSON, Morman, Cpl, Col Wm Johnson, Capt James R Rogers, E TN Drafted Mil

LAWSON, Nathan, Pvt, Col Wm Lillard, Capt Wm Hamilton, E TN Vol Inf

LAWSON, Robert, Artif, Col Jno Brown, Capt Jas Christian, E TN Mil Inf

LAWSON, Thomas, Pvt, Col Robert Steele, Capt James Randals, Inf

LAWTHER, William, Pvt, Brig Gen Thos Johnson, Capt Abraham Allen, Mil Inf

LAWYER, James, Agent, Lt Col Archer Cheatham, no Co Commander, Mtd Inf

LAX, Abraham, Pvt, Col S Copeland, Capt John Holshouser, Inf

LAX, John, 1 Sgt, Col R C Napier, Capt Early Benson, Mil Inf; apptd Ord Sgt from 1 Sgt

LAX, John, 1 Sgt, Col Wm Metcalf, Capt Thomas Marks, Mil Inf; promoted to Ens

LAX, Solomon, Pvt, Col Samuel Bayless, Capt Branch Jones, E TN Draft Mil

LAXON, John, Pvt, Col Thos Benton, Capt Wm J Smith, Vol Inf

LAXTON, Thomas, Pvt, Col Wm Johnson, Capt James Tunnell, E TN Mil

LAY, Bartley, Pvt, Col Edwin Booth, Capt John Slatton, E Tn Mil

LAY, David, Pvt, Capt Ebenezer Kirkpatrick, Mil Inf; deserted

LAY, James, Cpl, Col William Y Higgins, Capt James Hambleton, Mtd Gunmen

LAY, William, Pvt, Col S Bunch, Capt Jno English, E TN Draft Mil

LAYDON, George, Pvt, Col Wm Pillow, Capt Isiah Renshaw, Inf

LAYGAW (LAGAW), Rich, Pvt, Col Ewen Allison, Capt Jacob Hoyal, E Tn Mil

LAYMAN, Amanuel, Pvt, Col Samuel Bayless, Capt Jonathan Waddle, E TN Mil

LAYMAN, Joseph, Pvt, Col Samuel Bayless, Capt Jonathan Waddle, E TN Mil

LAYMASTER, Jno M, Pvt, Col Thos McCrory, Capt Wm Dooley, Inf

LAYNE, William, Pvt, Col Wm Hall, Capt Abraham Bledsoe, Vol Inf

LAYTON, Joshua, Pvt, Col Philip Pipkin, Capt Henry M Newlin, Mil Inf

LEA, Thomas, Pvt, Col John Williams, Capt David Vance, Mtd Mil

LEA, William, Pvt, Col Wm Pillow, Capt Isaiah Renshaw, Inf

LEACH, Asa, Cpl, Col Alexander Loury, Capt Gabriel Martin, Inf; discharged for inability

LEACH, Asbel, Pvt, Col A Cheatham, Capt George G Chapman, Inf

LEACH, George, Pvt, Col Jas Raulston, Capt Mathew Cowan, Inf; d 2-15-1815

LEACH, Henry, Pvt, Col John Coffee, Capt Fred Stump, Cav

LEACH, James, Pvt, Col S Copeland, Capt J Holshouser, Inf

LEACH, James, Pvt, Col Samuel Bunch, Capt Andrew Breden, E TN Mil; transferred to Capt Bacon Co

LEACH, James, Pvt, Col Thos Benton, Capt Wm Moore, Vol Inf

LEACH, James, Sgt, Col Thos Williamson, Capt Beverly Williams, Vol Mtd Gunmen

LEACH, John, 1 Cpl, Maj Wm Russell, Capt Mackie, Vol Mtd Gunmen

LEACH, John, Pvt, Col Samuel Bunch, Capt Andrew Breden, E TN Mil; transferred to Capt J Berry

LEACH, John, Pvt, Col Thos Williamson, Capt Geo

## Enlisted Men, War of 1812

Mitchie, 2nd Regt TN Vol Mtd Gunmen

LEACH, Joshua, Cpl, Col S Copeland, Capt John Holshouser, Inf

LEACH, Josiah, Dmr, Col A Loury, Capt Martin, Inf; appointed Wgnr

LEACH, William, Ffr, Col A Cheatham, Capt Geo G Chapman, Inf

LEADBETTER, George, Pvt, Col John Brown, Capt Charles Lewin, E TN Vol Mtd Inf

LEAGUE, Samuel, Pvt, Col Wm Johnson, Capt Elihu Milliken, 3rd Regt E TN Mil; substitute for Hail

LEAK, William, Pvt, Col Wm Johnson, Capt Jas Stewart, E TN Drafted Mil

LEAKS, Elias, Pvt, Col A Lowry, Capt A Rains, Inf

LEAKY, Henry, Pvt, Col Ewen Allison, Capt Jacob Hoyal, E TN Mil; transferred to Capt McPherson

LEAKY, Jeremiah, Pvt, Maj Wm Russell, Capt Geo Mitchie, Vol Mtd Gunmen

LEAKY, Joshua, Pvt, Col N T Perkins, Capt J B Quarles, Vol Mtd Inf

LEAMON, Green, Pvt, Regt Commander omitted, Capt Wm Henderson, Spies

LEAMON, Henry, Pvt, Regt Commander omitted, Capt Wm Henderson, Spies

LEATH, George, Pvt, Col John Williams, Capt Sam Bunch, Mtd Vol

LEATH, James, Pvt, Col John Williams, Capt Sam Bunch, Mtd Vol

LEATHERDALE, David, Pvt, Col Samuel Wear, Capt Jas Gillespie, E TN Vol Inf

LEATHERDALE, John, Sgt, Lt Col L Hammond, Capt Jas Craig, Inf

LEATHERDALE, Robert, Pvt, Col John Brown, Capt Jas Preston, E TN Mil Inf

LEATHERDALE, Robert, Pvt, Col John Brown, Capt John Trimble, E TN Mtd Gunmen

LEATHERDALE, William, Pvt, Col John Brown, Capt Jas Preston, E TN Mil Inf

LEATHERS, William, Pvt, Brig Gen Thos Johnson, Capt Robt Carson, Inf

LEATHERWOOD, Thomas, Pvt, Col Thos Benton, Capt Lewen, E TN Vol Mtd Inf

LEATLE, George, Pvt, Col John Williams, Capt Samuel Bunch, Mtd Vol

LEAVEN, L Ball, Pvt, Col Samuel Bunch, Capt Wm Jobe, E TN Vol Mtd Inf

LEBO, Daniel, Pvt, Col Samuel Bunch, Capt Sol Dobkins, E TN Mil; deserted 3-4-1814

LEBOW, Daniel, Pvt, Col Samuel Bunch, Capt John Houk, E TN Mil; joined from Capt Dobkins Co

LEBOW, Isaac, Pvt, Col Wm Lillard, Capt Thos Sharpe, 2nd Regt Inf

LEBOW, Joseph, Pvt, Col Samuel Bunch, Capt Jas Cumming, E TN Vol Mtd Inf

LECE, John, Pvt, Col John Cocke, Capt James Gray, Inf

LEDBETTER, Ephraim, Pvt, Col Wm Metcalf, Capt Wm Sitton, Mil Inf

LEDBETTER, George W, Pvt, Col Wm Pillow, Capt John H Anderson, Vol Inf

LEDBETTER, James, Pvt, Col A Loury, Lt Col L Hammond, Capt Thos Delaney, Inf

LEDBETTER, John, Pvt, Col Edward Bradley, Capt John Kennedy, Riflemen; AWOL 12-12-1813

LEDBETTER, John, Pvt, Col Philip Pipkin, Capt John Robertson, Mil Inf

LEDBETTER, Merrell, Blksmth, Maj Wm Russell, Capt Wm Russell, Vol Mtd Gunmen

LEDBETTER, Milerton, Sgt, Col R H Dyer, Maj Wm Russell, Capt Wm Russell, Mtd Gunmen

LEDBETTER, Millinton, Pvt, Maj Wm Russell, Capt Wm Russell, Vol Mtd Gunmen

LEDBETTER, Washington, Pvt, Col Philip Pipkin, Capt Eb Kirkpatrick, Mil Inf

LEDBETTER, Western, Pvt, Col John K Wynne, Capt John Porter, Inf

LEDFORD, William, Pvt, Regt Commander omitted, Capt John Crane, Mtd Inf

LEDGER (LEGER), Peter, Pvt, Col Samuel Bayless, Capt Jos B Bacon, E TN Mil

LEDGERWOOD, James, Pvt, Col Samuel Bayless, Capt Joseph Hale, E TN Mil

LEDGERWOOD, Samuel, Pvt, Col Edwin Booth, Capt John Sharpe, E TN Mil

LEE, Benjamin, Pvt, Col Philip Pipkin, Capt Eb Kirkpatrick, Mil Inf

LEE, C, Pvt, Col Thos Benton, Capt Geo Caperton, Inf

LEE, Cador, Pvt, Col Thos Benton, Capt Geo Caperton, Vol Inf; substituted for Russell Bean

LEE, Curry, Pvt, Col Jas Raulston, Capt Jas West, Inf

LEE, David, Pvt, Col John Brown, Capt Wm D Neilson, E TN Vol Mil

LEE, Edward J, Pvt, Col Thos McCrory, Capt Thos Gordon, Inf; deserted 11-18-1813?

LEE, Ephraim, Pvt, Col Philip Pipkin, Capt David Smith, Inf

LEE, Ephraim, Pvt, Col Philip Pipkin, Capt Wm Mackay, Mil Inf

LEE, Gardner, Cpl, Col Samuel Bunch, Capt Daniel Yarnell, E TN Mil

LEE, Gashom, Pvt, Col R C Napier, Capt Drury Adkins, Mil Inf

LEE, George, Pvt, Col John Cocke, Capt James Gray, Inf

LEE, Gorsham, Pvt, Col Robt Steele, Capt Samuel Maxwell, Mil Inf; transferred 3-14-1814

LEE, Guy, 2 Cpl, Col Jas Raulston, Capt Robinson, Inf

LEE, Henry T, Cpl, Col R H Dyer, Capt James White, Vol Mtd Gunmen

LEE, Henry, Pvt, Maj Wm Woodfolk, Capt James Turner, Inf

LEE, Herbert, Pvt, Col Robt M Dyer, Capt Robt Evans, Vol Mtd Gunmen

LEE, Herbert, Pvt, Maj Gen A Jackson, Capt Joe Parrish, Arty

LEE, Hert J, Pvt, Col A Cheatham, Capt James Giddins, Inf; transferred to the Arty

LEE, Hiram, Pvt, Col Samuel Bayless, Capt Branch Jones, E TN Drafted Mil

LEE, Isaac, Pvt, Regt Commander omitted, Capt Archibald McKinney, Cav

LEE, James, Pvt, Regt Commander omitted, Capt Elijah Rushing, Det of Inf

LEE, James, Pvt, Regt Commander omitted, Capt Jno

Miller, Spies
LEE, Jesse, Pvt, Maj Wm Woodfolk, Capt James C Neil, Inf
LEE, Jesse, Pvt, Maj Wm Woodfolk, Capt James Turner, Inf
LEE, Jesse, Pvt, Maj Wm Woodfolk, Capt John Sutton & Capt A Dudney, Inf; appointed Hospital Stewart
LEE, John, 1 Sgt, Gen Andrew Jackson, Capt Wm Russell, Mtd Spies
LEE, John, Pvt, Col A Cheatham, Capt Richard Benson, Inf
LEE, John, Pvt, Col Philip Pipkin, Capt John Robertson, Mil Inf
LEE, John, Pvt, Col R C Napier, Capt Drury Adkins, Mil Inf
LEE, John, Pvt, Col R H Dyer, Capt James Wyatt, Vol Mtd Gunmen; d 1-29-1815
LEE, John, Pvt, Col S Copeland, Capt David Williams, Inf
LEE, John, Pvt, Col T McCrory, Capt Abel Willis, Mil Inf
LEE, John, Pvt, Maj Wm Woodfolk, Capt John Sutton, Capt Abraham Dudney, Inf
LEE, John, Pvt, Regt Commander omitted, Capt Gray, Inf
LEE, Joseph, Pvt, Maj Gen Wm Carroll, Col James Raulston, Capt Wiley Huddleston, Inf
LEE, Joshua, Cpl, Maj Gen A Jackson, Col Thos Williamson, Capt Robert Steele, Vol Mtd Gunmen; promoted from Pvt
LEE, Joshua, Pvt, Col John K Wynne, Capt John Porter, Inf
LEE, Levi, 5 Sgt, Col James Raulston, Capt Henry West, Mil Inf
LEE, Levi, Pvt, Col Robert Steele, Capt James Bennett, Mil Inf; transferred to the Arty
LEE, Levi, Pvt, Maj Gen A Jackson, Col A Cheatham, Capt Wm Creel, Inf
LEE, Lewis H, Pvt, Col R H Dyer, Capt James White, Vol Mtd Gunmen
LEE, Lewis H, Tptr, Col R H Dyer, Capt James White, Vol Mtd Gunmen; d 1-30-1815
LEE, Loyd, Pvt, Col R C Napier, Capt Thomas Gray, Mil Inf
LEE, Loyd, Pvt, Regt Commander omitted, Capt Elijah Rushing, Det of Inf
LEE, Robert, Pvt, Col John K Wynne, Capt James Holleman, Inf
LEE, Robert, Pvt, Regt Commander omitted, Capt Elijah Rushing, Det of Inf
LEE, Samuel, Pvt, Col Ewen Allison, Capt Jonas Loughmiller, Mil; joined from Capt Griffin, transferred to McPherson
LEE, Samuel, Sgt, Col S Bunch, Capt Jones Griffin, E TN Drafted Mil
LEE, Samuel, Sgt, Col Samuel Bunch, Capt Geo McPherson, E TN Mil; joined from Capt Griffin's Co
LEE, Simpson, Pvt, Maj Gen A Jackson, Capt Hugh Kerr, Mtd Rangers
LEE, Stephen, 2 Sgt, Col Samuel Bunch, Capt William Jobe, E TN Vol Mtd Inf
LEE, Stephen, Pvt, Col Philip Pipkin, Capt Ebenezer Kirkpatrick, Mil Inf
LEE, Thomas D, Pvt, Col Thomas Williamson, Capt Beverly Williams, Vol Mtd Gunmen
LEE, Thomas, 1 Cpl, Maj John Childs, Capt James Cummings, E TN Vol Mtd Inf
LEE, Thomas, Pvt, Col John Cocke, Capt John Dalton, Inf
LEE, Thomas, Pvt, Col S Copeland, Capt Alexander Provine, Mil Inf
LEE, William, Pvt, Col T McCrory, Capt A Metcalf, Mil Inf
LEE, William, Pvt, Col Thomas Benton, Capt Benj Hewett, Vol Inf
LEE, William, Pvt, Col Thomas Benton, Capt Isaiah Renshaw, Vol Inf; transferred from Capt Hewett's Co
LEE, William, Pvt, Col Thomas Williamson, Capt John Dobbins & Capt John Doak, Vol Mtd Gunmen; replaced Arbin McAdam
LEE, William, Pvt, Maj John Childs, Capt James Cummings, E TN Vol Mtd Inf
LEE, William, Pvt, Regt Commander omitted, Capt Archibald McKinney, Cav
LEE (LEIGH), John W, Pvt, Maj Gen Wm Carroll, Capt Francis Ellis, Inf
LEECH, James, 4 Sgt, Col William Pillow, Capt William Moore, Inf
LEECH, James, Pvt, Col Thomas Benton, Capt William Moore, Vol Inf
LEECH, John, Cpl, Col Samuel Bunch, Capt Jno English, E TN Drafted Mil
LEECH, Joshua, Pvt, Col William Pillow, Capt William Moore, Inf
LEEK, James, 1 Sgt, Col A Loury, Capt J Williamson, W TN Mil
LEEK, James, 1 Sgt, Col L Hammond, Capt J N Williamson, 2 Regt Inf
LEEK, James, 1 Sgt, Col L Hammons, Capt Thomas Williamson, Inf
LEEK, John, Pvt, Col Edwin Booth, Capt John Sharp, E TN Mil
LEEK, Samuel, Pvt, Col William Higgins, Capt Adam Dale, Mtd Gunmen
LEEKEY, Christopher, Pvt, Col Ewen Allison, Capt Jacob Hoyal, E Tn Mil; trans to Capt Register's Co
LEEMAN, Henry, Pvt, Col R H Dyer, Capt Thomas Jones, Vol Mtd Gunmen; deserted
LEEPER, Hugh, Pvt, Col Samuel Bunch, Capt James Cumming, E Tn Vol Mtd Inf
LEEPER, John, Pvt, Col Ewin Allison, Capt Jonas Loughmiller, Mil; wounded 4-27-1814
LEEPER, William D, Tptr, Col R H Dyer, Capt Glen Owen, TN Vol Mtd Gunmen
LEETH, Ebenezer jr, Pvt, no Regt Commander, Capt Wm Henderson, Spies
LEETH, Ebenezer, Pvt, Regt Commander omitted, Capt John Roper & Capt Wm Lillard, E TN Vol Inf
LEETH, Ebenezer, Pvt, no Regt Commander, Capt Wm Henderson, Spies
LEETH, George jr, Pvt, Col Wm Lillard, Capt John Roper, E TN Vol Inf
LEETH, George sr, Pvt, Col Wm Lillard, Capt John Roper, E TN Vol Inf
LEETH, James, Pvt, Col Wm Lillard, Capt John Roper, E

## Enlisted Men, War of 1812

Tn Vol Inf

LEETH, Josiah, Col Samuel Bunch, Capt George Gregory, E TN Draft Mil; apptd waggoner

LEETLE, George, Pvt, no Regt Commander, Capt Wm Henderson, Spies

LEFEW, Joseph, Pvt, Col Samuel Bayless, Capt Joseph Rich, E Tn Inf

LEGAN, Martin, Pvt, Col Philip Pipkin, Capt James Blakemore, Mil Inf

LEGAND, Elisha, Pvt, Regt Commander omitted, Capt Jos Williams, Mil Cav

LEGATE, James, Pvt, Col A Cheatham, Capt Wm Johnson, Inf

LEGATT, James, Col Thomas Williams, Capt Wm Martin, Vol Mtd Gunmen

LEGERWOOD, James, Pvt, Col Samuel Bunch, Capt Nathan Gibbs, E Tn Draft Mil; trans to Capt Duncan's Co

LEGG, Samuel, Pvt, Col Ewin Allison, Capt Laughmiller, Mil

LEGG, Samuel, Pvt, Col Samuel Bayless, Capt Branch Jones, E TN Draft Mil

LEGG, Samuel, Pvt, Col Samuel Bunch, Capt Frances Berry, E Tn Mil; trans to Capt Griffin's Co

LEGG, Samuel, Pvt, Maj John Childs, Capt John Childs, E Tn Vol Mtd Inf

LEGG, Wesley, Pvt, Maj John Chiles, Capt Price, Vol Mtd Gunmen

LEGG, William, Pvt, Col Wm Lillard, Capt Zacheus Copeland, Branch omitted; apptd 1 Sgt

LEGGE (LEIG), Hosea, Ffr Maj, Col Wm Metcalf, no Co Commander, 1 Reg W TN Mil Inf; no svce performed

LEGGET (LEGGAT), John, Pvt, Lt Col Hammond, Capt James Craig, Inf

LEGGETT, Daniel, Pvt, Col A Loury, Capt George Sarver, Inf; died 2-28-1814

LEGON, Henry, Pvt, Col Wm Hall, Capt Wm L Alexander, Vol Inf

LEGRAND, John O, Pvt, Maj Gen Andrew Jackson, CApt Joseph Kirkpatrick, Mtd Gunmen

LEGRAND, Obediah, Pvt, Col James Raulston, Capt Elijah Haynie, Inf

LEIBER, Phillip, Cpl, Col Wm Johnson, Capt James Tunnell, E TN Mil

LEIGHTON, James, Pvt, Maj James Porter, Capt Samuel Cowan, Cav

LEIPER, Samuel, Pvt, Col Wm Hall, Capt Henry M Newlin, Inf

LEIPER, William, Pvt, no Regt Commander, Capt John Gordon, Mtd Spies

LEMANS, Henry, Pvt, Col John Coffee, Capt Larkin Terrell, Vol Cav

LEMANS, Henry, Pvt, Col N T Perkins, Capt John B Quarles, Vol Mtd Inf

LEMANS, John, Pvt, Col Philip Pipkin, Capt John Robertson, Mil Inf

LEMAR, George, Pvt, Col Edwin Booth, Capt Jno Lewis, E Tn Mil

LEMAR, William, Pvt, Col John Brown, Capt Hugh Barton, Regt E TN Mil Inf

LEMASTEN, Hugh, Pvt, Col A Cheatham, Capt Richard Benson, Inf

LEMASTER, Samuel, Pvt, Col John Cocke, Capt John Weakley, Inf

LEMLOCK, William, Pvt, Col A Loury, Capt Arahel Raines, Inf

LEMMINGS, Jesse, Pvt, Col Samuel Bunch, Capt Wm Jobe, E Tn Vol Mtd Inf

LEMMON, John, Pvt, Col Wm Lillard, Capt Wm McLin, E TN Inf

LEMMON, Orran, Pvt, Col James Raulston, Maj Gen Wm Carroll, Capt Edward Robinson, Inf

LEMMONS, John, 1 Sgt, Col Wm Hall, Capt John Moore, Vol Inf

LEMMONS, John, Pvt, Col Samuel Bayless, Capt Branch Jones, E TN Draft Mil

LEMMONS, Joshua, Pvt, Col Samuel Bayless, Capt Branch Jones, E Tn Vol Inf Drafted

LEMMONS, Levi, Pvt, Col Wm Lillard, Capt John Neatherton, E TN Vol Inf

LEMMONS, Samuel, Pvt, Col Wm Lillard, Capt John Neatherton, E TN Vol Inf

LEMMONS, Thomas, Pvt, Col Wm Johnston, Capt Joseph Kirk, Mil

LEMMONS, William, Pvt, Col R H Dyer, Capt Ephram Dickson, TN Vol Mtd Gunmen

LEMMONS, William, Pvt, Col Wm Johnson, Capt Henry Hunter, E TN Mil

LEMON, Henry, Pvt, Col John Coffee, Capt James Terrell, Vol Cav

LEMONS, Charles, Pvt, Col John Brown, Capt Charles Lewin, E Tn Vol Mtd Inf

LEMONS, M Samuel, Pvt, Col Edwin Booth, Capt omitted, E Tn Mil

LEMONS, Thomas, Pvt, Col Samuel Bayless, Capt Jesse Landen, E TN Mil

LEMONS, William sr, Sdlr, Col R H Dyer, Capt Ephraim Dickson, Tn Vol Mtd Gunmen; killed in battle 12-23-1814

LEMONS, William, Pvt, Col Newton Cannon, Capt John B Densey, Mtd Gunmen

LEMUEL, _____, Pvt, no other information

LENARD, George, Pvt, Regt Commander omitted, Capt Edwin S Moore, Mtd Riflemen

LENARD, Robert, Pvt, Regt Commander omitted, Capt Edwin S Moore, Mtd Riflemen

LENOIR, John P, QM Sgt, Col Robt H Dyer, no Co Commander, TN Vol Mtd Gunmen; died 1-6-1815 of battle wounds

LENOIR, Peterson, QM Sgt, Col Robert H Dyer, no Co Commander, TN Vol Mtd Gunmen

LENORD, John, Pvt, Col Wm Lillard, Capt Benj H King, E TN Vol Inf

LENORE, Pierson (Peterson), Pvt, Col Thos Williamson, Capt John Hutchings, Vol Mtd Gunmen; promoted to QM Sgt 1 Regt

LENOX, John, 1 Lt, Col Wm Y Higgins, Capt Samuel Allen, Mtd Tunmen; killed in battle 1-24-1814

LENOX, Samuel, Pvt, Col Philip Pipkin, Capt Peter Searcy, Mil Inf

LENSEY, Caleb, Pvt, Col John K Winn, Capt John Spinks,

Inf
LENSEY, Edward, Pvt, Col Philip Pipkin, Capt Peter Searcy, Mil Inf; deserted
LENSTON, Thomas William, Pvt, Col John Coffee, Capt Chas Kavanaugh, Cav
LENTON, John, Cpl, Col John Coffee, Capt Chas Kavanaugh, Cav
LENTZE, John, Pvt, Col Edwin Booth, Capt John Lewis, E Tn Mil
LENVILLE, Worly, Pvt, Col Thos Benton, Capt Wm J Smith, Vol Inf
LEONARD, Collen, Cpl, Col John K Wynne, Capt John Porter, Inf
LEONARD, Collin, Sgt, Col R H Dyer, Capt James Wyatt, Vol Mtd Gunmen
LEONARD, Griffith, Sgt, Col John K Wynne, Capt John Porter, Inf; wounded at Talledega 11-9-1813
LEONARD, Hezekiah, Pvt, Col A Lowry, Lt Col L Hammond, Capt Thos Delaney, Inf
LEONARD, Hezekiah, Pvt, Col Robt H Dyer, Capt James Wyatt, Vol Mtd Gunmen; deserted
LEONARD, Jacob, Pvt, Col Wm Metcalf, Capt Wm Sitton, Mil Inf
LEONARD, John, Pvt, Col John K Wynne, Capt John Porter, Inf
LEONARD, John, Pvt, Col Wm Metcalf, Capt Obadiah Waller, Mil Inf
LEONARD, Joshua, Pvt, Col Thos Benton, Capt Wm J Smith, Vol Inf
LEONARD, Joshua, Pvt, Col Wm Pillow, Capt Wm J Smith, Vol Inf
LEONARD, Samuel, Sgt, Col John K Wynne, Capt John Porter, Inf; died in service
LEONARD, William, Pvt, Col John K Wynne, Capt John POrter, Inf
LEONARD, William, Pvt, Col Robert Steele, Capt Richard M Ratton, Mil Inf
LEONARD, William, Pvt, Col Wm Metcalf, Capt Andrew Patterson, Mil Inf
LEPAN, Andy, Pvt, Gen A Jackson, Capt J Carvan, Branch omitted
LEPAN, Andy, Pvt, Lt Col Henry Bryan, Co Commander omitted, Inf
LERAY, William, Pvt, Gen Jackson, Capt Wm Russell, Mtd Spies
LERD, John, Pvt, Col R C Napier, Capt John Chism, Mil Inf
LERUE, George, Pvt, Col Wm Johnson, Capt Jas R Rogers, E TN Draft Mil
LES, Luke, Pvt, Col John Williams, Capt Wm Walker, Mtd Mil
LES, Pryor, Pvt, Col S Bunch, Capt Thomas Mann, E TN Vol Mtd Inf
LESLEY, George, Pvt, Col R H Dyer, Capt Jos Williams, Vol Mtd Gunmen
LESLEY, John, Pvt, Col Thos Williamson, Capt Robt Moore, Vol Mtd Gunmen
LESPEN, Elihu, Pvt, Col Wm Lillard, Capt Thos Sharpe, 2nd Regt Inf
LESTER, Holland, Pvt, Lt Col A Cheatham, Co Commander omitted, Mtd Inf

LESTER, Joseph, Pvt, Col William Hall, Capt Jas Hambleton, Vol Inf
LESTER, Joseph, Pvt, Lt Col Henry Bryan, Co Commander omitted, Inf
LESTER, Reuben, Cpl, Col Wm Johnson, Capt Chris Cook, E TN Mil
LESTER, Whitehead, Pvt, Col A Cheatham, Capt Jas Giddins, Inf
LESTER, Whitehead, Pvt, Col Thos Benton, Capt Jas McEwen, Vol Inf
LESTER, William, Pvt, Col John Brown, Capt John Chiles, E TN Vol Mtd Inf
LESTES (LYSLES), Seth, Dmr, Maj Wm Woodfolk, Capt Abraham Dudney & Capt John Sutton, Inf; d 12-4-1814
LETERDALE, John, Sgt, Col L Hammond, Capt Jas Craig, 2nd Regt W TN Mil
LETREL, Vincent, Pvt, Col S Copeland, Capt Wm Douglass, Inf
LETSENGER, George, Pvt, Col Jas Raulston, Capt Mathew Neal, Inf
LETSINGER, John, Pvt, Maj John Chiles, Capt Chas Conway, E TN Mtd Gunmen; Regimental Co Knox
LETTIN (LEYTON), Thomas, Pvt, Lt Col L Hammond, Capt James Craig, Inf
LETTLE, Ebenezer jr, Pvt, Regt Commander omitted, Capt Wm Henderson, Spies
LETTO, William, Pvt, Col John Coffee, Capt Fred Stump, Cav
LEVE, David B, Pvt, Col L Hammond, Capt J N Williamson, 2nd Regt Inf
LEVEL, John, Sgt, Col John Brown, Capt Wm D Neilson, E TN Vol Mil
LEVEN, John, Pvt, Col N Cannon, Capt Thomas Yardley, Mtd Riflemen
LEVERSON, Thomas, Pvt, Col Hammond, Capt J N Williamson, 2nd Regt Inf
LEVERTON, John, Pvt, Col Samuel Wear, Capt Simeon Perry, E TN Vol Mtd Inf
LEVERTON, Thomas, Pvt, Col A Lowry, Capt J N Williamson, W TN Mil
LEVI, James, Pvt, Col Robt H Dyer, Capt Robt Evans, Vol Mtd Gunmen; transferred to Capt Cowan's Co
LEVI, Thomas, Pvt, Col Robt H Dyer, Capt Robt Evans, Vol Mtd Gunmen
LEVINGSTON, David, Pvt, Col Edwin Booth, Capt John Sharp, E TN Mil; transferred from Capt Vernon's Co
LEVY, Benjamin, Pvt, Regt Commander omitted, Capt Arch McKinney, Cav
LEVY, James, Pvt, Maj Wm Russell, Capt John Cowan, Vol Mtd Gunmen
LEW, John Roberts, 4 Sgt, Regt Commander omitted, Capt Jas Terrill, Cav; transferred to Morris Co
LEWELING, John, Pvt, Col Samuel Bunch, Capt John Houk, E TN Mil; transferred to Capt English's Co
LEWER, Andrew, Pvt, Col John Brown, Capt Wm White, E TN Inf
LEWIS, Aaron, Pvt, Col John Coffee, Capt Michael Molton, Cav

## Enlisted Men, War of 1812

LEWIS, Aaron, Pvt, Col Robt H Dyer, Capt Jos Williams, Vol Mtd Gunmen

LEWIS, Allen, Pvt, Col John Cocke, Capt John Weakley, Inf

LEWIS, Allen, Pvt, Col John K Wynne, Capt Robert Breden, Inf; deserted 12-26-1813

LEWIS, Allen, Pvt, Col R H Dyer, Capt James White, Vol Mtd Gunmen

LEWIS, Allen, Tptr, Maj Gen Andrew Jackson, Capt John Crane, Mtd Gunmen

LEWIS, Ambrose, Mus, Col N T Perkins, Capt John B Quarles, Vol Mtd Inf

LEWIS, Andrew, Pvt, Col John Alcorn, Capt John J Winston, Mtd Riflemen

LEWIS, Benjamin, Pvt, Col R C Napier, Capt Edward Neblett, Mil Inf

LEWIS, Charles, Pvt, Col Philip Pipkin, Capt John Robertson, Mil Inf

LEWIS, Crow, Pvt, Regt Commander omitted, Capt Jos Williams, Mil Cav

LEWIS, Daniel, Pvt, Col Philip Pipkin, Capt John Robertson, Mil Inf

LEWIS, David, Pvt, no other information

LEWIS, Earle, Pvt, Col R C Napier, Capt Drury Adkins, Mil Inf

LEWIS, Eli, Pvt, Col William Lillard, Capt John Roper, E TN Vol Inf

LEWIS, Elijah, Sgt, Col Robert Steele, Capt Richard M Ratton, Mil Inf; deserted 4-29-1814

LEWIS, Gabriel, Pvt, Col Samuel Bayless, Capt James Churchman, E TN Mil

LEWIS, George R, Blksmth, Col R H Dyer, Capt James White, Vol Mtd Gunmen

LEWIS, George R, Pvt, Col R H Dyer, Capt James White, Vol Mtd Gunmen

LEWIS, George, Pvt, Col R H Dyer, Capt Joseph Williams, Vol Mtd Gunmen; d 2-15-1815

LEWIS, George, Pvt, Col Wm Lillard, Capt John Roper, E TN Vol Inf

LEWIS, Henry, Pvt, Col Edwin Booth, Capt John Lewis, E TN Mil

LEWIS, Henry, Pvt, Col Philip Pipkin, Capt George Mebane, Mil Inf

LEWIS, Henry, Pvt, Col T McCrory, Capt A Metcalf, Mil Inf

LEWIS, Hugh, Pvt, Col R H Dyer, Capt Cuthbert Hudson, Vol Mtd Gunmen; d 2-14-1815

LEWIS, James M, Sgt, Col Newton Cannon, Capt Francis Jones, Mtd Riflemen

LEWIS, James, Pvt, Col John Coffee, Capt Michael Molton, Cav; promoted to Cpl

LEWIS, James, Pvt, Col Robt H Dyer, Capt Bethel Allen, Vol Mtd Gunmen

LEWIS, James, Pvt, Col S Copeland, Capt Richard Sharp, Mil Inf; transferred to the Arty

LEWIS, James, Pvt, Col William Metcalf, Capt John Barnhart, Mil Inf

LEWIS, James, Pvt, Maj Gen A Jackson, Capt Joel Parrish, Arty

LEWIS, James, Pvt, Regt Commander omitted, Capt Jas Williams, Mil Cav

LEWIS, James, Pvt, Regt Commander omitted, Capt Jos Williams, Mil Cav

LEWIS, Jesse, 3 Cpl, Col Edwin Booth, Capt John Sharp, E TN Mil

LEWIS, Joel, Sgt, Col A Cheatham, Capt Richard Benson, Inf

LEWIS, John A, Pvt, Col N T Perkins, Capt George Eliot, Mil Inf

LEWIS, John, Pvt, Col Samuel Bayless, Capt Branch Jones, E TN Mil Drafted

LEWIS, John, Pvt, Col Thomas Benton, Capt George Caperton, Vol Inf; substituted Daniel Barker

LEWIS, John, Pvt, Lt Col Richard Napier, Co Commander omitted, Inf

LEWIS, John, Sgt, Col John Coffee, Capt Michael Molton, Cav

LEWIS, Joshua, Pvt, Col Robt Dyer, Capt Isaac Williams, Vol Mtd Gunmen

LEWIS, Joshua, Sgt, Col Robt Jarmon, Capt Nathan Peoples, Inf

LEWIS, Levi, Pvt, Col Edwin Booth, Capt Porter, Drafted Mil

LEWIS, Levi, Pvt, Col William Hall, Capt Henry M Newland, Inf

LEWIS, Marcija, Pvt, Col S Copeland, Capt William Douglass, Inf

LEWIS, Mikajah, Pvt, Col William Hall, Capt Henry M Newland, Inf

LEWIS, Mordica, 4 Cpl, Regt Commander omitted, Capt Jas Haggard, Mtd Gunmen

LEWIS, Mordica, Cpl, Regt Commander omitted, Capt Jas Haggard, Mtd Gunmen

LEWIS, Moses, Pvt, Col Samuel Bayless, Capt Branch Jones, E TN Drafted Mil

LEWIS, Norborun, Sgt, Col Newton Cannon, Capt Francis Jones, Mtd Riflemen

LEWIS, Norbourn, 3 Sgt, Gen Andrew Jackson, Capt Wm Russell, Mtd Spies

LEWIS, Price, Pvt, Col William Hall, Capt John Kennedy, Vol Inf

LEWIS, Samuel, Pvt, Col John Coffee, Capt Michael Molton, Cav

LEWIS, Samuel, Pvt, Col Samuel Bayless, Capt James Landen, E TN Mil

LEWIS, Solomon, Pvt, Col William Lillard, Capt William Hamilton, E TN Vol Inf

LEWIS, Thomas, 4 Sgt, Col James Raulston, Capt Daniel Newman, Inf

LEWIS, Tipton, Cor, Col Newton Cannon, Capt Francis Jones, Mtd Riflemen

LEWIS, Tipton, Pvt, Gen A Jackson, Capt Wm Russell, Mtd Spies

LEWIS, Washington, Pvt, Lt Col Jno Edmonson, Co Commander omitted, Cav

LEWIS, William, 2 Cpl, Col James Raulston, Capt James A Black

LEWIS, William, Pvt, Col Alex Loury, Capt Jas Kincaid, Branch Srvce omitted

LEWIS, William, Pvt, Col John Cocke, Capt Bird Nance, Inf

LEWIS, William, Pvt, Col Wm Lillard, Capt Wm Hamil-

ton, Branch Srvce omitted
LEWIS, William, Pvt, Maj John Childs, Capt John Stephens, E TN Vol Mtd Inf
LEWIS, William, Pvt, Regt Commander omitted, Capt Jas Haggard, Mtd Gunmen
LEWRY, Robert sr, Pvt, Col John Brown, Capt Wm Christian, E TN Mil Inf
LEYTON, Teal, Pvt, Col Jno Brown, Capt Lunsford Oliver, E TN Mil
LIBY, William, Pvt, Col Edward Bradley, Capt John Moore, Vol Inf; deserted 11-19-1813
LIEBER, Samuel, Cpl, Col Wm Johnston, Capt J Tunnell, E TN Mil
LIEVERAY, John, Pvt, Col Alex Loury, Capt John Looney, W TN Inf
LIFFORD, John, Pvt, Col Wm Lillard, Capt Wm Hamilton, E TN Vol Inf
LIFORD, John, Pvt, Col Samuel Bayless, Capt John Brook, E TN Mil
LIGGET, Henry, Sgt, Col Edwin E Booth, Capt Alex Biggs, Inf
LIGGETT, William, Pvt, Regt Commander omitted, Capt Archibald McKinney, Cav
LIGGON, Abner W, Pvt, Col P Pipkin, Capt John Strother, Mil; d 12-17-1814
LIGGON, Blackman, Pvt, Col Thos Williamson, Capt A M Metcalf, Vol Mtd Gunmen; d 4-16-1815
LIGGON, Paschal, Pvt, Col P Pipkin, Capt John Strother, Mil; attached to Capt D Smith, d 11-11-1814
LIGHT, Jacob, Pvt, Col Wm Johnson, Capt Benj Powell, E TN Mil; AWOL
LIGHT, John, Cpl, Col E Allison, Capt J Hoyal, E TN Mil; transferred to Capt Register's Camp
LIGHT, John, Pvt, Col Samuel Bayless, Capt Jos Goodson, E TN Mil
LIGHT, John, Pvt, Col Samuel Bunch, Capt Jas Penny, E TN Mtd Inf
LIGHT, John, Sgt, Col Samuel Bunch, Capt Francis Register, E TN Mil; joined from Capt Harval's Co
LIGHT, Obadiah, Pvt, Col E Allison, Capt J Hoyal, E TN Mil; transferred to Capt Register's Co
LIGHT, Obadiah, Pvt, Col S Bunch, Capt Francis Register, E TN Mil; joined from Capt Hoyle's Co
LIGHT, Obadiah, Pvt, Col Samuel Bayless, Capt Jos Goodson, E TN Mil
LIGHT, William, Pvt, Col E Allison, Capt J Loughmiller, Mil
LIGHT, William, Pvt, Col R C Napier, Capt D Adkins, Mil Inf
LIGHTFOOT, Thomas, Pvt, Regt Commander omitted, Capt Gray, Inf
LIGHTFOOT, William (Wilson), Pvt, Lt Col Leroy Hammond, Capt James Craig, Inf
LIGIN, James, Pvt, Col P Pipkin, Capt David Smith, Inf
LIGON, Henry, Pvt, Col Wm Hall, Capt Wm Alexander, Vol Inf
LIGON (LEGGAN), Henry, Pvt, Col Edward Bradley, Capt Wm Lauderdale, Vol Inf
LIKENS, Peter, Pvt, Col Wm Johnson, Capt Benj Powell, E TN Mil; d 11-13-1814
LILAS, William, Pvt, Col John Brown, Capt Jas Standifer,
E TN Vol Mtd Mil
LILBOURN, Andrew, Pvt, Col Wm Lillard, Capt Jacob Hartsell, E TN Vol Inf
LILE, Malachi, Pvt, Col Wm Metcalf, Capt Wm Mullin, Mil Inf
LILES, David, Cpl, Col Wm Johnston, Capt J R Rogers, E TN Drafted Mil
LILES, David, Pvt, Col Jas Raulston, Capt H West, Inf
LILES, Seth, Pvt, Col J K Wynne, Capt Jas Holleman, Inf
LILLARD, Abraham, Pvt, Col Samuel Bayless, Capt B Jones, E TN Mil
LILLARD, James, Pvt, Col Jno Williams, Capt Samuel Bunch, Mtd Vol
LILLARD, James, Pvt, Col Samuel Bayless, Capt B Jones, E TN Drafted Mil
LILLARD, John, Pvt, Col J Brown, Capt Chas Lewin, E TN Vol Mtd Inf
LILLES, Jesse, Pvt, Col Wm Hall, Capt H Newland, Inf
LILLEY, William, Pvt, Col Thos Williamson, Capt Thos Scurry, Vol Mtd Gunmen
LILLEY (LIELY), William, Pvt, Col Wm Hall, Capt John Moore, Vol Inf
LIME (LION), Nathaniel, Cpl, Col Wm Johnson, Capt Elihu Milliken, 3rd Regt E TN Mil
LINCH, Alford, Pvt, Col Samuel Bayless, Capt John Brock, E TN Mil
LINCH, Elbert, Pvt, Col Sam Bayless, Capt John Brock, E TN Mil; furloughed for inability
LINCH, Isaac, Pvt, Col Wm Johnson, Capt C Cook, E TN Mil; joined from Capt Hunter's
LINCH, John, 1 Sgt, Maj Gen Wm Carroll, Col Jas Raulston, Capt E Robinson, Inf
LINCH, John, Pvt, Col J K Wynne, Capt B Prince, Inf
LINCOLN (LINKHOM), Joseph, Pvt, Lt Col L Hammond, Capt Jas Tubb, Inf
LINDER, John, Pvt, Col John Cocke, Capt Jos Price, Inf
LINDIN, John, Pvt, Col Sam Bunch, Capt John Houk, E TN Mil
LINDSAY, Charles, Pvt, Regt Commander omitted, Capt Wm Henderson, Spies
LINDSAY, James, Pvt, Col Wm Metcalf, Capt Thomas Marks, Mil Inf
LINDSEY, Joachim, Pvt, no other information
LINDSEY, John, Cpl, Col Samuel Wear, Capt Rufus Morgan, E TN Vol Inf; promoted from a Pvt
LINDSEY, Joseph, Pvt, Maj Wm Woodfolk, Capt James C Neil, Inf
LINDSEY, Lemuel, Pvt, Col Edwin E Booth, Capt John McKamey, E TN Mil
LINDSEY, Moses, Sgt, Col Samuel Wear, Capt Rufus Morgan, E TN Vol Inf; reduced to ranks
LINDSEY, Thomas, Pvt, Col Wm Metcalf, Capt Thomas Marks, Mil Inf
LINDSEY, William L, Pvt, Col Thos Williamson, Capt Robert Moore, Vol Mtd Gunmen
LINDSEY, William, Pvt, Maj Wm Woodfolk, Capt Abraham Dudney, Inf
LINE, William, Pvt, Col Wm Johnson, Capt Elihu Milliken, 3rd Regt E TN Mil
LINGAR, John, Pvt, Col Samuel Bunch, Capt Moses, E TN Drafted Mil; transferred to Capt Houk's Co

## Enlisted Men, War of 1812

LINGIMPETTER, John, Pvt, Col Samuel Bayless, Capt James Churchman, E TN Mil

LINGIN, John, Pvt, Col Samuel Bunch, Capt Jno Houk, E TN Mil

LINING, Isaac, Pvt, Col Samuel Bayless, Capt James Churchman, E TN Mil

LINING, John, Pvt, Col Samuel Bayless, Capt James Churchman, E TN Mil

LINK, Bird, Pvt, Col A Loury, Capt J N Williamson, W TN Mil

LINK, Bird, Pvt, Col Leroy Hammonds, Capt Joseph N Williamson, 2nd Regt Inf

LINN, Ntahan, Pvt, Lt Col Leroy Hammond, Capt James Craig, Inf

LINSEY, Caleb, Pvt, Col Thos Williamson, Capt Thos Williamson, Vol Mtd Gunmen

LINSEY, John, 4 Sgt, Col Wm Metcalf, Capt Wm Sitton, Mil Inf

LINSEY, John, Pvt, Col Samuel Bunch, Capt Isaac Williams, E TN Mil

LINSEY, Joseph, Pvt, Col Thos McCrory, Capt William Dooley, Inf

LINSEY, William, Drm Maj, Maj Wm Woodfolk, Separate Bn of W TN Mil

LINSEY, William, Pvt, Col Wm Johnson, Capt Henry Hunter, E TN Mil

LINSTER, Thomas W, Pvt, Maj Gen Wm Carroll, Col Jas Raulston, Capt Edward Robinson, Inf

LINSTER, Thomas W, Sgt, Col Jno Coffee, Capt Charles Kavanaugh, Cav

LINSTER, Will, Pvt, Col Jno Coffee, Capt Robt Jetton, Cav

LINSTER (LINSTON), John W, Cpl, Col Jno Coffee, Capt Charles Kavanaugh, Cav

LINTHICUM, Edward, Pvt, Col S Copeland, Capt John Holshouser, Inf

LINTON, Allen, Ffr, Col Thos B Benton, Capt Thos Williamson, Vol Inf

LINTON, Alsom, Pvt, Col Thos H Benton, Capt Thos Williamson, Vol Inf

LINTON, John, 3 Cpl, Col Thos H Benton, Capt Thos Williamson, Vol Inf

LINTON, John, Cpl, Col Thos H Benton, Capt Thos Williamson, Vol Inf

LINVILLE, William, Cpl, Col Jas Raulston, Capt Elijah Haynie, Inf

LINVILLE, Worly, Pvt, Col Thos H Benton, Capt Wm J Smith, Vol Inf

LION (LINE), Nathaniel, Cpl, Col Wm Johnson, Capt Elihu Milliken, 3rd Regt E TN Mil

LIONS, Robert, Pvt, Maj Gen Andrew Jackson, Capt Thos Williamson & Capt Robt Steele, Vol Mtd Gunmen

LIPS, Jonathan, Pvt, Col Ewen Allison, Capt Adam Winsell, E TN Drafted Mil

LIPSCOMB, John, Pvt, Col R C Napier, Capt Samuel Ashmore, Mil Inf

LISBY, Nathan, Pvt, Regt Commander omitted, Capt Jas Haggard, Mtd Gunmen

LISENBAY, Charles, Pvt, Col Wm Lillard, Capt William McLin, E TN Inf

LISENBAY, William, Pvt, Col Wm Lillard, Capt William McLin, E TN Inf

LISLE, George, Pvt, Col Wm Metcalf, Capt Bird L Hurt, Mil Inf

LITNER, Christian, Pvt, Col John Williams, Capt David Vance, Mtd Mil

LITTERAL, George, Pvt, Col Wm Johnson, Capt James Tunnell, E TN Mil

LITTLE, Andrew, Cpl, Col Edwin E Booth, Capt John McKamey, E TN Mil

LITTLE, George, Pvt, Col Newton Cannon, Capt Andrew Patterson, Mtd Riflemen

LITTLE, Harmon, Pvt, Col G W Steel, Capt James Randals, Inf; AWOL 4-28-1814

LITTLE, Henry, Pvt, Col A Cheatham, Capt Charles Johnson, Inf; d 4-25-1814

LITTLE, Isaac, 1 Sgt, Col Thos H Benton, Capt James McEwen, Vol Inf; promoted to QM Sgt

LITTLE, Isaac, Cpl, Regt Commander omitted, Capt D Mason, Cav

LITTLE, Isaac, Pvt, Col Wm Lillard, Capt Wm McLin, E TN Inf

LITTLE, Isaac, QM Sgt, Commander omitted, 2nd Regt TN Vol Inf

LITTLE, Isaac, Sgt, Col Samuel Bayless, Capt Jonathan Waddle, E TN Mil

LITTLE, Jacob, Pvt, Col Samuel Bayless, Capt Jonathan Waddle, E TN Mil; d 4-10-1815 in service

LITTLE, James, Pvt, Col Wm Johnson, Capt Christopher Cook, E TN Mil; d 11-1-1814

LITTLE, James, Pvt, Col Wm Johnson, Capt Joseph Kirk, Mil

LITTLE, John F, Pvt, Col N T Perkins, Capt Philip Pipkin, Mtd Riflemen

LITTLE, John, Pvt, Col A Cheatham, Capt James Giddens, Inf

LITTLE, John, Pvt, Col Wm Lillard, Capt Benjamin H King, E TN Vol Inf

LITTLE, Josiah, Pvt, Col John Brown, Capt John Trimble, E TN Mtd Gunmen

LITTLE, Meril, Pvt, Maj Gen Wm Carroll, Capt Wiley Huddleston, Inf; d 2-14-1815

LITTLE, Neal, Pvt, Col Thomas Benton, Capt Jas McEwen, Vol Inf

LITTLE, Robert, Pvt, Col Phillip Pipkin, Capt John Strother, Mil

LITTLE, Samuel, Pvt, Col N Cannon, Capt John Handley, Mtd Riflemen

LITTLE, Samuel, Pvt, Col Thomas Benton, Capt Jas McFerrin, Vol Inf; deserted 1-4-1813 from camp near Nashville

LITTLE, Stephen, Pvt, Maj Wm Woodfolk, Capt Dudney & Capt John Sutton, Inf; appointed Artif

LITTLE, Thomas, Pvt, Col Loury, Lt Col Leroy Hammond, Capt Thomas Delaney, Inf

LITTLE, Thomas, Pvt, Col Robt Steele, Capt John Chitwood, Mil Inf

LITTLE, Valentine, Pvt, Col Ewen Allison, Capt William King, Drafted Mil

LITTLE, William, Pvt, Col Samuel Wear, Capt John Stephens, E TN Vol Inf

*Enlisted Men, War of 1812*

LITTLE, William, Pvt, Col Thomas Benton, Capt Geo Caperton, Vol Inf
LITTLEFIELD, John, Pvt, Col John Coffee, Capt Robert Jetton, Cav
LITTLEFIELD, John, Pvt, Col S Copeland, Capt Moses Thompson, Inf
LITTLETON, Charles, Pvt, Col Wm Johnson, Capt Benj Powell, E TN Mil
LITTLETON, Darnall (Darnel), Ffr, Maj Wm Woodfolk, Capt Abraham Dudney & Capt John Sutton, Inf
LITTLETON, Darnold, Pvt, Maj Wm Woodfolk, Capt Abraham Dudney, Inf
LITTLETON, Henry, Pvt, Col A Lowry, Capt Gabriel Martin, Inf
LITTLETON, Isaac, Pvt, Col N Cannon, Capt Martin, Mtd Gunmen; furloughed with a lame horse
LITTLETON, Moses, Pvt, Col Thos Williamson, Capt Beverly Williams, Vol Mtd Gunmen
LITTLETON, Reubin, Pvt, Col John Cocke, Capt John Dalton, Inf
LITTLETON, William, Pvt, Col John Cocke, Capt Richard Crunk, Inf
LITTON, Cabel, Pvt, Gen A Jackson, Capt Cowan, Branch Srvce omitted
LITTON, Caleb, Pvt, Lt Col Henry Bryan, Co Commander omitted, Inf
LITTON, Caleb, Pvt, Regt Commander omitted, Capt Josiah Askey, Inf
LITTON, James, Sgt, Col Thos Benton, Capt Jas McFerrin, Vol Inf
LITTON, Thomas, Pvt, Col Wm Johnson, Capt Jas Tunnell, 3rd Regt E TN Mil; mustered sick absent and died 11-15-1814
LITTRELL, Robert, Pvt, Col Thos Williamson, Capt Robt Steele, Maj Gen A Jackson, Vol Mtd Gunmen
LIVESAY, Jesse, Blksmth, Regt Commander omitted, Capt Arch McKenney, Cav
LIVIERS, James, Pvt, Col Wm Lillard, Capt Hugh Martin, E TN Vol Inf
LIVINGSTON, Preston, Pvt, Col John Williams, Capt Samuel Bunch, Mtd Vol
LIVINGSTON, Robert, Pvt, Col R H Dyer, Capt Jos Williams, Vol Mtd Gunmen
LIVINGSTON, Thomas, Pvt, Col S Copeland, Capt Williams, Inf
LIVINGSTON, Thomas, Pvt, Col William Hall, Capt John Kennedy, Vol Inf
LLOYD, James, Pvt, Col John Coffee, Capt David Smith, Vol Cav
LOCK, Francis, Cpl, Col A Lowry, Capt Geo Sarver, Inf
LOCK, George, Pvt, Regt Commander omitted, Capt Wm Henderson, Spies
LOCK, Joel, Pvt, Col John Alcorn, Capt Frederick Stump, Cav
LOCK, John, Pvt, Col John Cocke, Capt Jas Gault, Inf
LOCK, John, Pvt, Maj William Russell, Capt John Cowan, Vol Mtd Gunmen
LOCK, Joseph, Pvt, Col Jas Raulston, Capt Henry West, Inf
LOCK, Richard S, Pvt, Col Thos Benton, Capt Robt Cannon, Inf

LOCK, Samuel, Pvt, Col Jas Raulston, Capt Henry West, Inf
LOCK, Thomas B, 2 Cpl, Col John Cocke, Capt Jas Gault, Inf; d 4-1-1815 on steam boat at New Orleans
LOCK, Thomas, Pvt, Col John K Wynne, Capt B E Prince, Inf; d 12-9-1813
LOCKARD, James, 3 Cpl, Col Thos Benton, Capt William Moore, Vol Inf
LOCKARD, Samuel, Cpl, Col Thos Benton, Capt William Moore, Vol Inf
LOCKARD (LACKARD), Samuel, 3 Cpl, Col William Pillow, Capt William Mooer, Inf
LOCKART, Charles, Pvt, Lt Col A Cheatham, Capt Gabriel Martin, Inf
LOCKART, William, Sgt, Col Robt H Dyer, Capt Robt Edmondson, TN Vol Mtd Gunmen
LOCKE, John G, Pvt, Col Robt Steele, Capt Jas Bennett, Mil Inf
LOCKE, William, Pvt, Col N Cannon, Capt John B Dempsey, Mtd Gunmen
LOCKET, Benjamin, Pvt, Col Edwin Booth, Capt Richard Marshall, Drafted Mil; discharged for inability
LOCKEY, James, QM Sgt, Col John Brown, E TN Vol
LOCKHARD, James, Cpl, Col Thos Benton, Capt Wm Moore, Vol Inf
LOCKHART, Hugh, Artif - Blcksmth, Col Thos Williamson, Capt Richard Tate, Vol Mtd Gunmen; in place of Thos Thompson
LOCKHART, John, Pvt, Col Philip Pipkin, Capt Ebenezer Kirkpatrick, Mil Inf; transferred to Capt Smith for Tom Lockhart
LOCKHART, John, Pvt, Col S Copeland, Capt Jas Tait, Inf
LOCKHART, Thomas, Pvt, Col Philip Pipkin, Capt David Smith, Inf
LOCKHORN, Axim, Pvt, Col Edwin Booth, Capt McKenney, E TN Mil
LOCKHORN, Joel, Pvt, Col Edwin Booth, Capt McKenney, E TN Mil; deserted 1-6-1815
LOCKLEAR, Major, Pvt, Col A Lowry, Capt Jas Kincaid, Inf
LOCKMILLER, Gabriel, Pvt, Col Wm Lillard, Capt Wm Gillenwater, E TN Inf
LOCKNER, Christopher, Pvt, Col Samuel Bunch, Capt Geo McPherson, E TN Mil
LOCKTROLL, John, Pvt, Col Philip Pipkin, Capt Ebenezer Kirkpatrick, Mil Inf; transferred to Capt Smythe
LODE, Joseph, Pvt, Maj James Porter, Capt John H Anderson, Branch Srvce omitted
LOE, Acquilla, 3 Sgt, Maj John Childs, Capt Charles Conway, E TN Mtd Gunmen
LOE, John, Pvt, Col S Copeland, Capt Alexander Province, Mil Inf
LOEH, William, Pvt, no other information
LOFLAND, William, 2 Sgt, Regt Commander omitted, Capt David Smith, Cav Vol; d 10-30-1815
LOFLAND, William, Sgt, Col John Coffee, Capt David Smith, Vol Cav
LOFLEN, Joseph, Pvt, Col Thomas McCrory, Capt Samuel B McKnight, Inf

## Enlisted Men, War of 1812

LOFTON, Thomas, Far, Col Thos Williamson, Capt James Pace, Vol Mtd Gunmen

LOFTON, Thomas, Pvt, Col John Alcorn, Capt Alexander McKeen, Cav

LOFTY, Abel, Pvt, Col Samuel Bayless, Capt Branch Jones, E TN Drafted Mil

LOGAN, Alexander, Pvt, Col John Brown, Capt John Trimble, E TN Mtd Gunmen

LOGAN, Alexander, Pvt, Col Samuel Bunch, Capt Edward Buchanan, E TN Drafted Mil

LOGAN, Claibourn, Pvt, Maj Wm Woodfolk, Capt James C Neil, Inf

LOGAN, David, Pvt, Col Wm Johnson, Capt Christopher Cook, E TN Mil

LOGAN, David, Pvt, Col Wm Johnson, Capt Joseph Kirk, Mil

LOGAN, Henry, Pvt, Col John Brown, Capt John Trimble, E TN Mtd Gunmen

LOGAN, Henry, Pvt, Maj John Childs, Capt John Stephens, E TN Vol Mtd Inf

LOGAN, John, Pvt, Col Samuel Wear, Capt James Gillespie, E TN Vol Inf

LOGAN, John, Pvt, Col T McCrory, Capt A Metcalf, Mil Inf

LOGAN, John, Pvt, Maj Gen A Jackson, Capt Hugh Kerr, Mtd Rangers

LOGAN, Reuben, Pvt, Maj Wm Russell, Capt John Cowan, Vol Mtd Gunmen

LOGAN, Samuel, Pvt, Col Wm Lillard, Capt Robert McCalpin, E TN Inf

LOGAN, William, Asst Forage Master, Maj Gen John Cocke, E TN Vol Mil

LOGAN, William, Pvt, Col John K Wynne, Capt William Carruthers, W TN Inf

LOGAN, William, Pvt, Col Philip Pipkin, Capt David Smith, Mil Inf

LOGAN, William, Pvt, Col Philip Pipkin, Capt Ebenezer Kirkpatrick, Mil Inf; deserted 9-20-1814

LOGGINS, Dixon, Pvt, Col N T Perkins, Capt Geo W Marr, Vol Mtd Inf

LOGGINS, Martin, Pvt, Col T McCrory, Capt Jas Shannon, Mil Inf

LOGGINS, Samuel, Pvt, Regt Commander omitted, Capt Archibald McKinney, Cav

LOGGINS, William, 2 Sgt, Col R C Napier, Capt Edward Neblett, Mil Inf

LOHNER, Daniel, Cpl, Col Samuel Bayless, Capt Joseph Goodson, E TN Mil

LOKEY (LOOKEY), John, Pvt, Maj Wm Woodfolk, Capt James Neil, Inf

LOLLARD, James, Pvt, Regt Commander omitted, Capt Smith, Vol Inf

LOLLER, James, 2 Cpl, Col Wm Pillow, Capt William J Smith, Vol Inf

LOLLER, James, Pvt, Col Thomas Benton, Capt William J Smith, Vol Inf

LOLLER, James, Pvt, Col Thos Benton, Capt Wm J Smith, Vol Inf

LOMAN, Samuel, Sgt, Lt Col Wm Phillips, Co Commander omitted, Inf

LOMAX, Samuel, Pvt, Col Philip Pipkin, Capt Peter Searcy, Mil Inf

LOMAX, Theophelus, Pvt, Col S Bunch, Capt Jno Hawk, E TN Mil; transferred to Capt English Co

LOMAX, Theopholis, Pvt, Col S Bunch, Capt Jno English, E TN Drafted Mil

LOMAX, Thomas, Pvt, Col Wm Johnson, Capt Andrew Lawson, E TN Drafted Mil; d 11-18-1814

LOMICK (LOMIX), John, Pvt, Lt Col L Hammonds, Capt James Craig, Inf

LOMOX, William, Pvt, Col Thos Williamson, Capt Thomas Porter, Vol Mtd Gunmen

LONAS, Adam, Pvt, Col Wm Lillard, Capt Jacob Dyke, Vol Inf; unable to perform duty

LONAS, Henry, Pvt, Col John Brown, Capt Allen I Bacon, E TN Mil Inf

LONAS, Henry, Pvt, Col Samuel Wear, Capt John Chiles, E TN Vol Inf

LONAS, Jacob, Pvt, Col Samuel Wear, Capt John Chiles, E TN Vol Inf

LONDON, Amos, Pvt, Col Philip Pipkin, Capt David Smith, Inf

LONDRUM, Josiah, Pvt, Col John Cocke, Capt Joseph Price, Inf; d 1-14-1815

LONG, Alexander, Pvt, Col S Copeland, Capt Richard Sharp, Mil Inf

LONG, Alexander, Pvt, Col Wm Lillard, Capt George Argenbright, E TN Vol Riflemen

LONG, Anderson, Pvt, Maj William Woodfolk, Capt James C Neil, Inf

LONG, Anderson, Pvt, Maj William Woodfolk, Capt James Turner, Inf; transferred to Capt A Pearce, replaced A Flower

LONG, Aron, Pvt, Brig Gen T Johnson, Capt Robt Carson, Inf

LONG, Benjamin, Pvt, Col Newton Cannon, Capt Andrew Patterson, Mtd Riflemen; promoted to Sgt

LONG, Benjamin, Pvt, Regt Commander omitted, Capt Archibald McKenney, Cav

LONG, Charles, Pvt, Col Thos Williamson, Capt Thomas Scurry, Vol Mtd Gunmen

LONG, David, Pvt, Col Samuel Bunch, Capt Jas Cummings, E TN Vol Mtd Inf

LONG, George, Pvt, Col Edwin Booth, Capt Vernon, Branch Srvce omitted

LONG, George, Pvt, Col Wm Hall, Capt John Kennedy, Vol Inf

LONG, George, Pvt, Col Wm Lillard, Capt Geo Argenbright, E TN Vol Riflemen

LONG, Hardy, Pvt, Col Samuel Bayless, Capt Joseph Rich, E TN Inf; substitute for Wm McGill

LONG, Henry, Pvt, Col N T Perkins, Capt John Doak, Vol Mtd Gunmen

LONG, Henry, Pvt, Col Wm Lillard, Capt Jacob Dyke, Vol Inf; deserted

LONG, Henry, Pvt, Maj Gen Carroll, Col Wm Metcalf, Capt John Jackson, Inf

LONG, Hyram, Pvt, Col N T Perkins, Capt John Doak, Vol Mtd Gunmen

LONG, Isaac, Pvt, Col Robt H Dyer, Capt Robt Evans, Vol Mtd Gunmen

LONG, Isaac, Pvt, Col Wm Metcalf, Capt Wm Sitton, Mil

Inf; promoted to Cpl & d 3-25-1815
LONG, Jacob, Pvt, Col Alexander Loury, Lt Col Leroy Hammonds, Capt Arahel Rains, Inf
LONG, Jacob, Pvt, Col Wm Johnston, Capt Joseph Kirk, Mil; transferred
LONG, Jacob, Sgt, Col Wm Johnston, Capt Henry Hunter, E TN Mil
LONG, James, Hospital Surgeon Mate, Maj Gen Carroll, TN Mil
LONG, James, Pvt, Col John Cocke, Capt Byrd Nance, Inf
LONG, James, Pvt, Col John Coffee, Capt Charles Kavanaugh, Cav
LONG, James, Pvt, Col John Williams, Capt Ray Bunch, Mtd Vol
LONG, James, Pvt, Col N T Perkins, Capt Matthew Patterson, Mtd Vol
LONG, James, Pvt, Col Robert Braden, Capt John K Winn, Inf
LONG, James, Pvt, Col Samuel Bunch, Capt James Cummings, E TN Vol Mtd Inf
LONG, James, Pvt, Col Thomas McCrory, Capt Gordon, Inf; deserted 11-18-1813
LONG, James, Pvt, Regt Commander omitted, Capt James Terrill, Cav Vol
LONG, James, Pvt, Regt Commander omitted, Capt Larkin Terrill, Cav
LONG, John, Pvt, Col Robt Steele, Capt Robt Chitwood, Mil Inf
LONG, John, Pvt, Col Wm Johnson, Capt David McKamy, E TN Drafted Mil
LONG, John, Pvt, Col Wm Johnson, Capt Henry Hunter, E TN Mil
LONG, John, Pvt, Col Wm Johnson, Capt Joseph Kirk, Mil
LONG, John, Pvt, Col Wm Johnson, Capt Wm Cook, E TN Mil
LONG, John, Pvt, Regt Commander omitted, Capt Geo Smith, Spies
LONG, Joseph, Pvt, Col John Williams, Capt Samuel Bunch, Mtd Vol
LONG, Joseph, Pvt, Col Wm Johnson, Capt Elihu Milliken, 3rd Regt E TN Mil
LONG, Joseph, Pvt, Maj Childs, Capt John Conway, E TN Mtd Gunmen; Regimental Co - Knox
LONG, Joseph, Pvt, Maj John Childs, Capt John Conway, E TN Vol Mtd Inf; furnished James Duffield as a substitute
LONG, Matthew P, Pvt, Col John K Wynne, Capt Bayless E Prince, Inf
LONG, Moses, Pvt, Col Samuel Bunch, Capt Isaac Williams, E TN Mil; deserted 1-22-1814
LONG, Patrick, 3 Cpl, Col Wm Metcalf, Capt Thomas marks, Mil Inf; promoted to 1 Sgt
LONG, Portman, Pvt, Col Samuel Bayless, Capt Joseph Rich, E TN Inf
LONG, Robert, Pvt, Col John Cocke, Capt Bird Nance, Inf
LONG, Samuel, Pvt, Col N T Perkins, Capt Geo W Marr, Mtd Vol
LONG, Simon E, Pvt, Col Robt H Dyer, Capt Ephraim Dickson, 1st TN Mtd Gunmen
LONG, Simon E, Pvt, Regt Commander omitted, Capt Ephraim Dickson, Branch Srvce omitted
LONG, Thomas D, Pvt, Col Phillip Pipkin, Capt John Strother, Mil
LONG, Thomas, Pvt, Col Robt H Dyer, Capt Ephraim Dickson, 1st TN Mtd Vol Gunmen
LONG, Thomas, Sgt, Col Loury, Capt Brice Martin, Inf; a substitute for Peyton Shaw
LONG, Tobias, Pvt, Col John Brown, Capt Jessie G Reany, Mtd Gunmen
LONG, William C, Pvt, Col Thomas McCrory, Capt Wm Dooley, Inf
LONG, William C, Pvt, Col Wm Metcalf, Capt Bird L Hurt, Mil Inf
LONG, William, Pvt, Col John Brown, Capt Wm D Neilson, E TN Vol Mil
LONG, William, Pvt, Col Phillip Pipkin, Capt John Strother, Mil
LONG, William, Pvt, Col Robt H Dyer, Capt James McMahon, 1st TN Mtd Gunmen; d 1-21-1815
LONG, William, Pvt, Col Samuel Wear, Capt James Gillespie, E TN Vol Inf
LONG, William, Pvt, Col Thomas Williamson, Capt Cook & Crane, Vol Mtd Gunmen
LONGBOTTOM, Joseph, Pvt, Col Samuel Bunch, Capt John English, E TN Drafted Mil
LONGBOTTOM, Joseph, Pvt, Col Samuel Bunch, Capt John Houk, E TN Mil; joined from Capt English Co, discharged for inability
LONGMIRE, William, 3 Cpl, Col Wm Metcalf, Capt Obediah Waller, Mil Inf; d 2-20-1815
LOOKE, Jacob C, Pvt, Col John Coffee, Capt John Baskerville, Cav
LOOKEY (LOKEY), John, Pvt, Maj Wm Woodfolk, Capt James C Neil, Inf
LOOKINGBILL, John, Pvt, Col Wm Johnson, Capt Joseph Scott, E TN Drafted Mil
LOOKINGBILL, John, Pvt, Col Wm Lillard, Capt James Lillard, E TN Inf Vol
LOONAY, Peter, Pvt, Regt Commander omitted, Capt Geo Smith, Spies
LOONE, _____, Pvt, Col Thomas Benton, Capt Geo Capeston, Inf
LOONEY, Absalom, Pvt, Col Wm Lillard, Capt Geo Argenbright, E TN Vol Riflemen
LOONEY, Arthur G, Pvt, Maj John Childs, Capt Jas Cummings, E TN Vol Mtd Inf
LOONEY, Arthur, Pvt, Col Ewen Allison, Capt J Loughmiller, Mil; transferred to Capt Griffin's Co
LOONEY, Arthur, Pvt, Col S Bunch, Capt J Griffin, E TN Drafted Mil; joined from Capt Loughmiller's Co
LOONEY, Benjamin, Pvt, Col Edwin Booth, Capt John Slatton, E TN Mil; appointed Hospital Stewart
LOONEY, David R, Pvt, Col S Bunch, Capt J Griffin, E TN Drafted Mil; furloughed for inability
LOONEY, David, Pvt, Col N Cannon, Capt Jas Walton, Mtd Riflemen
LOONEY, David, Sgt, Col E Allison, Capt J Loughmiller, Mil; joined Capt Griffin Co
LOONEY, Elisha, Pvt, Col L Hammond, Capt Jas Tubb, Inf

## Enlisted Men, War of 1812

LOONEY, Henry, Pvt, Col N T Perkins, Capt John Doak, Vol Mtd Riflemen

LOONEY, Isaac, 3 Sgt, Col Jno Coffee, Capt J W Byrn, Cav

LOONEY, John, Sgt, Regt Commander omitted, Capt Jno Gordon, Mtd Spies

LOONEY, Michael, Cpl, Col N Cannon, Capt Wm Edward, Regt Command

LOONEY, Michael, Pvt, Maj John Childs, Capt Chas Cummings, E TN Vol Mtd Inf

LOONEY, Moses, Mus, Col John Brown, Capt Wm White, E TN Mil Inf

LOONEY, Moses, Pvt, Col Edwin Booth, Capt Geo Winton, E TN Mil

LOONEY, Moses, Pvt, Col N T Perkins, Capt John Doak, Vol Mtd Gunmen

LOONEY, Moses, Pvt, Regt Commander omitted, Capt Daniel Yarnell, E TN Mil; discharged for inability, substitute

LOONEY, Moses, Pvt, Regt Commander omitted, Capt Wm Henderson, Spies

LOONEY, Peter, 1 Maj, Col John Brown, Co Commander omitted, E TN Mtd Gunmen

LOONY, Joseph, Pvt, Col N T Perkins, Capt John Doak, Vol Mtd Gunmen

LOONY, Moses, Pvt, Col John Brown, Capt Jas Preston, E TN Mil Inf

LOOR, Daniel, Pvt, Col Wm Metcalf, Capt John Cunningham & Capt Alex Hill, Mil Inf

LOOTHER, Laurence, Cpl, Col Thos Williamson, Capt John Crane & Capt Jas Cook, Vol Mtd Gunmen

LOOTY (LEETY), Jacob, Pvt, Lt Col L Hammond, Col Alex Loury & Capt Thos Wells, Inf

LOPPS, Andrew, Pvt, Col Thos Williamson, Capt Richard Tate, Vol Mtd Gunmen

LORAINE, George, Pvt, Regt Commander omitted, Capt Wm Henderson, Spies

LORANCE, Alexander, Pvt, Col Thos Benton, Capt I Renshaw, Vol Inf

LORANCE, Allison, Pvt, Col Thos Benton, Capt Jas McFerrin, Vol Inf; transferred to Capt Renshaw

LORANCE, Jesse, Pvt, Col Wm Hall, Capt Brice Martin, Vol Inf; refused to march

LORANTS, David, Pvt, Col Robt Steele, Capt John Chitwood, Mil Inf; transferred to Capt Creel

LORANTS, David, Pvt, Maj Gen A Jackson, Col A Cheatham, Capt Wm Creel, Inf

LORE, Christopher E, Pvt, Col Thos Williamson, Capt John Doak & John Dobbins, Vol Mtd Gunmen; substituted Abe Sumers

LORN, Jesse, Pvt, Col Thos Williamson, Capt Thos Porter, Vol Mtd Gunmen

LOSSOMS, James, Pvt, Regt Commander omitted, Capt J Askey, Inf

LOTHNER, John, Cpl, Col S Bunch, Capt Geo McPherson, E TN Mil; joined from Capt Everett's Co

LOTT, Arthur, Pvt, Col Jas Raulston, Capt M Neale, Inf

LOTT, John, Pvt, Col Samuel Bayless, Capt J Waddle, E TN Mil

LOUDERMILK, Solomon, Pvt, Col S Bunch, Capt Jno McNare, E TN Mil; attached to Capt Duncan's Co

LOUDON, ___, Private Waiter to Lt Hill, Lt Col L Hammond, Capt Thos Wells, Branch Srvce omitted

LOUGHLEN, Young, 2 Sgt, Brig Gen Johnson, Capt Robt Carson, Inf

LOUGHLIN, Alexander, Pvt, Col Wm Lillard, Capt Hugh Martin, E TN Vol Inf; Wgnr

LOUGHMILLER, Frederick, Pvt, Col John Williams, Capt Samuel Bunch, Mtd Vol

LOUGHMILLER, Henry, Pvt, Col Wm Lillard, Capt Geo Argenbright, E TN Vol Riflemen

LOUGHMILLER, John, Pvt, Col Wm Lillard, Capt Geo Argenbright, E TN Vol Riflemen

LOUGHMILLER, Jonas, Pvt, Col John Williams, Capt Samuel Bunch, Mtd Vol

LOUR, Peter, Pvt, Col Samuel Bunch, Capt Wm Houston, E TN Vol Mtd Inf

LOURY, Samuel, Pvt, Col Samuel Wear, Capt Jesse Cole, Vol Inf

LOVE, Charles, Pvt, Col Samuel Bayless, Capt Jos Hale, E TN Mil

LOVE, David B, Pvt, Col Alex Loury, Capt J N Williamson, W TN Mil

LOVE, David, Pvt, Col P Pipkin, Capt David Smith, Inf

LOVE, David, Pvt, Col Thos Benton, Capt Geo Caperton, Vol Inf; Lewis Comsey substituted

LOVE, David, Pvt, Col Wm Higgins, Capt Wm Doake, Mtd Riflemen; deserted 1-14-1814

LOVE, Edwin, Pvt, Col R C Napier, Capt Andrew McCarty, Mil Inf

LOVE, James, Far, Col R H Dyer, Capt Jas Wyatt, Vol Mtd Gunmen

LOVE, Jesse, Pvt, Col Jas Raulston, Capt Henry Hamilton, Inf; also served Maj Gen Carroll

LOVE, John, Pvt, Col John Brown, Capt Wm White, E TN Vol Mtd Inf

LOVE, John, Pvt, Col Wm Johnson, Capt Jas Rogers, E TN Drafted Mil

LOVE, Joseph, Pvt, Col N T Perkins, Capt Matthew Johnston, Mil Inf

LOVE, Mathew, Pvt, Col Wm Hall, Capt Brice Martin, Vol Inf

LOVE, Samuel, Pvt, Col N T Perkins, Capt M Patterson, Mtd Vol

LOVE, Samuel, Pvt, Maj Gen Wm Carroll, Col James Raulston, Capt Wiley Huddleston, Inf

LOVE, Willam, Pvt, Maj Wm Woodfolk, Capt Abner Pearce, Inf

LOVEALL, Joseph, Pvt, Col Samuel Bayless, Capt Joseph Goodson, E TN Mil

LOVEDY, Henry, Pvt, Regt Commander omitted, Capt John Porter & Capt Edwin Booth, Drafted Mil

LOVEL, Gidion, Pvt, Col John Cocke, Capt Samuel Caruthers, Inf

LOVEL, William, Pvt, Col N T Perkins, Capt Pipkin, Mtd Riflemen

LOVELACE, James, Cpl, Col Samuel Bunch, Capt George McPherson, E TN Mil; joined for Capt Everett's Co

LOVELACE, James, Pvt, Col Ewin Allison, Capt Adam Winsell, E TN Drafted Mil

## Enlisted Men, War of 1812

LOVELACE, William, Cpl, Col Ewin Allison, Capt Adam Winsell, E TN Drafted Mil

LOVELACE, William, Pvt, Col Samuel Wear, Capt Jesse Cole, Vol Inf

LOVELADY, John, Pvt, Col Samuel Bunch, Capt John English, E TN Drafted Mil

LOVELADY, John, Pvt, Col Samuel Bunch, Capt John Houk, E TN Mil; transferred to Capt English's Co

LOVELADY, John, Pvt, Col Thomas H Benton, Capt Benj Hewitt, Vol Inf

LOVELADY, John, Pvt, Col Thomas H Benton, Capt Robert Cannon, Inf; transferred from Capt Hewitt's Co

LOVELADY, Thomas, Pvt, Col Thomas H Benton, Capt Benjamin Hewitt, Vol Inf; AWOL 12-10-1812

LOVELADY, Thomas, Pvt, Col Thomas H Benton, Capt Isaiah Renshaw, Vol Inf

LOVELAME, William, Pvt, Col Samuel Bayless, Capt James Landen, E TN Mil

LOVELL, David, Pvt, Col Thomas H Williamson, Capt Thomas Scurry, Vol Mtd Gunmen

LOVELL, Joshua, Pvt, Col Philip Pipkin, Capt James Blakemore, Mil Inf

LOVELL, William, Pvt, Col Thomas H Williamson, Capt Richard Tate, Vol Mtd Gunmen

LOVING, James, Pvt, Maj Woodfolk, Capt Abraham Dudney & Capt John Sutton, Inf

LOVING, Walter, Sgt, Col James Raulston, Capt Henry Hamilton, Inf; also under Maj Gen Wm Carroll

LOVING, Warner, Pvt, Col N T Perkins, Capt Mathew Patterson, Mtd Vol

LOVING, Warner, Pvt, Col Thomas H Williamson, Capt Richard Tate, Vol Mtd Gunmen

LOVLESS, Thomas, Pvt, Col Samuel Bayless, Capt Solomon Hendricks, E TN Mil

LOW, Acquilla June, Pvt, Col John Brown, Capt John Chiles, E TN Vol Mtd Inf

LOW, Elijah, Pvt, Col Samuel Wear, Capt John Chiles, E TN Vol Inf

LOW, George, Pvt, Col John Cocke, Capt James Gray, Inf

LOW, John, Pvt, Col Edwin E Booth, Capt Marshall, Drafted Mil

LOW, John, Pvt, Col Samuel Bayless, Capt Solomon Hendrix, E TN Mil; d 3-15-1815

LOW, John, Pvt, Col Samuel Bunch, Capt Edward Buchanan, E TN Drafted Mil

LOW, John, Pvt, Col Samuel Wear, Capt Rufus Morgan, E TN Vol Inf

LOW, Michael, Pvt, Col Edwin E Booth, Co Commander omitted, Drafted Mil

LOW, Nathan, Pvt, Col Samuel Wear, Capt Rufus Morgan, E TN Vol Inf

LOW, William, Sgt, Col Samuel Bayless, Capt Joseph Hale, E TN Mil; reduced to the ranks and died

LOWDEN, John, 5 Cpl, Maj Gen Wm Carroll, Capt Ellis, Inf

LOWDERMICK, Henry, Pvt, Col Samuel Bayless, Capt Joseph Bacon, E TN Mil

LOWE, Andrew, Cpl, Col Wm Booth, Capt Vernon, E TN Mil

LOWE, David, Pvt, Col Wm Metcalf, Capt Andrew Patterson, Mil Inf

LOWE, George, Pvt, Col Samuel Wear, Capt James Gillespie, E TN Vol Inf

LOWE, Isaac, Sgt, Col Samuel Wear, Capt John Chiles, E TN Vol Inf

LOWE, John, 3 Cpl, Maj John Chiles, Capt Reuben Tipton, E TN Vol Mtd Inf

LOWE, John, Pvt, Col Samuel Wear, Capt James Tedford, E TN Vol Inf

LOWE, John, Pvt, Col Wm Johnson, Capt David McKamy, E TN Drafted Mil

LOWE, Stephen, Pvt, Col Samuel Wear, Capt John Chiles, E TN Vol Inf

LOWE, Thomas, Pvt, Col Samuel Wear & Col Samuel Bunch, Capt Wm Mitchell, E TN Mtd Inf

LOWE (LEA), Pernet (Pormit), Pvt, Col Samuel Wear, Co Commander omitted, E TN Vol Inf

LOWERY, James S, Mus, Col Thomas H Benton, Capt George W Gibbs, Vol Inf

LOWERY, Joseph S, Ffr, Col Thos H Benton, Capt George Gibbs, Vol Inf

LOWEY, Alexander, Pvt, Col Jas Raulston, Capt Charles Wade, Inf

LOWLER (LOLLER), Stephen, Pvt, Col James Raulston, Capt Mathew Cowan, Inf

LOWMUND, William, Cpl, Gen Andrew Jackson, Capt Wm Russell, Mtd Spies

LOWNY, Green B, Pvt, Lt Isaac Barrett, Capt Nathan Davis, Inf

LOWRANCE, Alexander, Pvt, Col Thomas H Benton, Capt Isaiah Renshaw, Vol Inf

LOWREY, James, Pvt, Col Wm Metcalf, Capt Andrew Patterson, Mil Inf

LOWRY, Adam, Pvt, Col R C Napier, Capt Samuel Ashmore, Mil Inf

LOWRY, Andrew, Cpl, Col John Brown, Capt Wm Christian, E TN Mil Inf

LOWRY, Andrew, Sgt, Col Edwin E Booth, Capt Vernon, E TN Mil

LOWRY, Daniel, Pvt, Col R H Dyer, Capt Ephraim Dickson, TN Vol Mtd Gunmen

LOWRY, Isaac, Pvt, Col R C Napier, Capt Thomas Gray, Mil Inf

LOWRY, Jacob, Sgt, Col John Brown, Capt McKamy, E TN Mtd Gunmen

LOWRY, James, Pvt, Col R C Napier, Capt Thomas Preston, Mil Inf

LOWRY, Robert jr, Cpl, Col Edwin E Booth, Capt Vernon, E TN Mil

LOWRY, Robert sr, Cpl, Col Edwin E Booth, Capt Vernon, E TN Mil

LOY, George, Cpl, Col Wm Y Higgins, Capt Thomas Eldridge, Mtd Gunmen

LOY, James, Pvt, Col Wm Y Higgins, Capt Thomas Eldridge, Mtd Gunmen

LOY, Peter, Pvt, Col Samuel Wear, Capt John Doak, E TN Vol Inf

LOYD, Daniel, Pvt, Col Philip Pipkin, Capt Peter Searcy, Mil Inf

LOYD, Ephraim, Pvt, Col Philip Pipkin, Capt Ebenezer Kirkpatrick, Mil Inf

## Enlisted Men, War of 1812

LOYD, George, Pvt, Col John K Winn, Capt Wm McCall, Inf

LOYD, James, Pvt, Col Philip Pipkin, Capt Henry M Newlin, Mil Inf; replaced by Hail Loyd

LOYD, James, Pvt, Col Robt H Dyer, Capt Thomas Jones, Vol Mtd Gunmen

LOYD, James, Pvt, Maj Gen A Jackson, Col A Cheatham, Capt William Creel, Inf

LOYD, James, Pvt, Regt Commander omitted, Capt David Smith, Cav Vol

LOYD, Joel M, Pvt, Col James Raulston, Capt Mathew Neal, Inf; d 1-26-1814

LOYD, John, Pvt, Col A Loury, Lt Col L Hammond, Capt Thomas Delaney, Inf

LOYD, John, Pvt, Col Samuel Bayless, Capt Solomon Hendricks, E TN Mil; died

LOYD, Jordon, Cpl, Lt I Barrett, Capt Nathan Davis, Inf

LOYD, Lewis, Pvt, Col A Cheatham, Capt James Giddens, Inf

LOYD, Talton, Pvt, Col James Raulston, Capt Henry West, Inf

LOYD, Thomas, Pvt, Col John K Wynne, Capt John Porter, Inf

LOYD, Thomas, Pvt, Col Thomas Benton, Capt Isaiah Renshaw, Vol Inf

LOYD, Thomas, Pvt, Col Thomas Williamson, Capt Giles Burdett, Vol Mtd Gunmen

LOYD, Thomas, Pvt, Col Wm Johnson, Capt Christopher Cook, E TN Mil

LOYD, Thomas, Pvt, Col Wm Johnson, Capt Joseph Kirk, Mil

LOYD, Thomas, Pvt, Col Wm Pillow, Capt Isaiah Renshaw, Inf

LOYD, William, Pvt, Col R C Napier, Capt James McMurry, Mil Inf

LOYD, William, Pvt, Col Samuel Bayless, Capt Joseph Hale, E TN Mil; reduced from Sgt, d 1-29-1815

LOYD, William, Pvt, Maj Wm Carroll, Capt John Jackson & Capt A Metcalf, Inf

LUALLEN, Andrew, Pvt, Col Edwin Booth, Capt Richard Marshall, Drafted Mil

LUALLEN, John, Pvt, Maj Gen A Jackson, Capt Joseph Kirkpatrick, Mtd Gunmen

LUALLEN, William, Pvt, Col Edwin Booth, Capt Richard Marshall, Drafted Mil

LUARK, John, Tptr, Col Samuel Bayless, Capt James Landen, E TN Mil

LUCAS, Abel, Pvt, Col Wm Pillow, Capt Thomas Williamson, Vol Inf

LUCAS, Abel, Pvt, Regt Commander omitted, Capt Edwin S Moore, Mtd Riflemen

LUCAS, Abel, Pvt, Regt Commander omitted, Capt Thos Williamson, Det of TN Vol Inf; transferred to Moore's Mtd Inf

LUCAS, Andrew, Pvt, Brig Gen Thos Washington, Capt Jno Crawford, Mtd Inf

LUCAS, George, Pvt, Col John K Wynne, Capt Robt Breden, Inf

LUCAS, George, Pvt, Col Thomas Williamson, Capt James Cook & Capt John Crane, Vol Mtd Gunmen; d 2-24-1814

LUCAS, Isaac, Pvt, Col Jno Coffee, Capt Frederick Stump, Cav

LUCAS, Isaac, Pvt, Col John Alcorn, Capt Frederick Stump, Cav

LUCAS, John, Pvt, Col L Hammond, Capt J N Williamson, 2nd Regt Inf

LUCAS, John, Pvt, Col Newton Cannon, Capt David Hogan, Mtd Gunmen

LUCAS, John, Pvt, Col Wm Johnson, Capt Benjamin Powell, E TN Mil; d 11-7-1814

LUCAS, John, Tptr, Regt Commander omitted, Capt Edwin S Moore, Mtd Riflemen

LUCAS, Parker, Pvt, Col T Williamson, Capt James Cook & Capt John Crane, Vol Mtd Gunmen

LUCAS, Peter W, Pvt, Col Newton Cannon, Capt William Edward, Regt Command

LUCAS, Robert, Pvt, Col Robert Steele, Capt James Bennett, Mil Inf

LUCAS, William jr, Pvt, Col Newton Cannon, Capt David Hogan, Mtd Gunmen

LUCAS, William, Pvt, Col Robert Steele, Capt James Bennett, Mil Inf

LUCAS, William, Pvt, Lt Col Jno Edmonson, Co Commander omitted, Cav

LUCAS (LOOKES), John, Pvt, Col A Loury, Capt J N Williamson, W TN Mil

LUCE, Abner, 2 Cpl, Col Wm Metcalf, Capt Wm Mullin, Mil Inf

LUCE, Abner, Pvt, Col Wm Metcalf, Capt John Barnhart, Mil Inf; transferred to Capt Mullins' Co

LUCETOR, Jonathan, Pvt, Col Samuel Bunch, Capt Edward Buchanan, E TN Drafted Mil; transferred from Capt Duncan's Co

LUCK, James, Pvt, Col Newton Cannon, Capt John Harpole, Mtd Gunmen

LUCKEY, Christian, Pvt, Col Samuel Bunch, Capt Francis Register, E TN Mil; joined from Capt Hoyles Co, d 7-8-1814

LUCKEY, John, Cpl, Col Newton Cannon, Capt James Walton, Mtd Riflemen

LUCKY, Hiram, Pvt, Col J K Wynn, Capt Jas Cole, Inf

LUCKY, Hiram, Sgt, Col S Copeland, Capt James Tait, Inf

LUKERAY, William, Pvt, Col R C Napier, Capt Drury Adkins, Mil Inf

LUKES, Edward, Pvt, Lt Col Jno Edmonson, Co Commander omitted, Cav

LUM, David, Pvt, Col John Cocke, Capt John Dalton, Inf

LUMBLEY, Thomas, Pvt, Col P Pipkin, Capt Geo Mebane, Mil Inf

LUMBLEY (LUMLEY), Thomas, Pvt, Col Thos Benton, Capt I Renshaw, Vol Inf

LUMFORD, Ephriam, Pvt, Col Wm Johnson, Capt H Hunter, E TN Mil; substitute for Daniel Reece

LUMFORD, Joshua, Pvt, Regt Commander omitted, Capt David Smith, Cav Vol

LUMFORD, Samuel, Pvt, Regt Commander omitted, Capt David Smith, Cav Vol

LUMKINS, Robert, Pvt, Col S Bunch, Capt Daniel Yarnell, E TN Mil

LUMLEY, Green, Pvt, Col John Cocke, Capt Geo Barnes, Inf

## Enlisted Men, War of 1812

LUMLEY, Thomas, Pvt, Col Thos Benton, Capt I Renshaw, Vol Inf

LUMPKIN, James, Mus, Col Samuel Wear, Capt John Childs, E TN Vol Inf

LUNEY, Moses, Pvt, Col S Bunch, Capt Daniel Yarnell, E TN Mil; substitute for M Carnes discharged for inability

LUNG, James, Pvt, Col Samuel Bunch, Capt Jas Penny, E TN Mtd Inf

LUNGINS (LONGINS), John, Pvt, Col P Pipkin, Capt John Robertson, Mil Inf

LUNSFORD, Joshua, Pvt, Col John Coffee, Capt David Smith, Vol Cav

LUNSFORD, Lewis, Pvt, Col John K Wynne, Capt John Porter, Inf; deserted 10-11-1813

LUNSFORD, Samuel, Pvt, Col Jas Raulston, Capt M Neele, Inf; d 2-10-1815

LUNSFORD, Samuel, Pvt, Col John Coffee, Capt D Smith, Vol Cav

LUNTEFORD, Elam, Pvt, Regt Commander omitted, Capt Smith, Vol Inf

LUNTSFORD, Berry, Pvt, Regt Commander omitted, Capt Smith, Vol Inf

LUNTSFORD, Eton, Pvt, Col Thos Benton, Capt Wm Smith, Vol Inf

LUNY, Peter, Pvt, Regt Commander omitted, Capt Geo Smith, Spies

LURLEY, Henry, Pvt, Regt Commander omitted, Capt Jos Williams, Mil Cav

LURNLY (LUMLY), Thomas, Pvt, Col Wm Pillow, Capt I Renshaw, Inf

LUSBY, Henry, Pvt, Col N Cannon, Capt David Hogan, Mtd Gunmen; transferred to Capt Molton's Co

LUSBY, Henry, Pvt, Regt Commander omitted, Capt Jos Williams, Mil Cav

LUSBY, Nathan, Pvt, Maj Wm Russell, Capt Wm Chism, Vol Mtd Gunmen

LUSK, James, Pvt, Maj John Chiles, Capt John Stephens, E TN Vol Mtd Inf

LUSK, John, Pvt, Regt Commander omitted, Capt Larkin Ferrell, Inf

LUSTER, James D, Pvt, Col Robert Steele, Capt Jas Shenault, Mil Inf

LUSTER, Reuben, Cpl, Col Wm Johnston, Capt Jos Kirk, Mil

LUSTER, Stokeley D, Cpl, Col Ewen Allison, Capt Jonas Loughmiller, Mil

LUSTER, Thomas, Pvt, Col Wm Lillard, Capt Benj King, E TN Vol Inf

LUSTER, White, Pvt, Col Thos Williamson, Capt Wm Tate, Vol Mtd Gunmen

LUTER, Holland, Sgt, Col Alex Loury, Capt G Martin, Inf

LUTER, Jonathan, Pvt, Col Wm Johnston, Capt Jas Rogers, E TN Drafted Mil

LUTER, Mathew, Pvt, Col A Cheatham, Capt R Benson, Inf

LUTERELLE, Martin, Wagon Master, Brig Gen Geo Doherty, E TN Mil

LUTHER, George, Pvt, Col N Cannon, Capt I Williams, Mtd Riflemen

LUTON, Lemuel, Pvt, Regt Commander omitted, Capt Gray, Inf

LUTRELL, Lewis, Sgt, Col John Brown, Capt John Childs, E TN Mtd Vol Maj; promoted to Adjt?

LUTRELL, Shelton, Pvt, Col S Copeland, Capt John Holshouser, Inf

LUTRELL, Thomas, Pvt, Col S Copeland, Capt J Houlshouser, Inf

LUTTON, John L, Pvt, Col Wm Hall, Capt Brice Martin, Vol Inf

LUTTRELL, George, Cpl, Col Wm Johnston, Capt Jas Tunnell, E TN Mil

LUTTRELL, Richard, Pvt, Col Edwin Booth, Capt John Sharp, E TN Mil

LUTTRELL, Silas, Pvt, Col Edwin Booth, Capt John Lewis, E TN Mil

LUTY, David, 3 Cpl, Col N T Perkins, Capt M Johnston, Mil Inf

LYLE, Becheth, Pvt, Col Thos Williamson, Capt J Hutchings, Vol Mtd Gunmen

LYLE, Daniel, Cpl, Col Wm Lillard, Capt Thos McChristian, E TN Vol Inf

LYLES, James, Pvt, Col J Cocke, Capt J Price, Inf

LYLES, John, Pvt, Col N T Cannon, Capt John Hanley, Mtd Riflemen

LYLES (LILES), Daniel, Pvt, Col J Cocke, Capt J Price, Inf

LYME, James, Pvt, Maj Gen Wm Carroll, Col Jas Raulston, Capt Henry Hamilton, Inf

LYN, Amos, Pvt, Col Thos Williamson, Capt Jas Cook & Capt John Crane, Vol Mtd Gunmen

LYNCH, David, Pvt, Col Wm Lillard, Capt Wm Hamilton, E TN Vol Inf

LYNCH, George L, Pvt, Col T McCrory, Capt A Metcalf, Mil Inf

LYNCH, Isaac, Pvt, Col Wm Johnston, Capt J Kirk, Mil

LYNCH, Jacob, Pvt, Col Wm Metcalf, Capt O Waller, Mil Inf

LYNCH, James, Pvt, Col Thos Benton, Capt Thos Williamson, Vol Inf

LYNCH, James, Pvt, Col Wm Lillard, Capt Thomas Sharpe, 2nd Regt Inf; deserted 10-29-1813

LYNCH, James, Sgt, Col R C Napier, Capt Andrew McCarty, Mil Inf

LYNCH, James, Sgt, Col Wm Pillow, Capt Thos Williamson, Vol Inf

LYNCH, John, Pvt, Col John Cocke, Capt John Dalton, Inf

LYNCH, John, Pvt, Regt Commander omitted, Capt Jos Williams, Mil Cav

LYNCH (LINCH), Henry, 2 Cpl, Col J Cocke, Capt J Price, Inf; reduced to the ranks

LYNN, John W, Pvt, Col P Pipkin, Capt Ebenezer Kirkpatrick, Mil Inf

LYNTES (LINTZ), Martin, Pvt, Col Samuel Bayless, Capt Joseph Hale, E TN Mil

LYNTON (LINTON), Alson, Ffr, Col Wm Pillow, Capt Thos Williamson, Vol Inf

LYON, Andy, Pvt, Lt Col H Bryan, Capt John Weakley, Mil Inf

LYON, Asher, 5 Cpl, Col Wm Johnson, Capt Andrew Lawson, E TN Drafted Mil

LYON, Jacob, Pvt, Col John Williams, Capt David Vance,

Mtd Mil

LYON, Jacob, Pvt, Col S Bunch, Capt Thomas Mann, E TN Vol Inf

LYON, Nathaniel, Pvt, Maj John Chiles, Capt Daniel Price, E TN Vol Mtd Inf

LYON, Peter, Pvt, Col R H Dyer, Capt Samuel White, Vol Mtd Gunmen

LYON, Robert, Pvt, Col R H Dyer, Capt Thos B Haynie, Vol Inf

LYON, William, Pvt, Col Newton Cannon, Capt David Hogan, Mtd Gunmen

LYONS, Castleton, 1 Sgt, Gen Andrew Jackson, Capt Jas Reed, Inf

LYONS, Daniel, Pvt, Maj Wm Carroll, Capt Lewis Dillahunty & Capt Daniel M Bradford, Vol Inf

LYONS, Nathaniel, 2 Cpl, Col Samuel Wear, Capt Daniel Price, E TN Vol Inf

LYONS, Patrick, Pvt, Col Wm Johnson, Capt Andrew Lawson, E TN Mil Drafted; appointed QM Sgt

LYONS, William, Pvt, Lt Col Jno Edmonson, Co Commander omitted, Cav

LYSLEY (LOSLLEY), Thomas, Pvt, Col John Cocke, Capt James Gault, Inf

LYTAKER, Peter, 2 Sgt, Col Thos Bradley, Capt James Hambleton, Vol Inf

LYTAKER, Peter, Sgt, Col Wm Hall, Capt James Hambleton, Vol Inf

LYTAKER, Peter, Sgt, Lt Col Henry Bryan, Co Commander omitted, Inf

LYTLE, Cyrus, 4 Sgt, Regt Commander omitted, Capt Jos Williams, Mil Cav

LYTLE, Cyrus, Sgt, Regt Commander omitted, Capt Jos Williams, Mil Cav

LYTLE, James, Pvt, Col Thos Williamson, Capt James Cook & Capt John Crane, Vol Mtd Gunmen

LYTLE, Neal, Pvt, Col Thos H Benton, Capt James McEwen, Vol Inf

LYTLE, William, Pvt, Col Thos H Benton, Capt George Caperton, Vol Inf

LYTLE, William, Pvt, Regt Commander omitted, Capt James Cowan, Inf

MABEN, George, Pvt, Col Newton Cannon, Capt Wm Martin, Mtd Gunmen

MABERRY, Benjamin, Pvt, Col John Alcorn, Capt Wm Locke, Cav

MABERRY, Daniel, Pvt, Col Jno Coffee, Capt Alexander McKeen, Cav

MABERRY, James, Pvt, Col Wm Hall, Capt Jno Kennedy, Vol Inf

MABERRY, John, Pvt, Col John Alcorn, Capt Wm Locke, Cav

MABERRY, Theoderick, Pvt, Col Jno Coffee, Capt Blackman Coleman, Cav

MABERRY, Theodone, Pvt, Col Jno Coffee, Capt Wm Locke, Cav

MABERRY, Timothy, Pvt, Col Jno Coffee, Capt Alexander McKeen, Cav

MABERRY, Timothy, Pvt, Col Wm Hall, Capt Henry M Newlin, Inf; transferred to Cav, substitute for Isaac Vanboose

MABERRY, William, Pvt, Col Jno Coffee, Capt Robert Jetton, Cav

MABIN, David, Cpl, Col Thos Williamson, Capt James Pace, Lt James Nealy, Vol Mtd Gunmen

MABREE, Orran, Pvt, Col Wm Hall, Capt John Moore, Vol Inf; substitute for Wm Albonson

MABRY, Benjamin, Pvt, Col Edward Bradley, Capt Abraham Bledsoe, Riflemen

MABRY, John, Pvt, Col Wm Hall, Capt Travis C Nash, Inf

MABRY, Thomas I, Pvt, Col Thos Benton, Capt James McEwen, Vol Inf

MABRY (MAYBERRY), Daniel, Cpl, Col Alexander Loury, Capt James Kincaid, Inf

MABURY, Cornelius, Pvt, Col R C Napier, Capt James McMurry, Mil Inf

MACANALY, Jessey, Pvt, Col Thos Benton, Capt George Caperton, Inf; substitute for A Caperton

MACAULEY, Charles, Pvt, Col Wm Hall, Capt Henry M Newlin, Inf; refused to appear

MACCLANEHAN, Robert, Sgt, Col Wm Johnson, Capt James Tunnell, E TN Mil

MACE, Henry, Pvt, Col Jas Raulston, Capt Wiley Huddleston, Branch Srvce omitted

MACE, Henry, Pvt, Maj Gen Wm Carroll, Capt Wiley Huddleston, Inf

MACK, James M, 1 Sgt, Col R C Napier, Capt Samuel Ashmore, Mil Inf

MACK, Robards, Pvt, Col Wm Metcalf, Capt Wm Mullins, Mil Inf

MACKAFEE, John, Pvt, Col S Copeland, Capt Alexander Provine, Mil Inf; deserted 2-4-1814

MACKEY, Isaac, Pvt, Col S Copeland, Capt G W Stell, Mil Inf

MACKEY, John, Pvt, Maj Wm Russell, Capt Wm Chism, Vol Mtd Gunmen

MACKEY, William, Cpl, Maj Wm Russell, Capt Wm Chism, Vol Mtd Gunmen

MACKLIN, James S, Ffr, Col James Raulston, Capt James A Black, Inf; no service performed

MACKLIN, John, Pvt, Regt Commander omitted, Capt Edwin S Moore, Mtd Riflemen

MACKY, James, Pvt, Col Alexander Loury, Capt James Kincaid, Inf

MACKY, William, Pvt, Col Wm Johnson, Capt David McKamy, E TN Drafted Mil

MACKY (MCKEY), William, Sgt, Col Wm Pillow, Capt John H Anderson, Vol Inf

MADDEN, James, 3 Cpl, Col Wm Pillow, Capt Wm J Smith, Vol Inf

MADDEN, Wilson, Pvt, Lt Col Archer Cheatham, Capt Meredith Walker, Inf

MADDEN (MADING), Absolom, Sgt, Col Jno Coffee, Capt Michael Molton, Cav

MADDIN, George, Pvt, Col Ewen Allison, Capt John Hampton, Mil

MADDIN, Samuel, Pvt, Col Ewen Allison, Capt John Hampton, Mil

MADDIN (MADDING), Daniel, Pvt, Col Edward Bradley, Capt Brice Martin, Vol Inf; wounded at Talledega 11-9-1813 & furloughed

MADDOCKS, John, Pvt, Col John Alcorn, Capt Thomas Bradley, Vol Cav

## Enlisted Men, War of 1812

MADDON (MADUR), David, Pvt, Col Samuel Bayless, Capt John Brock, E TN Mil

MADDOX, Daniel, Pvt, Col Jno Brown, Capt Lunsford Oliver, E TN Mil

MADDOX, Nathan, Pvt, Col Samuel Wear, Capt John Chiles, E TN Vol Inf

MADDUX, Joseph, Pvt, Col Wm Lillard, Capt Wm Lillard, E TN Vol Inf

MADDUX, Nathaniel, Pvt, Col Wm Lillard, Capt Wm Lillard, E TN Vol Inf

MADEN, Samuel, Pvt, Lt Col Richard Napier, Co Commander omitted, Inf

MADERY (MADARY), James, Pvt, Col Wm Metcalf, Capt Obidiah Waller, Mil Inf

MADLOCK, Isham, Pvt, Col Wm Johnson, Capt Henry Hunter, E TN Mil; substitute for D McNabb

MADRILL, Robert, Pvt, Col Samuel Bayless, Capt Branch Jones, E TN Drafted Mil

MAGA, James, Pvt, Col Jno Brown, Capt Wm Christian, E TN Mil Inf

MAGEE, John, Pvt, Col Edwin Booth, Capt Thos Porter, Drafted Mil

MAGEE (MCGEE), John, Pvt, Col Thomas H Williamson, Capt Joseph Williams, Vol Mtd Gunmen

MAGEE (MCGEE), John, Pvt, Col Thos Williamson, Capt Beverly Williams, Vol Mtd Gunmen

MAGILL, Thomas, Sgt, Col Ewen Allison, Capt Jacob Hoyal, E TN Mil

MAGILL, William, Pvt, Col Ewen Allison, Capt Jacob Hoyal, E TN Mil

MAGINIS, William H, Pvt, Col Wm Pillow, Capt Wm Moore, Inf

MAGINNIS, William, Pvt, Col Thos Benton, Capt Wm Moore, Vol Inf

MAGNIS, Robert, Pvt, Col Wm Johnson, Capt Elihu Milliken, 3rd Regt E TN Mil

MAGONAGH, Floyd, Pvt, Col Samuel Wear, Capt Joseph Calloway, Mtd Inf

MAHAFFY, Martin, Pvt, Col Wm Johnson, Capt Elihu Milliken, 3rd Regt E TN Mil; never appeared

MAHAHE (MAHEHEE), Elisha, Pvt, Col John Cocke, Capt Joseph Price, Inf

MAHAHE (MAHEHEE), Thomas, Pvt, Col John Cocke, Capt Joseph Price, Inf

MAHAN, Alexander, Pvt, Col Thos Benton, Capt Thos Williamson, Vol Inf; deserted

MAHAN, Archimidus, Pvt, Col Samuel Wear, Capt Simeon Perry, E TN Vol Mtd Inf

MAHAN, John, Cpl, Col Samuel Bunch, Capt Jno Hawk, E TN Mil

MAHAN, John, Pvt, Col Samuel Bunch, Capt Jno English, E TN Drafted Mil

MAHAN, William, Pvt, Col Wm Y Higgins, Capt Thos Eldridge, Mtd Gunmen

MAHEHEE (MAGAHE), Elisha, Pvt, Col John Cocke, Capt Joseph Price, Inf

MAHER, Moses, Pvt, Col Wm Johnston, Capt James R Rogers, E TN Mil; substitute

MAHON, John, Pvt, Col Samuel Wear, Capt Simeon Perry, E TN Vol Mtd Inf

MAHON (MAHAN), Edward, Pvt, Col Samuel Wear, Capt Simeon Perry, E TN Vol Mtd Inf

MAIBRY, James, Pvt, Col Wm Hall, Capt John Kennedy, Vol Inf

MAIDWELL, Charles, Pvt, Col James Raulston, Capt Daniel Newman, Inf

MAIDWELL, John, Pvt, Col James Raulston, Capt Daniel Newman, Inf

MAIGRAVES, Samuel, Pvt, Col Jno Brown, Capt Wm D Neilson, Regt E TN Vol Mil

MAINLEY, Beverly, Pvt, Regt Commander omitted, Capt D Deadrick, Arty

MAINOR, James, Pvt, Col Robert Steele, Capt Richard M Ratton, Mil Inf

MAINS, Hugh, Pvt, Col Samuel Wear, Capt Jesse Cole, Vol Inf

MAINS, Hugh, Pvt, Col Wm Johnson, Capt Henry Hunter, E TN Mil; substitute for George Oliver

MAINS, Thomas, Pvt, Col Wm Johnson, Capt Henry Hunter, E TN Mil

MAINYARD, John, Pvt, Col A Loury, Capt Arahel Rains, Inf

MAIR, Christopher, Pvt, Col Samuel Bayless, Capt James Churchman, E TN Mil; transferred to Capt Millikin's Co

MAIR, Johnson, Pvt, Col Samuel Bayless, Capt James Landen, E TN Mil

MAITE, Michael, Pvt, Col Samuel Bunch, Capt Geo McPherson, E TN Mil; deserted

MAJORS, John, Pvt, Col Edwin Booth, Capt George Winton, E TN Mil

MAJORS, Rowland, Pvt, Col Edwin Booth, Capt John Sharp, E TN Mil

MAJORS, Thomas, Pvt, Col Ewen Allison, Capt Wm King, Drafted Mil

MAJORS, William, Pvt, Col S Copeland, Capt John Holshouser, Inf

MAKISSICK, John, Pvt, Col Edwin Booth, Capt Porter, Drafted Mil

MALCOM, George, Pvt, Col Samuel Wear, Capt John Stephens, E TN Vol Inf

MALCOM, John, Pvt, Col S Bunch, Capt Isaac Williams, E TN Mil

MALCOM, William, Pvt, Col John Williams, Capt Wm Walker, Vol

MALCOM, William, Pvt, Col Wm Lillard, Capt John Roper, E TN Vol Inf

MALLARD, James, Pvt, Col James Raulston, Capt Mathew Neal, Inf

MALLARD, John, 4 Sgt, Col Wm Metcalf, Capt Andrew Patterson, Mil Inf; killed 12-28-1814 below New Orleans

MALLECOAT, Phillip, Pvt, Col Wm Johnston, Capt Henry Hunter, E TN Mil

MALLERY, Samuel, Sgt, Regt Commander omitted, Capt Geo Smith, Spies

MALLERY, Willie, Pvt, Regt Commander omitted, Capt Jas Haggard, Mtd Gunmen

MALLOCK, Valentine, Sgt, Col Wm Hall, Capt John Kennedy, Vol Inf

MALLONCE, John, Pvt, Col Ewen Allison, Capt John Hampton, Mil

MALLORY, Benjamin, Pvt, Col John Cocke, Capt John Weakley, Inf
MALLORY, Wyley, Pvt, Col John Cocke, Capt John Weakley, Inf
MALONE, Amos, Pvt, Col Wm Johnson, Capt Joseph Scott, E TN Drafted Mil
MALONE, David, Pvt, Col James Raulston, Capt James A Black, Inf
MALONE, Isaac, Pvt, Col Wm Johnson, Capt Joseph Scott, E TN Drafted Mil
MALONE, James, Cpl, Col S Copeland, Capt John Dawson, Inf
MALONE, Jeremiah, Pvt, Col S Copeland, Capt Wm Douglass, Inf
MALONE, Lewis, Pvt, Col Wm Metcalf, Capt Obidiah Waller, Mil Inf
MALONE, Samuel, Pvt, Col S Copeland, Capt John Dawson, Inf
MALONE, Samuel, Pvt, Maj Gen Wm Carroll, Col James Raulston, Capt Elijah Haynie, Inf
MALONE, Thomas D, 5 Sgt, Col Philip Pipkin, Capt John Strother, Mil; attached to Capt Smith, transferred back
MALONE, William, Pvt, Gen A Jackson, Capt Hugh Kerr, Mtd Rangers
MALONEY, David, Pvt, Col Wm Johnson, Capt Wm Alexander, Det E TN Drafted Mil
MALONEY, Edward, Pvt, Col Wm Johnson, Capt Wm Alexander, Det of E TN Drafted Mil
MALONEY, John, Pvt, Col Wm Lillard, Capt Robert Maloney, E TN Vol Inf
MALONY, David, Cpl, Col Jno Brown, Capt Jas Preston, E TN Mil Inf; deserted
MALUGEN, James, Pvt, Col Robt Dyer, Capt Joseph Williams, Vol Mtd Gunmen
MALUGIN, James, Pvt, Col Robert Dyer, Capt Cuthbert Hudson, Vol Mtd Gunmen
MALUGIN, John, Pvt, Col Robert Dyer, Capt Cuthbert Hudson, Vol Mtd Gunmen
MANACO, John, Pvt, Col John Cocke, Capt Samuel Carothers, Inf
MANAGHAN, Thomas, Pvt, Col S Bunch, Capt Jones Griffin, E TN Drafted Mil; joined Capt Loughmiller's Co
MANAHAM, James, Pvt, Col John Coffee, Capt Alexander McKeen, Cav
MANAS, George, Pvt, Col Wm Lillard, Capt Wm Gillenwater, E TN Inf
MANBRY, Thomas J, Pvt, Col Thos Benton, Capt Jas McEwen, Vol Inf
MANCON, John, Pvt, Gen Johnston, Capt Oban, Inf
MANDAL, Eloderick, Pvt, Col Wm Hall, Capt John Moore, Vol Inf
MANDRALL, John, Pvt, Col Jno Coffee, Capt John Baskerville, Cav
MANDRELL, John, Pvt, Col John Alcorn, Capt John Baskerville, Vol Inf
MANER, Andrew, Pvt, Maj Wm Russell, Capt Wm Russell, Vol Mtd Gunmen
MANESS, Isam, Pvt, Col S Bayless, Capt Solomon Hendrick, E TN Mil

MANEY, Robert, Pvt, Maj John Childs, Capt Jas Conway, E TN Mtd Gunmen
MANEY, William, Pvt, Col Wm Johnson, Capt James McKamey, E TN Drafted Mil; substitute for John Ewing
MANIER, Samuel, Cpl, Col T McCrory, Capt Jas Shannon, Mil Inf
MANIFOLD, Henry, Pvt, Col S Wear, Capt S Bowman, Mtd Inf
MANIFOLO, Benjamin, Cpl, Col S Wear, Capt Samuel Bowman, Mtd Inf
MANIS, George, Pvt, Col Edwin Booth, Capt George Winton, E TN Mil
MANKUSS, Benjamin, Pvt, Col Wm Lillard, Capt Robt Maloney, E TN Vol Inf
MANLEY, Benjamin, Pvt, Col S Bunch, Capt N Gibbs, E TN Drafted Mil
MANLEY, Chapman W, 2 Sgt, Col Phillip Pipkin, Capt Wm MacKay, Mil Inf
MANLEY, Cornelius, Pvt, Col Jno Coffee, Capt Fredrick Stump, Cav
MANLEY, David, Pvt, Col S Bunch, Lt Jno Harris, E TN Mil
MANLEY, Jepe, Pvt, Jos Williams, Co Commander omitted, Mil Cav
MANLEY, Jesse, Far, Col N Cannon, Capt Thomas Yardley, Mtd Riflemen
MANLEY, Jesse, Pvt, Col Thomas Williamson, Capt James Pace & Capt James Nealy, Vol Mtd Gunmen
MANLEY, Lipe, Pvt, Regt Commander omitted, Capt Jos Williams, Mil Cav
MANN, Gilbert, Pvt, Col John Williams, Capt Wm Walker, Vol
MANN, John, Pvt, Regt Commander omitted, Capt Rains, Inf
MANN, Robert, Pvt, Brig Gen Johnson, Capt Allen, Mil Inf
MANN, Robert, Sgt, Col John Brown, Capt Allen I Bacon, Mil Inf
MANNEN, Job, Pvt, Col Thos Dyer, Capt Joseph Williams, Vol Mtd Gunmen
MANNEN, John, Pvt, Maj Gen Carroll, Capt Ellis, Inf; d 1-24-1815
MANNERS, Michael, Pvt, Col Jas Raulston, Capt Robinson, Inf
MANNING, Charles, Pvt, Col John Cocke, Capt Nance, Inf; subsitute for Henry Gill
MANNING, David, Pvt, Col Alexander Loury, Col Leroy Hammonds, Capt Thomas Wells, Inf
MANNING, David, Pvt, Col John Brown, Capt Charles Lewin, E TN Vol Mtd, Inf
MANNING, Edward, Pvt, Col John Cocke, Capt George Barnes, Inf; d 3-3-1815
MANNING, Ephraim, Pvt, Col T McCrory, Capt Isaac Patton, Mil Inf; transferred to Capt Gordon's Spies
MANNING, Ephraim, Pvt, Regt Commander omitted, Capt Jno Gordon, Mtd Spies
MANNING, John, Pvt, Col Geo Mebane, Co Commander omitted, Mil Inf

MANNING, John, Pvt, Regt Commander omitted, Capt Gray, Inf
MANNING, Joseph, Pvt, Col R C Napier, Capt Jas McMurray, Mil Inf
MANNING, Joseph, Pvt, Col Wm Johnson, Capt Andrew Lawson, E TN Drafted Mil
MANNING, Peter, Pvt, Col Edwin Booth, Capt John McKamay, E TN Mil
MANNON, Ephraim, Pvt, Col Wm Metcalf, Capt John Barnhart, Mil Inf
MANNON, Henry, Pvt, Col Edwin Booth, Capt Porter, Drafted Mil
MANNON, John, Pvt, Col S Bunch, Capt Isaac Williams, E TN Mil
MANOR, James, Pvt, Col Philip Pipkin, Capt Ebenezer Kirkpatrick, Mil Inf; deserted
MANOR, Levi M, Pvt, Col Wm Hall, Capt John Kennedy, Vol Inf
MANOR, Levi W, Pvt, Col Edward Bradley, Capt John Kennedy, Riflemen; AWOL at Ft Strother
MANRING, Twory, Pvt, Col Robert Steele, Capt John Chitwood, Mil Inf
MANSCON, Joel, Pvt, General Johnston, Capt Oban, Inf
MANSEON, Inmanneul, Pvt, Gen Johnston, Capt Daniel Oban, Inf
MANSFIELD, Anderson, Ffr, Col John Wynn, Capt Porter, Inf
MANSFIELD, Joseph, Pvt, Col Jno Brown, Capt Allen I Bacon, E TN Mil Inf
MANSFIELD, Thomas, Pvt, Col Edwin E Booth, Capt John Lewis, E TN Mil
MANSHER, Lewis, Cpl, Col Thomas Williamson, Capt Wm Martin, Vol Mtd Gunmen
MANSKER, Casper, Pvt, Col Thomas Williamson, Capt Wm Martin, Vol Mtd Gunmen
MANSKER, John, Pvt, Col John Wynn, Capt Wm McCall, Inf
MANSKER, Lewis M, Pvt, Col Thomas Williamson, Capt Wm Martin, Vol Mtd Gunmen
MANSKER, William, Pvt, Col John K Wynn, Capt Wm McCall, Inf
MANSON, Kames, Pvt, Gen Johnston, Capt Daniel Oban, Inf
MANTEETH, Robert, Pvt, Col S Bayless, Capt Hale, E TN Mil
MANUE, Cudbirth, Pvt, Regt Commander omitted, Capt Archibald McKamey, Cav
MANUS, Alexander, Pvt, Col Wm Johnson, Capt Joseph Kirk, Mil
MANUS, Thomas, Pvt, Col Ewin Allison, Capt Winsell, E TN Drafted Mil
MANYHAM, Thomas, Pvt, Col Ewen Allison, Capt Jonas Loughmiller, Mil; transferred to Capt Griffin's
MAPLES, Ephraim, Pvt, Col David Bunch, Capt Isaac Williams, E TN Mil
MAPLES, Ephraim, Pvt, Col Samuel Bunch, Capt Isaac Williams, E TN Mil
MAPLES, Isaah, Pvt, Col Samuel Wear, Capt Simon Perry, E TN Vol Mtd Inf
MAPLES, Jesse, Cpl, Col Booth, Capt Thomas Porter, Drafted Mil
MAPLES, Thomas, Pvt, Col Samuel Bunch, Capt Isaac Williams, E TN Mil
MAPLES, William, Sgt, Col Samuel Wear & Col Samuel Bunch, Capt Wm Mitchell, E TN Mtd Inf
MAR (MAN), George, Pvt, Col Wm Johnson, Capt Benj Powell, E TN Mil; substitute for Stephen Shiplet
MARABLE, Branton, Pvt, Col Newton Cannon, Capt Ota Cantrell, W TN Mtd Inf
MARABLE, Travis, Sgt, Col Newton Cannon, Capt Ota Cantrell, W TN Mtd Inf
MARAELE, Jacob, Pvt, Col Wm Metcalf, Capt John Cunningham & Capt Alexander Hill, Mil Inf
MARBURY, Joseph, Pvt, Col Samuel Bunch, Capt Daniel Yarnell, E TN Mil
MARCH, Daniel, Pvt, Col John Brown, Capt Hugh Barton, E TN Inf
MARCHAIN, John, Pvt, Col R C Napier, Capt James McMurray, Mil Inf
MARCHANT, Edward, 2 Cpl, Regt Commander omitted, Lt James Berry, Mtd Riflemen; promoted to 1 Cpl
MARCHANT, Edward, Pvt, Regt Commander omitted, Lt James Berry, Mtd Riflemen; promoted to 2 Cpl
MARCHANT, John, Pvt, Col Robert Steele, Capt John Chitwood, Mil Inf; transferred to the Arty
MARCHANT, John, Pvt, Regt Commander omitted, Capt Joel Parrish, Arty
MARCHBANK, Burwell, Pvt, Col John Brown, Capt James Preston, E TN Mil Inf
MARCHBANK, Joel, Pvt, Regt Commander omitted, Lt Scott, Det of Inf
MARCHEL, Benjamin, Pvt, Col Wm Johnson, Capt Elihu Milliken, 3rd Regt E TN Mil
MARCKUM, James, Pvt, Col Stephen Copeland, Capt G W Steele, Mil Inf; transferred to the Arty
MARCUM, Abner, Pvt, Col Robt Steele, Capt James Randals, Inf
MARCUM, George, Pvt, Col James Raulston, Capt Mathew Neal, Inf; promoted to Sgt
MARCUM, John, Pvt, Col S Copeland, Capt Jon Biles, Inf
MARCUM, John, Pvt, Maj Gen Carroll, Col Wm Metcalf, Capt John Jackson, Inf; d 1-9-1814
MARCUM, Samuel, Pvt, Col Robt H Dyer, Capt Robt Jones, Vol Mtd Gunmen
MARCUS, Philip, Pvt, Col Alexander Loury, Capt John Looney, W TN Inf
MARE, John, Pvt, Col S Copeland, Capt Wm Douglas, Inf
MARE (MAN), George, Pvt, Col Wm Johnson, Capt Benj Powell, E TN Mil; substitute for Stephen Shiplet
MARELE, Jacob, Pvt, Col Wm Metcalf, Capt John Cunningham & Capt Alexander Hill, Mil Inf
MARES, James, Pvt, Col S Copeland, Capt Wm Douglass, Inf
MARGADY, Russell, Pvt, Col James Raulston, Capt Henry West, Inf
MARIAN, Daniel, Pvt, Col Samuel Bunch, Capt Solomon Dobkins, E TN Drafted Mil; deserted
MARIGN, John, Pvt, Col Thomas McCrory, Capt James Shannon, Mil Inf
MARION, Moses, Pvt, Col Samuel Bunch, Capt Jones Griffin, E TN Drafted Mil; joined from Capt Longmiller's Co

## Enlisted Men, War of 1812

MARION, Samuel, Pvt, Col Samuel Bunch, Capt John Houk, E TN Mil; joined from Capt Dobbins Co, discharged for inability

MARK, Asberry, Pvt, Col Wm Johnson, Capt David McKamey, E TN Drafted Mil

MARK, Henry, Pvt, Col William Lillard, Capt George Keys, E TN Inf

MARK, John, Cpl, Col S Bayless, Capt James Landen, E TN Mil

MARKBERRY, Francis, Sgt, Col Francis Baily, Capt Branch Jones, E TN Drafted Mil

MARKHAM, Absolem, Pvt, Col James Raulston, Capt Daniel Newman, Inf

MARKHAM, David, Pvt, Col Dyer, Maj Russell, Capt Isaac Williams, Separate Bn 1st Regt TN Mtd Vol Gunmen

MARKHAM, James, Pvt, Col Edward Bradley, Capt Abraham Bledsoe, Riflemen

MARKHAM, James, Pvt, Col Thomas Williamson, Capt Thomas Scurry, Branch Srvce omitted

MARKHAM, James, Pvt, Col Wm Hall, Capt Abraham Bledsoe, Vol Inf

MARKHAM, Jasper, Pvt, Col Nicholas T Perkins, Capt George Eliot, Mil Inf

MARKHAM, John, Pvt, Col Thomas Williamson, Capt Thomas Scurry, Vol Mtd Gunmen

MARKHAM, Nathaniel, Pvt, Col James Raulston, Capt Daniel Newman, Inf

MARKHAM, Peter, Sgt, Col Samuel Bunch, Capt John Houk, E TN Mil; joined from Capt Dobbins' Co

MARKHAN, David M, Cpl, Col Alexander Loury, Capt James Kincaid, Inf

MARKIM, Thomas, Pvt, Col S Copeland, Capt Wm Douglass, Inf

MARKLAND, Nathan B, Pvt, Col John Williams, Capt Wm Walker, Vol

MARKRUM, James, Pvt, Col Wm Hall, Capt Abraham Bledsoe, Vol Inf

MARKUM, James, Pvt, Joel Parrish (no rank), Arty

MARKUM, Peter, Sgt, Col Samuel Bunch, Capt Solomon Dobkins, E TN Drafted Mil; transferred to Capt Hanks Co

MARKUS, John, Pvt, Col Thomas Benton, Capt Wm J Smith, Vol Inf

MARLBORG, Wesley, Pvt, Col John Cocke, Capt John Weakley, Inf

MARLER, Avery, Ffr, Maj Wm Woodfolk, Capt Daniel Ross, Inf; Ffr under Capt Ross, Dmr under Capt McCally

MARLER, Joseph, Pvt, Col Allison, Capt Allen, E TN Mil

MARLEY, Robert, 3 Cpl, Maj John CHiles, Capt Chas Conway, E TN Mtd Gunmen

MARLIN, Edward, Pvt, Col A Cheatham, Capt James Giddens, Inf

MARLIN, Elisha, Pvt, Col Ewen Allison, Capt Wm King, Drafted Mil; deserted 1-11-1814

MARLIN, Henry, Pvt, Col Robert Steele, Capt Samuel Maxwell, Mil Inf

MARLIN, James, Pvt, Col Jno Coffee, Capt Chas Kavanaugh, Cav; AWOL

MARLIN, James, Pvt, Col Jno Coffee, Capt Robert Jetton, Cav

MARLIN, James, Pvt, Col John Alcorn, Capt Robert Jetton, Vol Cav

MARLIN, John, Pvt, Col John Alcorn, Capt Robert Jetton, Vol Cav

MARLIN, William, Pvt, Col Edwin Booth, Capt John McKamey, E TN Mil

MARLIN, William, Pvt, Col Newton Cannon, Capt Wm Edwards, Regt Command

MARLIN, William, Pvt, Col R C Napier, Capt Thos Preston, Mil Inf

MARLIN (MARLON), James, 2 Cpl, Col Philip Pipkin, Capt George Mebane, Mil Inf

MARLIN (MARLON), Joseph, 2 Cpl, Col Philip Pipkin, Capt George Mebane, Mil Inf

MARLIN (MORLEN), John, Pvt, Col Jno Coffee, Capt Robert Jetton, Cav

MARLONE, Alfred P, Pvt, Col R H Dyer, Capt Robert Edmonston, 1st TN Vol Mtd Gunmen

MARLORN, Basdal, Pvt, Col Thos Williamson, Capt Beverly Williams, Vol Mtd Gunmen

MARLORN, James, Pvt, Col Thos Williamson, Capt Beverly Williams, Vol Mtd Gunmen

MARLOW, James, Pvt, Col Jno Coffee, Capt Robert Jetton, Cav

MARLOW, James, Pvt, Col John K Winn, Capt John Spinks, Inf

MARLOW, James, Pvt, Col Thos Williamson, Capt Beverly Williams, Vol Mtd Gunmen

MARLOW, Payton, Pvt, Col Thos Williamson, Capt Robert Moore, Vol Mtd Gunmen

MARLOW, Richard, Pvt, Col Newton Cannon, Capt John Harpole, Mtd Gunmen

MARLOW, Richard, Pvt, Col Thos Williamson, Capt Robert Moore, Vol Mtd Gunmen

MARLOW, Stephen, Pvt, Col James Raulston, Capt Haynie, Maj Gen Carroll, Inf

MARLOW, William, Pvt, Col Phillip Pipkin, Capt Ebenezer Kirkpatrick, Mil Inf

MARMEN, John, Pvt, Maj Gen Carroll, Capt Ellis, Inf

MARNEY, Samuel, Pvt, Col John Brown, Capt Allen I Bacon, E TN Mil Inf

MARR, John, Pvt, Col Wm Lillard, Capt Wm Lillard, Inf Vol

MARR, Lloyd, Pvt, Col Jas Raulston, Capt James Cowan, Inf

MARR, William, Pvt, Col Thos Benton, Capt Isaah Renshaw, Vol Inf; joined for Capt Hewett Co

MARREN, Daniel, Pvt, Col R H Dyer, Capt James Wyatt, Vol Mtd Gunmen

MARRILL, Boze, Cpl, Col Wm Hall, Capt Abraham Bledsoe, Vol Inf

MARRS, James, Pvt, Col Wm Metcalf, Capt Bird L Hurt, Mil Inf

MARRS, Will, Pvt, Col Thos Benton, Capt Isaah Renshaw, Vol Inf; trans to Capt Hewett's Co

MARRS, William, Pvt, Col Thos Benton, Capt Benj Hewett, Vol Inf

MARRS, William, Pvt, Col Wm Pillow, CApt Isiah Renshaw, Inf

MARS, Griffin, Pvt, Col Wm Metcalf, Capt Andrew Pat-

- 325

## Enlisted Men, War of 1812

terson, Mil Inf
MARS, Loya, Pvt, Col Wm Johnson, Capt Elihu Milliken, 3 Regt E Tn Mil
MARS, Samuel, Pvt, Col Phillip Pipkin, CApt Ebenezer Kirkpatrick, Mil Inf
MARSH, Gravaner, Pvt, Col Wm Lillard, Capt Wm McLin, E Tn Inf
MARSH, William, Pvt, Lt Col L Hammond, Col Alexander Loury, Capt Thos Delaney, Inf
MARSHAL, Ayers, Col John Williams, Capt Wm Walker, Vol ?
MARSHAL, Joel, Pvt, Col Wm Johnson, Capt James Tunnell, E TN Mil
MARSHAL, Joseph, Pvt, Col Samuel Bunch, Capt James Cummings, E TN Vol Mtd Inf; died 12-8-1813
MARSHALL, Benjamin, Pvt, Col Samuel Bunch, Capt Francis Berry, E Tn Mil
MARSHALL, Eli, Pvt, Col John K Winn, Capt Wm McCall, Inf
MARSHALL, Goodrum, Pvt, Col Thos Benton, Capt Henry L Douglass, Vol Inf
MARSHALL, Henry, Pvt, Col Ewen Allison, Capt J Loughmiller, Mil; trans to Capt Griffin's Co
MARSHALL, Henry, Pvt, Col S Bunch, Capt Jones Griffin, E TN Draft Mil; joined from Capt Longmiller Co
MARSHALL, Israel, Pvt, Col John K Winn, Capt John Spinks, Inf
MARSHALL, Jesse, Pvt, Col Thos Williamson, Capt Wm Metcalf, Vol Mtd Gunmen
MARSHALL, John, Pvt, Col R H Dyer, Capt Cuthbert Hudson, Vol Mtd Gunmen
MARSHALL, John, Pvt, Col Wm Lillard, Capt Wm Gillenwater, E TN Inf
MARSHALL, Leaven, Sgt, Col Newton Cannon, CApt Isaac Williams, Mtd Riflemen
MARSHALL, Mark, Pvt, Col Edwin Booth, Capt Richard Marshall, Drafted Mil
MARSHALL, Richard, Pvt, Col Jas Raulston, Capt Mathew Neal, Inf
MARSHALL, Robert, Pvt, Col Jno Coffee, Capt Thos Bradley, Vol Cav
MARSHALL, Robert, Pvt, Col John Alcorn, Capt Thos Bradley, Vol Inf
MARSHALL, Robert, Pvt, Col John K Winn, Capt John Spinks, Inf; trans to Capt Bradley's Co
MARSHALL, Stocton, Pvt, Col Edwin Booth, Capt Alexander Biggs, Inf; died 12-15-1814
MARSHALL, William, Pvt, Col John Cocke, Capt Bird Nance, Inf
MARSHALL, William, Pvt, Col Samuel Bunch, Capt James Cummings, E Tn Vol Mtd Inf
MARSHALL, William, Pvt, Maj Gen Wm Carroll, Col Jas Raulston, Capt Wiley Huddleston, Inf
MARTEN, James, Pvt, Col Samuel Wear, Capt John Stephens, E TN Vol Inf
MARTEN, Samuel, Pvt, Col Thos Benton, Capt Benj Hewett, Vol Inf
MARTEN, Stephen, Pvt, Col Samuel Wear, Capt Robert Doak, E TN Vol Inf
MARTEN, Thomas, Cpl, Col Jno Coffee, Capt John W Byrns, Cav
MARTERS, John, Pvt, Maj Gen A Jackson, Capt John Craine, Mtd Gunmen
MARTIAL, Elie, Pvt, Col Edward Bradley, Capt Wm Lauderdale, Vol Inf
MARTIAL, Hardy, Pvt, Col Edward Bradley, Capt Wm Lauderdale, Vol Inf
MARTIAL, Hardy, Pvt, Col Wm Hall, Capt Wm L Alexander, Vol Inf
MARTIAL, Jesse, Pvt, Col Edward Bradley, Capt Wm Lauderdale, Vol Inf
MARTIAL, Jesse, Pvt, Col Wm Hall, Capt Wm L Alexander, Vol Inf
MARTIAL, William, Pvt, Col Edward Bradley, Capt Harry L Douglass, Vol Inf
MARTIN, Ambrose, Pvt, Col R C Napier, Capt Edward Neblett, Mil Inf
MARTIN, Andrew, Pvt, Col A Loury, Capt Gabriel Martin, Inf
MARTIN, Andrew, Pvt, Col John K Wynne, Capt Robert Breden, Inf
MARTIN, Benjamin, Pvt, Regt Commander omitted, Capt Gray, Inf
MARTIN, Caffey, Pvt, Col Thomas Benton, Capt William J Smith, Vol Inf
MARTIN, Daniel, Pvt, Col A Cheatham, Maj Gen A Jackson, Inf
MARTIN, Daniel, Pvt, Col S Copeland, Capt John Holshouser, Inf
MARTIN, Daniel, Pvt, Col Samuel Bunch, Capt Joseph Duncan, E Tn Drafted Mil; trans to Capt English
MARTIN, David, 1 Cpl, Col Wm Metcalf, Capt Alexander Hill & Capt John Cunningham, Mil Inf; promoted to 2 Sgt
MARTIN, David, Pvt, Col James Raulston, Capt Daniel Newman, Inf
MARTIN, David, Pvt, Col John K Wynne, Capt James Cole, Inf
MARTIN, David, Pvt, Col Newton Cannon, Capt James Walton, Mtd Riflemen
MARTIN, David, Pvt, Col Samuel Bunch, Capt Jno English, E TN Draft Mil
MARTIN, Elisha, Pvt, Col Edwin Booth, Capt John Lewis, E Tn Mil
MARTIN, Elisha, Pvt, Col T McCrory, Capt Jas Shannon, Mil Inf
MARTIN, George W, Pvt, Col Thos Williamson, Capt Anthony M Metcalf, Vol Mtd Gunmen
MARTIN, George W, Sgt, Capt Wm Carroll, Maj Gen A Jackson, Vol Inf
MARTIN, George, Pvt, Col Edwin Booth, Capt John Lewis, E TN Mil
MARTIN, George, Pvt, Col Thos H Benton, Capt Geo W Gibbs, Vol Inf
MARTIN, George, Pvt, Regt Commander omitted, Capt Gray, Inf
MARTIN, Hugh, Pvt, Col Wm Lillard, Capt Jacob Hartsell, E Tn Vol Inf
MARTIN, Isaac, Pvt, Col John Williams, Capt David Vance, Mtd Mil
MARTIN, James G, Pvt, Col Philip Pipkin, Capt Wm

## Enlisted Men, War of 1812

Mackay, Mil Inf

MARTIN, James H, Pvt, Col Thomas Williamson, Capt James Cook & Capt John Crane, Vol Mtd Gunmen

MARTIN, James H, Pvt, Col Wm Y Higgins, Capt John B Cheatham, Mtd Riflemen

MARTIN, James H, Pvt, Lt Col Archer Cheatham, Co Commander omitted, 6th Brig Inf

MARTIN, James, Ffr, Col Wm Metcalf, Capt Alexander Hill & Capt John Cunningham, Mil Inf; promoted to Ffr Maj

MARTIN, James, Pvt, Col R C Napier, Capt John Chism, Mil Inf; transferred to the Arty

MARTIN, James, Pvt, Col S Copeland, Capt John Holshouser, Inf

MARTIN, James, Pvt, Col William Hall, Capt John Moore, Vol Inf

MARTIN, James, Pvt, Col Wm Metcalf, Capt John Barnhart, Mil Inf; d 2-8-1815

MARTIN, James, Pvt, Gen Andrew Jackson, Capt Joel Parrish, Arty

MARTIN, James, Pvt, Regt Commander omitted, Capt James Cowan, Inf

MARTIN, Jesse, Pvt, Col A Loury, Capt J N Williams, W TN Mil

MARTIN, Jesse, Pvt, Col Samuel Bunch, Capt Joseph Duncan, E TN Drafted Mil; joined from Capt Harris's Co

MARTIN, Jesse, Pvt, Col Wm Y Higgins, Capt John B Cheatham, Mtd Riflemen

MARTIN, Jessee, Pvt, Lt Col Archer Cheatham, Co Commander omitted, 6th Brig Inf

MARTIN, John D, Pvt, Regt Commander omitted, Capt D Mason, Cav

MARTIN, John H, 2 Sgt, Col Wm Hall, Capt Brice Martin, Vol Inf

MARTIN, John I, QM Sgt, Col Newton Cannon, TN Vol Mtd Riflemen

MARTIN, John L, Pvt, Col Newton Cannon, Capt James Walton, Mtd Riflemen; appointed QM Sgt

MARTIN, John L, Pvt, Col Wm Hall, Capt Brice Martin, Vol Inf; promoted to Maj of 2nd Regt

MARTIN, John L, Pvt, Gen Andrew Jackson, Capt William Russell, Mtd Spies

MARTIN, John S, Sgt, Regt Commander omitted, Capt James Cowan, Inf

MARTIN, John, Pvt, Col Edwin E Booth, Capt John Porter, Drafted Mil

MARTIN, John, Pvt, Col John Cocke, Capt Bird Nance, Inf; discharged by Court Martial 11-16-1814

MARTIN, John, Pvt, Col R C Dyer, Maj Wm Russell, Capt Wm Russell, Vol Mtd Gunmen

MARTIN, John, Pvt, Col Samuel Bayless, Capt Branch Jones, E TN Drafted Mil

MARTIN, John, Pvt, Col Samuel Bunch, Capt Andrew Breden, E TN Mil

MARTIN, John, Pvt, Col Samuel Copeland, Capt James Tait, Inf

MARTIN, John, Pvt, Col Samuel Wear, Capt John Stephens, E TN Vol Inf

MARTIN, John, Pvt, Col Samuel Wear, Capt Rufus Morgan, E TN Vol Inf

MARTIN, John, Pvt, Gen Andrew Jackson, Capt D Deaderick, Arty

MARTIN, John, Pvt, Maj James P Porter, Capt James Anderson, Cav

MARTIN, John, Rank omitted, Maj Gen John Cocke, TN Vol Mtd Gunmen

MARTIN, Jonathan, Pvt, Col Newton Cannon, Capt Francis Jones, Mtd Riflemen

MARTIN, Joseph, Pvt, Col John Coffee, Capt Charles Kavanaugh, Cav; AWOL

MARTIN, Joseph, Pvt, Col William Pillow, Capt Jas McFerrin, Inf; substitute for B Gilliand

MARTIN, Lewis, Pvt, Col Alexander Loury, Capt George Sarver, Inf

MARTIN, Merrit, Pvt, Maj Gen Andrew Jackson, Col Thomas H Williamson, Capt Robert Steele, Vol Mtd Gunmen

MARTIN, Michael, Pvt, Col S Copeland, Capt Robert Evans, Mil Inf

MARTIN, Moses, Pvt, Col Edwin E Booth, Capt John Sharp, E TN Mil

MARTIN, Nathan, Pvt, Col William Y Higgins, Capt Samuel A Allen, Mtd Gunmen

MARTIN, Oliver, Sgt, Regt Commander omitted, Capt James Craig, Inf

MARTIN, Orsamus A, Pvt, Col Wm Lillard, Capt Maloney, E TN Vol Inf

MARTIN, Patrick H, Pvt, Col Thomas H Williamson, Capt Wm Metcalf, Vol Mtd Inf; promoted to Adjt in Col T Williamson

MARTIN, Patrick H, Pvt, Regt Commander omitted, Capt D Deadrick, Arty

MARTIN, Patrick, Pvt, Col A Cheatham, Co Commander omitted, Inf

MARTIN, Richard, Pvt, Col Edwin E Booth, Capt Thomas Porter, Drafted Mil

MARTIN, Richard, Pvt, Col James Raulston, Capt Daniel Newman, Inf; d 2-5-1815

MARTIN, Richard, Pvt, Col John Alcorn, Capt Thomas Bradley, Vol Inf

MARTIN, Richard, Pvt, Col Robert Steele, Capt James Randals, Inf

MARTIN, Richard, Pvt, Regt Commander omitted, Capt James Cowan, Mtd Inf

MARTIN, Robert, Cpl, Col A Loury, Capt Hammond & Capt Arahel Rains, Inf

MARTIN, Robert, Pvt, Col William Lillard, Capt Thomas Sharpe, 2nd Regt Inf; deserted

MARTIN, Robert, Pvt, Maj John Chiles, Capt John Stephens, E TN Vol Mtd Inf

MARTIN, Samuel N, Pvt, Regt Commander omitted, Capt D Mason, Cav

MARTIN, Samuel N, Vol Mtd Gunmen, Col Thomas H Williamson, Capt Wm Martin, Vol Mtd Gunmen

MARTIN, Samuel, Pvt, Col R H Dyer, Capt James McMahon, TN Vol Mtd Gunmen

MARTIN, Samuel, Pvt, Col R H Dyer, Maj Wm Russell, Capt Wm Russell, Vol Mtd Gunmen

MARTIN, Samuel, Pvt, Col Thomas H Benton, Capt George Caperton, Vol Inf

MARTIN, Samuel, Pvt, Regt Commander omitted, Capt James Cowan, Inf
MARTIN, Samuel, Sgt Maj, Col Edwin E Booth, Co Commander omitted, E TN Mil
MARTIN, Signal, Pvt, Lt Col Leroy Hammond, Capt Wall, Inf
MARTIN, Thomas, Pvt, Col Edward Bradley, Capt Wm Brice Martin, Vol Inf
MARTIN, Thomas, Pvt, Col John Coffee, Capt Charles Kavanaugh, Cav
MARTIN, Thomas, Pvt, Col John Coffee, Capt George Byron, Cav
MARTIN, Thomas, Pvt, Col S Bayless, Capt John Brock, E TN Mil
MARTIN, Thomas, Pvt, Col Wm Hall, Capt Brice Martin, Vol Inf; refused to march, waiter for Maj Wm Martin
MARTIN, Thomas, Pvt, Col Wm Metcalf, Capt John Barnhardt, Mil Inf
MARTIN, William B, Sgt, Maj James Porter, Capt James Anderson, Cav
MARTIN, William, Pvt, Col Edwin E Booth, Capt Marshall, Drafted Mil
MARTIN, William, Pvt, Col James Raulston, Capt Mathew Neale, Inf
MARTIN, William, Pvt, Col John Alcorn, Capt Bradley, Branch Srvce omitted
MARTIN, William, Pvt, Col Newton Cannon, Capt William Edwards, Regt Command
MARTIN, William, Pvt, Col R C Napier, Capt Early Benson, Mil Inf
MARTIN, William, Pvt, Col R C Napier, Capt Edward Neblett, Mil Inf
MARTIN, William, Pvt, Col Robert Dyer, Capt Thomas White, Vol Mtd Gunmen
MARTIN, William, Pvt, Col S Bunch, no other information
MARTIN, William, Pvt, Col Samuel Bunch, Capt Edward Buchanan, E TN Mil
MARTIN, William, Pvt, Col William Hall, Capt Brice Martin, Vol Inf
MARTIN, William, Pvt, Col Wm Lillard, Co Commander omitted, E TN Inf
MARTIN, William, Pvt, Maj John Chiles, Capt John Stephens, E TN Vol Mtd Inf
MARTIN, William, Pvt, Maj William Woodfolk, Capt Ezekial Ross & Capt McCully, Inf
MARTIN, William, Pvt, Maj Wm Russell, Co Commander omitted, Vol Mtd Gunmen
MARTIN, William, Pvt, Maj Wm Woodfolk, Capt Abner Pearce, Inf; joined by transfer from Capt Dudney's Co
MARTIN, William, Pvt, Maj Wm Woodfolk, Co Commander omitted, Inf; transferred to Capt A Pearce
MARTIN, Wyly, Pvt, Regt Commander omitted, Capt Sam Bunch, Branch Srvce omitted
MARTIN, _____, Pvt, Col L Hammond, Capt J N Williamson, 2 Regt Inf
MARTON, John Sam, Pvt, Col Higgins, Capt Dale, Mtd Gunmen
MARTON, John, Cpl, Col Higgins, Capt Dale, Mtd Gunmen
MARTY, Daniel, Pvt, Regt Commander omitted, Capt Wm J Smith, Branch Srvce omitted
MARVELL, William, Pvt, Col Wm Hall, Capt Wallace, Inf
MASER, Jacob, Pvt, Col Edwin Booth, Capt Marshall, Drafted Mil
MASER, Michael, Pvt, Col Edwin Booth, Capt Marshall, Drafted Mil
MASER, Solomon, Pvt, Col Edwin Booth, Capt Marshall, Drafted Mil
MASES, Samuel, Pvt, Col William Johnson, Capt Andrew Lawson, E TN Drafted Mil; substitute for Joshua Simmons
MASEY, Charles, 1 Sgt, Col Edwin Booth, Capt John Sharpe, E TN Mil
MASH, Joel, Pvt, Maj Gen Carroll, Capt Ellis, Inf
MASH, Obidiah, Pvt, Col T McCrory, Capt William Dooley, Inf
MASHEL, Thomas, Pvt, Col S Bayless, Capt Hale, E TN Mil
MASON, Abraham, Sgt, Col Wm Pillow, Capt Mason, Vol Inf
MASON, Abram, 1 Sgt, Col Thomas Benton, Capt N Cannon, Inf
MASON, Asa, Pvt, Col A Cheatham, Capt Richard Benson, Inf
MASON, Charles, 3 Sgt, Lt Col Leroy Hammonds, Capt Thomas Wells, Inf
MASON, Coleman, Pvt, Col John Cocke, Capt Nance, Inf
MASON, Edmond, Pvt, Col S Wear, Capt Price, E TN Vol Inf
MASON, Edmond, Pvt, Maj Childs, Capt Price, Vol Mtd Gunmen
MASON, Gilbert, Pvt, Col N Cannon, Capt Thomas Yardley, Mtd Riflemen
MASON, Gilford, Pvt, Col Thomas Williamson, Capt John Crane, Vol Mtd Gunmen
MASON, Henry, Pvt, Col Thomas Williamson, Capt Crane & Capt Cook, Vol Mtd Gunmen; d 2-11-1815
MASON, Isaac, Sgt, Col A Cheatham, Co Commander omitted, Inf
MASON, James, Pvt, Col John Winn, Capt Robert Bradin, Inf
MASON, John, Pvt, Col Edwin Booth, Capt Porter, Drafted Mil
MASON, John, Pvt, Col William Johnston, Capt Henry Hunter, E TN Mil
MASON, Nathaniel, Pvt, Col John Williams, Capt David Vance, Mil
MASON, Phillip, Pvt, Col John Cocke, Capt Richard Crunk, Inf
MASON, Phillip, Pvt, Col William Higgins, Capt A Cheatham, Mtd Riflemen
MASON, Robert, Pvt, Lt Col Richard Napier, Co Commander omitted, Inf
MASON, Sion, Pvt, Col A Cheatham, Capt Richard Benson, Inf
MASON, Thomas, Pvt, Col Thomas Benton, Capt N Cannon, Vol Inf

## Enlisted Men, War of 1812

MASON, Thomas, Pvt, Col William Pillow, Capt Joseph Mason, Vol Inf

MASONER, George, Pvt, Col Ewen Allison, Capt Thomas Wilson, E TN Drafted Mil; appointed Wgnr

MASONER, Peter, Pvt, Col Ewen Allison, Capt Jacob Hoyal, E TN Mil

MASONGALE, John, Pvt, Regt Commander omitted, Capt Samuel Bunch, Branch Srvce omitted

MASSA, Isaac, Pvt, Col Philip Pipkin, Capt David Smith, Inf

MASSEE, Adam, Sgt, Regt Commander omitted, Capt Smith, Vol Inf

MASSEE, Samuel, Cpl, Col John Winn, Capt John Spinks, Inf

MASSEE, Thomas, Sgt, Regt Commander omitted, Capt Smith, Vol Inf

MASSENGALE, Blake, Pvt, Regt Commander omitted, Capt Josiah Askew, Inf

MASSENGALE, Levi, Pvt, Regt Commander omitted, Capt Gray, Inf

MASSENGATE, Blacke, Pvt, Regt Commander omitted, Capt Gray, Inf

MASSEY, Adam, 2 Sgt, Col Thomas Benton, Capt William J Smith, Vol Inf

MASSEY, Adam, Sgt, Col Thomas Benton, Capt William J Smith, Vol Inf

MASSEY, Drury, Pvt, Lt Col L Hammond, Capt James Craig, Inf

MASSEY, Isaac, Pvt, Ens Wm Pegran, Col Philip Pipkin, Capt David Smythe, W TN Mil

MASSEY, James, Pvt, Col William Lillard, Capt James Lillard, E TN Vol Inf

MASSEY, Jeremiah, Pvt, Col R H Dyer, Capt Joseph Williams, Vol Mtd Gunmen

MASSEY, Joel, Pvt, Col R H Dyer, Capt Joseph Williams, Vol Mtd Gunmen

MASSEY, John B, 1 Cpl, Brig Gen Thos Johnston, Capt Robert Carson, Inf

MASSEY, John, Pvt, Col Samuel Bayless, Capt Joseph Goodson, E TN Mil

MASSEY, John, Pvt, Regt Commander omitted, Capt Josiah Askew, Inf

MASSEY, Sevier, Pvt, Col Samuel Bayless, Capt Branch Jones, E TN Mil Drafted

MASSEY, Stephen, Pvt, Col Ewen Allison, Capt Jacob Hoyal, E TN Mil; deserted

MASSEY, Stephen, Pvt, Col Samuel Bayless, Capt Joseph Hale, E TN Mil; substitute for Jacob Smith

MASSEY, Thomas, 1 Sgt, Col Thos Benton, Capt Wm J Smith, Vol Inf

MASSEY, Thomas, Pvt, Col Newton Cannon, Capt George Brandon, Mtd Riflemen

MASSEY, Thomas, Pvt, Col Thomas Benton, Capt William J Smith, Vol Inf

MASSEY, William, Pvt, Col John K Wynne, Capt Robert Breden, Inf

MASSEY, William, Pvt, Maj Gen Wm Carroll, Col James Raulston, Capt Edward Robinson, Inf; d 3-4-1815

MASSIE, Peter, Pvt, Col Samuel Wear, Capt Joseph Calloway, Mtd Inf

MASSIMORE, Jacob, Pvt, Col Ewen Allison, Capt Jacob Hoyal, E TN Mil; transferred to Capt McPherson's

MASSINGALE, Alfred, Sgt, Col Wm Y Higgins, Capt Thomas Eldridge, Mtd Gunmen

MASSINGALE, George, Pvt, Col William Johnson, Capt Andrew Lawson, E TN Drafted Mil

MASSINGALE, James, Pvt, Col Wm Lillard, Capt Benjamin King, E TN Vol Inf; detached as QM Sgt

MASSINGALE, Joseph, QM Sgt, Col Wm Lillard, E TN Vol Mil

MASSY, Sims, Pvt, Col Edward Bradley, Capt Abraham Bledsoe, Riflemen

MASSY, Stephen, Pvt, Col Samuel Bunch, Capt Henry Stephens, E TN Mtd Inf

MASSY, Stephen, Pvt, Col William Johnston, Capt Joseph Kirk, Mil

MASSY, Thomas, Pvt, Col Wm Johnston, Capt James Stewart, E TN Drafted Mil

MATES, Henry, Dmr, Col Wm Johnson, Capt James Stewart, E TN Drafted Mil

MATHAS, James, Pvt, Maj Gen Wm Carroll, Capt Francis Ellis, Inf

MATHAS (MATHIS), Drury, Pvt, Col John Cocke, Capt James Gray, Inf

MATHENA, James, Pvt, Maj John Chiles, Capt Charles Conway, E TN Mtd Gunmen

MATHENY, Elijah, Pvt, Col Samuel Bunch, Capt James Penny, E TN Mtd Inf

MATHENY, John, Pvt, Regt Commander omitted, Capt Gray, Inf

MATHENY, Luke, Pvt, Col R H Dyer, Maj William Russell, Capt William Russell, Vol Mtd Gunmen

MATHENY, Samuel, Pvt, Col Samuel Bayless, Capt Joseph Hale, E TN Mil

MATHENY, William, Pvt, Col John Cocke, Capt Bird Nance, Inf

MATHENY, William, Pvt, Col Wm Metcalf, Capt Alexander Hill & Capt John Cunningham, Mil Inf

MATHENY, William, Pvt, Col Wm Metcalf, Capt Wm Mullin, Mil Inf

MATHEWS, Absolem, Pvt, Col Edwin Booth, Capt Richard Marshall, Drafted Mil

MATHEWS, Absolem, Pvt, Col Thos Benton, Capt Wm J Smith, Vol Inf

MATHEWS, Archibald, Pvt, Col John K Wynne, Capt James Cole, Inf

MATHEWS, Benjamin, Pvt, Col Edwin Booth, Capt Ricahrd Marshall, Drafted Mil

MATHEWS, Daniel, Pvt, Col Edwin Booth, Capt Richard Marshall, Drafted Mil

MATHEWS, David, Pvt, Col Edwin Booth, Capt Alexander Biggs, Inf

MATHEWS, David, Pvt, Col Edwin Booth, Capt Richard Marshall, Drafted Mil

MATHEWS, Drury, Pvt, Regt Commander omitted, Capt Gray, Inf

MATHEWS, Drury, Pvt, Regt Commander omitted, Capt Josiah Askew, Inf

MATHEWS, Ebenezer, Sgt, Col Ewen Allison, Capt Henry McCray, E TN Mil

MATHEWS, Ezekiel, Pvt, Col William Hall, Capt Abra-

- 329

## Enlisted Men, War of 1812

ham Bledsoe, Vol Inf
MATHEWS, George, 2 Sgt, Col Wm Y Higgins, Capt Samuel A Allen, Mtd Gunmen
MATHEWS, Jacob, Pvt, Col Jno Coffee, Capt Alexander McKeen, Cav
MATHEWS, James, Pvt, Col T McCrory, Capt Abel Willis, Mil Inf; killed 11-9-1813? at Talledega
MATHEWS, James, Pvt, Col William Metcalf, Capt Thomas Marks, Mil Inf
MATHEWS, James, Pvt, Maj Gen A Jackson, Col A Cheatham, Capt Wm Creel, Inf
MATHEWS, Jeremiah, Pvt, Regt Commander omitted, Capt Jno Miller, Spies; transferred to Capt Russel's Spies
MATHEWS, John, Pvt, Col A Cheatham, Capt George G Chapman, Inf
MATHEWS, John, Pvt, Col Robert Steele, Capt James Shinault, Mil Inf
MATHEWS, John, Pvt, Col Thomas Williamson, Capt James Cook & Capt John Crane, Vol Mtd Gunmen; d 3-27-1815
MATHEWS, Joseph, Pvt, Col Wm Hall, Capt Travis C Nash, Inf
MATHEWS, Joseph, Pvt, Regt Commander omitted, Capt Hugh Kerr, Mtd Rangers
MATHEWS, Lazarus, Pvt, Col John Cocke, Capt James Cole, Inf
MATHEWS, Lemuel, Pvt, Col Alexander Loury, Lt Col L Hammonds, Capt Arahel Rains, Inf
MATHEWS, Lewis, Pvt, Col R H Dyer, Capt James McMahon, 1st TN Vol Mtd Gunmen
MATHEWS, Lewis, Pvt, Col Thomas McCrory, Capt Sam'l B McKnight, Inf
MATHEWS, Moses, Pvt, Regt Commander omitted, Capt Ephraim Dickson, Branch Srvce omitted
MATHEWS, Pointer, Pvt, Col Ewen Allison, Capt Henry McCray, E TN Mil
MATHEWS, Preston, Pvt, Col John K Winn, Capt James Cole, Inf; deserted
MATHEWS, Richard, Pvt, Col S Copeland, Capt David Williams, Inf
MATHEWS, Richard, Pvt, Col Thomas Williamson, Capt James Cook & Capt John Crane, Vol Mtd Inf; d 4-1-1815
MATHEWS, Thomas, Pvt, Col Robert Steele, Capt James Shinault, Mil Inf
MATHEWS, William E, Pvt, Col John Cocke, Capt Bird Nance, Inf
MATHEWS, William, Dmr, Col Philip Pipkin, Capt John Robertson, Mil Inf; deserted
MATHEWS, William, Pvt, Brig Gen Thos Johnson, Capt Robert Carson, Inf
MATHEWS, William, Pvt, Col S Copeland, Capt James Tait, Inf
MATHEWSON, John, Pvt, Col John Cocke, Capt James Gray, Inf
MATHIAS, Ezekiel, Dmr, Col Joseph Hale, Capt Abraham Bledsoe, Vol Inf
MATHIAS, Stephen, 1 Cpl, Col Philip Pipkin, Ens Wm Pegram, Det of David Smith Co W TN Mil
MATHIAS, Stephen, Pvt, Col Philip Pipkin, Capt David Smith, Inf
MATHIAS, Thomas, 3 Sgt, Col Philip Pipkin, Ens Wm Pegram, Det of David Smith Co W TN Mil
MATHIAS, Thomas, Sgt, Col Philip Pipkin, Capt David Smith, Inf
MATHIONS, George, Pvt, Col Samuel Bayless, Capt Solomon Hendrix, E TN Mil
MATHIS, Broten, Pvt, Col Wm Johnson, Capt James R Rogers, E TN Drafted Mil
MATHIS, Joseph, Pvt, Col William Johnson, Capt Joseph Scott, E TN Drafted Mil
MATHIS, Joseph, Pvt, Col Edward Bradley, Capt Travis Nance, Vol Inf
MATHIS, Luke, Sdlr, Regt Commander omitted, Capt Edwin S Moore, Mtd Riflemen
MATHIS, Richard, Pvt, Col Thos Williamson, Capt Richard Tate, Vol Mtd Gunmen
MATHIS, Richard, Pvt, Col Wm Pillow, Capt Thos Williamson, Vol Inf
MATHIS, Robert, Pvt, Col Samuel Bunch, Capt Isaac Williams, E TN Mil
MATHIS, Thomas, Pvt, Col Samuel Bayless, Capt Jonathan Waddle, E TN Mil
MATHIS (MATHEWS), Isaac, Pvt, Maj Gen William Carroll, Capt Francis Ellis, Inf
MATHIS (MATHEWS), William, Pvt, Col Alexander Loury, Capt Gabriel Martin, Inf
MATHORN, George, Pvt, Col William Lillard, Capt Benjamin King, E TN Vol Inf
MATHORN, Henry, Pvt, Col Samuel Bayless, Capt James Landen, E TN Mil
MATHS, Adam, Pvt, Col John K Winn, Capt John Porter, Inf; killed at Talledega 11-9-1813
MATLOCK, B James, Pvt, Maj Gen Wm Carroll, Capt Francis Ellis, Inf; promoted to Cpl
MATLOCK, Benjamin, Pvt, Col R H Dyer, Capt Joseph Williams, Vol Mtd Gunmen
MATLOCK, Benjamin, Pvt, Regt Commander omitted, Capt James Craig, Inf
MATLOCK, Berry, Pvt, Col Robert Steele, Capt John Chitwood, Mil Inf
MATLOCK, Bird, Pvt, Regt Commander omitted, Capt James Haggard, Mtd Gunmen
MATLOCK, Byrd, Pvt, Col Robert Jarmon, Capt Nathan Peoples, Inf
MATLOCK, Byrd, Pvt, Regt Commander omitted, Capt William Teas, 6th Brig Inf
MATLOCK, Charles, Pvt, Regt Commander omitted, Capt James Haggard, Mtd Gunmen
MATLOCK, David, 4 Sgt, Col William Hall, Capt John Kennedy, Vol Inf
MATLOCK, David, Sgt, Col William Hall, Capt John Kennedy, Branch Srvce omitted
MATLOCK, Henry, Pvt, Col John Williams, Capt Wm Walker, Vol
MATLOCK, Henry, Pvt, Col Samuel Wear, Capt Jesse Cole, Vol Inf
MATLOCK, Isaac, Pvt, Col Edwin Booth, Capt John McKamey, E TN Mil
MATLOCK, Isham, Cpl, Col Wm Johnson, Capt Henry Hunter, E TN Mil; transferred to Capt Millican's

MATLOCK, Isham, Pvt, Col Samuel Wear, Capt Jesse Cole, Vol Inf
MATLOCK, James, Pvt, Col Robert Steele, Capt Richard M Ratton, Mil Inf
MATLOCK, John, Pvt, Col S Bunch, Capt Jno Hauk, E TN Mil; discharged for inability
MATLOCK, John, Pvt, Col Samuel Bunch, Capt Thos Mann, E TN Vol Mtd Inf
MATLOCK, Moses, Pvt, Col Robert Dyer, Capt Thomas Jones, Vol Mtd Gunmen; substitute for Jas Carter
MATLOCK, Moses, Pvt, Regt Commander omitted, Capt Jos Haggard, Mtd Gunmen
MATLOCK, Nicholas, Pvt, Col S Bunch, Capt Daniel Yarnell, E TN Mil
MATLOCK, Ransom, Pvt, Col William Johnson, Capt Henry Hunter, E TN Mil; attached to the Corps of Wgnrs
MATLOCK, Ranson, Pvt, Col S Wear, Capt Cole, Vol Inf
MATLOCK, Seofield?, Pvt, Col Ewen Allison, Capt Allen, E TN Mil
MATLOCK, Smith, Pvt, Col R Jarmon, Capt T Hamilton, Inf
MATLOCK, Smythe, Pvt, Col R C Dyer, Capt Joseph Williamson, Vol Mtd Gunmen
MATLOCK, Valentine, Pvt, Col Edward Bradley, Capt John Kennedy, Riflemen
MATLOCK, Vanlentin, Sgt, Col Wm Hall, Capt John Kennedy, Vol Inf
MATLOCK, William, Cpl, Col James Raulston, Capt James Hamilton, Inf
MATLOCK, William, Pvt, Col John Wynn, Capt William McCall, Inf
MATLOCK, William, Pvt, Col R T Perkins, Capt John B Quarles, Vol Mtd Inf
MATLOCK, William, Pvt, Col Robert Dyer, Capt Thomas Jones, Vol Mtd Gunmen
MATLOCK, William, Pvt, Col S Wear, Capt Jesse Cole, Vol Inf
MATLOCK, William, Pvt, Maj Gen Jackson, Col A Cheatham, Capt William Creel, Inf
MATLOCK, Zachariah, Pvt, Col S Copeland, Capt Moses Thompson, Inf
MATRITH, William, Pvt, Col John Cocke, Capt John Weakley, Inf
MATSON, John, Pvt, Col S Bunch, Capt Isaac Williams, E TN Mil
MATTHEWS, Absolam, Pvt, Col Thomas Benton, Capt Wm J Smith, Vol Inf
MATTHEWS, Cornelius, Pvt, Col Thos McCrory, Capt Jas Shannon, Mil Inf
MATTHEWS, David, Pvt, Col Alexander Loury, Capt Leroy Hammonds & Capt Raines, Inf
MATTHEWS, Jeremiah, Pvt, Regt Commander omitted, Capt John Miller, Spies; transferred to Capt Russell's Spies
MATTHEWS, Joe, Pvt, Gen Andrew Jackson, Capt Hugh Kerr, Mtd Rangers
MATTHEWS, Moses, Pvt, Col Robert Dyer, Capt Ephraim Dickson, TN Mtd Vol Gunmen; no service performed
MATTHEWS, Samuel, Pvt, Gen A Jackson, Capt Wm Russell, Mtd Spies
MATTHEWS, William, Pvt, Col Edward Bradley, Capt John Moore, Vol Inf
MATTHEWS, William, Pvt, Lt Col L Hammonds, Capt James Craig, Inf
MATTOX, Matthew, Pvt, Col S Bayless, Capt Branch Jones, E TN Drafted Mil
MATTOX, Nathan, Pvt, Col William Johnson, Capt James Tunnell, E TN Mil; d 12-15-1814
MATTOX (MATTHEW?), ____, Cpl, Col Lillard, Capt John Neatherton, E TN Vol Inf
MAURY, Abel V, Pvt, Lt James Berry, Co Commander omitted, Mtd Riflemen
MAURY, Eland, Cpl, Regt Commander omitted, Capt Robert Evans, Spies
MAURY, James H, Pvt, Col R T Perkins, Capt Mathew Johnston, Mil Inf
MAURY, James H, Pvt, Col Thos Benton, Capt Jas McEwen, Vol Inf
MAURY, John, Pvt, Regt Commander omitted, Capt Jno Miller, Spies
MAURY, Tom, Pvt, Brig Gen Jas White, Co Commander omitted, Spies
MAURY, William H, Pvt, Col R C Napier, Capt Early Benson, Mil Inf; d 4-2-1814
MAXAY, Bennet, Sgt, Col Thomas Williamson, Capt Richard Tate, Vol Mtd Gunmen
MAXEY, Bennett, Pvt, Col John Coffee, Capt Daniel Ross, Mtd Gunmen
MAXEY, Bennett, Pvt, Col Thomas Williamson, Capt Thomas Scurry, Vol Mtd Gunmen
MAXEY, William P, Sgt, Col Wm Metcalf, Capt Barnhart, Mil Inf
MAXFIELD, Benjamin, Sgt, Col William Lillard, Capt Thomas Sharpe, Inf
MAXFIELD, Isaac, Pvt, Col S Bunch, Capt Jno English, E TN Drafted Mil; substitute for English Barton
MAXFIELD, Isaac, Pvt, Col S Bunch, Capt Samuel Richardson, E TN Drafted Mil
MAXWELL, David, Pvt, Col Thos Williamson, Capt Thos Scurry, Vol Mtd Gunmen
MAXWELL, Ephraim, Pvt, Col Edward Bradley, Capt John Kennedy, Vol Inf
MAXWELL, Ephraim, Pvt, Col Wm Hall, Capt John Kennedy, Vol Inf
MAXWELL, George, Pvt, Col Samuel Bunch, Capt James Cummings, E TN Vol Mtd Inf
MAXWELL, James, Pvt, Col Philip Pipkin, Capt Henry M Newlin, Mil Inf
MAXWELL, James, Pvt, Col Thos Benton, Capt Thos Williamson, Vol Inf
MAXWELL, James, Pvt, Col Wm Pillow, Capt Thomas Williamson, Vol Inf
MAXWELL, John, Ffr, Col William Hall, Capt John Kennedy, Vol Inf
MAXWELL, John, Pvt, Col John Brown, Capt John Trimble, E TN Mtd Inf
MAXWELL, John, Pvt, Maj Wm Russell, Capt John Trimble, Vol Mtd Gunmen
MAXWELL, Robert, Pvt, Col William Metcalf, Capt

William Sitton, Mil Inf
MAXWELL, Simpson, Pvt, Maj Gen William Carroll, Col James Raulston, Capt Wiley Huddleston, Inf
MAXWELL, William, Pvt, Col Ewen Allison, Capt James Allen, E TN Mil
MAXWELL, William, Pvt, Col N T Perkins, Capt George Eliot, Mil Inf
MAXWELL, William, Pvt, Col Samuel Bunch, Capt Joseph Duncan, E TN Drafted Mil; joined from Capt Allen's Co
MAXWELL, William, Pvt, Col T McCrory, Capt Thos K Gordon, Inf
MAXWELL, William, Pvt, Col William Metcalf, Capt William Sitton, Mil Inf
MAY, Benjamin, Pvt, Col Samuel Bunch, Capt James Cumming, E TN Vol Mtd Inf
MAY, Benjamin, Pvt, Regt Commander omitted, Capt Thomas Gray, Inf
MAY, Cradock H, Pvt, Col A Loury, Capt George Sarver, Inf; deserted
MAY, Daniel, Pvt, Col Robert Steele, Capt Samuel Maxwell, Mil Inf
MAY, Demsey, Pvt, Col John Cocke, Capt Samuel M Caruthers, Inf
MAY, Francis, Pvt, Col John Brown, Capt Allen I Bacon, E TN Mil
MAY, George, Pvt, Col Archer Cheatham, Capt Hugh Birdwell, Inf
MAY, James, Pvt, Col Samuel Bunch, Capt Jno English, E TN Drafted Mil; joined from Capt Duncan's Co
MAY, John, Cpl, Col John Alcorn, Capt Alexander McKeen, Cav; promoted from Pvt
MAY, John, Pvt, Col Ewen Allison, Capt John Hampton, Mil
MAY, John, Pvt, Col Philip Pipkin, Capt Ebenezer Kirkpatrick, Mil Inf; deserted
MAY, John, Pvt, Col Robert Steele, Capt James Randals, Inf
MAY, Jonathan, Pvt, Col R H Dyer, Capt Joseph Williams, Vol Mtd Gunmen
MAY, Jonathan, Sgt, Regt Commander omitted, Capt Thos Gray, Inf
MAY, LeRoy, Asst Topographer, Maj Gen Andrew Jackson, Div of TN Mil; resigned 3-14-1814
MAY, Meede, Pvt, Col Philip Pipkin, Capt James Blakemore, Mil Inf
MAY, Obediah, Pvt, Col Robert Steele, Capt James Randals, Inf
MAY, Obediah, Pvt, Col Thos Benton, Capt Geo W Gibbs, Vol Inf
MAY, Obidiah, Pvt, Col William Pillow, Capt John H Anderson, Vol Inf; deserted
MAY, Peter, Pvt, Col Thos Benton, Capt Benj Reynolds, Vol Inf
MAY, Peter, Pvt, Col Wm Johnson, Capt Andrew Lawson, E TN Drafted Mil
MAY, Reynolds, Pvt, Col Samuel Bunch, Capt Jno English, E TN Drafted Mil
MAY, Robert, Pvt, Col A Cheatham, Capt Hugh Birdwell, Inf
MAY, Robert, Pvt, Col Edward Bradley, Capt Travis Nash, Vol Inf
MAY, Robert, Pvt, Col Thos Benton, Capt Isaiah Renshaw, Vol Inf; transferred to Nash
MAY, Robert, Pvt, Col William Hall, Capt Travis C Nash, Inf
MAY, Thomas, Blksmth, Col Robert Dyer, Capt Isaac Williams, Vol Mtd Gunmen
MAY, Thomas, Pvt, Col Ewen Allison, Capt Henry McCray, E TN Mil; discharged by surgeon
MAY, Tom, Pvt, Lt Col Richard Napier, Co Commander omitted, Inf
MAY, William P, Pvt, Regt Commander omitted, Capt D Deadrick, Arty
MAY, William W, Pvt, Col N T Perkins, Capt Philip Pipkin, Mtd Riflemen
MAY, William, Pvt, Col James Raulston, Co Commander omitted, Inf
MAY, William, Pvt, Col John Brown, Capt Charles Lewin, E TN Vol Mtd Inf
MAY, William, Pvt, Col Thomas Williamson, Capt Robert Moore, Vol Mtd Gunmen
MAY, William, Pvt, Col William Metcalf, Capt Bird L Hurt, Mil Inf
MAY, Woodson, Pvt, Brig Gen T Johnston, Capt Robert Carson, Inf
MAYARS, Henry, Pvt, Col Samuel Bunch, Capt Francis Register, E TN Mil; joined from Capt King's Co
MAYBERRY, Benjamin, Pvt, Col Edward Bradley, Capt Abraham Bledsoe, Branch Srvce omitted
MAYBERRY, Benjamin, Pvt, Col John Coffee, Capt Blackman Coleman, Cav
MAYBERRY, David, Pvt, Col R H Dyer, Capt James McMahon, TN Vol Mtd Gunmen
MAYBERRY, David, Pvt, Col Robert Steele, Capt James Randals, Inf
MAYBERRY, George, Pvt, Col John Brown, Capt Charles Lewin, E TN Vol Mtd Inf
MAYBERRY, Jacob, Pvt, Col John Brown, Capt Charles Lewin, E TN Vol Mtd Inf
MAYBERRY, Jacob, Pvt, Col Samuel Bunch, Capt John Inman, E TN Vol Mtd Inf
MAYBERRY, John, 4 Sgt, Brig Gen William Johnson, Capt Robert Carson, Inf
MAYBERRY, John, Pvt, Col Edwin E Booth, Capt Isaiah Renshaw, Vol Inf; transferred to Nashville
MAYBERRY, Joseph, Pvt, Col Samuel Bunch, Capt Joseph Duncan, E TN Drafted Mil; joined from Capt Yarnell Co
MAYBERRY, Joseph, Pvt, Regt Commander omitted, Capt Daniel Yarnell, E TN Mil
MAYBERRY, Samuel, 1 Cpl, Col John Coffee, Capt Blackman Coleman, Cav
MAYBERRY, William, Pvt, Col John Alcorn, Capt Jetton, Vol Cav
MAYBOROUGH, William, Pvt, Col John Coffee, Capt Robert Jetton, Cav
MAYER, Abraham, Pvt, Col Samuel Bayless, Capt John Brock, E TN Mil
MAYER, John, Cpl, Col Samuel Bayless, Co Commander omitted, E TN Inf
MAYERS, Christopher, Pvt, Col Samuel Bunch, Capt

## Enlisted Men, War of 1812

John Houk, E TN Mil; joined for Capt Berry Co
MAYES, John, 3 Cpl, Maj John Chiles, Capt Daniel Price, Vol Mtd Gunmen
MAYES, John, Cpl, Maj John Chiles, Capt Daniel Price, E TN Vol Mtd Inf
MAYES, John, Pvt, Col Samuel Wear, Capt Daniel Price, E TN Vol Inf
MAYFIELD, A B, Pvt, Col T McCrory, Capt Wm Dooly, Inf; transferred to Gordon's Spies
MAYFIELD, A B, Sgt, Regt Commander omitted, Capt John Gordon, Mtd Spies
MAYFIELD, Charles, Pvt, Col Ewin Allison, Capt Jacob Hoyal, E TN Mil; joined by transfer from Capt McPherson's Co
MAYFIELD, Charles, Pvt, Col S Bunch, Capt George McPherson, E TN Mil
MAYFIELD, Elias, Pvt, Regt Commander omitted, Capt D Mason, Cav
MAYFIELD, Elijah, Pvt, Col John Cocke, Capt John Weakley, Inf; enlisted in the regular service
MAYFIELD, Elijah, Pvt, Col Thomas H Benton, Capt Newton Cannon, Inf
MAYFIELD, Elijah, Tptr, Col Newton Cannon, Capt Gabriel Martin, Mtd Gunmen
MAYFIELD, Eliss, Pvt, Col Thomas H Williamson, Capt William Martin, Vol Mtd Gunmen
MAYFIELD, George, Pvt, Col William Pillow, Capt Thomas Williamson, Branch Srvce omitted; transferred to Capt Gordon's Co
MAYFIELD, George, Pvt, Regt Commander omitted, Capt John Gordon, Mtd Spies
MAYFIELD, George, Sgt, Gen Thos Washington, Capt John Crawford, Inf
MAYFIELD, Isaac, Pvt, Col T McCrory, Capt Isaac Patton, Mil Inf
MAYO, Valentine, Pvt, Col John Williams, Capt William Walker, E TN Vol
MAYO, William, Pvt, Col John Williams, Capt William Walker, Vol
MAYS, Dudley, Pvt, Col Samuel Bunch, Lt John Harris, E TN Mil
MAYS, Gooden, Cpl, Col William Lillard, Capt Thomas Sharpe, 2nd Regt Inf
MAYS, James, Pvt, Col Robert Steele, Capt James Randals, Inf
MAYS, Jesse, Pvt, Maj Gen Wm Carroll, Col Wm Metcalf, Capt John Jackson, Inf
MAYS, John, Pvt, Col John Cocke, Capt Samuel Caruthers, Inf
MAYS, John, Pvt, Col John Coffee, Co Commander omitted, Cav
MAYS, John, Pvt, Col S Bunch, Lt John Harris, E TN Mil; furnished a substitute
MAYS, Mede, Pvt, Col Thomas Bradley, Capt John Wallace, Vol Inf
MAYS, Mede, Pvt, Col Wm Hall, Capt John Wallace, Inf
MAYS, Richard, Pvt, Col Samuel Bayless, Capt John Brock, E TN Mil
MAYS, Samuel, Pvt, Col Wm Lillard, Capt Zacheus Copeland, E TN Vol Inf
MAYS, William W, Pvt, Col R H Dyer, Capt Robert Evans, Vol Mtd Gunmen
MAZE, David, Pvt, Col R C Napier, Capt John Chism, Mil Inf
MCADAIR, Thomas, Pvt, Col Wm Hall, Capt Wm Alexander, Vol Inf
MCADAMS, George, Pvt, Col Robert Dyer, Capt Jas McMahon, TN Vol Mtd Gunmen
MCADAMS, George, Pvt, Gen Andrew Jackson, Capt Nathan Davis, Inf
MCADAMS, Hugh, Sgt, Col John K Wynne, Capt John Porter, Inf
MCADAMS, Irwin, Pvt, Col Thomas Williamson, Capt John Dobbins & Capt Doak, Vol Mtd Gunmen
MCADAMS, James, 4 Cpl, Col Wm Metcalf, Capt Obidiah Walker, Mil Inf
MCADAMS, John, Pvt, Col John Wynn, Capt John Porter, Inf
MCADAMS, Robert, Pvt, Col John Allison, Capt Henry McCray, E TN Mil
MCADAMS, Thomas, Pvt, Col Edward Bradley, Capt Wm Lauderdale, Vol Inf
MCADAMS, William A, Pvt, Col John Alcorn, Capt Fredrick Stump, Cav; transferred to Capt Gordon's Co of Spies
MCADAMS, William B, Pvt, Regt Commander omitted, Capt John Gordon, Mtd Spies; promoted to Sgt
MCADAMS, William R, Sgt, Col Thomas Williamson, Capt Geo Mitchie, TN Vol Mtd Gunmen
MCADAMS, William R, Sgt, Maj William Russell, Capt Geo Mitchie, Vol Mtd Gunmen
MCADAMS, William, Sgt, Regt Commander omitted, Capt Jno Gordon, Mtd Spies
MCADOE, John, Pvt, Lt Col Jno Edmonson, Co Commander omitted, Cav
MCADOE, _____, Pvt, Lt Col Richard Napier, Co Commander omitted, Inf
MCADON, Samuel, Pvt, Col N Cannon, Capt David Hogan, Mtd Gunmen
MCADOO, David, Pvt, Col Robt Dyer, Capt Joseph Williams, Vol Mtd Gunmen
MCADOO, John, Pvt, Col Jno Brown, Capt Hugh Barton, E TN Mil Inf
MCADOO, John, Pvt, Col R H Dyer, Capt Joseph Williams, Vol Mtd Gunmen
MCADOO, William, Pvt, Col Jno Brown, Capt Hugh Barton, E TN Mil Inf
MCADOO, William, Pvt, Maj Wm Russell, Capt Geo Mitchie, Vol Mtd Gunmen
MCADOW, William, Pvt, Col Thomas Williamson, Capt Geo Mitchie, Regt TN Vol Mtd Gunmen
MCAFEE, Azariah, Pvt, Col Thos Benton, Capt Jas McEwen, Vol Inf
MCAFEE, Ezerial, Pvt, Col Wm Pillow, Capt C E McEwen, Vol Inf
MCAFEE, John, Sgt Maj, Col Samuel Bunch, Co Commander omitted, E TN Mil
MCAFEE, John, Sgt, Col S Bunch, Capt N Gibbs, E TN Drafted Mil
MCAFEE, Thomas, Pvt, Col S Wear, Capt John Stephens, Branch Srvce omitted
MCAHILLEY, Richard, Pvt, Gen Andrew Jackson, Capt

## Enlisted Men, War of 1812

Nathan Davis, Inf
MCALEB, Hiram, Pvt, Col R C Napier, Capt John Chism, Mil Inf; substitute for Thomas Stone
MCALESTEN, James, Pvt, Col S Wear, Capt Geo Gillespie, E TN Vol Inf
MCALISTER, David, Pvt, Regt Commander omitted, Capt Archibald McKinney, Cav
MCALLISTER, Andrew, Pvt, Col S Bayless, Capt Jas Churchman, E TN Mil
MCALLISTER, Athiel, Cpl, Col S Bunch, Capt Joseph Duncan, E TN Drafted Mil; transferred to Capt Buchanan Co
MCALLISTER, David, Pvt, Col N Cannon, Capt Jas Walton, Mtd Riflemen
MCALLISTER, John, 3 Cpl, Col Wm Metcalf, Capt Andrew Patterson, Mil Inf
MCALLISTER, John, Pvt, Col Thos Dyer, Capt Cuthbert Hudson, Vol Mtd Gunmen
MCALLISTER, John, Pvt, Col Wm Johnson, Capt Wm Alexander, E TN Drafted Mil
MCALLISTER, Michael, Pvt, Col R C Napier, Capt Drury Adkins, Mil Inf
MCALLISTER, Nathaniel, Pvt, Col Wm Pillow, Capt Jas McFerrin, Inf
MCALLY, Andrew, Pvt, Col Wm Johnson, Capt Elihu Milliken, Regt E TN Mil
MCALPHINE, Thomas, Pvt, Col N Cannon, Capt John Hanley, Mtd Riflemen
MCALPIN, John, Pvt, Brig Gen Johnston, Capt Allen, Mil Inf
MCAMISH, Alexander, Cpl, Col S Bayless, Capt Hale, E TN Mil
MCAMY, Joseph, Pvt, Col Thomas Williamson, Capt Giles Burdette, Vol Mtd Gunmen
MCANALLY, John, Pvt, Col John Brown, Capt Wm D Neilson, E TN Vol Mil
MCANALLY, John, Pvt, Col John Cocke, Capt Bird Nance, Inf
MCANALLY, Jonathan, Pvt, Col Wm Lillard, Capt Thomas Sharp, 2nd Regt Inf
MCANDERSON, Robert, Pvt, Maj Jas Porter, Capt Jas Anderson, Cav
MCANT, David, Pvt, Col Phillip Pipkin, Capt Henry Newlin, Mil Inf
MCARNISH, James, Pvt, Col S Bayless, Capt Hale, E TN Mil
MCARNISH, Joseph, Pvt, Col Ewen Allison, Capt Jacob Hoyal, E TN Mil
MCARNY, Joseph, Pvt, Col Thomas Williamson, Capt Giles Burdett, Vol Mtd Gunmen
MCARTER, Moses, Pvt, Col Edwin Booth, Capt John Porter, Drafted Mil
MCARTHUR, Daniel, Pvt, Col S Bunch, Capt John Hauk, E TN Mil; deserted 1-18-1814
MCAULISTER, Nathaniel, Pvt, Col Thos Benton, Capt Jas McFerrin, Vol Inf; deserted 1-4-1812
MCAULLY, Samuel, Pvt, Col John Brown, Capt William White, E TN Vol Mtd Inf
MCBAIN, Samuel, Pvt, Col N Cannon, Capt Wm Edwards, Command
MCBATH, Alexander, Pvt, Col S Bunch, Capt Jno McNare, E TN Mil
MCBATH, Andrew, Pvt, Maj John Childs, Capt Reuben Tipton, E TN Vol Mtd Inf; Regimental Co Knox
MCBATH, Thomas, Ffr, Col S Bunch, Capt Jno McNare, E TN Mil; appointed Ffr Maj
MCBAY, Hugh, Cpl, Col Ewen Allison, Capt Thomas Wilson, E TN Drafted Mil
MCBAY (MABBY), Obadiah, Pvt, Col Philip Pipkin, Capt John Strother, Inf
MCBEE, John, Pvt, Col Philip Pipkin, Capt Ebenezer Kirkpatrick, Mil Inf; deserted 9-24-1814
MCBEE, John, Sgt, Col Wm Johnson, Capt Henry Hunter, E TN Mil
MCBEE, Levi L, Pvt, Col Samuel Wear, Capt Rufus Morgan, E TN Vol Inf
MCBEE, Samuel, Pvt, Col Samuel Wear, Capt Joseph Calloway, Mtd Inf
MCBEE, Samuel, Pvt, Col Wm Metcalf, Capt Barbee Collins, Mil Inf
MCBEE, William, Pvt, Col Wm Metcalf, Capt Barbee Collins, Mil Inf
MCBETH, Thomas, Ffr Maj, Col Samuel Bunch, Maj Alexander Smith, E TN Mil
MCBORY, Hugh, Pvt, Col Wm Pillow, Capt C E McEwen, Branch Srvce omitted; deserted 11-13-1813
MCBRANT, Spencer, Pvt, Maj John Childs, Capt John Stephens, E TN Vol Mtd Inf
MCBRIDE, Abram, Pvt, Regt Commander omitted, Capt L Ferrell, Inf
MCBRIDE, Allen, Pvt, Col Samuel Bunch, Capt Jno English, E TN Drafted Mil
MCBRIDE, Barzilla, Pvt, Col Philip Pipkin, Capt James Blakemore, Mil Inf
MCBRIDE, Charles, Pvt, Col Thos Williamson, Capt Richard Tate, Vol Mtd Gunmen
MCBRIDE, Edward, Pvt, Col Robert R Dyer, Capt James Wyatt, Vol Mtd Gunmen
MCBRIDE, Edward, Pvt, Col Wm Metcalf, Capt Obidiah Waller, Mil Inf
MCBRIDE, Francis, Cpl, Col T McCrory, Capt Wm Dooley, Inf
MCBRIDE, Francis, Pvt, Col Thos Benton, Capt Benjamin Reynolds, Vol Inf
MCBRIDE, Francis, Pvt, Commanders omitted, Mtd Rangers
MCBRIDE, Hugh, Pvt, Col L Hammonds, Capt Geo Sarver, Inf; substituted by Henry Rule
MCBRIDE, Hugh, Pvt, Col Philip Pipkin, Capt John Robertson, Mil Inf
MCBRIDE, James, Pvt, Col Robt H Dyer, Capt Ephraim D Dickson, TN Vol Mtd Gunmen; no service performed
MCBRIDE, James, Pvt, Col Samuel Wear, Capt John Doak, E TN Vol Inf
MCBRIDE, Jesse, Pvt, Col Robt Steele, Capt James Shenault, Mil Inf
MCBRIDE, John, Dmr, Col A Loury, Capt John Looney, 2nd Regt W TN Mil; d 3-30-1815
MCBRIDE, John, Pvt, Col John K Wynne, Capt John Porter, Inf

MCBRIDE, John, Pvt, Col John K Wynne, Capt Wm Willson, Inf; attached to Capt Porter's Co
MCBRIDE, John, Pvt, Col Newton Cannon, Capt John B Demsey, Mtd Gunmen
MCBRIDE, John, Pvt, Col T McCrory, Capt Wm Dooley, Inf
MCBRIDE, John, Sgt, Col Robt H Dyer, Capt Ephraim D Dickson, TN Mtd Vol Gunmen
MCBRIDE, Joseph, Pvt, Maj Wm Carroll, Capt Lewis Dillahunty & Capt Daniel M Bradford, Vol Inf
MCBRIDE, Patrick, Pvt, Lt Col L Hammonds, Capt Arahel Rains, Inf
MCBRIDE, Patrick, Pvt, Maj Gen Wm Carroll, Col Wm Metcalf, Capt John Jackson, Inf
MCBRIDE, Samuel B, Pvt, Col Wm Metcalf, Capt Bird L Hurt, Mil Inf; d 3-5-1815
MCBRIDE, Samuel, 2 Sgt, Col R C Napier, Capt Samuel Ashmore, Mil Inf
MCBRIDE, Samuel, Mus, Col T McCrory, Capt Wm Dooley, Inf
MCBRIDE, Samuel, Pvt, Col Thomas Benton, Capt Benj Reynolds, Vol Inf
MCBRIDE, Thomas, Pvt, Col Thos Benton, Capt Wm Moore, Vol Inf
MCBRIDE, Thomas, Pvt, Col Wm Hall, Capt Henry M Newland, Inf
MCBROOM, Thomas, Pvt, Col Wm Lillard, Capt Wm Gillenwater, E TN Inf
MCBROOM, William, Pvt, Col Samuel Bunch, Lt Jno Harris, E TN Mil; deserted 4-24-1814
MCBROWN, Thomas, Pvt, Col Samuel Bunch, Capt Thomas Mann, E TN Vol Mtd Inf
MCCABE, Robert L, Pvt, Col Wm Johnson, Capt James R Rogers, E TN Drafted Mil
MCCABE, Robert, Pvt, Col Jno Brown, Capt Wm D Neilson, E TN Vol Mil
MCCABLE, James H, Pvt, Col S Copeland, Capt Ellen Wilkinson, Mil Inf
MCCABLE, James, Cpl, Maj William Russell, Capt John Trimble, Vol Mtd Gunmen
MCCABLE, James, Pvt, Col Samuel Wear, Capt James Gillespie, E TN Vol Inf
MCCAFEE, Azariah, Pvt, Col Robt Steele, Capt John Chitwood, Mil Inf
MCCAFEE (MCCAPEE), John, Pvt, Col Robert Steele, Capt John Chitwood, Mil Inf
MCCAFEE (MCCAPEE), Luke, Pvt, Col Robert Steele, Capt John Chitwood, Mil Inf
MCCAFFERTY, Green, Sgt, Gen A Jackson, Capt Nathan Davis, Inf
MCCAFFERTY, James, Pvt, Col N T Perkins, Capt Mathew Johnson, Mil Inf
MCCAIN, James, Pvt, Col Robert Steele, Capt Samuel Maxwell, Mil Inf
MCCAIN, Robert, Pvt, Lt I Barrett, Capt Nathan Davis, Inf
MCCALAUGH, Jno, Pvt, Regt Commander omitted, Capt Jas Haggard, Mtd Gunmen
MCCALEB, Hiram, Cpl, Lt Col Wm Phillips, Co Commander omitted, Inf
MCCALEB, Hiram, Pvt, Gen Thomas Johnson, Capt Daniel Oban, 36th Inf
MCCALEB, John, Pvt, Col James Raulston, Capt Daniel Newman, Inf
MCCALEB, John, Pvt, Gen Thomas Johnson, Capt Daniel Oban, 36th Inf
MCCALEB, Samuel, Pvt, Maj John Chiles, Capt Charles Conway, E TN Mtd Gunmen
MCCALEP, Alfred, Pvt, Col John Cocke, Capt John Dalton, Inf; substitute for Wm Morris
MCCALL, Dunkin, Pvt, Col Wm Johnson, Capt Benjamin Powell, E TN Mil
MCCALL, John, Pvt, Regt Commander omitted, Capt Wm McLin & Capt Wm Lillard, E TN Inf
MCCALL, Robert, Pvt, Col Wm Lillard, Capt Wm McLin, E TN Inf
MCCALL, Thomas, Pvt, Col R H Dyer, Capt Jas McMahon, 1st TN Vol Mtd Gunmen
MCCALL, Wilie, Pvt, Col Thos Williamson, Capt William Martin, Vol Mtd Gunmen
MCCALL, William C, Pvt, Col Samuel Wear, Capt Rufus Morgan, E TN Vol Inf
MCCALL, William, Cpl, Col Philip Pipkin, Capt Ebenezer Kirkpatrick, Mil Inf; promoted to Sgt
MCCALL, William, Pvt, Col Robert Steele, Capt Samuel Maxwell, Mil Inf
MCCALL, William, Pvt, Col Samuel Bunch, Capt F Register, E TN Mil; joined from Capt McPherson Co
MCCALL, William, Pvt, Col Samuel Bunch, Capt George McPherson, E TN Mil
MCCALL, William, Pvt, Regt Commander omitted, Capt Jas Terrill, Cav; killed at battle of Talledega 11-9-1813
MCCALLASTER, David, Pvt, Col R H Dyer, Capt Cuthbert Hudson, Vol Mtd Gunmen; promoted to Cpl
MCCALLASTER, John, Cpl, Col R H Dyer, Capt Cuthbert Hudson, Vol Mtd Gunmen
MCCALLISTER, William, Pvt, Regt Commander omitted, Capt Archibald McKinney, Cav
MCCALLON, James, 5 Cpl, Col Wm Johnson, Capt David McKamy, E TN Drafted Mil
MCCALLON, James, Pvt, Maj John Chiles, Capt John Stephens, E TN Vol Mtd Inf
MCCALLON, Joh, Pvt, Col Wm Johnson, Capt David McKamy, E TN Drafted Mil
MCCALLON, John, Pvt, Maj John Chiles, Capt John Stephens, E TN Vol Mtd Inf
MCCALLY, James, Pvt, Col Wm Metcalf, Capt Bird L Hurt, Mil Inf
MCCALOUGH, Jno M, Pvt, Regt Commander omitted, Capt Jas Haggard, Mtd Gunmen
MCCALPIN, Henry, Pvt, Col Wm Lillard, Capt Robert McCalpin, E TN Inf
MCCALPIN, John, Pvt, Col Wm Lillard, Capt Robert McCalpin, E TN Inf
MCCAMISH, Robert, Pvt, Col Wm Lillard, Capt Robert Maloney, E TN Vol Inf
MCCAMISH, Samuel, Pvt, Col Wm Lillard, Capt Robert Maloney, E TN Vol Inf
MCCAMISH, Thomas, Pvt, Col Wm Lillard, Capt Robt Maloney, E TN Vol Inf
MCCAMPBELL, James M, Pvt, Maj James Porter, Co

- 335

## Enlisted Men, War of 1812

MCCAMPBELL, John, 1 Cpl, Col S Bunch, Capt Jno McNare, E TN Mil — Commander omitted, Cav
MCCAMPBELL, Samuel S, Pvt, Maj James Porter, Co Commander omitted, Cav
MCCAMPBELL, William, Pvt, Col Samuel Wear, Capt James Tedford, E TN Vol Inf
MCCAMPBELL, ____, Tptr, Maj James Porter, Co Commander omitted, Cav
MCCAN, Michael, 1 Sgt, Col S Bunch, Capt James Cummings, E TN Vol Mtd Gunmen; Regimental Co Hawkins, appointed QM Sgt
MCCAN, Michael, QM Sgt, Col S Bunch, E TN Mil
MCCANCE, James, 2 Sgt, Col S Bunch, Capt James Cumming, E TN Vol Mtd Gunmen
MCCANCE, John, Pvt, Col S Bunch, Capt James Cumming, E TN Vol Mtd Inf
MCCANDLESS, David, 2 Sgt, Col Thos McCrory, Capt Thos Gordon, Inf
MCCANDLESS, James, Tptr, Regt Commander omitted, Capt Nathan Farmer, Mtd Riflemen
MCCANDLESS, John, 4 Sgt, Col Thos McCrory, Capt Thos Gordon, Inf
MCCANDLESS, Samuel, 1 Cpl, Col Thos McCrory, Capt Thos Gordon, Inf
MCCANDLESS, Thomas F, Cpl, Regt Commander omitted, Capt Nathan Farmer, Mtd Riflemen
MCCANDLESS, William, Pvt, Col N T Perkins, Capt Mathew Johnson, Mil Inf
MCCANDLESS, William, Pvt, Regt Commander omitted, Capt Joel Parrish, Branch Srvce omitted
MCCANDLEY, Daniel, Tptr, Col John Brown, Capt Jesse G Reany, Mtd Gunmen
MCCANE, Edward, Pvt, Col Wm Johnson, Capt James R Rogers, E TN Drafted Mil
MCCANE (MCCLANE), James, Pvt, Col Philip Pipkin, Capt Wm MacKay, Mil Inf
MCCANLESS, David, Pvt, Col Thos Williamson, Capt John Doak & Capt John Dobbins, Vol Mtd Gunmen
MCCANLESS, Samuel, Tptr, Maj Gen A Jackson, Col Thos Williamson, Capt Robert Steele, Vol Mtd Gunmen
MCCANLEY, John, Pvt, Col Samuel Bunch, Capt Edward Buchanan, E TN Mil
MCCANLEY, John, Pvt, Regt Commander omitted, Capt John Crane, Mtd Inf
MCCANLEY, Robert, Pvt, Col Edwin E Booth, Capt Samuel Thompson, Mil
MCCANLEY, Thomas, Pvt, Maj John Chiles, Capt John Stephens, E TN Vol Mtd Inf
MCCANLY, Dennis, 2 Cpl, Col James Raulston, Capt Mathew Cowan, Inf
MCCANN, Michael, 2 Sgt, Col John Williams, Capt David Vance, Mtd Mil
MCCANNON, ____, Pvt, Col Alexander Loury, Capt John Looney, W TN Inf; deserted 10-15-1841
MCCARGUE (HARGUE), Lewis, Pvt, Regt Commander omitted, Capt David Mason, Cav
MCCARLEY, Moses, Sgt, Col Thos Williamson, Capt John Crane & Capt James Cook, Vol Mtd Gunmen; promoted from Cpl
MCCARLEY, Thomas, Pvt, Col Wm Hall, Capt Henry M Newlin, Inf; complaining of disability
MCCARLEY, Wesley, Pvt, Col Thos Williamson, Capt James Cook & Capt John Crane, Vol Mtd Gunmen
MCCARMAC, James, Cpl, Col R H Dyer, Capt Bethel Allen, Vol Mtd Gunmen
MCCARMACK, James, Pvt, Maj Gen A Jackson, Col A Cheatham, Capt Wm Creel, Inf; transferred to Wagon Guard
MCCARMON, Cornelius, Pvt, Col Leroy Hammond, Capt Jas Tubb, Inf; transferred to John Looney
MCCAROL, John, Pvt, Col John Coffee, Capt Robert Jetton, Cav
MCCARREL, Talton, Pvt, Col Samuel Bayless, Capt Joseph Rich, E TN Inf
MCCARRELL, John, Pvt, Col Samuel Wear, Capt James Gillespie, E TN Vol Inf
MCCARRIEL, Francis, Pvt, Col Philip Pipkin, Capt John Robertson, Mil Inf
MCCARROLL, Abner, 3 Sgt, Col John K Wynne, Capt Bayless E Prince, Inf
MCCARROLL, George, Pvt, Col A Loury & Col Leroy Hammond, Capt Arahel Raines, Inf; exchanged for John Spear in Chisholm's
MCCARROLL, James, Pvt, Col Samuel Wear, Capt Bowman, Mtd Inf
MCCARROLL, John, 1 Sgt, Regt Commander omitted, Capt Jos Williams, Mil Cav
MCCARROLL, John, Sgt, Regt Commander omitted, Capt Jas Williams, Mil Cav
MCCARROLL, Simeon, Pvt, Col Samuel Bunch, Capt Joseph Duncan, E TN Drafted Mil; joined from Capt Yarnel Co
MCCARROLL, Simon, Pvt, Col S Bunch, Capt Daniel Yarnell, E TN Mil
MCCARROLL, William, Pvt, Col John Cocke, Capt Joseph Price, Inf
MCCART, Robert, Pvt, Col Edwin E Booth, Capt McKamy, E TN Mil
MCCARTER, Moses, Pvt, Col Wm Lillard, Capt John Roper, E TN Vol Inf
MCCARTER, Thomas, Pvt, Col John Brown, Capt James Preston, Regt E TN Mil Inf
MCCARTNEY, Andrew, Pvt, Col R H Dyer, Capt James Wyatt, Vol Mtd Gunmen
MCCARTNEY, Andrew, Pvt, Col S Copeland, Capt G W Steele, Mil Inf
MCCARTNEY, James, Sgt, Col Wm Johnson, Capt David McKamey, E TN Drafted Mil
MCCARTNEY, John, Pvt, Col Samuel Wear, Capt James Tedford, E TN Vol Inf
MCCARTNEY, John, Pvt, Maj Wm Russell, Capt John Tremble, Vol Mtd Gunmen
MCCARTNEY, Joseph, Pvt, Col James Raulston, Capt Henry Hamilton, Inf; also under Maj Gen Wm Carroll
MCCARTNEY, Robert, Pvt, Col Wm Y Higgins, Capt James Hambleton, Mtd Gunmen; promoted to Sgt, d 1-30-1814

## Enlisted Men, War of 1812

MCCARTY, Amos, Ffr Maj, Col Wm Hall, Co Commander omitted, 1st Regt TN Vol

MCCARTY, Janett, Pvt, Lt Col Henry Bryan, Co Commander omitted, Inf

MCCARTY, John L, Pvt, Col Samuel Wear, Co Commander omitted, Vol Inf

MCCARTY, Robert J, Pvt, Maj John Chiles, Capt James Cummings, E TN Vol Mtd Inf

MCCARTY, William, Ffr, Col Wm Johnson, Capt David McKamy, E TN Drafted Mil

MCCARTY, William, Pvt, Col Wm Johnson, Capt Elihu Milliken, 3rd Regt E TN Mil

MCCARVER, Hubbard, Pvt, Col R H Dyer, Maj Wm Russell, Capt Wm Russell, Vol Mtd Gunmen

MCCARVER, John, Pvt, Col R H Dyer, Capt Wm Russell, Vol Mtd Gunmen

MCCARVER, William, Pvt, Col Samuel Bunch, Capt James Cummings, E TN Vol Mtd Inf

MCCARY, George, Pvt, Col Ewin Allison, Capt Jacob Hoyal, E TN Mil; deserted 3-6-1814

MCCASLIN, Andrew, Pvt, Col R H Dyer, Capt Glen Owen, TN Vol Mtd Gunmen

MCCASLIN, Isaac, Pvt, Regt Commander omitted, Capt Edwin S Moore, Mtd Riflemen

MCCASLIN, James, Pvt, Col R H Dyer, Capt Glen Owen, TN Vol Mtd Gunmen; substituted by Edward Swanson

MCCASLIN, John, Pvt, Col R H Dyer, Capt Glen Owen, TN Vol Mtd Gunmen

MCCASLIN, Webster, Pvt, Col John Cocke, Capt John Dalton, Branch Srvce omitted

MCCASLINS, Isaac, Pvt, Regt Commander omitted, Capt Edwin S Moore, Mtd Riflemen

MCCAY, Samuel, Pvt, Col R H Dyer, Co Commander omitted, Vol Mtd Gunmen

MCCA___, Robert, Pvt, Col John Cocke, Capt John Dalton, Inf

MCCEARLEY, James, Pvt, Regt Commander omitted, Capt John Crain, Mtd Gunmen

MCCEARLEY, John, Pvt, Maj Gen Andrew Jackson, Capt John Craine, Mtd Gunmen

MCCEARLEY, Westley, Pvt, Gen Andrew Jackson, Capt John Craine, Mtd Gunmen

MCCEE, Hugh, Pvt, Col Leroy Hammond, Capt James Tubb, Inf

MCCHESTER, James, Pvt, Col Wm Lillard, Capt Zacheus Copeland, E TN Vol Inf

MCCHRISTIAN, David, Pvt, Col Wm Lillard, Capt Thomas McChristian, E TN Vol Inf

MCCHRISTIAN, James, Pvt, Col Wm Metcalf, Capt Barbee Collins, Mil Inf

MCCLAIN, Benjamin, Pvt, Col R H Dyer, Maj Wm Russell, Capt Wm Russell, Vol Mtd Gunmen

MCCLAIN, Benjamin, Sgt & Cpl, Col Thomas H Benton, Capt George W Gibbs, Vol Inf

MCCLAIN, Benjamin, Sgt, Col Thomas H Benton, Capt George W Gibbs, Vol Inf

MCCLAIN, Hacket, Pvt, Col Wm Metcalf, Capt Wm Mullins, Mil Inf

MCCLAIN, Hackett, Pvt, Col Philip Pipkin, Capt Thomas Scurry, Mil Inf

MCCLAIN, James, Sgt, Col Wm Lillard, Capt James Lillard, E TN Vol Inf

MCCLAIN, John, Pvt, Col R H Dyer, Capt Joseph Williams, Branch Srvce omitted

MCCLAIN, John, Pvt, Col Thomas H Benton, Capt C E McEwin, Vol Inf

MCCLAIN, Robert, Pvt, Col Wm Booth, Capt Porter, Drafted Mil

MCCLAIN, William, Pvt, Col W Booth, Capt John Lewis, E TN Mil

MCCLAIN, William, Pvt, Maj Wm Russell, Capt Wm Chism, Vol Mtd Gunmen

MCCLANAHAN, David, Pvt, Maj Gen Carroll, Capt Francis Ellis, Inf

MCCLANAHAN, Elisha, Pvt, Col John Cocke, Capt George Barnes, Inf; joined at Clarksville

MCCLANAHAN, Francis, Pvt, Col Leroy Hammond, Capt James Craig, Inf

MCCLANAHAN, Francis, Pvt, Maj William Woodfolk, Capt Abner Pearce, Inf; transferred from Capt Neil's Camp

MCCLANAHAN, James, Pvt, Col Leroy Hammond, Capt James Craig, Inf

MCCLANAHAN, James, Pvt, Col Samuel Bunch, Capt George Gregory, E TN Mil Inf

MCCLANAHAN, John, Pvt, Col Samuel Bunch, Capt George Gregory, E TN Drafted Mil

MCCLANAHAN, John, Pvt, Col Samuel Bunch, Capt John English, E TN Drafted Mil; furloughed for inability

MCCLANAHAN, Joseph, Pvt, Col R C Napier, Capt Thomas Gray, Mil Inf; on detachment as Wgnr

MCCLANAHAN, Joseph, Pvt, Col Samuel Bunch, Capt Samuel Richardson, E TN Drafted Mil; substitute for Robt Harris

MCCLANAHAN, Joseph, Pvt, Maj Robert Cooper, Co Commander omitted, Mtd Riflemen

MCCLANAHAN, Joseph, Pvt, Regt Commander omitted, Capt Samuel Richardson, E TN Drafted Mil

MCCLANAHAN, William, Pvt, Col John Cocke, Capt Samuel Caruthers, Inf

MCCLANE, James, Pvt, Col Philip Pipkin, Capt Wm Mackay, Mil Inf

MCCLANE, John, Pvt, Col Newton Cannon, Capt Wm Marlin, Mtd Gunmen

MCCLANE, John, Pvt, Col Thomas H Benton, Capt James McEwin, Vol Inf

MCCLANE, John, Pvt, Col Wm Hall, Capt Henry Newland, Inf; refused to appear

MCCLANE, John, Pvt, Col Wm Metcalf, Capt Andrew Patterson, Mil Inf

MCCLANNAHAN, Mathew, Pvt, Col Newton Cannon, Capt Ota Cantrell, W TN Mtd Inf; transferred to Evan's Co

MCCLARED, Daniel, Pvt, Col Newton Cannon, Capt John B Dempsey, Mtd Gunmen

MCCLAREN, Thomas, Pvt, Col Newton Cannon, Capt Wm Martin, Mtd Gunmen; wounded 11-3-1813

MCCLARIN, Robt, Pvt, no other information

MCCLARON, John, Pvt, Col Newton Cannon, Capt John Dempsey, Mtd Gunmen

## Enlisted Men, War of 1812

MCCLARY, Robert W, 2 Sgt, Col Samuel Bunch, Capt Wm Houston, E TN Vol Mtd Inf

MCCLARY, Robert, Pvt, Regt Commander omitted, Capt Edwin S Moore, Mtd Riflemen

MCCLARY, Samuel, Pvt, Col John Cocke, Capt Bird Nance, Inf; cleared by court martial

MCCLEAN, John, Pvt, Col John Edmonson, Co Commander omitted, Cav

MCCLEARY, Joseph, Pvt, Col Samuel Bunch, Capt John Nance, E TN Mtd Inf

MCCLEARY, Joseph, Pvt, Lt Col Henry Bryan, Co Commander omitted, Inf

MCCLEARY, Thomas, Sgt, Col Samuel Wear, Capt Samuel Bowman, Mtd Inf

MCCLEARY, William, Pvt, Col Wm Lillard, Capt Wm Gellenwater, E TN Inf

MCCLEGO, Blackman, Pvt, Col Samuel Bunch, Capt Joseph Duncan, E TN Drafted Mil; trans to Capt English Co

MCCLELAND, George, Pvt, Regt Commander omitted, Capt L Ferrell, Inf

MCCLELLAN, Isaac B, Cpl, Col EWin Allison, Capt Henry McCray, E TN Mil; promoted to Adjt

MCCLELLAN, James W, 2 Lt, Col Edwin E Booth, Capt John McKamy, E TN Mil

MCCLELLAN, John, Pvt, Brig Gen Joseph White, no other Commander listed, Spies

MCCLELLAN, Joseph, Pvt, Col Samuel Bunch, Capt Francis Berry, E TN Mil, attached to Capt Richardson Co

MCCLELLAN, William B, Cpl, Regt Commander omitted, Capt Edward S Moore, Mtd Riflemen

MCCLELLAND, Francis, Pvt, Lt Col Richard Napier, no other information

MCCLELLAND, William, Pvt, Col Richard Napier, Capt Drury Adkins, Mil Inf

MCCLENAHEN, Joseph, Pvt, Col Samuel Bunch, Capt Edward Buchannan, E TN Mil

MCCLENDON, David, Pvt, Col S Copeland, Capt Alexander Provine, Mil Inf

MCCLENDON, John, Pvt, Col S Copeland, Capt Richard Sharp, Mil Inf

MCCLENEHEN, Adams, Pvt, Col Allison, Capt Allison, E TN Mil

MCCLENEHEN, Lacey, Pvt, Col Ewin Allison, Capt SAmuel Allen, E TN Mil

MCCLENNAN, William, Pvt, Col R C Napier, Capt Early Benson, Mil Inf

MCCLEWELL, William, Pvt, Col John Brown, Capt Allen I Bacon, E TN Mil Inf

MCCLILLAN, John, Pvt, Brig Gen Jas White, no Co Commander, Apptd Spy

MCCLINDON, Davis, Pvt, Col James Raulston, Capt Charles Wade, Inf

MCCLINTIE, James, Sgt, Col John Brown, Capt Lunsford Oliver, E TN Mil

MCCLINTOCK, Robert, Sgt, Col Robt Dyer, Capt Isaac Williams, Vol Mtd Gunmen

MCCLISH, James, Pvt, Col John Alcorn, Capt Robert Jetton, Vol Cav

MCCLISH, James, Pvt, Col John Coffee, Capt Robert Jetton, Cav

MCCLISTER, William, Cpl, Col Samuel Bayless, Capt Jas Churchman, E TN Mil

MCCLOUD, Andrew, Pvt, Col Samuel Wear, Capt John Bayless, Mtd Inf

MCCLOUD, Angus, Pvt, Col Leroy Hammonds, Capt James Craig, Inf

MCCLOUD, Isham, Pvt, Col Samuel Wear, Capt Jesse Cole, Vol Inf

MCCLOUD, James, Pvt, Col Edwin Booth, Capt John Lewis, E TN Mil

MCCLOUD, James, Pvt, Col Samuel Wear, Capt John Bayless, Mtd Inf

MCCLUNG, David, Pvt, Col John Alcorn, Capt John Winston, Mtd Riflemen

MCCLUNG, Francis, Pvt, Col J Alcorn, Capt J Winston, Mtd Riflemen

MCCLUNG, Hugh, Pvt, Col Wm Johnston, Capt Wm Alexander, E TN Draft Mil

MCCLUNG, James, Pvt, Col John Brown, Capt John Chiles, E TN Vol Mtd Inf

MCCLUNG, Lasley, Pvt, Col John Alcorn, Capt John J Winston, Mtd Riflemen

MCCLUNG, Montgomery, Pvt, Col John Alcorn, Capt John J Winston, Mtd Riflemen

MCCLUNG, Patrick, Cpl, Col Samuel Wear, Capt Jas Gillespie, E TN Vol Inf

MCCLUNG, William, Pvt, Col John Alcorn, Capt John J Winston, Mtd Riflemen

MCCLURE, Auston, Pvt, Regt Commander omitted, Lt Jas Berry, Mtd Riflemen

MCCLURE, Ewing, Pvt, Col Wm Lillard, Capt Wm McLin, E TN Inf

MCCLURE, Henry, Pvt, Col N Cannon, Capt Martin, Mtd Gunmen

MCCLURE, Henry, Pvt, Col Thos Benton, Capt Robt Cannon, Inf

MCCLURE, Henry, Tptr, Col Thos Williamson, Capt William Martin, Vol Mtd Gunmen

MCCLURE, Huston, Pvt, Regt Commander omitted, Lt James Berry, Mtd Riflemen

MCCLURE, James, Pvt, Col Robt Steele, Capt Jas Bennett, Mil Inf

MCCLURE, James, Pvt, Maj Wm Woodfolk, Capt Jas C Neil, Inf

MCCLURE, John, 2 Sgt, Col Wm Johnson, Capt David McKamy, E TN Draft Mil

MCCLURE, John, Pvt, Col A Cheatham, Capt Wm Smith, Inf; trans to Capt Parrish Arty Co

MCCLURE, John, Pvt, Col John Brown, Capt John Trimble, E TN Mtd Gunmen

MCCLURE, John, Pvt, Col Robt Steele, Capt Jas Bennett, Mil Inf

MCCLURE, Robert, Pvt, Col Samuel Bayless, Capt Jonathan Waddell, E TN Mil

MCCLURE, Samuel, Cpl, Maj Gen A Jackson, Col Thos Williamson, Capt Robt Steele, Vot Mtd Gunmen

MCCLURE, Samuel, Pvt, Col N T Perkins, Capt John B Quarles, Vol Mtd Inf

MCCLURE, William, Cpl, Col Wm Johnson, Capt Benj Powell, E TN Mil

## Enlisted Men, War of 1812

MCCLURE, William, Pvt, Regt Commander omitted, Capt Gray, Inf
MCCLURG, John, Pvt, Col Edwin Booth, Capt Samuel Thompson, Mil
MCCLURG, William, 1 Cpl, Col Edwin Booth, Capt Alex Biggs, Inf
MCCLURGE, Samuel, Pvt, Maj John Chiles, Capt John Stephens, E TN Vol Mtd Inf
MCCLUSKEY, Alexander, Pvt, Col Edwin Booth, Capt Samuel Thompson, Mil
MCCLUSKEY, George B, Pvt, Gen A Jackson, Capt Russell, Mtd Spies
MCCLUSKEY, David, Pvt, Col N Cannon, Capt Francis Jones, Mtd Riflemen
MCCLUSKY, David, Pvt, Maj Wm Russell, Capt John Cowan, Vol Mtd Gunmen
MCCLUSKY, George B, Pvt, Col N Cannon, Capt Francis Jones, Mtd Riflemen
MCCLUSKY, John, Pvt, Col N Cannon, Capt Francis Jones, Mtd Riflemen
MCCLUSKY, John, Pvt, Maj John Chiles, Capt Daniel Price, E TN Vol Mtd Inf
MCCLUSKY, William, Pvt, Maj Wm Russell, Capt John Cowan, Vol Mtd Gunmen
MCCOLEMAN, William, Pvt, Col Thos Benton, Capt Thos Williamson, Vol Inf
MCCOLLISTER, David, Pvt, Regt Commander omitted, Capt Archibald McKenney, Cav
MCCOLLISTER, Ethiel, Sgt, Col Samuel Bunch, Capt Edward Buchanan, E TN Draft Mil; trans to Capt Duncan's Co
MCCOLLISTER, William, Pvt, Regt Commander omitted, Capt Arch McKinney, Cav
MCCOLLOCK, David, 3 Sgt, Col Thos McCrory, Capt Thos K Gordon, Inf
MCCOLLOUGH, Henry, Ffr, Col Wm Johnson, Capt Jas Stewart, 3 Regt E TN Mil
MCCOLLOUGH, John H, Pvt, Col John K Wynne, Capt James Cole, Inf
MCCOLLOUGH, Samuel, 2 Sgt, Maj John Chiles, Capt Jas Cummings, E TN Vol Mtd Inf; Regt from Hawkins Co
MCCOLLOUGH, Samuel, Pvt, Col Samuel Bunch, Capt Jones Griffin, E TN Draft Mil
MCCOLLOUGH, Samuel, Tptr, Commanders omitted, E Tn Vol Mtd Inf
MCCOLLOUGH, William, Tptr, Maj John Chiles, Capt Jas Cummings, E TN Vol Mtd Inf
MCCOLLUM, John, Pvt, Regt Commander omitted, Capt Archibald McKenney, Cav
MCCOLLUM, Thomas, Sdlr, Col R H Dyer, Capt Robert Evans, Vol Mtd Gunmen
MCCOLLUM, William, Ffr, Col Thos Benton, Capt Thos Williamson, Vol Inf
MCCOLLUM, William, Pvt, Regt Commander omitted, Capt Arch McKenney, Cav
MCCOLM (MCCOLLUM), Alexander, Pvt, Col Robt Steele, Capt Jas Randals, Inf
MCCOLM (MCCOLLUM), Daniel, Pvt, Col Philip Pipkin, Capt Wm Mackay, Mil Inf; died 11-11-1814
MCCOLM (MCCOLLUM), Thresher, Pvt, Col Philip Pipkin, Capt Wm MacKay, Mil Inf; died 11-11-1814

MCCOLOUGH, John, Pvt, Regt Commander omitted, Capt Jas Haggard, Mtd Gunmen
MCCOMAC, George, Pvt, Maj Gen Jackson, Capt Craine, Mtd Gunmen
MCCOMAC, Richard B, Pvt, Maj Gen Jackson, Capt Craine, Mtd Gunmen
MCCOMB, James, Pvt, Col Wm Johnson, Capt Jas R Rogers, E TN Draft Mil
MCCOMB, John L, Surgeon Mate, Col Samuel Bayless, no Co Commmander, 4 Regt E TN Mil
MCCOMBS, Robert, R M Sgt, Col Thos McCrory, no Co Commander, 2 Regt TN Mil
MCCOMBS, Robert, Sgt, Col Thos McCrory, Capt John Reynolds, Mil Inf
MCCOMIGIL, Eli, Pvt, Col Thos Benton, Capt Jas McFerrin, Vol Inf
MCCONKEY, John, Sgt, Col William Johnson, Capt Joseph Scott, E TN Draft Mil
MCCONKEY, Samuel, Cpl, Col Samuel Bunch, Capt F Register, E TN Mil; joined from Capt King's Co
MCCONKEY, Samuel, Ffr, Col Samuel Bayless, Capt James Landen, E TN Mil
MCCONKS, Samuel, 3 Cpl, Col Ewen Allison, Capt Wm King, Draft Mil
MCCONN, James, Pvt, Col John Coffee, Capt James Terrill, Vol Cav
MCCONNEL, Samuel, Pvt, Regt Commander omitted, Capt Ephraim Dickson, Branch omitted
MCCONNELL, Alfred, Pvt, Col A Loury, Capt George Sarver, Inf
MCCONNELL, Alfred, Pvt, Col Edward Bradley, Capt Wm Lauderdale, Vol Inf
MCCONNELL, Archibald, Pvt, Col Wm Metcalf, Capt Bird L Hurt, Mil Inf
MCCONNELL, James, Pvt, Col Edward Bradley, Capt John Kennedy, Riflemen; AWOL
MCCONNELL, James, Pvt, Col John Williams, Capt Wm Walker, Vol
MCCONNELL, James, Pvt, Col Robert H Dyer, Capt Ephraim D Dickson, TN Mtd Vol Gunmen
MCCONNELL, James, Pvt, Col SAmuel Wear, Capt Rufus Morgan, E TN Vol Inf
MCCONNELL, John, Pvt, Maj Wm Russell, Capt John Trimble, Vol Mtd Gunmen
MCCONNELL, Samuel, Pvt, Col John Brown, Capt Wm White, E TN Vol Mtd Inf
MCCONNELL, Samuel, Pvt, Col Robt H Dyer, Capt Ephraim D Dickson, TN Mtd Vol Gunmen
MCCONNELL, Samuel, Sgt, Maj Wm Russell, Capt John Trimble, Vol Mtd Gunmen
MCCONNELL, Thomas, Pvt, Col John Williams, Capt Wm Walker, Vol
MCCONNELL, Walter, Pvt, Col N T Perkins, Capt Mathew Johnson, Mil Inf
MCCONNELL, William, Maj Wm Russell, Capt John Trimble, Vol Mtd Gunmen
MCCONNELL, William, Pvt, Maj John Childs, Capt Charles Conway, E TN Mtd Gunmen; Regt from Roane Co

- 339

## Enlisted Men, War of 1812

MCCONNICO, Jason, Pvt, no other information
MCCORD, Allison, Pvt, Col Thos Williamson, Capt Martin, Vol Mtd Gunmen
MCCORD, Ambrose, Pvt, no other information
MCCORD, Ashael, Pvt, Col Wm Hammond, Capt James Cowan, Mtd Inf
MCCORD, Azil, Pvt, Maj Wm Russell, Capt John Cowan, Vol Mtd Gunmen
MCCORD, Harry, Pvt, Maj Wm Russell, Capt John Cowan, Vol Mtd Gunmen
MCCORD, James, Pvt, Col Robt Steele, Capt Robt Campbell, Mil Inf
MCCORD, Joseph, Pvt, Col Edwin Booth, Capt Porter, Drafted Mil
MCCORD, William, Pvt, Col S Copeland, Capt David Williams, Inf
MCCORKLE, Henry, Pvt, Col John Brown, Capt Wm White, E Tn Vol Mtd Inf
MCCORKLE, Joseph, Asst Wgnmstr, Brig Gen N Taylor, no other information
MCCORKLE, Joseph, Pvt, Col Wm Johnson, Capt Joseph Scott, E TN Drafted Mil; promoted to asst wgnmstr
MCCORMACH, Absolom, Pvt, Col T McCrory, Capt Thomas K Gordon, Inf
MCCORMACK, George jr, Pvt, Col John Alcorn, Capt Frederick Stump, Cav
MCCORMACK, George sr, Far, Col John Alcorn, Capt Frederick Stump, Cav
MCCORMACK, James G, Pvt, Col Wm Metcalf, Capt Thos Marks, Mil Inf
MCCORMACK, James, Pvt, Col Philip Pipkin, Capt David Smith, Inf; deserted
MCCORMACK, James, Pvt, Col Robt Steele, Capt John Chitwood, Mil Inf; also served in Capt Creel's Co
MCCORMACK, James, Sgt, Col R H Dyer, Capt Bethel Allen, Vol Mtd Gunmen
MCCORMACK, John B, Pvt, Col Wm Pillow, Capt C E McEwen, Vol Inf
MCCORMACK, John, Pvt, Col Wm Metcalf, Capt Thos Marks, Mil Inf
MCCORMACK, Jurdon, Pvt, Col John Wynne, Capt John Porter, Inf
MCCORMACK, William, Pvt, Col Ewen Allison, Capt Joseph Everett, E TN Mil; trans to Capt Griffin's
MCCORMELL, William, Pvt, Col John Brown, Capt Wm White, E TN Mil Inf
MCCORMIC, William, Pvt, Col John Brown, Capt Jas Preston, E TN Mil Inf
MCCORMICK, Andrew, Sdlr, Col Thomas Scurry, Capt Thomas Williamson, Vol Mtd Gunmen
MCCORMICK, George jr, Pvt, Col Jno Coffee, Capt Frederick Stump, Cav
MCCORMICK, George sr, Pvt, Col Jno Coffee, Capt Frederick Stump, Cav
MCCORMICK, John M, Pvt, Col Philip Pipkin, Capt Wm Mackay, Mil Inf
MCCORMICK, Samuel, Pvt, Col Thos Williamson, Capt John Doak & Capt John Dobbins, Vol Mtd Gunmen
MCCORMICK, William, Pvt, Col Samuel Bunch, Capt Jones Griffin, E TN Draft Mil; joined from Capt Everett's Co
MCCORRY, Alexander, Pvt, Col Wm Johnson, Capt Christopher Cook, E TN Mil
MCCORRY, Thomas, ADC, Brig Gen James White
MCCOWAN (MCKOWN), Alexander, Pvt, Lt Col L Hammonds, Capt James Tubb, Inf
MCCOWEN, Malcomb, Pvt, Col Wm Metcalf, Capt Obidiah Waller, Mil Inf
MCCOWN, John, Pvt, Maj John Childs, Capt Charles Conway, E TN Mtd Gunmen
MCCOWN, Sampson, Pvt, Col N T Perkins, Capt John B Quarles, Vol Mtd Inf
MCCOY, Abraham, Pvt, Col Wm Lillard, Capt John Neatherton, E TN Vol Inf; Wgnr
MCCOY, Alexander, Pvt, Col Wm Hall, Capt Henry M Newland, Inf
MCCOY, Amos, Pvt, Col Jno Coffee, Capt Robert Jetton, Cav
MCCOY, Cornelius, Pvt, Col Wm Johnson, Capt Christopher Cook, E TN Mil
MCCOY, Cornelius, Pvt, Col Wm Johnson, Capt Joseph Kirk, Mil; substitute
MCCOY, Daniel, 3 Cpl, Regt Commander omitted, Capt Jas Terrill, Cav
MCCOY, Daniel, 3 Sgt, Regt Commander omitted, Capt Jas Terrill, Cav
MCCOY, Daniel, Pvt, Col Ewen Allison, Capt Thomas Wilson, E TN Drafted Mil
MCCOY, Daniel, Pvt, Col Jno Coffee, Capt Jas Terrill, Vol Cav
MCCOY, Daniel, Pvt, Col Philip Pipkin, Capt Wm Mackay, Inf
MCCOY, Daniel, Pvt, Col Samuel Bayless, Capt Solomon Hendrix, E TN Mil
MCCOY, Daniel, Pvt, Col Samuel Bunch, Capt Geo McPherson, E TN Mil; joined from Capt Wilson's Co
MCCOY, David, Pvt, Col Jno Coffee, Capt Robert Jetton, Cav
MCCOY, David, Pvt, Col John Alcorn, Capt Robert Jetton, Vol Cav
MCCOY, Fleming, Pvt, Col Jno Brown, Capt Jas Standifer, E TN Vol Mtd Mil
MCCOY, Freling, Pvt, Col Wm Johnson, Capt Joseph Scott, E TN Drafted Mil
MCCOY, Henry, Pvt, Col Samuel Bunch, Capt James Penny, E TN Mtd Inf
MCCOY, Henry, Pvt, Col Wm Johnson, Capt Christopher Cook, E TN Mil
MCCOY, Henry, Pvt, Col Wm Johnson, Capt Joseph Kirk, Mil
MCCOY, Henry, Pvt, Regt Commander omitted, Capt Edwin S Moore, Mtd Riflemen
MCCOY, Jacob, Pvt, Col Samuel Bunch, Capt Wm Jobe, E TN Vol Mtd Inf
MCCOY, James H, Pvt, Col Wm Hall, Capt Abraham Bledsoe, Vol Inf
MCCOY, James, Pvt, Col Edwin E Booth, Capt John Slatton, E TN Mil
MCCOY, James, Pvt, Col Robert Steele, Capt John Chit-

## Enlisted Men, War of 1812

wood, Mil Inf
MCCOY, James, Pvt, Col Wm Hall, Capt Abraham Bledsoe, Vol Inf
MCCOY, John, Pvt, Col Isaac Williams, Capt Samuel Bunch, Mtd Vol
MCCOY, John, Pvt, Col John Cocke, Capt Bird Nance, Inf; d 3-16-1815
MCCOY, John, Pvt, Col Samuel Bunch, Capt James Cummings, E TN Vol Mtd Inf
MCCOY, John, Pvt, Col Wm Johnson, Capt Elihu Milliken, 3rd Regt E TN Mil
MCCOY, John, Pvt, Col Wm Lillard, Capt Robert McCalpin, E TN Inf
MCCOY, John, Sgt, Col Wm Johnson, Capt Benjamin Powell, E TN Mil; promoted from Cpl
MCCOY, Joseph, Pvt, Col Philip Pipkin, Capt Henry M Newlin, Mil Inf
MCCOY, William, Pvt, Col Samuel Bayless, Capt Joseph Goodson, E TN Mil
MCCRABB, Joseph, Pvt, Col Wm Lillard, Capt George Keys, E TN Inf
MCCRACKEN, Eli, Pvt, Col Thos McCrory, Capt Jno Reynolds, Mil Inf
MCCRACKEN, Ephraim, Pvt, Maj Gen Wm Carroll, Col Wm Metcalf, Capt John Jackson, Inf
MCCRACKEN, George, Pvt, Col Thos McCrory, Capt Jno Reynolds, Mil Inf
MCCRACKEN, John L, Pvt, Col N T Perkins, Capt Mathew Johnson, Mil Inf
MCCRACKEN, John, Pvt, Brig Gen Thos Washington, Co Commander omitted, Mtd Inf
MCCRACKEN, John, Pvt, Col Alexander Loury, Capt James Kincaid, Inf
MCCRACKEN, John, Pvt, Col Wm Lillard, Capt Wm McLin, E TN Inf
MCCRACKEN, Joseph, Pvt, Col Thos Williamson, Capt John Doak & Capt John Dobbins, Vol Mtd Gunmen
MCCRACKEN, Joseph, Pvt, Maj Gen Wm Carroll, Col Wm Metcalf, Capt John Jackson, Inf
MCCRACKEN, Joseph, Sgt, Col Thos McCrory, Capt Jno Reynolds, Mil Inf
MCCRACKEN, Robert, Pvt, Col Samuel Bayless, Capt Jonathan Waddle, E TN Mil
MCCRACKEN, Samuel, Pvt, Col Robert Steele, Capt Robert Campbell, Mil Inf
MCCRACKIN, John, Pvt, Col Jno Coffee, Capt Chas Kavanaugh, Cav; AWOL
MCCRACKIN, Samuel, Pvt, Col Samuel Bayless, Capt Joseph B Bacon, E TN Mil
MCCRACKING, Thomas, Pvt, Col A Cheatham, Capt James Giddins, Inf
MCCRADY, William, Pvt, Col John Cocke, Capt John Dalton, Inf
MCCRAIG, Samuel, Pvt, Col R H Dyer, Capt Isaac Williams, Vol Mtd Gunmen
MCCRAIG, William, Sgt, Regt Commander omitted, Capt Archibald McKinney, Cav; promoted to Sgt Maj in Col Perkins Regt
MCCRAIRY, Robert, Pvt, Col Jas Raulston, Capt James A Black, Inf

MCCRARY, John, Pvt, Col Jno Coffee, Capt Robert Jetton, Cav
MCCRAVEN, James, Pvt, Regt Commander omitted, Capt Archibold McKinney, Cav
MCCRAVEY, John, Pvt, Col R H Dyer, Capt Ephraim Dickson, 1st TN Mtd Vol Gunmen; d 2-21-1815
MCCRAVEY, John, Pvt, Regt Commander omitted, Capt Ephraim Dickson, Branch Srvce omitted
MCCRAW, Matox, Pvt, Col Wm Johnson, Capt Benjamin Powell, E TN Mil
MCCRAY, John S, Pvt, Lt Col Jno Edmonson, Co Commander omitted, Cav
MCCRAY, Philip, S Sgt, Col Wm Johnson, Capt Christopher Cook, E TN Drafted Mil
MCCRAY, Philip, Pvt, Col Ewen Allison, Capt Henry McCray, E TN Mil; transferred from Capt Hampton & to Capt Register
MCCRAY, Philip, Pvt, Col Wm Lillard, Capt Jacob Hartsell, E TN Vol Inf
MCCRAY, Philip, Sgt, Col S Bunch, Capt Francis Register, E TN Mil; joined from Capt McCrea's Co
MCCRAY, William, Sgt, Col Ewen Allison, Capt Henry McCray, E TN Mil
MCCREA, Phillip, Sgt, Col Ewen Allison, Capt John Hampton, Mil; transferred to Capt McCrea's Co
MCCREARY, John, Pvt, Col Jno Coffee, Capt Robert Jetton, Cav
MCCREE, David M, Pvt, Regt Commander omitted, Capt Jas Terrill, Cav
MCCREE, Moses, Pvt, Col John Alcorn, Capt John Baskerville, Vol Inf
MCCREGER, Harris, Sgt, Regt Commander omitted, Capt Gray, Inf
MCCRELIS, Robert, Pvt, Col Alexander Loury, Capt Geo Sarver, Inf; substitute for Joseph Easley
MCCRELIS, Robert, Pvt, Col Thos Benton, Capt Jas Renshaw, Vol Inf
MCCRELLIS, Robert, Pvt, Col Jno Coffee, Capt Henry Byron, Cav
MCCRORY, Alexander, Pvt, Col John Coffee, Capt Henry Byron, Cav
MCCRORY, Francis, Pvt, no other information
MCCRORY, Hugh, Pvt, Col R H Dyer, Capt Cuthbert Hudson, Vol Mtd Gunmen
MCCRORY, Hugh, Pvt, Col Thos Benton, Capt Jas McEwen, Vol Inf
MCCRORY, Hugh, Sdlr, Col R H Dyer, Capt Cuthbert Hudson, Vol Mtd Gunmen; appointed Sdlr from Pvt
MCCRORY, Robert, Pvt, Col Robert H Dyer, Capt Ephraim Dickson, TN Mtd Vol Gunmen
MCCRORY, Robert, Pvt, Maj Gen Andrew Jackson, Capt Joseph Kirkpatrick, Mtd Gunmen
MCCRORY, Thomas, Pvt, Brig Gen Thos Washington, Capt Jno Crawford, Mtd Inf
MCCROSKEY, Robert, Cpl, Col S Bunch, Capt Jno Hawk, E TN Mil
MCCROSKEY, William, Pvt, Col S Wear, Capt John Stephens, E TN Vol Inf
MCCUE, James, Pvt, Col Wm Metcalf, Capt Thomas Marks, Mil Inf

## Enlisted Men, War of 1812

MCCULACK, Henry, Ffr, Col Wm Johnson, Capt Jas Stewart, E TN Drafted Mil
MCCULLA, William, Pvt, Col William Lillard, Capt Wm Hamilton, E TN Vol Inf
MCCULLAK, John D, Cpl, Col Wm Johnson, Capt Benj Powell, E TN Mil
MCCULLEY, Joseph, 1 Cpl, Col John Cocke, Capt John Weakley, Inf
MCCULLOCK, Alexander, Pvt, Col Wm Metcalf, Capt Barbee Collins, Mil Inf
MCCULLOCK, David, Pvt, Col Thomas Williamson, Capt James Pace, Lt James Neeley, Vol Mtd Gunmen
MCCULLOCK, David, Pvt, Maj Gen Jackson, Col Thomas Williamson, Capt Robert Steele, Vol Mtd Gunmen
MCCULLOCK, James, Pvt, Col Ewen Allison, Capt Jacob Hoyal, E TN Mil
MCCULLOCK, John, Pvt, Regt Commander omitted, Capt Wm Peacock, Cav
MCCULLOCK, Joseph, Cpl, Col S Wear, Capt Joseph Calloway, Mtd Inf
MCCULLOCK, Moses, Pvt, Col Ewen Allison, Capt Henry Hoyal, E TN Mil
MCCULLOUGH, Alexander, Pvt, Col Wm Johnson, Capt Jas Rogers, E TN Mil
MCCULLOUGH, Elijah, Ffr, Col Wm Lillard, Capt George Argenbright, E TN Vol Riflemen
MCCULLOUGH, John, Pvt, Col Wm Johnson, Capt David McKamy, E TN Drafted Mil
MCCULLY, Joseph, 1 Cpl, Col John Cocke, Capt John Weakley, Inf
MCCULLY, William, Pvt, Col Joseph Kirkpatrick, Maj Gen Jackson, Mtd Gunmen
MCCULLY, William, Pvt, no Regt Commander, Capt Gordon, Mtd Spies
MCCULOUGH, William, Pvt, Col Wm Johnson, Capt David McKamy, E TN Drafted Mil; deserted
MCCUMMINS, Richard W, Pvt, no Regt Commander, Capt Geo Smith, Spies
MCCURBY, Robert, Pvt, Col Phillip Pipkin, Capt David Smith, Inf; died 11-2-1814?
MCCURDY, David, Dmr, Maj Wm Woodfolk, Capt James Neil, Inf
MCCURDY, James, Pvt, Col John K Wynn, Capt Wm Caruthers, W TN Inf
MCCURE, Robert, Pvt, Col S Wear, Capt Rufus Morgan, E Tn Vol Inf
MCCURRY, Jonathan, Pvt, Col Wm Johnson, Capt David McKamy, E TN Drafted Mil
MCCURRY, Joseph, Cpl, Col Edwin Booth, Capt Samuel Thompson, Mil
MCCURRY, Samuel, Pvt, Col S Booth, Capt Samuel Thompson, Mil; died 3-13-1815
MCCURRY, William, Pvt, Col Phillip Pipkin, Capt Geo Mebane, Mil Inf
MCCUTCHAN, William, Pvt, Regt Commander omitted, Capt Thos Williamson, Branch omitted
MCCUTCHEN, Robert, Pvt, Regt Commander omitted, Capt Archibald McKinney, Cav
MCCUTCHEN, Samuel, Pvt, Col N T Perkins, Capt Mathew Johnson, Mil Inf
MCCUTCHEON, John, Pvt, no Regt Commander, Capt Gordon, Mtd Spied
MCCUTCHEON, Robert, Pvt, Regt Commander omitted, Capt Archibald McKinney, Cav
MCCUTCHEON, Samuel, Pvt, Col A Loury, Capt J N Williamson, W TN Mil
MCCUTCHEON, William, Pvt, Col William Pillow, Capt Thomas Williamson, Vol Inf
MCCUTCHER, James, Pvt, Col Robert Dyer, Capt Robert Edmonston, TN Vol Mtd Gunmen
MCCUTCHIN, Robert, Pvt, Col John Coffee, Capt Charles Kavanaugh, Cav
MCCUTCHIN, Samuel, Pvt, Col Robert Steele, Capt James Randals, Inf
MCDANIEL, Alexander, Pvt, Col Newton Cannon, Capt John Hanley, Mtd Riflemen
MCDANIEL, Alexander, Pvt, Col Thos Benton, Capt Benj Hewett, Vol Inf; later joined Capt Geo Caperton's Co
MCDANIEL, Alexander, Pvt, Col Wm Lillard, Capt Zacheus Copeland, E TN Vol Inf
MCDANIEL, Allen, Pvt, Col John K Wynne, Capt James Cole, Inf
MCDANIEL, Allen, Pvt, Col N T Perkins, Capt Geo Eliot, Mil Inf
MCDANIEL, Allen, Pvt, Col Samuel Bunch, Capt F Register, E TN Mil
MCDANIEL, Archibald, Pvt, Col Thomas Benton, Capt James McEwen, Vol Inf
MCDANIEL, Bryan, Pvt, Col Samuel Wear, Capt Samuel Bowman, Mtd Inf
MCDANIEL, Daniel C, Pvt, Lt Col L Hammonds, Capt James Tubb, Inf
MCDANIEL, Daniel, Pvt, Col A Loury, Capt Arahel Rains, Lt Col L Hammonds, Inf
MCDANIEL, Daniel, Sgt, Col Jno Brown, Capt Allen I Baco, E TN Mil Inf
MCDANIEL, Edward, Pvt, Col Wm Johnson, Capt Benj Powell, E TN Mil
MCDANIEL, Elijah, Pvt, Maj Wm Russell, Capt Wm Chism, Vol Mtd Gunmen
MCDANIEL, George, Pvt, Regt Commander omitted, Capt Gray, Inf
MCDANIEL, Henry B, Pvt, Lt Col L Hammond, Capt James Tubb, Inf
MCDANIEL, Henry B, Pvt, Maj Gen A Jackson, Capt Joseph Kirkpatrick, Mtd Gunmen
MCDANIEL, Henry, 5 Cpl, Col James Raulston, Capt Mathew Cowan, Inf
MCDANIEL, Henry, Pvt, Regt Commander omitted, Capt L Ferrell, Inf
MCDANIEL, Jacob, Pvt, Col Edwin Booth, Capt John Sharp, E TN Mll
MCDANIEL, James, 5 Cpl, Col Philip Pipkin, Capt Geo Mebane, Mil Inf
MCDANIEL, James, Pvt, Col Samuel Bayless, Capt James Churchman, E TN Mil
MCDANIEL, James, Pvt, Col Samuel Wear, Capt Rufus Morgan, E TN Vol Inf
MCDANIEL, James, Pvt, Col Wm Metcalf, Capt Obidiah

## Enlisted Men, War of 1812

Waller, Mil Inf; trans to Capt Marks Co
MCDANIEL, Jeremiah, Pvt, Col John Williams, Capt David Vance, Mtd Mil
MCDANIEL, John, Cpl, Col Philip Pipkin, Capt Ebenezer Kirkpatrick, Mil Inf
MCDANIEL, John, Pvt, Col Robert Steele, Capt John Chitwood, Mil Inf
MCDANIEL, John, Pvt, Col Samuel Wear, Capt Rufus Morgan, E TN Vol Inf
MCDANIEL, John, Sgt, Col Samuel Bunch, Capt Joseph Duncan, E TN Drafted Mil; joined from Capt Buchanan's Co
MCDANIEL, Joseph, Pvt, Col Edward Bradley, Capt Wm Lauderdale, Vol Inf
MCDANIEL, Joseph, Pvt, Col James Raulston, Capt Daniel Newman, Inf; died 2-8-1815
MCDANIEL, Joseph, Pvt, Col Wm Hall, Capt Wm L Alexander, Vol Inf
MCDANIEL, Joseph, Pvt, Maj Wm Russell, Capt Wm Chism, Vol Mtd Gunmen
MCDANIEL, Loury, Pvt, Col A Loury, Capt J N Williamson, W TN Mil
MCDANIEL, Mosby, Pvt, Col N T Perkins, Capt Mathew Johnson, Mil Inf
MCDANIEL, Mosely, Pvt, Maj Gen Wm Carroll, Capt Lewis Dillahunty & Capt Daniel M Bradford, Vol Inf
MCDANIEL, Richard, Pvt, Col A Cheatham, Capt James Giddens, Inf
MCDANIEL, Robert, Pvt, Col A Loury, Capt Arahel Rains, Inf
MCDANIEL, Robert, Pvt, Maj Gen A Jackson, Col T Williamson, Capt Robert Steele, Vol Mtd Gunmen
MCDANIEL, Samuel, Pvt, Regt Commander omitted, Capt Arch McKinney, Cav
MCDANIEL, Squire B, Pvt, Col T McCrory, Capt Wm Dooley, Inf
MCDANIEL, Squire B, Pvt, Col Thos Benton, Capt Benj Reynolds, Vol Inf
MCDANIEL, Thomas, Pvt, Col Samuel Bunch, Capt Francis Berry, E TN Mil
MCDANIEL, Thomas, Pvt, Regt Commander omitted, Capt Jno Miller, Spies
MCDANIEL, William, Cpl, Col John Alcorn, Capt Thomas Bradley, Vol Cav
MCDANIEL, William, Cpl, Maj William Woodfolk, Capt James C Neil, Inf
MCDANIEL, William, Pvt, Col Phillip Pipkin, Capt John Robertson, Mil Inf
MCDANIEL, William, Pvt, Col Wm Metcalf, Capt Barbee Collins, Mil Inf
MCDANIEL, William, Pvt, Maj Wm Russell, Capt Wm Chism, Vol Mtd Gunmen
MCDANNOLD, Alexander, Pvt, Col Wm Pillow, Capt Geo Caperton, Inf
MCDAVALD, James, Pvt, Maj Gen A Jackson, Capt Wm Carroll, Vol Inf; received in place of Flemming Ward
MCDAVID, William, Pvt, Gen Jno Coffee, Co Commander omitted, Mtd Spies
MCDAVID, William, Pvt, Maj Wm Russell, Capt Wm Russell, Vol Mtd Gunmen; transferred to Capt Bean's Co
MCDAVID, William, Pvt, Regt Commander omitted, Capt James Cowan, Mtd Inf
MCDERMIT, Jacob, Pvt, Col John Coffee, Capt James Terrill, Vol Inf
MCDERMIT, Jacob, Pvt, Col Thos Williamson, Capt Beverly Williams, Vol Mtd Gunmen
MCDERRIN, John, Pvt, Col A Loury, Capt J Williamson, W TN Mil
MCDOELL, Elijah, 3 Sgt, Col Wm Hall, Capt Henry M Newland, Inf
MCDOLE, Archibald, Pvt, Col A Cheatham, Capt James Giddens, Inf
MCDOLE, Archibald, Pvt, Col Thomas Benton, Capt James McEwen, Vol Inf
MCDOLE, Shadrick M, Pvt, Col R C Napier, Capt Early Benson, Mil Inf
MCDONALD, Archibald, Pvt, Col Wm Pillow, Capt C E McEwen, Vol Inf
MCDONALD, David, Pvt, Col Robt Steele, Capt James Randals, Inf; AWOL 4-28-1814
MCDONALD, Edward, Pvt, Col Wm Johnson, Capt Benj Powell, Branch Srvce omitted
MCDONALD, Edward, Pvt, Col Wm Metcalf, Capt Alexander Hill & Capt John Cunningham, Mil Inf
MCDONALD, Elisha, Pvt, Col Samuel Wear, Capt John Doak, E TN Vol Inf
MCDONALD, Francis, Pvt, Lt Col L Hammond, Capt James Craig, Inf
MCDONALD, James, Pvt, Col Wm Metcalf, Capt Thomas Marks, Mil Inf
MCDONALD, Jamey, Pvt, Regt Commander omitted, Capt Edwin S Moore, Mtd Riflemen
MCDONALD, John, Pvt, Col S Copeland, Capt Wm Evans, Mil Inf
MCDONALD, John, Pvt, Col Samuel Wear, Capt John Doak, E TN Vol Inf
MCDONALD, John, Pvt, Col Thos Williamson, Capt James Cook & Capt John Dobbins, Vol Mtd Gunmen
MCDONALD, John, Pvt, Maj Wm Woodfolk, Capt John Sutton & Capt Abraham Dudney, Inf
MCDONALD, Joseph, Cpl, Col S Copeland, Capt Alexander Province, Mil Inf
MCDONALD, Joseph, Pvt, Col Thos Williamson, Capt Thomas Scurry, Vol Mtd Gunmen; d 2-17-1815
MCDONALD, Nath, Pvt, Col Wm Johnson, Capt James Stewart, E TN Mil
MCDONALD, Nathaniel, Pvt, Col Philip Pipkin, Capt Ebenezer Kirkpatrick, Mil Inf
MCDONALD, Squire B, Pvt, Col Thos Benton, Capt Benj Reynolds, Vol Inf
MCDONALD, Stephen, Pvt, Col Thos Williamson, Capt Thomas Scurry, Vol Mtd Gunmen
MCDONALD, Thomas, Pvt, Col S Copeland, Capt Wm Evans, Mil Inf
MCDONALD, Thomas, Pvt, Col Wm Johnson, Capt Benj Powell, E TN Mil; substitute for John Gonis
MCDONALD, William, Pvt, Col Robert Steele, Capt

Samuel Maxwell, Mil Inf
MCDONALD, William, Pvt, Maj Wm Woodfolk, Capt John Sutton & Capt Abraham Dudney, Inf
MCDONNALD, Daniel, Pvt, Col R H Dyer, Maj Wm Russell, Capt Wm Russell, Vol Mtd Gunmen
MCDONNALD, Squire B, Pvt, Col Thos Benton, Capt Benj Reynolds, Vol Inf
MCDONNALD, William A, Pvt, Maj Wm Russell, Capt Wm Russell, Vol Mtd Gunmen
MCDONNALL, William, Pvt, Col Jno Coffee, Capt Thos Bradley, Vol Cav
MCDONOUGH, Andrew, Pvt, Col Edwin Booth, Capt Vernon, E TN Mil
MCDOUGAL, James, Pvt, Col Robt Steele, Capt James Randals, Inf
MCDOUGALE, Aron, Pvt, Col John K Wynne, Capt Wm Carruthers, W TN Inf
MCDOUGALE, Aron, Pvt, Col John K Wynne, Capt Wm Wilson, Inf; transferred to Capt Caruthers Co
MCDOWEL, Archibald, Pvt, Col Wm Higgins, Capt Stephen Griffith, Mtd Riflemen
MCDOWEL, John, Pvt, Col Samuel Bunch, Capt Jno English, E TN Drafted Mil
MCDOWEL, John, Pvt, Col Samuel Bunch, Capt John Dobbins, E TN Mil; transferred to Capt English
MCDOWEL, John, Pvt, Col Samuel Wear, Capt John Stephens, E TN Vol Inf
MCDOWELL, James A, Pvt, Col John K Wynne, Capt John Porter, Inf
MCDOWELL, James, Pvt, Col A Loury, Capt Gabriel Martin, Inf
MCDOWELL, John, Pvt, Col Thos Benton, Capt Wm J Smith, Vol Inf
MCDOWELL, Joseph, Pvt, Col Wm Hall, Capt Henry M Newland, Inf
MCDOWELL, Nathan jr, Pvt, Col Wm Lillard, Capt Thomas Sharpe, 2nd Regt Inf
MCDOWELL, Nathan, Pvt, Col Wm Johnson, Capt James Stewart, E TN Drafted Mil; substitute
MCDOWELL, Robert, Pvt, Lt Col L Hammonds, Capt Arahel Rains, Inf
MCDUFFY, Neal, Pvt, Col Samuel Bayless, Capt Solomon Hendricks, E TN Mil
MCDUGALD, Hugh, 4 Sgt, Col Wm Metcalf, Capt Bird L Hurt, Mil Inf
MCELDRY, Samuel, Pvt, Col John Williams, Capt Wm Walker, Vol
MCELDRY, Samuel, Pvt, Col Samuel Wear, Capt John Chiles, E TN Vol Inf
MCELDRY, Samuel, QM, Commander omitted, E TN Vol Mtd Inf Bn
MCELDRY, Samuel, Sgt, Col John Brown, Capt John Childs, E TN Vol Mtd Gunmen
MCELDRY, Thomas, Sgt, Col Samuel Wear, Capt John Childs, E TN Vol Inf
MCELHANEY, Joseph, Pvt, Col Phillip Pipkin, Capt John Strother, Mil; attached to Capt David Smith
MCELHANY, Joseph, Pvt, Col A Cheatham, Capt Wm Smith, Inf
MCELHANY, Joseph, Pvt, Col John Cocke, Capt James Gault, Inf

MCELRATH, William, Pvt, Lt Col Henry Bryan, Co Commander omitted, Inf
MCELRIGHT, William, Pvt, Col John Cocke, Capt John Weakley, Inf
MCELROY, Alexander, Pvt, Col Jno Coffee, Capt Jno W Byrn, Cav
MCELROY, Archibald, Pvt, Col Thos Williamson, Capt John Dobbins & Capt John Doak, Vol Mtd Gunmen
MCELRUTH, William, Pvt, no other information
MCELSWORTH, John, Sgt, Col Jas Raulston, Capt H Hamilton, Inf; also under Maj Gen Carroll
MCELWICE, Thomas, Pvt, Col R C Napier, Capt John Chism, Mil Inf
MCELWORTH, Joseph, Pvt, Col Jas Raulston, Capt H Hamilton, Inf
MCELYA, Henry, Pvt, Col Wm Johnson, Capt H Hunter, E TN Mil; deserted 12-1814
MCELYCA, Daniel, Pvt, Col J K Winn, Capt Jno Spinks, Inf; d 11-22-1813
MCELYEA, John, Pvt, Col R C Napier, Capt Andrew McCarty, Mil Inf; on command as Wgnr
MCELYEA (MCELYRA), John, Pvt, Col Jas Raulston, Capt Chas Wade, Inf
MCENLILEY, Richard, Pvt, Col Wm Metcalf, Capt Thos Marks, Mil Inf
MCENTOCH, John, Pvt, Col P Pipkin, Capt John Strother, Mil; deserted 9-20-1814
MCENTURF, Casper, Pvt, Col Samuel Wear, Capt Robert Doak, E TN Vol Inf
MCENTURF, Jacob, Pvt, Col S Wear, Capt R Doak, E TN Vol Inf
MCEWEN, Alexander, 1 Sgt, Col Wm Pillow, Capt Jas McFerrin, Inf
MCEWEN, Christopher, Cpl, Regt Commander omitted, Capt David Mason, Cav
MCEWEN, Ephraim, Cpl, Regt Commander omitted, Capt D Mason, Cav
MCEWEN, John, Pvt, Col Thos Benton, Capt I Renshaw, Vol Inf
MCEWIN, David E, Pvt, Regt Commander omitted, Capt D Mason, Cav; promoted to Sgt & then 1 Lt
MCEWIN, Ephraim, Pvt, Regt Commander omitted, Capt D Mason, Cav
MCEWIN, James, Sgt, Col John Cocke, Capt Geo Barnes, Inf
MCEWIN, John L, 2 Sgt, Lt Col L Hammonds, Capt Alex Loury, Capt Thos Wells, Inf
MCEWING, James, Pvt, Col N Cannon, Capt Martin, Mtd Gunmen
MCEWING, Joseph, Sgt, Col N Cannon, Capt Martin, Mtd Gunmen; promoted from Pvt
MCFADDEN, James, Pvt, Col T H Benton, Capt Jas McEwen, Vol Inf
MCFADDEN, Thomas, Pvt, Col Wm Hall, Capt W L Alexander, Vol Inf; AWOL
MCFADDEN, William, Pvt, Col John Coffee, Capt David Smith, Vol Cav
MCFADDEN, William, Sgt, Lt Col Jno Edmonson, Co Commander omitted, Cav
MCFADDIN, James, Pvt, Regt Commander omitted, Capt

## Enlisted Men, War of 1812

Jos Williams, Mil Cav

MCFADDIN, William, Pvt, Regt Commander omitted, Capt David Smith, Cav

MCFADDINS, Ralph F, Pvt, Col Thos Williamson, Capt Richard Tate, Vol Mtd Gunmen

MCFADEN, James, Cpl, Col R H Dyer, Capt Robt Edmonson, TN Vol Mtd Gunmen

MCFADEN, James, Pvt, Col R H Dyer, Capt Robt Edmonston, 1st TN Vol Mtd Gunmen; d 2-5-1815 (not the Cpl of the same Co)

MCFADEN, John, Pvt, Col R H Dyer, Capt Robt Edmonston, 1st TN Vol Mtd Gunmen

MCFADEN, William, Pvt, Col R H Dyer, Capt Robt Edmonston, 1 TN Vol Mtd Gunmen

MCFADING, James, Pvt, Regt Commander omitted, Capt Jos Williams, Mil Cav

MCFALL, Daniel, Pvt, Col S Copeland, Capt S George, Inf

MCFALL, Elisha, Pvt, Col P Pipkin, Capt John Strother, Mil

MCFALL, George, Pvt, Col Robt Steele, Capt Robt Campbell, Mil Inf

MCFALL, Henry, Pvt, Col J Cocke, Capt J Price, Inf

MCFALL, Patrick, Pvt, Col Jno Brown, Capt Hugh Barton, E TN Mil Inf

MCFALL, Patrick, Pvt, Maj J Childs, Capt Chas Conway, E TN Mtd Gunmen

MCFALL, Samuel, 1 Sgt, Col J K Wynne, Capt B E Prince, Inf

MCFARLAN, James, Pvt, Col T H Benton, Capt Jas McFerrin, Vol Inf

MCFARLAND, Arthur, Pvt, Col S Copeland, Capt G W Stell, Mil Inf

MCFARLAND, David, Pvt, Col Wm Pillow, Capt John H Anderson, Vol Inf

MCFARLAND, George, Pvt, Col S Bunch, Capt E Buchanan, E TN Mil

MCFARLAND, George, Pvt, Maj Jno Childs, Capt Jno Stephens, E TN Vol Mtd Inf

MCFARLAND, James, Pvt, Col Jno Coffee, Capt Robt Jetton, Cav

MCFARLAND, John, Pvt, Maj Gen A Jackson, Col A Cheatham, Capt Wm Creel, Inf

MCFARLAND, Joseph, Pvt, Col E Allison, Capt J Hoyal, E TN Mil

MCFARLAND, Robert, Pvt, Maj Gen Andrew Jackson, Capt Wm Carroll, Vol Inf

MCFARLAND, William, Pvt, Col A Loury, Capt James Kincaid, Inf

MCFARLANE, Archilles, Pvt, Col John Coffee, Capt David Smith, Vol Cav

MCFARLANE, Harvey, Pvt, Col Samuel Bayless, Capt Joseph Goodson, E TN Mil

MCFARLEN, James, Pvt, Col Wm Pillow, Capt James McFerrin, Inf

MCFARLEN, Andrew, Pvt, Col R H Dyer, Capt Robt Edmondston, TN Vol Mtd Gunmen

MCFARLIN, Caleb, Pvt, Col Newton Cannon, Capt George Brandon, Mtd Riflemen

MCFARLIN, George, Pvt, Col Wm Lillard, Capt Jacob Dyke, Vol Inf

MCFARLIN, John, Pvt, Col Thomas H Williamson, Capt Beverly Williams, Mtd Gunmen

MCFARLIN, Thomas, Pvt, Col Newton Cannon, Capt George Brandon, Mtd Riflemen

MCFARLING, James, Pvt, Col Thomas H Benton, Capt James McFerrin, Vol Inf

MCFARREN, Thomas, Pvt, Col Thomas H Bradley, Capt Gabriel Martin, Vol Inf

MCFARREN, Walter, Pvt, Col Archer Cheatham, Capt Wm Smith, Inf

MCFARRIN, Thomas, Pvt, Col Wm Hall, Capt Brice Martin, Vol Inf

MCFEARSON, Jesse, Sgt, Col Wm Johnson, Capt James Rogers, E TN Drafted Mil

MCFEELY, Neele, Sgt, Maj Wm Russell, Capt John Cowan, Vol Mtd Gunmen

MCFERRAN, William, Pvt, Col Thomas H Williamson, Capt James Pace, Lt James Neely, Vol Mtd Gunmen; dismissed muster date

MCFERRIN, John, Pvt, Col T McCrory, Capt Isaac Patton, Mil Inf

MCFERRIN, Martin, Pvt, Col Newton Cannon, Capt Ota Cantrell, W TN Mtd Inf

MCFERRIN, Reuben, Pvt, Col James Raulston, Capt Mathew Cowan, Inf

MCFERRIN, William, 4 Sgt, Col Wm Pillow, Capt James McFerrin, Inf

MCFERRIN, William, Pvt, Col Samuel Wear, Capt Samuel Bayless, Mtd Inf

MCFERRIN, William, Pvt, Col Thomas H Benton, Capt James McFerrin, Vol Inf

MCFERRIN, _____, Pvt, Col L Hammond, Capt J N Williams, 2nd Regt Inf

MCFERSON, Thomas, Pvt, Col Wm Hall, Capt Brice Martin, Vol Inf

MCGAFFEN, Robert, Pvt, Col Samuel Bunch, Capt Daniel Yarnell, E TN Mil

MCGAHA, Aaron, Pvt, Col S Bunch, Capt James Cummings, E TN Vol Mtd Inf

MCGAHAY, John, Pvt, Col Wm Johnson, Capt Christopher Cook, E TN Mil

MCGAHAY, William, Pvt, Col Samuel Wear, Capt John Stephens, E TN Vol Inf

MCGANAHEY, James, Pvt, Col N T Perkins, Capt James McMahon, Mtd Gunmen

MCGANGHAY, James, 4 Cpl, Col Wm Johnson, Capt David McKamy, E TN Drafted Mil

MCGANGHY, Abner, Pvt, Regt Commander omitted, Capt Nathan Farmer, Mtd Riflemen

MCGANHEY, John, Pvt, Col Wm Johnson, Capt Joseph Kirk, Mil

MCGARRAHAH, Thomas, Pvt, Col James Raulston, Capt Mathew Cowan, Inf

MCGAVOCK, Jacob, Pvt, Regt Commander omitted, Capt D Deaderick, Arty

MCGAVOCK, James, Pvt, Col John Cocke, Capt John Dalton, Inf

MCGAVOCK, John, Pvt, Regt Commander omitted, Capt D Deadrick, Arty

MCGEA, Samuel, Pvt, Col Philip Pipkin, Capt Peter Searcy, Mil Inf

## Enlisted Men, War of 1812

MCGEE, Abraham, Pvt, Regt Commander omitted, Capt Archibald McKinney, Cav

MCGEE, Adam, Pvt, Regt Commander omitted, Capt Elijah Rushing, Det of Inf

MCGEE, Asa, Pvt, Regt Commander omitted, Capt Archibald McKinney, Cav

MCGEE, Charles, Pvt, Maj Wm Russell, Capt John Cowan, Vol Mtd Gunmen

MCGEE, Gentry, Sgt, Col N T Perkins, Capt John B Quarles, Vol Mtd Inf

MCGEE, George, Pvt, Col Samuel Bayless, Capt Jonathan Waddle, E TN Mil

MCGEE, Jacob, Pvt, Col Wm Johnson, Capt John McKamy, E TN Drafted Mil

MCGEE, James, Pvt, Col Edwin E Booth, Capt Thompson, Mil

MCGEE, Richard, Pvt, Maj Gen Andrew Jackson, Col Thomas H Williamson, Capt Robert Steele, Vol Mtd Gunmen

MCGEE, Robert, Pvt, Col Samuel Bunch, Capt Jones Griffin, E TN Drafted Mil

MCGEE, Samuel, Pvt, Col P Pipkin, Capt Peter Searcy, Mil Inf

MCGEE, Thomas, Pvt, Regt Commander omitted, Capt Thomas Gray, Inf

MCGEE, William, Pvt, Maj Gen A Jackson, Col A Cheatham, Capt Wm Creel, Inf

MCGEE, William, Pvt, Regt Commander omitted, Capt Gray, Inf

MCGEEHE, John, Pvt, Col John Cocke, Capt James Gray, Inf

MCGEEHE, Thomas, Pvt, Col Alexander Loury, Capt James Kincaid, Inf

MCGEEHEE, James, Pvt, Col S Copeland, Capt John Holshouser, Inf

MCGEHEE, John, Pvt, Col Alexander Loury, Lt Col Leroy Hammonds, Capt Thomas Delaney, Inf

MCGEHEE, Samuel, Pvt, Lt Col Leroy Hammonds, Col Alexander Loury, Capt Thomas Delaney, Inf

MCGENIS, William, Pvt, Col N Cannon, Capt Newton Patterson, Mtd Riflemen; transferred to Moore's Co

MCGHABREY, Robert, Pvt, Maj Wm Russell, Capt John Trimble, Vol Mtd Gunmen

MCGHEE, William, Pvt, Maj Robert Cooper, Co Commander omitted, Mtd Riflemen

MCGHIMMUR, Aaron, Pvt, Col Wm Lillard, Capt Thomas Sharpe, Inf

MCGILL, David, 3 Sgt, Brig Gen Thomas Johnson, Capt Robert Carson, Inf

MCGILL, David, Pvt, Col John K Wynn, Capt Wm Carothers, Inf W TN

MCGILL, Hugh, Pvt, Col Samuel Wear, Capt James Gillespie, E TN Vol Inf

MCGILL, James, Pvt, Col A Loury, Capt J N Williamson, W TN Mil

MCGILL, James, Pvt, Col Thomas Williamson, Capt John Williamson, Vol Mtd Gunmen

MCGILL, John, Pvt, Col Robert Steele, Capt Jas Randals, Inf

MCGILL, Roaling, Pvt, Col S Bayless, Capt Jas Churchman, E TN Mil; transferred to Capt Millikin Co

MCGILL, Robert, Pvt, Col Wm Johnson, Capt David McKamey, E TN Drafted Mil

MCGILL, Roland, Pvt, Col Wm Johnson, Capt Elihu Millikin, E TN Mil; transferred from Capt Hunter Co

MCGILL, Thomas, Pvt, Col Leroy Hammonds, Capt Jas Craig, Inf

MCGILL, William, Pvt, Col S Bunch, Capt S Richardson, E TN Drafted Mil

MCGILL, William, Pvt, Col S Wear, Capt James Gillespie, E TN Vol Inf

MCGILL, William, Pvt, Regt Commander omitted, Capt Samuel Richardson, E TN Drafted Mil

MCGINLEY, John, Cpl, Col S Bunch, Capt Edward Buchanan, E TN Drafted Mil

MCGINNIS, Abraham, Pvt, Col A Loury, Capt Leroy Hammonds & Capt Arahel Raines, Inf

MCGINNIS, Alexander, Pvt, Col Jas Raulston, Capt Robinson & Capt Major Carroll, Inf

MCGINNIS, John, Pvt, Col S Bayless, Capt J Waddell, E TN Mil

MCGINNIS, Joseph, Pvt, Col Wm Lillard, Capt Jacob Hartsell, E TN Vol Inf

MCGINNIS, Moses, Cpl, Col Wm Lillard, Capt Thomas Sharpe, E TN Inf

MCGINNIS, Robert, Pvt, Col S Bayless, Capt Jones, E TN Drafted Mil

MCGINNIS, Robert, Pvt, Col Wm Johnson, Capt Elihu Milliken, E TN Mil; transferred to Capt Jones Co

MCGINNIS, William H, Pvt, Col Robert Steele, Capt John Chitwood, Mil Inf

MCGINNIS, William H, Pvt, Col Thos Benton, Capt Moore, Vol Inf

MCGINTRY, Alexander, Pvt, Col Ewen Allison, Capt Henry McCray, E TN Mil

MCGIRK, Andrew, Pvt, Col Wm Lillard, Capt Thomas McChristian, E TN Vol Inf

MCGLANNEY, Lovern, Pvt, Col Wm Y Higgins, Capt James Hambleton, Mtd Gunmen; wounded 1-22-1814

MCGLAUGHLAN, Samuel, Pvt, Maj Wm Russell, Capt Isaac Williams, TN Vol Mtd Gunmen

MCGLAUGHLIN, Joseph, Pvt, Col John Alcorn, Capt Robt Jetton, Vol Cav

MCGLAUGHTON, Absolom, Pvt, Col N Cannon, Capt Isaac Williams, Mtd Riflemen

MCGLAUGHTON, John, Pvt, Col R C Napier, Capt Thomas Preston, Mil Inf

MCGLOMERY, Severn, Pvt, Maj Wm Russell, Capt Fleman Hodges, Vol Mtd Gunmen; substitute for Wm Stockton

MCGLOUGH, Alexander, Pvt, Col R C Napier, Capt Drury Adkins, Mil Inf

MCGLOUGHLIN, Abraham, Pvt, no other information

MCGLOUGHTON, John, Pvt, Col R C Napier, Capt Thos Preston, Mil Inf

MCGONEGAL, Eli, Pvt, Col Wm Pillow, Capt Jas McFerrin, Inf; deserted 11-19-1813

MCGOWAN, David, Pvt, Col Wm Pillow, Capt Geo Caperton, Inf

## Enlisted Men, War of 1812

MCGOWAN, James, Cpl, Col R C Napier, Capt Andrew McCarty, Mil Inf
MCGOWAN, John, Pvt, Col Thos Benton, Capt Geo Caperton, Inf
MCGOWAN, John, Pvt, Col Wm Pillow, Capt Geo Caperton, Inf
MCGOWAN, Samuel, Sgt, Maj Gen Jackson, Capt Allen, Mil Inf
MCGRAW, John, Dmr, Maj Gen Jackson, Capt Carroll, Vol Inf; may be Ffr
MCGRAW, Joseph, Pvt, Col Wm Hall, Capt Moore, Vol Inf; substitute of Andrew Robinson
MCGREER, David W, Pvt, Regt Commander omitted, Capt Jas Ferrill, Cav
MCGREGOR, Harris, Pvt, Col R C Napier, Capt Gray, Mil Inf
MCGREGOR, Harris, Pvt, Regt Commander omitted, Capt Elijah Rushing, Inf
MCGREGOR, John, Pvt, Col R C Napier, Capt Gray, Mil Inf
MCGREGOR, John, Sgt, Regt Commander omitted, Capt Abner Pearce, Branch Srvce omitted
MCGRIRK, Isaac, Pvt, Col S Bunch, Capt Francis Berry, E TN Mil; promoted to Sgt
MCGUAIR, John, Pvt, Col John Coffee, Capt Blackman Coleman, Cav
MCGUARY, Pleasant, Pvt, Gen Roberts, Capt Benj Reynolds, Branch Srvce omitted
MCGUIN, David, Pvt, Col S Bunch, Capt James Penney, E TN Mtd Inf
MCGUIN, John, Pvt, Lt Col Archer Cheatham, Co Commander omitted, Mtd Inf
MCGUIRE, Cornelius, Pvt, Col John K Wynne, Capt James Cole, Inf
MCGUIRE, Cornelius, Pvt, Col Samuel Bunch, Capt Geo Gregory, E TN Drafted Mil
MCGUIRE, Elijah, Pvt, Col Philip Pipkin, Capt Henry M Newlin, Mil Inf
MCGUIRE, George, 4 Sgt, Col Edward Bradley, Capt Abraham Bledsoe, Riflemen
MCGUIRE, George, Pvt, Col Wm Hall, Capt Abraham Bledsoe, Vol Inf
MCGUIRE, Henry, Pvt, Col Edwin E Booth, Capt Alexander Biggs, Inf
MCGUIRE, Isaac, Pvt, Maj Wm Russell, Capt Wm Chism, Vol Mtd Gunmen
MCGUIRE, James, Pvt, Col John Brown, Capt Jesse G Reany, Mtd Gunmen
MCGUIRE, James, Pvt, Col N Cannon, Capt Martin, Mtd Gunmen
MCGUIRE, James, Pvt, Richardson (Rank omitted), Gunmen
MCGUIRE, John, Pvt, Col A Loury, Capt Geo Sarver, Inf
MCGUIRE, John, Pvt, Regt Commander omitted, Capt Geo Smith, Spies
MCGUIRE, Josiah, Pvt, Col Samuel Bunch, Capt Joseph Duncan, E TN Drafted Mil
MCGUIRE, Nicholas, Pvt, Col Samuel Bunch, Capt Joseph Duncan, E TN Drafted Mil
MCGUIRE, Silas, 5 Cpl, Col Philip Pipkin, Capt Peter Searcy, Mil Inf

MCGUIRE, Silas, Pvt, Col T McCrory, Capt Thos K Brodon, Inf
MCGUIRE, William, Pvt, Col Edwin Booth, Capt Vernon, E TN Mil
MCGUIRE, William, Pvt, Col Jno Brown, Capt Wm Christian, E TN Mil Inf
MCGUNN, William, Pvt, no other information
MCHANY, Henry, Pvt, Col Robt Steele, Capt James Randals, Inf; deserted 3-5-1814
MCHENRY, John, Pvt, Lt Col Jno Edmonson, Co Commander omitted, Cav
MCHENRY, John, Sgt & Cpl, Col John Coffee, Capt Michael Molton, Cav
MCHENRY, Roberts, Pvt, Col Edwin Booth, Capt John Lewis, E TN Mil
MCHOON, Zachariah, Pvt, Col Wm Lillard, Capt John Neatherton, E TN Vol Inf
MCILLHINAY, John, Pvt, Col A Cheatham, Capt Geo G Chapman, Inf
MCILROY, Micajah, Pvt, Maj Wm Russell, Col Robt H Dyer, Capt Wm Russell, Vol Mtd Gunmen
MCILWAINE, John, Pvt, Col Wm Metcalf, Capt Wm Mullin, Mil Inf
MCINEER, Daniel, Pvt, Col Philip Pipkin, Capt John Robertson, Mil Inf
MCINIS, George, Pvt, Col Edward Bradley, Capt Brice Martin, Vol Inf
MCINNIS, George, Pvt, Col Wm Hall, Capt Brice Martin, Vol Inf
MCINNIS, Hugh, 1 Lt, Col S Copeland, Capt Allen Wilkinson, Mil Inf
MCINTIE, Archibald, Pvt, Maj Wm Woodfolk, Capt Ezekial Ross & Capt McCulley, Branch Srvce omitted
MCINTIRE, Archibald, Pvt, Col S Copeland, Capt Wm Hodges, Inf
MCINTIRE, Duncan, Pvt, Col Philip Pipkin, Capt Henry M Newlin, Mil Inf
MCINTIRE, John T, Sgt, Col Samuel Bunch, Capt Andrew Breden, E TN Mil; appointed Sgt Maj
MCINTOSH, Daniel, Pvt, Col Samuel Bayless, Capt Solomon Hendrix, E TN Mil; deserted from the garrison 12-15-1814
MCINTOSH, Daniel, Pvt, Maj Gen A Jackson, Capt Wm Carroll, Vol Inf
MCINTOSH, James, Pvt, Col John Cocke, Capt Richard Crunk, Inf
MCINTOSH, Nimrod, Pvt, Lt Col L Hammond, Capt James Craig, Inf
MCINTOSH, William, Pvt, Col James Raulston, Capt James A Black, Inf
MCINTOSH, William, Pvt, Lt Col Jno Edmonson, Co Commander omitted, Cav
MCINTURF, George, Pvt, Col Ewen Allison, Capt John Hampton, Mil
MCINTURF, George, Pvt, Col Wm Johnson, Capt Henry Hunter, E TN Mil
MCINTURF, Israel, Pvt, Col Ewen Allison, Capt Adam Winsell, E TN Draft Mil
MCINTURF, Thomas jr, Pvt, Col Ewen Allison, Capt Adam Winsell, E TN Draft Mil

## Enlisted Men, War of 1812

MCINTURF, Thomas, Pvt, Col Samuel Bunch, Capt F Register, E TN Mil; joined from Capt Winsel's Co
MCJOHN, John, Pvt, Brig Gen Jas White, no Co Commander, Appted Spy
MCJONES, Walter, 3 Cpl, Col Wm Lillard, Capt George Keys, E TN Inf
MCJONES, Walter, Pvt, Col S Bunch, Capt S Richerson, E TN Draft Mil; deserted
MCJONES, Walter, Pvt, Col Samuel Richardson, Capt English, E TN Draft Mil
MCKAIN, Samuel, Sgt, Col Thos Williamson, Capt Robert Moore, Vol Mtd Gunmen; appted Cor
MCKAMEY, James, Pvt, Col Newton Cannon, Capt John B Demsey, Mtd Gunmen
MCKAMEY, James, Pvt, Gen Andrew Jackson, Capt Hugh Kerr, Mtd Rangers
MCKAMY, Francis, Pvt, Col Newton Cannon, Capt John B Demsey, Mtd Gunmen
MCKAMY, James, 4 Sgt, Col Wm Johnson, Capt David McKamy, E TN Drafted Mil
MCKAMY, William, 4 Sgt, Col Edwin Booth, Capt Alexander Biggs, Inf
MCKAUGHAN, Archibald, Pvt, Col Robt Steele, Capt James Bennett, Mil Inf
MCKAY (MCKEE), Alexander, Pvt, Maj John Chiles, Capt John Stephens, E TN Vol Mtd Inf
MCKEAN, James K, 3 Sgt, Regt Commander omitted, Capt Jas Terrill, Cav
MCKEARBY, Ezekid, 2 Sgt, Col Wm Metcalf, Capt Thos Marks, Mil Inf
MCKEE, James, Pvt, Col John Cocke, Capt George Barnes, Inf
MCKEE, James, Pvt, Col R H Dyer, Capt Isaac Williams, Vol Mtd Gunmen
MCKEE, John, Pvt, Col Wm Lillard, Capt Robert Maloney, E TN Vol Inf
MCKEE, John, Sgt, Col Samuel Wear, Capt James Gillespie, E TN Vol Inf; promoted from Cpl
MCKEE, Joseph, Pvt, Col Alexander Loury, Capt James Kincaid, Inf
MCKEE, Lewis, Pvt, Col Jas Raulston, Capt Jas A Black, Inf
MCKEE, Robert, Pvt, Col Thos Benton, Capt Benjamin Reynolds, Vol Inf
MCKEE, Samuel, Pvt, Col Jno Coffee, Capt David Smith, Vol Cav
MCKEE, William, Cpl, Col Thos Benton, Capt George Gibbs, Vol Inf
MCKEE, William, Pvt, Col Jno Coffee, Capt David Smith, Vol Cav; deserted
MCKEE, William, Pvt, Col Samuel Wear, Capt Simeon Perry, E TN Vol Mtd Inf
MCKEE, William, Pvt, Col Wm Lillard, Capt S Copeland, E TN Vol Inf; drove baggage wagon
MCKEEHAN, George, Pvt, Col Wm Lillard, Capt Jacob Dyke, Vol Inf
MCKEEHAN, James, Pvt, Maj John Chiles, Capt Reuben Tipton, E TN Vol Mtd Inf; Regimental Co - Knox
MCKEEN, James K, 2 Cpl, Col Jno Coffee, Capt James Terrill, Vol Cav
MCKEHAN, Thomas, Pvt, Col Edwin E Booth, Capt John Porter, Drafted Mil
MCKELDRY, Samuel, Pvt, Maj John Chiles, Capt Reuben Tipton, E TN Vol Mtd Inf; promoted to Regt QM
MCKELLY, William, Pvt, Col Philip Pipkin, Capt George Mebane, Mil Inf; deserted from Ft Jackson 9-20-1814
MCKELRY, John, Pvt, Col Thos Williamson, Capt James Pace, Lt James Neely, Vol Mtd Gunmen
MCKENDRY, Malcom, Pvt, Regt Commander omitted, Capt James Gray, Inf
MCKENLEY, Daniel, Pvt, Col Newton Cannon, Capt Wm Martin, Mtd Gunmen
MCKENLEY, William, Pvt, Maj John Chiles, Capt Reuben Tipton, E TN Vol Mtd Inf
MCKENNEY, George, Pvt, Regt Commander omitted, Capt Archibald McKinney, Cav
MCKENNEY, Robert, Pvt, Maj Robert Cooper, Co Commander omitted, Mtd Riflemen
MCKENNEY, Robert, Sgt, Col Ewen Allison, Capt Thomas Wilson, E TN Drafted Mil
MCKENNIE, Joseph, Cpl, Col John Cocke, Capt Samuel M Caruthers, Inf
MCKENNIE, Samuel, Pvt, Col Wm Metcalf, Capt Wm Mullins, Mil Inf
MCKENNY, John, Pvt, Col N T Perkins, Capt Mathew Johnson, Mil Inf
MCKENNY, John, Pvt, Col Wm Johnson, Capt Elihu Milliken, 3rd Regt E TN Mil
MCKENSEY, Cornelius, Pvt, Col Philip Pipkin, Capt Ebenezer Kirkpatrick, Mil Inf
MCKENSEY, James, Pvt, Col Jno Coffee, Capt John W Byrns, Cav
MCKENSEY, Malcolm, Pvt, Col John Cocke, Capt James Gray, Inf; d 2-23-1815
MCKENZIE, Daniel, Pvt, Regt Commander omitted, Capt Jno Miller, Spies
MCKEON, James K, 2 Cpl, Col Jno Coffee, Capt Jas Terrill, Vol Cav
MCKEON, James, 3 Sgt, Regt Commander omitted, Capt Jas Terrill, Cav
MCKERGAN, Thomas, Pvt, Col Edwin Booth, Capt John Slatton, E TN Mil
MCKERTY, John, Pvt, Col Thos Williamson, Capt James Pace, Lt James Nealy, Vol Mtd Gunmen
MCKETHEN, Robert, Cpl, Col R C Napier, Capt Thos Preston, Mil Inf
MCKEY, James, Pvt, Col R H Dyer, Capt Cuthbert Hudson, Vol Mtd Gunmen
MCKEY, James, Pvt, Lt Col Richard Napier, Co Commander omitted, Inf
MCKEY, William, Pvt, Col Thos Benton, Capt George Gibbs, Vol Inf
MCKEY (MACKY), William, Sgt, Col Wm Pillow, Capt John H Anderson, Vol Inf
MCKIMIE, Samuel, Pvt, Col Wm Metcalf, Capt Wm Mullins, Mil Inf
MCKIMOR, William, Pvt, Regt Commander omitted, Capt Nathan Davis, Lt I Barrett, Inf
MCKINDLEY, John, Pvt, Col Wm Lillard, Capt John Roper, E TN Vol Inf

## Enlisted Men, War of 1812

MCKINELY, Robert, Pvt, Col Philip Pipkin, Capt David Smith, Mil Inf
MCKINLEY, David, Pvt, Col Edwin Booth, Capt Vernon, E TN Mil
MCKINLEY, James, Pvt, Col Alexander Loury, Lt Col Leroy Hammonds, Capt Thomas Delany, Inf
MCKINLEY, John, Pvt, Col Alexander Loury, Lt Col Leroy Hammonds, Capt Thomas Delany, Inf
MCKINLEY, Simmons, Pvt, Col Alexander Loury, Lt Col L Hammonds, Capt Thos Delany, Inf
MCKINNEY, Alexander, Pvt, Col A Loury, Capt J N Williamson, W TN Mil
MCKINNEY, Alexander, Pvt, Col Wm Metcalf, Capt Thos Marks, Mil Inf
MCKINNEY, Archibald, Pvt, Col Thos Williamson, Capt Richard Tate, Vol Mtd Gunmen; transferred to Capt Donelson
MCKINNEY, Archibald, Pvt, Col Wm Hall, Capt John Moore, Vol Inf
MCKINNEY, Archibold, Pvt, Col Jno Coffee, Capt Chas Kavanaugh, Cav
MCKINNEY, Charles, Surgeon Mate, Col Wm Higgins, 2nd Regt Mt Vol
MCKINNEY, Collier, Pvt, Regt Commander omitted, Capt Archibald McKamy, Cav
MCKINNEY, Collin, Pvt, Col John Coffee, Capt Charles Kavanaugh, Cav
MCKINNEY, Collin, Pvt, Col Thomas Williamson, Capt Richard Tate, Vol Mtd Gunmen; transferred to Capt Donelson
MCKINNEY, Daniel, Pvt, Col A Lowry, Capt John Williams, W TN Mil
MCKINNEY, Evan, Pvt, Maj Robert Cooper, Co Commander omitted, Mtd Riflemen
MCKINNEY, George, Pvt, Col Thomas Williamson, Capt Richard Tate, Vol Mtd Gunmen
MCKINNEY, George, Pvt, Regt Commander omitted, Capt Archibald McKamey, Cav
MCKINNEY, Isaac, Pvt, Regt Commander omitted, Capt Abner Pearce, Inf
MCKINNEY, James, Pvt, Col John Williams, Capt Samuel Bunch, Mtd Vol
MCKINNEY, James, Pvt, Col Robert Steele, Capt Samuel Maxwell, Mil Inf
MCKINNEY, James, Pvt, Col Samuel Bunch, Capt Jno English, E TN Drafted Mil
MCKINNEY, John, Pvt, Col Leroy Hammond, Capt James Craig, Inf
MCKINNEY, John, Pvt, Col Wm Lillard, Capt Zacheus Copeland, E TN Vol Inf
MCKINNEY, John, Pvt, Col Wm Metcalf, Capt Thomas Marks, Mil Inf
MCKINNEY, John, Pvt, Regt Commander omitted, Capt Robert Evans, Mtd Spies; transferred to Capt McKamy Co
MCKINNEY, John, Surgeon's Mate, Col John Alcorn, TN Vol Cav; resigned 11-16-1813
MCKINNEY, Mathew, Pvt, Maj John Childs, Capt Charles Conway, E TN Mtd Gunmen; promoted to Cpl & reduced to ranks
MCKINNEY, Reuben, Pvt, Col Edwin Booth, Capt John McKamey, E TN Mil
MCKINNEY, Reubin, Pvt, Col John Brown, Capt Wm D Neilson, E TN Vol Mil
MCKINNEY, Robert, Pvt, Col R C Napier, Capt Thomas Gray, Mil Inf
MCKINNEY, Robert, Pvt, Col Wm Metcalf, Capt Thomas Marks, Mil Inf
MCKINNEY, Samuel, Pvt, Col John Alcorn, Capt John Winston, Mtd Riflemen
MCKINNEY, Samuel, Pvt, Col Leroy Hammond, Capt J N Williamson, 2nd Regt Inf
MCKINNEY, Seth, Pvt, Col Samuel Wear, Capt Joseph Calloway, Mtd Inf
MCKINNEY, Thomas, Pvt, Col John Brown, Capt Wm D Neilson, E TN Vol Mil
MCKINNEY, Thomas, Sgt, Col John Alcorn, Capt John Winston, Mtd Riflemen
MCKINNEY, Vincent, Pvt, Col Samuel Bayless, Capt James Churchman, E TN Mil
MCKINNEY, William, Pvt, Maj John Childs, Capt John Conway, E TN Mtd Gunmen; reduced from Cpl
MCKINNIE, John, Pvt, Regt Commander omitted, Capt Nathan David, Lt I Barrett, Inf
MCKINNIE, Wiley (Willie), Pvt, Col James Raulston, Maj Sam Carroll, Capt Elija Haynie, Inf
MCKINNIS, George, Pvt, Col Wm Hall, Capt Brice Martin, Vol Inf
MCKINNIS, John, Pvt, Col Thomas McCrory, Capt Anthony Metcalf, Mil Inf
MCKINNY, William, Pvt, Maj Wm Russell, Capt Fleman Hodges, Vol Mtd Gunmen
MCKINSEY, James, Pvt, Col John Alcorn, Capt John W Byrn, Cav
MCKINSEY, Rolly, Pvt, Col Newton Cannon, Capt Isaac Williams, Mtd Riflemen; died 11-18-1813 (1 roll says 11-10-1813)
MCKINSEY, Turner, Pvt, Col William Wallace, Capt John Hall, Inf
MCKISACK, William, Pvt, Col Edwin Allison, Capt James Allen, E TN Mil
MCKISICK, Daniel, Pvt, Col Newton Cannon, Capt John B Demsey, Mtd Gunmen
MCKISICK, Daniel, Pvt, Col Thomas Benton, Capt Benjamin Hewitt, Vol Inf
MCKISICK, Daniel, Pvt, Col Thomas Benton, Capt Isaah Renshaw, Vol Inf; joined from Capt Hewitt's Co
MCKISICK, David, Sgt, Col Thomas Benton, Capt Benj Hewitt, Vol Inf
MCKISICK, Edward, Sgt, Col Thomas Williamson, Capt Thomas Scurry, Vol Mtd Gunmen
MCKISICK, John, Pvt, Col Thomas Benton, Capt Benjamin Hewitt, Vol Inf
MCKISICK, John, Sdlr, Col Newton Cannon, Capt James B Demsey, Mtd Gunmen
MCKISICK, Joseph, Pvt, Col Newton Cannon, Capt John B Demsey, Mtd Gunmen
MCKISICK, Joseph, Pvt, Col Thomas Benton, Capt Benjamin Hewit, Vol Inf
MCKISSACK, Archibald, Pvt, Col Wm Metcalf, Capt Thomas Marks, Mil Inf
MCKISSICK, Daniel, Pvt, Col Thomas Benton, Capt

Isaah Renshaw, Vol Inf; trans to Capt Hewitt's Co
MCKISSICK, David, Pvt, Col Thomas Benton, Capt Isaah Renshaw, Vol Inf; trans to Capt Hewitt's Co
MCKISSICK, Davis, Pvt, Col Newton Cannon, Capt James Demsey, Mtd Gunmen
MCKISSICK, Davis, Pvt, Col Thomas Benton, Capt Isaah Renshaw, Vol Inf; joined from Capt Hewitt's Co
MCKISSICK, John, Pvt, Col Thomas Benton, Capt Isaah Renshaw, Vol Inf; joined from Capt Hewitt's Co
MCKISSICK, Joseph, Pvt, Col Thomas Benton, Capt Isaah Renshaw, Vol Inf; joined from Capt Hewitt's Co
MCKITCHAN, James, Pvt, Col Samuel Bayless, Capt Joseph B Bacon, E TN Mil
MCKLEASY, Giles, Pvt, Maj Wm Russell, Capt John Cowan, Vol Mtd Gunmen
MCKLEHANEY, David, Pvt, Col Wear, Capt Simon Perry, E TN Vol Mtd Inf
MCKNIGHT, Alexander, Pvt, Col Newton Cannon, Capt George Brandon, Mtd Riflemen
MCKNIGHT, David, 3 Sgt, Col John Coffee, Capt Alexander McKeen, Cav
MCKNIGHT, James, Pvt, Col Leroy Hammonds, Capt Thomas Wells, Inf; also under Col Lowery
MCKNIGHT, James, Pvt, Col Pillow, Lt Mason, Vol Inf
MCKNIGHT, James, Pvt, Col Thomas Benton, Capt Newton Cannon, Inf
MCKNIGHT, James, Pvt, Regt Commander omitted, Capt Archibald McKamey, Cav
MCKNIGHT, James, Pvt, Regt Commander omitted, Capt E Moore, Mtd Riflemen
MCKNIGHT, John, Pvt, Col Wm Metcalf, Capt O Waller, Mil Inf
MCKNIGHT, Joseph, Pvt, Regt Commander omitted, Capt Archibald McKenney, Cav
MCKNIGHT, Robert, Pvt, Col A Cheatham, Capt Chas Johnson, Inf
MCKNIGHT, Samuel B, Pvt, Col Thos Benton, Capt Robt Cannon, Inf
MCKNIGHT, Samuel B, Pvt, Col Wm Pillow, Lt Jos Mason, Vol Inf
MCKNIGHT, Thomas, Pvt, Col S Copeland, Capt Moses Thompson, Inf
MCKNIGHT, William, Pvt, Regt Commander omitted, Capt E S Moore, Mtd Riflemen; trans from Lt Berry's Camp
MCKONOLDS, David, Pvt, Col Samuel Wear, Capt Jas Tedford, E TN Vol Inf
MCKORKELL, Andrew, Pvt, Col A Cheatham, Capt Chas Johnson, Inf
MCKOWN, Alexander, Pvt, Col Thos McCrory, Capt Anthony Metcalf, Mil Inf
MCKULLEY, James, Pvt, Col E E Booth, Capt J McKamey, E TN Mil
MCLAIN, Alexander, Pvt, Col Samuel Bayless, Capt J B Bacon, E TN Mll
MCLAIN, Robert, Pvt, Col N Cannon, Capt Ota Cantrell, W Tn Mtd Inf; promoted to Sgt
MCLANE, Benjamin, Sgt, Col Wm Pillow, Capt John Anderson, Vol Inf
MCLASKEY, George, Pvt, Col Thos Benton, Capt Geo Caperton, Vol Inf
MCLASKY, William, Pvt, Col T Benton, Capt G Caperton, Vol Inf
MCLAUGHLAN, William B, Pvt, Col S Copeland, Capt S George, Inf
MCLAUGHLEN, Steth, 3 Sgt, Col T Benton, Capt Jas McFerrin, Vol Inf
MCLAUGHLEN, Thomas, Pvt, Col Wm Hall, Capt T C Nash, Inf
MCLAUGHLIN, Elijah, Pvt, Col E Bradley, Capt T B Haynes, Vol Inf
MCLAUGHLIN, Elijah, Sgt, Col Wm Hall, Capt Henry Newlin, Inf
MCLAUGHLIN, John, Pvt, Col Wm Higgins, Capt S Griffith, Mtd Riflemen
MCLAUGHLIN, Samuel, Pvt, Col Wm Hall, Capt T C Nash, Inf
MCLEAN, Alexander, Sgt, Gen Jackson, Capt Hugh Kerr, Mted Rangers
MCLEAN, John, Pvt, Col N T Perkins, Capt Jas McMahon, Mtd Gunmen
MCLEHANY, John, Pvt, Maj Wm Russell, Capt F Hodges, Vol Mtd Gunmen
MCLEMORE, Moses, Cpl, Gen Andrew Jackson, Capt Nathan Davis, Inf
MCLEMORE, Robert, Pvt, Col R H Dyer, Capt Glen Owen, 1 TN Vol Mtd Gunmen
MCLENDON, Bright, Pvt, Col N T Perkins, Capt R Pipkin, Mtd Riflemen; wounded 1-24-1814
MCLENDON, Dennis, Pvt, Col N T Perkins, Capt P Pipkin, Mtd Riflemen
MCLENDON, Lewis, Pvt, Col Jno Winn, Capt Jno Spinks, Inf; deserted
MCLEON, John, Pvt, Regt Commander omitted, Capt Gray, Inf
MCLESTER, Joseph, Pvt, Col Samuel Bayless, Capt B Jones, E TN Draft Mil
MCLEYA (MCELYEA), Hugh, Pvt, Col A Cheatham, Capt R Benson, Inf
MCLIN, Benjamin, Pvt, Col E Allison, Capt H McCray, E Tn Mil; discharged by surgeon
MCLIN, David, Pvt, Col E Allison, Capt H McCray, E TN Mil; trans to Capt Register's Co
MCLIN, Joseph, Sgt, Col Wm Lillard, Capt Geo Keys, E TN Inf
MCLIN, William, Capt, Col Wm Lillard, Co Commander omitted, Inf
MCLISH, John, Pvt, Col R H Dyer, Capt Glen Owen, TN Vol Mtd Gunmen
MCLOUGHLIN, Thomas, Pvt, no other information
MCLOUGHLON, Samuel, Pvt, Col E Bradley, Capt T Nash, Vol Inf
MCLURE, Robert, Pvt, Col J Winn, Capt J Holleman, Inf; deserted
MCLUSKEY, George, Pvt, Col Thos Benton, Capt Geo Caperton, Inf
MCMAHAN, Abraham, Pvt, Col Thos Benton, Capt Wm Moore, Vol Inf
MCMAHAN, David, Pvt, Col John Alcorn, Capt Robert Jetton, Vol Cav
MCMAHAN, George, Pvt, Col S Bunch, Capt Jno Houk,

## Enlisted Men, War of 1812

E TN Mil; trans to Capt English's Co
MCMAHAN, James, Cpl, Maj Wm Russell, Capt John Trimble, Vol Mtd Gunmen
MCMAHAN, James, Pvt, Col E Booth, Capt John Slatton, E TN Mil
MCMAHAN, James, Pvt, Col Thomas Williamson, Capt John Hutchings, Vol Mtd Gunmen
MCMAHAN, James, Pvt, Col Wm Johnson, Capt Joseph Kirk, Mil
MCMAHAN, James, Pvt, Regt Commander omitted, Capt Jas Terrill, Cav Vol; later promoted to Cpl
MCMAHAN, John, Pvt, Col John Brown, Capt Jas McKamy, E TN Mtd Gunmen
MCMAHAN, John, Pvt, Maj Wm Russell, Capt John Trimble, Vol Mtd Gunmen
MCMAHAN, Redmon, Pvt, Col Edwin Booth, Capt John Porter, Drafted Mil
MCMAHAN, Samuel, Pvt, Regt Coimmander omitted, Capt Jas Terrill, Cav
MCMAHAN, William, Pvt, Col John Brown, Capt John Trimble, E TN Mtd Gunmen
MCMAHAN, William, Pvt, Col S Wear, Capt Jas Tedford, E Tn Vol Inf
MCMAHAN, William, Pvt, Col Wm Higgins, Capt James Hambleton, Mtd Gunmen
MCMAHON, David, Pvt, Col Wm Hall, Capt T C Nash, Inf
MCMAHON, Richard, 1 Sgt, Col John Coffee, Capt Jas Terrell, Vol Cav
MCMAHON, Richard, Pvt, Col Wm Hall, Capt Henry Newlin, Inf
MCMAHON, Thomas, Pvt, Col S Bunch, Capt James Penney, E Tn Mtd Inf
MCMAKEN, Andrew, Pvt, Gen Andrew Jackson, Capt Nathan Davis, Inf
MCMAKIN, Hugh, Pvt, Col Alexander Loury, Capt John Looney, W TN Inf
MCMAKIN, James, Pvt, Col Wm Johnson, Capt Christopher Cook, E Tn Mil
MCMAMIS, Joseph, Sgt, Col S Bunch, Capt Joseph Duncan, E Tn Drafted Mil; died 4-13-1814
MCMAN, Jacob, Pvt, Col John Cocke, Capt Ricahrd Crunk, Inf
MCMANN, James, QM Sgt, Col S Bunch, Co Commander omitted, E TN Mil
MCMANNIN, John, Pvt, Col Alexander Loury, Capt John Looney, W Tn Inf
MCMEANS, James R, Pvt, Lt Col Jno Edmonson, Co Commander omitted, Cav
MCMEANS, Jonas, Pvt, Col Wm Johnson, Capt Christopher Cook, E Tn Mil
MCMEKIN, Andrew, Ens, Col Alexnder Loury, Capt John Looney, W TN Mil
MCMI, Andrew, Pvt, Maj Wm Woodfolk, Capt James Neil, Inf
MCMICHAEL, John, Pvt, Maj Gen Carroll, Col Metcalf, Capt Jackson, Inf
MCMICHLE, Jesse, Pvt, Col Philip Pipkin, Capt Ebenezer Kirkpatrick, Mil Inf; deserted
MCMICKEN, Robert, Sgt, Col T McCrory, Capt A Metcalf, Inf

MCMICKLE, Jesse, Pvt, Col Philip Pipkin, Capt Ebenezer Kirkpatrick, Mil Inf; deserted
MCMILLEN, Andrew, 3 Cpl, Col S Bunch, Capt Jno McNare, E TN Mil; later attached to Capt Berry's Co
MCMILLEN, Daniel, Pvt, Col R C Napier, Capt Thomas Gray, Mil Inf
MCMILLEN, James, Pvt, Col Edwin Booth, Capt Samuel Thompson, Mil
MCMILLEN, John, Pvt, Col Jas Raulston, Capt Mathew Neal, Inf
MCMILLEN, John, Pvt, Col Thos Benton, Capt Henry Douglas, Vol Inf
MCMILLEN, Paul, Pvt, Col John Coffee, Capt Blackman Coleman, Cav
MCMILLIAM, Hugh, Sgt, Maj Wm Woodfolk, Capt Abner Pearce, Inf
MCMILLIAN, Alexander, 4 Sgt, Col Edwin Booth, Capt John Sharpe, E TN Mil
MCMILLIAN, Andrew, Pvt, Col Thos Benton, Capt Benj Hewett, Vol Inf; refused to march
MCMILLIAN, James, Adjt, Col John Brown, no Co Commander, E Tn Vol
MCMILLIAN, John, Pvt, Col S Wear, Capt Samuel Bowman, Mtd Inf
MCMILLIAN, Malcon, Pvt, Regt Commander omitted, Capt Gray, Inf
MCMILLIAN, Paul, Pvt, Col John Alcorn, Capt Wm Locke, Cav
MCMILLIAN, Thomas, Ens, Col Wm Johnson, Capt Henry Hunter, E TN Mil; trans to Capt Kirk Co
MCMILLIAN, William, Pvt, Col S Wear, Capt Daniel Price, E TN Vol Inf
MCMILLIAN, William, Pvt, Col Thos Benton, Capt Wm Moore, Vol Inf
MCMILLIM, Gilbert, Pvt, Col John Cocke, Capt Gray, Inf
MCMILLIN, Malcolm, Sgt, Col Jas Raulston, Capt Elijah Haynie, Inf
MCMILLIN, Malcom, Pvt, Col T Leroy Hammonds, Capt James Craig, Inf
MCMILLIN, William, Pvt, Col Thos Benton, Capt Wm Moore, Vol Inf
MCMILLIN, William, Pvt, Col Wm Pillow, Capt Wm Moore, Inf
MCMILLON, John, Pvt, Col Alexander Loury, Capt Geo Saver, Inf
MCMILLON, John, Pvt, Col Edward Bradley, Capt Abraham Bledsoe, Riflemen; deserted
MCMILLON, John, Pvt, Col Edward Bradley, Capt John Bledsoe, Riflemen; deserted
MCMILLON, William, Pvt, Maj John Childs, Capt Daniels Price, E TN Mtd Inf
MCMIN, Jesse, Pvt, Col Wm Metcalf, Capt Barbee Collins, Mil Inf
MCMIN, William, Pvt, Col Wm Metcalf, Capt B Collins, Mil Inf; died 12-23-1813
MCMINEWAY, John, Cpl, Col N T Cannon, Capt Ota Cantrell, W TN Mtd Inf; deserted
MCMINN, James, Pvt, Col E Booth, Capt Jno Slatton, E TN Mil
MCMINN, James, Pvt, Col Thomas Williamson, Capt

## Enlisted Men, War of 1812

John Hutchings, Vol Mtd Gunmen
MCMINN, Joseph, Pvt, Col Samuel Bunch, Capt Jno Cummings, E TN Vol Mtd Gunmen
MCMINNANY?, John, 3 Sgt, Col Jas Cocke, Capt B Nance, Inf
MCMORRIS, Alexander, Pvt, Col P Pipkin, Capt E Kirkpatrick, Mil Inf
MCMULLAN, Thoephelus, Pvt, Col S Copeland, Capt D Williams, Inf
MCMULLEN, James, Pvt, Col Robert Steele, Capt J Chitwood, Mil Inf
MCMULLEN, Thomas, Pvt, Col Robert Steele, Capt J Chitwood, Mil Inf
MCMUN, James, Pvt, Col S Bunch, Capt N Gibbs, E TN Drafted Mil; appointed QM Sgt
MCMUN, James, QM Sgt, Col Samuel Bunch, Maj Alex Smith, E TN Mil
MCMUN, John, Pvt, Regt Commander omitted, Capt David Smith, Cav
MCMUNAY, Albert, Pvt, Col A Cheatham, Capt Geo Chapman, Inf
MCMUNN, Jacob, Pvt, Col R Steele, Capt Jas Shenault, Mil Inf
MCMURRAY, Archibald, Cpl, Col E Booth, Capt A Biggs, Inf; promoted from Pvt
MCMURRAY, Robert, Pvt, Regt Commander omitted, Capt Jno Williams, Mil Cav
MCMURRAY, Samuel, Pvt, Col R C Napier, Capt J McMurray, Mil Inf; promoted to Wagon Master in the 1st Regt
MCMURRAY, Samuel, Pvt, Maj Jno Chiles, Capt Jno Stephens, E TN Vol Mtd Inf; d 3-14-1815
MCMURRAY, Samuel, Pvt, Regt Commander omitted, Capt J Terrill, Cav
MCMURREY, John, Cpl, Col J K Winn, Capt Wm McCall, Inf
MCMURREY, John, Pvt, Col Thomas Williamson, Capt A M Metcalf, Vol Mtd Gunmen
MCMURREY, James, Pvt, Col R H Dyer, Capt Jos Williams, Vol Mtd Gunmen
MCMURRY, James, Pvt, Col S Copeland, Capt Jno Biles, Inf; d 4-1-1814
MCMURRY, John, Pvt, Col Samuel Wear, Capt Jno Stephens, E TN Vol Inf
MCMURRY, John, Sgt, Col Thos Williamson, Capt Thos Scurry, Vol Mtd Gunmen
MCMURRY, Robert, Pvt, Col Jno Brown, Capt Jno Trimble, E TN Mtd Gunmen
MCMURRY, Robert, Pvt, Col Samuel Wear, Capt Jno Stephens, E TN Vol Inf
MCMURRY, Robert, Pvt, Regt Commander omitted, Capt Jos Williams, Mil Cav
MCMURRY, Samuel, Pvt, Regt Commander omitted, Capt Jas Terrill, Cav
MCMURRY, Thomas, Pvt, Col Wm Johnston, Capt D McKamy, E TN Drafted Mil
MCMURRY, William, Pvt, Col R H Dyer, Capt Jos Williams, Vol Mtd Gunmen
MCMURRY, William, Sdlr, Col N T Cannon, Capt Thos Yardley, Mtd Riflemen
MCMURTREE, Alexander, Pvt, Col Robt Steele, Capt Jas Bennett, Mil Inf
MCMURTRY, Henry, Pvt, Col Thos Williamson, Capt Robt Moore, Vol Mtd Gunmen
MCMURTRY, James, Pvt, Col R H Dyer, Capt Jos Williams, Vol Mtd Gunmen; d 2-6-1815
MCMURTRY, John, Pvt, Col Ewen Allison, Capt Thos Wilson, E TN Drafted Mil
MCMURTRY, John, Pvt, Col R H Dyer, Capt Jos Williams, Vol Mtd Gunmen
MCMURTRY, John, Pvt, Col T H Benton, Capt Benj Hewett, Vol Inf; out of state
MCMURTRY, John, Pvt, Col Thos Williamson, Capt Robt Moore, Vol Mtd Gunmen
MCMURTRY, John, Pvt, Maj Wm Russell, Capt F Hodges, Vol Mtd Gunmen; substitute for Jas Romines
MCMURTRY, Joseph, Pvt, Col Ewen Allison, Capt Thos Wilson, E TN Drafted Mil
MCNABB, Absolom, Pvt, Col Samuel Bunch, Capt Ed Buchanan, E TN Mil; transferred from Capt Duncan's Co
MCNABB, Absolom, Pvt, Col Samuel Bunch, Capt Jos Duncan, E TN Drafted Mil; transferred to Capt Buchanan's Co
MCNABB, Andrew, Pvt, Col Jno Brown, Capt Jno Trimble, E TN Mtd Gunmen
MCNABB, Battist, Pvt, Col Samuel Bunch, Capt Wm Jobe, E TN Vol Mtd Inf
MCNABB, David, Pvt, Col Jno Brown, Capt Wm D Neilson, E TN Vol Mil
MCNABB, David, Pvt, Col Wm Johnston, Capt Henry Hunter, E TN Mil
MCNABB, Eli, Pvt, Col Jno Brown, Capt Wm D Neilson, E TN Vol Mil
MCNABB, Elijah, Pvt, Col Jno Brown, Capt Wm D Neilson, E TN Vol Mil; substitute for Matthew English
MCNABB, George, Pvt, Col Samuel Bunch, Capt Wm Jobe, E TN Vol Mtd Inf
MCNABB, John, Pvt, Col J K Wynn, Capt Jas Cole, Inf
MCNABB, John, Pvt, Col L Hammons, Capt A Rains, Inf
MCNABB, John, Pvt, Col Samuel Bunch, Capt Wm Jobe, E TN Vol Mtd Inf
MCNABB, John, Pvt, Col Samuel Wear, Capt Jas Gillespie, E TN Vol Inf
MCNABB, Nathaniel, Pvt, Col S Bunch, Capt Wm Houston, E TN Mil; substituted by Thos Cary
MCNABB, Thomas, Pvt, Col Wm Johnson, Capt Jas R Rogers, E TN Drafted Mil
MCNABB, William, Pvt, Col Wm Johnson, Capt Jas R Rogers, E TN Drafted Mil
MCNABB, William, Pvt, Maj Wm Russell, Capt Jno Tremble, Vol Mtd Gunmen
MCNAIR, David, Pvt, Brig Gen Jas White, Co Commander omitted, Spy
MCNAIR, John, Pvt, Brig Gen Jas White, Co Commander omitted, Brig of E TN Mil Spies
MCNAIR, John, Pvt, Col Jno Williams, Capt Wm Walker, Vol
MCNAIRE, John, Pvt, Col Philip Pipkin, Capt William Mackay, Mil Inf

## Enlisted Men, War of 1812

MCNALL, William, Pvt, Col Jno Brown, Capt Wm D Neilson, E TN Vol Mil

MCNAMER, John, Pvt, Col T McCrory, Capt Jno Reynolds, Mil Inf

MCNARE, Price, Pvt, Col S Bunch, Capt Daniel Yarnell, E TN Mil; transferred to Capt McNare's Co

MCNARE, Price, Pvt, Col Samuel Bunch, Capt John McNare, E TN Mil; attached to Capt Duncan's Co

MCNARE, Price, Pvt, Col Samuel Bunch, Capt Joseph Duncan, E TN Drafted Mil; joined from Capt McNare's Co

MCNATT, Benjamin, Pvt, Col John Cocke, Capt James Gray, Inf

MCNATT, Leaven, Pvt, Regt Commander omitted, Capt Nathan Davis, Lt I Barrett, Inf

MCNATT, Solomon, Pvt, Regt Commander omitted, Capt James Gray, Inf

MCNATT, William, 5 Sgt, Maj Wm Woodfolk, Capt Mathew Neal, Inf; substitute for Wm Knott, promoted from Pvt

MCNAVE, Price (Bruce), Pvt, Col Wm Joihnson, Capt James Stewart, E TN Drafted Mil

MCNAW, Edward, Pvt, Col Samuel Bunch, Capt George Gregory, E TN Drafted Mil

MCNEACE, Hope H, Pvt, Col Newton Cannon, Capt Ota Cantrell, W TN Mtd Inf

MCNEACE, Jonas, Pvt, Col Wm Johnston, Capt Joseph Kirk, Mil; substitute for James McColm

MCNEAL, John, 6 Cpl, Col Wm Johnson, Capt Andrew Lawson, E TN Drafted Mil; d 11-28-1814

MCNEAL, John, Pvt, Col John K Wynne, Capt James Holleman, Inf

MCNEAL, John, Pvt, Col Wm Lillard, Capt George Keyes, E TN Inf

MCNEAL, Thomas, Pvt, Col N T Perkins, Capt James McMahon, Mtd Gunmen

MCNEAL (MCNAIL), Edward H, Sgt, Col Thomas H Williamson, Capt Wm Martin, Vol Mtd Gunmen

MCNEALEY, Ezekial, Pvt, Col Philip Pipkin, Capt Henry Newlin, Mil Inf

MCNEALEY, John, Pvt, Col Leroy Hammond, Capt James Tubb, Inf

MCNEALEY, Robert, Pvt, Col John Brown, Capt Wm White, E TN Mil Inf

MCNEALY, Isaac, Blksmth, Col Thomas H Williamson, Capt James Pace, Lt Neely, Vol Mtd Gunmen

MCNEALY, James, Pvt, Col Thos H Williamson, Capt James Pace, Lt Nealey, Vol Mtd Gunmen; d 3-6-1815

MCNEECE, Hope M, Pvt, Col Leroy Hammond, Capt J N Williamson, 2nd Regt Inf

MCNEECE, Jesse, Pvt, Col Samuel Bunch Capt, Francis Register, E TN Mil

MCNEECE, John, Pvt, Col Samuel Bunch, Capt George McPherson, E TN Mil; unable to perform duty

MCNEECE, William, Pvt, Col S Bunch, Capt George McPherson, E TN Mil

MCNEECE, William, Pvt, Col S? Bunch, Capt Francis Register, E TN Mil

MCNEECE, William, Pvt, Col Wm Lillard, Capt Robt Maloney, E TN Vol Inf; unable to perform duty

MCNEELEY, Moses, Pvt, Regt Commander omitted, Capt George Smith, Spies

MCNEELY, James, Pvt, Col Samuel Bunch, Capt Francis Register, E TN Mil

MCNEELY, Samuel, Pvt, Col Philip Pipkin, Capt Ebenezer Kirkpatrick, Mil Inf

MCNEELY, William, Pvt, Regt Commander omitted, Capt George McPherson, Branch Srvce omitted

MCNEES, Hopehull?, Pvt, Col Thomas H Benton, Capt Henry L Douglas, Vol Inf

MCNEICE, Job, Pvt, Col Edwin Allison, Capt McCray, E TN Mil

MCNEICE, Joseph, Pvt, Col Wm Johnson, Capt Benjamin Powell, E TN Mil

MCNEICE, Josiah, Pvt, Col Samuel Bunch, Capt James Penny, E TN Mtd Inf

MCNEIL, John, 4 Cpl, Col Edwin Allison, Capt Joseph Everett, E TN Mil; deserted

MCNELLY, Charles, Pvt, Col Samuel Wear, Capt John Stephens, E TN Vol Inf

MCNELLY, John, Pvt, Col Samuel Wear, Capt John Stephens, E TN Vol Inf

MCNETTLES, James, Pvt, Col Robert Steele, Capt James Bennett, Mil Inf

MCNEW, Edward, Pvt, Col Samuel Bunch, Capt John Houk, E TN Mil

MCNIEU, Hope H, Pvt, Col A Loury, Capt J N Williamson, W TN Mil

MCNIEW, Churville, Pvt, Col Edwin E Booth, Capt Vernon, E TN Mil

MCNIGHT, David, Sgt, Col John Alcorn, Capt Alexander McKeen, Cav

MCNIGHT, James, Pvt, Regt Commander omitted, Capt Edwin S Moore, Mtd Riflemen

MCNIGHT, John, Pvt, Col Samuel Wear, Capt Joseph Calloway, Mtd Inf

MCNIGHT, Lewis, Pvt, Col Newton Cannon, Capt George Bradon, Mtd Riflemen

MCNIGHT, Moses, 2 Cpl, Col Newton Cannon, Capt George Bradon, Mtd Riflemen

MCNIGHT, Thomas P, Sgt, Regt Commander omitted, Capt Edwin S Moore, Mtd Riflemen

MCNIGHT, William, Pvt, Col Newton Cannon, Capt George Brandon, Mtd Riflemen

MCNIGHT, William, Pvt, Lt Col Jas Berry, Co Commander omitted, Mtd Riflemen; transferred to Moore Co

MCNITT, Charles, Pvt, Col John K Winn, Capt Wm Wilson, Inf; transferred to Capt Caruthers Co

MCNOBLE, Elijah, Pvt, Col John Brown, Capt Wm White, Regt E TN Mil Inf; transferred to Capt Nelson's Co

MCNUT, Joseph, Pvt, Col Thomas H Benton, Capt Benjamin Reynolds, Vol Inf

MCNUTE, Joseph, Pvt, Col Thomas H Benton, Capt Jos McNute, Vol Inf

MCNUTT, Charles, Pvt, Col John K Winn, Capt Wm Carothers, W TN Inf

MCNUTT, George, Pvt, Col Edwin E Booth, Capt John Sharp, E TN Mil

MCNUTT, James, Pvt, Col Newton Cannon, Capt James

## Enlisted Men, War of 1812

Walton, Mtd Riflemen
MCNUTT, Peter, Pvt, Col Edwin E Booth, Capt John Sharpe, E TN Mil
MCNUTT, Robert, Pvt, Col Samuel Wear, Capt Samuel Bowman, Mtd Inf
MCNUTT, William, Pvt, Maj John Chiles, Capt Charles Conway, E TN Mtd Gunmen
MCPEAK, James, Pvt, Col R C Napier, Capt Samuel Ashmore, Cav
MCPEAK, John, Cpl, Col A Cheatham, Capt Charles Johnson, Inf
MCPEAK, John, Far, Col John Coffee, Capt Blackman Coleman, Cav
MCPEAKE, Henry, Cpl, Col John Alcorn, Capt Wm Locke, Cav
MCPEARSON, Jonathan, Pvt, Col John Cocke, Capt John Dalton, Inf; d 2-14-1815
MCPEET, Daniel, Pvt, Col S Copeland, Capt Moses Thompson, Inf
MCPETERS, Jonathan, 1 Lt, Col Samuel Bunch, Capt John Inman, E TN Vol Mtd Inf
MCPHEREN, Andrew, Pvt, Col Wm Johnson, Capt James Stewart, E TN Mil
MCPHERRAN, Andrew, Pvt, Col Wm Lillard, Capt Robert Maloney, E TN Mil Vol Inf
MCPHERRAN, James, Pvt, Col Wm Lillard, Capt Robert Maloney, E TN Vol Inf
MCPHERRAN, Samuel, Pvt, Col Wm Lillard, Capt Robert Maloney, E TN Vol Inf; unable to perform duty
MCPHERRAN, William, Pvt, Col Wm Lillard, Capt Robert Maloney, E TN Vol Inf; unable to perform duty
MCPHERSON, Andrew, Pvt, Col Samuel Bunch, Capt N Gibbs, E TN Drafted Mil
MCPHERSON, Andrew, Pvt, Col Wm Johnson, Capt James Stewart, E TN Drafted Mil
MCPHERSON, Bartlett, Pvt, Col John Brown, Capt Wm White, E TN Mil Inf
MCPHERSON, Elijah, Pvt, Col John Brown, Capt Wm White, Regt E TN Mil
MCPHERSON, George, Pvt, Col John Brown, Capt Wm White, E TN Mil Inf
MCPHERSON, Isaac, Cpl, Col John Brown, Capt James McKamy, E TN Mtd Gunmen
MCPHERSON, James, Pvt, Col John Brown, Capt Wm White, E TN Vol Mtd Inf
MCPHETRIDGE, William, Cpl, Col Samuel Bayless, Capt Joseph Rich, E TN Inf
MCPHILIP, John M, Pvt, Col Wm Hall, Capt Abraham Bledsoe, Vol Inf
MCPICK (MCPEAK), Henry, 3 Cpl, Col John Coffee, Capt Blackman Coleman, Cav
MCPIKE, Jesse, Pvt, Col Samuel Bunch, Capt Wm Jobe, E TN Vol Mtd Inf
MCPIPE, James, Pvt, Col Wm Johnson, Capt Christopher Cook, E TN Mil
MCQHIRTER, George W, Pvt, Col Edward Bradley, Capt Harry L Douglass, Vol Inf
MCQHIRTER, John, Pvt, Col R C Napier, Capt Andrew McCarty, Mil Inf
MCQUAIY, John, Pvt, Col John Alcorn, Capt Wm Locke, Cav
MCQUARY, Micajah, 6 Cpl, Col Wm Metcalf, Capt Wm Mullin, Mil Inf
MCQUARY, Pleasant, Pvt, Col Thos Benton, Capt Benj Reynolds, Vol Inf
MCQUEEN, John, Pvt, Gen A Jackson, Capt Wm Russell, Mtd Spies
MCQUEEN, Qilliam, Pvt, Col Samuel Bunch, Capt Jones Griffin, E TN Drafted Mil; joined from Capt Everett's Co, deserted
MCQUEEN, William, Pvt, Col Ewen Allison, Capt Adam Winsell, E TN Drafted Mil
MCQUIG, John, Pvt, Col John Coffee, Capt Blackman Coleman, Cav
MCQUILKIN, Robert, Pvt, Maj Gen A Jackson, Capt Wm Carroll, Vol Inf
MCQUILTY, Jesse, Pvt, Col Thos Benton, Capt Geo Caperton, Vol Inf
MCQUIRE, David, Pvt, Capt Nathan Davis, Lt I Barrett, Inf
MCQUISTER, Joseph, Pvt, Col Samuel Bunch, Capt Geo Gregory, E TN Drafted Mil; furnished a substitute
MCRAW, Joseph J, Sgt, Col Edward Bradley, Capt John Moore, Vol Inf
MCREA, Duncan, Sgt, Maj Cooper, Co Commander omitted, 26th TN Regt Mtd Riflemen
MCREA, Moses, Pvt, Col Thos Williamson, Capt Thomas Scurry, Vol Mtd Gunmen
MCREE, John, Pvt, Col R H Dyer, Capt Robert Edmonston, TN Vol Mtd Gunmen
MCREYNOLDS, John, 3 Sgt, Col Samuel Bunch, Capt Wm Houston, E TN Vol Mtd Inf
MCROBERTS, William, Cpl, Col Edwin Booth, Capt John Lewis, E TN Mil; promoted to Sgt
MCROY, James H, Pvt, Col Edward Bradley, Capt Abraham Bledsoe, Riflemen; deserted
MCRUNNELLS, Joseph, Pvt, Col Edward Bradley, Capt John Wallace, Vol Inf; deserted
MCRUNOLD, Thomas B, Sgt, Col Newton Cannon, Capt Andrew Patterson, Mtd Riflemen; reduced to the ranks
MCSPEDDON, John N, 2 Sgt, Col Philip Pipkin, Capt John Robertson, Mil Inf
MCSPEDDON, Samuel, Cpl, Col Wm Lillard, Capt Thos McChristian, E TN Vol Inf
MCSPUDDIN, James, Cpl, Col S Bunch, Capt Geo Gregory, E TN Drafted Mil
MCSWINE, Samuel, Sgt, Col John Cocke, Capt Joseph Price, Inf; d 2-27-1815
MCTEER, Montgomery, Pvt, Col Wm Johnson, Capt David McKamy, E TN Drafted Mil
MCTEER, Robert, Pvt, Col Wm Johnson, Capt David McKamy, E TN Drafted Mil; substitute for John Hansel
MCTIER, William, 1 Sgt, Maj John Childs, Capt James Cummings, E TN Vol Mtd Inf
MCTREER, John M, Pvt, Col Wm Johnson, Capt David McKamy, E TN Drafted Mil
MCULLER, Robert, Pvt, Col R C Napier, Capt John Chism, Mil Inf

MCVAY, Daniel, Pvt, Col Wm Lillard, Capt Geo Keys, E TN Inf
MCVAY, Eli, Pvt, Col Samuel Bunch, Capt Jones Griffin, E TN Drafted Mil; deserted
MCVAY, Eli, Pvt, Col Wm Johnson, Capt Benj Powell, E TN Mil
MCVAY, James, Pvt, Col Jno Brown, Capt Lunsford Oliver, E TN Mil
MCVAY, James, Pvt, Col Wm Johnson, Capt Benj Powell, E TN Mil
MCVAY, Levi, Pvt, Col Edwin Booth, Capt John Slatton, E TN Mil
MCVAY (MCVEAY), James, Pvt, Col John Brown, Capt James McKamy, E TN Mtd Gunmen
MCVEY, Joseph, Pvt, Maj John Childs, Capt James Cummings, E TN Vol Mtd Inf
MCWHARTON, Benjamin, Pvt, Col Wm Y Higgins, Capt James Hambleton, Mtd Gunmen
MCWHENNEY, Mathew, Cpl, Maj John Chiles, Capt Chas Conway, E TN Mtd Gunmen
MCWHERTER, Moses, Tptr, Col Newton Cannon, Capt James Walton, Mtd Riflemen
MCWHINNEY, William, Cpl, Maj John Chiles, Capt Chas Conway, E TN Mtd Gunmen
MCWHINNY, Thomas, Pvt, Col Samuel Wear, Capt Rufus Morgan, E TN Vol Inf
MCWHIRTER, Abner, Pvt, Col John K Wynne, Capt John Porter, Inf
MCWHIRTER, Francis, Pvt, Maj Wm Russell, Col R H Dyer, Capt Isaac Williams, Separate Bn 1st Regt TN Vol Mtd Gunmen
MCWHIRTER, George F, Sgt, Col S Copeland, Capt G W Stell, Mil Inf
MCWHORTER, Samuel, QM Sgt, Gen John Coffee, TN Vol Mtd Inf
MCWILLIAMS, Hugh, Pvt, Col R C Napier, Capt Samuel Ashmore, Mil Inf
MCWILLIAMS, James, Pvt, Col John Williams, Capt Samuel Bunch, Mtd Vol
MCWILLIAMS, James, Sgt, Col Samuel Bayless, Capt James Churchman, E TN Mil
MCWILLIAMS, John, Pvt, Col Wm Johnson, Capt Joseph Scott, E TN Drafted Mil
MEAD, John, Pvt, Col John Brown, Capt Wm White, E TN Vol Mtd Inf
MEADER, Thomas, 2 Sgt, Col William Hall, Capt Abraham Bledsoe, Branch Srvce omitted
MEADOR, Bennett, Pvt, Lt Col Leroy Hammond, Capt James Tubb, Inf; deserted
MEADOR, James, Pvt, Lt Col Hammonds, Capt James Tubb, Inf
MEADOUR, Jeptha, Pvt, Col Alexander Loury, Capt George Sarver, Inf
MEADOW, Allen, Pvt, Col R C Napier, Capt Andrew McCarty, Mil Inf
MEADOW, Allen, Pvt, Maj Gen Wm Carroll, Col James Raulston, Capt Elijah Haynie, Inf
MEADOW, Eli, Pvt, Col S Copeland, Capt Allen Wilkinson, Mil Inf
MEADOW, James, Pvt, Col James Raulston, Capt Elijah Haynie, Inf; d 2-4-1815
MEADOW, John, Pvt, Col S Copeland, Capt Allen Wilkinson, Mil Inf
MEADOW, Jonas, Cpl, Col James Raulston, Capt Elijah Haynie, Inf; d 1-30-1815
MEADOW, Thomas, 2 Sgt, Col Wm Hall, Capt Abraham Bledsoe, Vol Inf
MEADOW, William, Pvt, Maj Gen Carroll, Col James Raulston, Capt Elijah Haynee, Inf
MEADOWS, Ambrose, Pvt, Col Thomas Williamson, Capt Anthony Metcalf, Vol Mtd Gunmen
MEADOWS, Anderson, Pvt, Col R C Napier, Capt Early Benson, Mil Inf
MEADOWS, Asa, Pvt, Col Thomas McCrory, Capt Anthony Metcalf, Mil Inf
MEADOWS, Elijah, Sgt, Col Edward Bradley, Capt Thomas B Haynes, Vol Inf
MEADOWS, Isham, Pvt, Col James Raulston, Capt Mathew Neale, Inf
MEADOWS, John, Pvt, Col Thomas Williamson, Capt Anthony Metcalf, Vol Mtd Gunmen
MEADOWS, Litester, Pvt, Regt Commander omitted, Capt Nathan Farmer, Mtd Riflemen
MEADOWS, Pleasant, Pvt, Col William Johnson, Capt Benjamin Powell, E TN Mil
MEADOWS, Willis G, Dmr, Col Thomas McCrory, Capt Thomas Gordon, Inf
MEADOWS, Willis G, Sgt, Col Thomas Williamson, Capt Cook & Capt John Dobbins, Vol Mtd Gunmen
MEADS, Daniel, Pvt, Col William Lillard, Capt Zacheus Copeland, E TN Vol Inf
MEADVILLE, James, Pvt, Maj Woodfolk, Capt Abner Pearce, Inf
MEAK, John, Pvt, no other information
MEALONE (MALONE), James, Pvt, Lt Col Leroy Hammond, Capt James Craig, Inf
MEAN, Abraham, Pvt, Col William Johnson, Capt Christopher Cook, E TN Mil
MEANICK, Griffin, Pvt, Col R Jarman, Capt I Hamilton, Inf
MEANLY, Beverly H, Pvt, Maj Gen Andrew Jackson, Capt William Carroll, Vol Inf
MEANS, Andrew, Pvt, Col S Copeland, Capt Allen Williams, Inf
MEANS, Benjamin, Pvt, Col William Hall, Capt John Kennedy, Vol Inf; substituted by Joshua Stephens
MEANS, Elijah, Pvt, Col S Copeland, Capt Allen Williams, Mil Inf
MEANS, John, 1 Cpl, Col William Johnson, Capt David McKamey, E TN Drafted Mil
MEANS, Ormand, Pvt, Col Samuel Wear, Capt James Tedford, E TN Vol Inf
MEANS, Ormand, Sgt, Col Edwin E Booth, Capt Biggs, Inf
MEANS, Samuel, Pvt, Lt Col Hammond & Lt Col Lowry, Capt Thomas Wells, Inf
MEAREDETH, William, Pvt, Maj Wm Woodfolk, Capt Abner Pearce, Inf
MEARLES, David, Pvt, Col Robert Steele, Capt Richard Ratton, Mil Inf
MEARLES, Levi, Pvt, Col A Cheatham, Capt Charles Johnson, Inf

MEARRICK, Griffin, Pvt, Col Robert Jarmon, Col I Hamilton, Mtd Inf
MEASE, John, Pvt, Col William Hall, Capt Henry Newland, Inf
MEASLES, William, Pvt, Col James Cummings, Maj Chiles, E TN Mtd Inf
MEASLES, William, Pvt, Col Samuel Bunch, Capt Jones Griffin, E TN Drafted Mil
MEAZLES, Henry, Pvt, Regt Commander omitted, Capt Elijah Rushing, Det of Inf
MEBANE, David, Pvt, Col Newton Cannon, Capt Thomas Yardley, Mtd Riflemen
MECHUM, Spencer, Pvt, Col Alexander Loury, Capt Gabriel Martin, Inf
MEDCALF, Calloway, Pvt, Maj William Woodfolk, Capt Abner Pearce, Inf
MEDDLETON, William, 2 Cpl, Col William Metcalf, Capt John Cunningham & Capt John Hill, Mil Inf
MEDFORD, Isam, Pvt, Maj William Russell, Capt Fleman Rodgers (Hodges?), Vol Mtd Gunmen
MEDFORD, John, Pvt, Brig Gen Johnson, Capt Robert Carson, Inf
MEDFORD, Jonathan, Pvt, Col Thomas Benton, Capt Isaiah Renshaw, Vol Inf
MEDLICK, John, Pvt, Col Samuel Bunch, Capt Edward Buchanan, E TN Mil
MEDLIN, Britten, Pvt, Col Thomas Benton, Capt William J Smith, Vol Inf
MEDLIN, Hardy, Pvt, Col Edwin Booth, Capt Richard Marshall, Drafted Mil
MEDLIN, William, Pvt, Col Robert Steele, Capt John Chitwood, Mil Inf
MEDLOCK, Joab, Pvt, Col William Johnson, Capt Joseph Kirk, Mil
MEDLOCK, John, Pvt, Col Robert H Dyer, Capt Robert Edmundston, 1st TN Mtd Gunmen
MEDLOCK, Littlebury, Pvt, Col John K Wynne, Capt John Spinks, Inf
MEDOR (MEADOR), Bennett, Pvt, Col Leroy Hammond, Capt James Tubb, Inf; deserted
MEDOR (MEADOR), James, Pvt, Lt Col Leroy Hammond, Capt James Tubb, Inf
MEDUS, Jason, Sgt, Col Robert Steele, Capt Samuel Maxwell, Mil Inf
MEEDHAM, John, Pvt, Col Edward Bradley, Capt Brice Martin, Vol Inf; waiter to Capt Martin
MEEK, Adam, Pvt, Col Newton Cannon, Capt John Dempsey, Mtd Gunmen
MEEK, Alexander, 1 Sgt, Col Samuel Wear, Capt Joseph Calloway, Mtd Inf
MEEK, Daniel, Cpl, Col John Brown, Capt John Childs, E TN Vol Mtd Gunmen; appointed from Pvt
MEEK, Hays, Pvt, Col Newton Cannon, Capt John Hanley, Mtd Riflemen
MEEK, James, Pvt, Maj Gen Carroll, Col James Raulston, Capt Wiley Huddleston, Inf
MEEK, John, Pvt, Col Samuel Wear, Capt John Bayless, Mtd Inf
MEEK, Joseph, Pvt, Col Samuel Wear, Capt John Bayless, Mtd Inf
MEEK, Robert, Pvt, Col Samuel Bunch, Capt N Gibbs, E TN Drafted Mil
MEEK, Sm S C, Pvt, Col Newton Cannon, Capt John Demsey, Mtd Gunmen
MEEK, William, Pvt, no other information
MEEKS, Moses, Pvt, Lt Col Richard Napier, Co Commander omitted, Inf
MEENES, William D, Sgt, Lt Col Jno Edmonson, Co Commander omitted, Cav
MEESER, Phillip, Pvt, Col Ewen Allison, Capt Jonas Loughmiller, Mil; transferred to Capt Griffin Co
MEGEHE, Stephen, Pvt, Col Wm Hall, Capt John Moore, Vol Inf
MEGEHEE, William, Pvt, Col Philip Pipkin, Capt William Mackay, Mil Inf
MELAM, Jesse, Pvt, Col Samuel Bayless, Capt James Landen, E TN Mil
MELLEN, John, Pvt, Col A Loury, Capt George Sarver, Inf
MELLON, Terry, Pvt, Col Samuel Wear, Capt John Bayless, Mtd Inf
MELLON (MELTON), William, Pvt, Maj William Woodfolk, Capt Ezekial Ross & Capt McCulley, Inf
MELONE, Charles, Pvt, Col Edwin Booth, Capt Richard Marshall, Drafted Mil; discharged for inability
MELONE, Lewis, Pvt, Col Thomas Benton, Capt Henry L Douglass, Vol Inf
MELONE, Mark, Pvt, Col R H Dyer, Maj William Russell, Capt William Russell, Vol Mtd Gunmen
MELOY, Hugh, Pvt, Col Ewen Allison, Capt Thomas Wilson, E TN Drafted Mil; deserted 3-4-1814
MELSON, Elijah, Pvt, Col William Metcalf, Capt William Sitton, Mil Inf
MELTON, Carter, Pvt, Col Edwin Booth, Capt Samuel Thompson, Mil
MELTON, Elisha, Pvt, Col William Hall, Capt Henry M Newland, Inf
MELTON, Henry, Pvt, Col John Cocke, Capt Joseph Price, Inf; substitute for Jas Palmer
MELTON, Henry, Pvt, Regt Commander omitted, Capt James Craig, Inf
MELTON, Jacob, Pvt, Brig Gen Thos Johnson, Capt Abraham Allen, Mil Inf; d 2-27-1814
MELTON, James (John), Pvt, Col John Cocke, Capt Joseph Price, Inf
MELTON, James, Pvt, Maj Gen A Jackson, Capt William Carroll, Vol Inf
MELTON, James, Pvt, Regt Commander omitted, Capt James Craig, Inf
MELTON, John, Pvt, Col Samuel Bunch, Capt Andrew Breden, E TN Mil; transferred to Capt Bacon's Co
MELTON, Michael, Cpl, Maj William Russell, Capt Isaac Williams, Separate Bn of TN Vol Mtd Gunmen
MELTON, Michael, Pvt, Col R H Dyer, Capt Isaac Williams, 1st Regt TN Vol Mtd Gunmen
MELTON, Thomas, Pvt, Col Edward Bradley, Capt Abraham Bledsoe, Riflemen
MELTON, Thomas, Pvt, Col William Hall, Capt Abraham Bledsoe, Vol Inf
MELTON, William, Pvt, Col S Copeland, Capt Alexander Provine, Mil Inf

## Enlisted Men, War of 1812

MELTON (MILTON), Henry, Pvt, Col John Cocke, Capt Samuel Caruthers, Inf

MELUGAN, James, Pvt, Regt Commander omitted, Capt Jas Haggard, Mtd Gunmen

MELUGAN, Joseph, Pvt, Regt Commander omitted, Capt Jas Haggard, Mtd Gunmen; promoted to Sgt

MELVANEY, Henry, Pvt, Col John Williams, Capt David Vance, Mtd Mil

MELVIN, Andrew, Pvt, Col Thos Williamson, Capt Richard Tate, Vol Mtd Gunmen

MELVIN, Edmond, Pvt, Col Thos Williamson, Capt Richard Tate, Vol Mtd Gunmen

MELVIN, William, Pvt, Col A Loury, Capt J N Williamson, W TN Mil

MENAFEE, William, Sgt, Regt Commander omitted, Capt Arch McKinney, Cav

MENASCO, James, Pvt, Lt Col L Hammond, Capt James Craig, Inf

MENDINALL, William, Pvt, Col Samuel Bunch, Capt Jno Hawk, E TN Mil; joined from Capt Gregory Co

MENDINGALE, John, Pvt, Maj John Childs, Capt James Cummings, E TN Vol Mtd Inf

MENDINGALL, Samuel, Pvt, Maj William Russell, Capt Fleman Hodges, Vol Mtd Gunmen

MENDINGHALL?, _____, Pvt, Col Samuel Bunch, Capt Geo Gregory, E TN Drafted Mil

MENECE (MENEESE), John, Pvt, Col R H Dyer, Capt Thomas Jones, Vol Mtd Gunmen

MENEES, Benjamin, Pvt, Regt Commander omitted, Capt Jno Crane, Mtd Inf

MENEES, William, Sgt, Lt Col Jno Edmonson, Co Commander omitted, Cav

MENEESE, Benjamin W, Pvt, Col Thos Williamson, Capt James Cook & Capt John Crane, Vol Mtd Gunmen

MENEFEE, William, 4 Sgt, Maj John Childs, Capt Charles Conway, E TN Mtd Gunmen

MENEFIELD, Nimrod, Pvt, Col Jno Gordon, Co Commander omitted, Mtd Spies; promoted to Sgt

MENEFIELD, Nimrod, Sgt, Regt Commander omitted, Capt Jno Gordon, Mtd Spies

MENESE (MENEESE), Henry, Pvt, Col R H Dyer, Capt Thomas Jones, Vol Mtd Gunmen

MENESS, Benjamin W, Pvt, Lt Col Archer Cheatham, Co Commander omitted, 6th Brig Inf

MENESS, Isaac, Pvt, Lt Col Archer Cheatham, Co Commander omitted, Inf

MENESSE, James, Pvt, Col Thos Williamson, Capt James Cook & Capt John Crane, Vol Mtd Gunmen

MENICH, Adam, 3 Cpl, Col Samuel Bunch, Capt William Jobe, E TN Vol Mtd Inf

MENICK, Peter, Pvt, Col Samuel Bunch, Capt Geo McPherson, E TN Mil; joined from Capt Wilson's Co

MENIS, Samuel, Pvt, Col Samuel Wear, Capt James Tedford, E TN Vol Inf

MENIS, Thomas, Pvt, Col Samuel Wear, Capt James Tedford, E TN Vol Inf

MENIS (MINIS), John, 3 Cpl, Col William Johnson, Capt David McKamy, E TN Drafted Mil

MEPER (MISSER), John, Pvt, Col William Lillard, Capt Geo Argenbright, E TN Vol Riflemen

MERCER, James, Pvt, Col John Cocke, Capt Joseph Price, Inf

MERCER, Thomas, Pvt, Col Robert Steele, Capt Robert Campbell, Mil Inf

MERCER, Thomas, Pvt, Col Wm Lillard, Capt William McLin, E TN Inf

MERCHANT, David, Pvt, Col Newton Cannon, Capt Isaac Williams, Inf; d 12-20-1813

MERCHANTS, John, Tptr, Maj William Russell, Capt Isaac Williams, Separate Bn Vol Mtd Gunmen

MEREDITH, Junior, Pvt, Col Philip Pipkin, Capt David Smith, W TN Mil; attached to Capt John Strother's Co

MEREDITH, Richard, Lt, Col Samuel Wear, Capt John Chiles, E TN Vol Inf

MEREDITH, Samuel, 1 Sgt Maj, Col John Coffee, Co Commander omitted, TN Vol Cav

MEREDITH, Samuel, Pvt, Col Jas Raulston, Capt Henry West, Inf

MERIDETH, Bradley, Pvt, Col Jas Raulston, Capt Henry West, Inf

MERIDETH, James, Pvt, Col John Cocke, Capt Samuel M Caruthers, Inf

MERIDETH, James, Pvt, Col Wm Pillow, Capt Wm Moore, Inf

MERIDETH, Thomas, Pvt, Col John Cocke, Capt George Barnes, Inf

MERIDITH, Samuel, Pvt, Col Jno Coffee, Capt Jno Baskerville, Cav; promoted

MERIMAN, Elisha, Pvt, Col William Johnson, Capt James Tunnell, E TN Mil

MERIMAN, James June, Pvt, Col Wm Johnson, Capt James Tunnel, E TN Mil; substitute for James Allen June

MERIMAN, James sr, Pvt, Col Wm Johnson, Capt James Tunnell, E TN Mil; substitute for L Graves

MERIMAN, Malchi?, Pvt, Col Wm Johnson, Capt James Tunnell, E TN Mil; substitute for Robert Cozby

MERONY, Henry, Cpl, Col Newton Cannon, Capt James Walton, Mtd Riflemen

MERPHEY, Wiley, Pvt, Col William Johnson, Capt Elihu Milliken, 3rd Regt E TN Mil; never appeared

MERRAL, Caleb, Col Ewen Allison, Capt William King, Drafted Mil; promoted

MERRAL, Nathan, Pvt, Col Ewen Allison, Capt James King, Drafted Mil

MERRET, Edgecomb, Pvt, Col William Johnson, Capt Joseph Scott, E TN Drafted Mil

MERRET, George, Pvt, Col Samuel Bunch, Capt James Cummings, E TN Vol Mtd Inf

MERRETT, Silas, Pvt, Col James Raulston, Capt Jas M Black, Inf

MERRIDETH, William, Pvt, Col Alexander Loury, Capt James Kincaid, Inf

MERRIDITH, Juno, Cpl, Col Philip Pipkin, Capt David Smith, Inf

MERRIMAN, William, Pvt, Col Jno Brown, Capt John Chiles, E TN Vol Mtd Inf

MERRIMON, John, Pvt, Col Edwin Booth, Capt John

-357

## Enlisted Men, War of 1812

Lewis, E TN Mil
MERRIMORE, Charles, Pvt, Col John Brown, Capt Jesse G Reany, Mtd Gunmen
MERRIT, John, Pvt, Maj William Woodfolk, Capt Ezekial Ross & Capt McCulley, Inf
MERRITT, Thomas, Pvt, Col William Lillard, Capt Benjamin King, E TN Vol Inf
MERRIWEATHER, Douglas, Pvt, Lt Col Henry Bryan, Co Commander omitted, Inf
MERRYMAN, Briant, Pvt, Col William Johnson, Capt James Tunnell, E TN Mil
MERRYMAN, James sr, Pvt, Col William Johnson, Capt James Tunnell, 3rd Regt E TN Mil; d 11-22-1814
MERRYMAN, Jeremiah, Pvt, Col A Loury, Lt Col L Hammonds, Capt Arahel Rains, Inf
MERRYMAN, Jesse, Pvt, Maj Gen William Carroll, Col James Raulston, Capt Edward Robinson, Inf
MERRYMAN, William, Pvt, Col Edwin Booth, Capt Vernon, E TN Mil
MESERMORE, Jacob, Pvt, Col S Bunch, Capt Geo McPherson, E TN Mil; joined from Capt Hoyale Co, d 6-18-1814
MESSER, Asa, Dmr, Lt Col L Hammonds, Capt Thomas Delaney, Inf
MESSER, James, Pvt, Col Thomas Benton, Capt William Moore, Vol Inf
MESSER, John, Pvt, Col Ewen Allison, Capt Thos McCrory, E TN Mil
MESSER, John, Pvt, Col Samuel Bayless, Capt James Landen, E TN Mil
MESSER, John, Pvt, Regt Commander omitted, Capt David Vance & Capt Jno Williams, E TN Mtd Vol
MESSER, Joseph, Pvt, Col Samuel Bayless, Capt Jonathan Waddle, E TN Mil
MESSER, Philip, Pvt, Col Samuel Bunch, Capt Jones Griffin, E TN Drafted Mil; joined from Capt Longmiller's Co
MESSOR, Abner, Pvt, Col Edwin Booth, Capt Alexander Biggs, Inf
METHENY, Charles, Pvt, Lt Col Henry Bryan, Co Commander omitted, Inf
METHENY, Charles, Pvt, Regt Commander omitted, Capt James Cowan, Mtd Inf
METHENY, Charles, Pvt, Regt Commander omitted, Capt James Gray, Inf
METHENY, Colin, Pvt, Regt Commander omitted, Capt James Gray, Inf
METHENY, Luke, Pvt, Maj William Woodfolk, Capt James C Neil, Inf
METHVEN, James, Sgt, Col Samuel Bunch, Capt Francis Register, E TN Mil
METICAN, John, Pvt, Regt Commander omitted, Capt Wm Mitchel, Spies
METLOCK, Joab, Pvt, Col Wm Johnson, Capt Christopher Cook, E TN Mil
METLOCK, Smith, Pvt, Col Robert Jarman, Capt I Hamilton, Mtd Inf
MEWS, Richard, Pvt, Col Robert Steele, Capt James Shenault, Mil Inf
MEZELL, Henry, Pvt, Regt Commander omitted, Capt Thos Gray, Inf

MICHEAL, John, Pvt, Col Thos Dyer, Capt Robert Edmonston, TN Vol Mtd Gunmen
MICHEAL, Nave, Pvt, Col Edwin Booth, Capt Alexander Biggs, Inf
MICHEAL, William, Pvt, Col William Lillard, Capt James Sharp, 2nd Regt Inf
MICHIE, William, Pvt, Maj William Russell, Capt Geo Michie, Vol Mtd Gunmen
MICKIE, James, Sgt, Col N Cannon, Capt John Harpole, Mtd Gunmen; promoted to Ens
MICKLINBERRY, George, Pvt, Col Jno Coffee, Capt John Baskerville, Cav; AWOL
MIDDLEDITH, Cyrus, Pvt, Col Phillip Pipkin, Capt William Mackay, Mil Inf
MIDDLETON, Crane, Pvt, Col Alexander Loury, Capt Gabriel Martin, Inf
MIDDLETON, Drury, Pvt, Regt Commander omitted, Capt Archibald McKinney, Cav
MIDDLETON, John, Pvt, Col John Brown, Capt Allen I Bacon, E TN Mil Inf
MIDDLETON, Washington, Pvt, Col Edwin Booth, Capt James Sharpe, E TN Mil
MIDLIN, Littleton, Pvt, Col Jas Raulston, Capt Chas Wade, Inf
MIGHT (WRIGHT), Ellis G, Sgt, Col William Johnson, Capt Christopher Cook, E TN Mil
MIGRADY, James, Pvt, Col Ewen Allison, Capt Byrons, Cav
MILAM, Edward, Pvt, Col S Bayless, Capt Jonathan Waddle, E TN Mil
MILAN, James, Pvt, Regt Commander omitted, Capt Gray, Inf
MILAN, John, Pvt, Regt Commander omitted, Capt Elijah Rushing, Inf
MILAN, Robert, Pvt, Col S Bayless, Capt Johnathan Waddell, E TN Mil
MILAN, Solomon, Pvt, Regt Commander omitted, Capt Gray, Inf
MILAN, Thomas, Sgt, Col John K Wynn, Capt William Wilson, Inf
MILAN, Thomas, Sgt, Col John Wynn, Capt Porter, Inf; promoted from Pvt
MILES, Alexander, Pvt, Col John Cocke, Capt John Weakley, Inf
MILES, Charles, Pvt, Regt Commander omitted, Capt James H Haggard, Mtd Gunmen
MILES, Hartwell, Pvt, Col T McCrory, Capt Jas Sharnon, Mil Inf; transferred to Capt Gordon's Spies
MILES, James, Cpl, Col S Wear, Capt Joseph Calloway, Mtd Inf
MILES, James, Pvt, Col S Bunch, Capt Jas Cunningham, E TN Vol Mtd Inf
MILES, John, Cpl, Col William Metcalf, Capt Barbee, Mil Inf; d 1-15-1815
MILES, John, Cpl, Regt Commander omitted, Capt Edwin S Moore, Mtd Riflemen
MILES, John, Pvt, Maj William Woodfolk, Capt James Neil, Inf
MILES, Joseph, Pvt, Col William Metcalf, Capt Barbee Collins, Mil Inf
MILES, Landers, Pvt, Col Thos Benton, Capt Benj Rey-

## Enlisted Men, War of 1812

MILES, Richard, Pvt, Lt Col Jno Edmonson, Co Commander omitted, Cav
MILES, Saunders, Pvt, Col Thos Benton, Capt Benj Reynolds, Vol Inf
MILES, Thomas, Pvt, Col Philip Pipkin, Capt John Strother, Mil; attached to Capt D Smith & returned
MILES, William, Pvt, Col Robert Dyer, Capt Joseph Williams, Vol Mtd Gunmen
MILES, William, Pvt, Col S Bunch, Capt James Cunningham, E TN Mil Inf
MILES, William, Pvt, Col S Copeland, Capt John Holshouser, Inf
MILICAN, William, Pvt, Col William Johnson, Capt Henry Hunter, E TN Mil; transferred to Capt Williams Co
MILIKIN, Cornelius, Pvt, Col S Bunch, Capt Jno English, E TN Drafted Mil
MILKAUKS, Joseph, Pvt, Col S Bayless, Capt Joseph Goodson, E TN Mil
MILLAR, Daniel jr, Pvt, Col Robert Steele, Capt Samuel Maxwell, Mil Inf
MILLARD, George, Cpl, Col William Johnson, Capt Joseph Scott, E TN Drafted Mil
MILLARD, George, Pvt, Col William Johnson, Capt Joseph Scott, E TN Drafted Mil; promoted to Cpl
MILLARD, Levi, Cpl, Col S Bayless, Capt James Landen, E TN Mil
MILLARD, Nathaniel, Pvt, Col John Wynn, Capt John Porter, Inf; wounded 11-9-1813? at Talledega
MILLARD, Ociah, Pvt, Col William Lillard, Capt George Keys, E TN Inf
MILLARD, Samuel, Cpl, Col Robert Dyer, Maj William Russell, Capt William Russell, Branch Srvce omitted
MILLARD, Samuel, Pvt, Col S Copeland, Capt David Williams, Inf
MILLARD, Samuel, Pvt, Col T McCrory, Capt Isaac Patton, Mil Inf
MILLARD, Samuel, Pvt, Col William Lillard, Capt George Keys, E TN Inf
MILLARD, Timothy, Pvt, Col Philip Pipkin, Capt David Smith, W TN Mil; attached to Capt John Strother Co
MILLEGAN, James, Pvt, Col Thos Williamson, Capt Geo Mitchie, 2nd Regt TN Vol Mtd Gunmen
MILLEGAN, James, Pvt, Maj William Russell, Capt Geo Mitchie, Vol Mtd Gunmen
MILLER, Abraham, Pvt, Col Samuel Bunch, Capt James Penny, E TN Mtd Inf
MILLER, Abraham, Pvt, Col Wm Y Higgins, Capt Thomas Eldridge, Mtd Gunmen
MILLER, Adam, Pvt, Col Samuel Wear, Capt Rufus Morgan, E TN Vol Inf
MILLER, Alexander, Pvt, Col John Cocke, Capt John Weakley, Inf
MILLER, Alexander, Pvt, Col Philip Pipkin, Ens William Pegram, Det of Capt David Smythe Co of W TN Mil
MILLER, Carolinas, Pvt, Col John Brown, Capt John Trimble, E TN Mtd Gunmen
MILLER, Carolines, Pvt, Col Samuel Bunch, Capt Joseph Duncan, E TN Drafted Mil; substitute for Jesse Huffman
MILLER, Charles, Pvt, Col John Cocke, Capt Bird Nance, Inf; substitute for Charles Mathany
MILLER, Charles, Pvt, Regt Commander omitted, Capt James Craig, Inf
MILLER, Christopher, Pvt, Col William Lillard, Capt Jacob Dyke, Vol Inf
MILLER, Cullenas, Pvt, Maj John Childs, Capt Reuben Tipton, E TN Vol Mtd Inf
MILLER, Daniel sr, Pvt, Col Robert Steele, Capt Samuel Maxwell, Mil Inf
MILLER, David, Pvt, Col James Raulston, Capt James A Black, Inf
MILLER, David, Pvt, Col S Copeland, Capt John Dawson, Inf
MILLER, David, Pvt, Col William Johnson, Capt Henry Hunter, E TN Mil
MILLER, Edmund, Pvt, Col R C Napier, Capt Drury Adkins, Mil Inf
MILLER, Edward, Pvt, Lt Col Richard Napier, Co Commander omitted, Inf
MILLER, Francis, Pvt, Col Samuel Bayless, Capt Jonathan Waddell, E TN Mil
MILLER, Garland, Pvt, Maj William Russell, Capt James Cowan, Vol Mtd Gunmen
MILLER, Garlin, Pvt, Regt Commander omitted, Capt Wm Mitchell, Spies
MILLER, George L, Pvt, Lt Col L Hammond, Capt Thomas Wells, Inf; also under Col A Loury, enlisted in the Regular Army
MILLER, George, Cpl, Regt Commander omitted, Capt James Cowan, Inf
MILLER, George, Pvt, Col Samuel Bunch, Capt Jno English, E TN Drafted Mil
MILLER, George, Pvt, Col Samuel Bunch, Capt Jno Hawk, E TN Mil; joined from Capt English's Co
MILLER, George, Pvt, Col Samuel Bunch, Capt Moses, E TN Drafted Mil; transferred to Capt John English Co
MILLER, George, Pvt, Col Samuel Bunch, Capt Samuel Richardson, E TN Drafted Mil; transferred to Capt English
MILLER, George, Pvt, Col Samuel Wear, Capt Samuel Bowman, Mtd Inf
MILLER, Harmon, Pvt, Col Ewen Allison, Capt Jonas Loughmiller, Mil
MILLER, Harmon, Pvt, Col S Bunch, Capt Jones Griffin, E TN Drafted Mil
MILLER, Henry, Pvt, Col John Alcorn, Capt Wm Locke, Cav
MILLER, Henry, Pvt, Col John Brown, Capt Allen I Bacon, E TN Mil Inf
MILLER, Henry, Pvt, Col John Coffee, Capt Blackman Coleman, Cav
MILLER, Henry, Pvt, Col Robert Steele, Capt James Bennett, Mil Inf
MILLER, Henry, Pvt, Col William Hall, Capt John Kennedy, Vol Inf

## Enlisted Men, War of 1812

MILLER, Henry, Pvt, Col William Lillard, Capt William McLinn, E TN Inf
MILLER, Henry, Pvt, Maj William Russell, Capt Isaac Williams, Separate Bn TN Vol Mtd Gunmen
MILLER, Henry, Pvt, Regt Commander omitted, Capt Jno Crane, Mil Inf
MILLER, Isaac, 2 Sgt, Col Wm Metcalf, Capt Wm Sitton, Mil Inf
MILLER, Isaac, Pvt, Col Ewen Allison, Capt Henry McCray, E TN Mil; transferred to Capt Hampton's Co
MILLER, Isaac, Pvt, Col Ewen Allison, Capt John Hampton, Mil; attached from Capt McCrea's
MILLER, Isaac, Pvt, Col Robert Steele, Capt James Bennett, Mil Inf
MILLER, Isaac, Pvt, Col Samuel Bunch, Capt Geo Gregory, E TN Drafted Mil
MILLER, Jacob, Pvt, Col N T Perkins, Capt James McMahan, Mtd Gunmen
MILLER, Jacob, Pvt, Col Samuel Bayless, Capt James Churchman, E TN Mil
MILLER, Jacob, Pvt, Col Wm Lillard, Capt Geo Keys, E TN Inf
MILLER, James, Pvt, Col James Raulston, Capt Daniel Newman, Inf; d 1-21-1815
MILLER, James, Pvt, Regt Commander omitted, Capt Jno Miller, Spies
MILLER, Jesep, Pvt, Col Thomas McCrory, Capt James Shannon, Mil Inf
MILLER, John, Cpl, Col Samuel Bayless, Capt Branch Jones, E TN Drafted Mil
MILLER, John, Cpl, Lt Col Leroy Hammond, Co Commander omitted, Inf
MILLER, John, Pvt, Col A Cheatham, Capt George Chapman, Inf
MILLER, John, Pvt, Col A Loury, Capt J N Williams, W TN Mil
MILLER, John, Pvt, Col Edwin E Booth, Capt George Winton, E TN Mil
MILLER, John, Pvt, Col John Brown, Capt James Preston, Regt E TN Mil Inf
MILLER, John, Pvt, Col Robert Steele, Capt Samuel Maxwell, Mil Inf
MILLER, John, Pvt, Col Samuel Bayless, Capt James Churchman, E TN Mil
MILLER, John, Pvt, Col Samuel Bayless, Capt Joseph Rich, E TN Inf
MILLER, John, Pvt, Col Samuel Bunch, no other information
MILLER, John, Pvt, Col Samuel Wear, Capt James Gillespie, E TN Vol Inf
MILLER, John, Pvt, Col Samuel Wear, Capt Jesse Cole, Vol Inf
MILLER, John, Pvt, Col Thomas H Benton, Capt Henry L Douglas, Vol Inf
MILLER, John, Pvt, Col Thomas H Benton, Capt William Smith, Vol Inf
MILLER, John, Pvt, Col Thomas H Williamson, Co Commander omitted, Vol Mtd Gunmen
MILLER, John, Pvt, Col William Johnson, Capt James Stewart, E TN Drafted Mil
MILLER, John, Pvt, Col William Johnson, Capt James Stewart, E TN Mil
MILLER, John, Pvt, Col William Lillard, Capt Hugh Martin, E TN Vol Inf
MILLER, John, Pvt, Col William Pillow, Capt William Smith, Vol Inf
MILLER, John, Pvt, Lt Col LeRoy Hammons, Capt James Craig, Inf
MILLER, John, Pvt, Lt Col Leroy Hammons, Capt Arahel Raines, Inf; attached to Capt Kincaid Co
MILLER, John, Pvt, Maj John Chiles, Capt James Cowan, E TN Mtd Gunmen
MILLER, Joseph H, Pvt, Col Thomas McCrory, Co Commander omitted, 2nd Regt TN Mil; joined Capt James Shannon's Co
MILLER, Joseph, Pvt, Col John Brown, Capt Allen I Bacon, Regt E TN Mil Inf
MILLER, Joseph, Pvt, Col R C Napier, Capt Thomas Gray, Mil Inf
MILLER, Joseph, Pvt, Maj William Woodfolk, Capt Abraham Dudney, Inf
MILLER, Joseph, Pvt, Regt Commander omitted, Capt Abner Pearce, Inf
MILLER, Lewis, Pvt, Col Thomas H Williamson, Capt Giles Burdette, Vol Mtd Gunmen
MILLER, Mark, Pvt, Col R H Dyer, Capt James McMahon, TN Vol Mtd Gunmen
MILLER, Martin, Pvt, Col Edwin E Booth, Capt George Winton, E TN Mil
MILLER, Martin, Pvt, Col Ewin Allison, Capt Henry McRay, E TN Mil; deserted 3-4-1814
MILLER, Martin, Pvt, Col Samuel Wear, Capt Daniel Price, E TN Vol Inf
MILLER, Mathew, Cpl, Col Newton Cannon, Capt Thomas H Yardley, Mtd Riflemen; d 12-1813
MILLER, Nathaniel, Pvt, Col John Brown, Capt Wm D Neilson, Regt E TN Vol Mil
MILLER, Nathaniel, Pvt, Col Thomas H Williamson, Capt John Hutchins, Vol Mtd Gunmen
MILLER, Nathaniel, Sgt, Col Edwin E Booth, Capt John McKamy, E TN Mil; d 11-29-1814 in service
MILLER, Nelson, Pvt, Col William Johnson, Capt Henry Hunter, E TN Mil; transferred to Capt Millican's Co
MILLER, Nelson, Pvt, Col William Lillard, Capt Thomas Sharpe, 2nd Regt Inf
MILLER, Nelson, Pvt, Col Wm Johnson, Capt Elihu Milliken, 3rd Regt E TN Mil; transferred to Capt Hunter's Co
MILLER, Pleasant, Pvt, Col S Bunch, Capt N Gibbs, E TN Drafted Mil
MILLER, Pleasant, Pvt, Col Samuel Bunch, Capt Daniel Yarnell, E TN Drafted Mil
MILLER, Pleasant, Pvt, Col Samuel Bunch, Capt Joseph Duncan, E TN Drafted Mil; joined from Capt Gibbs Co
MILLER, Pleasant, Pvt, Maj John Chiles, Co Commander omitted, E TN Mtd Gunmen; Regimental Co - Knox
MILLER, Pleasant, Pvt, Regt Commander omitted, Capt William Walker & Capt John Williams, Vol

## Enlisted Men, War of 1812

MILLER, Robert, Pvt, Col Ewin Allison, Capt Loughmiller, Mil

MILLER, Robert, Pvt, Col Newton Cannon, Capt Thomas Yardley, Mtd Gunmen

MILLER, Robert, Pvt, Col Samuel Bunch, Capt Jones Griffin, E TN Drafted Mil

MILLER, Samuel H, Pvt, Col Newton Cannon, Capt Hamby, Mtd Riflemen

MILLER, Samuel, Pvt, Col A Loury, Capt Arahel Raines, Inf

MILLER, Samuel, Pvt, Col John Alcorn, Capt Thomas Bradley, Vol Cav

MILLER, Samuel, Pvt, Col John Coffee, Capt Thomas Bradley, Vol Cav

MILLER, Samuel, Pvt, Col William Lillard, Co Commander omitted, E TN Vol Inf

MILLER, Samuel, Pvt, Gen Andrew Jackson, Capt William Russell, Mtd Spies

MILLER, Samuel, Pvt, Regt Commander omitted, Capt John Miller, Spies

MILLER, Solomon, Pvt, Col John K Wynn, Capt Jas Cole, Inf

MILLER, Stephen, Pvt, Col William Metcalf, Capt Bird L Hurt, Mil Inf

MILLER, Tabias, Pvt, Regt Commander omitted, Capt Robert Evans, Mtd Spies

MILLER, Thomas H, Sgt, Regt Commander omitted, Capt William Walker & Capt John Williams, Branch Srvce omitted

MILLER, Thomas, Pvt, Col John Cocke, Capt Bird Nance, Inf

MILLER, Thomas, Pvt, Col Philip Pipkin, Capt David Smith, Inf; deserted

MILLER, Thomas, Pvt, Col Samuel Bunch, Capt David Vance, E TN Mtd Inf

MILLER, Thomas, Pvt, Col Samuel Wear, Capt Robert Doak, E TN Vol Inf

MILLER, Tobias, Rank omitted, Col Newton Cannon, Capt Brice Martin, Mtd Gunmen

MILLER, William D, Pvt, Col S Bunch, Capt James Penny, E TN Mil Inf

MILLER, William D, Pvt, Col Wm Johnson, Capt Jas Rogers, E TN Drafted Mil

MILLER, William L, Pvt, Col John Coffee, Capt Daniel Ross, Mtd Riflemen

MILLER, William S, Pvt, Col Thomas Williamson, Capt Anthony Metcalf, Vol Mtd Gunmen

MILLER, William, Cpl, Col William Pillow, Capt Jas Raulston, Inf

MILLER, William, Pvt, Col Edwin Booth, Capt John Marshall, Drafted Mil

MILLER, William, Pvt, Col Ewen Allison, Capt John Hampton, Mil

MILLER, William, Pvt, Col N Cannon, Capt Thomas Yardley, Mtd Riflemen

MILLER, William, Pvt, Col S Bunch, Capt Jones Griffin, E TN Drafted Mil; deserted

MILLER, William, Pvt, Col T McCrory, Capt Jas Shannon, Inf; wounded at Battle of Tilledgean?

MILLER, William, Pvt, Regt Commander omitted, Capt Jno Miller, Spies

MILLER, William, Sgt, Col S Copeland, Capt David Williams, Mil Inf

MILLER, William, Sgt, Lt Col Richard Napier, Co Commander omitted, Inf

MILLER (MILLS), Alexander, Pvt, Col John Cocke, Capt John Weakley, Inf

MILLERS, James, Pvt, Regt Commander omitted, Capt Jno Miller, Spies

MILLERS, Williams, Pvt, Regt Commander omitted, Capt Jno Miller, Spies

MILLIBARGER, J, 5 Sgt, Col Edwin Booth, Capt John Sharp, E TN Mil

MILLIBERGER, William, Pvt, Col Edwin Booth, Capt John Porter, Mil

MILLICAN, John, Pvt, Regt Commander omitted, Capt Wm Mitchell, Spies

MILLICAN, Julis, Pvt, Col Jno Brown, Capt Hugh Barton, E TN Mil Inf

MILLICAN, William, Pvt, Col Jno Brown, Capt Jas Preston, E TN Mil Inf

MILLIGAN, John, Pvt, Col Wm Metcalf, Capt Bird Hurt, Mil Inf

MILLIGAN, Robert, Pvt, Gen Andrew Jackson, Capt Hugh Kerr, Mtd Rangers

MILLIGAN, William, Pvt, Col S Copeland, Capt Moses Thompson, Inf

MILLIKEN, Cornelius, Dmr, Col Ewen Allison, Capt Allen, E TN Mil

MILLIKEN, Ezekiel, Pvt, Col S Bunch, Capt Daniel Yarnell, E TN Mil

MILLIKEN, Hiram, Pvt, Col S Bayless, Capt Jones, E TN Drafted Mil

MILLIKEN, Isaac, Pvt, Lt I Barrett, Capt Nathan Davis, Inf

MILLIKEN, John, Pvt, Lt Col Leroy Hammonds, Capt Alexander Loury & Capt Delaney, Inf

MILLIKEN, Samuel D?, Ens, Col Robert Steele, Capt John Chitwood, Mil Inf, Res omitted

MILLIKEN, William, Pvt, Col Wm Johnson, Capt Elihu Millikin, E TN Mil

MILLIKIN, Alexander, Pvt, Col S Bunch, Capt John Stephens, E TN Mil Inf

MILLIKIN, Samuel, Pvt, Col William Lillard, Capt Jacob Dyke, Vol Inf

MILLIN (MEDLIN), Willson, Pvt, Col Jas Raulston, Capt Chas Wade, Inf

MILLION, Jacob, Pvt, Col Ewen Allison, Capt T McCrory, E TN Mil; transferred to Capt McPheron's Co

MILLISICK, Joseph, Dmr, Col Ewen Allison, Capt Jonas Loughmiller, Mil

MILLS, Aaron, Pvt, Col William Lillard, Capt Jacob Dyke, Vol Inf

MILLS, Anderson, Pvt, Gen Andrew Jackson, Maj Wm Carroll, Col Wm Metcalf, Inf

MILLS, Charles, Pvt, Regt Commander omitted, Capt Jas Haggard, Mtd Gunmen

MILLS, David, Pvt, Col John Coffee, Capt Jas Terrell, Vol Cav; joined Capt Stumps Co

MILLS, David, Pvt, Col Phillip Pipkin, Capt John Strother, Mil; attached to Capt D Smith, deserted

- 361

## Enlisted Men, War of 1812

MILLS, Edmond, Pvt, Col R H Dyer, Capt Cuthbert Hudson, Vol Mtd Gunmen

MILLS, Gibson, Pvt, Col R C Napier, Capt Edward Neblett, Mil Inf

MILLS, Griffin, Pvt, Col R T Perkins, Capt George Marr, Mtd Vol

MILLS, Henry, Pvt, Regt Commander omitted, Capt S Bunch, Branch Srvce omitted

MILLS, James, 3 Sgt, Maj John Chiles, Capt Daniel Price, Vol Mtd Gunmen

MILLS, James, Cpl, Maj Gen Jackson, Col Thomas Williamson, Capt Robert Steele, Vol Mtd Gunmen; promoted from Pvt

MILLS, James, Pvt, Col William Y Higgins, Capt William Doak, Mtd Riflemen

MILLS, James, Sgt, Maj John Chiles, Capt Daniel Price, E TN Vol Mtd Inf

MILLS, Joel, Pvt, Col John Cocke, Capt Joseph Price, Inf; d 1-17-1815

MILLS, John, Cpl, Col Wm Johnson, Capt Jas Tunnell, E TN Mil

MILLS, John, Pvt, Col R H Dyer, Capt Cuthbert Hudson, Vol Mtd Gunmen

MILLS, John, Sgt, Maj Gen Jackson, Col Thomas Williamson, Capt Robert Steele, Vol Mtd Gunmen; appointed from Pvt

MILLS, Thomas, Pvt, Col Thomas Benton, Capt Benj Reynolds, Vol Inf

MILLS, Wesly, Pvt, Maj Gen Jackson, Col Thomas Williamson, Capt Robert Steele, Vol Mtd Gunmen

MILLS, William, Cpl, Col Wm Johnson, Capt James Tunnell, E TN Mil

MILLS, William, Pvt, Col Edwin Booth, Capt John Slatton, E TN Mil

MILLS, William, Pvt, Col Samuel Wear, Capt Joseph Calloway, Mtd Inf

MILLS, William, Pvt, Col Thomas Benton, Capt Wm Moore, Vol Inf

MILLS, William, Pvt, Col Thos Benton, Capt Wm Moore, Vol Inf

MILLS, William, Pvt, Col Wm Johnson, Capt James Tunnell, 3rd Regt E TN Mil; d 3-1-1815

MILLS, William, Pvt, Col Wm Johnson, Capt Jas Tunnell, E TN Mil

MILLS, William, Pvt, Regt Commander omitted, Capt John Williams & Capt Samuel Bunch, Vol

MILLS (MILES), David A, Pvt, Col Thomas H Benton, Capt Benjamin (James?) Reynolds, Vol Inf

MILMOUN, John, Pvt, Col John Cocke, Capt Samuel Caruthers, Inf

MILOM, William, Pvt, Col Thos McCrory, Capt Jas Shannon, Mil Inf; wounded at battle of Talledega

MILSAP, Edward, Pvt, Col Samuel Bayless, Capt Branch Jones, E TN Drafted Mil

MILSAP, Hicks, Pvt, Col Alexander Loury, Lt Col L Hammonds, Capt Thos Delaney, Inf

MILSAP, Isaac, Pvt, Col Wm Johnson, Capt James Rogers, E TN Drafted Mil; substitute

MILSAP, John, Pvt, Col Wm Johnson, Capt Andrew Lawson, E TN Drafted Mil

MILSAP, Jonathan, Pvt, Col Samuel Bayless, Capt Branch Jones, E TN Drafted Mil

MILSAP, Reuben, Sgt, Col John K Winn, Capt John Porter, Inf

MILSAP, William, Pvt, Col William Lillard, Capt William Lillard, E TN Vol Inf

MILSOM, Peter, Pvt, Col Newton Cannon, Capt John Hanley, Mtd Riflemen

MILSOP, Hicks, Dmr, Col Alexander Loury, Lt Col L Hammonds, Capt Thomas Delaney, Inf

MILSOPS, Isaac, Pvt, Col William Lillard, Capt William Lillard, E TN Vol Inf

MILSOPS, Robert, Pvt, Col Wm Lillard, Capt Wm Lillard, E TN Vol Inf

MILSOPS, Thomas, Pvt, Col William Lillard, Capt William Lillard, E TN Vol Inf

MILTIBARGER, Jacob, 5 Sgt, Col Edwin Booth, Capt John Sharp, E TN Mil

MILTON, Cooper, Pvt, Col Samuel Bayless, Capt Joseph Hale, E TN Mil

MILTON, Terry, Pvt, Col Samuel Bayless, Capt Joseph Hale, E TN Mil

MILTON, William, Pvt, Col John Brown, Capt Hugh Barton, E TN Mil Inf

MILUM, John, Pvt, Col John Cocke, Capt Samuel M Caruthers, Inf

MILUM, Samuel, Pvt, Col John Cocke, Capt Samuel M Caruthers, Inf

MIMBS, John, Cpl, Col Wm Metcalf, Capt Barbee Collins, Mil Inf

MIMS, Albert, Pvt, Col Wm Johnson, Capt Joseph Kirk, Mil

MINCHY (MINCHER), Richard, Pvt, Maj William Woodfolk, Capt Abraham Dudney, Capt John Sutton, Inf

MINER, Henry, Pvt, Col Wm Hall, Capt James Hambleton, Vol Inf

MINER, John, Pvt, Col Wm Hall, Capt James Hambleton, Vol Inf

MINETT (MINOT), Marlin, Pvt, Col Samuel Wear, Capt Joseph Calloway, Mtd Inf

MINICK, Adam, Pvt, Col John Brown, Capt Charles Lewin, E TN Vol Mtd Inf

MINICK, Petty, Pvt, Col Ewen Allison, Capt Thomas Wilson, E TN Drafted Mil

MINIS (MENIS), John, 3 Cpl, Col Wm Johnson, Capt David McKamy, E TN Drafted Mil

MINNIS (MINNIZ), Thomas, Pvt, Maj Wm Russell, Capt John Trimble, Vol Mtd Gunmen

MINOR, Daniel L, Pvt, Col John Cocke, Capt James Gray, Inf; also a Ffr

MINOR, Henry, Pvt, Lt Col Jno Edmonson, Co Commander omitted, Cav

MINOR, John, Pvt, Regt Commander omitted, Capt David Smith, Cav Vol

MINOR, Levi W, Pvt, Col Wm Hall, Capt John Kennedy, Vol Inf

MINOR, Thomas D, 4 Sgt, Maj Gen Andrew Jackson, Capt Joseph Kirkpatrick, Mtd Riflemen

MINOT (MINET), Marlin, Pvt, Col Samuel Wear, Capt Joseph Calloway, Branch Srvce omitted

MINOTT (MYNATT), Martin, Pvt, Maj John Chiles,

## Enlisted Men, War of 1812

Capt Daniel Price, E TN Vol Mtd Inf
MINTON, John, Pvt, Col Jas Raulston, Capt Edward Robinson, Inf
MINTON, John, Pvt, Maj Gen Wm Carroll, Col Jas Raulston, Capt Edward Robinson, Inf
MINUS, John, Pvt, Col R H Dyer, Capt Thos Jones, Vol Mtd Gunmen
MIRACK (MERACK), Green, Pvt, Col A Cheatham, Capt Richard Benson, Inf
MIRES, Adam, Pvt, Col Thos Williamson, Capt Beverly Williams, Vol Mtd Gunmen
MIRES, Elisha, Pvt, Col Wm Hall, Capt John Wallace, Inf
MIRES, John, Pvt, Col R C Napier, Capt Early Benson, Mil Inf
MIRES, Miles, Pvt, Col Wm Hall, Capt John Wallace, Inf
MIRES, Philip, Sgt, Col Thos Benton, Capt George Gibbs, Vol Inf; promoted from 2 Sgt
MIRES, Thomas, Pvt, Col N T Perkins, Capt George Eliot, Mil Inf
MISSE, Jesse, Pvt, Col John Alcorn, Capt Thomas Bradley, Vol Cav
MISSENGALE, James, Pvt, Regt Commander omitted, Capt Askew, Inf
MISSER, Jonas, Pvt, Col John Cocke, Capt Joseph Price, Inf; d 2-20-1815
MISSIKER, Reuben, Pvt, Col A Cheatham, Capt Birdwell, Inf
MITCHEL, Daniel, Pvt, Col Alexander Loury, Capt J N Williamson, W TN Mil
MITCHELL, Adam, Pvt, Col Samuel Bunch, Capt D G Vance, E TN Mtd Inf
MITCHELL, Andrew, Pvt, Col R C Napier, Capt Jno Chism, Mil Inf
MITCHELL, Andrew, Pvt, Col Wm Hall, Capt Henry Newlin, Inf
MITCHELL, Archibald, Pvt, Col Jno Alcorn, Capt Jno Baskerville, Vol Inf
MITCHELL, Archibald, Pvt, Col Jno Coffee, Capt Jno Baskerville, Cav
MITCHELL, Berry, Pvt, Maj Jno Childs, Capt Daniel Price, E TN Mtd Inf
MITCHELL, Blewford, Cpl, Col S Copeland, Capt S George, Inf
MITCHELL, Bradston, Pvt, Col Wm Johnson, Capt E Milliken, 3rd Regt E TN Mil
MITCHELL, Braxton, Pvt, Col Samuel Bayless, Capt Jas Churchman, E TN Mil; transferred from Capt Millikan's Co
MITCHELL, Charles B, Pvt, Col Samuel Bayless, Capt Branch Jones, E TN Mil Drafted
MITCHELL, Charles, Pvt, Col Jno Brown, Capt Wm D Neilson, E TN Vol Mil
MITCHELL, Daniel, Pvt, Col L Hammond, Capt J N Williamson, 2nd Regt Inf
MITCHELL, Elijah, Pvt, Col P Pipkin, Capt David Smith, Mil Inf
MITCHELL, Elijah, Sgt, Col Wm Lillard, Capt Thos Sharpe, 2nd Regt Inf
MITCHELL, George, Pvt, Col R H Dyer, Capt C Hudson, Vol Mtd Gunmen; transferred from Capt Joseph Williams Co

MITCHELL, George, Pvt, Col R H Dyer, Capt Jos Williams, Vol Mtd Gunmen; transferred to Capt Hunter's Co
MITCHELL, Greenberry, Pvt, Col E Booth, Capt Jno Slatton, Branch Srvce omitted
MITCHELL, Ichabod, Pvt, Col Thos Williamson, Capt Robert Moore, Vol Mtd Gunmen
MITCHELL, Ichabod, Pvt, Regt Commander omitted, Capt Geo Smith, Spies
MITCHELL, Isaac, Pvt, Col T McCrory, Capt Isaac Patton, Mil Inf
MITCHELL, James, 1 Cpl, Col Thos Benton, Capt G W Gibbs, Vol Inf
MITCHELL, James, Cpl, Col E Allison, Capt Jno Hampton, Mil
MITCHELL, James, Cpl, Col Thos Benton, Capt G W Gibbs, Vol Inf
MITCHELL, James, Cpl, Col Thos Benton, Capt G W Gibbs, Vol Inf; promoted from Pvt
MITCHELL, James, Pvt, Col Jno Coffee, Capt Jas Terrell, Vol Cav; United States service
MITCHELL, James, Pvt, Col John Coffee, Capt Jas Terrill, Vol Cav
MITCHELL, James, Pvt, Col Thos Williamson, Capt Jno Doak & Capt Jno Dobbins, Vol Gunmen
MITCHELL, James, Pvt, Col Wm Johnson, Capt Andrew Lawson, E TN Drafted Mil
MITCHELL, James, Pvt, Col Wm Lillard, Capt J Hartsell, E TN Vol Inf
MITCHELL, James, Pvt, Maj Wm Woodfolk, Capt Abner Pearce, Inf
MITCHELL, Jesse, Pvt, Col Alex Loury, Capt Jas Kincaid, Inf
MITCHELL, Jesse, Pvt, Col Wm Metcalf, Capt Thos Marks, Mil Inf
MITCHELL, Jesse, Pvt, Regt Commander omitted, Capt Gray, Inf
MITCHELL, John C, Pvt, Col William Hall, Capt John Wallace, Inf
MITCHELL, John, Pvt, Col Alex Loury, Lt Col L Hammond, Capt Thos Delaney, Inf
MITCHELL, John, Pvt, Col N T Cannon, Capt Jno Hanley, Mtd Riflemen
MITCHELL, John, Pvt, Col R H Dyer, Capt C Hudson, Vol Mtd Gunmen
MITCHELL, John, Pvt, Col R H Dyer, Capt Jas McMahon, TN Vol Mtd Gunmen; promoted to Cpl
MITCHELL, John, Pvt, Col S Bunch, Capt Jno Houk, E TN Mil; joined from Capt Dewises Co
MITCHELL, John, Pvt, Col Samuel Bayless, Capt J Waddell, E TN Mil
MITCHELL, John, Pvt, Col William Hale, Capt Wallace, Inf
MITCHELL, John, Pvt, Col Wm Higgins, Capt Wm Doake, Mtd Riflemen; promoted to QM Sgt
MITCHELL, John, Pvt, Col Wm Lillard, Capt J Hartsell, E TN Vol Inf
MITCHELL, John, Pvt, Col Wm Lillard, Capt Wm Gillenwater, E TN Inf
MITCHELL, John, Pvt, Gen Andrew Jackson, Capt Nathan Davis, Inf

- 363

## Enlisted Men, War of 1812

MITCHELL, John, Pvt, Maj Jno Childs, Capt Daniel Price, E TN Vol Mtd Inf

MITCHELL, John, Pvt, Regt Commander omitted, Capt Jas Haggard, Mtd Gunmen

MITCHELL, John, QM Sgt, Col Wm Higgins, Co Commander omitted, 2nd Regt Mtd Vol

MITCHELL, Luke, Pvt, Col Phillip Johnson, Co Commander omitted, E TN Mil

MITCHELL, Mathew, Pvt, Col John Coffee, Capt David Smith, Vol Cav; deserted

MITCHELL, Mathew, Pvt, Col Thomas Williamson, Capt Christopher Cook & Capt Daniel Ross, Vol Mtd Gunmen

MITCHELL, Miles, Pvt, Col Thomas Williamson, Capt Beverly Williams, Vol Mtd Gunmen; d 4-18-1815

MITCHELL, Nathaniel, 2 Sgt, Col William Lillard, Capt James Lillard, E TN Vol Inf

MITCHELL, Nelson, Pvt, Col William Johnson, Capt Andrew Lawson, E TN Drafted Mil; substitute for Thomas Mitchell

MITCHELL, Quillen, Pvt, Col John Childs, Capt Daniel Price, E TN Vol Mtd Inf

MITCHELL, Randolph, Pvt, Brig Gen Johnson, Capt Robert Carson, Inf

MITCHELL, Randolph, Pvt, Maj William Russell, Capt Flemin Hodges, Vol Mtd Gunmen

MITCHELL, Robert M, Pvt, Col Alexander Loury, Lt Col Leroy Hammonds, Capt Thomas Delaney, Inf

MITCHELL, Robert, Pvt, Col Edward Bradley, Capt Harry Douglas, Vol Inf

MITCHELL, Robert, Pvt, Col Thomas Benton, Capt Henry Douglas, Vol Inf

MITCHELL, Robert, Pvt, Col William Lillard, Capt James Hamilton, E TN Vol Inf; deserted

MITCHELL, Samuel B, Pvt, Col Samuel Bunch & Col Samuel Wear, Capt Wm Mitchell, Branch Srvce omitted

MITCHELL, Samuel, Pvt, Col William Lillard, Capt Robert Maloney, E TN Vol Inf

MITCHELL, Samuel, Pvt, Regt Commander omitted, Capt Jos Haggard, Mtd Gunmen

MITCHELL, Stephen, Pvt, Col S Copeland, Capt John Dawson, Inf

MITCHELL, Thomas C, Pvt, Col Thomas Williamson, Capt James Pace, Lt Nealey, Vol Mtd Gunmen; appointed Sgt Maj

MITCHELL, Thomas C, Pvt, Regt Commander omitted, Capt Wm Mitchell, Spies

MITCHELL, Thomas C, Sgt Maj, Col Robert H Dyer, Co Commander omitted, TN Vol Mtd Gunmen

MITCHELL, Thomas, Pvt, Col Edward Bradley, Capt Harry Douglas, Vol Inf

MITCHELL, Thomas, Pvt, Col Samuel Benton, Capt John Reynolds, Vol Inf

MITCHELL, William, 2 Cpl, Col Samuel Bunch, Capt William Houston, E TN Vol Mtd Inf

MITCHELL, William, Pvt, Col Newton Cannon, Capt Thos Yardley, Mtd Riflemen; promoted to Capt

MITCHELL, William, Pvt, Col Samuel Bayless, Capt Jonathan Waddell, E TN Mil

MITCHELL, William, Pvt, Col Samuel Wear, Capt John Bayless, Mtd Inf

MITCHELL, William, Pvt, Col Thomas McCrory, Capt Isaac Patton, Mil Inf

MITCHELL, William, Pvt, Col William Lillard, Capt Thomas Sharpe, 2nd Regt Inf

MITCHELL, William, Pvt, Maj John Childs, Capt Daniel Price, E TN Vol Mtd Inf

MITCHELL, Zadock, Cpl, Col Stephen Copeland, Capt G W Stell, Mil Inf

MITCHIL, George, Capt, Col Thos Williamson, Maj William Russell, TN Vol Mtd Gunmen

MITTENBERGER, William, Pvt, Col Samuel Bunch, Capt John English, E TN Draft Mil

MITTON (MELTON), Thomas, Pvt, Col John Wynne, Capt James Cole, Inf

MIXAM, John, Pvt, Col Newton Cannon, Capt John Hanley, Mtd Riflemen

MIXAM, Noah, Pvt, Maj William Woodfolk, Capt Abner Pearce, Inf

MIZE, Henry, Pvt, Maj William Woodfolk, Capt Abner Pearce, Inf

MOATS, Henry, Dmr, Col William Johnson, Capt James Stewart, 3 Regt E TN Mil

MOATS, Henry, Pvt, Col Samuel Wear, Capt John Childs, E Tn Vol Mil

MOBIAS, William, Pvt, Col Wm Johnson, Capt James Blakemore, Mil Inf

MOBLEY, Edward, Pvt, Col Wm Metcalf, Capt Wm Mullins, Mil Inf

MOBLY, David, Pvt, Col Leroy Hammonds, Capt Alexandria Loury & Capt Thomas Well, Inf

MOBLY, Luke, Pvt, Maj Gen Carroll, Col William Metcalf, Capt John Jackson, Inf

MOCK, Samuel, Pvt, Col Samuel Bunch, Capt F Register, E TN Mil

MOCORS, David, Pvt, Col Ewin Allison, Capt Jacob Hoyal, E TN Mil; joined from Capt McPherin's Co

MODGLING, Wright, Pvt, Col John Cocke, Capt James Gault, Inf

MOFFETT, Ephraim, Pvt, Col S Copeland, Capt Wm Douglass, Inf

MOFFETT, Robert, Pvt, Col William Hall, Capt Abraham Bledsoe, Vol Inf

MOFFETT, Thomas, Pvt, Col Samuel Bayless, Capt Joseph Rich, E TN Inf

MOFFITT, Samuel, Pvt, Col Wm Johnson, Capt Henry Hunter, E Tn Mil

MOFORD, Jonathan, Pvt, Col Thomas Benton, Capt Isiah Renshaw, Vol Inf

MOGERS, Henry, Pvt, Col Wm Johnson, Capt James Kirk, Mil

MOGERS, John, Pvt, Col Wm Johnson, Capt Joseph Kirk, Mil

MOLCOSTER, Christopher, Pvt, Col John Cocke, Capt Daniel Price, Inf; enlisted US Svce

MOLDEN, Blake, Pvt, Col Philip Pipkin, Capt Henry M Newlin, Mil Inf

MOLEN, Samuel, Pvt, Col R H Dyer, Capt Joseph Williams, 1 Regt TN Vol Mtd Gunmen

MOLSBY, David, Pvt, Col William Lillard, Capt Wm Gillenwater, E Tn Inf
MOLTON, Michael C, Pvt, Col John Coffee, Capt Michael Molton, Cav
MOLTON, Michael, Pvt, Lt Col Jno Edmonson, Co Commander omitted, Cav
MOLTON, Michale, Pvt, Regt Commander omitted, Capt William Peacock, Cav
MOND, John M, Pvt, Col John Cocke, Capt Richard Crunk, Inf
MONDAY, William, QM Sgt, Col R C Napier, no Co Commander, 1 Regt W TN Mil
MONDRALL, John, Pvt, Col John Coffee, Capt John Baskerville, Cav
MONDS, Job, Pvt, Col SAmuel Wear, Capt John Chiles, E TN Vol Inf
MONDS, Richard, Cpl, Col Wm Johnson, Capt James Stewart, 3 Regt E TN Mil
MONEY, Benjamin, Pvt, Col T McCrory, Capt William Dooley, Inf
MONEY, Benjamin, Pvt, Col Thomas Benton, Capt Benj Reynolds, Vol Inf
MONEY, John, Ffr, Col A Loury, Capt John Looney, 2 Regt W TN Mil
MONIS (MANIS), Bartly, Pvt, Col Ewen Allison, Capt James Loughmiller, Mil
MONIS (MANIS), Daniel, Pvt, Col Ewen Allison, Capt Jonas Loughmiller, Mil
MONROE, George, 2 Surgeon Mate, Col Jas Raulston, Co Commander omitted, W TN Mil Inf
MONROE, William, Cpl, Col Jno Coffee, Capt Daniel Ross, Mtd Gunmen
MONTEETH, George, Sgt, Col Samuel Bayless, Capt Joseph Hale, E TN Mil
MONTGOMERY, Alexander, Pvt, Col John Wynn, Capt Butler, Inf
MONTGOMERY, Andrew, Pvt, Brig Gen T Washington, Capt Jno Crawford, Inf
MONTGOMERY, David, Pvt, Col N T Perkins, Capt James McMahan, Mtd Gunmen
MONTGOMERY, David, Pvt, Maj Gen Wm Carroll, Col Wm Metcalf, Capt John Jackson, Inf
MONTGOMERY, Hugh, Pvt, Regt Commander omitted, Capt James Cowan, Inf
MONTGOMERY, James, 1 Cpl, Col Wm Pillow, Capt Geo Caperton, Inf
MONTGOMERY, James, 2 Cpl, Col Thomas Benton, Capt Geo Caperton, Vol Inf
MONTGOMERY, James, Pvt, Col Edwin E Booth, Capt Alexander Biggs, Inf
MONTGOMERY, James, Pvt, Col N T Perkins, Capt James McMahan, Mtd Gunmen
MONTGOMERY, James, Pvt, Gen Andrew Jackson, Capt William Russell, Mtd Spies
MONTGOMERY, James, Pvt, Regt Commander omitted, Capt James Cowan, Inf
MONTGOMERY, James, Sgt, Maj William Russell, Capt John Cowan, Vol Mtd Riflemen
MONTGOMERY, John A, Asst Fgmstr, Maj Gen John Cocke, no Co Commander, E Tn Vol Mil
MONTGOMERY, John, Cpl, Col Jno Coffee, Capt John W Byrns, Cav
MONTGOMERY, John, Cpl, Col John Alcorn, Capt John W Byrns, Cav; wounded in Talledega Battle 11-8-1813
MONTGOMERY, John, Pvt, Col N T Perkins, Capt James McMahan, Mtd Gunmen
MONTGOMERY, John, Pvt, Col Samuel Wear, Capt James Gillespie, E TN Vol Inf
MONTGOMERY, John, Pvt, Col T Williamson, Lt Nealry, Capt James Pace, Vol Mtd Gunmen
MONTGOMERY, John, Sgt, Col Edwin Booth, Capt Porter, Drafted Mil
MONTGOMERY, John, Sgt, Maj James Porter, Capt Jos Anderson, Cav; later apptd Asst QM
MONTGOMERY, Newman, Pvt, Col Jno Brown, Capt Hugh Barton, E TN Mil Inf
MONTGOMERY, Robert, Cpl, Col John Winn, Capt Butler, Inf
MONTGOMERY, Robert, Pvt, Col Philip Pipkin, Capt Ebenezer Kirkpatrick, Mil Inf
MONTGOMERY, Robert, Pvt, Maj William Woodfolk, Capt James Turner, Inf
MONTGOMERY, Samuel, Pvt, Col Samuel Wear, Capt James Gillespie, E TN Vol Inf
MONTGOMERY, Stephen, Pvt, Col Thos Williamson, Capt Anthony M Metcalf, Vol Mtd Gunmen
MONTGOMERY, Thomas, Col Edwin E Booth, Capt Alexander Biggs, Inf
MONTGOMERY, Thomas, Pvt, Col John Coffee, Capt David Smith, Vol Cav, deserted
MONTGOMERY, Thomas, Pvt, Col Wm Higgins, Capt Samuel A Allen, Mtd Gunmen
MONTGOMERY, William, Cpl, Maj William Russell, Capt John Cowan, Vol Mtd Gunmen
MONTGOMERY, William, Pvt, Col Thomas Benton, Capt Thomas Williamson, Vol Inf
MONTGOMERY, William, Pvt, Col Thos Benton, Capt Thos Williamson, Vol Inf
MONTGOMERY, William, Pvt, Col Wm Pillow, Capt Thomas Williamson, Vol Inf
MONTGOMERY, William, Pvt, Regt Commander omitted, Capt Geo Smith, Spies
MONTGOMERY, William, Sgt, Col Edwin E Booth, Capt Porter, Drafted Mil
MONTGOMERY, William, Sgt, Maj Jas P H Porter, Capt Jas Anderson, Cav
MOODY, Robert, Pvt, Col Edward Bradley, Capt Abraham Bledsoe, Riflemen; deserted
MOODY, Robert, Pvt, Col Wm Hall, Capt Abraham Bledsoe, Vol Inf
MOODY, Thomas, Pvt, Gen Andrew Jackson, Capt Nathan Davis, Inf
MOOLER, Frederick, Pvt, Col Jno Brown, Capt Wm D Neilson, E TN Vol Mil
MOOMAN, Randolph, Pvt, Col Edwin Booth, Capt John McKamey, E TN Mil
MOON, Jesse, Pvt, Col Samuel Bayless, Capt Branch Jones, E TN Draft Mil
MOON, John H, Pvt, Col Newton Cannon, Capt John Hanley, Mtd Riflemen; trans to Capt Dempsey Co
MOON, Joseph, Pvt, Col William Lillard, Capt William

## Enlisted Men, War of 1812

Lillard, E Tn Vol Inf
MOON, Richard, Pvt, Col Philip Pipkin, Capt David Smith, Inf
MOON, Richard, Pvt, Col Philip Pipkin, Capt Wm Mackay, Mil Inf
MOON, Richard, Pvt, Regt Commander omitted, Capt L Farrell, Inf
MOON, William, Pvt, Col John K Winn, Capt James Cole, Inf; trans to Capt Russell
MOON, William, Pvt, Gen Andrew Jackson, Capt William Russell, Mtd Spies
MOONEY, John, Pvt, Col S Copeland, Capt John Biles, Inf
MOONEY, Sampson, 2 Sgt, Col Jas Raulston, Capt Daniel Newman, Inf
MOONEYHAM, James, Pvt, Col John Brown, Capt Charles Lewin, E Tn Vol Mtd Inf
MOONKEY, John, Pvt, Col Wm Johnson, Capt Joseph Scott, E Tn Draft Mil
MOOR, Asg?, Pvt, Regt Commander omitted, Capt Nathan Farmer, Mtd Riflemen
MOOR, James, Pvt, Col Thos Benton, Capt Geo Caperton, Inf
MOOR, John H, Pvt, Col Newton Cannon, Capt John B Demsey, Mtd Gunmen; trans from Capt Hamby's Co
MOOR, John, Pvt, Col A Cheatham, Capt James Giddens, Inf
MOOR, Loderick, Pvt, Col Edward Bradley, Capt Thos B Haynie, Vol Inf
MOORE, Aaron, Pvt, Col Thos Williamson, Capt Giles Burdett, Vol Mtd Gunmen
MOORE, Alexander, Pvt, Col Thos Williamson, Capt James Cook & Capt John Crane, Vol Mtd Gunmen
MOORE, Alfred, Pvt, Col Edward Bradley, Capt Abraham Bledsoe, Riflemen; deserted
MOORE, Alfred, Pvt, Col John Alcorn, Capt Alexander McKeen, Cav
MOORE, Alfred, Pvt, Col John Coffee, Capt Alexander McKeen, Cav
MOORE, Allen, Pvt, Col N T Perkins, Capt John Doak, Vol Mtd Inf
MOORE, Allen, Pvt, Col Thos Benton, Capt Wm Moore, Vol Inf
MOORE, Allen, Pvt, Col Wm Pillow, Capt Wm Moore, Inf
MOORE, Andrew, Pvt, Col R H Dyer, Capt Robert Edmonston, 1 TN Vol Mtd Gunmen
MOORE, Andrew, Pvt, Col Samuel Bunch, Capt Jones Griffin, E TN Draft Mil; deserted
MOORE, Aron, 4 Cpl, Col Thos Williamson, Capt Giles Burdett, Vol Mtd Gunmen
MOORE, Asa, Pvt, Regt Commander omitted, Capt Nathan Farmer, Mtd Riflemen
MOORE, Bennett, 4 Sgt, Col R C Napier, Capt John Chism, Mil Inf
MOORE, Britton, Pvt, Col Wm Metcalf, Capt Alexander Hill & Capt John Cunningham, Mil Inf
MOORE, Charles B, Pvt, Col R C Napier, Capt Thomas Gray, Mil Inf
MOORE, Daniel R, Pvt, Regt Commander omitted, Capt Archibold McKinney, Cav
MOORE, Daniel, Pvt, Col Samuel Bayless, Capt Branch Jones, E Tn Draft Mil
MOORE, David A, Pvt, Col Wm Pillow, Capt C E McEwen, Vol Inf
MOORE, David, Cpl, Maj William Carroll, Capt Daniel M Bradford, Capt Lewis Dillahunty, Vol Inf
MOORE, David, Pvt, Col John Alcorn, Capt Robert Jetton, Vol Cav
MOORE, David, Pvt, Col John Coffee, Capt Robert Jetton, Cav
MOORE, David, Pvt, Regt Commander omitted, Capt Archibold McKinney, Cav
MOORE, Demarcus, Pvt, Col Thos Williamson, Capt James Pace & Capt James Neely, Vol Mtd Gunmen
MOORE, Elijah, Pvt, Col Samuel Bunch, Capt George Gregory, E TN Draft Mil
MOORE, Elisha, Pvt, Col Wm Lillard, Capt Brice Martin, E Tn Vol Inf
MOORE, Ephraim, Pvt, Col Samuel Bunch, Co Commander omitted, E TN Mil
MOORE, Ephriam D, Pvt, Col Thomas H Williams, Capt Robert Moore, Vol Mtd Gunmen; trans to Lt Col Bean's Spies
MOORE, Ezekiel, Pvt, Col John Alcorn, Capt John Winston, Mtd Riflemen
MOORE, Francis, Pvt, Col A Loury, Capt George Sarver, Inf
MOORE, French, Pvt, Col T McCrory, Capt Thomas Gordan, Inf; deserted
MOORE, French, Pvt, Col Thomas H Williamson, Capt Robert Steele, Vol Mtd Gunmen
MOORE, George D, Pvt, Col Wm Pillow, Capt John Anderson, Vol Inf
MOORE, George L, Pvt, Col Samuel Bunch, Capt George Gregory, E TN Draft Mil; disch for inability
MOORE, George, Pvt, Col John Brown, Capt Hugh Barton, E Tn Mil Inf
MOORE, George, Pvt, Col John Brown, Capt Wm D Neilson, Regt E TN Vol Mil
MOORE, George, Pvt, Col John Coffee, Capt Alexander McKeen, Cav
MOORE, George, Pvt, Col Samuel Wear, Capt Jesse Cole, Vol Inf
MOORE, George, Pvt, Col Thomas H Williamson, Capt Beverly Williams, Vol Mtd Gunmen; trans to Lt Bean's Co
MOORE, George, Pvt, Gen John Coffee, no Co Commander, Mtd Spies
MOORE, Golehew, Pvt, Col Samuel Bunch, Capt James Cummings, E Tn Vol Mtd Inf
MOORE, Harris(on), Pvt, Col Zacheus Copeland, Capt John Dawson, Inf
MOORE, Harver (Harvan), Pvt, Col James Raulston, Capt Edward Robinson, Inf
MOORE, Haynes, Pvt, Col Edwin E Booth, Capt David McKamy, E Tn Mil
MOORE, Henry, Pvt, Col John Alcorn, Capt John F Winston, Mtd Riflemen

MOORE, Henry, Pvt, Col John Cocke, Capt James Gray, Inf; enlisted in regular svce
MOORE, Henry, Pvt, Eol Edwin E Booth, Capt George Winton, E Tn Mil
MOORE, Henry, Sgt, Col Thomas H Benton, Capt John Moore, Vol Inf
MOORE, Hezekiah, Pvt, Col John Brown, Capt Wm White, E Tn Mil Inf
MOORE, Isaac, Pvt, Col Robert Steele, Capt Richard Ratton, Mil Inf
MOORE, Isham, Pvt, Col T McCrory, Capt Isaac Patton, Mil Inf; transferred to Capt Shannon's Co
MOORE, Isham, Pvt, Col T McCrory, Capt Jas Shannon, Mil Inf
MOORE, Isham, Pvt, Col Wm Metcalf, Capt Marks, Mil Inf
MOORE, Israel, 1 Sgt, Col Thomas Bradley, Capt John Wallace, Vol Inf
MOORE, Israel, 1 Sgt, Col Wm Hall, Capt John Wallace, Inf
MOORE, Israel, Pvt, Col Thomas H Williamson, Capt Thomas Scurry, Vol Mtd Gunmen
MOORE, Issac, Sgt, Col R H Dyer, Capt James Wyatt, Vol Mtd Gunmen
MOORE, James, 2 Cpl, Col A Loury, Co Commander omitted, 2nd Regt W TN Mil
MOORE, James, 4 Sgt, Col John Cocke, Capt John Dalton, Inf
MOORE, James, Cpl, Lt Jas Berry, Co Commander omitted, Mtd Riflemen
MOORE, James, Pvt, Col John Alcorn, Capt McKeen, Cav; killed 11-3-1813
MOORE, James, Pvt, Col John Coffee, Capt McKeen, Cav
MOORE, James, Pvt, Col R H Dyer, Capt Robert Edmondson, TN Vol Mtd Gunmen
MOORE, James, Pvt, Col Samuel Wear, Capt Robert Doak, E TN Vol Inf
MOORE, James, Pvt, Col Stephen Copeland, Capt Richard Sharp, Mil Inf
MOORE, James, Pvt, Col Thomas H Benton, Capt George Caperton, Vol Inf
MOORE, James, Pvt, Col William Hall, Capt Abraham Bledsoe, Vol Inf
MOORE, James, Pvt, Col Wm Hall, Capt Abraham Bledsoe, Vol Inf
MOORE, James, Pvt, Col Wm Lillard, Capt Jacob Dyke, Vol Inf
MOORE, James, Pvt, Col Wm Pillow, Capt C E McEwen, Vol Inf
MOORE, James, Pvt, Maj Gen William Carroll, Col James Raulston, Capt Edward Robinson, Inf
MOORE, James, Pvt, Maj John Chiles, Capt Reuben Tipton, E TN Vol Mtd Inf
MOORE, James, Sgt Maj, Gen John Coffee, Co Commander omitted, TN Vol Mtd Gunmen
MOORE, James, Sgt, Regt Commander omitted, Capt James Cowan, Inf
MOORE, Jeptha, Pvt, Gen A Jackson, Col Thos H Williams, Col Robert Steele, Vol Mtd Gunmen
MOORE, Joab, Pvt, Maj John Chiles, Capt Cummings, Vol Mtd Inf; furnished John Brotton as a substitute
MOORE, John, Cpl, Col Samuel Bunch, Capt F Register, E TN Mil
MOORE, John, Pvt, Col A Loury, Capt J N Williamson, W TN Mil
MOORE, John, Pvt, Col Edwin Booth, Capt Alexander Biggs, Inf
MOORE, John, Pvt, Col Ewen Allison, Capt Jacob Hoyal, E TN Mil; appointed Cpl
MOORE, John, Pvt, Col Ewen Allison, Capt Joseph Everett, E TN Mil; discharged for sickness by Gen Doherty
MOORE, John, Pvt, Col John Coffee, Capt David Smith, Vol Cav
MOORE, John, Pvt, Col John Coffee, Capt Michael Molton, Cav; absent out of state
MOORE, John, Pvt, Col John K Wynne, Capt Robert Breden, Inf; deserted 10-25-1813
MOORE, John, Pvt, Col R C Napier, Capt Drury Adkins, Mil Inf
MOORE, John, Pvt, Col R H Dyer, Capt Bethel Allen, Vol Mtd Gunmen
MOORE, John, Pvt, Col Robert H Dyer, Capt James Wyatt, Vol Mtd Gunmen
MOORE, John, Pvt, Col Samuel Bayless, Capt James Churchman, E TN Mil
MOORE, John, Pvt, Col Samuel Wear, Capt James Gillespie, E TN Vol Inf
MOORE, John, Pvt, Col T McCrory, Capt Isaac Patton, Mil Inf
MOORE, John, Pvt, Col T Williamson, Capt John Doak & Capt John Dobbins, Vol Mtd Gunmen; two John Moores in same unit
MOORE, John, Pvt, Col Thos Benton, Capt James McFerrin, Vol Inf
MOORE, John, Pvt, Col Wm Hall, Capt John Moore, Vol Inf; substituted Wm Moore
MOORE, John, Pvt, Col Wm Johnson, Capt Joseph Scott, E TN Drafted Mil; d 12-10-1814
MOORE, John, Pvt, Col Wm Pillow, Capt James McFerrin, Inf; furloughed by the Doctor
MOORE, John, Pvt, Lt Col L Hammond, Capt James Tubb, Inf
MOORE, John, Pvt, Maj Gen Wm Carroll, Col James Raulston, Capt Edward Robinson, Inf
MOORE, John, Pvt, Maj John Childs, Capt Charles Conway, E TN Mtd Gunmen; Regimental Co - Blount
MOORE, John, Pvt, Regt Commander omitted, Capt David Smith, Cav; transferred to the Inf
MOORE, John, Sgt, Brig Gen Thos Johnson, Capt Allen, Mil Inf
MOORE, John, Sgt, Col John Alcorn, Capt Alexander McKeen, Cav
MOORE, Jon A, Pvt, Col Wm Lillard, Capt Wm Hamilton, E TN Vol Inf
MOORE, Joseph H, Pvt, Col William Johnson, Capt James R Rogers, E TN Drafted Mil
MOORE, Joseph, Pvt, Col A Cheatham, Capt Charles Johnson, Inf
MOORE, Joseph, Pvt, Col Newton Cannon, Capt Wm Edwards, Regt Command

MOORE, Joseph, Pvt, Col T Williamson, Capt John Doak & Capt John Dobbins, Vol Mtd Gunmen
MOORE, Joseph, Pvt, Regt Commander omitted, Capt Jno Crane, Mtd Inf
MOORE, Josiah, Pvt, Col Wm Metcalf, Capt Wm Sitton, Mil Inf; d 1-28-1815
MOORE, Levi, Pvt, Col Newton Cannon, Capt Isaac Williams, Mtd Riflemen
MOORE, Liza, Pvt, Col Edward Bradley, Capt John Wallace, Vol Inf
MOORE, Loderick, Pvt, Col Thos Williamson, Capt John Doak & Capt John Dobbins, Vol Mtd Gunmen
MOORE, Loderick, Tptr, Col Thos Williamson, Capt John Doak & Capt John Dobbins, Vol Mtd Gunmen
MOORE, Marcus D, Pvt, Col Thos Williamson, Capt James Pace, Lt Nealy, Vol Mtd Gunmen
MOORE, Marcus, Sgt, Col Thos Williamson, Capt Robt Moore, Vol Mtd Gunmen; promoted from Pvt
MOORE, Mason (Morgan), Pvt, Col John Coffee, Capt David Smith, Vol Cav
MOORE, Mason, Pvt, Col R H Dyer, Capt Bethel Allen, Vol Mtd Gunmen
MOORE, Mathew, Pvt, Col Samuel Bayless, Capt John Brock, E TN Mil
MOORE, Mathew, Pvt, Col Thos Benton, Capt Thos Williamson, Vol Inf
MOORE, Mathew, Pvt, Col Wm Pillow, Capt Thos Williamson, Vol Inf
MOORE, Moses, Pvt, Col Ewen Allison, Capt John Brock, E TN Mil; deserted
MOORE, Nathaniel W, Pvt, Col R H Dyer, Capt Thomas Jones, Vol Mtd Gunmen
MOORE, Nathaniel, Pvt, Col Wm Lillard, Capt Jacob Dyke, Vol Inf
MOORE, Nathaniel, Pvt, Maj Gen Wm Carroll, Col James Raulston, Capt Edward Robinson, Inf
MOORE, R, QM Sgt, Col John Coffee, TN Vol Cav
MOORE, Reuben, QM Sgt, Col S Copeland, 3rd Regt TN Mil
MOORE, Richard, Pvt, Col Samuel Bayless, Capt John Brock, E TN Mil
MOORE, Richard, Pvt, Col Thos Williamson, Capt Thos Scurry, Vol Mtd Gunmen
MOORE, Richard, Pvt, Col Wm Lillard, Capt Thos Sharpe, 2nd Regt Inf
MOORE, Robert E, Cpl, Brig Gen Thomas Washington, Capt John Crawford, Mtd Inf
MOORE, Robert I, Pvt, Col N T Perkins, Capt Wm Johnston, Mil Inf
MOORE, Robert, Cpl, Col Alexander Loury, Capt George Sarver, Inf
MOORE, Robert, Cpl, Col Alexander Loury, Capt George Sarver, Inf; promoted
MOORE, Robert, Cpl, Col Thos Williamson, Capt John Doak & Capt John Dobbins, Vol Mtd Gunmen
MOORE, Robert, D V Mar (?), Col John Alcorn, Field Staff
MOORE, Robert, Pvt, Col John Alcorn, Capt John Baskerville, Vol Inf
MOORE, Robert, Pvt, Col John Coffee, Capt Alex McKean, Cav
MOORE, Robert, Pvt, Col John Coffee, Capt J W Byrn, Cav
MOORE, Robert, Pvt, Col John Coffee, Capt John Baskerville, Cav
MOORE, Robert, Pvt, Col N T Perkins, Capt John Doak, Vol Mtd Gunmen
MOORE, Robert, Pvt, Col Philip Pipkin, Capt James Blackmore, Mil Inf
MOORE, Robert, Pvt, Col Thos Williamson, Capt Robert Moore, Vol Mtd Gunmen
MOORE, Robert, Pvt, Col Wm Johnson, Capt Elihu Millikin, 3rd Regt E TN Mil
MOORE, Robert, Pvt, Gen Andrew Jackson, Capt Hugh Kerr, Mtd Rangers
MOORE, Robert, Pvt, Regt Commander omitted, Capt George Smith, Spies
MOORE, Robert, Q T (?), Col Robert H Dyer, no other information
MOORE, Robert, QM Sgt, Col John Coffee, TN Vol Cav & Mtd Gunmen
MOORE, Robert, QM, Col John Alcorn, TN Vol Cav
MOORE, Robert, Sgt, Col Thos Williamson, Capt James Pace, Lt Nealy, Vol Mtd Gunmen
MOORE, Samuel, Cpl, Col Samuel Bayless, Capt J B Bacon, E TN Mil
MOORE, Samuel, Pvt, Col John Barton, Capt Hugh Barton, Regt E TN Mil Inf
MOORE, Samuel, Pvt, Col N T Perkins, Co Commander omitted, Vol Mtd Gunmen
MOORE, Samuel, Pvt, Col S Copeland, Capt John Biles, Inf
MOORE, Samuel, Pvt, Regt Commander omitted, Capt John Crawford, Spies; transferred to Capt Runnell's Co
MOORE, Simon, Pvt, Maj Wm Russell, Capt I Williams, Separate Bn TN Vol Mtd Gunmen
MOORE, Spencer, Pvt, Maj Gen William Carroll, Col James Raulston, Inf
MOORE, Thomas, Pvt, Col Alexander Loury, Capt John Looney, W TN Inf
MOORE, Thomas, Pvt, Col R H Dyer, Capt A Allen, Vol Mtd Gunmen
MOORE, Thomas, Pvt, Gen Andrew Jackson, Capt Hugh Kerr, Mtd Rangers
MOORE, Thomas, Pvt, Regt Commander omitted, Capt James Craig, Inf
MOORE, Thompson, Cpl, Col Edwin Booth, Capt George Winton, E TN Mil
MOORE, Thompson, Pvt, Col John Brown, Capt Jas Preston, Regt E TN Mil Inf
MOORE, Warren, Pvt, Col John Winn, Capt John Spinks, Inf
MOORE, Whitfield, Cpl, Col Thomas Williamson, Capt Robert Moore, Vol Mtd Gunmen
MOORE, William H, Pvt, Col William Johnson, Co Commander omitted, E TN Drafted Mil; substitute
MOORE, William H, Pvt, Regt Commander omitted, Capt Archibald McKinney, Cav
MOORE, William L, Pvt, Col Wm Metcalf, Capt Andrew

## Enlisted Men, War of 1812

Patterson, Mil Inf; d 1-28-1815
MOORE, William, Pvt, Brig Gen Thomas Washington, Capt John Crawford, Inf
MOORE, William, Pvt, Col A Loury, Lt Col Wm Hammond, Capt Thomas Delaney, Inf
MOORE, William, Pvt, Col Edward Bradley, Capt John Moore, Vol Inf
MOORE, William, Pvt, Col Edwin E Booth, Capt John McKamy, E TN Mil
MOORE, William, Pvt, Col James Raulston, Capt Mathew Neale, Inf
MOORE, William, Pvt, Col John Cocke, Co Commander omitted, Inf
MOORE, William, Pvt, Col John Coffee, Capt John Baskerville, Cav
MOORE, William, Pvt, Col Joseph Hale, Capt John H Moore, Vol Inf; substitute for John Moore
MOORE, William, Pvt, Col R H Dyer, Capt Glen Owen, TN Vol Mtd Gunmen
MOORE, William, Pvt, Col R H Dyer, Co Commander omitted, Vol Mtd Gunmen
MOORE, William, Pvt, Col Samuel Bayless, Capt Churchman, E TN Mil
MOORE, William, Pvt, Col Samuel Bunch, Capt Joseph Duncan, E TN Drafted Mil
MOORE, William, Pvt, Col Thomas H Benton, Capt C E McEwin, Vol Inf
MOORE, William, Pvt, Col Thomas H Benton, Capt James McEwin, Vol Inf
MOORE, William, Pvt, Col Thomas H Williams, Capt Robert Moore, Vol Mtd Gunmen
MOORE, William, Pvt, Col William Lillard, Capt John Roper, E TN Vol Inf
MOORE, William, Pvt, Col William Pillow, Capt C E McEwin, Vol Inf
MOORE, William, Pvt, Col Wm Johnson, Capt James Rogers, E TN Drafted Mil
MOORE, William, Pvt, Col Wm Metcalf, Capt Alexander Hill & Capt John Cunningham, Mil Inf; d 2-7-1815
MOORE, William, Pvt, Maj Wm Russell, Capt John Cowan, Vol Mtd Gunmen
MOORE, William, Sgt, Col Wm Lillard, Capt Jacob Dyke, Vol Inf
MOORES, Joshua, Pvt, Col R H Dyer, Capt Bethel Allen, Vol Mtd Gunmen
MOORES, Richard, Pvt, Col Wm Lillard, Capt Wm Hamilton, E TN Vol Inf
MOORLOCK, George, Pvt, Col Ewen Allison, Capt Jonas Loughmiller, Mil; transferred to Capt McPherson's Co
MOORS, John, Pvt, Regt Commander omitted, Capt David Smith, Cav Vol; transferred to the Inf
MOOSELEY, Thomas, Pvt, Col Samuel Bunch, Capt Jones Griffin, Branch Srvce omitted; deserted
MOOSELY, Henry, Pvt, Col Samuel Bunch, Capt Jones Griffin, E TN Drafted Mil; deserted
MORE, Abraham, Pvt, Col Wm Johnson, Capt Joseph Kirk, Mil
MORE, John, Pvt, Col L Hammond, Capt J N Williamson, 2nd Regt Inf

MOREBEN, James, Pvt, Col Jno Coffee, Capt Robert Jetton, Cav
MOREHEAD, Charles, Pvt, Col Thos Williamson, Capt Thos Porter, Vol Mtd Gunmen
MOREHEAD, Henry, Sgt, Col Thos Williamson, Capt Thos Porter, Vol Mtd Gunmen; promoted from Pvt
MOREHEAD, Jacob, Pvt, Col Thos Williamson, Capt Thos Porter, Vol Mtd Gunmen
MOREHEAD, Jacob, Pvt, Lt John Harris, Co Commander omitted, Det of Inf
MOREHEAD, John, Pvt, Col Thos Williamson, Capt Thos Porter, Vol Mtd Gunmen
MOREHEAD, William, Pvt, Col John Cocke, Capt Samuel Caruthers, Inf
MOREHEAD, William, Pvt, Lt John Scott, Co Commander omitted, Det of Inf
MORELAND, Samuel, Pvt, Maj Wm Russell, Capt Isaac Williams, Separate Bn of TN Vol Mtd Gunmen
MORELAND, William jr, Pvt, Col Wm Johnson, Capt Henry Hunter, E TN Mil; left at Camp Ross as Band Guard
MORELAND, William sr, Pvt, Col Wm Johnson, Capt Henry Hunter, E TN Mil
MORELOCK, George, Pvt, Col Samuel Bunch, Capt Geo McPherson, E TN Mil; joined from Capt Loughmiller's Co
MORELOCK, Samuel, Cpl, Col Wm Johnson, Capt Benj Powell, E TN Mil; discharged for inability
MORELOCK, William jr, Pvt, Col Wm Johnson, Capt Henry Hunter, E TN Mil
MORGAN, Archibald, Pvt, Col A Cheatham, Capt Geo G Chapman, Inf
MORGAN, Archibald, Pvt, Col Philip Pipkin, Capt John Strother, Mil; deserted
MORGAN, Armstead H, Pvt, Col Philip Pipkin, Capt John Strother, Mil
MORGAN, Benjamin, Pvt, Col John K Wynne, Capt Bayless E Prince, Inf
MORGAN, Charles, Pvt, Col Edwin Booth, Capt Vernon, E TN Mil; joined from Capt Sharp's Co
MORGAN, Daniel, Pvt, Col John Alcorn, Capt John Baskerville, Vol Inf
MORGAN, George, Pvt, Maj Gen A Jackson, Capt Wm Carroll, Vol Inf; absent from the state
MORGAN, Gideon, Pvt, Col John Williams, Capt William Walker, Vol
MORGAN, Henry, Pvt, Col Wm Hall, Capt John Moore, Vol Inf
MORGAN, Henry, Pvt, Col Wm Metcalf, Capt Thomas Marks, Mil Inf
MORGAN, Henry, Sgt, Col S Copeland, Capt John Holshouser, Inf
MORGAN, James, Far, Maj Wm Russell, Capt Isaac Williams, Separate Bn of TN Vol Mtd Gunmen; also under Col R H Dyer
MORGAN, James, Pvt, Col Newton Cannon, Capt Isaac Williams, Mtd Riflemen
MORGAN, John, 3 Cpl, Col John Cocke, Capt Joseph Price, Inf
MORGAN, John, Dmr, Col Philip Pipkin, Capt John

-369

## Enlisted Men, War of 1812

Strother, Mil
MORGAN, John, Pvt, Col Edwin Booth, Capt Vernon, E TN Mil
MORGAN, John, Pvt, Col James Raulston, Capt Daniel Newman, Inf
MORGAN, John, Pvt, Col Jno Coffee, Capt Frederick Stump, Cav
MORGAN, John, Pvt, Col John Alcorn, Capt Fred Stump, Cav
MORGAN, John, Pvt, Col John Brown, Capt Wm White, E TN Vol Mtd Inf
MORGAN, John, Pvt, Col John Cocke, Capt Bird Nance, Inf
MORGAN, John, Pvt, Col T McCrory, Capt A Metcalf, Mil Inf
MORGAN, John, Pvt, Regt Commander omitted, Lt John Scott, Det of Inf
MORGAN, Joseph, Pvt, Col Edwin Booth, Capt Richard Marshall, Drafted Mil
MORGAN, Joseph, Pvt, Col James Raulston, Capt Mathew Cowan, Inf; d 2-15-1815
MORGAN, Joseph, Pvt, Col R C Napier, Capt Edward Neblett, Mil Inf
MORGAN, Joseph, Pvt, Col R H Dyer, Capt James McMahon, TN Vol Mtd Gunmen
MORGAN, Joseph, Pvt, Maj Gen William Carroll, Col James Raulston, Capt Elijah Haynie, Inf
MORGAN, Joseph, Pvt, Maj Wm Russell, Capt Isaac Williams, Separate Bn TN Vol Mtd Gunmen
MORGAN, Mathew, Pvt, Lt Col L Hammond, Capt Arahel Rains, Inf
MORGAN, Nathan, Pvt, Col John Wynne, Capt John Porter, Inf
MORGAN, Nathaniel, Pvt, Col A Loury, Lt Col L Hammond, Capt Arahel Rains, Inf
MORGAN, Nathaniel, Pvt, Col Wm Lillard, Capt Hugh Martin, E TN Vol Inf
MORGAN, Silas, Pvt, Regt Commander omitted, Capt Wyatt Fussell, Det of Inf
MORGAN, Simon, Pvt, Maj Gen Wm Carroll, Col Wm Metcalf, Capt John Jackson, Inf
MORGAN, Solomon, Pvt, Col Ewen Allison, Capt Wm King, Drafted Mil
MORGAN, Solomon, Pvt, Col Philip Pipkin, Capt Ebenezer Kirkpatrick, Mil Inf; deserted
MORGAN, Thomas, Pvt, Col James Raulston, Capt Mathew Cowan, Inf; d 1-22-1815
MORGAN, Thomas, Pvt, Col Samuel Bunch, Lt Jno Harris, E TN Mil
MORGAN, William, Pvt, Col Ewen Allison, Capt Wm King, Drafted Mil
MORGAN, William, Pvt, Col Samuel Bunch, Capt Geo McPherson, E TN Mil; joined from Capt Everett Co
MORGAN, William, Pvt, Col Samuel Bunch, Capt William Jobe, E TN Vol Mtd Inf
MORGAN, William, Pvt, Col Wm Lillard, Capt Wm Hamilton, E TN Vol Inf
MORGAN, William, Pvt, Lt Col Archer Cheatham, Capt Meredith Walker, Inf
MORGAN, William, Pvt, Regt Commander omitted, Capt James Cowan, Mtd Inf; d 2-16-1814
MORGAN, Willis, Dmr, Col Wm Johnson, Capt Wm Alexander, Det of E TN Drafted Mil
MORGAN, Willis, Pvt, Col John Cocke, Capt John Weakley, Inf
MORGIN, Lewis, Ffr, Col Wm Johnson, Capt Wm Alexander, Det of E TN Drafted Mil
MORIS, Boze, Pvt, Col Edward Bradley, Capt Abraham Bledsoe, Riflemen
MORLOCK, Jocob, Pvt, Col Ewen Allison, Capt Joseph Everett, E TN Mil
MORPHET, Robert, Pvt, Col William Hall, Capt Abraham Bledsoe, Vol Inf
MORPHINES, James, Pvt, Col Robert Steele, Capt James Randals, Inf
MORPHUS, Ezekiel, Pvt, Col Wm Metcalf, Capt Thomas Marks, Mil Inf
MORRELL, Reece, Pvt, Col John K Winn, Capt Bailey Butler, Inf
MORRELL, Samuel, Pvt, Col S Copeland, Capt Jno Holshouser, Inf
MORRICE, Loveit, Pvt, Col Alexander Loury, Capt James Kincaid, Inf
MORRICE, Martin, Pvt, Col Samuel Bunch, Capt Wm Houston, E TN Vol Mtd Inf
MORRIDAY, Junior, Pvt, Lt Col Leroy Hammonds, Capt Thomas Delaney, Inf
MORRIDAY, William, 3 Cpl, Col R H Dyer, Capt Robert Evans, Vol Mtd Gunmen
MORRIS, Allen, Pvt, Col Wm Johnson, Capt Christopher Cook, E TN Mil
MORRIS, Allen, Pvt, Col Wm Johnson, Capt Joseph Kirk, Mil; substitute
MORRIS, Allen, Pvt, Col Wm Lillard, Capt Wm Hamilton, E TN Vol Inf
MORRIS, Amos, 2 Sgt, Col Alexander Loury, Lt Col Leroy Hammonds, Capt Thomas Delaney, Inf
MORRIS, Boze, Pvt, Col Edward Bradley, Capt Abraham Bledsoe, Riflemen
MORRIS, Boze, Pvt, Col Wm Hall, Capt Abraham Bledsoe, Vol Inf
MORRIS, Carter, Pvt, Col John Cocke, Capt Joseph Price, Inf
MORRIS, Charles, Pvt, Col John Cocke, Capt Joseph Price, Inf
MORRIS, Charles, Sdlr, Col Newton Cannon, Capt Andrew Patterson, Mtd Riflemen
MORRIS, Claiborne, Ffr, Col Edward Bradley, Capt Wm Lauderdale, Vol Inf
MORRIS, Claiborne, Pvt, Col Wm Hall, Capt Wm L Alexander, Vol Inf; also a Ffr
MORRIS, Daniel, Pvt, Col Wm Metcalf, Capt John Barnhart, Mil Inf; d 2-8-1815
MORRIS, David W, Pvt, Col Newton Cannon, Capt James Walton, Mtd Riflemen
MORRIS, Edward, Pvt, Col S Copeland, Capt Wm Douglass, Inf
MORRIS, Elijah, 2 Cpl, Col Wm Lillard, Capt Wm Gillenwater, E TN Vol Inf
MORRIS, Elijah, 2 Cpl, Maj John Chiles, Capt James Cummings, E TN Vol Mtd Inf

## Enlisted Men, War of 1812

MORRIS, Ennis, Pvt, Col Philip Pipkin, Capt Wm Mackay, Mil Inf

MORRIS, Enos, Pvt, Col John Coffee, Capt Daniel Ross, Mtd Gunmen

MORRIS, Esau D, Pvt, Col Robert Steele, Capt Samuel Maxwell, Mil Inf

MORRIS, George, Pvt, Col Edward Bradley, Capt Brice Martin, Vol Inf

MORRIS, George, Pvt, Col Edward Bradley, Capt Wm Lauderdale, Vol Inf

MORRIS, George, Pvt, Col Wm Hall, Capt Brice Martin, Vol Inf

MORRIS, George, Pvt, Col Wm Hall, Capt Wm L Alexander, Vol Inf

MORRIS, Hannah, Pvt, Regt Commander omitted, Capt Samuel Richardson, E TN Drafted Mil; deserted 4-11-1814

MORRIS, Hardy S, Pvt, Col Wm Lillard, Capt Hugh Martin, E TN Vol Inf

MORRIS, Hezekiah, Pvt, Col Wm Metcalf, Capt Wm Sitton, Mil Inf

MORRIS, Isaac, Pvt, Col Alexander Loury, Capt George Sarver, Inf

MORRIS, Isaac, Pvt, Col John Alcorn, Capt John W Byrns, Cav

MORRIS, Isaac, Pvt, Col John Coffee, Capt John W Byrns, Cav

MORRIS, Isaac, Pvt, Col Wm Hall, Capt John Moore, Vol Inf

MORRIS, Isaac, Pvt, Lt Col Archer Cheatham, Capt Meredith Walker, Inf

MORRIS, Jacob, Pvt, Col Samuel Bunch, Capt George McPherson, E TN Mil; joined from Capt Griffin's Co

MORRIS, Jacob, Sgt, Col Ewen Allison, Capt Jonas Loughmiller, Mil; transferred to Capt Griffin's Co

MORRIS, James, Pvt, Col Edward Bradley, Capt Thos B Haynie, Vol Inf

MORRIS, James, Pvt, Col Edwin Booth, Capt Vernon, E TN Mil

MORRIS, James, Pvt, Col R H Dyer, Capt Bethel Allen, Vol Mtd Gunmen; d 2-21-1815

MORRIS, James, Pvt, Col Samuel Bunch, Capt Francis Berry, E TN Mil; attached to Capt Richardson's Co

MORRIS, James, Pvt, Col Wm Johnson, Capt John Tunnell, E TN Mil; substitute for Abner Farmer, has not appeared

MORRIS, Jefferson D, Pvt, Col John K Winn, Capt James Holleman, Inf

MORRIS, Jesse, Pvt, Col N T Perkins, Capt George W Marr, Mtd Vol Inf

MORRIS, Jesse, Pvt, Col R H Dyer, Capt Bethel Allen, Vol Mtd Gunmen

MORRIS, Jesse, Pvt, Col Wm Hall, Capt John Wallace, Inf

MORRIS, Jesse, Pvt, Lt Col Archer Cheatham, Capt Meredith Walker, Inf

MORRIS, John H, Pvt, Col Robert Dyer, Capt Bethel Allen, Vol Mtd Gunmen

MORRIS, John H, Pvt, Col Thos Benton, Capt Robert Caperton, Vol Inf

MORRIS, John, Cpl, Col S Bunch, Capt Francis Berry, E TN Mil; attached to Capt English Co

MORRIS, John, Pvt, Col A Cheatham, Capt Chapman, Inf

MORRIS, John, Pvt, Col John Wynn, Capt John Spinks, Inf

MORRIS, John, Pvt, Col S Bunch, Capt Jno English, E TN Drafted Mil; transferred to Capt English Co

MORRIS, John, Pvt, Col Thos Benton, Capt Robert Caperton, Inf

MORRIS, Jordan, Pvt, Col Wm Metcalf, Capt Hill & Capt John Cunningham, Mil Inf

MORRIS, Joseph, Pvt, Col S Wear, Capt John Childs, E TN Vol Inf

MORRIS, Joseph, Pvt, Col Thomas Williamson, Capt Wm Martin, Vol Mtd Gunmen

MORRIS, Joseph, Pvt, Col Thos Dyer, Capt Thomas White, Vol Mtd Gunmen

MORRIS, Joshua, Pvt, Col James Raulston, Capt James Cowan, Inf; d 1-28-1815

MORRIS, Mercer, Pvt, Col Robert Dyer, Capt Thomas Jones, Vol Mtd Gunmen

MORRIS, Misser, Pvt, Col A Cheatham, Capt Birdwell, Inf

MORRIS, Morris, Pvt, Col John Coffee, Capt Henry Bryan, Cav; promoted to Cpl then Capt

MORRIS, Morris, Pvt, Lt Col Jno Edmonson, Co Commander omitted, Cav; against Creek Indians

MORRIS, Neuburn, Pvt, Maj Gen Carroll, Col James Raulston, Capt John Robertson, Inf

MORRIS, Newman, Pvt, Col Edward Bradley, Capt Lauderdale, Vol Inf

MORRIS, Newman, Pvt, Col Wm Hall, Capt William Alexander, Vol Inf

MORRIS, Nickolas, Pvt, Regt Commander omitted, Capt Jas Haggard, Mtd Gunmen

MORRIS, Nimrod, Pvt, Col S Copeland, Capt John Dawson, Inf; d 3-15-1814

MORRIS, Oliver, 3 Cpl, Col Jno Brown, Capt William White, E TN Mtd Inf Vol

MORRIS, Oliver, Pvt, Col T McCrory, Capt Jno Shannon, Mil Inf

MORRIS, Reuben, Pvt, Col S Bunch, Capt Jas Cunningham, E TN Mtd Vol Inf

MORRIS, Reubin, Pvt, Col Ewen Allison, Capt Jonas Loughmiller, Mil

MORRIS, Richard, Pvt, Col S Bayless, Capt James Landen, E TN Mil

MORRIS, Robert, 4 Sgt, Col Jno Coffee, Capt Alexander McKeen, Cav

MORRIS, Robert, Blksmth, Col Jno Coffee, Capt Michael Molton, Cav

MORRIS, Robert, Pvt, Col Philip Pipkin, Capt John Robertson, Mil Inf

MORRIS, Robert, Pvt, Col William Lillard, Capt William Gillenwater, E TN Inf

MORRIS, Samuel, Pvt, Col Jno Coffee, Capt Michael Molton, Cav

MORRIS, Spencer, Pvt, Maj Gen Carroll, Col Jas Raulston, Capt Edward Robinson, Inf

MORRIS, Thomas, Pvt, Col Thomas Williamson, Capt

## Enlisted Men, War of 1812

Thomas Porter, Vol Mtd Gunmen
MORRIS, Thomas, Pvt, Col William Johnson, Capt Henry Hunter, E TN Mil
MORRIS, William, Pvt, Col Cannon, Capt Demsey, Mtd Gunmen
MORRIS, William, Pvt, Col Jas Raulston, Capt Jas A Black, Inf
MORRIS, William, Pvt, Col Jno Coffee, Capt Robert Jetton, Cav
MORRIS, William, Pvt, Col John Coffee, Capt Michael Molton, Cav
MORRIS, William, Pvt, Col John Coffee, Capt Robert Jetton, Cav
MORRIS, William, Pvt, Regt Commander omitted, Capt Jno Crane, Mtd Inf
MORRIS (MARRIS), Jesse, Pvt, Col John Cocke, Capt Richard Crunk, Inf
MORRISET, John, Pvt, Col Edwin Booth, Capt John Slatton, E TN Mil; appointed Forage Master
MORRISON, Alexander, Pvt, Col Edwin Booth, Capt John Porter, Drafted Mil
MORRISON, Andrew, Pvt, Col Jas Raulston, Capt John Black, Inf
MORRISON, Daniel, Pvt, Regt Commander omitted, Capt David Smith, Cav Vol
MORRISON, Danile, Pvt, Col John Cocke, Capt Joseph Price, Inf; substitute for Josiah Morrison
MORRISON, Edward, Ffr, Col Edwin Booth, Capt George Winton, E TN Mil
MORRISON, George, Pvt, Col Ewen Allison, Capt Jonas Loughmiller, Mil; transferred to Capt McPherson Co
MORRISON, George, Pvt, Col Samuel Bunch, Capt Geo McPherson, E TN Mil; joined from? Capt Loughmiller Co
MORRISON, James, Pvt, Col John Wynn, Capt Jas Cole, Inf; deserted
MORRISON, John, Ffr, Col John Cocke, Capt John Weakley, Inf
MORRISON, John, Pvt, Col S Wear, Capt Jas Tedford, E TN Vol Inf
MORRISON, John, Pvt, Col William Higgins, Capt Samuel Allen, Mtd Gunmen
MORRISON, John, Pvt, Col William Lillard, Capt Jacob Dyke, Vol Inf
MORRISON, Josiah, Pvt, Col John Cocke, Capt Joseph Price, Inf
MORRISON, Mathew, 2 Cpl, Col William Lillard, Capt Hugh Martin, E TN Vol Inf
MORRISON, Miles, Pvt, Col John Cocke, Capt Samuel Caruthers, Inf
MORRISON, Moses, Pvt, Col Ewen Allison, Capt Jonas Loughmiller, Mil; transferred to Capt Griffin Co
MORRISON, Thomas, Pvt, Col Samuel Bunch, Capt Edward Buchanan, E TN Mil
MORRISON, Thomas, Pvt, Regt Commander omitted, Capt Jas Williams, Mil Cav; d 11-28?-1813
MORRISON, William, 1 Cpl, Col William Lillard, Capt Hugh Martin, E TN Vol Inf
MORRISON, William, Pvt, Col Ewen Allison, Capt John Hampton, Mil; discharged by Gen Doherty for inability
MORRISON, William, Pvt, Col Samuel Bayless, Capt Joseph Rich, E TN Inf
MORRISON, William, Pvt, Col Wm Y Higgins, Capt Samuel A Allen, Mtd Gunmen
MORRISON, William, Pvt, Lt Col Jno Edmondson, Co Commander omitted, Cav
MORRISON, William, Pvt, Maj Porter, Capt Samuel Cowan, Cav
MORRISON, William, Pvt, Regt Commander omitted, Capt Jno Miller, Spies
MORRISS, Elijah, Pvt, Col William Lillard, Capt Robert McCalpin, E TN Inf; unable to perform duty
MORRISS, Gideon, Pvt, Maj Gen Andrew Jackson, Capt John Crane, Mtd Gunmen
MORRISS, James B, Pvt, Col Wm Hall, Capt John Kennedy, Vol Inf
MORRISS, John, Pvt, Col John Winn, Capt William Carruthers, W TN Inf
MORRISS, Mathew, Pvt, Maj Gen A Jackson, Capt John Crane, Mtd Gunmen; wounded at Ft Strother, since dead 2-1-1814
MORROW, Daniel, Pvt, Col Ewen Allison, Capt Joseph Everett, E TN Mil
MORROW, David, Pvt, Col A Loury, Capt J N Williamson, W TN Mil
MORROW, James, Pvt, Col James Raulston, Capt Elijah Haynie, Inf; d 2-5-1815
MORROW, James, Pvt, Lt Col Henry Bryan, Co Commander omitted, Inf
MORROW, James, Pvt, Regt Commander omitted, Capt James Cowan, Inf
MORROW, James, Sgt, Col Samuel Bunch, Capt Joseph Duncan, E TN Drafted Mil
MORROW, John, 2 Cpl, Maj John Childs, Capt Daniel Price, E TN Vol Mtd Inf
MORROW, John, 2 Cpl, Maj John Childs, Capt Daniel Price, Vol Mtd Gunmen
MORROW, John, Dmr, Maj Gen Wm Carroll, Col James Raulston, Capt Edward Robinson, Inf
MORROW, John, Pvt, Col S Copeland, Capt Moses Thompson, Inf
MORROW, John, Pvt, Col Thos Benton, Capt Henry L Douglass, Vol Inf
MORROW, John, Pvt, Col Wm Lillard, Capt Zacheus Copeland, E TN Vol Inf
MORROW, John, Pvt, Col Wm Metcalf, Capt Barbee Collins, Mil Inf
MORROW, John, Pvt, Maj John Chiles, Capt James Cummings, E TN Vol Mtd Inf; deserted
MORROW, Robert, Pvt, Col R H Dyer, Capt Betheal Allen, Vol Mtd Gunmen
MORROW, Samuel, Pvt, Col John Cocke, Capt Gray, Inf
MORROW, Thomas, Pvt, Lt Col Archer Cheatham, Capt Meredith Walker, Inf
MORROW, William, Pvt, Maj Gen Wm Carroll, Col James Raulston, Capt Elijah Haynie, Inf
MORROW, ____, Pvt, Col L Hammond, Capt J N Williamson, 2nd Regt Inf
MORROW (MARROW), David, 1 Sgt, Col Philip Pipkin, Capt John Strother, Mil

## Enlisted Men, War of 1812

MORTON, Asa, Blksmth, Col R H Dyer, Capt Thomas Jones, Vol Mtd Gunmen; d 3-17-1815

MORTON, David, Pvt, Col John Brown, Capt Hugh Barton, E TN Mil Inf

MORTON, Jacob, Pvt, Col A Loury, Capt J N Williamson, W TN Mil

MORTON, Jesse, Cpl, Col Samuel Bunch, Lt Jno Harris, E TN Mil

MORTON, Jesse, Pvt, Col N T Perkins, Capt Philip Pipkin, Mtd Riflemen

MORTON, John, Cpl, Col R H Dyer, Capt Bethel Allen, Vol Mtd Gunmen

MORTON, John, Pvt, Col Thos Benton, Capt Geo Caperton, Vol Inf; AWOL

MORTON, Joseph, Pvt, Maj William Russell, Capt John Trimble, Vol Mtd Gunmen

MORTON, Nicholas, Pvt, Col Wm Johnson, Capt Joseph Scott, E TN Drafted Mil

MORTON, Silas, 1 Cpl, Lt Col Hammonds, Capt James Kincaid, Inf

MORTON, Silas, Pvt, Col A Cheatham, Capt Charles Johnson, Inf

MORTON, Silas, Pvt, Col A Loury, Capt James Kincaid, Inf; appointed Cpl

MORTON, Thomas, Pvt, Col John Cocke, Capt John Dalton, Inf; d 3-20-1815

MORTON, Thomas, Pvt, Col John Coffee, Capt Thomas Bradley, Vol Cav

MOSBEY, John, 4 Cpl, Col John Cocke, Capt Bird Nance, Inf

MOSELEY, Daniel, Pvt, Col T Williamson, Capt A Metcalf, Vol Mtd Gunmen

MOSELEY, Isaac, Pvt, Col Samuel Bayless, Capt James Landen, E TN Mil

MOSELEY, John, Pvt, Col Wm Lillard, Capt Hugh Martin, E TN Vol Inf; deserted

MOSELEY, Thomas, Pvt, Col Thos Williamson, Capt John Crane & Capt James Cook, Vol Mtd Gunmen

MOSELY, Gillam, Pvt, Col John Cocke, Capt Bird Nance, Inf

MOSELY, John, Pvt, Col Wm Hall, Capt John Wallace, Inf

MOSELY, Thomas, Pvt, Col Wm Higgins, Capt A Cheatham, Mtd Riflemen

MOSER, Christopher, Pvt, Col Wm Metcalf, Capt John Barnhart, Mil Inf; d 3-13-1815

MOSER, George, Pvt, Col Edwin Booth, Capt Porter, Drafted Mil

MOSER, Henry, Sgt, Col Newton Cannon, Capt John Harpole, Mtd Gunmen

MOSER, John, Pvt, Col Wm Metcalf, Capt John Barnhart, Mil Inf

MOSER, Nicholas, Pvt, Col Samuel Bunch, Capt Andrew Breden, E TN Mil

MOSES, Asa, Pvt, Col A Loury, Lt Col L Hammond, Capt Thos Delaney, Inf

MOSES, Christopher, Pvt, Col Wm Johnson, Capt Elihu Milliken, 3rd Regt E TN Mil; transferred from Capt Churchman's Co

MOSES, James, Pvt, Col Edwin Booth, Capt Samuel Thompson, Mil

MOSES, James, Tptr, Col John Alcorn, Capt Frederick Stump, Cav

MOSES, James, Tptr, Col John Coffee, Capt Frederick Stump, Cav

MOSES, Joshua, Pvt, Col R H Dyer, Capt James Wyatt, Vol Mtd Gunmen; substitute for Jesse Street

MOSES, Peter, Pvt, Col Samuel Bunch, Capt Joseph Duncan, E TN Drafted Mil; joined from Capt Howell Co

MOSIER, Adam, Pvt, Col Samuel Bunch, Capt Jno English, E TN Drafted Mil

MOSLEY, Archibald, Pvt, Col Wm Metcalf, Capt Andrew Patterson, Mil Inf

MOSLEY, Henry, Pvt, Col R C Napier, Capt Edward Neblett, Mil Inf

MOSLEY, Henry, Pvt, Col Wm Johnson, Capt Benjamin Powell, E TN Mil

MOSLEY, John T, Pvt, Col Alexander Loury, Lt Col Leroy Hammonds, Capt Thomas Wells, Inf

MOSLEY, Thomas, Pvt, Regt Commander omitted, Capt Jas Williams, Mil Cav

MOSLEY, William, Pvt, Col Wm Lillard, Capt Hugh Martin, E TN Vol Inf; deserted

MOSS, Arnold, Pvt, Col Edwin Booth, Capt Richard Marshall, Drafted Mil

MOSS, Benjamin, Pvt, Col R H Dyer, Capt William White, Vol Mtd Gunmen; d 2-27-1815

MOSS, Cato, Pvt, Col Wm Hall, Capt John Wallace, Inf; substituted by Jos Moss

MOSS, David, Pvt, Col Thos Williamson, Capt Beverly Williams, Vol Mtd Gunmen; d 3-19-1815

MOSS, Edward, Pvt, Col Wm Metcalf, Capt Obidiah Waller, Mil Inf

MOSS, George, Pvt, Col Wm Lillard, Capt George Keyes, E TN Inf

MOSS, Gessum, Pvt, Col Wm Hall, Capt John Wallace, Inf

MOSS, Jesum, Pvt, Col Edward Bradley, Capt John Wallace, Vol Inf

MOSS, John P, Sgt, Col John Coffee, Capt Edward Bradley, Vol Cav

MOSS, Mathew, Pvt, Col Wm Metcalf, Capt Obidah Waller, Mil Inf

MOSS, Robert, Pvt, Col John Coffee, Capt James Terrill, Vol Cav

MOSS, Thomas B L, Pvt, Col John K Winn, Capt Robert Braden, Inf; promoted to QM Sgt in the 1st Regt

MOSS, Thomas B S, QM Sgt, Col John K Winn, 1st Regt TN Mil

MOSS, William, Pvt, Col John Alcorn, Capt Edward Bradley, Vol Cav

MOSS, William, Pvt, Col Robert Steele, Capt James Shenault, Mil Inf

MOSSES, Peter, Cpl, Col Samuel Bunch, Lt Jno Harris, E TN Mil

MOTERY (MALLORY), Will, Pvt, Col John Coffee, Capt John Baskerville, Cav

MOTHERAL, Joseph, Pvt, Col T T Perkins, Capt Mathew Patterson, Mtd Vol

MOTHEREL, James, Pvt, Regt Commander omitted,

## Enlisted Men, War of 1812

Capt Edwin S Moore, Mtd Riflemen
MOTHERHEAD, Simon, Pvt, Col R H Dyer, Capt Robert Evans, Vol Mtd Gunmen
MOTHRELL, John, Pvt, Maj Wm Carroll, Capt Lewis Dillahunty & Capt Daniel M Bradford, Vol Inf
MOTLOW, James A, Pvt, Regt Commander omitted, Capt Jos Williams, Mil Cav
MOUL, Jacob, Pvt, Col Wm Lillard, Capt Hugh Martin, E TN Vol Inf; deserted
MOULTON, Samuel, 2 Mate, Col Thos McCrory, 3rd Regt TN Mil
MOUNES, Elisha, Pvt & Ffr, Col Ewen Allison, Capt Jonas Loughmiller, Mil
MOUNT, John, Pvt, Col Samuel Wear, Capt Samuel Bowman, Mtd Inf
MOUNT, William, Pvt, Col John K Winn, Capt Wm McCall, Inf
MOUNTAIN, James, Pvt, Col Robert Steele, Capt Samuel Maxwell, Mil Inf
MOURNER, Walter, Pvt, Col Samuel Bunch, Capt Solomon Dobkins, E TN Drafted Mil; transferred to Capt English
MOURNING, Joseph, Pvt, Col Wm Lillard, Capt Wm Hamilton, E TN Vol Inf
MOURNING, Walter, Pvt, Col Samuel Bunch, Capt Jno English, E TN Drafted Mil; joined from Capt Dobkin's Co
MOURNING (MORIN), Samuel, Pvt, Col Jas Raulston, Capt Charles Wade, Inf
MOWDY (MANDY), John, Pvt, Col William Lillard, Capt George Keyes, E TN Inf
MOWRY, John, Pvt, Col John Brown, Capt John Chiles, E TN Vol Mtd Inf
MOWRY, Samuel, Pvt, Col John Brown, Capt John Chiles, E TN Vol Mtd Inf
MOYERS, William, Pvt, Col Ewin Allison, Capt Jacob Hoyal, E TN Mil; died 4-8-1814
MOZIER, Philip, Pvt, Col Ewen Allison, Capt Wm King, Drafted Mil; deserted
MUCKELROY, Micajah, Pvt, Col S Copeland, Capt Richard Sharp, Mil Inf
MUCKLEROY, Archibold, Pvt, Col Thos Williamson, Capt John Doak & Capt John Dobbins, Vol Mtd Gunmen
MUCKLEROY, Giles, Pvt, Gen Andrew Jackson, Capt Wm Russell, Mtd Spies
MUCKLEROY, Micajah, Pvt, Col Thos Williamson, Capt John Doak & Capt John Dobbins, Vol Mtd Gunmen; substituted David Youst
MUCKLEROY, William, Pvt, Col Thos Williamson, Capt Giles Burdett, Vol Mtd Gunmen
MUCKLEROY, William, Pvt, Col Thos Williamson, Capt Giles Burdett, Vol Mtd Gunmen; two Wm Muckleroy's on the roll
MULHERIN, Charles, 2 Mate, Col S Copeland, 3rd Regt TN Mil
MULHERN, James, Pvt, Maj Gen A Jackson, Col A Cheatham, Capt William Creel, Inf; promoted to Sgt in the 4th Regt
MULHERRIN, Charles, Pvt, Col R H Dyer, Capt Thomas Jones, Vol Mtd Gunmen

MULHOLLAND, William, Pvt, Regt Commander omitted, Capt Geo Smith, Spies
MULKY, John, Sdlr, Col Newton Cannon, Capt George Brandon, Mtd Riflemen
MULLEN, Joseph, Pvt, Maj Wm Woodfolk, Capt Ezekial Ross & Capt McCulley, Inf
MULLEN, Logan, Pvt, Col John K Winn, Capt James Holleman, Inf
MULLENDON, William, Pvt, Col Samuel Wear, Capt Simeon Perry, E TN Vol Mtd Inf
MULLENS, Loan, Pvt, Col P Pipkin, Capt J Robertson, Mil Inf
MULLENS, Nichols, Pvt, Col Wm Hall, Capt Jno Kennedy, Vol Inf
MULLER, John, Pvt, Col Alex Loury, Capt Jas Kincaid, Inf
MULLIN, Thomas, Pvt, Col Ewen Allison, Capt J Loughmiller, Mil
MULLINIA?, William, Pvt, Col Wm Johnson, Capt Jos Scott, E TN Drafted Mil
MULLINS, Elijah, Pvt, Col P Pipkin, Capt J Robertson, Mil Inf
MULLINS, James, Pvt, Col P Pipkin, Capt Jno Smith, Inf
MULLINS, James, Pvt, Col Samuel Bayless, Capt Jos Rich, E TN Inf
MULLINS, Jesse, Pvt, Col S Bunch, Capt F Register, E TN Mil; joined from Capt McPherson's Co
MULLINS, Jesse, Pvt, Col S Bunch, Capt Geo McPherson, E TN Mil
MULLINS, John, Pvt, Col Jno Brown, Capt Jas McKamey, E TN Mtd Gunmen
MULLINS, John, Pvt, Col Samuel Bayless, Capt John Brock, E TN Mil
MULLINS, John, Pvt, Col Samuel Bayless, Capt Jos Rich, E TN Inf
MULLINS, John, Pvt, Gen Andrew Jackson, Capt Hugh Kerr, Mtd Rangers
MULLINS, Joshua, Pvt, Col Samuel Bayless, Capt S Hendrix, E TN Mil
MULLINS, Nicholas, Pvt, Col Wm Hall, Capt Jno Kennedy, Vol Inf
MULLINS, William, Pvt, Col J K Wynn, Capt Jas Cole, Inf; deserted
MULLINS, William, Pvt, Col Wm Lillard, Capt Geo Keys, E TN Inf; deserted
MULLINS, William, Pvt, Regt Commander omitted, Capt Hugh Kerr, Mtd Rangers
MULUGHAN, John, Pvt, Col Robert Dyer, Capt Cuthbert Hudson, Vol Mtd Gunmen
MULVANY, Christian, Pvt, Col Wm Johnson, Capt Jas Stewart, E TN Drafted Mil
MULVANY, Henry, Sgt, Col Samuel Wear, Capt Samuel Bowman, Mtd Inf
MUNAHAN, John, Pvt, Col Wm Lillard, Capt Wm Gillenwater, E TN Inf
MUNCHER, John, Cpl, Col Wm Johnson, Capt C Cook, E TN Mil
MUNCHER, John, Cpl, Col Wm Johnson, Capt Jos Kirk, Mil
MUNCHER, John, Pvt, Col S Bunch, Capt F Register, E TN Mil; deserted

MUND, Dunkin, Pvt, Col Samuel Bayless, Capt S Hendricks, E TN Mil
MUNDINE, Charles, Pvt, Col P Pipkin, Capt Jas Blakemore, Mil Inf
MUNEY, John B, Pvt, Brig Gen N Taylor, Capt Wm Henderson, Spies
MUNFOLD, George, Cpl, Col Wm Johnson, Capt J R Rogers, E TN Draft Mil
MUNGAR, William, Pvt, Col E E Both, Capt Jno McKamey, E TN Mil
MUNGER, Henry, Pvt, Col Wm Johnston, Capt J R Rogers, E TN Draft Mil
MUNGLE, John, Pvt, Lt Col Hammond, Capt Jas Tubb, Inf
MUNN, James, Cpl, Col Samuel Wear, Capt Jesse Cole, Vol Inf
MUNSHER, John, Pvt, Col Wm Johnston, Capt Jos Kirk, Mil
MUNSON, Philip L, Pvt, Col Samuel Wear, Capt Jno Stephens, E TN Vol Inf
MURDICK, John, Sgt, Col E Booth, Capt Jno McKamey, E TN Mil
MURDOCK, William, Cpl, Col T H Benton, Capt G W Gibbs, Vol Inf
MURFREY, Mathias B, Pvt, Col N T Perkins, Capt M Johnston, Mil Inf
MURPHEY, David, Pvt, Col Wm Metcalf, Capt Thos Marks, Mil Inf
MURPHEY, Dennis, Pvt, Col Ed Bradley, Capt J Kennedy, Riflemen; AWOL
MURPHEY, James, Cpl, Col S Bunch, Capt Jno Houk, E TN Mil; disch at Knoxville
MURPHEY, James, Pvt, Col E Boothe, Capt J Porter, Drafted Mil
MURPHEY, James, Pvt, Col Thos Williamson, Capt A Metcalf, Vol Mtd Gunmen
MURPHEY, John, Pvt, Col Jno Cooke, Capt Jno Weakley, Inf
MURPHEY, Levi, Pvt, Lt Col Leroy Hammond, Capt Jas Craig, Inf; died 2-11-1815
MURPHEY, Thomas, Pvt, Col Wm Metcalf, Capt Thos Marks, Mil Inf
MURPHEY, Uriah C, Pvt, Col T H Benton, Capt G W Gibbs, Vol Inf
MURPHEY, Uriah E, Pvt, Col T H Benton, Capt G W Gibbs, Vol Inf
MURPHEY, William, Pvt, Col R C Napier, Capt E Benson, Mil Inf
MURPHIE, John, Pvt, Col Wm Johnston, Capt Wm Alexander, Det E TN Draft Mil
MURPHREE, Martin, Cpl, Col E Booth, Capt Geo Winton, E TN Mil
MURPHREE, Uriah C., Sgt, Col Robert Steele, Capt Richard M Ratton, Mil Inf
MURPHREY, Robert, Pvt, Col Jno Cocke, Capt Jno Weakley, Inf
MURPHY, Benjamin, Cpl, Col Edwin Booth, Capt Porter, Drafted Mil
MURPHY, Daniel, Pvt, Regt Commander omitted, Capt Gray, Inf
MURPHY, Daniel, Pvt, Regt Commander omitted, Capt Josiah Askew, Inf
MURPHY, George, Cpl, Col R C Napier, Capt Andrew McCarty, Mil Inf
MURPHY, Hugh, Pvt, Maj John Chiles, Capt John Stephens, E TN Vol Mtd Inf
MURPHY, James, Pvt, Col John Williams, Capt Wm Walker, Vol
MURPHY, James, Pvt, Maj John Chiles, Capt Reuben Tipton, E TN Vol Mtd Inf
MURPHY, John W, Pvt, Col Wm Metcalf, Capt Bird L Hurt, Mil Inf; died 4-8-1815
MURPHY, John, Cpl, Col Wm Johnson, Capt Wm Alexander, Det E TN Draft Mil
MURPHY, John, Pvt, Col Jno Brown, Capt Jas Preston, E TN Mil Inf
MURPHY, John, Pvt, Col Jno Coffee, Capt John Baskerville, Cav
MURPHY, John, Pvt, Col John Cocke, Capt John Weakley, Inf
MURPHY, John, Pvt, Col S Copeland, Capt Allen Wilkinson, Mil Inf
MURPHY, John, Pvt, Col Wm Lillard, Capt Geo Argenbright, E TN Vol Riflemen
MURPHY, John, Pvt, Lt Col Jno Edmonson, Co Commander omitted, Cav
MURPHY, Robert, Sgt, Col Edwin Booth, Capt Porter, Drafted Mil
MURPHY, Robertson, Pvt, Col John Cocke, Capt John Weakley, Inf
MURPHY, Robertson, Pvt, Lt Col Jno Edmonson, Co Commander omitted, Cav
MURPHY, Samuel L, Pvt, Col A Cheatham, Capt Richard Benson, Inf
MURPHY, Samuel, Pvt, Col Samuel Wear, Col Samuel Bunch, Capt Wm Mitchell, E TN Mtd Inf
MURPHY, Silas, Pvt, Col Wm Johnson, Capt James R Rogers, E TN Draft Mil
MURPHY, Thomas, Pvt, Col Samuel Bunch, Capt James Penny, E TN Mtd Inf
MURPHY, Thomas, Pvt, Col Wm Lillard, Capt Geo Argenbright, E TN Vol Riflemen
MURPHY, Uriah, Pvt, Maj John Childs, Capt Reuben Tipton, E TN Vol Mtd Inf; Regt from Knox
MURPHY, Will, Pvt, Col Jno Coffee, Capt John Baskerville, Cav
MURPHY, William, Pvt, Col John Alcorn, Capt John Baskerville, Vol Inf
MURPHY, William, Pvt, Col Samuel Wear, Capt Rufus Morgan, E TN Vol Inf
MURPHY, William, Pvt, Col Thos Williamson, Capt Thos Scurry, Vol Mtd Gunmen
MURRAIN, John, Pvt, Col Samuel Bunch, Capt Edward Buchanan, E Tn Mil
MURRAIN, John, Pvt, Col Samuel Bunch, Capt Joseph Duncan, E TN Draft Mil; joined from Capt Buchanan's Co
MURRAIN, Robert, Pvt, Col Samuel Bunch, Capt Edward Buchanan, E TN Mil
MURRAIN, Robert, Pvt, Col Samuel Bunch, Capt Joseph Duncan, E TN Mil; joined from Capt Buchanan's Co

## Enlisted Men, War of 1812

MURRAY, Christopher, Pvt, Col Samuel Bunch, Capt Geo McPherson, E TN Mil; deserted
MURRAY, Iabash, Pvt, Col Samuel Bunch, Capt Jno Hawk, E TN Mil; joined from Capt English Co; disch inability
MURRAY, James, Sgt, Maj Wm Woodfolk, Capt Abraham Dudney & Capt John Sutton, Inf
MURRAY, Jobias, Pvt, Col Samuel Bunch, Capt Jno English, E Tn Draft Mil
MURRAY, Joseph, Pvt, Col A Cheatham, Capt Richard Benson, Inf
MURRAY, Joseph, Pvt, Col Samuel Bunch, Capt F Register, E Tn Mil
MURRAY, Joseph, Pvt, Col Samuel Bunch, Capt Geo McPherson, E TN Mil; deserted
MURRAY, Thomas, Pvt, Col Samuel Bunch, Capt Geo McPherson, E TN Mil; deserted
MURRAY, Thomas, Pvt, Col Samuel Bunch, Capt Jno Hawk, E Tn Mil; trans from Capt English's Co
MURRAY, ___, Pvt, Regt Commander omitted, Capt Geo Smith, Spies
MURRELL, Israel (Isaac), Pvt, Col Newton Cannon, Capt John Hanley, Mtd Riflemen
MURRELL, John, Pvt, Col S Copeland, Capt William Hodges, Inf
MURRELL, John, Pvt, Col Samuel Bunch, Capt Jno English, E Tn Draft Mil
MURRELL, Richard, Pvt, Maj Wm Russell, Capt Fleman Hodges, Vol Mtd Gunmen
MURRELL, Samuel, Pvt, Col Samuel Bunch, Capt Geo Gregory, E TN Draft Mil
MURRELL, Will, Pvt, Col John Coffee, Capt James Terrill, Vol Cav
MURRELL, William, Pvt, Col Wm Cheatham, Capt Hugh Virdwell, Inf
MURREN, James, Pvt, Col Edwin Booth, Capt Samuel Thompson, Mil
MURREN, John, Pvt, Col Edwin Booth, Capt Samuel Thompson, Mil
MURREY, John B, Pvt, Regt Commander omitted, Capt Wm Anderson, Spies
MURRIN, Henry, Pvt, Col Samuel Wear, Capt John Stephens, E TN Vol Inf
MURRIN, John, Pvt, Col Wm Metcalf, Capt Bird L Hurt, Mil Inf; died 12-30-1814
MURRIN, Robert, Pvt, Col Samuel Wear, Capt John Stephens, E Tn Vol Inf
MURRIN, Robert, Pvt, Regt Commander omitted, Capt Samuel Bunch, Branch omitted
MURRY, Abel V, Pvt, Col Newton Cannon, Capt John Hanley, Mtd Riflemen
MURRY, Amos, Pvt, Col John Brown, Capt Allen I Bacon, E Tn Mil Inf
MURRY, Bland, Pvt, Col John Alcorn, Capt John W Byrns, Cav; trans to Capt Evans Co
MURRY, Christopher, Pvt, Col Ewen Allison, Capt Jacob Hoyal, E TN Mil; joined from Capt McPherson's Co
MURRY, Christopher, Pvt, Col Samuel Bayless, Capt James Landen, E Tn Mil
MURRY, David, Pvt, Col Samuel Wear, Capt Robert Doak, E TN Vol Inf
MURRY, Edward, Pvt, Col Woodfolk, Capt Abraham Dudney & Capt John Sutton, Inf
MURRY, George, Pvt, Col William Lillard, Capt Robert McCalpin, E TN Inf
MURRY, James, 4 Sgt, Col Robert H Dyer, Capt Thos Jones, Vol Mtd Gunmen
MURRY, James, Pvt, Col Samuel Bunch, Capt John English, E TN Draft Mil
MURRY, John B, Pvt, Col Samuel Wear, Capt Rufus Morgan, E Tn Vol Inf
MURRY, John, Pvt, Col James Raulston, Capt Charles Wade, Inf
MURRY, John, Pvt, Col SAmuel Bayless, Capt Jonathan Waddell, E TN Mil
MURRY, John, Pvt, Maj Gen Carroll, Capt Francis Ellis, Inf
MURRY, John, Pvt, Maj Wm Woodfolk, Capt Abraham Dudney, Inf
MURRY, Joshua, Pvt, Col Samuel Bunch, Capt John English, E Tn Draft Mil
MURRY, Robert, 1 Sgt, Col John Cocke, Capt James Gault, Inf; died 2-9-1814 (SB 1815)
MURRY, Simon, Pvt, Col James Raulston, Capt Charles Wade, Inf; died 2-8-1815
MURRY, Thomas D, Pvt, Col Samuel Wear, Capt Rufus Morgan, E TN Vol Mil
MURRY, Thomas, Pvt, Col Ewin Allison, Capt Jacob Hoyal, E TN MIl; joined from Capt McPherson's Co
MURRY, Thomas, Pvt, Col Samuel Bunch, Capt John English, E TN Draft Mil
MURRY, Urial, Sgt, Col Wm Lillard, Capt Henry West, E TN Mil Inf
MURRY, William, 1 Cpl, Col James Raulston, Capt Henry West, Inf
MURRY, William, Pvt, Col Newton Cannon, Capt John Hanley, Mtd Riflemen
MURRY, William, Pvt, Col Samuel Bayless, Capt Joseph Rich, E TN Inf
MURRY, William, Pvt, Maj Woodfolk, Capt Abraham Dudney & Capt John Sutton, Inf
MURS, Allen, Pvt, Col Alexander Loury, Capt Geo Saver, Inf
MURSELL, Richard, Pvt, Col Ewin Allison, Capt Joseph Everett, E TN Mil
MUSCHEWHITE, John, Pvt, Col Samuel Bayless, Capt Joseph Goodson, E TN Mil
MUSE, Joseph, Pvt, Col John Williams, Capt William Walker, Vol
MUSE, Thomas, Pvt, Maj Woodfolk, Capt Daniel Ross, Capt McCalley, Inf
MUSGROVE, Edward, Pvt, Col Wm Johnson, Capt Joseph Scott, E TN Draft Mil
MUSGROVE, John, Pvt, Col Allison, Capt Samuel Allen, E Tn MIl
MUSGROVE, John, Pvt, Col Wm Lillard, Capt Benjamin King, E Tn Vol Inf
MUSGROVE, Jonas, Pvt, Col Thomas Williamson, Capt Robert Steele, Vol Mtd Gunmen
MUSGROVE, Thomas, Pvt, Col Thos Williamson, Capt

## Enlisted Men, War of 1812

Robert Steele, Vol Mtd Gunmen
MUSIC, Reuben, Pvt, Col S Copeland, Capt Alexander Provine, Mil Inf
MUSIN, William, Pvt, Col Samuel Bayless, Capt James Landen, E Tn Mil
MUSS, William, Pvt, Col Wm Lillard, Capt John Roper, E Tn Vol Inf
MYARS, Henry, Pvt, Col Thos Johnson, Capt James Cook, E TN Mil
MYARS, John, Pvt, Col John Brown, Capt Wm Christian, E TN Mil Inf
MYARS, John, Pvt, Col Samuel Bunch, Capt Francis Register, E TN Mil; joined from Capt Wilson Co
MYARS, John, Pvt, Col William Johnson, Capt Christopher Cook, E Tn Mil
MYERS, Charles, Pvt, Col Ewin Allison, Capt Thomas Wilson, E Tn Draft Mil
MYERS, Christopher, Pvt, Col Ewin Allison, Capt Joseph Everett, E TN Mil; deserted
MYERS, Christopher, Pvt, Col Samuel Bunch, Capt Francis Berry, E TN Mil
MYERS, Daniel, Pvt, Col Wm Lillard Lillard, Capt Benjamin King, E Tn Vol Inf
MYERS, David, Pvt, Col John K Wynne, Capt Baily Butler, Inf
MYERS, Elias, Pvt, Regt Commander omitted, Capt Edwin S Moore, Mtd Riflemen
MYERS, Elias, Tptr, Col John Coffee, Capt Daniel Ross, Mtd Gunmen
MYERS, Elisha, Pvt, Col Thomas Williamson, Capt Thomas Scurry, Vol Mtd Gunmen
MYERS, Frederick, Pvt, Col Ewin Allison, Capt William King, Draft Mil
MYERS, Frederick, Pvt, Col Wm Lillard, Capt Robert McCalpin, E TN Inf
MYERS, Henry, Pvt, Col Ewin Allison, Capt Joseph Everett, E Tn Mil
MYERS, Henry, Pvt, Col Ewin Allison, Capt Thomas King, Draft Mil
MYERS, Henry, Pvt, Col Ewin Allison, Capt Thomas Wilson, E Tn Draft Mil
MYERS, Henry, Pvt, Col John K Wynne, Capt Baily Butler, Inf
MYERS, Henry, Pvt, Col Wm Lillard, Capt George Keys, E Tn Inf
MYERS, Jacob, Pvt, Col Ewin Allison, Capt Henry McCray, E TN Mil
MYERS, Jacob, Pvt, Col William Lillard, Capt Jacob Dyke, Vol Inf; unable to perform duty
MYERS, John jr, Pvt, Col Ewing Allison, Capt Thos Wilson, E TN Draft Mil
MYERS, John, Pvt, Col Ewin Allison, Capt Thomas Wilson, E TN Draft Mil
MYERS, John, Pvt, Col Wm Lillard, Capt Thomas King, E TN Vol Inf
MYLES, Hartwell, Pvt, Regt Commander omitted, Capt John Gordon, Mtd Spies
MYNATE, William, Pvt, Col Edwin Booth, Capt Richard Sharp, E TN Mil
MYNATT, Buckner, Pvt, Col Bradley, Capt Moore, Vol Inf
MYNATT, Martain, Pvt, Col John Childs, Capt Daniel Price, E TN Vol Mil
MYNATT, Martin, Pvt, Maj Childs, Capt Daniel Price, Mtd Gunmen
MYNATT, Richard, 2 Sgt, Col Samuel Wear, Capt Robt Price, E TN Vol Inf
MYNATT, Silas, Pvt, Col Samuel Wear, Capt Robert Price, E TN Vol Mtd Inf
MYNATT, Thomas, Pvt, Col Edwin Booth, Capt Richard Sharp, E TN Mil
MYNATT, William C, Pvt, Col John Williams, Capt William Walker, Vol
MYRAC, Ridley, Pvt, Col Edward Bradley, Capt John Moore, Vol Inf
MYRAC, Sterling, Pvt, Col Edward Bradley, Capt John Moore, Vol Inf
MYRES, Adam, Pvt, Col Wm Johnston, Capt Jas Tunnell, E TN Mil
MYRES, John, Pvt, Col Jas Raulston, Capt James Cowan, Inf
MYRICK, Buckner, Pvt, Col Wm Hall, Capt John Moore, Vol Inf
MYRICK, Lemmel, Pvt, Col A Cheatham, Capt Smith, Inf
MYRICK, Moland, Cpl, Col A Cheatham, Capt Smith, Inf
MYRICK, Ridley, Pvt, Col Wm Hall, Capt Moore, Vol Inf
MYRICK, Walter, Pvt, Col John Coffee, Capt Blackman Coleman, Cav
NABLET, William, Pvt, Col Wm Metcalf, Capt Thomas Marks, Mil Inf
NAIL, Acquilla, Pvt, Maj John Childs, Capt Charles Conway, E TN Mtd Gunmen; Regt from Knox Co
NAIL, Alex, Pvt, Col Jno Brown, Capt Jas Standifer, E TN Vol Mil
NAIL, Archibald, 5 Cpl, Col Wm Metcalf, Capt Thomas Marks, Mil Inf
NAIL, Archibald, Pvt, Col John Coffee, Capt Edward Bradley, Vol Cav
NAIL, Archibald, Pvt, Col Philip Pipkin, Capt Henry Newlin, Mil Inf; deserted
NAIL, Charles, Pvt, Col Phillip Pipkin, Capt David Smith, Mil Inf
NAIL, George C, Pvt, Regt Commander omitted, Capt Nathan Farmer, Mtd Riflemen
NAIL, Ichabald, Pvt, Col J Alcorn, Capt Thomas Bradley, Vol Cav
NAIL, James C, Pvt, Col Robert Steele, Capt John Chitwood, Mil Inf; transferred to the Arty
NAIL, James C, Pvt, Col T McCrory, Capt William Dooley, Inf
NAIL, James, Cpl, Col Jno Brown, Capt Jas Preston, E TN Mil Inf; promoted from Pvt
NAIL, James, Pvt, Regt Commander omitted, Capt J Parrish, Branch Srvce omitted
NAIL, John L, Pvt, Col J Alcorn, Capt Thomas Bradley, Vol Cav
NAIL, John L, Pvt, Regt Commander omitted, Capt Nathan Farmer, Mtd Riflemen; transferred to the Arty
NAIL, John, Cpl, Col Edward Bradley, Capt Elijah _____, Vol Inf
NAIL, John, Pvt, Regt Commander omitted, Capt J Parrish, Branch Srvce omitted

## Enlisted Men, War of 1812

NAIL, Joseph, 1 Sgt, Maj John Childs, Capt Chas Conway, E TN Mtd Gunmen
NAIL, Mathew, Pvt, Col John Brown, Capt William White, E TN Vol Mtd Inf; promoted to QM Sgt
NAIL, Mathew, Pvt, Col John Williams, Capt David Vance, Mtd Mil
NAIL, Mathew, QM Sgt, Col John Brown, E TN Vol Mtd Gunmen
NAIL, Nathaniel, Pvt, Col John Williams, Capt David Vance, Mtd Mil
NAIL, Nicholas, Pvt, Col John Brown, Capt Charles Lewin, E TN Vol Mtd Inf
NAIL, Reuben, Pvt, Col Edward Bradley, Capt Early Benson, Mil Inf
NAIL, Reuben, Pvt, Col Robert Williamson, Capt Robert Steele, Vol Mtd Gunmen
NAIL, Samuel, Pvt, Col John Coffee, Capt Edward Bradley, Vol Cav
NAIL, Thomas, Cpl, Col Edwin Booth, Capt Vernon, E TN Mil
NAIL, William, Pvt, Col Wm Hall, Capt Henry Newlin, Inf
NAILER, James, Pvt, Maj Wm Russell, Capt William Chism, Vol Mtd Gunmen
NAIR, John M, Pvt, Brig Gen Jas White, no other information
NAIR, Price M, Pvt, Col Wm Johnson, Capt Jas Stewart, E TN Mil
NALE, Robert, Pvt, Col John Williams, Capt S Bunch, Mil Vol
NALLS, Alexander, Pvt, Lt Col Richard Napier, Co Commander omitted, Inf
NALLY, Reuben, Pvt, Lt Col Richard Napier, Co Commander omitted, Inf
NANCE, Phillip, Pvt, Col S Bayless, Capt John Brock, E TN Mil; furloughed for inability
NANCE, Reuben, 4 Sgt, Col N Cannon, Capt John Demsey, Mtd Gunmen
NAPIER, J W, QM, Col R C Napier, W TN Mil
NARE, Jonathan, Pvt, Col S Bunch, Capt Francis Register, E TN Mil
NARRED, Larkin, Pvt, Lt Col Henry Bryan, Co Commander omitted, Inf
NASH, Daniel, Pvt, Col S Bunch, Capt Geo McPherson, E TN Mil; joined from? Capt Register Co
NASH, George R, Pvt, Col Jno Coffee, Capt Blackman Coleman, Cav
NASH, George, Pvt, Col Jno Coffee, Capt Blackman Coleman, Cav
NASH, John, 1 Sgt, Col Jno Coffee, Capt Blackman Coleman, Cav
NASH, John, 3 Sgt, Maj John Childs, Capt Jas Cunningham, E TN Vol Mtd Inf
NASH, John, Pvt, Col Robert Dyer, Capt James Wyatt, Vol Mtd Gunmen
NASH, John, Pvt, Col S Bunch, Capt Jas Cunningham, E TN Vol Mtd Inf
NASH, John, Pvt, Col Wm Lillard, Capt Thomas Sharpe, 2nd Regt Inf
NASH, John, Sgt, Col John Alcorn, Capt Wm Locke, Cav
NASH, Jonathan, Pvt, Col S Bunch, Capt Geo McPherson, E TN Mil; joined from? Capt Register's Co
NASH, Thomas, Pvt, Col John Alcorn, Capt William Locke, Cav
NASH, Thomas, Pvt, Col John Coffee, Capt Blackman Coleman, Cav
NASH, Thomas, Pvt, Col S Bayless, Capt Joseph Rich, E TN Inf
NASH, Thomas, Pvt, Col Wm Hall, Capt William Alexaner, Vol Inf
NASH, Thomas, Pvt, Maj Wm Russell, Capt John Cowan, Vol Mtd Gunmen
NASH, William, Pvt, Col Ewen Allison, Capt Joseph Everett, E TN Mil; furnished a substitute
NATEN (NOLEN), George, Sgt, Col Ewen Allison, Capt Wm King, Drafted Mil
NATION, Abraham, Pvt, Col Thos Benton, Capt Benjamin Reynolds, Vol Inf; refused to march
NATION, Eli, Pvt, Col Wm Metcalf, Capt Bird L Hurt, Mil Inf
NATION, Joel, Pvt, Col Jno Brown, Capt Hugh Barton, E TN Mil Inf
NATIONS, Abraham, Pvt, Col R C Napier, Capt Early Benson, Mil Inf
NATIONS, Christopher, Pvt, Col Wm Johnston, Capt Joseph Kirk, Mil; never appeared
NATIONS, Christopher, Pvt, Col Wm Metcalf, Capt Bird L Hurt, Mil Inf
NATIONS, James, Pvt, Col Thos Williamson, Capt Robt Steele, Vol Mtd Gunmen
NATIONS, Nathaniel, Cpl, Col N T Perkins, Capt John B Quarles, Vol Mtd Inf
NATIONS, Nathaniel, Pvt, Maj Gen A Jackson, Col Thos Williamson, Capt Robt Steele, Vol Mtd Gunmen
NATIONS, Thomas, 4 Sgt, Col A Loury, Capt John Looney, 2nd Regt W TN Mil
NATT, James, Pvt, Capt Nathan Davis, Lt I Barrett, Inf
NAVE, Abraham, Pvt, Col John Brown, Capt Charles Lewin, E TN Vol Mtd Inf
NAVE, Abraham, Pvt, Col Wm Lillard, Capt John Roper, E TN Vol Inf
NAVE, Cornelius, Pvt, Col T McCrory, Capt Thos K Gordon, Inf
NAVE, Henry, Pvt, Col John Brown, Capt Charles Levin, E TN Vol Mtd Inf
NAVE, Henry, Pvt, Col Samuel Bunch, Capt Wm Jobe, E TN Vol Mtd Inf
NAVE, Jacob, Pvt, Col John Brown, Capt Charles Lewin, E TN Vol Mtd Inf
NAVE, John, Ffr, Col T McCrory, Capt Thos K Gordon, Inf
NAVE, Samuel, Pvt, Col Samuel Bunch, Capt Joseph Duncan, E TN Drafted Mil; transferred to Capt Buchanan's Co
NAWL, William, Pvt, Col John Winn, Capt Wm Carruthers, W TN Inf
NEACE, Phillip, Pvt, Col Ewen Allison, Capt Thomas Wilson, E TN Drafted Mil
NEAL, Andrew, Pvt, Col R H Dyer, Capt Ephraim D Dickson, TN Mtd Vol Gunmen
NEAL, Benjamin, Pvt, Col Samuel Bayless, Capt James Churchman, E TN Mil; d 3-28-1815

## Enlisted Men, War of 1812

NEAL, Benjamin, Pvt, Col Wm Metcalf, Capt Obidiah Waller, Mil Inf

NEAL, Braxton, Pvt, Col Wm Metcalf, Capt Obidah Waller, Mil Inf; d 2-15-1814

NEAL, Ezekiel, 1 Sgt, Col Wm Metcalf, Capt Wm Sitton, Mil Inf; d 1-30-1815

NEAL, Henry, Pvt, Col R C Napier, Capt James McMurry, Mil Inf

NEAL, Isam, Pvt, Col Philip Pipkin, Capt Henry M Newlin, Mil Inf

NEAL, Jacob, Pvt, Col Newton Cannon, Capt John Harpole, Mtd Gunmen

NEAL, Jacob, Pvt, Col T Williamson, Capt Beverly Williams, Vol Mtd Gunmen; d 2-25-1815

NEAL, James, Pvt, Col Thos Williamson, Capt William Martin, Vol Mtd Gunmen

NEAL, James, Pvt, Col Wm Metcalf, Capt Obidah Waller, Mil Inf; d 2-15-1815

NEAL, James, Pvt, Col Wm Pillow, Capt Thos Williamson, Vol Inf

NEAL, Jeremiah, Pvt, Col Samuel Bunch, Capt Francis Berry, E TN Mil; attached to Capt Gregory Co

NEAL, Jerimiah, Pvt, Col Samuel Bunch, Capt Geo Gregory, E TN Drafted Mil

NEAL, Jesse, Pvt, Col John Wynne, Capt John Spinks, Inf

NEAL, John, Pvt, Col John Cocke, Capt Bird Nance, Inf; discharged by Court Martial

NEAL, Robert, Pvt, Col Newton Cannon, Capt John Harpole, Mtd Gunmen

NEAL, Stephen, Pvt, Regt Commander omitted, Sgt John Patton, Det of Inf

NEAL, Thomas, Pvt, Col William Hall, Capt John Wallace, Inf

NEAL, William, Pvt, Col S Copeland, Capt Wm Evans, Mil Inf

NEAL, Zephaniah, Pvt, Col James Raulston, Capt Charles Wade, Inf

NEAL (NALE), Samuel, Pvt, Col Jno Coffee, Capt Robert Jetton, Cav

NEAL (NEIL), Jesse, Pvt, Col A Loury, Lt Col L Hammond, Capt Thomas Wells, Inf

NEALE, Andrew, 4 Cpl, Col R C Napier, Capt Early Benson, Mil Inf; promoted from Pvt

NEALE, James, Pvt, Col Newton Cannon, Capt Wm Martin, Mtd Gunmen

NEALE, Thomas, Pvt, Col Edward Bradley, Capt John Wallace, Vol Inf

NEALE, Thomas, Pvt, Col Newton Cannon, Capt Ota Cantrell, W TN Mtd Inf

NEALE, Turner, Pvt, Col Newton Cannon, Capt Ota Cantrell, W TN Mtd Inf

NEALY, James, Pvt, Col Edward Bradley, Capt Abraham Bledsoe, Riflemen

NEARGANT, William, Sgt, Col Jno Coffee, Capt Robert Jetton, Cav

NEATHERTON, Moses, Pvt, Col Wm Lillard, Capt John Neatherton, E TN Vol Inf

NEATON, William, Pvt, Col Wm Pillow, Capt Thos Williamson, Vol Inf

NEDWER (NEDEREER), Samuel, Pvt, Col Wm Lillard, Capt Benj H King, E TN Vol Inf

NEDWER (NEDERER), Jacob sr, Pvt, Col Wm Lillard, Capt Wm Lillard, Capt Benj H Kings, E TN Vol Inf

NEDWER (NEDERER), Jacob, Pvt, Col Wm Lillard, Capt Benj H Kings, E TN Vol Inf

NEEDHAM, Enoch, Pvt, Col Robert Steele, Capt Robt Campbell, Mil Inf

NEEDHAM, Isaac, Cpl, Col Robt Steele, Capt Robt Campbell, Mil Inf

NEEDHAM, John, Pvt, Col Samuel Bunch, Capt S Richardson, E TN Drafted Mil

NEEDHAM, John, Pvt, Regt Commander omitted, Capt Sam'l Richardson, E TN Drafted Mil; substitute for Robert Farris

NEEDHAM, Lewis, Pvt, Col R C Napier, Capt Andrew McCarty, Mil Inf

NEEL, Benjamin, Sgt, Col S Bunch, Capt George Gregory, E TN Drafted Mil

NEEL, James, Pvt, Col S Bunch, Capt Francis Register, E TN Mil; deserted

NEEL, Stoddard, Pvt, Col Samuel Bayless, Capt Joseph Goodson, E TN Mil

NEELLEY (NULLEY), Thomas, Cpl, Col Thomas McCrory, Capt Samuel McKnight, Inf

NEELLY, Joseph, Pvt, Col Newton Cannon, Capt George Brandon, Mtd Riflemen

NEELLY, Robert, Cor, Col R H Dyer, Capt Robert Edmondson, TN Vol Mtd Gunmen; d 11-2-1814

NEELY, Charles L, Pvt, Col Perkins, Capt Wm Johnson, Mil Inf

NEELY, Charles, Pvt, Regt Commander omitted, Capt James Terrell, Cav; promoted to Lt in Col Perkins Regt

NEELY, George, 3 Sgt, Col A Loury, Co Commander omitted, 2nd Regt W TN Mil; promoted to QM with the Chickasaws

NEELY, George, Pvt, Col Thomas H Benton, Capt C E McEwin, Vol Inf

NEELY, George, Pvt, Regt Commander omitted, Capt C E McEwin, Vol Inf; transferred to Capt Gordon's Spies

NEELY, George, Pvt, Regt Commander omitted, Capt John Crawford, Inf

NEELY, George, Pvt, Regt Commander omitted, Capt John Gordon, Mtd Spies

NEELY, Hugh, Pvt, Col Wm Metcalf, Capt A Hill & Capt John Cunningham, Mil Inf

NEELY, Hugh, Pvt, Col Wm Metcalf, Capt Wm Mullins, Mil Inf

NEELY, Isaac I, Pvt, Col Thomas H Benton, Capt James McEwin, Vol Inf; AWOL

NEELY, Issac, Pvt, Col Thomas H Benton, Capt James McEwin, Vol Inf

NEELY, James A, Pvt, Col Philip Pipkin, Capt Wm McKay, Mil Inf; transferred to Capt Mebane

NEELY, James S, Pvt, Col Thomas McCrory, Capt Samuel McKnight, Inf; promoted to Sgt Maj in Col McCrory's Regt

NEELY, James S, Sgt Maj, Col Thomas McCrory, Co Commander omitted, 2nd Regt TN Mil

NEELY, James, Pvt, Col Thomas Bradley, Capt Abraham

## Enlisted Men, War of 1812

Bledsoe, Riflemen
NEELY, James, Pvt, Col Thomas H Williamson, Capt Wm Martin, Vol Mtd Gunmen
NEELY, John C, Pvt, Col Thomas H Williamson, Capt Wm Martin, Vol Mtd Gunmen
NEELY, John, Cpl, Col Samuel Bunch, Capt Francis Berry, E TN Mil
NEELY, John, Pvt, Col Wm Pillow, Capt Thomas H Williamson, Vol Inf; transferred to Capt Gordon's Spies
NEELY, John, Pvt, Regt Commander omitted, Capt John Gordon, Mtd Spies
NEELY, Joseph, Pvt, Col N T Perkins, Capt Mathew Patterson, Mtd Vol
NEELY, Joshua, Pvt, Col Philip Pipkin, Capt John Robertson, Mil Inf; deserted 9-20-1814
NEELY, Pollas, Sgt, Col R C Napier, Capt Andrew McCarty, Mil Inf
NEELY, Robert, Blksmth, Col R H Dyer, Capt James McMahon, TN Vol Mtd Gunmen
NEELY, Robert, Dmr, Col Edward Bradley, Capt Wm Lauderdale, Vol Inf
NEELY, Robert, Dmr, Col Wm Hall, Capt Wm Alexander, Vol Inf
NEELY, Samuel, Pvt, Col A Loury, Capt John Looney, W TN Inf; d 2-4-1814
NEELY, Samuel, Pvt, Gen Andrew Jackson, Capt Nathan Davis, Inf
NEELY, Samuel, Pvt, Regt Commander omitted, Capt N Davis, Mil Inf
NEELY, William, Cpl, Col Thomas McCrory, Capt John Reynolds, Mil Inf; promoted from a Pvt
NEELY, William, Pvt, Col S Bunch, Capt George McPherson, E TN Mil
NEELY, William, Tptr, Col R H Dyer, Capt Thomas Jones, Vol Mtd Gunmen
NEIGHBOURS, Benjamin, Pvt, Col William Y Higgins, Capt Samuel Allen, Mtd Gunmen
NEIL, Cornelius, Pvt, Col Samuel Bunch, Capt George Gregory, E TN Drafted Mil
NEIL, Jacob, Pvt, Col Ewin Allison, Capt Allen, E TN Mil
NEIL, Jacob, Pvt, Col S Copeland, Capt Alexander Provine, Mil Inf
NEIL, James O, Pvt, Regt Commander omitted, Lt James Berry, Mtd Riflemen
NEIL, Joseph, Pvt, Col Samuel Bayless, Capt John Brock, E TN Mil
NEIL, Thomas A, Pvt, Maj William Russell, Capt John Trimble, Vol Mtd Gunmen
NEIL, Thomas, Pvt, Col A Loury, Capt James Kincaid, Inf
NEILL, Charles, Pvt, Regt Commander omitted, Capt Jas Terrill, Cav; promoted to Lt in Col Perkins Regt
NEILL, George A, Pvt, Regt Commander omitted, Capt Ephraim Dickson, Branch Srvce omitted
NEILL, James, Pvt, Col Thomas H Williamson, Capt John Dobbins & Capt John Doak, Vol Mtd Gunmen
NEILSON, George D, Pvt, Col John Brown, Capt Wm D Neilson, Regt E TN Vol Mil
NEILSON, James, QM Sgt, Col Wm Metcalf, 1st Regt W TN Mil Inf; promoted from the lines
NEILSON, William D, Pvt, Col T McCrory, Co Commander omitted, Inf
NELMS, Samuel, Pvt, Col Philip Pipkin, Capt Ebenezer Kirkpatrick, Mil Inf
NELMS, Thomas, Pvt, no other information
NELMS (NILMES), William, Pvt, Col R H Dyer, Capt Wm White, Vol Mtd Gunmen
NELSON, Ambrose, Pvt, Col John Cocke, Capt Bird Nance, Inf; d 2-22-1815
NELSON, Beverly, Pvt, Col Newton Cannon, Capt Thos Yardley, Mtd Riflemen
NELSON, David, Pvt, Col Wm Lillard, Capt Wm McLin, E TN Inf; deserted
NELSON, George D, Cpl, Col Samuel Bayless, Capt Joseph Hale, E TN Mil; promoted from Pvt
NELSON, Isaac, Pvt, Maj William Russell, Capt John Cowan, Vol Mtd Gunmen
NELSON, Isaac, Pvt, Regt Commander omitted, Capt James Cowan, Mtd Inf
NELSON, James, Pvt, Col R H Dyer, Maj Wm Russell, Capt Wm Russell, Vol Mtd Gunmen
NELSON, James, Pvt, Col Wm Johnson, Capt Andrew Lawson, E TN Drafted Mil; substitute for Jas Harvey
NELSON, James, Pvt, Col Wm Metcalf, Capt Barbee Collins, Mil Inf; promoted to QM Sgt
NELSON, James, Pvt, Maj Wm Carroll, Capt Wm Metcalf, Capt John Jackson, Inf
NELSON, James, Sgt, Col Philip Pipkin, Capt George Mebane, Mil Inf
NELSON, John, Cpl, Col Ewen Allison, Capt Jacob Hoyal, E TN Mil; transferred from Capt McPherson's Co
NELSON, John, Cpl, Col John Alcorn, Capt Wm Locke, Cav
NELSON, John, Cpl, Col Samuel Bunch, Capt Geo McPherson, E TN Mil
NELSON, John, Pvt, Col Ewen Allison, Capt Wm King, Drafted Mil
NELSON, John, Pvt, Col Wm Lillard, Capt Thos McChristian, E TN Vol Inf
NELSON, John, Pvt, Gen A Jackson, Capt Hugh Kerr, Mtd Rangers
NELSON, John, Pvt, Maj John Chiles, Capt Chas Conway, E TN Mtd Gunmen; substitute for Wm Jones
NELSON, John, Pvt, Maj John Chiles, Capt Chas Conway, E TN Vol Mtd Inf
NELSON, John, Pvt, Maj William Russell, Capt John Cowan, Vol Mtd Gunmen
NELSON, John, Pvt, Regt Commander omitted, Capt James Cowan, Inf
NELSON, John, Sgt, Col John Brown, Capt Wm White, E TN Inf
NELSON, John, Sgt, Regt Commander omitted, Capt Jno Miller, Spies
NELSON, Joseph H, Pvt, Col Samuel Bunch, Capt James Penny, E TN Mtd Inf
NELSON, Mark, Pvt, Maj Wm Russell, Capt Wm Russell, Vol Mtd Gunmen
NELSON, Moses, Cpl, Col Samuel Bayless, Capt Jonathan Waddle, E TN Mil
NELSON, Moses, Pvt, Col Ewen Allison, Capt Henry

## Enlisted Men, War of 1812

McCray, E TN Mil; transferred to Capt Register's Co

NELSON, Moses, Pvt, Col Samuel Bunch, Capt F Register, E TN Mil; joined from Capt McCrea's Co

NELSON, Nial, Pvt, Col Ewen Allison, Capt John Hampton, Mil

NELSON, Pleasant, 1 Sgt, Col Thos Benton, Capt Benj Reynolds, Vol Inf

NELSON, Preston, Pvt, Regt Commander omitted, Capt James Cowan, Mtd Inf

NELSON, Robert D, Pvt, Col Ewen Allison, Capt Thos Wilson, E TN Drafted Mil

NELSON, Samuel, Pvt, Col Thos Benton, Capt George Gibbs, Vol Inf

NELSON, Southway, Pvt, Col Wm Johnson, Capt Andrew Lawson, E TN Drafted Mil

NELSON, Thomas, Pvt, Col John Brown, Capt John Chiles, E TN Vol Mtd Inf

NELSON, Thomas, Pvt, Col John Coffee, Capt Blackman Coleman, Cav

NELSON, William, 4 Cpl, Col Alexander Loury, Lt Col L Hammonds, Capt Thomas Wells, Inf

NELSON, William, Pvt, Col Isaac Williams, Capt Thos Wilson, E TN Drafted Mil

NELSON, William, Pvt, Col Samuel Bayless, Capt Jonathan Waddle, E TN Mil

NELSON, William, Pvt, Col Samuel Bunch, Capt Jones Griffin, E TN Drafted Mil; joined from Capt Wilson Co

NELUMS, Jacob, Pvt, Maj Gen A Jackson, Col Thos Williamson, Capt Robert Steele, Vol Mtd Gunmen

NEPPER (NIPPER), William, Pvt, Col Alexander Loury, Capt Gabriel Martin, Inf

NERANITH, Thomas, Pvt, Col Philip Pipkin, Capt James Blakemore, Mil Inf; substitute for John Panky

NESBETT, John, Sgt, Lt Col L Hammonds, Capt James Craig, Inf

NESBETT, Nathan, Cpl, Col R H Dyer, Capt Isaac Williams, Vol Mtd Gunmen

NESBETT, Nathan, Sgt, Col R C Napier, Capt Drury Adkins, Mil Inf

NESBIT, Jeremiah, Pvt, Lt Col Richard Napier, Co Commander omitted, Inf

NESBIT, John, Pvt, Lt Col Richard Napier, Co Commander omitted, Inf

NESBIT, Joseph, Pvt, Lt Col Richard Napier, Co Commander omitted, Inf

NESBIT, Nathan, Pvt, Lt Col Richard Napier, Co Commander omitted, Inf

NESBIT, Nathan, Pvt, Regt Commander omitted, Capt Jos Williams, Mil Cav

NESBIT, Tom, Cpl, Lt Col Richard Napier, Co Commander omitted, Inf

NESBITT, John, Pvt, Regt Commander omitted, Capt Jos Williams, Mil Cav

NESBITT, John, Sgt, Col L Hammonds, Capt James Craig, 2nd Regt W TN Mil

NESBITT, Nathan, Pvt, Regt Commander omitted, Capt Jos Williams, Mil Cav

NESBITT, Robert, Cpl, Col R C Napier, Capt Drury Adkins, Mil Inf

NESBITT, Robert, Pvt, Lt Col Richard Napier, Co Commander omitted, Inf

NESBITT, Robert, Pvt, Regt Commander omitted, Capt Jos Williams, Mil Cav

NESMITTEL, Alexander, Pvt, Col John Brown, Capt Allen I Bacon, E TN Mil Inf

NESTER, John, Pvt, Col Samuel Bunch, Capt N Gibbs, E TN Drafted Mil

NETHERLY, William, Pvt, Col Ewen Allison, Capt Adam Winsell, E TN Drafted Mil

NETHERLY, William, Pvt, Col Samuel Bayless, Capt Solomon Hendricks, E TN Mil

NETHERLY, William, Pvt, Col Samuel Bunch, Capt F Register, E TN Mil; joined from Capt Winsel's Co

NEUGENT, William, Sgt, Col Jno Coffee, Capt Robert Jetton, Cav

NEVEL, John, Pvt, Col Robert Dyer, Capt James Wyatt, Vol Mtd Gunmen

NEVINS, Isaac, Pvt, Col John Cocke, Capt Geo Barnes, Inf

NEVINS, Isaac, Pvt, Col T McCrory, Capt Jno Reynolds, Mil Inf

NEVINS, Robert, Pvt, Col S Copeland, Capt David Williams, Inf

NEVINS, William, Pvt, Col S Copeland, Capt David Williams, Inf

NEW, Jacob, Pvt, Col T McCrory, Capt Jas Shannon, Mil Inf

NEW, John, Pvt, Lt Col L Hammond, Capt James Tubb, Inf

NEW, John, Pvt, Maj Wm Woodfolk, Capt McCulley & Capt Ezekial Ross, Inf

NEW, Samuel, Pvt, Col Edward Bradley, Capt Harry L Douglass, Vol Inf

NEW, Samuel, Pvt, Col Thomas Benton, Capt Harry L Douglass, Vol Inf

NEW, Spencer, Pvt, Col A Loury, Capt J N Williamson, W TN Mil

NEWBERRY, Alexander, Pvt, Regt Commander omitted, Capt James Cowan, Mtd Inf

NEWBERRY, David, Pvt, Col Wm Lillard, Capt William Gillenwater, E TN Mil

NEWBERRY, James, Pvt, Regt Commander omitted, Capt James Cowan, Mtd Inf

NEWBERRY, William, Pvt, Col Samuel Bayless, Capt Joseph Hale, E TN Mil

NEWBURY, James, Pvt, Col R H Dyer, Maj William Russell, Capt Wm Russell, Vol Mtd Gunmen

NEWCOME, William, Cpl, Col A Cheatham, Capt Wm Creel, Inf

NEWEL, James, Pvt, Col Wm Metcalf, Capt Bird L Hurt, Mil Inf; d 1-4-1815

NEWEL, Joseph, Pvt, Col James Raulston, Capt Daniel Newman, Inf

NEWEL, Thomas, Pvt, Col Wm Hall, Capt John Moore, Vol Inf

NEWEL, William, Pvt, Col Wm Hall, Capt John Moore, Vol Inf

NEWELL, Hiley, Sgt, Regt Commander omitted, Capt James Craig, Inf

NEWELL, Isaac J, Pvt, Col John Wynn, Capt Butler, Inf
NEWELL, Thomas, Pvt, Col A Loury, Capt James Kincaid, Inf
NEWHOUSE, Isaac, Pvt, Col Samuel Bayless, Capt James Landen, E TN Mil
NEWLAN, Eli, Pvt, Col S Copeland, Capt David Williams, Inf
NEWLAN, Jesse, Pvt, Regt Commander omitted, Capt Nathan Farmer, Mtd Riflemen
NEWLAND, John, Pvt, Col R H Dyer, Capt James White, Vol Mtd Gunmen
NEWLEN, Joseph, Pvt, Col Samuel Wear, Capt Jesse Cole, Vol Inf
NEWLIN, Henry M, Capt, Col Philip Pipkin, Capt Henry M Newlin, Mil Inf, Res omitted
NEWLIN, Henry M, Capt, Col Wm Hall, Capt Henry M Newlin, Branch Srvce omitted
NEWLIN (NEWLAND), Jesse, Sgt, Col Wm Hall, Capt Henry M Newlin, Inf
NEWMAN, Alexander, Pvt, Col Edwin Booth, Capt Richard Marshall, Drafted Mil
NEWMAN, Charles, Pvt, Col Samuel Wear, Capt Samuel Bowman, Mtd Inf
NEWMAN, Conrad, Pvt, Col Edwin Booth, Capt John McKamey, E TN Mil
NEWMAN, Daniel, Capt, Col James Raulston, Capt Daniel Newman, Inf
NEWMAN, Daniel, Pvt, Col T McCrory, Capt Thos K Gordon, Inf
NEWMAN, Edmunds, Pvt, Col Edwin Booth, Capt Porter, Drafted Mil
NEWMAN, George, Pvt, Col T McCrory, Capt Wm Dooley, Inf
NEWMAN, Hamander, Cpl, Col Wm Lillard, Capt Thos McChristian, E TN Vol Inf
NEWMAN, Henry, 3 Cpl, Col Samuel Bunch, Capt Jno McNare, E TN Mil; attached to Capt Duncan's Co
NEWMAN, Henry, Cpl, Col Edwin Booth, Capt John Lewis, E TN Mil; promoted from Pvt
NEWMAN, Henry, Cpl, Col Samuel Bunch, Capt Joseph Duncan, E TN Drafted Mil; joined from Capt McNare's Co
NEWMAN, Henry, Pvt, Col John Williams, Capt Wm Walker, Vol
NEWMAN, Isaac, Pvt, Col Samuel Bunch, Capt Isaac Williams, E TN Mil
NEWMAN, James, Pvt, Col Samuel Wear, Capt John Doak, E TN Vol Inf
NEWMAN, John, Pvt, Col S Wear, Capt Samuel Bowman, Mtd Inf
NEWMAN, John, Pvt, Col Samuel Wear, Capt John Doak, E TN Vol Inf
NEWMAN, Joseph, Pvt, Maj William Carroll, Capt Daniel Bradford & Capt Dillahunty, Vol Inf
NEWMAN, Owen, Pvt, Col S Bunch, Capt Daniel Yarnell, E TN Mil
NEWMAN, William, Pvt, Col Isaac Williams, Capt S Bunch, Mil Vol
NEWMAN, William, Pvt, Col John Wynn, Capt Wm Carothers, W TN Inf; transferred to Capt Holinman Co
NEWMAN, William, Pvt, Col S Bunch, Capt Jones Griffin, E TN Drafted Mil; joined from Capt Williams Co
NEWMAN, William, Pvt, Col William Metcalf, Capt Barbee Collins, Mil Inf
NEWSOM, Davenport, Pvt, Col William Y Higgins, Capt Adam Dale, Mtd Gunmen
NEWSOM, Davenport, Pvt, Maj Gen Wm Carroll, Capt Robinson, Inf
NEWSOM, Green B, Pvt, Col Phillip Pipkin, Capt John Strother, Mil
NEWSOM, Lawrence, Pvt, Col John Cocke, Capt Gault, Inf; d 4-12-1815
NEWSOM, Levy, Pvt, Col William Lillard, Capt Keys, E TN Inf
NEWSOM, Robert, Pvt, Col T McCrory, Capt Jno Reynolds, Mil Inf
NEWSOM, Solomon, Cpl, Col A Cheatham, Capt Wm Smith, Inf
NEWSOM, William, Pvt, Lt Col Leroy Hammonds, Capt Alexander Loury & Capt Wells, Inf
NEWSOM, William, Pvt, Regt Commander omitted, Capt Joel Parrish, Arty
NEWSOME, Henry, Pvt, Col Alexander Loury, Capt James Kincaid, Inf; d 2-19-1815
NEWTON, Benjamin, Pvt, Col Alexander Loury, Capt Alexander Hammonds & Capt Raines, Inf
NEWTON, Henry, Pvt, Col Ewen Allison, Capt William King, Drafted Mil
NEWTON, Isham, Pvt, Col Robert Dyer, Capt James Wyatt, Vol Mtd Gunmen
NEWTON, John, 1 Sgt, Col Thos Benton, Capt Jas McFerrin, Vol Inf
NEWTON, John, Sgt, Col Thos Benton, Capt Jas McFerrin, Vol Inf
NEWTON, Larkin, Sgt, Col John Cocke, Capt George Barnes, Inf
NEWTON, Lemmel, Pvt, Col S Bayless, Capt James Landen, E TN Mil
NEWTON, Robert, Pvt, Col R T Perkins, Capt Phillip Pipkin, Mtd Riflemen
NEWTON, William, Pvt, Col John Wynn, Capt John Porter, Inf
NEWTON, William, Pvt, Col N Cannon, Capt John Hanley, Mtd Riflemen
NEWTON, William, Pvt, Col Thos Benton, Capt Isaac Williams, Vol Inf
NIBLET, William, Pvt, Regt Commander omitted, Capt David Smith, Cav
NIBLETT, Stephen, Pvt, Col R T Perkins, Capt Geo Mars, Mtd Vol
NICELY, David, Pvt, Col S Bunch, Capt S Richardson, E TN Drafted Mil
NICELY, John, Pvt, Col S Bunch, Capt Geo McPherson, E TN Mil
NICHOLS, Bird, Pvt, Col T McCrory, Capt A Metcalf, Mil Inf
NICHOLS, David, Pvt, Col William Carroll, Capt Jackson & Capt A Metcalf, Inf; d 2-4-1815
NICHOLS, Davis, Cpl, Col William Russell, Capt John Cowan, Vol Mtd Gunmen

## Enlisted Men, War of 1812

NICHOLS, Elijah, Pvt, Col Robert Steele, Capt Jas Shenault, Mil Inf

NICHOLS, George, Pvt, Col Jno Brown, Capt Wm Christian, E TN Mil Inf

NICHOLS, George, Pvt, Col N Cannon, Capt Francis Jones, Mtd Riflemen

NICHOLS, James, Cpl, Col Wm Metcalf, Capt Barbee Collins, Mil Inf

NICHOLS, Jesse, Pvt, Col Robert Steele, Capt Jas Shenault, Mil Inf

NICHOLS, Joel, Pvt, Col Phillip Pipkin, Capt Balkeman, Mil Inf; replaced by Jas Altman

NICHOLS, Joel, Pvt, Col T McCrory, Capt A Metcalf, Mil Inf

NICHOLS, John, 2 Sgt, Col Wm Metcalf, Capt B L Hurt, Mil Inf

NICHOLS, John, 4 Sgt, Col Metcalf, Capt Wells, Mil Inf

NICHOLS, John, Cpl, Maj William Russell, Capt John Cowan, Vol Mtd Gunmen

NICHOLS, John, Pvt, Col S Copeland, Capt George, Inf

NICHOLS, Jonathan, 4 Cpl, Col N Cannon, Capt Geo Brandon, Mtd Riflemen

NICHOLS, Jordon, Pvt, Col William Metcalf, Capt William Mullen, Mil Inf

NICHOLS, Lawrence, Pvt, Col Robert Steele, Capt John Chitwood, Mil Inf

NICHOLS, Lemel, Cpl, Col John Alcorn, Capt Alexander McKeen, Cav; promoted to Sgt

NICHOLS, Lemmel, 1 Cpl, Col Jno Coffee, Capt Alexander McKeen, Cav

NICHOLS, Mathew, Sgt, Col S Copeland, Capt William Hodges, Inf

NICHOLS, Moses, Pvt, Col Wm Metcalf, Capt Wm Sitton, Mil Inf

NICHOLS, Robert, Pvt, Col P Pipkin, Capt Jno Blakemore, Mil Inf

NICHOLS, Solomon, Pvt, Col N T Cannon, Capt F Jones, Mtd Riflemen

NICHOLS, Solomon, Pvt, Maj Wm Woodfolk, Capt Jas Neil, Inf

NICHOLS, Terry, Cpl, Col N T Cannon, Capt F Jones, Mtd Riflemen

NICHOLS, Thomas, Pvt, Maj Wm Russell, Capt I Wiliams, Separate Bn of TN Vol Mtd Gunmen; under Col R H Dyer

NICHOLS, William, Pvt, Col John Brown, Capt Wm Christian, E TN Mil Inf

NICHOLS, William, Pvt, Col N T Cannon, Capt Geo Brandon, Mtd Riflemen

NICHOLS, William, Pvt, Col N T Cannon, Capt Jno Hanley, Mtd Riflemen

NICHOLS, William, Pvt, Col P Pipkin, Capt H M Newlin, Mil Inf

NICHOLSON, John I, Pvt, Col Wm Hale, Capt Jno Kennedy, Vol Inf

NICHOLSON, John I, Tptr, Col Jno Coffee, Capt Jas Terrill, Vol Cav

NICHOLSON, John J, Pvt, Col Wm Hall, Capt Jas Kennedy, Vol Inf

NICHOLSON, John jr, Pvt, Maj Wm Russell, Capt F Hodges, Vol Mtd Gunmen; substitute for Sam'l Bradley

NICHOLSON, John sr, Pvt, Maj Wm Russell, Capt F Hodges, Vol Mtd Gunmen; substitute for Sam'l M Ray

NICHOLSON, John, Pvt, Col Thos Benton, Capt Benj Reynolds, Vol Inf

NICHOLSON, Nicholas, Pvt, Lt Col Jno Edmonson, Co Commander omitted, Cav

NICHOLSON, Nicholson, Pvt, Lt Col A Cheatham, Capt Gabriel Martin, Mtd Inf

NICHOLSON, Wesley, Pvt, Maj Wm Russell, Capt F Hodges, Vol Mtd Gunmen; substitute for John Burleson

NICHOLSON, William, Sgt, Col S Copeland, Capt G W Stell, Mil Inf

NICHOLSON, Wych, Pvt, Col J R Winn, Capt Wm Caruthers, W TN Inf; transferred to Capt Holliman's Co

NICHOLSON, Wyche, Pvt, Col S Copeland, Capt R Sharp, Mil Inf

NICKELSON, Wythe, Pvt, Col J K Winn, Capt Jas Holleman, Inf

NICKERSON, John, 1 Lt, Col R C Napier, Capt Jno Chism, Mil Inf

NICKERSON, William M, Pvt, Col Thomas Williamson, Capt Robert Moore, Vol Mtd Gunmen

NICKINS, James, Pvt, Col Jno Raulston, Capt Thos Wade, Inf

NICKINS, Samuel, Pvt, Col Jas Raulston, Capt Chas Wade, Inf

NICKINS, William, Pvt, Col N T Cannon, Capt Wm Edwards, Regt Command

NICKOLAS, Agrippa, Pvt, Col T McCrory, Capt McKnight, Inf

NICKOLAS, Coalman, Ffr, Col Phillip Pipkin, Capt Geo Mebane, Mil Inf

NICKOLAS, Isaac, Pvt, Col N Cannon, Capt Martin, Mtd Gunmen

NICKOLAS, Thomas, Pvt, Col S Copeland, Capt David Williams, Inf

NICKOLAS, William, Pvt, Col A Cheatham, Capt R Benson, Inf

NICKOLAS, William, Pvt, Col S Copeland, Capt David Williamson, Inf

NICKOLS, Benjamin, Pvt, Col S Bunch, Capt William Jobe, E TN Vol Mtd Inf

NICKOLS, Bird, Pvt, Col T McCrory, Capt A Metcalf, Mil Inf

NICKOLS, Charles, Pvt, Col S Bayless, Capt Jones, E TN Drafted Mil

NICKOLS, James, Pvt, Maj Wm Woodfolk, Capt Jas Neil, Inf

NICKOLS, Jesse, 1 Cpl, Col Wm Johnson, Capt C Cook, E TN Mil

NICKOLS, Joel, 5 Cpl, Lt Col L Hammond, Capt Jas Tubb, Inf; substitute for Jas Altum

NICKS, Abraham D, Pvt, Regt Commander omitted, Capt Ephraim Dickson, Branch Srvce omitted

NICKS, Absolom D, Pvt, Col R H Dyer, Capt E Dickson, 1st TN Mtd Vol Gunmen; no service performed

NICKS, Doke, Pvt, Col Wm Metcalf, Capt Jno Jackson,

- 383

Inf
NICOLS, James, Pvt, Col Wm Metcalf, Capt B Collins, Mil Inf
NICOLS, Thomas, Pvt, Col Alex Loury, Lt Col Hammonds, Capt Thos Delaney, Inf
NIDIFER, Jacob, Pvt, Col Wm Johnson, Capt Jno Scott, E TN Drafted Mil; substitute for Jas Blemis
NIDINS, Wilson, Pvt, Col Wm Johnston, Capt E Milliken, 3rd Regt E TN Mil
NIELE, Thomas, Pvt, Col Thomas Williamson, Capt Jno Hutchings, Vol Mtd Gunmen
NIELL, Samuel, Pvt, Col Thomas H Williamson, Capt Scurry, Vol Mtd Gunmen
NIGHT, Allen, Pvt, Col Wm Metcalf, Capt Jno Barnhart, Mil Inf
NIGHT, James A, Pvt, Col Wm Johnson, Capt Jas Tunnell, 3rd Regt E TN Mil; d 1-19-1814, substitute for Wm Hinton
NIGHT, John A, Pvt, Col Wm Johnson, Capt Jas Tunnell, E TN Mil; substitute for Benj Cannon
NIGHT, John, Pvt, Col Jno Alcorn, Capt Wm Locke, Cav
NIGHT, John, Pvt, Col Jno Coffee, Capt B Coleman, Cav
NIGHT, Thomas, Pvt, Col Samuel Wear, Capt Jno Stephens, E TN Vol Inf
NIGHT, Thomas, Pvt, Lt Col A Cheatham, Capt Gabriel Martin, 6th Brig Mtd Inf
NIGHT, William, 1 Sgt, Col R C Napier, Capt E Neblett, Mil Inf
NILES, Jesse, Pvt, Col E Bradley, Capt H L Douglass, Vol Inf
NIPP, Daniel, Pvt, Col E Allison, Capt J Hoyal, E TN Mil; transferred to Capt McChereon's Co
NIPPER, Jordan, Pvt, Col Wm Lillard, Capt Thomas Sharpe, 2nd E TN Regt Inf
NIPPER, Jordon, Pvt, Col Samuel Bayless, Capt Jos Rich, E TN Inf
NISELY, James, Pvt, Col Wm Johnson, Capt H Hunter, E TN Mil
NIVANS, John, 2 Sgt, Col P Pipkin, Ens Wm Pegram, Det of Capt David Smith's Camp of W TN Mil
NIVENS, Joseph, Pvt, Col Wm Metcalf, Capt Alex Hill & Capt John Cunningham, Mil Inf
NIX, Caleb, Pvt, Col S Copeland, Capt Jno Dawson, Inf
NIX, Robert, Pvt, Col S Copeland, Capt Jno Holshouser, Inf
NIXON, John B, Pvt, Col Jno Cocke, Capt B Nance, Inf
NIXON, John, Pvt, Col Wm Metcalf, Capt B Hurt, Mil Inf
NIXON, Robert R, Pvt, Col Wm Metcalf, Capt B Hurt, Mil Inf; deserted
NIXON, Robert, 2 Sgt, Col P Pipkin, Capt Jas Blakemore, Mil Inf
NIXON, Robert, 3 Sgt, Col S Copeland, Capt John Dawson, Inf
NIXON, William, Pvt, Col R H Dyer, Capt Jas McMahon, 1st TN Vol Mtd Gunmen
NOAH, Abraham, Pvt, Gen Jackson, Capt Wm Russell, Mtd Spies
NOAKES, Jesse, Pvt, Col Jno Cocke, Capt Geo Barnes, Inf
NOBLES, Luke, Pvt, Col Wm Metcalf, Capt Wm Sitton, Mil Inf
NOBLES, Nathaniel, Pvt, Col Philip Pipkin, Capt Wm Mackay, Mil Inf
NOBLES, Nathaniel, Pvt, Col Wm Pillow, Capt C E McEwen, Vol Inf
NOBLET, William, Pvt, Col John Wynne, Capt Wm Wilson, Inf
NOBLET, William, Pvt, Col Wm Johnson, Capt Wm Alexander, Det of E TN Drafted Mil
NOBLET, William, Pvt, Col Wm Pillow, Capt C E McEwen, Vol Inf
NOBLETT, John, Pvt, Lt I Barrett, Capt Nathan Davis, Inf
NOBLY, John, Pvt, Col T McCrory, Capt Isaac Patton, Mil Inf
NOE, David R, Pvt, Col Samuel Bunch, Capt Isaac Williams, Mtd Vol
NOE, George, Pvt, Col Samuel Bunch, Capt Thos Mann, E TN Vol Mtd Inf; appointed Wagon Master
NOE, George, Wagon Master, Maj Gen John Cocke, E TN Vol Mtd Inf
NOE, Jacob, Sgt, Col Samuel Bunch, Capt Isaac Williams, Mtd Vol
NOE, Joseph, Pvt, Col S Copeland, Capt Solomon George, Inf
NOE, Peter, Cpl, Col S Copeland, Capt Solomon George, Inf
NOEL, Alfred, Pvt, Col Wm Lillard, Capt Wm Hamilton, E TN Vol Inf
NOEL, Elijah, Pvt, Maj Gen Wm Carroll, Capt Henry Hamilton, Inf
NOEL, Thomas, Pvt, Col Edward Bradley, Capt John Moore, Vol Inf
NOEL, William, Pvt, Maj Gen Wm Carroll, Capt Henry Hamilton, Inf
NOGGLE, David, Pvt, Col Wm Lillard, Capt Robert Maloney, E TN Vol Inf; unable to perform duty
NOKES, Thomas, Pvt, Regt Commander omitted, Capt Jno Gordon, Mtd Spies
NOKY, Thomas, Pvt, Col A Loury, Capt James Kincaid, Inf
NOLAN, Peyton, Pvt, no other information
NOLAN, Thomas, Pvt, Col John Williams, Capt Wm Walker, Vol
NOLAND, Abraham, Pvt, Col John Alcorn, Capt Frederick Stump, Cav; transferred to Capt Evan's Spies
NOLAND, Benjamin, Pvt, Commanders & Branch Srvce omitted; sent home for health (unable to do military duty)
NOLAND, David, Pvt, Col Wm Johnson, Capt James R Rogers, E TN Drafted Mil
NOLEN, Abraham, Pvt, Regt Commander omitted, Capt Robt Evans, Mtd Spies
NOLEN, Golsby, Pvt, Col Thos Benton, Capt Thos Williamson, Vol Inf
NOLEN, Goolsby, Pvt, Col Wm Pillow, Capt Thos Williamson, Vol Inf
NOLEN, James, Pvt, Col Wm Metcalf, Capt John Barnhart, Mil Inf
NOLEN, Thomas, Pvt, Col N T Perkins, Capt John B Quarles, Vol Mtd Inf
NOLEN, William, Pvt, Col Newton Cannon, Capt Wm Martin, Mtd Gunmen
NOLEN (NOLINS), John, Pvt, Col Newton Cannon, Capt

## Enlisted Men, War of 1812

Andrew Patterson, Mtd Riflemen
NOLER, Micajah, Pvt, Brig Gen T Johnson, Capt Robert Carson, Inf
NOLIN, Robert, Blksmth, Regt Commander omitted, Capt Robt Evans, Mtd Spies
NOLIN, Robert, Pvt, Col John Coffee, Capt Daniel Ross, Mtd Gunmen; transferred to Capt Evans Co
NOLIN, Thomas, Pvt, Col Thos Benton, Capt Thos Williamson, Vol Inf
NON, Jeremiah, Pvt, Col Wm Johnson, Capt James Stewart, E TN Mil
NORIS, David, Pvt, Col Wm Johnson, Capt James Stewart, E TN Mil
NORIS, Jeremiah, Pvt, Col Wm Johnston, Capt James Stewart, E TN Mil
NORMAN, Aaron, Pvt, Col Samuel Bunch, Capt Andrew Breden, E TN Mil
NORMAN, Daniel, Pvt, Col Thos Williamson, Capt James Pace, Lt Nealy, Vol Mtd Gunmen
NORMAN, Elisha, Pvt, Col Robert Steele, Capt John Chitwood, Mil Inf
NORMAN, Henry, Pvt, Col Jno Coffee, Capt Alexander McKeen, Cav; substituted Nathaniel Henderson
NORMAN, Hiram, Pvt, Col Edwin Booth, Capt Richard Marshall, Drafted Mil
NORMAN, John, Cpl, Col Newton Cannon, Capt Francis Jones, Mtd Riflemen
NORMAN, Levi, Pvt, Col John Alcorn, Capt Robt Jetton, Vol Cav
NORMAN, Nathan, Pvt, Col John Cocke, Capt John Weakley, Inf
NORMAN, Pleasant, Pvt, Col Samuel Bayless, Capt Joseph Rick, E TN Inf
NORMAN, Prestley, Pvt, Col John Cocke, Capt George Barnes, Inf
NORMAN, Robert, Pvt, Col Wm Metcalf, Capt Andrew Patterson, Mil Inf
NORMAN, Thomas, Pvt, Col Robert Steele, Capt James Randals, Inf; AWOL
NORMAN, Thomas, Pvt, Col Wm Metcalf, Capt Wm Sitton, Mil Inf
NORMAN, Wiley, Pvt, Maj John Childs, Capt Charles Conway, E TN Mtd Gunmen; Regimental Co Anderson
NORMAN, William, Pvt, Col Jno Coffee, Capt Robert Jetton, Cav
NORMAN, William, Pvt, Col Newton Cannon, Capt Francis Jones, Mtd Riflemen
NORMAN, William, Pvt, Col Philip Pipkin, Capt David Smith, Mil Inf
NORMAN, William, Pvt, Col T McCrory, Capt Jno Reynolds, Mil Inf; died 1-2-1814?
NORMAN, William, Pvt, Maj John Childs, Capt Charles Conway, E TN Mtd Gunmen; Regt from Anderson Co
NORMAND, Mathews, Pvt, Col Wm Lillard, Capt Geo Argenbright, E TN Vol Riflemen
NORMEN, Isaac, Pvt, Brig Gen T Johnson, Capt Robert Carson, Inf
NORR (NOON), Jeremiah, Pvt, Col Wm Johnson, Capt James Stewart, E TN Draft Mil

NORRID, Larkin, Pvt, Regt Commander omitted, Capt Jas Haggard, Mtd Gunmen
NORRID, Priestly, Pvt, Maj Gen Andrew Jackson, Capt Wm Carroll, Vol Inf
NORRIS, David, Pvt, Col Wm Johnson, Capt James Stuart, E TN Draft Mil
NORRIS, Ezekiel, Pvt, Regt Commander omitted, Capt James Williams, Mil Cav
NORRIS, Garland, Pvt, Col Samuel Bayless, Capt Jonathan Waddell, E TN Mil
NORRIS, Garrett, Pvt, Col Samuel Bayless, Capt Joseph Bacon, E TN Mil
NORRIS, Harmon, Pvt, Col S Bunch, Capt S Rickerson, E Tn Draft Mil; deserted
NORRIS, James, Pvt, Col R H Dyer, Capt Cuthbert Hudson, Vol Mtd Gunmen; died 2-12-1815
NORRIS, James, Pvt, Col Samuel Bunch, Capt S Richardson, deserted
NORRIS, James, Pvt, Regt Commander omitted, Capt Samuel Richardson, E TN Draft Mil
NORRIS, Jepe, Pvt, Commanders omitted, Mil Cav
NORRIS, Jeremiah, Pvt, Col Wm Johnson, Capt James Stewart, E TN Draft Mll
NORRIS, Jesse, Pvt, Col John Coffee, Capt Michael Molton, Cav
NORRIS, Jesse, Pvt, Col R H Dyer, Capt Joseph Williams, Vol Mtd Gunmen
NORRIS, John, Pvt, Col Thomas McCrory, Capt Isaac Patton, Mil Inf; deserted
NORRIS, Life, Pvt, Regt Commander omitted, Capt Jos Williams, Mil Cav
NORRIS, Nicholas, Pvt, Regt Commander omitted, Capt James Haggard, Mtd Gunmen
NORRIS, R, Pvt, Col S Bunch, Capt S Richardson, E TN Draft Mil
NORRIS, Robert, Blksmth, Regt Commander omitted, Capt James William, Mil Inf
NORRIS, Robert, Pvt, Lt Col John Edmondson, Co Commander omitted, Cav
NORRIS, Robert, Pvt, Regt Commander omitted, Capt Wm Peacock, Branch omitted
NORRIS, Thomas, Cpl, Col Newton Cannon, Capt Wm Edwards, Regt Command
NORRIS, Thomas, Pvt, Col S Bunch, Capt Samuel Richardson, E TN Draft Mil
NORRIS, William, Pvt, Col A Cheatham, Capt Richard Benson, Inf
NORRIS, William, Pvt, Col John Cocke, Capt John Dalton, Inf
NORRIS, William, Pvt, Col R H Dyer, Capt Joseph Williams, Vol Mtd Gunmen
NORRIS, William, Pvt, Col S Bunch, Capt S Richardson, E TN Draft Mil
NORRIS, William, Pvt, Col Samuel Bayless, Capt Joseph Bacon, E TN Mil
NORRIS, William, Pvt, Lt Col John Edmondson, Co Commander omitted, Cav
NORRIS, William, Pvt, Regt Commander omitted, Capt John Crane, Mtd Inf
NORRIS, William, Sgt, Col Thomas McCrory, Capt Abel Willis, Mil Inf

- 385

NORROD, Edward, Pvt, Unit Commanders omitted, Det of Inf
NORROD, Larken, Pvt, Lt Col Bryan, Co Commander omitted, Inf
NORROD, Larkin, Pvt, Regt Commander omitted, Capt Askew, Inf
NORROD, Samuel, Pvt, Unit Commanders omitted, Det of Inf of 26 Regt
NORSWORTHY, Willis, Pvt, Col R H Dyer, Capt Joseph Williams, Vol Mtd Gunmen
NORTEN, John, Pvt, Col N T Perkinsw, Capt John Doak, Vol Mtd Gunmen
NORTEN, Nicholas, Pvt, Col Edwin E Booth, Capt Porter, Draft Mil
NORTH, Gabriel, Pvt, Col Samuel Bayless, Capt Joseph Hale, E TN Mil
NORTHCUT, Alexander, Pvt, Col S Copeland, Capt Thompson, Inf
NORTHCUT, Archibald, Pvt, Col Wm Metcalf, Capt Obediah Waller, Mil Inf
NORTHCUT, John, Pvt, Col Wm Metcalf, Capt Alexander Hill & Capt John Cunningham, Mil Inf
NORTHCUTT, Isaac, Pvt, Col John K Wynne, Capt John Porter, Inf
NORTHWORTHY, Willis, Pvt, Regt Commander omitted, Capt James Craig, Inf
NORTON, John, 1 Lt, Col Wm Metcalf, Capt Obediah Waller, Mil Inf
NORTON, Sampson, Pvt, Col Wm Metcalf, Capt Obediah Waller, Mil Inf
NORTON, William, Blksmth, Col John Alcorn, Capt Robert Jetton, Vol Cav
NORTON, William, Pvt, Col John Coffee, Capt Robert Jetton, Cav
NORTON, William, Pvt, Col Samuel Wear, Capt Samuel Bunch, Capt Wm Mitchell, E TN Mtd Inf
NORTON, William, Pvt, Col Wm Metcalf, Capt Barbee Collins, Mil Inf
NORVELL, Isaac, Pvt, no other information
NORVELL, Joseph, Pvt, Gen Andrew Jackson, Capt D Deadrick, Arty
NORVELL, Kiley, Sgt, Regt Commander omitted, Capt James Craig, Mil Inf
NORVELL, William, Pvt, Col James Raulston, Capt Mathew Neale, Inf
NORVILL, John P, Pvt, Col Perkins, Capt McMahan, Mtd Gunmen
NORVILL, Thomas, Ffr, Col S Bunch, Capt Jno Hauk, E Tn Mil; joined from Capt Davis' Co
NORVILL, Thomas, Ffr, Col S Bunch, Capt Moses, E TN Draft Mil; trans to Capt John Houk Co
NORVILLE, Nathaniel, Cpl, Col Thomas Williamson, Capt John Hutchings, Vol Mtd Gunmen
NORWOOD, Charles W, Pvt, Maj John Childs, Capt John Stephens, E TN Vol Mtd Inf
NORWOOD, John, Pvt, Col Robert Dyer, Capt William Russell & Capt Maj William Russell, Vol Mtd Gunmen
NORWOOD, John, Pvt, Col William Higgins, Capt Samuel Allen, Mtd Gunmen
NORWOOD, Richard, 4 Sgt, Col William Higgins, Capt Samuel Allen, Mtd Gunmen
NORWOOD, William, Pvt, Gen Jackson, Capt J Reed, Inf
NOTHUN, John, Pvt, Col S Bayless, Capt Joseph Goodson, E TN Mil
NOTSON, Nicholas, Pvt, Col Edwin Booth, Capt George Winton, E TN Mil
NOTSON, Nicholas, Pvt, Col S Bunch, Capt Thomas Mann, E TN Vol Mtd Inf
NOWELL, Isaac G, Pvt, Col Wm Metcalf, Capt Sitton, Mil Inf
NOWELL, James, Pvt, Col John K Winn, Capt Robert Braden, Inf
NOWELL, Riley, Pvt, Col John Cocke, Capt Joseph Price, Inf; died 3-5-1815
NOWLAND, Henry, Pvt, Col R T Perkins, Capt John Doak, Vol Mtd Gunmen
NOWLAND, John, Pvt, Col Leroy Hammonds, Capt Geo Saver, Inf
NOWLEN, Jabas, Pvt, Regt Commander omitted, Capt Efrain Dickson, Branch omitted
NOWLEN, John, Pvt, Col Alexander Loury, Capt Geo Saver, Inf
NOWLIN, Abraham, Far, Col Robert Dyer, Capt Thos White, Vol Mtd Gunmen; killed in battle 12-25-1814
NOWLIN, George, Pvt, Col Thos Benton, Capt Geo Caperton, Inf
NOWLIN, Goldsberry, Pvt, Col Thos Benton, Capt Thomas Williamson, Vol Inf
NOWLIN, Iabas, Pvt, Maj William Russell, Capt Isaac Williams, TN Mtd Vol Gunmen
NOWLIN, James, Pvt, Maj William Russell, Capt Isaac Williams, TN Mtd Vol Gunmen
NOWLIN, John, Pvt, Col Robert Dyer, Capt Ephraim Dickson, TN Mtd Vol Gunmen; trans to Capt Williams' Co
NOWLIN, Lile, Pvt, Col N Cannon, Capt Andrew Patterson, Mtd Riflemen
NOWLIN, Paten (Payten), Pvt, Col N Cannon, Capt Andrew Patterson, Mtd Riflemen
NOX, Squire, Pvt, Col John Cocke, Capt James Gault, Inf
NUBY, Jeremiah, Pvt, Maj William Russell, Capt William Chism, Vol Mtd Gunmen
NUCHOLS, Starling, Pvt, Col Alexander Loury, Capt Gabriel Martin, Inf
NUCUM, David, Pvt, Col S Bayless, Capt Branch Jones, E TN Drafted Mil
NUGEUT, John, Pvt, Col John Alcorn, Capt Robert Jetton, Vol Cav
NUMAN, William, Pvt, Col John Wynne, Capt James Holleman, Inf; deserted
NUN, Elisha, Pvt, Col S Bunch, Capt Solomon Dobbins, E TN Drafted Mil
NUN, John, Pvt, Lt Col Hammonds, Col Alexander Loury, Capt Thomas Wells, Inf
NUN, Zephaniah, Pvt, Col William Metcalf, Capt Andrew Patterson, Mil Inf
NUNERY, Nathan, Pvt, Col John Cocke, Capt Samuel Caruthers, Branch omitted; died 3-22-1815
NUNLLY, Archilles, Pvt, Col Phillip Pipkin, Capt David Smith, Inf

## Enlisted Men, War of 1812

NUNLY, John, Pvt, Col Wm Pegram, Capt Phillip Pipkin, Branch omitted
NUNN, John, Pvt, Maj William Russell, Capt Isaac Williams, TN Vol Mtd Gunmen
NUNN, Thomas, Pvt, Col N Cannon, Capt Gabriel Martin, Mtd Gunmen
NUNN, Thomas, Pvt, Maj William Russell, Capt Isaac Williams, TN Mtd Vol Gunmen; joined by trans from Capt Dickson
NUNN, William, Pvt, Col Edwin Booth, Capt John Slatton, E TN Mil
NUNNERLY, Archibald, Col Phillip Pipkin, Capt David Smith, Inf; deserted
NURMITH, John, Pvt, Col William Higgins, Capt Thomas Eldridge, Mtd Gunmen
NUSOM, William, Pvt, Col A Cheatham, Gen Jackson, Capt Creel, Inf; trans to Capt Gidden's Co
NUSOM, William, Pvt, Col R C Napier, Capt Edward Neblett, Mil Inf
NUT, Jesse, Pvt, Col John Brown, Capt Charles Lewin, E TN Vol Mtd Inf
O'BRAN, Peter, 3 Cpl, Maj William Woodfolk, Capt James C Neil, Inf
O'DANIEL, Henry, Pvt, Regt Commander omitted, Capt Jas Craig, Mil Inf
O'DONALD, John, Pvt, Col Thos Benton, Capt N Gibbs, Vol Inf
O'DONEAL, Tate, Pvt, Col John Coffee, Capt David Smith, Vol Cav
O'DONNELL, John, Pvt, Col Thos Benton, Capt N Gibbs, Vol Inf
O'KELLEY, Benjamin S, Cpl, Col S Copeland, Capt Richard Sharp, Mil Inf
O'NEAL, Curtis, Pvt, Col P Pipkin, Capt Jas Blakemore, Mil Inf
O'NEAL, Jacob, Pvt, Col S Bunch, Capt Jno English, E TN Draft Mil
O'NEAL, Peter, Sgt, Col Wm Hall, Capt Jas Hambleton, Vol Inf
O'NEILL, James, Pvt, Regt Commander omitted, Capt Jas Terrill, Cav
OAKLEY, Armistead, Pvt, Col John K Winn, Capt Robert Bradin, Inf
OAKLEY, Armstead, Pvt, Col A Loury, Capt Gabriel Martin, Inf
OAKLEY, Jesse, Pvt, Col Philip Pipkin, Capt W Mackay, Mil Inf
OAKLEY, William, Pvt, Regt Commander omitted, Capt Jas Terrill, Cav
OAKS, Isaac, Pvt, Col Samuel Bunch, Capt Isaac Williams, E TN Mil
OAKS, Isaac, Pvt, Col Samuel Bunch, Capt Jno Houk, E TN Mil; joined from Capt Williams' Co
OAKS, Isaac, Pvt, Col Wm Johnson, Capt James Tunnell, E Tn Mil
OAKS, John, Pvt, Col Samuel Bayless, Capt Joseph B Bacon, E TN Mil; died 2-15-1814
OAKS, Josiah, Pvt, Col Wm Johnson, Capt James Tunnell, E TN Mil
OAKS, Richard, Pvt, Col Samuel Bayless, Capt Joseph B Bacon, E TN Mil

OANCE, Joseph, Pvt, Col Samuel Wear, Capt Rufus Morgan, E TN Vol Inf
OANSBY, Walter, Pvt, Col John Cocke, Capt Richard Crunk, Inf
OAR, Greenbury, Pvt, Col John K Winn, Capt Wm McCall, Inf
OAR, James, Pvt, Col N T Perkins, Capt John B Quarles, Vol Mtd Inf
OARE, John, Pvt, Col John K Winn, Capt John Porter, Inf
OARNUM, William, Pvt, Col Samuel Bunch, Capt F Register, E TN Mil; joined from Capt Loughmiller's Co
OAZLEY, John, Pvt, Col Jas Raulston, Capt James A Black, Inf
ODAIR, John, Pvt, Col Thos Benton, Capt Wm Moore, Vol Inf
ODAM, Jacob, Pvt, Lt Col L Hammonds, Capt James Craig, Inf
ODAM, John W, Pvt, Col R H Dyer, Maj Wm Russell, Capt William Russell, Vol Mtd Gunmen
ODAM, Lewis, Pvt, Col Thos Benton, Capt Wm Moore, Vol Inf
ODAM (ODUM), Lewis, Pvt, Col Wm Pillow, Capt Wm Moore, Inf
ODANIEL, William, Pvt, Col Wm Johnson, Capt James Tunnell, E TN Mil
ODEHFORD, John, Pvt, Regt Commander omitted, Capt Jos Williams, Mil Cav
ODELL, James, Pvt, Col John K Winn, Capt John Spinks, Inf
ODELL, Jeremiah, Pvt, Col Thos McCrory, Capt Abel Willis, Mil Inf; wounded 11-9-1813
ODELL, Jeremiah, Pvt, Col Wm Lillard, Capt Wm Lillard, E Tn Vol Inf
ODELL, William jr, Pvt, Col Wm Lillard, Capt Wm Lillard, E Tn Vol Inf
ODELL, William sr, Pvt, Col Wm Lillard, Capt Wm Lillard, E TN Vol Inf
ODELL, William, Pvt, Col Edward Bradley, Capt Abraham Bledsoe, Riflemen
ODELL (ODLE), John, 3 Sgt, Col Wm Lillard, Capt Jacob Hartsell, E TN Vol Inf
ODEN, John, Pvt, Col Jno Brown, Capt Wm D Neilson, E TN Vol Mil; deserted
ODEN, John, Pvt, Col Wm Johnson, Capt James R Rogers, E Tn Draft Mil
ODEN, Lewis, Pvt, Col Edwin Booth, Capt John McKamey, E Tn Mil
ODEN, Thomas, Pvt, Col Edwin Booth, Capt John McKamey, E Tn Mll
ODENEAL, Levi, Pvt, Col Wm Lillard, Capt Wm Lillard, E TN Vol Inf
ODENEAL, Tate, 2 Lt, Col R H Dyer, Capt Robert Edmonston, 1 TN Vol Mtd Gunmen; killed 1-4-1815
ODENEAL, Tate, Pvt, Col John Coffee, Capt John W Byrns, Cav
ODERN, Demsey, Pvt, Maj Wm Woodfolk, Capt Ezekial Ross & Capt McCully, Inf
ODIL (ODLE), Anderson, Pvt, Col Philip Pipkin, Capt Wm Mackay, Mil Inf
ODLE, Caleb, Pvt, Col Edwin Booth, Capt John Porter,

- 387

## Enlisted Men, War of 1812

ODLE, Enoch, Pvt, Col Thos Benton, Capt William J Smith, Vol Inf Drafted Mil
ODLE, Isaac, Pvt, Col Samuel Bayless, Capt Jos B Bacon, E TN Mil
ODLE, James, Pvt, Col Ewen Allison, Capt John Hampton, Mil
ODLE, Job (Joab), Pvt, Maj Wm Woodfolk, Capt Abraham Dudney & Capt John Sutton, Inf
ODLE, John, Pvt, Col Ewen Allison, Capt John Hampton, Mil
ODLE, Joseph, Pvt, Col S Copeland, Capt David Williams, Inf
ODLE, Murfee, Pvt, Lt Col L Hammonds, Col Alexander Loury, Capt Thomas Wells, Inf
ODLE, Reuben, Pvt, Col Samuel Bayless, Capt Jonathan Waddle, E TN Mil
ODLE, Solomon, Pvt, Col Philip Pipkin, Capt John Strother, Mil Inf
ODLE, William, Pvt, Col Ewen Allison, Capt John Hampton, Mil
ODLE, William, Pvt, Col Samuel Bayless, Capt Branch Jones, E Tn Draft Mil
ODLE, William, Pvt, Col Wm Hall, Capt Abraham Bledsoe, Vol Inf
ODOM, Britton (Burton), Pvt, Col T McCrory, Capt A Metcalf, Mil Inf
ODUM, Burton, Pvt, Col T McCrory, Capt A Metcalf, Mil Inf
ODUM, Eli, Sgt, Gen John Coffee, Co Commander omitted, Mtd Spies
ODUM, John W, Sgt, Maj William Russell, Capt William Russell, Vol Mtd Gunmen
ODUM, Lewis, Pvt, Col Thos Benton, Capt Wm Moore, Vol Inf
ODUM, Moses, Cpl, Col S Copeland, Capt Robert Steele, Mil Inf
ODUM (ODAM), Lewis, Pvt, Col Wm Pillow, Capt Wm Moore, Inf
OFFICER, James, Sgt, Regt Commander omitted, Capt John Miller, Spies
OFTENER, Henry, Pvt, Col Thos Benton, Capt Wm Moore, Vol Inf
OGALSBAY, William, Pvt, Col N T Perkins, Capt John Doak, Vol Mtd Gunmen
OGDEN, Isaac, Pvt, Col R C Napier, Capt Andrew McCarty, Mil Inf
OGLE, John, Pvt, Col Wm Johnson, Capt Andrew Lawson, E TN Draft Mil
OGLE, Thomas, Pvt, Col Wm Johnson, Capt Andrew Lawson, E TN Draft Mil
OGLESBEE, Reubin, Pvt, Col R C Napier, Capt Edward Neblett, Mil Inf
OGLESBY, Peter, Pvt, Col Wm Johnson, Capt James Stewart, E TN Draft Mil
OGLEVIE, Elisha, Cpl, Col Robert Steele, Capt Robert Campbell, Mil Inf
OINT, Belitha, Pvt, Col Robert Jarmon, Capt Nathan Peoples, Inf
OKELLEY (OAKLEY), Armstead, Pvt, Col A Loury, Capt Gabriel Martin, Inf
OKENTUCKYD, Cherokee, Pvt, Col John Brown, Capt Jesse G Rainey, Mtd Gunmen
OKILLEWOOD, James, Pvt, Col T McCrory, Capt Jas Shannon, Mil Inf
OLANT, William, Pvt, Regt Commander omitted, Capt Jos Williams, Mil Cav
OLD, Henry, 3 Cpl, Lt Col L Hammond, Col A Loury, Capt Thomas Delaney, Inf
OLD, Jordon P, Pvt, Col Thos Benton, Capt James McEwen, Vol Inf
OLDFIELD, William, Pvt, Col John K Wynn, Capt Wm Carothers, W TN Inf
OLDHAM, Conaway, Pvt, Lt Col H Bryan, Co Commander omitted, Inf
OLDHAM, Connoway, Pvt, Col William Hall, Capt James Hambleton, Vol Inf
OLDHAM, E R, Pvt, Col Edward Bradley, Capt James Hambleton, Vol Inf
OLDHAM, Elias, Pvt, Col Thos Benton, Capt Geo Caperton, Vol Inf
OLDHAM, Elisha B, Pvt, Col Wm Hall, Capt James Hambleton, Vol Inf
OLDHAM, George, Pvt, Col Samuel Wear, Col Samuel Bunch, Capt Wm Mitchell, E TN Mtd Inf
OLDHAM, Greenlee, Pvt, Col A Metcalf, Capt Wm Sitton, Mil Inf
OLDHAM, Greenlee, Pvt, Col Thos Benton, Capt Wm Moore, Vol Inf
OLDHAM, Jesse, 2 Sgt, Col Philip Pipkin, Capt Ebenezer Kirkpatrick, Mil Inf; promoted to 1 Sgt
OLDHAM, John, Pvt, Col Samuel Wear, Col Samuel Bunch, Capt Wm Mitchell, E TN Mtd Inf
OLDHAM, Moses, Pvt, Col Thos Williamson, Capt Richardson Tate, Vol Mtd Gunmen
OLDHAM, Moses, Pvt, Regt Commander omitted, Capt Archibald McKinney, Cav
OLDHAM, Washington, Pvt, Lt Col L Hammond, Capt Thomas Delaney, Inf; also under Col A Loury
OLDS, Jordon R, Pvt, Col Thos Benton, Capt James McEwen, Vol Inf
OLEGRAN, John, Pvt, Maj Wm Woodfolk, Capt Ezekiel Ross & Capt McCulley, Inf
OLESUTTEYATE, Cherokee, Pvt, Col John Brown, Capt Jesse G Rainey, Mtd Gunmen
OLIGNER, Daniel, Pvt, Col Samuel Bayless, Capt James Landen, E TN Mil
OLINGER, David, Cpl, Col Wm Johnson, Capt Christopher Cook, E TN Mil
OLINGER, David, Pvt, Col Wm Johnson, Capt Joseph Kirk, Mil
OLINGER, George, Pvt, Col Samuel Wear, Capt Rufus Morgan, E TN Vol Inf
OLINGER, Henry, Pvt, Col Wm Lillard, Capt Robert McCalpin, E TN Inf
OLINGER, Jacob, Pvt, Col Samuel Wear, Capt Rufus Morgan, E TN Vol Inf
OLIVER, Durret, 4 Sgt, Col Edwin Booth, Capt Richard Marshall, Drafted Mil
OLIVER, Eli, Pvt, Col John Brown, Capt Allen I Bacon, E TN Mil Inf
OLIVER, Frederick, Pvt, Col Thos Williamson, Capt John

## Enlisted Men, War of 1812

Doak & Capt John Dobbins, Vol Mtd Gunmen
OLIVER, George, Pvt, Maj Gen Wm Carroll, Capt Wiley Huddleston, Inf
OLIVER, Henry, Sdlr, Regt Commander omitted, Capt A McKenney, Cav
OLIVER, Jeremiah, Pvt, Col N Cannon, Capt H Martin, Mtd Gunmen
OLIVER, Joel, Pvt, Col Wm Johnson, Capt Jas Rogers, E Tn Draft Mil
OLIVER, John, Pvt, Col E Allison, Capt A Winsell, E TN Draft Mil
OLIVER, John, Pvt, Col P Pipkin, Capt P Searcy, Mil Inf
OLIVER, Samuel, Pvt, Col Jas Raulston, Capt Jas Black, Inf; died 12-18-1814
OLIVER, Thomas M, Pvt, Regt Commander omitted, Capt Jas Haggard, Mtd Gunmen
OLIVER, William, Sgt, Col Wm Johnson, Capt Jas Rogers, E TN Draft Mil
OLIVIS, Nashariah, Pvt, Regt Commander omitted, Capt Geo Smith, Spies
OLLIVER, George, Pvt, Col E Allison, Capt A Winsell, E TN Draft Mil
OLLIVER, Henry, Sdlr, Col R H Dyer, Capt Glen Owen, 1 TN Vol Mtd Gunmen
OLLIVER, John, Pvt, Col R H Dyer, Capt Glen Owen, TN Vol Mtd Gunmen
ONEAL, Charles, Pvt, Col P Pipkin, Capt D Smith, Inf
ONEAL, Hastin, Pvt, Col Jno Brown, Capt Chas Lewin, E TN Vol Mtd Inf
ONEAL, Isom, Pvt, Col P Pipkin, Capt H M Newlin, Mil Inf
ONEAL, James, Pvt, Col Jno Coffee, Capt Jas Terrell, Vol Cav
ONEAL, James, Pvt, Col P Pipkin, Capt Jas Blakemore, Mil Inf
ONEAL, Jeremiah, Pvt, Col Jas Raulston, Capt Jas Black, Inf; died 12-18-1814
ONEAL, Peter, 4 Sgt, Col Ed Bradley, Capt Jas Hambleton, Vol Inf
ONEAL, Thomas H, Pvt, Col Wm Hall, Capt Jas Hambleton, Vol Inf
ONEAL, Thomas, Pvt, Col Samuel Bunch, Capt Thos Mann, E TN Vol Mtd Inf
ONEIL, Durias, Pvt, Col Samuel Bayless, Capt B Jones, E TN Draft Mil
ONEIL, James, Pvt, Regt Commander omitted, Lt Jas Berry, Mtd Riflemen
ORANGE, Bird, Pvt, Lt Col L Hammond, Capt Jas Tubb, Inf
ORANGE, Yearby, 5 Cpl, Col P Pipkin, Capt Jas Blakemore, Mil Inf
ORANGE, Zephaniah, Pvt, Lt Col L Hammond, Capt Jas Tubb, Inf
OREAR, Robert, Pvt, Col William Metcalf, Capt Alex Hill & Capt Jno Cunningham, Mil Inf
OREAR, William, Pvt, Col R H Dyer, Capt William Russell, Maj William Russell, Vol Mtd Gunmen
ORFORD, Isaac, Pvt, Col Thos Williamson, Maj Gen Jackson, Capt Robert Steele, Vol Mtd Gunmen; died 12-22-1814
ORGAN, Benjamin, Pvt, Col R H Dyer, Capt Robert Edmonston, 1 TN Vol Mtd Gunmen
ORGAN, Bennett, Pvt, Col Jno Coffee, Capt Thos Bradley, Vol Cav
ORGAN, Simpson, Pvt, Col Jno Coffee, Capt Thos Bradley, Vol Cav
ORICK, James, Pvt, Col E Booth, Capt Jno Slatton, E TN Mil
ORLEANS, George, Pvt, Col Thos Benton, Capt Thos Williamson, Vol Inf
ORMBY, James J, Pvt, Col A Cheatham, Capt R Benson, Inf
ORMBY, James, Pvt, Col A Cheatham, Capt R Benson, Inf
ORNEAL, Thomas, Pvt, Col S Bunch, Capt S Richardson, E TN Draft Mil; deserted
ORR, Alexander, Pvt, Col Jas Raulston, Capt Jas Black, Inf
ORR, Azaniah, Cpl, Col Samuel Bunch, Capt Jos Duncan, E TN Draft Mil
ORR, James, Pvt, Col J Alcorn, Capt Thomas Bradley, Vol Cav; promoted to Surgeon's Mate
ORR, James, Pvt, Col R H Dyer, Capt Jas McMahon, 1 TN Vol Mtd Gunmen
ORR, Marks, Pvt, Maj William Russell, Capt Jas Trimble, Vol Mtd Gunmen
ORR, Phillip, Pvt, Col N T Perkins, Capt Wm Johnston, Mil Inf
ORR, Robert, Pvt, Col N T Cannon, Capt Geo Brandon, Mtd Riflemen
ORR, Sample, Pvt, Maj Jno Childs, Capt Jno Stephens, E TN Vol Mtd Inf
ORR, Samuel, Pvt, Col Samuel Bunch, Capt E Buchanan, E TN Mil; joined from Capt Duncan's
ORR, William, Cpl, Col E Booth, Capt Geo Winton, E TN Mil
ORR, William, Pvt, Col E Booth, Capt Samuel Thompson, Mil
ORR, William, Pvt, Col John Brown, Capt James Preston, E TN Mil Inf
ORRICK, Joel, Pvt, Col Wm Higgins, Capt Wm Doak, Mtd Riflemen
ORRICK, John, Cpl, Col Wm Higgins, Capt Wm Doake, Mtd Riflemen
ORRICK, John, Pvt, Col Robert Steele, Capt Robert Campbell, Mil Inf
ORTANY, Lewis, Pvt, Col John Cocke, Capt Geo Barnes, Inf
ORTING, Pvt, Col R C Napier, Capt D Adkins, Mil Inf
ORTNER, Jacob, Pvt, Lt Col L Hammond, Capt James Craig, Inf
ORTON, Joseph, Pvt, Col Jno Cocke, Capt Jno Dalton, Inf
ORTON, Samuel, Pvt, Col Jno Cocke, Capt Jno Dalton, Inf
OSBORN, Alfred M, 3 Sgt, Regt Commander omitted, Capt D S Deadrick, Branch omitted
OSBORN, Edward, Pvt, Col Wm Metcalf, Capt B Collins, Mil Inf
OSBORN, Eli, Pvt, Maj Wm Woodfolk, Capt E Ross & Capt McMulley, Inf
OSBORN, Jesse, Pvt, Col Wm Metcalf, Capt Barbee Collins, Mil Inf

OSBORN, John, Pvt, Col John Cocke, Capt Richard Crunk, Inf
OSBORN, William, Pvt, Col Wm Metcalf, Capt Barbee Collins, Mil Inf
OSBURN, Abner, Pvt, Col Robert Dyer, Capt Jas McMahan, TN Vol Mtd Gunmen
OSBURN, Alfred M, Pvt, Maj Gen A Jackson, Capt William Carroll, Vol Inf
OSBURN, Benjamin, Pvt, Col Edward Bradley, Capt Moore, Vol Inf
OSBURN, Edward, Pvt, Col William Pillow, Capt Geo Caperton, Inf
OSBURN, John, Pvt, Col John Winn, Capt John Porter, Inf
OSBURN, John, Pvt, Regt Commander omitted, Capt Nathan Farmer, Mtd Riflemen
OSBURN, Thomas, Pvt, Col Edward Bradley, Capt John Moore, Vol Inf; deserted
OSBURN, Thomas, Pvt, Col John Winn, Capt William Willson, Inf; later attached to Capt Porter Co
OSBURN, William, Pvt, Regt Commander omitted, Capt L Ferrell, Inf
OSCENDINE, Archibald, Pvt, Col Wm Hall, Capt John Kennedy, Vol Inf
OSMENT, James, Pvt, Col Edward Bradley, Capt Harry Douglas, Vol Inf
OSMENT, James, Pvt, Col Thos Benton, Capt Harry Douglas, Branch omitted
OSTEAN, George, Pvt, Col Thos Benton, Capt Thomas Williamson, Vol Inf
OSTEEN, Dickinson, Pvt, Col Jas Raulston, Capt Henry Hamilton, Inf; also served under Maj Gen Carroll
OSTEEN, George, Pvt, Col Wm Metcalf, Capt Obidiah Waller, Mil Inf
OSTEEN, Isaac, Pvt, Col Phillip Pipkin, Capt William Mackay, Mil Inf
OSTEEN, John, Pvt, Lt Col Hammonds, Col Alexander Loury, Capt Thomas Wells, Inf
OSTEEN, Samuel, Pvt, Col Phillip Pipkin, Capt John Strother, Mil
OSTEEN, Samuel, Pvt, Col William Pillow, Capt Joseph Mason, Vol Inf
OTENAQUA, Cherokee, Pvt, Col John Brown, Capt Jesse Rainey, Mtd Gunmen
OTINGER, David, Pvt, Col Ewen Allison, Capt Nelson, E TN Drafted Mil
OTTERY, Lewis, Pvt, Col John Cocke, Capt George Barnes, Inf; died 2-4-1815
OUNSBAND, John, Rank omitted, Col John Cocke, Capt Richard Crunk, Inf
OUTLAW, Alexander S, Pvt, Col John Williams, Capt William Walker, Vol
OUTLAW, George, Pvt, Col R C Napier, Capt Edward Neblett, Mil Inf
OUTLAW, John, Pvt, Col Jno Coffee, Capt John Basskerville, Cav
OUTLAW, Seth, Pvt, Col R T Perkins, Capt Geo Marr, Mtd Vol
OUTLAW, Seth, Pvt, Col Wm Hall, Capt John Moore, Vol Inf
OVAR (O'BARR), Daniel, Pvt, Col Wm Metcalf, Capt John Barnhardt, Mil Inf

OVAR (O'BARR), Daniel, Pvt, Col Wm Metcalf, Capt John Barnhart, Mil Inf
OVERALL, Isaac H, Pvt, Col Robert Dyer, Capt Thomas Jones, Vol Mtd Gunmen
OVERALL, Robert, Pvt, Brig Gen Johnson, Capt Robert Carson, Inf
OVERBY, Alexander, Pvt, Col S Bayless, Capt Solomon Hendrick, E TN Mil
OVERBY, Anderson, Pvt, Col Jas Raulston, Capt Henry Hamilton, Inf; also served under Maj Gen Carroll
OVERBY, Anderson, Pvt, Col John Winn, Capt William McCall, Inf
OVERBY, Dury, Pvt, Col Jas Raulston, Capt Henry Hamilton, Inf; also served under Maj Gen Carroll
OVERBY, Lemmel, Pvt, Col Williamson Thomas, Capt Joseph Williams, Vol Mtd Gunmen
OVERBY, Nicholas, Pvt, Col William Hall, Capt John Moore, Vol Inf
OVERHOLDER, Jacob, Pvt, Col S Bunch, Capt F Register, E TN Mil; joined from Capt McCrea's Co
OVERHOLSTON, Jacob, Pvt, Col Ewen Allison, Capt Henry McCray, E TN Mil; trans to Capt Register Co
OVERSHINE, John, Pvt, Col William Metcalf, Capt John Cunningham & Capt Hill, Mil Inf
OVERSTREET, Robert, Pvt, Col R T Perkins, Capt George Eliot, Mil Inf
OVERTON, Arthur, Pvt, Col T McCrory, Capt Jas Reynolds, Mil Inf
OVERTON, Benjamin, Pvt, Col William Hall, Capt Abraham Bledsoe, Vol Inf
OVERTON, David, Cpl, Col Robert Dyer, Capt James Wyatt, Vol Mtd Gunmen
OVERTON, David, Pvt, Col Robert Steele, Capt John Chitwood, Mil Inf
OVERTON, Elisha, Pvt, Col William Lillard, Capt Hugh Martin, E TN Vol Inf
OVERTON, Gabriel, Pvt, Col Robert Dyer, Capt Cuthbert Hudson, Vol Mtd Gunmen; died 3-26-1815
OVERTON, James, Pvt, Col Wm Hall, Capt John Kennedy, Vol Inf
OVERTON, Westberry, Pvt, Col Jas Raulston, Maj William Carroll, Capt Robinson, Inf
OVERTURF, Philip, Pvt, Col Jas Raulston, Capt Henry West, Inf
OVERTURFT, John, Pvt, Col R T Perkins, Capt Robert Doak, Vol Mtd Gunmen
OWEN, Baxter, Pvt, Col Philip Pipkin, Capt Ebenezer Kirkpatrick, Mil Inf
OWEN, Charles, Pvt, Col Wm Johnson, Capt Joseph Scott, E TN Draft Mil
OWEN, Daniel, Pvt, Col Wm Lillard, Capt Wm Gillenwater, E TN Inf
OWEN, David, Pvt, Col Wm Hall, Capt Travis C Nash, Inf
OWEN, Edmund, Cpl, Col Thos Benton, Capt Thos Williamson, Vol Inf
OWEN, Frederick, Pvt, Col Wm Pillow, Capt Thos Williamson, Vol Inf
OWEN, James, Pvt, Maj Wm Carroll, Capt Lewis Dillahunty & Capt Daniel M Bradford, Vol Inf
OWEN, John, Pvt, Col Ewen Allison, Capt James Allen, E

## Enlisted Men, War of 1812

OWEN, Joshua, Pvt, Col Wm Metcalf, CApt John Barnhart, Mil Inf TN Mil

OWEN, Peter, Pvt, Col Wm Pillow, Capt Thos Williamson, Vol Inf

OWEN, Quinley, Pvt, Maj William Woodfolk, Capt Ezekiel Ross, Inf

OWEN, Rubin, Pvt, Col Thos Benton, Capt Thos Williamson, Vol Inf

OWEN, Samuel, Surgeon Mate, Col Thos McCrory, 2 Regt TN Mil; trans from Capt John Demsey Co

OWEN, Shadrick, Pvt, Col Samuel Bunch, Capt John Inman, E TN Vol Mtd Inf

OWEN, Stephen, Pvt, Col Newton Cannon, Capt John Demsey, Mtd Gunmen

OWEN, Thomas, Pvt, Col Wm Pillow, Capt Thos Williamson, Vol Inf

OWEN, Urbin, Pvt, Maj Wm Carroll, Capt Lewis Dillahunty, Capt Daniel W Bradford, Vol Inf

OWEN, William C, Sgt, Maj Gen A Jackson, Capt Wm Carroll, Vol Inf

OWEN, William jr, Pvt, Col Samuel Bayless, Capt John Brock, E TN Mil

OWEN, William sr, Pvt, Col S Bayless, Capt John Brock, E TN Mil

OWEN, William, Pvt, Col John Brown, Capt Wm White, E TN Mil Inf

OWEN, William, Pvt, Col Wm Lillard, Capt Wm Gillenwater, E TN Inf

OWENS, James H, Col Robert Steele, Capt James Randals, Inf

OWENS, Jeremiah, Pvt, Col James Raulston, CApt Charles Wade, Inf

OWENS, John, Pvt, Col Edwin Booth, Capt John Lewis, E TN Mil

OWENS, John, Pvt, Col Ewen Allison, Capt Joseph Everett, E TN Mil; disch for inability

OWENS, John, Pvt, Col John Brown, Capt James McKamy, E TN Mtd Gunmen

OWENS, Martin, Pvt, Col A Loury, Capt James Kincaid, Inf; died 1-18-1815?

OWENS, Newman, Pvt, Regt Commander omitted, Capt Dan'l Yarnell, E TN Mil; enlisted Reg Army 1-12-1814

OWENS, Reuben, Sgt, Col Ewen Allison, Capt Adam Winsell, E TN Draft Mil

OWENS, Robert, Pvt, Col Samuel Bunch, Capt Jno English, E TN Draft Mil

OWENS, Robert, Pvt, Col Thos Williamson, Capt Anthony Metcalf, Vol Mtd Gunmen

OWENS, Samuel, Pvt, Col John Brown, Capt James McKamy, E TN Gunmen

OWENS, Samuel, Pvt, Col Wm Lillard, Capt Hugh Martin, E Tn Vol Inf; unable to do duty

OWENS, Samuel, Pvt, Maj William Carroll, Capt Lewis Dillahunty, Capt Daniel M Bradford, Vol Inf

OWENS, Stephen, Pvt, Lt Col Jno Edmonson, Co Commander omitted, Cav

OWENS, Steward, Pvt, Col Samuel Bunch, Capt Isaac Williams, E TN Mil

OWENS, Thomas, Pvt, Col Edwin Booth, Capt Geo Winton, E TN Mil

OWENS, Thomas, Pvt, Col R H Dyer, Capt E D Dickson, TN Mtd Vol Gunmen

OWENS, Thomas, Pvt, Col Wm Johnson, Capt Andrew Lawson, E TN Draft Mil

OWENS, Thomas, Pvt, Col Wm Johnson, Capt Wm Alexander, Det of E TN Draft Mil

OWENS, Thomas, Pvt, Maj John Chiles, Capt John Stephens, E TN Vol Mtd Inf

OWENS, Urlin, Pvt, Col Thos Benton, Capt Thos Williamson, Vol Inf

OWENS, Waller, Pvt, Col Samuel Wear, Capt Rufus Morgan, E TN Inf

OWENS, Walter, Pvt, Regt Commander omitted, Capt Wm Henderson, Spies

OWENS, William, Pvt, Col A Loury, Capt James Kincaid, Inf; died 3-3-1815

OWENS, William, Pvt, Col Philip Pipkin, Capt Mackay, Mil Inf; trans to Capt Mebane

OWENS, William, Sgt, Col John K Winn, Capt Bailey Butler, Inf; deserted

OWENS, Wilson, Pvt, Col John Brown, Capt Hugh Barton, Regt E TN Mil Inf

OWENS (OENS), Daniel, Pvt, Col Edwin Booth, Capt John Slatton, E TN Mil

OWENS (OENS), James, Pvt, Col William Johnson, Capt Henry Hunter, E TN Mil; deserted

OWENSBY, Thomas, Pvt, Col John K Winn, Capt Bailey Butler, Inf

OWIN, George, 1 Cpl, Maj Gen Wm Carroll, Capt Wiley Huddleston, Inf

OWINGS, Jacob, Pvt, Col S Bunch, Capt John Houk, E TN Mil; joined from Capt Davis Co

OWINGS, Luallwood, Pvt, Col Thomas McCrory, Capt Thomas Gordon, Inf

OXENDINE, Archibald, Pvt, Col Wm Hall, Capt John Kennedy, Vol Inf

OXENDINE, David, Pvt, Col Robert Steele, Capt Samuel Maxwell, Mil Inf

OXENDINE, Stephen, Pvt, Col James Raulston, Capt Mathew Cowan; never mustered into svce

PACE, Alsa, Pvt, Col Jno Coffee, Capt Frederick Stump, Cav

PACE, Dempsey, Pvt, Lt Col A Cheatham, Capt Meredith Walker, Mtd Inf

PACE, Gideon, 3 Cpl, Col John K Winn, Capt Bayless Prince, Inf

PACE, Hardy, Pvt, Col John K Winn, Capt Bayless Prince, Inf

PACE, Hermine, Pvt, Col Newton Cannon, Capt John Harpole, Mtd Gunmen

PACE, John, 4 Sgt, Col John Cocke, Capt John Weakley, Inf

PACE, John, Pvt, Col Thos Williamson, Lt James Nealy, Capt James Pace, Vol Mtd Gunmen; died 1-9-1815

PACE, Kenchen, Sgt, Col Newton Cannon, Capt Thos Yardley, Mtd Riflemen

PACE, Thomas, Pvt, Col Philip Pipkin, Capt Ebenezer Kirkpatrick, Mil Inf

PACE, William, Pvt, Col Philip Pipkin, Capt E Kirkpa-

## Enlisted Men, War of 1812

trick, Mil Inf; deserted
PACE, William, Pvt, Lt Col A Cheatham, Co Commander omitted, 5 Brig Mtd Inf
PACE, William, Sgt, Col Thos Benton, Capt Isiah Renshaw, Vol Inf
PACE, William, Sgt, Col Wm Pillow, Capt Isiah Renshaw, Inf
PACE, Wilson, Pvt, Col Newton Cannon, Capt Thos Yardley, Mtd Riflemen
PACK, Benjamin, Pvt, Col R H Dyer, Capt Robert Evans, Vol Mtd Gunmen
PACK, Jeremiah, Pvt, Col John K Winn, Capt Wm Caruthers, W TN Inf; trans to Capt Holliman's Co
PACK, John, 4 Cpl, Col Wm Lillard, Capt Wm Gillenwater, E TN Vol Inf
PADGET, Francis, Pvt, Col Ewen Allison, Capt James Allen, E TN Mil
PAEDY, William, Pvt, Col Jno Brown, Capt Wm Christian, E TN Mil Inf
PAGE, David E, 6 Cpl, Col John Cocke, Capt James Gault, Inf
PAGE, David, Pvt, Capt Jno Crawford, Gen Thomas Washington, Mtd Inf
PAGE, James, Pvt, Col John Williams, Capt Wm Walker, Vol
PAGE, James, Pvt, Col Samuel Wear, Capt James Gillespie, E TN Vol Inf
PAGE, James, Pvt, Maj John Chiles, Capt John Stephens, E TN Vol Mtd Inf
PAGE, James, Pvt, Regt Commander omitted, Capt Nathan Peoples, Inf
PAGE, John, Pvt, Col S Copeland, Capt Wm Evans, Mil Inf
PAGE, John, Pvt, Regt Commander omitted, Capt Nathan Peoples, Inf
PAGE, Joiles, Pvt, Col R H Dyer, Capt Robert Evans, Vol Mtd Gunmen; dismissed from svce
PAGE, Joseph, Pvt, Col Thos Benton, Capt Thos Williamson, Vol Inf
PAGE, Nathan, Pvt, Col Wm Johnson, Capt Christopher Cook, E TN Mil
PAGE, Nathan, Pvt, Col Wm Johnson, Capt Joseph Kirk, Mil
PAGE, Nathaniel, Pvt, Col Wm Johnson, Capt Elihu Milliken, 3 Regt E Tn Mil
PAGE, Robert, Pvt, Col John Brown, Capt Jesse C Reany, Mtd Gunmen
PAGE, Robert, Pvt, Col R H Dyer, Capt Robert Evans, Vol Mtd Gunmen
PAGE, Robert, Pvt, Col Wm Johnson, Capt Elihu Milliken, 3 Regt E TN Mil
PAGGET, William, Pvt, Col Wm Lillard, Capt Jno Neatherton, E Tn Vol Mil
PAIN, George, Pvt, Col S Copeland, Capt James Tait, Inf; died 4-26-1814
PAIN, John, 2 Sgt, Col Thos Williamson, Capt Giles Burdett, Vol Mtd Gunmen
PAIN, John, Pvt, Col John K Winn, Capt Wm Carothers, W TN Inf; deserted
PAIN, Samuel, Pvt, Col Wm Johnson, Capt Stuart, E TN Draft Mil

PAIN, William, Pvt, Col Ewen Allison, Capt J Loughmiller; trans to Capt McPherson's Co
PAINE, Henry, Pvt, Col Wm Lillard, Capt Wm Hamilton, E TN Vol Inf
PAINE, Israel, Cpl, Col Samuel Bayless, Capt Joseph Rich, E TN Inf
PAINE, Jacob, 1 Sgt, Col John Cocke, Capt Bird Nance, Inf
PAINE, James, Pvt, Col R C Napier, Capt Early Benson, Mil Inf
PAINE, James, Pvt, Col Thos McCrory, Capt John Reynolds, Mil Inf
PAINE, John, Pvt, Col John Brown, Capt Lunsford Oliver, E Tn Mil
PAINE, Joseph, Pvt, Col Wm Hall, Capt John Wallace, Inf
PAINE, Matthew, Pvt, Gen A Jackson, Capt Wm Russell, Mtd Spies
PAINE, Micajah, 3 Cpl, Col N T Perkins, Capt James McMahon, Mtd Gunmen
PAINE, Nelson, Pvt, Col R H Dyer, Capt Robt Edmonston, 1 TN Vol Mtd Gunmen
PAINE, Thomas, Pvt, Maj Wm Russell, Capt Wm Chism, Vol Mtd Gunmen
PAINE, William, Pvt, Col R C Napier, Capt Early Benson, Mil Inf
PAINE (PAYNE), John, Pvt, Col Wm Johnson, Capt James Tunnell, E Tn Mil
PAINTE, Ezekiel, Pvt, Maj Wm Woodfolk, Capt James Turner, Inf
PAINTER, Adam, Pvt, Col Wm Lillard, Capt Wm McLin, E Tn Inf
PAINTER, David, Pvt, Col Ewen Allison, Capt Henry McCray, E TN Mil; trans to Capt Register's Co
PAINTER, David, Pvt, Col Samuel Bunch, Capt F Register, E TN Mil
PAINTER, Jacob, Pvt, Col Samuel Bayless, Capt Jonathan Waddle, E TN Mil
PAINTER, John, Ffr, Col Thos Benton, Capt Wm Moore, Vol Inf
PAINTER, John, Pvt, Col Wm Metcalf, Capt William Sitton, Mil Inf
PAINTER, John, Pvt, Col Wm Pillow, Capt Wm Moore, Inf
PAINTER, Joseph, Pvt, Col S Wear, Capt John Stephen, E TN Vol Inf
PAINTER, William, Pvt, Col S Bayless, Capt Johnathan Waddle, E TN Mil
PAIR, Matthew, Pvt, Col Edwin Booth, Capt John McKamey, E TN Mil
PAISLY, Moses, Ffr, Col Thos Benton, Capt Jas McFerrin, Vol Inf
PAISLY, Samuel, Pvt, Col Jas Raulston, Capt Chas Wade, Inf
PALIT, Charles, Pvt, Col S Wear, Capt William Mitchell & Capt S Bunch, E TN Mtd Inf
PALLEN, Archibald, Pvt, Col Jas Raulston, Capt Chas Wade, Inf
PALMER, Francis R, Pvt, Col Thomas Williamson, Capt John Moore, Vol Mtd Gunmen; trans to Lt Bean's Spies
PALMER, John, Cpl, Col Russell Williams, Capt Isaac

## Enlisted Men, War of 1812

Williams, Vol Mtd Gunmen
PALMER, John, Pvt, Col S Wear, Capt Jesse Cole, Vol Inf
PALMER, John, Pvt, Regt Commander omitted, Capt James Gray, Inf
PALMER, John, Pvt, Regt Commander omitted, Capt Jas Haggard, Mtd Gunmen; promoted to Fgmstr
PALMER, Phillip, Pvt, Col Robert Dyer, Capt Bethel Allen, Vol Mtd Gunmen
PALMER, Thomas, Pvt, Col S Bunch, Capt Joseph Duncan, E TN Drafted Mil; joined from Capt Allen's Co
PALMER, Thomas, Pvt, Col Wm Hall, Capt Travis Nash, Inf
PALMER, William N, Pvt, Col S Copeland, Capt Moses Thompson, Inf
PALMER, William, Pvt, Col Jas Raulston, Capt Jas Black, Inf
PALMER, William, Pvt, Col Phillip Pipkin, Capt Jas Blackmore, Mil Inf; deserted
PALMER, William, Pvt, Col S Wear, Capt Samuel Bowman, Mtd Inf
PALMER, Wilson L, Pvt, Col S Copeland, Capt Moses Thompson, Inf
PALMER (PARMER), Richard, Pvt, Col Thos Benton, Capt George Gibbs, Vol Inf
PANADESE, John, Pvt, Regt Commander omitted, Capt James Gray, Inf
PANE, Ashell, Chap, Col Edwin Booth, Co Commander omitted, E TN Mil
PANE, Moses, Pvt, Col Thomas Williamson, Capt Giles Burdett, Vol Mtd Gunmen
PANGLE, Andrew, Pvt, Col Samuel Bunch, Capt Simeon Perry, E TN Mil
PANGLE, Isaac, Pvt, Col John Williams, Capt William Walker, Vol
PANKEY, John, Pvt, Col John Brown, Capt Jas McKamy, E TN Mtd Gunmen
PANKEY, Stephen, Pvt, Col John Brown, Capt Jesse Reamy, Mtd Gunmen; died in svce 5-6-1814
PANKY, Joseph, Cpl, Col Alexander Loury, Capt Geo Saver, Inf
PANKY, Joseph, Pvt, Col John Alcorn, Capt Alexander McKeen, Cav
PANKY, Joseph, Pvt, Col Wm Hall, Capt John Wallace, Inf
PANKY, Lewis, 4 Cpl, Col R T Perkins, Capt George Eliot, Mil Inf
PANKY, Riley, Pvt, Col S Bunch, Capt Francis Berry, E TN Mil; died 4-20-1814
PANKY, Smith, Pvt, Col Jno Brown, Co Commander omitted, E TN Vol Mil
PANNEL, John, Pvt, Col Jno Brown, Capt Wm D Neilson, E TN Vol Mil
PANNEL, Thomas, Pvt, Col William Lillard, Capt Argenbright, E Tn Vol Riflemen
PANNELL, Samuel, Pvt, Col William Higgins, Capt Thomas Eldridge, Mtd Gunmen
PANNELL, Thomas, Cpl, Col William Johnson, Capt Benj Powell, E Tn Mil
PANTER, John, Pvt, Col Edwin Booth, Capt Alexander Biggs, Inf; appt Cpl

PAOMEORY, Francis, Pvt, Lt Jesse Bean, Gen John Coffee, Mtd Spies
PARCHMAN, Aquilly, Pvt, Col Wm Metcalf, Capt Thomas Marks, Mil Inf
PARE, Jacob, Pvt, Col Ewin Allison, Capt Joseph Everett, E TN Mil
PARE, James, 2 Cpl, no other information
PARHAM, Johnston, Pvt, Col Wm Johnson, Capt Jas Tunnell, E TN Mil
PARHAM, Thomas, Cpl, Col Edwin Booth, Capt Vernon, E Tn Mil
PARISH, David, Cpl, Col John Coffee, Capt Edward Bradley, Vol Cav
PARISH, Joel, Secty, Maj Gen Jackson, TN Mil
PARITT, William S, Pvt, Col Jas Raulston, Capt Henry West, Inf
PARK, Robert, Pvt, Col R T Perkins, Capt Jas McMahan, Mtd Gunmen
PARKER, Andrew, Pvt, Col Edward Bradley, Capt John Moore, Vol Inf
PARKER, Andrew, Pvt, Col Wm Hall, Capt John Moore, Vol Inf
PARKER, Aquille, Pvt, Col S Bayless, Capt James Launden, E TN Mil
PARKER, Archibald, Pvt, Col Phillip Pipkin, Capt John Robertson, Mil Inf; deserted
PARKER, Archibald, Pvt, Col Wm Hall, Capt Brice Martin, Vol Inf
PARKER, Benjamin, Pvt, Gen Johnston, Capt Daniel Oban, Inf
PARKER, Berry, Pvt, Col Thomas Williamson, Capt A Metcalf, Vol Mtd Gunmen; died 1-9-1815
PARKER, Charles, Pvt, Col Robert Steele, Capt Robert Campbell, Mil Inf
PARKER, Daniel, Pvt, Col T McCrory, Capt Jas Shannon, Mil Inf
PARKER, Daniel, Pvt, Col Thomas Williamson, Capt James Pace, Lt James Neeley, Vol Mtd Gunmen; died 1-3-1815
PARKER, Edward, Pvt, Col James Raulston, Maj Gen Wm Carroll, Capt Elijah Haynie, Inf
PARKER, Elijah, Pvt, Col T McCrory, Capt Jas Shannon, Branch omitted
PARKER, Everet, Pvt, Maj Wm Woodfolk, Capt Ezekial Ross, Inf
PARKER, Isaac, Pvt, Gen Thos Johnston, Capt Daniel Oban, 36 Inf
PARKER, James jr, Pvt, Col James Raulston, Maj Gen Wm Carroll, Inf
PARKER, James, Pvt, Col James Raulston, Capt Elijah Haynie, Branch omitted
PARKER, James, Pvt, Col Jno Williams, Capt David G Vance, E TN Mtd Vols
PARKER, James, Pvt, Col John K Winn, Capt Robert Bradin, Inf
PARKER, James, Pvt, Col John Williams, Capt David Vance, Mtd Mil
PARKER, James, Pvt, Col Samuel Bunch, Capt David G Vance, E TN Mtd Inf
PARKER, James, Pvt, Col Samuel Bunch, Capt S Richerson, Branch omitted

-393

PARKER, James, Pvt, Col Wm Lillard, Capt Thos Sharpe, 2 Regt Inf; deserted
PARKER, Jesse, Pvt, Lt Col L Hammond, Capt Thos Delaney, Inf; also under Col A Loury
PARKER, John C, Pvt, Maj Gen A Jackson, Capt John Craine, Mtd Gunmen
PARKER, John S, Sgt, Col Edwin Booth, Capt Vernon, E TN Mil
PARKER, John, Pvt, Col Jno Brown, Capt Jas Preston, E TN Mil Inf
PARKER, John, Pvt, Col John Coffee, Capt John Baskerville, Cav
PARKER, John, Pvt, Col S Copeland, Capt John Biles, Inf
PARKER, John, Pvt, Col Samuel Bunch, Capt John Dobbins, E TN Draft Mil
PARKER, John, Pvt, Lt Col Archer Cheatham, Co Commander omitted, Mtd Inf
PARKER, John, Pvt, Regt Commander omitted, Capt Archibald McKinney, Cav
PARKER, John, Pvt, Regt Commander omitted, Capt Chas Kavanaugh, Branch omitted
PARKER, John, Pvt, Regt Commander omitted, Capt Saml A Allen, Pack Horse Guard
PARKER, Joseph, Pvt, Brig Gen T Johnson, Capt Robert Carson, Inf
PARKER, Joseph, Pvt, Col Thos Williamson, Capt Anthony M Metcalf, Vol Mtd Gunmen; dismissed
PARKER, Joshua, Pvt, Col Thos Williamson, Capt Robert Steele, Vol Mtd Gunmen
PARKER, Josiah, Sgt, Col Ewen Allison, Capt John Hampton, Mil
PARKER, Lemuel, Pvt, Col R H Dyer, Capt Bethel Allen, Vol Mtd Gunmen; died 2-6-1815
PARKER, Leonard, Pvt, Gen Andrew Jackson, Capt D Deaderick, Arty; trans to Pack Horse Co
PARKER, Moses, Pvt, Col Edward Bradley, Capt James Hambleton, Vol Inf
PARKER, Moses, Pvt, Col Wm Hall, Capt Jones Hambleton, Vol Inf; joined at Clarksville
PARKER, Nathan, Pvt, Col James Raulston, Capt Charles Wade, Inf
PARKER, Nathan, Pvt, Regt Commander omitted, Capt Gray, Inf
PARKER, Nathaniel, Pvt, Col Edward Bradley, Capt Wm Lauderdale, Vol Inf
PARKER, Nathaniel, Pvt, Col Wm Hall, Capt Wm L Alexander, Vol Inf
PARKER, Peter, Pvt, Col John K Winn, Capt James Cole, Vol Inf
PARKER, Richard, Pvt, Col Thos Williamson, Capt A Metcalf, Vol Mtd Gunmen; dismissed
PARKER, Richard, Pvt, Maj Gen Wm Carroll, Col Wm Metcalf, Capt John Jackson, Mil
PARKER, Roland, Pvt, Maj John Chiles, Capt Chas Conway, E Tn Mtd Gunmen; died 2-28-1815
PARKER, Rolly, Pvt, Col Jno Brown, Capt Wm Christian, E TN Mil Inf
PARKER, Stephen, Pvt, Col R C Napier, Capt Thos Gray, Mil Inf
PARKER, Warmack, Pvt, Col Wm Hall, Capt Brice Martin, Vol Inf
PARKER, Wilburn, Pvt, Col Wm Metcalf, Capt Andrew Patterson, Mil Inf; died 2-22-1815
PARKER, William, Pvt, Col Edward Bradley, Capt Wm Lauderdale, Vol Inf
PARKER, William, Pvt, Col Ewen Allison, Capt Joseph Everett, E TN Mil; trans to Capt Richardson
PARKER, William, Pvt, Col Jno Coffee, Capt Robt Jetton, Cav
PARKER, William, Pvt, Col Robert Steele, Capt Richard M Ratton, Mil Inf; deserted
PARKER, William, Pvt, Col S Copeland, Capt Allen Wilkinson, Mil Inf
PARKER, William, Pvt, Col Samuel Bayless, Capt James Landen, E TN Mil
PARKER, William, Pvt, Col Samuel Bunch, Capt S Richerson, E TN Draft Mil
PARKER, William, Pvt, Col Wm Johnson, Capt Christopher Cook, E TN Mil
PARKER, William, Pvt, Col Wm Johnston, Capt Joseph Kirk, Mil
PARKER, William, Pvt, Col Wm Pillow, Capt Wm Moore, Inf
PARKER, William, Pvt, Lt Col L Hammond, Capt James Tubb, Inf
PARKER, Willie, Pvt, Col John Cocke, Capt John Weakley, Inf
PARKER, Womack, Pvt, Col Edward Bradley, Capt Brice Martin, Vol Inf
PARKER, Womack, Pvt, Col Thos Williamson, Capt A Metcalf, Vol Mtd Gunmen
PARKER, Zachariah, Pvt, Col Wm Metcalf, Capt Thos Marks, Mil Inf
PARKERSON, John, Pvt, Col Robert Steele, Capt Richard Ratton, Mil Inf
PARKERSON, Richard A, Pvt, Col S Copeland, Capt John Dawson, Inf
PARKES, Abner, Pvt, Col Samuel Wear, Capt James Gillespie, E TN Vol Inf
PARKES, Robert, Pvt, Col Wm Pillow, Capt Wm Moore, Inf
PARKES, William, Pvt, Col Thomas H Bent, Capt Wm Moore, Vol Inf
PARKEY, John, Pvt, Col Phillip Pipkin, Capt Jas Blackmore, Mil Inf
PARKHAM, Allen, Pvt, Col Edwin E Booth, Capt Vernon, E Tn Mil
PARKHURST, Elijah, Pvt, Col Thomas H Williamson, Capt Wm Metcalf, Vol Mtd Gunmen
PARKILL, John, Cpl, Col Wm Johnson, Capt Wm Alexander, Det of E TN Draft Mil
PARKISON, John, Pvt, Col Wm Pillow, Capt Wm Smith, Vol Inf
PARKS, Andrew, Sgt, Col Wm Lillard, Capt Maloney, E TN Vol Inf
PARKS, Benjamin, Pvt, Col Thomas H Williamson, Capt Richard Tate, Vol Inf
PARKS, Benjamin, Pvt, Regt Commander omitted, Capt D Mason, Cav
PARKS, George, Pvt, Col R H Dyer, Maj Wm Russell, Vol Mtd Gunmen
PARKS, Hugh, Pvt, Col R H Dyer, Capt McMahon, TN

## Enlisted Men, War of 1812

PARKS, James, Cpl, Col Newton Cannon, Capt Gabriel Martin, Vol Mtd Gunmen
PARKS, James, Pvt, Maj William Woodfolk, Capt Abraham Dudney & Capt John Sutton, Inf
PARKS, James, Sgt Maj, Col John Brown, no Co Commander, Regt E TN Vol
PARKS, John, Pvt, Col John Brown, Capt Hugh Barton, Reg E Tn Mil Inf
PARKS, John, Pvt, Lt Col A Cheatham, Capt Meredith Walker, Mtd Inf
PARKS, Marshall, Pvt, Regt Commander omitted, Capt D Mason, Cav
PARKS, Phillip, Pvt, Col Wm Johnson, Capt Andrew Lawson, E TN Draft Mil
PARKS, Robert, Pvt, Col John Coffee, Capt Byrn, Cav
PARKS, Robert, Pvt, Col Thomas H Benton, Capt Wm Moore, Vol Inf
PARKS, Samuel, Pvt, Maj James P H Porter, Capt Samuel Cowal, Mil Cav
PARKS, Will, Pvt, Col Thomas H Benton, Capt Wm Moore, Vol Inf
PARKS, William, Cpl, Col John Coffee, Capt Charles Kavanaugh, Cav
PARKS, William, Pvt, Col Thomas H Benton, Capt Wm Moore, Vol Inf
PARMER, John, Pvt, Col Newton Cannon, Capt David Hogan, Mtd Gunmen
PARNELL, Thomas, Pvt, Maj Wm Carroll, Col Wm Metcalf, Capt Jackson, Inf
PARR, Isham, Pvt, Col Newton Cannon, Capt Hanby, Mtd Riflemen
PARRADICE, John, Col Wm Metcalf, Capt John Barnhart, Mil Inf
PARRE (PERRY), Joshua, Pvt, Col R H Dyer, Capt Robert Evans, Vol Mtd Gunmen
PARRISH, Ezekial, Pvt, Lt Cole, Capt Richard Napier, Inf
PARRISH, Fountain, Pvt, Regt Commander omitted, Capt D Mason, Cav
PARRISH, Hasel, Cpl, Col John Coffee, Co Commander omitted, Cav
PARRISH, Howel, Pvt, Col John Coffee, Capt Michael Molton, Cav
PARRISH, Wyatt, Pvt, Col R H Dyer, Capt Joseph Williams, Vol Mtd Gunmen
PARRISS, Morgen, 5 Sgt, Maj Gen Wm Carroll, Capt Wiley Huddleston, Inf
PARROT, Benjamin, Pvt, Col T McCrory, Capt A Metcalf, Mil Inf
PARROT, James, Pvt, Col Samuel Wear, Capt Robert Doak, E TN Vol Mil
PARROT, Joseph, Pvt, Col Wm Lillard, Capt James Lillard, E Tn Vol Inf
PARROT, Reuben, Pvt, Col Samuel Wear, Capt Robert Doak, E Tn Vol Inf
PARROT, Samuel, Pvt, Col Wm Pillow, Capt John Anderson, Vol Inf
PARRY, Simeon, Pvt, Regt Commander omitted, Capt Larkin, Inf
PARSLEY, Moses, Pvt, Col Wm Pillow, Capt James McPherrin, Inf
PARSLEY, Williams, Pvt, Col Wm Johnson, Capt Jas Stewart, E TN Drafted Mil
PARSON, John, Sgt, Col Wm Lillard, Capt Jacob Dyke, Vol Inf
PARSON, Major, Pvt, Gen Andrew Jackson, Capt Wm Russell, Mtd Spies
PARSON, Thomas, Pvt, Gen Andrew Jackson, Capt Wm Russell, Mtd Spies
PARSONS, Benjamin P, Pvt, Col R H Dyer, Capt Robert Evans, Vol Mtd Gunmen
PARSONS, Benjamin T, Pvt, Col John Coffee, Capt Ezekiel Ross, Mtd Gunmen
PARSONS, Ewen, Pvt, Col John E Williams, Capt Wm Walker, Vols
PARSONS, John, Cpl, Col Samuel Bunch, Capt John Houk, E TN Mil
PARSONS, John, Pvt, Col Edwin Booth, Capt Vernon, Branch omitted
PARSONS, Joseph, Pvt, Col Samuel Bunch, Capt Jno Houk, E Tn Mil; disch at Knoxville
PARSONS, Major, Pvt, Maj Wm Russell, Capt John Cowan, Vol Mtd Gunmen
PARSONS, Peter, Pvt, Col John Williams, Capt Wm Walker, Vols
PARSONS, Thomas, 1 Sgt, Col Edwin Booth, Capt Richard Marshall, E TN Mil
PARSONS, William, Cpl, Col Ewen Allison, Capt Adam Winsell, E TN Draft Mil
PARTCHMENT, James, Pvt, Regt Commander omitted, Capt Jas Reed, Inf
PARTEN, Hightown, Pvt, Col Thos McCrory, Capt Thos Gordon, Inf
PARTEN, James, Pvt, Col Wm Metcalf, Capt Thos Marks, Mil Inf
PARTIN, Jesse, Pvt, Col G W Steel, Capt James Randals, Inf
PARTLOWE, Thomas, Pvt, Col N T Perkins, Capt John B Quarles, Vol Mtd Inf
PASCHAL, John sr, Pvt, Col R H Dyer, Capt Bethel Allen, Vol Mtd Gunmen
PASCHAL, Samuel, Pvt, Col R H Dyer, Capt Bethel Allen, Vol Mtd Gunmen; died 1-5-1815
PASCHALL, John jr, Pvt, Col R H Dyer, Capt Bethel Allen, Vol Mtd Gunmen; died 1-27-1815
PASKELL, Isaah, Pvt, Col John K Winn, Capt John Spinks, Inf
PASKELL, Samuel, Pvt, Col Thos McCrory, Capt A Metcalf, Mil Inf
PASSINS, Elijah O, Pvt, Col Jas Raulston, Capt James A Black, Inf
PASSLY, Moses, Ffr, Col Thos Benton, Capt James McFerrin, Vol Inf
PATE, Booker, Pvt, Col Jas Raulston, Capt Mathew Cowan, Inf
PATE, Charles, Pvt, Col Samuel Bunch, Capt John Inman, E Tn Vol Mtd Inf
PATE, Elisha, Pvt, Col Jas Raulston, Capt Mathew Cowan, Inf
PATE, George, Pvt, Col Samuel Bunch, Capt Geo McPherson, E TN Mil; joined from Capt King's Co

## Enlisted Men, War of 1812

PATE, George, Pvt, Maj John Chiles, Capt John Stephens, E Tn Vol Mtd Inf
PATE, Isaac, Pvt, Col Wm Hall, Capt John Kennedy, Vol Inf
PATE, Jeremiah, Cpl, Col Thos McCrory, Capt A Metcalf, Mil Inf
PATE, Jeremiah, Cpl, Col Thos McCrory, Capt Sam B McKnight, Inf
PATE, John, 2 Cpl, Col Wm Metcalf, Capt Thos Marks, Mil Inf
PATE, John, Pvt, Col R C Napier, Capt Early Benson, Mil Inf
PATE, John, Pvt, Col S Copeland, Capt John Dawson, Inf
PATE, Persons E, 4 Sgt, Col Philip Pipkin, Capt Wm Mackay, Mil Inf
PATE, Persons, Pvt, Regt Commander omitted, Capt D Mason, Cav
PATE, Solomon, Pvt, Col S Copeland, Capt Solomon George, Inf
PATE, Solomon, Pvt, Col Thos Benton, Capt Wm Moore, Vol Inf; 2 Regt Inf
PATE, Stephen, Pvt, Col John Alcorn, Capt John Winston, Mtd Riflemen
PATE, Thomas, Pvt, Col S Bunch, Capt Jno English, E TN Draft Mil; joined from Capt William's Co
PATE, William, Pvt, Col N T Perkins, Capt John B Quarles, Vol Mtd Inf
PATE, William, Rank omitted, Col John Cocke, Capt Richard Crunk, Inf
PATE (PAIT), William, Pvt, Col Philip Pipkin, Capt George Mebane, Mil Inf
PATERSON, John, Pvt, Col Samuel Bunch, Co Commander omitted, E Tn Mil
PATERSON, Tryan, Pvt, Col Samuel Wear, Capt Simeon Perry, E Tn Vol Mtd Inf
PATEY, Eli, Pvt, Col Jas Raulston, Maj Gen Wm Carroll, Capt Edward Robinson, Inf
PATEY, Eli, Pvt, Col S Copeland, Capt Wm Hodges, Inf
PATEY, Jesse, Pvt, Col Jas Raulston, Maj Gen Wm Carroll, Capt Edward Robinson, Inf; died 2-16-1815
PATILLO, George, Pvt, Col Philip Pipkin, Capt E Kirkpatrick, Mil Inf; deserted
PATON, Robert, Pvt, Col Alexander Loury, Capt Gabriel Martin, Inf
PATON, William, Cpl, Col Thos Benton, Capt Isiah Renshaw, Vol Inf
PATRICK, Caleb, Pvt, Col Edward Bradley, Capt Abraham Bledsoe, Riflemen
PATRICK, Caleb, Pvt, Col Jas Raulston, Capt Mathew Neal, Inf
PATRICK, Caleb, Pvt, Col Wm Hall, Capt Abraham Bledsoe, Vol Inf
PATRICK, James, Pvt, Col Newton Cannon, Capt George Brandon, Mtd Riflemen
PATRICK, James, Pvt, Col Wm Johnson, Capt James Stewart, E TN Mil
PATRICK, John T, Sgt, Regt Commander omitted, Capt Edwin S Moore, Mtd Riflemen
PATRICK, John, Pvt, Regt Commander omitted, Capt Larkin Ferrell, Inf
PATRICK, Lewis, Pvt, Regt Commander omitted, Capt Larkin Ferrell, Inf
PATRICK, Mas, Pvt, Col Wm Johnson, Capt James Stewart, E TN Draft Mil
PATRICK, Paul, Pvt, Col Philip Pipkin, Capt Ebenezer Kirkpatrick, Mil Inf
PATRICK, Willie, Pvt, Col Samuel Bunch, Capt James Cummings, E TN Vol Mtd Inf; Regt from Hawkins Co
PATRICK, Willie, Pvt, Col Samuel Bunch, Capt Jones Griffin, E TN Draft Mil
PATRICK, Willie, Pvt, Maj John Chiles, Capt James Cummings, E TN Vol Mtd Inf
PATTEN, John, Pvt, Col R C Napier, Capt Thos Preston, Mil Inf
PATTERN, John, Sgt, Col John Coffee, Lt Col Wm Phillips, 36th Reg TN Mil, Hickman Co?
PATTERSON, Alexander, Cpl, Col Philip Pipkin, Capt Geo Mebane, Mil Inf
PATTERSON, Alexander, Pvt, Col John Cocke, Capt Geo Barnes, Inf
PATTERSON, Alexander, Pvt, Col Wm Lillard, Capt Wm McLin, E Tn Inf
PATTERSON, Alexander, Pvt, Gen Wm Johnston, Capt Daniel Oban, 36 Inf
PATTERSON, Alexander, Sgt, Col Thos Williamson, Capt Thos Porter, Vol Mtd Gunmen; died 1-22-1815
PATTERSON, Andrew, Pvt, Brig Gen T Johnson, Capt Robert Carson, Inf
PATTERSON, Andrew, Pvt, Col S Bunch, Capt Thos Mann, E TN Vol Mtd Inf
PATTERSON, Archibald, Pvt, Maj Wm Russell, Capt John Cowan, Vol Mtd Gunmen
PATTERSON, Barnet M, Pvt, Col Thos Benton, Capt James McEwen, Vol Inf
PATTERSON, Benjamin, Pvt, Col John Cocke, Capt Samuel Caruthers, Inf; died 2-14-1815
PATTERSON, Benjamin, Pvt, Gen A Jackson, Capt David Deaderick, Arty
PATTERSON, Bernard M, Pvt, Col Thos Benton, Capt James McEwen, Vol Inf; promoted to Sgt Maj
PATTERSON, Bernard, Sgt Maj, Commanders omitted, 2 Regt TN Vol
PATTERSON, Charles, Pvt, Col Edwin Booth, Capt Porter, Drafted Mil
PATTERSON, David W, Pvt, Col Wm Metcalf, Capt John Barnhart, Mil Inf
PATTERSON, Francis, Sgt Maj, Col Samuel Bunch, no Co Commander, E TN Mil
PATTERSON, George, Pvt, Col Robert Steele, Capt Robt Campbell, Mil Inf
PATTERSON, Hugh, Pvt, Col Thos Williamson, Capt A Metcalf, Vol Mtd Gunmen
PATTERSON, Jacob, Blksmth, Col R H Dyer, Capt James McMahon, TN Mtd Vol Gunmen; killed in battle 12-23-1814
PATTERSON, James, Cpl, Col Newton Cannon, Capt James Walton, Mtd Riflemen
PATTERSON, James, Pvt, Col Newton Cannon, Capt Andrew Patterson, Mtd Riflemen
PATTERSON, James, Pvt, Col Thos Williamson, Capt

## Enlisted Men, War of 1812

Wm Martin, Vol Mtd Gunmen
PATTERSON, James, Pvt, Maj John Chiles, Capt Daniel Price, Vol Mtd Gunmen
PATTERSON, John, Cpl, Col A Cheatham, Capt Charles Johnson, Inf
PATTERSON, John, Pvt, Col Edward Bradley, Capt Brice Martin, Vol Inf
PATTERSON, John, Pvt, Col Philip Pipkin, Capt Geo Mebane, Mil Inf
PATTERSON, John, Pvt, Col Samuel Bunch, Capt Jno English, E TN Draft Mil; joined from Capt Williams' Co
PATTERSON, John, Pvt, Col Wm Johnson, Capt Elihu Milliken, Regt E TN Mil
PATTERSON, John, Pvt, Maj John Chiles, Capt Charles Conway, E TN Mtd Gunmen
PATTERSON, Joseph, Pvt, Col John Alcorn, Capt Wm Locke, Cav
PATTERSON, Joseph, Pvt, Col John Coffee, Capt Blackman Coleman, Cav
PATTERSON, Malcolm, Pvt, Col John Alcorn, Capt Wm Locke, Cav
PATTERSON, Malcolm, Pvt, Col Thos Benton, Capt Henry L Douglass, Vol Inf
PATTERSON, Mark, Pvt, Col A Cheatham, Capt Geo Chapman, Inf
PATTERSON, Marlin, Pvt, Regt Commander omitted, Capt Nathan Peoples, Inf
PATTERSON, Nathan, Pvt, Col N T Perkins, Capt Mathew Patterson, Mtd Vol
PATTERSON, Nathaniel, Pvt, Regt Commander omitted, Capt James Cowan, Mtd Inf
PATTERSON, Patrick, Sgt Maj, Brig Gen Thos Johnston, no Co Commander, Branch omitted
PATTERSON, Robert C, Cpl, Col Wm Pillow, Lt Mason, Vol Inf
PATTERSON, Robert C, Pvt, Col Thos Benton, Capt Robert Cannon, Inf
PATTERSON, Robert, Pvt, Col John Brown, Capt Hugh Barton, E TN Mil Inf
PATTERSON, Robert, Pvt, Col, N T Perkins, Capt John Doak, Vol Mtd Gunmen
PATTERSON, Samuel, Pvt, Maj Gen Wm Carroll, Capt Wiley Huddleston, Inf
PATTERSON, Silas, Pvt, Col Wm Johnson, Capt Andrew Lawson, E TN Draft Mil
PATTERSON, Solomon, Pvt, Col John Cocke, Capt John Dalton, Inf
PATTERSON, Thomas, 1 Sgt, Col Samuel Bunch, Capt Thos Mann, E TN Vol Mtd Inf; promoted to Sgt Maj
PATTERSON, Thomas, Pvt, Col R H Dyer, Capt Ephraim Dickson, TN Mtd Vol Gunmen
PATTERSON, Thomas, Sgt, Col A Metcalf, Capt John Barnhart, Mil Inf; died 1-12-1815
PATTERSON, Thomas, Sgt, Col Wm Higgins, Capt Adam Dale, Mtd Gunmen
PATTERSON, William T, 2 Sgt, Maj Gen Wm Carroll, Capt Francis Ellis, Inf
PATTERSON, William, Pvt, Col James Raulston, Capt James A Black, Inf
PATTERSON, William, Pvt, Col John Cocke, Capt James Gault, Inf
PATTERSON, William, Pvt, Col N T Perkins, Capt John B Quarles, Vol Mtd Inf
PATTERSON, William, Pvt, Regt Commander omitted, Capt D Mason, Cav
PATTON, David, Pvt, Col Wm Pillow, Capt Isiah Renshaw, Inf
PATTON, Elias, Pvt, Col Thomas McCrory, Capt William Dooley, Inf
PATTON, George, Pvt, Gen Andrew Jackson, Capt David Deadrick, Arty
PATTON, George, Sdlr, Col Jno Coffee, Capt Alexander McKeen, Cav
PATTON, George, Sdlr, Col John Alcorn, Capt Alexander McKeen, Cav; trans to Arty
PATTON, James, Pvt, Col N Cannon, Capt John Demsey, Mtd Gunmen
PATTON, James, Pvt, Col Thos Benton, Capt Benj Hewett, Vol Inf
PATTON, James, Pvt, Col Thos Benton, Capt Jas Renshaw, Vol Inf; joined from Capt Hewett
PATTON, James, Pvt, Gen Jackson, Capt William Russell, Mil Spies; died 11-23-1813 of wounds
PATTON, John C, Pvt, Lt T Barrett, Capt Nathan Davis, Branch omitted
PATTON, John, Cpl, Col John Cocke, Capt Samuel Carothers, Inf
PATTON, John, Cpl, Col Thos Benton, Capt Benj Hewett, Vol Inf
PATTON, John, Pvt, Col John Alcorn, Capt T McCrory, E TN Mil
PATTON, John, Pvt, Col John Winn, Capt William Willson, Inf; trans to Capt Cole's Co
PATTON, John, Pvt, Col John Wynn, Capt Jas Cole, Inf
PATTON, John, Pvt, Col N Cannon, Capt John Patterson, Mtd Riflemen
PATTON, John, Pvt, Col Thomas Williamson, Capt Doak & Capt John Dobbins, Vol Mtd Gunmen
PATTON, John, Pvt, Col William Metcalf, Capt Andrew Patterson, Mil Inf; died 2-2-1815
PATTON, John, Pvt, Lt T Barrett, Capt Nathan Davis, Inf
PATTON, John, Sgt, Commanders omitted, Inf
PATTON, Josiah, Pvt, Col Wm Hall, Capt John Kennedy, Vol Inf
PATTON, Mathew, Pvt, Col John Coffee, Capt Charles Kavanaugh, Cav
PATTON, Moses, Pvt, Col T McCrory, Capt William Dooly, Inf
PATTON, Richard T, Pvt, Col John Winn, Capt Robert Braden, Inf
PATTON, Richard T, Pvt, Col R C Napier, Capt Drury Adkins, Mil Inf
PATTON, Robert H, QM, Col S Bunch, Maj Alexander Smith, E TN Mil
PATTON, Robert, Pvt, Col A Cheatham, Capt Geo Chapman, Inf
PATTON, Robert, Pvt, Col John Allison, Capt Nelson, E TN Drafted Mil; apptd QM
PATTON, Robert, Pvt, Col T McCrory, Capt Jas Shannon, Mil Inf

PATTON, Samuel R, Pvt, Maj John Childs, Capt Daniel Price, E TN Mil Inf; in Gen Coffee Brig
PATTON, Samuel, Rank omitted, Col Wm Johnson, Capt Jas Stewart, E Tn Drafted Mil
PATTON, Thomas, Cpl, Maj Gen A Jackson, Capt William Carroll, Vol Inf
PATTON, Thomas, Pvt, Col Alexander Loury, Capt Arahel Rains & Capt Leroy Hammonds, Inf
PATTON, Thomas, Pvt, Col Phillip Pipkin, Capt William Mackey, Mil Inf
PATTON, Thomas, Pvt, Col S Wear, Capt Joseph Calloway, Mtd Inf
PATTON, Thomas, Pvt, Col T McCrory, Capt Isaac Patton, Mil Inf
PATTON, Thomas, Pvt, Col Wm Johnson, Capt Jas Tunnell, E Tn Mil
PATTON, William C, Pvt, Col S Bunch, Capt Jno Harris, E TN Mil
PATTON, William, Cpl, Col Thos Benton, Capt Benj Hewett, Vol Inf
PATTON, William, Cpl, Col Thos Benton, Capt Jas Renshaw, Vol Inf; joined from Capt Hewett Co
PATTON, William, Pvt, Col R C Napier, Capt Jas McMurry, Mil Inf
PATTON, William, Pvt, Col S Bunch, Capt Jas Duncan, E TN Drafted Mil; joined from Capt Howell's Co
PATTON, William, Pvt, Col William Pillow, Capt Jas Renshaw, Inf
PATTON, William, Pvt, Col Wm Johnson, Capt Jas Stewart, E TN Drafted Mil
PATTON, William, Pvt, Maj Gen A Jackson, Capt William Carroll, Vol Inf
PATTON, _____, Pvt, Col John Wynne, Capt John Porter, Inf
PAUL, Adley, Pvt, Col Edwin Booth, Capt John Lewis, E TN Mil
PAUL, Elias, Pvt, Col Thos Benton, Capt Henry Douglas, Vol Inf
PAUL, William, Pvt, Col John Brown, Capt John Childs, E TN Vol Mtd Inf
PAXTON, David, Pvt, Col Ewen Allison, Capt Edward Bradley, Vol Cav
PAXTON, John, Pvt, Col T McCrory, Capt Jas Shannon, Mil Inf
PAXTON, Thompson, Pvt, Col William Pillow, Capt C E McEwen, Vol Inf
PAYER, William, Pvt, Maj Robert Cooper, Co Commander omitted, Mtd Riflemen
PAYNE, Chesby, Pvt, Col William Higgins, Capt James Hambleton, Mtd Gunmn
PAYNE, Colison, Pvt, Col S Copeland, Capt John Dawson, Inf
PAYNE, Daniel, Cpl, Col Robert Dyer, Capt Jas McMahon, TN Mtd Vol Inf
PAYNE, Ephraim, Pvt, Col Phillip Pipkin, Capt Jas Renshaw, Mil Inf
PAYNE, George, Pvt, Col Robert Dyer, Capt Allen, Vol Mtd Gunmen
PAYNE, James, Pvt, Col James Raulston, Maj Gen Wm Carroll, Capt Edward Robinson, Inf
PAYNE, James, Pvt, Col S Copeland, Capt John Dawson, Inf
PAYNE, John B, Pvt, Col S Copeland, Capt Moses Thompson, Inf
PAYNE, John, Pvt, Col John K Wynne, Capt Wm Wilson, Inf; trans to Capt Caruthers Co
PAYNE, John, Pvt, Col Samuel Bunch, Capt S Richerson, E TN Draft Mil; deserted
PAYNE, John, Pvt, Col Wm Metcalf, Capt Thos Marks, Mil Inf
PAYNE, John, Pvt, Lt Col L Hammond, Capt Arahel Rains, Inf
PAYNE, Jonathan, Pvt, Col John Cocke, Capt John Dalton, Inf; died 2-11-1815
PAYNE, Joseph, Pvt, Col R H Dyer, Capt Ephraim D Dickson, TN Mtd Vol Gunmen; no svce performed
PAYNE, Joseph, Pvt, Col Thos Williamson, Capt Robert Moore, Vol Mtd Gunmen
PAYNE, Joseph, Pvt, Regt Commander omitted, Capt Ephraim Dickson, Branch omitted
PAYNE, Landa, Pvt, Col Samuel Bunch, Capt Jno Hawk, E TN Mil
PAYNE, Major, Pvt, Col Samuel Bunch, Capt S Richerson, E TN Draft Mil; deserted
PAYNE, Robert, Pvt, Col A Lowry, Capt John Looney, W TN Inf
PAYNE, Robert, Pvt, Col Edward Bradley, Capt Abraham Bledsoe, Riflemen
PAYNE, Robert, Pvt, Col Wm Hall, Capt Abraham Bledsoe, Vol Inf
PAYNE, Samuel, Pvt, Col Ewen Allison, Capt Wm King, Draft Mil
PAYNE, Thomas H, Pvt, Col Newton Cannon, Capt James Walton, Mtd Riflemen
PAYNE, William, Pvt, Col Wm Metcalf, Capt Chas Marks, Mil Inf
PAYNE, William, Pvt, Col Wm Metcalf, Capt John Barhart, Mil Inf; died 4-2-1815
PAYNE, William, Sgt, Col Samuel Bunch, Capt Geo McPherson, E TN Mil; joined from Capt Griffin Co
PAYNE (PAIN), William, Pvt, Col Ewen Allison, Capt James Laughmiller, Mil; trans to Capt McPherson Co
PAYNE (PAINE), John, Pvt, Col Wm Johnson, Capt James Tunnell, E TN Mil
PAYNER, Sercy, Pvt, Col Thos Williamson, Lt Jas Neely, Capt Jas Pace, Vol Mtd Gunmen
PAYSINGER, John, Pvt, Col Ewen Allison, Capt Thos Wilson, E TN Draft Mil
PAYSINGER, John, Pvt, Col Jas Raulston, Maj Gen Wm Carroll, Capt Jas Robinson, Inf
PAYSINGER, John, Pvt, Col Samuel Bunch, Capt Jones Griffin, E Tn Draft Mil; joined from Capt Wilson's Co
PAYSINGER, Michael, Pvt, Col Ewen Allison, Capt Nelson, E TN Draft Mil
PAYTON, George, Sgt, Col John Cocke, Capt Samuel N Caruthers, Inf
PAYTON, John H, Pvt, Col Jno Coffee, Capt John W Byrn, Cav

## Enlisted Men, War of 1812

PEACE, Pleasant, Pvt, Maj Wm Russell, Capt Fleman Hodges, Vol Mtd Gunmen

PEACH, James, Pvt, Col Wm Johns, Capt James Stuart, E TN Draft Mil

PEACOCK, Henry, Pvt, Maj Wm Woodfolk, Capt James Neil, Inf

PEACOCK, John, Pvt, Lt Col L Hammond, Capt James Craig, Inf

PEAKE, John, Pvt, Col R H Dyer, Capt Cuthbert Hudson, Vol Mtd Gunmen

PEAKE, John, Pvt, Col Samuel Copeland, Capt G W Stell, Mil Inf

PEARCE, Arthur, Pvt, Col T Williamson, Capt Wm Martin, Vol Mtd Gunmen

PEARCE, Charles, Pvt, Col James Raulston, Capt Henry Hamilton, Inf; also served under Maj Gen Wm Carroll

PEARCE, David, Pvt, Maj Wm Woodfolk, Capt Abner Pearce, Inf

PEARCE, James, Pvt, Col SAmuel Wear, Capt Joseph Calloway, Mtd Inf

PEARCE, John, Pvt, Col Philip Pipkin, Capt Peter Searcy, Mil Inf; deserted

PEARCE, John, Pvt, Col Wm Johnson, Capt Christopher Cook, E Tn Mil

PEARCE, John, Pvt, Maj Gen A Jackson, Capt John Craine, Mtd Gunmen

PEARCE, Joseph, Pvt, Col Wm LiHard, Capt Robert McCalpin, E Tn Inf

PEARCE, Nathan, Pvt, Col Samuel Wear, Capt Jesse Cole, Vol Inf

PEARCE, Richard, Pvt, Col Thos Benton, Capt James McEwen, Vol Inf

PEARCE, Solomon, Pvt, Col Samuel Wear, Capt John Chiles, E TN Inf

PEARCE, Stokely D, Sgt, Col Edward Bradley, Capt Travis Nash, Vol Inf

PEARCE, William, Pvt, Col Wm Lillard, Capt Robt Maloney, E TN Vol Inf

PEARCE, William, Sgt, Regt Commander omitted, Capt Gray, Inf

PEARCY, John, Pvt, Col Newton Cannon, Capt Wm Edwards, Regt Command

PEARS, William, Pvt, Col A Loury, Capt James Kincaid, Inf

PEARSALE, Benjamin, Pvt, Col John Coffee, Capt Michael Molton, Cav

PEARSILL, Abil, Sgt, Sgt, Regt Commander omitted, Capt Alex McKean, Branch omitted

PEARSOLL, Benjamin, Cpl, Regt Commander omitted, Capt Jos Williams, Mil Cav; promoted to Cor

PEARSOLL, Benjamin, Pvt, Regt Commander omitted, Capt Jos Williams, Mil Cav; promoted to Cpl

PEARSON, Daniel, Pvt, Col T McCrory, Capt Jno Reynolds, Mil Inf

PEARSON, Henry, Pvt, Col Jno Coffee, Capt John W Byrn, Cav

PEARSON, Henry, Pvt, Col Samuel Bunch, Capt James Cummings, E TN Vol Mtd Inf

PEARSON, Howell, Pvt, Col Thomas H Williamson, Capt Joseph Williams, Vol Mtd Gunmen

PEARSON, James, Pvt, Col Thomas H Williamson, Co Commander omitted, Vol Mtd Gunmen

PEARSON, John, Sgt, Col Samuel Bunch, Capt Edward Buchanan, E TN Drafted Mil

PEARSON, Robert, Pvt, Col Wm Johnson, Capt James Rogers, E TN Mil Drafted

PEARSON, Thomas, Pvt, Col Wm Johnson, Capt James Tunnell, E TN Mil

PEAY, Elias, Pvt, Col Newton Cannon, Capt Gabriel Martin, Mtd Gunmen

PEAY, Nathaniel, Pvt, Col Thomas H Benton, Co Commander omitted, Vol Inf

PEBILLER, Lewis, Pvt, Col Ewin Allison, Capt Joseph Everett, E TN Mil; deserted 3-4-1814

PEBLES, Howell, Cpl, Col Thos H Benton, Capt Jas McEwin, Vol Inf

PECK, James H, Asst Top Engineer, Brig Gen Nathan Taylor, no other information

PECK, James H, W Topograph Col Eng, Brig Gen N Taylor, no other information

PECK, John, Pvt, Regt Commander omitted, Capt James Cowan, Mtd Inf

PECK, L Moses, Pvt, Col Wm Lillard, Capt Thomas McChristian, E TN Vol Inf

PECK, Nathaniel, 4 Lt, Gen Andrew Jackson, Capt D Deadrick, Arty

PECK, Nathaniel, Pvt, Gen Andrew Jackson, Capt Wm Carroll, Branch Srvce omitted

PECK, Willie B, Sgt, Col Samuel Bayless, Capt Joseph Goodson, E TN Mil

PEDIGRUE, Hance, Pvt, Col Wm Lillard, Capt Hugh Martin, E TN Vol Inf

PEEBLES, Howell, Cpl, Col Thomas H Benton, Capt James McEwin, Vol Inf

PEEBLES, Howell, Pvt, Regt Commander omitted, Capt D Mason, Cav

PEEK, John, Pvt, Col Wm Johnson, Co Commander omitted, E TN Drafted Mil; deserted

PEEK, Moses L, QM, Brig Gen Nathaniel Taylor, Drafted Mil (3rd Regt E TN Drafted?)

PEELS, John, Pvt, Maj Wm Woodfolk, Capt Ezekial Ross, Inf

PEEPLES, Cordy C, Dmr, Col A Loury, Capt J N Williams, W TN Mil

PEEPLES, Cordy C, Ffr, Col Leroy Hammonds, Capt Joseph Hammond & Capt Thomas H Williamson, Inf

PEGRAM (PEGRIM), William, Sgt, Col Philip Pipkin, Capt David Smith, Mil

PELLAM, Jesse, Pvt, Col Edwin E Booth, Capt John McKamy, E TN Mil

PELSON (PULSON), John, Pvt, Col Wm Johnson, Capt James Rogers, E TN Drafted Mil

PEMBERTON, Benjamin, 2 Sgt, Col Wm Lillard, Capt Benjamin King, E TN Vol Inf

PEMBERTON, Ezekiel, Pvt, Col Wm Lillard, Capt Benjamin King, E TN Vol Inf

PEMBERTON, Joshua, Pvt, Col James Raulston, Capt Charles Wade, Inf; promoted to Cpl

PEMINGTON, David, Pvt, Col S Copeland, Capt Wm Douglas, Inf

- 399

## Enlisted Men, War of 1812

PEMSON, Henry, Pvt, Col John Alcorn, Capt Pyms, Cav
PENCE, Adam, Pvt, Col Samuel Bayless, Capt James Churchman, E TN Mil; d 3-28-1815
PENDERGRASS, Richard, Pvt, Col Thomas H Williamson, Capt Robert Moore, Vol Mtd Gunmen
PENDLETON, Asa, 1 Cpl, Col A Loury, Lt Col Leroy Hammond, Capt Thos Delaney, Inf
PENDLETON, William, Pvt, Col Edwin E Booth, Capt James McKamy, E TN Mil
PENEHOUSE, Daniel, Pvt, Maj Gen Wm Carroll, Col James Raulston, Capt Wm Robinson, Inf
PENILTON, Benjamin, Pvt, Col Copeland, Capt Wm Douglass, Inf
PENLAND, Noble, Pvt, Col Newton Cannon, Capt Demsey, Mtd Gunmen; wounded 11-9-1813
PENN, James, Pvt, Col Philip Pipkin, Capt MacKay, Mil Inf
PENN, John, Pvt, Col Wm Lillard, Capt Thomas Sharpe, 2nd Regt Inf
PENN, William, Pvt, Col Wm Lillard, Capt Thomas Sharpe, 2nd Regt Inf
PENNEL, John, Pvt, Col Samuel Wear, Capt James Gillespie, E TN Vol Inf
PENNEL, Samuel, Pvt, Maj Wm Russell, Co Commander omitted, Vol Mtd Gunmen
PENNINGTON, Andrew, Pvt, Col Wm Pillow, Capt James Anderson, Vol Inf
PENNINGTON, William, Pvt, Col R H Dyer, Capt James McMahon, TN Vol Mtd Gunmen
PENNY, John, Cpl, Brig Gen Wm Johnson, Capt Abraham Allen, Mil Inf
PENNY, John, Pvt, Maj Gen Wm Carroll, Capt Francis Ellis, Inf
PENTECOST, Morgan R, Cpl, Col A Loury, Co Commander omitted, Inf
PENTECOST, Morgan, Pvt, Col Thomas Bradley, Capt Abraham Bledsoe, Riflemen
PEOPLES, Cordy C, Ffr, Col L Hammond, Capt J N Williamson, 2nd Regt Inf
PEOPLES, George, Pvt, Col Thomas Williamson, Capt Robert Moore, Vol Mtd Gunmen; transferred to Lt Bean's Spies
PEOPLES, George, Pvt, Gen John Coffee, Co Commander omitted, Mtd Spies
PEOPLES, William, Pvt, Col R C Napier, Capt Andrew McCarty, Mil Inf
PEPPER, Nathaniel, Pvt, Col John Cocke, Capt Richard Crunk, Inf
PEPPER, William B, Pvt, Col Thos McCrory, Capt Thos Gordon, Inf
PEPPER, William, Pvt, Col John K Winn, Capt Andrew Braden, Inf
PERCE (PEARCE), Zion, Cpl, Col Wm Johnson, Capt Henry Hunter, E TN Mil
PERCER, Robert, Pvt, Brig Gen Thos Johnson, Capt Robert Carson, Inf
PERET, Lewis, Pvt, Col Wm Johnson, Capt David McKamy, E TN Drafted Mil
PERFEPILL, Jacob, Pvt, Col Samuel Bunch, Capt Francis Berry, E TN Mil; attached to Capt Gregory's Co
PERINE, Antheney, Pvt, Col Wm Lillard, Capt Thomas McChristian, E TN Vol Inf
PERINE, Mathew, Pvt, Col Wm Lillard, Capt Thomas McChristian, E TN Vol Inf
PERKINS, Absolom, Pvt, Col R C Napier, Co Commander omitted, Mil Inf
PERKINS, Absolum, Pvt, Gen Thomas Washington, Capt John Crawford, Mtd Inf
PERKINS, Charles H, QM Sgt, Lt Col L Hammonds, 2nd Regt W TN Mil; in place of Robert Johnson
PERKINS, Charles, 1 Mate, Col Thos McCrory, 3rd Regt TN Mil
PERKINS, Charles, Surgeon Mate, Col N T Perkins, 1st Regt TN Mtd Vol
PERKINS, Charles, Surgeon Mate, Col Thos McCrory, 2nd Regt TN Mil
PERKINS, Constantine, Pvt, Regt Commander omitted, Capt D Deaderick, Pack Horse Co
PERKINS, David, Pvt, Col Alexander Loury, Lt Col L Hammonds, Capt Arahel Rains, Inf
PERKINS, Elijah, Pvt, Col A Cheatham, Capt Chas Johnson, Inf
PERKINS, Ephraim, Pvt, Col Thos Benton, Capt Wm J Smith, Vol Inf
PERKINS, Ephraim, Pvt, Col Wm Pillow, Capt Wm J Smith, Vol Inf
PERKINS, Ephraim, Pvt, Regt Commander omitted, Capt Wm J Smith, Vol Inf; deserted
PERKINS, Ephram, Pvt, Maj Gen Wm Carroll, Capt Francis Ellis, Inf; substitute for Abr Triber
PERKINS, George, Cpl, Col L Hammonds, Capt James Craig, 2nd Regt W TN Mil
PERKINS, Hardin, Pvt, Col Wm Pillow, Capt C E McEwen, Vol Inf
PERKINS, James, Pvt, Regt Commander omitted, Capt Askew, Inf
PERKINS, John P, Pvt, Col N T Perkins, Col Wm Johnson, Mil Inf
PERKINS, John, Pvt, Col Newton Cannon, Capt Ota Cantrell, W TN Mtd Inf; deserted
PERKINS, Joseph, Pvt, Col Alexander Loury, Capt John Looney, W TN Inf
PERKINS, Levi, Pvt, Col Robert Steele, Capt Richard M Ratton, Mil Inf
PERKINS, Levi, Pvt, Col S Bunch, Capt F Register, E TN Mil
PERKINS, Major, Pvt, Col N Cannon, Capt John Hanley, Mtd Riflemen
PERKINS, Moses, Pvt, Maj Wm Russell, Col R H Dyer, Capt Isaac Williams, 1st Regt TN Vol Mtd Gunmen; Separate Bn Gunmen
PERKINS, Moses, Pvt, Regt Commander omitted, Capt Samuel Allen, Inf; Pack Horse Guards
PERKINS, Nicholas, Pvt, Gen Thos Washington, Capt Jno Crawford, Mtd Inf
PERKINS, Nicholas, S Mate, Col Ewen Allison, E TN Mil
PERKINS, Robert, Pvt, Col A Cheatham, Capt Wm Johnson, Inf
PERKINS, Robert, Pvt, Col N Cannon, Capt Wm Martin, Mtd Gunmen
PERKINS, Thomas H, Pvt, Col Newton Cannon, Capt Wm Martin, Mtd Gunmen; promoted to QM Sgt

## Enlisted Men, War of 1812

PERKINS, Thomas H, Pvt, Regt Commander omitted, Capt Edwin S Moore, Mtd Riflemen; promoted to Sgt on Col R Steele

PERKINS, Thomas H, QM Sgt, Col Newton Cannon, TN Vol Mtd Gunmen

PERKINS, Thomas H, Sgt Maj, Col Robert Steele, Co Commander omitted, 4th Regt TN Mil

PERKINS, William P, 4 Sgt, Col Thos Benton, Capt James McEwen, Vol Inf

PERKINS, William P, Sgt, Col Thos Benton, Capt James McEwen, Vol Inf

PERKINS, William, Pvt, Maj Wm Russell, Capt Isaac Williams, Separate Bn TN Vol Mtd Gunmen

PERKINS, Wright, Pvt, Col R H Dyer, Capt Cuthbert Hudson, Vol Mtd Gunmen

PERKINSON, John, Pvt, Col Thos Benton, Capt Wm J Smith, Vol Inf

PERRIS, Drury, Pvt, Col N T Perkins, Capt George Eliot, Mil Inf

PERRY, Alexander, 5 Sgt, Col Wm Metcalf, Capt Thomas Marks, Mil Inf

PERRY, Alexander, Pvt, Col R H Dyer, Capt James McMahon, TN Vol Mtd Gunmen

PERRY, Bird, Pvt, Col Wm Johnson, Capt James Stewart, E TN Mil

PERRY, Bud, Pvt, Col Wm Johnson, Capt James Stewart, E TN Drafted Mil

PERRY, Charles B, Pvt, Maj Wm Carroll, Capt Lewis Dillahunty & Capt Daniel M Bradford, Vol Inf

PERRY, Charles, Pvt, Col John Alcorn, Capt Jno W Byrns, Cav

PERRY, Edward, Pvt, Col Samuel Bayless, Capt John Brock, E TN Mil

PERRY, Eli, Pvt, Col Wm Johnson, Capt Elihu Milliken, 3rd Regt E TN Mil; transferred from Capt Hunter's Command

PERRY, Ely, Pvt, Col Wm Johnson, Capt Henry Hunter, E TN Mil; substitute for Jno Dunlap, transferred to Capt Milliken

PERRY, George, Pvt, Col John Cocke, Capt Sam M Caruthers, Inf

PERRY, George, Pvt, Lt Col A Cheatham, Co Commander omitted, 6th Brig Inf

PERRY, Horatio G, 1 Sgt, Col Wm Johnson, Capt Andrew Lawson, E TN Drafted Mil

PERRY, James, Pvt, Col Edwin Booth, Capt Sam Thompson, Mil

PERRY, James, Pvt, Col R C Napier, Capt Samuel Ashmore, Mil Inf

PERRY, James, Pvt, Regt Commander omitted, Capt James Gray, Inf

PERRY, Jesse, Pvt, Col John Coffee, Capt Robert Jetton, Cav; enlisted in the regular army

PERRY, John, Pvt, Col Philip Pipkin, Capt Ebenezer Kirkpatrick, Mil Inf

PERRY, John, Pvt, Col R C Napier, Capt Samuel Ashmore, Mil Inf

PERRY, John, Pvt, Col Thos Williamson, Capt Richard Tate, Vol Mtd Gunmen

PERRY, John, Pvt, Col Wm Hall, Capt Abraham Bledsoe, Vol Inf

PERRY, John, Rank omitted, Col R H Dyer, Capt James McMahon, TN Vol Mtd Gunmen; d 12-6-1814

PERRY, Joseph, Pvt, Col Wm Johnson, Capt Jas Stewart, E TN Drafted Mil; substitute

PERRY, Joshua, Pvt, Col T McCrory, Capt Isaac Patton, Branch Srvce omitted

PERRY, Kinchen, Pvt, Lt Col Leroy Hammonds, Capt Jas Craig, Inf

PERRY, Levin, Pvt, no other information

PERRY, Littleton, Pvt, Col Thomas Williamson, Capt Richard Tate, Vol Mtd Gunmen

PERRY, Luke, Pvt, Col S Bayless, Capt John Brock, E TN Mil

PERRY, Nathaniel, Pvt, Regt Commander omitted, Capt Edwin S Moore, Mtd Riflemen

PERRY, Nofflet, Pvt, Col John Coffee, Capt Henry Byron, Cav

PERRY, Noflet, Pvt, Col John Alcorn, Capt Henry Bryan, Cav

PERRY, Obadiah, Cpl, Col Alexander Loury, Capt Geo Saver, Inf

PERRY, Obadiah, Pvt, Col Edward Bradley, Capt John Moore, Vol Inf; deserted 11-19-1813

PERRY, Obediah, Pvt, Col Wm Hall, Capt John Moore, Vol Inf

PERRY, Richardson, Pvt, Col John Cocke, Capt John Dalton, Inf; d 4-16-1815

PERRY, Richardson, Pvt, Col Williamson, Capt Williams, Vol Mtd Gunmen

PERRY, Robert sr, Pvt, Col John Cocke, Capt Samuel Carothers, Inf

PERRY, Robert, Cpl, Col John Cocke, Capt Samuel Caruthers, Inf

PERRY, Robert, Pvt, Col A Cheatham, Capt Richard Benson, Inf

PERRY, Robert, Sgt, Lt Col A Cheatham, Co Commander omitted, Brig Mtd Inf

PERRY, Simeon, Pvt, Col John Alcorn, Capt Henry Byrns, Cav

PERRY, Simeon, Pvt, Col Robert Steele, Capt Jas Randal, Inf

PERRY, Simeon, Pvt, Maj Gen A Jackson, Col A Cheatham, Inf

PERRY, Simon, Pvt, Col Jno Coffee, Capt Henry Byron, Cav

PERRY, Siom L, Pvt, Col Nicholas Perkins, Capt Mathew Johnston, Mil Inf

PERRY, Thomas A, 2 Sgt, Col Wm Johnson, Capt Andrew Lawson, E TN Drafted Mil

PERRY, Thomas A, 3 Sgt, Col S Wear, Capt Sieom? Perry, E TN Vol Mtd Inf; promoted from Cpl

PERRY, Thomas A, Pvt, Col Wm Johnson, Capt David McKamey, E TN Drafted Mil; transferred to Capt Lawson for J McCullon

PERRY, Thomas, Pvt, Col A Cheatham, Capt Richard Benson, Inf

PERRY, Thomas, Pvt, Col Phillip Pipkin, Capt John Strother, Mil

PERRY, Thomas, Pvt, Col William Johnson, Capt Benj Powell, E TN Mil

PERRY, Thorton, Pvt, Col Philip Pipkin, Capt William

## Enlisted Men, War of 1812

Mackay, Mil Inf
PERRY, William, Pvt, Col R H Dyer, Capt James McMahon, TN Vol Mtd Gunmen
PERRY, William, Pvt, Lt Col A Cheatham, Co Commander omitted, Brig Mtd Inf
PERRYMAN, Joshua, Cpl, Col John Brown, Capt William White, E TN Mil Inf
PERSELL, Abel, Pvt, Col John Alcorn, Capt Alexander McKeen, Cav
PERSLEY, Jacob, Pvt, Col S Wear, Capt Jas Tedford, E TN Vol Inf
PERSON, George W, Cpl, Col John Cocke, Capt James Gault, Inf; transferred from Capt Patterson for W Hughs
PERSON, John, Pvt, Col Wm Johnson, Capt Elihu Milliken, E TN Mil
PERSON, Robert, Pvt, Col John Cocke, Capt George Barnes, Inf
PETERMAN, George, Pvt, Col T McCrory, Capt Abel Willis, Mil Inf
PETERS, Abraham, Pvt, Col S Bunch, Capt Geo McPherson, E TN Mil; joined from Capt King's Co
PETERS, Absolom, Pvt, Col Ewen Allison, Capt William King, Drafted Mil
PETERS, Bruten, Pvt, Col William Johnston, Capt Henry Hunter, E TN Mil
PETERS, Enanuel, 2 Sgt, Col William Lillard, Capt John Neatherton, Branch Srvce omitted
PETERS, Henry, Pvt, Col Edwin Booth, Capt Richard Marshall, Drafted Mil
PETERS, Isaac, Pvt, Col Edwin Allison, Capt William King, Drafted Mil
PETERS, Isaac, Pvt, Col S Bunch, Capt Geo McPherson, E TN Mil; joined from Capt King's Co
PETERS, James, Pvt, Col Edwin Allison, Capt Adam Winsell, E TN Drafted Mil; discharged for inability
PETERS, Joshua, Pvt, Maj Wm Woodfolk, Capt A Tuner, Inf
PETERS, Samuel, Far, Col N Cannon, Capt John Demsey, Mtd Gunmen
PETERS, Thomas, Pvt, Col John Brown, Capt Lunsford Oliver, E TN Mil
PETERS, Tobias, Cpl, Col S Bunch, Capt Robert Breden, E TN Mil
PETERSON, Andrew, Sgt, Lt Col Jno Edmonson, Co Commander omitted, Cav
PETERSON, Hiram, Pvt, Col S Wear, Capt Rufus Morgan, E TN Vol Inf
PETERSON, Joseph, Pvt, Col John Williams, Capt Wm Walker, Vol
PETERSON, Joseph, Pvt, Col Samuel Wear, Capt John Bayless, Mtd Inf
PETERSON, Morton, Pvt, Col Edwin Booth, Capt John Sharp, E TN Mil
PETERSON, William, Pvt, Col Edwin Booth, Capt John Lewis, E TN Mil
PETERSON, William, Pvt, Col Samuel Wear, Capt Rufus Morgan, E TN Vol Inf
PETIT, George, Pvt, Col Samuel Bayless, Capt Joseph Hale, E TN Mil

PETIT, Nehemiah, Pvt, Col Wm Johnson, Capt Joseph Scott, E TN Drafted Mil; substitute for Stephen Smith
PETNER, Adam, Pvt, Maj John Porter, Capt James Cowan, Cav; substituted in place of Alex McColn
PETREE, Adam, Pvt, Col Samuel Bayless, Capt John Brock, E TN Mil
PETRY, John, Pvt, Col Samuel Bayless, Capt Joseph Rich, E TN Inf
PETTETT, George, Pvt, Col Samuel Bunch, Capt Geo McPherson, E TN Mil; joined from Capt Register Co
PETTIT, George, Pvt, Col Samuel Bunch, Capt F Register, E TN Mil
PETTITT, Benjamin, 2 Cpl, Maj Gen Wm Carroll, Col James Raulston, Capt Wiley Huddleston, Inf
PETTUS, William H, Pvt, Col Thos Benton, Capt James Hambleton, Vol Inf
PETTY, Alexander, Pvt, Col Wm Pillow, Capt Isaiah Renshaw, Inf
PETTY, Alfred, 3 Sgt, Col Wm Metcalf, Capt Barbee Collins, Mil Inf
PETTY, Alfred, Pvt, Col Newton Cannon, Capt David Hogan, Mtd Gunmen
PETTY, Alfred, Pvt, Col R C Napier, Capt Drury Adkins, Mil Inf
PETTY, Ambrose, Pvt, Col Thos Benton, Capt Isaiah Renshaw, Vol Inf
PETTY, George, Pvt, Maj Cooper, Co Commander omitted, Mtd Riflemen
PETTY, Isham, 3 Sgt, Col John Cocke, Capt Joseph Price, Inf
PETTY, James, Pvt, Col John Wynne, Capt James Holleman, Inf
PETTY, William, Pvt, Col John Cocke, Capt Wm Caruthers, Inf
PETTY, William, Pvt, Lt Col L Hammond, Capt James Craig, Inf
PETTYJOHN, Abraham, Pvt, Col T McCrory, Capt Anthony Metcalf, Mil Inf
PETTYJOHN, Samuel, 2 Sgt, Col Wm Pillow, Capt Wm J Smith, Vol Inf
PETTYJOHN, Samuel, 3 Sgt, Col Thos Benton, Capt Wm J Smith, Vol Inf
PETTYJOHN, Samuel, Sgt, Col Thos Benton, Capt Wm J Smith, Vol Inf
PEW, Daniel, Pvt, Col Samuel Bunch, Capt Joseph Duncan, E TN Drafted Mil; joined from Capt Gibbs Co
PEW, Jesse, Pvt, Lt Col L Hammond, Capt James Tubb, Inf
PEW, Joel, Pvt, Col Philip Pipkin, Capt Henry M Newlin, Mil Inf; deserted from Ft Williams
PEW, Thomas, Pvt, Col Philip Pipkin, Capt Henry M Newlin, Mil Inf
PEW, William, Pvt, Col Thos Benton, Capt Wm Moore, Vol Inf; AWOL
PEWET, Hartwell, Pvt, Col John Cocke, Capt John Dalton, Inf
PEWET, Joel, Pvt, Col Samuel Bunch, Capt Edward Buchanan, E TN Mil; transferred from Capt

## Enlisted Men, War of 1812

Duncan's Roll
PEWETT, Thomas, Pvt, Col John Cocke, Capt Samuel Caruthers, Inf
PEWIS, Miles, Pvt, Col John Cocke, Capt John Dalton, Inf
PEYTON, Henry, Pvt, Col Thos Benton, Capt Benjamin Reynolds, Vol Inf; refused to march
PEYTON (PAYTON), Goerge Y, 1 Sgt, Col John Cocke, Capt Samuel N Caruthers, Inf
PHAGEN, James, Pvt, Col Wm Lillard, Capt Zacheus Copeland, E TN Vol Inf
PHARICE, John, Pvt, Col John Cocke, Capt James Gault, Inf
PHARIS, William, Pvt, Col James Raulston, Capt John Cowan, Inf
PHARR, Adam, Pvt, Maj Wm Russell, Capt Wm Chism, Vol Mtd Gunmen
PHARR, Samuel, Pvt, Col Wm Hall, Capt Abraham Bledsoe, Vol Inf
PHELANG, Richard C, 1 Sgt, Col John Coffee, Capt Fred Stump, Cav
PHELISTER, Win (William), Pvt, Col Thos Williamson, Capt John Hutchings, Vol Mtd Gunmen
PHELON, Richard C, Sgt, Col Wm Metcalf, Capt John Barnhart, Mil Inf
PHELPS, Charles, Pvt, Col John Cocke, Capt Bird Nance, Inf
PHELPS, Dadock, Pvt, Col John Cocke, Capt Bird Nance, Inf
PHELPS, Daniel, Pvt, Col John Cocke, Capt Bird Nance, Inf
PHELPS, David, Pvt, Col Thos Benton, Capt Geo W Gibbs, Vol Inf
PHELPS, David, Pvt, Col Wm Pillow, Capt John H Anderson, Vol Inf
PHELPS, Henry, Pvt, Col Thos Williamson, Capt Beverly Williams, Vol Mtd Gunmen
PHELPS, John, Pvt, Col Thos Williamson, Capt Beverly Williams, Vol Mtd Gunmen
PHELPS, Joshua, Pvt, Maj Wm Woodfolk, Capt James Turner, Inf
PHELPS, Kelan, Pvt, Col S Copeland, Capt John Holshouser, Inf
PHELPS, Silas, Pvt, Col Newton Cannon, Capt Ota Cantrell, W TN Mtd Inf
PHELPS, Zadock, Pvt, Col Newton Cannon, Capt Ota Cantrell, W TN Mtd Inf; deserted
PHENEHOUSE, Daniel, Pvt, Maj Gen Wm Carroll, Col James Raulston, Capt Edward Robinson, Inf
PHIBBS, Richard, Pvt, Col Jno Brown, Capt Hugh Barton, E TN Mil Inf
PHIBBS, Richard, Pvt, Maj John Childs, Capt Charles Conway, E TN Mtd Gunmen; d 1-28-1815
PHIELDING, Richard C, Sgt, Col John Alcorn, Capt Fred Stump, Cav
PHILHOF, Timothy, Pvt, Col Samuel Bayless, Capt John Brock, E TN Mil; furloughed & never returned
PHILIP, John M, Pvt, Col Jas Raulston, Capt Charles Wade, Inf
PHILIP, Robert, Pvt, Col Wm Lillard, Capt Arganbraight, E TN Vol Riflemen
PHILIPS, Benjamin, Pvt, Col John Cocke, Capt James Gault, Inf
PHILIPS, Benjamin, Pvt, Col Wm Lillard, Capt Hugh Martin, E TN Vol Inf
PHILIPS, John M, Pvt, Col Wm Hall, Capt Abraham Bledsoe, Vol Inf
PHILIPS, John, Pvt, Col Wm Lillard, Capt Geo Argenbright, E TN Vol Riflemen
PHILIPS, John, Pvt, Col Wm Lillard, Capt Wm Hamilton, E TN Vol Inf
PHILIPS, Jonathan, Pvt, Col Jas Raulston, Capt Jas A Black, Inf
PHILIPS, Samuel, Pvt, Col John Cocke, Capt John Dalton, Inf
PHILIPS, Thomas, Cpl, Col Robert Steele, Capt Samuel Maxwell, Mil Inf; deserted
PHILIPS, Thomas, Pvt, Col Thos Benton, Capt Isiah Renshaw, Vol Inf
PHILIPS, Thomas, Pvt, Col Wm Pillow, Capt Isiah Renshaw, Inf
PHILLIP, Beverly, Pvt, Col N T Perkins, Capt James McMahan, Mtd Gunmen
PHILLIP, Thomas, Pvt, Col Thos Benton, Capt Isiah Renshaw, Vol Inf
PHILLIPPS, Micajah, Pvt, Col Samuel Bunch, Capt Francis Berry, E TN Mil; attached to Capt Houk's Co
PHILLIPPS, Micajah, Pvt, Col Samuel Bunch, Capt Jones Houk, E TN Mil; joined from Capt Berry Co
PHILLIPS, Abraham, Pvt, Col S Bunch, Capt Jno Houk, E TN Mil
PHILLIPS, Andrew, Pvt, Col Wm Johnson, Capt Henry Hunter, E TN Mil
PHILLIPS, Benjamin, Pvt, Col Thos Williamson, Capt James Cook & Capt Jno Crane, Vol Mtd Gunmen
PHILLIPS, Benjamin, Pvt, Gen A Jackson, Capt Wm Russell, Mtd Spies
PHILLIPS, Charles, 2 Cpl, Col Ewen Allison, Capt Wm King, Drafted Mil
PHILLIPS, David, 3 Cpl, Col Thos Benton, Capt George Gibbs, Branch Srvce omitted
PHILLIPS, David, Cpl, Col Thos Benton, Capt George Gibbs, Vol Inf
PHILLIPS, David, Dmr, Maj Wm Woodfolk, Capt Ezekial Ross, Inf; Ffr under Capt McCulley
PHILLIPS, David, Pvt, Col Alexander Loury, Capt James Kincaid, Inf
PHILLIPS, David, Pvt, Col Jno Coffee, Capt Alexander McKeen, Cav
PHILLIPS, Eben, Pvt, Col John Coffee, Capt Jno Baskerville, Inf
PHILLIPS, George, Pvt, Col Jas Raulston, Capt James Black, Inf
PHILLIPS, George, Pvt, Col John Alcorn, Capt Robert Jetton, Vol Cav
PHILLIPS, George, Pvt, Col John Coffee, Capt Robert Jetton, Cav
PHILLIPS, George, Pvt, Col Samuel Bayless, Capt James Landen, E TN Mil
PHILLIPS, Ivy, Pvt, Col John Cocke, Capt James Gault, Inf
PHILLIPS, Ivy, Pvt, Col Thos McCrory, Capt Jas Shan-

non, Mil Inf
PHILLIPS, James, Pvt, Col S Copeland, Capt John Holshouser, Inf
PHILLIPS, James, Pvt, Col Thos Williamson, Capt Wm Martin, Vol Mtd Gunmen; transferred to Capt Doak Co
PHILLIPS, John M, Pvt, Col Edward Bradley, Capt Abraham Bledsoe, Riflemen
PHILLIPS, John M, Pvt, Col R C Napier, Capt James McMurray, Mil Inf
PHILLIPS, John M, Pvt, Col Wm Hall, Capt Abraham Bledsoe, Vol Inf
PHILLIPS, John, Cpl, Col Wm Y Higgins, Capt Adam Dale, Mtd Gunmen
PHILLIPS, John, Pvt, Col Ewen Allison, Capt James Allen, E TN Mil
PHILLIPS, John, Pvt, Col Ewen Allison, Capt Wm King, Drafted Mil
PHILLIPS, John, Pvt, Col Samuel Bayless, Capt Jos B Bacon, E TN Mil; appointed Artif
PHILLIPS, John, Pvt, Col Wm Hall, Capt John Wallace, Inf; substituted by Joseph Phillips
PHILLIPS, John, Pvt, Col Wm Johnson, Capt Jas R Rogers, E TN Mil; substitute
PHILLIPS, Jonas, Pvt, Col Samuel Bayless, Capt Branch Jones, E TN Drafted Mil
PHILLIPS, Joseph, Pvt, Col S Bunch, Capt Jno Houk, E TN Mil
PHILLIPS, Joseph, Pvt, Col Wm Hall, Capt John Wallace, Inf; substitute for John Phillips
PHILLIPS, Lewellyn, Pvt, Col A Cheatham, Capt Geo G Chapman, Inf
PHILLIPS, Lewis, Pvt, Col Thos Benton, Capt George Gibbs, Vol Inf; AWOL
PHILLIPS, Martin, Pvt, Col S Copeland, Capt James Tait, Inf
PHILLIPS, Moses, Pvt, Col Samuel Bayless, Capt Branch Jones, E TN Drafted Mil
PHILLIPS, Nathan B, Pvt, Maj Wm Russell, Capt John Cowan, Vol Mtd Gunmen
PHILLIPS, Nathan, Pvt, Col Wm Johnson, Capt Henry Hunter, E TN Mil; transferred to Millican's Camp
PHILLIPS, Noah, Pvt, Col Wm Hall, Capt W L Alexander, Vol Inf
PHILLIPS, Peter, Pvt, Col John Coffee, Capt Michael Molton, Cav
PHILLIPS, Pleasant, Pvt, Col Ewin Allison, Capt John Hampton, Mil
PHILLIPS, Pleasant, Pvt, Col Samuel Bunch, Capt F Register, E TN Mil; transferred to Capt Hampton's Co
PHILLIPS, Richard, Cpl, Col Alexander Loury, Capt James Kincaid, Inf
PHILLIPS, Robert, Pvt, Col Wm Johnson, Capt James Rogers, E TN Mil
PHILLIPS, Royal, Pvt, Col Ewin Allison, Capt John Hampton, Mil; transferred to Capt Register Co
PHILLIPS, Royal, Pvt, Col Samuel Bunch, Capt F Register, E TN Mil; transferred to Capt Hampton's Co
PHILLIPS, Samuel M, Pvt, Col Wm Metcalf, Capt Thomas Marks, Mil Inf
PHILLIPS, Samuel, Cor, Col Thos Williamson, Capt John Hutchings, Vol Mtd Gunmen
PHILLIPS, Samuel, Cor, Maj Gen John Cocke, Co Commander omitted, TN Vol Mtd Gunmen
PHILLIPS, Samuel, Pvt, Col Wm Johnson, Capt Henry Hunter, E TN Mil; d 3-5-1815
PHILLIPS, Solomon, Pvt, Col Ewen Allison, Capt Wm King, Drafted Mil
PHILLIPS, Thomas, Pvt, Col Thos Bradley, Capt Harry L Douglass, Vol Inf
PHILLIPS, Thomas, Pvt, Col Wm Metcalf, Capt Thos Marks, Mil Inf
PHILLIPS, Thomas, Pvt, Regt Commander omitted, Capt Jas Terrill, Cav
PHILLIPS, William B, Pvt, Col Robert Steele, Capt James Shenault, Mil Inf
PHILLIPS, William, Mus, Col Edward Bradley, Capt Harry L Douglass, Vol Inf
PHILLIPS, William, Pvt, Col N T Perkins, Capt Andrew Patterson, Mtd Vol
PHILLIPS, William, Pvt, Col Thomas Benton, Capt H L Douglass, Vol Inf
PHILLIPS, William, Pvt, Col Thos McCrory, Capt Jas Shannon, Mil Inf
PHILLIPS, William, Pvt, Col Wm Lillard, Capt Thomas Sharp, 2nd Regt Inf
PHILLIPS, William, Pvt, Maj Wm Woodfolk, Capt Ezekial Ross, Inf
PHILLPOTT, Horatio, Sgt Maj, Col Wm Higgins, Co Commander omitted, 2nd Regt Mtd Vol
PHILPOT, Reuben, Pvt, Col John Brown, Capt James Preston, E TN Mil
PHINEY, Waid, 2 Cpl, Col James Raulston, Capt Henry West, Inf
PHIPPS, Edward E, 3 Sgt, Col Samuel Bunch, Capt James Cummings, E TN Vol Mtd Gunmen
PHIPPS, James, Pvt, Col Wm Hall, Capt John Wallace, Inf; substitute in place of ___ Bush
PHIPPS, James, Pvt, Col Wm Lillard, Capt Thomas Sharp, 2nd Regt Inf
PHIPS, Solomon, Pvt, Col Samuel Bunch, Capt Francis Register, E TN Mil; joined from Capt King's Co
PIBLENER, Lewis, Pvt, Everett Upton (Rank omitted), no other information
PICKARD, Alexander, Pvt, Col Robert H Dyer, Capt James McMahan, 1st TN Vol Mtd Gunmen
PICKARD, Craig, Pvt, Col Robert H Dyer, Capt James McMahan, 1st TN Mtd Gunmen
PICKARD, Isaac, Pvt, Col Robert H Dyer, Capt James McMahan, 1st TN Vol Mtd Gunmen
PICKEL, Johnathan, Pvt, Col Samuel Wear, Capt Samuel Bowman, Mtd Inf
PICKENS, Henry, Pvt, Col John K Wynne, Capt John Porter, Inf
PICKENS, Henry, Pvt, Col Wm Lillard, Capt Benjamin King, E TN Vol Inf
PICKENS, John, Pvt, Col N T Perkins, Capt John Doak, Vol Mtd Gunmen
PICKENS, Joseph, Pvt, Col Robt Dyer, Capt James Wyatt, Vol Mtd Gunmen
PICKENS, Joseph, Pvt, Gen Andrew Jackson, Capt Wil-

## Enlisted Men, War of 1812

liam Russell, Mtd Spies

PICKENS, Joseph, Pvt, Regt Commander omitted, Capt John Gordon, Mtd Spies

PICKENS, Mathew, Pvt, Col N T Perkins, Capt John Doak, Vol Mtd Gunmen

PICKERING, Charles H, Sgt, Col A Loury, Capt Gabriel Martin, Inf; appointed QM Sgt

PICKERING, Charles, QM Sgt, Lt Col Hammonds, 2nd Regt W TN Mil

PICKERING, Spencer, Pvt, Lt Col Archie Cheatham, Co Commander omitted, Mtd Inf

PICKERING, Spencer, Pvt, Lt Col Jno Edmunson, Co Commander omitted, Cav

PICKERING, William, Pvt, Col Wm Hall, Capt John Wallace, Inf

PICKET, Allon, Cpt, Col Wm Johnson, Capt James Stewart, 3rd Regt E TN Mil

PICKETT, Abel, Pvt, Maj John Childs, Capt Daniel Price, Vol Mtd Gunmen

PICKETT, James, Pvt, Col Newton Cannon, Capt Francis Jones, Mtd Riflemen

PICKETT, John, Pvt, Col R H Dyer, Capt Joseph Williams, Vol Mtd Gunmen

PICKETT, William, Pvt, Col John Cocke, Capt George Barnes, Inf

PICKINS, John, Pvt, Col N T Perkins, Capt John Doak, Vol Mtd Gunmen

PICKINS, Robert B, Pvt, Gen Jackson, Col Thos Williamson, Capt Robert Steele, Vol Mtd Gunmen

PICKINS, William, Pvt, Col R C Napier, Capt Samuel Ashmore, Mil Inf

PICKLE, Henry, Pvt, Col John Brown, Capt Wm White, E TN Mtd Inf

PICKLE, James, Pvt, Col Thomas Benton, Capt Thos Williamson, Vol Inf

PIE, Nathaniel, Pvt, Col Thos Benton, Capt Isaiah Renshaw, Vol Inf; joined from Capt Hewett's Co

PIERCE, Allen, Pvt, Col John Brown, Capt John Chiles, E TN Vol Mtd Inf

PIERCE, Author, Pvt, Col Wm Hall, Capt Travis Nash, Inf

PIERCE, Benjamin, Pvt, Regt Commander omitted, Capt Geo Smith, Spies

PIERCE, Charles, Pvt, Col John Alcorn, Capt John W Byrns, Cav

PIERCE, Charles, Pvt, Col Leroy Hammonds, Capt Thos Wells, Inf

PIERCE, Daniel, Pvt, Col Samuel Bayless, Capt Joseph Hale, E TN Mil

PIERCE, Elijah, Pvt, Col John K Wynne, Capt Robert Braden, Inf

PIERCE, George, Pvt, Col John Coffee, Capt Daniel Ross, Mtd Gunmen

PIERCE, George, Pvt, Regt Commander omitted, Capt Geo Smith, Spies

PIERCE, Hardy, Pvt, Col Samuel Bayless, Capt Solomon Hendrix, E TN Mil

PIERCE, Hashial (Hosea), Pvt, Col John Cocke, Capt Joseph Price, Inf

PIERCE, Isaac, Pvt, Col Thos Williamson, Capt Robert Moore, Vol Mtd Gunmen

PIERCE, Jeremiah, Pvt, Maj John Childs, Capt Charles Conway, E TN Mtd Gunmen

PIERCE, Jesse, Pvt, Col Philip Pipkin, Capt David Smith, Mil Inf

PIERCE, Jesse, Pvt, Col Philip Pipkin, Ens Wm Pegram, Det of David Smith Co of TN Mil

PIERCE, Jesse, Pvt, Col R C Napier, Capt Edward Neblett, Mil Inf

PIERCE, John, Pvt, Col Wm Johnson, Capt Joseph Kirk, Mil

PIERCE, Philip, Pvt, Col Philip Pipkin, Co Commander omitted, Mil Inf

PIERCE, Richard, Pvt, Col Thomas H Benton, Co Commander omitted, Vol Inf

PIERCE, Richard, Pvt, Col Wm Y Higgins, Capt Stephen Griffith, Mtd Riflemen

PIERCE, Robert, Pvt, Col Samuel Bayless, Capt Joseph Hale, E TN Inf

PIERCE, Robert, Pvt, Col Wm Lillard, Capt Robert McCalpin, E TN Inf; deserted

PIERCE, Samuel, Pvt, Col Philip Pipkin, Capt Henry Newlin, Mil Inf; deserted

PIERCE, Solomon, Cpl, Col Edwin E Booth, Capt John Lewis, E TN Mil

PIERCE, Stokely, Pvt, Col Wm Hall, Capt Travis Nash, Inf

PIERCE, Stokley D, Ens, Col A Loury, Capt James Kincaid, Inf

PIERCE, Weston, Pvt, Col Samuel Bayless, Capt Joseph Hale, E TN Mil

PIERCE, William, Pvt, Regt Commander omitted, Capt George Smith, Spies

PIERCE (PEARCE), Lewis, Pvt, Col Wm Lillard, Capt Robert McCalpin, E TN Inf; deserted 10-30-1813

PIERCEFIELD, Henry, Pvt, Col Edwin E Booth, Capt John Sharp, E TN Mil

PIERCEFIELD, Thomas, Pvt, Col S Bunch, Capt S Richardson, E TN Drafted Mil

PIERCEFIELD, Thomas, Pvt, Regt Commander omitted, Capt S Richardson & Capt S Bunch, Branch Srvce omitted; deserted

PIERCY, James, Pvt, Col Thomas Benton, Capt George Caperton, Vol Inf

PIERSON, Benjamin, Sgt, Col S Bunch, Capt John Houk, E TN Mil; discharged at Knoxville

PIERSON, Henry, Pvt, Col Philip Pipkin, Capt David Smith, Inf

PIERSON, Isaac, Pvt, Col Philip Pipkin, Capt David Smith, Inf; deserted

PIERSON, James, Pvt, Regt Commander omitted, Capt George Smith, Spies

PIERSON, John, Pvt, Col Philip Pipkin, Capt David Smith, Inf

PIERSON, John, Pvt, Col Samuel Wear, Capt James Tedford, E TN Vol Inf

PIERSON, John, Pvt, Col Wm Higgins, Capt Adam Dale, Mtd Gunmen

PIERSON, William, Pvt, Col John Crane, Co Commander omitted, Mtd Inf

PIERSON, William, Pvt, Col S Copeland, Capt John Holshouser, Inf

PIEU (PUGH), David, Pvt, Col Philip Pipkin, Capt

- 405

## Enlisted Men, War of 1812

George Mebane, Mil Inf
PIGG, James, Cpl, Col A Loury, Co Commander omitted, Inf
PIGG, James, Pvt, Col Thomas H Benton, Capt James McEwen, Vol Inf
PIGG, James, Pvt, Col Wm Pillow, Capt James McEwen, Vol Inf
PIKE, James, Pvt, Col R C Napier, Capt James McMurry, Mil Inf
PIKE, James, Pvt, Col S Copeland, Capt David Williams, Mil Inf
PIKE, John, Pvt, Regt Commander omitted, Capt John Crane, Mtd Inf
PIKE, William B, Cpl, Col Edward Bradley, Capt Wm Lauderdale, Vol Inf
PIKE, William B, Pvt, Col Wm Hall, Capt Wm Alexander, Vol Inf
PIKE, William, 1 Cpl, Col John Cocke, Capt Richard Crunk, Inf
PILANT, Elisha, Pvt, Col Thos Williamson, Capt Jas Cook & Capt Jno Crane, Vol Mtd Gunmen
PILANT, Kincher, Pvt, Col E Allison, Capt Jonas Loughmiller, Mil
PILES, James, Pvt, Col R H Dyer, Capt Jas White, Vol Mtd Gunmen
PILES, Leonard P, Pvt, Col N T Perkins, Capt A Patterson, Mtd Vol
PILES, Leonard, Pvt, Col T McCrory, Capt A Willis, Mil Inf
PILES, William, Pvt, Col Sam'l Bunch, Capt F Berry, E TN Mil
PILLAR, William E, Pvt, Col Thos Benton, Capt W J Smith, Vol Inf
PILLAR, William E, Pvt, Col Wm Pillow, Capt W J Smith, Vol Inf
PILLAR, William E, Pvt, Regt Commander omitted, Capt Smith, Vol Inf
PILLER, William E, Pvt, Col Thos Benton, Capt W J Smith, Vol Inf
PILLMORE, Woodson, Pvt, Col S Copeland, Capt A Wilkinson, Mil Inf
PILLOW, Claiborne, Pvt, Col Wm Metcalf, Capt B Hurt, Mil Inf; promoted to Surgeon's Mate
PILLOW, Claiborne, Sgt Maj, Col Wm Metcalf, 1st Regt W TN Mil Inf; promoted from the lines
PILLOW, John, Pvt, Regt Commander omitted, Capt D Mason, Cav
PILLOW, William E, Pvt, Regt Commander omitted, Capt Smith, Branch Srvce omitted
PILLOW, William, Pvt, Col R C Napier, Capt A McCarty, Mil Inf
PILLOW, William, Pvt, Commanders omitted, 2nd Regt TN Vol Inf; promoted to Lt Col, wounded 11-9-1813
PINKERTON, David, Sgt, Col Jno Cocke, Capt Jno Dalton, Inf
PINKERTON, David, Sgt, Col Thos Williamson, Capt R Tate, Vol Mtd Gunmen
PINKERTON, James, Pvt, Regt Commander omitted, Capt Archibald McKinney, Cav
PINKERTON, Thomas, Pvt, Col Jno Alcorn, Capt Robert Jetton, Vol Cav
PINKERTON, Thomas, Pvt, Col Jno Coffee, Capt Robt Jetton, Cav
PINKERTON, Thomas, Pvt, Col Wm Metcalf, Capt Wm Sitton, Mil Inf
PINKLEY, George H, Pvt, Col J K Winn, Capt B Butler, Inf
PINKLEY, John, Pvt, Col Alex Loury, Capt G Martin, Inf
PINKSON, David, Pvt, Col Jno Cooke, Capt Jas Gault, Inf
PINKSTON, David, Pvt, Col Sam'l Bayless, Capt J Goodson, E TN Mil
PINKSTON, Hugh, Pvt, Col T McCrory, Capt Jas Shannon, Mil Inf
PINKSTON, Mathew, Cpl, Col Thos Williamson, Capt Wm Martin, Vol Mtd Gunmen
PINNELTON, James, Cpl, Col S Copeland, Capt Wm Douglass, Inf
PINNEY, John, Pvt, Maj Gen Wm Carroll, Capt F Ellis, Inf; substitute for Willis Dawson
PINSON, Duke, Pvt, Brig Gen Thos Johnston, Capt A Allen, Mil Inf
PINSON, Isaac, Pvt, Col P Pipkin, Capt D Smith, W TN Mil; on extra duty as Blksmth, attached to John Strothers Co
PINSON, John, Pvt, Col Thos Williamson, Capt R Tate, Vol Mtd Gunmen
PINSON, Nathan G, 1 Lt, Col N T Perkins, Capt Jno Doak, Mtd Riflemen
PINTARD, John M, Pvt, Col R C Napier, Capt Jas McMurrey, Mil Inf; transferred to the Arty
PINTARD, John, Pvt, Regt Commander omitted, Capt Joel Parrish, Arty
PIOT, John, Sgt, Col Sam'l Bayless, Capt Jos Rich, E TN Inf; promoted from Pvt
PIPKIN, Enos, Pvt, Col R H Dyer, Capt Jas McMahon, 1st TN Vol Mtd Gunmen
PIPKIN, Thomas B, Pvt, Col N T Perkins, Capt P Pipkin, Mtd Riflemen
PIPKIN, Thomas B, Pvt, Regt Commander omitted, Capt Rich'd Boyd, Branch Srvce omitted
PIPKIN, Thomas, Pvt, Brig Gen Thos Washington, Capt Jno Crawford, Mtd Inf
PIPKIN, Thomas, Pvt, Regt Commander omitted, Capt Jno Crawford, Mtd Mil
PIPPANT, Francis, Pvt, Col Jno Brown, Capt Allen I Bacon, E TN Mil Inf
PIPPENS, Jesse, Pvt, Col Edwin Booth, Capt Jno McKamey, E TN Mil
PIPPIN, William (Willis), Pvt, Col Jas Raulston, Capt M Cowan, Inf
PIPPIN, Willis, Pvt, Col J K Winn, Capt Jas Holleman, Inf
PIPPS, Eldridge, Pvt, Col T McCrory, Capt Isaac Patton, Mil Inf
PIROW, William, Pvt, Gen A Jackson, Capt Hugh Kerr, Mtd Rangers
PIRTLE, Samuel, Pvt, Col Jas Raulston, Capt Jas Black, Inf
PISTOLE, James, Pvt, Col P Pipkin, Capt Jas Blakemroe, Mil Inf
PISTOLL, William, Pvt, Col R H Dyer, Capt B Allen, Vol Mtd Gunmen

## Enlisted Men, War of 1812

PITCHFORD, John, Pvt, Col R H Dyer, Capt Jas Williams, Vol Mtd Gunmen
PITCHFORD, John, Pvt, Lt Col Richard Napier, Co Commander omitted, Inf
PITCHFORD, John, Pvt, Regt Commander omitted, Capt Jas Williams, Mil Cav
PITCHFORD, John, Sgt, Col R C Napier, Capt D Adkins, Mil Inf
PITCOCK, John, Cpl, Col S Copeland, Capt S George, Inf
PITCOCK, Stephen, Pvt, Col William Lillard, Capt Jacob Hartsell, E TN Vol Inf
PITMAN, William, Pvt, Col Alexander Loury, Capt Leroy Hammonds & Capt Arahel Rains, Inf
PITMAN, William, Pvt, Col Phillip Pipkin, Capt Henry Newlin, Mil Inf
PITNER, John, Pvt, Brig Gen N Taylor, Capt Wm Henderson, Spies
PITNER, John, Pvt, Regt Commander omitted, Capt L Ferrell, Inf
PITNER, Michael, Pvt, Col Thomas Williamson, Capt Beverly Williams, Vol Mtd Gunmen
PITT, Benjamin, Pvt, Col Thomas Williamson, Capt Thomas Scurry, Vol Mtd Gunmen
PITT, James, Pvt, Col Thos Williamson, Capt Thomas Scurry, Vol Mtd Gunmen
PITT, Sterling, Pvt, Col Thomas Williamson, Capt Thomas Scurry, Vol Mtd Gunmen
PITT, William, Pvt, Col Thomas Williamson, Capt Thomas Scurry, Vol Mtd Gunmen
PITTS, Ezekiel, Pvt, Col A Cheatham, Capt Wm Smith, Inf
PITTS, Jidy, Pvt, Col John K Wynn, Capt Robert Breden, Inf
PITTS, Lunford C, Hospital Surgeon's Mate, Maj Gen Wm Carroll, TN Mil; replaced Wm Rucker
PITTS, Lunsford C, 1 Surgeon Mate, Col S Copeland, Inf
PITTS, Lunsford C, QM Sgt, Col Edward Bradley, TN Vol Inf
PITTS, Lunsford C, Surgeon Mate, Col Edward Bradley, TN Vol Inf
PITTS, Lunsford E, 1 Surgeon's Mate, Col Jas Raulston, W TN Mil Inf; appointed Hospital Surgeon
PITTS, Thomas, 1 Lt, Col Edward Bradley, Capt Travis Nash, Vol Inf
PITTS, Thomas, Pvt, Col John Cocke, Capt Richard Crunk, Inf
PITTS, William, Pvt, Col John Wynn, Capt Robert Breden, Inf
PLACE, Peter, Pvt, Col Edwin Booth, Capt John Lewis, E TN Mil
PLADS, Richard, Cpl, Lt Col Leroy Hammonds, Capt Joseph Williamson, Inf; promoted to Regt QM
PLANT, John, Sgt, Col R N Dyer, Capt Joseph Williamson, Vol Mtd Gunmen
PLANT, Robert, Pvt, Col Phillip Pipkin, Capt John Strother, Mil
PLANT, William, Cpl, Col Robert Dyer, Capt Joseph Williams, Vol Mtd Gunmen; d 3-1-1815
PLANT, William, Pvt, Regt Commander omitted, Capt Jno Williams, Mil Cav
PLASTER, Isaac, Pvt, Col John Alcorn, Capt Henry Byrns, Cav
PLASTER, Isaac, Pvt, Regt Commander omitted, Capt John Crane, Mtd Inf
PLASTER, John, Pvt, Gen Jackson, Col Thomas Williamson, Capt Robert Steele, Vol Mtd Gunmen
PLASTERS, Isaac, Pvt, Col R C Napier, Capt Thomas Preston, Mil Inf
PLASTERS, Isaac, Pvt, Lt Col A Cheatham, Co Commander omitted, Mtd Inf
PLATT, Roswell, Pvt, Col Edward Bradley, Capt James Hambleton, Vol Inf
PLATT, Roswell, Pvt, Col Wm Hall, Capt James Hambleton, Vol Inf
PLEELER, Pleasant, Pvt, Col Thos Benton, Capt Jas Renshaw, Vol Inf
PLUMBLY, Archibald, Pvt, Col John Winn, Capt Bailey Butler, Inf; deserted
PLUMLEY, Archibald, Pvt, Col Jas Raulston, Capt Henry West, Inf; d 1-7-1815
PLUMLEY, Joseph, Pvt, Maj John Childs, Capt Daniel Price, E TN Mtd Inf
PLUMLEY, Thomas, Pvt, Col William Metcalf, Capt Andrew Patterson, Mil Inf
PLUMMER, Hillery C, Dmr, Col Thos Benton, Capt Thomas Williamson, Vol Inf
PLUMMER, Hillery C, Dmr, Col William Pillow, Capt Thomas Pillow, Vol Inf
PLUMMER, John, Pvt, Lt Col A Cheatham, Co Commander omitted, Mtd Inf
PLUMMER, John, Pvt, Lt Col Jno Edmonson, Co Commander omitted, Cav
POE, Claiburn, Pvt, Col S Copeland, Capt George, Inf
POE, Jesse, 2 Sgt, Col John Brown, Capt Charles Lewin, E TN Mtd Inf
POE, Larkin, Pvt, Col Jas Raulston, Capt Mathew Cowan, Inf
POE, Lindsey, Pvt, Col S Bunch, Capt Jno English, E TN Drafted Mil
POE, Polaskey, Pvt, Col S Bunch, Capt William Jobe, E TN Vol Mtd Inf
POE, Stephen, Pvt, Col Ewen Allisn, Capt Allen, E TN Mil
POE, Stephen, Pvt, Gen Jackson, Capt Hugh Kerr, Mtd Rangers
POE, Stephen, Pvt, Maj Wm Russell, Capt Fleman Hodges, Vol Mtd Gunmen
POE, William, Pvt, Gen Jackson, Capt Hugh Kerr, Mtd Rangers
POE, William, Pvt, Maj Wm Russell, Capt Fleman Hodges, Vol Mtd Gunmen
POGUE, Reuben H, Pvt, Col William Lillard, Capt William Hamilton, E TN Vol Inf; substitute for Luke Perry
POGUE (POUGE), Samuel, Pvt, Maj Gen Wm Carroll, Col Wm Metcalf, Capt John Jackson, Inf
POINDEXTER, John, Pvt, Col Edwin Booth, Capt John Slatton, E TN Mil
POINDEXTER, John, Pvt, Col John K Winn, Capt Bailey Butler, Inf; deserted 11-9-1813
POINDEXTER, Samuel, Pvt, Col Jas Raulston, Capt Henry West, Inf
POINTER, James, Pvt, Col N Cannon, Capt Isaac Wil-

## Enlisted Men, War of 1812

liams, Mtd Riflemen; deserted 10-10-1813
POINTER, Joseph, Pvt, Col Thomas Williamson, Capt John Hutchings, Vol Mtd Gunmen
POLESTON, Richard, Pvt, Col S Bunch, Capt John English, E TN Drafted Mil
POLITE, Mark, Pvt, Col R C Napier, Capt James McMurry, Mil Inf
POLK, Benjamin D, Pvt, Col Wm Hall, Capt Henry D Newlin, Inf
POLK, Benjamin, Pvt, Col N T Perkins, Capt James McMahon, Mtd Gunmen
POLK, Coin L, 1 Cpl, Col Wm Hall, Capt Henry D Newlin, Inf
POLK, Evan L, 1 Cpl, Col N T Perkins, Capt James McMahon, Mtd Gunmen
POLK, Evan, Cpl, Col Wm Hall, Capt Henry D Newlin, Inf
POLK, John, Pvt, Col R C Napier, Capt Samuel Ashmore, Mil Inf
POLK, John, Pvt, Col S Copeland, Capt Moses Thompson, Inf
POLK, John, Pvt, Regt Commander omitted, Capt James Gray, Inf
POLK, Richard, 2 Cpl, Col Thomas H Benton, Capt Newton Cannon, Vol Inf
POLK, Richard, Cpl, Col Wm Pillow, Lt Joseph Mason, Vol Inf
POLK, William, Pvt, Col R C Napier, Capt Samuel Ashmore, Mil Inf
POLK, William, Pvt, Lt Col Wm Phillips, Co Commander omitted, Inf
POLK, William, Pvt, Maj Robert Cooper, Co Commander omitted, Mtd Riflemen
POLLAND, Caleb D, Pvt, Col John Cocke, Capt John Dalton, Inf
POLLAND, John, Pvt, Col R H Dyer, Capt Robert Edmondson, TN Vol Mtd Gunmen
POLLAND, John, Pvt, Regt Commander omitted, Capt James Cowan, Mtd Inf
POLLARD, Samuel, Pvt, Col John Cocke, Capt George Barnes, Inf
POLLARD, Thomas P, Sgt, Col Thomas H Williamson, Capt James Pace & Capt Nealy, Vol Mtd Gunmen; d 1-13-1815
POLLOCK, Benjamin H, Ffr, Col Philip Pipkin, Capt Peter Searcy, Mil Inf; enlisted in 3rd Rifle Regt
POLLOCK, Benjamin H, Pvt, Regt Commander omitted, Capt Archibald McKinney, Cav
POLLOCK, John, Cpl, Col John K Winn, Capt Wm Carothers, W TN Inf; promoted from Pvt
POLLOCK, John, Cpl, Col Robert Steele, Capt James Shenault, Mil Inf
POLLOCK, Presley, Pvt, Col Edward Bradley, Capt James Hambleton, Vol Inf
POLLOCK, Robert, Pvt, Regt Commander omitted, Capt Archibald McKinney, Cav
POLLOCK, Robert, Rank omitted, Capt Charles Kavanaugh, no other information
POLLOCK, William, Pvt, Col Phillip Pipkin, Capt Henry M Newlin, Mil Inf
POLLOCK, William, Pvt, Col Robert Steele, Capt James

Shenault, Mil Inf
POLLOCK, William, Pvt, Maj Wm Woodfolk, Capt Abner Pearce, Inf; transferred from? Capt Nail's Co
POLSTON, John, Pvt, Lt Col Leroy Hammond, Capt Thomas Delaney, Inf
POMENTER, Theopolus, Pvt, Col Wm Johnson, Capt Benjamin Powell, E TN Mil; promoted to Sgt
PONDS, Benjamin, Pvt, Col A Loury, Capt Gabriel Martion, Inf
PONDS, Elijah, Pvt, Col Thomas H Williamson, Capt Moore, Vol Mtd Gunmen
PONDS, William, Pvt, Maj Gen Wm Carroll, Capt Henry Hamilton, Inf
POOL, Alexander, Pvt, Brig Gen Wm Johnson, Capt Robert Carson, Inf
POOL, Armstead P, Cpl, Col S Copeland, Capt Alexander Provine, Mil Inf
POOL, Asa, Pvt, Col Thomas H Benton, Capt George Caperton, Vol Inf; refused to march
POOL, John, Pvt, Col N T Perkins, Co Commander omitted, Mtd Vol
POOL, Patrick, Pvt, Maj Woodfolk, Capt James C Neil, Inf
POOL, William, 5 Sgt, Col John Cocke, Capt John Weakley, Inf
POOL, William, Cpl, Col Robert Steele, Capt James Shenault, Mil Inf
POOLE, Asa, Pvt, Lt Col Archer Cheatham, Capt Gabriel Martin, Mtd Vol
POOLE, Asa, Pvt, Lt Col John Edmondson, Co Commander omitted, Mtd Cav
POOLE, Young, Pvt, Col John K Winn, Capt Bailey Butler, Inf
POOR, Benjamin, Pvt, Col John Brown, Capt Wm White, E TN Vol Mtd Inf
POOR, Jeremiah, Pvt, Maj John Chiles, Capt Charles Conway, E TN Mtd Gunmen
POPE, Elias F, Sgt Maj, Col Robert H Dyer, Co Commander omitted, Regt TN Vol Mtd Gunmen
POPE, Elias F, Sgt, Regt Commander omitted, Capt Robert Edmondson, TN Vol Mtd Gunmen
POPE, Hardy, Pvt, Col Newton Cannon, Capt James Walton, Mtd Riflemen
POPE, Humphrey, Pvt, Col Edward Bradley, Co Commander omitted, Vol Inf
POPE, Humphrey, Pvt, Col Wm Hall, Capt Wm L Alexander, Vol Inf
POPE, Jacob, Pvt, Col Wm Johnson, Capt David McKamy, E TN Drafted Mil; d 12-3-1814
POPE, James, Pvt, Col Newton Cannon, Capt James Walton, Mtd Riflemen
POPE, John, Pvt, Col John Coffee, Capt John Dalton, Inf
POPE, Jonathan, Pvt, Col John Brown, Capt Jesse G Reany, Mtd Gunmen
POPE, Silas, 1 Cpl, Lt Col L Hammonds, Capt James Tubb, Inf
POPPOY, Nathaniel, Pvt, Col Samuel Bayless, Capt Jos B Bacon, E TN Mil
PORCH, Henry, Pvt, Regt Commander omitted, Capt Nathan Farmer, Mtd Riflemen; wounded 3-27-

*Enlisted Men, War of 1812*

1814 & d 3-28-1814
PORCH, John, Pvt, Col Thos Williamson, Capt John Doak & Capt John Dobbins, Vol Mtd Gunmen
PORKS, John, Pvt, Col Wm Y Higgins, Capt Wm Doake, Mtd Riflemen
PORTER, Alexander, Sgt, Col Edwin Booth, Capt Thos Porter, Drafted Mil
PORTER, Amos I, 1 Cpl, Col Wm Metcalf, Capt Andrew Patterson, Mil Inf
PORTER, Christopher, Pvt, Lt Col L Hammonds, Capt Arahel Rains, Inf
PORTER, Christopher, Sgt, Col Alexander Loury & Col Leroy Hammonds, Capt Arahel Rains, Inf; reduced to the ranks
PORTER, David, Pvt, Col A Cheatham, Capt Birdwell, Inf
PORTER, Hugh, 2 Lt, Brig Gen Jackson, Capt Robert Carson, Inf
PORTER, John H, 5 Sgt, Col Philip Pipkin, Capt Peter Searcy, Mil Inf
PORTER, John, 3 Cpl, Col Samuel Wear, Capt Simeon Perry, E TN Vol Mtd Inf
PORTER, John, Pvt, Col N T Perkins, Capt Wm Johnson, Mil Inf
PORTER, John, Pvt, Col Robert Steele, Capt John Chitwood, Mil Inf; deserted
PORTER, Minor, Cpl, Col Wm Johnson, Capt James R Rogers, E TN Mil Drafted
PORTER, Minrod, Pvt, Col Thos McCrory, Capt Wm Dooly, Inf
PORTER, Reece, Pvt, Col Thos Williamson, Capt John Doak & Capt John Dobbins, Vol Mtd Gunmen
PORTER, Reese, Pvt, Col John Coffee, Capt Robert Jetton, Cav
PORTER, Reese, Pvt, Regt Commander omitted, Capt Nathan Davis, Mil Inf
PORTER, Reese, Pvt, Regt Commander omitted, Capt Robert Evans, Mtd Spies
PORTER, Robert, Pvt, Maj Gen A Jackson, Col Thos Williamson, Capt Robert Steele, Vol Mtd Gunmen
PORTER, Russell, Pvt, Gen Andrew Jackson, Capt Nathan Davis, Inf
PORTER, Samuel, Pvt, Maj John Porter, Capt James Cowan, Cav
PORTER, Stephen, Pvt, Col John K Winn, Capt John Porter, Inf
PORTER, Stephen, Pvt, Col Samuel Bunch, Capt James Penny, E TN Mtd Inf
PORTER, Thomas C, Pvt, Col John Coffee, Capt James Terrell, Vol Cav; delinquent
PORTER, Thomas, Pvt, Col John K Winn, Capt Bailey Butler, Inf
PORTER, Thomas, Pvt, Col Thos Benton, Capt James McEwen, Vol Inf
PORTER, Thomas, Pvt, Regt Commander omitted, Capt Garrett Lane, Mtd Riflemen
PORTER, Thomas, Pvt, Regt Commander omitted, Capt Robert Evans, Mtd Spies
PORTER, Tom, Sgt, Regt Commander omitted, Capt Samuel Allen, Pack Horse Guards
PORTER, William, Pvt, Col N T Perkins, Capt Wm Johnson, Mil Inf
PORTER, William, Pvt, Col Samuel Wear, Capt Simeon Perry, E TN Vol Mtd Inf
PORTER, William, Pvt, Col Thos McCrory, Capt Samuel B McKnight, Inf
PORTER, William, Pvt, Lt Col A Cheatham, Capt Gabriel Martin, Mtd Inf
PORTERFIELD, Charles, Pvt, Col Jas Raulston, Capt James A Black, Inf
PORTERFIELD, John, Pvt, Col S Copeland, Capt Moses Thompson, Inf
PORTERFIELD, Samuel H, Pvt, Col S Copeland, Capt Moses Thompson, Inf
PORTERFIELD, Samuel, Pvt, Col Samuel Bayless, Capt James Landen, E TN Mil
PORTERFIELD, William W, Pvt, Col Jas Raulston, Capt James Black, Inf
PORTERS, Thomas, Pvt, Col N T Perkins, Capt Mathew Patterson, Mtd Vol Inf; AWOL
PORTWOOD, Micajah, Pvt, Col Edwin Booth, Capt Vernon, E TN Mil; joined after discharge from Gen Taylor's Brig
PORTWOOD, Micajah, Pvt, Col Wm Johnson, Capt James Tunnell, E TN Mil
PORTWOOD, Page, 4 Cpl, Maj John Chiles, Capt Charles Conway, E TN Mtd Gunmen
PORTWOOD, Page, Pvt, Col John Brown, Capt Hugh Barton, E TN Mil Inf
PORY, David C, Pvt, Col Wm Lillard, Capt Wm Hamilton, E TN Vol Inf
POSEY, Joseph H, Pvt, Col S Bunch, Capt James Griffin, E TN Drafted Mil
POSEY, Moses M, Pvt, Col Wm Johnson, Capt James Tunnell, E TN Mil
POSSONS (POSSINS), Thomas S, Pvt, Col Newton Cannon, Capt John B Demsey, Mtd Gunmen
POSTON, Richard, Pvt, Col S Copeland, Capt David Williams, Mil Inf
POSTON, Richard, Pvt, Col Wm Hall, Capt James Hambleton, Vol Inf
POTEET, George, Cpl, Col Thos Williamson, Capt John Doak & Capt John Dobbins, Vol Mtd Gunmen; d 1-12-1815
POTEET, James, Pvt, Col R C Napier, Capt Early Benson, Mil Inf
POTEET, James, Pvt, Maj Wm Woodfolk, Capt James C Neil, Inf
POTEET, John, Pvt, Col R C Napier, Capt Early Benson, Mil Inf
POTEET, William, Pvt, Col Wm Metcalf, Capt Thos Marks, Mil Inf
POTEETE, William, Pvt, Col R C Napier, Capt Early Benson, Mil Inf
POTETE, George, Pvt, Col John Wynne, Capt Wm McCall, Inf
POTS, Henry, Pvt, Col A Cheatham, Capt James Giddins, Inf
POTTELLO, George, Pvt, Col John Wynne, Capt Butler, Inf
POTTER, Absalom, Pvt, Col John Brown, Capt Wm White, E TN Mil Inf

## Enlisted Men, War of 1812

POTTER, Absolem, Pvt, Maj John Chiles, Capt Charles Conway, E TN Mtd Gunmen; Regimental Co - Roane

POTTER, Dornton, Pvt, Col Thos Williamson, Capt John Doak & Capt John Dobbins, Vol Mtd Gunmen

POTTER, Eldridge, Pvt, Col Samuel Bayless, Capt Joseph Hale, E TN Mil

POTTER, Ephraim, Cpl, Lt Col L Hammond, Capt James Craig, 2nd Regt W TN Mil

POTTER, James, Pvt, Col A Loury, Capt James Kincaid, Inf

POTTER, James, Pvt, Maj Wm Woodfolk, Capt Abraham Dudney, Inf

POTTER, James, Pvt, Maj Wm Woodfolk, Capt James Turner, Inf; transferred to Capt Sutton

POTTER, John, Pvt, Col John Brown, Capt Wm White, E TN Vol Mtd Inf

POTTER, John, Pvt, Col R C Napier, Capt Edward Neblett, Mil Inf

POTTER, Solomon, Pvt, Maj John Chiles, Capt Chas Conway, E TN Mtd Gunmen

POTTER, Thomas, Pvt, Col John Brown, Capt Wm White, E TN Mil Inf

POTTER, Thomas, Pvt, Col S Copeland, Capt Wm Evans, Inf

POTTER, William, Pvt, Col R H Dyer, Capt Isaac Williams, Vol Mtd Gunmen

POTTER, William, Pvt, Col Samuel Bayless, Capt Branch Jones, E TN Mil

POTTER, William, Pvt, Regt Commander omitted, Capt Garrett Lane, Mtd Riflemen

POTTER, Zachriah, Sgt, Maj Wm Woodfolk, Capt James Turner, Inf

POTTS, Abner, Pvt, Col Thos Williamson, Capt Richard Tate, Vol Mtd Gunmen

POTTS, Amos, Pvt, Maj Wm Russell, Capt Wm Chism, Vol Mtd Riflemen

POTTS, Leama, Sgt, Col John Cocke, Capt George Barnes, Inf; d 2-18-1815

POTTS, Robert, Pvt, Col John Cocke, Capt George Barnes, Inf

POTTS, Stringer, Ffr, Col John Cocke, Capt James Gault, Inf

POTTS, William, Pvt, Col A Loury, Capt Gabriel Martin, Inf

POUGE, Samuel, Pvt, Maj Gen Carroll, Col Wm Metcalf, Capt Jackson, Inf

POULSON (PELSON), John, Pvt, Col Wm Johnson, Capt James R Rogers, E TN Drafted Mil

POURES, Thomas H, Pvt, Col Wm Hall, Capt John Wallace, Inf

POWE, James, Pvt, Col Samuel Bayless, Capt John Brock, E TN Mil

POWEL, William B, 1 Cpl, Col Philip Pipkin, Capt John Strothers, Mil

POWELL, Allen, Pvt, Col Newton Cannon, Capt James Walton, Mtd Riflemen

POWELL, Benjamin, Pvt, Col John Brown, Capt John Chiles, E TN Vol Mtd Inf

POWELL, Dempsey, Pvt, Col Newton Cannon, Capt James Walton, Mtd Riflemen

POWELL, Elijah, Pvt, Col James Raulston, Capt Henry Hamilton, Inf

POWELL, Exum, Pvt, Col John Cocke, Capt Geo Barnes, Inf

POWELL, Green, Pvt, Col John Cocke, Capt Geo Barnes, Inf; d 1-18-1814

POWELL, Green, Pvt, Col Wm Johnson, Capt Elihu Milliken, 3rd Regt E TN Mil

POWELL, Hardin, Pvt, Col Wm Metcalf, Capt Richard Benson, Mil Inf

POWELL, Isham, Pvt, Col T McCrory, Capt Samuel B McKnight, Inf

POWELL, Isom, Pvt, Col R C Napier, Capt Andrew McCarty, Mil Inf

POWELL, James, Pvt, Col T McCrory, Capt A Metcalf, Mil Inf

POWELL, Jesse, Pvt, Col Newton Cannon, Capt James Walton, Mtd Riflemen

POWELL, John A, Cpl, Col Newton Cannon, Capt Andrew Patterson, Mtd Riflemen

POWELL, John A, Pvt, Col Thos Benton, Capt Benj Reynolds, Vol Inf

POWELL, John, Pvt, Col A Loury, Capt John Looney, W TN Inf; enlisted in the regular service

POWELL, John, Pvt, Col Newton Cannon, Capt James Walton, Mtd Riflemen

POWELL, John, Pvt, Maj Gen Wm Carroll, Capt Lewis Dillahunty & Capt Daniel M Bradford, Vol Inf

POWELL, Lewis, Pvt, Col Wm Metcalf, Capt Barbee Collins, Mil Inf

POWELL, Martin, Pvt, Col Wm Metcalf, Capt Andrew Patterson, Mil Inf; wounded 12-28-1814 & d 1-27-1815

POWELL, Mathew, 4 Sgt, Maj Gen Jackson, Capt John Craine, Mtd Gunmen

POWELL, Mathew, Sgt, Col Thos Williamson, Capt John Crane & Capt James Cook, Vol Mtd Gunmen

POWELL, Nathan, Pvt, Col A Cheatham, Capt Hugh Virdwell, Inf

POWELL, Nathan, Pvt, Col John Cocke, Capt James Gray, Inf

POWELL, Nathaniel L, Pvt, Col J K Winn, Capt B Butler, Inf

POWELL, Obadiah, Pvt, Col Wm Metcalf, Capt Jas Barnhart, Mil Inf

POWELL, Peter, Pvt, Col Wm Hall, Capt H M Newlin, Inf

POWELL, Richard, Pvt, Col R H Dyer, Capt Jos Williams, Vol Mtd Gunmen

POWELL, Thomas, Pvt, Col Wm Higgins, Capt S Griffith, Mtd Riflemen

POWELL, William, Pvt, Col A Cheatham, Capt Geo Chapman, Inf

POWELL, William, Pvt, Col Alex Loury, Lt Col L Hammonds, Capt Thos Delaney, Inf

POWELL, William, Pvt, Col Jno Cocke, Capt B Nance, Inf

POWELL, William, Pvt, Col Wm Metcalf, Capt Wm Mullin, Mil Inf

POWELL, William, Pvt, Col Wm Pillow, Capt C E McEwen, Vol Inf

POWER, Jesse, Pvt, Col Wm Higgins, Capt S Griffith, Mtd Riflemen

POWER, Martin, Pvt, Col Wm Higgions, Capt S Griffith, Mtd Riflemen
POWER, Richardson, Pvt, Col Wm Lillard, Capt Geo Keys, E TN Inf
POWERS, Charles, Pvt, Col E Booth, Capt Richard Marshall, Drafted Mil; discharged for inability
POWERS, Edward, Pvt, Brig Gen A Jackson, Col J H Williamson, Capt J H Williamson, Vol Mtd Gunmen
POWERS, Elisha, Pvt, Regt Commander omitted, Capt Jas Craig, Mil Inf
POWERS, Levi, Pvt, Maj Gen A Jackson, Col Thos Williamson, Capt Robert Steele, Vol Mtd Gunmen
POWERS, Robert, Pvt, Col N T Perkins, Capt Wm Johnston, Mil Inf
POWERS, Thomas, Pvt, Lt Col L Hammond, Capt Jas Craig, Inf
POWERS, William, Pvt, Col J Coffee, Capt M Molton, Cav
POWERS, Willis, Pvt, Brig Gen Wm Johnson, Capt A Allen, Mil Inf
POWLEY, William, Cpl, Col S Bunch, Capt Jno English, E TN Drafted Mil
POYTON, Elias, Cpl, Col Robert Steele, Capt Robert Campbell, Mil Inf
PRADEY, Burrell, Pvt, Col E Booth, Capt Geo Winton, E TN Mil
PRADEY, Burrell, Pvt, Col P Pipkin, Capt E Kirkpatrick, Mil Inf
PRAT, William, Pvt, Col Philip Pipkin, Capt E Kirkpatrick, Mil Inf; transferred to Capt Smith
PRATER, Andrew, Pvt, Col R H Dyer, Maj Wm Russell, Capt Wm Russell, Vol Mtd Gunmen
PRATER, Philip, Pvt, Col Jno Cocke, Capt Geo Barnes, Inf
PRATT, Constant, Pvt, Col Wm Lillard, Capt Robert Maloney, E TN Vol Inf
PRATT, Samuel, Pvt, Regt Commander omitted, Capt D Mason, Cav; promoted to Sgt
PRATT, Thomas, Pvt, Col S Bunch, Capt Jones Griffin, E TN Drafted Mil; discharged for inability
PRATT, William, Pvt, Col P Pipkin, Ens Wm Pegram, Det of Capt David Smythe Co of W TN Mil
PRATT, William, Pvt, Col T McCrory, Capt A Metcalf, Mil Inf
PRATT, William, Pvt, Lt I Barrett, Capt N Davis, Inf
PRECHETT, Enoch, Pvt, Regt Commander omitted, Capt Archibald McKenney, Cav
PREEDY, Richard, Pvt, Col Edwin Booth, Capt Vernon, E TN Mil
PREEDY, Thomas, Pvt, Col Edwin Booth, Capt Vernon, E TN Mil
PRELL, Willis, Pvt, Col A Loury, Capt Geo Sarver, Inf
PRENS, Reuben, Pvt, Col Samuel Bunch, Capt Geo McPherson, E TN Mil; joined from Capt Winsel's Co
PRENTICE, John, Pvt, Col Samuel Wear & Col Samuel Bunch, Capt Wm Mitchell, E TN Mtd Inf
PRESSLEY, James, Pvt, Col A Loury, Lt Col L Hammond, Capt Thos Wells, Inf
PRESTON, Ezekiel, Pvt, Lt Col L Hammond, Capt James Craig, Inf
PRESTON, James, Pvt, Col Jno Brown, Capt Jas Preston, E TN Mil Inf
PRESTON, Jesse, Pvt, Col John Brown, Capt Jas Preston, E TN Mil Inf
PREVOT, Noel, Pvt, Col Samuel Bunch, Capt Jno English, E TN Drafted Mil
PREWET, David, Pvt, Col Edwn Booth, Capt Rich'd Marshall, Drafted Mil; discharged for inability
PREWET, Silas, Pvt, Col Jno Coffee, Capt John Baskerville, Cav
PREWETT, George H, Pvt, Regt Commander omitted, Capt David Mason, Branch Srvce omitted; promoted to Cpl & reduced
PREWETT, James, Pvt, Col T McCrory, Capt Thos K Gordon, Inf; deserted
PREWETT, John B, Pvt, Col J Coffee, Capt Alexander McKeen, Cav
PREWETT, John B, Pvt, Col Thos Benton, Capt Benj Reynolds, Vol Inf
PREWETT, John W, Cpl, Regt Commander omitted, Capt Archibald McKinney, Cav
PREWETT, Silas, Pvt, Col John Alcorn, Capt John Baskerville, Vol Inf
PREWETT, Valantine, Pvt, Regt Commander omitted, Capt Archibald McKinney, Cav
PREWETT, William W, Pvt, Regt Commander omitted, Capt Archibald McKinney, Cav
PREWIT, Andrew, Pvt, Col Edwin Booth, Capt John McKamey, E TN Mil
PREWIT, Charles, Pvt, Col John Brown, Capt Wm White, E TN Vol Mtd Inf
PREWIT, Elisha, Pvt, Col Samuel Bunch, Capt Andrew Breden, E TN Mil; transferred to Capt J Berry's Co
PREWIT, John B, Pvt, Col Thos Benton, Capt Benj Reynolds, Vol Inf
PREWIT, John, Dmr, Col Samuel Bayless, Capt James Churchman, E TN Mil
PREWIT, Noah, Pvt, Col William Johnson, Capt Benj Powell, E TN Mil
PREWITT, John M, Pvt, Col Wm Higgins, Capt Thos Eldridge, Mtd Gunmen
PRICE, Auger, Pvt, Col Robert Dyer, Maj William Russell, Capt William Russell, Vol Mtd Gunmen
PRICE, Benjamin, Pvt, Col Wm Metcalf, Capt Hill & Capt John Cunningham, Mil Inf
PRICE, Daniel, Cpl, Maj John Childs, Capt Daniel Price, Vol Mtd Gunmen
PRICE, David, Pvt, Col Alexander Loury, Capt James Kincaid, Inf
PRICE, Dorsey, Pvt, Col Ewen Allison, Capt John Hampton, Mil; transferred from? Capt Register
PRICE, Edmon, Pvt, Maj John Childs, Capt Daniel Price, E TN Vol Inf
PRICE, Edward, Pvt, Col Edwin Booth, Capt John McKamey, E TN Mil; d 2-10-1815
PRICE, Edward, Pvt, Col John Brown, Capt John Childs, E TN Vol Mtd Inf
PRICE, Elijah (Elisha), 2 Sgt, Col Jas Raulston, Capt James Cowan, Inf

PRICE, Elijah, Pvt, Col Jas Raulston, Capt James Cowan, Inf
PRICE, Elijah, Pvt, Gen Andrew Jackson, Capt Nathan Davis, Inf
PRICE, F John, Pvt, Col Edwin Booth, Capt John McKamey, E TN Mil
PRICE, George, Pvt, Maj William Russell, Capt William Chism, Vol Mtd Gunmen
PRICE, Hugh, Pvt, Col William Metcalf, Capt Hill & Capt John Cunningham, Mil Inf
PRICE, James, Rank omitted, Maj John Childs, Capt John Stephens, E TN Vol Mtd Inf
PRICE, John, Pvt, Col John Alcorn, Capt William Locke, Cav
PRICE, John, Pvt, Col William Lilllard, Capt Robert Maloney, E TN Vol Inf
PRICE, John, Pvt, Col Wm Hall, Capt John Moore, Vol Inf
PRICE, John, Pvt, Maj William Russell, Capt William Chism, Vol Mtd Gunmen
PRICE, John, Pvt, Regt Commander omitted, Capt Wm Locke, Branch Srvce omitted
PRICE, John, Pvt, Regt Commander omitted, Sgt Wyatt Fussell, Inf
PRICE, Jonathan, Pvt, Col T McCrory, Capt Jno Reynolds, Mil Inf
PRICE, Joseph, Blksmth, Col Thomas Williamson, Capt Thomas Scurry, Vol Mtd Gunmen
PRICE, Joseph, Pvt, Col Alexander Loury, Capt James Kincaid, Inf
PRICE, Joshua, Pvt, Col Thos Dyer, Capt Joseph Williams, Vol Mtd Gunmen
PRICE, Josiah, Pvt, Col S Bayless, Capt Joseph Goodson, E TN Mil
PRICE, Luke, Pvt, Maj Wm Woodfolk, Capt Abraham Dudney & Capt Sutton, Inf; deserted 9-28-1814
PRICE, Martin, Pvt, Col Robert Dyer, Maj Wm Russell, Capt Wm Russell, Vol Mtd Gunmen
PRICE, Meridith, Pvt, Maj William Russell, Capt William Chism, Vol Mtd Gunmen
PRICE, Michael, Pvt, Col Jas Raulston, Capt Mathew Cowan, Inf
PRICE, Michael, Pvt, Regt Commander omitted, Capt L Ferrell, Inf
PRICE, Richard, Pvt, Col Thos Benton, Capt George Gibbs, Vol Inf; promoted to Cpl
PRICE, Richard, Sgt, Col John Wynne, Capt Jas Cole, Inf; wounded 11-9-1813 & sick absent
PRICE, Robert, 2 Cpl, Brig Gen Thomas Johnson, Capt Robert Carson, Inf
PRICE, Robert, Pvt, Col Robert Dyer, Capt Glen Owen, TN Vol Mtd Gunmen
PRICE, Simon, Pvt, Col Thos Benton, Capt Benj Hewett, Vol Inf
PRICE, Simon, Pvt, Col Thos Benton, Capt Jas Renshaw, Vol Inf
PRICE, Simon, Pvt, Regt Commander omitted, Capt Jas Renshaw, Vol Inf
PRICE, Solmon, Pvt, Col Jno Brown, Capt Hugh Barton, E TN Mil Inf
PRICE, Solomon, Pvt, Col Wm Metcalf, Capt William Sitton, Mil Inf
PRICE, Thomas, Pvt, Col S Bayless, Capt Jonathan Waddle, E TN Mil
PRICE, William, Pvt, Col Alexander Loury, Capt Geo Saver, Inf
PRICE, William, Pvt, Col Jno Brown, Capt Jas Preston, E TN Mil Inf
PRICE, William, Pvt, Col William Johnson, Capt William Alexander, E TN Drafted Mil
PRICE, William, Pvt, Maj John Childs, Capt John Stephens, E TN Vol Mtd Inf
PRICE, William, Pvt, Maj William Russell, Capt William Chism, Vol Mtd Riflemen
PRICE, William, Pvt, Maj Wm Woodfolk, Capt McCutley, Inf
PRICE, William, Pvt, Regt Commander omitted, Capt Samuel Allen, Pack Horse Guards
PRICE, Wilson, Pvt, Col Alexander Loury, Capt Geo Saver, Inf
PRICHARD, Benjamin, Pvt, Lt Col L Hammond, Capt James Tubb, Inf
PRICHARD, Enock, Pvt, Regt Commander omitted, Capt Jno Crawford, Mtd Mil
PRICHETT, Jarrod C, Pvt, Col A Cheatham, Capt Chas Johnson, Inf
PRIDE, Allen, Pvt, Col John Brown, Capt James McKamy, E TN Mtd Gunmen
PRIDE, Thomas, Pvt, Col Wm Higgins, Capt Thos Eldridge, Mtd Gunmen
PRIDE, Thomas, Pvt, Maj Wm Russell, Capt Fleman Hodges, Vol Mtd Gunmen
PRIDE, Wesley, Pvt, Maj Wm Russell, Capt John Trimble, Vol Mtd Gunmen
PRIDE, William, Pvt, Col John Brown, Capt John Trimble, E TN Mtd Inf
PRIEST, James, Pvt, Regt Commander omitted, Capt D Mason, Cav
PRIEST, John, Pvt, Col A Cheatham, Capt James Giddens, Inf
PRIEST, John, Pvt, Maj Gen Wm Carroll, Capt Wm Carroll, Vol Inf
PRIEST, Moses, Pvt, Col John Cocke, Capt Griffin, Inf
PRIEST, Moses, Pvt, Col John Cocke, Capt John Dalton, Inf; paid on Capt Dan'l M Bradford's roll
PRIEST, Moses, Pvt, Maj Wm Carroll, Capt Lewis Dillahunty & Capt Daniel Bradford, Vol Inf
PRIEST, Richard, Pvt, Gen Andrew Jackson, Capt Hugh Kerr, Mtd Rangers
PRIEST, Thomas, Pvt, Lt Col L Hammond, Capt A Loury & Capt Thos Wells, Inf
PRIESTLEY, William, Secretary Maj Gen, Maj Gen Wm Carroll, TN Mil
PRIESTLY, William, Cpl, Col Wm Lillard, Capt Geo Keyes, E TN Inf
PRIGMORE, John, Pvt, Col Ewen Allison, Capt James Laughmiller, Mil
PRIGMORE, Jonathan, Pvt, Col Edwin Booth, Capt John Slatton, E TN Mil
PRIM, Kinsey, Pvt, Col S Copeland, Capt Alexander Province, Mil Inf
PRIMM, Green, Pvt, Col John Cocke, Capt James Gault, Inf

## Enlisted Men, War of 1812

PRIMMER, James, Pvt, Col Samuel Wear, Capt Jesse Cole, Vol Inf
PRINCE, George, Pvt, Brig Gen T Johnson, Capt Robert Carson, Inf
PRINCE, Gilbert, Pvt, Col A Loury, Capt John Looney, W TN Inf
PRINCE, Jeremiah, 4 Cpl, Col Philip Pipkin, Capt Henry Newlin, Mil Inf
PRINE, Hierum (Hyram), Pvt, Col Samuel Bayless, Capt Solomon Hendrix, E TN Mil
PRINE, Samuel, Pvt, Col John Wynne, Capt James Cole, Inf
PRING, Nicholas, Pvt, Col Ewen Allison, Capt John Hampton, Mil
PRINT, James, Pvt, Col Samuel Wear, Capt Joseph Calloway, Mtd Inf
PRINT, William W, Pvt, Col Samuel Wear, Capt Joseph Calloway, Mtd Inf
PRINTICE, Zacheriah, Pvt, Col Samuel Wear, Capt Simeon Perry, E TN Vol Mtd Inf
PRINTICE, Zachriah, Sgt, Col Samuel Bunch, Capt John Howk, E TN Mil; discharged for inability
PRIOR, Samuel, Pvt, Col James Raulston, Capt Chas Wade, Inf
PRIOR, William, Pvt, Regt Commander omitted, Capt Geo Smith, Spies
PRIOR, William, Pvt, Regt Commander omitted, Capt Hampton, Branch Srvce omitted
PRIOR, William, Sgt, Col Ewen Allison, Capt John Hampton, Mil; promoted from Pvt, transferred to McPherson's Co
PRIOR (PRYOR), Joseph, Pvt, Maj Wm Woodfok, Capt Abraham Dudney & Capt John Sutton, Inf
PRISTLEY, James, Pvt, Maj Wm Carroll, Capt Lewis Dillahunty & Capt Daniel Bradford, Vol Inf
PRITCHARD, Enoch, Pvt, Brig Gen Thos Washington, Capt Jno Crawford, Mtd Inf
PRITCHARD, Henry, Pvt, Col Wm Metcalf, Capt Bird L Hurt, Mil Inf
PRITCHARD, James, Pvt, Col Robert Steele, Capt Robt Campbell, Mil Inf
PRITCHARD, James, Pvt, Lt John Scott, Co Commander omitted, Det of Inf
PRITCHELL, Enoch, Rank omitted, Capt Chas Kavanaugh, no other information
PRITCHET, Thomas, Pvt, Col Philip Pipkin, Capt Henry M Newlin, Mil Inf
PRITCHETT, Charles, Pvt, Col Wm Lillard, Capt Wm McLin, E TN Inf
PRITCHETT, Enoch, Pvt, Regt Commander omitted, Capt Archibald McKinney, Cav
PRITCHETT, James, Pvt, Col Philip Pipkin, Capt Henry M Newlin, Mil Inf; deserted
PRITCHETT, Thomas J, Pvt, Regt Commander omitted, Capt Edwin S Moore, Mtd Riflemen
PRIVAE, Stephen, Pvt, Col Wm Metcalf, Capt Obidah ____, Mil Inf
PRIVAT, Joel, Pvt, Col Samuel Bunch, Capt Joseph Duncan, E TN Drafted Mil; transferred to Capt Buchanan Co
PRIVAT, Namel, Pvt, Col Samuel Bunch, Capt Jno Hawk,
E TN Mil; joined from Capt English Co
PROBART, Robert C, Pvt, Lt Col Jno Edmonson, Co Commander omitted, Cav
PROBAST, Robert C, Pvt, Lt Col A Cheatham, Co Commander omitted, Mtd Inf
PROCK, William, Pvt, Col A Loury, Capt Gabriel Martin, Inf
PROCTER, Benjamin, Pvt, Lt Col L Hammond, Capt Thomas Delaney, Inf; d 1-15-1814
PROCTOR, Jeremiah, Pvt, Col A Metcalf, Capt Obidiah Waller, Mil Inf
PROCTOR, John, Pvt, Col A Loury, Capt Gabriel Martin, Inf
PROCTOR, Micajah, Pvt, Col Thos Williamson, Capt John Doak & Capt John Dobbins, Vol Mtd Gunmen
PROCTOR, William, 1 Cpl, Col A Metcalf, Capt Obidiah Waller, Mil Inf
PROFFIT, David, Pvt, Col Samuel Bayless, Capt Solomon Hendrix, E TN Mil
PROFIT, William, Cpl, Col Samuel Bayless, Capt Joseph Hale, E TN Mil
PROPHET, John, Pvt; Col Ewen Allison, Capt Joseph Everett, E TN Mil
PROPHET, Robert, Sgt, Col Samuel Bayless, Capt Joseph Hale, E TN Mil
PROVANCE, Henry, Ffr, Col Edwin Booth, Capt John Slatton, E TN Mil
PROVANCE, John, Ffr, Col S Bunch, Capt James Griffin, E TN Drafted Mil; deserted
PROVANCE, Thomas, Dmr, Col Edwin Booth, Capt John Slatton, E TN Mil
PROVINE, John, Ffr, Col Ewin Allison, Capt Hampton, Mil; attached from Capt Grffin Co
PROVINE, John, Pvt, Col Edwin E Booth, Capt John McKamey, E TN Mil; deserted
PROVINE, John, Pvt, Col S Bunch, Capt Jones Griffin, E TN Drafted Mil; joined from Capt Solomon Dobkins Co
PROVINE, John, Pvt, Col Wm Johnson, Capt Joseph Kirk, Mil; never appeared
PRUDE, James, Pvt, Col S Copeland, Capt Wm Douglas, Inf
PRUDE, John, Pvt, Col S Copeland, Capt Wm Douglas, Inf
PRUIT, John, Pvt, Col Samuel Wear, Capt Joseph Calloway, Mtd Inf
PRUITE, John, Pvt, Maj John Russell, Capt John Cowan, Vol Mtd Gunmen
PRUITE, William W, Pvt, Maj Wm Russell, Capt John Cowan, Vol Mtd Gunmen
PRYOR, Green, Pvt, Col John Brown, Capt Wm White, E TN Vol Mtd Inf
PRYOR, Green, Pvt, Col Wm Pillow, Capt C E McEwin, Vol Inf
PRYOR, Jeremiah, Pvt, Col John K Wynn, Capt James Hollman, Inf
PRYOR, John, Pvt, Col Edwin E Booth, Capt Marshall, Drafted Mil
PRYOR, Peter, Pvt, Col Wm Pillow, Co Commander omitted, Vol Inf

## Enlisted Men, War of 1812

PRYOR, Phillip, Pvt, Col Edwin E Booth, Capt John McKamy, E TN Mil
PRYOR, Samuel N, Pvt, Col Edwin E Booth, Capt Marshall, Drafted Mil
PRYOR, Samuel, Pvt, Regt Commander omitted, Capt Joseph Kirkpatrick, Mtd Gunmen
PRYOR, William C, Pvt, Regt Commander omitted, Capt Joel Parrish, Branch Srvce omitted
PRYOR, William, Pvt, Col A Cheatham, Capt Wm Johnson, Inf
PRYOR, William, Pvt, Col John Brown, Capt Wm White, E TN Vol Inf
PRYOR, William, Pvt, Col R H Dyer, Capt Owen, TN Vol Mtd Gunmen
PRYOR, William, Pvt, Col Wm Lillard, Capt Jacob Hartsell, E TN Vol Inf
PUCKET, Allen, Cpl, Col Wm Johnson, Capt James Stewart, E TN Drafted Mil
PUCKET, Luke, Pvt, Col Wm Metcalf, Capt Marks, Mil Inf
PUCKET, Peter, Pvt, Col Samuel Bunch, Capt Solomon Dobkins, E TN Drafted Mil; deserted
PUCKETT, Andrew L, Pvt, Col Thos Benton, Capt George Gibbs, Vol Inf
PUCKETT, Andrew S, 3 Sgt, Col Thos Benton, Capt Geo Gibbs, Vol Inf
PUCKETT, Douglas, Pvt, Col Wm Johnson, Capt Elihu Milliken, 3rd Regt E TN Mil
PUCKETT, Douglas, Pvt, Col Wm Johnson, Capt James Stewart, E TN Drafted Mil; d 3-18-1815
PUCKETT, Douglass, Pvt, Col Wm Lillard, Capt Zacheus Copeland, E TN Inf
PUCKETT, Drury, Pvt, Col Thos Benton, Capt Geo Gibbs, Vol Inf; AWOL
PUCKETT, Henry (Harvey), Pvt, Regt Commander omitted, Capt D Mason, Cav
PUCKETT, Henry, 1 Cpl, Col Leroy Hammond, Capt Thomas Wells & Capt A Loury, Inf; promoted to Sgt
PUCKETT, Jacob, Pvt, Brig Gen Johnson, Capt Allen, Mil Inf
PUCKETT, Jarrad, 2 Cpl, Col Leroy Hammonds, Capt Thomas Wells, Inf
PUCKETT, Joniah D, Pvt, Col John Cocke, Capt Joseph Price, Inf
PUCKETT, Luke, Pvt, Col Wm Metcalf, Capt William Russell, Mil Inf
PUCKETT, Peter, Pvt, Col S Bunch, Capt Jno Hauk, E TN Mil; discharged for inability
PUCKETT, Rice, Pvt, Col S Bayless, Capt Branch Jones, E TN Drafted Mil
PUCKETT, Robert, Pvt, Regt Commander omitted, Capt D Mason, Cav; d 12-30-1813
PUCKETT, William S, Pvt, Col T McCrory, Capt A Willis, Mil Inf
PUGH, Daniel, Cpl, Col S Bunch, Capt N Gibbs, E TN Drafted Mil; transferred to Capt Duncan's Co
PUGH, David, Pvt, Col Phillip Pipkin, Capt R T Perkins, Mtd Riflemen
PUGH, Henry, Pvt, Regt Commander omitted, Capt Thos Gray, Inf
PUGH, James, Pvt, Col Thomas Williamson, Capt Wm Martin, Vol Mtd Gunmen
PUGH, John, Pvt, Col S Copeland, Capt Moses Thompson, Inf
PUGH, Rees, Pvt, Col S Copeland, Capt John Dawson, Inf
PUGH, William, Pvt, Col John K Wynn, Capt John Porter, Inf
PUGH (PIEU), David, Pvt, Col Phillip Pipkin, Capt Geo Mebane, Mil Inf
PULLAM, Isham, Pvt, Col Robert Steele, Capt Jas Randals, Inf; AWOL
PULLEN, David, Pvt, Col S Copeland, Capt Allen Wilkinson, Mil Inf
PULLEN, Jesse, Pvt, Col John Coffee, Capt Henry Bryan, Cav
PULLEN, Jesse, Sgt, Regt Commander omitted, Capt Geo Smith, Spies
PULLEN, William, Pvt, Regt Commander omitted, Capt Nathan Farmer, Mtd Riflemen
PULLEY, Isham, Pvt, Col Robert Dyer, Capt Thomas Jones, Vol Mtd Gunmen; d 1-10-1815
PULLIAM, James H, Pvt, Col Wm Metcalf, Capt William Sitton, Mil Inf
PULLIN, Elisha, Pvt, Col R C Napier, Capt Samuel Ashmore, Mil Inf
PULLIN, Leroy, Pvt, Col S Bunch, Capt S Richardson; E TN Drafted Mil
PUMROY, William, Pvt, Col A Cheatham, Capt Charles Johnson, Inf
PUNCHARD, William, 2 Maj, Col Robert Steele, TN Mil
PURDEN, Alexander, Pvt, Maj William Woodfolk, Capt James Neil, Inf
PURDOM, John, Pvt, Col S Bunch, Capt F Register, E TN Mil; joined from Capt McPherson Co
PURDOM, John, Pvt, Col S Bunch, Capt Geo McPherson, E TN Mil; transferred to Capt Register Co
PURDON, Alexander, Pvt, Maj Woodfolk, Capt Abner Pearce, Inf; transferred from? Capt Nail's Co
PURKEEPILE, Jacob, Pvt, Col S Bunch, Capt Geo Gregory, E TN Drafted Mil
PURKEPILE, George, Pvt, Col William Lillard, Capt Robert McCalpin, E TN Inf; deserted
PURKEPILE, ____, Pvt, Col William Lillard, Capt S Copeland, E TN Vol Inf
PURMIT, Moses H, 2 Lt, Col Wm Metcalf, Capt John Patterson, Mil Inf
PURRIS, William, Pvt, Col John Williams, Capt William Walker, Vol
PURSEL, Hardy, Pvt, Col Jas Raulston, Capt Henry West, Inf
PURSELL, Abel, 2 Sgt, Col Jno Coffee, Capt Alexander McKeen, Cav
PURSELL, Abel, Pvt, Gen Jno Coffee, Lt Jesse Bean, Mtd Spies
PURSELL, William, Sgt, Col Ewen Allison, Capt Joseph Everett, E TN Mil
PURSLEY, Jacob, Pvt, Col S Wear, Capt Jas Tedford, E TN Vol Inf
PURSLEY, Robert, Pvt, Col Edward Bradley, Capt Brice Martin, Vol Inf
PURSLEY, Robert, Pvt, Col Wm Hall, Capt Brice Martin,

## Enlisted Men, War of 1812

Vol Inf
PURSLEY, William, Pvt, Col S Wear, Capt Rufus Morgan, E TN Vol Inf
PURTLE, John, Pvt, Col John Alcorn, Capt Edward Bradley, Vol Cav
PURTLE, Nathaniel, Pvt, Regt Commander omitted, Capt John Gray, Inf
PURVIS, Drury, Pvt, Col Phillip Pipkin, Capt Jas Blackmore, Mil Inf
PURVIS, William, Pvt, Col Williams, Capt Wm Walker, Vol
PUSHING, Abel, Pvt, Col John Cocke, Capt John Gray, Inf
PUSLEY, Robert, Pvt, Col Wm Hall, Capt Brice Martin, Vol Inf
PUTLEY, John, Pvt, Col S Bunch, Capt Jno Houk, E TN Mil; transferred to Capt Duncan Co
PUTMAN, Simeon, Cpl, Maj William Woodfolk, Capt Abraham Dudney, Inf; promoted to Sgt Maj
PUTMAN, Simeon, Sgt Maj, Maj Wm Woodfolk, W TN Mil
PUTTY, John, Pvt, Col S Bunch, Capt Joseph Duncan, E TN Drafted Mil; transferred to Capt Buchanan Co
PUTTY, John, Pvt, Col Samuel Bunch, Capt Edward Buchanan, E TN Mil; joined from Capt Duncan Co
PYBUS, William, Pvt, Col John Cocke, Capt Geo Barnes, Inf; joined at Clarksville, d 2-6-1815
PYLAND, Joseph, Pvt, Col Edwin Booth, Capt John Slatton, E TN Mil
PYOTT, Samuel, Pvt, Regt Commander omitted, Capt Thos Gray, Inf
PYRM, Charles, Pvt, Col A Loury, Lt Col L Hammond, Capt Thos Wells, Inf
PYRON, Allen, Pvt, Col Newton Cannon, Capt John Hanby, Mtd Riflemen; wounded 11-9-1813 at Talledega
PYRON, Richard, Pvt, Col Newton Cannon, Capt John Hanby, Mtd Riflemen
QUADS, Abram, Pvt, Col Wm Johnson, Capt Elihu Milliken, 3rd Regt E TN Mil
QUAIN, Timothy, Pvt, Col Edwin Booth, Capt Samuel Thompson, Mil
QUALLS, Cannon, Pvt, Col Philip Pipkin, Ens Wm Pegram, Det of Capt Smythe Co of W TN Mil
QUALLS, Eli, Pvt, Regt Commander omitted, Capt Nathan Peoples, Inf
QUALLS, James, Pvt, Col S Copeland, Capt John Dawson, Inf
QUALLS, Roland, Pvt, Col Wm Lillard, Capt Robt McCalpin, E TN Inf
QUAREY, John, Pvt, Col Wm Metcalf, Capt Wm Mullen, Mil Inf
QUARLES, Cannon, Pvt, Col Philip Pipkin, Capt David Smith, Mil Inf; deserted
QUARRINGTON, James, Pvt, Col Wm Metcalf, Capt Barbee Collins, Mil Inf
QUEEN, Adam, Pvt, Col Thos Benton, Capt Wm Smith, Vol Inf
QUEEN, John, Pvt, Col R H Dyer, Capt James McMahon, TN Vol Mtd Gunmen

QUESENBERRY, James, Pvt, Col S Copeland, Capt Moses Thompson, Inf
QUESENBURY, John, Pvt, Col S Copeland, Capt Moses Thompson, Inf
QUIERY, John, Pvt, Col Wm Metcalf, Capt Wm Sitton, Mil Inf
QUIET, James, Pvt, Col Wm Lillard, Capt Benj King, E TN Vol Inf
QUIET, William, 3 Cpl, Col Wm Lillard, Capt Benj H King, Branch Srvce omitted
QUIET, William, 3 Cpl, Lt Col Wm Snodgrass, Ens Gregg, Det of Inf of 2nd Regt Vol E TN Mil
QUILLAN, Charles, Pvt, Col Robert Steele, Capt John Cheetwood, Mil Inf; transferred to Capt Creel
QUILLAN, William, Pvt, Col A Cheatham, Capt James Giddens, Inf
QUILLEN, Charles, Pvt, Col R H Dyer, Capt James Wyatt, Vol Mtd Gunmen
QUILLEN, Charles, Pvt, Maj Gen A Jackson, Col A Cheatham, Capt Wm Creel, Inf
QUILLIAN, Charles, Pvt, Col Newton Cannon, Capt David Hogan, Mtd Gunmen; d 11-30-1813
QUIMBEY, Aaron, 4 Cpl, Col Ewen Allison, Capt Joseph Everett, E TN Mil
QUIMBEY, Burrel B, Pvt, Col Wm Metcalf, Capt Bird L Hurt, Mil Inf
QUIMY, Burwell B, Sgt, Col Robert Steele, Capt Robert Campbell, W TN Mil Inf
QUIMY, Russell B, 6 Cpl, Col Wm Metcalf, Capt Bird L Hurt, Mil Inf; promoted to Cpl
QUIN, Voluntine, Pvt, Col Philip Pipkin, Capt Henry M Newlin, Mil Inf; d 9-23-1814 at Ft Deposit
QUIN, William P, Pvt, Maj Gen A Jackson, Col Thos Williamson, Capt Robert Steele, Vol Mtd Gunmen
QUIN (QUENN), William, Dmr, Col Wm Hall, Capt Henry M Newlin, Inf
QUINLEY, Owen, Pvt, Col Edward Bradley, Capt Harry L Douglass, Vol Inf
QUINLY, Owen, Pvt, Col Thos Benton, Capt Henry Douglass, Vol Inf
QUINN, Allman jr, Pvt, Col Ewen Allison, Capt James Allen, E TN Mil; discharged for inability
QUINN, Allman, Pvt, Col Ewen Allison, Capt James Allen, E TN Mil
QUINN, Bartlett, Cpl, Col Ewen Allison, Capt James Allen, E TN Mil
QUINN, Enoch, Pvt, Col Samuel Bunch, Capt Dan'l Yarnell, E TN Mil
QUINN, James, Pvt, Col Samuel Bunch, Capt Jno English, E TN Drafted Mil; joined from Capt Davis's Co
QUINN, James, Pvt, Maj Gen A Jackson, Col Thos Williamson, Capt Robert Steele, Vol Mtd Gunmen; d 3-10-1815
QUINN, John, Pvt, Col Samuel Bunch, Lt Jno Harris, E TN Mil
QUINN, Joshua, Sgt, Col Ewen Allison, Capt James Allen, E TN Mil
QUINN, William, Pvt, Col Philip Pipkin, Capt Geo Mebane, Mil Inf
QUINN (QUEENE), James, Pvt, Col Samuel Bunch, Capt

## Enlisted Men, War of 1812

Moses, E TN Drafted Mil; transferred to Capt John English Co

RABB, Harris, Pvt, Col John Alcorn, Capt John Baskerville, Vol Inf

RABOURN, John, Cpl, Col Alexander Loury, Capt Leroy Hammonds & Capt Rains, Inf

RABURN, Howell, Pvt, Regt Commander omitted, Lt John Scott, Inf

RACKLEY, Silas, Dmr, Col Phillip Pipkin, Capt Jas Blackmore, Mil Inf

RACKLY, Allen, Pvt, Col S Copeland, Capt Moses Thompson, Inf

RADER, John, Pvt, Col William Lillard, Capt Robt Dyer, Vol Inf

RADER, John, Pvt, Col Wm Lillard, Capt Robt McCalpin, E TN Inf

RADER, Michael, Pvt, Col S Bayless, Capt Hale, E TN Mil

RADER, Peter, Pvt, Col S Bayless, Capt Hale, E TN Mil

RADER, Peter, Pvt, Col William Lillard, Capt Robert Dyer, Vol Mil Inf

RADFORD, Jesse, Pvt, Col Robert Dyer, Capt Glen Owen, TN Vol Mtd Gunmen; d 1-7-1815

RADFORD, John, Pvt, Col Thomas Williamson, Capt Brice Martin, Vol Mtd Gunmen

RADFORD, John, Pvt, Regt Commander omitted, Capt Archibald McKinney, Cav; d 3-10-1814

RADFORD, ____, Pvt, Col Thomas Williamson, Capt Brice Martin, Branch Srvce omitted; d 1-19-1815

RAGAN, Ahimas, Pvt, Col S Bunch, Capt Edward Buchanan, E TN Mil

RAGAN, Benjamin, Pvt, Regt Commander omitted, Capt Edwin S Moore, Mtd Riflemen

RAGAN, Daniel R, Pvt, Col S Bunch, Capt F Register, E TN Mil

RAGAN, Daniel R, Pvt, Col Samuel Bunch, Capt Geo McPherson, E TN Mil; joined from? Capt Register Co

RAGAN, David, Cpl, Maj Jas P H Porter, Capt Samuel Cowan, E TN Mil Cav

RAGAN, David, Pvt, Col S Bunch, Capt Jno Houk, E TN Mil

RAGAN, Ephraim, Pvt, Col S Wear, Capt John Childs, E TN Vol Inf

RAGAN, James, Pvt, Col A Cheatham, Capt Wm Smith, Inf

RAGAN, James, Pvt, Col Edward Bradley, Capt Brice Martin, Vol Inf

RAGAN, James, Pvt, Col John Alcorn, Capt Wm Locke, Cav

RAGAN, James, Pvt, Col S Bunch, Capt Jno Houk, E TN Mil; disch at Knoxville

RAGAN, James, Pvt, Col Wm Hall, Capt Brice Martin, Vol Inf

RAGAN, Jesse, Pvt, Col John Winn, Capt Bailey Butler, Inf

RAGAN, John Cpl, Maj John Childs, Capt John Stephens, E TN Vol Mtd Inf

RAGAN, John, Cpl, Col Robert Dyer, Capt Thomas Jones, Vol Mtd Gunmen

RAGAN, John, Pvt, Col T McCrory, Capt Isaac Patton, Mil Inf

RAGAN, John, Pvt, Col William Lillard, Capt George Argenbright, E TN Vol Riflemen

RAGAN, John, Pvt, Col Wm Hall, Capt Brice Martin, Vol Inf

RAGAN, Lewis, Pvt, Regt Commander omitted, Capt Joseph Williams, Mil Cav

RAGAN, Nathan, Pvt, Col Alexander Loury, Capt Geo Saver, Inf

RAGAN, Nathan, Pvt, Col Alexander Loury, Capt James Kincaid, Inf

RAGAN, Owen, Pvt, Col William Lillard, Capt Robert Maloney, E Tn Vol Inf

RAGAN, Peter, Pvt, Col S Wear, Capt Joseph Calloway, Mtd Inf

RAGAN, Powel, Pvt, Col S Bunch, Capt Jno English, E TN Drafted Mil

RAGAN, Samuel, Pvt, Col John Alcorn, Capt William Locke, Cav

RAGAN, William, Pvt, Col John Williams, Capt David Vance, Mil

RAGAN, William, Pvt, Col R C Napier, Capt Drury Adkins, Mil Inf

RAGANS, Henry, Pvt, Col Wm Johnson, Capt Jas Stewart, E TN Drafted Mil

RAGEN, James, Pvt, Col William Johnson, Capt Elihu Millikin, TN Mil

RAGEN, Jedithen, Pvt, Maj Wm Woodfolk, CApt Ross & Capt McCully, Inf

RAGLAND, John, Pvt, Col Wm Hall, Capt Brice Martin, Vol Inf

RAGLE, Adam, Pvt, Col Ewen Allison, Capt Joseph Everett, E TN Mil

RAGLE, George, Pvt, Col Ewen Allison, CApt Joseph Everett, E Tn Mil

RAGLIN, William, Pvt, Col A Cheatham, Capt Birdwell, Inf

RAGOR, John, Pvt, Col Thos Williamson, Capt Giles Burdett, Vol Mtd Gunmen

RAGSDALE, Asa, Pvt, Maj William Woodfolk, Capt Daniel Ross, Inf

RAGSDALE, Berry, Pvt, Col Robert Steele, Capt Jas Bennett, Mil Inf

RAGSDALE, Beryman, Pvt, Regt Commander omitted, Capt Askew, Inf

RAGSDALE, Clement, Pvt, Col William Higgins, Capt A Cheatham, Mtd Riflemen

RAGSDALE, Daniel, Pvt, Col Jas Raulston, Capt Jas Black, Inf

RAGSDALE, Daniel, Pvt, Col Robert Steele, Capt John Chitwood, Mil Inf; promoted to wgnmstr

RAGSDALE, Edward, Sgt, Col William Johnson, Capt Benj Powell, E TN Mil

RAGSDALE, James, Pvt, Col A Cheatham, Capt Charles Johnson, Inf

RAGSDALE, Joel, Pvt, Col A Cheatham, Capt Richard Benson, Inf

RAGSDALE, Lancaster, Pvt, Lt Col Leroy Hammonds, Capt Thomas Wells, Inf

RAGSDALE, Levi, Blksmth, Col John Coffee, Capt Chas Kavanaugh, Cav

RAGSDALE, Levi, Pvt, Regt Commander omitted, Capt

## Enlisted Men, War of 1812

Archibald McKinney, Cav
RAGSDALE, Lewis, Pvt, Col A Loury, Capt Gabriel Martin, Inf
RAGSDALE, Peter, Cpl, Col Wm Higgins, Capt Thos Eldridge, Mtd Gunmen
RAGSDALE, Robert, Tptr, Col John Coffee, Capt Chas Kavanaugh, Cav
RAGSDALE, Samuel, Pvt, Col John Alcorn, Capt Thos Bradley, Vol Cav
RAGSDALE, Thomas, Pvt, Col John Coffee, Capt Chas Kavanaugh, Cav; AWOL
RAGSDALL, Jeremiah, Pvt, Col Wm Pillow, Capt Geo Caperton, Inf
RAGSDOLL, David, Pvt, Col Jno Brown, Capt Jas Preston, E Tn Mil Inf
RAIGLER, Sawyers, 1 Cpl, Col John Cocke, Capt James Gault, Inf
RAINBOLT, John, Pvt, Col Samuel Bayless, Capt Solomon Hendrix, E TN Mil
RAINER, Henry, Pvt, Col Thos Williamson, CApt Robt Moore, Vol Mtd Gunmen
RAINES, Robert, Pvt, Maj Wm Woodfolk, Capt Abraham Dudney & Capt John Sutton, Inf
RAINES (RAIBY), John, Pvt, Col Edwin Booth, Capt John Slatton, E Tn Mil; deserted
RAINEY, David, Pvt, Regt Commander omitted, Capt Geo Smith, Spies
RAINEY, Isaac, Pvt, Lt I Barrett, Capt Nathan Davis, Inf
RAINEY, Jesse G, Bn? QM, Brig Gen Thos Coulter, no Co Commander, E TN Draft Mil
RAINEY, John, Pvt, Maj Gen Wm Carroll, Col Wm Metcalf, Capt John Jackson, Mil
RAINEY, Robert, Pvt, Col Wm Hall, Capt Henry M Newlin, Inf
RAINEY, Thomas, Pvt, Col Wm Hall, Capt Henry Newlin, Inf
RAINKEN, Elisha, Pvt, Col S Copeland, Capt John Holshouser, Inf
RAINS, George, Pvt, Col Samuel Bunch, Capt Jno English, E TN Draft Mil
RAINS, Joel, Pvt, Col John Brown, Capt Chas Lewin, E TN Vol Mtd Inf
RAINS, William, Pvt, Col Thos Benton, Capt Geo Gibbs, Vol Inf
RAINS, William, Pvt, Col Thos Benton, Capt Geo W Gibbs, Vol Inf
RAINS, William, Pvt, Col Wm Pillow, CApt John H Anderson, Vol Inf
RAINWATER, Burrell, Pvt, Regt Commander omitted, Capt Gray, Inf
RAINWATER, James, Pvt, Col Samuel Bayless, Capt James Churchman, E Tn Mil
RAINWATER, James, Pvt, Col Samuel Bunch, Capt Geo Gregory, E Tn Draft Mil
RALPH, Alexander, Pvt, Col James Raulston, Capt Henry Hamilton, Inf; also served under Gen Wm Carroll
RALPH, Alexander, Pvt, Col Wm Higgins, Capt Adam Dale, Mtd Gunmen
RALPH, Anderson, Pvt, Col R H Dyer, Capt Bethel Allen, Vol Mtd Gunmen
RALPH, Anderson, Pvt, Col Wm Higgins, Capt Adam Dake, Mtd Gunmen
RALPH, John, Pvt, Col A Loury, Capt Geo Sarver, Inf
RALPH, Josiah, Pvt, Col Samuel Bunch, Capt James Cummings, E TN Vol Mtd Inf
RALPH, Josiah, Pvt, Col Wm Lillard, Capt Hugh Martin, E Tn Vol Inf
RALPH, Thomas, Pvt, Col James Raulston, Capt Henry Hamilton, Inf; also served under Gen Wm Carroll
RALPH, Thomas, Pvt, Col T McCrory, Capt Jno Reynolds, Mil Inf
RALPH, William, Pvt, Col Wm Lillard, Capt Geo Argenbright, E TN Vol Riflemen
RALSTON, John, Pvt, Col R H Dyer, Capt James White, Vol Mtd Gunmen
RAMBO, Elias, Pvt, Col John Wynne, Capt Wm Carothers, W TN Inf
RAMBO, Elias, Pvt, Col John Wynne, Capt Wm Willson, Inf; trans to Capt Caruthers Co
RAMER, Adam, Pvt, Col Thos Benton, Capt Isaiah Renshaw, Vol Inf
RAMEY, John, Pvt, Col Wm Metcalf, Capt Wm Sitton, Mil Inf
RAMSAY, Elijah, Ens, Brig Gen T Johnson, Capt Allen, Mil Inf
RAMSAY, John D, Pvt, Col Wm Metcalf, Capt Bird L Hurt, Mil Inf
RAMSAY, John, Pvt, Regt Commander omitted, Capt Jas Terrill, Cav
RAMSAY, Obadiah, Pvt, Col T McCrory, Capt John Reynolds, Mil Inf
RAMSEY, Alexander, Pvt, Col Wm Hall, Capt John Kennedy, Vol Inf
RAMSEY, David, Pvt, Col John Cocke, Capt Geo Barnes, Inf; died 4-4-1815
RAMSEY, John, 4 Sgt, Maj Gen Wm Carroll, Col James Raulston, Capt Wiley Huddleston, Inf
RAMSEY, John, Pvt, Col John Coffee, Capt James Terrell, Vol Cav
RAMSEY, John, Pvt, Col T McCrory, Capt Samuel B McKnight, Inf; died 11-8-1813
RAMSEY, John, Sgt, Col Jno Brown, Capt Wm Standifer, E Tn Mil Inf
RAMSEY, Robert H, Pvt, Col Wm Hall, Capt Henry M Newlin, Inf
RAMSEY, Robert, Pvt, Col A Loury, Capt John Looney, W TN Inf
RAMSEY, William D, Pvt, Col Alexander Loury, Capt James Kincaid, Inf
RAMSEY, William G, Pvt, Col Alexander Loury, Capt John Looney, W TN Inf
RAMSEY, William H, Pvt, Col R H Dyer, Capt James McMahon, TN Vol Mtd Gunmen
RAMSEY, William, Cpl, Col Samuel Bayless, Capt Branch Jones, E TN Draft Mil
RAMSEY, William, Pvt, Col Ewen Allison, Capt James Allen, E TN Mil
RAMSEY, William, Pvt, Col John Brown, Capt James McKamy, E TN Mtd Gunmen
RAMSEY, William, Pvt, Col S Copeland, Capt Moses Thompson, Inf; enlisted Regular Svce 1-30-1814
RAMSEY, William, Pvt, Col Samuel Wear, Col Samuel

- 417

*Enlisted Men, War of 1812*

Bunch, Capt Wm Mitchell, E TN Mtd Inf
RAMSEY, William, Pvt, Col Thos Williamson, Capt Richard Tate, Vol Mtd Gunmen
RAMSEY, William, Pvt, Col Wm Johnson, Capt Benjamin Powell, E Tn Mil; died 11-18-1814
RANDALE, John, Pvt, Col Jarmon, Capt Isiah Hamilton, Inf
RANDALL, Greenberry, 2 Sgt, Maj Gen A Jackson, Capt John Craine, Mtd Gunmen
RANDALS, John, Cpl, Col Samuel Wear, Col Samuel Bunch, Capt Wm Mitchell, E TN Mtd Inf
RANDLE, Edmond, Pvt, Col R C Napier, Capt Thos Gray, Mil Inf
RANDLE, Edmond, Pvt, Regt Commander omitted, Capt Elijah Rushing, Det of Inf
RANDLE, Harry, Pvt, Regt Commander omitted, Capt James Gray, Inf
RANDLE, James, Pvt, Regt Commander omitted, Capt James Gray, Inf
RANDLE, Thomas, Pvt, Lt Col Henry Bryan, Co Commander omitted, Inf
RANDLE, Thomas, Pvt, Maj Cooper, Co Commander omitted, Mtd Riflemen
RANDLE, Thomas, Pvt, Regt Commander omitted, Capt Jas Cowan, Inf
RANDLE, William, Pvt, Lt Col Henry Bryan, Co Commander omitted, Inf
RANDLE, William, Pvt, Maj Cooper, Co Commander omitted, 26 TN Regt Mtd Riflemen
RANDLE, William, Pvt, Regt Commander omitted, Capt James Gray, Inf
RANDLE, Wilson, Pvt, Maj Cooper, Co Commander omitted, 26 TN Regt Mtd Riflemen
RANDLE, Wilson, Pvt, Regt Commander omitted, Capt Jas Cowan, Inf
RANDLES, Samuel, Pvt, Col Wm Lillard, Capt Jacob Hartsell, E Tn Vol Inf
RANDOL, Thomas, Pvt, Regt Commander omitted, Capt Jno Haggard, Mtd Gunmen
RANDOL, William, Pvt, Regt Commander omitted, Capt Jas Haggard, Mtd Gunmen
RANDOLPH, Hezekiah, Pvt, Col Wm Lillard, Capt Wm Lillard, E Tn Vol Inf
RANDOLPH, Joel, Cpl, Col S Copeland, Capt John Dawson, Inf
RANDOLPH, Rex A, Pvt, Col R C Napier, Capt John Chism, Mil Inf
RANDOLPH, Rex A, Pvt, Col R H Dyer, Capt James McMahon, 1 TN Vol Mtd Gunmen
RANDOLPH, Robert, Pvt, Maj John Chiles, Capt Charles Conway, E Tn Mtd Gunmen
RANDOLPH, Thomas J, 1 Sgt, Col Jas Raulston, Capt Daniel Newman, Inf
RANDOLPH, William, Pvt, Col Samuel Bayless, Capt Joseph Goodson, E Tn Mil
RANDOLPH, William, Pvt, Col Wm Lillard, Capt Wm Lillard, E TN Vol Inf
RANEY, Archibold, Pvt, Col Wm Hall, Capt John Kennedy, Vol Inf
RANKEN, Thomas, Pvt, Col Wm Lillard, Capt Thos McChristian, E Tn Vol Inf

RANKIN, C William, Pvt, Col Samuel Bunch, Capt Francis Berry, E TN Mil
RANKIN, James, Pvt, Col Edward Bradley, Capt Wm Lauderdale, Vol Inf
RANKIN, John M, Pvt, Col Samuel Bayless, Capt Joseph Hale, E Tn Mil
RANKIN, John M, Pvt, Col Samuel Wear, Capt James Tedford, E Tn Vol Inf
RANKIN, John P, Cpl, Col Samuel Bayless, Capt Joseph Goodson, E Tn Mil
RANKIN, John, Cpl, Col Samuel Bunch, Capt Geo Gregory, E Tn Draft Mil
RANKIN, John, Pvt, Col Samuel Wear, Capt John Stephens, E Tn Vol Inf
RANKIN, Samuel, Pvt, Col Samuel Bunch, Capt Edward Buchanan, E Tn Mil
RANKINS, James, Pvt, Col Philip Pipkin, Capt E Kirkpatrick, Mil Inf; deserted
RANKINS, James, Pvt, Col Wm Hall, Capt Wm L Alexander, Vol Inf
RANKINS, Jesse, Pvt, Col Wm Hall, Capt Wm L Alexander, Vol Inf
RANKINS, Moses, Pvt, Gen Andrew Jackson, Capt Nathan Davis, West S Inf
RANKINS, Samuel L, Pvt, Col Samuel Bunch, Capt Francis Berry, E TN Mil
RANNALS, Jesse, Tptr, Col N T Perkins, Capt Mathew Patterson, Mtd Vol Inf
RANSHAW, Benjamin, Pvt, Col Thos Benton, Capt Isiah Renshaw, Vol Inf
RANSOM, John, Pvt, Col Alexander Loury, Capt James Kincaid, Inf
RANSOM, John, Pvt, Col John Alcorn, Capt Alexander McKeen, Cav
RANSOM, William, Pvt, Col John Alcorn, Capt Alexander McKeen, Cav
RANSON, John, Pvt, Col J K Winn, Capt Wm Carruthers, W Tn Inf
RANYAN, George, Pvt, no other information
RAPE, Jacob, Pvt, Col R H Dyer, Capt Robert Evans, Vol Mtd Gunmen
RAPE, John, Pvt, Col Wm Metcalf, Capt Wm Mullin, Mil Inf
RAPE, Peter, Pvt, Col R H Dyer, Capt Robert Evans, Vol Mtd Gunmen
RAPER, Charles, Pvt, Regt Commander omitted, Capt Jas Haggard, Mtd Gunmen
RAPER (ROPER), William, Pvt, Maj Wm Russell, Capt John Trimble, Vol Mtd Gunmen
RAPP, Daniel, Pvt, Col Ewen Allison, Capt J Loughmiller, Mil
RARDEN, Alexander, Pvt, Regt Commander omitted, Lt Jas Berry, Mtd Riflemen
RASBERRY, George, Pvt, Col Philip Pipkin, Capt William Mackay, Mil Inf
RASBURY, John, Pvt, Col John Cocke, Capt James Gray, Inf
RASPBERRY, William, Rank omitted, Col Newton Perkins, Capt Philip Pipkin, Mtd Riflemen
RATER (RECTOR), Kenner, Pvt, Col Samuel Wear, Col Samuel Bunch, Capt Wm Mitchell, E Tn Mtd Inf

## Enlisted Men, War of 1812

RATHER, Asa, Pvt, Col Jno Brown, Capt Wm D Neilson, E TN Vol Mil

RATHER, Asa, Pvt, Col Wm Johnson, Capt Jas Rogers, E TN Draft Mil

RATHER, Benjamin, Pvt, Col Thos Williamson, Lt Jas Nealy, Capt Jas Pace, Vol Mtd Gunmen

RATHER, John, Pvt, Col Jno Brown, Capt Allen T Bacon, E TN Mil Inf

RATHER, John, Pvt, Maj Jno Childs, Capt Chas Conway, E TN Mtd Gunmen

RATHER, William, Pvt, Regt Commander omitted, Capt D Deaderick, Arty

RATLIFF, Joshua, Pvt, Col Thos Williamson, Capt Thos Scurry, Vol Mtd Gunmen

RATS, Godfrey, Pvt, Col P Pipkin, Capt H M Newlin, Mil Inf

RATTON, John A, Pvt, Col Robert Steele, Capt R M Ratton, Mil Inf

RAULINGS, Joshua, Pvt, Col N T Cannon, Capt Wm Edwards, Regt Command

RAULSTON, Mitchell, Pvt, Col S Bunch, Capt Jno Hauk, E Tn Mil; disch for inability

RAUSON, Ephraim, Pvt, Maj Jno Chiles, Capt Jno Stephens, E TN Vol Mtd Inf

RAWLINGS, James, Pvt, Col Wm Hale, Capt Wm Alexander, Vol Inf

RAWLINGS, Rhodarn, Pvt, Col Jno Raulston, Capt M Neale, Inf

RAWLINS, James, Pvt, Col Wm Hall, Capt Wm Alexander, Vol Inf

RAWLS, Alexander, Far, Col Thos Williamson, Capt Jno Crane & Capt Jas Cook, Vol Mtd Gunmen

RAWLS, Alexander, Pvt, Lt Col Archer Cheatham, Co Commander omitted, 6 Brig Mtd Inf

RAWLS, James, Pvt, Col Thos Williamson, Capt Jno Crane & Capt Jas Cook, Vol Mtd Gunmen

RAWSON, John, Pvt, Col Thos Benton, Capt Wm Smith, Vol Inf

RAWSON (ROSIN), James, Pvt, Col Wm Metcalf, Capt B Collins, Mil Inf

RAY, Abner, Pvt, Col Saml Bayless, Capt Jos Bacon, E Tn Mil

RAY, Alexander, Pvt, Col A Loury, Capt J N Williamson, W TN Mil

RAY, Alexander, Pvt, Col L Hammond, Capt J N Williamson, 2 Regt Inf

RAY, Andrew B, 1 Sgt, Col E Booth, Capt Alex Biggs, Inf

RAY, Archibald, Pvt, Col P Pipkin, Capt Geo Mebane, Mil Inf

RAY, Daniel, Pvt, Col J K Winn, Capt Wm Carothers, W Tn Inf; deserted

RAY, David, Blksmth, Col R H Dyer, Capt E C Dickson, TN Mtd Vol Gunmen

RAY, George, Pvt, Maj Wm Woodfolk, Capt A Dudney & Capt Jno Sutton, Inf; promoted to Cpl

RAY, Hugh, Pvt, Col Wm Lillard, Capt Robt McCalpin, E Tn Inf; deserted

RAY, Hugh, Pvt, Regt Commander omitted, Capt Ephraim Dickson, Branch omitted

RAY, Jacob, Pvt, Col S Copeland, Capt Jas Tait, Inf

RAY, John, Pvt, Brig Gen Thos Washington, Capt Jno Crawford, Mtd Inf

RAY, John, Pvt, Col E Booth, Capt Alex Biggs, Inf

RAY, John, Pvt, Col Wm Metcalf, Capt Jas Barnhart, Mil Inf

RAY, John, Pvt, Maj Wm Russell, Capt Wm Chism, Vol Mtd Riflemen

RAY, Joseph, Pvt, Col E Booth, Capt Saml Thompson, Mil

RAY, Joseph, Pvt, Col N T Perkins, Capt J S Quarles, Vol Mtd Inf

RAY, Joseph, Pvt, Col S Copeland, Capt Jas Tait, Inf

RAY, Joseph, Pvt, Col Saml Wear, Capt Jas Gillespie, E TN Vol Inf

RAY, Lewis, Pvt, Col E Booth, Capt Jno Thompson, Mil

RAY, Lewis, Pvt, Col N T Cannon, Capt John Harpole, Mtd Gunmen

RAY, Richard, Pvt, Col A Loury, Capt J N Williamson, W TN Mil

RAY, Richard, Pvt, Col L Hammond, Capt J N Willismon, 2 Regt Inf

RAY, Richard, Pvt, Col T McCrory, Capt Isaac Patton, Mil Inf

RAY, Samuel M, Pvt, Col Wm Higgins, Capt Jas Hambleton, Mtd Gunmen

RAY, Samuel, Pvt, Col Saml Wear, Capt Jno Stephens, E TN Vol Inf

RAY, Samuel, Pvt, Col Wm Lillard, Capt Sharpe, 2 Regt Inf

RAY, Samuel, Pvt, Maj Wm Russell, Capt F Hodges, Vol Mtd Gunmen

RAY, Stephen, Sgt, Col P Pipkin, Capt Geo Mebane, Mil Inf

RAY, Thomas, 4 Cpl, Col Jno Coffee, Capt Jas Terrell, Vol Cav

RAY, Thomas, Cpl, Col S Copeland, Capt Jas Tate, Inf

RAY, Thomas, Pvt, Col Samuel Bayless, Capt Jos Bacon, E Tn Mil

RAY, Thomas, Pvt, Maj Wm Woodfolk, Capt Jas Tunner, Inf

RAY, William, Pvt, Col E Booth, Capt Alex Biggs, Inf

RAY, William, Pvt, Col R H Dyer, Capt E Dickson, TN Mtd Vol Gunmen

RAY, William, Pvt, Col T McCrory, Capt Jas Shannon, Mil Inf

RAY, William, Pvt, Col Thos Williamson, Capt Beverly Williams, Vol Mtd Gunmen

RAY, William, Pvt, Col Wm Pillow, Capt Thos Williamson, Vol Inf

RAY (ROY), David, Pvt, Col N T Cannon, Capt J B Dansey, Mtd Gunmen

RAYBOURN, James, Pvt, Col Edward Bradley, Capt John Kennedy, Riflemen

RAYBOURNE, Thomas, Pvt, Col John Brown, Capt Wm White, E TN Vol Mtd Inf

RAYBURN, Henry, Pvt, Col T McCrory, Capt Thos K Gordon, Inf

RAYBURN, Joel, Pvt, Col John Wynne, Capt John Porter, Inf

RAYBURN, John, Pvt, Col Robt Steel, Capt John Cheetwood, Mil Inf

RAYNES, Reuben, Pvt, Regt Commander omitted, Capt

- 419

Gray, Inf
RAYNOLDS, James, Pvt, Maj Wm Woodfolk, Capt Abraham Dudney & Capt John Sutton, Inf
RAYOR, Jacob, Pvt, Col Thos Williamson, Capt Giles Burdett, Vol Mtd Gunmen
RAZOR, Peter, Pvt, Col Ewen Allison, Capt Adam Winsell, E TN Draft Mil; trans to Capt McAny's Co Mtd Gunmen
RAZZER (RAIZER), Eli, Pvt, Col Samuel Wear, Capt Jesse Col, Vol Inf
REA, Robert, Pvt, Col Newton Cannon, Capt James Walton, Mtd Riflemen
REA (RAY), James, Pvt, Lt Col L Hammond, Capt James Tubb, Inf
REACE, David, Pvt, Col Thos Bneton, Capt Wm J Smith, Vol Inf
REACE, Jacob, Pvt, Col Samuel Bayless, Capt James Churchman, E TN Mil
REACE, John, Pvt, Col Ewen Allison, Capt James Laughmiller, Mil; joined from Capt Griffin Co
REACE, Robert, Cpl, Col S Copeland, Capt James Tate, Branch omitted
READ, Andrew, Pvt, Regt Commander omitted, Capt Archibald McKinney, Cav; trans to Capt Johnson Co
READ, Andrew, Sgt, Col John Cocke, Capt John Dalton, Inf
READ, Charles, Pvt, Col Samuel Bayless, Capt Joseph Hale, E Tn Mil
READ, Clement N, Surgeon Mate, Col John Coffee, no Co Commander, TN Vol Cav & Mtd Riflemen
READ, David, Pvt, Col John Wynne, Capt James Cole, Inf
READ, David, Pvt, Col R H Dyer, Capt Robt Edmonston, TN Mtd Vol Gunmen
READ, Edmund, Pvt, Col A Cheatham, Capt Chas Johnson, Inf
READ, George, Pvt, Cpl Elisha Green, Mtd Spies
READ, Guilford D, Pvt, Col R H Dyer, Capt Bethel Allen, Vol Mtd TN Gunmen
READ, Henry, Pvt, Col N T Perkins, Capt James McMahan, Mtd Gunmen
READ, James B, Pvt, Col Wm Hall, Capt Henry M Newlin, Inf; under age & objected to by his father
READ, James, Pvt, Col Edward Bradley, Capt John Moore, Vol Inf
READ, James, Pvt, Col R H Dyer, Capt Bethel Allen, Vol Mtd Gunmen
READ, James, Pvt, Regt Commander omitted, Capt Jas Haggard, Mtd Gunmen
READ, John C, Pvt, Regt Commander omitted, Capt Jos Williams, Mil Cav; died 12-26-1813
READ, John H, Pvt, Regt Commander omitted, Lt Richard Napier, Inf
READ, John jr, Pvt, Regt Commander omitted, Capt Jas Haggard, Mtd Gunmen
READ, John sr, Pvt, Regt Commander omitted, Capt Jas Haggard, Mtd Gunmen
READ, John, Cpl, Col Edward Bradley, Capt John Moore, Vol Inf; deserted
READ, John, Pvt, Col A Loury, Capt James Kincaid, Inf
READ, John, Pvt, Col S Copeland, Capt Jas Tait, Inf
READ, John, Pvt, Lt Col L Hammond, Capt Thos Delaney, Inf; also under Col Loury
READ, John, Surgeon's Mate, Regt Commander omitted, 2 Regt TN Vol Inf
READ, Joseph, Cpl, Col Wm Hall, Capt John Moore, Vol Inf
READ, Robert, Pvt, no other information
READ, Samuel, 5 Cpl, Maj John Chiles, Capt John Stephens, E Tn Vol Mtd Inf
READ, Samuel, Pvt, Col Edward Bradley, Capt John Moore, Vol Inf; deserted
READ, Samuel, Sgt, Col John Brown, Capt John Trimble, E TN Mtd Gunmen
READ, William, Pvt, Col Newton Cannon, Capt John B Demsey, Mtd Gunmen
READ, Zenas, Pvt, Col N T Perkins, Capt John B Quarles, Vol Mtd Inf
READ (REED), Sion S, 2 Sgt, Col Jno Coffee, Capt Blackman Coleman, Cav
READ (REEDE), Edmond, Cpl, Col Thos Williamson, Capt Wm Martin, Vol Mtd Gunmen; died 2-16-1815
READE, Hugh, Pvt, Col Wm Hall, Capt John Kennedy, Vol Inf
READE, Isaac, Pvt, Col Jno Cocke, Capt Richard Crunk, Inf
READE, John, Pvt, Maj Wm Russell, Capt Isaac Williams, Separate Bn TN Vol Mtd Gunmen; under Col Dyer 1 Regt
READER, Rite A, 1 Cpl, Col A Cheatham, Capt James Gid;dens, Inf; trans to Arty
READER, Robert, Pvt, Col Ewen Allison, Capt Jacob Hoyal, E TN Mil; transferred to Capt Register 4-27-1814
READER, William, Pvt, Col Edwin Booth, Capt John Sharp, E TN Mil
READING, Alford S, Pvt, Lt Col Jno Edmonson, Co Commander omitted, Cav
READING, Augustus, Pvt, Maj Andrew Jackson, Capt John Crane, Mtd Gunmen
READING, Tobias, Pvt, Col John Cocke, Capt George Barnes, Inf; d 1-19-1815
READINS, George, Pvt, Col William Higgins, Capt Allen, Mtd Gunmen
REAGAN, Charles, Sgt, Col Edwin Booth, Capt Samuel Thompson, Mil
REAGAN, Henry, Pvt, Col Wm Johnson, Capt David McKamey, E TN Drafted Mil
REAGAN, Joseph, Pvt, Col Wm Johnson, Capt John McKamey, E TN Drafted Mil
REAGLE, Abraham, Pvt, Col William Lillard, Capt Brice Martin, E TN Vol Inf
REAMS, Boling, Pvt, Col John Cocke, Capt James Gault, Inf
REAMS, John, Pvt, no other information
REAMS, Joshua, Pvt, Regt Commander omitted, Capt D Mason, Arty
REAMY, John, Artif, Regt Commander omitted, Capt Jesse Reamy & Capt John Brown, Mtd Gunmen
REAR, John, Pvt, Col S Bunch, Capt Edward Buchanan, E TN Mil; transferred from Capt Duncan's Co

REASONER, Nicholas, Pvt, Col S Wear, Capt Jesse Cole, Vol Inf
REATEN, Yearby, Pvt, Col Stephen Copeland, Capt William Evans, Mil Inf
REATHERFORD, John, Pvt, Col John Coffee, Capt John Baskerville, Cav
REAVES, Conery, Pvt, Col Robert Dyer, Capt William Russell, Vol Mtd Gunmen
REAVES, Drury, Pvt, Col Robert Dyer, Capt Robert Evans, Vol Mtd Gunmen
REAVES, Elijah, Pvt, Col R C Napier, Capt Samuel Ashmore, Mil Inf
REAVES, George, Cpl, Col Robert Dyer, Capt Robert Evans, Vol Mtd Gunmen
REAVES, Hambleton, Pvt, Col Thomas Benton, Capt William Smith, Vol Inf
REAVES, Hooks, Pvt, Col S Copeland, Capt Alexander Provine, Mil Inf
REAVES, Jeremiah, Pvt, Col Jas Raulston, Capt Jas Black, Inf
REAVES, John, Cpl, Col Robert Dyer, Capt Robert Evans, Vol Mtd Gunmen; promoted from Pvt
REAVES, John, Pvt, Brig Gen Johnson, Capt Allen, Mil Inf
REAVES, John, Pvt, Col Robert Dyer, Capt Glen Owen, TN Vol Mtd Gunmen
REAVES, John, Pvt, Col T McCrory, Capt Jas Shannon, Mil Inf
REAVES, John, Pvt, Col T McCrory, Capt Wm Metcalf, Mil Inf
REAVES, Jordon, Pvt, Col S Copeland, Capt G W Stell, Mil Inf
REAVES, Levi, Pvt, Col Robert Steele, Capt Robert Campbell, Mil Inf
REAVES, Peter, Pvt, Col R C Napier, Capt Andrew McCarty, Mil Inf
REAVES, Reuben, Pvt, Maj Wm Woodfolk, Co Commander omitted, Inf
REAVES, Samuel, Pvt, Brig General Johnson, Capt Allen, Mil Inf; promoted to Wgn Master
REAVES, Samuel, Pvt, Col William Lillard, Capt Jacob Dyke, Vol Inf; deserted
REAVES, Thomas, Pvt, Maj Gen Jackson, Capt William Carroll, Vol Inf
REAVES, Timothy, Pvt, Col S Copeland, Capt Jacob Stell, Mil Inf
REAVES, Timothy, Pvt, Maj Gen Jackson, Col A Cheatham, Capt Creel, Inf; transferred to Capt Stell Co
REAVES, William S, Pvt, Col R C Napier, Capt Andrew McCarty, Mil Inf; transferred to the Arty
REAVES, William, Pvt, Col Robert Dyer, Capt Jacob Evans, Vol Mtd Gunmen
REAVES, William, Pvt, Col Wm Metcalf, Capt Obidiah Waller, Mil Inf
REAVES, William, Pvt, Maj Gen Jackson, Capt Daniel Oban, Inf
REAVES, William, Pvt, Maj Gen Jackson, Capt William Carroll, Vol Inf
REAVES, William, Pvt, Regt Commander omitted, Capt Joel Parrish, Branch Srvce omitted
REAVES, William, Sgt, Col John Cocke, Capt John Carothers, Inf
REAY, Samuel, Pvt, Col T McCrory, Capt Isaac Patton, Mil Inf; promoted to Sgt
RECORD, John H, Pvt, Col Thos Benton, Capt John Reynolds, Vol Inf
RECORD, Sion, Pvt, Col Thos Benton, Capt John Reynolds, Vol Inf
RECORD, Sion, Sgt, Col N Cannon, Capt Andrew Patterson, Mtd Riflemen; reduced to the ranks
RECTOR, Aquiller, Pvt, Col Wm Johnson, Capt Elihu Milliken, E TN Mil
RECTOR, Cumberland, Pvt, Col Jno Brown, Capt Jas Preston, E TN Mil Inf
RECTOR, Enock, Pvt, Col John Brown, Capt William White, E TN Vol Mtd Inf; d 4-13-1814
RECTOR, John, Sgt, Col Edwin Booth, Capt Richard Marshall, Drafted Mil
RECTOR, Kerner, Sgt, Col Jarman, Capt Hamilton, Inf
RECTOR, Lewis, Pvt, Col Jno Brown, Capt Lunsford Oliver, E TN Mil
RECTOR, Presley, Pvt, Col Jno Brown, Capt Jas Preston, E TN Mil Inf; deserted
REDDELL, Maraduke, Pvt, Col Alexander Loury, Capt Geo Saver, Inf
REDDICK, John, Pvt, Col John Winn, Capt William McCall, Inf
REDDIN, John, Pvt, Col Thomas Williamson, Capt Thomas Porter, Vol Mtd Gunmen
REDDIN (READING), Edward, Pvt, Col A Loury, Capt Arahel Rains, Inf
REDDINS, Isaac jr, Pvt, Col John Cocke, Capt Wm Caruthers, Inf
REDDIT, Marmaduke, Pvt, Col Edward Bradley, Capt Abraham Bledsoe, Riflemen
REDDITT, M D, Pvt, Col Alexander Loury, Capt Geo Saver, Inf
REDDY, Henry, Pvt, Gen Andrew Jackson, Capt Nathan Davis, Mtd Inf
REDDY, James, Pvt, Col Jas Raulston, Capt Elijah Haynie, Inf
REDDY, John, Pvt, Col Samuel Wear, Capt Rufus Morgan, E TN Vol Inf
REDDY, Lewis, Pvt, Col Samuel Bunch, Capt John Houk, E TN Mil; joined from Capt Gregory's Co
REDDY, _____, Pvt, Col S Bunch, Capt Jno Hauk, E TN Mil; joined from? Capt Williams Co
REDENOR, Davis, Pvt, Col Edwin Booth, Capt Richard Marshall, Drafted Mil
REDENOR, John, Pvt, Col Edwin Booth, Capt Richard Marshall, Drafted Mil; discharged for inability
REDFERN, Elisha, Pvt, Col Thos McCrory, Capt Joseph Sharmon, Mil Inf
REDFERN, Isaac, Sgt, Col Thos McCrory, Capt Jos Sharmon, Mil Inf
REDFERN, James, Sgt, Col Leroy Henry, Capt Gabriel Martin, Inf
REDMAN, James, Pvt, Col Samuel Wear, Capt Jesse Cole, Vol Inf
REDMAN, John, Cpl, Col Samuel Bunch, Capt Joseph Duncan, E TN Drafted Mil; joined from Capt

## Enlisted Men, War of 1812

Howell's Co
REDMAN, William, Cpl, Col Samuel Bayless, Capt John Brock, E TN Mil
REDMON, John, Pvt, Col Samuel Bunch, Lt John Harris, E TN Mil
REDMOND, William, Pvt, Col William Johnson, Capt David McKamy, E TN Drafted Mil
REDWINE, Willie, Pvt, Col Samuel Wear, Capt Robert Doak, E TN Vol Inf
REECE, Caleb, Pvt, Col Samuel Bayless, Capt Joseph Rich, E TN Inf; d 2-13-1815
REECE, David, Pvt, Col Thomas Benton, Capt Wm J Smith, Vol Inf
REECE, John, Pvt, Col William Lillard, Capt John McCalpin, E TN Inf
REECE, John, Sgt, Col Samuel Bunch, Capt John Griffin, E TN Drafted Mil
REECE, Joseph, Pvt, Col Samuel Bunch, Capt Jones Griffin, E TN Drafted Mil; discharged for inability
REECE, Murphey, Pvt, Maj Gen Jackson, Capt Joseph Kirkpatrick, Mtd Gunmen
REECE, Robert D, Pvt, Col Alexander Loury, Capt John Looney, W TN Inf
REECE, Roger, Pvt, Col Samuel Bayless, Capt Joseph Rich, E TN Inf
REECE, Solomon, Ffr Maj, Col Thomas McCrory, Co Commander omitted, 2nd Regt TN Mil
REECE, William, Pvt, Col Samuel Bunch, Capt Samuel Richerson, E TN Drafted Mil
REED, Abraham, Pvt, Col Edwin Booth, Capt John Lewis, E TN Mil
REED, Allen, Pvt, Col Edwin Booth, Capt Richard Marshall, Drafted Mil
REED, Andrew, Pvt, Col John Cocke, Capt John Dalton, Inf
REED, Andrew, Pvt, Col N T Perkins, Capt Matthew Johnson, Mil Inf
REED, Clement A, Pvt, Col John Coffee, Capt Blackman Coleman, Cav; promoted to Surgeon's Mate
REED, Clement A, Surgeon's Mate, Col John Alcorn, Co Commander omitted, TN Vol Cav
REED, Daniel, Pvt, Regt Commander omitted, Capt L Ferrell, Inf
REED, David, 1 Sgt, Col Thomas McCrory, Capt John Gordon, Inf; appointed from Pvt
REED, Davis, Pvt, Col N P Perkins, Capt John Doak, Vol Mtd Gunmen
REED, Davis, Pvt, Col Phillip Pipkin, Capt John Strother, Mil; deserted
REED, Edmond, Pvt, Col Newton Cannon, Capt Ota Cantrell, W TN Mtd Inf
REED, Elisha, Pvt, Col William Hall, Capt James Hambleton, Vol Inf
REED, Elisha, Pvt, Lt Col Henry Bryan, Co Commander omitted, Inf
REED, George C, Pvt, Col Robert H Dyer, Capt Ephraim Dickson, 1st TN Mtd Gunmen
REED, George W, Pvt, Col Samuel Bunch, Capt Joseph Duncan, Branch Srvce omitted; promoted from Cpl
REED, George W, Pvt, Col Samuel Wear, Capt Jas Gillespie, E TN Vol Inf
REED, George, Pvt, Col Edwin Booth, Capt John Porter, Drafted Mil
REED, George, Pvt, Col Samuel Wear, Capt John Chiles, E TN Vol Inf
REED, George, Pvt, Col William Lillard, Capt John Neatherton, E TN Vol Inf
REED, George, Pvt, Col William Woodfolk, Capt James C Neil, Inf
REED, George, Tptr, Maj John Childs, Capt Charles Conway, E TN Mtd Gunmen; Regt Co Knox
REED, Henry, Pvt, Col Wm Lillard, Capt Thos Martin, E TN Vol Inf
REED, Isaac, Pvt, Col Edwin Booth, Capt John Lewis, E TN Mil
REED, Isaac, Pvt, Col Phillip Pipkin, Capt E Kirkpatrick, Mil Inf; deserted
REED, Jacob, Pvt, Col Edwin Booth, Capt John Lewis, E TN Mil
REED, Jacob, Pvt, Col Wm Johnson, Capt James Stewart, E TN Mil
REED, Jacob, Pvt, Col Wm Johnson, Capt John Stuart, E TN Drafted Mil
REED, James, Pvt, Col A Cheatham, Capt Richard Benson, Inf
REED, James, Pvt, Col Edwin Booth, Capt Geo Winton, E TN Mil; transferred from Capt Jos Rich
REED, James, Pvt, Col James Raulston, Capt Elijah Haynie, Inf; enlisted in the regular service
REED, James, Pvt, Col Samuel Bayless, Capt Joseph Rich, E TN Inf; transferred to Capt Winters Co
REED, James, Pvt, Col Wm Hall, Capt John Moore, Vol Inf
REED, James, Pvt, Col Wm Johnson, Capt Wm Alexander, Det of E TN Drafted Mil
REED, Jesse, Pvt, Col Stephen Copeland, Capt Wm Evans, Mil Inf
REED, John A, Pvt, Col Phillip Pipkin, Capt John Strother, Mil
REED, John, Pvt, Col N T Perkins, Capt John Doak, Vol Mtd Gunmen
REED, John, Pvt, Col Newton Cannon, Capt Ota Cantrell, W TN Mtd Inf
REED, John, Pvt, Col Samuel Wear, Capt John Wiles, E TN Vol Inf
REED, John, Pvt, Col Thos Williamson, Capt Thos Scurry, Vol Mtd Gunmen
REED, John, Sgt, Brig Gen Thos Washington, Capt John Crawford, Mtd Inf
REED, Love, Pvt, Col Wm Lillard, Capt Hugh Martin, E TN Vol Inf
REED, Michell, Pvt, Col S Bunch, Capt John Houk, E TN Mil
REED, Robert, 1 Cpl, Col R C Napier, Capt Jno Chism, Mil Inf
REED, Robert, Pvt, Col N T Cannon, Capt Geo Brandon, Mtd Riflemen
REED, Robert, Pvt, Col N T Cannon, Capt Isaac Williams, Mtd Riflemen
REED, Robert, Pvt, Col T McCrory, Capt Wm Dooly, Inf; transferred to Gordon's Spies

## Enlisted Men, War of 1812

REED, Robert, Pvt, Regt Commander omitted, Capt D Mason, Cav

REED, Samuel, Dmr, Col Wm Hall, Capt Jno Moore, Vol Inf

REED, Samuel, Pvt, Col John Cocke, Capt Jno Dalton, Inf

REED, Samuel, Pvt, Col Samuel Wear, Capt Jno Stephen, E TN Vol Inf

REED, Samuel, Pvt, Col Wm Hall, Capt H M Newlin, Inf

REED, Samuel, Pvt, Maj Wm Russell, Capt Jas Cowan, Vol Mtd Gunmen

REED, Sion S, Sgt Maj, Gen John Coffee, TN Vol Mtd Gunmen

REED, Solomon, Pvt, Col Jno Brown, Capt Jno Chiles, E TN Vol Mtd Inf

REED, Thomas, Pvt, Col E Booth, Capt Jno Sharp, E TN Mil

REED, Thomas, Pvt, Col Wm Hall, Capt H M Newlin, Inf

REED, Thomas, Pvt, Col Wm Metcalf, Capt Wm Sitton, Mil Inf

REED, William P, Pvt, Col Samuel Wear, Capt Jas Gillespie, E TN Vol Inf

REED, William, Pvt, Col A Cheatham, Capt Richd Benson, Inf

REED, William, Pvt, Col E Booth, Capt Jno Sharp, E TN Mil

REED, William, Pvt, Col N T Cannon, Capt I Williams, Mtd Riflemen

REED, William, Pvt, Col P Pipkin, Capt E Kirkpatrick, Mil Inf; deserted

REED, William, Pvt, Col S Copeland, Capt Richard Sharp, Mil Inf; deserted

REED (READ), Sion S, 2 Sgt, Col John Coffee, Capt B Coleman, Cav

REEDE, Bailey, Pvt, Col E Bradley, Capt T B Haynie, Vol Inf

REEDE, Charles C, Sdlr, Col Thos Williamson, Capt Wm Martin, Vol Mtd Gunmen; d 2-21-1815

REEDE, John, Pvt, Col Jno Coffee, Capt M Molton, Cav

REEDE, Sion, Pvt, Col Thos Williamson, Capt Jno Hutchings, Vol Mtd Gunmen; promoted to Sgt Maj in 2nd Regt

REEDE, Thomas, Sgt, Col E Bradley, Capt T B Haynie, Vol Inf

REEDER, Benjamin, Pvt, Brig Gen Thos Washington, Capt Jno Crawford, Mtd Inf

REEDER, William, Pvt, Col Wm Johnson, Capt Benj Powell, E TN Mil

REEDER, Wright, 2 Cpl, Regt Commander omitted, Capt Joel Parrish, Branch Srvce omitted

REEDY, Lewis, Pvt, Col S Bunch, Capt Geo Gregory, E TN Drafted Mil; appointed Wgnr

REEDY, Thomas, Pvt, Col S Bunch, Capt Jno English, E TN Drafted Mil

REESE, Alsey, Pvt, Maj Gen A Jackson, Capt Jos Kirkpatrick, Mtd Gunmen

REESE, Charles T, Pvt, Col Thos Williamson, Capt Jno Hutchings, Vol Mtd Gunmen

REESE, Charles, Pvt, Regt Commander omitted, Capt Jno Gordon, Mtd Spies; wounded 5-1-1814

REESE, Solomon, Pvt, Col R H Dyer, Capt E Dickson, TN Mtd Vol Gunmen; no service performed

REEVES, Elijah, Pvt, Col P Pipkin, Capt Wm Mackay, Mil Inf

REEVES, Elisha, Pvt, Col Wm Metcalf, Capt Jno Barnhart, Mil Inf

REEVES, George, Pvt, Col Jno Coffee, Capt Danl Ross, Mtd Gunmen

REEVES, George, Pvt, Col Wm Lillard, Capt J Dyke, Vol Inf

REEVES, James, Pvt, Col Wm Lillard, Capt Jno Roper, E TN Vol Inf

REEVES, Jeremiah, Pvt, Col Jas Raulston, Capt Jas Black, Inf

REEVES, John, Pvt, Col Thos Benton, Capt Benj Reynolds, Vol Inf

REEVES, John, Pvt, Col Wm Lillard, Capt J Dyke, Vol Inf

REEVES, Moses, Pvt, Col Wm Lillard, Capt J Dyke, Vol Inf

REEVES, Samuel, Pvt, Col Wm Lillard, Capt Jno Roper, E TN Vol Inf

REEVES, William, Pvt, Col Jno Coffee, Capt Danl Ross, Mtd Gunmen

REFFENT, Jeffrey, Pvt, Col P Pipkin, Capt H M Newlin, Mil Inf; d 11-15-1814

REGAN, James, Sgt, Col S Bunch, Capt Jno Houk, E TN Mil

REGAN, Lewis, Pvt, no other information

REGGAN (RIGGIN), John, 1 Lt, Col Wm Metcalf, Capt B Collins, Mil Inf

REGGS, Jesse, Pvt, Col Wm Lillard, Capt Z Copeland, E TN Vol Inf

REGINS, Thomas, Pvt, Col T McCrory, Capt Jas Shannon, Mil Inf

REGION, Joel, Pvt, Col R H Dyer, Capt Robt Evans, Vol Mtd Gunmen

REGION, Joel, Pvt, Col Wm Pillow, Capt C E McEwen, Vol Inf

REGNA, John, Rank omitted, Maj Jno Chiles, Capt Chas Conway, E TN Mtd Gunmen

REGNEY, Henry, Pvt, Col Saml Wear, Capt Jno Chiles, E TN Vol Inf

REID, Hugh, Pvt, Col Wm Hall, Capt Jno Kennedy, Vol Inf

REID, Josiah, Cpl, Gen Andrew Jackson, Capt Nathan Davis, Inf

REID, Robert, Pvt, Regt Commander omitted, Capt Jno Gordon, Mtd Spies

REID, Samuel, Pvt, Col John Wynne, Capt Wm Carothers, W TN Inf

REIFF, Jacob, Tptr, Col John Alcorn, Capt Thos Bradley, Vol Cav

REINS, William, Tptr, Maj Wm Russell, Capt Wm Chism, Vol Mtd Gunmen

RELLOW, Daniel, Pvt, no other information

RELOUGH, David, Pvt, Gen T Johnston, Capt David Oban, 36th Inf

REMMINGTON, Joseph, Pvt, Col Samuel Wear, Capt Samuel Bowman, Mtd Inf

RENE, Benjamin, Pvt, Col Samuel Wear, Capt Jesse Cole, Vol Inf

RENFRO, Lewis, Pvt, Col Samuel Bunch, Capt Wm Houston, E TN Vol Mtd Inf

- 423

RENFRO (RENTFROM), John, Pvt, Col A Loury, Capt John Looney, W TN Inf
RENFROE, Jesse, Pvt, Col Philip Pipkin, Capt Ebenezer Kirkpatrick, Mil Inf; deserted
RENFROE, John, Pvt, Col John Brown, Capt W D Neilson, E TN Vol Mil
RENFROE, Stephen, Pvt, Col Samuel Bunch, Capt S Richerson, E TN Drafted Mil
RENGO (RINGO), William, Cpl, Col Thos Benton, Capt Benj Renshaw, Vol Inf
RENN, David, Pvt, Col R H Dyer, Capt Robert Evans, Vol Mtd Gunmen
RENNICK, William, Pvt, Regt Commander omitted, Capt Robt Evans, Mtd Spies
RENOE, Fleming, Pvt, Col Samuel Bunch, Capt Geo Gregory, E TN Drafted Mil
RENOE, Hezekiah, Pvt, Col Samuel Bunch, Capt George Gregory, E TN Drafted Mil
RENOE, Thomas, Pvt, Col Samuel Bunch, Capt Jno Hawk, E TN Mil; joined from Capt Gregory Co
RENSHAW, Benjamin, Pvt, Maj Gen Wm Carroll, Capt Francis Ellis, Inf
RENSHAW, Elijah, Cpl, Maj Gen Wm Carroll, Capt Francis Ellis, Inf; promoted from Pvt
RENSHAW, John, Pvt, Col Wm Pillow, Capt Benj Renshaw, Inf
RENTFRO, John, Pvt, Col N T Perkins, Capt John Doak, Vol Mtd Gunmen
RENTFRO, Mark, Sgt, Col John Brown, Capt Jesse Reany, Mtd Gunmen
REP, Benjamin Herring, Pvt, Regt Commander omitted, Capt David Smith, Cav Vol
REPLAGE, Frederick, Cpl, Col Newton Cannon, Capt Thos Yardley, Mtd Riflemen; AWOL
REPLEY, Samuel, Sgt, Col Samuel Bunch, Capt Francis Register, E TN Mil
RESDON, Benjamin, Pvt, Col Ewen Allison, Capt Wm King, Drafted Mil
RETESIDE, John, Pvt, Col Wm Lillard, Capt Geo Argenbright, E TN Vol Riflemen
REUBLE, John G, Sgt, Col Wm Lillard, Capt Jacob Hartsell, E TN Vol Inf
REVEN, Jacob, Pvt, Lt I Barrett, Capt Nathan Davis, Inf
REYNALDS, James, Pvt, Maj John Chiles, Capt Daniel Price, E TN Vol Mtd Inf
REYNOLDS, Clement, Pvt, Col Wm Lillard, Capt Robt Maloney, E TN Vol Inf
REYNOLDS, George, 4 Cpl, Col Wm Lillard, Capt Geo Argenbright, E TN Vol Riflemen
REYNOLDS, George, Pvt, Col A Loury, Capt J N Williamson, W TN Mil
REYNOLDS, George, Pvt, Col R H Dyer, Capt Glen Owen, TN Vol Mtd Gunmen; d 3-13-1815
REYNOLDS, Gideon, Pvt, Col Jno Brown, Capt Hugh Barton, E TN Mil
REYNOLDS, Henry, Pvt, Col Samuel Bayless, Capt Jones Landen, E TN Mil; deserted
REYNOLDS, Henry, Pvt, Col Wm Lillard, Capt Geo Argenbright, E TN Vol Riflemen
REYNOLDS, Houston, Pvt, Maj John Chiles, Capt Chas Conway, E TN Mtd Gunmen; Regimental Co - Anderson
REYNOLDS, Ireby, Pvt, Col Samuel Bunch, Capt Jones Griffin, E TN Drafted Mil; furloughed home for inability
REYNOLDS, Isaac, Pvt, Col T McCrory, Capt Thos K Gordon, Inf
REYNOLDS, Jacob, Pvt, Maj John Chiles, Capt Chas Conway, E TN Mil Gunmen; Regimental Co - Knox
REYNOLDS, James B, Pvt, Lt Col Jno Edmonson, Co Commander omitted, Cav
REYNOLDS, James, Pvt, Col Wm Pillow, Capt Geo Caperton, Inf
REYNOLDS, James, Pvt, Lt I Barrett, Capt Nathan Davis, Inf
REYNOLDS, James, Pvt, Maj John Chiles, Capt Daniel Price, Vol Mtd Gunmen
REYNOLDS, James, Pvt, Regt Commander omitted, Capt Gray, Inf
REYNOLDS, Jesse, Pvt, Col A Loury, Capt J N Williamson, W TN Mil
REYNOLDS, Jesse, Pvt, Lt Col L Hammond, Capt J N Williamson, 2nd Regt Inf
REYNOLDS, Jley?, Pvt, Col Ewen Allison, Capt Joseph Everett, E TN Mil; deserted
REYNOLDS, John, Pvt, Col S Copeland, Capt Fleman Hodges, Inf
REYNOLDS, John, Pvt, Col Samuel Bunch, Capt Andrew Breden, E TN Mil; transferred to Capt Bacon Co
REYNOLDS, John, Pvt, Col Samuel Bunch, Capt James Penney, E TN Mtd Inf
REYNOLDS, John, Pvt, Lt I Barrett, Capt Nathan Davis, Inf
REYNOLDS, Joseph C, Pvt, Col Jas Raulston, Capt Henry Hamilton, Inf; also under Maj Gen Carroll
REYNOLDS, Joseph, Pvt, Regt Commander omitted, Capt James Gray, Inf
REYNOLDS, Josiah, Pvt, Maj Gen Wm Carroll, Col Jas Raulston, Capt Edward Robinson, Inf
REYNOLDS, Mark, Pvt, Col R C Napier, Capt Drury Adkins, Mil Inf
REYNOLDS, Mark, Pvt, Col R H Dyer, Capt Jos Williams, Vol Mtd Gunmen
REYNOLDS, Reubin, Pvt, Col Newton Cannon, Capt Wm Martin, Mtd Gunmen
REYNOLDS, Samuel, Pvt, Col Ewen Allison, Capt Jacob Hoyal, E TN Mil
REYNOLDS, Stephen, Pvt, Col Wm Lillard, Capt Thomas Sharpe, 2nd Regt Inf
REYNOLDS, Thomas, 4 Sgt, Col N T Perkins, Capt Mathew Johnson, Mil Inf; wounded 1-1814? at Ft Strother
REYNOLDS, Thomas, Pvt, Col Edwin Booth, Capt Samuel Thompson, Mil
REYNOLDS, Thomas, Pvt, Col R H Dyer, Maj Wm Russell, Capt Wm Russell, Vol Mtd Gunmen
REYNOLDS, Wilford (Williard), Pvt, Col John Cocke, Capt George Barnes, Inf
REYNOLDS, William T, Pvt, Col R H Dyer, Capt Jos Williams, Vol Mtd Gunmen
REYNOLDS, William, Pvt, Col R H Dyer, Capt James

## Enlisted Men, War of 1812

McMahon, 1st TN Vol Mtd Gunmen
REYNOLDS, William, Pvt, Gen Andrew Jackson, Capt Nathan Davis, Inf
REYNOLDS, ____, Pvt, Col L Hammond, Capt J N Williamson, 2nd Regt Inf
RHEA, Andrew, 6 Cpl, Maj Gen Wm Carroll, Col Jas Raulston, Capt Edward Robinson, Inf
RHEA, Archibold, Pvt, Col S Copeland, Capt Wm Hodges, Inf
RHEA, Archibold, Pvt, Col Samuel Bunch, Lt Jno Harris, E TN Mil
RHEA, Archibold, Pvt, Maj Jas P H Porter, Capt Samuel Cowan, Cav
RHEA, George, Pvt, Col Thos McCrory, Capt A Willis, Mil Inf
RHEA, John, 4 Cpl, Col Jas Raulston, Maj Wm Carroll, Capt Edward Robinson, Inf
RHEA, John, Pvt, Col Samuel Bunch, Capt Joseph Duncan, E TN Drafted Mil; transferred to Capt Buckhanon's Co
RHEA, Looney, Pvt, Col Samuel Wear, Capt John Stephens, E TN Vol Inf
RHEA, Robert, Pvt, Col Isaac Williams, Capt Samuel Bunch, Mtd Vol
RHEA, Robert, Pvt, Col Samuel Bunch, Capt Joseph Duncan, E TN Drafted Mil
RHEA, Robert, Pvt, Col Samuel Wear, Capt Samuel Bayless, Mtd Inf
RHEA, Robert, Pvt, Col Wm Johnson, Capt David McKamy, E TN Drafted Mil; substituted for Wm Kelburne
RHEA, Robert, Pvt, Maj Gen Carroll, Col Jas Raulston, Capt Edward Robinson, Inf
RHEA, Robert, Pvt, Maj Jas P H Porter, Capt Samuel Bunch, E TN Mil Cav
RHEA, Robert, Pvt, Maj Jas P H Porter, Capt Samuel Cowan, Cav
RHEA, Silas, Pvt, Col Jno Brown, Capt Wm Christian, E TN Mil Inf
RHEA, William, 1 Cpl, Col Thos Benton, Capt Wm J Smith, Vol Inf; promoted from Pvt
RHEA, William, 4 Sgt, Col Wm Pillow, Capt Wm J Smith, Vol Inf
RHEA, William, Cpl, Regt Commander omitted, Capt Wm J Smith, Vol Inf
RHEA, William, Pvt, Col Samuel Wear, Capt Rufus Morgan, E TN Vol Inf
RHEA, William, Pvt, Col Thos Benton, Capt Thos Williamson, Vol Inf
RHOADES, Alexander, Pvt, Col Philip Pipkin, Capt E Kirkpatrick, Mil Inf; deserted
RHOADES, Samuel, Pvt, Col Edward Bradley, Capt Travis Nash, Vol Inf
RHOADS, Richard, Pvt, Col Wm Hall, Capt Travis Nash, Inf
RHOAN, Daniel C, Pvt, Col Samuel Wear, Capt Samuel Bunch, Capt Wm Mitchell, E TN Mtd Inf
RHODES, Isaac, Pvt, Col Thos McCrory, Capt Wm Dooly, Inf
RHODES, James R, Pvt, Col John Cocke, Capt John Dalton, Inf
RHODES, James, Dmr, Col Wm Hall, Capt John Wallace, Inf
RHODES, John, Pvt, Col John K Winn, Capt Wm McCall, Inf
RHODES, John, Pvt, Col R H Dyer, Capt James McMahon, 1st TN Vol Mtd Gunmen
RHODES, John, Pvt, Col Wm Metcalf, Capt Obidiah Waller, Mil Inf
RHODES, Richard, Pvt, Col Thos McCrory, Capt Isaac Patton, Mil Inf
RHODES, Richard, Pvt, Lt I Barrett, Capt Nathan Davis, Mil
RHODES, Samuel, Pvt, Col Wm Hall, Capt Travis Nash, Inf; unfit for service
RHODES, Thomas W, Pvt, Col Ewen Allison, Capt John Hampton, Mil
RHODES, Thomas, Pvt, Col Jno Coffee, Capt Alexander McKeen, Cav
RHODES, Thomas, Pvt, Maj Gen A Jackson, Capt J Kirkpatrick, Mtd Gunmen
RHODES, Thomas, Pvt, Regt Commander omitted, Capt Jno Gordon, Mtd Spies; wounded 2?-27-1814
RHODES, Thomas, Pvt, Regt Commander omitted, Capt Jno Williams, Mil Cav
RHODES, William, Pvt, Col John Cocke, Capt George Barnes, Inf; d 1-19-1815
RHODES, William, Pvt, Lt I Barrett, Capt Nathan Davis, Inf
RHUDOLPH, Frederick, Pvt, Regt Commander omitted, Capt James Cowan, Inf
RIAL, William, Pvt, Col Robert Steele, Capt James Bennett, Mil Inf
RICE, Able, Ffr, Col Philip Pipkin, Capt Henry M Newlin, Mil Inf
RICE, Balden, Pvt, Regt Commander omitted, Capt Geo Smith, Spies
RICE, Baldson, Pvt, Col R T Perkins, Capt Francis Eliot, Mil Inf
RICE, Benjamin, Pvt, Maj Gen Andrew Jackson, Capt Joseph Kirkpatrick, Mtd Gunmen; wounded 1-27-1814
RICE, Charles, Pvt, Maj John Childs, Capt Jas Cunningham, E TN Vol Mtd Inf
RICE, Elijah, Pvt, Col John Alcorn, Capt Henry Bryan, Cav; deserted
RICE, Elijah, Pvt, Col John Winn, Capt Wm Caruthers, W TN Inf
RICE, George, Pvt, Col S Wear, Capt Robert Doak, E TN Vol Inf
RICE, George, Pvt, Col Thos Benton, Capt John Reynolds, Vol Inf
RICE, Henry, Pvt, Col Phillip Pipkin, Capt John Robertson, Mil Inf
RICE, Jacob, Pvt, Col Alexander Loury, Capt James Kinciad, Inf
RICE, James, Pvt, Col John Winn, Capt Robert Brader, Inf; deserted
RICE, James, Pvt, Col Phillip Pipkin, Capt Ebenezer Kirkpatrick, Mil Inf
RICE, James, Pvt, Col Thos Benton, Capt John Reynolds, Vol Inf

## Enlisted Men, War of 1812

RICE, James, Pvt, Col William Pillow, Capt C E McEwen, Vol Inf
RICE, James, Pvt, Col Wm Metcalf, Capt Thomas Marks, Mil Inf; d 1-22-1815
RICE, Joel, Pvt, Col T McCrory, Capt William Dooley, Inf
RICE, Joel, Pvt, Gen Andrew Jackson, Capt D Deadrick, Arty
RICE, John B, Pvt, Col John Brown, Capt Wm D Neilson, E TN Vol Mil
RICE, John M, Pvt, Col Wm Hall, Capt Abraham Bledsoe, Vol Inf
RICE, John, Cpl, Col Robert Dyer, Capt Isaac Williams, Vol Mtd Gunmen
RICE, John, Pvt, Col Everett Griffin, no other information
RICE, John, Pvt, Col Ewin Allison, Capt Joseph Everett, E TN Mil
RICE, John, Pvt, Col John Alcorn, Capt Henry Byrums, Cav
RICE, John, Pvt, Col John Coffee, Capt Henry Byrun, Cav
RICE, John, Pvt, Col Johnson, Capt Milliken, E TN Mil; appointed Adjt
RICE, John, Pvt, Col William Johnson, Capt Benj Powell, E TN Mil
RICE, John, Pvt, Col William Lillard, Capt William Hamilton, E TN Vol Inf
RICE, John, Pvt, Regt Commander omitted, Sgt Wyatt Fussell, Inf
RICE, Kenas, Pvt, Regt Commander omitted, Capt Geo Smith, Spies
RICE, Kenass, Pvt, Col Thomas Williamson, Capt John Moore, Vol Mtd Gunmen
RICE, Laban, Pvt, no other information
RICE, Larkin, Pvt, Col Thos Benton, Capt Geo Caperton, Vol Inf
RICE, Larkin, Pvt, Col Thos Dyer, Capt Wm Russell, Vol Mtd Gunmen
RICE, Larkin, Pvt, Col William Pillow, Capt Geo Caperton, Inf
RICE, Lenard, Pvt, Col William Metcalf, Capt William Sitton, Mil Inf
RICE, Lewis, Pvt, Col John Williams, Capt S Bunch, Mil Vol
RICE, Martin, Pvt, Col William Johnson, Capt Christopher Cook, E TN Mil
RICE, Martin, Pvt, Col William Johnson, Capt Joseph Kirk, Mil
RICE, Mathew, Pvt, Col Thomas Williamson, Capt Robert Moore, Vol Mtd Gunmen
RICE, Nathan, Pvt, Col Edward Bradley, Capt Harry Douglas, Vol Inf
RICE, Nathaniel, Pvt, Col Thos Benton, Capt Henry Douglas, Vol Inf
RICE, Nicholas, Pvt, Col William Metcalf, Capt Bird Hurt, Mil Inf
RICE, Robert, Pvt, Col John Brown, Capt Wm D Neilson, E TN Vol Mil
RICE, Roland, Pvt, Col Phillip Pipkin, Capt Peter Searcy, Mil Inf
RICE, Simon, Pvt, no other information
RICE, Solomon, Mus, Col T McCrory, Capt William Dooly, Inf; promoted to Ffr Maj
RICE, Stephen, Pvt, Col William Lillard, Capt William Hamilton, E TN Vol Inf
RICE, Theadrick B, Pvt, Col N Cannon, Capt Francis Jones, Mtd Riflemen
RICE, Thomas, Pvt, Col Jas Raulston, Capt Chas Wade, Inf
RICE, William, Pvt, Col John Coffee, Capt Michael Molton, Cav
RICE, William, Pvt, Col John Wynne, Capt Robt Bradin, Inf; deserted
RICE, William, Pvt, Col Philip Pipkin, Capt Wm Mackay, Mil Inf
RICE, William, Pvt, Col Thomas Williamson, Capt Jas Cook & Capt Crane, Vol Mtd Gunmen
RICE, William, Pvt, Col William Higgins, Capt Allen, Mtd Gunmen
RICE, William, Pvt, Col Wm Metcalf, Capt Wm Sitton, Mil Inf
RICE, William, Pvt, Maj Wm Woodfolk, Capt Daniel Ross, Inf
RICE, William, Pvt, Regt Commander omitted, Capt Jos Williams, Mil Cav
RICE, William, Pvt, Regt Commander omitted, Capt Jos Williams, Mil Cav; deserted
RICEY, Joseph, Sgt, Maj William Russell, Capt William Chism, Vol Mtd Gunmen
RICH, John, Pvt, Maj Gen Carroll, Capt Wiley Huddleston, Inf
RICH, Joseph, Pvt, Maj William Russell, Capt Geo Mitchell, Vol Mtd Gunmen
RICH, Thomas, Pvt, Col William Pillow, Capt Geo Caperton, Inf
RICH, William, Pvt, Col Edward Bradley, Capt John Kennedy, Riflemen
RICH, William, Pvt, Col Wm Hall, Capt John Kennedy, Vol Inf
RICHARD, Abraham, Pvt, Col Wm Lillard, Capt Wm McLin, E TN Inf
RICHARD, Dick, Servant, Col Philip Pipkin, 1st Regt TN Mil; servant to 2nd Maj Alex Raulston
RICHARD, Isaac, Pvt, Col Samuel Bunch, Capt Jno Hawk, E TN Mil
RICHARD, Jacob, Pvt, Col R C Napier, Capt James McMurray, Mil Inf
RICHARD, Jesse, Pvt, Col Samuel Bayless, Capt Joseph B Bacon, E TN Mil
RICHARD, Jonathan, Pvt, Col A Loury, Capt John Looney, W TN Inf
RICHARD, Nathaniel, Pvt, Col A Loury, Capt John Looney, W TN Inf
RICHARD, William, Pvt, Col A Loury, Capt John Looney, W TN Inf
RICHARDS, Aaron, Pvt, Col Wm Lillard, Capt Wm Gillenwater, E TN Inf
RICHARDS, Gabriel, Tptr, Col John Brown, Capt Wm White, E TN Vol Inf Mtd
RICHARDS, Hiram, Pvt, Col Thomas Benton, Capt James McEwen, Vol Inf
RICHARDS, Hiram, Pvt, Col Thos Benton, Capt James McEwen, Vol Inf
RICHARDS, Robert R, Pvt, Col Thos Benton, Capt James

## Enlisted Men, War of 1812

McEwen, Vol Inf
RICHARDS, Stephen, Pvt, Col John Brown, Capt Jesse G Reany, Mtd Gunmen
RICHARDS, Will M, Pvt, Col John Coffee, Capt James Terrell, Vol Cav
RICHARDS, William, Sgt, Col N T Perkins, Capt John B Quarles, Vol Mtd Riflemen
RICHARDS, Willis, Pvt, Col Phillip Pipkin, Capt David Smith, W TN Mil; attached to Capt John Strother's Co
RICHARDSON, Aaron, Pvt, Col Samuel Bunch, Capt Andrew Breden, E TN Mil
RICHARDSON, Abel, Pvt, Col Edward Bradley, Capt John Kennedy, Riflemen
RICHARDSON, Abel, Pvt, Maj Wm Woodfolk, Capt Ezekial Ross & Capt McCulley, Inf
RICHARDSON, Able, Pvt, Col Wm Hall, Capt John Kennedy, Vol Inf
RICHARDSON, Allen, Cpl, Col R C Napier, Capt Samuel Ashmore, Mil Inf
RICHARDSON, Allen, Pvt, Maj Gen A Jackson, Capt Wm Carroll, Vol Inf
RICHARDSON, Amos, Pvt, Col Thos Benton, Capt Benj Reynolds, Vol Inf
RICHARDSON, Amos, Pvt, Col Wm Hall, Capt John Kennedy, Vol Inf
RICHARDSON, Benjamin, Pvt, Col James Raulston, Capt Mathew Cowan, Inf
RICHARDSON, Benjamin, Pvt, Maj Wm Woodfolk, Capt Abraham Dudney & Capt John Sutton, Inf
RICHARDSON, Booker, Sgt, Col R H Dyer, Capt Robt Evans, Vol Mtd Gunmen
RICHARDSON, Daniel, 5 Cpl, Col L Hammond, Capt J N Williamson, 2nd Regt Inf
RICHARDSON, Daniel, Cpl, Col A Loury, Capt J N Williamson, W TN Mil
RICHARDSON, Daniel, Pvt, Col N T Perkins, Capt Philip Pipkin, Mtd Riflemen
RICHARDSON, Daniel, Pvt, Col Philip Pipkin, Capt John Robertson, Mil Inf
RICHARDSON, Daniel, Pvt, Col Wm Hall, Capt Henry M Newlin, Inf
RICHARDSON, David, Pvt, Col Wm Lillard, Capt Benj H King, E TN Vol Inf
RICHARDSON, Fisher, Pvt, Col James Raulston, Capt Charles Wade, Inf; d 2-10-1815
RICHARDSON, Henry, Pvt, Col R H Dyer, Capt Robt Evans, Vol Mtd Gunmen
RICHARDSON, Isaac, Pvt, Col S Copeland, Capt Wm Evans, Mil Inf
RICHARDSON, James, 1 Cpl, Col Samuel Bunch, Capt Thos Mann, E TN Vol Mtd Inf
RICHARDSON, James, Pvt, Col Ewen Allison, Capt Joseph Everett, E TN Mil; transferred to Capt McPherson's
RICHARDSON, James, Pvt, Col Wm Metcalf, Capt Wm Mullen, Mil Inf
RICHARDSON, John, Pvt, Col A Cheatham, Capt James Giddens, Inf
RICHARDSON, John, Pvt, Col James Raulston, Capt Daniel Newman, Inf
RICHARDSON, John, Pvt, Col Thos Williamson, Capt Thos Porter, Vol Mtd Gunmen
RICHARDSON, John, Pvt, Regt Commander omitted, Capt McPherson, Branch Srvce omitted; King's Roll
RICHARDSON, John, Sgt & Cpl, Col Ewen Allison, Capt Adam Winsell, E TN Drafted Mil
RICHARDSON, May, Pvt, Maj Gen A Jackson, Col Thos Williamson, Capt Robert Steele, Vol Mtd Gunmen
RICHARDSON, Nathaniel, Pvt, Col Ewen Allison, Capt Joseph Everett, E TN Mil
RICHARDSON, Samuel, Pvt, Col John Coffee, Capt Michael Molton, Cav
RICHARDSON, Samuel, Pvt, Col S Bayless, Capt James Landen, E TN Mil; d 3-10-1815
RICHARDSON, Samuel, Pvt, Regt Commander omitted, Capt Jos Williams, Mil Cav
RICHARDSON, Thomas, Pvt, Col Jas Raulston, Capt James Cowan, Inf; d 2-28-1815
RICHARDSON, Wiley, Pvt, Col William Pillow, Capt C E McEwen, Vol Inf
RICHARDSON, William (Wiley), 3 Cpl, Col Thos Benton, Capt John Reynolds, Vol Inf
RICHARDSON, William, Cpl, Col Thos Benton, Cap John Reynolds, Vol Inf
RICHARDSON, William, Pvt, Col Phillip Pipkin, Capt R T Perkins, Mtd Riflemen
RICHARDSON, William, Pvt, Col S Copeland, Capt Holshouser, Inf
RICHARDSON, William, Pvt, Col Wm Metcalf, Capt William Mullen, Mil Inf
RICHARDSON, Willie, Pvt, Gen Roberts, Co Commander omitted, Mtd Rangers
RICHARDSON, Willis, Pvt, Col N Cannon, Capt William Edwards, Regt Command
RICHARDSON, Willis, Pvt, Col Phillip Pipkin, Capt Henry Newlin, Mil Inf; transferred to Capt Strother
RICHARDSON, Willis, Pvt, Col R C Napier, Capt Samuel Ashmore, Mil Inf
RICHER, Jacob, Pvt, Col William Lillard, Capt Jacob Dyke, Vol Inf
RICHERDSON, John, Pvt, Col Ewen Allison, Capt William King, Drafted Mil
RICHERSON, Ansil, Pvt, Col Thos Williamson, Capt John Dobbins & Capt Doak, Vol Mtd Gunmen
RICHERSON, Ezekiel, Pvt, Col Thomas Williamson, Capt Doak & Capt John Dobbins, Vol Mtd Gunmen
RICHERSON, George, Cpl, Col Edwin Booth, Capt Richard Marshall, Drafted Mil; discharged for inability
RICHERSON, James, Pvt, Col S Bunch, Capt Geo McPherson, E TN Mil; joined from? Capt Everett
RICHERSON, John, 3 Sgt, Col Edwin Booth, Capt Richard Marshall, Drafted Mil
RICHERSON, John, Pvt, Col S Bunch, Capt Everett, Branch Srvce omitted
RICHERSON, Lewis, Pvt, Col Edwin Booth, Capt Richard Marshall, Drafted Mil

RICHERSON, Mason, Pvt, Col John Coffee, Capt Daniel Ross, Mtd Gunmen
RICHERSON, Rucker, Pvt, Maj Gen Jackson, Col A Cheatham, Capt Creel, Inf
RICHEY, John, Pvt, Col Wm Johnson, Capt David McKamey, E TN Drafted Mil
RICHEY, John, Pvt, Gen Jackson, Capt Hugh Kerr, Mtd Rangers
RICHEY, John, Pvt, Phillip Pipkin, Capt John Strother, Mil
RICHEY, Thomas, Cpl, Gen Andrew Jackson, Capt Hugh Kerr, Mtd Rangers
RICHEY, Thomas, Pvt, Regt Commander omitted, Capt John Trimble, Gunmen
RICHEY, William, Pvt, Col Jno Coffee, Capt Frederick Stump, Cav
RICHIE, James, Pvt, Col Robert Steele, Capt Samuel Maxwell, Mil Inf; deserted
RICHLY, Gideon, Pvt, Col S Wear, Capt Jas Tedford, E TN Vol Inf
RICHMON, John, Pvt, Col Edwin Booth, Capt John McKamey, E TN Mil
RICHMOND, Andrew, Pvt, Maj Gen Jackson, Capt Joseph Kirkpatrick, Mtd Gunmen
RICHMOND, Isaac, Pvt, Col Philip Pipkin, Capt John Robertson, Mil Inf
RICKER, Martin, Pvt, Col William Lillard, Capt Jacob Dyke, Vol Inf
RICKET, John, Pvt, Col Jas Raulston, Capt Elijah Haynie, Inf
RICKET, John, Pvt, Col S Wear, Capt Joseph Calloway, Mtd Inf
RICKET, Reuben, Pvt, Col S Bunch, Capt N Gibbs, E TN Drafted Mil
RICKET, William, Pvt, Col Phillip Pipkin, Capt Henry Newlin, Mil Inf
RICKETT, Abel, Pvt, Maj John Childs, Capt Daniel Price, E TN Mtd Inf
RICKETT, Willis, Pvt, Col S Bunch, Capt John Harris, E TN Mil; d 2-2-1814
RICKETTS, David, Cpl, Maj William Russell, Capt William Chism, Vol Mtd Gunmen
RICKETTS, Richard, Pvt, Col Thomas Williamson, Capt Doak & Capt John Dobbins, Vol Mtd Gunmen
RIDDLE, James, Cpl, Col S Bunch, Capt Joseph Duncan, Branch Srvce omitted; joined from Capt Allen's Co
RIDDLE, James, Pvt, Col S Bayless, Capt I Bacon, E TN Mil
RIDDLE, John, Pvt, Col S Copeland, Capt Solomon George, Inf
RIDDLE, John, Pvt, Gen Andrew Jackson, Capt Nathan Davis, Inf
RIDDLE, Orange, Pvt, Col N Cannon, Capt John Harpole, Mtd Gunmen
RIDDLE, Samuel T, Cpl, Col S Copeland, Capt William Hodges, Inf
RIDDON, Lewis, Pvt, Col John Cocke, Capt Bird Nance, Inf
RIDENHOUS, Henry, Pvt, Col William Johnson, Capt Benj Powell, E TN Mil
RIDENOR, David, Pvt, Col S Bunch, Capt Andrew Breden, E Tn Mil; disch for inability
RIDER, Alexander, Cpl, Col S Wear, Capt Geo Gillespie, E Tn Vol Inf
RIDER, John, Pvt, Col S Wear, Capt Geo Gillespie, E TN Vol Inf
RIDER, Richard, Pvt, Col Thomas Williamson, Capt Doak & Capt Dobbins, Vol Mtd Gunmen
RIDGE, Alexander (Cherokee), Pvt, Brig Gen Jas White, Co Commander omitted, Appt Spy
RIDGE, Amos, Pvt, Col J K Wynn, Capt Jas Cole, Inf
RIDGE, John (Cherokee), Pvt, Brig Gen Jas White, Co Commander omitted, Spies
RIDGEWAY, John, Pvt, Regt Commander omitted, Capt Jas Gordon, Mtd Spies
RIDGEWAY, John, Pvt, Regt Commander omitted, Capt Jas Williams, Mil Cav
RIDGEWAY, Jonathan, Pvt, Regt Commander omitted, Capt Jno Gordon, Spies
RIDING, Harman, Pvt, Col P Pipkin, Capt Geo Mebane, Mil Inf
RIDING, James, Pvt, Lt Col L Hammond, Capt Jas Tubb, Inf
RIDLEY, Henry, 3 Cpl, Col Wm Hall, Capt T C Nash, Inf
RIDLEY, Henry, Sgt, Col N T Cannon, Capt Martin, Mtd Gunmen
RIDLEY, Jacob, Pvt, Lt I Barrett, Capt Nathan Davis, Inf
RIDLEY, James, Pvt, Col N T Cannon, Capt Martin, Mtd Gunmen; apptd an Artif
RIDLEY, Robert, Pvt, Col J K Winn, Capt Jas Holleman, Inf
RIDLEY, Samuel, Sgt, Col N Cannon, Capt Geo Martin, Mtd Gunmen; apptd an Artif
RIDLEY, Vincent, Sgt, Gen Roberts, Co Commander omitted, Mtd Rangers
RIDLEY, William, Pvt, Brig Gen Thos Washington, Capt Jno Crawford, Mtd Inf
RIDLEY, William, Pvt, Col T McCrory, Capt Jas Shannon, Mil Inf
RIED, Adam, 4 Cpl, Col E Bradley, Capt John Kennedy, Riflemen
RIEFF, Jacob, Tptr, Col Jno Coffee, Capt Thos Bradley, Vol Cav
RIEFF, Joseph, Cpl, Col Jno Coffee, Capt Thos Bradley, Vol Cav
RIGGINS, Thomas, Pvt, Col Wm Lillard, Capt Thos Sharpe, 2 Regt Inf
RIGGINS (REGANS), William, Pvt, Col P Pipkin, Capt Jno Robertson, Mil Inf
RIGGLE, George W, Pvt, Col Wm Johnson, Capt Wm Alexander, Det of E TN Draft Mil
RIGGS, David, 2 Cpl, Col Wm Metcalf, Capt O Waller, Mil Inf
RIGGS, Gedion, Pvt, Col Thos Benton, Capt Robert Cannon, Inf
RIGGS, Jesse, Sgt, Col S Bunch, Capt Geo McPherson, E TN Mil; trans to Capt Hoyles Co
RIGGS, John, Pvt, Col Wm Lillad, Capt Z Copeland, E TN Vol Inf
RIGGS, Levi, Pvt, Col S Bunch, Capt Geo Gregory, E TN Draft Mil

## Enlisted Men, War of 1812

RIGGS, Watson, Pvt, Col S Copeland, Capt Jas Tait, Inf

RIGGS, William, Pvt, Col R H Dyer, Capt Thos Jones, Vol Mtd Gunmen

RIGHT, David, Pvt, Col Wm Lillard, Capt Wm Hamilton, E Tn Vol Inf

RIGHT, David, Pvt, Maj William Russell, Capt Geo Mitchie, Vol Mtd Gunmen

RIGHT, Edward, Pvt, Col S Bunch, Capt Jno English, E TN Draft Mil

RIGHT, James, Pvt, Col Alexander Loury, Lt Col L Hammonds, Capt A Rains, Inf

RIGHT, James, Pvt, Col N T Perkins, Capt M Patterson, Mtd Vol

RIGHT, Larkin, Pvt, Col Thos Williamson, Capt Jas Cook & Capt Jno Crane, Vol Mtd Inf

RIGHT, Obadiah, Pvt, Col Alex Loury, Lt Col L Hammonds, CApt A Rains, Inf

RIGHT, Reason, Pvt, Col Wm Lillard, Capt Wm Hamilton, E Tn Vol Inf

RIGHT, Richard, Pvt, Col S Bunch, Capt Jno English, E TN Draft Mil

RIGHT, Robert, Pvt, Maj Gen Carroll, Capt W Huddleston, Inf; died 1-29-1815

RIGHT, Wiley, Pvt, Maj Jno Childs, Capt Danl Price, Vol Mtd Gunmen

RIGHT, William, Pvt, Col P Pipkin, Capt P Searcy, Mil Inf

RIGHT (WRIGHT), Thompson, Pvt, Col Thos Williamson, Capt Thos Porter, Vol Mtd Gunmen

RIGHTSELL, John, Sgt, Col Wm Johnson, Capt Benj Powell, E Tn Mil

RIGNEY, George, Pvt, Col S Bunch, Capt Danl Narnell, E Tn Mil; deserted

RIGNEY, George, Pvt, Col Samuel Bunch, Capt Jno Duncan, E Tn Draft Mil; joined from Capt Yarnell Co

RIGNEY, William, Pvt, Col Jno Brown, Capt Jno Chiles, E TN Vol Mtd Inf

RIGSBY, Right, Pvt, Col Jas Raulston, Capt E Hanie, Branch omitted

RIKER (RUKER), Frederick, Pvt, Col Samuel Bayless, Capt Jos Hale, E TN Mil

RIKER (RUKER), George, Pvt, Col Saml Bayless, Capt Jos Hale, E TN Mil

RILEY, Anderson, Pvt, Col Alex Loury, Capt Geo Sarver, Inf

RILEY, Anderson, Pvt, Col J K Winn, Capt Robert Braden, Inf

RILEY, Barney, Pvt, Col Alexander Loury, Capt Geo Sarver, Inf

RILEY, Henry, Pvt, Col Alexander Loury, Capt Geo Sarver, Inf

RILEY, James, Pvt, Col Alex Loury, Capt Geo Sarver, Inf

RILEY, James, Pvt, Col S Copeland, Capt S George, Inf

RILEY, John, Pvt, Col S Copeland, Capt Jno Holshouser, Inf

RILEY, Robert, Pvt, Col Edwin Booth, Capt John Lewis, E Tn Mil

RILEY, Samuel, Pvt, Col John Alcorn, Capt John Winston, Mtd Riflemen

RILEY, Stephen, Pvt, Col Wm Johnson, Capt James Tunnell, E Tn Mil

RINCHART, Abram, Pvt, Col Wm Hall, Capt James Hambleton, Vol Inf

RINCHART, Jacob, Pvt, Col Wm Hall, Capt James Hambleton, Vol Inf; joined at Clarksville

RINCHART, Jacob, Pvt, Col Wm Lillard, Capt Robert McCalpin, E TN Inf

RINCHEART, Jacob, Pvt, Col Thos Bradley, Capt James Hambleton, Vol Inf

RINEHART, John jr, Pvt, Col Ewen Allison, CApt John Hampton, Mil

RINEHART, John sr, Pvt, Col Ewen Allison, Capt John Hampton, Mil

RINEHEART, John, Pvt, Brig Gen Thos Johnson, Capt Abraham Allen, Mil Inf

RING, William, Pvt, Col Thos Benton, Capt Isiah Renshaw, Vol Inf

RING, William, Pvt, Col Wm Hall, Capt Abraham Bledsoe, Vol Inf

RINGE, Nathaniel, Pvt, Col Thos Benton, Capt Isiah Renshaw, 2 Regt Vol Inf

RINGS, Nathaniel, Pvt, Col Wm Pillow, Capt Isiah Renshaw, Inf

RINGS, William, Pvt, Col Wm Pillow, Capt Isiah Renshaw, Inf

RINKER, Philip, Pvt, Col Wm Johnson, Capt Joseph Kirk, Mil

RINNINGTON, Joseph, Pvt, Maj Wm Russell, Capt John Trimble, Vol Mtd Gunmen

RIP, Nelson Alford, Pvt, Brig Gen Thos Washington, Capt Jno Crawford, Mtd Inf

RIPLEY, Samuel, Pvt, Col Samuel Bunch, Capt F Register, E Tn Mil

RIPPITTO, John, Pvt, Maj John Chiles, Capt Charles Conway, E Tn Mtd Gunmen; Regt from Bledsoe Co

RISEN (RIZEN), Joh, Pvt, Lt Col L Hammonds, Capt James Tubb, Inf; died 2-12-1815

RISHARDSON, Daniel, 5 Cpl, Lt Col L Hammonds, Capt Thos Williamson, Inf

RITCH, Thomas, Pvt, Maj Wm Russell, Capt John Cowan, Vol Mtd Gunmen

RITCHE, William, Sgt, Col John Alcorn, Capt Frederick Stump, Cav

RITCHER, Thomas, Pvt, Col Jno Brown, Capt John Trimble, E Tn Mtd Gunmen; died 4-12-1814

RITCHEY, David, 4 Sgt, Col Samuel Wear, Capt Jos Calloway, Mtd Inf

RITCHIE, Daniel, Pvt, Col S Copeland, Capt Allen Wilkinson, Mil Inf

RITCHIE, David, Pvt, Col S Copeland, Capt Allen Wilkinson, Mil Inf

RITCHIE, Peter, Pvt, Col Robert Steele, Capt Samuel Maxwell, Mil Inf; deserted

RITCHIE, Robert T, Pvt, Col John Brown, Capt John Trimble, E TN Mtd Inf

RITE, John, Pvt, Col Wm Y Higgins, Capt James Hambleton, Mtd Gunmen; wounded 6-22-1814

RITE, Robertson, Pvt, Col Philip Pipkin, Capt George Mebane, Mil Inf

RITE (RIGHT), John, Pvt, Col Philip Pipkin, Capt George Mebane, Mil Inf

## Enlisted Men, War of 1812

RITE (RIGHT), Joseph, Pvt, Col Philip Pipkin, Capt George Mebane, Mil Inf

RITTER, Daniel, Pvt, Col John K Winn, Capt Robert Bradin, Inf

RIVERS, Joel F, Pvt, Col R H Dyer, Capt Robt Edmonston, TN Vol Mtd Gunmen

ROACH, Aaron, Pvt, Maj John Chiles, Capt Charles Conway, E TN Mtd Gunmen, Regt from Knox Co

ROACH, Abraham, Pvt, Col S Bunch, Capt Jno English, E TN Draft Mil; joined from Capt Howell's Co

ROACH, Absolom, Pvt, Col Samuel Bunch, Lt John Harris, E TN Mil

ROACH, Drury, Pvt, Col Wm Lillard, Capt Thos Sharpe, 2 Regt Inf

ROACH, Elija, Pvt, Col Thos Benton, Capt Thos Williamson, Vol Inf

ROACH, Ellsey, Pvt, Col Thomas Benton, Capt Thos Williamson, Vol Inf

ROACH, Elsey, Pvt, Col Wm Pillow, Capt Thos Williamson, Vol Inf

ROACH, James, Pvt, Brig Gen Thos Johnson, Capt Abraham Allen, Mil Inf

ROACH, John, Cpl, Col Samuel Wear, Capt John Stephens, E TN Vol Inf

ROACH, John, Pvt, Col Edward Bradley, Capt Harry L Douglass, Vol Inf

ROACH, John, Pvt, Col Samuel Wear, Capt Robert Doak, E Tn Vol Inf

ROACH, John, Sgt, Col Samuel Bunch, Capt Joseph Duncan, E Tn Drafted Mil

ROACH, Stephen, Pvt, Col Jas Raulston, Capt Henry Hamilton, Inf; also served under Maj Gen Carroll

ROACH, William, Pvt, Col Jas Raulston, Capt Charles Wade, Inf

ROACH, William, Pvt, Col Samuel Bunch, Capt Jones Griffin, E Tn Draft Mil

ROACH, William, Pvt, Maj John Chiles, Capt Charles Conway, E TN Mtd Gunmen; Regt from Knox Co

ROACH, Wilson, Pvt, Col Ewen Allison, Capt J Loughmiller, Mil; joined from Capt Griffin's Co

ROADES, Ephraim, Pvt, Col A Cheatham, Capt Charles Johnson, Inf

ROADES, Hazel, Pvt, Regt Commander omitted, Capt Robert Evans, Mtd Spies; trans to Capt Russell's Co

ROADS, Abner, Pvt, Col Alexander Loury, Capt J N Williamson, W TN Mil

ROADS, Abner, Pvt, Lt Col L Hammond, Capt J N Williamson, 2 Regt Inf

ROADS, Andrew, Pvt, Col Thos McCrory, Capt Thos Gordon, Inf; deserted

ROADS, Henry, Pvt, Col Edwin Booth, Capt John Slatton, E Tn Mil

ROADS, James, Pvt, Col Thos McCrory, Capt Thos Gordon, Inf

ROADS, John, Pvt, Col Edwin Booth, Capt John Lewis, E Tn Mil

ROADS, Levi, Sgt, Col Edwin Booth, Capt John Slatton, E Tn Mil

ROADS, Thomas, Pvt, Col Ewin Allison, Capt Jos Longmiller, Mil

ROADS, William, Pvt, Col Edwin Booth, Capt Geo Slatton, E Tn Mil

ROADS (RODES), Isaac, Pvt, Lt Col L Hammond, Capt James Tubb, Inf

ROAN, Andrew, Pvt, Col Wm Johnson, Capt Jas Stewart, E Tn Mil

ROAN, James, Cpl, Col John Alcorn, Capt Edward Bradley, Vol Cav

ROAN, James, Pvt, Col John Coffee, Capt Edward Bradley, Vol Cav

ROANE, Andrew, Pvt, Col William Johnson, Capt Jas Stewart, E Tn Drafted Mil

ROANE, James, Ens, Col S Copeland, Capt Alexander Provine, Mil Inf

ROANE, Josiah, Sgt Maj, Col S Bunch, no Co Commander, E TN Mil

ROANE, Samuel, Sgt Maj, Col S Copeland, no Co Commander, TN Mil Inf

ROARK, Asa, Sgt, Col James Raulston, Capt Elijah Haynie, Inf

ROARK, John, Cpl, Col Jas Raulston, Capt Elijah Haynie, Inf

ROARK, Moses, Pvt, Lt Col Henry Bryan, Co Commander omitted, Inf

ROARK, Moses, Pvt, Regt Commander omitted, Capt James Cowan, Inf

ROARK, Samuel, Pvt, Col Wm Hall, Capt Geo Martin, Vol Inf

ROARK, Thomas, Pvt, Maj William Russell, Capt John Trimble, Vol Mtd Gunmen

ROARK, Timothy, Pvt, Maj Gen Carroll, Capt Wiley Huddleston, Inf

ROBARD, Mack, Pvt, Col Wm Metcalf, Capt William Mullen, Mil Inf

ROBARTS, Isaac, Cpl, Col Edwin Booth, Capt George Winton, E TN Mil; trans from Capt James Farmer Co

ROBARTS, Isaac, Pvt, Col Stephen Copeland, Capt William Evans, Inf

ROBASON, John, Pvt, Col Robert Steele, Capt Jas Randal, Inf

ROBB, Harris, Pvt, Col Thomas Williamson, Capt Thomas Scurry, Vol Mtd Gunmen

ROBB, Samuel, Pvt, Col Thomas Williamson, Capt Thomas Scurry, Vol Mtd Gunmen; died 2-14-1815

ROBBERTS, Robert, Pvt, Col Philip Pipkin, Capt Geo Mebane, Mil Inf; deserted

ROBBINS, Charles, Pvt, Col Johnson, Capt Allen, Mil Inf

ROBBINS, Thomas, Pvt, Col Philip Pipkin, Capt Jackson, Mil Inf

ROBBINS, Thomas, Pvt, Col Phillip Pipkin, Capt Geo Mebane, Mil Inf

ROBBS, Edward, Pvt, Col Ewen Allison, Capt Allen, E TN Mil

ROBBS, Edward, Pvt, Col S Bunch, Capt Jno English, E TN Drafted Mil; joined from Capt Allen Co

ROBBS, Samuel, Pvt, Col Nicholas Perkins, Capt George Eliot, Mil Inf

ROBERD, William, Pvt, Col S Bayless, Capt Hale, E TN Mil

ROBERSON, Isaac, Pvt, Col Edwin Booth, Capt John

430 -

## Enlisted Men, War of 1812

Sharp, E Tn Mil

ROBERSON, John, Pvt, Col S Bayless, Capt Solomon Hendrix, E Tn Mil

ROBERSON, John, Pvt, Col William Hall, Capt Abraham Bledsoe, Vol Inf

ROBERSON, John, Sgt, Col John Brown, Capt Wm Christian, E Tn Mil Inf

ROBERSON, Julius, Sgt, Col Edward Bradley, Capt John Kennedy, Vol Inf

ROBERSON, William, Sgt, Col Jno Brown, Capt Wm Christian, E Tn Mil Inf

ROBERSON, William, Sgt, no Regt Commander, Ens Wm Pegram, E TN Mil; det of Capt David Smith

ROBERT, Bradley, Cpl, Col Wm Hall, Capt Geo Martin, Vol Inf

ROBERT, Charles, Pvt, Col Jas Raulston, Capt Elijah Haynie, Inf

ROBERT, Jesse, 5 Cpl, Col Wm Metcalf, Capt Alexander Hill & Capt John Cunningham, Mil Inf; promoted to 2 Sgt

ROBERTS, Aaron, Pvt, Col S Bunch, Capt Jno English, E Tn Drafted Mil

ROBERTS, Abraham, Pvt, Col Wm Sharpe, Capt Thos Lillard, Inf

ROBERTS, Amos, Pvt, Col Wm Johnson, Capt Elihu Milliken, E TN Mil; trans to Capt McKamy Co

ROBERTS, Andrew, Pvt, Maj John Childs, Capt Daniel Price, Vol Mtd Gunmen

ROBERTS, Burkars, Pvt, Maj John Childs, Capt Chas Conway, E TN Mtd Gunmen; Regt from Roane Co

ROBERTS, David, Pvt, Col Robert Dyer, Capt William Evans, Vol Mtd Gunmen

ROBERTS, Edward, Pvt, Col John Brown, Capt Wm White, E TN Mil Inf

ROBERTS, Graham, Pvt, Col Robert Dyer, Capt Wm Russell, Vol Mtd Gunmen

ROBERTS, Isaac, Col William Higgins, Capt Stephen Griffith, Mtd Riflemen

ROBERTS, Isaac, Pvt, Maj William Woodfolk, Capt Abraham Dudney, Inf

ROBERTS, Isaac, Pvt, Maj Wm Woodfolk, Capt Jas Turner, Inf

ROBERTS, Isam, Pvt, Col Wm Johnson, Capt Elihu Millikin, TN Vol Mil

ROBERTS, Jacob, Dmr, Col Wm Johnson, Capt Jas Tunnell, E Tn Mil

ROBERTS, James, Dmr, Col R C Napier, Capt John Chism, Mil Inf

ROBERTS, James, Pvt, Col Alexander Loury, Capt Leroy Hammonds & Capt Raines, Inf

ROBERTS, James, Pvt, Col Edwin Booth, Capt Samuel Thompson, Mil

ROBERTS, James, Pvt, Col Ewen Allison, Capt James Laughmiller, Mil

ROBERTS, James, Pvt, Col John Wynn, Capt Jas Cole, Inf

ROBERTS, James, Pvt, Col Wm Johnson, Capt Elihu Millikin, E TN Mil

ROBERTS, James, Pvt, Col Wm Lillard, Capt Jacob Dykes, Vol Inf

ROBERTS, James, Pvt, Lt Col L Hammond, Col A Loury, Capt Thos Wells, Inf

ROBERTS, Jeptha, Pvt, Col Wm Lillard, Capt Thomas Sharpe, 2 Regt Inf

ROBERTS, Jeremiah, Pvt, Col R H Dyer, Capt Thos Jones, Vol Mtd Gunmen

ROBERTS, Jesse, Cpl, Col S Copeland, Capt James Tait, Inf

ROBERTS, Jesse, Pvt, Col A Cheatham, Capt Geo G Chapman, Inf

ROBERTS, John C, Pvt, Maj John Chiles, Capt Chas Conway, E TN Mtd Gunmen

ROBERTS, John D, Pvt, Col John Brown, Capt Allen I Bacon, E TN Mil Inf

ROBERTS, John jr, Pvt, Col John Coffee, Capt James Terrell, Vol Cav

ROBERTS, John, 4 Cpl, Col Ewen Allison, Capt Wm King, Drafted Mil

ROBERTS, John, Cpl, Col Samuel Wear, Capt John Bayless, Mtd Inf

ROBERTS, John, Pvt, Col Wm Johnson, Capt James Stewart, E Tn Draft Mil

ROBERTS, John, Pvt, Maj John Childs, Capt Daniel Price, Vol Mtd Gunmen; Regt from Roane Co

ROBERTS, John, Pvt, Maj John Chiles, Capt Chas Conway, E Tn Mtd Gunmen

ROBERTS, John, Pvt, Maj John Chiles, Capt Daniel Price, E TN Vol Mtd Inf

ROBERTS, John, Pvt, Maj Wm Russell, Capt Geo Mitchie, Vol Mtd Gunmen

ROBERTS, John, Sgt, Regt Commander omitted, Capt Edwin S Moore, Mtd Riflemen

ROBERTS, John, jr, Pvt, Col R H Dyer, Capt Thos Jones, Vol Mtd Gunmen

ROBERTS, John, sr, 4 Sgt, Regt Commander omitted, Capt Jas Terrill, Cav; trans to Capt Moore's Co

ROBERTS, John, sr, Pvt, Col John Coffee, Capt James Terrell, Vol Cav

ROBERTS, John, sr, Sgt, Col R H Dyer, Capt Thos Jones, Vol Mtd Gunmen

ROBERTS, Joshua, Cpl, Col John Brown, Capt Wm White, E Tn Mll Inf

ROBERTS, Joshua, Pvt, Col Samuel Bunch, Capt F Register, E Tn Mil; trans to Capt Bacon's

ROBERTS, Joshua, Pvt, Col Wm Johnson, Capt James R Rogers, E Tn Draft Mil

ROBERTS, Jozedic, Pvt, Col Samuel Wear, Capt Daniel Price, E Tn Vol Inf

ROBERTS, Lewis, Pvt, Col Samuel Bayless, Capt James Landen, E Tn Mil

ROBERTS, Mark, Pvt, Col T McCrory, Capt Wm Dooley, Inf

ROBERTS, Mathew S, Cpl, Regt Commander omitted, Capt Edwin S Moore, Mtd Riflemen

ROBERTS, Mathew, Pvt, Col R H Dyer, Capt Thos Jones, Vol Mtd Gunmen

ROBERTS, Nathan, Pvt, Regt Commander omitted, Capt Jas Cowan, Inf

ROBERTS, Ninson, Pvt, Col Jno Brown, Capt Hugh Barton, Branch omitted

ROBERTS, Peter P, Sgt Maj, Col John Cocke, no Co Commander, 2 Regt W Tn Mll Inf

- 431

## Enlisted Men, War of 1812

ROBERTS, Peter, Pvt, Col Wm Metcalf, Capt Barbee Collins, Mil Inf
ROBERTS, Peter, Pvt, Maj Wm Woodfolk, Capt John Sutton, Inf; died 12-3-1814
ROBERTS, Philip, Pvt, Maj John Chiles, Capt Chas Conway, E TN Mtd Gunmen; Regt from Roane Co
ROBERTS, Richard, Pvt, Col S Copeland, Capt David Williams, Inf
ROBERTS, Riland, Pvt, Col Wm Metcalf, Capt Barbee Collins, Mil Inf
ROBERTS, Robert S, Sgt, Col Edwin Booth, Capt John McKamey, E Tn Mil
ROBERTS, Robert, Pvt, Maj Gen Wm Carroll, Capt F Ellis, Inf
ROBERTS, Shadrick, Pvt, Col Ewen Allison, Capt James Laughmiller, Mil; deserted
ROBERTS, Shadrick, Pvt, Col John Brown, Capt Hugh Barton, E Tn Mil Inf
ROBERTS, Silas, Sgt, Col Robert Steele, Capt Samuel Maxwell, Mil Inf
ROBERTS, Thomas, 1 Surgeon Mate, Col John Cocke, 3 Regt W Tn Mll Inf
ROBERTS, Thomas, 2 Surgeon Mate, Col R C Napier, 1 Regt W Tn Mil
ROBERTS, Thomas, Col Robert Steele, Capt Samuel Maxwell, Mil Inf
ROBERTS, Thomas, Col Samuel Bunch, Capt Andrew Breden, E Tn Mil
ROBERTS, Thomas, Pvt, Col Jno Coffee, Capt John W Byrn, Cav
ROBERTS, Thomas, Pvt, Col John Coffee, Capt David Smith, Vol Cav
ROBERTS, Thomas, Pvt, Col Samuel Bunch, Capt Jones Griffin, E Tn Draft Mil; deserted
ROBERTS, Thomas, Pvt, Regt Commander omitted, Capt Archibald McKinney, Cav
ROBERTS, Thomas, Surgeon's Mate, Col Newton Cannon, TN Vol Mtd Gunmen
ROBERTS, Tom N, Pvt, no other information
ROBERTS, William A, Pvt, Col Jno Coffee, Capt John Baskerville, Cav
ROBERTS, William A, Pvt, Col John Alcorn, Capt John Baskerville, Vol Inf
ROBERTS, William H, 1 Cpl, Regt Commander omitted, Capt James Haggard, Mtd Gunmen; trans to Capt Molton's Co
ROBERTS, William H, Pvt, Lt Col Richard Napier, Co Commander omitted, Inf
ROBERTS, William H, Pvt, Regt Commander omitted, Capt James Williams, Mil Cav
ROBERTS, William, 3 Sgt, Col Samuel Bunch, Capt David Vance, E TN Mtd Inf
ROBERTS, William, Pvt, Col Samuel Bunch, Capt Isaac Williams, Mtd Vol
ROBERTS, William, Pvt, Col Wm Metcalf, Maj Gen Wm Carroll, Capt John Jackson, Inf
ROBERTS, William, Pvt, Col Wm Pillow, Capt Geo Caperton, Inf
ROBERTS, William, Pvt, Maj Wm Woodfolk, Capt Abner Pearce, Inf
ROBERTS, William, Sgt, Col Jno Brown, Capt Allen I Bacon, TN Mil Inf; promoted from Cpl
ROBERTS, Willis, Pvt, Col Robert Steele, Capt James Shenault, Mil Inf
ROBERTSON, Abel, Pvt, Col John Cocke, Co Commander omitted, Inf
ROBERTSON, Abraham, Pvt, Col John Coffee, Capt Michael Molton, Cav; deserted
ROBERTSON, Andrew, 1 Cpl, Col James Raulston, Capt Charles Wade, Inf
ROBERTSON, Andrew, 2 Sgt, Col Wm Hall, Capt John Moore, Vol Inf
ROBERTSON, Burton, Pvt, Col Philip Pipkin, Capt George Mebane, Mil Inf
ROBERTSON, Charles, Pvt, Col Edwin Booth, Co Commander omitted, E TN Mil
ROBERTSON, Christopher, Pvt, Capt Adam Dale & Capt W Y Higgins, Mtd Gunmen; died of wounds rec 1-22-1814 at Emuckford
ROBERTSON, Cullen, Pvt, Col Thomas H Williamson, Capt John Cocke & Capt John Crane, Vol Mtd Gunmen
ROBERTSON, Daniel, Pvt, Col John Williams, Capt David Vance, Mtd Mil
ROBERTSON, Daniel, Pvt, Col Samuel Wear, Capt John Chiles, E Tn Vol Inf
ROBERTSON, Daniel, Pvt, Maj John Chiles, Capt Charles Conway, E TN Mtd Gunmen
ROBERTSON, Darius, Pvt, Col John Cocke, Capt Richard Crunk, Inf; died 4-5-1815
ROBERTSON, David G, Pvt, Col R C Napier, Capt James McMurry, Mil Inf; died 3-14-1814
ROBERTSON, Edward, Pvt, Capt Adam Dale & Capt Wm Y Higgins, Mtd Gunmen
ROBERTSON, Eli, Pvt, Col Wm Y Higgins, Capt Samuel Allen, Mtd Gunmen
ROBERTSON, Eli, Pvt, Lt Col Wm Phillips, no other information
ROBERTSON, Elijah, Pvt, Col Philip Pipkin, Capt John Robertson, Mil Inf
ROBERTSON, Elijah, Pvt, Col Samuel Wear, Capt Simeon Perry, E TN Vol Inf; reduced from Sgt
ROBERTSON, Elisha, Pvt, Col Edward Bradley, Capt Wm Lauderdale, Vol Inf
ROBERTSON, Elisha, Pvt, Col Jarman, Capt Hamilton, Inf
ROBERTSON, Elisha, Pvt, Col Philip Pipkin, Capt John Strother, Mil
ROBERTSON, Enoch, Pvt, Col Wm Johnson, Capt Andrew Lawson, E Tn Draft Mil
ROBERTSON, Fulton, Pvt, Col Philip Pipkin, Capt George Mebane, Mil Inf
ROBERTSON, George, Pvt, Col S Copeland, Capt Wm Evans, Mil Inf
ROBERTSON, Hardy, Pvt, Col John Alcorn, Capt John W Byrne, Cav
ROBERTSON, Hardy, Pvt, Col John Coffee, Capt John Byrn, Cav
ROBERTSON, Henry, Cpl, Col John Alcorn, Capt John Winston, Mtd Riflemen
ROBERTSON, Hezekiah, Pvt, Col James Raulston, Capt ELijah Haynie, Inf

## Enlisted Men, War of 1812

ROBERTSON, Hezekiah, Pvt, Col Philip Pipkin, Capt Henry Newlin, Mil Inf

ROBERTSON, Isaac, Pvt, Lt Col L Hammond, Capt Thos Delaney, Inf; also under Col A Loury

ROBERTSON, James R, Pvt, Col N T Perkins, Capt Philip Pipkin, Mtd Riflemen

ROBERTSON, James, Pvt Brig Gen T Johnson, Capt Robert Carson, Inf

ROBERTSON, James, Pvt, Col Edwin Booth, Capt Geo Winton, E TN Mil

ROBERTSON, James, Pvt, Col John Cocke, Capt Richard Crunk, Inf

ROBERTSON, James, Pvt, Col John Wynne, Capt Wm Carothers, W Tn Inf

ROBERTSON, James, Pvt, Col R C Napier, Capt Drury Adkins, Mil Inf

ROBERTSON, James, Pvt, Col T Johnson, Capt Benj Powell, E TN Mil; trans to Capt Cumming

ROBERTSON, John A, Pvt, Col N T Cannon, Capt Jno Hanley, Mtd Riflemen

ROBERTSON, John N, Pvt, Col Wm Lillard, Capt Z Copeland, E TN Vol Inf

ROBERTSON, John, 4 Sgt, Regt Commander omitted, Capt David Smith, Cav

ROBERTSON, John, Pvt, Col A Cheatham, Co Commander omitted, Mtd Inf

ROBERTSON, John, Pvt, Col A Loury, Capt Geo Sarver, Inf

ROBERTSON, John, Pvt, Col A Loury, Capt John Looney, W TN Inf

ROBERTSON, John, Pvt, Col E Booth, Capt Geo Winton, E TN Mil

ROBERTSON, John, Pvt, Col Edward Bradley, Capt Abraham Bledsoe, Riflemen

ROBERTSON, John, Pvt, Col S Copeland, Capt Solomon George, Inf

ROBERTSON, John, Pvt, Col Samuel Bayless, Capt Joseph Hale, E Tn Mil

ROBERTSON, John, Pvt, Col Samuel Bayless, Capt Joseph Rich, E TN Inf

ROBERTSON, John, Pvt, Col Thos Benton, Capt Wm Smith, Vol Inf

ROBERTSON, John, Pvt, Col Wm Hall, Capt Abraham Bledsoe, Vol Inf

ROBERTSON, John, Pvt, Col Wm Hall, Capt Henry M Newlin, Inf

ROBERTSON, John, Pvt, Col Wm Lillard, Capt Zacherus Copeland, E TN Vol Inf

ROBERTSON, John, Pvt, Col Wm Metcalf, Capt Wm Sitton, Mil Inf

ROBERTSON, John, Pvt, Col Wm Pillow, Capt Wm I Smith, Vol Inf

ROBERTSON, John, Pvt, Lt Col Jno Edmonson, Co Commander omitted, Cav

ROBERTSON, John, Pvt, Lt Col L Hammond, Capt James Tubb, Inf

ROBERTSON, John, Pvt, Lt Col L Hammond, Capt Jas Tubb, Branch omitted

ROBERTSON, John, Pvt, Regt Commander omitted, Capt I Ferrell, Inf

ROBERTSON, Joseph, Pvt, Col E Allison, Capt Jos Everett, E TN Mil

ROBERTSON, Joseph, Pvt, Col E Booth, Capt Alex Biggs, Inf

ROBERTSON, Jules, Pvt, Col Wm Hall, Capt Jno Kennedy, Vol Inf

ROBERTSON, Julius, Sgt, Col S Copeland, Capt Wm Evans, Mil Inf

ROBERTSON, Lawson, Pvt, Maj Gen A Jackson, Capt Wm Carroll, Vol Inf

ROBERTSON, Linsey, Pvt, Col Wm Johnson, Capt Jas Rogers, E TN Draft Mil

ROBERTSON, Lott, Pvt, Col Jas Raulston, Capt E Haynie, Inf

ROBERTSON, Mark, Pvt, Col E Booth, Capt A Biggs, Inf

ROBERTSON, Michael, Pvt, Col Wm Metcalf, Capt Wm Sitton, Mil Inf

ROBERTSON, Michael, Pvt, Cpl Elisha Green, Mtd Spies

ROBERTSON, Michael, Pvt, Maj Wm Woodfolk, Capt Jas Hall, Inf

ROBERTSON, Nathaniel, Pvt, Col Jno Cocke, Capt Geo Barnes, Inf

ROBERTSON, Redrick, Pvt, Col R H Dyer, Capt Jas Wyatt, Vol Mtd Gunmen

ROBERTSON, Rerdon, Pvt, Col Wm Hall, Capt Jno Kennedy, Vol Inf

ROBERTSON, Richard, Pvt, Col Wm Metcalf, Capt Wm Sitton, Mil Inf

ROBERTSON, Risdel, Pvt, Col E Booth, Capt Vernon, E TN Mil

ROBERTSON, Robert A, Pvt, Col Thos Benton, Capt Geo Caperton, Vol Inf; joined from Capt Hewett's Co

ROBERTSON, Robert, Cpl, Maj Wm Russell, Capt Jno Tremble, Vol Mtd Gunmen

ROBERTSON, Robert, Pvt, Col Jno Cocke, Capt Geo Barnes, Inf

ROBERTSON, Robert, Pvt, Col Thos Benton, Capt Benjamin Hewett, Vol Inf

ROBERTSON, Robert, Pvt, Col Wm Johnson, Capt Jno Tunnell, 3 Regt E TN Mil; died 11-4-1814

ROBERTSON, Samuel, Pvt, Col R E Dyer, Capt Jos Williams, Vol Mtd Gunmen

ROBERTSON, Samuel, Pvt, Col S Bunch, Capt S Robinson, E TN Draft Mil

ROBERTSON, Squire, Pvt, Regt Commander omitted, Capt Gray, Inf

ROBERTSON, Stephen, Pvt, Col Wm Hall, Capt Jno Kennedy, Vol Inf

ROBERTSON, Thomas, Pvt, Maj Wm Woodfolk, Capt A Pearce, Inf; transferred from Capt Dudney's Co

ROBERTSON, Thomas, Pvt, Maj Wm Woodfolk, Capt Jas Neil, Inf

ROBERTSON, William, 3 Cpl, Col E Bradley, Capt Jno Kennedy, Riflemen; AWOL

ROBERTSON, William, 4 Sgt, Col P Pipkin, Capt David Smith, W TN Mil; transferred from Capt Jno Strothers

ROBERTSON, William, Pvt, Col J K Winn, Capt Wm McCall, Inf

ROBERTSON, William, Pvt, Col Jno Cocke, Capt B Nance, Inf

ROBERTSON, William, Pvt, Col Jno Cocke, Capt Jos

## Enlisted Men, War of 1812

Price, Inf
ROBERTSON, William, Pvt, Col Jno Coffee, Capt Jno Baskerville, Cav
ROBERTSON, William, Pvt, Col John Cocke, Capt James Gault, Inf
ROBERTSON, William, Pvt, Col N T Cannon, Capt Martin, Mtd Gunmen
ROBERTSON, William, Pvt, Col P Pipkin, Capt Jno Strother, Mil
ROBERTSON, William, Pvt, Col R H Dyer, Capt B Allen, Vol Mtd Gunmen
ROBERTSON, William, Pvt, Col R H Dyer, Capt Thos Jones, Vol Mtd Gunmen; d 3-20-1815
ROBERTSON, William, Pvt, Regt Commander omitted, Capt Jas Askew, Inf
ROBERTSON, William, Sgt, Col P Pipkin, Capt D Smith, Mil Inf
ROBERTSON, Winfrey, Pvt, Col Wm Lillard, Capt Thos Sharpe, 2nd Regt Inf
ROBERTSON, Zachariah, 3 Sgt, Col P Pipkin, Capt Jno Robertson, Mil Inf
ROBERTSON, Zachariah, Pvt, Regt Commander omitted, Capt Edwin S Moore, Mtd Riflemen
ROBINS, John, Pvt, Regt Commander omitted, Capt Jas Gray, Inf
ROBINS, Michael, Pvt, Col Edwin E Booth, Capt Richard Marshall, Drafted Mil
ROBINSON, Abner, Pvt, Col R H Dyer, Capt Ephraim Dickson, TN Mtd Gunmen
ROBINSON, Abraham, Pvt, Col R H Dyer, Capt Cuthbert Hudson, Vol Mtd Gunmen
ROBINSON, Abraham, Pvt, Lt Col Leroy Hammond, Capt James Craig, Inf
ROBINSON, Alex, Pvt, Regt Commander omitted, Capt John Gordon, Mtd Spies
ROBINSON, Alexander, Pvt, Col John K Wynne, Capt John Porter, Inf; transferred to Capt Gordon's Spies
ROBINSON, Alexander, Pvt, Col John K Wynne, Capt Prince, Inf
ROBINSON, Alexander, Sgt, Maj Wm Woodfolk, Capt Abner Pearce, Inf
ROBINSON, Allen, Pvt, Col James Raulston, Capt James Neale, Inf; d 1-3-1815
ROBINSON, Andrew, Cpl, Col James Raulston, Capt Henry Hamilton, Inf; also under Maj Gen Wm Carroll
ROBINSON, Andrew, Pvt, Col S Copeland, Capt Robert Steele, Mil Inf
ROBINSON, Archibald, Pvt, Col S Copeland, Co Commander omitted, Inf
ROBINSON, Augerrtus, Pvt, Maj William Russell, Capt Wm Mitchell, Vol Mtd Gunmen
ROBINSON, Breashears, Pvt, Col Wm Johnson, Capt Rogers, E TN Drafted Mil
ROBINSON, Charles D, Pvt, Col Thomas H Williamson, Capt Wm Metcalf, Vol Mtd Gunmen
ROBINSON, Charles P, Pvt, Regt Commander omitted, Capt David Smith, Cav Vol
ROBINSON, Culson, Pvt, Col Newton Cannon, Capt James Walton, Mtd Riflemen

ROBINSON, Daniel, Pvt, Lt Col Leroy Hammond, Capt James Craig, Inf
ROBINSON, David, Pvt, Col James Raulston, Capt Mathew Neale, Inf
ROBINSON, David, Pvt, Col S Copeland, Capt Wm Hodges, Inf
ROBINSON, Enoch, Pvt, Col Wm Johnson, Capt Scott, E TN Drafted Mil; transferred from Capt Lawson
ROBINSON, Field, Pvt, Col Samuel Bayless, Capt Joseph Rich, E TN Inf
ROBINSON, George, Pvt, Col S Bunch, Capt Francis Register, E TN Mil
ROBINSON, Henry, Pvt, Col Newton Cannon, Capt James Walton, Mtd Riflemen
ROBINSON, Isaac, Pvt, Col Samuel Wear, Capt Daniel Price, E TN Inf
ROBINSON, Jacob, Pvt, Col Wm Johnson, Capt Rogers, E TN Drafted Mil
ROBINSON, James, Pvt, Col Ewen Allison, Capt John Hampton, Mil
ROBINSON, James, Pvt, Col S Copeland, Capt John Dawson, Inf
ROBINSON, James, Pvt, Maj John Chiles, Capt James Cummings, E TN Vol Mtd Inf; transf from Capt Powell's Co of TN Mil
ROBINSON, John C, Pvt, Col Jno Coffee, Capt John W Byrn, Cav
ROBINSON, John W, Pvt, Col S Copeland, Capt Wm Hodges, Inf
ROBINSON, John W, Pvt, Maj John Chiles, Capt James Cummings, E TN Vol Mtd Inf
ROBINSON, John, Pvt, Col John Brown, Capt Jesse G Reany, Mtd Gunmen
ROBINSON, John, Pvt, Col John Coffee, Capt David Smith, Vol Cav
ROBINSON, John, Pvt, Col John K Cocke, Capt James Gault, Inf
ROBINSON, John, Pvt, Col S Copeland, Capt G W Steel, Mil Inf
ROBINSON, John, Pvt, Col Samuel Bunch, Capt S Richardson, E TN Drafted Mil; discharged for inability
ROBINSON, John, Pvt, Maj Gen Wm Carroll, Col James Raulston, Capt Edward Robinson, Inf
ROBINSON, John, Sgt, Col Samuel Bunch, Capt John Inman, E TN Vol Mtd Inf
ROBINSON, Joseph, Pvt, Col Samuel Bunch, Capt John English, E TN Drafted Mil
ROBINSON, Joseph, Pvt, Col Wm Lillard, Capt Jacob Dyke, Vol Inf
ROBINSON, Michael, Pvt, Col John Brown, Capt John Trimble, E TN Mtd Gunmen
ROBINSON, Peter, Pvt, Col S Copeland, Capt Wm Hodges, Inf
ROBINSON, Peter, Pvt, Regt Commander omitted, Capt Wm Hodges, Branch Srvce omitted
ROBINSON, Richard, Pvt, Col Jno Brown, Capt Wm D Neilson, E TN Vol Mil
ROBINSON, Robert, Pvt, Col Samuel Bunch, Capt F Register, E TN Mil
ROBINSON, Robert, Pvt, Col Wm Lillard, Capt Jacob

## Enlisted Men, War of 1812

Dyke, Branch Srvce omitted; unable to perform duty
ROBINSON, Samuel B, 5 Sgt, Maj Gen Wm Carroll, Col Jas Raulston, Capt Edward Robinson, Inf
ROBINSON, Samuel L, Pvt, Col John Cocke, Capt James Gault, Inf; d 2-4-1815
ROBINSON, Thomas, Cpl, Col S Copeland, Capt Moses Thompson, Inf
ROBINSON, Thomas, Pvt, Col Newton Cannon, Capt James Walton, Mtd Riflemen
ROBINSON, Thomas, Pvt, Col R C Napier, Capt Thos Gray, Mil Inf
ROBINSON, Thomas, Pvt, Col Samuel Bunch, Capt Jones Griffin, E TN Mil
ROBINSON, Vest, Pvt, Col Thos Williamson, Capt James Pace, Lt James Nealy, Vol Mtd Gunmen
ROBINSON, William, Pvt, Col Edwin Booth, Capt Samuel Thompson, Mil
ROBINSON, William, Pvt, Col John Alcorn, Capt Jno Baskerville, Vol Inf
ROBINSON, William, Pvt, Col R H Dyer, Capt Cuthbert Hudson, Vol Mtd Gunmen
ROBINSON, William, Pvt, Col Samuel Wear, Capt John Stephens, E TN Vol Inf
ROBINSON, William, Pvt, Regt Commander omitted, Capt John Gordon, Mtd Spies
ROBINSON, William, Sgt, Col Samuel Bayless, Capt Joseph Rich, E TN Inf
ROCHELL, James, Pvt, Col Newton Cannon, Capt James Walton, Mtd Riflemen
ROCHHOLD, Francis, Pvt, Col Ewen Allison, Capt John Hampton, Mil; transferred to Capt Mcrea's Co
ROCKHOLT, Francis, Pvt, Col Ewen Allison, Capt Henry McCray, E TN Mil; transferred to Capt Hampton's Co
RODDEN, Jacob, Pvt, Regt Commander omitted, Capt James Gray, Inf
RODDEY, Philip, Pvt, Col Thos McCrory, Capt A Metcalf, Mil Inf
RODDLY, James, Cpl, Col S Copeland, Capt Allen Wilkinson, Mil Inf
RODDY, Andrew, Pvt, Col Samuel Wear, Capt Joseph Calloway, Mtd Inf
RODDY, Andrew, Pvt, Maj John Chiles, Capt Reuben Tipton, E TN Vol Mtd Inf; Regimental Co - Blount
RODDY, James, Pvt, Col Samuel Wear, Capt Joseph Calloway, Mtd Inf
RODDY, Jesse, Pvt, Col John Brown, Capt John Trimble, E TN Mtd Inf
RODDY, John, Pvt, Maj John Chiles, Capt John Chiles, E TN Mtd Inf; Regimental Co - Blount
RODDY, John, Pvt, Maj John Chiles, Capt Reuben Tipton, E TN Vol Mtd Inf; Regimental Co - Blount
RODDY, Phillip, Pvt, Col Thos McCrory, Capt A Metcalf, Mil Inf
RODDYE, Isaac, Pvt, Col Samuel Bunch, Capt Wm Houston, E TN Vol Mtd Inf
RODEN, Abedaigo, Pvt, Col John Brown, Capt William White, E TN Mil Inf
RODEN, Greenbury, Pvt, Col Newton Cannon, Capt David Hogan, Mtd Gunmen
RODER, Isaac sr, Pvt, Col John Cocke, Capt Sam M Caruthers, Inf
RODES, Abner, Pvt, Col Thos Williamson, Capt A Metcalf, Vol Mtd Gunmen
RODES, Abram, Pvt, Col Jno Coffee, Capt Alexander McKeen, Cav
RODES, Hazel, Pvt, no other information
RODES, Hazie, Pvt, Col John Alcorn, Capt John Winston, Mtd Riflemen
RODES, Henry, Pvt, Col Thos Williamson, Capt A Metcalf, Vol Mtd Gunmen
RODES, Thomas, Pvt, Col Jno Coffee, Capt Alexander McKeen, Cav
RODES, Thomas, Pvt, Col John Coffee, Capt Michael Molton, Cav
RODGER, William H, Pvt, Col Alexander Loury, Lt Col L Hammonds, Capt Thomas Wells, Inf
RODGERS, Abraham, Pvt, Col R H Dyer, Capt Robert Edmonston, 1st TN Mtd Vol Gunmen
RODGERS, Andrew, Pvt, Col Jarmon, Capt Isiah Hamilton, Inf
RODGERS, Andrew, Pvt, Col Wm Johnson, Capt David McKamy, E TN Drafted Mil
RODGERS, Andrew, Pvt, Regt Commander omitted, Capt Wm Teas, 6th Brig Inf
RODGERS, Armistead, Pvt, Regt Commander omitted, Capt George Smith, Spies
RODGERS, Brinkley M, Pvt, Col Thos Williamson, Capt Beverly Williams, Vol Mtd Gunmen
RODGERS, Charles, Pvt, Col N T Perkins, Capt Mathew Johnson, Mil Inf
RODGERS, David, Sgt, Col Samuel Bayless, Capt James Landen, E TN Mil
RODGERS, Elijah, Cpl, Col Ewen Allison, Capt John Hampton, Mil
RODGERS, George, Pvt, Col R H Dyer, Capt Joseph Williams, 1st Regt TN Vol Mtd Gunmen
RODGERS, George, Pvt, Col Wm Lillard, Capt John Roper, E TN Vol Inf
RODGERS, George, Pvt, Maj William Russell, Capt Isaac Williams, Separate Bn of TN Vol Mtd Gunmen
RODGERS, Isaac, Pvt, Col R H Dyer, Maj William Russell, Capt Isaac Williams, Separate Bn of TN Vol Mtd Gunmen
RODGERS, Jacob, Pvt, Col John Cocke, Capt James Gray, Inf
RODGERS, John, Pvt, Col S Copeland, Capt Wm Evans, Mil Inf
RODGERS, John, Pvt, Col Samuel Bunch, Capt James Penny, E TN Mtd Inf
RODGERS, John, Pvt, Col Samuel Wear, Capt Wm Gillespie, E TN Vol Inf
RODGERS, John, Pvt, Maj Wm Woodfolk, Capt Abraham Dudney, Inf; d 3-28-1815
RODGERS, John, Pvt, Maj Wm Woodfolk, Capt James Turner, Inf
RODGERS, Jonah, Pvt, Capt Nathan Davis, Lt I Barrett, Inf
RODGERS, Jonathan, Pvt, Col R H Dyer, Capt Joseph Williams, Vol Mtd Gunmen

- 435

RODGERS, Joseph, Cpl, Col R H Dyer, Capt Joseph Williams, 1st Regt TN Vol Mtd Gunmen
RODGERS, Joseph, Pvt, Col James Raulston, Capt Daniel Newman, Inf
RODGERS, Joseph, Pvt, Col Samuel Bayless, Capt James Landen, E TN Mil
RODGERS, Joseph, Pvt, Col Samuel Wear, Capt John Chiles, E TN Vol Inf
RODGERS, Joseph, Pvt, Maj Wm Russell, Capt Isaac Williams, Separate Bn of TN Vol Mtd Gunmen
RODGERS, Joseph, Pvt, Regt Commander omitted, Capt Wm Teas, 6th Brig Inf
RODGERS, Levi, Pvt, Maj Wm Russell, Capt Wm Chism, Vol Mtd Gunmen
RODGERS, Mansun, Pvt, Col Samuel Bayless, Capt Joseph Goodson, E TN Mil
RODGERS, Patterson, Pvt, Col Samuel Wear, Capt James Gillespie, E TN Vol Inf
RODGERS, Peter, Pvt, Col Newton Cannon, Capt John Harpole, Mtd Gunmen
RODGERS, Robert, 5 Sgt, Maj Gen Wm Carroll, Capt F Ellis, Inf
RODGERS, Robert, Pvt, Col Thomas Benton, Capt James McFerrin, Vol Inf
RODGERS, Samuel, Cpl, Col Newton Cannon, Capt Isaac Williams, Mtd Riflemen
RODGERS, Samuel, Pvt, Col Wm Pillow, Capt Mason, Vol Inf
RODGERS, Spencer, Pvt, Col Philip Pipkin, Capt Henry M Newlin, Mil Inf
RODGERS, Thomas A, 2 Sgt, Col John Williams, Capt David Vance, Mtd Mil
RODGERS, Thomas, Pvt, Regt Commander omitted, Capt Robert Evans, Mtd Spies
RODGERS, Uriah W, Pvt, Col Thomas Williamson, Capt Beverly Williams, Vol Mtd Gunmen
RODGERS, William, Pvt, Col N T Perkins, Capt James McMahan, Mtd Gunmen
RODGERS, William, Pvt, Col R H Dyer, Capt James McMahan, TN Vol Mtd Gunmen
RODGERS, William, Pvt, Col Samuel Wear, Capt James Gillespie, E TN Vol Inf
RODGERS, William, Pvt, Col Samuel Wear, Capt John Chiles, E TN Vol Inf
RODGERS, William, Pvt, Maj Wm Russell, Capt Isaac Williams, Separate Bn of TN Vol Mtd Gunmen; also under Col R H Dyer
ROE, John, Pvt, Col R H Dyer, Capt B Allen, Vol Mtd Gunmen
ROE, Laurence, Pvt, Maj Wm Carroll, Capt L Dillahunty & Capt Danl Bradford, Vol Inf
ROE, Samuel, Pvt, Col R H Dyer, Capt Jas Wyatt, Vol Mtd Gunmen
ROESBERRY, Thomas, Pvt, Col Wm Johnson, Capt Jas Tunnell, E TN Mil
ROGAN, Benjamin, Cpl, Col Jno Alcorn, Capt F Stump, Cav
ROGERS, Alex, Pvt, Col John Brown, Capt Standifer, E TN Vol Mtd Mil
ROGERS, Anderson, Pvt, Col Jno Brown, Capt Wm D Neilson, E TN Vol Mil

ROGERS, Andrew, Pvt, Col Wm Johnson, Capt Jas Rogers, E TN Mil
ROGERS, Armstead, Pvt, Regt Commander omitted, Capt Geo Smith, Spies
ROGERS, Benjamin, Pvt, no other information
ROGERS, Britton, Pvt, Col Thos Williamson, Capt Thos Scurry, Vol Mtd Gunmen
ROGERS, Cordi, Cpl, Col S Copeland, Capt A Wilkinson, Mil Inf
ROGERS, Daniel, Cpl, Maj John Porter, Capt Mathew Cowan, Cav
ROGERS, David, Pvt, Col Wm Hall, Capt Travis Nash, Inf
ROGERS, David, Pvt, Col Wm Metcalf, Capt Bird Hurt, Mil Inf
ROGERS, Edward C, Pvt, Regt Commander omitted, Capt Larken Ferrell, Inf
ROGERS, Edward, Pvt, Col N Cannon, Capt John Handley, Mtd Riflemen
ROGERS, Edward, Pvt, Regt Commander omitted, Capt Thomas Gray, Inf
ROGERS, Elijah, Pvt, Col William Johnson, Capt Andrew Lawson, E TN Drafted Mil
ROGERS, Elijah, Sgt, Col S Copeland, Capt David Williams, Mil Inf
ROGERS, Elisha, Pvt, Col Jas Raulston, Capt Chas Wade, Inf; d 1-6-1815
ROGERS, Elisha, Pvt, Col S Bunch, Capt Francis Berry, E TN Mil
ROGERS, Elisha, Pvt, Maj Gen Jackson, Capt Joseph Kirkpatrick, Mtd Gunmen
ROGERS, Ezekiel, Pvt, Col Ewen Allison, Capt T McCrory, E TN Mil; deserted 3-4-1814
ROGERS, George, Pvt, Col S Wear, Capt S Bunch & Capt Wm Mitchell, E TN Mtd Inf
ROGERS, George, Pvt, Lt Col Wm Phillips, Co Commander omitted, Inf
ROGERS, Henry, Pvt, Col Jas Raulston, Capt Jas Black, Inf
ROGERS, Isaac, Pvt, Col Edward Bradley, Capt Travis Nash, Vol Inf
ROGERS, Isaac, Pvt, Col John Cocke, Capt John Weakley, Inf
ROGERS, Isaac, Pvt, Col Wm Hall, Capt Travis Nash, Inf
ROGERS, Isaac, Pvt, Lt I Barrett, Capt Nathan Davis, Inf
ROGERS, Isom, Pvt, Regt Commander omitted, Sgt Wyatt Fussell, Inf
ROGERS, James R, Pvt, Maj Porter, Capt Jas Anderson, Cav
ROGERS, James, Pvt, Col S Bunch, Capt William Houston, E TN Vol Mtd Inf
ROGERS, James, Pvt, Col William Higgins, Capt James Hambleton, Mtd Gunmen
ROGERS, James, Sgt, Col S Copeland, Capt William Douglas, Inf
ROGERS, Jeditlen, Pvt, Maj Woodfolk, Capt Rose & Capt McCully, Inf
ROGERS, Jeremiah, Pvt, Col William Johnson, Capt Andrew Lawson, E TN Drafted Mil
ROGERS, Jesse, Cpl, Col Wm Johnson, Capt Jas Stewart, E TN Drafted Mil
ROGERS, Jesse, Cpl, Col Wm Johnson, Capt Jas Stewart,

## Enlisted Men, War of 1812

ROGERS, Jesse, Pvt, Col Ewen Allison, Capt William King, Drafted E TN Mil

ROGERS, Jesse, Pvt, Col Jas Raulston, Capt Henry West, Inf

ROGERS, John, Pvt, Col S Bunch, Capt Edward Buchanan, E TN Mil

ROGERS, John, Pvt, Col S Bunch, Capt William Houston, E TN Vol Mtd Inf

ROGERS, John, Pvt, Col Thos Benton, Capt Thos Williamson, Vol Inf; d 1-23-1814?

ROGERS, John, Pvt, Col Wm Johnson, Capt Jas Stewart, E TN Drafted Mil

ROGERS, John, Pvt, Maj Wm Woodfolk, Capt Jas Turner, Inf

ROGERS, Johnathan, Pvt, Regt Commander omitted, Capt Jos Williams, Mil Cav

ROGERS, Jonathan, Pvt, Col Thomas Williamson, Capt Thomas Scurry, Vol Mtd Gunmen; d 2-21-1815

ROGERS, Joseph, Pvt, Col Alexander Loury, Capt Leroy Hammonds & Capt Raines, Inf; attached to Gen Taylor's Life Guard

ROGERS, Joseph, Pvt, Col Samuel Bunch, Capt Joseph Duncan, E TN Drafted Mil

ROGERS, Larkin, Cpl, Col William Higgins, Capt Stephen Griffith, Mtd Riflemen

ROGERS, Larkin, Pvt, Col Thos Benton, Capt William Moore, Vol Inf

ROGERS, Larkin, Pvt, Col William Pillow, Capt William Moore, Inf

ROGERS, Levi, Pvt, Maj William Woodfolk, Capt Ross & Capt McCully, Inf

ROGERS, Levin, Cpl, Col Wm Johnson, Capt Jas Rogers, E TN Drafted Mil

ROGERS, Lorcain, Pvt, Col Thos Benton, Capt Geo Moore, Vol Inf

ROGERS, Lot, Pvt, Col S Bunch, Capt Edward Buchanan, E TN Mil

ROGERS, Mason, Pvt, Col S Bunch, Capt Francis Berry, E TN Mil

ROGERS, Mason, Pvt, Col S Bunch, Capt Jno Houk, E TN Mil; joined from Capt Berry's Co

ROGERS, Mathew, Pvt, Regt Commander omitted, Capt Geo Smith, Spies

ROGERS, Micujah, Pvt, Maj John Porter, Capt Jas Anderson, Cav

ROGERS, Patterson, Pvt, Col John Brown, Capt William White, E TN Mil Inf

ROGERS, Raily, Pvt, Col Johnson, Capt Hamilton, Inf

ROGERS, Raleigh, Pvt, Maj John Porter, Capt Jno Anderson, Cav

ROGERS, Robert, Pvt, Col John Alcorn, Capt George Winton, Mtd Riflemen

ROGERS, Robert, Pvt, Col William Higgins, Capt Doak, Mtd Riflemen

ROGERS, Rowland, Pvt, Col S Bunch, Capt Francis Berry, E TN Mil

ROGERS, Samuel I, Cpl, Col S Bunch, Capt John Reynolds, Vol Inf

ROGERS, Samuel, 2 Cpl, Col Thos Benton, Capt John Reynolds, Vol Inf

ROGERS, Samuel, Cpl, Col John Alcorn, Capt Henry Bryan, Cav

ROGERS, Samuel, Pvt, Col Jno Coffee, Capt Bryan, Cav; promoted to Cpl

ROGERS, Samuel, Pvt, Col Samuel Bunch, Capt William Houston, E TN Vol Mtd Inf

ROGERS, Samuel, Pvt, Col Thos Benton, Capt N Cannon, Inf

ROGERS, Sion, Pvt, Col John Cocke, Capt Geo Price, Inf

ROGERS, Solomon, Pvt, Col Thos Benton, Capt John Reynolds, Vol Inf

ROGERS, Solomon, Sgt, Gen Andrew Jackson, Capt Nathan Davis, Inf

ROGERS, Stanton, Pvt, Col James Raulston, Capt Henry Hamilton, Inf; d 12-25-1814, also under Maj Gen Wm Carroll

ROGERS, Stephen, Pvt, Col Edwin Booth, Capt Samuel Thompson, Mil

ROGERS, Tavener, Pvt, Col S Copeland, Capt Richard Sharp, Mil Inf

ROGERS, Thomas, Pvt, Col Newton Cannon, Capt Thos Yardley, Mtd Riflemen; transferred to Capt Evans Spies

ROGERS, Thomas, Pvt, Col Wm Lillard, Capt Wm Hamilton, E TN Vol Inf

ROGERS, Thomas, Pvt, Regt Commander omitted, Capt Jos Williams, Mil Cav

ROGERS, Vinson, Pvt, Col Edwin Booth, Capt Alexander Biggs, Inf

ROGERS, William, Cpl, Col John Cocke, Capt Geo Barnes, Inf

ROGERS, William, Pvt, Col Ewen Allison, Capt Wm King, Drafted Mil

ROGERS, William, Pvt, Col Philip Pipkin, Capt Peter Searcy, Mil Inf

ROGERS, William, Pvt, Col William Higgins, Capt John Doak, Mtd Riflemen

ROGERS, William, Pvt, Col Wm Lillard, Capt Wm Gillenwater, E TN Inf

ROGERS, William, Pvt, Col Wm Lillard, Capt Wm McLin, E TN Inf

ROGERS, William, Sgt, Col Edwin Booth, Capt Samuel Thompson, Mil; appointed from Pvt

ROGGERS, Isaac, Pvt, Col John Cocke, Capt John Weakley, Inf

ROGGERS, Jesse, Pvt, Col John Cocke, Capt Samuel Caruthers, Inf; d 1-18-1815

ROISON (RISON), William, Pvt, Maj Gen Wm Carroll, Col James Raulston, Inf; d 2-3-1815

ROLAND, Frederick, Pvt, Col Philip Pipkin, Capt Ebenezer Kirkpatrick, Mil Inf

ROLAND, Sherrad, Pvt, Col S Copeland, Capt Wm Douglas, Inf

ROLIN, Roberts, Pvt, Col Wm Metcalf, Capt Barbee Collins, Mil Inf

ROLINS, Thomas, Pvt, Col Philip Pipkin, Capt Geo Mebane, Mil Inf

ROLLEN, John, Pvt, Col T McCrory, Capt Jno Reynolds, Mil Inf

ROLLING, Jordon, Pvt, Col T McCrory, Capt Jas Shannon, Mil Inf

- 437

*Enlisted Men, War of 1812*

ROLLINGS, Joshua, Pvt, Col Thos Williamson, Capt Thos Scurry, Vol Mtd Gunmen
ROLLINS, Benjamin, Pvt, Col Newton Cannon, Capt Francis Jones, Mtd Riflemen
ROLLINS, Benjamin, Pvt, Col R H Dyer, Maj Wm Russell, Capt Wm Russell, Vol Mtd Gunmen
ROLLINS, Joshua H, Pvt, Col R C Napier, Capt Thos Preston, Mil Inf
ROLLINS, William, Pvt, Col Samuel Bunch, Capt S Richardson, E TN Drafted Mil
ROLLS, Alexander, Pvt, Col John Alcorn, Capt Fred Stump, Cav
ROLLS, John, Pvt, Maj Gen Wm Carroll, Capt Wiley Huddleston, Inf
ROLONG (ROLING), Abram, Pvt, Col N T Perkins, Capt Mathew Johnston, Mil Inf
ROLS, Alexander, Pvt, Col Jno Coffee, Capt Fred Stump, Cav
ROLSTER (ROLSTON), George, Pvt, Col Samuel Wear, Capt James Gillespie, E TN Vol Inf
ROLSTON, John, Cpl, Col R H Dyer, Capt James White, Vol Mtd Gunmen
ROLSTON, William, Pvt, Col John Cocke, Capt John Dalton, Inf
ROMINE, Aaron, Pvt, Col Newton Cannon, Capt John Harpole, Mtd Gunmen
ROMINES, Aron, Pvt, Col S Copeland, Capt G W Stell, Mil Inf
ROMINES, James, Pvt, Gen Andrew Jackson, Capt J Read, Inf
ROMINS, Peter, Pvt, Col A Loury, Lt Col L Hammond, Capt Arahel Rains, Inf
ROMNER (RUMINER), Daniel, Pvt, Col Thomas Williamson, Capt James Pace, Lt Nealy, Vol Mtd Gunmen
RONEY, John, Pvt, Maj Gen Wm Carroll, Col James Raulston, Capt Henry Hamilton, Inf
RONINE, Samuel, Pvt, Col Wm Lillard, Capt John Roper, E TN Vol Inf
ROOF, George, Pvt, Col T McCrory, Capt Thos K Gordon, Inf; deserted
ROOK, Benjamin, Pvt, Col S Copeland, Capt John Biles, Inf
ROOK, Daniel, Pvt, Col Philip Pipkin, Capt John Strother, Mil
ROOK, Jacob, Pvt, Col A Loury, Capt James Kincaid, Inf
ROOK, John, Pvt, Col R H Dyer, Capt Robt Edmonston, TN Vol Mtd Gunmen
ROOKE, John, Pvt, Col John Cocke, Capt Joseph Price, Inf
ROOKE, Samuel, Pvt, Col John Brown, Capt John Trimble, E TN Mtd Inf
ROOKS, Hezekiah, Pvt, Col Samuel Bunch, Capt S Richardson, Branch Srvce omitted
ROOKS, Savern, Pvt, Col Ewen Allison, Capt Jacob Hoyal, E TN Mil; transferred to Capt Register's Co
ROOKS, Sovereign, Pvt, Col Samuel Bunch, Capt F Register, E TN Mil; joined Hoyal's Co
ROOMS, Joshua, Pvt, Col S Bunch, Capt Geo McPherson, E TN Mil; transferred to Capt Register's Co

ROORK, Samuel, Sgt, Maj Wm Russell, Capt John Trimble, Vol Mtd Gunmen
ROPE, James W, Sgt, Col Samuel Bunch, Capt Isaac Williams, E TN Mil
ROPE, James W, Sgt, Regt Commander omitted, Capt Isaac Williams, E TN Mil
ROPER, Charles, Pvt, Regt Commander omitted, Capt Jas Haggard, Mtd Gunmen
ROPER, David N, 4 Cpl, Col John Cocke, Capt Richard Crunk, Inf
ROPER, David, Pvt, Col Samuel Bunch, Capt Edward Buchanan, E TN Mil
ROPER, Ewel, Pvt, Col Samuel Bunch, Capt Edward Buchanan, E TN Mil
ROPER, George W, Pvt, Col A Cheatham, Capt Chas Johnson, Inf
ROPER, John, Cpl, Col Thomas Williamson, Capt A Metcalf, Vol Mtd Gunmen
RORACK (ROWARK), Owen, Pvt, Col R H Dyer, Maj Wm Russell, Capt Wm Russell, TN Vol Mtd Gunmen
RORK, James, Pvt, Col Wm Johnson, Capt Benj Powell, E TN Mil
ROSE, Alexander, Pvt, Col R H Dyer, Capt Joseph Williams, Vol Mtd Gunmen
ROSE, Alexander, Pvt, Lt Col L Hammond, Capt James Craig, Inf
ROSE, Basil (Bazzel), Pvt, Col John Cocke, Capt Richard Crunk, Inf
ROSE, Benjamin, Pvt, Col Wm Johnston, Capt Joseph Kirk, Mil; never appeared
ROSE, Bennet, Sgt, Maj Wm Russell, Capt Wm Chism, Vol Mtd Gunmen
ROSE, Daniel, Pvt, Col Wm Hall, Capt Brice Martin, Vol Inf
ROSE, Elisha, Pvt, Col Edwin Booth, Capt Porter, Drafted Mil
ROSE, James, Pvt, Col Philip Pipkin, Capt John Strother, Mil
ROSE, James, Pvt, Col Wm Higgins, Capt John B Cheatham, Mtd Riflemen
ROSE, James, Pvt, Maj Wm Russell, Capt Fleman Hodges, Vol Mtd Gunmen
ROSE, John, Pvt, Col Samuel Bunch, Capt David G Vance, E TN Mtd Inf
ROSE, Joseph, Pvt, Col John Wynne, Capt Butler, Inf; deserted
ROSE, Joseph, Pvt, Col Thos Williamson, Capt A Metcalf, Vol Mtd Gunmen
ROSE, Joseph, Pvt, Maj Wm Woodfolk, Capt Abraham Dudney, Inf; also under Capt John Sutton
ROSE, Little B, Pvt, Col John Cocke, Capt John Weakley, Inf
ROSE, Martin, Pvt, Col John Cocke, Capt Richard Crunk, Inf; d 2-14-1815
ROSE, McKinsey, Pvt, Col Samuel Bunch, Capt Jno Hawk, E TN Mil
ROSE, N B, Brig QM, Maj Gen Andrew Jackson, no other information
ROSE, Neel B, Pvt, Col John Coffee, Capt Blackman Coleman, Cav; promoted to QM

## Enlisted Men, War of 1812

ROSE, Richard, Dmr, Col John Cocke, Capt Richard Crunk, Inf
ROSE, Richard, Pvt, Col A Loury, Capt Gabriel Martin, Inf
ROSE, Washington, Pvt, Maj Wm Woodfolk, Capt James Turner, Inf
ROSE, Wilie, Pvt, Col A Loury, Capt Gabriel Martin, Inf
ROSE, William, Pvt, Col Newton Cannon, Capt James Walter, Mtd Riflemen
ROSE, William, Pvt, Col R H Dyer, Capt Bethel Allen, Vol Mtd Gunmen
ROSEBOROUGH, Samuel, Pvt, Col Wm Metcalf, Capt Wm Sitton, Mil Inf
ROSS, Abraham, Sgt, Col R C Napier, Capt Thos Gray, Mil Inf
ROSS, Alex, Pvt, Col Newton Cannon, Capt David Hogan, Mtd Gunmen
ROSS, Alexander, 3 Cpl, Regt Commander omitted, Capt Jas Haggard, Mtd Gunmen
ROSS, Allen, Pvt, Col Newton Cannon, Capt John Harpole, Mtd Gunmen
ROSS, Allen, Pvt, Regt Commander omitted, Capt Gray, Inf
ROSS, Charles, Pvt, Col John Cocke, Capt James Gray, Inf; promoted to Cpl
ROSS, Charles, Pvt, Regt Commander omitted, Capt Gray, Inf
ROSS, Daniel, Pvt, Col A Loury, Capt Gabriel Martin, Inf
ROSS, Ezekiel, 4 Sgt, Col R C Napier, Capt James McMurray, Mil Inf
ROSS, Francis, Pvt, Col Newton Cannon, Capt John Hamby, Mtd Riflemen
ROSS, Francis, Pvt, Regt Commander omitted, Capt Geo Smith, Spies
ROSS, George, Cpl, Col Edward Bradley, Capt Harry L Douglass, Vol Inf
ROSS, George, Pvt, Col Thomas Benton, Capt Henry L Douglass, Vol Inf
ROSS, Hugh P, Pvt, Col S Copeland, Capt Wm Douglas, Inf
ROSS, Hugh P, Pvt, Col Thomas H Benton, Capt Benjamin Hewitt, Vol Inf
ROSS, Hugh R, Pvt, Col Thomas H Benton, Capt Robert Cannon, Inf; transferred from Capt Hewet's Co
ROSS, Issac M, Cpl, Col Newton Cannon, Co Commander omitted, Mtd Riflemen
ROSS, Issac W, Pvt, Col Thomas H Benton, Capt John Howell, Vol Inf
ROSS, Issac W, Pvt, Col Thomas W Benton, Capt Newton Cannon, Inf; transferred from Hewett's Co
ROSS, Issac, Pvt, Col Thomas H Benton, Capt C E McEwin, Vol Inf
ROSS, Issac, Pvt, Regt Commander omitted, Capt James Gray, Inf
ROSS, Jacob (Joab), Pvt, Col R C Napier, Capt Early Benson, Mil Inf
ROSS, James F, Pvt, Col Thomas H Williamson, Capt Richard Tate, Vol Mtd Gunmen; transferred from Capt Hewitt's Co
ROSS, James N, Cpl, Col Newton Cannon, Capt Andrew Patterson, Mtd Riflemen
ROSS, James, Pvt, Col Edwin E Booth, Capt Marshall, Drafted Mil
ROSS, James, Pvt, Col Robert Steele, Capt Robert Campbell, Mil Inf
ROSS, James, Pvt, Col Thomas H Benton, Capt Benjamin Hewett, Vol Inf
ROSS, James, Pvt, Col Thomas H Williamson, Capt Giles Burdette, Vol Mtd Gunmen
ROSS, James, Pvt, Lt Col John Edmondson, Co Commander omitted, Cav
ROSS, James, Sgt, Col Ewin Allison, Capt Jacob Hoyal, E TN Mil
ROSS, Joe, Pvt, Gen Andrew Jackson, Capt James Read, Inf
ROSS, John G, Sgt, Col Edwin E Wear, Capt Rufus Morgan, E TN Vol Inf
ROSS, John, Pvt, Col Ewin Allison, Capt Ewin Allison, Mil; deserted
ROSS, John, Pvt, Col John K Winn, Co Commander omitted, Inf
ROSS, John, Pvt, Col Samuel Wear, Capt Bowman, Mtd Inf; deserted
ROSS, John, Pvt, Col Thomas H Benton, Capt Benjamin Hewett, Vol Inf
ROSS, John, Pvt, Col Wm Johnson, Capt Henry Hunter, E TN Mil
ROSS, John, Pvt, Regt Commander omitted, Capt James Gray, Inf
ROSS, Joseph, Pvt, Col Samuel Wear, Capt James Cole, Vol Inf
ROSS, Joshua, Pvt, Col John Cocke, Capt John Weakley, Inf
ROSS, Little B, Pvt, Col John Cocke, Capt John Weakley, Inf
ROSS, Martin, Pvt, Col Wm Lillard, Capt Thomas Sharpe, 2nd Regt Inf
ROSS, Robert, Pvt, Maj Wm Woodfolk, Capt Mathew Neale, Inf
ROSS, Samuel, Cpl, Col Samuel Bunch, Capt Edward Buchanan, E TN Drafted Mil; transferred from Capt Duncan's Co
ROSS, Samuel, Sgt, Col Samuel Bunch, Capt Joseph Duncan, E TN Drafted Mil; transferred to Capt Buchanan's Co
ROSS, Solomon, Pvt, Regt Commander omitted, Capt James Gray, Inf
ROSS, Theodore, Pvt, Col S Copeland, Capt Moses Thompson, Inf
ROSS, Thomas B, Pvt, Col A Loury, Capt George Sarver, Inf
ROSS, Thomas, Pvt, Regt Commander omitted, Capt John Cowan, Inf
ROSS, Tucker T, Pvt, Col A Loury, Capt John Looney, 2nd Regt W TN Mil
ROSS, Valentine G, Pvt, Col A Loury, Capt George Sarver, Inf
ROSS, William J, Pvt, Col Thomas H Benton, Capt Robert Cannon, Inf; transferred from? Capt Hewett's Co
ROSS, William N, Pvt, Regt Commander omitted, Capt James Gray, Inf
ROSS, William T, Pvt, Col Newton Cannon, Capt Andrew

## Enlisted Men, War of 1812

ROSS, William T, Pvt, Col Thomas H Benton, Capt Benjamin Hewett, Vol Inf
ROSS, William, Pvt, Col A Loury, Capt George Sarver, Inf
ROSS, William, Pvt, Col Ewin Allison, Capt Jacob Hoyal, E TN Mil
ROSS, William, Pvt, Col John Brown, Capt John Chiles, E TN Mtd Inf
ROSS, William, Pvt, Col R C Napier, Capt Early Benson, Mil Inf
ROSSIN, Joseph, Pvt, Col Wm Metcalf, Capt Barbee Collins, Mil Inf
ROSSON, Simeon, Pvt, Col Robert Steele, Capt Richard M Ratton, Mil Inf
ROSSON, William, Cpl, Col Robert Steele, Capt John Chitwood, Mil Inf
ROSSON (ROSSIN), Elisha, Pvt, Col Wm Pillow, Capt Wm Moore, Inf; Regt Co - Lincoln
ROSSOU, Joseph, Pvt, Col A Cheatham, Co Commander omitted, Mtd Inf
ROSSWELL, Miles, Pvt, Col Thos H Benton, Capt Thomas Williamson, Vol Inf
ROTHEWELL, James, Pvt, Col S Bunch, Capt John English, E TN Drafted Mil; joined from Capt Allen's Co
ROTHWELL, James, Pvt, Col Ewin Allison, Capt James Allen, E TN Mil
ROUCE (ROUSE), John, Pvt, Col A Loury, Capt James Kincaid, Inf
ROUDER, Mashack, Pvt, Col Wm Johnson, Capt James R Rogers, E TN Drafted Mil
ROUNDTREE, Tuner, Pvt, Col Newton Cannon, Capt James Walton, Mtd Riflemen
ROUT, John, Pvt, Col Samuel Bunch, Capt Francis Berry, E TN Mil
ROUTH, James, Pvt, Col Samuel Wear, Capt Samuel Bowman, Mtd Inf
ROUTH, Jeremiah, Pvt, Col Samuel Bunch, Capt Isaac Williams, E TN Mil
ROUTH, Jeremiah, Pvt, Col Samuel Bunch, Capt Jno English, E TN Drafted Mil; joined from Capt Williams Co
ROUTH, Stephen, Pvt, Col Samuel Bunch, Capt Isaac Williams, E TN Mil
ROUTH, Stephen, Pvt, Col Samuel Bunch, Capt Jno Hawk, E TN Mil; joined from Capt Williams Co
ROUTON, Joseph, Pvt, Col Philip Pipkin, Capt Geo Mebane, Mil Inf
ROW, James, Pvt, Col T McCrory, Capt A Willis, Mil Inf
ROW, Mansfield W, Pvt, Maj Wm Woodfolk, Capt Ezekial Ross, Capt McCulley, Inf
ROW, Stephen W, Pvt, Col T McCrory, Capt A Willis, Mil Inf
ROWARK, David, Pvt, Col Wm Lillard, Capt Wm Hamilton, E TN Vol Inf
ROWDEN, Abednego, Pvt, Col Edwin Booth, Capt John McKamey, E TN Mil; deserted
ROWDEN, John, Pvt, Maj Wm Russell, Capt Wm Chism, Vol Mtd Riflemen
ROWDEN, William E, Pvt, Col Wm Johnson, Capt Wm Alexander, Det of E TN Drafted Mil
ROWDIN, Mashack, Pvt, Col Edwin Booth, Capt John McKamey, E TN Mil
ROWE, James, Pvt, Col Wm Metcalf, Capt William Mullen, Mil; d 2-8-1815
ROWE, James, Pvt, Col Wm Metcalf, Capt William Sitton, Mil Inf
ROWE, John, Pvt, Gen Andrew Jackson, Capt Nathan Davis, Inf
ROWE, Joseph, Pvt, Col R C Napier, Capt Early Benson, Mil Inf
ROWLAND, Charles, Pvt, Col Wm Metcalf, Capt Barbee Collins, Mil Inf
ROWLAND, George, 2 Cpl, Maj William Russell, Capt R C Napier, Vol Mtd Gunmen
ROWLAND, George, Cpl, Col N Cannon, Capt Jas Walton, Mtd Riflemen; wounded 11-2-1813 & furloughed
ROWLAND, George, Pvt, Col Robert Dyer, Capt Allen, Vol Mtd Gunmen
ROWLAND, James, Pvt, Col Robert Dyer, Capt Allen, Vol Mtd Gunmen
ROWLAND, John, Pvt, Brig Gen Thos Washington, Capt Jno Crawford, Inf
ROWLAND, John, Pvt, Col S Bunch, Capt Jno Houk, E TN Mil
ROWLAND, Richardson, Pvt, Col Jno Coffee, Capt Edward Bradley, Vol Cav
ROWLAND, William, Pvt, Maj William Carroll, Capt Daniel Bradford & Capt Dillahanty, Vol Inf
ROWLEY, James, Pvt, Lt Col John Edmonson, Co Commander omitted, Cav
ROWLIN, George, Pvt, Col Thos Benton, Capt Geo Caperton, Vol Inf
ROWTON, William D, 2 Sgt, Col Philip Pipkin, Capt Geo Mebane, Mil Inf
ROY, John, Pvt, Col A Cheatham, Capt James Giddins, Inf
ROY, John, Pvt, Col Edward Bradley, Capt Travis Nash, Vol Inf
ROY, John, Pvt, Col N Cannon, Capt Martin, Mtd Gunmen; wounded 11-9-1813 at Talledega and furloughed
ROY, Thomas, 4 Cpl, Col Jno Coffee, Capt Jas Terrell, Vol Cav
ROY, William L, Pvt, Lt Col Richard Napier, Co Commander omitted, Inf
ROY, Willie, Pvt, Regt Commander omitted, Lt James Berry, Mtd Riflemen
ROY, _____, Servant, Col Robert Dyer, TN Vol Mtd Gunmen; private servant to Maj Chas Kavanaugh
ROYAL, George, Pvt, Col S Bayless, Capt Joseph Rich, E TN Inf
ROYAL, James, Pvt, Col S Copeland, Capt Allen Wilkerson, Mil Inf; transferred to the Arty
ROYAL, John, Pvt, Col Phillip Pipkin, Capt John Robertson, Mil Inf
ROYER, Charlie, Pvt, Col Wm Lillard, Capt John Roper, E TN Vol Inf
ROYER, John, Pvt, Col S Bunch, Capt Geo Gregory, E TN Drafted Mil
ROYER, John, Pvt, Col W Johnson, Capt Jas Stewart, E

## Enlisted Men, War of 1812

ROYER, John, Pvt, Col Wm Johnson, Capt Jas Stewart, E TN Mil; d 12-13-1814
ROYSTER, Abraham, Pvt, Col Wm Hall, Capt James Hambleton, Vol Inf
RUCCO, Jacob, Pvt, Col S Bunch, Capt F Register, E TN Mil
RUCKER, Edmond, Pvt, Col Thos Dyer, Capt Jones, Vol Mtd Gunmen
RUCKER, Felix, Pvt, Col Edward Bradley, Capt Travis Nash, Vol Inf
RUCKER, Felix, Pvt, Col Thos Benton, Capt Jas Renshaw, Branch Srvce omitted
RUCKER, Felix, Pvt, Col Wm Hall, Capt Travis Nash, Inf
RUCKER, James, Pvt, Col N Cannon, Capt Thomas Yardley, Mtd Riflemen
RUCKER, Jesse, Pvt, Col S Wear, Capt Geo Gillespie, E TN Vol Inf
RUCKER, Jonathan, Cpl, Col John Cocke, Capt George Barnes, Inf
RUCKER, Pascal, Pvt, Col S Wear, Capt S Bayless, Mtd Inf
RUCKER, S R, Pvt, Col N Cannon, Capt Thomas Yardley, Mtd Riflemen
RUCKER, Samuel, Cpl, Col N Cannon, Capt Thomas Yardley, Mtd Riflemen
RUCKER, William, Pvt, Col William Lillard, Capt Thomas Sharpe, Inf
RUDD, Elijah, Pvt, Maj John Childs, Capt John Stephens, E TN Vol Mtd Inf
RUDD, James, Pvt, Col Alexander Loury, Capt John Looney, W TN Inf
RUDD, William, Pvt, Col S Wear, Capt Geo Gillespie, E TN Vol Inf
RUDDER, Robert, Pvt, Col S Bunch, Capt F Register, E TN Mil
RUDDER, Samuel, Pvt, Col William Johnson, Capt Christopher Cook, E TN Mil
RUDDER, Samuel, Pvt, Col William Johnson, Capt Joseph Kirk, Mil
RUDOLPH, Elijah, Pvt, Regt Commander omitted, Capt Jas Cowan, Inf
RUDOLPH, Elijah, Pvt, Regt Commander omitted, Capt Jas Haggard, Mtd Gunmen
RUDOLPH, Fredrick, Pvt, Col Robert Dyer, Capt Robert Edmonston, TN Vol Gunmen
RUDOLPH, Fredrick, Pvt, Lt Col Henry Bryan, Co Commander omitted, Inf
RUDOLPH, John, Pvt, Brig Gen Johnson, Capt Allen, Mil Inf
RUDOLPH, Michael, Pvt, Lt Col Henry Bryan, Co Commander omitted, Inf
RUDOLPH, Michael, Pvt, Regt Commander omitted, Capt Jas Cowan, Inf
RUDOLPH, Peter, Pvt, Brig Gen Johnston, Capt Allen, Mil Inf
RUDOPH, Elijah, Pvt, Lt Col Henry Bryan, Co Commander omitted, Inf
RUFF, Joseph, Sgt, Col John Alcorn, Capt Edward Bradley, Vol Cav
RUFFIN, Ginn, Pvt, Lt Col Leroy Hammonds, Capt Jas Craig, Inf; deserted
RULE, Aaron, Pvt, Col Alex Loury, Capt Geo Sarver, Inf
RULE, Henry, Pvt, Col Alex Loury, Capt Geo Sarver, Inf
RULE, John, Pvt, Col Aex Loury, Capt Geo Sarver, Inf
RULE, Solomon, Pvt, Col N T Perkins, Capt Geo Eliot, Mil Inf
RULEMAN, Jacob, Pvt, Maj Wm Woodfolk, Capt E Ross, Inf
RULER, Jacob, Pvt, Col Jno Brown, Capt Wm White, E TN Mil Inf
RUMINER, Daniel, Pvt, Col Thomas Williamson, Capt James Pace, Lt James Nealy, Vol Mtd Gunmen
RUMNIOR, John, Pvt, Col Thos Benton, Capt I Renshaw, Vol Inf
RUNION, Isaac, Pvt, Col Jno Brown, Capt Wm Christian, E TN Mil Inf
RUNIONS, Riah, Pvt, Col Saml Bunch, Capt S Dobkins, E Tn Draft Mil
RUNNALDS, Benjamin, Pvt, Col P Pipkin, Capt H M Newlin, Mil Inf
RUNNALDS (RUNNEL), John, Pvt, Col Wm Lillard, Capt Robt McCalpin, E Tn Inf
RUNYAN, Joseph, Cpl, Col E Booth, Capt Porter, Drafted Mil
RUPHIN (RURHIN), Philip, Pvt, Maj John Chiles, Capt Chas Conway, E TN Mtd Gunmen
RUPPELL, John, Pvt, Gen Andrew Jackson, Capt Nathan Davis, Inf
RUSH, Churchel, Sgt, Col Samuel Bayless, Capt Joseph Goodson, E TN Mil
RUSH, John, Pvt, Col E Booth, Capt Alex Biggs, Inf
RUSHING, Abel, Pvt, Col John Cocke, Capt James Gray, Inf
RUSHING, Daniel, Pvt, Col Jno Coffee, Capt M Molton, Cav
RUSHING, David, Pvt, Lt Col Jno Edmonson, Co Commander omitted, Cav
RUSHING, Dennis, Cpl, Col Jno Cocke, Capt Jas Gray, Inf
RUSHING, John, Pvt, Maj Wm Russell, Capt I Williams, 1 Regt TN Vol Gunmen
RUSHING, Mark, Pvt, Regt Commander omitted, Capt J Askew, Inf
RUSHING, Mathew, Pvt, Col John Cocke, Capt James Gault, Inf
RUSHING, Matthew, Pvt, Col R H Dyer, Capt E D Dickson, TN Mtd Vol Gunmen; no svce performed
RUSHING, Phillip, Pvt, Col John Brown, Capt Wm U Neilson, E TN Vol Mil
RUSHING, Richard, Pvt, Col Jno Coffee, Capt M Molton, Cav
RUSHING, Richard, Pvt, Regt Commander omitted, Capt Joseph Williams, Mil Cav
RUSHING, Thomas, Pvt, Col Alex Loury, Cap G Martin, Inf
RUSHING, Willes, Pvt, Col John Cocke, Capt James Gray, Inf
RUSHION, Philip, Pvt, Maj Jno Childs, Capt Jas Cummings, E Tn Mtd Gunmen; Regt from Roane Co
RUSK, Robert, Pvt, Col John Coffee, Capt John Byrn,

## Enlisted Men, War of 1812

Cav; deserted
RUSS, Joseph, Pvt, Col Thos Benton, Capt Geo Gibbs, Vol Inf
RUSS, Josiah, Pvt, Col Thos Benton, Capt Geo Gibbs, Vol Inf
RUSSE, James, Cpl, Col Ewen Allison, Capt James Allen, E TN Mil
RUSSEL, Andrew, Pvt, Col Wm Johnson, Capt Jas Stewart, E TN Mil
RUSSEL, Henry, Pvt, Col A Cheatham, Capt Chas Johnson, Inf
RUSSEL, Henry, Pvt, Col Thos Benton, Capt Robert Cannon, Inf
RUSSEL, Henry, Pvt, Lt Col L Hammond, Capt Thos Wells, Inf; also under Col A Loury
RUSSEL, Henry, Pvt, Regt Commander omitted, Capt James Cowan, Inf
RUSSEL, Jeremiah, Pvt, Col A Loury, Lt Col L Hammond, Capt Thomas Wells, Inf
RUSSELL, Aaron, Pvt, Col Ewen Allison, Capt Jos Everett, E TN Mil; transferred to Capt Griffin
RUSSELL, Aaron, Pvt, Col S Bunch, Capt Jones Griffin, E TN Drafted Mil; joined from Capt Everett's Co
RUSSELL, Aaron, Pvt, Col Wm Lillard, Capt Geo Keyes, E TN Inf
RUSSELL, Abraham, Pvt, Commanders & Branch Srvce omitted; d 11-23-1813 at Talledega
RUSSELL, Absolem, Pvt, Col Thos Benton, Capt Geo Caperton, Vol Inf
RUSSELL, Alexander, Pvt, Col Jno Coffee, Capt Robert Jetton, Cav
RUSSELL, Alexander, Pvt, Col John Alcorn, Capt Robert Jetton, Vol Cav
RUSSELL, Andrew, Pvt, Col Wm Johnson, Capt Jas Stuart, E TN Drafted Mil
RUSSELL, Andrew, Pvt, Maj John Chiles, Capt Chas Conway, E TN Mtd Gunmen; Regimental Co Knox
RUSSELL, Arnold, Pvt, Regt Commander omitted, Capt John Gordon, Branch Srvce omitted
RUSSELL, Arnold, Pvt, Regt Commander omitted, Capt Robert Evans, Mtd Spies
RUSSELL, Benjamin, Pvt, Col Ewen Allison, Capt H McCray, E TN Mil; transferred to Capt Register Co
RUSSELL, Benjamin, Pvt, Col S Bunch, Capt F Register, E TN Mil; joined from Capt McCrea's Co
RUSSELL, Benjamin, Pvt, Col Samuel Bayless, Capt J B Bacon, E TN Mil
RUSSELL, David, Pvt, Col Thos McCrory, Capt Wm Dooly, Inf
RUSSELL, Edmond, Private Servant, Maj Wm Russell, Separate Bn of TN Vol Mtd Gunmen; Servant to Maj Russell
RUSSELL, Edmond, Pvt, Maj Wm Russell, Capt Jno Cowan, Vol Mtd Gunmen
RUSSELL, Edward, Pvt, Col Robert Steele, Capt Cheetwood, Mil Inf
RUSSELL, Edward, Pvt, Col Wm Lillard, Capt Robert Maloney, E TN Vol Inf
RUSSELL, Edward, Pvt, Regt Commander omitted, Capt Jas Cowan, Inf
RUSSELL, Elain, Pvt, Col John Wynne, Capt John Porter, Inf
RUSSELL, Elam, Pvt, Col J K Wynne, Capt Abel Willson, Inf; attached to Capt Porter's Co
RUSSELL, Elam, Pvt, Col Wm Metcalf, Capt O Waller, Mil Inf
RUSSELL, Elijah, Pvt, Col Samuel Bayless, Capt Solomon Hendrix, E TN Mil
RUSSELL, Emmett, Pvt, no other information
RUSSELL, George, 4 Sgt, Gen A Jackson, Capt Wm Russell, Mtd Spies
RUSSELL, George, Pvt, Col Newton Cannon, Capt Francis Jones, Mtd Riflemen
RUSSELL, George, Pvt, Col Samuel Bunch, Capt Daniel Yarnell, E TN Mil
RUSSELL, George, Pvt, Col Wm Hall, Capt Abraham Bledsoe, Vol Inf
RUSSELL, George, Pvt, Maj John Chiles, Capt Chas Conway, E TN Mtd Gunmen; Regimental Co - Knox
RUSSELL, George, Pvt, Maj Wm Russell, Capt Geo Michie, Vol Mtd Gunmen
RUSSELL, George, Pvt, Regt Commander omitted, Capt Jas Cowan, Inf
RUSSELL, Henry, Pvt, Col Wm Pillow, Capt Geo Caperton, Inf
RUSSELL, Henry, Pvt, Col Wm Pillow, Lt Mason, Vol Inf
RUSSELL, Isaac, Pvt, no other information
RUSSELL, Isam jr, Pvt, Col R H Dyer, Maj Wm Russell, Capt Wm Russell, Vol Mtd Gunmen
RUSSELL, Isham, Cpl, Col John Wynne, Capt John Porter, Inf
RUSSELL, Isham, Sgt, Col R H Dyer, Maj Wm Russell, Capt Wm Russell, Vol Mtd Gunmen
RUSSELL, James H, Pvt, Maj Cooper, Co Commander omitted, Mtd Riflemen
RUSSELL, James R, Pvt, Brig Gen Wm Johnson, Capt Robt Carson, Inf
RUSSELL, James, 3 Sgt, Col William Pillow, Capt William J Smith, Vol Inf
RUSSELL, James, Pvt, Col A Loury, Lt Col L Hammons, Capt Arahel Rains, Inf
RUSSELL, James, Pvt, Col R H Dyer, Capt James White, Vol Mtd Gunmen; d 3-1-1815
RUSSELL, James, Pvt, Col R H Dyer, Capt Robert Evans, Vol Mtd Gunmen
RUSSELL, James, Pvt, Maj Wm Russell, Capt Geo Mitchie, Vol Mtd Gunmen
RUSSELL, James, Pvt, Regt Commander omitted, Capt Robert Evans, Mtd Spies
RUSSELL, James, Sgt, Col Thos Benton, Capt Wm J Smith, Vol Inf
RUSSELL, James, Sgt, Regt Commander omitted, Capt Smith, Vol Inf
RUSSELL, Jeremiah, Pvt, Col John Wynne, Capt John Porter, Inf
RUSSELL, Jeremiah, Pvt, Col John Wynne, Capt Wm Willson, Inf; attached to Capt Porter Co
RUSSELL, John jr, Pvt, Col John Brown, Capt Jesse G Reany, Mtd Gunmen

## Enlisted Men, War of 1812

RUSSELL, John, Cpl, Col John Brown, Capt Jesse G Reany, Mtd Gunmen
RUSSELL, John, Pvt, Col John Brown, Capt James McKamey, E TN Mtd Gunmen
RUSSELL, John, Pvt, Col R H Dyer, Maj Wm Russell, Capt Wm Russell, Vol Mtd Gunmen
RUSSELL, John, Pvt, Col Thos Benton, Capt Geo Caperton, Vol Inf; out of state
RUSSELL, John, Pvt, Col Wm Johnson, Capt Joseph Scott, E TN Drafted Mil; d 12-25-1814
RUSSELL, John, Pvt, Regt Commander omitted, Capt Jas Cowan, Inf
RUSSELL, Lanceford, Pvt, Col Wm Pillow, Capt Geo Caperton, Inf
RUSSELL, Lemuel, Pvt, Lt Col L Hammond, Capt James Craig, Inf
RUSSELL, Lewis, Pvt, Col R H Dyer, Maj Wm Russell, Capt Wm Russell, Vol Mtd Gunmen
RUSSELL, Lewis, Pvt, Maj W Russell, Capt John Trimble, Vol Mtd Gunmen; transferred to Capt Wm Russell's Co
RUSSELL, Lewis, Pvt, Regt Commander omitted, Capt Jas Cowan, Inf
RUSSELL, Major, Pvt, Col Ewen Allison, Capt Joseph Everett, E TN Mil; transferred to Capt Griffin Co
RUSSELL, Major, Pvt, Col Samuel Bunch, Capt Jones Griffin, E TN Drafted Mil; joined from Capt Everett's Co
RUSSELL, Majro?, Pvt, Col Wm Lillard, Capt Geo Keyes, E TN Inf
RUSSELL, Martin, Pvt, Col Ewen Allison, Capt Adam Winsell, E TN Drafted Mil
RUSSELL, Martin, Pvt, Col Samuel Bunch, Capt F Register, E TN Mil
RUSSELL, Moses sr, Pvt, Col John Brown, Capt James McKamey, E TN Mtd Gunmen
RUSSELL, Moses, Pvt, Col Ewen Allison, Capt Joseph Everett, E TN Mil; transferred to Capt Griffin Co
RUSSELL, Moses, Pvt, Col John Brown, Capt James McKamey, E TN Mtd Gunmen
RUSSELL, Moses, Pvt, Col S Bunch, Capt James Griffin, E TN Drafted Mil; joined from Capt Everett's Co
RUSSELL, Moses, Pvt, Col Wm Johnson, Capt Elihu Milliken, 3rd Regt E TN Mil
RUSSELL, Nathan, Pvt, Col A Loury, Lt Col L Hammond, Capt Arahel Rains, Inf
RUSSELL, Nicholas, Pvt, Col William Johnson, Capt Henry Hunter, E TN Mil
RUSSELL, Robert, Pvt, Col Jno Coffee, Capt Robert Jetton, Cav
RUSSELL, Robert, Pvt, Col John Alcorn, Capt Robert Jetton, Vol Cav
RUSSELL, Robert, Pvt, Col William Lillard, Capt Robert Maloney, E TN Vol Inf
RUSSELL, Samuel, 4 Cpl, Col William Pillow, Capt Geo Caperton, Inf
RUSSELL, Samuel, Pvt, Col Thomas Benton, Capt Geo Caperton, Inf
RUSSELL, Seth, Pvt, Col A Cheatham, Capt Charles Johnson, Inf
RUSSELL, Thomas, Pvt, Col N Cannon, Capt David Hogan, Mtd Gunmen
RUSSELL, Thomas, Pvt, Col S Bayless, Capt Solomon Hendrick, E TN Mil
RUSSELL, Thomas, Pvt, Col S Wear, Capt Jesse Cole, Vol Inf
RUSSELL, Thomas, Pvt, Col William Lillard, Capt Robert Maloney, E TN Vol Inf
RUSSELL, William sr, Pvt, Col Thos Benton, Capt Geo Caperton, Inf
RUSSELL, William, Pvt, Col Edwin Booth, Capt John Lewis, E TN Mil
RUSSELL, William, Pvt, Col John Brown, Capt Wm White, E TN Mil Inf
RUSSELL, William, Pvt, Col N Cannon, Capt Thomas Yardley, Mtd Riflemen
RUSSELL, William, Pvt, Col S Bayless, Capt Hale, E TN Mil
RUSSELL, William, Pvt, Col S Copeland, Capt John Holshouser, Inf; transferred to the Arty
RUSSELL, William, Pvt, Col S Wear, Capt Geo Gillespie, E TN Vol Inf
RUSSELL, William, Pvt, Col Thos Benton, Capt Geo Caperton, Inf
RUSSELL, William, Pvt, Col Thos Benton, Capt Geo Caperton, Vol Inf
RUSSELL, William, Pvt, Col Thos Benton, Capt Geo Caperton, Vol Inf; two Wm Russell's on same roll
RUSSELL, William, Pvt, Col William Lillard, Capt Wm McLin, E TN Inf
RUSSELL, William, Pvt, Col William Pillow, Capt Geo Caperton, Inf
RUSSELL, William, Pvt, Regt Commander omitted, Capt James Cowan, Mtd Inf
RUSSELL, William, Pvt, Regt Commander omitted, Capt Joel Parrish, Branch Srvce omitted
RUSSELL, William, Sgt, Col Robert Dyer, Maj William Russell, Capt William Russell, Vol Mtd Gunmen
RUSSELL, York, Private Servant, Maj Wm Russell, Separate Bn of TN Vol Mtd Gunmen; Servant to Maj Russell
RUSSEY, John, Pvt, Col Thos Benton, Capt Geo Caperton, Inf; out of state
RUSSIAN, John P, Pvt, Col Phillip Pipkin, Capt Peter Searcy, Mil Inf
RUSSLY, John, 2 Sgt, Gen Jackson, Capt William Russell, Mtd Spies
RUST, Jerry, Pvt, Gen Andrew Jackson, Capt Joel Parrish, Arty
RUST, William, Pvt, Col Wm Metcalf, Capt Bird Hurt, Mil Inf
RUST (RUSK), Robert, Pvt, Col John Coffee, Capt D Smith, Vol Cav
RUTH, Isaac, Pvt, Maj John Childs, Capt Daniel Price, E TN Vol Mtd Inf
RUTHERFORD, Benjamin D, Sgt, Col Robert Dyer, Capt Robert Edmonson, TN Vol Mtd Gunmen
RUTHERFORD, Benjamin, Pvt, Col John Brown, Capt Chas Levin, E TN Vol Mtd Inf
RUTHERFORD, Benjamin, Pvt, Col William Johnson, Capt Christopher Cook, E TN Mil
RUTHERFORD, Berryman, Pvt, Col William Johnson,

*Enlisted Men, War of 1812*

Capt Joseph Kirk, Mil
RUTHERFORD, Charles, Pvt, Col S Bunch, Capt Inman, E TN Vol Mtd Inf
RUTHERFORD, Ellett, Pvt, Col S Bunch, Capt F Register, E TN Mil
RUTHERFORD, James, 6 Cpl, Col Wm Johnson, Capt Elihu Milliken, 3rd Regt E TN Mil
RUTHERFORD, James, Pvt, Col Ewin Allison, Capt John Baskerville, Vol Inf
RUTHERFORD, James, Pvt, Col N T Perkins, Capt Mathew Johnson, Mil Inf
RUTHERFORD, James, Pvt, Col Thomas Bunch, Capt Wm Jobe, E TN Vol Mtd Inf
RUTHERFORD, James, Pvt, Maj John Chiles, Capt Daniel Price, E TN Vol Mtd Inf
RUTHERFORD, John, Pvt, Col John Alcorn, Capt John Baskerville, Vol Inf; wounded 11-9-1813 & on furlough
RUTHERFORD, John, Pvt, Col John Cocke, Capt John Weakley, Inf
RUTHERFORD, John, Pvt, Col John K Wynn, Capt Bayless E Prince, Inf
RUTHERFORD, John, Pvt, Col Samuel Bunch, Capt John Inman, E TN Vol Mtd Inf
RUTHERFORD, Joseph, Pvt, Col S Bunch, Capt N Gibbs, E TN Drafted Mil; transferred to Capt Englishman's Co
RUTHERFORD, Joseph, Pvt, Col Samuel Bunch, Capt James Penny, E TN Mtd Inf
RUTHERFORD, Joseph, Pvt, Col Samuel Bunch, Capt Joseph Duncan, E TN Drafted Mil; joined from Capt Gibbs Co
RUTHERFORD, Joseph, Pvt, Col Wm Johnson, Capt Elihu Millikin, 3rd Regt E TN Mil
RUTHERFORD, Joseph, Pvt, Regt Commander omitted, Capt Joseph Duncan & Capt Samuel Bunch, E TN Drafted Mil
RUTHERFORD, Mark, 3 Sgt, Col Samuel Wear, Capt Daniel Price, E TN Vol Inf
RUTHERFORD, Rhadford, Pvt, Regt Commander omitted, Capt Thomas Gray, Inf
RUTHERFORD, Robert, Pvt, Col A Loury, Capt Gabriel Martin, Inf
RUTHERFORD, Robert, Pvt, Col Robert Steele, Capt James Shenault, Mil Inf
RUTHERFORD, Samuel M, Sgt, Col James Raulston, Capt Elijah Haynie, Inf
RUTHERFORD, Samuel, Pvt, Col S Bunch, Capt Daniel Yarnell, E TN Mil
RUTHERFORD, Thomas, Pvt, Col A Loury, Capt James Kincaid, Inf
RUTHERFORD, Thomas, Pvt, Col John Brown, Capt James Preston, Regt E TN Mil Inf
RUTHERFORD, William, Pvt, Col S Bunch, Capt N Gibbs, E TN Drafted Mil; transferred to Capt Duncan Co
RUTHERFORD, William, Pvt, Col Wm Johnson, Capt Wm Alexander, Detachment of E TN Drafted Mil
RUTLEDGE, Alexander, Pvt, Col Robert Steele, Capt Jas Bennett, Mil Inf
RUTLEDGE, Alexander, Pvt, Col S Copeland, Capt Moses Thompson, Inf
RUTLEDGE, Benjamin, Pvt, Col Wm Metcalf, Capt Hill & Capt Cunningham, Mil Inf
RUTLEDGE, Charles, Pvt, Col John Winn, Capt Bailey Butler, Inf
RUTLEDGE, Davis, Pvt, Brig Gen Thomas Johnson, Capt Robert Carson, Inf
RUTLEDGE, Elijah, Pvt, Col Jas Raulston, Capt Chas Wade, Inf
RUTLEDGE, Elijah, Pvt, Col Thos Benton, Capt Henry Douglas, Vol Inf
RUTLEDGE, Henry, Pvt, Maj Wm Woodfolk, Capt Abraham Dudney, Inf
RUTLEDGE, John, Pvt, Col John Winn, Capt Bailey Butler, Inf; transferred to Pack Horse Guards
RUTLEDGE, Robert, Pvt, Maj William Woodfolk, Capt James Neil, Inf
RUTLEDGE, Samuel J, Pvt, Col Thomas H Benton, Capt Benj Reynolds, Vol Inf
RUTLEDGE, Samuel J, Pvt, Col Thos Benton, Capt John Reynolds, Vol Inf
RUTLEDGE, Samuel, Pvt, Col T McCrory, Capt William Dooly, Inf
RUTLEDGE, Samuel, Pvt, Gen Roberts, Co Commander omitted, Mtd Rangers
RUTLEDGE, William, Pvt, Col A Cheatham, Capt Wm Johnson, Inf
RUTLEDGE, William, Pvt, Col T McCrory, Capt Wm Dooley, Inf
RUTLEDGE, William, Pvt, Col Wm Lillard, Capt George Keyes, E TN Inf; appointed Regt QM
RUTLEDGE, William, QM, Col Wm Lillard, E TN Vol Mil
RYAN, Abner, Pvt, Col S Bunch, Capt S Richardson, E TN Drafted Mil
RYAN, Fuller, Pvt, Col Samuel Bayless, Capt Joseph Rich, E TN Inf
RYAN, Fuller, Pvt, Col Wm Lillard, Capt Zacheus Copeland, E TN Vol Inf; deserted
RYAN, John, Pvt, Col Wm Johnston, Capt Joseph Kirk, Mil
RYAN, John, Pvt, Regt Commander omitted, Capt John Cowan, Inf
RYAN, Joseph, Pvt, Col Newton Cannon, Capt Ota Cantrell, W TN Mtd Inf
RYAN, Joseph, Pvt, Col Philip Pipkin, Capt John Robertson, Mil Inf
RYBOUR, Samuel H D, Pvt, Col John Coffee, Capt David Smith, Vol Cav; promoted to Sgt
RYBOURNE, James H, Pvt, Col John Coffee, Capt John W Byrn, Cav
RYBOURNE, Samuel H D, Pvt, Col John Edmondson, Co Commander omitted, Cav
RYBURN, Samuel H P, Pvt, Col Wm Hall, Capt James Hambleton, Vol Inf
RYCHARD, George, Pvt, Regt Commander omitted, Capt Wm McLin, E TN Inf
RYE, Benjamin, Pvt, Col R C Napier, Capt Edward Neblett, Mil Inf
RYE, George W, Pvt, Col James Raulston, Capt Elijah Haynie, Inf

## Enlisted Men, War of 1812

RYE, Solomon, Pvt, Col R C Napier, Capt Edward Neblett, Mil Inf

RYEN, Reuben, Pvt, Col Philip Pipkin, Capt John Robertson, Mil Inf; deserted

RYLAND (RILAND), John, Pvt, Col Wm Johnson, Capt Andrew Lawson, E TN Drafted Mil; substitute for Jos Shiel

RYLEY, Joseph, Pvt, Col N T Perkins, Capt Mathew Patterson, Vol Mtd Inf

RYMAL, Jacob, Pvt, Col S Bunch, Capt Francis Register, E TN Mil

RYNEHART, Jacob, Pvt, Col Wm Hall, Capt James Hambleton, Vol Inf

SADDLER, Caliborn, Pvt, Col Philip Pipkin, Capt David Smith, Inf; deserted

SADLER, George, Pvt, Col John Alcorn, Capt John Winston, Mtd Riflemen

SADLER, Henry, 1 Lt, Col James Raulston, Capt Mathew Cowan, Inf

SADLER, Thomas, Pvt, Col Wm Metcalf, Capt Andrew Patterson, Mil Inf; d 2-8-1815

SAFFELL, John, Pvt, Col Edwin Booth, Capt Samuel Thompson, Mil

SAFFLE, John, Pvt, Col Samuel Bunch, Capt Joseph Duncan, E TN Drafted Mil; joined from Capt Buchanan's Co

SAFFORD, Isham, Pvt, Col T McCrory, Capt Isaac Patton, Mil Inf; deserted

SAFTON, Miles, Pvt, Regt Commander omitted, Capt Gray, Inf

SAGRLY, Joseph, Pvt, Col Wm Pillow, Capt James McFerrin, Inf; deserted

SAILING, Daniel, Pvt, Col Wm Metcalf, Capt Andrew Patteson, Mil Inf

SAILING, John, Pvt, Col Wm Metcalf, Capt Andrew Patterson, Mil Inf

SAILOR, Daniel, Pvt, Brig Gen Wm Johnson, Capt Robt Carson, Inf; discharged for want of arms

SAILOR, William, Dmr, Col Samuel Bayless, Capt Joseph Goodson, E TN Mil

SALES, John, Pvt, Maj Wm Russell, Capt Wm Chism, Vol Mtd Riflemen

SALESBERRY, Isaac, Pvt, Col Philip Pipkin, Capt James Blakemore, Mil Inf

SALESBURY, James, Pvt, Col Wm Pillow, Capt C E McEwen, Vol Inf

SALEY (SAILING), Jacob, Pvt, Col A Loury, Lt Col L Hammond, Capt Thos Delaney, Inf; enlisted in the U S Service

SALINIS, William, Pvt, Col Wm Johnson, Capt Henry Hunter, E TN Mil

SALISBURY, James, 2 Sgt, Col A Cheatham, Capt James Giddins, Inf

SALISBURY, James, Cpl, Maj Wm Carroll, Capt Lewis Dillahunty & Capt Daniel Bradford, Vol Inf; promoted to 5 Sgt

SALISBURY, James, Pvt, Regt Commander omitted, Capt D Mason, Cav

SALMON, John W, Sgt, Col Philip Pipkin, Capt John Robertson, Mil Inf

SALMONS, William, Pvt, Col Wm Johnson, Capt Shockley, E TN Mil

SALMONS (SAMMONS), Robert, Pvt, Col Philip Pipkin, Capt David Smith, Inf

SALMONS (SAMMONS), Robert, Pvt, Col Philip Pipkin, Capt Geo Smith, Inf

SALVAGE, Preston, Pvt, Col Edward Bradley, Capt John Kennedy, Riflemen; AWOL

SAMES, John, Pvt, Col Samuel Bayless, Capt James Landen, E TN Mil

SAMMONS, William, Pvt, Col Wm Lillard, Capt Thos Sharpe, 2nd Regt Inf

SAMONS, Robert, Pvt, Col Philip Pipkin, Capt Wm Mackay, Mil Inf

SAMPLE, John, Pvt, Col Samuel Wear, Capt John Bayless, Mtd Inf

SAMPLE, William, Pvt, Regt Commander omitted, Capt Mason, Cav

SAMPLES, Alexander, Pvt, Col Ewen Allison, Capt James Allen, E TN Mil

SAMPLES, Charles, Pvt, Col Edwin Booth, Capt Alexander Biggs, Inf

SAMPLES, David, Pvt, Col William Lillard, Capt Robert McCalpin, E TN Inf

SAMPLES, William, Pvt, Col Samuel Wear, Capt Rufus Morgan, E TN Vol Inf

SAMPSON, Ephraim, Pvt, Col T McCrory, Capt Isaac Patton, Mil Inf

SAMPSON, George, Forage Master, Maj Gen Wm Carroll, Co Commander omitted, TN Mil

SAMPSON, George, Pvt, Col N T Perkins, Capt Geo Eliot, Mil Inf

SAMPSON, Jesse, Pvt, Maj Gen Wm Carroll, Col James Raulston, Capt Edward Robinson, Inf; d 3-19-1815

SAMPSON, Micajah, Pvt, Maj Gen A Jackson, Col T Williamson, Capt Robert Steele, Vol Mtd Gunmen

SANDERS, Abraham, Pvt, Col Wm Johnson, Capt Joseph Scott, E TN Drafted Mil

SANDERS, Aron, Pvt, Col S Copeland, Capt James Tait, Inf

SANDERS, Aron, Pvt, Col S Copeland, Capt James White, Inf

SANDERS, Daniel, Pvt, Lt Col A Cheatham, Capt Ben Elliott, Mtd Inf

SANDERS, David, Pvt, Col Wm Metcalf, Capt Andrew Patterson, Mil Inf; d 2-25-1815

SANDERS, Eli, Pvt, Col N T Perkins, Capt John Doak, Vol Mtd Gunmen

SANDERS, Elijah, 6 Cpl, Col James Raulston, Capt Henry West, Mil Inf

SANDERS, Elisha, Pvt, Col John Coffee, Capt Blackman Coleman, Cav

SANDERS, Fayette, Cpl, Col Thos Williamson, Capt Thos Scurry, Vol Mtd Gunmen

SANDERS, Gabriel, Pvt, Col A Loury, Capt Gabriel Martin, Inf

SANDERS, Gabriel, Pvt, Col Wm Hall, Capt John Kennedy, Vol Inf

SANDERS, George, Pvt, Col R H Dyer, Capt Robert Evans, Vol Mtd Gunmen

-445

## Enlisted Men, War of 1812

SANDERS, Isaac, Pvt, Col A Loury, Capt Gabriel, Inf
SANDERS, Isaac, Pvt, Col John Wynne, Capt Robt Braden, Inf
SANDERS, Jacob, Pvt, Col James Raulston, Capt Elijah Haynie, Inf
SANDERS, James, Pvt, Col A Cheatham, Capt Richard Benson, Inf
SANDERS, James, Pvt, Col A Loury, Capt Gabriel Martin, Inf
SANDERS, James, Pvt, Col John Coffee, Capt Alexander McKeen, Cav
SANDERS, James, Pvt, Col Wm Metcalf, Capt Andrew Patterson, Mil Inf; d 2-21-1815
SANDERS, John L, Pvt, Col Wm Hall, Capt Brice Martin, Vol Inf
SANDERS, John S, Sgt, Col S Copeland, Capt Allen Wilkinson, Mtd Inf
SANDERS, John, Pvt, Col Samuel Bunch, Capt F Register, E TN Mil
SANDERS, John, Pvt, Col T McCrory, Capt Jno Reynolds, Mil Inf
SANDERS, Jordan, Pvt, Col T Williamson, Capt A Metcalf, Vol Mtd Gunmen
SANDERS, Nathan, Pvt, Col N T Perkins, Capt John Doak, Vol Mtd Gunmen
SANDERS, Reuban, Pvt, Col Thos Benton, Capt Geo Caperton, Vol Inf
SANDERS, Robert, Pvt, Lt Col Archer Cheatham, Capt Ben Elliott, Mtd Inf
SANDERS, Southey, Pvt, Col Wm Metcalf, Capt B Collins, Mil Inf
SANDERS, Thomas, Pvt, Col E Bradley, Capt Brice Martin, Vol Inf; killed 11-9-1813 at Talledega
SANDERS, Thomas, Pvt, Col S Copeland, Capt Jno Biles, Inf
SANDERS, William, Pvt, Col Thos Williamson, Capt Jno Doak & Capt Jno Dobbins, Vol Mtd Gunmen
SANDERS, William, Pvt, Lt Col Archer Cheatham, Capt Ben Elliott, Mtd Inf
SANDERSON, Daniel, Pvt, Col Thos Williamson, Capt Robert Moore, Vol Mtd Gunmen
SANDERSON, Edward, Pvt, Col Thomas Williamson, Capt Thomas Scurry, Vol Mtd Gunmen
SANDERSON, James, Pvt, Col E Bradley, Capt Jas Hambleton, Vol Inf
SANDERSON, James, Pvt, Col Wm Hall, Capt Jas Hambleton, Vol Inf
SANDERSON, John, Pvt, Col Thos Williamson, Capt Robert Moore, Vol Mtd Gunmen
SANDERSON, John, Pvt, Regt Commander omitted, Capt Geo Smith, Spies
SANDERSON, Nathaniel, Pvt, Col Wm Hall, Capt Jas Hambleton, Vol Inf
SANDERSON, Nathaniel, Pvt, Lt Col Henry Bryan, 1 Maj Robert Searcy, Inf
SANDERSON, Robert, Pvt, Col E Bradley, Capt Jas Hambleton, Vol Inf
SANDERSON, Thomas, Pvt, Col E Bradley, Capt Jas Hambleton, Vol Inf
SANDERSON, Thomas, Pvt, Col S Copeland, Capt G W Stell, Mil Inf

SANDFORD, Benjamin, Pvt, Col John Cocke, Capt Jas Gault, Inf; d 4-7-1815
SANDFORD, George, Pvt, Col Jno Cocke, Capt Jas Gault, Inf
SANDLING, William, Pvt, Col Wm Metcalf, Capt B Collins, Mil Inf
SANDORS, James, Pvt, Col Jno Cocke, Capt B Nance, Inf
SANDS, Edmund, Pvt, Col Wm Johnson, Capt Andrew Lawson, E TN Drafted Mil; d 11-30-1814
SANDS, George, Pvt, Col Thos Williamson, Capt B Williams, Vol Mtd Swordsmen; d 1-7-1815
SANDS, Isaac, Pvt, Col Samuel Bayless, Capt J Waddle, E TN Mil
SANDS, John, Pvt, Col S Bunch, Capt Geo McPherson, E TN Mil; joined Capt Register's Co
SANDS, Joseph, Pvt, Col S Bunch, Capt S Richardson, E TN Drafted Mil
SANDS, Thomas, Pvt, Col S Bunch, Capt F Register, E TN Mil; joined from Capt McPherson's Co
SANDS, Thomas, Pvt, Col S Bunch, Capt Geo McPherson, E TN Mil
SANFORD, James, Pvt, Col Jno Cocke, Capt B Nance, Inf
SAPP, Alexander, Pvt, Col E Booth, Capt Miles Vernon, E TN Mil
SAPP, Alexander, Pvt, Col Jno Brown, Capt Wm Christian, E TN Mil Inf
SAPPINGTON, James M, Pvt, Col Jno Brown, Capt Wm D Neilson, E TN Vol Inf; deserted
SAPPINGTON, John, Pvt, Col S Bunch, Capt N Gibbs, E TN Drafted Mil; transferred to Capt Duncan's Co
SAPPINGTON, John, Pvt, Col Samuel Bunch, Capt Jos Duncan, E TN Drafted Mil; joined from Capt Gibb's Co
SAPPINGTON, Thomas, 1 Surgeon's Mate, Col Alexander Loury, Lt Col Leroy Hammons, 2nd Regt W TN Mil
SARGEANT, Johnson, Pvt, Maj Wm Russell, Capt Geo Mitchie, Vol Mtd Gunmen
SARGEANT, William, Pvt, Col Wm Pillow, Capt Geo Caperton, Inf
SARRATE (SARATT), Joseph, Pvt, Col N T Cannon, Capt Ota Cantrell, W TN Mtd Inf
SARRET, Wilson, Pvt, Col Thos Williamson, Capt B Williams, Vol Mtd Gunmen
SARTIN, Isaac, Cpl, Col Jno Brown, Capt Hugh Barton, E TN Mil Inf
SARTIN, Jacob, Pvt, Col Samuel Bunch, Capt Andrew Breden, E TN Mil; transferred to Capt Bacon's Co
SARTIN, John, Pvt, Gen A Jackson, Capt Hugh Kerr, Mtd Rangers
SASSEAN, William, Pvt, Maj John Chiles, Capt R Tipton, E TN Vol Mtd Inf; Regt Co - Jefferson
SASSUN, Randolph, Pvt, Col William Lillard, Capt John Roper, E TN Vol Inf
SASSUN, William, Pvt, Col Wm Lillard, Capt John Roper, E TN Vol Inf
SATERFIELD, Levi, Sgt, Col Wm Lillard, Capt Thomas Sharpe, 2nd Regt Inf
SATERFIELD, Peter, 5 Sgt, Col A Loury, Capt J Thompson, W TN Mil
SATERFIELD, Peter, 5 Sgt, Lt Col L Hammons, Capt

## Enlisted Men, War of 1812

Joseph Williamson, Inf
SATERFIELD, Peter, Pvt, Col L Hammond, Capt J N Williamson, 2nd Regt Inf
SATERFIELD, Peter, Pvt, Lt Col L Hammond, Capt Thomas Wells, Inf
SATHIETE, William, Pvt, Col Samuel Wear, Capt James Gillespie, E TN Vol Inf
SATTERFIELD, Hosea, Pvt, Col S Bunch, Capt S Richerson, E TN Drafted Mil
SATTERFIELD, Larry, Pvt, Col John Cocke, Capt James Gray, Inf
SAULTS, John, Pvt, Col John Allison, Capt T McCrory, E TN Mil; transferred to Capt McPherson's Co
SAUNDERS, A B, Sgt Maj, Col R H Dyer, no other information
SAUNDERS, Alexander, Pvt, Brig Gen James White, Co Commander omitted, Spies
SAUNDERS, Augusta B, Pvt, Col Robert Dyer, Capt James McMahon, TN Vol Mtd Gunmen
SAUNDERS, Augustus B, Pvt, Regt Commander omitted, Capt Archibald McKinney, Cav; promoted to Sgt Maj
SAUNDERS, Augustus, Pvt, Regt Commander omitted, Capt David Deadrick, Arty
SAUNDERS, Daniel, Sgt, Maj Carroll, Capt Bradford & Capt Dillahaunty, Vol Inf
SAUNDERS, David, Pvt, Col Wm Metcalf, Capt Andrew Patterson, Mil Inf; d 2-25-1814
SAUNDERS, Eli, Pvt, Col R T Perkins, Capt Doak, Vol Mtd Gunmen
SAUNDERS, Elisha, Pvt, Col N Cannon, Capt Ota Cantrell, W TN Mtd Inf
SAUNDERS, Ezekiel, Pvt, Regt Commander omitted, Capt David Smith, Cav Vol
SAUNDERS, Franklin, Pvt, Maj Gen A Jackson, Capt Carroll, Vol Inf
SAUNDERS, George, Pvt, Col A Cheatham, Capt James Giddins, Inf
SAUNDERS, George, Pvt, Maj Wm Woodfolk, Capt James Neil, Inf
SAUNDERS, Isaac, Pvt, Col N Cannon, Capt Ota Cantrell, E TN Mtd Inf
SAUNDERS, Isaac, Pvt, Lt Col Archer Cheatham, Capt Ben Elliott, Mtd Inf
SAUNDERS, James, Pvt, Col John Cocke, Capt Bird Nance, Inf
SAUNDERS, John L, 1 Cpl, Regt Commander omitted, Capt David Smith, Cav
SAUNDERS, John S, Cpl, Col John Coffee, Capt John Smith, Vol Cav
SAUNDERS, John S, Pvt, Col Wm Hall, Capt Brice Martin, Vol Inf
SAUNDERS, John, Pvt, Col John Cocke, Capt Richard Crunk, Inf
SAUNDERS, Sotherland, Pvt, Col Wm Metcalf, Capt Barbee Collins, Mil Inf
SAUNDERS, Thomas, Pvt, Col John Coffee, Capt Robert Jetton, Cav
SAUNDERS, Thomas, Sgt, Col John Alcorn, Capt Robert Jetton, Vol Cav
SAUNDERS, Thomas, Sgt, Col R T Perkins, Capt Mathew Patterson, Mtd Vol; AWOL
SAUNDERS, Thomsa, Pvt, Col N Cannon, Capt John Dempsey, Mtd Gunmen
SAUNDERS, West, 3 Sgt, Col John Cocke, Capt James Gault, Inf
SAUNDERS, William, Pvt, Col John Cocke, Capt George Barnes, Inf
SAUNDERSON, Eli, Cpl, Col S Bunch, Capt Jno English, E TN Mil Drafted
SAURY, Henry, Pvt, Col Philip Pipkin; Capt Henry Newlin, Mil Inf
SAUTTS, John, Pvt, Col S Bunch, Capt John McPherson, E TN Mil; joined from? Capt McCray's Co
SAVAGE, George, 4 Cpl, Col S Bunch, Capt Jas Cunningham, Branch Srvce omitted
SAVAGE, John, Pvt, Maj Gen Carroll, Capt Wiley Huddleston, Inf
SAVAGE, Joshua, Pvt, Col John Cocke, Capt Richard Crunk, Inf
SAVAGE, Joshua, Pvt, Col Philip Pipkin, Capt John Strother, Mil; deserted
SAVAGE, Kindrel, Pvt, Col James Raulston, Capt Wiley Huddleston, Inf; d 1-17-1815
SAVAGE, Robert, Pvt, Col T McCrory, Capt A Willis, Mil Inf
SAVELY, William, Pvt, Col Thomas Williamson, Capt Robert Moore, Vol Mtd Gunmen
SAWAL, Jesse, Pvt, Col William Lillard, Capt Thomas McChristian, E TN Vol Inf
SAWYER, Dempsey, Pvt, Col Robert Steele, Capt Jas Bennett, Mil Inf
SAWYER, Dempsey, Pvt, Col Wm Metcalf, Capt William Mullen, Mil Inf
SAWYER, Demsey, Pvt, Col Philip Pipkin, Capt John Robertson, Mil Inf
SAWYER, Demsey, Pvt, Col Wm Metcalf, Capt William Mullen, Mil Inf
SAWYER, Thomas, Pvt, Col Wm Metcalf, Capt William Mullen, Mil Inf
SAWYERS, Dempsey, Pvt, Col John Coffee, Capt Daniel Ross, Mtd Gunmen
SAWYERS, Ethan, Pvt, Col S Bunch, Capt N Gibbs, E TN Drafted Mil
SAWYERS, James, 2 Cpl, Col John Cocke, Capt Bird Nance, Inf
SAWYERS, James, Pvt, Col A Cheatham, Capt Wm Smith, Inf
SAWYERS, James, Pvt, Col N Cannon, Capt Ota Cantrell, W TN Mtd Inf
SAWYERS, Thomas, Pvt, Col Wm Metcalf, Capt William Mullen, Mil Inf
SAWYERS, William P, Pvt, Col Robert Dyer, Capt James Wyatt, Vol Mtd Gunmen
SAWYERS, William, Pvt, Col John Williams, Capt William Walker, Vol
SAWYERS, William, Pvt, Col S Wear, Capt Robert Doak, E TN Vol Inf
SAWYERS, William, Pvt, Col S Wear, Capt S Bayless, Mtd Inf
SAXTON, Jeremiah, Pvt, Col S Wear, Capt Jesse Cole, Vol Inf

## Enlisted Men, War of 1812

SAYNER, Thomas, Pvt, Lt John Scott, Co Commander omitted, Inf
SCAGGS, James jr, Pvt, Col S Wear, Capt S Bayless, Mtd Inf
SCAGGS, James, Pvt, Maj John Childs, Capt Chas Conway, E TN Mtd Gunmen; Regimental Co - Knox
SCAGGS, James, Pvt, Regt Commander omitted, Capt S Bunch & Capt Isaac Williams, Mtd Vol
SCAGGS, James, Sgt, Col S Wear, Capt S Bayless, Mtd Inf
SCAGGS, Stephen M, Sgt, Col S Wear, Capt S Bayless, Mtd Inf
SCAGGS, Wesley, Pvt, Col A Loury, Lt Col L Hammond, Capt Arahel Rains, Inf
SCAGGS, Wesley, Pvt, Col A Loury, Lt Col L Hammonds, Capt Arahel Rains, Inf
SCAGGS, William, Pvt, Col Thomas Johnston, Capt Joseph Kirk, Mil
SCALES, Anthony, Mus, Col Edward Bradley, Capt Harry L Douglass, Vol Inf
SCALES, Henry, Pvt, Gen Andrew Jackson, Capt Nathan Davis, Inf
SCALES, John, Pvt, Brig Gen T Washington, Capt John Crawford, Mtd Inf
SCARBERRY, James, Pvt, Col James Raulston, Capt Daniel Newman, Inf
SCARBERRY, James, Pvt, Col Samuel Wear, Capt John Chiles, E TN Vol Inf
SCARBERRY, William, Ffr, Col Samuel Bunch, Capt Andrew Breden, E TN Mil
SCARBERRY, William, Pvt, Col James Raulston, Capt Daniel Newman, Inf
SCARBOROUGH, Alexander, Pvt, Regt Commander omitted, Capt Thos Gray, Inf
SCARBOROUGH, David, Pvt, Col Samuel Bunch, Capt Andrew Breden, E TN Mil
SCARBOROUGH, Howell, Pvt, Col S Copeland, Capt Richard Sharp, Mil Inf
SCARBOROUGH, Robert, Pvt, Col Samuel Bunch, Capt Andrew Breden, E TN Mil
SCARRAT, Joseph, Pvt, Col Wm Metcalf, Capt Alexander Hill & Capt John Cunningham, Mil Inf
SCHOLDS (SCALDS), John, Pvt, Col John Cocke, Capt James Gray, Inf; d 1-20-1815
SCHREINSHER, James, Dmr, Col Wm Metcalf, Capt Alexander Hill & Capt John Cunningham, Mil Inf
SCISCO, John, Pvt, Regt Commander omitted, Capt Jno Miller, Spies
SCISMORE, William, Pvt, Col John Wynne, Capt James Holleman, Inf
SCOALS, Nathaniel, Pvt, Col A Loury, Capt James Kincaid, Inf
SCOBEY, Nathaniel, Pvt, Col A Loury, Capt James Kincaid, Inf
SCOGGINS, Jesse, Cpl, Col Robt Steele, Capt James Randals, Inf
SCOGGINS, Russell, Pvt, Regt Commander omitted, Capt Wm Mitchell, Spies
SCOLDS, John, Pvt, Col John Alcorn, Capt John Baskerville, Vol Inf
SCORRY, Joseph, Pvt, Maj Gen John Cocke, Co Commander omitted, TN Vol Mtd Gunmen
SCOT, Edmanuel, Pvt, Col S Copeland, Capt Alexander Provine, Mil Inf
SCOT, James, Pvt, Gen Andrew Jackson, Capt Nathan Davis, Inf
SCOTCUP, Thomas, Pvt, Col Jas Raulston, Capt Henry Hamilton, Inf; also under Maj Gen Wm Carroll
SCOTT, Adam, Pvt, Col Wm Metcalf, Capt Wm Mullin, Mil Inf
SCOTT, Adam, Pvt, Col Wm Metcalf, Capt Wm Sitton, Mil Inf
SCOTT, Alexander, Dmr, Col Jno Brown, Capt Hugh Barton, E TN Mil Inf
SCOTT, Alexander, Pvt, Col John Cocke, Capt Geo Barnes, Inf; joined at Clarksville
SCOTT, Alexander, Pvt, Col John Cocke, Capt James Gault, Inf
SCOTT, Andrew, 1 Sgt, Col Wm Lillard, Capt Thos McChristian, E TN Vol Inf
SCOTT, Elijah, Pvt, Col Samuel Bayless, Capt Joseph Goodson, E TN Mil
SCOTT, Francis, Pvt, Col Newton Cannon, Capt John Harpole, Mtd Gunmen
SCOTT, Hubard, Pvt, Col Jno Coffee, Capt Alexander McKeen, Cav
SCOTT, Isaac, Pvt, Col John Coffee, Capt Chas Kavanaugh, Cav
SCOTT, James, Pvt, Col John Brown, Capt James Standifer, Regt E TN Vol Mtd Mil
SCOTT, James, Pvt, Col Newton Cannon, Capt John Harpole, Mtd Gunmen
SCOTT, James, Pvt, Col Samuel Wear, Capt John Childs, E TN Vol Inf
SCOTT, James, Pvt, Col Wm Johnson, Capt David McKamy, E TN Drafted Mil
SCOTT, James, Pvt, Maj Jno Childs, Capt Chas Conway, E TN Mtd Gunmen
SCOTT, James, Pvt, Maj Wm Woodfolk, Capt J C Niel, Inf
SCOTT, James, Sgt, Regt Commander omitted, Capt Jos Williams, Mil Cav
SCOTT, Jesse, Pvt, Col S Bunch, Capt S Richardson, E TN Drafted Mil
SCOTT, Jesse, Pvt, Col Thos Williamson, Capt Jno Hutchings, Vol Mtd Gunmen
SCOTT, John, 5 Cpl, Maj Gen Wm Carroll, Col Jas Raulston, Capt E Robinson, Inf
SCOTT, John, Pvt, Col Jno Brown, Capt Allen I Bacon, E TN Mil Inf
SCOTT, John, Pvt, Col P Pipkin, Capt Wm Mackay, Mil Inf
SCOTT, John, Pvt, Col S Bunch, Capt Geo McPherson, E TN Mil
SCOTT, John, Pvt, Col Sam'l Bayless, Capt Jno Brock, E TN Mil
SCOTT, John, Pvt, Col Thos Benton, Capt H L Douglass, Vol Inf
SCOTT, John, Pvt, Col Wm Johnson, Capt C Cook, E TN Mil
SCOTT, John, Pvt, Col Wm Johnson, Capt Jos Kirk, Mil
SCOTT, John, Sgt, Col Jno Brown, Capt Hugh Barton, E TN Mil Inf
SCOTT, Joseph, Pvt, Col Alex Loury, Capt Jno Looney,

## Enlisted Men, War of 1812

W TN Inf
SCOTT, Joseph, Pvt, Col R C Napier, Capt D Adkins, Mil Inf
SCOTT, Mathew, Pvt, Maj Wm Woodfolk, Capt E Ross & Capt McCulley, Inf
SCOTT, Nehemiah, Pvt, Lt Col Richard Napier, Co Commander omitted, Inf
SCOTT, Obadiah, Pvt, Maj Wm Woodfolk, Capt Jas Neil, Inf
SCOTT, Reuben, Pvt, Col Wm Johnson, Capt Jas Stewart, E TN Drafted Mil
SCOTT, Robert, Pvt, Gen Andrew Jackson, Capt Nathan Davis, Mtd Inf
SCOTT, Robert, Pvt, Lt Col Richard Napier, Co Commander omitted, Inf
SCOTT, Rosemond, Pvt, Maj Gen Wm Carroll, Capt F Ellis, Inf
SCOTT, Samuel jr, Pvt, Col Sam'l Bayless, Capt Jas Landen, E TN Mil
SCOTT, Samuel sr, Pvt, Col Sam'l Bayless, Capt Jno Landen, E TN Mil
SCOTT, Samuel, Pvt, Col R H Dyer, Capt Thos Jones, Vol Mtd Gunmen; arm broken two places in action 12-23-1814
SCOTT, Samuel, Pvt, Regt Commander omitted, Capt Edwin S Moore, Mtd Riflemen
SCOTT, Simon, Pvt, Col P Pipkin, Capt Jno Strother, Mil
SCOTT, Stallard, Pvt, Col Jno Coffee, Capt McKeen, Cav
SCOTT, Thomas, Pvt, Col Wm Johnson, Capt Elihu Milliken, 3rd Regt E TN Mil
SCOTT, Wilie, Pvt, Col N T Cannon, Capt Jno Harpole, Mtd Gunmen
SCOTT, Wilie, Pvt, Col Samuel Wear, Capt Jno Chiles, E TN Vol Inf
SCOTT, William, Cpl, Regt Commander omitted, Capt Archibald McKenney, Cav
SCOTT, William, Dmr, Col Jno Brown, Co Commander omitted, E TN Vol
SCOTT, William, Pvt, Brig Gen Thos Washington, Capt Jno Crawford, Mtd Inf
SCOTT, William, Pvt, Col E Allison, Capt Wm King, Drafted Mil
SCOTT, William, Pvt, Col E Booth, Capt A Biggs, Inf
SCOTT, William, Pvt, Col J K Winn, Capt Wm Carothers, W TN Inf
SCOTT, William, Pvt, Col Jno Brown, Capt Jas Standifer, E TN Vol Mtd Mil
SCOTT, William, Pvt, Col Jno Coffee, Capt Chas Kavanaugh, Cav
SCOTT, William, Pvt, Col Thos Benton, Capt Geo Caperton, Vol Inf
SCOTT, William, Pvt, Col Wm Metcalf, Capt Thos Marks, Mil Inf
SCOTT, William, Sgt, Col R H Dyer, Capt Glen Owen, TN Vol Mtd Gunmen
SCRAGGIN, David, Pvt, Col Wm Johnson, Capt James Tunnell, E TN Mil
SCRIBNER, Benjamin, Pvt, Col Wm Y Higgins, Capt James Hambleton, Mtd Gunmen
SCRIBNER, Benjmain, Pvt, Maj Gen Wm Carroll, Col Jas Raulston, Capt Edward Robinson, Inf
SCRIBNER, William, Pvt, Col Philip Pipkin, Capt Henry M Newlin, Mil Inf
SCRIVENER, James, Pvt, Col Edwin E Booth, Capt John Porter, Drafted Mil
SCRIVENER, James, Pvt, Col R H Dyer, Capt Bethel Allen, Vol Mtd Gunmen
SCRIVENER, Moses, Pvt, Col R H Dyer, Capt Bethel Allen, Vol Mtd Gunmen
SCRIVENER, Reuben, Pvt, Regt Commander omitted, Capt Jacob Prewett, Mtd Vol Pack Horse Guards
SCRIVINOR, Benjamin, Pvt, Maj Gen Wm Carroll, Col James Raulston, Capt Edward Robinson, Inf
SCRIVNER, Jonathan, Pvt, Col John Brown, Capt Wm D Neilson, Regt E TN Vol Inf
SCROGGINS, Russell, Pvt, Col Newton Cannon, Capt Francis Jones, Mtd Riflemen
SCRUCHFIELD, Alfred, Pvt, Col Wm Johnson, Capt James Stewart, E TN Drafted Mil
SCRUCHFIELD, Jesse, Pvt, Col Wm Johnson, Capt James Stewart, E TN Drafted Mil
SCRUFIELD, Zopheus, Pvt, Col Wm Johnson, Capt James Stewart, E TN Drafted Mil
SCRUGGS, Allen, Pvt, Maj Gen Andrew Jackson, Col Thomas H Williamson, Capt Robert Steele, Vol Mtd Gunmen
SCRUGGS, Allen, Pvt, Regt Commander omitted, Capt Abner Pearce, Inf
SCRUGGS, Edward, Pvt, Col Robert Steele, Capt James Randals, Inf
SCRUGGS, Elisha, Pvt, Col R C Napier, Capt Thomas Gray, Mil Inf
SCRUGGS, Isaac B, Pvt, Col John Coffee, Capt Charles Kavanaugh, Cav
SCRUGGS, Isaac, Pvt, Col Robert Steele, Capt James Randals, Inf
SCRUGGS, James, Sgt, Col John Brown, Capt Hugh Barton, Regt E TN Mil Inf
SCRUGGS, James, Sgt, Col Samuel Bunch, Capt James Penny, E TN Mtd Inf
SCRUGGS, Micajah, Pvt, Col Robert Steele, Capt Richard M Ratton, Mil Inf
SCRUGGS, Nathan, Sgt, Col John Cocke, Capt James Gault, Inf; promoted from Pvt
SCRUGGS, Western W, Pvt, Col A Loury, Lt Col Leroy Hammond, Capt Thomas Wells, Inf
SCRUGGS, William, Pvt, Col Ewin Allison, Capt Jacob Hoyal, E TN Mil
SCRUGGS, William, Pvt, Col John Brown, Capt Hugh Barton, Regt E TN Mil Inf
SCUDDER, Henry, Pvt, Col R H Dyer, Capt Bethel Allen, Vol Mtd Gunmen
SCUDDER, Mathis (Mathias), Pvt, Col T McCrory, Capt A Metcalf, Mil Inf; wounded at Talledega 11-9-1813
SCUDDER, Ralph, Pvt, Maj Gen Wm Carroll, Col Jas Raulston, Capt E Robinson, Inf
SCUDDER, Thomas, Pvt, Maj Wm Woodfolk, Capt E Ross & Capt McCulley, Inf
SCUGGS (SKEGGS), Archibald, Pvt, Maj Wm Woodfolk, Capt Abraham Dudney and Capt Jno Sutton, Inf

SCURLOCK, Joshua, Cpl, Col Thos Williamson, Capt B Williams, Vol Mtd Gunmen
SCURLOCK, Thomas, Pvt, Col Jno Coffee, Capt J W Byrn, Cav
SCURRY, Thomas, Pvt, Maj Gen John Cocke, Co Commander omitted, TN Vol Mtd Gunmen
SEABOLT, Lewis, Pvt, Col Philip Pipkin, Capt Henry Newlin, Mil Inf
SEABOLT, Lewis, Pvt, Col Wm Higgins, Capt Thos Eldridge, Mtd Gunmen
SEABOURN, Christopher, Pvt, Col Thomas Williamson, Capt Richard Tate, Vol Mtd Gunmen
SEABURN, James, Pvt, Col Samuel Bunch, Capt Wm Jobe, E TN Vol Mtd Inf
SEABURN, Richard, Pvt, Maj John Chiles, Capt Chas Conway, E TN Mtd Gunmen
SEACREST, Leroy, Pvt, Col A Loury, Lt Col Leroy Hammond, Capt Thomas Wells, Inf
SEAGRAVES, Bennet, Dmr, Col Philip Pipkin, Capt Ebenezer Kirkpatrick, Mil Inf
SEAGRAVES, Duncan, Pvt, Brig Gen Washington, Capt Jno Crawford, Mtd Inf
SEAHORN, Gabriel, Pvt, Col Robt Steel, Capt John Cheetwood, Mil Inf
SEAHORN, Hugh, Pvt, Maj John Childs, Capt Reuben Tipton, E TN Vol Mtd Inf; Regt from Jefferson Co
SEALE, James, Pvt, Col A Cheatham, Capt Geo Chapman, Inf
SEALS, Hezekiah, Pvt, Col Samuel Bunch, Capt James Cummings, E TN Vol Mtd Inf
SEALS, Jeremiah, Pvt, Col Samuel Bunch, Capt Jones Griffin, E TN Draft Mil; deserted
SEALS, Jeremiah, Pvt, Col Wm Johnson, Capt Benj Powel, E Tn Mil
SEALS, Peter, Pvt, Col Wm Johnson, Capt Benj Powell, E TN Mil
SEALS, Solomon, Pvt, Col Samuel Bunch, Capt Jones Griffin, E TN Draft Mil; deserted
SEALS, Solomon, Pvt, Col Wm Johnson, Capt Benj Powell, E TN Mil
SEALS, Solomon, Pvt, Gen T Johnston, Capt David Oban, 36 Inf
SEALS, William, Pvt, Col Thos Williamson, Capt A Metcalf, Vol Mtd Gunmen
SEARCA, Jacob, Sdlr, Col John Alcorn, Capt John Byrn, Cav
SEARCA, Jacob, Sdlr, Col John Coffee, Capt John Byrn, Cav
SEARCY, James, Sgt, Col Wm Hall, Capt John Moore, Vol Inf
SEARCY, Peter, Cpl, Col Philip Pipkin, Capt Peter Searcy, Mil Inf
SEARCY, William, Pvt, Col John K Winn, Capt John Spinks, Inf
SEARS, John, Pvt, Col Wm Johnson, Capt James Tunnell, E TN Mil
SEAT, Benjamin P, Pvt, Regt Commander omitted, Capt Francis Ellis, Inf; also under Maj Gen Wm Carroll
SEAT, Green, Pvt, Col John Cocke, Capt James Gault, Inf
SEAT, John, Pvt, Col R H Dyer, Capt Thomas Jones, Vol Mtd Gunmen
SEAT, John, Pvt, Col Thomas H Benton, Capt Newton Cannon, Inf
SEAT, Joseph, Pvt, Col Thomas H Benton, Capt Newton Cannon, Inf
SEAT, Robert, Pvt, Col R H Dyer, Capt Thomas Jones, Vol Mtd Gunmen
SEATON, Alexander, Pvt, Col Edwin E Booth, Capt Samuel Thompson, Mil
SEATON, James, Pvt, Col Edward Bradley, Co Commander omitted, Riflemen
SEATON, William, Pvt, Col Wm Johnson, Capt James Tunnell, E Tn Mil; notified & never appeared
SEAWELL, Lewis, Pvt, Col Thomas H Benton, Capt Benjamin Hewett, Vol Inf
SEAWELL, William, Pvt, Col Thomas H Benton, Capt Benjamin Hewett, Vol Inf
SEAWELL (SEWELL), Jesse, Pvt, Col Thos Benton, Capt Wm Moore, Vol Inf
SEAY, William, Pvt, Gen Andrew Jackson, Capt David Deadrick; trans to Horse Pack
SEAY, William, Pvt, Regt Commander omitted, Capt Daniel Yarnell, E Tn Mil
SEBINAL, Frederick, Pvt, Col John Alcorn, Capt John Winston, Mtd Riflemen
SECRIST, Abram, Pvt, Col Thomas H Benton, Capt James McEwen, Vol Inf
SEE, James, Pvt, Regt Commander omitted, Capt John Miller, Spies
SEE, William, Pvt, Col T McCrory, Capt Wm Metcalf, Mil Inf
SEEDON, Joseph, Pvt, Col S Bunch, Capt Francis Register, E Tn Mil
SEELS (SEALS), Anthony, Ffr Maj, Maj Wm Woodfolk, Co Commander omitted, Separate Bn of W TN Mil
SEELY (SEEBY), George, Pvt, Col Thos Benton, Capt Geo W Gibbs, Mtd Gunmen
SEET, James, Pvt, Col A Loury, Capt J N Williamson, W TN Mil
SEET, James, Pvt, Col Wm Pillow, Lt Mason, Vol Inf
SEET, John, Pvt, Col A Loury, Capt J N Williamson, W TN Mil
SEET, John, Pvt, Col Wm Pillow, Lt Mason, Vol Inf
SEET, Joseph, Pvt, Col Wm Pillow, Lt Mason, Vol Inf
SEET, _____, Pvt, Col L Hammond, Capt J N Williamson, 2 Regt Inf
SEGAND, Elisha, Pvt, Regt Commander omitted, Capt Jos Williams, Mil Cav
SEGRES, William, Pvt, Lt Col L Hammond, Capt Thos Wells, Inf; also Col A Loury
SEHORN, Jacob, Pvt, Col Wm Lillard, Capt Thos McChristian, E TN Vol Inf
SEISMORE, William, Pvt, Col John Wynne, Capt James Holleman, Inf
SEJIANT, William, Pvt, Col Thos Benton, Capt Geo Caperton, Vol Inf
SELF, Ashburn, Pvt, Col R H Dyer, Capt Isaac Williams, Vol Mtd Gunmen
SELF, Levi, Pvt, Col Edwin Bunch, Capt Vernon, E TN Mil
SELF, Milihicideek, Pvt, Col Philip Pipkin, Capt Eben-

ezer Kirkpatrick, Mil Inf
SELF (SWIFT), Parks, Pvt, Col Philip Pipkin, Capt E Kilpatrick, Mil Inf; apptd Cpl
SELLARS, James, Pvt, Col Samuel Bunch, Capt S Richerson, E TN Draft Mil
SELLARS, John, Pvt, Col John Wynne, Capt John Porter, Inf
SELLARS, John, Sgt, Col John Wynne, Capt Wm Willson, Inf
SELLARS, Nathan, Pvt, Maj John Childs, Capt Reuben Tipton, E TN Vol Mtd Inf; Regt from Jefferson Co
SELLARS, Robert, Pvt, Col John Wynne, Capt John Porter, Inf
SELLARS, Silas, Pvt, Lt Col Archer Cheatham, Capt Gabriel Martin, Mtd Inf
SELLARS, Thomas, Pvt, Lt Archer Cheatham, Capt Gabriel Martin, Mtd Inf
SELLERS, James, Pvt, Col Samuel Bunch, Capt S Richardson, E TN Draft Mil
SELLERS, John, Pvt, Col R C Napier, Capt Samuel Ashmore, Mil Inf
SELLERS, Robert, Pvt, Col John Wynne, Capt Wm Willson, Inf; trans to Capt Porter's Co
SELLERS, Samuel, Pvt, Lt Col Richard Napier, Co Commander omitted, Inf
SELLERS, Samuel, Sgt, Col Samuel Wear, Capt Joseph Calloway, Mtd Inf
SELTON, Emy, Pvt, Col T Williamson, Capt A Metcalf, Vol Mtd Gunmen
SELTON, Ezra, Pvt, Col T Williamson, Capt A Metcalf, Vol Mtd Gunmen
SELVAFAGE, Archibald, Pvt, Col Edwin Booth, Capt Richard Marshall, Draft Mil; disch on acct of inability
SELVAGE, George, Sgt, Col Wm Johnson, Capt Jas Rogers, E TN Drafted Mil
SELVIDGE, Preston, Pvt, Col S Copeland, Capt William Evans, Mil Inf
SELVIDGE, William, Pvt, Col S Copeland, Capt William Evans, Mil Inf
SENSEBOUGH, Jacob, Pvt, Col Wm Lillard, Capt Geo Argenbright, E Tn Vol Riflemen
SENTON (SEXTON), Robert, Pvt, Col R H Dyer, Capt Bethel Allen, Vol Mtd Gunmen
SENTRE, John, Pvt, Col A Loury, Capt Geo Sarver, Inf
SEREICHFIELD, Jesse, Pvt, Col Wm Johnson, Capt James Stewart, E Tn Mil
SERGEANT, Johnson, Pvt, Regt Commander omitted, Capt James Cowan, Mtd Inf
SERGEANT, Temple, Pvt, Regt Commander omitted, Capt James Cowan, Mtd Inf
SERGEANT, William L, Sgt, Maj Wm Russell, Capt Wm Chism, Vol Mtd Gunmen
SERGEANT, William, Pvt, Brig Gen T Washington, Capt Jno Crawford, Mtd Inf
SERGEANT, William, Pvt, Col Thos Benton, Capt Geo Caperton, Inf
SERIECHFIELD, Zopher, Pvt, Col Wm Johnson, Capt James Stewart, E Tn Mil
SERISHCHFIELD, Alfred, Pvt, Col Wm Johnson, Capt James Stewart, E TN Mil

SERITHFIELD, Henry, Pvt, Col SAmuel Wear, Capt John Doak, E Tn Vol Inf
SERRAT, James, Pvt, Col Wm Metcalf, Capt Alexander Hill, Capt John Cunningham, Mil Inf
SERRER, Archibald, Cpl, Col Wm Hall, Capt John Kennedy, Vol Inf
SERRER, John, Pvt, Col Wm Hall, Capt John Kennedy, Vol Inf
SERRER, William, Cpl, Col Wm Hall, Capt John Kennedy, Vol Inf
SESTER, James, Sgt, Col A Loury, Lt Col L Hammond, Capt Thos Wells, Inf
SETTON, Jeffrey, 3 Cpl, Col Edward Bradley, Capt Brice Martin, Vol Inf; promoted from Pvt
SEVEIR, James, Pvt, Col Samuel Bayless, Capt Solomon Hendrix, E Tn Mil
SEVIER, James, Pvt, Col Ewen Allison, Capt Adam Winsell, E Tn Draft Mil
SEVIER, James, Pvt, Col S Bunch, Capt F Register, E Tn Mil; joined from Winsel's Co
SEVIER, John F, Pvt, Col Wm Lillard, Capt Benj King, E Tn Vol Inf
SEVIER, John, Pvt, Col Samuel Bunch, Capt James Penny, E Tn Mtd Inf
SEVIERE, Charles, 2 Maj, Col Thos McCrory, 2 Regt TN Mil; in command of Gen Jackson
SEVIERS, Frederick, Pvt, Col Edwin Booth, Capt Richard Marshall, Drafted Mil; died 1-27-1815
SEVILLE, Joseph, Pvt, Col Wm Lillard, Capt John Roper, E Tn Vol Inf
SEWAL (SEWELL), Jesse, Pvt, Col James Raulston, Maj Gen Wm Carroll, Capt Wiley Huddleston, Inf
SEWEL, Jesse, Pvt, Col Samuel Bunch, Capt Jno English, E Tn Draft Mil; joined from Capt Gregory's Co
SEWEL, Jesse, Pvt, Col Thos Benton, Capt Wm Moore, Vol Inf
SEWELL, Benj C, Pvt, Col Newton Cannon, Capt John Harpole, Mtd Gunmen
SEWELL, George, Pvt, Col R C Napier, Capt Andrew McCarty, Mil Inf
SEWELL, John B, Pvt, Col Newton Cannon, Capt John Harpole, Mtd Gunmen
SEXTON, Aron, Pvt, Col Wm Johnson, Capt Jas Tunnell, E Tn Mil
SEXTON, Britton, Pvt, Regt Commander omitted, Capt Gray, Inf
SEXTON, James, Pvt, Col N Cannon, Capt Francis Jones, Mtd Riflemen
SEXTON, John G, Pvt, Lt Col Leroy Hammonds, Capt Rains, Inf
SEXTON, John, Pvt, Col S Bunch, Capt Jno English, E TN Drafted Mil
SEXTON, John, Pvt, Col Wm Johnson, Capt Jas Tunnell, E Tn Mil
SEXTON, Martin, Pvt, Col Wm Metcalf, Capt Barbee Collins, Mil Inf
SEXTON, Miles, Pvt, Regt Commander omitted, Capt Gray, Inf
SEXTON, Moses, Pvt, Col William Johnson, Capt Jas Tunnell, E Tn Mil; reduced from Cpl
SEXTON, Samuel, 4 Sgt, Col Wm Metcalf, Capt Barbee

## Enlisted Men, War of 1812

Collins, Mil Inf
SEXTON, Samuel, Pvt, Col N Cannon, Capt Francis Jones, Mtd Riflemen
SEXTON, William, Pvt, Col William Johnson, Capt Jas Tunnell, E Tn Mil
SHACHELFORD, Daniel, Sgt, Col N Cannon, Capt Ota Cantrell, W Tn Mil Inf
SHACKLEFORD, David, Pvt, Col S Bunch, Capt Solomon Dobbins, E Tn Drafted Mil; deserted
SHACKLEFORD, Hiram, Pvt, Col S Bunch, Capt Jno Houk, E Tn Mil; joined from Capt Dobbins' Co
SHACKLEFORD, Lewis, Pvt, Col S Bunch, Capt Solomon Dobbins, E Tn Mil; disch for inability
SHACKLEFORD, William, Pvt, Col William Johnson, Capt Elihu Millikin, E Tn Mil
SHADDEN, James, Pvt, Col Robert Steele, Capt Samuel Maxwell, Mil Inf; on command as wagon guards
SHADDEN, James, Pvt, Col Thos Benton, Capt William Smith, Vol Inf
SHADDEN, James, Pvt, Regt Commander omitted, Capt Smith, Vol Inf
SHADDEN, William, Pvt, Col William Pillow, Capt William Smith, Vol Inf
SHADDON, James, 4 Sgt, Col William Hall, Capt Henry Newlin, Inf
SHADDON, John, Pvt, Col Jno Brown, Capt Jas Standifer, E Tn Vol Mtd Mil
SHAFER, Jacob, Pvt, Col Ewen Allison, Capt Allen E TN Mil; died 2-12-1814
SHAHAN, John, Sgt, Col S Bunch, Capt Jno Houk, E TN Mil; disch on acct of inability
SHAHORN, Thomas, Pvt, Col S Wear, Col S Bunch, Capt Mitchell, E Tn Mtd Inf
SHAIFER, Josiah S, Pvt, Col Thomas Williamson, Capt Cook & Capt John Crane, Vol Mtd Gunmen
SHAIN, William, Cpl, Col Thomas Williamson, Capt Robert Moore, Vol Mtd Gunmen; promoted from Pvt
SHALTON, Parks, Pvt, Col Wm Johnson, Capt David McKamey, E Tn Drafted Mil
SHANER, John, Pvt, Col William Billard, Capt George Argenbright, E Tn Vol Riflemen
SHANKLE, George, Pvt, Maj William Russell, Capt Wm Russell & Capt Robert Dyer, Vol Mtd Gunmen
SHANKLE, George, Pvt, Regt Commander omitted, Capt L Ferrell, Inf
SHANKLE, Jesse, Pvt, Col John Wynne, Capt Bailey Butler, Inf
SHANKLE, John, Pvt, Col John Wynne, Capt Bailey Butler, Inf
SHANKLIN, John, Pvt, Col Wm Metcalf, Capt Barbee Collins, Mil Inf; died 3-10-1815
SHANKLIN, Robert, Pvt, Col John Coffee, Capt David Smith, Vol Cav
SHANKS, Moses, Pvt, Col S Bayless, Capt Jonathan Waddle, E Tn Mil
SHANKS, Nicholas, Cpl, Col S Bunch, Capt F Register, E Tn Mil
SHANKS, Nicholas, Pvt, Col S Bunch, Capt Geo McPherson, E TN Mil; joined from Capt Register
SHANNON, Andrews, Pvt, Col Edwin Booth, Capt John McKamey, E Tn Mil
SHANNON, Archibald, Pvt, Col Thomas Benton, Capt Henry Douglas, Vol Inf
SHANNON, Archibald, Pvt, Col Thomas Williamson, Capt Beverly Williams, Vol Mtd Gunmen
SHANNON, Charles, Pvt, Col Edwin Booth, Capt John Lewis, E Tn Mil
SHANNON, David, Pvt, Col R T Perkins, Capt Mathew Patterson, Mtd Vol
SHANNON, Hugh, Pvt, Col Alexander Loury, Capt Geo Martin, Inf; apptd wgnr
SHANNON, James, Pfr, Col Philip Pipkin, Capt John Robertson, Mil Inf
SHANNON, James, Pvt, Col John Cocke, Capt Richard Crunk, Inf
SHANNON, James, Pvt, Col Robert Jarman, Capt Nathan Peoples, Mil Inf
SHANNON, James, Pvt, Col S Bunch, Capt F Register, E Tn Mil; deserted
SHANNON, James, Pvt, Col S Bunch, Capt Geo McPherson, E Tn Mil; joined from Capt Register's Co
SHANNON, John, Pvt, Col Wm Johnson, Capt Jas Tunnell, E Tn Mil
SHANNON, Robert, Cpl, Col N Cannon, Capt Geo Martin, Mtd Gunmen; wounded 11-3-1813
SHANNON, Robert, Pvt, Col Jno Brown, Capt Jas Standifer, E TN Vol Mil
SHANNON, Robert, Pvt, Col Thomas Williamson, Capt Beverly Williams, Vol Mtd Gunmen
SHANNON, Samuel, Pvt, Col N Cannon, Capt Geo Martin, Mtd Gunmen
SHANNON, Thomas, Pvt, Col R T Perkins, Capt Doak, Vol Mtd Inf
SHANNON, William, Pvt, Col Edward Bradley, Capt Thos B Haynie, Vol Inf
SHANNON, William, Pvt, Col Jno Brown, Capt Lunsford Oliver, E Tn Mil
SHANNON, William, Pvt, Col S Bunch, Capt James Penny, E Tn Mtd Inf
SHARFER, Josiah L, Pvt, Col Thomas Williamson, Capt Cook & Capt John Crane, Vol Mtd Gunmen
SHARP, Addison, Pvt, Maj John Childs, Capt John Stephens, E TN Vol Mtd Inf
SHARP, Alexander, 4 Sgt, Maj John Childs, Capt John Stephens, E Tn Vol Mtd Inf
SHARP, Alexander, Sgt, Col Samuel Wear, Capt John Stephen, E Tn Vol Inf
SHARP, Cyrus, Pvt, Col John Alcorn, Capt John Baskerville, Vol Inf; killed 11-9-1813 at Talledega
SHARP, Cyrus, Pvt, Col John Alcorn, Capt Wm Locke, Cav
SHARP, Cyrus, Pvt, Col John Coffee, Capt Blackman Coleman, Cav
SHARP, Daniel, Pvt, Col Wm Johnson, Capt Benj Powell, E Tn Mil
SHARP, Elisha, Pvt, Col Wm Johnson, Capt Joseph Scott, E Tn Draft Mil
SHARP, George, Pvt, Col Samuel Bunch, Capt Jno English, E TN Draft Mil
SHARP, George, Pvt, Col Wm Johnson, Capt James Tunnell, E TN Mil

## Enlisted Men, War of 1812

SHARP, Gibs H (Giles H), Pvt, Col T McCrory, Capt A Metcalf, Mil Inf
SHARP, Jacob, Pvt, Col Samuel Bunch, Capt Jno English, E Tn Draft Mil
SHARP, James D, Pvt, Col A Loury, Capt J N Williamson, W Tn Mil
SHARP, James D, Pvt, Col John Coffee, Capt Michael Molton, Cav
SHARP, James D, Pvt, Col L Hammond, Capt J N Williamson, 2 Regt Inf
SHARP, James D, Pvt, Regt Commander omitted, Capt Jas Williams, Mil Cav
SHARP, James D, Pvt, Regt Commander omitted, Capt Jas Williamson, Mil Cav; deserted
SHARP, James D, Sgt, Col N T Perkins, Capt Mathew Patterson, Mtd Vol
SHARP, James, Pvt, Col Thos Benton, Capt Geo Caperton, Inf
SHARP, John, Pvt, Col A Loury, Capt John Looney, W TN Inf
SHARP, John, Pvt, Col James Raulston, Capt James A Black, Inf
SHARP, John, Pvt, Col John Brown, Capt Chas Lewin, E TN Vol Mtd Inf
SHARP, John, Pvt, Col Thos Benton, Capt Geo Caperton, Vol Inf
SHARP, John, Pvt, Col Wm Johnson, Capt James Tunnell, E TN Mil
SHARP, John, Pvt, Lt Col L Hammond, Capt James Craig, Inf
SHARP, Joshua, Pvt, Col Philip Pipkin, Capt Henry M Newlin, Mil Inf
SHARP, Levi, Pvt, Col Samuel Bunch, Lt Jno Harris, E TN Mil
SHARP, Nehemiah, Pvt, Col Wm Metcalf, Capt Bird L Hurt, Mil Inf
SHARP, Nicholas, Pvt, Col Wm Johnson, Capt James Tunnell, E TN Mil
SHARP, Richard, Pvt, Col Samuel Bunch, Capt Jno English, E TN Draft Mil
SHARP, Thomas, Pvt, Col R C Napier, Capt Early Benson, Mil Inf
SHARP, William, Pvt, Col A Loury, Lt Col L Hammond, Capt Thos Wells, Inf
SHARP, William, Sgt, Maj Wm Russell, Capt Isaac Williams, Separate Bn Vol Mtd TN Gunmen
SHARP, Williams, Pvt, Col John Alcorn, Capt Wm Locke, Cav
SHARPE, George, Pvt, Col Wm Lillard, Capt Wm Hamilton, E TN Vol Inf
SHARPE, John, Sgt, Col A Cheatham, Capt Wm Smith, Inf
SHARPE, John, Sgt, Col Samuel Wear, Capt John Doak, Branch omitted
SHARPE, Martin, Pvt, Col Wm Lillard, Capt Wm Hamilton, E TN Inf Vol
SHARPE, Powell, Pvt, Col Wm Lillard, Capt Wm Hamilton, E TN Vol Inf
SHARPE, William, Cpl, Col Samuel Wear, Capt John Doak, E TN Vol Inf
SHARPE, William, Sgt, Col Wm Lillard, Capt Thos Sharpe, 2 Regt E TN Inf
SHAVER, Charles, Pvt, Col A Loury, Capt Geo Sarver, Inf
SHAVER, Charles, Pvt, Col Edward Bradley, Capt Abraham Bledsoe, Riflemen; deserted
SHAVER, Jacob, Cpl, Col James Raulston, Capt Mathew Neal, Inf
SHAVER, Joseph, Pvt, Col A Loury, Capt Geo Sarver, Inf
SHAVER, Joseph, Pvt, Col Samuel Bunch, Capt F Register, E TN Mil
SHAW, George M, Pvt, Col T McCrory, Capt Samuel B McKnight, Inf
SHAW, Henry, Pvt, Maj Gen Wm Carroll, Capt Lewis Dillahunty & Capt Bridges, Vol Inf; died 1-3-1815
SHAW, James, Pvt, Col John K Wynne, Capt Thomas Williamson, Inf; trans to Capt Caruthers Co
SHAW, James, Pvt, Col R H Dyer, Capt Ephraim Dickson, TN Vol Mtd Gunmen
SHAW, James, Pvt, Col R H Dyer, Capt James McMahon, TN Vol Mtd Gunmen; later apptd Cpl
SHAW, James, Pvt, Lt Col A Cheatham, Capt Ben Elliott, Mtd Inf
SHAW, Jeremiah, Pvt, Col Philip Pipkin, Capt James Blakemore, Mil Inf
SHAW, Jesse, 4 Sgt, Col James Raulston, Capt Charles Wade, Inf
SHAW, John, Pvt, Col John Cocke, Capt George Barnes, Inf
SHAW, John, Pvt, Col Robert Steele, Capt James Bennett, Mil Inf
SHAW, John, Pvt, Maj Gen Wm Carroll, Capt Lewis Dillahunty, Capt Bridges, Vol Inf
SHAW, John, Sgt, Col S Copeland, Capt Fleman Hodges, Inf
SHAW, Josiah, Pvt, Regt Commander omitted, Capt Robert Evans, Mtd Spies
SHAW, Paten, Pvt, Col A Loury, Capt Gabriel Martin, Inf
SHAW, Robert, Cpl, Col John Brown, Capt John Childs, E TN Vol Mtd Gunmen
SHAW, William, Pvt, Col A Cheatham, Capt Birdwell, Inf
SHAW, William, Pvt, Col John Cocke, Capt Richard Crunk, Inf
SHAW, William, Pvt, Col Leroy Hammond, Capt James Tubb, Inf
SHAW, William, Pvt, Col N T Perkins, Capt John Doak, Vol Mtd Inf
SHAW, William, Pvt, Col Thomas H Williamson, Capt Robert Moore, Vol Mtd Gunmen
SHEAMORE, Thomas, Pvt, Col S Bunch, Capt John English, E TN Draft Mil
SHEAR, James, Pvt, Col John Cocke, Capt Bird Nance, Inf
SHEARAL, Thomas M, 1 Sgt, Col Wm Lillard, Capt Jacob Hartsell, E TN Vol Inf
SHEDDON, John, Pvt, Col Wm Lillard, Capt Thomas McChristian, E TN Vol Inf
SHEFFEY, Samuel, Pvt, Col Ewin Allison, Capt John Hampton, Mil
SHEFFIELD, Ephraim, Pvt, Col R H Dyer, Capt Ephraim Dickson, TN Vol Mtd Gunmen; no svce per-

formed
SHEFFIELD, Jason, Pvt, Col R H Dyer, Capt Ephraim Dickson, TN Vol Mtd Gunmen; no svce performed
SHEFFIELD, Matthew, Pvt, no other information
SHEHBOON, Lewis, Pvt, Lt Col James Cole, Co Commander omitted, Inf
SHEHON, John, Pvt, Col R C Napier, Capt Drury Adkins, Mil Inf
SHEHORN, John, Pvt, Regt Commander omitted, Capt Jos Williams, Mil Cav
SHELBURN, James, Pvt, Col Thomas H Williamson, Capt Wm Martin, Vol Mtd Gunmen
SHELBY, Charles, Pvt, Col N T Perkins, Capt Marr, Mtd Vol
SHELBY, Eli, Pvt, Col Philip Pipkin, Capt John Robertson, Mil Inf
SHELBY, Eli, Pvt, Col Wm Johnson, Capt John Cook, E TN Mil
SHELBY, Henry, 2 Qt? Sgt, Col John Cocke, Co Commander omitted, 2 Regt W TN Mil Inf
SHELBY, Henry, Sgt Maj, Col Nicholas T Perkins, no Co Commander, 1 Regt TN Mtd Vol
SHELBY, Isaac, Pvt, Capt Thos Williamson & Capt James Pace, Lt James Neely, Vol Mtd Gunmen
SHELBY, Isaac, Pvt, Regt Commander omitted, Capt Wm Mitchell, Spies
SHELBY, Jacob, Tptr, Maj John Childs, Capt Reuben Tipton, E TN Vol Mtd Inf; Regt from Jefferson Co
SHELBY, John H, 1 Sgt, Col John Cocke, Capt John Weakley, Inf
SHELBY, Thomas P, 2 Sgt, Col John Cocke, Capt John Weakley, Inf
SHELBY, Thomas T, Pvt, Col John Cocke, Capt John Weakley, Inf; died 3-9-1815
SHELBY, William, Pvt, Regt Commander omitted, Capt Joe Williams, Mil Cav; deserted
SHELDEN, Thomas, Pvt, Col S Bunch, Capt Inman, E TN Vol Mtd Inf
SHELFER, Michael, Pvt, Col Wm Metcalf, Capt Andrew Patterson, Mil Inf; d 1-28-1815
SHELHORN, John, Pvt, Col Wm Hall, Capt Alexander, Vol Inf
SHELL, Isaac, Cpl, Col S Copeland, Capt William Evans, Mil Inf
SHELL, Isaac, Pvt, Col Edward Bradley, Capt John Kennedy, Riflemen
SHELL, Isaac, Pvt, Col S Copeland, Capt William Douglas, Inf
SHELL, Isaac, Pvt, Col Wm Hall, Capt John Kennedy, Vol Inf
SHELL, John, Pvt, Col S Wear, Capt Rufus Morgan, E TN Vol Inf
SHELL, John, Pvt, Col William Lillard, Capt Benj King, E TN Vol Inf
SHELL, John, Pvt, Col Wm Hall, Capt John Kennedy, Vol Inf
SHELL, Lewis, Pvt, Col Booth, Capt John Sharp, E TN Mil
SHELL, Samuel, Pvt, Col Wm Metcalf, Capt Jas Cunningham & Capt Hill, Mil Inf

SHELLBURN, John P, Pvt, Regt Commander omitted, Capt D Mason, Cav
SHELLER, Martin, Pvt, Col Jno Brown, Capt Hugh Barton, E TN Mil Inf
SHELLEY, Isaac, Pvt, Col N Cannon, Capt Ota Cantrell, Mil Inf; transferred to Mitchell Co
SHELLS, John M, Pvt, no other information
SHELLY, Jacob, Pvt, Col Sam'l Wear, Capt Jos Calloway, Mtd Inf
SHELLY, James, Pvt, Col William Lillard, Capt Robert Maloney, E TN Vol Inf
SHELLY, Jeremiah, Pvt, Col Sam'l Bunch, Capt H Stephens, E TN Mtd Inf; transferred to Capt Zachariah Copeland's Co
SHELLY, Jonathan, 2 Cpl, Maj Jno Childs, Capt R Tipton, E TN Vol Mtd Inf; Regt Co - Jefferson
SHELLY, Jonathan, Pvt, Col Sam'l Wear, Capt Jos Calloway, Mtd Inf
SHELLY, William, Pvt, Lt Col Richard Napier, Co Commander omitted, Inf
SHELTON, David, 3 Sgt, Col E Bradley, Capt B Martin, Vol Inf; promoted from a Pvt
SHELTON, Drury, Pvt, Col Alex Loury, Lt Col L Hammonds, Capt Thos Delany, Inf
SHELTON, Elijah, Pvt, Col S Copeland, Capt Jno Holshouser, Inf
SHELTON, Ezeriah, Pvt, Col Sam'l Bayless, Capt Jos Rich, E TN Inf
SHELTON, George, Pvt, Col R H Dyer, Capt C Hudson, Vol Mtd Gunmen; d 1-21-1815
SHELTON, George, Pvt, Col R H Dyer, Capt Jos Williams, Vol Mtd Gunmen
SHELTON, Gilbert, Pvt, Col Robt Jarmon, Capt Nathan Peoples, Mil Inf
SHELTON, James, 2 Cpl, Col E Bradley, Capt B Martin, Vol Inf
SHELTON, James, 3 Cpl, Col Wm Hall, Capt B Martin, Vol Inf
SHELTON, James, Cpl, Col Thos Williamson, Capt A Metcalf, Vol Mtd Gunmen; promoted from a Pvt
SHELTON, James, Pvt, Col J K Wynne, Capt Robert Bradin, Inf
SHELTON, James, Pvt, Col P Pipkin, Capt Jno Strother, Mil
SHELTON, James, Pvt, Col S Bunch, Capt Geo McPherson, E TN Mil; joined from Capt Griffin's Co
SHELTON, James, Pvt, Col Thos Williamson, Capt Wm Metcalf, Vol Mtd Gunmen
SHELTON, Joel, Pvt, Col R H Dyer, Capt C Hudson, Vol Mtd Gunmen
SHELTON, Joel, Pvt, Col R H Dyer, Capt Jos Williams, Vol Mtd Gunmen
SHELTON, John, Cpl, Col Saml Wear, Capt Jno Childs, E TN Vol Inf
SHELTON, Palestine, Pvt, Maj Jno Childs, Capt Chas Conway, E TN Mtd Gunmen; Regt Co - Anderson
SHELTON, Peter, Pvt, Col M Molton, Capt Wm Sitton, Mil Inf
SHELTON, Philmore, Pvt, Col Thos Williamson, Capt Jno Doak & Capt Jno Dobbins, Vol Mtd Gunmen
SHELTON, Richard, Pvt, Col Wm Johnson, Capt H

## Enlisted Men, War of 1812

Hunter, E TN Mil
SHELTON, Scrulan, Pvt, Col Sam'l Bunch, Capt A Breden, E TN Mil; discharged for inability
SHELTON, Scurvin, Pvt, Maj Jno Childs, Capt Chas Conway, E TN Mtd Gunmen; Regt Co - Anderson
SHELTON, William, Pvt, Col Sam'l Wear, Capt Jno Childs, E TN Vol Inf
SHELTON, William, Pvt, Regt Commander omitted, Capt Robt Evans, Mtd Spies
SHENAULT, Ruben, Ffr, Col P Pipkin, Capt E Kirkpatrick, Mil Inf
SHENAULT, Thomas, Pvt, Col S Copeland, Capt Jno Holshouser, Inf
SHEP, William, Pvt, Col Thos Williamson, Capt Thos Porter, Vol Mtd Gunmen
SHEPHERD, John, Pvt, Col Alex Loury, Lt Col L Hammons, Capt A Rains, Inf
SHEPHERD, Stephen, Pvt, Col P Pipkin, Capt E Kirkpatrick, Mil Inf
SHEPHERD, William, Pvt, Col Thos Williamson, Capt Wm Martin, Vol Mtd Gunmen
SHEPPARD, Howardson, Pvt, Col Jno Alcorn, Capt Alex McKeen, Cav
SHEPPARD, Thornton, Pvt, no other information
SHEPPERD, James, Pvt, Col Wm Pillow, Capt Jno Anderson, Vol Inf
SHERAN, Charles, Pvt, Col Wm Johnson, Capt Benj Powell, Branch Srvce omitted
SHERLBY, Adam, Pvt, Col Samuel Bayless, Capt Solomon Hendricks, E TN Mil
SHEROD, Sterling, Pvt, Col John Cocke, Capt Bird Nance, Inf
SHERON, Jarret, Pvt, Col Newton Cannon, Capt Andrew Patterson, Mtd Riflemen
SHERON, Richard, Pvt, Regt Commander omitted, Capt James Gray, Inf
SHERRAN, Charles, Pvt, Col Wm Johnson, Capt Benjamin Powell, E TN Mil
SHERRELL, George, Pvt, Regt Commander omitted, Capt James Cowan & Capt Thomas Porter, Cav
SHERRELL, Hiram, Pvt, Col Thomas H Benton, Capt Smith, Vol Inf
SHERRELL, Hiram, Pvt, Col Wm Pillow, Capt Wm Smith, Vol Inf
SHERRILL, Charles K, Pvt, Col Edwin E Booth, Capt Vernon, E TN Mil
SHERRILL, Samuel B, Pvt, Col Wm Metcalf, Capt Barbee Collins, Mil Inf
SHERRILL, _____, Pvt, Col Thomas H Benton, Capt Smith, Vol Inf
SHERROD, Lemuel, Pvt, Maj Wm Carroll, Capt Jackson & Capt Wm Metcalf, Inf
SHERROD, Robert, Pvt, Col Wm Y Higgins, Capt John Cheatham, Mtd Riflemen
SHERROD, Samuel, Pvt, Col T McCrory, Co Commander omitted, Mil Inf
SHERROLL, Andrew P, Pvt, Col T McCrory, Capt Abel Willis, Mil Inf
SHERWOOD, Jonathan, Pvt, Col John Coffee, Capt Blackman Coleman, Cav
SHERWOOD, Samuel, Pvt, Col Thomas Williamson,

Capt James Pace, Lt James Neely, Vol Mtd Gunmen
SHETTLES, Phillip, Pvt, Col Thomas H Benton, Capt Wm Smith, Vol Inf
SHETTLES, Phillip, Pvt, Col Wm Pillow, Capt Wm Smith, Vol Inf
SHICKEL, Martin, Pvt, Col Newton Cannon, Capt Francis Jones, Mtd Riflemen
SHIEFFIELD, Nathan, Pvt, Col Wm Metcalf, Capt William Sitton, Mil Inf
SHIELDS, Arnet, Pvt, Col Samuel Wear, Capt Simeon Perry, E TN Vol Mtd Inf
SHIELDS, James, Pvt, Col John Brown, Capt John Childs, E TN Vol Mtd Inf
SHIELDS, John, Pvt, Col William Johnson, Capt Christopher Cook, E TN Mil
SHIELDS, John, Pvt, Col William Lillard, Capt Robert Maloney, Vol E TN Inf
SHIELDS, John, Pvt, Col Wm Johnson, Capt Joseph Kirk, Mil
SHIELDS, Jonathan, Pvt, Col William Higgins, Capt James Hambleton, Mtd Gunmen
SHIELDS, William B, Pvt, Gen Andrew Jackson, Capt Nathan Davis, Mtd Inf
SHIELDS, William, Pvt, Col Ewin Allison, Capt Jacob Hoyal, E TN Mil
SHIELDS, William, Pvt, Col S Bayless, Capt I Bacon, E TN Mil; promoted to Wagon Master
SHIELDS, William, Pvt, Regt Commander omitted, Capt Wm McLin, E TN Inf
SHIELDS, William, Wagon Master, Brig Gen Geo Doherty, E TN Mil
SHIELDS, Zachariah, Pvt, Col S Bayless, Capt Johnathan Waddle, E TN Mil
SHIKKLE, Joseph, Pvt, Col Wm Y Higgins, Capt Stephen Griffith, Mtd Riflemen
SHILTON, Gilbert, Pvt, Col John Cocke, Capt Joseph Price, Inf
SHINALT, John, Pvt, Col Thomas Williamson, Capt John Hutchings, Vol Mtd Gunmen
SHINAULL, Reuben, Pvt, Lt Col Leroy Hammonds, Capt Thomas Kelaney, Inf
SHINAULT, John, Pvt, Col John Winn, Capt Wm Carothers, W TN Inf
SHINAULT, John, Pvt, Col Robert Steele, Capt Jas Shinault, Mil Inf
SHINAULT, William, Sgt, Col Robert Steele, Capt Jas Shinault, Mil Inf
SHINFROCK, Henry, Pvt, Col Wm Johnson, Capt Jas Stewart, E TN Mil; d 12-13-1814
SHIP, Simon, Pvt, Col Thos Benton, Capt Jas Renshaw, Vol Inf; d 3-30-1813
SHIP, William, Pvt, Lt Col A Cheatham, Capt Gabriel Martin, Mtd Inf
SHIP, William, Pvt, Lt Col Jno Edmonson, Co Commander omitted, Cav
SHIPBY, Warner, Cpl, Col William Johnston, Capt Henry Hunter, E TN Mil; transferred to Capt Millikin Co
SHIPE, Henry, Pvt, Maj John Childs, Capt Daniel Price, Vol Mtd Gunmen
SHIPLEY, Adam, Cpl, Regt Commander omitted, Capt

- 455

## Enlisted Men, War of 1812

Samuel Richardson, E TN Drafted Mil
SHIPLEY, Adam, Pvt, Col S Bayless, Capt I Bacon, E TN Mil
SHIPLEY, Adam, Pvt, Col S Bunch, Capt F Register, E TN Mil
SHIPLEY, Adam, Pvt, Col S Bunch, Capt S Robinson, E TN Drafted Mil
SHIPLEY, James, Pvt, Col Ewen Allison, Capt John Hampton, Mil
SHIPLEY, James, Pvt, Col Wm Johnson, Capt Andrew Lawson, E TN Drafted Mil
SHIPLEY, Jesse, Pvt, Col S Bunch, Capt David Vance, E TN Mil Inf
SHIPLEY, Joseph, Cpl, Col S Wear, Capt Rufus Morgan, E TN Vol Inf
SHIPLEY, Joseph, Hospital Stewart, Col Edwin Booth, Co Commander omitted, E TN Mil
SHIPLEY, Peter, Pvt, Col Edwin Booth, Capt John Sharp, E TN Mil
SHIPLEY, Rauleigh, Pvt, Col S Bayless, Capt John Brock, E TN Mil
SHIPLEY, Samuel, Pvt, Col S Bayless, Capt James Landen, E TN Mil
SHIPLEY, Tidan, Pvt, Col Sam'l Bayless, Capt Jno Brock, E TN Mil
SHIPLEY, Tolbert, Sgt, Col Sam'l Bayless, Capt Jno Brock, E TN Mil
SHIPLEY, Varnes, Pvt, Col Wm Johnson, Capt E Milliken, 3rd Regt E TN Mil; transferred from Capt Hunter's Co
SHIPLEY, _____, Pvt, Col S Bunch, Capt Geo McPherson, E TN Mil; also w/Capt Register
SHIPLY, Aquila, Pvt, Col Wm Lillard, Capt Geo Keyes, E TN Inf
SHIPLY, Joseph, Sgt, Col E Booth, Capt Jno Lewis, E TN Mil; promoted to Hospital Stewart
SHIPLY, Richard, Pvt, Col Wm Lillard, Capt Geo Keyes, E TN Inf
SHIPMAN, Daniel, Cpl, Col Robert Steele, Capt Bennett, Mil Inf
SHIPMAN, Isaac, Pvt, Col Robt Steele, Capt Jas Bennett, Mil Inf
SHIPP, Daniel, 3 Cpl, Col N T Perkins, Capt Jno Doak, Vol Mtd Gunmen
SHIPP, Josiah, Pvt, Regt Commander omitted, Capt Elisha Green, Mtd Spies
SHIPPEN, Archibald, Pvt, Col Thos Williamson, Capt Thos Scurry, Vol Mtd Gunmen
SHIPPY, Ely, Pvt, Col Sam'l Bayless, Capt Jas Landen, E TN Mil
SHIPS, Lewis, Pvt, Col Thos Williamson, Capt Jas Pace & Capt Jas Nealy, Vol Mtd Gunmen
SHIRES, James, Pvt, Col A Cheatham, Capt H Birdwell, Inf
SHIRROD, John, Pvt, Lt Col Edmonson, Co Commander omitted, Mtd Inf
SHITTELSWORTH, Philip, Pvt, Col Jas Raulston, Capt M Cowan, Inf
SHIVERS, Isiah, Pvt, Lt Col Archer Cheatham, Capt M Walker, Inf
SHIVERS, Jonas, Far, Maj Gen A Jackson, Capt Jno Craine, Mtd Gunmen
SHIVERS, Thomas, Pvt, Col Jno Coffee, Capt F Stump, Cav
SHIVERS, Thomas, Pvt, Col Jno Coffee, Capt Jas Terrell, Vol Cav
SHOAT, Thomas, 2 Cpl, Col James Raulston, Capt Henry Hamilton, Inf; also under Maj Gen Wm Carroll
SHOCKLEY, Ephraim, Cpl, Col Robt Steele, Capt Richard Randal, Inf
SHOCKLEY, Isham, Pvt, Col Robt Steele, Capt R M Randals, Inf
SHOCKLEY, Richard, Pvt, Col Samuel Bayless, Capt Joseph Rich, E TN Inf
SHOCKLY, Caleb, Pvt, Col Wm Johnson, Capt Henry Hunter, E TN Mil
SHOCKLY, Thomas, Pvt, Col Wm Johnson, Capt Henry Hunter, E TN Mil
SHOEMAKE, Edmond, Pvt, Col John Cocke, Capt Samuel M Caruthers, Inf
SHOEMAKE, William, Pvt, Col James Raulston, Capt John Cowan, Inf
SHOEMAKER, Henry, Pvt, Col Samuel Bayless, Capt Joseph Rich, E TN Inf
SHOEMAKER, Jeremiah, Pvt, Col M Lillard, Capt Hugh Martion, E TN Vol Inf
SHOEMAKER, John, Sgt, Col Samuel Bunch, Capt Andrew Breden, E TN Mil; promoted from Pvt
SHOEMAKER, Moses, Pvt, Col John Brown, Capt Wm White, E TN Vol Mtd Inf
SHOEMAKER, Thomas, Pvt, Col John Brown, Capt Wm White, E TN Mil Inf
SHOEMAKER, William, Pvt, Col John Brown, Capt Wm White, E TN Vol Mtd Inf
SHOEMAN, William G, Pvt, Col T McCrory, Capt Jas Shannon, Mil Inf
SHOEMATE, Thomas, Pvt, Col Wm Metcalf, Capt Wm Mullin, Mil Inf
SHOFNER, Michael, Pvt, Col Edwin Booth, Capt Richard Marshall, Drafted Mil
SHOFNER, Michael, Pvt, Col Samuel Bunch, Capt Andrew Breden, E TN Mil; transferred to Capt I Berry's Co
SHOOK, Abraham, Pvt, Col Thos Williamson, Capt John Hutchings, Vol Mtd Gunmen; d 12-10-1814
SHOOK, Harmon, Pvt, Col Wm Johnson, Capt David McKamy, E TN Drafted Mil
SHOOK, Isaac, Pvt, Col Wm Johnson, Capt James Stuart, E TN Drafted Mil
SHOOKMAN, Thomas, Pvt, Col Samuel Wear, Capt John Doak, E TN Vol Inf
SHOOLMAN, Thomas, Pvt, Col Wm Johnson, Capt Benj Powell, E TN Mil
SHOOPMAN, Michael, Pvt, Col Samuel Wear, Capt John Doak, E TN Vol Inf
SHOOPMAN, William, Pvt, Col Samuel Wear, Capt John Doak, E TN Vol Inf
SHOOTMAN, William, Pvt, Col Edwin Booth, Capt Richard Marshall, Drafted Mil
SHOPSHIRE, Walter, Pvt, Col Edwin Booth, Capt John Slatton, E TN Mil
SHORE, Abiram, Pvt, Col R H Dyer, Maj Wm Russell,

## Enlisted Men, War of 1812

SHORES, John, Pvt, Col R H Dyer, Capt Robt Evans, Vol Mtd Gunmen; d 2-23-1815
SHORES, William, Pvt, Col Wm Metcalf, Capt Obidiah Waller, Mil Inf; d 2-24-1815
SHORT, Aaron, Pvt, Col John Brown, Capt James McKamey, E TN Mtd Gunmen
SHORT, Benjamin, Pvt, Col Thos Williamson, Capt John Doak & Capt John Dobbins, Vol Mtd Gunmen
SHORT, Elisha, 5 Cpl, Col James Raulston, Capt Henry West, Inf
SHORT, Enos, Pvt, Maj Wm Russell, Capt Geo Mitchie, Vol Mtd Gunmen
SHORT, Isaac, Pvt, Col Edward Bradley, Capt John Moore, Vol Inf; deserted
SHORT, Isaac, Pvt, Col Wm Hall, Capt John Moore, Vol Inf
SHORT, John, Pvt, Col Samuel Wear, Capt James Gillespie, E TN Vol Inf
SHORT, Josiah, Pvt, Col Wm Johnson, Capt James Tunnell, E TN Mil
SHORT, Theophelus, Pvt, Col N T Perkins, Capt John B Quarles, Vol Mtd Inf
SHORT, Thomas, Pvt, no other information
SHORT, William, Pvt, Col Jno Coffee, Capt Frederick Stump, Cav
SHORT, William, Pvt, Col John Brown, Capt Wm White, E TN Mil Inf
SHORTER, James, Cpl, Col Robert Steele, Capt John Cheetwood, Mil Inf
SHOTT, Hugh, Pvt, Col Samuel Wear, Capt James Tedford, E TN Vol Inf
SHOUGH, John, Pvt, Col Samuel Bunch, Capt Isaac Williams, Mtd Vol
SHOULDERS, William, Pvt, Col James Raulston, Capt Henry Hamilton, Inf; also under Maj Gen Wm Carroll
SHOULTS, David, Pvt, Col Wm Johnson, Capt Christopher Cook, 3rd Regt E TN Mil; transferred to Capt Hunter's Co
SHOURE, Henry, Pvt, Regt Commander omitted, Capt Thos Gray, Inf
SHOUSE, Daniel, Pvt, Regt Commander omitted, Capt Wm Teas, 6th Brig Inf
SHRADLING?, William, Pvt, Col Samuel Wear, Co Commander omitted, Mtd Inf
SHROPSHIRE, Walter, 2 Sgt, Col Wm Lillard, Capt George Argenbright, E TN Vol Riflemen
SHROWE, John, Pvt, Col Wm Johnson, Capt David McKamy, E TN Drafted Mil
SHRYGLEY, Samuel, Sgt, Col R H Dyer, Capt James McMahon, TN Vol Mtd Gunmen
SHUFFIELD, Isham, Cpl, Col Jno Cocke, Capt Jas Gault, Inf; d 1-10-1815
SHUKKLE, William, Pvt, Col Wm Y Higgins, Capt Stephen Griffith, Mtd Riflemen
SHULES, David, Pvt, Col Wm Johnson, Capt Joseph Kirk, Mil
SHULES, Jacob, Pvt, Col Wm Johnson, Capt Elihu Milliken, 3rd Regt E TN Mil
SHULL, Abraham, Pvt, Col S Bunch, Capt Isaac Williams, E TN Mil
SHULL, Abraham, Pvt, Col S Bunch, Capt John English, E TN Drafted Mil; joined from Capt Williams Co
SHULL, Absolom, Pvt, Col S Bunch, Capt I Williamson, E TN Mil
SHULLEY, Jacob, Pvt, Col S Bunch, Capt John English, E TN Drafted Mil; joined from Capt F Berry's Co
SHULLY, Jeremiah, Pvt, Col Wm Lillard, Capt S Copeland, E TN Vol Inf
SHULLY, Jonathan, Pvt, Col Wm Lillard, Capt James Lillard, E TN Inf Vol
SHULTS, David, Pvt, Col Wm Johnson, Capt Henry Hunter, E TN Mil
SHULTS, Kamason, Pvt, Col Samuel Wear & Col Samuel Bunch, Capt Wm Mitchell, E TN Mtd Inf
SHULTZ, Benjamin, Pvt, Col John Brown, Capt Wm White, Regt E TN Mil Inf
SHUMAKE, Andrew, Pvt, Col Wm Metcalf, Capt Bird L Hurt, Mil Inf; d 1-2-1815
SHUMATE, Fielding, Pvt, Col Thomas H Williamson, Capt Richard Tate, Vol Mtd Gunmen
SHUMATE, Fielding, Pvt, Regt Commander omitted, Lt James Berry, Mtd Riflemen
SHUMATE, Robert, 1 Cpl, Col John Cocke, Capt Wm Caruthers, Inf; reduced to the ranks
SHUMATER, Thomas, Pvt, Col Thomas H Williamson, Capt Wm Sitton, Capt Richard Tate, Vol Mtd Gunmen
SHUMATER, Thomas, Pvt, Col Wm Metcalf, Capt Wm Sitton, Mil Inf
SHUSTEED, William, Pvt, Col Robert Steele, Capt James Bennett, Mil Inf
SHUTE, George A, Pvt, Col Thomas H Benton, Capt James McEwin, Vol Inf
SHUTE, Phillip, Pvt, Regt Commander omitted, Capt L Ferrell, Inf
SHUTTON, James, Pvt, Col Ewin Allison, Capt Thomas Wilson, E TN Drafted Mil
SIBINAL, Frederick, Pvt, Col John Alcorn, Capt George Winston, Mtd Riflemen
SICKES, Jonas, Dmr, Col Wm Hall, Capt Travis Nash, Vol Inf
SIEBER, Samuel, Pvt, Col Wm Johnson, Capt James Tunnell, E TN Mil
SIGLAR, Henry, Pvt, Col Samuel Bayless, Capt Solomon Hendricks, E TN Mil
SIGLER, Henry, Pvt, Col Samuel Wear, Capt Jesse Cole, Vol Inf
SIGLER, John S, Pvt, Maj Gen Andrew Jackson, Col Thomas McCrory, Capt Isaac Patton, 2nd Regt TN Mil
SIKES, Jonas, Cpl, Col Edward Bradley, Co Commander omitted, Vol Inf; promoted from Pvt
SIKES, Terrel, Pvt, Maj Gen Wm Carroll, Col James Raulston, Capt Edward Robinson, Inf
SILAS, Jesse, Pvt, Col Edwin Booth, Capt John Lewis, E TN Mil; d 2-8-1815
SILCOCKE, James, Pvt, Col Jno Cocke, Capt Jos Price, Branch Srvce omitted
SILLAVAN, Ezekiel, Pvt, Col Sam'l Wear, Capt Dan'l Price, E TN Vol Inf

- 457

## Enlisted Men, War of 1812

SILLAVAN, William, Pvt, Col Sam'l Wear, Capt Dan'l Price, E TN Vol Inf
SILLMAN, John, Pvt, Gen Wm Johnston, Capt Dan'l Oban, 36th Inf
SILLMAN, Thomas, Pvt, Col Jno Cocke, Capt Sam'l Caruthers, Inf
SILMON, Abner, Pvt, Col R H Dyer, Maj Wm Russell, Capt Wm Russell, Vol Mtd Gunmen
SILMON, Benjamin, Pvt, Col R H Dyer, Maj Wm Russell, Capt Wm Russell, Vol Mtd Gunmen
SILMON, Eli, Pvt, Col Thos Williamson, Capt Jno Hutchings, Vol Mtd Gunmen
SILVAY, Samuel, Pvt, Col E Booth, Capt Jno McKamey, E TN Mil
SILVERTOOTH, Jacob, Pvt, Maj Wm Russell, Capt Geo Mitchie, Vol Mtd Gunmen
SIMANS, John, Pvt, Col Sam'l Wear, Capt Jas Tedford, E TN Vol Inf
SIMERLY, William, Pvt, Col Wm Johnson, Capt H Hunter, E TN Mil
SIMKINS, William, Pvt, Col William Pillow, Capt Jos Mason, Vol Inf
SIMMERLY, Henry, Pvt, Col E Allison, Capt A Winsell, E TN Drafted Mil
SIMMERLY, Henry, Pvt, Col S Bunch, Capt F Register, E TN Mil; joined from Capt Winsel's Co
SIMMERLY, Henry, Pvt, Col Sam'l Wear, Capt Jesse Cole, Vol Inf
SIMMERLY, John, Pvt, Col Sam'l Wear, Capt Jesse Cole, Vol Inf
SIMMONS, Alfred, Pvt, Col S Bunch, Capt S Richardson, Branch Srvce omitted
SIMMONS, Alsed, Pvt, Col S Wear, Capt Simeon Perry, E TN Vol Mtd Inf
SIMMONS, Christopher, Pvt, Lt Col L Hammonds, Capt Jas Tubb, Branch Srvce omitted
SIMMONS, Edward, Pvt, Col Thos Benton, Capt Thos Williamson, Vol Inf
SIMMONS, Edward, Pvt, Regt Commander omitted, Capt Jno Crane, Mtd Inf
SIMMONS, Elisha, Pvt, Regt Commander omitted, Capt Jos Williams, Mil Cav
SIMMONS, Elisha, Sdlr, Col Jno Coffee, Capt M Molton, Cav
SIMMONS, Isaac, Pvt, Col Jno Cocke, Capt Jos Price, Inf
SIMMONS, Isham, Cpl, Regt Commander omitted, Capt Sam'l Richardson, E TN Drafted Mil
SIMMONS, Isham, Pvt, Col S Bunch, Capt S Roberson, E TN Drafted Mil
SIMMONS, Jacob, Pvt, Col J K Wynne, Capt Wm Carothers, W TN Inf
SIMMONS, Jacob, Pvt, Col J K Wynne, Capt Wm Wilson, Inf; transferred to Capt Caruthers Co
SIMMONS, James, Pvt, Col A Cheatham, Capt Richard Benson, Inf
SIMMONS, James, Pvt, Col Jno Coffee, Capt M Molton, Cav
SIMMONS, James, Pvt, Col S Bunch, Capt Jno Harris, E TN Mil
SIMMONS, James, Pvt, Col S Bunch, Lt Jno Harris, E TN Mil
SIMMONS, James, Pvt, Regt Commander omitted, Capt Jos Williams, Mil Cav
SIMMONS, Joel, Pvt, Col T McCrory, Capt A Metcalf, Mil Inf
SIMMONS, John H, Pvt, Col William Pillow, Capt Geo Caperton, Inf
SIMMONS, John, Pvt, Col Alexander Loury, Capt Geo Sarver, Inf
SIMMONS, John, Pvt, Col E Allison, Capt J Loughmiller, Mil; transferred to Capt McPhersons' Co
SIMMONS, John, Pvt, Col Jno Williams, Capt David Vance, Mtd Mil
SIMMONS, John, Pvt, Col S Bunch, Capt Geo McPherson, E TN Mil; joined from Capt Loughmiller's Co
SIMMONS, John, Pvt, Col S Bunch, Capt Jno Harris, E TN Mil
SIMMONS, John, Pvt, Col S Bunch, Capt Jno Houk, E TN Mil; joined from? Capt Gregory Co
SIMMONS, John, Pvt, Col Saml Bunch, Capt Jos Duncan, E TN Drafted Mil
SIMMONS, John, Pvt, Col Thos Benton, Capt Geo Caperton, Vol Inf
SIMMONS, John, Pvt, Col Wm Metcalf, Capt Wm Mullin, Mil Inf
SIMMONS, John, Pvt, Gen A Jackson, Capt Nathan Davis, Inf
SIMMONS, John, Pvt, Gen Andrew Jackson, Capt Nathan Davis, Inf
SIMMONS, John, Pvt, Lt Col Archer Cheatham, Capt Meredith Walker, Inf
SIMMONS, Jonathan, Pvt, Col S Bunch, Capt Jno Harris, E TN Mil
SIMMONS, Jonathan, Pvt, Col Saml Bunch, Capt Jos Duncan, E TN Drafted Mil; joined from Capt Howel's Co
SIMMONS, Joseph, Pvt, Regt Commander omitted, Capt Jos Williams, Mil Cav
SIMMONS, Lemuel, Pvt, Col T McCrory, Capt T Gordon, Inf
SIMMONS, Luke, Pvt, Col A Cheatham, Capt Rich'd Benson, Inf
SIMMONS, Marvel, Pvt, Col P Pipkin, Capt Geo Mebane, Mil Inf; deserted
SIMMONS, Mathew, Pvt, Col John Wynne, Capt John Spinks, Inf
SIMMONS, Micajah, Pvt, Col S Bunch, Capt Jno Harris, E TN Mil
SIMMONS, Nathan, Pvt, Maj Gen Wm Carroll, Col Jas Raulston, Capt E Haynie, Inf
SIMMONS, Richard, Pvt, Col Wm Lillard, Capt Thos Sharpe, 2nd Inf
SIMMONS, Robert, Pvt, Maj Gen Wm Carroll, Capt Ellis, Inf
SIMMONS, Thomas, 1 Cpl, Col Wm Lillard, Capt Wm Gillenwater, E TN Vol Inf
SIMMONS, Thomas, Pvt, Col J K Wynne, Capt Jno Porter, Inf; deserted
SIMMONS, Thomas, Pvt, Col S Bunch, Capt Jno English, E TN Drafted Mil; joined from Capt Gibbs Co
SIMMONS, Thomas, Pvt, Col S Bunch, Capt N Gibbs, E

TN Drafted Mil; transferred to Capt Duncan's Co
SIMMONS, Thomas, Pvt, Regt Commander omitted, Capt Jno Crane, Mtd Inf
SIMMONS, Tom, Pvt, Lt Col Archer Cheatham, Capt Meredith Walker, Inf
SIMMONS, William, Pvt, Col A Cheatham, Capt Richard Benson, Inf
SIMMONS, William, Pvt, Col Jno Cocke, Capt Jas Gault, Inf
SIMMONS, William, Pvt, Col S Bunch, Capt Jas Cummings, E TN Vol Mtd Inf
SIMMONS, William, Pvt, Col Wm Metcalf, Capt Barbee Collins, Mil Inf; d 3-22-1815?
SIMMONS, William, Pvt, Maj John Childs, Capt John Cunningham, E TN Vol Mtd Inf
SIMMONS, William, Pvt, Maj John Childs, Capt John Stephens, E TN Vol Mtd Inf
SIMON, Christopher, Pvt, Col Leroy Hammonds, Capt Jas Tubb, Branch Srvce omitted
SIMONS, Jacob, Pvt, Col Wm Johnson, Capt David McKamey, E TN Drafted Mil; deserted
SIMONS, John, Pvt, Col Leroy Hammonds, Capt Jas Tubb, Inf; enlisted in the regular service
SIMONS (SIMMONS), John, Pvt, Col Wm Metcalf, Capt Wm Mullin, Mil Inf
SIMPSON, Abel, Pvt, Col Robert Steele, Capt Campbell, Mil Inf
SIMPSON, Archibald, Pvt, Col Thos Benton, Capt Henry Douglas, Vol Inf
SIMPSON, Charles, 1 Surgeon Mate, Col Wm Hall, Co Commander omitted, TN Vol
SIMPSON, Charles, Pvt, Col Thos Benton, Capt Geo Caperton, Inf; promoted to Surgeon's Mate
SIMPSON, David, Pvt, Regt Commander omitted, Capt Richard Sharpe & Capt William Lillard, Inf
SIMPSON, Elijah, Cpl, Col Thos Benton, Capt Henry Douglas, Vol Inf
SIMPSON, George, Pvt, Col Philip Pipkin, Capt Geo Newlin, Mil Inf
SIMPSON, Gilbert, Pvt, Col N Cannon, Capt Thomas Yardley, Mtd Riflemen; killed 11-3-1813 at Tallehache
SIMPSON, James, Pvt, Col Leroy Loury, Capt Raines, Inf
SIMPSON, James, Pvt, Col William Johnson, Capt Andrew Lawson, E TN Drafted Mil
SIMPSON, Jermiah, Pvt, Col William Hall, Capt John Moore, Vol Inf
SIMPSON, John, Pvt, Col Bunch, Capt S Bunch, Mtd Vol
SIMPSON, John, Pvt, Col Williams, Capt Vance, Mtd Mil
SIMPSON, John, Pvt, Col Wm Hall, Capt Geo Martin, Vol Inf
SIMPSON, John, Pvt, Maj William Russell, Capt Williams, TN Vol Mtd Gunmen
SIMPSON, Robert, Pvt, Col Edward Bradley, Capt Geo Martin, Vol Inf
SIMPSON, Thomas, Pvt, Col R C Napier, Capt Early Benson, Mil Inf
SIMPSON, Thomas, Pvt, Col Thomas Williamson, Capt A Metcalf, Vol Mtd Gunmen; d 1-1-1815
SIMPSON, Valentine, Pvt, Col John Brown, Capt John Childs, E TN Vol Mtd Inf

SIMPSON, William M, Pvt, Col Thos Benton, Capt N Cannon, Inf
SIMPSON, William, Pvt, Col Alexander Loury, Capt Peter Looney, W TN Inf
SIMPSON, William, Pvt, Col N Cannon, Capt Thomas Yardley, Mtd Riflemen
SIMPSON, William, Pvt, Col R T Perkins, Capt Johnston, Mil Inf
SIMPSON, William, Pvt, Col Richard Tate, Capt Thomas Williamson, Vol Mtd Gunmen
SIMPSON, William, Pvt, Col S Wear, Capt Doak, E TN Vol Inf
SIMPSON, William, Pvt, Col Wm Lillard, Capt Roper, E TN Vol Inf
SIMPSON, William, Pvt, Maj Carroll, Capt Dillahunty & Capt Bradford, Vol Inf
SIMPSON, William, Pvt, Maj Gen Carroll, Col Jas Raulston, Capt Robinson, Inf
SIMPSON, Zachariah, Pvt, Col John Alcorn, Capt William Locke, Cav
SIMPSON, _____, Surgeon's Mate, Col Newton Cannon, TN Vol Mtd Gunmen
SIMS, Abraham, Pvt, Col R C Napier, Capt Early Benson, Mil Inf
SIMS, Alexander, Pvt, Col Wm Hall, Capt Geo Hambleton, Vol Inf
SIMS, Alexander, Pvt, Col Wm Hall, Capt James Hambleton, Vol Inf
SIMS, Alexander, Sgt, Maj Robert Searcy, Capt Henry Bryan, 2nd Inf
SIMS, Alfred, 4 Sgt, Col Philip Pipkin, Capt Geo Newlin, Mil Inf
SIMS, James, Pvt, Col John Coffee, Capt Fredrick Stump, Cav
SIMS, James, Pvt, Gen Carroll, Capt Ellis, Inf; d 3-2-1815
SIMS, John H, Pvt, Regt Commander omitted, Capt Geo Smith, Spies
SIMS, John, Pvt, Col S Bunch, Capt Gregory, Branch Srvce omitted
SIMS, John, Pvt, Col S Wear, Capt John Stephens, E TN Vol Inf
SIMS, John, Pvt, Col Thos Benton, Capt Geo Caperton, Inf
SIMS, John, Pvt, Regt Commander omitted, Capt Geo Smith, Spies
SIMS, Martin, Pvt, Col Robert Dyer, Capt Ephraim Dickson, TN Mtd Vol Gunmen
SIMS, Martin, Sgt, Col S Copeland, Capt Richard Sharp, Mil Inf
SIMS, Newton, Pvt, Col Wm Hall, Capt Geo Hambleton, Vol Inf
SIMS, Robert, Pvt, Col Alexander Loury, Capt Geo Sarver, Inf
SIMSON, William, Pvt, Col S Bunch, Capt Jno English, E TN Drafted Mil
SINCLAIR, Charles, Pvt, Col Samuel Bunch, Capt Jno English, E TN Drafted Mil
SINCLAIR, Hugh, Pvt, Col R H Dyer, Capt James McMahan, TN Vol Mtd Gunmen
SINCLAIR, James, Pvt, Col N T Perkins, Capt John B Quarles, Vol Mtd Inf

*Enlisted Men, War of 1812*

SINCLAIR, Joseph, Pvt, Col Samuel Wear, Capt John Childs, E TN Vol Inf
SINGLAR, Amos, 5 Sgt, Col John Cocke, Capt Richard Crunk, Inf
SINGLETARY, David, Pvt, Col Wm Metcalf, Capt Wm Mullen, Mil Inf
SINGLETARY, John, Pvt, Col Wm Metcalf, Capt Wm Mullen, Mil Inf; deceased
SINGLETON, Edward, Blksmth, Col Jno Coffee, Capt Frederick Stump, Cav
SINGLETON, Edward, Blksmth, Col John Alcorn, Capt Frederick Stump, Cav
SINGLETON, James, Pvt, Regt Commander omitted, Capt Sam'l Cowan, Branch Srvce omitted
SINGLETON, William, Pvt, Col A Loury, Capt James Kincaid, Inf
SINGLETON, William, Pvt, Maj Wm Woodfolk, Capt Abner Pearce, Inf; transferred from Capt Neil's Co
SINGLETON, William, Pvt, Maj Wm Woodfolk, Capt James C Neil, Inf
SINKS, Jesse, Pvt, Col John Cocke, Capt Joseph Price, Inf
SINNER (SINON), William, Pvt, Col Philip Pipkin, Capt David Smith, Inf
SINNER (SINON), William, Rank omitted, Col Philip Pipkin, Capt Mullen, Mil Inf
SIRELY, Absolom, Pvt, Col Samuel Wear, Capt Simeon Perry, E TN Vol Mtd Inf
SISCO, James, Pvt, Col Wm Johnson, Capt James R Rogers, E TN Drafted Mil
SISCO, John, Pvt, Regt Commander omitted, Capt Jno Miller, Spies
SISK, Joel, Pvt, Col R H Dyer, Maj Wm Russell, Capt Wm Russell, Vol Mtd Gunmen
SISSOME, William, Pvt, Col Robt Steele, Capt Robt Campbell, Mil Inf
SITTER, Jeffrey, 3 Cpl, Col Wm Hall, Capt Brice Martin, Vol Inf
SITTON, Jeffrey, 3 Cpl, Col Wm Hall, Capt Brice Martin, Vol Inf
SITTON, Jeffrey, Pvt, Col Wm Hall, Capt Brice Martin, Vol Inf; reduced from Cpl
SITTON, Jehu (Jahur) L, Pvt, Col Wm Hall, Capt Brice Martin, Vol Inf
SITTON, Jesse, Pvt, Col Wm Metcalf, Capt Wm Sitton, Mil Inf
SITTON, John L, Pvt, Col Edward Bradley, Capt Brice Martin, Vol Inf
SITTON, Phillip, Pvt, Col Edward Bradley, Capt Brice Martin, Vol Inf
SITTON, Phillip, Pvt, Col Wm Hall, Capt Brice Martin, Vol Inf
SKAGGS, James, Pvt, Col Jno Williams, Capt Sam'l Bunch, E TN Mtd Vol
SKAGGS, Stephen, Pvt, Col T Williams, Capt Wm Walker, Vol
SKEELERS, William, Pvt, Col Wm Johnson, Capt Elihu Milliken, 3rd Regt E TN Mil
SKEEN, Elijah, Pvt, Col Samuel Bunch, Capt Joseph Duncan, E TN Drafted Mil; joined from Capt Buchanan Co

SKEEN, Elisha, Pvt, Col Samuel Bunch, Capt Edward Buchanan, E TN Mil
SKEENS, John, Pvt, Col Wm Lillard, Capt Thos McChristian, E TN Vol Inf
SKELITON, Joseph, Pvt, Col John Cocke, Capt James Gault, Inf; d 2-17-1815
SKELLERN, George, Pvt, Col Edwin Booth, Capt Vernon, E TN Mil
SKELLY, Jacob, Pvt, Col Samuel Bunch, Capt Francis Berry, E TN Mil; attached to Capt English Co
SKELTON, Alexander, Pvt, Col Wm Lillard, Capt Geo Argenbright, E TN Vol Riflemen
SKELTON, William, Pvt, Col Wm Lillard, Capt Geo Argenbright, E TN Vol Riflemen
SKIDMORE, Abraham, Pvt, Col Wm Metcalf, Capt Andrew Patterson, Mil Inf
SKILES, Ephraim, Pvt, Col John Brown, Capt Jesse G Reany, Mtd Gunmen; discharged for inability
SKILES, George, Ens, Col James Raulston, Capt Mathew Cowan, Inf
SKILES, James, Pvt, Col John Brown, Capt Jesse Reany, Mtd Gunmen
SKILES, John, Pvt, Col Samuel Bayless, Capt Joseph Goodson, E TN Mil
SKILETON, Joseph, Pvt, Col A Cheatham, Capt Chas Johnson, Inf
SKILLEN, George, Pvt, Col Wm Johnson, Capt James Tunnell, E TN Mil
SKILLEN, Isaac, Pvt, Col Wm Lillard, Capt Geo Keyes, E TN Inf
SKILLERN, James, Pvt, Col John Brown, Capt Jesse G Reany, Mtd Gunmen
SKILLERN, William, Pvt, Col Thos Benton, Capt Henry L Douglass, Vol Inf
SKINER, Ebenezer, Pvt, Maj Wm Woodfolk, Capt Ezekial Ross & Capt McCulley, Inf
SKINNER, Ebenezer, Pvt, Col R C Napier, Capt Thos Gray, Mil Inf
SKINNER, Ebenezer, Pvt, Lt Col L Hammond, Capt James Craig, Inf
SKINNER, Ebenezer, Pvt, Regt Commander omitted, Capt Abner Pearce, Inf
SKINNER, Ebenezer, Pvt, Regt Commander omitted, Capt Askew, Inf
SKINNER, Jesse, Pvt, Lt Col A Cheatham, Capt Gabriel Martin, Mtd Inf
SKINNER, John, Pvt, Col Jno Coffee, Capt Fred Stump, Cav
SKINNER, William, Pvt, Col Samuel Bunch, Capt Dan'l Yarnell, E TN Mil
SKIPPER, Jacob, Pvt, Col Robt Steele, Capt Robt Campbell, Mil Inf
SKIPPER, William, Pvt, Col R C Napier, Capt James McMurray, Mil Inf
SKYLES, William, Pvt, Col John Brown, Capt Jesse G Reany, Mtd Gunmen
SLADE, Benazah, 2 Cpl, Col N T Perkins, Capt John Doak, Vol Mtd Gunmen
SLAGER (SLIGER), Adam, Pvt, Col Wm Johnson, Capt Andrew Lawson, E TN Drafted Mil
SLATER, David H, Pvt, Col T Williamson, Capt James

Pace, Lt Nealy, Vol Mtd Gunmen; dismissed day of mustering in
SLATTON, Ambrose, Pvt, Col Edwin Booth, Capt John Sharpe, E TN Mil
SLATTON, John, Pvt, Col S Bunch, Capt Jas Cunningham, E TN Vol Mtd Inf
SLATTON, John, Pvt, Col Samuel Bunch, Capt James Cummings, E TN Vol Mtd Inf
SLAUGHTER, Abraham, Pvt, Col Wm Johnson, Capt Joseph Scott, E TN Drafted Mil
SLAUGHTER, Francis, Blksmth, Col R H Dyer, Capt Robt Evans, Vol Mtd Gunmen
SLAUGHTER, John, Pvt, Maj Wm Russell, Capt Fleman Hodges, Vol Mtd Gunmen
SLAUGHTER, Joseph, Pvt, Maj Wm Russell, Capt Fleman Hodges, Vol Mtd Gunmen
SLAUGHTER, Martin, Cpl, Col Wm Johnson, Capt Joseph Scott, E TN Drafted Mil
SLAUGHTER, Rheuben, Sgt, Maj Gen A Jackson, Capt Jos Kirkpatrick, Mtd Gunmen
SLAVIN, John, Pvt, Lt Col L Hammond, Capt James Tubb, Inf
SLEAGLE, John, Pvt, Col Wm Lillard, Capt Jacob Hartsell, E TN Vol Inf
SLEDGE, Henry, Pvt, Col A Cheatham, Capt Chas Johnson, Inf
SLEEDER, John, Pvt, Col T Williamson, Capt James Pace, Lt Nealy, Vol Mtd Gunmen
SLEIGLER, John L, Pvt, Col T McCrory, Capt Isaac Patton, Mil Inf
SLEMONS, William, Pvt, Col Wm Lillard, Capt Wm McLin, E TN Inf
SLENE, Joseph, Pvt, Col Samuel Wear, Capt Jesse Cole, Vol Inf
SLEWARD, Roberson, Pvt, Col Edward Bradley, Capt Wm Lauderdale, Vol Inf
SLICKER, George, Sgt, Col T McCrory, Capt Isaac Patton, Inf
SLIGER (SLAGER), Adam, Pvt, Col Wm Johnson, Capt Andrew Lawson, E TN Drafted Mil
SLOAME, John, Pvt, Regt Commander omitted, Capt Archibald McKinney, Cav
SLOAN, Archibald, 2 Cpl, Col Wm Johnson, Capt David McKamey, E TN Drafted Mil
SLOAN, Archibald, Pvt, Col John Coffee, Capt Chas Kavanaugh, Cav
SLOAN, James, Pvt, Col Samuel Wear, Capt James Tedford, E TN Vol Inf
SLOAN, James, Pvt, Maj Wm Russell, Capt John Trimble, Vol Mtd Gunmen
SLOAN, James, Pvt, Regt Commander omitted, Capt Mason, Cav
SLOAN, John, Pvt, Maj Wm Russell, Capt John Tremble, Vol Mtd Gunmen
SLOAN, Joseph, Pvt, Col Ewen Allison, Capt Adam Winsell, E TN Drafted Mil
SLOAN, Joseph, Pvt, Col S Bunch, Capt F Register, E TN Mil; joined Winsel's Co
SLOAN, Thomas, Pvt, Col John Wynne, Capt Wm Carothers, W TN Inf
SLOANE, John, Pvt, Regt Commander omitted, Capt Archibald McKinney, Cav
SLOUN, Joiah R, Pvt, Lt Col Leroy Hammonds, Capt Jas Tubb, Inf
SLOUN, Jonah, Pvt, Lt Col Alexander Hammonds, Capt Jas Tubb, Inf
SLOVER, Jacob, Pvt, Col S Bunch, Capt Geo Gregory, E TN Drafted Mil
SLOWN, Josiah R, Pvt, Lt Col L Hammond, Capt Jas Tubbs, Inf
SLOWN, Josiah, Pvt, Lt Col L Hammonds, Capt Jas Tubb, Inf
SMALING, Robert, Sgt, Col William Hunter, Capt Henry Hunter, E TN Mil
SMALL, Daniel, Pvt, Col R T Perkins, Capt Quarles, Vol Mtd Inf
SMALL, George, Pvt, Col John Wynne, Capt John Porter, Inf
SMALL, Henry, Pvt, Maj William Russell, Capt Mitchell, Vol Mtd Gunmen
SMALL, Henry, Pvt, Regt Commander omitted, Capt James Cowan, Inf
SMALL, James, Pvt, Col S Bayless, Capt Branch Jones, E TN Drafted Mil
SMALL, John, Pvt, Regt Commander omitted, Capt N Gibbs, Vol Inf
SMALL, Robert, Cpl, Col Edwin Booth, Capt McKinney, E TN Mil
SMALLEN, William, Pvt, Col S Bayless, Capt Solomon Hendrix, E TN Mil
SMALLEY, Joshua, Pvt, Col Philip Pipkin, Capt Henry Newlin, Mil Inf
SMALLING, Nathaniel, Pvt, Col Ewen Allison, Capt Adam Winsell, E TN Drafted Mil
SMALLING, Robert, Pvt, Gen Jackson, Capt Hugh Kerr, Mtd Rangers
SMALLING, Robert, Pvt, Regt Commander omitted, Capt Hugh Kerr, Mtd Rangers
SMALLING, Samuel, Pvt, Col Ewen Allison, Capt Adam Winsell, E TN Drafted Mil
SMALLING, Solomon, Pvt, Col Ewen Allison, Capt Adam Winsell, E TN Drafted Mil
SMALLWOOD, Elisha, Pvt, Col S Copeland, Capt Thomas Williams, Inf
SMALLWOOD, John, Pvt, Col Thos Benton, Capt Geo Gibbs, Vol Inf
SMART, Bennet, Pvt, Col Thomas Williamson, Capt John Crane & Capt Cook, Vol Mtd Gunmen
SMART, David H, Pvt, Col A Cheatham, Capt Geo Chapman, Inf
SMART, David H, Pvt, Col Thomas Williamson, Capt Cook & Capt Geo Crane, Vol Mtd Gunmen
SMART, John, Pvt, Col Robert Dyer, Maj William Russell, Capt William Russell, Vol Mtd Gunmen
SMART, John, Pvt, Col Wm Hall, Capt Henry Newlin, Inf
SMART, John, Pvt, Maj Wm Woodfolk, Capt Ross & Capt McCulley, Inf
SMART, Joseph, Cpl, Col S Copeland, Capt Alexander Provine, Mil Inf; promoted from Pvt
SMART, Joseph, Pvt, Col Jas Raulston, Capt Jas Raulston, Inf
SMART, Peters, Sgt, Col John Cocke, Capt Richard

## Enlisted Men, War of 1812

Crunk, Inf
SMART, Phillip, Sgt, Col S Copeland, Capt Alexander Provine, Mil Inf; promoted to Sgt Maj
SMART, Sam, Pvt, Gen Andrew Jackson, Capt Nathan Davis, Inf
SMEDDY, William, Ffr, Col Thomas Benton, Capt William Smith, Vol Inf
SMELCER, Joseph, Cpl, Col S Bayless, Capt Joseph Goodson, E Tn Mil
SMIDBY, Robert, Pvt, Col Everett Upton, no other information
SMIDDY, Reuben, Pvt, Col S Wear, Capt Doak, E TN Vol Inf
SMIDDY, Robert, Pvt, Col Ewen Allison, Capt Joseph Everett, E TN Mil; deserted
SMIDDY, William, Ffr, Col Thos Benton, Capt William Smith, Vol Inf
SMIDDY, William, Ffr, Regt Commander omitted, Capt Richard Smith, Vol Inf
SMIDLY, William, Pvt, Col Alexander Loury, Capt Gabriel Martin, Inf
SMIDLY, William, Pvt, Col Alexander Loury, Capt Geo Martin, Inf
SMILEON, John, Pvt, Col S Copeland, Capt David Williams, Inf
SMILEY, Alexander, Pvt, Col William Lillard, Capt Gabriel Martin, E TN Vol Inf
SMILEY, Hugh B, Pvt, Maj William Russell, Capt William Russell, TN Vol Mtd Gunmen; trans from Capt Dickson
SMILEY, Joseph, Pvt, Col William Lillard, Capt Gabriel Martin, E TN Vol Inf
SMILEY, Sawyer, Pvt, Col William Lillard, Capt McCulpin, E Tn Inf; died 1-4-1814
SMILEY, Thomas, Pvt, Regt Commander omitted, Capt James Cowan, Inf
SMILLING, Lemmuel, Dmr, Col Wm Metcalf, Maj Gen Carroll, Capt Jackson, Inf
SMITH, Aaron, Pvt, Gen Andrew Jackson, Capt Nathan Davis, Mtd Inf
SMITH, Abner, Cpl, Maj Gen Wm Carroll, Capt John Jackson & Capt Wm Metcalf, Mil Inf
SMITH, Abraham, Pvt, Col Edward Bradley, Capt Wm Lauderdale, Vol Inf
SMITH, Abraham, Pvt, Col N T Perkins, Capt John Doak, Vol Mtd Gunmen
SMITH, Abraham, Pvt, Col Wm Hall, Capt Wm Alexander, Vol Inf
SMITH, Abraham, Pvt, Lt Col Hammonds, Capt Thomas Delaney, Inf
SMITH, Abraham, Pvt, Maj Gen Andrew Jackson, Capt Joseph Kirkpatrick, Mtd Gunmen
SMITH, Abraham, Pvt, Maj Wm Woodfolk, Capt Ezekiel Ross & Capt McCully, Inf; reduced from Sgt
SMITH, Alexander, Ffr, Col Wm Metcalf, Capt Wm Sitton, Mil Inf
SMITH, Alexander, Pvt, Lt Col Leroy Hammonds, Capt Thomas Delaney, Inf
SMITH, Alijah, Pvt, Col S Copeland, Capt Thomas Williamson, Mil Inf
SMITH, Allen, Cpl, Col John K Wynne, Capt John Spinks, Inf
SMITH, Allen, Pvt, Col Philip Pipkin, Capt Wm Mackay, trans to Capt Searcy
SMITH, Allen, Pvt, Col Robert Steele, Capt Samuel Maxwell, Mil Inf
SMITH, Allen, Pvt, Maj Gen Wm Carroll, Capt Lewis Dillahunty & Capt Daniel Bradford, Vol Inf
SMITH, Andrew, Pvt, Brig Gen Thos Johnson, Capt Abraham Allen, Mil Inf
SMITH, Andrew, Pvt, Col John Coffee, Capt Michael Molton, Cav
SMITH, Andrew, Pvt, Col N T Perkins, Capt Mathew Johnston, Mil Inf
SMITH, Andrew, Pvt, Col Wm Hall, Capt John Wallace, Inf
SMITH, Andrew, Pvt, Col Wm Metcalf, Capt Bird L Hurt, Mil Inf
SMITH, Andrew, Pvt, Lt Col Napier, Co Commander omitted, Inf
SMITH, Andrew, Pvt, Regt Commander omitted, Capt Jas Williams, Mil Inf
SMITH, Archibald, Pvt, Col James Raulston, Maj Gen Wm Carroll, Capt Elijah Haynie, Inf
SMITH, Archibald, Pvt, Col John K Wynne, Capt Bayless E Prince, Inf
SMITH, Archilles, Pvt, Col R H Dyer, Capt Robert Evans, Vol Mtd Gunmen
SMITH, Aron, Pvt, Regt Commander omitted, Capt James Haggard, Mtd Gunmen
SMITH, Arthur, Pvt, Col Ewin Allison, Capt Joseph Everett, E TN Mil
SMITH, Asa, Pvt, Col Wm Y Higgins, Capt Stephen Griffin, Mtd Riflemen
SMITH, B Samuel, Pvt, Col Samuel Bunch, Capt Henry Stephens, E TN Mtd Inf
SMITH, Barnet, Pvt, Col Wm Lillard, Capt Zacheus Copeland, E TN Vol Inf
SMITH, Barthet, Pvt, Col Wm Hall, Capt Wm Alexander, Vol Inf
SMITH, Bartlett, Cpl, Col Thomas Bradley, Capt Wm Lauderdale, Vol Inf
SMITH, Bartlett, Pvt, Col Wm Hall, Capt Wm Alexander, Vol Inf
SMITH, Benjamin F, Pvt, Col John Coffee, Capt John W Byrn, Cav
SMITH, Benjamin F, Pvt, Regt Commander omitted, Capt David Smith, Cav; also 2 Cpl
SMITH, Benjamin, Pvt, Col A Loury, Capt Gabriel Martin, Inf
SMITH, Benjamin, Pvt, Col John Coffee, Capt David Smith, Vol Cav
SMITH, Benjamin, Pvt, Col N T Perkins, Capt John B Quarles, Mtd Inf
SMITH, Benjamin, Pvt, Col R H Dyer, Capt Cuthbert Hudson, Vol Mtd Gunmen; died 11-28-1814
SMITH, Benjamin, Pvt, Col R H Dyer, Capt Thomas White, Vol Mtd Gunmen
SMITH, Benjamin, Pvt, Col Samuel Bayless, Capt Joseph Goodson, E TN Mil
SMITH, Benjamin, Pvt, Col Samuel Bunch, Capt Simeon Perry, E TN Mil

## Enlisted Men, War of 1812

SMITH, Benjamin, Pvt, Col Wm Johnson, Capt Joseph Scott, E TN Draft Mil
SMITH, Benjamin, Sgt Maj-Paymaster, Gen John Coffee, TN Vol Mtd Gunmen
SMITH, Bennet, Pvt, Col Wm Hall, Capt Travis Nash, Inf; not legally notified or enrolled
SMITH, Bird, Pvt, Col James Raulston, Capt Daniel Newman, Inf
SMITH, Briant, Pvt, Col Ewin Allison, Capt Jonas Loughmiller, Mil; trans from Capt Griffin
SMITH, Briant, Pvt, Col Samuel Bunch, Capt Jones Griffin, E TN Draft Mil
SMITH, Burton, Pvt, Col John Cocke, Capt Richard Crunk, Inf
SMITH, Burwell, Pvt, Col Samuel Bayless, Capt John Brock, E TN Mil
SMITH, Caswell, Pvt, Maj Robert Cooper, Co Commander omitted, Mtd Riflemen
SMITH, Caswell, Pvt, Regt Commander omitted, Capt Thos Gray
SMITH, Charles M, Pvt, Col Isaac Williams, Capt Samuel Bunch, Mtd Vol
SMITH, Charles, Pvt, Col John Cocke, Capt James Gault, Inf; died 2-6-1815
SMITH, Charles, Pvt, Col S Copeland, Capt Moses Thompson, Inf
SMITH, Charles, Pvt, Maj Gen Wm Carroll, Capt Wiley Huddleston, Inf
SMITH, Charles, Sgt, Col Wm Johnston, Capt Christopher Cook, E TN Mil
SMITH, Charles, Sgt, Col Wm Johnston, Capt Joseph Kirk, Mil
SMITH, Cornelius, Pvt, Col S Bunch, Capt Francis Register, E TN Mil
SMITH, Cornelius, Pvt, Col Samuel Bunch, Capt George McPherson, E TN Mil; joined from Capt Register's Co
SMITH, Cornelius, Pvt, Col Wm Lillard, Capt Jacob Dyke, Vol Inf; unable to perform duty
SMITH, Daniel, Pvt, Col John Cocke, Capt Richard Crunk, Inf
SMITH, Daniel, Pvt, Col N T Perkins, Capt Jas McMahan, Mtd Gunmen
SMITH, Daniel, Sgt, Col Ewin Allison, Capt Adam Winsell, E TN Drafted Mil
SMITH, David, Pvt, Col Edward Bradley, Capt Harry L Douglas, Vol Inf
SMITH, David, Pvt, Col S Bunch, Capt Nathan Gibbs, E TN Draft Mil
SMITH, David, Pvt, Col Samuel Bayless, Capt John Brock, E TN Mil; died 2-8-1815
SMITH, David, Pvt, Col Thos H Williamson, Capt James Pace & Lt James Nealey, Vol Mtd Gunmen; died 2-10-1815
SMITH, David, Pvt, Col Wm Johnson, Capt David McKamy, E TN Draft Mil
SMITH, David, Pvt, Gen Jackson, Capt Hugh Kerr, Mtd Rangers
SMITH, David, Pvt, Maj John Childs, Capt Reuben Tipton, E TN Vol Mtd Inf; Regt from Jefferson Co
SMITH, Edward, 1 Cpl, Col Samuel Bunch, Capt Wm Jobe, E TN Vol Mtd Inf
SMITH, Edward, Pvt, Col R H Dyer, Capt Robert Evans, Vol Mtd Gunmen
SMITH, Edward, Pvt, Col Wm Lillard, Capt Thomas Sharpe, 2 Regt Inf
SMITH, Edward, Pvt, Regt Commander omitted, Capt Jos Williams, Mil Cav
SMITH, Eli, Sgt, Col Samuel Wear, Co Commander omitted, E TN Vol Inf
SMITH, Elijah jr, Pvt, Col Thomas H Benton, Capt James McFerrin, Vol Inf
SMITH, Elijah sr, Pvt, Col Thomas H Benton, Capt James McFerrin, Vol Inf
SMITH, Elijah, Cpl, Col Edward Bradley, Capt Elijah Haynie, Vol Inf
SMITH, Elijah, Pvt, Col Samuel Bayless, Capt John Brock, E TN Mil
SMITH, Elijah, Pvt, Col Thomas H Benton, Capt James McFerrin, Vol Inf
SMITH, Elijah, Pvt, Col Wm Hall, Capt Henry Newland, Inf
SMITH, Elijah, Pvt, Col Wm Pillow, Capt James McFerrin, Inf
SMITH, Elisha, Pvt, Col John K Wynne, Capt Wm Carothers, W TN Inf
SMITH, Eliza, Pvt, Lt Col Richard Napier, Co Commander omitted, Inf
SMITH, Eneves, Pvt, Col James Raulston, Capt Daniel Newman, Inf
SMITH, Ezekiel, Pvt, Col Ewin Allison, Co Commander omitted, E TN Mil; deserted 3-4-1814
SMITH, Ezekiel, Pvt, Col S Bunch, Capt Jones Griffin, E TN Drafted Mil; discharged for inability
SMITH, Ezekiel, Pvt, Col Samuel Bayless, Capt Solomon Hendrix, E TN Mil
SMITH, Fielding, Pvt, Col John Cocke, Capt John Weakley, Inf
SMITH, Francis R, Pvt, Col S Copeland, Capt Moses Thompson, Inf
SMITH, Francis, 1 Sgt, Col Wm Metcalf, Capt Andrew Patterson, Mil Inf
SMITH, Francis, Pvt, Regt Commander omitted, Capt Jos Williams, Mil Cav
SMITH, Fredrick, Cpl, Col John Cocke, Capt James Gray, Inf; d 2-2-1815
SMITH, Fredrick, Cpl, Lt Col Henry Bryan, Maj Robert Searcy, Inf
SMITH, Fredrick, Sgt, Col S Bayless, Capt Joseph Goodson, E TN Mil
SMITH, Gabriel, Pvt, Col John Cocke, Capt James Gault, Inf
SMITH, George B, Pvt, Col Jno Brown, Capt Wm D Neilson, E TN Vol Mil
SMITH, George, 1 Cpl, Col Philip Pipkin, Capt Geo Mebane, Mil Inf
SMITH, George, Pvt, Col Alexander Loury, Capt Leroy Hammonds & Capt Raines, Inf; transferred to Capt Chism
SMITH, George, Pvt, Col Ewen Allison, Capt Jonas Loughmiller, Mil; joined from Capt Griffin
SMITH, George, Pvt, Col John Cocke, Capt James Gray,

SMITH, George, Pvt, Col John Wynne, Capt Geo Breden, Inf
SMITH, George, Pvt, Col S Bayless, Capt I Bacon, E TN Mil
SMITH, George, Pvt, Col Thomas Williamson, Capt Giles Burdett, Vol Mtd Gunmen
SMITH, George, Pvt, Maj Gen Jackson, Capt John Crane, Mtd Gunmen; d 1-8-1814
SMITH, George, Pvt, Maj John Childs, Capt Jas Cunningham, E TN Vol Mtd Inf
SMITH, George, Pvt, Maj William Russell, Capt John Chism, Vol Mtd Riflemen
SMITH, George, Pvt, Regt Commander omitted, Capt Elijah Rushing, Inf
SMITH, George, Sgt, Col Edwin Booth, Capt John Sharp, E TN Mil
SMITH, Georgy, Pvt, Col S Bunch, Capt Jones & Capt Griffin, E TN Drafted Mil
SMITH, Gregory, Pvt, Col S Bunch, Capt Geo McPherson, E TN Mil
SMITH, Hamliaso, Pvt, Col Samuel Bunch, Capt Thos Mann, E TN Vol Mtd Inf
SMITH, Harris, Pvt, Col John Wynne, Capt John Spinks, Inf
SMITH, Hartwell, Pvt, Col Philip Pipkin, Capt Blakemore, Mil Inf
SMITH, Henry, Pvt, Col Ewen Allison, Capt Wm King, Drafted Mil
SMITH, Henry, Pvt, Col Samuel Bunch, Capt F Register, E TN Mil
SMITH, Henry, Pvt, Col T McCrory, Capt Jas Shannon, Mil Inf
SMITH, Henry, Pvt, Maj Gen Wm Carroll, Col James Raulston, Capt Elijah Haynie, Inf
SMITH, Henry, Pvt, Maj Wm Woodfolk, Capt Ezekial Ross & Capt McCulley, Inf
SMITH, Henry, Pvt, Regt Commander omitted, Capt Gray, Inf
SMITH, Hezekiah, Pvt, Col Wm Lillard, Capt Jacob Dykes, Vol Inf; deserted
SMITH, Hezekiah, Pvt, Regt Commander omitted, Capt Geo Smith, Spies
SMITH, Ira, Pvt, Col Wm Hall, Capt John Kennedy, Vol Inf
SMITH, Irie, Pvt, Col Wm Hall, Capt John Kennedy, Vol Inf
SMITH, Isaac, Pvt, Col A Loury, Lt Col L Hammond, Capt Arahel Rains, Inf; transferred to Capt Chisholms
SMITH, Isaac, Pvt, Col John Brown, Capt John Childs, E TN Vol Mtd Inf
SMITH, Isaac, Pvt, Col John Cocke, Capt Samuel M Caruthers, Inf
SMITH, Isaac, Pvt, Col Samuel Bunch, Capt Geo Gregory, E TN Drafted Mil
SMITH, Isaac, Pvt, Col Samuel Wear, Capt Rufus Morgan, E TN Vol Inf; unable to perform duty
SMITH, Isaac, Pvt, Col Thos Johnston, Capt Daniel Oban, 36th Inf
SMITH, Isaac, Pvt, Col Wm Johnson, Capt Elihu Milliken, 3rd Regt E TN Mil
SMITH, Isaac, Pvt, Col Wm Johnson, Capt James Stewart, E TN Drafted Mil
SMITH, Isaac, Pvt, Maj Wm Russell, Capt Wm Chism, Vol Mtd Riflemen
SMITH, Isaac, Sgt, Col T McCrory, Capt Jas Shannon, TN Mil
SMITH, Isakiah, Pvt, Col Ewen Allison, Capt Jacob Hoyal, E TN Mil
SMITH, Isham, 4 Sgt, Col Wm Hall, Capt Travis C Nash, Vol Inf
SMITH, Isham, Pvt, Col Wm Lillard, Capt Thos Sharpe, 2nd Regt Inf
SMITH, Jack, Sgt Maj, Col John Coffee, TN Vol Cav
SMITH, Jacob C, Pvt, Regt Commander omitted, Capt Mason, Cav
SMITH, Jacob, Cpl, Col Robt Steele, Capt James Bennett, Mil Inf
SMITH, Jacob, Pvt, Col John Wynne, Capt Butler, Inf; deserted
SMITH, Jacob, Pvt, Col R C Napier, Capt Samuel Ashmore, Mil Inf
SMITH, Jacob, Pvt, Col Samuel Bayless, Capt John Brock, E TN Mil
SMITH, Jacob, Pvt, Col Thos Williamson, Capt James Cook & Capt John Crane, Vol Mtd Gunmen
SMITH, Jacob, Pvt, Col Wm Johnson, Capt Christopher Cook, E TN Mil
SMITH, Jacob, Pvt, Maj Wm Woodfolk, Capt Abraham Dudney & Capt John Sutton, Inf
SMITH, James A, Pvt, Col Philip Pipkin, Capt David Smith, Inf
SMITH, James H, Pvt, Regt Commander omitted, Capt Archibald McKinney, Cav
SMITH, James M, Pvt, Col Wm Metcalf, Capt Thos Marks, Mil Inf
SMITH, James M, Pvt, Col Wm Metcalf, Capt Wm Mullin, Mil Inf
SMITH, James, 1 Cpl, Col Samuel Bunch, Capt Henry Stephen, E TN Mtd Inf
SMITH, James, Cpl, Col T McCrory, Capt Abel Willis, Mil Inf; promoted from Pvt
SMITH, James, Pvt, Col A Loury, Lt Col L Hammond, Capt Thos Delany, Inf
SMITH, James, Pvt, Col Edwin Booth, Capt John Sharp, E TN Mil
SMITH, James, Pvt, Col John Alcorn, Capt Thos Bradley, Vol Cav
SMITH, James, Pvt, Col John Wynne, Capt Bayless E Prince, Inf
SMITH, James, Pvt, Col John Wynne, Capt John Porter, Inf
SMITH, James, Pvt, Col Philip Pipkin, Capt John Robertson, Mil Inf
SMITH, James, Pvt, Col R C Napier, Capt Edward Neblett, Mil Inf
SMITH, James, Pvt, Col S Bunch, Capt Jno English, E TN Drafted Mil
SMITH, James, Pvt, Col Samuel Bunch, Capt Edward Buchanan, E TN Mil
SMITH, James, Pvt, Col Samuel Bunch, Capt James

Penny, E TN Mtd Inf
SMITH, James, Pvt, Col Samuel Bunch, Capt Joseph Duncan, E TN Drafted Mil; joined from Capt Yarnell's Co
SMITH, James, Pvt, Col Samuel Wear, Capt John Doak, E TN Vol Inf
SMITH, James, Pvt, Col Wm Hall, Capt James Hambleton, Vol Inf
SMITH, James, Pvt, Col Wm Metcalf, Capt John Barnhart, Mil Inf
SMITH, James, Pvt, Maj Wm Russell, Capt Wm Chism, Vol Mtd Riflemen
SMITH, James, Pvt, Regt Commander omitted, Capt Gray, Inf
SMITH, Jasper, Pvt, Col S Copeland, Capt John Holshouser, Inf
SMITH, Jeremiah, Dmr, Col John Cocke, Capt Samuel M Caruthers, Inf
SMITH, Jeremiah, Pvt, Maj Gen A Jackson, Capt Joseph Kirkpatrick, Mtd Gunmen; killed 1-22-1814
SMITH, Jesse, Pvt, Col Edwin Booth, Capt John Sharpe, E TN Mil
SMITH, Jesse, Pvt, Col Samuel Bunch, Capt Jno McNare, E TN Mil; attached to Capt Duncan's Co
SMITH, Jesse, Pvt, Col Samuel Bunch, Capt Joseph Duncan, E TN Drafted Mil; joined from Capt McNare's Co
SMITH, Jesse, Pvt, Maj James Porter, Capt James Anderson, Cav
SMITH, Joel, Pvt, Col John Cocke, Capt Geo Barnes, Inf
SMITH, Joel, Pvt, Col R H Dyer, Capt Cuthbert Hudson, Vol Mtd Gunmen
SMITH, John jr, Pvt, Col John Coffee, Capt Blackman Coleman, Cav
SMITH, John jr, Pvt, Col John Coffee, Capt James Terrell, Vol Cav
SMITH, John jr, Pvt, Col Wm Johnson, Capt Joseph Scott, E TN Drafted Mil
SMITH, John sr, Pvt, Col Edward Bradley, Capt John Kennedy, Riflemen; AWOL
SMITH, John sr, Pvt, Col John Coffee, Capt James Terrell, Vol Cav
SMITH, John, 1 Sgt, Col Samuel Bunch, Capt David G Vance, E TN Mtd Inf
SMITH, John, 2 Sgt Maj, Col John Coffee, TN Vol Cav
SMITH, John, 2 Sgt Maj, Col John Coffee, TN Vol Cav & Mtd Gunmen
SMITH, John, 3 Cpl, Col Philip Pipkin, Capt John Robertson, Mil Inf
SMITH, John, Cpl, Col John Brown, Capt John Childs, E TN Vol Mtd Gunmen
SMITH, John, Maj Gen A Jackson, Col Thos Williamson, Capt Robt Steele, Vol Mtd Gunmen
SMITH, John, Pvt, Brig Gen T Johnston, Capt Abraham Allen, Mil Inf
SMITH, John, Pvt, Col Edwin Booth, Capt John Charpe, E TN Mil
SMITH, John, Pvt, Col Ewen Allison, Capt Wm King, Drafted Mil
SMITH, John, Pvt, Col James Raulston, Capt James A Black, Inf
SMITH, John, Pvt, Col Jno Brown, Capt Wm D Neilson, Regt E TN Vol Mil
SMITH, John, Pvt, Col John Alcorn, Capt Wm Locke, Cav
SMITH, John, Pvt, Col John Coffee, Capt Blackman Coleman, Cav
SMITH, John, Pvt, Col John Coffee, Capt David Smith, Vol Cav
SMITH, John, Pvt, Col John Wynne, Capt John Porter, Inf
SMITH, John, Pvt, Col John Wynne, Capt John Spinks, Inf
SMITH, John, Pvt, Col N T Perkins, Capt James McMahan, Mtd Gunmen
SMITH, John, Pvt, Col Philip Pipkin, Capt David Smith, Inf
SMITH, John, Pvt, Col Philip Pipkin, Capt John Robertson, Mil Inf
SMITH, John, Pvt, Col Philip Pipkin, Capt John Strother, Mil
SMITH, John, Pvt, Col Philip Pipkin, Capt Peter Searcy, Mil Inf
SMITH, John, Pvt, Col R H Dyer, Capt Ephraim Dickson, TN Vol Mtd Gunmen
SMITH, John, Pvt, Col Robt Steele, Capt James Bennett, Mil Inf
SMITH, John, Pvt, Col Samuel Bayless, Capt John Brock, E TN Mil
SMITH, John, Pvt, Col Samuel Bayless, Capt Joseph _____, E TN Mil
SMITH, John, Pvt, Col Samuel Bunch, Capt F Register, E TN Mil
SMITH, John, Pvt, Col Samuel Wear, Capt John Doak, E TN Vol Inf
SMITH, John, Pvt, Col Samuel Wear, Capt John Stephens, E TN Vol Inf
SMITH, John, Pvt, Col Thos Benton, Capt Geo W Gibbs, Vol Inf
SMITH, John, Pvt, Col Thos Benton, Capt Wm J Smith, Vol Inf
SMITH, John, Pvt, Col Wm Hall, Capt John Kennedy, Vol Inf
SMITH, John, Pvt, Col Wm Johnson, Capt Benj Powell, E TN Mil
SMITH, John, Pvt, Col Wm Johnson, Capt Christopher Cook, 3rd Regt E TN Mil; joined from Capt E Milliken's Co
SMITH, John, Pvt, Col Wm Johnson, Capt Elihu Milliken, 3rd Regt E TN Mil
SMITH, John, Pvt, Col Wm Metcalf, Capt Alexander Hill & Capt John Cunningham, Mil Inf
SMITH, John, Pvt, Col Wm Metcalf, Capt Bird L Hurt, Mil Inf
SMITH, John, Pvt, Col Wm Metcalf, Capt Obidah Waller, Mil Inf; d 2-20-1815
SMITH, John, Pvt, Lt Col Jno Edmonson, no other information
SMITH, John, Pvt, Lt Col L Hammond, Capt James Craig, Inf
SMITH, John, Pvt, Maj John Childs, Capt Chas Conway, E TN Mtd Gunmen

SMITH, John, Pvt, Maj Wm Russell, Capt Geo Mitchie, Vol Mtd Gunmen
SMITH, John, Pvt, Maj Wm Woodfolk, Capt Abner Pearce, Inf
SMITH, John, Pvt, Maj Wm Woodfolk, Capt James Neil, Inf; d (date illegible)
SMITH, John, Pvt, Regt Commander omitted, Capt Jas Terrill, Cav
SMITH, John, Pvt, Regt Commander omitted, Capt Wm Mitchell, Spies
SMITH, Jno W N A, Pvt, Col Jno Coffee, Capt Jno W Byrn, Cav
SMITH, John A, Pvt, Col Samuel Bunch, Capt Edward Buchanan, E TN Mil
SMITH, John A, Pvt, Col Samuel Bunch, Capt Joseph Duncan, E TN Drafted Mil; joined from Capt Buchanan Co
SMITH, John A, Pvt, Gen Andrew Jackson, Capt Hugh Kerr, Mtd Rangers
SMITH, John C, Pvt, Col S Copeland, Capt Moses Thompson, Inf; deserted
SMITH, John D, 1 Cpl, Col Philip Pipkin, Capt David Smith, W TN Mil; promoted to 5 Sgt, attached to Capt Jno Strother
SMITH, John F, Sgt, Regt Commander omitted, Capt Mason, Cav
SMITH, John I, 1 Sgt, Col Wm Pillow, Capt Wm J Smith, Vol Inf
SMITH, John I, Pvt, Col Thos Benton, Capt Wm J Smith, Vol Inf
SMITH, John J, Pvt, Col Samuel Bayless, Capt James Landen, E TN Mil
SMITH, John J, Pvt, Col Thos Benton, Capt Wm J Smith, Vol Inf
SMITH, John M, 1 Cpl, Col Wm Hall, Capt John Moore, Vol Inf
SMITH, John M, Pvt, Col N T Perkins, Capt Geo Marr, Mtd Vol
SMITH, John S, Pvt, Col Philip Pipkin, Capt David Smith, W TN Mil; attached to Capt John Strother's Co
SMITH, John S, Pvt, Col S Copeland, Capt Richard Sharp, Mil Inf; deserted
SMITH, John W A, Pvt, Col John Coffee, Capt David Smith, Vol Cav
SMITH, John W, Pvt, Regt Commander omitted, Capt G Lane, Mtd Riflemen
SMITH, John, Pvt, Col Philip Pipkin, Capt Wm Mackay, Mil Inf
SMITH, John, Pvt, Lt Col Henry Bryan, Maj Robt Searcy, Inf
SMITH, John, Sgt, Col Philip Pipkin, Capt Ebenezer Kirkpatrick, Mil Inf
SMITH, Jonah, Pvt, Col Wm Lillard, Capt Thos Sharpe, 2nd Inf
SMITH, Jonathan H, Pvt, Col R H Dyer, Capt Robt Edmonston, TN Vol Mtd Gunmen
SMITH, Jonathan H, Pvt, Col Thos Benton, Capt James McEwen, Vol Inf
SMITH, Jonathan, Pvt, Col Philip Pipkin, Capt David Smith, Inf; attached to Capt John Strother Co

SMITH, Jonathan, Pvt, Maj Wm Woodfolk, Capt Abraham Dudney & Capt John Sutton, Inf
SMITH, Joseih, Pvt, Col R C Napier, Capt Edward Neblett, Mil Inf
SMITH, Joseph, Pvt, Col A Loury, Capt Gabriel Martin, Inf
SMITH, Joseph, Pvt, Col A Loury, Capt J N Williamson, W TN Mil
SMITH, Joseph, Pvt, Col Edwin Booth, Capt Samuel Thompson, Mil
SMITH, Joseph, Pvt, Col Jno Brown, Capt Lunsford Oliver, E TN Mil
SMITH, Joseph, Pvt, Col John Wynne, Capt John Porter, Inf; deserted
SMITH, Joseph, Pvt, Col L Hammond, Capt J N Williamson, 2nd Regt Inf
SMITH, Joseph, Pvt, Col Philip Pipkin, Capt James Blakemore, Mil Inf
SMITH, Joseph, Pvt, Col Samuel Bunch, Capt Daniel Yarnell, E TN Mil
SMITH, Joseph, Pvt, Col Samuel Bunch, Capt S Richardson, Branch Srvce omitted
SMITH, Joseph, Pvt, Col Wm Johnson, Capt Joseph Scott, E TN Drafted Mil
SMITH, Joseph, Pvt, Lt Col Jno Edmonson, Co Commander omitted, Mtd Inf
SMITH, Joshua R, Pvt, Col John Cocke, Capt Joseph Price, Inf
SMITH, Josiah, Pvt, Col R H Dyer, Capt Bethel Allen, Vol Mtd Gunmen
SMITH, Josiah, Pvt, Regt Commander omitted, Capt David Smith, Cav
SMITH, Kenchen, Pvt, Col T Williamson, Capt Beverly Williams, Vol Mtd Gunmen
SMITH, Kensey, Pvt, Col Samuel Wear, Capt Daniel Price, E TN Vol Inf
SMITH, Larkin, Pvt, Col R H Dyer, Capt Bethel Allen, Vol Mtd Gunmen
SMITH, Lemeon, Pvt, Col John Brown, Capt Lunsford Oliver, E TN Mil
SMITH, Levi, Dmr, Col Samuel Bayless, Capt Branch Jones, E TN Mil Drafted
SMITH, Luke, 2 Lt, Col John Cocke, Capt Bird Nance, Inf, Res omitted; d 3-20-1815
SMITH, Mathew, Pvt, Col Wm Johnson, Capt James R Rogers, E TN Drafted Mil
SMITH, Mathew, Pvt, Maj Jones Porter, Capt James Anderson, Cav
SMITH, Mathias, Pvt, Col R H Dyer, Capt James McMahan, TN Vol Mtd Gunmen
SMITH, Merril, Pvt, Col Samuel Bunch, Lt Jno Harris, E TN Mil
SMITH, Michael, Pvt, Maj John Childs, Capt Chas Conway, E TN Mtd Gunmen; Regt Co - Knox
SMITH, Michael, Pvt, Regt Commander omitted, Capt Elijah Rushing, Det of Inf
SMITH, Moses, Pvt, Col Samuel Wear, Capt Daniel Price, E TN Vol Inf
SMITH, Moses, Pvt, Col Wm Johnson, Capt Henry Hunter, E TN Mil
SMITH, Moses, Pvt, Col Wm Lillard, Capt Robt Mc-

## Enlisted Men, War of 1812

SMITH, Calpin, E TN Inf
SMITH, Mumphoid, Pvt, Regt Commander omitted, Capt Jas Haggard, Mtd Gunmen; transferred to Capt Molton's Co
SMITH, Mumphoid, Pvt, Regt Commander omitted, Capt Jos Williams, Mil Cav
SMITH, Nathan, Pvt, Col S Copeland, Capt James Tait, Inf
SMITH, Nathan, Pvt, Col Wm Johnson, Capt James R Rogers, E TN Drafted Mil
SMITH, Nathaniel, 4 Sgt, Col John Williams, Capt Daniel Vance, Mtd Mil; promoted to Ens
SMITH, Neal, Ffr, Col James Raulston, Capt Chas Wade, Inf
SMITH, Nehemiah, Pvt, Col John Cocke, Capt John Dalton, Inf
SMITH, Neil, 5 Cpl, Col James Raulston, Capt Chas Wade, Inf
SMITH, Nelson, Pvt, Maj Wm Russell, Capt Isaac Williams, Separate Bn of TN Vol Mtd Gunmen
SMITH, Nimrod, Pvt, Col Wm Johnson, Capt James Stewart, E TN Mil Drafted
SMITH, Peter, Pvt, Col Samuel Bayless, Capt Joseph Rick, E TN Inf; transferred to Capt Milliken's Co
SMITH, Peter, Pvt, Col Wm Johnson, Capt Elihu Milliken, 3rd Regt E TN Mil; transferred from Capt Churchman's Co
SMITH, Peter, Pvt, Col Wm Lillard, Capt Thos Sharpe, 2nd Regt Inf
SMITH, Phieldin, Pvt, Lt Col Henry Bryan, Maj Robt Searcy, Inf
SMITH, Phillip, Pvt, Maj James Porter, Capt James Anderson, Cav
SMITH, Poindexter, Pvt, Col John Wynne, Capt John Spinks, Inf
SMITH, Pracus, Pvt, Col James Raulston, Capt Daniel Newman, Inf
SMITH, Randolph, Pvt, Col Jno Brown, Capt Jas Preston, E TN Mil Inf
SMITH, Randolph, Pvt, Col John Cocke, Capt Geo Barnes, Inf
SMITH, Randolph, Pvt, Col Wm Johnson, Capt Elihu Milliken, 3rd Regt E TN Mil
SMITH, Renny, Pvt, Col Wm Hall, Capt John Kennedy, Vol Inf
SMITH, Reuben, Pvt, Col Edward Bradley, Capt John Kennedy, Riflemen
SMITH, Richard, Pvt, Col J K Wynne, Capt Robt Bradin, Inf
SMITH, Richard, Pvt, Col Jno Cocke, Capt Jno Weakley, Inf
SMITH, Richard, Pvt, Col Jno Williams, Capt D Vance, Mtd Mil
SMITH, Richard, Pvt, Col N T Cannon, Capt Francis Jones, Mtd Riflemen
SMITH, Richard, Pvt, Col N T Cannon, Capt Martin, Mtd Gunmen; wounded 11-3-1813 & d 11-9-1813
SMITH, Richard, Pvt, Col N T Perkins, Capt M Johnston, Mil Inf
SMITH, Richard, Pvt, Col Sam'l Bunch, Capt D Vance, E TN Mtd Inf
SMITH, Rinery, Pvt, Col Wm Hall, Capt John Kennedy, Vol Inf
SMITH, Robert, Pvt, Col Jno Coffee, Capt B Coleman, Cav
SMITH, Robert, Pvt, Col Thos H Benton, Capt Jas McEwen, Vol Inf
SMITH, Robert, Pvt, Maj Gen A Jackson, Col A Cheatham, Capt Wm Creel, Inf
SMITH, Robert, Pvt, Maj Jno Childs, Capt Jas Cummings, E TN Vol Mtd Inf
SMITH, Robert, Sgt, Col Wm Pillow, Capt C E McEwen, Vol Inf
SMITH, Samuel, Cpl, Col N T Cannon, Capt Martin, Mtd Gunmen; promoted from Pvt
SMITH, Samuel, Pvt, Col E Allison, Capt Jos Everett, E TN Mil; deserted
SMITH, Samuel, Pvt, Col Jno Alcorn, Capt Wm Locke, Cav
SMITH, Samuel, Pvt, Col Jno Cocke, Capt Jno Dalton, Inf; promoted from Pvt to Sgt
SMITH, Samuel, Pvt, Col Jno Cocke, Capt Jno Weakley, Inf; d 1-29-1815
SMITH, Samuel, Pvt, Col Jno Coffee, Capt B Coleman, Cav
SMITH, Samuel, Pvt, Col Saml Bayless, Capt Jos Hale, E TN Mil; joined from Capt Jones Co
SMITH, Samuel, Pvt, Col Saml Bunch, Capt Jones Griffin, E TN Drafted Mil; joined from Capt Everett's Co
SMITH, Samuel, Pvt, Col Samuel Bayless, Capt Branch Jones, E TN Drafted Mil; transferred to Capt Hale's Co
SMITH, Samuel, Pvt, Col Thos Benton, Capt Robt Cannon, Inf
SMITH, Samuel, Pvt, Col Thos Williamson, Capt Jno Hutchings, Vol Mtd Gunmen; promoted to 2 Lt
SMITH, Samuel, Pvt, Col Wm Lillard, Capt Benj King, E TN Vol Inf
SMITH, Samuel, Pvt, Maj Gen A Jackson, Capt J Craine, Mtd Gunmen
SMITH, Samuel, Pvt, Maj Wm Carroll, Capt L Dillahunty & Capt Danl Bradford, Vol Inf
SMITH, Samuel, Tptr, Maj Wm Russell, Capt Geo Mitchie, Vol Mtd Gunmen
SMITH, Sion, Pvt, Col Jno Cocke, Capt Saml Caruthers, Inf
SMITH, Stephen, Mus Dmr, Col Wm Johnson, Capt Jas Rogers, E TN Drafted Mil
SMITH, Stephen, Pvt, Col Robt Steele, Capt Robt Campbell, Mil Inf
SMITH, Stephen, Pvt, Col Wm Higgins, Capt Thos Eldridge, Mtd Gunmen
SMITH, Stephen, Pvt, Col Wm Johnson, Capt Jas Rogers, E TN Drafted Mil
SMITH, Sterling (Starling), Pvt, Col Jno Cocke, Capt Rich'd Crunk, Inf
SMITH, Sterling, Pvt, Col Saml Bayless, Capt S Hendrix, E TN Mil
SMITH, Thomas B, Pvt, Col Jno Coffee, Capt Robt Jetton, Cav
SMITH, Thomas, Cpl, Col Sam'l Wear, Capt Jno Stephens, E TN Vol Inf

## Enlisted Men, War of 1812

SMITH, Thomas, Ffr, Col E Booth, Capt Saml Thompson, Mil

SMITH, Thomas, Pvt, Col Alex Loury, Lt Col L Hammons, Capt A Rains, Inf

SMITH, Thomas, Pvt, Col E Allison, Capt Jos Everett, E TN Mil; deserted

SMITH, Thomas, Pvt, Col Jno Coffee, Capt Alex McKeen, Cav

SMITH, Thomas, Pvt, Col Jno Coffee, Capt Danl Ross, Mtd Gunmen

SMITH, Thomas, Pvt, Col N T Perkins, Capt Jas McMahan, Mtd Gunmen; killed 1-24-1814

SMITH, Thomas, Pvt, Col P Pipkin, Capt Wm McKay, Mil Inf

SMITH, Thomas, Pvt, Col S Bunch, Capt Jones Griffin, E TN Drafted Mil; joined from Capt Everett's Co

SMITH, Thomas, Pvt, Col Sam'l Wear, Capt Jas Gillespie, E TN Vol Inf

SMITH, Thomas, Pvt, Col Saml Bayless, Capt S Hendrix, E TN Mil

SMITH, Thomas, Pvt, Col Saml Bunch, Capt Jas Penny, E TN Mtd Inf

SMITH, Thomas, Pvt, Col Wm Hall, Capt Jno Moore, Vol Inf

SMITH, Thomas, Pvt, Col Wm Metcalf, Capt Wm Mullins, Mil Inf

SMITH, Thomas, Pvt, Maj Gen A Jackson, Capt Wm Carroll, Vol Inf

SMITH, Thomas, Pvt, Maj Gen Wm Carroll, Col Wm Metcalf, Capt Jno Jackson, Inf

SMITH, Thomas, Pvt, Maj Wm Woodfolk, Capt A Dudney, Inf

SMITH, Thomas, Pvt, Maj Wm Woodfolk, Capt J C Neil, Inf

SMITH, Thomas, Sgt, Maj Wm Carroll, Capt Dan'l Bradford & Capt L Dillahunty, Vol Inf; promoted to Ens

SMITH, Thomas, Sgt, Maj Wm Woodfolk, Capt A Dudney & Capt Jno Sutton, Inf; promoted from Pvt

SMITH, Turner, Pvt, Col Wm Lillard, Capt J Hartsell, E TN Vol Inf

SMITH, Washington, Pvt, Col Jno Cocke, Capt Geo Barnes, Inf; d 1-18-1815

SMITH, Will, Pvt, Col Jno Coffee, Capt Byrn, Cav

SMITH, William H, Pvt, Col Jno Brown, Capt Wm D Neilson, E TN Vol Mil; promoted to Deputy QM

SMITH, William, 1 Cpl, Regt Commander omitted, Capt Jas Terrill, Cav

SMITH, William, Asst Dept QM Gen, Maj Jno Cocke, E TN Mil Vol

SMITH, William, Cpl, Col Wm Johnson, Capt E Milliken, 3rd Regt E TN Mil

SMITH, William, Cpl, Maj Wm Woodfolk, Capt Jas Neil, Inf

SMITH, William, Pvt, Col Alex Loury, Lt Col L Hammond, Capt Thos Wells, Inf

SMITH, William, Pvt, Col E Allison, Capt Jas Allen, E TN Mil

SMITH, William, Pvt, Col E Allison, Capt Wm King, Drafted Mil

SMITH, William, Pvt, Col E Booth, Capt Vernon, E TN Mil

SMITH, William, Pvt, Col E Bradley, Capt H L Douglass, Vol Inf

SMITH, William, Pvt, Col Jno Brown, Capt Hugh Barton, E TN Mil Inf

SMITH, William, Pvt, Col Jno Cocke, Capt Jno Dalton, Inf

SMITH, William, Pvt, Col Jno Coffee, Capt David Smith, Vol Cav

SMITH, William, Pvt, Col Jno Edmonson, Lt Col Archer Cheatham, Mtd Inf

SMITH, William, Pvt, Col Jno Williams, Capt Sam'l Bunch, Mtd Vol

SMITH, William, Pvt, Col N T Perkins, Capt Geo Eliot, Mil Inf

SMITH, William, Pvt, Col P Pipkin, Capt E Kirkpatrick, Mil Inf; deserted

SMITH, William, Pvt, Col R H Dyer, Capt Robt Evans, Vol Mtd Gunmen; KIA 12-23-1814

SMITH, William, Pvt, Col S Bunch, Capt Isaac Williams, E TN Mil

SMITH, William, Pvt, Col S Bunch, Capt Jno English, E TN Drafted Mil

SMITH, William, Pvt, Col S Bunch, Capt Jno McNare, E TN Mil

SMITH, William, Pvt, Col S Copeland, Capt Jno Holshouser, Inf

SMITH, William, Pvt, Col Sam'l Wear, Capt R Morgan, E TN Vol Inf

SMITH, William, Pvt, Col Saml Bayless, Capt S Hendrix, E TN Mil

SMITH, William, Pvt, Col Thos Benton, Capt H L Douglass, Vol Inf

SMITH, William, Pvt, Col Thos Williamson, Capt Jas Doak & Capt Jno Dobbins, Vol Mtd Gunmen

SMITH, William, Pvt, Col Wm Hall, Capt Jas Hambleton, Vol Inf

SMITH, William, Pvt, Col Wm Hall, Capt Jno Kennedy, Vol Inf

SMITH, William, Pvt, Col Wm Hall, Capt T C Nash, Inf

SMITH, William, Pvt, Col Wm Johnson, Capt Jas Tunnell, E TN Mil; promoted to Sgt and reduced to the ranks

SMITH, William, Pvt, Col Wm Johnson, Capt Jas Tunnell, E TN Mil; two Wm Smith's on this roll

SMITH, William, Pvt, Col Wm Lillard, Capt Geo Argenbright, E TN Vol Riflemen

SMITH, William, Pvt, Col Wm Lillard, Capt Hugh Martin, E TN Vol Inf

SMITH, William, Pvt, Col Wm Lillard, Capt Wm Hamilton, E TN Vol Inf

SMITH, William, Pvt, Col Wm Lillard, Capt Z Copeland, E TN Vol Inf

SMITH, William, Pvt, Col Wm Metcalf, Capt B Hurt, Mil Inf

SMITH, William, Pvt, Maj Wm Russell, Capt Wm Chism, Vol Mtd Riflemen

SMITH, William, Pvt, Maj Wm Woodfolk, Capt A Pearce, Inf; transferred from Capt Wail's Co

SMITH, William, Pvt, Maj Wm Woodfolk, Capt Jas Neil, Inf; reduced from Cpl

SMITH, William, Pvt, Regt Commander omitted, Capt

## Enlisted Men, War of 1812

David Cook, Cav Vol
SMITH, William, Pvt, Regt Commander omitted, Capt David Smith, Cav
SMITH, William, Pvt, Regt Commander omitted, Capt Geo Smith, Spies
SMITH, William, Pvt, Regt Commander omitted, Capt Robt Evans, Mtd Spies; transferred to Capt Russell's Co
SMITH, William, Pvt, no other information; d 4-1-1814
SMITH, William, Sgt, Col Thos Williamson, Capt Jno Hutchings, Vol Mtd Gunmen
SMITH, Willis, Pvt, Col N T Perkins, Capt M Patterson, Mtd Vol
SMITH, Wiolliam, Pvt, Col Jno Brown, Capt Jno Childs, E TN Mtd Inf
SMITH, Wyett, Pvt, Regt Commander omitted, Capt Wm Mitchell, Spies
SMITH, Zachariah, Pvt, Col E Booth, Capt Geo Winton, E TN Mil; transferred from Capt Millikan's Co
SMITH, Zachariah, Pvt, Col Jno Brown, Capt Jas Preston, E TN Mil Inf
SMITH, Zachariah, Pvt, Col Sam'l Bayless, Capt Jos Bacon, E TN Mil
SMITH, Zachariah, Pvt, Col Wm Johnson, Capt E Milliken, 3rd Regt E TN Mil; transferred to Capt Winton's Co
SMITHERMAN, Lewis, Pvt, Col Edward Bradley, Capt Travis Nash, Vol Inf
SMITHERMAN, Samuel, Pvt, Col Wm Hall, Capt Travis Nash, Inf
SMITHERMON, Lewis, Pvt, Col Wm Hall, Capt Travis C Nash, Inf
SMITHERMON, William, Pvt, Col Wm Hall, Capt Travis Nash, Inf
SMITHERY, James, Pvt, Col Wm Metcalf, Capt Alexander Hill & Capt John Cunningham, Mil Inf
SMITHERY, Phillip, Pvt, Col Ewen Allison, Capt Thos Wilson, E TN Drafted Mil; deserted
SMITHSON, John, Pvt, Col Wm Metcalf, Capt Alexander Hill & Capt John Cunningham, Mil Inf
SMITHSON, William, Pvt, Regt Commander omitted, Capt Geo Smith, Spies
SMOTHERMAN, Edmund, Pvt, Col R C Napier, Capt James McMurray, Mil Inf
SMOTHERMAN, John, Pvt, Col Thos Williamson, Capt Richard Tate, Vol Mtd Gunmen
SMOTHERMAN, William, Pvt, Col Thos Williamson, Capt Richard Tate, Vol Mtd Gunmen
SMOTHERS, Jacob, Pvt, Col John Wynne, Capt Wm McCall, Inf
SMOTHERS, John, Pvt, Col Philip Pipkin, Capt Geo Mebane, Mil Inf
SMOTHERS, John, Pvt, Col Robt Steele, Capt Robert Campbell, Mil Inf
SMOTHERS, Thomas, Ffr, Col Jas Raulston, Capt Henry Hamilton, Inf; also under Maj Gen Carroll
SMOTHERS, William, Pvt, Col John Wynne, Capt McCall, Inf
SMYLEY, Thomas, Pvt, Regt Commander omitted, Capt Jas Cowan, Mtd Inf
SMYTH, Burton, Pvt, Col A Cheatham, Capt Chapman, Inf
SMYTHE, Isaac, Pvt, Col A Cheatham, Capt Chapman, Inf
SMYTHE, John A, Pvt, Col S Wear, Capt John Stephen, E TN Vol Inf
SNAPP, George, Pvt, Col Wm McLin, Col Wm Lillard, E TN Inf
SNEED, Allen, Pvt, Col John Brown, Capt Jas McKamy, E TN Mtd Gunmen
SNEED, Burrel, Pvt, Col Wm Metcalf, Capt John Barnhart, Mil Inf
SNEED, Constant F, QM Sgt, Col Robert Dyer, Vol Mtd Gunmen
SNEED, Constantine, Pvt, Col Robert Dyer, Capt Robert Edmonson, TN Vol Mtd Gunmen; appointed QM Sgt
SNEED, George, Pvt, Col Wm Johnston, Capt Wm Rogers, E TN Drafted Mil
SNEED, James P, Pvt, Col William Pillow, Capt C E McEwen, Vol Inf
SNEED, John, Pvt, Col Wm Johnston, Capt Wm Rogers, E TN Drafted Mil
SNEED, William, Pvt, Col Robert Steele, Capt Samuel Maxwell, Mil Inf
SNEED, William, Pvt, Regt Commander omitted, Lt John Scott, Inf
SNELL, Isaac, Pvt, Col Wm Hall, Capt John Kennedy, Vol Inf
SNELL, Larin, Pvt, Lt Col Phillip (Pipkin?), Co Commander omitted, Inf
SNELL, Lewis, Pvt, Col Williams, Capt Pate, Vol Mtd Gunmen
SNELL, Lewis, Pvt, Gen Johnston, Capt Oban, Inf
SNIDER, Christopher, Pvt, Col S Bayless, Capt Solomon Hendricks, E TN Mil
SNIDER, David, Pvt, Col Edwin Booth, Capt Thompson, Mil
SNIDER, George, Pvt, Maj John Childs, Capt John Stephens, E TN Mtd Inf
SNIDER, Jacob, Pvt, Col E Allison, Capt Jos Everett, E TN Mil
SNIDER, Jacob, Pvt, Col E Booth, Capt Saml Thompson, Mil
SNIDER, John, Cpl, Col E Booth, Capt Saml Thompson, Mil
SNIDER, John, Pvt, Col Saml Wear, Capt Jas Tedford, E TN Vol Inf
SNIDER, Michael, Pvt, Col Saml Wear, Capt Jno Stephens, E TN Vol Inf
SNIDER, Peter, Pvt, Col Wm Johnson, Capt H Hunter, E TN Mil
SNIDER, Thomas, Pvt, Maj Jno Childs, Capt Jno Stephens, E TN Vol Mtd Inf
SNODDERLY, George, Cpl, Col Saml Wear, Capt Robt Doak, E TN Vol Inf
SNODDERLY, Jacob, Pvt, Col E Booth, Capt Thos Porter, Drafted Mil
SNODDY, Adam, Pvt, Col Thos Williamson, Capt Thos Scurry, Vol Mtd Gunmen
SNODDY, David, Pvt, Col Thos Williamson, Capt Thos Scurry, Vol Mtd Gunmen

## Enlisted Men, War of 1812

SNODDY, James, Pvt, Col Wm Lillard, Capt Z Copeland, E TN Vol Inf
SNODGRASS, George, Pvt, Col Thos Williamson, Capt Jno Doak & Capt Jno Dobbins, Vol Mtd Gunmen
SNODGRASS, George, Pvt, Col Wm Lillard, Capt Jas Lillard, E TN Inf Vol
SNODGRASS, James, Pvt, Col Wm Lillard, Capt Wm Lillard, E TN Inf Vol
SNODGRASS, John, 2 Sgt, Col Wm Lillard, Capt Z Copeland, E TN Vol Inf
SNODGRASS, John, Pvt, Col Wm Metcalf, Capt B Collins, Mil Inf
SNODGRASS, William, Pvt, Col Saml Wear, Capt Danl Price, E TN Vol Inf
SNODGRASS, William, Pvt, Col Wm Johnson, Capt Jas Rogers, E TN Drafted Mil
SNOW, Eli, Pvt, Col Thos Williamson, Capt Jno Doak & Capt Jno Dobbins, Vol Mtd Gunmen
SNOW, James, Pvt, Col P Pipkin, Capt Jas Blakemore, Mil Inf
SNOW, Joseph, Ffr, Col S Copeland, Capt Wm Hodges, Inf
SNOW, Leroy, Sgt, Lt Col L Hammonds, Capt Jos Williamson, Inf
SNOW, Levi, 2 Sgt, Col L Hammond, Capt J N Williamson, 2 Regt Inf
SNOW, Levi, Pvt, Col T McCrory, Capt Jas Shannon, Mil Inf
SNOW, Levy, 2 Sgt, Col A Loury, Capt I Williamson, W TN Mil
SNOW, William, Pvt, Col T McCrory, Capt T Gordon, Inf
SNOWDEN, Jacob, Pvt, Col Edward Bradley, Capt Travis Nash, Vol Inf
SNOWDEN, Jacob, Pvt, Col Wm Hall, Capt Travis Nash, Inf
SNOWDEN, John, Pvt, Col Thos Benton, Capt George Gibbs, Vol Inf
SOAP, George, Pvt, Col Thos Benton, Capt Geo Caperton, Inf
SOAP, George, Pvt, Col William Pillow, Capt Geo Caperton, Inf
SOAP, Joseph, 3 Sgt, Col N Cannon, Capt Geo Brandon, Mtd Riflemen
SOARY, Horatio, Cpl, Col A Cheatham, Capt Thos Benson, Inf
SOFFLE, John, Pvt, Col S Bunch, Capt Edward Buchanan, E TN Mil
SOLOMON, Abraham, Pvt, Capt Richard Sharp, Col William Lillard, Inf
SOLOMON, Austin, Pvt, Col A Cheatham, Capt Chapman, Inf
SOLOMON, Goodman, Pvt, Col S Bayless, Capt Joseph Rich, Inf
SOLOMON, Henry, Pvt, Col William Lillard, Capt Richard Sharp, Inf
SOLOMON, Humphreys, Pvt, Col S Bunch, Lt Jno Harris, E TN Mil
SOLOMON, James, Pvt, Col S Bayless, Capt Jones, E TN Drafted Mil
SOLOMON, William, Pvt, Col Leroy Hammonds, Capt Raines, Inf

SOMERS, William, Pvt, Col William Johnson, Capt Andrew Lawson, E TN Drafted Mil
SOMMERVILL, Robert M, Pvt, Col Jno Coffee, Capt Molton, Cav; absent out of state
SORELLS, Joseph, Pvt, Maj Gen Carroll, Capt Jackson & Capt Wm Metcalf, Inf
SORELS, Richard, Pvt, Col Wm Metcalf, Capt Wm Waller, Mil Inf
SORRY, Allen, Pvt, Col R C Napier, Capt Edward Neblett, Mil Inf
SOUDER, Emanuel, Pvt, Col S Bayless, Capt John Brock, E TN Mil
SOUDERS, Jacob, Pvt, Col S Wear, Capt Doak, E TN Vol Inf
SOUELS, Joseph, Pvt, Col S Copeland, Capt Richard Sharp, Mil Inf
SOUGS, Willsby, Pvt, Col Wm Metcalf, Capt Geo Sitton, Mil Inf
SOULS, William, Pvt, Col Ewen Allison, Capt William King, Drafted Mil
SOUNGS, Allen, Pvt, Col Wm Metcalf, Capt Geo Sitton, Mil Inf
SOUT, William, Pvt, Col John K Wynne, Capt James Cole, Inf
SOUTH, Philip, Pvt, Col Alexander Loury, Capt John Looney, W TN Inf
SOUTHALL, James, Pvt, Col John Cocke, Capt John Dalton, Inf; d 2-16-1815
SOUTHERLAND, James, Cpl, Col S Bayless, Capt Joseph Rich, E TN Inf
SOUTHERN, Archiles, Pvt, Col Thomas Williamson, Capt John Crane & Capt Cook, Vol Mtd Gunmen
SOUTHERN, Archiles, Sgt, Col A Cheatham, Co Commander omitted, Inf
SOUTHERN, John, Pvt, Col Philip Pipkin, Capt Jas Robertson, Mil Inf; d 12-30-1814
SOUTHERN, William, Pvt, Lt Col A Cheatham, Capt G Martin, Mtd Inf
SOUTHERN, William, Pvt, Lt Col John Edmonson, Co Commander omitted, Cav
SOWARD, Henry, Pvt, Col Edwin Booth, Capt John Lewis, E TN Mil; d 2-8-1815
SOWELL, Jesse, Pvt, Col S Bunch, Capt Geo Gregory, E TN Drafted Mil
SOWELL, Newton, Pvt, Col S Copeland, Capt John Holshouser, Inf
SOWELL, William, Pvt, Col Thos Benton, Capt Geo Caperton, Vol Inf; joined from? Capt Howette
SPAN, Christian, Pvt, Col Ewin Booth, Capt Richard Marshall, Drafted Mil
SPAN, Terrell, Pvt, Col A Cheatham, Capt Wm Smith, Inf; discharged for inability
SPARKES, Isaac, Pvt, Regt Commander omitted, Capt Wm Teas, 6th Brig Inf
SPARKMAN, William, Cpl, Col R H Dyer, Capt James McMahan, TN Mtd Vol Gunmen
SPARKS, Absolom, Pvt, Col Ewen Allison, Capt Jonas Loughmiller, Mil
SPARKS, Bailey, Pvt, Regt Commander omitted, Capt Wm Teas, 6th Brig Inf
SPEACE, Thomas, 3 Cpl, Col A Loury, Capt J William-

## Enlisted Men, War of 1812

son, W TN Mil
SPEACE, Thomas, 3 Cpl, Col L Hammond, Capt J N Williamson, 2nd Regt Inf; transferred to Pack Horse Dept
SPEAK, Thomas, Pvt, Col A Loury, Capt John Looney, W TN Inf; d 12-6-1814
SPEAKS, Hiram, Pvt, Col Wm Higgins, Capt Stephen Griffith, Mtd Riflemen
SPEAKS, Richmond, Pvt, Col Wm Higgins, Capt Stephen Griffith, Mtd Riflemen
SPEAKS, William, Pvt, Col Wm Higgins, Capt Stephen Griffith, Mtd Riflemen
SPEAR, Isaac, Surgeon Mate, Maj Gen Wm Carroll, TN Mil
SPEAR, Jesse, 3 Cpl, Col Wm Lillard, Capt Wm Gillenwater, E TN Vol Inf
SPEARS, David, Pvt, Col Edwin Booth, Capt Richard Marshall, Drafted Mil
SPEARS, Edward, Ffr, Col A Loury, Lt Col L Hammond, Capt Arahel Rains, Inf
SPEARS, Edward, Pvt, Col L Hammonds, Capt Arahel Rains, Inf
SPEARS, Isaac, Surgeon's Mate, Commanders omitted, E TN Vol Mtd Gunmen
SPEARS, James, Pvt, Col John Cocke, Capt Bird Nance, Inf
SPEARS, Jesse, Pvt, Col Wm Higgins, Capt Samuel A Allen, Mtd Gunmen
SPEARS, John, Pvt, Col Samuel Wear, Capt Joseph Calloway, Mtd Inf
SPEARS, John, Pvt, Col Wm Johnson, Capt James Tunnell, E TN Mil
SPEARS, John, Pvt, Lt Col L Hammond, Capt Arahel Rains, Inf
SPEARS, John, Pvt, Maj Wm Russell, Capt Wm Chism, Vol Mtd Riflemen
SPEARS, Thomas, Pvt, Col Wm Johnson, Capt Joseph Scott, E TN Drafted Mil
SPEARS, William, Pvt, Col S Copeland, Capt John Dawson, Inf
SPENCE, Charles, Pvt, Col S Copeland, Allen Wilkinson, Mil Inf
SPENCE, Daniel, Pvt, Col John Cocke, Capt Bird Nance, Inf
SPENCE, David, Pvt, Col N T Perkins, Capt Philip Pipkin, Mtd Riflemen
SPENCE, David, Pvt, Col Philip Pipkin, Capt Wm Mackay, Mil Inf; d 11-1814
SPENCE, John, Cpl, Col Edward Bradley, Capt John Moore, Vol Inf; deserted
SPENCE, John, Ffr, Col Wm Hall, Capt John Moore, Vol Inf
SPENCE, Jordon, Pvt, Col Thos Williamson, Capt Beverly Williams, Vol Mtd Gunmen; deserted
SPENCE, Peter, Pvt, Col Philip Pipkin, Capt Peter Searcy, Mil Inf
SPENCE, William, Pvt, Col John Cocke, Capt Bird Nance, Inf
SPENCER, Benjamin D, Pvt, Regt Commander omitted, Capt Jos Williams, Mil Cav
SPENCER, Benjamin, Pvt, Col John Cocke, Capt James Gray, Inf
SPENCER, Benjamin, Pvt, Col Thos Benton, Capt James McEwen, Vol Inf
SPENCER, Benjamin, Pvt, Col Wm Metcalf, Capt Wm Mullin, Mil Inf
SPENCER, Benjamin, Pvt, Regt Commander omitted, Capt Jas Williams, Mil Cav
SPENCER, Benjamin, Sgt, Col Wm Pillow, Capt C E McEwen, Vol Inf
SPENCER, Clark, Pvt, Col John Coffee, Capt Michael Molton, Cav
SPENCER, Clark, Pvt, Col R H Dyer, Capt Joseph Williams, Vol Mtd Gunmen; promoted to Sgt
SPENCER, Clark, Pvt, Lt Col R C Napier, Co Commander omitted, Inf
SPENCER, Clark, Pvt, Regt Commander omitted, Capt Jas Williams, Mil Cav
SPENCER, Henry, Cpl, Col Samuel Bunch, Capt F Register, E TN Mil; joined from Capt McCrea's Co
SPENCER, James, Pvt, Col John Brown, Capt Jesse G Rainey, Mtd Gunmen
SPENCER, James, Pvt, Col R C Napier, Capt Early Benson, Mil Inf
SPENCER, James, Pvt, Col S Copeland, Capt Wm Hodge, Inf
SPENCER, Jesse, Ffr, Col A Loury, Capt Gabriel Martin, Inf
SPENCER, John, Pvt, Col John Cocke, Capt James Gray, Inf
SPENCER, John, Pvt, Col R H Dyer, Capt Bethel Allen, Vol Mtd Gunmen
SPENCER, John, Pvt, Lt Col Richard C Napier, Co Commander omitted, Inf
SPENCER, John, Pvt, Regt Commander omitted, Capt Jas Haggard, Mtd Gunmen
SPENCER, John, Sgt, Regt Commander omitted, Capt Gray, Inf
SPENCER, Michael, Pvt, Col S Copeland, Capt Solomon George, Inf
SPENCER, Moses, Pvt, Maj Gen Wm Carroll, Col Jas Raulston, Capt Edward Robinson, Inf
SPENCER, Rencher, Pvt, Col James Raulston, Capt Chas Wade, Inf
SPENCER, Thomas, Pvt, Col Wm Metcalf, Capt Bird L Hurt, Mil Inf
SPERE, Thomas, 3 Cpl, Lt Col L Hammond, Capt Joseph N Williamson, Inf
SPERYERS, Thomas, Pvt, Col Wm Johnson, Capt Joseph Scott, E TN Drafted Mil
SPICER, Claiborne, Pvt, Col R C Napier, Capt Drury Adkins, Mil Inf
SPIDDLY (SPRADLY), John, Pvt, Col Samuel Bayless, Capt John Brock, E TN Mil
SPINALL, Reuben, Pvt, Brig Gen Johnson, Capt Robert Carson, Inf
SPIVY, James, Pvt, Col Jas Raulston, Capt John Cowan, Inf
SPIVY, James, Pvt, Col Robt Steele, Capt Samuel Maxwell, Mil Inf
SPIVY, William, Pvt, Maj Wm Woodfolk, Capt Abraham Dudney & Capt John Sutton, Inf

SPOON, Abraham, Pvt, Col Samuel Bunch, Capt S Richardson, E TN Draft Mil
SPOOR, Cornelius F, Adj, Regt Commander omitted, Bn E TN Vol Mtd Inf
SPRADLEN, Obadiah, Pvt, Col A Loury, Capt Geo Sarver, Inf
SPRADLIN, James, Pvt, Maj Wm Russell, Capt Wm Chism, Vol Mtd Riflemen
SPRADLIN, William, Pvt, Col A Loury, Lt Col L Hammond, Capt Arahel Rains, Inf
SPRADLIN, William, Pvt, Maj Wm Russell, Capt Wm Chism, Vol Mtd Riflemen
SPRADLING, James, Pvt, Col Samuel Bunch, Capt Jones Griffin, E TN Draft Mil; trans to Capt Dobkins' Co
SPRADLING, John, Pvt, Col Samuel Bunch, Capt John Dobkins, E TN Draft Mil; deserted
SPRADLING, Obadiah, Pvt, Col Samuel Wear, Capt Joseph Calloway, Mtd Inf
SPRAGAN, Thomas, Pvt, Col Samuel Bunch, Capt Edward Buchanan, E TN Mil
SPRAGAN, William, Pvt, Col Samuel Bunch, Capt Edward Buchanan, E TN Mil
SPRAGGANS, Asa, Pvt, Col Edwin Booth, Capt Alexander Biggs, Inf
SPRAGGANS, Elisha, Pvt, Col Edwin Booth, Capt Alexander Biggs, Inf
SPRAT, John, Pvt, Col Thos Benton, Capt James McEwen, Vol Inf
SPRATT, Blythe, Pvt, Regt Commander omitted, Lt Jas Berry, Mtd Riflemen
SPRATT, John, Pvt, Col John Alcorn, Capt Wm Locke, Cav
SPRATT, John, Pvt, Col Thos Benton, Capt James McEwen, Vol Inf; see remakr on Capt Wm Carroll
SPRATT, Joseph, Pvt, Col Thomas H Benton, Capt James McEwin, Vol Inf
SPRATT, Joseph, Pvt, Regt Commander omitted, Capt Archibald McKinney, Cav
SPRATT, Joseph, Pvt-Far, Col R H Dyer, Capt Glen Owen, TN Vol Mtd Gunmen
SPRATT, Samuel, Pvt, Regt Commander omitted, Capt Archibald McKinney, Cav
SPRING, Aron, Pvt, Col Jas Raulston, Capt James Black, Inf
SPRING, Moses, Pvt, Col Jas Raulston, Capt James A Black, Inf
SPRING, Valentine, Pvt, Col John Brown, Capt Wm Christian, Regt E TN Mil Inf
SPRINGFIELD, James, Pvt, Col Thos Benton, Capt Geo Biggs, Vol Inf
SPRINGS, James, Pvt, Col Wm Johnson, Capt Andrew Lawson, E TN Draft Mll
SPROGGINS, Thomas, Pvt, Col Samuel Bunch, Capt Joseph Duncan, E TN Drafted Mil; joined from Capt Buckhanon's Co
SPROGGINS, William, Pvt, Col Samuel Bunch, Capt Joseph Duncan, E TN Drafted Mil; joined from Capt Bukhown's Co
SPROUL, John, Pvt, Col Wm Y Higgins, Capt James Hambleton, Mtd Gunmen

SPROUS, Aaron, Pvt, Maj Wm Woodfolk, Capt Ezekiel Ross, Inf
SPROWEL, John, Pvt, Col Wm Lillard, Capt Geo Argenbright, E TN Vol Inf
SPROWEL, Zephemi, 3 Cpl, Col Wm Hall, Capt Henry Newlin, Inf
SPROWL, John, Pvt, Col Samuel Wear, Capt Joseph Calloway, Mtd Inf
SPURLOCK, Francis, Pvt, Col James Raulston, Capt Mathew Cowan, Inf
SPURLOCK, Harry, Pvt, Col James Raulston, Capt Mathew Cowan, Inf; died 1-26-1815
SPURLOCK, Joseph, Pvt, Col A Loury, Capt Peter Looney, W TN Inf
SPURLOCK, Miles, Pvt, Regt Commander omitted, Capt L Ferrell, Inf
SQUIB, Caleb, Pvt, Col Wm Johnson, Capt Andrew Lawson, E TN Draft Mil
SRADER, Christopher, Pvt, Col S Bunch, Capt Isaac Williams, E TN Mil
SRADLING, William, Pvt, Col Samuel Wear, Capt Joseph Calloway, Mtd Inf
ST CLAIR, William, Pvt, Col Wm Hall, Capt John Kennedy, Vol Inf
STACEY, John, Sgt, Col Robert Steele, Capt Burnette, Mil Inf
STACKS, John, Pvt, Col Thomas H Benton, Capt Benjamin Reynolds, Vol Inf
STACKS, William, Pvt, Col Wm Metcalf, Capt Andrew Patterson, Mil Inf; died 2-23-1815
STACY, Thomas, Cpl, Col Wm Pillow, Capt C E McEwen, Vol Inf
STACY, Thomas, Pvt, Col Thos Berton, Capt James McEwen, Vol Inf
STACY, William, Cpl, Col S Copeland, Capt Richard Sharp, Mil Inf
STAFFORD, Abel, Pvt, Maj Wm Russell, Capt John Tremble, Vol Mtd Gunmen
STAFFORD, Benjamin, Pvt, Col Samuel Bunch, Capt Jno Hawk, E? TN Mil
STAFFORD, Bird, Pvt, Col Jas Raulston, Capt Henry West, Inf; died 2-24-1815
STAFFORD, Cain, Cpl, Lt Col L Hammond, Capt James Tubbe, Inf
STAFFORD, James, Pvt, Col Samuel Bunch, Capt Isaac Williams, Mtd Vol
STAFFORD, John, Pvt, Lt Col L Hammond, Capt James Craig, Inf; died 1-5-1815
STAFFORD, John, Pvt, Lt Col L Hammond, Capt James Tubb, Inf
STAFFORD, Samuel, Pvt, Col Thos Williamson, Capt A Metcalf, Vol Mtd Gunmen; died 3-28-1815
STAFFORD, Stephen, Pvt, Lt Col L Hammond, Capt James Tubb, Inf
STAFFORD, Thomas, Pvt, Col Edward Bradley, Capt Brice Martin, Vol Inf
STAFFORD, Thomas, Pvt, Col Robt Steele, Capt James Randals, Inf
STAFFORD, Thomas, Pvt, Col Wm Hall, Capt Brice Martin, Vol Inf
STAFFORD, William, Pvt, Col John Wynne, Capt James

Cole, Inf
STAFFORD, Williams, Pvt, Col R H Dyer, Capt Cuthbert Hudson, Vol Mtd Gunmen
STAFFORD, ____, Servant, Col Philip Pipkin, 1 Regt TN Mil; servant to Regt Surgeon Wm Winne
STAGGS, William, Pvt, Col Wm Hall, Capt Travis C Nash, Inf
STAGGS, William, Pvt, Col Wm Johnson, Capt Christopher Cook, E TN Mil
STAIR, George, Pvt, Col Ewen Allison, Capt Joseph Everett, E TN Mil
STAIR, Joseph, Pvt, Col Samuel Bunch, Capt David G Vance, E TN Mtd Inf
STAL (STEELE), James, Pvt, Col R H Dyer, Capt James White, Vol Mtd Gunmen
STALCUP, Isaac, Pvt, Col A Loury, Capt Geo Sarver, Inf; later apptd Cpl
STALCUP, James, Pvt, Col John Alcorn, Capt John Baskerville, Vol Inf
STALEY, Frederick, Pvt, Lt Col Henry Bryan, Maj Robt Searcy, Inf
STALEY, John, Pvt, Brig Gen Wm Johnson, Capt Allen, Mil Inf
STALIONS, Sharod, Pvt, Col Wm Hall, Capt John Moore, Vol Inf
STALKUP, Isaac, Pvt, Col Edward Bradley, Capt John Moore, Vol Inf
STALLINGS, Elisha, Pvt, Col John Alcorn, Capt John W Byrns, Cav
STALLINGS, John, Pvt, Col S Copeland, Capt Wm Hodges, Inf
STALLION, Elias, Pvt, Col Wm Metcalf, Capt Wm Sitton, Mil Inf
STALLION, Elisha, Pvt, Col Jno Coffee, Capt John W Byrn, Cav
STALY (STOLEY), Frederick, Pvt, Col John Cocke, Capt John Weakley, Inf; died 2-7-1815
STAMBLEY, Daniel, Pvt, Col R H Dyer, Capt Robt Edmonston, TN Vol Mtd Gunmen
STAMPS, George, Pvt, Col R H Dyer, Maj Wm Russell, Capt Wm Russell, Branch omitted
STAMPS, Hosea, Pvt, Col R H Dyer, Maj Wm Russell, Capt Wm Russell, Vol Mtd Gunmen
STAMPS, James, Pvt, Maj Wm Russell, Capt Geo Mitchie, Vol Mtd Gunmen
STAMPS, Stanford, Pvt, Maj Wm Woodfolk, Capt Abraham Dudney, Inf
STAMPS, Timothy, Pvt, Col R H Dyer, Capt Wm Russell, Vol Mtd Gunmen
STAMPS, Timothy, Pvt, Col Robt Steele, Capt Richard M Raton, Mil Inf
STAMPS, William, Pvt, Col A Loury, Capt Arahel Rains, Inf
STANBERRY, Samuel, Pvt, Col Ewen Allison, CApt Henry McCray, E TN Mil
STANBURY, Ezekiel, Pvt, Col Wm Johnson, Capt Christopher Cook, E TN Mil
STANBURY, Ezekiel, Pvt, Col Wm Johnston, Capt Joseph Kirk, Mil
STANDAFER, William, Pvt, Regt Commander omitted, Capt Jno Gordon, Mtd Spies

STANDEFER, Anderson, Pvt, Col A Loury, Lt Col L Hammond, Capt Thos Delaney, Inf
STANDERFORD, Stephen, Sgt, Gen A Jackson, Capt Hugh Kerr, Mtd Rangers
STANDFIELD, Ashley, Cpl, Regt Commander omitted, Capt Archibald McKenney, Cav
STANDFIELD, George, Pvt, Col A Loury, Lt Col L Hammond, Capt Thos Wells, Inf
STANDFIELD, Goodloe, Pvt, Regt Commander omitted, Capt Archibald McKinney, Cav
STANDFIELD, James, Pvt, Col Wm Lillard, Capt Hugh Martin, E TN Mtd Vol Inf
STANDFORD, George, Pvt, Col Wm Metcalf, Capt Thos Marks, Mil Inf
STANDFORD, Hugh, Pvt, Col Philip Pipkin, Capt John Strother, Mil; deserted
STANDIFER, John, Pvt, Col Edward Bradley, Capt Wm Lauderdale, Vol Inf
STANDIFER, John, Pvt, Col Wm Hall, Capt Wm L Alexander, Vol Inf
STANDIFER, William, 1 Cpl, Col Wm Hall, Capt W L Alexander, Vol Inf
STANDIFER, William, Pvt, Col Newton Cannon, Capt John Harpole, Mtd Gunmen; joined Capt Gordon's spies
STANDIFER, William, Col Thos Benton, Capt Isiah Renshaw, Vol Inf; trans to Nash
STANDIFORD, Stephen, Sgt, Regt Commander omitted, Capt Hugh Kerr, Mtd Rangers
STANDLEY, John, Pvt, Maj Wm Woodfolk, Capt Ezekial Ross & Capt McCulley, Inf
STANDRIDGE, Zeph, Pvt, Col Edwin Booth, Capt Alexander Biggs, Inf
STANDSBERRY, William, Pvt, Col Wm Lillard, Capt Wm Gillenwater, E TN Inf
STANFIELD, Ashley, Pvt, Col John Coffee, Capt John Baskerville, Cav
STANFIELD, Ashley, Sgt, Col Philip Pipkin, Capt Ebenezer Kirkpatrick, Mil Inf
STANFIELD, David, Pvt, Lt Col L Hammonds, Capt Thos Delaney, Inf; also under Col A Loury
STANFIELD, John, Pvt, Col Ewen Allison, Capt Joseph Everett, E TN Mil
STANFIELD, John, Pvt, Col Samuel Bunch, Capt Jones Griffin, E TN Draft Mil; joined from Capt Everett's Co
STANFIELD, John, Pvt, Col Wm Lillard, Capt Hugh Martin, E TN Vol Inf
STANFIELD, Marmaduke, Pvt, Col R H Dyer, Capt Robt Edmonston, TN Mtd Vol Gunmen
STANFIELD, Marmaduke, Pvt, Col Thos Williamson, Capt Richard Tate, Vol Mtd Gunmen
STANFIELD, Marmaduke, Pvt, Col Thos Williamson, Capt Wm Martin, Vol Mtd Gunmen
STANFIELD, Samuel, Cpl, Col Samuel Bayless, Capt Joseph Goodson, E TN Mil
STANFORD, Lucas, Pvt, Col John Wynne, Capt Bayless Prince, Inf
STANFORD, Thomas, Pvt, Col Philip Pipkin, Capt James Blakemore, Mil Inf
STANFORD, William, Pvt, Col S Copeland, Capt Wm

## Enlisted Men, War of 1812

Hodge, Inf; deserted
STANIEL, Jesse, Sgt, Col A Cheatham, Capt Chas Johnson, Inf
STANIFER, William, Pvt, Col Wm Hall, Capt Travis C Nash, Inf
STANIFOLK, Benjamin, Pvt, Col Edwin Booth, Capt John Sharp, E TN Mil; died 2-23-1815
STANIFPHER, William, Cpl, Col Edward Bradley, Capt Travis Nash, Vol Inf
STANLEY, Abraham, Pvt, Regt Commander omitted, Capt Gray, Inf
STANLEY, David, Blksmth, Col N T Perkins, Capt Mathew Patterson, Mtd Vol
STANLEY, David, Pvt, Col Philip Pipkin, Capt Wm Mackay, Mil Inf
STANLEY, James, Pvt, Col Samuel Bunch, Capt Thos Mann, E TN Vol Mtd Inf
STANLEY, John, Pvt, Col Samuel Wear, Capt John Doak, E TN Vol Inf
STANLEY, Joseph, Pvt, Col John Cocke, Capt Geo Barnes, Inf
STANLEY, Noble, Pvt, Col A Cheatham, Capt Geo S Chapman, Inf
STANLEY, Page, Pvt, Col Edwin Booth, Capt John Sharp, E TN Mil
STANLEY, Rhode, Pvt, Col John Brown, Capt Hugh Barton, E TN Mil Inf
STANLEY, Richard, Pvt, Col A Cheatham, Capt Geo G Chapman, Inf
STANLEY, William, Pvt, Col Wm Johnson, Capt Christopher Cook, E TN Mil
STANLEY, William, Pvt, Col Wm Johnston, Capt Joseph Kirk, Mil
STANLEY, Wright, Sgt, Regt Commander omitted, Capt Danl Eason, Cav
STANLY, James, Pvt, Brig Gen T Johnson, Capt Robt Carson, Inf
STANSBERRY, Elijah, Pvt, Col S Bayless, Capt Jonathan Waddle, E TN Mil
STANSBUARY, Samuel, Pvt, Maj Wm Woodfolk, Capt Abner Pearce, Inf
STANTON, Champ, Pvt, Col Jas Raulston, Capt Mathew Cowan, Inf
STANTON, Charles, Pvt, Col Wm Hall, Capt John Kennedy, Vol Inf
STANTY, Benjamin, Pvt, Col Wm Metcalf, Capt John Barnhart, Mil Inf; trans to artif
STAPLES, Charles H, 4 Cpl, Col Edward Bradley, Capt Abraham Bledsoe, Riflemen
STAPLES, Charles H, Pvt, Col Philip Pipkin, Capt William Mackey, Mil Inf
STAPLES, Charles, Pvt, Col S Copeland, Capt William Evans, Mil Inf
STAPLES, James, Pvt, Col William Lillard, Capt George Argenbright, E Tn Vol Riflemen
STAPLES, James, Pvt, Col Wm Johnson, Capt Benj Powell, E TN Mil
STAPLES, Richard, Pvt, Col Wm Johnson, Capt Benj Powell, E TN Mil
STAR, Isaac, Pvt, Lt Col H Bryan, Capt Jno Weakley, Mil Inf

STAR, Isaac, Pvt, Lt Col Henry Bryan, Capt? Robt Searcy, Inf
STARELY, Elijah, Pvt, Maj Wm Woodfolk, Capt Abner Pearce, Inf
STARK, Benjamin, Pvt, Col William Johnson, Capt Joseph Scott, E TN Drafted Mil
STARK, James W, Pvt, Col Alexander Loury, Capt Gabriel Martin, Inf
STARK, James W, Pvt, Col John Wynne, Capt Robert Bradin, Inf
STARK, Jesse, Pvt, Col S Copeland, Capt David Williams, Inf
STARKS, David, Cpl, Col Thos Williams, Capt Crane & Capt Jas Cook, Vol Mtd Gunmen; died 2-10-1815
STARKS, Ephraim, Cpl, Col Thos Williamson, Capt Crane & Capt Jas Cook, Vol Mtd Gunmen
STARKS, James, 3 Cpl, Col John Cocke, Capt Richard Crunk, Inf
STARKS, James, Cpl, Col Thos Williamson, Capt Crane & Capt Jas Cook, Vol Mtd Gunmen; died 2-10-1815
STARKS, Perry B, Pvt, Col Thomas Williamson, Capt Robert Moore, Vol Mtd Gunmen
STARKS, Thomas W, 2 Cpl, Col John Cocke, Capt Richard Crunk, Inf
STARKS, Walter W, Sgt, Col John Wynne, Capt Robt Bradin, Inf
STARKY, John, Pvt, Col A Loury, Col L Hammons, Capt Arahel Rains, Inf; died at Ft Montgomery
STARLING, Thomas, Pvt, Col Wm Johnson, Capt Elihu Milliken, 3 Regt E TN Mil; trans to Capt Rich's Co
STARNES, Adam, Pvt, Col Wm Hall, Capt Abraham Bledsoe, Vol Inf
STARNES, Adams, Pvt, Col Edward Bradley, Capt Abraham Bledsoe, Riflemen
STARNES, David, 3 Sgt, Col Edward Bradley, Capt Abraham Bledsoe, Riflemen
STARNES, David, Sgt, Col Wm Hall, Capt Abraham Bledsoe, Vol Inf
STARNES, Frederick, Pvt, Col Wm Lillard, Capt Jacob Hartsell, E TN Vol Inf
STARNES, Jacob, Cpl, Col Samuel Bayless, Capt Jonathan Waddle, E TN Mil
STARNES, John, Pvt, Col Wm Lillard, Capt Wm Gillenwater, E TN Inf
STARNES, John, Pvt, Col Wm Lillard, Capt Wm McLin, E TN Inf
STARR, James, Pvt, Col S Wear, Capt Doak, E TN Vol Inf
STARRETT, Benjamin, Pvt, Col Cannon, Capt Isaac Williams, Mtd Riflemen
STARRETT, Benjamin, Pvt, Maj William Russell, CApt Isaac Williams, TN Vol Mtd Gunmen
STARRETT, Joseph, Pvt, Col N Cannon, Capt Isaac Williams, Mtd Riflemen
STATLER, Abraham, Pvt, Col William Pillow, Capt Jas McFerrin, Inf
STATON, John, Pvt, Col John Brown, Capt Jesse Reamy, Mtd Gunmen
STAUNTON, John, Pvt, Col S Bayless, Capt John Brock, E TN Mil
STEAKLY, Daniel, Pvt, Col S Bayless, Capt Jas Church-

## Enlisted Men, War of 1812

man, E TN Mil
STEALE, James T, Sgt, Col Thos Benton, Capt George Gibbs, Vol Inf
STECKS (STACKS), Martin, Pvt, Col Thos H Benton, Capt Benj Reynolds, Vol Inf
STEEDMAN, John, Pvt, Col S Bayless, Capt James Landen, E TN Mil; died 2-18-1815
STEEGAL, Martin, Pvt, Col Ewen Allison, Capt Allen, E TN Mil
STEEGALL, Martin, Pvt, Regt Commander omitted, Capt Joseph Duncan, E TN Drafted Mil; joined from Capt Allen's Co
STEEL, Aaron, Pvt, Col Thos McCrory, Capt McKnight, Inf
STEEL, Alexander, Pvt, Col A Loury, Capt J N Williamson, E TN Mil
STEEL, Andrew, Pvt, Gen Andrew Jackson, Capt Jas Reed, Inf
STEEL, Archibald B, Pvt, Col Jas Raulston, Capt Chas Wade, Inf
STEEL, David, Pvt, Col Ewen Allison, Capt Wm King, Drafted Mll
STEEL, Elijah, Pvt, Col A Loury, Capt J N Williamson, W TN Mil
STEEL, George A, Pvt, Col Thos Benton, Capt Jas McEwen, Vol Inf
STEEL, James B, Pvt, Gen Jackson, Capt J Read, Inf
STEEL, James T, 1 Sgt, Col Thos Benton, Capt Geo Gibbs, Vol Inf
STEEL, John, Pvt, Col Thos Benton, Capt Geo Smith, Vol Inf
STEEL, John, Pvt, Col Thos Benton, Capt Wm Smith, Vol Inf
STEEL, John, Pvt, Col Wm Pillow, Capt Geo Smith, Vol Inf; deserted
STEEL, Joseph, Pvt, Col Wm Higgins, Capt Saml Allen, Mtd Gunmen
STEEL, Michael, Pvt, Col T McCrory, Capt Saml McKnight, Inf
STEEL, Richard, Pvt, Col Wm Lillard, Capt Geo Argenbright, E TN Vol Riflemen
STEEL, Samuel, 1 Sgt, Col Philip Pipkin, Capt John Robertson, Mil Inf
STEEL, Samuel, Pvt, Col John Coffee, Capt Daniel Ross, Mtd Gunmen
STEEL, _____, Pvt, Col Leroy Hammonds, Capt J N Williams, Inf
STEELE, Alexander, Pvt, Col Alexander Loury, Capt Arahel Raines, Inf
STEELE, George, Pvt, Lt Col Hammonds, Capt Jas Craig, Inf
STEELE, James L, Sgt, Col Thos Benton, Capt Geo Gibbs, Vol Inf
STEELE, John S, Pvt, Maj Jas Porter, Capt Jas Anderson, Cav
STEELE, Richard, Pvt, Maj John Childs, Capt Jas Cummings, E TN Vol Mtd Inf
STEELE, William, Pvt, Col Newton Cannon, Capt John B Demsey, Mtd Gunmen
STEGALL, Benjamin, Pvt, Col A Loury, Capt J N Williamson, W Tn Mil

STEGALL, Mathew, Pvt, Col Saml Bayless, Capt Branch Jones, E TN Draft Mil
STEINE, William, Pvt, Col John Coffee, Capt Blackman Coleman, Cav
STELL, John, Cpl, Col Newton Cannon, Capt Ota Cantrell, W TN Mtd Inf
STELL, Littlebury, Pvt, Col Newton Cannon, Capt Ota Cantrell, W TN Mtd Inf
STELL, Samuel, Pvt, Col Thos Benton, Capt James McFerrin, Vol Inf
STENAPHER, Benjamin, Pvt, Col Wm Johnson, Capt Jas R Rogers, E TN Draft Mil
STENNELL, George, 3 Sgt, Col Thos Benton, Capt Henry L Douglass, Vol Inf
STENNETT, Benjamin, Pvt, Col N T Perkins, Capt Mathew Patterson, Mtd Vol
STENNETT, Benjamin, Pvt, Col R H Dyer, Capt Robt Evans, Vol Mtd Gunmen
STENNETT, George, Pvt, Col Edward Bradley, Capt Harry L Douglass, Vol Inf
STENNETT, John, Pvt, Col N T Perkins, Capt Mathew Patterson, Mtd Vol
STENNETT, William H, Cpl, Lt Col L Hammond, Capt Jas Craig, Inf
STEP, Abraham, Pvt, Col A Loury, Lt Col L Hammons, Capt Arahel Rains, Inf
STEP, James, Pvt, Lt Col L Hammons, Capt Arahel Rains, Inf
STEP, John, Cpl, Col Saml Bayless, Capt Jos Goodson, E TN Mil
STEP, John, Pvt, Col Saml Bayless, Capt Branch Jones, E TN Draft Mil; trans to Capt Goodson's Co
STEP, John, Pvt, Col Wm Johnson, Capt Elihu Milliken, 3 Regt E TN Mil
STEP, Robert, Pvt, Col A Loury, Lt Col L Hammons, Capt Arahel Rains, Inf
STEPHAN, Joshua, Pvt, Col Wm Hall, Capt John Kennedy, Vol Inf
STEPHEN, Abraham, Pvt, Col John Williams, Capt Wm Walker, Mtd Mil
STEPHEN, John, Pvt, Col Philip Pipkin, Capt John Strother, Mil
STEPHEN, Larkin, Pvt, Col Samuel Bunch, Capt Jno English, E TN Drafted Mil; furloughed for inability
STEPHEN, Patton, Pvt, Col L Hammond, Capt Arahel Rains, Inf
STEPHEN, Vachel, Pvt, Col Wm Metcalf, Capt A Patterson, Mil Inf
STEPHENS, Benjamin, Pvt, Col Edward Bradley, Capt John Kennedy, Riflemen; AWOL
STEPHENS, Charles, Pvt, Col John Cocke, Capt Richard Crunk, Inf
STEPHENS, Daniel, Pvt, Col R H Dyer, Maj Wm Russell, Capt Wm Russell, Vol Mtd Gunmen
STEPHENS, David, Pvt, Col Wm Johnson, Capt Joseph Scott, E TN Drafted Mil
STEPHENS, Edward, 6 Cpl, Col Philip Pipkin, Capt Ebenezer Kirkpatrick, Mil Inf; promoted to 2 Sgt
STEPHENS, Edward, Pvt, Col N T Perkins, Capt Mathews Johnston, Mil Inf

- 475

## Enlisted Men, War of 1812

STEPHENS, Edward, Pvt, Regt Commander omitted, Capt Gray, Inf
STEPHENS, Edwin, Pvt, Col R C Napier, Capt Thos Gray, Mil Inf; d 4-26-1814
STEPHENS, Ezekiel, Pvt, Brig Gen T Johnson, Capt Allen, Mil Inf
STEPHENS, Ezekiel, Pvt, Col John Cocke, Capt John Weakley, Inf
STEPHENS, Garison, Pvt, Col S Copeland, Capt John Dawson, Inf
STEPHENS, George, Pvt, Col John Cocke, Capt James Gray, Inf
STEPHENS, George, Pvt, Regt Commander omitted, Capt Jas Cowan, Mtd Inf
STEPHENS, Henry, Pvt, Col John Williams, Capt Wm Walker, E TN Mtd Vol
STEPHENS, Holstein, Pvt, Col Samuel Wear, Capt Henry Stephens, E TN Vol Inf
STEPHENS, James, Pvt, Col A Cheatham, Capt James Giddens, Inf
STEPHENS, James, Pvt, Col Newton Cannon, Capt Geo Brandon, Mtd Riflemen
STEPHENS, James, Pvt, Col Philip Pipkin, Capt Henry M Newlin, Mil Inf; substitute for John Gosset
STEPHENS, James, Pvt, Col Wm Metcalf, Capt Barbee Collins, Mil Inf
STEPHENS, Jeremiah, Pvt, Maj Wm Woodfolk, Capt Abner Pearce, Inf
STEPHENS, John, 4 Sgt, Lt Col L Hammond, Capt James Tubb, Inf; d 3-9-1815
STEPHENS, John, Pvt, Col James Raulston, Capt Mathew Cowan, Inf
STEPHENS, John, Pvt, Col N T Perkins, Capt Mathew Johnston, Mil Inf
STEPHENS, John, Pvt, Col Newton Cannon, Capt Jas Walton, Mtd Riflemen
STEPHENS, John, Pvt, Col S Copeland, Capt Wm Evans, Mil Inf
STEPHENS, John, Pvt, Col Samuel Bunch, Capt Wm Jobe, E TN Vol Mtd Inf
STEPHENS, John, Pvt, Col Wm Lillard, Capt Wm McLin, E TN Inf
STEPHENS, John, Pvt, Maj Wm Russell, Capt Geo Mitchie, Vol Mtd Gunmen
STEPHENS, Jonathan, Pvt, Col R C Napier, Capt Thos Gray, Mil Inf
STEPHENS, Joshua, Pvt, Col S Copeland, Capt Wm Evans, Mil Inf
STEPHENS, Josiah sr, Pvt, Col Thos Benton, Capt Geo Caperton, Inf
STEPHENS, Laomi jr, Pvt, Col Thos Williamson, Capt Wm Martin, Vol Mtd Gunmen
STEPHENS, Laomi sr, Pvt, Col Thos Williamson, Capt Wm Martin, Vol Mtd Gunmen; d 2-21-1815
STEPHENS, Larkin, Pvt, Col Samuel Bunch, Capt Moses, E TN Mil Drafted; transferred to Capt John English Co
STEPHENS, Orkiles, Pvt, Maj Gen Wm Carroll, Capt Wiley Huddleston, Inf
STEPHENS, Phillip, Pvt, Col Wm Johnson, Capt James Rogers, E TN Mil

STEPHENS, Rachell, Cpl, Col R C Napier, Capt Thos Preston, Mil Inf
STEPHENS, Samuel, Pvt, Regt Commander omitted, Capt Jas Cowan, Mtd Inf
STEPHENS, Shadarack, Pvt, Col Edwin Booth, Capt John McKamey, E TN Mil
STEPHENS, Shadrack, Pvt, Col Jno Brown, Capt Wm White, E TN Vol Mtd Inf
STEPHENS, Squire, Pvt, Col R C Napier, Capt Thos Preston, Mil Inf
STEPHENS, Sutton, Pvt, Regt Commander omitted, Capt Larkin Ferrill, Mil Inf
STEPHENS, Thomas W, Pvt, Col Sam'l Bunch, Capt W? Stephens, E TN Mil Inf
STEPHENS, Washington, Pvt, Col Jno Brown, Capt Wm White, E TN Mtd Vol Inf
STEPHENS, William, Pvt, Col N T Perkins, Capt M Johnston, Mil Inf
STEPHENS, William, Pvt, Maj Jno Childs, Capt Jno Stephens, E TN Vol Mtd Inf
STEPHENS, Zachariah, Pvt, Col Sam'l Bayless, Capt Jos Bacon, E TN Mil
STEPHENSON, Alexander, Pvt, Col Wm Johnson, Capt Elihu Milliken, 3rd Regt E TN Mil
STEPHENSON, Edward, Pvt, Col John Alcorn, Capt Thos Bradley, Vol Cav
STEPHENSON, Henry, Pvt, Col Samuel Bunch, Capt Jno English, E TN Drafted Mil; joined from Capt Duncan's Co
STEPHENSON, Henry, Pvt, Col Samuel Bunch, Capt Joseph Duncan, E TN Drafted Mil; transferred to Capt English's Co
STEPHENSON, James M, Pvt, Col Samuel Bunch, Capt Joseph Duncan, E TN Drafted Mil
STEPHENSON, James W, 3 Sgt, Col Philip Pipkin, Capt Henry M Newlin, Mil Inf; deserted
STEPHENSON, James, Pvt, Col Samuel Wear, Capt Rufus Morgan, E TN Vol Inf
STEPHENSON, John, 4 Cpl, Regt Commander omitted, Capt Brice Martin, Vol Inf
STEPHENSON, John, Pvt, Col John Brown, Capt Allen I Bacon, E TN Mil Inf
STEPHENSON, John, Pvt, Col Wm Metcalf, Capt Wm Mullin, Mil Inf
STEPHENSON, S, Pvt, Col A Loury, Capt Arahel Rains, Inf
STEPHENSON, Watson, 2 Sgt, Col Philip Pipkin, Capt Henry M Newlin, Mil Inf
STEPHENSON, William, Pvt, Col Samuel Bayless, Capt Joseph B Bacon, E TN Mil
STEPHENSON, William, Pvt, Col Samuel Wear, Capt John Childs, E TN Vol Inf
STEPHENSON, William, Pvt, Col Thos Williamson, Capt A Metcalf, Vol Mtd Gunmen
STEPHENSON, William, Sgt, Col R H Dyer, Capt Robt Evans, Vol Mtd Gunmen
STEPHENSON, Zachariah, Pvt, Col Edwin Booth, Capt Richard Marshall, Drafted Mil
STEPLES, Charles H, 4 Cpl, Col Edward Bradley, Capt Abraham Bledsoe, Riflemen
STEPTOE, Simon, Pvt, Col R C Napier, Capt James

## Enlisted Men, War of 1812

McMurry, Mil Inf
STEPTON, Simon, Pvt, Col A Loury, Capt Geo Sarver, Inf
STERGUS, Wallace, 2 Surgeon's Mate, Col Archer Cheatham, 2nd Regt TN
STERLING, John, Pvt, Col Samuel Bunch, Capt Edward Buchanan, E TN Mil
STERLING, John, Pvt, Col Samuel Bunch, Capt Joseph Duncan, E TN Drafted Mil; joined from Capt Buchanan Co
STERLING, Thomas, Pvt, Col Edwin Booth, Capt Alexander Biggs, Inf
STERLING, Thomas, Pvt, Col Samuel Bayless, Capt Joseph Rich, E TN Inf; joined from Capt Milliken's Co
STERLING, Thomas, Pvt, Col Wm Johnson, Capt Elihu Milliken, 3rd Regt E TN Mil
STERNS, David, 3 Sgt, Col Wm Hall, Capt Abraham Bledsoe, Vol Inf
STERNS, George, Pvt, Col Wm Johnson, Capt Elihu Milliken, 3rd Regt E TN Mil
STERNS, Jacob, Pvt, Col Wm Lillard, Capt Thos McChristian, E TN Vol Mil Inf
STERNS, Moses, Pvt, Maj Wm Woodfolk, Capt Ezekial Ross, Capt McCulley, Inf
STEVENS, Bartholomew, Pvt, Col Philip Pipkin, Capt Wm Mackay, Mil Inf
STEVENS, Charles, Pvt, Col Wm Pillow, Capt C E McEwin, Vol Inf
STEVENS, George, Pvt, Regt Commander omitted, Capt James Cowan, Mtd Inf
STEVENS, Henry, Pvt, Col John Williams, Capt Wm Walker, Vol
STEVENS, James, Pvt, Regt Commander omitted, Capt Mason, Cav; discharged sick
STEVENS, Joel, Pvt, Regt Commander omitted, Capt D Mason, Cav
STEVENS, John, Pvt, Col T McCrory, Co Commander omitted, Mil Inf
STEVENS, Lewis, Pvt, Regt Commander omitted, Capt D Mason, Cav
STEVENS, Samuel, Pvt, Regt Commander omitted, Capt James Cowan, Mtd Inf
STEVENS, Suttin, Pvt, Regt Commander omitted, Capt L Ferrell, Inf
STEVENS, William, Pvt, Regt Commander omitted, Capt D Mason, Cav; discharged for ill health
STEVENSON, Giles, Pvt, Col John Cocke, Capt John Dalton, Inf
STEVENSON, John, 4 Cpl, Col Wm Hall, Capt Brice Martin, Vol Inf
STEVENSON, Williamson, Pvt, Col S Copeland, Capt Allen Wilkinson, Mil Inf
STEVINS, John, Pvt, Col Samuel Copeland, Capt Wm Jobe, E TN Vol Mtd Inf
STEWARD, Abraham, Pvt, Gen Andrew Jackson, Capt Hugh Kerr, Mtd Rangers
STEWARD, Adam, Pvt, Gen Andrew Jackson, Capt Nathan Davis, Branch Srvce omitted
STEWARD, John, Pvt, Col Thomas Williamson, Capt John Dobbins & Capt Cook, Vol Mtd Gunmen

STEWARD, Roberson, Pvt, Col Edward Bradley, Capt Wm Lauderdale, Vol Inf
STEWARD, Robert A, Sgt, Col Wm Johnson, Capt James Rogers, E TN Drafted Mil
STEWARD, Robert, Pvt, Col Wm Pillow, Capt Wm Smith, Vol Inf
STEWARD, Robert, Pvt, Regt Commander omitted, Capt David Vance & Capt John Williams, Mtd Mil
STEWARD, Robert, Pvt, Regt Commander omitted, Capt Wm I Smith, Branch Srvce omitted
STEWARD, Saber (Sabre), Pvt, Col A Loury, Capt J N Williamson, W TN Mil
STEWARD, Thomas, Pvt, Col N T Perkins, Capt John Quarles, Vol Mtd Inf
STEWARD, Thomas, Pvt, Gen Andrew Jackson, Capt Nathan Davis, Inf
STEWARD, William, Cpl, Col Edwin Booth, Capt John Slatton, E TN Mil
STEWARD, William, Pvt, Col John Alcorn, Capt John Byrns, Cav
STEWARD, _____, Pvt, Col L Hammond, Capt J N Williamson, 2nd Regt Inf
STEWART, Alexander, Pvt, Col John K Wynne, Capt John Spinks, Inf
STEWART, Alexander, Pvt, Col Richard Napier, Capt Early Benson, Mil Inf
STEWART, Andrew, Cpl, Col John K Wynne, Capt Wm Wilson, Inf
STEWART, Andrew, Pvt, Col John K Wynne, Capt John Porter, Inf
STEWART, Andrew, Pvt, Col Samuel Bunch, Capt Robert Breden, E TN Mil
STEWART, Andrew, Pvt, Col Thomas H Williamson, Capt James Cook & Capt John Dobbins, Vol Mtd Gunmen; d 2-2-1815
STEWART, Anthony, Pvt, Col Wm Lillard, Capt George Argenbright, E TN Vol Riflemen
STEWART, Arthur, Pvt, Regt Commander omitted, Capt Archibald McKinney, Cav
STEWART, Dempsey, Pvt, Col John Cocke, Capt John Weakley, Inf
STEWART, Dempsey, Pvt, Regt Commander omitted, Capt John Crane, Mtd Inf
STEWART, Edward, Cpl, Col John Brown, Capt John McKamy, E TN Mtd Gunmen
STEWART, Edward, Pvt, Col Edwin E Booth, Capt Vernon, E TN Mil
STEWART, Elisha, Pvt, Col James Raulston, Capt Daniel Newman, Inf
STEWART, Evans, Pvt, Col Edwin E Booth, Capt John Slatton, E TN Mil
STEWART, George, Pvt, Col Samuel Bunch, no other information
STEWART, George, Sgt, Col Edwin E Booth, Capt John McKamy, E TN Mil; promoted from the ranks
STEWART, Harbert, Pvt, Col Samuel Bunch, Capt Edward Buchanan, E TN Mil; deserted
STEWART, James W, Sgt, Col Newton Cannon, Capt Thomas Yardley, Mtd Riflemen
STEWART, James, Pvt, Col T McCrory, Capt A Willis, Mil Inf; transferred to Pack Horse Co

## Enlisted Men, War of 1812

STEWART, James, Pvt, Col Wm Hall, Capt James Raulston, Vol Inf
STEWART, James, Pvt, Col Wm Johnson, Capt Jas Rogers, E TN Mil
STEWART, James, Pvt, Maj William Woodfolk, Capt Ezekiel Ross & Capt McCulley, Inf
STEWART, James, Steward, Col Samuel Bunch, E TN Mil
STEWART, Jesse, Pvt, Maj Wm Woodfolk, Capt John Sutton & Capt Dudney, Inf; no service performed
STEWART, John R, Pvt, Col Wm Johnson, Capt Benjamin Powell, E TN Mil
STEWART, John, Pvt, Col A Cheatham, Capt Wm Smith, Inf
STEWART, John, Pvt, Col James Raulston, Capt Henry Hamilton, Inf; also under Maj Gen Wm Carroll
STEWART, John, Pvt, Col James Raulston, Capt James Black, Inf
STEWART, John, Pvt, Col N T Perkins, Capt Wm Johnston, Mil Inf
STEWART, John, Pvt, Col Samuel Wear, Capt James Gillespie, E TN Vol Inf
STEWART, John, Pvt, Col Thomas H Williamson, Capt John Doak & Capt John Dobbins, Vol Mtd Gunmen
STEWART, John, Pvt, Col Wm Metcalf, Capt Bird L Hurt, Mil Inf
STEWART, John, Pvt, Col Wm Metcalf, Capt Marks, Mil Inf
STEWART, John, Pvt, Maj Wm Woodfolk, Capt Abner Pearce, Inf
STEWART, Joshua, Pvt, Capt Nathan Davis, Lt I Barrett, Inf
STEWART, Larney, Pvt, Col Phillip Pipkin, Capt James Blakemore, Mil Inf
STEWART, Lasurous, Pvt, Gen Andrew Jackson, Capt Hugh Kerr, Mtd Rangers
STEWART, Lazereth, Pvt, Col Wm Hall, Capt Henry M _____, Inf; refused to march
STEWART, Matthew, Cpl, Gen Andrew Jackson, Capt Hugh Kerr, Mtd Rangers
STEWART, Micus, Pvt, Col John Alcorn, Capt Wm Locke, Cav
STEWART, Murdock, Pvt, Col S Copeland, Capt Allen Wilkinson, Mil Inf
STEWART, Patton (Peyton), Pvt, Col Wm Hall, Capt John Wallace, Inf
STEWART, Peterson, Pvt, Col Wm Hall, Capt Wm Alexander, Vol Inf; AWOL
STEWART, William, Pvt, Brig Gen T Johnson, Capt Allen, Mil Inf
STEWART, William, Pvt, Capt Nathan Davis, Lt I Barrett, Inf
STEWART, William, Pvt, Col Thos Benton, Capt Henry L Douglass, Vol Inf
STEWART, William, Pvt, Col Wm Pillow, Capt Wm Moore, Inf
STEWART, William, Pvt, Lt Col Wm Phillips, Co Commander omitted, Inf
STEWART, William, Pvt, Maj Gen A Jackson, Capt Joseph Kirkpatrick, Mtd Gunmen

STEWART (STUART), William, Pvt, Col Thomas H Benton, Capt William Moore, Vol Inf
STEWART (STUART), William, Pvt, Col Thos Benton, Capt Wm Moore, Vol Inf
STILES, David, Pvt, Col S Copeland, Capt John Dawson, Inf
STILES, Enoch, Pvt, Col S Copeland, Capt Wm Hodge, Inf
STILES, John, Pvt, Col R H Dyer, Capt Bethel Allen, Vol Mtd Gunmen
STILES, John, Pvt, Col S Copeland, Capt Wm Hodge, Inf
STILES, Sam, Pvt, Col Newton Cannon, Capt James Walton, Mtd Riflemen
STILES, Samuel, Pvt, Col S Copeland, Capt Wm Hodge, Inf
STILES, William, Pvt, Col Wm Higgins, Capt Adam Dale, Mtd Gunmen
STILL, Freeman, Pvt, Col E Booth, Capt Richd Marshall, Drafted Mil; discharged for inability
STILL, George W, Pvt, Col John Alcorn, Capt Thos Bradley, Vol Cav
STILL, James, Pvt, Col Saml Bunch, Capt A Breden, E TN Mil
STILLMAN, Mathias, Pvt, Col J K Wynne, Capt Wm Wilson, Inf; transferred to Capt Caruthers Co
STINE, Andrew, Pvt, Col Saml Bayless, Capt Jos Hale, E TN Mil
STINE, John, Pvt, Col Saml Bayless, Capt Jos Hale, E TN Mil
STINET, James, Pvt, Col Wm Johnson, Capt Jas Stewart, E TN Mil
STINNEL, George, Pvt, Col Thos Benton, Capt H Douglass, Vol Inf
STINNEL, Samuel, Pvt, Col E Booth, Capt Vernon, E TN Mil
STINNETT, William, Cpl, Col L Hammond, Capt Jas Craig, 2nd Regt W TN Mil
STINSON, James, Pvt, Regt Commander omitted, Capt Archibald McKenney, Cav
STINSON, John, Pvt, Col Thomas Benton, Capt Wm Smith, Vol Inf
STINSON, Mutney, Pvt, Gen A Jackson, Capt Hugh Kerr, Mtd Rangers
STINSON, Samuel, Pvt, Col Thos Benton, Capt Wm Smith, Vol Inf
STINSON, Whitley, Cpl, Maj Wm Russell, Capt F Hodges, Vol Mtd Gunmen
STINSON, Whitley, Pvt, Regt Commander omitted, Capt Hugh Kerr, Mtd Rangers
STINSON, William, Cpl, Col E Booth, Capt Saml Thompson, Mil
STOBAUGH, John, Pvt, Col Thos Benton, Capt Thos Williamson, Vol Inf
STOBAUGH, John, Pvt, Col Wm Pillow, Capt Thos Williamson, Vol Inf
STOBOUGH, James, Pvt, Col Thos Williamson, Capt Thos Porter, Vol Mtd Gunmen
STOBOUGH, John, Pvt, Col Thos Williamson, Capt Thos Porter, Vol Mtd Gunmen
STOBUCK, John, Pvt, Col R H Dyer, Capt Robt Edmonston, TN Vol Mtd Gunmen

## Enlisted Men, War of 1812

STOBUCK, John, Pvt, Maj Gen A Jackson, Col A Cheatham, Capt Wm Creel, Inf
STOCKARD, Nathan, Pvt, Col Alcorn, Capt Wm Locke, Cav
STOCKARD, Nathan, Pvt, Col Wm Metcalf, Capt Wm Mullin, Mil Inf
STOCKARD, Stephen, Pvt, Col Jno Cocke, Capt Jno Dalton, Inf
STOCKARD, William, Cpl, Col Jno Alcorn, Capt Wm Locke, Cav
STOCKART, Nathan, Pvt, Col Wm Metcalf, Capt Wm Mullin, Mil Inf
STOCKHILL, John, Pvt, Maj Wm Russell, Capt Wm Chism, Vol Mtd Riflemen
STOCKTON, Benjamin, Pvt, Maj Wm Russell, Capt F Hodges, Vol Mtd Gunmen
STOCKTON, Nathaniel, Pvt, Col Jno Coffee, Capt B Coleman, Cav
STOCKTON, William, Pvt, Col Jno Coffee, Capt B Coleman, Cav
STOCKTON, Willis, Pvt, Col Jno Brown, Capt Jno Trimble, E TN Mtd Gunmen
STOGAN, Thomas, Pvt, Col E Booth, Capt Jno McKamey, E TN Mil
STOKE, John, Pvt, Col S Bunch, Capt F Register, E TN Mil; deserted
STOKE, John, Pvt, Col S Bunch, Capt Geo McPherson, E TN Mil; joined from Capt Register Co
STOKE, Martin, Pvt, Col Thos Benton, Capt Benj Reynolds, Vol Inf
STOKES, Abner, Pvt, Regt Commander omitted, Capt Gray, Inf
STOKES, David, Pvt, Col Alex Loury, Capt Jno Looney, W TN Inf
STOKES, John, Pvt, Col Alex Loury, Capt Jno Looney, W TN Inf
STOKES, John, Pvt, Col Jas Raulston, Capt M Cowan, Inf
STOKES, Jordan D, Pvt, Col R H Dyer, Capt E Allen, Vol Mtd Gunmen
STOKES, Martin, Pvt, Col Thos Benton, Capt Benj Reynolds, Vol Inf
STOKES, William, Pvt, Col A Cheatham, Capt Wm Smith, Inf
STOKES, William, Pvt, Col R H Dyer, Maj Wm Russell, Capt Wm Russell, Vol Mtd Gunmen
STOKES, William, Pvt, Col Thos Williamson, Capt Jas Pace, Lt Jas Nealy, Vol Mtd Gunmen
STOLEY (STALY), Frederick, Pvt, Col Jno Cocke, Capt Jno Weakley, Inf; d 2-7-1815
STOLTZ, Soloman, Pvt, Col A Cheatham, Capt R Benson, Inf
STONE, Daniel, Pvt, Col Wm Lillard, Capt Thos Sharpe, 2nd Regt Inf
STONE, David, Pvt, Col A Loury, Lt Col L Hammonds, Capt A Rains, Inf
STONE, Drury, 2 Sgt, Col Wm Hall, Capt Wm Alexander, Vol Inf
STONE, George, Pvt, Col Saml Bunch, Capt Jos Duncan, E TN Drafted Mil
STONE, James, Pvt, Col Jno Coffee, Capt B Coleman, Cav
STONE, James, Pvt, Maj Gen Wm Carroll, Col Wm Metcalf, Capt Jno Jackson, Inf
STONE, James, Pvt, Regt Commander omitted, Capt David Mason, Cav
STONE, Joel, Pvt, Col Wm Higgins, Capt Jas Hambleton, Mtd Gunmen
STONE, John, Dmr, Col Saml Bayless, Capt Jno Brock, E TN Mil; d 1-30-1815 in service
STONE, John, Drm Maj, Col Jno Cocke, Co Commander omitted, 2nd Regt W TN Mil Inf
STONE, John, Pvt, Col Jno Coffee, Capt B Coleman, Cav
STONE, John, Pvt, Col N T Cannon, Capt D Hogan, Mtd Gunmen; wounded at Tallihatchee 11-3-1813
STONE, John, Pvt, Col Saml Bunch, Capt E Buchanan, E TN Mil; joined from Capt Duncan's Co
STONE, John, Pvt, Col Saml Bunch, Capt Jos Duncan, E TN Drafted Mil; transferred to Capt Buckhannon's Co
STONE, John, Pvt, Col Wm Johnson, Capt Jas Stewart, E TN Mil
STONE, John, Pvt, Maj Wm Woodfolk, Capt Jas Neil, Inf
STONE, John, Pvt, Regt Commander omitted, Capt Jno Crane, Mtd Inf
STONE, John, Pvt, Regt Commander omitted, Capt Wm Henderson, Spies
STONE, Marvel, Sgt, Lt Col Richard Napier, Co Commander omitted, Inf
STONE, Micajah, Pvt, Maj Wm Woodfolk, Capt Jas Turner, Inf
STONE, Nicholas C, Pvt, Col Jno Cocke, Capt Richd Crunk, Inf
STONE, Reuben, Pvt, Col Saml Bayless, Capt Jno Brock, E TN Mil
STONE, Saml, Pvt, Col N T Cannon, Capt Jno Demsey, Mtd Gunmen
STONE, Thomas, Pvt, Brig Gen Johnson, Capt Robt Carson, Inf; discharged for want of arms
STONE, Thomas, Pvt, Col A Cheatham, Capt Geo Chapman, Inf
STONE, Thomas, Pvt, Col Dyer, Capt Jas McMahan, TN Vol Mtd Gunmen
STONE, Thomas, Pvt, Col N T Cannon, Capt Jno Demsey, Mtd Gunmen
STONE, Thomas, Pvt, Col Napier, Capt Jno Chism, Mil Inf
STONE, Uriah, Sgt, Col R H Dyer, Capt Ephraim Dickson, TN Vol Gunmen; reduced to the ranks
STONE, William H, Cpl, Col Robert Dyer, Capt Glen Owen, TN Vol Mtd Gunmen
STONE, William, 1 Cpl, Col John Cocke, Capt Bird Nance, Inf
STONE, William, Pvt, Col James Raulston, Capt Mathew Neale, Inf
STONE, William, Pvt, Col John Alcorn, Capt Thomas Bradley, Vol Cav
STONE, William, Pvt, Col Newton Cannon, Capt John B Dempsey, Mtd Gunmen
STONE, William, Pvt, Lt Col Leroy Hammonds, Co Commander omitted, Inf
STONE (STILL), Green, 3 Cpl, Col Jno Cocke, Capt B Nance, Inf; d 1-26-1815
STONECEIPHER, John, Pvt, Col John Brown, Capt Wm

White, E TN Vol Mtd Inf
STONECIPHER, Samuel, Pvt, Col John Brown, Capt Wm White, E TN Mtd Inf
STONECYPHER, Daniel, Pvt, Col Edwin E Booth, Capt John McKamy, E TN Mil
STONER, Abraham, Pvt, Col Samuel Wear & Col Samuel Bunch, Capt Wm Mitchell, E TN Mtd Inf
STORER, Jacob, Pvt, Regt Commander omitted, Capt Wm Henderson, Spies
STORY, Henry, Pvt, Maj Gen Wm Carroll, Capt Francis Ellis, Inf
STORY, James, Pvt, Lt Col Leroy Hammond, Capt James Craig, Inf
STORY, Vincent, Ffr, Col R C Napier, Capt Andrew McCarty, Mil Inf
STORY, William, Pvt, Col S Copeland, Capt John Holshouser, Inf
STORY, William, Sgt, Col Samuel Bayless, Capt Branch Jones, E TN Mil Drafted
STOUT, Abraham, Pvt, Maj John Porter, Capt James Anderson, Cav
STOUT, Benjamin C, 2 Sgt, Maj John Childs, Capt Charles Conway, E TN Mtd Gunmen; Regt Co - Roan
STOUT, Benjamin C, Pvt, Regt Commander omitted, Capt John Williams & Capt Wm Walker, Vol
STOUT, Benjamin, Pvt, Col Thomas Williamson, Capt James Pace, Lt James Nealy, Vol Mtd Gunmen
STOUT, David, Pvt, Col Wm Johnson, Capt Henry Hunter, E TN Mil
STOUT, George, Pvt, Col Edwin Allison, Capt Winsell, E TN Drafted Mil; discharged for inability
STOUT, Henry, Pvt, Col Ewin Allison, Capt Adam Winsell, E TN Drafted Mil; deserted
STOUT, Joseph, Pvt, Col S Booth, Co Commander omitted, Drafted Mil
STOUT, Moses, Pvt, Col Samuel Bayless, Capt Joseph Hale, E TN Mil
STOUT, Moses, Pvt, Col Samuel Wear, Co Commander omitted, E TN Vol Inf; deserted
STOUT, Moses, Pvt, Col Wm Johnson, Capt James Tunnell, E TN Mil; deserted
STOUT, William, Pvt, Maj Gen Wm Carroll, Capt Wiley Huddleston, Inf
STOVALL, Elijah H, Pvt, Col Thomas H Benton, Capt George Caperton, Inf
STOVALL, Elisha, Pvt, Col Wm Pillow, Capt George Caperton, Inf
STOVALL, George H, Pvt, Col R H Dyer, Capt Wm Russell, Vol Mtd Gunmen
STOVALL, Joseph, Pvt, Col Thomas Williamson, Capt Wm Martin, Vol Mtd Gunmen
STOVALL, Thomas, Pvt, Col James Raulston, Capt Mathew Neale, Inf
STOVER, Daniel, Sgt, Col Samuel Wear, Capt Jesse Cole, Vol Inf
STOVER, Elijah, Pvt, Col Wm Johnson, Capt Andrew Lawson, E TN Drafted Mil
STOVER, Jacob, Pvt, Col Ewin Allison, Capt Adam Winsell, E TN Drafted Mil
STOVER, Jacob, Pvt, Col John Brown, Capt Charles Lewin, E TN Mtd Inf
STOVER, Jacob, Pvt, Col S Bunch, Capt George McPherson, E TN Mil; joined from? Capt Lewin's Co
STOVER, Jacob, Pvt, Regt Commander omitted, Capt Wm Henderson, Spies; d 1-20-1815
STOVER, Lewis, Pvt, Col Wm Metcalf, Capt Wm Mullin, Mil Inf
STOVER, Lewis, Pvt, Col Wm Metcalf, Capt Wm Sitton, Mil Inf
STOW, John, Pvt, Col Wm Johnson, Capt Stewart, E TN Drafted Mil
STOWE, Abraham, Pvt, Maj Wm Woodfolk, Capt Abraham Dudney & Capt John Sutton, Inf
STRAIN, John, 2 Lt, Col Edwin E Booth, Capt Alexander Biggs, Inf
STRAITOR, Jacob, Pvt, Col Wm Hall, Capt Abraham Bledsoe, Vol Inf
STRAND, Jesse, Pvt, Col Archer Cheatham, Capt Ben Elliott, Mtd Inf
STRAND, Joseph, Cpl, Col Samuel Wear, Capt Jesse Cole, Vol Inf
STRANGE, Coleman, Pvt, Col Stephen Copeland, Capt Wm Hodges, Inf
STRANGE, John, Pvt, Col Ewin Allison, Capt Abraham Allen, E TN Mil
STRANGE, Joseph, Pvt, Col Wm Lillard, Capt John Neatherton, E TN Inf
STRANGHAN, Stephen, 4 Cpl, Col Thomas McCrory, Capt Thomas Gordon, Inf
STRANGHON, Tapley, Pvt, Col Wm Metcalf, Capt Marks, Mil Inf
STRANLER, Samuel, Pvt, Col Wm Pillow, Capt C E McEwin, Vol Inf
STRATER, Adam, Pvt, Col Wm Hall, Capt Travis C Nash, Inf
STRATOR, Jacob, Pvt, Col Wm Hall, Capt Abraham Bledsoe, Vol Inf
STRATTON, Ambrose, Pvt, Col Samuel Wear, Capt Robert Doak, E TN Vol Inf
STRATTON, James, Pvt, Col James Raulston, Co Commander omitted, Inf; also under Maj Gen Wm Carroll
STRAWN, James, Pvt, Col Wm Metcalf, Capt Wm Sitton, Mil Inf
STRAWN, Stephen, Pvt, Col Wm Metcalf, Capt Wm Sitton, Mil Inf
STREAUTH, John, Pvt, Col Thos Benton, Capt Thos Williamson, Vol Inf
STREET, James, Pvt, Col Wm Hall, Capt Wm L Alexander, Vol Inf
STREET, James, Pvt, Col Wm Metcalf, Capt John Barnhart, Mil Inf
STREET, Jesse, Pvt, Col R H Dyer, Capt James Wyatt, Vol Mtd Gunmen
STREET, Joseph, Pvt, Col Wm Metcalf, Capt Obidiah Waller, Mil Inf; d 4-3-1815
STREET, Solomon, Pvt, Col Wm Metcalf, Capt Wm Sitton, Mil Inf
STREET, William jr, Pvt, Regt Commander omitted, Capt James Cowan, Mtd Inf
STREET, William, Cpl, Regt Commander omitted, Capt James Cowan, Mtd Inf

## Enlisted Men, War of 1812

STRENGTH, John, Pvt, Col Thos Benton, Capt Thos Williamson, Vol Inf
STRICKLAIN, Stephen, Pvt, Col A Cheatham, Capt Geo Chapman, Inf
STRICKLAN, Harmen, Pvt, Col A Cheatham, Capt Geo Chapman, Inf
STRICKLAN, James, Pvt, Col R H Dyer, Capt B Allen, Vol Mtd Gunmen
STRICKLAND, Samuel, Pvt, Col Wm Metcalf, Capt Bird Hurt, Mil Inf
STRICKLER, Samuel, Pvt, Col William Lillard, Capt Hugh Martin, E TN Vol Inf
STRICKLIN, Edmond, Pvt, Col Charles Lewis, Co Commander omitted, E TN Vol Mtd Inf
STRICKLIN, Edmond, Pvt, Col S Wear, Capt Simeon Perry, E TN Vol Mtd Inf
STRICKLIN, Jacob, Ens, Col Ewen Allison, Capt Joseph Everett, E TN Mil
STRICKLIN, John, Pvt, Col Wm Metcalf, Capt John Cunningham & Capt Hill, Mil Inf
STRICKLIN, Jonathan, Pvt, Col John Wynne, Capt John Breden, Inf
STRICKLIN, Seth, Pvt, Col Wm Metcalf, Capt John Cunningham & Capt Hill, Mil Inf
STRICKLIN, William, Pvt, Col Wm Metcalf, Capt Hill & Capt John Cunningham, Mil Inf
STRICKLING, Harman, Pvt, Col Alexander Loury, Capt Gabriel Martin, Inf
STRICKLING, John, Pvt, Col Alexander Loury, Co Commander omitted, Inf
STRICKLING, Warren G, 1 Cpl, Col Jas Raulston, Capt Geo Black, Branch Srvce omitted
STRICKLINGER, Ezekiel, Pvt, Col Wm Metcalf, Capt Geo Sitton, Mil Inf; d 2-8-1815
STRINGER, Joseph, Pvt, Col A Cheatham, Capt Charles Johnson, Inf
STRINGER, Joseph, Pvt, Col John Cocke, Capt James Gault, Inf
STRINGER, Joseph, Pvt, Col N Cannon, Capt Martin, Mtd Gunmen
STRINGER, William B, Pvt, Col Ewen Allison, Capt T McCrory, E TN Mil
STRINGER, William, Pvt, Col S Wear, Capt Daniel Price, E TN Vol Inf
STRINGFELLOW, James, Pvt, Col Thos Benton, Capt Geo Gibbs, Vol Inf
STRINGFELLOW, John, Pvt, Col John Alcorn, Capt John Winston, Mtd Riflemen
STRINGFELLOW, Richard E, Pvt, Col T McCrory, Capt Isaac Potts, Mil Inf
STRINGFELLOW, Richard, Pvt, Maj John Childs, Capt Chas Conway, E TN Mtd Gunmen
STRINGFELLOW, Thomas, Pvt, Col John Alcorn, Capt Chas Winston, Mtd Riflemen
STRINGFELLOW, William, 4 Cpl, Lt Col Leroy Hammonds, Capt Joseph Williamson, Inf; transferred to Pack Horse Dept
STRINGFELLOW, William, Cpl, Col A Loury, Capt J N Williams, W TN Mil
STRONG, David T, Pvt, Col S Wear, Capt Robert Doak, E TN Vol Inf

STRONG, George, Pvt, Col Robert Steele, Capt Jas Shenault, Mil Inf
STRONG, John, Pvt, Col Philip Pipkin, Capt Jas Mackey, Mil Inf
STRONG, John, Pvt, Col S Copeland, Capt William Hodge, Inf
STRONG, John, Pvt, Col William Pegram, Capt Philip Pipkin, W TN Mil
STRONG, Mastion, Pvt, Col William Johnson, Capt Jas Rogers, E TN Drafted Mil
STRONG, Nathan, Pvt, Col John Alcorn, Capt Chas Winston, Mtd Riflemen
STRONG, Thomas, Pvt, Col John K Wynne, Capt William McCall, Inf
STRONG, Thomas, Pvt, Lt Col Leroy Hammonds, Capt Jas Tubb, Inf
STRONG, William, Pvt, Col John Cocke, Capt James Gray, Inf
STRONG, William, Pvt, Col William Higgins, Capt Adam Dale, Mtd Gunmen
STROTHER, Benjamin, Pvt, Col Perkins, Capt Geo Mars, Mtd Vol
STROTHER, James, Pvt, Col Jno Coffee, Capt Henry Byran, Cav
STROTHER, John, Principle Photographer, Maj Gen Andrew Jackson, no other information
STROTHER, Orlando S, Pvt, Col William Pillow, Capt Geo Caperton, Inf
STROTHER, Robert, Cpl, Col Thomas Williamson, Capt Pace, Lt Nealy, Vol Mtd Gunmen
STROTHER, Robert, Pvt, Col Jno Coffee, Capt Henry Byran, Cav
STROWD, Allen, Cpl, Col William Pillow, Capt Jas Renshaw, Inf
STROWD, Christopher, Pvt, Col S Bayless, Capt Hale, E TN Mil
STROWD, James, Pvt, Col John Cocke, Capt George Barnes, Inf
STROWD, James, Pvt, Col S Bayless, Capt Solomon Hendricks, E TN Mil
STROWD, Jesse, Pvt, Col Robert Dyer, Capt Cuthbert Hudson, Vol Mtd Gunmen
STROWD, Jesse, Pvt, Lt Col A Cheatham, Capt Benj Elliott, Mtd Inf
STROWD, John, Pvt, Col John Cocke, Capt George Barnes, Inf
STROWD, John, Pvt, Col Thomas Williamson, Capt John Hutchings, Vol Mtd Gunmen
STROWD, Thomas, Pvt, Col R T Perkins, Capt Mathew Patterson, Mtd Vol
STROWD, William, Pvt, Col Thomas Williamson, Capt Jas Cook & Capt Crane, Vol Mtd Gunmen
STUARD, John, Pvt, Maj William Russell, Capt Fleman Hodges, Vol Mtd Gunmen
STUARD, Patrick, Pvt, Lt Col Leroy Hammonds, Capt Jas Tubbs, Inf
STUART, Aaron, Pvt, Col N Cannon, Capt John Harpole, Mtd Gunmen
STUART, Alexander, Pvt, Col Robert Dyer, Capt Jones, Mtd Vol Gunmen
STUART, David, Pvt, Col S Bayless, Capt Solomon

Hendricks, E TN Mil
STUART, Ducan, Pvt, Col R C Napier, Capt Andrew McCarty, Mil Inf
STUART, Elisha, Pvt, Col Edwin Booth, Capt John Slatton, E TN Mil
STUART, Isaac, Pvt, Lt Col Hammonds, Capt George Tubb, Inf
STUART, John, Pvt, Col John Brown, Capt James Preston, Regt E TN Mil Inf
STUART, John, Pvt, Col John Wynne, Capt Bailey Butler, Inf; deserted
STUART, John, Pvt, Col R C Napier, Capt Drury Adkins, Mil Inf
STUART, John, Pvt, Col Robert Steele, Capt John Chitwood, Mil Inf
STUART, John, Pvt, Col Wm Johnson, Capt John McKamy, E TN Drafted Mil
STUART, John, Pvt, Maj Wm Woodfolk, Capt Anthony Turner, Inf
STUART, Joseph, Cpl, Maj P H Porter, Capt James Anderson, E TN Cav
STUART, Robert, Pvt, Col Samuel Bayless, Capt Solomon Hendrix, E TN Mil
STUART, Robert, Pvt, Col Thomas H Benton, Capt Wm Smith, Vol Inf
STUART, Robert, Pvt, Regt Commander omitted, Capt Smith, Vol Inf
STUART, William, 4 Sgt, Col Edwin E Booth, Capt Harry L Douglas, Vol Inf
STUART, William, Pvt, Col John Alcorn, Capt John Baskerville, Vol Inf
STUART, William, Pvt, Col Thomas H Benton, Capt Wm Moore, Vol Inf
STUART, William, Pvt, Col Wm Johnson, Co Commander omitted, E TN Mil
STUART, William, Pvt, Maj Wm Woodfolk, Capt James Turner, Inf
STUBBLEFIELD, Benjamin, Pvt, Col Edward Bradley, Capt Wm Lauderdale, Vol Inf
STUBBLEFIELD, Garrison, Pvt, Col Wm Hall, Capt Wm Alexander, Vol Inf
STUBBLEFIELD, Jeremiah, Pvt, Col Wm Metcalf, Capt Wm Sitton, Mil Inf
STUBBLEFIELD, Lemmuel, Pvt, Col John Coffee, Co Commander omitted, Cav; also under Capt John Baskerville
STUBBLEFIELD, Stephen, Pvt, Col Samuel Bunch, Capt James Cummings, E TN Vol Mtd Inf
STUBBLEFIELD, William, Pvt, Col Wm Hall, Capt Wm Alexander, Vol Inf
STUBBLEFIELD, Woodruff, Pvt, Col Wm Hall, Capt Wm Alexander, Vol Inf
STUBBS, Aron, Pvt, Col John Brown, Capt Wm White, Regt E TN Mil Inf
STUBBS, Everet, Pvt, Col John Brown, Capt Wm White, E TN Vol Inf; d 4-27-1814
STUBS, George, Pvt, Maj Wm Russell, Capt Wm Mitchell, Vol Mtd Gunmen
STUDDART, John, Pvt, Regt Commander omitted, Capt G Law, Riflemen
STULSE, John, Pvt, Col Wm Lillard, Capt Robert McCalpin, E TN Inf
STUMP, John, Pvt, Col John Alcorn, Capt Frederick Stump, Cav
STURDIVEN, Benjamin, Pvt, Col John Coffee, Capt Ezekiel Ross, Branch Srvce omitted
STURGEON, James, Pvt, Maj John Childs, Capt James Cumming, E TN Vol Mtd Inf
STURGUS, Wallace, Surgeon's Mate, Col Philip Pipkin, 1st Regt TN Mil
STURGUS, William, Pvt, Col John Wynne, Capt James Cole, Inf
STURGUS, William, Pvt, Gen A Jackson, Capt Wm Russell, Mtd Spies
SUATSEL, John, Pvt, Col Wm Johnston, Capt Joseph Kirk, Mil
SUGARS, Nathan, Pvt, Col S Bunch, Lt John Harris, E TN Mil
SUGS, William, Pvt, Maj Gen Wm Carroll, Capt Francis Ellis, Inf; deserted
SUILEVANT, Charles, Pvt, Col A Loury, Capt James Kincaid, Inf
SUINDLE, George C, Pvt, Col Jas Raulston, Capt Daniel Newman, Inf
SUITER, William, Pvt, Col R H Dyer, Capt Beverly Williams, Vol Mtd Gunmen
SULIVAN, Elijah, Pvt, Col Wm Metcalf, Capt Bird L Hurt, Mil Inf
SULIVAN, Frederick S, Pvt, Col Thomas H Williamson, Capt James Pace, Lt James Nealey, Vol Mtd Gunmen
SULIVAN, Reuben, Pvt, Maj Wm Woodfolk, Capt Ezekiel Ross, Inf
SULIVAN, Simeon, Pvt, Col Thomas H Williams, Capt Richard Tate, Vol Mtd Gunmen
SULIVANT, Russell, Pvt, Col John Cocke, Capt Bird Nance, Inf
SULLENS, Joseph, Cpl, Col Edwin E Booth, Capt James McKamy, E TN Mil
SULLI, Kelly, Pvt, Col Leroy Hammons, Capt Arahel Rains, Inf
SULLIVAN, Bennet, Pvt, Col R C Napier, Capt James McMurry, Mil Inf
SULLIVAN, Burnet, Pvt, Maj Wm Woodfolk, Capt Ezekiel Ross, Inf
SULLIVAN, Daniel, Pvt, Brig Gen Thomas Johnson, Capt Robert Carson, Inf
SULLIVAN, Daniel, Pvt, Col S Copeland, Capt John Biles, Inf
SULLIVAN, Daniel, Pvt, Col S Copeland, Capt John Holshouser, Inf; transferred to Capt B Biles Co
SULLIVAN, Edmund (Edward), Pvt, Col A Loury, Capt George Sarver, Inf
SULLIVAN, Elijah, 4 Cpl, Col N T Perkins, Capt Mathew Patterson, Mtd Vol
SULLIVAN, Elisha, Pvt, Col Thomas Bradley, Capt John Moore, Vol Inf
SULLIVAN, Elisha, Pvt, Col Wm Hall, Capt John Moore, Vol Inf
SULLIVAN, Ezekiel, Cpl, Col S Bunch, Capt Robert Breden, E TN Mil; transferred to Capt Bacon's Co
SULLIVAN, Frederick, Pvt, Col John Alcorn, Capt

## Enlisted Men, War of 1812

McKeen, Cav
SULLIVAN, George, Pvt, Col Leroy Hammond, Capt James Craig, Inf
SULLIVAN, Holland, Pvt, Col Edward Bradley, Capt Wm Douglas, Vol Inf
SULLIVAN, Holland, Pvt, Col Thomas H Benton, Capt Wm Douglas, Vol Inf
SULLIVAN, Isaac C, Pvt, Col Wm Hall, Capt Brice Martin, Vol Inf
SULLIVAN, James, Dmr, Col Edwin E Booth, Capt Vernon, E TN Mil
SULLIVAN, James, Pvt, Col Leroy Hammond, Capt James Tubb, Inf
SULLIVAN, James, Pvt, Col T McCrory, Capt Jno Reynolds, Branch Srvce omitted
SULLIVAN, Jeremiah, Cpl, Col Thomas H Williamson, Capt Richard Tate, Vol Mtd Gunmen
SULLIVAN, John, Pvt, Col Edwin Booth, Capt John Sharp, E TN Mil
SULLIVAN, John, Sgt, Col John Wynne, Capt James Cole, Branch Srvce omitted
SULLIVAN, Jordan, Pvt, Col Jas Raulston, Capt Mathew Cowan, Inf
SULLIVAN, Levi, Pvt, Col Edward Bradley, Capt Harry L Douglas, Vol Inf
SULLIVAN, Levi, Pvt, Col Thos Benton, Capt Henry L Douglass, Vol Inf
SULLIVAN, Richard, Cpl, Col John Coffee, Capt Daniel Ross, Mtd Gunmen
SULLIVAN, Samuel, Pvt, Col Wm Johnson, Capt Wm Alexander, Det of E TN Drafted Mil
SULLIVAN, Simeon, Pvt, Col Thos Williamson, Capt Richard Tate, Vol Mtd Gunmen
SULLIVAN, William, Pvt, Col Wm Higgins, Capt Adam Dale, Mtd Gunmen
SULLIVAN, Zachariah, Pvt, Col Wm Hall, Capt James Hambleton, Vol Inf
SULLIVAN, Zachariah, Pvt, Lt Col Henry Bryan, Maj Robert Searcy, Inf
SUMEN, Smith, Pvt, Regt Commander omitted, Capt Sam Allen, Pack Horse Guards
SUMERS, Arden, Pvt, Col John Coffee, Capt Thos Bradley, Vol Cav
SUMERS, Thomas, Pvt, Maj Gen Wm Carroll, Capt Francis Ellis, Inf
SUMMER, Jacob, Far, Col John Coffee, Capt Daniel Ross, Mtd Gunmen
SUMMERFORD, Peter, Pvt, Col Samuel Wear, Capt James Gillespie, E TN Vol Inf
SUMMERS, Abraham, Pvt, Col Thos Williamson, Capt John Doak & Capt John Dobbins, Vol Mtd Gunmen
SUMMERS, Alexander, Pvt, Col Wm Hall, Capt John Wallace, Inf
SUMMERS, Arden, Cpl, Col John Alcorn, Capt Thos Bradley, Vol Cav
SUMMERS, Basley, Pvt, Col Wm Hall, Capt John Wallace, Inf
SUMMERS, Bazdol (Boswell), Pvt, Col Philip Pipkin, Capt Geo Mebane, Branch Srvce omitted
SUMMERS, Daniel R, Pvt, Col Robt Steele, Capt John Cheetwood, Mil Inf
SUMMERS, George, Pvt, Col Jas Raulston, Capt James A Black, Inf
SUMMERS, George, Pvt, Col Philip Pipkin, Capt John Robertson, Mil Inf
SUMMERS, Isaac, Pvt, Col Ewen Allison, Capt John Hampton, Mil
SUMMERS, Isaac, Pvt, Col John Wynne, Capt John Porter, Inf
SUMMERS, Isaiah (Isaac), Pvt, Col Wm Hall, Capt John Wallace, Inf
SUMMERS, James B, Pvt, Col S Copeland, Capt Moses Thompson, Inf
SUMMERS, James, Pvt, Col R C Napier, Capt Thos Gray, Mil Inf
SUMMERS, John, 2 Cpl, Col Thos Williamson, Capt Giles Burdett, Vol Mtd Gunmen
SUMMERS, John, Pvt, Col John Brown, Capt John Trimbel, E TN Mtd Gunmen
SUMMERS, John, Pvt, Col John Cocke, Capt Geo Barnes, Inf
SUMMERS, Johnston, Pvt, Col Ewen Allison, Capt John Hampton, Mil; died 5-21-1814
SUMMERS, Peter, Pvt, Col A Loury, Capt Gabriel Martin, Inf
SUMMERS, Thomas, Pvt, Col Robt Steele, Capt Robt Campbell, Mil Inf
SUMMERS, Thomas, Pvt, Col Thos Williamson, Capt John Doak & Capt John Dobbins, Vol Mtd Gunmen
SUMMONS, Elisha, Pvt, Col Jarmon, Capt Hamilton, Inf
SUMNER, Talton, Pvt, Col A Cheatham, Capt Chas Johnson, Inf
SUMNER, Talton, Pvt, Col Philip Pipkin, Capt Wm Mackay, Mil Inf
SUMPTER, Benjamin, Pvt, Col Wm Lillard, Capt Wm Hamilton, E TN Vol Inf
SUMPTER, Henry, Pvt, Col Samuel Bunch, Capt Wm Houston, E TN Vol Mtd Inf; trans to Capt Hamilton's Co
SUMPTER, Henry, Pvt, Col Wm Johnson, Capt Christopher Cook, E TN Mil
SUMPTER, Henry, Pvt, Col Wm Johnston, Capt Joseph Kirk, Mil
SUMPTER, Henry, Pvt, Col Wm Lillard, Capt Wm Hamilton, Branch omitted
SUMPTER, James, Pvt, Col Samuel Bunch, Capt N Gibbs, E TN Draft Mil
SUMPTER, James, Pvt, Maj John Childs, Capt Chas Conway, E TN Mtd Gunmen
SUMPTER, John, Pvt, Col Samuel Bunch, Capt Jno Hawk, E TN Mil; joined from Capt Dobkins Co
SUMPTER, John, Pvt, Col Samuel Bunch, Capt John Dobkins, E TN Draft Mil; trans to Capt English
SUMPTER, John, Pvt, Col Samuel Bunch, Capt Wm Houston, E TN Vol Mtd Inf; trans to Capt Hamilton's Co
SUMPTER, John, Pvt, Col Wm Lillard, Capt Wm Hamilton, E TN Vol Inf
SUMPTER, William, Pvt, Col Saml Bunch, Capt N Gibbs, E TN Draft Mil; to Regular Army 1-20-1814

- 483

SUNDERLAND, Nathan, Pvt, Col Robt Steel, Capt Richard Randals, Inf; joined Regular Army 2-3-1814
SUNDERLAND, Solomon, Pvt, Col Samuel Bayless, Capt James Churchman, E TN Mil
SURGENT, Thomas, Sgt, Regt Commander omitted, Capt Saml Richardson, E TN Draft Mil
SURGEONOR, Abraham, Pvt, Col Samuel Bunch, Capt Jno Hawk, E TN Mil; disch at Knoxville
SUSONG, Andrew, Pvt, Col Wm Lillard, Capt Geo Keyes?, E TN Inf
SUTERS, Joshua, Pvt, Regt Commander omitted, Lt John Scott, Det Inf
SUTHERLAND, Daniel, Pvt, Col Edwin Booth, Capt Vernon, E TN Mil; died 12-21-1814
SUTHERLAND, George, Pvt, Col Wm Johnson, Capt Benj Powell, E TN Mil; disch for inability
SUTHERLAND, James, Pvt, Lt Col Hammond, Capt Tubb, Inf
SUTHERLAND, James, Sgt, Col Wm Johnson, Capt James Tunnell, E TN Mil
SUTHERLAND, John, Pvt, Col McCrory, Capt McKnight, Inf
SUTHERLAND, John, Pvt, Col Raulston, Capt West, Inf
SUTHERLAND, Thomas, Pvt, Col Metcalf, Capt Hurt, Mil Inf
SUTHERLAND, Thomas, Pvt, Col Raulston, Maj Gen Carroll, Capt Haynie, Inf
SUTHERN, Isaah, Pvt, Col Napier, Capt Chism, Mil Inf
SUTLER, Francis, Pvt, Col Higgins, Capt Cheatham, Mtd Riflemen
SUTLER, Marcus, Pvt, Col Higgins, Capt Cheatham, Mtd Riflemen
SUTOR, Lawrence, Pvt, Lt Col A Cheatham, Capt Gabriel Martin, Mtd Inf
SUTOR, Lawrence, Pvt, Lt Col John Edmonson, Co Commander omitted, Cav
SUTTLE, Francis, Pvt, Col Cocke, Capt Weakley, Inf; died 2-15-1815
SUTTLES, Henry, Pvt, Col Pipkin, Capt Smith, Inf
SUTTLES, Lemuel, Pvt, Col Pipkin, Capt Newlin, Mil Inf
SUTTON, Edmund, Pvt, Col Wynne, Capt Butler, Inf
SUTTON, James, Pvt, Col Wynne, Capt Carothers, W TN Inf
SUTTON, John, Pvt, Col Ewin Allison, Capt Jas Allen, E TN Mil
SUTTON, John, Pvt, Col Johnson, Capt Powell, E TN Mil
SUTTON, John, Pvt, Col Philip Pipkin, Capt Jas Blakemore, Mil Inf
SUTTON, Rowland, Pvt, Col Thos Benton, Capt Henry Douglass, Vol Inf; joined Capt Bradley's Cav
SUTTON, Samuel, Pvt, Col Samuel Bunch, Capt James Penny, E TN Mtd Inf
SUTTON, Stephen, Pvt, Lt Col Hammonds, Capt Arahel Rains, Inf
SUTTON, William, Pvt, Col Alexander Loury, Lt Col Leroy Hammonds, Capt Arahel Rains, Inf
SWAFFORD, Abraham, Pvt, Col Jno Brown, Capt Wm Christian, E TN Mil Inf
SWAFFORD, Alexander, Pvt, Col Edwin E Booth, Capt Vernon, E TN Mil
SWAFFORD, David B, Pvt, Col Samuel Bayless, Capt James Landen, E TN Mil
SWAFFORD, James, Pvt, Col Wm Johnson, Capt Jas Tunnell, 3 Regt E TN Mil
SWAFFORD, John, Cpl, Col Alexander Loury, Capt Brice Martin, Inf
SWAFFORD, Moses, Pvt, Col Wm Johnson, Capt Jas Tunnell, E TN Mil; died 11-24-1814
SWAFFORD, William, Pvt, Col Wm Johnson, Capt Benj Powell, E TN Mil
SWAFORD, Larkin, Pvt, Col Jas Raulston, Capt Mathew Cowan, Inf
SWAGGARTY, Stokely, Pvt, Col Edwin Booth, Capt John Sharp, E TN Mil
SWAIN, Uriah, Pvt, Col Wm Y Higgins, Capt John B Cheatham, Mtd Riflemen
SWALLOW, Jacob, Sgt, Col S Copeland, Capt David Williams, Mil Inf
SWAN, Edward, Pvt, Maj Gen Wm Carroll, Capt Francis Ellis, Inf; died 3-12-1815
SWAN, George, Pvt, Col N T Perkins, Capt John B Quarles, Vol Mtd Inf
SWAN, John D, Cpl, Col Saml Wear, Capt Rufus Morgan, E TN Vol Inf
SWAN, John, Pvt, Col Samuel Wear, Capt Rufus Morgan, E TN Vol Inf; reduced from Sgt
SWAN, Robert, Pvt, Col Edwin Booth, Capt John Lewis, E TN Mil
SWAN, Uriah, Pvt, Col John Cocke, Capt Richard Crunk, Inf
SWAN, Uriah, Pvt, Lt Col A Cheatham, Capt Meredith Walker, Inf
SWAN, William, Sgt, Col Edwin Booth, Capt John Lewis, E TN Mil; promoted to QM Sgt
SWANEY, Edmond, Pvt, Col Philip Pipkin, Capt Blakemore, Mil Inf; deserted
SWANEY, James, Pvt, Col Wm Metcalf, Capt Obidiah Waller, Mil Inf
SWANN, Daniel, Pvt, Col Jno Brown, Capt Jas Preston, E TN Regt Mil Inf
SWANN, Moses, Sdlr, Col Jno Coffee, Capt Robt Jetton, Cav
SWANSON, Edward, Pvt, Col Robt H Dyer, Capt Glen Owen?, Vol TN Mtd Gunmen
SWANSON, Peter, Pvt, Col Thos Williamson, Maj Gen Andrew Jackson, Capt Robt Steele, Vol Mtd Gunmen
SWANSON, Richard, Pvt, Regt Commander omitted, Capt David Mason, Cav
SWATSELL, Henry, Cpl, Col Wm Allison, Capt Thos Wilson, E TN Draft Mil
SWATSELL, Jacob, Pvt, Col Samuel Bayless, Capt Joseph Hale, E TN Mil
SWATSELL, John, Pvt, Col Wm Johnson, Capt Chris Cooke, E TN Mil; died 11-10-1814
SWATSELL, Joseph, Pvt, Col Ewen Allison, Capt Thos Wilson, E TN Draft Mil
SWATZEL, Henry, Pvt, Col Wm Lillard, Capt Robt McCalpin, E TN Inf
SWATZEL, Jacob, Pvt, Col Wm Lillard, Capt Robt McCalpin, E TN Inf
SWATZEL, Joseph, Pvt, Col Wm Lillard, Capt Robt

## Enlisted Men, War of 1812

McCalpin, E TN Inf

SWEAN, Lutter, Pvt, Col Wm Hall, Capt Henry Newlin, Inf

SWEARA, Richard, Pvt, Col John Brown, Capt Wm White, Regt E TN Mil Inf

SWEARENGER, Hugh, Pvt, Maj Wm Woodfolk, Capt John Sutton, Inf

SWEARENGERN, William, Pvt, Col Edwin Booth, Capt Saml Thompson, Mil

SWEAT, Nathan, Pvt, Col S Bunch, Capt Jno English, E TN Drafted Mil

SWEAT, William, Pvt, Col Jas Raulston, Capt Jas Black, Inf; lived Campbell Co--died 1816

SWEAT, William, Pvt, Col S Bunch, Capt Jno English, E TN Drafted Mil

SWEENEY, Nathan, Pvt, Regt Commander omitted, Capt Thos Sharp & Capt Wm Lillard, Inf

SWEET, Alexander, Pvt, Col Ewin Allison, Capt Wm King, Drafted Mil

SWEETEN, John, Cpl, Regt Commander omitted, Capt Porter & Capt Edwin Booth, Drafted Mil

SWEETON, John, Pvt, Col S Bunch, Capt Jno English, E TN Drafted Mil

SWELLERAN, Zachariah, Pvt, Col Edward Bradley, Capt Geo Hambleton, Vol Inf

SWETHERLAND, Thomas, Pvt, Col Jas Raulston, Capt Maj Gen Carroll(!), Inf

SWICHER, Henry H, Pvt, Col John Cocke, Capt John Dalton, Inf

SWIDDY, William, Pvt, Col Wm Pillow, Capt Wm Smith, Vol Inf

SWIER, John, Pvt, Col Wm Hall, Capt John Kennedy, Vol Inf

SWIER, William, 4 Cpl, Col Wm Hall, Capt John Kennedy, Vol Inf

SWIFT, Absolom, 1 Cpl, Maj Gen Carroll, Capt Ellis, Inf

SWIFT, Absolom, Pvt, Regt Commander omitted, Capt Jas Haggard, Mtd Gunmen

SWIFT, Harry, Pvt, Col Jas Raulston, Capt Jas Cowan, Inf

SWIFT, Parks, Pvt, Col Philip Pipkin, Capt Ebenezer Kirkpatrick, Mil Inf; apptd Cpl

SWIFT, Thomas, Pvt, Regt Commander omitted, Capt Jas Haggard, Mtd Gunmen

SWIFT, William, Pvt, Col John Cocke, Capt Richd Crunk, Inf

SWIN, Archibald, Cpl, Col Wm Hall, Capt John Kennedy, Vol Inf

SWINDLE, Jesse, Pvt, Col S Copeland, Capt John Holehouser, Inf

SWINDLE, Joel, Pvt, Col John Wynne, Capt John Porter, Inf

SWINGFIELD, Richard, Pvt, Col S Wear, Capt John Childs, E TN Vol Inf

SWINGLE, Joseph, Dmr, Col Jas Raulston, Capt Chas Wade, Inf

SWINGLEY, Joseph, Sgt, Col John Wynne, Capt John Spinks, Inf

SWINGSTON, Samuel, Pvt, Col Wm Metcalf, Capt Geo Sitton, Mil Inf

SWINGSTON, Thomas, Pvt, Col Edward Hall, Capt John Kennedy, Vol Inf

SWINGSTON, William, Pvt, Col Edward Hall, Capt John Kennedy, Vol Inf; unfit for svce

SWINHER, James, Pvt, Regt Commander omitted, Capt Mason, Cav; promoted Sgt

SWINNEY, Edward, Pvt, Col Philip Pipkin, Capt Jas Blackmore, Mil Inf; deserted

SWINNEY, Joel, Pvt, Col A Loury, Capt Geo Saver, Inf

SWISHER, Henry H, Cpl, Col John Cocke, Capt John Dalton, Inf

SWISHER, Henry, Pvt, Regt Commander omitted, Capt D Mason, Branch omitted

SWISHER, Michael, Pvt, Col Edwin Booth, Capt Richd Sharpe, E TN Mil

SWOBE, George, Pvt, Maj Wm Russell, Capt Mitchell, Vol Mtd Gunmen

SWOKE, William, Pvt, Maj Wm Russell, Capt Mitchell, Vol Mtd Gunmen

SYKES, Warren, Pvt, Col John Cocke, Capt Joseph Price, Inf

SYMOUS, John, Pvt, Col Wm Johnson, Capt Elihu Millikin, E TN Mil; trans from Capt Churchman Co

SYMS, Jeffry, Pvt, Col R C Napier, Capt Edward Neblett, Mil Inf

SYPPET, Jesse, Pvt, Col Wm Metcalf, Capt Hill & Capt Cunningham, Mil Inf

SYPRETT, Lawrence, Pvt, Regt Commander omitted, Capt Archibald McKamey, Cav

SYPRETT, Stephen, Pvt, Regt Commander omitted, Capt Archibald McKamey, Cav

SYTHE (SYTLE), Cyrus, Pvt, Regt Commander omitted, Capt J N Williams, Mil Cav

TABER, John H, Pvt, Col Wm Metcalf, Capt Thos Marks, Mil Inf

TABER, Robert, Pvt, Col Philip Pipkin, Capt Peter Search, Mil Inf

TABER, Williams, Pvt, Col A Loury, Capt J N Williamson, W TN Mil

TABLE, John, Pvt, Col John Brown, Capt John Childs, E TN Vol Mtd Gunmen

TABLER, John, Pvt, Maj John Childs, Capt Daniel Price, E TN Mtd Inf Vol

TABLER, Malkiah, Pvt, Col Edwin Booth, Capt John Sharp, E TN Mil

TABLER, William, 4 Cpl, Maj John Childs, Capt Danl Price, E TN Vol Mtd Inf

TABLER, William, Pvt, Col Saml Wear, Capt Danl Price, E TN Vol Inf

TABOR, John, Pvt, Col Wm Metcalf, Capt Wm Mullins, Mil Inf

TABOR, William, Pvt, Col L Hammond, Capt J N Williamson, 2 Regt Inf

TABS (TOLER), Joel, Pvt, Col Jas Raulston, Maj Gen Wm Carroll, CApt Elijah Haynie, Inf

TACKER, William, Pvt, Col Edward Bradley, Capt ELijah Haynie, Vol Inf

TACKER, William, Pvt, Col Wm Hall, Capt Henry M Newlin, Inf

TACKETT, James, Col Wm Pillow, Capt John Anderson, Vol Inf

TACKETT, James, Pvt, Col Thos Benton, Capt Geo W Gibbs, Vol Inf

TACKETT, John, Pvt, Col Saml Bayless, Capt John Brock, E TN Mil
TACKETT, William, Pvt, Col James Raulston, Capt Jas A Black, Inf
TADE, John, Pvt, Col T McCrory, Capt A Willis, Mil Inf
TAFF, George, Pvt, Col Saml Bayless, Capt James Churchman, E TN Mil
TAFF, James, Pvt, Col Saml Bayless, Capt James Churchman, E TN Mil
TAFF, John, Pvt, Col John Brown, Capt Chas Lewin, E TN Vol Mtd Inf
TAFF, John, Pvt, Col Wm Lillard, Capt John Roper, E TN Vol Inf
TAGUE, John, Pvt, Col Ewen Allison, CApt Adam Winsell, E TN Draft Mil
TAGUE, John, Pvt, Col Jas Raulston, Capt Jas A Black, Inf
TAILER (TAYLOR), Gabriel, Pvt, Col Wm Hall, Capt Henry Newlin, Inf; refused to appear
TAILOR, Frederick, Pvt, Maj Wm Woodfolk, Capt Abner Pearce, Inf
TAILOR, Richard, Pvt, Col Edwin Booth, Capt John Sharp, E TN Mil
TAIT, John, Pvt, Col Wm Metcalf, Capt Wm Mullins, Mil Inf
TAIT, Larken, Pvt, Lt Col Richd Napier, Co Commander omitted, Inf
TAIT, Richard, Sgt, Regt Commander omitted, Capt Jno Forgon, Mtd Spies
TAIT, Zachariah, Pvt, Col R H Dyer, Capt Jas White, Vol Mtd Gunmen
TAIT (TATE), George, Pvt, Col Jas Raulston, Capt Jas Cowan, Inf; promoted to Fife Maj
TALANT, Jonathan, Pvt, Col Edwin Booth, Capt John McKamey, E TN Mil
TALANT, William, Pvt, Col Edwin Booth, Capt John McKamey, E TN Mil
TALBERT, William, Pvt, Col Jas Raulston, Capt Chas Wade, Inf
TALBERT, William, Pvt, Col John Coffee, Capt Thos Bradley, Vol Cav
TALBERT (TALBOT), Notley, Pvt, Col Jas Raulston, Capt Chas Wade, Inf
TALBERT (TALBOT), William, Pvt, Col Philip Pipkin, Capt David Smith, Inf
TALBOT, James R, Pvt, Maj Wm Woodfolk, Capt Abraham Dudney, Inf; also under Capt John Sutton
TALBOT, John, Pvt, Maj Gen A Jackson, Capt Wm Carroll, Vol Inf
TALBOT, John, Pvt, Maj Wm Woodfolk, Capt Abraham Dudney, Inf
TALBOTT, William, Cpl, Col Thos Williamson, Capt A Metcalf, Vol Mtd Gunmen
TALLENT, Thomas, Pvt, Col Wm Johnson, Capt Jas R Rogers, E TN Draft Mil
TALLENTS, John, Pvt, Maj Wm Woodfolk, Capt Abner Pearce, Inf; deserted
TALLEY, Bannester, Pvt, Col Wm Metcalf, Capt Wm Mullin, Mil Inf
TALLEY, Bird T, Pvt, Col T McCrory, Capt Isaac Patton, Mil Inf
TALLEY, John, Pvt, Regt Commander omitted, Capt Jas Cowan, Mtd Inf
TALLEY, Richard, Pvt, Maj Wm Woodfolk, Capt Jas Neal, Inf
TALLEY, Thomas, Pvt, Col Ewen Allison, Capt Jos Everett, E TN Mil; trans to Capt Griffin's Co
TALLEY, William, Pvt, Regt Commander omitted, Capt Jas Cowan, Mtd Inf
TALLY, Daniel, Pvt, Col S Copeland, Capt Alexander Provine, Mil Inf
TALLY, Hobson, Pvt, Col Philip Pipkin, Capt Ebenezer Kirkpatrick, Mil Inf
TALLY, John, Pvt, Regt Commander omitted, Capt Jas Cowan, Mtd Inf
TALLY, Newman, Pvt, Maj Wm Woodfolk, Capt Ezekial Ross, Inf; also under Capt McCully
TALLY, Thomas, Pvt, Col S Bunch, Capt F Register, E TN Mil
TALLY, William, Pvt, Col Jas Raulston, Capt Chas Wade, Inf
TALLY, William, Pvt, Col R H Dyer, Capt Jas McMahan, TN Vol Mtd Gunmen
TALLY, William, Pvt, Col S Copeland, Capt Wm Evans, Mil Inf
TALLY, William, Pvt, Regt Commander omitted, Capt Jas Cowan, Mtd Inf
TAMAHILL, John, Pvt, Col A Loury, Capt J N Williamson, W TN Mil; died 11-13-1814
TAMEHILL, John, Pvt, Col L Hammons, Capt J N Williamson, 2 Regt Inf; died 11-13-1814
TAMER, Henry, Pvt, Col Wm Johnson, Capt Joseph Hunter, E TN Mil
TAMER, Joseph, Sgt, Col R McCrory, Capt John Shannon, Mil Inf
TANKERLY, John B?, Pvt, Regt Commander omitted, Lt Jas Berry, Mtd Riflemen
TANKERLY, John, Pvt, Col R H Dyer, Capt Ephraim D Dickson, TN Mtd Vol Gunmen; trans t Capt Williams Co
TANKERSLEY, George, Pvt, Col A Cheatham, Capt Jas Giddens, Inf
TANKERSLEY, George, Pvt, Col Thos H Williamson, Capt Wm Martin, Vol Mtd Gunmen
TANKERSLEY, John B, Pvt, Col Newton Cannon, Capt Wm Martin, Mtd Gunmen; trans to Capt Evans Co of Spies
TANKERSLEY, John B, Pvt, Maj Wm Russell, Capt Isaac Williams, Separate Bn TN Vol Mtd Gunmen; trans from Capt Dickson
TANKERSLEY, John H, QM Sgt, Maj Wm Russell, Separate Bn of TN Mtd Gunmen
TANKERSLEY, John R, Pvt, Col John Coffee, Capt Chas Kavanaugh, Cav
TANKERSLEY, John R, Pvt, Regt Commander omitted, Capt R Evans, Spies
TANKERSLEY, John R, Pvt, Regt Commander omitted, Lt Jas Berry, Mtd Riflemen; trans from Lt Hogan's Co
TANKERSLEY, John, Pvt, Regt Commander omitted, Capt Robt Evans, Mtd Spies
TANKERSLEY, Richard, Pvt, Col A Cheatham, Capt Wm Johnson, Inf

TANKERSLEY, Richard, Sgt, Col Thos H Williamson, Capt Wm Martin, Vol Mtd Gunmen
TANKERSLEY, William, Pvt, Col Wm Johnson, Capt Henry Hunter, E Tn Mil
TANKERSLEY, William, Pvt, Col Wm Johnson, Capt Jos Hunter, E TN Mil
TANKERSLY, Charles, Pvt, Regt Commander omitted, Capt Nathan Farmer, Mtd Riflemen
TAPLEY, Harbert, Pvt, Col R C Napier, Capt Thos Preston, Mil Inf
TAPPER, John, Cpl, Col Thos H Benton, Capt Geo Gibbs, Vol Inf
TARBER, Benjamin, Far, Col Thos H Williamson, Capt Thos Scurry, Vol Mtd Gunmen
TARKINGTON, Benjamin, Pvt, no other information
TARKINGTON, Jesse, Pvt, no other information
TARKINGTON, Joshua, Pvt, no other information
TARKINGTON, Silvenus, Pvt, Col R H Dyer, Capt Glen Owen, TN Vol Mtd Gunmen
TARKINGTON, Silvenus, Pvt, Maj Wm Russell, Capt Isaac Williams, TN Vol Mtd Gunmen; trans from Capt Owen
TARNALER, Ezekiel, Pvt, Lt Col Leroy Hammond, Capt Thos Delaney, Inf
TARNER, John, Pvt, Col A Cheatham, Capt Geo Chapman, Inf
TARPLEY, Edward, Pvt, Col John Cocke, Capt Barnes, Inf
TARPLEY, Henry, Pvt, Col Edward Bradley, Capt Harry L Douglas, Vol Inf
TARPLEY, John, Pvt, Col John Cocke, Capt Jas Gault, Inf; died 4-10-1815
TARPLEY, Pleasant, Pvt, Col Edward Bradley, Capt Harry L Douglas, Vol Inf
TARPLEY, Seth T, Pvt, Col Jas Raulston, Capt Jas Neale, Inf
TARPLEY, Steth T, Pvt, Col Edward Bradley, CApt Harry L Douglas, Vol Inf
TARPLEY, William, Pvt, Col Saml Bunch, Capt Danl Parnell, E TN Mil; disch for inability
TARPLEY, William, Pvt, Col Wm Johnson, Capt Jas Stewart, E TN Mil
TARRANT, Francis D, Pvt, Col Saml Bayless, Capt Jos Goodson, E TN Mil
TARRANTS, James, Pvt, Col John Cocke, Capt Danl Price, Inf
TARRANTS, Leonard, Pvt, Col Thos H Benton, Capt Geo Caperton, Vol Inf
TARVER, Edmund D, Sgt, Col Saml Copeland, Capt G W Steele, Mil Inf
TARVER, Silus, Cpl, Col S Copeland, Capt Still, Mil Inf
TARWATER, David, Pvt, Col Saml Wear, Capt Jos Calloway, Mtd Inf
TARWATER, Lewis, Pvt, Col Thos H Benton, Capt Geo W Gibbs, Vol Inf
TASSEL, David, 3 Sgt, Col Wm Metcalf, Capt Hill & Capt John Cunninghm, Mil Inf; d 12-24-1814
TATAM, Edward, Pvt, Col Thomas Williamson, Capt Richard Tate, Vol Mtd Gunmen
TATAM, Isaiah, Pvt, Col Thomas Williamson, Capt Richard Tate, Vol Mtd Gunmen
TATE, David M, Cpl, Col Thos Williamson, Capt Richard Tate, Vol Mtd Gunmen
TATE, David, Pvt, Col S Bunch, Capt Mann, E TN Vol Mtd Inf
TATE, David, Pvt, Col Williams, Capt Vance, Mtd Mil
TATE, Edward, Ens, Col Ewen Allison, Capt Jonas Loughmiller, Mil; joined Capt McPherson Co
TATE, Edward, Pvt, Col S Bunch, Capt Geo McPherson, E TN Mil; joined from? Capt Loughmiller
TATE, Edward, Pvt, Col S Bunch, Capt Mann, E TN Vol Mtd Inf; promoted to 1 Sgt
TATE, George, Ffr, Col Jas Raulston, Capt Chas Wade, Inf
TATE, Isaac, Pvt, Col Edwin Booth, Capt Geo Biggs, Inf
TATE, James, Ffr Maj, Col James Raulston, Co Commander omitted, W TN Mil Inf
TATE, John K, Pvt, Col S Bunch, Capt Mann, E TN Vol Mtd Inf
TATE, John, Pvt, Col Wm Metcalf, Capt William Mullen, Mil Inf
TATE, Joseph, Tptr, Col Thomason, Capt Richard Tate, Vol Mtd Gunmen
TATE, Larkin, Pvt, Col R C Napier, Capt Drury Adkins, Mil Inf
TATE, Thomas T, Pvt, Maj John Childs, Capt Jas Cunningham, E TN Mtd Inf
TATE, William, Pvt, Col Edwin Booth, Capt Geo Biggs, Inf
TATE, Zachariah, 2 Lt, Col Robert Dyer, Capt Thomas White, Vol Mtd Gunmen; promoted from Sgt
TATE, Zachariah, Pvt, Col S Bayless, Capt Yale, E TN Mil
TATEM, Peter, Pvt, Col Wm Metcalf, Capt William Mullen, Mil Inf
TATOM, William, Pvt, Col R C Napier, Capt Drury Adkins, Mil Inf
TATOM, William, Pvt, Lt Col Richard Napier, Co Commander omitted, Inf
TATTOM, John, Pvt, Lt Col Richard Napier, Co Commander omitted, Inf
TATTON, Benjamin, Pvt, Col Wm Hall, Capt John Kennedy, Vol Inf
TATUM, Henry, Pvt, Col John Brown, Capt Reamy, Mtd Gunmen
TATUM, Howell, Principle Eng, Maj Gen Andrew Jackson, TN Mil; appointed Prinicple Topographer
TATUM, Ira, Pvt, Maj Wm Woodfolk, Capt Ross & Capt McCulley, Inf
TATUM, Isaiah, Pvt, Col Edward Bradley, Capt Travis Nash, Vol Inf
TATUM, Isaiah, Pvt, Col Wm Hall, Capt Travis Nash, Inf
TATUM, James, Principle Wagon Master, Maj Gen Andrew Jackson, TN Mil
TATUM, Jesse, Pvt, Col Wm Hall, Capt Travis Nash, Inf
TATUM, Jonathan, Pvt, Col William Higgins, Capt Allen, Mtd Gunmen
TATUM, Nathaniel, Pvt, Col N Cannon, Capt Hanley, Mtd Riflemen
TATUM, Peter, Pvt, Col Wm Metcalf, Capt William Mullen, Mil Inf
TAYERS, Lewis, Pvt, Col William Lillard, Capt John

## Enlisted Men, War of 1812

Neatherton, E TN Vol Inf
TAYLOR, Abraham, Pvt, Col John Cocke, Capt James Gault, Inf; d 1-21-1815
TAYLOR, Abraham, Pvt, Col Thomas Williamson, Capt Beverly Williams, Vol Mtd Gunmen
TAYLOR, Adley, Pvt, Col S Wear, Capt Morgan, E TN Vol Inf
TAYLOR, Alexander, 6 Cpl, Col Jas Raulston, Capt Jas Black, Inf
TAYLOR, Alexander, Pvt, Col Jas Raulston, Capt Jas Black, Inf; reduced from Cpl
TAYLOR, Alien, Pvt, Col A Loury, Capt John Looney, W TN Inf; transferred
TAYLOR, Allen, Pvt, Lt Col Leroy Hammonds, Capt Jas Tubb, Inf; transferred from Capt John Looney
TAYLOR, Allen, Pvt, Lt Col Richard Napier, Co Commander omitted, Inf
TAYLOR, Allen, Pvt, Regt Commander omitted, Capt Benj Reynolds, Mtd Rangers
TAYLOR, Anderson, Pvt, Col Edward Bradley, Capt Harry Douglas, Vol Inf
TAYLOR, Anderson, Pvt, Col Thos Benton, Capt Henry Douglas, Vol Inf
TAYLOR, Armisted, Cpl, Col William Pillow, Capt John Anderson, Vol Inf
TAYLOR, Barillia, Pvt, Col William Higgins, Capt Dale, Branch Srvce omitted
TAYLOR, Benjamin, Pvt, Col S Bunch, Capt Edward Buchanan, E TN Mil
TAYLOR, Berry, Pvt, Col William Pillow, Capt William Smith, Vol Inf; deserted
TAYLOR, Britian, Pvt, Col N Cannon, Capt John Harpole, Mtd Gunmen
TAYLOR, Britian, Pvt, Col S Copeland, Capt Moses Thompson, Inf
TAYLOR, Britten, 4 Cpl, Col Thomas Benton, Capt Henry Douglas, Vol Inf
TAYLOR, Brittian, Far, Col Thomas Williamson, Capt Beverly Williams, Vol Mtd Gunmen; transferred to Lt Bean's Spies
TAYLOR, Cal, Pvt, Regt Commander omitted, Capt J Parrish, Branch Srvce omitted
TAYLOR, Charles, Cpl, Col S Bunch, Capt Edward Buchanan, E TN Drafted Mil
TAYLOR, Charles, Pvt, Col Jno Coffee, Capt Robert Jetton, Cav
TAYLOR, Cornellium, Cpl, Col Jas Raulston, Capt ? Haynie, Inf
TAYLOR, Daniel, 3 Sgt, Col Samuel Bunch, Capt Thomas Mann, E TN Mtd Inf Vol
TAYLOR, Daniel, Cpl, Col S Copeland, Capt Jno Holshouser, Inf
TAYLOR, David, Pvt, Col S Copeland, Capt Jno Dawson, Inf
TAYLOR, Densey, Cpl, Col Thos McCrory, Capt Saml B McKnight, Inf
TAYLOR, Edmond, Pvt, Col R H Dyer, Capt Jos Williams, Vol Mtd Gunmen
TAYLOR, Edward, Pvt, Col Alex Loury, Capt Jas Kincaid, Inf
TAYLOR, Edward, Pvt, Col Wm Lillard, Capt Geo Keyes, E TN Inf
TAYLOR, Edwin, Pvt, Lt Col Richard Napier, Co Commander omitted, Inf
TAYLOR, Elas, Pvt, Col Wm Pillar, Capt Geo Caperton, Inf
TAYLOR, Eli, Pvt, Col Thos Benton, Capt Geo Caperton, Inf
TAYLOR, Ellison, Pvt, Col Thos Benton, Capt I Renshaw, Vol Inf; transferred to Nash
TAYLOR, Ellison, Pvt, Col Wm Hall, Capt T C Nash, Inf
TAYLOR, Eloy, Pvt, Col Thos Benton, Capt Geo Caperton, Vol Inf
TAYLOR, Eloy, Pvt, Regt Commander omitted, Capt Geo Caperton, 2nd Regt Vol Inf
TAYLOR, Epps, Pvt, Maj Gen Wm Carroll, Col Wm Metcalf, Capt John Jackson, Inf
TAYLOR, Fielden, Pvt, Col R C Napier, Capt Jas McMurrey, Mil Inf
TAYLOR, Francis, Pvt, Col Wm Metcalf, Capt Jno Barnhart, Mil Inf
TAYLOR, Gabriel, Pvt, Col A Cheatham, Capt Richd Benson, Inf; transferred to the Arty
TAYLOR, Gabriel, Pvt, Gen Andrew Jackson, Capt Joel Parrish, Arty
TAYLOR, Gabriel, Pvt, Maj Gen Wm Russell, Capt F Hodges, Vol Mtd Gunmen
TAYLOR, George, Pvt, Col Jno Brown, Capt Lunsford Oliver, E TN Mil
TAYLOR, George, Pvt, Col S Bunch, Capt A Breden, E TN Mil
TAYLOR, George, Pvt, Col S Bunch, Capt Jno Houk, TN Mil
TAYLOR, George, Pvt, Col Samuel Bunch, Capt Thos Mann, E TN Vol Mtd Inf
TAYLOR, George, Pvt, Col T McCrory, Capt Jno Reynolds, Mil Inf; transferred from Capt Shannon's Co
TAYLOR, George, Pvt, Col Thos Williamson, Capt Metcalf, Vol Gunmen
TAYLOR, George, Pvt, Gen Jno Coffee, Co Commander omitted, Mtd Spies
TAYLOR, George, Pvt, Regt Commander omitted, Lt Jesse Bean, Mtd Spies
TAYLOR, Grant, Pvt, Col Thos Benton, Capt Geo Caperton, Vol Inf
TAYLOR, Grant, Pvt, Col Wm Pillar, Capt Geo Caperton, Inf; transferred to Capt Russell's Co
TAYLOR, Grant, Pvt, Gen A Jackson, Capt Wm Russell, Mtd Spies
TAYLOR, Henry, 2 Sgt, Maj Gen Wm Carroll, Col Jas Raulston, Capt Ed Robinson, Inf
TAYLOR, Henry, Pvt, Col Saml Wear, Capt Jno Bayless, Mtd Inf
TAYLOR, Hubert, Pvt, Regt Commander omitted, Capt Abner Pearce, Inf
TAYLOR, Isaac, Pvt, Col J Alcorn, Capt Thos Bradley, Vol Cav
TAYLOR, Isaac, Pvt, Col P Pipkin, Capt David Smith, Inf; deserted
TAYLOR, Isaac, Pvt, Col Wm Higgins, Capt Saml Allen, Mtd Gunmen

## Enlisted Men, War of 1812

TAYLOR, Isaac, Pvt, Col Wm Lillard, Capt Benj King, E TN Vol Inf
TAYLOR, Jacob, Pvt, Col Wm Hall, Capt Jno Moore, Vol Inf
TAYLOR, Jacob, Pvt, Col Wm Johnson, Capt L Hunter, E Tn Mil
TAYLOR, Jacob, Pvt, Regt Commander omitted, Capt Ed Bradley & Capt Jno Moore, Vol Inf
TAYLOR, James, 4 Cpl, Col Jno Brown, Capt Chas Lewis, E TN Mtd Inf
TAYLOR, James, Pvt, Col Jno Cocke, Capt Jas Gray, Inf
TAYLOR, James, Pvt, Col N Cannon, Capt Jas Walton, Mtd Riflemen
TAYLOR, James, Pvt, Col N T Perkins, Capt Geo Marr, Mtd Vol
TAYLOR, James, Pvt, Col Thos Benton, Capt Geo Caperton, Vol Inf
TAYLOR, James, Pvt, Col Thos Williamson, Capt A Metcalf, Vol Mtd Gunmen
TAYLOR, James, Pvt, Col Wm Lillard, Capt Geo Argenbright, E TN Vol Riflemen
TAYLOR, James, Pvt, Maj Jno Childs, Capt Jno Stephens, E TN Vol Mtd Inf; d 1-19-1815
TAYLOR, James, Sgt, Lt Col Henry Bryan, Co Commander omitted, Inf
TAYLOR, Jeremiah, Pvt, Col E Allison, Capt Wm King, Drafted Mil; AWOL
TAYLOR, Jesse, Pvt, Col Jno Brown, Capt Wm White, E TN Mil Inf
TAYLOR, Jesse, Pvt, Col Jno Cocke, Capt Geo Barnes, Inf
TAYLOR, Jesse, Pvt, Maj Wm Carroll, Capt Lewis Dillahunty & Capt D Brafford, Vol Inf
TAYLOR, Joel, 3 Sgt, Brig Gen Jno Coffee, TN Vol Mtd Gunmen
TAYLOR, John M, Pvt, Col Edward Bradley, Capt Abraham Bledsoe, Riflemen
TAYLOR, John M, Pvt, Col Wm Hall, Capt Abraham Bledsoe, Vol Inf
TAYLOR, John, Pvt, Col Edward Bradley, Capt John Moore, Vol Inf
TAYLOR, John, Pvt, Col Jno Brown, Capt Jas Preston, E TN Mil
TAYLOR, John, Pvt, Col John Brown, Capt Wm White, E TN Mil Inf
TAYLOR, John, Pvt, Col Samuel Bunch, Capt S Richardson, E TN Drafted Mil
TAYLOR, John, Pvt, Col Samuel Bunch, Capt Wm Jobe, E TN Vol Mtd Inf
TAYLOR, John, Pvt, Col Wm Hall, Capt John Moore, Vol Inf
TAYLOR, Jonathan, Pvt, Col John Wynne, Capt Robt Bradin, Inf
TAYLOR, Joseph, Pvt, Col T Williamson, Capt Robt Moore, Vol Mtd Gunmen
TAYLOR, Joseph, Pvt, Col T Williamson, Capt Wm Martin, Vol Mtd Gunmen
TAYLOR, Joseph, Pvt, Lt Col Archer Cheatham, no other information
TAYLOR, Joseph, Pvt, Maj Gen A Jackson, Col A Cheatham, Capt Wm Creel, Inf
TAYLOR, Joseph, Pvt, Maj Wm Russell, Capt Flemen Hodges, Vol Mtd Gunmen
TAYLOR, Joseph, Pvt, Regt Commander omitted, Capt James Cowan, Mtd Inf
TAYLOR, Joseph, Pvt, Regt Commander omitted, Capt James Terrill, Cav
TAYLOR, Joseph, Sgt, Col N Cannon, Capt James Walton, Mtd Riflemen; wounded by accident 10-3-1813
TAYLOR, Josiah, Pvt, Col Jas Raulston, Capt James A Black, Inf
TAYLOR, Josiah, Pvt, Maj Wm Russell, Capt Fleman Hodges, Vol Mtd Gunmen
TAYLOR, Larkin, Pvt, Col A Cheatham, Capt Chas Johnson, Inf
TAYLOR, Lee, Pvt, Col A Loury, Capt Geo Sarver, Inf
TAYLOR, Lee, Pvt, Col Thos Benton, Capt Geo Caperton, Vol Inf; out of state
TAYLOR, Lerory, Pvt, Col Ewen Allison, Capt Adam Winsell, E TN Drafted Mil
TAYLOR, Leroy, Pvt, Col Samuel Bunch, Capt Geo McPherson, E TN Mil
TAYLOR, Leroy, Pvt, Gen Andrew Jackson, Capt Wm Russell, Mtd Spies
TAYLOR, Levi, Pvt, Col John Alcorn, Capt Robt Jetton, Vol Cav
TAYLOR, Levy, Pvt, Col Jno Coffee, Capt Robt Jetton, Cav
TAYLOR, Martin, Pvt, Col Jno Coffee, Capt Robt Jetton, Cav
TAYLOR, Martin, Pvt, Col John Alcorn, Capt Robt Jetton, Vol Cav
TAYLOR, Micajah, Pvt, Col Robt Steele, Capt Robt Campbell, Mil Inf
TAYLOR, Michael, Pvt, Col John Cocke, Capt Geo Barnes, Inf
TAYLOR, Nathan, Pvt, Gen Andrew Jackson, Capt Nathan Davis, Inf
TAYLOR, Ovan, Pvt, Lt Col Archer Cheatham, Capt Gabriel Martin, Inf
TAYLOR, Peter, Cpl, Regt Commander omitted, Capt Hamilton, Spies
TAYLOR, Peter, Cpl, Regt Commander omitted, Capt Wm Henderson, Spies
TAYLOR, Redden, Pvt, Col T McCrory, Capt Samuel B McKnight, Inf
TAYLOR, Robert, Pvt, Col Samuel Wear, Capt Simeon Perry, E TN Vol Mtd Inf; reduced from Sgt
TAYLOR, Samuel, Pvt, Col Ewen Allison, Capt Joseph Everett, E TN Mil; transferred to Capt Griffin's Co
TAYLOR, Samuel, Pvt, Col Jno Brown, Capt Lunsford Oliver, E TN Mil
TAYLOR, Samuel, Pvt, Col Samuel Bayless, Capt James Landen, E TN Mil
TAYLOR, Samuel, Pvt, Col Samuel Bunch, Capt Jones Griffin, E TN Drafted Mil
TAYLOR, Solomon, Pvt, Col A Cheatham, Capt Richard Benson, Inf
TAYLOR, Stephen, Sgt, Col Wm Johnson, Capt Joseph Scott, E TN Drafted Mil; promoted to Sgt Maj
TAYLOR, Telden, Pvt, Col A Loury, Capt Geo Sarver, Inf

- 489

## Enlisted Men, War of 1812

TAYLOR, Thomas, Pvt, Col A Cheatham, Capt James Giddens, Inf

TAYLOR, Thomas, Pvt, Col Ewen Allison, Capt Jacob Hoyal, E TN Mil

TAYLOR, Thomas, Pvt, Col John Alcorn, Capt John Baskerville, Vol Inf

TAYLOR, Thomas, Pvt, Col John Cocke, Capt Geo Barnes, Inf

TAYLOR, Thomas, Pvt, Col John Coffee, Capt James Terrell, Vol Cav

TAYLOR, Thomas, Pvt, Col Philip Pipkin, Capt Geo Mebane, Mil Inf

TAYLOR, Thomas, Pvt, Col Samuel Bunch, Capt Geo McPherson, E TN Mil; joined from Capt Hoyle's Co

TAYLOR, Thomas, Pvt, Col Thos Williamson, Capt John Doak & Capt John Dobbins, Vol Mtd Gunmen

TAYLOR, Thomas, Pvt, Douglas McKisson (Rank omitted), no other information

TAYLOR, Thornton, Pvt, Col Edward Bradley, Capt Travis Nash, Vol Inf

TAYLOR, Thornton, Pvt, Col Wm Hall, Capt Travis Nash, Inf

TAYLOR, William, 2 Cpl, Maj John Childs, Capt John Stephens, E TN Vol Mtd Inf

TAYLOR, William, Pvt, Col Edward Bradley, Capt John Kennedy, Riflemen

TAYLOR, William, Pvt, Col Jas Raulston, Capt Daniel Newman, Inf

TAYLOR, William, Pvt, Col Jas Raulston, Capt Elijah Haynie, Inf

TAYLOR, William, Pvt, Col John Alcorn, Capt Robert Jetton, Vol Cav

TAYLOR, William, Pvt, Col John Brown, Capt John Chiles, E TN Vol Mtd Inf

TAYLOR, William, Pvt, Col John Coffee, Capt Daniel Ross, Mtd Gunmen

TAYLOR, William, Pvt, Col Newton Cannon, Capt James Walton, Mtd Riflemen; wounded 11-2-1813?

TAYLOR, William, Pvt, Col Thos Benton, Capt Wm Moore, Vol Inf

TAYLOR, William, Pvt, Col Wm Johnson, Capt Benjamin Powell, E TN Mil

TAYLOR, William, Pvt, Maj Wm Woodfolk, Capt James Turner, Inf

TAYLOR, William, Pvt, Regt Commander omitted, Capt James Cowan, Mtd Inf

TAYLOR, William, Pvt, Regt Commander omitted, Capt James Craig, Mtd Inf

TAYLOR, William, Pvt, Regt Commander omitted, Capt James Gray, Inf

TAYLOR, William, Pvt, Regt Commander omitted, Capt Jos Williams, Mil Cav

TAYLOR, Wilson, Pvt, Maj Wm Carroll, Capt Lewis Dillahunty & Capt Daniel Bradford, Vol Inf

TAYLOR, Zachariah, Pvt, Lt Col Archer Cheatham, no other information

TAYS, John, Pvt, Col Edwin E Booth, Capt John Sharp, E TN Mil

TAYS, John, Pvt, Col John Coffee, Capt Ezekial Ross, Mtd Gunmen

TAYS, John, Pvt, Col Wm Metcalf, Capt Wm Mullin, Mil Inf

TAYS, John, Pvt, Maj Gen Wm Carroll, Col Jas Raulston, Capt Edward Robinson, Inf

TAYS, John, Pvt, Maj Wm Woodfolk, Capt James C Neil, Inf

TAYS, Robert, Pvt, Col S Bunch, Capt John English, E TN Drafted Mil

TAZE, Robert, Pvt, Col S Bunch, Capt N Gibbs, E TN Drafted Mil; transferred to Capt English Co

TEA, James, Pvt, Regt Commander omitted, Capt Nathan Peoples & Capt Robert Jarmon, Inf

TEACH, Thomas, Sgt, Col S Bunch, Capt N Gibbs, E TN Drafted Mil; promoted to Sgt Maj

TEACHER, Casey, Pvt, Col S Wear, Capt Rufus Morgan, E TN Vol Inf

TEAD, Peter, Pvt, Regt Commander omitted, Capt Davis Deadrick, Branch Srvce omitted

TEAFERTILLO, Henry, Pvt, Col John K Wynne, Capt Bailey Butler, Inf

TEAFERTILLO, John, Pvt, Col John K Wynne, Capt Bailey Butler, Inf; deserted

TEAGUE, Jacob, Pvt, Col Wm Johnson, Capt Andrew Lawson, E TN Drafted Mil

TEAL, George, 4 Cpl, Col James Raulston, Capt Mathew Cowan, Inf

TEAL, John, Pvt, Col Samuel Wear, Capt James Gillespie, E TN Vol Inf

TEAL, Robert, Pvt, Col John Coffee, Capt John Baskerville, Cav

TEAL, Samuel, Pvt, Col Wm Johnson, Capt McKamy, E TN Drafted Mil

TEAL, Timothy, Pvt, Maj Gen Wm Carroll, Capt John Jackson, Inf

TEASE, Joseph, Pvt, Col John Coffee, Capt Charles Kavanaugh, Cav

TEASLEY, George, Cpl, Lt Col Henry Bryan, Co Commander omitted, Inf

TEAVAULT, Jesse, Pvt, Col Samuel Wear, Capt James Gillespie, E TN Vol Inf

TEAWALT, Jesse, Pvt, Maj John Childs, Capt John Stephens, E TN Vol Mtd Inf

TEDDER, John, 2 Sgt, Col Jno Brown, Capt Jas Standifer, E TN Vol Mtd Mil

TEDDER (TIDDOR), Elisha, Pvt, Col Philip Pipkin, Capt George Mebane, Mil Inf

TEDFORD, George, Pvt, Maj Wm Woodfolk, Capt James C Neil, Inf

TEDFORD, George, Sgt, Col Edwin Booth, Capt Samuel Thompson, Mil

TEDFORD, James jr, Pvt, Col Samuel Wear, Capt James Tedford, E TN Vol Inf

TEDFORD, James, Pvt, Col Edwin Booth, Capt Alexander Biggs, Inf

TEDFORD, James, Pvt, Lt Col L Hammond, Capt James Craig, Inf

TEDFORD, John, Pvt, Col Jas Raulston, Capt James Cowan, Inf

TEDFORD, John, Pvt, Col S Copeland, Capt Wm Hodges, Inf

TEDFORD, John, Sgt, Col Samuel Wear, Capt James

Tedford, E TN Vol Inf
TEDFORD, William, Pvt, Col John K Wynne, Capt Bailey Butler, Inf
TEDFORD, William, Pvt, Col R H Dyer, Capt Cuthbert Hudson, Vol Mtd Gunmen
TEDO, William, Pvt, Brig Gen Thos Johnson, Capt Robert Carson, Inf; discharged for want of arms
TEED, Peter W, Orderly Sgt, Maj Gen Andrew Jackson, Col Thos McCrory, Capt Isaac Patton, Inf
TEED, Peter W, Pvt, Regt Commander omitted, Capt Archibald McKinney, Cav
TEED, Peter, Pvt, Regt Commander omitted, Capt D S Deadrick, Arty
TEEFFILLER, John, Pvt, Col Philip Pipkin, Capt David Smith, Inf
TEEL, Alexander, Pvt, Col Jas Raulston, Capt Mathew Neel, Inf
TEFERTILLER, John, Pvt, Col Philip Pipkin, Capt Wm Mackay, Mil Inf
TELFORD, Robert, 1 St, Col Thos Benton, Capt Henry L Douglass, Vol Inf
TELFORD, Robert, Sgt, Col Edward Bradley, Capt Henry Douglass, Vol Inf
TELFORD, Thomas, Cpl, Col John Wynne, Capt John Spinks, Inf
TELLERS, Henry G, Pvt, Regt Commander omitted, Capt Nathan Peoples, Inf
TEMPLE, Demsey, Pvt, Col Thos Williamson, Capt John Hutchings, Vol Mtd Gunmen
TEMPLE, James, Pvt, Col Wm Lillard, Capt Robert Maloney, E TN Vol Inf
TEMPLE, Reddock, Pvt, Col A Cheatham, Capt James Giddens, Inf
TEMPLETON, Absolom, Pvt, Col Wm Lillard, Capt Jacob Dykes, Vol Inf
TEMPLETON, Absolom, Sgt, Col Samuel Bunch, Capt Francis Register, E TN Mil
TEMPLETON, Archibold, Pvt, Col N T Perkins, Capt John Doak, Vol Mtd Gunmen
TEMPLETON, James, Pvt, Col Newton Cannon, Capt John E Demsey, Mtd Gunmen; wounded 11-3-1813
TENNERSON, Abraham, Pvt, Col Thos Benton, Capt Isiah Renshaw, Vol Inf
TENNESON, Edmond, Pvt, Col Thos Benton, Capt Isiah Renshaw, Vol Inf; transferred to McFerran
TENNESON, Solomon, Pvt, Col Newton Cannon, Capt George Brandon, Mtd Riflemen
TENNESSON, Edmond, Pvt, Col John Coffee, Capt Robert Jetton, Cav
TENNISON, Edmon, Pvt, Col Thos Benton, Capt James McFerrin, Vol Inf
TENNISON, Edmund, Pvt, Col John Alcorn, Capt Robert Jetton, Vol Cav
TENNISSON, Joseph, Pvt, Col Thos Williamson, Capt James Pace, Lt James Neal, Vol Mtd Gunmen
TENPAN, James, Sgt, Regt Commander omitted, Capt James Gray, Inf
TENPAN, Jesse, Pvt, Regt Commander omitted, Capt Gray, Inf
TENTALLER, John, Pvt, Col Philip Pipkin, Capt David Smith, Inf
TEPTON, Jacob, Pvt, Col Wm Hall, Capt John Kennedy, Vol Inf
TERCE, Solomon, Ffr, Col A Loury, Capt James Kincaid, Inf
TERRELL, George, Pvt, Col Philip Pipkin, Capt Jas McMahon, Mtd Gunmen
TERRILL, Edmund, Pvt, Regt Commander omitted, Capt Jas Terrill, Cav; promoted to Sgt Maj in Col Alcomia Regt
TERRY, Clement, Pvt, Col John Brown, Capt Jesse Reamy, Mtd Gunmen
TERRY, David, Pvt, Col Robt Dyer, Capt Robert Edmonston, TN Vol Mtd Gunmen; d 1-25-1815
TERRY, James, Pvt, Col Wm Metcalf, Capt Andrew Patterson, Mil Inf
TERRY, Jesse, Pvt, Col Jno Brown, Capt Jas Standifer, E TN Vol Mtd Mil
TERRY, Joseph, Pvt, Col S Copeland, Capt David Williams, Inf
TERRY, Joseph, Pvt, Col Wm Johnson, Capt Wm Stewart, E TN Mil
TERRY, Noel, Pvt, Col John Cocke, Capt Samuel Carothers, Inf
TERRY, Stephen, Pvt, Col Jno Coffee, Capt David Smith, Vol Cav
TERRY, Stephen, Pvt, Col Jno Coffee, Capt Henry Bryan, Cav
TERRY, William, Pvt, Col John Wynne, Capt John Spinks, Inf
TERRY, William, Pvt, Maj Wm Woodfolk, Capt Dudney & Capt John Sutton, Inf
TERRY, William, Sgt, Col S McCrory, Capt Abel Willis, Mil Inf; promoted from Cpl
THACKER, Abraham, Pvt, Col Robt Steele, Capt Richard Ratton, Mil Inf
THACKER, John, Pvt, Col R C Napier, Capt Edward Neblett, Mil Inf
THACKER, John, Pvt, Col Wm Metcalf, Capt Bird Hurt, Mil Inf
THACKER, Petris, Pvt, Col S Bunch, Capt S Robertson, E TN Drafted Mil; deserted
THACKER, Pettis, Pvt, Col S Bunch, Capt S Richardson, E TN Drafted Mil; deserted
THACKSTON, James, Pvt, Col John Wynne, Capt Bayless Prince, Inf
THACKSTON, Job, Pvt, Col John Wynne, Capt Bayless Prince, Inf
THAL, Edward, Pvt, Maj Wm Woodfolk, Capt Mathew Neale, Inf
THARLTON, John, Sgt, Col S Wear, Capt John Childs, E TN Vol Inf
THARP, David, Pvt, Col William Johnson, Capt Elihu Millikin, E TN Mil
THARP, Henry, Pvt, Col Thomas Williamson, Capt John Crane & Capt Cook, Vol Mtd Gunmen
THARP, James, Pvt, Col S Bunch, Capt F Register, E TN Mil
THARP, James, Pvt, Col Wm Johnson, Capt Andrew Lawson, E TN Drafted Mil
THARP, Jonathan, Pvt, Col S Wear, Capt Joseph Cal-

- 491

## Enlisted Men, War of 1812

loway, Mtd Inf
THARP, Lewis, Pvt, Col S Bunch, Capt Jones Griffin, E TN Drafted Mil; discharged for inability
THARP, Moses, Pvt, Col John Wynne, Capt Wm Carothers, W TN Inf
THASLEY, Peter, Pvt, Col Thos Bradley, Capt James Hambleton, Vol Inf
THASLEY, Peter, Pvt, Col Wm Hall, Capt James Hambleton, Vol Inf
THATCH, Thomas H, Sgt Maj, Col S Bunch, Maj Alexander Smith, E TN Mil
THATCHER, Carey, 1 Sgt, Maj John Childs, Capt Reuben Tipton, E TN Vol Mtd Inf; Regimental Co - Knox
THAXTON, Thomas, Pvt, Regt Commander omitted, Capt L Ferrell, Inf
THAXTON, William, Cpl, Col S Copeland, Capt William Douglass, Inf
THERMAN, Dickerson, Pvt, Col Wm Lillard, Capt Geo Argenbright, E TN Riflemen
THERMAN, Thomas, Cpl, Col Wm Lillard, Capt Geo Argenbright, E TN Riflemen
THEVEATT, James, Cpl, Col Robert Dyer, Capt Allen, Vol Mtd Gunmen
THOMAS, Abraham, Pvt, Col Edwin Booth, Capt Vernon, E TN Mil
THOMAS, Adam, Pvt, Col S Copeland, Capt Wilkinson, Mil Inf
THOMAS, Andrew, Pvt, Col John Cocke, Capt Jas Gault, Inf
THOMAS, Archibald, 1 Sgt Mate, Col Archer Cheatham, no Co Commander, 2 Regt of TN
THOMAS, Archibald, Sgt, Col Wm Higgins, Capt A Cheatham, Mtd Riflemen
THOMAS, Benjamin, Cpl, Col Leroy Hammonds, Capt Jas Craig, W TN Mil
THOMAS, Benjamin, Pvt, Col S Bunch, Capt Isaac Williams, E TN Mil
THOMAS, Benjamin, Pvt, Col Wm Johnson, Capt Andrew Lawson, E TN Drafted Mll
THOMAS, Bible, Pvt, no other information; deserted
THOMAS, Daniel, Pvt, Col Thos Benton, Capt Geo Gibbs, Vol Inf
THOMAS, Daniel, Pvt, Col Wm Pillow, Capt Anderson, Vol Inf
THOMAS, Daniel, Pvt, Maj Wm Russell, Capt John Chism, Vol Mtd Gunmen
THOMAS, David, Dmr, Col Edwin Booth, Capt John McKamey, E TN Mil
THOMAS, David, Pvt, Col Ewen Allison, Capt Wm King, Draft Mil
THOMAS, Elijah, Pvt, Col Edwin Booth, Capt Porter, Drafted Mil
THOMAS, Ellis, Sgt, Col Saml Wear, Col Saml Bunch, Capt Wm Mitchell, E TN Vol Inf; apptd 1 Sgt
THOMAS, Ephraim, Pvt, Col Philip Pipkin, Capt Jas Blakemore, Mil Inf
THOMAS, Fredrick, Pvt, Col Wm Johnson, Capt David McKamy, E TN Draft Mil
THOMAS, George, 1 Cpl, Col Thos Benton, Capt Benj Reynolds, Vol Inf
THOMAS, George, 2 Cpl, Col John Brown, Capt Chas Levin, E TN Mtd Inf
THOMAS, George, Cpl, Col Thos Benton, Capt Benj Reynolds, Vol Inf
THOMAS, George, Pvt, Col Wm Hall, Capt John Moore, Vol Inf
THOMAS, George, Pvt, Gen Roberts, Capt Benj Reynolds, Mtd Rangers
THOMAS, Hamilton, Sgt, Col Wm Pillow, Capt John H Anderson, Vol Inf
THOMAS, Henry, Pvt, Col Thos Williamson, Capt A Metcalf, Vol Mtd Gunmen
THOMAS, Humphrey, Pvt, Lt Col L Hammond, Capt James A Tubb, Inf
THOMAS, Isaac, Pvt, Col Wm Lillard, Capt Benj H King, E TN Vol Inf
THOMAS, Isaac, Pvt, Maj Wm Woodfolk, Capt Abner Pearce, Inf
THOMAS, Isaac, Pvt, Maj Wm Woodfolk, Capt John Sutton, Inf
THOMAS, Jacob, Pvt, Col Samuel Bunch, Capt Edward Buchanan, E TN Mil
THOMAS, James, Pvt, Col Edward Bradley, Capt Harry L Douglass, Vol Inf
THOMAS, James, Pvt, Col Philip Pipkin, Capt Geo Mebane, Mil Inf
THOMAS, James, Pvt, Regt Commander omitted, Capt Saml Richardson, E TN Drafted Mil
THOMAS, Jessie, Pvt, Col Jas Raulston, Capt Mathew Cowan, Inf
THOMAS, Job H, Pvt, Col Thos McCrory, Capt Wm Dooly, Inf
THOMAS, John C, 4 Sgt, Col R C Napier, Capt Edward Neblett, Mil Inf
THOMAS, John C, Cpl, Col R H Dyer, Capt Robt Edmonston, TN Vol Mtd Gunmen
THOMAS, John, Pvt, Col R H Dyer, Capt Thos Jones, Vol Mtd Gunmen
THOMAS, John, Pvt, Col Samuel Bunch, Capt Geo Gregory, E TN Drafted Mil
THOMAS, John, Pvt, Col Samuel Wear & Col Samuel Bunch, Capt Wm Mitchell, E TN Mtd Inf
THOMAS, John, Pvt, Col Thos Benton, Capt James McFerrin, Vol Inf
THOMAS, John, Pvt, Lt Col Jno Edmonson, Co Commander omitted, Cav
THOMAS, John, Pvt, Regt Commander omitted, Capt Archibald McKinney, Cav
THOMAS, Joseph, Cpl, Col Wm Pillow, Capt John H Anderson, Vol Inf
THOMAS, Joseph, Pvt, Col Jas Raulston, Capt Elijah Haynie, Inf
THOMAS, Joseph, Pvt, Col Samuel Wear, Capt John Doak, E TN Vol Inf
THOMAS, Joseph, Pvt, Col Thos Benton, Capt Geo W Gibbs, Vol Inf
THOMAS, Lewis, Pvt, Col Philip Pipkin, Capt John Strother, Mil
THOMAS, Louis (Lewis), Pvt, Col Philip Pipkin, Capt Ebenezer Kirkpatrick, Mil Inf
THOMAS, Luke, Sdlr, Col John Alcorn, Capt John Baskerville, Vol Inf

## Enlisted Men, War of 1812

THOMAS, Luke, Sdlr, Col John Coffee, Capt John Baskerville, Cav

THOMAS, Maraday, Pvt, Maj Gen Wm Carroll, Col James Raulston, Capt Elijah Haynie, Inf

THOMAS, Mark, Pvt, Col John Cocke, Capt James Gault, Inf; d 3-10-1815

THOMAS, Mark, Pvt, Col Thos Benton, Capt Thos Williamson, Vol Inf

THOMAS, Nathan, Pvt, Regt Commander omitted, Capt Gray, Inf

THOMAS, Robert, Pvt, Maj Wm Woodfolk, Capt Ezekial Ross & Capt McCulley, Inf

THOMAS, Samuel, Pvt, Maj Wm Russell, Capt Wm Chism, Vol Mtd Riflemen

THOMAS, Samuel, Pvt, Regt Commander omitted, Capt G Lane, Mtd Riflemen

THOMAS, Stephen, Pvt, Col Wm Lillard, Capt John Roper, E TN Vol Inf

THOMAS, Thomas, Pvt, Col Philip Pipkin, Capt Henry M Newlin, Mil Inf

THOMAS, William, Pvt, Col A Loury, Capt Arahel Rains, Inf

THOMAS, William, Pvt, Col Edwin Booth, Capt Samuel Thompson, Mil

THOMAS, William, Pvt, Col R H Dyer, Capt Cuthbert Hudson, Vol Mtd Gunmen

THOMAS, William, Pvt, Col S Copeland, Capt Alexander Provine, Mil Inf

THOMAS, William, Pvt, Col Samuel Bunch, Capt Isaac Williams, E TN Mil; deserted 1-23-1814

THOMAS, William, Pvt, Col Thomas McCrory, Capt Isaac Patton, Mtd Inf

THOMAS, William, Pvt, Col Wm Hall, Capt James Hambleton, Vol Inf

THOMAS, William, Pvt, Col Wm Hall, Capt Wm L Alexander, Vol Inf

THOMAS, William, Pvt, Col Wm Johnson, Capt Elihu Milliken, 3rd Regt E TN Mil

THOMAS, William, Pvt, Lt Col Richard Napier, Co Commander omitted, Inf

THOMAS, William, Pvt, Maj Wm Woodfolk, Capt Ezekial Ross & Capt McCulley, Inf

THOMAS, Willie, Pvt, Col Jas Raulston, Capt Henry Hamilton, Inf

THOMAS, Young, Pvt, Col R H Dyer, Capt Robert Edmondson, TN Vol Mtd Gunmen

THOMASON, Edmund, Pvt, Col R H Dyer, Capt Bethel Allen, Vol Mtd Gunmen

THOMASON, Jeremiah, Pvt, Col R H Dyer, Capt Ephraim Dickson, TN Vol Mtd Gunmen

THOMASON, John, 1 Cpl, Col James Raulston, Capt Mathew Cowan, Inf

THOMASON, John, Pvt, Col Wm Y Higgins, Capt Samuel Allen, Mtd Gunmen

THOMASON, Mark, Pvt, Col John Cocke, Capt John Weakley, Inf

THOMASON, Mark, Pvt, Col John K Wynne, Capt Bayless Prince, Inf

THOMASON, Mark, Pvt, Regt Commander omitted, Capt Gray, Inf

THOMASON, Richard, Pvt, Regt Commander omitted, Capt James Gray, Inf

THOMASON, William, Pvt, Col Thomas H Williamson, Capt Wm Metcalf, Vol Mtd Gunmen

THOMASON, William, Pvt, Col Wm Metcalf, Capt Wm Sitton, Mil Inf

THOMASTON, Joseph, Pvt, Col John Cocke, Capt James Gray, Inf

THOMPSON, Aaron, Pvt, Col Wm Lillard, Capt Robert McCalpin, E TN Inf

THOMPSON, Abram, Blksmth, Col Newton Cannon, Capt Thomas Yardley, Mtd Riflemen

THOMPSON, Adam, Pvt, Regt Commander omitted, Capt Wm McLin & Capt Wm Lillard, E TN Inf

THOMPSON, Alexander, Pvt, Lt Col Hammond, Capt Thomas Wells, Inf

THOMPSON, Andrew, Pvt, Col John Brown, Capt Wm Christian, Regt E TN Mil Inf

THOMPSON, Andrew, Pvt, Col Thomas H Benton, Capt Wm Smith, Branch Srvce omitted

THOMPSON, Andrew, Pvt, Col Thoms H Benton, Capt Wm Smith, Vol Inf

THOMPSON, Andrew, Pvt, Col Wm Johnson, Capt James Tunnell, E TN Mil

THOMPSON, Andrew, Pvt, Regt Commander omitted, Capt David Smith, Vol Inf

THOMPSON, Archibald, Pvt, Col John Alcorn, Capt John W Byrns, Cav

THOMPSON, Archibald, Pvt, Col John Coffee, Capt John W Byrns, Cav

THOMPSON, Azariah, Sgt, Col R H Dyer, Capt Ephram Dickson, TN Mtd Vol Gunmen

THOMPSON, Benjamin, Pvt, Gen Andrew Jackson, Capt Wm Russell, Mtd Spies

THOMPSON, Blackburn, Pvt, Col Wm Johnson, Capt James Tunnell, E TN Mil

THOMPSON, Charles, Pvt, Maj Wm Woodfolk, Capt Abner Pearce, Inf; transferred from Capt Abraham Dudney Co

THOMPSON, Charles, Pvt, Maj Wm Woodfolk, Capt Mathew Neale, Inf

THOMPSON, David, 2 Sgt, Col Wm Hall, Capt Travis C Nash, Inf

THOMPSON, David, Pvt, Col N T Perkins, Co Commander omitted, Mtd Vol

THOMPSON, David, Pvt, Col Newton Cannon, Capt Thomas Yarkley, Mtd Riflemen

THOMPSON, David, Pvt, Col S Copeland & Col James Tait, Co Commander omitted, Inf

THOMPSON, David, Pvt, Col Samuel Wear, Capt James Gillespie, E TN Vol Inf; deserted

THOMPSON, David, Pvt, Col Samuel Wear, Capt John Childs, E TN Vol Inf

THOMPSON, David, Pvt, Col Williams, Capt David Vance, Mtd Mil

THOMPSON, Elbert H, Sgt, Col John Alcorn, Capt John F Winston, Mtd Riflemen

THOMPSON, Elijah, Sgt, Col John Allison & Col Ewin Allison, Capt Thomas Wilson, E TN Drafted Mil

THOMPSON, Frederick, Pvt, Col Thomas H Williamson, Capt James Tait, Vol Mtd Gunmen; d 2-9-1815

THOMPSON, George M, Pvt, Col R H Dyer, Capt Wm

- 493

## Enlisted Men, War of 1812

THOMPSON, Harmon, Pvt, Col Wm Johnson, Capt James Tunnell, E TN Mil
THOMPSON, Henry D, Pvt, Col John Alcorn, Capt Robert Jetton, Vol Cav
THOMPSON, Henry D, Pvt, Col John Coffee, Capt Robert Jetton, Cav
THOMPSON, Henry, Pvt, Col Wm Lillard, Capt McCalpin, E TN Inf
THOMPSON, Henry, Pvt, Col Wm Y Higgins, Capt James Hambleton, Mtd Gunmen
THOMPSON, Henry, Pvt, Regt Commander omitted, Capt John Gordon, Mtd Spies
THOMPSON, Isaac, Pvt, Col Wm Lillard, Capt Wm McLin, E TN Inf
THOMPSON, Jacob, Pvt, Brig Gen Thomas Washington, Capt John Crawford, Inf
THOMPSON, Jacob, Regt QM, Col Philip Pipkin, Co Commander omitted, 1st Regt TN Mil
THOMPSON, Jahoiada, Pvt, Col Saml Bunch, Capt Andrew Breden, E TN Mil
THOMPSON, James jr, Pvt, Col Jno Coffee, Capt Alex McKeen, Cav
THOMPSON, James sr, Pvt, Col Jno Coffee, Capt Alex McKeen, Cav
THOMPSON, James, 4 Cpl, Col James Raulston, Capt Henry West, Inf
THOMPSON, James, Pvt, Col John K Wynne, Capt James Cole, Inf
THOMPSON, James, Pvt, Col N T Perkins, Capt John B Quarles, Vol Mtd Inf
THOMPSON, James, Pvt, Col R H Dyer, Capt Joseph Williams, Vol Mtd Gunmen
THOMPSON, James, Pvt, Col S Bunch, Capt Edward Buchanan, E TN Mil
THOMPSON, James, Pvt, Col Samuel Wear, Capt John Childs, E TN Vol Inf
THOMPSON, James, Pvt, Col Thos Benton, Capt Isaiah Renshaw, Vol Inf
THOMPSON, James, Pvt, Col Wm Pillow, Co Commander omitted, 2nd Regt TN Vol Inf; transferred to the 39 W TN Inf
THOMPSON, James, Pvt, Maj Wm Russell, Capt John Chism, Vol Mtd Riflemen
THOMPSON, James, Pvt, Regt Commander omitted, Capt James Smith, Mil Cav
THOMPSON, James, Pvt, Regt Commander omitted, Capt James Williams, Mil Cav
THOMPSON, James, Pvt, Regt Commander omitted, Capt Wm Mitchell, Spies
THOMPSON, James, Sgt, Col Samuel Bunch, Capt Jas Penny, E TN Mtd Inf
THOMPSON, Jenans, Pvt, Col S Copeland, Capt John Biles, Inf
THOMPSON, Jesse, Pvt, Col Newton Cannon, Capt George Brandon, Mtd Riflemen
THOMPSON, Jesse, Pvt, Col Newton Cannon, Capt Thos Yardley, Mtd Riflemen
THOMPSON, Jesse, Pvt, Maj John Childs, Capt John Stephens, E TN Vol Mtd Inf
THOMPSON, John, Cpl, Col Thos McCrory, Capt John Reynolds, Mil Inf
THOMPSON, John, Pvt, Col Alexander Loury, Capt John Looney, W TN Inf
THOMPSON, John, Pvt, Col John Brown, Capt Wm White, Regt E TN Mil Inf
THOMPSON, John, Pvt, Col Robt H Dyer, Capt Len Owen, TN Vol Mtd Gunmen
THOMPSON, John, Pvt, Regt Commander omitted, Capt Nathan Davis, Lt I Barratt, Branch Srvce omitted
THOMPSON, Joseph A, Pvt, Regt Commander omitted, Capt Geo Smith, Spies
THOMPSON, Joseph jr, Pvt, Col John Alcorn, Capt Alex McKeen, Cav; transferred to Mitchell's Spies
THOMPSON, Joseph, Pvt, Col S Copeland, Capt John Biles, Inf
THOMPSON, Joseph, Pvt, Col Thos Benton, Capt Robt Cannon, Inf; transferred to Capt McKains Co
THOMPSON, Joseph, Pvt, Regt Commander omitted, Capt W Mitchell, Spies
THOMPSON, Joseph, Sdlr, Col Newt Cannon, Capt Wm Martin, Mtd Gunmen
THOMPSON, Loyal B, 1 Sgt, Col Sam Bunch, Capt John McNair, E TN Mil
THOMPSON, Mark, Pvt, Col John Cocke, Capt John Weakley, Inf
THOMPSON, Martin, Ffr Maj, Col Sam Bayless, Co Commander omitted, 4th Regt E TN Mil; d 2-1-1815
THOMPSON, Maston, Ffr, Col Sam Bayless, Capt Joseph Rich, E TN Inf; promoted to Ffr Maj
THOMPSON, Moses, Pvt, Col Philip Pipkin, Capt Henry M Newlin, Mil Inf; d 9-24-1814 at Ft Williams
THOMPSON, Moses, Pvt, Col S Copeland, Capt John Biles, Inf
THOMPSON, Nathan O, Pvt, Regt Commander omitted, Capt Jos Williams, Mil Cav
THOMPSON, Nathan, Pvt, Regt Commander omitted, Capt Jas Haggard, Mtd Gunmen; transferred to Capt Molton Co
THOMPSON, Neill, Pvt, Col Jas Raulston, Capt Jas Black, Inf
THOMPSON, Nicholas, Pvt, Col R C Napier, Capt James McMurry, Mil Inf
THOMPSON, Nicholas, Pvt, Lt Col A Cheatham, Capt Gabriel Martin, Mtd Inf
THOMPSON, Nicholas, Pvt, Lt Col Jno Edmonson, Co Commander omitted, Cav
THOMPSON, Philip, Sgt, Col Thos Benton, Capt Jas McEwen, Vol Inf
THOMPSON, Reuben, Pvt, Col Newt Cannon, Capt John Demsey, Mtd Gunmen
THOMPSON, Robert, Cpl, Maj Wm Woodfolk, Capt A Dudney, Inf
THOMPSON, Robert, Pvt, Col N T Perkins, Capt Philip Pipkin, Mtd Riflemen
THOMPSON, Robert, Pvt, Col Sam Wear, Capt John Stephens, E TN Vol Inf
THOMPSON, Robert, Sgt, Col Sam Wear, Capt Jas Gillespie, E TN Vol Inf
THOMPSON, Samuel, Pvt, Col Robert Steele, Capt Jas Randals, Inf

## Enlisted Men, War of 1812

THOMPSON, Samuel, Pvt, Col Thos Benton, Capt Isaiah Renshaw, Inf
THOMPSON, Samuel, Pvt, Col Wm Pillow, Capt Isaiah Renshaw, Inf
THOMPSON, Shared, Pvt, Col Robt M Dyer, Capt Robt Evans, Vol Mtd Gunmen
THOMPSON, Solomon, Pvt, Col Thos Benton, Capt Isaiah Renshaw, Vol Inf
THOMPSON, Swan, Cpl, Col Wm Y Higgins, Capt Jas Hambleton, Mtd Gunmen; wounded 1-22-1814 and present
THOMPSON, Terry, Pvt, Col John W Wynne, Capt Wm McCall, Inf
THOMPSON, Thomas A, Sgt, Col Thos Williamson, Capt Anthony Metcalf, Vol Mtd Gunmen
THOMPSON, Thomas F, Orderly Sgt, Col Newton Cannon, Capt John Demsey, Mtd Gunmen
THOMPSON, Thomas, Artif, Col Thos Williamson, Capt Richard Tate, Vol Mtd Gunmen
THOMPSON, Thomas, Pvt, Col Edwin Booth, Capt Saml Thompson, Mil
THOMPSON, Thomas, Pvt, Col Newt Cannon, Capt Wm Martin, Mtd Gunmen
THOMPSON, Thomas, Pvt, Col Saml Bunch, Capt Jas Penny, E TN Mtd Inf
THOMPSON, Thomas, Pvt, Col Williamson, Capt Richard Tate, Vol Mtd Gunmen
THOMPSON, Thomas, Pvt, Col Wm Metcalf, Capt Wm Mullin, Mil Inf
THOMPSON, Thomas, Pvt, Regt Commander omitted, Capt Nathan Farmer, Mtd Riflemen
THOMPSON, Wallace, Pvt, Col Saml Bunch, Capt Edward Buchanan, E TN Mil
THOMPSON, William C, Pvt, Col T McCrory, Capt Isaac Patton, Mil Inf
THOMPSON, William, 3 Sgt, Col A Loury, Lt Col L Hammond, Capt Thos Delaney, Inf
THOMPSON, William, Cpl, Col Samuel Wear, Capt James Gillespie, E TN Vol Inf; promoted from Pvt
THOMPSON, William, Pvt, Brig Gen Thos Washington, Capt Jno Crawford, Mtd Inf
THOMPSON, William, Pvt, Col A Loury, Capt James Kincaid, Inf
THOMPSON, William, Pvt, Col Jno Brown, Capt Wm Christian, E TN Mil Inf
THOMPSON, William, Pvt, Col John Coffee, Capt Chas Kavanaugh, Cav; AWOL
THOMPSON, William, Pvt, Col N T Perkins, Capt Geo W Marr, Mtd Vol
THOMPSON, William, Pvt, Col R H Dyer, Capt Joseph Williams, Vol Mtd Gunmen
THOMPSON, William, Pvt, Col R H Dyer, Capt Robt Evans, Vol Mtd Gunmen; elected to Tptr
THOMPSON, William, Pvt, Col S Copeland, Capt John Holshouser, Inf
THOMPSON, William, Pvt, Col Thos Williamson, Capt John Doak & Capt John Dobbins, Vol Mtd Gunmen
THOMPSON, William, Pvt, Col Thos Williamson, Capt Robt Moore, Vol Mtd Gunmen
THOMPSON, William, Pvt, Col Thos Williamson, Capt Thos Porter, Vol Mtd Gunmen
THOMPSON, William, Pvt, Col Wm Hall, Capt Henry M Newlin, Inf
THOMPSON, William, Pvt, Col Wm Johnston, Capt Joseph Kirk, Mil; never appeared
THOMPSON, William, Pvt, Gen Andrew Jackson, Capt Joel Parrish, Arty
THOMPSON, Zachariah, Pvt, Maj Wm Russell, Capt Wm Chism, Vol Mtd Riflemen
THORNBERRY, John, Sgt, Col Samuel Wear, Capt James Gillespie, E TN Vol Inf
THORNTON, Barnet, Pvt, Col Saml Bayless, Capt Jas Churchman, E TN Mil
THORNTON, Barnet, Pvt, Col Saml Bunch, Capt Geo Gregory, E TN Regt
THORNTON, Barnett, Pvt, Col Saml Bunch, Capt Jno Hawk, E TN Mil
THORNTON, Daniel, Pvt, Col Saml Bunch, Capt Geo Gregory, E TN Draft Mil; disch for inability
THORNTON, James, Pvt, Col R H Dyer, Capt Wm Russell, Vol Mtd Gunmen
THORNTON, John W, Pvt, Col R H Dyer, Capt Robt Evans, Vol Mtd Gunmen
THORNTON, Luke, Pvt, Col S Copeland, Capt Allen Wilkinson, Mil Inf
THORNTON, Nelson, Pvt, Col Saml Bunch, Capt Jas Penney, E TN Mtd Inf
THORNTON, Thomas J, Pvt, Col R H Dyer, Capt Robt Evans, Vol Mtd Gunmen
THORNTON, William, Pvt, Col R H Dyer, Capt Wm Russell, Vol Mtd Gunmen
THORNTON, Yancey, Pvt, Lt Col Wm Phillips, no other information
THORNTON, Yancey, Pvt, Maj Cooper, Co Commander omitted, Mtd Riflemen
THORP, James, Cpl, Col Wm Lillard, Capt Wm McLin, E TN Inf
THRASHER, Benjamin F, Sgt, Col Edwin Booth, Capt John Lewis, E TN Inf
THRASHER, Isaac, Pvt, Col Wm Lillard, Capt Jacob Hartsell, E TN Vol Inf
THRASHER, John, Pvt, Brig Gen T Johnson, Capt Robt Carson, Inf
THRASHER, John, Pvt, Maj Wm Woodfolk, Capt Jas Nail, Inf
THRASHER, John, Pvt, Regt Commander omitted, Capt Nathan Davis, Lt I Barrett, Inf
THRASHER, Thomas, Pvt, Maj Wm Russell, Capt Geo Mitchie, Vol Mtd Gunmen
THRASHER, William, Pvt, Col Thos Benton, Capt Wm Moore, Vol Inf
THREADFORD, James, Pvt, Lt Col L Hammond, Capt Jas Craig, Inf
THREAT, Isham, Pvt, Brig Gen T Johnson, Capt Abraham Allen, Mil Inf
THREAT, John, Pvt, Col John Cocke, Capt Joseph Price, Inf
THRESHER, Isaac, Pvt, Col Wm Johnson, Capt Andrew Lawson, E TN Draft Mil
THRESHER, Joseph, Cpl, Col Wm Higgins, Capt John Doake, Mtd Riflemen

## Enlisted Men, War of 1812

THROGMARTON, Reuben, Pvt, Col John Cocke, Capt Jas Gray, Inf; enlisted Regular Army 11-22-1814

THROGMORTEN, William, Pvt, Col Philip Pipkin, Capt Peter Searcy, Mil Inf; deserted

THROOP, Charles, Pvt, Col John Wynne, Capt John Porter, Inf

THRURSVILE, William, Pvt, Col Wm Johnson, Capt Jas Stewart, E TN Draft Mil

THRUWETT, William, Pvt, Col Wm Johnson, Capt Jas Stewart, E TN Draft Mil

THUDGILL, William, Pvt, Col A Loury, Capt Jas Kincaid, Inf; (Threadgill)

THURCATT, John, Pvt, Col John Wynne, Capt Bayless E Prince, Inf

THURMAN, Flemming B, Pvt, Col A Loury, Capt John Looney, W TN Inf

THURMAN, Fountain, 3 Cpl, Col Wm Metcalf, Capt Wm Sitton, Mil Inf

THURMAN, Graves, Pvt, Col Philip Pipkin, Capt Wm Mackey, Mil Inf

THWEAT, Isham, Pvt, Col John Cocke, Capt John Dalton, Inf

THWEAT (TREAT), William K, Pvt, Col John Cocke, Capt John Dalton, Inf; died 1-16-1815

THWEATT, Henry, Pvt, Col R H Dyer, Capt Bethel Allen, Vol Mtd Gunmen; died 2-28-1815

TIAWELL, Robert, Pvt, Col R C Napier, Capt Drury Adkins, Mil Inf

TIBB (TIBBS), John, Pvt, Col Wm Johnson, Capt Benj Powell, E TN Mil

TIDDOR (TEDDER), Elisha, Pvt, Col Philip Pipkin, Capt Geo Mebane, Mil Inf

TIDFORD, Knott, Pvt, Col R H Dyer, Capt Cuthbert Hudson, Vol Mtd Gunmen; died 2-7-1815

TIDWELL, Absolom, Pvt, Col Robt Steele, Capt John Chitwood, Mil Inf

TIDWELL, Mark, Pvt, Maj William Russell, Capt John Chism, Vol Mtd Gunmen

TIDWELL, Mott, Pvt, Col Robt Dyer, Capt Cuthbert Hudson, Vol Mtd Gunmen

TIDWELL, Robert, Pvt, Col Robt Dyer, Capt Cuthbert Hudson, Vol Mtd Gunmen

TIDWELL (TIDFORD), Quilla, Pvt, Col Robt Dyer, Capt Cuthbert Hudson, Vol Mtd Gunmen

TIFHTILLER, Joseph, Pvt, Col S Bunch, Capt Edward Buchanan, E TN Mil

TIGARD, Elisha, Pvt, Regt Commander omitted, Capt Jos Williams, Mil Cav

TIGERD, Hugh, Pvt, Col Jas Raulston, Capt Wiley Huddleston, Inf

TIGNER, Edward, Pvt, Col T McCrory, Capt Isaac Patton, Mil Inf; deserted

TILFORD, John, Pvt, Col John Alcorn, Capt Edward Bradley, Vol Cav

TILFORD, John, Pvt, Col Thos Benton, Capt Henry Douglas, Vol Inf

TILFORD, John, Pvt, Col Thos Williamson, Capt Beverly Williams, Vol Mtd Gunmen

TILFORD, Robert, 1 Sgt, Col Thos Benton, Capt Henry Douglas, Vol Inf

TILFORD, Robert, Pvt, Gen Andrew Jackson, Capt Nathan Davis, Inf

TILFORD, Thomas, Pvt, Gen Andrew Jackson, Capt Nathan Davis, Inf

TILISON, Spencer, Pvt, Col Wm Lillard, Capt Robt McCalpin, E TN Inf

TILLERY, Thomas, 1 Cpl, Col Philip Pipkin, Capt Jas Blakemore, Mil Inf; deserted

TILLET, William, Pvt, Col Robt Dyer, Capt Evans, Vol Mtd Gunmen

TILLEY, George, Pvt, Col John Wynne, Capt Wm McCall, Inf

TILLEY, John, Pvt, Col Wm Metcalf, Capt Andrew Patterson, Mil Inf

TILLEY, Lewis, Pvt, Col Jas Raulston, Capt Nathan Neal, Inf; died 2-1-1815

TILSON, John, Pvt, Col Wm Lillard, Capt Jacob Hartsell, E TN Vol Inf

TIMA, Noah, Pvt, Col John Cocke, Capt Geo Barnes, Inf

TIMS, Jabas, Dmr, Col S Copeland, Capt Moses Thompson, Inf

TINDAL (TINDELL), Joshua, Pvt, Col Wm Johnson, Capt Jas Stewart, E TN Drafted Mil

TINDALL, Robert, 5 Cpl, Maj John Childs, Capt Chas Conway, E TN Mtd Gunmen

TINDLE, Samuel, Pvt, Col N Cannon, Capt Isaac Williams, Mtd Riflemen

TINDLE, Samuel, Pvt, Col Thos Williamson, Capt John Hutchings, Vol Mtd Gunmen

TINER, Jesse, Pvt, Col Thos Benton, Capt Benj Reynolds, Vol Inf

TINER, Jesse, Pvt, Col Wm Pillow, Capt Jas McEwen, Vol Inf

TINER, Lewis, Pvt, Col Thos Benton, Capt Benj Reynolds, Vol Inf

TINES, Jesse, Pvt, Col Wm Metcalf, Capt Bird Hurt, Mil Inf

TINES, John, Pvt, Col John Cocke, Capt John Weakley, Inf

TINKER, Abraham, Pvt, Col Wm Lillard, Capt Jacob Hartsell, E TN Vol Inf

TINKLE, Robert, Pvt, Col N Cannon, Capt John Handley, Mtd Riflemen

TINNER, John, Blksmth, Col Robt Dyer, Capt Robt Edmonston, TN Mtd Gunmen; died 1-31-1815

TINNER, Lawrence, Pvt, Col Wm Hall, Capt Jas Hambleton, Vol Inf

TINNERY, Larry, Pvt, Lt Col H B Bryan, Capt Jas Hamilton, Mil Inf

TINNING, William A, Pvt, Col John Wynne, Capt Wm McCall, Inf

TINOR, John, Pvt, Col John Cocke, Capt John Weakley, Inf

TINSELY, Cornelius, Pvt, Col R C Napier, Capt Preston, Mil Inf

TINSELY, Phillip, Ffr, Col Wm Hall, Capt Henry Newlin, Inf

TINSLEY, Moses, Pvt, Col Jas Raulston, Capt Mathew Neil, Inf

TIPIT, William, Pvt, Col John Brown, Capt Jas Preston, E TN Mil Inf

TIPPER, Joshua, Pvt, Col S Copeland, Capt John Dawson,

## Enlisted Men, War of 1812

Inf
TIPPER, Kenchen, Pvt, Col Wm Metcalf, Capt Andrew Patterson, Mil Inf
TIPPET, Benjamin, 2 Sgt, Col John Brown, Capt Wm White, E TN Mtd Inf
TIPPIT, Benjamin, 2 Cpl, Col John Brown, Capt Jas Standifer, E TN Vol Mil Inf
TIPPIT, William, Pvt, Col Wm Johnson, Capt Wm Alexander, E TN Drafted Mil
TIPPS, Benjamin, Pvt, Col Jno Brown, Capt Hugh Barton, E TN Mil Inf
TIPPS, George, Pvt, Maj Wm Russell, Capt Wm Russell, Vol Mtd Gunmen
TIPPS, John, Pvt, Col Wm Metcalf, Capt Geo Sitton, Mil Inf; died 1-6-1815
TIPPS, Peter, Pvt, Col Thos Benton, Capt Wm Moore, Vol Inf
TIPPY, John, Pvt, Col R T Perkins, Capt Phillip Pipkin, Mtd Riflemen
TIPS, Peter, 2 Cpl, Col Wm Pillow, Capt Wm Moore, Inf
TIPTON, Abraham, 3 Sgt, Col Ewen Allison, Capt Wm King, Drafted Mil
TIPTON, Abraham, Sgt, Col S Wear, Capt Jesse Cole, Vol Inf
TIPTON, Alexander, Sgt, Col S Wear, Capt Jesse Cole, Vol Inf
TIPTON, Benjamin, Pvt, Col S Wear, Capt Joseph Calloway, Mtd Inf
TIPTON, Edward, Pvt, Col R T Perkins, CApt Phillip Pipkin, Mtd Riflemen; killed 1-20-1814
TIPTON, Isaac, Pvt, Col Saml Wear, Capt Jos Calloway, Branch omitted
TIPTON, Isaac, Pvt, Maj Jno Childs, Capt R Tipton, E TN Vol Mtd Inf; Regt from Blount Co
TIPTON, Jacob, Pvt, Col E Allison, Capt A Winsell, E TN Draft Mil
TIPTON, Jacob, Pvt, Col Ed Bradley, CApt Jno Kennedy, Riflemen
TIPTON, Jacob, Pvt, Col Jno Williams, Capt Wm Walker, E TN Mtd Vol
TIPTON, Jacob, Pvt, Col S Bunch, Capt F Register, E TN Mil; joined from Capt Winsel's Co
TIPTON, Jacob, Pvt, Col Saml Wear, Capt Jos Calloway, Mtd Inf
TIPTON, Jacob, Pvt, Col Wm Hall, Capt Jno Kennedy, Vol Inf
TIPTON, James, 2 Sgt, Maj Gen A Jackson, Capt Kirkpatrick, Mtd Gunmen
TIPTON, John, Pvt, Col Saml Wear, Capt Jos Calloway, Mtd Inf
TIPTON, John, Pvt, Maj Jno Childs, Capt R Tipton, E TN Vol Mtd Inf; Regt from Blount Co
TIPTON, Jonathan, Pvt, Maj Jno Childs, Capt R Tipton, E TN Vol Mtd Inf; Regt from Blount Co
TIPTON, Joseph, Pvt, Col Saml Bunch, Capt E Buchanan, E TN Mil
TIPTON, Joseph, Pvt, Lt Col L Hammons, Capt A Rains, Inf; attached to Gen Taylor's Life Guard
TIPTON, Joshua, Blksmth, Col Thos Williamson, Capt Williams, Vol Mtd Gunmen; died 4-20-1815
TIPTON, Reuben, Pvt, Col Jno Brown, Capt Jno Childs, E TN Vol Mtd Inf
TIPTON, Reuben, Sgt, Col Jno Williams, Capt Saml Bunch, Mtd Vol
TIPTON, Samuel, Pvt, Col Saml Bayless, Capt S Hendrix, E TN Mil
TIPTON, Samuel, Pvt, Col Wm Johnson, Capt D McKamy, E TN Draft Mil
TIPTON, William sr, Pvt, Col Saml Wear, Capt Jos Calloway, Mtd Inf
TIPTON, William, Pvt, Col Saml Wear, Capt Jos Calloway, Mtd Inf
TIPTONS, Abraham, Pvt, Col Jno Williams, Capt Wm Walker, Mtd Vol
TIRPIN (TURPIN), Mathew, Pvt, Col Robt Steele, Capt Jas Shenault, Mil Inf
TITSON, Joseph, Pvt, Col Saml Bayless, Capt J Waddle, E TN Mil
TITSON, Thomas, Pvt, Col S Bayless, Capt J Waddle, E TN Mil
TITSWORTH, Frederick, Pvt, Col E Allison, Capt Jos Everett, E TN Mil; trans to Capt McPherson's Co
TITSWORTH, Frederick, Pvt, Col S Bunch, Capt Geo McPherson, E TN Mil; joined from Capt Everett's Co
TITTLE, Anthony, Pvt, Col Alex Loury, Lt Col L Hammons, Capt A Rains, Inf
TITTLE, John, Pvt, Col Wm Johnson, Capt A Lawson, E TN Draft Mil
TITUS, Ebenezer, Pvt, Col Wm Pillow, Capt Thos Williamson, Vol Inf
TITUS, George, Pvt, Col N Cannon, Capt Hemby, Mtd Riflemen; trans to Capt Evans' Co of Spies
TITUS, George, Pvt, Regt Commander omitted, Capt Robt Evans, Mtd Spies
TIVIG, Timothy, Pvt, Col N Cannon, Capt Ota Cantrell, W TN Mtd Inf
TOBS (TOLER), Joel, Pvt, Col Jas Raulston, Maj Gen Wm Carroll, Capt E Haynie, Inf
TODD, Aaron, Pvt, Col N Cannon, Capt Geo Brandon, Mtd Riflemen
TODD, Asa, Pvt, Col Wm Hale, Capt A Bledsoe, Vol Inf
TODD, Benjamin, Pvt, Col N Cannon, Capt Geo Brandon, Mtd Riflemen
TODD, Cornelius, Pvt, Col A Cheatham, Capt Chas Johnson, Inf
TODD, David, Pvt, Col S Bunch, Capt Jones Griffin, E TN Draft Mil
TODD, Edmond, Pvt, Col N Cannon, Capt Ota Cantrell, W TN Mtd Inf
TODD, Isaac, Pvt, Col S Bunch, Capt Geo Gregory, E TN Draft Mil
TODD, Isaac, Pvt, Col S Bunch, Capt Jno Houk, E TN Mil; joined from Capt Gregory's Co
TODD, Isaac, Pvt, Col Saml Bayless, Capt B Jones, E TN Draft Mil; trans from Capt Hale's Co
TODD, Isaac, Pvt, Col Saml Bayless, Capt Jos Hale, E Tn Mil
TODD, James, Pvt, Lt Col L Hammond, Capt Jas Craig, Inf
TODD, Jesse, Pvt, Col Saml Bayless, Capt B Jones, E TN Draft Mil

## Enlisted Men, War of 1812

TODD, Reuben, Pvt, Maj Wm Woodfolk, Capt A Pearce, Inf
TODD, Robert, Pvt, Col A Cheatham, Capt C Johnson, Inf
TODD, Robert, Pvt, Col N Cannon, Capt Geo Brandon, Mtd Riflemen
TODD, Williamson, Fife Maj, Col Jno Brown, Co Commander omitted, E TN Vol
TODHUNTER, Dickerson, Pvt, Col J E? Wynne, Capt Jas Holleman, Inf; deserted
TODHUNTER, Dickinson, Pvt, Col J M Wynne, Capt Geo Carothers, W TN Inf; trans to Capt Holliman's Co
TODHUNTER, Dickson, Pvt, Lt Col L Hammond, Capt Thos Delaney, Inf
TOLAND, Isaac, Pvt, Col R H Dyer, Capt Jos Williams, Vol Mtd Gunmen
TOLAND, Jacob, Pvt, Regt Commander omitted, Capt Jas Craig, Mtd Inf
TOLAR (TOLOR), Lewis, Pvt, Col Jno Cocke, Capt Jno Weakley, Inf
TOLLER, Charles, Pvt, Col N Cannon, CApt Geo Brandon, Mtd Riflemen; trans to the pack horses dept
TOLLER, John, Pvt, Col Thos Williamson, Capt Robert Moore, Vol Mtd Gunmen
TOLLETT, Henry, Pvt, Col E Booth, Capt Vernon, E TN Mil
TOLLIVER, Zachariah, Pvt, Col Thos Williamson, Capt Richd Tate, Vol Mtd Gunmen
TOLLY, Robert, Pvt, Gen Thos Johnston, Capt Danl Oban, 36 Inf; reenlisted 1812
TOM, Joseph, Cpl, Gen Andrew Jackson, Capt Nathan Davis, Inf
TOM, William, Pvt, Gen Andrew Jackson, Capt Nathan Craig, Inf
TOMBLIN, John, Pvt, Col A Cheatham, Capt James Giddens, Inf
TOMBOLIN, Gale, Pvt, Col Robt Steele, Capt Jas Randals, Inf
TOMBOLIN, Lace, Pvt, Col Philip Pipkin, Capt David Smith, Inf
TOMBS, Nathan, Pvt, Col John Wynne, Capt Jas Cole, Inf; deserted
TOMILSON, Uriah, Pvt, Col John Cocke, Capt Jas Gray, Inf
TOMILSTON, John, Pvt, Col N T Perkins, Capt Geo W Marr, Mtd Vol
TOMILSTON, Peter, Pvt, Col N T Perkins, Capt Geo W Marr, Vol Mtd
TOMLIN, Charles, 1 Sgt, Col A Cheatham, Capt Jas Giddens, Inf
TOMLIN, Charles, 1 Sgt, Col Philip Pipkin, Capt Wm Mackay, Mil Inf
TOMLIN, Charles, Pvt, Brig Gen T Washington, Capt Jno Crawford, Inf
TOMLIN, Charles, Pvt, Col Thos Benton, Capt Jas McEwen, Vol Inf; (Tomblin)
TOMLIN, Charles, Pvt, Col Wm Pillow, Capt C E McEwen, Vol Inf
TOMLIN, James, Pvt, no other information
TOMLIN, Jesse, Pvt, Col Thos Benton, Capt Benj Reynolds, Vol Inf

TOMLIN, John, Cpl, Brig Gen T Washington, Capt Jno Crawford, Inf
TOMLIN, Nicholas, Pvt, no other information
TOMLIN, Nicholas, Sgt, Col R H Dyer, Capt Glen Owen, TN Vol Mtd Gunmen
TOMLIN, Nicholas, Sgt, Col Wm Pillow, Capt C E McEwen, Vol Inf
TOMLINSON, Henry, Cpl, Col T McCrory, Capt Saml B McKnight, Inf
TOMLINSON, Henry, Pvt, Col Thos Williamson, Capt John Hutchines, Vol Mtd Gunmen; died 3-13-1815
TOMLINSON, James, Pvt, Col Wm Metcalf, Capt Bird L Hurt, Mil Inf
TOMLINSON, Jesse, Pvt, Col Thos Benton, Capt Benj Reynolds, Vol Inf
TOMLINSON, Uriah, Pvt, Col John Cocke, Capt Jas Gray, Inf
TOMLINSON, William, Pvt, Regt Commander omitted, Capt Gray, Inf
TOMMERSON, John, Pvt, Col Jas Raulston, Capt Mathew Cowan, Inf
TOMPKINS, Harrison, Pvt, Col John Cocke, Capt Joseph Price, Inf
TOMPKINS, Harrison, Pvt, Lt Col John Edmondson, Co Commander omitted, Cav
TOMPKINS, Isaac, Dmr, Col Philip Pipkin, Capt Wm Mackay, Mil Inf; also a Ffr
TOMPKINS, John, 3 Sgt, Col N T Perkins, Capt Geo Eliot, Mil Inf
TOMPSON, James, Blksmth, Col Newt Cannon, CApt John B Demsey, Mtd Gunmen
TONEY, Berry, Pvt, Col Wm Metcalf, Capt Bird L Hurt, Mil Inf
TONEY, Noel, Pvt, Col John Cocke, Capt Saml M Caruthers, Inf
TONGATE, Martin, 1 Sgt, Col Philip Pipkin, Capt Henry Newlin, Mil Inf
TOOL, William, Pvt, Col Saml Wear, Capt Jas Gillespie, E TN Vol Inf
TOOMEY, James, Pvt, Col Edwin Booth, Capt Porter, Drafted Mil
TORRENTINE, Alexander, 1 Sgt, Col S Copeland, Capt John Biles, Inf
TOSH, William, Pvt, Col John Wynne, Capt Jas Holleman, Inf
TOSH (TASK), Guy, Pvt, Col Jas Raulston, Capt Mathew Cowan, Inf
TOTTY, Mathew, Pvt, Col A Loury, Capt Jas Kincaid, Inf
TOTTY, Robert, Pvt, Lt Col L Hammond, Capt Jas Craig, Inf; apptd Cpl
TOTTY, William, Pvt, Col N T Perkins, Capt Philip Pipkin, Mtd Riflemen
TOUR, Joseph, Cpl, Regt Commander omitted, Capt Nathan Davis, Mil Inf; AWOL
TOUR, William, Pvt, Regt Commander omitted, Capt Nathan Davis, Mil Inf; AWOL
TOW, James, Pvt, Col Ewen Allison, Capt Jas Allen, E TN Mil; deserted
TOW, John, Pvt, Col Ewen Allison, Capt Jas Allen, E TN Mil

## Enlisted Men, War of 1812

TOWNS, Edmond, Pvt, Col Thos Williamson, Capt Wm Metcalf, Vol Mtd Gunmen
TOWNSEND, Andrew, Pvt, Col A L Loury, Lt Col L Hammonds, Capt Arahel Rains, Inf
TOWNSEND, Green J, Pvt, Maj Wm Carroll, Capt Lewis Dillahunty & Capt Danl Bradford, Vol Inf; apptd Cpl
TOWNSEND, Green J, Sgt, Col A Cheatham, Capt Wm Creel, Inf; trans to Arty
TOWNSEND, Green, Pvt, Regt Commander omitted, Capt Parrish, Arty
TOWNSEND, Joseph, Pvt, Col Edward Bradley, Capt John Kennedy, Riflemen; AWOL
TOWNSEND, Joseph, Pvt, Maj Gen Wm Carroll, Capt Wiley Huddleston, Inf; died 1-17-1815
TOWNSEND, Joshua, 4 Cpl, Col N T Perkins, Capt John Doak, Vol Mtd Gunmen
TOWNSEND, Nathaniel, Pvt, Col Edward Bradley, Capt John Kennedy, Riflemen
TOWNSEND, Stephen, 3 Sgt, Maj Gen Wm Carroll, Col Jas Raulston, Capt Wiley Huddleston, Inf; died 1-5-1815
TOWNSEND, William, 3 Cpl, Regt Commander omitted, Capt Wm Russell, Mtd Spies
TOWNSEND, William, Sgt, Col Philip Pipkin, Capt John Robertson, Mil Inf
TOWNSLEY, James, Pvt, Col Saml Wear, Capt Jas Gillespie, E TN Vol Inf
TOYLER, Lewis, Pvt, Col John Cocke, Capt John Weakley, Inf
TRACEY, Timothy, Pvt, Col Thos Williamson, Capt Beverly Williams, Vol Mtd Gunmen
TRACY, Paris, Pvt, Col Philip Pipkin, Capt Henry Newlin, Mil Inf; died 9-20-1814
TRACY, Timothy, 2 Cpl, Gen John Coffee, Co Commander omitted, Mtd Spies
TRACY, Timothy, Pvt, Col Newton Cannon, Capt John Harpole, Mtd Gunmen
TRACY, Timothy, Pvt, Col Thos Benton, Capt Henry L Douglass, Vol Inf
TRACY, Timothy, Pvt, Gen Jno Coffee, Lt Jesse Bean, Mtd Spies
TRACY, William, Pvt, Col Wm Hall, Capt John Moore, Vol Inf
TRAIL, Basil, Pvt, Col Jas Raulston, Capt Mathew Neal, Inf; died 4-10-1815
TRAIL, Bassel, 2 Sgt, Col R C Napier, Capt Jas McMurray, Mil Inf
TRAILLER, James, Pvt, Col N T Perkins, Capt Mathew Patterson, Vol Mtd Gunmen
TRAKY, Hyram, Pvt, Col N T Perkins, Capt Geo Marr, Mtd Vol
TRAMEL, Peter, Pvt, Col Samuel Bayless, Capt Jas Churchman, E TN Mil
TRAMELL, Dennis, Pvt, Col Edwin Booth, Capt Saml Thompson, Mil
TRAMMELL, James, Pvt, Col Wm Pillow, Capt Thos Williamson, Vol Inf
TRAVIS, Beverly, Pvt, Col S Copeland, Capt David Williams, Mil Inf
TRAVIS, John, Pvt, Col Thos Bradley, Capt Jas Hambleton, Vol Inf
TRAVIS, John, Pvt, Col Wm Hall, Capt Jas Hambleton, Vol Inf
TRAVIS, John, Pvt, Lt Col Henry Bryan, Co Commander omitted, Inf
TRAVIS, Thomas, Cpl, Col Wm Hall, Capt Jas Hambleton, Vol Inf
TRAVIS (TERCE), Solomon, Pvt, Col Alexander Loury, Capt Jas Kincaid, Inf; also Ffr
TRAYLOR, James, Pvt, Col Thos McCrory, Capt Isaac Patton, Mil Inf; deserted
TREADEWAY, Ezekiel, Pvt, Lt Col L Hammond, Capt Thos Delaney, Inf
TREADEWELL, David, Pvt, Gen A Jackson, Capt Wm Russell, Mtd Spies; wounded 1-22-1815
TREADWELL, Daniel, 4 Sgt, Col John Coffee, no other information
TREADWELL, Daniel, Sgt, Regt Commander omitted, Capt Robt Evans, Mtd Spies
TREAL, John, Pvt, Col John Brown, Capt Lunsford Oliver, E TN Mil
TREAT (THWEAT), William I, Pvt, Col John Cocke, Capt John Dalton, Inf; died 1-16-1815
TREBLE, Abraham, Sgt, Col R C Napier, Capt Thos Preston, Mil Inf
TREDWAY, John, Pvt, Col Saml Bunch, Capt Jas Cummings, E TN Vol Mtd Inf
TREGDEN, Solomon, Pvt, Col Saml Bunch, Capt Thos Mann, E TN Vol Mtd Inf
TRENOR, Edward, Cpl, Col Alexander Loury, Capt John Looney, 2 Regt W TN Mil
TRENT, Jesse, Pvt, Col Edwin Booth, Capt John Slatton, E Tn Mil
TRENT, Robert, Pvt, Maj John Childs, Capt Jas Cummings, E TN Vol Mtd Inf
TRENT, Samuel, Pvt, Col Edwin Booth, Capt John Slatton, E TN Mil
TREWETT, Henry M, Pvt, Gen Thos Johnson, Capt Danl Oban, 36 Inf
TREWITT, William, Pvt, Col R H Dyer, Capt Bethel Allen, Vol Mtd Gunmen
TRIBBET, Robert, Pvt, Col Wm Johnson, Capt Jos Scott, E TN Draft Mil
TRIBLE, Isaiah, Pvt, Maj Wm Woodfolk, Capt Ezekial Ross & Capt McCulley, Inf
TRIBUTE, Robert, Pvt, Col Wm Johnson, Capt Jos Scott, E TN Draft Mil
TRICE, Lewis, Pvt, Col John K Wynne, Capt Bayless Prince, Inf
TRICE, Namfill, Pvt, Lt Col Henry Bryan, Co Commander omitted, Inf
TRICE, Robert, Pvt, Lt Col Henry Bryan, Co Commander omitted, Inf
TRICE, Wampill, Pvt, Regt Commander omitted, Capt Jas Cowan, Mtd Inf
TRICKER, John, Pvt, Col Saml Wear, Capt Jos Calloway, Mtd Inf
TRIM, Elijah, Pvt, Col Thos Benton, Capt Benj Reynolds, Vol Inf
TRIMBLE, David, Pvt, Col Thos Williamson, Capt Jas Cook & Capt John Crane, Vol Mtd Gunmen

- 499

TRIMBLE, George W, Pvt, Col A Cheatham, Capt Jas Giddens, Inf
TRIMBLE, John, 2 Sgt, Col Wm Metcalf, Capt Obidiah Waller, Mil Inf
TRIMBLE, John, Pvt, Col John Williams, Capt Saml Bunch, Mtd Vol
TRIMBLE, John, Pvt, Col Saml Bunch, Capt Thos Mann, E TN Vol Mtd Inf
TRINKLE (TRIMBLE), Henry, Pvt, Col Saml Bunch, Capt Andrew Breden, E TN Mil
TRIPLET, Nimrod, Pvt, Col Thos Benton, Capt Wm Moore, Vol Inf
TRIPLETT, Nimrod, Pvt, Col Robt Steele, Capt John Chitwood, Mil Inf; deserted
TROBAUGH, Jacob, Sgt, Col Ewen Allison, Capt Thomas Wilson, E TN Drafted Mil
TROBEAUGH, John, Pvt, Col R H Dyer, Capt Bethel Allen, Vol Mtd Gunmen
TROBOUGH, Daniel, Cpl, Col Ewen Allison, Capt Thomas Wilson, E TN Drafted Mil; appointed Adjt
TROBUCK, Henry, Pvt, Lt Col L Hammonds, Capt James Tubb, Inf
TROBUCK, John, Pvt, Col R H Dyer, Capt Bethel Allen, Vol Mtd Gunmen
TROLLINGER, Henry, Pvt, Col Phillip Pipkin, Capt Edward Robinson, Mil Inf
TROLLINGER, John, 4 Cpl, Col Philip Pipkin, Capt Edward Robinson, Mil Inf; promoted from Pvt
TROLLINGER, John, Pvt, Col Phillip Pipkin, Capt Edward Robinson, Mil Inf
TROLTER, David, Pvt, Col Williams, Capt Vance, Mil
TROOP, Charles, Cpl, Col Thomas Williamson, Capt Richard Tate, Vol Mtd Gunmen; d 2-17-1815
TROOP, Francis, Cpl, Col Thomas Williamson, Capt Richard Tate, Vol Mtd Gunmen
TROTMAN, Thomas, Pvt, Col John Wynne, Capt James Holleman, Inf; deserted
TROTT, Henry, Pvt, Col Jno Coffee, Capt Blackman Coleman, Cav
TROTTER, David, Pvt, Col William Johnson, Capt Christopher Cook, E TN Mil
TROTTER, David, Pvt, Col William Johnson, Capt Jas Stewart, E TN Mil
TROTTER, David, Pvt, Col William Johnson, Capt Joseph Kirk, Mil
TROTTER, David, Pvt, Col Wm Johnson, Capt Jas Stewart, E TN Drafted Mil
TROTTER, Isaac, Cpl, Col Edwin Booth, Capt Geo Biggs, Inf; promoted from Pvt
TROTTER, Joseph, Asst Forage Master, Brig Gen N Taylor, no other information; promoted to Principal Forage Master
TROTTER, Joseph, Pvt, Col William Johnson, Capt Andrew Lawson, E TN Drafted Mil; appointed Forage Master
TROTTER, William, Pvt, Col John Cocke, Capt Joseph PRice, Inf; d 1-29-1815
TROTTER, William, Pvt, Maj John Childs, Capt John Stephens, E TN Vol Mtd Inf
TROUP, Francis, Pvt, Col William Pillow, Capt Thomas Williamson, Vol Inf

TROUSDALE, James, Pvt, Col Jno Coffee, Capt John Baskerville, Cav
TROUSDALE, John, Pvt, Col John Cocke, Capt Joseph Price, Inf
TROUSDALE, John, Pvt, Regt Commander omitted, Capt Gray, Inf
TROUSDALE, William, Cpl, Col John Cocke, Capt Joseph Price, Inf
TROUSDALE, William, Pvt, Col Thomas Williamson, Capt Thomas Scurry, Vol Mtd Gunmen
TROUSDALE, William, Pvt, Regt Commander omitted, Capt Jas Haggard, Mtd Gunmen
TROUT, Benjamin, Pvt, Col Philip Pipkin, Capt Geo Mebane, Mil Inf; furloughed for losing his eyesight
TROUT, George, Pvt, Col S Wear, Capt S Bayless, Mtd Inf; discharged - unable to perform duty
TROUT, Henry, Pvt, Col Thomas Williamson, Capt Beverly Williams, Vol Mtd Gunmen
TROUT, John, Pvt, Col S Bunch, Capt N Gibbs, E TN Drafted Mil
TROUT, John, Pvt, Regt Commander omitted, Capt Samuel Richardson, E TN Drafted Mil
TROUT, Thomas, Pvt, Col John Wynne, Capt Geo Spinks, Inf
TRUE, John, Pvt, Col William Higgins, Capt Thomas Eldridge, Mtd Gunmen
TRUETT, Lewis, Pvt, Col S Copeland, Capt G W Stell, Mil Inf
TRULL, Nathan, Pvt, Col John Cocke, Capt James Gault, Inf; d 1-31-1815
TRULL, William, Pvt, Col S Bunch, Capt Isaac Williams, E TN Mil; transferred to Capt Houk's Co
TRULL, William, Pvt, Col S Bunch, Capt Jno Houk, E TN Mil; joined from? Capt Williams
TRUMAN, Alexander, Pvt, Regt Commander omitted, Capt Jas Haggard, Mtd Gunmen
TRUNIS, Green H, Pvt, Gen Jackson, Capt William Russell, Mtd Spies
TRUNSTON, Peter, Pvt, Col Thos Dyer, Capt Jas McMahon, TN Vol Mil? Gunmen
TRUS, George, Sgt, Col William Higgins, Capt Thomas Eldridge, Mtd Gunmen
TRUSLER, John, Pvt, Col S Bunch, Capt Jones Griffin, E TN Drafted Mil; joined from Capt Loughmiller's Co
TRUSLEY, John, Pvt, Col Edwin Booth, Capt Geo Slatton, E TN Mil
TRUSLEY, John, Pvt, Col Ewen Allison, Capt Jonas Loughmiller, Mil; transferred to Capt Griffin Co
TRUSSELL, Harrison, Pvt, Col Robert Dyer, Capt Thomas Jones, Vol Mtd Gunmen
TRUSSELL, Nathew, Pvt, Col A Cheatham, Capt Chapman, Inf
TRUSSETT, Benjamin, Pvt, Col A Cheatham, Capt Chapman, Inf
TRUSTY, Anseylin, Pvt, Col Edward Bradley, Capt Richard Douglas, Vol Inf
TUBB, Aquilla, Pvt, Col John Cocke, Capt Joseph Price, Inf
TUBB, Elias, 2 Cpl, Col John Wynne, Capt Joseph Price,

## Enlisted Men, War of 1812

TUBB, James, Pvt, Brig Gen Johnston, Capt Allen, Mil Inf
TUBB, Joel, Pvt, Col John Cocke, Capt Joseph Price, Inf; promoted to Sgt
TUBB, John, Pvt, Col John Cocke, Capt Geo Carothers, Inf
TUBBS, David, Pvt, Col Williamson, Capt Porter, Vol Mtd Gunmen
TUBBS, Isaac, Pvt, Col Philip Pipkin, Capt John Roberson, Mil Inf
TUBBS, William, Pvt, Col Wm Metcalf, Capt John Collins, Mil Inf
TUCKER, Archibald, Pvt, Col Edwin Booth, Capt Geo Slatton, E TN Mil; d 12-28-1814
TUCKER, Benjamin, Pvt, Col Thomas Williamson, Capt Beverly Williams, Vol Mtd Gunmen; transferred to Lt Bean's Spies
TUCKER, Benjamin, QM Sgt, Col A Cheatham, Co Commander omitted, Regt of TN Mil
TUCKER, Campbell, Pvt, Col A Cheatham, Capt Geo Smith, Inf
TUCKER, Campbell, Sgt, Col Alexander Loury, Capt James Kincaid, Inf
TUCKER, Daniel S, Pvt, Col Wm Metcalf, Capt John Barnhart, Mil Inf; d 2-7-1815
TUCKER, Drury, Pvt, Col Edward Bradley, Capt Elijah Haynie, Vol Inf
TUCKER, Drury, Pvt, Col Wm Hall, Capt Henry Newlin, Inf
TUCKER, Elijah, Pvt, Col Philip Pipkin, Capt Ebenezer Kirkpatrick, Mil Inf
TUCKER, Green, Pvt, Col Williamson, Capt Joseph Williams, Vol Mtd Gunmen
TUCKER, Henry, Pvt, Col R C Napier, Capt Early Benson, Mil Inf
TUCKER, James, 5 Cpl, Col Samuel Wear, Capt Joseph Calloway, Mtd Inf
TUCKER, James, Pvt, Col John Cocke, Capt George Barnes, Inf; d 12-21-1814
TUCKER, James, Pvt, Col Thos Benton, Capt James McFerrin, Vol Inf; AWOL
TUCKER, James, Pvt, Col Wm Higgins, Capt John Doake, Mtd Riflemen
TUCKER, Joel, Pvt, Col Edwin Booth, Capt Porter, Drafted Mil
TUCKER, John, Pvt, Col A Loury, Capt Geo Sarver, Inf
TUCKER, John, Pvt, Col Edwin Booth, Capt Geo Winton, E TN Mil; transferred from Capt Milliken's Co
TUCKER, John, Pvt, Col Ewen Allison, Capt Henry McCray, E TN Mil; deserted
TUCKER, John, Pvt, Col Ewen Allison, Capt James Loughmiller, Mil
TUCKER, John, Pvt, Col R C Napier, Capt Drury Adkins, Mil Inf
TUCKER, John, Pvt, Col Samuel Bunch, Capt Jones Miller, E TN Drafted Mil; joined from Capt Loughmiller's Co
TUCKER, John, Pvt, Col Thos Williamson, Capt James Cook & Capt John Crane, Vol Mtd Gunmen
TUCKER, John, Pvt, Col Wm Johnson, Capt James K Rogers, E TN Mil

TUCKER, John, Pvt, Col Wm Johnston, Capt Elihu Milliken, 3rd Regt E TN Mil; transferred to Capt Winton's Co
TUCKER, Jonathan, Pvt, Col Wm Lillard, Capt Jacob Hartsell, E TN Vol Inf
TUCKER, Joseph, Pvt, Col John Cocke, Capt John Dalton, Inf
TUCKER, Lemuel, Pvt, Col S Copeland, Capt John Holshouser, Inf
TUCKER, Lewis, Pvt, Col John Cocke, Capt John Dalton, Inf; d 3-13-1815
TUCKER, Mathew, Pvt, Col S Copeland, Capt John Holshouser, Inf
TUCKER, Obadiah A, Pvt, Col Wm Lillard, Capt Thos Sharpe, 2nd Spy Inf
TUCKER, Samuel, Pvt, Col James Raulston, Capt James A Black, Inf
TUCKER, Stephen, Pvt, Lt Col L Hammond, Capt Thos Wells, Inf; also under Col A Loury
TUCKER, Wiley, Pvt, Col Wm Johnson, Capt Elihu Milliken, 3rd Regt E TN Mil; joined from Capt Goodson's Co
TUCKER, William B, Pvt, Col R H Dyer, Capt Ephraim D Dickson, TN Vol Mtd Gunmen; no service performed
TUCKER, William, Cpl, Col Samuel Bunch, Capt Isaac Williams, E TN Mil
TUCKER, William, Pvt, Col John Cocke, Capt Geo Barnes, Inf
TUCKER, William, Pvt, Col Samuel Wear, Capt Simeon Perry, E TN Vol Mtd Inf
TUCKER, William, Pvt, Col T McCrory, Capt John Reynolds, Mil Inf
TUCKER, William, Sgt, Col Samuel Bunch, Capt Jno Hawk, E TN Mil; joined from Capt Williams Co
TUCKNESS, Henry, Pvt, Col R H Dyer, Capt Robert Edmondson, TN Vol Mtd Gunmen
TUGGLE, Henry, Pvt, Col R H Dyer, Capt Bethel Allen, Vol Mtd Gunmen
TULL, Nicholas, Pvt, Col John Alcorn, Capt Frederick Stump, Branch Srvce omitted
TULLOCK, John L, Pvt, Col Samuel Bunch, Capt Joseph Duncan, E TN Drafted Mil; transferred to Capt Buchanon's Co
TUMBLER (TUMBLEN), John, Pvt, Col Wm Lillard, Capt George Keys, E TN Inf
TUMBLESON, David, Pvt, Col Robert Steele, Capt James Randals, Inf
TUMLESON, Dave, Pvt, no other information
TUMMING, Samuel, Pvt, Col Samuel Bunch, Capt Duncan, E TN Drafted Mil
TUMMINS, Edward, Pvt, Col S Bunch, Capt John Moore, E TN Mil
TUMPOW, Robert, Pvt, Maj Wm Russell, Capt Wm Chism, Vol Mtd Gunmen
TUNE, James, Pvt, Col T McCrory, Capt Isaac Patton, Mil Inf
TUNE, Lewis, Pvt, Col R H Dyer, Capt Glen Owen, TN Vol Mtd Gunmen
TUNEL, James, Pvt, Col John Williams, Capt Wm Walker, Mtd Vol

- 501

## Enlisted Men, War of 1812

TUNER, Jacob, Pvt, Col Samuel Wear, Capt Samuel Bowman, Mtd Inf
TUNIS, William, Pvt, Col Wm Johnson, Capt Andrew Lawson, E TN Drafted Mil
TUNLAP (TUNLEY), John, Pvt, Col Wm Hall, Capt John Kennedy, Inf
TUNLEY, George, Sgt Maj, Col Wm Lillard, Co Commander omitted, E TN Vol Mil
TUNLEY, James, Pvt, Col S Bunch, Capt Jno English, E TN Drafted Mil; joined from Capt Gibbs
TUNNELL, James, Pvt, Col John Brown, Capt Hugh Barton, Regt E TN Mil Inf
TUNNELL, Luther, Pvt, Col John Brown, Capt Hugh Barton, Regt E TN Mil Inf
TUNNING, Robert, Pvt, Col A Loury, Capt George Sarver, Inf
TUNSTALL, Edward, Pvt, Col John Cocke, Capt John Weakley, Inf
TUNSTALL, James, Pvt, Regt Commander omitted, Capt Jos Williams, Mil Cav
TUNSTATE, Thomas, QM, Brig Gen Thomas Johnston, no other information
TUPPER, John, Pvt, Regt Commander omitted, Capt Wm Russell, Mtd Spies
TUR, James M, Pvt, Maj James Porter, Capt Samuel Cowan, Cav
TURBERVILLE, Absolem, Pvt, Col John Brown, Capt John Childs, E TN Vol Mtd Inf
TURBERVILLE, Benjamin, Pvt, Col Thomas H Benton, Capt Thomas H Williamson, Vol Inf
TURBERVILLE, Willis, Pvt, Col Thomas H Benton, Capt Thomas Williamson, Vol Inf
TURBEVILLE, William, Pvt, Col Thomas H Benton, Capt Thomas Williamson, Vol Inf
TURLEY, John, Pvt, Col Thomas H Booth, Capt Vernon, E TN Mil
TURNAGE, George, Pvt, Col Thomas H Benton, Capt George W Gibbs, Vol Inf; deserted for the United State Rifle Regt
TURNAGE, Isaac, Pvt, Col Philip Pipkin, Capt John Robertson, Mil Inf
TURNAGE, Isaac, Pvt, Col Wm Pillow, Capt C E McEwin, Vol Inf
TURNAGE, James, Pvt, Col R H Dyer, Capt Glen Owen, TN Vol Mtd Gunmen
TURNAGE, Thomas, Pvt, Col A Cheatham, Capt James Giddens, Inf
TURNAGE, Thomas, Pvt, Col R H Dyer, Capt Evans, Vol Mtd Gunmen
TURNAGE, Thomas, Pvt, Col T McCrory, Capt Isaac Patton, Mil Inf
TURNAGE, Thres, Pvt, no other information
TURNAGE, William, Pvt, Col R H Dyer, Capt Glen Owen, TN Vol Mtd Gunmen
TURNAGE, William, Pvt, Col Thomas H Benton, Capt C E McEwen, Vol Inf
TURNBALL, William, Pvt, Col Wm Hall, Capt Brice Martin, Vol Inf
TURNBOW, Hugh, Pvt, Col R C Napier, Co Commander omitted, Mil Inf
TURNBOW, Isaac, Pvt, Regt Commander omitted, Capt Hugh Kerr, Mtd Rangers
TURNBULL, William, Pvt, Col Thomas Bradley, Capt Gabriel Martin, Vol Inf
TURNBULL, William, Pvt, Col Wm Hall, Capt Brice Martin, Vol Inf
TURNER, Berryman, Pvt, Maj Gen Wm Carroll, Col James Raulston, Capt Elijah Haynie, Inf
TURNER, Bird, Pvt, Col Thomas H Williamson, Capt Thomas Scurry, Vol Mtd Gunmen; no service performed
TURNER, Caleb, Pvt, Col Wm Y Higgins, Capt Thomas Eldridge, Mtd Gunmen
TURNER, Caleb, Pvt, Maj Wm Russell, Capt Fleman Hodges, Vol Mtd Gunmen
TURNER, Charles, Pvt, Regt Commander omitted, Capt Thomas Gray, Inf
TURNER, Daniel, Pvt, Col Edwin E Booth, Capt John McKamy, E TN Mil
TURNER, Elisha, 2 Cpl, Regt Commander omitted, Capt James Williams, Mil Cav
TURNER, George, Pvt, Col Thos Williamson, Capt Geo Mitchie, 2nd Regt TN Vol Mtd Gunmen
TURNER, George, Pvt, Col Wm Johnson, Capt James Tunnell, E TN Mil
TURNER, George, Pvt, Maj Wm Russell, Capt Geo Mitchie, Vol Mtd Gunmen
TURNER, Hamner, Pvt, Regt Commander omitted, Capt Nathan Farmer, Mtd Riflemen
TURNER, Henry, Pvt, Col Newton Cannon, Capt James Walton, Mtd Riflemen
TURNER, Henry, Pvt, Col S Copeland, Capt Wm Hodges, Inf
TURNER, Henry, Pvt, Lt Col L Hammond, Capt James Tubb, Inf; deserted
TURNER, Howard W, Sgt, Col R H Dyer, Capt Joseph Williams, Vol Mtd Gunmen
TURNER, Howard, Tptr, Regt Commander omitted, Capt Jos Williams, Mil Cav
TURNER, Howel W, Tptr, Col John Coffee, Capt Michael Molton, Cav
TURNER, James, Pvt, Col John Williams, Capt Wm Walker, Mtd Mil
TURNER, James, Pvt, Col Philip Pipkin, Capt Peter Searcy, Mil Inf
TURNER, James, Pvt, Col Samuel Bayless, Capt Brown Jones, E TN Mil
TURNER, James, Pvt, Col Samuel Wear & Col Samuel Bunch, Capt Wm Mitchell, E TN Mtd Inf
TURNER, James, Pvt, Regt Commander omitted, Capt Abner Pearce, Inf
TURNER, Jeffrey, Pvt, Col John Cocke, Capt James Gray, Inf
TURNER, Jesse, Pvt, Col John Brown, Capt John Childs, E TN Vol Mtd Inf
TURNER, Jesse, Pvt, Col John Cocke, Capt James Gray, Inf
TURNER, John M, Sgt, Col Thos Williamson, Capt Robt Moore, Vol Mtd Gunmen; d 1-11-1815
TURNER, John, Pvt, Col A Loury, Capt Geo Sarver, Inf
TURNER, John, Pvt, Col John Alcorn, Capt John Burns, Cav

## Enlisted Men, War of 1812

TURNER, John, Pvt, Col John Coffee, Capt John W Byrne, Cav

TURNER, John, Pvt, Col John Wynne, Capt James Holleman, Inf

TURNER, John, Tptr, Col R H Dyer, Capt Joseph Williams, Vol Mtd Gunmen

TURNER, Joseph, Pvt, Col Wm Pillow, Capt C E McEwen, Vol Inf

TURNER, Joseph, Pvt, Col Wm Pillow, Capt Thos Williamson, Vol Inf

TURNER, Nathan, Pvt, Col Edwin Booth, Capt John McKamey, E TN Mil

TURNER, Nathan, Pvt, Col Samuel Bayless, Capt Branch Jones, E TN Drafted Mil

TURNER, Philip, Pvt, Col John Alcorn, Capt John W Byrns, Cav

TURNER, Philip, Pvt, Col Thos Williamson, Capt Robt Moore, Vol Mtd Gunmen

TURNER, Robert, Pvt, Maj Wm Carroll, Capt Lewis Dillahunty & Capt Daniel M Bradford, Vol Inf

TURNER, Robert, Surgeon Mate, Col Jas Raulston, W TN Mil Inf

TURNER, Samuel, Pvt, Col Thos Benton, Capt James McEwen, Vol Inf

TURNER, Samuel, Tptr, Lt Col Jno Edmonson, Co Commander omitted, Cav

TURNER, Thomas, Pvt, Col P Pipkin, Capt H Newlin, Mil Inf

TURNER, Will, Pvt, Col Jno Coffee, Capt Jas Terrell, Vol Cav

TURNER, William, 1 Cpl, Col S Bunch, Capt Moses, E TN Drafted Inf; transferred to Capt John Hauk's Co

TURNER, William, Cpl, Col R H Dyer, Capt Jos Williams, Vol Mtd Gunmen

TURNER, William, Far, Col Jno Coffee, Capt Jno Baskerville, Cav

TURNER, William, Pvt, Col Jno Coffee, Capt Danl Ross, Mtd Gunmen

TURNER, William, Pvt, Col R C Napier, Capt Saml Ashmore, Mil Inf

TURNER, William, Pvt, Col S Bunch, Capt Jno Houk, E TN Mil; joined from Capt Davis's Co

TURNER, William, Pvt, Col Thos Williamson, Capt Jno Hutchings, Vol Mtd Gunmen

TURNER, William, Pvt, Col Thos Williamson, Capt Thos Scurry, Vol Mtd Gunmen

TURNER, William, Pvt, Col Wm Johnson, Capt Benj Powell, E TN Mil

TURNER, William, Pvt, Col Wm Johnson, Capt H Hunter, E TN Mil

TURNER, William, Pvt, Col Wm Metcalf, Capt B Hurt, Mil Inf

TURNER, William, Pvt, Lt Col A Cheatham, Capt G Martin, Mtd Inf

TURNER, William, Pvt, Lt Col A Cheatham, Co Commander omitted, Mtd Inf

TURNER, William, Pvt, Lt Col Jno Edmonson, Capt Gabriel Martin, Cav

TURNER, Willie, Pvt, Col S Copeland, Capt Moses Thompson, Inf

TURNERY, Larry, Pvt, Lt Col Henry Bryan, Co Commander omitted, Inf

TURNEY, Daniel, Sgt, Col Wm Higgins, Capt Adam Dale, Mtd Gunmen

TURNEY, Henry, Pvt, Col R H Dyer, Capt B Allen, Vol Mtd Gunmen; d 2-28-1815

TURNEY, Henry, Pvt, Col Wm Higgins, Capt Jas Hambleton, Mtd Gunmen

TURNEY, Isaac, Pvt, Col T McCrory, Capt A Metcalf, Mil Inf

TURNEY, Joseph, Pvt, Maj Wm Russell, Capt Geo Mitchie, Vol Mtd Gunmen

TURNEY, Peter, Pvt, Col Wm Higgins, Capt A Dale, Mtd Gunmen; wounded 1-22-1814 and absent

TURNEY, Samuel, Pvt, Col P Pipkin, Capt D Smith, Inf

TURNEY, Samuel, Pvt, Col P Pipkin, Capt Wm Mackey, Mil Inf

TURNHAM, Isaac, Pvt, Gen A Jackson, Capt Hugh Kerr, Mtd Rangers

TURNHAM, Joseph, Pvt, Col S Copeland, Capt Alex Provine, Mil Inf

TURNKEY, John, Pvt, Col Wm Hall, Capt Jno Kennedy, Vol Inf

TURNLEY, George, Sgt Maj, Col Wm Lillard, Capt Z Copeland, E TN Vol Inf

TURNLEY, James, Sgt, Col S Bunch, Capt Geo Gregory, E TN Drafted Mil; promoted from Cpl

TURPIN, Aaron, Dmr, Col Jno Cocke, Capt Geo Barnes, Branch Srvce omitted; d 2-4-1815

TURPIN, Henry, Pvt, Col N Cannon, Capt Jno Demsey, Mtd Gunmen

TURPIN, Henry, Pvt, Col P Pipkin, Capt H Newlin, Mil Inf

TURPIN, Henry, Pvt, Regt Commander omitted, Lt Jos Berry, Mtd Riflemen

TURPIN, Martin, Pvt, Col E Booth, Capt Richd Marshall, Drafted Mil; discharged for inability

TURPIN, Mathew S, Pvt, Maj Wm Russell, Capt I Williams, Separate Bn TN Vol Mtd Gunmen

TUSLER, William, 2 Cpl, Col Wm Lillard, Capt Benj King, E TN Vol Inf

TUSSEY, Jonathan, Pvt, Col Wm Lillard, Capt Geo Keyes, E TN Inf

TUTEN, Obid, Pvt, Col Jno Brown, Capt Wm D Neilson, E TN Vol Mil

TUTEN, Wyley, Cpl, Col Jno Brown, Capt Wm D Neilson, E TN Vol Mil; promoted from a Pvt

TUTEN, Zachariah, Pvt, Col Jno Brown, Capt Wm D Neilson, E TN Vol Mil

TUTT, Michael, Pvt, Col Wm Johnson, Capt Benj Powell, E TN Mil

TUTTLE, David, Pvt, Col Thos Benton, Capt Benj Reynolds, Vol Inf

TUTTLE, Ichabod, Pvt, Gen A Jackson, Capt Jas Reed, Branch Srvce omitted

TWIDWELL, John, 1 Cpl, Maj Gen Wm Carroll, Col Jas Raulston, Capt Robinson, Inf

TWINER, Joseph, Pvt, Col P Pipkin, Capt Wm McKay, Mil Inf

TWITTY, William, Pvt, Col J K Wynne, Capt Jas Holleman, Inf

TWITTY, William, Pvt, Col Robt Steele, Capt Jas Bennett, Mil Inf
TYGART, Hugh, Pvt, Regt Commander omitted, Capt Larkin Ferrill, Mil Inf
TYGART, John, Pvt, Regt Commander omitted, Capt Larkin Ferrell, Inf
TYLER, James, Pvt, Col Wm Hall, Capt Jas Hambleton, Vol Inf
TYLER, Stephen, Pvt, Col Saml Booth, Capt Thos Porter, Drafted Mil
TYNCH, George, Pvt, Col Saml Bunch, Capt Breden, E TN Mil
TYNER, Jesse, Cpl, Col R C Napier, Capt Saml Ashmore, Mil Inf
TYNER, Jesse, Pvt, Col Wm Metcalf, Capt B Hurt, Mil Inf
TYNER, John, Pvt, Gen Andrew Jackson, Capt Nathan Davis, Inf
TYNES, Samuel, Pvt, Col Wm Hale, Capt Jas Hambleton, Vol Inf
TYNES, Samuel, Pvt, Gen Andrew Jackson, Capt Nathan Davis, Inf
TYRE, John M, Pvt, Col N T Perkins, Capt Geo Eliot, Mil Inf
TYRE, Nathaniel, Pvt, Col Wm Lillard, Capt Jno Neatherton, E TN Vol Inf
TYRE, Richard, Pvt, Col N T Perkins, Capt Geo Eliot, Mil Inf
TYRE, Wright, Pvt, Col N T Perkins, Capt Geo Marr, Mtd Vol
TYRE, Wright, Pvt, Col Wm Hall, Capt Jno Wallace, Inf
TYREE, Garland, Pvt, Lt Col L Hammond, Capt Jas Tubb, Inf
TYREE, Jesse, Pvt, Col P Pipkin, Capt David Smith, Inf; deserted
TYREE, John, Pvt, Col J K Wynne, Capt Jas Holleman, Inf
TYREE, John, Pvt, Col R H Dyer, Capt B Allen, Vol Mtd Gunmen
TYREE, John, Pvt, Col S Bunch, Capt Geo Gregory, E TN Drafted Mil
TYREE, John, Pvt, Col S Bunch, Capt Jno English, E TN Drafted Mil
TYRELL, Edmund, Sgt Maj, Col Jno Coffee, TN Vol Cav
TYTUS, George, Pvt, Regt Commander omitted, Capt Robt Evans, Spies
UBANKS, John, Pvt, Col Thos Williamson, Capt Robt Moore, Vol Mtd Gunmen
UMPHRIES, William, Pvt, Col Wm Johnson, Capt Henry Hunter, E TN Mil
UNDERHILL, Daniel, Pvt, Col John Cocke, Capt John Dalton, Inf
UNDERHILL, Samuel, Pvt, Col Edward Bradley, Capt Harry Douglass, Vol Inf
UNDERWOOD, Abner, Regt QM, Col Jno Brown, Regt E TN Vol
UNDERWOOD, Benjamin jr, Pvt, Col Wm Johnson, Capt Jas Stewart, E TN Mil
UNDERWOOD, Benjamin sr, Pvt, Col Wm Johnson, Capt Jas Stewart, E TN Drafted Mil
UNDERWOOD, Britsen, Pvt, Col Wm Johnson, Capt Jas Stewart, E TN Mil
UNDERWOOD, Britton, Pvt, Col Wm Johnson, Capt Jas Stewart, E TN Drafted Mil
UNDERWOOD, Enoch, Pvt, Col Edwin Booth, Capt John Sharp, E TN Mil; d 1-3-1815
UNDERWOOD, George, Pvt, Col John Brown, Capt Wm White, E TN Vol Mtd Inf
UNDERWOOD, George, Pvt, Col Samuel Wear, Capt Samuel Bowman, Mtd Inf
UNDERWOOD, John, Pvt, Brig Gen Thos Johnston, Capt Abraham Allen, Mil Inf
UNDERWOOD, Nimrod, Pvt, Col Wm Johnson, Capt Andrew Lawson, E TN Drafted Mil
UNDERWOOD, Perry, Pvt, Col A Cheatham, Capt Chas Johnson, Inf
UNDERWOOD, Richard, Cpl, Col Sam Bayless, Capt James Landon, E TN Mil
UNDERWOOD, Richard, Pvt, Col Wm Lillard, Capt Benj H King, E TN Vol Inf
UNDERWOOD, Thomas, Pvt, Col John Cocke, Capt John Weakley, Inf
UNDERWOOD, Willis, Pvt, Lt Col Leroy Hammonds, Capt Thos Delaney & Capt Alex Loury, Inf
UPCHURCH, Samuel, Pvt, Col Thos Williamson, Capt Bev Williams, Vol Mtd Gunmen
UPTON, David, Pvt, Col S Copeland, Capt Allen Wilkinson, Mil Inf
UPTON, James, 3 Sgt, Maj Gen Carroll, Col Jas Raulston, Capt Edward Robinson, Inf
UPTON, Jesse, Pvt, Col Wm Johnson, Capt Jas Rogers, E TN Drafted Mil
UPTON, Joseph, Pvt, Col Ed Bradley, Capt Brice Martin, Vol Inf
UPTON, Stephen, Pvt, Maj Gen Carroll, Col Jas Raulston, Capt Wiley Huddleston, Inf
UPTON, William, Pvt, Col Sam Bunch, Col John Williams, Mtd Vol
URGUHART, Neil, Pvt, Maj Wm Woodfolk, CApt Abner Pearce, Inf
USERY, Larkin, Pvt, Col Jno Coffee, Capt John W Byrn, Cav
USHER, John, Pvt, Col John Brown, Capt Lunsford Oliver, E TN Mil
USHER, John, Pvt, Col Saml Bunch, Capt Andrew Breden, E TN Mil; died 4-8-1814
USRY, Phillip, Pvt, Col Wm Metcalf, Capt Obidiah Waller, Mil Inf
USRY, Richard, Pvt, Col Wm Metcalf, Capt Obidiah Waller, Mil Inf; trans from Capt Jackson
USRY, Thomas, Pvt, Col Thos Williamson, Maj Gen Jackson, Capt Robt Steele, Vol Mtd Gunmen
USRY, Warren, Pvt, Col Wm Metcalf, Capt O Waller, Mil Inf
USRY, William, Pvt, Col Thos Williamson, Maj Gen Jackson, Capt Robt Steele, Vol Mtd Gunmen
USSERY, Larkin, Pvt, Col John Coffee, Capt David Smith, Vol Cav
USSERY, William B, Pvt, Col Thos Benton, Capt Geo Gibbs, Vol Inf
USSERY, William, Pvt, Col Thos Benton, Capt Geo Gibbs, Vol Inf
USTLETON, James, Pvt, Col T McCrory, Capt John Reynolds, Mil Inf

## Enlisted Men, War of 1812

USURY, Richard, Pvt, Col Wm Metcalf, Capt John Jackson, Inf; trans to Capt Waller
UTLEY, Seth, Pvt, Regt Commander omitted, Capt Jas Gray, Inf
UTTER, James, Cpl, Col John Brown, Capt John Trimble, E TN Mtd Gunmen
UTTER, Joseph, Pvt, Col Sam Wear, Capt Jas Gillespie, E TN Vol Inf
UTTER, Samuel, Pvt, Col John Brown, Capt John Trimble, E TN Mtd Inf
UTTER, William, Pvt, Col Wear, Capt Jas Gillespie, E TN Vol Inf
UTTINGER, George, Pvt, Col Saml Bayless, Capt Branch Jones, E TN Draft Mil
UTTINGER, Peter, Ffr, Col Saml Bayless, Capt Branch Jones, E TN Draft Mll
UZRA, Hutchens, Pvt, Col Wm Hall, Capt Henry Newland, Inf
UZZELL, Elisha, Pvt, Col N Cannon, Capt Wm Marlin, Mtd Gunmen; trans to Capt Evans Co of Spies
UZZELL, Jourdan, Pvt, Col Jno Coffee, Capt John W Byrns, Cav
VALENTINE, Thomas, Pvt, Col Thos Williamson, Capt Thos Scurry, Vol Mtd Gunmen
VALENTINE, William, Pvt, Col R H Dyer, Capt Joseph Williams, Vol Mtd Gunmen
VALES, John, Pvt, Col Jas Raulston, Capt Henry West, Inf
VALES, Samuel, Pvt, Col Jas Raulston, Capt Henry West, Inf
VALIENT, James, Pvt, Col Wm Higgins, Capt Thos Eldridge, Mtd Gunmen
VALINT (VALUNT?), Robert L, Pvt, Gen Andrew Jackson, Capt Hugh Kerr, Mtd Rangers
VAM, Edmund, Pvt, Col William Lillard, Capt John Neatherton, E TN Vol Inf
VANATTA, Samuel, Pvt, Col W Higgins, Capt Abener Dale, Branch omitted
VANBEBBER, James, Dmr, Col Wm Lillard, Capt Wm Hamilton, E TN Vol Inf; armorer
VANBEBBLER, Isaac, Pvt, Col Wm Lillard, Capt Wm Hamilton, E TN Vol Inf
VANBEBBLER, Jacob, Pvt, Col Wm Lillard, Capt Wm Hamilton, E TN Vol Inf
VANBIBBER, John, Pvt, Col Saml Bayless, Capt John Brock, E TN Mil; died 2-11-1815
VANCE, Daniel, Pvt, Col Saml Bunch, Capt Jos Duncan, E TN Drafted Mil; joined from Capt McNare's Co
VANCE, David G, Asst Wgnmstr, Brig Gen N Taylor, Branch Srvce omitted
VANCE, David, Pvt, Col Saml Bunch, Capt Jno McNare, E TN Mil; trans to Capt Duncan's Co
VANCE, David, Pvt, Col Wm Lillard, Capt Benj H King, E TN Vol Inf
VANCE, Hanns, Pvt, Col Samuel Bayless, Capt Joseph Hale, E TN Mil
VANCE, Jacob, Pvt, Col Wm Hall, Capt John Moore, Vol Inf
VANCE, Robert, Pvt, Col Ewen Allison, Capt Adam Winsell, E TN Drafted Mil
VANCE, Robert, Pvt, Col Samuel Wear, Capt Joseph Calloway, Mtd Inf
VANCE, Samuel, Pvt, Col Philip Pipkin, Capt James Blakemore, Mil Inf
VANCE, Samuel, Pvt, Col Samuel Bunch, Capt S Richardson, E TN Drafted Mil; discharged for inability
VANCE, Samuel, Pvt, Col Samuel Bunch, Capt Saml Richardson, E TN Drafted Mil
VANCE, William K, Sgt, Col John Williams, Capt David G Vance, E TN Mtd Vol
VANCE, William, Pvt, Col John Williams, Capt Wm Walker, Mtd Inf
VANCE, William, Pvt, Col Wm Metcalf, Capt Thos Marks, Mil Inf
VANDEPENTER, Jacob, Cpl, Col Samuel Bunch, Capt John Dobkins, E TN Drafted Mil; discharged for inability
VANDERGRIFF, Jacob, Pvt, Col Wm Johnson, Capt Henry Hunter, E TN Mil
VANDERGRIFF, Jarad, Pvt, Col Samuel Bunch, Capt Jno English, E TN Drafted Mil
VANDERGRIFF, Leonard, Pvt, Col Edwin Booth, Capt Richard Marshall, Drafted Mil
VANDERGRIFF, Leonard, Pvt, Col Samuel Bunch, Capt Jno McNare, E TN Mil
VANDERGRIFT, Jacob, Pvt, Col Ewen Allison, Capt Adam Winsell, E TN Drafted Mil
VANDERPOOL, Abner (Abraham), Pvt, Col Samuel Bayless, Capt John Brock, E TN Mil
VANDERPOOLE, Anthony, Pvt, Col Samuel Wear, Capt John Doak, E TN Vol Inf
VANDERPOOLE, Wincent, Pvt, Col Samuel Wear, Capt John Doak, E TN Vol Inf
VANDERSTATER, John, Sgt, Col Samuel Bayless, Capt James Landen, E TN Mil
VANDERVENTER, Abraham, Pvt, Col Samuel Bayless, Capt James Landen, E TN Mil
VANDUREN, John, 5 Sgt, Col Philip Pipkin, Capt Wm Mackay, Mil Inf
VANDYKE, John, Cpl, Col Samuel Wear, Capt John Chiles, E TN Vol Inf
VANDYKE, Thomas, Hospital Sgt, Brig Gen Geo Doherty, E TN Mil
VANHOEY, John, Pvt, Col T McCrory, Capt A Metcalf, Mil Inf
VANHOOK, Loyd, Pvt, Maj Gen Wm Carroll, Col James Raulston, Capt Edward Robinson, Inf
VANHOOK, Robert, Pvt, Col Wm Hall, Capt Brice Martin, Vol Inf
VANHOOSE, Azor, Pvt, Col Thos Williamson, Capt James Pace, Lt Nealy, Vol Mtd Gunmen
VANHOOSE, Isaac, Dmr, Col Wm Hall, Capt John Kennedy, Vol Inf
VANHOOSE, Isiah, Pvt, Col Jno Coffee, Capt Alexander McKeen, Cav
VANHOOSE, Mathious, Pvt, Col Samuel Bayless, Capt James Churchman, E TN Mil
VANHOOVER, Isaac, Dmr, Col A Loury, Col L Hammonds, Capt Arahel Rains, Inf
VANHOOZER, Valentin, 5 Sgt, Col James Raulston, Capt Chas Wade, Inf
VANHOSER, Jacob, Pvt, Col Philip Pipkin, Capt George

## Enlisted Men, War of 1812

Mebane, Mil Inf; deserted
VANHOZER, William, Pvt, Col Samuel Bunch, Capt Jno Hawk, E TN Mil; joined from Capt Berry's Co
VANHUZER, Squire, Pvt, Maj Wm Woodfolk, Capt Abner Pearce, Inf
VANN, David G, Private Wagon Master, Brig Gen N Taylor, no other information
VANPELT, Jesse, Pvt, Col Edwin Booth, Capt Vernon, Mil Inf
VANSANT, John, Pvt, Col Robert Steele, Capt Jas Bennett, Mil Inf
VANTRESSE, Valentine, Pvt, Col T McCrory, Capt A Metcalf, Mil Inf
VANZAYE, Azow, Pvt, Col Thomas Williamson, Capt Nealy & Capt Pate, Vol Mtd Gunmen
VARMEN, Nehemiah, Pvt, Col John Cocke, Capt Richard Crunk, Inf; detached to the Artif Dept
VARNAIL, Joe, Cpl, Col S Wear, Capt Geo Mitchell, E TN Mtd Inf
VARNAL, William, 1 Cpl, Regt Commander omitted, Capt Jos Williams, Mil Cav
VARNEL, Joseph, Pvt, Regt Commander omitted, Capt William Henderson, Spies
VARNER, George, Pvt, Col Edwin Booth, Capt Geo Winton, E TN Mil; died in service 1-22-1815
VARNER, Jacob, Pvt, Col S Bunch, Capt Jno Houk, E TN Mil; joined from? Capt English Co
VARNER, Jacob, Pvt, Col S Bunch, Capt Moses, E TN Drafted Mil; transferred to Capt John English Co
VARNER, James, Sgt, Col Edwin Booth, Capt George Winton, E TN Mil
VARNER, John, Pvt, Col John Brown, Capt Trimble, E TN Mil Inf
VARNER, John, Pvt, Maj William Russell, Capt John Trimble, Vol Mtd Gunmen
VARNER, Joseph, Pvt, Col N Cannon, Capt Jas Walton, Mtd Riflemen
VARNON, Miles, Pvt, Col Jno Brown, Capt Wm Christian, E TN Mil Inf
VARNON, Thomas, Pvt, Col Jno Brown, Capt Wm Christian, E TN Mil Inf
VARREL, James, Pvt, Col Wm Lillard, Capt Robert McCalpin, E TN Inf
VAUGH, Archibald, Pvt, Col T McCrory, Capt Isaac Patton, Mil Inf; deserted
VAUGH, Archibald, Pvt, Col Wm Metcalf, Capt John Barnhart, Mil Inf
VAUGH, Benjamin, Pvt, Col William Higgins, Capt Thomas Eldridge, Mtd Gunmen
VAUGH, Jacob, Pvt, Col Jno Coffee, Capt Michael Molton, Cav
VAUGH, William, Pvt, Col William Higgins, Capt Thomas Eldridge, Mtd Gunmen
VAUGHN, Allen, Pvt, Col Edwin Booth, Capt Geo Slatton, E TN Mil
VAUGHN, Allen, Pvt, Col Ewen Allison, Capt Loughmiller, Mil; transferred to Capt Griffin Co
VAUGHN, Allen, Pvt, Col S Bunch, Capt Jones Griffin, E TN Drafted Mil; joined from Capt Jones Griffin
VAUGHN, Daniel, Pvt, Lt Col Hammonds, Capt Thomas Wells, Inf
VAUGHN, David, Cpl, Col R C Napier, Capt Edward Neblett, Mil Inf
VAUGHN, David, Cpl, Col Robert Dyer, Capt Robert Edmonston, TN Mtd Gunmen
VAUGHN, Edmond W, Pvt, Col Thomas Williamson, Capt Robert Moore, Vol Mtd Gunmen
VAUGHN, Edmund W, Sgt, Col T McCrory, Capt Isaac Patton, Inf; promoted to Sgt
VAUGHN, Edmund, Pvt, Col Robert Dyer, Maj William Russell, Capt William Russell, Vol Mtd Gunmen
VAUGHN, Elisha, Pvt, Col John Cocke, Capt Geo Barnes, Inf
VAUGHN, Gideon, Pvt, Col Thomas Williamson, Capt Robert Moore, Vol Mtd Gunmen
VAUGHN, Henry, Pvt, Col Robert Dyer, Capt James Wyatt, Vol Mtd Gunmen
VAUGHN, Isaac, Pvt, Col S Bunch, Capt Jno English, E TN Drafted Mil; joined from? Capt Duncan Co
VAUGHN, Jacob, Pvt, Lt Col Jno Edmonson, Co Commander omitted, Cav
VAUGHN, James, Pvt, Col Jno Coffee, Capt Jas Terrell, Vol Cav
VAUGHN, James, Pvt, Col Robt Dyer, Maj William Russell, Capt William Russell, Vol Mtd Gunmen
VAUGHN, James, Pvt, Col Thomas Williamson, Capt Beverly Williams, Vol Mtd Gunmen; d 1-13-1815
VAUGHN, Jesse, Pvt, Col S Bunch, Capt Joseph Duncan, E TN Drafted Mil; transferred to Capt English
VAUGHN, Jesse, Pvt, Col William Lillard, Capt William Gillenwater, E TN Inf
VAUGHN, John M, Pvt, Col William Lillard, Capt George Keys, E TN Inf
VAUGHN, John R, Pvt, Lt Col J Edmondson, Capt Robert Moore, Vol Mtd Gunmen
VAUGHN, John, Pvt, Col S Wear, Capt Joseph Calloway, Mtd Inf
VAUGHN, John, Pvt, Col Wm Metcalf, Capt Hill & Capt Cunningham, Mil Inf
VAUGHN, Paul, Pvt, Col John Coffee, Capt Ezekial Ross, Mtd Gunmen
VAUGHN, Robert, Pvt, Col William Higgins, Capt Stephen Griffith, Mtd Riflemen
VAUGHN, Samuel, Pvt, Col Thomas Williamson, Capt Robert Moore, Vol Mtd Gunmen
VAUGHN, Stephen, Pvt, Col Robert Dyer, Maj William Russell, Capt William Russell, Vol Mtd Gunmen
VAUGHN, Thomas, Cpl, Col Edwin Allison, Capt Jonas Loughmiller, Mil
VAUGHN, Thomas, Sgt, Col Edwin Booth, Capt Geo Slatton, E TN Mil
VAUGHN, William, Cpl, Col Edwin Booth, Capt Geo Slatton, E TN Mil
VAUGHN, William, Pvt, Col Ewin Allison, Capt Jonas Loughmiller, Mil; joined from King, transferred to Capt McPherson
VAUGHN, William, Pvt, Col S Bunch, Capt Geo McPherson, E TN Mil; joined from? Capt Longmiller Co
VAUGHN, William, Pvt, Lt Col A Cheatham, Capt Gabriel Martin, Mtd Inf
VAUGHN, William, Pvt, Lt Col A Cheatham, Co Com-

## Enlisted Men, War of 1812

mander omitted, Mtd Inf
VAULS, William 3 Cpl, Col R T Perkins, Capt Phillip Pipkin, Mtd Riflemen
VAULT, John, Pvt, Col John Cocke, Capt Jas Gault, Inf; died 3-24-1815
VAULX, James, Pvt, Maj Gen A Jackson, Capt Wm Carroll, Vol Inf
VAUN, Archibold, Master Sgt, Col Thos McCrory, no Co Commander, 2 Regt TN Mil
VAUN, David, Pvt, Regt Commander omitted, Capt Jos Williams, Mil Cav
VAUN, Harwell, Pvt, Col A Cheatham, Capt Jas Giddens, Inf
VAUN, Jacob, Pvt, Col Edward Bradley, Capt John Moore, Vol Inf
VAUN, John, Pvt, Col Wm Johnson, Capt Jas R Rogers, E TN Draft Mil
VAUN, Samuel, Pvt, Col Wm Pillow, Capt Geo Caperton, Inf
VEITCH, Amos, Pvt, Col Edwin Booth, Capt Richd Marshall, Drafted Mil
VENABLE, Joseph M, 1 Surgeon Mate, Brig Gen John Coffee, TN Vol Mtd Gunmen
VENABLE, Joseph, Pvt, Col Alexander Loury, Lt Col L Hammond, Capt Thos Wells, Inf
VENABLE, Richard, Pvt, Col Wm Metcalf, Capt Andrew Patterson, Mil Inf; died 3-26-1815
VENABLE, Richard, Sgt, Col Newton Cannon, Capt Andrew Patterson, Mtd Riflemen
VENABLE, Richard, Sgt, Col R H Dyer, Capt Ephraim Dickson, 1 TN Mtd Vol Gunmen
VENABLE, Samuel, Pvt, Col Newton Cannon, Capt Andrew Patterson, Mtd Riflemen
VENABLE, Thomas, Pvt, Col Newton Cannon, Capt Andrew Patterson, Mtd Riflemen
VENATA (VANATA), Christopher, Pvt, Col John Cocke, Capt Jas Gault, Inf
VENDAGE, John, Pvt, Col A Cheatham, Capt Jas Giddens, Inf
VENSANT, Abraham, Pvt, Maj Wm Russell, Capt Geo Mitchie, Vol Mtd Gunmen
VENSANT, Jacob, Pvt, Col Thos Benton, Capt Geo Caperton, Inf
VENTER, John B, Pvt, Col John Cocke, Capt Jas Gray, Inf
VENTERS (VENTRUS), Asa, Pvt, Col Thos Williamson, Capt Anthony Metcalf, Vol Mtd Gunmen
VERKIN (VERHUN), William, Pvt, Col John Cocke, Capt John Weakley, Inf
VERNON, Nehemiah, Pvt, Col John K Wynne, Capt Robt Braden, Inf
VERNON, Solomon, Pvt, Col Wm Johnson, Capt Jas Stewart, E TN Draft Mil
VERNUM, William, Cpl, Col Ewen Allison, Capt Jonas Loughmiller, Mil; trans to Capt Griffin's Co
VEST, James, Pvt, Col Wm Lillard, Capt Jacob Hartsell, E TN Vol Inf
VEST, Robertson, Pvt, Col Newton Cannon, Capt Ota Cantrell, W TN Mtd Inf
VICK, Argentine, Pvt, Col Jas Raulston, Maj Gen Wm Carroll, Capt Edward Robinson, Inf
VICK, John, Pvt, Col Wm Metcalf, Capt John Barnhart,
Mil Inf
VICK, Lewis, Pvt, Col S Copeland, Capt John Dawson, Inf
VICK, Nathan, Pvt, Col R H Dyer, Capt Robt Edmonston, 1 TN Vol Mtd Gunmen
VICK, Pilgrim, Pvt, Col Jas Raulston, Maj Gen Wm Carroll, Capt Edward Robinson, Inf
VICK, Pilgrim, Pvt, Col S Copeland, Capt John Dawson, Inf
VICK, Roland, Pvt, Col Philip Pipkin, Capt John STrother, Mil
VICK, William, Pvt, Lt Col L Hammond, Capt Jas Tubb, Inf
VICKERS, William, Pvt, Col Philip Pipkin, Capt Peter Searcy, Mil Inf
VICKERY, Azle, Pvt, Col Thos McCrory, Capt A Willis, Mil Inf
VICKERY, John, Pvt, Col Thos McCrory, Capt A Willis, Mil Inf
VICKERY, Richard, Pvt, Col Philip Pipkin, Capt John Robertson, Mil Inf
VICKORY, Charles, Pvt, Col Saml Bayless, Capt Branch Jones, E TN Draft Mil
VICKORY, Michael, Pvt, Col Saml Bayless, Capt Branch Jones, E TN Draft Mil
VIMOR, George, Pvt, Regt Commander omitted, Capt N Peoples, Inf
VIMOR, Teard, Pvt, Col Jarmon, Capt N Peoples, Inf
VINCE, William, Pvt, Col John Williams, Capt Wm Walker, Vol
VINCEN, James, Pvt, Col Jas Raulston, Capt James Cowan, Inf
VINCEN, Jurdan, Pvt, Col John K Wynne, Capt John Porter, Inf
VINCENT, Amos, Pvt, Col Wm Y Higgins, Capt Jas Hambleton, Mtd Gunmen
VINCENT, Archibold, Pvt, Col Thos McCrory, Capt Saml B McKnight, Inf
VINCENT, Benjamin G, 4 Cpl, Col Wm Hall, Capt John Wallace, Inf
VINCENT, Berry, Pvt, Col Robt Steele, Capt John Chitwood, Mil Inf
VINCENT, Edmund, Pvt, Col N T Perkins, Capt Geo Eliot, Mil Inf
VINCENT, Francis A, Pvt, Col Ewen Allison, CApt Jos Everett, E TN Mil
VINCENT, James, Pvt, Col John K Wynne, Capt Wm McCall, Inf
VINCENT, Michell, Pvt, Col Wm Hall, Capt John Wallace, Inf
VINCENT, Thomas, Pvt, Col R H Dyer, Maj Wm Russell, Capt Wm Russell, Vol Mtd Gunmen
VINCENT, Thomas, Pvt, Col Wm Lillard, Capt Hugh Martin, E TN Vol Inf
VINCENT, Wilie, Pvt, Regt Commander omitted, Capt Geo Smith, Spies
VINCENT, William, Pvt, Col Thos Williamson, Capt Wm Metcalf, Vol Mtd Gunmen
VINEGAN, George, Pvt, Col Robt Steele, Capt Jas Shinault, Mil Inf
VINERS, John S, Pvt, Col John Cocke, Capt Jas Gray, Inf; died 1-25-1815

## Enlisted Men, War of 1812

VINES, David, Pvt, Col Edwin E Booth, Capt John Slatton, E TN Mil

VINEY, Andrew, Sgt, Col Edwin Booth, Capt Vernon, E TN Mil; died 1-2-1815

VINEYARD, George Pvt, Maj Gen Andrew Jackson, Capt John Crane, Mtd Gunmen

VINEYARD, George, Pvt, Col John Cocke, Capt George Barnes, Inf

VINEYARD, Josiah, Pvt, Col John Cocke, Capt John Weakley, Inf

VINSEN, Edward, Cpl, Col Thos H Williamson, Capt Thos Scurry, Vol Mtd Gunmen

VINSON, Bental, Pvt, Col Thos Williamson, Capt Thos Scurry, Vol Mtd Gunmen

VINSON, Berry, Pvt, Col Wm Metcalf, Capt Obediah Waller, Mil Inf

VINSON, David, Pvt, Col John K Wynne, Capt Wm Caruthers, W TN Inf

VINSON, Henry, Pvt, Col John Cocke, Capt Jas Gray, Inf

VINSON, James, Pvt, Col John Cocke, Capt Jas Gray, Inf

VINSON, John, Pvt, Col R H Dyer, Capt Ephraim Dickson, TN Mtd Vol Gunmen

VINSON, Jordan, Pvt, Col John Wynne, Capt Wm Wilson, Inf; trans to Capt Porter's Co

VINSON, Stokley, Cpl, Col Thos H Williamson, Capt Thos Scurry, Vol Mtd Gunmen

VINSON, William, Pvt, Col Wm Lillard, Capt Jas Lillard, E Tn Inf Vol

VINSON, William, Sgt, Col John Cocke, Capt Geo Barnes, Inf; died 2-18-1815

VINSON, Willie, Cpl, Regt Commander omitted, Capt Geo Smith, Spies

VINVERET, Launcelot, Pvt, Maj Wm Woodfolk, Capt Ezekiel Ross & Capt McCulley, Inf

VINYARD, George, Pvt, Col SAml Bunch, Capt John Houk E Tn Mil; joined from Capt Gregory's Co

VINYARD, George, Pvt, Col Saml Bunch, Capt Geo Gregory, E TN Draft Mll

VINYARD, Issah, Pvt, Col John Cocke, Capt John Weakley, Inf

VINYARD, James, Pvt, Col Saml Wear, Capt Simeon Perry, E TN Vol Inf; deserted

VINYARD, John, Pvt, Col Saml Bunch, Capt S Robertson, E TN Draft Mil

VINYARD, Nicholas, 1 Cpl, Maj John Childs, Capt Danl Price, E TN Vol Mtd Inf

VINYARD, Nicholas, Sgt, Col S Bunch, Capt S Robertson, E TN Draft Mil

VINYARD, William, Pvt, Maj John Childs, Capt Danl Price, E TN Mtd Inf Vol

VIRTIAM, William, Pvt, Col John Cocke, Capt John Weakley, Inf

VISER, John L, Sgt, Col Wm Hall, Capt Jas Hambleton, Vol Inf

VITITO, Thomas, Pvt, Col Wm Lillard, Capt Thos Sharpe, 2 Regt Inf

VIVRETT, Micajah, Pvt, Col Jas Raulston, Capt Chas Wade, Inf

VIZER, John L, Pvt, Lt Col H Bryan, Co Commander omitted, Inf

VIZER, Peter, Pvt, Regt Commander omitted, Capt Jas Hamilton, Branch omitted

VIZER, William, Pvt, Lt Col H Bryan, Co Commander omitted, Inf

VOORHIES, John, Pvt, Col Wm Metcalf, Capt Bird L Hurt, Mil Inf

VORHIES, David, Pvt, Col A Loury, Capt John Looney, W TN Inf

VOSS, William, Pvt, Col R H Dyer, Capt James McMahon, TN Vol Mtd Gunmen

VOWELL, Thomas, Pvt, Col John Brown, Capt Lunsford Oliver, E TN Mil

VYSER, John L, 3 Sgt, Col Edward Bradley, Capt James Hambleton, Vol Inf

VYSER, John L, Pvt, Col Wm Hall, Capt James Hambleton, Vol Inf

VYSER, Peter, Pvt, Col Edward Bradley, Capt James Hambleton, Vol Inf

VYSER, Peter, Pvt, Col Wm Hall, Capt James Hambleton, Branch Srvce omitted

VYSER, William, 3 Cpl, Col Edward Bradley, Capt James Hambleton, Vol Inf

VYSER, William, Pvt, Col Wm Hall, Capt James Hambleton, Vol Inf

WADDELL, David, Pvt, Col Robt Steele, Capt Jones Bennett, Mil Inf

WADDLE, Daniel, Pvt, Col Ewen Allison, Capt Joseph Everett, E TN Mil; deserted

WADDLE, Daniel, Pvt, Col Samuel Bunch, Capt Jones Griffin, E TN Drafted Mil; joined from Capt Everett's Co

WADDLE, David, Pvt, Col Samuel Bayless, Capt James Landen, E TN Mil

WADDLE, John sr, Sgt, Col Ewen Allison, Capt Jonas Loughmiller, Mil

WADDLE, John, Pvt, Col Ewen Allison, Capt Jonas Loughmiller, Mil

WADDLE, John, Pvt, Col Wm Lillard, Capt Geo Keyes, E TN Inf

WADDLE, Robert, Pvt, Col Ewen Allison, Capt Jonas Loughmiller, Mil

WADDLE (WADALE), Amos, Pvt, Maj Gen A Jackson, Col T Williamson, Capt Robt Steele, Vol Mtd Gunmen

WADE, David, Pvt, Col Philip Pipkin, Capt John Strother, Mil; d 11-11-1814

WADE, Edward, Pvt, Lt Col Henry Bryan, Co Commander omitted, Inf

WADE, Hampton, Pvt, Col Jno Williams, Capt Wm Walker, E TN Mtd Vol

WADE, James G, Pvt, Col Philip Pipkin, Capt John Robertson, Mil Inf

WADE, Lawson, Pvt, Col Thos Williamson, Capt Robt Moore, Vol Mtd Gunmen

WADE, Patter, Pvt, no other information

WADE, Peter, Pvt, Col Philip Pipkin, Capt John Strother, Inf; attached to Capt D Smith

WADE, Peter, Pvt, Col Philip Pipkin, Ens Wm Pegram, Det of Capt David Smith Co of W TN Mil

WADE, Richard, Pvt, Col S Roberts, Capt Jno English, E TN Drafted Mil; joined from Davis Co, furloughed for inability

## Enlisted Men, War of 1812

WADE, Robert, Pvt, Brig Gen T Johnston, Capt Allen, Mil Inf

WADE, Walter, Pvt, Col John Alcorn, Capt Wm Locke, Cav

WADKINS, John M, Cpl, Col Jas Raulston, Capt Henry Hamilton, Inf; also under Maj Gen Wm Carroll

WADKINS, John, Pvt, Col Philip Pipkin, Capt John Strother, Mil

WADKINS, Phelip, Sgt, Col Thos Williamson, Capt Robt Moore, Vol Mtd Gunmen; promoted from Cpl

WADKINS, Tedrick, Pvt, Col S Copeland, Capt Moses Thompson, Inf

WADLEY, John, Pvt, Col Edward Bradley, Capt Travis Nash, Vol Inf

WADLY, John, Pvt, Col Wm Hall, Capt Travis C Nash, Inf

WADSWORTH, Thomas, Pvt, Col Wm Metcalf, Capt Wm Mullin, Mil Inf

WAGEL (WAGAL), Adam, Pvt, Col Wm Johnson, Capt Benj Powell, E TN Mil; d 2-12-1815

WAGGONER, A, Pvt, Col Wm Higgins, Capt John Doak, Mtd Riflemen

WAGGONER, David, Pvt, Col Thos Williamson, Capt Richard Tate, Vol Mtd Gunmen

WAGGONER, Frederick, Pvt, Col Ewen Allison, Capt Adam Winsell, E TN Drafted Mil

WAGGONER, George, 3 Sgt, Col Samuel Bunch, Capt J N McNare, E TN Mil

WAGGONER, Henry, Pvt, Col Edwin Booth, Capt John Sharp, E TN Mil

WAGGONER, Jacob, Pvt, Col R H Dyer, Capt Thos Jones, Vol Mtd Gunmen

WAGGONER, Jacob, Pvt, Col Wm Lillard, Capt Benj King, E TN Vol Inf

WAGGONER, Jacob, Pvt, Lt Col Wm Snodgrass, Ens Gregg, Det of Inf of 2nd Regt of E TN Mil Vol

WAGGONER, Jacob, Pvt, Maj Gen A Jackson, Capt John Craine, Mtd Gunmen

WAGGONER, Jesse, Pvt, Col Samuel Bunch, Capt S Richerson, E TN Drafted Mil

WAGGONER, John, Pvt, Col N T Perkins, Capt James McMahon, Mtd Gunmen

WAGGONER, John, Pvt, Col R H Dyer, Capt James McMahon, TN Vol Mtd Gunmen

WAGGONER, John, Pvt, Col Robt Steele, Capt Robt Campbell, Mil Inf; transferred to the Arty Co

WAGGONER, John, Pvt, Col Wm Lillard, Capt Benj H King, E TN Vol Inf

WAGGONER, John, Pvt, Lt Col Wm Snodgrass, Ens Gregg, Det of Inf of 2nd Regt E TN Vol Mil

WAGGONER, John, Pvt, Regt Commander omitted, Capt Joel Parrish, Arty

WAGGONER, Peter, Pvt, Col Edwin Booth, Capt John Sharp, E TN Mil

WAGGONER, Peter, Pvt, Maj Wm Russell, Capt Geo Mitchie, Vol Mtd Gunmen

WAGGONER, Philip, Pvt, Col Philip Pipkin, Capt Wm Mackay, Mil Inf

WAGGONER, Samuel, Pvt, Col Samuel Bayless, Capt Joseph Rich, E TN Inf

WAGGONER, Samuel, Pvt, Col Samuel Bunch, Capt S Richerson, E TN Drafted Mil; discharged for inability

WAGGONER, Solomon, Sgt, Col Newton Cannon, Capt Francis Jones, Mtd Riflemen

WAGGONER, Thomas, Pvt, Col Samuel Bunch, Capt S Richerson, E TN Drafted Mil

WAGGONER, William, Pvt, Col Wm Metcalf, Capt John Barnhart, Mil Inf

WAID, Richard, Pvt, Col Samuel Bunch, Capt Moses, E TN Drafted Mil; transferred to Capt John English Co

WAIGHT, Lemuel, Pvt, Col Newton Cannon, Capt Ota Cantrell, W TN Mtd Inf

WAIR, William, Pvt, Gen Wm Johnston, Capt David Oban, 36th Inf

WAITS, John B, Pvt, Col A Loury, Lt Col L Hammonds, Capt Arahel Rains, Inf

WAITY, Allen, Cpl, Col John Wynne, Capt James Cole, Inf

WAKEFIELD, Charles, Pvt, Col N T Perkins, Capt John Doak, Vol Mtd Gunmen

WAKEFIELD, Henry, Pvt, Col T Williamson, Capt A Metcalf, Vol Mtd Gunmen; d 1-13-1815

WAKEFIELD, William, Pvt, Col S Copeland, Capt Allen Wilkinson, Mil Inf

WALDEN, David, Pvt, Col Jno Coffee, Capt John W Byrn, Cav

WALDEN, James, Pvt, Regt Commander omitted, Capt James Cowan, Mtd Inf

WALDEN, John, Pvt, Col Newton Cannon, Capt Ota Cantrell, W TN Mtd Inf

WALDEN (WALLING), David, Pvt, Col John Coffee, Capt David Smith, Vol Cav

WALDON, William, Pvt, Col John Cocke, Capt Bird Nance, Inf

WALDON, William, Pvt, Col Robt Steele, Capt James Bennett, Mil Inf

WALDROPE, Claibourn, Pvt, Col John Cocke, Capt Geo Barnes, Inf

WALDROPE, Ezekiel, Pvt, Col John Cocke, Capt Samuel M Caruthers, Inf

WALDROPE, Michael, Pvt, Regt Commander omitted, Capt Archibald McKenny, Cav

WALDRUM, John, Pvt, Col James Raulston, Capt Mathew Neale, Inf

WALERS, George, Pvt, Col Wm Johnson, Capt Elihu Milliken, 3rd Regt E TN Mil

WALES, Andrew, Pvt, Lt Col Jno Edmonson, Co Commander omitted, Cav

WALKENS, Isaac, Pvt, Col Wm Lillard, Capt Thos McChristian, E TN Vol Inf

WALKER, Achilles, Pvt, Lt Col Richard Napier, Co Commander omitted, Inf

WALKER, Anderson, Pvt, Col Wm Hall, Capt James Hambleton, Vol Inf

WALKER, Anderson, Pvt, Lt Col Jno Edmonson, Co Commander omitted, Cav

WALKER, Andrew, Pvt, Col A Loury, Capt Geo Sarver, Inf

WALKER, Andrew, Pvt, Col S Copeland, Capt Wm Douglass, Inf

WALKER, Asa, Pvt, Col Philip Pipkin, Capt Peter Searcy,

WALKER, Audley P, Pvt, Col John Brown, Capt James McKamy, E TN Mtd Gunmen
WALKER, Benjamin P, Pvt, Regt Commander omitted, Lt Jesse Bean, Branch Srvce omitted
WALKER, Benjamin, Pvt, Lt Col Richard Napier, Co Commander omitted, Inf
WALKER, Benjamin, Pvt, Regt Commander omitted, Capt Jno Miller, Spies
WALKER, Buckley, Cpl, Col Philip Pipkin, Capt John Robertson, Mil Inf
WALKER, Buckley, Pvt, Col Edward Bradley, Capt John Kennedy, Riflemen
WALKER, Buckner, Pvt, Col Wm Johnson, Capt James Stewart, E TN Mil
WALKER, Chad, Pvt, Col John Cocke, Capt John Weakley, Inf
WALKER, Charles, Cpl, Col Wm Johnson, Capt Elihu Milliken, 3rd Regt E TN Mil; promoted to QM Sgt
WALKER, Charles, Pvt, Col Thos Williamson, Capt Thos Scurry, Vol Mtd Gunmen
WALKER, Charles, Pvt, Lt Col Henry Bryan, Co Commander omitted, Inf
WALKER, Charles, Pvt, Maj Wm Russell, Capt John Trimble, Vol Mtd Gunmen
WALKER, Charles, QM Sgt, Col Wm Johnson, 3rd Regt E TN Drafted Mil
WALKER, Charley, Cpl, Col John Cocke, Capt Samuel M Caruthers, Inf
WALKER, Clayton, Cpl, Col T McCrory, Capt Isaac Patton, Inf
WALKER, Clayton, Pvt, Col A Cheatham, Capt James Giddens, Inf
WALKER, Daley, Pvt, Col Samuel Bunch, Capt N Gibbs, E TN Drafted Mil
WALKER, David, Far, Regt Commander omitted, Capt Edwin S Moore, Riflemen
WALKER, David, Pvt, Col Thos Benton, Capt Isiah Renshaw, Vol Inf
WALKER, David, Pvt, Col Wm Metcalf, Capt John Barnhart, Mil Inf
WALKER, Edward, Far, Col R H Dyer, Capt Bethel Allen, Vol Mtd Gunmen
WALKER, Edward, Pvt, Col Edwin Booth, Capt John Slatton, E TN Mil
WALKER, Elias R, Pvt, Regt Commander omitted, Capt Lane, Mtd Riflemen
WALKER, Elias, Pvt, Col Ewen Allison, Capt John Hampton, Inf
WALKER, Elias, Pvt, Col Jno Walker, Capt David Vance, Mtd Mil
WALKER, Elijah, Pvt, Col Philip Pipkin, Capt Peter Searcy, Mil Inf
WALKER, Elisha, Pvt, Regt Commander omitted, Capt Garrett Lane, Mtd Riflemen
WALKER, Gabriel L, Sgt, Col A Cheatham, Capt Chas Johnson, Inf
WALKER, George, Pvt, Col Edwin Booth, Capt John Sharp, E TN Mil
WALKER, Hance H, Pvt, Col Thos Benton, Capt Robt Cannon, Inf
WALKER, Hardridge, 3 Sgt, Col Wm Hall, Capt James Hambleton, Vol Inf
WALKER, Hugh, Pvt, Col Jno Coffee, Capt Fred Stump, Cav
WALKER, Isah, Pvt, Col Ewen Allison, Capt Wm King, Drafted Mil
WALKER, Israel, Pvt, Col Wm Y Higgins, Capt Thos Eldridge, Mtd Gunmen
WALKER, Jacob, Pvt, Col R C Napier, Capt Drury Adkins, Mil Inf
WALKER, James, Cpl, Lt Col Archer Cheatham, Co Commander omitted, Cav
WALKER, James, Cpl, Lt Col Jno Edmonson, Co Commander omitted, Cav
WALKER, James, Far, Regt Commander omitted, Capt David Smith, Cav
WALKER, James, Pvt, Col Edwin Booth, Capt Alexander Biggs, Inf
WALKER, James, Pvt, Col John Cocke, Capt George Barnes, Inf
WALKER, James, Pvt, Col John Coffee, Capt David Smith, Vol Cav
WALKER, James, Pvt, Col John Coffee, Capt John Byrns, Cav
WALKER, James, Pvt, Col R H Dyer, Capt Joseph Williams, Vol Mtd Gunmen; d 3-28-1815
WALKER, James, Pvt, Col Samuel Bayless, Capt James Churchman, E TN Mil; joined from Capt Milliken's Co
WALKER, James, Pvt, Col Wm Johnson, Capt Elihu Milliken, 3rd Regt E TN Mil; transferred to Capt Churchman's Co
WALKER, James, Pvt, Col Wm Johnson, Capt James Stewart, E TN Drafted Mil
WALKER, James, Pvt, Col Wm Johnson, Capt James Stewart, E TN Mil
WALKER, James, Pvt, Col Wm Lillard, Capt Jacob Dyke, Vol Inf
WALKER, James, Pvt, Maj John Childs, Capt Charles Conway, E TN Mtd Gunmen
WALKER, James, Pvt, Regt Commander omitted, Capt Jas Terrill, Cav
WALKER, James, Pvt, Regt Commander omitted, Capt Jno Gordon, Spies
WALKER, James, Pvt, Regt Commander omitted, Capt Nathan Farmer, Mtd Riflemen
WALKER, James, Sdlr, Col R H Dyer, Capt Robert Edmonston, 1 TN Vol Mtd Gunmen
WALKER, James, Sdlr, Regt Commander omitted, Capt David Smith, Vol Cav
WALKER, James, Sgt, Col A Cheatham, Capt Birdwell, Inf
WALKER, James, Sgt, Col John K Wynne, Capt Bailey Butler, Inf
WALKER, Jeremiah, Pvt, Col Ewen Allison, Capt Jonas Loughmiller, Mil; transferred to Capt McPherson's Co
WALKER, Jeremiah, Pvt, Col Samuel Bunch, Capt Geo McPherson, E TN Mil; joined from Capt Loughmiller Co
WALKER, Jesse, Pvt, Col Edwin Booth, Capt John Slat-

## Enlisted Men, War of 1812

ton, E TN Mil
WALKER, Jesse, Pvt, Col R H Dyer, Capt Joseph Williams, 1st Regt TN Vol Mtd Gunmen
WALKER, Job, 2 Cpl, Col Wm Hall, Capt Travis C Nash, Inf
WALKER, Joel, Pvt, Col John Brown, Capt James McKamy, E TN Mtd Gunmen
WALKER, John B, Pvt, Lt Col Jno Edmonston, Co Commander omitted, Cav
WALKER, John B, Sgt, Col R H Dyer, Capt Cuthbert Hudson, Vol Mtd Gunmen
WALKER, John H, 2 Sgt, Col John Cocke, Capt Samuel Caruthers, Inf
WALKER, John M, Sgt, Regt Commander omitted, Capt D Mason, Cav
WALKER, John O, Pvt, Col Wm Johnson, Capt James Stewart, E TN Mil
WALKER, John S, Pvt, Col Wm Lillard, Capt Jacob Hartsell, E TN Vol Inf
WALKER, John, 1 Sgt, Col Samuel Wear, Capt Simeon Perry, Mtd Inf; promoted from Cpl
WALKER, John, Cpl, Col Edwin Booth, Capt Thos Porter, Drafted Mil
WALKER, John, Pvt, Col John Alcorn, Capt John W Byrns, Cav
WALKER, John, Pvt, Col John K Wynne, Capt Wm Carothers, W TN Inf
WALKER, John, Pvt, Col Philip Pipkin, Capt Peter Searcy, Mil Inf
WALKER, John, Pvt, Col Thos Williamson, Capt Giles Burdett, Vol Mtd Gunmen
WALKER, John, Pvt, Col Wm Hall, Capt James Hambleton, Vol Inf
WALKER, John, Pvt, Col Wm Johnson, Capt James Stewart, E TN Drafted Mil
WALKER, John, Pvt, Col Wm Metcalf, Capt Thomas Marks, Mil Inf
WALKER, John, Pvt, Maj John Childs, Capt James Cummings, E TN Vol Mtd Inf
WALKER, John, Pvt, Maj Wm Russell, Capt George Mitchie, Vol Mtd Gunmen
WALKER, John, Pvt, Maj Wm Russell, Capt Isaac Williams, Separate Bn of Vol Mtd Gunmen
WALKER, John, Pvt, Regt Commander omitted, Capt Garrett Lane, Mtd Riflemen
WALKER, John, Pvt, Regt Commander omitted, Capt Jno Miller, Spies
WALKER, John, Sgt, Col Wm Lillard, Capt Robert McCalpin, E TN Inf
WALKER, John, Sgt, Lt Col Wm Phillips, Co Commander omitted, Inf
WALKER, John, Tptr, Col R H Dyer, Capt Cuthbert Hudson, Vol Mtd Gunmen
WALKER, Joseph, Pvt, Col John Brown, Capt James McKamy, E TN Mtd Gunmen
WALKER, Joseph, Pvt, Col Newton Cannon, Capt John B Demsey, Mtd Gunmen
WALKER, Joseph, Pvt, Col Wm Johnson, Capt Elihu Milliken, 3rd Regt E TN Mil
WALKER, Joseph, Pvt, Maj Gen Wm Carroll, Capt Francis Ellis, Inf

WALKER, Joseph, Pvt, Regt Commander omitted, Capt Robert Evans, Spies
WALKER, Martin D, Pvt, Maj Wm Russell, Capt Isaac Williams, Separate Bn of TN Vol Mtd Gunmen
WALKER, Mathew, Pvt, Col A Cheatham, Capt Richard Benson, Inf
WALKER, Mikajah, Pvt, Col Edwin Booth, Capt John Slatton, E TN Mil
WALKER, Nathaniel, Pvt, Gen Andrew Jackson, Capt Nathan Davis, Inf
WALKER, Noah, Cpl, Col Thomas H Benton, Capt C E McEwen, Vol Inf
WALKER, Noah, Cpl, Col Wm Pillow, Capt C E McEwen, Vol Inf
WALKER, Patterson, Pvt, Col Wm Metcalf, Capt John Barnhart, Mil Inf; d 2-28-1815
WALKER, Philip, Cpl, Col R H Dyer, Capt Ephraim Dickson, TN Vol Mtd Gunmen; promoted from Pvt
WALKER, Philip, Pvt, Regt Commander omitted, Capt Archibald McKinney, Cav
WALKER, Robert M, Pvt, Col Wm Metcalf, Capt John Barnhart, Mil Inf
WALKER, Robert, Pvt, Col Samuel Wear, Capt John Stephens, E TN Vol Inf
WALKER, Robert, Pvt, Col Wm Y Higgins, Capt Stephen Griffith, Mtd Riflemen
WALKER, Samuel R, Tptr, Col John Brown, Capt Archibald McKinney, E TN Mtd Gunmen
WALKER, Samuel S, Pvt, Col John Brown, Capt James McKamy, E TN Mtd Gunmen
WALKER, Samuel, Pvt, Col John Brown, Capt James Standifer, E TN Vol Mtd Mil
WALKER, Samuel, Pvt, Col John Brown, Capt John Trimble, E TN Mtd Gunmen
WALKER, Samuel, Pvt, Col S Bunch, Capt John English, E TN Drafted Mil
WALKER, Samuel, Pvt, Col Wm Johnson, Capt Henry Hunter, E TN Mil; transferred to Stuart Co
WALKER, Samuel, Pvt, Col Wm Johnson, Capt James Stewart, E TN Drafted Mil
WALKER, Samuel, Pvt, Lt Col Leroy Hammons, Capt Thomas Delaney, Inf
WALKER, Samuel, Pvt, Regt Commander omitted, Capt Archibald McKinney, Cav
WALKER, Samuel, Sgt, Col John Alcorn, Capt Robert Jetton, Vol Inf
WALKER, Silvester, Pvt, Col R C Napier, Co Commander omitted, Mil Inf
WALKER, Simeon L, Pvt, Maj Gen Wm Carroll, Capt Francis Ellis, Inf
WALKER, Sylvanus, Pvt, Col Philip Pipkin, Capt Peter Searcy, Mil Inf
WALKER, Thomas, Pvt, Col Edwin E Booth, Capt Alexander Biggs, Inf
WALKER, Thomas, Pvt, Col Philip Pipkin, Capt Peter Searcy, Mil Inf
WALKER, Thomas, Pvt, Col Robert Steele, Capt John Chitwood, Mil Inf
WALKER, Thomas, Pvt, Col Samuel Bayless, Capt Joseph Bacon, E TN Mil

WALKER, Thomas, Pvt, Regt Commander omitted, Lt John Scott, Det of Inf
WALKER, Washington, Pvt, Col T McCrory, Capt Dooly, Inf
WALKER, Wiley, 5 Sgt, Col Philip Pipkin, Capt James Blakemore, Mil Inf
WALKER, William H, Pvt, Col T Johnson, Capt David McKamey, E TN Drafted Mil
WALKER, William, Cpl, Col Philip Pipkin, Co Commander omitted, Mil Inf; also under Capt James Blakemore
WALKER, William, Cpl, Col Wm Metcalf, Capt John Barnhart, Mil Inf; d 1-12-1815
WALKER, William, Pvt, Brig Gen Thomas Johnson, Capt Abraham Allen, Mil Inf
WALKER, William, Pvt, Col A Cheatham, Capt Benj Elliott, Mtd Inf
WALKER, William, Pvt, Col A Cheatham, Capt Charles Johnson, Inf
WALKER, William, Pvt, Col James Allen, Capt Jonas Loughmiller, Mil
WALKER, William, Pvt, Col James Raulston, Capt Daniel Newman, Inf
WALKER, William, Pvt, Col John Cocke, Capt John Weakley, Inf
WALKER, William, Pvt, Col John K Wynne, Capt Wm Caruthers, W TN Inf
WALKER, William, Pvt, Col N T Perkins, Capt John Quarles, Vol Mtd Inf
WALKER, William, Pvt, Col R H Dyer, Capt Thomas White, Vol Mtd Gunmen
WALKER, William, Pvt, Col Robert Steele, Capt John Chitwood, Mil Inf
WALKER, William, Pvt, Col S Bunch, Capt John McNore, E TN Mil
WALKER, William, Pvt, Col Samuel Wear, Capt Rufus Morgan, E TN Vol Inf
WALKER, William, Pvt, Col T McCrory, Capt Isaac Patton, Mil Inf; transferred to Gordon's Spies
WALKER, William, Pvt, Col Thomas H Williamson, Capt George Mitchie, 2nd Regt TN Vol Mtd Gunmen
WALKER, William, Pvt, Col Thomas H Williamson, Capt Thomas Porter, Vol Mtd Gunmen
WALKER, William, Pvt, Col Wm Johnson, Capt David McKamy, E TN Drafted Mil
WALKER, William, Pvt, Col Wm Johnson, Capt James Stewart, E TN Drafted Mil
WALKER, William, Pvt, Col Wm Johnson, Capt James Stewart, E TN Mil
WALKER, William, Pvt, Maj Gen Andrew Jackson, Capt Wm Carroll, Vol Inf
WALKER, William, Pvt, Maj James Porter, Capt Samuel Cowan, Cav
WALKER, William, Pvt, Maj Wm Russell, Capt Joseph Williams, Separate Bn TN Vol Mtd Gunmen
WALKER, William, Pvt, Regt Commander omitted, Capt Jno Crane, Mtd Inf
WALKER, William, Pvt, Regt Commander omitted, Capt John Gordon, Mtd Spies
WALKER, William, Pvt, Regt Commander omitted, Capt Wm Henderson, Spies
WALKER, William, Rank omitted, Maj Wm Russell, Capt George Mitchie, Vol Mtd Gunmen
WALKER, Willis, Cpl, Col R H Dyer, Capt Cuthbert Hudson, Vol Mtd Gunmen; promoted to Sgt
WALKER, _ance H, Sgt, Col Newton Cannon, Capt Wm Martin, Mtd Gunmen; promoted from Cpl, wounded 11-3-1813
WALKER (WARPAR), John, Pvt, Col Samuel Bayless, Capt John Brock, E TN Mil
WALL, Drury, Pvt, Col Thos Williamson, Capt Wm Martin, Vol Mtd Gunmen
WALL, H, Pvt, Col Newton Cannon, Capt Wm Edwards, Regt Command; discharged for inability
WALL, Henry, Pvt, Col Philip Pipkin, Capt John Robertson, Mil Inf
WALL, Henry, Pvt, Regt Commander omitted, Capt Gray, Inf
WALL, Hugh, Pvt, Col Thos Williamson, Capt Thos Scurry, Vol Mtd Gunmen
WALL, John, Pvt, Col Wm Pillow, Capt Isaiah Renshaw, Inf
WALL, Maddleton, Pvt, Col Samuel Bayless, Capt Branch Jones, E TN Drafted Mil
WALL, Scroggin, Pvt, Regt Commander omitted, Lt Jas Berry, Mtd Riflemen
WALLACE, Archibald, Pvt, Col R C Napier, Capt James McMurry, Mil Inf
WALLACE, David, Pvt, Col Jno Brown, Capt Hugh Barton, E TN Mil Inf
WALLACE, David, Pvt, Col R C Napier, Capt Thos Preston, Mil Inf
WALLACE, Davis, Pvt, Col Wm Lillard, Capt Wm McLin, E TN Inf
WALLACE, Ezekiel, Pvt, Col John Coffee, Capt Chas Kavanaugh, Cav
WALLACE, James, Pvt, Col Edward Bradley, Capt John Wallace, Vol Inf
WALLACE, James, Pvt, Col James Raulston, Capt Mathew Neale, Inf
WALLACE, James, Pvt, Col John Brown, Capt John Trimble, E TN Mtd Gunmen
WALLACE, James, Pvt, Col Wm Hall, Capt John Wallace, Inf
WALLACE, Jesse, Pvt, Maj P H Porter, Capt Samuel Cowan, Inf
WALLACE, John, Pvt, Brig Gen T Johnston, Capt Robt Carson, Inf
WALLACE, John, Pvt, Col Jno Brown, Capt Hugh Barton, E TN Mil Inf
WALLACE, John, Pvt, Col John Cocke, Capt James Gray, Inf
WALLACE, John, Pvt, Col John Cocke, Capt Joseph Price, Inf; d 2-16-1815
WALLACE, Jonathan, Pvt, Col Newton Cannon, Capt Thos Yardley, Mtd Riflemen
WALLACE, Jonathan, Sgt, Col Thos Williamson, Capt James Pace, Lt Nealy, Vol Mtd Gunmen
WALLACE, Joseph, Pvt, Col Edward Bradley, Capt John Wallace, Vol Inf
WALLACE, Joseph, Pvt, Col Wm Hall, Capt John Wallace, Inf

## Enlisted Men, War of 1812

WALLACE, Robert B, 3 Sgt, Col Ewen Allison, Capt Joseph Everett, E TN Mil; transferred to Capt McPherson's Co

WALLACE, Robert B, Sgt, Col Samuel Bunch, Capt Geo McPherson, E TN Mil; joined from Capt Everett's Co

WALLACE, Samuel, Pvt, Col A Loury, Capt James Kincaid, Inf

WALLACE, Samuel, Pvt, Col Jno Brown, Capt Hugh Barton, E TN Mil Inf

WALLACE, Samuel, Pvt, Col John Coffee, Capt Alexander McKeen, Cav

WALLACE, Samuel, Pvt, Col N T Perkins, Capt Geo Eliot, Mil Inf; wounded & furloughed 2-7-1814

WALLACE, Samuel, Pvt, Col Thos Williamson, Capt Robt Moore, Vol Mtd Gunmen

WALLACE, Thomas, Pvt, Col John Cocke, Capt Joseph Price, Inf

WALLACE, William jr, Pvt, Col Newton Cannon, Capt Thos Yardley, Mtd Riflemen

WALLACE, William sr, Pvt, Col Newton Cannon, Capt Thos Yardley, Mtd Riflemen

WALLACE, William, Pvt, Col Thos Benton, Capt James McEwen, Vol Inf

WALLACE, William, Pvt, Maj Jas P H Porter, Capt Saml Cowan, E TN Mil Cav

WALLACE, William, Pvt, Maj John Childs, Capt John Stephens, E TN Vol Mtd Inf

WALLEN, Aaron, Pvt, Col Edwin Booth, Capt Alex Biggs, Inf; deserted

WALLEN, Benjamin, Pvt, Gen John Coffee, Co Commander omitted, Mtd Spies

WALLEN, Davis, 6 Cpl, Col Edwin Booth, Capt John Sharp, E TN Mil

WALLEN, Jesse, Pvt, Col L Hammonds, Capt Jas Tubbs, Inf

WALLER, Eli, Pvt, Col Thos Williamson, Capt Robt Moore, Vol Mtd Gunmen

WALLER, John, 6 Cpl, Maj Gen Wm Carroll, Capt Francis Ellis, Inf

WALLER, Richard, Pvt, Col John Cocke, Capt Bird Nance, Inf; enlisted in the regular service

WALLER (WOLLER), William, Pvt, Col Wm Lillard, Capt Geo Keyes, E TN Inf

WALLICE, Isaac, Pvt, Col Philip Pipkin, Capt John Strother, Mil; deserted

WALLICE, James, Pvt, Col Samuel Wear, Capt James Tedford, E TN Vol Inf

WALLICE, Robert, Pvt, Col Jno Brown, Capt James McKamy, E TN Mtd Gunmen

WALLIN, Thomas, Pvt, Col Wm Johnson, Capt Henry Hunter, E TN Mil

WALLING (WALDEN), David, Pvt, Col John Coffee, Capt David Smith, Vol Cav

WALLIS, Adam, Pvt, Col A Loury, Capt Geo Sarver, Inf

WALLIS, David B, Pvt, Col Edwin Booth, Capt Alexander Biggs, Inf; deserted

WALLIS, James, Pvt, Col Thos Benton, Capt James McFerrin, Vol Inf; transferred from Capt Hewett's Co

WALLIS, Levi, Pvt, Col Philip Pipkin, Capt Ebenezer Kirkpatrick, Mil Inf

WALLIS, Richard, Pvt, Col John Cocke, Capt Bird Nance, Inf

WALLIS, Samuel, Pvt, Col Thos Benton, Capt James McFerrin, Vol Inf; transferred from the Cav

WALLIS, Thomas, Pvt, Col John Coffee, Capt Chas Kavanaugh, Cav

WALLIS (WALLACE), John, Pvt, Lt Col L Hammond, Capt Arahel Rains, Inf

WALLS, Burgess, Pvt, Col R C Napier, Capt Edward Neblett, Mil Inf

WALLS, Drury, Pvt, Regt Commander omitted, Lt Jas Berry, Mtd Riflemen

WALLS, Noah, Pvt, Col Thos Williamson, Capt James Pace, Lt Nealy, Vol Mtd Gunmen

WALLS, Richard, Pvt, Lt Col L Hammonds, Capt Jas Tubbs, Inf; enlisted in the regular service

WALLS, Scoggin, Pvt, Regt Commander omitted, Lt Jas Berry, Mtd Riflemen

WALLS, William, Pvt, Col A Cheatham, Capt Chas Johnson, Inf

WALT, Jacob A, Pvt, Col Thos Benton, Capt Wm Moore, Vol Inf

WALT, John A, Pvt, Col Thos Benton, Capt Wm Moore, Vol Inf

WALTER, John, Sdlr, Col Newt Cannon, Capt Jas Walton, Mtd Riflemen

WALTERS, Absolom, Pvt, Col Wm Lillard, Capt John Ruper, E TN Vol Inf; deserted

WALTERS, Joseph, Pvt, Regt Commander omitted, Capt Hugh Kerr, Mtd Rangers

WALTERS, Oliver, Sgt, Regt Commander omitted, Capt Jas Craig, Mil Inf

WALTERS, Thomas, Pvt, Col Thos Benton, Capt Geo Gibbs, Vol Inf

WALTERS, Thomas, Pvt, Lt Col L Hammonds, Capt Jas Tubbs, Inf

WALTERS, William, Pvt, Col Wm Lillard, Capt John Ruper, E TN Vol Inf

WALTHALE, Richard B, Pvt, Regt Commander omitted, Capt D S Deadrick, Arty

WALTHALL, R B, Pvt, Gen Andrew Jackson, Capt D Deadrick, Arty

WALTHALL, Richard, Pvt, Regt Commander omitted, Capt Joel Parrish, Arty

WALTHALL, Thomas B, Pvt, Regt Commander omitted, Capt D Mason, Cav

WALTON, George, Pvt, Maj Wm Russell, Capt Geo Mitchie, Vol Mtd Gunmen

WALTON, Harris, Pvt, Col Ed Bradley, Capt Wm Lauderdale, Vol Inf

WALTON, Harris, Pvt, Col Wm Hall, Capt Wm Alexander, Vol Inf

WALTON, Henry, Pvt, Col Edwin Booth, Capt John Lewis, E TN Mil

WALTON, Ira, Pvt, no other information

WALTON, James, Pvt, Col Edwin Booth, Capt John Lewis, E TN Mil

WALTON, Josiah, 1 Sgt, Col Jno Coffee, Capt John W Byrns, Cav

WALTON, Killis, Pvt, Regt Commander omitted, Capt

## Enlisted Men, War of 1812

Nathan Farmer, Mtd Riflemen
WALTON, Thomas, Pvt, Col A Loury, Lt Col L Hammonds, Capt Thos Wells, Inf
WALTON, William, Pvt, Col N T Perkins, Capt Mathew Patterson, Mtd Vol
WANHAM, Thomas, Pvt, Col Thos Williamson, Capt Thos Porter, Vol Mtd Gunmen; d 2-12-1815
WANTLAND, Marshal, Pvt, Col Wm Lillard, Capt Geo Keyes, E TN Inf
WARD, Anthony, Pvt, Maj Wm Woodfolk, Capt Ezekial Ross & Capt McCully, Inf
WARD, Asa, Pvt, Col John Cocke, Capt Sam Caruthers, Inf
WARD, Benjamin, Pvt, Col John Coffee, Capt Blackman Coleman, Cav
WARD, Benjamin, Pvt, Col S Bunch, Capt Francis Berry, E TN Mil; deserted
WARD, Benjamin, Pvt, Col S Bunch, Capt Geo Gregory, E TN Drafted Mil; transferred to Capt F Perry's Co
WARD, Dickin, Pvt, Col Edward Bradley, Capt Brice Martin, Vol Inf
WARD, Dickin, Pvt, Col Wm Hall, Capt Brice Martin, Vol Inf
WARD, Edward, Pvt, Lt Col Henry Bryan, Co Commander omitted, Inf
WARD, Eli, Pvt, Col Wm Metcalf, Capt Bird Hurt, Mil Inf; d 12-31-1814
WARD, Fleming, Pvt, Maj Gen Jackson, Capt Wm Carroll, Vol Inf
WARD, George, 3 Cpl, Maj Wm Russell, Capt Geo Mitchie, Vol Mtd Gunmen
WARD, Henry R, Artif, Col Thos Williamson, Capt Richard Tate, Vol Mtd Gunmen
WARD, Henry R, Far, Col N T Perkins, Capt Philip Pipkin, Mtd Riflemen
WARD, Henry, Pvt, Col John Cocke, Capt Bird Nance, Inf
WARD, Hezekiah, Pvt, Col R C Napier, Capt Saml Ashmore, Mil Inf
WARD, Isham, Pvt, Maj Wm Russell, Capt Wm Chism, Vol Mtd Gunmen
WARD, James, Pvt, Col R C Napier, Capt Sam Ashmore, Mil Inf
WARD, James, Pvt, Col Robert Steele, Capt Samuel Maxwell, Mil Inf; transferred
WARD, James, Pvt, Col Wm Johnson, Capt Jas Stewart, E TN Drafted Mil
WARD, James, Pvt, Col Wm Metcalf, Capt John Cunningham & Capt Alex Hill, Mil Inf
WARD, Jesse, Pvt, Col Wm Johnson, Capt Jas Stewart, E TN Mil
WARD, Jesse, Pvt, Regt Commander omitted, Lt John Harris, Det of Inf
WARD, John, Pvt, Col R C Napier, Capt Benson, Mil Inf
WARD, John, Pvt, Maj Jno Childs, Capt R Tipton, E TN Vol Mtd Inf; Regt Co - Knox
WARD, Jonathan, Pvt, Col R H Dyer, Capt Jos Williams, 1st Regt Vol Mtd Gunmen
WARD, Labon, Pvt, Col Saml Bunch, Capt Jas Penney, E TN Mtd Inf
WARD, Manoah, Pvt, Maj Wm Woodfolk, Capt Jas Turner, Inf
WARD, Mathew, Pvt, Col N T Perkins, Capt Jno Quarles, Vol Mtd Inf
WARD, Philip, Pvt, Maj Gen Andrew Jackson, Col A Cheatham, Capt Wm Creel, Inf
WARD, Richard, Pvt, Col Wm Johnson, Capt H Hunter, E TN Mil
WARD, Simeon, Pvt, Maj Wm Woodfolk, Capt Abner Pearce, Inf; promoted to Cpl
WARD, Thomas, Pvt, Col Thos Benton, Capt Geo Caperton, Inf
WARD, Thomas, Pvt, Gen A Jackson, Capt Hugh Kerr, Mtd Rangers
WARD, Thomas, Pvt, Regt Commander omitted, Capt Thos Gray, Inf
WARD, William, Pvt, Col E Booth, Capt Jno Lewis, E TN Mil
WARD, William, Pvt, Col J K Wynne, Capt R Bradin, Inf
WARD, William, Pvt, Col Jno Cocke, Capt Jos Price, Inf
WARD, William, Pvt, Col Wm Hall, Capt Jas Hambleton, Vol Inf
WARD, William, Pvt, Maj Wm Russell, Capt F Hodges, Vol Mtd Gunmen
WARDEN, Charley, Pvt, Col Robt Steele, Capt Jas Bennett, Mil Inf
WARDEN, John, Cpl, Col Saml Wear, Capt Jesse Cole, Vol Inf
WARDON, Hugh, Pvt, Col Saml Bayless, Capt S Hendricks, E TN Mil
WARDON, William, Pvt, Col Wm Metcalf, Capt Jno Barnhart, Mil Inf; d 1-12-1815
WARE, Jonathan, Pvt, Col Wm Higgins, Capt Thos Eldridge, Mtd Gunmen
WARE, Robert, Pvt, Col R C Napier, Capt D Adkins, Mil Inf
WARE, William, Pvt, Col Jno Coffee, Capt Alex McKeen, Cav
WARE, William, Pvt, Col P Pipkin, Capt Jas Blakemore, Vol Inf
WARE, William, Pvt, Col Robt Steele, Capt Robt Campbell, Mil Inf
WARFORD, Samuel, Pvt, Col P Pipkin, Capt Jas Blakemore, Mil Inf
WARMACK, David, Pvt, Col Jno Cocke, Capt Jas Gray, Inf
WARMACK, Mahel, Pvt, Col Wm Metcalf, Capt A Patterson, Mil Inf
WARMACK, William, Pvt, Col S Copeland, Capt Jno Biles, Inf
WARMACK, William, Pvt, Col Wm Metcalf, Capt A Patterson, Mil Inf
WARMICK, Werton, Pvt, Col Wm Johnson, Capt Jas Stewart, E TN Mil
WARMOCK, Hiram, Pvt, Regt Commander omitted, Capt Gray, Inf
WARMOCK, John, Pvt, Col J K Wynne, Capt Jas Cole, Inf
WARMOCK, William, Pvt, Col Thos Benton, Capt H Douglass, Vol Inf
WARMUCK, William, Pvt, Col Wm Metcalf, Capt B Collins, Mil Inf
WARNELL, Ricahrd, Pvt, Col Robt Steele, Capt Jas Ben-

## Enlisted Men, War of 1812

WARNER, Mars, Pvt, Col R H Dyer, Capt E Dickson, TN Vol Mtd Gunmen
WARNER, Richard, Pvt, Col R H Dyer, Capt E Dickson, TN Mtd Vol Gunmen
WARNER, William, Pvt, Col N Cannon, Capt A Patterson, Mtd Riflemen
WARNER, William, Pvt, Col R H Dyer, Capt E Dickson, TN Mtd Vol Gunmen
WARNICK, Henry, Pvt, Col Wm Johnson, Capt H Hunter, E TN Mil
WARNICK, Hiram, Pvt, Col R C Napier, Capt Thos Gray, Mil Inf
WARRAN, Michal, Pvt, Col E Allison, Capt Jas King, Drafted Mil; promoted to Cpl
WARREN, Burrell, Pvt, Col Thos Williamson, Capt Wm Martin, Vol Mtd Gunmen
WARREN, Daniel, Pvt, Col Jno Cocke, Capt Geo Caruthers, Inf
WARREN, Daniel, Pvt, Col Jno Coffee, Capt Thos Bradley, Vol Cav
WARREN, Daniel, Pvt, Col Thos Benton, Capt Geo Caperton, Vol Inf; AWOL
WARREN, Daniel, Pvt, Regt Commander omitted, Capt Thos Gray, Inf
WARREN, Edward, Sgt, Col Jno Brown, Capt Wm White, E TN Mil Inf
WARREN, Elisha, Pvt, Col Jas Raulston, Capt Jas Black, Inf
WARREN, Humphrey, Pvt, Maj Wm Russell, Capt Geo Mitchie, Vol Mtd Gunmen
WARREN, Isom, Pvt, Col P Pipkin, Capt P Searcy, Mil Inf
WARREN, Jacob, Cpl, Col E Booth, Capt Jno McKamey, E TN Mil
WARREN, James S, Pvt, Regt Commander omitted, Sgt Jno Patton, Inf
WARREN, James, Pvt, Col Alex Loury, Capt Jas Kincaid, Inf; d 2-3-1815
WARREN, James, Pvt, Col Thos Benton, Capt Jas McFerrin, Vol Inf
WARREN, James, Pvt, Lt Col L Hammond, Capt Thos Wells, Inf
WARREN, Jesse, Cpl, Col Jno Coffee, Capt Thos Bradley, Vol Cav
WARREN, John D, Pvt, Col R H Dyer, Capt Glen Owen, 1st TN Vol Mtd Gunmen
WARREN, John D, Pvt, Col Wm Pillow, Capt C E McEwen, Vol Inf
WARREN, John jr, Pvt, Col A Cheatham, Capt George G Chapman, Inf
WARREN, John sr, Pvt, Col A Cheatham, Capt George Chapman, Inf
WARREN, John, 1 Sgt, Col Samuel Bunch, Capt Wm Jobe, E TN Vol Mtd Inf
WARREN, John, Pvt, Col John Coffee, Capt Thomas Bradley, Vol Cav
WARREN, John, Pvt, Col Philip Pipkin, Capt Peter Searcy, Mil Inf
WARREN, Samuel, 5 Sgt, Col John Cocke, Capt James Gault, Inf
WARREN, Samuel, Pvt, Col John Alcorn, Capt Robert Jetton, Vol Cav
WARREN, Samuel, Pvt, Col John Coffee, Capt Robert Jetton, Cav
WARREN, William, Dmr, Col Thos Benton, Capt James McFerrin, Vol Inf
WARREN, William, Pvt, Col Wm Pillow, Capt John H Anderson, Vol Inf
WARREN, William, Pvt, Lt Col L Hammond, Capt James Craig, Inf
WARREN, Zachariah, 3 Cpl, Col Wm Metcalf, Capt John Cunningham & Capt Alexander Hill, Mil Inf
WARRIN, Daniel, Pvt, Col Thos Benton, Capt George Caperton, Inf
WARRIN, Joseph, Pvt, Col Thos Benton, Capt James McFerrin, Vol Inf; AWOL
WARRIN, Sebert, Pvt, Col Alexander Loury, Capt Gabriel Martin, Inf
WARTERBARGER, Jacob, Pvt, Col Ewen Allison, Capt Henry McCray, E TN Mil
WARTHAM, John, Pvt, Lt Col Henry Bryan, Co Commander omitted, Inf
WARWICK, Weston, Pvt, Col Wm Johnson, Capt James Stewart, E TN Drafted Mil
WASEE, Cherokee, Pvt, Col John Brown, Capt Jesse Rainey, Mtd Gunmen
WASHAM (WORSHAM), Jeremiah, Pvt, Col John Brown, Capt Jesse Rainey, Mtd Gunmen
WASHAM (WORSHAM), Jeremiah, Pvt, Col R H Dyer, Capt James Wyatt, Vol Mtd Gunmen
WASHAM (WORSHAM), William, Pvt, Col R H Dyer, Capt James Wyatt, Vol Mtd Gunmen
WASHBURN, John, Pvt, Col Wm Y Higgins, Capt James Hambleton, Mtd Gunmen
WASHBURN, Lewis, Pvt, Col R H Dyer, Capt Bethel Allen, Vol Mtd Gunmen
WASHBURN, Samuel, Pvt, Col John Coffee, Capt Alexander McKeen, Inf; gone to Georgia
WASHBURN, Samuel, Pvt, Col Thos Benton, Capt Isiah Renshaw, Vol Inf
WASHBURN, Thomas, 3 Sgt, Col Thos Williamson, Capt Giles Burdett, Vol Mtd Gunmen
WASHER, Peter, Pvt, Col Philip Pipkin, Capt John Strother, Mil; deserted
WASHINGTON, James, Cpl, no other information
WASHINGTON, Richard, Pvt, Lt Col Jno Edmonson, Co Commander omitted, Cav
WASHMAN, Joshua, Pvt, Col Samuel Bunch, Capt S Richardson, E TN Drafted Mil
WASHTON, Samuel, Pvt, Col Wm Pillow, Capt Isiah Renshaw, Inf
WASON, Elijah, Pvt, Col Jas Raulston, Capt James Cowan, Inf; d 3-27-1815
WASSAN, Abner G, 3 Sgt, Col John Coffee, Capt James Terrill, Vol Cav
WASSON, Abner G, Sgt Maj, Col John K Wynne, 1st Regt TN Mil
WATERHOUSE, Richard G, Pvt, Col John Williams, Capt Wm Walker, Mtd Mil
WATERS, Alsten, Pvt, Col Wm Metcalf, Capt Thomas Marks, Mil Inf
WATERS, Champly, Pvt, Col Wm Lillard, Capt Thomas

- 515

## Enlisted Men, War of 1812

WATERS, George W, Pvt, Col Wm Metcalf, Capt John Barnhart, Mil Inf
WATERS, George W, Sgt, Col A Cheatham, Capt Birdwell, Inf
WATERS, George, Pvt, Col Thos Williamson, Capt Beverly Williams, Vol Mtd Gunmen
WATERS, John, Pvt, Col Wm Lillard, Capt Thos Sharpe, 2nd Regt Inf
WATERS, Thomas, Pvt, Col Thos Benton, Capt George Gibbs, Vol Inf
WATERS, Thomas, Pvt, Col Wm Hall, Capt Brice Martin, Vol Inf
WATERS, Wilson T, Pvt, Col Edward Bradley, Capt Harry L Douglass, Vol Inf
WATERS, Wilson T, Pvt, Col Thos Williamson, Capt Beverly Williams, Vol Mtd Gunmen
WATIKINS, Archibold, Sgt, Col Newton Cannon, Capt James Walton, Mtd Riflemen
WATKINS, Benjamin, Pvt, Col Wm Johnson, Capt Andrew Lawson, E TN Drafted Mil
WATKINS, Benjamin, Pvt, Maj Gen Wm Carroll, Capt Wiley Huddleston, Inf
WATKINS, Ichabad, Pvt, Col Jarmon, Capt I Hamilton, Inf
WATKINS, Isaac, Pvt, Col William Johnson, Capt Andrew Lawson, E TN Drafted Mil
WATKINS, Isaiah, Pvt, Col Robt Dyer, Capt Joseph Williams, Vol Mtd Gunmen
WATKINS, Jacob, Pvt, Col N T Perkins, Capt Philip Pipkin, Mtd Riflemen
WATKINS, James, 1 Sgt, Col Wm Metcalf, Capt Wm Mullen, Mil Inf
WATKINS, Jesse, Pvt, Col Wm Johnson, Capt Jas Tunnell, E TN Mil
WATKINS, John, Pvt, Col A Cheatham, Capt Richard Benson, Inf
WATKINS, John, Pvt, Maj Gen Carroll, Capt Ellis, Inf
WATKINS, Joseph, 1 Sgt, Col Wm Metcalf, Capt Wm Mullen, Mil Inf
WATKINS, Micajah, Pvt, Col A Loury, Capt J N Williamson, W TN Mil
WATKINS, Micajah, Pvt, Col Leroy Hammonds, Capt J N Williamson, 2 Regt Inf
WATKINS, Milton, Pvt, Col John Alcorn, Capt Winston, Mtd Riflemen
WATKINS, Philip, Pvt, Col Thos Williamson, Capt Robert Moore, Vol Mtd Gunmen
WATKINS, Samuel, 4 Cpl, Col R T Perkins, Capt Phillip Pipkin, Mtd Riflemen
WATKINS, Samuel, 5 Sgt, Col Wm Metcalf, Capt Wm Mullen, Mil Inf
WATKINS, Thomas G, 4 Sgt, Col John Coffee, Capt Blackman Coleman, Cav
WATKINS, Thomas W, Pvt, Col John Alcorn, Capt Wm Locke, Cav
WATKINS, William M, Pvt, Maj Carroll, Capt Dillahunty, Capt Bradford, Branch omitted
WATKINS, William, Pvt, Col Edwin Booth, Capt Porter, Drafted Mil
WATSON, Christopher, Pvt, Col Wm Hall, Capt John Kennedy, Vol Inf; enlisted in U S (service?)
WATSON, David, Pvt, Col Ewen Allison, Capt Wilson, E TN Drafted Mil
WATSON, David, Pvt, Col Thos Benton, Capt Thos Williamson, Vol Inf
WATSON, David, Pvt, Col Wm Metcalf, Capt Hill & Capt Cunningham, Mil Inf; elected 1 Cpl
WATSON, David, Pvt, Col Wm Pillow, Capt Thos Williamson, Vol Inf
WATSON, Elijah, Pvt, Col S Bayless, Capt Jas Landen, E TN Mil
WATSON, George, Pvt, Col Wm Pillow, Co Commander omitted, Vol Inf; died 1-24-1814
WATSON, George, Pvt, Lt Col A Cheatham, Capt Gabriel Martin, Mtd Inf
WATSON, George, Pvt, Lt Col Jno Edmonson, Co Commander omitted, Cav
WATSON, Hardy, Ffr, Col Jas Raulston, Capt Mathew Neal, Inf
WATSON, Henry, Pvt, Col Wm Lillard, Capt Thos Sharpe, Inf
WATSON, James, Pvt, Col John Wynne, Capt Jas Holleman, Inf
WATSON, John, Pvt, Col John Brown, Capt White, E TN Vol Mtd Inf
WATSON, John, Pvt, Col R T Perkins, Capt Phillip Pipkin, Mtd Riflemen
WATSON, John, Pvt, Col Wm Johnson, Capt Wm Alexander, E Tn Drafted Mil
WATSON, John, Pvt, Maj Carroll, Capt Daillahunty & Capt Bradford, Vol Inf
WATSON, Mathew, Pvt, Lt Col A Cheatham, Capt Gabriel Martin, Mtd Inf
WATSON, Peter, Pvt, Col Wm Metcalf, Capt Cunningham & Capt Hill, Mil Inf
WATSON, Samuel, Pvt, Col R C Napier, Capt McMurry, Mil Inf
WATSON, Samuel, Pvt, Col Thos Williamson, CApt A Metcalf, Vol Mtd Gunmen
WATSON, Thomas, Pvt, Col S Bunch, Capt Mann, E TN Vol Mtd Inf
WATSON, William, 3 Cpl, Col S Bunch, Capt Wm Houston, E Tn Vol Mtd Inf
WATSON, William, Pvt, Col Robt Dyer, Capt Jos Williams, Vol Mtd Gunmen
WATT, George A, Pvt, Lt Col L Hammonds, Capt Delaney, Inf
WATT, Pyrham, Pvt, Col John Brown, Capt John Childs, E TN Vol Mtd Inf
WATT, Robert, Pvt, Col R T Perkins, Capt Doak, Vol Mtd Gunmen
WATTER, Thomas, Pvt, Col Wm Hall, Capt Hugh Martin, Vol Inf
WATTERS, Joseph, Pvt, Gen Jackson, Capt Hugh Kerr, Mtd Rangers
WATTS, Adam, Pvt, Col S Bayless, Capt Jonathan Waddle, E TN Mil
WATTS, George William, Cpl, Col Wm Metcalf, Capt John Barnhart, Mil Inf
WATTS, George, Pvt, Col Philip Pipkin, Capt Henry Newlin, Mil Inf; deserted

WATTS, George, Sgt, Col Robert Steele, Capt Wm Russell, Mil Inf
WATTS, James, Pvt, Col R C Napier, Capt McMurry, Mil Inf
WATTS, John, Pvt, Capt Nathan Davis, Lt I Barrett, Inf
WATTS, Lewis, Pvt, Col Edward Bradley, Capt Wm Lauderdale, Vol Inf
WATTS, Lewis, Pvt, Col Jas Raulston, Capt Mathew Neal, Inf
WATTS, Lot, Pvt, Maj Wm Woodfolk, Capt Abner ____, Inf
WATTS, Mason, Pvt, Col Jas Raulston, Capt Mathew Cowan, Inf
WATTS, Mason, Pvt, Col Robt Steele, Capt Saml Maxwell, Mil Inf; deserted
WATTS, Reuben, Pvt, Col Wm Hall, Capt Wm Alexander, Inf
WATTS, Robert, Pvt, Maj Wm Woodfolk, Capt Abner Pearce, Inf
WATTS, Samuel, Pvt, Col Robt Dyer, Capt Jas Wyatt, Vol Mtd Gunmen
WATTS, Solomon, Pvt, Col John Wynne, Capt Porter, Inf
WATTS, Solomon, Pvt, Col Robt Dyer, Capt Jas Wyatt, Vol Mtd Gunmen
WATTS, William, Pvt, Col John Alcorn, Capt Bryans, Cav
WATWOOD, George, 3 Cpl, Col Philip Pipkin, Capt John Strother, Mil; deserted
WATWOOD, John, Pvt, Gen Brig Johnson, Capt Allen, Mil Inf
WATWOOD, John, Pvt, Maj Gen Wm Carroll, Capt Francis Ellis, Inf
WAUMAN (WARMAN), Joseph, Cpl, Col Edwin Booth, Capt Richd Marshall, Drafted Mll
WAY, Nathaniel, Pvt, Col Thos Williamson, Capt Richd Tate, Vol Mtd Gunmen
WAY (WRAY?), James, Pvt, Col R C Napier, Capt Edward Neblett, Mil Inf
WAYLAND, Henry, Sdlr, Col R H Dyer, Capt Jos Williams, Vol Mtd Gunmen
WEAGER, Henry, Pvt, Col Wm Pillow, Capt Isaiah Renshaw, Inf
WEAGER, William, Pvt, Col SAml Bayless, Capt Branch Jones, E TN Draft Mil
WEAKLEY, Benjamin, Pvt, Lt Col Jno Edmonson, Co Commander omitted, Cav
WEAKLEY, Imph, Pvt, Regt Commander omitted, Capt Jos Williams, Mil Cav
WEAKLEY, Joseph, Pvt, Regt Commander omitted, Capt Jos Williams, Mil Cav
WEAKLEY, Robert, Pvt, Col Edward Bradley, Capt Jas Hambleton, Vol Inf
WEAKLEY, Robert, Pvt, Col Wm Hall, Capt Jas Hambleton, Vol Inf
WEAKLEY, Sam, Pvt, Lt Col Jno Edmonson, Co Commander omitted, Cav
WEAKLEY, William, Pvt, Col Philip Pipkin, Capt John Strother, Mil
WEAKS, James, Pvt, Maj Wm Russell, Capt Geo Mitchie, Vol Mtd Gunmen
WEAKS, Solomon, Sgt, Col Newton Cannon, Capt Jas Walton, Mtd Riflemen; died accidentally
WEAR, Benjamin, Pvt, Regt Commander omitted, Capt Jas Cowan, Mtd Inf
WEAR, David, 3 Sgt, Col Wm Lillard, Capt Thos McChristian, E TN Vol Inf
WEAR, George, Pvt, Col Saml Wear, Capt John Bayless, Mtd Inf
WEAR, Hugh, Pvt, Col Ewen Allison, Capt Henry McCray, E TN Mil
WEAR, Hugh, Pvt, Col Saml Wear, Capt Jas Gillespie, E TN Vol Inf
WEAR, Jacob, Pvt, Col Saml Bunch, Capt Jones Griffin, E TN Draft Mll
WEAR, John S, Pvt, Col Saml Wear, Capt John Stephens, E TN Vol Inf
WEAR, John, 2 Sgt, Col Saml Wear, Capt Simeon Perry, Mtd Inf
WEAR, John, Pvt, Col Edwin Booth, Capt Alexander Biggs, Inf; left as Wgnr
WEAR, John, Pvt, Col Jno Brown, Capt Jas Preston, E TN Mil Inf
WEAR, John, Pvt, Col John Alcorn, Capt John Baskerville, Vol Inf; transferred to Capt Speices? Co
WEAR, Samuel, Pvt, Col Saml Wear, Capt Jas Tedford, E Tn Vol Inf
WEAR, Samuel, Pvt, Col Wm Lillard, Capt Thos McChristian, E Tn Vol Inf; wgnr to Co
WEAR, Thomas, Pvt, Col Samuel Wear, Capt James Gillespie, E TN Vol Inf
WEAR, William, Pvt, Col Samuel Wear, Capt John Stephens, E TN Vol Inf
WEAR (WEIR), Samuel, Pvt, Col Saml Bunch, Capt Edward Buchanan, E Tn Mil
WEARE, John, Pvt, Col Edwin Booth, Capt John Sharp, E TN Mil; detailed as Wgnr
WEAS, Samuel, Pvt, Col John Coffee, Capt Alexander McKeen, Cav
WEASE, John, Pvt, Col Samuel Bunch, Capt Geo McPherson, E TN Mil; joined from Capt Wilson's Co
WEASE (WEAR), William, Pvt, Col Samuel Wear, Capt Daniel Price, E TN Vol Inf
WEATHERFORD, Benjamin H, Sgt, Maj Wm Woodfolk, Capt James Turner, Inf
WEATHERFORD, Benjamin, Pvt, Col S Copeland, Capt David Williams, Inf
WEATHERFORD, Helkiah, Pvt, Col A Loury, Capt James Kincaid, Inf
WEATHERFORD, John, Pvt, Regt Commander omitted, Capt Elijah Rushing, Det of Inf
WEATHERFORD, Thomas, Pvt, Col A Loury, Capt James Kincaid, Inf; d 2-20-1815
WEATHERFORD, William, Pvt, Col John Cocke, Capt James Gray, Inf
WEATHERINTON, William, Pvt, Lt Col L Hammond, Capt Thos Wells, Inf; also under Col A Loury
WEATHERLY, Isaiah, Pvt, Col Robt Steele, Capt Robt Campbell, Mil Inf
WEATHERLY, Joseph, Pvt, Col Jas Raulston, Capt Daniel Newman, Inf; killed 12-28-1814
WEATHERSPOON, Harrison, 4 Cpl, Col Philip Pipkin,

Capt Geo Mebane, Mil Inf; deserted
WEATLEY, William, Pvt, Col Wm Hall, Capt John Moore, Vol Inf
WEAVER, Craven, Pvt, Col A Cheatham, Capt Birdwell, Inf
WEAVER, Craven, Pvt, Col Thomas H Williamson, Capt Richard Tate, Vol Mtd Gunmen
WEAVER, Daniel, Pvt, Col William Y Higgins, Capt James Hambleton, Mtd Gunmen
WEAVER, Frederick, Sdlr, Regt Commander omitted, Capt Jos Williams, Mil Cav
WEAVER, Frederick, Tailor, Regt Commander omitted, Capt Isaac Williams, Mil Cav
WEAVER, Hartwell, Pvt, Col R H Dyer, Capt Isaac Williams, Vol Mtd Gunmen
WEAVER, Jacob, Pvt, Col Wm Higgins, Capt Stephen Griffith, Mtd Riflemen
WEAVER, John, Pvt, Col John Cocke, Capt John Dalton, Inf
WEAVER, John, Pvt, Col John Coffee, Capt John Baskerville, Cav
WEAVER, John, Pvt, Col John K Wynnne, Capt William Wilson, Inf; transferred to Capt Caruthers Co
WEAVER, John, Pvt, Col Robert Steele, Capt Richard M Ratton, Mil Inf; promoted to Sgt
WEAVER, Joseph, Pvt, Col John K Wynne, Capt Wm Wilson, Inf
WEAVER, Joseph, Sgt, Col John K Wynne, Capt Wm Carothers, W TN Inf
WEBB, Benjamin, Sgt, Col Edward Bradley, Capt Travis Nash, Vol Inf
WEBB, Boen, Pvt, Col Thomas H Williamson, Capt Isaac Williams, Vol Mtd Gunmen
WEBB, Cornelius, Pvt, Col Newton Cannon, Capt John Hanly, Mtd Riflemen
WEBB, Cornelius, Pvt, Col R H Dyer, Capt James Wyatt, Vol Mtd Gunmen
WEBB, Cornelius, Pvt, Regt Commander omitted, Capt Archibald McKinney, Cav
WEBB, Daniel, Pvt, Col Samuel Bunch, Capt John Inman, E TN Vol Mtd Inf
WEBB, Edward, Pvt, Col John K Wynne, Capt James Cole, Inf; d 12-15-1813
WEBB, Fielding, Pvt, Col John K Wynne, Co Commander omitted, Inf; d 12-25-1813
WEBB, George, Pvt, Col Newton Cannon, Capt Hamby, Mtd Riflemen
WEBB, George, Pvt, Col R H Dyer, Co Commander omitted, Vol Mtd Gunmen
WEBB, Hugh, Pvt, Col Wm Hall, Capt Travis Nash, Inf
WEBB, Hugh, Sgt, Col Thomas Bradley, Co Commander omitted, Vol Inf; promoted from Pvt
WEBB, Jacob, 5 Cpl, Col Wm Metcalf, Capt Andrew Patterson, Mil Inf
WEBB, Jacob, Pvt, Col Philip Pipkin, Capt Strother, Mil Inf
WEBB, Jacob, Pvt, Col S Copeland, Capt Biles, Inf
WEBB, Jacob, Pvt, Col S Copeland, Capt Provine, Mil Inf; transferred to Capt Poelin's Co
WEBB, Jacob, Pvt, Col Wm Y Higgins, Co Commander omitted, Mtd Gunmen
WEBB, Jacob, Pvt, Regt Commander omitted, Capt Alex Provine, Branch Srvce omitted

WEBB, James, 2 Cpl, Regt Commander omitted, Capt S Copeland & Capt Biles, Inf
WEBB, James, Pvt, Col A Cheatham, Capt Benson, Mtd Riflemen
WEBB, James, Pvt, Col Newton Cannon, Capt Andrew Patterson, Mtd Riflemen
WEBB, James, Pvt, Col Newton Cannon, Capt Hamby, Mtd Riflemen
WEBB, James, Pvt, Col R H Dyer, Capt Ephraim Dickson, TN Mtd Vol Gunmen
WEBB, James, Pvt, Col S Bunch, Capt S Richardson, E TN Drafted Mil
WEBB, James, Pvt, Col Thomas Benton, Capt Moore, Vol Inf
WEBB, James, Pvt, Col William Y Higgins, Capt Samuel Allen, Mtd Gunmen
WEBB, James, Pvt, Col Wm Johnson, Capt Benjamin Powell, E TN Mil
WEBB, James, Pvt, Regt Commander omitted, Capt Archibald McKinney, Cav
WEBB, Jesse T, Pvt, Col Philip Pipkin, Capt Ebenezer Kirkpatrick, Mil Inf; deserted
WEBB, Jesse, Pvt, Col Edwin E Booth, Capt Porter, Drafted Mil
WEBB, Jesse, Pvt, Col S Bunch, Capt John Houk, E TN Mil; joined from? Capt Dobbins Co
WEBB, Jesse, Pvt, Col Samuel Bunch, Capt Solomon Dobkins, E TN Mil Drafted; transferred to Capt Houk's Co
WEBB, Jesse, Pvt, Gen Andrew Jackson, Capt Nathan Davis, Inf
WEBB, John B, Cpl, Lt Col L Hammons, Capt A Rains, Inf
WEBB, John P, Pvt, Col Wm Pillow, Capt I Renshaw, Inf; deserted
WEBB, John, 2 Cpl, Col P Pipkin, Capt Jno Strother, Mil
WEBB, John, Pvt, Col E Booth, Capt R Marshall, Drafted Mil; discharged for inability
WEBB, John, Pvt, Col P Pipkin, Capt H Newlin, Mil Inf
WEBB, John, Pvt, Col S Copeland, Capt Jas Tait, Inf
WEBB, John, Pvt, Col Sam'l Bayless, Capt Jas Landen, E TN Mil
WEBB, John, Pvt, Col Wm Hall, Capt Travis Nash, Inf
WEBB, John, Pvt, Maj Jno Childs, Capt R Tipton, E TN Vol Mtd Inf; Regt Co - Knox
WEBB, Joseph, Pvt, Col Ewen Allison, Capt Allen, E TN Mil
WEBB, Joseph, Pvt, Col S Bunch, Capt Dan'l Yarnell, E TN Mil; enlisted in the regular troop
WEBB, Joseph, Pvt, Col Wm Lillard, Capt H Martin, E TN Vol Inf
WEBB, Joseph, Pvt, Col Wm Lillard, Capt Jno Roper, E TN Vol Inf
WEBB, Littleberry, Pvt, Col R C Napier, Capt Richd Benson, Mil Inf
WEBB, Mosby, Sgt, Maj Wm Woodfolk, Capt A Pearce, Inf
WEBB, Richard, Pvt, Col T McCrory, Capt A Willis, Mil Inf
WEBB, Ross, 3 Lt, Col Thos Williamson, Capt Wm Moore, Vol Mtd Gunmen, Res omitted; d 2-23-

## Enlisted Men, War of 1812

1815
WEBB, Ross, Pvt, Col N Cannon, Capt Jno Harpole, Mtd Gunmen
WEBB, Solomon, Pvt, Col Wm Hall, Capt T C Nash, Inf
WEBB, Thomas, Pvt, Col Jno Brown, Capt Chas Lewin, E TN Vol Mtd Inf
WEBB, Thomas, Pvt, Col Saml Wear, Capt Porter, E TN Vol Mtd Inf
WEBB, William, Pvt, Col E Booth, Capt Saml Thompson, Mil
WEBB, William, Pvt, Col J K Wynne, Capt Jas Cole, Inf
WEBB, William, Pvt, Col Saml Bayless, Capt Jas Churchman, E TN Mil; transferred to Capt Milliken's Co
WEBB, William, Pvt, Col Wm Johnson, Capt E Milliken, 3rd Regt E TN Mil; transferred from Capt Churchman's Co
WEBB, William, Pvt, Col Wm Metcalf, Capt Thos Marks, Mil Inf
WEBB, Woodson, Pvt, Maj Wm Woodfolk, Capt E Ross, Inf; also under Capt McCulley
WEBB (WEBBER), Josiah, Pvt, Col Alex Loury, Capt Jas Kincaid, Inf
WEBBER, Bernard, Pvt, Maj Wm Woodfolk, Capt E Ross & Capt McCulley, Inf
WEBBER, Isaiah, Pvt, Maj Wm Woodfolk, Capt E Ross & Capt McCulley, Inf
WEBBER, John, Pvt, Col Alex Loury, Capt Jas Kincaid, Inf
WEBBER, John, Pvt, Col S Copeland, Capt S George, Inf
WEBSTER, John M, Pvt, Col Jno Alcorn, Capt F Stump, Cav; deserted
WEBSTER, Moses, Pvt, Col Wm Metcalf, Capt Jno Barnhart, Mil Inf
WEBSTER, Ratis, Pvt, Col Wm Lillard, Capt Wm Gillenwater, E TN Inf
WEBSTER, Richard, Pvt, Col Saml Wear, Capt E Cole, Vol Inf
WEEDING, Richard, Pvt, Col Wm Lillard, Capt Thos Sharpe, 2nd Regt Inf
WEEKS, Charles, Pvt, Regt Commander omitted, Capt E Rushing, Det of Inf
WEEKS, James jr, Pvt, Col N Cannon, Capt F Jones, Mtd Riflemen
WEEKS, John, Pvt, Col N Cannon, Capt F Jones, Mtd Riflemen
WEEKS, John, Pvt, Maj Gen Wm Carroll, Col Jas Raulston, Capt E Haynie, Inf
WEEKS, Rodes, Pvt, Col N Cannon, Capt Jas Walton, Mtd Riflemen
WEEL, Lewis, Pvt, Regt Commander omitted, Capt L Ferrell, Inf
WEESE, John, Pvt, Col S Bunch, Capt Jno English, E TN Drafted Mil; transferred to Capt Wilson's Co
WEESE (WESE), John, Pvt, Col Wm Johnson, Capt David McKamy, E TN Drafted Mil
WEIR, John, Pvt, Col E Booth, Capt Geo Winton, E TN Mil; d 1-28-1815 in service
WELCH, Benjamin, Pvt, Col A Cheatham, Capt Chas Johnson, Inf
WELCH, Benjamin, Pvt, Col Thos Williamson, Capt Richd Tate, Vol Mtd Gunmen
WELCH, Daniel, Pvt, Col Jno Williams, Capt Jno Williams, E TN Mtd Vol
WELCH, Daniel, Sgt, Regt Commander omitted, Capt Henderson, Spies
WELCH, David, Pvt, Col P Pipkin, Capt P Searcy, Mil Inf
WELCH, Isaac, Pvt, Col R Steele, Capt Saml Maxwell, Mil Inf; deserted
WELCH, James, Pvt, Col P Pipkin, Capt Jno Robertson, Mil Inf
WELCH, James, Pvt, Col Saml Bunch, Capt F Berry, E TN Mil
WELCH, James, Pvt, Col T McCrory, Capt A Metcalf, Mil Inf
WELCH, James, Pvt, Col T McCrory, Capt Wm Metcalf, Mil Inf
WELCH, James, Pvt, Col Wm Metcalf, Capt Thos Marks, Mil Inf
WELCH, James, Pvt, Maj Wm Woodfolk, Capt E Ross & Capt McCulley, Inf
WELCH, John, Cpl, Col Wm Johnson, Capt Jos Scott, E TN Drafted Mil; promoted to Sgt
WELCH, John, Pvt, Col James Raulston, Capt Daniel Newman, Inf
WELCH, John, Pvt, Col Jno Brown, Capt Chas Lewin, E TN Vol Mtd Inf
WELCH, John, Pvt, Col N T Perkins, Capt Jno Doak, Vol Mtd Inf
WELCH, John, Pvt, Col Robt Steele, Capt James Shinault, Mil Inf
WELCH, John, Pvt, Col Samuel Bunch, Capt Henry Stephens, E TN Mtd Inf
WELCH, John, Pvt, Maj Wm Woodfolk, Capt A Dudney & Capt Jno Sutton, Inf; appointed Artif
WELCH, Jonathan, Pvt, Col John Cocke, Capt Samuel Caruthers, Inf; d 2-11-1815
WELCH, Jonathan, Pvt, Regt Commander omitted, Capt Gray, Inf
WELCH, Tanley, Pvt, Col Samuel Bayless, Capt John Brock, E TN Mil
WELCH, Thomas, Pvt, Col A Cheatham, Capt Geo G Chapman, Inf
WELCH, William, Pvt, Col Jas Raulston, Capt Daniel Newman, Inf
WELCH, William, Pvt, Col Thos Williamson, Capt John Doak & Capt John Dobbins, Vol Mtd Gunmen
WELDEN, William, Cpl, Col Samuel Wear, Capt John Stephens, E TN Vol Inf
WELDON, Daniel, Pvt, Col Edwin Booth, Capt John McKamey, E TN Mil
WELDON, William, Pvt, Maj John Childs, Capt John Stephens, E TN Vol Mtd Inf
WELDS, Samuel, Cpl, Col Samuel Wear, Capt Jesse Cole, Vol Inf
WELL, John, Cpl, Col Thos Williamson, Capt Robt Steele, Vol Mtd Gunmen
WELLET, Robert, Pvt, Col Philip Pipkin, Capt Henry M Newlin, Mil Inf
WELLINGTON, Archelous, Pvt, Col Philip Pipkin, Capt John Robertson, Mil Inf
WELLS, Aaron, Pvt, Col Edwin Booth, Capt John Slatton, E TN Mil

## Enlisted Men, War of 1812

WELLS, Andrew W, Pvt, Col Wm Pillow, Capt Thos Williamson, Vol Inf
WELLS, Andrew, Pvt, Col Edwin Booth, Capt Porter, Drafted Mil
WELLS, Andrew, Pvt, Col Samuel Wear, Capt Porter, E TN Vol Mtd Inf
WELLS, Archibald, Pvt, Col Newton Cannon, Capt Ota Cantrell, W TN Mtd Inf
WELLS, Bryant, Pvt, Regt Commander omitted, Capt Archibald McKinney, Cav
WELLS, Burrell, Pvt, Col S Copeland, Capt Wm Hodges, Inf
WELLS, Charles, Cpl, Col Thos Benton, Capt James McFerrin, Vol Inf
WELLS, Charles, Cpl, Col Wm Pillow, Capt James McFerran, Inf; reduced to the ranks
WELLS, Daniel, Pvt, Col Edwin Booth, Capt John Slatton, E TN Mil
WELLS, David, Pvt, Col Jno Coffee, Capt Fred Stump, Cav
WELLS, David, Sgt, Col John Alcorn, Capt Fred Stump, Cav; promoted from Pvt
WELLS, Edmond, Pvt, Col John Coffee, Capt Chas Kavanaugh, Cav
WELLS, Edmund, Sgt, Regt Commander omitted, Capt Archibald McKinney, Cav; promoted from Pvt
WELLS, George, Pvt, Col Samuel Wear, Capt Joseph Calloway, Mtd Inf
WELLS, George, Pvt, Maj John Childs, Capt Reuben Tipton, E TN Vol Mtd Inf; Regt Co - Knox
WELLS, Jacob, Pvt, Col Wm Johnson, Capt James Stewart, E TN Mil
WELLS, John J, Pvt, Col R H Dyer, Capt Isaac Williams, Vol Mtd Gunmen
WELLS, John S, Pvt, Col Samuel Bunch, Capt James Cummings, E TN Vol Mtd Inf
WELLS, John, Pvt, Col Robt Steele, Capt James Randals, Inf
WELLS, John, Pvt, Maj John Childs, Capt Reuben Tipton, E TN Mtd Inf; Regt Co - Jefferson
WELLS, Jonathan, Pvt, Col T McCrory, Capt Chas K Gordon, Inf
WELLS, Joshua S, Cpl, Col Samuel Bayless, Capt Joseph Hale, E TN Mil
WELLS, Lamb (Lemuel), Pvt, Lt Col L Hammond, Capt Thomas Wells, Inf; also under Col A Loury, enlisted Regular Service
WELLS, Roland, Pvt, Regt Commander omitted, Lt John Scott, Det of Inf
WELLS, Samuel, Pvt, Col John Coffee, Capt Chas Cavanaugh, Cav
WELLS, Samuel, Pvt, Regt Commander omitted, Capt Archibald McKinney, Cav
WELLS, Stephen, Pvt, Col John Brown, Capt John Childs, E TN Vol Mtd Inf
WELLS, Thomas F, Pvt, Col Jno Williams, Capt Wm Walker, E TN Mtd Vol
WELLS, Thomas F, Pvt, Col Thos Williams, Capt Wm Walker, Mtd Vol
WELLS, Thomas H, Pvt, Col Robt Steele, Capt John Cheetwood, Mil Inf; transferred to Capt Creel

WELLS, Thomas, Pvt, Col A Loury, Capt J N Williamson, W TN Mil
WELLS, Thomas, Pvt, Lt Col L Hammond, Capt J N Williamson, 2nd Regt Inf
WELLS, Thomas, Pvt, Regt Commander omitted, Capt Archibald McKinney, Cav
WELLS, William H, 3 Cpl, Col John Cocke, Capt John Calton, Inf
WELLS, William H, Pvt, Col John Coffee, Capt Chas Kavanaugh, Cav
WELLS, William, Pvt, Col A Cheatham, Capt Wm Smith, Inf
WELSH, Daniel, Pvt, Col Samuel Bunch, Capt Isaac Williams, Mtd Vol
WELSH, William, Pvt, Col Philip Pipkin, Capt Peter Searcy, Mil Inf
WELTY, John, Pvt, Col Wm Johnson, Capt Christopher Cook, E TN Mil
WELTY, John, Pvt, Col Wm Johnston, Capt Joseph Kirk, Mil
WENDHAM, William, Sgt, Col Jas Raulston, Capt Henry Hamilton, Inf; also under Maj Gen Wm Carroll
WENFORD, Robert, Pvt, Col S Copeland, Capt Wm Hodges, Inf
WENKERS, Aron, Pvt, Col Jno Edmonson, Co Commander omitted, Cav
WENKLE, Daniel, Pvt, Lt Col L Hammond, Capt Thos Wells, Inf
WENOHAM, Sherrod, Pvt, Regt Commander omitted, Capt Gray, Inf
WERAY, James, Pvt, Col Philip Pipkin, Capt William Mackay, Mil Inf
WERE, William, Pvt, Col John Alcorn, Capt Alexander McKeen, Cav
WERMINGTON, Edwin, Pvt, Col Thomas Williamson, Capt Thomas Scurry, Vol Mtd Gunmen
WEST, Absolom, Pvt, Col Wm Johnson, Capt Jas Rogers, E TN Drafted Mil; discharged for inability
WEST, Asa, Pvt, Brig Gen Johnson, Capt Robert Carson, Inf
WEST, Basil, Pvt, Col Jno Coffee, Capt Blackman Coleman, Cav
WEST, Bozelle, Tptr, Col John Alcorn, Capt William Locke, Cav
WEST, Daniel, Pvt, Col Alexander Loury, Co Commander omitted, Inf
WEST, Daniel, Pvt, Col Jas Raulston, Capt Mathew Neale, Inf
WEST, David, 3 Sgt, Col Edward Bradley, Capt Geo Bledsoe, Riflemen
WEST, David, Pvt, Col Wm Hall, Capt Geo Bledsoe, Vol Inf
WEST, George, Pvt, Col Jno Coffee, Capt Michael Molton, Cav
WEST, Irwin, Pvt, Col Robert Steele, Capt Jas Bennett, Mil Inf
WEST, Isaac, Pvt, Col John Wynne, Capt Wm Carothers, W TN Inf; deserted
WEST, Isaac, Pvt, Col T McCrory, Capt A Willis, Mil Inf
WEST, Isaac, Pvt, Lt Col Jno Edmonson, Co Commander omitted, Cav

## Enlisted Men, War of 1812

WEST, Isaac, Pvt, Regt Commander omitted, Capt Nathan Davis, Lt I Barrett, Inf
WEST, Jacob, Pvt, Col Jno Coffee, Capt John Baskerville, Cav
WEST, James, Pvt, Col S Copeland, Capt William Hodges, Inf
WEST, John, Pvt, Col Edward Bradley, Capt John Kennedy, Riflemen
WEST, John, Pvt, Col John Wynne, Capt James Holleman, Inf
WEST, John, Pvt, Maj Gen Carroll, Capt Ellis, Inf
WEST, Logan, Sgt, Brig Gen Thos Washington, Capt Jno Crawford, Mtd Inf
WEST, Moses, Pvt, Col Wm Johnson, Capt Elihu Milliken, E TN Mil
WEST, Robert, Pvt, Col John Alcorn, Capt John Baskerville, Vol Inf
WEST, Samuel, Pvt, Col Jno Coffee, Capt John Baskerville, Cav
WEST, Thomas L, Pvt, Regt Commander omitted, Capt David Mason, Cav
WEST, Thomas, Pvt, Col John Wynne, Capt Robert Braden, Inf
WEST, Thomas, Pvt, Col S Bunch, Capt F Register, E TN Mil
WEST, William, Pvt, Col Edwin Booth, Capt Thompson, Mil
WEST, William, Pvt, Col S Copeland, Capt Thompson, Inf
WEST, William, Pvt, Col William Lillard, Capt Benj King, E TN Vol Inf
WEST, William, Sgt, Col Wm Johnson, Capt Elihu Milliken, E TN Mil
WESTBROOK, Samuel, Pvt, Col R T Perkins, Capt Mathew Patterson, Mtd Vol
WESTBROOK, Wesley, Pvt, Col Wm Metcalf, Capt William Mullen, Mil Inf
WESTERMAN, Charles, Pvt, Regt Commander omitted, Capt Nathan Davis, Lt Isaac Barrett, Inf
WESTERMAN, John W, Pvt, Col Robert Dyer, Capt Joseph Williams, TN Vol Mtd Gunmen
WESTERMAN, John, Cpl, Maj Russell, Capt Williams, Vol Mtd Gunmen
WESTERMAN, William, Pvt, Maj William Russell, Capt William, TN Mtd Gunmen
WESTLY, Henderson, Pvt, Col S Copeland, Capt Geo Evans, Inf; attached to Wgnr
WESTLY, Hugh, Pvt, Col Wm Hall, Capt Henry Newlin, Inf
WESTMORELAND, John, Pvt, Col Wm Hall, Capt John Kennedy, Vol Inf; could not be notified
WESTMORELAND, John, Pvt, Maj Gen Carroll, Capt Wiley Huddleston, Inf
WESTON, Fredrick, Pvt, Col R C Napier, Capt Gray, Mil Inf
WESTON, Jesse, Pvt, Col John Cocke, Capt Gray, Inf
WESTON, John, Pvt, Col William Higgins, Capt James Hamberton, Mtd Gunmen
WESTON, William, Pvt, Col William Lillard, Capt Maloney, E TN Vol Inf
WETHERLY, William, Pvt, Col Wm Johnson, Capt Henry Hunter, E TN Mil
WHALEN, John, Pvt, Col William Pillow, Capt Geo Caperton, Inf
WHALEN, John, Sgt, Col S Bunch, Capt Geo Gregory, E TN Drafted Mil
WHALEY, Alexander, Ffr, Col John Brown, Capt Wm D Neilson, E TN Vol Mil
WHALEY, Elisha, Pvt, Col S Copeland, Capt William Hodges, Inf
WHALEY, Felix, Pvt, Col Newton Cannon, Capt John B Demsey, Mtd Gunmen; transferred to Capt Carother's Co
WHALEY, John, Pvt, Col Edwin Booth, Capt John Winston, E TN Mil
WHALEY, William, Ffr, Regt Commander omitted, Capt Porter & Capt Edwin Booth, Drafted Mil
WHALEY, William, Pvt, Col A Cheatham, Capt William Johnson, Inf
WHALIN, John, Pvt, Col Thos Benton, Capt Geo Caperton, Inf
WHALY, Philip, Pvt, Col John K Wynne, Capt Samuel Carothers, W TN Inf
WHARTON, Archibold, Pvt, Col John K Wynne, Capt James Holleman, Inf; deserted
WHARTON, Archibold, Pvt, Col John K Wynne, Capt Wm Carothers, W TN Inf
WHARTON, David, Cpl, Col R H Dyer, Co Commander omitted, 1st TN Mtd Vol Gunmen
WHATBY, Elijah, Pvt, Col R C Napier, Capt James Gray, Mil Inf
WHEALEY, Middleton, Pvt, Col Wm Johnson, Capt Andrew Lawson, E TN Drafted Mil
WHEARD, Jacob, Pvt, Col Samuel Bunch, Capt Jno English, E TN Drafted Mil
WHEAT, Hazzy, Pvt, Col John Brown, Capt Allen I Bacon, E TN Mil Inf
WHEAT, Josiah, Pvt, Col Wm Y Higgins, Capt Thos Eldridge, Mtd Gunmen
WHEATE, Levy, Pvt, Col Edwin Booth, Capt John McKamey, E TN Mil
WHEATISKA, Cherokee, Pvt, Col John Brown, Capt Jesse G Rainey, Mtd Gunmen
WHEDLEY, John, Pvt, Col R H Dyer, Capt Robt Edmonston, 1st TN Vol Mtd Gunmen
WHEELER, Edward B, Pvt, Col S Copeland, Capt Moses Thompson, Inf
WHEELER, Elijah, Pvt, Col Jas Raulston, Capt James Cowan, Inf
WHEELER, Erasters, Pvt, Maj Wm Carroll, Capt Lewis Dillahunty & Capt Daniel M Bradford, Vol Inf
WHEELER, Greenebery, Pvt, Col Samuel Bunch, Capt David Vance, E TN Mtd Mil; apprentice to David G Vance
WHEELER, John, Pvt, Col John Williams, Capt Samuel Bunch, Mtd Vol
WHEELER, John, Pvt, Col Samuel Wear, Capt Joseph Calloway, Mtd Inf
WHEELER, John, Pvt, Col Wm Johnson, Capt Elihu Milliken, 3rd Regt E TN Mil
WHEELER, Jonathan, Cpl, Col John Brown, Capt John Trimble, E TN Mtd Gunmen

*Enlisted Men, War of 1812*

WHEELER, Jonathan, Cpl, Col Samuel Wear, Capt James Tedford, E TN Vol Inf
WHEELER, Nimrod, Pvt, Maj John Childs, Capt Charles Conway, E TN Mtd Gunmen
WHEELER, William, Pvt, Col Alexander Loury, Lt Col L Hammond, Capt Thomas Delaney, Inf
WHEELER, William, Pvt, Col Ewen Allison, Capt John Hampton, Mil
WHEELER, William, Pvt, Col John Cocke, Capt Samuel Caruthers, Inf
WHEELER, William, Pvt, Col Samuel Wear, Capt John Stephens, E TN Vol Inf
WHEELER, William, Pvt, Maj John Chiles, Capt Reuben Tipton, E TN Vol Mtd Inf; Regt Co - Blount
WHEEMING, Thomas, Pvt, Col Wm Johnson, Capt Christopher Cook, E TN Mil
WHELER, John, Pvt, Col Wm Johnson, Capt Andrew Lawson, E TN Drafted Mil
WHELOCK, Enock, Pvt, Col Samuel Bunch, Capt David G Vance, E TN Mtd Inf
WHERRY, Jonathan, 1 Sgt, Col Newton Cannon, Capt George Brandon, Mtd Riflemen
WHERRY, Simon, Pvt, Col Alexander Loury, Capt George Sarver, Inf
WHESENHUNT, Henry, Pvt, Col Edwin Booth, Capt John Slatton, E TN Mil
WHETLEY, Taylor, Pvt, Col Newton Cannon, Capt James Walton, Mtd Riflemen
WHILBY, John, Pvt, Col A Cheatham, Capt James Giddens, Inf
WHILEHEAR, Robert, Sgt, Lt Col Archer Cheatham, Co Commander omitted, 6th Brig Mtd Inf
WHILY, Briton, Pvt, Col S Copeland, Capt G W Steel, Mil Inf
WHINNERY, Thomas, Pvt, Col Wm Johnson, Capt Joseph Kirk, Mil
WHINNEY, Abraham, Pvt, Capt Nathan Davis, Lt I Barrett, Inf
WHIPPLE, Pray, Pvt, Lt Col A Cheatham, Co Commander omitted, 6th Brig Mtd Inf
WHISING, William, Pvt, Col John Brown, Capt Allen I Bacon, E TN Mil Inf
WHITAEER?, David, Pvt, Col Philip Pipkin, Capt Henry M Newlin, Mil Inf
WHITAKER, Benjamin, Pvt, Col Newton Cannon, Capt John Hanley, Mtd Riflemen
WHITAKER, Burton, Pvt, Col John Coffee, Capt Frederick Stump, Cav
WHITAKER, Burton, Tptr, Regt Commander omitted, Capt Jas Terrill, Cav
WHITAKER, James, Pvt, Lt Col A Cheatham, Capt Benjamin Elliott, 6th Brig Mtd Inf
WHITAKER, John, Pvt, Col S Copeland, Capt David Williams, Inf
WHITAKER, Rice W, Sgt, Col Samuel Bunch, Capt Solomon Dobkins, E TN Drafted Mil
WHITAKER, Samuel, Pvt, Col Alexander Loury, Lt Col L Hammond, Capt Thos Delaney, Inf
WHITAKER, Thomas, Pvt, Col Newton Cannon, Capt John Hanley, Mtd Riflemen
WHITE, Abraham D, Pvt, Col Samuel Wear, Capt Samuel Bayless, Mtd Inf
WHITE, Absolem, Pvt, Col John Brown, Capt James McKamy, E TN Mtd Gunmen; deserted
WHITE, Adam, Pvt, Col Wm Lillard, Capt Jacob Hartsell, E TN Vol Inf
WHITE, Alexander E, Pvt, Col N T Perkins, Capt John Doak, Vol Mtd Gunmen
WHITE, Alexander, Pvt, Col Thos Williamson, Capt John Doak & Capt John Dobbins, Vol Mtd Gunmen
WHITE, Alfred M, Pvt, Col R H Dyer, Capt James McMahon, 1st TN Vol Mtd Gunmen; no service performed
WHITE, Alfred, Pvt, Col Wm Hall, Capt Travis C Nash, Inf
WHITE, Alfred, Pvt, Gen Andrew Jackson, Capt D Deadrick, Arty; appointed Armorer
WHITE, Andrew, Sgt, Col N T Perkins, Capt James McMahan, Mtd Gunmen
WHITE, Arther, Pvt, Col N T Perkins, Capt Mathew Patterson, Mtd Vol
WHITE, Arthur, Pvt, Maj Gen A Jackson, Col Wm Carroll, Vol Inf
WHITE, Arthur, Pvt, Regt Commander omitted, Capt Jas Terrill, Cav
WHITE, Benjamin jr, Pvt, Col Samuel Bunch, Capt Isaac Williams, Mtd Vol
WHITE, Benjamin sr, Pvt, Col Samuel Bunch, Capt Isaac Williams, Mtd Vol
WHITE, Benjamin, Pvt, Col John Brown, Capt James McKamy, E TN Mtd Gunmen
WHITE, Benjamin, Pvt, Col R C Napier, Capt Andrew McCarty, Mil Inf
WHITE, Breant, Pvt, Col John Brown, Capt Wm White, E TN Mil Inf
WHITE, Cain G, Sgt, Col Thos Williamson, Capt John Doak & Capt John Dobbins, Vol Mtd Gunmen; appointed from Cpl
WHITE, Carrol, Pvt, Col Wm Metcalf, Capt Thos Marks, Mil Inf
WHITE, Charles, Pvt, Col Edward Bradley, Capt Wm Lauderdale, Vol Inf
WHITE, Charles, Pvt, Col L Hammond, Capt James Craig, Inf
WHITE, Charles, Pvt, Col R C Napier, Capt Thos Preston, Mil Inf
WHITE, Charles, Pvt, Col Wm Johnson, Capt Benj Powell, E TN Mil
WHITE, Charles, Pvt, Maj Gen A Jackson, Capt Ebenezer Kirkpatrick, Mtd Gunmen
WHITE, Daniel, Pvt, Maj Gen A Jackson, Capt Wm Carroll, Vol Inf
WHITE, David, Pvt, Col Ewen Allison, Capt Thos Wilson, E TN Drafted Mil
WHITE, David, Pvt, Col John Cocke, Capt John Weakley, Inf; d 1-8-1815
WHITE, David, Pvt, Col Samuel Bayless, Capt Jonathan Waddle, E TN Mil
WHITE, Edward, Pvt, Col T McCrory, Capt Wm Dooly, Inf
WHITE, Elisha, Pvt, Col Philip Pipkin, Capt James Blakemore, Mil Inf

## Enlisted Men, War of 1812

WHITE, Elisha, Pvt, Regt Commander omitted, Capt Jas Reed, Inf
WHITE, Fielding L, Pvt, Col John Cocke, Capt Geo Barnes, Inf
WHITE, Fielding, Pvt, Col John Wynne, Capt Robt Bradin, Inf
WHITE, George, Pvt, Col Samuel Bunch, Capt John McKamy, E TN Mil
WHITE, Henry, Pvt, Col R H Dyer, Capt Robt Edmonston, TN Vol Mtd Gunmen; d 1-25-1815
WHITE, Henry, Pvt, Gen Andrew Jackson, Capt Nathan Davis, Inf
WHITE, Holland, Pvt, Col Wm Pillow, Capt C E McEwen, Vol Inf
WHITE, Isaac, Pvt, Col N T Perkins, Capt Mathew Johnston, Mil Inf
WHITE, Isaac, Pvt, Col Samuel Wear, Capt John Stephen, E TN Vol Inf
WHITE, Isaac, Pvt, Col Thos Benton, Capt James McEwen, Vol Inf
WHITE, Isaiah, Pvt, Col Thos Benton, Capt Robt Cannon, Inf
WHITE, Jabez, Sgt, Col Wm Metcalf, Capt John Barnhart, Mil Inf
WHITE, Jacob, Pvt, Col Samuel Bayless, Capt Solomon Hendrix, E TN Mil; reduced from Cpl
WHITE, James H, Pvt, Col Wm Johnson, Capt James Stewart, E TN Drafted Mil
WHITE, James, Pvt, Col Ewen Allison, Capt James Allen, E TN Mil
WHITE, James, Pvt, Col John Cocke, Capt Geo Barnes, Inf
WHITE, James, Pvt, Col Newton Cannon, Capt John B Demsey, Mtd Gunmen
WHITE, James, Pvt, Col Robt Steele, Capt Robt Campbell, Mil Inf
WHITE, James, Pvt, Col S Copeland, Capt John Biles, Inf
WHITE, James, Pvt, Col Thos Williamson, Capt A Metcalf, Vol Mtd Gunmen
WHITE, James, Pvt, Col Wm Johnson, Capt David McKamy, E TN Drafted Mil
WHITE, James, Pvt, Col Wm Lillard, Capt Wm McLin, E TN Inf
WHITE, James, Pvt, Regt Commander omitted, Capt Benj Reynolds, Mtd Rangers
WHITE, James, Pvt, Regt Commander omitted, Capt Jas Craig, Mil Inf
WHITE, James, Sgt, Col T McCrory, Capt Samuel B McKnight, Inf
WHITE, Jeremiah, Pvt, Col Philip Pipkin, Capt David Smith, Inf
WHITE, Jeremiah, Pvt, Col T McCrory, Capt A Metcalf, Mil Inf
WHITE, Jesse, Sgt, Commanders omitted, E TN Mil Inf
WHITE, John L, Pvt, Col J K Wynne, Capt Jno Porter, Inf
WHITE, John L, Pvt, Col N T Perkins, Capt M Patterson, Mtd Vol
WHITE, John L, Pvt, Col Thos Williamson, Capt Jno Doak & Capt Jno Dobbins, Vol Mtd Gunmen
WHITE, John T, Pvt, Col Thos Benton, Capt Benj Reynolds, Vol Inf
WHITE, John, Pvt, Col E Booth, Capt Richd Marshall, Drafted Mil
WHITE, John, Pvt, Col James Raulston, Capt Chas Wade, Inf; d 3-15-1815
WHITE, John, Pvt, Col Jas Raulston, Capt Danl Newman, Inf
WHITE, John, Pvt, Col Jno Alcorn, Capt Jno Baskerville, Vol Inf
WHITE, John, Pvt, Col Jno Brown, Capt Standifer, E TN Vol Mtd Mil
WHITE, John, Pvt, Col Jno Coffee, Capt Jno Baskerville, Cav
WHITE, John, Pvt, Col John Brown, Capt Chas Lewin, E TN Vol Mtd Inf
WHITE, John, Pvt, Col John Brown, Capt James McKamy, E TN Mtd Gunmen
WHITE, John, Pvt, Col N T Perkins, Capt John Doak, Vol Mtd Gunmen
WHITE, John, Pvt, Col S Copeland, Capt Jno Holshouser, Inf
WHITE, John, Pvt, Col Saml Bunch, Capt E Buchanan, E TN Mil
WHITE, John, Pvt, Col Samuel Bayless, Capt Solomon Hendrix, E TN Mil
WHITE, John, Pvt, Col Samuel Bunch, Capt Henry Stephens, E TN Mtd Inf
WHITE, John, Pvt, Regt Commander omitted, Capt Archibald McKinney, Cav
WHITE, John, Pvt, Regt Commander omitted, Capt Geo Smith, Spies
WHITE, Jonah, Pvt, Regt Commander omitted, Capt Archibald McKinney, Cav
WHITE, Jonathan D, 5 Sgt, Col E Booth, Capt Richd Marshall, Drafted Mil
WHITE, Joseph, Pvt, Col Robt Steele, Capt Jas Randals, Inf
WHITE, Joshua, Cpl, Col Wm Metcalf, Capt Jno Barnhart, Mil Inf; d 1-12-1815
WHITE, Joshua, Pvt, Col R H Dyer, Capt C Hudson, Vol Mtd Gunmen
WHITE, Josiah, Pvt, Col Wm Pillow, Capt Jos Mason, Vol Inf
WHITE, Josiah, Pvt, Regt Commander omitted, Capt A McKenney, Cav
WHITE, Lemuel, Pvt, Brig Gen Thos Washington, Capt Jno Crawford, Inf
WHITE, Lewis, Pvt, Col Jno Cocke, Capt Geo Barnes, Inf
WHITE, Lunden, Pvt, Col R C Napier, Capt Thos Preston, Mil Inf
WHITE, Medy, Pvt, Col R H Dyer, Capt C Hudson, Vol Mtd Gunmen
WHITE, Moses, Pvt, Col Saml Wear, Capt Jno Chiles, E TN Vol Inf
WHITE, Moses, Pvt, Regt Commander omitted, Capt Wm Walker & Capt John Williams, Mtd Mil
WHITE, Muse, Pvt, Col Jno Williams, Co Commander omitted, Mtd Vol
WHITE, Nathan, Pvt, Col Thos Williamson, Capt Thos Scurry, Vol Mtd Gunmen
WHITE, Peter, Pvt, Col Saml Wear, Capt Jos Calloway, Mtd Inf

WHITE, Peter, Pvt, Col Wm Johnson, Capt Wm Alexander, E TN Drafted Mil
WHITE, Reese, Pvt, Col P Pipkin, Capt David Smith, Inf
WHITE, Riley, Pvt, Regt Commander omitted, Capt Jas Craig, Mil Inf
WHITE, Robert, Pvt, Col P Pipkin, Capt E Kirkpatrick, Mil Inf
WHITE, Ruse P, Pvt, Col Robt Steele, Capt Jas Randals, Inf
WHITE, Samuel B, Pvt, Col Wm Hall, Capt Martin, Vol Inf; refused to march
WHITE, Samuel W, Sgt, Col Thomas Williamson, Co Commander omitted, 2nd Regt Vol Mtd Gunmen QM Corps
WHITE, Samuel, Pvt, Col J K Wynne, Capt Jas Cole, Inf; deserted
WHITE, Samuel, Pvt, Col Jas Raulston, Capt D Newman, Inf
WHITE, Samuel, Pvt, Col S Copeland, Capt Jno Holshouser, Inf
WHITE, Samuel, Pvt, Col Thos Williamson, Capt A Metcalf, Vol Mtd Gunmen
WHITE, Samuel, Pvt, Regt Commander omitted, Capt Nathan Davis, Lt I Barrett, Inf
WHITE, Samuel, Sgt, Col P Pipkin, Capt David Smith, Mil Inf
WHITE, Samuel, Sgt, Col Robt Steele, Capt Jas Randals, Inf
WHITE, Stephen F, 1 Sgt, Col Wm Hall, Capt T Nash, Inf
WHITE, Stephen, Pvt, Col Jno Alcorn, Capt F Stump, Cav
WHITE, Tery, Pvt, Col Wm Lillard, Capt J Hartsell, E TN Vol Inf
WHITE, Thomas B, Pvt, Col A Cheatham, Capt Jas Giddens, Inf
WHITE, Thomas, Pvt, Col E Booth, Capt Porter, Drafted Mil
WHITE, Thomas, Pvt, Col Saml Wear & Col S Bunch, Capt Wm Mitchell, E TN Mtd Inf
WHITE, Thomas, Pvt, Col Saml Wear, Capt R Morgan, E TN Vol Inf
WHITE, William R, Pvt, Maj John Childs, Capt John Stephens, E TN Vol Mtd Inf
WHITE, William, Aide-De-Camp, Maj Gen Wm Carroll, Co Commander omitted, TN Mil
WHITE, William, Cpl, Col S Bunch, Capt Isaac Williams, E TN Mil
WHITE, William, Pvt, Col John Alcorn, Capt John Winston, Mtd Riflemen
WHITE, William, Pvt, Col John Cocke, Capt Joseph Price, Inf
WHITE, William, Pvt, Col N Cannon, Capt Ota Cantrell, W TN Mtd Inf
WHITE, William, Pvt, Col N T Perkins, Capt Jno Doak, Vol Mtd Gunmen
WHITE, William, Pvt, Col R C Napier, Capt Thos Preston, Mil Inf
WHITE, William, Pvt, Col R H Dyer, Capt C Hudson, Vol Mtd Gunmen
WHITE, William, Pvt, Col Robt Steele, Capt Jas Randals, Inf
WHITE, William, Pvt, Col S Wear, Capt Jno Stephens, E TN Vol Inf
WHITE, William, Pvt, Col Saml Wear, Capt Rufus Morgan, E TN Vol Inf
WHITE, William, Pvt, Col Thos Benton, Capt Geo Caperton, Vol Inf; out of state
WHITE, William, Pvt, Col Wm Johnson, Capt David McKamy, E TN Drafted Mil; deserted
WHITE, William, Pvt, Col Wm Lillard, Capt Robt Maloney, E TN Vol Inf
WHITE, William, Pvt, Lt Col Wm Snodgrass, Ens Gregg, Inf 2nd Regt E TN Vol Mil
WHITE, Willis, Pvt, Col R T Perkins, Capt Philip Pipkin, Mtd Riflemen
WHITE, Willis, Pvt, Col Thos Benton, Capt Robert Moore, Vol Inf
WHITE, Willis, Pvt, Col William Pillow, Capt Robert Moore, Inf
WHITE, Willson, Pvt, Col Wm Metcalf, Capt John Barnhart, Branch Srvce omitted
WHITECOTTON, James, Pvt, Col S Bayless, Capt Joseph Rich, E TN Inf
WHITECOTTON, William, Pvt, Col S Bayless, Capt Joseph Rich, E TN Inf
WHITED, John, 2 Sgt, Col Ewen Allison, Capt Joseph Everett, E TN Mil; transferred to Capt Griffin Co
WHITEFIELD, Anat, Pvt, Col Thos Benton, Capt McFerrin, Vol Inf
WHITEFIELD, Ansil, Pvt, Col William Pillow, Capt Jas McFerrin, Inf
WHITEHEAD, Jacob, Pvt, Col A Cheatham, Capt Wm Johnson, Inf
WHITEHEAD, John, Pvt, Col S Wear, Capt Jesse Cole, Vol Inf
WHITEHEAD, Lazarus, Pvt, Col John Wynne, Capt John Carothers, W TN Inf
WHITEHEAD, Lazarus, Pvt, Col John Wynne, Capt William Wilson, Inf; transferred to Capt Carothers Co
WHITEHEAD, Lazarus, Pvt, Col Robert Dyer, Capt Ephraim Dickson, TN Mtd Vol Gunmen
WHITEHEAD, Robert, Pvt, Col William Higgins, Capt A Cheatham, Mtd Riflemen
WHITEHEAD, Robert, Sgt, Lt Col A Cheatham, Capt Benj Elliott, Mtd Inf
WHITEHEAD, Thomas, Pvt, Col Ewen Allison, Capt Adam Winsell, E TN Drafted Mil
WHITEHEAD, William, Pvt, Col Ewen Allison, Capt Adam Winsell, E TN Drafted Mil
WHITEHEAD, William, Pvt, Col S Bunch, Capt Moses, E TN Drafted Mil
WHITEHOUSE, Asa, Pvt, Gen Jackson, Col A Cheatham, Capt Creel, Inf; transferred to the arty
WHITEKER, Burton, Tptr, Regt Commander omitted, Capt Jas Terrill, Cav
WHITEKER, David, Pvt, Maj Wm Woodfolk, Capt Abner Pearce, Inf
WHITEKER, Thomas, Pvt, Lt Col Hammonds, Capt Delaney, Inf
WHITEMORE, Gower, Pvt, Maj Gen Carroll, Col Jas Raulston, Capt Edward Robertson, Inf; d 1-30-1815
WHITESIDE, Thomas, Pvt, Col John Walker, Capt

## Enlisted Men, War of 1812

Vance, Mtd Mil
WHITESIDY, William, Pvt, Regt Commander omitted, Capt Gray, Inf
WHITFIELD, Ancil, Pvt, Col Thos Benton, Capt McFerrin, Vol Inf
WHITFIELD, Ancil, Pvt, Col Thos Benton, Capt Richard McFerrin, Vol Inf
WHITFIELD, Killebrew, Pvt, Regt Commander omitted, Capt Davis Smith, Cav Vol
WHITFIELD, William, Pvt, Col John Wynne, Capt Bayless Prince, Inf
WHITLEDGE, Thomas, Pvt, Col R C Napier, Capt Edward Neblett, Mil Inf
WHITLEHUNT, Henry, Pvt, Col Wm Lillard, Capt S Copeland, E TN Vol Inf
WHITLEY, Benjamin, Pvt, Col Jas Raulston, Capt Geo Black, Inf
WHITLEY, Joab, Pvt, Col Thomas Williamson, Capt Richard Tate, Vol Mtd Gunmen; d 2-10-1815
WHITLEY, Marcus, Pvt, Col S Copeland, Capt Moses Thompson, Inf
WHITLEY, Samuel, Pvt, Maj William Russell, Capt Mitchell, Vol Mtd Gunmen
WHITLEY, Taylor, Pvt, Maj Wm Woodfolk, Capt Sutton & Capt Dudney, Inf
WHITLEY, Thomas, Pvt, Regt Commander omitted, Capt Askew, Inf
WHITLOCK, Henry M, Pvt, Maj Carroll, Capt Dillahunty & Capt Bradford, Vol Inf
WHITLOCK, James, Pvt, Col Jas Raulston, Capt Geo Black, Inf
WHITLOCK, John, Pvt, Col Wm Johnson, Capt Andrew Lawson, E TN Drafted Mil
WHITLOCK, William, Pvt, Col Jas Raulston, Capt Geo Black, Inf; d 2-5-1815
WHITMORE, Jacob, Cpl, Col S Wear, Capt Doak, E TN Vol Inf
WHITNEY, Aaron, Pvt, Col Jas Raulston, Capt Henry West, Inf
WHITSETT, Absolom, Cpl, Col John Wynne, Capt Porter, Inf
WHITSETT, James, Pvt, Col John Alcorn, Capt William Locke, Cav
WHITSETT, Joseph, Pvt, Col A Cheatham, Capt Wm Smith, Inf; discharged for want of arms
WHITSIBLE, James, Pvt, Col John Coffee, Capt Blackman Coleman, Cav
WHITSON, Abraham, Pvt, Col William Lillard, Capt John Neatherton, E TN Vol Inf
WHITSON, Allen, Pvt, Col Wm Metcalf, Capt Gill & Capt Cunningham, Mil Inf
WHITSON, David, Pvt, Maj John Childs, Capt Chas Conway, E TN Mtd Gunmen
WHITSON, Harrison, Pvt, Col Alexander Loury, Capt Hammonds & Capt Rains, Inf
WHITSON, James, Pvt, Regt Commander omitted, Capt Jas Terrill, Cav
WHITSON, Jeremiah, Pvt, Col John Brown, Capt John Childs, E TN Vol Mtd Inf
WHITSON, Jesse, Pvt, Col Ewen Allison, Capt Adam Winsell, E TN Drafted Mil
WHITSON, John, Pvt, Col S Copeland, Capt G W Stell, Mil Inf
WHITSON, John, Pvt, Maj Wm Woodfolk, Capt Arahel Ross & Capt McCully, Inf
WHITSON, Joseph, Pvt, Col Wm Higgins, Capt John Doake, Mtd Riflemen
WHITSON, Thomas, Pvt, Col N T Perkins, Capt James McMahan, Mtd Inf
WHITSON, Thomas, Pvt, Col Wm Lillard, Capt Jacob Hartsell, E TN Vol Inf; discharged at Knoxville, unfit for duty
WHITSON, William H, Pvt, Col John Coffee, Capt Blackman Coleman, Cav
WHITSON, William, Pvt, Col John Alcorn, Capt William Locke, Cav
WHITSON, William, Pvt, Col William Lillard, Capt Jacob Hartsell, E TN Vol Inf
WHITSON, William, Pvt, Regt Commander omitted, Capt Jas Terrell, Cav
WHITTEN, Archibald, Pvt, Col S Bunch, Capt Jno Hawk, E TN Mil
WHITTEN, Elijah, Pvt, Col Wm Johnson, Capt James Tunnell, 3rd Regt E TN Mil; promoted to Cpl, d 11-21-1814
WHITTENBARGAR, Daniel, Pvt, Col Samuel Bunch, Capt Joseph Duncan, E TN Drafted Mil
WHITTENBARGER, Mathew, Sgt, Col Samuel Wear, Capt James Gillespie, E TN Vol Inf
WHITTIKER, Thomas, Pvt, Col Wm Johnson, Capt Andrew Lawson, E TN Drafted Mil
WHITTINGTON, Azariah, Pvt, Col Jas Raulston, Capt Mathew Neale, Inf
WHITTINGTON, Joseph, Pvt, Col Jas Raulston, Capt Mathew Neale, Inf
WHITTLE, George, Pvt, Col Samuel Wear, Capt Simeon Perry, E TN Vol Mtd Inf
WHITTLE, John, Pvt, Col Samuel Wear, Capt Simeon Perry, E TN Vol Mtd Inf
WHITTLE, Ninion, Pvt, Col John Cocke, Capt Geo Barnes, Inf
WHITTLE, Robert, Pvt, Col Jno Coffee, Capt Robt Jetton, Cav
WHITTOCK, Henry M, 1 Cpl, Col John Cocke, Capt John Dalton, Inf
WHITTON, Ambros, Pvt, Col Philip Pipkin, Capt Geo Mebane, Mil Inf
WHITTON, Elijah, Pvt, Col Wm Johnson, Capt James Tunnell, E TN Mil; reduced from Cpl
WHITWELL, Thomas, Pvt, Maj Gen Wm Carroll, Capt Francis Ellis, Inf
WHITWORTH, Edmund, Pvt, Col Robt Steele, Capt James Shinualt, Mil Inf
WHITWORTH, Jacob, Pvt, Col R H Dyer, Capt Ephraim D Dickson, TN Vol Mtd Gunmen
WHITWORTH, Jacob, Sgt, Maj Wm Woodfolk, Capt James C Neil, Inf
WHITWORTH, James, Pvt, Col James Raulston, Capt Chas Wade, Inf
WHITWORTH, John, Pvt, Col Philip Pipkin, Capt John Strother, Mil
WHITWORTH, Joseph S, Pvt, Col John Cocke, Capt John

Weakley, Inf
WHITWORTH, Philmore, Pvt, Col R C Napier, Capt Edward Neblett, Mil Inf
WHITWORTH, Samuel, Pvt, Maj Wm Woodfolk, Capt James C Neil, Inf
WHITWORTH, Samuel, Pvt, Maj Wm Woodfolk, Capt John Sutton, Inf
WHITWORTH, Samuel, Pvt, Regt Commander omitted, Capt Geo Smith, Spies
WHOOBURY, Jesse B, Pvt, Col A Loury, Capt J N Williamson, W TN Mil
WHOOTEN, James D, Pvt, Col John Cocke, Capt Geo Barnes, Inf; promoted to 2 Sgt
WHORTON, David, Pvt, Col R C Napier, Capt John Chism, Mil Inf
WHORTON, David, Pvt, Col Wm Hall, Capt Henry M Newlin, Inf
WHORTON (HORTON), Caleb, Pvt, Col Philip Pipkin, Capt Henry M Newlin, Mil Inf
WHYTUS, Eser, Pvt, Regt Commander omitted, Capt Joel Parrish, Arty
WIATT, Daniel, Pvt, Col Philip Pipkin, Capt Peter Searcy, Mil Inf
WIATT, James, Cpl, Col A Loury, Capt Gabriel Martin, Inf
WIATT, Martin, Pvt, Regt Commander omitted, Capt G Lane, Mtd Riflemen
WIATT, Samuel, Pvt, Col Philip Pipkin, Capt James Blakemore, Mil Inf
WIATT (WYATT), Daniel, Pvt, Col John Cocke, Capt James Gray, Inf; d 3-9-1815
WIDENER, Henry, Pvt, Maj John Childs, Capt John Stephens, E TN Vol Mtd Inf
WIER, John, Pvt, Col Wm Johnson, Capt David McKamy, E TN Drafted Mil
WIGG, Mathew, Pvt, Col Thos Benton, Capt James McEwen, Vol Inf
WIGGANS, Blake, Pvt, Col Philip Pipkin, Capt Peter Searcy, Mil Inf
WIGGER (WIGOR), Henry, Pvt, Col A Loury, Capt James Kincaid, Inf
WIGGINGTON, John, Pvt, Lt Col L Hammonds, Capt Arahel Rains, Inf
WIGGS, Mathew, Pvt, Col Thos Benton, Capt James McEwen, Vol Inf
WIGINGTON, John, Pvt, Col John Wynne, Capt James Cole, Inf
WIGOR (WIGGER), Henry, Pvt, Col A Loury, Capt James Kincaid, Inf
WILBORN, Chapley R, Pvt, Maj Wm Russell, Capt Isaac Williams, Separate Bn of TN Vol Mtd Gunmen
WILBORN, Tarlton, Pvt, Col R H Dyer, Capt David Wyatt, Vol Mtd Gunmen
WILBOURNE, Carlton, Pvt, Col S Copeland, Capt John Holshouser, Inf
WILBOURNE, Thomas, Pvt, Maj Gen Wm Carroll, Col Jas Raulston, Capt Elijah Haynie, Inf
WILBURN, Colton, Pvt, Col Newton Cannon, Capt John Hanley, Mtd Riflemen
WILBURN, John, Pvt, Col A Cheatham, Capt James Giddens, Inf

WILCOCKS, James, Pvt, Col Thos Williamson, Capt Richard Tate, Vol Mtd Gunmen
WILCOCKSON, David, Pvt, Regt Commander omitted, Capt Wm Henderson, Spies
WILCOCON, James, Sgt, Col Samuel Bunch, Capt Jno Hawk, E TN Mil; joined from Capt Williams Co
WILCOX, James, Pvt, Col Ewin Allison, Capt Thomas McCrory, E TN Mil; transferred to Capt Register's Co
WILCOX, James, Pvt, Col Samuel Bunch, Capt F Register, E TN Mil; joined from Capt McCrea's Co
WILCOXER, David, Pvt, Regt Commander omitted, Capt Wm Henderson, Spies
WILCOXSOM, Isaac, Pvt, Col Wm Metcalf, Capt Marks, Mil
WILDAIR, Daniel, Pvt, Maj Wm Russell, Capt Wm Hodges, Vol Mtd Gunmen
WILDER, David, Pvt, Col Edwin E Booth, Capt Samuel Thompson, Mil
WILDER, David, Pvt, Col James Cummings, Co Commander omitted, E TN Vol Inf
WILDER, James, Pvt, Col Edwin E Booth, Capt John Slatton, E TN Mil
WILDER, James, Pvt, Col Samuel Bunch, Capt James Cummings, E TN Mil
WILDER, Jeremiah, Pvt, Col S Copeland, Capt John Biles, Inf
WILDER, Thomas, Pvt, Col S Bunch, Capt Isaac Bunch, Mtd Vol
WILDER, William, Pvt, Maj John Childs, Capt James Cummings, E TN Vol Inf
WILDERMAN, James, Pvt, Maj William Russell, Co Commander omitted, Vol Mtd Gunmen
WILDS, Samuel, Pvt, Col Samuel Bayless, Capt Solomon Hendricks, E TN Mil
WILEMAN, John, Pvt, Col R H Dyer, Maj William Russell, Capt William Russell, Vol Mtd Gunmen
WILES, Samuel, Pvt, Col R C Napier, Capt Samuel Ashmore, Mil Inf; d 4-10-1814
WILES, William, Pvt, Col Thomas Benton, Capt Benjamin Reynolds, Vol Inf
WILEY, Alexander, Pvt, Regt Commander omitted, Capt James Gordon, Branch Srvce omitted
WILEY, Andrew, Pvt, Col Samuel Bunch, Lt John Harris, E TN Mil
WILEY, George, Pvt, Col Ewin Allison, Capt Abraham Allen, E TN Mil
WILEY, Jacob, Pvt, Col Wm Lillard, Capt John Neatherton, E TN Vol Inf
WILEY, Samuel, Pvt, Col John Coffee, Capt Frederick Stump, Cav
WILEY, Samuel, Sgt, Col R H Dyer, Capt Thomas White, Vol Mtd Gunmen; promoted from Cpl
WILEY, Vincent, Pvt, Col John Alcorn, Capt William Locke, Cav
WILEY, Wyatt, Pvt, Col Phillip Pipkin, Capt William Mackay, Mil Inf
WILFORD, Joseph, Pvt, Col Samuel Bayless, Capt John Brock, E TN Mil
WILHELM, Jacob, Pvt, Col S Bunch, Capt John Houk, E TN Mil

## Enlisted Men, War of 1812

WILHELM, Job, Pvt, Col John Houks, Capt Francis Berry, Branch Srvce omitted

WILHELM, Jobe, Pvt, Col Samuel Bunch, Capt Berry, E TN Mil; attached to Capt Houk's Co

WILHELMS, Andrew, Pvt, Col John Brown, Capt James Preston, Regt E TN Mil Inf

WILHITE, James, Pvt, Col Wm Lillard, Capt John Roper, E TN Vol Inf

WILIX, Robert, Col Wm Johnson, Capt John McKamy, E TN Drafted Mil

WILKER, George, Pvt, Col Edwin E Booth, Co Commander omitted, E TN Mil

WILKER, James, Pvt, Maj John Childs, Capt Daniel Price, Mtd Gunmen

WILKERSON, Archibald, Pvt, Col Wm Hall, Capt Brice Martin, Vol Inf

WILKERSON, Elijah, Pvt, Col A Loury, Capt James Kincaid, Inf

WILKERSON, John, 3 Cpl, Col Samuel Wear, Capt Daniel Price, E TN Vol Inf

WILKERSON, Perry, 2 Sgt, Maj John Chiles, Capt Reuben Tipton, E TN Vol Mtd Inf

WILKERSON, William J, Pvt, Col N T Perkins, Capt Mathew Patterson, Mtd Vol

WILKES, Benjamin, Sgt, Col John Coffee, Co Commander omitted, Mtd Gunmen

WILKES, John, Pvt, Regt Commander omitted, Capt Edwin S Moore, Cav

WILKINS, Thomas, Pvt, Col Wm Johnson, Capt Benjamin Powell, Branch Srvce omitted

WILKINS, William C, Pvt, Col Wm Metcalf, Capt Wm Mullins, Mil Inf

WILKINS, Willis, Cpl, Col Wm Pillow, Capt Isiaha Renshaw, Inf

WILKINS, Willis, Sgt, Col Thos H Benton, Capt Isah Renshaw, Vol Inf

WILKINS, Witts, Sgt, Col Thos H Benton, Capt Isiah Renshaw, Vol Inf

WILKINSON, Areha, Pvt, Col Thomas Bradley, Co Commander omitted, Vol Inf

WILKINSON, Benjamin, Pvt, Col N T Perkins, Capt George Eliot, Mil Inf

WILKINSON, Benjamin, Pvt, Col Thomas Williamson, Capt Thomas Scurry, Vol Mtd Gunmen

WILKINSON, Daniel, Pvt, Col Thomas Williamson, Capt Wm Metcalf, Vol Mtd Gunmen

WILKINSON, Elijah, Pvt, Brig Gen Challie? Johnson, Capt Robert Carson, Inf

WILKINSON, James, Pvt, Regt Commander omitted, Capt Alexander Provine, Mil Inf

WILKINSON, Jesse, Pvt, Regt Commander omitted, Capt Joel Parrish, Arty

WILKINSON, John, Pvt, Col Thomas McCrory, Capt Isaac Patton, Mil Inf

WILKINSON, Perry, 2 Sgt, Maj John Childs, Capt Reuben Tipton, E TN Vol Mtd Inf; Regt Co - Jefferson

WILKINSON, Thomas, Pvt, Col LeRoy Hammond, Capt J N Williams, 2nd Regt TN

WILKINSON, Uriah, Pvt, Col John Brown, Capt Allen I Bacon, Regt E TN Mil

WILKS, Benjamin, Pvt, Col Samuel Bunch, Capt Edwin S Moore, Mtd Riflemen

WILKS, Daniel, Pvt, Col Newton Cannon, Capt Wm Martin, Mtd Gunmen

WILKS, John, Pvt, Col Thos Benton, Capt Benj Reynolds, Vol Inf

WILKS, John, Pvt, Col Thos McCrory, Capt Wm Dooley, Inf

WILKS, John, Pvt, Regt Commander omitted, Capt Edwin S Moore, Mtd Riflemen

WILKS, William, Pvt, Col Wm Metcalf, Capt Bird L Hurt, Mil Inf

WILLARD, James, Pvt, Col S Copeland, Capt Moses Thompson, Inf

WILLARD, Joel, Pvt, Col S Copeland, Capt Moses Thompson, Inf; killed 3-27-1814 in battle of Tehopeca

WILLBOURN, Johnson, Pvt, Maj Wm Russell, Capt Isaac Williams, Separate Bn of TN Vol Mtd Gunmen

WILLBURN, William, Pvt, Col Robert Steele, Capt John Chitwood, Mil Inf

WILLCOCKSON, David, Pvt, Col Samuel Wear, Capt Simeon Perry, E TN Mtd Inf

WILLCOCKSON, David, Pvt, Gen Nathan Taylor, Capt Wm Henderson, Spies

WILLCOCKSON, James, 2 Cpl, Col Samuel Wear, Capt Simeon Perry, E TN Vol Mtd Inf; reduced from Sgt

WILLEBY, Benjamin, Pvt, Col Ewen Allison, Capt Jacob Hoyal, E TN Mil

WILLET, Robert, Pvt, Col Philip Pipkin, Capt Henry M Newlin, Mil Inf

WILLET, William, Pvt, Col Robert Steele, Capt John Chitwood, Mil Inf

WILLETT, Edward, Pvt, Col Ewen Allison, Capt Adam Winsell, E TN Drafted Mil

WILLETT, Edward, Pvt, Col Samuel Bunch, Capt Geo McPherson, E TN Mil; joined from Capt Winsell's Co

WILLEY, Alexander, Pvt, no other information

WILLEY, John, Pvt, Col Thos McCrory, Capt Wm Dooley, Inf

WILLEY, Thomas, Pvt, Col R H Dyer, Capt Wm White, Vol Mtd Gunmen

WILLEY, Willis, Pvt, Col R C Napier, Capt Drury Adkins, Mil Inf

WILLFORD, Thomas, Pvt, Brig Gen Wm Johnson, Capt Abraham Allen, Mil Inf

WILLHITE, George, Pvt, Col Samuel Wear, Capt Robert Doak, E TN Vol Inf

WILLHITE, James, Pvt, Col Wm Lillard, Capt Jacob Hartsell, E TN Vol Inf

WILLHITE, Philip, Pvt, Col Wm Lillard, Capt Robert McCalpin, E TN Inf

WILLIAMS, Aaron, Pvt, Col John K Wynne, Capt James Cole, Inf

WILLIAMS, Abb (Albert, Abel), Pvt, Col Thos Benton, Capt Henry L Douglass, Vol Inf

WILLIAMS, Abel, Pvt, Col Edward Bradley, Capt Harry L Douglass, Vol Inf

WILLIAMS, Adam, Pvt, Col R H Dyer, Capt Wm Russell, Vol Mtd Gunmen

- 527

## Enlisted Men, War of 1812

WILLIAMS, Alex, 3 Cpl, Col Jno Brown, Capt Jas Standifer, E TN Mtd Mil
WILLIAMS, Allen, Pvt, Lt Col L Hammond, Capt James Craig, Inf; d 2-11-1815
WILLIAMS, Anderson, Cpl, Col Thos McCrory, Capt Anthony Metcalf, Mil Inf
WILLIAMS, Anderson, Pvt, Col Thos Williamson, Capt A M Metcalf, Vol Mtd Gunmen
WILLIAMS, Arter, Tptr, Col R H Dyer, Capt Robt Edmonston, 1st TN Vol Mtd Gunmen
WILLIAMS, Arther, Pvt, Col John Coffee, Capt John W Byrns, Cav
WILLIAMS, Arthur, Pvt, Col John Coffee, Capt David Smith, Vol Cav
WILLIAMS, Arthur, Pvt, Lt Col Jno Edmonston, Co Commander omitted, Cav
WILLIAMS, Barnett, Pvt, Col S Copeland, Capt David Williams, Inf
WILLIAMS, Basil, Pvt, Col S Copeland, Capt John Biles, Inf
WILLIAMS, Benjamin, Pvt, Col Jas Raulston, Capt Henry Hamilton, Inf
WILLIAMS, Benjamin, Pvt, Col John Brown, Capt Lunsford Oliver, E TN Mil
WILLIAMS, Benjamin, Pvt, Col R C Napier, Capt Early Benson, Mil Inf; attached to the Arty
WILLIAMS, Benjamin, Pvt, Gen Andrew Jackson, Capt Wm Russell, Mtd Spies
WILLIAMS, Benjamin, Pvt, Regt Commander omitted, Capt Jno Crane, Inf
WILLIAMS, Benjamin, Pvt, Regt Commander omitted, Capt Joel Parrish, Arty
WILLIAMS, Bennett, Pvt, Col Ewen Allison, Capt John Hampton, Mil
WILLIAMS, Beverly, Capt, Col Thos Williamson, Capt Beverly Williams, Vol Mtd Gunmen
WILLIAMS, Cabel, Pvt, Lt Col Archer Cheatham, Co Commander omitted, Inf
WILLIAMS, Cabel, Pvt, Lt Col Wm Phillips, Co Commander omitted, Inf
WILLIAMS, Caleb, Pvt, Maj Robert Cooper, Co Commander omitted, 26th Regt Mtd Riflemen
WILLIAMS, Charles, Pvt, Col Alexander Loury, Capt George Sarver, Inf
WILLIAMS, Charles, Pvt, Col John Cocke, Capt James Gray, Inf; d 2-15-1815
WILLIAMS, Charles, Pvt, Col John K Wynne, Capt Bailey Butler, Inf; deserted
WILLIAMS, Charles, Pvt, Col Wm Pillow, Capt C E McEwen, Vol Inf
WILLIAMS, Charles, Pvt, Lt Col L Hammond, Capt Thos Delaney, Inf
WILLIAMS, Charles, Pvt, Maj Gen Wm Carroll, Capt Wiley Huddleston, Inf
WILLIAMS, Charles, Pvt, Regt Commander omitted, Capt James Gray, Inf
WILLIAMS, Claibourn, Pvt, Col N T Perkins, Capt John Doak, Vol Mtd Gunmen
WILLIAMS, Clement, Pvt, Col Samuel Wear, Capt Samuel Bowman, Mtd Inf
WILLIAMS, Daniel H, QM, Brig Gen Thos Johnson, no other information
WILLIAMS, Daniel, Pvt, Col R H Dyer, Capt Ephraim Dickson, 1st TN Mtd Vol Gunmen; d 1-31-1815
WILLIAMS, Daniel, Pvt, Gen Andrew Jackson, Capt D Deadrick, Arty
WILLIAMS, David F, Pvt, Lt Col Jno Edmonson, Capt Wm Peacock, Cav
WILLIAMS, David W, Pvt, Col Wm Lillard, Capt Jacob Dykes, Vol Inf
WILLIAMS, David, Cpl, Col Philip Pipkin, Capt Ebenezer Kirkpatrick, Mil Inf; resigned and deserted
WILLIAMS, David, Cpl, Col Sam Bayless, Capt Jos Goodson, E TN Mil
WILLIAMS, David, Pvt, Col Jno Coffee, Capt John Baskerville, Cav
WILLIAMS, David, Pvt, Col Sam Wear, Capt Jas Gillespie, E TN Vol Inf; unable to perform duty
WILLIAMS, David, Pvt, Col Samuel Bayless, Capt Branch Jones, E TN Drafted Mil
WILLIAMS, David, Pvt, Maj Gen Andrew Jackson, Capt Jos Kirkpatrick, Mtd Gunmen
WILLIAMS, Edward, Pvt, Col A Loury, Capt J N Williamson, W TN Mil
WILLIAMS, Edward, Pvt, Col L Hammons, Capt J N Williamson, 2nd Regt Inf
WILLIAMS, Edward, Pvt, Col Robert Dyer, Capt James Wyatt, Vol Mtd Gunmen
WILLIAMS, Edward, Pvt, Col Robt Steele, Capt John Chitwood, Mil Inf
WILLIAMS, Eldred, Sgt, Col A Cheatham, Capt Wm Creel, Inf; transferred to the Arty
WILLIAMS, Elijah jr, Pvt, Col Newt Cannon, Capt Isaac Williams, Mtd Riflemen
WILLIAMS, Elijah, Pvt, Col John Alcorn, Capt John W Byrne, Cav
WILLIAMS, Elijah, Pvt, Col Wm Hall, Capt Abraham Bledsoe, Vol Inf
WILLIAMS, Elijah, Pvt, Col Wm Johnson, Capt Elihu Milliken, 3rd Regt E TN Mil; deceased 2-1-1815
WILLIAMS, Elijah, Pvt, Maj Wm Russell, Capt Isaac Williams, Separate Bn of TN Mtd Gunmen Vol
WILLIAMS, Elisha, Pvt, Col N T Perkins, Capt Mathew Patterson, Mtd Vol
WILLIAMS, Elisha, Pvt, Col Philip Pipkin, Capt Ebenezer Kirkpatrick, Mil Inf; transferred to Capt Blakemore
WILLIAMS, Elisha, Pvt, Col Philip Pipkin, Capt Mackay, Mil Inf
WILLIAMS, Elisha, Pvt, Col Robt Dyer, Capt Glenn Owen, 1st TN Vol Mtd Gunmen
WILLIAMS, Elisha, Pvt, Col Thos McCrory, Capt Jas Shannon, Mil Inf
WILLIAMS, Elisha, Pvt, Col Thos Williamson, Capt Beverly William, Vol Mtd Gunmen
WILLIAMS, Enox, Pvt, Col Sam Bayless, Capt Jos Hale, E TN Mil
WILLIAMS, Etheldred, Pvt, Maj Gen Jackson, Capt Wm Carroll, Vol Inf
WILLIAMS, Etheldridge, Pvt, Regt Commander omitted, Capt Joel Parrish, Arty
WILLIAMS, Ethelred, Cpl, Col John Coffee, Capt David

## Enlisted Men, War of 1812

Smith, Vol Cav
WILLIAMS, Ezekiel, Cpl, Maj Wm Russell, Capt Isaac Williams, Separate Bn of Vol Mtd Gunmen
WILLIAMS, Ezekiel, Pvt, Col Robt Dyer, Capt Isaac Williams, 1st Regt TN Vol Mtd Gunmen
WILLIAMS, Ezekiel, Pvt, Col S Copeland, Capt John Biles, Inf; promoted to Cpl
WILLIAMS, Francis, Pvt, Col Jas Raulston, Capt Daniel Newman, Inf
WILLIAMS, Francis, Pvt, Col Sam Bayless, Capt Jos Rich, E TN Inf
WILLIAMS, Francis, Pvt, Col Sam Wear, Capt Jesse Cole, Vol Inf
WILLIAMS, G B, Pvt, Col Newt Cannon, Capt Wm Edwards, Regt Command
WILLIAMS, George, Dmr, Maj Wm Carroll, Capt D Bradford & Capt L Dillahunty, Vol Inf
WILLIAMS, George, Drm Maj, Col Thos McCrory, 2nd Regt TN Mil
WILLIAMS, George, Pvt, Col John Coffee, Capt Blackman Coleman, Cav
WILLIAMS, George, Pvt, Col Wm Johnson, Capt David McKamy, E TN Drafted Mil
WILLIAMS, George, Pvt, Col Wm Johnson, Capt Jas Rogers, E TN Mil
WILLIAMS, George, Pvt, Col Wm Metcalf, Capt Thos Marks, Mil Inf
WILLIAMS, George, Pvt, Col Wm Pillow, Capt Thos Williamson, Vol Inf
WILLIAMS, George, Pvt, Maj Wm Russell, Capt John Trimble, Vol Mtd Gunmen
WILLIAMS, George, Surgeon Mate, Gen John Coffee, TN Vol Mtd Inf
WILLIAMS, Gideon G, Pvt, Col Wm Pillow, Capt Thos Williamson, Vol Inf; promoted to Sgt
WILLIAMS, Gideon G, Sgt Maj, Col Wm Pillow, Co Commander omitted, 2nd Regt TN Vol Inf
WILLIAMS, Gideon, Pvt, Gen Andrew Jackson, Capt D Deaderick, Arty
WILLIAMS, Gideon, Pvt, Regt Commander omitted, Capt D S Deaderick, Arty
WILLIAMS, Godfrey, Pvt, Col Sam Wear, Capt Jesse Cole, Vol Inf
WILLIAMS, Green, Pvt, Col Philip Pipkin, Capt Henry Newlin, Mil Inf
WILLIAMS, Green, Pvt, Col Wm Johnson, Capt Andrew Lawson, E TN Drafted Mil
WILLIAMS, Green, Pvt, Col Wm Johnson, Capt Elihu Milliken, 3rd Regt E TN Mil
WILLIAMS, Harden, Pvt, Col S Copeland, Capt Jas Tait, Inf
WILLIAMS, Henry, Pvt, Col Jas Raulston, Capt Henry Hamilton, Inf; also under Maj Gen Carroll
WILLIAMS, Henry, Pvt, Col Newt Cannon, Capt Wm Edwards, Regt Command
WILLIAMS, Henry, Pvt, Col S Copeland, Capt John Biles, Inf
WILLIAMS, Henry, Pvt, Regt Commander omitted, Capt Jas Craig, Branch Srvce omitted
WILLIAMS, Henry, Sgt, Regt Commander omitted, Lt Jas Berry, Mtd Riflemen; promoted from Cpl
WILLIAMS, Hiram, Pvt, Maj Gen Jackson, Capt Jos Kirkpatrick, Mtd Gunmen; killed 1-22-1814
WILLIAMS, Isaac, Cpl, Col Robt Dyer, Capt Glenn Owen, 1st TN Vol Mtd Gunmen
WILLIAMS, Isaac, Pvt, Col Philip Pipkin, Capt David Smythe, Inf; transferred to Capt John Strothers Co
WILLIAMS, Isaac, Pvt, Col Thos Williamson, Capt James Pace, Lt Nealy, Vol Mtd Gunmen
WILLIAMS, Isaac, Pvt, Regt Commander omitted, Capt Nathan Farmer, Mtd Riflemen
WILLIAMS, Isaac, Pvt, Regt Commander omitted, Capt Philip Pipkin, Ens Wm Pegram, Det of Capt David Smythe Co of W TN Mil
WILLIAMS, Isom (Isham), Pvt, Col Philip Pipkin, Capt Peter Searcy, Mil Inf; deserted
WILLIAMS, Jacob, Pvt, Col N T Perkins, Capt James McMahan, Mtd Gunmen
WILLIAMS, James A, Sgt, Col A Loury, Lt Col L Hammonds, Capt Arahel Rains, Inf; promoted from a Pvt
WILLIAMS, James jr, Pvt, Col Wm Hall, Capt John Kennedy, Vol Inf
WILLIAMS, James sr, Pvt, Col Wm Hall, Capt John Kennedy, Vol Inf
WILLIAMS, James, Ffr, Maj Wm Woodfolk, Capt James C Neil, Inf
WILLIAMS, James, Pvt, Col A Loury, Lt Col L Hammonds, Capt Arahel Rains, Inf
WILLIAMS, James, Pvt, Col Edward Bradley, Capt John Kennedy, Riflemen
WILLIAMS, James, Pvt, Col Edwin Booth, Capt John Lewis, E TN Mil
WILLIAMS, James, Pvt, Col Edwin Booth, Capt Samuel Thompson, Mil
WILLIAMS, James, Pvt, Col Newton Cannon, Capt Isaac Williams, Mtd Riflemen
WILLIAMS, James, Pvt, Col Philip Pipkin, Capt David Smith, Mil Inf
WILLIAMS, James, Pvt, Col R H Dyer, Capt Glen Owen, TN Vol Mtd Gunmen
WILLIAMS, James, Pvt, Col R H Dyer, Maj Wm Russell, Capt Wm Russell, Vol Mtd Gunmen
WILLIAMS, James, Pvt, Col S Copeland, Capt John Dawson, Inf
WILLIAMS, James, Pvt, Col Samuel Bunch, Capt Edward Buchanan, E TN Mil
WILLIAMS, James, Pvt, Col Samuel Bunch, Capt Isaac Williams, Mtd Vol
WILLIAMS, James, Pvt, Col Samuel Bunch, Capt James Cummings, E TN Vol Mtd Inf
WILLIAMS, James, Pvt, Col Samuel Bunch, Capt Jno Hawk, E TN Mil; transferred to Capt Williams Co
WILLIAMS, James, Pvt, Col Wm Hall, Capt John Kennedy, Vol Inf
WILLIAMS, James, Pvt, Col Wm Johnson, Capt Andrew Lawson, E TN Drafted Mil
WILLIAMS, James, Pvt, Col Wm Johnson, Capt Christopher Cook, E TN Mil
WILLIAMS, James, Pvt, Col Wm Johnston, Capt Joseph Kirk, Mil
WILLIAMS, James, Pvt, Col Wm Lillard, Capt Wm

## Enlisted Men, War of 1812

Hamilton, E TN Vol Inf
WILLIAMS, James, Pvt, Col Wm Lillard, Capt Wm Lillard, E TN Inf Vol
WILLIAMS, James, Pvt, Col Wm Metcalf, Capt Wm Sitton, Mil Inf
WILLIAMS, James, Pvt, Gen Andrew Jackson, Capt D Deaderick, Arty; transferred to the Mil
WILLIAMS, James, Pvt, Regt Commander omitted, Capt David Smith, Cav Vol
WILLIAMS, James, Pvt, Regt Commander omitted, Capt I Parrish, Arty
WILLIAMS, James, Pvt, Regt Commander omitted, Capt Jno Crane, Mtd Inf
WILLIAMS, James, Rank omitted, Col Wm Metcalf, Capt Wm Mullin, Mil Inf
WILLIAMS, James, Sgt, Col S Copeland, Capt Allen Williams, Mil Inf
WILLIAMS, Jason, Pvt, Col S Copeland, Capt Robt Steele, Mil Inf
WILLIAMS, Jeremiah, Pvt, Gen Andrew Jackson, Capt Nathan Davis, Inf
WILLIAMS, Jerry, Pvt, Regt Commander omitted, Capt Patterson, Branch Srvce omitted
WILLIAMS, Jesse C, Pvt, Col John Coffee, Capt Thos Bradley, Vol Cav
WILLIAMS, Jesse C, Pvt, Col Thos Williamson, Capt Beverly Williams, Vol Mtd Gunmen
WILLIAMS, Jesse, Pvt, Col A Loury, Lt Col L Hammond, Capt Arahel Rains, Inf
WILLIAMS, Jesse, Pvt, Col Jas Raulston, Capt Daniel Newman, Inf
WILLIAMS, Jesse, Pvt, Col John Cocke, Capt Geo Barnes, Inf
WILLIAMS, Jesse, Pvt, Col John Wynne, Capt John Spinks, Inf
WILLIAMS, Jesse, Pvt, Col R H Dyer, Capt David Wyatt, Vol Mtd Gunmen
WILLIAMS, Jesse, Pvt, Col Wm Metcalf, Capt Wm Mullin, Mil Inf
WILLIAMS, Jesse, Pvt, Col Wm Metcalf, Capt Wm Sitton, Mil Inf
WILLIAMS, Joe, Sgt, Lt Col Jno Edmonson, Capt Wm Peacock, Cav
WILLIAMS, Joel, Pvt, Lt Col A Cheatham, Capt Meredith Walker, Mtd Inf
WILLIAMS, Joel, Pvt, Lt Col Phillips, Co Commander omitted, Inf
WILLIAMS, Joel, Pvt, Maj Cooper, Co Commander omitted, 26th TN Regt Mtd Riflemen
WILLIAMS, John C, Pvt, Col Leroy Hammonds, Capt Arahel Rains, Inf
WILLIAMS, John J, Pvt, Col S Copeland, Capt Tait, Inf
WILLIAMS, John T, Pvt, Col Thomas Williams, Capt John Hutchings, Vol Mtd Gunmen
WILLIAMS, John W, Pvt, Regt Commander omitted, Capt Jas Cowan, Mtd Inf
WILLIAMS, John, 5 Cpl, Col Philip Pipkin, Capt Ebenezer Kirkpatrick, Mil Inf; promoted to Sgt
WILLIAMS, John, Pvt, Col A Cheatham, Capt Richard Benson, Inf
WILLIAMS, John, Pvt, Col Edward Bradley, Capt William Lauderdale, Vol Inf
WILLIAMS, John, Pvt, Col John Cocke, Capt Gray, Inf; d 2-5-1815
WILLIAMS, John, Pvt, Col John Cocke, Capt John Weakley, Inf
WILLIAMS, John, Pvt, Col John Cocke, Capt Samuel M Caruthers, Inf
WILLIAMS, John, Pvt, Col Newton Cannon, Capt John Harpole, Mtd Gunmen
WILLIAMS, John, Pvt, Col Philip Pipkin, Capt Geo Mebane, Mil Inf
WILLIAMS, John, Pvt, Col Philip Pipkin, Capt Wm Pegram, W TN Mil
WILLIAMS, John, Pvt, Col R C Napier, Capt Thomas Preston, Mil Inf
WILLIAMS, John, Pvt, Col R H Dyer, Capt David Wyatt, Vol Mtd Gunmen
WILLIAMS, John, Pvt, Col R T Perkins, Capt McMahon, Mtd Gunmen
WILLIAMS, John, Pvt, Col Robert Dyer, Capt Ephraim Dickson, TN Mtd Gunmen
WILLIAMS, John, Pvt, Col Robert Steele, Capt Jas Randals, Inf
WILLIAMS, John, Pvt, Col S Wear, Capt Geo Gillespie, E TN Vol Inf
WILLIAMS, John, Pvt, Col S Wear, Capt S Bayless, Mtd Inf
WILLIAMS, John, Pvt, Col T McCrory, Capt Wm Dooley, Inf
WILLIAMS, John, Pvt, Col Thos Benton, Capt Geo Caperton, Inf
WILLIAMS, John, Pvt, Col Thos Benton, Capt Geo Caperton, Vol Inf
WILLIAMS, John, Pvt, Col Wm Hall, Capt William Alexander, Vol Inf
WILLIAMS, John, Pvt, Col Wm Johnson, Capt Benj Powell, E TN Mil
WILLIAMS, John, Pvt, Col Wm Johnson, Capt Jas Rogers, E TN Drafted Mil
WILLIAMS, John, Pvt, Col Wm Lillard, Capt Thomas Sharpe, Inf
WILLIAMS, John, Pvt, Col Wm Metcalf, Capt Bird Hurt, Mil Inf
WILLIAMS, John, Pvt, Col Wm Pillow, Capt Geo Caperton, Inf
WILLIAMS, John, Pvt, Col Wm Walker, Capt John Williams, Mtd Mil
WILLIAMS, John, Pvt, Lt Col A Cheatham, Co Commander omitted, 6th Brig Mtd Inf
WILLIAMS, John, Pvt, Lt Col Henry Bryan, Co Commander omitted, Inf
WILLIAMS, John, Pvt, Maj John Chiles, Capt Chas Conway, E TN Mtd Gunmen
WILLIAMS, John, Pvt, Maj William Russell, Capt John Trimble, Vol Mtd Gunmen
WILLIAMS, John, Pvt, Maj Wm Woodfolk, Capt Abner Pearce, Branch Srvce omitted
WILLIAMS, John, Pvt, Regt Commander omitted, Capt James Cowan, Mtd Inf
WILLIAMS, John, Pvt, Regt Commander omitted, Capt Thos Gray, Inf

## Enlisted Men, War of 1812

WILLIAMS, John, Pvt, Regt Commander omitted, Lt John Scott, Det of Inf

WILLIAMS, John, Sgt, Col S Bunch, Capt Francis Berry, E TN Mil

WILLIAMS, Jonathan, Pvt, Col S Copeland, Capt Wilkinson, Mil Inf

WILLIAMS, Jonathan, Pvt, Col Wm Bradley, Capt John Kennedy, Riflemen

WILLIAMS, Jonathan, Pvt, Col Wm Johnson, Capt Elihu Milliken, E TN Mil

WILLIAMS, Jonathan, Pvt, Maj William Russell, Capt Geo Mitchell, Vol Mtd Gunmen

WILLIAMS, Jordon, Pvt, Col John Cocke, Capt Geo Barnes, Inf; d 1-24-1815

WILLIAMS, Joseph N, Pvt, Lt Col Hammonds, Capt Raines, Inf

WILLIAMS, Joseph, Pvt, Col A Cheatham, Capt Birdwell, Inf

WILLIAMS, Joseph, Pvt, Col Jas Raulston, Capt Henry Hamilton, Inf; also under Maj Gen Carroll

WILLIAMS, Joseph, Pvt, Col Johnson, Capt Jas Tunnell, E TN Mil

WILLIAMS, Joseph, Pvt, Col Robert Dyer, Capt Dickson, Branch Srvce omitted

WILLIAMS, Joseph, Pvt, Maj Gen Carroll, Capt? Wiley Huddleston, Inf; d 1-7-1815

WILLIAMS, Joseph, Sgt, Col Wm Metcalf, Capt Jackson & Capt Carroll, Inf

WILLIAMS, Joseph, Sgt, Lt Col Jno Edmonson, Co Commander omitted, Cav

WILLIAMS, Josiah, Pvt, Col Thos Benton, Capt Geo Caperton, Inf

WILLIAMS, Lea, 2 Sgt, Col S Bunch, Capt Moses, E TN Drafted Mil

WILLIAMS, Lewis, Pvt, Maj Carroll, Capt Dillahunty & Capt Bradford, Vol Inf

WILLIAMS, Mathew, Pvt, Col John Alcorn, Capt Fredrick Stump, Cav

WILLIAMS, Mathew, Pvt, Col Jon Coffee, Capt Fredrick Stump, Cav

WILLIAMS, Matthew, Pvt, Lt Col Henry Bryan, Co Commander omitted, Inf

WILLIAMS, Millikin, Pvt, Col S Bunch, Capt Mann, E TN Vol Mtd Inf; deserted

WILLIAMS, Morgan, Pvt, Col Thos Dyer, Capt James Wyatt, Vol Mtd Gunmen

WILLIAMS, Moses, Pvt, Col Philip Pipkin, Capt Henry Newlin, Mil Inf

WILLIAMS, Moses, Pvt, Col Philip Pipkin, Capt Smith, Inf

WILLIAMS, Moses, Pvt, Col Philip Pipkin, Capt William Mackay, Mil Inf

WILLIAMS, Nathan, Pvt, Col Thos Williamson, Capt Robt Moore, Vol Mtd Gunmen

WILLIAMS, Oliver, Pvt, Col Philip Pipkin, Capt David Smith, Mil Inf

WILLIAMS, Owen, Pvt, Col Philip Pipkin, Capt David Smith, Inf

WILLIAMS, Patrick, Pvt, Col Wm Johnson, Capt Andrew Lawson, E TN Drafted Mil

WILLIAMS, Paul, Pvt, Regt Commander omitted, Capt James Cowan, Mtd Inf

WILLIAMS, Peter, Pvt, Col John Cocke, Capt James Gault, Inf; d 11-31-1815

WILLIAMS, Phileeon, Cpl, Col Thos Williamson, Capt Thos Porter, Vol Mtd Gunmen; promoted from Pvt

WILLIAMS, Philip, Pvt, Col John Cocke, Capt John Weakley, Inf; also a Dmr

WILLIAMS, Phillip E, Pvt, Col Newton Cannon, Capt Francis Jones, Mtd Riflemen

WILLIAMS, Phillip, Pvt, Col Thos Benton, Capt Geo Caperton, Vol Inf

WILLIAMS, Ralph, Pvt, Col John Wynne, Capt Wm Carothers, W TN Inf

WILLIAMS, Real, Sgt, Regt Commander omitted, Capt G Lane, Mtd Riflemen

WILLIAMS, Reese, Pvt, Col Wm Johnson, Capt Henry Hunter, E TN Mil

WILLIAMS, Richard, Pvt, Col R H Dyer, Capt Joseph Williams, Vol Mtd Gunmen; promoted to Cpl

WILLIAMS, Robert F, QM Sgt, Col Robt Steele, Co Commander omitted, 4th Regt TN Mil

WILLIAMS, Robert, 1 Sgt, Col Philip Pipkin, Capt Henry M Newlin, Mil Inf; d 12-19-1814

WILLIAMS, Robert, Pvt, Col A Loury, Capt Geo Sarver, Inf

WILLIAMS, Robert, Pvt, Col Ewen Allison, Capt Henry McCray, E TN Mil; deserted

WILLIAMS, Robert, Pvt, Col Jas Raulston, Capt Henry West, Inf

WILLIAMS, Robert, Pvt, Col R C Napier, Capt Drury Adkins, Mil Inf

WILLIAMS, Robert, Pvt, Col R C Napier, Capt Early Benson, Mil Inf

WILLIAMS, Robert, Pvt, Col Samuel Bunch, Capt Wm Jobe, E TN Vol Mtd Inf

WILLIAMS, Robert, Pvt, Maj Gen Wm Carroll, Col Jas Raulston, Capt Edward Robinson, Inf

WILLIAMS, Robert, Pvt, Maj Wm Russell, Capt John Trimble, Vol Mtd Gunmen

WILLIAMS, Robert, QM Sgt, Col Philip Pipkin, 1st Regt TN Mil; promoted from Sgt

WILLIAMS, Samuel, Cpl, Col Wm Metcalf, Capt Barbee Collins, Mil Inf

WILLIAMS, Samuel, Pvt, Col Ewen Allison, Capt Jonas Loughmiller, Mil; transferred to Capt Griffin's Co

WILLIAMS, Samuel, Pvt, Col R H Dyer, Maj Wm Russell, Capt Isaac Williams, Separate Bn of TN Vol Mtd Gunmen

WILLIAMS, Samuel, Pvt, Col Samuel Bayless, Capt Jonathan Waddle, E TN Mil

WILLIAMS, Samuel, Pvt, Col Samuel Bunch, Capt Jones Griffin, Branch Srvce omitted; joined from Capt Loughmiller's Co

WILLIAMS, Sherod, Cpl, Col Newton Cannon, Capt Francis Jones, Mtd Riflemen

WILLIAMS, Silas, Cpl, Col Wm Lillard, Capt Wm Hamilton, E TN Vol Inf

WILLIAMS, Simon, Pvt, Col T McCrory, Capt A Metcalf, W TN Mil Inf

## Enlisted Men, War of 1812

WILLIAMS, Solomon, Pvt, Lt Col Henry Bryan, Co Commander omitted, Inf
WILLIAMS, Solomon, Pvt, Regt Commander omitted, Capt Jas Haggard, Mtd Gunmen
WILLIAMS, Sterling, Pvt, Col Edwin Booth, Capt Richard Marshall, Drafted Mil
WILLIAMS, Stewart, Pvt, Col Ewen Allison, Capt Henry McCray, E TN Mil; discharged by a surgeon
WILLIAMS, Terry (Jerry?), Pvt, Col Newton Cannon, Capt Andrew Patterson, Mtd Riflemen
WILLIAMS, Terry, Pvt, Regt Commander omitted, Capt Edwin S Moore, Mtd Riflemen
WILLIAMS, Thomas L, Pvt, Col Jno Williams, Capt Wm Walker, Mtd Mil
WILLIAMS, Thomas, 3 Cpl, Regt Commander omitted, Capt Jos Williams, Mil Cav
WILLIAMS, Thomas, Cpl, Col Newton Cannon, Capt Francis Jones, Mtd Riflemen
WILLIAMS, Thomas, Pvt, Col Edward Bradley, Capt John Kennedy, Branch Srvce omitted
WILLIAMS, Thomas, Pvt, Col Ewen Allison, Capt Jacob Hoyal, E TN Mil; deserted
WILLIAMS, Thomas, Pvt, Col J K Wynne, Capt Robt Bradin, Inf; d 12-19-1813
WILLIAMS, Thomas, Pvt, Col Newton Cannon, Capt John Harpole, Mtd Gunmen
WILLIAMS, Thomas, Pvt, Col R H Dyer, Maj Wm Russell, Capt Wm Russell, Vol Mtd Gunmen
WILLIAMS, Thomas, Pvt, Col Samuel Bunch, Capt James Penny, E TN Mtd Inf
WILLIAMS, Thomas, Pvt, Col Thos Benton, Capt Thos Williamson, Vol Inf
WILLIAMS, Thomas, Pvt, Col Thos Williamson, Capt Robt Moore, Vol Mtd Gunmen
WILLIAMS, Thomas, Pvt, Col Wm Hall, Capt John Kennedy, Vol Inf
WILLIAMS, Thomas, Pvt, Col Wm Johnson, Capt Elihu Milliken, 3rd Regt E TN Mil; transferred to Capt Hunter's Co
WILLIAMS, Thomas, Pvt, Col Wm Johnson, Capt Henry Hunter, E TN Mil
WILLIAMS, Thomas, Pvt, Col Wm Pillow, Capt Thos Williamson, Vol Inf
WILLIAMS, Thomas, Pvt, Lt Col Archer Cheatham, Co Commander omitted, 6th Brig Mtd Inf
WILLIAMS, Thomas, Pvt, Lt Col Richard Napier, Co Commander omitted, Inf
WILLIAMS, Thomas, Pvt, Maj Wm Russell, Capt Geo Mitchie, Vol Mtd Gunmen
WILLIAMS, Vincent, Pvt, Col Wm Higgins, Capt Jno Cheatham, Mtd Riflemen
WILLIAMS, William F, Sgt, Col John Coffee, Capt Wm J Smith, Vol Cav
WILLIAMS, William, 3 Sgt, Col S Copeland, Capt Jno Biles, Inf
WILLIAMS, William, Pvt, Col Alex Loury, Capt G Martin, Inf
WILLIAMS, William, Pvt, Col E Allison, Capt Allen, E TN Mil
WILLIAMS, William, Pvt, Col E Allison, Capt J Loughmiller, Mil
WILLIAMS, William, Pvt, Col Ed Bradley, Capt Jas Hambleton, Vol Inf
WILLIAMS, William, Pvt, Col J K Wynne, Capt B Butler, Inf
WILLIAMS, William, Pvt, Col J K Wynne, Capt Jas Holleman, Inf
WILLIAMS, William, Pvt, Col Jno Alcorn, Capt Thomas Bradley, Vol Cav
WILLIAMS, William, Pvt, Col Jno Brown, Capt Chas Lewin, E TN Vol Mtd Inf
WILLIAMS, William, Pvt, Col N Cannon, Capt Thos Yardley, Mtd Riflemen
WILLIAMS, William, Pvt, Col N Cannon, Capt Wm Edwards, Regt Command
WILLIAMS, William, Pvt, Col N T Perkins, Capt Jas McMahan, Mtd Inf
WILLIAMS, William, Pvt, Col N T Perkins, Capt M Johnston, Mil Inf
WILLIAMS, William, Pvt, Col R H Dyer, Capt I Williams, 1st Regt TN Vol Mtd Gunmen
WILLIAMS, William, Pvt, Col Saml Bunch, Capt Jas Duncan, E TN Drafted Mil; joined from Capt Allen's Co
WILLIAMS, William, Pvt, Col Thos Benton, Capt Geo Caperton, Vol Inf
WILLIAMS, William, Pvt, Col Wm Lillard, Capt Jno Neatherton, E TN Vol Inf
WILLIAMS, William, Pvt, Col Wm Metcalf, Capt O Waller, Mil Inf
WILLIAMS, William, Pvt, Col Wm Pillow, Capt Caperton, Inf
WILLIAMS, William, Pvt, Regt Commander omitted, Capt Edwin S Moore, Mtd Riflemen
WILLIAMS, William, Pvt, Regt Commander omitted, Capt Elijah Rushing, Det of Inf
WILLIAMS, William, Pvt, Regt Commander omitted, Capt Jas Haggard, Mtd Gunmen
WILLIAMS, William, Rank omitted, Col J K Wynne, Capt Jno Porter, Inf
WILLIAMS, William, Sgt, Col N Cannon, Capt I Williams, Mtd Riflemen
WILLIAMS, William, Sgt, Maj Wm Russell, Capt I Williams, Separate Bn of TN Vol Mtd Gunmen
WILLIAMS, Williamson, Pvt, Col Thos Williamson, Capt B Williams, Vol Mtd Gunmen
WILLIAMS (WILSON), Solomon, Pvt, Col Jas Raulston, Capt Henry West, Inf
WILLIAMSON, James, Pvt, Col James Raulston, Capt M Cowan, Inf
WILLIAMSON, James, Pvt, Col T McCrory, Capt A Metcalf, Mil Inf
WILLIAMSON, John S, Pvt, Maj Gen A Jackson, Capt Wm Carroll, Vol Inf
WILLIAMSON, John W, 1 Cpl, Col P Pipkin, Capt Wm Mackay, Mil Inf
WILLIAMSON, John, Pvt, Col Jno Cocke, Capt B Nance, Inf; discharged by Court Martial
WILLIAMSON, John, Pvt, Col Jno Coffee, Capt A McKeen, Cav; discharged for inability
WILLIAMSON, John, Pvt, Regt Commander omitted, Capt David Mason, Branch Srvce omitted

## Enlisted Men, War of 1812

WILLIAMSON, Joseph, Pvt, Col T McCrory, Capt Wm Metcalf, Mil Inf
WILLIAMSON, Levi, Pvt, Col Thomas Bradley, Capt John Kennedy, Riflemen; AWOL at Ft Strother
WILLIAMSON, Thomas, Pvt, Maj Wm Russell, Capt Geo Mitchie, Vol Mtd Gunmen
WILLIAMSON, William W, Pvt, Regt Commander omitted, Capt David Mason, Branch Srvce omitted
WILLIE, Allen F, Pvt, Col Philip Pipkin, Capt Peter Searcy, Mil Inf
WILLIE, Jodiah, Pvt, Col John Coffee, Capt James Terrell, Vol Cav
WILLIE, Willis, Pvt, Col James Raulston, Capt Henry Hamilton, Inf; also under Maj Gen Wm Carroll, d 1-18-1815
WILLIFORD, David, Pvt, Regt Commander omitted, Capt Larkin Ferrill, Mil Inf; transferred
WILLIFORD, Jeremiah, Pvt, Col Leroy Hammond, Capt James Tubb, Inf
WILLIFORD, John, Pvt, Col A Loury, Capt Gabriel Martin, Inf
WILLIFORD, John, Pvt, Col John K Wynne, Capt Bayless E Prince, Inf
WILLIFORD, Jordon, Pvt, Brig Gen Wm Johnson, Capt Robert Carson, Inf
WILLIFORD, Thomas, Pvt, Col John K Wynne, Capt Bayless E Prince, Inf
WILLIFORD, William, Pvt, Brig Gen Wm Johnson, Capt Robert Carson, Inf
WILLIFRED, Thomas, Pvt, Lt Col Henry Bryan, Co Commander omitted, Inf
WILLIS, Andrew W, Pvt, Col Thomas H Benton, Capt Thomas Williamson, Vol Inf
WILLIS, Armstead, Pvt, Col Wm Booth, Capt John Slatton, E TN Mil
WILLIS, Barnabas, Pvt, Regt Commander omitted, Capt L Ferrell, Inf
WILLIS, Brimet, Pvt, Col S Copeland, Capt William Hodges, Inf
WILLIS, Daniel, Pvt, Col A Cheatham, Capt Charles Johnson, Inf
WILLIS, Daniel, Pvt, Col Philip Pipkin, Capt James Blakemore, Mil Inf
WILLIS, Henry, Pvt, Maj Gen Wm Carroll, Capt Wiley Huddleston, Inf
WILLIS, Jacob, Pvt, Col Thomas Bradley, Capt John Wallace, Vol Inf
WILLIS, Jacob, Pvt, Col Wm Hall, Capt John Wallace, Inf
WILLIS, James, Pvt, Col R H Dyer, Capt Joseph Williams, Vol Mtd Gunmen
WILLIS, James, Pvt, Maj Wm Woodfolk, Capt Abner Pearce, Inf
WILLIS, John, Pvt, Col Thomas Williamson, Capt Robert Moore, Vol Mtd Gunmen
WILLIS, Josiah, Pvt, Col John Coffee, Capt James Terrell, Vol Cav
WILLIS, Larkin, Pvt, Col Samuel Bunch, Capt John Williams, Mtd Vol
WILLIS, Malachia C, Sgt, Col R C Napier, Capt Thomas Preston, Mil Inf
WILLIS, Thomas, Pvt, Col Wm Lillard, Capt Thomas Sharpe, 2nd Regt Inf
WILLIS, William, Pvt, Col Thomas H Benton, Co Commander omitted, Vol Inf
WILLIS, William, Pvt, Col Wm Lillard, Capt Thomas Sharpe, 2nd Regt Inf
WILLIS, William, Pvt, Col Wm Metcalf, Co Commander omitted, Mil Inf
WILLIS, William, Pvt, Col Wm Pillow, Capt Thomas Williams, Vol Inf
WILLIS (WILEY), Vincent, Pvt, Col John Coffee, Capt Blackman Coleman, Cav
WILLMORE, Willie, Pvt, Col S Copeland, Capt Allen Wilkinson, Mil Inf
WILLS, Andrew W, Pvt, Col Thomas H Benton, Capt Thomas Williamson, Vol Inf
WILLS, David, Pvt, Col I Hamilton, Capt Jarman, Inf
WILLS, David, Pvt, Col John Coffee, Capt James Terrell, Vol Cav
WILLS, Jacob, Pvt, Col Samuel Bunch, Capt John E Williams, Mtd Vol
WILLS, Martin, Far, Regt Commander omitted, Capt James Haggard, Mtd Gunmen
WILLS, Samuel, Pvt, Regt Commander omitted, Capt Archibald McKinney, Cav
WILLS, Thomas P, Pvt, Col A Cheatham, Capt Wm Creel, Inf
WILLSON, Adam, Pvt, Col Samuel Wear & Col Samuel Bunch, Capt Mitchell, E TN Mtd Inf
WILLSON, Benjamin, Pvt, Gen Andrew Jackson, Capt Hugh Kerr, Mtd Rangers
WILLSON, Bennett, Pvt, Col S Bunch, Capt Moses, E TN Mil Drafted
WILLSON, David, Pvt, Col Thomas H Benton, Co Commander omitted, Vol Inf
WILLSON, Greenberry, Pvt, Col Wm Johnson, Capt James Tunnell, E TN Mil
WILLSON, Gregory, Pvt, Col A Cheatham, Capt Wm Johnson, Inf
WILLSON, Isac, Sgt, Col Wm Johnson, Capt James Stewart, 3rd Regt E TN Mil
WILLSON, James, Pvt, Col Wm Y Higgins, Capt James Hambleton, Mtd Gunmen
WILLSON, Joel, Pvt, Maj Gen Andrew Jackson, Col A Cheatham, Capt Wm Creel, Inf
WILLSON, John, Cpl, Regt Commander omitted, Capt John Dempsey, Branch Srvce omitted
WILLSON, John, Pvt, Col Isaac Williams, Capt Samuel Bunch, Mtd Vol
WILLSON, Joseph, Pvt, Col John Coffee, Capt Michael Molton, Cav; excused for being a Justice of the Peace
WILLSON, Thomas, Pvt, Col A Cheatham, Capt Charles Johnson, Inf
WILLSON, Thomas, Pvt, Col James Raulston, Capt Henry Hamilton, Inf; also under Maj Gen Wm Carroll
WILLY, William A, Pvt, Gen Andrew Jackson, Capt Wm Russell, Mtd Spies
WILMOT, Stephen, Pvt, Col Wm Johnson, Capt Benj Powell, E TN Mil; d 11-17-1814
WILMOT, Thomas, Pvt, Col Wm Johnson, Capt Ben-

## Enlisted Men, War of 1812

jamin Powell, Branch Srvce omitted; d 11-17-1814
WILMOTH, Abraham, Pvt, Col Philip Pipkin, Capt George Mebane, Mil Inf; deserted
WILMOUTH, Abraham, Pvt, Col John Cocke, Capt George Barnes, Inf
WILMOUTH, Stephen W, Pvt, Col Wm Lillard, Capt Geo Argenbright, E TN Vol Riflemen
WILSON, Aaron J, Pvt, Maj Wm Woodfolk, Capt James C Neil, Inf
WILSON, Aaron, Pvt, Col John K Wynne, Capt James Cole, Inf; deserted
WILSON, Abel, Pvt, Col S Bunch, Capt S Richardson, E TN Drafted Mil
WILSON, Alexander, Pvt, Col N T Perkins, Capt John Doak, Vol Mtd Inf
WILSON, Alexander, Pvt, Col R H Dyer, Capt Jos Williams, Vol Mtd Gunmen
WILSON, Amos, Pvt, Col Samuel Wear, Capt Rufus Morgan, E TN Vol Inf
WILSON, Archaless, Pvt, Col Alexander Loury, Lt Col L Hammond, Capt Thos Wells, Inf
WILSON, Benjamin, Pvt, Col John Cocke, Capt Saml M Caruthers, Inf
WILSON, Benjamin, Pvt, Col John Coffee, Capt Blackman Coleman, Cav
WILSON, Benjamin, Pvt, Col Wm Johnson, Capt Henry Hunter, E TN Mil
WILSON, Benjamin, Pvt, Col Wm Y Higgins, Capt Adam Dale, Mtd Gunmen
WILSON, Boyd, Pvt, Col R C Napier, Capt Early Benson, Mil Inf
WILSON, Daniel, Pvt, Col Wm Metcalf, Capt Wm Mullin, Mil Inf
WILSON, David, 2 Sgt, Col Wm Metcalf, Capt Andrew Patterson, Mil Inf
WILSON, David, Pvt, Col Thos Benton, Capt James McEwen, Vol Inf
WILSON, David, Pvt, Col Wm Johnson, Capt Christopher Cook, E TN Mil
WILSON, David, Pvt, Col Wm Johnson, Capt Joseph Kirk, Mil
WILSON, Ebin, Pvt, Col Newton Cannon, Capt John B Dempsey, Mtd Gunmen
WILSON, Ephraim, Pvt, Col Wm Lillard, Capt Robert Maloney, E TN Vol Inf
WILSON, George, 1 Cpl, Col Thos Williamson, Capt Giles Burdett, Vol Mtd Gunmen
WILSON, George, Pvt, Col Ewen Allison, Capt Jacob Hoyal, E TN Mil
WILSON, George, Pvt, Col Wm Pillow, Capt Thos Williamson, Vol Inf
WILSON, Harden, 1 Sgt, Col Wm Y Higgins, Capt Saml A Allen, Mtd Gunmen
WILSON, Hugh, Pvt, Col Ewen Allison, Capt Jacob Hoyal, E TN Mil
WILSON, Hugh, Pvt, Col Robert Steele, Capt Samuel Maxwell, Mil Inf
WILSON, Isaac, Pvt, Gen Andrew Jackson, Capt Nathan Davis, Inf
WILSON, Isaac, Sgt, Col Wm Johnson, Capt James Stewart, E TN Drafted Mil
WILSON, Israel, Pvt, Regt Commander omitted, Capt James Cowan, Mtd Inf
WILSON, James L, Cpl, Col Newton Cannon, Capt Andrew Patteson, Mtd Riflemen; reduced to the ranks
WILSON, James M, Pvt, Col Newton Cannon, Capt Andrew Patterson, Mtd Riflemen
WILSON, James, 6 Cpl, Col Philip Pipkin, Capt Peter Searcy, Mil Inf
WILSON, James, Cpl, Col John Alcorn, Capt Jno Baskerville, Vol Inf
WILSON, James, Cpl, Col John Coffee, Capt Jno Baskerville, Cav
WILSON, James, Pvt, Col Edwin Booth, Capt John Sharp, E TN Mil
WILSON, James, Pvt, Col G W Steel, Capt James Randals, Inf
WILSON, James, Pvt, Col N T Perkins, Capt Mathew Patterson, Mtd Vol
WILSON, James, Pvt, Col Philip Pipkin, Capt George Mebane, Mil Inf
WILSON, James, Pvt, Col R C Napier, Capt Andrew McCarty, Mil Inf
WILSON, James, Pvt, Col S Copeland, Capt John Holshouser, Inf
WILSON, James, Pvt, Col Samuel Wear, Capt Daniel Price, E TN Vol Inf
WILSON, James, Pvt, Col Wm Lillard, Capt Thos Sharpe, 2nd Regt Inf
WILSON, James, Pvt, Gen A Jackson, Capt Nathan Davis, Inf
WILSON, James, Pvt, Gen A Jackson, Capt Wm Russell, Mtd Spies
WILSON, James, Pvt, Maj Gen A Jackson, Col Thos Williamson, Capt Robert Steele, Vol Mtd Gunmen
WILSON, James, Pvt, Regt Commander omitted, Capt Archibold McKinney, Cav
WILSON, James, Pvt, Regt Commander omitted, Capt Charles Kavanaugh, Branch Srvce omitted
WILSON, James, Pvt, Regt Commander omitted, Capt G Lane, Mtd Riflemen
WILSON, James, Pvt, Regt Commander omitted, Capt James Cowan, Mtd Inf
WILSON, Jason, Pvt, Regt Commander omitted, Capt David Mason, Cav; furloughed for health
WILSON, Jesse, Pvt, Col John K Wynne, Capt James Cole, Inf; deserted
WILSON, Joel, Pvt, Col Thos McCrory, Capt Saml B McKnight, Inf
WILSON, Joel, Pvt, Col Wm Metcalf, Capt Bird L Hurt, Mil Inf
WILSON, John W, Pvt, Col Wm Lillard, Capt Robt Maloney, E TN Vol Inf
WILSON, John, 1 Sgt, Col Jno Coffee, Capt Jetton, Cav
WILSON, John, 4 Cpl, Col Newton Cannon, Capt John B Demsey, Mtd Gunmen
WILSON, John, Cpl, Col Samuel Bayless, Capt Solomon Hendricks, E TN Mil; reduced to the ranks
WILSON, John, Pvt, Col Alexander Loury, Capt Looney,

## Enlisted Men, War of 1812

WILSON, John, Pvt, Col Jno Williams, Capt Samuel Bunch, E TN Mtd Vol
W TN Inf
WILSON, John, Pvt, Col John Alcorn, Capt Jetton, Vol Cav; d 12-8-1813
WILSON, John, Pvt, Col John Cocke, Capt James Gault, Inf
WILSON, John, Pvt, Col John Coffee, Capt Blackman Coleman, Cav
WILSON, John, Pvt, Col Philip Pipkin, Capt Kirkpatrick, Mil Inf
WILSON, John, Pvt, Col R H Dyer, Capt Ephraim Dickson, 1st TN Mtd Vol Gunmen
WILSON, John, Pvt, Col S Bayless, Capt Rich, E TN Inf
WILSON, John, Pvt, Col S Wear, Capt Jas Tedford, E TN Vol Inf
WILSON, John, Pvt, Col Samuel Bunch, Capt Jno English, E TN Drafted Mil
WILSON, John, Pvt, Col Samuel Bunch, Capt Jno Houk, E TN Mil; joined from Capt English's Co
WILSON, John, Pvt, Col Wm Johnson, Capt Benj Powell, E TN Mil
WILSON, John, Pvt, Col Wm Johnson, Capt Wm McKamey, E TN Drafted Mil
WILSON, John, Pvt, Col Wm Metcalf, Capt Bird Hurt, Mil Inf
WILSON, John, Pvt, Col Wm Y Higgins, Capt Stephen Griffith, Mtd Riflemen
WILSON, John, Pvt, Regt Commander omitted, Capt David Mason, Cav
WILSON, John, Pvt, Regt Commander omitted, Capt Jno Miller, Spies
WILSON, John, Pvt, Regt Commander omitted, Capt Nathan Farmer, Mtd Riflemen
WILSON, John, Sgt, Col Edwin Booth, Capt Lewis, W TN Inf
WILSON, John, Sgt, Col John Alcorn, Capt Jetton, Vol Cav
WILSON, Jonathan, Pvt, Col N T Perkins, Capt George Eliot, Mil Inf
WILSON, Joseph J, Pvt, Col Samuel Bunch, Capt James Penny, E TN Mtd Inf
WILSON, Joseph L, Pvt, Col Wm Metcalf, Capt Thos Marks, Mil Inf
WILSON, Joseph, Pvt, Col Ewen Allison, Capt Adam Winsell, E TN Drafted Mil
WILSON, Joseph, Pvt, Col John Cocke, Capt James Gault, Inf
WILSON, Joseph, Pvt, Col John K Wynne, Capt James Holleman, Inf; deserted
WILSON, Joseph, Pvt, Col Philip Pipkin, Capt David Smith, Inf
WILSON, Joseph, Pvt, Col Philip Pipkin, Capt Wm Mackay, Mil Inf
WILSON, Joseph, Pvt, Lt Col Wm Phillips, Co Commander omitted, Inf
WILSON, Joseph, Pvt, Maj Wm Russell, Capt John Trimble, Vol Mtd Gunmen
WILSON, Landen C, Pvt, Col John K Wynne, Capt Bailey Butler, Inf
WILSON, Leven, Pvt, Col Thos Williamson, Capt George Mitchie, 2nd Regt TN Vol Mtd Gunmen
WILSON, Leven, Pvt, Maj Wm Russell, Capt George Mitchie, Vol Mtd Gunmen
WILSON, Mark, Pvt, Col Thos Williamson, Capt Wm Martin, Vol Mtd Gunmen
WILSON, Marlin, Sgt, Col Thos Williamson, Capt James Pace, Lt James Neely, Vol Mtd Gunmen
WILSON, Mathew, Pvt, Regt Commander omitted, Capt Nathan Farmer, Mtd Riflemen
WILSON, Michael, Pvt, Maj Wm Woodfolk, Capt Ezekial Ross & Capt McCulley, Inf
WILSON, Moses, Pvt, Col Edwin Booth, Capt John Lewis, E TN Mil
WILSON, Moses, Pvt, Col Thos Williamson, Capt Thos Scurry, Vol Mtd Gunmen
WILSON, Peter, Pvt, Col John Brown, Capt Charles Lewin, E TN Vol Mtd Inf
WILSON, Petty, Pvt, Regt Commander omitted, Capt John Scott, Det of Inf
WILSON, Robert, Dmr, Col John Cocke, Capt James Gault, Inf
WILSON, Robert, Far, Col R H Dyer, Capt Jos Williams, Vol Mtd Gunmen
WILSON, Robert, Pvt, Col Edwin Booth, Capt Alexander Biggs, Inf
WILSON, Robert, Pvt, Col John Cocke, Capt John Weakley, Inf
WILSON, Robert, Pvt, Col N T Perkins, Capt Mathew Patterson, Mtd Vol
WILSON, Robert, Pvt, Col Philip Pipkin, Capt David Smith, Mil Inf
WILSON, Robert, Pvt, Col Samuel Bunch, Capt Joseph Duncan, E TN Drafted Mil
WILSON, Robert, Pvt, Col Samuel Wear, Capt James Tedford, E TN Vol Inf
WILSON, Samuel D, Pvt, Col N Cannon, Capt Martin, Mtd Gunmen
WILSON, Samuel, 1 Cpl, Col Edward Bradley, Capt John Wallace, Vol Inf
WILSON, Samuel, 1 Cpl, Col S Copeland, Capt John Biles, Inf
WILSON, Samuel, 4 Sgt, Col John Coffee, Capt Robert Jetton, Cav
WILSON, Samuel, Cpl, Col John Brown, Capt John Trimble, E TN Mtd Gunmen
WILSON, Samuel, Cpl, Col John K Wynne, Capt Wm McCall, Inf
WILSON, Samuel, Pvt, Col John Alcorn, Capt Robt Jetton, Vol Cav; wounded 11-9-1813?
WILSON, Samuel, Pvt, Col Samuel Bunch, Capt Jones Griffin, E TN Drafted Mil
WILSON, Samuel, Pvt, Regt Commander omitted, Capt D Mason, Cav
WILSON, Samuel, Sgt, Col John Coffee, Capt Robert Jetton, Cav; promoted from Pvt
WILSON, Thomas, Pvt, Col John Wynne, Capt James Cole, Inf
WILSON, Thomas, Pvt, Maj John Chiles, Capt Chas Conway, E TN Mtd Gunmen
WILSON, Thomas, Pvt, Regt Commander omitted, Capt D Mason, Cav

## Enlisted Men, War of 1812

WILSON, Tilden, Pvt, Col Thos Williamson, Capt Thos Scurry, Vol Mtd Gunmen

WILSON, William W, 2 Sgt, Lt Col L Hammond, Capt Joseph N Williamson, 2nd Regt Inf; promoted from 3 Sgt

WILSON, William, Dmr, Col Thos Benton, Capt Isaiah Renshaw, Vol Inf

WILSON, William, Pvt, Col A Cheatham, Capt Richard Benson, Inf

WILSON, William, Pvt, Col Edwin Booth, Capt Richard Marshall, Drafted Mil; d 3-22-1815

WILSON, William, Pvt, Col Ewen Allison, Capt Jacob Hoyal, E TN Mil

WILSON, William, Pvt, Col Newton Cannon, Capt John B Demsey, Mtd Gunmen

WILSON, William, Pvt, Col Philip Pipkin, Capt David Smith, Ens Wm Pegram, Det of W TN Mil

WILSON, William, Pvt, Col Philip Pipkin, Capt David Smith, Inf

WILSON, William, Pvt, Col R H Dyer, Capt Bethel Allen, Vol Mtd Gunmen; d 2-25-1815

WILSON, William, Pvt, Col Samuel Bunch, Capt Jones Griffin, E TN Drafted Mil; deserted

WILSON, William, Pvt, Col Samuel Wear, Capt John Stephens, E TN Vol Inf

WILSON, William, Pvt, Col Samuel Wear, Capt Samuel Bowman, Mtd Inf

WILSON, William, Pvt, Col Thos Williamson, Capt John Doak & Capt John Dobbins, Vol Mtd Gunmen

WILSON, William, Pvt, Col Thos Williamson, Capt Richard Tate, Vol Mtd Gunmen

WILSON, William, Pvt, Col Wm Johnson, Capt James Tunnell, E TN Mil

WILSON, William, Pvt, Regt Commander omitted, Capt G Lane, Mtd Riflemen

WILSON, William, Pvt, Regt Commander omitted, Capt James Cowan, Mtd Inf

WILSON, William, Sgt, Col A Loury, Capt J Williamson, W TN Mil

WILSON, Willie, Pvt, Col Thos Williamson, Capt Thos Porter, Vol Mtd Gunmen; d 2-12-1815

WILSONE, John, Pvt, Regt Commander omitted, Capt Jno Miller, Spies

WILSSO, Simon, Pvt, Col T McCrory, Capt John Reynolds, Mil Inf

WILY, Samuel, Cpl, Col John Alcorn, Capt Frederick Stump, Cav; promoted from Pvt

WIMBERLEY, George, Sgt Maj, Col Archer Cheatham, Co Commander omitted, 3rd Regt TN

WIMBERLY, George, Pvt, Regt Commander omitted, Capt Jas Haggard, Mtd Gunmen

WIMBERLY, Melice, Pvt, Col John Alcorn, Capt Wm Locke, Cav

WIMBS, Hardy, Pvt, Col Philip Pipkin, Capt John Strother, Mil

WIMBS, William, Pvt, Col Philip Pipkin, Capt John Strother, Mil

WIMS, John, Pvt, Col R H Dyer, Capt Cuthbert Hudson, Vol Mtd Gunmen

WINAGER, Adam, Pvt, Col Wm Lillard, Capt Geo Argenbright, E TN Vol Riflemen

WINAGER, Andrew, Pvt, Col Wm Lillard, Capt Geo Argenbright, E TN Vol Riflemen

WINAGER, Samuel, Pvt, Col Wm Lillard, Capt Geo Argenbright, E TN Vol Riflemen

WINDALL, Andrew, Pvt, Col Samuel Bunch, Capt Henry Stephens, E TN Mtd Inf

WINDALL, William N, 2 Sgt, Col Samuel Bunch, Capt Henry Stephens, E TN Mtd Inf

WINDAM, Reuben, Pvt, Col John Alcorn, Capt John Winston, Mtd Riflemen

WINDLE, Joseph H, Asst District Paymaster, no other information

WINDORS, John, Pvt, Col Philip Pipkin, Capt Henry M Newlin, Mil Inf

WINEGAR, Adam, Pvt, Col Wm Johnson, Capt Benj Powell, E TN Mil

WINEGAR, Jacob, Pvt, Col Wm Lillard, Capt Geo Argenbright, E TN Vol Riflemen

WINEGAR, Peter, Pvt, Col Ewen Allison, Capt Jonas Loughmiller, Mil; transferred to Capt McPherson Co

WINEGAR, Peter, Pvt, Col Samuel Bunch, Capt Geo McPherson, E TN Mil; joined from Capt Loughmiller's Co

WINFIELD, Joseph, Pvt, Col A Cheatham, Capt Geo G Chapman, Inf

WINFIELD, Joseph, Pvt, Maj Gen Wm Carroll, Capt John Jackson & Capt A Metcalf, Inf

WINFORD, Benjamin, Pvt, Col Newton Cannon, Capt John Harpole, Mtd Gunmen

WINFORD, Michael S, Pvt, Col Thos Benton, Capt Geo Caperton, Inf

WINFORD, Smith, Cpl, Col Newton Cannon, Capt Francis Jones, Mtd Riflemen

WINFREY, Valentine, Pvt, Col N T Perkins, Capt Mathew Patterson, Mtd Vol

WINFREY, Wilson, Pvt, Maj Gen Wm Carroll, Col James Raulston, Capt Elijah Haynie, Inf

WINFRY, John, Pvt, Col Philip Pipkin, Capt E Kirkpatrick, Mil Inf

WINGATE, William, Pvt, Col John Coffee, Capt Michael Molton, Cav

WINGATE, William, Pvt, Regt Commander omitted, Capt Jos Williams, Mil Cav

WINGFIELD, Joseph, Pvt, Maj Gen Wm Carroll, Col Wm Metcalf, Capt John Jackson, Inf

WINGORE, Thomas, Pvt, Col Jno Coffee, Capt John W Byrn, Cav; deserted

WINKERS, Aron, Pvt, Lt Col John Edmondson, Co Commander omitted, Cav

WINKLE, Abraham, Pvt, Col Samuel Bayless, Capt Jonathan Waddle, E TN Mil

WINKLE, Mathew, Pvt, Col Wm Lillard, Capt Maloney, E TN Inf; unable to perform duty

WINN, C Coleman, Pvt, Col Samuel Bunch, Capt Henry Stephens, E TN Mtd Inf

WINN, Coleman, Pvt, Col Samuel Bayless, Capt Jones, E TN Drafted Mil

WINN, Dennis, Pvt, Col R C Napier, Capt Early Benson, Mil Inf; d 3-10-1814

WINN, Iham, Sgt, Col John Alcorn, Capt Thomas Bra-

## Enlisted Men, War of 1812

dley, Vol Cav; promoted to Ens
WINN, James T, Pvt, Col John Alcorn, Capt Thomas Bradley, Vol Cav
WINN, Peter, 5 Cpl, Col John Coffee, Capt Blackman Coleman, Inf
WINN, Peter, Sgt, Col John Alcorn, Capt Wm Locke, Cav
WINN, Thomas, Pvt, Lt Col Leroy Hammond, Co Commander omitted, Inf; transferred to Capt Looney's Co
WINN, Wilson, Pvt, Regt Commander omitted, Capt John Gordon, Mtd Spies
WINNER, Samuel, Pvt, Maj Gen Wm Carroll, Capt Lewis Dillahunty & Capt Daniel Bradford, Vol Inf
WINNINGHAM, Sherard, Pvt, Col Philip Pipkin, Capt Peter Searcy, Mil Inf
WINSELL, Jermine, Pvt, Col Thomas McCrory, Capt John Reynolds, Mil Inf
WINSET, Amos, Pvt, Col John Cocke, Capt James Gault, Inf
WINSET, Daniel, Pvt, Lt Col Leroy Hammond, Capt Thomas Wells, Inf
WINSET, John, Pvt, Col John Cocke, Capt James Gault, Inf
WINSET, William, Pvt, Lt Col Leroy Hammond, Capt Thomas Wells, Inf; joined from Capt Raines Co
WINSETT, Asa, 5 Cpl, Col John Cocke, Capt James Gault, Inf
WINSETT, Martin, Pvt, Lt Col A Cheatham, Co Commander omitted, Mtd Inf
WINSETTE, Martin, Pvt, Lt Col John Edmondson, Co Commander omitted, Cav
WINSTEAD, Benjamin, Pvt, Col Wm Metcalf, Capt Bird Hurt, Mil Inf
WINSTEAD, Charles, Sgt, Regt Commander omitted, Capt Jas Haggard, Mtd Gunmen
WINSTEAD, Johnston, Pvt, Col Thos Benton, Capt John Reynolds, Vol Inf
WINSTEAD, Samuel, Pvt, Col Wm Metcalf, Capt Bird Hurt, Mil Inf
WINSTON, Isaac, Pvt, Col John Alcorn, Capt Winston, Mtd Riflemen
WINSTON, Lewis, Pvt, Regt Commander omitted, Capt D Deadrick, Arty
WINSTONE, John, Pvt, Col Thomas Williams, Capt John Hutchings, Vol Mtd Gunmen
WINTER, Sam, Cpl, Regt Commander omitted, Capt Nathan Davis, Lt Isaac Barrett, Inf
WINTER, Stephen, Sgt, Col Edwin Booth, Capt Porter, Drafted Mil
WINTERS, Aaron, Pvt, Lt Col Jno Edmonson, Co Commander omitted, Cav
WINTERS, Aaron, Pvt, Maj Gen Jackson, Capt Jno Craine, Mtd Gunmen
WINTERS, Caleb jr, Pvt, Regt Commander omitted, Capt Jno Crane, Mtd Inf
WINTERS, Caleb, Pvt, Maj Gen Jackson, Capt Crane, Mtd Gunmen
WINTERS, Christopher, Pvt, Col S Bayless, Capt Hale, E TN Mil
WINTERS, Isaac, Pvt, Col John Wynne, Capt Geo Bradin, Inf

WINTERS, James, Pvt, Col T McCrory, Capt Gordon, Inf
WINTERS, Josiah, Pvt, Maj Gen Jackson, Capt Craine, Mtd Gunmen
WINTERS, Moses, Pvt, Lt Col Jno Edmonson, Co Commander omitted, Cav
WINTERS, Moses, Pvt, Maj Gen Jackson, Capt Craine, Mtd Gunmen
WINTERS, Moses, Pvt, Regt Commander omitted, Capt Jno Crane, Mtd Inf
WINTERS, Nathan, Pvt, Maj Gen Jackson, Capt Craine, Mtd Gunmen
WINTERS, Samuel, Pvt, Col Thos Benton, Capt Jas Hewett, Vol Inf
WINTERS, Samuel, Pvt, Col Thos Benton, Capt Jas Renshaw, Vol Inf; transferred from? Capt Hewett's Co
WINTERS, Samuel, Pvt, Col William Pillow, Capt Jas Renshaw, Inf
WINTON, Stephen, Pvt, Maj William Russell, Capt John Chism, Vol Mtd Gunmen
WION, John, Dmr, Col William Lillard, Capt Geo Argenbright, E TN Vol Riflemen
WIOTT, Frank, Pvt, Col N Cannon, Capt Hamby, Mtd Riflemen
WIOTT, James, Pvt, Col N Cannon, Capt Hamby, Mtd Riflemen
WIRICK, Henry, Pvt, Col Wm Johnson, Capt Henry Hunter, E TN Mil; transferred to Kirk's Co
WISDOM, Francis, Pvt, Col Jas Raulston, Capt West, Inf
WISDOM, Francis, Pvt, Col Thomas _____, Capt John Dobbins & Capt Doak, Vol Mtd Gunmen
WISE, Benjamin, Pvt, Col S Bayless, Capt Hale, E TN Mil
WISE, Benjamin, Pvt, Col Wm Lillard, Capt Robert Maloney, E TN Vol Inf; unable to perform duty
WISE, Carver William, Pvt, Col S Bayless, Capt Hale, Branch Srvce omitted
WISE, Henry, Cpl, Maj Wm Woodfolk, Co Commander omitted, Inf
WISE, James, Pvt, Col S Bunch, Capt Edward Buchanan, E TN Mil
WISE, John, Pvt, Col Ewen Allison, Capt Thos Wilson, E TN Drafted Mil
WISE, John, Pvt, Col Jno Coffee, Capt Chas Kavanaugh, Cav
WISE, John, Pvt, Col Thos Benton, Capt Benj Hewett, Vol Inf
WISE, John, Pvt, Col Thos Benton, Capt Jas Renshaw, Vol Inf; joined from? Capt Hewett
WISE, John, Pvt, Regt Commander omitted, Capt Archibald McKinney, Cav
WISE, Joseph, Cpl, Regt Commander omitted, Capt Archibald McKinney, Cav
WISE, Joseph, Pvt, Col Samuel Bayless, Capt Branch Jones, E TN Drafted Mil
WISE, Simon, Pvt, Col Samuel Bayless, Capt Branch Jones, E TN Drafted Mil
WISE, Step, Pvt, Col Robt Steele, Capt Samuel Maxwell, Mil Inf
WISEMAN, Jonathan, Pvt, Col S Copeland, Capt Beverly Wilkinson, Mtd Inf
WISENER, John, Pvt, Col Wm Metcalf, Capt Thos Marks,

## Enlisted Men, War of 1812

WISENER, Martin, Pvt, Col Thos Williamson, Capt Wm Martin, Vol Mtd Gunmen Mil Inf
WISER, Jacob, Pvt, Col Wm Lillard, Capt Hugh Martin, E TN Vol Inf
WIT, William, Pvt, Col Thos Benton, Capt Geo Caperton, Inf
WITECAR, Thomas, Pvt, Col William Lillard, Capt Jacob Hartsell, E TN Vol Inf; unfit for duty
WITHERAN, James, Pvt, Col Thos Benton, Capt Geo W Gibbs, Vol Inf
WITHERAN, Richard, Pvt, Col Thos Benton, Capt Geo W Gibbs, Vol Inf
WITHEROW, James, Pvt, Col Thos Benton, Capt Geo W Gibbs, Vol Inf
WITHEROW, Richard, Pvt, Col Thos Benton, Capt Geo W Gibbs, Vol Inf
WITHERS, Hugh H, Cpl, Col R H Dyer, Capt Ephraim D Dickson, TN Vol Mtd Gunmen
WITHERS, Hugh, Pvt, Col Newton Cannon, Capt Wm Edwards, Regt Command
WITHERS, Thomas, Pvt, Col Jas Raulston, Capt Mathew Neale, Inf
WITHERSPOON, John, Blksmth, Col Newton Cannon, Capt Geo Brandon, Mtd Riflemen
WITHERSPOON, Samuel G, Pvt, Col S Copeland, Capt Moses Thompson, Inf
WITHROW, James, Pvt, Col Wm Pillow, Capt John H Anderson, Vol Inf
WITHROW, Richard, Pvt, Col Wm Pillow, Capt John Anderson, Vol Inf
WITT, Charles, Cpl, Col Edwin Booth, Capt Geo Winton, E TN Mil
WITT, Daniel, Cpl, Col Samuel Bunch, Capt Francis Berry, E TN Mil; promoted
WITT, Daniel, Cpl, Col Samuel Bunch, Capt Jno English, E TN Drafted Mil; joined from Capt Gregory's Co
WITT, Daniel, Pvt, Col Samuel Bunch, Capt Francis Berr, E TN Mil; promoted to Sgt in English's Co
WITT, Ealy, Pvt, Col Wm Lillard, Capt Thos McChristian, E TN Vol Inf
WITT, Ely, Pvt, Col Samuel Bayless, Capt James Churchman, E TN Mil
WITT, Enoch, Pvt, Col Wm Lillard, Capt Zacheus Copeland, E TN Vol Inf
WITT, Harmon, 1 Cpl, Col Wm Lillard, Capt Zacheus Copeland, E TN Vol Inf
WITT, James, Pvt, Col Wm Lillard, Capt John Roper, E TN Vol Inf
WITT, James, Pvt, Col Wm Lillard, Capt Zacheus Copeland, E TN Vol Inf
WITT, James, Pvt, Maj John Chiles, Capt Chas Conway, E TN Mtd Gunmen
WITT, Joshua, Pvt, Col Edward Bradley, Capt John Kennedy, Riflemen; AWOL
WITT, Lewis, Pvt, Regt Commander omitted, Capt Larkin Ferrell, Mil Inf
WITT, Reuben, Pvt, Maj Wm Woodfolk, Capt Abraham Dudney & Capt John Sutton, Inf; deserted
WITT, Reuben, Pvt, Maj Wm Woodfolk, Capt James Turner, Inf

WITT, Robert, Pvt, Col Wm Johnson, Capt David McKamy, E TN Drafted Mil
WITT, Silas, Pvt, Maj John Chiles, Capt Reuben Tipton, E TN Vol Mtd Inf; Regt Co - Jefferson
WITTED, John, Pvt, Col Samuel Bunch, Capt Jones Griffin, E TN Drafted Mil; joined from Laughmiller, left for inability
WITTENBARGER, John, Pvt, Col Samuel Wear, Capt Daniel Price, E TN Vol Inf
WITTION, Redman, Pvt, Col Jno Brown, Capt Hugh Barton, E TN Mil Inf
WITTS, John, Pvt, Maj John Chiles, Capt Reuben Tipton, E TN Vol Mtd Inf
WOLF, George W, Sdlr, Col N T Perkins, Capt Philip Pipkin, Mtd Riflemen
WOLF, George, Pvt, Col Samuel Bunch, Capt Jno McNars, E TN Mil; attached to Capt Berry's Co
WOLF, George, Sgt, Col Wm Johnson, Capt James Stewart, E TN Drafted Mil
WOLF, Henry, Pvt, Col Wm Lillard, Capt Geo Keyes, E TN Inf
WOLF, James, Pvt, Maj John Childs, Capt John Stephens, E TN Vol Mtd Inf
WOLF, Jerimiah, Pvt, Regt Commander omitted, Capt Danl Yarnell, E TN Mil
WOLF, John, Pvt, Col John Wynne, Capt Wm Wilson, Inf; transferred to Capt Caruthers Co
WOLF, John, Pvt, Col Samuel Bayless, Capt Branch Jones, E TN Drafted Mil
WOLF, John, Pvt, Col Samuel Bunch, Capt Edward Buchanan, E TN Mil
WOLF, Joseph, Pvt, Col Samuel Bayless, Capt Jonathan Waddle, E TN Mil
WOLF, Peter, Pvt, Col Samuel Bayless, Capt Joseph Rich, E TN Inf
WOLF, Toias?, Pvt, Col S Copeland, Capt John Biles, Inf
WOLFE, Jeremiah, Pvt, Col Samuel Bunch, Capt Danl Yarnell, E TN Mil
WOLFE, John, Pvt, Regt Commander omitted, Capt Edward Buchanan, Branch Srvce omitted
WOLFE, William, Pvt, Regt Commander omitted, Capt D Mason, Cav
WOLFENBARGER, Jacob, Mus, Col Samuel Bunch, Capt John Dobkins, E TN Drafted Mil; deserted
WOLFENBARGER, Joseph, Pvt, Col Wm Lillard, Capt Thos Sharpe, 2nd Regt Inf
WOLFINBERGER, Jacob, Dmr, Col Ewen Allison, Capt John Hampton, Mil; transferred from Capt Dobbins' Co
WOLK, George, Sgt, Col Wm Johnson, Capt James Stewart, 3rd Regt E TN Mil
WOLLARD, Churchwell, Pvt, Col R H Dyer, Capt James McMahon, TN Vol Mtd Gunmen
WOLLARD, Nathaniel, Pvt, Col R H Dyer, Capt James McMahon, TN Vol Mtd Gunmen
WOLLARD (WOOLARD), William, Pvt, Col R H Dyer, Capt James McMahon, TN Vol Mtd Gunmen
WOLLIN, John, Pvt, Col John Alcorn, Capt Joseph Everett, E TN Mil; deserted
WOLSEL, Isreal, Pvt, Col S Bunch, Capt Geo McPherson, E TN Mil

## Enlisted Men, War of 1812

WOLSEY, Fathais, Pvt, Col S Bunch, Capt F Register, E TN Mil; deserted

WOLSEY, Isreal, Pvt, Col S Bunch, Capt F Register, E TN Mil

WOLSEY, William, Pvt, Col S Bunch, Capt Penny, E TN Mtd Inf

WOLSEY, ____, Pvt, Col S Bunch, Capt Geo McPherson, E TN Mil; joined from? Capt Register Co

WOMACK, David, Pvt, Col John Cocke, Capt Gray, Inf

WOMACK, Josiah, Pvt, Regt Commander omitted, Capt Nathan Davis, Lt I Barrett, Inf; d 3-12-1814

WOMBLE, Jesse, Pvt, Col S Bunch, Capt S Richardson, E TN Drafted Mil

WOMBLE, Joshua, Pvt, Col S Bunch, Capt S Richardson, E TN Drafted Mil

WOMMACH, John, Sgt, Col Alexander Loury, Capt Rains, Inf

WOOD, Absolm, Pvt, Col John Wynne, Capt Bailey Butler, Inf

WOOD, Alexander, Pvt, Col Wm Lillard, Capt Wm Lillard, E TN Inf

WOOD, Allen, Pvt, Col Wm Metcalf, Capt Sitton, Mil

WOOD, Archibald, Pvt, Col Thos Benton, Capt Jas Caperton, Inf

WOOD, Archibald, Sdlr, Col Thomas Williamson, Capt Robert Moore, Vol Mtd Gunmen

WOOD, Benjamin, Pvt, Col John Wynne, Capt Wood, Inf

WOOD, Charles, 2 Cpl, Col Thos Benton, Capt Geo Caperton, Inf

WOOD, Charles, 4 Sgt, Col Thos Benton, Capt Geo Caperton, Inf

WOOD, Charles, Cpl, Col Thos Benton, Capt Geo Caperton, Vol Inf

WOOD, Clement, Pvt, Col Edwin Booth, Capt Lewis, E TN Mil

WOOD, Curtis, Cpl, Col Robert Steele, Capt Jas Bennett, Mil Inf

WOOD, Fleming P, 1 Cpl, Col A Loury, Capt J Williams, W TN Mil

WOOD, Hennury P, 1 Cpl, Lt Col Hammonds, Capt Joseph Williamson, Inf

WOOD, Hiram, Cpl, Col Robert Steele, Capt John Chitwood, Mil Inf

WOOD, Hiram, Pvt, Col T McCrory, Capt Isaac Patton, Mil Inf

WOOD, Isom, Pvt, Col Philip Pipkin, Capt Jas Blackmore, Vol Inf

WOOD, James B, Sgt, Col John Alcorn, Capt George Winston, Mtd Riflemen

WOOD, James, Pvt, Col Jno Brown, Capt Hugh Barton, E TN Mil Inf; deserted

WOOD, James, Pvt, Col Philip Pipkin, Capt Allen, Vol Mtd Gunmen

WOOD, James, Pvt, Col Wm Johnson, Capt Jas Stewart, E TN Drafted Mil

WOOD, John, 2 Cpl, Col S Bunch, Capt William Jobe, E TN Vol Mtd Inf

WOOD, John, Pvt, Col John Wynne, Capt Bailey Butler, Inf

WOOD, John, Pvt, Col Philip Pipkin, Capt Geo Blackmore, Branch Srvce omitted; deserted

WOOD, John, Pvt, Col S Bunch, Capt Robert Breden, E TN Mil

WOOD, John, Pvt, Col Wm Lillard, Capt Jacob Hartsell, E TN Vol Inf

WOOD, John, Pvt, Col Wm Metcalf, Capt Bird Hurt, Mil Inf

WOOD, John, Pvt, Lt Col Leroy Hammonds, Capt Jas Craig, Inf

WOOD, John, Pvt, Regt Commander omitted, Capt Nathan Davis, Lt I Barrett, Branch Srvce omitted

WOOD, John, Sgt, Col Robert Steele, Capt Richard Ratton, Mil Inf

WOOD, Joseph, Pvt, Col N Cannon, Capt Edwards, Command

WOOD, Joseph, Pvt, Col N Cannon, Capt John Harpole, Mtd Gunmen

WOOD, Joseph, Pvt, Col S Bayless, Capt I Bacon, E TN Mil

WOOD, Levi, Pvt, Regt Commander omitted, Capt Jas Terrell, Cav

WOOD, Mason, Pvt, Col Robert Dyer, Capt Allen, Vol Mtd Gunmen

WOOD, Mosey, Pvt, Lt Col Hammonds, Capt Thomas Delaney, Inf

WOOD, Owen, Pvt, Col Leroy Loury, Capt James Kincaid, Inf

WOOD, Reuben, Pvt, Col John Cocke, Capt Bird Nance, Inf

WOOD, Reuben, Pvt, Col S Bunch, Capt Robert Steele, Mil Inf

WOOD, Robert, Pvt, Col R T Perkins, Capt Quarles, Mtd Inf

WOOD, Smith, Pvt, Col Thomas Williamson, Capt Robert Moore, Vol Mtd Gunmen

WOOD, Stephen, 3 Cpl, Col John Cocke, Capt James Gault, Inf

WOOD, Thomas, Pvt, Col Phillip ____, Capt Geo Mebane, Mil Inf

WOOD, Thomas, Pvt, Col Robert Steele, Capt Jas Bennett, Mil Inf

WOOD, Thomas, Pvt, Col S Copeland, Capt Tait, Inf

WOOD, Thompson, 4 Sgt, Col John Cocke, Capt James Gault, Inf

WOOD, West, Pvt, Regt Commander omitted, Capt J N Williams, Mil Cav

WOOD, West, Sgt, Col John Coffee, Capt Mitchell Molton, Cav

WOOD, William, Pvt, Col Philip Pipkin, Co Commander omitted, Mil Inf

WOOD, William, Pvt, Regt Commander omitted, Capt Nathan Davis, Lt I Barrett, Inf

WOOD, William, Sgt, Col S Copeland, Capt Richard Sharp, Mil Inf; promoted from a Pvt

WOOD, Zachariah, Pvt, Col John Allison, Capt Jonas Loughmiller, Mil; transferred to Capt McPherson Co

WOODALL, Joe, Pvt, Regt Commander omitted, Capt Joel Parrish, Arty

WOODALL, Joseph, 2 Cpl, Col Edward Bradley, Capt John Kennedy, Riflemen

WOODALL, Joseph, Pvt, Col S Copeland, Capt Wm

## Enlisted Men, War of 1812

Evans, Mil Inf; transferred to the Arty Co
WOODALL, Joseph, Pvt, Col Wm Hall, Capt John Kennedy, Vol Inf
WOODALL, Joseph, Pvt, Maj Gen Jackson, Capt Joel Parrish, Branch Srvce omitted
WOODALL, Thomas, Pvt, Col Wm Johnson, Capt David McKamy, E TN Drafted Mil; deserted
WOODALL, William, 3 Sgt, Col Wm Lillard, Capt Geo Argenbright, E TN Vol Riflemen
WOODARD, Charles, Pvt, Col Jno Brown, Capt Jas Preston, E TN Mil Inf
WOODARD, Henry, Pvt, Col Philip Pipkin, Capt James Blakemore, Mil Inf
WOODARD, James, Pvt, Col R H Dyer, Capt Wm White, Vol Mtd Gunmen
WOODARD, John, Pvt, Col John Brown, Capt Jas Preston, E TN Mil Inf
WOODARD, John, Pvt, Col Wm Y Higgins, Capt James Hambleton, Mtd Gunmen
WOODARD, William, Pvt, no other information
WOODART, Jeremiah, Pvt, Maj Wm Russell, Capt John Trimble, Vol Mtd Gunmen
WOODBEE, Eppy, Pvt, Col Samuel Bayless, Capt Solomon Hendricks, E TN Mil
WOODBERRY, Jesse B, Pvt, Col L Hammond, Capt J N Williamson, 2nd Regt Inf
WOODCOCK, Maraday, Pvt, Col Jas Raulston, Capt Elijah Haynie, Inf
WOODCOCK, Mark, Cpl, Col Jas Raulston, Capt Elijah Haynie, Inf; d 1-30-1814
WOODCOCK, William, Pvt, Col Jas Raulston, Capt Elijah Haynie, Inf; d 2-23-1815
WOODDY, William, Pvt, Col Edwin E Booth, Capt Samuel Thompson, Mil
WOODELL, James, Pvt, Col Thomas McCrory, Co Commander omitted, Inf
WOODEN, William, Pvt, Col Wm Metcalf, Capt John Barnhart, Mil; d 1-12-1815
WOODFEN, Samuel, Cpl, Col Thomas Williamson, Capt John Hutchings, Vol Mtd Gunmen
WOODFIN, Moses, Pvt, Col John K Wynne, Capt Wm Carothers, W TN Inf
WOODIE, James, Pvt, Col Thomas Williamson, Capt Wm Martin, Vol Mtd Gunmen
WOODLAND, Samuel, Pvt, Col Philip Pipkin, Capt Mackey, Mil Inf
WOODLEY, Jacob, Pvt, Col Thomas H Benton, Capt George Gibbs, Vol Inf
WOODLEY, Jacob, Pvt, Col Wm Pillow, Capt John Anderson, Vol Inf
WOODLEY, John, Pvt, Maj Wm Russell, Capt Wm Chism, Vol Mtd Gunmen
WOODRIDGE, Edward, Pvt, Col Philip Pipkin, Capt David Smith, Mil Inf
WOODS, Archibald, Pvt, Col S Bunch, Capt George Gregory, E TN Drafted Mil; enlisted in the 39th US Regt
WOODS, Archibald, Pvt, Col Thomas H Benton, Capt George Caperton, Vol Inf
WOODS, Charles, 4 Sgt, Col Wm Pillow, Capt George Caperton, Inf
WOODS, Elijah, Pvt, Col Ewen Allison, Capt Joseph Everett, E TN Mil; transferred to Capt McPherson's Co
WOODS, Flemins P, 1 Cpl, Col L Hammond, Capt J N Williamson, 2nd Regt Inf
WOODS, Isac, Pvt, Col Wm Metcalf, Capt Marks, Mil Inf
WOODS, Israel, Pvt, Col R H Dyer, Maj Wm Russell, Capt Wm Russell, Vol Mtd Gunmen
WOODS, James, Pvt, Col Wm Johnson, Capt Jas Stewart, E TN Mil
WOODS, Joel, Pvt, Maj John Chiles, Capt Reuben Tipton, E TN Vol Inf; Regt from Jefferson Co
WOODS, John, Pvt, Col Thos Bradley, Capt Travis Nash, Vol Inf
WOODS, John L, Pvt, Col Thos Williamson, Capt Wm Metcalf, Vol Mtd Gunmen
WOODS, John, Pvt, Col John Coffee, Capt Alexander McKeen, Cav
WOODS, John, Pvt, Maj Wm Woodfolk, Capt Jas Turner, Inf; reduced from dmr
WOODS, John, Pvt, Regt Commander omitted, Capt Jas Cowan, Mtd Inf
WOODS, John, Wgnmstr, Maj Gen John Cocke, E TN Vol
WOODS, Joseph B, Pvt, Col Saml Wear, Capt Jas Gillespie, E TN Vol Inf
WOODS, Joseph, Pvt, Col Wm Lillard, Capt Geo Argenbright, E TN Vol Riflemen
WOODS, Joshua, Pvt, Col S Copeland, Capt George, Inf
WOODS, Joshua, Pvt, Maj Gen Andrew Jackson, Capt John Craine, Mtd Gunmen; wounded 1-22-1814
WOODS, Peter, Pvt, Col R H Dyer, Maj Wm Russell, Capt Wm Russell, Vol Mtd Gunmen
WOODS, Richard M, Pvt, Col John Williams, Capt David G Vance, E TN Mtd Vol
WOODS, West, Pvt, Col John Coffee, Capt Michael Molton, Cav
WOODS, William M, Pvt, Col Thos Benton, Capt Benj Reynolds, Vol Inf
WOODS, William, Pvt, Col John Cocke, Capt Saml M Caruthers, Inf
WOODS, Williams, Pvt, Col T McCrory, Capt Thos K Gordon, Inf
WOODS, Wyly, Sgt, Col Saml Bunch, Capt John Inman, E TN Vol Mtd Inf
WOODSON, Obadiah, Pvt, Col Newton Cannon, Capt Jas Walton, Mtd Riflemen
WOODSWORTH, Thomas, Pvt, Col Wm Metcalf, Capt Wm Mullins, Mil Inf
WOODWARD, Solomon, Pvt, Col Wm Metcalf, Capt Andrew Patterson, Mil Inf
WOODY, Jacob, Pvt, Col Thos Benton, Capt Geo W Gibbs, Vol Inf
WOODY, James, Pvt, Col Saml Wear, Capt Jas Gillespie, E Tn Vol Inf
WOODY, Nicholas, Pvt, Col Ewen Allison, Capt Allen, E TN Mil
WOODY, Nicholas, Pvt, Col Saml Bunch, Capt Jos Duncan, E TN Draft Mil
WOODY, Oliver, Pvt, Col Wm Hall, Capt Henry M Newlin, Inf
WOODY, Silas, Pvt, Col Saml Bunch, Capt Jos Duncan, E

Tn Draft Mil; joined from Capt Allen's Co
WOODY, William, Pvt, Col Jas Raulston, Maj Gen Wm Carroll, Capt Edward Robinson, Inf
WOODY, Zachariah, Pvt, Col Saml Bunch, Capt Geo McPherson, E Tn Mll; joined from Capt Loughmiller Co
WOOLARD, Swain W, Pvt, Col Wm Metcalf, Capt Bird L Hurt, Mil Inf
WOOLFE, John, Pvt, Col John Wynne, Capt Wm Carothers, W TN Inf; deserted
WOOLLARD, Church, Pvt, Col Edward Bradley, Capt Thos B Haynie, Vol Inf
WOOLSAY, Samuel, Pvt, Col John Wynne, Capt Robt Bradin, Inf
WOOLSEY, Noah, Pvt, Col Saml Bayless, Capt Jos Hale, E TN Mil
WOOLSEY, Stephen, Pvt, Col Robt Steele, Capt Saml Maxwell, Mil Inf
WOOLSEY, Stephen, Sgt, Col John Wynne, Capt Jas Holleman, Inf
WOOLSEY, Thomas, Pvt, Col Philip Pipkin, Capt John Strother, Mll
WOOLZ, Elijah, Pvt, Col Saml Bunch, Capt Geo McPherson, E TN Mll; joined from Capt Register's Co
WOOSLEY, Nathan, Pvt, Col Thos Benton, Capt Henry L Douglass, Vol Inf
WOOSLEY, Oliver, Pvt, Col Edwin Booth, Capt John Slatton, E TN Mll
WOOTAN, Jonathan, Pvt, Maj Wm Russell, Capt Wm Chism, Vol Mtd Gunmen
WOOTEN, Daniel, Pvt, Col A Loury, Capt John Looney, W TN Inf
WOOTEN, John, Sgt, Col Jas Raulston, Capt Mathew Neal, Inf; died 1-1-1815
WOOTEN, William, Pvt, Maj Wm Russell, Capt Geo Mitchie, Vol Mtd Gunmen
WOOTON, John, Pvt, Col Edward Bradley, Capt Wm Lauderdale, Vol Inf
WORD (WARD), Pleasant, Pvt, Col Philip Pipkin, Capt Henry M Newlin, Mil Inf; promoted to 3 Sgt
WORDLY, Pvt, Col A Cheatham, Capt Chas Johnson, Inf
WORDON, John, 6 Cpl, Col Saml Bayless, Capt Solomon Hendrix, E TN Mil; died 12-24-1814
WORK, Flemment (Flemming), Pvt, Col Jno Brown, Capt Wm D Neilson, Regt E TN Vol Mil
WORK, Samuel, Pvt, Col R H Dyer, Capt Robt Evans, Vol Gunmen
WORLEY, David, Pvt, Col Saml Bayless, Capt Jas Landen, E TN Mil
WORLEY, Elijah, Pvt, Col Saml Bayless, Capt Jas Landen, E TN Mil
WORLEY, George, Pvt, Col Wm Lillard, Capt Robt Maloney, E TN Vol Inf
WORLEY, Henry, Pvt, Col R H Dyer, Capt Cuthbert Hudson, Vol Mtd Gunmen
WORLEY, Hiram, Pvt, Col Ewen Allison, Capt Adam Winsell, E TN Draft Mil
WORLEY, John, Pvt, Col Ewen Allison, Capt Adam Winsell, E TN Draft Mil
WORLEY, Willis, Pvt, Col Wm Johnson, CApt Elihu Milliken, 3 Regt E TN Mil

WORMICK, John, Pvt, Col Saml Wear, Capt John Porter, E TN Vol Mtd Inf
WORNICK, John, Pvt, Col Philip Pipkin, Capt Geo Mebane, Mil Inf
WORNNINGTON, Edward, Pvt, Col Philip Pipkin, Capt John Robertson, Mil Inf
WORTHAM, Joseph L, Pvt, Col Newton Cannon, Capt Andrew Patterson, Mtd Riflemen
WORTHAN, James L, Pvt, Col R H Dyer, Capt Ephraim D Dickson, TN Mtd Vol Gunmen
WORTHAN, John, Cpl, Col R H Dyer, Maj Wm Russell, Capt Wm Russell, Vol Mtd Gunmen
WORTHAN, John, Pvt, Col Philip Pipkin, Capt David Smith, Inf
WORTHAN, Silvester, Sgt, Col Newton Cannon, Capt Francis Jones, Mtd Riflemen
WORTHAN, William, Pvt, Col Philip Pipkin, Capt David Smith, Inf
WORTHAN, William, Pvt, Col Philip Pipkin, Capt Francis Smith, Inf
WORTHINGTON, Abraham, Pvt, Col R H Dyer, Capt Jas McMahan, TN Vol Mtd Gunmen
WORTHINGTON, James, Pvt, Col Jno Brown, Capt Jas Standifer, E TN Vol Mtd Mil; died 12-3-1813
WORTHINGTON, James, Pvt, Col Saml Bunch, Capt Isaac Williams, Mtd Vol
WORTHINGTON, Jesse, Pvt, Col Jno Brown, Capt Jas Standifer, E TN Vol Mtd Mil
WORTHINGTON, Robert, Pvt, Col Jno Brown, Capt Jas Standifer, E TN Vol Mtd Mil
WORTHINGTON, William, Pvt, Col Saml Bunch, Capt Isaac Williams, Mtd Vol
WORTHWERTH, Willis, Pvt, Regt Commander omitted, Capt Jas Craig, Mil Inf
WOTEN, David, Pvt, Col A Cheatham, Capt Jas Giddins, Inf
WOTEN, George, Pvt, Col A Cheatham, Capt Jas Gidden, Inf
WOTSON, David, Pvt, Col S Bayless, Capt Jos Rich, E TN Inf
WRAY, Archibald, Pvt, Maj Gen Jackson, Capt Kirkpatrick, Mtd Gunmen
WRAY, James, Pvt, Col Philip Pipkin, Capt Mackey, Mil Inf
WRAY, John, Pvt, Maj Gen Jackson, Capt Jos Kirkpatrick, Mtd Gunmen
WRAY, Robert, Pvt, Col R C Napier, Capt Edward Neblett, Mil Inf
WREN, David jr, Pvt, Col Robt Dyer, Capt Evans, Vol Mtd Gunmen; died 11-12-1812
WREN, James, Pvt, Col Philip Pipkin, Ens Wm Pegram, W TN Mil
WREN, William, Pvt, Col Jno Coffee, Capt Danl Ross, Mtd Gunmen
WREY, Isaac, Pvt, Col Robt Dyer, Capt Evans, Vol Mtd Gunmen; died 2-24-1814
WRICE, John, Pvt, Col S Bunch, Capt Jones Griffin, E TN Drafted Mll
WRIGHT, Barlet, Pvt, Col John Wynne, Capt Jas Cole, Inf
WRIGHT, Bird, Sgt, Col Edward Bradley, Capt Wm Lauderdale, Branch omitted

WRIGHT, Byrd, Sgt, Col Wm Hall, Capt Wm Alexander, Vol Inf
WRIGHT, Christopher, Pvt, Col Edward Bradley, Capt Elijah Haynie, Vol Inf
WRIGHT, Christopher, Pvt, Col Wm Hall, Capt Henry Newlin, Inf
WRIGHT, Christopher, Pvt, Regt Commander omitted, Capt Jno Gordon, Mtd Spies
WRIGHT, Daniel, Pvt, Col John Alcorn, Capt John Baskerville, Vol Inf
WRIGHT, David, Pvt, Regt Commander omitted, Capt Jas Cowan, Mtd Inf
WRIGHT, Elijah, Cpl, Col Jas Raulston, Capt Mathew Neal, Inf
WRIGHT, Elijah, Pvt, Col Robt Dyer, Capt Jas Wyatt, Vol Mtd Gunmen
WRIGHT, Elijah, Pvt, Col S Bunch, Capt Vance, E TN Mtd Inf
WRIGHT, Ellis G, Sgt, Col Wm Johnston, Capt Jos Kirk, Mil
WRIGHT, George, Pvt, Col Edward Bradley, Capt John Moore, Vol Inf
WRIGHT, George, Pvt, Col Robt Dyer, Capt Cuthbert Hudson, Vol Mtd Gunmen; died 2-1-1815
WRIGHT, Hollis, Pvt, Col Thos Benton, Capt Thos Williamson, Vol Inf
WRIGHT, Isaac, Pvt, Col N Cannon, Capt Hamby, Mtd Riflemen
WRIGHT, Isaac, Pvt, Col Thos Williamson, Capt Beverly Williams, Vol Mtd Gunmen
WRIGHT, Isaac, Pvt, Col Thos Williamson, Capt Dobbins & Capt Doak, Vol Mtd Gunmen
WRIGHT, Jacob, Pvt, Col Thos Williamson, Capt Doak & Capt John Dobbins, Vol Mtd Gunmen
WRIGHT, Jacob, Pvt, Lt Col Hammonds, Capt Geo Tubb, Inf; died 2-25-1815
WRIGHT, Jacob, Sgt, Col Robt Dyer, Capt Jas Wyatt, Vol Mtd Gunmen
WRIGHT, James jr, Pvt, Col Edwin Booth, Capt Geo Slatton, E TN Mil
WRIGHT, James sr, Pvt, Col Edwin Booth, Capt Geo Slatton, E TN Mil
WRIGHT, James, Pvt, Col S Bayless, Capt Jones, E TN Drafted Mil; died 2-20-1815
WRIGHT, James, Pvt, Col Wm Metcalf, Capt Wm Mullens, Mil Inf
WRIGHT, James, Pvt, Regt Commander omitted, Capt Sam Allen, Pack Horse Guards
WRIGHT, Jeremiah, Pvt, Col Phillip Pipkin, Capt Geo Smith, Mil Inf
WRIGHT, John A, Pvt, Col S Bunch, Capt Duncan, E TN Drafted Mil
WRIGHT, John, Pvt, Col Jas Raulston, Capt Henry Hamilton, Inf
WRIGHT, John, Pvt, Col Jas Raulston, Capt Henry West, Inf
WRIGHT, John, Pvt, Col Jno Brwon, Capt Hugh Barton, E TN Mil Inf
WRIGHT, John, Pvt, Col Philip Pipkin, Capt Jackson, Mil Inf
WRIGHT, John, Pvt, Col R C Napier, Capt McCarty, Mil Inf
WRIGHT, John, Pvt, Col Robt Steele, Capt Robt Campbell, Mil Inf
WRIGHT, John, Pvt, Col S Bunch, Lt Jno Harris, E TN Mil
WRIGHT, John, Pvt, Col S Wear, Capt Jesse Cole, Vol Inf
WRIGHT, John, Pvt, Col Thos Benton, Capt Jas McEwen, Vol Inf; missing
WRIGHT, John, Pvt, Col Wm Lillard, Capt Maloney, E TN Vol Inf; wgnr
WRIGHT, John, Pvt, Lt Col Jno Edmondson, Co Commander omitted, Cav
WRIGHT, John, Pvt, Maj John Childs, Capt Chas Conway, E TN Mtd Gunmen
WRIGHT, John, Pvt, Maj Wm Russell, Capt John Trimble, Vol Mtd Gunmen
WRIGHT, John, Pvt, Regt Commander omitted, Capt ELijah Rushing, Inf
WRIGHT, Joseph, Pvt, Col Wm Metcalf, Capt Wm Mullen, Mil Inf
WRIGHT, Linsey, Pvt, Col Edwin Booth, Capt Geo Biggs, Inf
WRIGHT, Payton, Pvt, Col Thos Williamson, Capt Cook & Capt Crane, Vol Mtd Gunmen
WRIGHT, Perryan, Pvt, Col S Bunch, Capt A Breden, E TN Mil
WRIGHT, Peyton, Pvt, Lt Col Archer Cheatham, Co Commander omitted, Mtd Inf
WRIGHT, Richard, 2 Cpl, Col R C Napier, Capt E Benson, Mil Inf
WRIGHT, Richard, Pvt, Regt Commander omitted, Capt Jas Ross English, Branch omitted
WRIGHT, Riding, Pvt, Maj Wm Woodfolk, Capt E Ross & Capt McCulley, Inf
WRIGHT, Robert, Pvt, Regt Commander omitted, Lt Jno Scott, Inf
WRIGHT, Robertson, Pvt, Col Ed Bradley, Capt Brice Martin, Vol Inf
WRIGHT, Robertson, Pvt, Lt Col L Hammond, Capt Jas Tubb, Inf
WRIGHT, Samuel, 1 Sgt, Col Saml Bayless, Capt S Hendrix, E TN Mil
WRIGHT, Samuel, Pvt, Col Alex Loury, Capt Jno Looney, W TN Inf
WRIGHT, Solomon, Pvt, Col Jas Raulston, Capt E Haynie, Inf
WRIGHT, Thomas A, Pvt, Col Jas Raulston, Capt H Hamilton, Inf; also served under Maj Gen Carroll
WRIGHT, Thomas, Pvt, Col Saml Bunch, Capt Jos Duncan, E TN Drafted Mil
WRIGHT, Thomas, Pvt, Col Thos Benton, Capt Thos Williamson, Vol Inf
WRIGHT, Thomas, Pvt, Col Wm Pillow, Capt Thos Williamson, Vol Inf
WRIGHT, Thomas, Pvt, Lt Col Richd Napier, Co Commander omitted, Inf
WRIGHT, Thomas, Pvt, Maj Jno Childs, Capt R Tipton, E TN Vol Mtd Inf; Regt from Knox Co
WRIGHT, Thompson, Pvt Mus, Col Wm Pillow, no other information
WRIGHT, Thompson, Pvt, Col Ed Bradley, Capt Brice Martin, Vol Inf

## Enlisted Men, War of 1812

WRIGHT, Thompson, Pvt, Col Jno Alcorn, Capt Alex McKeen, Cav
WRIGHT, Thompson, Pvt, Col P Pipkin, Capt Jas Blakemore, Mil Inf
WRIGHT, William, 1 Cpl, Col Jas Raulston, Co Commander omitted, W TN Mil Inf
WRIGHT, William, 4 Sgt, Col Wm Hall, Capt Travis Nash, Inf
WRIGHT, William, Cpl, Col Jas Raulston, Capt M Neal, Inf
WRIGHT, William, Pvt, Col Jno Cocke, Capt Geo Barnes, Inf
WRIGHT, William, Pvt, Col P Pipkin, Capt P Searcy, Mil Inf
WRIGHT, William, Pvt, Col Saml Bayless, Capt Branch Jones, E TN Draft Mil
WRIGHT, William, Pvt, Col Thos Benton, Capt Geo Caperton, Inf
WRIGHT, William, Pvt, Col Wm Higgins, Capt Thos Eldridge, Mtd Gunmen
WRIGHT, William, Pvt, Col Wm Johnston, Capt Jos Kirk, Mil; never appeared
WRIGHT, William, Pvt, Col Wm Metcalf, Capt Jno Cunningham & Capt Alex Hill, Mil Inf
WRIGHT, William, Pvt, Col Wm Pillow, Capt Geo Caperton, Inf
WRIGHT, William, Pvt, Regt Commander omitted, Capt ELijah Rushing, Inf
WRIGHT, William, Pvt, Regt Commander omitted, Lt Jno Scott, Inf
WRIGHT, William, Sgt, Col Ed Bradley, Capt Travis Nash, Vol Inf
WRIGHT, Wylea, Pvt, Col Wm Lillard, Capt Thos McChristian, E TN Vol Inf
WRIGHT (MIGHT), Ellis G, Sgt, Col William Johnson, Capt Christopher Cook, E TN Mil
WRIGHTSELL, William, 3 Cpl, Col Saml Bayless, Capt S Hendrix, E TN Mil; died 4-23-1815
WRINKLE, Henry, Pvt, Col Saml Wear, Capt Saml Bowman, Mtd Inf
WRINKLE, Jacob, Pvt, Col Saml Wear, Capt Saml Bowman, Mtd Inf
WRITE, William C, Sgt, Col T McCrory, Capt A Metcalf, Mil Inf
WRITE (RITE), Wesley I, Sgt, Col Saml Bayless, Capt Jos Hall, E TN Mil
WROE, Thomas, Dmr, Col Jno Brown, Capt Wm D Neilson, E TN Vol Mil
WRY, Absolom, Pvt, Col Jno Cocke, Capt Jos Price, Inf
WRY, Benjamin, 7 Cpl, Col Jno Cocke, Capt Jos Price, Inf; promoted from Pvt
WRY, Isaac, Pvt, Col J K Wynne, Capt Bayless Prince, Inf
WRY, Joseph, Sgt, Col J K Wynne, Capt Bayless Prince, Inf
WRYE, George W, Pvt, Maj Gen Wm Carroll, Capt E Haynie, Inf
WUMBLE, Redding, Pvt, Regt Commander omitted, Capt Geo Smith, Spies
WURRELL, William, Pvt, Col Wm Hall, Capt Jno Wallace, Inf
WYATT, Abraham, Pvt, Regt Commander omitted, Capt Jos Askew, Inf
WYATT, Carey, Pvt, Maj Jno Chiles, Capt Jos Price, Mil Inf
WYATT, Daniel, Pvt, Col Jno Cocke, Capt Jas Gray, Inf
WYATT, Daniel, Pvt, Regt Commander omitted, Capt Jos Askew, Inf
WYATT, Edwin, Pvt, Col E Booth, Capt Jno Lewis, E TN Mil; promoted Surgeon of 5 Regt Mil
WYATT, Ezekiel, Pvt, Col R H Dyer, Capt Bethel Allen, Vol Mtd Gunmen
WYATT, James, Mus, Col Edwin Booth, Capt Richd Marshall, Drafted Mil
WYATT, James, Pvt, Col Wm Higgins, Capt Jno Doake, Mtd Riflemen
WYATT, James, Pvt, Col Wm Higgins, Capt Thos Eldridge, Mtd Gunmen
WYATT, James, Pvt, Regt Commander omitted, Capt Archibald McKinney, Cav
WYATT, Joseph, Cpl, Col John Alcorn, Capt John Winston, Mtd Riflemen
WYATT, Joseph, Pvt, Col Ewen Allison, Capt Wm King, Draft Mil
WYATT, Joseph, Pvt, Col John Alcorn, Capt Thos Bradley, Vol Cav
WYATT, Joseph, Pvt, Col John Brown, Capt Lunsford Oliver, E TN Mil
WYATT, Joseph, Sgt Maj, Col Wm Y Higgins, 2 Regt Mtd Vol
WYATT, Martin, Pvt, no Regt Commander, Capt Garrett Lane, Mtd Riflemen; acting as Pack Horse Guards
WYATT, Robert, Pvt, Regt Commander omitted, Capt Jas Gray, Inf
WYATT, Solomon, Pvt, Col Philip Pipkin, Capt Peter Searcy, Mil Inf
WYATT, Thomas E, Asst Adjt Gen, Maj Gen Andrew Jackson, Div of TN Mil
WYATT, Thomas E, Pvt, Col John Alcorn, Capt Thos Bradley, Vol Cav
WYATT, Thomas E, Pvt, Maj Gen A Jackson, Capt Wm Carroll, Vol Inf
WYATT, Thomas, Cpl, Regt Commander omitted, Capt Askew, Inf
WYATT, W, Surgeon Mate, Col R H Dyer, no Co Commander, Branch omitted
WYATT, William, Pvt, Col Edwin Booth, Capt Saml Thompson, Mil
WYATT, William, Pvt, Regt Commander omitted, Capt Jas Gray, Inf
WYATT, William, Sgr (Surgeon?) Mate, Col Wm Pillow, 2 Regt TN Vol Inf
WYETT, Francis, Pvt, Col R H Dyer, Capt Jas Wyatt, Vol Mtd Gunmen
WYGENTON, Nathan, Pvt, Col Jas Raulston, Capt Mathew Neal, Inf
WYLEY, Thomas, Pvt, Col John Brown, Capt Wm White, E TN Vol Mtd Inf; disch for inability
WYLY, Abraham, Pvt, Col Saml Bayless, Capt Branch Jones, E TN Draft Mil
WYLY, Alexander, Pvt, Col John Brown, Capt Jas Standifer, E TN Vol Mtd Mil
WYN, Henry, Cpl, Col John Alcorn, Capt John W Byrn,

## Enlisted Men, War of 1812

Cav; wounded at Talledega 11-9-1813 & died 11-12-1813

WYNN, Isham, Sgt, Col John Coffee, Capt Thos Bradley, Vol Cav

WYNN, James T, Pvt, Col John Coffee, Capt Thos Bradley, Vol Cav

WYNN, James T, Sgt Maj, Col R C Napier, 1 Regt W TN Mil

WYNN, Peter, Pvt, Col John Coffee, Capt John W Byrn, Cav

WYNNE, Henry, Pvt, Col John Coffee, Capt John W Byrn, Cav

WYNNE, James T, Pvt, Col S Copeland, Capt G W Steel, Mil Inf; promoted to Sgt Maj 1 Regt

WYNNE, Richard, Pvt, Col Alexander Loury, Capt Geo Sarver, Inf

WYOTT, Martin, Pvt, Col R C Napier, Capt Jas Gray, Mil Inf

WYOTT, Robert, Pvt, Col R C Napier, Capt Jas Gray, Mil Inf

WYRICK, Frederick, Pvt, Col Wm Lillard, Capt Thos Sharpe, 2 Regt Inf

WYRICK, Henry, Pvt, Col Wm Johnson, Capt Christopher Cook, E TN Mil

WYRICK, William, Pvt, Col Wm Lillard, Capt Ben H King, E TN Vol Inf

WYZER, Jacob, Pvt, Lt Wm Snodgrass, Ens Gregg, Det of Inf of 2 Regt E TN Vol Mil

YADEN, William P, Cpl, Col Saml Bayless, Capt John Broack, Branch omitted

YAGER, Abner, Pvt, Col Wm Metcalf, Capt Wm Sitton, Mil Inf

YAGER, Daniel, Pvt, Col Saml Bayless, Capt Jonathan Waddle, E TN Mil

YAGER, Lewis, 4 Cpl, Col Wm Metcalf, Capt Wm Sitton, Mil Inf

YAGER, Reuben, Pvt, Col Wm Metcalf, Capt Wm Sitton, Mil Inf; died 1-11-1815

YAKELEY, Samuel, 5 Cpl, Col Saml Bayless, Capt Solomon Hendrix, E TN Mil

YANCEY, Philip, Cpl, Gen Andrew Jackson, Capt Nathan Davis, Inf

YANCEY, Philips, 6 Cpl, Col Wm Metcalf, Capt Thos Marks, Mil Inf

YANCY, Garland, Pvt, Col Jas Raulston, Capt Mathew Neale, Inf; died 2-6-1815

YANCY, John, Dmr, Col Philip Pipkin, Capt David Smith, Inf; det of W TN Mil

YANCY, Joseph, Pvt, Col Jas Raulston, Capt Mathew Neale, Inf; died 1-20-1815

YANCY, Philip, Cpl, Regt Commander omitted, Capt Nathan Davis, Mil Inf

YANCY, Sheriff S, Pvt, Col John Cocke, Capt Geo Barnes, Inf

YANDALL, John, Sgt, Col John Wynne, Capt Wm McCall, Inf

YARBER, Malber, Pvt, Col Wm Johnson, Capt Jos Kirk, Mil

YARBERRY, Edward, Pvt, Col Wm Hall, Capt John Moore, Vol Inf

YARBOR, Mathew, Pvt, Col Wm Johnson, Capt Christopher Cook, E TN Mil

YARBOROUGH, Absolom, 2 Sgt, Col A Loury, Capt John Looney, 2nd Regt W TN Mil

YARBOROUGH, Ambrose (Amber), Pvt, Maj Gen Wm Carroll, Col Wm Metcalf, Capt John Jackson, Inf

YARBOROUGH, Edward, Pvt, Col Edward Bradley, Capt John Moore, Vol Inf

YARBOROUGH, Jesse, Pvt, Brig Gen Thos Washington, Capt Jno Crawford, Inf

YARBOROUGH, Jesse, Pvt, Col Wm Hall, Capt Henry M Newlin, Inf

YARBOROUGH, Moses, Pvt, Lt Col Jno Edmonson, Co Commander omitted, Cav

YARBOROUGH, Robert, Pvt, Brig Gen T Washington, Capt Jno Crawford, Mtd Inf

YARBOROUGH, Robert, Pvt, Col N T Perkins, Capt John Doak, Vol Mtd Gunmen

YARBOW, Moses, Pvt, Col Samuel Bayless, Capt Solomon Hendrix, E TN Mil

YARBROUGH, James, 4 Sgt, Col John Cocke, Capt Joseph Price, Inf

YARBROUGH, Jesse, Pvt, Col Edward Bradley, Capt Thos B Haynie, Vol Inf

YARBROUGH, Jesse, Pvt, Maj Gen Wm Carroll, Col Wm Metcalf, Capt John Jackson, Inf; d 1-18-1815

YARBROUGH, Joel, Pvt, Col John Coffee, Capt Michael Molton, Branch Srvce omitted; deserted

YARBROUGH, John, Pvt, Col T McCrory, Capt Thos K Gordon, Inf

YARBROUGH, Nathan, Pvt, Col R C Napier, Capt Thos Gray, Mil Inf

YARBROUGH, Nathan, Pvt, Regt Commander omitted, Capt Gray, Inf

YARDLEY, Benjamin, Pvt, Col Jno Coffee, Capt Alexander McKeen, Inf

YARNALL, Aaron, Master Artif, Maj Gen John Cocke, Co Commander omitted, E TN Mil

YARNELL, Aaron, Pvt, Col Samuel Wear, Capt John Chiles, E TN Vol Inf

YARNELL, Aron, Master Artif, Div of Maj Gen John Cocke, Co Commander omitted, E TN Mil

YASBERRY, Edward, Pvt, Col Wm Hall, Capt John Moore, Vol Inf

YATES, Charles, Pvt, Col A Loury, Capt Gabriel Martin, Inf

YATES, Charles, Pvt, Col Wm Higgins, Capt A Cheatham, Mtd Riflemen

YATES, Daniel, Pvt, Col A Cheatham, Capt Charles Johnson, Inf

YATES, Daniel, Pvt, Col A Loury, Capt James Kincaid, Inf

YATES, Daniel, Pvt, Col Jas Raulston, Capt Henry West, Inf; d 2-16-1814

YATES, Daniel, Pvt, Maj Wm Woodfolk, Capt James C Neil, Inf

YATES, Elias, Pvt, Col Robt Steele, Capt James Shinault, Mil Inf

YATES, Elijah, Pvt, Col Wm Metcalf, Capt John Barnhart, Mil Inf

YATES, James, Pvt, Col Wm Higgins, Capt A Cheatham, Mtd Riflemen

## Enlisted Men, War of 1812

YATES, John, Pvt, Col John Cocke, Capt Richard Crunk, Inf

YATES, Joshua, Pvt, Maj Wm Russell, Capt Geo Mitchie, Vol Mtd Gunmen

YATES, Lewis, Pvt, Col A Loury, Capt Gabriel Martin, Inf

YATES, Nicholas, Pvt, Col Ewen Allison, Capt Jacob Hoyal, E TN Mil

YATES, Robert, Pvt, Col Ewen Allison, Capt Allen, E TN Mil; d 4-11-1814

YATES, Samuel, Pvt, Regt Commander omitted, Capt Nathan Davis, Lt I Barrett, Inf

YATES, William, Pvt, Col Wm Higgins, Capt A Cheatham, Mtd Riflemen

YEAGER, Abner, Pvt, Col S Copeland, Capt John Holshouser, Inf

YEAGER, Ira, Pvt, Col S Copeland, Capt John Holshouser, Inf

YEAKLEY, Henry, Pvt, Col Ewen Allison, Capt Joseph Everett, E TN Mil; deserted

YEAKLEY, Richard, Pvt, Col Ewen Allison, Capt Joseph Everett, E TN Mil; deserted

YEARLY, William, Pvt, Col Thos Williamson, Capt James Pace, Lt Nealy, Vol Mtd Gunmen

YEAROUT, John, Pvt, Col Samuel Bunch, Capt Edward Buchanan, E TN Mil; transferred from Capt Duncan's Co

YEAROUT, John, Pvt, Col Samuel Bunch, Capt Joseph Duncan, E TN Drafted Mil; transferred to Capt Buchanan Co

YEARWOOD, Isaac, Pvt, Col Thos Benton, Capt Wm Moore, Vol Inf

YEARWOOD, Isaac, Pvt, Col William Pillow, Capt William Moore, Inf

YEAT, William, Pvt, Col John Brown, Capt Chas Lewin, E TN Vol Mtd Inf

YELL, Archibald, Sgt, Col Thomas Williamson, Capt John Hutchings, Vol Mtd Gunmen

YELL, James, Pvt, Col Thomas Williams, Capt John Hutchings, Vol Mtd Gunmen

YELL, Percy, Pvt, Col Thomas Williamson, Capt John Hutchings, Vol Mtd Gunmen

YEOBANKS, Robert, Pvt, Col S Copeland, Capt John Hutchings, Inf

YEWENS, John, Pvt, Col S Copeland, Capt John Holshouser, Inf

YIELDING, Francis, Cpl, Col Robert Dyer, Maj William Russell, Capt William Russell, Vol Mtd Gunmen

YOES, Nathan, Pvt, Col John Winn, Capt Robert Bradin, Inf

YOKELY, John, Pvt, Col S Bayless, Capt James Landen, E TN Mil

YOKELY, William, Pvt, Col S Bayless, Capt James Landen, E TN Mil

YORK, Aron, Pvt, Col Wm Johnson, Capt Jas Tunnell, E TN Mil; d 1-15-1815

YORK, James, Pvt, Col Thomas Williamson, Capt Thomas Scurry, Vol Mtd Gunmen

YORK, James, Pvt, Maj Wm Woodfolk, Capt Abraham Dudney, Inf

YORK, Jeremiah, Pvt, Col S Bunch, Capt Robert Breden, E TN Mil; transferred to Capt Bacon's Co

YORK, Jeremiah, Pvt, Maj John Childs, Capt Chas Conway, E TN Mtd Gunmen

YORK, John, 2 Sgt, Regt Commander omitted, Capt J Prewitt, Mtd Vol

YORK, John, Pvt, Col N Cannon, Capt John Demsey, Mtd Gunmen; wounded 11-9-1813 & returned home

YORK, John, Pvt, Col Robert Dyer, Co Commander omitted, TN Mtd Vol Gunmen

YORK, John, Pvt, Col Thomas Williamson, Capt Tate, Vol Mtd Gunmen

YORK, John, Pvt, Regt Commander omitted, Capt Jno Dempsey, Branch Srvce omitted

YORK, John, Sgt, Col S Bayless, Capt I Bacon, E TN Mil

YORK, Jonathan, Pvt, Col R T Perkins, Capt Quarles, Vol Mtd Inf

YORK, Jonathan, Pvt, Col Thomas Williamson, Capt Robert Steele, Vol Mtd Gunmen

YORK, Richard, Pvt, Col Jas Raulston, Capt Robinson, Capt Carroll, Branch Srvce omitted

YORK, Richard, Pvt, Gen Carroll, Col Jas Raulston, Capt Elijah Haynie, Inf

YORK, Robert, Rank omitted, Col Philip Pipkin, Capt Kirkpatrick, Mil Inf

YORK, Thomas, Pvt, Col Wm Johnson, Capt Jas Rogers, E TN Drafted Mil

YORK, Uriah, Pvt, Regt Commander omitted, Capt J Prewitt, Mtd Vol; pack horse guards

YORK, William, Pvt, Col Hammonds, Capt Delaney, Inf; two William Yorks

YORK, William, Pvt, Lt Col Leroy Hammonds, Capt Geo Tubb, Inf

YORK, William, Pvt, Lt Col Leroy Hammonds, Capt Thomas Delaney, Inf

YOST, Andrew, 2 Sgt, Col S Bunch, Capt Jno McNore, E TN Mil

YOUNG, Alexander, Pvt, Brig Gen Johnson, Capt Carson, Inf; discharged for want of arms

YOUNG, Alexander, Pvt, Col Wm Metcalf, Capt Hill & Capt Cunningham, Mil Inf

YOUNG, Archibald, 2 Sgt, Col Wm Hall, Capt Henry Newlin, Inf

YOUNG, Archibald, Pvt, Col Wm Higgins, Capt Adam Dale, Mtd Gunmen

YOUNG, Archibald, QM Sgt, Col Jas Raulston, W TN Mil Inf

YOUNG, Archibald, Sgt, Col Edward Bradley, Capt Elijah Haynie, Vol Inf

YOUNG, Arthur G, Pvt, Col S Bunch, Capt John Cunningham, E TN Vol Mtd Inf

YOUNG, Baxter (Baxtor), Cpl, Regt Commander omitted, Capt Geo Smith, Spies

YOUNG, Beverly, Sgt, Col Alexander Loury, Capt Geo Saver, Inf; reduced to the ranks

YOUNG, Carter, Pvt, Col S Bunch, Capt Geo Bredin, E TN Mil; transferred to Capt Bacon's Co

YOUNG, Daniel, Pvt, Col A Cheatham, Capt Charles Johnson, Inf; transferred to Capt Moor's Co

YOUNG, Daniel, Pvt, Col Thomas Williamson, Capt John Dobbins & Capt Doak, Vol Mtd Gunmen

YOUNG, Daniel, Pvt, Regt Commander omitted, Capt

## Enlisted Men, War of 1812

Edwin S Moore, Cav; transferred from? Capt Jno Story Regt
YOUNG, David, Pvt, Col S Copeland, Capt George, Inf
YOUNG, Ebenezer, 5 Cpl, Col Wm Metcalf, Capt Bird Hurt, Mil Inf
YOUNG, Edmond, Pvt, Col N Cannon, Capt John Demsey, Mtd Gunmen
YOUNG, Edward, 2 Cpl, Col John Brown, Capt William White, E TN Vol Mtd Inf; deserted
YOUNG, Eli, Pvt, Col John Winn, Capt James Holleman, Inf
YOUNG, Ephraim, Pvt, Col T McCrory, Capt Jas Shannon, Branch Srvce omitted
YOUNG, Ewin, Pvt, Col Williams, Capt Vance, Mtd Mil
YOUNG, Ewing, Pvt, Regt Commander omitted, Capt Jas Terrill, Cav Vol
YOUNG, Francis, Pvt, Col Jas Raulston, Capt Geo Black, Inf
YOUNG, Francis, Pvt, Col S Bunch, Capt Jno Harris, E TN Mil
YOUNG, Hardway, Pvt, Col Jas Raulston, Capt Elijah Haynie & Capt Carroll, Branch Srvce omitted
YOUNG, Harvey, Cpl, Col R T Perkins, Capt Quarles, Vol Mtd Inf
YOUNG, Henry, 2 Cpl, Col Wm Hall, Capt William Alexander, Vol Inf
YOUNG, Henry, Pvt, Col Alexander Loury, Capt Geo Saver, Inf; joined the Arty
YOUNG, Henry, Pvt, Col Robert Dyer, Capt James Wyatt, Vol Mtd Gunmen
YOUNG, Henry, Sgt, Col Edward Bradley, Capt William Lauderdale, Vol Inf
YOUNG, Isaac, Sgt, Col S Copeland, Capt Wm Douglas, Inf
YOUNG, James H, Pvt, Col Thomas H Williamson, Capt Robert Moore, Vol Mtd Gunmen
YOUNG, James W, Pvt, Col S Bunch, Capt David Vance, E TN Mtd Inf
YOUNG, Jesse, Pvt, Lt Col Leroy Hammonds, Capt James Craig, Inf
YOUNG, John L, 4 Sgt, Col John Cocke, Capt Richard Crunk, Inf
YOUNG, John, Pvt, Col Edwin E Booth, Capt John McKamy, E TN Mil
YOUNG, John, Pvt, Col John Cocke, Capt George Barnes, Inf
YOUNG, John, Pvt, Col John Coffee, Capt Thomas Bradley, Vol Cav
YOUNG, John, Pvt, Col Newton Cannon, Capt Gabriel Martin, Mtd Gunmen
YOUNG, John, Pvt, Col R C Napier, Co Commander omitted, Mil Inf
YOUNG, John, Pvt, Col R H Dyer, Maj Wm Russell, Capt Wm Russell, Vol Mtd Gunmen
YOUNG, John, Pvt, Col S Copeland, Capt Wm Douglas, Inf
YOUNG, John, Pvt, Col Thomas H Benton, Capt William Moore, Vol Inf
YOUNG, John, Pvt, Col Wm Lillard, Capt George Keyes, Branch Srvce omitted; deserted 10-30-1813
YOUNG, John, Pvt, Col Wm Metcalf, Capt Waller, Mil Inf

YOUNG, John, Pvt, Maj Gen Wm Carroll, Capt Wiley Huddleston, Inf
YOUNG, John, Pvt, Maj Wm Russell, Capt John Trimble, Vol Mtd Gunmen
YOUNG, Joseph S, Pvt, Col John K Wynne, Capt John Porter, Inf
YOUNG, Joseph, Pvt, Col Thomas H Benton, Capt James McFerrin, Vol Inf
YOUNG, Joseph, Pvt, Col Wm Metcalf, Capt Bird L Hurt, Mil Inf
YOUNG, Joseph, Pvt, Col Wm Pillow, Capt James McFerrin, Inf; deserted
YOUNG, Larkin, Pvt, Col Edwin E Booth, Capt Porter, Drafted Mil
YOUNG, Lawrence, Pvt, Col Wm Metcalf, Capt William Mullins, Mil Inf
YOUNG, Manson, Pvt, Col Leroy Hammond, Capt James Tubb, Inf
YOUNG, Manson, Pvt, Col S Copeland, Capt Allen Wilkinson, Mil Inf
YOUNG, Mathew M, Pvt, Col Samuel Wear, Capt James Tedford, E TN Vol Inf
YOUNG, Mathew, Sgt, Maj Wm Russell, Capt John Trimble, Vol Mtd Gunmen
YOUNG, Michael, Cpl, Col A Cheatham, Capt Charles Johnson, Inf
YOUNG, Nicholas, Pvt, Col Robert Steele, Capt James Bennett, Inf
YOUNG, Parker, Pvt, Maj Wm Woodfolk, Capt Ezekiel Ross, Inf; deserted
YOUNG, Peter, Pvt, Col Samuel Bunch, Capt Joseph Duncan, E TN Drafted Mil; joined from Capt Buchanan's Co
YOUNG, Robert B, Sgt, Col Samuel Wear, Capt James Tedford, E TN Vol Inf
YOUNG, Robert, Pvt, Col A Loury & Col Leroy Hammond, Capt Arahel Rains, Inf; deserted
YOUNG, Robert, Pvt, Col Thomas H Williamson, Capt James Pace, Lt James Nealy, Vol Mtd Gunmen
YOUNG, Samuel, 3 Sgt, Col Newton Cannon, Capt David Hogan, Mtd Gunmen
YOUNG, Samuel, Pvt, Col Thomas H Williamson, Capt James Pace, Lt James Nealy, Vol Mtd Gunmen
YOUNG, Samuel, Pvt, Col Wm Johnson, Capt James Tunnell, E TN Mil; notified & never appeared (transferred)
YOUNG, Samuel, Pvt, Regt Commander omitted, Capt John Gordon, Mtd Spies
YOUNG, Samuel, Sgt, Col Leroy Hammond, Capt James Craig, 2nd Regt W TN Mil
YOUNG, Samuel, Sgt, Lt Col Leroy Hammond, Capt James Craig, Inf
YOUNG, Sirous (Cyrus), Sgt, Col Thomas Williamson, Capt Wm Metcalf, Vol Mtd Gunmen
YOUNG, Sirous, Sgt, Col Thomas Williamson, Capt Wm Metcalf, Vol Mtd Gunmen
YOUNG, Thomas, Cpl, Col Thomas McCrory, Capt James Shannon, Mil Inf
YOUNG, Thomas, Pvt, Col John Alcorn, Capt John Baskerville, Vol Inf
YOUNG, Thomas, Pvt, Col John Coffee, Capt John

## Enlisted Men, War of 1812

Baskerville, Cav
YOUNG, Thomas, Pvt, Col Newton Cannon, Capt David Hogan, Mtd Gunmen
YOUNG, Thomas, Pvt, Col R H Dyer, Maj Wm Russell, Capt Wm Russell, Vol Mtd Gunmen
YOUNG, Thomas, Pvt, Maj Gen Wm Carroll, Capt Francis Ellis, Inf
YOUNG, Thomas, Pvt, Maj Wm Woodfolk, Capt Ezekiel Ross, Inf; deserted
YOUNG, William W, 4 Sgt, Col Philip Pipkin, Capt James Blakemore, Mil Inf
YOUNG, William jr, Pvt, Col Thomas Williams, Capt Samuel Bunch, Mtd Vol
YOUNG, William sr, Pvt, Col John Williams, Capt Samuel Bunch, Mtd Vol
YOUNG, William, Pvt, Col Edward Bradley, Capt Wm Lauderdale, Vol Inf
YOUNG, William, Pvt, Col John Alcorn, Capt John Baskerville, Vol Inf
YOUNG, William, Pvt, Col Philip Pipkin, Capt James Blakemore, Mil Inf; AWOL
YOUNG, William. Pvt, Col Thomas H Williamson, Capt James Cook & Capt John Dobbins, Vol Mtd Gunmen
YOUNG, William, Pvt, Col Wm Johnson, Capt John McKamy, E TN Drafted Mil; d 11-18-1814
YOUNG, William, Pvt, Regt Commander omitted, Capt Edwin S Moore, Mtd Riflemen; d 4-2-1814
YOUNG, Willis, Pvt, Col R H Dyer, Maj Wm Russell, Capt Wm Russell, Vol Mtd Gunmen
YOUNGBLOOD, Allen, Pvt, Col S Copeland, Capt Wm Douglass, Inf
YOUNGBLOOD, William, Pvt, Brig Gen Thos Johnson, Capt Robt Carson, Inf
YOUNGER, James N, Pvt, Col Alex Loury, Lt Col L Hammond, Capt Thos Wells, Inf
YOUNGER, Samuel, Pvt, Lt Col Leroy Hammond, Capt Thomas Wells, Inf; d 10-18-1814 at Deposit
YOUNT, David, Pvt, Col Thos Williamson, Capt Jno Doak & Capt Jno Dobbins, Vol Mtd Gunmen
YOUNT, Jacob, Pvt, Col Saml Bunch, Capt Ed Buchanan, E TN Mil; d 3-29-1814
YOUNT, Peter, Pvt, Col Saml Bunch, Capt Ed Buchanan, E TN Mil
YOUREE, David, Pvt, Col N Cannon, Capt Geo Brandon, Mtd Riflemen
YOWS, John, Pvt, Col Thos Williamson, Capt Jas Cook & Capt John Crane, Vol Mtd Gunmen
ZACHARY, Gilbert, Pvt, Col Edwin Booth, Capt Jno Sharp, E TN Mil
ZACHARY, William, Pvt, Col Saml Bayless, Capt Jos Rich, E TN Inf
ZACHERY, Joseph W, Pvt, Col Jno Coffee, Capt B Coleman, Cav
ZACHERY, Josiah W, Pvt, Col Jno Alcorn, Capt Wm Locke, Cav
ZEANS, Samuel, Sgt, Col Wm Lillard, Capt Jno Roper, E TN Inf
_____, Abraham, Servant, Col Robert H Dyer, Co Commander omitted, Regt of TN Vol Mtd Gunmen; servant for Surgeon Fore
_____, Anthony (Negro), Waiter, Col William Metcalf, 1 Regt W TN Mil Inf
_____, Archee, Servant, Gen John Coffee, TN Vol Mtd Gunmen; Servant to Jas Armstrong Surgeon
_____, Bandy, Servant to Gen Coffee, no other information
_____, Ben (Negro), Waiter, Col James Raulston, Co Commander omitted, W TN Mil Inf
_____, Ben, Servant to Gen John Coffee, no other information
_____, Bill (Negro servant), Maj William Woodfolk, Co Commander omitted, Separate Bn W TN Mil
_____, Bob, Waiter, Col Jas Raulston, Co Commander omitted, W TN Mil Inf; served Lt Col Williams left with his master
_____, Bobb, Servant, Col Samuel Bayless, Capt Jonathan Waddell, E TN Mil; Col Samuel Bayless servant
_____, Bryan, Private Servant, Col Wm Metcalf, 1st Regt W TN Mil Inf; waiter to Wm K Rencker
_____, Bryant, Waiter, Maj Gen Wm Carroll, TN Mil; waiter to Wm R Rucker Hospital Surgeon Mate
_____, Buck, Waiter to John H Burton, Col John Cocke, Co Commander omitted, 2nd Regt W TN Mil
_____, Caroline, Waiter to Col Booth, Col Edwin Booth, Capt John Lewis, E TN Mil
_____, Cato, Waiter to Col Cocke, Co Commander omitted, 2nd Regt W TN Mil Inf; negro
_____, Charles, Pvt Servant, Col Robert Dyer, Capt Robert Evans, Vol Mtd Gunmen
_____, Charles, Pvt Waiter for Capt Thomas Wells, Lt Col Leroy Hammonds, Inf
_____, Charles, Pvt Waiter, Lt Col Leroy Hammonds, 2 Regt W TN Mil; pvt waiter for Doc. Sappington
_____, Charles, Pvt waiter to Capt Childs, Col John Brown, E TN Mtd Inf Vol
_____, Charles, Pvt, Col Thomas Williamson, Capt William Martin, Vol Mtd Gunmen; pvt servant to Lt Saml Martin
_____, Charles, Servant to Gen John Coffee
_____, Charles, Waiter to Capt William Mullin, Col William Metcalf, Mil Inf
_____, Charles, Waiter to Maj Childs, E TN Vol Mtd Inf
_____, Cheater, Pvt Servant, Col Philip Pipkin, Capt John Robertson, Mil Inf
_____, Condea, Servant, Lt Lewis Green, no other information
_____, Daniel (David), Waiter, Col Jas Raulston, Capt Mat Neal, Inf; waiter to Capt Neal
_____, Daniel, Waiter, Col Wm Metcalf, Chap George Foster, 1st Regt W TN Mil Inf; d 1-2-1815
_____, David, Private Waiter, Col John Brown, Co Commander omitted, E TN Vol Mtd Gunmen; waiter to Col Brown
_____, David, Waiter, Col Thomas Williamson, Capt Thomas Scurry, Vol Mtd Gunmen; private servant of Capt Scurry
_____, David, Waiter, Maj William Russell, Capt Isaac Williams, Vol Mtd Gunmen
_____, Dick, Waiter, Brig Gen Bird Smith, Maj Gen Wm Carroll, 2nd Brig TN Mil; waiter to Gen Bird Smith

-547

## Enlisted Men, War of 1812

\_\_\_\_, Edmond (Edward), Servant, Col Samuel Bayless, Capt Johnathan Waddell, E TN Mil; Maj Wm Roadman's Servant

\_\_\_\_, Emanuel, Waiter, Maj Gen William Carroll, TN Mil; waiter to Asst Adjt Gen Bazie Shord, killed 1-1815

\_\_\_\_, Frank, Servant, Gen John Coffee, Co Commander omitted, E TN Vol Mtd Gunmen; servant for Maj Wm Mitchell

\_\_\_\_, Fredrick, Servant, Col Pipkin, Co Commander omitted, 1st Regt TN Mil; servant to Adjt John C Hicks

\_\_\_\_, Gabriel, Servant, Col Philip Pipkin, 1st Regt TN Mil; servant to Col Pipkin

\_\_\_\_, George, Capt's Pvt Waiter, Col Metcalf, Capt Hurt, Mil Inf

\_\_\_\_, George, Waiter to Capt Looney, W TN Inf

\_\_\_\_, Gran--?, Pvt Servant to G W Martin of 2 Regt TN Vol Mtd Gunmen of Coffee Brig

\_\_\_\_, Green, Servant, Brig Gen John Coffee, E TN Mtd Gunmen; servant to Maj Martin

\_\_\_\_, Green, Servant, Gen John Coffee's Brig, TN Vol Mtd Gunmen; servant to Lt George W Martin

\_\_\_\_, Harrison, Private Servant to Lt Tyre, Col Alex Loury, Capt George Sarver, Inf

\_\_\_\_, Harry, Servant to Col Pipkin, 1st Regt TN Mil

\_\_\_\_, Henry, Waiter, Maj Gen Wm Carroll, TN Mil; waiter to Wm Carroll

\_\_\_\_, Isaac & Jack, Servants, Gen John Coffee, no Co Commander, TN Vol Mtd Gunmen; private servants to Col Geo Smith

\_\_\_\_, Isaac, Waiter, Col Edwin Booth, Capt Vernon, E TN Militia; Brig Chap waiter

\_\_\_\_, Isaac, Waiter, Col Thos \_\_\_\_, Capt Thomas Scurry, Vol Mtd Gunmen; pvt servant

\_\_\_\_, Isaac, Waiter, Maj Gen Wm Carroll, no Co Commander, TN Mil; waiter to Anthonyh C Robertson

\_\_\_\_, Isham, Servant, Brig Gen John Coffee, no Co Commander, E TN Vol Mtd Gunmen; servant to Simpson Harris

\_\_\_\_, Ishmael, Servant, Col R H Dyer, no Co Commander, Regt TN Vol Mtd Gunmen; pvt servant of Lt Col Melton

\_\_\_\_, Jack & Issac, Servants, Gen John Coffee, TN Vol Mtd Gunmen; pvt servant to Lt Col Geo Smith

\_\_\_\_, Jack & Sterling, Servants, Gen John Coffee, Ten Vol Mtd Gunmen; pvt servant of Col Williamson

\_\_\_\_, Jack (Negro), Waiter, Col Wm Metcalf, no Co Commander, 1 Regt W TN Mil Inf; waiter to Wm Wood

\_\_\_\_, Jack, Pvt Waiter, Col Wm Johnson, 3 Regt E TN Mil; QM Moses L Peck pvt servant

\_\_\_\_, Jack, Pvt, Col Wm Johns, 3 Regt E TN Mil; Col Wm Johnson's Pvt Waiter

\_\_\_\_, Jack, Servant to Dr Lawson, 2 Regt W TN Mil; Nurse, surgeon

\_\_\_\_, Jack, Servant, Col Alexander Loury, no Co Commander, Mil; Dr Lawson's nurse servant

\_\_\_\_, Jack, Servant, Col R H Dyer, no Co Commander, Regt TN Vol Mtd Gunmen; servant of Col Gibson

\_\_\_\_, Jack, Servant, Gen John Coffee, TN Vol Mtd Gunmen; private servant of Col Williamson

\_\_\_\_, Jackson, Waiter, Maj Gen Wm Carroll, TN Mil

\_\_\_\_, Jacob (Negro), Waiter, Col Wm Metcalf, 1st Regt W TN Mil Inf; Waiter to Lt Col James Henderson

\_\_\_\_, Jacob, Waiter, Col E Booth, Capt Vernon, E TN Mil; Gen Coutlon's Waiter

\_\_\_\_, James, Waiter, Col Edwin Booth, Capt John Lewis, E TN Mil

\_\_\_\_, Jep, Servant, Gen John Coffee, TN Vol Mtd Gunmen; private servant to Lt Col Geo Eliot

\_\_\_\_, Jesse (Negro), Waiter, Maj Wm Woodfolk, Separate Bn of W TN Mil

\_\_\_\_, Jesse, Waiter, Col T Williamson, Capt John Hutchings, Vol Mtd Gunmen; waiter to Capt Hutchings

\_\_\_\_, Jim (Negro), Private Servant, Col Wm Metcalf, W TN Mil Inf; Waiter to Alexander Perryman QM

\_\_\_\_, Joe, Servant, Brig Gen John Coffee, E TN Vol Mtd Gunmen; servant to Maj McCullock

\_\_\_\_, John, Waiter to Lt Col Jarman, Col John Cocke, W TN Mil Inf

\_\_\_\_, John, Waiter, Col Robert H Dyer, Capt Thomas Jones, Vol Mtd Gunmen; waiter to Capt Jones

\_\_\_\_, Joseph, Waiter, Brig Gen Geo Doherty, E TN Mil; private waiter to Adison Carrick (Asst Dept A M Gen'l)

\_\_\_\_, Jupiter, Servant, Col Robert H Dyer, Regt of TN Vol Mtd Gunmen; private servant to Lt Col Lauderdale

\_\_\_\_, Lee, Servant, Col Philip Pipkin, 1st Regt TN Mil; servant to Col Pipkin AWOL 10-20-1814 from Ft Strother

\_\_\_\_, Leeds (Negro), Waiter, Col Jas Raulston, W TN Mil Inf; waiter to Chap Samuel Hodge

\_\_\_\_, Lewis, Waiter, Col Robert H Dyer, Capt Jos Williams, Vol Mtd Gunmen; waiter to Lt N Scott

\_\_\_\_, Lewis, Waiter, Maj Gen Wm Carroll, TN Mil; waiter to Andrew Hynes (Capt & Aide de Camp)

\_\_\_\_, Lieu, Waiter, Maj Wm Russell, Capt I Williams, Separate Bn of TN Vol Mtd Gunmen; waiter to Lt I Baird

\_\_\_\_, London (Negro), Private Servant, Col Wm Metcalf, 1st Regt W TN Mil Inf; private servant to Lewis Dillahunty

\_\_\_\_, Luke, Waiter, Maj Gen Wm Carroll, TN Mil; waiter to Maj Gen Carroll

\_\_\_\_, Mage, Servant, Col Philip Pipkin, 1st Regt TN Mil; servant to 1 Maj Jasper Smith

\_\_\_\_, Martin, Pvt Waiter, Brig Gen N Taylor, no other information

\_\_\_\_, Martin, Waiter, Maj Gen Wm Carroll, no Co Commander, TN Mil; Waiter for Jas Long

\_\_\_\_, Mat?, Servant, Col Robert H Dyer, TN Vol Mtd Gunmen; servant of Col Dyer

\_\_\_\_, Mat?, Waiter to QM Cocke, Col John Cocke, 2nd Regt W TN Mil Inf

\_\_\_\_, Ned, Servant, Brig Gen John Coffee, E TN Mtd Gunmen; servant to Lt D Hays

\_\_\_\_, Nelson, Waiter, Col Jas Raulston, Capt Mathew Neal, Inf; waiter to Lt Anthony

\_\_\_\_, Nickla, Servant, Gen John Coffee, TN Vol Mtd Gunmen; servant to Lt John Smith (Adjt?)

## Enlisted Men, War of 1812

\_\_\_\_\_, Patrick, Waiter, Maj Wm Russell, Capt John Cowan, Vol Mtd Gunmen; Servant to Capt Cowan

\_\_\_\_\_, Pete, Servant, Gen John Coffee, TN Vol Mtd Gunmen; Servant to Jas Armstrong Surgeon

\_\_\_\_\_, Peter, Private Waiter, Gen N Taylor, Branch Srvce omitted; private waiter to Maj Jno Russell

\_\_\_\_\_, Peter, Waiter, Col Robert Dyer, Capt Jas McMahon, TN Vol Mtd Gunmen; servant to Col Dyer

\_\_\_\_\_, Peter, Waiter, Maj Gen Jackson, Col Thos Williamson, Capt Robt Steele, Vol Mtd Gunmen; served Capt Robt Tate

\_\_\_\_\_, Peter, Waiter, Maj Gen Wm Carroll, TN Mil; waiter to Samuel Hogg (Hospital Surgeon)

\_\_\_\_\_, Primus, Waiter, Maj Gen Wm Carroll, TN Mil; waiter to C Manton (Judge Advocate)

\_\_\_\_\_, Radick (Negro), Waiter to Adjt Prince, Col John Cocke, W TN Mil Inf

\_\_\_\_\_, Robert, Pvt Waiter, Col Wm Johnson, E TN Mil; Pvt servant to Lt Col Thos E Clark

\_\_\_\_\_, Robert, Waiter, Col Samuel Bunch, E TN Mil; Pvt waiter to T C Clark

\_\_\_\_\_, Sam'l, Pvt, Lt Col Hammonds, Capt Wells, Inf

\_\_\_\_\_, Sam, Negro Waiter, Col James Raulston, W TN Mil Inf; waiter to Col Raulston

\_\_\_\_\_, Sam, Waiter, Maj Wm Russell, Capt Fleman Hodges, Vol Mtd Gunmen; waiter to Capt T Hodges

\_\_\_\_\_, Sampson, Servant, Col Philip Pipkin, 1st Regt TN Mil; servant to S Mate Allen Sutton

\_\_\_\_\_, Sampson, Waiter, Maj Gen Wm Carroll, TN Mil; waiter to Robert Hays (Asst Insp Gen)

\_\_\_\_\_, Seazer, Pvt Waiter, Regt Commander omitted, Capt Wm Johnson, 3 Regt E TN Mil; Dr Spencer Gibbons pvt waiter

\_\_\_\_\_, Solomon, Waiter to Bayless E Prince, Col John Cocke, W TN Mil Inf

\_\_\_\_\_, Stephen, Waiter, Maj Gen Wm Carroll, TN Mil; waiter to P Grayson

\_\_\_\_\_, Sterling, Servant, Gen John Coffee, TN Vol Mtd Gunmen; private servant of Col Williamson

\_\_\_\_\_, Thomas, Waiter, Maj Gen Wm Carroll, TN Mil; Waiter to Hospital Surgeon

\_\_\_\_\_, Thomas, Waiter, Maj Wm Carroll, TN Mil; Waiter to Chas Manton

\_\_\_\_\_, Thornton, Pvt Waiter to Doc Carden, Col Edwin Booth, Capt John Sharp, E TN Mil

\_\_\_\_\_, Tom, Servant, Brig Gen John Coffee, E TN Volt Mtd Gunmen; Servant to Maj Parrish

\_\_\_\_\_, Tom, Servant, Lt Col L Hammonds, 2 Regt TN Mil; Servant to Maj Wm C Smart

\_\_\_\_\_, Tom, Waiter, Col Alex Loury, 2 Regt W TN Mil; Waiter to W C Smart

\_\_\_\_\_, Tom, Waiter, Maj Wm Russell, Capt Williams, Separate Bn TN Vol Mtd Gunmen; Waiter to Capt I Williams

\_\_\_\_\_, Washington, Negro Waiter, Col Jas Raulston, W TN Mil Inf; waiter to Maj Watkins

\_\_\_\_\_, William, Negro Waiter, Col Jas Raulston, W TN Mil Inf; waiter to Maj Abbets

\_\_\_\_\_, William, Negro Waiter, Col John Cocke, 2nd Regt W TN Mil Inf; waiter to Maj Burton

\_\_\_\_\_, Willis, Negro Servant, Maj Wm Woodfolk, Separate Bn W TN Mil; servant to Lt Wilson